Also Available:

THE NEW INTERPRETER'S® BIBLE:
A COMMENTARY IN TWELVE VOLUMES

THE NEW INTERPRETER'S® BIBLE INDEX

THE NEW INTERPRETER'S® STUDY BIBLE

THE PASTOR'S® BIBLE STUDY:
A NEW INTERPRETER'S® SERIES

THE NEW INTERPRETER'S® BIBLE
OLD TESTAMENT SURVEY

THE NEW INTERPRETER'S® BIBLE
NEW TESTAMENT SURVEY

THE NEW INTERPRETER'S® DICTIONARY OF THE BIBLE

A-C

VOLUME 1

EDITORIAL BOARD

THE NEW INTERPRETER'S® DICTIONARY OF THE BIBLE

A-C

VOLUME 1

ABINGDON PRESS

Nashville

THE NEW INTERPRETER'S® DICTIONARY OF THE BIBLE
A-C
VOLUME 1

Library of Congress Cataloging-in-Publication Data

The New Interpreter's Dictionary of the Bible.
    p. cm.
  Includes bibliographical references.
  ISBN 0-687-05427-3 (alk. paper)
  1. Bible--Dictionaries. I. Abingdon Press.

  BS440.N445 2006
  220.3--dc22

2006025839

ISBN-10: 0-687-05427-3   ISBN-13: 978-0-687-05427-5

PUBLICATION STAFF

Project Director: Paul N. Franklyn
Project Manager: Marianne Blickenstaff
Reference Editor: Heather R. McMurray
Production Editor: Alicia Benjamin-Samuels
Contracts Manager: Linda Spicer
Production Design Manager: Ed Wynne
Typesetter: Gayl Hinton
NewInterpreters.com Web Developer: Justyn Hunter
Process Analyst: Rebecca Burgoyne
Print Procurement: Clara Stuart
Marketing Manager: Teresa Alspaugh

EXECUTIVE STAFF

President and Publisher: Neil M. Alexander
Senior Vice President, Publishing: Harriet Jane Olson
Vice President, Abingdon Press: Tammy Gaines

1 2 3 4 5 6 7 8 9 10 – 06 07 08 09 10 11 12 13 14 15

MANUFACTURED IN THE UNITED STATES OF AMERICA

ACKNOWLEDGEMENTS

Art Resource, NY: ART Figure 13a

Todd Bolen/Bible Places: ABILA Figure 1; ARCHITECTURE, NT Figure 2;
BETHLEHEM Figure 1; BETH-SHAN Figure 1, 2; CAESAREA MARITIMA Figure 1, 2;
CAESAREA PHILIPPI Figure 1; CORINTH Figure 1

Reuben G. Bullard Jr., Karak Resources Project: CAPITAL Figure 1

Kevin Butcher: BAALBECK Figure 1

Cameraphoto Arte, Venice/Art Resource, NY: ART Figure 4

David W. J. Gill: ARCHITECTURE, NT Figure 1; ATHENS Figure 1, 2; CRETE Figure 1

David Graf: ARAB, ARABIA, ARABIANS Figure 1, 2

Axel Hausmann and Günter Müller: CATERPILLAR Figure 1

Ze'ev Herzog: ARCHITECTURE, OT Figure 1, 2

John C. H. Laughlin: ARCHAEOLOGY Figure 1, 2, 3, 4, 5, 6, 7, 8, 9; CITY Figure 2

Erich Lessing/Art Resource, NY: AKHENATEN Figure 1; ALPHABET Figure 1;
AMARNA, TELL EL Figure 1; ART Figure 3, 11; ASSYRIA AND BABYLONIA Figure 3, 5, 6, 7

Madaba Plains Project AMMON, AMMONITES Figure 2 illustrated by Peter Erhard

Marcus Milwright: CASTLE Figure 1

Nimatallah/Art Resource, NY: ART Figure 12

The Philadelphia Museum of Art/Art Resource, NY: ART Figure 14

Réunion des Musées Nationaux/Art Resource, NY: ASSYRIA AND BABYLONIA Figure 4

Leen and Kathleen Ritmeyer: AKELDAMA Figure 1

Scala/Art Resource, NY: ART Figure 2, 7, 8, 9, 10; ASSYRIA AND BABYLONIA Figure 2

SEF/Art Resource, NY: ART Figure 1

L. E. Stager ARCHITECTURE, OT Figure 3

Vassilios Tzaferis: CAPERNAUM Figure 1, 2

David Ussishkin: CITY Figure 1 illustrated by Judith Dekel

Vanni/Art Resource, NY: ART Figure 5, 6

John Mark Wade, Kavak Resources Project: AMMON, AMMONITES Figure 1

CONSULTANTS

ARCHAEOLOGY CONSULTANT

JOHN LAUGHLIN
Averett University
Danville, VA

CONSULTING READERS

ERIC ELNES
Scottsdale Congregational United Church of Christ
Scottsdale, AZ

DOTTIE ESCOBEDO-FRANK
CrossRoads United Methodist Church
Phoenix, AZ

RENAE EXTRUM-FERNANDEZ
Walnut Creek First United Methodist Church
Walnut Creek, CA

TYRONE GORDON
St. Luke Community United Methodist Church
Dallas, TX

KEVASS J. HARDING
Dellrose United Methodist Church
Wichita, KS

JAMES A. HARNISH
Hyde Park United Methodist Church
Tampa, FL

JUDI K. HOFFMAN
Edgehill United Methodist Church
Nashville, TN

ROBERT JOHNSON
Windsor Village United Methodist Church
Houston, TX

CHAN-HIE KIM
Upland, CA

SUNGHO LEE
Korean United Methodist Church of Santa Clara Valley
San Jose, CA

MERRY HOPE MELOY
Doylesburg, PA

H. MITCHELL SIMPSON
University Baptist Church
Chapel Hill, NC

EVELENE SOMBRERO NAVARRETE
Holbrook United Methodist Church
Holbrook, AZ

MARIELLEN SAWADA-YOSHINO
San Jose United Methodist Church
San Jose, CA

CONTRIBUTORS

REIDAR AASGAARD
University of Oslo
Oslo, Norway

JUDITH Z. ABRAMS
MAQOM
Houston, TX

PAUL ACHTEMEIER
Union Theological Seminary &
Presbyterian School of Christian Education
Richmond, VA

JAMES S. ACKERMAN
Indiana University
Bloomington, IN

SUSAN ACKERMAN
Dartmouth College
Hanover, NH

SAMUEL L. ADAMS
Yale University
North Branford, CT

BEN C. AKER
Assemblies of God Theological Seminary
Springfield, MO

DALE C. ALLISON, JR.
Pittsburgh Theological Seminary
Pittsburgh, PA

CHERYL ANDERSON
Garrett-Evangelical Theological Seminary
Evanston, IL

GARY A. ANDERSON
University of Notre Dame
Notre Dame, IN

KEVIN L. ANDERSON
Asbury College
Wilmore, KY

DEBORAH A. APPLER
Moravian Theological Seminary
Bethlehem, PA

M. KATHRYN ARMISTEAD
Abingdon Press
Nashville, TN

WILLIAM ARNAL
University of Regina
Regina, Canada

BILL T. ARNOLD
Asbury Theological Seminary
Wilmore, KY

PETER ARZT-GRABNER
Universität Salzburg
Salzburg, Austria

RICHARD ASCOUGH
Queen's Theological College
Kingston, Canada

DAVID E. AUNE
University of Notre Dame
Notre Dame, IN

HECTOR I. AVALOS
Iowa State University
Ames, IA

ANNALISA AZZONI
Vanderbilt University
Nashville, TN

JO-ANN BADLEY
Newman Theological College
Edmonton, Canada

WILMA ANN BAILEY
Christian Theological Seminary
Indianapolis, IN

JILL BAKER
Brown University
Old Saybrook, CT

WILLIAM H. BARNES
Minneapolis, MN

JOHN BARTON
University of Oxford, Oriel College
Oxford, England

JUDITH R. BASKIN
University of Oregon
Eugene, OR

DAVID R. BAUER
Asbury Theological Seminary
Wilmore, KY

RICHARD BAUTCH
St. Edward's University
Austin, TX

EHUD BEN ZVI
University of Alberta
Edmonton, Canada

MARIAN OSBORNE BERKY
Anderson University
Anderson, IN

JOHANNES BEUTLER, SJ
Pontificio Instituto Biblico
Roma, Italy

BRYAN D. BIBB
Furman University
Greenville, SC

BRUCE C. BIRCH
Wesley Theological Seminary
Washington, DC

J. TED BLAKLEY
University of St. Andrews
St. Andrews, UK

L. GREGORY BLOOMQUIST
St. Paul University
Ottawa, Canada

DARRELL L. BOCK
Dallas Theological Seminary
Dallas, TX

ROLAND BOER
Monash University
Melbourne, Australia

HELEN K. BOND
New College, University of Edinburgh
Mound Place, Scotland

SUSAN E. BOND
Claremont Graduate University
Claremont, CA

ODED BOROWSKI
Emory University
Atlanta, GA

WALTER C. BOUZARD
Wartburg College
Waverly, IA

MARY PETRINA BOYD
Coupeville, WA

KENT BRAMLETT
University of Toronto
Toronto, Ontario, Canada

MARC BRETTLER
Brandeis University
Waltham, MA

VALERIE J. BRIDGEMAN-DAVIS
Memphis Theological Seminary
Memphis, TN

PAMELA BRIGHT
Concordia University
Montreal, Canada

BUZZ BROOKMAN
North Central University
Minneapolis, MN

MICHAEL JOSEPH BROWN
Emory University
Atlanta, GA

RICHARD BURRIDGE
King's College
Strand, UK

DENISE K. BUELL
Williams College
Williamstown, MA

NANCY CALVERT-KOYZIS
King's University College
Hamilton, Ontario, Canada

GREG A. CAMP
Fresno Pacific University
Fresno, CA

DEBORAH CANTRELL
Vanderbilt University
Nashville, TN

GREG CAREY
Lancaster Theological Seminary
Lancaster, PA

WARREN CARTER
St. Paul School of Theology
Kansas City, MO

TONY W. CARTLEDGE
Biblical Recorder
Raleigh, NC

JOSEPH R. CATHEY
Dallas Baptist University
Godley, TX

KATHY J. CHAMBERS
Vanderbilt University
Nashville, TN

MARK A. CHANCEY
Southern Methodist University
Dallas, TX

EMILY R. CHENEY
Athens, GA

BRUCE CHILTON
Bard College
Annandale-On-Hudson, NY

L. JULIANA M. CLAASSENS
Baptist Theological Seminary at Richmond
Richmond, VA

TREVOR COCHELL
Baylor University
Waco, TX

CHANNA COHEN STUART
Free University Amsterdam
Culemborg, The Netherlands

GARY COLLEDGE
University of St. Andrews
St. Andrews, UK

RAYMOND F. COLLINS
The Catholic University of America
Lanham, MD

EDGAR W. CONRAD
University of Queensland
Corinda, Australia

CRISTINA CONTI
Buenos Aires, Argentina

COLLEEN CONWAY
Seton Hall University
South Orange, NJ

EDWARD M. COOK
Cincinnati, OH

JOAN E. COOK, S.C.
Sisters of Charity of Cincinnati
Silver Spring, MD

STEVE COOK
Vanderbilt University
Nashville, TN

ROBERT B. COOTE
San Francisco Theological Seminary
San Anselmo, CA

J. BLAKE COUEY
Princeton Theological Seminary
Princeton, NJ

J. R. C. COUSLAND
University of British Columbia
Vancouver, Canada

SIDNIE W. CRAWFORD
University of Nebraska-Lincoln
Lincoln, NE

TIMOTHY G. CRAWFORD
Bluefield College
Bluefield, VA

R. ALAN CULPEPPER
McAfee School of Theology
Mercer University
Atlanta, GA

MARY ROSE D'ANGELO
University of Notre Dame
Notre Dame, IN

FREDERICK W. DANKER
Emeritus, Christ Seminary-Seminex
St. Louis, MO

MAXWELL J. DAVIDSON
Morling College
Eastwood, New South Wales, Australia

LINDA DAY
Pittsburgh, PA

L. J. DE REGT
United Bible Societies
Den Haag, The Netherlands

KRISTIN DE TROYER
Claremont School of Theology
Claremont, CA

J. ANDREW DEARMAN
Austin Presbyterian Theological Seminary
Austin, TX

MARK DELCOGLIANO
Candler School of Theology, Emory University
Decatur, GA

WILL DEMING
The University of Portland
Portland, OR

DAVID DESILVA
Ashland Theological Seminary
Ashland, OH

JESSICA L. TINKLENBERG DEVEGA
Berkeley Preparatory School
Tampa, FL

WILLIAM G. DEVER
Bedford Hills, NY

LAMOINE DEVRIES
Missouri State University
Springfield, MO

DEVORAH DIMANT
University of Haifa
Mount Carmel, Israel

ROBERT A. DIVITO
Loyola University of Chicago
Chicago, IL

FRED W. DOBBS-ALLSOPP
Princeton Theological Seminary
Princeton, NJ

MARY KAY DOBROVOLNY, RSM
Vanderbilt University
Nashville, TN

TERENCE L. DONALDSON
Wycliffe College, University of Toronto
Toronto, Canada

F. GERALD DOWNING
Chorley, UK

DAVID J. DOWNS
Princeton Theological Seminary
Princeton, NJ

JOEL F. DRINKARD, JR.
The Southern Baptist Theological Seminary
Louisville, KY

CHERYL A. KIRK-DUGGAN
Shaw University
Raleigh, NC

JAMES D. G. DUNN
University of Durham
Durham, UK

RUBEN R. DUPERTUIS
Centre College
Danville, KY

NICOLE WILKINSON DURAN
Villanova University
Villanova, PA

JENNIE EBELING
University of Evansville
Evansville, IN

TERRY W. EDDINGER
Carolina Evangelical Divinity School
Winston-Salem, NC

GÖRAN EIDEVALL
Göteborg University
Göteborg, Sweden

PAMELA EISENBAUM
Iliff School of Theology
Denver, CO

YOEL ELITZUR
Herzog College
Alon Shevut, Israel

CASEY D. ELLEDGE
Gustavus Adolphus College
St. Peter, MN

PAUL ELLINGWORTH
King's College
University of Aberdeen
Aberdeen, UK

MARK W. ELLIOTT
University of St. Andrews
St. Andrews, UK

JAMES D. ERNEST
Baker Academic
Caledonia, MI

CRAIG EVANS
Acadia Divinity College
Wolfville, Canada

KATHLEEN FARMER
United Theological Seminary
Dayton, OH

MARK FINNEY
St. Mary's College
University of St. Andrews
St. Andrews, UK

PETER M. FISCHER
Göteborg University
Göteborg, Sweden

JOHN T. FITZGERALD
University of Miami
Coral Gables, FL

LEANN FLESHER
American Baptist Seminary of the West
Berkeley, CA

CAROLE R. FONTAINE
Andover Newton Theological School
Newton Centre, MA

MARY F. FOSKETT
Wake Forest University
Winston-Salem, NC

TERENCE E. FRETHEIM
Luther Seminary
Saint Paul, MN

MARK FRETZ
Lancaster, PA

STEVEN FRIESEN
University of Texas
Austin, TX

ANN FRITSCHEL
Wartburg Theological Seminary
Dubuque, IA

LAWRENCE FRIZZELL
Seton Hall University
South Orange, NJ

SUSANA DE SOLA FUNSTEN
Claremont Graduate University
Claremont, CA

FRANCISCO GARCÍA-TRETO
Trinity University
San Antonio, TX

BEVERLY R. GAVENTA
Princeton Theological Seminary
Princeton, NJ

HEIDI S. GEIB
Vanderbilt University
Nashville, TN

JEFFREY B. GIBSON
Harry S. Truman College
Chicago, IL

GARY GILBERT
Claremont McKenna College
Claremont, CA

WILLIAM K. GILDERS
Candler School of Theology
Emory University
Atlanta, GA

DAVID W. J. GILL
University of Wales Swansea
Swansea, UK

MARK D. GIVEN
Missouri State University
Springfield, MO

BETH GLAZIER-MCDONALD
Centre College
Danville, KY

ROBERT GNUSE
Loyola University of New Orleans
New Orleans, LA

JOHN GOLDINGAY
Fuller Theological Seminary
Pasadena, CA

PAUL W. GOOCH
Victoria University
University of Toronto
Toronto, Canada

MICHAEL J. GORMAN
Saint Mary's Seminary and University
Baltimore, MD

LESTER L. GRABBE
University of Hull
Hull, UK

DAVID F. GRAF
University of Miami
Coral Gables, FL

JOEL B. GREEN
Asbury Theological Seminary
Wilmore, KY

LEONARD J. GREENSPOON
Creighton University
Omaha, NE

JAMES P. GRIMSHAW
Carroll College
Waukesha, WI

DENNIS E. GROH
Illinois Wesleyan University
Bloomington, IL

MAYER GRUBER
Ben-Gurion University of the Negev
Beer-sheva, Israel

CHRISTINE E. GUDORF
International University
Miami, FL

MICHAEL O. GUINAN
Franciscan School of Theology
Berkeley, CA

JUDITH M. GUNDRY-VOLF
Yale University Divinity School
New Haven, CT

DONALD A. HAGNER
Fuller Theological Seminary
Pasadena, CA

GILDAS HAMEL
University of California Santa Cruz
Santa Cruz, CA

VICTOR HAMILTON
Asbury College
Wilmore, KY

MEREDITH BURKE HAMMONS
Vanderbilt University
Nashville, TN

PHILLIP HARLAND
Concordia University
Montreal, Canada

DANIEL J. HARRINGTON, SJ
Weston Jesuit School of Theology
Cambridge, MA

HANNAH HARRINGTON
Patten University
Oakland, CA

J. GORDON HARRIS
North American Baptist Seminary
Sioux Falls, SD

AXEL HAUSMANN
Munich University
Munich, Germany

DANIEL HAWK
Ashland Theological Seminary
Ashland, OH

RALPH K. HAWKINS
Bethel College
Mishawaka, IN

DAVID M. HAY[†]
Coe College
Cedar Rapids, IA

JOHN H. HAYES
Candler School of Theology
Emory University
Atlanta, GA

CHARLES W. HEDRICK
Missouri State University
Springfield, MO

PAMELA HEDRICK
Wheeling Jesuit University
Wheeling, WV

[†]*deceased*

PETRA HELDT
Jerusalem University College
Jerusalem, Israel

GINA HENS-PIAZZA
Jesuit School of Theology
Berkeley, CA

ZE'EV HERZOG
Tel Aviv University
Ramat Aviv, Israel

RICHARD S. HESS
Denver Seminary
Littleton, CO

THEODORE HIEBERT
McCormick Theological Seminary
Chicago, IL

RICHARD H. HIERS
University of Florida
Gainesville, FL

CAROLYN HIGGINBOTHAM
Christian Theological Seminary
Indianapolis, IN

CRAIG HILL
Wesley Theological Seminary
Washington, DC

MARTHA HIMMELFARB
Princeton University
Princeton, NJ

T. R. HOBBS
International Baptist Theological Seminary
Hamilton, Canada

KENNETH G. HOGLUND
Wake Forest University
Winston-Salem, NC

SUSAN HOLLIS
SUNY Empire State College
Penfield, NY

MICHAEL HOLMES
Bethel University
St. Paul, MN

PAUL K. HOOKER
Presbytery of St. Augustine
Jacksonville, FL

DAVID HOPKINS
Wesley Theological Seminary
Washington, DC

LESLIE J. HOPPE, O.F.M.
Catholic Theological Union
Chicago, IL

HEIDI J. HORNIK
Baylor University
Waco, TX

FRED L. HORTON
Wake Forest University
Winston-Salem, NC

BONNIE G. HOWE
Dominican University of California
Oakland, CA

LARRY HURTADO
University of Edinburgh
Edinburgh, UK

JEREMY M. HUTTON
Princeton Theological Seminary
Princeton, NJ

SUSAN E. HYLEN
Vanderbilt University
Nashville, TN

TAL ILAN
Free University of Berlin
Berlin, Germany

STUART IRVINE
Louisiana State University
Baton Rouge, LA

BRIAN P. IRWIN
Knox College
Toronto School of Theology
Toronto, Canada

GLENNA S. JACKSON
Otterbein College
Westerville, OH

DAVID JENSEN
Austin Presbyterian Theological Seminary
Austin, TX

ANDY JOHNSON
Nazarene Theological Seminary
Kansas City, MO

EARL JOHNSON
Siena College
Loudonville, NY

MARSHALL JOHNSON
Minneapolis, MN

PHILIP S. JOHNSTON
Wycliffe Hall
Oxford University
Oxford, UK

WILLIAM JOHNSTONE
University of Aberdeen
Aberdeen, UK

F. STANLEY JONES
California State University, Long Beach
Long Beach, CA

JUDITH JONES
Wartburg College
Waverly, IA

A. HEATH JONES III
Nashville, TN

STEPHAN JOUBERT
Pretoria, South Africa

NYASHA JUNIOR
Princeton Theological Seminary
Princeton, NJ

JOEL KAMINSKY
Smith College
Northampton, MA

BRAD E. KELLE
Point Loma Nazarene University
San Diego, CA

JOHN KESSLER
Tyndale Seminary
Toronto, Canada

ANN E. KILLEBREW
The Pennsylvania State University
University Park, PA

KYOUNG-JIN KIM
University of Cheonan
Seoul, Korea

HYUN CHUL PAUL KIM
Methodist Theological School in Ohio
Delaware, OH

URIAH Y. KIM
Hartford Seminary
Hartford, CT

WILLIAM KLASSEN
University of Waterloo
Waterloo, Canada

RALPH W. KLEIN
Lutheran School Of Theology At Chicago
Chicago, IL

RAZ KLETTER
Tel-Aviv, Israel

SHERI KLOUDA
Southwestern Baptist Theological Seminary
Fort Worth, TX

A. BERNARD KNAPP
University of Glasgow
Glasgow, UK

ERNST AXEL KNAUF
University of Berne
Berne, Switzerland

GARY KNOPPERS
The Pennsylvania State University
University Park, PA

YOSHITAKA KOBAYASHI
Adventist International Institute of Advanced Studies
Silang, Philippines

JOHN T. KOENIG
General Theological Seminary
New York, NY

CRAIG KOESTER
Luther Seminary
St. Paul, MN

JENNIFER L. KOOSED
Albright College
Reading, PA

EDGAR KRENTZ
Lutheran School of Theology at Chicago
Chicago, IL

KAH-JIN JEFFREY KUAN
Pacific School of Religion
Berkeley, CA

ROBERT KUGLER
Lewis & Clark College
Portland, OR

JACQUELINE E. LAPSLEY
Princeton Theological Seminary
Princeton, NJ

JOHN LAUGHLIN
Averett University
Danville, VA

JOHN I. LAWLOR
Grand Rapids Theological Seminary
Grand Rapids, MI

EUNNY LEE
Princeton Theological Seminary
Princeton, NJ

MARY JOAN WINN LEITH
Stonehill College
Easton, MA

JOEL LEMON
Candler School of Theology
Emory University
Atlanta, GA

JUTTA LEONHARDT-BALZER
Ludwig-Maximilians Universität
Munich, Germany

JOHN R. LEVISON
Seattle Pacific University, School of Theology
Seattle, WA

GREGORY L. LINTON
Great Lakes Christian College
Lansing, MI

DAVID R. LIPOVITCH
University of Toronto
Toronto, Canada

ODED LIPSCHITS
Tel Aviv University
Tel Aviv, Israel

KENNETH D. LITWAK
Asbury Theological Seminary
Wilmore, KY

RICHARD N. LONGENECKER
McMaster University
Hamilton, Canada

FRANCISCO LOZADA, JR.
University of the Incarnate Word
San Antonio, TX

LAMONTTE M. LUKER
Lutheran Theological Seminary
Columbia, SC

HARRY O. MAIER
Vancouver School of Theology
Vancouver, Canada

BRUCE MALINA
Creighton University
Omaha, NE

CLAUDE F. MARIOTTINI
Northern Baptist Theological Seminary
Lombard, IL

I. HOWARD MARSHALL
King's College, University of Aberdeen
Aberdeen, UK

LUTHER MARTIN
University of Vermont
Burlington, VT

RALPH P. MARTIN
Fuller Theological Seminary
Pasadena, CA

ERIC F. MASON
Judson College
Elgin, IL

STEVEN D. MASON
LeTourneau University
Longview, TX

VICTOR H. MATTHEWS
Missouri State University
Springfield, MO

STEVEN R. MATTHIES
Southport Presbyterian Church
Indianapolis, IN

GERALD L. MATTINGLY
Johnson Bible College
Knoxville, TN

S. DEAN MCBRIDE
Union Theological Seminary &
Presbyterian School of Christian Education
Richmond, VA

BYRON R. MCCANE
Wofford College
Spartanburg, SC

P. KYLE MCCARTER, JR.
Johns Hopkins University
Baltimore, MD

C. MARK MCCORMICK
Stillman College
Tuscaloosa, AL

LEE MARTIN MCDONALD
Acadia Divinity College
Acadia University
Wolfville, Canada

THOMAS A. MCGINN
Vanderbilt University
Nashville, TN

STEVEN L. MCKENZIE
Rhodes College
Memphis, TN

JAMES A. METZGER
Vanderbilt University
Nashville, TN

CAROL MEYERS
Duke University
Durham, NC

PAMELA J. MILNE
University of Windsor
Windsor, Canada

MARCUS MILWRIGHT
University of Victoria
Victoria, Canada

MARGARET M. MITCHELL
University of Chicago Divinity School
Chicago, IL

PHILIP G. MONROE
Biblical Seminary
Hatfield, PA

MILTON C. MORELAND
Rhodes College
Memphis, TN

STEVE MOTYER
London School of Theology
Northwood, UK

HANS-FRIEDRICH MUELLER
Union College
Schenectady, NY

GUNTHER MULLER
Hebrew University Hadasseh Medical School
Jerusalem, Israel

JEROME MURPHY-O'CONNOR
École Biblique et Archéologique Française
Jerusalem, Israel

LYTTON MUSSELMAN
Old Dominion University
Norfolk, VA

WILLIAM H. MYERS
Ashland Theological Seminary
Ashland, OH

GUY NAVE
Luther College
Decorah, IA

RICHARD D. NELSON
Perkins School of Theology
Southern Methodist University
Dallas, TX

MICHAEL W. NEWHEART
Howard University School of Divinity
Washington, DC

JUDITH H. NEWMAN
Emmanuel College

University of Toronto
Toronto, Canada

JAMES NOGALSKI
Gardner-Webb University
Boiling Springs, NC

ED NOORT
University of Groningen
Groningen, The Netherlands

MICHAEL OBLATH
Pacific School of Religion
Berkeley, CA

GERBERN OEGEMA
McGill University
Montreal, Canada

DENNIS OLSON
Princeton Theological Seminary
Princeton, NJ

SUSANNE OTTO
Aalen, Germany

SHARON PACE
Marquette University
Milwaukee, WI

KIM PAFFENROTH
Iona College
New Rochelle, NY

EUNG CHUN PARK
San Francisco Theological Seminary
San Anselmo, CA

GEORGE PARSENIOS
Princeton Theological Seminary
Princeton, NJ

DALE PATRICK
Drake University
Des Moines, IA

PHEME PERKINS
Boston College
Chestnut Hill, MA

DAVID L. PETERSEN
Candler School of Theology
Emory University
Atlanta, GA

THOMAS E. PHILLIPS
Point Loma Nazarene University
San Diego, CA

ALBERT PIETERSMA
University of Toronto
Toronto, Canada

JOHN J. PILCH
Georgetown University
Washington, DC

PIERLUIGI PIOVANELLI
University of Ottawa
Ottawa, Canada

JORGE PIXLEY
Seminario Teologico Bautista-Managua
Managua, Nicaragua

ELIZABETH E. PLATT
University of Dubuque Theological Seminary
Dubuque, IA

BEATE PONGRATZ-LEISTEN
Princeton University
Princeton, NJ

ADAM L. PORTER
Illinois College
Jacksonville, IL

DEVADASAN PREMNATH
St. Bernard's School of Theology & Ministry
Rochester, NY

JEAN-FRANÇOIS RACINE
Jesuit School of Theology at Berkeley
Berkeley, CA

PAUL REDDITT
Georgetown College
Georgetown, KY

RUTH REESE
Asbury Theological Seminary
Wilmore, KY

BARBARA REID
Catholic Theological Union
Chicago, IL

RAYMOND H. REIMER
North American Baptist Seminary
Sioux Falls, SD

ADELE REINHARTZ
University of Ottawa
Ottawa, Canada

DAVID M. REIS
University of Oregon
Eugene, OR

BENNIE H. REYNOLDS III
The University of North Carolina at Chapel Hill
Chapel Hill, NC

VICTOR RHEE
Talbot School of Theology
Biola University
La Mirada, CA

JAMES N. RHODES
Saint Michael's College
Colchester, VT

SUZANNE RICHARD
Gannon University
Erie, PA

LEEN AND KATHLEEN RITMEYER
Hawthorndene, Australia

GREGORY A. ROBBINS
University of Denver
Denver, CO

J.J.M. ROBERTS
Princeton Theological Seminary
Princeton, NJ

GNANA ROBINSON
Peace Trust High Ground
Nagercoil, India

JEFFREY S. ROGERS
First Baptist Church, Greenville
Greenville, SC

GARY O. ROLLEFSON
Whitman College
Walla Walla, WA

MARK R. RONCACE
Wingate University
Wingate, NC

CHRISTOPHER ROWLAND
University of Oxford, Queen's College
Oxford, UK

RODNEY S. SADLER, JR.
Union Theological Seminary &
Presbyterian School of Christian Education
Richmond, VA

KATHARINE DOOB SAKENFELD
Princeton Theological Seminary
Princeton, NJ

LINDA SCHEARING
Gonzaga University
Fairfield, WA

BRIAN B. SCHMIDT
University of Michigan
Ann Arbor, MI

TAMMI J. SCHNEIDER
Claremont Graduate University
Claremont, CA

MICHAEL J. SCHUFER
Claremont Graduate University
Claremont, CA

EILEEN M. SCHULLER
McMaster University
Hamilton, Canada

STEVEN J. SCHWEITZER
University of Notre Dame
Notre Dame, IN

JOANN SCURLOCK
Elmhurst College
Elmhurst, IL

ALAN F. SEGAL
Barnard College
Columbia University
New York, NY

C. L. SEOW
Princeton Theological Seminary
Princeton, NJ

ITZHAQ SHAI
Bar-Ilan University
Ramat Gan, Israel

L. JEAN SHELDON
Pacific Union College
Angwin, CA

TOM SHEPHERD
Union College
Lincoln, NE

PHILLIP MICHAEL SHERMAN
Maryville College
Maryville, TN

MARY E. SHIELDS
Trinity Lutheran Seminary
Columbus, OH

STEPHEN J. SHOEMAKER
University of Oregon
Eugene, OR

RONALD SIMKINS
Creighton University
Omaha, NE

MATTHEW L. SKINNER
Luther Seminary
St. Paul, MN

P. OKTOR SKJAERVO
Harvard University
Cambridge, MA

CHRIS M. SMITH
Bethany University
Scotts Valley, CA

DENNIS SMITH
Phillips Theological Seminary
Tulsa, OK

LEIVY SMOLAR
Union Theological Seminary &
Presbyterian School of Christian Education
Richmond, VA

MARION L. SOARDS
Louisville Presbyterian Theological Seminary
Louisville, KY

WILL SOLL
Webster University
St. Louis, MO

ELNA SOLVANG
Concordia College
Moorhead, MN

SUSANNA W. SOUTHARD
Vanderbilt University
Nashville, TN

F. SCOTT SPENCER
Baptist Theological Seminary at Richmond
Richmond, VA

PAUL SPILSBURY
Canadian Theological Seminary
Calgary, Canada

ZDRAVKO STEFANOVIC
School of Theology Walla Walla College
College Place, WA

ERIC C. STEWART
Indiana University South Bend
South Bend, IN

D. MATTHEW STITH
Community Presbyterian Church
West Fargo, ND

LAURENCE H. STOOKEY
Wesley Theological Seminary
Washington, DC

JAMES R. STRANGE
Candler School of Theology
Emory University
Atlanta, GA

WILLIAM D. STROKER
Drew University
Madison, NJ

JOHN T. STRONG
Missouri State University
Springfield, MO

JERRY L. SUMNEY
Lexington Theological Seminary
Lexington, KY

STEPHEN E. TABACHNICK
University of Memphis
Memphis, TN

ROBERT TANNEHILL
Methodist Theological School in Ohio
Delaware, OH

JOAN E. TAYLOR
University of Waikato
Hamilton, New Zealand

TOM THATCHER
Cincinnati Christian University
Cincinnati, OH

ANTHONY THISELTON
University of Nottingham
Nottingham, UK

BONNIE THURSTON
Pittsburgh Theological Seminary
Pittsburgh, PA

WESLEY IRWIN TOEWS
Canadian Mennonite University
Winnipeg, Canada

JORGE TORREBLANCA
Universidad Adventista Del Plata
Entre Rios, Argentina

PHILIP H. TOWNER
United Bible Societies
Reading, UK

W. SIBLEY TOWNER
Kilmarnock, VA

JOSEPH L. TRAFTON
Western Kentucky University
Bowling Green, KY

PAUL TREBILCO
University of Otago
Dunedin, New Zealand

JULIO TREBOLLE
Ciudad Universitaria
Madrid, Spain

ALLISON A. TRITES
Acadia Divinity College
Wolfville, Canada

DAVID TROBISCH
Bangor Theological Seminary
Bangor, ME

PATRICIA K. TULL
Louisville Presbyterian Theological Seminary
Louisville, KY

GRAHAM H. TWELFTREE
School of Divinity
Regent University
Virginia Beach, VA

FIDELE KWASI UGIRA
Kinshasa, Congo

JUSTIN S. UKPONG
University of Uyo
Uyo, Nigeria

OMER SERGEY
Tel Aviv University
Tel Aviv, Israel

EVELINE J. VAN DER STEEN
East Carolina University
Greenville, NC

KAREL VAN DER TOORN
Universiteit van Amsterdam
Amsterdam, The Netherlands

ROBERT E. VAN VOORST
Western Theological Seminary
Holland, MI

JOHANNA VAN WIJK-BOS
Louisville Presbyterian Theological Seminary
Louisville, KY

JAMES C. VANDERKAM
University of Notre Dame
Notre Dame, IN

MICHAEL G. VANZANT
Mount Vernon Nazarene University
Mount Vernon, OH

ANDREW VAUGHN
Gustavus Adolphus College
Saint Peter, MN

OSVALDO VENA
Garrett-Evangelical Theological Seminary
Evanston, IL

BURTON L. VISOTZKY
Jewish Theological Seminary of America
New York, NY

ROBERT W. WALL
Seattle Pacific University
Seattle, WA

HAROLD C. WASHINGTON
Saint Paul School of Theology
Kansas City, MO

NANCY WEATHERWAX
University of Missouri-Columbia
Columbia, OH

DOROTHY JEAN WEAVER
Eastern Mennonite Seminary
Harrisonburg, VA

JO BAILEY WELLS
Duke Divinity School
Durham, NC

STEPHEN WESTERHOLM
McMaster University
Hamilton, Canada

DAVID S. WILLIAMS
University of Georgia
Athens, GA

PETER (P.J.) WILLIAMS
King's College, Aberdeen University
Aberdeen, UK

TIMOTHY M. WILLIS
Pepperdine University/Seaver College
Mailbu, CA

KEVIN A. WILSON
Lithuania Christian College
Kretingos, Lithuania

VINCENT L. WIMBUSH
Claremont Graduate University
Claremont, CA

JOHN D. WINELAND
Kentucky Christian University
Grayson, KY

DEREK E. WITTMAN
Baylor University
Waco, TX

LISA M. WOLFE
United Theological Seminary
Dayton, OH

AL WOLTERS
Redeemer University College
Ancaster, Canada

FOOK KONG WONG
Hong Kong Baptist Theological Seminary
New Territory, China

TELFORD WORK
Westmont College
Santa Barbara, CA

ARCHIE WRIGHT
Regent University
Virginia Beach, VA

J. EDWARD WRIGHT
University of Arizona
Tucson, AZ

SEUNG AI YANG
St. Paul Seminary School of Divinity
University of St. Thomas
St. Paul, MN

KHIOK-KHNG YEO
Garrett-Evangelical Theological Seminary
Evanston, IL

THOMAS YODER NEUFELD
Conrad Grebel University College
Waterloo, Canada

K. LAWSON YOUNGER, JR.
Trinity International University
Deerfield, IL

RANDALL W. YOUNKER
Seventh Day Adventist Theological Seminary
Andrews University
Berrien Springs, MI

A. W. ZWIEP
Vrije Universiteit
Amsterdam, The Netherlands

General Editor's Preface

On behalf of the Editorial Board, I welcome you to the company of users of *The New Interpreter's*® *Dictionary of the Bible*, a five-volume set offering the best in contemporary biblical scholarship. This new dictionary stands in the continuing tradition of the Interpreter's® series, developed for church and synagogue teachers and preachers and with the goal of supporting congregations and all students of the Bible as they seek to learn and grow.

Comprehensive in scope: The dictionary covers all the persons and places mentioned in the Bible. It contains a full range of articles on the cultural, religious, and political contexts of the Bible in the ancient Near East and the Greco-Roman world, and it offers many articles explaining key methods of biblical interpretation. *Theological* in focus: The dictionary includes numerous articles on theological and ethical themes and concepts important to understanding the biblical witness.

The original *Interpreter's Dictionary of the Bible*, published in the 1960s, remained a key reference tool for pastors and teachers for nearly half a century. Yet it was of course a product of its time. Biblical scholarship moved an enormous distance in the intervening years, in knowledge of the literature and culture of the ancient world, and in the development of new approaches that have opened fresh horizons of interpretation, for individual books of the Bible, and for many theological concepts. Study of the Dead Sea Scrolls, of ancient Gnostic documents, and of extra-biblical prophetic texts from the ancient Near East are but a few of the many areas in which scholarship focused on extra-biblical texts has developed new data of great significance for understanding the Bible. Increased attention to gender, ethnicity, and economic class offers new insights into previously neglected aspects of the culture of the biblical world, which in some cases leads to striking new perspectives on biblical texts. Archaeology teams up with a wide range of natural sciences to develop methods that give greater insight into ancient community life in addition to military upheavals. Newly discovered inscriptions and artifacts shed new light on biblical history and on religious beliefs and practices of ancient Israel and early Christianity. Recent progress in the analysis of Hebrew poetry, in understanding of Greek rhetoric, in theories of characterization, as well as new models of social-scientific analysis and cultural studies offer new avenues of inquiry in support of theological reading of the biblical text. To account for these and many other exciting developments, we have produced an entirely new dictionary rather than a revision of the old. While there may not be new information on certain obscure biblical persons or places, the major articles, almost without exception, introduce fresh material and even entirely new topics that were not on the 1960s scholarly horizon.

Of course these many changes in biblical studies have not taken place in a vacuum. The world itself has also changed greatly. As we move through the 21st cent., we face a world grown smaller by speed of communication, yet in many ways politically and economically more fragmented (or at least we are more aware of the fragmentation) than ever before. Ecologically we face a possibly precarious future; factionalism and hostility seems on the increase within and among some religious and racial/ethnic groups, even as signs of reconciliation and search for common ground blossom in unexpected places. While such issues will not be addressed directly on every page, it is the aim of this dictionary to enable wise use of the biblical tradition in theological and ethical approaches to these difficult issues.

As the knowledge of the world surrounding the Bible and also methods for studying the Bible have expanded and changed, so also has the profile of the leaders in biblical scholarship. *The New Interpreter's Dictionary* contributors number approximately 900 women and men in more than 40 different countries from Australia to Africa, from the Americas to Europe, Asia, and the Middle East. Chosen for their scholarly expertise and publication in the areas of their articles, they are identified with Catholic, Orthodox, Jewish, and many different Protestant traditions; they range in personal commitment from conservative to liberal and come from many racial/ethnic and cultural backgrounds. The wide scope of the contributors' contexts reflects the global scope of biblical scholarship of the 21st cent.

The Editorial Board took joint responsibility for nominating the wide range of authors who have contributed to this dictionary. Meetings, followed by numerous conference calls and innumerable rounds of email communication enabled comment and consensus building around the hundreds of nominees. Access to such a global span of contributors was greatly eased by computer and internet technology that could not have been feasible even a decade ago, with a website through which more than 7,100 articles were moved seamlessly and without paper from author to press and then through the various editorial stages. All but the very briefest articles were reviewed for content, balance of perspective, and accessibility by at least one member of the editorial board, and web and email facilitated discussion with authors of any proposed revisions. In addition, experienced pastors were recruited for further review of select longer articles, as an additional check on the readability and theological usefulness of the material for the intended audience.

In guidelines for authors and editors, this project has emphasized openness and generosity to various points of view. In an era when the very notion of one right answer to every question is itself increasingly called into question, we have asked our authors to offer their own perspectives on their topics while still including a clear and charitable presentation of significant alternative scholarly viewpoints. The editors are grateful to the authors for their willingness to write in this style, which will provide a fuller interpretive context for readers who are seeking an introduction to a subject.

As General Editor, it is my joy to express appreciation to the entire Editorial Board for their untiring efforts. The Board itself reflects something of the ecclesial, cultural, and racial/ethnic diversity, as well as the range of scholarly expertise that we have worked to bring to fruition in our contributing authors. Thanks, then, to Samuel Balentine, Brian Blount, Joel Green, Kah-Jin Jeffrey Kuan, Pheme Perkins, and Eileen Schuller for all that each of you has brought to our common work; and thanks to Paul Franklyn and Marianne Blickenstaff of Abingdon Press, who have shepherded this long process with intelligence, imagination, and love.

KATHARINE DOOB SAKENFELD, GENERAL EDITOR

FEATURES OF
THE NEW INTERPRETER'S® DICTIONARY
OF THE BIBLE

A. The Main Entry

1. Title. Main entries are set in a bold font and highlighted in red. In most instances, where more than one person or place in the Bible shares a name, one article covers all instances of that proper name. For example, the article on JOSHUA will include Joshua, high priest and Joshua, son of Nun. However, in some instances, where the subject material is especially important, we divide articles between experts in various fields, to obtain the best treatments. For example, instead of one article on Abraham, we have ABRAHAM, NT and ABRAHAM, OT.

The articles are listed in alphabetical letter (rather than word) order, with rare exceptions; e.g., when listing all of the entries pertaining to BAAL some minor content sequencing was required.

2. Pronunciation. If the main entry is a person or place in the Bible, it is followed by a preferred pronunciation that is endorsed by the Society of Biblical Literature and derived from the *Bible Pronunciation Guide* (ed. William O. Walker, 1989). The following pronunciation key is a useful guide to the sounds that are intended by the preferred pronunciation.

a	cat	ihr	ear	ou	how
ah	father	j	joke	p	pat
ahr	lard	k	king	r	run
air	care	kh	ch as in German *Buch*	s	so
aw	jaw	ks	vex	sh	sure
ay	pay	kw	quill	t	toe
b	bug	l	love	th	thin
ch	chew	m	mat	*th*	then
d	do	n	not	ts	tsetse
e, eh	pet	ng	sing	tw	twin
ee	seem	o	hot	uh	ago
er	error	oh	go	uhr	her
f	fun	oi	boy	v	vow
g	good	oo	foot	w	weather
h	hot	*oo*	boot	y	young
hw	whether	oor	poor	z	zone
i	it	or	for	zh	vision
i	sky				

Stress accents are printed after stressed syllables. ′ is a primary stress. ‵ is a secondary stress.

3. Biblical Languages. The editors think it important for a dictionary to make the original biblical languages a part of appropiate entries. To satisfy those readers who are trained in

Hebrew, Aramaic, and Greek, the key terms are rendered in the original language as part of the main-entry heading. A transliteration is provided in the heading, and also with the first occurrence of any Hebrew or Greek font that is introduced in the body of an article. The transliteration style is based on the "general purpose" guide in the *SBL Handbook of Style*. For some students of the ancient languages, the transliteration style functions as a pronunciation guide, though this dictionary makes no attempt to reconcile English pronunciations with ancient-language transliterations.

4. Outline. Entries with more than 2,000 words ordinarily have an outline to help the reader navigate the information contained in the article.

5. Cross References. In the body of the main entry a reader will encounter words presented in all CAPITALS to signal that this topic exists as a separate entry in the dictionary. It would diffuse the purpose of special emphasis to signal a cross reference through capitalization for every person or place in the Bible. The capitalized cross reference means that information in another article is available to enhance the reader's understanding of a concept or to further explain the meaning of a technical term.

More than 1,300 main entries in the dictionary are linked with cross-references to specific articles that pertain to the person, place, or topic. One of the risks of publishing five volumes over the course of several years is the potential of including "blind" cross references that lead the reader to another cross reference rather than to an article. Great care is taken in our database to prevent this frustration for the reader; if any blind references occur (perhaps if an article failed to appear) we will correct the link upon reprint.

6. Bibliography. This dictionary is not intended as a technical reference tool; therefore, entries do not contain detailed citations within the body of the article, nor footnotes at the end. However, a limited number of technical articles contain parenthetic citations of an author's name, with bibliographic reference at the end of the entry. Bibliographies for articles are necessarily short and select. Works published before the mid-20th cent. generally are avoided in favor of more current works that build on earlier publications.

B. Main Entry List

The definitions included in this dictionary are written in a style that is accessible to students, pastors, and teachers of the Bible. Style decisions are based on the needs, interests, and skills in the primary audience. A group of consulting readers (all pastors of churches) aided us in vetting these articles for comprehension and usefulness in their daily tasks.

We began with the main entries from *The Interpreter's Dictionary of the Bible* (1964, 1975). We subtracted from this list several hundred King James Version spellings of persons, places, and obsolete terms, and replaced these with spellings or terms found in the *New Revised Standard Version* of the Bible. To the list of entries we added terms from other theological handbooks and Bible dictionaries, as well as topics recommended by members of the editorial board and authors. Author input was crucial as we responded to suggestions about dated topics, emerging trends, and more recently published primary sources.

The authors have moved away from the word-study approach that dominated biblical scholarship when the *Interpreter's Dictionary* was published. Scholars have learned that literary context is more important for present day Bible readers than etymology (word origins) or later theological notions of what a word means. A Bible dictionary, like any other dictionary, indexes single words or phrases that label people, places, and subjects. The challenge for the author of a Bible dictionary article is to convey (within the limited word count) the diverse range of meaning that can be represented by major terms.

AARON, AARONITE air′uhn אַהֲרֹן ʾaharon; אַהֲרֹן bene ʾaharon בֵּית אַהֲרֹן betʾaharon]. 1. AARON. The elder brother of Moses, eventually considered to be the primary ancestor of the Jerusalem priesthood. In preexilic texts, Aaron appears in non-priestly roles as Moses' spokesperson and assistant. In materials from the Second Temple period, he is presented as the first ancestor from whom the priestly families of the Jerusalem Temple descended and paradigm for the office of high priest. Claiming Aaronic ancestry played a decisive role in conflicts among groups competing for priestly legitimacy.

Those portions of the Pentateuch generally thought to be preexilic (attributed to J and E) do not present Aaron as a priest or priestly ancestor, in contrast to the portrayal of the later Priestly Writer (P). In preexilic texts Aaron is primarily the elder brother of Moses (Exod 6:20; 7:7) and thus brother of Miriam (Exod 15:20).

As God equips Moses for confrontation with Pharaoh, Aaron is provided as his spokesperson. Aaron's role is explained to Moses using the metaphor of a prophet as one who speaks for God (Exod 4:14-16) and illustrated in the scene described in Exod 4:27-31. Elsewhere Aaron functions as an assistant for Moses, so that "Moses and Aaron" work together as a team throughout the final form of Exod 5–12 as the conflict with Pharaoh and the plagues reach their culmination. During a battle with the Amalekites, Aaron links up with the otherwise obscure Hur (Exod 24:14) to support Moses' hands while Joshua fights (Exod 17:8-13). Aaron is present at Sinai, but not as a priest (Exod 19:24). With his two sons, Aaron joins the elders in seeing God and eating and drinking during the covenant ceremony described in Exod 24, but it is Moses who performs the priestly actions (vv. 6, 8). Aaron also appears as Moses' assistant in the P narrative of the miraculous provision of water from the rock at Meribah (Num 20:2-13). Aaron's non-priestly role in the exodus tradition is summed up by Mic 6:4, "I sent before you Moses, Aaron, and Miriam."

Although it is impossible to say anything about Aaron as an actual historical figure, his name is of Egyptian derivation ("the name [of the god] is great"), like other names associated with Israel's earliest priesthood (Moses, Phinehas, Hophni). His traditional gravesite was Mount Hor in Edom (Num 20:12, 22-29, called Moserah, "Chastisement," in Deut 10:6). Like Moses, he died outside of the land of promise as a punishment (Deut 32:50).

In P and Chronicles, Aaron is presented as the ancestor of the Jerusalem priesthood and the original and model high priest. He is declared to be a descendant of Levi through Kohath (Exod 6:16-25), but his offspring are exalted above the other Levite families in possessing the sole right to priesthood (Num 3:5-10). Laws instituting the priesthood and sacrificial cult are applied to "Aaron and his sons," a phrase that directly corresponds to the priesthood of the Second Temple. Exodus 28–29 and Lev 1–8 inaugurate and regulate their vestments, ordination, and sacrificial functions. Leviticus 21 guards their holiness, and Num 18 promotes their prerogatives in contrast to the lower status Levites. Numbers 6:22-27 grants them authority to bless the people with a distinctive benediction. These texts read back the later priesthood of the Jerusalem temple into the desert period and attach it securely to the sons of Aaron.

Although certain priests were more important than others in preexilic Jerusalem, the office of high priest as such emerged as a new development in the Second Temple. This office combined political and religious leadership and was achieved through family succession. In P, Aaron embodies and personifies the figure of the high priest. His rich vestments are described in Exod 28 and his exclusive responsibilities in the Day of Atonement ritual in Lev 16.

The final form of the OT portrays a straightforward and settled priestly reality. Aaron was the ancestor of all legitimate priests through his sons Eleazar and Ithamar (Num 3:1-4), and the office of high priest belonged to the family line descended from Zadok, whom Solomon appointed (1 Kgs 2:35; see ZADOK, ZADOKITES). However, it is clear that actual developments were much more complicated, involving struggles among rival priestly groups both inside and outside Jerusalem. Eventually, a particular faction's ability to claim Aaronic descent became the decisive factor in advancing and maintaining its privileges. Numerous theories have attempted to untangle these convoluted developments, but no consensus has emerged.

At an early stage, not all Israelite priests were regarded as descendants of Aaron, but rather bore the title Levite (Deut 18:1-8; 33:8-11; Judg 17) or considered Moses as their ancestor (Judg 18:30; perhaps the "Mushites" of Num 3:33; 26:58). No unambiguous line of priestly descent connects Aaron (and his son Eleazar and grandson Phinehas) with the priests mentioned in Samuel and Kings (Eli and his family and Zadok). Significantly, Aaron is almost completely absent from the DEUTERONOMISTIC HISTORY and the prophetic books (including that of the priest Ezekiel).

Rivalries between priestly groups are reflected in the story of the objections that Aaron and Miriam raise with Moses over his Cushite wife in Num 12: "Has the Lord spoken only through Moses? Has he not spoken through us also?" (v. 2). Aaron and Miriam give voice to claims of legitimacy that the story undermines by asserting Moses' unique status as one to whom the LORD relates "face to face" (v. 8). Miriam is severely punished with leprosy, apparently a harsh rejection of any priestly entitlements that may have been claimed by women cultic personnel. Numbers 16 legitimizes Aaron's exclusive priestly rank in opposition to rival claims by Levite groups personified by Korah "son of Levi" (vv. 1, 5-11). Korah's dreadful death (vv. 32-33) stresses that only "the descendants of Aaron" (v. 40) can perform the priestly act of offering incense. When they do so, however, it serves as an effective intercession (vv. 47-48). Similarly, 2 Chr 26:16-21 describes the punishment of King Uzziah for encroaching on the cultic rights of "the descendants of Aaron" (v. 18). The budding of Aaron's staff in Num 17 also authenticates the Aaronic priesthood over against its rivals. *See* AARON'S ROD.

Significantly, the GOLDEN CALF incident (Exod 32 and Deut 9) associates Aaron with the cult of the calf image practiced in Bethel and founded by Jeroboam I, first monarch of the Northern Kingdom (compare Exod 32:4, 8 with 1 Kgs 12:28). This could indicate that the priests of Bethel claimed Aaronic descent, or it might be a libel against the Aaronic priests by a competing faction represented by the "sons of Levi" who display such commendable zeal (Exod 32:25-29). First Kings 12:31 asserts that the Bethel priesthood was non-Levitical. Again, this could be a false vilification of the Aaronites or an indication that they were not yet claiming a Levite background. Some sort of connection between Aaron and the Bethel priesthood is suggested by the circumstance that the burial site of his son Eleazar was thought to be in Ephraim (Josh 24:33) and the association of Eleazar's son Phinehas with Bethel in Judg 20:26-28. Another hint is the perplexing correlation between Aaron's sons Nadab and Abihu and Jeroboam's sons Nadab and Abijah, all of whom suffer premature deaths (Lev 10:1-2; 1 Kgs 14:1, 17; 15:25, 28).

Genealogical traditions in Ezra and Nehemiah also advance claims and negotiate tensions between rival priestly groups. The most trustworthy list of those who returned from exile, that of Ezra 2 (Neh 7), makes no mention of either Aaron or Zadok in describing the four families of Jerusalem priests. In contrast, the genealogy of Ezra insists on his Aaronic and Zadokite descent (Ezra 7:1-5). Scholars generally agree that the Zadokite Jerusalem priesthood advanced its claim to Aaronic descent only in the Second Temple period. Ezekiel 44, for example, advances Zadokite prerogatives without

mentioning Aaron. The Chronicler supplements and rewrites Samuel and Kings to incorporate mention of Aaron and the Aaronic priesthood. Examples are 1 Chr 24:1-3 which makes Zadok a son of Eleazar son of Aaron and 2 Chr 13:9-10 where Jeroboam is accused of excluding not only Levites but also Aaronic priests. The sequence in 1 Chr 6:3-15, 50-53 presents the final resolution of the genealogical question: "Aaron . . . Eleazar . . . Phinehas . . . Ahitub . . . Zadok." *See* PRIESTS AND LEVITES.

2. The Aaronites were sons or house of Aaron. Descendants of Aaron, who emerged as the sole legitimate claimants to priesthood. Priestly office was not originally limited to Aaronites. Exodus 32 and Num 12, 16–17 witness to rivalries between Aaronites and other groups claiming priestly prerogatives. The Priestly Writer and Chronicles confirm that, by the Second Temple period, all legitimate priests were considered Aaronites. *See* P, PRIESTLY WRITERS; PRIESTS AND LEVITES.

Bibliography: Frank M. Cross. "The Priestly Houses of Early Israel." *Canaanite Myth and Hebrew* (1973) 195–215; Gary N. Knoppers. "Aaron's Calf and Jeroboam's Calves." *Fortunate Are the Eyes That See: Essays in Honor of David Noel Freedman*, ed. A. B. Beck, *et al.* (1995) 92–104. Richard D. Nelson. *Raising Up a Faithful Priest* (1993).

RICHARD D. NELSON

AARON'S STAFF [מַטֶּה matteh]. In Exodus, Aaron's staff appears alongside the staff of Moses as an instrument of power in the confrontation with Pharaoh and the plagues. The final form of the text exhibits some confusion between these staffs. Texts featuring Aaron's staff are assigned to the Priestly writer (*See* DOCUMENTARY HYPOTHESIS): Exod 7:8-12 (becoming a snake), 19 (Nile into blood); 8:1-2 [E 5-6] (frogs), 12-13 [E 16-17] (gnats).

In Num 17, a staff representing Levi is inscribed with Aaron's name. It blossoms, proving the placement and preeminence of the Aaronites within Levi as the only legitimate priests. It was preserved in the sanctuary as a warning to rival factions. *See* AARON.

RICHARD D. NELSON

AB [אָב ʾav]. Fifth month in the Hebrew calendar, mentioned in the Talmud but not in the OT. *See* CALENDAR.

ABADDON uh-bad'uhn [אֲבַדּוֹן ʾavaddon; Ἀβαδδών Abaddōn]. Abaddon, a proper noun from the root אבד ʾbd (perish), is translated as (the place of) destruction. It clearly refers to the underworld and is found six times in the OT, most often in wisdom literature (Job 26:6; 28:22; 31:12; Prov 15:11; 27:20; Ps 88:11). In the

NT, it is personified as the angel of the bottomless pit (Apollyōn = destroyer) who reigns as king over the demonic locusts of Rev 9:3-11. In late Jewish literature it came to be known as the place in Sheol for the punishment of the wicked. *See* DEAD, ABODE OF THE; DEMON; DESTROYER; PIT; SHEOL.

LEANN SNOW FLESHER

ABAGTHA uh-bag'thuh [אֲבַגְתָא 'avaghtha']. One of the seven EUNUCHS assigned to take VASHTI to AHASUERUS'S banquet in order to display her beauty (Esth 1:10). Eunuchs were high officials in the Persian court, fulfilling several roles. This group of seven functions as chamberlains for the king, carrying his message from one part of the palace to another. They may not have been literal eunuchs, for the word becomes a title as well as a common noun in the Persian period. Abagtha's name may come from the Iranian word gabata, "fortunate one."

SIDNIE WHITE CRAWFORD

ABANA ab'uh-nuh [אֲבָנָה 'avana]. A river, now called Barada, that orignates in the Anti-Lebanon Mountains. It flows southeastward through DAMASCUS, terminating in the marshy lake Bahret el-Kibliyeh. ELIJAH sends NAAMAN, army captain of King Aram, to cure his leprosy in the JORDAN RIVER. Naaman retorts that the Abana and Pharpar rivers of Damascus are preferable (2 Kgs 5:12).

ABANDON [נָטַשׁ natash, עָזַב 'azav; ἀφίημι aphiēmi, ἐγκαταλείπω enkataleipō]. The translations of several verbs in Hebrew (natash, 'azav) and Greek (aphiēmi, enkataleipō) mean to *leave behind* or *forsake*. Such verbs sometimes appear together in parallelism in the same verse, showing their equivalence (e.g., Ps 94:14; Jer 12:7; Heb 13:5). Different English versions will translate the same verse using *abandon, leave,* or *forsake* interchangeably (e.g., Prov 4:2; Isa 1:4; Rev 2:4).

These verbs sometimes apply to purely human relations, such as one person abandoning another (Josh 10:6), or people leaving the land empty to lie fallow (Lev 26:43). But the most frequent biblical usage is to describe the relationship between people and God, usually in a way that shows the people neglecting or damaging the relationship. The Israelites are often described as having abandoned God to take up idol worship (Deut 29:25; 32:15; Judg 2:13; 2 Chr 12:5; 15:2) thus breaking the covenant with God (Jer 22:9). In response to such faithlessness, God sometimes abandons the Israelites to their enemies (Num 32:15; 1 Chr 28:9; 2 Chr 12:5; 15:2). In the NT, such abandonment by people is not national, but individual: Jesus accuses some of the Pharisees of abandoning the commandment of God to follow merely human rules (Mark 7:8), an individual Christian church is admonished for losing its love of God (Rev 2:4), and the readers are exhorted not to lose their confidence in their faith (Heb 10:35). When speaking of God abandoning Israel or the faithful, the verb is often negated, so as to show God's steadfast loyalty, even in the face of human failure. The reader is assured that God will not abandon Israel (Deut 4:31; Ps 94:14), or that, even though God has abandoned them in the past because of their faithlessness, God will never again do so (Isa 54:7). For individuals, this is expressed as confidence that God will not abandon believers in their time of need (Ps 16:10; Acts 2:27, 31; 2 Cor 4:9). Even when the individual feels abandoned by God, as expressed most vividly in Jesus' cry on the cross (Matt 27:46; Mark 15:34), the implication is that this is fleeting and God will never permanently abandon such a person (Ps 22:1-5). Overall, the verbs usually highlight the sinful weakness of people, contrasted with the abiding love and righteousness of God.

KIM PAFFENROTH

ABARIM MOUNTAINS ab'uh-rim [הָר הָעֲבָרִים har ha'avarim; ὄρος Αβαριμ oros Abarim]. A range across the Jordan extending from its highest peak, Mount NEBO, in the north to the Arabian Desert (Num 27:12; 33:47-48; Deut 32:49; Jer 22:20). The northern part is also known as PISGAH, identified as the place where BALAAM blessed Israel the second time (Num 23:14), Moses saw the Land (Deut 34:1), and Jeremiah hid the ark (2 Macc 2:4-5).

CHANNA COHEN STUART

ABBA ah'buh [ἀββά abba]. The transliterated Aramaic word abba appears three times in the NT, always as an address to God and always with the translation ὁ πατήρ ho patēr (the father). Paul attributes the cry ἀββά ὁ πατήρ abba ho patēr to the spirit in the hearts of believing communities, interpreting it as evidence of their adoption as God's sons and heirs (Gal 4:6, Rom 8:15). Mark 14:36 attributes this cry to Jesus—before Jesus' arrest, he pleads: "Abba, Father all things are possible to you. Take this cup from me. But not what I will, but what you do."

Some 20th cent. interpreters made the use of the word *Abba* as an address for God, which is distinct from Jewish understandings of God. The case was most fully argued by Joachim Jeremias' essay *Abba* (1966), which developed and expanded a two-page article by Gerhard Kittel, originally published in the same year as his Nazi pamphlet on the "Jewish Question" (1933). Kittel interpreted *Abba* as deriving from baby talk, concluding that the "Father-child relationship to God" taught by Jesus, "far surpasses any possibilities of intimacy assumed in Judaism, introducing indeed something which is wholly new" (*TDNT* 1, 6).

Although Jeremias' claims for this word have made a major impact on Christian theology, some scholars questioned his case almost immediately. Better understandings of both the history of Aramaic and of Judaism at the time of Christian origins have further undermined it. Two Dead Sea texts demonstrate that Jews before and during Jesus' time could address God as father in Jeremias' individual, personal sense (4Q372: *Apocryphon of Joseph* 1, 14–25 and 4Q460 frg. 5, col. 1, 1–5). Also problematic are the identification of *Abba* with baby talk, and the claim that Jesus always addressed God as *Abba*.

Gal 3:26–4:7 offers a starting point for reinterpreting. This address is the Spirit's testimony that believers are no longer like children but are God's (adult) sons and heirs, a status that overcomes the distinctions Jew and Greek, slave and free, male and female. Mark 14:36 represents "Abba, Father" as exemplary spiritual prayer. The Gospels attribute forms of *father* (not *Abba*) to Jesus with increasing frequency. Whether in Jesus' use or the Gospels' theology, *father* should be seen as appealing to widespread forms of Jewish, Greek and Roman piety, and perhaps as resisting the Roman emperors' title *pater patriae*. See ANTI-SEMITISM; GOD, NAMES OF; GOD THE FATHER; SONS OF GOD.

Bibliography: James Barr. "Abba Isn't Daddy." *JTS* 39 (1988) 28–47; Mary Rose D'Angelo. "Abba and 'Father': Imperial Theology and the Traditions about Jesus." *JBL* 111 (1992) 611–630; Joachim Jeremias. *Abba: Studien zur neutestamentlichen Theologie und Zeitgeschichte* (1966); Eileen Schuller. "4Q372 1: A Text about Joseph." *RQ* 14 (1990) 343–70.

MARY ROSE D'ANGELO

ABDA ab´duh [עַבְדָּא ʿavdhaʾ]. Adoniram's father (1 Kgs 4:6); Shammua's son among the Levites who returned to Jerusalem after the exile (Neh 11:17; compare 1 Chr 9:16). See LEVITES; SOLOMON.

ABDEEL ab´dee-uhl [עַבְדְּאֵל ʿavdheʾel]. "Servant of God." Shelemiah's father, mentioned to identify Shelemiah, who was unable to serve Jehoiakim by arresting Jeremiah and Baruch, since God hid them (Jer 36:26).

ABDI ab´di [עַבְדִּי ʿavdi]. 1. A Levite from the clan of Merari, he was father of Kishi and grandfather of Ethan, appointed as one of the head temple singers by David (1 Chr 6:44 [Heb. 6:29]; 15:17).

2. The Levite father of Kish. Kish was chosen to help King Hezekiah with religious reforms (2 Chr 29:12).

3. One of the descendants of Elam who divorced his foreign wife after the people returned from the exile (Ezra 10:26).

CLAUDE F. MARIOTTINI

ABDIAS, APOSTOLIC HISTORY OF. The *Apostolic History of Abdias* is the name an early editor (Wolfgang Lazius, 1552) gave to a comprehensive Latin collection of lives and martyrdoms of the apostles. The manuscripts apparently present the work, which has not yet been critically edited, anonymously under the title "Miracles of the Apostles" or "Martyrdoms of the Apostles."

An epilogue to the account of Simon and Jude states that Abdias, the bishop of Babylon who was ordained by the apostles, wrote the deeds of the apostles in Hebrew, which were translated by his disciple Eutropius into Greek and arranged into ten books by Africanus. A preceding paragraph in this account states that a Craton or Grathon composed his narrative of Simon and Jude in ten books, which Julius Africanus is said to have translated into Latin. Some of these details seem to have been copied from an earlier work, but they might have also been intended to apply to the new work as a whole—hence the attribution to Abdias.

The collection seems to date from the end of the sixth century and to derive from the region of the Franks. Its value lies in its use of older sources not preserved elsewhere.

F. STANLEY JONES

ABDIEL ab´dee-uhl [עַבְדִּיאֵל ʿavdhiʾel]. "Servant of God." Guri's son and Ahi's father (1 Chr 5:15) in the Gadite tribe's genealogy, mighty warriors whom God favored. See GAD, GADITES.

ABDON ab´duhn [עַבְדּוֹן ʿavdon]. 1. A minor judge, i.e., a tribal leader in pre-monarchical Israel, Judg 12:13-15, from Pirathon (Farʿata) on Mount Ephraim. His wealth was so extreme that he could provide donkeys for each of his 40 children and those 30 of his grandchildren who were of riding age. The donkey was a luxury item in ancient Israel's tribal society: it did not produce wool nor consumable (kosher) milk or meat, and was of no use in plowing.

2. A levitical city in the tribal territory of Asher, Josh 21:30, to be identified with Khirbet ʿAbda in the Plain of Acco. Throughout the Iron Age, the material culture of Acco and its plain was Phoenician.

ERNST AXEL KNAUF

ABEDNEGO uh-bed´ni-goh. See DANIEL, BOOK OF; FURNACE; SHADRACH, MESHACH, ABEDNEGO; SONG OF THE THREE JEWS.

ABEL ay´buhl [הֶבֶל hevel; Ἄβελ Abel]. The second son of Adam and Eve (Gen 4:2), Abel appears only as the brother slain by CAIN because God preferred Abel's offering to Cain's (Gen 4:1-16). Commentators connect the name Abel with the Hebrew noun hevel, meaning "vapor, breath" (e.g., Isa 57:13; Ps 144:4) which would denote Abel's ephemeral life, underscored by the absence of any mention of offspring. The brothers are introduced by their occupations: Abel was a shepherd, Cain a farmer, but the story is best understood as a primeval individual narrative rather than reflecting tribal strife or competition between occupations. God's preference for Abel's gifts is left unexplained. The emphasis is placed on Cain's distress, jealousy, and disregard for God's warning. The murder of Abel "in the field," far from an inhabited area where Abel could cry for help, highlights Cain's villainy and Abel's innocence. Abel's blood cries from the earth suggesting defilement of the soil (Num 35:33-34), so Cain is expelled from the land (Gen 4:10-11). According to *1 En.* 22:19-20 and 85:3-4, even after death Abel's spirit continues to complain about his own childless death and Cain. In *1 Enoch* Abel is already the prototype of the murdered innocent as he is in Matt 23:35 (Luke 11:51). In Heb 11:4 he is portrayed as the first man of faith, recognized as such by God's acceptance of his offering.

Bibliography: U. Cassuto. *A Commentary on the Book of Genesis, Part I* (1961); V. P. Hamilton. *The Book of Genesis Chapters 1–17* (1990); N. Sarna. *Genesis: The JPS Torah Commentary* (1989); C. Westermann. *Genesis 1–11* (1984).

DEVORAH DIMANT

ABEL-BETH-MA'ACAH　ay'buhl-beth-may'uh-kuk [אָבֵל בֵּית־מַעֲכָה 'avel beth ma'akhah]. Tell 'Abil al-Qamh is a prominent 35-acre mound, six mi. south of modern Metulla, identified with biblical 'Abel-Beth-Ma'acah on Israel's northern border, conquered by the Aramaean BEN-HADAD in the early 9th cent. BCE (1 Kgs 15:20), and in the late 8th cent. BCE by TIGLATH-PILESER III (2 Kgs 15:29). It is mentioned in the Egyptian "EXECRATION texts" of the 19th and 18th cent. BCE, on the lists of Thutmosis III, and in the Egyptian AMARNA LETTERS.

Bibliography: W. G. Dever. "'Abel-beth-Ma'acah: 'Northern Gateway of Ancient Israel.'" L. T. Geraty and L. G. Herr, eds. *The Archaeology of Jordan and Other Studies Presented to Siegfried H. Horn* (1986).

WILLIAM G. DEVER

ABEL-KERAMIM　ay'buhl-ker'uh-mim [אָבֵל כְּרָמִים 'avel keramim]. A town marking the limit of Jephtah's pursuit of the Ammonites (Judg 11:33). It could be identified with SAHAB SE of Amman. The name of "Abil" for a place in the vicinity of Sahab is still attested during the Islamic conquests. This boundary indicates that Jephtah beat the Ammonites from their northwestern border to their southeastern outposts. *See* AMMON, AMMONITES.

ERNST AXEL KNAUF

ABEL-MAIM　ay'buhl-may'im. *See* ABEL-BETH-MA'ACAH.

ABEL-MEHOLAH　ay'buhl-mi-hoh'luh [אָבֵל מְחוֹלָה 'avel mekholah]. An Iron Age town in the Jordan Valley,

south of BETH-SHEAN. According to its biblical spelling, the name means "meadow of dancing." Originally, however, it may have been written as 'avel maklah (pronounced Abel-mahlah), and thus it would have denoted a meadow that once belonged to the Manassite clan of Mahlah (Num 26:33). In any case, the name is one of several compound toponyms formed with 'avel. Others include Abel-mizraim, Abel-maim, Abel-keramim, Abel-shittim, and Abel-beth-maacah.

Abel-meholah was probably the hometown of ADRIEL son of Barzillai, "the Meholathite," who was married to MERAB, the older daughter of Saul (1 Sam 18:19). More notably, it was the hometown of ELISHA (1 Kgs 19:16, 19-20), where he likely lived with his parents and subsisted by farming.

Gideon and three hundred Israelite troops routed a Midianite army in the vicinity of the hill of Moreh, in the Jezreel Valley (Judg 7:1, 19-22), the Midianites fleeing "as far as the border of Abel-meholah."

The third biblical reference, 1 Kgs 4:7-19, presents a system of twelve officials and districts for providing food to the royal household of Solomon. Verse 12 lists it among the official and selected towns of the fifth district.

Various proposals for the location of Abel-meholah include sites on both sides of the Jordan River. The most likely candidate is Tell Abu Sus, on the west bank of the Jordan at the southern edge of the Beth-shean Valley, approximately 2 km below the confluence of the Jordan and the Wadi Yabis. Surface pottery at the site indicates occupation during the Early Bronze, Middle Bronze II, Late Bronze II, Iron I and II, Byzantine, and Arabic periods.

Bibliography: Z. Kallai. *Historical Geography of the Bible: The Tribal Territories of Israel* (1986).

STUART IRVINE

ABEL-MIZRAIM　ay'buhl-miz'ray-im [אָבֵל מִצְרַיִם 'avel mitsrayim]. "Meadow of Egypt." Alternate name for ATAD (Gen 50:11).

ABEL-SHITTIM　ay'buhl-shit'im [אָבֵל הַשִּׁטִּים 'avel hashittim]. *Meadow* or "brook of the acacias." Campsite on Moabite plains near Jordan River (Num 33:49). Later shortened to Shittim. *See* SHITTIM.

ABGARUS, EPISTLES OF CHRIST AND. An apocryphal exchange with the Edessan king in a narrative preserved independently in Eusebius' *Church History*, the *Doctrine of Addai*, and Greek papyri. Jesus responds to Abgar's request for healing that he will send a disciple after he has been taken up.

F. STANLEY JONES

ABHOR [בָּאַשׁ ba'ash, גָּעַל ga'al, קוּץ quts, שָׁקַץ shiqqets, תָּאַב ta'av, תָּעַב ta'av; βδελύσσομαι bdelyssomai]. These verbs have a wide variety of applications that range from sexual offenses (quts, Lev 20:23) to idolatrous practices and other cultic irregularities (ga'al, Lev 26:30; shiqqets // ta'av, Deut 7:26; ta'av, Ezek 16:25; 1 Kgs 21:26), from food prohibitions (shiqqets, Lev 11:11, 13, 43) to moral and ethical faults (ta'av, Pss 5:7; 119:163; Amos 5:10; Mic 3:9; ba'ash, Prov 13:15).

Underlying all these verbs is the notion of behavior or actions that are ethically or ritually abhorrent either to the deity or to human beings. The character and values of both people and God are revealed by what each "abhors." Alienated from God, Job is also alienated from friends who abhor (ta'av) him (Job 19:19; 30:16). In spite of all Yahweh has done, Israel abhors (ga'al) Yahweh's statutes (Lev 26:43) by running after other gods and sacrificing on their high places (Lev 26:30). Yahweh, however, will not abhor (ga'al) his people "so as to destroy them utterly" (Lev 26:44). According to Mic 3:9, the corrupt leadership of Israel abhors (ta'av) justice. Yahweh abhors (ta'av) the bloodthirsty and deceitful (Ps 5:7), but admonished Israel not to abhor (ta'av) the Edomites, their kin. Yahweh also told them not to abhor the Egyptians because the people of Israel were aliens residing in Egypt (Deut 23:7).

In Leviticus, the call to be holy "for I the Lord am holy" (20:26) requires separation from all that is abhorrent to the deity. This includes Canaanite practices such as worship of Molech, magic, and numerous sexual offenses. "Because they [the Canaanites] did all these things, I abhorred them" (quts, Lev 20:23). In addition, Israel is warned not to "bring abomination" on itself by eating unclean food (shiqqets, Lev 11:11, 13, 43; 20:25). Similarly, in Deut 7:26, practices associated with the nations are to be utterly detested (shiqqets) and abhorred (ta'av). These verbs establish the boundaries of the covenant community by excluding the practices of other nations. The nemesis of behavior that fails to respect such boundaries is the deity's anger, punishment, and exclusion. "I will abhor you" (ga'al, Lev 26:30). Conversely, following the deity's demands ensures God's continuing presence and favor. "I will place my dwelling in your midst, and I shall not abhor you" (ga'al, Lev 26:11). In the NT, Paul speaks of abhorring (bdelyssomai) idols in Rom 2:22.

BETH GLAZIER-MCDONALD

ABI ay'bi [אֲבִי 'avi]. "My father." Shortened form of ABIJAH (2 Kgs 18:2; compare 2 Chr 29:1).

ABI-ALBON ay'bi-al'buhn [אֲבִי־עַלְבוֹן 'avi 'alvon]. One of David's mighty warriors (2 Sam 23:31). Parallel text in 1 Chr 11:32 and the LXX translation of 2 Sam 23:31 have "ABIEL the Arbathite."

ABIASAPH uh-bi'uh-saf [אֲבִיאָסָף 'avi 'asaf]. Descendant of Levi and Korah who, with his household, left Egypt with Moses (Exod 6:24). In 1 Chr 9:19 and 26:1 modifications of the name as "Ebisaph" (אֶבְיָסָף 'eveyasaf), and "sons of Asaph"(בְּנֵי אָסָף bene 'asaf) refer to Abisaph's role as a gatekeeper in the temple.

ABIATHAR uh-bi'uh-thar [אֶבְיָתָר 'evyathar]. Perceiving David as a rival for the crown and suspecting that descendants of the priest ELI were supporting David's cause, Saul commanded that all the priests in Nob be slaughtered (1 Sam 22:6-19). Only one escaped, fleeing to David's camp and taking the EPHOD, a powerful reminder of the SHILOH shrine tradition, with him. The survivor was Abiathar, great-grandson of Eli. His presence as David's priest from earliest times was crucial in swinging popular support to David.

After David established the United Monarchy in Jerusalem, a second priest, ZADOK, emerged as Abiathar's partner. We know the many years of Abiathar's faithful service to David, but the narrator offers no scenes to contrast the characters of the two priests until the struggle for succession erupts, with David on his death-bed. ADONIJAH, supported by Abiathar and most of the old guard, is described negatively (1 Kgs 1:5-7). SOLOMON remains silent, and Zadok and the new guard support his candidacy (1 Kgs 1:7-10). Solomon eventually finds a reason to execute all of his rival's supporters except for Abiathar, whom he banishes to Anathoth, outside Jerusalem (1 Kgs 2:13-46).

The editors of Samuel and Kings intended to show how and why religious leadership of Israel would be stripped away from one priestly family and given to another. The physical and spiritual blindness of Eli, accompanied by the ritual and ethical sins of his sons, were finally requited by the banishment of Abiathar and the empowerment of Zadok in Jerusalem (1 Sam 1:13-14; 2:12-25, 27-36; 3:2-3; 1 Kgs 2:26-27).

Bibliography: Frank M. Cross. *Canaanite Myth and Hebrew Epic* (1973).

JAMES S. ACKERMAN

ABIB ay'bib [אָבִיב 'aviv]. First month in Hebrew calendar when Passover was celebrated (Exod 12:21-28; 13:3-10). After the Babylonian exile, it was renamed Nisan. *See* CALENDAR.

ABIB, TEL tel ay'bib [תֵּל אָבִיב tel 'aviv]. A place in Babylonia in the vicinity of the CHEBAR, where exiles from Judah lived (Ezek 3:15). A cuneiform tablet from Nippur mentions the river Chebar as naru kabaru, "Fat River." The people harvested barley when the ears became "full and fat" (*CAD* K 8:5 kabaru). Since the river Chebar means "full and fat (ears of barley)," the exiled Judahites might have called the nearby place tel 'aviv, which means, "mound of young ears of barley." However, the name tel 'aviv closely resembles the Akkadian expression til abubi "ruins made by the FLOOD" (*CAD* A 1:78). The Babylonians often referred to the flood when they saw a large area of the devastated ruins, saying kıma til abubi "like the ruin of the flood." However, if the Hebrew ʾaviv refers to the Akkadian word abbu "washout (caused by a flooded river)" (*CAD* A 1:47-48), til abbi may refer to a smaller washed-out area of the washed riverbank caused by a local flood.

YOSHITAKA KOBAYASHI

ABIDA uh-bi´duh [אֲבִידָע ʾavidhaʿ]. Grandson of KETURAH and ABRAHAM, Abida appears as the fourth of five sons of MIDIAN in the matching genealogical lists of Gen 25:4 and 1 Chr 1:33. The name literally means "(my) father knows." A traditional association with the Arabian tribe of Ibadidi is questionable.

ABIDAN uh-bi´duhn [אֲבִידָן ʾavidhan]. The name means "the (divine) father judges." During the census taken by Moses in the wilderness, Abidan son of GIDE-ONI represented the tribe of Benjamin (Num 1:11). Likewise, he led the Benjaminite troops encamped west of the tabernacle (Num 2:22; 10:24) and presented offerings on the ninth day of the dedication of the tabernacle altar (Num 7:60, 65). Some passages describe Abidan as a נָשִׂיא (nasiʾ, PRINCE).

SUSANNA W. SOUTHARD

ABIDE [לִין lin; μένω menō]. To *abide* is to stay, tarry, or dwell, to turn aside from a journey, to remain in a place, or to seek shelter. Metaphorically, *abide* refers to being in God's care: "Let me abide (lin) in your tent forever" (Ps 61:4). Abiding in God's tent requires that one honor the LORD and do what is right (Ps 15:1-5). A term sometimes translated *abide* is גּוּר gur, "sojourn," to be a guest or a stranger seeking shelter and protection (*see* SOJOURNER). Those who abide (gur) in the shadow of Shaddai take refuge and are delivered from pestilence and destruction (Ps 91:1). *Abiding* is an important concept for discipleship in the Johannine literature. The disciples who *abide* (menō) in Jesus abide also in God's love (1 John 4:13-16). Jesus is the vine, and the disciples *abide* in Jesus like branches that bear fruit (John 15:4-11). Bearing fruit adds an element of responsibility: in order to bear fruit, the disciples must love others (John 15:12-17; 1 John 4:16-21) and follow God's commandments (1 John 2:6; 3:24). *See* BRANCH; FRUIT OF THE SPIRIT; LOVE IN THE NT; VINE, VINEYARD.

MARIANNE BLICKENSTAFF

ABIEL ay´bee-uhl [אֲבִיאֵל ʾaviʾel]. 1. Abiel, a descendant of BENJAMIN and son of ZEROR, was the father of KISH and the grandfather of SAUL (1 Sam 9:1). In 1 Chr 8:29 and 9:35 his name appears as JEIEL. This lineage is confused by other passages where Abiel is the father of NER (1 Sam 14:51) and Ner is said to be father of Kish and father of Saul (1 Chr 8:33; 9:35-39). One

resolution is to correct 1 Sam 9:1 to read, "Abiel was the grandfather of Kish."

2. An Arbathite from BETH-ARABAH (Josh 15:6, 61), Abiel was a member of the "Thirty," a group of warriors who supported David (1 Chr 11:32). In a list of David's mighty men he is called ABIALBON (2 Sam 23:31).

CLAUDE F. MARIOTTINI

ABIEZER ay´bi̵ee´zuhr [אֲבִיעֶזֶר ʾaviʿezer]. Also known as IEZER (Num 26:30). The compound name means "Father is help." The OT refers to two individuals by the name Abiezer. 1. A descendant from MANASSEH, tentatively identified as the son of GIL-EAD, progeny of MACHIR, and probably corresponding to Iezer, one of Gilead's sons, from the Iezerites mentioned in Num 26:30. The Abiezerites were the family of GIDEON and assigned an inheritance west of the Jordan. Initially, the Abiezerites assisted Gideon, a judge and deliverer of Israel, in warfare with the Midianites. But they withdrew their support following tribal conflicts with the Ephraimites, who were excluded from the military campaign.

2. A Benjaminite warrior, a native of ANATHOTH, which was home to ABIATHAR the priest. His eventual descendant was the prophet JEREMIAH. Abiezer belonged to a select number of fighters loyal to the throne, bodyguards known as DAVID'S CHAMPIONS. According to 1 Chr 27:12, Abiezer served as an officer in charge of one of David's twelve monthly levies of 24,000 men in the ninth month. However, the historicity of the account remains in doubt, portraying David's military strength from an idealistic perspective.

SHERI L. KLOUDA

ABIGAIL ab´uh-gayl [אֲבִיגַיִל ʾavighayil, אֲבִגַיִל ʾavighayal]. Possibly meaning "my (divine) father rejoices." 1. Wife of NABAL the Carmelite who later marries DAVID; mother of David's son CHILEAB (2 Sam 3:3; Daniel in 1 Chr 3:1). Neither Abigail nor Chileab appear in the accounts of David's kingship after the period in Hebron. In 1 Sam 25 she appears wise, politically effective and prophetic. Abigail's "good understanding" (v. 3), judgment (v. 33*a*), speaking and hospitality contrast with the churlish Nabal (fool). These are all qualities reflected in the "woman of valor" in Prov 31:10-31. She acts quickly to placate David's anger at Nabal. Through her speech, Abigail aligns herself with David while diffusing tension and averting violence. In a prophetic proclamation that anticipates Nathan's oracle in 2 Sam 7:11, 16, Abigail assures David that Yahweh will make him a "sure house" (v. 28). After Yahweh strikes Nabal dead, David sends messengers to Abigail and she becomes his wife (1 Sam 25:42).

2. Sister or half-sister of David and Zeruiah, wife of Ithra the Israelite (2 Sam 17:25) or Jether the Ishmaelite (1 Chr 2:17). Absalom appointed her son Amasa

commander of the army in place of Joab. The MT of 2 Sam 17:25 says that she is the daughter of Nahash, but some Greek texts say she is the daughter of Jesse.

ELNA K. SOLVANG

ABIHAIL ab′uh-hayl [אֲבִיחַיִל, ʾavikhayil]. Meaning "the Father is might," Abihail is the name of several individuals in the OT. 1. Descended from MERARI, the youngest son of LEVI, Abihail is the father of ZURIEL mentioned in the third census list of Moses (Num 3:14-39).

2. Wife of ABISHUR from the house of JUDAH and descended from JERAHMEEL (1 Chr 2:29).

3. A Gadite mentioned in the genealogy of 1 Chr 5:11-17.

4. The wife of JERIMOTH, mother of MAHALATH, and daughter of ELIAB (2 Chr 11:18). The passage is ambiguous: some versions (KJV) suggest that Abihail and Mahalath were both King REHOBOAM's wives. Abihail's father, Eliab, and her husband, Jerimoth, were among David's sons, thus Mahalath married David's grandson Rehoboam, although among David's household intermarriage appears unusual.

5. Father of Queen ESTHER, the wife of King AHASUERUS; uncle of MORDECAI, the priest (Esth 2:15; 9:29).

SHERI L. KLOUDA

ABIHU uh-bi′hyoo [אֲבִיהוּא ʾavihuʾ]. The second of four sons of Elisheba and Aaron (Exod 6:23; Num 3:2; 26:60; 1 Chr 6:3; 24:1), appointed to priestly service (Exod 28:1). Abihu appears in hierarchy just below Moses and Aaron and with them ascended the mountain and "saw the God of Israel" (Exod 24:1, 9-11). Abihu and Nadab disgraced Aaron when they "offered strange fire before Yahweh which he had not commanded them" and were consumed by fire from Yahweh (Lev 10:1-7; compare Num 3:4; 26:61; 1 Chr 24:2).

Bibliography: B. D. Bibb. "Nadab and Abihu Attempt to Fill a Gap: Law and Narrative in Leviticus 10:1-7." *JSOT* 96 (2001) 83–99; W. Houston. "Tragedy in the Courts of the Lord: A Socio-Literary Reading of the Death of Nadab and Abihu." *JSOT* 90 (2000) 31–39.

WESLEY TOEWS

ABIHUD uh-bi′huhd [אֲבִיהוּד ʾavihudh]. The third son of BELA, the firstborn son of BENJAMIN (1 Chr 8:3). Some emend the text to read "GERA the father of EHUD (אֲבִי אֵחוּד ʾavi ʾekhudh)," which follows the genealogy of Judg 3:15 and connects to the list of Ehud's descendents (1 Chr 8:6a).

ABIJAH uh-bi′juh [אֲבִיָּה ʾaviyyah]. 1. A son of Becher and the grandson of BENJAMIN (1 Chr 7:8).

2. The daughter of MACHIR (1 Chr 2:21), she was the wife of HEZRON, a man from the tribe of Judah. After the death of Hezron in Caleb-ephrathah, Abijah gave birth to Ashhur, the father of Tekoa (1 Chr 2:24). The LXX offers a different reading in 1 Chr 2:24. Some translations, following the LXX, correct the text and eliminate Abijah as a proper name (compare RSV).

3. The second son of SAMUEL (1 Sam 8:2; 1 Chr 6:28 [Heb. 6:13]). When Samuel became old, he appointed his two sons, Abijah and his older brother Joel, to serve as judges in BEERSHEBA. However, Abijah and his brother took bribes and perverted justice. Their corrupt behavior created much discontent among the people and led the elders of the nation to demand a king to reign over Israel (1 Sam 8:4-5).

4. A descendant of AARON, he was one of the leaders of the 24 courses or divisions into which the priesthood was divided in the days of David (1 Chr 24:10; *see* PRIESTS AND LEVITES). The priestly divisions were formed from representatives of the houses of Eleazar and Ithamar, the sons of Aaron, and were selected to serve in the Temple by the casting of lots. Abijah was the leader of the eighth division. Zacharias, the father of John the Baptist, a priest belonging to the division of Abijah, was serving in the temple when an angel of the Lord appeared to him (Luke 1:5).

5. A son of JEROBOAM I, and probably the heir apparent of the first king of the Northern Kingdom. Abijah became gravely ill and since the illness threatened his life, Jeroboam sent his wife in disguise to the prophet AHIJAH of Shiloh with a present in order to consult the prophet concerning the healing of the child. Ahijah was the prophet who tore his garment into twelve pieces and gave Jeroboam ten pieces to symbolize God's decision to give him ten tribes after the division of the kingdom (1 Kgs 11:29-40). Despite Ahijah's blindness and because of a divine revelation, the prophet was told that a woman was coming to visit him and that she was the king's wife. When the king's wife arrived, Ahijah pronounced an oracle of doom against Jeroboam's house because of his religious reforms. Ahijah announced to her the end of Jeroboam's kingship and the complete extermination of his dynasty. The prophet also announced that Abijah would die and be the only one of all of the men of the house of Jeroboam to go to his grave in peace and be mourned in Israel. When Jeroboam's wife returned home, Abijah died as soon as she approached the threshold of her house in Tirzah. Abijah was buried with honors and all Israel mourned for him, just as Ahijah had prophesied (1 Kgs 14:1-18). The LXX presents a variant account of the visit of Jeroboam's wife to Ahijah. This variant story may represent a different tradition that was circulated in the Northern Kingdom.

6. The second king of Judah after the division of the kingdom. Abijah was the son of REHOBOAM, and grandson of Solomon (1 Chr 3:10). Abijah is portrayed differently in Kings and Chronicles. In Kings he is called

Abijam ("My Father is Yam"), a possible reference to Yam, the West Semitic god of the sea (1 Kgs 14:31; 15:1-8). The DEUTERONOMIC HISTORIAN also portrays Abijah as an evil king who did not follow in the ways of David and whose reign was allowed because of God's promise to David (1 Kgs 15:3-5). The Chronicler gives a positive representation of Abijah. According to the Chronicler, his victory against Jeroboam occurred because of his faithfulness to God (2 Chr 13:2-21).

Rehoboam appointed Abijah "chief prince among his brothers" and heir of his throne because of his love for his wife Maacah, even though Abijah was not his firstborn (2 Chr 11:18-22). The biblical text is not very clear about the identity of Abijah's mother. In 1 Kgs 15:2 the Deuteronomic Historian declares that his mother was MAACAH, the daughter of Abishalom (compare 2 Chr 11:20, 22), but in 2 Chr 13:2 the Chronicler says that his mother's name was MICHAIAH, the daughter of Uriel of Gibeah. Maacah and Michaiah are variations of the same name; and Abishalom is in all likelihood ABSOLOM, the son of David. Since the word *daughter* can also refer to a granddaughter or a great-granddaughter, it is possible, therefore, that Uriel of Gibeah married TAMAR, the beautiful daughter of Absalom (2 Sam 14:27), and by her had Maacah, who was thus the daughter of Uriel and granddaughter of Absalom. The reference to Abijah's wives and children indicates he had a large harem: he had fourteen wives, twenty-two sons, and sixteen daughters (2 Chr 13:21).

Abijah was appointed as the successor to the throne of Judah during the lifetime of his father Rehoboam. Rehoboam had many children from his wives and concubines. Thus, Abijah was named the successor in order to ensure a peaceful transition to the throne. Abijah became king in the eighteenth year of Jeroboam, king of Israel, and he reigned three years (2 Chr 12:16; 13:1, 2).

At the beginning of his reign, Abijah made an attempt at bringing the ten tribes that composed the Northern Kingdom under the control of Judah (2 Chr 13:3-19). The battle between Israel and Judah took place in Zemaraim, in the hill country of Ephraim. In the battle, the army of Jeroboam was twice the size of the army of Abijah (1 Chr 13:3). The large numbers of soldiers in the two armies represent the Chronicler's view that the victory in the battle belongs to the Lord.

Before the battle, Abijah made a lengthy speech to Jeroboam and the people of Israel in which he reminded the people that God had made a covenant with David, giving his family the right of ruling over the people of Israel forever, and that Jeroboam was king because he had rebelled against the house of his master. According to Abijah, Jeroboam's war against Judah was a war against "the kingdom of the Lord in the hand of the sons of David" (2 Chr 13:8). Abijah boldly announced victory because God was the one leading the army of Judah (1 Chr 13:12). While Abijah was speaking, Jeroboam attacked. Confronted by a superior army, the people of Judah cried to the Lord and God gave Abijah and his army an overwhelming victory over Jeroboam's army. Abijah defeated Jeroboam and took the cities of Bethel, Jeshanah, and Ephron and their villages. Because of his faithfulness to God, Abijah ended his days enjoying peace and prosperity and by having many children.

7. The wife of King AHAZ of Judah and the daughter of Zechariah, Abijah was the mother of King HEZEKIAH (2 Chr 29:1). Her name appears in 2 Kgs 18:2 as Abi, the abbreviated form of the name.

8. One of the twenty-one priests who affixed his signatures to the document made by Nehemiah in which the signatories pledged to keep the law (Neh 10:7 [Heb. 10:8]).

9. A priest who returned from the Babylonian exile with ZERUBBABEL and JESHUA the priest (Neh 12:4). Abijah was the father of Zichri, who was one of the heads of the ancestral house of Abijah in the days of JOIAKIM, the high priest at the time of Ezra (Neh 12:17).

CLAUDE F. MARIOTTINI

ABIJAM uh-bi'juhm [אֲבִיָּם 'aviyyam]. "Father of the sea." He was the son of Maacah and Rehoboam. He reigned over Judah 915–13 BCE while Jereboam ruled over the northern kingdom of Israel (1 Kgs 15:1, 7, 8). Called ABIJAH in parallel text at 2 Chr 13:1-22.

ABILA ["Αβιλα Abila]. Abila is one of the Greco-Roman cities joined together in a loose-knit confederation of cities known as the DECAPOLIS. Abila is not mentioned directly in the NT but the group occurs in the report that Jesus traveled through and ministered to people from the Decapolis (Matt 4:25; Mark 5:20; 7:31).

Todd Bolen/Bible Places
Figure 1: Abila Byzantine church on Umm el Amad

Abila has been identified with Tel Abil (Quailbah) in northern Jordan located about 10 mi. north-northeast of Irbid and about 3 mi. south of Wadi Yarmuk. Three lines of evidence support the conclusion that Quailbah is Abila of the Decapolis. First, the site corresponds well with the geographic evidence from the ancient authors Eusebius and Jerome who state that Abila is 12 mi. from Gadara (Eusebius, *Onom.* 32.16). Second, the modern Arabic name Tel Abil preserves the ancient name. Third, the "Abila Stone," a Greek inscription that mentions Abila, was discovered during excavations at the site in 1984.

Evidence that Abila was a part of the Decapolis come from two lines of evidence. First, Abila is listed in Ptolemy's 2nd cent. CE list of 18 Decapolis cities (*Geogr.* 5.14) even though it does not appear on Pliny's 1st cent. list *Natural History.* Second, an inscription dated to 133 or 134 CE from Tayibeh, near Palmyra, mentions an Agathangelos from Abila of the Decapolis (*CIG* 4501).

The word *Abila* comes from the Semitic word Abel (אָבֵל ʾavel). Abel means a place of a perennial stream. Abila has a perennial stream and a long occupational history, so it is reasonable to suggest it as the candidate of one of the biblical Abels. Abila could be the site of ABEL-MEHOLAH, the home of ELISHA (Judg 7:22; 1 Kgs 4:12; 19:16), or it could be ABEL-BETH-MA'ACAH (2 Sam 20:14-15; 1 Kgs 15:20; 2 Kgs 15:29).

The strategic location of Abila is demonstrated by Antiochus III's campaign against the city during the Hellenistic period (ca. 218 BCE). Polybius records that Antiochus III conquered the city along with Pella and Gadara (*see* GADARA, GADARENES).

Abila is famous for its large number of ancient tombs. Several painted Roman tombs are among the finest examples known in the Middle East.

Abila was occupied continuously from the Chalcolithic period until Ottoman times. The city flourished during the 2nd cent. CE through the Byzantine period and was home to at least five Byzantine churches, a Roman theater, a bath complex, numerous tombs in an extensive necropolis, and 3 underground water channels that lead from the spring, Ain Quailbah.

Bibliography: John Wineland. *Ancient Abila: An Archaeological History* (2001).

JOHN WINELAND

ABILENE ab'uh-lee'nee ['Αβιληνή Abilēnē]. A region in the Anti-Lebanon mountain range that derived its name from Abila (Souq Wadi Barada), its chief city, which was located NE of Mount Hermon, some 18 mi. to the NW of Damascus on the way to Heliopolis (Baalbek). This Abila is to be distinguished from other places with the same name, such as Abila of the Decapolis (Tell Abil) and Peraean Abila (Tell al-Kuffrein).

During the Hellenistic period this region became part of the area controlled by the Ituraeans when they succeeded in occupying the entire Beqa'a valley and the surrounding territory. The southward expansion of their realm from Lebanon into Galilee was checked by

the Hasmonean king, Aristobulus I, who defeated the Ituraeans in 104 BCE and annexed a portion of their land to Judea. From ca. 85 to 40 BCE, the Ituraeans were led by the brigand chieftain, Ptolemy, the son of Mennaeus, who retained control of most of his domain in ca. 64 by bribing the Roman general Pompey and later allied himself with the descendants of Aristobulus II (d. ca. 49), befriending his son Antigonus and marrying his daughter Alexandra. Ptolemy's son, Lysanias, also supported Antigonus, who rose to power in Judea on the strength of a Parthian invasion in 40 BCE. Cleopatra VII later used that Parthian connection to denounce Lysanias, who was executed in 37–36 BCE by Mark Antony. As part of a major land redistribution project, Antony gave Cleopatra a large part of Lysanias' vast domain, which she in turn leased to Zenodorus (probably a relative of Lysanias). Although he retained power following Actium (31 BCE), his realm was reduced in size when Augustus, unhappy with Zenodorus' reign, gave a large portion to Herod the Great, who had dealt with Ituraea in the 40s when he was governor of Coele-Syria. At Zenodorus' death in 20 BCE, Herod received most of what remained of the Ituraean's tetrarchy. Whether this included Abilene is debated, with some scholars arguing that it came under Herod's control and others contending that it remained an Ituraean principality. If Abilene was part of Herod's kingdom, it almost certainly reverted to the descendants of Lysanias after Herod's death, for in ca. 28 CE another Lysanias was ruling over Abilene as tetrarch (Luke 3:1), a reign that is confirmed by epigraphic evidence. At that point, however, the tetrarchy of Abilene could be distinguished from that of Ituraea (Luke 3:1). Abilene subsequently came under the control of Herod Agrippa I (37–44 CE), thanks to his friendship with Gaius and Claudius. Nine years after Agrippa's death, Claudius transferred control of this region to Herod Agrippa II, who retained it in his realm until his death in the 90s, after which it was annexed to the Roman province of Syria.

Bibliography: M. Sartre. *The Middle East under Rome* (2005); E. Schürer. *The History of the Jewish People.* Vol. 1 (1973–87) 561–73.

JOHN T. FITZGERALD

ABIMAEL uh-bim'ay-uhl [אֲבִימָאֵל ʾavimaʾel]. One of Joktan's thirteen sons, descendants of Noah's son Shem (Gen 10:21-31) and from whom Abraham descended (1 Chr 1:17-27).

ABIMELECH uh-bim'uh-lek [אֲבִימֶלֶךְ ʾavimelek]. Abimelech is identified as the King of Gerar in association with Abraham in Gen 20:1-19; 21:22-34 and with Isaac in Gen 26:1-11. In both cases, the "wife-sister" motif is employed, whereby the patriarch tries to save himself from some perceived threat by claiming his wife is his sister (also Abram in Egypt [Gen 12:10-20]).

Scholars ponder the reason for three such similar stories, and which is "original" or "earliest," and whether the same Abimelech appears in both stories or if the name is a title. Literary approaches consider how the stories differ because in Abraham's situation, the deity protects Abimelech from touching Sarah (Gen 18:5). This is especially important since the deity recently told the couple that Sarah would bear a child the following year (Gen 17:16; 18:10) and Abraham receives compensation from the king (Gen 20:14-16). Isaac's case differs as Rebekah already had borne children (Gen 25:24), and Isaac fears anyone in Gerar might take her (Gen 25:10). Abimelech negotiates water rights with both Patriarchs (Gen 21:22-34; 26:26-33).

The reference to Abimelech as king of the Philistines (Gen 26:1) appears anachronistic, because the Philistines presumably arrive in the area in the mid 12th cent. BCE. Solutions include: using this as proof the narrative is not historical; considering the reference is to an earlier wave of Philistines; or considering the reference as one later readers would have understood, which also explains why the area of Gerar is referred to as the land of the Philistines with Abraham (Gen 21:34).

Abimelech is the first to attempt kingship, beginning Israel's conflict over the idea and role of kingship. Abimelech was the son of Gideon/Jerubbaal, the previous judge (Judg 6:1–8:35). Gideon/Jerubbaal had seventy sons through numerous wives, and a Shechemite woman, usually translated as "concubine," bore a son who he named Abimelech, a common Syro-Palestinian name which means, "my father is king." The name, considered by some to be a throne name, lends irony to the story from a literary perspective.

Following his father's death, Abimelech proposes kingship to his mother's family in Shechem based on their bloodlines. The Shechemites accept and give him seventy shekels to hire worthless fellows who kill his brothers "on one stone" at his father's house, with the exception of the youngest who survives by hiding (Judg 9:4-5). After the Shechemites proclaim Abimelech king, Jotham, the surviving brother, returns to offer a prophetic fable condemning Abimelech's actions, promotion to kingship, and a critique of kingship (Judg 9:7-20).

The text states that Abimelech ruled over Israel for three years, though only Shechem pronounces him king. This implies that contrary to Gideon/Jerubbaal's statements, his sons ruled Israel. Despite his kingship in Shechem, Abimelech never appears in Shechem, so that after three years, when something happens between Abimelech and the citizens of Shechem, and ambushes were established against him, he was not in the city (Judg 9:22-25). Instead, Gaal, son of Ebed (translated as "loathsome son of a slave"), gains the confidence of the Shechemites, which ultimately leads to a battle between Abimelech and the city where Abimelech destroys the city of Shechem.

Abimelech then turns to destroy the city of Thebez (Judg 9:50). As he was about to destroy the fortified tower, a woman drops a millstone on his head. He asks his attendant to kill him so that they will not say that a woman killed him, ensuring that this story is later repeated precisely as an example of a woman killing a warrior (2 Sam 11:18-21).

The text does not portray Abimelech sympathetically; this is clear in the reference that Elohim returned to Abimelech the bad that he had done to his father (Judg 9:56). Reasons for his negative evaluation include: the deity did not call him, he tried to establish kingship, and he murdered his brothers. This sorry tale fits into the downward spiral of the book of Judges and ties in, ironically, with his father's story because Gideon/Jerubbaal was first introduced beating wheat in a winepress (Judg 6:11); the Midianite general he fights was killed at a winepress (Judg 7:25); and a wine festival marks the beginning of the end for Abimelech (Judg 7:25); Gideon/Jerubbaal fights because of his brothers' ("sons of his mother") death (Judg 8:19) while Abimelech gains kingship through his mother, and kills his brothers through his father; Gideon/Jerubbaal's oldest son is too timid to kill the captured foreign leader (Judg 8:20) and Jotham, Abimelech's youngest brother, is saved only because he hides, and, after delivering his fable, again flees (Judg 9:5-21). *See* GIDEON; JERUBBAAL; KING, KINGSHIP; PHILISTINES; SHECHEM, SHECHEMITES.

TAMMI SCHNEIDER

ABINADAB uh-bin'uh-dab [אֲבִינָדָב 'avinadhab] A personal name, meaning "My father is noble." 1. Father of Eleazar, Uzzah, and possibly Ahio (his brother). Men moved the ark from BETH-SHEMESH to the "house (palace/temple) of Abinadab on the hill" at Kiriath-jearim (1 Sam 7:1; 1 Chr 13:7) or Baale-Judah (2 Sam 6:3, 4).

2. Second son of David's father JESSE (1 Sam 16:8; 1 Chr 2:13). He and his brothers Eliah and Shamma were soldiers in Saul's camp opposing the Philistines (1 Sam 17:13).

3. Son of SAUL, third- or fourth-born son and sixth child born to AHINOAM (1 Sam 14:49-50; 1 Chr 8:33-39; 9:38-44). His name only appears together with Eshbaal in Chronicles.

J. GORDON HARRIS

ABINOAM uh-bin'oh-uhm [אֲבִינֹעַם 'avino'am]. "My Father is delight." Barak's father who lived in the city Kedesh in the region Naphtali (Judg 4:6, 12; 5:1, 12).

ABIR. *See* HABIRU, HAPIRU.

ABIRAM uh-bi'ruhm [אֲבִירָם, 'aviram; Ἀβειρών Abeirōn]. 1. A Reubenite involved with Korah's challenge of the exclusive priestly leadership of Moses and

Aaron (Num 16; also *see* Num 11–12). God settled the dispute by destroying the rebels, their families, and their possessions. The narrative reflects tensions between the priestly classes.

For contemporary readers, the story raises theological questions concerning God's punishment of the people for reasons that may seem insignificant. Abiram illustrates Israel's waywardness and the reasons to avoid God's wrath (Deut 11:6; Ps 106:17; Sir 45:18).

2. The son of Hiel of Bethel (1 Kgs 16:34), who rebuilt Jericho contrary to divine command; thereby costing his sons' lives (Josh 6:26). *See* AARONITE; DATHAN; KORAH; LEVITE.

LISA MICHELE WOLFE

ABIR YA'AQOB [אֲבִיר יַעֲקֹב 'avir ya'aqov]. A divine epithet, "the MIGHTY ONE of Jacob," among the northern tribes of Israel (Gen 49:24) and connected with the ark, originally the emblem of God in the north (Ps 132:2, 5). Apparently a designation of EL, the Canaanite high god, it may once have been understood to mean "the Bull of Jacob"—"bull" being a military designation for the DIVINE WARRIOR. A variant form, 'avir yisra'el, is attested in Isa 1:24, where it is associated with "LORD OF HOSTS," a designation of God originating from the northern central sanctuary at SHILOH, where the ark was located (1 Sam 4:3).

C. L. SEOW

ABISHAG ab'uh-shag [אֲבִישַׁג 'avishagh]. A young Shunnamite brought to serve David in his old age (1 Kgs 1:3) either as a nurse, concubine, or wife. The text states that David did not know her sexually, which emphasizes his weakened state. She stands in contradistinction to the vocal BATHSHEBA who inquires about SOLOMON's kingship (1:15) while Abishag watches. After David's death, his older son ADONIJAH requests to marry Abishag (2:17). Solomon interprets this request as a threat to his kingship and orders Adonijah's death (2:22-25).

HEATHER R. MCMURRAY

ABISHAI uh-bi'shi [אֲבִישַׁי 'avishay]. The *ay/ai* ending usually indicates a hypocoristic shortening of a longer-phrased name: perhaps "[Divine] Father (avi) is peace." If so, his formal name would be "Absalom." *See* NAMES. Son of David's sister Zeruiah, brother of Joab and Asahel (1 Chr 2:13-17). Whereas Joab was commander of David's army, Abishai was chief of its striking nucleus, renowned for his boldness and courage (2 Sam 21:15-17; 23:18-19).

More than any other character Abishai is depicted as David's alter ego, the consistent voice of his dark side, who advocates use of violence to advance David's honor and self-interest. At one point David refers to Abishai as his "satan/adversary/tester/tempter" (2 Sam 19:22). In each case, ironically, Abishai's intervention elicits a royal response that serves to highlight what is best about David (1 Sam 26:6-12; 2 Sam 16:9-14; 19:16-23). In David's last moments, however, we witness Abishai's voice in triumph as the king's dark side makes its final appearance (1 Kgs 2:5-9). Solomon will have no compunctions about carrying out the violence first urged by Abishai, and kingship in Israel will no longer be subject to David's usual self-restraint.

Bibliography: D. M. Gunn. *The Story of King David: Genre and Interpretation. JSOTSup* 6 (1982); R. Polzin. *David and the Deuteronomist: A Literary Study of the Deuteronomistic History* (1993).

JAMES S. ACKERMAN

ABISHALOM uh-bish'uh-luhm. *See* ABSALOM.

ABISHUA uh-bish'oo-uh [אֲבִישׁוּעַ 'avishu'a]. 1. A son of BELA, and grandson of BENJAMIN (1 Chr 8:4), although Abishua does not appear in Benjamin's genealogies in Gen 46:21 and Num 26:38-40 or among the sons of Bela in 1 Chr 7:7.

2. The son of PHINEHAS and great-grandson of AARON the priest. Abishua was the father of BUKKI. According to the genealogy of Aaron, Abishua served as the fourth High Priest of Israel (1 Chr 6:4-5 [Heb. 5:30-31], 50 [Heb. 6:35]). He was one of the ancestors of EZRA (Ezra 7:5).

CLAUDE F. MARIOTTINI

ABISHUR uh-bi'shuhr [אֲבִישׁוּר 'avishur]. A Judahite of the Hezron family, son of SHAMMAI and brother of Nadab. He, his wife ABIHAIL, and sons Ahban and Molid appear in the list of Jerahmeel's descendants (1 Chr 2:25-33).

ABITAL uh-bi'tuhl [אֲבִיטַל 'avital]. "My father is dew." One of David's wives, who bore his fifth son Shephatiah (2 Sam 3:4; 1 Chr 3:3).

ABITUB uh-bi'tuhb [אֲבִיטוּב 'avituv]. "My father is goodness." One of Shaharaim's two sons, by his wife Hushim, as mentioned in Benjamin's genealogy (1 Chr 8:11).

ABIUD uh-bi'uhd [Ἀβιούδ Abioud]. In Jesus' genealogy, Zerubbabel's son and Eliakim's father (Matt 1:13).

ABNER ab'nuhr [אַבְנֵר avner]. Abner's name ("father [is] Ner") identifies his paternal patronage. Traditionally Abner is a relative of Saul, either as a cousin or possibly an uncle (1 Sam 14:50). Consistent with the practice of placing members of the extended royal family in positions of authority, Abner plays a prominent role in both Saul and Ishbaal's reigns. Abner serves as Israel's army commander under Saul (14:51). He also appears as a functionary in the king's court, investigating the identity of the young lad who slew Goliath, and later introducing David before the king (1 Sam 17:55-57). Abner even enjoys an esteemed place at the king's table alongside David and the king's son, Jonathan (1 Sam 20:25). He also functions as the king's bodyguard (1 Sam 26:13-25). In this capacity however, he receives David's reprimand for failing to live up to his responsibilities (1 Sam 26:13-16). Following the death of Saul on Mount Gilboa, Abner plays an instrumental role in elevating Ishbaal as successor to the throne and establishing him at MAHANAIM (2 Sam 2:8-9), far removed from David's territory in Hebron.

During his service to Ishbaal, two crises develop, altering Abner's relationship to the king. First, a national struggle develops when Abner meets David's forces, led by Joab, in a battle at Gibeon (2 Sam 2:12-14). Both sides assign twelve men to fight in the battle. When all twenty-four die, precipitating a draw, new hostilities erupt; Joab and his brothers pursue Israel's commander, though Abner ultimately ends up killing Asahel, Joab's brother. This deed has fatal future consequences for Abner. Next, a domestic predicament develops, severing Abner's fidelity to Ishbaal. Against royal decorum, Abner goes in to Rizpah, a concubine of the royal house, for which he receives rebuke from Ishbaal (2 Sam 3:6). Only the king has a right to sexual relations with the royal concubines.

The potential political overtones of this action are confirmed in a parallel tradition. In 2 Sam 16:21-22, Absalom has relations with ten concubines of the royal household in conjunction with his attempted coup on David's kingship. Hence, Abner's actions may have been viewed as more than a breach in protocol. His failure to respect the limits of his prerogatives as the king's officer may also be interpreted as his ambition for the throne.

Consequent to Ishbaal's rebuke, Abner vows retaliation by pledging to promote David's kingship over all Israel and Judah. Abner's meeting and subsequent alliance with Judah's leader gains credibility when David appoints Jaasiel, Abner's son, as head over the house of Benjamin (1 Chr 27:21). Joab is unhappy and skeptical about the new kinship between Abner and David. He tries to convince David that Abner is on a reconnaissance mission on Ishabaal's behalf (2 Sam 3:24-25). Unable to convince David of Abner's spurious intentions, Joab takes matters into his own hands. He lures Abner out of the city to Hebron for a conversation. There, Joab slays Abner at the city gate (2 Sam 3:26-27).

Joab's motive for the murder of Abner appears two-fold. Tradition confirms that the death of Abner by Joab's sword finally avenges the death of his brother Asahel at Gibeon (2 Sam 3:27). David's new interest in Abner as commander of Saul and Ishbaal's armies, however, may have also been perceived as a threat to Joab's post. Hence, the end of Abner short-circuits any threat to Joab as leader of David's forces.

When David hears of Abner's death, he interprets it as an act of blood revenge for which he curses Joab and his whole house (2 Sam 3:38-39). Whether out of respect for Abner as blood relative of Saul, or for a matter of political expediency, David approves the burial of Abner at Hebron, accompanied by a display of public mourning (2 Sam 3:31-32).

Tradition documents a part of David's own lament over Abner (2 Sam 3:34). This display of grief by Judah's leader exonerates David of any blame for the death of this son of Israel. Moreover, the opportunity to honor Abner in death serves David's political agenda. The end of Abner signals the end of opposition to David's eventual kingship over Israel. When Ishbaal dies, his head is reported to have been entombed with Abner's remains (2 Sam 4). Hence, with the burials of both Abner and Ishbaal, the house of Saul's kingship is both figuratively and literally laid to rest.

GINA HENS-PIAZZA

ABODE OF THE DEAD. *See* DEAD, ABODE OF THE; SHEOL.

ABOMINATION [תּוֹעֵבָה toʿavah, שִׁקּוּץ shiqquts, שָׁקַץ shaqats, פִּגּוּל pigul; βδέλυγμα bdelugma]. Three terms in the OT can be translated "abomination." The most important of these is toʿavah, which occurs 117 times in the OT and refers to that which is repulsive to another person, usually Yahweh. The verb תָּעַב taʿav occurs 22 times, meaning "to abhor, loathe, or detest"; "to commit abominable deeds"; "to be loathed, detestable"; or "to be abhorred." The etymology of toʿavah has yet to be determined with certainty. The term probably derives from the root yʿv, related to ʿyv, "darken, contaminate, stain" (compare Lam 2:1), and may have its origins in Arabic.

The LXX usually translates toʿavah as bdelygma, with the sense of abhorrence and repugnance. Often, especially in the prophets, toʿavah is equated with ἀνομία anomia ("lawlessness") a purely ethical concept, and, although it is translated in Wisdom literature as bdelygma and sometimes even as ἀκάθαρτος akathartos or ἀκαθαρσία akatharsia ("impure"), the emphasis nevertheless remains ethical rather than cultic.

Toʿavah in the OT can refer to what is loathsome to either God or humans. For example, shepherds are an abomination to the Egyptians (Gen 46:34); the psalmist is an abomination to his former friends (Ps 88:8 [Heb. 88:9]); turning away from evil is loathsome to fools (Prov 13:19). The term is used primarily to denote that which is repugnant to God. Many instances deal with idolatry and pagan practices directly and are sometimes referred to collectively as "abominations of the nations" (Deut 18:9; 1 Kgs 14:31; 2 Kgs 16:3; 21:2; 2 Chr 33:2; 36:14). These repulsive pagan practices include worship of idols (Deut 7:25), human sacrifice (Deut 12:31; Ezek 16:22), cultic prostitution (1Kgs 14:23-24) and witchcraft (Deut 18:12). Sometimes to'avah is a synonym for the idol itself, e.g., the god Milcom is referred to as "the abomination of the Ammonites" (2 Kgs 23:13; compare Isa 44:19). Other cultic abominations deal with the incorrect worship of Yahweh, including defective sacrifices (Deut 17:1) and invalid offerers (Deut 23:19). Forbidden meats are called abominations, and by observance of dietary restrictions Israel is kept necessarily separate from her pagan neighbors (Deut 14:2-8; *see* CLEAN AND UNCLEAN).

Various unethical attitudes and behavior are repugnant to God as well because they are incompatible with his character and values. Several of these are categorized as to'avah, including false weights (Deut 25:13-16), prayer from the wicked (Prov 28:9), transvestism (Deut 22:5), and remarriage with a divorcee (Deut 24:4). Proverbs lists seven abominations, including pride, lying, murder, evil plots, false testimony, and strife (Prov 6:16-19). Leviticus orders Israel not to engage in any of a number of abominable sexual relations and warns that the former inhabitants of the land were expelled on account of these sins (Lev 18:26-30; compare Ezek 22:11).

Certain acts are reprehensible to the deity and labeled "abomination" also in Egyptian wisdom literature, where false weights are an abomination of the god Ra (Wisdom of Amenemope 18:15-19:3). Also, a Phoenician inscription warns potential grave robbers not to open a sarcophagus, since that would be "an abomination to Astarte" (KAI 13.6).

Sheqets and shiqquts, too, can be translated "abomination." Sheqets denotes certain forbidden foods (compare Lev 11:10-19); shiqquts refers specifically to illicit cult objects. Daniel's "abomination causing desolation" is in this latter category (Dan 11:31; 12:31; compare Matt 24:15; Mark 13:14; *see* ANTIOCHUS, ABOMINATION OF DESOLATION). The verbal root shqts, on the other hand, is a general term and functions as a synonym of t'v.

Another term for "abomination," pigul, has a technical usage and denotes sacrificial flesh that is not eaten in the prescribed time. For example, the thank offering is restricted in that offerers have only one day to eat its meat, forcing them to include family and friends in the feast (Lev 7:18). If food remains, it is labelled pigul and must be destroyed.

When the NT writers use the term bdelygma, it usually refers to evil and evildoers (compare the lists of various types of sinners in Tit 1:16; Rev 21:8). The word emphasizes the repugnance that God, unlike human beings, feels toward evil (compare Luke 16:15). The description of the "great whore" Babylon in Revelation links abomination with sexual sins (Rev 17:1-5; compare Lev 18).

HANNAH K. HARRINGTON

ABOMINATION OF DESOLATION [שִׁקּוּצִים מְשֹׁמֵם shiqqutsim meshomem; βδέλυγμα ἐρημώσεως bdelygma erēmōseōs]. This phrase, with variations, is derived from Dan 9:27; 11:31; and 12:11; with a parallel in 8:13. In Dan 9:27, the term *abomination* (shiqqutsim) is plural. Elsewhere in Daniel *abomination* is singular (שִׁקּוּץ shiqquts). The phrase in Greek appears in 1 Macc 1:54 (bdelygma erēmōseōs parallel to LXX of Dan 11:31), and again in Matt 24:15, and Mark 13:14 (τὸ βδέλυγμα τῆς ἐρημώσεως to bdelygma tēs erēmōseōs), parallel to LXX of Dan 12:11.

In the OT the concept of abomination is linked to four Hebrew words: תּוֹעֵבָה to'evah, "something abominable, detestable"; פִּגּוּל pigul, sacrificial meat more than three days old, of which eating was forbidden; shiqquts, "something abominable"; and שָׁקַץ shaqats, "to detest" (*see* ABOMINATION). These words refer to God's revulsion toward practices counter to his expressed will. The two ideas most commonly associated with abomination are uncleanness (particularly in Lev 11) and idolatry, with shiqquts and shaqats especially linked to idolatry. The NT's use of bdelygma ties it to idolatry and uncleanness.

The meaning of the term *desolation* (שָׁמֵם shamem) suggests two ideas: being deserted or desolate, and the resulting psychological state of a people horrified at the outcome. The Greek noun ἐρήμωσις erēmōsis is a rare word meaning "devastation, destruction, desolation" and is related to the more common adjective ἔρημος erēmos, "abandoned, empty, desolate."

The combination of the words into the phrase "abomination of desolation" established a new semantic field of meaning. The participle of "to desolate" in Hebrew can serve as a verb, a noun, or an adjective. Some scholars opt for a nominal usage ("desolater"), others for the adjectival usage ("desolating"). The LXX phrase uses the genitival form and suggests the adjectival usage, "the desolating abomination." However, Dan 9:27 is more problematic. The Hebrew words do not form a phrase, and in Greek bdelygma is singular, linked to the plural of erēmōsis. The NASB translates the phrase nominally with "on the wing of abominations will come one who makes desolate." The NRSV translates it more adjectively, "on a wing of the temple he will set up an abomination that causes desolation."

A. OT Interpretation

The majority of scholars believe that the abomination of desolation refers to the destructive work of the Seleucid king, ANTIOCHUS IV EPIPHANES. According to some ancient Jewish sources, in 167 BCE Antiochus sought to destroy the practice of Judaism. He outlawed circumcision and the observance of the Sabbath. He forced idolatrous practices on the people and desecrated the Temple in Jerusalem by placing an altar to Zeus on the altar of burnt offering. First Maccabees labels the last action the "abomination of desolation" (1 Macc

1:54; Josephus, *Ant.* 12.248-264). Swine, which are unclean according to Levitical law, were offered as sacrifices on this pagan altar (2 Macc 6:1-5). Some scholars maintain that the phrase shiqqutsim meshomem is a contemptuous deformation of the name of the Phoenecian god בַּעַל שָׁמֵם ba'al shamem.

The sacrilege was reversed by the amazing triumph of Jewish forces under the leadership of Judas Maccabeus and the rededication of the Temple in 164 BCE, exactly three years to the day (25 Kislev) from the time of the desecration (1 Macc 4; Josephus, *Ant* 12.316-322). Josephus connects the desecration of the Temple with the desolation of the sanctuary prophesied by Daniel 408 years before (*Ant* 12.316-322).

Some scholars maintain that Dan 11:1-39 gives a rather clear delineation of the history of the Seleucid and Ptolemaic dynasties as *vaticinium ex eventu*. In the verses following, the author tries but fails to predict the future. If this position is taken, then the "little horn powers" of Dan 7 and 8 and the "desolater" of Dan 9 are all depictions of Antiochus IV. Critics of this position note that none of the numerical figures in Daniel (Dan 7:25; 8:14; 9:24-27; 12:11-12) fits exactly with the desecrating work of Antiochus IV or the chronology of the Seleucid empire, nor do all the historical details of Dan 8 seem to match Antiochus.

A variety of alternative interpretations have been suggested. Many of the Protestant Reformers identified the little horns of Dan 7 and 8 as a reference to the Papacy. Some scholars see Dan 9:24-27 fulfilled in the ministry of Jesus Christ, with the abomination of desolation occurring at the time of the Roman destruction of Jerusalem under Titus in 70 CE. Others link the prophecy of the desolator to an eschatological coming of the antichrist.

B. NT Usage

In the NT the phrase to bdelygma tēs erēmōseōs appears only in Matt 24:15 and Mark 13:14 (*see* ESCHATOLOGY OF THE NT). However, the concept of abomination and linkages to Dan 7–8 are also found in Luke 21; 2 Thess 2; and in Rev 12–13; 17; 21.

Two things are strikingly clear in Jesus' eschatological discourse. He describes the abomination of desolation in the future and makes no mention of any fulfillment in the past. The abomination is the sign for the Christian disciples in Judea to flee to the mountains (Matt 24:16; Mark 13:14). The abomination is said to stand where it should not, implying the desecration of a holy place.

Some scholars suggest that this abomination of desolation is the setting up of Roman standards for pagan worship within the Temple precincts at the fall of Jerusalem in 70 CE (but this would seem to be too late for the flight of the disciples). Others note the Zealots' atrocities during the siege of Jerusalem (though this seems difficult to harmonize with the concept of "standing"). Other suggestions include a statue of Titus set up on the side of the desolated Temple (disputed historically), statues or standards erected by Pilate and Hadrian (too early or late), or Caligula's command for his statue to be placed in the Temple (never fulfilled). An end-time fulfillment in the coming of the antichrist is also suggested, linked to 2 Thess 2 and Rev 12–13; 17.

Commentators note that the inexact correspondence between the eschatological discourse and the events of the revolt of 66–70 CE militates against the claims of some that the discourse is a remembrance of events rather than prophecy of future events. The discourse is also found in Luke but without the phrase "abomination of desolation." Instead, the evangelist speaks of Jerusalem being surrounded by armies prior to its desolation (erēmōsis, Luke 21:20). Perhaps this is the earliest interpretation of the Markan phrase "abomination of desolation" and deserves primacy of consideration for explaining how the sign was fulfilled.

Jesus' words concerning the abomination of desolation are often seen as a reapplication of the text of Daniel. While the writings of Josephus suggest such reapplication (*Ant* 10.263-281), Matthew and Mark give no suggestion of a dual application. In the absence of such evidence it seems preferable to see Jesus' words as oriented only toward the future.

Bibliography: John J. Collins. *Daniel* (1993); Desmond Ford. *The Abomination of Desolation in Biblical Eschatology* (1979); Robert Gundry. *Mark: A Commentary on His Apology for the Cross* (1993); Johan Lust. "Cult and Sacrifice in Daniel: The Tamid and the Abomination of Desolation." *The Book of Daniel: Composition and Reception.* Vol. 2 (2001); J. Barton Payne. "The Goal of Daniel's Seventy Weeks." *JETS* 21 (1978) 97–115; Paul Redditt. "Calculating the 'Times': Daniel 12:5-13." *Perspectives in Religious Studies* 25 (1998) 373–79; Paul Redditt. "Daniel 9: Its Structure and Meaning." *CBQ* 62 (2000) 236–49; Steven Weitzman. "Plotting Antiochus's Persecution." *JBL* 123(2004) 219–34.

TOM SHEPHERD

ABORTION. The Bible contains no direct references to abortion. Infanticide was the preferred method of birth limitation in the ancient world, because it allowed for sex selection and was not dangerous to maternal life and health. Other available methods of abortion were life threatening to the mother. Infanticide is denounced in Jer 7:30-34. The OT tends toward pronatalism, when presenting infertility as a tragedy for women, as well as for families and tribes (Hos 9:14; Ps 127:3). Yet Exod 21:22-25 requires only monetary damages for causing a woman to miscarry, but life for life and eye for eye when further harm falls to the woman. The legal material in Exodus became the scriptural basis of Jewish teaching that personhood begins when the fetus emerges from the mother's womb. Jeremiah and the psalmist imply identification between the fetus and the later person: "Before I formed you in the womb I knew you, and before you were born I consecrated you" (Jer 1:5; also Ps 139:13-16). Some abortion opponents elevate these verses over Exod 21, and further understand fetuses as among the weak and needy whom, as God commands, should be protected (e.g., Ps 82:3-4). *See* ONAN.

CHRISTINE E. GUDORF

ABOT. *See* SAYINGS OF THE FATHERS.

ABRAHAM, APOCALYPSE OF. The document is an APOCRYPHAL and APOCALYPTIC book about ABRAHAM's conversion from idolatry to the one true God and his temporary heavenly journey. It was probably composed in Palestine between 70 and 100–150 CE by a Jewish author. It is contemporary with the *Fourth Book of Ezra*, the Second or *Syriac Apocalypse of Baruch*, and the book of Revelation. It is one of the earliest examples of Jewish *merkavah* mysticism, the mystical interpretations of the heavenly chariot in Ezek 1–2, which became prominent in the later Hekhalot literature of talmudic times. Despite its Jewish origin, its reception history has mainly been in Orthodox Christianity. The book is important for the fields of biblical studies, NT, early Judaism, and especially for the study of apocalypticism and tradition history.

The Apocalypse has been handed down in six complete surviving Old Church Slavonic (or Old Bulgarian) manuscripts made in Russia after 1300 CE as well as several other fragmentary versions. Its original language may have been Hebrew or Aramaic or Greek with Hebraisms. There are very few indications in the book that point to a historical context or relevance (*see*, however, 28:3 and 29:2). The apocalyptic character is unmistakable (pseudepigraphy, visions, revelations, eschatology, and a heavenly journey). The theology is directed against paganism and highlights the importance of monotheism.

The provenance is closest to Pharasaic-Rabbinic circles, as there is little affinity with the thought and practice of other Jewish religious groups of the period. In general, it has to be assumed that the Apocalypse was written as a reaction or answer to the tumultuous social and religious times after the destruction of the Second Temple in 70 CE and the ultimate pagan dominance of Jerusalem and Israel. The author clearly wanted to warn his audience not to be influenced by the idolatry spread by the Roman army, but to stay within the boundaries of Jewish monotheism.

The book contains 31 chs. with a Haggadah on Abraham's conversion from his father Terah's idolatry to his belief in the one true God (chs. 1–8), and a midrash on Gen 15:9-11 (in chs. 9–31), which begins with a description of Abraham's ascent into heaven (10–16).

During his journey, Abraham receives seven visions, dealing with the throne of God (17–18), the stars of heaven (19–20), the creation (21–22), Adam and Eve (23–24), the idol (25–26), the heathens (27–28), and the last day (29–31).

Before the last day comes, a battle will take place, in which the heathens will kill many, set the temple on fire, and plunder the holy vessels. However, in the same way that his father Terah's idol was consumed by fire, at the end of days also they will be destroyed by fire. Judgment and the punishment of the earth will follow (29) with a number of "plagues" modeled after the 10 plagues in Exod 7–10 (30). Then the righteous will live and rule as kings and judges. After the vision, Abraham returns to earth and is called "God's Chosen One" (31).

There is no Messiah figure in the Apocalypse, although the expected life of the righteous as kings and judges does disclose some of the future expectations of the author, namely that there will be a time of righteousness after a period of idolatry and war. This future hope could very well fit in a situation after the destruction of the Second Temple and a time of great distress and uncertainty in the decades to come, during which the people hoped for what was lacking most: a time of righteousness, as exemplified by "our father Abraham."

In all of this, the life of Abraham functions namely as the sole example and role model of the importance of turning away from idolatry, of the belief in the one true God and of righteousness as the theological center of a new social code still to be developed. This message, then, is all dressed in the attire of the images and popular beliefs of those days, namely in visions, revelations, and heavenly journeys.

Bibliography: R. Rubienkiewicz. "The Apocalypse of Abraham." *The Old Testament Pseudepigrapha.* J. H. Charlesworth, ed. Vol. 1 (1983) 681–705.

GERBERN S. OEGEMA

ABRAHAM, CHILDREN OF. Designation given to the children of Israel, who are, by extension, children of his grandfather, Abraham, the father of the nation. But, through Ishmael, Arabs are also children of Abraham. In a spiritual sense, Jews, Muslims, and Christians are all his children (Gal 3:6-9).

In the context of the covenant, the change of the name from Abram to Abraham is supposed to connote that he will be "father of a multitude," but the name should then be *ab-hamon* instead of *ab-raham*, which philologically is only an expansion of *ab-ram*, meaning "(my) father (is) exalted."

In keeping with the concerns of the Gospel of Matthew, Jesus' genealogy starts with Abraham. Jesus rebukes Abraham's children for not behaving like such (Matt 3:9; Luke 3:8; John 8:33-47). Remarkably, Jesus applied the designation to a woman. He called the bent woman he healed on the Sabbath "daughter of Abraham" (Luke 13:16).

CRISTINA CONTI

ABRAHAM, NT AND EARLY JUDAISM ay'bruh-ham אַבְרָהָם 'avraham, אַבְרָם 'avram; Ἀβρααμ Abraam, Ἀβραμ Abram].

A. Abraham in Early Judaism

For the ancient Jewish sources Abraham is the celebrated ancestor of the Jews (*Pss. Sol.* 9:17; *3 Macc* 6:3; 4Q176 1-2i10; *m. Gitttin* 89a). Even in quotations of non-Jewish decrees he is called the father of the Jews (Josephus, *Ant.* 12.226; 14.255). Throughout early Jewish literature the fundamental importance of the Abraham narrative lies in God's covenant with Abraham (*Jub.* 12:22-24; 14:17-20; 15:3-16; *4 Ezra* 3:13-15; *2 Bar.* 57:1. 4Q378 22i4; 4Q393 3, 7; Sir 44:19-21). God has chosen Abraham and his seed as his own (*Pss. Sol.* 9:15-19; *T. Levi* 15:4). Abraham is regarded as the "friend of God" (Isa 41:8; 2 Chr 20:7; *Jub.* 19:9; Philo, *Sobr* 55-56). The importance of Abraham is sometimes extended from the Jews to the whole world: God has promised that Abraham will be a father and blessing of the nations (Sir 44:19-21; *Jub.* 24:11).

The biblical account can be expanded. Abraham is described as refusing to participate in constructing the tower of Babel (*L.A.B.* 6:3). As an experienced astronomer he is the first to oppose idolatry and to venerate the one God whose wisdom and power are evident in the order of the heavens (*Jub.* 12:1-21; 21:3-5; Philo, *Drunkenness* 94; *Migration* 176–197; *Heir* 275–283; *Dreams* 1:52-54; Josephus, *Ant.* 1.155–57; *Apoc. Ab.* 1–8). As such he is the first proselyte (*b. Tanhuma* 32a). Abraham is raised above the heavens (*L.A.B.* 18:5). Apocalyptic expectations are also linked with the figure of Abraham: Abraham receives knowledge about the end of times (*4 Ezra* 3:13-15). After death he becomes immortal and like the angels (Philo. *Sacrifices* 5). Abraham welcomes the faithful martyr (*4 Macc.* 13:18). His grave in Hebron is venerated (Josephus, *J.W.* 4.531).

The figure of Abraham is presented as a model for imitation in two ways, one emphasizes his faith and the other his steadfastness in trials. On the basis of the passage Gen 15:6, Philo emphasizes Abraham's faith in God as the basis of his righteousness. Abraham is the ideal of the man who trusts in God (*Alleg. Interp.* 3.228; *Migration* 44; *Heir* 8-9, 90-95; *Names* 177–186). The sacrifice of Isaac is treated as a thank-offering for the blessing already received (*Unchangeable* 4; *Dreams* 1.194-95). This view is not shared by other Jews. Particularly since the Maccabean revolt, the mere descent from Abraham is not regarded as sufficient (*4 Macc.* 14:20; 16:15-23; 18:1-2, 20-23). Abraham's merits are highlighted. He obeys God's will (*Jub.* 18:15-16;

CD III, 2-3). Abraham's righteousness is also seen in his trust in God, which proves itself in his trials and miracles (*Jub.* 11:18-22; 19:8; *m. Avot* 5:3). Abraham's willingness to sacrifice his son demonstrates his piety (1 Macc 2:50-52; Josephus, *Ant.* 1.222-36, compare 7.333). Abraham proved worthy of God's blessing, and with his blessing Jews have inherited his obligation (*m. Avot* 5:19). Thus, one can forfeit Abraham's blessing through wrong behavior (*m. Avot* 3:11; CD III, 3-20).

Abraham is regarded as righteous and just, even without sin (*Jub.* 23:10; *Pr. Man.* 8). His observance of the divine law is perfect (*Jub.* 23:10; Sir 44:19-20; Jdt 8:26; 1 Macc 2:52; *Jub.* 6:19; 15:1-2; *4 Macc.* 16:20; *2 Bar.* 57:1. Philo, *Migration* 130-31), even though the Torah had not yet been written (*Jub.* 16:28; *2 Bar.* 57:2). For Philo, Abraham is an "unwritten law" (*Abraham*, 275–76). In the Dead Sea Scrolls, Abraham's circumcision is seen as indicating observance of the whole torah (CD XVI, 6). God himself taught Abraham to sacrifice (4Q158 4-6), and the observance of the purity laws is also associated with the "covenant of Abraham" (CD XII, 11).

In Hellenistic Judaism Abraham is a model, even of the Greek virtues (Wis 10:5-6; *4 Macc.* 16:20; *Sib. Or.* 3:218. Philo, *Abraham* 13; *Cherubim* 40; *Worse* 59; *Posterity* 62, 75-76; *Sobr.* 17; *Migration* 125; *Prelim. Studies* 23, 35; Josephus, *Ant.* 1.148-256, esp. 256; *J.W.* 5.380). The Jewish people inherit Abraham's virtues along with his promise (Philo, *Sacrifices* 43 on Gen 25:5; Josephus, *Ant.* 1.289, 346; 2.229, 318; 3.87; 4.4; 5.97, 113; 8.155; 11.169). In Philo's allegorical writings, Abraham is the wise man who learns by teaching, not by nature or by practice (*Cherubim* 7, 10, 45; *Unchangeable* 4; *Dreams* 1.160, 166-70; *Moses* 1.76). Abraham can never be wrong. Thus his laughter at the promise of Isaac's birth (Gen 17:15f.) must be the joy of the wise man (*Alleg. Interp.* 3.217-19; *Cherubim* 106; *Worse* 124; *Names* 154–166).

These texts demonstrate that in postexilic Judaism Abraham is remembered as father of the Jews. He is a model of faith and an example of good behavior. God's blessing and the covenant with Abraham are the foundation of Jewish identity.

B. Abraham in the NT

Next to Moses Abraham is the most frequently named figure from the OT. As in other early Jewish texts, Abraham is the ancestor of the Jews (Matt 1:1-2; Luke 13:16; 16:24ff.; 19:9; Acts 13:26; Rom 4:1; 11:1). New Testament writings acknowledge Abraham's centrality in salvation history: Abraham receives the covenant and the promise of God's support for his descendants (Luke 1:55, 73; Acts 3:25; 7:2, 17). God is frequently called the God of Abraham and Isaac and Jacob, particularly when God's abiding presence with his people is expressed (Matt 22:32; Mark 12:26 par.; Luke 16:22 ff.; 20:38; Acts 3:13; 7:32). Abraham is not simply important as a past example. He is the symbol of future blessing for his true descendants (Matt 8:11; Luke 13:28; 16:19-31; Heb 2:16; 6:13). This blessing is seen as fulfilled in Abraham's descendant Jesus (Matt 1:1–2:17; Luke 3:34; Gal 3:16). The epistle to the Hebrews interprets Abraham's tithe offering to MELCHIZEDEK (Gen 14) as proof that the priesthood of Melchizedek—symbolizing Christ—is superior to the priesthood of the Levites (Heb 7:1-10).

Key NT texts refer to Abraham in arguments concerning the meaning of God's promise to Abraham and the role of the Jews and of the Torah's observance for Christians. As in many Jewish writings of the time, Abraham's children are not identified with everyone of Jewish ancestry. John the Baptist preaches that any child of Abraham must show honest repentance (Matt 3:9; Luke 3:8). Similarly, biological descent from Abraham is no reason for a superior position in the Christian community (2 Cor 11:22).

Paul opposes Jewish Christians who link being the seed of Abraham to the observance of the Torah (Rom 4, 2). Paul still regards Abraham's blessing as permanent for the Jews and expects all Israel to be ultimately saved (Rom 9–11; Gal 3:14). Ethnic descent and Torah observance, however, no longer define the seed of Abraham, only the spirit and faith in Christ (Rom 4:9; 9:7; Gal 3:7-9, 22, 29). The way is open for believing Gentiles, because Abraham, the first proselyte, believed in God and trusted God's promise before he was circumcised (Rom 4:2, 12-25; Gal 3:6–8, 18). Similarly, Hebrews praises Abraham for the faith, which led him to obey God's call, to leave his home and to trust in God's promise of numerous descendants (Heb 11:8-12).

This interpretation of Abraham's faith as the basis for God's blessing did not remain undisputed, even among Christians. The epistle of James, in the only NT reference to the binding of Isaac, insists that Abraham received the blessing because of his works, his obedience, which made a "friend of God" (Jas 2:21-24).

The dispute over who is the true descendant of Abraham is approached in the most polemical way in John's Gospel. The Johannine Jesus concedes that the Jews are the "seed of Abraham" (John 8:37) but denies that they are "children of Abraham" (John 8:39-40), because they reject Jesus, who is more than Abraham (John 8:52-59). By contrast, Abraham obeyed God and received the blessing (John 8:39f.). Abraham's reward and his joy was to see the day of Jesus (John 8:56). Abraham's joy here is an allusion to his laughter at the promise of God's blessing in Gen 17:17.

Thus, in the NT, as in early Judaism, it is God's blessing of Abraham that is the source of salvation. Not all the physical descendants of Abraham, however, receive this blessing, as the blessing is not exclusively related to physical descent, but to trust in God. In early Judaism this idea leads to the conclusion that some Jews are not regarded as children of Abraham. The main interest of the Christian texts is not to exclude anyone but to

include gentiles in the Jewish blessing and covenant. The interpretation of the figure of Abraham is the focal point of the emerging Christian self-definition in its relationship with and departure from other early Jewish interpretations. *See* DEAD SEA SCROLLS; JOSEPHUS, FLAVIUS; PHILO OF ALEXANDRIA; QUMRAN.

Bibliography: William Baird. "Abraham in the NT: Tradition and the New Identity." *Int* 42 (1988) 367–79; G. Walter Hansen. *Abraham in Galatians: Epistolary and Rhetorical Contexts* (1989); Jeffrey S. Siker. *Disinheriting the Jews: Abraham in Early Christian Controversy* (1991).

JUTTA LEONHARDT-BALZER

ABRAHAM, OT ay´bruh-ham [אַבְרָהָם ʾavraham, אַבְרָם ʾavram]. Abraham, the "first" of the Genesis patriarchs, is the progenitor of three major religious traditions (Judaism, Christianity, and Islam). As such, he has lived up to the meaning of his name ("the father of a multitude," according to Gen 17:5). His earlier name, Abram (probably "exalted father"), is used exclusively in Gen 11:26–17:5 (Neh 9:7). He is given his new identity in view of a divinely recharacterized covenant relationship (Gen 17:1-8).

The primary texts that portray the story of Abraham are recorded in Gen 11:26–25:11. They depict various episodes in the patriarch's life, from his birth (11:26) to his death and burial (25:7-10). These texts often mirror each other (e.g., the endangering of Sarah in 12:10-20 and 20:1-18; the covenant in 15:7-21 and 17:1-8), providing the reader with differing perspectives on Abraham and his family as well as the development of God's purposes in and through them. His calling by God is presented in 12:1-3 as having a particular relationship to the content of Gen 1–11, namely, "all the families of the earth" (*see* "families" in 10:5, 20, 31-32). God's call of Abraham may be described as a divine strategy in the service of a universal purpose, namely, the salvation of all the earth that had fallen under the sway of human sin and its disastrous effects. Abraham is an initially exclusive divine choice or election for the sake of a maximally inclusive end.

Little is known of Abraham prior to his call. Genealogical references establish Abraham's lineage as a descendant of Shem, and more specifically, Eber (or the Hebrews; Gen 11:10-26). Subsequent texts are concerned to show that he is ethnically related to various Arabian (25:1-6, 12-18) and Aramean (22:20-24) groups, "the children of Lot" (Moabites and Ammonites, 19:30-38), as well as the descendants of his son Isaac (Jacob, the progenitor of the twelve tribes of Israel, and Esau, the progenitor of the Edomites, Gen 36). His Mesopotamian origins are made clear by the several references to Ur of the Chaldees (probably south of modern Baghdad), from which the family of his father Terah traveled to Haran (in SE Turkey) on their way to Canaan. There they settled until the death of Terah (11:32), at which point God's command to Abraham calls him, in effect, to complete the journey to Canaan. Continued family links with Haran are evident in the search for a wife for Isaac (Gen 24) and in the Jacob story (Gen 29–31).

Abraham's birth and early years in Ur are minimally noted (11:27-31; 15:7; Acts 7:2-4). Joshua 24:2-3 implies that God called Abraham out of an idolatrous situation in which his father served other gods (so also the Qur'an). It is not altogether clear whether Abraham also did so (see Isa 51:2); that he was a monotheist is certainly not stressed. Later Jewish literature expands upon this early life, linking him, for example, to a vocation in astronomy, for which Chaldea was famous. His father Terah's move from Ur "to go into the land of Canaan" (11:31) may help explain Abraham's immediate response to God's call in 12:4. But God's extensive promises to him in 12:2-3 may have been most decisive in generating his responsiveness. Promise is the leitmotiv of the Genesis narrative, reinforced by the pervasive use of this theme by both OT and NT references to Abraham. In other words, it is God's word and deed, especially unconditional promises, with which the narrative is most prominently concerned. Abraham's faith is created by these promissory words (15:6) and so his faithfulness is an indispensable, but secondary, feature of the narrative.

A. The Story of Abraham
B. Historical Issues
C. Theological Emphases
  1. Abraham's God
  2. God's promises to Abraham
    a. Son
    b. Land
    c. Nation, name, kings, descendants
    d. Blessing
    e. Presence
  3. Abraham as sinful and faithful human being
D. Abraham Throughout the OT
Bibliography

A. The Story of Abraham

The narratives initially have a lively interest in the journeys of Abraham and his family, bringing him into contact with every major part of the land of promise and with every neighboring people. The first chapters (12–14; 15:7-21) focus on the divine promise of a land. Initially, he moves through the entire land, from Haran to Shechem to Bethel to the Negeb, and finally to Egypt (12:4-20). After negotiating over land with Lot (at Bethel), he settles in the Hebron area (13:1-18), from where he engages in military activity in protection of Lot (Gen 14). The resultant blessing on the part of the otherwise unknown priest-king Melchizedek (14:18-20) demonstrates that God can work through outsiders to bless the people of God (12:3, "I will bless those who bless you," assumes that the non-chosen have the powers of creational blessing).

The next major section in the Abrahamic cycle focuses on the son that God has promised. The issue is introduced by Abraham (15:1-2), to whom God responds with the promise of a direct heir (15:3-5). After an apparent fulfillment in the birth of Ishmael through Sarah's slave girl, Hagar (Gen 16), God moves to a more precise promise of a son with Sarah as the mother, though with special consideration for the future of Ishmael and his family (17:15-20). The "covenant" with Abraham, first focused on the land (15:7-21), is now recharacterized as being "between me [God] and you." God will "be their God" and this covenant is "everlasting." This introduces a heightened sense of the relationship between Abraham (and his family) and God; with a new name (17:1, El Shaddai), God's own identity is now bound up with this family.

The cycle moves through several problematic incidents, from Abraham's repeated endangerment of SARAH (20:1-18; see 12:10-20), to disbelief on the part of both Abraham and Sarah (17:15–18:15), toward the fulfillment of the promise of a son through Sarah (21:1-7). The story of Sodom and Gomorrah (18:16–19:38) provides a catastrophic interlude that illustrates both that potential blessing may come to "outsiders" through the Abrahamic family and the seriousness with which God takes moral evil, while at the same time exhibiting a lively concern for justice and the plight of the innocent. This story exhibits a remarkably interactive relationship between Abraham and God (especially 18:22-32), and God acts to deliver Lot and his family because "God remembered Abraham" (19:29).

The next section (21:9–22:19) is climactic, consisting primarily of two parallel stories regarding the potential loss of the sons of Abraham, first Ishmael to the wilderness (21:8-21), then Isaac as a burnt offering (22:1-19). Yet, both are delivered, as "God was with the boy" Ishmael (21:20), and the angel of the Lord stops Abraham from completing the sacrifice of Isaac (22:12-14). Moreover, to both sons God makes promises regarding continuing life and community (21:13, 18; 22:15-18). Both Isaac and Ishmael return to bury their father (25:9) and the fulfillment of divine promises to both sons is reported (25:12-18, 19-26). The narrative concludes with reports of the death of Sarah and Abraham's purchase of a burial plot (Gen 23)—an initial installment of the gift of land, the obtaining of a suitable wife (Rebekah) for Isaac (Gen 24), a notice regarding Abraham's third family (25:1-6), and the report of Abraham's death and burial (25:7-11).

Abraham's three wives bear him eight children. In addition to Sarah, Hagar is given by Sarah to be his "wife" (16:3), and she bears Ishmael. After Sarah's death, Abraham takes another "wife," named Keturah (25:1), who bears him six additional children. Genesis

25:6 refers to both Hagar and Keturah as "concubines," probably because of their secondary standing within Abraham's household, recognized in that their children are less than full heirs of Abraham, as they are given gifts and "sent away" (25:6). At the same time, these children were a part of the fulfillment of the promise that he would become the father of a multitude of nations (17:5-6; *see* 25:2-4; 12-18). Besides Isaac, however, only Ishmael among Abraham's other children is the recipient of promises (17:20; and 16:10; 21:13, 18). Remarkably, God makes commitments to those who stand outside of the family of Abraham and Isaac.

B. Historical Issues

Historical issues with respect to the Abrahamic narratives are complex. The literary vehicle used in these texts is that of a story of the past; Israel understood these ancestral figures as part of its pre-exodus heritage. At the same time, these stories portray matters that would normally not be a part of any public record (Gen 14 is something of an exception); rather, they portray the complex relationships of family life (they are sometimes called "family narratives"). The genealogical materials show some chronological interest on the part of the narrators, though the details are notoriously difficult to interpret.

Although the ancient writers were not concerned to reconstruct a history of this early era, modern scholars have picked up that interest, working with biblical and extra-biblical data. This task has been made difficult by the nature of the texts themselves as well as by the difficulties in assessing the import of extra-biblical parallels. As a result, scholarly reconstructions of this ancestral period have had mixed results (*see* van Seters; Thompson; Millard). Various ancient Near Eastern parallels to ancestral names, customs, and modes of life have been overdrawn at times; yet, the parallels may be sufficient to claim that these texts carry some authentic memories of a 2nd millennium setting and are not simply a product of ancient imaginations. The historical task remains exceptionally difficult and Abraham remains at best an elusive figure (the earliest extra-biblical reference to the name is in a 10th cent. Egyptian text set in the Negeb, a common setting for Abraham in the biblical texts). In a general way, it is common to date the time of the ancestors in the first half of the 2nd millennium (2000–1500 BCE).

The place of Abraham as the progenitor of the Israelite people is complex and disputed. Contrary to the canonical arrangement of Israel's ancestors, Jacob would seem to be the progenitor of Israel. Jacob, not Abraham, is given the name Israel; Jacob is the "wandering Aramaean" in the credo of Deut 26:5-9. For these and other reasons, it is often thought that Abraham may not have been literally the "father" of all Israelites. That is, his story may have been prefaced to the story of Jacob because of his relationship to certain southern tribal groups, later known as Judah (note Abraham's special connections to Hebron and Beersheba, though he establishes altars across the land, *see* Gen 12:6-8). At some point these groups were integrated into the main Jacob-Joseph tribal association (in the north, later called Israel), and their progenitor was in time given an honored place in the classical genealogical framework. The united monarchy, when northern and southern tribal configurations were unified, is commonly suggested as a time for such a combination of the traditions. Hence, it may be that Abraham was the progenitor of only some of the tribes that became a part of the larger Israelite people. The construction of the Abraham-Isaac-Jacob framework, then, would enable all the major tribal groups that made up the Israelite peoples to be related to the ancestral heritage. This linkage of ancestral figures, while probably not literally genealogical, does recognize the complex roots of Israel's foundations and stakes a claim with respect to the continuity of their various historical experiences and their faith in the same God.

Some tension exists in the narrative regarding Abraham's wealth and social standing. On the one hand, the general image of Abraham in the narrative is that of a nomadic shepherd of modest means (compare his ability to travel with apparent ease). On the other hand, in Gen 14 he has an army of soldiers in his retinue and in Gen 23:6 he is "a mighty prince." Moreover, many servants were part of his household (14:14; 17:23-27; 18:7; 24:2, 35, 59). The one servant named (Eliezer) was perhaps the leader of this group of servants, and would have been Abraham's heir in the absence of his own children (15:2-3); he is probably the servant commissioned by Abraham to seek a wife for Isaac (Gen 24). It is not clear at what point these servants were acquired, but at least some of them (probably including Hagar) were given to him by Egypt's pharaoh (Gen 12:16), along with other gifts that certainly advanced his wealth if they did not establish it in the first place (the pharaoh seems to acknowledge Abraham as a person of considerable social standing). Abraham's status was also acknowledged by Abimelech, who further increased his wealth in the wake of this negative encounter (20:14). Elements of both a settled and a nomadic culture seem to be combined, perhaps reflecting a complex history in the transmission of these texts.

One dimension of these texts often cited in this discussion is the nature of the religion of Abraham and his family (*see* Cross). The religious (and other) expressions of these chapters are often distinctive from later Israelite practices (*see* Moberly). From this it seems clear that later Israelites did not simply read their own religious lives back into these texts (though, strikingly, nothing seems incompatible with Israel's later faith). One apparent memory of practice from pre-exodus times includes references to the worship of God under various forms of the name El (El Elyon, El

Shaddai, El Olam, El Bethel), referred to as the God of my/our/your father(s), the God of Abraham, the God of Isaac, and the God of Jacob (*see* Gen 16:13; 21:33; 33:20; El is the name of the high god in the Canaanite pantheon). This ancestral God was a personal deity who accompanied this family on its journeys, providing care and protection. The conversations between God and the members of this family are described in terms that would be characteristic of everyday personal interactions. The personal nature of this relationship is evident, for example, in the almost complete absence of religious institutions independent of family life—e.g., no temple, priesthood, or sacrificial system (important for later Israel at one time or another). Worship was practiced independent of existing (Canaanite) shrines and revolved around the particular needs of the family, with the patriarch functioning in whatever priestly responsibilities might be in order (e.g., building an altar; sacrificing; praying, blessing, *see* 12:7-8; 13:4, 18). The legitimacy of the worship of non-Israelite individuals is at least implicitly acknowledged in the Melchizedek episode (14:18-20). God was not considered limited to activity in and with Abraham and his family, but that is the focus of these narratives.

Some traditions understand Yahweh as a name for God, revealed only at the time of Moses (Exod 3:14, 16; 6:2-3) and that El was an earlier name for God. These texts, however, generally understand El to be an alternate name or epithet for Yahweh (e.g., Abraham understands Melchizedek's "God Most High (El Elyon)" to be identified with Yahweh; 14:18-20). The frequent use of Yahweh in Genesis is anachronistic in some ways, but it conveys an important theological conviction: the God whom the family of Abraham worshiped under the name El is to be identified with Yahweh. It may be concluded that the revelation of the name Yahweh to Moses meant a genuine advancement in the understanding of God that the ancestors had, without standing in significant contradiction thereto.

The complex history of the origins and formation of the Abrahamic texts is also of interest. The common assumption is that these texts developed over the course of Israel's history in the hands of authors and editors (e.g., JEDP *see* DOCUMENTARY HYPOTHESIS), who told and retold these stories and shaped them to speak to several generations of Israelites. So, traditionally, the Yahwist is associated with the concerns of the united monarchy (David, Solomon), while the Priestly writer has often been understood to address Israel in Babylonian exile. More recently, efforts have been made to relate the present form of the Pentateuch to the concerns of the Jewish community in the post-exilic period. However one resolves these particular hypotheses, it is likely that an ongoing "rolling" body of Abrahamic material was continually supplemented and used again and again to speak to communities of faith. As such, these texts are hermeneutically layered, with many possible settings in view over time, though they are difficult to sort out.

This effort has often been pursued with larger bodies of texts (such as J or P; *see* Brueggemann and Wolff); such work has also been pursued at the level of individual texts. For example, correspondences may be observed between various episodes in Israel's history and texts revealing of the life of the Abrahamic family. Abraham's journey into Egypt (12:10-20) has many parallels with Israel's later journey into Egypt and its hardships related to the Pharaoh. Such parallels suggest that the Abrahamic narratives at times have been composed with a view to later events in Israel's history. Or, the dialogue between Abraham and God with respect to saving the cities of Sodom and Gomorrah because of the number of righteous within it (18:16-33) might be related to the siege of Jerusalem by the Babylonians in 587 BCE. Should not the righteous in the city mean that God would save the city for their sake? The story of the binding of Isaac (22:1-19) might also be interpreted in terms of the fall of Jerusalem. Faithful Israelites, like Abraham, have been put to the test in midst of a judgment that has killed many of their children. With the loss of so many children, is there a future for Israel? What then happens to God's promise to Abraham? To have these promises so regularly punctuate the narrative would have been important for such an audience, so tempted to despair. It is striking that the promises—land, nationhood, name, descendants, presence—are so attuned to the exiles' future as a people. That "descendants" are referred to thirteen times in chap. 17 alone would surely be noticed. Like Abraham, they would be living short of fulfillment; but promises generate hope in God's possibilities. The key would be their trust in the God who keeps promises.

C. Theological Emphases
1. Abraham's God

Abraham's God is a down-to-earth God. God appears at Abraham's tent door in the form of a human being (Gen 18:1-2) and eats with him. God enters into a genuine dialogue with Abraham about the future of Sodom and Gomorrah (18:16-32). Abraham's God takes the human participant seriously, engaging what Abraham says and does. God's relationship with Abraham occurs in and through various divine modes of speaking and presence, from vision (15:1-6) to appearance in human form (18:16-33). It is likely that the "angel of the Lord" is a way of speaking of such a divine appearance (compare 16:7-11 with 16:13). Moreover, this God establishes a covenant with Abraham in specific response to his doubts and his questions (Gen 15).

At the same time, Abraham's God is not a big human being, however mysterious. The God of the Abraham narratives is transcendent as well as immanent. God calls Abraham to a responsibility that is universal in scope—all the families of the earth are the focus of this

God's interests (12:3). God has a world in view, not just some local issue. This God has all people in view, not just an elect people, however important they are in God's purposes. Even more, God makes promises on which people can depend and that word of God has the power to create faith in human beings, with the result that a genuine and faithful relationship comes clearly into view (15:6). This is a God whose word has such power that lives and worlds are changed for good. Moreover, God puts Abraham to the test, commanding him to sacrifice the son of the very promise that God had articulated (22:1-19). In addition, God brings judgment on the sin of the world, and Sodom and Gomorrah are destroyed forever, except in memory (Gen 19).

Notably, God interacts not only with Abraham but also with outsiders such as Hagar (Gen 16:7-14) and Abimelech (20:3-6). The call of Abraham does not narrow God's channel of activity down to a history of salvation. God remains active in every sphere of life. Abraham frequently encounters outsiders: Egyptians (Pharaoh, 12:10-20; Hagar, 16:1; 21:9); other empires, including pre-Israelite rulers of Jerusalem (14); Sodom and Gomorrah (18–19); Canaanites (20; 21:22-34); Hittites (23); and Aramaeans (24; see also 19:37-38; 25:1-18). This interest is certainly related to the call to be a blessing to such families (12:2-3). How well this call is fulfilled may be discerned by the various ways in which Abraham relates to these peoples. Both positive (Sodom and Gomorrah, 18:23-33) and negative (Abimelech and his family, 20) models are developed. These outsiders, in turn, respond in ways that are theologically sophisticated and in their behaviors often put the chosen family to shame. We encounter a Melchizedek, who mediates the blessing of Abraham's God on Abraham (14); a Hagar, the only person in the Bible who, in view of her experience with God, gives God a new name (16:13); an Abimelech, who exemplifies a fear of God in a way that calls Abraham to account for his deeds and who serves as his confessor (20) and offers a theological interpretation of events (21:22-23; see 26:28-29).

2. God's promises to Abraham

Promise stands at the beginning of Abraham's story (12:1-3), creating his faith and generating the basic shape of his life. God's promises are decisive for the future of Abraham and his family and, through them, all the world's families. Having given promises, God is committed to a certain future, and so the future changes for God as well. God's promises to Abraham also stand at the climax of his story (22:16-18) and are repeated at key junctures (chs. 12, 13, 15, 17-18, 24). Alongside promises to the chosen line stand promises to Hagar/Ishmael (16–17, 21) and Abimelech (20:7); that God engages in acts of promising outside the Israelite community of faith provides, at the least, an important link between insider and outsider in their experience of God.

The major promises made by God to Abraham are:

a. Son. Interpreters often consider the promise of a son to Abraham to be the oldest, enhanced over the years by other promises. This process extends the promises beyond Abraham's own lifetime to an open future. These promises continue to play a key role for Abraham *as promises*, quite apart from fulfillment, giving direction to his life and a shape to his hopes and dreams.

b. Land. The promise of a land (12:7) provides the initial focus for the story, with a choice of lands given to Lot (ch. 13), the threat provided by surrounding empires and the links to Jerusalem (ch. 14), and the sealing of this promise in covenant (15:7-21). This theme is reinforced at the end of the story in the purchase of a burial site (ch. 23).

c. Nation, name, kings, descendants. These promises are stated at various points, to both Sarah (17:16) and Abraham (17:3-6). The first three are fulfilled in the Davidic empire. As for descendants, fulfillment is more complicated. Literally, it centers on Isaac, but it also includes descendants through the lines of Hagar/Ishmael and the children by Keturah (25:1-6). Even more, the legacy of Abraham includes not only Jews, but also Christians (see Rom 4) and Muslims, who track their descendance through Hagar and Ishmael (the Qur'an has over 250 references to Abraham).

d. Blessing. This promise is given a central place in the call of Abraham (12:1-3) and commonly appears throughout his story. Blessing encompasses the promises noted above, as well as creational realities such as life and fertility, which all of God's creatures experience independent of their knowledge of God. Such blessings are life-enabling and life-sustaining, but finally insufficient for the fullest possible life. And so, the *promise* of blessing brings focus and intensity to God's specific activity in and through the chosen family that finally has redemption in view for all families.

e. Presence. The promise of blessing to Abraham (12:2) and to Sarah (17:16) implies an ongoing presence of God in their lives, as does the new formulation in 17:7-8, "I will be God to you and to your descendants after you."

3. Abraham as sinful and faithful human being

Abraham continues in the train of the sinful creatures imaged in the first chapters of Genesis. God establishes a new beginning with Abraham (and Sarah), but does not perfect them before working in and through them. Abraham demonstrates this reality almost immediately by endangering his wife Sarah with a claim that she is his sister (12:10-20). This act is repeated later in the encounter with Abimelech (20:1-18), who will call Abraham to account for his behaviors: "you have done things to me that ought not to be done" (20:9). Moreover, both Abraham and Sarah evidence their sinfulness in their disbelieving response to God's promises regarding a son (17:17; 18:12).

Abraham is also a faithful and responsible human being. For example, Abraham is called by God and, without hesitation, leaves family and friends and heads for Canaan (12:1-4), and obeys God's call to sacrifice his son in the face of a seeming contradiction of the promise (22:1-19). This "test" of Abraham is intended, not to kill Isaac, but to test his faithfulness (so that *God* may know, v. 12). Abraham's fidelity is necessary in order for God's purposes to move forward in and through him. While God's command (in view of the promise) is bizarre, Abraham's response is informed by a conviction that God can be trusted finally to save Isaac (22:5, 8). Isaac's response in "walking on" with his father shows he believes his father's trust is well placed. The provision of a ram for the sacrifice, and God's overriding of the original command with another, confirm Abraham's trust. Because of the faithfulness of Abraham with respect to his son, God's promises to him are renewed (22:16-18).

Abraham's faithful response to God's promise is explicitly lifted up in Gen 15:6: Abraham "believed the Lord, and the Lord reckoned it to him as righteousness" (this text becomes paradigmatic for what the NT means by faith, Rom 4; Gal 3–4). This text in context demonstrates that questions and doubts can appropriately accompany faith, as do Abraham's questions with respect to Sodom and Gomorrah (18:25). Abraham's intercessory advocacy on behalf of Sodom and Gomorrah is understood to be a sign of faithfulness. Indeed, Abraham's response to God in these various contexts is such that later texts will refer to Abraham as God's "friend" (Isa 41:8; 2 Chr 20:7; James 2:23). The striking testimony regarding Abraham in Gen 26:5 is a witness to human responsibility: Abraham "obeyed my voice and kept my charge, my commandments, my statutes, and my laws" (and this before Mount Sinai; compare 26:3-5, 24).

The future is shaped not simply by the God who promises but also by the way in which Abraham responds (*see* 22:15-18). Abraham is not passive, as if the drama were shaped solely by God's will and word. Indeed, his initiatives (e.g., his questioning of God) and those of others (e.g., Sarah's efforts to give Abraham a child through Hagar) are not signs of a lack of faith; rather, they illustrate the depth of God's engagement with and commitment to human beings as the instruments of the divine purpose. Human beings can neither preserve nor annul God's promises, for God will keep promises; but their words and deeds will have much to say in how that promise moves toward fulfillment. Human beings make a difference to God and to the shape the future takes.

D. Abraham Throughout the OT

Beyond Genesis, the name Abraham occurs forty-two times in the OT (in fifteen books), though never in specific association with any of the Genesis stories. The one story that is referenced repeatedly (Sodom and Gomorrah, e.g., Jer 23:14) is never linked with Abraham. The subsequent OT references to Abraham, sometimes called the "servant" of God, are associated primarily with the promises of land and descendants (e.g., Num 32:11; Deut 1:8; 6:10; 9:5; 34:4; Ps 105:6, 9, 42). The formula, "The God of Abraham" (e.g., Exod 4:5; 1 Kgs 18:36; 1 Chr 29:18) repeatedly links Israel with Abraham's God. Indeed, Israel is known as "the people of the God of Abraham" (Ps 47:9); Abraham was considered Israel's "father" (Isa 51:2).

God's promises to Abraham are repeated to Isaac (26:3-4, 24) and to Jacob (28:4, 13-14; 35:11-12), through Joseph to the twelve sons of Jacob (50:24), and to Moses and the people of Israel (Exod 6:3-8; 33:1). Indeed, Moses understands that God's covenant with Abraham takes precedence over the covenant with Israel at Sinai (Exod 32:13), remaining in place in spite of Israel's apostasy. Other texts make similar claims (e.g., Lev 26:42; Deut 4:31; 2 Kgs 13:23; Jer 33:26; Mic 7:20; Gal 3:29).

Remarkably, the faithfulness of Abraham (15:6), so prominent in the NT portrayal (Rom 4), receives minimal attention in the OT beyond the Abrahamic cycle (e.g., Gen 26:5). Post-biblical Judaism will give prominence to Abraham's obedience and to his monotheistic beliefs. Islam will stress Abraham's rejection of idolatrous practices and stake a claim with respect to his foundational witness to monotheism. *See* AMRAPHEL; CHEDORLAOMER; FAITH; HAGAR; HEBRON; ISHMAEL; JUSTIFICATION; LABAN; LOT; MAMRE; MELCHIZEDEK; PATRIARCHS; PENTATEUCH; REBEKAH; RIGHTEOUSNESS, OT; SARAH.

Bibliography: Walter Brueggemann and H. W. Wolff. *The Vitality of Old Testament Traditions.* 2nd Ed (1982); Frank Moore Cross. "Yahweh and the God of the Patriarchs." *HTR* 55 (1962) 225–59; Terence E. Fretheim. "The Book of Genesis." *NIB* 1 (1994) 321–674; J. G. Janzen. *Abraham and All the Families of the Earth: A Commentary on Genesis 12–50* (1993); A. R. Millard and D. J. Wiseman. *Essays on the Patriarchal Narratives* (1983); R. W. L. Moberly. *The Old Testament of the Old Testament: Patriarchal Narratives and Mosaic Yahwism* (1992); A. Pagolu. *The Religion of the Patriarchs* (1998); Thomas L. Thompson. *The Historicity of the Patriarchal Narratives: The Quest for the Historical Abraham* (1974); John van Seters. *Abraham in History and Tradition* (1975); Claus Westermann. *Genesis 12–50: A Commentary* (1985).

TERENCE FRETHEIM

ABRAHAM'S BOSOM [κόλπας Ἀβραάμ kolpas Abraam]. A metaphorical reference to the familial belonging, honor, and repose the righteous enjoy in the afterlife. The expression only occurs in Luke 16:22. It is not a synonym for paradise (though note the confusion in *T. Ab.* 20:14a). Instead it represents the blessed state of the righteous who join the PATRIARCHS in

PARADISE after death. Transport to Abraham's bosom may have an antecedent in the ancient idea of being gathered to one's ancestors (Gen 25:8). Other texts express the hope that the patriarchs welcome the righteous dead into HEAVEN (4 Macc 13:17; *Apoc. Zeph.* 9:1-5). The metaphor of the bosom can signify filial intimacy (John 1:18, where the NRSV renders kolpas as "heart"), or the close association and honor of reclining next to someone important at a meal (John 13:23; *see* RECLINE). If being in Abraham's bosom involves reclining at the MESSIANIC BANQUET with the patriarchs (Matt 8:11; Luke 13:28-29), this would mark a fitting reversal for poor Lazarus who had previously been unwelcome at the rich man's table (Luke 16:19-21). The idea of being in Abraham's bosom or in the embrace of the patriarchs continued to be used in Christian and rabbinic writings of the blessedness and rest experienced by the faithful at death.

KEVIN L. ANDERSON

ABRAHAM, TESTAMENT OF. The *Testament of Abraham* first came to the attention of Western academics with the publication in 1892 of the critical edition of M. R. James. In contrast to the meager report in Gen 25:7-10, the book imaginatively recounts the dramatic circumstances of Abraham's death. When the day for the patriarch to depart this life draws near, God sends an angel, the Commander-in-chief Michael, to tell the philanthropist to set his affairs in order. But Abraham refuses to co-operate. Eventually, after Abraham breaks a series of bargains with God, Death, taking over the role of the ineffectual Michael, tricks the patriarch into giving up his soul. Abraham never makes his testament.

The comedic work circulated in Greek, Coptic, Arabic, Slavonic, and Romanian. There are two recensions, one shorter, one longer. The latter is usually closer to the original story, even though its language is often medieval. While Christians rewrote the *T. Ab.*, so much so that the original cannot be recovered, the various textual traditions probably derive from a Jewish text written in Greek in Egypt, presumably in Alexandria, before the middle of the 2nd cent. CE.

Despite recurrent interaction with Scripture, the *T. Ab.* does not promote a canon-centered piety. Central scriptural themes are conspicuously absent, and the story itself fails to follow the Bible. The *Testament* communicates not through exegesis but through a new, imaginative narrative, which again and again contradicts Genesis. So while it regularly echoes and finds inspiration in the Bible, the *Testament* goes its own way. Instead of making Scripture the last word, it creatively exploits it for novel ends.

The central issue in the *Testament* is Death, and the focus on Abraham is ultimately incidental. The patriarch is not, so to speak, his biblical self but rather every individual, the human being faced with death, who is, no matter how pious, anxious about quitting this life.

Abraham never comes to terms with his own death, which is why he never makes a testament. The patriarch is denial incarnate. He is all too slow to recognize Michael and fathom his mission. Then, once he does fathom his identity, he refuses to co-operate with him. Then he makes a deal on which he reneges. Then he delays the inevitable by quizzing Death about multiple matters. And when slipping away at the end, he is still telling Death to depart. Indeed, at his dying moment he is fantasizing about getting well (20:8-9). So from beginning to end Abraham runs from reality. He never comes to terms with the fact that his death is at hand.

Although the *Testament* candidly displays the human denial of death, it does so with humor and sympathy, and it is ultimately optimistic, at least for all those whose bad deeds do not exceed their good deeds. Abraham may, like everyone else, fear death, but wisdom recognizes that the world is ultimately "futile" (1:7) and that leaving it is, for the saved, to exchange suffering, grief, and groaning for peace, fervent joy, and eternal life (20:15). Death may appear hideous (as in ch. 17), but beyond death is the world to come. The *Testament* copes with death-related anxiety by teaching that death is not the end but instead the beginning of a better existence.

Despite the somber topic and the serious theological questions that it addresses, *Testament* is less instruction than it is entertainment. The lighthearted parody of testamentary literature is full of irony, and the text should recurrently move readers to laugh. It does this largely through irony, through the disparity between its picture of Abraham and that of the Bible and subsequent tradition. From Genesis, Abraham is a paradigm of faith, obedience, and sagacity. In the *Testament*, which mocks naive genuflection before scriptural heroes, the patriarch does not exercise much faith in God nor display obedience. He does not even show much sense: it takes him, despite a talking tree and tears turning into jewels, a ludicrously long time to figure out what is going on, and even then he refuses to face the inevitable. The man who interceded for Sodom and Gomorrah also acts against character by slaughtering sinners in ch. 10. So the Abraham of the *Testament* is not the revered Abraham of tradition but his all-too-human opposite. His confrontation with mortality turns him unexpectedly into an obtuse, stubborn old man who exercises not the blind obedience of Gen 22 but self-centered defiance.

Bibliography: Dale C. Allison, Jr. *The Testament of Abraham* (2003).

DALE C. ALLISON, JR.

ABRAM ay´bruhm [אַבְרָם ʾavram]. "Exalted father." The name of Abraham in Gen 11:26–17:4; 1 Chr 1:27; and Neh 9:7. *See* ABRAHAM.

ABRON ay´bruhn [Ἀβρωνά Abrōna]. A brook whose towns Holofernes destroyed all the way to the sea (Jdt 2:24). Sometimes identified as the Chaboras River.

ABRONAH uh-broh´nuh [עַבְרֹנָה ʿavronah]. One of the exodus itinerary sites visited by the Israelites as they traveled between the WILDERNESS OF SINAI and YAM SUF (Num 33:34-35). Late sources locate Abronah close to Yam Suf and EZION-GEBER.

ABSALOM ab´suh-luhm [אַבְשָׁלוֹם ʾavshalom]. "Absh-alom," with its variant form "Abishalom" (see 1 Kgs 15:2, 10) is a theophoric name, "(my) Father is peace (or well-being)."

According to 2 Sam 3:3, Absalom was the third of the sons of DAVID born in Hebron. His mother was MAACAH, daughter of Talmai, king of Geshur, whose marriage to David was probably the result of a political alliance. She was also was the mother of TAMAR, who was raped by AMNON, Absalom's eldest half-brother. Absalom had three sons, whose names are not given, and a daughter also named Tamar, who "was a beautiful woman" (2 Sam 14:27). There is a confusing reference in 1 Kgs 15 to "Maacah daughter of Abishalom," mother of Abijam and Asa, son and grandson of Rehoboam who reigned in Jerusalem after him. Since almost certainly a daughter of Absalom would have been born long before Rehoboam, those references present a conundrum with no clear solution. The note that begins in 2 Sam 14:25 describes Absalom's physical appearance in regal terms reminiscent of what 1 Sam 9:2 and 10:23 say about Saul—he was tall and handsome—and adds a special emphasis on the abundance and thickness of his hair, foreshadowing the circumstances of his death in 2 Sam 18:9.

Absalom plays a major role in the narrative that has come to be known as the "Throne Succession" of David (2 Sam 9-20; 1 Kgs 1–2) where his presence, as much as his absence in exile or in death, provides a core element of the plot from 2 Sam 13:1 to 19:10. In 2 Sam 13:1, the author places Absalom immediately before the reader by identifying Tamar as his sister, thus making it clear that Amnon's rape of Tamar is an attack on Absalom as well. Tamar finds refuge, presumably for the rest of her life, in Absalom's house-hold. While David does nothing in response to the outrage, Absalom waits, and after two years pass he sets in motion a revenge plot that results in the murder of Amnon. Absalom immediately flees to Geshur, where he stays three years under the protection of King Talmai, his maternal grandfather. As David's grief over Amnon subsides, his yearning for exiled Absalom increases. This situation provides the context for Joab's first intervention into Absalom's story. David's kinsman and general, JOAB, tricks David into allow-ing Absalom to return, in a manner reminiscent of Nathan's ruse after the Bathsheba affair. Joab coaches

a widow from Tekoa to tell David a fictitious story about one of her sons killing another, and the resultant threat to the life of the living one by her avenging relatives (14:14). David recognizes Joab's hand in the deception, but agrees to allow Absalom's return, and Joab himself brings Absalom back from Geshur. Absa-lom remains banned from David's presence for two years, until he forces the issue by having his servants set fire to a field belonging to Joab, who had refused to talk to him about a return to court.

While a formal reconciliation with David follows, Absalom's behavior shows him eager to seize the throne. He acts as a politician, enhancing his image by enlarging and militarizing his entourage. He publicly criticizes the administration of justice in his father's courts and promises better if he were in charge. He acts as a "man of the people" refusing the obeisance required by custom from those who approached him. In four years (not forty, as the Masoretic Text reads) of this sort of activity, "Absalom stole the hearts of the people of Israel" (15:6), and plotted his revolt. Absalom was personally estranged from David, and he may have blamed him for not punishing Amnon. From the beginning of his rebellion, Absalom counted on the support of many of the political leaders of Israel and Judah, which may point to growing popular dis-content with David.

Pretending to fulfill a vow made in exile, Absa-lom rallies his supporters to Hebron, and there has himself proclaimed king. Notable among the leaders who joined Absalom was AHITOPHEL of Giloh, one of David's wisest counselors. David recognizes Ahitophel as a real threat (15:31) and makes plans to counteract him (15:32-34) in David's flight from Jeru-salem. David leaves behind several important officials loyal to him, charged with sending him information and buying him time for his retreat and eventual counterattack. Notable among these is HUSHAI the Archite, David's counselor, whose specific mission is to insinuate himself into Absalom's court and counter Ahitophel's advice. On the strength of that advice, Absalom has a tent pitched on the roof of the royal palace, and spends the night with ten concubines that David had left behind. Ahitophel intended this as an act of political rape (16:21). Hushai was able to countermand the second piece of advice, namely that Absalom send Ahitophel with 12,000 men in immedi-ate pursuit of David, to attack and kill him before he has time to regroup. Hushai's counsel was to wait until all Israel "from Dan to Beer-sheba" can gather under Absalom's leadership and then go after David. David has enough time to cross the Jordan, reach Mahanaim, and gather troops and provisions for the decisive battle with his son.

The battle takes place in the "forest of Ephraim," an otherwise unknown location East of the Jordan. David ordered Joab, Abishai, and Ittai, his three commanders, to deal gently with Absalom (18:5), an order that Joab notoriously ignores. Absalom is captured when his hair becomes entangled in the low branches of an oak. Joab kills him while he hangs there. In one of the most poignant scenes of the narrative, David mourns and weeps "O my son Absalom, my son, my son Absalom! Would I had died instead of you, O Absalom, my son, my son!" (18:33). Joab tells the king he must stop and allow his troops to celebrate their victory and return him to his throne in Jerusalem.

FRANCISCO GARCÍA-TRETO

ABSTINENCE. A variety of Hebrew and Greek terms exhort refraining from eating some or all foods to express devotion, to strengthen another's faith (1 Tim 4:3; Zech 7:3), or refraining from association with certain people (Acts 15:20, 29), certain passions, and from sexual activity during war, for purification (1 Pet 2:11) or preparation for the end times. *See* FASTING.

ABU GHOSH. *See* GHOSH, ABU.

ABU HAWAM. *See* HAWAM, ABU.

ABUBUS uh-boo'buhs ['Αβοῦβος 'Aboubos]. Father of Jericho's governor Ptolemy, who married Simon Maccabeus' daughter and murdered Simon Maccabeus and his two sons (1 Macc 16:11-16).

ABUNDANCE [רֹב rov; περίσσευμα perisseuma]. Abundance refers to a large quantity or a plentiful amount of either material or non-material entities. In biblical texts it often connotes an amount over and above basic needs or expectations.

The OT refers frequently to the abundance of God's "steadfast love" (Pss 5:7; 69:13; 106:7, 45; Isa 63:7; Lam 3:32), and the God of Israel is consistently described as "abounding in [i.e., having an abundance of] steadfast love" (Exod 34:6; Num 14:18; Neh 9:17; Pss 86:5, 15; 103:8; 145:8; Joel 2:13; Jonah 4:2).

In the OT, an abundance of material possessions (wealth) is sometimes referred to as a gift from God (Deut 8:18; 25:11) or a reward for piety (Prov 3:9-10; 22:4), righteousness (Prov 15:6) or hard work and good planning (Prov 10:4; 21:5). But OT texts also acknowledge that an abundance of wealth could be gained in unacceptable ways (Prov 13:23; 21:6; 28:20), and the prophets often condemned those who had accumulated their abundance at the expense of others (Amos 5:11; 8:4-10; Isa 5:8-10).

The NT attitude toward material abundance is best characterized by Jesus' parable of "The Rich Fool," which is preceded by the warning, "Take care! Be on your guard against all kinds of greed, for one's life does not consist in the abundance of possessions" (Luke 12:15-21). Material abundance is far less important

than having "life" and having it "abundantly" (John 10:10).

The most congruent story in all four Gospels is that of the feeding of the five thousand (Matt 14:15-21; Mark 6:30-44; Luke 9:12-17; John 6:3-14). A seemingly small amount (five loaves and two fish) becomes an abundance of food for a great multitude (with twelve baskets of scraps left over). Thus, Jesus redefines abundance: when you share what little you have, it turns out to be more than enough.

KATHLEEN A. FARMER

ABUSE. *See* SEXUAL ABUSE.

ABYSS uh-bis' [ἄβυσσος abyssos]. In the Apocrypha, abyss is the region of the deep often contrasted with the earth and the heavens (Sir 1:3; 16:18; 24:5, 29; 42:18). In the NT, abyss is the abode of demons (Luke 8:31) or the abode of the dead (Rom 10:7).

ACACIA uh-kay'shuh [שִׁטָּה shittah, שִׁטִּים shittim]. A tree or shrub common in the desert areas of Egypt, Arabia, Sinai, and Negev. The word occurs 28 times in the OT, all in the plural form **shittim** except once in the singular form **shittah** (Isa 41:19). Acacia trees generally grow to a height of 3–5 m (10–15 ft.), but some grow as tall as 15 m (50 ft.). Acacias have yellow flowers and green leaves, which become darker in color over time. Due to its exceptional durability, *Acacia raddiana* was used for the ARK OF THE COVENANT, the furnishings of the TABERNACLE, and the ALTAR (Exod 25–27; 30; 35-38; compare Deut 10:3). Other uses for acacia wood include gate doors, charcoal, and Egyptian mummy coffins; acacia leaves and fruit are used as fodder. *Acacia senegal* is a source for gum arabic. This word also occurs in reference to places, such as ABEL-SHITTIM, "meadow of the acacias" (Num 33:49), where the acacia trees may have been abundant (Num 25:1; Josh 2:1; Mic 6:5). Acacia, along with six other desert trees, depicts the imagery of the wondrous renewal of the wilderness (Isa 41:19). Some scholars propose to link the burning bush Moses saw (Exod 3:2) with *Acacia nilotica* because of its shiny appearance. *See* BUSH, BURNING; PLANTS OF THE BIBLE.

Bibliography: Nogah Hareuveni. *Tree and Shrub in Our Biblical Heritage* (1984); Michal Zohary. *Plants of the Bible* (1982).

HYUN CHUL PAUL KIM

ACCAD ak'ad [אַכַּד 'akkadh]. A city, Sumerian name Agade, in northern BABYLONIA, listed in Gen 10:10 among the main cities of the kingdom of Nimrod in the land of Shinar. Possibly founded by Sargon in the 24th cent. BCE, Accad became the dynastic capital until its fall in the 22nd cent. BCE, recorded in the Sumerian "Curse of Agade." The city was never rebuilt and its site has never been identified. *See* AKKADIAN; ASSYRIA; SUMER.

ANNALISA AZZONI

ACCENT, GALILEAN. Acts 2:7 and Mark 14:70 (‭א‬ B C D *al*) imply that the speech of a Galilean could be distinguished from that of a Judean. Matthew 26:73 and Mark 14:70 (A N Θ *al*) state this explicitly. However, in the absence of contemporary evidence it is unclear whether the distinguishing traits were phonetic, rhythmic, lexical, idiomatic, morphological or syntactic, or a combination of these. *Eruvin* 53*a-b* eulogizes Judeans for their precision in pronunciation while censuring Galileans for failing to distinguish the gutturals ʾaleph, ʿayin, and kheth. The plausibility that Galileans did not always distinguish gutturals in Aramaic (and by implication Hebrew) is increased by clearer evidence that their geographical neighbors, the Samaritans, failed to distinguish gutturals.

P. J. WILLIAMS

ACCENTS, LINGUISTIC, MUSICAL, POETIC. *See* MASORETIC ACCENTS.

ACCEPTANCE. Acceptance is a biblical theme touching on several aspects of divine-human and human-human relationships, and associated with a range of Hebrew and Greek terms. Its basic signification is social, arising from hierarchical power-relationships within which *acceptance* can have great social meaning. Esther's perilous entry into the presence of King Ahasuerus could have resulted in her immediate death (Esth 4:11), but her acceptance signaled the king's willingness to grant her request "even to the half of my kingdom" (Esth 5:3). Transferred metaphorically into the divine-human sphere, acceptance by God signals the ultimate social security. Paul significantly uses the language of admission to a royal court in Rom 5:1-2: "since we are justified by faith, we have peace with God through our Lord Jesus Christ, through whom we have obtained access to this grace in which we stand."

In the OT the priestly strand of thought links acceptability closely with sacrifice. Because acceptance by God depends on the offering of acceptable sacrifices, the conditions of acceptability are carefully prescribed (Exod 28:38; Lev 1:3; 22:27, etc.). But there is no exact cause-and-effect relationship between offering correct sacrifices and obtaining acceptance by God. In Gen 4:4 it is not "Abel's offering" that God accepts but "Abel and his offering." The author of Hebrews spots this subtle difference: Because of his "greater" sacrifice we can conclude that Abel himself was "righteous" before God, unlike Cain (Heb 11:4).

This gentle critique of the sacrificial cult—sacrifices do not *make* people acceptable, but confirm that they are *already* acceptable, because God does not turn them away—bursts into full bloom with the prophets, who inveigh against false confidence in sacrifices (e.g., Isa 1:10-15; Jer 6:20; Mic 6:6-8). It underlies also the story of the acceptance of Moses in Exod 32–34: the sin of Israel is expiated not by sacrifice but by Moses' intercession, and Israel's continuation in the covenant depends wholly upon God's mercy (Exod 33:19; 34:6-7). It reappears in Ps 51, where the repentant sinner knows that he is accepted by God quite apart from the cult (Ps 51:16-17).

Thus, the stage is set for the NT, where suddenly Gentiles are acceptable to God in a new way. Cornelius revolutionizes Peter's thinking about the conditions of acceptability (Acts 10:35). Out of this surprising "act" of the Holy Spirit is born the Pauline gospel of equal justification: Jews and Gentiles, without distinction, are made acceptable to God through Christ by faith (e.g., Rom 3:28-30). The *rationale* for this gospel is Jesus' acceptance of social outcasts (e.g., Mark 1:40-45; Luke 19:1-10). The *condition* is acceptance of Christ by us (Col 2:6; John 1:10-13)—a strange reversal of the social hierarchy. And the *consequence* must be acceptance of each other, in spite of all differences of status and nationality (Rom 14:1-12; 15:9-11; 16:3-16; 1 Cor 11:20-21, 33-34). The sacrificial cult is now explicitly recast and re-expressed in terms of the *ethical life* of the community—praise and practical service are the sacrifices acceptable to God (Heb 13:15-16). *See* INCLUSIVE, EXCLUSIVE; JUSTIFICATION; RIGHTEOUSNESS; SACRIFICES AND OFFERINGS.

STEVE MOTYER

ACCESS [προσαγωγή *prosagōgē*]. A key term in Rom 5:2, where Paul summarizes the effects of JUSTIFICATION by faith: "we have peace with God through our Lord Jesus Christ, through whom we have obtained access to this grace in which we stand." The term reappears in similar contexts in Eph 2:18; 3:12. It is likely that the term draws on "court" imagery, connoting "access through the royal chamberlain into the king's presence" (Dunn). The social significance of such access is that first-century Mediterranean culture depended on a reciprocal system of material benefit and social honor, which bound clients and patrons together in mutual dependence. That "access"—often mediated by influential brokers—was essential in the system. The letter to the Hebrews suggests that Christ as "mediator" (Heb 8:6; 12:24) gives us "entrance" (εἴσοδος, *eisodos*) into the heavenly Sanctuary (Heb 10:19), and Christ enables us to "approach the throne of grace" (Heb 4:16).

Bibliography: J. D. G. Dunn. *Romans 1–8.* WBC 38a (1988); David A. deSilva. *Honor, Patronage, Kinship and Purity: Unlocking New Testament Culture* (2000).

STEVE MOTYER

ACCO, AKKO ak′oh [עַכּוֹ ʿakko; Ακχω Akchō, Πτολεμαις Ptolemais]. A port city on the coast of Israel, eight mi. north of Mount Carmel and thirty mi. south of Tyre. It is the best natural port on the coast of Israel, and well situated for inland trade through the Jezreel Valley. It served this purpose from an early date, and is mentioned as an important Egyptian holding in the Amarna letters (14th cent. BCE).

The only reference to Acco in the OT is a note in Judg 1:31 that the tribe of Asher "did not drive out the inhabitants of Acco," an indication that the Canaanite settlement there was well established and strong. Indeed, throughout the Israelite period Acco was a Phoenician city, dominated by Tyre and Sidon to the north. Like all of the cities in this region, it was ruled in turn by the Assyrian, Babylonian, and Persian empires. The city was conquered by Alexander the Great in his swing through Palestine on the way to Egypt. After his death, it became part of the Seleucid Empire, but was captured for a time by the Ptolemies in the 3rd cent. BCE, who renamed it Ptolemais, as it is called in the books of the Maccabees and in Acts 21:7.

The city of Ptolemais served as a capital of the Seleucid empire. First Macc 5:21-24 reports that in the time leading up to the purging of Jerusalem in 164 BCE, Simon handed the Greeks a decisive defeat in Galilee, chasing them as far as the gate of Ptolemais. First Macc 10 describes the rule of Alexander Balas who arrived in Ptolemais and claimed kingship there around the year 153 BCE. He was opposed by Demetrius, who attempted to recruit the support of the Maccabean leader Jonathan. Alexander outbid Demetrius by appointing Jonathan to be High Priest. Alexander defeated Demetrius and made peace with Ptolemy VI, who gave Alexander his daughter Cleopatra in marriage. The text notes that Ptolemy "celebrated her wedding at Ptolemais with great pomp, as kings do" (1 Macc 10:58). Jonathan made the trip from Jerusalem for the occasion, bringing silver and gold for the two Greek kings (v. 60). The three leaders enjoyed each other's company, ignoring the jeers of certain "malcontents" from Israel (v. 61). Years later, Jonathan was taken prisoner in the city after he was led there deceitfully by Tryphon, who finally killed him (1 Macc 12:44-48, 13:23).

The city of Acco is important as a site of battle between the Crusaders and the Muslims. Thousands of people died fighting for this city during the 12th and 13th cent. CE, and it was the last city given up by the Crusaders. A 50 acre site (Tell el-Fukhar) was excavated between 1973 and 1989 by Moshe Dothan.

BRYAN D. BIBB

ACCURSED [חֵרֶם kherem; ἀνάθεμα anathema, ἀνάθημα anathēma, κατάθεμα katathema, καταρά-ομαι kataraomai, κατάρα katara, ἐπάρατος eparatos, ἐπικατά epikata, ἐπικατάρατος epikataratos]. The noun is rendered "accursed," "under ban," "devoted for destruction," "devoted thing" by various versions (e.g., Deut 7:26; Josh 6:17-18; 7:1, 11-13, 15; 22:20). The word usually has a negative connotation of putting something under complete destruction. It also carries a positive sense of "gifts" or "offerings" dedicated for the service of God (e.g., Lev 27:28; Num 18:14; Ezek 44:29). Other words with a negative connotation are אָרוּר ʾarur (Ps 119:21; Jer 48:10), קָלָל qalal (e.g., Deut 21:23; Isa 65:20), זְעוּמָה ze‘umah (Mic 6:10), מַעַל ma‘al (1 Chr 2:7).

The idea of "accursed" is expressed by anathema (Rom 9:3; 1 Cor 16:22; Gal 1:8, 9; 1 Cor 12:3 [accursed]), kakathema (Rev 22:3 [accursed]), kataraomai (accursed—Matt 25:41; Mark 11:21; curse—Luke 6:28; Rom 12:14; Jas 3:9), katara (curse Gal 3:10, 13; cursed Heb 6:8; cursing Jas 3:10; accursed 2 Pet 2:14), eparatos (John 7:49 [accursed]), epikataratos (Gal 3:10, 13 [cursed]). With the exception of anathēma ("gifts dedicated") in Luke 21:5, these terms have a negative force. Some examples of the accursed are: 1. Proclaimer of different gospel (Gal 1:8, 9); 2. Those who rely on the work of the law (Gal 3:10); 3. Anyone who does not love Jesus (1 Cor 16:22); 4. False prophets/teachers (2 Pet 2:14). See ANATHEMA; BLASPHEMY; BLESSINGS AND CURSINGS; DEVOTED; EXCOMMUNICATION; OATH.

VICTOR RHEE

ACCUSER. See SATAN.

ACHAIA uh-kay′yuh. The province of Achaia, formed after the incorporation of Greece in the Roman Empire (146 BCE), covered the area of the Peloponnese and southern mainland Greece. The term Achaians was used in the Homeric epics to refer to the Greeks, and in classical Greece Achaia was a distinct area in the northern Peloponnese. Macedonia, located north of Achaia, formed a separate province at certain times, such as after the Augustan reforms in 27 BCE. The province consisted of a series of cities, such as Argos, Athens and Sparta, which continued to maintain a strong Greek identity. Major sanctuaries which attracted visitors from across the Greek-speaking world included Olympia, Delphi, and Isthmia. Corinth, refounded in 44 BCE, became the provincial capital and seat of the Roman governor, which is where Paul encounters Gallio (Acts 18:12). Patras, in the northern Peloponnese, was another major colony. Parts of the province are described by the Augustan writer Strabo in books 8 and 9 of his Geography. A 2nd cent. CE view of the province can be obtained from the travel-writer Pausanias. Christian communities within the province seem to have worked together, responding to food-shortages at Jerusalem (Rom 15:26), and the main church seems to have been in Corinth (2 Cor 1:1).

Bibliography: David W. J. Gill. "Achaia." *The Book of Acts in Its Graeco-Roman Setting* (1994) 433–53.

DAVID W. J. GILL

ACHAICUS uh-kay´uh-kuhs [Ἀχαϊκός Achaikos]. Bracketed with STEPHANAS and FORTUNATUS in 1 Cor 16:17 as one of the three long-standing Christian converts from Corinth who traveled to Paul in Ephesus. They caused him delight, "raised his spirits" (16:18), helped compensate for his missing Corinth, and may have brought the letter to which Paul alludes in 7:1. "The Achaean" suggests a name suitable for a present or former slave, originally from somewhere other than Achaea.

ANTHONY THISELTON

ACHAN ay´kan [עָכָן ʿakhan, alternatively: ACHAR עָכָר ʿakhar]. The patriarch of a Judahite family stoned to death for taking and hiding devoted items from Jericho (Josh 7:1-26). Achan's story offers a sophisticated reflection on the danger of violating Israel's internal boundaries. Achan represents a Canaanized insider who brings what is outside (and different) into the midst of the community. Israel's survival as a nation is imperiled by hidden difference, a point made by interweaving themes of divine anger, national defeat, sacrilege, discovery, and punishment.

Achan's name derives from no known Semitic root and may be an intentional alteration of *Achar* (compare 1 Chr 2:7). *Achar* (calamity) corresponds to the language of punishment issued by JOSHUA and fits the etiological connection made with the VALLEY OF ACHOR (7:25-26). Achan, however, may constitute a cryptic reference to CANAAN, as the roots of the two terms share the same consonants but in different order.

L. DANIEL HAWK

ACHAR ay´kahr [עָכָר ʿakhar]. Carmi's son, called "the troubler of Israel" because he had violated the BAN (1 Chr 2:7). Some manuscripts read ACHAN.

ACHBOR ak´bohr [עַכְבּוֹר ʿakhbor]. 1. Father of the Edomite king, BAAL-HANAN (Gen 36:38-39; 1 Chr 1:49).

2. King JOSIAH's courtier who accompanies HILKI-AH on his quest to have HULDAH authenticate the Book of the Law (2 Kgs 22:12, 14). This could be the father of ELNATHAN (Jer 26:22; 36:12).

HEATHER R. MCMURRAY

ACHIM ay´kim [Ἀχίμ achim]. Son of Zadok and father of Eliud in Matthew's genealogy of Jesus (Matt 1:14).

ACHIOR ay´kee-ohr [Ἀχιώρ Achiōr]. In the book of JUDITH, the commander of the Ammonite army who is abandoned as a traitor by the Assyrians and taken captive by the people of Bethulia. A "righteous Gentile," Achior rehearses Jewish history and theology in impressive detail (Jdt 5:5-21), sides with the Jews in the battle, corroborates Judith's conquest (Jdt 14:5-8), and ultimately converts to Judaism (14:10). *See* GENTILES; JUDITH, BOOK OF.

LINDA DAY

ACHISH ay´kish [אָכִישׁ ʾakhish]. 1. The son of MAOCH and king of the Philistine city of GATH (1 Sam 21:27-29) who gives David ZIKLAG. From there David launches attacks against Israel's enemies, while telling Achish that he attacked Judah. The other Philistine lords do not trust David, so Achish sends David away before the Philistines fight the Israelites in Saul's final battle at Mount Gilboa (1 Sam 31).

2. The king of Gath when two servants of SHIMEI flee to Gath (1 Kgs 2:39-40). Shimei's pursuit of these servants leads to his death because he violates his oath to SOLOMON.

HEATHER R. MCMURRAY

ACHOR ay´kohr [עָכוֹר ʿakhor]. A valley located on the escarpment that rises near the northwest tip of the Dead Sea. Although the precise location of the valley is in dispute, it was well known in the biblical period, constituting a segment of the boundary between Judah and Benjamin (Josh 15:7). The valley's name, meaning *disaster*, suggests a particularly inhospitable area. The valley came to be associated with the execution of Achan and his family (Josh 7:24-26), although the name of the site probably predates the association. Both Isaiah and Hosea look to Achor's transformation into a fertile valley as a metaphor of divine restoration (Isa 65:10; Hos 2:15).

L. DANIEL HAWK

ACHSAH ak´suh [עַכְסָה ʿakhsah]. The daughter of CALEB who asked for and received springs of water in the NEGEB (Josh 15:13-19; Judg 1:11-15). Achsah exemplifies the aggressive initiative necessary for possessing the land promised by God and in so doing presents a feminine counterpoint to her father (Josh 4:6-12). Within Joshua, the grant of land she receives undercuts the equation of land with male ownership and anticipates a larger grant of land to other women, namely ZELOPHEHAD'S daughters. *See* ALLOTMENT OF LAND; LAND.

L. DANIEL HAWK

ACHSHAPH ak´shaf [אַכְשָׁף ʾakhshaf]. A city state in the coalition of hostile northern Canaanite kings (Josh 11:1) that became part of the territory of Asher (Josh 19:25). The city state appears in numerous ancient documents: Egyptian Execration Texts (20th–18th cent. BCE), the Karnak List of Towns conquered by Tutmose III (15th cent. BCE), the Tell el-Amarna Letters (ca. 14th cent. BCE) and the Papyrus Anastasi 1 (13th cent. BCE). Achshaph probably was in the plain of Acco.

J. GORDON HARRIS

ACHZIB ak′zib [אַכְזִיב ʾakhziv]. 1. A town of the tribe of Judah (Josh 15:44) in the Shephelah. Micah mentions it among several cities of the foothills using paronomasia or puns to indicate that Assyria would conquer them before Jerusalem (Mic 1:14). The town may be connected with the birthplace of Judah's son, Shelah. His mother was Bathshua, daughter of a Canaanite. His birth city was identified as CHEZIB (כְּזִיב keziv), a variant of Achzib (Gen 38:1-5).

2. A tell on the Mediterranean coast north of Acco that remained a Canaanite city during the period of the Judges (Josh 19:29; Judg 1:31). Excavations reveal that it existed in the MB, was sacked twice in the LB, and flourished in the 8th cent. BCE until 701 BCE when it was conquered by Sennacherib of Assyria. After the 6th cent. BCE it became a Phoenician city.

J. GORDON HARRIS

ACQUIRE [קָנָה qanah]. The primary sense of the verb qanah is concrete and economic, referring to the acquisition of property: most often real estate (Gen 33:19; Lev 25:30; 2 Sam 24:21; Jer 32:7ff.; etc.), but also livestock (2 Sam 12:3; 24:24), construction materials (2 Kgs 12:13; 22:6), spices (Isa 43:24), a loincloth (Jer 13:2, 4), a jug (Jer 19:1), etc. It is not uncommon for it to be accompanied by an explicit reference to monetary payment or some other form of compensation (Gen 33:19; 47:19; 2 Sam 24:24; Amos 8:6; etc.). Hence, the verb often takes on the specialized meaning of "to purchase" and functions as an antonym of "to sell" (Gen 47:19; Lev 25:14; Deut 28:68; Isa 24:2; Ezek 7:12).

In proverbial wisdom, the verb is applied to the intellectual realm to commend the acquisition of wisdom and knowledge (Prov 1:5; 4:5, 7; 15:32; 16:16; 17:16; 18:15; 19:8; 23:23; compare Sir 16:24; 51:25, 28). The economic nuance of the word is sometimes exploited to depict wisdom as a valuable commodity and to promise that those who acquire wisdom will profit by it: "Buy truth, and do not sell it; buy wisdom, instruction, and understanding" (Prov 23:23). "How much better to get wisdom than gold! To get understanding is to be chosen rather than silver" (Prov 16:16).

People may also be "acquired." The verb is used for the purchase of slaves (Gen 39:1; 47:19-23; Exod 21:2; Lev 22:11; 25:44-45, 50; Deut 28:68; Amos 8:6; Eccl 2:7; see SLAVERY), the acquisition of a wife (Ruth 4:5, 10), and the ransom of a prisoner (Neh 5:8). Old Testament laws pertaining to slaves were designed to protect Hebrew indentured servants from perpetual servitude, stipulating that they were to be released

every 7th year (Exod 21:1-11; compare Deut 15:12-15). However, foreigners and resident aliens could be acquired as permanent slaves (Lev 25:44-45). The usage in Ruth 4 is sometimes seen as evidence of the practice of MARRIAGE by purchase (i.e., through the payment of a bride-price). More likely, the language of "to acquire as wife" is determined by its immediate context, where marriage is linked to the "acquisition" of land (Ruth 4:5, 8-10). Detached from that context, the more typical language of "to take as wife" is employed (Ruth 4:13), suggesting that the choice of the former idiom is a matter of stylistic uniformity. A similar usage is attested also in Mishnaic Hebrew, where "acquire" is used for marriage—but only in contexts where the marriage occurs as a part of a larger commercial transaction involving the purchase or transfer of property.

God occurs as the subject of "acquire" in a number of poetic texts that bring together the notions of divine ownership and redemption (qanah//gaʾal Exod 15:13, 16; Pss 74:2; 78:54; Isa 11:11). As in other Semitic languages, the Hebrew verb qanah may also mean "to (be)get/bear" or "to create" (Deut 32:6; Ps 139:13; Prov 8:22; compare Gen 4:1b). The title שָׁמַיִם וָאָרֶץ קֹנֵה qoneh shamayim waʾarets "creator of heaven and earth" in Gen 14:19, 22 reflects a divine epithet widely attested in West Semitic. The participle קֹנֵה qoneh is usually understood to mean "creator," but it may mean "possessor" or "lord" of the earth (compare Isa 1:3, where בַּעַל baʿal "master" parallels qoneh).

EUNNY LEE

ACRE. See WEIGHTS AND MEASURES.

ACROSTIC. A poetic device where the initial signs of each line spell something meaningful. In Mesopotamian poetry, a message is spelled out, while the Bible always spells out the alphabet. Biblical acrostics, found only in the OT, reflect the existence of two different orders for the ALPHABET. Most are in Psalms and Lam 1–4; the end of Proverbs contains the famous acrostic "a capable wife." Psalm 119, an eight-fold alphabetic acrostic, is the most complex biblical acrostic. Some acrostics are incomplete or broken (e.g., Nah 1; Pss 9–10; 145; Prov 24:1-12; 29:22-27).

The purpose of acrostics is debated. Some scholars believe that they reflect a formal poetic technique, balancing a highly structured form with the creativity of poetry; others suggest that they facilitate memorization; some claim that acrostics reflect scribal training or pedagogical purposes, while others suggest that they express totality, or may even reflect ancient magical uses of the alphabet. Most likely, no single function explains all of the uses of acrostics, which developed into more diverse types in post-biblical Hebrew (including Ben Sirah and several compositions known from the Dead Sea Scrolls) and early Christian literature. See POETRY, HEBREW.

Bibliography: Victor Avigdor Hurowitz. "Proverbs 29:22-27: Another Unnoticed Alphabetic Acrostic." *JSOT* 92 (2001) 121–25; William Michael Soll. "Babylonian and Biblical Acrostics." *Bib* 69 (1988) 305–23.

MARC ZVI BRETTLER

ACT FAITHLESSLY. There are two main Hebrew verbs variously translated as to be or act faithlessly, treacherously, deceitfully, or unfaithfully (מָעַל ma'al, בָּגַד baghad). They both describe a situation common in the OT of the people not being trustworthy or not keeping their commitments to one another or to God. The equivalent verb in Greek (ἀπιστέω apisteō) does not carry the same connotations, but means something more like "disbelieve."

Faithless, sinful dealings between people are frequently decried in the Bible (e.g., Exod 21:8; Judg 9:23; Job 6:15; Ps 59:5; Prov 2:22; Jer 12:6; Hab 1:13). Even more frequent are the accusations against the people for their being treacherous toward God by breaking the covenant and commandments, especially those prohibiting idolatry (e.g., Lev 26:40; Num 31:16; Deut 32:51; Josh 22:16; 1 Sam 14:33; 1 Chr 10:13; 2 Chr 12:2; Ezra 10:2; Neh 1:8; Ps 78:57; Jer 5:11; Ezek 14:13; Dan 9:7). Transgressions against other people are also described as acts of faithlessness toward God (Lev 6:2; Num 5:6; Hos 6:7; Mal 2:10-16). Sexual infidelity, either on the wife's part (Num 5:12, 27), or by a man visiting a prostitute (Prov 23:28) is deemed an especially defiling form of faithlessness. It is often incorporated into the description of Israel's faithlessness toward God, as though Israel is the wayward wife and God is the wronged husband (1 Chr 5:25; Jer 3:8, 11, 20; Hos 5:7). Comparisons are sometimes made to nonhuman entities, as when an untrustworthy person is compared to a toothache (Prov 25:19), and when wealth or wine is said to be untrustworthy (Hab 2:5). In the Bible the phrase is meant to emphasize people's sinfulness and their inability to keep promises. Human faithlessness is contrasted with God's complete trustworthiness; one can rely on God's promises and commitments.

KIM PAFFENROTH

ACTS, BOOK OF. See ACTS OF THE APOSTLES.

ACTS OF ANDREW AND MATTHIAS. *See* ANDREW AND MATTHIAS (MATTHEW), ACTS OF.

ACTS OF BARNABAS. *See* BARNABAS, ACTS OF.

ACTS OF JOHN. *See* JOHN, ACTS OF.

ACTS OF PAUL AND THECLA. *See* PAUL AND THECLA, ACTS OF.

ACTS OF PETER. *See* PETER, ACTS OF.

ACTS OF SOLOMON, BOOK OF THE. *See* BOOKS REFERRED TO IN THE BIBLE.

ACTS OF THOMAS. *See* THOMAS, ACTS OF.

ACTS OF THE APOSTLES. The Acts of the Apostles narrates the early witness of the church to the resurrection of Jesus, beginning with the events of the Ascension and Pentecost in Jerusalem and continuing through Paul's arrival in Rome. Written by the author of the Gospel of Luke, Acts extends the evangelist's story of God's salvation through Jesus Christ both to the people of Israel and to the Gentiles.

A. Structure of Acts

The book of Acts lends itself to several different structural analyses. Because the figures of Peter and Paul loom large in the story, the book can be read as consisting of Part I (chs. 1–12), in which Peter is the main character, and Part II (chs. 13–28), in which Paul is the main character. Another conventional way of understanding the structure of Acts is to view it through the geographical spread of the church's witness, with the programmatic statement of 1:8 as a key. On this view, following the introduction in Acts 1, Acts 2–9 form the first part of the book, which traces the witness in Jerusalem, Judea, and Samaria, and chs. 10–28 constitute the second part, which traces the witness "to the ends of the earth."

These proposals are both helpful guides for first

readings of Acts, but neither one does justice to Luke's intricate story. If Acts divides itself into the accounts of Peter and then of Paul, it is hard to understand why the early chapters include almost nothing distinctive about Peter's biography or his attitudes. More important, the 2 parts of the story overlap in odd ways, with the first narration of Paul's conversion appearing in what is supposed to be Peter's half of the story (Acts 9:1-30) and with Peter appearing at the Jerusalem Council, which takes place in what is supposed to be Paul's half of the story (Acts 15:1-35). Similar problems arise with any straightforward geographical analysis of the structure of Acts, since there are several occasions when witnesses for the gospel encounter believers in locations that have not been mentioned earlier (e.g., 9:32, 36; 21:3-4). Most significantly, when Paul arrives in Rome, he is greeted by believers in that massively important location without anything that indicates how or when the witness arrived in Rome (28:14-15).

Instead of analyzing the structure of Acts simply in terms of personnel or places, it is instructive to examine the unfolding of the narrative. Two events may be regarded as pivotal: the inclusion of Cornelius and his household (10:1–11:18) and the final-defense speech of Paul (26:1-23). Both of these events are pivotal to the story in the sense that the surrounding narrative dramatically leads up to them and later must account for their consequences. The first scene establishes God's unilateral and unequivocal judgment that the Gentiles also are included within the scope of the gospel; the second scene declares Paul's innocence and faithfulness as a witness to God's offer of the gospel to Jew and Gentile alike. With these two events as keys to analyzing Luke's story, the following structure emerges:

Prologue 1:1–2:47
Part I   Acts 3:1–15:35
           Preparation 3:1–9:43
           Climactic Event 10:1–11:18
           Denouement 11:19–15:35
Part II   Acts 15:36–28:31
           Preparation 15:36–25:27
           Climactic Event 26:1-32
           Denouement 27:1–28:31

B. Detailed Analysis

1. Historical concerns

a. Authorship, audience, and date of composition. Perhaps as early as the late 2nd cent., Christian tradition identifies Luke as the author of both the Gospel of Luke and the Acts of the Apostles, although nowhere in either volume does the author's name appear. Further, tradition identifies this particular Luke as a physician who traveled with Paul. Eusebius, writing early in the 4th cent., describes Luke as "of Antiochene parentage and a physician by profession," who knew not only Paul but all of the apostles. Although the single authorship of both the Third Gospel and Acts is rarely questioned,

the notion that the author was named Luke and was a physician and companion of Paul rests on two assumptions, both of which are problematic. First, it assumes that the so-called "we" passages in Acts derive from an actual account composed by someone who traveled with Paul. The "we" passages are those sections of the book in which the narration suddenly shifts from third person to first person, as happens for the first time at 16:10: "When he had seen the vision, we immediately tried to cross over to Macedonia" (16:10-17; 20:5-15; 21:1-18; 28:1-16). This notion that the "we" passages come from Luke himself has been seriously questioned by critical scholarship (*see* below, "Sources"). Second, the traditional identification associates the companion of Paul, inferred from the "we" passages, with the Luke referred to in Col 4:14; 2 Tim 4:11; and Phlm 24. These are very loose textual connections, however. Philemon 24 simply lists Luke as one of Paul's fellow workers, along with Mark, Aristarchus, and Demas. Second Timothy 4:11 mentions Luke being with Paul and Col 4:14 mentions "Luke, the beloved physician." Yet many scholars question the Pauline authorship of both 2 Timothy and Colossians (*see* PASTORAL LETTERS and COLOSSIANS), which at least undermines the weight of the references.

Given the fragility of this evidence, scholars customarily employ the name "Luke" for the author in deference to tradition, but they turn to the text itself for whatever information it may yield about the author. In the opening lines of the Gospel the author uses a masculine verbal form in self-reference, which means that the author is almost certainly a man (παρηκολουθηκότι parēkolouthēkoti; "after investigating" Luke 1:3). Already in the infancy narratives and often elsewhere in both volumes, Luke gives evidence of extensive knowledge of the SEPTUAGINT, the OT in Greek translation. That could mean that Luke himself is Jewish. It could also mean that he is a Gentile who was persuaded by Christian proclamation after a long history of association with the synagogue, either as a proselyte to Judaism or as a regular observer of synagogue services (a "god-fearer"). The variety of narrative and rhetorical conventions present in the book and its dramatic and vivid style probably mean that Luke was well-educated, although educational level and social standing are not readily correlated in the Greco-Roman world.

Attempts to identify the audience of Luke–Acts begin with the opening lines of both volumes, where Luke explicitly addresses himself to "Theophilus." Luke provides no other information about his addressee. The name means "lover of God" or "beloved of God," and students of Luke–Acts have often concluded that Theophilus is a symbolic name, so that Theophilus represents anyone who has come to believe in the gospel and who seeks to know about it. Attractive as this conclusion is, there is not widespread evidence in this period for symbolic dedications. There was, however, the frequent practice of dedicating a book to a prominent or well-placed individual, with the expectation that the dedicatee would provide for its further distribution. Given that custom, it seems likely that, whomever the individual Theophilus is, Luke composes his work in the hope of a significantly larger audience than this one individual.

As in the case of learning something about the authorship of Acts, then, the text itself is searched for clues about the audience. Given the breadth of Luke's narrative, ranging as it does from Palestinian village life to philosophical discourses in Athens and on to house arrest in Rome, confident statements about Luke's audience are unlikely to be forthcoming. What is certain is that Luke's extended audience understands Greek (probably through hearing it read rather than through reading it, in view of the low rate of literacy and the expense involved in copying manuscripts). Given the content of both volumes, the audience appears to consist of people who are already Christians. (To be sure, the term *Christian* is anachronistic, although it appears already in Acts 11:26 as an epithet hurled at believers.) Little in the narrative would be inviting for those who do not already know something about the kingship of David, e.g., or the hope of a Messiah for Israel. Given the way in which Luke draws on OT traditions, both explicitly and implicitly, the audience is itself either acquainted with the OT or, more likely, Luke is employing his narrative to inform them.

These observations raise the difficult question of whether Luke's audience consists of Gentile or Jewish followers of "the Way" (Acts 9:2; 18:25; 19:9, 23; 22:4; 24:14, 22). Once again the breadth and complexity of Luke's story challenges easy answers. Although the early chapters of Acts, with their focus on Jerusalem, may suggest a Jewish audience, scenes in Athens and Antioch may be read as addressing the concerns of Gentile believers. A few small details might tip the scales in favor of a Gentile audience, as when Luke refers to the entirety of Palestine by the name "Judea" (e.g., Luke 1:5; 4:44; Acts 2:9; 10:37), or when he describes Sadducees and Pharisees in ways that would be superfluous for Jewish readers (Acts 23:8). An attractive conclusion might be that a significant portion of Luke's audience consists of "GOD-FEARERS," people who were informed about Jewish teaching and practice through the synagogue (*see* Acts 15:21) and who were well represented among early followers of "the Way." Nevertheless, even a brief consideration of the evidence reinforces the conclusion that ascertaining the ethnic composition of the intended audience for this volume is an extremely complex affair.

As with authorship and audience, there is also little evidence upon which to estimate the date of composition for Acts. At first glance, it might seem that Acts was composed while Paul was still alive, since he remains in custody at the end of the volume

(28:30-31), awaiting a trial before Caesar. Yet there are indications in the narrative that Luke knows of Paul's death (20:22-24, 38; 21:11-14), so that the narrative ending of Acts does not necessarily correlate with the time of composition. One secure date is offered by the procuratorship of Festus, who takes part in Paul's trial in Acts 25 and who becomes procurator ca. 59 CE. In addition, Luke almost certainly composed the Gospel before Acts, and the Gospel itself was likely written only after the destruction of the Jerusalem Temple in 70 CE (*see* Luke 19:41-44; 21:20-24). Taken together, then, these indications point to composition no earlier than the mid- to late 70s. Acquaintance with and usage of Acts by Christian writers can be traced, with some confidence, to the middle of the 2nd cent., implying that it must have been both composed and circulated before that time. That time frame suggests to many scholars a date of writing sometime in the 80s or 90s of the 1st cent.

b. Purposes. Since Luke is the only one of the four evangelists whose Gospel is accompanied by an account of events following the crucifixion and resurrection, the question of what prompted Luke to write this second volume is a matter of some significance. Because of its narrative form, it might be thought to offer an institutional history or a biography of Peter and Paul, but the highly selective nature of the scenes included and omitted undermines that theory. Specific sections of Acts lend themselves to theories about the need to respond to some misinterpretation of Christianity. For example, the fact that in some passages representatives of the Roman Empire appear to respond protectively to Christian witnesses (e.g., 18:12-17; 23:16-30; 27:1-3, 42-44) prompts the theory that Luke writes to secure the protection of Rome for the fledgling church; or the long series of Paul's trials and defense speeches are read as reflecting a need to defend Paul to Jewish Christians who regard him as an apostate to Judaism (chps. 21–26). Such explanations of the book's purpose generally fail because they account well for only one relatively small segment of what is a long and multifaceted story.

In a general sense, Luke's purpose can be understood as catechetical, in that he seeks to instruct believers, particularly Gentile believers, in the fundamentals of their tradition. To be sure, Luke has not composed a textbook or a curriculum for formal classroom use, but much of the content and shape of both the Gospel and Acts would serve well to consolidate those who are relatively new to the faith.

Within the general rubric of catechesis, two overarching aspects of the story stand out as significant and may suggest specific concerns for Luke's audience. First, Luke–Acts devotes massive attention to the history of God's dealings with Israel. This is evident from beginning to end in Luke's Gospel, as even a casual glance at the story of Jesus' birth or the resurrection narrative will confirm. Acts also concerns God's dealings with Israel. The motif is most obvious in the early events that take place in Jerusalem, since Peter's early sermons present Jesus as the fulfillment of God's promises to Israel, and Stephen's long recounting of Israel's history likewise places Jesus within that framework. The chapters that follow the Jerusalem Council place more emphasis on the gospel's inclusion of Gentiles, but God's history with Israel returns importantly in Paul's defense speeches and in the final scene of the book. If Acts is a kind of catechesis, then the shape of that catechesis has to do with God's actions for Israel in the past and the way in which those actions now incorporate Gentiles alongside Jews. Especially if the Lukan audience does contain a number of Gentile believers, then Luke wishes his Gentile audience to understand that the story of Jesus Christ makes no sense apart from the context of God's ongoing history with Israel, a history that now reaches out to include them as well. As the Jerusalem Council makes clear, these Gentiles believers do not need to become Jews themselves, but they do need to be grounded in Israel's story.

One reason for the desire to place both Jews and Gentiles within the story of Israel is that Gentiles may find that their former religious practices exert an enormous pull. An important feature of Acts concerns the discrediting of other gods. As early as Stephen's speech, Luke reminds his audience that God does not reside in houses constructed by human beings (7:48), a conventional claim about Israel's God that takes on a polemical cast when placed before by a Gentile audience. When a healing at Lystra prompts the inhabitants to mistake Paul and Barnabas for Hermes and Zeus, Paul responds with an explicit attack on the "worthless" things that are worshiped as divine (14:8-20). The Areopagus speech brings this attack to its full volume (17:22-31), and the riot in Ephesus reveals the passion with which one of those same gods is defended (19:23-41). The Jerusalem Council results in agreement that Gentiles must foredate idolatry (15:20, 29). Given the ubiquity of the gods and the ubiquity of opportunities to pay them honor and service, many Gentiles who were drawn to Christian belief and practice may have found the continuing attraction of those other gods extremely powerful. In common with other early Christian writers (notice Rev 2:20-23; 1 Cor 8:1-6), Luke fiercely rejects any hint of syncretism.

c. Questions of historical accuracy and reliability. Because Acts presents itself as a narrative of historical events, and also because there is no source parallel to it from the earliest period of the church's life, students of Christianity long tried to reconstruct the history of the early church by using information gleaned from this book. Much of 20th cent. scholarship on the book of Acts focused on such historical investigation, with vigorous debates ensuing, in which some staunchly defended the accuracy of Luke's account and others critiqued it. When framing the question of historical accuracy, it is important to distinguish exactly what kind of information is being sought and what information Luke might reasonably provide.

In a number of instances, Luke does seem to make factual errors. In 5:36, GAMALIEL refers to an attempted revolt led by someone named Theudas, an incident confirmed by the account of JOSEPHUS (*Ant.* 18.1-10; 20.97-98; *J.W.* 2.117-18; 7.252-53), but located by him in the mid-40s, well after the scene in Acts 5 might have taken place. Many other details of the story, particularly the names of Roman officials, do find confirmation in contemporaneous historical works. There are also some larger motifs in the story that may well reflect Luke's shaping of events. During Paul's travels, he regularly begins his witnessing in synagogues, finds himself in conflict with Jews as a result of that activity, and also finds Gentiles who are receptive to Christian preaching (13:13-52; 14:1-7; 17:1-10, 11-15; 18:5-17). Precisely because that pattern is so regular, readers suspect that the history has been conformed to Luke's understanding. That is in no way surprising, since it is an unavoidable feature of narration; neither Luke nor anyone else could tell everything that happened, so the selection involved in any narration already shapes that narration.

Given that inescapable shaping of narratives, the use of Acts for reconstructing the chronology of PAUL's life and witness is particularly difficult. In Acts 17, Paul begins his work in Thessalonica in the synagogue, where there are both Jewish and Gentile converts, but 1 Thessalonians yields no evidence that the congregation there contains Jewish believers. Paul's letters say nothing of his education or his birth in Tarsus, and their comments about his conversion are quite restricted. Luke's account of the Jerusalem Council is exceedingly difficult to coordinate with Paul's comments in Gal 2. As a result of these problems, the more cautious procedure is to employ Paul's letters as primary sources and to use Acts only to corroborate or supplement what is gleaned from the correspondence.

2. Cultural contexts

Whatever questions persist about the historicity of Luke's account of the spread of the Christian witness, Acts offers its readers a vibrant portrait of the multiplicity of cultures in the 1st cent. world. The historical location of Luke–Acts is that of the ROMAN EMPIRE. Although Rome seldom enters the narrative explicitly before Acts 19:21, the empire directly controls every city and territory named in the whole of Luke–Acts. At several points the story proceeds on the tacit assumption that the legal processes of the empire can be trusted, as when Paul insists on being treated according to the standards promised to Romans citizens (16:35-40; 22:25) or when he appeals to the emperor for a hearing based on his Roman citizenship (25:10,

21; 26:32). The constant travel that frames the second half of Acts reflects the relative stability of this period and the safety of the ubiquitous road system. Not everything is innocuous, to be sure. The proconsul GALLIO pays no attention to the charges brought against Paul, but he also pays no attention to the public beating of Sosthenes (18:12-17). The public outrage in Ephesus is quelled only when the town clerk utters a less than subtle threat about what might happen if residents were charged with rioting (19:23-41).

Paul and his coworkers often receive fair, even protective, treatment from local leaders who are, however remotely, representatives of Rome—such as Claudius Lysias who safely removes Paul from Jerusalem (22:22-29; 23:16-31), Agrippa and Festus who patiently hear Paul's defense (25:13–26:32), and the centurion Julius who is charged with transporting Paul to Rome (27:3, 43). This pattern is often understood to reflect Luke's desire to curry favor with Rome, that he writes to seek the support or protection of Rome for the emerging church. Yet the evidence is not univocal. The governor Felix, while keeping Paul in custody for 2 years, seeks out conversation with him in the hopes of receiving a bribe (24:24-27). And the letter Claudius Lysias writes to Felix about Paul does not entirely coincide with the incidents that had preceded it, for Lysias is also protecting himself even while protecting Paul (23:26-30). In addition, Peter's words to the Roman centurion Cornelius—that Jesus Christ is "Lord of all"—sharply conflict with the empire's understanding of its own place (*see also* 17:1-9). The conflicting evidence about Luke's stance toward Rome reflects Luke's total focus on the narration of God's actions in the event of Jesus Christ; that focus in turns means Luke assesses everyone and everything solely by the standard of the gospel. Luke is not apolitical; instead, he understands that power (and therefore politics) belongs to God. For him, therefore, the assumption that Rome has power or is powerful would be a false assumption, even a delusion (as in Acts 4:19-20; 5:27-42).

Within the sphere of Roman control, Greek culture has an ongoing impact, as is evidenced most basically in the Greek language Luke writes. That Paul himself knows Greek gains him the attention of the tribune in Jerusalem, who fears that he may be a rebellious Egyptian (21:37-38). The journeying motif that preoccupies much of Acts as well as Luke's Gospel has counterparts in Greek literature, beginning with Homer, of course, and extending well past Luke's time. In particular, the extended account of Paul's journey to Italy by ship, complete with the storm and shipwreck and the uncertain welcome by local inhabitants, is a standard feature of Greek literature. Of the many scenes that reflect the assumptions and values of Greek culture, perhaps none is more important than Paul's sermon in Athens, introduced by the fickleness of Athenian intellectuals, cast as a conversation with Epicureans and Stoics, and

located in the heart of Greek civilization. Peter and John may be recognized in Jerusalem as "uneducated and ordinary men" (4:13), but Luke shows that the gospel is fully equipped for encounter with Greek culture.

However imbued Acts is with the world of Greece and Rome, Luke's grand story begins in Jerusalem with the story of Zechariah's priestly service, and that location is never entirely left behind, no matter how much territory is covered by the time the reader reaches Acts 28. The formative early scenes of the church's life are not only located geographically in Jerusalem but culturally as well. The early sermons in Jerusalem introduce Jesus by placing him in the history of Israel; Peter can explain who Jesus is by appeal to Moses and David, and especially to God's promises in Scripture. The religious authorities resist the preaching of Peter and attempt to silence it, but the conflict is that between two understandings of Judaism. The crisis posed by the neglect of certain widows in the community reflects the scriptural mandate to care for the widow and the orphan. Even Stephen's sharp attack on the Jews of Jerusalem reinforces the Jewishness of this story, both by its rehearsal of Israel's history and by its prophetic tone.

To be sure, once persecution forces believers to flee Jerusalem (8:1), and especially after Paul and Barnabas begin their work together, the locations and cultural settings change. Yet the Jewish matrix of Luke's story never disappears from view. Most obviously, Jerusalem provides the location for both the Council of Acts 15 and the first stage of Paul's arrest and trial. In addition, synagogues regularly serve as the beginning point of Paul's work in various cities. That pattern is not abandoned, even in the imperial city of Rome, where the closing scene of the entire two-volume work finds Paul in conversation with Jews. The large sweep of the narrative works as a confirmation of Paul's claim to Agrippa that he had always behaved faithfully to "the prophets and Moses."

3. Literary features
a. Genre. While widespread agreement exists that Acts belongs to the general category of historiography, several proposals have emerged that attempt to specify the genre of Acts more narrowly. A more precise definition of the genre of Luke's second volume might help to understand the larger function of this book, a book without parallel in the NT. Several proposals about genre articulate a place for Acts within historiographical writing (historical monograph, apologetic history, general history, institutional history). Some read Acts as the history of the successors of Jesus, so that Acts continues Luke's biography of Jesus. Other proposals place Acts more closely to the ancient novel rather than to history.

Reasons for these varying proposals are not difficult to find. The distinctions among genres are quite fluid, and it is highly unlikely that a writer as skilled as Luke was constrained by the conventions of any single genre. In fact, individual features of each of these genres appear within the lines of Acts. For example, the shipwreck that finds Paul on the island of Malta and welcomed by local inhabitants has counterparts in a number of ancient novels. On the other hand, the speeches that form an important part of the book have their literary home in historiography. It is more helpful, then, to explore the multiple genres that constitute Acts rather than to read the book through a single lens.

b. Sources. In the opening lines of Luke's Gospel, he explicitly refers to previous accounts of "the events that have been fulfilled among us" and to his own careful investigation. If the words of this preface stand over both the Gospel and Acts, then Luke himself seems to indicate that he has used earlier sources in the writing of both volumes. Many NT scholars agree that the composition of the Gospel reflects the use of earlier written or oral sources (*see* SYNOPTIC PROBLEM), and deduce from that fact the probability that Luke also had written or oral sources at his disposal for the composition of Acts. One conventional approach identifies sources as arising from local church traditions, so that the church at Antioch, for example, might be represented by a source recounting its history. The early chapters, on the other hand, might come from a source connected with the church at Jerusalem.

The uniqueness of Acts in the NT constitutes a major problem for various source proposals, and attempts to separate sources in Acts have dwindled in recent decades. Unlike the Gospel of Luke, which has parallels in Matthew and Mark and occasionally the Gospel of John, the book of Acts has no parallels with which to compare or contrast. While some events related in Acts may be identified with passages in the letters of Paul (e.g., Acts 15 and Gal 2), there are very few such common reports, and they are notoriously difficult to analyze for comparative purposes. Another challenge that faces any attempt to analyze the sources of Acts is that Luke's own vocabulary and style pervade the entire book. References to divine necessity or to the boldness of the church's witness are not confined to single portions of the text. At the very least, this means that Luke freely edited any sources he employed, which renders the isolation of those sources improbable.

An important challenge to the observation about Luke's style and vocabulary pervading the book arises with the "we" passages. At several places in Acts, and without any introductory comment or explanation, the narrator shifts from third person into first person plural. This takes place first when the narrator inexplicably changes from describing the travels of "they" (Paul, Silas, and Timothy) through Phrygia and Galatia, to the determination that "we" should cross into Macedonia (16:6, 10). Later, as Paul begins his final journey to Jerusalem, the narration shifts its explanation of the travel of Paul from "he" and "they," when "we"

intrude to sail with him to Troas (20:5-15; *see also* 21:1-18; 27:1–28:16). Readers of Acts have traditionally and understandably deduced that these sections of the book come from an eyewitness account, either an account written by Luke himself, or that of someone else who traveled with Paul. What argues against this assumption is that even in the "we" sections, the literary style and vocabulary cohere with that of the larger narrative. In addition, research into the compositions of ancient historians undermine the assumption that a change in narration indicates a change in sources.

It is best to conclude that, whatever written or oral sources Luke may have used, including the "we" source, they are no longer available for analysis. That conclusion does not mean that Luke wrote Acts without reference to any earlier accounts, but it does mean that readers of Acts will do better to refrain from attempting reconstruction of Luke's treatment of his sources.

c. Literary characteristics. The elusive nature of the genre and sources of Acts in no way detracts from the effectiveness of Luke's story, which engages readers with a variety of storytelling techniques and traditions. To begin with, Luke draws deeply on the OT. The sermons of Peter and Paul's first sermon in Pisidian Antioch interpret Jesus by means of prominent figures drawn from the OT, most especially Moses and David (e.g., 2:29-32; 3:22-23; 13:36-37). Stephen's inflammatory speech in Acts 7 recalls several important OT recitals of God's actions on behalf of Israel and Israel's persistent rebellion, as in Joshua's recollection of events leading up to the conquest (Josh 24:2-13) and the recollections of it in Pss 78, 105, 106, and 135. The healings by Elijah and Elisha in an upper room (1 Kgs 17:17-24; 2 Kgs 4:18-37; *see also* Luke 7:11-17; 8:41-42, 49-56) are recast in Peter's healings of Aeneas and Dorcas (Acts 9:32-43).

Luke draws effectively on non-Jewish literary traditions as well. The scene in Lystra, when Paul and Barnabas are mistaken for gods, shows the influence of numerous accounts of gods appearing in human form and taking mortals by surprise (14:8-18). Similarly, the role assigned to Rhoda in Acts 12 plays off of comic accounts involving a female servant who is both confused and confusing to others. The dramatic account of the storm and shipwreck that comprises Acts 27 is such a standard feature of Greco-Roman literature that it becomes a target of satirists. The extensive use that Luke makes of the speeches also reflects Greco-Roman practice.

These various literary influences come together in a story that is crafted for maximum effect. To begin with, Luke ties together the narrative of the Gospel with that of Acts by presenting many important scenes in Acts that parallel earlier events in the Gospel. The story of Jesus' ascension offers an excellent example of such parallels, since it serves to close Luke's Gospel and to open the story of Acts. The healings carried out by Peter (3:1-10; 9:32-43) and later by Paul (14:8-11) recall Jesus's own role as healer. Stephen's death as the wrongful death of an innocent person replays that of Jesus. In particular, Stephen prays for Jesus to receive his spirit, just as Jesus himself submits his spirit to God (Luke 23:46; Acts 7:59; and *see also* Ps 31:5). A further link between the two scenes comes as Stephen's vision of Jesus standing at God's right hand fulfills Jesus' declaration to the council at his trial (Luke 22:69).

Another important instance in which Acts re-presents elements of Luke's Gospel appears in the parallels between Jesus' journey to Jerusalem and that of Paul to Jerusalem and Rome. Both begin with a clear declaration of intent; as Jesus "set his face to go to Jerusalem" (Luke 9:51), later Paul resolves "in the Spirit" that he must go to Jerusalem and then to Rome (19:21). Each journey is punctuated by reminders of the destination that lies ahead. Although Paul's does not culminate in crucifixion, there are hints that death awaits him in Rome.

In addition to these parallels between Acts and Luke's Gospel, Luke also makes extensive use of repetition internal to Acts itself. Repetition, whether of entire scenes or of elements of them, underscores the importance of events, especially for early audiences, most of whom were hearing the narrative read aloud rather than reading it for themselves. The most elaborate instance of repetition, both of single elements and of whole scenes, appears in the Cornelius account in 10:1–11:18. Peter three times sees the vision involving all sorts of animals, clean and unclean (10:9-16). The men who come to Peter from Cornelius repeat what Cornelius (and the reader) has already learned in 10:1-9, but Cornelius repeats it again himself in vv. 30-33. As if this elaborate presentation were not enough, Luke has Peter recount the entire event again before believers in Jerusalem in 11:1-18. The whole event is then replayed yet again as part of the discussion at the Apostolic Council (15:7-11).

Another prominent instance of repetition is that of Paul's conversion, which Luke narrates three times (in chs. 9, 22, 26) and in three distinct ways that reflect the particular context of each narration. The sermons of Peter in Jerusalem and Paul's initial sermon at Pisidian Antioch also repeat, and thereby reinforce, one another in their interpretation of Jesus' place in Israel's history, their accusation against Jerusalem Jews for crucifying Jesus, and their explanation of God's role in events (2:14-36; 3:12*b*-26; 13:16*b*-41). The stories of Paul's witness in various cities are sometimes hard to distinguish from one another because they repeat the pattern of proclamation, acceptance of the gospel by some, and resistance to the gospel by others, a resistance that often propels Paul out of town.

Continuing a pattern employed in the Third Gospel (*see*, e.g., 2:25-48), Acts pairs stories involving male characters with those involving female characters, thus making for yet another form of repetition. Instead of compressing the story of Ananias and Sapphira into a single event, Luke first explains what happened to Ananias and then how the same demise overtook Sapphira (5:1-11). The two vignettes at the conclusion of Acts 9 likewise recount first the healing of Aeneas (9:32-35) and then that of Dorcas (9:36-43).

Luke's treatment of individual characters often fascinates and puzzles readers. He does not display a modern interest in character study or character development; instead, his characters enter and exit the narrative to play a specific role within the larger story of God's actions on behalf of Israel and the Gentiles. Nevertheless, the use of vivid detail enlivens some of Luke's characters, such as the Ethiopian eunuch, a powerful member of the court of Ethiopia, who actively seeks out the gospel (8:26-40). Later, Paul encounters "a slave-girl who had a spirit of divination and brought her owners a great deal of money by fortune-telling" (16:16). With a single line, Luke tips off readers to both the girl's situation and the avarice of her owners.

Consistent with his subordination of human agents to the larger story of God's actions, Luke frequently introduces characters only to have them disappear. Considerable care is taken with the story of Matthias's selection as the replacement for Judas (1:15-26), creating the expectation that Matthias will play some significant role, yet his name never again appears in the book of Acts. In the same way, Luke recounts the selection of seven men who are charged with caring for the widows, but only two of them enter the story again, Stephen and Philip (6:1-6). Perhaps most striking is Luke's treatment of Peter, whose work is crucial in Jerusalem, yet after the Jerusalem Council he simply disappears from sight.

In at least two instances, Luke creates small and elegant introductions for characters who will become important parts of the story; he does so by introducing the character, then allowing the character to disappear and then reappear when that character has a larger role to play. Barnabas initially comes on the scene in Acts 4, when Luke reports that he sold a parcel of land and then gave the proceeds to be used by the community, placing the funds at the feet of the apostles (4:36-37). Nothing more is reported about Barnabas until after Paul's conversion, when he mysteriously reappears in Jerusalem, where he vouches for Paul's truthfulness when he is in danger (9:26-30). He again disappears from the narrative until 11:22 to ascertain what has happened in Antioch and subsequently seeks Paul's assistance. From that point on until the separation in 15:36-41, he and Paul form a team. A similar pattern obtains with the introduction of Paul (as Saul), whose initial appearance at the death of Stephen (7:59–8:1, 3) is followed by a disappearance and then by his return in ch. 9 in the first account of his conversion.

d. Significant themes. Several important themes

recur in the narrative in service of its larger catechetical and theological concerns. Perhaps the most obvious is the theme of promise and fulfillment. As was the case already in Luke's Gospel (Luke 1:13-17, 19-20, 31-33, 35-37, 54-55), the story opens with a series of promises, in this case promises from and about the risen Jesus. Jesus himself instructs the apostles to wait in Jerusalem for the fulfillment of "the promise of the Father," namely, the gift of the Holy Spirit (Acts 1:4). He also promises the witness that is to take place in "Jerusalem, in all Judea and Samaria, and to the ends of the earth" (1:8). In addition, Jesus' ascension is marked by the promise of his eventual return (1:11). The fulfillment of the promise of the Holy Spirit begins at Pentecost, with the dramatic outpouring on those gathered in Jerusalem, but the outpouring of the Holy Spirit continues to take place throughout Acts (e.g., 4:31; 8:15-17; 10:44; 19:6-7). The promise of the witness "to the ends of the earth" similarly begins to be fulfilled at Pentecost and continues throughout the book. Although the promise of Jesus' return is not fulfilled in the pages of Acts, the expectation of Jesus' return exerts its influence on the story (as in 17:30-31).

Acts continues to interpret Jesus himself as the fulfillment of God's own promises. Peter begins his Pentecost speech by quoting from Joel and interpreting the outpouring of the Holy Spirit as the fulfillment of Joel's words (2:16); he later identifies Jesus as the fulfillment of God's promise regarding David's offspring (2:29; *see also* 2:39). Peter's second speech identifies Jesus with the prophet-like-Moses whom God had promised to Israel (3:22). In his first speech at Pisidian Antioch Paul begins with a recital of Israel's history and interprets the resurrection itself as the fulfillment of God's promise (13:16-41). Likewise, Paul's final defense speech declares to Agrippa that he is on trial solely because of his "hope in the promise made by God, to our ancestors" (26:6).

To say that this is a story of promises does not mean that the fulfillment of those promises is met with approval and ready acceptance. Early on, the religious authorities in Jerusalem are unprepared to welcome the fulfillment of God's promises, since they are troubled by the people's warm response to Peter's preaching of the resurrection (4:1-3; 5:18). A similar rejection dogs Paul's travels and results in his arrest and trial. It is not only outsiders who find the fulfillment of the promises unacceptable, however. The story of the church's own resistance to the conversion of the gentiles indicates that even those who are part of "the Way" do not welcome the fulfillment of this particular promise to "those that are far off" (Acts 2:39). (*See* PROMISE.)

This resistance to the fulfillment of the promises is related to a second significant theme in Acts, namely, the relationship between resistance to the gospel and its growth. Luke repeatedly narrates incidents in which attempts to silence or confine Christian preaching results instead in its further spread. The religious leaders in Jerusalem explicitly warn Peter and John against preaching further in Jesus' name (4:13-22), but the community immediately joins in prayer and receives the gift of the Spirit and of boldness (4:23-31). Following the second arrest, they are flogged and warned against preaching further (5:39-40), but they persist in preaching and their numbers increase (5:41–6:1). The outbreak of persecution that follows Stephen's death propels all but the apostles out of Jerusalem, which in turn prepares the way for the witness in Samaria (8:1b-4). Later on, there are those who resist Paul's witness in the various cities of his travels, but when they succeed in forcing him from one city, he simply moves on to another.

The most developed instance of resistance that results in further proclamation is that of the church's enemy, Saul. Already at the end of Luke's introduction of Saul, he emerges as an ardent persecutor of the church (8:3). When he returns in Acts 9, he is actively seeking to extend that persecution outside of Jerusalem (matching the proclamation of the gospel that has moved outside Jerusalem in Acts 8). Of course, by the end of the story in Acts 9, Saul is no longer the persecutor; his encounter with the risen Jesus brings about his reversal, and he now emerges as an equally ardent proclaimer of the gospel who is himself being persecuted (9:19b-30). The retellings of this event in Acts 22 and 26 draw further attention to this radical reversal in Paul's life, since both accounts emphasize both the intensity of his resistance to the gospel and his divine calling to preach that same gospel. (*See* CHRISTIANS, PERSECUTION OF.)

This emphasis on the persistence of preaching introduces yet another theme, that of the boldness (παρρησία *parrhēsia*) of the witnesses. As early as Pentecost, Peter describes his own proclamation about Jesus as an act of boldness (2:29; NRSV: confidently), and the Jerusalem authorities who question Peter and John see this boldness in their responses (4:13). In the scene that follows, after the two have been released and have returned to their fellow believers, the gathered community prays together. Notably, they do not pray for protection or for the overthrow of their enemies but for boldness of speech (4:29) and for the presence of God in "signs and wonders." Luke reports that, following this prayer, the place itself is shaken and all are filled with the Spirit and also that they "spoke the word of God with boldness" (4:31). This boldness of speech becomes a hallmark of the activity of the witnesses. Paul and Barnabas "boldly" confront those Jews in Pisidian Antioch who speak out against their preaching (13:46). In Iconium, the pair preaches "boldly for the Lord" (14:3). Apollos speaks "boldly" in the synagogue of Ephesus regarding "the Way of the Lord" (18:26), as Paul does in Corinth (19:8). Following the climactic speech before Agrippa, Paul declares that he has spoken boldly (26:26; NRSV: freely). Given this pattern, it is not surprising that Luke concludes the entire book with the observation that Paul, although confined to his own lodging, continued to preach and teach "with all boldness and without hindrance" (28:31). By doing so, Luke indicates that even confinement will not bring an end to Christian proclamation. (*See* BOLDNESS, CONFIDENCE IN FAITH.)

A final theme that plays a significant role in Acts concerns the proper use of money or possessions. Acts does not contain the explicit teaching about money or possessions that is found in the Gospel of Luke. The warnings of John the Baptist (Luke 3:10-14) and the teachings of Jesus about wealth (e.g., Luke 12:13-21; 16:11-13, 19-31; 18:22-25) have no clear counterpart in Acts. Instead of teaching directly, Luke shows indirectly that possessions are opportunities for service, even as the greed for possessions constitutes a serious threat. The well-known stories of the sharing of goods in the Jerusalem community draws on a Greco-Roman convention according to which friends share their property, but those stories also make clear that this friendship extends to real property, that the owning of property is subordinated to the community generated by the gospel (2:44-45; 4:32-37).

Although that particular practice does not obtain outside of Jerusalem, Luke does report favorably on a number of disciples (or those who become disciples) who use their possessions wisely on behalf of others. One reason for the deep grief that envelopes Peter when he arrives at the home of Dorcas is that "she was devoted to good works and acts of charity," and she made clothing for the widows in the community (9:36, 39). Cornelius, even prior to his conversion, is described as someone who "gave alms generously to the people" (10:2; *see also* Luke 7:1-10). In Philippi, Paul meets Lydia of Thyatira, who deals in the luxury good of purple cloth, and who insists on offering the hospitality of her household to Paul and others (16:11-15, 40).

If Luke is careful to draw attention to acts of generosity, he is equally careful to draw attention to those who appear to be motivated by avarice. This thread in the story begins as early as the brief report about Judas, who "acquired a field with the reward of his wickedness" (1:18). Although Luke attributes to Satan the act of Ananias and Sapphira, who withhold funds they have declared for the common purse, the story nevertheless displays the dire consequences attached to such deceit about money (5:1-11). Simon Magus is explicitly said to have offered money to Peter and John so that he might receive the power to convey the Holy Spirit (8:14-24), and the owners of the slave girl are incensed when Paul expels her demon and renders her incapable of making money for them (16:16-24). The riot in Ephesus erupts because of Demetrius's fear that Christian preaching would disrupt their local trade in the business of Artemis (19:23-41). The Roman official Felix seeks out conversation with Paul, in the hope of receiving a bribe (24:26). (*See* WEALTH.)

This pervasive theme about the responsible and irresponsible disposition toward possessions may help to explain two otherwise odd details in the story. Toward the end of his speech to the Ephesian elders in Miletus, Paul comments that he has never taken money from anyone and quotes an otherwise unknown saying of Jesus: "It is more blessed to give than to receive" (20:33-35). Since the plot has not included any accusation of malfeasance against Paul, the comment seems out of place. Given Luke's larger concern about the proper use of possessions, however, it makes sense that this intensely pastoral speech, a speech that marks the end of Paul's work among believers, should touch on the question of money. Luke's teaching about extends even to the last lines of the book, since he reports that Paul lived in Rome, under arrest, but "at his own expense" (28:30).

C. Theological and Religious Significance of Acts
1. "Plan of God" and "Will of God"

Although it is conventional to speak of the Acts of the Apostles as the story of the church or the story of Peter and Paul, the overarching theological preoccupation of Acts is with God. Already with the two phrases "plan of God" and "will of God," Luke's theological concerns come to expression. Luke uses "word of God" to refer to the content of the gospel itself, as when Sergius Paulus seeks to hear "the word of God" from Barnabas and Paul (13:7; *see also* 4:31; 13:44; 16:32). "Plan of God" has to do with the intention and oversight of God that comprehends both the life and ministry of Jesus and the way in which the witness to Jesus' resurrection makes its way through the Mediterranean world. Peter declares that God's plan included even the act of those Jerusalem Jews who killed Jesus (2:23), and Paul summarizes his preaching as comprising the "whole purpose [i.e., plan] of God" (20:27; *see also* 4:28; 5:38; 13:36). See WILL OF GOD.

These phrases reveal the comprehensive nature of Luke's understanding of the role of God, fundamental to which is the understanding that God is the God of Israel. Peter's Pentecost speech connects Jesus with the prophecy of Joel as well as with the story of David (2:16, 24-36). Peter later speaks of "the God of Abraham, the God of Isaac, and the God of Jacob, the God of our ancestors" (3:13). Stephen's speech consists of a lengthy rehearsal of God's history with Israel. To be sure, when Paul addresses Gentiles in Lystra and in Athens, he does not begin with God's history with Israel, but even on those occasions Israel's understanding of God as creator makes its way into the text. In Luke's presentation of the gospel and its witness, God's action on behalf of human salvation is profoundly related to God's repeated initiative to rescue and redeem Israel.

God's faithfulness to the promises of Scripture replays God's covenant faithfulness in the OT.

Understanding that God is the God of Israel is essential for Acts, but it is equally essential to understand that God is the Father of Jesus, the one who sent him, who attested Jesus through his deeds, and through whose own foreknowledge and plan Jesus was crucified. Most important for Luke, God is the one who raised Jesus from the dead. All of these actions convey what must be known about Jesus, but they also convey what must be known about God. That is to say, while Israel's history is necessary for understanding Acts, Israel's history does not appear in Luke's story on its own, apart from its relationship to Jesus. This comes to expression early on, in Peter's speeches, since Israel's history serves as a framework for explaining Jesus' identity. Even Stephen's long rehearsal of the history of Israel in Acts 7 finally makes reference to Jesus, and there are hints throughout the speech of the relationship between Jesus and the patriarchs. Because of the extensive use of prophetic imagery in Acts, it is tempting to read the history of Israel in this book as if Jesus were simply one more in the line of the prophets. Yet, Jesus is both the "prophet-like-Moses" (3:22) and more than that; he is God's very agent of salvation.

In addition to being the God of Israel and the Father of Jesus Christ, in Acts God is also the God who includes the Gentiles. There are hints of this radical act of inclusion early on in the church's life in Jerusalem (2:39; 3:25; and *see* Luke 2:32), as well as in the story of the Ethiopian eunuch (8:26-40), but this feature of God's character comes to full expression in the account of Peter and Cornelius in 10:1–11:18. As Peter reluctantly recognizes what the heavenly voice means when it declares that God makes clean, he draws the only possible conclusion: "God shows no partiality" (10:34). The statement is particularly revealing, because it is one of the only times when Luke employs a principle or an abstraction in his description of God. After the Cornelius event, when Peter rehearses the Cornelius story for believers in Jerusalem, those believers draw the conclusion again: "Then God has given even to the Gentiles the repentance that leads to life" (11:18). Later on, Paul and others frequently depict their labor as God's own activity among the Gentiles: God "had opened a door of faith for the Gentiles" (14:27; *see also* 15:4, 12; 21:19). God is the God of Israel, the God who raised Jesus from the dead, and the God who acts decisively to include the Gentiles.

A final element in Luke's characterization of God has to do with the community of believers: God is the God who acts among and through those who are called to believe in Jesus' name. (Here, as elsewhere, the actions attributed to "God" also include those of Jesus and the Spirit, as the actions of the three are profoundly intertwined in Acts; *see* below). The story of Acts is not, in the first instance, a story about the church or its apostles or its leaders, but a story about God's own actions through those people. This claim intersects with the claim that God is the God of Israel, of course, since both the apostles and many early believers are themselves Jews. Divine direction begins even before the ascension, with the instruction given to the apostles. It extends to include the rescue of all those caught in the storm with Paul in Acts 27. Divine direction includes the selection and empowerment of the witnesses, the specific instructions for their labor, and strengthening of Paul during his captivity and trial.

2. The continuing presence of Jesus

Consistent with the characterization of God as the God of Israel, much of Luke's presentation of Jesus has to do with him as the one who fulfills Israel's hopes. This comes to expression in the sermons of both Peter and Paul, especially in Paul's final speech before Agrippa, where he characterizes the gospel itself as what Israel has hoped for (26:6-8). The title "Messiah" or "Anointed One" serves to point to this connection between Jesus and the hopes of Israel (as at 2:36; 3:17-21).

Luke regularly connects Jesus with Israel's hope by reference to Jesus' resurrection. The early speeches of Peter in Jerusalem forcefully insist that God raised Jesus in spite of the rejection of Jerusalem Jews that led to his crucifixion, and by way of fulfilling God's ancient promises (2:30; 3:18). Likewise, Paul's initial sermon at Pisidian Antioch interprets Jesus' resurrection as the fulfillment of God's promise (13:32-41). This understanding of the resurrection as the hope that extends back to Israel's ancestors and finds its fulfillment in Jesus Christ comes to the surface again in an important way in Paul's final defense speeches (*see* 23:6; 24:15, 21; and esp. 26:6-8, 22-23).

Scripture plays a crucial role in Luke's affirmation that Jesus is God's fulfillment of Israel's hope. Peter introduces Jesus as David's successor and as the "prophet-like-Moses" (2:29-36; 3:22). Peter's speeches also draw on the Psalms to explain Jesus' death and resurrection (e.g., Ps 16:8-11 in Acts 2:25-28; Ps 16:10 in 2:31; Ps 110:1 in 2:34-35). Luke does more than merely offer citations, however. Stephen's speech recounts the biblical story of Israel in a way that draws attention to both God's faithfulness to the promise and Israel's rejection. Even if Stephen does not specifically include Jesus' ministry, he does clearly draw a line between Israel's earlier pattern of rejection and the rejection of Jesus (and of Stephen as well; *see* 7:51-53). In addition, general references to the law and the prophets (3:18; 24:14; 26:22; 28:23) and to arguing from Scripture (17:2) reinforce Luke's identification of Jesus as the fulfillment of Israel's hope.

Jesus is God's fulfillment of Israel's hopes, but Jesus is also, for Luke, identified both with God and with the Holy Spirit. The narrative constructs this identification in at least three ways. First, and perhaps most obvious, Acts associates Jesus with God through the frequent reference to the name of Jesus. Healings are carried out through Jesus' name (3:6, 16; 4:7-12; 16:18; *see also* 4:30). People who repent and believe are baptized in Jesus' name (2:38; 8:12, 16; 19:5), salvation is declared through the name (2:21; 4:12), witnesses bear and suffer for the name (5:41; 9:15). Given Luke's familiarity with Scripture, this pattern probably reflects something more than the conviction that having a person's name is effective; references to Jesus' name and its power actually identify him with God (see, e.g., Gen 21:33; Deut 12:11; 1 Kgs 18:24-25; 2 Kgs 5:11; Ps 20:1; Zech 13:9).

Second, the risen and ascended Jesus is associated with God and the Spirit by means of their shared location. When the opening scene of Acts depicts Jesus' ascension to heaven, it identifies heaven as Jesus' current location ("This Jesus, who has been taken up from you into heaven, will come in the same way as you saw him go into heaven"; 1:11). Peter's Pentecost speech reinforces that location with its claim that Jesus is now "exalted at the right hand of God," and that Jesus pours out the Holy Spirit on gathered believers from that place (2:33-35; *see also* 3:21). Just prior to his death, Stephen sees Jesus "standing at the right hand of God" (7:54-58). These repeated assertions of Jesus' location are theological affirmations: just as God was with Jesus in his ministry (10:38), now Jesus is with God.

Third, Luke connects Jesus with God and the Spirit through their actions, which are inextricably related to one another. In several passages, the three are connected, as if they cannot be spoken of apart from one another. A telling instance takes place in the Pentecost speech, when Peter identifies Jesus as the one who received the Holy Spirit from God and poured it out on those present (2:33). Later on, Peter announces to Cornelius and his household that God was "preaching peace by Jesus Christ" and that God anointed Jesus with the Spirit (10:36-37). On the occasion of Paul's farewell address to the Ephesian elders, he urges them to care for the church, reminding them that the Holy Spirit had made them overseers of "the church of God" that God obtained with "the blood of his own" (NRSV: the blood of his own Son; 20:28).

Luke presents Jesus as the fulfillment of Israel's hope and as inextricably related to both God and the Spirit. Luke also presents Jesus as present and active in the church's witness. Following the ascension, Jesus can scarcely be present in the same way as he is in Luke's first volume, and some interpretations of Acts emphasize the absence of Jesus and the church or the Spirit as Jesus' "replacement." Some remarkable strands in the narrative undermine the notion of Jesus' absence, however. In the first verse of Acts, Luke characterizes his first volume as concerning "the things Jesus began to do and to teach" (author's trans., emphasis added), sig-

naling to the audience that in this book also Jesus will be acting and teaching. When the risen Jesus instructs the apostles (v. 2) and identifies them as his witnesses, he also implies that their own teaching and preaching is, in effect, Jesus' work. To be sure, Jesus enters the narrative directly only at Paul's conversion, where he charges Paul with persecuting, not the church but Jesus himself (9:4). The repetition of this charge in the subsequent reiterations of Paul's conversion (22:7; 26:14) gives it greater force. Two further texts offer important reinforcement of this notion of Jesus' presence. When Peter goes to the ailing Aeneas, he does not cure him in Jesus' name but announces: "Jesus Christ heals you" (9:34). Most important, in 26:23, Paul declares that Jesus is the one who is proclaiming light to Israel and the Gentiles. In Luke's understanding, it is entirely possible for Jesus to be at the right hand of God and simultaneously at work in Christian witness and work.

3. The empowering Spirit

From the opening lines of the book of Acts, the HOLY SPIRIT is present and active in a bewildering array of roles. Yet tracing the various activities of the Holy Spirit in Acts is a frustrating undertaking, both literarily and theologically, since what seems to be a pattern of the Spirit's activity in one place (e.g., 2:38) is overturned in another place (10:44). In addition, the actions attributed to the Spirit in one place are actions attributed to God or to Jesus in other places. With respect to God, Jesus, and the Spirit, then, they are so identified with one another in Acts that the emergence of trinitarian language is readily understandable.

One role the Spirit plays in Acts is that of connecting events to Israel's history through the prophetic voice of the Spirit in Scripture. Peter declares that the need to replace the betrayer Judas is attested by the Holy Spirit speaking through the Psalms (1:16-21). Later, the gathered community in Jerusalem similarly hear in Ps 2 the voice of the Spirit (4:25-26). At the conclusion of the book, Paul identifies the Holy Spirit as the one who spoke through the prophet Isaiah (28:25).

Perhaps most prominently in Acts, the Spirit serves to empower believers. At Pentecost, it empowers the multiplication of speech that in turn inaugurates the witness of Peter's initial sermon. The several roles of the Spirit in these opening scenes replays the Spirit's role in the conception of Jesus, in Elizabeth's recognition of Mary's pregnancy, the canticles of Zechariah, and the life of Simeon (Luke 1:35, 41, 67; 2:25-26). In turn, that empowerment echoes the empowering work of the Spirit in the OT (*see*, e.g., Judg 3:10; 11:29; 1 Sam 10:10; 19:23).

Peter's citation from the prophet Joel indicates that the empowerment brought about by the Spirit in this new moment will be a comprehensive empowerment. It will fall upon "all flesh," "your sons and your daughters," "young men," and "old men" (2:17-18).

That word finds its initial fulfillment in the response to Peter's speech, since what Peter announces is that the Spirit is not for the few, an elite group of prophets, but for all those whom God calls (2:38-39). While not predictable or consistent in this or other matters, Acts does on numerous occasions depict the gift of the Spirit to believers (see 8:15; 17; 9:17; 19:6).

Occasionally, Luke describes an individual as being full of the Spirit as well as joy, faith, or wisdom (6:3, 5, 10; 11:24; 13:52). Such descriptions function as recommendations for the individual who is to undertake a particular role. Reference to the Spirit demonstrates that joy, faith, and wisdom are not personality characteristics of these individuals; they are gifts of the Spirit. In that sense, these descriptions resemble Paul's description of the SPIRITUAL GIFTS (see 1 Cor 12:4-11; Rom 12:4-8); what these individuals undertake becomes possible only because they have received from the Spirit gifts of faith, wisdom, or joy.

In some instances, Luke reports on the Spirit's empowerment by means of the laying on of hands, a gesture familiar from the OT (e.g., Deut 34:9). Peter and John travel to Samaria, to bestow the Spirit on the Samaritans by the LAYING ON OF HANDS (8:17), and Ananias lays hands on Saul (9:17). Paul later lays hands on some disciples who have received only water baptism, so that they may receive the Spirit (19:1-7). The frequency of this practice does not make it routine or predictable, which is the conclusion maliciously drawn by Simon Magus (8:9-13, 18-24). The fact that the apostles lay on hands to bestow the Spirit also does not mean that the Spirit is at their disposal, as Peter learns in the Cornelius account, when he and his companions are amazed to see that the Spirit falls even on the Gentiles (10:44-48; 11:15-18).

In Acts the Spirit is also the inaugurator of the witness, in addition to being an agent of empowerment. The Spirit commands Philip to go and join the chariot of the Ethiopian eunuch and later sends Philip to Caesarea (8:29, 40). It directs Peter to go to the home of Cornelius, despite Peter's resistance (10:19-20). The initial work of Barnabas and Paul begins when the Holy Spirit instructs the Antioch church to commission them (13:1-3). Paul later reminds the Ephesian elders that they were appointed by the Holy Spirit (20:28). Paul's final journey to Jerusalem and then Rome finds him bound to the Spirit (20:22). The Spirit witnesses alongside the witnesses to the gospel (5:32; 15:8, 28); the Spirit witnesses to Paul about his own future (20:23).

4. Church

Among the important contributions of Luke's second volume is its portrait of the church. Even prior to Pentecost, women and men come together in Jerusalem to pray (1:12-14). In many places, Luke refers to these people as the ekklēsia (e.g., 5:11; 9:31; 15:22; 20:17). On other occasions, he refers to them as "the

Way," or as "disciples." Luke is also the only NT writer to use the term CHRISTIAN, although the term emerges as an epithet hurled at believers from those on the outside (11:26).

Luke's understanding of the church's origins is clear: the church comes into being as evidence of God's plan and God's activity in the world. The church draws its existence entirely from God's intervention. The gathering in Jerusalem prior to Pentecost directly results from the command of the risen Jesus (1:4), and it is the Spirit's arrival that prompts Peter's initial sermon, which in turn elicits the faith of 3,000 people. Even Luke's vivid description of the Jerusalem community at the end of Acts 2 stands bracketed by comments about God's activity (2:38, 47). Acts routinely depicts the activity of the church as being directed by, and sometimes corrected by, God and God's agents. In the story of the Ethiopian eunuch, an angel directs Philip to a deserted place in the middle of the day when travel would be unusual, then the Spirit instructs Philip to run to the chariot, and afterward the Spirit whisks Philip away to Azotus (8:26-40). Similarly, the risen Jesus appears to commission Paul as a witness and then must overcome the resistance of Ananias. Most significantly, the inclusion of Gentiles comes about as a result of multiple divine interventions and in the face of considerable resistance from those within the church, including Peter himself. There are some occasions when believers themselves take initiative, as when Peter declares the necessity of replacing Judas and when the Jerusalem community attends to the crisis in distributing food to widows. (Even on these occasions, however, the decisions that result involve prayer.) In the vast majority of instances, however, the church takes its orders from God.

Primary among the activities of the church is DOXOLOGY, the praise of God. Luke ascribes to believers a broad vocabulary of amazement, awe, rejoicing, joy, praise, and prayer. Doxology begins with the response to the dramatic invasion of the Holy Spirit at Pentecost and appears also in the description of the Jerusalem community at the end of Acts 2. Doxology extends to Paul's final journey, with the thanksgiving he offers before the meal on ship and the thanksgiving for safe arrival in Rome. Luke's portrait of the Gentiles includes their response of joy to the proclamation of the gospel (13:48-52; 16:34; see also 8:8); he also attributes joy to those Jewish believers who witness the Gentiles' response (11:23; 13:52; 15:3). The single comment made about the Ethiopian eunuch after his baptism is that he "went on his way rejoicing" (8:39). Later Christian tradition holds that the eunuch went home to Ethiopia to proclaim the gospel, a tradition that coheres well with the Lukan story of joyous response to the gospel.

Brought into existence by God and continually giving thanks to God, the church's task is to offer a bold witness to the world. That WITNESS takes its most obvious form in the proclamation of the gospel throughout the cities of the Mediterranean, beginning from Jerusalem, Judea, and Samaria, and extending to the "ends of the earth" (1:8). Luke often characterizes this proclamation as involving boldness of speech (*see* §B.3.d above), yet the witness also involves teaching (*see* 18:26; 28:31). Witness does not always involve speech alone. It can take place through healings (see, e.g., 5:12; 9:32-35, 36-42; 19:11-12), as well as in the confrontation of magicians and others who act against the gospel or seek to profit from it (as in 13:4-12; 19:13-20).

The witness of the church also takes the form of mutual responsibility in a community of believers. The early stories in Jerusalem attribute a number of functions to that community, including worship, the sharing of meals, and the sharing of possessions. The community is connected by bonds that are theological, liturgical, and social, and those connections all derive from God's intervention, as is clear in 2:42-47.

Although Acts does not detail the formation of Christian groups outside Jerusalem, the formation of Christian communities does continue to play an important role in the story, especially in the narration of Paul's journey from Ephesus to Jerusalem in Chs. 20:1–21:16. There Luke includes three scenes of community life—the scene involving Eutychus (20:7-12), the farewell address to the Ephesian elders (20:17-38), and the gathering at Philip's home in Caesarea (21:8-14)—each of which shows groups of believers with strong ties to one another. A major feature of Paul's sermon in Acts 20 is the responsibility of the leaders to protect the community from harm.

a. Leadership and witness. Acts opens with the risen Jesus instructing the group referred to as apostles, and this term for those who stand at the center of the community in Jerusalem persists during the first half of Acts (e.g., 1:26; 2:37, 42-43; 5:2; 8:1; 11:1). The risen Jesus promises that these apostles will become the "witnesses" to his resurrection. They come to apply that term to themselves (see, e.g., 3:15; 10:41; 13:31), and Paul's work also is characterized as that of witnessing (22:15, 20; 23:11; 26:16, 22). Students of Luke often refer to these apostles and witnesses as the "leaders" of the church, but that language is somewhat misleading. Acts does not present a drama about the leadership of human beings or about the successors of Jesus. To be sure, the careful decision that there must be a replacement for the apostle Judas suggests the world of leaders and their successors. Yet it is revealing that the replacement for Judas, Matthias, never again appears in the pages of Acts. Understanding Acts as a story about successors or human leaders becomes even more difficult as the story unfolds. For example, in Acts 12, when an angel releases Peter from prison and imminent death, Peter goes directly to greet a gathering of believers. Afterward, Luke comments that Peter

"went to another place," with no hint about why Peter left or where he went. Peter does appear briefly at the Jerusalem Council in Acts 15, but afterward there is no further mention of him in the book. The brief part James plays in Acts 15 and the single reference to him in Acts 21 scarcely renders him a central figure in the narrative. And, given Luke's obvious knowledge of the OT, he must have known stories about succession that might have been recast had he wanted to show the "mantle" passing from Peter to James, but he has not done so.

Because the second half of the book focuses extensively on Paul's activity, he might be regarded as the real exception, the major hero of Luke's story. The extended account of his arrest, captivity, and trial in Jerusalem and Caesarea finds Paul alone, with no other believers or community of believers surrounding him, as if he were the focus of the narrative. Even here, however, Luke attributes Paul's situation to the divine plan, shifting attention away from Paul and toward God who sends him (see, e.g., 19:21; 20:22; 23:11). In addition, the major speeches in this section recount Paul's activity when he was the church's persecutor, reminding readers that Paul became a witness only after his own intense resistance to the gospel was overcome by Jesus himself (22:3-21; 26:1-23). Paul is presented, then, not as a hero or leader but as the "slave of the Most High God" (16:17).

b. Women and men. Luke draws attention to the presence of women in this story, and he appears to do so deliberately (9:2, 36; 17:34; 21:5). The earliest post-Ascension gathering of believers for prayer includes women, with Jesus' mother, Mary, identified by name. Mary, the mother of John Mark, and Lydia serve the witness by making their households available for gatherings and for hospitality, a crucial need of the emerging community (12:12; 16:15, 40). The disciple Dorcas provides for widows in Joppa (9:36-43), Priscilla joins Aquila in completing the instruction of Apollos (18:24-28), and Philip's unnamed daughters are among the prophets (21:9). On the other hand, Sapphira joins her husband in deceit, so that women are also included among those who misunderstand and misappropriate (5:1-11).

Despite the presence of women in this narrative, they have little voice in Acts. Peter may anticipate the outpouring of the Holy Spirit on male and female alike (2:17-18), but women's speech is reported indirectly and seldom quoted. Perhaps more telling, Peter stipulates that the replacement for Matthias must be a male (ἀνήρ anēr; 1:21), and the apostles later agree that that males should be selected to assist in the distribution of food (6:3). This specification stands in contrast with the leadership of women as reflected in Paul's letters (*see* especially the women identified in Rom 16).

It is helpful to consider these features of Acts in their larger literary context, where female characters largely function as the possessions of fathers and husbands. Many are described solely as mothers or portrayed in terms of their physical appearance (as, for example, in *Roman Antiquities* of Dionysius of Halicarnassus or in Chariton's novel *Callirhoe*). Few of Luke's women appear only as wives or daughters (although *see* Drusilla in 24:24 and Bernice in 26:13, 23; 26:30). Consistent with Luke's larger program, women are either believers in the gospel, or they are its opponents. In some cases, they act generously with respect to others, as in the case of Dorcas and Lydia. They may also offer instruction or be endowed with prophetic gifts, as in the case of Philip's daughters, even if the content of their speech is never heard. When Luke introduces characters, whether male or female, he places them in relationship to the gospel. What is important in Luke's assessment is where people stand in relationship to the gospel.

5. Israel, the Law, and the Jewish mission

What is often referred to as Luke's understanding of Israel is actually a set of several interrelated issues. Given the lengthy and complicated nature of Luke's story, it is not surprising that several of these issues tend to become confused with one another. Luke's history of Israel and its place in the divine plan may be quite different from Luke's understanding of Jewish law, or his depiction of Jews (individual or corporate), or his understanding of the future of Christian witness among Jews. In addition, asking whether Luke's treatment of any of these questions is "positive" or "negative" imposes a simplistic option on a grand, textured story.

That God intends Jesus Christ for the salvation of Israel is a theme that pervades the book of Acts, beginning with Peter's Pentecost speech and extending through Paul's final declaration that his own captivity is for "the hope of Israel" (28:20). In this sense, Acts follows seamlessly on the Gospel of Luke, which opens with repeated declarations that the coming of Jesus Christ has to do with nothing less than the salvation of Israel. As early as Gabriel's announcement to Zechariah, Luke characterizes John the Baptist as one who "will turn many of the people of Israel to the Lord their God." Mary learns from the annunciation of Gabriel and in turn herself announces in the MAGNIFICAT that Jesus comes as the heir "of his ancestor David" and that his birth signals God's assistance to Israel (*see also* Luke 1:68-79; 2:11, 25-26, 32*b*, 38).

That permanent connection between God and Israel does not necessarily prompt a uniform endorsement of Jewish law, about which Luke's understanding is not easily discovered. Matters of law observance enter Acts most explicitly in relationship to Stephen, to the Jerusalem Council's discussion of the inclusion of Gentiles, and to Paul. Stephen and Paul are both accused of speaking against the law and the Temple (6:11, 13; 21:21, 28), but it is important to note that neither one

makes defense of the law or his own law observance an important feature of his response (although *see* 23:1; 24:13-14). The Jerusalem Council decides that Gentiles must observe some basic practices having to do with idolatry and sexual immorality, but the discussion on that occasion does not concern the virtues of the LAW or the necessity of its maintenance by believers (15:1-35). When Paul circumcises Timothy, whose mother is Jewish, he appears to do so for fear of Jewish resistance to Timothy as a coworker rather than because of his own commitment to maintaining the law (16:1-3). In these events there is not so much a firm endorsement of the law as an introduction of the law to serve other concerns, such as showing the injustice carried out against Stephen and Paul or reinforcing the need for Gentiles to avoid blatantly offensive behavior. The law does not appear to be a central Lukan concern in and of itself.

Luke does display concern for the response of Jews to the Christian witness, and that response is sharply divided. The leadership in Jerusalem undertakes to silence Peter and John as early as Acts 3. When the witness moves outside Jerusalem, Jews in other locations consistently divide between those who are willing to hear and those who not only reject but seek to silence Christian witness. On three separate occasions, Paul announces that he will turn to the ggentiles (13:44-52; 18:5-7; 28:23-28), and it is possible to read those three declarations in diametrically opposing ways. Because the book—indeed the whole of Luke–Acts—ends following the third such declaration, the third may signal the end of witness among Jews. The third may also mean, on the other hand, what is customary in prophetic judgment of Israel: that Jews are being called to repentance. The final lines of the book indicate that Paul will welcome all who come to him, both Jews and Gentiles. Luke is able to affirm both that Israel belongs irrevocably to God and that many Jews have failed to respond to the salvation God initiated in Jesus Christ, in the same way that he asserts both that human beings failed when they crucified Jesus and that the crucifixion was part of God's plan.

6. A place for the gentiles

God's faithfulness to Israel does not mean that God's care is restricted to Israel. As early as the promise of the witness to "the ends of the earth" (1:8) and the promise to "all who are far away" (2:39), Luke makes it clear that the gospel extends as far as humanity can be found. This extension is anticipated already in the birth narratives of Luke's Gospel, when Simeon's canticle celebrates in Jesus' birth the arrival of God's own "salvation," and "a light for revelation to the Gentiles" (Luke 2:32; *see also* Acts 26:23). Because it is the devout Gentile Cornelius whose conversion forces the church to acknowledge God's inclusion of Gentiles, it might be thought that only those Gentiles who are already well-disposed to Israel's God will be deemed acceptable. Yet the proconsul Sergius Paulus (13:4-12), the Philippian jailer and his household (16:25-35), and Dionysius and Damaris (17:34) are among those who "turn to the Lord" without any indication that they have previously been associated with the synagogue or its people. As James concludes at the Jerusalem Council, it is God who looks "favorably on the Gentiles, to take from among them a people for his name" (15:14).

Among Jews, the response of Gentiles to Christian proclamation is divided. Some Gentiles understand and are receptive, not only those noted above but the ones included in the summary statements of 13:48 and 28:28. On the other hand, the Gentiles of Lystra reveal themselves to be fickle (14:8-20), those of Athens are mere gadflies (17:21), and those of Ephesus vigilant to protect their deity Artemis and her city (19:23-41). There is also frequent reference to the many gods served by Gentiles, a feature that should not be surprising, as the non-Jewish world was replete with gods and their worship. The Jerusalem Council agrees that it is essential for Gentile believers to observe those elements of Jewish law that are most closely associated with the prevention of idolatry (15:19-20, 29; 21:25). Here, as throughout the Acts of the Apostles, Luke conveys the urgency and the all-encompassing character of God's action for human salvation and the urgency of a corresponding obedience on the part of those whom God calls.

Bibliography: Loveday Alexander. *The Preface to Luke's Gospel: Literary Convention and Social Context in Luke 1:1-4 and Acts 1:1* (1993); C. K. Barrett. *A Critical and Exegetical Commentary on the Acts of the Apostles 1–14* (1994). C. K. Barrett. *A Critical and Exegetical Commentary on the Acts of the Apostles 15–28* (1998); F. F. Bruce. *The Acts of the Apostles: The Greek Text with Introduction and Commentary.* 3rd ed. (1990); F. F. Bruce. *Commentary on the Book of the Acts: The English Text with Introduction, Exposition and Notes.* NICNT. Rev. ed. (1987); Henry Joel Cadbury. *The Making of Luke–Acts.* 2nd ed. (1958); John Carroll. *Response to the End of History: Eschatology and Situation in Luke–Acts* (1988); Richard J. Cassidy. *Society and Politics in the Acts of the* Apostles (1987); Hans Conzelmann. *Acts of the Apostles* (1987); Charles H. Cosgrove. "The Divine ΔEI in Luke–Acts." *NovT* 26 (1983) 168–90; Martin Dibelius. *Studies in the Acts of the Apostles* (1956; rep. 1999); Joseph A. Fitzmyer. *The Acts of the Apostles* (1998); Susan Garrett. *The Demise of the Devil: Magic and the Demonic in Luke's Writings* (1989); Beverly Roberts Gaventa. *The Acts of the Apostles* (2003); Beverly Roberts Gaventa. *From Darkness to Light: Aspects of Conversion in the New Testament* (1986); Ernst Haenchen. *The Acts of the Apostles: A Commentary* (1971); Jacob Jervell. *Luke and the People of God: A New Look at Luke–Acts* (1972); Luke Timothy Johnson. *The Acts of the Apostles* (1992); Gerhard A. Krodel. *Acts* (1986); K. Lake and H. J. Cadbury. *English Translation and Commentary.* Vol. 4 of *The Beginnings of Christianity* (1933); Daniel Marguerat. *The First Christian Historian: Writing the "Acts of the Apostles"* (2002). Gail R. O'Day. "Acts." *Women's Bible Commentary* (1998) 394–402; Ivoni Richter Reimer. *Women in the Acts of the Apostles: A Feminist Liberation Perspective* (1995); Paul Schubert. "The Final Cycle of Speeches in the Book of Acts." *JBL* 87 (1968) 1–16; Paul Schubert. "The Place of the Areopague Speech in the Composition of Acts." *Transitions in Biblical Scholarship* (1968); Turid Karlsen Seim. *The Double Message: Patterns of Gender in Luke–Acts* (1994); Marion L. Soards. *The Speeches in Acts: Their Content, Context, and Concerns* (1994); F. Scott Spencer. *Acts. Readings* (1997); Charles H. Talbert. *Reading Acts: A Literary and Theological Commentary on the Acts of the Apostles* (1997); Robert Tannehill. *The Narrative Unity of Luke–Acts. Volume 2: The Acts of the Apostles* (1990, 1994); Joseph B. Tyson, ed. *Luke–Acts and the Jewish People: Eight Critical Perspectives* (1988); Joseph B. Tyson. *Luke, Judaism, and the Scholars: Critical Approaches to Luke–Acts* (1999); Robert W. Wall. "The Acts of the Apostles." *The New Interpreter's Bible* (2002) 12:3-368; Bruce Winter, ed. *The Book of Acts in Its First Century Setting* (1993–96).

BEVERLY ROBERTS GAVENTA

ADADAH ad'uh-duh [עַדְעָדָה ʿadheʿadha]. A town located on the Edomite boundary of southern Judah (Josh 15:22). Since the town is translated as Αρουηλ (Arouēl) in LXX[B], scholars have concluded that perhaps the ר (r) was misconstrued as ד (d) in the original reading of ערערה, an alternate spelling for AROER.

ADAH ay'duh [עָדָה ʿadhah]. A woman's name, meaning *to adorn.* 1. Adah and LAMECH were the parents of JABAL, whose descendants lived in tents and raised livestock (Gen 4:19-20), and JUBAL the musician (Gen 4:21). Lamech confesses murder to Adah and his other wife, ZILLAH (Gen 4:23).

2. Esau's Canaanite wife (Gen 36:2). She was the mother of Esau's firstborn son ELIPHAZ (Gen 36:15) and through him the mother of the Edomite clans, Teman, Omar, Zepho, Kenaz, Korah, Gatam, and Amalek (36:15-16). She and Esau's household moved to the hill country of Seir in Edom (36:6-7). *See* ESAU; LAMECH.

LISA MICHELE WOLFE

ADAIAH uh-day'yuh [עֲדָיָה ʿadhayah; Αδια Adia, Αδαια Adaia]. 1. A native of BOZKATH in Judah (Josh 15:29), the father of JEDIDAH and maternal grandfather of King JOSIAH (2 Kgs 22:1).

2. A member of the Levitical family of GERSHOM;

son of ETHNI; father of ZERAH and an ancestor of ASAPH (1 Chr 6:41 [Heb. 6:26]).

3. Son of SHIMEI (1 Chr 8:21) and one of the leaders of the tribe of Benjamin in Jerusalem before Judah's exile (1 Chr 8:28).

4. Father of MAASEIAH, one of the 5 commanders of hundreds who joined in a coup against Queen ATHALIAH, usurper of Judah's throne (2 Chr 23:1).

5. Son of JOIARIB and father of HAZAIAH and an ancestor of Maaseiah, who was one of the tribal leaders of Judah in Jerusalem after the exile (Neh 11:5).

6. A priest, son of JEROHAM (1 Chr 9:12; Neh 11:12), probably of the Levitical family of Gershom (compare 1 Chr 6:41 [Heb. 6:26]), who returned from exile and settled in Jerusalem.

7. Son of BANI, an Israelite who divorced his Gentile wife after the exile (Ezra 10:29; 1 Esd 9:30).

8. Son of BINNUI an Israelite forced to divorce his Gentile wife after the exile (Ezra 10:39).

CLAUDE F. MARIOTTINI

ADALIA uh-day'lee-uh [אֲדַלְיָא *'adhalya'*]. One of HAMAN's sons hung on the gallows (Esth 9:8).

ADAM [אָדָם *'adham;* Ἀδάμ Adam]. The figure of Adam, who is so ubiquitous in Western literature, occupies a very narrow piece of ground in the OT. Indeed, even if we expand our textual purview to include the NT, his role remains limited. He is never mentioned by name in any explicit fashion in the Gospels. It is to the Apostle Paul that we can attribute the starting point for the prominence of this figure (*see* esp., Rom 5 and 1 Cor 15). For Paul, Adam becomes the crucial piece of his soteriological scheme. Adam as "first man" becomes the source of sin and death that Jesus, the "last man," overcomes. Once this schema is in place, no understanding of Christ's salvific work can sidestep the figure of Adam; he assumes center stage in every subsequent Christian anthropology.

In the OT, Adam's presence is limited to the first several chapters of Genesis. But even here, he is rarely identified by the personal name "Adam." Rather, he is most often referred to by the more generic title, "man." This semantic problem is not unique, however, to this figure in Gen 1–11. Other "personal" names are clearly not such in the conventional sense, but rather indicate larger abstract concepts (e.g., Eve, "life-giving one," Enosh, "humankind," and Noah, "rest"). This is a phenomenon that is particularly in evidence in Gen 1–11 and rather rare elsewhere in the Bible.

The first unambiguous reference to Adam as a personal name does not occur until Gen 4:1, though many translators locate such a usage already at 2:20, 3:17 and 3:21 (in each of these three cases the consonantal text of the Hebrew original will allow for the more generic meaning "man"). The reason for this is that the word *'adham* in Hebrew is the common noun for man or mankind and is never used as a personal name except in these chapters. This point is worthy of some emphasis; no Hebrew speaker in the biblical period would have thought this word refers to an actual person. The usage of this common noun as a personal name is the literary invention of the biblical author. The reason for this unusual usage of a common noun as a personal name is to advance the notion of the representative nature of this first human being. He represents all human beings who would necessarily stem from him. Whatever happens to Adam has repercussions for all humankind.

The name *Adam* is intimately tied to his origin according to the creation account in the Yahwistic or "J" account (Gen 2:4*b*–3:24): "God formed man from the dust of the ground." Here the words for man and ground are understood as having a common etymological origin: *'adham* (human) comes from אֲדָמָה *adamah* (earth). God forms, or better molds, this ground into the shape of a human person. God is imagined here as a potter who works with clay and concludes his work by animating it with his very own breath (*see* J, YAHWIST).

The name of the location that Adam is brought into is Eden. Since this name has deep associations with the concepts of blessing and life, it is altogether possible that our author presumes that if the first human couple had remained there they would not have died. This does not mean that they were created immortal; in fact just the opposite. They were created mortal but had they been able to remain in Eden, eternal life would have been conferred upon them. The location of Adam and Eve is the determinative variable—Eden confers "life"—not the ontological status of the human being. In any event, it is certainly significant that only when they are driven into exile to the east of Eden and the door is forever closed for reentry is their mortal status made clear: "By the sweat of your face you shall eat bread until you return to the ground for out of it you were taken; you are dust and to dust you shall return" (Gen 3:19).

The status of Adam as a special being among God's other creatures is made in several ways. First, Adam is animated by the infusion of the divine breath. Second, Adam names the animals. This is an indication of his lordship over them and so the animals often proceed before Adam with bowed heads in early Christian art and commentary. Though Genesis only hints at this sort of notion, the domestication of the wild animals becomes an important theme in later eschatological and apocalyptic literature (*see* Isa 11:1-9; 65:17-25). On the basis that last things must mirror first things, later interpretive traditions would describe the origin of strife within the animal kingdom and the origin of the carnivore as rooted in the rebellion of Adam and Eve (*see Apoc. Mos.*, 10–12). In Eden, the conditions described by Isa 11 and 65 held sway.

But lordship of Adam and Eve over other created life does not entail destructive domination. Some readers with an empassioned environmental consciousness have asserted that the roots of our ecological crisis reside in the biblical doctrine of Adam's lordship over creation, which meant his power to do with the created order whatever he saw fit to do. But the act of calling the animals by name invokes the images of a protector and steward rather than a dictatorial ruler. This is made very clear in the story of Jonah. In this tale the fate of man and beast are inextricably linked. Because domestic animals lived in close proximity to human beings, should human civilization fall so would the animals. Indeed our author makes a special point of declaring that God had mercy on Nineveh because of the great number of people and animals that dwelled therein (Jonah 4:11).

A third manner of indicating the special status of the human person is by way of their gender. To be sure, the person's animals also possess gender, but the fact that the Bible passes over this detail in silence is significant. Here the biblical writer has in mind the unique form of companionship and lifelong marital bonds that have no counterpart in the animal world (Gen 2:24). As a result, man is not considered complete until he is rendered in his full sexual complementarity: "This at last is bone of my bones and flesh of my flesh; this one shall be called woman (אִשָּׁה ʾishah) for out of man (אִישׁ ʾish) this one was taken" (Gen 2:23; Tob 8:6).

Fourth, but by no means last, humanity is singled out from the rest of creation by being made the subject of a command that is tied to the faculty of moral discernment (what the Bible calls "the knowledge of good and evil"). In linking that status of humankind to the keeping of a commandment, the story of the garden of Eden shows a rather broad parallel to Israel's national story as Jewish midrashic tradition was wont to point out. Both Adam, and Eve as well as Israel, are subject to a divine edict. Adam's was a single command, while Israel subjected herself to the totality of the Torah. Violation of this edict will entail exile from a land of life and beatitude. God makes this explicit when he conveys the command to Adam (Gen 2:16-17); whereas Moses conveys the same idea when he exhorts Israel to obedience just before their entrance into the promised land: "See, I am setting before you today a blessing and a curse: the blessing if you obey the commandments [. . .] and the curse if you do not obey the commandments" (Deut 11:26-27). Keeping the commandments will yield a life of blessing in a land flowing with milk and honey; disobedience will bring in its wake the curse of exile and death.

One problem that has long perplexed readers of the story is whether Adam and Eve would have attained moral discernment had they not eaten of the tree. The position of the ancient Gnostics that has been adapted by many moderns is that God was jealous of these creatures and withheld knowledge until they had sinned and became mortal (see Gen 3:22, which offers some support). Though there is some ambiguity in the Genesis account, it is more likely that the Bible imagines that moral discernment would have been granted to Adam and Eve but by other means. Because of the rapidity of their fall, we will never know what they might have been. This view is more in keeping with the rest of Biblical teaching that regards wisdom as a gift that only God can bestow and then, only to those who fear him.

In any event it is clear that as a result of attaining moral discernment by improper means Adam and Eve are driven from Eden. This makes the story of the fall very much like the other tales found in Gen 1–11: Humankind comes upon natural goods by improper means. So in Gen 4 we are witness to the founding of cities, musical instruments, and the tools of agriculture —all which were thought to be the result of a divine gift elsewhere in the ANE—as the result of the murderous offspring of Cain. Our narrative is not scoring points to the favor of some sort of primitivism (à la Rousseau). Cities, music, and agriculture are all items worthy of praise elsewhere in the Bible. The point is that these benefactions originate by sinful means, as does the moral consciousness of man. They will only be put to beneficial use by God's dramatic intervention into history to elect the nation Israel.

In the priestly account of creation (Gen 1:1–2:4a) the account of the creation of humankind is more brief. Here the key motif is that humankind is created in the image and likeness of God (1:26). It is worth emphasizing that the status of this first being as the "image and likeness" is not limited to the male gender. The parallelistic form of expression rules that out:

So God created humankind (adam) in his image,
In the likeness of God he created them;
Male and female he created them (1:27).

What is conveyed by the notion of image is not clear. Because the terms *image* and *likeness* are terms for images or statues, one possibility is that "image" refers to some sort of physical resemblance. Though this may seem far-fetched, one should remember that the Priestly source is quite fond of anthropomorphic language to highlight the dignity of humanity. In the tabernacle narrative (Exod 25–31; 35–40), for example, the making of a dwelling for God is described in terms analogous to the creation of the universe. As God *fashions* the world in which humans will dwell, so the Israelites *fashion* a shrine in which God will dwell. But perhaps more significant for P than some sort of physical resemblance is the establishment of humankind as *rulers* over the created order (Gen 1:28). As God *rules* over the heavens, so human beings as his image (literally his "representatives" in as much as a statue *re-presents* a living being in a different form) hold sway over the earth.

In early Jewish and Christian tradition, this motif was pushed in two different directions. Since human beings are distinguished from the animal kingdom by language and the capacity for abstract thought that it confers, the primary sense of image and likeness must reside in the rational faculties of the human animal. Human beings, though weaker than the animals, can rule over them due to their higher wisdom. This became an especially productive in Christian exegesis because the rational faculty of humankind is defined by his λόγος logos (literally meaning "word" but having the extended sense of "rationality"). In this way the imagery of Gen 1 was thought to impinge on the definition of Christ in John 1:1 as the divine *Logos* ("In the beginning was the Word . . .").

The notion of the image could also retain its physical characteristics in early Jewish and Christian interpretation. If human beings looked like God in any fashion is was because they were enveloped in a glorious light. In one Rabbinic tradition—subsequently adopted by almost all Christian interpreters—Adam and Eve were adorned in garments of light. The animals had to hold their heads down as they passed before them due to the brilliance of their light. This light was lost upon their fall but would return at the resurrection when the righteous would shine in heaven like stars.

Because the beginning of time was thought to mirror the end of time, many biblical traditions about the eschaton were read back into the stories about creation. Thus the Isaianic traditions about the peace that would reign in the animal kingdom became a part of the conventional depiction of Eden. Though Genesis is silent about the relationship of Sabbath to human culture, the rest of the Jewish Bible is not. This lead to the creation of numerous Jewish traditions as to how Adam kept the first Sabbath day. Indeed, the differences that exist between traditional Jewish and Christian readers of these chapters are almost invariably grounded in the different visions the two traditions have regarding the eschaton.

In the Pauline epistles, Adam becomes a type for Jesus Christ, the "second Adam," who reverses the exile and death brought by the "first" Adam (1 Cor 15:22, 45; Rom 5:14). *See* CREATION; EDEN, GARDEN OF; EVE; HUMANITY, OT; SECOND ADAM.

Bibliography: Gary A. Anderson. *The Genesis of Perfection: Adam and Eve in Jewish and Christian Imagination* (2001); James Barr. *The Garden of Eden and the Hope of Immortality* (1993); Phyllis Bird. "'Male and Female He Created Them': Gen 1:27b in the Context of the Priestly Account of Creation." *HTR* 74 (1981) 129–59; Robert A. Di Vito. "The Demarcation of Divine and Human Realms in Genesis 2–11." *Creation in the Biblical Traditions*, ed. R. J. Clifford and J. J. Collins (1992) 39–56; R. W. L. Moberly. "Did the Serpent Get It Right?" *JTS* 39 (1988) 1–27; Susan Niditch. *Chaos to Cosmos: Studies in Biblical Patterns of Creation* (1985); Michael E. Stone. *A History of the Literature of Adam and Eve* (1992); Howard Wallace. *The Eden Narrative* (1985).

GARY A. ANDERSON

ADAM AND EVE, LIFE OF. A pseudepigraphic text that narrates the adventures of the progenitors of humankind after the fall and their subsequent expulsion from the Garden of Eden. This Midrash of Gen 3 has been preserved in at least two different textual forms: a Greek one, also called *Apocalypse of Moses*, and a Latin one. The Latin version begins with a lengthy description of the penitence of Adam in the Jordan and Eve in the Tigris River, where Satan successfully deceives her a second time (Latin 1–22, absent in the Greek). Then, after Cain's murder of his brother Abel, Eve gives birth to Seth (Latin 23–24 // Greek 1–4). Adam informs Seth about the vision of the Lord that he saw when he was taken up to the heavenly Paradise (Latin 25–29, absent in the Greek), and then, on his deathbed he tells the story of the original sin to his sons and daughters and sends Seth forth to search for the oil of mercy from the Garden of Eden (Latin 30–44 // Greek 5–14). At this point the Greek text inserts Eve's own recollection of the fall (Greek 15–30, absent in Latin). Both forms come to an end with the description of the death of Adam, the assumption of his soul to the heavenly Paradise, and the burial of his body—together with his son Abel and, a few days after, his wife Eve—on the spot where he had been created (Latin 45–51 // Greek 31–43).

The parallels that the Latin form—especially a newly discovered manuscript—shared with the Armenian and Georgian versions, point out the existence of a more developed Greek text, presently lost. Among the most debated issues in contemporary research there is the question of ascertaining whether or not such a fuller form of the *Life of Adam and Eve* was the original one. Thus, de Jonge and Tromp argue for the primacy of the preserved Greek text, while Anderson and Stone argue for the text that was used by the translators of the Latin, Armenian, and Georgian versions. Concerning the question of the Jewish or Christian origins of the *Life of Adam and Eve*, a new consensus is growing around de Jonge's original suggestion to see it as the work of a Christian author. The question as to whether or not this author used ancient Jewish traditions and sources is still under debate.

The influence that the *Life of Adam and Eve* has exerted on literature, art, and culture is enormous. The *Apocalypse of Adam* (NHC V, 5), the *Testament of Adam*, the *Cave of Treasures*, the *Conflict of Adam and Eve with Satan*, and the *Discourse on Abbatôn, the Angel of Death* are all connected with the traditions found in the *Life of Adam and Eve*.

One can even see the indirect influence of this text on Milton's *Paradise Lost*.

Bibliography: Gary A. Anderson, Michael E. Stone. *A Synopsis of the Books of Adam and Eve* (1994); Gary A. Anderson, Michael E. Stone, and Johannes Tromp, ed. *Literature on Adam and Eve: Collected Essays* (2000); Marinus de Jonge. *Pseudepigrapha of the Old Testament as Part of Christian Literature: The Case of the Testaments of the Twelve Patriarchs and the Greek Life of Adam and Eve* (2003); Marinus de Jonge, and Johannes Tromp. *The Life of Adam and Eve and Related Literature* (1997); Michael E. Stone. *A History of the Literature of Adam and Eve* (1992).

PIERLUIGI PIOVANELLI

ADAM, APOCALYPSE OF. The 5th tractate in a codex from the mid-4th cent. that contains Coptic translations of Gnostic texts. Originally composed in Greek in the late 2nd or early 3rd cent. CE, this work was unknown until the Nag Hammadi discovery. The text claims to be a revelation that Adam gave to his son Seth; angels subsequently inscribed it on high mountain rock. Three blocks of material in *Apoc. Adam* may have been drawn from different sources: 1) Adam's version of how the "god who created us" divided Adam and Eve to deprive them of divine glory and eternal life; 2) a revelation that Adam received from three angelic beings concerning the fate of his descendants; and 3) a stylized catalog of thirteen false explanations for the origin of the divine Illuminator.

The first two blocks of material draw upon apocryphal traditions concerning Adam: the Watchers and Noah, which are comparable to *1 En.* and *L.A.E.* Speculation concerning the Nephilim of Gen 6:1-4 underlies the insistence that sexual passions (*epithumia*) deprive humans of their immortality and subject them to the authority of the god who created and rules the material world. The mythic elements in the thirteen false explanations are unclear. Possible allusions include legends of Solomon and the demons; the birth of Mithras from a rock; the birth of one of the Muses; the woman clothed with the sun of Rev 12, and, perhaps, the Word of John 1:1-18 in the final instance.

The *Apocalypse of Adam* follows a simple outline:

I. Introduction: Adam teaches Seth in Adam's 700th year (of his death, Gen 5:4 LXX) (V, 64, 1-6).

II. Adam and Eve lose their divine glory. When the wrathful creator divides them, they are subject to death. Glory departs to Seth and his seed (V, 64, 6, 65, 25).

III. Adam's dream vision: three angelic beings will reveal the fate of the seed to whom life has gone (65, 26–66, 8).

IV. Creator responds by deepening the entanglement with desire and death; birth of Cain (V, 66, 9–67, 14).

V. Revelation as "salvation history" of the Sethians and the sons of Noah. Noah has a covenant with creator, but 400,000 sons of Ham and Japheth defect and join undefiled Sethians. Each of creator's attempts against Sethians (flood and fire) is foiled by angelic rescue (V, 67, 14–76, 7).

VI. Coming of the Illuminator to leave behind immortal, Gnostic race. Hostile lower powers can only punish the "flesh of the man on whom the holy spirit has come" (V, 76, 8–77, 18).

VII. Powers use the name in error; thirteen false explanations concerning the Illuminator's origins (V, 77, 19–83, 4).

VIII. Apocalyptic judgment scene: those doomed to die acknowledge Gnostic truth. Condemned by angels for defiled baptism (V, 83, 4–86, 26).

IX. Conclusion: true angelic revelation not written in a book, given by Adam to Seth (V, 85, 1-31).

Since *Apoc. Adam* lacks the speculative detail of Gnostic texts like *Ap. John*, it may have been composed for neophytes.

Bibliography: George W. MacRae. "The Apocalypse of Adam." *Nag Hammadi Codices V, 2–5.* NHS XI (1979) 151–95.

PHEME PERKINS

ADAM, CITY ad′uhm [אָדָם ʾadham]. A Transjordanian city, described as "beside ZARETHAN," south of the meeting of the JABBOK and JORDAN rivers and modern Tell ed-Damiyeh, where the Jordan's waters miraculously arose upstream from the Israelites, allowing them to cross the river on dry land (Josh 3:16). Hosea denounces certain priests' disloyalty to Yahweh and murderous activities at the city (Hos 6:7).

ADAM, SECOND ad′uhm. *See* SECOND ADAM.

ADAMAH ad′uh-muh [אֲדָמָה ʾadhamah]. A fortified city in the tribe of NAPHTALI (Josh 19:36). Adamah should not be identified with Adam in Transjordan (Josh 3:16) or with Adami-neqeb (Josh 19:33). Its location remains largely unknown despite suggestions of 7 km west of the SEA OF GALILEE, at MADON (Josh 11:1; 12:19), and 7 km north of CAPERNAUM.

J. GORDON HARRIS

ADAMANT [שָׁמִיר shamir]. In the OT, ADAMANT is a metaphor for Israel's resistance to God's word (Zech 7:12); see the LXX translation ἀπειθής apeithes ("disobedience"). ADAMANT is a gemstone of unknown composition with the attribute of extreme hardness. Ancient writers were possibly referring to emery. Current usage of ADAMANT is synonymous with DIAMOND.

ELIZABETH E. PLATT

ADAMI-NEKEB [אֲדָמִי הַנֶּקֶב ʾadhami hanneqev]. A city between Mount Tabor and the Sea of Galilee, which is on the border of the inheritance of Naphtali (Josh 19:32-39). Neqeb means "to pierce" or "a pass." The Bible refers to Adami of the narrow pass to separate it from Adam of the ford. Some Greek manuscripts take this as two separate locations.

J. GORDON HARRIS

ADAR ay′dahr [אֲדָר ʾadhar, Ἀδαρ Adar]. Twelfth month in the postexilic Hebrew CALENDAR when completion of the rebuilt Temple (Ezra 6:14-16), Purim (Esth 9:1-32), and Nicanor's defeat (2 Macc 15:36) were celebrated.

ADASA ad′uh-suh [Ἀδασά Hadasa, Ἀδασά Adasa]. Village where JUDAS MACCABEUS defeated the Syrian general Nicanor in 160/1 BCE (1 Macc 7:40-45). Josephus locates it near Beth Horon (*Ant.* 12.408), and it is often identified with Khirbet ʿAdaseh (165:139), along the ancient roadway running between Jerusalem and Beth Horon. *See* NICANOR.

J. R. C. COUSLAND

ADBEEL ad′bee-uhl [אַדְבְּאֵל ʾadhbeʾel]. One of ISHMAEL's twelve sons (Gen 25:13; 1 Chr 1:29); eponymous ancestor of an Arabian tribe often identified with the people of Idibaʾilu, who became subjects of TIGLATH-PILESER III (called PUL in 2 Kgs 15:19) ca. 735 BCE. They probably were located southwest of the DEAD SEA. *See* ARAB, ARABIA, ARABIAN.

ADDAN ad′uhm [אַדָּן ʾaddan]. Place in Babylonia whose exiles could not prove their ancestry as Israelites (Ezra 2:59). Addon (אַדּוֹן ʾadhon) in Neh 7:61. *See* CHERUB.

ADDAR ad′ahr [אַדָּר ʾaddar]. 1. One of the nine sons of BELA (1 Chr 8:3), the first-born son of Benjamin.

2. A town near the WILDERNESS OF ZIN listed along with HEZRON and others as southern boundary markers for the territory allotted to the tribe of JUDAH (Josh 15:1-4). In the parallel version (Num 34:1-5) the two town names are combined as HAZAR-ADDAR.

A. HEATH JONES III

ADDER [פֶּתֶן pethen, צִפְעֹנִי tsifʿoni, צֶפַע tsefaʿ]. A general term for a poisonous snake, although it is difficult to know which species of VIPER is intended. The term is invoked most often metaphorically, comparing a poisonous snake to wine that bites without warning (Prov 23:32), to God's punishment upon a rebellious people (Jer 8:17), and to the hostile wickedness of Israel's enemies (Deut 32:33 NRSV "asps"). *See* ASP; FIERY SERPENT OR POISONOUS SNAKE.

BRYAN D. BIBB

ADDI ad′i [Ἀδδί Addi]. 1. A leader of returnees from the Babylonian exile who collectively agreed to divorce their foreign wives (1 Esd 9:31).

2. An ancestor of Jesus (Luke 3:28). The name Addi is not included in the genealogical parallels of Ezra 10:25-44 and Matt 1:2-16, respectively.

ADDITIONS TO DANIEL. *See* DANIEL, ADDITIONS TO.

ADDITIONS TO ESTHER. *See* ESTHER, ADDITIONS TO.

ADDON ad′uhn. *See* ADDAN.

ADER, KHIRBET ay′duhr. Located on the Central Plateau in TRANSJORDAN near the ancient KING'S HIGHWAY just N of Kerak (7 km), Khirbet Ader is best known as a settlement site in the Early Bronze IV period (2300–2000 BCE), a so-called "nomadic interlude" following urban collapse throughout the S. Levant. Multiphase occupational levels were found, including house remains with typical Early Bronze IV degenerate red-slipped and burnished pottery. Unfortunately, before excavation, an apparent tripartite temple with altar and menhirs was destroyed due to building activity in modern Ader, which sits atop the ruins.

Excavation also uncovered wall fragments from the Iron IIC period (7th–6th cent. BCE) and a city wall and tower from the Late Roman/Byzantine periods, when the site was known as Adara. Texts reference a medieval site as well. *See* JORDAN.

Bibliography: W. F. Albright. "Soundings at Ader: A Bronze Age City of Moab." *BASOR* 53 (1934) 13–18; R. L. Cleveland. "The Excavation of the Conway High Place (Petra) and Soundings at Khirbet Ader." *AASOR* 34–35 (1960) 59–97; S. Richard. "The Early Bronze Age in the Southern Levant." *Near Eastern Archaeology: A Reader.* S. Richard, ed. (–2003).

SUZANNE RICHARD

ADIDA ad′uh-duh [Ἀδιδά Adida]. Town built and fortified by Simon Maccabeus, located in the low hills (Shephelah) four miles east of Lydda (1 Macc 12:38; 13:13). Probably the town HADID.

ADIEL ay′dee-uhl [עֲדִיאֵל ʿadhiʾel]. 1. Father of AZMAVETH, who was David's royal treasurer (1 Chr 27:25).

2. One of SIMEON's tribal leaders (1 Chr 4:36) who, in the days of HEZEKIAH, led the conquest of GEDOR (or GERAR) to find pasture for their flock (1 Chr 4:38-40).

3. A priest, son of JAHZERAH and the father of MAASAI, from the house of IMMER, qualified to serve in the Temple upon returning from exile (1 Chr 9:12).

ADIN ay′din [עָדִין ‘adhin]. The ancestor of 454 Jews; (Ezra 2:15; 8:6; Neh 7:20; 10:16) (1 Esd 5:14) who returned to Jerusalem with ZERUBBABEL or with EZRA.

CLAUDE F. MARIOTTINI

ADINA ay′uh-nuh [עֲדִינָא ‘adhina’]. The son of Shiza; a Reubenite leader listed among David's warriors (1 Chr 11:42).

ADJURATION [שָׁבַע shava‘, ἐξορκίζω exorkizō, ὁρκίζω orkizō]. An appeal mandating a person to speak or act under oath (e.g., 1 Kgs 2:42). Also, the demons' appeal for leniency (Mark 5:7); the exorcist's authoritative pronouncement (Acts 19:13), or a specific formula over evil spirits. See DEMON; EXORCISM; OATH.

ADLAI ad′li [עֶדְלָי ‘adhlay]. The father of SHAPHAT, who was in charge of David's royal herds in the valleys (1 Chr 27:29).

ADMAH ad′muh [אַדְמָה ’adhema]. Located in the Siddim Valley at the southernmost tip of the Dead Sea–Canaanite territory in the region of Sodom and Gomorrah (Gen 10:19). Admah's King Shinab and the other kings of that area rebelled against King Chedorlaomer's Edomite coalition, which ended with Chedorlaomer's destructive victory including the capture of Abram's nephew Lot (Gen 14:1-16). Elsewhere, Admah represents punishment that the Lord will either inflict (Deut 29:23) or mercifully abandon (Hos 11:8) in response to Israel's covenant disobedience. See CHEDORLAOMER; GOMORRAH; SIDDIM; VALLEY OF SODOM.

LISA MICHELE WOLFE

ADMATHA ad-may′thuh [אַדְמָתָא ’adhmatha’]. One of "the seven officials of Persia and Media, who had access to the king," AHASUERUS (Esth 1:14). (The LXX lists only three names.) These officials advised the king to banish Queen VASHTI, an action that led to the elevation of ESTHER (Esth 1:19-20). See ESTHER, BOOK OF.

ADMIN ad′min [Ἀδμιν Admin]. An ancestor of Jesus, Aminadab's father (Luke 3:33).

ADMONITIONS OF IPU-WER. See IPU-WER, ADMONITIONS OF.

ADNAH ad′nuh [עַדְנָה ‘adhenah]. 1. Judahite military commander during the reign of JEHOSHAPHAT (2 Chr 17:14).

2. Manassite who deserted SAUL and joined DAVID prior to Saul's death (1 Chr 12:20).

ADONAI, ADONAY ad′oh-ni′ [אָדוֹן ’adhon Lord; אֲדֹנָי ’adhonay My Lord; κύριος kyrios]. Lord was an epithet of God (Josh 3:11). The term began as a title;

however, Adonai became an alternate name for YHWH (יהוה see YAHWEH; TETRAGRAMMATON), often used in parallelism with Yahweh or as a substitute for it, when Yahweh was deemed too sacred to be pronounced. Subsequently, when the MASORETES added vowel points to the text, the tetragrammaton appeared with the vowels for Adonai. See NAMES OF GOD.

C. L. SEOW

ADONI-BEZEK uh-doh′ni-bee′zek [אֲדֹנִי בֶזֶק ’adhoni vezeq]. A Canaanite king who was defeated by the invading tribes of Judah and Simeon at Bezek during the conquest of Canaan (Judg 1:5-7). His name means "Lord of Bezek" and could be a variation of ADONI-ZEDEK, a king mentioned in Joshua (Josh 10:1-3). Adoni-Bezek endured the same humiliation (the amputation of his thumbs and toes) to which he subjected 70 kings he had conquered. Adoni-Bezek interpreted his defeat and mutilation as God's retribution. His story is similar to other accounts in Judges of divine retribution taken on enemies through the actions of human agents (Eglon 3:19-22; Sisera, 4:19-21; Abimelech, 9:53-54; the Philistines, 16:25-30).

FIDEL KWASI UGIRA

ADONIJAH ad′uh-ni′juh [אֲדֹנִיָה ’adhoniyyah, אֲדֹנִיָהוּ ’adoniyahu]. 1. David's fourth son, born in Hebron by his wife Haggith (2 Sam 3:4). First Kings 1–2 narrates Adonijah's failed bid to succeed DAVID as king of Israel. Since Adonijah's three older brothers were dead, he was ideally positioned as the rightful heir, but his younger brother Solomon was a formidable rival, due in part to the political skill of Solomon's mother BATHSHEBA.

Rather than seeking David's approval of his plan, Adonijah acts without his knowledge or permission, and gathers the royal house for a sacrificial feast at En-rogel, excluding Solomon and his supporters. The prophet NATHAN sends Bathsheba to ask David how it is that "Adonijah has become king" without David's knowledge (1 Kgs 1:11, 18). By appealing to the old king's sense of honor, Bathsheba and Nathan convince David to declare that Solomon should be anointed king (1 Kgs 1:32-35). When it becomes clear that the tide has turned, Adonijah flees to the Temple and refuses to come out without Solomon's promise to spare him. After David's death, however, Adonijah again shows his lack of political acuity by asking Solomon for ABISHAG, the concubine who had comforted David in his infirmity. Solomon interprets this as a subtle bid for kingship and has Adonijah killed, despite his earlier promise.

2. Judean leader from the time of Jehoshaphat (2 Chr 17:8) and Ezra (Neh 10:16).

3. A leader who set his seal on Ezra's covenant.

BRYAN D. BIBB

ADONIKAM ad′uh-ni′kuhm [אֲדֹנִיקָם ’adhoniqam]. The head of a non-priestly clan returning to Judah from Babylonia in several lists in Ezra-Nehemiah. One list includes those said to come up with Zerubbabel and Joshua during the reign of Darius (Ezra 2:13; Neh 7:18); another, those with Ezra in the reign of Artaxerxes (Ezra 8:13). *See* EZRA; NEHEMIAH.

LESTER L. GRABBE

ADONIRAM ad'uh-ni'ruhm [אֲדֹנִירָם 'adhoniram]. Adoniram, son of ABDA, was a Solomonic official in charge of the corvee-force (1 Kgs 4:6; 5:14). The incumbent of that office under Solomon's father, DAVID, is called Adoram in 2 Sam 20:24, the same name for the office-holder under Solomon's son and successor, REHOBOAM (1 Kings 12:18). Various textual witnesses, however, read Adoniram instead of Adoram in these cases, thus prompting some scholars to suggest either that Adoram is a variant of Adoniram and, indeed, that the same person might have held the office over the reigns of three kings—a remarkably but not impossibly long tenure.

The name of the official under Rehoboam is recorded as Hadoram in 2 Chr 10:18, and there, again, some Greek manuscripts and the Syriac version have Adoniram. The name Adoram/Hadoram may indicate a foreign origin, for it praises the god Haddu/Addu ("Haddu/Addu is Exalted"), a storm deity known in Canaanite religion by his epithet, BAAL (lord). Thus, Adoniram is an understandable alternative to the foreign-sounding Adoram/Hadoram, perhaps a more acceptable alternative to Yahwists.

C. L. SEOW

ADONI-ZEDEK uh-doh'ni -zee'kuhm [אֲדֹנִי־צֶדֶק 'adhoni tsedheq; Ἀδωνιβεζεκ Adōnibezek]. "My Lord is righteous" or "My Lord is Zedek." The Jebusite king of Jerusalem led a coalition of the kings from Jerusalem, Hebron, Jarmuth, Eglon, and Lachish—against GIBEON (Josh 10). Calls for help brought JOSHUA on a forced march all night. The biblical account records that Yahweh killed soldiers with hailstones as they fled, and at Joshua's request, caused the sun and moon to stand still until the army could finish slaughtering panic-stricken coalition soldiers (Josh 10:11-13). The five kings hid in a cave at MAKKEDAH. Joshua took them from the cave and hanged them on five trees (Josh 10:16-27). Some associate Adoni-Zedek with Adoni-Bezek (see the Greek), a Canaanite judge in Judg 1, but that is unlikely. *See also* ADONI-BEZEK.

J. GORDON HARRIS

ADOPTION [υἱοθεσία huiothesia]. Although adoption has long been a significant metaphor in Christian theology, its occurrence as a specific term in the Bible is infrequent. The term, huiothesia, or "adoption as a SON" (literally, "to have the place of a son"), occurs 5 times in the NT but not at all in the LXX and other contemporaneous Jewish writing. No Hebrew

equivalent appears in the Hebrew of the OT. Paul uses huiothesia metaphorically 4 times in his extant letters (Rom 8:15; 8:23; and 9:4; Gal 4:5) and the author of Ephesians refers to huiothesia once (Eph 1:5). Because the language of adoption is employed explicitly by Paul, scholars have sought to determine whether Paul's use of huiothesia is indicative of a primarily Jewish, or Greco-Roman milieu. The practice of adoption by both Greeks and Romans has been clearly established. However, scholars continue to debate whether adoption as a formal legal arrangement was practiced in ancient Israel and early Judaism.

A. Adoption in Ancient Israel and Early Judaism
B. Adoption in Ancient Greece and Rome
C. The Pauline Metaphor
Bibliography

A. Adoption in Ancient Israel and Early Judaism

Whereas the OT refers to the guardianship of foundlings and orphans by adults other than a child's birth parents, it is difficult to determine whether ancient Israel allowed for adoption as a formal arrangement in which children, especially sons, would be legally recognized as the heirs of their adoptive fathers. It is clear that ancient Jewish law provided adult males without legitimate male offspring at least 2 means of acquiring proper heirs. In the first instance, Jewish legislation recognized formal processes for granting male children who had been born outside of marriage legitimacy as heirs. In the second situation, levirate marriage allowed for the continuation of a deceased man's lineage through the subsequent union of his widow and his surviving brother (Deut 25:5-10). Sons produced in levirate marriage were the legal children, heirs, and progenitors of their mother's deceased husband. In both cases, Jewish law ensured that inheritance would proceed along biologically defined familial lines and according to legally recognized blood ties; perhaps in light of such means, adoption as a formal legal institution was generally unnecessary in ancient Israel.

However, other biblical phrases functioned as adoption formulae, and important biblical narratives illustrate the practice of adoption. The CODE OF HAMMURABI (laws 185, 186, and 190), the Laws of Eshnunna, and numerous Babylonian and Mesopotamian documents attest to the common practice of adoption in the ancient Near East. In light of such evidence, well-known biblical declarations attributed to the God of Israel, "You are my son" (Ps 2:7) and "I will be his Father" (2 Sam 7:14), as well as specific metaphors employed by biblical writers (Ezek 16:1-7) have been read comparatively as adoption language. Indeed, biblical writers might have used adoption imagery and language precisely in order to confirm Israel's legitimacy and right to inheritance. If adoption was practiced in ancient Judaism, Jewish tradition serves as a good framework for understanding Paul's references to huiothesia.

Eliezer, Moses, Obed, and Esther are among the biblical characters whom scholars have identified as likely subjects of adoption. The example of Eliezer is especially illustrative of how concern for inheritance dominated ancient Israel's interest in securing legitimate sons. After the childless Abraham makes the slave Eliezer his heir, the divine voice instructs Abraham that it will be his "own son," not Eliezer, who will serve as his heir (Gen 15:4). This story shows not only how adoption was motivated by the need for an heir but how it could be annulled by the subsequent arrival of a son legitimately born to an adoptive FATHER.

A few Jewish inscriptions in Rome, a reference from the Aramaic papyri and an adoption deed in Egypt also suggest that Jewish families sometimes adopted children. Whether such practice reflects Jewish legislation specifically, though, is unclear.

B. Adoption in Ancient Greece and Rome

Owing to Paul's use of adoption as a theological metaphor in Galatians and Romans (Rom 8:15, 23; and 9:4; Gal 4:5), scholars have looked to both Greek and Roman practices of adoption as the relevant contexts for understanding Paul. Used primarily as a means of circumventing the rules governing succession, especially when the deceased had no immediate sons who could serve as his direct heirs, adoption was a legal and fairly common practice in ancient Greece. It usually involved the adoption of a male blood relation who could carry on the family line and cult. While its practice was rooted in the desire to ensure such continuity, it was motivated also by an accompanying determination to delimit inheritance along familial blood ties.

The Greeks allowed for three ways of adopting: an adoptive father could name and register an adoptee by way of a formal ceremony; an adoption could be enacted according to a will; an adoption could be arranged posthumously by the kin or heirs of the deceased. Whichever the case, the adoption had no legal bearing on the relationship between an adoptee and birthmother. Neither did it establish a legal relationship between an adoptee and the adoptive father's wife or daughters. In sum, the adoptive relationship had limited legal impact on familial ties and obligations. Evidence from Athens indicates, in fact, that in some cases, adoptions were probationary and could be annulled. That adoption was pertinent primarily for testamentary purposes is evidenced by its decline by the 4th cent. BCE, when Greek law allowed for means other than adoption by which inheritance could be managed and protected.

In contrast, under Roman law adoption had a far greater legal reach. It was a well-known practice, as adoption created the familial relations that Julius Cae-

sar, Augustus, and Tiberias shared. Adoption was not only a means of establishing inheritance, it was a tool for creating alliances among powerful families.

Roman law recognized two kinds of adoption: *adrogatio* and *adoptio*. The first concerned the adoption of a person who was *sui iuris*, that is, not under the *potestas*, or legal power, of another. The second involved the adoption of someone who was *alieni iuris*, or under *potestas*. In cases of *adoptio*, adoption involved the annulment of the former *potestas* and the establishment of *potestas* under the adoptive *paterfamilias*. In both cases, adoption established a radical reconfiguration of familial relations. Not only were former familial ties legally erased, with those under the *potestas* of the adrogated coming under the new *postestas* of the adoptive father, all former debts and obligations were canceled. In regard to Roman law and customs, the adoptee was recognized as the full child of the adoptive *paterfamilias*. No legal distinction was made between adopted children and those born to a *paterfamilias*.

Evidence suggests that Romans adopted both sons and daughters. However, as in Greek adoption (and possibly in cases of Israelite or Jewish adoption), males were likely adopted in order to secure heirs. Whereas important familial alliances could be established through the adoption of sons or daughters, females were unlikely to have been adopted primarily for the purpose of establishing heirs.

C. The Pauline Metaphor

Although some see antecedents for Paul's adoption language in Jewish tradition, it resonates more with the Roman practice of *adoptio*. Paul's metaphor clearly stresses the transformed identity of the believer who has been brought into a new relationship with God. The suggestion that Paul's theological use of adoption language was shaped by Roman practice accords well with what scholars know of Paul's immediate social and political context. Moreover, though the establishment and enforcement of Roman law throughout the empire was complex and varied, Paul's hearers were likely to have been at least somewhat familiar with Roman forms of adoption. However, Paul's metaphor also extends beyond the concrete expressions of its practice. Whereas his use of huiothesia presupposes the image of adopted sons who function also as heirs, Paul clearly intends to include both male and female believers in his characterization of Christians as those who are fully heirs and children of God. *See* CHILD, CHILDREN; DAUGHTER; FAMILY; HAMMURABI, CODE OF; HEIR; INHERITANCE; LAW IN EARLY JUDAISM; LAW IN THE NT; LAW IN THE OT; SON.

Bibliography: Kathleen E. Corley. "Women's Inheritance Rights in Antiquity and Paul's Metaphor of Adoption." *A Feminist Companion to Paul,* ed. Amy-Jill Levine with Marianne Blickenstaff (2004) 98–121;

Francis Lyall. *Slaves, Citizens, Sons: Legal Metaphors in the New Testament* (1984); Meir Malul. "Adoption of Foundlings in the Bible and Mesopotamian Documents: A Study of Some Legal Metaphors in Ezekiel 16:1-7." *JSOT* 46 (1990) 97–126; Janet L. R. Melnyk, "When Israel Was a Child: Ancient Near Eastern Adoption Formulas and the Relationship between God and Israel." *History and Interpretation: Essays in Honor of John Hayes*, ed. M. Patrick Graham, et al. (1993) 245–59; Shalom M. Paul. "Adoption Formulae: A Study of Cuneiform and Biblical Legal Cases." *Maarav* 2/2 (1979–1980) 173–85; James M. Scott. *Adoption as Sons of God: An Exegetical Investigation into the Background of* huiothesia *in the Pauline Corpus* (1992).

MARY FOSKETT

ADORA uh-doh´ruh. *See* ADORAIM.

ADORAIM ad´-uh-ray´im [אֲדוֹרַיִם ʾadhorayim; Ἀδωραί Adōrai, Ἀδωρά Adōra]. City in southern Israel, dating from the Bronze Age, one of fifteen later fortified by REHOBOAM (2 Chr 11:9). In the Hellenistic period, Adora and Marisa were the principal Idumean cities. In 143/2 BCE Tryphon invaded Judea near Adora in an unsuccessful attempt to subdue SIMON MACCABEUS (1 Macc 13:20). JOHN HYRCANUS later (ca. 126/5 BCE) captured Adora and Marisa and, according to Josephus, compelled their inhabitants to be circumcised and accept the Jewish law (*Ant.* 13.257-258). Adora is the modern DURA (152:101), situated about 6 miles southwest of HEBRON.

J. R. C. COUSLAND

ADORAM uh-doh´ruhm. *See* ADONIRAM.

ADORATION. *See* WORSHIP, EARLY JEWISH; WORSHIP, NT, CHRISTIAN; WORSHIP, OT.

ADRAMMELECH uh-dram´uh-lek [אַדְרַמֶּלֶךְ ʾadhramelekh]. A deity mentioned in 2 Kgs 17:31. The king of Assyria deported peoples from Babylon, Cuthah, Avva, Hamath, and Sepharvaim, and settled them in the cities of Samaria, to replace the Israelites, who had been previously deported to Assyria. Here these peoples continued their worship of foreign gods. While the other groups are simply described as making idols, the Sepharvaites are singled out as the ones who burned children in sacrifice to Adrammelech and ANAMMELECH, the "gods of Sepharvaim." Unfortunately, this episode does not have any supporting evidence, and no convincing identification has been proposed for Adrammelech, despite various attempts to explain its West Semitic sounding name, nor for the toponym Sepharvaim, which may be located in Syria, since it is mentioned near Hamath.

ANNALISA AZZONI

ADRAMYTTIUM ad´ruh-mit´ee-uhm [Ἀδρα-μυττηνός Adramyttēnos]. An ancient port city along the coast of the Roman province Asia (now Turkey). A commercial ship from Adramyttium bound for the Asian coast carried Paul, ARISTARCHUS, and JULIUS the Centurion from Caesarea to Myra on the first leg of their journey to Rome (Acts 27:2).

ADRIA, SEA OF ay´dree-uh [Ἀδρίας Adrias]. An arm of the Mediterranean Sea located between the Apennine peninsula in the west (Italy), the Balkan peninsula in the east (former Yugoslavia and Albania), and the Ionian Sea in the south, known today as the Adriatic Sea. This body of water that stretches some five hundred miles from southeast to northwest is dangerous for travel in winter due to storms caused by strong northeast winds, locally called *bura*.

On his way to Rome, the apostle Paul traveled on a boat that "was driven up and down" the sea of Adria for two weeks ending in a shipwreck (Acts 27:27). Josephus wrote that the boat on which he traveled "sank in the midst of the sea of Adria" (Josephus, *Vita* 3).

Certain geographical terms in Acts 27–28 lead to a conclusion that the name *Adria* is used in this text in a much wider sense than the Adriatic Sea of today. Thus, in NT times, the part of the Mediterranean between Crete and Malta, as far as Sicily was loosely called Adria.

This conclusion is confirmed by several references to Adria used by ancient writers, such as Strabo, who considered the Ionian Sea to be a part of the Adriatic Sea. The name derives from Atria, an old Etruscan city located in the delta of the Po River (in today's Italy).

ZDRAVKO STEFANOVIC

ADRIEL ay´dree-uhl [עַדְרִיאֵל ʿadhriʾel]. The son of BARZILLIA and husband of either MERAB (1 Sam 18:19) or MICHAL (some Hebrew and Greek manuscripts, 2 Sam 21:8), King SAUL's daughters. DAVID presents Adriel's five sons to the Gibionites for execution because of Saul's transgression against them, a transgression unrecorded in 1 Samuel.

HEATHER R. MCMURRAY

ADULLAM uh-duhl´uhm [עֲדֻלָּם ʿadhullam; Οδολλαμ Odollam]. A city in the southern SHEPHELAH (Josh 15:35) commonly identified with the unexcavated site, Tell esh Sheikh Madhkûr. Adullam guarded a route from the coastal plain to the highlands of Judea.

A character named Hirah is identified as an Adullamite in the story of Judah and Tamar (Gen 38:1, 12, 20). The book of Joshua includes Adullam's king in a list of conquered local rulers (Josh 12:15) and states that the city was later allotted to the tribe of Judah (Josh 15:35). Fleeing Saul, David hid in "the cave of Adullam" (1 Sam 22:1-2), which later became a "stronghold" (v. 4) for him and his "mighty men" (2 Sam 5:17; 23:13-17; 1 Chr 11:15).

Adullam was among the cities fortified by Rehoboam in the face of Shishak's impending invasion of Palestine (ca. 918 BCE) (2 Chr 11:7), and Micah mourns Adullam (Mic 1:15), possibly in anticipation of the invasion of Sennacharib (2 Kgs 18:13 = 2 Chr 32:1). Following the exile, Adullam was one of the places where the returning Judeans settled (Neh 11:30). Later, Judas Maccabeus and his army found refuge there during the Maccabean revolt (2 Macc 12:38).

RALPH K. HAWKINS

ADULTERY [נָאַף naʾaf; μοιχεία moicheia]. The term in the Bible is used in a variety of contexts, including legal, prophetic, gospel, and epistolary texts. Adultery may be defined as a man having sex with another man's wife, or a married woman having sex with ("lying with") a man other than her husband. The term is also at times metaphorical.

A. Old Testament

The two terms or phrases consistently used for adultery in the OT are naʾaf ("to commit adultery") and "to lay with one's neighbor's wife." There is some semantic overlap between naʾaf and זָנָה zanah, "to whore" or "to prostitute." Some married or widowed women are accused of committing zanah instead of naʾaf (compare Gen 38.24).

1. Legal contexts

Both versions of the TEN COMMANDMENTS include a prohibition against committing adultery (Exod 20:14; Deut 5:18). The key to the determination of whether a sexual act is adultery or not appears to be the *woman's* marital status. The term *wife* includes affianced women: a woman engaged to be married is called the "neighbor's wife" (Deut 22:23-24). Both parties are condemned to death (compare Lev 20:10; Deut 22:24). The method of death is not specific in Leviticus; in Deuteronomy, it is stoning (compare John 8.4). Lying with an unmarried woman is not termed adultery and carries different consequences: a payment to the father and marriage to the woman without the possibility of divorce (Deut 22:29). Reflective of a social situation in which women are objects of exchange between men, in all cases, the subject of the law is the man, and the offense is against another man: a man commits adultery with someone else's wife (fiance); the woman is called an adulteress.

2. The prophets

The prophets include adultery in catalogues of prohibited actions dealing with social justice and maintenance of proper community relationships. A surprising number of texts (compare Hos 4:2; Jer 7:9; 9:2; 23:14; 29:23; Mal 3:5) use the term in parallel with lying, deception, theft, and oppressing the poor. Several texts connect adultery with bloodshed (compare Hos 4:2;

Ezek 16:8; 23:37, 45). Ezekiel uses stronger terminology to describe adultery; instead of "to lie with," the language is to "defile" (Ezek 18:6, 11, 15; 33:26) or "commit an abomination with" (Ezek 22:11). Finally, there is a significant connection between adultery and the land: the land mourns as a result of adultery (Jer 23:10; Hos 4:2-3), and adultery pollutes the land (Jer 3:1-5, 8, 9).

3. Other

In Proverbs, the adulteress is compared with the "strange woman." In one instance, the term "strange woman" is translated "adulteress" in the NRSV (Prov 6:7). In these contexts, adulteresses are pictured as seducing young men from following the way of wisdom. As in the prophets, the language used to describe the woman's acts links adultery with deceit (compare Prov 6:7, 32; 7:19-20; 30:20; also Ps 50:18 and Job 24:15).

B. New Testament

Like the OT, adultery often appears in catalogues equivalent to the Ten Commandments (Matt 5:27; 15:19; 19:18; Mark 7:22; 10:19; Luke 18:11, 20; Rom 2:22; 13:9; 1 Cor 6:9; and Jas 2:11). Also in accord with the OT, adultery is a forbidden activity because of damage to the community. The community issue is clearest in Rom 13:9, and Jas 4:4.

In Jesus' teachings on divorce in the synoptic gospels, the scope of adultery is expanded: if a divorced man marries another woman, or a man marries a woman who has been divorced by her husband, they commit adultery (moicheia) (Matt 19:9; Mark 10:11-12; Luke 16:18; compare Rom 7:3). Matthew 5:32 extends the category even further: a man who divorces his wife "causes her to commit adultery."

Finally, adultery is used metaphorically. First, 2 Pet 2:14 describes the sinner as having "eyes full of adultery." Here, in congruence with the connection between adultery and deceit in the OT, adultery is linked with insatiability, enticement, and greed. Jesus also calls the generation to whom he is preaching "an evil and adulterous generation." In Matthew (12:29; 16:4), the label is placed on those who ask for a sign, while in Mark (8:38) the "adulterous and sinful generation" are those who are ashamed of Jesus' words. *See* DIVORCE; FORNICATION; HOSEA, BOOK OF; MARRIAGE; TRIAL BY ORDEAL

MARY E. SHIELDS

ADUMMIM uh-duhm'im [אֲדֻמִּים ʾadhummim]. The root adam means "red," and in the plural means "big red" or "red places." Red rock formations form the northern boundary of Judah (Josh 15:7). The southern border of the tribe of Benjamin, from Enshemesh to Geliloth, is opposite the ascent of Adummim (Josh 18:17). The site once was a stronghold between Jerusalem and Jericho. Adummim may have referred to other locations: Adami-Nekeb and the Horns of Hattin.

J. GORDON HARRIS

ADVENT. Advent comes from the Latin *adventus*, "coming." The Vulgate uses this expression to translate the Greek word παρουσία, parousia, which means "coming" or "presence," and more often than not refers to the eschatological coming of the Lord Jesus Christ (1 Thess 3:13; 4:15; 5:23; 2 Thess 2:1), or of the Lord (1 Thess 4:15; Jas 5:7, 8), or of the Son of Man (Matt 24:27, 37, 39), or simply to "his coming" (1 Cor 15:23; 1 Thess 2:19; 2 Pet 3:4; 1 John 2:28). In Acts 7:52 *adventus* translates the word ἔλευσις, eleusis, "coming," but in this context it refers to Christ's first advent. The season of Advent begins the fourth Sunday before Christmas and focuses on the past, the coming of Christ at the incarnation, and on the future, his coming as judge at the PAROUSIA.

OSVALDO VENA

ADVERSARY [ἀντίδικος antidikos]. Plaintiff in a lawsuit (Matt 5:25; Luke 12:58, 18:3); Satan (1 Pet 5:8). *See* SATAN.

ADVISE [יָעַץ yaʿats, עֵצָה ʿetsah; βουλή boulē, συμβουλεύω symbouleuō, γνώμη gnōmē]. The biblical usage of advisement illustrates the necessity of counsel and discernment as part of all human decision-making. Advisors are plentiful throughout the Scriptures, but discerning the wisdom of their counsel seems not so easy. For every Jethro offering godly counsel (Exod 18:19), there are numerous Ahithophels who provide foolish counsel (2 Sam 16:20), and even those who provide counsel in an effort to destroy (Ezra 4:5). Though the contemporary imagery of advice and counsel is closer to therapeutic dialogue, it is clear that the biblical imagery does not reflect this neutral advice. Either one's counsel/opinion is of the Lord or reflects personal desires.

Throughout the OT, the Hebrew word yaats, and its variant etsah, appear most frequently (168 times) to connote the broad activity of consultation and advisement of one to another. For example, King Rehoboam (1 Kgs 12) seeks advice from the elders as to how he should treat those who were asking for relief from his father Solomon's heavy taxation. He receives two opposing consultations, which illustrates that even though godly advice is present, God allows individuals to listen to their own desires and plans (e.g., Pss 5:10; 81:12; Jer 7:24). A few times, advisement comes in the form of prophetic prediction, as when Balaam predicts what Israel will do to Balak's kingdom (Num 24:14), but more frequently it suggests both perception and purpose (motivation) for carrying out a plan of action. Advisement does not always require advisor/advisee relationships. It is possible for an individual to deliberate or consider the best plan on his or her own (e.g., 2 Sam 24:13).

Advisement in the NT is expressed by the giving and receiving of advice in order to proceed toward a particular goal. Such consultation is not neutral but devises plans to achieve a desired goal. The Greek words boulē (Luke 7:30; 23:51; Acts 2:23; 4:28; 5:38; 13:36; 20:27; 27:12; 42; 1 Cor 4:5; Eph 1:11; Heb 6:17) and its variant, symbouleuō (Matt 26:4; John 18:14; Acts 9:23; Rev 3:18) connote the giving or receiving of advice. One cannot read the NT texts that express this kind of consultation without noticing the stark contrast between the will of God and the plans of people. There are numerous references to religious leaders taking counsel in their plots to kill Jesus or one of his followers (boulē or symbouleuō, Matt 12:14; 22:15; 26:4; 27:1; John 11:53; 18:14; Acts 5:33). Peter declares that the conspiracy to kill Jesus succeeds only as part of God's plan (boulē Acts 2:23). Gamaliel recognizes the foolishness of trying to deter those doing God's will (boulē) and so advises caution in punishing Peter and John (Acts 5:38-39).

The word gnōmē (e.g., Rev 17:13, 17) is more often used to express self-advisement or personal judgment. Paul adjures the Corinthians to be of the same mind and purpose (1 Cor 1:10). Paul gives his personal judgment (1 Cor 7:40; 2 Cor 8:10) or asks the counsel of another (Phlm 14). *See* COUNSEL, COUNSELOR.

PHILIP G. MONROE

ADVOCATE [παράκλητος paraklētos]. The NRSV translation of paraklētos, variously translated as *Counselor* (KJV) and *Comforter* (NIV). In the NT it appears only in the Johannine literature. In the Gospel of John it is Jesus' name for the HOLY SPIRIT, whom the Father (or Jesus) will send to the disciples to be Jesus' presence in the world after his return to the Father (14:16, 26; 15:26-27; 16:7b-11, 12-15). In 1 John it describes Jesus' role for the sinner (2:1). *See* COMFORTER; COUNSELOR; HOLY SPIRIT; PARACLETE.

MICHAEL WILLETT NEWHEART

AEGEAN. The Aegean is a sea, which lies to the east of mainland GREECE, and to the west of Turkey. Its southern boundary is the island of CRETE (part of the Roman province of Crete and Cyrenaica), which separates it from the MEDITERRANEAN. Its northern boundary is MACEDONIA. The Aegean was served by important ports such as the PIRAEUS (for Athens) and CENCHREAE (for Corinth), both for the province of ACHAIA; and EPHESUS and MILETUS, for the province of Asia. The Aegean is dotted with islands that include the Cyclades in the south, the Northern and Southern Sporades (including the island of Cos), and Samothrace.

DAVID W. J. GILL

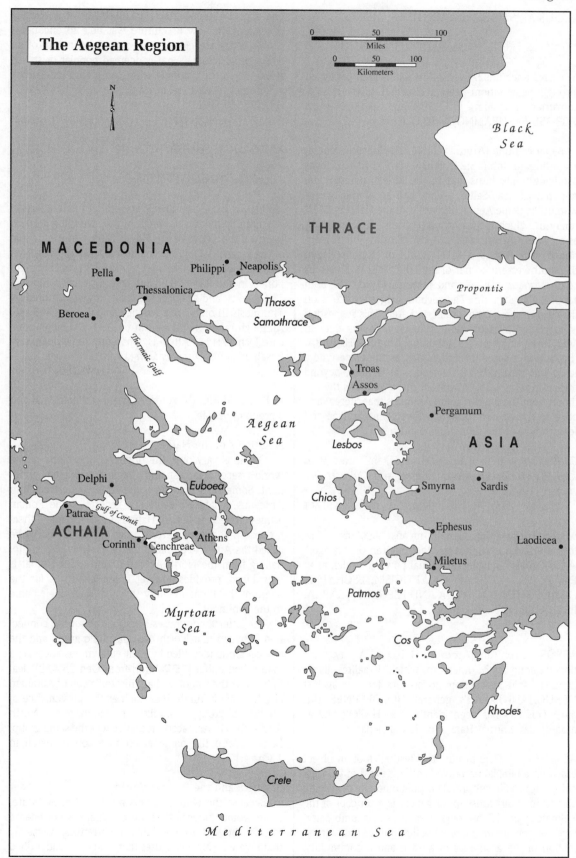

The Aegean Region

AELIUS ARISTIDES. *See* ARISTIDES, AELIUS.

AEMILIUS PAULLUS. *See* PAULLUS, AEMILIUS.

AENEAS i-nee´uhs [Αἰνέας Aineas]. A man paralyzed for eight years whom Peter healed and whose healing converted all residing in LYDDA and SHARON (Acts 9:33-35). *See* HEALING; MIRACLES.

AENON ee´nuhn [Αἰνών Ainōn]. The location where, according to John 3:23, JOHN THE BAPTIST was baptizing while Jesus was in the Judean countryside. Aenon was near Salim, and it had an abundance of water. The name Aenon derives from the Hebrew עֵנַיִם ʿenayim, which means "double spring." It is uncertain as to where Aenon was, but two sites are often mentioned. The first is 6–8 mi. south of Scythopolis, in the southwestern corner of the DECAPOLIS. Eusebius (*Onomasticon* 40:1-4), and Jerome (*Epistle* 73) both support this location. The second suggested site is on the eastern side of the Jordan, in Perea. This suggestion is supported by a 6th cent. map on a church floor in MEDEBA, which places Aenon opposite BETHABARA. (Bethabara is sometimes identified as the place where Jesus was baptized; it is referred to as Bethany beyond Jordan in John 1:28.) Also from the 6th cent. is the tradition from the pilgrim guide Antonius that there was a cave on the eastern location where John baptized and Jesus stayed at the time of his baptism.

Bibliography: John J. Rousseau and Rami Arav. *Jesus and His World: An Archaeological and Cultural Dictionary* (1995).

MICHAEL WILLETT NEWHEART

AEON [αἰών aiōn]. Literally means "age," as in historical era. Jesus alludes to "the children of this age." *Aeon* can also indicate a spiritual power or ruler, as in Eph 2:2. *See* AGE; APOCALYPTICISM; ESCHATOLOGY OF THE APOCRYPHA AND PSEUDEPIGRAPHA; ESCHATOLOGY OF THE NT.

GREG CAREY

AESORA i-soh´ruh [Αἰσωρά Haisōra]. A city mentioned along with others to which Israelites living in Judah sent instructions to prepare for war against NEBUCHADNEZZAR's general HOLOFERNES (Jdt 4:4). This city has been identified as HAZOR and as modern-day Khirbet Hazzur or Tell el-Qedah.

AESTHETICS. The beauty and aesthetics of an object based on a biblical narrative is often devoid of its original context and culture. The phenomenon of placing objects in an art museum or gallery is a concept of the Enlightenment. Those objects such as catacomb paintings that remain *in situ* provide the most accurate information of the aesthetics of an age and a community. The appeal and success of an object of art is entirely dependent on how its culture was able to encounter it. Aesthetics are closely linked to the function of an object or structure. What is deemed popular or stylish at one period of history is often considered indecorous at another period of history. *See* ART; CARVING; CRAFTS; DESIGN.

HEIDI J. HORNIK

AETIOLOGY. *See* ETIOLOGY.

AFFLICTION. *See* SUFFERING.

ʿAFFULA, EL. The ruins of ancient ʿAffula are largely obscured by the development of the sprawling modern town on the slopes of the Hill of Moreh in the middle of the Jezreel Valley. The name probably derives from Semitic ʿophel, "hill/citadel." ʿAffula is probably mentioned in the 19th/18th cent. BCE Egyptian EXECRATION texts, and again in the list of towns captured by Thutmosis III on his first Asiatic campaign in 1468 BCE. Although rarely mentioned in the Hebrew Bible (compare Josh 17:11), ʿAffula is apparently remembered by Eusebius in his *Onomasticon* (14.20; as "Arbela").

WILLIAM G. DEVER

AFRICA, AFRICAN. A term applied to a continent and a group of people.

A. Origins of the Name

Opinions vary over the origins of the name of the world's second largest and the first populated continent. Some hold that the name Africa is derived from Africanus, a late 3rd cent. BCE general of the Roman armies charged to pursue Hannibal to Carthage. Others propose that the name originates with a Berber tribe called the Afri, the plural of the term *Afer*. This group, hailing from the North African region around what is now Libya, provides another potential source for the name of the Roman colony that that gave their name to the continent.

The latter theory raises questions about the connection between that North African ethnic group and the biblical group identified by their eponymous ancestor, a man called Epher [עֵפֶר ʿefer] from Gen 25:4. Biblical Epher was the son of Midian, himself a son of Abraham and his wife Keturah. Inasmuch as the provenience of the biblical group would likely be the deserts of North Africa, the Genesis account may reflect the same group. Epher is also the name given to a son of Ezrah in 1 Chr 4:17.

B. Africa and the Biblical World

Because the word *Africa* is not found in Scripture, some would suppose that the continent is considered an afterthought to the biblical narratives. Certainly there were no biblical figures that would have identified themselves as African, because the term was not applied to the continent until the post-biblical period. Further, due to the tendency for identity to be based upon tribal and national identity markers, it is unlikely that any biblical figure would have conceived of their identity with as universal an identity marker as "African." Africa and Africans are terms that would have been meaningless in the period when the OT and NT were composed.

However, the Bible deals with countless places and people that present-day readers would deem "African." Contemporary readers would generally consider many countries mentioned in the Bible such as Cush, Ethiopia, Egypt, Seba, and Put as continental African nations. These nations frequently recur in biblical narratives as allies and enemies of the people of Israel/Judah and their God. Similarly, nationals from these countries are heroes (e.g., EBED-MELECH, TIRHAKAH) and villains (e.g., PHARAOH, ZERAH) in the stories about the survival of Yahweh's people. Despite the absence of the name Africa, nations within the borders traditionally ascribed to this continent, are well represented on the pages of Scripture.

Some scholars think that the traditional boundaries for Africa and African people may be too narrowly delimited, curtailing the continent in the northeastern corner of Egypt at the Sinai peninsula. Due to certain geographical factors, there are legitimate reasons to question the validity of the traditional boundaries and to argue for the inclusion of the Levant as a part of continental Africa. Though deemed the bridge "between" Asia and Africa, rarely has Western scholarship seriously addressed the location of this region "within" Africa.

The story of the Bible unfolds principally on the African continent, a region of the world typically described as the LEVANT, the Near East, or the Middle East. The land of Palestine actually sits on the two continental plates that comprise the African continent. The line where these plates converge is marked by an enormous valley, the Great Rift Valley that begins in the north as the Jordan Valley and extends through Red Sea as far south as Lake Tanganyika in southeastern Africa. Israel/Judah rest upon the African Continental plate, as does the rest of the landmass comprising Cis-Jordan; while Trans-Jordan is founded upon the Arabo-Nubian Continental plate. Consistent with this identification are the indigenous flora and fauna of Palestine typifying African botanical and zoological forms. Similarly, climate and geology are also akin to other portions of the African continent. In fact, in an effort to define the world from the perspective of Europe, the imprecise designations Near East and Middle East have been deemed "Eurocentric" concepts. More problematic is the separation of not just Libya and Egypt, but all of Palestine from their African contexts as though the Near or Middle East was a continental unit unto itself. Maps of the Biblical world tend to reinforce such thinking,

having as their southwestern extreme Lower Egypt, and rarely illustrating beyond Upper Egypt as far as Cush. This "de-Africanization" of the Bible has helped perpetuate the myth of Africa as a primitive continent.

C. Africa in Biblical Studies

Though the term *Africa* does not occur in the Bible, there are a few typical strategies for addressing the role that Africa and Africans play in Scripture. One strategy is simply to deny that the Bible addresses Africa at all. Proponents of this opinion tend to deny that known African peoples in Scripture are actually African, choosing instead to label them "Semitic" or "Near Eastern." In part, the principal result of this line of reasoning is the creation of a zone devoid of continental affiliation, which is called the Near or Middle East. While this concept has been helpful for demonstrating certain cultural continuities between Levantine societies over time, it has also served to isolate these from other African cultures that share similar traits and social structures.

A second strategy, developed around the sons of Noah's second son Ham, introduced in Gen 10:6-20, is to determine that this lineage, and generally this line alone, presents characters that moderns would deem African. Works emphasizing the Hamite origins of African peoples tend to misapply the anachronistic concept of "race" to the Bible, suggesting that the "Table of Nations" in Gen 10 represents an accurate assessment of the development of racial human sub-species groups. Though this argument has proven useful to diaspora Africans arguing for a "stolen legacy" of greatness, it has also been used by their ideological foes to justify their oppression. By misappropriating the "Curse of Canaan" from Gen 9:18-27, and transforming it into a "Curse on Ham," Europeans were able to theologically justify the enslavement of all African people as Ham's descendants.

A third strategy is to associate all of Africa with CUSH or its Greek equivalent, ETHIOPIA. Favored by "Ethiopianists" and many other diaspora African groups, Cush, or more commonly Ethiopia, became synonymous with the entire continent, in a similar manner to the way Ethiopia was used as a globalizing term for dark-skinned Africans by Hellenistic authors. In this way the glorious story of the Cushites/Ethiopians becomes the history of contemporary, diaspora African peoples. For these groups, passages such as Ps 68:31 [Heb. 68:32], Amos 9:7, and Zeph 3:10 signify the special relationship that Yahweh has with Africans. Yet this strategy also presents difficulties, because it universalizes the narrative of a particular east African group and applies it to all contemporary diaspora Africans, even though most diaspora Africans in the Western world are descendants of people from western African nations (with their own distinctive histories). Another concern is that by elevating Cush as the African quintessence, the histories of other African nations in the Bible, such as Egypt, Put, Seba, Sheba, and even Israel/Judah are ignored.

To fully appreciate the role Africa and its people play in Scripture is to move beyond Western stereotypes of the "dark continent" and embrace the diversity of what is Africa and African. African nations consist of more than just Cush; they include Egypt, Canaan, Edom, Libya, Arabia, Midian, and even Israel and Judah. African peoples are not only those who are deeply pigmented with broad facial features but include people of various hews, with different phenotypes, and varying physical traits. A globalizing African identity cannot be assumed to have imposed certain distinctive ways of being on those from this vast continent; instead people from Africa can be appreciated for the multiplicity of ways that they express their identities on the pages of the Bible. Those who exegete the Bible should recognize that the Promised Land itself is a prime piece of African real estate, at the very heart of the biblical story. *See* AFRICAN INTERPRETATION; AFROCENTRIC INTERPRETATION; ARAB, ARABIA, ARABIANS; CANAAN; CUSH, CUSHITE; CUSHAN; CUSHITE WIFE, MOSES'; EDOM; EGYPT; ETHIOPIA; ISRAEL, GEOGORAPHY OF; LEVANT; LIBYA; MIDIAN, MIDIANITES.

RODNEY S. SADLER, JR.

AFRICAN INTERPRETATION. Africa is the cradle of systematic interpretation of the Bible in Christianity. The earliest such attempt is traced to Origen who started the Alexandrian school of exegesis in Alexandria, Egypt, in the 3rd cent. CE using allegorical techniques to read the Bible (*see* ORIGEN). This method was replaced in the Western church in the 18th through the 20th cent. by the historical and literary critical methods that reached modern Africa in the 20th cent. Four kinds of methods are currently practiced in Africa—the allegorical method practiced by the Coptic Orthodox Church in North Africa, the historical-critical method and the literary-critical method practiced in sub-Saharan Africa and particularly by the whites in South Africa, and the contextual method practiced by black African scholars. Since the first 3 are more widely used outside Africa and can be studied through a cross-reference, I shall exclude them from consideration here. The last, which is characterized by a creative encounter between the Bible and the African context, shall be the focus of this essay. It is categorized into 2 exegetical paradigms: inculturation, which is rooted in the indigenous religious culture of the people, and liberation, rooted in the secular culture. The following 7 *models*—the first 4 belonging to the inculturation paradigm and the last 3 the liberation paradigm—may be identified.

A. Comparative Model

Modern biblical studies in sub-Saharan Africa originated during a period of widespread condemnation of African religion and culture by the Christian missionaries of the 19th and 20th cent. African scholars responded with research that sought to legitimate African religion and culture vis-à-vis Christianity. Their comparative studies demonstrated continuities and discontinuities between biblical material and African culture and religion. The continuities showed that African culture and religion are not opposed to Christianity, while the discontinuities indicated that the relationship between the 2 is dialectical. For example, Kwesi Dickson highlights the conceptual presence of "corporate personality" in both the Bible and African culture. He also acknowledges discontinuity, pointing out that while in the Bible the prophets preached God's openness toward the gentiles, in African culture such openness to other people is absent. Unfortunately, while this approach helped articulate the values of African religion and culture in a Christian context, it was often too apologetic in its defense of the African traditions and too polemical in its perspective on Christianity. It also demonstrated little concern for hermeneutical or secular application. Nevertheless, as a result of this approach, in the 1970s, African Traditional Religion and culture came to be understood as a *preparation for the gospel*.

B. Africa-in-the-Bible Model

This model is concerned with the presence of Africa and African peoples in the Bible and the significance of such presence. Some studies in this model have shown African influence on the religion of the Hebrew Patriarchs, and some have highlighted the contribution of Egypt in the biblical story. For example, Egypt is highlighted as a place of refuge for Jesus at his birth. Other studies have corrected the impression that North Africa belongs to the Middle East and challenged the negative stereotypes about African peoples embedded in certain traditional readings of some biblical texts (e.g., *see* the study by David Adamo). Though this model is disinterested in either theological or social engagement, it has created a strong awareness of the importance of African nations and peoples in the biblical story (*see* AFRICA; CUSH; EGYPT; ETHIOPIA).

C. Evaluative Model

This model engages in dialogue between the Bible and the African context. The following approaches are used: evaluation of elements of African culture in the light of biblical witness; interpreting biblical texts with concepts from African culture; applying the meaning of biblical texts to African contexts; and studying biblical texts to discover biblical models that support inculturation of Christianity in Africa. The model operates from the classical understanding of exegesis as the recovery of text meaning, and hermeneutics as the application of that meaning to a particular contemporary context. An example of the first approach is John Mbiti's—the most commonly applied model today. Through its use,

African culture and religion came to be seen in the 1980s as *indispensable resources in the interpretation of the Bible.*

D. Inculturation Hermeneutics Model

None of the previous inculturation models pays sufficient attention to social issues. Inculturation hermeneutics seeks to redress this failing by adopting a *holistic approach to culture.* The religious and secular aspects of culture are treated as though they were interconnected. This model operates at the point where academic and ordinary readings of the Bible meet. While its methodology is rooted in the ordinary people's approach to the Bible, its conceptual framework of interpretation is informed by African sociocultural perspectives. The Bible is read through an African sociocultural grid. This makes the African context the *subject* of interpretation. Hermeneutics is understood as the process whereby a community of readers who are critically aware of their context interacts with the historically located text. The basic hermeneutic theory is that the *meaning of a text is a function of the interaction between the text in its social-historical context, and a community of readers in their contemporary contexts.* For example, see J. Ukpong's reading of the parable of the shrewd manager (Luke 16:1-13).

E. Liberation Theology Model

The liberation paradigm, to which the last three models belong, uses the Bible as a resource for struggle against oppression. The liberation theology model focuses on political and economic oppression, while the next 2 focus on gender and racial oppression, respectively. The story of God's liberation of the Hebrews in the book of Exodus is the grounding text for the hermeneutics of political liberation. God's call on Israel to take special care of the poor among them, and deal justly with all (*see* Exod 23:11; Amos 2:6-7; 5:21-24), and Jesus' concern for the poor (*see* Luke 4:18-19; 6:20-21) provide the grounding for the hermeneutics of economic liberation. These and similar texts are read against the background of neocolonialism and economic oppression in Africa (e.g., *see* Canaan Banana reading). Liberation hermeneutics has raised awareness about secular issues as a matter of theological concern, and the idea of injustice as a structural phenomenon. However, it has been criticized for lack of attention to religious-cultural issues like witchcraft, spirit possession, etc., which are also pressing issues in Africa.

F. Feminist Theology Model

This model uses the Bible as a resource for struggle against women's oppression. Five interrelated approaches expressing two main concerns—a critique of androcentrism both in the Bible and in biblical interpretation, and a recovery of muted voices of women in the Bible—are discernible. One approach, such as

M. Odeyoye's reading, challenges conventional hermeneutics by which scripture is interpreted in androcentric terms. A second critiques and reinterprets those biblical texts that are oppressive to women or portray them as inferior to men. A third highlights texts that show the positive role of women in the Bible. A fourth enquires into the basic biblical theological orientation that can function as a guide to interpreting both the negative and positive biblical texts about women. A fifth interprets biblical texts from the perspective of African women's experience. Feminist hermeneutics has problematized many biblical texts and raised awareness about women's oppression as a matter of theological concern.

G. Black Theology Model

Black theology uses the Bible as a resource in the struggle against apartheid that prevailed in South Africa until 1994. "Black" includes ethnic blacks, Indians, and colored people in South Africa who were discriminated against during the apartheid regime. Black theology, such as Desmond Tutu's, heightens black consciousness to the point that the blacks become critically aware of their situation of oppression and the need to struggle against it. Suitable biblical texts like the exodus story are read against the background of oppressive actions of the apartheid regime to show how the Bible sides with the oppressed against the oppressor. Black theology made a significant contribution to the demise of apartheid in South Africa. The *Kairos Document,* an anti-apartheid statement issued in 1985 by both black and white concerned theologians in South Africa motivated the international community to take up stringent action against the apartheid regime. In postapartheid South Africa, black theology seeks liberation from the legacy of apartheid for fullness of life, reconciliation and integration. *See* AFROCENTRIC INTERPETATION; BIBLICAL CRITICISM; BIBLICAL INTERPRETATION, HISTORY OF; CULTURAL HERMEUTICS; CULTURAL STUDIES; FEMINIST INTERPRETATION; IDEOLOGICAL CRITICISM; LIBERATION THEOLOGY; WOMANIST INTERPRETATION.

Bibliography: David Adamo. "Ethiopia in the Bible." *African Christian Studies* 8:2 (1992) 51–64; Canaan Banana, *The Gospel According to the Ghetto* (1981); Kwesi Dickson. "Continuity and Discontinuity between the Old Testament and African Life and Thought." in Kofi Appiah-Kubi and Sergio Torres ed., *African Theology en Route* (1970) 95–108; John Mbiti. "Is Jesus Christ in African Religion?" John S. Pobee, ed. *Exploring Afro-Christology* (1992) 21–30; Mercy Oduyoye."Violence against Women: A Challenge to Christian Theology." *Journal of Inculturation Theology* 1:1 (1994) 47–70; Desmond Tutu. *Hope and Suffering* (1986); Justin S. Ukpong. "Parable of the Shrewd Manager, Luke 16:1-13." *Semeia* 73 (1995) 189–210.

JUSTIN S. UKPONG

AFRICAN-AMERICAN INTERPRETATION. *See* AFRO-CENTRIC INTERPRETATION.

AFROCENTRIC INTERPRETATION. African American interpretation of the Bible is varied and conflicting, layered and complex, dynamic and evolving. It should be understood as a reflection of a people's interpretation of the worlds they were forced to negotiate, and the shape of the worlds they made for themselves. Although it has origins and valences that are normally understood to be appropriate to a particular historical period, especially the 1970s and 1980s—and their rather intense discourses and politics of identity formation, the term *afrocentric* can be used in this article as an appropriate handle to refer to interpretation in all its variety and development, popular and academic, over a long period of time. This suggests that *afrocentric* biblical interpretation is interpretation not so much of any particular orientation or content, but that interpretation that is of, for, and by the people now called "African Americans."

Since no one person, organization, historical period, situation, or orientation in the past or present can capture the complexity of the phenomenon of afrocentric biblical interpretation, a useful way to understand such interpretation is in terms of a schema of historical "readings." Such a schema does not capture all engagements; it intends only to isolate and explain patterns and currents that are reflective of sentiments and practices and orientations of a large segment of the people.

- A. First Reading: Awe and Fear—Initial Negotiation of the Bible and the New World
- B. Second Reading: Critique and Accommodation
- C. Third Reading: Critique from the Margins
- D. Fourth Reading: Fundamentalism or Leaving Race Behind
- E. Drawing the Circle More Widely: or Women's Reading

A. First Feading: Awe and Fear

From the beginning of their captive experience in what became the United States, peoples of African descent, most of whom were made to be slaves, were confronted with the missionizing efforts to convert them to the religions of the white slavocracy. These (mostly Christian) religions or denominations—especially Anglicanism—were for the most part the establishment religions of the landed gentry; they did not appeal much to the slaves. Numerous testimonies from clerics, teachers, and missionaries of the 18th and 19th cent. register frustration and shock over the Africans' lack of understanding of and uneasy socialization into white religious orientations. The formality and the literacy presupposed by these cultures—in catechetical training and Bible study, for example—clearly at first frustrated the "conversion" of the African slave masses. Not only were the Africans,

on the whole, according to custom and law, deemed incapable of meeting the presupposed literacy requirements, they did not seem emotionally disposed toward the orientations of the establishment religions.

The Bible did have a place in these initial missionary efforts. But that place was not primary: its presence was indirect, embedded within catechetical materials, or muted and domesticated within doctrinaire or catechetical, and mostly formal, preaching. The Africans' introduction to "the Scriptures," by whatever agency, would have been difficult. Cultures steeped in oral traditions at first generally find curious and odd the concept of the spiritual circumscribed by a book, then certainly difficult to accept and fathom; later, perhaps, they may find it awesome and fascinating.

B. Second Reading: Critique and Accommodation

It was not until the late 18th cent., with the growth of nonestablishment, evangelical, free-church, and camp-meeting revivalist movements in the North and South, that the mostly enslaved Africans began to engage the Bible on a large scale. Finding themselves directly appealed to by the new evangelicals and revivalists in vivid, emotional, biblical language, and noting that nearly the entire white world explained its power and authority by appeal to the Bible, the Africans could hardly fail to be drawn closer to it. They embraced the Bible, transforming it from the Book of the religion of the white aristocratic slavers and lower-class exhorters into a source of psychic-spiritual power, a source of inspiration for learning and affirmation, and into a language capable of articulating strong hopes and veiling stinging critique.

From the late 18th cent. through the end of slavery, the period of Reconstruction, and into the modern civil rights era of the 1950s and 1960s, a great majority of African Americans continued their engagement with or readings of the Bible that reflected major dynamics in the self-understandings and orientations. The founding of the independent churches and denominations beginning in the late 18th cent. historically postdates and logically presupposes the cultivation of certain identifiable African diaspora religious worldviews and orientations. The Bible played a fundamental role, if not *the* fundamental role, in the cultivation and articulation of such worldviews and orientations. It was discovered as a type of language world full of drama and proclamation such that the African slave or freedperson could be provided with certain powerful rhetoric and visions that fired the imagination and articulated hope, struggle, and resistance.

During this period one of the most popular readings of the Bible was one in which the Protestant canon provided the rhetoric and visions of prophetic critique, the blueprints for "racial uplift," and social and political peace (integration) as the ultimate goal—all profoundly confused with uses having to do with personal salvation. This "reading"—both of the Bible and of American culture—expressed considerable ambivalence. It was both critical and accommodationist. On the one hand, its respect for the Protestant canon reflected its desire to accommodate and be included within the American (socioeconomic, political, and religious) mainstream. On the other hand, its interpretation of the Bible was on the whole from a social and ideological location "from below," and reflected a blistering critique of Bible-believing, slave-holding, racist America. Important personalities—from Frederick Douglass to Martin Luther King Jr.—are among the powerful articulators of the reading. But the popular sources, some anonymous, some by not-very-well-known individuals—the songs, conversion narratives, poetry, prayers, diaries, and the like—are a truer, more powerful reflection of this phenomenon.

C. Third Reading: Critique from the Margins

Another reading was cultivated in the early decades of the 20th cent., primarily in the urban centers of the North and South. It reflected the sentiments of displaced and disoriented rural and small-town residents who migrated to the big cities in search of better job opportunities. These individuals formed new religious communities that gave them a sense of solidarity missing in the "mainline" churches.

A very different reading of the Bible is in evidence among many in such groups, one that was also reflective of a different attitude about society and culture. It was a more critical, even radical attitude about America: there was little hope of full integration into the mainstream. America was seen as racist and arrogant: its "mainstream" religious groups—including the African American groups—were seen as worldly and perfidious. The engagement of the Bible and of other religious texts clearly reflects this attitude. Such engagement was associated with a number of groups—the Garvey Movement, Father Divine and the Peace Mission Movement, the Black Jews, the Nation of Islam, the Spiritual churches, the Pentecostal movement, among the most prominent. What they had in common were sensibilities, attitudes about the world, which were reflected not only in their more radial (race-inflected) interpretation of the (Protestant-delimited) Bible but also in their acceptance of other esoteric authoritative texts that, of course, justified their sensibilities and agenda. Many of them focused, to degrees far beyond anything on record among the African American establishment churches, on the utter perfidy of whites (e.g., Nation of Islam, Garvey Movement), as well as the salvation of African peoples (e.g., Black Jews).

D. Fourth Reading: Fundamentalism or Leaving Race Behind

Another African American reading of the Bible and American culture emerged as a dominant one in the late 20th cent. Sometimes called fundamentalism, it was and continues to be in many respects a reaction to both the accommodationist and the separatist readings discussed above. Its use of the Bible is a sharp departure from the traditional African American engagement of the Bible. To be sure, African Americans have historically been evangelical in their religious sensibilities, including the attachment of primary importance to the Bible as guide. Yet they have historically exhibited more playfulness than doctrinalism and moralism in their engagement of the Bible. The letters of the Bible were less important than the evocative power of the stories, poetry, and prophetic proclamations. In the African American rapprochement with white fundamentalist and evangelical groups of more recent decades, the basis of the interpretive engagement has shifted from historical and cultural experience, from being race-specific (as with the mainstream groups) or radical (as with the "sects" and "cults"), to being (as it is claimed) "Bible-based," that is, focused upon true doctrine in the letters of the Bible, thereby relativizing racial identity and experience. In much the same way that the rise of fundamentalism among whites in the early decades of the 20th cent. represented a rejection of modernism, so within the world of African Americans a turn toward (supposedly nonracial) fundamentalism represents a rejection of African Americans' historical experiences.

E. Drawing a Wider Circle or Women's Reading

In evidence throughout the history of African American readings of the Bible are the special readings of African American women. From Phillis Wheatley to modern womanist and other interpreters, women are part of each of the readings distinguished above. But across each of these readings, differences in historical periods, locations, classes, and other factors notwithstanding, collectively women have for the most part added special emphases. Especially poignant among them is the radical challenge of consistency in prophetic communal self-judgment as African American religious communities struggle to apply the divine moral imperative of inclusiveness to gender relations. *See* BIBLICAL INTERPRETATION, HISTORY OF; IDEOLOGICAL INTERPRETATION; SLAVERY; WOMANIST INTERPRETATION.

VINCENT WIMBUSH

AFTERLIFE. Virtually every human culture has told myths or designed rituals or elaborated conceptions of the afterlife, which signifies the continued existence of human beings after death. These begin with funerals and dignified disposal of the corpse, but also include commemoration and ritual attempts to effect a beatific afterlife. Belief in an afterlife may be older than the human race itself, as Neanderthal gravesites already contain grave goods, as do most burials of our proper species. Many cultures bury with their dead provisions for a journey or other items needed by the living apparently believing that the dead take up residence elsewhere. But some believe that the objects retain important aspects of the identity of the deceased so that they cannot be bequeathed to others. Other burial rites that involve placating, feeding or honoring the dead indicate the belief that the deceased have become ghosts, spirits or demons. As such, the dead may be a source of danger or blessing to the human community. Often we simply do not know specifically what a culture believed based on the evidence of its interments. We are lucky when we have the literature of a culture and can link burials with rituals and beliefs concerned with the afterlife.

Egypt held elaborate views of the afterlife, depending on mummification of the corpse as well as inhumation in pyramids or tombs, usually supervised by the temple priesthood of Osiris. Besides preserving the corpse, ritual texts on pyramids, coffins, and papyri tell us that the mummy was aided in its journey to the *Duat*, the afterlife realm, by the actions of the priesthood, the grand edifices, and the elaborate spells. At first, we have records only of the Pharaoh's journey to exalted status. He was identified with Horus during life and Osiris afterwards and so participated in the life of the gods. Hieroglyphic texts help him ascend to heaven using the pyramid as a ladder. Eventually, by the New Kingdom (starting ca.1580 BCE), an afterlife was also achieved by members of the court, bureaucrats, and retainers—all those whose hearts were judged lighter than a feather, in the ordeal narrated in *The Egyptian Book of the Dead,* ch. 125, which is frequently illustrated in papyrus scrolls (*see* BOOK OF THE DEAD; EGYPT). Court officials are frequently seen enjoying the life of a wealthy Egyptian in their afterlife. Egypt shows us clearly that even monolithic cultures could maintain different and, to some extent, conflicting views of the afterlife at the same time. Such ambiguities continue even through modern times in every complex culture.

The afterlife was depicted more pessimistically in Mesopotamia and Canaan. The dead were virtually imprisoned in an underworld city, where they could be restrained from causing damage to the living. The dead could be appeased by proper funeral ceremonies and regular memorial offerings. The Epic of Gilgamesh dealt with death and afterlife in seemingly contradictory ways. The most famous version today seeks to comfort Gilgamesh for losing his friend Enkidu to death and then losing his quest for immortality. The comforts offered are the glories of city life, as well as the pleasures of clean clothing, leisure, wife and children. Other versions continue the adventures of Gilgamesh in the underworld where he appears later to become a underworld judge of equity (*see* GILGAMESH, EPIC OF). Similar notions can be found in Canaan. Specially glorified dead (rp‘ym, Hebrew refaʾim) might be

recalled to the presence of the living in carefully supervised ritual occasions. At Ugarit, the mrzkh (*marzih*) commemoration, held at intervals after the death of an important personage, was a copious drinking bout, wherein the living, the grateful dead, and the gods might meet and be glorified (KTU i.20:I-II).

Israelite culture contrasts with the great cultures of the ancient Near East in that there is little description of an afterlife. Genesis 2–3 contains no discussion of the afterlife, though it narrates how humans came to die. Though archaeology shows that the burial customs of the Israelites were almost indistinguishable from Canaanites, the Bible hardly refers to the rich myths that embody the Canaanite or Mesopotamian sense of afterlife. The Bible uniquely uses the term שְׁאוֹל sheʾol for the underworld, which is usually translated into Greek as HADES. The spirits of the dead (רְפָאִים refaʾim) dwell in SHEOL (Isa 14:9; Job 26:5; Prov 9:18) and usually have no relationship with the living or with God. The dead cannot praise God (Ps 30:9) or experience God's saving presence (Ps 88:10-12; Isa 38:18-19). The OT speaks of "sleeping with one's ancestors" (Gen 25:18; 47:30), a reference which may refer to burial of the remains in the family tomb (2 Kgs 22:20) and other times appears to refer to the whole process of entering the afterlife, as Jacob is "gathered" several weeks before his body is buried in the land of Israel (Gen 50:1-13). To make matters even more complicated, Ugarit contained a group of divinized royal dead who were called the "gathered" ones (qabusi, KTU I.16I). There is little indication that the OT writers believed that a deceased person's individual consciousness was specially marked for immortality, though ghosts might be recalled and asked for oracles (1 Sam 28). The term גֵּי הִנֹּם ge hinnom ("the valley of Hinom," in Greek, γέεννα geenna "Gehenna") refers to a large ravine just SW of Jerusalem, putatively the site of the idolatrous practice of passing children through fire (2 Kgs 23:10; 2 Chr 28:3; 33:6; Jer 7:31; 32:35), understood in the NT as a fiery abyss (*see* GEHENNA).

Even though Saul employed a medium to summon the shade of Samuel (1 Sam 28:3-19), necromancy (a form of divination through spirits of the dead) was treated as one of many forms of idolatry (Lev 19:26; 20:6; Deut 18:10-11; Isa 8:19-22). The prohibition in Lev 19:26 alludes to practices of divination in which the shades of the dead are summoned up, somewhat similar to the séance performed by Odysseus (Homer, *Odyssey* 10.535–37; 11.25–50). Some scholars think that spirits (אֹבוֹת ʾovoth and יִדְּעֹנִים yiddʿonim) were part of a cult of ancestors, the אֱלֹהִים ʾelohim of Isa 8:19–22. An oracle against Egypt (Isa 19:1-15) mocks the Egyptians' attempts to ward off disaster by consulting the dead, because such practices are futile. The term sheʾol and the name of King Saul (shaʾul שָׁאוּל) share the same root, usually meaning "ask" or "inquire" in Hebrew. The story of Saul's sin in seeking a séance with the medium of Endor describes the ghost of Samuel as an *elohim*, a god (1 Sam 28:13), hinting that ghosts may have been more widely sought out for oracles and that biblical editors despised the practice, even if the ghost were as venerable as Samuel (*see* ENDOR, MEDIUM OF; NECROMANCY). In Hebrew, *marzeah* (mrzkh), a drinking party, cognate with Ugaritic *marzih*, was condemned by the prophets, suggesting that the silence of the Bible on the afterlife may also have been part of the attempt to stamp out these abhorred practices (*see* Amos 6:4-7; Jer 16:5-9).

The books of Job and Ecclesiastes both question a beatific afterlife. But some psalms and other prophetic texts hint that God will bring God's righteous close (Ps 115:16-18; Isa 38:18-19). Perhaps this too is to be compared to the Hebrew phrase that the righteous dead will be "gathered to their ancestors in peace" (e.g., Gen 25:8; 49:33). But other verses in Psalms also deny that the dead sing praises to God (Pss 88 and 115:17).

Since God holds the power of life and death for both individuals and nations, some passages in the OT anticipate rescue from death (Ps 16:10-11). Psalm 49:10-20 consigns the fools to the dismal realm of Sheol while the wise, who endured suffering in this life, will be ransomed by God. Though OT texts generally do not signal a shift in Israelite beliefs about the afterlife, they later provided warrant for such views. For example, Ezek 37 presents a resurrection scene, with flesh, then skin appearing to cover bone, but this is a prophetic parable, not a depiction of the destiny awaiting the dead. Similarly, Isa 26:19, "the dead will live, their corpses will rise," is a powerful image for the renewal of a devastated people.

These OT passages also provide a framework that distinguishes the emerging Jewish and early Christian vision of the afterlife from philosophical accounts of immortality. The Bible has no provision for a separable soul that is the seat of understanding or consciousness and is naturally immortal, notions familiar to readers of Plato (e.g., *Phaedo*). Nor can a pleasant afterlife among the gods be secured by ritual initiation into the mysteries popular in the Greco-Roman world, such as that of Isis and Osiris (*see* Apuleius, *The Golden Ass*, Book 11; Plutarch, "On Isis and Osiris," *Moralia* 531c-384c) or Mithras (Porphyry, *De antro nympharum* 6; *see* GREEK RELIGION AND PHILOSOPHY; MYSTERY RELIGIONS; ROMAN RELIGION). For Jews and early Christians, the afterlife requires an expression of God's creative power to endow humanity with immortality. Consequently, Jewish and early Christian authors emphasize the reward enjoyed by the righteous more than they do the punishment of the wicked who remain in Sheol (e.g., Dan 12:1-3; 1 Thess 4:13-18; Rev 2:7, 10, 17; 3:5, 21; 20:11-21:27). In order to bestow life on the faithful, God must reassemble the body torn apart by death (Ezek 37:1-14), or provide a new kind of body in continuity with the old (1 Cor 15:36-57).

Nevertheless, during postexilic times both Persian and Greek ideas of the afterlife were influential in Jewish culture. Platonic notions of the immortality of the soul influenced the new Hellenistic-Roman Jewish aristocracy (e.g., Philo, *Sacr.* 5; *Gig.* 14, etc; Josephus, *J.W.* 7.341). Zoroastrian resurrection might have influenced Second Temple Judaism, though evidence of a channel of transmission is lacking. Philo preferred a single, non-repeatable life to the Platonic reincarnation, which has no support in the Bible. Jewish conceptions of resurrection were adopted by small, millenarian cult groups at first.

The earliest biblical reference to resurrection is Dan 12:3, an apocalyptic passage predicting that, at the nearing end of the world, some will receive resurrection while others, presumably martyrs and leaders, will "shine like the dome of the sky . . . like stars forever." Some exegetes interpret that image as a reference to astral immortality or to inclusion among the angels. The martyr traditions in 2 Macc 7 emphasize the physical character of resurrection. In a new act of creation, God will provide bodies for those who suffered rather than deny their religion. Their persecutors have no hope of resurrection. Thus resurrection first appears as reward for the righteous (Dan 12:2). Other evidence of an afterlife in Jewish circles comes from Enoch traditions (possibly datable as early as the 3rd cent. BCE). During a cosmic journey, the seer sees the places of future punishment, the distinctive storage places for the souls of the wicked and righteous as well as paradise and the tree of life to be given to the righteous (*1 En.* 21-24). Wisdom (1st cent. CE) affirms the immortality of the righteous who suffer persecution from the wicked (Wis 2–5).

These pictures of an afterlife which reflects God's vindication of the righteous and punishment of the wicked have been adopted in the NT. The passion narratives view Jesus as a martyr or the embodiment of the suffering righteous person. In that context, both Jesus and his followers might expect to be raised up to new life at the time of judgment just as Dan 12:2-3 predicted They might also anticipate resting peacefully until that time. But they could not anticipate resurrection of a single individual prior to the end-time. If Jesus has been raised from the dead, then his death and resurrection mark a transition to the end of days, at which point others will be raised. Matt 27:52-53 depicts the dead rising in their tombs to symbolize that belief.

For Paul, the afterlife of all believers is dependent on Christ, for they come to be in Christ (Phil 3:20-21; 2 Cor 3:18-4:6). Though Paul is not clear on the state of the dead prior to the consummation, he suggests that they remain at peace with Christ in some sense (Phil 1:21-25; 2 Cor 5:1-10). The canonical gospels depict Jesus' risen state as bodily in the physical sense (Luke 24:36-42; John 20:26-27), familiar from the martyr traditions. Faced with Christians who denied bodily resurrection in 1 Cor 15, Paul distinguishes between the experiences of bodily mortality and subjection to sin typical of this life, from the Spirit-endowed body of resurrection (1 Cor 15:41, 50). The former, which Paul refers to as "flesh" cannot inherit God's kingdom. The latter will bear the true image of God manifest in the risen Christ (1 Cor 15:42-57; *see* BODY; FLESH IN THE NT).

Elsewhere, the message of the afterlife is closely tied to the fulfillment of divine justice (e.g., 1 and 2 Peter) and to God's restoration of the cosmos (e.g., Revelation). The nature of human existence between death and the final resurrection is indeterminate in the NT; the Gospel of Luke, e.g., seems to support an immediate passage from this life to the next (16:22; 23:42-43), whereas a text like 1 Thess 4:13-17 outlines a vision of the end where those in Christ, both living and dead, meet him in the air.

Rabbinic Judaism used the term תחית המתים tekhiyath hametim for resurrection and described "the world to come" (עולם הבא 'olam haba') often as the return of "all Israel" to its homeland forever (*see* Isa 60 in *mi Sanh.* 10), though they excluded notorious sinners from this reward and praised those sinners believed to have repented. Furthermore, they confined their discussion of resurrection to the interpretation of the first five books of Torah, removing visionary experience from the discussion entirely. To live more easily within a world that was largely not-Jewish, the rabbis predicated that "the righteous of all nations," not merely Jews alone, "have a place in the world to come." (*t. Sanh.* 13:2). The rabbis, like the Christians, eventually worked the immortality of the soul into their descriptions of the afterlife by suggesting that it was immortality of the soul that persons received at death, while resurrection of the body awaited the last judgment.

The Quran, which builds on all previous conceptions, suggests that the dead remain in their graves in a semi-sensate state called the *Barzakh* where they do penance for their sins (Quran, Fatiha, 22:7; 23:100-102). The time in the grave thus serves as a kind of purgatory. But only the righteous will be resurrected on the Day of Judgment. Martyrs, however, claim direct entrance into paradise (Quran 29:52, 57-58; also 56:1-26) and in later Islam, mystics claim the same, based on the bliss achievable through mystic contemplation. *See* BURIAL; DEAD, ABODE OF THE; DEATH, NT; DEATH, OT; IMMORTALITY; RESURRECTION, EARLY JEWISH; RESURRECTION, NT; RESURRECTION, OT; SHEOL.

Bibliography: A. J. Avery-Peck and J. Neusner. *Judaism in Late Antiquity*, pt. 4: *Death, Life-after Death, Resurrection and the World-to-Come in the Judaisms of Antiquity* (2000); R. Bauckham. *The Fate of the Dead* (1998); Elizabeth Bloch-Smith. *Judahite Burial Practices and Beliefs about the Dead* (1992); Pheme Perkins. *Resurrection: NT Witness and Contemporary Reflection* (1984); Alan F. Segal. *A History of the Afterlife in Western Religion* (2004); C. Setzer. *Resurrection of the Body in Early Judaism and Early Christianity* (2004); N. T. Wright. *The Resurrection of the Son of God* (2003).

ALAN F. SEGAL

AGABUS agʹuh-buhs [Ἄγαβος Hagabos]. A Judean prophet whose visions involve Saul/Paul (Acts 11:27-30; 21:10-14). In Acts 11:27-30 Agabus arrives in Antioch with a group of prophets from Jerusalem to meet with the disciples. He predicts a worldwide famine during the reign of Claudius (41–54 CE). In response, church elders send relief to the Judean believers through Barnabas and Saul. In Caesarea (21:10-14), Agabus uses Paul's belt to graphically demonstrate his prophecy that Paul will be bound by the Jews and delivered to the Romans. Agabus is partially correct; Paul is bound by the Jews, but the Romans actually rescue him and bind him in chains to protect him from the violent crowd (21:27-40). Tradition identifies Agabus as one of the Seventy and a martyr at Antioch.

HEIDI S. GEIB

AGAG, AGAGITE ayʹgag, ayʹguh-g*i*t [אגג 'aghagh].
1. King mentioned in Balaam's third oracle (Num 24:7). The king is likely legendary, though some equate him with Agag (2).

2. King of the Amalekites, Israel's traditional enemy (Exod 17:8-16; Esth 3:1 for the Agagite HAMAN). SAMUEL orders Saul to devote Agag, the Amalakites, and their possesions to destruction (1 Sam 15). Saul and the Israelites spare Agag and the finest Amalekite possessions, supposedly for sacrific to God (1 Sam 15:15, 21). God in turn rejects Saul, for the second time, for his disobediance (*see* 1 Sam 13). Samuel executes Agag. According to Pseudo-Philo's more negative portrayal of Saul (*L.A.B.* 58), Saul spares Agag out of greed for his treasaures. The Lord orders Samuel to let Agag's wife live long enough to bear a son to be Saul's stumbling block; Agag's son kills Saul (*L.A.B.* 65). According to Josephus, Samuel orders someone else to kill Agag (*Ant.* 6.155). *See* AMALEK, AMALEKITE; DESTROY, UTTERLY; SAUL, SON OF KISH.

HEATHER R. MCMURRAY

3. A term used to describe ESTHER's and Mordecai's archenemy, HAMAN (Esth 3:1, 10), connecting him to Saul's arch enemy, AGAG, the king of Amalek (just as MORDECAI, descendant of BENJAMIN, is connected to Saul). Haman becomes subject to the divine instructions to wipe out Agag's descendants (1 Sam 15:8). *See* AMALEK, AMALEKITE.

NICOLE WILKINSON DURAN

AGAPE [ἀγάπη agapē]. Agape occurs 116 times as a noun and 143 times as a verb in the NT and is by far the most frequently used word for love. Its NT meaning has its origins in the OT. Jesus reiterates the commands of Deut 6:5 and Lev 19:18 to love the Lord your God with all your heart, soul, and mind, and to love your neighbor as yourself, and he makes these two commands the interpretive lens through which the law and the prophets should be understood (Matt 22:40). The command to "love your neighbor" is repeated in almost every major segment of the NT (e.g., Rom 13:9; Jas 2:8) and generally forms a "rule of love" that governs the life of NT believers. Agape love in the NT is oriented toward both God and neighbor.

Agape is demonstrated by the ministry, death, and resurrection of Jesus. Jesus is loved by and loves the Father, and part of his ministry is to connect his followers to the Father's love (John 14:23). Paul states that "God proves his love toward us in that while we were still sinners Christ died for us" (Rom 5:8).

The sacrificial love of Jesus Christ as well as his commands to love one another (John 13:34), to love one's neighbor (Matt 22:39), and to love one's enemies (Matt 5:44) form the basis for the ethic of love that permeates the NT. Believers are called to a life imitating God, who makes himself known in Jesus as "the one who loved us and gave himself up for us" (Eph 5:1-2).

This ethic of love was demonstrated in shared agape meals or feasts. While the word agape is used more frequently in the 2nd and 3rd cent. to describe such meals, there is one example in the epistle of Jude (v. 12). These meals were most likely occasions at which believers shared food, wine, teaching, and praise of God. In the earliest example that we have of this feast, there is already abuse and division being caused by the way in which it is celebrated. The opponents in Jude were using the feast to further their own purposes rather than living out of the other-centered ethic of love that should have defined their life together.

The agape meal should be interpreted in the context of other NT meals. Jesus showed love by eating with all who welcomed him, from Pharisees (Luke 7:36-50) to tax collectors and sinners (Matt 9:9-10), and by proclaiming a kingdom where the least become the guests of honor at the great feast (Luke 14:15-24). Like Yahweh (Exod 16), Jesus miraculously provides bread for his followers (John 6:1-14), and there is such an abundance of food that there are leftovers.

These meals are precursors to the final meal that Jesus eats with his disciples in which he identifies the bread as his body and the cup as a new covenant made with his blood. The bread and cup are tangible markers of his sacrifice. Each time that his followers reenact that meal, they remember and proclaim Jesus' death until he returns (1 Cor 11:23-26). The meals of the early Christians were to be a setting in which the dynamics of love were lived out; however, almost from the beginning this was a struggle (e.g., Acts 6:1-6; 11:1-3; 15:1-5; 1 Cor 11:17-34). Despite the struggle to live the Christian life, Paul encourages the believers at Corinth to pursue agape as the "more excellent way" to live together (1 Cor 12:31–13:13). Love of God and neighbor is the aim for those who desire to live within the body of Christ. See LORD'S SUPPER; LOVE IN THE NT; LOVE IN THE OT; MEALS.

Bibliography: Colin Grant. "For the Love of God: Agape." *JRE* 24 (2001) 3–21; Gene Outka. "Theocentric *Agape* and the Self: An Asymmetrical Affirmation in Response to Colin Grant's Either/Or." *JRE* 24 (2001) 35–42; Dennis E. Smith. *From Symposium to Eucharist: The Banquet in the Early Christian World* (2003); Ceslaus Spicq. *Agape in the New Testament* (1965).

RUTH ANNE REESE

AGATE [שְׁבוֹ shevo; ἀχάτης achatēs, χαλκηδών chalkēdōn]. The eighth stone of the high priest's BREASTPIECE (Exod 28:19; 39:12). AGATE is a variety of chalcedony displaying distinct, irregular banding in a variety of colors and translucencies (banded agate) or containing inclusions appearing as delicate leaves (moss agate). AGATE was used very early in the ANE for beads and seals. The Hebrew is probably a loan word from the Akkadian, subu, defined as "precious stone." The LXX has achatēs in Exod 28:19. AGATE is the third gem of twelfth adorning the foundation wall of the New Jerusalem (Rev 21:19; chalkēdōn).

ELIZABETH E. PLATT

AGATHOCLES. The regent who ruthlessly and oppressively ruled Egypt after Ptolemy Philopater died in 203 BCE, since the son who succeeded Philopater at the time was only six years old. Along with Sosibius he assumed guardianship of the boy. His governing produced revolts (see Dan 11:9-13).

AGE [αἰών aiōn]. The division of history into a series of preordained "ages" figures prominently in several ancient Jewish and Christian texts. The oldest extant Jewish apocalypses, Daniel (notably in chs. 7 and 9) and *1 Enoch* (esp. 91:11-17; 93:1-10), present schematic divisions of history. This theme continues into later apocalypses such as 4 Ezra, the *Apoc. Ab.*, and Rev 6:10-11; 20:2-10.

In the NT the synoptic Jesus distinguishes between this age (or TIME) and the age to come (Matt 12:32; Mark 10:30; Luke 18:30; 20:34-35), while Paul expresses antagonism toward the "wisdom" and the "rulers" of "the present evil age" (e.g., 1 Cor 2:6; Gal 1:4). See AEON; APOCALYPTICISM; ESCHATOLOGY IN EARLY JUDAISM; ESCHATOLOGY OF THE NT; ESCHATOLOGY OF THE OT.

GREG CAREY

AGEE ay´gee [אַגֵא ’aghe’]. Agee the Hararite was the father of SHAMMAH, a warrior among the three (ELEAZER, Shammah, and JOSHEB) who commanded under David (2 Sam 23:11). Some scholars have tried to emend the name, but support for the name as it appears in the text is provided in IQSam.

AGIA ay´gee-uh [Αὐγία Aygia]. Wife of Jaddus and daughter of BARZILLAI (1 Esd 5:38). The descendants of Agia and JADDUS could not document their descent from the preexilic priesthood (Neh 7:64). David favored Agia's family (2 Sam 17:27; 19:31-40; 1 Kgs 2:7).

AGING [שָׁנִים shanim ("years"), יָמִים yamim ("days"); ἡλικία hēlikia ("age, life span, stature")]. In the Bible, aging is not so much a chronology of years as a representation of life stages that determine a person's level of respect, economic value, and role in society (Lev 27:1-8; Jer 6:11; Matt 6:27; Luke 12:25).

A. Old Testament

Sometimes Scripture notes aging by listing age as a span of years. The generations of Adam in Gen 5:1-32 contain long life spans, and the genealogy of Enoch explains why he did not live as long as other ancestors (Gen 5:23-24). Shem's genealogy links him to Haran (Gen 11:30-32) and place names in northwest Mesopotamia, the area of Abraham and kinsmen. Genesis genealogies divide a life span as: the time before having a son, the time in which children were born, and the days (years) before death (Gen 5; 11:10-32). Genesis includes parallel Babylonian lists that attribute even longer life spans to Mesopotamian kings.

The OT indicates the importance of ancestors by attributing to them long lives. Adam lived 130 years before Seth was born, and he died 800 years later (Gen 5:4-5). Methuselah lived the longest, 969 years; Noah lived to be 950 years old (350 years after the flood). Abraham lived to 175 years. Isaac lived to be180 years old; Jacob, 147 years; Joseph, 110 years; Moses, 120 years; and Joshua, 110 years. On the other hand, some people were limited to a shorter lifespan because of their forbidden marriages (Gen 6:1-3). In actuality, archaeological analysis of ancient bone fragments indicates that life expectancy was relatively short due to disease, accidents, and war.

The Bible records that David and Solomon both reigned forty years (1 Kgs 2:11; 1 Chr 29:27; 1 Kgs 11:42; 2 Chr 9:30). The age at death was indicated in general terms such as "good old age, full of days." The actual life span of these kings probably was not very long. Kings and Chronicles also mention the actual age of kings at death (2 Chr 25:1; 2 Kgs 14:2; 2 Chr 21:5; 2 Kgs 15:2) and show that these kings lived ordinary life spans (averaged 54.7 years). The stages of a king's life are: age at accession, age at birth of successor, age at accession of son as coregent, and age at death.

The Bible describes aging as four seasons of life—childhood, youth, young married or maturity, and elderly (Jer 51:22)—or as five seasons: small child, youth (maturity begins at thirteen, Gen 17:25), adult men and women (זָקֵן zaqen), elder and aged (יָמִים מְלֵא mele’ yamim, Jer 6:11). Life lived to the fourth quarter of life (70–80 years, Ps 90:10) may indicate a full life, but few people in the Bible lived to that age.

The economic value of an aging member of society appears in a scale for equivalent payments of vows (Lev 27:1-8). The Bible reflects the worth of a person's work capacity at life's stages as grounds for payment of vows. These values are calculated in shekels of silver and may represent the cost of a slave at various times in life (Wenham 1978).

Equivalent for a	Male	Female
1 month–5 years old	5	3 (shekels)
5–20 years old	20	10
20–60 years old	50	30
Over 60 years old	15	10

The peak of male and female value (20–60 years) indicates the period of family leadership roles: the years of hard work, parenting, and family instruction. Men of this age could be conscripted for military service (Num 1:3, 20, 22; 26:2, 4; 2 Chr 25:5). A drop in the value of both genders at age 60 indicates that they retired or were unable to work by that age.

Physical disabilities frequently lowered an older person's capacity to perform hard tasks for the family. A diminished ability to have children lowered the value of men and especially women (Gen 18:11-12). Isaac stated that because his eyes were dim in his old age and he could not see (Gen 27:1-2), he needed to bless Esau as the new head of the household.

B. New Testament

The NT says little about the physical process of aging. The Gospel of Luke follows the child Jesus as he moves from birth to youth and illustrates Jesus at age twelve teaching and answering questions in the Temple, amazing the crowds, and upsetting his parents by his independence. The age of Jesus follows those prescribed in the law and corresponds with moving the family back to Nazareth. Jesus grew (αὐξάνω auxanō), was filled with wisdom, and enjoyed the favor of God (Luke 2:40). Luke summarizes the aging of Jesus as increasing in wisdom and in years (hēlikia), and in divine and human favor (Luke 2:52). Growth (hēlikia) is used for stature (Matt 6:27; Luke 12:25; Eph 4:13).

While an elderly man is a πρεσβύτης presbytēs (Luke 1:18; Titus 2:2), and an elderly woman a πρεσβῦτις presbytis (Titus 2:3), the NT more often describes aging as spiritual maturity or the responsibility of leadership. Paul refers to himself as an older man or "elder" (presbytēs) ministering to a "child," Onesimus (Phlm 9-10). The elder, experienced Christian is the nurturer of the new believer. Leaders of the people are frequently referred to as "elders" (πρεσβύτερος presbyteros; e.g., Matt 15:2; Mark 7:3-5; Luke 7:3; Acts 2:17; Rev 7:11, 13). In the epistles of John, the "Elder" (presbyteros; 2 John 1; 3 John 1) refers to his readers as "children" (τέκνον teknon). He writes to three different generations: children (teknon), fathers (πατήρ patēr), and youth (νεανίσκος neaniskos) (1 John 2:12-14). The words for these generations are in masculine form but remain relevant for both genders.

C. Early Judaism

The literature of Judaism provides a number of descriptions that provide a context for early Christian views of aging. Philo speaks about aging as seven-year stages of growth for men (*Creation*, 34–36). The first seven years bring the growth of teeth, the second stage (to age 14) the capacity of emitting seed. In the third stage (to age 21), the beard grows. Men become stronger during the fourth stage (age 28), and the fifth brings ripeness for marriage (by age 35). The sixth set of seven years (to age 42) sees the bloom of under-standing, and the seventh (age 49), improvement of the mind and reason. The eighth stage (age 56) represents the perfecting of understanding and reason. The ninth (age 63) brings forbearance, gentleness, and the taming of passions. The tenth stage (age 70) is the end of life.

The fourth division (*Neziqin*) of the Mishnah out-lines the aging process as life transitions: five-year-olds are fit for the Scripture, ten-year-olds for the Mishnah, and thirteen-year-olds for obeying the Commandments. Fifteen is the age for the Talmud, eighteen for the bridal chamber, twenty for pursuing a calling, thirty for authority, forty for discernment, fifty for counsel, sixty to be an elder, seventy for grey hair, eighty for special strength, ninety for bowed back, and one hundred as one who has already died (*Avot* 5:21). These sayings indicate that youth is for studying and learning and that leadership potential comes with age. *See* GENEAL-OGY; GROWTH; LIFE; OLD AGE.

Bibliography: J. G. Harris. *Biblical Perspectives on Aging: God and the Elderly* (1987); A. Malamat. "Longevity: Biblical Concepts and Some Ancient Near Eastern Parallels." *AfO* 19 (1982) 215–18; G. J. Wen-ham. "Leviticus 27:28 and the Price of Slaves." *ZAW* 90 (1978) 264–65.

J. GORDON HARRIS

AGNOSTIC, AGNOSTICISM [ἀγνωσία agnōsia, ἄγνωστος agnōstos]. A position that the mind can-not know with absolute certainty God's existence and nature. T. H. Huxley coined the term, referring to the Athenians' worship of the "unknown god" (Acts 17:23). Precursors to this position include Protagoras, Socrates, and Isocrates and more recently, D. Hume and I. Kant.

AGONY. *See* GETHSEMANE; PASSION NARRATIVES; SUFFERING AND EVIL.

AGORA [רְחֹב rekhov; ἀγορά agora]. Few references to the "agora," or "public square" occur in the OT. Typically it denotes a wide, open area near the city gate. It depicts the site of formal and informal assembly (Prov 1:20), public lament, celebration, or socializing (Prov 7:12), judging (Ps 55:11), and even sleeping, if shelter was unavailable (Gen 19:2). In NT times, the well-known agora or "marketplace" functioned as the nerve center of public life, commonly characterized by busy crowds.

In the eleven NT occurrences of "agora," a clear distinction emerges: all Gospel references follow the OT with its Near Eastern sense of "marketplace," similar to bazaars of contemporary oriental towns and cities (Matt 11:16; 20:3; 23:7; Mark 6:56; 7:4; 12:38; Luke 7:32; 11:43; 20:46). It is the place that Jewish laborers gather for daily hire (Matt 20:3), a common place for children to play (Luke 7:32; Matt 11:16), and a forum for religious leaders to seek public honor (Matt 23:7; Mark 12:38; Luke 11:43; 20:46).

Mark's Gospel contrasts the sick with religious lead-ers in the Galilean agora. Jesus heals the ill and impure (6:56), while the Pharisees and scribes require ritual purification before eating food from the same market-place (7:4).

The remaining uses of "agora" occur in Acts (16:19; 17:17). Both refer to the central square of the arche-typal Greek city. The Hellenistic square was surrounded not only by markets but by stoas, temples, pillars, altars, and statues of the emperor cult. Most significant of the Hellenistic innovations, the agora replaced the typical Palestinian city gate as the focal point of activity, inte-grating the functions of marketplace *and* civic center.

The Hellenistic agora's judicial function is obvious in Luke's vivid depiction of Paul and Silas being forc-ibly dragged "into the marketplace" and set before "authorities" (Acts 16:19). Use of "authorities" (τοὺς ἄρχοντας, tous archontas) and the more specific term *magistrates* (τοῖς στρατηγοῖς tois stratēgois in v. 20) for those pronouncing judgment in the agora is widely attested in Greek literature (Epictetus, *Dis-courses* 2, 1, 26; Herodotus, *Persian Wars*, 5:38).

Luke's final reference to the agora is significant. The narrative takes an unforeseen shift in Athens, which is the culturally and intellectually quintessential Hel-lenistic city. Paul's missionary efforts now focus deliber-ately upon the epicenter of Greco-Roman life, the city square (Acts 17:17). Scant attention is paid to Paul's evangelistic efforts in Athens' synagogue. Luke focuses instead on Paul's persistent and indiscriminate reasoning (διελέγετο dielegeto) with passersby in a historic and symbolic encounter between the divine word and the gentile world.

Paul's dialogic teaching style recalls that of Socrates, and another Socratic echo relates to the place Paul, Socrates, and contemporary philosophers all publicized their reasoned discourse, the Greek agora (*see* Plato, *Apol.* 1.17C; 17.30B; Diogenes, *Lives* 2.21; Xenophon, *Mem.* 1.1.10). Set within Athens' celebrated city square, Paul's message and style poignantly convey the universal thrust and scope of his mission.

CHRIS M. SMITH

AGRAPHA [ἄγραφα agrapha]. An agraphon (literally, "not written") is a saying attributed to the earthly Jesus that has not been transmitted in the earliest version of the four canonical Gospels. This is a designation primarily of location, not of judgment concerning origin, historical or theological value. "Extracanonical sayings of Jesus" has the same meaning. In the following discussion, the two designations will be used interchangeably.

Agrapha include relatively short sayings, but also parables and sayings set in brief narrative settings, often referred to as apothegms or pronouncement stories. Certain types of materials attributed to Jesus are usually excluded, such as sayings of the child Jesus in the infancy gospels, lengthy revelatory discourses between Jesus and one or more of his disciples, and sayings of the pre-existent Christ or of the risen Christ, whether in the NT itself or in other early Christian writings.

Extracanonical sayings of Jesus, in terms of their forms, are relatively analogous to those of the synoptic tradition and may be grouped under the same categories. Most of these sayings may be categorized using the form-critical designations developed by Rudolph Bultmann.

A. Sources and Collections

The sources of extracanonical sayings of Jesus are numerous and varied: 1. NT writings other than the gospels

2. Manuscripts of the gospels containing additions or significant variations

3. Quotations found in early Christian literature, such as the church fathers, church orders, and early liturgies

4. Manuscripts or fragments of non-canonical writings, usually designated NT apocrypha

5. Manichaean and Mandaean writings

6. Ancient Jewish writings, including the *Toledot Jesu*

7. The Qur'an and other Muslim writings. Sayings from 6 and 7 are usually not included because of their later date

The Nag Hammadi corpus contains some documents of particular importance. Deservedly, *Gos. Thom.* has received much attention since its publication in 1959.

It is a collection of some 114 sayings, about one half of which have parallels in the canonical tradition. This is the largest single extant ancient extracanonical collection of sayings of Jesus.

There is thus no fixed corpus of extracanonical sayings of Jesus. Further study of known materials and the discovery of new ones will likely add to the number of sources, as well as to the number of individual sayings.

B. Research and the Value of the Agrapha

A major academic emphasis has been the quest for "authentic" sayings, i.e., sayings viewed as having been spoken by the historical Jesus. After surveying the larger corpus of sayings, J. Jeremias considers 18 (21 in the first edition) to be potentially authentic and treats them in terms of their religious significance. O. Hofius reduced the 18 to 9 and had doubts about some of the 9.

In its quest for the teachings of the historical Jesus, the Jesus Seminar placed *Gos. Thom.* on a par with the canonical Gospels. In several instances the version of a parable in Thomas is viewed as more likely original with Jesus than those in the canonical versions. Two parables, the parables of the assassin and the woman with a jar (*Gos. Thom.* 97 and 98), not paralleled in the canonical tradition, are considered likely to have originated with Jesus. The Seminar considers none of the short sayings unparalleled in the canonical gospels likely to be from the historical Jesus.

Other studies have focused on the processes of the formation of extracanonical sayings in order to identify ways in which Jesus' teachings were shaped and adapted in early Christianity. Bultmann used numerous examples from the agrapha to show that the tendencies in the development of the tradition, which he identified in the canonical materials, continued in extracanonical writings.

The search for potentially authentic sayings of Jesus, important as that may be, cannot be viewed as the main value of the agrapha. Their importance lies more in their broadening our understanding of the various ways in which traditions of Jesus' teachings developed within early Christianity. This would include showing: 1) How the teachings of Jesus have been shaped by the community contexts of which the gospel writers were a part or from which they drew their materials, as well as 2) The specific processes of the modification of sayings of Jesus when compared with versions of the same sayings likely to have been preserved in earlier forms, including explanatory additions and analogous formulations. Thus, in broadening our understanding of the full picture of the early history of the Jesus tradition, the agrapha are of considerable value, particularly to the historian but also to the theologian.

Bibliography: W. Bauer. *Das Leben Jesu im Zeitalter der neutestamentlichen Apokryphen* (1909); R. Bultmann.

History of the Synoptic Tradition (1963); James H. Charlesworth and Craig Evans. "Jesus in the Agrapha and Apocryphal Gospels." *Studying the Historical Jesus: Evaluations of the State of Current Research.* Leiden (1994); John Dominic Crossan. *In Fragments: The Aphorisms of Jesus* (1983); John Dominic Crossan. *Sayings Parallels* (1986); Robert W. Funk. *New Gospel Parallels.* 2 vols. (1985); John Dominic Crossan, Roy W. Hoover and The Jesus Seminar. *The Five Gospels* (1993); O. Hofius. "Unknown Sayings of Jesus." *The Gospel and the Gospels,* ed. Peter Stuhlmacher (1991); J. Jeremias. *Unknown Sayings of Jesus.* Rev. ed. (1964); Robert J. Miller, ed. *The Complete Gospels* (1994); William D. Stroker. *Extracanonical Sayings of Jesus: Texts, Translations, and Notes* (1989); L. Wright. *Alterations of the Words of Jesus as Quoted in the Literature of the Second Century* (1952).

WILLIAM D. STROKER

AGRARIAN. *See* AGRICULTURE.

AGRICULTURE. Agriculture embraces the multitudinous and diverse activities by which human communities endeavor to sustain themselves through the exploitation of plants to produce food, feed, and other crops (fibers and oils). In common parlance, agriculture, the "cultivation of fields," encompasses arboriculture, the "cultivation of trees" (e.g., the date palm) and horticulture, the "cultivation of gardens" (e.g., vegetables such as the cucumber). In the Levant, agriculture-based subsistence has nearly always included a component of pastoralism (herding of animals).

A. Mediterranean Mixed Economy
B. Olive Processing
C. Plowing
D. Sowing
E. Weeding
F. Harvesting
G. Threshing
H. Viticulture
Bibliography

Twenty-first cent. farmers and home gardeners must be careful not to read their experience of farming back into the ancient world. Three aspects of ancient agriculture reveal the reality behind this caution. First and foremost stands the inherent social character of work in the fields. The conduct of agriculture responded to a much broader band of non-economic, social, cultural, and political factors than is the case today. Second, ancient farming families and farmhands confronted their tasks with a tool kit consisting nearly exclusively of hand tools and implements, which, needless to say, were untouched by the Industrial Revolution. With some rare exceptions, the Iron Age tool kit was already at least two millennia old and would remain stable for

another two millennia. In further distinction from current industrial and postindustrial societies, agricultural labors occupied by far the greatest portion of the work undertaken by the vast majority of the residents of Palestine. Second place went to the related activities surrounding food preparation. The ancient agrarian society of Palestine not only lacked many other employment opportunities as well as a labor market to access them, it demanded as many hands as could be mustered in order to provision the society. The high labor demand resulted in part from the fact that the environmental givens were hardly ideal—no garden of Eden (Gen 2) or even well-watered plain (Gen 13). Moreover, the variability of the requisite rainfall made agricultural production tenuous at best. During many periods, the pattern and quantity of precipitation demanded significant human alteration of the landscape in the form of terraces, embankments, and reservoirs. Given the demands and overall preoccupation with rain-fed agriculture, it is no surprise that biblical literature incorporates a high view of labor (the human in place in the garden "to till and to keep" [Gen 2.15]) in its definition of the essence of a human being.

Though the contemporary experience of agriculture offers little guidance, it is still possible to understand the nature of the ancient agricultural system. Ancient literature, such as the Bible and the Sumerian "Farmer's Instruction," offers some help, as do the Greek and Roman treatises on botany and farming (e.g., Hesiod, Theophrastus, and Varro). The most important source consists in analogy with the activities of premodern farming in Palestine itself. The observations of prewar and more modern ethnographers must be critically examined, but often witness to the substantial continuity of agricultural practice between the ancient and preindustrial eras.

The character of Mediterranean agriculture, with its constellation of field, orchard, garden, and pasture, rests on the complex interaction of variable environmental, demographic, and technical circumstances. The interrelationship of these three parameters is crucial. The use of sundry tools and the adoption of various patterns of work relate to the amount of labor available for agricultural tasks. But the labor supply is not strictly a matter of counting heads because different cultural/historical environments affect how much time workers spend in the fields. The relative integration of any region into broader socioeconomic entities plays no small role in determining the focus of labor's efforts (e.g., the variety of crops). Not least, the natural environment weighs in especially strongly on Palestine's partially marginal landscape. Climatic conditions (rainfall and temperature), soil, vegetation, and topography make greater or lesser demands on labor to farm successfully. All of this renders the agricultural landscape of Palestine in biblical times a rather complex canvas resistant to generalization.

A. Mediterranean Mixed Economy

Nevertheless, Palestine's agriculture generally represents a variety of what has come to be known as the Mediterranean mixed economy. With roots stretching back to the very earliest permanent villages, the emergence of full-fledged Mediterranean agriculture and pastoralism coincided with Palestine's first urban period, the Early Bronze Age. Farming focused on the all-important grains—wheat and barley—as well as legumes (chickpeas and lentils). Aboriculture included Fig, Date Palm, Grape, and the queen of trees, the OLIVE, in its repertoire. SHEEP and GOATS naturally dominated the faunal menagerie, joined by the DONKEY (a transport beast) and an increasing presence of the OX, the bovine power source for the plow.

The basic structure of the Mediterranean mixed economy rests on the region's sharp climatic biseasonality. Five months of rainless summer bake the soil hard. The winter rains—beginning in November and petering out in April—must fall to inaugurate the plowing of the fields. Throughout most of the region precipitation is ample, above the 200 mm level necessary for dry farming, yet it is squeezed into a short five month rainy season. Moreover, throughout most of the Levant rainfall is notoriously erratic. The frustrating rainfall regime elicited a variety of coping strategies, from field techniques to exchange systems. Farmers attempted to diversify their productive base so as not to depend too greatly upon any one pursuit. Farmers diversified especially by the cultivation of tree and vine crops whose environmental preferences at the same time matched the region's mountainous and jumbled geography characterized by limited expanses of level land. Plains and valley bottoms were always the focus of agricultural efforts, but farming extended into the highland regions, where terrain was perfectly suited to horticulture. Heavier rainfall and hilly topography demanded terrace construction to stabilize hillside soils and control runoff. Despite their many benefits, especially the retention of rainwater, the widespread adoption of terraces was regularly limited by the high labor costs demanded by their construction and maintenance. Short-term challenges preoccupied subsistence-oriented agriculturalists. Yet terraced-based horticultural development held the key to any long-term highland agricultural tenancy. Like pastoralism, horticulture complemented rain-fed grain cultivation. Many of its products were storable (dried dates, wine and raisins, olive oil, and fig cakes) and made essential dietary contributions (e.g., sugar and fat). Arboriculture provided a resource subject to a somewhat different set of environmental hazards than field crops whose yields were not only erratic, but notably meager. Moreover, the transportability of tree and vine products facilitated the creation of specialized regional economies and interregional exchange.

The building, dismantling, and rebuilding of the Mediterranean mixed economy has stamped the ebb and flow of Levantine civilization since the Early Bronze Age. Such subsistence pattern oscillations represent movements along an increasingly well-understood and documented pastoral-agricultural continuum. At one end of this spectrum, periods of high intensity agriculture manifest relatively higher population densities, settlement patterns with recognizable central places, specialization of production in agricultural, industrial, and pastoral pursuits, including the production of market oriented goods, integration into interregional and international trading networks, and heightened investments in permanent production facilities, transportation, food storage, and water and soil management. At the spectrum's other end, periods of agricultural abatement produce low-intensity constellations dominated by subsistence-oriented nomadic pastoralists. A relatively lower sedentary population density clings to a decentralized landscape with fewer settled towns and villages, while nonsedentary folk spread out in seasonal encampments. Regional isolation dampens trade, and production for auto consumption produces few large-scale permanent facilities.

Many factors are associated with movement along this continuum. Agricultural intensification is propelled by population growth, centralization, expanding markets and international trade, bureaucratic direction, and innovation. Abatement is connected to environmental degradation, population decline, loss of trading opportunities, political disintegration, and military defeat. The Iron Age marked a particularly sharp and well-documented spike in the course of Levantine agricultural history. The Palestinian region is particularly well documented. There, settlement patterns signal a thoroughgoing intensification of agricultural subsistence. The crucial context of this agricultural trajectory was the expansion of the Assyrian empire and the florescence of Mediterranean trade. Increasing population density, growing urbanization and centralization, and burgeoning international trade and militarization contributed to the agricultural industrialization and commercialization. Olive OIL and WINE production flourished. Terrace technology spurted forward, reclaiming denuded hillside slopes. The terraces were accompanied by hundreds of rock-cut presses throughout highland regions where vintners produced wine at both industrial sites (e.g., Gibeon, north of Jerusalem) and dispersed farmsteads. The addition of a beam to the presses advanced pressing technology, adding leverage to extract grape juice and olive oil more proficiently. Signs of bureaucratic management of production and distribution took the form of royally stamped wine jar handles. The enormous concentration of olive oil production facilities at 7th cent. Ekron on the southern Palestinian coast superbly manifests the economic benefits of proximity to the sea and the access it afforded to Mediterranean commerce. The overall intensification stretched even to the arid lands of the Negeb where runoff farming created elaborate wadi terraces, catchments, and even diversion systems to trap a meager rainfall. With its emphasis on commodity production, Iron Age agricultural intensification supplies a signal instance of urban manipulation of the economy. The ambitions of agricultural intensification supplanted the subsistence-oriented objectives of villages.

Whether village-centered or royally managed, the agricultural world of ancient Israel, Judah, and the other small tribal kingdoms dominated the lives of its rural inhabitants. Responding to risk by diversifying productive pursuits packed the agricultural year from the onset of the rains until the last drop of oil was decanted from the press vats. One ancient witness to the conduct of agriculture engraved his perceptions on the 10th cent. limestone tablet known as the GEZER CALENDAR. This month-by-month list preserves our fullest ancient Palestinian record of the farmer's annual work regimen. The list of agricultural seasons reads:

line 1: two months of [olive] harvest;
line 1-2: two months of sowing;
line 2: two months of late sowing;
line 3: a month of hoeing weeds;
line 4: a month of harvesting barley;
line 5: a month of harvesting and [measur]ing;
line 6: two months of cutting [grapes];
line 7: a month of [collecting] summer fruit.

Since cultivators hardly need (and could not read) a "to do" list to tell them when to pick olives and so forth, the calendar more probably represents a scribal enumeration of agricultural activities for the purpose of administration and taxation. Its data line up well with ethnographic observations of the preindustrial patterns of, as well as biblical references to, farming operations.

B. Olive Processing

The Gezer Calendar opens the agricultural year with what is for all intents and purposes the last act of the previous growing season, the harvest of ripe olives during the period immediately before the rainy season. The olive fruit set occurred six to eight months earlier, just subsequent to the end of the rains. The almost carefree maintenance of the olive during the year [like the fig] was balanced by a fairly complex harvest and processing picture [like the grape]. However, the demands of harvest did not entail any urgency. There was no incentive to gather olives at their peak; they did not become markedly less valuable and, unlike many fruits, e.g., the apple, did not drop from their branch while waiting for a tardy harvester who might have been occupied otherwise. The harvesting of olives entailed a mix of three methods: primarily beating the tree branches with sticks [תָּחְבֹּט thakhbot: Deut 24:20; נֹקֶף noqef Isa 17:6, 24:13], but also pruning branches to speed the process and reach inaccessible fruits, and picking. Most

olives were destined for the press. It remains unclear whether the ancients ate olives without pickling—ameliorating the fruit's extraordinarily bitter taste—a practice clearly attested first in the Hellenistic period.

The process of extracting and purifying olive oil involves three steps and a few facilities. First, the olives must be crushed. Oversized mortars may have performed this task during the Iron Age during which era, there is nothing in the archaeological record even remotely resembling the round-stone crushing machines familiar in the Hellenistic period and beyond. Likely, however, well before the Hellenistic period a more simply wrought cylindrical stone was rolled over olives spread out on a hard surface cut into bedrock in order to crush them. The second step in the oil extraction process involved pressing crushed olives by placing heavy stone weights upon woven baskets filled with crushed olives. Such a method would not have been very efficient since only the dead weight of the stone would have exerted pressure to expel the oil. By the 8th cent. BCE, orchard workers equipped the PRESS with a BEAM anchored in a wall above the baskets of crushed olives. Draped with stone weights, the beam pressed down upon the stones that covered the baskets with a substantially greater force. The pressing operation produced a mixture of one part olive oil and four to five parts water. The final stage of processing olives provided for the separation of the oil from the water facilitated by the rising of the oil to the top of the mixture. Olive oil required no further processing after separation. The workers transferred the oil to ceramic vessels and sent it on to its destination.

C. Plowing

Though the olive harvest tops the Gezer Calendar list, plowing of the cereal fields was the first operation of the agricultural year. Decisive among the determinants of the conduct of plowing was the farmer's decision regarding timing. On land that had been fallowed the previous year, the hard, sun-baked soil made plowing unfeasible. Working the field had to wait until the rains softened its surface. Land recently cropped could be plowed earlier. Yet for all intents and purposes, the coming of the winter rains initiated the agricultural year. Ideally, fields received two plowings: the first rendered the soil more porous to the continuing rains and uprooted fast-starting weeds. The second plowing would be linked to planting, making final preparation for sowing. The verb חרש khrsh is the most frequent term for the plowing of fields destined to be sown with cereals. Its abundance and semantic generality make it available for metaphorical employment, e.g., those who plow evil and sow mischief reap them (Job 4:8). Plowing was a slow and difficult operation that taxed the operator of the plow as well as the draft animals.

The basic determinant of plowing efficiency was the traction PLOW (מַחֲרֶשְׁתוֹ makhareshothu, only in 1 Sam

13:20-21), consisting of a long plow beam connected to an elbow-shaped share beam at the end of which the farmer affixed a bronze or iron plow point. The plower's strength and skill endeavored to keep the plow point at a level depth. The strength and endurance of the draft animals determined the speed of the traction plow. The customary plowing team of two yoked oxen could cultivate during the course of the whole season somewhere between eight and fifteen hectares. The amount of arable land that the yoked cattle steered by a single plower could prepare in a day ranged between 2,035 and 4,000 sq.m (an area about an acre [4,047 sq.m] in size).

D. Sowing

While not an arduous undertaking, sowing demanded a great deal of concentration, and modern analogies stress the skill required of the sower who dispersed wheat, barley, or lentil seed handful by handful over the prepared field. In general, the urgency of getting a crop started grew as the winter progressed and the window of opportunity shrank. The labor demands of plowing and sowing could easily become burdensome toward the end of the approximately four-month season. Since the frequency of rain within the rainy season was unpredictable, a strategy of "staggered sowing" spread the risk arising from a prolonged hiatus of rain after plowing and sowing began. Staggered sowing was not generally the most efficient crop production strategy (e.g., it may have increased the amount of time lost in travel to the fields), but it represented a balance of weather expectations, limited labor, and tenured experience with the difficulties of subsistence farming. With no crop, however, did sowing add hugely to the labor load of the farming family. Sowing was, however, a momentous act. With the low yield rates of antiquity, a farming family would cast nearly one-fifth of its grain stores into the breeze and onto the earth where it faced an uncertain future. The broadcasting season deserves its sobriquet "the days of hope." Isaiah's reference (55:10) to the beneficial rain "yielding seed for sowing and bread for eating" expresses well the competition between grain that would become flour and that destined to be returned to the earth.

E. Weeding

Besides competing for water, nutrients, and sun, the weeds that invaded grain and pulse fields complicated harvest. They retarded the progress of the harvesters who must have watched for such prickly invaders as the three-star thistle. More significantly, weeds could have added greatly—up to one-third by weight—to the burden of moving harvested crops to the threshing floor and then bedeviled the process of winnowing and sifting. Once carted home, adulterated stores of seeds were a great frustration for whomever must clean the grain before grinding it into flour. Some weed seeds (such as darnel, which harbors a noxious fungus) were, in fact, poisonous, and the breadmaker could ill afford their presence in the flour.

Weeding the fields was, consequently, a necessary agricultural operation. Weeders attacked their adversaries with hoes or by handpicking during the late-winter/early-spring weeks while the weeds were still immature. The Gezer Calendar listed a time of weeding directly after conclusion of plowing and sowing. Weeding demanded neither intense preoccupation nor a tight schedule. Undertaken in the growing seasonal warmth, weeding time offered a welcome break from winter's overcast skies and chilling temperatures. In premodern Palestine, women constituted the greatest proportion of weeders. Some weeds naturally ended up on the menus of village kitchens and in mangers as animal fodder.

F. Harvesting

The cereal harvest represents the most conspicuous agricultural operation in the Bible. References run the gamut from the book of Ruth's portrayal of the barley harvest, through prophetic predictions of disaster (Jer 5:17), legislation (Deut 24:19), moral instruction (Prov 20:4), its metaphorical deployment (Ps 126:5), notably in parables of the climatic time (Joel 3:13; Matt 3:12; 13:39; 2 Esd 4:39), and its calendrical and liturgical presence as the Feast of Weeks (Pentecost). Likewise, the grain harvest is the most intense process of the entire year, demanding the greatest labor input over the shortest period of time and commandeering nearly every available hand within a village. While harvest could be a season of joy (Isa 9:3), it meant long days of drudgery.

The OT's main term for the cereal HARVEST, קָצַר qatsar (verb) and קָצִיר qatsir (noun), is shared by the Gezer Calendar, which enumerates two months of harvesting beginning, as is appropriate, with the BARLEY harvest. The harvest festival (PENTECOST) celebrated the end of the GRAIN harvest fifty days after the first sheaf of barley came out of the fields. The LXX translates these two words with θερίζω (therizō) and θερισμός (therismos).

Unfortunately, no technical development ameliorated backbreaking harvest labor or relieved the season's labor intensity. Its only tool, the SICKLE, remained unchanged in form and basic design throughout the biblical period. Flint blades slowly gave way to iron over the course of the period of the monarchy, but no movement occurred toward the introduction of the long-handled, long-bladed SCYTHE.

Adding to the staggering quantity and exhausting quality of the labor demanded by harvest was the farming family's or field owner's sense of urgency to gather the ripe stands of cereals before they would fall prey to accidental fire, an invasion of predatory insects, thievery, or the advance of pastoralists and their hungry herds. The only relief for the laborer came in the form of communal cooperation. Reciprocal labor exchange devices are common among agricultural communities that experience great seasonal fluctuations in labor demand, and observers report that the premodern families and villages of Palestine did help one another during the cereal harvest.

G. Threshing

The harvest per se represented only the first step in a complex series of operations that made field crops available for storage, distribution, and consumption by the community. Once harvesters cut the grain, bound sheaves or collected loose ears, workers transported the whole product to the threshing ground, usually located near the village. Before the threshing ground could serve as a site for laborious processing of the harvest, it demanded its own share of labor. Farmers had initially to construct the curvilinear ground, which then required regular maintenance. While some sites may have been merely ordinary outcrops of bedrock or pieces of ground beaten hard through years of use, all were specially prepared for their function. Farmers often enclosed them with a low stone wall—to keep out animals and contain the stalks—and repaired their surfaces with patches of clayey soil. Before the arrival of the grain, workers cleared the threshing yard of stones, perhaps scraped and rolled it (compare the "roof rollers" often found by excavators), and by all means swept it clean. Both modern observations and biblical hints suggest that the communal facilities were the predominant pattern (e.g., the threshing grounds of the town of Keilah [1 Sam 23:1]; the one upon which Boaz sleeps [Ruth 3:2]; the one at the gate of Samaria [1 Kgs 22:10]). The inefficient transportation technology spurred the creation of a number of threshing floors, located propitiously for winnowing but at no great distance from the fields. Sheaves of harvested stalks were bulky and difficult to manage, especially when compared with sacks of cleaned grain. Yet the social benefit of communal cooperation joined with security to encourage the prevalence of communal threshing yards.

Workers spread harvested stalks evenly on the threshing ground. They carried out the initial threshing—the process of separating the ears from the stalks and disarticulating the cereal spikelets from their spikes—by use of the threshing sledge, a ca .75-m wide sled of boards bearing pieces of sharp flint, basalt, or metal teeth on its bottom side. Attached to the sledge by ropes, donkeys, oxen, or camels walked a circular path around the ground guided by a worker who rode the sledge. Threshing could also succeed without the sledge by use of a yoked group of animals that trampled the amassed grain as they walked round and round.

Attendants repeatedly turned the pile and tossed additional stalks into the path of the thresher. The bulky material was soon reduced to a carpet of straw and grain spikelets. Workers raked the accumulation to remove the longest straws and other coarse products, carted off these bulky residues, and piled the spikelets and unrakeable straw to the side. Additional sheaves were threshed until the whole harvest stood ready for the next step, winnowing, to separate "the wheat from the chaff" (Luke 3:17). Threshing gave way to winnowing, and winnowing to sieving, and sieving to some form of packaging for transport to storage. Once threshing produced a pile of spikelets, ear fragments, and pieces of straw, winnowing separated the heavier spikelets from the straw and chaff. Winnowing involved tossing the threshing-ground mixture into the breeze, which caught and displaced the lighter particles a greater distance from the pile. The threshing yard was located with an eye to the direction of the summer's breeze, and workers winnowed their harvest when the wind came up in a steady, gust-free strength appropriate to the weight of the plant materials. The aim was to separate, not to eliminate, the lighter residue which, like all the other products of the harvest, found a usage as fodder or an additive to building materials or potter's clay.

The winnowing fork became the winnowing shovel as the process progressively sorted the mixture. The next step utilized a series of sieves to isolate the spikelets and catch the larger fragments of the ear that had not blown away. The finest sieves would catch the spikelets and let other, smaller objects, notably weed seeds, pass through. By the end of summer, farmers could view the result of the whole year's investment of labor—a relatively clean pile of grain or lentils and various grades of straw and chaff.

But the harvest labor was not yet over. The second month of harvesting as listed by the Gezer Calendar (text reconstructed) includes "measuring." Undoubtedly this refers to the process that gauged the overall size of the harvest and apportioned it according to contractual arrangements, perhaps including the exactions of taxes.

Work with the spikelets was not yet complete, of course: preparation of various cereal-based foodstuffs demanded a further cleaning of the harvest, processing by grinding, pounding, or soaking in water and preparing food, one meal at a time. The absence of reliable and convenient means of food preservation forced those who cooked (predominantly females) to start anew with each meal, making food preparation a ceaseless preoccupation. The processing into flour for bread was the inescapable daily task of cooks during every season of fieldwork. Nourished by a renewed store of field crops, farmers could then turn their attention to the ripening products of the vineyard.

H. Viticulture

The cultivation of grapes provides some of the most arresting images in the whole Bible, notably the repeated scene of rural security "under vine and fig tree" (Mic 4; Isa 2; and 1 Kgs 5) and the abandoned farmhands of Job 24, as well as others (e.g., the vineyard of Isa 5, the vine of Ezek 19, the basket of figs in Jer 24, the withered fig tree of Mark 11, and the blood-spattered vintner of Isa 63). While most deal with harvest and processing of grapes, these tasks are the culmination of devotion to viticulture in the gaps of the farmers' preoccupation with field crops. While an established vineyard or fig orchard did not call for the massive labor commitment required for the annual cultivation of grains and legumes, the products of the grapevine demanded labor-intensive processing in expressly created facilities. Moreover, establishing vineyards de novo was costly and labor intensive. Many of the necessities of this process—shared by the olive, fig, almond, and pomegranate as well—appear in Isaiah's Song of the Vineyard (5:1-7). They range from site selection (fertile hill) and preparation (hoed it and cleared it of stones) through securing planting stock (choice vines), planting, and training the vines (not mentioned), creation of water collection installations (not mentioned), construction of processing and storage facilities (hewed a winepress), and perimeter wall construction (its wall) to protect the plot, especially at the early stages of growth, from the depradations of roaming herbivores. The ground preparation was clearly the most arduous of all activities. Apart from any required tree and brush clearance, the sloping hillside may have invited or required the creation of terraces.

Terracing is the technique of the creation of arable land behind a stone wall built laterally across a hillside or valley bottom (embankments). The construction of terraces created leveled surfaces that chiefly aimed to control runoff. The control of runoff reduced soil erosion from the hillside and, above all, enhanced the penetration of water into the soil, the key to replenishing the soil water bank.

The preparation of the terrace soil for planting also required considerable effort and skill. In order to preserve the qualities of the cultivated varieties, vines, and other fruit-bearing trees were not propagated by seed but by setting out slips, cuttings from mature stock that had been rooted in specially tended nurseries. Grafting cuttings from cultivated varieties onto wild plants also played a role.

Vines required the greatest degree of attention among fruit-bearers after having been set out in a vineyard. Vines demanded careful pruning and support so as to achieve a desired habit. The vintner, equipped with specialized knowledge—had to see that the vines were trained either into a standing habit—possibly supported by wooden props—or along the ground supported by a few carefully positioned stones. The latter habit is better suited to conserving moisture since the plants lie low and escape much of the desiccating wind. Ezekiel 17:6 appears to refer to this method of training.

Once established, the VINEYARD again outdistanced the other fruit-bearers with respect to the amount of tending required. As partial compensation, the VINE also repaid its planter with substantial yields three to

five years after being set out. The fig required twice that time, while the lag time for the olive was twice again as long, climbing to upward of twenty years. The vine reached middle age at about twenty and had lost most of its vigor by fifty. The life cycle of fruit-bearing vines and trees represented a determinative factor in the decision to invest the land and labor. Establishing an orchard indefinitely subtracted land from the production of cereal and legume staples or pastoral pursuits at the same time as it demanded a sizeable commitment of labor with no immediate subsistence gain.

The labor committed to an established vineyard paralleled the vine's growth cycle. From bud break to leaf fall and in between as well, vine tenders plowed or hoed to control weeds and increase rainfall infiltration, pruned and desuckered to channel the plant's energy productively, harvested and processed the grapes, and replaced unhealthy vines. Apart from the harvest, pruning absorbed the greatest share of energy. Pruning determined the number of flower clusters likely to form during of the next growing season and thereby set the overall potential yield of each vine (John 15:2 specifically links pruning to yield enhancement).

GRAPE harvest was a time of urgency, communal collaboration, and public celebration. The harvester moved through the vineyard cutting off individual bunches at the stem, placing them in some sort of container, probably a basket (Deut 26:5, Jer 24:2; and Amos 8:1), and eventually delivered the grapes to the field pressing station. Some grapes became table grapes to be eaten immediately, and workers spread others out in the sun to produce storable raisins. The major portion of the harvest found its way to the press. Winemaking was a technically simple process. Equipment and installations designed for making WINE were plentiful throughout the grape-growing regions of Palestine.

Winepresses were ordinarily field installations hewn out in bedrock in close proximity to the vineyard, and consisted of a treading basin and a collection vat. After workers removed the stems from the clusters, they placed the grapes in the treading basin to be crushed. Biblical Hebrew uses a standard verb for walking in the specialized sense to signify or to denote the process of treading grapes. The one who supplied the foot power is called a "treader" (Isa 16:10; 63:2; Amos 9:12; Neh 13:15) and the finite verb denotes the process itself (Judg 9:27; Job 24:11; Isa 16:10, 63; Jer 48:13, and Lam 1:15). The feet were the perfect crushing tools, because they liberated the juice of the grape without crushing the bitter pips. The treading basin slope downward toward one end where a narrow conduit lead the juice, now separated from the skins, into the collection vat. There the yeast that naturally accompanied the grape already started the process of fermentation. Soon the workers decanted the juice into jars—the lees remain in the sump—where the yeast then multiplied in an oxygen-restricted context that triggered the production of ethanol. When fermentation ended, the vintner stoppered the wine jars, and workers loaded them on donkeys and hauled them off to caves where the wine matured in the cool.

All aspects of the tending, harvesting, and processing of the other common fruit-bearers demanded far less specialized knowledge and attention and occasioned much less anxiety than the activities associated with the vineyard. The demand of harvesting diverged most widely. By far the most simple and least demanding was the fig tree. Drying was the only processing activity required, and the harvest was especially unrushed and drawn out since the fruit of the fig tree ripened not at once but in two stages at the beginning and end of summer

The only special demand of FIG production related to its curious pollination system involving symbiosis with a tiny wasp that reproduces in the flowers [turned galls] of the male tree. For a significant production of fruit from the female tree, the galls must be brought into proximity with the flowering female fig at the correct moment. Despite the lack of data on this practice, given the apparent importance of the fig in the diet and economy of Palestine, it is likely that fig growers (Amos 7:14) knew how to manage its quirky pollination.

Though biblical literature contains numerous references to the fig—reflective of its value and its "sweet" contribution to the diet—the activities of its rather minimal labor demands do not play any part. The same holds true for the ALMOND; DATES; POMEGRANATE.

Bibliography: Oded Borowski. *Agriculture in Iron Age Israel* (1987); David C. Hopkins. *The Highlands of Canaan: Agricultural Life in the Early Iron Age* (1985); Oystein LaBianca. *Sedentarization and Nomadization: Food System Cycles at Hesban and Vicinity in Transjordan* (1990); Aren M. Maeir. *The Rural Landscape of Ancient Israel* (2003); David W. Tandy and Walter C. Neal. *Hesiod's Work and Days* (1996).

DAVID HOPKINS

AGRIPPA uh-grip´uh [Ἀγρίππας *Agrippas*]. The name of two 1st cent. Herodian kings. Both appear briefly in Acts, although most of our information comes from Josephus and archaeological sources. 1. Agrippa I: Born in 10 or 11 BCE, Julius Agrippa I was the grandson of Herod I (and the son of Aristobulus and Berenice). He grew up in Rome, where he made a number of influential contacts at court. Agrippa's youthful extravagance was notorious; he fell into debt and fled the city but was helped by both his brother-in-law Antipas and the Roman governor of Syria, L. Pomponius Flaccus (subsequently quarrelling with both), and Tiberius' sister-in-law Antonia, who finally paid off his debts. The young man returned to Rome and began to cultivate

the friendship of Gaius (Caligula), but was jailed by Tiberius on suspicion of sedition. When Gaius became emperor, he released Agrippa and made him king over the predominantly Gentile former territories of his uncle Philip, adding those of Antipas in 39. After Gaius' assassination in 41, Agrippa helped Claudius secure the throne and was rewarded with the lands of Samaria and Judea and consular status. He was now king of all the territories once ruled by his grandfather.

Josephus presents him as a practicing Jew (*Ant.* 19.331); and it is true that he rebuilt parts of Jerusalem and supported the Jewish cause in Rome, using his influence in 40 CE to block Gaius' attempt to erect a statue of himself in the guise of Jupiter in the Temple (*J.W.* 2.185-203, *Ant.* 18.261-308; Philo, *Embassy* 207–333). Yet his upbringing meant that his primary attachment was always to Rome rather than his ancestral traditions. Like his grandfather, he enjoyed donating statues, buildings, and games to cities outside his realm.

Acts 12:1-4 (incorrectly naming him Herod) maintains that Agrippa had James Zebedee killed "with the sword," a punishment that suggests that he held the apostle responsible for civil disorder. Later, he arrested Peter, perhaps again for stirring up apocalyptic expectations (though Peter was miraculously released, 12:6-11). As a result of these measures, the remaining disciples seem to have fled the city, and leadership of the church passed to James, the brother of Jesus.

Agrippa died at Caesarea in 44 CE after a short illness. Acts 12:20-30 and Josephus (*Ant.* 19.343-52) recount how, at a festival in honor of the emperor, the king was acclaimed by the people as a god and, failing to stifle their enthusiasm, was struck down by a debilitating disease. Acts notes that he was "eaten by worms" sets the king alongside other impious characters visited by divine retribution. Agrippa left one surviving son, Agrippa II (see below) and three daughters. After Agrippa's death, Roman procurators governed Judea until the outbreak of the revolt in 66 CE.

2. Agrippa II: Born in 27 or 28 CE in Rome, Marcus Julius Agrippa II, son of Agrippa I and Cypros, was brought up at the court of Claudius. He was considered too young to rule over his father's extensive territories in 44 CE, but was instead appointed king of Chalcis in about 49 CE. Shortly afterward, he exchanged Chalcis for Philip's former territories, to which Nero later added parts of Galilee and Peraea. He showed a particular interest in Jerusalem and its Temple, and succeeded to his father's right to appoint high priests (a right that he used with some enthusiasm).

After the death of her second husband, his sister Berenice and her two sons came to live with him at court in Panias (renamed Neronias in honor of the emperor), an arrangement that led to rumors of incest. The two royals greeted Festus in Caesarea when he arrived as procurator of Judea in 60 CE. On the same occasion they heard Paul's defense. Acts uses Agrippa as a witness to Paul's innocence—the king is impressed by the apostle's eloquence and declares that he could have been released had he not appealed to Caesar (Acts 25:13–26:32).

When the Jewish revolt broke out in 66 CE, Agrippa supported Rome. Later, Vespasian rewarded him for his loyalty with further territories and the symbols of praetorian rank. He and Berenice (now Titus' mistress) came to Rome in 75 CE where they initially enjoyed great prestige. Under Domitian, however, Agrippa's lands were reduced. He died in 100, having never married and leaving no children. *See also* BERENICE; FESTUS, PORCIUS.

Bibliography: D. R. Schwartz. *Agrippa I* (1990); N. Kokkinos. *The Herodian Dynasty* (1998); D. C. Braund. *Rome and the Friendly King* (1987).

HELEN K. BOND

AGUR ay´guhr [אָגוּר ʾaghur]. Agur, "son of JAKEH," is either the proper name or the title (Assembler or Gatherer) of the speaker in Prov 30. The NRSV translates מַשָּׂא massaʾ (30:1) as "oracle," but it also could be a clan name (MASSA) that traces Agur's ancestry back to ISHMAEL (Gen 25:14; 1 Chr 1:30). Agur speaks ironically, mocking those who claim to have inside knowledge about "the holy ones" (30:3). The rhetorical questions in 30:4 are examples of truly unanswerable questions, making the point that it is not wise to pretend to have answers to every conceivable question.

Bibliography: P. Franklyn. "The Sayings of Agur: Piety or Skepticism?" *ZAW* (1983).

KATHLEEN A. FARMER

AH! [הִנֵּה hinneh; ἰδού idou]. As a demonstrative particle, adverb, or interjection, *Ah* is a translation of the exclamation "behold!" found in the NRSV and several other English translations (including REB, NAB, and JPS). The exclamation prefaces some of the prophets' oracles of woe: "Ah, sinful nation!" (Isa 1:4; *see also* 5:8, 11, 18, 21, 22; Hos 12:8; Amos 5:7; Nah 3:1; Zeph 3:1) and against enemies (Isa 33:1; Zeph 2:5). The prophets Jeremiah and Ezekiel use it as a prayerful address: "Ah, Lord God!" (Jer 1:6; 4:10; 14:13; 32:17; Ezek 4:14; 9:8; 11:13; 20:49). The exclamation poetically describes feelings of love between bride and bridegroom: "Ah! you are beautiful, my love!" (Song 1:15-16).

J. GORDON HARRIS

AHAB ay´hab [אַחְאָב ʾakhʾav]. Ahab was king of Northern Israel (ca. 875–854), succeeding his father Omri. He married Jezebel, daughter of King Ethbaal of Sidon. Jehu murdered Ahab's seventy sons in Samaria (2 Kgs 10), and his daughter (or sister) Athaliah ruled

Judah prior to her murder (2 Kgs 11:1–16, 20). The DEUTERONOMISTIC HISTORIAN considers him Northern Israel's worst king (1 Kgs 16:30, 33; 21:25; Mic 6:16), comparing him to Manasseh of Judah (2 Kgs 21:3), though extra-biblical, archaeological, and some biblical texts depict a wealthy ruler of a powerful state.

   A. Sources
     1. Biblical sources
     2. Extra-biblical sources
       a. Monolith Inscription
       b. The Mesha Stele
       c. The Tel Dan Inscription
     3. Archaeological sources
   B. Domestic Policy
   C. Foreign Policy

A. Sources
1. Biblical sources
The main biblical texts about Ahab are 1 Kgs 16:29–22:40, with the exception of ch. 19, though he and his family are named elsewhere.

The negative biblical references to Ahab dominate the text's presentation of him. First Kings 16:30, 33; 21:25 label him the worst king of Israel, and 2 Kgs 21:3 likens him to the worst of the Judean kings, Manasseh. The text names some of his offensive actions by noting that he married Jezebel, served, worshiped, and erected an altar to Baal in the temple of Baal that he built in Samaria (1 Kgs 16:31-32), and made a sacred post (1 Kgs 16:33). The text also includes stories that reveal Ahab as petty, mean, and weak by taking instruction from his foreign wife, Jezebel (1 Kgs 21). Because of the negative statements made about him in the text, other stories, such as those concerning Elijah, the battle between the prophets and the priests of Baal, and his death in battle are treated as further reflecting his evil ways, despite impressing even the Israelite Deity with some of his actions, thereby staying the disaster to befall Israel from his reign to that of his son (1 Kgs 21:29).

2. Extra-biblical sources
a. The Monolith Inscription. The Monolith Inscription refers to Ahab of Israel and is the earliest reference to someone from the Bible as a historical contemporary. According to the inscription, the Assyrian king Shalmaneser III faced a coalition of twelve states at the battle of Qarqar, including Israel, ruled by Ahab. The inscription claims Ahab provided 2,000 chariots and 10,000 soldiers, the largest contingent of the coalition. The coalition included members that, according to the biblical text, Israel were in conflict with: Hadadezer of Damascus, and Irhuleni, king of Hamath. While at best the battle was a nonresounding victory (contra the inscriptions claim) since neither Hamath nor Damascus

were taken, the alliance could not hold, and in Shalmaneser III's eighteenth year Israel, ruled by Jehu, offered tribute to Assyria.

b. The Mesha Stele. Ahab is not named in this inscription, discovered in the ancient capital of the Moabites, but since his father Omri is referred to explicitly, as is "his son," Ahab is the assumed ruler mentioned in the 9th cent. inscription about Mesha, the king of Moab (referred to in 2 Kgs 3:4). The inscription claims Omri "humbled" Moab as did his son who followed him.

c. The Tel Dan Inscription. The Tel Dan inscription is an Aramaic inscription discovered at the site of Tel Dan in Israel. Only fragments of the stele exist, making it difficult to piece together all relevant people in the text, although Ahab may be mentioned. The stele probably refers to Hazael's capture of parts of Israel, and Hazael appears to claim to have killed Jehoram, son of Ahab, king of Israel (contra 2 Kgs 9:24). Ahab's name appears in a break in the text and is reconstructed because he is the father of Jehoram.

3. Archaeological sources

Archaeological excavations in Israel have revealed a wealth of material dated to the period of Ahab, and there is a debate about the attribution of material traditionally dated to Solomon that some now argue is Omride. The Omride/Ahab material includes the site of Samaria, probably founded by Omri. First Kings 22:39 claims Ahab built an "ivory house." While no house with ivory walls has been uncovered, ivory plaques were discovered at Samaria that probably decorated the palace, thereby supporting the biblical claim. Excavations at Samaria also unearthed a fortified casemate wall ascribed to Ahab's reign. Other sites that Ahab completed or developed into fortifications are located in strategically important locations such as Hazor, Dan, and Megiddo. Both Hazor and Megiddo reveal pillared buildings, which were either used as storage facilities or stables, and complexly engineered water systems that allowed the inhabitants safe access to their water sources during a siege.

The most recent excavations at Megiddo lay at the heart of attempts to redate material traditionally ascribed to the period of Solomon to the reign of Omri and/or Ahab. The site of Jezreel, also a capital of the Northern Kingdom, was occupied for only a short period in the 9th cent., thereby providing archaeologists with a unique case where distinctive pottery styles can be used as dating indicators for the period of the Omrides at other sites. The pottery correlates with that found at Megiddo in levels for palaces traditionally dated to Solomon, thus opening up the debate about what material belongs to the Omrides versus Solomon. While the data used focuses on issues concerning archaeology, the debate also addresses the larger issue of how to correlate archaeology with the Bible and, particularly relevant for Ahab, how the biblical text depicts Israel's history.

B. Domestic Policy

Ahab ruled Israel for twenty-two years (1 Kgs 16:29), a fairly long time for an ancient Near Eastern monarch, especially a king of Israel. Thus some of his policies must have been positive for him to retain his hold on the throne despite the negative evaluation he receives from the text.

The text begins by noting Ahab's marriage to a Phoenician woman. This presumably leads him to erect altars to Baal, setting up his negative evaluation in the eyes of the text that would consider such actions strict violations against the biblical Deity. Yet there is no evidence that Ahab himself was under the control of other deities: his children both have Yahweh names; he heeds the words of Elijah and Micaiah; and he places Obadiah, who the text stresses reveres the Deity (1 Kgs 18:3), in charge of his palace. Instead, the text depicts Jezebel as the one committing most of the crimes of the Ahab administration, thereby using her as an example (deserved or not) of the range of problems that occur when marrying a foreigner and allowing a woman too much control.

One major incident during Ahab's reign concerns a famine that strikes Israel, particularly Samaria. Ahab, the king, is described as physically exploring the country for grass to feed the horses and mules (1 Kgs 18). When Elijah and Ahab meet, Elijah charges Ahab and his father's house with forsaking the Deity's commandments and going after Baalim. Elijah calls for the meeting on Mount Carmel between all Israel and prophets of Baal and Asherah, described as "eating at Jezebel's table" (1 Kgs 18:19), thereby stressing Jezebel not Ahab.

The meeting on Mount Carmel further highlights the problem the text has with Jezebel. Ahab sends the order, as Elijah demands, and when Elijah addresses the people they refuse to take a stand. After the prophets of Baal lose the contest and are slaughtered, the drought ends with a heavy downpour. After Ahab tells the news to Jezebel, it is a message from her to Elijah that causes him to flee.

Jezebel also controls Ahab in the Naboth incident. Ahab wants a vineyard belonging to Naboth so he can build a vegetable garden (1 Kgs 21:1-2). A weak Ahab is depicted as whining, moping, and allowing his wife to control the situation, even writing letters in his name with his seal. There is a twist in the Ahab described, because when Elijah confronts him, he fasts, lays in sackcloth, and walks about so subdued that even the Deity decides not to bring the disaster during his reign (1 Kgs 21:29).

The Naboth incident may reflect other historical issues. The story about Naboth's vineyard may reveal the conflict between the biblical tribal laws where the land must stay in the tribe (Lev 25:23; Num 36:5-9) versus Ahab's attempts to gain more control of his own kingdom. Some consider the Baal incident an example of Ahab trying to provide for both the adherents of the Israelite deity and Canaanites under his hegemony. The text also notes that he built an ivory palace and fortified towns, both confirmed by archaeology, thus revealing that he took some care of those under his control and had the financial resources to do so.

C. Foreign Policy

The data about Ahab reveal a ruler active on both the regional as well as international stage. There are fewer regional battles compared with previous and following kings, though the limited biblical material about Ahab's international dealings as compared with the extra-biblical material highlights how the Bible has an agenda and avoids data that would stray from it, further supporting the contention that Ahab was more powerful than the biblical text would imply.

There are no accounts of border skirmishes with Judah during Ahab's reign; instead, according to the biblical text, one of the critiques of King Jehoshaphat of Judah is that he submitted to Ahab (1 Kgs 22:49). This relationship leads Jehoshaphat to fight a battle against Aram with Ahab (1 Kgs 22 and 2 Chr 18) and ally himself by marriage to Ahab's (2 Chr 18:1) daughter (2 Kgs 8:18), or his sister (2 Chr 22:2).

Ahab's wife further highlights the use of marriage forming political alliances. Jezebel is identified as a daughter of the king of the Sidonians. While the marriage is used as a foil by the biblical writers, it reflects continuing positive relationships with at least the city of Sidon, if not all the Phoenician coastal cities. There are also no reported problems with Israel's other coastal neighbor, the Philistines. Israelite control over the Moabites is maintained under Ahab, admitted by the Moabite's themselves in the Mesha Stele.

The only regional conflict during Ahab's reign appears in two biblical reports of problems concerning the Arameans. The first concerns an invasion of Israel from the Aramean kingdom of Damascus (1 Kgs 20), though many scholars consider the placement of this story to be a mistake and argue that it better reflects a later period. The second is also complicated and concerns Ahab's death. According to 1 Kgs 22:29-38, Ahab, joined by Jehoshaphat of Judah, fought the Arameans at the city of Ramoth-Gilead, where Ahab dies from his wounds. First Kgs 22:40 contradicts this by using the terminology used to refer to nonviolent deaths for Ahab. Thus, at best, there were no major regional conflicts in the reign of Ahab, or at the worst, there was one with a recent coalition member.

The conflict during Ahab's reign, with historical documentation, was against Shalmaneser III, something not reported by the biblical text. There is no reason to doubt the veracity of the coalition members in Shalmaneser III's inscription, though the victory claim is debatable. If Israel and the Arameans battled (1 Kgs 20), it was forgotten in light of the Assyrian threat, and forgotten following the battle (1 Kgs 22). The battle against Assyria took place at Qarqar, not on Israel's border. Ahab appears as one of the strongest members of a coalition of regional states consolidating in the face of the rising power of Assyria. He is depicted as a leader with both wealth and strength.

The OT depicts Ahab as a ruler swayed by his foreign wife to carry out acts contrary to the commands of his deity. This picture contrasts with that drawn from extra-biblical references, biblical references (and lack of references), and archaeology of a leader ruling over a financially strong, politically powerful state with peaceful borders. *See* JEZEBEL; MESHA INSCRIPTION; OMRI.

TAMMI J. SCHNEIDER

AHARAH uh-hair´uh [אַחְרַח ʾakharakh]. The third son of Benjamin (1 Chr 8:1); probably a corruption of AHIRAM (אֲחִירָם ʾakhiram) (Num 26:38). *See* ROSH.

AHARHEL uh-hahr´hel [אֲחַרְחֵל ʾakharkhel]. Son of the Judahite, HARUM (1 Chr 4:8). The LXX reading (ἀδελφοῦ Ρηχαβ adelphou Rēchab) presupposes רָחָב אֲחִי ʾakhi rakhav, "brother of Rahab."

AHASBAI uh-haz´bi [אֲחַסְבַּי ʾakhasbay]. A Maacathite, the father of ELIPHELET, one of David's mighty warriors known as the "Thirty" (2 Sam 23:34). Eliphelet was probably a Judean from the clan of MAACAH (1 Chr 2:48; 4:19) since most of David's warriors came from southern Judah. It is also possible that he came from ABEL BETH-MAACAH near Dan (2 Sam 20:14). Since the city once belonged to the ARAMEANS (2 Sam 10:6), Eliphelet may have been one of the foreigners who fought with David. In the parallel list (1 Chr 11:35-36), his name appears as UR, either a different name or evidence of textual corruption.

CLAUDE F. MARIOTTINI

AHASHTARITES uh-hash´tuh-rīts [אֲחַשְׁתָּרִי ʾakhashtari]. "HAAHASHTARI" (1 Chr 4:6) is either the name of one of the four sons of ASSHUR and his wife NAARAH from the tribe of Judah, or the name of a Judahite clan, "the Ahashtarites." The name may be of Persian origin.

AHASUERUS uh-has´yoo-er´uhs [אֲחַשְׁוֵרוֹשׁ, ʾAkhashverosh; Ασυηρος Asyēros]. This figure most likely was intended to reflect XERXES I, Achaemenid king of Persia, who reigned 486–465 BCE. *Ahasuerus* is the Hebraicized rendering of the Persian name Xšayāršan, which was rendered into Greek (and from that into English) as *Xerxes*. Ezra 4:6 provides a temporal reference to Ahasuerus's reign, when the people of the land render complaint against the returning exiles.

The most prominent appearance of Ahasuerus is in the book of Esther. Though certain details reflect what is known about Xerxes (e.g., his luxurious palace, his requirement of tribute from his subjects, his large harem), in this story Ahasuerus is essentially a fictional construct of a well-known historical figure. King Ahasuerus rules a large territory, "from India to Ethiopia" (Esth 1:1). After banishing his first queen for insubordination, he chooses his next queen (the Jewish Esther) by means of a kingdom-wide contest. Easily manipulated, he agrees first to a plot of genocide against the Jews, and then to his queen's request for the Jews' self-defense. Ahasuerus is drawn with mixed moral character. He is foolish, fond of parties, dependent upon the advice of others, and easily angered. Yet he is also generous and loving, trusting, and welcoming of foreigners into the Persian kingdom.

There are brief mentions of an Ahasuerus as the father of Darius the Mede in Dan 9:1, and as a ruler who, along with Nebuchadnezzar, destroys Nineveh in Tob 14:15. Both of these references are historically and logically problematic. *See* ARTAXERXES; ESTHER, BOOK OF; XERXES.

LINDA DAY

AHAVA uh-hay'vuh [אַהֲוָא *'ahawa'*]. Rendezvous point where Ezra gathered exiled Judahites to embark on their trip from Babylon back to Palestine. The biblical text mentions Ahava only in Ezra 8, once as a town/settlement (v. 15) and twice as a river/canal (vv. 21, 31). Although Ezra 8:17 mentions sending representatives from Ahava to "the place called Casiphia" (*see* CASIPHIA), neither site has been reliably identified. Scholars posit different locations for Ahava (e.g., Opis, Awa-na, Itu), all within 200 km of Babylon and probably along tributaries of either the Tigris or Euphrates rivers.

MARK J. H. FRETZ

AHAZ ay'haz [אָחָז *'akhaz*; Αχαζ *Achaz*]. Judean king from the 8th cent. BCE, under whom Judah became an Assyrian vassal. Assyrian sources indicate that his full name was Jehoahaz ("the LORD has seized"). According to 2 Kgs 16:2, Ahaz succeeded his father Jotham when he was twenty and reigned sixteen yrs. Chronological problems make it difficult to determine the dates of his reign, traditionally assigned by scholars to 735–15 BCE, although some prefer 743–27 BCE. Based upon Assyrian records, he had become king by around 734 BCE. The biblical material provides conflicting dates for the accession of his successor Hezekiah (727 BCE according to 2 Kgs 18:9-10; 715 BCE according to 2 Kgs 18:13). More problematic, 2 Kgs 18:2 gives Hezekiah's age at the beginning of his reign as twenty-five, which would make Ahaz eleven years old when his son was born. A prophetic oracle in Isa 14:28-32, dated to the year of Ahaz's death, may describe the death of the Assyrian king Tiglath-pileser III. If so, it would help to establish 727 BCE as the end of Ahaz's reign, but this interpretation is uncertain.

Three OT texts depict Ahaz in detail, each portraying him negatively. Following standard regnal formulas, 2 Kgs 16 opens with the indictment that "he did not do what was right in the sight of the LORD" (v. 2), in contrast to his four immediate predecessors (2 Kgs 12:2; 14:3; 15:3, 34). Instead of emulating his ancestor David, Ahaz followed apostate northern kings and the pagan pre-Israelite inhabitants of the land by sacrificing his son and worshiping at religious shrines that were regarded as illicit by the Deuteronomistic authors of 1–2 Kings (vv. 3-4). Two episodes from Ahaz's reign follow. In vv. 5-9, he survives a threatened attack from the coalition of Israel and Aram (*see* SYRO-EPHRAIMITE WAR). Although their siege of Jerusalem proves unsuccessful, they seize the territory of Elath from Judah. In response to this threat, Ahaz appeals to TIGLATH-PILE-SER, who conquers the Aramean capital Damascus and deposes the Israelite ruler Pekah. The second episode (vv. 10-18) concerns Temple renovations undertaken by Ahaz. Most significantly, he replaces the bronze altar installed by Solomon with a new stone altar, based upon one he had seen in Damascus. Other changes, the precise nature of which is unclear, are carried out upon orders from the Assyrian king.

Despite the narrator's condemnation of Ahaz, these actions do not necessarily appear objectionable. Although the Syro-Ephraimite invasion implies divine judgment against Ahaz, it does not succeed. The narrator indicates displeasure with Ahaz's appeal to Tiglath-pileser by referring to his tribute as a "bribe" (NRSV, "present"), perhaps because he took treasure from the Temple to pay it. Similar actions, however, are attributed to the godly Hezekiah (2 Kgs 18:15). Although submission to Assyria compromised Judah's political independence—Judah would remain an Assyrian vassal for nearly a century—at least in the short term it saved the nation from military disaster. Nothing in the text suggests that Ahaz's new altar represented the introduction of Assyrian religious customs, as some scholars have suggested, or that he sacrificed to foreign deities upon it. Indeed, the text describes the new altar in neutral language, which may reflect the historical sources used by the author. The charge that Ahaz imitated the kings of Israel could suggest that it was an affront to God, similar to the altar erected by Jeroboam I (1 Kgs 12:32–13:5). Perhaps the fault lies in modifying the Solomonic layout of the Temple, albeit to make ostensible improvements. The tension between the narrator's condemnation of Ahaz and the ambiguity of his actions produces a subtle, suggestive text, relying upon connections with other stories in Kings for its argumentative force. Ahaz's reign marks the beginning of an alternating pattern of wicked and righteous monarchs in 2 Kings, culminating in the reign of the ideal ruler Josiah. In particular, Ahaz serves as a foil to Hezekiah, who removed the high places (2 Kgs 18:4) and rebelled against Assyrian authority (2 Kgs 18:7); his actions also foreshadow the reign of Manasseh, whom the author of Kings regards more negatively than any other Judean monarch (2 Kgs 21:2-9).

While 2 Chr 28 is based upon 2 Kgs 16, the Chronicler has significantly recast the narrative to remove any ambiguity, leaving no doubt concerning Ahaz's wickedness. In addition to the indictments in 2 Kgs 16:2-4, Ahaz becomes guilty of Baal worship and repeated child sacrifice (vv. 2-4). The text explicitly states that God used Israel and Aram to punish Ahaz. They defeat Ahaz in separate attacks and take many captives, while additional Edomite and Philistine raids result in substantial loss of territory (vv. 5-8, 17-19). The Chronicler does not allow Ahaz to benefit from his appeal to Assyria, explicitly noting that the Assyrian King "oppressed him instead of strengthening him" (v. 20). The Chronicles version also charges Ahaz with the worship of Aramaean deities upon his new altar, a desperate concession to idolatry that only compounded his troubles (vv. 22-24). He ultimately closes the Temple and builds altars "in every corner of Jerusalem" and high places "in every city of Judah" (vv. 24-25). For the Chronicler, who especially emphasizes royal patronage of the Temple, this action represents a virtually unpardonable sin. The chapter ends with the note that Ahaz was not buried in the royal tombs (v. 27), presumably because of his unsurpassed evil, another detail unique to this account. Within 1–2 Chronicles Ahaz surpasses Manasseh as the most wicked king of Israel, just as Hezekiah surpasses Josiah as the most godly. Indeed, Hezekiah's extensive religious reforms in 2 Chronicles begin with the reversal of Ahaz's suppression of Temple worship (2 Chr 29:3, 7, 16, 19).

Isaiah 7:1-17 is concerned with Ahaz's actions during the Syro-Ephraimite war and considerably supplements the other accounts. In particular, we learn that the coalition intended to depose Ahaz and replace him with a puppet ruler, "the son of Tabeel" (v. 6). The prophetic narrative depicts an encounter between Ahaz and Isaiah on the eve of the conflict. Ahaz is terrified by the threat to his kingdom ("the heart of Ahaz . . . shook as the trees of the forest shake before the wind," v. 2). Isaiah appeals to the traditions of God's support for Jerusalem and the Davidic monarch to exhort him to trust God (vv. 4-9). When Ahaz refuses his offer of a sign under the guise of piety, the prophet becomes disappointed in his lack of faith but gives him a sign nonetheless: the birth of a child named Immanuel, perhaps Ahaz's son but more likely the prophet's. The child's birth establishes a concrete time limit for the end of the Syro-Ephraimite war, although the text ends with an ominous allusion to Assyrian domination of Judah, which is probably a later addition (vv. 10-17). While Isa 7 does not portray Ahaz as utterly reprobate, its portrait is hardly flattering, for Ahaz appears weak, fearful, and ultimately faithless. As with 2 Kings and 2 Chronicles,

the character of Ahaz may serve as a foil in Isaiah for Hezekiah, whose faith during Sennacherib's siege of Jerusalem is depicted in Isa 36–39.

As already noted, an inscription of Tiglath-pileser III lists "Jehoahaz, the Judahite" among Syro-Palestinian kings who paid tribute to Assyria (*COS* 2.117D). Ahaz's name also appears on two purported artifacts from ancient Judah: the seal of one of his royal officials and a seal impression from Ahaz himself. Neither artifact came from controlled excavations, however, and their authenticity remains suspect; the latter especially is a probable forgery. None of these extrabiblical materials adds significantly to our knowledge of Ahaz, but they remind us that his reign constituted only a small part of the ancient Near Eastern political picture in the late 8th cent. BCE. Against this background, his actions make sense according to the standards of political expediency. Ahaz is vilified in 2 Kings and 2 Chronicles, though he preserved the kingdom of Judah and the Davidic royal line against considerable threats. The same authors laud Hezekiah, whose actions brought the nation to the brink of political disaster. The irony reveals the sometimes counterintuitive character of the theological criteria (based in worship practices) by which these writers evaluate the kings of Israel and Judah.

Bibliography: Peter R. Ackroyd. "The Biblical Interpretations of the Reigns of Ahaz and Hezekiah." *In the Shelter of Elyon: Essays on Ancient Palestinian Life and Literature in Honor of G. W. Ahlström* (1984); Ehud Ben Zvi. "A Gateway to the Chronicler's Teaching: The Account of the Reign of Ahaz in 2 Chr 28, 1–27." *SJOT* 7 (1993) 216–49; Robert Deutsch. "First Impressions: What We Learn from King Ahaz's Seal." *BAR* 24/3 (1998) 54–56, 62; Klaas A. D. Smelik. "The Representation of King Ahaz in 2 Kings 16 and 2 Chronicles 28." *Intertextuality in Ugarit and Israel* (1998).

J. BLAKE COUEY

AHAZIAH ay′huh-zi′uh [אֲחַזְיָהוּ ’akhazyahu]. 1. Ahaziah succeeded his father Joram (2 Kgs 8:25), ruling Judah for one year (ca. 843–842) because he was the remaining son (2 Chr 22:1). His mother, Athaliah, the daughter of Omri (2 Kgs 8:26) or Ahab (2 Kgs 8:18), relates him to Israel and a negative evaluation by the text (2 Kgs 8:27). He battles Hazael of Aram with Joram, Ahab's son, who Ahaziah visits in Jezreel when ill from his wounds (2 Kgs 8:29; 9:16). While there, Jehu mounts his coup against Joram. In Kings, Ahaziah is shot on his chariot, flees to Megiddo where he dies, and is buried in Jerusalem (2 Kgs 9:27-28). In Chronicles, Jehu's forces catch Ahaziah hiding in Samaria and kill him (2 Chr 22:9), and in the Tel Dan inscription, Hazael claims to kill Ahaziah. Upon Ahaziah's death, Athaliah kills the princes and rules Judah while Joash, Ahaziah's son, is hiding (2 Kgs 11:3).

2. Ahaziah (ca. 852–851) succeeded his father, Ahab (1 Kgs 22:40), ruling Israel for two years (1 Kgs 22:52). The text evaluates him negatively because he acts like both parents and worships Baal (1 Kgs 22:53-54). In Kings, Jehoshaphat of Judah rejects Ahaziah's proposal to join a shipping venture (1 Kgs 22:48-51). In 2 Chr the same incident has Jehoshaphat entering a partnership with Ahaziah (2 Chr 20:35). A prophet prophesies against Jehoshaphat claiming the Deity will break up their work and the ships are destroyed (2 Chr 20:36-37). In the Elijah cycle, Ahaziah falls through the lattice of his chamber at Samaria and is injured (2 Kgs 1:2). He sends messengers to Baal-zebub, the god of Ekron, and Elijah rebukes them for seeking advice outside of Israel and prophesies that Ahaziah will not recover (2 Kgs 1:2-4). Ahaziah dies (2 Kgs 1:17) with no son (2 Kgs 1:17).

TAMMI J. SCHNEIDER

AHBAN ah´ban [אֶחְבָּן ʾakhban]. One of the sons of Abishur, of Judah, in the genealogy of Jerahmeel (1 Chr 2:29).

AHER ay´huhr [אַחֵר ʾakher]. The Benjaminite father of HUSHIM (1 Chr 7:12), possibly a textual error (compare LXX and Gen 46:23). *See* AHIRAM.

AHI ay´hi [אֲחִי ʾakhi]. Perhaps an abbreviation of AHIJAH. Ahi means "brother of Yah." Rather than a proper name, ʾakhi can mean simply, "his brother." 1. The name of ABDIEL's son in the Gadite tribe (1 Chr 5:15). 2. One of SHEMER's sons in Asher's tribe (1 Chr 7:34).

AHIAH uh-hi´uh [אֲחִיָּה ʾakhiyah]. Variant of AHIJAH [אֲחִיָּהוּ ʾakhiyahu]. According to Neh 10:26 (Heb 10:27), a leader who supported Nehemiah's reform.

AHIAM uh-hi´uhm [אֲחִיאָם ʾakhiʾam]. The son of Sharar (2 Sam 23:33) or Sachar the Hararite (1 Chr 11:35); one of David's "Thirty." *See* HARARITE; SHARAR.

AHIAN uh-hi´uhn [אַחְיָן ʾakhyan]. "Fraternal." One of SHEMIDA's four sons in the tribe of MANASSEH (1 Chr 7:19). In the LXX, the name has several variants.

AHIEZER ay´hi-ee´zuhr [אֲחִיעֶזֶר ʾakhiʿezer]. Meaning "the (divine) brother helps." 1. Son of AMMISHADDAI who represented the tribe of DAN during Moses' census (Num 1:12), presented offerings for the tabernacle altar's dedication (Num 7:66, 71), and led the Danite troops (Num 2:25; 10:25). 2. Head of the Benjaminite archer/slingers who joined David at ZIKLAG (1 Chr 12:3).

AHIHUD uh-hi´huhd [אֲחִיהוּד ʾakhihudh]. "Brother of majesty." 1. SHELOMI's son and a leader of the ASHER tribe who received a portion of land according to Moses' allocations (Num 34:27). 2. Son of the Benjaminite GERA or HEGLAN (1 Chr 8:7). 3. In possibly a corrupted spelling, BELA's third son and Benjamin's grandson, although the name may instead be a word describing Gera as the father of EHUD (1 Chr 8:3-4).

AHIJAH uh-hi´juh [אֲחִיָּהוּ ʾakhiyahu; Αχια Achia] 1. A priest, a great-grandson of Eli, priest at Shiloh. According to 1 Sam 14, Ahijah accompanied King Saul and his troops when they were at Gibeah, defending Israel against the Philistines. His apparent function was to make inquiries of God, for which purpose he carried an EPHOD (v. 3), or bore the ARK (v. 18), and manipulated the URIM AND THUMMIM (vv. 36-42). Ahijah apparently had a brother named Ahimelech (a priest at Nob), since both were sons of Ahitub (compare 1 Sam 14:3 with 22:9, 11). However, some scholars treat these as two variant names for one person (Ahijah meaning "brother of Yahweh" and Ahimelech meaning "brother of the king"), or explain that the Yahwistic name Ahijah displaced the name Ahimelech because of the latter's possible association with the Canaanite deity Molech. Ahijah also appears in the genealogy of Ezra in 2 Esd 1:2.

2. A high official in king Solomon's administration who served as secretary, together with his brother Elihoreph (1 Kgs 4:3).

3. A prophet from Shiloh who gave Jeroboam divine authorization to lead the northern tribes in secession from Davidic rule (1 Kgs 11:26-40; compare 2 Chr 10:15). Ahijah's oracle announced Yahweh's intention 1) to tear away ten tribes from Solomon's kingdom after his death, because Solomon had forsaken Yahweh to worship other gods, 2) to preserve a diminished kingdom of one tribe for Solomon's son out of loyalty to David, 3) to make Jeroboam king over the ten tribes, and 4) to establish an enduring dynasty for Jeroboam if he would keep God's commandments, as David had done. The oracle is puzzling because it does not account for the twelfth Israelite tribe.

Ahijah also has a role in an account concerning the illness of Jeroboam's son (1 Kgs 14:1-18). Jeroboam sent his wife to inquire of Ahijah. Ahijah responded that the child would die. However, his simple response concerning their son is couched within a massive oracle of judgment against Jeroboam, which predicts the end of his dynasty because of his sin in making other gods and leading Israel to sin.

These two accounts bear the imprint of the Deuteronomists. It is possible that a Shilonite tradition still shows through the work of the Deuteronomists, namely, a tradition calling for loyalty to Yahweh alone and tolerating no iconography other than the cherubim and ark. That Ahijah the prophet was from Shiloh, an important old Israelite sanctuary, may be very significant. A few biblical texts assert (Ps 78:60-72) or imply (Jer 7:14; 26:6) that Yahweh had rejected Shiloh in favor of Jerusalem, which may reflect an ancient tension between the two sanctuaries. It appears that Ahijah did oppose Solomon, and later Jeroboam, out of jealousy for the sanctuary at Shiloh. Solomon had dismissed Abiathar, descendant of the Shilonite priests (1 Sam 20:20 plus 14:3), from the priesthood in Jerusalem. Jeroboam had exalted Bethel and Dan as royal sanctuaries and installed the bull iconography in both, rather than refurbishing Shiloh with its cherubim and ark.

Ahijah's activity in rejecting and designating kings on behalf of Yahweh follows a pattern within Samuel–Kings. Samuel initially anointed Saul as king (1 Sam 9:27–10:1; 11:14-15), later announced Yahweh's rejection of Saul (1 Sam 13:8-15; 15:10-35), and then anointed David to succeed him (1 Sam 16:1-13). The prophet Nathan played a role in establishing Solomon as king (1 Kgs 1:11-40). The prophet Jehu rejected Baasha's kingship (1 Kgs 16:1-4), Elijah rejected Ahab's (1 Kgs 21:17-24), and Elisha sent an unnamed prophet to anoint Jehu as king and to commission him to destroy the house of Ahab (2 Kgs 9:1-10).

Ahijah, as a prophetic character, has an important function within the Deuteronomistic History in that he 1) explains the dissolution of the Davidic kingdom as the outcome of divine sanction against Solomon, 2) accents the theme concerning Yahweh's continuing loyalty to David by preserving a diminished dynasty in Jerusalem, and 3) establishes the theme concerning the sin of Jeroboam which continues unbroken throughout the account concerning the kings in Israel.

The LXX includes a supplement after 3 Kgs 12:24 that offers abbreviated and divergent versions of the accounts pertaining to Ahijah. It places the account about the illness and death of Jeroboam's son shortly after it tells of Jeroboam's return from Egypt. Immediately after that follows an account about Shemaiah (not Ahijah) designating Jeroboam as king over the ten seceding tribes. It is doubtful that this supplement offers an independent witness since it appears to have been composed from the materials preserved within the MT.

4. The father of Baasha. Baasha became the third king of Israel after he overthrew Nadab, the son of Jeroboam I (1 Kgs 15:27, 33; 21:22; and 2 Kgs 9:9).

5. The fourth son of Jerahmeel, son of Hezron, son of Perez, son of Judah by Tamar according to the Chronicler's genealogy (1 Chr 2:25).

6. The second son of Ehud, son of Bela, son of Benjamin, according to the Chronicler's genealogy (1 Chr 8:7).

7. One of David's renowned warriors according to the Chronicler's list (1 Chr 11:36). A parallel list at 2 Sam 23:24-38 does not include Ahijah, but the two lists also diverge in many other respects.

8. A Levite in David's time who had charge of the treasuries of the house of God, according to the Hebrew of 1 Chr 26:20. However, the Greek reads "their brothers," referring to the Levites, and this may be the better reading.

9. One of the officials who signed a written agreement to observe God's law on behalf of the postexilic community in Judea (Neh 10:26 [Heb. 10:27]). English translations spell the name as "Ahiah."

Bibliography: S. L. McKenzie. *The Trouble with Kings* (1991); W. I. Toews. *Monarchy and Religious Institution in Israel under Jeroboam I* (1993).

WESLEY TOEWS

AHIJAH THE SHILONITE, PROPHECY OF. *See* AHIJAH 3: BOOKS REFERRED TO IN THE BIBLE.

AHIKAM uh-hi´kuhm [אֲחִיקָם ʾakhiqam]. The son of Shaphan (2 Kgs 22:12) and father of Gedaliah (2 Kgs 25:22), Ahikam was an official of King Josiah sent to the prophetess HULDAH after the lawbook was found (2 Kgs 22:14; 2 Chr 34:20). Afterward, he protected Jeremiah against JEHOIAKIM and his followers (Jer 26:24).

AHIKAR, AHIQAR uh-hi´kahr [Ἀχιάχαρος Achiacharos]. From the Aramaic ʾakhiqr, meaning "the (divine) brother is glorious." An advisor to the Assyrian kings Sennacherib and Esarhaddon, the subject of the *Book of Ahikar*, which contains the story of Ahikar and his nephew Nadin, as well as the proverbs Ahikar taught. The story may be based on an actual historical figure of the Assyrian period. It must have originated between the time of Esarhaddon (681–69 BCE) and the date of the earliest extant text in the late 5th cent. BCE. A cuneiform text dated to 165 BCE refers to one of the scholars of Esarhaddon's court as "the one the Ahlamu (Arameans) call Ahikar."

The earliest known form of the *Book of Ahikar* is contained in a papyrus palimpsest of fourteen columns discovered on the island of Elephantine in Upper Egypt (*see* PALIMPSEST; PAPYRUS, PAPYRI). The 5th cent. BCE text is fragmentary and the end is lost; what remains is the oldest extant literary work written in Aramaic. Of the later forms of the *Book* from the early centuries CE, those written in Syriac, Armenian, and Arabic are the oldest and most important. A Greek version (using different names) was included in the *Life of Aesop*.

According to the legend, Ahikar, the wise counselor of Assyria, had no son. He adopted his nephew Nadin (or Nadan) and taught him wisdom in a series of proverbs. When the aged Ahikar retired from his post, Nadin replaced him, but through jealousy falsely accused his adopted father of treason. Esarhaddon condemned Ahikar to death, but a sympathetic king's officer allowed him to go into hiding instead. Later, when Ahikar's wisdom is again needed in the kingdom, he reappeared to serve the king and to denounce the perfidy of Nadin.

In all forms of the *Book*, the Ahikar tale provides a framework for a series of proverbs and short parables in the Near Eastern wisdom tradition. The proverbs are only loosely linked to the tale and probably originated separately. The Elephantine proverbs are written in a slightly different dialect than the story, which may point to their origin in one of the independent Aramaean kingdoms of Syria in the 8th–7th cent. BCE.

Ahikar and his nephew are mentioned in the book of Tobit, where Ahikar is referred to as Tobit's nephew (1:21) and therefore an Israelite. Ahikar's "son" is called Nadab in the Greek versions of Tobit, but a Tobit text from Qumran attests the original name Nadin (ndn). Ahikar supported Tobit when the latter fell into disgrace (1:22; 2:10) and Ahikar's own fall and restoration are mentioned in Tob 14:10. One of Ahikar's proverbs, with a slight difference of wording, appears in Tob 4:17. *See* ELEPHANTINE PAPYRI; TOBIT, BOOK OF; WISDOM IN THE ANE.

Bibliography: J. C. Greenfield. "The Wisdom of Ahiqar." *Wisdom in Ancient Israel*, ed. J. Day, R. Gordon, H. G. M. Williamson (1997) 43–54; J. Rendel Harris. A. S. Lewis, F. C. Conybeare. "The Story of Ahikar." *APOT* 2:715–784; J. Lindenberger. "Ahiqar." *OTP* 2:479–507; B. Porten and A. Yardeni. *Textbook of Aramaic Documents from Ancient Egypt. Vol. 3* (1993).

EDWARD M. COOK

AHILUD uh-hi´luhd [אֲחִילוּד ʾakhiludh]. Father of Jeshoshaphat, recorder during the reign of David and Solomon (2 Sam 8:16; 20:24; 1 Kgs 4:3). Ahilud was also the father of Baana, one of the twelve officers of Solomon (1 Kgs 4:12). Scholars believe that these two Ahiluds were the same person.

AHIMAAZ uh-him´ay-az [אֲחִימַעַץ ʾakhimaʿats]. 1. The son of Zadok, David's chief priest, who plays an important role in the royal house's victory over the rebellious son Absalom (2 Sam 15–18). After David has to flee from Jerusalem, he sends Ahimaaz and Jonathan, the son of Abiathar, to observe and report Absalom's doings to David in hiding (15:27-37). Their report of Absalom's military strategy (after hiding for a time in a well to escape detection) enable David to prepare for the final decisive victory (17:17-20). After the death of Absalom, Ahimaaz demands that he be allowed to give David the news after a messenger had already been dispatched. He outruns the first messenger to David, but then only tells David the good news that Absalom's forces had been defeated. He pretends to know nothing of Absalom's fate, and leaves it to the original messenger to give David the bad news that

Absalom is dead (18:28-29). The literary presentation of Ahimaaz is thick with irony and ambiguity.

2. The father of Saul's wife, Ahinoam (1 Sam 14:50).

3. Solomon's son-in-law, one of the twelve district officials (1 Kgs 4:15).

BRYAN D. BIBB

AHIMAN uh-hi´muhn [אֲחִימָן ʾakhiman]. 1. Descendant of ANAK (Num 13:22; Josh 15:14; Judg 1:10). Anak was said to be one of the giants called NEPHILIM (Num 13:33; Gen 6:4). Twelve spies sent by Moses to investigate the land of Canaan encounter Ahiman and the Anakim. Ahiman, Sheshai, and Talmai were probably leaders of the Anakim conquered by the tribes.

2. Ahiman was the name of a Levite who was one of four gatekeepers in the Second Temple (1 Chr 9:17). Nehemiah 11:19 excludes Ahiman and Shallum from the list of gatekeepers.

J. GORDON HARRIS

AHIMELECH uh-him´uh-lek [אֲחִימֶלֶךְ ʾakhimelekh]. 1. A priest during the time of Saul. The insurgent David comes to the sanctuary at NOB and tells Ahimelech that Saul had sent David on a secret mission and that he needs bread for his men and a sword (1 Sam 21:1-9). Ahimelech gives him some of the holy bread used in the sanctuary and the only sword in the place, the one that had belonged to Goliath. When word reaches Saul by means of a spying official, DOEG the Edomite, he summons Ahimelech, son of AHITUB of the lineage of ELI, and accuses him of conspiring with the rebellious David (1 Sam 22:9-19). Saul does not believe Ahimelech's genuine protestations of innocence and has all of the priests killed. The guardsmen refuse such a grim task, and only Doeg the Edomite obeys, killing a total of eighty-five priests. Ahimelech's son ABIATHAR escapes and allies himself with David.

2. A Hittite who would not follow David into Saul's camp (1 Sam 26:6).

3. "Ahimelech, son of Abiathar" who helped Zadok organize the priestly class (1 Chr 18:16; 24:3-6). This name perhaps should be reversed to refer to Abiathar himself.

BRYAN D. BIBB

AHIMOTH uh-hi´moth [אֲחִימוֹת ʾakhimoth]. "My brother is Mot (death)." ELKANAH's son, a descendant of KOHATH within the Levite tribe (1 Chr 6:25). In 1 Chr 6:35, "son of Mahath" suggests that the name may be Ahimahath. Also it may be a shortened form of AHIMELECH.

AHINADAB uh-hin´uh-dab [אֲחִינָדָב ʾakhinadhav]. According to 1 Kgs 4:14, the son of IDDO and one of Solomon's officers, in charge of the southern part of Transjordan.

AHINOAM uh-hin'oh-uhm [אֲחִינֹעַם 'akhino'am]. 1. Daughter of AHIMAAZ, wife of King SAUL, mother of JONATHAN, ISHVI, MALCHISHUA, MERAB, and MICHAL (1 Sam 14:49-50).

2. One of DAVID's wives, a JEZREELITE. She and David's CARMELITE wife ABIGAIL are with him in GATH. Both are captured by the AMALEKITES at ZIKLAG. She may be the same woman as Saul's wife Ahinoam (1 Sam 25:43; 27:3; 30:5; 2 Sam 2:2; 3:2; 1 Chr 3:1).

HEATHER R. MCMURRAY

AHIO uh-hi'oh [אַחְיוֹ 'akhyo]. 1. AMINADAB's (ABINADAB's) son and UZZAH's brother (2 Sam 6:3; 1 Chr 13:7) who assisted in carrying the ark of God (LXX: "his brother").

2. ELPAAL's son in the Benjamin tribe (LXX^A/LXX^L: "their brothers") (1 Chr 8:14).

3. JEIEL and MAACAH's son in the Benjamin tribe (1 Chr 8:31; 9:37).

AHIQAR uh-hi'kahr. *See* AHIKAR, AHIQAR.

AHIRA uh-hi'ruh [אֲחִירַע 'akhira']. Son of Enam, leader (PRINCE) of the NAPHTALI tribe, assigned to assist Moses in the census (Num 1:15). Numbers 7:78-83 describes his offering on behalf of his tribe. Ahira was also in charge of the miltary troops of Naphtali from Sinai to Palestine (Num 10:27).

AHIRAM uh-hi'ruhm [אֲחִירָם 'akhiram]. Ahiram is the third of BENJAMIN's five sons who would inhabit the land with his family, the Ahiramites, according to the census list in Num 26:38. Probable variant spellings are AHARAH, Benjamin's third son (1 Chr 8:1); AHER, father of HUSHIM of the family of Benjamin (1 Chr 7:12); and EHI, the sixth of ten sons of Benjamin (Gen 46:21).

JOAN COOK

AHISAMACH uh-his'uh-mak [אֲחִיסָמָךְ 'akhisamakh]. The name literally means "my (divine) brother has supported." From the tribe of Dan, Ahisamach was the father of OHOLIAB, one of the skilled workers assigned to design and make the tabernacle and its furnishings (Exod 31:6; 35:34; 38:23).

AHISHAHAR uh-hish'uh-hahr [אֲחִישָׁחַר 'akhishakhar]. One of the sons of BILHAN, of the family of Jediael, Ahishahar was a Benjaminite warrior who was the chief of a subclan of Jediael according to the genealogy found in 1 Chr 7:10-12a. Some scholars doubt the authenticity of this genealogy.

AHISHAR uh-hi'shahr [אֲחִישָׁר 'akhishar]. "My brother has sung." Overseer of Solomon's palace household (1 Kgs 4:6). *See* CHAMBERLAIN.

AHITHOPHEL uh-hith'uh-fel [אֲחִיתֹפֶל 'akhithofel]. A counselor of David and supporter of Absolom in his rebellion. Ahithophel is remembered as a person of great political and military wisdom. He speaks with authority, and when leaders follow his advice they prosper and when they do not they fail. Speaking with him "was as if one consulted the oracle of God," so he was highly valued first by David and then by Absolom (2 Sam 16:23).

After David flees Jerusalem, Ahithophel gives Absolom the excellent advice to sleep with all of David's concubines publicly, thus displaying royal authority among the people (16:21-22). He also suggests that Absolom should immediately send him with soldiers to overrun David's demoralized troops and to kill only the king, which would have settled the coup (17:1-3). His advice is overruled by that of Hushai the Archite who argues that Absolom should take the time to muster troops from all of Israel before crushing David's supporters utterly (17:11-13). David, however, had sent Hushai as a spy to undermine the good advice of Ahithophel. When Ahithophel's advice is not accepted, he knows that Absolom's coup cannot prevail, so he goes to his home and commits suicide (17:23).

The reference to Ahithophel's wisdom in 2 Sam 16:23 brings up the important issue of how kings gathered and processed tactical information. In the ancient world, kings always consulted prophets to tell them what would unfold in the future and whether their plans would succeed or fail. This was a delicate process, and at Mari there is record of kings dividing prophets into several groups so that they could be asked the same question independently. Prophecy was so politically sensitive that official prophets were sworn to an oath of silence. The role of Ahithophel is striking in that his ability to predict the outcome of events is comparable to the foretelling of the prophets, though he acts without any divine revelation. His skill is purely political and intellectual, and in his character is the beginning of a long tension between religious and political factors in forming royal policy.

BRYAN D. BIBB

AHITUB uh-hi'tob [אֲחִיטוּב 'akhituv; Ἀχιτώβ Achitōb]. "My (divine) brother is good." 1. Father of AHIJAH in 1 Sam 14:3, but father of AHIMELECH and grandfather of ABIATHAR in 1 Sam 22:9-22.

2. Father of ZADOK and grandfather of AHIMAAZ (2 Sam 8:17; 1 Chr 6:8-9, 52-53; 18:16).

3. Father (1 Chr 6:12; Ezra 7:2) or grandfather of a different Zadok (1 Chr 9:11; Neh 11:11).

4. Ancestor of JUDITH (Jdt 8:1).

SUSANNA W. SOUTHARD

AHLAB ah'lab [אַחְלָב 'akhlav]. City in the region of Asher where the Canaanites were allowed to remain

(Judg 1:31), northeast of Tyre, near the coast; also called MAHALAB (Josh 19:29).

AHLAI ahʹlī [אַחְלָי ʾakhlay]. 1. The son of SHESHAN (1 Chr 2:31). However, 1 Chr 2:34-5 says Sheshan had no sons, only daughters, and he gave an Egyptian servant, JARHA, to his daughter as a husband, and she gave birth to a son named ATTAI. Explanations vary. Perhaps the name Sheshan appears in two different genealogies: the genealogy of the descendants of JERAHMEEL (1 Chr 2:25-33) and the genealogy of Seshan's descendants (1 Chr 2:34-41). Or perhaps Ahlai was Sheshan's daughter.

2. The father of ZABAD, one of David's warriors who gave their full support to his kingship (1 Chr 11:41).

CLAUDE F. MARIOTTINI

AHLAMU. See ARAM, ARAMEANS.

AHOAH uh-hohʹuh [אֲחוֹחַ ʾakhoakh]. Son of BELA and grandson of BENJAMIN in the Benjamin tribe (1 Chr 8:4), the name may have originally been AHIJAH (אֲחִיָּה ʾakhiyah). The same person is referred to as AHIAH in 1 Chr 8:7.

AHOHI, AHOHITE uh-hohʹhit [אֲחוֹחִי ʾakhokhi]. Father of DODO and grandfather of ELEAZAR (2 Sam 23:9). Appellation for warriors: ZALMON, one of THE THIRTY (2 Sam 23:28); ILAI (1 Chr 11:29); and DODAI (1 Chr 27:4), in each case perhaps indicating geographical origin or descent from Ahohi or Ahoah (1 Chr 11:12).

AHRIMAN [Ἀρειμάνιος Areimanios, Ἀριμάνης Arimanēs]. In Zoroastrianism, Ahriman is the Persian evil spirit Angra Mainyu, whose counterpart is the good spirit Ahura Mazda (Ormuzd). This may have influenced the late-developing notion of Satan as personified evil in Judaism and Christianity. See PERSIA, HISTORY AND RELIGION OF; ZOROASTER.

AHUMAI uh-hyooʹmi [אֲחוּמַי ʾakhumay]. Ahumai is listed as a descendant of Judah and a son of JAHATH and grandson of REAIAH (1 Chr 4:2). In the LXX the name is Αχιμι (Achimi), Αχιμαι (Achimai), or Αχ(ε)ιμ(ε)ι (Ach(e)im(e)i).

AHURA MAZDA. Name of the supreme god of the ancient Iranians (Persians), notably the Achaemenids (550–330 BCE), whose empire included the territories inhabited by the Jews. The terms *Mazdean* (Mazdayasnian) and *Mazdaism* (= Zoroastrian, Zoroastrianism) are derived from the name. The word **ahura** equals Old Indic **asura**, a title given to several gods, and **maz-dā** means literally "he who places (all things, gifts, etc.) in (his) mind." The epithets, therefore, originally meant approximately "all-knowing (ruling) lord," but by the Achaemenid period, Ahuramazdā was probably just a name, which in Sasanian times (224–651 CE) was reduced to Ohrmazd (Hormizd).

Ahura Mazda brought the ordered cosmos into being by "thinking order (asha)" and "thinking the creation," in an ordering sacrifice by which he set everything in its proper place, heaven above, earth below, the sun in the sky, etc., and he is the ruler of the ordered, sunlit cosmos. He also fashioned, like a carpenter, humans and other beings.

In the oldest texts, the GATHAS, Ahura Mazda's principal opponent is the cosmic deception (**druj**), representing darkness and chaos, but later it is Angra Manyu (Ahrimen), the Evil Spirit. Ahura Mazda is surrounded by several gods and godesses, among them Miara, who clears the path for the rising sun; Anāhitā, goddess of the heavenly waters and fertility; Sraosha, opponent of Wrath (Aēshma), demon of darkness, etc. He is the father of the heavenly fire and the six Life-giving Immortals (amesha spentas), among them Best Order (Asha Vahishta, Ardwahisht), the cosmic order manifested in the sunlit heavenly spaces, and Life-giving Humility (Spentā armaiti, Spandarmad), the earth and his spouse.

By the 3rd–4th cent. CE, Ohrmazd and Ahrimen were thought by some to have been twin brothers. In this belief, proscribed by Sasanian, as well as Manichean, theologians, their common progenitor was Time (Zurwan), who conceived them upon sacrificing in vain for a thousand years to obtain a son and doubting the efficacy of his sacrifice. In the GATHAS, however, the original twins are **spenta manyu**, "the Life-giving Spirit," and **angra manyu**, perhaps, "the black *or* destructive spirit."

In Sasanian cosmogony, Ohrmazd and Ahrimen are separate, both existing in time without beginning, Ohrmazd above in light and goodness, Ahrimen below in darkness and destruction. It has been suggested that this dualistic worldview may have influenced similar ideas in Jewish thought, especially as reflected in some texts in the Dead Sea Scrolls.

In the AVESTA, Ahura Mazda conveys his will to living beings through Zarathustra, but in the Achaemenid inscriptions through the kings, who believed they had been chosen by Ahuramazda and called upon and sacrificed to him among "all the gods" as their special protector. This is depicted in rock reliefs, which show the king standing in front of a fire altar, above which hovers the image of Ahura Mazda in the winged sun disk symbolizing the cosmic order and with the ring of royalty in his outstretched hand. See PERSIA, HISTORY AND RELIGION OF.

Bibliography: P. O. Skjærvø. "Ahura Mazda and armaiti, Heaven and Earth, in the Old Avesta." *JAOS* 122 (2002) 399–410.

P. OKTOR SKJÆRVØ

AHUZZAM uh-huh´zuhm [אֲחֻזָּם ʾakhuzzam]. "Possessor." A son of Ashhur in Judah's genealogy (1 Chr 4:6). *See* ASHHUR.

AHUZZATH uh-huh´zath [אֲחֻזַּת ʾakhuzzath]. Friend of the king Abimelech of Gerar. Although the term *friend* is often used, the connotation is more that of royal advisor. Ahuzzath and Phicol accompanied their sovereign when he wished to make a covenant with Isaac at Beersheba (Gen 26:26). ABIMELECH and Phicol also make a covenant with Abraham in Gen 21, but Ahuzzath does not appear in this narrative.

MEREDITH BURKE HAMMONS

AHZAI ah´zi [אַחְזָי ʾakhzay]. Son of Meshillemoth, a priest in Jerusalem when Nehemiah rebuilt the city's walls (Neh 11:13; 1 Chr 9:12 has יַחְזֵרָה yakhzerah, JAHZERAH).

AI *i* [עַי ʾay]. Trying to correlate archaeological material remains with biblical texts is a legitimate enterprise for excavators and biblical exegetes. However, such correlation must not be assumed in advance. This methodological principle is relevant in dealing with the dramatic story of the destruction of biblical Ai by Joshua and the "Israelites" (Joshua 7–8). Placed in the larger context of the conquest of Canaan by Israel, we are told that the Israelites killed "12,000" people (8:25) and that the "city" was burned and its king's body thrown into the city gate (8:24-29).

Biblical Ai today is almost universally identified with Khirbet et-Tell ("ruin of the tell") which is located about 9 mi. northeast of Jerusalem. However, the archaeological history of et-Tell suggests a very different story from that in the Bible. Major archaeological excavations were conducted here by J. Marquet-Krause (d. 1936) between 1933 and 1935, and by Joseph A. Callaway (d. 1988) from 1964 to 1976. Both excavators concluded that et-Tell had two major periods of occupation: the Early Bronze Age (ca. 3100–2400 BCE) and Iron Age I (ca. 1220–1050 BCE). Of ten strata that were identified, eight belong to the EBA.

During most of its EBA history, et-Tell was a large (ca. 27.5 acres) fortified city that included temples, industrial remains, and residential buildings. This phase of the city's history came to a violent end around 2400 BCE, perhaps by the Egyptians. The site was then abandoned until 1200 BCE when a small (ca. 3 acres) un-walled farming village was built here. By then the name of the EBA city was no longer known, thus the name "Ai," which is traditionally translated as "ruin" or "heap." While two phases of Iron I occupation were identified by Callaway, et-Tell remained a very small farming community during its entire Iron I history, clearly indicating that it was an agricultural, pastoralist community very similar

to other Canaanite farming villages. The end of the Iron I village came around 1050 BCE when the site was abandoned. Houses were left standing, and no evidence was found of burning as told in the biblical story. Callaway estimated the population at this time to be no more than 150 people, not the 12,000 mentioned in the Bible.

Because the archaeological history of et-Tell does not fit at all with the biblical story, various scenarios have been suggested. They vary from arguing that a story of the destruction of Bethel, which did occur at the end of the Late Bronze Age, somehow got transferred to Ai, to locating biblical Ai someplace other than at et-Tell. Other nearby sites have been excavated, but there are no Late Bronze Age or Iron Age I remains that can be correlated with the biblical story.

The story of Ai is part of the DEUTERONOMISTIC HISTORY (Joshua–2 Kings), which means that its literary date and function must be discussed within that context. Thus, the story has more to do with the theological concerns of its author(s) than with the actual history of the site.

Bibliography: Joseph A. Callaway. *Pottery from the Tombs at Ai (et-Tell)* (1964); Joseph A. Callaway. "New Evidence on the Conquest of Ai." *JBL* 1968 (87) 312–20; Joseph A. Callaway. *The Early Bronze Age Sanctuary at Ai (et-Tell)* (1972). Joseph A. Callaway. *The Early Bronze Age Citadel and Lower City at Ai (et-Tell): A Report of the Joint Archaeological Excavations to Ai (et-Tell)* 2 (1980). Ziony Zevit. "The Problem of Ai: New theory rejects the battle as described in Bible but explains how story evolved." *BAR* 11 (1985) 58–69.

JOHN C. H. LAUGHLIN

AIAH ay´yuh [אַיָּה ʾayyah]. The name means *hawk*. 1. One of Zibeon's sons, brother of Anah (Gen 36:24; 1 Chr 1:40), of the Horite clan from Edom.

2. The father of RIZPAH, Saul's concubine. She became a pawn in the politics surrounding Saul's reign (2 Sam 3:6-11; 21:8-14). *See* SAUL, SON OF KISH; ZIBEON.

LISA MICHELE WOLFE

AIATH ay´yath. *See* AI.

AIJALON ay´juh-lon [אַיָּלוֹן ʾayyalon]. 1. A city allotted to the tribe of Dan (Josh 19:42; Judg 1:35), mentioned as Aialuna in the Amarna Letters, and identified with modern Yalo, about fourteen m. northeast of Jerusalem. During the settlement period its inhabitants were subjected to forced labor by the house of Joseph (Josh 1:35). Joshua once commanded the sun to stand still at Gibeon and the moon in the valley of Aijalon (Josh 10:12). The tribe of Benjamin was associated with Aijalon (1 Chr 8:13), perhaps indicating the absorption of a portion of Danites into Benjamin. Aijalon was designated a Kohathite Levitical city (Josh 21:24; 1 Chr 6:66-70 [Heb. 6:51-55]), listed among the Ephraimite cities. The Israelite army of Saul and Jonathan defeated the Philistines at Aijalon (1 Sam 14:31), which was later fortified by Rehoboam against possible invasion from the Northern Kingdom (2 Chr 11:10). A south wall inscription of the Great Temple of Amon at Karnak lists Aijalon among 156 cities of Judah conquered by Pharaoh Shishak (2 Chr 12:2-12). In the 8th cent. BCE, during the reign of Ahaz, Aijalon was conquered by the Philistines (2 Chr 28:18).

2. A city of the tribe of Zebulun where Elon was buried (Judg 12:12). The location of this place is unknown.

CLAUDE F. MARIOTTINI

AIJELETH-SHAHAR ay´juh-leth-shay´hahr הַשַּׁחַר אַיֶּלֶת ʾayyeleth hashakhar]. A phrase in the title of Ps 22 with uncertain significance. *See* MUSIC.

ʿAYIN [ע ʿ]. The 16th letter of the Hebrew alphabet, which derives from the original Semitic word, *ʿayn-, "eye." *See* ALPHABET.

ʿAIN GHAZAL. *See* GHAZAL, ʿAIN.

ʿAJJUL, TELL EL. This city, of which 12 hectares is preserved, is located north of Wadi Gaza. Excavations were undertaken in the 1930s by W. M. F. Petrie, and since 1999 by P. M. Fischer and M. Sadeq. The historical identification is ambiguous, but the Canaanite "Sharuhen" is a good candidate. This wealthy cosmopolitan city flourished between the 17th and 14th cent. BCE. The rich finds, which include gold and silver jewelry and precious stones, armors and weapons of bronze, incised bone plaques, the largest number of scarabs in the Levant, and a rich repertoire of imported pottery, demonstrate trading connections with Cyprus, Egypt, Syria, Upper Euphrates, Anatolia, Crete, and Mycenae. The city was certainly *the* trade center in the Southern Levant from where goods were distributed all over the eastern Mediterranean, and therefore one of the most influential cities in the area during the late Middle and Late Bronze Ages. There are stray finds from the Iron Age and later periods.

Bibliography: P. M. Fischer. "The Preliminary Chronology of Tell el-ʿAjjul." Vol. 2. *SCIEM* (2000); P. M. Fischer and M. Sadeq. "Tell el-ʿAjjul 2000. Second Season Preliminary Report." *Egypt and the Levant* 12 (2002) 109–53.

PETER M. FISCHER

AKAN ay´kan עֲקָן ʿaqan]. Grandson of Seir the Horites. Brother of Uz (Gen 36:27). *See* JAAKAN.

AKEDAH. The Akedah refers to Abraham *binding* אֶת־יִצְחָק יַעֲקֹד ya´aqodh eth-yitskhaq) his son Isaac in preparation for laying him on the altar as a burnt offering (Gen 22:9) or to the entire story. God's command to Abraham to sacrifice Isaac, his "only son" whom he loves, is called a "test" (Gen 22:1). Abraham, unhesitatingly and not knowing it is a test, is obedient to the command and takes Isaac on a three-day journey to the place God shows him (Mount Moriah). On the way, Abraham assures a questioning Isaac that God will provide, thereby exhibiting trust that God would somehow remain faithful to the promise (Gen 17:19-21). With no resistance from Isaac, Abraham "binds" him and *then* lays him on the altar (Gen 22:9). The angel of the Lord, however, intervenes and commands Abraham to stay his knife-filled hand. A ram is offered instead of Isaac. Inasmuch as Isaac is not said to return with Abraham (Gen 22:19), an early interpretation (in both Jewish and Christian circles) supposed that Isaac was actually killed and later was resurrected from the dead (already evident in Heb 11:17-19).

This story is not mentioned again in the OT, but it soon becomes a commonly interpreted text in both Judaism and Christianity (Wis 10:5; Sir 44:20; 1 Macc 2:52; 4 Macc 13:12; 14:20; 16:20; 18:11; *Jub.* 17:15-18; 18:16; Heb 11:17-19; Jas 2:21; Philo; Pseudo Philo; Josephus). In both Jewish and Christian sources, a strong emphasis was placed on Abraham's obedience and, sometimes secondarily, his faith. It is striking that the NT references to the story are infrequent and are not linked to the crucifixion. In subsequent Christian thought (e.g., Eusebius), the story is seen as a type of the sacrifice of Jesus. It is likely that Jewish and Christian interpreters of this text have been influenced by one another from early times. A common interpretation of the Quranic version of the story has Ishmael replace Isaac.

Bibliography: Edward Kessler. *Bound by the Bible: Jews, Christians and the Sacrifice of Isaac* (2004).

TERENCE E. FRETHEIM

AKELDAMA uh-kel´duh-muh. In Aramaic, Akeldama, means, Field of Blood, and is usually identified as the area at the southeast end of the Hinnom Valley, where it joins the Kidron Valley, east of the Old City of Jerusalem. Its scriptural origin is in Matt 27:3-9 as the potters field bought with the blood money of Judas to bury strangers in (*see* Acts 1:18-19). The identification of this area with Akeldama was made as early as the 3rd cent. CE.

In this very location, however, is a complex of magnificent tombs decorated in the style of the Second Temple, far too ornate for the tombs of foreigners. In the past century and a half, these tombs were investigated by Tobler, Macalister, and Dalman. Josephus, in his description of the circumvallation wall the Roman commander Titus built around Jerusalem, mentions "the tomb (monument) of Ananus (Annas) the high priest" (Josephus, *J. W.* 5.506), precisely at the site known as Akeldama. This record, together with the outstanding style of these tombs, makes their identification as belonging to the wealthy family of Annas clearly warranted. The true Akeldama is more likely to have been located farther to the north, at the head of the Refaim Valley where clay deposits necessary to the work of a potter could be found.

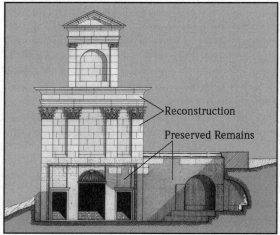

Leen and Kathleen Ritmeyer

Figure 1: The tomb of Annas the High Priest at "Akeldama": A reconstruction of the most elaborate tomb at Akeldama. Masonry blocks found above the triple-gated entranceway point to a former superstructure. This would accord well with the description of the monument of Annas mentioned as located in this area by Josephus, in his description of the siege-wall built by Titus around the city. It also echoes the decoration of the nearby Temple Mount where the priestly family of Annas served.

AKHENATEN. Akhenaten (Amenhotep IV), tenth king of the 18th Egyptian dynasty, is credited with founding the world's first monotheistic religion. His accomplishments have passed into history under the name AMARNA, after the site of his capital, Tell el-Amarna. The historical era incorporating the reigns of Akhenaten and his successors Smenkhkare, Tutankhamen, and Ay is often termed the *Amarna period.*

A. History of the Reign

Originally named Amenhotep after his father, Akhenaten was the second son of Amenhotep III and his chief wife Tiye. The details of his early life and his ascension to the throne remain obscure. Most scholars accept the theory that Amenhotep IV served as co-regent in the last two years of his father's reign, although arguments for a lengthy co-regency, or none at all, persist.

The chronology of the New Kingdom remains uncertain, especially for the Amarna period. Probable dates for his reign are 1355–1338 BCE, although a reign as early as 1377–1361 is possible. *See* EGYPT § B Chronology.

Estimates of Akhenaten vary. Some dismiss him as a reclusive religious fanatic. Others consider him a ruthless autocrat who used religion as a cover for the elimination of every rival power base.

In his fifth regnal year, he changed his name from Amenhotep "Amun is satisfied" to Akhenaten "Beneficial for Aten" to reflect a key program of his reign, devotion to the god Aten. One month later he announced plans to establish a new capital city, also named after Aten: AKHETATEN "Horizon of Aten." The unfolding of his program over the next twelve years transformed Egypt in what has been called the Amarna revolution.

Akhenaten's revolution did not extend to international affairs. Throughout the Amarna period, Egypt maintained a conventional foreign policy that preserved its status in the imperial brotherhood and its sphere of influence in Asia and Nubia. The few minor rebellions were suppressed with a minimum of effort.

International relations during the reign of Akhenaten are better documented than those of any other era of Egyptian history, thanks to the discovery of the archive of diplomatic correspondence at Tell el-Amarna. The AMARNA LETTERS attest to Egypt's interactions with imperial powers and vassal states in western Asia.

Akhenaten's chief wife Nefertiti bore him six daughters: Meritaten, Meketaten, Ankhesenpaaten, Neferneferuaten Tasherit, Neferneferure, and Setepenre. A secondary wife Kiya was the mother of a seventh daughter and perhaps also the future king Tutankhamen.

Akhenaten was succeeded by the enigmatic Smenkhkare, whom many scholars believe was none other than Queen Nefertiti. The much beloved Nefertiti is replaced as chief royal wife by her eldest daughter Meritaten in inscriptions from the last years of Akhenaten's reign. One theory suggests that Meritaten's role was purely ceremonial and reflected Nefertiti's promotion to co-regent.

Smenkhkare's brief rule was followed by that of Tutankhamen, the husband (and perhaps half-brother) of Akhenaten's daughter Ankhesenpaaten. Tutankhamen soon transferred the capital back to Memphis, and Akhenaten's mummy was moved to the Valley of the Kings at Thebes. His tomb reliefs and grave goods at Amarna were deliberately damaged. The claim that the male mummy found in the sarcophagus of Queen Kiya in tomb KV 55 is that of Akhenaten is unproved.

B. The "Heretic King"

Although Akhenaten is known as the "heretic king" for his religious revolution, he broke with tradition in many areas. He attempted to reshape the whole of Egyptian society by imposing his own vision of political relations, art, and religion. The undermining of traditional structures and values served to reassert the absolute authority of the pharaoh.

1. Political revolution

Akhenaten radically reshaped the political landscape by moving the capital city from Memphis to

Akhetaten (Tell el-Amarna) and replacing the traditional bureaucracy with "upstarts," young men from outside the nobility.

Akhenaten chose a remote, uninhabited site for his new capital. The move was not a retreat from reality, but a strategic realignment of power. The location allowed Akhenaten to construct the city according to his own vision and to fill it with his own handpicked corps of officials, "nobodies" who were loyal to him alone. The old structures, physical and social, were left behind in Memphis, as were the families who had run the bureaucracy for generations. The move solidified pharaonic control over every governmental department.

2. Artistic revolution

The art of Akhenaten's reign broke with the established canons of Egyptian art in ways that have been termed expressionistic and manneristic, after movements in modern Western art. The new canons seem to emphasize intimacy, emotion, and movement over the static idealized scenes of conventional Egyptian art. The royal family is depicted sharing intimate moments and affectionate embraces. Occasionally figures in motion turn toward the viewer as the artist experiments with frontal perspectives. Most striking are the distorted human figures with their elongated heads and necks, swollen bellies, and spindly limbs.

The reasons for this revolution have been widely debated. A long-standing theory holds that the human figures are based on a realistic portrait of Akhenaten who refused to allow his artists to conceal his genetic deformities behind a traditional idealized image. The depictions of nature and family life can also be interpreted as realistic. An opposing theory characterizes Amarna art as an expressionistic style based on diagonal axes. The artistic revolution derives from Akhenaten's theology that rejected the static eternal world of the gods in favor of an emphasis on nature and immediacy.

3. Religious revolution

Akhenaten rejected the traditional polytheism of Egypt, promoting instead the worship of the sun god Aten as universal creator and sole deity and suppressing the worship of all other gods. This revolution proceeded in steps. Early in the reign Aten could be depicted using conventional iconography as the hawk-headed sun god Re-Harakhty. His epithets included references to the gods Re-Harakhty and Shu: "Re-Harakhty who rejoices in the horizon, in his name of Shu which is in the sun-disk." After year nine, the epithets were altered by replacing the divine names with "ruler" and "light" respectively. Iconographic representations employing human or animal forms were also eschewed in favor of a simple sun disk with rays terminating in hands. These hands, which offer life in hieroglyphic form to the king and queen, were the only permitted anthropomorphism.

Figure 1: Pharaoh Amenophis IV (Akhenaten). Part of a monumental statue from Karnak, Egypt; Egyptian Museum, Cairo, Egypt.

The final step in the revolution was the suppression of the worship of other deities. Akhenaten closed their temples and had their names and images defaced. Even the word *gods* was erased from monuments. The concept of plural gods was anathema to the new religion. Aten was not the chief god of the Egyptian pantheon; he was the only god. The suppression focused especially on the god Amun, previously the most important and powerful of the Egyptian cults.

Despite his depiction as a rayed sun disk, the god Aten was not identical with the sun disk. Except when abbreviated in names, the god was always distinguished from the physical sun disk by the adjective *living*. Aten was the living sun disk, the solar energy that creates and sustains the universe.

In some ways Aten was a distant impersonal god, without mythology or anthropomorphic form, visible only as rays of sunlight. Only Akhenaten had direct access to Aten. In the iconography of Amarna, the royal family worshiped Aten. Everyone else worshiped his divine son Akhenaten. Together Aten, Akhenaten, and Nefertiti formed a new divine triad, displacing all other divine triads, such as Amun-Mut-Khonsu and Osiris-Isis-Horus.

At the same time the worship of Aten focused on the present rather than the eternal, the tangible physical world rather than the mysterious divine realm. Aten was omnipresent like sunlight, giving life to the whole earth every day. His cult was conducted in open-air shrines exposed to the sunlight, a radical departure from the mysterious rites conducted in the dark inner sancta of traditional processional temples.

Aten was the first god to be accorded the symbols of kingship. He was the first deity to have his epithets inscribed in cartouches. Previously only the names of the king and queen were surrounded by a cartouche. He was also the first to celebrate a royal jubilee, or sed-fest. In regnal year three Akhenaten celebrated his jubilee jointly with Aten at Karnak.

4. Atenism and biblical monotheism

The theory deriving biblical monotheism from Akhenaten's religious revolution is fraught with problems. Despite the shared features of aniconism and rigorous monolatry, the two religions are more different than they are alike. Aten is fundamentally a sun god, even at his most de-mythologized. Yahweh, the god of Israel, is at home on the mountaintop, first at Sinai and later at Zion. His theophanies are accompanied by volcanic eruptions, earthquakes, and thunderstorms.

Furthermore, the events that followed the death of Akhenaten make it unlikely that memory of his religious innovations were preserved for any length of time. Within a generation his successors undertook to erase any evidence of his reign or his revolutions. The name of Akhenaten was expunged from the official record. Akhetaten was abandoned. The temples of the traditional Egyptian deities were reopened, and the cult of Amun was restored to prominence. *See* AMARNA, TELL EL-; EGYPT; PHARAOH.

Bibliography: Cyril Aldred. *Akhenaten, King of Egypt* (1988); Jan Assmann. *Akhanyati's Theology of Light and Time* (1992); Rita E. Freed, Yvonne J. Markowitz, and Sue H. D'Auria, eds. *Pharaohs of the Sun: Akhenaten, Nefertiti, Tutankhamen* (1999); Erik Hornung. *Akhenaten and the Religion of Light* (1999); William J. Murnane. *Texts from the Amarna Period in Egypt* (1995); Donald B. Redford. *Akhenaten, the Heretic King* (1984); Nicholas Reeves. *Akhenaten: Egypt's False Prophet* (2001).

CAROLYN R. HIGGINBOTHAM

AKHETATEN. Literally "Horizon of Aten," was founded on virgin soil by the 18th dynasty, Egyptian king Akhenaten as his capital city and the sacred precinct of the sun-god Aten. The sacred precinct of Akhetaten is delimited by boundary stelae describing its founding. It spanned the Nile and comprised the capital city, temples, tombs, villages, and agricultural fields. Shortly after the death of Akhenaten, the capital returned to Thebes, and most of its residents left.

The extensively excavated site, approximately 250 miles north of Thebes, is better known by the modern designation Tell el-Amarna. *See* AKHENATEN; AMARNA, TELL ELI EGYPT.

CAROLYN R. HIGGINBOTHAM

AKITU. An ancient Mesopotamian festival tied to the equinoxes, agriculture, and lunar phases. At the ritual's beginning, a city's god was escorted out of the city to reside in the Akitu house for 11 days. Throughout the ceremony, worshipers gave a range of offerings, specified by day and time. At the festival's closing, the god was ushered back into the city in a majestic ceremonial procession. This ritual included a specific role for the king, and in its later occurrences included the reading of ENUMA ELISH, a Mesopotamian creation story.

While it was often celebrated twice a year, in some cases the Akitu became a single NEW YEAR festival. The ceremony was pervasive throughout Mesopotamia, and its details varied according to time and place. It is attested in numerous documents from the mid-3rd millennium to the mid-3rd cent. BCE.

Most scholars assert that the parting of the city's god symbolized chaos, while the triumphant return highlighted the god's restoration of cosmic order. Some have additionally noted political aspects of the ritual related to its particular socio-historical settings.

Analogies to ancient Israel include the biannual festivals specified in Exod 23:16, and speculation that the Babylonian Akitu influenced the timing and content of Israel's New Year celebrations. (*See* Exod 12:2; Lev 23:23-25; 25:9; Ezek 40:1).

Bibliography: Mark E. Cohen. *The Cultic Calendars of the Ancient Near East* (1993). Benjamin D. Sommer. "The Babylonian Akitu Festival: Rectifying the King or Renewing the Cosmos?" *JANES* 27 (2000) 81–95.

LISA MICHELE WOLFE

AKIVA, RABBI. A rabbinic sage in Jewish Palestine during the late 1st through early 3rd cent. CE; Akiva ben Yosef was the subject of many hagiographic legends (*see* HAGIOGRAPHA). It is impossible to accurately determine his biography. He is depicted as having humble, shepherding origins, and coming to TORAH study late in life. Rabbi Akiva subsequently disdained those ignorant of rabbinic law. Legend records his marriage to Rachel, the daughter of a wealthy leader of the Jewish community, and his abandonment of her for many years to study Torah. Upon his return, accompanied by large numbers of disciples, he credited his wife by telling them, "Yours and mine are hers." Many of the details of the Akiva legend parallel those of his biblical namesake, JACOB. Rabbinic legends report poignant tales of Akiva's martyrdom at the hands of Roman torturers (although this is disputed by other tales of his death elsewhere in the rabbinic corpus).

Akiva's abundant opinions in the arcana of rabbinic law (*see* HALACHAH) often espouse conservative positions. He often was the "swing vote" between the Gamalielite dynasty and disciples of JOHANAN BEN ZAKKAI. Rabbi Akiva is reported to be the master of

Rabbi Meir and in that role, one of the first organizers of rabbinic opinions into what would become the MISHNAH.

Rabbi Akiva was renowned for his legal prowess as a biblical exegete. He advanced a system of expanding or limiting the purview of scriptural verses. Akiva viewed the Bible as a code to be deciphered, believing that nothing in the Divine Writ is superfluous. This hermeneutic was in opposition to the so-called school of Rabbi Ishmael, which held that the Torah should be understood as normative human discourse. *See* ISHMAEL, RABBI.

Bibliography: H. L. Strack and G. Stemberger. *Introduction to the Talmud and Midrash* (1992).

BURTON L. VISOTZKY

AKKADIAN. East Semitic language spoken in ancient Mesopotamia and belonging to the larger Afroasiatic linguistic family. Attested from the mid-3rd millennium BCE, Akkadian borrowed its cuneiform writing system from the unrelated SUMERIAN language. Beginning with the second millennium, Akkadian appeared in northern and southern branches, respectively known as Assyrian and Babylonian. While Assyrian was discontinued after the fall of Assyria in 625 BCE, Babylonian is attested into the 1st cent. BCE. *See* ACCAD; ASSYRIA; BABYLONIA; SUMER.

ANNALISA AZZONI

AKKO. *See* ACCO, AKKO.

AKKUB ak´uhb [עַקּוּב *'aqquv*]. In 1 Chr 3:24, Akkub is a son of ELIOENAI, a postexilic member of the Davidic line through King JEHOIACHIN. The name *Akkub* also represents the head of a family of postexilic temple gatekeepers (1 Chr 9:17; Ezra 2:42; Neh 7:45; 11:19; 12:25) and the head of a family of temple servants (Ezra 2:45). According to Neh 8:7, Akkub was an expounder of the law. *See* NETHINIM.

STEVEN D. MASON

AKRABATTENE ak´ruh-bat´uh-nee [Ἀκραβαττήνη *Akrabattēnē*]. Variously identified as a stronghold or toparchy, (compare with Josephus *J.W.* 2.235; 4:551), southeast of Shechem. While this may be the site of Judas Maccabeus' defeat of the Idumeans (1 Macc 5:3), the Akrabattene in Idumea, south of Hebron, cannot be excluded.

J. R. C. COUSLAND

AKRABBIM, AKRABBIN uh-krab´im [עַקְרַבִּים *'aqrabbim*]. "The Scorpion Pass" or "Ascent of Scorpions" (ma'aleh 'aqrabbim) is an area southwest of the DEAD SEA (Num 34:4; Josh 15:3; Judg 1:36). Akrabattene in 1 Macc 5:3 could be the same place, although Josephus mentions an area with this name as being in SAMARIA.

ALABASTER [שֵׁשׁ *shesh*; ἀλάβαστρος *alabastros*]. The name *alabaster* derives from the city of Alabastron, which was famous for the manufacture of vases and amphorae made for the perfume trade. There are two varieties of alabaster: the oriental alabaster, a carbonate of lime (hydrated calcium carbonate), which is still mined in Egypt (now referred to as onyx) and is harder than modern alabaster (3 on the measure of hardness scale vs. 2) and the chalky alabaster (hydrated calcium sulphate). Chalky alabaster was formed during the Miocene period as the sediments of calcium sulphate contained in seawater underwent a process of concentration forming into stalagmites. A soft white stone, alabaster is more easily carved than marble and thus ideal for intricate decoration, sculpture work, and the creation of small containers for precious oils and perfumes. A questionable translation in Song 5:15 (NRSV) compares the lover's legs to "alabaster columns," but it is probably better to equate them with sturdy "marble pillars" (NIV). In the synoptic story of the anointing of Jesus' head (Matt 26:7; Mark 14:3), a woman breaks off the neck of an alabaster flask that contains NARD, a very expensive luxury import from India, and pours the cooling substance over his forehead. A similar story appears in Luke 7:37 in which a woman brings an alabaster jar of PERFUME to anoint Jesus' feet as an act of supplication and respect. In both cases, the precious character of the perfume is accented by its alabaster container.

VICTOR H. MATTHEWS

ALALAKH. Alalakh is ancient Tell Atchana, located at the SE corner of the fertile Hatay Plain, on the Orontes River. In Greco-Roman times the city of Antioch, to the west of Alalakh, dominated the region, as Antakya does today. Excavated by Sir Leonard Woolley in the 1930s and again in 1947, it has since 2003 been the object of renewed digging under the direction of the University of Chicago Oriental Institute. At Tell Atchana, seventeen strata date from 3100 BCE to 1200 BCE, with particular interest given to levels VII (ca. 17th cent.) and IV (ca. 15th cent.), wherein hundreds of cuneiform tablets were unearthed. Level VII provided important links in Mesopotamian chronology and Yarimlim's multiroomed palace, not unlike those of MARI and of Knossos. From the last stratum of ca. 1200 BCE the cuneiform-decorated statue of Idrimi was excavated. This cuneiform presereves a 15th cent. BCE prose narrative that has been compared to the story of David's rise in 1 Samuel (*COS* 1.148). Like David, IDRIMI claims to be rightful heir but must nevertheless flee his kingdom and live among neighbors (Emar and then Ammia in Canaan) until he can return and reestablish his rule. This initiates the period covered by the Level IV cuneiform tablets. Under Idrimi and his successors, Alalakh governs the kingdom of Mukish that lies immediately north of Ugarit. Unlike the cities in Canaan, however, the social structure betrays strong Hurrian influence. Further, the Hapiru, a social class despised in the Amarna letters from Palestine, hold high offices at Alalakh. As at Nuzi and Ugarit, comparisons of customs in Gen 12–50 have been criticized as not unique to the Bronze Age, but they nevertheless remain in a unique concentration. These include the transferal of firstborn inheritance to another (*AT* 92.15-19; *COS* 3.101B; Gen 15:2-3; 48:13-14, 22), a betrothal gift to the wife's father (*AT* 17.4-6; *COS* 3.101A; Gen 34:12), provisions for barrenness (*AT* 93; *COS* 3.101C; Gen 16:1-4), and the related inheritance rights of women (AT 7; *COS* 3.129). International treaties, land grants, and exchanges of property (*AT* 1–3, 6, 52, 456; *COS* 2.127–29; 2.136; 3.99B; 2.137) anticipate biblical covenants, exchanges of towns (1 Kgs 11:11), and the structure of the book of Joshua as a land grant.

Bibliography: M. Dietrich and O. Loretz. "Die Inschrift der Statue des Königs Idrimi von Alalah." *UF* 13 (1981) 201–68; R. S. Hess. "The Bible and Alalakh." *Mesopotamia and the Bible: Comparative Explorations* (2002); R. S. Hess. "The Book of Joshua as a Land Grant." *Bib* 83 (2002) 493–506; D. J. Wiseman. *The Alalakh Tablets* (1953); D. J. Wiseman. "Abban and Alalah." *JCS* 12 (1958) 124–29.

RICHARD S. HESS

ALCIMUS al´si-muhs [Ἄλκιμος Alkimos]. Alcimus (a Greek name corresponding to the Hebrew name Yakim) was a high priest in Jerusalem during the events leading up to the Maccabean Revolt. Our main sources of information about Alcimus are 1 Macc 7, 9; 2 Macc 14, additional information in Josephus's *Ant.* 12 and 20, and the rabbinic midrash *Genesis Rabbah.* The two main sources condemn Alcimus. For instance, in 1 Maccabees he is described as the leader of "renegade and godless men of Israel" (7:5) and his death in "great agony" is attributed to divine punishment for having removed a wall in the Temple (9:54-56). Second Maccabees states that Alcimus "had willfully defiled himself" (14:3). Both of these sources also identify Alcimus as being a Hellenizer and an opponent of Judas Maccabeus (1 Macc 7:5-6; 2 Macc 14:6). Since they display ardent pro-Judas tendencies, many scholars treat their characterizations of Alcimus with some skepticism. Regardless of Alcimus's relative degree of Hellenizing, which is difficult to ascertain because of the tendencies of our sources, he could claim descent from Aaron and his legitimacy on those lines was acknowledged even by those who opposed him on other grounds. Alcimus may have died of a stroke (*see* the description of his paralysis in 1 Macc 9:55). Upon his death in 159 BCE the position of high priest remained vacant for several years. Eventually, Judas's brother Jonathan filled the position in 152 BCE when he was appointed by Alexander Balas, son of Antiochus IV.

DAVID S. WILLIAMS

ALEMA al´uh-muh [Ἄλειμοι Aleimoi]. Location in Gilead where Judas Maccabeus liberated captive Jews imprisoned by the surrounding Gentiles (1 Macc 5:26, 44). Although the Greek (᾿en Alemois) could suggest Alema was a region, it was more likely a fortified city, sometimes identified with the modern site ʿAlma on the plain of Hauran.

J. R. C. COUSLAND

ALEMETH al´uh-meth [עָלֶמֶת ʿalemeth]. 1. The grandson of Benjamin through Becher (1 Chr 7:8).

2. Saul's descendant through Jonathan's son Meribbaal (Mephibosheth). In the genealogies he is listed as either the son of Jehoaddah (1 Chr 8:36) or Jarah (1 Chr 9:42).

3. A levitical city in Benjamin (1 Chr 6:60; Heb 6:45).

HEATHER R. MCMURRAY

ALEF [א ʾalef]. The first letter of the Hebrew alphabet, which derives from the Semitic name *ʾalf-, meaning "ox." This Hebrew letter is also the symbol used to represent the 4th cent. CE Greek manuscript called Codex Sinaiticus. *See* ALPHABET; SINAITICUS, CODEX.

ALEPPO CODEX. Oldest known complete manuscript of the OT, written ca. 920 CE in Palestine, a valuable source document for the Masoretic textual tradition. It was kept in the synagogue of Aleppo, Syria (therefore its name), which was set on fire by rioters in 1948; the codex was thought to be destroyed, but two-thirds of it were recovered. *See* MASORA; TEXT CRITICISM, OT.

ALEXANDER BALAS, EPIPHANES al´ig-zan´duhr i-pif´uh-neez [Ἀλέξανδρος ὁ Βάλας Alexandros ho Balas, Ἐπιφανής Epiphanēs]. Alexander Epiphanes, also referred to as "Balas," was a pretender to the Seleucid throne and was able to take it from Demetrius I. He claimed that he was the son of Antiochus IV Epiphanes and was apparently believed by a sufficient number of his countrymen to assume the kingship of the Seleucid kingdom. According to the author of 1 Macc, in 152 BCE, he landed at Ptolemais on the coast of Syria in 152 BCE and was welcomed by the people as their new king (*see* 1 Macc 10:1–11:19). He soon after made an alliance with Jonathan Maccabeus, leader and high priest of the Jews in order to help him defeat his rival to the throne, Demetrius I. For his friendship Jonathan was given a series of titles normally reserved for Greeks only, including *friend of the king*, *brother*, and *first friend*, and a gold broach that was customarily given to cousins of the king. Demetrius I feared the loss of his kingdom and likewise sought an alliance with Jonathan, but his offers were refused because of a lack of trust and also Demetrius's earlier cruelties to the Jews. Alexander, who was also the son-in-law of

Ptolemy Philometer VI of Egypt, defeated Demetrius I and was a ruler of the Seleucid Dynasty from roughly 151 to 145 BCE.

In 145, King Ptolemy VI of Egypt invaded Palestine reportedly to assist Alexander Balas, but when he discovered a plot against him by Alexander Balas, he withdrew his daughter, gave her in marriage to the son of Demetrius I, Demetrius II, and sought his support in battle against Alexander Balas with the promise of restoring his father's kingdom to his new son-in-law. According to Josephus, he came with his forces and by deception and trickery defeated the Seleucid king in battle (*Ant.* 13.106–19). When Alexander Balas fled to Arabia, an Arabian chief beheaded him. Ptolemy VI, having been seriously wounded in battle, died soon thereafter and Demetrius II, the son of Demetrius I, became the new Seleucid king. This turn of events led to several civil wars and hastened the disintegration of the Seleucid Empire.

Bibliography: Martin Hengel. *Judaism and Hellenism: Studies in Their Encounter in Palestine during Early Hellenistic Period* (1974); Simon Price. "The History of the Hellenistic Period." *The Oxford History of the Classical World* (1986).

LEE MARTIN MCDONALD

ALEXANDER, FALSE TEACHER, COPPERSMITH

al´ig-zan´duhr [Ἀλέξανδρος ὁ χαλυεὺς Alexandros ho chalkeus]. Alexander was a common name in antiquity and the same is true in the NT (e.g., Mark 15:21; Acts 4:6; 19:33; 1 Tim 1:20; 2 Tim 4:14). One identified as Alexander was a coppersmith who apparently lived in Troas (2 Tim 4:13) and is also likely the same person mentioned with Hymenaeus who "suffered shipwreck in the faith" (1 Tim 1:19-20). In 2 Tim 4:14, Paul refers to him as one who caused him "great harm," perhaps as Paul's accuser before the Roman authorities that led to Paul's arrest (compare with Acts 21:27). It may be that this Alexander was also guilty of the heresy of Hymenaeus, who is condemned along with Philetus for spreading the teaching that the resurrection had already taken place, that is spiritualizing the resurrection hope of the church, or emphasizing a realized eschatology (2 Tim 2:17). It was unusual for the early Christians to mention the names of heretics in the early church, and this appears to be an early exception. For instance, Ignatius (ca. 115) refused to identify in writing the names of heretics who also denied the faith (*Smyrn.* 5:3). This was Paul's earlier practice.

Alexander the coppersmith may have come from Ephesus to Troas (or returned to Troas), which is mentioned just prior to the reference to Alexander (2 Tim 4:13). There was a special guild of coppersmiths at Troas. As a result of his heresy and the harm he caused to Paul and the church, he was "handed over to Satan" (1 Tim 1:20; compare 1 Cor 5:5) and assured that the Lord (Christ or God) will judge him (2 Tim 4:14). There is another Alexander, a Jew, mentioned in Acts 19:33-34, who tried to make a defense before the crowd in the theater, but he is not likely the same Alexander referred to in the Pastoral Epistles.

Bibliography: J. D. Quinn, W. C. Wacker. *First and Second Letters to Timothy.* ECC (2000); I. H. Marshall. *Pastoral Epistles.* ICC. 2004; M. Dibelius, H. Conzelmann. *Pastoral Epistles.* Hermeneia (1982).

LEE MARTIN MCDONALD

ALEXANDER JANNAEUS, JANNEUS al´ig-zan´dulr

[Ἀλέξανδρος ὁ Ἰανναῖος Alexandros ho Iannaios]. In the Hasmonean Dynasty, following the death of John Hyrcanus in 103 BCE, his oldest son, Aristobulus I (104–03) came to the throne but was quickly ousted by his brother, Alexander Jannaeus (103–76 BCE). He was known as a violent and cruel man. He brought a Hellenistic monarchy to the Jewish people. He was opposed both by the Nabataen Arabs and subsequently by the Pharisees both for his aggression and abuse of the office of high priest, as well as lack of concern for the Torah. According to Josephus, he is most known for his atrocities against the Pharisees whose families he slaughtered before their eyes and crucified them while he and his concubines feasted as they watched the executions (*Ant.* 13.379-83). This was the first time a Jew used this cruel form of punishment introduced by the Romans. He lived a long life and on his deathbed he bequeathed his throne to Salome Alexandra (76–67 BCE) and advised her to make peace with the Pharisees. See Josephus, *Ant.* 13.320-364, 372–407; and 20.242.

LEE MARTIN MCDONALD

ALEXANDER OF ABONOTEICHOS al´ig-zan´duhr

a-bahn-o´tay-kus [Ἀλέξανδρος Ἀβωνοτειχίτος Alexandros Abōnoteichitos]. Second cent. CE prophet of Glycon, a manifestation of Asclepius in the form of a snake. Many came to consult him and participate in the mysteries, but Christians and EPICUREANS were specifically excluded as unbelievers. Lucian of Samosata wrote against him in his *Alexander, or the False Prophet.*

MARK DELCOGLIANO

ALEXANDER OF EPHESUS al´ig-zan´duhr [Ἀλέξαν-

δρος Alexandros]. Fearing that Paul's converts would prevent the highly profitable worship of ARTEMIS, a crowd of Ephesians rallied in opposition. Jews in the crowd pushed the unknown Alexander to speak; he was drowned out by the crowd's support for Artemis. Alexander's identity and narrative purpose are unclear in Eph 19:33-34.

HEIDI S. GEIB

ALEXANDER OF JERUSALEM al´ig-zan´duhr [Ἀλέξανδρος Alexandros]. Alexander, originally a bishop in Cappadocia, became bishop of Jerusalem ca. 212 CE (EUSEBIUS, *Hist. eccl.* VI) and founded the library later used by Eusebius himself. A friend of ORIGEN, whom he ordained to the priesthood and defended against Demetrius, Origen's bishop, he suffered martyrdom in the Decian persecution.

MARK DELCOGLIANO

ALEXANDER POLYHISTOR al´ig-zan´duhr [Ἀλέξανδρος Πολυΐστορας Alexandros Poluistoras]. Greek polymath (ca. 105–35 BCE) whose fragmentary *On the Jews* (preserved in Eusebius, *Praep. ev.* IX, 17f. and Clement of Alexandria, *Strom.* I, 21, 130) contains several otherwise unknown quotations from earlier authors who wrote on the early history of the Jews and elaborated the biblical accounts.

ALEXANDER, SON OF SIMON OF CYRENE al´ig-zan´duhr [Ἀλέξανδρος Alexandros]. Alexander, the son of SIMON of Cyrene, is mentioned only once in the Bible (Mark 15:21). He is known only in relation to his father and his brother RUFUS. Mark's inclusion of Alexander's and his brother's names, coupled with the elimination of these names in the Matthean and Lukan parallels, have led some scholars to conclude that Alexander and Rufus may have been members of Mark's community or part of the community of the author of Mark's passion source.

ERIC C. STEWART

ALEXANDER THE GREAT al´ig-zan´duhr [Ἀλέξανδρος Alexandros]. Alexander III, son of Philip II of Macedon, was born in July of 356 BCE. He was educated by Aristotle, who gave him his appreciation for culture and philosophy. Alexander learned military strategy as commander of a portion of his father's armies. After Philip's assassination, Alexander garnered support from influential generals and led his army of some 40,000 to victories in the east as far as India and to the south as far as Egypt. He had conquered Darius's Achaemenid Empire by the remarkable age of 24. During his many conquests (334–23 BCE), Palestine also fell under Greek control. Revolutionizing cultural, linguistic, religious, and political changes significantly influenced the Mediterranean world for centuries and paved the way for the advance of Christian missions.

The opening sentences of *1 Maccabees* (ca. 104–100 BCE) poignantly describe the enormous impact that Alexander made on the ancient world:

> He fought many battles, conquered strong-holds, and put to death the kings of the earth. He advanced to the ends of the earth, and plundered many nations. When the earth became quiet before him, he was exalted, and his heart was lifted up. He gathered a very strong army and

ruled over countries, nations, and princes, and they became tributary to him (1 Macc 1:2–4).

As a result of these conquests, the Greek language was spoken almost everywhere in the Mediterranean world. There was a move toward syncretism of architectural and religious heritages of the Greek and Oriental peoples that is commonly called "Hellenization." Josephus (ca. 90 CE) tells of Alexander's involvement in the Jewish and Samaritan conflicts in Palestine and the establishment of the Samaritan temple on Mount Gerizim (*Ant.* 11.304-47). He further reports that Alexander bowed himself before the God of the Jews in the presence of the priests of Jerusalem and read the Book of Daniel to confirm that the Greeks would defeat Darius (11.333, 337). The rabbinic Jews report more of Alexander's activities (*b. Tamid* 31*b*-32*b*; *Gen. Rab.* 61:7).

Alexander reportedly gave a speech that emphasized the brotherhood and reconciliation of all persons to some 9,000 "dignitaries and notables of all races" at Opis, a town on the Tigris River in 324 BCE. The speech undoubtedly contains embellishments from Eratosthenes, of the library of Alexandria in Egypt, as well as Ptolemy, one of Alexander's most loyal generals. The contents of the speech have been repeated in various contexts that suggest an element of authenticity. The Roman historian Flavius Arrian (ca. 130 BCE) reports: "And Alexander prayed for all sorts of blessings, and especially for harmony and fellowship in the empire between Macedonians and Persians" (Arrian, *Anab.* 7.11.9). Strabo claims that Alexander said that the real distinction between people was not race, but whether they were good or bad (*Geogr.* 1.4.9). (*See also* Plutarch, *Alex. fortuna* 1.6).

The spread of Greek language and culture may not have been a result of Alexander's vision for a unified world so much as his ambition to conquer and to fortify his military. In any case, the influence of Alexander the Great on the Greco-Roman world and upon the dissemination of the Christian proclamation cannot be overestimated.

Alexander died in May of 323 BCE in Babylon and was buried in Alexandria by Ptolemy, one of his generals. He was reportedly seen ascending to heaven. Alexander described himself as a son of Zeus-Ammon and spread the story that his true father was divine. Roman emperor worship in the 1ˢᵗ cent. CE has its roots in Alexander's claim to divinity. *See* EMPEROR WORSHIP; HELLENISM; GREEK RELIGION AND PHILOSOPHY.

Bibliography: R. L. Fox. *Alexander the Great* (1997).

LEE MARTIN MCDONALD

ALEXANDRA SALOME [Ἀλέξανδρα Σαλώμη Alexandra Salōmē]. A Jewish queen of the Hasmonean dynasty between 76–67 BCE. Alexandra Salome was the last fully independent Hasmonean monarch. She inherited the throne from her husband, Alexander Jannaeus (r. 103–76 BCE). On ascending the throne she reversed his internal policies, favoring the Pharisees over the Sadducees. Her international politics included appeasement of the Armenian Mithridates and a failed attempt to take Damascus. Since she was a woman and could not serve as high priest, as her predecessors had done, she nominated her son Hyrcanus II for the office. On her death a war of succession between him and her other son, Aristobulus II, broke out and brought in its wake Roman intervention, effectively ending Hasmonean rule and the independence of Judaea.

The Jewish historian Josephus provides most of our information about this queen. He only knows her Greek name—*Alexandra*. Despite the fact that she was a woman, Josephus' appraisal of her reign is surprisingly positive. Her Hebrew name, cited here and elsewhere as Salome, is a scholarly deduction from the many faulty versions of her name found in rabbinic literature. The rabbis also failed to comment on her gender and praised her reign profusely, as a time of God's bounty to his people. Recently it has been ascertained that the queen is also mentioned in the literature of Qumran, where her Hebrew name is correctly preserved as slmzywn. The members of the Qumran sect, unlike Josephus and the rabbis, viewed the reign of the queen as violent and illegitimate. *See* ALEXANDER JANNAEUS, JANNEUS; ARISTOBULUS; HASMONEANS; HYRCANUS; JOSEPHUS, FLAVIUS; PHARISEES; QUMRAN; RABBINIC LITERATURE; SADDUCEES.

TAL ILAN

ALEXANDRIA al´ig-zan´dree-uh [Ἀλεξάνδρια Alexandria]. City in Egypt founded as an autonomous Greek polis by Alexander the Great (331 BCE), situated 14 mi. west of the Canopic branch of the Nile, in between the Mediterranean Sea and Lake Mareotis.

After Alexander's death (323 BCE), Ptolemy I Soter entombed his body here in the Soma (or Sema). Beautifying Alexandria as his royal seat, Ptolemy built the magnificent Mouseion (incorporating lecture halls, laboratories, gardens, observatories, and a zoo) and Library. By 200 BCE Alexandria was pre-eminent among Hellenistic cities as a trade center where East met West and as a powerhouse of science, literature, mathematics, and philosophy (*see* HELLENISM). Alexandria became part of the Roman Empire after Cleopatra VII and Mark Anthony were defeated by Octavian in the Battle of Actium (31 BCE).

Strabo, *Geogr.* 17, describes Alexandria as being 30 stadia (3.5 mi.) long and 7–8 stadia (1 mi.) wide. A rectangular grid plan was laid by Deinokrates of Rhodes, with two main streets: the Canopic Way, from the western necropolis (Gate of the Moon) to the east (Gate of the Sun), crossed by the Street of the Soma.

Alexandria boasted a grand Serapeum, Poseidium, Paneium, Caesareum/Sebasteion (*see* EMPEROR-WORSHIP), emporium, gymnasium, theater and extramural hippodrome.

On the island of Pharos was one of the Seven Wonders of the World: the tall lighthouse built by Sostratos the Cnidian in 297 BCE. Pharos was connected by a mole 1200 yards (7 stadia) long—the Heptastadion—which created dual harbors: the western Eunostos and eastern Great harbor. A third existed on Lake Mareotis.

Numerous tombs survive with decoration illustrative of the Greco-Egyptian character of the city. It was divided into five sectors (Α, Β, Γ, Δ, Ε), one mainly inhabited by Egyptians, two largely populated by Jews, with "Greeks" forming he largest body. Jewish intellectual life flourished, particularly the allegorical school of exegesis (*see* ALLEGORY) whose most famous exponent was PHILO JUDEUS (1st cent.). Numerous Greek texts in the corpus of intertestamental literature may have their provenance here. The SEPTUAGINT was apparently translated on Pharos.

APOLLOS, a Jew "instructed in the Way of the Lord" (Acts 18:24-28), came from Alexandria. Traditionally founded by St. Mark, the Christian community thrived throughout the Roman and Byzantine periods, with its catechetical school under Clement and Origen (2nd–3rd cent.), and with powerful bishops such as Athanasius and Cyril (4th–5th cent.). Alexandria was also a centre of GNOSTICISM, led by Basilides and his son Isidore (2nd–3rd cent.).

JOAN E. TAYLOR

ALEXANDRINUS, CODEX. Written in the 5th cent. CE, this codex is one of the most valuable Greek manuscripts of the OT and NT (see TEXT, NT; VERSIONS, ANCIENT). Its provenance is unknown, but its name derives from its earliest known location, Alexandria, Egypt. In 1627 the codex was sent as a gift to James I of England, and today it is housed in the British Library (Royal Mss 1 D. VIII = Nestle-Aland A or 02). It contains the Bible of the Catholic Canon, which includes the deuterocanonical books, and 3 and 4 Maccabees from the SEPTUAGINT; the Psalms of Solomon were originally included but are now missing. Of the NT, Matt 1:1–25:6; John 6:50–8:52; and 2 Cor 4:13–12:6 are missing; appended are *1 Clem.*, and *2 Clem.* up to 12:4. The text of Alexandrinus is considered one of the most valuable witnesses to the LXX. Concerning the NT, the codex was obviously copied from several manuscripts of varying value (very high for Acts and the Catholic Epistles, and higher in the Pauline Epistles and Revelation, but lower in the Gospels).

PETER ARZT-GRABNER

ALEXANDRIUM. *See* HERODIAN FORTRESSES.

ALGEBRA. *See* MATHEMATICS.

ALGUM al'guhm [אַלְגּוּם 'alghum]. A type of wood used in the construction of the Temple of Solomon (2 Chr 2:7; 9:10-11). It is likely that algum is an error of transposition for "ALMUG." The Septuagint translates the term as "pine."

ALI, TELL. Located at the southern end of the Sea of Galilee, this small site has a long, albeit interrupted, occupational sequence beginning in the Middle PPNB (8500–7500 BCE). It was one of the first sites to be re-inhabited in the Jordan Valley during the PPNC (6900–6350 BCE) (Garfinkel 1994), and habitation continued during the Jericho IX Pottery Neolithic (6350–5800 BCE), the Wadi Rabah phase (5500–4300 BCE), and the Chalcolithic period.

Bibliography: Y. Garfinkel. "The 'PPNC' Flint Assemblage from Tel ʿAli." Gebel and S. K. Kozlowski, eds. *Neolithic Chipped Stone Industries of the Fertile Crescent* (1994).

GARY O. ROLLEFSON

ALIAH al'ee-uh. *See* ALVAH.

ALIAN al'ee-uhn. *See* ALVAN.

ALIEN. *See* FOREIGN, FOREIGNER; SOJOURNER.

ALIENATION. The English word *alienation* expresses the concept of losing a once held privilege or intimate connection with others. The biblical imagery of alienation begins with the banishment of Adam and Eve from the Garden and their loss of direct communion with God. Their rebellion (Gen 3) initiates an expanding chasm between God and creation as well as between creatures. Cain is cut off from his family (Gen 4). Entire groups are estranged by language and geography (Gen 11). The remainder of the OT provides ample illustration of alienation. Jacob flees from his family due to his deception of Esau. Joseph's own brothers sell him into slavery. Egypt enslaves Israel. Moses names one of his sons, Gershom, *an alien there* (Exod 2:22), depicting his own exile. The kingdom of Israel is divided (1 Kgs 12) and then exiled, sending Israelites into Babylon as captives, cut off from the presence of God.

The NT affirms that sin alienates people from God. Ephesians 2:12 reminds readers that once they were cut off and excluded from the family of God. The text describes (ch. 4) the full effect of sin on human hearts: ignorance leading to callousness, greed, and ultimately to complete futility of mind and alienation from God.

Though human sin has brought about alienation, God's wrath against sin is the final cause of the separation. This is aptly illustrated when God tells Israel that they will know his displeasure (i.e., opposition, alienation) during their forty years in the desert (Num 14:34). However, not all estrangement is the result of personal iniquity. Disease (Lev 13:46) separated unclean from clean and God's people accepted a life of alien status while waiting for their promised deliverance (Heb 11:13).

The laments (e.g., Pss 13, 22, 39, 102, 107; Lamentations) depict a proper response to the crushing weight of being estranged from God. One cries out for relief (Ps 39:10), for forgiveness (Ps 51), for restoration (Lam 2:20), for understanding and wisdom (Pss 88, 90), for vindication (Hab 1:2-3; Lam 3:64), but ultimately one groans, waits, and worships God (Lam 3:24).

Though God's hand is in alienation, God is not indifferent to human suffering nor without rescue plan. Adam and Eve are cared for, even in their banishment. Abraham is promised that he and his alien offspring will be planted in the Land (Gen 17:8). Israel is given a priestly mediator. Aliens receive justice and mercy. Thirty discrete commands are given to the Israelites to treat foreigners the same as any other citizen (e.g., Exod 22:21; Jer 7:6; Ezek 22:29).

The ultimate picture of God's care for alienated people is evidenced in Jesus' atoning sacrifice for sinners—bringing humans into the holy of holies (Heb 10:19-20) and breaking the dividing wall of hostility (Eph 2:14). He is scapegoated (Lev 16:8-10) and experiences alienation from the Father to reconcile us to God's family and to each other (Eph 2:19; 2 Cor 5:18-21). *See* LIBERATION; RECONCILIATION; REJECT; SIN.

PHILIP G. MONROE

ALLA, DEIR. *See* DEIR ALLA, TELL.

ALLAMMELECH uh-lam'uh-lek [אַלַּמֶּלֶךְ 'allam-melekh]. Town, possibly situated in the Plain of Acco, given to the Asher tribe (Josh 19:26) when Joshua apportioned the remaining territories (Josh 18:10). *See* ASHER.

ALLEGORY. Allegory is a way of interpreting a text in terms of another reality or story, in order to lend new meaning.

A. Ancient Origins

In the ancient world, allegory was a way of making words say something other than what they appeared to mean. For example, in allegorical personification, the Greek gods Uranus, Chronos, and Zeus become the figures of One, Mind, and Soul. This allegorization of the Greek gods and their actions encouraged biblical interpreters to think in terms of depth behind language, even of the world and events depicted in Scripture. For example, the Septuagint's translations of the prophets become both more abstract and universal and future-oriented than the Hebrew (an exception is Isa 7:14, where the LXX has "virgin" rather than "young woman," and we read "breasts" rather than "loves" in Song 1:2 LXX).

Paul led the way for Christian allegory with his interpretation of two women (Hagar and Sarah, Gen 16:21) as two types of covenant in Gal 4:22-24 (*see* PAUL, THE APOSTLE). His stories were drawn from salvation history, not from fanciful imagination. The Bible never uses the term μῦθος mythos (tale, story, myth) except unfavorably (e.g., 1 Tim 1:4; 4:7), but Paul's narrative examples and his use of the word ἀλληγορέω allēgoreō ("I allegorize," Gal 4:24) gave the green light to future Christian allegorical interpreters of the Bible.

There was also a Stoic tradition of understanding texts as speaking on three levels: literal, moral, and metaphysical (*see* STOIC, STOICISM). This tradition was taken over and applied to the Bible by exegetes such as PHILO OF ALEXANDRIA and ORIGEN. In *Cels.* (1, 42), written ca. 250 CE, Origen notes that, just as one must read certain passages of Homer allegorically, one might need to approach the NT allegorically when a literal interpretation is unedifying. This suggests that truly wise texts intend themselves to be allegorized; allegory involves both writing and reading, both the expression and the interpretation. Jesus' parables also inspired allegories of NT passages. Bede (*On Figures and Tropes:* CCSL 123A) shows how the same perfection can be shown by an *allegoria facti* of Joseph's coat in Gen 37, and by the *allegoria verbi* of the burning lamps of Christ's teaching (Luke 12:35). Of course, such interpretation could be taken a bit far, such as suggesting that the grass trampled during the feeding of the five thousand (John 6:10) was concupiscence needing to be stamped on heavily.

B. The Triumph of Allegorical Reading of the Bible in Christian Late Antiquity

Allegorizing refers to interpreting according to the analogy of faith, the creedal doctrines that the church needs to know and believe for the fullness of salvation. The "tropological sense" means not just a "moral lesson," but what is to be done in the Christian life on the basis of membership in a community of grace. The "eschatological (or anagogical) sense" of these doctrines gave the OT more emphasis by continuing to speak at length about the judgment, the "Day of the Lord" and a new existence to come. Thus Origen can come to the meaning of the SONG OF SONGS for the individual believer only after he has built the ecclesiological foundation by treating the bride and groom as church and Christ (*see* BRIDE OF CHRIST). What Origen means by TYPOLOGY is usually allegory, even if it is biblical, since the historical sense of the text corresponds to heavenly truths (e.g, the Trinity), not just NT events. The spiritual is contained in the divinely inspired text. Allegory is not a hermeneutic, but each "sense" is a stage of teaching within Scripture appropriate to stages of readers or hearers. The soul reascends up the descending chain of revelation, although there

is no getting to the heavenly realm of truths and even to God without going through the story of Christ, his founding of the church, and his coming back for her. Thus the visible and the invisible are joined through the incarnational principle of the eternal gospel (Rev 14:6).

If typology is a congruence of events, then allegory is a congruence of words and concepts between Testaments. Allegory rests on typology because it follows divine revelation across both Testaments. Not all texts are candidates for allegorical interpretation owing to their nature (e.g., probably not most of Proverbs). To give such a spiritual interpretation means following the path of history of God's communication with God's people.

There were limits to allegory as suggested by the Golden Age of patristic exegesis (350–450 CE). For John Chrysostom, Paul did not really mean "allegory" as pagans would mean it but used the word "improperly," modifying its sense so as to rule out any suggestion of fiction in the biblical narratives (PL 26:389 on Gal 4:24; *see* CHRYSOSTOM, JOHN). The later church fathers preferred the less loaded word *theoria* as something not polar opposite to *allegoria*, but as an interpretation that operated with sentences, paragraphs, and stories rather than with words only. It is not wrong to think that they were looking for a text behind a text, and yet such a text was part of a historical movement, of salvation history. As Origen puts it (*Princ.* II, 3, 7), the heavenly world is mapped out by biblical histories. That the early church fathers considered *theoria* the more acceptable term for the spiritual sense than *allegoria* makes it clear that they believed such interpretation arises from within the text itself, and is not imposed by the reader or other external authority. For Diodore *theoria* is the raising of the spiritual sense from the literal sense. The *skopos* or intention of Scripture is the training (*paideia*) of the soul; the *Logos* is just as much in the OT as in the NT text.

C. The Contribution of Augustine

Allegory for Augustine was based on both words and events of the OT, not just one or the other. He did not allegorize the NT. Augustine believed that one should read all OT stories through the lens of the NT or else risk acquiring non-Christian morals. For Augustine, the NT is fully clear since there is no deceit in it, whereas there might be deceit in the OT. (*Against Lying* XII, 26). In any case, Augustine did not draw a moral lesson from Jacob's lying, nor David's having many wives; these are allegories. In his treatment of Ps 103 (104), Augustine clearly allegorizes the wings of the wind as souls.

We may find it odd when Augustine interprets Jacob's deceptive classification of Laban's cattle into a mystery (*Sermon* 4, 15; *City of God* 16, 37). But how else should he have understood the dark and objectionable passages of the Bible, unless he found in the words of Scripture the figure of an underlying truth? Wherever Augustine encountered obscurity or unworthiness in the Bible, he took this as a clue that the passage was not to be taken literally.

Augustine also insisted that one understands the dark places of Scripture by learning the biblical language (*On Christian Doctrine* 2, 30), but only after one has tried to understand the words literally, and while remaining aware of the danger of disconnecting allegory from the obvious meaning of a text (*De genesi ad litteram*) and of one's general exegetical shortcomings. For Augustine, there were two criteria for interpretation: love of God (*On the Trinity*) and neighbor, and, even more important, consonance with the Rule of Faith. Thus, a reader could find meaning that was not necessarily what the writer intended, presumably because God is the author who claims "copyright" for the use and meaning of his texts. Augustine believed that God likes to communicate in pictures rather than primarily in propositions and tightly reasoned argument. Allegory points us toward the eternal truths most clearly expressed in the NT. Allegory is a way of approaching an obscure OT text through the typological correspondence to events and figures in the NT, so that a connection is drawn with something of profound spiritual import and relevance to the Christian reader.

D. The Middle Ages: Allegory as Foundation of Spiritual Reading of Bible and World

In the Christian Middle Ages, Augustine's suggestion that biblical words signified things that in turn allegorically signified other things, was perhaps the most important single aspect of his teaching (*De Doctrina Christiana*). Not only words but things too are full of meaning, (Hugh, *Didascalion* VI, 14; Bonaventura, *Breviloquium*, Prol 4). The same images can be interpreted for good or for ill; e.g., "lion" can stand for both Christ and the devil (Rev 5:5; 1 Pet 5:8).

Allegory developed into the revelation of the spiritual meaning of the world, with the Bible as textbook for discovering hidden meanings in things of the world, all of which take their place in a story. To take a famous example from John Cassian (CSEL 13, 2, 404–7) on Gal 4:24, "Jerusalem" can be understood as the physical city according to the historical sense, the church of Christ according to the allegorical, the heavenly city of God according to the anagogical sense, and the soul of humanity according to the tropological (moral). These four senses correspond in turn to knowledge, revelation, prophecy, and teaching of 1 Cor 14:6.

"All creation speaks of God," wrote Hugh of St. Victor (*Didascalion* VI, 5), though of course the Bible led the way. Thus, angels' clothing in the Bible could stand for glory of resurrection bodies. Conrad of Hirsau developed this use of allegory: e.g., snow, while according to its form white and signifying purity of good works

(Ps 51:7; Isa 1:18), by nature is cold and signifies the extinguishing of lust. Bible and nature become commentaries on each other.

Even if for Thomas Aquinas, the plain sense of Scripture would be sufficient for establishing doctrine; allegory of OT passages had to do with reinforcing it. There was an awareness that unscrupulous Christians could abuse the Bible by taking it too literally. The OT has to be read through the NT. Alcuin (late 8th cent.), taught the warrior Charlemagne about the biblical uses of sword: the sword of God's Word and the sword of vengeance. Charlemagne has them both but he must avoid feuding.

The most famous mnemonic is attributed to Augustine of Dacia in his *Rotulus Pugillaris* (ca. 1260): "The letter teaches what happened, allegory what you should believe, the moral what you should do, and the anagogical where you are heading." Allegory was supremely about finding Christ in the Scriptures, and this was the basis of the other two spiritual senses. "What their exegesis was looking for was not 'metaphysical truths'; it was the traces of the living, personal, incarnate, vivifying Truth" (De Lubac, 1986).

Even those scholars for whom the Bible's literal sense mattered a great deal, such as Andrew of St. Victor, the allegorical was always the most Christian sense, with the moral sense contingent on the doctrinal understanding of the mysteries of the faith, rather than as something available to the natural person. Allegory is the doctrinal sense of it all; in terms of an architectural metaphor that became popular, the "edifice of doctrine" was required for the edification of the faith (Gregory the Great). Allegory would always serve an ethical construction; allegory is the walls, tropology (which can be anagogic or moral) is the roof. For monks such as Hugh of St. Victor, the uplift of the anagogical sense was a summons to contemplation.

Thomas Aquinas wanted to restrict allegory to Scripture only, but Dante advocated a "poet's allegory." The Bible did provide Dante with prime material for allegory, however. Dante, by making Virgil and biblical characters in his *Divine Comedy* more real people in their afterlife than they were in their earthly existence, did not so much secularize these people as show how human beings are most themselves in their end-state. What Dante seems to have done is, by allegorizing, make the figures of the blessed have something to say for now.

E. The Decline and Revisioning of Allegory

Martin Luther disdained allegory, not least where such readings made the Bible speak of abstract heavenly matters, detached from the everyday and sinful experience of the biblical writers and Luther's Christian flock. Such a detachment may well have been operative in the work of late medieval commentators. J. W. von Goethe (18th cent.) preferred the figural to the allegorical, seeing the general in the particular, rather than using a particular to illustrate a general, for Carl Jung (20th cent.) allegory was too "conscious" to be useful in reading sacred texts; it was mechanical rather than organic.

Today there is a new appreciation of allegory and its spiritual senses, because allegory allows a spiritual interpretation rather than a historical interpretation voided of anything other than academic relevance for the church. *See* ARCHETYPE; BIBLICAL INTERPRETATION, HISTORY OF; JESUS, METAPHORS FOR; LITERARY INTERPRETATION, NT; LITERARY INTERPRETATION, OT; METAPHOR IN THEOLOGY; TYPOLOGY.

Bibliography: David Dawson. *Allegorical Readers and Cultural Revision in Ancient Alexandria* (1992); David Dawson. *Christian Figural Reading and the Fashioning of Identity* (2002); Henri De Lubac. *Medieval Exegesis* (1998); Robert Lamberton. *Homer the Theologian: Neoplatonist Allegorical Reading and the Growth of the Epic Tradition* (1986); C. S. Lewis. *The Allegory of Love: A Study in Medieval Tradition* (1938); Jon Whitman. *The Dynamics of an Ancient and Medieval Technique* (1987); Frances Young. *Biblical Exegesis and the Formation of Christian Culture* (1997).

MARK W. ELLIOTT

ALLELUIA al'uh-loo'yuh. Translation of the Hebrew word halleluyah (הללויה) as it appears in the Latin Vulgate. *See* HALLELUJAH.

ALLIANCE בְּרִית berith, חָתַן khathan]. When Judah makes alliances with Ephraim or Aram (1 Kgs 15:19; 2 Chr 16:3), the word is berith, a term translated "covenant" in other contexts (*see* COVENANT, OT). Similarly, the "allies" of Abraham (Gen 14:13) are more literally the "masters of Abraham's berith: and in Obad 7 Edom's "allies" are the "men of your berith."

The NRSV uses "covenant," "treaty," and "compact" as well as "alliance" to refer to such political alliances. In Gen 21:22-34 Abraham and Abimelech make a berith following conflict over the use of a well, an agreement to live at peace with each other and not be in conflict over this issue (a key issue in wilderness areas); both parties seem to have equal standing in making the agreement. In Josh 9, the Gibeonites trick Israel into making a "treaty" with them (compare 1 Sam 11:1-2; 1 Kgs 5:12; 20:34; Isa 33:8; Hos 12:1). David and Abner make an alliance on the basis of which Abner will support David's bid for the throne and get Ephraim in general to come into alliance with him (2 Sam 3:12-13, 21; 5:3; in 1 Chr 11:3 the alliance-makers are implicitly Israel as a whole). The priest Jehoiada makes a compact with the palace and temple guards to crown the young Joash on the throne in place of his Baal-inclined mother Athaliah (2 Kgs 11:4; 2 Chr 23:1). The "empty oaths"

with which people "make covenants" in Hos 10:4 may refer to the agreements between people and king that the people fail to observe in that they keep assassinating their kings. In Ps 83:5 various peoples make a covenant to attack Israel, though the psalm says they are allying "against you [Yahweh]." Ephraim makes a "treaty" with Assyria (Hos 12:1). Daniel 9:27 refers to a berith that constitutes an alliance between reformist Jews and Greeks in the context of the Antiochene crisis. The "covenant of kinship" that Tyre failed to observe when it "delivered whole communities over to Edom" (Amos 1:9) likely refers to an alliance that put Tyre in kinship-type relationship with people whom it then betrayed by transporting them as slaves; treaty partners can refer to each other as brothers (compare 1 Kgs 20:31-34).

Other occurrences of "alliance" represent the verbs אָסַף 'asaf "gather together" (Judg 3:13) or חָתַן khathan "make a marriage alliance" (1 Kgs 3:1; 2 Chr 18:1; Dan 11:6, 23) or the noun מַסֵּכָה massekhah "weaving" (Isa 30:1).

JOHN GOLDINGAY

ALLOGENES [Ἀλλογενής Allogenēs]. A COPTIC treatise discovered at NAG HAMMADI (NHC 11, 3) in which Allogenes, whose name means "stranger" and who may represent SETH, records for his "son," Messos, the divine revelations he received. Through its monism the work perhaps displays some connection with the traditions of PLATO.

ALLON al'on [אַלּוֹן 'allon]. Naming meaning *oak*. Simeonite Son of Jedaiah and father of Shiphi (1 Chr 4:37), a priest at the time of King Hezekiah. *See* ELON; SIMEON, SIMEONITES.

ALLON-BACUTH al'uhn-bak'uhth [אַלּוֹן בָּכוּת 'allon bakhuth]. Located near BETHEL, the burial site of REBEKAH's nurse DEBORAH, was named Allon-Bacuth, which means "the oak of weeping" (Gen 35:8). This may be a literary allusion to the palm of Deborah in Judg 4:5.

ALLOTMENT OF LAND. According to the Bible, the areas of tribal settlement in the land of Canaan were determined by lot. The procedure followed the subjugation of the land and its kings and initiated the process by which the tribes occupied their territories. The allocation of land by lot completed the divine charge given to Joshua; that is, to bring the Israelites into their inheritance (Josh 1:6).

The casting of lots rendered the allocation of land as a sacred act and reinforced the conviction that God gave the land of Canaan to Israel (compare Josh 1:2, 3; 2:14; 5:6). The territory assigned by God through the lot became a tribe's "inheritance" (נַחֲלָה nakhalah) and "possession" (יְרֻשָּׁה yerushah). The former term (and its verbal equivalent) occurs forty-five times during the description of the allotments (Josh 13–21) and denotes the idea of a legitimate and perpetual claim. The latter, expressed by the verb yarash, signifies the actual occupation of the territory (Josh 1:11; 13:1; 18:3; 21:43 [Heb. 21:41]). Both modify as God's promise to give the land as an inheritance (Deut 4:21; 19:10; 20:16; 21:23; 24:4; 26:1), as a possession (Deut 3:18; 5:13; 12:1; 19:2, 14; 21:1), and as an inheritance to possess (Deut 15:4; 25:19). The ritual allocation of lands by lot therefore expressed the decision of the God who gave the land and thereby established each tribe's rightful claim of ownership to the territory it occupied.

The practice of assigning land by lot incorporated legal conventions well attested in ancient Near Eastern literature. There are particularly strong correlations with Mesopotamian texts that stipulate the means by which the estate of a patriarch can be divided among his heirs. The texts indicate that an estate remained the common property and responsibility of the heirs until they were ready to take their inheritances. When they decided to divide the estate, an administrator was appointed among the coheirs, the estate was dissolved, squatters were evicted, and the property was partitioned by lot. Farther afield, Greek colonial accounts report the division of newly acquired lands by lot after oracular consultation.

The book of Joshua reports that Joshua, along with Eleazar the priest, distributed the tribal inheritances by lot "as the Lord had commanded Moses" (14:2). The report looks back to two Mosaic directives, set prior to Israel's entry into Canaan, that implicitly link the nation and the land; the first (Num 26:52-56) occurs after an enumeration of the people who would enter Canaan, while the second (Num 34:13) occurs after a description of the boundaries of the land. The intent of the Mosaic commandments, however, is not entirely clear. Moses first declares that each tribe should be apportioned land in proportion to its population (26:53-54); large tribes should receive larger areas and small tribes smaller areas. Yet immediately thereafter, Moses decrees that the land should be apportioned by lot (v. 55). The two commands, then, appear to prescribe different decision-making procedures for allocating tribal territories, one human and the other divine. Although modern interpreters have suggested various explanations for this discrepancy, the best solution remains that of Abravanel, a medieval rabbinical scholar, who proposed that the general areas of settlement were determined by lot to avoid conflict among the tribes and, once determined, were adjusted accordingly relative to tribal populations.

The allotment of tribal lands in Joshua takes place in two distinct phases. The first, evidently set at Gilgal, relates the apportionment of land to the tribes of Judah, Ephraim, and the half-tribe of Manasseh and includes a number of anecdotes associated with the tribes (14:1–17:18). The second takes place at Shiloh, before the tent of meeting, and begins with a rebuke of the seven remaining tribes (18:1–19:51). Lying outside this scheme are two other tribal groups. The tribes that settle east of the Jordan (Reuben, Gad, and the half-tribe of Manasseh) ostensibly occupy lands outside the land the Lord promised to Israel (compare Josh 22:19). Their lands are not allocated by lot but are parceled out by Moses (Deut 3:12-17; Josh 13:8, 14, 29; 18:7), implicitly diminishing the claim of the territory the tribes occupy in the Transjordan. The second group, the tribe of Levi, does not receive land as an inheritance but does receive cities among the tribal possessions. The lot designates the cities and allocates them to the Levitical clans (Josh 21:4, 8, 9-10, 20, 40; compare Num 35:1-8).

The two-phase allotment of territory suggests a process that included the scaling back of claims and settlement. The description of remaining land that precedes the first allotment of territories (13:1-6) defines the land more extensively than the area actually covered by all the allotments. In other words, there is a discrepancy between the area of land that is "given" and the land actually occupied (compare Josh 1:4). Comparison of the individual allotments reveals a measure of overlap between the territories Judah, Ephraim, half-Manasseh (phase one) and the seven tribes (phase two). An editorial note explicitly reports that the inheritance of Simeon lay within the territory of Judah, and a number of the cities allotted to Simeon are listed in the southern district of the territory allotted to Judah (compare Josh 19:1-9 with 15:21-32). Likewise, some of the towns allotted to Dan appear also in the allotment of Judah (compare Josh 19:41-46 with 15:33, 45). In addition, the description of Manasseh's allotment reports the existence of Manassite cities within the territories of Issachar and Asher (Josh 17:11). As noted above, the designation of Levitical cities explicitly testifies to the practice of reserving a portion of one tribe's land for settlement by another. Finally, the challenge that the Cisjordanian tribes make to those in the Transjordan, that they take property for themselves west of the Jordan (Josh 22:19), implicitly confirms a procedure whereby some tribes might make room for others to settle within their lands. With these examples in mind, it is plausible that the major tribes successfully occupied lands originally allotted to them and that the second allocation, Shiloh, represents a longer, extended process by which the seven remaining tribes occupied at least some of the land already settled by Judah and the Joseph tribes.

The tribal allotments are reconfigured in Ezekiel's vision of the land, which presumes the more expansive boundaries (Ezek 47:13–48:7). Ezekiel approximates the roles of Moses and Joshua in the vision, both commanding that the land be allotted among the tribes as an inheritance and defining the geographical relationships between them. These relationships, however, are different from those prescribed in Joshua, and, corresponding to the idealized character of the vision, each tribal territory constitutes an equal portion. *See* CONQUEST; TRIBES, TERRITORIES OF.

Bibliography: E. Assis. "'How Long Are You Slack to Go to Possess the Land' (Jos. xviii 3): Ideal and Reality in the Distribution Descriptions in Joshua xiii–xix." *VT* 53 (2003) 1–25; N. C. Habel. *The Land Is Mine: Six Biblical Land Ideologies* (1995) 33–35, 54–75; A. M. Kitz. "Undivided Inheritance and Lot Casting in the Book of Joshua." *JBL* 119 (2000) 600–618; J. Milgrom. *Numbers.* JPS Torah Commentary (1990) 480–82.

L. DANIEL HAWK

ALLOY. *See* METALLURGY.

ALMIGHTY [παντοκράτωρ pantokratōr]. The term *Almighty* is derived from the Greek word pantokratōr, which is an interpretation of the Hebrew divine name shaddai. In the NT, the epithet appears mostly in the book of Revelation (*see also* 2 Cor 6:18).

The emphasis on divine sovereignty and power inherent in the term may have been intended as a response to the claim of universal power claimed by Alexander the Great and subsequent rulers in the Hellenistic and Roman empires. In the face of the threats and claims of divine superiority by hostile powers, the faithful emphasized that it is their God who is *Almighty. See* EL-SHADDA; GOD, NAMES OF.

C. L. SEOW

ALMODAD al-moh´dad [אַלְמוֹדָד ʾalmodhadh]. The first son of Joktan, a sixth generation descendant of Shem and one of seventy descendants of Noah (Gen 10:26). The listing of 6 generations highlights the importance of Almodad's branch of the family, from which Abraham was born (1 Chr 1:24). His family settled along the Arabian Peninsula during the population of the area after the flood, setting the stage for the migration from Ur that began the ancestral history.

JOAN E. COOK

ALMON al´muhn [עַלְמוֹן ʿalmon]. Almon is one of four towns allocated for the Levites out of Benjamin's portion (Josh 21:18), but it is not included in the list of Benjamin's towns in Josh 18:21-28. It may be the same as the town ALEMETH (1 Chr 6:60). Almon has been identified as Khirbet Almit northeast of Anata.

EMILY CHENEY

ALMOND [לוז luz, שָׁקֵד shaqedh]. Almonds (*Amygdalus communis*) were one of the gifts sent by Jacob to Egypt (Gen 43:11). The root shqd means "to watch, wake," a play on words used in Jer 1:11. Aaron's staff produced almonds overnight as a sign of Yahweh's choice (Num 17:8-23). The cups of the lamp stand in the Tabernacle looked like almond blossoms (Exod 25:33-34; 37:19-20). White hair is compared to the

almond (Eccl 12:5). The remains of almonds have been found at Iron Age Tel el-Ful (Gibeah) and Bethlehem.

Bibliography: Oded Borowski. *Agriculture in Iron Age Israel* (1987).

DAVID LIPOVITCH

ALMON-DIBLATHAIM al´muhn-dib´luh-thay´im [עַלְמֹן דִּבְלָתָיְמָה ʿalmon divlathayim]. Possibly the same as BETH-DIBLATHAIM (Jer 48:22), it is one of the sites the Israelites visited when traveling from KADESH-BARNEA to Moab (Num 33:46-47). The text situates it near the Wadi Zered, close to Moab's border with EDOM (Deut 2:13).

ALMS, ALMSGIVING [ἐλεημοσύνη eleēmosunē]. Almsgiving is a benevolent activity for the poor and needy given out of compassion, mercy, and pity. Alms can be money, food, or actions in kind. In fact the Hebrew word for alms, or almsgiving is not found in the OT. However, a spirit of charity pervades throughout the Torah and the pronouncements of the Prophets who advocate the rights of the poor. It is generally known that in LXX, eleēmosune does not mean almsgiving but righteousness or kindness of God (Ps 103:6; Isa 1:27; 28:17) and of humankind (Gen 47:29; Prov 19:22; 20:28; 21:21).

The origin of almsgiving is theologically founded on the exodus of the Israelites from Egypt. God is presented as frequently reminding the Israelites of this unique event, when God gave divine commandments on behalf of the widows, orphans, and strangers who represented the lower orders of society throughout the history of Israel (Deut 24:17-18; 10:18-20; 27:19; Exod 22:21-27).

One can enumerate several organized systems of relief or almsgiving directed specially to the well-being of the poor and destitute in the Torah, and these systems are emphasised by the rabbis in the MISHNAH. First, there is the prescription of the second tithe for the poor in the third and sixth year of every sabbatical cycle (Deut 14:28-29; 26:12). A second edict is related to the Sabbath law on cultivation of crops, by which God commanded the Israelites to let the land lie unploughed and unused during the seventh year, so that the poor might get food from it (Exod 23:10-11). A third edict concerns the regulations about the harvest which enabled the poor to claim "the three customary rights" that served to relieve the poor from hunger and starvation. A fourth edict is found in the decrees of the Year of Jubilee. If anyone who was impoverished had been forced to part with his inheritance, he could reclaim it in the Year of Jubilee (Lev 25:25-28). Also, interest loans were forbidden for the sake of the poor (*see* LOAN; MONEY), so that the poor were to borrow money at no cost, when needed (Lev 25:39-55): according to Leviticus if an impoverished Israelite should sell himself into slavery, he might have expected more favorable terms than the non-Israelite, and he was also entitled by the law to go free at the Jubilee.

Thus, it is clear that Judaism traces its practice of almsgiving back to Torah. Poor people in early Judaism were not wholly despised and neglected but remembered throughout its history (Deut 15:11). Accordingly, almsgiving was regarded later in Judaism as one of the three pillars of the world, along with the Torah and the Temple service.

In the NT, Jesus exhorts almsgiving in line with the teachings of the OT. According to the gospels, almsgiving to take care of the needs of the poor and the destitute is one of the characteristics which a disciple of Jesus should display. However, each evangelist approaches the issue from his own perspectives, so that the definition of almsgiving and the degree to which it is emphasized varies. Mark does not refer to eleēmosunē at all. Matthew makes use of it three times only in chapter 6 (Matt 6:2, 3, 4); his attribution does not appear to be a positive one because the term is mentioned as a part of Jesus' critique of the Pharisees' hypocrisy on prayer and fasting (Matt 6:1-16). In contrast, Luke's exhortations to almsgiving are positive admonitions (Luke 11:41/Matt 23:26; Luke 12:33/Matt 6:19-20).

Apart from these explicit references to almsgiving, Luke's repeated references to the poor (πτωχός ptōchos) in the Gospel of Luke may well disclose that he has a special interest in almsgiving. While Mark and Matthew make use of ptōchos five times in their gospels (Mark 10:21; 12:42, 43; 14:5, 7; Matt 5:3; 11:5; 19:21; 26:9, 11), and John refers to the term four times (John 12:5, 6, 8; 13:29), Luke refers to it nine times (Luke 4:18; 6:20; 7:22; 14:13, 21; 18:22; 19:8; 21:2, 3). Given Luke's particular concerns about wealth and poverty, it is not surprising that his work came to be called "the gospel for the poor" (Luke 4:18), which can be confirmed in Acts where eleēmosune is used eight times (3:2, 3, 10; 9:36; 10:2, 4, 31; 24:17).

It is rather surprising, however, that in the Pauline epistles the almsgiving motif is, when compared with the attention it receives in the gospels, poorly developed. There is no exhortation comparable to the one Jesus commands: "sell your possessions and give alms to the poor." The matter of the poor does not seem to be accentuated as a separate agenda. Instead it is mentioned in passing as Paul tackles the factionalism of the Corinthian church revealed in the improper institution of the Lord's supper (1 Cor 11:17-34).

Taking into account the bulk of material on the contribution, gifts, or financial aid (διακονία diakonia) of the Gentile churches for the Jerusalem Church (2 Cor 8–9), it appears that the motif of almsgiving in the Pauline epistles is less a personal and individual way of charity than it is an organizational and ecclesiastical way of doing good. Paul delivered money collected from the Gentile churches to the poverty-stricken Jerusalem church (Acts 11:27-29; Rom 15:25-27; Gal 2:10; 2 Cor 8:20; 9:13) perhaps as an attempt to build unity between the churches through spiritual congeniality.

It is generally acknowledged that James gives more explicit attention to almsgiving than Paul. Rigorous reproach of the wealthy (Jas 5:1-6), along with sympathetic concern for the poor and the needy (Jas 2:1-9), earn James' book the designation 'the Epistle for the Poor.'

Bibliography: Kyoung-Jin Kim. *Stewardship and Almsgiving in Luke's Theology* (1998).

KYOUNG-JIN KIM

ALMUG al´muhg [אַלְמֻג ʾalmugh, אַלְמֻגִּים ʾalmuggim; ξύλα ἀπελέκητα xyla apelekēta]. A type of wood used in the construction of the Temple of Solomon brought from Ophir by Hiram of Tyre. It was also used to make harps and lyres for the Temple (1 Kgs 10:11-12). In the account in the book of Chronicles this wood is called "ALGUM wood." The attestation of a cognate term (almg) in a list of raw materials from Late Bronze Age Ugarit suggests that almug is the correct reading and that algum is an error of transposition. The exact type of tree represented is still, however, uncertain. The LXX translates algum wood as xyla apelekēta, "unhewn or rough wood." Josephus (*Ant.* 1.176-78) says that it is a special pine wood. Almug is most commonly identified with red sandalwood (*Pterocarpus santalinus*) or white sandalwood (*Santalum album*) from India or Sri Lanka. These types of wood are used in manufacturing musical instruments and are known for their fine scent.

DAVID LIPOVITCH

ALOES al´ohz [אֲהָלִים ʾahalim, אֲהָלוֹת ʾahaloth; ἀλόη aloē]. References in the OT to aloes are most likely based on lign-aloes or eaglewood (*Aquilaria agallocha*), a tree that may grow to 120 ft. and is native to northern Burma and Malaysia. The fragrant resinous wood that was cut up into chips for transport by traders is, in fact, the result of a fungal disease that infects the tree. It was used, along with myrrh and cassia, to perfume robes (Ps 45:8 [9]) or, along with CINNAMON and MYRRH, to freshen the bed (Prov 7:17). While the resin has a distinct and pleasing odor, it is sweeter when burned as incense like FRANKINCENSE and myrrh (Song 4:14). Aloe was so prized that it forms part of Balaam's idyllic characterization of God's blessing of Israel's encampments (Num 24:6). There is an almost Eden-like quality to this exotic image of luxuriant trees, and flowing buckets that abundantly water their seed. The NT story of Nicodemus' use of myrrh and aloe to anoint Jesus' body after the crucifixion (John 19:39) refers to another plant (*Aloe vera*) native to southwest Arabia. The large quantity (100 lbs.) brought by Nicodemus is an indication of the honor he wished to bestow on the body. The yellowish leaf juice was drained and formed into hardened blocks for easy transport to markets where it was sold as an embalming spice and a purge. *See* PERFUME; PLANTS OF THE BIBLE; SPICES.

VICTOR H. MATTHEWS

ALPHA [α A a]. The first letter of the Greek alphabet. The letter derives from the Phoenician *ʾalp, the voiceless glottal stop, which was not needed in Greek, so the sign was put to use as a vowel letter representing a. In Rev 1:8 and 22:13, the letter is used (with ω, OMEGA, the last letter of the Greek alphabet) to emphasize both God and Christ as the source, creator, and redeemer of all existence. *See* ALPHABET; ALPHA AND OMEGA.

P. KYLE MCCARTER, JR.

ALPHA AND OMEGA [τὸ ἄλφα καὶ τὸ ὦ to alpha kai to ō]. The first and last letters of the Greek alphabet, used metaphorically as God's self-description (Rev 1:8; 21:6) and that of Jesus (Rev 22:13) in the visions of Revelation. These are the only occasions where God speaks directly in Revelation, and constitute portrayals of God and Christ as the beginning and the end of all things, fittingly occurring at the beginning and the end of the book itself. The phrase echoes the book's stress on defining God in terms of time, as in the similar phrase, "who was and is and is to come" (1:4). Clearly the apocalyptic focus of the book makes God's rule over time of primary concern. But "alpha and omega" also expresses Revelation's use of the phenomenon of writing as symbolic in itself. Existence and its meaning are seen as a text, a scroll that would have remained sealed and unread if not for the Christ, whose death enables him to open it (5:1-10). So Christ is the means by which the contents of the scroll are conveyed and, at the same time, he is the contents. God, and Christ as divine, is every letter of what is written in human experience, from creation to apocalypse. What will be, according to the scrolls that Revelation's narrator sees and even eats (5:1; 10:9), is in this sense a playing out of who God is, in relation to humanity.

NICOLE DURAN WILKINSON

ALPHABET. Despite their sometimes-striking differences in appearance, the myriad of alphabets, ancient and modern, are cousins, descendants of a common ancestor devised some 4,000 years ago. The proof of this kinship is the fact that all alphabets are based on a common principle, namely, that a single sign represents a single sound of a language. In most cases the alphabetic signs are graphic, so that an alphabet is a type of writing system. The signs of the earliest alphabet were *picto*graphic, but the pictures were soon simplified into abstract linear shapes, and the vast majority of subsequent alphabets have been linear. There are exceptions to this generality, such as the cuneiform alphabets of the Late Bronze Age, in which the letters are not linear (drawn) but formed of combinations of wedges pressed into clay; certain modern alphabets in which the letters are not linear or even graphic, such as the semaphore alphabet, in which the letters are signaled using flags or other devices; or the several forms of manual signing, in which the letters are represented by various positions of the hands and fingers. Apart from such exceptions,

though, alphabets tend to be graphic and linear, consisting of a discrete set of signs that represent in visual form the individual sounds of a language.

A. Origin of the Alphabet
B. Names and Letters of the Alphabet
C. Order of the Letters of the Alphabet
D. Early Development of the Alphabet
E. National Scripts of the Alphabet
F. Transmission of the Alphabet to Greece
Bibliography

A. Origin of the Alphabet

Writing systems were invented in Mesopotamia and Egypt over 5,000 years ago. However, these systems were not alphabets. Alphabetic writing, invented by speakers of a Semitic language, seems first to have appeared approximately one millennium later, as explained below. In their speech, every syllable began with a consonant. By devising a group of graphic signs corresponding to the consonantal sounds of their language, they were able to create a simple writing system that, even without vowel signs, represented their speech adequately. Although it would be incorrect to describe this first alphabet as borrowing from Egyptian writing, it seems clear that features of Egyptian writing inspired it. Of the various types of signs used in Egyptian hieroglyphics many were phonetic, representing one, two, or three consonantal sounds. The first of these groups—the uniconsonantal signs—were functionally alphabetic, since each of them corresponded to a single consonantal sound. If the Egyptian scribes had chosen to write only with the uniconsonantal signs, we might credit them with having invented the alphabet. They never did so, however, so that the invention was left to others, evidently speakers of a Semitic language who were familiar enough with the Egyptian system to recognize the advantage of adapting the "alphabetic" principal embedded in the uniconsonantal signs to their own needs. It follows that the historical context in which the alphabet was invented should be sought in a place where Semitic speakers lived in close contact with Egyptian culture, and in fact the oldest surviving alphabetic inscriptions derive from such a context.

The earliest examples of alphabetic writing so far discovered come from the Sinai peninsula and Upper Egypt. Most of these were found in the vicinity of Serābiṭ el-Ḥādem, a remote site in the southwestern Sinai about 12 mi. east of the Gulf of Suez and 55 mi. northwest of St. Catherine's monastery and the Jebel Musa. In pharaonic times the Serābiṭ plateau was the center of the primary Egyptian turquoise mining region and a principal seat of the worship of the goddess Hathor, "the Mistress of Turqoise." In 1904–05 Flinders Petrie conducted a survey of the mines and temple precinct, during which he examined and recorded not only a large number of Egyptian hieroglyphic inscriptions but also an enigmatic group of rock-cut graffiti that were not Egyptian. Petrie regarded these Proto-Sinaitic inscriptions, as they later came to be called, as a "local barbarism," but in a 1915 watershed study Alan Gardiner showed that they are written in a primitive form of the Semitic alphabet that is ancestral to the Phoenician script and its derivatives (see below). Noting the pictorial form of the Proto-Sinaitic signs, Gardiner was able to demonstrate further that the alphabet was invented as a pictographic system based on an acrophonic principle. To explain, each individual sign was drawn as a rudimentary picture of a common object, the name of which began with the consonantal sound that the sign was used to represent in writing. Thus, for example, a schematic sketch of the floor plan of a house represented *b*, the sound at the beginning of the early Semitic word for "house" (*bayt-), or a drawing of the wavy surface of a body of water represent *m*, the first sound in the early Semitic word for "water" (*maym- or *mawm-). Following this line of reasoning Gardiner was able to decipher a sequence of signs that occurs in a number of the inscriptions, especially those found in the temple precinct. The five-letter sequence is lbʿlt, in which Gardiner recognized the dedicatory phrase "to Baʿlat." Baʿlat, "the (divine) Lady," was the name or epithet of a major Semitic goddess, who was known to be identified with Hathor, the Egyptian goddess to whom the Serābiṭ shrine was dedicated.

Building on Gardiner's insight, W. F. Albright and other scholars were eventually able to identify with a high degree of probability the consonantal values of about half of the thirty or so Proto-Sinaitic signs. Even so, the alphabetic texts from Serābiṭ have so far resisted a comprehensive interpretation. Most of the inscriptions are in poor condition, and even the most extensively preserved have yielded to no more than partial decipherment. Nevertheless, the general character of the corpus seems well understood. Gardiner's lbʿlt, "to Baʿlat," is representative of the content of the inscriptions found in the sacred precinct, where dedicatory texts are to be expected, and a corresponding key word in the inscriptions from the mines is ʾrḥt, "expedition" (compare biblical Hebrew אֹרְחָת ʾōrḥāt, "travelling company, caravan, expedition," in Gen 37:25). This meaning of ʾrḥt (not "wild cow," as Albright supposed) is strongly favored by the analysis of the alphabetic texts from the mines in light of Egyptian hieroglyphic texts found in the same area; the latter frequently refer to or commemorate one of the many expeditions to the region, testifying to the faithfulness with which the leader of the expedition (usually the speaker in the text) carried out the wishes of the king who commissioned his project, and boasting of the success of the mission.

The date of the alphabetic texts from Serābiṭ el-Ḥādem is established by, among other things, the presence of one of the inscriptions (Sinai 345) alongside an Egyptian text on a small sphinx found in the temple precinct and now held in the British Museum. Leading historians of Egyptian art now agree that this object, with its bilingual inscription, is a product of the late Middle Kingdom, that is, the end of the Twelfth or the Thirteenth Dynasty—in short, the late 19th or early 18th cent. BCE. This date corresponds well with the fact that the great preponderance of references to Semitic participants in the Serābiṭ mining operations come from Egyptian inscriptions of the Middle Kingdom.

Primitive alphabetic inscriptions have also been found in Egypt proper. In the 1994–95 season of their survey of ancient inscriptions left in the desert roads west of ancient Thebes (modern Luxor), John and Deborah Darnell examined two non-Egyptian graffiti cut into the walls of a depression called the Wadi el-Ḥol ("Valley of Terror"), which lies roughly at the mid-point of the Luxor-Farshût road that transects the Qena bend of the Nile. The script of the two inscriptions is almost identical to that of the alphabetic texts from Serābiṭ el-Ḥādem, which, as already pointed out, probably date to the Egyptian Middle Kingdom, and the character of the Egyptian graffiti found in and near the Wadi el-Ḥol shows that this route was heavily trafficked by private individuals and lower-level government officials during the same period (the Twelfth and Thirteenth Dynasties). One of these travelers, a certain Bebi, who is known from other Middle Kingdom sources, is given the title "overseer of the expeditionary force of the Asiatics," and the presence in the region of "Asiatics" (Egyptian ʿЗm.w), that is, natives of Canaan and Syria and therefore most probably speakers of a Semitic language, provides the context for the appearance there of very early alphabetic texts.

The convergence of chronology between the primitive alphabetic inscriptions from the Sinai and the Thebaid, both of which might be dated to the late 19th or early 18th cent. BCE, suggests that the Serābiṭ el-Ḥādem and Wadi el-Ḥol inscriptions are likely to be roughly contemporary examples of a single, widespread phenomenon in Middle Kingdom Egypt and its provinces, in which "Asiatics," as the Egyptians called them, were living and producing documents in their own Semitic dialects, using an incipient writing system we now call the alphabet. Moreover, the well-preserved pictographic character of these earliest alphabetic inscriptions suggests that they were not far removed from the time at which the alphabet was actually invented. When compared to Egyptian hieroglyphic writing, various formal characteristics of the alphabetic letters themselves tend to point to a period overlapping from the latter part of the First Intermediate Period and the early part of the Middle Kingdom, that is, from the middle of the 21st to the first part of the 20th cent. BCE. Some Egyptologists have described this period as a time of innovation and experimentation in Egyptian writing or, to put it another way, a time when the rigidity of the rules for writing Egyptian were relaxed somewhat. There is some evidence of a substantial increase in Egyptian literacy in the Middle Kingdom, a phenomenon that seems confirmed by inscriptions left in the Wadi el-Hol in the late Middle Kingdom by low-ranking soldiers and individuals with relatively humble titles. This points to a broadening of literacy in which even foreigners may have found a way to participate.

When these special features of writing and literacy are considered together, they favor a hypothesis proposing the late First Intermediate or early Middle Kingdom as the time when the alphabet was invented—in round numbers, ca. 2000 BCE. At the same time, these features reinforce the probability, already noted, that the *place* of invention was a location where speakers of Semitic languages lived and Egyptian writing was abundant. It might seem most logical to seek a location for the birthplace of the alphabet in Syria-Canaan itself, since the inventors were evidently native to that region. On the other hand, since we must assign the alphabetic inscriptions from Sinai and Upper Egypt a Middle Kingdom date, and a time of invention even earlier, in the late First Intermediate–*early* Middle Kingdom, there is no *a priori* reason to look outside of Egypt itself, with its extensive "Asiatic" population, for the place of invention. And indeed Canaan and southern Syria in this period, the end of Early Bronze IV or beginning of Middle Bronze I, was not a hospitable environment for such an invention. The restoration of urban culture, which had collapsed at the end of the 3rd millennium, was not yet fully under way. The Egyptian tale of Sinuhe, dating to the mid-20th cent. BCE, indicates that there was *some* Egyptian presence in the hinterlands of southern Syria and northern Canaan at this time, but it is unlikely to have consisted of more than small communities of expatriates and refugees like Sinuhe himself. On the other hand, there is ample literary and archaeological evidence of the presence of Asiatics in large numbers in Egypt at this time. Already in the First Intermediate period they had begun to penetrate the Egyptian frontier, and the number burgeoned in the Middle Kingdom. Sometimes they came as refugees from hardships in Canaan, sometimes as skilled workers seeking Egyptian employment. Sometimes the Egyptians resisted their arrival, sometimes they were welcomed, and sometimes they came involuntarily as prisoners of war. But they were present in abundance in Middle Kingdom Egypt, and it now seems probable (not certain) that it was there, amid the highly literate culture of the Nile Valley, that Semitic-speaking Asiatics invented the alphabet that *mutatis mutandis* we still use today.

B. Names of the Letters of the Alphabet

The traditional names of the letters evidently survive from the time of the origin of the alphabet, being derived from the pictographs, which, according to the acrophonic principle, were used to represent the initial sounds of the objects they depicted. These old names survive in slightly variant form in the letter names of the Hebrew-Aramaic and Greek alphabets, both of which were derived from the Phoenician, as explained below.

The Hebrew-Aramaic letter names are given below, together with the original forms and, when they are known, the meanings of the names. The asterisk before the original names signifies that the word is a hypothetical showing the probable form that evolved into the letter names in Phoenician, Hebrew, Aramaic, Greek, and so on. Note that the traditional names are neither purely Canaanite (Phoenician) nor purely Aramaic, but show some dialect mixing—compare bet (contracted from original *bayt-) with ʿayin (uncontracted from original *ʿayn-).

Letter	Name	Original Name	Original Acrophonic Meaning
א	ʾalef	*ʾalp-	"ox"
ב	bet	*bayt-	"house"
ג	gimel	*gaml-	"throw-stick"
ד	dalet	*dalt-	"door," but the shape seems to derive from a by-form, *digg-, "fish"
ה	he	unknown	unknown
ו	waw	*waww-	"hook"
ז	zayin	*zayn	unknown, and the shape may derive from δ (delta), after δ merged with *z
ח	khet	*khayt- or *khit-	unknown, but the shape seems to derive from *harm, "fence," after *h merged with *kh
ט	tet	*tayt- or *tit-	unknown
י	yod	*yad-	"[fore]arm"
כ ך	kaf	*kaff-	"palm [of hand]"
ל	lamed	*lamd-	"ox-goad"
מ ם	mem	*maym-	"water"
נ ן	nun	*nun-	"serpent"[?], though the shape may derive from a by-form, *nakhsh-, "snake"
ס	samek	*samk-	unknown
ע	ʿayin	*ʿayn-	"eye"
פ ף	pe	unknown	unknown
צ ץ	tsade	unknown	unknown
ק	qof	unknown	unknown
ר	resh	*riʾsh-	"head"
שׁ, שׂ	shin, sin	*tann-	"composite bow"
ת	taw	*taww-	"[writer's] mark"

C. Order of the Letters of the Alphabet

The traditional ABC order of the alphabet as it is still known today is thousands of years old. Exactly how closely its origin approaches the invention of the alphabet 4,000 years ago is unknown, but it is very early. Essentially the same sequence is found in cuneiform texts from the 14th cent. BCE, found at Raš Šamra, ancient Ugarit, listing the letters of the alphabet in order. Such a text is called an abecedary. The Ugaritic abecedaries that follow the ABC order list the letters as follows: ʾa, b, g, ḫ, d, h, w, z, ḥ, ṭ, y, k, š, l, m, ḏ, n, z̧, s, ʿ, p, ṣ, q, r, t̪, ġ, t, ʾi, ʾu, ś. This sequence is identical to that of the later alphabet, as it is known from Canaanite and Hebrew-Aramaic abecedaries, except in two respects. First, since Ugaritic retained a larger consonantal inventory than later related languages, several consonants that would eventually merge with other consonants are still independent and hold their original position in the alphabet; these include ḫ (which would merge with ḥ as ח ḥet), š (which would merge with t as ש šin), ḏ (which would merge with z as ז zayin), z̧ (which would merge with ṣ as צ ṣade), ġ (which would merge with ʿ as ע ʿayin) and apparently ś (though the status of this sign is not entirely clear). Second, the Ugaritic alphabet has three ʾalep signs—marked as in a syllabic system for the accompanying vowels as ʾa, ʾi and ʾu—and the second and third of these signs are added at the end of the sequence.

In addition to the familiar ABC arrangement there is a second traditional order of the alphabet that is also quite ancient. This is the so-called halaḥam alphabet used in the writing of Classical Ethiopic (Ge'ez), which preserves the script and language traditions of the Old South Arabian peoples, whose inscriptions are attested as early as the 8th cent. BCE. The antiquity of this alternative alphabetic tradition is proven by its presence in two cuneiform abecedaries of the Late Bronze Age, found at Beth Shemesh in 1933 and at Raš Šamra in 1988. The order of the letters of the halaḥam alphabet is as follows: h, l, ḥ, m, q, w, s_2 (š or t̪), r, b, t, s_1 (š or t̪), k, n, ḫ, ṣ, s_3 (s), p, ʾ, ʿ, d, ġ, ṭ, z, ḏ, y, t, z̧.

D. Early Development of the Alphabet

Apart from the Palaeo-Alphabetic inscriptions from Serābiṭ el-Ḥādem and the Wadi el-Hol, very little alphabetic material survives from the Middle Bronze Age. The most probable candidate, which was found in 1929 at Gezer, is a small fragment of a ceramic cult stand, likely dating to the 17th cent. BCE and bearing three signs in an archaic alphabetic script highly reminiscent of that of the Proto-Sinaitic inscriptions. More recently, also at Gezer, alphabetic jar signs have been from a securely dated 16th cent. context. Two other poorly understood and, therefore, highly uncertain specimens, both of which should probably be dated to the end of the Middle Bronze or beginning of the Late Bronze Age, include the undeciphered signs on a plaque from Shechem and a bronze dagger from Lachish.

Surviving examples of archaic alphabetic or "Proto-Canaanite" script increase as we move into the Late Bronze Age. By this time the linear alphabetic signs had lost their original pictographic character, having been modified for convenience in writing into simpler, more abstract shapes. Writing could still be done from left to right or from right to left, as in the Palaeo-Alphabetic inscriptions, but with the loss of the pictorial character of the signs the option of vertical writing, a feature reminiscent of Egyptian hieroglyphic which had existed in the earlier period, was now abandoned. The site of LACHISH has been particularly productive of 13th cent. materials, including a bowl (Lachish Bowl No. 1) with at least five legible signs, a more recently discovered bowl fragment bearing two lines of Proto-Canaanite script, and especially the Lachish ewer, an eighteen-inch tall vessel with an eleven-letter inscription painted in red on its shoulder.

An idiosyncratic episode in the history of the alphabet occurred in Late Bronze Age Syria with ramifications that were felt as far south as central Canaan. The Bronze Age was the period of "Cuneiform Culture," when the indigenous Mesopotamian CUNEIFORM writing system was used so widely that it came to be thought as the international vehicle of diplomatic communication and literacy in general. In this spirit, sometime near the middle of the 2nd millennium BCE, the linear alphabet was adapted to the cuneiform medium, and an alphabet was designed for writing the letters with wedges on clay tablets. In particular, the excavations at Raš Šamra, ancient UGARIT on the Syrian coast, have recovered more than 1,500 tablets written in alphabetic cuneiform, bearing sometimes extensive texts of various types including letters, administrative documents, myths, rituals, and even abecedaries (see §C, Order of the Alphabet). A significant number of other tablets have been found in excavations to the south at Ras Ibn Hani, which may have been the summer residence of the royal family of Ugarit. Though extensive archives of the Ugaritic type have not been found at other sites, a scattering of alphabetic cuneiform tablets elsewhere in Syria (Tell Nebi Mend), Lebanon (Ṣarepta), and Israel (TAANACH, Naḥal Tavor and Beth-Shemesh) show that this cuneiform adaptation of the alphabet was not an isolated phenomenon.

Returning now to the linear Proto-Canaanite script at the time of the Late Bronze-Iron Age transition, we note that the late 13th and 12th cent. have yielded a number of brief ostraca and inscribed jar handles from sites in Canaan, Phoenicia and Syria, including Raddanah, Ṣarepta (bibical ZAREPATH), Tell el-Farʿah South (Qubur el-Walaydah), BETH-SHEMESH, and Revadim in the Valley of Sorek, among others. Of special importance is an inscribed storage jar fragment found in 1976 at ʿIzbet Ṣarṭah, a small site in Israel situated on a hill opposite Aphek at the edge of the Philistine Plain. The ʿIzbet Ṣarṭah ostracon was evidently a scribe's practice tablet, since it contains four lines of more or less random Proto-Canaanite signs. The fifth line, however, is an abecedary, that is, the letters of the alphabet written in sequence. The ʿIzbet Ṣarṭah abecedary, which is written from left to right, contains twenty-two signs, the same number of the fully developed Phoenician alphabet of the beginning of the Iron Age. The abecedary reads as follows: ʾ, b, g, d, h, w (?), ḥ, z, ṭ, y, k, l, [ ], n, s, p, ʿ, ṣ, q, r, š, t. Note that the sequence follows the traditional ABC order of the alphabet, except for transposition of zayin and ḥet—otherwise known only in the Tel Zayit abecedary (*see* §E. National Scripts of the Iron Age)—and ʿayin and pe, a reversal which is also known from the Tel Zayit and KUNTILLET ʿAJRUD abecedaries, as well as a group of biblical passages containing acrostic poetry (Lam 2:16–17; 3:46-51; 4:16-17; Ps 10: 6-8; Prov 31: 25-26 [LXX]).

In the last century of the 2nd millennium BCE, the

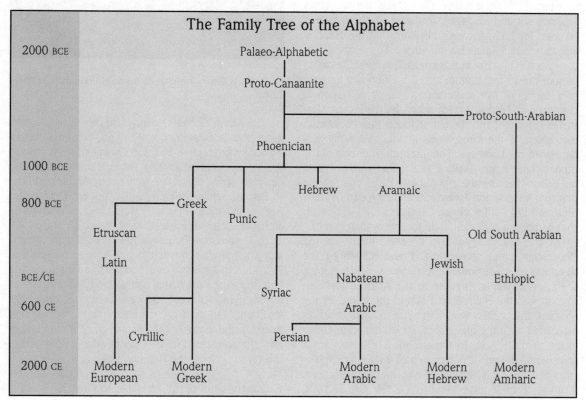

The Family Tree of the Alphabet

2000 BCE — Palaeo-Alphabetic — Proto-Canaanite — Proto-South-Arabian — Phoenician — 1000 BCE — Hebrew — Aramaic — 800 BCE — Greek — Punic — Etruscan — Old South Arabian — Latin — Jewish — BCE/CE — Nabatean — Ethiopic — Syriac — 600 CE — Arabic — Cyrillic — Persian — 2000 CE — Modern European — Modern Greek — Modern Arabic — Modern Hebrew — Modern Amharic

alphabet went through a rather rapid period of palaeographical development, as the individual letter forms acquired the basic shapes and traditional stances that would appear in the fully developed Phoenician alphabet and the national scripts of the Iron Age, and the direction of writing stabilized in a right to left direction. The evidence for these critical developments is ample because of a substantial group of brief but distinctive inscriptions engraved on bronze arrowheads. At least fifty of these arrowheads are known, published or in public and private collections awaiting publication, and palaeographically they span a period from the end of the 12th to the beginning of the 10th cent. BCE. Although only one was recovered in an official excavation, most of them are likely to have come from Lebanon or southern Syria and, in particular, the Biqaʿ Valley, the territory of the ancient kingdom of Amurru, with which many of the arrowheads are probably to be associated—all are inscribed with personal names, which are sometimes followed by the legend "king of Amurru" or the title of a high official, presumably of the court of Amurru. Among the most interesting of these artifacts is a group said to have come not from Lebanon but from the Judean Hills and the village of El-Ḥadr, southwest of Bethlehem; some of the blades from this horde bear the name of a certain Ben-ʿAnat, which is reminiscent of "Shamgar (son of) Ben-ʿAnat," who is mentioned as one of Israel's deliverers in Judg 3:31 and 5:6.

E. National Scripts of the Iron Age

The emergence in the 11th cent. BCE of a distinctive epigraphic tradition on the Lebanese littoral, the mature Phoenician script, is a major watershed in the history of the alphabet. On the one hand, the Phoenician alphabet was the direct heir to the Proto-Canaanite tradition of the 2nd millennium. The sequence of 11th cent. arrowheads shows the refinements of form and presentation that marked the transition. On the other hand, the Phoenician alphabet was the mediator of the Proto-Canaanite tradition to the national scripts of the Iron Age and, in this regard, the direct ancestor of the Aramaic and Hebrew scripts in Syria and Canaan respectively. This is shown by the fact that both Aramaic and Hebrew employed a twenty-two letter alphabet, which was entirely suited to the phonemic inventory of Phoenician but problematic for Old Aramaic and, to a lesser degree, for Hebrew. In Phoenician, for example, the consonants śin and šin have merged, but in Hebrew they remain distinct; and yet the Hebrew alphabet lacks separate śin and šin signs, so that a single sign must be used for both, a clear indication that the Hebrew alphabet was Phoenician in origin. The character of the Phoenician script at this crucial juncture, the beginning of the 1st millennium BCE, is well known because of a corpus of five major inscriptions from the royal cemetery at Byblos, which span the 10th cent. The earliest of these, and the oldest substantial Phoenician inscription, is the sarcophagus of King ʾAḥiram, who flourished ca. 1000 BCE. The inscriptions of two of the other Byblian kings, ʾAbibaal and ʾElibaal, are inscribed on objects bearing the images and cartouches of the first two kings of the Twenty-Second Egyptian dynasty, Shishak I (945–24 BCE) and Osorkon I (924–889 BCE), thus assuring a 10th cent. date for the Byblian corpus.

At the beginning of the 1st millennium BCE the Phoenician script spread inland and influenced the development of regional scripts that were developing there, eventually giving rise to the Aramaic tradition in Syria and the Hebrew tradition in the south. By the 9th cent. this process would give rise to national scripts associated with the new nation states that were taking shape in the region. In Canaan the 10th cent. was a transitional period. It is represented by a scattering of inscribed materials, including two major inscriptions.

One of these, the so-called GEZER CALENDAR, seems to be a scribal practice tablet in soft limestone; it lists the successive activities of the agricultural year. The other substantial 10th cent. inscription from Canaan is an abecedary found at TEL ZAYIT in the Judean Shephelah. It reads as follows: a, b, g, d, w, h, ḥ, z, ṭ, y, l, k, m, n, s, p, ʿ, ṣ, q, r, š, t. Note the transposition from the traditional order of the letters of he and waw, zayin and ḥet, kap and lamed, and ʿayin and pe. Some of these reversals, such as kap and lamed, seem likely to be mistakes, but others have known parallels: zayin and ḥet with the ʿIzbet Ṣarṭah abecedary and ʿayin and pe with numerous other sources (on both of these reversals, *see* §D. Early Development of the Alphabet). These 10th cent. inscriptions exhibit features that are directly ancestral to the Hebrew alphabet, which from the 9th cent., until its essential demise in the 6th cent., exhibited its own diagnostic features. It served as the national script of the Kingdoms of Israel and Judah, and it gave rise to its own daughter scripts, in particular Moabite and, whether directly or indirectly, Edomite.

Figure 1: Gezer Calendar; Archaeological Museum; Istanbul, Turkey.

The Aram. alphabet, which had developed its own distinctive features by the 9th cent., proved to be an especially productive tradition, giving rise not only to the Syriac tradition but also, through its Roman-period daughter script, Nabatean, to the early Arabic tradition, to Persian, and eventually to the modern Persian and Arabic alphabets. In the 8th cent. BCE, the Aramaic alphabet, along with the Aramaic language, was adopted by the Assyrian Empire as the medium of diplomatic and commercial correspondence and administration. The succeeding Babylonian and Persian Empires inherited it from the Assyrians, and its long and widespread history permitted it to displace a number of local script traditions. The Aramaic daughter traditions thus produced included not only Nabatean and Palmyrene, but also the so-called "square" script (the Jewish script) most familiar from the Hebrew Bible.

F. Transmission of the Alphabet to Greece

The Phoenician homeland was a narrow strip of land, never more than about 30 mi. wide, stretching along the coast west of the mountains of Lebanon. From an early date, therefore, the Phoenicians were a maritime people, sailing the Mediterranean and eventually establishing trading colonies on its islands and coastlands. This mercantile activity brought them into early contact with the Greeks, a circumstance that had far-reaching consequences for the history of the alphabet. Phoenician inscriptions dating to the 9th and 8th cent. have been found at maritime sites in Anatolia, Cyprus, Sardinia, Malta, Spain, and various ports of call in North Africa. This was the historical context in which the alphabet was introduced to the Greeks, who having borrowed it from the Phoenicians, passed it on to the Italic peoples (Etruscans and Romans), and eventually to the rest of Europe. In general, the modern alphabets of Western Europe are descended from this western Greek tradition via the Romans, while the modern alphabets of Greece itself and Eastern Europe, such as Cyrillic, are descended directly from the main (central and eastern) Greek tradition.

The Greeks openly acknowledged the Phoenician origin of the letters (γράμματα grammata), which they described as φοινίκης phoinikēs. Even without this testimony, however, the derivation from Phoenician is clear. As shown in the enumeration below, most of the names of the Greek letters are transparently Phoenician and mean nothing in Greek. Moreover, the earliest Greek inscriptions, which begin to appear in the 8th cent. BCE, are written in letters that bear a striking resemblance to their Phoenician prototypes of the same period. This seems to show that the Greek alphabet had become an independent tradition by ca. 800 BCE. Even so, certain characteristics of the earliest Greek scripts—including the option of writing from left to right or from right to left, certain irregularities in the stance ("rotation") of individual letters, and a few distinctive letter forms—seem to point to an earlier period of contact, no later than the 12th–11th cent., prior to the standardization of the Phoenician script, and some scholars have used this evidence to argue for an earlier date of borrowing.

In any case, the Greeks recognized that their language, because of its many vowel-initial consonants and other features, was less well suited than Phoenician to being written in a strictly consonantal script, and they devised an orthographic system that went well beyond the developing Semitic system of matres lectionis in representing vowels. With this crucial step, the introduction of a full system of vowel letters, the ancient invention of the alphabet was complete. The alphabet was now readily adaptable to the needs of almost any language. In particular, the Greeks chose six Semitic letters with consonantal sounds not needed for writing Greek and used them to represent vowels: ʾalep for a (short or long), he for short e, waw for u (long or short), ḥet for long e, yod for i, and ʿayin for short o (omega, the long o, had no Semitic prototype). The Greeks made other changes as well. Following the letters from alpha to tau, which are derived from the twenty-two letters of the Phoenician alphabet, they eventually added five others, including a second letter derived from the sixth Phoenician letter (upsilon from *waw) and four others without Phoenician prototypes. In the early centuries of its use the Greek alphabet was not uniform. There were several local or "epichoric" variations of the Greek alphabet with differing signs and sometimes with differing uses of the same signs. Following the 19th cent. classicist A. Kirchhoff, the principal groupings of the epichoric scripts are referred to as "green" (primitive), "blue," and "red," the latter two groups being distinguished especially by their use of the non-Phoenician signs. The "blue" scripts used the trident for ps and the X for chi, while the "red" scripts used the trident for chi and represented ps by a combination of signs (pi sigma or phi sigma), leaving the X form available for use as ks or x, which in the blue scripts was represented by the sign borrowed from

Phoenician *samk. By the early 4th cent., however, these local scripts were replaced by the alphabet of the Ionians, which was at home on the western coast of Asia Minor ("Ionia") and on many of the Aegean Islands, and which had been adopted in Athens near the end of the 5th cent. BCE, following the Peloponnesian War. Before this happened, however, Euboean traders, who used a "red" script, had carried their alphabet west to Italy, where it was adopted in turn by the Etruscans and the Romans. Since the modern Greek alphabet is a descendant of a "blue" alphabet, it has the familiar trident-form psi and X-form chi, while alphabets descended from the Roman preserve ancient "red" features, such as use of X for ks.

The names of the letters of the Greek alphabet are listed below with notes on their Phoenician origins.

Letter	Name	Phoenician	Notes On Origin
α	alpha	*ʾalp	The voiceless glottal stop was not needed in Greek, and the sign was put to use as a vowel letter representing a.
β	beta	*bet	
γ	gamma	*gaml	
δ	delta	*dalt or *dilt	
ε	epsilon	*hē	The simple h was not needed in Greek, and the sign was used as a vowel letter, originally representing e in general, but in the Ionian dialect, which was "psilotic," that is, lacking the aspirate [the so-called rough breathing], it was used for short e in contrast with eta, the long e. Greek e began to be called e psilon, "simple e," in the Middle Ages to distinguish it from ai, which had come to have the same pronunciation.
ς	fau/digamma	*waw[<*waww]	*waw[<*waww] was the prototype of two Greek letters, the consonantal fau representing v and the vocalic u, later upsilon. Fau came to be called digamma because of its F-shape, which resembled two gammas, and its use in western Greek scripts gave rise to the Roman letter f.

ζ	zeta	unknown	The exact name of the Phoenician prototype is unknown, but the name of the Greek letter probably arose from pattern leveling with eta and theta. The sound of the Phoenician letter is thought to have been a simple z, but it was adapted in Greek for the zd [or dz] of zeta.
η	eta	*khet	*khet, a voiceless fricative, was originally used for the Greek aspirate, but in the psilotic Ionian dialect, which lacked the aspirate, *khet became the vowel letter eta, representing long e in contrast with epsilon, the short e.
θ	theta	*tet	*tet, an emphatic t, was not needed in Greek, and the sign was used to represent the aspirated t [th].
ι	iota	*yod	*yod, the consonant y, was used in Greek as a vowel letter to represent i.
κ	kappa	*kap	
λ	lambda	*lamd	
μ	mu	*môm [<*mawm] or *mêm [<*maym]	
ν	nu	*nun	
ξ	xi	*samk	*samk gave its form to Greek xi, but not its sound; evidently *samk was a voiceless alveolar sibilant. The "blue" alphabets used it for the double consonant ks, which was otherwise written as kappa sigma but represented in some "red" alphabets by chi.
ο	omicron	*ʿên [<*ʿayn]	*ʿên [<*ʿayn], a voiced pharyngeal, was not need in Greek, and the sound was used as a voice letter, representing o; the Ionians used it as

			short o (o mikron, "little o") as distinct from omega, which represented long o (o mega, "big o").
π	pi	*pe	
σ	san	*tsade	Though Phoenician *sade is the source of its shape and position in the alphabet, the name of san seems to be derived from Phoenician *šin or *šan (*tann-), the form of which is preserved in sigma; the various archaic Greek scripts used either san or sigma as the simple s, but the Ionian usage, sigma, eventually become universal, as usual.
ϙ	koppa	*qop	*qop was widely used in the archaic Greece scripts as koppa, and before it was abandoned it penetrated via the western scripts into Italy, where it was preserved as Roman q.
ρ	rho		
σ, ς	sigma	*samk [*simk]	Phoenician *shin or *shan gave its form and position in the alphabet to sigma but its name to san; the source of the name sigma is uncertain, but some have derived it from Phoenician *samk [*simk ?].
τ	tau	*taww	
υ	upsilon	*waw	As already noted, *waw [<*waww] was the prototype not only of the consonant fau (w) but also the vowel u, later u psilon ["simple u," to distinguish it from oi, which had come to have the same pronunciation].
		[<*waww]	
φ	phi	none	No Phoenician prototype
χ	chi	none	The chi sign, which has no Phoenician prototype, represents kh in "blue" alphabets, but ks in some "red" alphabets.

| ψ | psi | none | The psi sign, which has no Phoenician proto-type, represents ps in "blue" alphabets, but kh in "red"alphabets. |
| ω | omega | none | No Phoenician prototype |

Bibliography: W. F. Albright. *The Proto-Sinaitic Inscriptions and Their Decipherment* (1969); F. M. Cross. *Leaves from an Epigrapher's Notebook. Collected Papers in Hebrew and West Semitic Palaeography and Epigraphy* (2003); J. C. Darnell, C. Dobbs-Allsop, M. J. Lundberg, D. K. McCarter, and B. Zuckerman. *Two Early Alphabetic Inscriptions from the Wadi el-Ḥol* (2005); D. Diringer. *The Alphabet. A Key to the History of Mankind.* 2 vols. 3rd ed. (1968); John F. Healey. *The Early Alphabet (Reading the Past)* (1990); A. H. Gardiner. *"The Egyptian Origin of the Semitic Alphabet."* JEA 3(1916) 1–16; L. Jeffery. *The Local Scripts of Archaic Greece.* Rev. ed. with supplement by A. Johnston (1990); A. Kirchhoff. *Studien zur Geschichte des griechischen Alphabets.* 4th ed. (1887); P. K. McCarter. *Ancient Inscriptions. Voices from the Biblical World* (1996); J. Naveh. *Early History of the Alphabet* (1982).

P. KYLE MCCARTER, JR.

ALPHAEUS al-fee'uhs [Ἀλφαῖος Halphaios]. Alphaeus, a Greek name common among 1st cent. Palestinian Jews, occurs 5 times in the NT to identify sons. (This parallels the use of abu, "son of," in modern Arabic.) The usage reflects patriarchal culture. (Note that Jesus, "Son of Mary" is thus unusual.) 1. In Mark 2:14 and *Gos. Pet.* 14:3 (where Levi appears with brothers Peter and Andrew), Alphaeus is father of LEVI, the tax collector or customs officer of Herod Antipas. Some manuscripts read "James," but textual evidence indicates this is probably scribal harmonization with 3:18. "Tax collector" and "sinner" are often synonymous in the synoptics, thus the son of Alphaeus is the first of many such both to host and to follow Jesus. (*See* Mark 2:15-17; Luke 5:27-39.)

2. In Mark 3:18 (Matt 10:3; Luke 6:15; Acts 1:13), JAMES (sometimes called "the less"), son of Alphaeus, is distinguished from James, son of Zebedee and brother of John. Without convincing evidence, this James has been associated with CLOPAS (John 19:25) or CLEOPAS (Luke 24:18). Of either father, nothing is known. *See* JAMES; TAX COLLECTOR.

BONNIE THURSTON

ALTAR [מִזְבֵּחַ mizveakh; θυσιαστηρίων thusiasterion]. A place for sacrifice, from the verb זָבַח zavakh, meaning "to slaughter." Offerings were sacrificed at the altar, and the people of God joined in celebrating the divine pleasure in this sacred and communal meal, a feast that they also shared with one another. In Greek the term thusiasterion bears the same relationship to the verb θύω thuō. The English term *altar* derives from the Latin designation of a high place.

References to the principal altars of Israel involve thematic and ritual patterns. They are best traced by following the development of phases in the growth of the OT, because that resolves the many references into differing usages of altars over time. The sources involved are conventionally called Yahwist, Elohist, Deuteronomist, and the Priestly. The interest here is not in defending the DOCUMENTARY HYPOTHESIS but in following the order in which narratives concerning altars were generated, collating them with the Prophets and Writings as we proceed. On that basis the NT's usage similarly unfolds.

A. Sacrifice to Yahweh, from Abraham through David
B. The Mosaic Covenant and its Altar
C. Prophets and Deuteronomic Lawgivers
D. Priestly Consolidation of the Prophetic Vision
E. The Altar for the End Time
F. Jesus' Altar and the Altar in Heaven
Bibliography

A. Sacrifice to Yahweh, from Abraham through David

Abram builds altars near Shechem and Bethel, and calls on the name of Yahweh there (Gen 12:6-8; 13:4), as he later does in Hebron among the oaks of Mamre (Gen 13:18). Isaac similarly builds an altar at Beersheba (Gen 26:23-25). In the cases of both Abram and Isaac, the building of the altar is motivated by an appearance of Yahweh to the patriarch (Gen 12:7; 26:24)

Abraham and Isaac make their altar in the midst of travel, using unhewn stone and earth. Destruction of more elaborate altars dedicated to other gods becomes imperative (Judg 2:1-2). The story of Gideon in particular links the visible presence of God with sacrifice, the triumph of Israel, the establishment of a named altar for Yahweh, and the removal of other altars, down to the detail that sacred trees are burned on Yahweh's altar to consume a bull (Judg 6:11-28). The commandment against making covenant with the inhabitants of the land, and the injunction to destroy their altars, pillars, and sacred trees (Exod 34:12-17; Judg 2:1-2) follows as a matter of course.

Throughout these stories, Yahweh takes part in a meal, which by his participation becomes a sacrifice. His participation might be direct or by means of an emissary or angel; in either case a simple rock can become an altar when it is the place where Yahweh enjoys an offering. In the story of Manoah (Judg 13:8-23), hospitality to Yahweh's emissary reaches its climax when "the flame went up from the altar to heaven, and the angel of the Yahweh went up in the altar's flame"

(Judg 13:20). Saul builds his first altar to Yahweh (1 Sam 14:31-35) as part of his effort to get Israelites during to campaign to cease eating their meat with blood: the mizbeakh here functions as a center of eating meat as well as a place of sacrifice, revealing how the two are intertwined.

Gideon exercised oracular powers after his sacrifice (Judg 6:33-40), and divine guidance is also offered in proximity to the altar, for Israel as a whole at Bethel in Judg 21:1-12. Abuse of the prerogatives of the altar will feature as key to the prophecy to Eli that his sons Hophni and Phinehas would die (1 Sam 2:27-36). Samuel takes their place, eventually building an altar in Ramah as part of his role as prophet, priest, and judge (1 Sam 7:17). David, guided by his seer Gad, offers sacrifice on an altar he builds in order to protect Jerusalem from plague (2 Sam 24:17-25), and the result is that "Yahweh was supplicated for the land."

B. The Mosaic Covenant and its Altar

Exod 20:24-25 has God require any stone altar should not be made with hewn stone, because that would pollute the structure. In particular, stepped altars are proscribed on the grounds that they are a pretext to show the nakedness of priests. The worship of Yahweh must be unlike that of other gods. For that reason, an altar should not be abused by a murderer as a place of refuge (Exod 21:14). By the same logic, the altar Abraham builds near Beersheba to sacrifice his son is not used for that purpose: human offerings are rejected, not because Abraham does not obey God, but because in his fear of God he learns that Yahweh desires the ram (Gen 22:1-19).

Jacob constructs an altar in Shechem, and gives it the name, "God, the God of Israel" (Gen 33:18-20), signaling a divine encounter. God's appearance to Jacob is explicitly the occasion of his building the altar at Bethel, which he calls "God of Bethel" (Gen 35:7). God demands the altar to mark where he had appeared to Jacob when the patriarch fled from his brother Esau (Gen 35:1), referring back to Gen 28:10-22, where a rough stone monument marks the place of the vision, and Jacob responds by making preparations that involve putting away other gods from his household (Gen 35:2-3).

As with Abraham, Isaac, and Jacob, God speaks with Moses. Moses builds an altar in response (Exod 17:14-16), which he names, memorializing enmity with Amalek. These themes are articulated more elaborately in Exod 24:4, 6, where the altar is a pivotal part of Moses' covenant sacrifice. The God of Israel actually appears to Moses, Aaron, Nadab, Abihu and seventy elders while they eat and drink during the course of sacrifice (Exod 24:9-11). That caps a scene in which Moses erects twelve standing stones together with the altar, representing the twelve clans of Israel that are about to accept the covenant whose wording Moses has written.

The covenantal significance of the standing stones in this scene is beyond dispute, yet it is noteworthy that arrangements with such stones configured around altars are a part of archaeological discoveries from the Iron Age. Twelve stones arranged around an altar provided points of reference for the relative positions of the sun, moon, and other heavenly bodies, so that sacrifices could be conducted at such installations at a precise, repeatable time. Even Balaam, although in the service of an enemy of Israel, is blessed by a vision of Israel's prosperity and dominance as a result of his offerings to Yahweh on sequences of seven altars (Num 23–24).

When Aaron makes an altar before the molten calf (Exod 32), it marks the height of his apostasy. Opposition to foreign cults and to degradations of Israel's worship especially concerns the early prophets. Elijah symbolizes their confrontational stance in the context on Mount Carmel, where by supernatural means his sacrifice on the altar to Yahweh he repairs—carefully using the twelve stones that represent Israel (1 Kgs 18:30-32) prevails over the prophets of Baal (1 Kgs 18:17-40). Elijah then slays the prophets of Baal, much as Moses dealt with the idolaters of his time.

The vehemence of these attacks is rooted in prophetic opposition to the kings in the Northern Kingdom of Israel. Jeroboam's altars in Bethel and Dan are associated with a proclamation that echoes Aaron's apostasy: "Behold your gods, Israel, which brought you up out of the land of Egypt" (I Kgs 12:26-33; compare v. 28 with Exod 32:4). Ahab is compared negatively even to this in his construction of an altar (1 Kgs 16:32-33) and his destruction of Yahweh's prophets and altars (1 Kgs 19:10, 14).

C. Prophets and Deuteronomic Lawgivers

Amos continued the prophetic attack on cultic sites opposed to Yahweh, especially at Bethel, linking that worship with social oppression (Amos 2:8; 3:14; 9:1); Hosea takes up the theme of judgment (Hos 8:11; 10:1-2; 12:11). In Judah, on the other hand, the establishment of the Temple in Jerusalem brought about a prophetic recognition of the presence of God there, sometimes with visionary confirmation (Isa 6:1-10). Nonetheless, Isaiah maintains the prophetic denunciation of foreign altars and even altars to Yahweh apart from the cult in Jerusalem (Isa 17:7-8; 27:9).

This trenchant distinction between all other sites and the single authorized sanctuary in Jerusalem governed the presentation in Deuteronomy, and in Deuteronomistic work associated with the last book of the Torah. Deuteronomy sets out an explicit program of the elimination of foreign sanctuaries and altars in favor of "the altar Yahweh your God" (Deut 12:2-7, 27; see also 7:5). The program includes not accommodating to styles of worship common among the peoples, such as planting a sacred grove near the altar (16:21).

Properly conducted worship permits Israelites to recite and maintain their identity as they keep the commandments and a priest offers their sacrifice at the altar (Deut 26:4-19). The words of the Torah are therefore of particular importance, and Moses instructs Israel to inscribe the words on stone and to set up an altar of whole stones on the other side of the Jordan (Deut 27:1-8). Likewise, teaching the Torah as well as offering on the altar becomes the special blessing conveyed through the clan of Levi (Deut 33:10). Joshua is described as fulfilling Moses instructions, including the construction of the altar on Mount Ebal (Josh 8:30-35; see Deut 27:4). Joshua also assigns the people of Gibeon manual tasks associated with the service of the altar (Josh 9:27).

Any altar outside of the place that Yahweh chooses is anathema as the site of an altar, and near civil war illustrates that (Josh 22:9-34) when Reuben, Gad, and part of Manasseh propose to build an altar. Only their agreement to use their edifice as a monument in Yahweh's honor rather than as a true altar for sacrifice averts violence. Jeroboam's rebellion is the epitome of this problem, and the altar is the target of a prophecy that one day: "Altar, altar, thus says Yahweh: Look, a son shall be born to the house of Davis, Josiah his name, and he will sacrifice upon you the priests of the high places who burn incense upon you, and men's bones will burn upon you" (1 Kgs 13:1-10, 2). A sign follows, in which Jeroboam's hand withers, the altar splits, and its ashes spill away, signaling divine displeasure.

The priest Jehoiada leads a revolt centered on the altar (2 Kgs 11:11; 12:9) that takes rule from the hand of the regent Athaliah and sees to the destruction of Baal's altars, idols, and priests (2 Kgs 11:18). His actions are the antithesis of Ahaz's, who orders change in the altar that accord with the design of Tiglathpileser's in Damascus (2 Kgs 16:10-16). Uriah the priest complies, including the arrangement that the bronze altar installed by Solomon (v. 14, see below) should be moved and reserved for the use of the king in divination. Even in Hezekiah's time, there are enough alternative sites to the Temple that the Assyrians claim that Hezekiah's removal of altars outside of Jerusalem is an affront to Yahweh (2 Kgs 18:22; Isa 36:7).

Manasseh the king is depicted (2 Kgs 21:1-18) in terms that make even Ahaz's abominations—and the Amorites' for that matter (v. 11)—pale in comparison. "He made his son pass through fire" (v. 6) and brought the prophecy that Jerusalem would be handed over to its enemies.

Just prior to the disastrous fulfillment of that prophecy, Josiah offers a brief respite of integrity, guided by a scroll found in the Temple (2 Kgs 23:1-20), probably some form of the present book of Deuteronomy; he destroys the places in the Hinnom Valley, where people made their sons and daughter pass through fire to the god Molech (2 Kgs 23:10), as well as cultic objects and altars constructed by Ahaz, Manasseh, and even Solomon (1 Kgs 23:12-13). Particularly, he fulfills the prophecy against Jeroboam. The hope that such repentance could turn away judgment survived up until the Babylonian destruction of the Temple. Jeremiah 17:1 speaks of Judah's sin as carved on the horns of their many altars, but in context there is still hope for both the altar and the city (Jer 17:24-27). Events, however, produced Judah's exile.

Although the association of Solomon with the idolatrous kings Ahaz and Manasseh might seem strange, it is coherent with the Deuteronomistic presentation. Solomon's greatness cannot be denied, but neither can his trespass on the purview of the Temple. He has people taken from the refuge secured by holding the horns of the altar; Joab is even murdered there (1 Kgs 1:50-53; 2:28-34). Solomon sacrifices and burns incense in high places, offering at Gibeon in particular, where Yahweh appears to him in a dream, and where Solomon makes his famous request for wisdom (1 Kgs 3:1-15). That story is closed by having Solomon return to Jerusalem, stand before the ark, and offer sacrifice, but the ambivalence remains that Solomon achieves what should not be achievable by means of the high places.

The Temple itself, however, is Solomon's construction; the system of courts and the arrangement of ark, sanctuary, and altars as well as their dedication and use are carefully described (1 Kgs 6-8; 8:22, 31, 54, 64; 9:25). It is of interest that even the stone for the house was prepared before it was shipped to the site, so that it imitated the construction of the altar (1 Kgs 6:7). A cedar altar covered with gold, presumably for incense (see below), is located in the sanctuary (6:20, 22; 7:48), as well as a bronze altar that could not contain all the sacrifices Solomon offered (1 Kgs 8:64), so that an additional area (implicitly, an altar of unhewn stones) was sanctified for the purpose. Although Solomon is described as offering sacrifice upon the altar three times a year, and burning incense (1 Kgs 9:25), he is led astray by his seven hundred wives and three hundred concubines to build high places for foreign gods, even Molech, whose devotes passed their children through fire (1 Kgs 11:1-8).

D. Priestly Consolidation of the Prophetic Vision

The Deuteronomists characterized the process of losing the Temple as virtually inevitable: the seeds of destruction were planted even with Solomon. But the unusual circumstances after the Exile that permitted Judeans to return to Jerusalem and rebuild their Temple included by a visionary movement that specified the pattern according to which restoration should proceed, giving Israel its Second Temple.

The conviction that the Temple and its altar were justly lost as a result of Israel's disobedience in no way diminished the pain of that loss. Ezekiel's position as both priest and prophet made him the pivot of a visionary recovery. He insisted in terms reminiscent of the punishment of Jeroboam that the altars of Israel had been justly defiled (Ezek 6:4-5, 13) specifically tying the altar as well as the altar of bronze in the Temple to Israel's abominations (8:5, 16; 9:2). Yet Ezekiel's vision also includes a specification of the Temple that is to be restored, and of its service. The sons of Zadok have its charge (40:46), because they alone of the Levites had not been implicated in the royal abominations that brought about the Temple's destruction (44:10-16). The "Prince" (no longer called a king) is also relegated; he eats bread before Yahweh, but does not offer sacrifice (Ezek 44:1-3). The placement, dimensions, and sanctification of altars are laid out (40:47; 41:22, here referring to the table; 43:13-27; 45:19); the promise of realizing this vision is that healing waters will issue to the south of the altar (47:1).

Similarities between Ezekiel and the HOLINESS CODE (Lev 17–26), as well as the Priestly source, generally have frequently been observed, but there is nothing like exact agreement (for example, in regard to the altar's measurements, which vary in ancient sources). The power of the combined prophetic and priestly perspective, however, comes through all these articulations. The altar and the whole Temple that contains the altar are God's alone, a reality inviolate in heaven whatever happens on the earth. For that reason, the altar is a place of supernatural power as well as of communion with God.

The nature of true worship had broken through even before Israel had inherited the land, and before Abraham had been called. Noah, endowed with the wisdom to offer only clean beasts, sacrifices to God on an altar (Gen 8:20–9:17) occasioning God's favor, marked by the divine bestowal of animals for food provided blood is not consumed, and the covenant that permits the world to endure.

No vision can compare with Moses' vision in the Priestly source. God gives him specific instructions including visionary disclosures for the altar: how it should be constructed of wood and bronze (Exod 27:1-8), how and who can approach it without the threat of death (Exod 28:42-43; see Lev 10:1-3), how its sanctity can safely be transferred to priests (Exod 29:10-39), and how it enables Israel to dwell with God in their midst (Exod 29:40-46). The actual layout of the altars, including a golden-covered altar for incense (Exod 30:1-10), and the relation of the principal altar to a basin for purification (Exod 30:18, 20), and the anointing of the altars (Exod 30:26-28) are all detailed, and the implementation of the visionary template by Bezazel is described (31:1-11; 37:25; 38:1-7, 30) as Moses sees to the realization of the visionary arrangement (35:15-16; 39:38-39; 40:5-33).

The book of Leviticus specifies the sacred choreography that is to transpire within the arrangement. For that reason, the altar features persistently, in Lev

1–9. As in Ezekiel, the king is called a prince, and his sacrifice for sin is under the strict control of a priest, and is comparable to that of an ordinary Israelite (Lev 4:22-35). It is the priests who have special access to the altar (Lev 10:12-15), because God placed Aaron and his sons there by Moses' own hands (Lev 8:1-30). They render a person with an outbreak of skin clean by means of sacrifice (Lev 14:20), and Aaron's descendant sees to the undiminished sanctity of the altar as the place where God meets his people (Lev 16:20)

E. The Altar for the End Time

The rebuilding of the Temple did not bring the supernatural triumph envisaged by Ezekiel and enshrined in the Holiness Code and the Priestly source of the Torah. Nonetheless, the book of Psalms, compiled during the period of the Second Temple, represents the joy experienced by worshippers around the altar, and their celebratory participation there with procession, dance, and music (Pss 26:6; 43:4; 51:19; 84:3; 118:27). At the same time, the context of several of these references in psalms (26:6; 51:19) make it plain beyond dispute that innocence and righteousness, purity that reaches to the heart, were associated with sacrifice on the altar.

As compared to Solomon's Temple, however, the Second Temple was not prepossessing. The altar was established and sacrifice offered even before the foundation of the new Temple was laid (Ezra 3:2-3), and arrangements were made for service on the altar (Neh 10:34), but those familiar with the first Temple wept at the dedication of the second (Ezra 3:12). The newly consecrated altar itself seemed to testify to the iniquities that had resulted in destruction. The altar proper is at issue in Lam 2:7, where is said to have been forsaken, and such a lament, articulated as a rebuke for continuing corruption, features also in Joel 1:13; 2:17; Mal 1:7, 10; 2:13.

A powerful prophetic response to this sense of an incomplete restoration came in the form of predicting the opening of the altar to all Israel, assisted by foreigners who are included in the festivity (Isa 56:6-8; 60:7-14). (This expectation reversed the direction of an earlier prophecy, in which an altar to Yahweh was to stand in Egypt; Isa 19:18-19. The colony at Elephantine shows how plausible an extension into Egypt may have seemed.) Zechariah became the preeminent prophet of this transformation of Jerusalem, so that the whole city would serve as an altar (14:20).

Robust though these hopes were, the proper use of the altar was also defended by looking backward, rather than forward. First Chronicles portrays David as careful in regard to sacrifice (1 Chr 16:40), as receiving the spectacular intervention of fire from heaven in the manner of Elijah (1 Chr 21:26), as avoiding the altar at Gib-eon (1 Chr 21:29–22:1), and as progressing far in preparations for constructing the Temple (1 Chr 28:18). 2 Chronicles details the choreography and drama around the altar to serve as precedents of worship given by Solomon (2 Chr 5:12; 6:12-13; 8:12-15), Hezekiah (29:12-36), and Josiah (35:16-19), and repeats standard functions of the altar, such as receiving oaths as well as sacrifice (2 Chr 6:22-23; 7:7; 1 Kgs 8:64). Similarly, when Solomon besought Yahweh at Gibon, he did so by means of the bronze altar that Bazazel had made (2 Chr 1:5-6). Yet the drama of punishment for crime against the altar is also heightened (26:16-23).

F. Jesus' Altar and the Altar in Heaven

The crisis of the abomination ANTIOCHUS EPIPH-ANES imposed on the altar is met in the Maccabean literature with a strong emphasis upon rededication and subsequent rejoicing in defiance of suffering and foreign persecution (1 Macc 1:20-23, 54, 59; 4:36–5:8; 6:7), and prayer before the rededicated altar is rewarded with victory (1 Macc 7:33-50). Supernatural power associated with the altar is celebrated (2 Macc 1:18-36; 2:1-23; 3:15-30; 10:5, 24-38; 14:30–15:36) despite the corruption associated with the abomination on the altar (2 Macc 4:14; 6:1-11; 14:3). Confidence in the altar's power, together with the ethical as well as cultic sanctity that demands the human response of purity, is also stressed in works apart from Maccabean literature (Tob 1:6; Jdt 4:3, 11; 8:24; 9:8; Wis 9:8; Sir 35:6; 47:9; 50:11, 15).

The NT sometimes refers favorably and in a similar idiom to the vitality of the altar (Luke 1:11; Jas 2:21), but Jesus' attitude is more specific and more pointed. He decries the abuses of the recent past that have killed prophets, especially Zechariah, whom he says perished between the altar and (Luke 11:49-51; Matt 23:34-36). Jesus' conviction that the altar was too sacred for oaths (Matt 23:16-22) was fully consistent with his insistence that the Temple was to fulfill Isaiah's prophecy and become a house of prayer for all peoples (Mark 11:17; Matt 21:13; Luke 19:46). His own intervention in the Temple (Mark 11:15-19; John 2:13-22; Matt 21:12-17; Luke 19:45-48) removed the vendors that, according to the prophecy of Zechariah (14:20-21), had no place near the altar.

Following his intervention in the Temple, Jesus taught that in his meals with his disciples, wine and bread became "blood" and "flesh" (Luke 22:15-20; John 6:52-59; 1 Cor 11:23-25; Mark 14:22-31; Matt 26–30), a surrogate for offerings at the altar. That belief persisted to the point that Paul directly equates those who preach the message of Jesus with priests who serve the altar and those who participate in the LORD'S SUP-PER with those who eat from the altar (1 Cor 9:13-14; 10:18). Paul also compares opposition to his preaching to those who pulled down Yahweh's altars during the time of Elijah (Rom 11:3). It is likely that Matt 5:23-24 reflects a similar conception of eucharistic worship as a gathering at the altar.

With the destruction of the Second Temple, the usage of the NT appropriated the altar all the more boldly and emphatically to the sacrifice of Jesus. Hebrews portrays Jesus as a true high priest, despite coming from the people of Judah rather than Levi (Heb 7:13), whose sacrifice once for all establishes an altar in heaven (Heb 13:10). Although Hebrews' articulation of this theme is masterful, and unusually literate among the writings of the NT, the theme itself was widespread. The altar in heaven is pivotally important within the visionary prophecy of John of Patmos (Rev 6:9; 8:3, 5; 9:13; 11:1; 14:18; 16:7), and the image is developed in even more detail than in Hebrews. *See* BABEL, TOWER OF; DOCUMENTARY HYPOTHESIS; HIGH PLACES; INCENSE ALTAR; SACRIFICE AND OFFERINGS; TEMPLE; WORSHIP IN THE OT; WORSHIP IN THE NT.

Bibliography: Gary A. Anderson. *Sacrifices and Offerings in Ancient Israel. Studies in their Social and Political Importance* (1987); Emmanuel Anati. *The Mountain of God: Har Karkom* (1986); Th. A. Busink. *Der Tempel von Jerusalem von Salomo bis Herodes. Eine archäologisch-historische Studie unter Berücksichtigung des westsemitischen Tempelbaus. 2. Band: Von Ezekiel bis Middot* (1980); Bruce Chilton. *The Temple of Jesus. His Sacrificial Program Within a Cultural History of Sacrifice* (1992); Menahem Haran. *Temples and Temple-Service in Ancient Israel. An Inquiry into the Character of Cult Phenomena and the Historical Setting of the Priestly School* (1978); Benjamin Mazar. *The Mountain of the LORD.* G. Cornfield, trans. (1975); Jacob Milgrom. *Studies in Cultic Theology and Terminology* (1983).

BRUCE CHILTON

ALTAR OF WITNESS. *See* WITNESS, ALTAR OF.

AL-ULA. *See* ULA, AL-.

ALUSH ayʹluhsh [אָלוּשׁ *ʾalush*]. An exodus itinerary site (Num 33:13-14) between Yam Suf and MOUNT SINAI whose proximity with REPHIDIM may imply an association with the AMALEKITES.

ALVAH alʹvuh [עַלְוָה *ʿalwah*, עַלְיָה *ʿalyah*]. According to Gen 36:40-43, Alvah is one of the clans of Esau/EDOM. The name appears as ALIAH in 1 Chr 1:51*b*-54. This may be the same as ALVAN/ALIAN, son of SHOBAL, in Gen 36:23 = 1 Chr 1:40. *See* ESAUITES.

ALVAN alʹvuhn [עַלְוָן *ʿalvan*]. Ancestor of a Horite subclan in Edom, first son of Shobal and grandson of Seir (Gen 36:23; Alian in 1 Chr 1:40).

ALWAYS [תָּמִיד *tamidh* כָּל-הַיָּמִים *kol hayyamim*; πάντοτε *pantote*, πᾶς *pas*]. The translation of numerous Hebrew and Greek words or phrases. In the OT it most often appears for tamid or kol hayyamim, literally "all the days." In the NT it usually renders **pantote** or phrases including pas, "all, every" (also the norm in the Deuterocanonicals).

Always can be used in multiple ways, but two are most common. It often denotes typical or habitual situations (e.g., the presence of the poor contrasted with Jesus' impending departure, Mark 14:7/Matt 26:11; John 12:8) or practices (Paul's prayers for fellow believers, Rom 1:9; 1 Cor 1:4; 1 Thess 1:2; Phlm 4; compare Col 1:3; 2 Thess 1:11). Also, the term frequently appears in exhortations to observe the law and proper teaching (e.g., Deut 11:1; 2 Kgs 17:37; Prov 6:21) or practice Christian behavior (1 Cor 15:58; Eph 6:18; Phil 4:4; Col 4:6; 1 Thess 5:15-16; 2 Tim 4:5). It appears in positive and negative proverbial sayings (Sir 27:11; Titus 1:12). In John, Jesus always obeys his Father (8:29), who in turn always hears the Son (11:42).

Always may convey certainty of God's promises or of some divine quality. Divine retribution should be expected by those who sin (Wis 14:31); alternately, one may take comfort knowing that God will not always show wrath (Isa 57:16; Ps 103:9). It connotes that God's promises concerning the Davidic dynasty are enduring (1 Kgs 11:36; Ps 89:21). As eternal, heavenly high priest, Jesus always makes intercession for believers (Heb 7:25), and his abiding presence with believers is assured (Matt 28:20).

ERIC F. MASON

'AM HA'ARETS [עַם הָאָרֶץ 'am ha'arets, הָאָרֶץ עַמֵּי 'amme ha'arets]. The phrase, which means "(the) people(s) of the land," occurs approximately seventy times in the OT, most often in the singular 'am ha'arets, although the plural 'amme ha'arets, is also common. It occurs frequently in the rabbinic literature.

What may have begun as a general term for any people who lived in a particular country (e.g., Israelites: 2 Kgs 25:3; non-Israelites: Num 14:9; plural, Deut 28:10) eventually became more specific in different contexts. Thus, some take it as referring to a social class, the lower stratum of society (2 Kgs 24:18), rural compared to urban. The dominant view, however, is that the phrase referred to the power-wielding segment of society (2 Kgs 25:19), those who possessed land or wealth and, therefore, power. The history of scholarship on the phrase shows that context must always determine its specific meaning.

Most striking, however, is the "semantic revolution" (Gunneweg) wherein the originally neutral or positive term became a pejorative. This happened in the postexilic period when the term was applied by the returning exiles to the residents of Palestine, whom they regarded as defiled through marriage with the Canaanites and involvement in paganism (e.g., Ezra 9:1, 11; 2 Chr 13:9).

In the rabbinic literature the phrase is used not in the sense of any social classification, but still negatively to refer to those who did not observe the purity laws or those who were simply ignorant concerning Torah. Those described by the Pharisees in John 7:49 as "this crowd which does not know the law" fit well the later rabbinic definition of "people of the land." *See* PEOPLE OF THE LAND.

Bibliography: A. H. J. Gunneweg. "'Am Ha-Eretz—A Semantic Revolution." *ZAW* 95 (1983) 437–40; E. W. Nicholson. "The Meaning of The Expression 'Am Ha-Eretz in the Old Testament." *JSS* 10 (1965) 59–66; A. Oppenheimer. *The 'Am Ha-Aretz: A Study in the Social History of the Jewish People in the Hellenistic-Roman Period.* ALGHJ 8 (1977).

DONALD A. HAGNER

AMAD ay'mad [עַמְעָד 'am'adh]. A town allocated to the Asher tribe (Josh 19:26). *See* ASHER.

AMAL ay'muhl [עָמָל 'amal]. A warrior son of Helem of the tribe of Asher (1 Chr 7:35). *See* HELEM.

AMALEK, AMALEKITES am'uh-lek, uh-mal'uh-kits [עֲמָלֵק 'amaleq; עֲמָלֵקִי 'amaleqi]. References to the people of Amalek, also known as Amalekites, are preserved only in the OT and traditions derived from it. They are one of the peoples living in and around Canaan and are described as opponents of the Israelites as they moved from Egypt into the wilderness. They remained enemies after Israel's settlement in the promised land. A deep-seated enmity existed between Amalek and Israel that pervades most references to them. There are hints of an old connection between Israel and Amalek (see Negev and Amalek below). Perhaps the enmity of the preserved sources is the result of prior connections gone sour.

1. Name, Origins, Geography

According to Gen 36:12, 16 (1 Chr 1:36), Amalek is the name of Esau's grandson, born to Eliphaz and his concubine Timna. This would make Amalek the eponymous ancestor of the population group bearing his name, following a pattern that also defines Canaanites, Ammonites, Moabites, and Israelites, each of whom bears the name of their ancestor. Esau, in turn, is the ancestor of the Edomites (Gen 36:1, 19, 43), a people living south and southeast of the Dead Sea. What these ancestor reports preserve about the early history of Amelekites and their relationship to the Edomites is not clear, but suggestive by way of geography and social structure. The Edomites had strong tribal and clan constituencies (Gen 36:19-30). Amalek, therefore, is likely a clan-based people, related by social structure (cooperative ventures and marriage?) and proximity to Edom and other groups known collectively as the children of the East (Judg 6:3, 33; 7:12). The Amalekites seem to inhabit the eastern and southern fringes between the wilderness and sedentary existence, moving around with their flocks and camels in search of pasture, land, and water. Edom too, in later references, is located in Negev or a region south of the Judean hill country.

These geographic and cultural contacts are reflected in narratives where Amalekites are paired with Ammon, Moab, and Midian in fighting against Israel, which first encounters them in the wilderness just after their departure from Egypt (Exod 17:8-16). One of Balaam's oracles names Amalek as the "first of nations" (Num 24:20). This might be recognition of their ancient status as a people, for which there is other evidence (1 Sam 27:8), or perhaps refer to their "firstness" in attacking Israel. The oracle about Amalek concludes with a prophecy of their destruction, a theme to be repeated in other encounters with them.

2. Amalek in the Wilderness

The account of the battle between Israel and Amalek in Exod 17:8-16, preserves a number of peculiar features. First, in the narrative storyline the Amalekites are the first opponents Israel meets in the wilderness, even before reaching Mt. Sinai. This would put them in territory also inhabited by Midian. The Midianite priest Jethro is Moses' father-in-law. Second, Joshua leads the Israelite forces in the route of Amalek. He does not have such a military leadership role again until the conquest of the land in the book that bears his name. Some scholars, therefore, have suggested that the account of fighting against Amalek is narrated out of sequence and belongs to a later time closer to the entrance into the promised land. Third, the enmity between Amalek and Israel is quite pronounced in the version of the account now preserved: "The Lord will have war against Amalek from generation to generation" (17:16). Moreover, the retrospective in Deut 25:17-19 recalls the attack on Israel and reminds hearers that "remembrance of Amalek shall be blotted out underneath the heavens." There is perhaps more than meets the eye in this first narrated encounter with Amalek.

According to Num 14:25-45, the Israelites were to avoid the Amalekites and Canaanites and not seek to enter the hill country of Canaan. In defiance of this instruction, an abortive attempt was made to enter the hill country through the Negev. They were repulsed at a place named Hormah (which means destruction) by the Amalekites and others.

3. Amalek in the Book of Judges

In the description of Eglon's oppression of the Benjaminites (Judg 3:12-30), Ammon and the Amalekites are in league with Moab. The report of the cooperative venture is brief, and the narrator does not expand on their respective roles, save in the case of the Moabite king. The account of struggles during the days of Gideon has the Midianites playing the primary oppressive role (Judg 6:1–7:25), with the Amalekites and the children of the East as a supporting cast (6:3, 33; 7:12). Midian is described as a numerous and imposing force, arranged in tent groups and accompanied by camels and livestock. They and their compatriots attacked Israel after the farmers had sown their crops (6:3-4). Gideon is introduced as someone preparing grain in a winepress in order to hide the produce from the Midianites. All this suggests that the tribal herdsmen of Midian and Amalek sought to take the agricultural produce of Israel by force in seasonal raids, and that they terrorized the Israelite farmers in the process. The semi-nomadic peoples of the East would have a symbiotic relationship with more sedentary inhabitants of the land based on their complementary economies. In good times there would be reciprocal exchange, and some peoples related to the semi-nomadic tribes would settle down to facilitate these contacts. Thus, one encounters occasional references to the land or city of the Amalekites in sedentary territory (1 Sam 27:8).

4. Saul and Amalek

The prophet-priest Samuel urged King Saul to strike the Amalekites and to destroy them and their possessions (1 Sam 15:1-7). This was an invitation to conduct "holy war" against Amalek and thus to devote the victory and spoils to the Lord. The subsequent fighting takes place in the wilderness area east of Egypt. Agag, the Amalekite king, is captured, along with spoils such as livestock. In defiance of the ban pronounced through Samuel, Saul and his forces neither execute Agag nor destroy the possessions of the Amalekites. This causes a rift between Samuel and Saul, since Samuel regards the sparing of Agag and the best of the livestock as disobedience to the word of the Lord. The account of Saul's disobedience in this regard is a reason for his rejection as king over Israel (1 Sam 15:8-30; 28:18). Saul subsequently executes Agag "before the Lord," but Samuel's next move is to go and anoint David as the next king over Israel (1 Sam 15:31–16:13; *see* Agag, Amalek, and Haman below).

5. David and Amalek

In his avoidance of King Saul, David and his warrior band lived in the rugged southern hill country and roamed through the wilderness of the Negev. These circumstances brought him into contact with the Philistines and semi-nomadic peoples like the Amalekites in his role of protector of other inhabitants in the region (1 Sam 27:8). His anger at the rebuff of Nabal (1 Sam 25:1-42; note especially v. 21) should be read in this context. The Amalekites, in turn, opposed David's presence and role in the region. They conducted a raid on the city of Ziklag, a gift of the Philistines to David, capturing property and kidnapping members of his family. David eventually gained the upper hand against them (1 Sam 30:1-25; 2 Sam 8:12).

6. Negev and Amalek

The place of Amalek in the wilderness region south of the Judean hill country has been previously noted. The Negev region is also part of the traditional tribal inheritance of Simeon. There is a report of fighting in the days of Hezekiah, king of Judah, in which the remnant of Amalek was destroyed (1 Chr 4:43). This is something of a final comment on a sad history.

There are also intriguing indications of a connection between the Kenites and the Amalekites in this general area. According to Judg 1:16, Moses' father-in-law was a Kenite whose descendants lived in the Negev south of Arad among the Amalekites (see also Judg 4:11). In the report of the fighting with the Amalekites, Saul commanded the Kenites living among them to depart lest they be destroyed (1 Sam 15:6). Elsewhere, Moses' father-in-law is a Midianite, mentioned in the context of the struggles with the Amalekites (Exod 17–18). It is difficult to unravel the historical and cultural connections between the Kenites, who were related to the Israelites, and the Amalekites, the inveterate enemy of the Israelites, but they seem to go back far in Israel's preserved memory.

7. Agag, Amalek, and Haman

In the book of Esther, Haman is the vile enemy of the Jews. He is described as an Agagite (Esth 3:1, 10; 8:3, 5; 9:24). The gentilic Agagite identifying Haman is obscure and thus difficult to place in context. It is the case that Agag is the only name preserved for an Amalekite, and possibly it is a dynastic name (Num 24:7) in their tribal society. It is then possible that the description of Haman as an Agagite is intended to connect him with the ancient enemy of the Jews. The Targum of Esther makes the connection specifically. Whether this was the intention of the narrator cannot be known for certain.

8. Amalek as Symbol of Evil and Genocide

In spite of the difficulties in reconstructing relations between Amalek and Israel, the tradition of enmity between them has remained a factor in post-biblical Judaism, with Amalek representing inveterate enemies who are to be opposed and, if possible, defeated. An annual reminder of "Amalekite" hostility has been rooted in the observance of Purim, a festival celebrating the deliverance of the Jews from the plot of Haman. *Mishnah Megillah* 30b commands that the story of the battle with Amalek (Exod 17:8-16) should be read during Purim, and various traditions of representing Amalekite as evil at Purim developed over time.

Bibliography: A. Sagi. "The Punishment of Amalek in Jewish Tradition: Coping with the Moral Problem." *HTR* 87 (1994) 323–46; Louis H. Feldman. *"Remember Amalek!": Vengeance, Zealotry, and Group Destruction in the Bible, According to Philo, Pseudo-Philo, and Josephus* (2004).

                                        J. ANDREW DEARMAN

AMAM ay´mahn [אֲמָם ʾamam]. A town allocated to the territory of the tribe of Judah (Josh 15:26).

AMANA uh-may´nuh [אֲמָנָה ʾamanah]. Mountain located near or in the Lebanon mountains and south of the valley of the Amana River (2 Kgs 5:12; Song 4:8). *See* ABANA.

AMANUENSIS. A technical term from the Latin meaning "of the hand," referring to one who copies documents for, or takes dictation from, another. In the OT, such a figure is known as a scribe (סֹפֵר sofer), a term that can include copyists as well as those who keep accounts, whether of finances (2 Kgs 12:11 [Eng. 12:10]; 2 Chr 24:11) or military conscripts (2 Kgs 25:19; 2 Chr 26:11; Jer 52:25). The prophet Jeremiah employed Baruch as an amanuensis to record the prophet's oracles and read them to the people of Judah (Jer 36:4-6, 17-18, 32). The late 7th cent. BCE Yavneh Yam ostracon, a legal plea by an agricultural laborer, likely testifies to the use of scribes in producing official documents on behalf of ordinary citizenry (*COS* 3.41). Egyptian papyri from the Ptolemaic and Roman periods, as well as the correspondence of Roman literati, provide evidence for the use of amanuenses (sg. γραμματεύς grammateus) in NT-era letter writing. It is clear that the apostle Paul dictated some of his letters to copyists, inserting closing words in his own hand as a sign of authenticity (1 Cor 16:21; Gal 6:11; Col 4:18; 2 Thess 3:17). A letter of Cicero in which the Roman statesman alludes to specific capabilities among his scribes has led some to see the use of different amanuenses behind the varying styles within the Pauline corpus (Cicero, *Att.* 333.3). *See* SCRIBE.

Bibliography: G. J. Bahr. "Paul and Letter Writing in the First Century." *CBQ* 28 (1966) 465–77; Richard N. Longenecker. "Ancient Amanuensis and the Pauline Epistles." Richard N. Longenecker and Merrill C. Tenney, eds. *New Dimensions in New Testament Study* (1974) 281–97.

                                        BRIAN PAUL IRWIN

AMARIAH am´uh-ri´uh [אֲמַרְיָה ʾamaryah]. 1. A LEVITE and HIGH PRIEST (1 Chr 6:7, 52 [Heb. 5:33; 6:37]), a descendant of AARON, he was the son of MERAIOTH and the father of AHITUB and the grandfather of ZADOK, the High Priest during David's reign.

2. A Levite and high priest and descendant of Aaron through ELEAZAR (1 Chr 6:11 [Heb. 5:37]), the son of AZARIAH (also high priest; 1 Chr 6:10 [Heb. 5:36]) and the father of Ahitub (II) and grandfather of Zadok (II), Amariah appears as an ancestor in EZRA's genealogy (Ezra 7:3; 1 Esd 8:2; 2 Esd 1:2).

3. A Levite from the KOHATHITEs clan, HEBRON's second son (1 Chr 23:19; 24:23), selected to serve among David's twenty-four Levite divisions.

4. A Levite called "the chief priest," active in the political and religious reforms of JEHOSHAPHAT and appointed to have authority over temple matters (2 Chr 19:11).

5. A Levite, one of the six people King HEZEKIAH appointed to distribute free will offerings to the Levites living in priestly cities outside of Jerusalem (2 Chr 31:15).

6. Son of Hezekiah (possibly King Hezekiah) and father of GEDALIAH and one of the ancestors of the prophet ZEPHANIAH (Zeph 1:1).

7. The son of SHEPHATIAH and father of ZECHARI-AH, a Judahite and descendant of the family of PEREZ. After the Babylonian exile, ATHAIAH, a descendant of Amariah was among those who settled in Jerusalem (Neh 11:4).

8. One of the priests who returned from Babylon with ZERUBBABEL (Neh 12:2), he appears to have been identical with the father of JEHOHANAN, one of the leaders of the ancestral houses in the days of the High Priest JOIAKIM (Neh 12:13).

9. A priest among those who signed a postexilic community agreement to keep the law of Moses (Neh 10:3).

10. A descendant of BINNUI and one of the Jews who divorced his Gentile wife whom he had married after the people's return from their exile in Babylon (Ezra 10:42).

CLAUDE F. MARIOTTINI

AMARNA LETTERS. The Amarna letters comprise the body of diplomatic correspondence from the reigns of the Egyptian pharaohs Amenophis III, AKHENATEN (Amenophis IV) and Tutankhamen. The letters are an important resource for the political history of the late 14th cent. BCE and for the development of the Canaanite language.

According to tradition, in 1887 a peasant woman digging in the ruins at Tell-el Amarna for sebakh, nutrient-rich decayed mud brick, unearthed several clay tablets inscribed in cuneiform script. She had stumbled upon the "Place of the Letters of the Pharaoh," the archive of diplomatic correspondence. However, the discovery actually occurred, the tablets soon found their way into the antiquities market and eventually into the collections of several European museums. Scholars had already identified Tell el-Amarna as AKHETATEN, the capital city of the 18th dynasty pharaoh Akhenaten, although exploration of the site had been largely limited to the boundary stelae and the tombs.

Ultimately 382 tablets or portions of tablets were recovered from Tell el-Amarna, 350 letters and 32 miscellaneous texts. With few exceptions, the letters were written in a provincial form of the Babylonian language, which served as the diplomatic lingua franca in the 2nd millennium BCE. The letters can be divided into two main categories: royal correspondence exchanged with other imperial powers, and vassal correspondence exchanged with subordinate states in western Asia. A few letters were also exchanged with the independent states of Arzawa (in southwestern Turkey) and Alashiya (on Cyprus).

The letters attest to international relations from the 30th year of Amenophis III to the first years of Tutankhamen, when the capital returned to Memphis and the city was abandoned. The earliest letters in the archive must have been transported from the old capital to the new when Akhetaten was founded in regnal year five of Akhenaten (Amenophis IV). For reasons unknown, the archive was left behind in the abandoned capital.

From the late 16th–12th cent. BCE, the ANE was dominated by the so-called club of great powers, a brotherhood of great kings. Membership in the brotherhood varied over time, but during the Amarna period comprised EGYPT, Mitanni (in northern Syria), Babylonia (in southern Iraq), Assyria (a former Mitannian vassal in northern Iraq between Mitanni and Babylonia) and Hatti (in eastern Turkey).

International diplomacy required the frequent exchange of letters, gifts, and princesses. The royal correspondence attests to all three facets, since the primary topics were gift exchange and interdynastic marriage. In the letters the great kings addressed each other as "brother" and described in great detail both the gifts accompanying the letter and the gifts received (or desired) from the other. They also negotiated interdynastic marriages and the concomitant wedding gifts.

The underlying structure of Egypt's Asian empire was a network of city-states, stretching from Byblos, Qadesh, and Amurru in the north to Ashkelon, Lachish, and Jerusalem in the south. Each city-state had its own ruler and controlled the surrounding agricultural land, including a number of villages. The city-state rulers were bound to Egypt as vassals and were required to deliver tribute, intelligence reports, and military support as demanded. Their allegiance was ensured by loyalty oaths, strategically placed garrisons, and hostages—their sons were educated at the Egyptian court.

The evidence of the correspondence suggests that a system of provinces overlay the city-state structure. Egyptian overseers were assigned to monitor developments in the empire and to collect the tribute. For the most part, however, the vassals were left to their own devices to manage the affairs of their city-states and to fend off incursions from greedy neighbors. The vassals frequently sought to enlist Egyptian support for their cause by warning that a neighboring city-state was becoming a threat to Egyptian sovereignty. Repeated complaints were lodged about the growing strength of Amurru, under the leadership of Abdi-Ashirta and his son Aziru, and of Shechem, under Labayu.

The stories in the OT books of Joshua and Judges presuppose a similar network of city-states, each controlling an agricultural hinterland and ruled by its own king. Although the precise composition of and balance of power within the network differs, a number of the city-states recur, including Megiddo, Shechem, Ashkelon, Jerusalem, and Lachish.

The vassal correspondence includes frequent warnings about the threat posed by the HABIRU or Apiru. The term is ill defined in the letters, but seems to refer to a broad class of individuals outside Canaanite society. The Habiru appear as landless men who survived by preying on caravans or by hiring themselves out as mercenaries. Their predations were a real threat to trade and to the security of outlying villages. City-state rulers complained to the Egyptians about peers whose armies incorporated Habiru mercenaries.

The origins of the Habiru who plagued the Canaanite city-states in the Amarna period are uncertain. They may have been casualties of environmental and economic decline who took refuge in the mountains when their farms could no longer sustain them.

Despite the apparent similarity between Habiru and HEBREW, the two words are etymologically and sociologically unrelated. As used in the biblical texts, Hebrew refers to an ethnicity rather than a social status.

The vassal correspondence preserves some of the earliest evidence for the Canaanite language. Although the language of the letters is, properly speaking, Babylonian, the provincial dialect often employs a morphology and syntax derived from Canaanite or another northwest Semitic language. Canaanite proper names and the occasional Canaanite word or phrase attest to developments in pronunciation. *See* AMARNA, TELL EL-; HABIRU, HAPIRU; LANGUAGES OF THE ANCIENT NEAR EAST.

Bibliography: Raymond Cohen and Raymond Westbrook, eds. *Amarna Diplomacy: The Beginnings of International Relations* (2000); Frederick J. Giles. *The Amarna Age: Western Asia.* The Australian Centre for Egyptology Studies 5 (1997); William L. Moran. *The Amarna Letters* (1992).

CAROLYN R. HIGGINBOTHAM

AMARNA, TELL EL. Tell el-Amarna is the modern name for the site where the 18th dynasty Egyptian king AKHENATEN built his sacred precinct and capital city AKHETATEN "Horizon of Aten." One of the best preserved ancient Egyptian urban sites, Tell el-Amarna has been extensively excavated, providing critical information about political and cultural developments in the late 14th cent. BCE, especially the Amarna revolution in religion and art. The cache of diplomatic correspondence from the site, known as the AMARNA LETTERS, has furthered the understanding of international relations in the period.

A. Identification
B. Exploration and Excavation
C. History of Occupation
D. Layout of the Sacred Precinct
    1. Central city
    2. Sites north of the central city
    3. Sites south of the central city
    4. Tombs
E. Important Finds
    1. Amarna letters
    2. Sculpture
    3. Architecture
    4. The great hymn to the Aten
Bibliography

A. Identification

Tell el-Amarna is a misnomer because the site is not, properly speaking, a *tell* (mound of ruins, *see* TEL, TELL). This modern designation apparently derives from the conflation of multiple local names reported by European visitors in the 18th and 19th cent.: Bene Amran (an Arab tribe resident in the region), et-Till (the largest village in the area) and perhaps also el-Amariya (another nearby village).

Tell el-Amarna is approximately 200 mi. south of Memphis and 250 mi. north of Thebes, in an area where the cliffs on the east side of the Nile suddenly recede from the riverbank to form a large desert "bay" about seven miles long and four miles deep. Although the name Tell el-Amarna is often used to specify the desert bay, where the city, temples and tombs were located, Akhenaten's sacred precinct incorporated the villages and fields on the west bank as well. A series of boundary stelae demarcated the borders of the sacred precinct. On the east bank the boundary followed the natural contours of the land. On the west bank, where the cliffs remain well back from the river, the northern and southern boundary lines extended due west from the respective points on the east.

B. Exploration and Excavation

The site of Tell el-Amarna has long been of interest to Europeans. It was visited many times in the 17th cent., most notably by Napoleon's expedition in 1799. Some of these early travelers published accounts of their visit to the site.

Modern archaeological investigation of the site began in the 19th cent. and has been conducted under the auspices of a number of sponsors, most notably the Egypt Exploration Society (EES), formerly the Egypt Exploration Fund (EEF). Early investigators, including John Gardner Wilkinson (1824–25) and Richard Lepsius (1843 and 1845), produced detailed plans of the city and tombs and drawings of some boundary stelae. The royal tomb was discovered and "cleared" by Alexandre Barsanti on behalf of the Egyptian Antiquities Service beginning in 1891, a process that destroyed at least as much as it preserved. The same season W. M. Flinders Petrie conducted the first serious scientific excavation of the town site. Norman de Garis Davies' EEF-sponsored expedition in 1901–07 made careful drawings of the tombs and stelae.

Ludwig Borchardt excavated the site for the Deutsche Orient-Gesellschaft in 1907–14. His most significant find was the workshop of the sculptor Thutmose, including the famous bust of Nefertiti now in the Ägyptisches Museum in Berlin. The EES sponsored expeditions in 1921–36 under a series of directors, including Thomas Eric Peet, Leonard Woolley, Henri Frankfort and John Pendlebury. Renewed excavations under the direction of Barry Kemp for the EES began in 1977. The royal tomb was reinvestigated by Geoffrey Martin in the 1970s.

C. History of Occupation

The primary period of occupation extended from the founding of Akhetaten during the reign of Akhenaten (14th cent. BCE) until the return of the capital to Memphis in the second or third year of Tutankhamen. Previous interest in the region seems to have focused on mineral resources rather than habitation. In the Middle/Upper Paleolithic the desert terraces near the later workmen's village were used for flint-working. Old Kingdom expeditions crossed the site en route to the alabaster quarries at Hatnub.

The fifteen boundary stelae which define the borders of Akhetaten indicate that it was founded in regnal year five. The city was ready for occupation by year eight or nine and functioned as the capital for the rest of Akhenaten's reign and for the brief reign of his successor Smenkhkare. The next king, Tutankhaten, soon changed his name to Tutankhamen and moved the capital back to Memphis. Shortly thereafter the city was abandoned. Many of the structures were dismantled and recycled as building materials at nearby Hermopolis.

Limited occupation continued for several centuries at a site near the riverbank. The sacred precinct outside the deserted workmen's village, where a late New Kingdom burial was found, may have served as a cemetery for the riverside settlement. The area was not extensively resettled until Late Roman times. There were two Coptic period settlements on the site, each with its own church, one in and around the north tombs and one in the southern area known as Kom el-Nana. The latter may have been a monastery.

D. Layout of the Sacred Precinct

The boundary stelae enclose a seven mile long area on both sides of the Nile. The west bank was used for cultivation. The primary residential, administrative, and religious sites stretched along the east bank. Private tombs were cut into the cliffs north and east of the city. In a wadi directly east of the central city lay the royal tomb.

Fifteen boundary stelae have been located. If there were originally more stelae, no trace of them remains. Some of the stelae are simple stelae with a depiction of the royal family carved in relief above a foundation inscription. Others form part of a rock shrine with statues of the royal family carved in the round. The inscriptions fall into two categories. Stelae K, M and X, all located

east of the river, bear the year five proclamation describing Akhenaten's discovery of the site and the proposed layout for the sacred precinct. The inscription on the other eleven stelae records the one year anniversary of the original proclamation and a renewal of the king's oath in regnal year eight.

1. Central city

The heart of AKHETATEN was the central city where the most important official activities, religious and administrative, were conducted. It was laid out in a grid with the royal road as its main axis.

The largest complex by far was the great ATEN temple, a large compound surrounded by an enclosure wall and incorporating two major sanctuaries and several smaller structures. Here Akhenaten was able to complete what he had originally undertaken at Karnak. There he had erected two structures in the shadow of the great temple of Amun-Re, the Gempaaten "The Aten is found" and the house of the *benben*, a symbol of the solar cult at Heliopolis. At Akhetaten the Gempaaten and the house of the *benben* became the centerpieces of a massive open air cult center for Aten complete with hundreds of altars and offering tables.

The king's house and the great palace lay on either side of the royal road south of the great Aten temple and were connected to each other via a bridge. Despite their names these structures were public reception halls where the king received foreign emissaries and Egyptian officials. The complex of administrative structures east of the king's house included the Place of the Letters of the Pharaoh where the king's diplomatic correspondence was stored.

South of the king's house was the small Aten temple which may have been intended to serve the traditional function of a royal mortuary temple.

2. Sites north of the central city

The royal road linked the central city with administrative and residential areas to the north, including the complex known today as the north city. The north city included a massive administrative center, numerous large villas, and the northern riverside palace which probably served as the principal royal residence.

The northern palace, an isolated structure between the north city and the central city, was the residence of Queen Meritaten, daughter of Akhetaten. Prior to her elevation to the status of chief royal wife, the residence belonged to another queen, either her mother the chief wife Nefertiti or Kiya a secondary queen.

Just north of the central city lay a residential quarter with densely packed houses of varying sizes. The area was still under development at the time the city was abandoned.

3. Sites south of the central city

A major residential and administrative area, known

today as the main city or south suburb, adjoined the central city to the south. Some residences doubled as workshops, e.g., the house/workshop of the sculptor Thutmose where the famous bust of Nefertiti was found.

The Amarna period enclosure at Kom el-Nana lay along the original route of the royal road as it extended due south from the central city. The partially excavated site featured two large shrines, a processional hall, and a bakery for the production of bread offering. The ancient name of the complex may have been the sunshade of Re of the great queen Nefertiti.

Further to the south and closer to the riverbank lay the dual enclosure called Maruaten. Both enclosures were laid out as garden shrines, the central feature of which was a rectangular pool. An inscription refers to "the sunshade of Re of the king's daughter Meritaten in the Meruaten in Akhetaten." It is unclear whether the name designated the entire complex or a portion of it.

4. Tombs

The royal tomb (Amarna tomb 26) was cut into the cliffs of the Wadi Abu Hasah el-Bahri east of the central city. The king's second daughter Meketaten was buried in a side chamber. The walls of the chamber depict the grieving family. Four other tombs (Amarna tombs 27–30), presumably intended for members of the royal family, were begun nearby.

There were two sets of private rock-cut tombs intended for the Amarna nobility. The north tombs (Amarna tombs 1–6) were cut into the cliffs northeast of the city. The south tombs (Amarna tombs 7–25) were in the cliffs east of the main city. The most historically important is tomb 25 which was prepared for Ay, the nobleman who succeeded Tutankhamen as pharaoh.

A walled settlement east of the central city housed the workmen and guards of the necropolis. Even though work stopped on the rock-cut tombs upon the death of Akhenaten, the workmen's village continued to prosper into the reign of Tutankhamen as the security center for the tombs.

Ordinary people did not rate a rock-cut tomb. Evidence suggests that they were buried in cemeteries on the desert floor southwest of the north tombs.

E. Important Finds

1. Amarna letters

A total of 382 clay tablets have been recovered from Tell el-Amarna, mostly diplomatic correspondence from the Place of the Letters of the Pharaoh in the central city. The letters document Egypt's relations with its vassals in western Asia and with independent states and imperial powers in Mesopotamia and the eastern Mediterranean. They also provide important information about the social and political context of Late Bronze Age Canaan.

2. Sculpture

The most famous sculpture from Tell el-Amarna is the painted bust of Nefertiti, which Borchardt unearthed in Thutmose's workshop. The bust was left behind because it was a sculptor's model, as were many other pieces found in that building. Alongside the models were a number of unfinished statues and heads. Statuettes of the royal family discovered in other homes probably belonged to family shrines in which the royal family was the focus of worship.

The reliefs carved on stelae and on the walls of the palaces, temples and tombs provide the primary visual expression of Akhenaten's religion. They include images of the royal family worshiping Aten, depicted as a sun-disk with rays ending in hands. The hands typically hold the hieroglyph for life before the noses of the king and queen, symbolizing Aten's gift of life.

Other reliefs depict Akhenaten and Nefertiti riding a chariot, perhaps illustrating their dramatic procession along the royal road from the northern riverside palace to the central city. Also depicted are formal official events, intimate family gatherings and scenes of everyday life.

Photo Credit: Erich Lessing / Art Resource, NY

Figure 1: Relief of royal family of Amenophis IV (Akhenaton) offering a sacrifice to Aton, the sun god. Egypt, 1350 BCE. Egyptian Museum, Cairo, Egypt.

3. Architecture

The residential quarters at Tell el-Amarna are among the most extensive ever excavated in Egypt. The homes of prominent citizens, often termed villas, share a remarkably consistent floor plan perhaps because they were built on virgin soil and did not have to be accommodated to pre-existing structures. Each house had a pillared central hall for the reception of guests. A row of entry rooms provided a buffer between the street and the interior. The private family quarters were in the rear of the building.

Archaeologists have unearthed a number of similar buildings from Late Bronze Age sites in southern Canaan. Often termed governor's houses, they more likely represent the emulation of Egyptian culture by vassal princes. Having been raised in the Egyptian court as hostages to ensure their fathers' loyalty, they aspired to live like high-ranking courtiers in the Nile Valley.

4. The great hymn to the Aten

The great hymn to the Aten is one of the most important literary expressions of Akhenaten's religion. Inscribed in the tomb of the future king Ay (Amarna tomb 25), the hymn celebrates the dependence of all creation on Aten as the source of life. Aten created the world and breathes life into each creature that is born. The world lives when Aten rises and dies when he sets.

The hymn has many parallels to Ps 104, especially verses 20–30. In that section of the psalm, human dependence on God is linked to the daily circuit of the sun. When the sun rises, the wild beasts retire to their dens, and human beings go out to work until the sun sets. The power of God to give or take life is further stressed in 104:29-30 in the metaphor of breath which God can either take away, resulting in death, or send forth, resulting in creation.

Because the Egyptian hymn and the Biblical psalm are separated by a vast gulf of time and space, it is highly unlikely that the author of Ps 104 ever read the great hymn to the Aten. Nonetheless, the hymn may have been known to the Canaanite literati of the Amarna period who drew upon its concepts and metaphors in the composition of their own creation hymns. By this mechanism Atenist influences passed into the literary world of ancient Israel. *See* EGYPT.

Bibliography: Barry J. Kemp. *Amarna Reports* (1984); Barry J. Kemp and Salvatore Garfi. *A Survey of the Ancient City of El-Amarna* (1993); Geoffrey T. Martin. *The Royal Tomb at el-Amarna*. Vol. 1–2 (1974–1989); William J. Murnane and Charles C. Van Siclen III. *The Boundary Stelae of Akhenaten* (1993).

CAROLYN R. HIGGINBOTHAM

AMASA [עֲמָשָׂא 'amasa']. 1. A military leader who led Absolom's troops during the rebellion (2 Sam 17:25). After the uprising had been crushed and ABSOLOM killed, David forgave Amasa's participation, and even put him in charge of the royal troops (19:13). This angered JOAB, and when the two men met on the road in pursuit of another rebel, Joab seized Amasa as

if to kiss him but then plunged a sword into his gut (20:8-12).

Why David would give the leader of rebel troops the highest position in the kingdom's military is an intriguing question. Most of all, David wanted to heal the division between the warring factions, and the elevation of Amasa paid off when he was able to persuade the army of Judah to support David's return to Jerusalem (19:14). David also may have been harboring resentment toward Joab for his role in the death of Absolom (18:14). David's bitterness about Joab's behavior shows in his parting words to Solomon, in which he asks his son to bring judgment on Joab for "retaliating in time of peace for blood that has been shed in war" (1 Kgs 2:5). Solomon uses this as his justification for Joab's execution (1 Kgs 2:32).

2. An Israelite soldier who opposes the taking of Judean booty in Israel's war with Judah during the time of Ahaz (2 Chr 28:12).

BRYAN D. BIBB

AMASAI uh-may'si [עֲמָשַׂי 'amasay]. 1. A Kohathite listed in the genealogies (1 Chr 6:25).

2. A Benjaminite or Judahite who was chief of David's Thirty (1 Chr 12:18), David's loyal band of warriors.

3. A priest appointed by David to blow the trumpet in front of the ark of the covenant (1 Chr 15:24).

4. The father of Mahath, a priest and Kohathite, who took part in the reforms of Hezekiah (2 Chr 29:12).

Amasai (1.) was also father to a man named Mahath, but because two centuries separate Amasai (1.) and Amasai (4.), they cannot be the same person. *See* MAASAI.

KEVIN A. WILSON

AMASHSAI uh-mash'si [עֲמַשְׁסַי 'amashsay; Αμεσσαι Amessai]. A postexilic priest, the son of Azarel and grandson of Ahzai (Neh 11:13). In a parallel account his name occurs as Maasai son of Adiel (1 Chr 9:12). Both lists trace him back to Immer, a Levitical priest descended from Eleazar (1 Chr 24:4, 14).

AMASIAH am'uh-si'uh [עֲמַסְיָה 'amasyah] "Yahu has carried." A commander in Jehoshaphat's army, a son of Zichri of Judah (2 Chr 17:16).

AMAW ay'maw [עַמּוֹ 'ammo]. In the NRSV, Amaw is named as the place where Balaam was residing when King Balak of Moab sent for him to curse the Israelites based on W. F. Albright's interpretation of 'ammo in Num 22:5. Varying textual versions scholars pose conflicting locations for Balaam's home and complicate the meaning of this passage. The Hebrew Masoretic Text simply reads, "the land of the sons of *his people*," אֶרֶץ בְּנֵי־עַמּוֹ, 'erets bene 'ammo; the LXX supports this reading (γῆς υἱῶν λαοῦ αὐτοῦ, gēs huiōn laou autou). The story line of Num 22:5 names this as the place Balaam was residing when King Balak of Moab sent for him to curse the Israelites

Albright's interpretation relies on his understanding of the term ʿammo in the Idrimi Inscription and Egyptian texts. He places Amaw east of Aleppo (in the area between Syria and Assyria), near the Euphrates River. The NRSV and several other translations rely on his interpretation and render ʿammo as "Amaw." The NRSV also identifies "the river" as the "Euphrates," though the Hebrew of Num 22:5 does not include that detail. (Deut 23:5 may also support this view of Amaw.)

Many scholars now dispute Albright's proposal. The Deir ʿAlla inscription records that Balaam was from Transjordan. That report concurs with the Latin Vulgate, Samaritan Pentateuch, and other versions of Num 22:5, which read "the land of the Ammonites." Layton has proposed that the river is the Jabbok, a location that would lend itself better to the setting of the narrative than one as far away as Aleppo. See BALAAM; DEIR ʿALLA; IDRIMI INSCRIPTION.

Bibliography: W. F. Albright. "Some Important Recent Discoveries: Alphabetic Origins and the Idrimi Statue." *BASOR* 118 (1950) 15–22; Scott C. Layton. "Whence Comes Balaam? Num 22, 5 Revisited." *Biblica* 73 (1992) 32–61; Baruch A. Levine. *Numbers 21–36.* AB 4A (2000) 148.

LISA MICHELE WOLFE

AMAZEMENT. *See* ASTONISHMENT, AMAZEMENT.

AMAZIAH amʹuh-ziʹuh [אֲמַצְיָהוּ ʾamatsyahu, אֲמַצְיָה ʾamatsyah]. 1. A descendant of DAVID, Amaziah was the ninth ruler of the Southern Kingdom of JUDAH. The brief record in 2 Kgs 14 includes several intriguing sketches of early triumphs and later failures with little commentary. The author of Chronicles follows this storyline with marked expansions.

According to 2 Kgs 12:21 and 14:2, Amaziah is enthroned at 25 after his father's murder by two officials, and reigns 29 years—a number considered implausibly high by scholars, who generally allot him 17 years beginning ca. 800 BCE. He receives qualified praise: "He did what was right in the sight of the LORD, yet not like his ancestor David" (2 Kgs 14:3). He is commended for showing his regard for justice by executing his father's assassins but sparing their children according to Mosaic law (Deut 24:16).

After defeating EDOM in battle, Amaziah sends word to King JEHOASH of Israel: "Let us look one another in the face" (2 Kgs 14:8), an ambiguous request usually read as a challenge. It is certainly taken as such by Jehoash, who scoffs with a parable comparing their relative strength to that of a cedar tree and a thornbush. But Amaziah persists, and they meet

for battle at BETH-SHEMESH, sixteen mi. southwest of Jerusalem. Amaziah is defeated, abandoned by his troops, and captured. Jehoash proceeds to Jerusalem, where he destroys about 400 cubits (600 ft.) of the city wall, raids the Temple and palace, and takes hostages, presumably in exchange for Amaziah himself. By coupling this defeat with Jehoash's clear reticence, the author suggests that Amaziah's defeat resulted from avoidable hubris.

Much later, 15 years after Jehoash's death, Amaziah is pursued by conspirators to LACHISH and assassinated. Juxtaposition with the prior story invites a connection between his disastrous foreign policy and the evidently widespread ire of his subjects; however, given the significant time gap, he could have been unpopular for other reasons. Along with Athaliah and his father Jehoash, Amaziah becomes the third ruler in a row assassinated by subjects. Despite continuing dissatisfaction with the dynasty, he is succeeded by his 16-year-old son Azariah (Uzziah).

Second Chronicles 25 expands the Edom episode, detailing the battle preparations, which include the hiring and, at a prophet's prompting, subsequent discharge of 100,000 Israelite soldiers. Enraged, the soldiers plunder several cities that are presumably Judahite, though they oddly include Samaria and Beth-horon. Amaziah, meanwhile, massacres twice as many Edomites as in the Kings story, throwing 10,000 from the pinnacle of Sela. But by worshiping Edomite gods he incurs divine wrath, precipitating his subsequent disasters. Whether these additions have any historical basis is unknown; the organization of Amaziah's life into periods of obedience/favor and rebellion/disfavor suggests that the author has added the idolatry episode as a theological explanation for Amaziah's misfortunes.

2. Levitical song leader (1 Chr 6:16; 31-32; 45).

3. Priest at Bethel who informed King Jeroboam of Amos' prophecy (Amos 7:10-13).

Bibliography: Patrick M. Graham. "Aspects of the Structure and Rhetoric of 2 Chronicles 25." *History and Interpretation* (1993) 78–89; Ann M. Vater Solomon. "Jehoash's Fable of the Thistle and the Cedar." *Saga, Legend, Tale, Novella, Fable* (1985) 126–32.

PATRICIA K. TULL

AMBASSADOR [מַלְאָךְ malʾakh, צִיר tsir; πρέσβευτής presbeytēs]. An ambassador is an official envoy between leaders. In the OT, JUDAH sends ambassadors to Egypt (Ezek 17:15) and Ethiopia (Isa 18:2). In both cases, the prophets condemn these political machinations, because they understand them as violations of Judah's covenant with Yaweh. In 1 Maccabees such diplomacy is neutrally regarded (9:70; 10:51). New Testament writers employ the term figuratively—they are ambassadors of Christ, carrying his message throughout the world (2 Cor 5:20; Eph 6:20; Phlm 1:9), though often delivering it "in chains" (from prison). *See* INTER-PRETER; MESSENGER; PRIESTS AND LEVITES.

JENNIFER L. KOOSED

AMBER [חַשְׁמַל khashmal; ἤλεκτρον ēlektron]. The English word used as a metaphor to describe a facet of brightness in the cloud and flashing fire in Ezekiel's vision (Ezek 1:4, 27; 8:2). This Hebrew noun of uncertain etymology is probably a loan word from another language; note that the Greek translation (LXX) uses ēlektron to label the bright flash in Ezekiel. Today AMBER is known as a fossilized resin produced by pine trees in the Oligocene period. It usually has yellow to brown coloring, but AMBER with white and red colorations is also known. In the ancient world, AMBER, primarily from the Baltic area, was used as a fragrance, a charm, and a medicine. It has been found in many archaeological excavations in the Levant.

ELIZABETH E. PLATT

AMBROSE. With the support of both orthodox and Arian leaders, Ambrose (ca. 339–397 CE) became bishop of Milan in 374 CE. Once in office, however, he capitalized upon his connections with Rome to oppose ARIANISM and other heresies. Although Ambrose's literary works occasionally reflect his interest in promoting orthodox theology, especially CHRISTOLOGY, BAPTISM, the EUCHARIST, and redemption, his primary concerns were practical rather than doctrinal. Thus, his writings often focus on moral and ascetic topics such as church order, ecclesiastical unity, and virginity. The liturgy he formulated became a template for later worship.

DAVID M. REIS

AMBROSIASTER. The name now given to an unknown mid-to-late 4th cent. CE Latin commentator on the Old Latin Version of the Pauline leters, long thought to be AMBROSE of Milan. His popular commentaries were used by AUGUSTINE, JEROME, and Pelagius. He is likely the author of *Quaestiones veteris et novi testamenti*, once attributed to AUGUSTINE.

MARK DELCOGLIANO

AMBUSH. Ambush is the act of deceiving and surprising an enemy by flanking its army on both sides and inflicting serious casualties on its soldiers. It is used to great effect in Joshua's assault on Ai (Josh 8) and in the Jewish forces' assault on the armies of Cestius Gallus (Josephus, *Ant.* 2.548). In the Bible "ambush" often becomes a metaphor for spiritual distress (Job 16:13; 19:12; 2 Cor 4:8). *See* BATTLE; WAR, METHODS, TACTICS, WEAPONS OF).

T. R. HOBBS

AMEN ah-men´ [אָמֵן ʾaman; ἀμήν amēn]. A term of ratification, *amen* has passed from Hebrew to Greek to English and other languages in transliteration but often untranslated. The Hebraic root indicates trustworthiness or firmness concerning what is said.

The sayings of Jesus in the Gospels are sometimes given emphasis by an introductory *amen* (e.g., Matt. 5:26; Luke 23:43). There *amen* is translated into English as "truly" [NRSV]. The Epistles use untranslated amens with some frequency, including Rom 1:25; Gal. 1:5; 1 Pet 4:11; and 1 Thess 5:28. Revelation 3:14 designates Christ himself as "the Amen, the faithful and true witness," with the implication that, in Christ, believers find authenticity and theincarnate ratification of God's covenant.

The Gospel of John uses a double *amen*, as in John 1:52—"very truly" (*see* Neh 8:6). First Corinthians 14:16 reveals that to say *amen* in the Christian assembly is to concur with that which has been spoken by another. This liturgical use of *amen* arose when no printed prayer books or hymnals existed, but congregational worship in synagogue and church had to actively involve all participants. Therefore, what an individual uttered in prayer or preaching was affirmed by the assembly; a congregational *amen* was one way of guaranteeing such participation.

Justin Martyr (ca. 100—ca. 165 CE) concluded his narration of the eucharistic rite with instructions that when the presider "has finished the prayers and the thanksgiving, all the people present give their assent by saying 'Amen.' Amen is Hebrew for 'So be it'" (*1 Apol.* 65:3-4).

Despite similarities in general design, across the long centuries of synagogue and church it is difficult to trace specific practices that have absolute continuity; but the liturgical use of the *amen* as a ratification seems constant in every era. Even so, new uses are found and sometimes discarded. For example: among Protestants, *amens* were not sung at the end of hymns. Later, the sung *amen* became popular, but only when the closing stanza was a Trinitarian doxology. Eventually *amens* were added to the majority of hymns—although not to certain categories, including "gospel songs" and Christmas carols.

More recently, the process has reversed. Some hymnals have dropped sung *amens* altogether for various reasons, but primarily because a congregational hymn is affirmed by all in the act of singing. Adding a ratification is deemed redundant. It would be more logical to ask everyone to sing an *amen* at the close of an anthem or solo, where congregational ratification would have functional meaning. Similarly, it is appropriate to have a unison *amen* at the close of a prayer spoken by one person; but for everyone to say *amen* at the end of the Lord's Prayer is pointless if all worshipers have uttered the prayer in unison. Still, such inconsistent usage is not likely to fall out of favor despite the dictates of theological logic.

Transliterated spellings of *amen* differ somewhat to conform to pertinent rules in the receiving language. Thus, when languages require that every word must end with a vowel, "amen" is rendered "ameni" in Tongan or "amine" in Maori, for example.

In English, pronunciation varies. Within the same congregation the word may be rendered AH-MEN after a hymn or prayer but AY-MEN when used to affirm personal testimonies or sermons. Differing pronunciations are determined by local or denominational practice, as well as by ethnic and regional tradition.

LAURENCE HULL STOOKEY

AMENEMOPE, INSTRUCTION OF ah´men-em´oh-pi. Although the several manuscripts preserving this piece of Egyptian wisdom literature are from a later date, it was likely composed in the 19th–20th dynasties (ca. 1305–1080 BCE). The instructions, set up as if a father were teaching his son, bring life and well-being to those who follow them and have parallels in the "Words of the Wise" (Prov 22:17–24:22). Scholars often assume a literary relationship between these two works while debating the precise nature of that relationship. The majority see the material in Proverbs as having drawn on the Instruction of Amenemope.

Bibliography: Miriam Lichtheim, *Ancient Egyptian Literature*, vol. 2 (1976) 146–63.

KEVIN A. WILSON

AMETHYST אַחְלָמָה ʾakhlamah; ἀμέθυστος amethystos]. This Hebrew term is of uncertain etymology. AMETHYST is the 9th stone in the high priest's breastpiece (Exod 28:19; 39:12). Amethystos is the 12th gem in the wall's foundation of the New Jerusalem (Rev 21:20). Especially in Egyptian archaeology, stones or glass gems ranging from light mauve to dark purple are found in beads and inlays of gold bracelets and pectorals. Today AMETHYST refers to a violet hued crystalline quartz.

ELIZABETH E. PLATT

AMI ay´mi. *See* AMON.

AMINADAB uh-min´uh-dab [Ἀμιναδάβ Aminadab]. 1. The son of ARAM and the father of NAHSON (Matt 1:4). The name is elsewhere rendered AMMINADAB. 2. The father of ESTHER (Add Esth 2:7, 15; 9:29). According to Hebrew manuscripts, Esther's father was ABIHAIL.

AMITTAI uh-mit´i [אֲמִתַּי ʾamitay]. The father of the prophet Jonah (2 Kgs 14:25; Jonah 1:1). The root, ʾamn, means "to be firm, reliable, faithful." The ay/ai ending usually indicates a shortening of a longer-phrased name. Thus: "Yahweh is faithful." *See* NAMES.

JAMES S. ACKERMAN

AMMAH am´uh [אַמָּה ʾammah]. A hill east of GIBEON where JOAB and DAVID's forces face ABNER and ISH-

BAAL's men. Abner, who killed Joab's brother ASAHEL while attempting to flee from the Battle of Gibeon, ironically appeals to Joab to end hostilities because of the close relationship between the two sides (2 Sam 2:24-32).

HEATHER R. MCMURRAY

AMMI am´i [עַמִּי ʿammi]. Ammi is the second name given to HOSEA and GOMER's son (Hos 2:1 = 2:3 in Heb.). Originally named LO-AMMI ("not my people") by God to reflect the broken covenant with the Northern Kingdom, the name was modified to Ammi ("my people") suggesting Israel's restoration.

AMMIDIANS uh-mid´ee-uhns [Ἀμμιδίοι Ammidioi]. Along with the Chadiasans, 442 belonging to these two groups returned from exile with Zerubbabel and other leaders (1 Esd 5:20). *See* GHADIASANS.

AMMIEL am´ee-uhl [עַמִּיאֵל ʾammiʾel] "My kinsman is God." 1. GAMALLI's son, the Dannite, chosen by Moses as one of the spies (Num 13:12).

2. Father of MACHIR who housed MEPHIBOSETH, JONATHAN's son, and later brought food for DAVID who fled from ABSALOM (2 Sam 9:4-5; 17:27).

3. Father of BATHSHUA (1 Chr 3:5; perhaps ELIAM, father of BATHSHEBA, 2 Sam 11:3).

4. OBED-EDOM's sixth son, one of the temple gatekeepers (1 Chr 26:5).

HEATHER R. MCMURRAY

AMMIHUD uh-mi´huhd [עַמִּיהוּד ʾammihudh]. "My relative is majesty." 1. An Ephraimite, the father of ELISHAMA (Num 1:10, 7:53), leader of the EPHRAIMITES (Num 2:18, 7:48, 10:22).

2. A member of the tribe of SIMEON (Num 34:20) who helped Moses apportion Canaan to the tribes.

3. A member of the tribe of NAPHTALI (Num 34:28), who helped apportion Canaan for Israel's tribes.

4. In 2 Sam 13:37, Ammihud (עַמִּיהוּר ʾammikhur) is the father of TALMAI, King of GESHUR, with whom Absalom found refuge from King David.

5. In 1 Chr 9:4, Ammihud is named as a postexilic Jerusalemite descended from Judah. *See* OMRI.

LISA MICHELE WOLFE

AMMINADAB uh-min´uh-dab [עַמִּינָדָב ʿamminadhav; Ἀμιναδάβ Aminadab]. 1. Amminadab ("my relative is generous, or noble") was the father of Elisheba, Aaron's wife (Exod 6:23), and the father of Nahshon, a Judahite leader (Num 1:7; 2:3; 7:12; 17, 10:14). His ancestry goes back to JUDAH and Tamar through Perez. His descendants include BOAZ (Ruth 4:19, 20; 1 Chr 2:10). The genealogies of Jesus include Amminadab (Luke 3:33; AMINADAB in Matt 1:4).

2. A LEVITE son of KOHATH (1 Chr 6:22 [Heb. 6:7]; in contrast *see* Exod 6:18; 1 Chr 6:2 [Heb. 5:28]).

3. Son of UZZIEL, who with other Levites was summoned to move the ark to Jerusalem (1 Chr 15:10, 11).

4. According to an ancient record from Ashurbanipal (ca. 668–633 BCE), Amminadabi was king of Beth-Ammon (*ANET*, 294).

LISA MICHELE WOLFE

AMMISHADDAI am-i-shad´*i* [עַמִּישַׁדָּי *'ammishadday*]. "My (divine) kin is SHADDAI." Ammishaddai appears in this text only as the father of AHIEZER, leader of the Danites (Num 1:12; 2:25; 7:66, 71; 10:25). Shaddai is often translated as "almighty." *See* ALMIGHTY GOD.

AMMIZABAD uh-miz´uh-bad [עַמִּיזָבָד *'ammizavadh*]. Son of BENAIAH, Ammizabad commanded his father's division of 24,000 troops, who were part of the monthly levy (1 Chr 27:6). Benaiah was the commander of The Thirty, also known as DAVID'S CHAMPIONS.

AMMON, AMMONITES am´uhn, am´uh-n*it*-es [עַמּוֹן בְּנֵי bene 'ammon; Ἀμμων Ammōn]. The Ammonites were a tribal people living east of the Jordan River. A reflection of their history is preserved in the name Amman, the modern capital of Jordan. In the OT the Ammonites are characteristically called the bene 'ammon, i.e., the descendants of Ammon. In the book of Genesis, the eponymous ancestor of the Ammonites is BEN-AMMI, who along with MOAB, is a product of an incestuous union between Lot and his two daughters. The etiological account in Gen 19:30-38 portrays two basic relationships. One is a claim of distant kinship between the Israelites and Ammon and Moab. The other relates Ammon to Moab. In the Iron Age and the period of regional nation-states (ca. 1000–580 BCE), the territories of Ammon and Moab abutted each other in TRANSJORDAN, and political relations between them and Israel or Judah varied between productive and antagonistic.

A. Geography and Demography

The territory inhabited by the Ammonites can be broadly described as that area north of the Arnon River (modern Wadi Mujib; *see* MUJIB, WADI EL) and south of the Jabbok River (Wadi Zarqa) which is also bounded by the Jordan River and the Dead Sea on the west and by the arid desert region on the east. Such a description requires considerable qualification, however, since other peoples also inhabited parts of the same region and at various times claimed portions of it as their own (below). With regard to a tribal people like the Ammonites, many of whom moved periodically with their flocks of sheep and goats, it is better to think of settlement patterns in a traditional homeland that expand and contract along with variations in rainfall and in response to security concerns. The tribal-based culture of the Ammonites would include urban development, i.e., some walled cities, and villages that cultivated

crops and not just supported animal husbandry. Both biblical and extra-biblical sources indicate that their political structure included monarchy.

In the center of modern Amman is the imposing citadel or mound that represented Rabbah, the capital of the nation-state of Ammon, during the Iron Age. The citadel is most likely the site of the Israelite siege depicted in 1 Sam 11, when Uriah the Hittite is killed. In the second half of the 20th cent., the modern city of Amman grew dramatically on the surrounding hills, and the construction boom resulted in the uncovering of a number of tombs with material culture from the Ammonite period. Among the artifacts are statues, pottery, jewelry, and inscribed objects. The last named items are part of a small but valuable collection of Ammonite inscriptions. Long-term excavations at Tall Hisban (HESHBON), Tall al 'Umayri, and Tall Jalul, continue to add to the understanding of Ammonite culture.

B. Old Testament

The Ammonites play a role in the biblical accounts of wilderness wandering and settlement in the promised land. Indeed, they are noted periodically throughout the historical and prophetic books, though less so in references to the postexilic period.

According to the summary given in Deut 2:19-37, the Israelite tribes approaching the Ammonites from the south were not to provoke the Ammonites or to take their land from them. Sihon, an Amorite king in the region from Heshbon, however, did come out against the Israelites and was defeated, and the Israelites took cities in the region belonging to his realm. The Ammonite settlements specifically referred to were along the Jabbok River and in the hill country (2:37). Although there are several historical difficulties associated with this summary, it does serve to explain the presence of Israelites in this region. The traditional tribal inheritances of Reuben and Gad (compare Num 32:32-38; Josh 22:1-34) are located in the area ascribed to Sihon.

The book of Judges portrays the Ammonites as one of the periodic oppressors of the Israelites. They are mentioned incidentally as cohorts with the Moabite king EGLON, who expanded his realm to include territory across the Jordan at the city of Palms, which is probably a reference to the city of Jericho (3:12-30). The Ammonites took the lead to expand their influence across the Jordan and in the hills of Gilead at the expense of the Israelites (10:6–12:7). In the exchanges between Jephthah and the Ammonites, Jephthah refers to Israelites who have lived three hundred years in the region that once belonged to Sihon (11:12-27; compare vs. 24-26). He asks why the Ammonites and their deity CHEMOSH did not regain these cities during that time. There are two striking elements in the manner in which Jephthah's message concludes. The first is the reference to Chemosh as an Ammonite deity (*see* the section on Ammonite Religion below). Elsewhere Chemosh is known as a Moabite deity. The second is the time span of 300 years, which seems unduly long. Regarding the first matter, it is possible that the passage reflects a late and clumsy effort on the part of an editor, who simply makes a historical mistake. One can then say the same thing about the chronological reference of three cent. Perhaps a late author or editor has approximated a period of settlement based on adding together lengths of oppression or rest given elsewhere in the book of Judges. On the other hand, the close relationship between Moab and Ammon may be behind the odd reference to Chemosh and the mention of Balak, king of Moab, in 11:24-25.

Both Saul and David fight against the Ammonites (1 Sam 11:1-13; 2 Sam 10:1–11:25; 12:26-31). Saul was able to muster an army and defeat the Ammonites led by Nahash. An expanded version of the account was discovered in a Hebrew manuscript of Samuel among the Dead Sea Scrolls (see end of 1 Sam 10 NRSV). In the case of David, the siege of the Ammonite capital Rabbah and subsequent control of Ammon is narrated in the context of the king's adultery with Bathsheba. After their defeat, David takes the Ammonite crown as a trophy. Several of the limestone statues from the Ammonite period discovered in the area of greater Amman depict either a king or deity wearing a prominent crown similar to the Egyptian Atef crown (fig. 1).

Figure 1: King or Deity Wearing Atef-style Crown, Amman Museum, Jordan.

Oracles against Ammon occur in several of the prophetic books (Amos 1:13-15; Jer 49:1-6; Ezek 21:20-32; 25:1-7; Zeph 2:8-10). These presuppose ongoing ten-

sions between Judah and Ammon, although Solomon had an Ammonite wife (1 Kgs 11:1; 14:31). BAALIS, an Ammonite king, reportedly conspired against Gedaliah, the governor of Judah appointed by the Babylonians in the aftermath of Jerusalem's downfall (Jer 40:14). In the postexilic period an Ammonite named Tobiah was influential in Jerusalem (Neh 2:10, 19; 3:35).

C. Ancient Near Eastern Context

Ammon is known from extra-biblical texts, including those that archaeologists and epigraphers define as Ammonite. For example, there are references to the Ammonites in neo-Assyrian texts from the time of TIGLATH-PILESER III. Among the corpus of Ammonite texts are references to rulers of Ammon that supplement the list of rulers named in either the Bible or the Assyrian annals. One name deciphered on a seal impression is baal yisha', possibly the Baalis known from a reference in Jer 40:14 (fig. 2).

Figure 2: Seal impression from ʿUmayri.

Archaeological research suggests that the Ammonite culture and kingdom flourished in the 7th or 6th cent. BCE. However, the Babylonians curtailed political expansion. The Ammonite city of Rabbah was renamed Philadelphia and included among the cities of the DECAPOLIS during the Hellenistic period. As the Nabatean culture (see NABATEANS) expanded from the south, it also made its influence felt in the land of Ammon.

D. Ammonite Religion

Three times MILCOM is described as the deity of the Ammonites (1 Kgs 11:5, 33; 2 Kgs 23:13). Such a description does not mean the Ammonites were monotheists, but suggests at least that the royal cult in Ammon venerated Milcom and that this deity was a defining element in Ammonite culture. These references are all in polemical contexts and it would be unwise to assume biblical "Milcom" reflects Ammonite pronunciation, but apparently the texts do preserve accurately the name/title of an Ammonite deity. Unvocalized Ammonite texts also preserve references to a deity mlkm. Milcom is derived from the root word מָלַךְ malakh, "to rule." The most common deity in Ammonite texts, however, is אֵל ʾel, which can be translated generically as "god" or specifically as a proper name. If the latter, then the Iron Age Ammonite cult likely preserved the worship of the Canaanite high god El, known from Bronze Age texts and cultures. In either case, Milcom/mlkm could be a title/epithet of ʾel, or a separate deity altogether.

Bibliography: Burton MacDonald and Randall Younker, eds. *Ancient Ammon* (1999).

J. ANDREW DEARMAN

AMNON am´non אַמְנוֹן ʾamnon]. 1. The firstborn son of DAVID and AHINOAM (2 Sam 3:2). His name, ironically, means *faithful.* Amnon rapes and discards his half-sister TAMAR (2 Sam 13; a violation of laws in Exod 22:16; Lev 18:9-11 and Deut 22:28-29; 27:22). David refuses to punish him, one of several stories of David's failure to hold himself and his family accountable to Israelite laws. In retribution ABSALOM, Tamar's full brother, orders his servants to kill Amnon.

2. A son of Shimon in the list of Judahite descendants (1 Chr 4:20).

Bibliography: John Van Seters. *In Search of History: Historiography in the Ancient World and the Origins of Biblical History* (1997).

HEATHER R. MCMURRAY

AMOK ay´mok עָמוֹק ʾamoq]. A priest and the ancestor of a priestly group who returned to Jerusalem with Zerubbabel from exile (Neh 12:7, 20).

AMON am´uhn אָמוֹן ʾamon; Ἡμείμ Ēmeim]. 1. One of the most important ancient Egyptian primordial gods, whose name, "the Hidden," is a possible reference to his mysterious nature. The suggestion that his name is connected to "wind" and "breath of life" is a matter of dispute, and is possibly based on the mistaken understanding that Amon's original nature was air; however, air, together with light and water, is simply one of the elements of Amon's immanent manifestation. The god is mostly represented as having a human form, with a characteristic headdress composed by two upright tall feathers, and his sacred animal is the ram. Amon is also associated with the deity Min, whose characteristics are virility and fertility.

Amon's first occurrence in Egyptian literature is in the Unas Pyramid Texts (PT 446) where the god is included, along with his feminine counterpart Amaunet, among the eight primeval gods and goddesses who constitute the Ogdoad of Hermopolis. From the 11th dynasty onward, Amon's influence becomes more localized, and the god is worshiped as the city-god of Thebes. Amon's primacy is stengthened throughout the New Kingdom, with the only exception the Amarna period, and particularly since the 18th dynasty, in his association with the sun god Ra, Amon is elevated to the role of chief god of the pantheon. In this new role he is venerated in the temple of Karnak as the state god of Egypt. During the 21st dynasty a new religious role was instituted as part of the cult of Amon: the title of "god's wife of Amon" was bestowed upon royal women, thus strengthening the connection between the royal family and the god. In the OT, Amon is mentioned directly in Jer 46:25, in an oracle in which Yahweh proclaims, through the words of the prophet, that he will punish "Amon from No (Thebes)" through Nebuchadnezzar of Babylon. Amon is also mentioned indirectly in Nah 3:8, where the sack of No-Amon ("city of Amon"), i.e., Thebes, perpetrated by the Assyrian Esarhaddon in 663 BCE, is an example for the Assyrians that their rule is similarly destined to failure.

ANNALISA AZZONI

2. Samaria's governor under King AHAB of Israel. Ahab turned the prophet Micaiah over to Amon and Joash (1Kgs 22:24-28).

3. King of Judah after the death of his father, Manasseh. Although the name means "faithful," Amon, like his father before him, worshiped other gods. Amon came to the throne at the age of twenty-two and reigned for two years (ca. 642–40), then was assassinated, possibly for pro-Assyrian policies (2 Kgs 21:19-26//2Chr 33:21-25). His assassins were put to death by the people, who subsequently placed Amon's son Josiah upon the throne.

4. Ēmeim in 2 Esd 17:59. One of Solomon's servants, whose descendants returned from the Babylonian exile (Neh 7:59; "Ami" in the par. at Ezra 2:57.

HEATHER R. MCMURRAY

AMORA, AMORAIM אֲמוֹרָא ʾamora', אֲמוֹרִים ʾamorim]. Babylonian Aramaic noun denoting "speaker." In Rabbinic literature the term designates 1) a rabbi's spokesperson, the functional equivalent of the modern teaching assistant; and 2) rabbis from the close of the MISHNAH (ca. 220 CE) to the end of antiquity (499 CE). To these people are attributed laws (halakhah), biblical commentary (midrash), prayers, poems, aphorisms, anecdotes, and declarations concerning theology, history, biology, medicine, folklore, etc. (HAGGADAH). These utterances appear in the two Talmuds and in midrashim (q.v.). The designation *speakers* may reflect the conviction that their teachings were composed and transmitted orally.

MAYER I. GRUBER

AMORITES am´uh-r*i*ts [אֱמֹרִי ’emori]. In the OT, *Amorite* is a term for inhabitants in and around the land of CANAAN. On occasion, it is used as a general reference to pre- and non-Israelite inhabitants; at other times it is used to describe a segment, that is, one population group among several, inhabiting the land of Canaan before the Israelite settlement in the land. In Mesopotamia, the Amurru (a cognate term) were peoples located to the west and north. Indeed, the etymology of Amurru indicates "west/western."

A. Old Testament

The term *Amorite(s)* occurs primarily in the Pentateuch and in the prophets in narrative accounts of Israel's history. In the ten times it is used outside of these two collections, the term is used in texts that refer to the role of the Amorites in the national storyline, which is described in Josh 24:8, 15-18. Beginning with the books of Samuel and Kings, the term is used less frequently.

The first employment of the name *Amorite* in the Pentateuch comes in the so-called Table of Nations in Gen 10. The NATIONS of the known world are grouped there according to descent from one of Noah's three sons: Shem, Ham, and Japhet. Canaan, the son of Ham, is the eponymous ancestor of Sidon, Heth (= Hittites), Jebusites, Amorites, Girgashites, Hivites, Arkites, Sinites, Arvadites, Zemarites, and Hamathites (10:15-18). Some of those named are obscure; nevertheless, a KINSHIP connection is made between these "families of Canaan" and the Amorites. Lists of pre-Israelite nations occur periodically in the Pentateuch and Former Prophets, but their number is not fixed. Deuteronomy 7:1 refers to the seven nations of the land whose territory is to be given over to Israel. Amorite is joined with Hittites, Jebusites, Girgashites, Hivites, Perizzites and Canaanites. All except the Perizzites are in the list of Canaanite families in Gen 10:15-8. One may encounter five peoples (Num 13:5), most frequently it is six (Exod 3:8, 17; 23:3; 33:2; 34:11), and occasionally it is seven (Deut 7:1; Josh 3:10) or even more (Gen 15:19-21). The representative number of seven nations survives in summary presentations (e.g., Acts 13:19).

Some references to the peoples of Canaan offer no geographic or cultural specificity except to the particularity of their name. Sometimes the terms for the people are overlapping or used synonymously (below). On occasion, however, some distinction is offered, as when the Amorites are associated with hills and mountains. For example, in Num 13:29 the Amalekites, another population group in the region, are associated with the Negev or southern reaches of the land of Canaan; the Hittites, Amorites, and Jebusites are placed in the hill country; and the Canaanites are linked with the Mediterranean coast and the Jordan River valley (cf. Deut 1:7; Josh 5:1; 11:3). The hills and tableland east of the Jordan are also associated with the Amorites, although some of this territory exceeds the boundaries of Canaan described in Num 34:1-12. Two kings of the Amorite peoples east of the Jordan are named in the accounts of occupation: Sihon from Heshbon and Og from Bashan (Num 21:21-25; Deut 4:47; 31:4; Ps 135:11). According to Num 21:13, the border between the Amorites and the Moabites was the Arnon River (modern Wadi Mujib). Heshbon is part of the tableland north of the Arnon and east of the Dead Sea. According to Num 32:39 Amorites inhabited Gilead, the forested hills east of the Jordan River. Bashan would be territory to the north and northeast of Gilead, where Og had established rule.

The covenant ceremony narrated in Gen 15:9-21 concludes with a description of the future for Abram's descendants, along with references to land that they will possess. In 15:16 the "iniquity of the Amorites" apparently refers inclusively to the inhabitants of the land. In 15:19-21, however, the Amorites are but one of ten peoples listed for the land between the river of Egypt and the Euphrates River. In Abram's own time, however, he had established good relations with some of the Amorites in the land (Gen 14:13). The prophet Amos stands in the tradition of referring generally to the pre-Israelite inhabitants as Amorites in the summary statement of 2:9, that God "destroyed the Amorite before them (= Israelites), although his height was like that of cedars and his strength like that of oaks." The summary of the national storyline in Joshua's final testament describes the inhabitants of the promised land west of the Jordan as "Amorites" and the deities worshiped there as "gods of the Amorites" (Josh 24:8, 15-18; Judg 6:10).

B. Ancient Near Eastern References

Mesopotamian sources from the late 3rd and 2nd millennium use the cognate term *Amurru* as one way to refer to the tribal peoples who live west of them. On the basis of these texts and some questionable judgments from the investigation of material culture, some scholars have reconstructed waves of Amorites coming and receding through the Fertile Crescent, and then linked them with the movement of Abraham and his family in the earlier part of the 2nd millennium BCE. This appears to be an overreach on the part of historical reconstruction, although the Mesopotamian texts do preserve a number of personal names of these "Amorites" that are related in form and syntax to names in the early biblical tradition. Egyptian documents from the Late Bronze Age give evidence of a kingdom in the southern Orontes Valley named Amurru. It was involved in the affairs of the region and linked diplomatically with Egypt.

Bibliography: H. B. Huffmon. *Amorite Personal Names in the Mari Texts: A Structural and Lexical Study* (1965); Victor H. Matthews. *Pastoral Nomadism in the Mari Kingdom* (1978).

J. ANDREW DEARMAN

AMOS, BOOK OF ay′muhs. Among the prophets in ancient Israel, Amos (עָמוֹס 'amos) was the first to be associated with a book that preserves his words. For the first time we see an extensive collection of recorded prophecies associated with a prophet. Paradoxically, however, very little personal information is available concerning the prophet himself in contrast to some of the earlier prophetic figures such as Ahijah, Elijah, and Elisha. Because of the paucity of the information, the available information has been subjected to close scrutiny.

    A. Person
        1. Origin
        2. Occupation
        3. Calling
    B. Book
        1. Literary features
        2. Outline of content
        3. Composition and structure
    C. Sociohistorical Context
        1. Colonization
        2. Regional specialization
        3. Demographics
        4. Trade and commerce
           a. The growth of urban centers
           b. Militarization
           c. Extraction of surplus
           d. Lifestyle of the upper class
           e. Trade and commerce
           f. Market condition
           g. Indebtedness of the peasants
           h. Role of the creditors
           i. Role of judicial courts
        5. Heart of the economic issue
    D. Key Themes
        1. End of Israel
        2. Day of Yahweh
        3. God as sovereign
        4. Social injustices
        5. Empty rituals
        6. Inevitable judgment
        7. Promise of restoration
    E. Contemporary Relevance
    Bibliography

A. Person

1. Origin

Amos came from a town about 15 km south of Jerusalem called Tekoa (1:1). Curiously, we have a prophet of Judean origin but functioning primarily in the north. This prompts Amaziah, the priest of Bethel, to admonish Amos to go back to where he came from (7:12). Why did Amos feel compelled to prophesy in the north while he probably had enough to worry about in the south? One explanation is his belief in the vision of a Davidic empire as the true destiny of Israel. Amos'

prophetic ministry relates primarily to the context of and issues raised by the first part of 8th cent. Israel and Judah.

2. Occupation

There is uncertainty surrounding Amos' occupation and thus his social location. Earlier characterizations of the prophet, which tended to be rather sentimental and romantic, envisioned him as a poor, lowly shepherd whose solitary life of herding made him a strong and meditative soul. Germane to this discussion is the reference to Amos as a נֹקֵד noqedh. Traditionally, the Hebrew term has been rendered as *shepherd*. But in light of the use of the same term with reference to the Moabite king, Mesha (2 Kgs 3:4, the only other use of the term), it is more likely that Amos was a *sheep breeder* than a simple shepherd. This would place Amos not among the poor but among people of some means. Although his position is probably not on par with the Moabite king in a socioeconomic sense, it is clear is that we have to abandon any notion of Amos as a poor country shepherd.

Another description used of Amos is בּוֹלֵס *boles*, often rendered as *dresser* of sycamore trees or mulberry figs. The fruit of the sycamore trees is not as sweet as the real figs, but through a process of pricking and tending the fruit could be made more edible. The references to Amos as a noqedh and boles may point to the double occupation of Amos as an owner of livestock and grower of mulberry figs.

3. Calling

Much discussion has centered on the verbless sentence in 7:14 attributed to Amos: "not a prophet; not (even) a son of a prophet." If one reads with a present tense of the verb *to be*, the sentence implies that Amos is disassociating himself from the prophetic guild, that is, from the professional group of prophets who enjoyed royal patronage. Thus, Amos declares that he is not a central prophet with any kind of position, status, or clout within the broader structures of the society. If one supplies the past tense of the verb *to be*—"I *was* not a prophet nor a son of prophet (to begin with)"—the implication is that Amos has become a prophet by virtue of his calling. Another possibility is to interpret the terms חֹזֶה khozeh ("seer/visionary") and נָבִיא navi' ("prophet") as conveying regional associations. Thus, khozeh is the Judean designation for the prophet and navi' the designation for prophet in the north. However one reads 7:14, Amos clearly insists on his right to exercise his prophetic vocation because of his calling.

B. Book

1. Literary Features

For a relatively small composition, the book of Amos is fairly complex in terms of its nature and literary history. The book incorporates a variety of literary materials including but not limited to judgment invectives (4:1-3; 5:7, 10-13, 18-24; 6:1-7), vision reports (7–9), biographic materials, hymnic fragments (4:13; 5:8ff.; 9:5ff.), and didactic materials (3:3-8). The occurrence of numerical sayings in the opening two chapters and the didactic style in 3:3-8 raise the question of Wisdom's influence on Amos. This is further supported by the intriguing reference to Joab sending for a "wise woman" from Tekoa (2 Sam 14:1-2).

From a rhetorical perspective, some of the sections within the book exhibit masterful use of techniques with tremendous effect. One classic instance stands at the very outset of the book where the *Oracles against Nations* in 1:1–2:5 are used as a set-up to render judgment against Israel (2:6b-8). As the intended Israelite audience is gloating in the fate of its neighbors, Amos lowers the boom when they least expect it. In another instance, Amos takes the popular expectation concerning the Day of Yahweh as an occasion for Israel's deliverance and turns it on its head (5:18-20).

2. Outline of content

The book opens with a superscription situating the context of Amos' prophetic ministry (1:1-2). The first major section to follow is the oracles addressed to Damascus, Gaza, Tyre, Edom, Ammon, Moab, and Judah, which culminates in the oracle against Israel. Amos 3:1–6:14 contain a variety of invectives, most of which are addressed to specific groups of people. This is followed by a series of vision reports—locusts (7:1-3); fire (7:4-6); plumb line (7:7-9); summer fruit (8:1-3); and Yahweh at the altar (9:1-6). Interspersed in the middle is the account of the confrontation at Bethel (7:10-17). Another set of oracles follows in 8:4-14 and 9:7-10. The book ends with a promise of restoration for the Davidic house in 9:11-15.

3. Composition and structure

The compositional history of the book is also complex. The scholarly approach to the growth of the book has been wide-ranging. Wolff proposes a complex six-layer redactional history. The first two levels comprise the words of Amos (3–6, most of the vision reports in 7–9, and the Oracles against the Nations, excluding 1:9-12 and 2:4-5). The third level (e.g., 7:10-19) is an early redaction provided by the circle of Amos' disciples. Wolff traces three additional redactional layers to the Josianic (e.g., the hymnic pieces in 4:13; 5:8-9; and 9:5-6), Deuteronomic (1:9-12; 2:4-5), and postexilic periods (9:11-15). Coote posits a simple scheme involving three layers of redaction pertaining to the 8th (stage A), 7th (stage B), and 6th (stage C) cent. BCE. Most scholarly treatments seem to agree on the concentration of 8th cent. materials in 3–6 and that the book in its final form also reflects editorial modifications from the 7th and 6th cent. Möller challenges the redactional approach to the book. He argues that the final form of the book presents the debate between Amos and the Israelites as a warning to the Judeans. Möller points to some interesting rhetorical features, which demarcate the book into nine sections. The initial section (OAN) is marked by the reoccurrence of "Thus says Yahweh." Each of the next three sections (3:1-15; 4:1-13; and 5:1-17) is introduced by "Hear/Listen." The two sections that follow (5:18-27 and 6:1-14) are introduced by the particle "Woe." The vision cum narrative sections in 7:1–8:3 are marked by "The Lord showed me." The phrase "Hear/Listen" is also found in 8:4-14, par. chs. 3, 4, and 5. The final section is introduced by the words "I saw the Lord," which mirrors "The Lord showed me." These rhetorical features might reflect a careful shaping of the materials to make a point. In addressing the compositional history, it is not necessary to settle on a particular number of editions. What is important, however, is to recognize the dynamics inherent in the transmissional history of materials from antiquity. Traditions survived due to a process of interpretation and appropriation involving the tradents and recipients. Hence, in the process of transmission, each layer of interpretation, even if it does not originate with the prophet, is just as critical in preserving the continuity of the prophetic message as the words of the prophet. The key to an understanding of these interpretive layers is a keen sense of the context and issues reflected explicitly or implicitly in the text. Using particular issues and context as an indicator may be a more helpful way to date the different layers of materials in the book.

The materials pertinent to the context and issues of 8th cent. Israel are concentrated to a large extent in chs. 3–6 (*see* below). At the front end of this nucleus stand the Oracles against the Nations—chs. 1–2. The collection of vision reports—chs. 7–9—brackets the nucleus at the other end. It is difficult to assign a precise date to the oracles, as they tend to contain a mix of old and new materials. Older materials were often used in later contexts, giving rise to newer synthesis. The oracles are used as a set-up for the condemnation of Israel. From a literary perspective, this section is a brilliant introduction to the detailed critique of social reality in 8th cent. Israel in chs. 3–6. The placement of the vision reports at the end of the book is somewhat unusual. One would expect them to come at the beginning. But in Amos's scheme, the trenchant critique in 3–6 only demonstrates why judgment is inevitable as illustrated through the vision reports in 7–9.

C. Sociohistorical Context

The superscription of the book places Amos's prophetic ministry during the reigns of Jeroboam II (786–746 BCE) in Israel and Uzziah (783–742) in Judah. Two aspects stand out about this period. First, the first part of 8th cent. was a period of unprecedented economic growth and political stability for Israel and Judah under Jeroboam II and Uzziah, respectively. Second, in light of the above, it is anomalous that the prophetic materials that relate to this period give the impression that not all was well. In fact, this is the period that also gives rise to the most number of and the most intense of prophetic oracles. This section will seek to address both aspects in some detail.

That the first part of the 8th cent. was a period of prosperity and growth can be substantiated by looking at some specific indicators: colonization, regional specialization, demographics, and trade and commerce.

1. Colonization

Jeroboam II and Uzziah were not only powerful in forging a strong state domestically, they were also able to expand into neighboring territories and wield control over their neighbors. Second Chronicles 26:6-8 describes a large-scale expansion of the Judean hegemony under Uzziah. According to this passage, the colonizing activity of Uzziah extended into (a) the Philistine cities of Gath, Jabneh, and Ashdod; (b) Gur-baal where the Arabs lived; and (c) Egypt. In 2 Chr 17:11 we read that the Philistines and the Arabs brought tributes and presents to Uzziah. The kings of Judah repeatedly made efforts to penetrate the Philistine plains with a view toward gaining control over the Philistine section of the Way of the Sea (*Via Maris*).

The *Via Maris* was a major trade route, which ran along the coast through the Philistine plain connecting Egypt with Mesopotamia and Anatolia. Some of the important cities along this section were Ashdod, Ashkelon, and Joppa. The main route continued in the direction of the Plain of Sharon and turned NE toward the Jezreel Valley. This section of the route, which went through the mountainous Ephraimite hill country, was very important. The passes on this road were strategically important as they could be blocked easily. One such pass opens into Megiddo. It is small wonder that Megiddo played such a major role in the fortification system of ancient Israel. Archaeological excavations at sites such as Tell Mor and Tell Nagila indicate a Judean presence in the Philistine territory.

The expansion eastward includes areas immediately east of the Jordan Valley, the Dead Sea, and the ʿArabah. The Transjordanian areas included the more prominent biblical places of Bashan, Gilead, Ammon, and Edom. The control of this region was keenly sought by many powers for centuries for two reasons: 1) its economic importance and 2) the trade route that plied through the length of the Transjordanian plateau. The economic importance of this region was in terms of its agricultural and herding resources. The King's Highway, which connected Egypt and Arabia with Syria and Mesopotamia, facilitated movement of goods and thereby generated income for those who controlled the trade route through tolls from caravans. Second Kings 14:25 reports that Jeroboam II "restored the border of Israel from the entrance of Hamath as far as the sea of

ʿArabah." Under Amaziah of Judah, the southernmost part of the highway came under Judean control (2 Kgs 14:7). His son and successor, Uzziah, is credited with the rebuilding of Elath (2 Chr 26:2).

From the point of view of climactic conditions and agricultural resources, the expansion into the Negev (area which slopes into the desert region) may seem inexplicable. Despite the climactic snags and topographical limitations, the Negev continued to attract the Judean kings as an avenue for territorial expansion. The Negev had its own advantages. First of all, most of the roads leading to Egypt, Arabia, and Edom passed through the Negev. This network of roads was, in fact, a means of conducting international and inter-regional commerce. Second, the Negev served as a defense frontier on the boundary. It was an effective buffer zone against infiltrating desert groups and other enemies. Third, the Negev gave access to the ʿArabah, whose economic importance was its rich copper mines. Finally, the Negev provided another settlement space for the excess population of the Judean kingdom. The network of trade routes, the system of strategically located fortresses, and the groups of settlements in the Negev region all point to the conclusion that this was a conscious and well-planned drive on the part of the Judean monarchy to colonize this area. Uzziah certainly becomes the prime candidate for such an initiative.

2. Regional specialization

Geographical conditions suited to particular crops and economic activities promote regional specialization. Second Chronicles 26:10 offers some clues concerning regional specialization in Judah under Uzziah. This passage reflects regional specialization with the promotion of herding in the steppes by building guard towers and providing water by means of hewn cisterns; intensive cultivation of staples like wheat and barley in the fertile plains where there was adequate supply of water; and development of viticulture in the hill country, which is best suited for it. In terms of geographic potential, Israel and Judah offer a striking variety. The various specialized economic activities included viticulture, olive orcharding, mining and metallurgy, dyeing and weaving, the perfume industry, and farming and herding.

3. Demographics

Another indicator of growth and development in the 8th cent. is the changes in demographics. The growth of economy brings about changes in the demographic pattern. The increase or decrease in economic activities unique to particular areas is bound to affect the population numbers. Even though paleodemographic studies are few and far in between, there have been some estimates on the basis of circumstantial and indirect information. One such avenue of information is the growth of cities. On the basis of the increased building activity seen in the 8th cent. levels of sites such as Hazor, Samaria, Tell Beit Mirsim, Tell el-Kheleifeh, Tell es-Saʾdiyah, Tell en-Nasbeh, Beersheba, Megiddo, Tell el-Hesi, and Jerusalem, it is possible to assume changes in the nature and number of the population.

4. Trade and commerce

The overall picture we derive is that of a thriving trade and commerce in the 8th cent. BCE. The available information indicates that interregional and international trade was initiated, maintained, and monopolized by the crown. It is precisely at the times when there was a strong centralized power that there was also thriving trade. The geopolitical advantage enjoyed by Israel and Judah in the 8th cent. enabled them to control trade and commerce through the control of trade routes. This had two very favorable outcomes for the elites. First, the entire trade enterprise was geared toward procuring items of interest and demand to the elites. This included strategic military items and other luxury items. Second, since the elites controlled the trade, they were also the beneficiaries of the lucrative trade enterprises. The profitable nature of inter-regional and international trade prompted the production of commodities or articles, which had good exchange value. Commodities such as wine and oil were worth more in terms of their exchange value per unit of volume and weight in comparison to grain. Hence wine and olive oil, the agricultural specialties of Palestine, were prominent items in export/import exchanges.

In discussions concerning 8th-cent. Israel and Judah, the question often neglected is: Who were the beneficiaries of this growth and prosperity, or at whose expense were such prosperity and growth achieved? The anomaly one needs to explain is this: Why do the most number and the most intense of prophetic oracles come from a period that enjoyed significant prosperity and growth? One explanation is that the growth and prosperity witnessed in the first part of the 8th cent. benefited only a small minority of the population: the members of the ruling class. Through an organized system of taxation, they were able to extract the economic surplus. The surplus went to support a life of leisure and luxury, which is characterized by palatial private residences, conspicuous consumption, use of luxury items such as fine linen, expensive ornaments and perfume, and nonproductive recreational activity. Considerable surplus was also invested in providing for military means in order to gain political control. Stronger political control results in greater socioeconomic benefit. This in turn enables the elite to invest even more in the military. And so goes the vicious cycle. The cumulative effect is the impoverishment of the peasantry, who constituted the majority of the population.

5. Heart of the economic issue

The heart of the issue in the 8th cent. socioeconomic reality is the growth of large estates in the hands of a minority class of landowners. The small plots of land to which the common peasants had access for residence and cultivation of staples were taken away by the landed elite. This phenomenon is related to and is a result of various factors.

a. The growth of urban centers. A market-oriented economy gives rise to the emergence of privileged social groups such as ruling class, officials of the royal administration, wealthy landowners, merchants, and moneylenders. Conversely, the whole market economy is geared toward catering to the whims and fancies of these privileged groups. The best of the goods and services flowed into a handful of urban centers. The importance of the urban center/city stems from its political (administrative and military), economic, and religious functions. The social groups associated with these various functions had to be supported. Being the productive base, the vast agricultural periphery was the main provider of goods and services to the urban centers. In the initial stages of the development of agrarian societies, this might have been an arrangement of mutual benefit. The primary producers provided goods and services in return for military protection. But with the balance of power tilted in favor of the ruling class, the mutual dependence soon degenerated into outright exploitation. The cities as administrative centers of the state functioned effectively in extracting the surplus from the rural areas. The urban centers virtually lived off the rural areas.

b. Militarization. The dominance of the ruling class over the peasant group is possible because of the military power of the former. There is a concerted effort to ensure that the state has a strong military force at its disposal. The ruling class understood the basic equation that the stronger one's military power, the more powerful one can be politically. The more political power one has, the more social and economic benefits one can derive.

c. Extraction of surplus. The systematic extraction of agricultural surplus was accomplished through a careful system of taxation. Two things are critical to the success of the taxation system. First, the highly organized nature of the operations of ruling aristocracy gives them an advantage even though they are a minority. Second, the ruling class can accomplish what it wants because it has the military power.

d. Life-style of the upper class. The extracted agricultural surplus went to support a life of leisure and luxury for the elite. Two key words, which describe the life-style of the upper class, are leisure and luxury.

e. Trade and commerce. One other area with significant impact at many levels is the growth of trade and commerce. In agrarian monarchies, trade and commerce is initiated, maintained, and monopolized by the royal group. Hence the beneficiaries of this enterprise are also the same group of people. In fact, interregional or international trade is geared toward procuring items that are of value and interest to this group. In this connection, the systematic development and control of trade routes is vital for the movement of goods as well as for generating revenues from trading caravans.

f. **Market condition.** This refers to the abuses/corrupt practices in the market situation. With the advent of a wider market orientation, drastic changes occur in the area of production. The demands of the market forces promote the cultivation of those crops that produce maximum economic advantage. This means that more and more lands are converted to producing commercial crops, leaving the staples, which the peasants needed for survival, in short supply. Consequently, peasants are forced to buy the staples in the market, which they once produced themselves. The merchants took advantage of the peasants' unfamiliarity with the market conditions and shortchanged them through unscrupulous tampering and deceit in the transactions.

g. **Indebtedness of the peasants.** Many factors drove the peasants into debt. First, the exactions in agricultural produce were heavy; sometimes more than half of the total produce. Prices tend to be the lowest at the time of the harvest. Illegal business practices on the part of the landowners further cut into the returns. Second, the peasants bore the brunt of much of the taxation to support the programs of the state. The energies of the peasants were expended on fulfilling their agricultural and state obligations. Third, when peasants are dependent primarily upon rain for agriculture, there are serious consequences. If the rains fail, then they are forced to borrow to feed the family. If the rains fail for subsequent seasons, then the peasant goes into deeper debt. Often, the peasants offered either the piece of land they owned or an article of value or a member of the family as collateral. Failure to repay mounting loans resulted in the foreclosure of land and/or being sold into debt slavery. Accumulation of land through debt instruments becomes a way of creating large estates.

h. **Role of the creditors.** The creditors and moneylenders play a critical role in the impoverishment of the peasantry. It is conceivable that the creditors and moneylenders were the landed elite themselves or a separate class within that group who specialized in that operation.

i. **Role of judicial courts.** The courts had the function of establishing justice—a concept that had a legal connotation of establishing who was in the right and what was right based on the principle of entitlement. But these courts had become the very instrument of subverting justice. Amos' critique reflects many of these aspects, as shown below.

D. Key Themes
1. End of Israel
Amos' preaching is shaped by his conviction that the end of Israel is inescapable. Rather than being a mere futuristic prediction, Amos' conviction is borne out of his keen observation of what was happening in the society. The prophet's message of judgment is anchored in a solid understanding of issues confronting his society.

2. Day of Yahweh
The overarching conceptual framework for Amos' message of judgment is the Day of Yahweh. In Israelite thinking, any event or momentous occasion that had the potential to change the course of human history could be designated as "day." Further, the "day" derived its significance by virtue of its association to the One whose moment it is. In its original usage, the "day of Yahweh" signaled God's intervention on behalf of Israel. In Amos' hands, it undergoes an unexpected twist. Yahweh will come not to rescue but to punish Israel. This is a shocking twist for Amos' contemporaries. But it speaks volumes for the creative imagination and powerful conviction of the prophet.

3. God as sovereign
Amos speaks with such conviction because of his submission to the sovereignty of God. He has a profound sense of who God is and what God desires. This is clearly illustrated by his use of the Day of Yahweh, a concept that conveys his fundamental belief in the sovereignty of God. This is also reflected in the use of the OAN. Even though the literary history of this genre is complex and the anti-nations sentiment uncomfortable, its theological intent is clear. God is the ultimate sovereign whose claim relativizes all other claims. No nation is to conduct itself as though it were a law unto itself. In order to understand this particular genre, it is important to keep in mind that the intended hearers of this speech were Israel and/or Judah, even though the addressee may be a foreign nation.

4. Social injustices
The name and message of Amos has become synonymous with the call for justice. What sets apart Amos' call for justice is its concrete and specific nature. For the 8th cent. prophets of Israel in general and Amos in particular, poverty or injustice or oppression is no accident. They speak with clarity and specificity, knowing what the oppression is, who the oppressors and the oppressed are. The afore-mentioned delineation of various aspects of the social reality of the 8th cent. is the backdrop for understanding Amos' critique. The very first oracle against Israel (2:6b-8) indicates whose side the prophet is on. This is an indictment of the conditions that led to the indebtedness of the peasant. Amos 3:9-11 is an indictment against the role of the urban centers in contributing to oppression. The opening lines here draw attention to the violent and oppressive crimes of the elite. The urban centers represent the prosperity and development achieved at the expense

of the rural periphery. The occurrence of "fortified palaces" four times in this passage is noteworthy, because such strongholds would be the residential quarters of the upper class or military officials. Amos 6:1-3 picks up the same concern. Verse 1 refers to the upper crust of the society. The reference to Kullani and Hamath is also revealing, because they were important commercial centers in Syria. The comparison between the Syrian and the Israelite centers is not only to show their function as commercial hubs but also to drive home the point that Israel will meet with a similar fate as Kullani and Hamath. The systematic extraction of surplus through taxation is reflected in 5:11-12 and 7:1. In most translations of 5:11, the verb is rendered in a more general sense meaning "to trample" or "tread." But there is adequate basis to emend it to read, "collect rent" or "tax." Whether one reads the reference in 7:1 to "king's mowing" as shorn wool or agricultural reaping, it is clear that the text is talking about the prime share of surplus taken by the crown.

Amos comments on various aspects of the life-style of the elite. The penchant for owning two separate mansions—one for summer and another one for winter —is mentioned in 3:15. Residences decorated with ivory carvings and furnishings became symbols of the elite's wealth and power. Amos 4:1-3, an indictment of the drinking habits of the Samrian women, makes it clear that the indulgent life-style was built upon the misery of the poor. Amos 6:4-7 is a classic statement on the elite's life-style. The key to grasping the force of this passage is the reference to מַרְזֵחַ marzeakh in v. 7. Most translations render it as "revelry." But no single word in English renders the full force of marzeakh. Marzeakh was a celebration held in honor of the dead. Plush furniture, indolent leisure, epicurean food, free-flowing wine, perfumed oil, and music were the hallmarks of this celebration. To Amos, marzeakh epitomizes the life-style of the elite. The prophet does not proceed without pointing to the adverse effects of this life on the poor. The elite do not seem to have the slightest concern "over the shattering of Joseph," which is a reference to the suffering majority. The prophet contrasts the luxury of the few with the suffering and oppression of the many. The abuses and corrupt practices in the market situation are picked up in 8:4-7. Amos isolates the practices of cheating with false measures and rigged scales. In addition, the merchants adulterated the goods by mixing chaff with the grain. That the victims of these fraudulent practices were the poor peasants is explicitly mentioned in v. 6.

The part played by the judicial courts in subverting justice to the poor is picked up in 5:7, 11. The courts had the function of establishing justice, but due to the venality of the elite, they perverted the justice they were meant to serve. The officials as well as the elite victimized the very groups that needed special protection. Old Testament legal texts stipulate a special concern for vulnerable groups such as the poor, the widows, the orphans, and the foreigners (Exod 22:22; 23:6; Deut 24:16). The prophetic commitment to this principle seems to presuppose these legal traditions. Amos 5:11 highlights how corruption was rampant among the court officials. In fact, it was so pervasive that those who dared to dispense justice and act with integrity were scorned by their colleagues. The conscientious officials incurred the wrath and scorn of both their peers and members of the elite.

5. Empty rituals

The meticulous observance of religious and cultic obligations with no real change of heart and upright conduct comes under indictment in 5:21-27. Amos is critical of the complacency that leads some to think that as long as they fulfilled their religious and cultic obligations all was right. For Amos, without a commitment to justice, religious observances were abominable to Yahweh. If religious observances do not result in or reflect commitment to social justice, then they are nothing more than empty rituals. This is part of the broader prophetic emphasis on the congruence between faith and practice or creed and deed.

6. Inevitable judgment

In looking at the path on which his contemporary society was heading, Amos is convinced that judgment is inevitable. After a few successful attempts at pleading on behalf of "Jacob" (7:2-3, 5-6), Amos conveys the message of irreversible doom by means of three different visions—plumb line (7:7-9), summer fruit (8:1-3), and a vision at the altar (9:1-3). The vision at the altar, in particular, portrays not only the inevitability of the judgment but also the relentless nature of the pursuit. In the vision reports, Amos uses evocative imagery and language to create powerful word pictures.

7. Promise of restoration

Most scholars assign 9:11-15 to an exilic redactor, because it presupposes the fall of the Davidic house. The promise of restoration relates to the reversal of the devastations surrounding 587 BCE. Whether or not this message of hope is integral to Amos' critique has been a subject of discussion. Prophetic critique is as much about dismantling as it is about building. Offering a word of hope is not out of character with prophetic imagination.

E. Contemporary Relevance

For a contemporary reader living in a postmodern cyber age, Amos' context and message may seem far removed. How are we to relate to a message given so long ago, in the context of an agrarian society? There are certain key points worthy of note. First, Amos' critique, like other prophetic voices of the 8th cent. Israel and Judah, is noteworthy for its understanding and analysis of his contemporary society and its issues. Amos does not resort to abstractions. His critique is grounded in the reality of suffering that affected the majority of the population. In fact, this is the driving force behind the prophet's uncompromising stance. Second, Amos is concerned with a more fundamental issue—does everyone have just and equitable access to the economic base? This is a fundamental question that can be posed irrespective of time, place, and society. Amos raises this question in relation to land, which is the primary means of the economic base for his society. For another society, it may be something else. But the basic question remains valid. Third, striving toward human liberation entails a struggle against various forms of oppression and injustice. As long as one is committed to this challenge, one can always learn and relearn something from the prophets.

Bibliography: M. Daniel R. Carroll. *Amos—The Prophet and His Oracles* (2002); Robert Coote. *Amos among the Prophets* (1981); John S. Holladay Jr. "The Kingdoms of Israel and Judah: Political and Economic Centralization in the Iron Age II A–B (ca. 1000–750 BCE)." *The Archaeology of Society in The Holy Land.* Thomas E. Levy, ed. (1995); Jörg Jeremias. *Book of Amos: A Commentary* (1998); Philip King. *Amos, Hosea, Micah: An Archaeological Commentary* (1988); Bernhard Lang. "The Social Organization of Peasant Poverty in Biblical Israel." *Anthropological Approaches to the Old Testament.* B. Lang, ed. (1985) 83–99; Karl Möller. *A Prophet in Debate. The Rhetoric of Persuasion in Amos* (2003); Shalom Paul. *Amos: A Commentary on the Book of Amos* (1991); David L. Petersen. *The Role of the Prophets* (1981); Max E. Polley. *Amos and the Davidic Empire. A Socio-Historical Perspective* (1989); D. N. Premnath. *Eighth Century Prophets: A Social Analysis* (2003); Robert Wilson. *Prophecy and Society in Ancient Israel* (1984); Hans W. Wolff. *Amos the Prophet* (1973).

DEVADASAN PREMNATH

AMOS ay′muhs [Ἀμώς *Amōs*]. Josiah's father; Manasseh's son (Matt 1:10). Manuscript evidence is divided between Amos and Amon. Amos with Asaph (Matt 1:8) symbolizes prophets and psalms within the Davidic genealogy.

AMOZ ay′muhz [אָמוֹץ *'amots*]. Isaiah's father (2 Kgs 19:2, 20; 20:1; 2 Chr 26:22; 32:20, 32; Isa 1:1; 2:1; 13:1; 20:2; 37:2, 21; 38:1). In rabbinical traditions, brother of Judean king Amaziah.

AMPHICTYONY. A league of groups, often characterized as twelve though numbers vary, that organized around a central religious shrine and cooperated in funding and administering the activities at that shrine. The term has its roots in classical Greece, and applies most famously to the Delphi amphictyony in the 6th cent. BCE. This group of twelve cities was formed around the shrine of Apollo at Delphi, and established a set of rules by which the partners would provide for the sanctuary and the roads that led to it (on a monthly rotating basis), and for political stability and peace among the members.

The model of Greek amphictyonies led scholars to posit that Israel had something like this during the period of the judges, the time between the settlement in Canaan and the establishment of the monarchy. Martin Noth argued that membership in the Israelite tribal league shifted over time, as seen in the different genealogies of Israel. Levi and Joseph are present in the earliest list (Gen 49), but in later lists (e.g., Num 26) Levi is omitted and Joseph is replaced with his two sons Manasseh and Ephraim. Levi's omission is connected with the fact that as a priestly tribe it had no land inheritance. Noth argued that the Israelite amphictyony rotated around a central sanctuary, and that the tribes gathered there yearly for a covenantal renewal ceremony (Josh 24). The actual site of that sanctuary changed, however, as the Ark of the Covenant moved from Shechem to Bethel, Gilgal, and Shiloh.

The model of the Israelite tribes as an amphictyony is no longer the consensus view. The historical reconstruction of such an entity depends too much on contestable literary analysis of the biblical text. Also, historians generally argue now that there was no political unity of "all Israel" until well into the monarchical period. Historians of religion have begun to emphasize the diversity and localization of the worship of Yahweh in early Israel. Rather than cooperating to move their sanctuary from place to place, it is more likely that particular groups developed their own regional shrines.

It is true, however, that Israel always considered itself to be composed of distinct tribes, and that some kind of tribal alliance must lie at the roots of the developing monarchy. Thus, the notion of a tribal league may still be a valuable metaphor, even if the full model cannot be applied to Israel intact.

BRYAN D. BIBB

AMPHIPOLIS am-fip′uh-lis [Ἀμφίπολις *Amphipolis*]. An ancient city in Macedonia on the east bank of the Strymon River about three mi. from the Aegean Sea. Paul and Silas passed through this city, and probably preached there, on his second missionary journey while traveling along the Egnatian Way from PHILIPPI to THESSALONICA (Acts 17:1). This route was the main overland connection between important ports that linked Greece and Italy.

Amphipolis is set on a hill with the river winding around below on three sides, and a wall protects it on the other (east) side. Its name "around the city" is derived from its geography (Thuc. 4.102). The city was founded as a colony of ATHENS in 436 BCE. It was captured by the Spartans in 424 BCE and returned to Athenian control in 421 BCE. Philip the Great occupied the city in 357 BCE. The Romans understood the strategic importance of the city that is located along the Egnatian Way. Amphipolis guarded the major bridge over the Strymon River. It was granted the status of a free city and became the residence of the Roman governor of Macedonia.

The city was known for its rich land and agricultural products such as wine, wood, olive oil, and wool. There are gold and silver mines in the area also. These made Amphipolis economically important. Several inscriptions and coins have been found at the site and excavations have opened several tombs from the Classical and Hellenistic periods. Four Byzantine churches, sections of the ancient city walls, and parts of the Roman aqueduct are preserved at the site.

JOHN WINELAND

AMPLIATUS am′pli-ay′tuhs [Ἀμπλιάτος Ampliatos]. A Christian greeted by Paul as "my beloved in the Lord" (Rom 16:8), whom Paul may have met and befriended in the eastern part of the Roman Empire. Some manuscripts include the shortened form "Amplian." The name is typical for slaves or freedmen, which is suggestive of Ampliatus' possible social background. This is probably not the same Ampliatus as found in the Roman catacomb of Domatilla. *See* PAUL, THE APOSTLE; ROMANS, LETTER TO THE; SLAVERY.

SUSANA DE SOLA FUNSTEN

AMRAM, AMRAMITES am′ram, am′ruh-m*it*s [עַמְרָם ʾamram, עַמְרָמִי ʾamrami]. 1. The father of AARON, MOSES, and MIRIAM (Exod 6:20; Num 26:59). Amram's father was KOHATH, one of Levi's sons (Exod 6:18-20; 1 Chr 6:2-3 [Heb. 5:27-29]).

2. Amramites were Kohathite Levites whose responsibilities for the sanctuary included caring for the ark and altars (Num 3:27-31; 1 Chr 23:13).

3. In Ezra 10:34, one of the priests who promised to reject their foreign wives. *See* SOCIOLOGY, ISRAELITE; TRIBE.

LISA MICHELE WOLFE

AMRAPHEL am′ruh-fel [אַמְרָפֶל ʾamrafel]. King of SHINAR, and one of the four kings led by CHEDORLAOMER in his western campaign against cities in the Dead Sea region (Gen 14). These two, along with Arioch and Tidal, fought against the kings of Sodom, Gomorrah, Admah, Zeboiim, and Bela (Zoar), who had allied in rebellion against Chedorlaomer.

Shinar is a name for Babylon, seen first in the Bible in the genealogy of nations in Gen 10:10 and in the story of the building of the tower of Babel (Gen 11:1-9). Earlier scholars identified Amraphel with Hammurapi based on a superficial similarity between their names. There is evidence that the story in Gen 14 has been constructed

from an ancient list of four rebellious kings called "the Chedorlaomer texts." Based on comparison with those texts, some identify Amraphel with the Babylonian king Marduk-apal-iddina from the 8th cent. BCE.

BRYAN D. BIBB

AMULETS [לַחַשׁ lakhash, בָּתֵּי הַנֶּפֶשׁ batte hannefesh]. Possibly from the verb lakhash "to charm." Small objects, often pierced for suspension from the neck or wrist, believed to provide protection from malevolent supernatural powers and/or to ensure health and good fortune. They could be constructed from an array of materials, from mouse bones and vegetable matter to precious metals and stones. Men, women, and children, and people from all social classes, wore amulets. They could also be interred with the dead. In many respects an amulet functioned as a material form of continuous prayer on the wearer's behalf. Activated by a religious specialist's ritual action, an amulet's power derived also from communal belief in its effectiveness (*see* MAGIC).

Amulets featured in the religious landscape not only of biblical Israel, but also of Second Temple and Mishnaic Judaism, and early Christianity. JEWELRY may have possessed amuletic qualities, and the Bible can hint with faint disdain at its more than merely ornamental function (Gen 35:4; Exod 32:3; Judg 8:21; Isa 3:18-21 **batte hannefesh** lit. "houses of life."). Yet the jewels on the high priest's breastplate (Exod 28:15-21) are clearly amuletic. The biblical text tacitly acknowledges the protective powers of one type of amulet, the personal signet (*see* SEALS AND SCARABS); in Song 8:6 the lover, worn "as a seal" against the beloved's heart, repels the force of death (*see also* Gen 38:24-26; Prov 6:21). Even God can wear (metaphorically) a signet ring (Jer 22:24). Among the many amulets from ancient Israelite sites, Egyptian-style amulets depicting the solar Eye of Horus or the protective spirit, Bes, seem to have been particularly popular. Both types may reflect in some way the official worship of Yahweh, as was probably true of the decorations on Israelite seals.

The most important amulets yet discovered in Israel are two tiny silver scrolls excavated in 1979 at Ketef Hinnom, a late 7th or early 6th cent. BCE burial site just outside Jerusalem. Before being permanently rolled up, each amulet was inscribed, probably by a professional scribe, with a short preface and the text of the so-called "Priestly Benediction" (Num 6:24-26). These inscriptions represent the oldest references to Yahweh found in Jerusalem and, more significantly, the earliest known documentation of texts that appear in the OT. Mention of the covenant in one of the amulets echoes Deut 7:9, and in the other Yahweh is addressed as the "Rebuker of Evil," affirming the amulet's protective function.

In the Second Temple period a similar dynamic animated the biblical passages contained inside תְּפִלִּים tefillim and מְזוּזוֹת mezuzoth (*see* PHYLACTERIES and MEZUZAH), amulets that fulfill, respectively, the commandments of Exod 13:16 (Deut 6:8) and Deut 6:9 (*see* Matt 23:5). Whether Paul (Gal 5:20) or other NT writers would have condemned amulets as sorcery (φαρμακεία pharmakeia; *see also* Acts 8:9; 19:11-19) is unclear but plausible, given the human tendency to dismiss what others do as magic and what one does oneself as correct ritual. Nevertheless, papyri of the first few centuries of the Common Era attest to Jewish and early Christian use of text-based amulets to thwart demonic (Jas 2:19) and other dangers.

Bibliography: C. Andrews. *Amulets of Ancient Egypt* (1994); G. Barkay, et al. "The Amulets from Ketef Hinnom." *BASOR* 334 (2004) 41–71; C. Herrmann. *Ägyptische Amulette aus Palästina/Israel, I–II* (1994–2002); O. Keel and C. Uehlinger. *Gods, Goddesses, and Images of God* (1998); M. Meyer, et al., eds. *Ancient Christian Magic* (1994); J. Naveh and S. Shaked. *Amulets and Magic Bowls* (1985).

MARY JOAN WINN LEITH

AMUQ PLAIN. A plain on the Orontes River, historically in the region of Syria but located today within the southern border of Turkey. The plain is bounded on the north and west by the Amanus Mountains and in the south by the Ghab Valley. The Orontes River flows south to north through the Ghab Valley to the Amuq Plain, where it turns to head toward the Mediterranean Sea. Because of its location on the Orontes and its proximity to Aleppo in the east, the plain has been a crossroads for travel for millennia. The two important cities of Alalakh and Antioch lie in the southern portion of the plain. *See* ORONTES RIVER; SYRIA.

KEVIN A. WILSON

AMZI am′zi [אַמְצִי ’amtsi]. 1. A Levite of Merari's family, son of Bani, father of Hilkiah and grandfather of Amaziah (1 Chr 6:30-31), ancestor of Ethan the musician (1 Chr 6:46).

2. A priest, son of Zechariah, an ancestor of Adaiah in Neh 11:12, but not mentioned among Adaiah's ancestors in 1 Chr 9:2.

ANAB ay′nab [עֲנָב ‘anav]. A city in the southern hill country, Anab was allotted to JUDAH (Josh 15:48-50). JOSHUA wiped out the Anakim/Anakites who lived in HEBRON, DEBIR, and Anab (Josh 11:21). The ancient city is identified with Khirbet ‘Unnab ets-Tsaghir, where Iron Age materials have been found.

ANAEL an′ay-uhl [Ἀναήλ Hanaēl]. Tobit's brother (Tob 1:21) whose son Ahikar served the kings Sennacherib and Esarhaddon. According to some manuscripts, the name is Hananael.

ANAFA, TEL. A small- to medium sized settlement in upper Galilee that was occupied from the Early Bronze Age

through the 1st cent. CE. The site was extensively excavated in nine seasons from 1968 to 1981. Tel Anafa is important as a setting that reveals the variety of cultural influences in upper Galilee during the Late Hellenistic and Early Roman periods when the town was at its most notable stage. To date, the site has not been definitively associated with any town that is named in ancient literary sources.

Tel Anafa is on the west side of the Golan Heights, near the Hula Basin, approximately ten mi. south of Tel Dan. The 10-meter high mound sits near significant ancient roads that connected Damascus to the Mediterranean coast at Tyre, and linked the upper Galilee to lucrative transdesert trade routes. In the Late Hellenistic period, the settlement expanded beyond the mound as the occupants took advantage of their location and the town flourished as a regional trade center.

Archaeologists from the University of Michigan and the University of Missouri found a large number of luxury items that date to the early 1st cent. BCE. Imported lamps, fine wares (red-slipped and Parthian green-glazed pottery), molded glass bowls, and exotic metal items reveal a town that was well connected to Hellenistic culture. Excavations exposed a bath complex and a large stucco building from this period. The building was lavishly constructed and decorated with Greek masonry techniques. There were two subsequent occupation phases, including its being reconstructed during the reign of Herod Phillip. The settlement became less significant through the Early Roman period. The town was permanently abandoned at the end of the 1st cent. CE. *See* GALILEE.

MILTON MORELAND

ANAGOGICAL. Anagogical interpretation finds meaning not in a text's literal sense but in its ability to lead readers to heavenly meanings. For example, Hebrews 4 takes Israel's rest in Canaan to anticipate the believer's eternal rest in heaven. Many medieval interpreters perceived anagogical significance as an implicit dimension of every biblical text. Roman Catholic teaching affirms anagogical interpretation as part of the "living reading of Scripture in the Church" (*Catechism* 115). *See* ESCHATOLOGY, NT; INTERPRETATION.

GREG CAREY

ANAH ay′nuh [עֲנָה ‘anah]. 1. The father of OHOLIB-AMAH, one of ESAU's Canaanite wives, Anah was son of ZIBEON and grandson of SEIR the HORITE (Gen 36:2; 1 Chr 1:40). Anah discovered some kind of water in the wilderness while tending his father's donkeys (Gen 36:24).

2. Anah is also named as a son of Seir (Gen 36:20; 1 Chr 1:38). One of the Horite clans bore Anah's name (Gen 36:29).

LISA MICHELE WOLFE

ANAHARATH uh-nay′huh-rath [אֲנָחֲרָת ’anakharath]. Town given to tribe of Issachar (Josh 19:19) when

Joshua apportioned the territories (Josh 18:10). Located south of EN-DOR. *See* ISSACHAR.

ANAIAH uh-nay´yuh [עֲנָיָה ʿanayah]. One of six men standing at Ezra's right hand when he read from the book of the law of Moses to the assembly (Neh 8:4). He is one of the leaders of the people who set their seal to the covenant (Neh 10:22).

ANAK, ANAKIM, ANAKITES ay´nak, an´uh-kim, an´uh-k*its* [עֲנָק ʿanaq, עֲנָקִים ʿanaqim, בְּנֵי עֲנָק bene ʿanaq, יְלִידֵי הָעֲנָק yelidhe haʿanaq]. 1. The son of Arba, named as the ancestor of the Anakim or Anakites (Josh 15:13, 21:11).

2. An area in or around HEBRON (also called Kiriath-arba, "the city of Arba") named for Anak. The area is in Judah's central hill country to the middle west of the Dead Sea, south of Jerusalem. Most references name CALEB as the conqueror of Anakite land (Josh 14:12, 15:13-14, 21:12; Judg 1:20). Joshua 21:11 reports that as part of the Levites' allotment of land, the city was settled by Aaronide Kohathites. A 19th or 18th cent. BCE fragment listing Egypt's enemies makes reference to the Asiatic iyʿaneq and its ruler (ANET 328). This may be related to the biblical references.

3. The inhabitants of Anak called Anakim and Anakites (the sons of Anak [bene ʿanaq], Num 13:22-28; Deut 1:28, 9:2). The spies to Cannan were frightened by the great stature of the Anakim, who were said to be descendents of the NEPHILIM (Gen 6:4; Num 13:33). In some places, the Anakim serve as a point of comparison for great height (Deut 2:10, 21); the word refers to "neck," hence "long-necked" or "tall." Joshua 11:21-22 attributes the destruction of the Anakim to Joshua instead of Caleb. This reference asserts that after Joshua's battles, these tall people remained only in Gaza, Gath, and Ashdod.

LISA MICHELE WOLFE

ANALOGY. Analogy is comparison using one concept to understand or explain aspects of another concept. A kind of structural parallelism, classic analogy follows an "A is to B as C is to D" pattern. Analogy can reveal conventional ways of understanding or create new category connections, which writers and readers then use to reason and interpret. Analogies in the biblical writings vary in degree of conventionality and elaboration. Metaphors are elaborated analogies; parables are extended analogies.

Analogies are often presented as identities: "God *is* light" (1 John 1:5). Isaiah uses scalar spatial concepts of higher and lower, and of "heavens" in comparison with the earth, to help readers understand differences between the LORD and his people: "For my thoughts are not your thoughts, nor are your ways my ways, says the LORD. For as the heavens are higher than the earth, so are my ways higher than your ways and my thoughts

than your thoughts" (Isa 55:8-9). The psalmist uses the experience of thirst to consider—and evoke emotions connected with—longing for God: "As a deer longs for flowing streams, so my soul longs for you O God. My soul thirsts for God, for the living God" (Ps 42:1-2*a*).

Contextual clues help us recognize analogies, but readers may not be aware of analogies as they read. Standard analogies can be deeply entrenched in a reading community's conceptual structure; "new" analogies may feel less deeply entrenched, but actually work with conventional frames. *See* METAPHOR; PARABLE; PARALLELISM; RHETORICAL CRITICISM; SIMILITUDE.

Bibliography: Mark Turner. *Reading Minds* (1993).

ANAMIM an´uh-mim [עֲנָמִים ʿanamim]. One of the offspring of EGYPT in the genealogy of nations, the descendants of NOAH, in Gen 10:1-32. This list demonstrates clearly one of the central purposes of ancestral genealogies and narratives, to explain the origins and relationships among various people groups. Anamim's father, Egypt, is the son of HAM, and brother to Cush, Put, and Canaan. This gives the line of Ham control over southwest Asia and north Africa. The children of Egypt all represent peoples in North Africa, although some are hard to identify, including Anamim. William F. Albright postulated that Anamim refers to CYRENE on the coast of Libya, and although this identification has not held up, that general area is most probable. *See* AFRICA, AFRICAN.

BRYAN D. BIBB

ANAMMELECH uh-nam´uh-lek [עֲנַמֶּלֶךְ ʿanammelekh]. A deity worshiped by the people of SEPHARVAIM who relocated to Samaria after 722 BCE and the reign of Sargon II. In Samaria, Anamemlech worship included child sacrifice (2 Kgs 17:31). Anammelech is associated with the Mesopotamian Ana and the Syrian Anath, as well as the deity ADRAMELECH.

ANAN ay´nuhn [עָנָן ʿanan]. A leader who placed his name on the sealed covenant document (Neh 10:26).

ANANI uh-nay´*i* [עֲנָנִי ʿanani]. Elioenai's seventh son (3:24) listed among David's and Zerubbabel's descendants in 1 Chr 3:1-24.

ANANIAH an´uh-n*i*´uh [עֲנַנְיָה ʿananeyah]. 1. The father of MAASEIAH, whose son, AZARIAH, participated in repairing the walls of Jerusalem near his own house under NEHEMIAH's leadership (Neh 3:23).

2. A Benjaminite village where Jewish exiles settled upon returning to the land (Neh 11:31-32), probably named for family members of Ananiah living there, hence the NT's name for the town, BETHANY ("house of Ananiah" = βηθανία Bēthania).

STEVEN D. MASON

ANANIAS an´uh-ni´uhs [Ἀνανίας Hananias]. 1. Ananias, together with his wife Sapphira, donated profits from a property sale to the Jerusalem church (Acts 4:34–5:1). However, this couple "kept back some of the proceeds" while claiming to contribute the full amount (5:2). When Peter exposed this pretense as a lie against God and the Holy Spirit, Ananias dropped dead on the spot. The same fate befell Sapphira, provoking "great fear" throughout the congregation (5:5, 11).

2. A disciple of Christ (Acts 9:10) and well-known adherent to the Jewish law (22:12), Ananias of Damascus was instrumental in transforming Saul of Tarsus from a violent opponent of the early church to its leading missionary (9:1-19; 22:12-16). Guided by a vision of the risen Lord, Ananias met Saul in Judas's house on Straight Street, restored Saul's sight and imparted the Spirit through laying on of hands, directed Saul to be baptized, and relayed his divine commission to be Christ's "witness" (22:15).

3. Appointed high priest by Herod Agrippa II in 48 CE, Ananias, the son of Nebedeus, presided over the Jewish council that judged Paul after his arrest in the Temple (Acts 23:1-5; 21:27–22:29). Upon hearing Paul's confession, Ananias ordered bystanders to strike Paul's mouth (23:1-2). In turn, Paul lashed back at Ananias, invoking God's discipline against "you whitewashed wall" (23:3). When challenged about his insolent response to the high priest, Paul claimed (feigned?) ignorance of Ananias's office. "Five days later," Ananias, along with some elders and a special prosecutor (Tertullus), presented their case against Paul to the Roman prefect, Felix, in Caesarea (24:1). Josephus reported Ananias's assassination in 66 CE by Manahem's band of Jewish rebels (*J.W.* 2.440-42; *Ant.* 20.103, 130-36).

F. SCOTT SPENCER

ANASIB an´uh-sib [Ἀνασείβ Anaseib]. Progenitor of a family group of priests who returned to Jerusalem after Darius conquered the Babylonians (1 Esd 5:24). Nine hundred seventy-two priests descended from Anasib through Jedaiah. Compare Ezra 2:36 and Neh 7:39.

ANATH ay´nath [עֲנָת ʿanath, Ugaritic ʿnt]. 1. Anath is a warrior goddess in Canaanite religion, the consort of the storm god Baal, with whom she twice joins to fight against, first, a dragonlike deity of the sea and, second, the Canaanite god of sterility and death. Anat was also a well-known warrior goddess in New Kingdom Egypt (ca. 1575–1087 BCE), depicted in one image as holding a sword and a shield and described in one text as part of a war chariot.

In the Bible, Anath's name appears only in a few place names (Anathoth, Beth-anoth, and Beth-Anath) and as a part of some personal names (Shamgar, son of Anath in Judg 3:31; 5:6, Anathoth, and Anthothijah). Anath's character as a warrior goddess, however, probably influenced the depictions of some of the Bible's warrior women, especially Deborah and Jael in Judg 5. They, similarly to Anath, fight alongside a male deity, Yahweh, who uses the storm as his weapon (Judg 5:4-5, 20-21). The woman of Thebez in Judg 9:50-57 also, like Anath, uses a millstone as a weapon to defeat an enemy. *See* ASHERAH; ASTARTE.

2. SHAMGAR's father (Judg 3:31; 5:6), although this may be a theophoric rather than a personal name.

SUSAN ACKERMAN

ANATHEMA uh-nath´uh-muh [ἀνάθεμα anathema]. The Greek occurs six times in the NT, but most English versions translate it "accursed." In the LXX **anathema** translates חרם khrm, DEVOTED (to God) for destruction. (Acts 23 relates to a dire OATH.) In Rom 9:3 Paul wishes to be "ACCURSED" if this could gain the salvation of the Jews. In Gal 1:8, 9, those who seduced others into illusion by preaching "a different Gospel" invite God's curse. In 1 Cor 16:22 "anathema" is the alternative to "loving the Lord," implying a covenant context. Most versions translate 1 Cor 12:3 "Let Jesus be cursed," but recently a few have urged that (Anathema Iēsous Ἀνάθεμα Ἰησοῦς) means "May Jesus curse." Authentic Christians do not resort to curse-prayers. *See* CURSE.

ANTHONY THISELTON

ANATHOTH an´uh-thoth [עֲנָתוֹת ʿanathoth; Ἀναθωθ Anathōth]. 1. A Levitical city within the territory of BENJAMIN (Josh 21:18; 1 Chr 6:60 [Heb. 6:45]) whose biblical name is preserved in the name of the modern village of Anata and whose probable site is Ras el-Kharrubeth. ABIATHAR was banished to Anathoth by SOLOMON because he supported ADONIJAH (1 Kgs 2:26). The city was the birthplace of the prophet JEREMIAH (Jer 1:1; 11:21-23; 29:27; 32:7-9), possibly linking Jeremiah to Abiathar. Anathoth was the native place of ABIEZER (2 Sam 23:27; 1 Chr 11:28) and JEHU, two of David's mighty men. Citizens of Anathoth returned with ZERUBBABEL from Babylonian exile (Ezra 2:23; Neh 7:27; 1 Esd 5:18).

2. The eighth of the nine sons of BECHER, the son of Benjamin (1 Chr 7:8).

3. One of the leaders in the postexilic community who signed a document pledging to keep God's law (Neh 10:19).

CLAUDE F. MARIOTTINI

ANCESTOR. *See* FATHER; GENEALOGY; MOTHER.

ANCESTOR WORSHIP. Ancestor worship and cults of the dead indicate acts intended to sustain, placate, or benefit from the dead, normally one's family members. Precision is difficult and the terms are used loosely, since some acts may have expressed respect or veneration rather than worship, or have involved little ritual. Provision for and prayer to the dead was widespread in the ancient Near East, and is occasionally noted in the OT. Many scholars think it was widely accepted within early Yahwism, that it was later proscribed, and that redactors recast the traditions leaving only occasional textual traces (e.g., Lewis). Others, however, contend that Yahwistic disapproval of such acts was indeed ancient, and that the apparent traces can be better explained (e.g., Johnston).

Numbers 25:2 records the Baal-Peor apostasy when Israelite men joined Moabite women in what Ps 106:28 calls (literally) "sacrifices of the dead." Ezekiel 43:7-9 probably condemns a pre-exilic royal ancestor cult, and Isa 57:6 a postexilic death cult (translating חֶלְקַת khalaqoth as "dead" rather than "smooth stones"; MT reads חַלְּקֵי־נַחַל khalleqe nakhal). Later references to grave offerings (Letter of Jer 27; Tob 4:17; Sir 30:18) imply a general practice.

More important, Deut 26:14 bars from the triennial tithe any food offered "to/for a deceased" (lemeth), implying a regular Israelite practice. But it is unclear whether this was a funerary feast for the living or a grave offering to the deceased, and if the latter, whether presented only at interment or regularly thereafter. It is also unclear whether the Deuteronomists abhorred the practice but felt unable to proscribe it completely, or whether, since they strongly proscribed other abhorrent practices, they considered it relatively harmless. Excavated Judahite graves usually contain jugs and bowls and there is some archaeological evidence of initial food offerings, but not clearly for continued sustenance.

Some scholars posit a death cult behind other passages. For instance, that in 1 Sam 28 the concluding meal was a cultic feast (מַרְזֵחַ marzeakh) attended by the ancestors; that in Ps 16:3 "the holy ones in the land (אֶרֶץ ʾerets)" were the powerful dead in the underworld; that in Ps 49:11 "naming" meant invoking the ancestors. Some also posit an ancestor cult behind various customs and institutions: the marzeakh, TERAPHIM, pillars, aspects of family life, family and other sacrifices, new moon assemblies, and certain burial notices. Some of these are possible, but many require significant rereading of the text and further difficulties. In particular, it is now widely accepted that the marzeakh was an occasion for social drinking, sometimes funerary, as in Jer 16:5, but more commonly not, as in Amos 6:7.

Whatever the beliefs and practices in popular Israelite religion in different periods, orthodox Yahwism was apparently little interested in the abode of the dead and was opposed to contacting them. *See* ABODE OF THE DEAD; NECROMANCY.

Bibliography: P. S. Johnston. *Shades of Sheol* (2002); T. J. Lewis. *Cults of the Dead in Ancient Israel and Ugarit* (1989).

PHILIP S. JOHNSTON

ANCHOR [ἄγκυρα ankura]. A weight dropped from a ship to hold the vessel in place. The earliest anchors were simply stones but later, the Romans developed more sophisticated styles involving iron or wood. A ship would generally have more than one anchor so that extra lines could be dropped in heavy seas, and in case the lines in use snapped and had to be replaced. Because they are made of such solid materials, anchors are among the most common artifacts brought to the surface by marine archaeologists. They provide a helpful typology for dating a shipwreck, although their durability makes them less suited to that task because they can be used long after their manufacture.

The Israelites were not sea-faring people, and their writings have very little to say about ships and sailing. The Greeks and Romans, however, mastered the sea from an early stage, and the busy traffic in the Mediterranean Sea aided the spread of the Christian message. Most references to anchors in the Bible occur in the narrative of Paul's shipwreck in Acts 27–28, including the last ditch effort to save the ship by cutting the anchors loose (27:40). Heb 6:19 evokes the metaphor of hope as "the anchor of the soul." *See* SHIPS AND SAILING, NT.

BRYAN D. BIBB

ANCIENT OF DAYS עַתִּיק יוֹמִין ʿattiq yomin; παλαιὸς ἡμερῶν palaios hēmerōn]. In his vision of divine judgment, the sage Daniel sees a celestial court, where a certain "Ancient of Days" sits enthroned to attend to the threat of cosmic chaos represented by terrible monsters arising from the sea (Dan 7:1-14). The mythological background of the vision is suggested by the plurality of thrones, which would have been occupied by other deities of the divine council.

The god ʾEl, whose name appears within Daniel's own (Daniʾel "My Judge is El"), is the supreme ruler of the Canaanite pantheon in mythology—El appears as an old god, sitting enthroned in both texts and iconography. In Ugaritic literature, this gray-haired god is called mlkh av hnm "king, father of years," that is, an ancient one. The deity in Daniel's vision is a white-haired being, sitting on a fiery, mobile throne that recalls the vision of Ezekiel (Ezek 1). In mythology, the threat to world order is represented by various sea monsters, while the young champion in El's council, who arises to meet the threat, is the storm god, Baal, known also as "the Rider of the Cloud. This champion's victory over the forces of chaos brought him kingship and dominion. It is interesting, therefore, that the champion in Daniel's vision is one who "comes with the clouds" (Dan 7:13) and his victory would also bring dominion and kingship (Dan 7:14).

C. L. SEOW

ANCIENT VERSIONS. *See* VERSIONS, ANCIENT.

ANDREW an′dr*oo* [Ἀνδρέας Andreas]. Andrew is first mentioned in the Gospel of Mark as the brother of Simon PETER (Mark 1:16). He appears twelve times in the

NT, four times in the Gospels among the lists of apostles (Mark 3:18; Matt 10:2; Luke 6:14; Acts 1:13), and always among the first four names in these lists (Peter, Andrew, James, and John). Among the Gospels, Mark and John give Andrew the most attention. In Mark's gospel, Andrew is one of the first disciples to be called by Jesus along with Peter (1:16-18), is present when Jesus cures Peter's mother-in-law (1:29-31), and is among a few (Peter, James, and John) to hear Jesus predict the destruction of the Temple (13:3-4). However, Matthew and Luke omit Andrew's name from these Markan stories, which may suggest they regard him as less important (Matt 8:14-15; 24:1-3; Luke 4:38-39; 21:5-7). In the Gospel of John, Andrew has a larger role: he first appears as the brother of Simon Peter and as a disciple of John, both of whom are from Bethsaida (1:35-40, 44); he is among the first to follow Jesus, is instrumental in bringing Peter to Jesus, and is the first disciple to recognize Jesus as the Messiah. He appears in John 6:1-14, asking Jesus how he would feed a multitude with very few provisions, which motivates Jesus to perform the miracle of the loaves and fish. His final appearance in John is in the story of the Greeks (12:20-34), who, coming from Bethsaida, encounter Philip and ask to see Jesus. Philip tells Andrew of their request, and they both inform Jesus. He is mentioned elsewhere only in Acts 1:13 among those in the upper room. Outside the NT, Andrew is found among some apocryphal writings. *See* ANDREW, ACTS OF; ANDREW AND MATTHIAS (MATTHEW), ACTS OF; ANDREW AND PAUL, ACTS OF; PETER AND ANDREW, ACTS OF.

Bibliography: F. Dvornik. *The Idea of Apostolicity in Byzantium and the Legend of the Apostle Andrew* (1958); M. R. James. *The Apocryphal New Testament* (1924) 337–63, 453–60, 472–75; D. R. McDonald. *The Acts of Andrew and The Acts of Andrew and Matthias in the City of the Cannibals* (1990); P. M. Peterson. *Andrew, Brother of Simon Peter, His History and His Legends* (1958).

FRANCISCO LOZADA, JR.

ANDREW AND MATTHIAS (MATTHEW), ACTS OF. Considered secondary in relation to the *Acts of Andrew,* the *Acts of Andrew and Matthias (Matthew)* survives in Greek, Syriac, and partly in Latin. It dates between the 3rd and 5th cent., though parts of the tale could be from the 2nd cent.

The story begins with the apostles casting lots to determine their country to evangelize. Matthias receives the land of the cannibals (ἀνθρωποφάγοι anthrōpophagoi). Upon arrival, Matthias is blinded, given poisonous drink, and imprisoned by the cannibals for future consumption. However, Matthias retains his senses and prays for help. Jesus appears in the form of a light and voice and informs Matthias that Andrew would rescue him. The next scene takes placed on a ship. Unknown to Andrew and his disciples, Jesus is the pilot. To ease their concern regarding the rough sea, the pilot (Jesus) asks Andrew to tell his disciples about those wondrous works that his Savior performed, such as the stilling of the storm. He does, and they are immediately calm. The pilot (Jesus) makes another request. He wants to know why the Jews do not believe in Jesus. Andrew tells a story about how Jesus and the Twelve went to a heathen temple and performed a miracle to convince Jewish priests of Jesus' true identity, but because their hearts were weakened the priests remained unconvinced. Andrew and other disciples also began to doubt the identity of Jesus. Therefore, Jesus took the Twelve into the desert and performed more miracles to restore their faith. Then Jesus and the Twelve returned to the heathen temple and caused a sphinx carved within the temple to come down. The priests failed to believe that Jesus is the Son of God. Jesus then asked the sphinx to call upon the twelve patriarchs of Israel to come to the temple to convince the priests, but the priests still would not believe. The story ends, and the pilot (Jesus) nearing land orders his angels to take Andrew and his men outside the city of the cannibals. Jesus and his angels return to heaven.

Andrew and his men awake and realize that Jesus was aboard the ship. They pray to Jesus to return, and he does, but this time in the form of a beautiful young child. After warning of the trials that await them in the city, Jesus departs. Andrew and his men rescue Matthias and others from impending death by way of a cloud. Andrew reproaches the devil and returns to the city. Andrew discovers that the angry cannibals are preparing to devour the soldiers, who guarded Matthias and others, and some old men. Before they can consume the victims, Andrew prays, and the executioners' hands turn to stone. The executioners next try to devour the children of the old men, and again their hands turn to stone after Andrew prays. The devil then appears in the guise of an old man and instructs the cannibals how to capture Andrew.

The story concludes with Andrew in prison being punished and humiliated. After several days of imprisonment, Andrew walks to a pillar with a statue on it and orders the statue to flood the city. He also orders Michael to encircle the city with fire so that no one can escape the flood and that all will be killed for their lack of faith. After nearly all are killed, Andrew orders the survivors to bring all of the dead to him so that he can revive them to life. They do so, and he constructs a church, baptizes all of them, and sets to depart. However, Jesus appears to Andrew again in the form of a beautiful child, reproves him from leaving, and orders him to stay seven more days.

Bibliography: M. R. James. *The Apocryphal New Testament* (1924) 337–63, 453–58, 472–75; D. R. McDonald. "The Acts of Andrew and Matthias and

The Acts of Andrew." *Semeia* 38 (1986) 9–26; D. R. McDonald. "Response to Jean-Marc Prieur." *Semeia* 38 (1986) 35–39; D. R. McDonald. *The Acts of Andrew and The Acts of Andrew and Matthias in the City of the Cannibals* (1990).

FRANCISCO LOZADA, JR.

ANDREW AND PAUL, ACTS OF. A brief NT apocryphal narrative, composed in Syriac but extant only in Coptic. It was written possibly in the 3rd or 4th cent. The narrative, recounts the journeys of Andrew and Paul and their fabulous encounters with non-Christians. The journey begins on a ship with Andrew healing a blind woman by accidentally touching her eyes with the cloak of Paul. It ends with Andrew making a dismembered child whole, resulting in the conversion of 2,700 Jews. *See* APOCRYPHA, NT.

Bibliography: F. H. Hallock. "An Apocalypse of SS. Andrew and Paul." *JSOR* 13 (1929) 190–94; M. R. James. "The Acts of Andrew and Paul." *The Apocryphal New Testament* (1924) 472–75.

FRANCISCO LOZADA, JR.

ANDREW, ACTS OF PETER AND. *See* PETER AND ANDREW, ACTS OF.

ANDREW, FRAGMENTARY STORY OF. M. R. James used this designation for a fragmentary account preserved in Paris Coptic MS 129, folio 87, and Leiden Coptic Insinger MS 51, that involves a woman, her child, and a talking dog, who refused to eat the child. The story has also been attributed to a form of the Acts of Andrew and Philemon since Philemon is mentioned, though this incident is not known in the other witnesses to this writing.

Bibliography: Oscar von, Lemm. "Koptische Miscellen LXVIII-LXXII." *Bulletin de l'Académie Impériale des Sciences de St.-Pétersbourg* (1910) 61–86.

F. STANLEY JONES

ANDRONICUS an-dron'uh-kuhs [Ἀνδρόνικος Andronikos]. The name occurs frequently in Greco-Roman antiquity. It is used to name four people pertinent to the Bible. 1. Regent in Antioch (171 BCE) when ANTIOCHUS IV Epiphanes warred against the rebellious people of Tarsus and Mallus. Bribed by MENELAUS with gold from the Jerusalem Temple treasury he killed the high priest ONIAS III. On his return Antiochus executed him when Jews and Greeks alike appealed against him (2 Macc 4:30-38).

2. A second official of Antiochus IV Epiphanes (2 Macc 5:23) placed in charge of the temple on Mt. GERIZIM when Antiochus invaded Samaria and Judea.

3. Under PTOLEMY Philometor, Andronicus, the son of Messalamus, represented the Jews of Jerusalem

and Judea in a dispute with the Samaritans over whose temple was the legitimate temple of God. He won the case by arguing from the Torah and the succession of priests (Josephus, *Ant.* 13.75-79).

4. Paul greets Andronicus and JUNIA, Jews who were in Christ before him and were imprisoned with him, as "prominent among the apostles" (Rom 16:7).

EDGAR KRENTZ

ANEM ay'nuhm [עָנֵם ʿanem]. A town and its pasture lands taken from the tribe of Manasseh and allocated to the Gershomites (1 Chr 6:73). In Josh 21:29 and 19:21 this town is designated as En-gannim. Present location is possibly ʿOlam or Khirbet ʿAnim. *See* EN-GANNIM; GERSHOM.

ANER ay'nuhr [עָנֵר ʿaner]. In Gen 14:13, Aner and his brothers MAMRE and ESHKOL join with Abram against CHEDORLAOMER, King of ELAM. Genesis Apocryphan (22:6) describes an active role for the brothers in battle. The reference to Aner as a Levitical city in Manasseh (1 Chr 6:70) is most likely a scribal error based on Josh 21:25, where the name is given as TAANACH.

ANGEL [מַלְאָךְ malʾakh; ἄγγελος angelos]. While Hebrew malʾakh and Greek angelos designate messengers both human and heavenly, in the English Bible, angels are spiritual beings. Despite considerable angelological development, often speculative, in the literature of the late Second Temple period, the general contours of NT angelology derive from ideas in earlier literature.

A. Early Angelology
  1. Terminology
  2. General concepts
  3. An angel of Yahweh
  4. The heavenly council
  5. The army of Yahweh
  6. Evil angels
B. The Exile and Beyond: A Developing Angelology
  1. Ezekiel
  2. Zechariah
  3. Terminology
  4. Relationship to early OT literature
  5. Naming and rank of angels
  6. Appearance and nature of angels
  7. Good and evil angels
  8. Eschatological functions of angels
  9. Fellowship with angels
C. Angels in the NT
  1. NT terminology
  2. Appearance and nature of angels

3. Roles in relation to the kingdom of God
   a. Angels and the person and work of Jesus
   b. Angels, humans, and the gospel
   c. Revelation by angels
   d. Evil angels
   e. Angels and judgment
Bibliography

A. Early Angelology

Though often mentioned elsewhere in the OT, angels are especially prominent in Genesis and Judges, and in Ezekiel and Zechariah from the exilic period. The importance of angels in Genesis and Judges indicates that belief in angels is ancient.

1. Terminology

Mal'akh, cognate with l'k ("to send") in several Semitic languages, means "a messenger." Of over 200 occurrences in the OT, about half designate humans (e.g., Gen 32:3; Num 20:14; Nah 2:13; Heb 14), and half spiritual beings, clearly distinguished in English as angels (e.g., Gen 16:7; Exod 32:34; 1 Kgs 13:18). The LXX translated mal'akh with angelos for both humans and angels. Sometimes angelos was also used when other Hebrew expressions such as bene ha'elohim בְּנֵי הָאֱלֹהִים (sons of God) were understood to mean angels (e.g., Job 1:6; 2:1; 38:7; NRSV, heavenly beings). Similarly, אֱלֹהִים 'elohim, gods, was interpreted as angels in Ps 138:1. The English word *angel* comes from the term angelos used in the LXX to designate heavenly beings.

A rich vocabulary developed along with a growing understanding of the nature and roles of angels. Designations such as angel of the LORD (or Yahweh, Gen 16:11; Judg 6:11); angel of God (Gen 21:17; 2 Sam 14:17); heavenly beings (bene' ha' elohim, sons of God; Job 1:6; 2:1; Pss 29:1; 89:5; Heb 6) and divine beings ('elohim, gods Ps 8:5; Heb 6; 82:1; 97:7) indicate angels' special connection to Yahweh. Holy ones (Job 5:1; Ps 89:5-7; Heb 6–8) implies purity and dedication to God.

Angels serve by doing God's will (Ps 103:1). They are called mighty (Ps 78:25), the host of heaven (1 Kgs 22:19), Yahweh's hosts (Josh 5:14-15; Pss 103:21; 148:2), and the host of the height (NRSV, host of heaven, Isa 24:21). Hosts (צְבָאוֹת tsiv'oth) is a military term, and can designate Israel's armies (Exod 12:41), the stars (tseva' Deut 4:19), and angels (1 Kgs 22:19). The common title "Yahweh of hosts (yhwh tseva'oth; 1 Sam 17:45; 1 Chr 11:9) refers in part to Yahweh's army of innumerable angels, and the title, "commander (שַׂר sar) of the army (or host) of the LORD" (Josh 5:14-15) indicates hierarchical rank.

The winged SERAPHIM (Isa 6:2, 6, 7) and cherubim (Exod 25:20; Ezek 10:2, 15) are classes of heavenly beings distinguishable from angels in general. While in early usage mal'akh meant messenger, later it was used for heavenly beings in general.

2. General concepts

Angels belong to heaven (Gen 28:12; Job 2:1-2; Ps 148:1-2; Isa 24:21), but can come to earth as Yahweh's servants, indistinguishable from humans. (They do not fly, contrary to common representation in Christian art.) Abraham "saw three men" (Gen 18:2). Yet the narrative states that Abraham negotiates directly with Yahweh concerning Sodom's fate (Gen 18:22-33). How or when he knew his visitors were not human is unclear. Jacob wrestled with "a man" (Gen 32:24, 30), while Gideon recognized his visitor's identity only when the angel made fire consume the meal Gideon prepared (Judg 6:21-22). Joshua, seeing a man with sword in hand, had to be told this was the commander of Yahweh's army (Josh 5:13-15). Manoah and his wife initially were unaware they were speaking with an angel (Judg 13:16, 19-20).

Angels are creatures (Ps 148:1-6). As mighty ones (גִּבֹּרֵי כֹחַ gibore khoakh Ps 103:20) doing God's bidding, they surpass humans in power and wisdom (2 Sam 14:17, 20). But despite their superiority to humans, angels are not to be worshiped (Josh 5:14); but they worship Yahweh (Pss 29:1-2; 103:21; 148:2). While usually only one or two encounter humans, angels are so numerous they are "the host of heaven" (1 Kgs 22:19; Pss 103:19-21; 148:2) and "God's camp" (Gen 32:1-2 [Heb. 32:2-3]). Myriads come with Yahweh from Sinai (Deut 33:2; Ps 68:17 [Heb. 68:18]).

Angels were primarily messengers, sometimes reporting to God about humans (Job 1:6; 2:1), but typically conveying messages from Yahweh. An angel promised Hagar many descendants (Gen 16:7-16; 21:17-19), instructed Abraham not to harm Isaac (Gen 22:11-14), and told Jacob to leave Laban (Gen 31:11-13). Angels announced Sodom's destruction (Gen 19:12-13) and the births of Isaac (Gen 18:10) and Samson (Judg 13:3). An angel was present at Moses' call to lead Israel out of Egypt (Exod 3:2). The commander of Yahweh's army confronted Joshua before the attack on Jericho (Josh 5:13-15), and an angel told Gideon Yahweh would deliver Israel from Midian (Judg 6). Elijah was given a message for Samaria (2 Kgs 1:3-4).

Beyond this basic role, angels acted more broadly as Yahweh's envoys, accomplishing specific tasks. The pestilence Yahweh sent following David's sin was executed by an angel (2 Sam 24:16-17), as was the rout of the Assyrians (2 Kgs 19:35). Consequently, angels can be called "destroying angels" (Ps 78:49).

Angels also perform sustaining roles, as when they provide guidance on journeys; e.g., in the search for a wife for Isaac (Gen 24:7). Elijah, fleeing from Jezebel, was given sustenance by an angel (1 Kgs 19:5-8). The angel Raphael accompanied Tobias in his journey to find a wife (Tob 5:1–12:22) and protected Tobias from a demon that intended to kill him (Tob 8:1-3). Angels also protected the whole nation in its exodus journey (Exod 23:20, 23; 32:34; 33:2). Yahweh had allocated a patron angel over each nation in the distribution of territories, according to Deut 32:8 (LXX; and 4QDeut 32:8, where ʾelohim, gods, corresponds to the LXX, angeloi, against Heb. bene yisraʾel, sons of Israel). Angels provide protection for the righteous in general (Ps 34:7 [Heb. 34:8]; Ps 91:11), for Israel in its wilderness journey (Exod 23:20), and for individuals such as Jacob (Gen 48:16-17).

3. An angel of Yahweh

The phrase malʾakh yhwh (either "an angel of Yahweh" or "the angel of Yahweh"), occurs 50 times in the OT, mostly in the earlier writings (e.g., Gen 16:7-11; 22:11; Exod 3:2; Num 22:22-35; Judg 2:1; 5:23; 2 Sam 24:16-17; 1 Kgs 19:5-7; 2 Kgs 1:1-16; 1 Chr 21:12-30; Ps 34:7 [Heb. 34:8]; Isa 37:36; Zech 1:11-12). The translation "an angel of the LORD" is preferable, despite a long-standing contrary tradition.

Some narratives show apparent merging of the angel and Yahweh, contrary to the normally clear distinction between messengers and those sending them. When Yahweh appeared to Abraham he saw three "men" (Gen 18:1-2). Then, the visitors having eaten, Yahweh spoke to Abraham (Gen 18:13), and also said he would go to Sodom and Gomorrah (Gen 18:21). Meanwhile, two of the men left for Sodom (Gen 18:22; 19:1), while Abraham continued speaking with Yahweh (Gen 18:23-33). Similar blurring occurs elsewhere (e.g., Judg 6:11-23; 13:3-23; Num 22:22-35). Various explanations have been suggested. Perhaps "angel" has been interpolated into the text out of embarrassment that Yahweh should seem to communicate directly with humans. Perhaps the activity of Yahweh's emissary is difficult to distinguish from his personal activity. Perhaps these occasions were theophanies. One effect of the ambiguity is that there can be no doubt Yahweh has spoken. Even while Yahweh's transcendence is maintained, humans meet Yahweh through angelic mediation.

4. The heavenly council

Heavenly angels do more than worship God. Yahweh has his divine council, corresponding to the ANE political organization of a king assisted by a royal court. Yahweh is praised "in the assembly of the holy ones" (קְדֹשִׁים בִּקְהַל biqhal qedhoshim; Ps 89:5 [Heb. 89:6]), and "feared in the council of the holy ones" (בְּסוֹד קְדֹשִׁים besodh qedhoshim Ps 89:7 [Heb. 89:8]). Prophets could be privy to council decisions. Thus Jeremiah laments how prophets have not stood in Yahweh's council (besodh yhwh; Jer 23:18) and so not proclaimed his words (Jer 23:22). Micaiah saw Yahweh enthroned with "the host of heaven" (צְבָא הַשָּׁמַיִם tsevaʾ hashamayim) around him. The council deliberated about who would entice Ahab into battle, and eventually Yahweh commissioned one volunteer to assist (1 Kgs 22:19-23). Yahweh pronounces judgment "in the divine council" (בַּעֲדַתאֵל

baʿadhath ʾel) "in the midst of the gods" (בְּקֶרֶב אֱלֹהִים beqerev ʾelohim; Ps 82:1).

5. The army of Yahweh

God is called "Yahweh of hosts" or "armies" (yhwh tsevaʾoth) over 240 times. Yahweh is head of Israel's armies (1 Sam 17:45), all the heavenly bodies (Deut 4:19), and the angelic host of heaven (1 Kgs 22:19), which is accountable to him (Isa 24:21-22). In Deut 33:2-3, despite textual issues, the sense seems to be that Yahweh comes from Sinai to Israel, accompanied by "myriads of holy ones," marching under his orders. Similarly, Yahweh, the warrior, advances victorious with thousands of chariots (Ps 68:17 [Heb. 68:18]). Military imagery is also used when the "commander of the army of the LORD" (sar tsevaʾ yhwh, Josh 5:14) confronts Joshua prior to Israel's conquest of Jericho. The angelic army has a critical role in certain later writings (1QM 13 x-xii; 1 En. 1:8-9; Rev 12:7).

6. Evil angels

Angels are essentially good, though not always perfect (Job 4:18). They praise Yahweh and fulfill Yahweh's commissions on earth. They can act against humans, as when Yahweh sent "destroying angels" against Egypt (Ps 78:49 מַלְאֲכֵי רָעִים malʾakhe raʿim; compare LXX, ἀγγέλων πονηρῶν angelōn ponērōn, "evil angels"). The psalmist prayed that an angel might pursue his enemies (Ps 35:5-6). An "evil spirit" from Yahweh came upon Saul (1 Sam 16:14-23) and a "lying spirit" was sent to Ahab's prophets (1 Kgs 22:19-23). These angels are not intrinsically evil, but are perceived as bringing evil. In Exod 4:24, Yahweh tried to kill Moses, but later tradition modified this to say it was an angel (LXX) or the evil spirit Mastemah (Jub. 48:2-4; see DEMON). Similarly, in 1 Chr 21:1, an angelic "adversary" (satan) incites David to conduct a census. The word satan does not designate the wicked angel, "Satan," of later texts, but designates human adversaries (1 Kgs 11:14), and the angel who opposed Balaam (Num 22:22, 32). When the angels presented themselves to Yahweh, it was "the adversary" (Job 1:6– 2:7, הַשָּׂטָן hassatan) who questioned Job's integrity. The same is true in the later Zech 3:1-2.

B. The Exile and Beyond: A Developing Angelology

Typically, the canonical prophets received communication directly from Yahweh, rather than by angelic mediation. This contrasts with many writings from the exile through the late Second Temple period. For example, in the pre-exilic Amos and exilic Jeremiah, angels are absent, while "Thus says the LORD," "says the LORD," and (in Jeremiah) "the word of the LORD came to me" are common. Parts of Ezekiel are similar, and outside of Zechariah's visions, all three expressions occur frequently. In the other prophets, angels feature only when events from Israel's past are recalled

(Isa 37:6; 63:9; Hos 12:4 [Heb. 12:5]), and with the seraphim in Isaiah's vision (Isa 6:1-7). Ezekiel and Zechariah are examples of transition between earlier angelology and developments in late Second Temple Judaism, combining the tradition of Yahweh's direct word with revelation mediated by angels.

The Babylonian exile precipitated unprecedented national crisis for Yahweh's covenant people, with loss of the land, Jerusalem, and the Temple. Writings from the exile and beyond draw upon a variety of genres to respond to this crisis, including the apocalypse, which offered reassurance for a devastated nation, using the heavenly journey and its messages from Yahweh's presence through a heavenly guide. Apocalypses such as *1–2 En.*, and 4 Ezra became increasingly important, offering certainty in the midst of despair by conveying a cosmic perspective from the throne room of Yahweh. References to angels occur unevenly in the centuries before and after the start of the Christian era literature, with few or none in Sirach, Wisdom of Solomon, *2 Baruch*, *Epistle of Jeremiah*, Susanna, 1–4 Maccabees, 1 Esdras, and *Psalms of Solomon*. By contrast, angels are prominent in Tobit, Jubilees, *4 Ezra*, *1 Enoch*, *2 Enoch*, *Testaments of the Twelve Patriarchs*, and much Qumran sectarian literature. Diverse theological and sociological concerns were involved.

1. Ezekiel

When the heavens opened for Ezekiel, he saw "visions of God" (Ezek 1:1) and "the likeness of the glory of the LORD" (Ezek 1:28). Burning coals were in the midst of four cherubim (Ezek 10:2, 20)—shining, winged living creatures with both human and animal features (Ezek 1:5-11)—moving in unison with the four spectacular wheels of the divine chariot throne. This vision set the context for various revelations received by Ezekiel through angelic mediation.

In the first series of visions, Ezekiel saw "a man clothed in linen, with a writing case" (Ezek 8:2; 9:2). The guide conducted Ezekiel to various locations associated with the Temple (Ezek 8:7, 14, 16), telling him to make certain observations and asking many questions (Ezek 8:6, 12, 15, 17). Those in Jerusalem who had lamented the abominations committed there were marked by the man with the writing case so they would be safe in the coming slaughter (Ezek 9:3-6). These features recur in later apocalypses such as *1 Enoch*.

In the second series, Ezekiel was brought by Yahweh to Israel. His guide was shining and bronzelike, "with a linen cord and a measuring reed" (Ezek 40:3) and meticulously measured the temple and its precincts (Ezek 40:1–44:5). Yahweh's glory filled the Temple (Ezek 44:4) and assured restoration.

2. Zechariah

Mal'akh (angel) occurs 18 times, and apart from Zech 12:8, all occur in the eight visions of Zech 1–6 concerning the defeat of the Jews' enemies (Zech 1:18-21 [Heb. 2:1-4]), judgment (Zech 5:1-4), exile (Zech 5:5-11), and future peace and prosperity for Yahweh's people and Jerusalem (Zech 1:7-17; 2:1-5; 3:1-10; 4:1-14; 6:1-8). Four angelic horsemen patrolled the earth and reported to the angel assisting the prophet, evoking the idea of the angelic army. Zechariah visited the heavenly council (Zech 3:1-10) when it dealt with a charge of impurity against the high priest, Joshua, brought by an accusing angel (hassatan, the adversary, rather than the NRSV's "Satan"). Features typical of apocalypses include an angelic intermediary and symbolism (e.g., horses, Zech 1:8; a lampstand and olive trees, Zech 4:1-3; horns, Zech 1:18-19). The seer's angelic guide (Zech 3:1; 5:5) asked questions, supplied the interpretations (Zech 5:1-3), and answered queries from the seer (Zech 5:5-6). Again, such information was reassuring, since it came from an angel close to Yahweh.

3. Terminology

Extensive angelological development resulted in a proliferation of terminology in this period. Angels are frequently spirits (רוחות rukhoth) 1QS 3 xviii; *1 En.* 15:4; *Jub.* 1:25; 2:2; *T. Levi* 4:1; *4 Ezra* 6:41), as well as spirits of holiness (רוחי קדש rkhy qdsh 1QH 8 xii), spirits of heaven (*1 En.* 15:10) and spirits of truth (אמת רוחי rkhy 'mth, 1QS 4 xxiii). Similarly, host is combined with other terms, as in host of knowledge (צבא דעת tsb' d'th, 1QH 18 xxiii) and everlasting host (צבא עד tsb' 'dh, 1QH 11 xiii). Angels are holy ones (qdshm, Zech 14:5; *1 En.* 1:9), holy watchers (Dan 4:13; וקדש ער 'r wqdsh *1 En.* 15:9) and host of holy ones (tsb' qdshm, 1QH 3 xxii). Other epithets include honored ones (נכבדים nkbdym, 1 QH 10 viii; *2 En.* 21:1, 3), princes (שרים srym, 4Q400 3 ii, 2), priests (כהנים khnym, 4Q403 1 xxi), authorities (εχουσια exousiai, *T. Levi* 3:8; *1 En.* 61:10), powers (δυναμεις dynameis, *2 En.* 20:1), and thrones (θρονοι thronoi, *T. Levi* 3:8; *2 En.* 20:1). In addition to cherubim and seraphim, there are spiritual beings called 'ofannim (*1 En.* 61:10; 71:7), related to the chariot wheels (אופנים 'ofannim) of Ezek 1:15-21.

4. Relationship to early OT literature

Angels basically fulfill the functions already encountered in the pre-exilic literature. They are created beings (Neh 9:6; *4 Ezra* 6:41; *Jub.* 2:2) who accompany travelers (Tob 5:17-22; 6:1), protect God's people (2 Macc 11:6; Ep Jer 1:7; 1QH 8 xi-xii) and individuals (*Jub.* 35:17; 2 Macc 10:29-30), and strengthen those overwhelmed at their presence (Dan 8:16-18; *4 Ezra* 5:15; 10:30; *1 En.* 14:13-14, 24-25; *2 En.* 21:3; cf. Ezek 2:2; 3:24). They are innumerable (*4 Ezra* 6:3; *2 Bar.* 48:10; 56:14; *1 En.* 1:9), the host of heaven (Neh 9:6; Sir 17:32; *Pr. Man.* 1:15; 1QH 3 xxxv; *1 En.* 104:6; 1QM 12 i, 7) and holy ones (Tob 11:14; 3 Macc 2:2; Sir 45:2; 42:17; Wis 3:9; *1 En.* 81:5; 1QS 11 viii), who praise God (Tob 8:15), and surround the divine throne (*1 En.* 14:8-25). They serve as guides and interpreters in apocalypses (Dan 9:21-22; *4 Ezra* 2:44-48; 10:28-40; *1 En.* 17:1; 19:1; 72:1). The destruction of the Assyrian army is recalled (Sir 48:21; 1 Macc 7:41; 2 Kgs 19:35), and angelic help can be invoked in battle (2 Macc 11:6). Angels on horseback ride against Apollonius, enemy of the Jerusalem Temple (4 Macc 4:10; Deut 33:2-3; 2 Kgs 2:12). God the warrior comes with innumerable angels to bring final judgment on the wicked (*1 En.* 1:3-9).

However, elaboration of earlier ideas also occurred. The teaching function encountered in Ezek 8–9; 40–48 is extensive in *1 Enoch*. Uriel teaches Enoch about the true solar calendar (*1 En.* 72:1; 74:2; 82:7). Angels are now directly involved in the functioning of the whole cosmos, controlling the luminaries under their leader, Uriel (*1 En.* 79:6), guiding the stars (*1 En.* 80:1), and managing the seasons, months, and days (*1 En.* 82:11) and natural phenomena generally (*Jub.* 2:2; *4 Ezra* 8:22; *1 En.* 60:17-21; 1QH 1 vi-xiii). In earlier writings, Yahweh controlled the heavenly bodies (Job 9:7; Isa 40:26), but now angels have delegated responsibility in running the universe, while the earlier belief about angels as national patrons (4QDeut 32:8 and LXX) is elaborated to explain Israel's great suffering at the hands of seventy angels (*1 En.* 85–90).

Angels are mediators, not just of revelation, but as intercessors with God on behalf of humans (*1 En.* 9:3; 15:2; 40:6; 99:3; Tob 12:12, 15; *T. Dan.* 6:2 [Heb. 6:3]; *T. Levi* 5:6). Such elaboration correlates with an increasing sense of God's transcendence, evident in the contrast between the earlier account in which Yahweh incites David to number the people (2 Sam 24:1), and the later 1 Chr 21:1 where it is Satan, now personified, who does this.

While it has often been supposed that there has been fundamental influence from outside sources, notably Zoroastrian dualism, this should not be overemphasized. The roots of the later angelology lie in the OT, though the idea of a leading evil angel, Satan, and an angelic host associated with him, seems at least partly attributable to such influence.

5. Naming and rank of angels

Rank among angels is prominent (compare Josh 5:14-15), with many angels bearing personal names. Two traditions developed, one with four archangels, Michael, Gabriel, Raphael, and Sariel (*1 En.* 9:1; 10:1, 4, 9, 11; 40:1-10; 1QM 9 xiv-xvi), or Phanuel (*1 En.* 40:9), or commonly Uriel (*Life of Adam and Eve* [Greek] 40:2). The other has seven (*1 En.* 20; 81:5-10; 87:2-3; 90:21-24; Tob 12:15), adding Uriel, Raguel, and Remiel (Jeremiel in *4 Ezra* 4:36) in *1 En.* 20. The only angels named in the OT are Gabriel (Dan 8:16; 9:21) and Michael, Israel's prince (Dan 10:13, 21; 12:1). *First Enoch* 82:13-20 has a highly complex list of names.

Qumran texts know the four-archangel tradition (1QM 9 xiv-xvi). Michael is probably identical with "the Prince of Light(s)" (1QS 3 xx; CD 5 xviii; 1QM 13 xi) and Melchizedek (11Q Melch 2 v-xiii). Songs of the Sabbath Sacrifice has seven chief princes and seven deputies over groups of angels involved in the heavenly worship (4Q403 1 i; Q400 3 ii, 2).

Leading angels who serve in God's immediate presence, like a king's chief ministers, are also called Angels of the Presence (*Jub.* 1:27, 29; 2:1, 18; *T. Levi* 3:4-8; *T. Jud.* 25:2; *1 En.* 40:1; Tob 12:15; 1QH 6 xii-xiii; 1QSb 4 xxv-xxvi). The antecedent is the angel in Isa 63:9 who had rescued Israel.

6. Appearance and nature of angels

No longer indistinguishable from humans, angels can be spectacular, radiant like the sun (*2 En.* 19:1), and frightening to humans (3 Macc 6:18; *4 Ezra* 14:3; *Jos. Asen.* 14:11). Handsome (2 Macc 3:26), dressed in white linen, sometimes with gold belts (Dan 10:5; 12:6; *T. Levi* 8:2; compare Ezek 9:2-3), they can ride horses with golden bridles (2 Macc 10:29-30). At least some fly (Dan 9:21; *4 Ezra* 14:3) and transport humans rapidly over great distances (Bel 1:36). They live forever (*1 En.* 15:4, 6), have special food (Wis 16:20; *4 Ezra* 1:19), and are even thought able to impart immortality to humans (*Jos. Asen.* 16:14). Frequently called spirits in Qumran literature (**rukhot**/**rukhe**; 1QS 3 xviii; 1QM 12 viii; 1QH 3 xxii-xxiii), they only seem to consume earthly fare when with humans (Tob 12:19; *T. Ab.* 4:9-10).

7. Good and evil angels

Speculation on Gen 6:1-4 understood the "sons of God" (bene 'elohim) as angels who sinned by marrying human women, thereby introducing sin into the world (*1 En.* 6-36). The fallen angels are called watchers, a term also used elsewhere for unfallen angels (Dan 4:13, 17, 23; *1 En.* 12:2-3; *Jub.* 4:15; 4QMessar 2 xvi-xviii), as well as fallen angels (*Jub.* 4:22; 7:21; *T. Naph.* 3:5; 1 Qap Gen ar 2 i, 16). The term watcher (Dan 4:13, Aramaic Dan 4:10; ('ir weqaddish, holy watcher) suggests that angels are always alert, being related to Aramaic, 'wr, to be awake. They are also called stars in another version of their fall (*1 En.* 86-88). *First Enoch* 6–36 has two literary strands, with leaders Shemihazah (*1 En.* 6:3, 7) and Asael (*1 En.* 8:1-4; 86:1) who introduced devastating evils to the world (*1 En.* 7–8). The spirits of the watchers' deceased giant offspring continue to wreak havoc (*1 En.* 10:9, 15) and are subject to Mastema, a leading evil spirit (*Jub.* 10:1-14; compare 48:1-2). Here is a clear angelic dualism, involving evil and good angels. Evil spirits are mentioned elsewhere in *Jub.* 11:4-5; 12:20; *T. Sim.* 4:9; *T. Levi* 18:12.

Qumran speculation on angels is markedly dualistic. The Angel of Darkness with his spirits (1QS 3 xx-xxi, 24) opposes the Prince of Lights (1QS 3 xx) (the Prince of Light in 1QM 17 vi-viii, and Michael, 1QM 13 x), who stands with the sons of light, the faithful sect members, against the angels of destruction led by Belial (1QM 1 i; 13 x-xii; 1QS 2 iv-v; CD 5 xvii-xix) and the humans who belong to them. The Angel of Darkness rules the wicked (1QS 3 xx-xxi). Presumably there is one leader of the evil angels, vaiously called Belial, the Angel of Darkness, Melchiresha (4Q'Amramb 2 iii; 4Q280 2 ii), Mastema (*Jub.* 10:8; 48:1-2; 1QM 13 xi), Satan and the devil *L.A.E.* 9-16). Satan is now a proper name and not just a noun meaning adversary as in earlier texts. Melchizedek, a good angel, corresponds to Melchiresha (11QMelch 2 v, viii, ix, xiii).

8. Eschatological functions of angels

Angelic involvement in Israel's military conflicts (2 Macc 10:29-31) is mirrored in the heavenly realm, as when Israel's protector, Michael, fights the princes of Egypt and Greece (Dan 10:13, 21; 12:1). In the War Scroll, the ultimate heavenly eschatological battle parallels the earthly conflict, as Michael and God's angels (1QM 3 x; 17 vi-viii) fight alongside the Qumran sect (1QM 1 x-xi; 12 vii-viii; 15 xiii-xiv), defeating both Belial's angels and the sect's human enemies (1QM 1 iv-vi; 3 ix; 13 i-ii; 16 ix). Similar ideas occur elsewhere (1QH 3 xix-xxxvi; 4Q402 7-10; 1QS 4 xviii-xix).

In *1 Enoch*, the theme of a final assize is highly developed. The fallen watchers are temporarily incarcerated (*1 En.* 27), and eventually judged (*1 En.* 90:22, 25; 91:21). Obedient angels execute the final judgment (*1 En.* 91:15), serving the summons, arresting the fallen angels (*1 En.* 10:11-13) and acting as prison warders to bring angels and human sinners to judgment (*1 En.* 90:20-26; 100:4). Angels serve the court by keeping books of evidence (*1 En.* 10:8; 89:61-63; 90:20; 100:10), speak to God on behalf of the righteous (*1 En.* 104:1), and execute the sentence on the fallen angels (*1 En.* 10:13; 90:24-26). Occasionally Qumran texts reflect similar themes, with angels of destruction punishing all people who belong to the Angel of Darkness (1QS 4 xi-xiv; CD 2 v-vii). Myriads of angels are present in the divine courtroom in Dan 7:10.

9. Fellowship with angels

One Enochic tradition anticipates that the righteous will eventually live with the angels (*1 En.* 104:1-6; *2 En.* 22). Elsewhere, transformation of the individual into angelic form is considered highly desirable (*2 En.* 22:7-10; *Apoc. Zeph.* 8:3). By contrast, the Qumran literature shows an inaugurated eschatology, the community joined in present communion with the angels (1QS 11 v-ix; CD 15 xv-xvii; 1QH 3 xxi-xxii; 6 xii-xiii; 11 xiii; 4Q181 1 i-vi; 1QSa 2 viii-ix).

C. Angels in the NT

Angels are most prominent in the Gospels, Acts, Hebrews, and Revelation, with occasional references in over half of the remaining NT books. The nature and roles of angels correspond closely to ideas already discussed, though the language is much more restrained than that of late Second Temple Judaism. Angels function in relation to God and the establishment of his kingdom, and so are involved with the Messiah and his people, the establishment of the church, and the consummation of God's purposes in the world. There is no interest in angels for their own sake.

1. NT terminology

The Greek angelos is now a term specific for angels, referring to human messengers only in Matt 11:10, and Jas 2:25. Angels are called holy ones (Jude 14), and stars (Rev 1:16, 20; 2:1; 3:1; the fallen watchers, *1 En.* 86–88), and the heavenly host (stratia, army; Luke 2:13; Acts 7:42). *Spirits* commonly refers to evil spirits (e.g., Matt 10:1; Luke 7:21; Gal 4:3; 1 Tim 4:1; Rev 16:14), but occasionally is used of humans (1 Cor 14:32; Heb 12:23; Rev 22:6) or good angels. Angels are spirits who serve God (Heb 1:14). God is the Father of spirits (Heb 12:9), and has seven spirits, corresponding to the seven Angels of the Presence (Rev 1:4; 3:1; 4:5). The tradition of four archangels may be recalled in Rev 7:1-2.

Archangel occurs twice (Jude 9; 1 Thess 4:6), and Michael (Jude 9) and Gabriel (Luke 1:19, 26) are the only angels named. Satan (Mark 4:15; Acts 5:3; Rev 20:2) occurs thirty-six times, now designating the leader of the fallen angels, also called Beelzebul (Matt 12:24), the ancient serpent (2 Cor 11:3; Rev 12:9; 20:2), Beliar (2 Cor 6:15 = Belial in Qumran texts), the dragon (Rev. 12:4; 13:2; 16:13; 20:2), and the devil (Matt 4:1; Eph 6:11). Apollyon (or Abaddon, Rev 9:11) is over the bottomless pit. Cherubim are mentioned in connection with the Israelite tabernacle (Heb 9:5), while the living creatures, presumably cherubim, are animal-like creatures protecting the divine throne (fourteen times in Revelation; e.g., Rev 4:6-9; 5:6-8).

In addition, there are rulers ($\dot{\alpha}\rho\chi\alpha\iota$ archai, Rom 8:38; Eph 6:12; Col 1:16; 2:15), authorities ($\epsilon\xi\text{ου}\sigma\iota\alpha\varsigma$ exousias, Eph 6:12; Col 1:16; 2:15; 1 Pet 3:22), cosmic powers (κοσμοκράτορεις kosmokratoreis) of this present darkness (Eph 6:12), powers ($\delta\text{υνάμεων}$ dynameōn, 1 Pet 3:22), dominions (κυριοτητες kyriotētes, Col 1:16) and spiritual forces ($\pi\text{νευματικα}$ pneumatika) of evil (Eph 6:12), although there is diversity of opinion about which of these terms refer to spiritual beings.

2. Appearance and nature of angels

Angels are readily distinguishable from humans (Acts 6:15), though they can be entertained without recognition (Heb 13:2). At Jesus' tomb they are men (Luke 24:4) and a young man (Mark 16:5), clothed in white (Mark 16:5; Matt 8:3-5; John 20:12; 2 Macc 3:26, 33-34; Rev 3:5), with dazzling appearance (Luke 24:4-7). The guards at the tomb (Matt 28:3-5) and the women (Mark 16:5-7; Luke 24:4-5) were terrified by them. Revelation describes angels as strikingly different from humans (Rev 10:1; 18:1), and one angel flies (Rev 14:6).

As created beings (John 1:3; Col 1:15-16), angels belong to God (Luke 2:15; 12:9; Acts 12:23; 27:23; Heb 1:6-7), and should not be worshiped (Col 2:18; Rev 22:8-9). Spiritual beings that serve God (Heb 1:14), with roles in the realm of nature (Rev 7:1-2; 8:7-12; 19:17), angels have delegated authority (Rev 18:1). As heavenly beings (Mark 12:25; 13:32; Luke 2:13, 15; John 1:51; Gal 1:8; Heb 12:22; Rev 14:6, 10), they surround God's throne as the divine council (Heb 12:22; Rev 3:5; 5:11; 7:11; 8:2) and worship him (Heb 1:6). They are exceedingly numerous (Matt 26:53; Heb 12:22; Jude 14; *1 En.* 1:9; Rev 5:11), holy (Mark 8:38; Acts 10:22; Rev 14:10), mighty (2 Pet 2:11; Rev 10:1; 18:21), immortal (Luke 20:36), with no need to reproduce (Matt 22:30). They have their own language (1 Cor 13:1) and limited knowledge (Matt 24:36).

3. Roles in relation to the kingdom of God

In Jewish belief, the Sinai Covenant Law was mediated by angels (Acts 7:38, 53; Gal 3:19; Heb 2:2; *Jub.* 1:27-29; Josephus, *Ant.* 15.136). Angels are also important in the inauguration of the New Covenant and the kingdom of God.

a. Angels and the person and work of Jesus. Angels are prominent in the critical events of the birth, temptations, and resurrection of the Messiah. The archangel Gabriel announced the birth of John the Baptist (Luke 1:11, 19), harbinger of the Messiah (Luke 1:13-20) and told Mary (Luke 1:26-38) and Joseph (Matt 1:18-20) of the birth of Jesus, the Messiah (Matt 1:21; Luke 1:31-33). An angel told the shepherds of Jesus' birth, and then the heavenly host praised God (Luke 2:9-15). An angel warned Joseph to flee to Egypt (Matt 2:13), advising him when to return (Matt 2:19-21) to settle in Nazareth (Matt 2:22-23).

At the outset of Jesus' messianic ministry (Matt 4:1-11), Satan unsuccessfully sought to divert him from the means appropriate to his mission, urging him to throw himself from the pinnacle of the Temple, given that angels would protect him (Ps 91:11-12). Angels ministered to him at the conclusion of these temptations, perhaps offering food, Jesus having earlier refused to convert stones to bread (Matt 4:11; compare 1 Kgs 19:5-8). In Gethsemane, Jesus could have called on twelve legions of angels, the heavenly army, for assistance (Matt 26:53).

An angel rolled back the stone (Matt 28:22) and announced Jesus' resurrection to the women (Matt 28:2-7; Mark 16:5-7; Luke 24:4-8). Christ was "seen by angels" (1 Tim 3:16), possibly a reference to their presence at the empty tomb or to his earthly life generally. In Hebrews, angelos occurs twelve times,

the majority of which are in Heb 1–2, where the Son's superiority to angels is argued (Heb 1:4). Angels worship the Son (Heb 1:6), for God's relationship to the Son is different from theirs (Heb 1:5). He sits at God's right hand, all his enemies ultimately to be defeated (Heb 1:13), though in the incarnation, the Son is temporarily lower than the angels (Heb 2:9). Angels serve for the sake of those saved through the Son (Heb 1:14).

b. Angels, humans, and the gospel. Angels assist God's servants in the spread of the gospel. An angel delivered the apostles from jail (Acts 5:19; 12:7-12), reassured Paul when he was endangered at sea (Acts 27:23), instructed and guided Philip so he could preach to the Ethiopian (Acts 8:26), and guided Cornelius to Peter, so the gospel reached the Gentiles (Acts 10:3, 22). Jesus spoke of children's guardian angels who continually see God's face (Matt 18:10) and angels carry a poor man into Abraham's presence at death (Luke 16:22). Paul attributed his "thorn in the flesh" to a "messenger of Satan" (2 Cor 12:7; angelos), perhaps not an evil angel, but one acting by divine permission, since God's purpose is involved. Angels control nature, at least while God's servants are marked so they will be safe (Rev 7:1-3; Heb 1:7). In the New Jerusalem, twelve angels protect the redeemed by guarding the gates (Rev 21:12).

Angels observe human affairs (1 Cor 4:9; 1 Tim 5:21), especially the drama of redemption (1 Pet 1:12), and rejoice whenever sinners repent (Luke 15:7). The saved join the community of heaven's angels (Heb 12:22). In Revelation, the seven churches have their individual angels (Rev 1:20; 2:1), while Corinthian women at worship require a "symbol of authority" on the head, enigmatically "because of the angels" (1 Cor 11:10). Eventually, humans will judge angels (1 Cor 6:3) and be over the coming world (Heb 2:5).

c. Revelation by angels. Typical of earlier apocalypses, angels feature prominently in Revelation. Angelos occurs 67 times out of 175 in the NT (including Luke 22:43). The seer, transported to heaven and in the company of angels, is shown mysteries (Rev 17:7) and things to come (Rev 1:1; 21:9), learning that angels convey the saints' prayers to God (Rev 8:3-4), that the redeemed will enjoy bliss with God (Rev 7:2-3) and that the kingdom's enemies will come under "the Lord and his Christ" (Rev 11:15; 18:1). Angels execute God's wrath (Rev 15:1), throw Satan into the pit (Rev 20:1-3), and make proclamations (Rev 5:2; 14:6, 8, 9). An angel instructs John to write about the marriage of the Lamb (Rev 19:9) and measures the New Jerusalem, thereby emphasizing the future security of God's people (Rev 21:9-27).

d. Evil angels. Spiritual dualism involving two unequal powers is a fundamental NT motif. Satan, principal enemy of the kingdom, is thrown down to the earth, along with his angelic retinue (Rev 12:9). He opposes Jesus' messianic work (Matt 4:1-11; 16:23), working against God's Spirit (Matt 12:24-29) and snatching the word from the hearers (Mark 4:15). Nevertheless, he is defeated through the disciples' ministry (Luke 10:18). He inspires people to oppose God (Luke 22:3, 31; John 13:27; Acts 5:3), is followed by unbelievers (Acts 26:18; 1 Tim 5:15; 1 John 3:8, 10; Rev 2:9; 3:9), tempts and deceives (1 Cor 7:5; 2 Cor 2:11; 11:14; 2 Thess 2:9) and opposes Paul (1 Thess 2:18).

Some angels that had sinned remain imprisoned until the judgment (2 Pet 2:4; Jude 6). But Satan and evil spirits or demons (Matt 10:1; Luke 7:21; Gal 4:3; 1 Tim 4:1; Rev 16:14) will wreak havoc on earth until judgment day (Rev 12:9) and God's people struggle against these evil spiritual forces (Eph 6:12). Moreover, just as Satan opposes God's kingdom on earth, his angels fight in the heavenly realm against Michael's army (Rev 12:3). Ultimately, Satan and his forces will be defeated, consigned eternally to the bottomless pit prepared for them (Rev 20:1-3, 7-10; Matt 25:41).

e. Angels and judgment. An angel effected present judgment by killing Agrippa, who had accepted the crowd's adulation (Acts 12:20-23). Angels will act significantly in future judgment, a theme encountered already in late Second Temple literature. They will execute God's wrath (Rev 14:14-20; 15:1; 16:1), witness the condemnation of those consigned to the lake of fire (Rev 14:10), and accompany the Son of Man when he returns in messianic judgment (Matt 16:27; 25:31; 2 Thess 1:7; Dan 7:13). Angelic reapers, like police making arrests, will separate the righteous and wicked (Matt 13:39, 41, 49), gather God's elect (Matt 24:31), and be present when the Son of Man informs the eschatological court of who has denied him before others (Luke 12:8-9; Rev 3:5). An angel will act as prison warden, executing sentence on Satan (Rev 20:1-3, 7, 10; 20:14-15). Ultimately, all enemies will be defeated, the kingdom of God will be unrivaled, and God will dwell with his people in the New Jerusalem (Rev 21:1-3). *See* ANGELIC HOST; APOCALYPSE; ARCHANGEL; BELIAL; CHERUBIM; DIVINE ASSEMBLY; GABRIEL; HOLY WAR; HOSTS; HOSTS OF HEAVEN; LORD OF HOSTS; MICHAEL; SATAN; SERAPHIM; WATCHER.

Bibliography: Christoph Auffarth and Loren T. Stuckenbruck, eds. *The Fall of the Angels* (2004); P. Benoit. "Pauline Angelology and Demonology: Reflexions on the Designation of the Heavenly Powers and on the Origin of Angelic Evil according to Paul." *RSB* 3 1 (Jan 1983) 1–18; Matthew Black. *"The Book of Enoch" or "1 Enoch"* (1985); Peter R. Carrell. *Jesus and the Angels: Angelology and the Christology of the Apocalypse of John* (1997); John J. Collins. "Powers in Heaven: God, Gods, and Angels in the Dead Sea Scrolls." John J. Collins and Robert A. Kugler, eds. *Reli-gion in the Dead Sea Scrolls* (2000) 9–28; Maxwell J. Davidson. *Angels at Qumran: A Comparative Study of 1 Enoch 1–36, 72–108 and Sectarian Writings from Qumran* (1992); Chris Forbes. "Paul's Principalities and Powers: Demythologizing Apocalyptic?" *JSNT* 82 (2001) 61–88; Stephen F. Noll. *Angels of Light, Powers of Darkness: Thinking Biblically about Angels, Satan, and Principalities* (1998); Christopher Rowland. *The Open Heaven: A Study of Apocalyptic Judaism and Early Christianity* (1982); W. A. VanGemeren. "The Sons of God in Genesis 6:1-4." *WTJ* 43 (1981) 320–48; Walter Wink. *Naming the Powers: The Language of Power in the New Testament.* Vol. 1 (1984).

MAXWELL JOHN DAVIDSON

ANGELIC HOST [צָבָא tsava'; στρατιᾶς stratias]. The Hebrew and Greek words mean *army* (Num 1:3; Deut 24:5), and the translation *host*, suggested by the image of many soldiers, designates both the stars (Deut 4:19; Neh 9:6; Ps 148:3-4; Acts 7:42) and the angels who surround God's throne (Deut 33:2; 1 Kgs 22:19; Ps 148:2; *4 Ezra* 6:3; Luke 2:13), praising him (Pss 29:1, 89:5; Heb 6; 148:2; Heb 1:6; 1QH 3:21-23; Rev 5:11; 7:11).

As Yahweh's council, the angelic host is analogous to an ancient Near Eastern royal court, and functions in judgment (Dan 7:10; *1 En.* 1:9; Jude 14). Micaiah saw Yahweh enthroned, consulting his council (1 Kgs 22:19 = 2 Chr 18:18). Prophets ought to learn from it (Jer 23:18-22). Yahweh is praised "in the assembly of the holy ones" (בִּקְהַל קְדֹשִׁים biqhal qedhoshim; Ps 89:5), feared "in the council of the holy ones" (בְּסוֹד קְדֹשִׁים besod qedhoshim, Ps 89:7; Heb 8), and pronounces judgment "in the divine council" (אֵל בַּעֲדַת ba'adhath 'el; compare 1QH III 21-22) among "the gods" (אֱלֹהִים 'elohim; Ps 82:1).

Early Israel saw Yahweh as head of its armies (1 Sam 17:45; 1 Sam 15:2). However, Yahweh is also over the angelic army (Deut 33:2-3; 2 Kgs 6:17; Ps 103:20-21). Jacob, met by angels, declared the place God's camp (Gen 32:1-2), while the commander of Yahweh's army (שַׂר צְבָא יְהוָה sar tseva' yhwh) confronted Joshua (Josh 5:14-15).

An angel announced the Savior's advent to the shepherds. Then a "multitude of the heavenly host" (πλῆθος στρατιᾶς οὐρανίου plēthos stratias ouraniou, Luke 2:13-15) appeared from heaven, glorifying God. Their presence anticipated the angelic protection available to the Messiah (Matt 4:6; 26:53).

In the Qumran *War Scroll*, the angelic host under Michael will fight against BELIAL and his hosts, mirroring the battle between the sectarians and their enemies (1QM XIII 10-12). In Revelation, Michael's angels fight the dragon's angels in heaven (Rev 12:7-9), throwing them down to earth where they oppose God's cause. Ultimately, the Word of God, as King of kings, is accompanied by the armies of heaven, and is victorious

(Rev-19:13-16). *See* ANGEL; DIVINE ASSEMBLY; DIVINE WARRIOR; SATAN; YAHWEH OF HOSTS.

Bibliography: Tremper Longman III and Daniel G. Reid. *God Is a Warrior* (1995); Patrick D. Miller. *The Divine Warrior in Early Israel* (1973); E. Theodore Mullen. *The Divine Council in Canaanite and Early Hebrew Literature: The Assembly of the Gods* (1980).

MAXWELL J. DAVIDSON

ANGELIC LITURGY. *See* SONGS OF THE SABBATH SACRIFICE.

ANGELS OF THE SEVEN CHURCHES [ἄγγελοι τῶν ἑπτὰ ἐκκλησιῶν angeloi tōn hepta ekklēsiōn]. Mentioned only in Rev 1:20 and addressed individually in letters to the churches (Rev 2:1, 8, 12, 18; 3:1, 7, 14), these angels have been identified as guardian angels of the churches and as heavenly personifications of the churches on earth. They have been seen as human leaders, such as bishops, or as messengers sent to John (Rev 1:4), and have been equated to stars (Rev 1:20). Approximately sixty references to angelos (ἄγγελος) in Revelation are to spiritual beings. *See* ANGEL; REVELATION, BOOK OF.

Bibliography: David E. Aune. *Revelation.* WBC 52 (1997).

MAXWELL J. DAVIDSON

ANGER [אַף ʾaf; θυμός thymos]. Anger is a strong feeling of displeasure or hostility that often provokes action against the person(s) or situations that arouse it.

A. Words for Anger

The Hebrew word most often translated "anger" is ʾaf (Gen 27:45). The dual form of this word denotes the nostrils, which may suggest that ʾaf implies the snort that can accompany anger. Among other words translated as "anger," חֵמָה khema (2 Sam 11:20) suggests the furious heat of anger; it is also translated "fury," "rage," and "heat." חָרוֹן kharon suggests something that blazes (חָרָה kharah, Gen 4:6); it is also translated "fury" and "heat" (*see* BURN, BURNING). עֶבְרָה ʿevrah suggests something that bursts out and overwhelms (עָבַר ʿavar Job 40:11); it, too, can be translated "fury." The word for wind or spirit, רוּחַ ruakh, is sometimes translated "anger" (Judg 8:3). כַּעַס kaʿas (Eccl 7:9) suggests vexation, a strong feeling that can be mixed up with frustration and grief (the same word in Eccl 1:18). קֶצֶף qetsef often suggests a stronger feeling of wrath (Esth 1:18). זַעַף zaʿaf suggests the raging of a storm (2 Chr 16:10). זַעַם zaʿam is usually reckoned to mean "indignation" (e.g., Jer 15:17). The most common NT word is thymos (Heb 11:27), which can also suggest passion or courage, and thus points to the strength of feelings involved in anger. ὀργή orgē (Jas 1:19) perhaps suggests an even stronger feeling—more often translated "wrath" (*see* WRATH; WRATH OF GOD).

B. The Dynamics of Anger

Biblical allusions to anger often refer to it simply as an aspect of being human, without necessarily suggesting a moral or theological judgment. It is part of a biblical understanding that by nature human beings get angry, as it is part of a biblical understanding that it is human nature to feel compassion or hatred or desire.

Anger is thus treated in the Bible as a natural response on the part of people who feel wronged. So Esau gets angry when Jacob swindles him (Gen 27:44-45), as does Jacob when Rachel treats him as responsible for her not having children (Gen 30:1-2), and Laban when he feels slighted (Gen 31:35). After his bride betrays his riddle, Samson goes home to his parents in hot anger (Judg 14:28)—he has been made a fool. Saul gets angry because of people's enthusiasm for David (1 Sam 18:8) and because of Jonathan's attitude to David (1 Sam 20:30). Abner gets angry at Ish-bosheth's implicit accusation of him (2 Sam 3:8). Naaman gets angry because he feels slighted (2 Kgs 5:11). Asa gets angry when challenged by a seer, as does Uzziah when challenged by the priests (2 Chr 16:10; 26:19). A man gets angry when his father has mercy on his brother in a way that seems unfair (Luke 15:28). Thus anger is a response to a sense that one has been personally devalued or slighted. One's human worth has been placed in question. A backbiting tongue therefore generates anger (Prov 25:23). So does jealousy—because it issues out of rejection, with its associated slight and shame (Prov 6:34). Paradoxically, it is possible to be angry with oneself (Gen 45:5)—because one has slighted oneself or dishonored oneself by one's action.

Loss of self-esteem is not the only reason for anger. Sanballat and others get angry at Nehemiah's wall building (Neh 4:1, 7 [Heb. 3:33; 4:1]); they are frustrated at the prospect of loss of power. The wicked get angry when faithful people do well (Ps 112:10).

Anger is also a natural response to the wronging of someone with whom one identifies. Jacob's sons are very angry when Shechem rapes their sister (Gen 34:7; compare 49:5-7), as is Potiphar when he believes Joseph has attempted to seduce his wife (Gen 39:19). Jonathan gets angry because of his father's hostility to David, and thus to him (1 Sam 20:34). In these instances, identifying with the person who has directly been wronged means one's own esteem has been imperiled.

This throws into relief the more selfless nature of the anger that arises on other occasions. Moses' anger burns hot when he sees the gold calf and the Israelites dancing (Exod 32:19); this seems to be an anger expressing concern for Yahweh's honor. The mayor of Shechem is angry at a plot to unseat Abimelech as king (Judg 9:30). Nahash the Ammonite's threat to maim and disgrace the people of Jabesh-gilead arouses furious anger in Saul (1 Sam 11:6). Elisha gets angry with the king when he falls short in what he implicitly asks of God (2 Kgs 13:19). People get angry with Jesus for breaking the Law when he heals on the Sabbath (John 7:23). Jesus gets angry at people who do not want him to heal on the Sabbath (Mark 3:5).

In light of the serious significance that can thus attach to anger, some humor or irony appears on other occasions when someone gets angry. Balaam gets angry when his donkey will not move (Num 22:27), and his employer gets angry when Balaam will not curse Israel (Num 24:10). Eliab gets angry because he thinks his brother is acting above his station (1 Sam 17:28). Ahasuerus gets angry because his wife Vashti refuses to show off her beauty before the guests at his banquet (Esth 1:12). Elihu gets angry at Job because he justifies himself, and at Job's three friends because they do not answer adequately (Job 32:2-5). Jonah gets angry when God has mercy on Nineveh and when, in turn, God makes his sheltering plant wither (Jonah 4:1-9).

C. The Trouble with Anger

Anger can carry negative consequences. A hot-tempered man stirs up strife, but the person who is slow to anger quiets contention (Prov 15:18). The people's anger leads them to cause trouble to others (Pss 55:3; 124:3). Anger causes strife and transgression (Prov 29:22; 30:33), is cruel and overwhelming (Prov 27:4), or brings devastation and persecution (Isa 14:6; Amos 1:11). Thus Yahweh warns Cain that his naturally angry response to his rejection means that sin is crouching at the door of his life, ready to pounce, and his anger indeed issues in the murder of Abel (Gen 4:5-8). Anger makes Potiphar put Joseph in prison (Gen 39:19; compare Gen 40:2; 41:10; 2 Chr 16:10) and leads Simeon and Levi to overreact in slaughtering the men in Shechem (Gen 49:5-6). Anger makes Balaam beat his donkey, and it makes Barak berate and sack Balaam (Num 22:27; 24:10). It makes Naaman refuse to take the action that will bring healing (2 Kgs 5:11-12). It makes Ahasuerus depose Vashti and hang Haman (Esth 1:12; 2:1; 7:10). It makes Job rage at God (according to Bildad, at least; Job 18:4). It makes a householder send a servant to jail (Matt 18:34). It makes Herod kill a whole town's children (Matt 2:16).

The anger of a powerful person is therefore something of which to be wary (Gen 44:18; 2 Sam 11:20; Dan 2:12; 3:13; Matt 22:7). Fortunately it is often the case that "a soft answer turns away wrath" (Prov 15:1), as Naaman's servants illustrate (2 Kgs 5:11-14). Likewise, when the Ephraimites are angered by not

having been summoned to a battle against the Midianites, Gideon is able to placate them with a conciliatory answer (Judg 8:1-3).

Anger can also have terrible consequences for oneself. This is so for Saul, and Gen 49:7 sees the scattering of Simeon and Levi in Israel as a fruit of their angry action. In fact, anger is just stupid (Eccl 7:9).

In the NT anger is often simply condemned (Matt 5:22; 2 Cor 12:20; Gal 5:20; Eph 4:31; Col 3:8; 1 Tim 2:8). Do not even get angry at wickedness, a psalm advises, because it leads to wrongdoing (Ps 37:8)—perhaps because anger leads to joining evildoers, or perhaps because it leads to taking action against them wrongly. Proverbs advises not to associate with angry people, or risk ending up like them (Prov 22:24-25).

D. The Value of Anger

At the same time, passages noted above show how Scripture recognizes the positive significance of anger. It can be an appropriate response to wrongdoing, and a response that provides the energy to take action against wrongdoing. Yahweh points out that if Job had enough overflowing anger he could put down the arrogant and wicked (Job 40:11-12). It is when Yahweh's spirit comes on him that Saul gets very angry at the Ammonites' treatment of the people of Jabesh-Gilead and takes spectacular action on their behalf (1 Sam 11:6-11). Nehemiah gets angry at oppression within the community and takes decisive action (Neh 5:6). Yahweh stirs up the Philistines' anger against Judah and they invade and pillage Judah, unwittingly implementing Yahweh's will (2 Chr 21:16-17). An exception proves the rule: David gets angry when he hears about Amnon's rape of Tamar (2 Sam 13:21), but he never does anything about it.

E. Ambiguity in References to Anger

Perhaps because Scripture focuses on simply recognizing that anger is an aspect of human nature, the writers often leave its interpretation ambiguous. Moses exits from his last confrontation with Pharaoh "in hot anger" and later gets angry at the Israelites (Exod 11:8; 16:20). Anger makes him hurl away and break the stones bearing the Decalogue, burn and grind up the calf, throw the powder into water, and make the Israelites drink it (Exod 32:19-20). Moses gets angry with Eleazar and Ithamar, then with the army officers, for not obeying Yahweh's word (Lev 10:16; Num 31:14), and also with Korah, Dathan, and Abiram for their criticisms of him (Num 16:15). Samuel gets angry when Saul has not obeyed Yahweh, but Samuel is also angry when, as a result of Saul's disobedience, Yahweh rejects Saul (1 Sam 15:10-11). David gets angry when Yahweh kills Uzzah because he reached out to steady the ark, but in his anger, David is also afraid of Yahweh (2 Sam 6:8-9).

There is a still broader ambiguity. Human anger does not effect God's righteousness (Jas 1:20). Like vengeance, anger is God's business (*see* WRATH OF GOD).

F. Controlling Anger

Scripture often refers to the importance of being slow to anger. The person who is slow to anger has great understanding, whereas a hasty temper exalts folly (Prov 14:29; *see* 19:11; 29:11; Jas 1:19). Although anger has a heat and a force that generates right action, this heat and force can also generate wrong action, or express itself against an object other than one that deserves it (2 Sam 12:5-6). Or it may generate action that goes too far: the community needs to safeguard against the hot anger of the avenger of blood in case he takes action when someone had killed a person accidentally (Deut 19:6). Jacob curses the particularly fierce anger of his sons that led to their slaughtering the men of Shechem (Gen 49:7). The trouble is that anger takes self-control—people who can be slow to anger are as impressive as powerful rulers (Prov 16:32).

Ephesians thus exhorts people to be angry, but not to sin (4:26)—even though the same letter also condemns anger (4:31). (The exhortation in Ephesians follows the Greek in Ps 4:4 LXX, but it is doubtful that the Hebrew refers to anger.) The statement, "Do not let the sun go down on your anger" (Eph 4:26), is a little puzzling, as the importance of being slow to anger might imply that letting the sun go down on your anger would give time for reflection, time to cool off. The force of anger does dissipate with time (Gen 27:44-45; Esth 2:1; 7:10), and while that may sometimes be for the worse (the impetus to do the thing that needs doing may be lost), it may well be for the better. Presumably Ephesians is exhorting people not to nurse anger when they ought to let it dissipate. It is the godless in heart who cherish anger (Job 36:13).

JOHN GOLDINGAY

ANGLE, THE an′guhl [הַמִּקְצוֹעַ hammiqtsoʿa]. An area in Jerusalem where Uzziah built towers to fortify the city (2 Chr 26:9). Ezer, Baruch, Binnui, and Palal restored sections opposite and near this portion of Jerusalem, probably located near the palace (Neh 3:19-20, 24-25). *See* CORNER GATE, ASCENT OF; JERUSALEM.

ANGUISH. *See* SUFFERING AND EVIL.

ANIAM uh-ni′uhm [אֲנִיעָם ʾaniʿam]. In Manasseh's genealogy, Shemida's fourth son (1 Chr 7:19).

ANIM ay′nim [עָנִים ʿanim]. A city in the southern hill country near DEBIR, Anim was allotted to Judah (Josh 15:50). The name means "springs." Scholars identify Anim with Khirbet Ghuwein et-Tahta.

ANIMAL APOCALYPSE. *See* ENOCH, FIRST BOOK OF.

ANIMAL WORSHIP. *See* TOTEMISM.

ANIMALS OF THE BIBLE [בְּהֵמָה behemah; κτῆνους ktēnous]. By the time the OT was composed, all the animals deemed useful to human beings in the ancient Near Eastern menagerie had been already domesticated. Therefore, the Israelites were not involved in domesticating and introducing new species to the domestic setting. By then there was a very clear division between wild animals (which could not be utilized for human benefit) and domestic animals.

  A. Sources of Information
  B. Domestic Animals
    1. Herd animals
      a. Sheep and goats
      b. Cows and bulls
    2. Draft and pack animals
      a. Donkey
      b. Camel
    3. Other animals
  C. Wild Animals
    1. Ungulates
    2. Other herbivores
    3. Carnivores
    4. Exotic animals
    5. Birds
    6. Marine animals
    7. Rodents, reptiles, and insects
  D. Animals in the Cult
  E. Mythical Animals
  F. Animals and Magic
  G. Animals in Biblical Literature
  Bibliography

A. Sources of Information

The Bible is replete with names of animals. To establish the identity of an animal, first a linguistic study of the term must be conducted; this includes comparison with other ancient and modern languages used in the region. The linguistic study should include ancient texts that have references to the animal, its place of habitation, and where applicable, its use by humans. Once the linguistic study is completed, a study of artistic representations reveals how the ancients depicted the animal. To finalize the process of identity, a survey of zoo-archaeological remains provides an historical record; the date of the sample can be compared with the dating of the texts (Borowski 1998, 29–37). The final result should yield the identity of the animal.

B. Domestic Animals

Domestic animals are those whose behavior and characteristics have been modified and shaped by human beings for different lengths of time, depending on the animal. The end result of domestication is to produce livestock that benefit humankind with a source of food, clothing, or labor.

1. Herd animals

a. Sheep (כֶּבֶשׂ keves; πρόβατον probaton, προβάτιον probation) and goats (עֵז ʿez; ἐρίφιον eriphion, ἔριφος eriphos) represented the largest group of animals raised in biblical societies. Both species were raised for their by-products, including milk, dung, wool, or hair. When slaughtered, they provide meat, skin, bones, and horns. All of these by-products could be used by the herders themselves or traded as surplus. These animals were kept in herds of various sizes. Herding was a major occupation of the Israelites and their neighbors. Most of the ancient flock-tending societies were not full-time nomads, but rather transhumant (semi-nomadic) or settled. This means that part of their time was devoted to agricultural pursuits since in both cases a home base was maintained. The size of the flocks was determined by the available resources such as water, grazing lands, and available space. (The story of Abraham and Lot illustrates conflict between herders who must share grazing lands [Gen 13:1-12]).

b. Cows and bulls. Other ruminants belonging to the Israelite domestic menagerie were cows (פָּרָה parah; βοῦς bous, δάμαλις damalis) and bulls or OXEN (פַּר/שׁוֹר sor/par; bous, βόειος boeios) These were kept in smaller numbers than goats and sheep and were raised only under settled conditions. While these animals also contributed by-products, their most important contribution was that of supplying traction in pulling plows, wagons, and carts.

2. Draft and pack animals

In addition to large cattle, various other animals, including equids and camels, provided locomotion, traction, and transportation. These animals supplied the muscle for hauling cargo and people from place to place.

a. Donkey. The most common among the draft and pack animals was the DONKEY (חֲמוֹר khammor; ὄνος onos), which can be considered the ancient off-road "truck" because of its ability to carry heavy loads in rough terrain and under very harsh conditions. Appreciation of the donkey can be seen by the fact that it was enumerated as war booty, and in certain cultures it was used for sacrifice when sealing a covenant (Borowski 1998, 90–99). In biblical folklore, a donkey is able to see the angel of the Lord standing in the path and so saves his master Balaam's life (Num 22:21-35). Saul, a herder of donkeys, is anointed king while searching for his lost animals (1 Sam 9:3–10:16). Jesus rode a donkey into Jerusalem (Matt 21:2-7; Luke 13:15). The HORSE (סוּס sus; ἵππος hippos) was considered a prestige animal. The one to receive the king's honor will ride a fine horse (Esth 6:8-11). Unlike the donkey that served

in multiple capacities, the horse was reserved mostly for military use either in the cavalry or for pulling chariots). Horsemen and chariots are described in 2 Sam 1:6; 8:4; 10:18; 2 Kgs 1:5; 4:26; 2 Kgs 2:12; 13:7, 14; 18:24; Dan 11:40; pharaoh's horses and chariots were thrown into the sea (Exod 15:1, 21). Horse-trading was a profitable enterprise that sometimes was monopolized by royalty; biblical tradition mentions Solomon's involvement in this endeavor (1 Kgs 10:28-29; 2 Chr 1:17). Ahab's chariot force is well attested in Assyrian records (Pritchard 1969, 278–79). The appearance of mythical horses portends catastrophes upon the earth: the white horse's rider comes to conquer; the red horse's rider takes peace from the earth; the black horse's rider bears a pair of scales; the pale green horse's rider brings death, famine, and pestilence (Rev 6:1-8).

Another equid that was hard at work was the MULE (פֶּרֶד peredh; ἡμίονος hēmionos [lit., "half donkey"]) or the hinny (פִּרְדָּה pirdah), both of which are hybrids of donkey and horse. The mule is sterile and cannot reproduce, thus it was always considered an expensive animal. Although it was considered a working animal (1 Kgs 18:5; Zech 14:15; Ps 32:9), it was also a riding animal good enough for a king (1 Kgs 33, 38, 44) and the king's sons (2 Sam 13:29; 18:9). Mules were highly valued, more so than sheep, oxen, and horses, and were listed in booty lists (Borowski 1998, 108-11).

b. Camel. Although the CAMEL (גָּמָל gamal; κάμηλος kamēlos) plays a prominent role in biblical narratives (Gen 12:14-16; 24:10-67; 31:17-35; 37:25; Matt 19:24), it seems that its appearance in the Patriarchal stories is anachronistic. However, its role in connection with the Gideon pericope (Judg 6-7) is more in tune with what scholars think about the date of its arrival in the Levant, i.e., during Iron Age I (Borowski 1998, 112–21). Camels were used for riding (Isa 21:7) and were given as royal presents (2 Kgs 8:9). Two humped (Bactrian) camels were offered as tribute as can be seen on the Black Obelisk of Shalmaneser III (858–24 BCE). They were also used for carrying cargo and large herds were considered part of the royal inventory (1 Chr 27:30). Although there is no mention in the Bible of the camel used in agriculture, its by-products (dung, milk, hair) were probably utilized.

3. Other animals

One of the common animals in the Israelite farmyard that was not associated with food production was the DOG (כֶּלֶב kelev; κυνάριον kynarion), which earned both respect and disparagement. Domestic dogs were used for hunting, herding (Isa 56:11), guarding (Isa 56:10), and companionship (Tob 6:2; 11:4). However, unmanaged dogs were well known in the biblical world and aroused ill feelings (Borowski 1998, 133-40). Murderers, idolators, and fornicators are likened to dogs (Rev 22:25). Carrion is to be thrown to the dogs (Exod 22:31), and dogs are known to consume other vile things (Prov 26:11; Luke 15:21). Jezebel's body is eaten by dogs (2 Kgs 9:35-36; *see also* 1 Kgs 16:4). Jesus alludes to non-Isarelites as scavenging dogs, but a woman pleads that even the dogs eat the crumbs from the table and so earns Jesus' favor (Matt 15:26-28). Another animal native to the region, but abhorred, was SWINE (חֲזִיר khazir; χοῖρος choiros). A proverb warns that a beautiful woman with no sense is like a gold ring in a pig's snout (Prov 11:22), and "pearls" should not be thrown before "swine" (Matt 7:6). Jesus casts out demons into a herd of swine (Matt 8:28-33; Mark 5:11-13; Luke 8:32-33). Twice the pig is mentioned as forbidden for consumption by Israelites (Lev 11:7; Deut 14:8), and the zoo-archaeological samples from Israelite sites definitely suggest that the ancient Israelite population adhered to this rule (Borowski 1998, 140–44. Although not mentioned in the biblical text, the CAT (αἴλουρος ailouros) must have been part of the Israelite domestic menagerie simply because it is known to have existed in the surrounding cultures of Egypt and Mesopotamia. Its ability to exterminate mice must have made the cat attractive. (Borowski 1998, 144–46.)

C. Wild Animals

A variety of wild animals roamed the biblical world. Some were feared; others were hunted for food. Some were considered exotic, and others were abhorred.

1. Ungulates

Several wild ungulate (hoofed), ruminant (chewing cud) animals are mentioned as permitted for consumption. The list in Deut 14:5 includes the following: אַיָּל 'ayyil, ἔλαφον elaphon; צְבִי tsevi, δορκάδα dorkada; יַחְמוּר yakhmur, βούβαλον boubalon; אַקּוֹ 'aqqo, τραγέλαφον tragelaphon; דִּישֹׁן dishon, πύγαργον pygargon; תְּאוֹ te'o, ὄρυγα orygma; and זָמֶר zemer, καμηλοπάρδαλιν kamēlopardalin, translated as "the deer, the gazelle, the roebuck, the wild goat, the ibex, the antelope, and the mountain-sheep" (NRSV) and "the HART, and the gazelle, and the roebuck, and the wild goat, and the pygarg, and the antelope, and the chamois" (ASV). The true identification of the Hebrew terms is not well known, but zoo-archaeological samples suggest that some of these animals should be identified as certain species of deer and gazelles; others might be identified with the IBEX and other bovids (cattle). *See* ROE.

2. Other herbivores

Two small herbivores are mention in the OT, שָׁפָן shafan or δασύπους dasypous, and אַרְנֶבֶת 'arneveth (Lev 11:5; Deut 14:7), both of which were considered unclean for consumption. The former might be identified as hyrax and the latter as hare (rabbit). Large herbivores such as the ELEPHANT (ἐλέφας elephas) appear in the Apocrypha (1 Macc 6:35, 46; 2 Macc 13:15; 3 Macc 5:45). Elephants, probably related to the Afri-

can (*Loxdonta Africana*), were prevalent in the Near East and were hunted mostly for their ivory (Borowski 1998, 195–96). Carved ivory objects were prestige items and were collected by kings and nobility, and collections of such were kept in great palaces (Amos 3:15; Ps 45:9). Another animal whose tusks were used for carving was the HIPPOPOTAMUS (ἱπποπόταμος hippopotamos), known in the Bible as behemoth (בְּהֵמוֹת) (Job 40:15-24), and described in great detail before Job to illustrate God's imagination.

3. Carnivores

A number of small and large carnivores were native to the region. Most of them are mentioned in the Bible and can be securely identified. Skeletal evidence of carnivores in Israelite cult sites is minimal. LION and BEAR bones were discovered near the altar at Dan. Other sites that yielded lion bones are pre-Israelite Jaffa and Philistine Miqne-Ekron. A small bronze lion figurine was discovered near the altar at Arad (Borowski 1998, 226–27). Although they were not exploited, they are recognized by the biblical authors, and many times are used when depicting a picture of a particular environment or as metaphors.

The LION, to which Judah was likened, was considered the fiercest (Gen 49:9). It appears in the Bible under several terms (אֲרִי 'ari, אַרְיֵה 'aryeh, לְבִי levi', לַיִשׁ layish, כְּפִיר kefir; λέων leōn) and is known to have roamed throughout Syria-Palestine (Borowski 1998, 196–200). Lions were considered a menace to herders (1 Sam 17:34-37) and travelers (1 Kgs 13:25-28; 20:36). Lion bones and lion images recovered at cult centers (Dan, Arad) suggest that the animal played a distinct role in worship practices.

A close relative of the lion, the LEOPARD (נָמֵר namer; πάρδαλις pardalis), was known as a swift (Hab 1:8) and fierce animal roaming through the mountainous regions of Palestine (Song 4:8). Its spots were its trademark (Jer 13:23).

Quite common in biblical times was the Syrian brown BEAR (דֹּב dov; ἄρκος arkos) that was prowling (Prov 28:15) in wooded areas (2 Kgs 2:23-24). Bears were known for their distinct growl (Isa 59:11) and presented a menace to herders and their herds (1 Sam 17:34-37). Bears who lost their young (2 Sam 17:8) were considered most dangerous.

Several small carnivores of the Canid family were extant throughout the region. In spite of its size, the WOLF (זְאֵב ze'ev; λύκος lukos), which was the ancestor of the domestic dog, was considered a fierce animal of prey: "Benjamin is a ravenous wolf, in the morning devouring the prey, and at evening dividing the spoil" (Gen 49:27). Jesus warns of false prophets in sheep's clothing who inwardly are ravenous wolves (Matt 7:15; see also Acts 20:29). The disciples go out like lambs among the wolves (Matt 10:16; Luke 10:3). Close relatives of the dog are the FOX (שׁוּעָל shu'al;

ἀλώπηξ alōpēx) and the JACKAL (תַּן tan), both of which were used as symbols of destruction (Song 2:15) and desolation since they were living among the ruins (Jer 10:22; Ezek 13:4). Jesus refers to the difficulty of his itinerate lifestyle by saying that even foxes have holes, but he has no place to rest (Matt 8:20). Samson uses foxes to burn his enemies' fields (Judg 15:4-5). The cunning reputation of the fox is highlighted when Jesus refers to Herod as a "fox" (Luke 13:32). Both foxes and jackals hunt small game such as rodents; they also eat lizards, insects, and fowl (Borowski 1998, 203-05).

A scavenger common to the region is the striped HYENA (צָבוֹעַ tsavoʿa, ὕαινα hyaina). In spite of its prevalence, its existence is recorded in the Bible only in place names such as "Valley of the Hyenas" (NRSV Balley of Zeboim גֵּי הַצְּבֹעִים gey hatsevoʿim), somewhere near Jerusalem (1 Sam 13:18).

4. Exotic animals

Exotic animals were owned by royalty and the nobility, probably as symbols of wealth and prestige. King Solomon is recorded as importing from distant lands APES and תֻּכִּיִּים tukkiyyim or πίθηκος pithēkos (1 Kgs 10:22//2 Chr 9:21). The latter term has been translated in various ways (peacocks or baboons in NRSV), none of which is certain. Also uncertain is the biblical reference to תַּחַשׁ takhash, whose hide was used in the construction of the tabernacle, and **takhash** skin is mentioned once for making shoes (Ezek 16:10).

5. Birds

A secondary dietary source of meat was BIRDS, several of which were allowed to be eaten and were sacrificed. Although not specifically listed as part of the menu, three wild birds are mentioned in the sacrifice lists and thus presumably were fit for consumption. These include the QUAIL (שְׂלָו selaw; ὀρτυγομήτρα ortygomētra, Exod 16:13), the DOVE (יוֹנָה yonah; περιστερά peristera, Lev 1:14), and TURTLEDOVE (תּוֹר tor; νεόσσιον neossion, Lev 5:7). The rock partridge (קֹרֵא qoreʾ; κόραξ korax, 1 Sam 26:20), which is related to the quail, was hunted and thus can be presumed to have been part of the diet. It seems that the chicken did not appear in the Levant before the 8th cent. BCE. By the Hellenistic period and later in the Roman period, the bird is well established and the male of the species, the COCK, is mentioned as the one to announce the arrival of the day (3 Macc 5:23; Matt 26:34, 74-75; Mark 14:30, 68-72; Luke 22:34, 60-61; John 13:38; 18:27). Before the introduction of the chicken to the Israelite farmyard, eggs were available in the wild where they were collected (Deut 22:6; Isa 10:14).

The Bible is very clear concerning birds that cannot be eaten. There are two lists of these birds; in Lev 11:13-19, twenty species are listed, and in Deut 14:12-18, twenty-one are enumerated. The common denominator of these birds is that they are birds of prey and feed on carrion, fish, and refuse (Borowski 1998, 149–151). Although not all of the birds listed can be identified with complete certainty, the lists include eagle, vulture, osprey, ostrich, owl, and more. The BAT (עֲטַלֵּף ʿatallef; νυκτερίς nukteris) is mentioned in both of the bird lists, though it is not a bird.

6. Marine animals

Unlike other animals, when the Bible refers to FISH, it is only by using the collective (דָּגָה/דָּג dagh/daghah; ἰχθύς ichthus, Exod 7:18). No names of particular fish are mentioned. There is no question that the Israelites consumed fish, as evident from zoo-archaeological samples, however, the treatment of fish in the Bible is generic. Fish were not among the sacrificial animals but were permitted for consumption. The rules for clean fish were very clear: "These you may eat, of all that are in the waters. Everything in the waters that has fins and scales, whether in the seas or in the streams—such you may eat … Everything in the waters that does not have fins and scales is detestable to you" (Lev 11:9, 12; *see also* Deut 14:9-10). Fish are mentioned frequently in the NT as a source of food and as a symbol of Jesus' providence (Matt 7:10, 14:17-19; 15:34-36; Mark 6:38-43; 8:7; Luke 5:6-9; 9:13-16; 11:11; 24:42; John 6:9-11; 21:5-13).

Fresh and salt water mollusks have been recovered from archaeological excavations, but the best known because of their by-product are purple dye producing mollusks *Murex brandaris*, *Murex trunculus*, and *Purpura haemostoma* (Borowski 1998, 176–80). These mollusks have been available on the eastern Mediterranean coast and were used for the production of two varieties of purple dye known in the Bible as אַרְגָּמָן ʾargaman and תְּכֵלֶת tekhelet. Dyed textiles were highly valued and are enumerated in lists of tribute and booty.

7. Rodents, reptiles, and insects

While in some cultures rodents such as the Guinea pig and the dormouse have been eaten, biblical rules abhorred them: "These are unclean for you among the creatures that swarm upon the earth: הַחֹלֶד holedh, γαλῆ galē; עַכְבָּר ʿakhbar, μῦς mys; צָב tsav, κροκόδειλος krokodeilos; אֲנָקָה ʾanaqah, כֹּחַ koakh, לְטָאָה letaʾah, חֹמֶט khomet, and תִּנְשֶׁמֶת tinshemeth (Lev 11:29-30). The names of these rodents vary in different Bible versions: for example, the LXX translates these Hebrew terms with a variety of Greek terms. The NRSV translates "the WEASEL, the MOUSE, the great lizard according to its kind, the GECKO, the land CROCODILE, the LIZARD, the sand lizard, and the chameleon." The problem of interpretation can be illustrated by the last name on this list; here tinshemeth is presented as a rodent or a reptile, while in Lev 11:18 and in Deut 14:16 tinshemeth is included in the list of unclean birds and is probably a member of the owl family. All reptiles (שֶׁרֶץ sherets) were forbidden from consumption. The rule is all-inclusive: "All creatures that swarm upon the earth are detestable; they shall not be eaten. Whatever moves on its belly, and whatever moves on all fours, or whatever has many feet, all the creatures that swarm upon the earth, you shall not eat; for they are detestable. You shall not make yourselves detestable with any creature that swarms; you shall not defile yourselves with them, and so become unclean" (Lev 11:41-43).

INSECTS were also forbidden for consumption with one broad exception: "All winged insects that walk upon all fours are detestable to you. But among the winged insects that walk on all fours you may eat those that have jointed legs above their feet, with which to leap on the ground. Of them you may eat: the locust according to its kind, the bald locust according to its kind, the cricket according to its kind, and the grasshopper according to its kind. But all other winged insects that have four feet are detestable to you" (Lev 11:20-23). The different types of grasshoppers belonging to the *Order Orthopter: Family Acrididae* were allowed. BEES were not eaten but their HONEY was highly prized. Another by-product, WAX, was also very useful (*see* INSECTS OF THE BIBLE).

D. Animals in the Cult

Animals played a highly important role in worship practices; some were sacrificed and others venerated. As with the cults of ancient Israel's neighbors, it was assumed that Yahweh appears on the back of an animal. In the Southern kingdom of Judah, he appeared on top of the mythical cherubim (see below); in the Northern Kingdom of Israel, Yahweh appeared on the back of a bull. In this connection, the references to "the bull of Jacob" (אֲבִיר יַעֲקֹב ʾavir yaʿakov Gen 49:24; Isa 49:26; Ps 132:2, 5) and "the bull of Israel" (יִשְׂרָאֵל אֲבִיר ʾavir yisraʾel Isa 1:24) can be understood. Yahweh's image as a bull is strengthened by the bronze bull figurine from the Iron Age I Israelite Bull Site in the Samaria region (Borowski 1998, 213–14).

The OT mentions the bull (פַּר par) as an animal common in sacrifices (Num 7). Other animals common in sacrifices were large CATTLE (בָּקָר baqar) and small cattle (צֹאן soʾn), the latter included sheep and goats. Sacrificial animals included adults as well as young, male as well as female, none with "a defect, anything seriously wrong; for that is abhorrent to the LORD your God" (Deut 17:1). A special type of sacrificial animal was the firstling of all ruminants (Lev 1:2; Num 7), which had to be at least a week old (Exod 22:29; Lev 22:27). Specially fattened animals (כָּרִים karim, Isa 34:6; מֵחִים mekhim, Ps 66:15; מְרִיא meriʾ, 1 Kgs 1:9) were also sacrificed.

Birds were also sacrificed, especially by those who could not afford a four-legged animal. Turtledoves or pigeons could be used as substitute (Lev 5:7; 12:8).

A special ritual described in Num 19 calls for the sacrifice of a red heifer. The ashes of the red heifer were used to purify ritually unclean people and vessels. Another ritual involving a heifer is described in Deut 21:1-9. When a corpse is discovered outside a settlement and the killer cannot be found, "the elders of that town shall bring the heifer down to a wadi with running water, which is neither plowed nor sown, and shall break the heifer's neck there in the wadi" (Deut 21:4). Then they shall wash their hands and declare, "Our hands did not shed this blood, nor were we witnesses to it. Absolve, O LORD, your people Israel, whom you redeemed; do not let the guilt of innocent blood remain in the midst of your people Israel" (vv. 7-8).

Some rituals required specific animals to be sacrificed. These include male goat yearlings (שָׂעִיר saʿir, עִזִּים ʿizzim, Num 7), young ruminants (שֶׂה seh, Exod 12:5), CALF (עֵגֶל ʿeghel, Lev 9:3), he-goats (עַתּוּד ʿattudh, Num 7), rams (אַיִל ʾayil, Num 7), and more. Certain parts of the animal were considered choice and were either burned completely or given to the priests.

A very distinct sacrifice was that of the Passover, which had to be performed with a yearling male without a blemish (Exod 12:5). The animal had to be selected beforehand and on the appropriate night was slaughtered, roasted, and completely consumed before sunrise. This feast was probably in celebration of the beginning of the grazing season (spring), and the sacrifice was the first culling of the herd.

With the exception of birds, wild animals are not included in the sacrificial lists even though many were permitted as food. While remains of domestic animals were recovered in Israelite cult centers, very few remains of wild animals were found. The presence of the latter is probably the result of consumption as food rather than being sacrificed.

E. Mythical Animals

Israelite culture was influenced by the surrounding cultures, and this was expressed in many ways. Literary and artistic works depicting fantastic animals found their way into Israelite culture. The CHERUBIM in the Jerusalem Temple are a good example of such mythological beings. Ezekiel describes them:

> They were of human form. Each had four faces, and each of them had four wings. Their legs were straight, and the soles of their feet were like the sole of a calf's foot; and they sparkled like burnished bronze. Under their wings on their four sides they had human hands. And the four had their faces and their wings thus: their wings touched one another; each of them moved straight ahead, without turning as they moved.

As for the appearance of their faces: the four had the face of a human being, the face of a lion on the right side, the face of an ox on the left side, and the face of an eagle; such were their faces. Their wings were spread out above; each creature had two wings, each of which touched the wing of another, while two covered their bodies (Ezek 1:5-14; *see also* 10:14).

Other mythological animals, which seem to have existed in the sea, including Rahab, Yamm, and Tannin (Isa 51:9; Ps 89:11; Job 9:13; 26:12), together with LEVIATHAN (Isa 27:1), threatened world order. The "great fish" that swallowed Jonah (Jonah 1:17) can be also considered a fantastic animal. Satyrs or "goat-demons" are also mentioned as disturbing the peace (Lev 17:7; Isa 13:21; 34:14; 2 Chr 11:15). Some particular animals, such as the serpent in the Garden of Eden (Gen 3:1-4) and Balaam's donkey (Num 22:21-30), had the gift of speech and used this ability to interact with humans (Borowski 2002, 304–06). A mythical BEAST with ten horns and seven heads, with bear's feet and a lion's mouth, and a beast that spoke like a dragon represent the enemies of the church (Rev 13:1-18).

F. Animals and Magic

In spite of proscriptions against using magic (Lev 19:26), the Israelites continued to practice it, and like their neighbors did it to some extent with animals. AUGURY, which is the ability to predict the future through observation of omens like the flight of birds, must have been practiced in ancient Israel, as suggested by the story of the FLOOD, where Noah used a raven and a dove to tell whether the water had subsided (Gen 8:9-12). This is echoed in Jeremiah: "Even the stork in the heavens knows its times; and the turtledove, swallow, and crane observe the time of their coming" (8:7).

The stories about Moses are replete with animal imagery, especially during his dealings with Pharaoh and through some of the plagues (frogs, gnats, flies, locust). Moses also used magic to heal those bitten by a SERPENT. He made a bronze snake, such that all who looked upon were saved (Num 21:4-9). That snake was destroyed by Hezekiah during his religious reforms (2 Kgs 18:4) (Borowski 2002, 420–22).

G. Animals in Biblical Literature

Animals played an important role in the various genres of biblical literature. They are used as omens in the Joseph story (Gen 41:132), when fat and lean cows appear in a dream. Upon interpretation, it is revealed that the cows represent years of plenty and of draught.

Animals appear in proverbs, parables, and riddles. Job asserts his right to complain by using a proverb comparing his situation to that of a braying donkey and lowing ox (Job 6:5). Proverbs utilizes animal behavior to convey messages related to human behavior. "Go to the ANT, you lazybones; consider its ways, and be wise. Without having any chief or officer or ruler, it prepares its food in summer, and gathers its sustenance in harvest" (Prov 6:6-8). Other animals used in proverbs include dogs, BADGERS, locusts, and snakes, among others. Certain animals are used as symbols of beauty: "Let your fountain be blessed, and rejoice in the wife of your youth, a lovely deer, a graceful DOE. May her breasts satisfy you at all times; may you be intoxicated always by her love" (Prov 5:18-19). The gazelle and the DEER as metaphors for beauty appear in several instances (Song 3:5; 4:5; 2 Sam 2:18).

Animals figure in parables, such as Nathan's telling King David about a rich man who robbed the one little lamb owned by a poor man. This parable was told in reaction to David's affair with Bathsheba and the killing of her husband Uriah (2 Sam 12:1-7). The image of SHEEP symbolizes the people of Israel, while Yahweh is their shepherd (Ps 23; 74:1). Sheep also figure in Jesus' parables as metaphors for human lives, with Jesus as shepherd (Matt 12:11-12; 18:12; 25:32-33; Mark 14:27; Luke 15:4-6; John 10:2-27; 21:16-17). A parable in Ezek 19:1-9 uses the lion as a metaphor for Judah, and the CUBs are kings of the House of David. The lion serves also as the subject of Samson's riddle (Judg 14:14-18): "Out of the eater came something to eat. Out of the strong came something sweet." The response given by the Philistines was: "What is sweeter than honey? What is stronger than a lion?" And since they used Samson's wife to get the answer, he countered them with another animal metaphor: "If you had not plowed with my heifer, you would not have found out my riddle."

DOGS play a mixed role; mostly they are depicted as pariahs (1 Sam 17:43), but sometimes they convey loyalty (Eccl 9:4). Humility was sometimes expressed by comparing oneself to a dog, as in the case of Hazael, who said: "What is your servant, who is a mere dog, that he should do this great thing?" To which Elisha answered, "The LORD has shown me that you are to be king over Aram" (2 Kgs 8:13). At times the simile was to a dead dog, as when Mephiboshet son of Jonathan meets King David and "He did obeisance and said, 'What is your servant, that you should look upon a dead dog such as I?'" (2 Sam 9:8; *see also* 1 Sam 24:15 [Heb. 24:14]).

Wild animals and birds provide much of the symbolic and metaphoric images. The fierce lion is a symbol of strength, retribution, destruction, and vengeance (Joel 1:6). The roar of the lion is like Yahweh's speech (Amos 3:8). In the blessing of Jacob to his sons, Judah is likened to a lion (Gen 49:9), and Dan to a snake (49:17). The image of the lion is used in the blessing of Moses to the tribes when describing the attributes of Gad (Deut 33:20), and Dan (33:22). There are many other instances where the image of the lion plays a role.

The eagle is the most respected bird in biblical imagery. Its speed (Jer 4:13), size (Jer 49:22; 17:3), and place of habitat (Job 39:27; Jer 49:16), made it an agent of rescue (Exod 19:4; Deut 32:11) and shelter (Ps 91:3-4). All these attributes allow Ezekiel to use the eagle's image in reference to both King Nebuchadnezzar (Ezek 17:2-6) and Pharaoh Psammetichus II (Ezek 17:7). Both the eagle and the lion were symbols of strength and nobility, as expressed in David's lament over Saul and Jonathan. "They were swifter than eagles, they were stronger than lions" (2 Sam 1:23).

INSECTS were also used in biblical references to provide images of attributes and entities. The ant is a model for diligence (Prov 6:6-8), while the spider's web is likened to something that should not be trusted (Job 8:14). The image of the locust becomes a symbol of devastation (Joel 1:4; 1 Kgs 8:37; Amos 4:9) and is invoked to portray enemy hordes (Judg 6:5). The bee serves as a symbol to the army troops of Assyria, while the fly symbolizes the Egyptian troops (Isa 7:18-19). The biblical wasp (Exod 23:28; Deut 7:20; Josh 24:12) might have been used as a metaphor for Egypt (Borowski 1983).

There are times when animals are in possession of a distinct knowledge that humans lack, such as the knowledge of Yahweh and divine accomplishments. Job, in his response to his friends, invokes appealing to the animals for such instruction: "But ask the animals, and they will teach you; the birds of the air, and they will tell you; ask the plants of the earth, and they will teach you; and the fish of the sea will declare to you. Who among all these does not know that the hand of the LORD has done this? In his hand is the life of every living thing and the breath of every human being" (Job 12:7-10). This is very reminiscent of Isaiah's exhortation, "The ox knows its owner, and the donkey its master's crib; but Israel does not know, my people do not understand" (Isa 1:3). *See* APE; ASS; BADGER; BATS; BEARS; BEASTS; BIRDS OF THE BIBLE; BIT; CALF; CAMEL; CARAVAN; CARRIAGE; CART; CAT; CATTLE; CHAMELEON; CHEETAH; CREATURES, LIVING; CROCODILE; CUB; DEER; DEN OF LIONS; DOE; DOG; DROMEDARY; ELEPHANT; FAWN; FOX; FURROW; GAZELLE; GECKO; GOAT; GOATHERD; GOATSKIN; GREAT LIZARD; HART; HEDGEHOG; HIND; HIPPOPOTAMUS; HORSE; HYENA; IBEX; INSECTS OF THE BIBLE; JACKAL; KID; LAND CROCODILE; LEECH; LEOPARD; LION; MALLOW; MOUSE; MULE; OX; ROCK BADGER; ROE; SAND LIZARD; SCALES, FISH; SHEEP, SHEEPFOLD; SHEEP-SHEARING, SHEEPSKIN; STALL; SWINE; WEASEL; WHALE; WHITE HORSE; WILD ASS; WILD BEASTS; WILD BOAR; WILD GOAT; WILD OX; WINNOW; WOLF.

Bibliography: O. Borowski. *Every Living Thing: Daily Use of Animals in Ancient Israel* (1998); O. Borowski.

"Animals in the Literature of Syria-Palestine" and "Animals in the Religion of Syria-Palestine." *A History of the Animal World in the Ancient Near East.* B. J. Collins, ed. (2002) 289–306, 405–24; J. B. Pritchard. *Ancient Near Eastern Texts Relating to the Old Testament* (1969).

ODED BOROWSKI

ANKHSHESHONQ, INSTRUCTION OF. The late Ptolemaic Instruction of Ankhsheshonq (or Onchshenshonqy), written in Demotic, presents the typical advice of an Egyptian father to his son on living a successful life. Although sometimes compared to Greek and Hebrew wisdom writings, it derives directly from mainstream Egyptian instructional materials. In its narrative frame, Ankhsheshonq, a high priest of the sun-god Re, learns of a plot to kill Pharaoh but does not report it. On its discovery, Ankhsheshonq is jailed but is granted his request to write out a collection of maxims, largely in monostichs on jar sherds, for his son (*AEL* III, 159–184; *LAE*[3], 497–529).

SUSAN HOLLIS

ANKLETS [עֶכֶס 'ekhes] Isaiah 3:18 and Jdt 10:4 describe women wearing anklets—bands of metal that encircled the ankle—along with other JEWELRY (e.g., BRACELETS, ARMLETS, RINGS). Anklets were worn to enhance women's beauty and perhaps to attract attention with their tinkling sound. According to Isa 3:18, anklets, along with all finery, will be stripped away and replaced by sackcloth on the day of judgment.

ANNA an'uh [Ἅννα Hanna]. 1. In the story of Tobit, Anna supports her blind husband by weaving (women's work), responds angrily when he challenges the reward she received for her work, weeps when her son leaves them for a long journey, grieves and watches when her son returns late, and rejoices when he returns with a wife. Anna dies at an old age and her son buries her with her husband. *See* Tobit.

2. Anna's story is narrated as a parallel to Simeon's in Luke's infancy narrative (2:36-38). They both praise God because they recognize Jesus as the Christ, but Anna's words are not included. Anna is described as a prophetess, like Miriam or Deborah in the OT, or like others in Acts who fulfill the prophecy of Joel (Acts 2:17). She is an Asherite, but "daughter of Phanuel" does not further identify her. Luke depicts her as pious, devoted to God, worshiping daily at the temple, praying, and fasting. She is very old, either 84, or widowed for 84 years (thus 105, if she was married at 14, as was customary). The latter is more likely. This characterization is like Judith (Jdt 16:23), and Elizabeth and Zechariah (Luke 1:6-7). Pious, celibate widows like Anna were important in the early church (1 Tim 5:3-16).

3. According to the post-biblical Christian tradition, Anna is the mother of Mary, so the grandmother of Jesus. Anna and her husband Joachim are elderly and pious Jews, but childless. An angel of the Lord answers their cries for a child. Anna promises to devote the child to the Lord. She subsequently bears a girl child and names her Mary. When Mary is three years of age, they take her to live in the temple. Any ambiguity about the miraculous conception of Mary is clarified in later literature. *See* JAMES, PROTEVANGELIUM OF; PSEUDO-MATTHEW, GOSPEL OF.

Bibliography: J. K. Elliott. "Anna's Age (Luke 2:36-37)." *NovT* 30 (1988): 100–102.

JO-ANN BADLEY

ANNAN an′uhn [Ἀννάν Annan]. Family head whose descendants sent their foreign wives and their children away as God's covenant required (1 Esd 9:32). *See* HARAM.

ANNAS an′uhs [Ἄννας Hannas]. Annas, son of Seth, was high priest from 6 to 15 CE. Later he continued to wield extraordinary power (Luke 3:2), interrogating Jesus (John 18), serving in the SANHEDRIN (Acts 4), and enjoying the distinction of being the only Jewish high priest to have five sons and one son-in-law (CAIAPHAS) follow him in office.

Bibliography: James C. VanderKam. *From Joshua to Caiaphas* (2004) 42–24.

JOHN T. FITZGERALD

ANNIAS uh-ni′uhs [Ἀννεις Anneis, Ἀννιας Annias]. The progenitor of a family who returned with Zerubbabel and other leaders to Jerusalem after the exile (1 Esd 5:16).

ANNIUTH uh-ni′uhth [Ἀννιουθ Anniouth]. A Levite (1 Esd 9:48). Named Bani (Neh 8:7). *See* BANI.

ANNIVERSARY. The term *anniversary* is absent from modern Bible translations with the exceptions of Deut 16:6 (NIV) and 4 Macc 1:10 (RSV, NRSV). However, there are a number of annual observances of significant events in biblical tradition. For example, the annual PASSOVER celebration "on the fourteenth day of the first month" (Num 28:16) commemorated Israel's deliverance from Egypt. The "first day of the seventh month" (Num 29:1) was New Year's Day (ROSH HA-SHANAH). It appears that during Babylonian captivity the Jews observed four annual fasts to remember the siege and fall of Jerusalem (Zech 7:1-7; 8:19). Christian commemorations focus more on events than specific dates (e.g., EASTER). *See* CALENDAR; CHRISTIAN YEAR; FEASTS AND FESTIVALS; NEW YEAR.

MARK RONCACE

ANNUNCIATION. The term *annunciation* is often used in reference to the Lukan birth narrative, wherein the angel Gabriel announces to the virgin Mary that she will give birth to Jesus (Luke 1:26-38). The annunciation type-scene is well attested in the Bible and consists of the following elements: 1. The future mother of a biblical hero is described as infertile, or BARREN or in Mary's case, a virgin (Gen 16:1; 29:31; Judg 13:2; Luke 1:7).

2. An ANGEL, a visitor from God, or an oracle announces that the woman will bear a son (Gen 15:4-5; 18:9-15; 30:22; Judg 13:3-7; Luke 1:13-17).

3. The woman conceives and gives birth (Gen 21:1-7; 30:23; Judg 13:24; Luke 1:24, 57).

The extracanonical Protoevangelium of James narrates a variation of the Lukan annunciation to Mary, and also includes an announcement of Mary's own birth. *See* INFANCY NARRATIVES; MAGNIFICAT.

Bibliography: Janice Capel Anderson. "Mary's Difference: Gender and Patriarchy in the Birth Narratives." *The Journal of Religion.* 67 (1987) 183–202; Robert Alter. "How Conventions Help Us Read: The Case of the Bible's Annunciation Type-Scene." *Prooftexts* 3 (1983) 115–30.

MARY FOSKETT

ANNUNUS an′yoo-nuhs [Ἀννοῦνος Announos]. One of the priests procured to return to Jerusalem with Ezra in order to serve in the Temple (1 Esd 8:48). He is not included in the parallel list in Ezra 8:19, one of several discrepancies in the accounts of Ezra 8 and 1 Esd 8.

ANOINT [מָשַׁח mashakh; χρίω chriō]. Anointing is the application of oil to a person or object by smearing, pouring, or sprinkling. Both the OT and NT refer to common, non-ritual, cosmetic or hygienic anointing (*see* e.g., Ruth 3:3; 2 Sam 12:20; Ezek 16:9; Amos 6:6; Ps 23:5; Matt 6:17; Luke 7:46). In most of its occurrences in the OT, *anoint* indicates the ritual application of oil to persons or objects to mark or effect a change of identity or status.

In the OT, anointing objects effects their consecration. Jacob anointed a standing stone at Bethel by pouring oil on it, establishing it as an abode of God's presence (Gen 28:18, 22; 31:13). In the Priestly tradition, the sacred "tent of meeting" and its appurtenances are anointed and consecrated with specially prepared sacred oil (Exod 30:22-29).

Most references to ritual anointing of persons in the OT connect it with kingship. In some texts anointing indicates the people's acceptance of a king (Judg 9:8, 15; 2 Sam 2:7; 5:3). Other texts represent it as marking God's selection of the monarch (1 Sam 9:16; 10:1; 16:1-13; 2 Kgs 9:3, 6, 12). In most of its occurrences, the noun "anointed one" (מָשִׁיחַ mashiakh, Messiah) appears with the Divine Name ("the LORD's anointed";

see 1 Sam 24:6; 26:9; 19:22) or with a possessive pronoun referring to God (*see* 1 Sam 2:10, 35; 12:3, 5; Ps 2:2; 20:6; 84:9; 89:38; 132:10, 17), indicating that anointing established a special relationship between the monarch and God. While humans performed the ritual act of anointing, people believe the source of the status given by anointing was directly from God.

According to OT priestly texts, Aaron was consecrated as head priest by anointing, and those of his descendants who follow him in this status are to be so consecrated (Exod 29:7; Lev 6:22; 16:32; 21:10). Thus, the head priest is referred to as "the anointed priest" (הַכֹּהֵן הַמָּשִׁיחַ hakkohen hammashiakh; Lev 4:3, 5, 16).

In the OT *anoint* does not always indicate a literal rite with oil, but can mean *appoint* or *designate* (Isa 61:1; Isa 45:1). This nonliteral usage carries over into the NT, where Jesus is regularly designated with the standard Greek translation of Hebrew **mashiakh**, Χριστός (**Christos**; Christ). In Acts 4:27 and 10:38, we are told that God anointed Jesus; in the Gospel of Luke, Jesus applies Isa 61:1 to himself (Luke 4:18, 21).

The practice of anointing the dead for burial (ἀλείφω **aleiphō**) is described in Mark 16:1, Luke 23:55-56, and John 19:39-40, when Jesus' followers come to prepare his body with spices. An unnamed woman anoints Jesus' feet with expensive oil, an act that Jesus equates with anointing his body before burial (Mark 4:18) and as a sign of great devotion (Luke 7:36-50). *See* BETHEL; BURIAL; CONSECRATE; OIL; SPICES.

WILLIAM K. GILDERS

ANOINTED, THE [מָשִׁיחַ **mashiakh**]. Anointing persons and objects with oil was a widespread practice in the ancient world to mark transitions (e.g., the liberation of a slave or the marking of a vassal). In the OT, anointing denoted an elevation in status, such as the inauguration of a king, the consecration of a priest, and the reincorporation of a leper into the community. The English word MESSIAH stems from the Hebrew word **mashiakh**. In Greek, the term becomes χριστός **christos** (from χρίω **chriō**, *annoint*). *See* ANOINT; CHRIST; MESSIAH, JESUS THE; MESSIAH, JEWISH; OIL.

JUDITH Z. ABRAMS

ANSWER [עָנָה **'anah**; ἀποκρίνομαι **apokrinomai**]. The word *answer* in Scripture can link God with prayers of intercession and petition. God responds graciously to human need (Matt 6:2, 25-34) and rewards persistent asking (Luke 11:9-13; 18:1-8). Psalms address God in the confidence that requests for help will be heard and dealt with mercifully. Psalm 86:7 is typical: "In the day of my trouble I call on you, for you will answer me" (*see also* 99:6-8; 118:5; 138:3; 143:1 and similarly Isa 58:9 and Joel 2:19). On occasion God is praised for answering Israel with acts of deliverance even before the people utter their requests (Ps 65:5; Isa 65:24).

In most cases the verbs for *answer* in the Bible ('**anah** in Hebrew; **apokrinomai** in Greek) refer to human conversations. Usually the accent is on responsiveness to a question, a request, or a command. Sometimes the words simply indicate that one or more interlocutors wish to keep a conversation going (2 Kgs 20:10) or begin a speech (Job 8:1; 11:1). This usage occurs regularly in the formula "he/she answered and said . . . " On the lips of Jesus it underlines his authoritative status. When Pharisees ask him whether it is lawful to divorce one's wife, Jesus' answer-saying becomes a question: "What did Moses command you?" Then, countering the chapter and verse response of his hearers, Jesus answers and says: "Because of your hardness of heart he wrote this commandment" (Mark 10:3-5; *see also* 11:29-30; 12:17, 29-31, 34; 14:48-49). This sovereign tone is most evident in John where **apokrinomai** turns up some forty times in his speeches, mostly in debates with authorities or instructions to disciples. In Matt 11:25, Jesus answers God with a prayer ("I thank you Father . . . because you have hidden these things from the wise and intelligent . . ."). Here the verb *answer* may indicate that the Holy Spirit has inspired Jesus' prayer (*see* Luke 10:21 [Q]).

Biblical authors think in terms of God answering prayer with the proviso that divine initiative and human responsiveness remain the prime realities. God's answers assume a relationship or call it into being, and may take forms that petitioners neither anticipate nor desire. God's response to Job's cry for justice comes out of a whirlwind and accuses him (Who is this . . . ? Gird up your loins . . . I will question you, and you shall declare to me"; Job 38:1). Jesus promises his followers that he will do whatever they ask in his name (John 14:13), but asking in Jesus' name unites them with the one who lays down his life for his friends (15:12-14). Both petition and response are shaped by the cross. In the Bible, God's answers are seen as ultimately redemptive; but they are also mysterious, often exceeding the reach of human understanding (Rom 11:33-36). *See* PRAYER.

JOHN KOENIG

ANT [נְמָלָה **nemalah**; μύρμηκης **myrēmēs**]. This insect crawls into the biblical text only twice, both times in the book of Proverbs (6:6; 30:25) where it is used to illustrate industriousness. There the ant exemplifies a key theme in wisdom literature—to be wise and prosperous, one need only observe the order of the natural world, then comport oneself accordingly. There are several species of indigenous harvesting ants, all of which exhibit the gathering and storing behavior described in Proverbs. *See* INSECTS OF THE BIBLE.

JENNIFER L. KOOSED

ANTAIOS [Ἀνταῖος **Antaios**]. Son of Poseidon and Gaia (Earth). A Libyan giant who forced strangers to wrestle him, killing them upon victory, and decorating Poseidon's temple with their skulls. During his 11th labor, HERACLES wrestled Antaios and defeated him after perceiving that Antaios gathered his strength by remaining in contact with the earth.

MICHAEL SCHUFER

ANTEDILUVIAN. Genesis 1–5 constitutes the antediluvian ("pre-flood") portion of the biblical narrative. Personal traits such as long life and wisdom are often associated with antediluvian figures in the Bible (e.g., Enoch) and other ancient literature (e.g., Utnapishtim in the Gilgamesh Epic). *See* FLOOD.

ANTELOPE [תְּאוֹ te'o]. The antelope is a ruminant with permanent hollow horns that does not fit into the common categories of domesticated bovine animals such as oxen, goats, and sheep. The difficulty in defining *antelope* from biblical days is revealed in the KJV translation of te'o as "wild ox" (Deut 14:5) and "wild bull" (Isa 51:20). Varieties of antelope have many different characteristics. Deuteronomy 14:5 declares the antelope, along with the common bovine, and the deer, the gazelle, the roebuck, the wild goat, the ibex, and the mountain sheep, as animals that the Israelites may eat. The most prevalent antelope in ancient Palestine was the gazelle, a graceful contrast to the cumbersome ox of the KJV translation. Other types of antelope probably inhabited ancient Israel. The LXX translates the Hebrew word in Deut 14:5 as ὄρυξ oryx, possibly meaning the antelope *oryx beatrix* or *oryx leucoryx*. Antelope were hunted as wild game; the large horns of the antelope made it easy to snare in nets (Isa 51:20). *See* ANIMALS OF THE BIBLE.

MICHAEL G. VANZANT

ANTHOTHIJAH an'thoh-th*i*'juh [עֲנְתֹתִיָּה 'anthothiyah]. According to Benjamin's genealogy in 1 Chr 8:1-40, he is one of Shashak's sons (8:24).

ANTHROPOLOGY, NT CULTURAL. Cultural anthropology is one of the social sciences that study human groups and human behavior in groups in a comparative way. Human groups range from small collectivities to large-scale societies. Cultural anthropology differs from sociology. As a rule sociologists study such groups and behaviors in their own society, while anthropologists do similar studies in alien societies. In order to carry out their study of alien groups, anthropologists must necessarily compare those groups with groups in their own society. As a result anthropological methods always entail comparison, implicit or explicit, with the scholar's own society. Since social systems consist of institutions, culture, and person types, anthropology attempts to understand and explain alien institutions and cultures. Focus on person types is called social or cross-cultural psychology (social psychology).

Social scientists observe the recurring patterns that human beings follow in-group behavior. Generalizations based on observations of such usual patterns of behavior provide a description of the norms of a given society. Norms enable members of a society to understand each other and predict what others will do in certain circumstances. Deviation from those norms produces social dissonance. This deviant behavior is called by various names: trespasses, sins, or crimes. A description of the institutions, values, and person types of a given society entails a description of predictable behaviors: modes of acting, perceiving, thinking, feeling, and the like. Sociology textbooks in the U.S. describe the societal patterns or norms of social interaction in the U.S., including selected normative patterns of evasion, that is, permissible crimes. Anthropologists, in contrast, seek to describe such patterns in their chosen society of study.

A fundamental presupposition of the social sciences is that meanings expressed in language, human interaction, or artifacts always derive from social system. And a fundamental presupposition of NT studies is that the NT documents come from the Eastern Mediterranean of the 1st cent. Hence to discover the 1st cent. meanings being communicated by and in the NT documents, one must attempt to recover an understanding of the social systems from which they derive. The chief tool for the study of alien social systems is the comparative orientation of cross-culturally oriented anthropology. Such anthropological study, however, must also be outfitted with the cross-temporal perspectives of history.

For instance, U.S. sociology deals with at least four basic social institutions (and subsets): family, economics, politics, and religion. Historians indicate that the separation of church and state (religion and politics) occurred for the first time in the 18th cent. as did the separation of bank/market and state (economics and politics). Anthropologists have frequently noted that peasant societies (presumably 1st cent. Mediterranean societies as well), with their perception of limited good, have a substantive economic system. *Substantive* means that economics is embedded in family (domestic economy) and government (political economy). Likewise, societies not directly influenced by the 18th cent. Euro-American idea of separation of church and state (e.g., Islamic countries) will have substantive religion. This means religion is coterminous with the whole of society embedded both in the family (domestic religion) and the state (political religion). Given that the NT anteceded the 18th cent. and its separations, the presumption is that in the time of the NT there existed domestic religion and political religion as well as domestic economy and political economy (but not formal religion or formal economy). Religious and economic concerns were realized through kinship and political norms. To proclaim the kingdom of God (theocracy) or to hail someone as king of Israel is to express political statements. To address one's fellows as *brothers* or *sisters*" in Christ is to describe others in kinship terms. Although most contemporary NT readers consider those documents to be about religion, they originated in social systems where religion was embedded in kinship and/or politics. Hence the documents are about kinship and/or politics in which religion is embedded. For this reason the use of modern sociology of religion based on religion as a formal, freestanding social institution will always produce inaccurate anachronistic (and ethnocentric) results.

More specifically, a number of anthropologists consider the Mediterranean to be a culture area. Traditional assessments of self, others, nature, time, space, and the deity are quite similar across the region. If with the help of historical awareness one removes the features of Constantine's political religious Christendom and the Talmud-based Jewish domestic religion, Medieval Christianity, the Reformation, the Enlightenment, Romanticism, and the Industrial Revolution, one can discover constant features available in isolated Mediterranean areas and discernable in ancient Mediterranean documents.

Furthermore, by studying isolated, contemporary Mediterranean groups, one can actually observe how traditional Mediterranean patterns and values play out. This furnishes a NT reader with scenarios for imagining what is going on in the interactions depicted in the documents. Some of these patterns and values include concern for honor or reputation (and no concern about psychological guilt), elite acquisition of honor through benefaction, collectivistic personality (with concern for group integrity over individual self-reliance), patronage as a systemic feature of interaction (with brokers and favors for clients), envy (and the evil eye) as social experience, visions and other ecstatic events, ways of sickening and healing, or gender as primary in self-definition.

The theological significance of this approach is rooted in the truism that all theology is analogy. All the comparisons used to describe God in the NT come from the social system of the authors. To understand NT theology, cultural anthropology is indispensable.

Bibliography: Bruce J. Malina. *The New Testament World: Insights from Cultural Anthropology.* 3rd ed. (2001); Bruce J. Malina. *The Social World of Jesus and the Gospels* (1996); Jerome H. Neyrey, ed. *The Social World of Luke Acts: Models for Interpretation* (1991); John J. Pilch. *Visions and Healing in the Acts of the Apostles: How the Early Believers Experienced God* (2004); John J. Pilch. *Healing in the New Testament: Insights from Medical and Mediterranean Anthropology* (2000); Richard L. Rohrbaugh, ed. *The Social Sciences and New Testament Interpretation* (1996).

BRUCE J. MALINA

ANTHROPOLOGY, NT THEOLOGICAL. The NT conceives of a human being as a psychophysical unity whose present and continuing existence depends entirely upon God.

The NT has no single or entirely consistent Anthropology. New Testament writers usually discuss the nature of humans only as a part of some larger theological discussion. When they do address anthropological issues, they are less concerned to define essences of which humans are composed and more to describe humanity's place in relation to God and one another, as well as humanity's relationship to all creation. New Testament writers are not interested in the metaphysics of Anthropology but in the possession of fully human existence in the presence of God.

New Testament writers use various terms to refer to different aspects of existence, often drawing on the OT. These terms often do not designate different parts of a person, but are different ways to speak of the whole. Each term has multiple meanings that sometimes stand in tension with one another.

> A. Hellenistic Anthropology
> B. Gospels and Acts
> C. Paul
> D. Other NT
> Bibliography

A. Hellenistic Anthropology

Interpreters have often assumed that Platonism's ideas of the soul are a primary background or source of NT Anthropology, perhaps because that is the view Gnosticism adopted. But Platonism's understanding that the soul and the material realm are in opposition to each other is distinctive in Hellenistic times. Epicureans and Stoics see both BODY and SOUL (whether ψυχή psychē or πνεῦμα pneuma) as material, with the latter composed of finer and more subtle matter, but still of matter. Within this outlook, body and soul (which is another form of a body) are dependent upon each other. Even those Hellenistic Jewish documents that clearly separate soul and body nearly all have unification of the two as the final state for the saved.

B. Gospels and Acts

In the Gospels, Jesus has a high view of humanity. Humans are more important than other parts of creation (Matt 6:25-30; 10:29-31), so important that their needs require an interpretation of Sabbath observance that allows them to be met (Matt 12:9-14; Mark 2:23-3:6; Luke 6:1-11; 13:10-17). As children of God humans have a special dignity that must be respected. Yet humans are obligated to serve God, who renders judgment on their behavior. Even the high standard of behavior Jesus demands in the Sermon on the Mount and on the Plain demonstrates a high view of humanity because Jesus assumes it is reasonable for God to expect that much from humans.

Still, humans have all turned away from God and their general inclinations are toward evil (Matt 7:11; 16:4; Luke 11:13, 29). In John, humans live in darkness and lack understanding (John 9:39-41; 12:40) and so they violate God's law (John 3:19; 7:19; 16:8-9). Yet Jesus' calls to repentance assume that humans can experience a change of heart that enables them to live according to God's will. Zaccheus (Luke 19:1-10), the parable of the Prodigal Son (Luke 15:11-24), and even in the good soil of the parable of the Sower (Mark 4:1-20; Matt 13:1-23; Luke 8:4-15) are examples of such change (compare Mark 3:31-35 where those who do God's will are Jesus' family).

The multiple ways the Gospels speak of God's judgment do not reflect a single anthropological metaphysic. The parable of the rich man and Lazarus imagines some immediate judgment that anticipates a future final determination (Luke 16:19-31). John, however, envisions a resurrection of all "from the grave" at the Parousia (5:28-29) and so does not, in this place, assume consciousness between death and Parousia. Likewise, Matthew has the queen of Sheba rise at the judgment (12:41-42). In Acts, Luke has Paul believe in the resurrection of all at the Parousia (24:5-15).

While Luke's parable envisions a bodily postmortem existence, elsewhere he assumes that the SPIRIT (pneuma) survives death apart from the body (8:55). But survival of the pneuma does not constitute the full existence the resurrection promises. The resurrected Christ assures the disciples that he is not a "ghost" (NRSV for pneuma) because he has "flesh and bone" (24:39). Similarly, Matthew and Luke assume that humans appear at judgment in bodily form because God has power over "soul" (psychē) and "body" (σῶμα sōma) there (Matt 5:27-30; 10:28; Luke 12:4). One is fully human in these texts only when embodied. Furthermore, psychē sometimes refers simply to LIFE (Matt 20:28; Mark 3:4; 10:45; Luke 6:9) or even to one's whole self (Matt 22:37; Mark 12:30, where it translates nefesh [נֶפֶשׁ]; Luke 12:19, 22; John 10:11), rather than designating some part of human nature.

John speaks of the gift of salvation as "life" or "eternal life" (ζωή zōē, 3:15-17). He asserts that only the Father and the Son have life in themselves, all others are granted life (5:25-29). Even when Jesus asserts that Abraham is among the living, as in Mark 12:26-27, Abraham is living because he is among those God has granted life, not because humans are immortal by nature (compare John 8:53-59).

C. Paul

Paul comments more extensively on Anthropology than other NT writers, but does not offer a systematic or comprehensive treatment. There are significant tensions among his anthropological assertions, and he gives the same anthropological term multiple meanings. Paul's categories are not philosophical or essen-

tialist, but relational and eschatological. Paul speaks of fully human existence in comparison with truncated existence, rather than of ontological components. Still, this fullness is bodily existence because humans are essentially bodily beings.

Paul's Anthropology is dependent on his eschatology in which the resurrection realizes God's fullest will for humanity. Human existence in the present is not what God intends because sin reigns in the world and even gains control within the will. So God acts to recreate the whole cosmos, including humanity. This new humanity that is a part of the new creation is of central importance for Paul's Anthropology. Since God declared the original creation good, the recreation of humanity will also be consistent with the good of humanity's current nature.

Paul views humans as mortal beings, particularly since the sin of Adam (Rom 5:12-21), who may be granted continuing existence by God. While all face God's judgment, condemnation may well mean extinction for most since Paul describes the gift of salvation as God's giving of life (Rom 4:7; 8:11; 1 Cor 15:22) and as eternal life (Rom 2:7; 5:21; Gal 6:8).

In 1 Cor 15, Paul rejects belief in the immortality of the soul. He argues for bodily existence as the full and final nature of human existence. The eschatological body will be a "spiritual body" (σῶμα πνευματικόν sōma pneumatikon) as opposed to a "natural body" (σῶμα ψυχικόν sōma psychikon). This eschatological body is composed of different material, but is no less a body (15:42-50). Fully human life requires this bodily aspect. There is no hint of any intermediate state here, only of resurrection of the dead to a new, immortal and glorious bodily life. The mortal is exchanged for the immortal (15:50-55; see also 1 Thess 4:13-18).

Paul's comments on the postmortem state in Phil 1:22-23 sound somewhat different. Here Paul says it is better for him to depart life "in the flesh" (σάρξ sarx) and so be "with Christ." This implies immediate fellowship with Christ but does not describe what sort of existence that may be, though his comments in 1 Corinthians suggest that it must be bodily.

Paul's eschatological assurances in the face of apostolic suffering in 2 Cor 4:16–5:10 present yet a different outlook. Paul's comments about the "inner person" and "outer person" recognize a duality in human existence (as does 2 Cor 12:1-7), but not an opposition between soul and body. In 5:1-10 he possesses a "building from God" in the postmortem state so that he will not be found naked. This implies something less than possession of the final embodied state, but still not complete lack of embodiment. This state is not satisfactory, nor is it the final will of God for humans, even though it implies fellowship with God. However, this may be an uncommon state of existence reserved for only a few. Throughout 2 Corinthians Paul distinguishes between the apostolic company and other Christians. That difference may be present here. Just as martyrs are present in heaven before others are raised in Rev 6:9-11, Paul may envision apostles being given an existence only few experience. If so, Paul's cryptic comments about this state of existence do not reflect his more general view of what happens at death. In any case, genuine and fully human existence requires bodiliness. Paul does not equate the essential self with the body alone, but wholeness and personal identity require bodiliness. Furthermore, people experience this fully human existence only at the Parousia, when the individual is raised together with Christ and all believers.

D. Other NT

Other NT writings also assume an Anthropology rather than explicate one. Sometimes they contrast present life in the *flesh* (sarx) with existence in the *spirit* (pneuma). When 1 Peter refers to the postmortem state of the saints and those who need to hear the preaching of Jesus, he calls them "spirits" (πνεύμασιν pneumasin; 3:18-19) and he says the saved live "in the spirit" (4:6). While he contrasts *flesh* and *spirit* as two realms of existence, this need not indicate that "flesh" is evil. However, 1 Pet 2:11 does set the "desires of the flesh" in opposition to the soul (psychē). Even here it is not just the "flesh," but desires that belong to the realm of the flesh, that opposes the psychē. And psychē probably does not designate some nonmaterial essence superior to the body because only a few lines earlier it refers to whole persons (3:20). Indeed, the only use of sōma in 1 Peter is a reference to the body of Christ. Still, 1 Peter assumes some duality in its anthropological remarks.

Hebrews also uses sōma to signify the whole self when referring to the sacrifice of Jesus' body (10:5-10). Again like 1 Peter, Hebrews speaks of saints who have died as "spirits" (πνεύματα pneumata). But this is not technical vocabulary because the writer also calls angels *spirits* (1:14, perhaps also 1:7 where the NRSV translates pneumata "winds"). And as in most of the NT, pneuma usually refers to the Holy Spirit rather than to an aspect of humanity (e.g., 2:4; 3:7). When Heb 4:12 says the word of God can divide soul (psychē) from spirit (pneuma), this is not ontological trichotomy, but use of metaphor to dramatize God's discernment of our innermost selves, as the following distinction between "thoughts and intentions of the HEART (καρδία kardia)" shows.

In Revelation John usually envisions a bodily resurrection of all to face judgment. There is no hint of an interim existence for anyone other than martyrs. Martyrs appear under the altar as psychas (ψυχὰς) who have not taken possession of their final state of existence (6:9-11; 20:4). Revelation also uses psychē more generally for life, even that of animals (8:9; 12:11; 16:3). Revelation calls the fate of those not among the saints "the second death" (e.g., 20:14), which may indicate that their fate is nonexistence.

While the NT writers espouse no specific metaphysical Anthropology and do not use precise vocabulary to address this topic, they do share a general view of humanity. They agree that humans are wholly dependent upon God and possess the fullness and wholeness of human existence only as bodily beings. They do not denigrate embodiment or the material realm because those who are fully human always partake of the material realm, even when that matter is the fine and subtle matter that makes up the eschatological "spiritual body." The NT sees humans as part of the creation and of extraordinary value because of the ways they are related to God. *See* AFTERLIFE; FLESH IN THE NT; HUMANITY, NT; MIND.

Bibliography: K. Berger. *Identity and Experience in the New Testament* (2003); R. Bieringer, V. Koperski, and B. Lataire, eds. *Resurrection in the New Testament* (2002); Rudolf Bultmann. *Theology of the New Testament.* Vol. 1 (1954); John W. Cooper. *Body, Soul and Life Everlasting: Biblical Anthropology and the Monism-Dualism Debate* Rev. Ed. (2000); Joel B. Green, ed. *What about the Soul? Neuroscience and Christian Anthropology* (2004); Robert Gundry. *Sōma in Biblical Theology: With Emphasis on Pauline Anthropology* (1976); Murray J. Harris. *Raised Immortal: Resurrection and Immortality in the New Testament* (1983); Robert Jewett. *Paul's Anthropological Terms: A Study of Their Use in Conflict Settings* (1971); R. N. Longenecker, ed. *Life in the Face of Death: The Resurrection Message of the New Testament* (1998); J. A. T. Robinson. *The Body: A Study in Pauline Theology* (1952); John Wright and P. Potter, eds. *Psyche and Soma: Physicians and Metaphysicians on the Mind-Body Problem from Antiquity to Enlightenment* (2000).

JERRY L. SUMNEY

ANTHROPOLOGY, OT CULTURAL. Also known as social or sociocultural anthropology, cultural anthropology is one of several subfields of the wider discipline of anthropology. It focuses on the cultural and social aspects of contemporary or recent populations. By collecting information about individual populations through fieldwork involving direct observation, it seeks to recognize and understand the diversity among human groups as well as the similarities in their lifeways, social forms and institutions, and inter-group and interpersonal dynamics. In its attempts to understand similarities among peoples, the comparative perspective in particular has long attracted biblical scholars.

The OT originates in and reflects the lives of real people living in real time, however removed it may be from them in its final canonical form. Yet the information in biblical texts at best provides only a partial and sometimes distorted glimpse of the ancient social contexts of the texts. Consequently, for more than two centuries, scholars have sought to fill the lacunae in our knowledge of ancient Israel by considering the data and theories of what is now known as cultural anthropology. They believe that inferences about people in the biblical world can be made on the basis of information about pre-modern peoples still visible in present or recent past. Although the analogical reasoning required for using such information to understand ancient society has its limitations, in that no two societies are ever exactly alike however strong their commonalities, it nonetheless provides interpretive possibilities that otherwise would be unavailable.

One of the most important functions of cultural anthropology in biblical research is to help scholars understand the context in which texts originate so that they can be evaluated in relation to the needs, values, and beliefs of their own time. That is, by learning about the cultural processes of the ancient Israelites, we can understand better what otherwise might seem bizarre and even unacceptable. Assumptions based on post-biblical interpretive traditions and on what we know in the world today need no longer be used anachronistically to appraise biblical texts.

The first and perhaps most influential scholar to apply the findings of cultural anthropology to biblical studies in a systematic way was the Scotsman William Robertson Smith. His extensive research on tribal groups in the Middle East led him to theorize about various customs and social structures of the Israelites, especially the role of animal sacrifice in group life. Although many of his proposals, published in the 1880s, have since been modified or discarded, his ideas about the relationship of the realities of the material world to the beliefs and practices of any people have had enduring significance.

Another European writing in the late 19th cent., the German Bernhard Stade, was also influential in his use of concepts from cultural anthropology. His book on Israelite history is notable for its attention to Israelite social and religious institutions as well as its political forms. In drawing on the theorists of his day, he posited that the power of the male head of the patriarchal family was integral to the organization of all social and religious institutions. His views were influential in his own day and well into the 20th cent.; some of the theories of Julius Wellhausen about ancient Israel and its religious development can be traced in part to Stade's work.

Both of these scholars, and others of their generation, held an evolutionary view of human society. They believed that the commonalities among diverse groups were the result of the fact that different peoples were moving through the same stage of cultural evolution in the same order. In its most general form, this meant that societies were thought to originate as bands, then become tribes, develop into chieftaincies, and ultimately form states. Late 20th century scholars have revealed the flaws in this scheme; but its basic distinctions among the forms of human socio-political organizations, from simple to complex, and its goal of understanding each of these "stages," continues to provide useful models for understanding the development of Israelite society. They indicate, for example, how important the great importance of the role of kinship, whether real or constructed, is in contributing to the stability and survival of pre-modern peoples; the prominence of the genealogies of the OT as well as the frequent references to families and tribes becomes comprehensible in this respect.

In addition to its contributions to our understanding Israelite political, social, and religious forms and their functions, cultural anthropology has played a significant role in other aspects of biblical study. It has revolutionized the study of specific phenomena mentioned in the Bible (e.g., prophecy, law, sacrifice, and marriage); and it has led to more nuanced analysis of various leadership positions that appear in OT texts. It also has shown how the powerful influence of honor and shame in the eastern Mediterranean and Semitic worlds has shaped biblical narratives and ideologies. And it has helped us understand how the individual is embedded in community in the biblical world more fundamentally than in contemporary modern life.

In recent decades, the rich anthropological literature on gender roles and dynamics has helped scholars analyze the role of female figures in the Bible in relation to the social realities of antiquity rather than according to present values. The lives of women in the biblical period have usually been evaluated according to the notions of patriarchal hierarchies that have dominated biblical studies since they were put forward by 19th cent. theorists; but evidence that women in traditional societies, including ancient Israel, have their own hierarchies that cross-cut those of men contests such interpretations. And the notion of women as powerless in patriarchal households has now been countered by the realization that the significant economic contributions of women to household life afforded them considerable personal, social, and even political power. *See* ANTHROPOLOGY, CULTURAL NT; ANTHROPOLOGY (NT); SOCIOLOGY, OT.

Bibliography: Charles E. Carter and Carol Meyers, eds. *Community, Identity, and Ideology: Social Science Approaches to the Hebrew Bible* (1996); John Rogerson. *Anthropology and the Old Testament* (1978).

CAROL MEYERS

ANTHROPOLOGY, OT THEOLOGICAL. A theological anthropology of the OT represents the effort to articulate the biblical conception of the human person, or subject, as expressed in the canonical books of the OT (אָדָם ʾadham "human being, humanity"; also אֱנוֹשׁ ʾenosh, "individual man, human being, mortal"). As such, it is concerned with a specific literary construction of humanness, which may or may not correspond precisely with the results of an anthropological investigation of the people "behind the book," insofar as the latter includes the totality of a culture's physical and symbolic representations of the human. In other words, a theological anthropology of the OT aims at understanding what it means to be a human subject in the view of those texts that are revelation for Jews and Christians alike.

A. Modernity and the OT
B. Engagement in a Social Identity
C. Personal Unity
D. Inner Depths
E. Heteronomy
F. The Paradox of Being Human
Bibliography

Of course, the OT contains neither a systematic reflection on anthropology nor an abstract definition of terms dealing with the human person as such. Therefore, a number of formulations are possible, bound as they all are to making explicit what is largely implicit in the discourses of various biblical genres. Even more, because the books of the Bible reflect the different historical circumstances of their writing, there will not be a single, standard conception of the human but multiple and sometimes even apparently conflicting conceptions that ultimately enrich the Bible's understanding.

A. Modernity and the OT

A comparison of the OT's construction of personal identity and that of the modern West reveals marked differences in the ways the human person may be conceived. At least since the Enlightenment, discourse about the "self" has largely displaced earlier forms of discourse about the human subject, including talk of a "soul," derived from ancient Greek anthropological models, so that people today speak generally not simply about themselves but about the self they "have" or the self they "are." It is clear that biblical writings know nothing of such language. This does not mean the people represented in the OT have no consciousness of self, as some older anthropological investigations insisted, but it does suggest that in the construction of personal identity salient features of modern identity, or personhood, are not valued by OT authors to the same degree. Among these features delineated by scholars of the modern Western identity are the autonomy, self-sufficiency, and self-responsible unity of the human person, its disengagement from the world by sharply defined personal boundaries, and the awareness of possessing "inner depths" that underlie self-expression and self-exploration. In fact, for modernity what is most important about the self is that sense of inwardness, or of having "inner depths," that for every person there is a world that lies "within" as well as a world "without," with this "inner" world holding the real key to one's "true" self. The pronounced individualism of modern times is grounded in just this, modernity's location of the self in the "depths" of interiority rather than in relationships to a larger social world. A very different construction of personal identity emerges in the OT: here the subject is: 1) deeply embedded, or engaged, in its social identity; 2) is comparatively decentered and porous with respect to personal boundaries; 3) is relatively transparent, socialized, and embodied (i.e., lacking in a sense of "inner depths"), and 4) achieves "authenticity" in a kind of heteronomy marked by obedience to, and dependence on, another.

B. Engagement in a Social Identity

In contrast to the relative atomism, self-sufficiency, and disengagement of the modern self from society, the ancient Israelite stands at the center of ever-widening circles of relation defined by kinship, beginning with the "family." The latter is not the modern nuclear family, for which Hebrew has no direct expression, but "the house of the father" (see Josh 7:14-18), the lineage headed by the oldest living paternal ancestor. So a basic "household" consisted ideally of at least four generations, and this household constituted the basic unit of social and political life in ancient Israel within which individuals established their personal identity. For the individual then, there were few alternatives. The system of unilineal descent through the father ensured that membership within a family was always unambiguous, since at any time the individual belonged to only one family line, the father's. This in turn maximized the amount of social control that the patriarchal family exerted over the individual (e.g., in the ownership of property), and in many periods the "father's house" and associated kin provided the only significant source of security and protection individuals enjoyed. Even more, since agricultural land was the principal source of income, the family, which collectively farmed the land and shared its produce, was the only domain of economic opportunity, just as, under the management of the *paterfamilias*, it provided the legal framework within which people lived, from childhood well on into adulthood.

Personally, socially, economically, and legally the individual was embedded in the family and enmeshed in obligations of kinship; and the extent to which this family solidarity implicated members in one another's fate is evident in the Bible (e.g., children bearing the father's sins, Exod 20:5; Ezek 18:1-3; obligations incumbent upon a clan "brother" as גֹּאֵל goʾel, "redeemer," Judg 8:18-21; 2 Sam 3:27; Lev 25:23-28), even if some of the theories formerly put forward to explain it (e.g., Israel's "corporate personality") now seem quaint. What is important for a theological anthropology is to see how the language and conceptuality of contemporary moral discourse, with its insistence on self-responsibility, autonomy, and personal freedom, find little resonance in the Bible. This is not because the ancient Israelite was incapable of authentic moral choice, but because within the horizon of the OT one ought to speak more of a "moral community" than a "personal morality" distinct from the social roles and practices of the community.

C. Personal Unity

The modern conviction of personal unity finds only a distant echo in the biblical construction of individual identity, even if the starting point, God's creation of the human as a **nefesh khayah** (נֶפֶשׁ חַיָה), "living being" (Gen 2:7), does not support any dualism of mortal body and immortal soul. That a conception of psychic wholeness and unity of personality is at home in the OT is not in dispute. Ancient Israelites could point to themselves as individual agents of acts by means of the pronoun *I* and would not hesitate to stay out of the path of a charging bull. The issue is how this psychic unity is conceived. Simply put, human faculties and bodily organs are represented as enjoying a measure of independence foreign to contemporary thought, as when "the eye of the adulterer waits for the twilight" (Job 24:15) or "my soul longs for...the courts of the LORD; my heart and my flesh sing for joy" (Ps 84:2). Here individual organs and body parts seem to operate almost as independent centers of activity and are even susceptible to moral judgment (Prov 12:22; Neh 9:8; Jer 5:23). In other words, what these and numerous other examples suggest is a depiction of subjectivity more as the sum of parts than as a whole, a complex and differentiated unity. That means it differs profoundly from the unity represented by Plato's localization of desire and emotion under the hegemony of reason in a center like the "soul," from which the individual's acts flow and from which one can assert reason's rule over one's total moral life. In fact, the closest the word **nefesh**, traditionally translated *soul*, comes to the Platonic concept is in its usage as the seat of a wide range of emotions or feelings. But none of these belong exclusively to **nefesh** and are found associated as well with **ruakh** (רוּחַ) *spirit*, and **lev** (לֵב) *heart*.

Going hand in hand with the lack of a center for the localization of human faculties and emotions is a marked permeability in the boundaries defining personal identity. This is evident in the use of **ruakh**, *wind* or *spirit*, to designate the driving force in a person for acts that are out of character. Thus the LORD's "spirit" empowers Samson (Judg 14:6) and turns the newly anointed Saul into a "different person" (1 Sam 10:6). Of course, they have not lost their "personal" identity; the point again is how that identity is conceived. For biblical anthropology God's initiative with the human

subject does not displace the latter's own capacity for personal action: it makes it "more" itself.

D. Inner Depths

If the most striking manifestation of the modern sense of interiority is the conviction that every person has "inner depths," marking that person as unique, its absence in the OT is equally striking. One does not look "within" to discover who one is. That is something one comes to through education, by learning concretely the roles one has in society and the status accompanying them. Self-knowledge, then, can be relatively unproblematic, as can, at least for the discerning, knowledge of another (Prov 20:5) because (apart from outright deception) people simply disclose who they are through their conduct (Prov 14:5). Or better, people are identified with their acts even as they are their body (only moderns "have" a body). That "explains" why physical defects can disqualify individuals from a priestly office (Lev 21:16-24) or even from entering the cultic community (Deut 23:1): in the absence of "inner depths" as a focal point of self-definition, there is no center "within" a self and apart from the body to be set over against a "real" self.

E. Heteronomy

Moderns demand autonomy. In the OT this demand is confronted with the equally insistent demands of traditional society, where the goals of a "permeable" individual are characteristically subordinated to those of the group. This subordination is never absolute any more than the demand for autonomy is. The point is that moderns locate authenticity in the rejection of any form of heteronomy even as the OT promotes it. For the latter, wisdom does not come to those who look "within" themselves for guidance but only to those who are willing to heed the authoritative voices of religious tradition (Prov 1:8-9). Indeed the conviction is that independent thought is actually bound to end in moral failure: "Trust in the Lord with all your heart, and do not rely on your own insight" (Prov 3:5). If today responsibility is synonymous with one's capacity for pure self-determination, for the OT only a species of heteronomy can be the basis of morality. So Jeremiah and Ezekiel both hope for the day when God will write the law directly into people's hearts (Jer 31:31-34; Ezek 36:25-27).

F. The Paradox of Being Human

These aspects of the biblical construction of the human person underlie basic and powerful beliefs. Among these is the unspoken conviction that the human person lives only in simultaneous relation to God, to others, and to the earth and, within these relationships, out of a kind of dialectical tension manifest in the contrast between humanity's dignity and special status in the world and humanity's ontological insufficiency and moral poverty. Indeed the paradox of the human situation comes to remarkable expression in a series of covenants where God, to whom "the whole earth" belongs (Exod 19:5), nevertheless is bound contractually by this human legal instrument to honor the claims of the clearly beholden human "partner."

That humanity's relationship to God is unique among all creatures is perhaps most explicit in humanity's creation in God's image (Gen 1:26-28), making the human the only sanctioned image of God in the OT, a status not even human sinfulness can abrogate (Gen 5:1-3; 9:6). Thereby, for the Priestly Writer, to see the human is in some sense to see the face of God, who at humanity's creation has chosen to exercise dominion over the earth and its creatures precisely through humanity (Gen 1:26-28; 2:19). Consequently, even in the most abject of conditions, the human subject remains empowered by God to act in the world with initiative, confidence, and authority, to such an extent that in the OT strikingly there is no real analogue for the extreme self-abasement and loss of personal agency one finds in the hymnic literature of the Dead Sea Scrolls. Being a "little lower than God" (Ps 8:6), the human can make a stand before no less a one than the Almighty and can, in the manner of numerous lament psalms, press claims for justice and mercy both, appealing like Job, not to any covenantal promises, but simply to its own righteousness (Job 31).

Yet this being who alone among creatures was brought into existence by God's breath of life remains dependent on that breath, always "of the earth" and destined "for the earth" (Gen 2:7; 3:19). Outside of the deuterocanonicals, only a few late texts in the OT (Isa 26:19; Dan 12:1-3) expand the horizon of the human subject's hopes for life beyond its days "in the flesh." For all its glory, "flesh" is not "spirit," says Isaiah, the human is not God (31:3).

Dependent upon God even for the possibilities of life earth provides, the human subject is not finally its own master, having been created to serve God (Gen 2:15). So it is service, above all, rather than self-fulfillment, that gives purpose and meaning to human life, and the obligation incumbent upon all to heed God's voice cannot be superseded or abridged in any way (Isa 45:9). While the OT has much to say about how that service gets specified, Micah sums it up eloquently: "to do justice, and to love kindness, and to walk humbly with your God" (Mic 6:8).

Of course, the other side of this sense of an all-pervasive responsibility before God is the fact of human failure and sin, the "flesh's" frailty not always being sharply distinguished from a certain moral weakness on the part of the human subject (Ps 78:39; Job 15:14-16; 25:4-6). So lively is Israel's experience of sin that the psalmist may even complain of being born "guilty" (Ps 51:5) even as "no one living is righteous before God" (Ps 143:2). This is no doctrine of original sin. Nonetheless,

such confessions highlight Israel's profound awareness of humanity's guilt before God and the universal need for forgiveness, the "totalizing" of human responsibility finding its corresponding expression in the attribution of all evil and misfortune to human moral failure (Gen 2–3). As terrifying as this conclusion about human responsibility for evil is, paradoxically it testifies all the same to the conviction that human beings have in life a fundamental choice to make and, what is more, that they have it within their power, by God's help, to effect the good. Such is the paradox of the human subject in the OT. See AUTONOMY; ETHICS IN THE OT.

Bibliography: Aubrey R. Johnson. *The Vitality of the Individual in the Thought of Ancient Israel* (1964); Carol A. Newsom. *The Self as Symbolic Space: Constructing Identity and Community at Qumran* (2004); Charles Taylor. *Sources of the Self: The Making of the Modern Identity* (1989); H. W. Wolff. *Anthropology of the Old Testament* (1974).

ROBERT A. DIVITO

ANTHROPOMORPHISM. Anthropomorphism (from ἄνθρωπος anthrōpos [*human*] and μορφή morphē [*form* or *nature*]) is the analogical application of human characteristics and actions to something that is not human. Scripture uses anthropomorphisms when it describes God as a person with humanlike feelings and actions.

Examples of anthropomorphic language for God abound in Scripture. God's mouth speaks truth with an effective, powerful voice (Deut 30:20; Ps 29:3; Isa 40:5, 24). God's eyes and ears watch over the earth and its inhabitants (Deut 11:12; Ps 34:15; Prov 15:3). God's face bestows blessing and honor (Gen 32:30; Num 6:25). God's hands create (Isa 64:8), hurt and heal (Job 5:18), hold (Ps 37:24; Luke 23:46), and guide (Ps 139:10). God is a warrior with a powerful right arm (Deut 4:34; Pss 44:3; 98:1); God also has the comforting arms of a mother (Isa 66:13).

God's actions are likened to various human social roles: Father, Lord, Shepherd, Healer, Potter, Judge, Liberator, and King. Ideal actions, feelings, and intentions appropriate to each social role are attributed to God. Thus the Lord is a shepherd who holds lambs close to God's heart (Isa 40:11). Then when Jesus says, "I am the Good Shepherd," readers may hear a claim to the divine quality of holding and caring (John 10:11, 14).

Too literal readings of anthropomorphisms neglect their metaphorical, analogical qualities. But properly understood, anthropomorphisms allow readers to experience God as personal, near, and engaged rather than abstract, remote, and aloof. See ANALOGY; GOD, FINGER OF; GOD, METAPHORS FOR; GOD, OT VIEW OF; JESUS, METAPHORS FOR; METAPHOR IN THEOLOGY.

BONNIE G. HOWE

ANTICHRIST (ἀντίχριστος antichristos). The Antichrist is the adversary of God and Christ that comes in the end times. According to some sources he deceives many into false faith, and according to others he persecutes the people of God. The word consists of the noun χριστός christos, meaning "anointed one" or "messiah," and the prefix ἀντί anti, which can mean either "against" or "in place of." Both meanings of the prefix are significant. Most writers depict the Antichrist as an opponent, who is "against Christ," but some also envision him imitating or putting himself "in place of" Christ and promoting false beliefs in place of the truth about Christ. The term *Antichrist* is not used in Revelation. It first appears in the Johannine Epistles (1 John 2:18, 22; 2 John 7), and writers from the 2nd cent. onward refer to the Antichrist as an agent of SATAN, who combines traits of the man of lawlessness (2 Thess 2:1-3), the beast (Rev 13:1-10), and other enemies of God.

A. Antecedents in Jewish Sources
  1. Daniel
  2. Other Jewish writings
B. New Testament
  1. Synoptic Gospels
  2. Second Thessalonians
  3. Johannine Epistles
  4. Revelation
C. Christian Writings from 100–500 CE
D. Later Developments
Bibliography

A. Antecedents in Jewish Sources

Traditions concerning Antichrist are Christian in origin, but they have antecedents in Jewish writings that expect this age to see increased wickedness and the rise of a tyrant before God ends the dominion of evil and establishes a righteous kingdom.

1. Daniel

The book of Daniel envisions a tyrant coming at the close of the age. The author depicts successive empires as four beasts: a lion, a bear, a leopard, and a ten-horned monster. From these empires arises the tyrant, pictured as a horn, who speaks haughtily against God and tries to alter the holy law. This oppressive ruler makes war against the holy ones, and for three and a half years they are under his power (Dan 7:19-27). Supremely arrogant, he presses upward to heaven and casts down the stars. He ends the practice of lawful burnt offering and sets up a desolating sacrifice. This tyrant marks the culmination of sin and wickedness, and his reign is characterized by deceit and destruction (8:9-11, 23-25; 9:27). Finally, however, God intervenes, breaks the oppressor's power, and establishes an everlasting kingdom (7:27; 8:25).

The tyrant's traits resemble those of ANTIOCHUS IV EPIPHANES, who suppressed observance of Jewish customs and turned the Jerusalem Temple into a sanctuary of Zeus in 167 BCE. By depicting the tyrant in visionary form, Daniel shaped the way writers in subsequent centuries thought of the end of the age. The themes of deception, violent persecution of the faithful, and desecration of the Temple appear in different ways in the NT and later writings.

2. Other Jewish Writings

Jewish apocalyptic writings envision sin and evil increasing throughout the present age, and some also refer to a particular figure as the leader of opposition to God. The DEAD SEA SCROLLS understand that the present age is under the dominion of Belial, the evil angel who leads other evil angels and reigns over the human sons of darkness. Belial is wicked but is ultimately subject to God, and God will even send Belial to punish apostates in the future (CD 8 ii). At the end of the age God's allies will defeat Belial and bring his reign to an end. Some scrolls picture this happening when the good angel Michael helps the sons of light defeat the wicked angel Belial and the sons of darkness (1QM 17 v-viii). In other scrolls God's agent is called Melchizedek or "king of righteousness" (11QMelch 2 xii-xiii) and the evil figure is Melchiresha or "king of wickedness" (4Q544). Although none of these angelic beings is a messiah, the opposition of good and evil figures has analogies to the contrast between Christ and Antichrist. Similar expectations for the final defeat of Belial or Beliar also appear in the *Testaments of the Twelve Patriarchs*, a Jewish work with Christian editing (*T. Levi* 3:3; 18:12; *T. Dan* 5:10-11).

A human tyrant is pictured rising up before the close of the age in some texts. Some writers focus on conditions in Israel, warning of debauched leaders spreading impiety until a terrible ruler comes to punish them for their sins. Bringing evil to its climax, he will persecute faithful Jews until some are forced to choose martyrdom, but God will intervene, establishing a righteous kingdom (*T. Mos.* 7–10). Other writers follow Daniel in picturing a series of empires oppressing the whole earth, with the last of these exhibiting the traits of the Roman Empire. The final king will be cruel and arrogant, fomenting ungodliness throughout his realm until the coming of God's messiah (*4 Ezra* 12:10-39; *2 Bar.* 36-40).

Supernatural opposition to God, along with threats of human tyranny, appears in the *Sibylline Oracles*. These texts envision this age culminating in a breakdown of the social and natural order, and the world falling under oppressive rule (*Sib. Or.* 3:75-92, 611-15). There are warnings that deceivers will appear and that the evil angel Beliar will do signs, even imitating God by raising the dead. Beliar is said to come from the *Sebastenoi*, the line of Augustus, recalling a tradition that expected the emperor Nero to return with destructive power. God, however, will destroy Beliar and his allies (2:154-173; 3:63-74; 5:28-34).

B. New Testament

The NT mentions a number of deceitful or evil figures in connection with the end times. The themes in these passages—violence, deception, and defilement of the Temple—are drawn together into a composite picture of the final enemy by later writers.

1. Synoptic Gospels

Jesus' discourse about the last days warns that several types of opponents will threaten the faithful. The faithful will be challenged to distinguish true from false claims. Since some will come in Jesus' name, claiming to be the Messiah, Jesus' followers must not be deceived by appearances (Mark 13:6; Matt 24:5). When wars and persecutions occur, false messiahs and false prophets will lead many astray by performing miracles to demonstrate their power. The faithful must therefore resist being swayed by signs and omens, and hold fast to the truth they have received (Matt 24:23-26; Mark 13:22). These so-called prophets and messiahs lure people into false beliefs through deception, but are not said to be the agents of violent persecution.

A sign of the end is that "the desolating sacrilege" will stand where it—or literally "he"—does not belong (Mark 13:14). The language recalls Dan 9:27, which tells of the desecration of the Temple. Some associate this sacrilege with the emperor Caligula's attempt to place a statue of himself in the Temple or with Roman troops acclaiming Titus emperor in the Temple compound in 70 CE (Josephus, *J.W.* 2.184-85; 6.316). In the later history of interpretation, many identified the sacrilege as the work of the Antichrist by linking it to the man of lawlessness in 2 Thess 2:3-4.

2. Second Thessalonians

This letter warns that rebellion against God will occur at the end of the age, before Christ's return from heaven. The rebellion will entail apostasy from true faith and lawless behavior. The mystery of lawlessness, which is already at work, will climax in "the man of lawlessness" (2 Thess 2:3). Also known as "the son of destruction," this figure will bring about the destruction of many by leading them away from the truth and thereby bringing them under divine condemnation. Finally, however, he will be destroyed by Christ (2:8-12).

If Christ is an agent of God, the man of lawlessness is said to be an agent of Satan (2:9). Currently restrained by an unnamed power, the lawless one will someday perform signs and beguile the world with lies. This sinister figure will show contempt for every type of worship and exalt himself above the so-called gods of the nations. He will also usurp divine prerogatives by taking his seat in the Temple of the true God, declaring himself to be God (2:4).

The meaning of this passage for readers living after the Temple's destruction in 70 CE is disputed. Futuristic interpreters expect the Temple to be rebuilt so that the lawless one can enter it. Others, however, suggest that the Temple is an image for the Christian community, as it is in other Pauline passages (1 Cor 3:16; 2 Cor 6:16; Eph 2:21), or that the temple is a heavenly one, or that the passage simply describes godless arrogance in apocalyptic language.

3. Johannine Epistles

The author of 1 John assumes that the devil has been active since the beginning of time and that the devil's works are manifest in human lawlessness (1 John 3:8; 5:19). The author also knows that a figure he calls Antichrist is to appear at the world's last hour, before the return of Christ. Although the term *antichrist* is used here for the first time in extant writings (2:18, 22; 4:3; 2 John 7), it conveys a traditional expectation of an outpouring of falsehood at the end of the age. Nothing is said here about the Antichrist engaging in violent persecution; attention centers on his role as the consummate deceiver.

Expectations concerning the Antichrist are fulfilled by the emergence of many false believers, all of whom are antichrists according to 1 John 2:18-19. Written in the context of a schism within the Christian community, 1 John recognizes that the spirit of Antichrist is at work in the people who depart from the truth of the Christian message they received. Rather than looking for a single Antichrist, these epistles hold that the Antichrist is present among the false believers collectively, and regard each person promoting false teaching as the Antichrist (1 John 2:22; 2 John 7).

The hallmark of Antichrist is denying that Jesus is the Messiah, who came in the flesh. What makes this teaching deceptive, from the author's perspective, is that it does not overtly reject Jesus, but presents a spiritualized form of the tradition, which denies Christ's humanity and effectively disallows the atoning significance of his death (1 John 2:2). The false prophets spreading this message are moved by the spirit of error, not the spirit of truth (4:1-6).

4. Revelation

Opponents of God and Christ are prominent in Revelation's visions. Of these the beast from the sea is most closely linked to the Antichrist tradition (Rev 13:1-10). The power behind the beast is Satan, pictured as a dragon with seven heads and ten horns. After being expelled from heaven by the angel Michael, Satan rages about the earth, persecuting the people of God (12:7-12). The agent of persecution is the beast who, like Satan, has seven heads and ten horns.

The beast combines the features of the four beasts envisioned by Daniel into one great adversary, resembling a leopard, bear, lion, and ten-horned monster (Rev 13:1-2). It tyrannizes the world, blaspheming God and making war on the faithful. This beast is the demonic counterpart to Christ the Lamb. If the Lamb was slain and yet lived, the same is said of the beast. But where the Lamb triumphs by faithful suffering, the beast triumphs by violent conquest. Where the Lamb redeems people of every nation to serve God, the beast oppresses people of every nation and makes them serve Satan (5:5-10; 13:1-10). The beast is identified with the cryptic number 666, which many now relate to the name "Nero Caesar," since the beast's violence against the church is like that of Nero.

The beast from the sea is allied with a beast from the land, who is a false prophet. This figure performs miracles to create an illusion of supernatural power, yet he lures people into false faith. He forces them to worship the first beast and bear its mark, and helps gather the kings of the earth for battle against God (13:11-18; 16:13-14). Another ally is the great harlot, who sits on the first beast with its seven heads. Since the heads represent seven mountains, the harlot has traits of Rome, the city set on seven hills. She also bears the name of Babylon, the city that destroyed the first Temple. Blasphemous, arrogant, and obsessed with luxury, the harlot slaughters the people of God (17:1-14).

These agents of evil begin their downfall when the beast turns against the harlot and destroys her (17:16). The beast and false prophet are then defeated by Christ, who subdues them with the sword from his mouth (19:11-21). Finally, Satan is bound for a thousand years before reappearing in league with Gog and Magog, powers whose names recall the adversaries mentioned in Ezek 38–39. They make a last attack against God's people, but are defeated by fire from heaven, and Satan is cast into the lake of fire (Rev 20:7-10).

Interpreters understand the beast and its allies differently, depending on the way they relate Revelation's visions to the world of time and space. From a historical perspective, the visions depict God's opponents in ways that reflect Rome and its emperors. Because the visions look to the final defeat of evil, futuristic interpreters have looked for an individual beast or Antichrist to come at the end of the age. Others, however, see in the beast an image of the evil that is operative at many times and places. Both of these latter interpretations emerge in the early centuries of the church.

C. Christian Writings from 100–500 CE

Traditions concerning Antichrist undergo several developments in this period. First, Christian writers define the coming adversary more clearly as the counterpart to Christ. The *Didache* recognizes that false prophets are a persistent problem, while warning that in the last days false prophets will multiply. Then the deceiver of the world will come as Son of God, giving the illusion of legitimacy by doing miracles. Unlike Jesus, however, this figure will commit iniquities (16:3-4). Further, *The Martyrdom and Ascension of Isaiah*, a Jewish work with Christian editing, expects the church to be persecuted in the end times by Beliar, a wicked angel who will come in the form of a king like Nero. Beliar will do miracles, but will be defeated by Christ and his angels (4:1-14).

Second, various biblical passages are combined into a composite picture of the Antichrist. Especially influential are Irenaeus (*Haer* 5:25-30) and Hippolytus (*Treatise on Christ and Antichrist*), who say that the Antichrist will sum up all evil, as Christ summed up all goodness. They expect the Antichrist to be of Jewish origin, from the tribe of Dan. Receiving power from the devil, the Antichrist will be an evil king, who will try to take God's place in the Temple (2 Thess 2:4). He will be the desolating sacrilege (Matt 24:15), the tyrant who persecutes the holy ones for three and a half years (Dan 7:24-25), and either the first or second beast in John's apocalypse (Rev 13:1-18).

Third, new elements are added. Some writers describe the Antichrist's physical appearance so that people might recognize him (*Apocalypse of Elijah* 3). Many conclude that the force restraining the Antichrist, according to 2 Thess 2:6-7, is the Roman Empire, and that the empire will therefore have to fall before the Antichrist's arrival. Later legends say that the last emperor will lay down his crown in Jerusalem just prior to the Antichrist's coming.

Fourth, some writers hold that Antichrist is not only an individual, who will come in the future, but is a power at work in many people in this age. This broader view of Antichrist is based on the Johannine Epistles, which said that many antichrists had come in the form of false believers (1 John 2:18, 22; 2 John 7). Accordingly, Tyconius and Augustine argue that heretics might deny Christ by their words, but even those who remain in the church can be Antichrist by denying Christ through hateful actions. Christians are, therefore, to examine themselves for signs of Antichrist.

D. Later Developments

Attempts to identify the Antichrist with known figures became more common during the 11th and 12th cent. Conflicts between the pope and emperor sometimes led each to denounce the other as Antichrist. Calls for reform within the church, especially by the radical Franciscans, prompted some to identify particular popes as Antichrist because of their worldliness. In the 16th cent., Martin Luther and John Calvin went further, identifying the institution of the papacy itself as the Antichrist. Many Protestants accepted this idea, but Roman Catholics typically argued that the Antichrist was to come at the end of time and was therefore not linked to the papacy.

Futuristic interpreters from the early 19th cent. onward modified the Protestant perspective by envisioning the Antichrist as a secular tyrant, like Napoleon or Hitler, rather than as the pope. Disillusioned with established Christianity, they came to see both Roman

Catholic and most Protestant churches as degenerate groups symbolized by the harlot of Revelation. They expect that true Christians will be "raptured" up to heaven in order to escape the coming tribulation. They anticipate that the Antichrist will establish one world government and try to control the world's currency. After rebuilding the Temple in Jerusalem, the Antichrist is expected to desecrate it before being defeated at the battle of Armageddon.

Traditions concerning Antichrist have offered vivid ways to think about evil in the world. Many have worked with a composite picture of the Antichrist, like that formulated in the 2nd and 3rd cent., but the NT writings themselves offer varied perspectives on the powers that oppose God and Christ. While many have expected the Antichrist to be an individual that is to come at the end of time, others have made important contributions by seeing in the Antichrist concept a broader tendency to resist God and Christ both inside and outside of the Christian community. *See* BELIAR; REVELATION, BOOK OF; SATAN.

Bibliography: Bernard McGinn. *Antichrist: Two Thousand Years of Human Fascination with Evil* (2000); L. J. Lietaert Peerbolte. *The Antecedents of Antichrist: A Traditio-Historical Study of the Earliest Christian Views on Eschatological Opponents* (1996).

CRAIG R. KOESTER

ANTIGONUS [Ἀντιγονος Antigonon]. Antigonus was a Hasmonean ruler installed by the Parthians (40–37 BCE). Greek and Hebrew inscriptions on his bronze coins show that he adopted the titles of king and high priest. Some coins bear temple-related imagery, including the earliest known artistic depiction of a menorah. Antigonus was ultimately defeated and executed by the Romans, who placed Herod on the throne. His death marked the end of the Hasmonean dynasty, the cessation of Parthian attempts to seize Palestine, the solidification of Roman control of the region, and the establishment of the Herodian line of client kings. *See* HASMONEANS; HEROD.

MARK A. CHANCEY

ANTI-JUDAISM. A term used to describe Christian critique of Judaism as a religion, i.e., Christian condemnations and denigrations of Jewish belief and practice. This polemic appears already in the NT, but anti-Judaism was greatly exacerbated by the sermons and commentaries of later church fathers. What some label anti-Jewish polemic in the NT, others label intra-Jewish polemic, since in the earliest period Christianity is not a fully established religion distinct from Judaism.

In the wake of the Holocaust, much reflection and debate has ensued about the relationship between theologically motivated Christian anti-Judaism and the racially motivated anti-Semitism that inspired Nazism. Some Christian theologians insisted that only the term

anti-Judaism was appropriate to describe Christianity's critique of Judaism while anti-Semitisim was the result of secularism, nationalism, and racism.

With greater historical and theological sophistication, however, the idea that Christian anti-Judaism was a wholly separate phenomenon from anti-Semitism lost credibility. There were too many lines of continuity and areas of overlap. Most historians and theologians now recognize that the long history of Christian anti-Jewish polemic fostered much of the hostility that made the Holocaust possible.

At the same time, there are significant differences between modern anti-Semitism and ancient Christian anti-Judaism. Nazism was not a Christian movement, and its brand of anti-Semitism was heavily influenced by pseudo-scientific theories of race that postdate the NT by centuries. Scholars of early Christianity often employ the term *anti-Judaism*, not to deny the ways in which NT texts contributed to anti-Semitism, but to maintain greater historical and sociological precision in describing the causes and motivations of anti-Jewish polemic. *See* ANTI-SEMITISM; HOLOCAUST AND BIBLICAL INTERPRETATION.

PAMELA EISENBAUM

ANTILEBANON an'tee-leb'uh-nuhn [Ἀντιλίβανον Antilibanon]. Parallel to the LEBANON range, the Anti-Lebanon mountains run north-south along the border between Lebanon and Syria, peaking to the south at Mount HERMON. In the Bible, only Judith mentions the range by name (Jdt 1:7).

ANTIMONY an'tuh-moh'nee [פוך pukh]. Antimony is the eyeliner of the ancient world, used for beautifying as well as protecting the eyes from the glare of the sun and from insects. The substance is made by pulverizing certain minerals (galena for black, malachite for green) into powder. In the Bible, it is a sign of wealth and luxury. Its use is implied in the translations of pukh as "paint" (2 Kgs 9:30; Jer 4:30). Jezebel puts it on defiantly to meet her murderers (2 Kgs 9:30). Jeremiah mentions it when he condemns the vanity of Jerusalem (4:30); Isaiah uses the term figuratively to describe Jerusalem's rebuilt walls (54:11; LXX anthrax, coal); and in 1 Chr 29:2 (LXX "precious stones" lithous poluteles), the cosmetic is listed with other items David has provided for the Temple. Job's third daughter receives the odd name Kerenhappuch, "horn of antimony" (קרן הפוך qeren happukh), perhaps because she is Job's newfound wealth, beauty, and happiness (42:14). *See* COSMETICS.

JENNIFER L. KOOSED

ANTINOMIAN, ANTINOMIANISM. The term *antinomianism* was coined by Martin Luther to name and refute Johann Agricola's view that allegedly repudiated the laws of the OT. The word derives from ἀντί anti plus νόμος nomos, even though antinomia in classical Greek simply meant conflict of laws or ambiguity in the law, not an ethos against the law. Antinomianism in Christian theology refers to a doctrine that states that, since grace is the sole foundation for salvation, the laws of the OT, ceremonial or moral, have no role or meaning for Christians. Paul's attitude toward the Torah is notoriously ambiguous, and the negative side of this ambiguity seems to have engendered the antinomian tendency of Marcion and subsequent Gnostic sects, and as a result an anti-Jewish hermeneutic in Christianity, whereas the positive side of it, which is later echoed by Matthew, James, and Hebrews, has reserved room for a more holistic appreciation of Paul's incorporation of his Jewish heritage in current NT scholarship. Even though the antinomian controversy during the Reformation period ended with Agricola's recantation of his position, antinomianism continued to be advocated by the Anabaptists in England and Anne Hutchinson in Colonial America. In general, Christianity has rejected antinomianism because it is regarded as damaging the unity of the Bible.

EUNG CHUN PARK

ANTIOCH, AT JERUSALEM an′tee-ok [Ἀντιοχεία Antiocheia]. JASON offered to pay 440 talents of silver to ANTIOCHUS IV Epiphanes in exchange for the high priesthood and an additional 150 talents if Antiochus would allow him to build a gymnasium and "to enroll the people of Jerusalem as citizens of Antioch" (2 Macc 4:9). A popular interpretation of this is that Jerusalem's name was changed to Antioch, and the residents were called "ANTIOCHIANS."

Bibliography: Robert Doran. "The Second Book of Maccabees." *NIB* Vol. 4 (1996); Victor Tcherikover. *Hellenistic Civilization and the Jews* (1959).

GREGORY L. LINTON

ANTIOCH, PISIDIAN an′tee-ok [Ἀντιοχεία Antiocheia]. A Roman colony in northern Pisidia. It is located on one of the main Roman roads heading east-west from Ephesus and up the Maeander valley, and then from Antioch eastwards to Iconium and across the Taurus mountains to Tarsus and Cilicia. Pisidian Antioch was connected to the coastal cities of Pamphylia (such as Side) by a new Roman road. The remains of the colony are located at the modern town of Yalvaç.

The origin of the city probably lies in the Hellenistic period when it was established by Seleucus I Nicator (312–280 BCE). The purpose was probably strategic as the city served to protect the road eastwards. Studies of the design of the temple at the extra-mural sanctuary of the local deity Mên Askaenos shows architectural similarities with the temple of Artemis at Magnesia on the Maeander, the city from which the settlers were drawn.

With the establishment of the Roman colony of Galatia, the emperor Augustus established a Roman colony at Antioch. Prosopographical studies have shown that some of the colonists had their origins in Italy. Among the structures in the city was a temple in the Corinthian style which seems to have housed the imperial cult. A copy of the *Res Gestae* of the emperor Augustus was cut onto the monumental gateway or *propylon.*

A set of gladiatorial games and wild animal hunts were established in the colony, probably in the mid-1st cent. CE by the benefactor Maximianus. It is probably these games, known as the Maximianeia, which were re-established in the late 2nd cent. CE and associated with the extra-mural cult of Mên Askaenos. This local male deity, represented by the crescent moon, became associated with the Roman female deity Luna, the personification of the moon.

The Roman governor of Cyprus, Sergius Paullus (Acts 13:7), had family estates in the region of Pisidian Antioch. Paullus may have given the introduction to Paul—who significantly changes his name from Saul at this point—who later traveled to the colony (Acts 13:14). The epistle to the Galatians is likely to have been addressed to churches, including those established at Pisidian Antioch.

Bibliography: B. Levick. *Roman Colonies in Southern Asia Minor* (1967); S. Mitchell and M. Waelkens. *Pisidian Antioch: the Site and its Monuments* (1998); W. M. Ramsay. "Colonia Caesarea (Pisidian Antioch) in the Augustan Age." *JRS* 6 (1916) 83–134.

DAVID W. J. GILL

ANTIOCH, SYRIAN an′tee-ok, sihr′ee-uhn [Ἀντιόχεια Antiocheia]. Antioch was the name of at least sixteen cities in the Greco-Roman period, five of which were located in SYRIA. The NT mentions Antioch of Pisidia (Acts 13; *see* ANTIOCH, PISIDIAN) and Antioch of Syria (Acts 6; 11; 13–15; 18; Gal 2; 2 Tim 3). The latter is also known as the Syrian Antioch or Antioch on the Orontes. It was the third largest city in the Greco-Roman world behind Rome and Alexandria (Egypt). It was added to the territory of Turkey in 1938 and it is now known as Antakya (Hatay).

Syrian Antioch was founded by one of Alexander the Great's officers, SELEUCUS I Nicator (ca. 300 BCE), who established the Seleucid Empire and dynasty. He named the city for his father ANTIOCHUS and established it as the western capital of his empire. The city had an abundant supply of water from the Orontes River and the springs of the southern suburb, Daphne. Several Jewish mercenaries were rewarded with land grants in the city by the Seleucids during the Hellenistic period.

When the Seleucid power waned, Antioch was taken by Tigranes of Armenia in 83 BCE. Pompey the Great conquered the city and established Roman control in 64 BCE and gave it free city status. Antioch became the capital of the new Roman province called

Syria. It emerged as a cosmopolitan center of commerce and as a meeting point of eastern and western cultures. Julius Caesar, Augustus, and Tiberius refurbished the city with the help of Herod the Great, who used his support as a demonstration of his loyalty to Rome.

The city of Antioch is mentioned several times in the NT. The disciples chose seven men, including Stephen and Nicolas from Antioch, to serve the Hellenists (Greek Jews) (Acts 6:5). Some Christians fleeing persecution in Jerusalem, following the stoning of Stephen, traveled as far as Phoenicia, Cyprus, and Antioch. In Antioch some of these refugees preached only to the Jews while others, originally from Cyprus, and Cyrene, preached to Greek-speaking Gentiles as well (Acts 11:19-21). This activity resulted in many new converts. When news of this growth reached the Jerusalem leaders, they dispatched Barnabus to assess the situation (Acts 11:22). Finding things in good order, Barnabus then traveled to Tarsus and brought Paul, a native of that city, back to Antioch (Acts 11:25).

The name *Christian* was first used at Antioch to describe the followers of Christ. It is not clear if this name was invented by the Christians of Antioch for themselves, or was a pejorative term coined by an outside group, or was some type of designation assigned by government officials (Acts 11:26). Agabus and other prophets from Jerusalem traveled to Antioch and predicted a famine in the Roman Empire. The Christians of Antioch collected funds for Judean famine relief and sent them with Paul and Barnabus to Jerusalem (Acts 11:27-30; *see* COLLECTION).

Paul and Barnabus were set apart as missionaries by the leaders of the church in Antioch. Paul used Antioch as the headquarters for his three missionary journeys. Antioch, with its mixed population, became the focal point of disputes over circumcision. These arguments prompted a meeting of leaders in Jerusalem often called the Council of Jerusalem and resulted in a letter being sent by the leaders of Jerusalem to the church in Antioch (Acts 15; *see* JERUSALEM, COUNCIL OF).

Little of the ancient city remains visible today except for some of the Roman walls and aqueducts. Excavations during the 1930s unearthed some 300 fine mosaics dating to the 2nd cent. *See* ANTIOCHIANS.

Bibliography: Glanville Downey. *A History of Antioch in Syria: From Seleucus to the Arab Conquest* (1961); Christine Kondoleon, ed. *Antioch: The Lost Ancient City* (2000).

JOHN WINELAND

ANTIOCHIANS an´tee-ok´ee-uhns [Ἀντιοχεῖς Antiocheis]. Citizens of ANTIOCH. JASON obtained the high priesthood from ANTIOCHUS IV by offering to pay 440 talents of silver (2 Macc 4:7-9) and an additional 150 talents if Antiochus would allow him to build a gymnasium and "enroll the people of Jerusalem

as citizens of Antioch" (2 Macc 4:9, 19). The interpretation varies. First, Antiochus IV imitated the Romans by establishing a republic, granting Jason permission to draw up a citizenship list of Hellenized Jews in Jerusalem (Goldstein). Second, a Hellenistic corporation centered on the gymnasium was established in Jerusalem, granting Jason authority to compile a roster of members who would enjoy the privileges of citizenship (Bickerman). Third, Jerusalem was reconstituted as a Greek *polis* named Antioch, and Jason received authority to organize the *demos,* the body of citizens of the newly established city (Tcherikover).

Bibliography: Elias Bickerman. *The God of the Maccabees: Studies on the Meaning and Origin of the Maccabean Revolt* (1979); Robert Doran. "The Second Book of Maccabees." NIB 4 (1996) 181–200; Jonathan A. Goldstein. *II Maccabees.* AB 41A (1983); Victor Tcherikover. *Hellenistic Civilization and the Jews* (1959).

GREGORY L. LINTON

ANTIOCHIS an-ti´uh-kis [Ἀντιοχις Antiochis]. Concubine of ANTIOCHUS IV Epiphanes whose gift of the cities of Tarsus and Mallus to her led to their inhabitants' revolt (2 Macc 4:30).

ANTIOCHUS an-ti´uh-kuhs [Ἀντιοχος Antiochos]. Antiochus was a frequent name of emperors of the Seleucids. The Seleucid dynasty had begun with Seleucus I (ca. 312–281 BCE) who had been over Alexander's elite guard. Much of the 3rd cent. BCE was dominated by the so-called "Syrian wars" between the Ptolemaic and Seleucid empires over Coele-Syria, which Ptolemy I had seized in 302.

1. Antiochus I Soter (281–61 BCE)

The son of Seleucus I. He had difficulties in securing his throne (in the so-called Syrian War of Succession, ca. 280–79 BCE), and Ptolemy II seems to have taken advantage of his temporary weakness to extend his possessions. Antiochus's troubles continued in the Celtic invasion of 278–77 BCE, following which he defeated the Gauls decisively in the "elephant battle" sometime between 275 and 270 BCE. We know little about the First Syrian War (274–71 BCE), but it seems to have caused little change with regard to Seleucid and Ptolemaic territories.

2. Antiochus II Theos (261–46 BCE)

The son of Antiochus I and instigator of the Second Syrian War (ca. 260–53 BCE) in which territory was gained in Asia Minor. Ptolemy II made peace by giving his daughter Berenice Syra in marriage to Antiochus. Antiochus's son by his first wife Laodice was recognized in Asia Minor as Seleucus II (246–25 BCE); however, a son (name unknown) by his second wife, Berenice, was

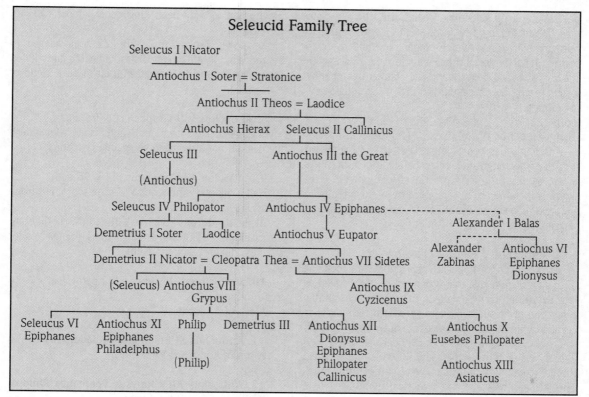

Seleucid Family Tree

Seleucus I Nicator

Antiochus I Soter = Stratonice

Antiochus II Theos = Laodice

Antiochus Hierax   Seleucus II Callinicus

Seleucus III   Antiochus III the Great

(Antiochus)

Seleucus IV Philopator   Antiochus IV Epiphanes - - - - - - - - - - - - - - - Alexander I Balas

Demetrius I Soter   Laodice   Antiochus V Eupator   Alexander Zabinas   Antiochus VI Epiphanes Dionysus

Demetrius II Nicator = Cleopatra Thea = Antiochus VII Sidetes

(Seleucus) Antiochus VIII Grypus   Antiochus IX Cyzicenus

Seleucus VI Epiphanes   Antiochus XI Epiphanes Philadelphus   Philip   Demetrius III   Antiochus XII Dionysus Epiphanes Philopater Callinicus   Antiochus X Eusebes Philopater

(Philip)   Antiochus XIII Asiaticus

accepted as the new ruler elsewhere, as well as being supported by the new Egyptian king Ptolemy III. This was the cause of the Third Syrian War or Laodicean War (246–241 BCE), from which the Ptolemies regained various territories.

Seleucus II's claim to the throne was now recognized in Babylon, but he left western Asia Minor under his brother Antiochus Hierax (ca. 246–26 BCE). Unfortunately, Hierax moved from coruler to rival: after a quarrel with his brother, he proclaimed himself king over the Seleucid realms. Thus, the conclusion of the Third Syrian War was the beginning of the so-called War of the Brothers (ca. 241–36 BCE) between Hierax and Seleucus II. Peace was eventually concluded between them (before 236 BCE), which allowed Antiochus Hierex to retain control over his territory. After further squabbles Hierax was murdered in 226 BCE; however, Seleucus II died not long afterward. Seleucus III (226/5–23 BCE) who succeeded to the throne wished to reassert Seleucid rule over Asia Minor but was killed in a campaign against Pergamum.

3. Antiochus III (223–187 BCE) the Great

The younger brother of Seleucus III became the new king, later known as Antiochus the Great. He set out to take Coele-Syria in what became known as the Fourth Syrian War (221–17 BCE) against the new Egyptian king Ptolemy IV Euergetes. From 220–18 BCE the Seleucid armies pushed continually southward, delayed mainly by various diplomatic maneuvers on the part of the Egyptians. Ptolemy used this period to assemble and train a large force. The decisive battle came in 217 BCE at Raphia in Palestine, at which Antiochus was defeated and forced to vacate his gains in Coele-Syria. The next fifteen years were marked by activities on the part of Antiochus to consolidate his empire in the west. Ptolemy IV died in 204 BCE, succeeded by Ptolemy V Epiphanes. Antiochus III saw his chance and initiated the Fifth Syrian War (202–200 BCE). In spite of clever generalship on the part of Scipio the Egyptian commander, the Ptolemaic cause was lost at the battle of Paneion in 200 BCE. Coele-Syria was now in Seleucid hands after a century of effort. Following one hundred years of Ptolemaic control, Judea had new rulers, and the immediate result seemed favorable. In gratitude for help received from the Jews in his taking Jerusalem, Antiochus issued a decree granting temporary relief from taxes (Josephus, *Ant.* 12.138-46). Antiochus III continued his expansion in Asia Minor and Thrace, however, this brought him into conflict with Rome who now had a major interest in the Greek East in the wake of the Second Punic War. Antiochus was defeated at Magnesia about 190 by the Romans; the terms of the treaty included not only a boundary of his kingdom at the Taurus mountains but also very stiff war reparations. To meet this expense, Antiochus took to raiding and robbing temples; it was in the course of an attack on the temple at Elymais that he was killed in 187 BCE.

Antiochus III's reign marks a transition in preoccupation for the Seleucids. Whereas the 3rd cent. had been focused on regaining Coele-Syria, the 2nd cent. was dominated by two concerns: 1) with trying to outmaneuver Rome, which came more and more to restrict the activities of the Seleucid rulers, and 2) with the rise of a rival dynasty and the resultant competion against each other for control of the weakening Seleucid empire.

4. Antiochus IV Epiphanes (175–64 BCE)

Antiochus III's son Seleucus IV (187–75 BCE) had a rather undistinguished reign before the throne was taken by his brother Antiochus IV Epiphanes. This figure is infamous in history, because of his attempt to suppress Judaism in Judah, and features prominently in Jewish literature.

5. Antiochus V Eupator (164–62 BCE)

At the death of Epiphanes his minor son took the throne for a short rule that was more or less dictated by regents. Antiochus was plotted against by his cousin, the eldest son of Seleucus IV, who murdered him and succeeded to the throne as Demetrius I Soter (162–50 BCE).

It was during the next couple of decades that a new dynasty claimed to be the rightful heir to the Seleucid Empire (some of whose rulers were named Antiochus). The struggle between the two rival dynasties was a godsend to the struggling Maccabean rulership who used it to establish an independent Jewish state. The first rival claimant was ALEXANDER BALAS (150–45 BCE). Both he and Demetrius wooed JONATHAN THE MACCABEE with concessions. After Demetrius I's death, his son attempted to retake his father's territory as Demetrius II (145–40, 129–26 BCE). Tryphon, a general of Alexander Balas, crowned Alexander's young son as Antiochus VI.

6. Antiochus VI. Epiphanes Dionysus (145–42 BCE)

A rival to Demetrius II. In the resulting engagement Demetrius was defeated, and Jonathan Maccabee was able to make gains by throwing his lot in with Antiochus VI. But in 143 Trypho captured and killed both Jonathan and Antiochus VI, taking the throne for himself (ca. 142–38 BCE). Demetrius II marched east in hopes of gaining assistance against Tryphon, but was taken prisoner by the Parthians.

7. Antiochus VII Sidetes (138–29 BCE)

Demetrius's wife Cleopatra sent for his brother to marry her and take the throne as Antiochus VII Sidetes. He attempted to bring Judah, now under the rule of Simon Maccabee, back under Seleucid control, but was defeated by Simon's sons. Some years later he besieged the Jewish ruler John Hyrcanus in Jerusalem in a dispute over Palestinian cities such as Joppa that Simon had taken from the Syrians, but agreement was finally reached. Antiochus VII was killed fighting for the Parthians and succeeded by his brother Demetrius

II who had already been king once before (145–40, 129–126 BCE).

Alexander Zabinas (ca. 128–122 BCE), alleged to be the son of Alexander Balas, defeated and killed Demetrius II, but he showed himself to be a friend of Hyrcanus I.

8. Antiochus VIII Grypus (126–96 BCE)

Succeeded Demetrius and soon ended Alexander's life. He did not attempt to go against Hyrcanus

9. Antiochus IX Cyzicenus (113–95 BCE)

Half-brother of Antiochus VIII who took the throne as a rival.

At the deaths of Antiochus VIII and IX, six different claimants for the throne fought among themselves for the next dozen years, including:

10. Antiochus X Eusebes Philopator (ca. 87–84 BCE)

A son of Antiochus IX.

11. Antiochus XI Epiphanes Philadelphus

A son of Antiochus VIII.

12. Antiochus XII Dionysus Epiphanes Philopator Callinicus (ca. 87–84 BCE)

During the reign of ALEXANDER JANNEUS (ca. 86 BCE) Judah was invaded by the army of yet another rival, a son of Antiochus XI. His aim, however, seems to have been only to march through to fight against Arabia. For a period of time (83–69 BCE), Tigranes, king of Armenia, took over Syria and ruled it until he was defeated by the Romans.

13. Antiochus XIII Asiaticus (ca. 65–64 BCE)

Placed briefly on the throne by the Romans but then removed by Pompey. Asiaticus was the last ruler over the Seleucid kingdom, which now came to an end, though it had been an empire in name only for many years. *See* DEMETRIUS; EPIPHANES; HASMONEANS; HYRCANUS I; JANNEUS (ALEXANDER); JONATHAN MACCABEUS; LYSIAS; MACCABEAN REVOLT; PTOLEMY; SELEUCID EMPIRE; SELEUCUS; SIMON MACCABEUS.

Bibliography: Lester L. Grabbe. *Judaism from Cyrus to Hadrian: Vol. I: Persian and Greek Periods*; *Vol. II: Roman Period* (1992); Susan Sherwin-White and Amélie Kuhrt. *From Samarkhand to Sardis: A New Approach to the Seleucid Empire* (1993).

LESTER L. GRABBE

ANTIPAS an′tee-puhs [Ἀντίπας *Antipas*] Abbreviation of Ἀντίπατρος *Antipatros*, Antipater. **1.** The second son of Herod I and Malthace, Antipas inherited Galilee and Perea on his father's death in 4 BCE. Luke 3:1 and

Matt 14:1 correctly identify him as "tetrach," though Mark 6:14-29 refers to him more loosely as "King." The NT calls him by his family name, "Herod."

Antipas divorced the daughter of Aretas IV of Nabataea in favor of his brother's wife, Herodias. Josephus maintains that his subsequent defeat in battle was popularly attributed to divine retribution for the death of John the Baptist whom Antipas had executed as a subversive (*Ant.* 18.116–120). Mark 6:14-28 and Matt 14:3-12 suggest that the dispute was over his marriage (which was unlawful, Lev 18:16), though the two accounts are not necessarily incompatible. Jesus grew up in Antipas' territory, but apart from Luke 13:31 seems to have avoided conflict. Luke 23:6-12 alone maintains that Jesus was tried before Antipas, though the historicity of this scene is questionable. Antipas was banished to Gaul in 39 CE.

2. *Herod's Father. See* ANTIPATER.

3. A martyr of the church at Pergamum, Rev 2:13.

Bibliography: H. W. Hoehner. *Herod Antipas* (1972).

HELEN K. BOND

ANTIPATER an-tip´uh-tuhr [Ἀντίπατρος Antipatros]. (ca. 100–43 BCE) 1. Father of Herod the Great. Antipater was descended from a wealthy and noble Idumean family that may have become Jewish under the forcible Judaization implemented by John Hyrcanus. Antipater's father, also named Antipater, was appointed stratēgos (governor) of Idumea by Alexander Jannaeus, and the younger Antipater appears to have succeeded him in this position at Marisa. Antipater's wife, Cyprus, was of noble, possibly royal, Nabatean lineage, and with her he had four sons and one daughter: Phasael, Herod, Joseph, Pheroras, and Salome.

Antipater played a pivotal role in the dynastic conflict between the Hasmonean brothers Hyrcanus and Aristobulus, the two sons of Alexander Jannaeus and Alexandra Salome. Antipater expanded his own sphere of influence by siding with the elder—and weaker—Hyrcanus, who had been compelled to cede his royal and high priestly rule to his more ambitious brother. Antipater agitated and intrigued on behalf of Hyrcanus, claiming that Aristobulus had usurped the lawful throne. He persuaded the Nabatean king Aretas III to enter the conflict, and helped orchestrate the defeat of Aristobulus and the return of Hyrcanus as both king and high priest. When Aristobulus retaliated, the Roman general Pompey intervened, besieging Aristobulus in Jerusalem. After capturing the city in 63 BCE, Pompey made Palestine tributary to Rome and confirmed Hyrcanus as the people's high priest. Thereafter, Antipater and Hyrcanus consistently upheld Roman interests and policies (as evidenced by the dismay expressed in *Pss. Sol.* 2, 8, 17). After Pompey's death in 48 BCE, Antipater became a staunch supporter of Julius Caesar, furnishing him with troops and aid, and even

fighting on his behalf. Caesar rewarded Antipater's devotion by appointing him as epitropos (procurator) of Judea in 47 BCE, and by making him a Roman citizen and exempting him from taxes. Despite ongoing Jewish resentment at his pro-Roman sympathies and Gentile heritage, Antipater managed to consolidate his power with ever increasing success. By nominating both Phasael and Herod as stratēgoi (governors) over Jerusalem and Galilee, respectively, he passed this legacy on to his sons. So, when in 43 BCE Antipater was poisoned by a jealous Jewish noble, Malichus, he left the way clear for his descendants to dominate Jewish politics for the next century.

Antipater had a genius for politics: he was courageous, opportunistic, and adept at reading prevailing political currents. He shrewdly played on his wealth, power, and influence to make himself a power broker, with the surprising result that he was actually able to displace the hereditary Hasmonean kings and install his own "half-caste" Idumean family in their stead.

Josephus's writings are our chief source for Antipater's life (*J.W.* 1.123-228; *Ant.* 14.8-284), but Eusebius and other Christian sources provide supplementary—if often unreliable—information.

2. One of two envoys sent by JONATHAN, then by SIMON MACCABEUS, to consolidate diplomatic ties with the Romans and Spartans (1 Macc 12:16; 14:22; Josephus, *Ant.* 13.169), Antipater may have belonged to an ambassadorial family (*see* 1 Macc 8:17).

Bibliography: Nikos Kokkinos. *The Herodian Dynasty: Origins, Role in Society and Eclipse.* JSPSup 30 (1998); Peter Richardson. *Herod: King of the Jews and Friend of the Romans* (1996); M. J. Smallwood. *The Jews Under Roman Rule* (1981).

J. R. C. COUSLAND

ANTIPATRIS an-tip´uh-tris [Ἀντιπατρίς Antipatris]. Located at the source of the YARKON RIVER, approximately 12 km (7.5 mi.) east of Tel Aviv, HEROD the Great enlarged and changed the name of the ancient city of APHEK to Antipatris to honor his father, ANTIPATER, in 9 BCE.

Although surrounded by rich agricultural land, the city had long been a fortified border town. The Zenon Papyri (259 BCE) mention it (as *Pegae*) as a guard post, and ALEXANDER JANNAEUS (103–76 BCE) fortified it with a moat (Josephus, *Ant.* 13.390; *J.W.* 1.99).

Archaeologists have identified the main street of Antipatris. Eight m wide, it had elevated sidewalks and was lined with shops. Herod built a new fortress on the acropolis. During the revolts that broke out at Herod's death in 4 BCE, rebels burned the city (Josephus, *J.W.* 2.513).

Antipatris was rebuilt, and the Romans used it as a military post. When they moved Paul from Jerusalem to CAESAREA, they stopped in Antipatris (Acts 23:31).

After surviving the Jewish Revolt (66–70 CE) with only minor damage, Antipatris grew to cover the entire thirty acre tell during the 3rd cent. CE. Inhabitants built large houses and decorated them with mosaics and also started building a small theater (*odeon*). The large earthquake of 363 CE destroyed the unfinished theater and leveled the town.

The city continued to be inhabited until the Ottoman period (remains of the Ottoman fortress built from 1572–74 are still visible), although mainly as a military post.

ADAM L. PORTER

ANTIPHRASIS. The use of a word or phrase to convey the opposite of its usual meaning. The quintessential biblical example is when Job's wife instructs, "Bless God and die!" (Job 2:9). Nearly all modern translations supply the word *curse* rather than the original Hebrew *bless*. See EUPHEMISM.

ANTI-SEMITISM. There are texts in the Christian canon that express hostility toward Jews and seemingly denigrate Judaism, sometimes severely. These texts have, at times, been interpreted by Christians in such a way as to promote anti-Semitism. Whether or not the term *anti-Semitism* should be used in regard to biblical literature is debatable. Because the term was not coined until the late 19th cent. in Germany and has racial connotations that do not necessarily apply to antiquity, most contemporary biblical scholars prefer to use the term ANTI-JUDAISM to describe texts that demean Jews or Judaism. At the same time, anti-Semitism is commonly used today to denote any antipathy toward Jews as Jews. Taken in this sense, there can be no doubt that biblical texts have been used to foster anti-Semitism, even if the biblical texts themselves cannot be properly labeled anti-Semitic.

The Gospels and Paul have been most influential in the promotion of Christian anti-Semitism. Because of the antagonistic role played by Jews in the story of Jesus' death, gospel texts were instrumental in the formulation of negative images of Jews. In all four Gospels, both Roman and Jewish authorities play a role in the crucifixion of Jesus. Over time the role of the Romans became insignificant while the role played by Jews became theologically critical (*see* PASSION NARRATIVES). The involvement of Jews in the death of Jesus ultimately coalesced into the charge of deicide, the notion that all Jews, past, present, and future, bear collective responsibility for killing Christ. The Passion play—an Easter liturgical tradition popular in the medieval period in which the story of Jesus' passion was dramatized—tended to emphasize the calumny of the Jews in the execution of Jesus, popularizing the portrayal of Jews as "Christ-killers." Certain passages from the Gospels became widely known proof-texts for illustrating Jewish culpability for the death of Jesus, such as "His blood be on us and on our children" (Matt 27:25).

The image of Jews as Christ-killers meant that Jews were not merely people who rejected Jesus; they rejected God and, as a result, God had rejected them. The mutual enmity between God and Jews consequently led to the perception that Jews were the agents and allies of Satan. Jesus appears to confirm this perspective in the Gospel of John when he says to his Jewish audience: "If God were your Father, you would love me, for I proceeded and came forth from God . . . . Why do you not understand what I say? It is because you cannot bear to hear my word. You are of your father the devil, and your will is to do your father's desires . . . . He who is of God hears the words of God; the reason why you do not hear them is that you are not of God" (John 8:42-47).

Certain passages in Paul's letters were also used to demonstrate that Jews were despised by God. In Gal 3:10, e.g., Paul says "all those who rely on works of the law are under a curse." Traditionally "those who rely on works of the law" was understood to refer to Jews. Here and elsewhere Paul was taken to mean that the giving of the Torah to Israel was a form of divine punishment—the result of the intractable obduracy of the Jews. Moreover, the image of Paul that developed in church tradition contributed to reading Paul's letters as anti-Jewish. Paul was understood to have converted from Judaism to Christianity, and his letters were perceived to reflect that experience. Paul's ostensibly negative statements about law were collectively taken as a wholesale rejection of Torah-centered Judaism in favor of Christ-centered Christianity. Paul's letters thus enabled the development of a Christian theology of Judaism, in which Judaism was portrayed as the antithesis of Christianity, the former being a legalistic religion of "works-righteousness," the latter a grace-filled religion of faith.

While passages from the NT have been most frequently utilized in the denigration of Judaism, OT passages have been similarly utilized. The ancient Israelite tradition of self-critique produced texts in which Israel acknowledges her guilt before God and God holds Israel to account, sometimes severely (e.g., Pss 50:12-23; 95:6-11; Hos 4:1–10:15; Isa 65:1-16). In a Christian context, historically removed from the world of ancient Israel, this rhetoric of self-critique was lost. Judgment oracles and other texts that describe divine retribution were instead read as condemnations of Jews, while promises and blessings were understood to pertain to Christians.

Post-Holocaust reflection of the late 20th cent. has led scholars to a new level of awareness about the problem of anti-Semitism and the NT. Biblical scholars have tried to distinguish between the biblical text itself and Christian interpretive tradition in an effort to show that many texts used to foster anti-Semitism have different and even positive interpretive possibilities, once the complexities of the historical context are taken into account. See ANTI-JUDAISM.

Bibliography: Paula Fredriksen and Adele Reinhartz. *Jesus, Judaism, and Christian Anti-Judaism: Reading the New Testament after the Holocaust* (2002); John Gager. *The Origins of Anti-Semitism: Attitudes Toward Judaism in Pagan and Christian Antiquity* (1985); Gavin I. Langmuir. *Toward a Definition of Antisemitism* (1990); Tod Linafelt. *A Shadow of Glory: Reading the New Testament after the Holocaust* (2002); Rosemary Radford Reuther. *Faith and Fratricide: The Theological Roots of Anti-Semitism* (1974); Marcel Simon. *Verus Israel: A Study of the Relations Between Christians and Jews in the Roman Empire* (135–425) (1985).

PAMELA EISENBAUM

ANTITHESIS. 1. A stylized balancing of two opposing ideas (Eccl 10:2; "The heart of the wise inclines to the right, but the heart of a fool to the left").

2. A rhetorical strategy for showing continuity and discontinuity by removing one word or phrase and substituting another (e.g., Gen 1:1 LXX ἐν ἀρχῇ ἐποίησεν ὁ θεός [en archē epoiēsen ho theos] becomes in John 1:1 ἐν ἀρχῇ ἦν ὁ λόγος [en archē ēn ho logos]).

3. The heuristic notion by which the Tübingen School of scholarship identified Paul's role in early Christianity.

L. GREGORY BLOOMQUIST

ANTONIA, FORTRESS an'toh'nee-uh [Ἀντονία Antonia]. Herod the Great built the Antonia at the northeast terminus of Jerusalem's Second Wall and named it for his patron Mark Antony. A short north-south wall tied it to the north wall of the Temple complex, but later the northern expansion of the Temple plaza put the Antonia on the northwest corner of the Temple fortifications. On that location a fortified structure had stood, previously called the Baris (Βάρις **Baris**, "large house" or "fortress," perhaps related to בִּירָה **birah** "fortress" or "citadel") probably erected by John Hyrcanus (134–104 BCE). Josephus tells us little about the use of the Baris except that it was the location of Aristobulus' (104–103 BCE) wrongful killing of his brother Antigonus and later served as a prison for Aristobulus's wife and sons (Josephus, *J.W.* 1.75, 118).

Although we have little information about the Baris, we have detailed descriptions of the Antonia from Josephus. The Antonia stood on a 50-cubit-high escarpment at the juncture of the Temple's northern and western stoa. The structure then rose another 40 cubits above its foundation. Smooth stones fastened to the escarpment produced both a pleasing effect and a defensive glacis that made attack from Bezetha, north of the structure, virtually impossible. Within the Antonia there were many different spaces, including baths, barracks, and courtyards, as though several cities had joined together in a single structure, and Josephus writes that it was like a royal palace. Each

corner of the building except the southeastern had a 50-cubit-high tower. The southeastern tower was 70 cubits high and provided an unrestricted view of the whole Temple complex to the soldiers stationed on the high tower. At the juncture of the northern and western stoa there were staircases leading to the Temple precincts in case the soldier had to make a hasty incursion to quell a disturbance (Josephus, *J.W.* 5.238–45).

Herod established the Antonia as his first major building project after taking control of the city in 37 BCE. After Antony's defeat at Actium in 31 CE, the Antonia remained the only structure in the empire that survived under Antony's name. Besides its defensive function, Josephus mentions that the Antonia served as a storage place for the high priestly vestments as its predecessor, the Baris, had previously served (Josephus, *Ant.* 15.377–491).

Tacitus describes the challenges Titus would have faced if he had attacked Jerusalem from the north (*Hist.* 5.11). He describes an outer wall, either a wall that ran approximately along the line of the present Old City wall or the wall that lies some 450 m north. The defenders of the city had ingeniously provided this wall with sharp curves and oblique angles that would make it possible for defenders to rain missiles from the flank on fighters scaling the wall. If attackers survived these defenses, they would still have to contend with additional walls behind them that surrounded the royal palace and rose to a great height, at the pinnacle of which stood the Tower Antonia. In point of fact, however, Titus did not attack from the north but from the west at the Tower of Hippicus. When he assaulted the Temple in 70 CE, he ordered his soldiers to raze the Antonia so that his troops could pour through the breech onto the Temple plaza (Josephus, *J.W.* 6.93).

The large paving stones in the basement of the Sisters of Zion Convent and the Convent of the Flagellation are often represented as the court of the Antonia and, possibly, the pavement where Jesus stood before Pilate according to John 19:13. These paving stones, however, belong to a later forum in Hadrian's Aelia Capitolina. The actual site of the Antonia probably lies somewhere beneath these stones. *See* GABBATHA; HADRIAN; JERUSALEM, WALLS OF; PRAETORIUM.

Bibliography: P. Benoit. "The Archaeological Reconstruction of the Antonia Fortress." Y. Yadin, ed., *Jerusalem Revealed* (1975) 87–89; Emmett Willard Hamrick. "The Northern Barrier Wall in Site T." *Excavations in Jerusalem 1961–1967.* Vol. 1. A. J. Tushingham, ed. (1985) 215–32; Duane W. Roller. *The Building Program of Herod the Great* (1998); C. J. Wightman. *The Walls of Jerusalem: From the Canaanites to the Mamluks* (1994).

FRED L. HORTON

ANTONY, MARK. See MARK ANTONY.

ANUB [עָנוּב ʿanuv]. In Judah's genealogy, he is Koz's son (1 Chr 4:8).

ANVIL [פַּעַם paʿam]. An instrument beaten upon with a hammer. The context provided in Isa 41:7 suggests that striking this instrument is related to smoothing with a hammer, so that working with this instrument represents the collaborative efforts of making idols.

ANXIETY [דְּאַג daʾegh, דְּאָגָה deʾaghah, כָּעַס kaʿas, עָצַב ʿatsav, חָרַד kharadh; μεριμνάω merimnaō, μέριμνα merimna, προμεριμνάω promerimnao, φροντίζω phrontizō, φρονέω phroneō]. Anxiety is distress or unease regarding present or impending ill. Although such unease is an inevitable element of human experience (Sir 40:1-2), biblical texts sometimes attempt to counteract it, at least when its object is economic or everyday life. Passages in both Testaments affirm that God's anxious care for human beings renders their anxious care for themselves redundant. Some texts further regard fretful worry as problematic because it is perceived as arising from a lack of trust in God or as diminishing such trust.

A. Terminology

The customary verb for "to worry" or "to be anxious" is daʾegh (1 Sam 9:5; 10:2; Jer 17:8; 42:6; Ps 38:19). Verbs with similar meaning include khaʿas, "to be vexed" (Ps 112:10; Eccl 7:9; Neh 3:33) and ʿatsav, "to be (deeply) worried" (1 Sam 20:3, 34; 2 Sam 19:3); and karadh, which usually means "tremble," means "to worry" in 2 Kgs 4:13. Deʾaghah is the most common noun for "anxiety" or "concern" (Prov 12:25; Jer 49:23; Ezek 4:16; 12:18-19; Sir 30:24; 34:1).

The most important NT word is the verb merimnaō, which means either "to be apprehensive" or "(unduly) concerned" (as five times in Matt 6:25-34) or, more positively, "to be anxious about" (1 Cor 7:32; Phil 2:20). The cognate noun, merimna, means "anxiety" or "worry" (Mark 13:22; Luke 21:34; 2 Cor 11:28; 1 Pet 5:7), the related ἀμέριμνος (amerimnos) "lack of concern" (Matt 28:14; 1 Cor 7:32). Promerimnaō indicates "worry beforehand" (Mark 13:11). Sometimes the verbs phrontizo and phroneo express unselfish concern or anxiety for others (Phil 4:10; Titus 3:8).

B. Anxiety in the OT

The Bible nowhere disparages the anxiety that inevitably arises from sincere concern for others (1 Sam 9:5; 10:2; 2 Kgs 4:13; 1 Esd 8:71; 2 Esd 3:3; Add Esth 14:1; 2 Macc 3:21). Nor does it criticize Hannah for her anxious desire to have a son (1 Sam 1:16). Her legitimate wish is in fact granted. Scripture further assumes that anxiety over one's sin is the appropriate response when it fosters repentance (Ps 51). Yet the OT knows that anxiety can be crippling because it can weigh down the human heart (Prov 12:25; Sir 30:24; 31:1-2).

Psalm 127 offers a brief theological critique of anxiety. Those who eat "the bread of anxious toil" are those who engage in restless activity for their own advantage. But they do not obtain what they seek, for human enterprise is vain without God's blessing. "Unless the Lord builds the house, those who build it labor in vain" (127:1). Anxious toil is futility unless it is has God's blessing.

A similar line of thought is implicit in Jer 17:7-8. "Those who trust in the Lord" are blessed because they are like a tree planted beside the water, a tree that sends its roots out into a stream, so that the heat does not trouble it, and its leaves stay green; and "in the year of drought it is not anxious." People who wisely trust in God will find that God meets the needs that have occasioned their anxiety. Such individuals are the counterparts of "those who trust in mere mortals and make mere flesh their strength," and who are thus like a shrub in the desert that never sees relief from its parched condition (17:5-6). It follows that anxiety will accompany those who trust human beings, and that those who instead trust God can find freedom from worry.

C. Anxiety in the NT

The NT elaborates this thought, above all in Matt 6:25-34 and Luke 12:22-31, which offer extended theological reflection on anxiety. Both passages open with an imperative not to worry about food and clothing. Several supporting arguments follow.

1) Food and clothing are not the most important things (Matt 6:25; Luke 12:23).
2) If God takes care of birds and lilies, surely God will all the more look after human beings (Matt 6:26, 28-30; Luke 12:24, 27-28).
3) Anxiety accomplishes nothing useful (Matt 6:27; Luke 12:25).
4) Worry about food and clothing characterizes pagans (Matt 6:32; Luke 12:30).
5) God knows what people need (Matt 6:32; Luke 12:30).
6) If one first seeks God's kingdom, Providence will ensure that one's true needs are met.

In its Matthean context, the section follows the exhortation to gather treasure not on earth but in heaven (Matt 6:19-21), the parable about the good and bad eye (6:22-23; this is about being generous; compare 20:15), and the parable of the two masters (6:24). All three logia have to do with one's disposition toward material possessions. Matthew 6:25-34 follows as encouragement. Serving God at the expense of money will create fretfulness about what one will eat, drink, and wear. Jesus, however, assures listeners that the heavenly Father cares for them, so they can lay aside anxiety. "Do not worry" means, in effect, "You need not worry." The conclusion in v. 34 (unique to Matthew) is an old proverb that worrying about tomorrow is foolish, for "tomorrow will bring worries of its own. Today's trouble is enough for today." This is not pessimism or Stoicism but recognition that with God one can be content with what is to hand, and that anxiety for tomorrow is needless because the compassionate God is Lord of the future.

Luke's handling of the material on care makes it less encouragement than warning. Luke 12:22-31 trails the parable of the rich fool who built larger barns for his grain and goods, only to die unexpectedly (12:13-21). It is in turn followed by a series of admonitions to store up treasure in heaven (12:32-34) and to be like slaves who are ready when their master returns, not like the unfaithful servant who misbehaves in his master's absence and so is later punished (12:35-48). In its Lukan context, 12:22-31 is an admonition to free oneself from worldly concerns in the face of eschatological judgment. The warning is repeated in 21:34: "Be on guard so that your hearts are not weighed down with . . . the worries of this life, and that day catch you unexpectedly."

As to what Jesus himself intended in his original composition, our best guess is that he was addressing individuals who, like the birds and flowers, were not toiling, that is, not working for a living. Certainly his words, which can leave the impression that prudential planning and hard work are unimportant, do not sound like advice for normal existence, peasant or otherwise. They rather imply abandonment of day-to-day life. On this reading, Jesus was addressing not everyone but a select group of disciples who lived according to the difficult way of life outlined in the missionary discourses; see Matt 10:7-16; Mark 6:6-13; Luke 9:1-6; 10:3-12. One can well imagine him trying to lighten their inevitable anxiety about food, drink, and clothing, things for which they were to make no provision.

Other synoptic texts also speak about anxiety. The interpretation of the parable of the sower includes a class of people in whom the word fails to thrive because "the cares of the world, and the lure of wealth, and the desire for other things come in and choke the word, and it yields nothing" (Mark 4:19; compare Matt 13:22; Luke 8:14). Mark 13:11 informs readers that, although they will stand trial, they need not worry beforehand what to say, because the Holy Spirit will speak through them (compare Matt 10:19-20). Luke 10:41 rebukes Martha for being anxious and distracted over many things, clarifying that only one thing is needful, heeding Jesus. All of these texts line up well with Matt 6:25-33 = Luke 12:22-31: anxiety is a problem to be overcome, and it is overcome through trust in God's care.

Paul offers a similar teaching. Although the apostle is naturally anxious about the well being of others (2 Cor 11:28; Phil 2:28), he recognizes that anxiety for worldly affairs detracts from Christian service and so should be impeded (1 Cor 7:32-34). Furthermore, he believes that, in the last analysis, followers of Jesus have nothing much to be anxious about. While the apostle may sigh with anxiety because he longs to leave his earthly tent and put on his heavenly clothing (2 Cor 5:1-5), he also rejoices and enjoins others to do the same and to put aside all worry (Phil 4:6). Even in prison he is content because of his faith in God's presence and God's future in Jesus Christ (2 Cor 12:10; Phil 4:11-13; compare Heb 13:5). First Peter 5:7 catches the Pauline spirit when it instructs readers to cast their anxieties on God because God cares for them.

D. Anxiety and Eschatology

Wisdom herself, according to Wis 7:23, is free of anxiety. Perhaps this notion derives in part from the circumstance, evident to all, that, if one is wise, one recognizes that anxiety of itself accomplishes nothing and can even debilitate. But Wis 7:23 probably also reflects the theological conviction that God is good, and that if one is wise enough to trust God, one's needs will be met (Ps 127:1-2; Jer 17:5-8). The problem with this, however, is that it is all too often the case that the saints' needs are not met. Sometimes they suffer terribly (1 Cor 11:16-29), and sometimes, like Jesus, they are tortured and killed. Everything can go wrong. So experience seems to give the lie to the belief that trust in God will resolve worldly cares.

This is one reason the NT has an eschatological horizon. The sources of anxiety cannot be wholly eradicated if this world is the end of the story. From one point of view, then, texts such as Luke 6:20-23, which promise God's future to those deprived in the here and now, aim to offset anxiety by offering the hope that, if one's needs are not met in this world, they will be met in the world to come. This is especially evident in Matt 10:26-31 and Luke 12:2-7. Here the "Do not worry" of Matt 6:25 and Luke 12:22 gives way to the nearly synonymous, "Do not be afraid" (Matt 10:31; Luke 12:7), and the focus moves from the present to the eschatological future, when all will be revealed (Matt 10:26-27; Luke 12:2-3) and the divine judgment will fall (Matt 10:28; Luke 12:4-5). In these texts, earthly circumstances, not even the death of the body, should not instigate anxiety; only one's standing before God matters. In this way worldly concerns cease to trouble and faith can free itself from misplaced anxiety.

DALE C. ALLISON, JR.

ANY, INSTRUCTION OF. In this Egyptian early New Kingdom text, a father instructs a son in the traditional Egyptian values for life, counseling moderate behavior in all his son's actions (see COS I, 110-115; AEL II, 135-146; LAE[3], 434-437; or ANET[3], 420-421 [excerpts]). Although this text presents traditional themes known from earlier and contemporaneous instructional texts (sometimes, inappropriately, called wisdom texts), it is notable for its conclusion: a contentious son does not accept his father's instructions because it is paternal advice. Nevertheless, Any's last word notes that bread is what counts, implying that right behavior provides the needed resources.

SUSAN HOLLIS

APAME uh-pay'mee [Ἀπάμη Apamē]. Apame is a concubine in the court of the Persian king DARIUS, who, after ZERUBBABEL's discourse on the strength of women, removes Darius's crown from his head, places it on hers, and slaps the king in the face (1 Esd 4:29-31). While the text identifies her as the daughter of Bartacus, scholarship has not determined if she is a historical person. The name also appears in Achaemenid and Hellenistic contexts.

JOHN S. COOK

APE [קוֹף qof]. A foreign word possibly from the Sanskrit kapi, is usually translated as "ape." In Hebrew it is probably a loanword from the Egyptian gif. The term appears in the OT twice, once in 1 Kgs 10:22 and in 2 Chr 9:21, both times in the descriptions of King Solomon's maritime expeditions to faraway lands from where his ships brought ". . . gold and silver, ivory, apes (qofim) and PEACOCKS. See ANIMALS OF THE BIBLE.

ODED BOROWSKI

APELLES uh-pel'eez [Ἀπελλῆς apellēs]. Second cent. CE disciple of MARCION who lived and taught in Rome and Alexandria and later broke with his teacher, rejecting his DOCETISM and DUALISM, while maintaining his denigration of the OT and mutilation of the NT. Fragments of Apelles' *Syllogisms* on the falsity of the OT are preserved in Ambrose's *De paradiso*, and his teaching is summarized in Tertullian, *Praescr.* 30.5–7; Hippolytus, *Haer.* 7.31; and Eusebius, *Hist. eccl.* 5.13.

MARK DELCOGLIANO

APHAIREMA uh-fair'uh-muh [Ἀφαίρεμα (-έρ) Aphairema (-er)]. OT territory of Ephraim. In Hellenistic times, along with Lydda and Rathamin, one of three toparchies annexed to Judea from Samaria by Alexander the Great, but later returned to Samaria by Antiochus IV. While both Demetrius I (1 Macc 10:30, 38) and Demetrius II (1 Macc 11:34) promised their restoration, Antiochus VI ultimately confirmed the gift (1 Macc 11:57). The town of Aphairema corresponds to the modern Et Tayyiba.

J. R. C. COUSLAND

APHEK ay'fek [אֲפֵק 'afeq]. Aphek is mentioned several times in the Bible as the name of a place (Josh 12:18; 13:14; 19:30; 1 Sam 4:1; 29:1; 1 Kgs 20:26, 30; 2 Kgs 13:17) and refers to varying locations. The name *Aphek*

comes from the Hebrew word אָפִיק afiq, which means "river bed," and, therefore, the name was given to sites located along rivers or next to springs. A different translation for the word was suggested by Albright, who claimed that Aphek came from the Assyrian apēqu and means *fortress*.

Aphek of the Sharon plain (Josh 12:18; 1 Sam 4:1, 12) is about 30 acres and lies at the headwaters of the Yarkon River. The city name appeared for the first time in the Middle Bronze Age, and it is mentioned among the cities conquered by the pharaohs Thutmose III and Amenhotep II. The archaeological excavations revealed a city continuously inhabited from the Chalcolithic to the Ottoman periods. Archaeological remains from the Early Bronze Age point to a fortified city. The Middle Bronze Age city included palaces, and was destroyed by the Egyptians at the end of the period. During the Late Bronze Age more palaces were built, and one served as the Egyptian governor's residence (several cuneiform tablets were found there). In the 12th cent. BCE the site was settled, probably by fishermen. The Philistines came to Aphek in the 11th cent. BCE and in the 10th cent. BCE the site became part of the Israelite entity.

Other places with this name are Aphek of Asher (Josh 19:29-30), which a few scholars identify with Tel Kurdana, and others with Tel Kabri; Aphek of Aram (1 Kgs 20:26; 2 Kgs 13:17), which should be located in the Aramean territory close to the border with Israel; and Aphek in Lebanon (Josh 13:4), northeast of Beirut; and Aphekah in Judah (Josh 15:23), in the Hebron vicinity.

ITZHAQ SHAI

APHEKAH uh-fee'kuh [אֲפֵקָה 'afeqah]. A city in the allotment Joshua gave Judah (Josh 15:53), most likely identical with APHEK (Josh 12:18) and Aphik (Judg 1:31). The king of this royal Canaanite city was defeated by Joshua and the Israelites (Josh 12:7, 18).

APHERRA uh-fer'uh [Ἀφερρά Apherra]. One of several heads of families who were descendants of Solomon's servants who altogether numbered 372 (1 Esd 5:34).

APHIAH uh-fi'uh [אֲפִיחַ 'afiakh]. A Benjaminite ancestor of King Saul (1 Sam 9:1).

APHIK ay'fik [אֲפִיק 'afikh]. City in the tribe of ASHER whose Canaanite inhabitants were not driven out (Judg 1:31). Place of worship of Aphrodite.

APHORISM. A universal truth expressed in pithy form, a maxim, proverb, or adage (e.g., Eccl 9:4: "whoever is joined with all the living has hope, for a living dog is better than a dead lion") or a rhetorical technique used to challenge or correct a significant word's presumed meaning. For example, when Jesus is asked, "Teacher, what good deed must I do to have eternal life?" Jesus aphorizes concerning good (agathos): "Why do you ask me about what is good? There is only one who is good. If you wish to enter into life, keep the commandments" (Matt 19:16-17).

L. GREGORY BLOOMQUIST

APHRAH af'ruh. *See* BETH-LE-APHRAH.

APHRAHAT. An early father of the Syriac Church, also known as the "Persian Sage," Aphrahat lived in Mesopotamia during the Sasanian dynasty of the Iranian Empire. His twenty-three *Demonstrations* (337–344 CE) provide valuable insights into pre-Nicene, non-Roman Christology as well as early Christian encounters with Judaism.

APIRU. *See* HABIRU, HAPIRU.

APIS ay'pis [חַף khaf; Ἄπις Apis]. Only Jer 46:15 refers to this bull, where the NRSV, following the LXX, divides the Hebrew as מַדּוּעַ נָס חַף maduaʿ nas khaf ("Why has Apis fled?"), instead of מַדּוּעַ נִסְחַף maduaʿ niskhaf. which the KJV translates as "Why are [they] swept away?" In their capital, Memphis, the Egyptians worshiped this bull as a fertility god, from at least the beginning of the First Dynasty. Considered a manifestation of the god Ptah, the bull was later known as the incarnation of the god Osiris. According to Herodotus a cow gave birth to Apis when a flash of lightning from heaven descended upon the cow. *See* BAAL.

EMILY CHENEY

APOCALYPSE uh-pok'uh-lips' [ἀποκάλυψις apokalypsis]. The Greek term *apocalypse* means "revelation" or "disclosure," from καλύπτω kalypto, "to cover, hide." An *apocalypse* consists of visions, auditions, and dreams, whereby the divine world and its secrets are uncovered, revealed, or opened up to the seer. The term *apocalypse* is often used in connection with the revelation of God and divine secrets, whether of heaven or the future of the world, found, for example, in: *Testaments of the Twelve Patriarchs* (Reuben 3:15; Judah 16:4; Joseph 6:6; Levi 1:2; 18:2; Benjamin 10:5); *Joseph and Aseneth* (16:7; 22:9), and Theodotion's version of Daniel (2:19, 47; 10:1; 11:35).

The word *apocalypse* is found in Luke 2:32 (from Isa 42:6; 49:6), and is part of Paul's description of his conversion (Gal 1:12). It seems to have a distinct eschatological dimension (1 Cor 1:7 compare 2 Thess 1:7; 1 Pet 1:7 compare 1:13 and 4:13). An apocalypse could be experienced both by the apostle himself and by members of the church (2 Cor 12:2ff.; Gal 2:2; 1 Cor 14:23). While there are similarities between several Jewish and Christian works, the extent of the similarities should not be overestimated. Luther correctly noted the difference between Revelation and Daniel (and other OT visionary literature) in his 1530 *Preface to the Book of Revelation*: he said that Revelation is an apocalypse "without either words or interpretations, but only with images and figures."

The words "Apocalypse of Jesus Christ" open the book of Revelation. The word *apocalypse* is only used once in Revelation, but it is clear throughout the rest of the book that this work is prophecy—and so in terms of its contents (there are many allusions to Ezekiel, Daniel, and other prophetic books, with their symbolic language and future hope) and its status (22:18)—that John regards his words as of the same authority and character as those of the earlier prophets.

The earliest Christian extra-canonical apocalypse, the *Shepherd of Hermas*, originated in Rome in the middle of the 2nd cent. CE, and is a collection of exhortations that result from the visionary's instruction by an angelic intermediary. *See* APOCALYPTICISM.

Bibliography: John J. Collins. *The Apocalyptic Imagination* (1998); Christopher Rowland. *The Open Heaven: A Study of Apocalyptic in Judaism and Early Christianity* (1982, 2003).

CHRISTOPHER ROWLAND

APOCALYPSE, ANIMAL. *See* ENOCH, FIRST BOOK OF.

APOCALYPSE, LITTLE. Name for chapters within books that tell about end time events (Isa 24-27; Mark 13; Matt 24; and Luke 21). *See* ISAIAH, BOOK OF.

APOCALYPSE OF ABRAHAM. *See* ABRAHAM, APOCALYPSE OF.

APOCALYPSE OF ADAM. *See* ADAM, APOCALYPSE OF.

APOCALYPSE OF BARUCH. *See* BARUCH, SECOND BOOK OF; BARUCH, THIRD BOOK OF.

APOCALYPSE OF ELIJAH. *See* ELIJAH, APOCALYPSE OF.

APOCALYPSE OF ENOCH. *See* ENOCH, FIRST BOOK OF; ENOCH, SECOND BOOK OF; ENOCH, THIRD BOOK OF.

APOCALYPSE OF EZRA. *See* ESDRAS, SECOND BOOK OF.

APOCALYPSE OF JOHN. *See* REVELATION, BOOK OF.

APOCALYPSE OF MOSES. *See* ADAM AND EVE, LIFE OF.

APOCALYPSE OF PAUL. *See* PAUL, APOCALYPSE OF.

APOCALYPSE OF PETER. *See* PETER, APOCALYPSE OF.

APOCALYPSE OF WEEKS. The *Apocalypse of Weeks* consists of two sections (91:10-18; 93:1-10), now divided and in reverse order, within the *Epistle of Enoch* (*1 En.* 91–105). Manuscript evidence from Qumran reveals that these sections once circulated in the correct order.

The *Apocalypse* divides Israel's history into ten "weeks," from creation to the final judgment. Ordinary history ends in the 7th week, when a righteous minority emerges from an "apostate generation." This depiction probably reflects the period just prior to or contemporaneous with the Maccabean Revolt (167–164 BCE). *See* ENOCH, FIRST BOOK OF.

GREG CAREY

APOCALYPSE OF ZEPHANIAH. *See* ZEPHANIAH, APOCALYPSE OF.

APOCALYPTICISM. *Apocalypticism* derives from ἀποκάλυψις apokalypsis, the Greek for unveiling or revelation. In 19th cent. German biblical scholarship the word *apokalyptik* gained currency as a way of describing a cluster of religious ideas, some of which were found in revelatory texts like Daniel and Revelation. Such ideas gained an important place in the discussion of Jewish and Christian theology. As a result, apocalypticism is frequently seen as a form of ESCHATOLOGY, with well-defined characteristics: 1) hope for a better world, and with a belief that God's kingdom will break into history, which then leads to history's end; 2) dualism (contrast between the present evil age and a glorious future; exotic symbolism (e.g., Dan 7); 3) an eschatological expectation in which a dramatic transformation of this sinful age will lead to the inauguration of a heavenly kingdom; 4) the stark contrast between the present evil age and the glorious future suggesting a sectarian ethos, in which communities (such as the one that produced texts like the War Scroll, 1QM, had cut themselves off from wider society and awaited a divine reordering of the world); 5) the imminent end of this world; 6) a deterministic view of history. The influence of the contents of the book of Revelation is apparent in much of this understanding, esp. Rev 6; 19:11-17, 21-2).

   A. Apocalypticism: Distinct Movement or
      Component of Jewish Religion
     1. The origins of apocalypticism
     2. Apocalypticism, merkavah mysticism, and
       early rabbinic Judaism
     3. Early Christianity and apocalypticism
     4. The influence of apocalypticism in Christian
       history
   B. Types of Apocalypticism
   Bibliography

A. Apocalypticism: Distinct Movement or
   Component of Jewish Religion

During the 20th cent., apocalypticism in Judaism and early Christianity was regarded as one religious current among others. The evidence suggests, however, that apocalypticism was a strand of all forms of Jewish religion. Priests, Pharisees, Essenes, and others shared what one might term an apocalyptic outlook. It is an outlook found in different forms in other religions in antiquity, and it is characterised by "higher wisdom through revelation" (Hengel). Apocalypticism is the belief that access to the divine mysteries comes through the discernment of divine secrets by dream, vision or audition rather than through the traditional practices of religion or the application of exegetical methods. This important feature is found in those texts that are usually labeled with the title APOCALYPSE and applies to the two canonical examples of this kind of literature, the books of Daniel and Revelation, even if in both these works eschatological mysteries predominate (*see* DANIEL, BOOK OF; REVELATION; BOOK OF).

The different apocalypses cover a wide range of topics, ranging from 1) the heavenly works (Dan 7:9; *1 En.* 14:8, 71; *Apoc. Ab.* 18, *T. Levi* 2, *3 Bar.*; Rev 4; *Ascen. Isa.*), 2) astronomy (*1 En.* 72; *2 En.* 23), 3) the course of history (Dan 8; *1 En.* 85; 91:12, 93, *T. Levi* 16, 4 Ezra 11, *2 Bar* 35, 53; *Apoc. Ab.* 27), and 4) human destiny (*Apoc. Ab.* 20, 4 Ezra 3:4, 7; *2 Bar.* 48). In this material the apocalyptic seer is offered a revelation direct from God through vision or through divine emissary. The divine truth is revealed to the seer, who then passes it on to all those to whom the seer chooses to make known this knowledge. The reader of such visionary texts is enabled to see the totality of human history from the divine perspective, and according to some apocalypses, their hopes for the future are on the verge of being realized (Dan 12:6; *4 Ezra* 14:10; *2 Bar.* 85:20).

One common feature of these texts (and other Second Temple Jewish texts, apart from the book of Revelation) is their pseudonymity. Though written by unknown writers, they are attributed to biblical characters such as Enoch, Abraham, or Moses, all of whom were believed to have a close relationship with the heavenly world. Thus on the basis of the interpretation of Gen 5:24, Enoch was believed to have been taken up to heaven, and Abraham was given promises of the future at several points in the biblical account (e.g., Gen 15:12-21). Moses' ascent up the mountain came in Jewish tradition to be equated with a heavenly ascent. Pseudepigraphy had a long history in Judaism for the later prophetic oracles. For example, the later chapters of Isaiah were written by late writers and added to the Isaianic corpus. Expansion of a corpus was a very common literary convention in antiquity and may have served as a means of enhancing the authority of the revelations committed to writing. Whether the apocalypses are merely literary creations or include the records of actual experiences is a matter of debate.

1. The origins of apocalypticism

Significant difference of opinion persists about the origins of apocalypticism. The mythology of Canaanite religion, which was such a potent influence on early Jewish theology, left relics in apocalyptic mythology. Indeed, the alternative account of the origin of evil in *1 En.* 6–11, briefly alluded to in Gen 6:4, indicates a rich mythological world, which was the mythological backdrop too much OT theology. Non-Jewish backgrounds have been canvased, and there is an obvious similarity between the views of history and the dualistic outlook of Persian religion. The world of late antiquity generally was one characterized by the quest for divine wisdom, which came through dreams and other forms of revelation.

Two accounts of apocalyptic origins perceive it as primarily a belief system that developed within Judaism. The first account of this internal development suggests that apocalyptic is the successor to the prophetic movement, and particularly to the future of hope of the prophets. The concern with human history and the vindication of Israel's hopes is said to represent the formulation of the prophetic hope in the changed circumstances of another age. Those who take this line stress the close links with prophecy but also point out the subtle change that took place in the form of that hope in apocalyptic literature. In prophetic eschatology the future arises out of the present, whereas in the apocalyptic literature the future is said to break into the present.

There is evidence of a subtle change that has taken place in the form of hope in the apocalyptic literature as compared with most of the prophetic texts in the Bible. It is often suggested that the future hope was placed on another plane, the supernatural and other-worldly (e.g., Isa 65–66; compare Rev 21 and *4 Ezra* 7:50), near the beginning of the Christian era. Its stress from first to last is on the supernatural and otherworldly, just as in Rev 21 the seer looks forward to a new heaven and new earth with the old creation passing away.

Some doubt whether the apocalypses do offer evidence of the "otherworldly" eschatology. Nevertheless, it is widely held that there existed in Judaism two types of future hope: a national eschatology found principally in the rabbinic texts, and otherworldly eschatology found principally in the apocalypses. The evidence from the apocalypses themselves, however, indicates that such a dichotomy cannot be easily substantiated. Apart from a handful of passages that are always cited as examples of otherworldly eschatology, the doctrine of the future hope as it is found in the apocalypses seems to be remarkably consistent with the expectation found in other Jewish sources. More evident is the subtle change of prophetic genre in the later chapters of Ezekiel, with its visions of a New Jerusalem, the highly symbolic visions of early chapters of Zechariah, the cataclysmic upheavals of the last chapters of the same

book, and the probably late eschatological chapters of Isa 24–27 and Isa 55–66. Also important is the emergence of the apocalyptic heavenly ascent evident in passages such as *1 En.* 14. The journey into heaven has its antecedents in the call visions of Ezekiel (Ezek 1 and 10) and Isaiah (Isa 6), as well as the parallel glimpses of the heavenly court in 1 Kgs 22 and Job 1–2.

The second account proposed for the origin of apocalyptic emphasizes the links with the wisdom literature of the OT, with its interest in understanding the cosmos and the ways of the world. Apocalypticism is concerned with knowledge, not only of the age to come but also of things in heaven (e.g., *1 En.* 72) and the mysteries of human existence. These interests are similar to features of the wisdom literature. Some readers can make a case that the concern with the destiny of Israel, so evident in parts of certain apocalypses, is hardly to be found in works like Ecclesiastes and Ben Sirach, both of which seem to discourage the kinds of speculations we find in the apocalypses (*see* Sir 3:21). Yet the interpretation of dreams, oracles, astrology, and the ability to divine mysteries concerning future events were the activities of certain wise men in antiquity. There is some trace of the role of such figures in the OT, e.g., in the Joseph stories in Genesis and Daniel. But the most obvious apocalyptic moment in the wisdom corpus is the opening and dramatic climax of the book of Job. The latter enables Job's entirely reasonable stance to be transcended and for Job to move from understanding on the basis of hearsay to one based on apocalyptic insight (Job 42:11).

Spatial categories form an important part of apocalyptic thought. Such categories are presupposed by several NT writers and indeed form part of the argument of one or two documents. In Ephesians, for example, the author speaks of a heavenly dimension to the church's existence. By his use of the phrase "in the heavenly places," he links the church with the exalted Christ (2:6). In the letter to the Hebrews an important part of the argument concerns the belief (which is based on the superiority of Christ's sacrifice) that Christ's offering of himself enabled him to enter not the earthly shrine but heaven itself, into the very presence of God (9:11, 24). This framework of contrast between the world below and the world above facilitates the writer's presentation of the saving work of Christ. Christ the heavenly pioneer has entered into the inner shrine, behind the veil (6:20). He has entered not into a sanctuary made with hands, a copy of the true one, but into heaven itself, to appear in the presence of God on behalf of his people.

2. Apocalypticism, merkavah mysticism, and early rabbinic Judaism

Apocalypticism may well have been an important component of nascent rabbinic Judaism. We see from hints in the MISHNAH that apocalyptic interests already existed in the tannaitic period, in *M. Hag.* 2:1, and needed to be controlled. The restrictions mentioned in the Mishnah concerned a speculative meditation on Gen 1 and Ezek 1, which might lead the expositor to visionary insight into the divine, akin to that enjoyed by Ezekiel (and earlier Isaiah). Such passages offered the exegete a glimpse into the heavenly world. Later Jewish texts indicate that cosmogony and theosophy played a very significant part in rabbinic theology (e.g., *b. Hag.* 12*a*). It is not always easy to reconstruct the history of Jewish mysticism from its obscure beginnings during the period of the Second Temple and into the *hekaloth* texts (which speak of the mystic's ascent through the heavenly palaces). In the rabbinic corpus we find that names of major teachers such as R. Yohanan ben Zakkai (*b. Hag.* 14*b*) and R. Akiba (e.g., in *b. Hag.* 14*b*–15*b*) are linked with apocalyptic, visionary activity. The scarcity of information about the nature of the mystical involvement does not allow us to reconstruct with any degree of certainty the character of this mystical interest. *See* MERKAVAH MYSTICISM.

3. Early Christianity and apocalypticism

In early Christianity, apart from the book of Revelation itself, visionary insight played an important part (Mark 1.10; Acts 10–11). Paul, e.g., writes about the centrality of the divine revelation (Gal 1:12, 16). For many NT writers vision equips them with insight hidden to others and privileges them to enjoy a role in history denied even to the greatest figures of the past (1 Pet 1:11-12).

Despite attempts over the years to play down the importance of apocalypticism in early Christianity, the indications suggest that its thought-forms and outlook were more typical of early Christianity than is often allowed. In the earliest period of Christianity, resort to the apocalyptic language and genre enabled the NT writers to have access to the privilege of understanding the significance of events and persons from the divine perspective. Apocalypticism, therefore, was the vehicle whereby the first Christians were able to articulate their deepest convictions about the ultimate significance of Jesus Christ in the divine purposes (*see* CHRISTOLOGY).

4. The influence of apocalypticism in Christian history

The book of Revelation was the catalyst in succeeding centuries for a variety of eschatological or apocalyptically inclined movements and readings of history. The popularity of apocalyptic ideas among movements such as Montanism led to a growing suspicion of the book. Apocalypticism was from the very start a thorn in the flesh of the wielders of ecclesiastical power in the centuries that followed, not least because it was such a central component of earliest Christian experience and self-definition from the very start of the Christian church.

An antiapocalyptic stand is apparent within early Christian theology, in which both future hope for this world, claim to visionary experience, and the allusive language of the book of Revelation manage to cut across the clearer parameters of an emerging theology, which put a greater weight on rationality and definition. Although in so many ways indebted to the structure and theology of the book of Revelation, these antiapocalyptic strands crystalized in Augustine's epoch-making *The City of God*. For Augustine the City of God is quite clearly a transcendent, heavenly reality despite its hidden presence in the midst of the earthly city. The coming of the heavenly city in all its fullness is not on the plane of history. It is at present hidden, but nowhere, and at no time, can the City of God become a reality in its totality in the midst of human affairs, because the values of the earthly city are utterly opposed to those of the City of God. In *The City of God* we find a questioning of simplistic attempts to discern from the complexities of the historical process evidence of the hand of God in human affairs. Augustine does this by espousing a sharp division between the earthly city and the city of God. The former is always characterised by corruption and violence and can never be identified in entirety with the City of God. All that can be hoped for is a modicum of peace and justice to ensure some kind of stability.

An important contribution was made by Augustine's attempt to make politics relative through eschatology, for thereby he refuses to sanctify any political arrangement. A theocracy is excluded this side of the kingdom of God. The church serves as a witness to the values of the eternal kingdom and thus as the organ whereby the injustices of the present age can be exposed. The church, however, can never be identified with the City of God, for it is also, to varying degrees corrupt, because of its participation in the values of the old order. The church can only point in the direction of the City of God. Yet at best, this task, complicated and beset with problems as it is, is its essential ministry of opposition to and critical reflection on fallible human arrangements. At worst, by insisting that the rule of the state, however limited, is a hedge against the effects of original sin, Augustine validated secular power and the church's reluctant but necessary subordination to it.

The legacy of Augustine's *City of God* is pervasive in Christian doctrine, but in the 12th cent. there emerged an influential reading of the book of Revelation by Joachim of Fiore, which was to use Revelation as a hermeneutical key to understand both Scripture and the whole of history. Joachim broke decisively from the Augustinian tradition by willingness to find significance in history. Joachim of Fiore's interpretation of Revelation (this is why any discussion of apocalypticism needs to take full account of this development) and his Trinitarian historicism, in which world history is divided into three ages corresponding to the three persons of the Trinity, provoked a very different attitude toward eschatology. The later Middle Ages was a period of such intense upheaval, fired by apocalyptic revivals. Eschatological events ceased to be some mysterious transcendent entities but ciphers of imminent historical possibilities. In the hands of Joachim's followers, their own contemporary history and part in it became the arena for the fulfillment of the eschatological promises. Contemporary events became the markers of eschatological fulfillment, since the apocalyptic symbols received their meaning in the contemporary persons and events. A good example of this can be found in 13th cent. Franciscan theology. Many Franciscans believed that they were living in the eschatological age, with St. Francis having a unique role in ushering in the final epoch of history. The opening of the sixth seal of the Apocalypse is linked with Francis and the rise of a new age of evangelical piety. Some even went so far as to identify the forces of evil as incarnate in the church, thereby identifying it with the whore of Babylon. As a result there emerged an eschatology that has profound influence on Western thought in the centuries to come, which is testimony to a historical eschatology that is linked to political change.

Though apocalypticism was generally frowned on by the magisterial Reformers (e.g., Luther initially outlined his reasons for relegating the book of Revelation to a subordinate place within the CANON OF THE NEW TESTAMENT, and Calvin wrote no commentary on this book), its importance in the 16th cent. should not be underestimated in words that echo much earlier (and later) assessments in the Christian tradition. It had a significant influence on radical Anabaptism at Muenster. The parallel link between Revelation and radical politics is particularly evident in the English Civil War writing of the 17th cent. For many, the rule of the beast is not merely eschatological but is seen in the political arrangements of the day, in the monarchy and those organs of state that maintained the hegemony of a social elite. Alongside this radical appropriation, there was a rich tradition of interpretation in which the careful exposition of the book was carried out in a more measured and less heated atmosphere, encouraging a long tradition of apocalyptic speculation. Chief among these was Joseph Mede (1586–1638), whose work had enormous influence on subsequent generations. The use of the Apocalypse as a repository of prophecies concerning the future was present from the start and reached an influential climax in Mede's work, but in the last 200 years it has become very much part of a growing trend of eschatological interpretation. A political and historical use of Revelation had a new lease of life at the time of the French Revolution. In William Blake's own prophecy, the images of Revelation are woven into the fabric of his own visionary mythology. Throughout the 1790s Blake's writing and designs return to the themes of prophetic struggle and the need to be aware of the dangers of the prophetic spirit degenerating into the apostasy of state religion.

The rise of historical scholarship led to a different perspective on the book, which focused more on past meaning rather than present use. Attention is paid entirely to the book in its ancient context. As well as detailed text-critical analysis there are lengthy quotations from ancient sources, including rabbinic parallels, which illuminate particular passages of Revelation. Early modern interpreters like Hugo Grotius (1583–1645) had argued that the book's meaning was almost entirely related to the circumstances of John's own day (the so-called "preterist method" of interpretation of Revelation).

B. Types of Apocalypticism

It is important to make distinctions among the various kinds of apocalyptic influence. There has been that fascination with prognostication about the future, which the ambiguities of prophetic texts, especially the book of Daniel, have set in train. Such an eschatological science is by no means the only characteristic form of apocalypticism. The impact of appeal to visions and other apparently more direct acquaintance with the divine, and information about God and the world is consistently and episodically a key aspect of religion. Speculation about the future on the basis of the close reading of sacred texts is a parallel phenomenon, open to question and debate like any other form of exegesis. The latter is not necessarily politically subversive. Indeed, not only is it characteristic of apolitical groups like the Jehovah's Witnesses, but it is also the dominant ideology of the most conservative political force in late 20th cent. American religion. The eschatological scenario in which the elect are raptured into heaven to save them from the catastrophe that is to befall the world is a key component of an increasing number of the world's Christians. In its present form it has its origins in the early 19th cent., but popularized by the Scofield Reference Bible at the beginning of the 20th cent. Similar to the detailed speculations of the followers of Joachim of Fiore, as they interpreted the Apocalypse, and Joseph Mede in the 17th cent., they believe that a biblically based eschatology can afford their generation a way of understanding where they are in the divine economy. With such eschatological maps we are a long way from the eschatological agnosticism of Augustine in *The City of God*, the text that has become the cornerstone for orthodox eschatology.

In the light of the way in which sectarian groups in the history of religions tend to be excessively dualistic and support their view of the world by appeal to apocalyptic knowledge, apocalypticism is often seen as the religiosity of a marginalized minority, oppressed by a powerful hierarchy, despairing of political change. It is true that in the Dead Sea Scrolls we find represented the ideology of a group that cut itself off from the rest of the nation to maintain its holiness. For Jews of the Second Temple period, however, the world they inhabited was one in which angels had communion with humans, and the privileged humans could have access to heaven. In believing this, Jews and Christians differed little from their contemporaries in the wider world of antiquity, save that they believed their God was superior to all the demons and spirits that existed. The Dead Sea Scrolls have demonstrated the way in which human history was seen as a struggle between the forces of light and darkness, in which angelic forces are mingled with their earthly counterparts in a vast cosmic drama that encompasses life in the present. Thus there opened up a door through which one might perceive the divine mysteries about past, present, and future—through mystical access to divine wisdom in the visions and dreams that are the very heart of apocalypticism.

The visionary element, the hope for the future, and the active participation in the inauguration of eschatological change, is endemic to religion and culture. Nor is this hope peculiar to Christianity, though it is the history of the Western church that has been particularly indebted to apocalypticism as a motor of theological ideas through the centuries. Judaism is traditionally viewed as a religion based on the interpretation and application of Torah in diverse situations. But from its very inception the apocalyptic and the mystical have been a necessary counterpoint to the practice that has been typical of Jewish identity. From the origins of the kabbalah via the various Hasidic and messianic movements, through the centuries apocalypticism is a key factor in Jewish religion. Indeed, at almost exactly the same time that Western Christianity was revitalized by the apocalyptic currents, which came about as the result of the influence of Joachim of Fiore, messianic mysticism, typified by David Abulafia, exercised analogous impact on Jewish life.

Visions are unproblematic, unless they result in "following other gods" (Deut 13:2), with the attendant departure from established custom and obligation. The problem of true and false prophecy is endemic to religion and has a long history in Judaism (Deut 13; 18; Jer 23:16). The appeal to visions brooks no dissent, for what is offered is apparently a bypassing of the rational to appeal to something more directly linked with the divine and therefore of greater authority. When this (as it often did) involved some kind of departure from habit and convention, the social dislocation caused by such an appeal was great. The three Abrahamic faiths are shot through with such appeals, whether it be the Torah given to Moses on Sinai and the imitation of that in later texts like the temple scroll, the Quran dictated to Muhammad by the archangel Gabriel, or the various visionary encounters that were decisive in the accounts of the origins of early Christianity, all exhibit both the creative and subversive potential of this form of apocalyptic religion.

Alongside the prognosticators, however, there is another group of apocalyptists, who either believe they have a role to play in bringing about the apocalypse or by their visionary conviction seek to encourage others to bring that to pass. In various texts of the NT the present becomes a moment of opportunity for transforming the imperfect into the perfect; history and eschatology become inextricably intertwined. In many of the stories told about Jesus, e.g., he is proclaiming the present as decisive in God's purposes and himself as the messianic agent for change. Paul's mission to the Gentiles was linked with the framework of an eschatological drama in which Paul is a crucial actor. For many of the NT writers, history is illuminated by apocalypse (e.g., 1 Cor 10:11; 1 Pet 1:11). This peculiar characteristic of early Christian writings, in which religious hope is actualized, connects the world of the NT writers and later apocalypticism, whether it be the followers of Joachim of Fiore, the Anabaptists of Muenster, or the English radicals who expected to inaugurate God's kingdom in England in the wake of the execution of Charles I.

One feature of some apocalyptic thinking and practice is that it represents a clear alternative to conventional wisdom and custom. Apocalyptic experience may challenge a traditional belief system. Apocalyptic experience was a motor of the early Christian movement. Early Christianity was not only indebted to apocalyptic terminology, its very identity was formed by the dialectical tension between the above and below, the present and the future. Apocalypticism has been part of the counterpoint of mainstream Christianity ever since. See ABRAHAM, APOCALYPSE OF; ABRAHAM, TESTAMENT OF; ADAM, APOCALYPSE OF; AMOS, BOOK OF; LITTLE APOCALYPSE; BARUCH, BOOK OF; DANIEL, BOOK OF; ELIJAH, APOCALYPSE OF; ENOCH, BOOKS OF; ESDRAS, BOOKS OF; HERMAS, SHEPHERD OF; JAMES, APOCALYPSE OF; JAMES, FIRST APOCALYPSE OF; JAMES, SECOND APOCALYPSE OF; JOEL, BOOK OF; JUBILEES, BOOK OF; MESSOS, APOCALYPSE OF; NOAH, APOCALYPSE OF; PAUL, APOCALYPSE OF; PETER, APOCALYPSE OF; PSEUDEPIGRAPHA; REVELATION, BOOK OF; SATAN; SOLOMON, PSALMS OF; THOMAS, APOCALYPSE OF; VIRGIN, APOCALYPSES OF THE; ZECHARIAH, BOOK OF; ZEPHANIAH, APOCALYPSE OF; ZOSTRIANOS, APOCALYPSE OF.

Bibliography: R. Bauckham. *The Theology of the Book of Revelation* (1993); J. H. Charlesworth. *The Old Testament Pseudepigrapha*, Vol. 1 (1983); J. J. Collins. *The Apocalyptic Imagination: An Introduction to the Jewish Matrix of Christianity.* 2nd ed. (1998); J. J. Collins. *The Encyclopedia of Apocalypticism. Vol. 1: The Origins of Apocalypticism in Judaism and Christianity* (1998); D. Hellholm. *Apocalypticism in the Mediterranean World and the Near East* (1989); M. Hengel. *Judaism and Hellenism* (1974); C. Hill. *The World*

Turned Upside Down (1972); M. Idel. *Messianic Mystics* (1999); J. Kovacs and C. Rowland. *The Book of Revelation: The Apocalypse of Jesus Christ* (2004); B. McGinn. *The Encyclopedia of Apocalypticism. Vol. 2 Apocalypticism in Western History and Culture* (1998); C. Rowland. *The Open Heaven* (1982); C. Rowland. *Revelation NIB* 12 (1998); S. Stein. *The Encyclopedia of Apocalypticism. Vol. 3 Apocalypticism in Western History and Culture* (1998); M. E. Stone. "Apocalyptic Literature." *Jewish Writings of the Second Temple Period* (1984) 383–441.

CHRISTOPHER ROWLAND

APOCRYPHA, DEUTEROCANONICALS. The Apocrypha is a collection of books written by Jewish authors between the 3rd cent. BCE and 1st cent. CE. Their identification as a discrete collection (set apart from the Pseudepigrapha, Dead Sea Scrolls, the works of Philo, etc.) is due largely to the high value placed on these books by Christian readers throughout the millennia and long-standing historic debates concerning their place in the Christian canon.

A. Definitions
B. Contents
C. Use, Collection, and Authority
D. Significance
Bibliography

A. Definitions

Apocrypha is the designation generally given to a particular collection of Jewish texts written between 250 BCE and 100 CE, some originally in Hebrew or Aramaic, the rest originally composed in Greek. These texts are set apart as a (somewhat) bounded collection distinct from the wealth of literature composed by Jews in the post-prophetic period largely as a result of the reading activity of Christians in the earliest centuries of the movement, who found these books to be helpful resources alongside the books of the Jewish canon (the Christian "OT") for articulating their own faith and for determining questions of ethics, and on account of inner-Christian debates concerning the boundaries of canon. The term *Apocrypha* itself is a transliteration of Greek word (ἀπόκρυφα apokrypha) meaning "hidden things," denoting the noncanonical status of these texts in the eyes of those who use this designation.

The term *deuterocanonical* is used mainly in Roman Catholic circles as a designation for the books included in the Catholic OT but excluded from the Jewish Bible (and hence Protestant OT). It does not imply, however, secondary status—any more than the second commandment has less authority than the first, or than Deuteronomy lags in normative weight behind the "first" statement of the Law in Exodus. Rather, it acknowledges the lateness of these texts, such that they were excluded from the collection of texts inherited by the early church from the

synagogue, and the lateness of the definitive affirmation of this body of literature as canonical (at the Council of Trent in 1546), while nevertheless affirming their authority as part of the broader canon of the Catholic Church.

B. Contents

The collection contains works in a variety of genres, most of which were already represented within the canon of the Jewish Scriptures, which therefore clearly served as a model for the authors of the Apocrypha. Together with the content of many of these books, which also shows a high level of reflection upon and interpretation of the Jewish Scriptures at many points, this imitative character signals their derivative nature, which may also help to account for their failure to enter the Jewish canon.

The Apocryphal/Deuterocanonical Books

Tobit

Judith

Esther (the Greek Version containing the additional chapters)

The Wisdom of Solomon

Sirach

Baruch

The Letter of Jeremiah

The Additions to Daniel
  The Prayer of Azariah and the Song of the Three Jews
  Susanna
  Bel and the Dragon

1 Maccabees

2 Maccabees

1 Esdras

The Prayer of Manasseh

Psalm 151

3 Maccabees

2 Esdras

4 Maccabees

Of great importance for our knowledge of key events in the postprophetic period are the historical books, which extend the "biblical" story, often in "biblical" idiom. First and Second Maccabees tell the story of the initiatives toward Hellenization (toward making Jerusalem more like a Greek city and Judea fully a part of the Greek world), the violent suppression of traditional Judaism, and the successful resistance on the part of martyrs who died rather than break faith with God and revolutionaries who restored political independence to Judea after centuries of Gentile domination.

First Maccabees is a dynastic history, tracing the rise of the Hasmonean house to power and legitimating its claim to rule. Second Maccabees, while certainly glorifying the Maccabean heroes, gives more of a theological interpretation to events, using the history to underscore the ongoing validity of Deuteronomistic theology. As long as Judeans keep the covenant, their lives remain stable and secure under God's protection. Initiatives to break the covenant to become more like the Gentile nations results in national disaster. A return to obedience (here, in the form of dying for the sake of God's law) restores God's favor.

Third Maccabees is something of a misnomer, as the book is concerned with a suppression of Judaism in Ptolemaic Egypt, God's miraculous deliverance of the loyal Jews, and the punishment of the relatively few apostate Jews at the hands of the faithful. It begins with an episode similar to the opening episode of 2 Maccabees and presents a plot that is closely parallel down to the establishment and promotion of a festival commemorating God's deliverance, suggesting its largely unhistorical (and derivative) nature (though it does bear witness to the tensions and hostility among traditional Jews, apostate Jews, and the dominant culture at its worst, as well as to ancient "anti-Gentilism"). Its chief goal seems to have been to offer a story that demonstrated God's availability to and care for Diaspora Jews, unmitigated by their distance from Judea.

Another important group, containing the books most treasured by early Christian writers, expands the body of wisdom literature, continuing the tradition of Proverbs, Ecclesiastes, and the "Wisdom Psalms." The Wisdom of Ben Sira contains the curriculum of a sage who directed a school in Jerusalem in the first quarter of the 2nd cent. BCE. Ben Sira taught his students to resist the tendencies toward assimilation to the Greek culture wherever this threatened diligent observance of the Torah, which for him remained the irreplaceable source of personal honor and national security, seen especially in his praise of Jewish heroes and censure of those who led Israel away from covenant loyalty. Far from being a burden or a manifestation of legalism, Torah was celebrated as God's special gift to Israel, God's gracing of Israel, a view that reverberates throughout this corpus. Alongside this general concern running throughout his work, he left behind a valuable body of reflections on providence and free will, prayer, temptation, forgiveness, and almsgiving, as well as the practical advice on how to succeed in "society" that his students expected. He thus provides important windows into social practices and relationships, such as the expectations of friends and patrons, management of the ancient household, proper behavior at symposia, and the dangers that must be navigated by the player in politics. His infamous reflections on women bear testimony to the elevation of silence, submissiveness, and chastity as primary values to be nurtured in women in his world.

Wisdom of Solomon, written in Greek in Egypt two centuries later, offers more thoroughly developed reflections on a few key topics: the trials of the righteous in this life and God's postmortem vindication of them in the sight of their persecutors, the role of Wisdom in creation and in the pious life, God's providential care for God's people and punishment of their enemies, and the folly of Gentile religion (including the ruler cult).

A third group includes thematic treatises, toward which wisdom literature is already tending in the Second Temple period. Letter of Jeremiah, the Hebrew original of which may date back to the late 4th cent. BCE, stresses the manufactured and artificial nature of Gentile idolatrous religion, seeking to insulate Jewish readers from being impressed by and drawn to the cults of the dominant culture. Fourth Maccabees, written in Greek in the middle half of the 1st cent. CE, presents itself as a philosophical treatise on the mastery of the passions, arguing that strict observance of the Jewish Law is the surest way to fulfill this Greek philosophical ideal and using the example of the Jewish martyrs during the Hellenizing Crisis of 168–166 BCE as its strongest proofs (hence the title, linking this book with the other books of the "Maccabees"). The author's mastery of Greek composition and rhetoric, and his familiarity with some of the intricacies of Greek philosophical debates, shows how fully "Hellenized" a Jew could be without sacrificing commitment to and observance of the Torah and its distinctive way of life.

A fourth category could be grouped together as expansions and reformulations of Scripture. First Esdras is a retelling of 2 Chr 35–36, Ezra, and parts of Nehemiah, probably originally composed in Hebrew or Aramaic in the 2nd or 1st cent. BCE. It gives a far more prominent role to Zerubbabel, first by including the originally unrelated story of the "contest of the three bodyguards" concerning what is the strongest force in the world (the winner is identified as Zerubbabel), second by absorbing Nehemiah's role into Zerubbabel's. The author may have set out to give a sense that David's throne had been restored in Zerubbabel, even though the latter was not officially a king.

The Greek version of Esther grew in stages and contains six substantial additions (often separated out as "The Additions to Esther") as well as minor changes throughout the text. These additions introduce a strongly theological element that was (strangely) lacking in the Hebrew version, showing dream visions and lengthy prayers introducing theological and ethical interpretation of the events of the story as well as the direct intervention of God. Esther's crossing of unacceptable boundaries (e.g., marrying the Gentile king, eating with Gentiles, and possibly participating in the worship of the king's gods) is dealt with in these additions, even while the boundary between Jew and Gentile is dramatically reaffirmed in God's providential care for the former, but not the latter. The additions also expand the texts of the edict against Jews and the edict rescinding the former action, providing windows into ancient anti-Judaism.

The Greek version of Daniel was also expanded to include two additional court stories and several liturgical pieces. Susanna glorifies the wisdom of the young Daniel, who is able to prevent a gross miscarriage of justice, while Bel and the Dragon shows an older Daniel successfully demonstrating the emptiness of Gentile religion and surviving the hostility of the Gentile priests. The Song of the Three Jews cast into the furnace becomes an occasion for the composition and introduction of liturgical texts. The Prayer of Azariah is a corporate confession of sin and plea for deliverance, predicated on the association of God's name with God's people; the Song of the Three Jews is a hymn praising God for his deliverance and calling upon the entire created order to join in God's praise. These four additions were composed prior to 100 BCE, the time of the translation of Daniel into Greek; some might predate the final form of Hebrew–Aramaic Daniel.

Other liturgical texts inspired by biblical events are included in the Apocrypha. Psalm 151 conflates two originally independent Hebrew psalms celebrating God's election of David and David's victory over Goliath, an important story for Jews surrounded by giant Gentile powers to remember. Prayer of Manasseh is a beautiful penitential psalm, placed on the lips of Judah's most wicked king (see 2 Chr 33:21-25), "recreating" his lost prayer (2 Chr 33:18-19) and giving expression to the boundless mercies of God.

Baruch is a mixed composition that fits broadly within the category of reformulation of biblical tradition. It opens with the prescription of a liturgy of repentance for Jews in Judea and the Diaspora, highly reminiscent of the penitential prayer in Dan 9 (which, however, may predate the final form of Daniel). A wisdom poem follows, reflecting the language of Job 28 and Deut 30, directing the reader back to the keeping of Torah as the path to national recovery. The last part of Baruch presents a lament by Jerusalem over her children and a reformulation of the prophetic message of hope, especially as found in Deutero-Isaiah and, in its final chapter, in *Pss. Sol.* 11. This highly derivative work provides a highly effective summary of the scriptural tradition as it pertains to Jewish life under Gentile domination.

The genre of folk tale or romance is represented by Tobit and Judith (3 Maccabees might properly be included here as well). Tobit, written in Aramaic possibly as early as the 3rd cent. BCE, is a tale of the lives of two interrelated families in the Eastern Diaspora that combines the motifs of several well-known folk tales. It is a vital witness to the ethics of Diaspora Jews, especially emphasizing almsgiving and other works of charity, the value of endogamy, and the value of kinship relations. It also bears witness to the theological developments of the period, including angelology and demonology, the affirmation of Deuteronomy's interpretation of national prosperity and misfortune (extending this to individuals), the explanation of individual suffering as a test of faithfulness (as in Job), and the eschatological restoration and exaltation of Jerusalem.

Judith is a piece of "historical fiction," reflecting many of the dynamics of the Maccabean Revolution but featuring Nebuchadnezzar as the Gentile king and Holofernes as his invading general rather than contemporary figures. After the town of Bethulia is besieged, Judith emerges as the heroine who will liberate her city, which she accomplishes by beheading Holofernes in his tent when he is drunk and trying to seduce her. Although featuring a female heroine and thus the potential land value of a "good woman," the book also bears witness to the persistence of traditional values concerning women: the greatest disgrace is to be killed by the hand of a woman, the weakest enemy; there is no virtue for women where their chastity has been compromised; even if Judith can emerge as a heroine in a crisis, her proper place remains outside the male sphere of governance. It remains a rich witness to the theology and ethics of the period, as well as the cultural dynamics of honor, shame, and the "proper" use of deceit.

Finally, the Apocrypha includes an example of the genre of apocalypse. Second Esdras is actually a composite work. The core (2 Esd 3–14 = *4 Ezra*) is a Jewish apocalypse written at the end of the 1st cent. CE. The author wrestles with major questions concerning God's providence and justice and the meaningfulness of election in the wake of the first Jewish Revolt (and Rome's continued prosperity). The solution is to be found first in God's postmortem rewarding of the pious and punishment of those who failed life's contest of keeping Torah, and second in the eschatological future when God's Messiah will indict Rome for her crimes and usher in an age of peace. The final episode concerns the restoration of the inspired text of the Scriptures and of a much broader number of books to be reserved for use only by the wise. The prologue and epilogue (2 Esd 1–2 = 5 Ezra; 2 Esd 15–16 = 6 Ezra) are Christian additions from the 2nd and 3rd cent. CE, the former showing clear dependence on Matthew and Revelation, the latter presenting a prophetic denunciation of Rome and her provinces during a period of persecution.

C. Use, Collection, and Authority

No book of the Apocrypha, save for the Wisdom of Ben Sira, appears to have been a serious candidate for inclusion in the Jewish canon, and the only reference to the canonicity of Ben Sira is a negative pronouncement (*t. Yad.* 2.13). Those that were composed in Greek (2–4 Maccabees and Wisdom of Solomon would have been excluded outright); the others, including Ben Sira, were known to have been written too late to be considered to have been imbued with the prophetic voice, believed to have lapsed in the postexilic period (1 Macc 4:46; 9:27; 14:41; Josephus, *Ag. Ap.* 1.40–41), differed from the texts already known in Palestine (i.e., the shorter versions of Daniel and Esther, the latter of which also invited considerable debate), or aroused objections on other grounds.

Nevertheless, there is widespread evidence concerning the value placed on, and use made of, these texts in early Judaism. Among the Dead Sea Scrolls were found fragments of Ben Sira (from two different copies; additional manuscript discoveries at Masada and the Cairo *genizah* augment this number considerably), Tobit (from five different copies), Letter of Jeremiah, and Psalm 151 (included in one of the *Psalms Scroll from Cave ll*), bearing witness at least to the reading of these texts in the first centuries BCE and CE and to their being sufficiently valued to merit copying and preservation. Ben Sira's words continue to be quoted by rabbis (though not always properly attributed to him) despite his noncanonical status. The popularity of the Feast of Dedication (Hanukkah) assured the survival of the stories of 1 and 2 Maccabees in the popular imagination, even though the texts were never canonical authorities. Indeed, the success of Hanukkah bears eloquent testimony to the authority and influence a text could have (in this case, 2 Maccabees with its two prefixed letters enjoining Jewish communities to observe this festival) without ever being considered a canonical text. There is no evidence to suggest that Diaspora Jews had a wider canon than their Judean coreligionists. The Septuagint codices sometimes mistakenly adduced as evidence for such an "Alexandrian canon" bear witness to Christian, not Jewish, collections of Scripture.

Jewish Christians, beginning with the founder of the early Christian movement, show an increasing tendency to value these texts as resources for faith, piety, and ethics. Sayings of Jesus (preserved in the Q stratum) about the necessity of forgiving others if one hopes to be forgiven by God and about almsgiving as the laying up of a treasure for the future resonate with the teaching of Ben Sira (compare Matt 6:12, 14-15 with Sir 28:2-4 and Luke 12:33; 18:22; and Matt 6:19-21 with Sir 29:9-12 [also Tob 4:8-10]). When Jesus is remembered to have invited people to take up his yoke, promising it to be easy and a sure path to rest, he sounds very much like the old sage inviting people to lodge in his school (compare Matt 11:28-30 with Sir 51:23, 26-27). James of Jerusalem resonates deeply with Ben Sira as he absolves God of all responsibility for temptation and human sin (Jas 1:13-14; Sir 15:11-12, 20), and discusses the dangers of the tongue (Jas 3:6, 9-12; Sir 22:27; 28:12). Jesus, James, and Paul (compare Rom 9:20-21 with Sir 33:12-13; Rom 12:15 with Sir 7:34) were all well positioned to have learned selected contents of Ben Sira, whether by direct engagement or through being taught by intermediaries who included

distinctive teachings of Ben Sira in their own teaching.

Early Christian authors found Wisdom speculation such as one finds in Wis 7:22-26; 8:4; 9:1-2, 9 to be of immense value as they pondered the preincarnate activity of the Son and his relationship with God the Father (see Heb 1:1-4; Col 1:15-20; John 1:1-3, 10-13). This stream of tradition would continue to shape the church's definition of the shared essence of the Father and the Son as well as the formulation of the doctrine of the Trinity. The martyrology of 2 and 4 Maccabees, aside from providing examples of faith valued by the early church (*see* Heb 11:35; Origen, *Exhortation to Martyrdom*), also provided resources for interpreting the death of Jesus as a ransom for sins that allowed the disobedient to experience a return to God's favor.

Christians in the 2nd and 3rd cent. noticed the traces of the Apocrypha in the NT and other valued texts such as the *Didache*. This contributed, no doubt, to the elevation of the apocryphal books in the estimation of the church, and the increasing tendency to quote from these books as "Scripture." This line of reasoning is nowhere made clearer than in Tertullian's suggestion that even *1 Enoch* should be regarded as canonical, since Jude makes use of it (*Cult. fem.* 1.3). The great 4th and 5th cent. codices of the Septuagint (Sinaiticus, Vaticanus, and Alexandrinus) also bear witness to the inclusion of apocryphal books in early Christian usage, although here, too, the evidence is mixed since the range of "additional" books varies from one to the other.

Nevertheless, many early church leaders voiced hesitancy to accept these books as canonical, especially when their Jewish neighbors did not. Origen addressed this issue explicitly, arguing that the God who bought the Christians with a price would also see to it that they received as scriptural precisely what God desired (*Ep. Afr.* 4–5). Even those who did exclude the additional books may well have adopted the Greek versions of Esther and Daniel as canonical (thus including the additions). Baruch and Letter of Jeremiah may have been included in this category as "Additions to Jeremiah."

The debate reached a critical point when Jerome urged the exclusion of the Apocrypha, including the additions to Daniel and Esther present in Greek versions, on the basis of his study of the Hebrew texts with a rabbi in Palestine. They would continue to be promoted as worthy of reading for edification, but not for the confirmation of doctrine. He was opposed by Augustine based on the majority practice of the church and on his desire to maintain unity with Christians in the East (where the estimation of the apocryphal books was less in dispute, and where local sees were given authority to establish their own practice in regard to the public reading of these texts). Indeed, Augustine's own use especially of Wisdom of Solomon and the Wisdom of Ben Sira shows that he regarded them as quite suitable for theological reflection and argument.

His position prevailed in the Western church, and is reflected in the eventual confirmation of the canonicity of 1 and 2 Maccabees, Wisdom, Ben Sira, Tobit, Judith, and the longer forms of Daniel, Esther, and "Jeremiah," although this continued to be questioned by such important voices as Gregory the Great, Hugh of St. Victor, and Cardinal Cajetan.

The Protestant Reformers, with their emphasis on "Scripture alone" as the basis for the establishment of doctrine, revived the objections of Jerome and others to the use of the Apocrypha as canonical authorities. In part, this was driven by the fact that several of the doctrines to which they particularly objected were founded on texts in the Apocrypha (the salvific effects of works of mercy: Tob 4:7-11; the idea of a treasury of merits against future dangers: Tob 4:8-11; Sir 29:9-12; atonement for the sins of the deceased: 2 Macc 12:39-45; the intercession of the saints: 2 Macc 15:12-14). Nevertheless, these Reformers continued to commend the apocryphal books as useful devotional literature and to publish them in a separate section in their Bibles. In Luther's words (from the preface to his German translation of the Apocrypha), they are "still both useful and good to read."

This finally led to the Catholic Church's official affirmation of the apocryphal books as "Deuterocanonical" at the Council of Trent in 1546. The Roman Catholic canon would exclude 1 Esdras, 2 Esdras, 3 and 4 Maccabees, Prayer of Manasseh, and Psalm 151 (though all but 4 Maccabees appear in Appendices to the Vulgate). The Greek Orthodox canon excludes only 2 Esdras and 4 Maccabees; the Slavonic Bible excludes only 4 Maccabees.

D. Significance

The books of the Apocrypha witness to the challenges to faith in the Second Temple period and the ways in which people of faith negotiated those challenges. Especially prominent is the challenge posed by Hellenism and the dual concern observed in many Jewish circles to adapt to the new environment and make full use of its resources while maintaining their cultural and religious identity, concerns that also emerge under the largely Jewish Christian leadership of the early Christian movement. Intertwined with this challenge, though not limited to it, is the challenge of continuing to find ways by which to make traditional resources meaningful in new circumstances. Thus the Apocryphal books invite the reader into the authors' selection, shaping, and interpretation of the resources of the Jewish Scriptures in the postprophetic period.

The Apocrypha are essential to the study of the environment of early Christianity, providing a set of first-order resources to aid understanding of the thought and practice of Judaism in the postprophetic period, and the ways in which critical events from the 2nd cent. BCE shaped Jewish consciousness, identity, and hope (in regard both to personal and national eschatology). They bear witness to the greater connection between Jesus and the movement he founded and the faith and practice of Judaism in the 1st cent. than is appreciated by people who "freeze" Judaism's development in the early postexilic period (i.e., stopping with their reading of the Jewish Scriptures or Protestant OT canon). They provide essential background on the social, cultural, and religious dynamics that provide the keys to understanding such phenomena as Saul's persecution of Jewish Christians, the offensiveness of Paul's Torah-free gospel, the sources of Jewish opposition to Pauline Christianity (and other chiefly "Hellenist" forms of Jewish Christianity), Judaizing Christian missionaries, and the church's rejection of a nationalistic eschatology. It is within these books that one gains access to the theological developments that laid important foundations for early Christian theology (e.g., the effective death of the righteous person, immortality and resurrection, speculation about the "person" of Wisdom, all of which have direct bearing on the development of Christology) as well as illumine the worldview embraced by early Judaism and early Christianity (e.g., in regard to angelology and demonology, in the expectation of divine intervention in response to prayer, and the like).

These gifts of the Apocrypha are less likely to be neglected in religious communities that affirm their canonical status. They can be valued as religious literature, however, even among religious communities that have purposefully excluded them from their canons. Because many of these texts were born from the struggle to discover the way of faithfulness in the midst of significant challenges, and indeed nurtured that faithfulness among their readers, they also commend themselves as devotional literature of the first order — devotional literature that has stood the test of time and has been repeatedly affirmed by the reading practices of Catholic and Orthodox communions. Even where they are not used as sources for theological reflection, they can be valued as worthy and serious conversation partners in the quest for theological truth, wrestling quite openly as they do with questions of perpetual interest.

Bibliography: R. Beckwith. *The Old Testament Canon of the New Testament Church: And Its Background in Early Judaism* (1985); M. Delcor. "The Apocrypha and Pseudepigrapha of the Hellenistic Period." *The Cambridge History of Judaism.* Vol. 2, ed. W. D. Davies and L. Finkelstein (1989) 409–503; D. A. DeSilva. *Introducing the Apocrypha: Context, Message, and Significance* (2002); D. J. Harrington. *Invitation to the Apocrypha* (1999); B. M. Metzger. *An Introduction to the Apocrypha* (1957); S. Meurer. *The Apocrypha in Ecumenical Perspective* (1991). H. L. Orlinsky. "The Canonization of the Hebrew Bible and the Exclusion of the Apocrypha." *Essays in Biblical Culture and Bible*

Translation (1974) 227–284; M. Silva and K. H. Jobes. *Invitation to the Septuagint* (2000); M. E. Stone, ed. *Jewish Writings of the Second Temple Period* (1984); A. C. Sundberg. *The Old Testament of the Early Church* (1964).

DAVID A. DESILVA

APOCRYPHA, NT. The NT Apocrypha (from the Greek ἀπόκρυφος apokryphos, plural ἀπόκρυφα apokrypha, meaning "hidden, secret") are a heterogeneous group of texts initially gathered together by European scholars in the 16th cent. Johann Albert Fabricius first published such a collection in his *Codex apocryphus Novi Testamenti* (1703). He sought to collect all the noncanonical printed narratives pertaining to the origins of Christianity, no matter if they were ancient or modern, authentic or counterfeit, of Christian, Jewish, or Muslim origin. The French priest Jacques-Paul Migne, the editor of the monumental *Patrologia Graeca* and *Latina*, also cast the net wide in his *Dictionnaire des apocryphes* (1856–1858).

In the 19th cent. the scientific study of this corpus began. In 1823 Johan Karl Thilo classified the apocryphal texts according to the literary genres of Gospels, Acts, Letters, and Apocalypses found in the NT. At the same time, the search for new Greek and Latin manuscripts prompted the rediscovery of ancient texts and the publication of critical editions of the writings already known. Constantin von Tischendorf first published the *Evangelia apocrypha* (1853; 2nd ed., 1876), the *Apocalypses apocryphae* (1866), and the *Acta apostolorum apocrypha* (1851), subsequently reedited by Richard A. Lipsius and Max Bonnet (1891–1903). Montague Rhodes James was the author of *The Apocryphal New Testament* (1924), which remained for many years the standard anthology in English.

Apocrypha, NT

Gospels, Birth and Infancy
Arabic Gospel of the Infancy
Armenian Gospel of the Infancy
Arundel Manuscript 404
Assumption of the Virgin
Joseph the Carpenter, History of
Infancy Gospel of Thomas
Protoevangelium of James
Pseudo-Matthew, Gospel of

Gospels, Ministry and Passion
Barnabas the Apostle, Book of the
    Resurrection of Christ by
Bartholomew, Gospel of
Descent into Hell, Christ's
Ebionites, Gospel of
Egyptians, Gospel of the
Hebrews, Gospel of the
Joseph of Arimathea, Narrative of
Judas, Gospel of
Mark, Secret Gospel of (?)
Nazareans, Gospel of
Peter, Gospel of
Philip, Gospel of
Pilate, Acts of (= Gospel of Nicodemus)
Pilate to Claudius, Letter of
Pilate and Herod, Letters of
Pilate to Tiberius, Letter of
Thomas, Gospel of

Dialogues, Jesus and Disciples
Apostles, Epistle of the
Bartholomew, Questions of
Freer Logion
James, Apocryphon of
James, First Apocalypse of
James, Second Apocalypse of
Jesus Christ, Wisdom of
Jeu, Two Books of
John, Apocryphon of
Mary, Gospel of
Peter, Apocalypse of (NHC VII,3)
Philip, Letter of Peter to
Pistis Sophia
Savior, Dialogue of the

Savior, Gospel of the
    (= Pap. Berol. 22220)
Thomas the Contender, Book of

Acts
Andrew, Acts of
Andrew and Matthew, Acts of
Andrew and Paul, Acts of
Andrew and Peter, Acts of
Barnabas, Acts of
Bartholomew, Martyrdom of
James, Acts of
John, Acts of
John, Acts of according to Prochorus
John, Acts of at Rome
Mark, Acts of
Matthew, Martyrdom of
Paul, Acts of
Paul and Thecla, Acts of
Paul, Martyrdom of
Peter, Acts of
Peter, Act of (BG 8502,4)
Peter and the Twelve, Acts of
Peter, Martyrdom of
Peter and Paul, Martyrdom of
Peter, Preaching of
Philip, Acts of
Pseudo-Abdias, Apostolic History of
Pseudo-Clementines
Simon and Jude, Martyrdom of
Thaddaeus, Acts of
Thomas, Acts of
Timothy, Acts of

Epistles
Abgar, Epistles of Christ and
Corinthians, Third Epistle to the
Laodiceans, Epistle to the
Lentulus, Epistle to
Paul and Seneca, Epistles of
Pseudo-Titus, Letter of

Teaching, Doctrine of
Addai, Doctrine of the Apostle
Paul, Prayer of the Apostle
Silvanus, Teachings of

Apocalypses
Adam, Apocalypse of
Elchasai, Book of
Esra, Fifth and Sixth Books of
Isaiah, Ascension of
Paul, Apocalypse of
Paul, Apocalypse of (NHC V,2)
Peter, Apocalypse of
Sibyilline Oracles (Christian)
Thomas, Apocalypse of
Virgin, Apocalypse of the
Zephaniah, Apocalypse of
    (= Apolypse of Sophonias)

Unidentified Gospel Fragments
PEgerton 2
POxy 840
POxy 1224
Papyrus Berolinensis 11710
Papyrus Cairensis 10735
Papyrus Merton 51
Fayyum Fragment
Strasbourg Coptic Papyrus 5-6

Lost Gospels, Titles from Ancient Authors
Adversaries of the Law and the
    Prophets, Gospel of the
Andrew, Gospel of
Apelles, Gospel of
Apostles, Memoria of
Bardesanes, Gospel of
Basilides, Gospel of
Cerinthus, Gospel of
Mani, Gospel of
Twelve Apostles, Gospel of the
    (Manichaean)
Valentinus, Gospel of

Related Subjects
Agrapha
Apostolic Constitutions and Canons
Diatessaron (or Tatian)
Marcion
Nag Hammadi

From the end of the 19th cent. new texts were identified among the thousands of fragmentary papyri and parchments unearthed in Egypt. Thus, in 1886–1887 a composite codex containing the Greek texts of *1 En.* 1–32 and large portions of the *Gospel* and the *Apocalypse of Peter* was discovered in the necropolis of Akhmim (ancient Panapolis), while several tiny fragments of previously unknown gospels were found among the Oxyrhynchus papyri. The climax of these discoveries was the discovery at Nag Hammadi (ancient Chenoboskion), in 1945, of thirteen codices (designated NHC I–XIII) containing forty-five Coptic texts. The majority were apocryphal texts (e.g., the *Gospel of Thomas*, the *Gospel of Philip*, the *Apocryphon of John*, the *Apocryphon of James*, the *Sophia of Jesus Christ*, the *Dialogue of the Savior*, the *First* and the *Second Apocalypse of James*, the *Coptic Apocalypse of Peter*, the *Coptic Apocalypse of Paul*, and the *Letter of Peter to Philip*) originally written in Greek by authors belonging to what we could label as the "Gnostic" wing of early Christianity.

During the 20th cent. the perspectives laid down by the German scholars Edgar Hennecke and Wilhelm Schneemelcher dominated research on the NT Apocrypha. Hennecke's *Neutestamentliche Apokryphen* (1904) was expanded and reedited. The sixth edition of Schneemelcher's *Neutestamentliche Apokryphen in deutscher Übersetzung*, also translated into English, appeared in 1989–1990. In this anthology texts are classified according to their literary genre and, normally, only those written before the end of 3rd cent. are taken into account. Thus, for example, to the genre "Gospels" belong the following texts: the *agrapha* or isolated sayings of Jesus (only seven are accepted instead of the eighteen listed by Joachim Jeremias); the fragments of unknown (e.g., the *Papyrus Egerton 2*, the *Fayyum Fragment*, and the *Secret Gospel of Mark*) and Jewish-Christian gospels (the *Gospel of the Nazareans*, the *Gospel of the Ebionites*, and the *Gospel of the Hebrews*); some major texts (the *Gospel of Thomas*, the *Gospel of Philip*, the patristic citations of the *Gospel of the Egyptians*, and the fragment of the *Gospel of Peter*); a series of conversations of the risen Jesus with the apostles (e.g., the *Epistula Apostolorum*, the *Dialogue of the Savior*, and the *First* and the *Second Apocalypse of James*); the infancy Gospels (e.g., the *Protevangelium of James*, the *Infancy Story of Thomas*, and some excerpts from the *Arabic Infancy Gospel* and the *Gospel of the Pseudo-Matthew*); and some Passion narratives (e.g., the *Abgar Legend*, the *Gospel of Nicodemus* or *Acts of Pilate*, and the *Gospel [Questions] of Bartholomew*). The writings relating to the apostles include: some apostolic pseudepigrapha (the citations of the *Kerygma Petri*, pseudo-Paul's *Epistle to the Laodiceans*, the *Correspondence between Seneca and Paul*, and the *Pseudo-Titus Epistle*); the apocryphal acts of the apostles written in the 2nd and the 3rd cent.

(the *Acts of Andrew*, the *Acts of John*, the *Acts of Paul* including *3 Corinthians*, the *Acts of Peter*, and the *Acts of Thomas*); the *Acts of Peter and the Twelve Apostles*, and a selection from the *Pseudo-Clementine Homilies* and *Recognitions*. Finally, the apocalypses take account of the following groups: the early Christian apocalypses (the *Ascension of Isaiah* and the *Apocalypse of Peter*); the apocalyptic prophecies (*5* and *6 Ezra*, a choice of the Christian *Sibylline Oracles*, and the fragments of the *Book of Elchasaï*); and the later apocalypses (the *Coptic Apocalypse of Peter*, the *Coptic Apocalypse of Paul*, the *Apocalypse of Paul*, and the *Apocalypse of Thomas*).

The literary and chronological criteria used to classify texts in this system are sometimes either inexact or questionable. Some texts, considered too "Gnostic" (e.g., the *Apocryphon of John*) or too late (e.g., the *Acts of Philip*), are only briefly mentioned, while other Christian writings (e.g., the *Odes of Solomon*) are omitted. Even the exceptional inclusion of later texts (e.g., the *Apocalypse of Paul*) may give readers the false impression that such writings are of interest only because they have preserved more ancient sources. Equally problematic is Schneemelcher's opinion that later texts are more "hagiographic" than "apocryphal," as if, after 300 CE, the narrative recollections of early Christian days were suddenly becoming too legendary to be considered as true apocryphal texts. As a matter of fact, the production of apocryphal texts never ceased and, from the 4th to the 6th cent., produced the great cycles of Jesus' Passion and Mary's death, not to mention the Coptic or Latin *Apocryphal Acts of the Apostles* of medieval collections. Picard's definition of apocryphal texts as Christian "mythologies"—i.e., "traditions about the origins of the same community which feels the need to retell and to adapt, from one epoch to another one, the story of its origins"—would encompass not only ancient and medieval texts, but also modern "Strange New Gospels" (e.g., Levi H. Dowling's *Aquarian Gospel*), novels (e.g., Nikos Kazantzakis's *The Last Temptation of Christ*), and movies (e.g., Mel Gibson's *The Passion of the Christ*). Accordingly, the most rewarding approaches to the phenomenon of "apocryphicity" try to locate them—with Koester, Ehrman, or Lapham—on a map of the theological, cultural, and historical trajectories of Christianity.

Unlike Hennecke and Schneemelcher, the Italian scholar Erbetta was much more inclusive in his selection of apocryphal texts and didn't hesitate to translate several late antique or early medieval works. The same position was taken by the members of the *Association pour l'étude de la literature apocryphe chrétienne* (AELAC), founded by Bovon and Geoltrain in 1981, with the participation of many Swiss, French, and Italian specialists. From the very beginning, the mission of the AELAC has been the publication of new and exhaustive critical editions and commentaries of ancient and medieval Christian apocryphal texts. Twenty-five years after its foundation, its results are impressive: fifteen volumes of the Corpus Christianorum, Series Apocryphorum (the *Acts of John*, the *Armenian Apocryphal Acts of the Apostles*, the *Acts of Andrew*, the *Ascension of Isaiah*, the *Gospel of the Pseudo-Matthew*, the *Acts of Philip*, the *Irish Infancy Gospels*, and the *Kerygma Petri*); eleven volumes of the paperback series Apocryphes (the *Gospel of Bartholomew*, the *Ascension of Isaiah*, the *Abgar Legend*, the *Odes of Solomon*, the *Epistula Apostolorum*, the *Dialogue between Solomon and Saturn*, the *Acts of Andrew*, the *Acts of Philip*, the *Gospel of Nicodemus*, the *Pseudo-Clementine Recognitions*, and the *Acts of Mar Mari*); fifteen volumes of the international *Apocrypha* journal; two volumes of the Pléiade anthology; Geerard's comprehensive *Clavisth*; and countless books, essays, projects, and collaborations.

In the English-speaking world, more energy has been devoted to the publication and study of the "Gnostic" apocryphal and nonapocryphal texts from Nag Hammadi. Especially important for NT studies are the traditions preserved by the *Gospel of Thomas* and the *Gospel of Mary*. Examination of Mary of Magdala as an apocryphal character proves to be instrumental for the understanding of the interactions between "Gnostic" and "Orthodox" narratives, earlier and later as well. The study of the progressive replacement of the Magdalene with Mary the mother as the true superstar of late antique apocryphal texts also opens the door to a reappraisal of some almost forgotten later traditions. Among the newly published texts, there are two previously little-known Passion Gospels: the Coptic fragmentary *Gospel of the Savior* (published by Hedrick and Mirecki, and subsequently reedited by Emmel) and the Ethiopic *Book of the Cock* (translated by Piovanelli). The Swiss scholar Rodolphe Kasser announced the imminent publication of a Coptic papyrus codex containing alternative versions of the *Epistle of Peter to Philip* and the *First Apocalypse of James* and, what is more appealing, the *Gospel of Judas*, a text known to Irenaeus and supposed to have been lost in 2004 by the Eighth International Congress of Coptic Studies. *See* COPTIC LANGUAGE; GNOSTICISM; NAG HAMMADI TEXTS.

Bibliography: Jan N. Bremmer, ed. *The Apocryphal Acts of Thomas* (2001); Bart D. Ehrman. *Lost Christianities: The Battles for Scripture and the Faiths We Never Knew* (2003); Keith J. Elliott. *The Apocryphal New Testament: A Collection of Apocryphal Christian Literature in an English Translation* (1993); Stephen Emmel. "Preliminary Reedition and Translation of the Gospel of the Savior: New Light on the Strasbourg Coptic Gospel and the Stauros Text from Nubia." *Apocrypha* 14 (2003) 9–53; Charles W. Hedrick and Paul A. Mirecki. *The Gospel of the Savior: A New Ancient Gospel* (1999); F. Stanley Jones, ed. *Which Mary? The Marys of Early Christian Tradition* (2002); Karen L. King. *The Gospel of Mary of Magdala: Jesus and the First Woman Apostle* (2003); Helmut Koester. *Ancient Christian Gospels: Their History and Development*. (1990); Fred Lapham. *An Introduction to the New Testament Apocrypha* (2003); Stephen L. Patterson. *The Gospel of Thomas and Jesus* (1993); Pierluigi-Piovanelli. "What Is a Christian Apocryphal Text and How Does It Work? Some Observations on Apocryphal Hermeneutics." *Nederlands Theologisch Tijdschrift* 59 (2005) 31–40; Pierluigi Piovanelli, ed. *Bringing the Underground to the Foreground: New Perspectives on Jewish and Christian Apocryphal Texts and Traditions* (2006); Wilhelm Schneemelcher, ed. *New Testament Apocrypha*. 2 vols. (1991–1992); Robert F. Stoops, ed. *The Apocryphal Acts of the Apostles in Intertextual Perspectives. Semeia* 80 (1997).

PIERLUIGI PIOVANELLI

APOCRYPHON OF JEREMIAH. *See* JEREMIAH, APOCRYPHON OF.

APOCRYPHON OF JOHN. *See* JOHN, APOCRYPHON OF; JOHN, SECRET BOOK OF.

APODICTIC, APODEICTIC. The term apodictic/apodeictic is credited to the German scholar, Albrecht Alt. Alt distinguished between laws that apply unconditionally, without reference to particular circumstances (apodictic laws), and those that describe specific conditions under which they apply (CASUISTIC LAWS). Apodictic laws tend to be commands that often fail to prescribe a punishment. Excellent examples of such laws are the Ten Commandments.

Alt found that apodictic laws were unique to ancient Israel and related to its cultic practices; whereas the casuistic laws, influenced by ancient Near Eastern practices, were not unique and were related to ancient Israel's secular legal system. Since Alt's groundbreaking work, apodictic laws are no longer thought to be solely Israelite in origin and their association with cultic traditions is questioned. Rather, OT laws, both apodictic and casuistic, are viewed as sacred because they express significant aspects of ancient Israel's responsibility in its covenantal relationship with Yahweh.

CHERYL B. ANDERSON

APOLLO [Ἀπόλλων Apollōn]. The twin brother of ARTEMIS and the son of ZEUS and Leto, Apollo became one of the most popular and esteemed of the Greek gods. The cult of Apollo reached across many boundaries of Mediterranean cultures, and it assigned a broad range of functions to the deity.

Apollo was associated with music, lyric poetry, the sun, and the protection of both crops and livestock. He could send and divert plagues. He was a god of healing and purification, although his son Asclepius grew to greater prominence as a healer by the time of Hellenism's onset, overshadowing but not entirely eliminating Apollo's reputation as one who cures. Most attention to Apollo focused on his role in prophecy and divination.

The *Homeric Hymn to Apollo* explains the god's connections to divination and the shrine at Delphi by telling the tale of Apollo killing the giant serpent, the PYTHON, that lived there. Thus the "Python spirit" (πνεῦμα Πύθων pneuma Pythōn) of Acts 16:16 refers to the slave girl's divinatory capacities. The oracle at Delphi enjoyed widespread fame as a place for inquirers to receive prophetic utterances from Apollo in the mouths and interpretations of his functionaries. Other sites offered similar opportunities for people to hear inspired messages delivered through the deity's priestesses and (much less commonly) priests. The nature of these oracular communications and the practices of the god's intermediaries varied significantly, although Apollonian divination generally was considered more restrained than the frenzied methods associated with the Cybele and Dionysus cults. Nevertheless, in contexts where the ecstatic behavior of Apollonian divination was familiar, the prophetic experiences of the early churches may have prompted some to emphasize the distinctive characteristics of the Holy Spirit's manifestations among Christians. Admonitions to the Corinthians concerning acceptable modes of congregational prayer, prophecy, and inspired speech (*see* 1 Cor 11:2-16; 14:21-33*a*, 39-40) may indicate attempts to contrast Christian prophecy with the mantic (and, to Paul, shameful or implicitly sexualized) utterances performed by the female prophets of Apollo and other deities throughout the Greco-Roman world.

Apollo's continuing importance in the Roman era is seen in Octavian's giving special devotion to the god and ordering the construction of a temple to Apollo on the Palatine in Rome in response to his victory over MARK ANTONY at Actium in 31 BCE. *See* GREEK RELIGION AND PHILOSOPHY.

MATTHEW L. SKINNER

APOLLODORUS, MYTHOGRAPHER [Ἀπολλόδωρος Apollodōros]. Author of the *Library* (*Bibliotheca*), a compilation of Greek myths from the world of the primal gods to Odysseus' death and an important source for the lives of the earliest Greek heroes. Its influence in antiquity rests upon its comprehensiveness and simplicity of style. Traditionally, authorship of the *Library* is attributed to Apollodorus of Athens (ca. 180, after 120 BCE), a polymath known for his *Chronicle* and *On the Gods*. Internal evidence, however, makes this impossible. While the text's authorship thus remains unknown, most scholars place it between the 1st cent. BCE and CE. *See* KOINE.

DAVID M. REIS

APOLLONIA ap´uh-loh´nee-uh [Ἀπολλωνία Appolōnia]. A Macedonian city named for the Greek god Apollo. Apollonia was centrally located on the Egnatian Way, the Roman-built east-west route for travel from Italy to the province of Asia. PAUL and SILAS passed through Apollonia on their way to THESSALONICA (Acts 17:1).

APOLLONIUS ap´uh-loh´nee-uhs [Ἀπολλώνιος Apollōnios]. 1. Son of Thraseas, governor of Coele-Syria and Phoenicia (2 Macc 3:5), who urged the despoiling of the temple treasury; 4 Macc 4:1-14 makes him the despoiler.

2. Son of Menestheus sent by Antiochus IV Epiphanes to commemorate Ptolemy VI Philometer's coronation in 172 BCE. Jason the high priest acclaimed Apollonius in Jerusalem en route (2 Macc 4:21-22).

3. Mysarch (i.e., commander of Antiochus IV's Mysian mercenaries), possibly to be identified with Apollonius (2) and/or (4). At Antiochus's behest, he seized Jerusalem by trickery in 168/7 BCE and constructed the fortified Akra to house Syrian troops (2 Macc 5:23-26; compare with 1 Macc 1:29-36).

4. Governor of Samaria (Josephus, *Ant.* 12.261, 287). Led a campaign against Judas Maccabeus in 166/5 BCE, and lost the battle and his life. Judas took his sword as a trophy (1 Macc 3:10-12).

5. Son of Gennaios, a regional governor who harassed the Jews (2 Macc 12:2).

6. Governor of Coele-Syria and Phoenicia. On behalf of Demetrius II (*not* Alexander Balas, as in Josephus, *Ant.* 13.87-88) he fought Jonathan Maccabeus in a major battle near Ashod in 146 BCE, and was decisively defeated (1 Macc 10:69-89).

J. R. C. COUSLAND

APOLLONIUS OF TYANA. *See* PHILOSTRATUS, FLAVIUS.

APOLLOPHANES ap´uh-lof´uh-neez [Ἀπολλοφάνης Apollophanēs]. An Ammonite killed with his brothers Chaereas and Timothy by "twenty young men" in Judas Maccabeus' army at Gazara (2 Macc 10:32-37; 1 Macc 5:6-8).

APOLLOS uh-pol´uhs [Ἀπολλῶς Apollōs, Ἀπολλώνιος Apollōnios]. According to LUKE, Apollos was a Jew and a native of ALEXANDRIA, "an eloquent man, well-versed in the scriptures" (Acts 18:24). Having received instruction in "the WAY of the Lord," Luke states that "he spoke with a burning enthusiasm and taught accurately the things concerning Jesus" (Acts 18:25*a-b*). This zeal and rhetorical proficiency impressed the Ephesians, who commended him to CORINTH, where he exercised a similar influence over that community (Acts 18:27–19:1). Luke's assertion that Apollos was deficient in the Holy Spirit makes him clearly subordinate to Paul (Acts 18:25c-26; cf. 19:1-7). This demotion perhaps reflects Apollos' popularity, a fact that Paul himself recognized (1 Cor 1:12; 3:4, 21-22). Because of Apollos' reputation in Corinth, Paul validates his work as a fellow servant of God and a "guardian," but ultimately elevates himself to the role of the Corinthians' father (1 Cor 3:5-15; 4:14-16). Even so, Paul's closing remarks demonstrate that while he and Apollos were in EPHESUS together, the two worked independently (1 Cor 16:12). The deutero-Pauline tradition places Apollos in CRETE (Titus 3:13), JEROME asserted that he became the bishop of CORINTH, and Luther argued that he was the author of Hebrews.

DAVID M. REIS

APOLLYON uh-pol'yuhn [Ἀπολλύων Apollyōn]. The name of the ruler of the abyss in Rev 9:11 and a Greek translation of the Hebrew name ABADDON, which means, literally, "Destroyer." Ancient Jewish and Christian writers use many names for the leader of the demons, including SATAN, BEELZEBUL, MASTEMA, and Semyaza.

APOLOGETICS. Derived from classical Greek usage, "apologetics" originally referred to a judicial defense (ἀπολογία apologia) against an accusation (κατηγορία katēgoria). Classical texts evidence these defenses (e.g., Plato, *Apol.* 28a and *Ep.* 7), while the strategies for defenses are extant in presentations of forensic rhetoric (e.g., Aristotle, *Rhet.* 1.10-15). It is incorrect to view simply any polemical passage as an *apologia*, especially given the agonistic nature of ancient rhetoric.

Apologetic terminology can be found in 1st cent. CE Christian literature (e.g., 2 Tim 4:16; 1 Pet 3:15; apologia; Luke 12:11; Acts 24:10 ἀπολογέομαι apologeomai). The narrative forms of classical *apologiai* are also present (e.g., the various defenses in Acts [e.g., 22:1-21], as well as Paul's epistolary defenses against accusations of false motives (e.g., 1 Thess 2:1-12) and of preaching an inadequate gospel (e.g., Galatians); compare also Josephus, *Against Apion*).

In the first two cent. BCE, however, "apologetics" began to experience a transformation as authors wove deliberative and epideictic rhetorical strategies and goals into (sometimes fictive) forensic contexts (e.g., Dionysius of Halicarnassus, *Antiquitates romanae*; Philo, *Hypothetica* and *Legatio ad Gaium*; Josephus, *Antiquities*; Luke and Acts [26:29]) with a view to creating etiologies and explanatory histories of origins. This evolution gave rise in the 2nd cent. CE (and beyond) to the clearly identifiable work of Christian "apologists" (e.g., Melito, Justin, Tatian) who authored increasingly sophisticated rhetorical (catechetical or propagandistic) presentations of Christian practice and doctrine, works that, drawing heavily on OT and NT biblical materials, have as their goal not a

defense and acquittal of their authors but a clear and even self-incriminating (martyrological) presentation to judicial figures (real or fictive) of Christian claims, often in rivalry with other claims.

L. GREGORY BLOOMQUIST

APOPHTHEGM. A transliterated Greek term with the general meaning *saying* (the plural form is *apophthegmata*), but has been used by some NT scholars as the specific designation for one category of originally oral sayings of Jesus that are embedded in a brief narrative context and which typically culminate in a pithy saying of Jesus. While Rudolf Bultmann preferred to designate these oral forms with the general term *apophthegmata*, Martin Dibelius favored the term *paradigm* (*example*), and Anglo-American scholars have preferred the designations "pronouncement story" (Vincent Taylor) or *chreia* (a Greek word meaning *anecdote*, considered an analogy to Gospel paradigms by Dibelius). For Bultmann, subtypes of the *apophthegmata* include controversy sayings (e.g., Mark 3:1-6), school sayings (e.g., Mark 12:28-34), and biographical *apophthegmata* (e.g., Luke 9:57-62). *See* FORM CRITICISM.

Bibliography: Rudolf Bultmann. *The History of the Synoptic Tradition* (1963).

DAVID E. AUNE

APOSTASY uh-pos'tuh-see [מְשׁוּבָה meshuvah; ἀποστασία apostasia]. The word *apostasy* derives from the Greek noun apostasia, which means "a standing away from" or "rebellion." Though originally referring to political or military rebellion, during the Greco-Roman period the noun also came to mean religious rebellion. The word *apostasy* has been used to translate different Hebrew words, the most common of which is meshuvah. Though this noun can bear a general negative sense, e.g., "waywardness" (Prov 1:32), it most frequently, particularly in the book of Jeremiah, signifies behavior in which Israel strays from its religious commitments. Jeremiah 2:19 uses the noun meshuvah, "apostasy," alluding to a graphic depiction of religious infidelity depicted earlier in that chapter (*see* 2:13). The idea of apostasy logically requires that an individual or group knew or agreed to a proper form of religious life.

Though the word meshuvah can stand in parallel with nouns such as "wickedness" and "transgressions" (e.g., Jer 2:19; 5:6), the arena of such misbehavior is normally religious, e.g., worshiping other gods, rather than ethical infractions. Hence, when Paul is accused of teaching Jews "to forsake Moses" (Acts 21:21), it was appropriate for the author to characterize Paul's activity as apostasia. (*See* also 2 Thess 2:3, for the use of the noun, there translated as "rebellion," also in a religious sense.) The Bible reports numerous instances of apostasy, though without using the aforementioned Hebrew and Greek vocabulary; e.g., Saul's "rebellion"

(1 Sam 15:22-23) and those who were "enlightened" but who had "fallen away" (Heb 6:4-6).

DAVID PETERSEN

APOSTLE uh-pos´uhl [ἀπόστολος apostolos]. Used in the NT, both as a general designation for someone authorized to act on behalf of another, or sent with a commission, and as a distinctive title for particular founding figures and church leaders.

    A. NT Usage
    B. Background and Origins
      1. *Apostolos* in Greek usage
      2. Parallels and influences
    C. Development of the Apostolate
    Bibliography

A. NT Usage

Of the seventy-nine appearances of the term, the majority are found in Luke–Acts and in letters attributed to Paul (thirty-four each). In Luke–Acts, *apostle* is used almost exclusively of the Twelve (usually the group as a whole), both during the time of Jesus and (with Matthias replacing Judas) after the resurrection. Unlike the other Synoptics, where *apostle* is used of the Twelve only in connection with a specific, limited mission (Matt 10:2; Mark 3:14 [var.]; 6:30), in Luke the term is a permanent title, bestowed by Jesus when the Twelve were chosen (Luke 6:13). In Acts 1:15-26, the fixed character of the "Twelve apostles" is indicated both by the need to fill the gap left by Judas' defection and in the criterion set out by Peter: Judas' replacement must have witnessed the ministry of Jesus "from the baptism of John" through to the resurrection and ascension (v. 22). This criterion would appear to disqualify Paul, who also differs from Luke's portrait of an apostle in the itinerant nature of his ministry; except for Peter, forced to leave Jerusalem because of persecution, apostles are resident in Jerusalem (e.g., Acts 8:1, 14; 9:27; 15:2). Nevertheless, Luke does not completely deny the term to Paul, twice referring to Paul and Barnabas as *apostles* in one particular account (Acts 14:4, 14). Many interpreters attempt to resolve this discrepancy by understanding the word in a generic sense (Paul and Barnabas as delegates of the Antioch church), but nothing in the passage itself (where "the apostles" appears without qualification) or in the earlier commissioning scene (Acts 13:1-4, where Luke could easily have used **apostellein**) encourages us to read the verse in this way. The discrepancy is not easily resolved.

Most occurrences of *apostle* in Paul's letters have to do with his own role and status. The term appears in the salutation of all but four of the letters attributed to him. In the undisputed epistles, his understanding of the criteria for apostleship becomes evident as he responds to those who question his legitimacy. An apostle is one who has seen the risen Lord (1 Cor 15:8-9; Gal 1:15-16), who has been commissioned by "Jesus Christ and God the Father" (Gal 1:1) to proclaim the gospel, and whose ministry is accompanied by "the signs of an apostle" (2 Cor 12:12)—not only "wonders and mighty works" (2 Cor 12:12) but also the fruit of apostolic labor represented by the converts themselves (1 Cor 9:2).

Paul's letters also provide important information about "those who were already apostles before [him]" (Gal 1:17). In contrast to Luke, Paul differentiates "the Twelve" and "the apostles": the list in 1 Cor 15:5-8 details separate resurrection appearances "to Cephas, then to the Twelve," and "to James, then to all the apostles." Since he elsewhere ascribes apostleship to Cephas/Peter (Gal 2:7-8), there is a certain overlap between the two groups. But the overlap is by no means complete. The parallel formulation seems to indicate that James (presumably the brother of Jesus) is to be counted as an apostle just as Cephas is numbered among the Twelve (*see also* Gal 1:19). Further, Paul ascribes the term to others who certainly were not part of the Twelve: Andronicus and Junia (Rom 16:7); Barnabas, apparently (1 Cor 9:6); perhaps Silvanus and Timothy (1 Thess 2:7). He also speaks contemptuously of certain "super apostles" (2 Cor 11:5; 12:11) or "false apostles" (2 Cor 11:13) who, along with those mentioned in Rev 2:2 and *Did.* 11:3-6, would presumably claim the title for themselves without the modifiers. What seems to be reflected in Paul's letters, then, is the existence of a larger group of apostles, constituted not through association with the earthly Jesus but on the basis of criteria similar to those claimed by Paul for himself.

As a group, the apostles constitute the first of the gifts with which the church has been endowed (1 Cor 12:28), a theme that reappears in Ephesians (4:11) alongside a more elevated conception—the apostles (and prophets) as the foundation of the church (Eph 2:20). A similar foundational role appears in Rev 21:14 (with Lukan echoes: "the twelve apostles of the Lamb"), in several other NT passages (2 Pet 3:2; Jude 17), and frequently in the apostolic fathers (esp. Ignatius).

In two other passages Paul uses **apostolos** in the generic sense of a delegate or agent—once of certain persons commissioned by "the churches" to participate in Paul's collection project (2 Cor 8:23) and once of Epaphroditus as an agent of the church in Philippi (Phil 2:25). A similar generic sense appears in John 13:16 ("an apostle is not greater than the one who sent him")—the only appearance of the word in John's Gospel.

Most of the eleven other occurrences of *apostle* have been commented on already. In addition, the term appears in the salutation of 1 and 2 Peter, in a manner reminiscent of Paul (e.g., "Peter an apostle of Jesus Christ"; 1 Pet 1:1). A unique use of the term is found in Hebrews (3:1), where it is used of Christ himself ("the apostle and high priest of our confession"). Any assessment of the NT material also needs to take account of the related term *apostleship* (ἀποστολή apostolē), found in Acts 1:25 and three times in Paul (Rom 1:5; 1 Cor 9:2; Gal 2:8).

B. Background and Origins
1. Apostolos in Greek usage
Although it is derived from the common verb ἀποστέλλειν (apostellein, to send), apostolos is relatively uncommon in Greek literature outside the NT and its sphere of influence. In classical and Hellenistic usage it is usually associated with seafaring or naval expeditions, most often with an impersonal reference: the sending of a ship or fleet (Lysias *Or.* 19.21); an embassy by ship (Herodotus *Hist.* 5.38); a naval squadron (Demosthenes *Cor.* 80, 107); a bill of lading (P.Oxy. 1197.13). Occasionally the term is used personally—e.g., of the commander of an expedition (Hesychius *Lex.*) or of a group of colonists (Dionysius of Halicarnassus *Ant. rom.* 9.59.2). Only in Herodotus (5th cent. BCE), however, do we find the term used of an individual who has explicitly been commissioned: e.g., a herald (kērux) sent to arrange a truce is referred to as an apostolos (*Hist.* 1.28).

The picture does not change when we turn to Hellenistic Jewish material. Apostolos appears just twice: once in Josephus (*Ant.* 17.300), referring to a delegation sent by the Jewish nation to the emperor; and once in the LXX (3 Kgdms 14:6), where the prophet Ahijah describes himself as one who was sent (shaluakh) by God to deliver a particular message.

Thus the early Christians seem to have taken a relatively rare word and made it part of their special vocabulary. Various attempts have been made to account for this development.

2. Parallels and influences
The earliest and most influential theory is that the roots of the NT apostolate are to be found, both semantically and conceptually, in the Jewish institution of the shaliakh (from שָׁלַח shalakh, "to send"). Appearing frequently in the Mishnah, a shaliakh is a legal agent who has been authorized to act on behalf of an individual or group in some way or another. Such an agent might arrange a betrothal (*m. Qidd.* 2.1), a divorce (*m. Git.* 4.1) or a business transaction (*t. Yebam.* 4.4). Agents of a court (*m. Git.* 3.6) or of the Jerusalem Sanhedrin (*m. Yebam.* 16.7) are also known as sheluhim. The institution was sufficiently well established in the Tannaitic period that it generated the maxim "a man's agent is as the man himself" (e.g., *m. Ber.* 5.5). According to this theory the term (in its Aramaic form shelikha') was introduced by Jesus himself, first when sending his disciples out on a limited mission, and then in a fresh commissioning after the resurrection. Subsequently, the rare word apostolos gained currency as an equivalent in the Greek-speaking church.

This theory has been vigorously criticized on two fronts. One criticism has to do with differences in substance: since the role of the shaliakh is temporary and pertains primarily to the legal and secular sphere, it fails to account for the early Christian apostolate at its most distinctive point—the apostle as a permanently appointed missionary. The second criticism concerns dating. The earliest evidence for the shaliakh institution is provided by the Mishnah (ca. 225 CE), which means that, even taking into account the character of the Mishnah as a compilation of tradition, there is no certain evidence that the institution existed in the time of Jesus.

These criticisms have been advanced in the service of several alternative theories. Schmithals has argued for a Gnostic origin, but the theory of a pre-Christian Gnosticism is doubtful in itself and there is little evidence for Gnostic use of the term. Others place more stress on the uniqueness of the Christian phenomenon, accounting for the term itself either by arguing that the sense of the term found in Herodotus continued to be present in *koine* Greek or by appealing to the influence of the LXX, where apostellein is often used with reference to divine commissioning (e.g., Isa 6:8; 61:1; Jer 7:25).

Except for Schmithals' theory, these suggestions of influence are not necessarily mutually exclusive. The shaliakh institution does not have to be dated later than the 1st cent. and it may well have been a factor. With respect to Greek usage, the NT writers themselves provide evidence for a generic, "secular" use of the term (2 Cor 8:23; Phil 2:25; John 13:16). Still, emphasis needs to be placed not on where the early Christians found the term but on what they did with it.

C. Development of the Apostolate
On the basis of the preceding discussion, a brief sketch can be attempted here. There is little reason to doubt either that Jesus appointed twelve disciples for a particular role or that this role included limited-term preaching missions in Galilee. Given the prevalence of "sending" language in Jesus' sayings, it is probable that he used the verb in connection with the missions of the disciples and at least possible that he used the noun form.

The resurrection experience, which brought the Jerusalem church into being, also brought into being a foundational group of community leaders. This group included the Twelve but was not restricted to them. One can only speculate about an Aramaic term for members of this group, but evidence from Paul indicates that Greek-speakers knew them as apostoloi (Gal 1:17). Paul's reference to Andronicus and Junia (certainly feminine; *see* JUNIA, JUNIAS) as being "among the apostles" (Rom 16:7) indicates that women were included, even if none of the women who first witnessed the resurrection is so described. Paul's letters provide evidence that as the Christian movement spread outside Judea and into the Hellenistic world an element of itinerancy was added, so that *apostoloi* were not only commissioned witnesses of the resurrection but also traveling missionaries. With his conviction that he had been sent to "the nations," however, Paul made itinerant mission so much a part of the *apostolos* concept that in subsequent centuries the Twelve themselves were transformed into resolute missionaries bringing the gospel to the farthest corners of the earth. This transformation bears witness also to Luke's contribution, who, in his concern for continuity and orderly development, took the idea of a foundational group of apostles, combined it with the memory of the Twelve disciples chosen by the earthly Jesus himself, and so produced the enduring conception of "the Twelve apostles."

Bibliography: F. H. Agnew. "On the Origin of the Term *Apostolos*." *CBQ* 38 (1976) 49–53; F. H. Agnew. "The Origin of the NT Apostle-Concept: A Review of Research." *JBL* 105 (1986) 75–96; Heinz O. Guenther. *The Footprints of Jesus' Twelve in Early Christian Traditions: A Study in the Meaning of Religious Symbolism* (1985); J. A. Kirk. "Apostleship Since Rengstorf: Towards a Synthesis." *NTS* 21 (1975) 249–64; J. B. Lightfoot. "The Name and Office of Apostle." *The Epistle of St. Paul to the Galatians* (1890) 92–101; Johannes Munck. "Paul, the Apostles, and the Twelve." *ST* 3 (1949) 96–110; Walter Schmithals. *The Office of Apostle in the Early Church* (1969); Rudolf Schnackenburg. "Apostles Before and During Paul's Time." *Apostolic History and the Gospel.* W. Ward Gasque and Ralph P. Martin, eds. (1970) 287–303.

TERENCE DONALDSON

APOSTLES, ACTS OF THE. *See* ACTS OF THE APOSTLES.

APOSTLES, EPISTLE OF THE. The title given to an apocryphal writing preserved in fullest form in Ethiopic (manuscripts from the 14th to the 20th cent.), partially in Coptic (4th–5th cent.), and fragmentarily in Latin (5th–6th cent.). The first half of the running head of the Latin pages reads "epistle" (*epistula*), but the remainder has not been preserved. The traditional designation "Epistle of the Apostles" may or may not be the original title of the work. Another possibility is that the opening words of the Ethiopic have preserved the title: "The Book of the Revelation of Jesus Christ to His Disciples." The *Epistle to the Apostles* was composed most probably in Greek, though recently Syriac has also been suggested. This writing was essentially unknown to Western scholarship before attention fell on the Coptic papyrus codex in 1895.

The *Epistle to the Apostles* does employ some epistolary formulas to present "for the whole world" what was revealed to the eleven apostles by Jesus Christ. It is written in the name of these apostles (Cephas is distinguished here from Peter) and directed to the churches of the east, west, north, and south "because of the false apostles Simon and Cerinthus." After an introduction that reviews the preexistence, incarnation, life, and fleshly resurrection of Christ (Peter, too, puts his finger into the marks of the nails in the Lord's hands), the writing records what Jesus told the apostles after his resurrection in the form of a revelatory dialogue. The main topics are the details of the incarnation, the resurrection of the flesh and the body, martyrdom, the nature of the afterlife, christological issues (the unity of the Son with the Father), Christ's mission to the underworld, the content, purpose, and inner workings of Christian proclamation, the place of Paul and the predominance of Christians of Gentile background, Christian "believers" who will not be saved and the attitude that is proper to take toward them, the signs of the end and the form of Christ's coming, and Christian ethics, community, and discipline.

Heavily imbued with the language of the Gospel of John, the *Epistle to the Apostles* can be understood as a late expression of the Johannine school in which the Johannine heritage is integrated with the gospels of Matthew, Mark, and Luke, and with Acts and Paul. John appears first in the list of apostles.

Thus, although Egypt and Syria have also been proposed for the origin of the *Epistle to the Apostles*, Asia Minor is most likely its home. It is possible that *Ep. Apos.* 15 promotes celebration of a Christian Passover in a form for which Asia Minor became infamous (Quartodecimanism): a fast in remembrance of Jesus' death through the night of the fifteenth of Nisan, broken by an agape-feast at the cock's crow. Furthermore, the text of the NT writings known by the *Epistle to the Apostles* is distinctly "Western" and displays an affinity with Irenaeus's text in its christological reading of John 1:13 in the singular (*Ep. Apos.* 3). Like Irenaeus, *Ep. Apos.* 3 also applies "over the cherubim" (Pss 80:1; 99:1) to Christ.

The justification of the role of Paul vis à vis the eleven apostles builds on the effort in Acts but clearly moves to a new level by having Christ himself proclaim in advance the appearance of Paul and the details of his mission. Hence, some scholars have suggested that the *Epistle to the Apostles* must derive from a Jewish Christian environment that would have demanded such a bold justification of Paul. But the *Epistle to the Apostles* is not Jewish Christian, nor does it seem to derive from a Jewish Christian background. Rather, the author is best understood as a Gentile Christian with a Johannine background who is arguing for an evolving consensus of the Great Church that was based on, alongside the Gospel of John and perhaps the Johannine letters, the OT, the synoptic Gospels, Acts, and the Paulines.

A date of ca. 172 CE may be conjectured for the *Epistle to the Apostles* This date allows the *Epistle to the Apostles* to be after the plague under Marcus Aurelius, which seems to be described in chs. 34–36, and before the coming of Christ predicted apparently for the year 180 CE in ch. 17. There are textual variants for the latter indication, however, and some scholars have urged that the *Epistle to the Apostles* should be dated before 150 CE, even as early as the first fifth of the 2nd cent.

The *Epistle to the Apostles* is important as a testimony to the reception of Acts, and it also perhaps presents an early attestation of the *Infancy Gospel of Thomas*. Later witnesses to the *Epistle to the Apostles* are not plentiful. It was used perhaps by the Apostolic Church Order, the Epistle of Pseudo-Titus, and the Testament of Our Lord and (most certainly) by another apocalypse preserved in Ethiopic and of uncertain date that also used the Testament of Our Lord and by the later Ethiopic tradition.

Bibliography: Charles E. Hill. "*The Epistula Apostolorum:* An Asian Tract from the Time of Polycarp." *JECS* 7 (1999) 1–53; Julian Hills. "Tradition and Composition in the 'Epistula Apostolorum.'" HDR 24 (1990); A. Stewart-Sykes. "The Asian Context of the New Prophecy and of Epistula Apostolorum." *VC* 51 (1997) 416–38.

F. STANLEY JONES

APOSTOLIC CONSTITUTIONS AND CANONS. The Apostolic Constitutions is an eight-volume compilation under the pseudonym Clement of Rome, who is said to have written at the request of the apostles. The last book closes with eighty-five canons that were circulated independently.

Books 1–6 expand on the Didascalia. Book 7 is based on the Didache and a set of Jewish prayers. Book 8 employs the Apostolic Tradition; the closing canons are partially adopted from previous synodal decisions.

The compiler is generally dated to ca. 380 CE, located in or around Antioch, and often identified with the interpolator of the letters of Ignatius of Antioch and with the author of the Commentary on Job, ascribed to a "Julian."

Bibliography: James Donaldson, ed. William Whiston, trans. "Constitutions of the Holy Apostles." Vol. 7. The Ante-Nicene Fathers (1979); Marcel Metzger. *Les Constitutions Apostoliques.* SC 320, 329, 336 (1985–87).

F. STANLEY JONES

APOSTOLIC COUNCIL. *See* JERUSALEM, COUNCIL OF.

APOSTOLIC FATHERS, CHURCH FATHERS. The phrase "Apostolic Fathers" is used to designate a collection of early Christian writings composed (for the most part) during the late 1st or early 2nd cent. CE. The writings in this collection form the earliest portion of a larger collection of texts often called the "Church Fathers" that includes Christian writings up through Isidore of Seville (d. 636) in the West and John of Damascus (d. ca. 750) in the East. While the phrase "apostolic fathers" seems to have been used in antiquity, and collections of early Christian writings existed during the Middle Ages, its modern significance may be traced to the 17th cent., when several collections of varying length were published. Most influential were those by Cotelier (1672), who gathered together works he attributed to "holy fathers who were active in apostolic times," and Wake (1693), who titled his collection "Apostolical Fathers." Both editors included *1 Clement, 2 Clement,* the letters of Ignatius, Polycarp's *Letter to the Philippians,* the *Martyrdom of Polycarp,* the *Epistle of Barnabas,* and the *Shepherd of Hermas.* Some of the documents in these early collections have since been omitted (e.g., the *Martyrdom of Ignatius,* the *Apostolic Constitutions,* or the Pseudo-Clementine *Recognitions*), and others have been added: the *Epistle to Diognetus* and the fragments of Papias and of Quadratus (by Gallandi in 1765), and the *Didache* (following its discovery in 1873). The form of the collection as it exists today—comprising eleven documents (*1–2 Clement, Martyrdom of Polycarp, Didache, Barnabas, Hermas, Diognetus*) or authors (Ignatius, Polycarp, Papias, Quadratus)—is clearly somewhat arbitrary. It possesses no particular unity or coherence with regard to chronology, content, or literary genre (the collection includes letters, a church handbook, a tract, a sermon, a martyrdom, an apocalypse, and an apology) and exists largely as a matter of tradition and convenience. Nonetheless, these writings are the earliest surviving documents written by authors (some known, some anonymous) now seen as early representatives of what would become, in the 4th and 5th cent., Christian Orthodoxy. Hence they are often labeled "proto-orthodox" writers, to distinguish them from representatives of other forms and expressions of Christianity that also flourished in the 2nd cent. It is this theological orientation, therefore, rather than genre, date, or content, that gives the collection whatever unity it now possesses.

Bibliography: Bart D. Ehrman. *The Apostolic Fathers.* 2 vols. LCL (2003) 24–25; Michael W. Holmes. *The Apostolic Fathers: Greek Texts and English Translations* (1999); Michael W. Holmes. *The Apostolic Fathers in English.* 3rd ed. (2005); Clayton N. Jefford. *Reading the Apostolic Fathers: An Introduction* (1996).

MICHAEL W. HOLMES

APOSTOLIC HISTORY OF ABDIAS. *See* ABDIAS, APOSTOLIC HISTORY OF.

APPAIM ap´ay-im [אַפַּיִם ’appayim]. Nadab's son and Ishi's father in the genealogy of the clan of Jerahmeel, a descendant of Judah and his daughter-in-law Tamar (1 Chr 2:30-31).

APPAREL. See CLOTH, CLOTHES.

APPEALS TO CAESAR BY PAUL.

Paul's appeal to Caesar (Acts 25:11) raises both historical and theological questions for interpreters of Acts. Historically, the initial problem is to determine the precise nature and function of the appeal to the emperor in Roman history and law. A right of Roman citizens under the empire, the appeal (*appellatio*) developed from the Roman custom of *provocatio* (Lat., "I call out"), a cry for help to the people of Rome in the face of a perceived injustice by a Roman magistrate. Scholarly disagreements persist about the timing of such appeals—whether permissible before a trial, in order to secure an alternate court, or only after the verdict and sentence were announced—as well as about the authority of a Roman provincial ruler to refuse an appeal. Literary evidence suggests that the appeal was somewhat flexible and that a ruler had the practical power, whether always strictly legal or not, to decide whether to grant the appeal, even against the advice of his council. A subsequent historical question, then, is whether the description in Acts is consistent with what can be known of *provocatio/appellatio* under the early empire. Although debated, the portrayal in Acts seems plausibly to lie within the range of known uses of *provocatio/appellatio*.

One may also ask how Paul's appeal to Caesar functions theologically. According to Acts, it is a "divine necessity" for Paul to reach Rome. Paul's appeal is therefore a means of accomplishing the divine plan to carry the gospel to the very heart of the empire. While interpreters sometimes suggest that Paul made his appeal in order to preserve his life, the narrative itself is not sanguine about Paul's release, hinting instead that Paul's witness to the gospel in Rome may take a form similar to that of Jesus in Jerusalem. Whereas attempts at a strictly historical reconstruction of Paul's motives for appeal discuss his presumed hope for acquittal by a less hostile court, the narrative suggests a theological concern for Paul's proclamation of Jesus and the kingdom of God before Caesar.

Bibliography: John Crook. *Law and Life of Rome.* (1967); Peter Garnsey. "The *lex Iulia* and Appeal Under the Empire." *JRS* 56 (1966) 167–89; A. H. M. Jones. *Studies in Roman Government and Law* (1968); Andrew W. Lintott. "*Provocatio* from the Struggle of the Orders to the Principate." *ANRW* I.2 (1972) 226–67; Fergus Millar. *The Emperor in the Roman World (31 BC–AD 337)* (1977); Brian Rapske. *The Book of Acts and Paul in Roman Custody* (1994); A. N. Sherwin-White. *Roman Society and Roman Law in the New Testament* (1963).

STEVEN ROBERT MATTHIES

APPHIA af´ee-uh [Ἀπφία Apphia]. A Christian woman mentioned in Paul's greeting to PHILEMON (Phlm 2) along with ARCHIPPUS as members of Philemon's house church. Perhaps they are related to Philemon as wife and son or as sister and younger brother. The name "Apphia" or "Aphphia" occurs in inscriptions from Phrygia.

PHEME PERKINS

APPHUS af´uhs [Ἀπφους Apphous]. An appellation for JONATHAN MACCABEUS, one of Mattathias' five sons. Means "cunning" (1 Macc 2:5).

APPIAN WAY ap´ee-uhn [ἡ Ἀππία ὁδός hē Appia hodos, Lat. *Via Appia*]. Called "the queen of roads" by the poet Statius, it ran 364 mi. from the Porta Capena at Rome to Brundisium, the chief Italian port for travel to Greece and eastward. Begun in 312 BCE, completed by 200 BCE, it was named after Appius Claudius, who built the stretch from Rome to Capua along which Paul later traveled from Puteoli (Acts 28:13), passing en route through the FORUM OF APPIUS and the THREE TAVERNS (Acts 28:15).

Bibliography: Ivana Della Portella, ed. *The Appian Way* (2004).

JOHN T. FITZGERALD

APPIUS, FORUM OF. See FORUM OF APPIUS.

APPLE [אישׁון 'ishon, תַּפּוּחַ tappuah; μῆλον mēlon]. Described as a sweet-tasting (Song 2:3), golden (Prov 25:11), and scented fruit (Song 7:8 [Heb. Song 7:9], whose tree provides shade (Song 2:3; 8:5) and physical sustenance (Song 2:5; Joel 1:12). Uncertainty surrounds the exact species (fig, date, quince, citrus, apricot, apple), yet the most probable candidate is the apricot (*prunus armeniaca*) because it best fulfills biblical descriptions and, unlike the common apple (*pyrus malus, malus pumila*), it was cultivated and grew wild in biblical Palestine and Syria. Alternatively, the tappuakh might be the indigenous, "apple-shaped" quince (*cydonia oblonga* L.). The quince, originating from Persia, is also fragrant and is used for medicinal purposes; however, it tastes sour, not sweet, as the apple is described. The Targum translates tappuakh in Song 2:3 as אתרוגא ('trwg') or citron, which is supported by Prov 25:11's description of "tappuakh of gold." Citrus, not native to the Near East, is a possible, though unlikely, translation. The LXX's μῆλον (mēlon) is translated "apple" (Prov 25:11; Song 2:3; 8:5; Joel 1:12) and "pomegranate" (Song 4:3; 6:7).

While the fruit of the tree in the middle of the garden of Eden (Gen 2:9, 17; 3:3-6) is unnamed, tradition designates it as the common apple (*see* EDEN, GARDEN OF). First, the Targum to the Song of Songs on 2:5 and 7:9 places the tappuakh in Eden where God's holy words are described as being sweet as the tappuakh in the garden of Eden. Drawing on Song 8:5, Rabbi

Aquila aligns the apple tree with "the tree of knowl-edge of good and evil" (Gen 2:9), which may be the source of Jerome's Latin translation: the Latin word for "evil," malum, is identical to mālum, the Latin word for "apple." These associations may have led the apple to become the symbol of the first temptation and the cause of human sin. See APPLE OF THE EYE; FRUIT.

Bibliography: Oded Borowski. *Agriculture in Iron Age Israel: The Evidence from Archaeology and the Bible* (1987); H. N. Moldenke and A. L. Moldenke. *Plants of the Bible* (1952).

DEBORAH A. APPLER

APPLE OF THE EYE אִישׁוֹן עַיִן 'ishon 'ayin, עַיִן בַּת bath 'ayin, בָּבַת עַיִן bavath 'ayin]. Several Hebrew terms are thus translated to indicate the eye's pupil or the eyeball, used metaphorically to designate something precious, vulnerable, and deserving of vigi-lant care. Deuteronomy 32:10 and Prov 7:2 use 'ishon 'ayin to denote, respectively, the preciousness of Israel to Yahweh and of the law to the faithful. In Ps 17:8 bath 'ayin invokes Yahweh's protection, while in Lam 2:18 it designates the eye as the locus of tears. Zecha-riah 2:8 [Heb. 2:12] uses bavath 'ayin to assert that injury done to Israel is tantamount to assaulting the eye of Yahweh.

JOHN KESSLER

APPOINT יָעַד ya'adh, שִׂים sim, פָּקַד paqadh; τίθημι tithēmi, ποιέω poieō]. Term used to translate several Hebrew and Greek words that mean designat-ing a time, place, or a person for a specific purpose. Complying with God's instructions, Moses appointed a specific time each year for festivals, especially for remembering God's deliverance of the Israelites out of Egypt during Passover (Lev 23:2-4, 44; Num 9:2-3; Exod 23:15). Moses also appointed places of refuge for persons who had committed unpremeditated murder (Exod 21:13). Appointing a person meant either that God was assigning that person to perform a specific leadership role or that God had sanctioned a leader to make the selection. For example, God appointed Moses and Aaron to lead the Israelites out of Egypt and Joshua to replace Moses (Num 27:16); but Moses, with God's direction, appointed the Levites to take care of the tabernacle (Num 1:50). Not only prophetic lead-ers and priests, but kings and judges are also referred to as appointed (1 Sam 13:14; 2 Sam 6:21; 7:10-11). Similarly, Paul refers to God as having appointed the civil authorities to their positions (Rom 13:2) and the Corinthian members to the roles of apostle, prophet, teacher, miracle worker, healer, helper, administrator, and speaker of tongues (1 Cor 12:28). Jesus is men-tioned as appointing his disciples (Mark 3:14) and seventy others (Luke 10:1) to heal and preach. Leaders of the early church continued to refer to their leaders as

having been appointed by God (2 Tim 1:11) or by other church leaders (Acts 14:23; 2 Cor 8:19; Titus 1:5).

EMILY CHENEY

APPROACH קָרֵב qarev, נָגַשׁ naghash; προσέρχο—μαι proserchomai]. A concept that indicates nearing the divine and the conditions that allow such risky access. In many cases, this has to do with the *myste-rium tremendum*, which expresses the awe-inspiring and fearsome presence of God.

Several passages illustrate the great care necessary to "approach" the divine. The Holiness Code warns that those priests with physical impairments were not "qualified" to present food offerings, or to enter the holiest part of the Temple (Lev 21:17 [qrb], 23 [ngsh]) and legislates against contamination by that which is considered unclean, including menstruating women and incestuous relationships (Lev 18:6, 14, 19 [qrb]). Job exclaims that were he to receive an audience with God, he would "approach" (qrb) the divine "like a prince." Through the prophet Isaiah, Yahweh invites the people to enter God's presence (ngsh) in order to hear news of divine help (41:1).

The Korahites transgressed the boundaries ensur-ing safety in regard to holiness (Num 16:5-40). No one other than Aaronites may enter the sanctuary and altar area (Num 18:3-22). The Zadokites receive the privilege of approaching the sanctuary, and the responsibility of preventing the holy and unclean from contaminating each other (Ezek 44:16).

The book of Hebrews picks up on this concept in discussing access to God through Jesus (Heb 4:16; 7:25; 10:22). See AARON; CLEAN AND UNCLEAN; HOLINESS CODE; KORAH; P, PRIESTLY WRITERS; ZADOK, ZADOKITES.

Bibliography: Rudolf Otto. *The Idea of the Holy: An Inquiry into the Non-Rational Factor in the Idea of the Divine and its Relation to the Rational* (1923).

LISA MICHELE WOLFE

APRON [σιμικίνθιον simikinthion]. In NT references a simikinthion was a workers' overgarment (Acts 19:12). See GIRDLE; LOINCLOTH.

APULEIUS. Author of *Metamorphoses*, known as *The Golden Ass*, important for understanding the Isis Mys-teries and the similarities of their rituals to Christian rituals.

AQABA, GULF OF ah'kuh-bah. In ancient times, the Elanitic Gulf. The body of water, about 100 mi. long and 15 mi. wide, lying between the Sinai Peninsula and Midian, and culminating in the south in the Straits of Tiran and the Red Sea, and in the north at the time of the Exodus in the settlements of Elath and Ezion-Geber (Num 33:35; Deut 2:8). In the time of Solomon, Ezion-

Geber (which may or may not be synonymous with the Ezion-Geber of the exodus), served as the harbor for his Red Sea fleet, which, manned by Phoenician sailors, traded with Arabia, Africa, and India (1 Kgs 9:26-28; 2 Chr 8:17-18). The barren coasts and seasonal winds of the Gulf and the strong currents at the Straits make sailing difficult. Jehoshaphat's fleet was wrecked while still at Ezion-Geber (1 Kgs 22:48). Trade also depended on whether the Israelites, the Edomites, or the Egyptians controlled Elath and Ezion-Geber.

STEPHEN E. TABACHNICK

AQHAT. In the Ugaritic Legend of Aqhat, he is Danel's son, whom Anath kills when Aqhat refuses to give her his bow in exchange for immortality and wealth.

AQIBA. *See* AKIBA, RABBI.

AQUEDUCT. *See* WATER WORKS.

AQUILA AND PRISCILLA ak´wi-luh, pri-sil´uh [Ἀκύλας Akylas, Πρίσκιλλα Priskilla]. A married couple; business and missionary associates of the Apostle Paul.

Priscilla (the diminutive form used in Acts 18:2, 18, 26) or Prisca (Rom 16:3; 1 Cor 16:19; 2 Tim 4:19) is cited before her husband in four of the six NT references, probably signaling her more prominent role in the early church. Both bear Latin names, and Aquila is identified as a Jewish "native of Pontus" (Acts 18:2). The Pauline Letters and Acts sketch the couple's work and travels across the eastern Mediterranean world, based in Rome, Corinth, and Ephesus.

Acts reports that Aquila and Priscilla left Rome as a result of Claudius Caesar's edict expelling Jews from the city (49 CE). They settled in Corinth where they plied their tent-making or leather-working trade and first welcomed fellow artisan Paul into their home and business (18:1-3). Since Paul did not evangelize them, they must have already embraced the Christian way before leaving Rome. After eighteen months in Corinth, the three missionaries sailed to Ephesus, where Priscilla and Aquila remained while Paul headed to Jerusalem (18:18-23). In Ephesus, the couple expounded "the Way of God . . . more accurately" to the eloquent philosopher-teacher Apollos (18:24-26), and established a church in their home (1 Cor 16:19). They further "risk[ed] their necks" defending Paul in some unspecified fashion and, after Claudius's death (54 CE), returned to Rome and again hosted a local congregation (Rom 16:3-5*a*).

In short, the NT portrays Aquila and Priscilla as mobile, relatively prosperous (enough to secure a home in urban centers), courageous, and hospitable early Christian leaders.

Bibliography: F. M. Gillman. *Women Who Knew Paul* (1992).

F. SCOTT SPENCER

AQUILA'S VERSION. One of three Jewish revisions of the LXX. Aquila's revision, known only in fragmentary form, follows the Hebrew text very closely. Aquila even reproduces Hebrew syntax in his translation—often resulting in atrocious Greek. The discovery of a Greek text of the Twelve Prophets at Nahal Hever in 1947 demonstrates that Aquila's revision was the consummation of a larger translational tendency among Greek-speaking Jews in antiquity toward highly literal translations of the OT.

PHILLIP MICHAEL SHERMAN

AR ahr (עָר ʿar). A location in MOAB considered a northern Moabite border marker on the edge of AMMONITE land along the ARNON River (Num 21:15; Deut 2:18-19). Before Ar was allotted to LOT's descendants, it was the home of the REPHAIM, known for their great stature (Deut 2:9-11, 20). Ar represents Moab's destruction in the poetry of Num 21:28 and Isa 15:1. Because of its similarity to the word *city* (עִיר ʿir), it may have had a representative meaning. Archaeology has not definitively established its location.

Bibliography: J. Maxwell Miller. "The Israelite Journey through (around) Moab and Moabite Toponymy." *JBL* 1084 (1989) 577–95.

LISA MICHELE WOLFE

ARA air´uh [אֲרָא ʾaraʾ]. One of the Asherite Jether's three sons and a warrior (1 Chr 7:38).

ARAB, ARABIAN, ARABIA [עֲרָב ʿarav, עַרְבִי ʿarvi; Ἀραβία Arabia]. The terms *Arab* and *Arabia* changed their meanings often in antiquity, including designations of sedentary cultures and urban dwellers. The name ʿarav is often derived from ʿaravah (עֲרָבָה, *desert,* Isa 35:1, 6; Jer 17:6), but its absence in either Akkadian or Arabic makes this proposal unlikely. The name appears in various forms in Assyrian from a base form of **Arrubu** and as **Arabaya** in Old Persian.

A. Geography
    1. *Arab* and *Arabia* in ancient Sources
    2. *Arab* and *Arabia* in modern times
    3. Areas of settlement
B. Religion
C. Languages and Scripts
    1. South Arabia
    2. North Arabia
D. History
    1. Tribal society
    2. Assyrian period
    3. Babylonian period
    4. Persian period
    5. Hellenistic period
    6. Roman period

E. Biblical References
  1. Old Testament
  2. Apocrypha
  3. New Testament
Bibliography

A. Geography

1. *Arab* and *Arabia* in Ancient Sources

The geographical designation *Arabia* does not appear in the OT, but *Arab* first appears in texts from the 8th cent. for the "people of the desert" (i.e. "nomads") stretching across the Sinai from the Suez to the Syrian desert to the Persian Gulf, and south into the Arabian Peninsula. The phrases "sons of the East" (**bene qedem**, as in Judg 6:3; 1 Kgs 4:30; *see* PEOPLE OF THE EAST) and "land of the East" (ʾerets ʿarav, Gen 25:6; Isa 2:6) appear to be used earlier for the Arabs and Arabia. Only later is the name *Arab* applied to a particular people and place. It refers, in retrospect, to the Ishmaelites and Midianites, and then to their successors, the Dedanites, Qedarites, and Sabaeans. In the NT and Josephus, *Arab* refers to the Nabateans of the Hellenistic and Roman eras.

In extra-biblical literature, *Arab* is used of various ethnic groups who inhabit a wide expanse of territory from Iran to Egypt. The Hapiru of the AMARNA LETTERS and the "sand-dwellers," or *Shoshu* of Egyptian texts in the second millennium BCE, have also been associated with a nomadic population, but these are generic categories, not ethnic designations. In the third millennium BCE, Mesopotamian sources designated Bahrain and the adjacent coastline as *Dilmun*, the legendary "home of the gods" famous from the Gilgamesh Epic. In South Arabian inscriptions, *Arab* appears in 40 texts to designate an external population, either from Najran or the desert, who were used as a military auxiliary force by the Sabean kings (*see* SABEANS) in the 1st to the 4th cent. CE. The recent proposal that *Arab* designates a community of camel-riding nomadic warriors united under the command of a divine hero cannot possibly cover the meaning of Arabs from the Assyrian to the Roman periods.

The knowledge of Arabia in antiquity is a late development. From the western perspective, it begins with Alexander's mission to add Arabia to his conquests. Babylonian records support the Greek sources in indicating that an exploratory campaign was launched, with a ship from Aqaba reaching Qanaʾ and the incense lands, but the ship from Babylon turned back in the Persian Gulf. Later, Ptolemy II (282–246 BCE) sent another exploratory mission into the Red Sea around 270 BCE. Later geographers must have used this official report, including Eratosthenes of Alexandria (ca. mid-3rd cent. BCE), who represents the whole Arabian Peninsula as Arabia Eudaimon ("Blessed or Prosperous Arabia"), separating it from Arabia Desert in the north by a route from Heliopolis through PETRA to Babylon (Strabo, *Geogr.* 16.767). The region of Eudaimon

includes farmers in the north, nomads in the center, and rain-blessed Yemen in the south.

In the Augustan age, the concept of *Arabia Eudaemon* was narrowed to the "incense" kingdoms of South Arabia in Yemen. Josephus considers the whole Arabian Peninsula as Arabia Felix (*Ant.* 1.239; *J.W.* 2.221, 385), as does Ptolemy of Alexandria in the mid-2nd cent. (*Geogr.* 5.17, 19; 6.7). Both former and later writers subsumed Nabataea into Arabia Desert. Ironically, the Peutinger Table—a Roman road map of the 5th cent. CE, based on earlier information—includes India and the Far East to China, but excludes completely the Arabian Peninsula.

2. *Arab* and *Arabia* in Modern Times

Although the term *Arabia* was used broadly in antiquity for various desert areas from Egypt to Mesopotamia, *Arabia* proper designates the vast Arabian Peninsula (the Jazirat al-ʿArab or "Island of Arabs"). The trapezoidal peninsula itself represents over a million square mi., some 2200 km (1400 mi.) in length and 1,200 km (750 mi.) in width at its widest points. The modern countries of Saudi Arabia, Yemen, Oman, the United Arab Emirates, Qatar, and Bahrain occupy the peninsula.

David Graf
Figure 1: Dumah

3. Areas of Settlement

The Arabian Peninsula was sparsely populated in antiquity and even until recently. Approximately one-fifth of the whole peninsula is inhabitable. In antiquity, the population centers were oases; Dumah (*see* Figure 1 above), Taymaʾ, and Dedan in North Arabia were prominent. Today's population is concentrated along the coastal areas: the Hijaz in the west, Yemen adjacent to the Indian Ocean in the south, and the eastern coasts adjacent to the Persian Gulf. The mountainous Hijaz (*Barrier*) along the western coasts is a long stretch of Precambrian exposures that forms the eastern part of the Arabian-Nubian shield, extending from Aqaba in the north to the Bab al-Mandab Strait in Yemen. The plain along the western coast is called the Tihana ("hot earth") and is 3–45 mi. wide, rising in low foothills to the mountainous Hijaz. Along the eastern coasts, the settled area is dominated by Hofuf in the al-Hasa oasis, its strong springs creating extensive canal-fed agriculture and the dates known as the finest in Arabia. The Yemen highlands in the south are the most fertile landscape in Arabia, the beneficiary of the summer monsoon rains. Its mountains rise between 7,000 and 12,000 ft. high, creating lush green valleys and large oases (like Marib), which merge into the arid inland plateau. A sophisticated irrigation system was created in antiquity to capture the seasonal rains. Frankincense and myrrh were grown in Hadramawt to the east, and the demand for these aromatics in Egypt, Mesopotamia, and the Mediterranean world produced a prospering and lucrative trade that made South Arabia famous in antiquity.

Large urban settlements at oases argue against the common assumption that the Arabs of antiquity were merely nomads. That a large portion of Arabia was occupied by CAMEL nomads living in tents is not to be questioned, but this image should not overshadow the various population centers that were the primary focus of the OT writers. The camel was indispensable for crossing the huge desert expanses between the scattered oases, but it should not be characterized as just the animal of nomads as it also functioned as a "beast of burden." Imperialist regions commonly characterized the "outsiders" beyond their control as "nomads," but emerging evidence for Arabia shows a symbiotic relationship existed between oasis dwellers and tent-dwelling nomads.

The rest of Arabia is dominated by desert. The Syrian Desert (*Hamad*) is in the north, between Palestine and Mesopotamia. Temperatures in the Arabian interior reach 50°C or more in the summer, and less than 150 millimeters of rain falls in a year. The largest of the Arabian deserts is the Rubʿal-Khali or "Empty Quarter"—almost 500,000 square km of sand dunes rising as high as 60 m—the very last part of the Arabian desert to be explored by westerners and the largest body of sand in the world.

B. Religion

Assyrian texts describe the pantheon of Arabian gods as consisting of six deities: ʿAtarsamayin (Ashtarte/Ishtar of the heavens), Daya, Nuhai, Ruldaiu (Ruda), Abbiʾliu, and Atarqurama. North Arabian Dumaitic texts from Sakakka preserve petitions to these deities. In the 5th cent. BCE, the Greek historian Herodotus says that the Arabs have only two deities, a fertility god named Oroltalt, who he associates with Dionysius, and Alilat, identified with Ruda and Allat. It is likely that this information came from the Arabs dwelling along the Mediterranean coast of northern Sinai, revealing the widespread nature of the cults.

Other evidence comes from two Aramaic stelae found at Taymaʾ, initially dated to the mid-6th cent.

BCE, but recently to the end of the 5th cent. BCE. The most recently found stele demonstrates close connections with the Lihyan dynasty at Dedan. The artistic reliefs on the stelae display influences from South Arabia, Mesopotamia and Egypt, suggesting further the cosmopolitan nature of the oasis. The gods mentioned on the stele appear local—slm, snglʾ, ʾshymʾ, an entirely different pantheon and cultural tradition than Dumah. The latter god is interesting, as it is the god of the exiles to Hamath in 2 Kgs 17:30, and the annals of Sargon II in 715 BCE indicate that Arabs were transplanted to Samaria. It is possible that Nabonidus' invading army had Arab contingents who introduced the deity to the oasis.

The main deity worshipped at Dedan was Dhu Ghabat, but Dedan was cosmopolitan, and the inscriptions from the settlement indicate the pantheon included the Arabian god Allah and the goddesses Allat, Han-ʿUzza, Han-ʾAktab (the Arabian counterpart to Nabu, the Mesopotamian god of writing), Qos (the chief god of the Edomites in Tranjordan), Baʿal-shamin (the Syrian god of Heaven), and Wadd (the chief god of the Mineans in south Arabia).

C. Languages and Scripts

Although Arabs are mentioned in cuneiform texts, the primary sources for North and South Arabia are the indigenous languages and script of pre-Islamic Arabia. These are separated into two distinct groups, North Arabian and South Arabian. The internal classification and relationships remain problematic, and subject to change with the steady increase of new finds.

1. South Arabia

The languages of South Arabia are named after the first millenium BCE kingdoms of Southwest Arabia located on the edge of the highlands of Yemen: Sabaic, Minaic or Madabic (formerly "Minean"), Qatabanic, and Hadramitic of the first millennium BCE. This group of languages also is sometimes called *Sayhadic* (i.e. the languages grouped around the Sayhad Desert in Yemen) and is characterized by 29 graphemes that function mainly as consonants. Sabaic, centered at Marib and Sirwah, was the most influential and longest lasting of the group, beginning sometime around the 8th cent. BCE and continuing at least until the latest dated text of 554/9 CE. The majority of the texts date between the 1st to the 4th cent. CE. Minaic was used between the 8th and 1st cent. BCE, but was less common than Sabaic. Minaic distribution is extensive as a result of commercial activities in the Hellenistic era, with texts stretching from a trading colony at Dedan to the Levant, Egypt, and Delos in the Aegean. The Qatabanic texts are centered at their capital at Timnaʾ, but extend to Bab al-Mandab on the Red Sea, until Saba and Hadramawt defeated Timnaʾ in the 2nd cent. CE. Hadramitic texts are to the east of the others, centered at the capital of Sabwa, but extending as far as Oman in far southeast Arabia. Another group of texts was produced by the kingdom of Himyar with its capital at Zafar during the 2nd to 4th cent. CE, at which time Himyar replaced Saba as the prominent power in South Arabia.

More than 10,000 inscriptions from South Arabia have been published. This corpus is diverse, comprised of monumental stone inscriptions, bronze plaques, coins, amulets, and even wooden sticks (on which a minuscule script was used). These texts are of political, economic, legal, and religious import, the latter including dozens of interesting penitential and expiatory ("confession") inscriptions, without parallels in the ANE, but closely approximate a much larger corpus of Greek texts from Lydia and Phrygia of the Roman imperial period.

2. North Arabia

The languages and scripts of North Arabia are even more diverse, and consequently even more difficult to categorize or characterize because of the disparity in the corpus and the laconic nature of the texts. Record-keeping and archives are a fundamental part of trading activity; hence forces for literacy in North Arabia centered around major oases and settled areas. Encounters with nomads at sanctuaries and rural markets may have facilitated the spread and distribution of the Arabian scripts, but this was a product of urban dwellers across North Arabia. North Arabian texts have been labeled "Southwest Semitic," but more recently have been categorized with Canaanite and Aramaic as "Central Semitic" (between Northwest Semitic and South Semitic). Some may date as early as the 13th cent. BCE, but are concentrated in North Arabia between the 8th cent. BCE and the 4th cent. CE, although surviving in the Najran area of Southwestern Arabia until the 7th cent. BCE. There are more than 40,000 of these inter-related texts, representing the largest attested literacy anywhere in the ancient Near East or Mediterranean world. Unfortunately most of the texts are of "graffiti" nature, contained merely names and patronyms, occasionally "tribal" associations and petitions to deities, and, most rarely, historical information, but without precise dates. Initially, most of the texts were produced at the major oases of North Arabia: Tayma', Dedan (Dadan in Neo-Babylonian texts and the LXX; modern al-ʿUla), and Dumah (modern al-Jawf), all of which were involved with the lucrative aromatic trade in frankincense and myrrh of South Arabia. The dispersal of these texts, in local varieties and derivative nature, is expansive, extending from Southern Mesopotamia, the interspersing deserts between the major oases, to the Lebanese coast, with a few isolated texts as far away as Pompeii in Italy.

North Arabian scripts were initially categorized as five types (A–E), but subsequent finds have forced revision and reappraisal. A is represented by the major oases scripts with names derived from them, Dumaitic (or Jawfitic), Taymanitic (from Tayma'), Dadanitic, as well as a few texts from eastern Arabia designated Hasaitic (after the al-Hasa region opposite Bahrain). A may have been more widely known. A Luwian inscription of King Yariris of Carchemish in Syria preserves his boast that he knew the "Taimani" writing, possibly referring to Taymanitic. The others types also have been given geographical labels, Najdi (B), Hijazi (C and D), and Tabuki (E) with South Thamudic designating scripts further south in the Najran region.

Both the older and newer divisions are problematic. The more than 10,000 Tabuki (E) Thamudic texts have been the most troublesome to classify, especially with the discovery of thousands of texts in the Hisma desert of southern Jordan. Sporadic finds of Thamudic texts appear throughout Transjordan as far north as southern Syria and Galilee, so it is geographically more extensive than the present category indicates. In addition, there are more than 20,000 Safaitic texts (a misnomer, as none are found in the Safa region southeast of Damascus), from the Syrian Desert. Both the Thamudic E and Safaitic texts are dated roughly to the 1st cent. BCE to the 4th cent. CE.

Aramaic texts begin to appear in NW Arabia in the last part of the second millenium BCE, probably as a result of the Babylonian King Nabonidus' stay at Tayma', but most of these date to the Persian and Hellenistic periods. A few Aramaic Nabataean texts date perhaps as early as the late 3rd cent. BCE. In the late 1st cent. BCE, there is a dramatic upsurge. After the Roman annexation of Nabataean in 106 CE, they dwindle; the last dated Nabataean Arabic inscription is 356 CE. During the 1st cent. BCE and early 1st cent. CE, the distribution of these texts extend from Syria and Lebanon to Yemen, but are concentrated between Petra and Al-ʿUla, and Jauf to the Nile, with the largest number—almost 4,000 texts—in the Sinai. When Nabataean Aramaic inscriptions first began to accumulate at the end of the 19th cent., it was observed that the onomasticon was dominated by Arabic names, with sporadic Arabisms in the grammar, orthography, and syntax intruding into the Aramaic texts. The presence of these elements led to the suggestion the Nabataeans wrote in Aramaic for public and monumental purposes, but privately spoke in their "mother" tongue of Arabic. In addition, there were several dozen Arabic loanwords that were isolated in the vocabulary of the inscriptions that supported the "Arabic" hypothesis, although mainly consisting of a specialized vocabulary for political, legal and funerary matters. If the spoken vernacular Arabic language surfaced, it was argued that it was only in only in "prestige" (i.e., Sabaic, Dedanitic and Aramaic) scripts and that Arabic replaced Aramaic slowly but progressively only after the dismemberment of the Nabataean kingdom.

But Arabic loanwords and linguistic elements have subsequently appeared in Aramaic texts from Petra, the papyri from Nehal Hever near the Dead Sea, and Egypt. This expanded the lexical use of Arabic to religious affairs, legal precedents, and land tenure, circumstances which suggested the Arabic substratum was far more substantial than previously recognized. In addition, texts written purely in Old Arabic began to appear throughout Arabia. A Nabataean inscription was discovered near ʿEin ʿAvdat in the Negev that preserved some lines of poetry in Arabic. Complete texts in Old Arabic written in Thamudic B preserve petitions to a Nabataean deity. These were found at Madaba and Uraynibah (30–40 km south of Amman, Jordan). Other Nabataean elements in the onomasticon suggest a date early in the 1st cent. CE. Since these lengthy stylized texts of more than 250 graphemes are written purely in the Old Arabic language, they suggest at least segments of the population within the Nabataean realm utilized Arabic as both a spoken and written language, transcribed in the local Thamudic E script typical of the Transjordan region. *Arab* has finally achieved the status of an ethnicon: people living in what is called *Arabia* who are called *Arab* by others, and who speak *Arabic*.

D. History

As with many cultures in the ancient Near East, there is no continuous narrative of the Arabs or Arabia. Their history must be pieced together from allusions and fleeting episodes in Assyrian, Babylonian, Persian, Hellenistic, and Roman periods. Although most of the pieces of this fragmentary mosaic are missing, they illuminate the references to Arabs in the OT. Of course the more than 50,000 inscriptions from the various Arab communities in antiquity are the primary records.

1. Tribal society

The infrastructure of Arab society is composed of tribal confederations. In the early Iron Age (1200–1000 BCE), the Assyrian and Arabian sources are silent. Archaeological evidence from an impressive fortified settlement at Qurayya in northwest Arabia near Tabuk has been connected with the Midaianite confederation, which appears in OT narratives. From the Assyrian to the Persian period, the Qedarite confederation dominated North Arabia. Although they appear to be centered at Dumah, their territory stretched north as far as Palmyra (Tadmor) in Syria, south to the Northern Hijaz, and later west to embrace Transjordan, the Negev and Sinai to the Suez canal. Their successor was the NABATAENS, who established a monarchy in the early Hellenistic period

In the mid-seventh century, the Assyrian records refer to an Arab "confederacy of ʿAtarsamin" suggesting tribes united around a central deity and shrine, such as the Greek amphictyony with proposed parallels with the twelve tribes of Israel and the Sumerian city states. The Thamudic confederation, mentioned first in the annals of King Sargon II in the Assyrian period, is men-

tioned as late as the Quran. Their legendary importance led to the pre-Islamic North Arabian inscriptions discovered in the region being named "Thamudic" by western scholars in the 19th cent., though only a few texts can be associated with the Thamudic confederacy.

The traditional assumption for an Arab presence in the Levant was that it was the last major migration of Semites from the Arabian Peninsula into the fertile Crescent in the pre-Islamic period. These Arabians purportedly arrived as nomads or bedouin, infiltrating the regions of settled cultures, before they integrated into sedentary life. Historians and linguists have now begun to express reservation about the "nomadic" thesis and expressed the need for another paradigm. When the Arabs first appear in the 9th cent. BCE, they are already an established fact, and the evidence for when and how any dramatic intrusion into the sedentary zone is took place is lacking.

2. Assyrian period

The first appearances of the term *Arab* in Assyrian sources is the reference to "Gindibuʾ the Arab," the commander of a thousand camels, who fought with a Damascene coalition of Syrian and Palestinian allies against the Assyrian army of Shalmaneser III at the battle of Qarqar (853 BCE). The homeland of Gindibu has been ascribed to Dumah in North Arabia, but southern Syria is just as likely the location. It is not until a century later that *Arabs* appear again in the Assyrian annals, but afterwards, they are regularly mentioned.

In the reign of Tiglath-Pileser III (744–727 BCE), he provides a list of 35 Aramean tribes he conquered in southern Babylonia. Of those listed in the region, the linguistic analysis of their tribal names suggests a possible Arabic identity for 16 of them, some of which seem to be nomadic, but others are clearly sedentary. Those conquered in Syria are integrated into the Assyrian administrative system. In 738 BCE, Tiglath-Pileser imposed tribute on Zabibe, Queen of the Arabs, along with the kings of Damascus, Hamath, Tyre, Byblos and Samaria, respectable company, thus signaling her importance. In 733 BCE, Tiglath-Pileser raided the camp of Samsi, Queen of the Arabs at Mt. Saqurri (perhaps Jebel al-Druz/ʿArab in the southern Haran of Syria). Samsi may have been Zabibe's successor. Her camp was despoiled; the tents of her people were burned, and she was forced to retreat to the desert. Included in the booty seized by the Assyrians were 5000 (bags) of spices, the earliest indication of the Arabian aromatics trade.

Sargon II (722–705 BCE) continued to pursue aggressive policies against the Arabs, defeating in 716 BCE the Thamud, Ibadidi, Marsimani, and Hayappi (OT EPHAH). The survivors were settled in Samaria and the region of Damascus. In the same year, Sargon received tribute from Samasi Queen of the Arabs, Pirʾu King of Egypt, and Itaʾamar the Sabean. Some letters from

Assyrian governors in western Syria in the Sargonid period indicate the *Arabs* in the region are integrated into the settled population and are familiar with imperial administration—their leaders employ scribes for communicating with the Assyrian court, and the Arab population Sargon governs is engaged in sedentary agriculture, pastoralism and stock breeding. By this time the Arab settlements in Bit-Dakkuri and Bit-Amukani emerged east of the Euphrates in Babylonia. A late 8th-cent. reference to caravans from Tayma' and Saba' provides another indication of the burgeoning commerce from Arabia.

In 703, in the region of the Assyrian king Sennecherib (705–681 BCE), a rebellion in Babylon was quelled. Basqanu the brother of the Qedarite queen Iati'e was captured. All the Arab towns mentioned are located in the western districts of Bit Dakkuri and Bit Amukani. In 691 BCE, another campaign was directed against TeTe'elunu the queen of the Qedarite Arabs, who was pursued to her center at Dumah, where her army was defeated. She was taken to Assyria as a captive , with "spices and precious stone" seized as booty. Another Arab leader Hazi'il was installed as ruler in her place, and was succeeded by his son Iauta'.

Under Esarhaddon (681–669 BCE), Tabuah, a captive of Sennecherib, returned to Dumah with the images of the Arab gods seized in the campaigns of 678 and 676 BCE. In Esarhaddon's campaign against Egypt in 671 BCE, the Arabs of the Sinai assisted the Assyrian army across the desert. In the reign of Asshurbanipal (668–627 BCE), Iauta' the Qedarite king revolted and was replaced by Abiyate' son of Sahri. The Qedarites had enjoyed the favor of Esarhaddon and Assurbanipal, and a treaty was signed with Iauta' in 652 BCE to continue the policy. In 644 CE, the last recorded Assyrian campaigns against the Arabs took place: the first against the Qedarite king Abiate' and Uiate, king of Su-mu-il (which some scholars phonetically equate with ISHMAEL) between Damascus and the Euphrates, and another devastating one against Natnu, king of the Nebayot, probably in North Arabia. The Assyrian texts of Asshurbanipal's campaigns against the Arabs are illustrated by the palace reliefs of the king from Nineveh.

In the Assyrian period, dramatic changes took place as Arabs moved across a wide geographical sphere that included the regions of central Syria, the Syrian Desert, central, east and northwest Arabia, southwestern Babylonia, the Hijaz, and the Northern Sinai. Arab rulers initially were queens and priestesses, wielding political power and authority, but gradually these were replaced by kings. There are signs that the campaigns also grew in ferocity, starting with tributary ventures and ending with vicious assaults, as rebellions increased. In the time of Tiglath-Pileser III, Arabic personal names appear rarely in Mesopotamian texts. However, as more Arabs moved into Mesopotamia in the 7th cent. BCE, Arab names become more common in texts. Artistic depic-

tions of Arabs also appear with notable variations in Assyrian reliefs probably first in the reign of Tiglath-Pileser III and thereafter until the reign of Asshurbanipal (668–627 BC).

3. Babylonian period

The Neo-Babylonian kings appear to have continued the aggressive policy of the Neo-Assyrian kings against the Arabs. Nebuchadnezzar in 599/98 BCE, directed a campaign against probably Qedar and other Arabs in the Syria Desert. The penetration of the Arabs into the Transjordanian kingdoms of Ammon, Moab and Edom is ascribed to this period, immediately after the fall of Jerusalem in 586 BCE.

Nebuchadnezzar's successor, Nabonidus (556–539 BCE), conducted a campaign even deeper into Arabia. In ca. 552 BCE, he departed from Babylon for the Haran in the region of the Upper Euphrates and then Tayma', where he remained for a decade. Nabonidius' route to Tayma' to northwest Arabia appears to have been directly south from Haran through Transjordan to his Arabian destination. A rock relief depicting a Neo- Babylonian king from Sela' in Edom is reasonably identified with Nabonidus, offering further support for his itinerary. Nabonidus killed the king of Tayma', and proceeded to conquer the oases to the west and south—Dedan, Fadak, Khaybar, Yadi', and Yathrib (Medina)—all the important oases along the trade route southward to the incense kingdoms of South Arabia, suggesting economic and political motives. The oasis at Tayma' was probably fortified and developed by Nabonidus in his stay, but his palace as never been located. The rise of the Persian King Cyrus the Great brought an end to Nabonidus' Arabian adventure, but the lasting residue is the spread of Aramaic, the language of the Babylonian scribes. Some Taymanite texts from the desert west of Tayma' are the product of Nabonius' personnel, MRDN, the servant of Nabonidus, and 'NDS', an overseer (ntrt). The names are unknown in the epigraphic North Arabian corpus, but the language syntax and morphology is close to Arabic, suggesting that they may be Babylonian Arabs that Nabonidus brought with him from Mesopotamia.

4. Persian period

Arabia appears in the "satrapal/provincial" lists of the Persian king Darius I (521–486 BCE), in conjunction with Assyria and Babylon, suggesting it refers to Arabia adjacent to southern Babylonia in eastern Arabia. This is confirmed by the statue of Darius I found at Susa that lists the satrapies in Egyptian hieroglyphs; Arabia appears here as Hagar, the designation for Thaj in East Arabia. These must be the tributary Arabs, in contrast to the independent Arabs who merely provide gifts of frankincense, i.e. the Qedarite Arabs in northwest Arabia (Herodotus 3.97).

For Herodotus, the whole region east of the Nile from Pelusium at the far eastern entry to the Delta along the Mediterranean to the Suez is called *Arabia* and is populated with Arabs (2.8, 15-19, 75, 124). The Delta border town of Daphnae (modern Defeneh) is even described as a garrison against Arabs and Syrians (2.30). This designation is supported by the LXX rendering of the phrase "Land of Goshen" as the "Arabia of Geshem the Arab" (Gen 45:10; 46:34). The connections with the OT "Geshem the Arab" (Neh 2:19; 6:1-2, 6) are supported by epigraphical and archaeological finds. A Dadanitic inscription from Al-ʿUla refers to a "Geshem son of Shhar and ʿAbd "governor of Dadan." The absence of the phrase "King of Qedar" prevents a positive identification with Geshem the Arab, but the fact that his name precedes that of the Governor of the Oasis is important. Evidence for the presence of Arabs in Southern Palestine has also emerged. Over a thousand Aramaic ostraca have been discovered near Beersheba and Hebron dating from 363 to at least 312/311 BCE. The ostraca are filled with Arabized Edomite and Arabic names, suggesting Arabs are already an integral part of the sedentary population.

At Tell el-Maskhuta, along the Wadi Thumilat canal connecting Memphis in the eastern Delta to the Suez canal and Red Sea, a sanctuary was found with silver bowls inscribed in Aramaic, three of which were votive offerings to Han-ʾIlat (the Arabian goddess Allat) by Arabs including "Qainu son of Geshem, King of Qedar," whose father is known from the OT and other sources. A hoard of thousands of Attic tetradrachma was also discovered at the shrine, reflecting the prosperity of trade flowing through this vital artery to the Nile from the Red Sea. The Qedarite contingent may have been stationed here to guard access and monitor traffic into and from the Nile. If these connections are accepted, then the Qederaite confederation controlled a vast territory precisely contiguous with the territory that later constituted the Nabataean kingdom.

5. Hellenistic period

During Alexander the Great's conquests, he encountered Arabs at various places and stages during his expedition. After Alexander's death, Arab troops regularly appear in the service of Seleucid kings of Syria: Antiochus III utilized Arab troops from the region of Rabbatamana (Amman), at the battle of Raphia in 217 BCE, and at the battle of Magnesia in 189 BCE. In 145 BCE, the Seleucid Alexander Balas sought refuge with an Arab dynast named Diocles at Abae (1 Macc 11:17) and his successor appears to be an Arab dynast named Imalcue (1 Macc 11:38-40; Malchus in Josephus, *Ant* 13.131), residing somewhere near Chalcis, on the Arabian border in North Syria.

Recent publications attest to the Nabataean dynasty in the 3rd cent. BCE. In the Milan Papyrus preserving the epigrams of the poet Posidippus of Pella (ca. 282–252 BCE) reference is made to a Nabataean king who was in charge of an Arabian fighting cavalry force, the

first attested Nabataean monarch. The next Nabataen king mentioned is a Nabataean inscription from the Haran (ca. 200 BCE). By the end of the 2nd cent., the Nabatean center at Petra had become internationally famous as a emporia involved in the incense trade. In 88/87, the Seleucid King Antiochus XII was killed in a campaign against the Nabateans led by Obodas I, and afterwards the Nabataean King Aretas III was placed in control of Damascus.

Arab presence in Egypt continued. By the 3rd cent. BCE, a nome (province in Egypt) named *Arabia* existed southwest of Pelusium. It is in the Suez region that two Nabataean inscriptions dating to 77 and 35 BCE were discovered, suggesting the caravan route leading from Tell el-Maskhuta across the Sinai to Petra was still in operation.

6. Roman period

After the eclipse of Seleucid power, the Roman legate Pompey's eastern campaign encountered a Syria ruled by petty kings and tyrants, whose kingdoms were ravaged by the Arabians. As a result, he united the realm, creating the Roman province of Syria, with the Arabs pushed to the east and south. East of Apamea was called Paropotamia, an area ruled by Arab phylarchs (tribal governors), and to the south, the land of the Scenitae Arabs, similar to the nomads in Mesopotamia. Pompey's attempts to conquer the Nabataens were unsuccessful. They were represented as clients by his successors, and they later offered military assistance to both Caesar at Alexandria in 47 BCE and Augustus for the expedition to Arabia Felix in 26/5 BCE. A number of newly discovered North Arabian Safaitic texts from northern Jordan refer to the Herodian dynasts and Roman officials of the early Roman imperial era, including Herod the Great and/or Herod Antipas, Philip the Tetrarch, King Agrippa (the I or II), and unspecified Roman administrators. In several texts reference is made to a conflict with the "Jews," who plundered and apparently set fire to a shrine, perhaps of Baal-Shamin, the deity invoked by the inscribers of the texts. The event has been associated with the revolt of the Arabs in the Trachonitis during the reign of Herod the Great in 12 BCE. Another text is dated to the year "Herod engaged in war," perhaps the war between Herod the Great and Arab rebels in the Trachonitis around 12 BCE (Josephus, *Ant.* 16.130; 273–276) or between Herod Antipas and Aretas IV sometime after 34 and before 37 CE (*Ant.* 18.109-115). Antipas (Herod in the NT; Matt 14:1-12 = Mark 6:14-29; Luke 13:31-32) was Tetrarch of Galilee and Peraea in Transjordan, and perhaps tried to seize his brother Philip's territory in the Syrian Haran after Philip's death. Nabataean interests were also at stake in this area, so the "war between the Nabataeans and the Jews" mentioned in another text may allude to the same conflict. Other inscriptions are dated to the year that "the people of the Haran complained to

Caesar (i.e. the Roman governor) about Philip" and "the year that Philip died." The "rebellion against King Agrippa" in another text could be either Agrippa I (37–44 CE) or, more likely, Agrippa II (50–ca. 94 CE), perhaps alluding to the First Jewish Revolt. Although the Nabateans were at times friendly with Herod the Great and his successors, it was an uneasy relationship that erupted frequently in conflict (Josephus, *Ant.* 16.274-284; 18.114-124), so it is no surprise the Nabataean king Malichus II provided troops to assist Rome during the Jewish Revolt in 66–70 CE (Josephus, *J.W.* 3.68).

E. Biblical References

1. Old Testament

The Proto-history of the Arabs is associated with HAGAR, Sarah's servant, with whom Abraham fathered ISHMAEL (Gen 16:5-16; 21:8-21). Thus Hagar became the legendary mother of the Ishmaelites, at odds with SARAH, the mother of ISAAC. The personal name of Hagar is familiar in Aramaic and ancient North Arabian (hgr/hgrw), and as the word for "town, city" in South Arabian. In a cuneiform text from Bahrain, it appears as a toponym (A-gar-rum), probably designating East Arabia. In the list of subject countries of the Darius I found at Susa, Hagar is used to designate the Persian province of *Arabaya*, somewhere adjacent to the Mesopotamian provinces. The most likely candidate is the huge settlement of Thaj in eastern Arabia, from which in the 3rd cent. BCE coins were minted with the name of the "king of Hagar." *Hagar* is preserved as the name for East Arabia in Christian and Muslim sources into the Middle Ages, suggesting that tradition associated Hagar with this region of Arabia.

The genealogical lists in Genesis of the sons of KETURAH (Gen 25:1-4) and Ishmael (Gen 25:13-15; 1 Chr 1:28-31) mention a number of Arabian tribes or toponymns without mentioning Arabs. They appear to be of different periods and purposes. *Keturah* (*qeturah*, "incense") appears to reflect the aromatics trade of South Arabia. Ishmael is more specifically represented as the eponymous ancestor of a confederation of twelve Arab tribes: Nebaioth, Kedar, Adbeel, Mibsam, Mishma, Dumah, Massa, Hadad, Tema, Jetur, Naphish, and Kedemah, who dwell between Havilah to Shur, i.e. Assyrian to Egypt. Assyrian inscriptions mention the various Arab tribes that appear in the biblical genealogies only beginning with the late 8th cent. BCE: Saba' (Gen 25:3, "Sheba"), Massa (Gen 25:14), the Haiappa (Gen 25:4, Ephah), Idibailui (Gen 25:13, Adbeel), Qidri (Gen 25:13, Kedar), and Nabaaiti (Gen 25:13, Nebaioth). Taymanitic inscriptions from the 6th/5th cent. BCE at Jebel Ghunaym, near the oasis mention both Massa' and Nabayat, and refer to a "war against Dedan." The major North Arabian oases appear in the OT during the same period: Tayma' (Isa 21:13, Tema), Adummatu (Isa 21:11, Dumah), Dedan (Isa 21:13), and Bazu (Jer 25:23, Buz). These allusions to the major tribes and settlements of Arabia in the eighth through the 5th cent. BCE, suggest the historical context for the genealogical lists in Genesis and Chronicles are a product of the same period. These later connections and associations argue against the view that the Ishmaelites were a nomadic tribe in south Palestine prior to 1000 BCE.

David Graf

Figure 2: Dedan

Some references to Arabs and Arabia in the 10th and 9th cent. have been considered later projections of Arabian developments into earlier periods by post 8th cent. editors. The prime example is the visit of the Queen of Sheba to the court of Solomon in the 10th cent. BCE, generally considered to be a later effort to embellish and enhance the reign of Solomonic (1 Kgs 10:1-10; 2 Chr 9:1-2). The Queen's camels bear "spices, gold, and precious stones," and Solomon receives tribute from all the "Kings of Arabia" (I Kgs 10:15 and 2 Chr 9:15), matters which appear anachronistic for the 10th cent. BCE. The earliest reference to the South Arabian state of Sheba is the reign of Tiglath-Pileser III, two centuries later. Furthermore, no queens are mentioned in any of the many royal inscriptions of South Arabia, but a string of queens are known from North Arabia, including Samsi. It is in connection with Queen Samsi in 733 BCE, during the reign of Tiglath-Pileser III, that Saba' is first mentioned in Assyrian texts. The legendary long journey from Marib to Jerusalem (over 1,500 mi. and a half year journey by camel caravan) has then remained questionable.

The discovery of an Assyrian text mentioning a camel caravan of Taymanites and Sabeans that was intersected at the middle Euphrates (8th cent. BCE) has infused new life into the debate, precisely when archaeological evidence is now beginning to mount for an earlier date for Sabean civilization. These developments perhaps provide a basis for reexamining other episodes in the OT that appear to be of similar questionable nature. JEHOSHAPHAT, the 9th cent. King of Judah, received tribute from the Philistines and Arabs (2 Chr 17:11), implying Arabs lived in the Negev. In the 8th cent. BCE, King UZZIAH of Judah led a campaign against Arabs in the town of Gur-baal (2 Chr 26:7); the location is disputed, with Sela' or Petra in Edom proposed. Since these events are recorded in Chronicles but not in Kings, the events are questionable. It should also be noted that the inclusion of "Arab and Dumah" among the towns of the hill country is purely a coincidental similarity in names, as both probably refer to villages southwest of Hebron—today Khirbet et-Rabiyeh and Dumah.

Beginning in the 8th cent., and afterwards, the major oases and tribes of North Arabia appear in the prophetic writings of the OT. In Isaiah's Oracle on Arabia, the caravans of Dedan and Tema are mentioned (Isa 21:13-16). Jeremiah mentions Dedan, Tema and Buz, and refers to the "kings of Arabia" and the "kings of the mixed tribes" that dwell in the Desert" (25:23-24). By this time, the word *Arab* is an ethnic term. In Ezekiel's later Oracle on Tyre, the traders of Dedan are cited along with the lambs, rams and goats of the Arabs of Kedar, and the spices, precious stones and gold from Sheba (Ezek 27:20-22). The Book of Job also mentions the caravans of Temen and traders of Dedan (6:19) and shows an intimate knowledge of the fauna and wild life of Arabia—lions, mountain goats, wild asses, wild ox, raven, ostriches, hawks and eagles are all mentioned (37:39–39:12). The older names of Ishmael and Midian have disappeared, replaced now by the term *Arab* and particular important locations within Arabia. When "Geshem the Arab" appears in the 5th cent. BCE (Neh 2:19; 4:7 [Heb. 4:1]; 6:1), the process is complete. *Arab* as a general term for desert dwellers that was replaced by particular toponyms in Arabia, is finally identified with a specific individual, Gashmu the King of Qedar.

2. Apocrypha

In 168 BCE, the former high priest Jason sought refuge with the "Arab tyrant Aretas" (2 Macc 5:8), probably the "King Aretas" in the Nabataean inscription from Elusa. Later, in 163 BCE, Judas and Jonathan had a friendly encounter with the Nabateans and with Arabs called Zabadeans in the vicinity of Damascus (1 Macc 5:25-26, 39; 12:31), whom Josephus identified as Nabataeans (*Ant.* 13.179). According to 2 Macc, Judas suffered an attack from 5000 tent-dwelling Arabs, with their 500 horsemen (12:10-12). In Judith, a Jewish novel set during the reign of Nebuchadnezzar, HOLOFERNES burned and looted the Midianite settlements on the southern borders of Japheth, "fronting toward Arabia" (2:25). In 2 Esd 15:25, the "hissing dragons" of Arabia are part of the apocalyptic imagery used by the author.

3. New Testament

In Acts 2:11, among the Jewish diaspora on Pentecost, were "Arabian Jews" perhaps from the northern Hijaz. *Arabia* at the time of Peter's address at Pentecost

is a loose term, and the possibilities are numerous. Evidence for a Jewish presence in Arabia includes a Nabataean tomb inscription for "Shubaytu son of 'Eli'u, a Jew" at Meda'in Salih (ancient Hegra) dated to 42 CE. There also was a Jewish community at Aden, at the SW corner of the Arabian Peninsula, attested by approximately 200 epitaphs, but less than half predate the 19th cent. CE. Their dating remains controversial. A rabbi from Aden was buried in Galilee in the 3rd cent. CE, so an earlier date for the Aden inscriptions remains possible.

After his conversion, Paul of Tarsus indicates that he went to Arabia, before returning to Damascus (Gal 1:17). The precise location of this "Arabia" is disputed, with proposals that the area was in the environs of Damascus (Justin, *Dial.* 78.10; some Greek texts add Arabia to Damascus), the Decapolis (Pliny, *Nat.* 16.74), the Nabataean capital at Petra, or the Sinai (Gal 4:25). The thrust of Paul's missionary activity was west, not east, so the visit to Arabia seems to be as a recluse, not as a missionary.

The description of his return, stay and escape from Damascus further complicates the matter. In Acts 9:10-19, Paul spent a period of time in Damascus at the home of Ananias preaching in the synagogues, where there was a large Jewish community (Josephus, *J.W.* 2.560, 7.368). His efforts infuriated the local Jews, and they plotted to have him killed. Paul escapes because the Christians lower him over the city wall in a basket (Acts 9:23-25). According to 2 Cor 11:32-33, Paul escaped over the city wall of Damascus in order to avoid the ethnarch of the Nabataean King Aretas IV (9 BCE–40 CE). The implication is that the Nabataean king was in charge of the entire city, not just the quarter where the Nabataeans resided. This has been related to the emperor Gaius Caligula's rather liberal policy of assigning to the client kings various territories in the East. The death of Aretas IV in 40 CE, provides the *terminus ad quem* for Paul's visit to Damascus, one of the rare firm chronological fixed points for the Apostle's activity.

Bibliography: A. R. Ansary. *Qaryat al-Fau: A Portrait of Pre-Islamic Civilisation in Saudi Arabia* (1981); Glen W. Bowersock. *Roman Arabia* (1983); Jean-Francois Breton. *Arabia Felix from the Time of the Queen of Sheba, Eighth Century B.C. to First Century A.D.* (1999); Richard Bulliett. *The Camel and the Wheel* (1990); R. Byrne. "Early Assyrian Contacts with Arabs and the Impact on Levantine Vassal Tribute." *BASOR* 331 (2003) 11–25; Israel Eph'al. *The Ancient Arabs: Nomads on the Borders of the Fertile Crescent, 9th–5th Centuries BC* (1982); David F. Graf. *Rome and the Arabian Frontier: from the Nabataeans to the Saracens* (1997); David F. Graf. "Language and Life-Style as Boundary Markers: The North Arabian Epigraphic Evidence." *Mediterranean Archaeology* 16 (2003) 27–56; David F. Graf.

"North Arabian Epigraphy and Demography." *La Topoi: Orient-Occident*, Supp 4 (2004) 319–40; David F. Graf and Michael Zwettler. "The North Arabian 'Thamudic E' Inscription from Uranibah West." BASOR 235 (2004) 53–89; Nigel Groom. *Frankincense and Myrrh: A Study of the Incense Trade* (1981); Hani Hayajneh. "First Evidence of Nabonidus in the Ancient North Arabian Inscriptioons from the region of Tayma'." *Proceedings of the Society for Arabian Studies* 31 (2001) 81–95; H. Klein-Franke. "Tombstones bearing Hebrew Inscriptions in Aden." *Arabian Archaeology and Epigraphy* 16 (2005) 161–82; Edward Lipinski. *The Aramaeans: Their Ancient History, Culture, Religion* (2000); M. C. A. Macdonald. "North Arabia in the First Millennium BCE." *CANE* (1995) 1355–1369; M. C. A. Macdonald. "Reflections on the Linguistic Map of pre-Islamic Arabia." *Arabian Archaeology and Epigraphy* 11 (2000) 28–79; Simo Parpola. *State Archives of Assyria*, Vol. I: *The Correspondence of Sargon II*, Part I, *Letters from Assyria and the West* (1987); Daniel T. Potts. "Thaj and the Location of Gerrha." *Proceedings of the Seminar for Arabian Studies* 14 (1984) 87–91; Julian Reade. "Assyrian Illustrations of Arabs." *Arabia and Its Neighbors: Essays on Prehistorical and Historical Developments Presented in Honour of Beatrice de Cardi*. C. Phillips, D. Potts, and S. Searight, eds. (1998) 221–32; Jan Retsö. *The Arabs in Antiquity: Their History from the Assyrians to the Umayyads* (2003); Jan Retsö. "When Did Yemen become *Arabia felix*?" *Proccedings of the Society for Arabian Studies* 33 (2003) 229–235; K. Schippmann. *Ancient South Arabia from the Queen of Sheba to the Advent of Islam* (2001); Hayim Tadmor. *The Inscriptions of Tiglath-Pileser III King of Assyria* (1994).

DAVID GRAF

ARABAH air′uh-buh [עֲרָבָה ʿaravah]. The modern identification of the Arabah is that land situated south of the DEAD SEA, extending to Elath (*see* ELATH, ELOTH; EZION-GEBER). This identification, however, does not exist in the OT. Rather, there, the Arabah is identified as the Jordan River Valley, including part, or all, of the Dead Sea. The Arabah, therefore, is also part of the Syrian-East African Rift that extends from Turkey to Mozambique.

Although frequently occurring in parallel with midhbar [מִדְבָּר, as in Isa 35:6 and Jer 17:6), the Arabah is often linked with other geographical locales. On the eastern side of the Jordan River, the Hebrew text identifies the Arabah of Moab (Num 22:1; 26:3, 63; 31:12; Deut 34:1; Josh 13:32). A location "east of Jordan" is also suggested in Deut 4:49 and Josh 12:1-3. Moreover, a Western identification of the Arabah is also suggested in the name "the Arabah of Jericho" (Josh 4:13; 5:10). There is also a general Western proximity reflected in other verses (Deut 11:30; Josh 8:14; 18:18; 2 Sam 2:29; 2 Kgs 25:4-5).

With these references in mind, it seems apparent that the biblical authors envisioned the entire Jordan River Valley, from Chinnereth to the Dead Sea, as part of the Arabah (Deut 1:7; Josh 11:2, 16). In addition, the Dead Sea itself is included within the Arabah. One of the several names attached to the Dead Sea is the "Sea of the Arabah" (Deut 3:17; 4:49; Josh 3:16). As it is common in the OT to identify bodies of water with the name of a bordering area, it is reasonable to identify the area bordering (and including) the Dead Sea on west and east as the Arabah.

The general region of the Arabah may be defined fairly specifically. The northern extent is to Chinnereth (Josh 11:2), being limited on the east and west by the expanse of the Jordan River Valley as one proceeds south (and perhaps by the mountains bordering the Dead Sea).

The common biblical phrase, the "way of/to X" is used in the text to designate a road leading to a particular locale, in this case, the Arabah. Just as with Deut 2:1, the "way of/to Yam Suf" is the path the Israelites initially take in order to bypass Mount Seir. Thus, they are heading south (*see* SEIR and SUPH). They then turn toward the northeast, away from Elath and away from the road heading north, i.e., the "way of/to the Arabah." They are commanded to take the "way of/to Moab," in other words, the northeast. Therefore, the southern limit of the Arabah is in the direction of the Dead Sea.

While not mentioned in the stories of the Israelite patriarchs, the Arabah plays a major role in several concurrent biblical stories. Lot settles there following his parting from Abraham. The narrative of Gen 14 takes place in the Dead Sea region, encompassing the Arabah. The stark landscape of the Arabah is highlighted in the story of Sodom and Gomorrah (Gen 19), as well as with Lot's flight with his family toward Zoar and the surrounding mountains (also Gen 19). When Jacob flees from Laban, he journeys through the Arabah (Gen 32). He wrestles there with a divine being prior to his reconciliation with Esau (Gen 33). The Arabah is also the final encampment of the Israelites prior to crossing into Canaan under Joshua's leadership. The region was located primarily within the boundaries of tribal Manasseh and Gad. As is the case with the Levant itself, which is perceived to be a bridge between Asia and Africa, so too does the Arabah play a role bridging many critical events and narratives portrayed in the OT.

Bibliography: Menashe Har-El. "The ʿAravah." *HS* 26 (1985) 219–23.

MICHAEL OBLATH

ARABAH, SEA OF air′uh-buh. *See* SALT SEA.

ARABAH, WADI air′uh-buh [נַחַל הָעֲרָבָה nakhal haʿaravah]. The Wadi ARABAH makes up one of the borders of Yahweh's punishment in Amos's vision of doom (Amos 6:14). It is often associated with the WADI ZERED, the crossing of which was the end of the Israelites' wandering in the wilderness (Num 21:12; Deut 2:13-14).

ARABIC GOSPEL OF THE INFANCY. *See* APOCRYPHA, NT; JAMES, PROTEVANGELIUM OF; THOMAS, GOSPEL OF.

ARAD air´ad [עֲרָד 'aradh]. Arad is a town in southern Palestine mentioned four times in the OT. The Israelite tribes, attempting to enter Canaan from the south, encountered the king of Arad who defeated them in neighboring Horma (Num 21:1; 33:40). The king of Arad is listed, however, among the conquered kings of Canaan (Josh 12:14). Finally the area of "Negeb Arad" was settled by the Kenites, the descendants of Hobab, Moses' father-in-law (Judg 1:16). The place name *Arad* appears twice in the list of Pharaoh Shishak (Shoshenq I) dated to 925 BCE ('arad rbt 'arad n-bt yrhm). Arad Rabat ("Greater Arad") is commonly identified with Tel Arad.

The site of Tel Arad is located on the northeastern edge of the Beer-sheba Valley. Its identification is secured through the preservation of the name as Tell 'Arad in Arabic. Excavations were begun in 1962 by Ruth Amiran (until 1984) who exposed parts of the "lower city," and Yohanan Aharoni (until 1967) who dug on the high tell. Ze'ev Herzog directed the exposure of the Iron Age gate area (1976) in conjunction with the development of the site by the Israeli National Parks Authority.

The "lower city" occupies an area of ca. 9 ha of a craterlike shape. This unusual topography is explained by the desire to catch runoff water inside the settlement. During the Chalcolithic Period (Stratum V) and Early Bronze IB (Stratum IV) the site was sparsely occupied. In the Early Bronze Age II (Strata III–I) a fortified city was erected protected by a 2.25 m wide city-wall with protruding semicircular towers. A main gate on the west offered the transit for loaded pack animals, while several narrow postern-gates allowed the farmers direct access to their fields. The dwellings in the city consisted of rounded compounds fenced by a wall that included a domestic broad-house, auxiliary rooms for storage and cooking, rounded or square platforms used as bases of granaries, and open spaces for penning the household's animals. Several larger broad-rooms were interpreted as two pairs of twin-temples, and a large residential unit was identified as a "palace." The validation of these presumptions must await further exposure of the site. The city was subject to piecemeal abandonment at the end of the EBII.

At the lowest point of the city, a shaft, over 4 m in diameter, had been hewn into the bedrock, reaching water level at a depth of 25 m. The wide diameter of the shaft suggests that it was dug already in the Early Bronze Age, and inadvertently groundwater level was met. The shaft was reused during the Iron Age and the Herodian Period.

After a gap of over 1,500 years the high summit was reoccupied. Herzog and Singer-Avitz relate the first settlement (Stratum XII, a village arranged as "enclosed settlement") to the Shoshenq I list, and thus date it to the second half of the 10th cent. BCE. The first fortress, ca. 50 m square, surrounded by a casemate wall (Stratum XI), was erected during the Late Iron Age IIA, in the 9th cent. BCE. In the 8th cent. BCE a new solid wall was built and utilized until the end of the fortress in the early 6th cent. BCE (Strata X–VI).

In Stratum X a temple was constructed at the northwest corner of the fortress. It consisted of a large forecourt with an offering altar, a broad-room main hall, and a niche protruding westward. In the niche were found a raised stone podium, a rounded stele, and two nicely curved stone "incense altars." A second stele, often misinterpreted as simultaneously used, was in fact inserted into the back wall of the niche. The temple was reused, with raised floors, in Stratum IX, but was deliberately dismantled at the end of Stratum IX. The stele and the incense altars were carefully buried under the floor. The absence of any sign of damage in the cult objects suggests to some scholars an act of a cultic reform at Arad, which may be associated with the reform attributed to King Hezekiah (2 Kgs 18:4; 2 Chr 31:1).

Over 200 inscriptions (OSTRACA) were found at Arad (Aharoni 1981), 131 in Hebrew and the rest in Aramaic, Greek, and Arabic. Most of the Hebrew inscriptions are from strata VII–VI in the 7th and early 6th cent. BCE. Many of them belong to the Elyashib, the commander of the fortress of Stratum VI.

Bibliography: Y. Aharoni. *Arad Inscriptions* (1981); R. Amiran, U. Paran, Y. Shiloh, R. Brown, Y. Tsafrir, and A. Ben-Tor. *Early Arad I: The Chalcolithic Settlement and Early Bronze Age City* (1978); R. Amiran, and O. Ilan. *Early Arad II: The Chalcolithic and Early Bronze IB Settlements and the Early Bronze II City—Architecture and Town Planning* (1996); Z. Herzog. "The Fortress Mound at Tel Arad: An Interim Report." *TA* 29 (2002) 3–109; N. Na'aman. "The Abandonment of Cult Places in the Kingdom of Israel and Judah as Acts of Cult Reform." *UF* 34 (2002) 585–602; L. Singer-Avitz. "Arad: The Iron Age Pottery Assemblages." *TA* 29 (2002) 110–214.

ZE'EV HERZOG

ARAD OSTRACA. A collection of more than a hundred inscribed potsherds found at Tell Arad in the eastern Negeb, deriving from the 10th–6th cent. BCE, whose content ranges from administrative and military information to various partial lists. Seventh-century inscriptions include references to a new king in Judah (Arad

88), the Edomites (Arad 40), and the Jerusalem Temple (Arad 18). Due to their fragmentary nature, very little historical information can be derived from them.

RALPH K. HAWKINS

ARADUS air´uh-duhs [Ἄραδος Arados]. Island city of North Phoenicia, to whose people the Roman Consul Lucius wrote assuring them of the Jews' allegiance (1 Macc 15:23). *See* ARVAD.

ARAH air´uh [אָרַח ʾarakh; Ἀρεε Aree] 1. One of the sons of ULLA from the line of ASHER (1 Chr 7:29).

2. The ancestor of a group of exiles who returned with ZERUBBABEL from Babylonian captivity (Ezra 2:5; Neh 7:10; 1 Esd 5:10).

ARAM, ARAMEANS air´uhm, air´uh-mee´uhn [אֲרָם ʾaram, אֲרַמִּי ʾarammi]. Semitic peoples who inhabited areas from the Middle Euphrates in Mesopotamia to the Orontes River and DAMASCUS in central and southern SYRIA. They were particularly active from ca. 1200–730 BCE. They never formed a unified kingdom but primarily existed as independent states that were loosely connected by language and culture.

In the OT, "Aram" stands as part of the compound names of particular kingdoms. The texts most commonly use the label *Aram*, however, to designate those peoples living immediately north of Israel and east of the Jordan River. The Bible presents the Arameans as having close cultural and political relationships with Israel, relationships that often oscillate between friendly and unfriendly. During the monarchical period (esp. 900–730 BCE), the Aramean kingdom of Damascus became one of the most powerful states in Syria-Palestine. In the OT literature relating to these years, Aram most frequently designates this kingdom in particular.

A. Sources
  1. Biblical texts
  2. Extra-biblical texts and archaeological data
B. Origins and Early History (pre-10th cent. BCE)
C. Arameans, Israelites, and Assyrians (10th–8th cent. BCE)
D. Culture and Religion
Bibliography

A. Sources

Sources of information for the Arameans include: biblical texts, consisting of scattered references and allusions; extra-biblical texts, including Aramaic, Assyrian, and Egyptian inscriptions; and archaeological data, including cultural artifacts and material remains.

1. Biblical texts

One of the OT's clearest, and perhaps most ancient, confessions of Israelite faith explicitly presents a historic connection between Israelites and Arameans: "A wandering Aramean was my ancestor" (Deut 26:5). Genesis 10:22, a text within the priestly table of nations, identifies Aram as a son of Shem, while Gen 22:21 presents Aram's origin as a grandson of Nahor, the brother of Abraham. Drawing upon different traditions, 1 Chr 7:34 introduces Aram as a son of Shemer, a descendant of Asher, while Amos 9:7 declares that the LORD brought the Arameans up from "Kir." Passages that associate the patriarchs and matriarchs with Arameans in the area of Haran (e.g., Bethuel in Gen 25:20 and Laban in Gen 31:20) further depict a connection between Aram and Israel.

The OT includes numerous other references to persons and events associated with Aram, as well as to historical interactions among Israel, Judah, and various Aramean kingdoms. Apart from some references to relatives of Isaac and Jacob in Gen 24 and 29, the obscure figure of "Cushan-rishathaim of Aram-Naharaim" in Judg 3, and occasional mentions within some prophetic books (e.g., Isa 7:2, 4-5; Jer 35:11; Ezek 16:57), the majority of references to Aram appear in Samuel and Kings, with parallels in 1 and 2 Chronicles. These references describe the interactions of various Aramean states and rulers with Israelite and Judean kings from Saul and David to Ahaz and Hoshea.

2. Extra-biblical texts and archaeological data

Extrabiblical non-Aramaic sources predominantly consist of Assyrian royal inscriptions, with some sporadic mentions in Egyptian and Ugaritic texts. The name "Damascus" appears, for example, in the AMARNA LETTERS (*COS* 3.93:243), and references to Arameans occur in Ugaritic texts in personal names and in the designation "fields of the Arameans." The Assyrian royal inscriptions provide the first incontestable references to the Arameans in the annals of Tiglath-pileser I (1114–1076 BCE). These describe the king's battles with Arameans living to the southwest of Assyria (*ANET* 275). The annals of Tiglath-pileser's son, Ashur-bel-kala (1073–1056 BCE), contain similar references. Assyrian descriptions of the Arameans also occur from the time of Ashur-dan II (934–912 BCE) through that of Ashurnasirpal II (883–859 BCE), Shalmaneser III (858–824 BCE), Adad-nirari III (810–783 BCE), and Tiglath-pileser III (744–727 BCE).

There are few documents from the Arameans themselves. These are not royal annals such as one finds in Assyria, nor king lists and chronicles such as one finds in Babylonia. Instead, nearly all the major sources are occasional royal inscriptions that come from the 9th cent. BCE.

Three of the most significant Aramaic texts come from the 9th cent. reign of Hazael, king of Aram Damascus. The Tel Dan Inscription (*COS* 2.39:161-62), a memorial stela discovered in the early 1990s, likely records Hazael's victories over Jehoram of Israel and Ahaziah of the "House of David," though the latter has been vigorously debated. Hazael's booty inscriptions

(*COS* 2.40:162-63)—two inscribed ivory plaques taken by the Assyrians as booty to Arslan-Tash (near Til Barsip) and Nimrud and an inscribed bronze ornament for a horse's head taken as booty to the Greek island of Samos—attest to Hazael's military campaigns.

From later in the 9th cent. or early in the 8th cent. comes the inscription of Zakkur king of Hamath and Lush (*COS* 2.35:155), which records his successful resistance against a coalition led by Hazael's son Ben-Hadad. The Melqart Stela (*COS* 2.33:152-53), a royal inscription erected by a king named Ben-Hadad, dedicated to the god Melqart, and found north of Aleppo, may also describe the efforts of Ben-Hadad son of Hazael to maintain control of territories north of Damascus, but scholars are divided over whether the king named in this text is Aramean or not (Mazar 1962, 112). The Sefire Treaties (*COS* 2.82:213-17), found just south of Aleppo, date from the mid-8th cent. BCE and represent the longest extant inscription in Old Aramaic. They describe a treaty between the king of Arpad and the king of the uncertain locale, "KTK."

Archaeological remains from Aramean, Israelite, and other territories also contribute to our knowledge of the Arameans. Additionally, portrayals of Aramean people appear on gates and walls of Assyrian and Aramean buildings.

B. Origins and Early History (pre-10th cent. BCE)

The question of Aramean origins and early history involves the years leading up to and including the 12th–11th cent. BCE. Their emergence coincides at the latest with changes in Syria-Palestine at the end of the Late Bronze Age (ca. 1200 BCE). Since the Arameans existed as loosely connected territorial kingdoms in various geographical areas, they at times evidence different origins and development. Particularly lacking is archaeological data for the material conditions in Syria and Mesopotamia that accompanied the rise of the Arameans. Hence, reconstruction must rely mainly upon textual references.

As described above, the OT preserves at least four traditions concerning the origins of the Arameans (Gen 10:22; 22:21; Amos 9:7; 1 Chr 7:34) and places Arameans in Haran as early as the time envisioned for Abraham and Isaac (ca. 2000 BCE). While some scholars maintain that these associations with Haran fit some contexts in Israelite history, biblical traditions of Aramean origins, especially those in the genealogies of Genesis, likely represent the OT's practice of relating all ethnic groups through common ancestry. They probably do not provide precise genealogical information concerning Aramean origins.

Possible references in non-Assyrian texts, which would describe pre-12th cent. origins, remain contested. Some scholars identify references to the names "Aram" and "Aramu" in 3rd millennium texts from Ebla, but these groups seem to be located in upper Mesopotamia, east of the Tigris. A potential reference occurs on an Egyptian statue base from Thebes as early as the time of Amenophis III, and Ugaritic texts from the 14th cent. may contain gentilics for Aram.

A central issue related to the origins of the Arameans concerns their connection with other groups mentioned in texts from before the 12th cent. Tiglath-pileser I links the Arameans with the "Akhlamu." The earliest use of this term for a population group stands in the Amarna letters, but it may also appear in texts from Mari and Ugarit. In the Assyrian texts, Akhlamu designates a seminomadic group on the fringes of Syrian and Mesopotamian society. Due to the geographical similarities and Assyrian pairings, many scholars see the Arameans as identical with or at least as a subgroup of the Akhlamu. If this identification is correct, it points to an origin for the Arameans in at least the Middle Bronze Age. This conclusion remains questionable, however, since some texts include references to both Akhlamu and Arameans independently, and Mesopotamian texts in general often pair the names of nomadic groups without suggesting identification.

The evidence favors the conclusion that the Arameans gradually emerged in Mesopotamia and Syria during the Late Bronze Age, at least 200 years before their initial encounters with Tiglath-pileser I. Scholars remain divided, however, over whether the Arameans were nomads who migrated into this region from the Syrian desert or pastoralist descendants of Amorite groups who had lived in Syria since the 18th cent. The older view—that the Arameans flooded into the region during a time of upheaval around 1250 BCE—has been challenged more recently for relying on an overly simplistic view of the development of nomadic groups into urban cultures and for lacking archaeological evidence for the displacement of populations around this time. The extrabiblical texts do not portray the Arameans as immigrants, and later Arameans occupy the same area as the earlier Amorites. In any case, Arameans filled the vacuum created by the collapse of the Hittite empire in approximately 1250 BCE.

For the remainder of the 12th and 11th cent.—the period of Aramean expansion following their initial emergence—information is sparse, especially for southern Syria. When the sources resume in the mid-10th cent., a variety of Aramean territorial states are in place around the Orontes River, Beqaʿ Valley, and northern Transjordan. While the Assyrian texts designate the groups in the Babylon area with the general term *Arameans*, they assume the political and geographical independence of the Syrian states and identify them by the specific names of the individual kingdoms.

C. Arameans, Israelites, and Assyrians (10th–8th cent. BCE)

Aramean history in the 10th–8th cent. unfolded in the context of the Assyrian Empire, and knowledge of it predominantly comes from Assyrian sources. By the beginning of the 10th cent., biblical and Assyrian texts describe conflicts of Israel and Assyria with several centralized states in Syria and upper Mesopotamia. The states included Bit-Adini, Arpad, Hamath, Aram-Zobah (*see* ZOBAH), and GESHUR.

Early information on the Aramean states in central and southern Syria is limited to the OT. Aram Zobah, located in the Beqaʿ Valley north of Damascus, was the most powerful Aramean state in the 11th–10th cent. and fought with Israel as early as the time of Saul (1 Sam 14:47). Second Samuel 10:6-19 says that David defeated a group of Arameans from Beth-rehob, Zobah, and Maccah, which had been hired by the Ammonites, and subsequently defeated another Aramean coalition led by Hadadezer, king of Zobah. In 2 Sam 8:3-12, perhaps a summary of 10:6-19 or perhaps a misplaced description of later battles, David struck down Hadadezer of Zobah, defeated the Arameans of Damascus who came to Hadadezer's aid, and placed garrisons in Damascus. If these traditions are in any way reliable, they provide the earliest OT references to a powerful Aramean kingdom and its interactions with Israel.

The OT's texts about Solomon then describe the emergence of Damascus in the 10th cent. as the primary Aramean kingdom in southern Syria. First Kings 11:23-25 indicates that Rezon broke away from Hadadezer of Zobah and became king in Damascus. Since there is no clear archaeological evidence for the arrival of the Arameans in Damascus, this tradition remains unconfirmed. Even if historical, it is unclear whether Rezon took Damascus away from Israel, Zobah, or Edom. In any case, the biblical texts depict Rezon as the ruler of Damascus in the third quarter of the 10th cent. and as a persistent adversary throughout Solomon's reign.

First Kings 15:18 gives the names of Rezon's successors throughout the rest of the 10th cent.: Hezion followed by Tab-Rimmon. King Asa of Judah's remark to a later Aramean king concerning a previous alliance between "my father and your father" (1 Kgs 15:19) may indicate that relations between Israel and Aram Damascus fluctuated between hostile and cooperative in the last half of the 10th cent. The available sources for Damascus between the mid-10th and mid-9th cent., however, are mainly limited to sporadic biblical references, which may be later and misplaced, with some Assyrian references. By the late 10th cent., Assyrian activity in the west began to reemerge under Assur-dan II (932–910 BCE) apparently to check any potential Aramean expansion.

The next major intersection of Israelite and Aramean history occurred during the reigns of Baasha of Israel and Asa of Judah (ca. 900 BCE). According to 1 Kgs 15:16-21, Ben-Hadad I, son of Tab-Rimmon, attacked Basha after Asa convinced him to break a standing alliance with Israel. The Aramean king then captured several cities in northern Israel. The biblical texts provide the only sources for these events, but a destruction

layer in stratum IV at Tell al-Qadi that dates to the first quarter of the 9th cent. may attest to the conquest. Outside of these events, Aramean activities in central and southern Syria during the first half of the 9th cent. are obscure. By the time sufficient biblical and Assyrian sources reemerge (ca. 860 BCE), Aram Damascus, under its new king Hadadezer (Adad-idri), stands as the major power in the west.

In 859–858 BCE, Shalmaneser III became king of Assyria. He campaigned against Bit-Adini and northern Syria from 858-855 BCE. Shortly thereafter (853–852 BCE), Shalmaneser encountered a south Syrian-Palestinian coalition led by Hadadezer of Damascus and including Ahab of Israel (*see* Monolith Inscription; *COS* 2.113A:261-64). The coalition met the Assyrians at Qarqar on the Orontes River and apparently stalled or defeated Shalmaneser, since Assyrian texts record no booty being taken and Shalmaneser pushes no farther west. This alliance fought Shalmaneser on three more occasions between 853 and 845 BCE, apparently scoring a victory or stalemate each time, and the Assyrian texts consistently picture Aram Damascus as the leading western power.

Assyrian texts portray Israel as an ally of Hadadezer during the reign of Ahab. The biblical materials concerning Ahab, however, especially 1 Kgs 20 and 22, make no mention of the battle of Qarqar, identify the Aramean king contemporary with Ahab as BEN-HADAD, not Hadadezer, and depict Israel and Aram as enemies during this period. Some scholars identify the Ben-Hadad in 1 Kgs 20 and 22 with Hadadezer and conclude that relations between Israel and Aram oscillated during the reigns of Omri and Ahab. Evidence for such hostilities during the time of Omri may appear in the Tel Dan Inscription's reference to a previous (pre–841 BCE) Israelite invasion of Aram Damascus, an invasion for which there is no confirming evidence (*COS* 2.39:161-62). Because of chronological and textual problems, the majority of interpreters conclude that 1 Kgs 20 and 22 are redactionally misplaced and actually refer to hostilities with an Aramean king Ben-Hadad in the later Jehu. Thus, all evidence points to Israelite and Aramean cooperation throughout the reign of Hadadezer of Damascus (ca. 880–843 BCE).

The situation changed in 843 BCE when Hazael took the throne of Aram Damascus. The Assyrian texts identified him as an usurper, who took control of Damascus upon the death of Hadadezer, and 2 Kgs 8:7-15 depicted him as murdering his predecessor, who is incorrectly identified as Ben-Hadad.

The reign of Hazael was the apex of Aram Damascus's power. Shortly after Hazael's accession, likely as a result of his aggression, fighting broke out between Israel and Aram at Ramoth-Gilead (2 Kgs 8:28-29; 9:14b-15a). Second Kings 9–10 then describe the takeover of the Samarian government by Jehu, who killed the kings of Israel and Judah. The Tel Dan Inscription, probably a memorial stela of Hazael, likely reflects these events, although the fragmentary stela attributes the killing of Jehoram and Ahaziah to the Aramean king and many of its details remain debated. Not long after these events, the Assyrians under Shalmaneser III moved westward to quell Hazael's expansion. Probably because of his local aggression, Hazael faced Assyria without a coalition. For 841 BCE, Assyrian texts recorded a campaign against Hazael alone in which Shalmaneser forced him to retreat but was unable to capture Damascus, although he did destroy the surrounding lands, cities, and villages. In the course of the campaign, Shalmaneser received tribute from Jehu of Israel, marking his submission to Assyria as a vassal.

Hazael survived further Assyrian campaigns in 838 and 837 BCE. Following the 837 campaign, however, Assyria entered a period of decline during the last four years of Shalmaneser (828–824 BCE) and the first three years of Shamshi-Adad (824–822 BCE). Hence, the three decades following 837 BCE saw no Assyrian campaigns to the west.

In the vacuum created by Assyria's weakness, Aram Damascus was able to expand unchecked. Biblical and extrabiblical texts suggest that Hazael constructed an Aramean empire that lasted into the reign of his successor (Ben-Hadad), that controlled all of Syria-Palestine, and that subjugated Israel and Judah. Yet the exact nature and extent of this empire remain contested. Extrabiblical sources such as the Tel Dan Inscription claim the Aramean king's ability to kill kings of Israel and Judah. Similarly, the Zakkur Stela points to Aramean influence in Hamath. Hazael's booty inscriptions refer to the king's crossing of the "river" and may indicate that Hazael even conducted offensive campaigns into Assyrian territory north of the Euphrates. Archaeological evidence of destruction at places like Jezreel also points to Aramean encroachment into the upper Jordan Valley.

Biblical texts relating to the reigns of Jehoahaz of Israel and Joash and Amaziah of Judah also indicate that Aramean hegemony reached unparalleled heights at this time. Second Kings 13:3 reports succinctly, "The anger of the LORD was kindled against Israel, so that he gave them repeatedly into the hand of King Hazael of Aram, then into the hand of Ben-Hadad son of Hazael." Second Kings 10:32-33 associates Israel's loss of territory in the Transjordan with Hazael's expansion, and 2 Kgs 12:17*a* suggests that Hazael subjugated the Philistine city of Gath and virtually all of the land west of the Jordan. The only major event reported by the biblical writers for the reign of Joash of Judah is that Hazael threatened Jerusalem and Joash paid him tribute not unlike a vassal (2 Kgs 12:17-18).

The available evidence suggests that Hazael at least dominated Israel and Judah and likely established an empire that included some Philistine kingdoms, Transjordan kingdoms, Tyre, and perhaps areas north of the Euphrates. Some scholars have questioned key points such as the identity of the entities on and implications of Hazael's booty inscriptions, and pointed out that other states in northern and central Syria did not cease to exist. It is a fair warning not to overstate the power of Damascus on the basis of its dominance over Israel. Nonetheless, it seems reasonable to conclude that Israel and Judah, and likely others, became vassal states to Aram Damascus. If 1 Kgs 20:14-15, 24 reflect conditions under the Jehu dynasty (*see* above), the "governors of the districts" and the "commanders" that replace kings—a system of organization previously unknown in Israel—may indicate that Hazael divided his dominated territories into administrative districts, of which Samaria would have been one.

At the end of the years 837–810 BCE, the Assyrian king Adad-nirari III (810–783 BCE) led a resurgence of Assyrian strength in the west. Although the date of Hazael's death is unknown, 2 Kgs 13:22 links it with the death of Jehoahaz of Israel and thus places it in the general timeframe of Assyria's resurgence (ca. 805 BCE). Extrabiblical Aramaic and Assyrian texts, as well as biblical texts (2 Kgs 6:24–7:20; 13, and probably 1 Kgs 20 and 22), indicate that three major developments took place during the reign of Hazael's son Ben-Hadad: 1) Adad-nirari III attacked Damascus; 2) Ben-Hadad suffered defeat north of Damascus; and 3) Israel threw off the Aramean yoke south of Damascus. The sources do not, however, yield certainty on the chronology of these events. Perhaps as early as 803 or as late as 796 BCE, the Assyrians attacked Damascus and collected tribute from Ben-Hadad (referred to in Assyrian texts with the title "mar'i," "lord"; compare Saba'a stela [*COS* 2.114E:274-75] and Rimah stela [*COS* 2.114F:275-76]). Before or after this confrontation, the Zakkur Stela recorded that Ben-Hadad unsuccessfully led a coalition of kings against Zakkur, king of Hamath and Lush, likely due to the latter's alliance with Assyria and the former's desire to maintain the Aramean control of the north.

The Arameans suffered similar losses to Israel. Second Kings 13:5 attributes Israel's escape from Aramean dominance to the coming of a "savior" sent by God; this could be a veiled reference to Adad-nirari III's return to the west. After paying tribute to reconfirm their pro-Assyrian status (*see* Rimah Stela), Israel scored at least three victories over Ben-Hadad (2 Kgs 13–14), although scholars continue to debate whether Jehoahaz or Joash should be credited with these victories.

There are no extant Aramean sources that indicate how long Ben-Hadad remained on the throne or what happened in the latter part of his reign. Following its resurgence under Adad-nirari III, Assyria experienced another period of decline from 782–745 BCE. Initially, however, this period afforded no opportunity for Aramean expansion. Control of the west remained in the hands of the powerful Assyrian governor Shamshi-ilu, who operated out of Bit-Adini. Assyrian texts indicate that Shamshi-ilu led another campaign against Damascus in 773–772 BCE. The king of Damascus at the time was Hadianu (ca. 775–750 BCE; see Pazarcik Stela; *COS* 2.114B:273), who was perhaps rebelling against Assyria but about whom nothing else is known. Additionally, 2 Kgs 14:28 says that Jeroboam II (788–748 BCE) dominated Damascus and Hamath, although the historical reliability and details of this claim remain vexing for scholars.

The death of Shamshi-ilu not long after 752–751 BCE removed any strong sense of Assyrian presence in the west, provided Aram Damascus another opportunity to assert dominance in Syria-Palestine, and ushered in the final era of power in Aramean history. Both Assyrian and biblical texts introduce Rezin (Aramaic, "Radyan"), the next king of Damascus, as the dominant political force in the area, who attempted to reestablish Hazael's earlier empire. Little is known of Rezin's reign before ca. 740 BCE, when he begins to appear in Assyrian annals. Yet 2 Kgs 15:37 and 16:6 suggest that Rezin encroached on Israelite territory as early as the final years of Jeroboam II, and the prophetic oracle against Damascus in Amos 1:3-5, which describes an Aramean invasion of Galilee, may date from this time (ca. 750 BCE). Contemporary Assyrian inscriptions credit Rezin with an extended domain of the "house of Hazael" (*COS* 2.117F:291).

The course of events changed in 744 BCE when TIGLATH-PILESER III took the throne of Assyria. He immediately undertook a series of campaigns and annexations designed to reestablish Assyrian control over the far reaches of the empire. He first recaptured territories in northern Syria like Arpad and Hamath (ca. 738 BCE). Although Rezin is recorded as paying tribute to Tiglath-pileser as early as 738 (*COS* 2.117A:284), this action should probably be seen as a nominal tribute designed to buy time, since Assyria remained occupied in the north. Throughout this same period, Rezin worked to construct a widespread, anti-Assyrian coalition to challenge the resurgent Tiglath-pileser and push for economic freedom from Assyria. Pekah of Israel apparently played a key part in these developments. Chronological difficulties with Pekah's reign suggest the possibility that he emerged as an Aramean-supported rival king, perhaps based in Gilead, in league with Rezin and his anti-Assyrian movement as early as the time of Jeroboam II. The various Assyrian lists of states that paid tribute and were subjugated during these years suggest that Rezin's coalition included Tyre, Ashkelon, Arabia, Gaza, and Israel.

When Pekah, probably with the support of Rezin, seized the throne in Samaria in 734 BCE (2 Kgs 15:25), the Northern Kingdom took its place among the rebellious states opposing Assyria's resurgence and precipitated a conflict between Damascus, Israel, and Judah referred to as the "Syro-Ephraimitic War" (734–731

BCE). Judah, under King Ahaz, refused to follow the Northern Kingdom's lead and pursued an independent course, an action that prompted a joint Israelite and Aramean siege of Jerusalem (2 Kgs 16:1-18; 2 Chr 28:1-25; Isa 7:1-17).

The attack on Jerusalem would prove to be Aram Damascus's last significant action. Although the precise sequence of these events remains debated, Tiglath-pileser III moved down the Mediterranean coast and attacked Philistia in 734–733 BCE before moving against Arabia and Tyre. These actions were followed by a decisive, two-year siege and capture of Damascus (733–731 BCE). Assyrian texts recorded the capture of 591 towns, the destruction of Damascus, the execution of Rezin, the deportation of parts of the population, and the provincialization of Aramean territories (*ANET* 283). This destruction marked the disappearance of an independent Aram Damascus from the stage of history.

Following the Syro-Ephraimitic war, Aramean groups intersected only briefly with Israelite history during the final years of the Northern Kingdom. In 720 BCE, Ilubiʾdi of Hamath led a coalition that challenged Assyrian dominance and included the city of Samaria. The new Assyrian king, Sargon II, quickly suppressed the revolt, and his actions marked the end of the main course of Aramean history in Syria Palestine. Aramean groups remained a significant political factor in the years after 720 BCE only in Babylonia. While Arameans in this area appear as rebels in the texts of Sennacherib (704–681 BCE), even they eventually assimilated into other population elements.

Throughout the following centuries, Damascus played a role as a provincial capital in the Persian period, an important city in the Hellenistic period, and a Nabatean capital in the Roman period. Indeed, various Aramean cities went on to have a storied history, yet they never again attained the political power they knew across the first six centuries of the Iron Age.

D. Culture and Religion

Because the Arameans existed as several groups in different areas, there was not a single Aramean culture. Adequate sources for fully reconstructing social, economic, and domestic life have not survived. Available texts depict an economy that mainly consisted of farming and animal husbandry, with some industry controlled by the royal administration. The clearest sources (registry documents from Haran) reveal a family structure that was patriarchal, with child care and food preparation as women's primary activities. The Aramean groups in the east seem to have maintained a more tribal structure, while the western Arameans developed territorial states governed by dynastic monarchies.

Perhaps also due to their diversity, Aramean groups made few lasting contributions to the culture of the ancient Near East. Nearly all their material culture—art, architecture, metalwork, etc.—was adapted from older traditions or contemporary neighbors. The primary cultural impact of the Arameans was the ARAMAIC language. By the mid-8th cent. Aramaic was the official diplomatic language of the Assyrian Empire, and some texts in the OT, most notably parts of Ezra and Daniel, are in Aramaic. Aramaic became a common spoken language in the Neo-Babylonian period and later the *lingua franca* of the Persian Empire. The language survived in various dialects into the Roman period, probably constituting the language spoken by Jesus of Nazareth.

Aramean religion shared the tradition and gods of broader West Semitic religion. The god HADAD was the main deity for many groups, especially for Aram Damascus, and was attested in both biblical and extra-biblical texts. The texts connected Hadad with the name "Raman" ("Thunderer"), which appears in the OT as "Rimmon" (2 Kgs 5:18; Zech 12:11). This is the only Aramean god to appear in the OT, although a stela at Bethsaida apparently venerates Hadad, and a sanctuary dedicated to Aramean gods has been discovered at Megiddo.

Hadad was a god of rain and thunderstorm, who was connected with fertility, yet neither biblical nor extrabiblical sources preserved a developed mythology for the deity. Ugaritic and Amarna texts mentioned a god called "Ba'lu-Haddu," and this deity may have functionally become two by the 1st millennium. Various Aramean texts invoked the names of other deities, notably the moon god Sin and Baal Shamayn. The veneration of Aramean gods included the practice of prophecy and the rite of funerary meals. *See* ARAM-MAACAH; ARAM-NAHARAIM; PADDAN-ARAM.

Bibliography: J. A. Brinkman. *A Political History of Post-Kassite Babylonia 1158–722 B.C.* (1968); R. Burns. *Damascus: A History* (2005); P. M. M. Daviau, J. Wevers, and M. Weigl. *The World of the Aramaeans.* 3 vols. (2001); J. C. Greenfeld. "Aspects of Aramean Religion." *Ancient Israelite Religion* (1987); E. Lipiński. *The Aramaeans: Their Ancient History, Culture, Religion* (2000); B. Mazar. "The Aramean Empire and Its Relations with Israel." *BA* 25 (1962) 98–120; W. Pitard, *Ancient Damascus: A Historical Study of the Syrian City-State from the Earliest Times until Its Fall to the Assyrians in 732 B.C.E.* (1987); W. Pitard. "Arameans." *Peoples of the Old Testament World* (1994).

BRAD E. KELLE

ARAMAIC LEVI DOCUMENT. The Aramaic Levi Document (henceforth ALD) is an early Jewish composition authored some time between the late 4th and early 2nd cent. BCE. Aramaic fragments dating as early as the Hasmonean period appear in the DEAD SEA SCROLLS (1Q21; 4Q213; 4Q213a; 4Q213b; 4Q214;

4Q214a; 4Q214b), and further Aramaic fragments from around the 10th cent. CE were found in the Cairo GENIZAH. An 11th cent. CE Mount Athos manuscript of the Greek TESTAMENTS OF THE TWELVE PATRIARCHS contains additions to the Testament of Levi that match some of the Aramaic material found at Qumran and Cairo. (A small Syriac fragment from the 9th cent. CE is also known.) ALD's provenance is assigned to various locales in the land of Israel, and some scholars (Drawnel for intance) think much of its content can be traced back to the Babylonian exile.

Because the document is attested so fragmentarily in such diverse locales and across such a long period, the chief challenge facing scholars has been determining its precise contents and order. A complete listing of the elements identified in the surviving fragments includes the following: episodes relating to the Dinah episode at Shechem (Gen 34), the sale of Joseph (Gen 37), a prayer of LEVI, travels of Levi to visit his father and grandfather, one or more visions, Levi's elevation to the priesthood (in a heavenly vision and by the hand of his father), instruction in priestly practice (including measurements for wood, salt, flour, oil, wince, and incense), a serial life history of Levi and his immediate descendants, and Levi's wisdom teaching. Not all commentators agree on the existence of each item on the foregoing list, let alone as to how the pieces should be ordered. However, the close affiliation between ALD and the *Testament of Levi* has prompted some to use the *Testament* as a guide for reconstructing ALD, while others reject that strategy for ordering ALD's fragments. All agree, though, that some form of ALD was a source for the *Testament of Levi*. Parts of it are also closely associated with *Jub.* 30–31, suggesting a direct relationship between the two works, or at least the possibility that they drew from the same pool of traditions about Levi (*see* JUBILEES, BOOK OF).

While all agree that ALD is concerned in general to address the Israelite priesthood and that it was important to the Qumran covenanters, more specific notions of its purpose vary. Some argue that it is a wisdom text intended to educate priests as administrators and rulers, and that it especially draws on metrology priests learned in a Babylonian setting. Others make no effort to address the work's purpose as a whole, although they note some of its specific aspects related to the priesthood. Others argue that ALD is part of a "Levi-Priestly tradition" extending back to Malachi and forward to the *Testament of Levi* that repeatedly uses traditions about Levi to take part in an ongoing debate over who should possess the priestly office and exercise its power. *See* PRIESTS AND LEVITES.

Bibliography: Henryk Drawnel. *An Aramaic Wisdom Text from Qumran* (2004); Jonas C. Greenfield, Michael E. Stone, Esther Eshel. *The Aramaic Levi Document: Edition, Translation, Commentary* (2004); Robert Kugler.

From Patriarch to Priest: The Levi-Priestly Tradition from Aramaic Levi to Testament of Levi (1996).

ROBERT KUGLER

ARAMAIC SCRIPT air´uh-may´ik. About 1100 BCE, the Arameans adopted the Canaanite/Phoenician script. Used locally at first, it became, under the Assyrian, Babylonian, and Persian empires, a medium of international communication. From the 3rd cent. BCE, various offshoots developed in the East (e.g., Syriac) and the West (e.g., Jewish [ancestor of modern Hebrew]). *See* ALPHABET.

MICHAEL D. GUINAN

ARAMAIC VERSION(S). *See* VERSIONS, ANCIENT; VERSIONS, SYRIAC.

ARAMAIC, ARAMAISM. Aramaic describes a cluster of closely related dialects that first appear ca. the 9th cent. BCE and continue in use down to today. It belongs to the subdivision of the Semitic languages commonly referred to as Northwest Semitic that also includes the Canaanite dialects, most notably, Hebrew. Aramaic is of special biblical importance: 1) it is actually used in both the OT (Gen 31:47; Jer 10:11; Ezra 4:8–6:18; 7:12-26; Dan 2:4–7:28) and the NT (Mark 5:41; 7:34; 15:34; Matt 27:46; 1 Cor 16:22; Rev 22:20); 2) it has supplied important nonbiblical texts of various kinds throughout almost the whole biblical period.

    A. Phases of Aramaic
        1. Old Aramaic (925–700 BCE)
        2. Official Aramaic (700–200 BCE)
        3. Middle Aramaic (200 BCE–200 CE)
        4. Late Aramaic (200–1200 CE)
        5. Modern Aramaic
    B. Aramaism
        1. OT
        2. NT
    Bibliography

A. Phases of Aramaic

Because of its use over such a long span of time, Aramaic is usually divided into periods or phases, based on both chronology and geography, but any such divisions, with their dates, have to be regarded as provisional (*See* Fitzmyer 1979, 57-84; Kaufman 1997).

1. Old Aramaic (925–700 BCE)

Beginning about 1200 BCE, the traditional great empires in the ancient Middle East (Egyptian, Hittite, and Assyrian) went into decline. This enabled smaller city-states in the land "in-between" to arise and consolidate their power. Among these were the Philistines, the Hebrews, the Phoenicians, and the Arameans.

The earliest texts (contemporary with the biblical period of the divided monarchy) are inscriptions on stone, pottery, and other imperishable material. Originally, the Arameans used the Canaanite (or Phoenician) alphabet, but eventually (ca. 750 BCE) began to develop their own. The extant texts reflect dialectical variation: northern (near the modern city of Zincirli), also called Samalian or Ya'udian; eastern (on the upper Habur River near ancient Gozan); and western, or standard (around the city of Aleppo). The first appears in the inscriptions of Hadad and Panamu; the second, in the bilingual (Akkadian-Aramaic) inscription on the statue (called both "image" and "likeness") found at Tell Fakhariyeh; the third, in the Melqart stele, the stele of King Zakkur (describing a god's miraculous delivery of the king from enemies with the intervention of a prophet), the treaty-covenants of Sefire, the Tell Dan inscription (containing most likely the earliest extra-biblical reference to the "house of David"), and the Bar Rakib inscriptions. The language of the Deir ʿAlla inscription from Jordan recounting a vision of Balaam, son of Beor (Num 22–24) has been debated considerably by scholars. It has features of both Canaanite and Aramaic; perhaps at this time and in this area, a clear dividing line did not yet exist (Layton and Pardee 1988).

2. Official Aramaic (700–200 BCE)

About 750 BCE, the Assyrians began to expand and initiated a new age of empire. The neighbors to their immediate west, the Arameans, felt their presence early, and the Aramaic language and script began to spread out. The Assyrians began using it, along with their own dialect of Akkadian. Pictorial representations often show two sets of scribes, one writing cuneiform with a clay tablet and stylus, and one writing Aramaic with a scroll and pen (*see ANEP* 235, 236). Aramaic also appears on Assyrian seals, weights, and business dockets. The Rabshakeh incident (2 Kgs 18:26) suggests that Aramaic was on its way to being a kind of international language.

Aramaic continued in use after the Assyrians were succeeded by the Neo-Babylonian (Chaldean) Empire. Thus a Philistine (or Phoenician?) king Adon wrote to Pharaoh in Egypt for help against the Babylonians, and he wrote in Aramaic! In the 19th cent. CE, excavations in Babylonia directed attention especially to this Neo-Babylonian-Chaldean Empire. Since the book of Daniel is set during that time, scholars then referred to the non-Hebrew language of that book (i.e., Aramaic) as "Chaldee" or "Chaldean." These terms are no longer in use but are met in older references.

In 539 BCE, Babylon fell to Cyrus, and the Persian Empire began. Under the Persians, Aramaic, as an official language for government matters, reached its widest expansion. From this time, Aramaic is attested in Egypt, Arabia, Palestine, Syria, parts of Asia Minor, Assyria, Babylonia, Armenia, and the Indus Valley. Of what was surely a vast corpus of administrative documents, only a portion has survived. The bulk is from

Egypt where the dry climate was especially conducive to the preservation of documents on papyrus and leather. Two collections are especially important, that of the Persian satrap (governor) of Egypt, Arsames (411–408 BCE) and that of the Jewish military garrison at Elephantine (Syene) (495–399 BCE), which includes official letters, family archives, administrative, legal, and literary documents. An important literary text is the Words of Ahiqar, an Assyrian sage, which contains many proverbs set within a narrative framework, an important example of Near Eastern wisdom literature. Religious practices (Sabbath and Passover) as well as a temple of Yahweh are mentioned. (*See* Porten 1992, 2003) This period coincides with the biblical return from exile and the postexilic time. The Aramaic letters of the book of Ezra relating to rebuilding the Temple in Jerusalem (4:8–6:18; 7:12-26) belong also to this period.

Despite the span of time and the geographical spread, the language of this period shows a striking homogeneity. While minor local differences appear sporadically, a literary standard form for both the language and its orthography developed that would last for centuries. It is this form of Aramaic that the student today usually learns first.

3. Middle Aramaic (200 BCE–200 CE)

In 334 BCE, Alexander (the Great) of Macedon, (356–323) crossed into Asia Minor and began his conquest of the Persian Empire. Having been himself a student of Aristotle, he was eager to spread Greek life and culture. The age of Hellenism had begun, and with it Greek replaced Aramaic as the international language. When the Romans took over in 63 BCE, Greek continued to be used.

While the standard literary Aramaic continued to have some influence, independent dialects began to appear. There were also regional developments in the Aramaic script. Texts surviving from this period are often divided into two groups. Some propose "epigraphic and canonical" (*See* Kaufman 1997, 116–17); others distinguish on a geographical basis, North Arabia and Palestine on the one hand, and Syria and Mesopotamia on the other (*See* Fitzmyer 1979, 61–62).

From North Arabia comes a large number of Nabatean inscriptions (e.g., burial inscriptions, legal documents). Almost all deal with matters of religion, and the bulk of them is from the region of Petra. The Nabateans, whose territory covered much of the ancient kingdoms of Edom and Moab, developed a distinctive script that was the direct ancestor of the Arabic alphabet. These inscriptions date from ca. 190 BCE–150 CE.

Jewish Palestinian Aramaic appears in a variety of finds: 1) the discoveries in the Dead Sea area, particularly Qumran and Wadi Murabba'at. About 25 percent of the Dead Sea Scrolls were written in Aramaic, notably the Genesis Apocryphon and the Targum of Job; 2) the Aramaic sections of the book of Daniel, if not a little earlier, belong here; 3) inscriptional material, e.g., on ossuaries, tombstones, and coins; 4) words and phrases in the NT and Josephus; 5) letters and documents from the time of the Second Jewish Revolt against Rome (132–135 CE), especially those connected with Simon Bar Kochba (Koseba). This dialect of Aramaic was most likely the first language of Jesus of Nazareth. (*See* Fitzmyer 1979, 6–10, 38–46). The Aramaic script that developed in this period became the basis for what is now known as the Hebrew square letter script.

Palmyra (Tadmor), a crossroads oasis in the north Syrian desert, has yielded several thousand inscriptions spanning roughly 44 BCE – 272 CE. They are primarily dedicatory, funerary, and religious; there is a lengthy one dealing with duty tariffs, and many of them are Greek bilinguals. They show a remarkable mixture of diverse elements: Aramaic, Babylonian, Phoenician, Syro-Palestinian, and Arabic. Farther north, in the area of Edessa (modern Urfa in southeastern Turkey), a number of "Old Syriac" votive and funerary inscriptions have been found. Finally, off to the east, near the Tigris River and the old city of Assur, lies the oasis center of Hatra. It has produced a number of dedicatory inscriptions, dating from the 1st to the 3rd cent. CE.

4. Late Aramaic (200–1200 CE)

A great deal of material survives from this period. While it used to be customary to divide it geographically into two, east and west, more recent studies propose a tri-partite division, west (Palestine), central (Syria), and east (Babylonia). Further distinctions are based on the particular religious group that passed on the various texts: Jewish, Christian, and Samaritan (in the west), and Mandean (in the east). The closing date of this period is elusive; proposals have included 700, 900, and 1200. In the early part of this period, Aramaic dialects were still in common use, but beginning in the 7th cent., with the rise of Islam, Arabic became more and more the spoken language. The Aramaic dialects became progressively languages of scholarship and religious activity, not unlike Latin in the Western Middle Ages.

Western (Palestinian) Aramaic appears in literature produced by three groups. Jewish Palestinian is used primarily in the Palestinian targums (e.g., Neofiti) and the Palestinian Talmud and Midrashim (also known as "Yerushalmi"). Christian Palestinian appears in some inscriptions but mostly in Bible translations, liturgical lectionaries, sermons, and biographies used by Melkite Christians. They are almost all translations from Greek and are written in a form of the Syriac script. The Samaritans, residing in the Shechem area, had their own Targum to the Pentateuch (in two recensions) as well as chronicles, sermons, and liturgical poetry, written in their own distinctive script.

Central (Syrian) Aramaic is virtually equivalent to Syriac, the dialect spoken in and around Edessa.

Recently, some late Jewish texts (e.g., Targum Pseudo-Jonathan) have also been classified here. From the 4th cent., Edessa became the center of a large and significant Christian population. Its theological school was an active participant (along with Antioch and Alexandria) in the acute debates (mostly christological) of the time. The body of literature in Syriac is larger than any other Aramaic dialect and includes a wide range of topics: Bible translations (notably, the Peshitta ("simple" or "common"), commentaries, and homilies; acts of the martyrs and saints; ascetical and spiritual literature; historiography and chronicles; legal texts (civil and ecclesiastical); philosophy (Syriac translations of Greek thinkers passed to the Arabs and through them eventually into the West); science (medicine, astronomy, geography, chemistry, mathematics); grammar, lexicography, rhetoric, and poetry. During the 5th and 6th cent., the Syriac church was split into two groups: the Western (or Jacobite) branch continued in the area of Edessa, while the Eastern (Nestorian) branch set up its center in Nisibis under Persian rule. From an earlier common script (Estrangela), the two branches developed each its own form, designated respectively "Jacobite" and "Nestorian." While traditional, these confessional terms are not really adequate. Each branch developed, for the first time, methods to indicate vowels, the Eastern using dots and the Western using stylized Greek letters.

Eastern (Babylonian) Aramaic appears in two forms. Jewish Babylonian Aramaic was the language of the Jewish community in Mesopotamia and appears especially in the Aramaic parts of the Babylonian Talmud. Mandaic was the language of the Mandeans, a non-Christian Gnostic group (manda⁽ is Aramaic for "knowledge"), perhaps with Palestinian origins, which settled very early in the regions near Babylon. They produced a large literature and also developed a distinctive alphabetic script.

5. Modern Aramaic

Some forms of Aramaic continue to be spoken today in various parts of the Middle East (Syria, Turkey, Iraq, and Iran) by Jews, Christians, Muslims, and Mandeans. In addition, many modern speakers of Aramaic, as victims of various forms of persecution, have taken refuge in other parts of the world, notably Europe and the United States. A large number of dialects are represented, and the task of classifying them is quite difficult. They all show heavy influences from surrounding languages, e.g., Arabic, Turkish, Kurdish, Persian (*See* Jastrow 1997; E. Yildiz 2000, 39–44).

In accord with the threefold division of Late Aramaic, a descendant of Western (Palestinain) Aramaic is still spoken in the largely Christian village of Maʾlula in the Antilebanon Range, northeast of Damascus. Central Aramaic appears in groups of both Western and Eastern Syriac Christians. East Aramaic survives in Mandaic, though the number of speakers is diminishing.

B. Aramaism

The question of Aramaisms arises in the study of both the OT and the NT. An Aramaism may be described as Aramaic interference in the vocabulary or syntax of the Hebrew or Greek. Aramaisms may arise from the normal process of "languages in contact." Hebrew and Aramaic were in use side by side for centuries during the OT period; and in 1st cent. Palestine, while Aramaic was most likely the primary language spoken, Greek was also known and used (*See* Fitzmyer 1979, 32–38). Or Aramaisms may arise from the process of translating originally Aramaic texts into Hebrew or Greek. The question however is a complex one.

1. Old Testament

In OT studies, the issue of Aramaisms has usually been tied to questions of dating. During the postexilic period, Aramaic became more and more the language of the people, so, it was argued, the presence of Aramaisms in a text is an indication of its late dating. Nuances are called for. What is called "biblical Hebrew" is a literary language; indications exist that the languages spoken "on the ground" displayed considerable dialectical variations. Some Aramaisms then may have no chronological significance at all: 1) those in poetic texts—in old texts (e.g., Exod 15), they could reflect ancient linguistic usages, in later ones, poets often use old and arcane vocabulary; 2) those in Wisdom texts like Proverbs and Job—wisdom material may have been circulated in Aramaic form before the Hebrew writers adapted them; 3) those that appear in books or narratives set in Northern Israel—the Hebrew of Israel had some dialectical features more in common with Aramaic to its immediate north than with Judean Hebrew to the south; and 4) those that occur in texts where Arameans play a prominent role—to impart an authentic atmosphere to the narrative. Some scholars prefer to call these "Aramaic-like" features (*See* Rendsburg 2003; Hurvitz 2003).

Some Aramaisms do reflect a late interference of Aramaic into Hebrew, but a combination of indications should be used. Three such criteria are often suggested: 1) biblical distribution—the documentation of the feature should be characteristic of distinctively late biblical texts; 2) linguistic contrast—the Aramaic features depart from more typical Hebrew usage in other OT books; and 3) external sources—the feature can be shown to have had widespread usage in Aramaic dialects in which it is thought to have originated (*See* Hurvitz 2003, 35).

2. New Testament

Aramaisms in the NT form one part of a larger concern about Aramaic and the NT. This question has a number of facets: 1) the nature of 1st–cent. Palestinian Aramaic (orthography, phonology, syntax, its spoken or literary character); 2) the Aramaic names, words, and phrases preserved in the NT and the writings of Josephus; 3) Aramaisms in NT Greek; 4) real or alleged mistranslations of a possible Aramaic substratum; 5) Aramaic literary forms that may be reflected in early confessions and hymns; 6) Aramaic and variant readings in the NT Greek textual tradition; 7) Jewish literary traditions and motifs found in the NT and known Aramaic literature; 8) the influence of Aramaic epistolography on some parts of the NT epistles (*See* Fitzmyer 1979, 1–27). These are complicated questions, and methodological rigor is called for in trying to sort through them.

Aramaisms in the Bible are real. While discoveries of Aramaic texts over the last cent. or so have greatly enriched our understanding, our knowledge of Aramaic, in whatever period, remains necessarily incomplete. New discoveries, which hopefully lie ahead, will always have to be taken into account.

Bibliography: Joseph A. Fitzmyer. *A Wandering Aramean: Collected Aramean Essays* (1979); Joseph A. Fitzmyer. "The Aramaic Language and the Study of the New Testament." *JBL* 99 (1980) 5–21; Avi Hurvitz. "Hebrew and Aramaic in the Biblical Period: The Problem of 'Aramaisms' in Linguistic Research on the Hebrew Bible." *Biblical Hebrew: Studies in Chronology and Typology* (2003) 24–37; Otto Jastrow. "The Neo-Aramaic Languages." *The Semitic Langauges* (1997) 334–77; Stephen A. Kaufman. "Aramaic," in *The Semitic Languages* (1997) 114–30; Scott C. Layton and Dennis Pardee. "Old Aramaic Inscriptions." in *BA* 51 (1988) 172–89; Bezalel Porten. "Elephantine and the Bible." *Semitic Papyrology in Context* (2003) 51–83; Gary A. Rendsburg. "Hurvitz Redux: On the Continued Scholarly Inattention to a Simple Principle of Hebrew Philology." *Biblical Hebrew: Studies in Chronology and Typology* (2003) 104–28.

MICHAEL D. GUINAN

ARAMEAN CONCUBINE פִּילַגְשׁוֹ הָאֲרַמִּיָּה pilaghsho ha'arammiyyah]. Manasseh's unnamed concubine who bore his sons Asriel and Machir (1 Chr 7:14).

ARAM-MAACAH air'uhm-may'uh-kuh אֲרַם מַעֲכָה 'aram ma'akhah]. A subdivision of Aram (1 Chr 19:6). *See* MAACAH.

ARAM-NAHARAIM air'uhm-nay-huh-ray'im נַהֲרַיִם אֲרַם 'aram naharayim; Μεσοποταμία Mesopotamia]. Literally, "Aram of the rivers," in the NRSV this name is sometimes transliterated (Gen 24:10; Judg 3:8; Ps 60:1) and other times identified as MESOPOTAMIA (Deut 23:4; 1 Chr 19:6) with the LXX, referring specifically to the area of the TIGRIS and EUPHRATES rivers.

A. HEATH JONES, III

ARAM-ZOBAH air'uhm-zoh'buh אֲרַם צוֹבָה 'aram tsovah]. A town mentioned in the superscription of Ps 60. *See* ZOBAH.

ARAN air'an אֲרָן 'aran]. Grandson of Seir, the Horite, and son of Dishan. A chief or a clan of the Horites (Gen 36:28; 1 Chr 1:42). *See* HARAN; OREN.

ARARAT air'uh-rat אֲרָרָט 'ararat]. Ararat refers to the mountainous area in ARMENIA surrounding Lake Van. Historical information about this area is found predominantly in Assyrian texts, which designate the region as Urartu. The Hebrew spelling is similar to the Assyrian, though the Hebrew used *a* rather than *u* vowels. References are made to the area and people of Urartu as early as the 13th cent. BCE, but the kingdom of Urartu existed only from the 9th to the late 7th /early 6th cent. BCE. Archaeological excavations in the area indicate that it was an advanced civilization. Its language, written in CUNEIFORM, is not related to any other known language (although some have suggested a relation to Hurrian). Urartu was at the height of its power in the 8th cent. BCE, and it is against this background that one should understand the allusion to Ararat in 2 Kgs 19:37//Isa 37:38 where it is recounted that the Assyrian king, Sennacherib, while "worshipping in the temple of his god Nisroch," was murdered by two of his sons who "escaped into the land of Ararat" (*see* ASSYRIA AND BABYLONIA). Allusion to the kingdom of Urartu is also made in Jer 51:27 where Ararat, along with Minni and Ashkenaz, is summoned as one of three kingdoms whom the LORD intends to use to vent wrath against Babylon for the wrong that it has committed against Zion. In addition to these two allusions to a historical Urartu (Ararat), Ararat is also mentioned in the well-known story of the FLOOD, in which Noah's ark is said to have come to rest on "the mountains of Ararat" (Gen 8:4; *see* ARK OF NOAH). Here the reference is to a general mountainous area in the region of Urartu rather than to a specific Mount Ararat, as it has come to be popularly understood. Reports of sightings of the Ark are as old as Josephus in the 1st cent. CE, who himself did not see the ark but who refers to others who recount seeing it, and as new as the photo that the National Aeronautic and Space Administration posted on its Web site on March 18, 2001, as a site that some claimed to be a picture of Noah's ark. Tradition has associated the more general reference to the "mountains of Ararat" in Gen 8:4 with a very specific Turkish mountain, Agri Dag, an extinct volcano 16,584 ft. above sea level on the northeastern border of Turkey. Since the story of Noah's ark in its Hebrew version is similar to other mythic traditional ancient Near Eastern flood stories such as the Gilgamesh Epic, it is probable that searches for vestiges of an actual ark are pointless (*see* GILGAMESH, EPIC OF).

Bibliography: P. E. Zimansky. *Ancient Ararat: A Handbook of Urartian Studies* (1998).

EDGAR W. CONRAD

ARATUS [Ἄρατος Aratos]. A Stoic poet (315–240 BCE) from Soli in Cilicia, educated in ATHENS. His astronomical poem *Phaenomena* was widely read and translated into Arabic and Latin. Its proem to Zeus is quoted by Paul in the AREOPAGUS speech, "For we too are his offspring" (Acts 17:28).

ARAUNAH uh-raw'nuh [אֲרַוְנָה 'arawnah, Ορνα Orna]. In 2 Sam 24 it is at the threshing floor of Araunah the Jebusite that Yahweh stops an angel just short of destroying Jerusalem. Upon King David's confession to having taken a census of the people, God tells David to erect an altar at the threshing floor. Araunah appears on the scene, and, recognizing David as the king, offers to give David the threshing floor, the oxen, the wood, and all of the other implements for the sacrifice. David declines the gift and insists on paying. Then the sacrifices are made, the destruction is averted, and a severe plague on the people is stemmed.

The name *Araunah* appears inconsistently in different manuscripts as 'aranyah (אֲרַנְיָה) and 'ornah (אוֹרְנָה), while in the parallel account (1 Chr 21) the name is consistently ORNAN ('ornan אָרְנָן). The LXX uses the name Orna in both accounts.

Etymologies of the name have led some to wonder whether Araunah was a Jebusite king. Others have seen Araunah's threshing floor as a Jebusite shrine, and the story as a political and cult move for the establishment of the Davidic rule and the future Temple.

A. HEATH JONES, III

ARBA ahr'buh [אַרְבַּע 'arba']. Arba was the greatest member of the Anakim, the race of GIANTS (Josh 14:15), and father of ANAK (Josh 15:13; 21:11). The word 'arba means "four" and may not be a personal name. The LXX states that the name Αρβοκ (Arbok) is the former name of the city of HEBRON and identifies it as the principal city of the Anakim. KIRIATH-ARBA, the ancient name of Hebron, may refer to the "city of four clans/districts or persons."

J. GORDON HARRIS

ARBATHITE ahr'buh-thit [עַרְבָתִי 'arvati]. Resident of the Arabah region in Israel or the town Beth-Arabah. Designation for Abi-albon, one of David's warriors (2 Sam 23:31; Abiel in 1 Chr 11:32).

ARBATTA ahr-bat'uh. Region whose Jewish populace was rescued from oppressive Gentiles by Simon Maccabeus and brought to Judea in 163 BCE. As 1 Macc 5:23 mentions both "Galilee and Arbatta," the latter may be identical with Josephus' Narbata, which he describes variously as a "district" or "toparchy" bordering on the territory of Caesarea (*J.W.* 2.291, 509). This would make Narbata an inland region, situated northwest of Samaria and south of Mount Carmel. Josephus further relates (*J.W.* 2.291) that Narbata served as a refuge for

the Jews of Caesarea during the First Jewish Revolt against Rome (66–70 CE).

J. R. C. COUSLAND

ARBELA ahr-bee'luh [Ἄρβηλα Arbēla]. Promontory situated three mi. northwest of Tiberias, usually identified with Khirbet Irbid (196:246), which is located on the southeast side of Wadi Hammam. In 161 BCE it served as a staging ground for Bacchides' as troops in his upcWoming battle with Judas Maccabeus (1 Macc 9:2; Josephus, *Ant.* 12.421). The numerous caves across from the wadi served as a refuge for the Jewish fugitives, and later (38 BCE) for those brigands opposed to Herod the Great. Josephus recounts how Herod affected their capture by lowering his soldiers down to the caves in huge boxes (*Ant.* 14.420–30; *J.W.* 1.309-13).

J. R. C. COUSLAND

ARBITE ahr'bit [אַרְבִּי 'arbi]. An appellation indicating that Paarai, a warrior among David's Thirty, resided in the town Arab (2 Sam 23:35).

ARCHAEOLOGY. Archaeology is a social science whose purpose is to help in understanding what it is to be human by a systematic study of the material remains of the past. On prehistoric sites (*see below*, §D.1) archaeology is often a sub-discipline of anthropology. On the other hand, in the case of the ancient Near East (or Middle East), archaeology is traditionally a branch of historical studies, which in Israel is particularly related to the world of the Bible. Some scholars have made archaeology as it is practiced in Israel an independent discipline.

Furthermore, while Israeli archaeologists have a very real interest in the archaeology of the biblical period, it is motivated usually by non-theological concerns, unlike American Protestant archaeologists who fostered the "Biblical Archaeology" movement of the twentieth century (*see below*). The optimism that characterized this movement, namely that archaeological data could be used to "prove the Bible true," began to wane quickly during the last half of the twentieth century when it became obvious that more and more archaeological data could not be reconciled with a literal reading of many biblical texts (e.g., the conquest stories in Joshua). Furthermore, many literary scholars are suggesting that the final dates for much of the Bible (e.g., the Pentateuch; the Deuteronomic History: Joshua, Judges, Samuel and Kings) are much later than the periods within which this material is set. This fact raises serious questions concerning the historicity and purpose(s) of such texts. The most archaeologists can do is tell us what happened in the past with suggested [non-theological] causes and consequences. They can neither confirm nor disconfirm the theological interpretation given these events by the biblical writers.

The material remains that archaeologists study were created both by human activity (artifacts) as well as by natural processes (ecofacts). During the last quarter of the twentieth century an enormous amount of archaeological data from all over the world was recovered. Much detail emerged from scientifically conducted excavations. Unfortunately, during the same period many archaeological sites were lost to modernization efforts in many countries, including Israel and other countries relevant for the biblical period. Furthermore, the looting of antiquity sites is an international scandal, and many valuable artifacts have been lost to the underground market and to private collectors. Forgeries related to the Bible are also a major concern. (For a famous 19th cent. example, see Silberman 1982, 131-146. *See* FORGERIES). While this survey will emphasize archaeology particularly in Israel, very important archaeological work has taken place over much of the Middle East beginning in the second half of the 20th century and continuing into the 21st cent.

A. Nomenclature: What to Call It
B. Field Research Designs and Methods
   1. Historical/political vs. anthropological
   2. Stratigraphy, pottery typology, and other methods of dating
C. Chronological Periods
D. Major Syntheses of Archaeological Periods of the Near East
   1. Prehistoric periods
      a. Paleolithic
         i. Lower Paleolithic
         ii. Middle Paleolithic
         iii. Upper Paleolithic
      b. Epipaleolithic
      c. Neolithic
      d. Chalcolithic
   2. Historic periods
      a. Early Bronze Age
      b. Middle Bronze Age
      c. Late Bronze Age
      d. Iron Age I
      e. Iron Age II
      f. Assyrian, Babylonian, and Persian Periods
      g. Hellenistic Period
      h. Roman Palestine
      i. Byzantine
      j. Early Islamic
      k. Middle Islamic; "Crusader"
      l. Late Islamic
E. The Archaeology of Israel
   1. Biblical archaeology
   2. Israeli archaeology
   3. Recovery of the cultures of related peoples
   4. Computers
F. Prospects for Dialogue

A. Nomenclature: What to Call It

While archaeological excavations are global in nature, and though various types of archaeology seem to have settled jargon for most scholars (e.g., Paleolithic, New World, Old World, Classical), what to call this activity in the modern state of Israel is controversial. The phrase "Biblical Archeology," though still popular and familiar to the general public, is in decline among most biblical scholars and professional archaeologists (*see* Davis 2004, but also Biran and Aviram 1993). As more and more archaeologists specialize in periods that are not directly related to the Bible (e.g., "Neolithic," Byzantine," "Islamic") other descriptions have been suggested. While "Syro-Palestinian Archaeology" is a phrase used by a minority of scholars, Israeli archaeologists frequently refer to the "Archaeology of Ancient Israel" (Ben-Tor 1992) or "Archaeology of the Land of the Bible" (Mazar 1990). Labels such as the "Archaeology of the Holy Land" or the "Archaeology of Palestine" no longer seem appropriate in light of the politics in the Middle East.

The archaeological legacy known from modern-day Israel ranges from Paleolithic remains that date back for well over a million years to abandoned 20th cent. military trenches. In the discussion that follows, the simple descriptive phrase, The Archaeology of Israel, refers to the archaeological field work that is relevant to any archaeological period that has been undertaken in the geographical region now known as the State of Israel. Because of current political realities, the geographical region known as the West Bank will also be included under this designation. Israel's neighbors, such as Jordan, Syria, Iraq, Iran, and Turkey, as well as other countries, also have departments of antiquities, and thus there is properly an Archaeology of Jordan, of Syria, Turkey, and so on. Within these broad categories can also be included the archaeological data that might be considered relevant to the world of the Bible (*see* §E.1).

B. Field Research Designs and Methods

1. Historical/political vs. anthropological

It is commonplace today in all archaeological projects to speak of multi-disciplinary staffs. Depending on the nature of the site, the amount of time the archaeologists have for field work, the question(s) that might be answered, and other factors (e.g., budget restrictions), any number of technical specialists may be involved with the project. These positions typically include computer technicians, geologists, bone specialists, plant specialists, environmentalists, ethnographers, and anthropologists. Particularly noteworthy is the emergence of "Environmental Archaeology." Not until the last half of the 20th cent. did archaeologists begin to try to understand the entire ecosystems in which past cultures lived. Such studies include careful analyses of floral (plant) and faunal (animal) remains, water resources and usage, forest depletions, sea level and climatic changes, and many other factors, such as annual rainfall amounts, that indicate how past humans interacted with the natural world around them. A classic example is the case of the Nabataeans who inhabited the harsh environment of Israel's Negev Desert over two thousand years ago. Environmental studies using aerial photographs have shown that by constructing ditches and cisterns to collect the sparse annual rainfall (less than an inch a year), the Nabataeans were able to provide their drinking water needs and create a thriving agricultural society that produced grapes, wheat, and olives.

Not all digs are equally staffed, but this specialization evolved under the influence of American archaeological theory and practice since the 1960s. It is dubbed the New Archaeology (sometimes called processual archaeology). Books and articles on the methods and research designs for archaeological projects have mushroomed, creating an enormous amount of archaeological jargon (*see* Renfrew and Bahn 2004; Trigger 1989). However, before most archaeologists who dig in the Middle East, including Israel, could learn and apply this new method to their field practices, it was supplanted by "post-processual" archaeology. The "new archaeology" placed great emphasis on the explanation for culture changes (not only the mere description of it). The post-processual scholars emphasize a variety of interpretive methods and are especially interested in the symbols and religion of past cultures. (On many of the issues and terms used in this discussion, *see* Renfrew and Bahn 2005.) The influence of these developments in field methods has been felt, and in some instances, thoroughly integrated into excavations taking place in Israel or neighboring countries such as Jordan.

On most digs field work is organized and carried out to answer specific questions that the excavator is trying to answer. In the past, many of these questions pertained to the historical-political history of the site. In Israel, this meant that most archaeologists focused on the major tells (artificial mounds reflecting periods of repeated occupation of a site, Fig 1.) which were believed to

contain the remains of cities mentioned in the Bible, related to remembered people and political events, especially destructions. Ignored were the thousands of villages, hamlets, and farmsteads where the vast majority of nameless people lived and died. This focus on tells has changed radically. Major tells are still important, of course, and some tells in Israel, such as Hazor, Megiddo, and Beth Shemesh, have been, or are currently being re-excavated. Others, such as Tel Rehov in the Jordan Valley, are being excavated for the first time. Yet there is also an increased interest in rural areas, especially as these are discovered through surface surveys. Particularly important are studies designed to show how the outlying villages and hamlets were related economically, socially, and politically to the larger towns and cities (this type of research is called "Central Place Theory"). Consequently, research goals designed more around anthropological models have proliferated. Today archaeologists seek to understand how long-term (a popular expression seen in much of the current literature is the French, *la longue durée*) changes in land use, environment, population growth, subsistence patterns, and a host of other issues, affected the lives of ordinary people and brought about cultural change.

Laughlin
Figure 2: Archaeological Site with "Grid"

2. Stratigraphy, pottery typology, and other methods of dating

The intense discussion over how to dig an archaeological site, brought on by the introduction of the so-called "baulk-debris" method of the late K. Kenyon, is over, though techniques are and should be constantly refined. All archaeologists working in the Near East employ this technique, which consists of dividing an archaeological site into a "grid" pattern that creates "baulks" (Fig. 2). Even those who once preferred the horizontal exposure afforded by "Architectural Archaeology," now universally use the "Kenyon" method (Fig. 3). Kenyon's technique provides the excavator a valuable snapshot of a site's stratigraphy, at least for that part of the site where the method is used. As a result of

Laughlin
Figure 1: Photo of Tell

Laughlin

Figure 3: Exposure of Iron Age architectural fragments from Hazor

Kenyon's influence, stratigraphical sections are a very common part of archaeological publications. Stratigraphy refers to the way an archaeological site is formed and assumes that a deposit or layer must be older than the one which covers it (Fig. 4). Thus, stratigraphical profiles allow for a relative chronological sequence of occupational periods. In some instances, Near Eastern tells have many such strata, and untangling them is one

Laughlin

Figure 4: "Stratigraphical Section"

of the greatest challenges facing the excavator. However, in the past, little consideration was given to how tells form. The process that creates a tell is now frequently included in the research. This process includes the natural topography of the site, foundation trenches, leveling and new construction, erosion, burrowing animals, environmental interactions, as well as destruction by various causes (*see* TEL, TELL). The history of the occupation of a site may be very complicated. Furthermore, the activity on different parts of the tell, dating to the same time, may differ. Each site is unique, and far-ranging conclusions based upon limited exposure can be misleading.

The first question asked of an archaeological discovery is usually, How old is it? A number of techniques, some of them very technical, can offer clues to answer the question. Among the more promising and emerging tools are thermoluminescence and electron spin resonance (ESR).

Both methods depend upon radioactive material still present in certain materials (such as sand and teeth). If these experimental methods prove to be reliable, they will be of tremendous value in dating remains for which other methods may not be appropriate.

However, since the Pottery Neolithic period (ca. 5500 BCE) the most common technique used by archaeologists to date their discoveries is pottery typology. Pottery remains are ubiquitous on all Near Eastern sites and even broken pieces (*sherds*) can be of diagnostic value. Following William Flinders Petrie's pioneering work at Tell el-Hesi in 1890, archaeologists have developed a reliable chronological ceramic typology. Based upon such factors as shape, decoration, clay type(s), and method of manufacture, expert ceramicists can date most recovered pottery within a hundred years of manufacture. This is especially true of the historic periods (*see* POTTERY). Pottery recovered from sites in Israel (and neighboring countries) is analyzed and cataloged from every conceivable angle. Pottery charts, photographs, and drawings are a major component of both preliminary and final publications of an excavation (Fig. 5).

Laughlin

Figure 5: Iron Age pottery from Dan

However, pottery remains may also give an excavator other kinds of very useful information. If properly studied and compared, the pottery can reveal an understanding of trade patterns, socioeconomic conditions of the people who made it, production and firing techniques, and other issues now of vital importance to excavators who are consciously attempting to recover all the "cultural" information possible from a site.

C. Chronological Periods

The absolute dates for the many chronological periods used in archaeological discussions have always been approximate, especially for the earlier periods. However, it is essential that anyone studying archaeology have some idea of the dates that archaeologists frequently employ. The table that follows is given for convenience and, in places, follows closely the dates published in the NEAEHL (Vol. 4:1529).

Chronological Chart of Major Archaeological Periods

Archaeological Period	Dates
Lower Paleolithic	1,400,000–250,000 BCE
Middle Paleolithic	250,000–45,000 BCE
Upper Paleolithic	45,000–18,000 BCE
Epipaleolithic (or Mesolithic)	18,000–8300 BCE (The latter part of this period, from ca. 12,000–9600 BCE, is often called the "Natufian Period" See below, §D.1.a.iii.b.)
Pre-pottery Neolithic (divided into Pre-Pottery Neolithic A-C)	8300–5500 BCE
Pottery Neolithic (also with sub-phases)	5500–4500 BCE
Chalcolithic	4500–3300 BCE (4000–3300 also called the "Ghassulian Phase")
Early Bronze Age I A-B	3300–3000 BCE
Early Bronze Age II	3000–2700 BCE
Early Bronze Age III	2700–2200 BCE
Early Bronze Age IV (also called "Intermediate Bronze" or "Middle Bronze I")	2200–2000 BCE
Middle Bronze Age I	2000–1750 BCE
Middle Bronze Age II	1750–1650 BCE
Middle Bronze Age III	1650–1550 BCE
Late Bronze Age I	1550–1400 BCE
Late Bronze Age II A	1400–1300 BCE
Late Bronze Age II B	1300–1200 BCE
Iron Age I A	1200–1150 BCE
Iron Age I B	1150–1000 BCE
Iron Age II A	1000–900 BCE
Iron Age II B	900–700 BCE
Iron Age II C	700–586 BCE
Babylonian and Persian Periods	586–332 BCE
Hellenistic Period	332–63 BCE
Early Roman	63 BCE–32 CE
Late Roman	132–324 CE
Byzantine Period (Usually divided into "Early" and "Late" sub-periods)	324–638 CE
Early Islamic (Umayyad and Abbasid)	638–1099 CE
Middle Islamic (Crusader and Ayyubid)	1099–1291 CE
Late Islamic (Fatimid and Mamluk)	1291–1516 CE
Ottoman Period	1516–1917 CE
Modern Period	post 1917 CE

D. Major Syntheses of Archaeology Periods of the Near East

As the table clearly illustrates, the division of past ages into the many different archaeological periods, to which all material remains are assigned, has been refined considerably since the Three Age System (Stone, Bronze, and Iron) became popular in the mid 19th cent. Furthermore, major publications synthesizing and interpreting the archaeological data from most of these periods have appeared since the 1980s. Many archaeological excavations and discoveries from the Near East since the 1970s have greatly increased the mass of data now available for study. These data come from all periods, Paleolithic to Modern, and are reported in a bewildering amount and variety of publications. Even with the help of computers it is well-nigh impossible for a single individual to keep track of all the excavations and publications now taking place, even in one country such as Israel. While helpful web site databases can usually be found on the internet, they should always be used critically.

This glut of available data is especially dense for persons who have a genuine interest in the archaeology of the Near East but are not professionals. The journal, *Biblical Archaeologist* (now *Near Eastern Archaeology*), contains a series of articles, with the general title of Archaeological Sources for the History of Palestine or ASHP (originally called Archaeological Sources for the Study of Palestine). These extensive summaries are ideal for non-specialists who are interested in trying to follow the progress of archaeology that takes place in the Near East, especially Israel. Each entry is written by a specialist and is accompanied by an extensive bibliography. Some of these periods may be more familiar to biblical students than others, but some familiarity with them, even if only rudimentary, is necessary if the archaeology of Israel, and even more so, the archaeology of the ancient Near East (ANE), are to be put into their broadest perspectives.

Furthermore, archaeological remains in the modern state of Israel (as well as other Middle Eastern countries) date to tens of thousands, and even hundreds of thousands of years, before Israel appeared on the scene. Biblical students should be most interested in these discoveries because they not only put into sharp relief the relatively brief period of the Israelites (six hundred years from ca. 1200–587 BCE), but also because even a passing acquaintance with these discoveries can serve as a healthy reminder that the world-view expressed through the Bible cannot be used uncritically as a source for ancient history. In addition, some familiarity with these other periods enhances a long-term view of archaeology in the region, which persuades us that ancient Israel is but one of many cultures that appeared and disappeared in the long human drama played out in this part of the world.

1. Prehistoric Periods

a. Paleolithic (ca. 1,400,000–18,000 BCE). The long Paleolithic Period, which is usually divided into three archaeological sub-periods (the Lower, Middle, and Upper Paleolithic) and into three geological sub-periods (the Lower, Middle and Upper Pleistocene, with the Lower being the earliest) spans well over a million years in Israel.

i. Lower Paleolithic (1,400,000–250,000 BCE): The oldest documented Acheulean deposit (an LP cultural tradition named after a place in France, Saint Acheul) known outside of Africa is Ubeidiya, a Paleolithic site located about two miles southwest of the Sea of Galilee. First excavated in the 1960s, thousands of stone implements (especially hand axes) have been recovered from some 60 layers of deposits, which have been dated between 1.4 and 1 million years old. The inhabitants, identified as *Homo ergaster* ("working man"; this species is sometimes called *Homo erectus*), survived mainly from a diet of meat as indicated by animal remains [e.g., rhinoceros, hippopotamus (scavenged), deer, and horse], which was supplemented with fruit and leaves. Thus, Ubeidiya offers many clues to the evolution and movement of early humans out of Africa (*see* Levy, ed. 1995; Bar-Yosef's Prehistoric Palestine, OEANE 4: 207–212).

ii. Middle Paleolithic (250,000–45,000 BCE). Several MP sites are known from the region stretching from Syria to Lebanon, and from Israel and Jordan. Many are located in caves (such as Amud, Qafzeh, Tabun and Kebara, all in north Israel), while others have been found beneath rock shelters (e.g., Abu Sif and Erq el-Ahmar, in the Judean Desert), and still others in open air sites (such as Biqat Quneitra located northeast of the Sea of Galilee). This period can be described as the last archaeological phase in which our own human ancestors were faced with any serious evolutionary rivals, such as the Neanderthals, for global domination. The human fossil remains from such sites as Amud, Qafzel, Skhul, Tabun and Kebara, are the oldest such fossils known today and are of primary importance in understanding the history of the biological evolution of modern humans.

iii. The Upper Paleolithic (45,000–18,000 BCE). The UP in Israel is represented by a number of caves or rock shelters, all of which are located in north Israel, either on or close to the Mediterranean coast (Tabun Cave, Kebara Cave, Neve David, Hefzibah, etc.) or near the Sea of Galilee (Amud, Qafzeh, Nahal Ein Gev). The material evidence indicates the inhabitants were mobile hunter-gathers who lived off such animal resources as gazelle, ibex, and deer. The presence of grinding tools may also indicate that their diet was supplemented with vegetables. This period is also distinguished by its lithic (stone) industry that included scrapers, blades, and many flakes.

b. Epipaleolithic [sometimes called the Mesolithic, or "Middle Stone" age (18,000–8300 BCE)]. Many sites dating to this period are found scattered throughout the Near East, from Mesopotamia to Syria, and from northern Israel to the Negev and Jordan (ancient Edom and Moab). The period from ca 12,000–9,600 BCE is called the Natufian era, a name derived from the discovery of this culture by Dorothy Garrod (d. 1968) in a cave located in the wadi en-Natuf in northern Israel. Since then, many discoveries from this period have led some authorities to conclude that the Natufian people were the first settled societies, a distinction traditionally reserved for inhabitants of the last phase of the long Stone Age, the Neolithic. An important Natufian site is Eynan (Mallaha, in Arabic), located in north Israel, on the west side of the Huleh basin. It was occupied throughout the long Natufian period.

Perhaps the most surprising discovery of an Epipaleolithic site occurred in 1989 on the southwestern shoreline of the Sea of Galilee. Called Ohalo II, this quarter acre site, submerged under water for thousands of years, surfaced during an extremely dry spell, when the lake's shoreline receded. Dated to ca. 18,000 BCE, the site contains the well-preserved remains of a village, whose huts had been constructed of brush and wood, and whose floors contained tens of thousands of seeds, representing over a hundred species of plants and fruits. The burial site of a man, estimated to be in his mid thirties, was also discovered. That such a village (Ohalo II) existed at this early date has raised serious questions concerning the important point in human evolution when humans made the transition from a hunter-gatherer lifestyle to one of village agriculturalists.

c. Neolithic (8300–4500 BCE). The Neolithic culture in the ANE is perhaps the better-known prehistoric period in Israel, due to the work of the late K. Kenyon at Jericho. Excavating there from 1952–1958, Kenyon recovered four Neolithic phases: Pre-pottery Neolithic A and B, and Pottery Neolithic A and B (the first two are also called Aceramic phases by some experts). In fact, Jericho still claims to be the oldest city in the world. The Neolithic period is also the beginning point for recent single volume syntheses of the archaeology of ancient Israel (e.g., Mazar 1990; Ben-Tor 1992). This point in time is misleading, however, given what is now known of much older periods that are briefly described above.

Since the time of Kenyon's work an enormous amount of additional data from a variety of Neolithic sites is documented. Concomitantly the cultural reconstructions of this period grow more complex as newer archaeological methods force a more multi-faceted and refined analysis of the period. For example, while Jericho still boasts the largest PPNA site yet discovered, excavations at other places, beginning in the 1980s, such as Jerf el Ahmar, Abu Hureya, and Mureybet (Syria), Göbekli Tepe and Çatalhöyük (Turkey), ʿAin Ghazal, and Khirbet Hammam (Jordan), have led some specialists to conclude that Jericho, as well as other Neolithic sites found in the Jordan Valley, were on the periphery with regard to Neolithic origins. Furthermore, applying post-processual methods to these discoveries, earlier interpretations, such as the cultic function of dozens of modeled skulls known from Jordan to Turkey, have been re-evaluated. It is now known that some of the skulls are from women and children not just men as previously believed. In addition to religious functions, the skulls may have had fertility or apotropaic (to ward off evil) meanings. No doubt as more data are recovered and analyzed, other creative suggestions and re-interpretations of the cultures from this period will occur. In addition, many of the more recently excavated sites are much larger than Neolithic Jericho (ca. 6 acre) and other Jordan Valley sites. These larger sites include ʿAin Ghazal (25–35 acre) and Çatalhöyük (30 acre). These larger cities also supported populations estimated to have been in the thousands. Particularly remarkable are the astounding art works (including painted walls and sculptured monoliths) from such places as Göbekli Tepe, Jerf el Ahmar and Çatalhöyük, as well as the anthropomorphic clay-twig statues (32 figures in two caches) discovered at ʿAin Ghazal, Jordan, during the 1980s (*see* GHAZAL, ʿAIN).

d. Chalcolithic (copper+stone) (ca. 4500–3300 BCE). This period produced distinct regional cultures ranging from the Golan in the north, which produced basalt pillar-statures to the metallurgy (copper) in the Beer-sheba region in the south. A spectacular example of the latter is the copper hoard found in the "Cave of the Treasure" near the Dead Sea by Pesah Bar-Adon in the early 1960s. Formal burial grounds also date to this period, including the hundreds of nawamis (stone structures) known from the southern Sinai Peninsula. For the first time large farming-villages appeared in Israel and Jordan and olives were domesticated. All of this evidence (and much more) suggests to experts that major social, political, and economic changes took place during this time characterized in part by craft specialization and a socially elite class that created "spatial hierarchies" called "chiefdoms." However, despite the remarkable achievements of this period and over a thousand years of existence, the end came rather quietly. Most sites appear simply to have been abandoned and never resettled (*see* Levy 1986).

2. Historic Periods (ca. 3400 BCE–present)

a. Early Bronze Age. (ca. 3400–2000 BCE). The EBA was the first major urbanized era in Israel (EBA II/III) and is characterized by social and economic stratification, witnessed by a large number of small occupied sites (1–2 acres) and several heavily fortified large (20–30 acres) cities, especially during the EBA III period, such as Ai (et-Tell), Aphek, Jericho, Arad, and others. This urbanization process reached its peak during EBA III (ca. 2700–2300 BCE) after which there was a major collapse of the EB city-state organization. The older view—that this collapse was brought about

by invaders, particularly the Amorites—is generally discarded by scholars in favor of internal processes. This important and complex period in the history of Israel is ably analyzed by S. Richard (1987).

b. Middle Bronze Age (ca. 2200–1550 BCE). The MBA is one of the best-known periods from Israel, due to the quantity as well as the quality of the preserved remains. This period witnessed the second major urbanized era in the country, with large fortified cities built throughout the land, such as Laish (Dan), Megiddo, Aphek, Lachish, and Hazor (and many others). Also dating to the MBA are historical texts containing the names of biblical cites such as Jerusalem, Hazor, and Shechem. These texts are known from Egypt ("Execration Texts") and from the Mesopotamian sites of Mari and Nuzi. Sometimes referred to as the "zenith" of the urban Canaanite era, the MBA is summarized by W. G. Dever (1987). The traditional association of this period with the biblical ancestor stories (patriarchs) has long been disputed.

c. The Late Bronze Age (1550–1200 BCE). The LBA is the label for the ultimate decline and death of the material culture of the Bronze Age. The LBA saw a drop both in the number and size of settlements. By the end of the period it has been estimated that 95 percent of the sites were 12.5 acres in size or less (43 percent were 2.5 acres or less). Among some of the most important architectural remains from this period are temples. Examples come from Hazor, Megiddo, Beth-shan, and Lachish. The temple known from Shechem is called a mighdol ("fortress") because of its enormous size (70 x 86' with walls 16' thick). The excavator at Shechem, the late G. Ernest Wright, identified this temple with that of El Berit ("god of the covenant") described in the book of Judges (9:46-49).

Also dating to the LBA is an important collection of clay tablets found in Egypt at a site known as Tell el-Amarna. Dating to the first half of the fourteenth century BCE, many of these texts came from vassal city-state rulers in Israel such as Labʾayu of Shechem and ʿAbda-heba of Jerusalem. These letters reflect a period of political chaos in Israel caused in part by a group of people identified as the ʿApiru. Whether or not there is any etymological connection between the terms ʿApiru and "Hebrew" (ʿivri) is debated.

What brought the LBA to an end is also a moot point among specialists. The decline of Egyptian control, coupled with general economic collapse in the Mediterranean basin, implies that the end came more as a whimper than a bang. The story of the exodus out of Egypt by Moses and the Israelites has also been traditionally linked to this time. Although conservative scholars continue to read this story as history, many archaeologists and biblical historians have observed that the story is making theological claims about the liberation of a people (*see* Leonard 1989).

d. Iron Age I (1200–1000 BCE). This seminal

period in the history of Israel was little documented during the 20th cent. But surveys and discoveries not only in Israel proper but also in other areas such as ancient Moab, Edom, and Ammon (all now in modern Jordan), shed considerable light on this period (*see* Block-Smith and Nakhai 1999). The connection of the Iron Age with early Israelites, while popular, is not accepted by all authorities. From where did the inhabitants come to populate the hundreds of Iron Age I villages that are now known in the Central Hill Country? How were they organized? What kind of cultic practices, if any, did they engage? The question of the origin of Israel remains controversial. Furthermore, many scholars reject the linking of the destruction of certain sites dating to the Late Bronze Age or early Iron Age I with the "conquest" stories in the Bible. While much more is known today archaeologically about the Iron Age I, it is an over simplification to identify the Iron Age I material remains of the Central Hill country of Israel as Israelite. Archaeology can, and has, gone a long way in helping students recover the culture of this period, but issues of ethnicity are complex in terms of what the archaeological record ought to look like. Furthermore, earlier archaeological ethnic markers once thought to denote the presence of Israelites in Iron Age I remains have been discarded. These include the so-called four-room house, the collared-rim store jar, and the pottery in general, all of which are now known to have had Late Bronze Age predecessors.

e. Iron Age II (1000–586 BCE). For readers who are primarily interested in what role, if any, archaeology can play in helping one better understand the Bible (in this case the Hebrew Bible or OT), the Iron Age II period is of ultimate significance. Historically (and biblically) speaking, this is the time of the kingdoms of Israel and Judah, the prophets, the Assyrian assault at the end of the 8th century BCE, and the Babylonian attack in 587/86 BCE. The amount and variety of archaeological realia dating to this period is immense and growing. They include massive architectural remains (gates, fortifications, palaces), remnants of rural villages, and ingenious water systems such as those at Jerusalem, Hazor, Megiddo, Beth Shemesh, and Gibeon. Of most importance, hundreds if not thousands of INSCRIPTIONS, including inscribed potsherds (OSTRACA) from such places as Arad (*see* ARAD OSTRACA), Lachish, and Samaria, as well as monumental inscriptions from Tel Dan, the Siloam Tunnel (Jerusalem), and the MOABITE STONE date to this period. All of this archaeological material, and much more unmentioned, is important for reconstructing and understanding the societies of both Israel and Judah.

Unlike an earlier generation of archaeologists who were pre-occupied with correlating material remains with political events and significant personages mentioned in the Bible, today there is growing interest in the daily lives of the masses of unnamed folk who made up the majority of the inhabitants of ancient Israel: the "poor of the land" (*see* Borowski 2003; King and Stager 2001). Knowledge gained from surveys and excavations clearly shows that most people during biblical times lived in small villages or farmsteads and hamlets. With a life expectancy of less than fifty years, these unnamed masses faced a daily challenge of survival, which was constantly threatened by drought and pestilence. In addition, the abuse and exploitation, to which they were often subjected by the wealthy and powerful, is frequently condemned by the biblical prophets (Isa 1:10-17; Amos 4:1; 5:10-11).

Also characteristic of these rural populations is "folk religion." There is growing literature on the subject of popular ancient Israelite religion, which is now understood to have been polytheistic until the Exile or later. The publications on this subject are vast. For orientation to some of the major issues see the following: Dever 2005; Kletter 2001; LaRocca-Pitts 2001; Miller 1989; Smith 2001; van der Toorn 1994; for an excellent summary of Iron Age II archaeology, *see* Herr 1997. The archaeological data now known include remains from family or local shrines stretching from Tel Dan in the north to Kuntillet ʿAjrud in the Negev. This material dates from the 12th through the 7th cent. BCE and includes **bamoth** ("high places" [Tel Dan]), **masseboth** (standing stones; Fig. 6; for both bamot and matsevoth see now LaRocca-Pitts 2001), clay female pillar figurines, identified with Asherah, the Great Mother Goddess (*see* Dever 2005; Kletter 2001), offering and incense stands, altars including "horned," figurines of various kinds including "horse and rider," good-luck charms, and very important inscriptions. Among the latter are those discovered at Khirbet el-Qôm (8th cent. BCE) and Kuntillet ʿAjrud (9th–8th cent. BCE)

Laughlin

Figure 6: Five masseboth found near the Iron Age II gate area, Tel Dan: 8th cent. BCE

which speak of "Yahweh" and his "a/Asherah." This mass of archaeological evidence (and there is a lot more) points to a polytheistic folk religion that existed among the illiterate masses that was very different from the monotheistic "book religion" (as it is sometimes called) known from the Bible. The role of women in this family or clan-oriented religion is emphasized (for orientation and bibliography, *see* Dever 2005).

Another serious archaeological and historical controversy for Iron Age II is the existence and extent of a Davidic and Solomonic monarchy. Archaeologically, this problem is defined by what is known (or, perhaps more to the point, what is not known) about Jerusalem during the 10th cent. BCE (the traditional date for David and Solomon). The date of certain pottery forms and controversies over the identification and dating of certain strata, especially at Megiddo, Hazor, and Gezer are part of this puzzle. While most specialists argue for a Davidic-Solomonic Jerusalem, others suggest that if such an "empire" existed it was hardly of biblical proportions (*see* Vaughn and Killebrew 2003). Based upon the material remains from the above sites (esp. gates and pottery) some archaeologists claim that a "Solomonic United Monarchy" can be defended (*see* esp. Dever 2001 and Mazar 1990, 368–402). However, other experts date these same archaeological data a hundred years later thus removing them from any discussion of a 10th cent. BCE empire (*see* particularly Finkelstein 2005; Finkelstein and Silberman 2001).

On the other hand, the question of whether or not David was a real historical figure was laid to rest for mainstream scholars with the discovery of the Tel Dan Stele (10th cent. BCE) in 1993. The Aramaic inscription makes reference to the "house of David."

f. The Assyrian, Babylonian, and Persian Periods (ca. 732–332 BCE). The Assyrian invasion of ancient Israel and Judah during the last half of the 8th cent. BCE changed dramatically the political and demographic makeup of these states, especially the former. By the end of the 8th cent., Assyria controlled most of the region. One of the best-documented casualties of this Assyrian assault is the conquest of Lachish, whose defeat is graphically portrayed on the walls of Sennacherib's palace at Nineveh. The Assyrians set up administrative centers at such places as Hazor, Megiddo, and Gezer. Archaeological evidence of their presence includes remains of palaces and other official buildings, cylinder seals, pottery, and imported metal bowls. By the end of the 7th cent. BCE, the capitol city of the Assyrian empire, Nineveh (612 BCE), had fallen to the Babylonians who would ultimately destroy Jerusalem in 586 and deport many of the upper class to Babylon (the "Exile"). However, the destruction was not total and such sites as Mizpah, Tell el-Ful (Gibeah?), and even Jerusalem, continued to exist with local populations.

The control of the region by Babylon was short lived and by 539 BCE, the first king of Persia, Cyrus (559–529 BCE), founded the Persian Empire. There was a revival of life in Israel spurred by the return of exiles to Jerusalem and elsewhere. While the archaeological evidence is not as clear as it is for other periods, the Persians administered the region from various cities such as Megiddo (for Galilee), Dor (the coastal region), Ashdod (Philistia), and Idumea (the Negev). This period is reflected in biblical texts such as Haggai, Zechariah, 1 and 2 Chronicles and Ezra and Nehemiah (Esther, placed in this period by its author, is problematic from a historical perspective). The presence of ethnic diversity and its perceived threat to the Jewish community are clearly indicated in books such as Nehemiah (10:31; 13:24) and Ezra (10; *see* Stern 2001).

g. Hellenistic Period (332–63 BCE). During this time there was continued general economic and population recovery begun during the preceding Persian period. Another characteristic of this period is the diversity of the population reflected in the material culture. Outside of the boundaries of what was known as Judah and Samaria, the influence of Greek culture ("Hellenization") was wide spread. Such sites as Tel Anafa and Banias (Panion), both in Upper Galilee, show clear Greek influences. At Banias a cult-shrine to the Greek god, Pan (thus the site's name, Panion), was established sometime during the 3rd cent. BCE (Fig. 7). Also at Dan, a site very close to Banias, there was a thriving Greek cult attested by an inscription that reads in part: "to the god who is in Dan" (this inscription is written in both Greek and Aramaic; Fig. 8).

At Tel Anafa remains of houses were discovered which are similar to the material culture known from the coastal regions, including the fancy table ware know as Eastern Segillata Ware which was imported from the Phoenician coast. By the 2nd cent. BCE, Greek influence was present even in traditional Jewish enclaves such as Jerusalem. Greek coins and the recovery of hundreds of stamped wine jar handles, many of them from Rhodes, point to increased Hellenization.

Laughlin

Figure 7: Cave of Pan at Banias: Caesarea Philippi.

By the time of the Antiochus IV Epiphanes (175–163 BCE), the situation was ripe for the Jewish rebellion that occurred under Mattathias of Modein (a small village located northwest of Jerusalem). Known as "The

Laughlin

Figure 8: Bilingual Hellenistic Inscription from Tel Dan.

Maccabean War" (Maccabeus ["hammer"] was the nickname of one of Mattathias's sons), this rebellion was first directed against the Jews who supported the Hellenizing policies of Antiochus, and then against Antiochus and his forces (*see* the apocryphal book, 1 Maccabees and the biblical book of Daniel). This clash between traditional Jewish practices and the Hellenized urban elite led to sectarian movements among the Jews, the most famous example of which is Qumran where the Dead Sea scrolls were found in 1947. The end of the Hellenistic period in Israel is usually dated with the arrival in Jerusalem of the Roman general, Pompey, in 63 BCE (*see* Berlin, 1997).

h. **Roman Palestine** (63 BCE–324 CE). Herod the Great (37–4 BCE) and his building programs are well documented, but other forces shaped this era, such as the Nabateans and the revolts (66–70 CE; 132–135 CE) against Rome after Herod's time. Rome domination involved the building of roads to make the movements of military forces easier and faster. (*see* Chaney and Porter 2001). A few scholars seek to integrate the archaeology of this period with NT texts (Crossan and Reed 2001; 2004; *see also* Reed 2000). These volumes illustrate the kind of dialogue that is long overdue between those who focus on texts and those who focus on material remains.

i. **Byzantine** (324–638 CE). The Byzantine era is one of the best archaeologically attested periods known with remains found on almost all antiquity sites in Israel. This includes the Judean desert where many monasteries were built and inhabited by Christian monks. This historically important period has recently been assessed, including a survey of major archaeological sites, and a discussion of many inscriptions known from this time (*see* Parker 1999). This is an important era for understanding the rise and spread of Christianity, documented by a burst of church-building following the arrival in Israel of Constantine's mother, Helena, in 325 CE.

j. **Early Islamic** (Umayyad–Abbasid, 630 [38]–1099 CE). Only towards the end of the 20th cent. has Islamic archaeology become a discipline in its own right. It is common to divide this period into three major sub-periods (early, middle, late) stretching from the seventh through the 15th cent. CE. The Umayyad era (661–749) brought substantive changes to the region including the construc-

tion of the famous Dome of the Rock in Jerusalem and the larger surrounding compound called the Haram esh-Sharif. Under Umayyad control Jerusalem became a major administrative center. This rich and luxurious period is reflected in the material remains from such sites as Khirbat al-Mafjar, near Jericho, and Khirbat al-Minyeh, located on the northwest shore of the Sea of Galilee. In the mid-8th cent. CE, the Abbasids moved the region's center to Iraq, where in 762 they founded the city of Baghdad. Political chaos followed with the rebellion of various tribes. One of the causalities of these conflicts was the destruction of the Church of the Holy Sepulchre in Jerusalem in 1009–10. The rich cultural heritage of this period includes art and architecture, inscriptions and textiles, coins and pottery (*see* Schick 1998).

k. **Middle Islamic; "Crusader"** (Frankish and Ayyubid, 1099–1291 CE). The conquest of Jerusalem by the Franks in 1099 to their final defeat by the Arabs in 1291, forever changed the political, social, and archaeological landscape of the area. Many sites in Israel (e.g., Acco, Caesarea Maritima, Jerusalem, Tiberias, and Banias) contain significant remains from this period. Perhaps one of the most important archaeological conclusions is that not only the urban areas but also the country-side (villages and hamlets) were occupied by the Franks at this time. A wealth of archaeological material is known from this period including the remains of many castles, the construction and restoration of churches (the Church of the Holy Sepulchre among them), and fine art work that includes wall painting, mosaics, and sculptures (Boas 1998).

l. **Late Islamic** (Fatimid and Mamluk, 1291–1516 CE). The Mamluks (also spelled Mameluke) were an army of slaves (from **mamluk**, the Arab word for slave) who gained political control over much of the Near East beginning in 1250 CE. Discoveries from such places as Banias (Caesarea Philippi), which had a sizable Mamlukan occupation, to Jerusalem and Beersheba, as well as Transjordanian sites such as Hisban, the rich material culture of these later periods has emerged from obscurity thanks to archaeologists. The remains include markets, courtyards, and pottery (Fig. 9). Their rule came to an end with the conquest of Syria by the Ottoman Turks in 1516 (*see* Walker 1999). In addition to the summaries of these

Laughlin

Figure 9: Mamluk courtyard from Banias

major archaeological periods known to have existed in Israel, ancient Moab also receives considerable attention by archaeologists. Projects are under way in the Karak region, also at Khirbat al-Mudayna, and via the Madaba Plains Project. Among contemporary issues is the question of Moabite ethnicity, especially during the biblical period (*see* several articles in *BA* 60, 1997).

E. The Archaeology of Israel

The following is a brief summary of the major archaeological issues for students of the Bible. More details can be found in the bibliography.

1. Biblical Archaeology

The rise and fall of so-called Biblical Archaeology is well-documented (Davis 2004 with bibliography). While this term is still popular and is part of the title of a highly successful magazine devoted to archaeology in the Near East, particularly Israel (*Biblical Archaeology Review*), it is usually associated with American Protestant archaeological efforts in Israel, which stretch from the 1920s to the 1960s is are intractably linked with W. F. Albright (d. 1970). There are many issues embedded, and it is easy to overly simplify, but many scholars insist that the fatal flaw in this approach is its assumption, whether consciously expressed or not, that the Bible's portrait of "what happened" in Israel's history is true empirically and scientifically, such that archaeological data, if rightly interpreted, can support that biblical portrait of history (*see* NIV Archaeological Study Bible 2004). Biblical archaeologists seek to validate historically biblical stories of the patriarchs, the story of the exodus out of Egypt, and especially the conquest of Canaan under the leadership of Joshua. Such goals, however sincerely conceived, miss the point and stretch the limits of what archaeology can prove or disprove.

On the other hand, there is an immense amount of archaeological data that date to the "biblical" period. Thus the extreme skepticism that characterizes some discussions vis-à-vis archaeology and the Bible is unwarranted (*see* particularly the controversy documented in Lemche 1998; Thomson 1999; Dever 2001; and Finkelstein 2005). While archaeology can provide a broad cultural overview of the world out of which the Bible came (e.g, the polytheistic context of folk religion in 1000–586 BCE), it has more difficulty when attempts are made to apply it to specific texts. Furthermore, archaeological data are constantly expanding, and will continue to do so in the future. No one can predict beforehand how such new data will force re-evaluations of earlier interpretations. Thus most, if not all, archaeological conclusions should be held tentatively and remain open to modification and/or rejection when new data and interpretations warrant it.

Archaeologists should always be motivated by the goal of recovering and recording as accurately as possible all of the available material remains left by past human behavior as well as by natural forces. When these data are analyzed and valid archaeological conclusions, especially those bearing upon historical questions, are published, then biblical experts can see if these data shed any light on matters of biblical interpretation.

The question is not whether archaeological data from the ANE, particularly from Israel, are important for biblical studies. Of course they are. Only archaeology can provide the material realia that offer clues to any interpretation of history, clues that are subject to the same biases as found in any other aspect of biblical interpretation. It is just as important to remember that the texts of the Bible cannot be read as an "objective" account of Israel's "history." Often it is only archaeological data that are contemporary with the events described by a biblical author. But even here there is often controversy. At what point can one be confident that the material world recovered by the archaeologists intersects the literary/theological world of the biblical author? Part of the answer to this question depends on the presumed dates for the biblical texts and their historicity (compare the examples listed above. Note also that the word history, in our modern usage of the term, does not appear in the Bible).

This persistent activity forces a re-evaluation of what archaeology can legitimately contribute to biblical studies. The perception persists that archaeologists excavate in Israel to find something spectacular related to the Bible. In the past, no small blame for this perception must be placed on the archaeologists themselves, for that was exactly what they were doing.

The future of "Biblical Archaeology" is still uncertain. The concept can be legitimate if both "text" experts and "dirt" experts do their work independently and then talk to one another. However, if the recent attempt to resurrect Biblical Archaeology becomes primarily a smokescreen for the hidden religious assumptions of its users, it will no more succeed than previous attempts. The scholar who goes to the field, looking for something to confirm prior beliefs about the Bible, will almost always find the "proof."

2. Israeli Archaeology

During the heyday of Biblical Archaeology, foreign schools conducted their own digs independently of the Israelis. With the maturation of the state of Israel, most excavations are controlled by the Israel Antiquities Authority (IAA), and even those excavations sponsored primarily by outside institutions are usually joint projects conducted in collaboration with Israeli archaeologists.

The following chart lists some of the major projects in the lands of the Bible. Many of these projects are still continuing. Due to the political realities in Israel (and elsewhere in the Middle East), the participation by American groups, especially colleges and universities has substantially subsided.

SITES (Alphabetical Order)	EXCAVATORS	DATES	DESCRIPTIONS/MAJOR DISCOVERIES
ACCO	Moshe Dothan	1973-1979	Middle Bronze Gate; fortifications; Late Bronze Age through Byzantine remains
AI (et-TELL)	Judith Marquet-Krause Joseph A. Callaway	Krause: 1933-1935 Callaway: Between 1964-1976	Large (27 a.) fortified Early Bronze Age City; Small (4-5 a) unfortified Iron Age I farming village. Site abandoned ca. 1050 BCE. Important site for "conquest" story
APHEK	Moshe Kochavi	1972-1985	Middle Bronze and Late Bronze Age Egyptian "palaces;" Canaanite city-state
ARAD	Y. Aharoni and Ruth Amiran	1962-1984	Major Early Bronze Age city; Iron Age Citadel; "YHWH" temple
AROER	Avraham Biran	1975-1972	Iron Age II-III structures; Herodian Remains
ASHDOD	Moshe Dothan	1962-1972	Philistine remains; "Ashdoda" figurine; seals with possible Philistine script
ASHKELON	Lawrence E. Stager	1985-	Large (150 a) fortified MBA Canaanite city. MBA silver coated calf; Philistine deposits; Persian remains including dog cemetery; Crusader city; site listed on Merneptah Stele (late 13th cent. BCE).
BANIAS (CAESAREA PHILIPPI)	Vassilios Tzaferis	1988-2000	Monumental Early Roman city; Palace of Agrippa II; huge Byzantine bathhouse; Crusader, Mamlukan remains
BATASH, TELL (TIMNAH)	Amihai Mazar and George Kelm	1977-1989	Fortified MB II town; Philistine occupation; Iron Age II town destroyed by Sennacherib in 701 BCE
BETHSAIDA	Rami Arav	1990-present	Iron Age II city and fortifications; "Bit Hilani" palace; Hellenistic-Early Roman; Middle Ages
BETH-SHEAN	Amihai Mazar	1989-1996	Refined previous known stratigraphy; Neolithic-Crusader periods. Egyptian administrative center during LBA
BETH-SHEBA	Yohanan Aharoni Z. Herzog	Aharoni: 1969-1976 Herzog: 1976	Well-preserved Iron Age II town
BETH-SHEMESH	Shlomo Bunimovitz and Zvi Lederman	1990-present	Iron Age I and II remains: 12th-7th cents. BCE. Major Iron Age II water installation
CAESAREA MARITIMA	Various directors over many years. Major underwater exploration begun in 1975 by Avner Raban (d. 2004), Haifa Univ. Caesarea Combined Expeditions project	Joint Project called the Combined Caesarea Expeditions Sponsored by Haifa Univ. and Univ. of Maryland:1988-present	Herod the Great's harbor and city; Byzantine, Early Islamic and Crusader remains. A major temple found.
CAPERNAUM	Vassilios Tzaferis	1982-1987	Greek Orthodox property; 2nd-3rd cent. CE Roman Bathhouse; Early Islamic gold hoard; Late Roman–Early Islamic architecture
CHORAZIN	Z. Yeivin	1980-1984	Byzantine village and synagogue
DAN (This is the longest continuous excavation ever conducted in Israel)	Avraham Biran	1967-2000	Neolithic-Byzantine; Major MBA fortifications including mud-brick arched gate and rampart walls; Iron Age II gates; "high place;" massebot; Tel Dan stele that mentions "house of David"
DEIR EL-BALAH	Trude Dothan	1989-1996	Fifty anthropoid clay coffins; LBA Egyptian outpost; Philistine, Israelite, Byzantine remains
DOR	Ephraim Stern; Ilan Sharon and Ayelet Gilboa	Stern: 1980-1991 Sharon and Gilboa, 2003-present	Massive brick wall, Iron Age I; other material from Iron II, Persian, Hellenistic (large temples), Roman
FARʿAH, TELL (POSSIBLY BIBLICAL TIRZAH)	Roland de Vaux	1946-1960	Occupied as early as Pre-pottery Neolithic Period; Important Iron Age II remains; if Tirzah, Omri's first capitol city.
GATH (Tell es-Safi)	Aren M. Maeir	1996-present	Major Philistine site; One of largest Iron II sites (over 120 acres); Important Iron Age II pottery and architectural remains
GEZER	G. Ernest Wright; W. G. Dever; Joe Seger	1964-1974; 1984; 1990	26 strata identified dating from Late Chalcolithic-Roman (Early Byzantine); MBA fortified Canaanite city (over 30 a.) with "High Place." Controversy over dating of Iron Age architectural remains (10th cent. BCE or later?); "Gezer Calendar;" Several violent destructions.

SITES (Alphabetical Order)	EXCAVATORS	DATES	DESCRIPTIONS/MAJOR DISCOVERIES
GIBEON (EL-JIB)	James B. Pritchard	1956-1962	Site located 5 m. N of Jerusalem; EBA IV occupation; No LBA town found; Iron Age remains include massive water system including the "Great Pool;" 31 Iron Age jar handles inscribed with gb'n (Gibeon).
HALIF, TELL (RIMMON?)	Joe D. Seger	Between 1976-1993	17 strata of occupation-Chalcolihtic-20th cent. Fortified EBA III city; Re-occupied during LBA and Iron Ages. Major destruction end of 8th cent. BCE. Strong case for identifying with biblical Rimmon
HAZOR	Y. Yadin Amnon Ben-Tor	Yadin: 1955-1958; Ben-Tor: 1990-present	Major Bronze, Iron Age architectural remains including Bronze Age temples; "Solomonic" gate and walls; huge Iron Age II water shaft
HERODIAN JERICHO	Ehud Netzer	1973-1983	Hasmonean palace; major Herodian palace complexes
HESBON (TALL HISBON)	S. H. Horn Lawrence T. Geraty Ø ystein S. LaBianca	1968-	Located in Jordan; No occupation pre-dating 12th cent. BCE. Iron Age II material, esp. 7th- 6th cent. BCE; Cave complex; Later material from Islamic and Mamluk periods. If biblical Hesbon, raises important questions about "Israelite Conquest."
ISKANDER, KHIRBET [the "ruin of Alexander (the Great")]	Suzanne Richard	1981-	East of Dead Sea. Important Early Bronze Age site
'IZBET SARTAH	Israel Finkelstein	1976-1978	Iron Age I-II settlements; inhabitants identified by excavator with population group that inhabited the Central Hill Country villages during the Iron Age I
JALUL, TELL	Randy Younker David Merling	1992-	3 miles east of Madaba, Jordan. Important Iron Age site (12th-8th cents. BCE). Persian remains.
JERUSALEM Since the early 1850s, well over 130 separate excavations have been conducted in Jerusalem. Many of these have been by foreign excavators, beginning with the Frenchman, F. De Sauley in 1849-51. However, much work has been, and still is, done by Israeli archaeologists. The list here is selective.	Ruth Amiran	1953-1960	Burial caves in West Jerusalem
	D. Ussishkin	1968-1971	Burial caves in Silwan Village
	Benjamin Mazar	1968-1978	Ophel Hill; southwest corner of Temple Mound: Second Temple period through Fatimid (10th – 11th cents. CE).
	R. Amiran and A. Eitan	1968-1969	"Tower of David," Old City
	N. Avigad	1969-1982	Jewish Quarter, Old City including the "Broad Wall" dated to the time of King Hezekiah, late 8th cent. BCE.
	G. Barkay	1975-1989	Ketef Hinnom, SW of Old City; 8th-6th cent BCE burial caves; silver "scrolls" with biblical text ("Levitical Blessing")
	Yigael Shiloh	1978-1984	City of David; many important discoveries from Chalcolithic down to Byzantine period. Among most controversial: date and function of "Stepped stone structure"
	Ronny Reich	1990-present	Various projects: work in "Warren's Shaft" (was not for drawing water as traditionally interpreted); Middle Bronze Age constructions protecting the Gihon Spring at foot of Ophel Hill; 2005, "Pool of Siloam"
JEZREEL	David Ussishkin John Woodhead	1990-1995	Royal town from time of Omride (9th cent. BCE); mound occupied up to 20th cent.
KARAK RESOURCES PROJECT (KRP)	Gerald Mattingly	1995-	Located in Karak district of central Jordan. Multidisplinary dig and survey with emphasis on use of natural resources by ancient and modern populations.
LACHISH	David Ussishkin	1973-1987	Major site with remains from many periods. Canaanite City-State; Late Bronze Age Fosse Temple; site violently destroyed ca. 1150 BCE (by whom is debated); large fortified Iron II city with large palace-fort; destroyed by Assyrians in 701 BCE; Assyrian siege ramp; royal storage jars with stamped handles; famous "Lachish Letters"
MEGIDDO	Israel Finkelstein, John Woodhead David Ussishkin	1994-present	Major re-excavation of this important tell; controversy over traditional dating of some remains to time of Solomon

SITES (Alphabetical Order)	EXCAVATORS	DATES	DESCRIPTIONS/MAJOR DISCOVERIES
MIQNE, TEL/EKRON	Trude Dothan; Seymour Gitin	1981-1995	Major Philistine city with Iron II olive oil industry
QASILE	Amihai Mazar	1971-1974; 1982-1992	Philistine city
RADDANA, KHIRBET	Joseph A. Callaway	Between 1969-1974	Small (less than 2 a.) Iron Age I Canaanite farming village with pillared houses; Important for understanding history of Central Hill Country; located short distance N of Jerusalem
RAMAT RACHEL	Oded Lipschits Oren Tal	Renewed excavations are due to begin in 2005	Judean palaces; Roman villa; Byzantine monastery
REHOV, TEL	Amihai Mazar	1997-present	In Bethshean Valley; major Early Bronze, Late Bronze and Iron Age I-III remains; important Iron Age II A material dating to 10th-9th cents. BCE
SEPPHORIS	Eric M. Meyers Carol L. Meyers James Strange Ehud Netzer K. G. Hogland	1976-1990s	Located 4 m N of Nazareth. Major Roman-Byzantine city; Jewish center of learning; Spectacular mosaics including "Mona Lisa of the Galilee" from Roman villa. Elaborate water system with aqueducts; many tombs.
SHILOH	Israel Finkelstein	1981-1964	MB, LB, Iron I and II; Hellenistic, Roman and Byzantine. Early "Israelite" cult site
TIBERIAS	Yizhar Hirschfeld	1989-present	"Cardo," marketplace; Late Roman structures; 6th cent. Synagogue; city gate
'UMEYRI, TALL AL	Lawrence T. Geraty; Larry G. Herr	1984-	Located in Jordan; Site is part of the Madaba Plains Project; Well preserved Iron Age I town; Persian administrative center with seals of Persian officials; site important for the history of Jordan and transition from LBA to Iron I settlements.
YOKNEAM (or JOKNEAM)	Amnon Ben-Tor	1977-1988	23 strata identified; major Iron Age remains. Prominent Arab and Crusader center. Town was part of a major regional study.

3. Recovery of the Cultures of Related Peoples

Archaeologists have recovered clues for several of the cultures of other peoples mentioned in the Bible, who played a direct role in the life of Israel. These include the Ammonites, Moabites, and Edomites (Jordan), and the Assyrians, Babylonians and Persians, as well as the Phoenicians and Philistines. The culture of the latter group, the Philistines, has especially come to light due to the excavations of Tel Miqne/Ekron, Ashkelon, Ashdod, Qasile, Dor, and now probably Gath (Tell es-Safi) (see Dothan 1982; Dothan and Dothan 1992; Ehrlich 1996).

4. Computers

Computers have obviously revolutionized the field of archaeology. Research, the processing of raw data, publications, and many other tasks are all changed because of the computer. Most of the change is certainly welcomed. However, the experts and onlookers seek a consistent way in which archeological data are made available via the computer. Many excavations now have their own Web site and can easily be accessed via internet search engines. However, internet sites, just as other sources of information (e.g., newspapers, T.V., libraries), should be used critically. The most reliable web sites for archaeology are probably those created and maintained by the sponsoring academic institutions.

F. Prospects for Dialogue

Archaeology as practiced in Israel is no longer the "hand-maiden" of the Bible. This is no way undermines the valid contributions that the discipline can make to biblical studies. Archaeological "facts" are interpretations of material remains, and interpretations differ. But the search for "proof" that the Bible is "true" or "false" is moribund.

Furthermore, the complexity of both biblical texts and archaeological realia has forced the recognition that experts in both fields need the input and insights of one another. Thus, for many years there has been a call for a dialogue between exegetes and excavators. Literary critics, for the most part, do not seem interested in the kind of questions archaeologists can answer, especially historical ones. At the same time, specialists in archaeological research have broadened out far beyond the limited confines of a "biblical archaeology." Nevertheless, there is room for optimism. It is only to be expected that more and more archaeological data will be discovered that date to the biblical period (taking this phrase to include both OT and NT eras). Literary scholars should have a special interest in knowing how these discoveries help them understand and interpret the world out of which their texts come. Sometimes archaeology can serve as a very helpful corrective to the biases of the biblical authors (as well as contemporary biblical scholars). A very clear example is what archaeologists have discovered relevant to the "religion" of Israel, which can be compared and contrasted with the "biblical" presentation of it, especially in the books of Deuteronomy, Joshua, and Judges (*see* above). On the other hand, archaeologists who have a very valid interest in the Bible need to take seriously what their literary counterparts can teach them about the history, composition, and interpretation of these texts. When both voices (the exegete and the excavator) are understood and treated fairly, perhaps then the Bible can be heard in its most authentic ancient, as well as modern, voice.

Bibliography: For further research about the life and land of the Bible, highly recommended are two multivolume works on archaeology: *The New Encyclopedia of Archaeological Excavations in the Holy Land*, E. Stern, ed., (4 vols., a 5th vol. forthcoming), 1993. (This publication replaces the earlier *Encyclopedia of Archaeological Excavations in the Holy Land*, 1977). Most entries are usually written by the site's excavator(s). The work is restricted to archaeological work conducted in Israel (as well as a few sites now in the modern state of Jordan).

The second publication is *The Oxford Encyclopedia of Archaeology in the Near East*, Eric M. Meyers, editor-in-chief (5 vols.), 1997. The strength of the OEANE is its broader perspective that includes essays on important archaeological work originating in Iran, Iraq, Syria, Jordan Egypt, and the Mediterranean world (see in particular the articles under the general heading: History of the Field. Also there are very helpful discussions on archaeological theory and method in OEANE. Another informative feature of this encyclopedia is the inclusion of numerous biographies of archaeologists and other scholars who made significant contributions to the world of Near Eastern archaeology.

Andrea M. Banning. "The Neolithic period: Triumphs of Architecture, Agriculture, and Art." *NEA* 61 (1998) 188–237; O. Bar-Yosef and F. Valla, eds. *The Natufian Culture in the Levant* (1991); Amnon Ben-Tor, ed. *The Archaeology of Ancient Israel* (1992); Andrea M. Berlin. "Between Large Forces: Palestine in the Hellenistic Period." *BA* 60 (1997) 2-51; Avraham Biran and Joseph Aviran, eds. *Biblical Archaeology Today, 1990. Proceedings of the Second International Congress on Biblical Archaeology Jerusalem, June-July 1990* (1993); Elizabeth Block-Smith and Beth Alpert Nakhai. "A Landscape Comes to Life: The Iron Age I." *NEA* 62 (1999) 62–92; 101–127; Adrian J. Boas. "The Frankish Period: A Unique Medieval Society Emerges," *NEA* 61 (1998) 138–173; Mark A. Chancy and Adam Porter. "The Archaeology of Roman Palestine." *NEA* 64 (2001) 164–203; Douglas R. Clark and Victor H. Matthews, eds. *One Hundred Years of American Archaeology in the Middle East Proceedings of the American Schools of Oriental Research Centennial Celebration,* *Washington, DC, April 2000* (2003); Michael D. Coogan, J. Cheryl Exum, and Lawrence E. Stager, eds. *Scripture and Other Artifacts: Essays on the Bible and Archaeology in Honor of Philip J. King* (1994); John Dominic Crossan and Jonathan L. Reed. *Excavating Jesus: Beneath the Stones, Behind the Texts* (2001); John Dominic Crossan and Jonathan L. Reed. *In Search of Paul: How Jesus's Apostle Opposed Rome's Empire with God' Kingdom. A New Vision of Paul's Words and World* (2004); Thomas W. Davis. *Shifting Sands: The Rise and Fall of Biblical Archaeology* (2004); William G. Dever. "The Middle Bronze Age: The Zenith of the Urban Canaanite Era." *BA* 50(1987) 149–177; William G. Dever. *Recent Archaeological Discoveries and Biblical Research* (1990); William G. Dever. *What Did the Biblical Writers Known & When Did They Know It? What Archaeology Can Tell Us About the Reality of Ancient Israel* (2001); William G. Dever. *Who Were the Early Israelites and Where Did They Come From?* (2003); William G. Dever, *Did God Have a Wife? Archaeology and Folk Religion in ancient Israel* (2005); Trude Dothan. *The Philistines and Their Material Culture* (1982); Trude Dothan and Moshe Dothan. *People of the Sea: The Search for the Philistines* (1992); Peter L. Drewett. *Field Archaeology An Introduction* (1999); Joel F. Drinkard, Gerald L. Mattingly, and J. Maxwell Miller, eds. *Benchmarks in Time and Culture Essays in Honor of Joseph A. Callaway* (1988); Carl S. Ehrlich. *The Philistines in Transition: a History from ca. 1000–730 BCE* (1996); Israel Finkelstein. *The Archaeology of the Israelite Settlement* (1988); Israel Finkelstein and Nadav Na'aman, eds. *From Nomadism to Monarchy: Archaeology and Historical Aspects of Early Israel* (1994); Israel Finkelstein and Neil Asher Silberman. *The Bible Unearthed: Archaeology's New Vision of Ancient Israel and the Origin of its Sacred Texts* (2001); Larry G. Herr. "The Iron Age II Period: Emerging Nations." *BA* 60 (1997) 114-183; James K. Hoffmeier and Allan Millard, eds. *The Future of Biblical Archaeology; Reassessing Methodology and Assumptions* (2004); Philip J. King and Lawrence E. Stager. *Life in Biblical Israel* (2001); Øystein S. LaBianca. *Hesban 1. Sedentarization and Nomadization: Food System Cycles at Hesban and Vicinity in Transjordan* (1990); John C. H. Laughlin. *Archaeology and the Bible* (2000); Elizabeth LaRocca-Pitts. *Of Wood and Stone: The Significance of Israelite Cultic Items in the Bible and Its Early Interpreters* (2001); Niels Peter Lemche. *The Israelites in History and Tradition* (1998); Albert J. Leonard. "The Late Bronze Age." *BA* 52 (1989) 4–39; Thomas E. Levy. "Archaeology Sources for the Study of Palestine: The Chalcolithic Period." *BA* 49 (1986) 82-108; Thomas E. Levy, ed. *The Archaeology of Society in the Holy Land* (1995); Amihai Mazar. *Archaeology of the Land of the Bible 10,000–586 B.C.E.* (1990); Amihai Mazar, ed. *Studies in the Archaeology of the Iron Age in Israel and Judah* (2001); Patrick D. Miller.

The Religion of Ancient Israel (1989); Steven Mithen. *After the Ice A Global History 20,00-5000 BC* (2004); P. R. S. Moorey. *A Century of Biblical Archaeology* (1991); Thomas S. Parker. "The Byzantine Period: An Empire's New Holy Land." *NEA* 62 (1999) 134–180; Mehmet Özdogan and Nezih Basgelen, eds. *Neolithic Turkey: The Cradle of Civilization* (1999); Susan Pollock and Reinhard Bernbeck, eds. *Archaeologies of the Middle East Critical Perspectives* (2005); Jonathan L. Reed. *Archaeology and the Galilean Jesus: A Re-examination of the Evidence* (2000); Colin Renfrew and Paul Bahn. *Archaeology Theories Methods and Practices.* 4th ed. (2004); Colin Renfrew and Paul Bahn, eds. *Archaeology The Key Concepts* (2005); Suzanne Richard. "The Early Bronze Age: The Rise and Collapse of Urbanism." *BA* 50 (1987) 22–43; Joe D. Seger, ed. *Retrieving the Past Essays on Archaeological Research and Methodology In Honor of Gus W. Van Beek* (1996); John J. Shea. "The Middles Paleolithic: Early Modern Humans and Neanderthals in the Levant." *NEA* 64 (2001) 38–64; Neil Asher Silberman, Neil Asher. *Digging for God & Country: Exploration, Archaeology, and the Secret Struggle for the Holy Land, 1799–1917* (1982); Neil Asher Silberman and Daniel B. Small, eds. *The Archaeology of Israel: Constructing the Past Interpreting the Present* (1997); Ephraim Stern. *Archaeology of the Land of the Bible. Volume II. The Assyrian, Babylonian, and Persian Periods 732–332 BCE* (2001); Thomas L. Thompson. *The Mythic Past* (1999); Bruce G. Trigger. *A History of Archaeological Thought* (1989); Bethany J. Walker. "Militarization to Nomadization: The Middle and Late Islamic Periods." *NEA* 62 (1999) 202–232.

JOHN C. H. LAUGHLIN

ARCHANGEL ahrk´ayn-juhl [ἀρχάγγελος archangelos]. Meaning chief angel, *archangel* occurs only twice in the Bible, though the idea is more widespread, and the archangels Michael and Gabriel are named in both testaments (1 Thess 4:16; Jude 1:9).

Christ's return will be accompanied by an unnamed archangel's victory shout (1 Thess 4:16), while Jude 1:9 calls Michael an archangel (reflecting a nonextant passage in the *Testament of Moses*). Michael a has special responsibility as protector of Israel (Dan 10:13, 20; 12:1; *1 En.* 20:5), and resists the angels who stand behind Persia and Greece and oppose Israel. In Second Temple Judaism, leading angels are associated with nations (*Jub.* 15:31-32; *1 En.* 89:59; 90:22-25; LXX Deut 32:8-9 and 4QDeut XXXII, 8-9). According to the *War Scroll*, Michael and his angels assist the sect in the eschatological battle with the wicked angel Belial and his armies, both human and angelic (1QM XVII; 5-8).

One Second Temple tradition has four archangels, Michael, Gabriel, Raphael, and Sariel (*1 En.* 9:1; 10:1, 4, 9, 11; 1QM IX,14-16), or Phanuel (*1 En.* 40:9) or commonly Uriel (*L.A.E.* [Gk.] 40:2). Another has seven (*1 En.* 20; 81:5-10; 87:2-3; 90:21-24; Tob 12:15),

adding the names Uriel, Raguel, and Remiel (probably Jeremiel in *4 Ezra* 4:36) in *1 En.* 20. In *Songs of the Sabbath Sacrifice*, seven chief princes and seven deputy princes are over groups of angels involved in the heavenly worship (4Q403 1 I; Q400 3 II, 2).

Gabriel interprets a vision of the end time for Daniel (Dan 8:16; 9:21), announces the births of John the Baptist (Luke 1:11-20) and Jesus (Luke 1:26-38), and stands "in the presence of God" (Luke 1:19). *Angels of the Presence* mentioned elsewhere in Jewish literature should be identified with archangels (1-QH VI, 12-13; 1QSb IV, 25-26; *Jub.* 1:27, 29; 2:1, 18; 15:27; 31:14; *T.-Levi* 3:5-8; *T. Jud.* 25:2; Tob 12:15), along with the Prince of Light (1QS III, 20; CD V, 17-19), the Angel of Truth (1QS III, 24), and possibly the angel Melchizedech (11QMelch). *See* ANGEL; ANGELIC HOST; GABRIEL; MICHAEL; WATCHER.

Bibliography: Matthew Black. *The Book of Enoch or 1 Enoch* (1985); Maxwell J. Davidson. *Angels at Qumran: A Comparative Study of 1 Enoch 1–36, 72–108 and Sectarian Writings from Qumran* (1992).

MAXWELL JOHN DAVIDSON

ARCHELAUS ahr´kuh-lay´uhs [Ἀρχέλαος Archelaos]. Herod Archelaus was the son of Malthake and Herod the Great. Along with younger brother Herod Antipas and half-brother Herod Phillip, he was educated in Hellenism among Roman elites in the capital of the empire. In 4 BCE his father divided up his kingdom and named Archelaus βασιλεύς basileus ("king." *J.W.* 1.665-69; *Ant.* 17.189-921) over Judea, Samaria, and Idumea (*Ant.* 17.317-20). This comprised about half of his father's kingdom that included the cities of Jerusalem, Caesarea, Sebaste, and Joppa. His brother Herod Antipas was made τετραάρχης tetraarchēs ("ruler of a fourth," but in the Roman Empire, ruler of any partial kingdom) over Galilee and Perea, while his half-brother Philip became tetraarchēs over the region east and north of the Sea of Galilee (Trachonitis, Batanea, Galonitis, Peneas, Auranitis, and the domain of Zenodorus). Archelaus' receiving a larger portion of Herod's kingdom than his brothers reflects the inheritance of the oldest son (Deut 21:17). Caesar Augustus reduced his title to ἐθνάρχης ethnarchēs ("ruler of a people," *Ant.* 17.317-20). Although a good administrator, the elites of his ethnarchy found him interpersonally incompetent: high-handed, autocratic, and insensitive to their social standards, notably in his appointments to the high priesthood of Jerusalem. A group of Judean and Samaritan elites successfully petitioned the emperor in Rome to have him removed. As a result Judea lost its last "king," since the ethnarchy of Archaelaus was made into a Roman province governed henceforth by a Roman procurator. Herod Archelaus himself was exiled to Vienne in southern Gaul (6 CE). *See* ETHNARCH; HEROD (FAMILY); TETRARCH.

Bibliography: K. C. Hanson. "The Herodians and Mediterranean Kinship." *BTB* 19 (1989) 75–84; 142–51. E. Mary Smallwood. *The Jews under Roman Rule: From Pompey to Diocletian.* 2nd ed. (1981).

BRUCE J. MALINA

ARCHER [מוֹרֶה moreh, בַּעַל חִצִּים baʿal khitsim, רַב rav, תֹּפֵשׂ קֶשֶׁת tofes qesheth, דֹּרֵךְ קֶשֶׁת dorekh qesheth, רֹבֵה קַשָּׁת roveh qashath; τοξότης toxotēs, κύριος τοξεύματου kyrios toxeumatou, ὁ τείνων τόξον ho teinōn toxon]. A soldier armed with bow and arrows, generally found in military contexts.

In the OT, archers appear as members of Israelite and non-Israelite groups, and were identified by the generic "archer" (moreh and baʿal khitsim; e.g., Gen 49:23; Job 16:13), or as "[one] grasping the bow," (tofes qesheth, Amos 2:15), "[those] treading (i.e., stringing) the bow" (dorekhe qasheth, e.g., Jer 46:9; 50:14; 51:3; 1 Chr 8:40), and possibly as "[one] shooting the bow" (roveh qashath, Gen 21:20). Some Israelite or Judean soldiers have bows (1 Sam 2:4). Philistine archers pressed Saul during the battle of Gilboa (1 Sam 31:3; 1 Chr 10:3), and an Aramean soldier killed the king of Israel with a bow (1 Kgs 22:34). The archers of the Egyptian ARMY were responsible for Josiah's death (2 Chr 35:23). Several individuals practice archery outside of an organized military context. Jonathan warns David by purporting to practice shooting arrows (1 Sam 20; also 2 Sam 1:22). Jehu kills Jehoram with bow and arrow (2 Kgs 9:24).

Iconographic evidence from the ancient Near East suggests that archers were variable in their position on the battlefield. They were stationed atop city walls under siege, or integrated with the infantry (e.g., 2 Sam 11:24; *ANEP*, figs. 362, 365, 368, 372, 373). The Assyrians trained soldiers to use the bow while on horseback; however, more commonly archers were stationed in chariots (e.g., 2 Kgs 9:24), a tactic attested in Egyptian and Assyrian art (*ANEP*, figs. 184, 190, 314, 315, 316). *See* BOW AND ARROW; WAR, METHODS, TACTICS, WEAPONS OF (BRONZE AGE THROUGH PERSIAN PERIOD); WAR, METHODS, TACTICS, WEAPONS OF (HELLENISTIC THROUGH ROMAN PERIODS).

JEREMY M. HUTTON

ARCHETYPE. An original or pattern that has been copied. The term derives from Platonic philosophy, where it refers to the ultimate realities that exist in the realm of perfect forms, of which all things in the physical world are imitations. Literary critics and folklorists use the term to refer to themes or motifs that recur in a variety of texts, generally carrying with them a stock set of ideas. The biblical authors appeal to archetypal images and stories that would remind the audience of a wide range of cultural values. Abraham, for example, often serves as an archetype to recall themes of faithfulness and covenant. Many stories in the Gospels associate Jesus with OT themes and storylines. An example appears in Acts 7, where Luke revisits Israelite history to justify the geographical and ethnic expansion of the church. *See* TYPOLOGY.

TOM THATCHER

ARCHEVITES ahr'kuh-vit [אַרְכְּוָי ʾarkeway, אַרְכְּוָיֵא ʾarkewaye]. The NRSV simply lists them as "inhabitants of [the Mesopotamian city of] ERECH" (Sumerian Uruk) among peoples resettled in and around SAMARIA by OSNAPPAR (probably the Assyrian king ASHURBANIPAL) who are signatories to REHUM's and SHIMSHAI's letter to the Persian king ARTAXERXES (Ezra 4:9).

ARCHIPPUS ahr-kip'uhs [Ἄρχιππος Archippos]. A Christian from Colossae greeted as an addressee in Phlm 2 and in the concluding greetings of Col 4:17. Since the letter to Philemon deals with a personal matter (Paul's intervention on behalf of Philemon's slave, Onesimus) and is to be read to the community assembled in Philemon's house, Archippus and Aphia appear to be related to Philemon or members of his household. However, the epithet, "our fellow-soldier" [συστρατιώτης sustratiōtēs, Phlm 2], indicates a role in the missionary efforts of Paul and Timothy. Paul uses the same word for Epaphroditus who had brought him assistance from the Philippian community (Phil 2:25). The reference in Col 4:17 suggests that Archippus had some independent responsibility for the spread of Christianity in the region. He is reminded to take care to complete the service [διακονία diakonia] that he had received in the Lord. It is impossible to determine from the context what that ministry was and whether the phrase is to be taken as encouragement, reminder, or reprimand. Since Paul, himself, had not been active in Colossae, Archippus may have been enlisted in local efforts of evangelization by Philemon or Epaphras (Phlm 23; Col 4:12).

PHEME PERKINS

ARCHISYNAGOGOS. *See* RULER OF SYNAGOGUE.

ARCHITE ahr'kit [אַרְכִּי ʾarki]. 1. Appellation for HUSHAI, a friend of King DAVID (2 Sam 15:32; 16:16; 17:5, 14; 1 Chr 27:33).

2. Name of a clan living in an area southwest of BETHEL and near ATAROTH, whose presence marked the southern boundary of the Joseph tribes (Josh 16:2).

EMILY CHENEY

ARCHITECTURE, NT. The NT does not describe any architecture in great detail. The most frequent and extended descriptions are of Herod's temple and of other public areas in Jerusalem. This does not mean, fortunately, that we are ignorant of architecture in NT times, only that the NT itself is not a very helpful resource for us. There are, however, many helpful resources. The writings of ancient historians such as Josephus and the discoveries of modern archaeology have done much to help us visualize the architecture of Roman Palestine. Recently, scholarship has devoted increasing energy to reconstructing the daily lives and relationships of ancient peoples and has extended our vision to domestic structures as well as to monumental ones (*see* JOSEPHUS, FLAVIUS). For this kind of investigation archaeology alone provides the most important data.

    A. Domestic Architecture
    B. Monumental Architecture
    Bibliography

A. Domestic Architecture

    Y. Hirschfeld has devised a simple nomenclature to describe domestic structures in Palestine, distinguishing three basic types: 1) the "simple house," 2) the "complex house," and 3) the "courtyard HOUSE." The most common domestic structure from the time of the NT was the "simple house," consisting of a single room often with another room on a second story. Simple houses ranged in size from 20 m^2 to as much as 200 m^2, with a courtyard lying either in front of or behind the structure. Materials for these houses were local, ranging from basalt stone in Capernaum to plastered mud brick in Aila (Aqaba). Most often the floor was of beaten earth, but in simple houses discovered under the CAPERNAUM synagogue the flooring was basalt. The houses were arranged in warrens of alleyways within the *insulae* of the town. Excavations have shown that the first-floor rooms sometimes served as a place of business, likely for those living on the next level (*see* SYNAGOGUE).

    Although some simple houses are quite basic, others are not. Two houses at Meiron, consisting of at least two domestic structures, were dubbed by excavators the "Patrician House" and the "Lintel House," respectively. These two buildings shared a common roof and the area of both structures together was 260 m^2. The noise and activity of the workshops and domiciles together must have suggested a busy and prosperous place to a visitor. Jewish ritual baths (מִקְוָאוֹת miqwa'oth) were sometimes present in large houses of the simple type, and public baths were usually accessible in the area to accommodate residents' ordinary personal needs (*see* MIQVAH, MIQVA'OTH). Additions to simple houses were perpendicular to the original structure.

    The "complex house" featured wings that extended to enclose an outside courtyard. Within such complex structures, a relatively large number of people could live and work within a relatively small surface "footprint." Complex houses may be simple houses expanded incrementally as the number of residents increased, or they may have been built as complex houses.

David W. J. Gill
Figure 1: Miqvah at Jericho

    The third type of house, the "courtyard house," came in two varieties: a traditional Palestinian type in which the enclosed courtyard has no columns, and the "peristyle house" that encloses its courtyard in classical Greco-Roman fashion with columns. Good archaeological examples of the traditional type would include both the Palatial Mansion and the Burnt House from the Jewish Quarter in Jerusalem. As its nickname suggests, the Palatial Mansion was beautifully appointed with mosaic floors, pools, and miqwa'oth, all cascading from the upper city into the Tyropoeon Valley below and covering some 600 m^2 in all. The Burnt House, so named because it was discovered beneath a thick destruction layer, was not as magnificent as the Palatial Mansion yet may have served the needs of a priestly family. The workshops in the cellar suggested the presence of some kind of industry at the site.

    The second variety of courtyard house, the peristyle house, is also a marker of wealth and prestige. Built in a classical style, such structures are invariably large, well decorated, and comfortable. To this variety belong, e.g., the Dionysius House at Sepphoris, the Colonnaded House in Jerusalem, and the Late Roman mansion at Aphek. Some of these great buildings may have functioned as meeting houses and/or hostels. There is probably no archaeological evidence that could decide the matter for us.

B. Monumental Architecture

    Beyond the walls of their own houses, however, people in NT Palestine enjoyed a vast display of grand and innovative public architecture, largely inspired and created by HEROD THE GREAT (r. 37–4 BCE). Herod not only succeeded in creating architecture in the Roman style all over Palestine but in some cases permanently changed the topography of the landscape to do so. One sees significant remains of his work at CAESAREA MARITIMA, JERUSALEM, SAMARIA, and the Wilderness of Judea. Although later rulers left important architectural marks on Palestine, it was Herod who recreated the land in his own image and in the image of his Roman patrons.

    Herod's building enterprises can be found in such far removed places as LAODICEA on the Sea, Syrian

ANTIOCH, and the islands of COS, DELOS, and LESBOS. His first such undertaking occurred on the island of RHODES where he had stopped on his way from Egypt to Rome in 40 BCE, before he was king. According to Josephus (*Ant.* 14.378), Herod paid for the reconstruction of the city of Rhodes and its industry out of his own pocket despite his meager resources. He also rebuilt the temple of APOLLO there, though this construction may have occurred later in his career (*J.W.* 1.424; *Ant.* 16.147). Even though Octavian founded the city of NICOPOLIS to celebrate his victory over Antony and Cleopatra at nearby Actium, it was Herod, who had been allied with Antony at the time of the battle, who, according to Josephus, built "most of the public structures" (*Ant.* 16.147).

Herod left his mark all over the eastern Mediterranean but nowhere more powerfully than in Palestine. The capstone of his efforts was his own seaside capital city, CAESAREA. After a brief period of construction (19–10/9 BCE), Herod celebrated the completion of his masterpiece with games, theater, prize fights, and musical competitions (*Ant.* 16.136). The great harbor consisted of a breakwater that opened only to the north founded upon massive cement blocks that had been floated out to their appointed places and then sunk. Josephus describes the entire inner harbor as having moorings for ships and places where sailors could sleep. The great circular enclosure was guarded by several towers, the greatest of which was named Drusus after a son-in-law of Caesar (*Ant.* 15.336-37). In the great theater near Herod's promontory palace, where Herod's grandson died many years later (*Ant.* 19.343-52; Acts 12:19-23), actors and musicians entertained cultured visitors while at the amphitheater north of the palace horse races, mock naval battles, and combat with beasts assuaged the appetites of others. Founded on an artificial hill above the harbor was a grand Corinthian colonnaded temple to Roma and Augustus (*see* TEMPLES, HEROD'S). A largely decorative city wall encircled the new capital.

Figure 2: Theater at Caesarea

Although Caesarea was Herod's crowning architectural achievement, the Herodian reconstruction of Jerusalem and its Temple to the Jewish God was no mean achievement. Once more, Herod showed no reluctance about shaping the topography of the place to suit his scheme. Whether it was paving over the 50 m escarpment beneath his Antonia fortress to creating massive retaining walls and filling them with soil to lift and flatten the Temple platform, Herod did not cower before the huge physical obstacles to his plans. Along the western city wall, Herod created his own residence, one that Josephus found difficult to describe because of its grandeur (*J.W.* 5.176). The structure's walls rose thirty cubits all around. Inside there were rooms for guests, lavishly arrayed with excellent furniture and vessels of silver and gold. Porticos shaded guests from the Middle Eastern sun while canals, gardens, and dove courts all conspired to soothe king and visitor alike (*J.W.* 5.176–82).

Herod's properties around JERICHO were also quite lavish. "NT Jericho" lies to the south of modern Jericho. Where the Wadi Qelt empties into the Jordan Valley, the HASMONEAN princes had had a palace that Herod later refurbished and expanded in his own style. A much larger peristyle structure than this stood to the south of the Wadi Qelt that included a large bath that initially misled excavators into thinking that the building was a GYMNASIUM. Finally, near the refurbished Hasmonean palace, a new grand structure arose in a style that softened sharp edges into curves. This differed from the squared Hellenistic style Herod had retained in his early reconstruction. A central peristyle surrounded the open courtyard. A hippodrome north of the palace and possibly a theater make it clear that Jericho was important to Herod's political life as well as his personal life.

The architectural contributions of Herod's successors are more difficult to estimate than those of Herod himself. ARCHELAUS, during his troubled reign over Judea (4 BCE–6 CE), diverted water from Naera to Jericho by means of aqueducts as well as to a large date-palm grove he had created nearby. He also rebuilt one of Herod's palaces at Jericho (*Ant.* 17.339-40). The major architectural successes of HEROD ANTIPAS, Archelaus' brother, tetrarch of the Galilee from 4 BCE until 39 CE, were the founding of a new capital city and the rebuilding of SEPPHORIS. The new capital of TIBERIAS arose on the southwest corner of the Sea of Galilee, and Antipas named it for the new emperor Tiberius. The only clue we receive about the nature of the palace in Tiberias comes from a story Josephus relates about coming to the city of Tiberias from Jerusalem with the demand that the grand accoutrements of Antipas' palace be destroyed because he had decorated it with images of living things contrary to the law (*Life* 65). Coins of the city suggest that there may have been both a temple to Zeus in Tiberias and a Serapion, but we do not know that Herod Antipas built them. Antipas also rebuilt Sepphoris, which, perhaps contrary to Antipas' own desire (*Life* 37), was the principal city of the GALILEE until the time of the First Jewish Revolt. Herod's son Philip (r. 4 BCE–33/34 CE) is remembered for his construction of a city called Caesarea (*see* CAESAREA PHILIPPI) near the cave of Pan and the temple of Augustus. A great building excavated there as well as the vaulted *horrea*, remind one of similar structures at CAESAREA MARITIMA, but the dating of them all is problematic.

Bibliography: Y. Hirschfeld. *The Palestinian Dwelling in the Roman-Byzantine Period* (1995); Eric M. Meyers. "The Problem of Gendered Space in Syro-Palestinian Domestic Architecture." *Early Christian Families In Context: An Interdisciplinary Dialogue* (2003) 44–69; Eric M. Meyers. "Roman-Period Houses from the Galilee: Domestic Architecture and Gendered Spaces." *Canaan, Ancient Israel, And Their Neighbors from the Late Bronze Age through Roman Palaestina* (2003) 487–99; Alexandra Rentzleff. "A Nabataean and Roman Domestic Area at the Red Sea Port of Aila." *BASOR* 331 (2003) 45–65; Peter Richardson. *Herod: King of the Jews and Friend of the Roman* (1996); D. W. Roller. *The Building Program of Herod the Great* (1998).

FRED L. HORTON

ARCHITECTURE, OT. Dictionary definitions of architecture refer to the science and art of building. Architecture involves both the technical aspects of construction and the aesthetics of design. Most of the structures of the biblical world were functional or utilitarian, and thus this article will focus on the construction techniques.

This article will focus on the geographical region of OT Canaan and Israel–Judah and on the OT time period, archaeologically the Middle and Late Bronze Ages (2200–1200 BCE), and Iron Ages I and II (1200–538 BCE), with a briefer discussion of earlier periods.

The inhabitants of the biblical world used the building materials most readily available for their construction. Mud brick was the most common material used throughout the biblical period in all areas. Field stone was often used in areas where it was readily available, and for monumental structures. Later monumental structures used hewn stone, including ashlar masonry. Timber was used for posts, beams, roof supports, and between stone courses in some structures.

A. Earliest periods
  1. Neolithic
  2. Chalcolithic
  3. Early Bronze Age
B. Middle–Late Bronze Age
  1. City planning
    a. Walls
    b. Gates
    c. Roads
  2. Domestic architecture
  3. Monumental architecture
    a. Palaces
    b. Temples
C. Iron Age
  1. City planning
    a. Walls and gates
    b. Plazas
    c. Water systems
  2. Domestic architecture

  3. Monumental architecture
    a. Palaces
    b. Temples
    c. Capitals
  4. Later influences
Bibliography

A. Earliest periods
1. Neolithic

Jericho in the Pre-Pottery Neolithic period shows an architectural sophistication already in the 9th–8th millennium BCE. Community planning and cooperation were required to construct a city wall, a rock-cut ditch in front of the wall, and a circular tower. The wall that surrounded the 10-acre mound was constructed of stone; it was 2 m thick, and is preserved in places to a height of 5.75 m. The ditch was cut into bedrock and was 9.5 m wide and 2.25 m deep. The tower was built of stone and located just inside the wall. It is preserved to a height of 7.75 m and has a diameter of 8.5 m. Most remarkable is a set of internal stairs within the tower leading from an opening at the base to the top. Extraordinary skill was necessary to create such a structure ca. 7800 BCE.

The wall, originally interpreted as defensive, is more recently interpreted as a flood-control device. The tower's function remains elusive. It is suggested that it was a watchtower or had cultic significance. Regardless of purpose, the architectural sophistication at so early a period remains quite remarkable.

Houses were primarily constructed of mud brick on stone foundations. Most had only one room. The floor plan varied from rectangular to oval or circular; many were cut two or three steps below the ground surface. The presence of door sockets indicates that the entrances had doors even at this early period. The architectural elements of Pre-Pottery Neolithic are apparently indigenous.

2. Chalcolithic

In the Chalcolithic Age, 5th–4th millennium BCE, the domestic structures are often composed of an enclosure wall and a courtyard with a rectangular broad-room house near the back. Hearths and silos are found in the courtyard. Most structures were constructed of mud brick on stone foundations.

The one structure designated as a shrine was found at EN-GEDI. It had an enclosure wall with two entrances into a large courtyard. One entrance was actually a gate house—almost a two-chamber gate. The shrine was a large broad-room building opposite the gate house; it had a semicircular altar and low benches. The other structure was a broad-room, possibly a priest's house. In the courtyard was a circular installation with a drain.

3. Early Bronze Age

By the Early Bronze Age, 3300–2200 BCE, more sophistication is evident in domestic and monumental structures. The Early Bronze Age is the era of the pyramids in Egypt, and the early city-states in Mesopotamia—Sumer and Old Kingdom Akkad—with large palaces, temples, and ziggurats. In Syria, Tell Mardikh-Ebla is the best example of monumental architecture.

Within CANAAN, Early Bronze domestic architecture is dominated by broad-room structures, often with smaller rooms connected. In many of the houses benches were found along the walls of the main room. Cooking hearths are found in a courtyard or unroofed portions of the house.

True gates with defensive towers are found as part of the city walls. The walls are of stone and/or mud brick often with towers at regular intervals; the gates are usually two chambered gates. Some sites such as MEGIDDO also have a glacis protecting the base and foundation of the wall. By Early Bronze III some city walls were 8–10 m thick.

The primary monumental structures are temples, as exemplified by the three adjacent Megiddo Stratum XV Broad-room Temples, 4040, 5192, and 5269. These three temples have nearly identical floor plans: a broad room with two columns to support the roof, and a porch in front also with two columns. Each temple has adjoining rooms to one side. A large circular altar adjacent to Temple 4040 probably predates the temples. One palace has been excavated at Megiddo. It had two wings separated by a corridor, inner courtyards, and ceremonial and private dwelling spaces. Most Early Bronze architectural features are considered indigenous.

B. Middle–Late Bronze Age

The Middle Bronze Age, especially Middle Bronze II represents the height of the Canaanite period. After a period of destruction and abandonment of most cities at the end of Early Bronze and Middle Bronze Age I, Middle Bronze Age II marks a new period of urban settlement. This new urban period marks the rise of the Canaanite city-states. Many of the architectural features of Middle Bronze in Canaan show influence from northern Syria.

1. City planning

a. Walls. Massive defensive systems are one characteristic of the Middle Bronze period. Walls are often 2–4 m thick, usually constructed of mud bricks on stone foundations and with towers at regular intervals. A glacis was often added to the base of the wall.

Sloping ramparts 25–40 m thick and 10–15 m high surround the city at sites including DAN, AKKO, HAZOR, and SCHECHEM. Some of the ramparts are constructed of layers of packed earth, others have a mud brick or stone core with earth packed around the core. At Hazor a rock-cut ditch outside the rampart further enhanced the defense of the city.

b. Gates. Since any opening in the defenses would be a weak point, gates received special protection. Towers with thick walls often flanked the gateway; pier walls narrow the passageway to limit access and provide a place to anchor doors. The passageway typically was wide enough for chariots to pass through. The towers often had stairways to give access to the roof. Door sockets have been found in several of the gates.

At Tel Dan a complete Middle Bronze gate was discovered. The entryway was paved with cobblestone leading up to the gate. The six-pier gate was fully preserved. The gate also has a true arch at the entrance. A set of stairs alongside the wall led from the gate, possibly to a pedestrian entrance. The six-pier gate like the one at Dan is the most common Middle Bronze gate in Canaan. Simpler four-pier gates are also found. Similar walls and defenses are found at numerous Canaanite city-states during the Middle Bronze Age such as Ashkelon, Hazor, Shechem, and Gezer. The six-pier gate apparently originated in Syria.

c. Roads. Middle Bronze Age towns often have roads dividing them into rectangular sections along with drainage systems and sewers. The combination indicates great care in planning to locate the drains and to provide proper gradiant (*see* ROAD).

2. Domestic architecture

The typical domestic dwelling of the Middle Bronze Age is the courtyard house. The simplest form of courtyard house has a walled courtyard entered directly from the street with the rooms of the house, often with two stories, in the back. An example of these houses is found in Stratum XII, Area B-B at Megiddo. The classic form of the courtyard house is found later in Middle Bronze and in Late Bronze; it has the courtyard surrounded by rooms on all sides. From the street one entered a room, often small, perhaps like an entrance hall, and from there into the courtyard. The other rooms were entered from the courtyard. Many examples of the patrician houses and palaces are just larger examples of the courtyard house (*see* HOUSE; HOUSEHOLD, HOUSEHOLDER).

3. Monumental architecture

a. Palaces. Canaan has relatively few monumental palaces excavated to date. Most have a similar floor plan to the typical courtyard house, differing primarily in size and complexity, and in the location of the palace near the temple or citadel. One palace at Megiddo has a large courtyard surrounded with small rooms on all sides. None of the Canaanite palaces compare with the much larger ones from northern Syria, such as Mari, Ugarit, and Alalakh.

b. Temples. The most common temple design in Middle Bronze Palestine is the symmetrical temple. This design has northern Syrian antecedents (*see* TEMPLES, SEMITIC). The walls are thick (some as much as 5 m-thick). The entrance is along the central axis and the holy of holies is at the end opposite the entrance. The temples have only one or two architectural elements; the cella or main room can be either long-room or broad-room. The holy of holies may be a niche in the back wall or a raised platform. Some temples have two towers in the front, somewhat like gate towers. The so-called MIGDAL Temple at SHECHEM has 5 m-thick walls; square towers flank the entrance. The porch has a single column in the middle. The cella is a long-room divided by two rows of octagonal limestone columns. The floor is of beaten lime plaster. A stele was placed on each side of the entrance. In the courtyard in front of the temple was a brick altar. The temple has been identified with the Temple of BAAL-BERITH and the Migdal-Shechem of Judg 9.

C. Iron Age

The end of Late Bronze Age marks another period of destruction and abandonment of many cities. Although a few cities continued after destruction without any lengthy period of abandonment, most were abandoned from the end of the Late Bronze Age until Iron II. Iron Age I witnessed the establishment of hundreds of small villages, many unfortified. Most of the cities were rebuilt only in Iron II.

1. City planning

In the Iron Age one town plan appears in a number of sites. The town walls typically follow the contour of the site. Just inside the gate was a plaza. From the plaza a peripheral road circled the town, at times with a single row of houses between the road and the city wall. Other roads radiated from the plaza through the town. Some administrative buildings were usually located near the plaza. Often the palace was located on the opposite side of the town on the highest ground, at times in a separate walled acropolis. In other cities, primarily capital or administrative cities, an orthogonal road plan divided the city into rectangular sections with roads that intersected at right angles.

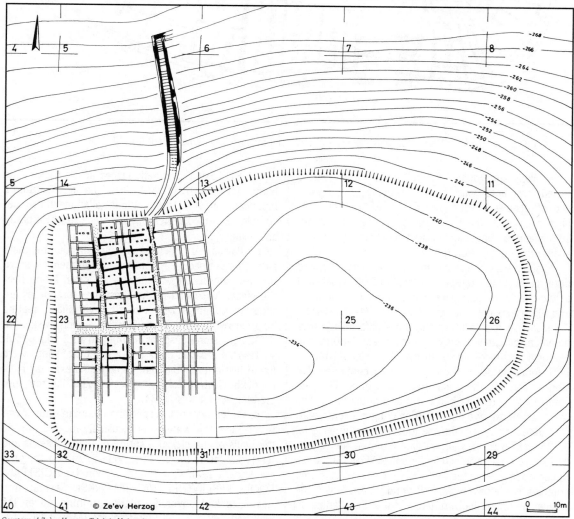

Courtesy of Ze'ev Herzog, Tel Aviv University

Figure 1: Grid City Plan of Tell es-Saʿidiyeh Str. V, Iron IIB, illustrating residential block of houses and orthogonal planning.

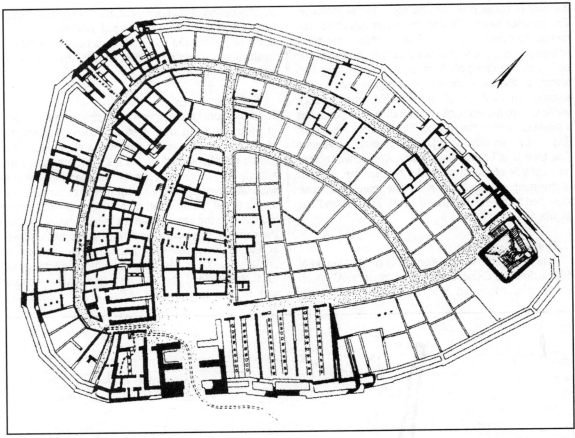

Courtesy of Ze'ev Herzog, Tel Aviv University

FIGURE 2: City Plan of Tel Beersheba with a four-chamber gate and casemate wall system. Str. II, Late 8th cent. BCE.

a. **Walls and gates.** City walls in the Iron Age are varied: casemate walls, filled casemates, solid walls, and offsets-insets walls (*see* CITY). Many city walls have a glacis at the base. The gates are also varied. Two-chamber, four-chamber, and six-chamber gates all appear throughout Iron II.

At some sites, the gate complex contained inner and outer gates. One example is Megiddo IVB, which had a two-chamber outer gate, which then gave indirect entry into a six-chamber gate (*see* CITY GATE; GATE). Tel Dan also has an inner and outer gate. In the area between the gates there was a canopied platform; the platform may have held a throne. Four sets of MASSE-BOT found close to these gates: two contained five stones each and the other two, four stones. The gate complex at Bethsaida had inner and outer gates. The outer gate had two towers protecting the entryway. An indirect entry led into the four-chamber inner gate. At 35 × 17.5 m, it is largest gate found in the region. The stone foundation and lower courses had mud brick upper courses covered with plaster. Inside the gate complex was a paved plaza. Beyond the plaza was the palace. Bethsaida had numerous cultic installations in front of the inner gate. To the right of the gate was a bamah (בָּמָה) or high place, with steps leading to the

top. A STELE was originally placed at the back of the bamah (*see* BAMAH, BAMOTH). The stele featured a bull-headed figure. Other cultic installations in the gate complex included benches, four other stelae, a basin, and a shelf.

b. **Plazas.** An open square just inside the main gate offered space for public and commercial activities. Storehouses or warehouses are often found near the plaza. At several of the sites, the storehouses are tripartite buildings with two rows of pillars creating long narrow, rooms. These may have been miskenoth (מִסְכְּנוֹת), storehouses as mentioned in 2 Chr 32:28. At Tel Dan a paved plaza and a section of shops were found just outside the gate complex. These may have been khutsoth (חוּצוֹת), street bazaars like the ones mentioned in 1 Kgs 20:34.

c. **Water systems.** A special problem in time of war is access to the water supply, usually located outside the walls of the city at a spring or well. Cisterns and reservoirs inside the city were one solution; large ones are known from Gezer and Gibeon (*see* CISTERN; POOL; RESERVOIR; WATERWORKS). Several Iron Age sites had covered galleries running under the wall and down to the water source (MEGIDDO, Tell es-Saidiyeh). Much more impressive are the systems cut down through earlier occupational levels and through bedrock to reach the water table. The systems included an entrance structure, a rock-hewn shaft with stairs, a stepped tunnel, and a water chamber or a horizontal tunnel to the water source (e.g., Megiddo, Hazor, Gezer, Gibeon). The Jerusalem water systems include at least three different systems: Warren's shaft, Siloam channel, and Hezekiah's tunnel. Warren's shaft included an entrance, a stepped tunnel and horizontal tunnel, a vertical shaft, and a tunnel connecting to the Gihon spring. The Siloam channel included both a rock-hewn channel and a rock-hewn tunnel. Hezekiah's tunnel system includes the tunnel itself connecting to the Gihon spring, the SILOAM pool, and an overflow channel.

2. Domestic architecture

The Iron Age, especially in Israel and Judah, is characterized by the four-room or pillared house. These structures typically have a broad-room across the back and two or three parallel long-rooms or areas in front. The entrance is usually in the center of the front area and enters a courtyard. The front spaces were often used for animal pens, storage, and workshops. The broad-room in the back was the private dwelling area. Since some of the parallel spaces are defined by a row of pillars, the house is also called a pillared house. Many of these houses had a second story over all or parts; the second story provided additional family space. Access to the second story was provided by stone or wooden stairs or ladders.

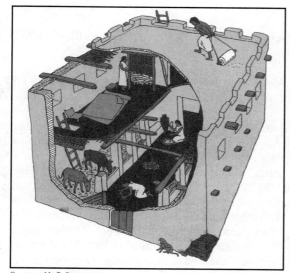

Courtesy of L. E. Stager

Figure 3: Four-room house.

3. Monumental architecture

a. Palaces. Several Iron Age II palaces have been found. The Omride palace in Samaria is the only example of a royal palace in the capital city of Israel or Judah. First constructed by OMRI, the complex was enlarged by AHAB. The palace complex is surrounded by a casemate wall on the summit of the mound. The remains have the finest ashlar masonry. Remains include official rooms, storerooms, and even a large pool along with many open courts. The discovery of the Samaria ivories within the complex indicates the elaborate decoration used in the buildings and furniture.

Other Iron II buildings termed palaces have been found at Hazor, Ramat Rahel, Megiddo, Lachish. The Lachish palace itself was built on a large podium. In addition to the podium where the palace was located, the palace complex included a large open court surrounded by storehouse buildings and other administrative buildings. The PALACE OF SOLOMON is described in 1 Kgs 7. The main room of the palace was the HALL of Pillars, 50 × 30 cubits. This room, probably with rows of pillars or columns, would seem to show Egyptian influence like the Hypostyle Hall at Karnak. The Hall of Pillars was probably a major reception hall for official functions. In front of the Hall of Pillars was a porch also with pillars. Apparently close to the Hall of Pillars was the Hall of the Throne, also called the Hall of Justice. Solomon's private dwelling is said to be in another court in the back of the hall. Also in the private area is the dwelling for Pharaoh's daughter, Solomon's wife. Thus the palace had at least two areas, a public ceremonial area and a private area. Within the palace compound there was at least one other structure, the Hall of the Forest of Lebanon with either three or four rows of pillars/columns. It was probably used for the largest ceremonial functions. Apparently the same type of fine ashlar construction was used on the palace as on other Iron Age palaces.

b. Temples. The only Iron II temple-sanctuaries found in Israel are at ARAD and at TEL DAN. The Arad sanctuary featured an open court with an altar of unhewn stone. Beyond the court one entered a broad-room cella. In back of the cella was the holy of holies. Steps led up to the holy of holies and two small carved limestone altars flanked the entrance. Inside the holy of holies were two standing stones (מַצֵּבוֹת matsevoth), one hewn and showing traces of red paint, the other unhewn.

The Tel Dan sacred area included a raised podium that was constructed of ashlar masonry in header-stretcher pattern. The temple was apparently built on this podium, but no remains exist. The excavator, Avraham Biran, argued that the podium was part of the beth bamoth (בֵּית בָּמוֹת House of High Places; *see* 1 Kgs 12:31). In the court area south of the temple was the foundation base of a large altar. A series of rooms enclosed the sacred temenos area on the west. The temple has been identified with Jeroboam's sanctuary for the gold calves mentioned in 1 Kgs 12.

An Iron Age temple at 'Ain Dara, Syria, has been discussed as having parallels to the Solomonic Temple. Although the 'Ain Dara temple can be described as tripartite, it has closer parallels to the Middle Bronze and Late Bronze symmetrical temples than it does to the Solomonic Temple. The ʿAin Dara temple is symmetrical with the entrance along the main axis. There are two primary architectural units: an antechamber and a main hall or cella. A raised platform across the back of the cella was the holy of holies. Both the antechamber and cella are broad-rooms. Two column bases were located just outside the entrance of the temple. Reliefs of lions and a sphinx decorated the exterior façade of the temple.

According to the description in 1 Kgs 6, the Solomonic Temple had a tripartite design. It was 60 × 20 × 30 cubits high. The porch (עֻלָם ʿulam) had two free-standing pillars (Jachin and Boaz); inside was the הֵכָל hekhal or holy place, a long-room in which the tables of showbread and the altar of incense were placed. The דְבִר devir or holy of holies was beyond the hekhal. It was a cube 20 cubits on a side in which the ark of the covenant was placed. Both the hekhal and devir had wood paneling and were gold covered. The temple was constructed of the finest ashlar masonry.

c. Capitals. Volute capitals (also called Proto-Aeolic and Proto-Ionic capitals) are one of the main decorative features that have been found in their archaeological context from Iron Age monumental construction. Over forty of these capitals have been excavated in Israel and Jordan. At least one of these capitals was found apparently where it had fallen from its original position atop a pier wall of the gate at Mudaybiʿ, Jordan. It was found facedown in the gateway directly in front of a pier wall, and exactly aligned with the pier. Five capitals or fragments have been found at that site. Other volute capitals have been found at Megiddo, Samaria, Hazor, Dan, Jerusalem, and Ramat Rahel in Israel and Amman, Jordan. These capitals would have sat on top of pillars, columns, or pier walls in gateways.

4. Later influences

Following the rise of the Neo-Assyrian Empire resulting in Assyrian domination of Israel and Judah, Assyrian influence of the architecture is also seen. The Assyrian buildings regularly have a central audience hall surrounded by rooms on all sides. Assyrian-style mud bricks are used in the construction. Shallow niches are found in many rooms; the floors are made of thick plaster. Many structures include a drainage system using terra-cotta pipes. Likewise, Persian influence is found in some structures following the rise of the Persian Empire after 539 BCE.

Bibliography: F. Braemer. *L'architecture domestique du Levant à l'âge du Fer* (1982); Th. Busink. *Der Tempel von Jerusalem* (1970); C. H. J. de Geus. *Towns in Ancient Israel and in the Southern Levant* (2003); Volkmar Fritz. "Paläste während der Bronze-und Eisenheit in Palästina." *ZDPV* 99 (1983) 1–42; Larry Herr. "Tripartite Pillared Buildings and the Market Place in Iron Age Palestine." *BASOR* 272 (1988) 47–67; Zeʾev Herzog. "Israelite City Planning Seen in the Light of Beer-Sheba and Arad Excavations." *Expedition* 20 (1978) 38–43; Zeʾev Herzog. *Das Stadttor in Israel und in den Nachbarlandern* (1986); Zeʾev Herzog. *Archaeology of the City* (1997); Aharon Kempinski and Ronny Reich. *The Architecture of Ancient Israel* (1992); R. Naumann. *Architektur Kleinasiens von ihren Anfängen bis zum Ende der hethitischen Zeit* (1971); Yigal Shiloh. "The Four Room House, Its Situation and Function in the Israelite City" *IEJ* 20 (1970) 180–190. Yigal Shiloh. "Elements in the Development of Town Planning in the Israelite City" *IEJ* 28 (1978) 36–51; Yigal Shiloh. *The Proto-Aeolic Capital and Israelite Ashlar Masonry* (1979); Yigal Shiloh. "The Casemate Wall, the Four Room House, and Early Planning in the Israelite City." *BASOR* 268 (1987) 3–15; G. R. H. Wright. *Ancient Building in South Syria and Palestine* (1997).

JOEL F. DRINKARD, JR.

ARCHIVES, HOUSE OF THE [Aram. בֵּית סִפְרַיָּא beth sifrayyaʾ]. A section of the royal treasury (Ezra 5:17) where official documents were stored, perhaps as early as the Late Uruk period (late 4th millennium BCE), although EBLA TEXTS provide the earliest archives found *in situ* (Early Bronze Age III, ca. 2400–2300 BCE). The number of archives in the Near East increased significantly in the 8th cent., reaching a zenith in the 7th cent. BCE. Searching the archives is a main theme of the book of Ezra, where the "house of the archives" is referenced both explicitly (6:1) and by allusion (2:62; 4:15; 19; 5:17).

RALPH K. HAWKINS

ARCHIVES OF MURASHU. *See* MURASHU, ARCHIVES OF.

ARCHONS, HYPOSTASIS OF. *See* HYPOSTASIS OF THE ARCHONS.

ARCTURUS ahrk-toorʾuhs [עָשׁ ʿash, עַיִשׁ ʿayish; Ἀρκτοῦρος Arktouros]. The first constellation of stars mentioned in Job 9:9 (ʿash; probably ʿayish = constellation, perhaps Great Bear) is thought by some, including the translators of the LXX, to refer to Arcturus (Alpha Bootis), the brightest star in the Northern Hemisphere and the fourth brightest star in the sky. The Greek name, Arcturus, means *Bear Watcher*, which references its apparent pursuit of Ursa Major around the pole. Others have suggested the references in Job refer to Ursa Major itself, nicknamed the Great Bear by several ancient societies including Babylon and Greece, each of which saw in the constellation the image of a she-bear, a portion of which is known to us as the Big Dipper. It is difficult to determine with any certainty which constellations of stars are being referred to in Job 9:9 and 38:31-32. *See* ASTROLOGY, ASTRONOMY.

LEANN SNOW FLESHER

ARD ahrd [אַרְדְּ ʾard, אַדָּר ʾadar; Αραδ Arad, Αδαρ Adar]. In Gen 46:21 Ard is listed as one of Benjamin's ten sons. Yet, in Num 26:40 and 1 Chr 8:3 he is listed as a grandson of Benjamin. The discrepancy calls into question the generational precision of the expression sons of in addition to raising the possibility that the phrase may simply represent clan affiliation. Some Greek and Hebrew texts represent Ard as something like Adar or ADDAR, the variants easily explained as a transposition of the Hebrew consonants resh (ר) and dalet (ד).

STEVEN D. MASON

ARDAT ahr´dat. Field where Ezra received a fourth vision about a mourning woman (2 Esd 9:26). May be derived from אֶרֶץ חָדָשׁ ʾrts khdsh, new land See ARAD.

ARDON ahr´don [אַרְדּוֹן ʾardon]. Caleb's son in the list of Judah's descendants (1 Chr 2:18).

AREINI, TELL EL. Named after an Arab sheikh buried on the tell, this important site is located in the southeastern coastal plain known as biblical Philistia. The remains were initially identified as Gath (Josh 19:13), one of the five cities of the Philistines. Recent archaeological activity has brought that identification into question. El-Areini's ancient name is still unknown. The site is located about 19 km from the coastal location of ASHKELON, also part of the Philistine realm. During the Early Bronze I period (ca. 3200–3100 BCE) the tell became the largest city in the southern plain. Occupation evidence from the 12th–6th cent. BCE portrays an important city in Philistia during the formation and existence of the Israelite monarchy. Intermittent occupation and burials continued through the Persian, Hellenistic, and Byzantine periods. The discovery of numerous figurines of the goddess ASTARTE reveals the Iron Age religious mindset of the inhabitants.

MICHAEL G. VANZANT

ARELI, ARELITES uh-ree´li [אַרְאֵלִי ʾareʾli]. Son of Gad, Jacob and Zilpah's son, who settled in Egypt (Gen 46:16). The progenitor of the Arelites (Num 26:17). See ARIEL.

AREOPAGITE air´ee-op´uh-git [Ἀρεοπαγίτης Areopagitēs]. A member of the Council of the Areopagus [lit. "the hill of Ares" or "Mars' Hill," from the Greek areios (Ἄρειος) and pagos (πάγος)], the main governing body of Athens. Acts 17 recounts Paul's conversion of DIONYSIUS the Areopagite (Acts 17:34), whose surname implies his membership on the council.

AREOPAGUS air´ee-op´uh-guhs [ὁ Ἄρειος πάγος ho Areios pagos] (Acts 17:19, 22). "The hill of Ares" (or "Mars' Hill"), a rocky height of 377 ft. in Athens located NW of the Acropolis and south of the Agora (see map under ATHENS), and the council that met there in ancient times.

A. Name and Origins

The Areopagus was named after Ares who, according to Pausanias (Descr. 1.28.5), was the first to be tried there for murder. According to one theory, the hill derived its name from the Arai (Ἀραί) or "Curses" associated with the Furies whose shrine was in a cave at the NE foot of the summit. As for the origins of the council, a mythological account has Athena convening the court to try Orestes for murder (Aeschylus, Eum. 11.397-753). In reality, it emerged from the aristocracy and was probably first simply called βουλή/boulē ("council"), but later (likely under Solon) renamed in connection with the hill to distinguish it from a new second council. Its official designation became "The Council of the Areopagus," though the simple term Areopagus was used of either the hill or the council.

B. History and Power

The council of the Areopagus probably functioned initially as an advisory board to the king. From time immemorial it possessed judicial authority in cases of homicide, but with the decline of the Athenian monarchy its jurisdiction expanded into every facet of corporate life. However, the development of democracy in Athens curtailed its influence considerably. Solon conducted a legislative reform in 594 BC, and established the Council of the 400, which assumed many of the functions of the Areopagus. Notoriously, Ephialtes stripped the Areopagus of its state judicial powers in 462/1 BCE, but left intact its inviolable authority in trials for homicide, wounding, and arson. Over the succeeding three centuries it gradually regained various state and judicial functions, including the authority to adjudicate in matters pertaining to military desertion, morals, and weights and measures. Under Roman rule the Areopagus reclaimed many of its former prerogatives as supreme court and governing authority in Athens. It intervened in a wide range of affairs including education, morality, philosophical lectures, and religious cults. In NT times Roman emperors formally recognized it as the highest ranking authority in Athens.

C. Paul before the Areopagus

Acts 17:16-34 recounts Paul's time in Athens during his second missionary venture. Two interpretive issues have been obtained regarding this setting:

1. The location of Paul's Areopagus appearance

Traditionally, Paul's Areopagus speech was believed to have been delivered on the very hill, before the time-honored council. However, modern consensus is that the council had not met on the hill since the 4th cent. BCE, but at the Royal Stoa in the Agora. The archaeological discovery of the Royal Stoa in the late 1960s has added credibility to this claim, if only circumstantially. The documentary evidence for this venue is a single reference in Demosthenes (*1 Aristog.* 25.23), but this merely attests that there were occasions when the council met in closed session at the Royal Stoa. Although Acts 17 does not establish the location of the Areopagus council (notwithstanding KJV's infelicitous "in the midst of Mars' hill," 17:22), it does portray Paul as standing before it. First, the use of the preposition *epi* in 17:19 indicates that Paul was brought not "*unto* Areopagus" (KJV) but "*in front of* the Areopagus" (NRSV), in keeping with Lukan usage elsewhere (compare 16:19; 17:6). Second, "in the midst of the Areopagus" (17:22) represents Paul's presence before the council, not a topographical location. Finally, the mention of "Dionysius the Areopagite" in 17:34 supports the contention that Paul had been given a hearing before the council.

2. The nature of the proceedings

The traditional view is that Paul stood trial before the Areopagus. Many modern scholars have found it difficult to maintain this view, given the courteous request in 17:19-20, the lack of formal charges, and the character of the summary following Paul's speech (17:32-34). However, Winter has clarified that Paul was summonsed, not to a criminal trial, but to a preliminary hearing in which his perceived status as a herald of foreign deities would be duly assessed by the Areopagus.

Bibliography: T. D. Barnes. "An Apostle on Trial." *JTS* 20 (1969) 407–19; C. J. Hemer, "Paul at Athens: A Topographical Note." *NTS* 20 (1973–74) 341–50; B. W. Winter. "On Introducing Gods to Athens: An Alternative Reading of Acts 17:18-20." *TynBul* 47 (1996) 71–90.

KEVIN L. ANDERSON

ARETALOGY [ἀρεταλογία *aretalogia*]. In the Hellenistic and Roman periods, the rarely attested Greek term **aretalogia** was used in reference to the practice of reciting the virtues and praiseworthy deeds or powers of a deity or deities. One who performed such sacred discourses for a deity, such as Isis or Sarapis, could be called an **aretalogos**, as at Delos (Suetonius, *Aug.* 4); this functionary is analogous to the better attested **theologos** (who composed or performed **theologia** in praise of the gods).

Scholars of Greek and Roman religions use *aretalogy* to refer to various sorts of materials, including inscriptions, that are aimed primarily at recounting the wonderful achievements of a particular god or gods. Some NT scholars adopted and adapted this modern usage in discussions of the literary genre of the Gospels and other Greek or Roman literature that described the teachings and deeds of a philosopher or "divine man" (θεῖος ἀνήρ *theios anēr*, e.g., Apollonius of Tyana). In particular, those who have followed the lead of M. Smith and M. Hadas argue that we can speak of aretalogy as a literary genre; that the aretalogy was distinguishable from the biography genre in some way; and that the Gospel of Luke or other Gospels are best described as aretalogies for the holy man and teacher, Jesus. A number of scholars have challenged this view, particularly since we lack consistent ancient uses of the term *aretalogy* in reference to a type of writing and because of difficulties associated with the scholarly "divine man" category itself. *See* GOSPELS, GENRE.

Bibliography: Richard A. Burridge. *What Are the Gospels: A Comparison with Graeco-Roman Biography.* 2nd ed. (2004); Morton Smith and Moses Hadas. *Heroes and Gods* (1965).

PHILIP A. HARLAND

ARETAS air'uh-tuhs [Ἀρέτας *Aretas*]. Dynastic name of a number of Nabatean (Arabian) kings.

1. Aretas I (ca. 170–160 BCE) was the first of the Nabatean dynasts mentioned in the historical record, where an inscription styles him as king (Aramaic mlk). According to 2 Macc 5:8, the high priest Jason was held by him in 168 BCE.

2. Aretas II (ca. 120–96 BCE) pledged to help Gaza fend off the siege of Alexander Jannaeus (Josephus *Ant.* 13.358-64).

3. Aretas III "Philhellene" (ca. 87–62 BCE) was invited by Coele-Syria and Damascus to become their ruler (ca. 84–72 BCE), Aretas became embroiled in territorial disputes with the Hasmoneans. In 82 BCE he defeated Alexander Jannaeus and, later, in the dynastic contest between Hyrcanus II and Aristobulus II, supported the former. In return, Hyrcanus promised to restore twelve cities captured by Alexander (Josephus, *Ant.* 14.18).

4. Aretas IV "Philopatris" (ca. 9 BCE–39 CE) was a long-lived king who presided over a period of notable prosperity in Nabatea. When Herod Antipas expelled his wife, Aretas's daughter, in favor of Herodias, Aretas sent a punitive expedition against him and secured a major victory. According to Josephus, the people regarded Herod's defeat as divine punishment for his execution of John the Baptist (*Ant.* 18.109-19). In 2 Cor 11:32-33 (*see* Gal 1:15-17) Paul describes his escape from Damascus when "the governor [ethnarch] under King Aretas" sought to capture him. Whether Aretas's ethnarch actually controlled the city or simply oversaw its resident Nabatean colony remains disputed.

Bibliography: G. W. Bowersock. *Roman Arabia* (1983).

J. R. C. COUSLAND

ARGOB AND ARIEH, ahr'gob air'ee-uh [אַרְגֹּב 'argov, Ἀργοβ *Argob*; אַרְיֵה 'aryeh, Ἀρια *Aria*]. The sentence structure in 2 Kgs 15:25 makes it difficult to determine whether ARGOB and ARIEH are two men who had conspired with the captain, PEKAH, to kill King PEKAHIAH or had been assassinated along with King Pekahiah.

ARIANISM. A 4th cent. theological system developed by the presbyter Arius (ca. 260–336 CE). To preserve the uniqueness of God, Arianism argued that the Son was a creation of the Father, not coeternal or of the same substance (homoousios). The councils of Nicea (325) and Constantinople (381) condemned Arianism's Christology. *See* TRINITY.

ARIARATHES air´ee-ahr´theez [Ἀριαράθης Ariarathēs]. Cappadocian king (163–130 BCE) to whom the Roman consul Lucius wrote a letter assuring him of the Jews' allegiance and requesting him not to join alliances against them (1 Macc 15:22).

ARIDAI air´uh-d*i* [אֲרִדַי ʾaridhay]. Haman's ninth of ten sons, all killed and hung on the gallows as part of the purging of Jewish enemies (Esth 9:9).

ARIDATHA air´uh-day´thuh [אֲרִידָתָא ʾaridatha']. Haman's sixth of ten sons, all killed and hung on the gallows as part of the purging of Jewish enemies (Esth 9:8).

ARIEH air´ee-uh [אַרְיֵה ʾaryeh]. Killed by Pekah (2 Kgs 15:25). *See* ARGOB and ARIEH.

ARIEL air´ee-uhl [אֲרִיאֵל ʾariʾel; Ἀριήλ Ariēl]. 1. Ariel is an obscure name for Jerusalem in Isa 29:1-8. While Yahweh fights against Jerusalem (vv. 1-4), punishment from Yahweh is suddenly unleashed against all the nations that make war against Ariel (vv. 5-8). Judging from the use of the word in Ezek 43:15-16 and line 12 of the Mesha inscription (COS 2, 137–38), Ariel means something like "altar hearth" and may designate the altar of burnt offering as a symbolic reference to Jerusalem in Isa 29. Yahweh threatens to make Jerusalem like an altar hearth; that is, it will become a place for sacrifice or slaughter (Isa 29:2). Ariel as a designation for Jerusalem may also be related to the etymology of ʾariʾel (lion of God) since Judah is called a lion's whelp in Gen 49:9. Others detect an allusion to har el (הַר אֵל har ʾel) that is, Jerusalem as the "mountain of God."

2. In 2 Sam 23:20 (1 Chr 11:22) Ariel may be a noun referring to a military hero, although the LXX, followed by NRSV, states that Benaiah struck down two sons of a person named Ariel.

3. One of nine leaders mentioned in Ezra 8:16 (Iduel in the par. text of 1 Esd 8:43).

RALPH W. KLEIN

ARIMATHEA air´uh-muh-thee´uh [Ἀριμαθία Arimathia]. According to all four Gospels Arimathea was the hometown of JOSEPH OF ARIMATHEA, who provided a tomb for Jesus (Matt 27:57; Mark 15:43; Luke 23:51; John 19:38). Its identification and location remain uncertain. Luke describes it as a "city of the Jews," not necessarily implying a Judean location. Eusebius and Jerome both identify Arimathea with RAMAH, in BENJAMIN (Josh 18:25) or EPHRAIM (1 Sam 1:1 = Armathaim in the LXX), the birthplace of SAMUEL (1 Sam 1:1, 19; 2:11), where a medieval monastery of Joseph of Arimathea was erected. Other proposals include RATHAMIN (1 Macc 11:34) and Ramathain (Josephus, *Ant.* 13.127). All of these proposals could refer to the same location. If Rathamin and Arimathea are identical, Luke's insistence upon the city's Jewishness may result from King Demetrios III's cession of territory from Samaria to Judea in 142 BCE (1 Macc 11:34).

GREG CAREY

ARIMATHEA, JOSEPH OF. *See* JOSEPH OF ARIMATHEA.

ARIOCH [אַרְיוֹךְ ʾaryokh; Ἀριωχ Ariōch]. 1. The king of Ellasar and one of four kings led by Chedorlaomer in his western campaign against cities in the Dead Sea region (Gen 14). These two, along with Amraphel and Tidal, fought against the kings of Sodom, Gomorrah, Admah, Zeboiim, and Bela (Zoar), who had allied in rebellion against Chedorlaomer. In light of Babylonian documents called "the Chedorlaomer texts," Arioch is sometimes identified with Tukulti-Ninurta I, who ruled Assyria in the 13th cent. BCE.

2. The name of a captain of Nebuchadnezzar's royal guard, who had been sent to kill all of the wise men in the country because no one could interpret the king's dream (Dan 2). Faced with execution, Daniel promises to explain the dream and Arioch takes him to Nebuchadnezzar.

3. The name of the king of the Elymeans (i.e., the Elamites) mentioned in Jdt 1:6.

BRYAN D. BIBB

ARISAI air´uh-s*i* [אֲרִסַי ʾarisay]. One of Haman's sons hung on the gallows (Esth 9:9).

ARISH, WADI EL. *See* EGYPT, WADI OF.

ARISTARCHUS air´is-tahr´kuhs [Ἀρίσταρχος Aristarchos]. One of the fellow workers (συνεργοί sunergoi) of Paul (Phlm 24). Colossians 4:10 describes him as a "fellow prisoner of war" (συναιχμάλωτος sunaichmalōtos), the sense of which is debated. The following verse probably includes him with Mark and Jesus/Justus as "of the circumcision." Most likely the same Aristarchus is mentioned three times in Acts. In 19:29, he is described as a Macedonian traveling companion (συνεκδήμους sunekdēmous) of Paul who was dragged into the theater during the riot in Ephesus. He is called a Thessalonian in the list of those accompanying Paul from Greece to Macedonia (20:4), and a Macedonian from Thessalonica traveling with Paul to Rome (27:2). Indeed, he may have been a constant companion of Paul from Ephesus to Rome.

MARK D. GIVEN

ARISTEAS, LETTER OF air´is-tee´uhs [Ἀριστεας Aristeas]. The *Letter of Aristeas* is the oldest and fullest extant account of the origins of the LXX, specifically the Greek translation of the Pentateuch. Thus, the 3rd cent. Christian writer Eusebius titled the document "Concerning the Translation of the Law of the Jews," even though this topic is relegated to a relatively few verses, namely, 9-11, 28-50, and 301-317 (out of a total of 322).

The *Letter* purports to be a contemporary account, composed in Alexandria, Egypt, from the reign of Ptolemy II (Philadelphus), who ruled from 285–247 BCE. The author identifies himself as Aristeas and addresses his remarks to his "brother," Philocrates. As related by Aristeas, the impetus for the translation came from the royal librarian Demetrius, who wished to add "the lawbooks of the Jews" in Greek to a collection numbering over 200,000 volumes (vv. 9-11). Ptolemy agreed and sent a letter to Eleazar, high priest in Jerusalem, requesting seventy-two elders (six from each tribe) "of exemplary lives, with the experience of the Law and ability to translate it" (v. 39). At the same time, Ptolemy released 100,000 Jews who had been transported in servitude to Egypt by his father.

The high priest acceded to this request and also sent "fine skins on which the Law had been written in letters of gold in Jewish characters" (v. 176). The central part of the *Letter* describes the gifts, banqueting, and conversation between the Egyptian monarch and his Jewish guests. At the end of a week Demetrius led the seventy-two translators across a jetty to an island identified as Pharos, where after exactly seventy-two days, they completed their task. The resulting document was read to the Jewish community, which received it with great acclaim and rejoicing, as did Ptolemy, who suitably rewarded each of the seventy-two for his labors.

Through the Middle Ages, the *Letter of Aristeas* was understood as an essentially historical account of how the first five books of the Septuagint came about. The Jewish historian Josephus (late 1st cent. CE) knew it, and the Alexandrian Jewish philosopher Philo (early 1st cent. CE) even adds some details, most notably that tourists of his day could visit Pharos as the site of an annual celebration to commemorate the work of the translators. Leaders in the early church, for whom the LXX came to be sacred writ, also knew the *Letter* and embellished it. Thus, although the earliest copies of the *Letter* itself date from the 11th cent. CE, there is no doubt that the *Letter* itself is of ancient date.

But is it historically accurate? Because of certain discrepancies—e.g., Demetrius was not the librarian at the time of Ptolemy II, and the LXX of the Five Books of Moses does not represent the work of one group or individual—there is uniform agreement today that the *Letter* cannot be the eyewitness account it claims to be. In all likelihood, it dates to the mid-2nd cent. BCE, that is, a century later than the events it appears to reflect. On the other hand, there is good linguistic evidence from the LXX of the Pentateuch itself that the Greek version of these books does indeed date to the first half of the 3rd cent. BCE, and the Jewish names mentioned in the Letter are compatible with this era.

Much attention has been paid to the *Letter's* assertion that the LXX owes its origins to royal decree as opposed to the internal needs of the Alexandrian Jewish community, where knowledge of the Hebrew language was quickly receding. A strong case can be made, both from the historical record and historical parallels, that in this instance internal and external exigencies coalesced, with the result that the Jews of Alexandria and their royal patron could well have worked together to produce this earliest written translation of the Hebrew Bible.

Near the end of the *Letter*, after the Greek text is proclaimed, the leaders of the Jewish community "commanded that a curse should be laid . . . on anyone who should alter the version by any addition or change to any part of the written text, or any deletion either" (v. 311). This episode brings to mind the ratification of the Torah by the Israelites at Mount Sinai (Exod 19 and 24) and strongly suggests that, at least as described by Aristeas, the Greek Pentateuch was held to have authority equal to that of the Hebrew Torah. It is likely that this view reflects the author's perception of events of his own day (mid-2nd cent. BCE), when rival Greek versions began to challenge the unique place held until then by the Greek Pentateuch of the 3rd cent.

The procedures adopted by the translators, as outlined in the *Letter*, accord well with translation-by-committee to this very day: "They set to completing their several tasks, reaching agreement among themselves on each by comparing versions. . . . The business of their meeting occupied them until the ninth hour [3:00 PM] of each day" (vv. 302–303). Only the luxury of their surroundings and their freedom from other commitments—"a magnificent building in a very quiet situation" (v. 301)—separate them from modern Bible translators. With the possible exception of the fact that seventy-two happened to be the number both of the translators and of the days of translation, a phenomenon very briefly noted by Aristeas (v. 307), there is nothing of the "miraculous" about the entire process that produced the Greek Pentateuch.

Philo saw the translators in a rather different light: they were "prophets and priests of the mysteries," who, "under inspiration, wrote . . . the same word for word, as though dictated to each by an invisible prompter." In Epiphanius, the level of embellishment reached its peak, with a narrative that places thirty-six pairs of translators in individual cells. Working in isolation, each pair completed its work in the same amount of time and with exactly the same results, such that comparison of the thirty-six texts found no discrepancy at all. Only divine oversight or intervention could produce such unanimity, it was asserted; this was in accord with the elevated status that the LXX enjoyed among early Christians.

Although scholars will continue to refine their understanding of Septuagintal origins, they are unlikely to dislodge the *Letter of Aristeas* from its literary and cultural importance or its centrality as a historical witness *see* SEPTUAGINT.

LEONARD GREENSPOON

ARISTEAS THE EXEGETE. Eusebius (*Praep. ev.* 9.25.1–4) quotes ALEXANDER POLYHISTOR, who cites *Concerning the Jews* by Aristeas the Exegete, a work otherwise unattested. The fragment discusses Job, and the Septuagint's supplement to Job provides the same information. If Aristeas used the LXX, he must have written between its completion and the time of Polyhistor (80–35 BCE). *See* JOB, BOOK OF.

Bibliography: Carl R. Holladay. *Fragments from Hellenistic Jewish Authors Volume 1: Historians* (1983).
KENNETH D. LITWAK

ARISTIDES. Second-century Athenian philosopher and apologist, whose defense of Christianity is the earliest preserved. Eusebius and Jerome ascribe to him a treatise addressed to the emperor Hadrian (ca. 124 CE). *Apology for Christians* traces humanity's quest for spiritual enlightenment among barbarians, Greeks, Jews, and Christians to demonstrate that Christians alone possess a true idea of the one God, a piety that evinces a superior morality. Aristides' work, according to Eusebius, was "preserved by many." Indeed, the text of the *Apology* has survived in two, fragmentary, 4th cent. Greek papyri, an Armenian version (published in 1878), and, most importantly in a 7th cent., Syriac translation discovered by J. R. Harris in 1889 on Mount Sinai. It was also reproduced in a lengthy section of the Greek novel *Barlaam and Josaphat* (8th or 10th cent.).

Bibliography: R. M. Grant. *Greek Apologists of the Second Century* (1988).
GREGORY ALLEN ROBBINS

ARISTIDES, AELIUS. A rhetorician and sophist (ca. 117–189 CE) trained in Athens and Pergamum, and an important source for Roman social and religious history. His works include public and private addresses, historical declamations, polemical essays, prose hymns, and *Sacred Discourses*.

Bibliography: P. W. van der Horst. *Aelius Aristides and the New Testament* (1980).

ARISTOBULUS air´is-tob´yuh-luhs [Ἀριστόβουλος *Aristoboulos*]. The son of Herod by his wife Mariamme, born shortly after 40 BCE (*J.W.* 2.12.4 §241; 1.22.2 §435). Our knowledge of his life comes almost entirely from the accounts of Josephus in the *Jewish War* and the *Antiquities of the Jews*. Mariamme was the granddaughter of the last Hasmonean ruler, Hyrcanus II, which means that in Aristobulus and his siblings the Herodian and the Hasmonean lines came together. Aristobulus was the younger of two brothers, though his elder brother Alexander was apparently only a year or two older. Aristobulus and Alexander are often mentioned together in Josephus's accounts, with Alexander usually taking the lead (*Ant.* 16.11.8 §401). Aristobulus and Alexander were educated in Rome, as was a common practice for the sons of eastern dynasts in this time, and the two youths even stayed for a time with Augustus Caesar (*Ant.* 15.10.1 §342).

In order to understand Aristobulus and his brother Alexander, one needs to be aware that Herod had their mother Mariamme executed (*J.W.* 1.22.4 §§441-44; *Ant.* 15.7.5 §§232-36). Herod's relationship to her was complex: he loved her dearly but with great jealousy (*J.W.* 1.22.2 §§435-36; *Ant.* 15.3.9 §§81-87; 15.7.1-4 §202-22). Her death occurred about 29 BCE when Aristobulus and his brother were still quite young, but the boys would resent the murder for the rest of their lives (*J.W.* 1.23.1 §445). Alongside this attitude was another that proved to be equally destructive: they saw themselves as heirs of the noble Hasmonean family and despised their Idumean relatives whom they saw as commoners (*Ant.* 15.3.9 §81; 15.7.4 §220). Some scholars think that they deemed Herod and his family as not being proper Jews. This last point was based on the fact that the Idumeans had converted to Judaism several generations earlier. From all accounts, the Herodian family conducted themselves religiously and ethnically as Jews, but many Jews may still have looked down on them as only "half Jews," despite the generations-long practice of Judaism. However, Josephus's accounts of Aristobulus and Alexander say nothing about this.

This attitude on the part of Aristobulus and his brother was a major contributing factor to their gaining powerful enemies at Herod's court, in the persons of Salome and Antipater. Since Salome (Herod's sister) had played a part in Mariamme's death by making accusations about her to Herod (*Ant.* 15.3.9 §§80-81; 15.7.3-4 §§213-31), it is hardly surprising that she developed a hatred for Mariamme's sons (*Ant.* 16.3.1-2 §§66-77). Their youthful outspokenness meant that it was easy for their enemies to accuse them before Herod, who believed such reports and decided to bring back Antipater to court.

For Aristobulus and Alexander, Antipater was even more dangerous than Salome. He was Herod's eldest son, born of the first wife Doris whom Herod had sent away when he married Mariamme (*J.W.* 1.12.3 §241; 1.22.1 §433). Herod brought Antipater back to court ca. 14 BCE to show the two brothers that there was no guarantee that one of them would succeed him on the throne (*Ant.* 16.3.3 §§78-86). Indeed, as time went on and Antipater cultivated his father's affections, Herod named Antipater in his will as heir and sent him to Rome to meet Augustus. Even from Rome Antipater continued the accusations against Aristobulus and his brother, until Herod finally brought them to Italy and accused them before Augustus (*J.W.* 1.23.2-3 §§449-54; *Ant.* 16.4.1-4 §§87-126). The Roman emperor, however, was moved by Alexander's speech in defense of himself and Aristobulus, and effected an emotional reconciliation between the young men and their father. When Herod returned to Jerusalem with all three of his sons, he designated Antipater as his first heir, followed by Alexander and Aristobulus (*J.W.* 1.23.5 457-66; *Ant.* 16.4.6 §§132-33).

Despite this brief respite, the next several years saw the court intrigues continue. Although Salome was no friend to Antipater, the combined verbal assault of the two of them had their effect on Herod, especially since Aristobulus and Alexander seemed to have remained rather naive about countering their enemies' attacks. Finally, ca. 7 BCE Herod had Aristobulus and his brother arrested and imprisoned (*J.W.* 1.27.1 §§534-35; *Ant.* 16.10.1-7 §§300-334). He consulted Augustus, who advised him to try them by a council composed of Herod's own relatives and some high-ranking Roman officials in the region. The brothers were condemned, and Herod had them strangled (*J.W.* 1.17.1-6 §§536-51; *Ant.* 16.10.9-11.7 §§351-94). They had been popular among the Jewish people, not least because their mother had been a prominent Hasmonean.

Despite some promise (though his brother apparently had more ability), Aristobulus had accomplished little in his life. His main claim to fame, however, was his children by Berenice, the daughter of Herod's sister Salome, including Agrippa I who would become the last king of Judah (41-44 CE); Herod of Calchis; and Herodias who became wife of the tetrarch Herod Antipas (alluded to in Mark 6:17-18, though with some errors). In spite of his treatment of their father, Herod took great care of his grandchildren. As for Antipater, his intrigues eventually caught up with him, and he was executed shortly before Herod's own death in 4 BCE. *See* HEROD, FAMILY.

LESTER L. GRABBE

ARISTOBULUS, LETTER TO [Ἀριστόβουλος Aristobulos]. A Letter from Palestinian Jews to Egyptian Jews contained in 2 Macc 1:10–2:18. The purpose of the letter is to encourage the Egyptian Jews to join with their Palestinian coreligionists in celebrating the purification of the Temple (2 Macc 1:18; 2:16). The letter purports to date from 164 BCE and alludes to the rededication of the Temple after its profanation by Antiochus IV Epiphanes in 167. It recounts, among other things, Antiochus's demise in Persia (2 Macc 1:11-17), Nehemiah's discovery and thanksgiving for the sacrificial fire that had been secreted before the exile (2 Macc 1:18-36), and Jeremiah's caching of the tent, ark, and incense altar in a cave (2 Macc 2:4-8). It closes with a thanksgiving and the above-mentioned invitation.

The sender is likely Judas Maccabeus, who ruled the Jewish people ca. 166–160 BCE. The letter's recipient is generally identified as Aristobulus, the earliest known Jewish philosopher, who was a counselor (didaskalos) to King Ptolemy, and fragments of whose work survive in Eusebius and Clement of Alexandria (*see* ARISTOBULUS). If the letter is genuine, it provides a revealing glimpse into the early Maccabean period. Many scholars, however, believe it to be a forgery, dating from 60 BCE or later. Its account of Antiochus's death disagrees with other ancient sources and with the account found in 2 Macc 9 itself; other features, such as its formula of greeting, are more characteristic of the 1st cent. BCE. *See* ARISTOBULUS, OT PSEUDEPIGRAPHA.

Bibliography: Carl R. Holladay. *Fragments from Hellenistic Jewish Authors.* Volume III. *Aristobulus* (1995).

J. R. C. COUSLAND

ARISTOBULOS, OT PSEUDEPIGRAPHA air´istob´yuh-luhs, soo´duh-pig´ruh-fuh [Ἀριστόβουλος Aristoboulos]. Fragments attributed to the Jewish-Hellenistic philosopher and exegete Aristobulus. There are five main fragments, all evidently derived from one lengthy exegetical work on the Torah (*Explanations of the Book of Moses*), dedicated by Aristobulus to "Ptolemy the King" (probably Ptolemy VI Philometor, ca. 180–45 BCE). Though undeniably limited, these excerpts represent the first extant examples of Jewish philosophy and hermeneutics, and are among the earliest writings to suggest that Moses and the prophets were the true fountainhead of Greek thought. Fragment 1 is contained in a larger excerpt of Anatolius's lost *On the Passover,* cited in Eusebius's *Ecclesiastical History,* while Fragments 2–5 occur in Eusebius' *Praeparatio Evangelica.* Clement of Alexandria's *Stromateis* also furnishes partial parallels.

Fragment 1 (*H.E.* VII 32, 17–18) concerns the calculation of the date of Passover. Aristobulus is the first to relate it to the appearance of the solar and lunar equinoxes.

Fragment 2 (*P.E.* VIII 10, 1–17) is the longest and outlines Aristobulus's allegorical method, with particular reference to the Torah's anthropomorphisms. He interprets the references to God's body metaphorically; God's "hands," for instance, really refer to his power, God's "standing" to his divine supremacy.

Fragment 3 (*P.E.* XIII 12, 1–2) maintains that both PLATO and Pythagoras derived many of their ideas from early Greek translations of the Torah.

Fragment 4 (*P.E.* XIII 13, 3–8) suggests that Orpheus, ARATUS, and other Greek philosophers appropriated Moses' understanding of God.

Fragment 5 (*P.E.* XIII 12, 9–16) discusses the Sabbath and argues for the universal sanctity of the number seven.

Bibliography: Carl R. Holladay. "Aristobulus." *Fragments from Hellenistic Jewish Authors.* Vol. 3 (1995).

J. R. C. COUSLAND

ARISTOTLE. Aristotle (b. 384–d. 322 BCE) was born in Stagira in northern Greece. His father, a physician in a Macedonian court, died while Aristotle was still a young boy. At seventeen he moved to Athens where he was a student at Plato's Academy for about twenty years. After his teacher's death, Aristotle left Athens, eventually working in the court of Philip II of Macedon, where he briefly tutored the young Alexander the Great. In the latter part of his life he returned to Athens where he ran his own school in what was called the Lyceum until just before his death.

Aristotle's prolific writings included works on logic, ethics, rhetoric, politics, and science. In contrast to Plato, who located reality and knowledge in abstract ideas or forms, for Aristotle the world could be comprehended through careful observation. In response to earlier arguments that identified reality as either form or matter, Aristotle posited that all things have a substance, which consists of both. Change, which Plato had difficulty accounting for, was central to Aristotle who viewed all activity and behavior as teleological or goal directed; that is, moving toward an ultimate end. Aristotle's influence on Christianity is considerable. Somewhat indirectly, Aristotle's writings left their mark on later Hellenistic and Roman thought, thus influencing later Jewish and Christian writers; his writings on rhetoric, for example, provide the principle categories for subsequent rhetorical theory and practice, and are invaluable for placing biblical literature in its Greco-Roman literary and cultural context. More directly, his writings became the central philosophical works for Medieval Christian thought.

RUBEN R. DUPERTUIS

ARIUS air´ee-uhs. Founder of ARIANISM, (d. 336 CE), was a presbyter of Alexandria when he disputed Bishop Alexander's doctrine of the "eternal" fatherhood and

sonship of God and Christ, a position continued by his successor bishop, Athanasius of Alexandria. Arius's counter-teaching—holding that the Son was a promoted deity temporally and qualitatively differing from the divinity of God the Father—was condemned at Nicea.

Fellow students or admirers of Lucian of Antioch joined Arius in this debate, including Asterios the Sophist (also called "the sacrificer" by his orthodox enemies), Eusebius of Nicomedia, and Eusebius of Caesarea.

Only hostile Orthodox sources, most importantly ATHANASIUS, preserve fragments of Arius' teachings (letters and the *Thalia,* a metrical collection of sayings). There once was a consensus that Arius's teachings were guided by the pagan philosophical concern to preserve the strictest monotheism by excluding the Son of God from "full" divinity. In contrast, whether the heart of early Arian theology is motivated by soteriological or theological concerns, a consensus is emerging that the controversy turned on how to interpret scriptural texts referring to sonship and fatherhood.

Bibliography: Lewis Ayers. *Nicaea and Its Legacy* (2004). Robert C. Gregg and Dennis E. Groh, *Early Arianism. A View of Salvation* (1981).

DENNIS E. GROH

ARK OF NOAH [תֵּבָה tevah; κιβωτός kibōtos]. Floating wooden box that enabled NOAH, his family, and the world's animals to survive the FLOOD. In Gen 6:14-16 God commands the building of the ark. Similar divine instructions and their execution can be found in the Epics of Atrahasis III i 20-33, ii 10-15, and Gilgamesh XI 24-31, 48-66 as well. Noah's ark is made of an unidentified type of tree translated as CYPRESS in the NRSV (עֲצֵי־גֹפֶר ʿatse ghofer, Gen 6:14). He seals the container with pitch (כֹּפֶר kofer = kuprum Gilg. XI 65, "bitumen"). The dimensions of 300 × 50 × 30 cubits (ca. 150 × 25 × 15 m) suggest a long container, contrary to the Mesopotamian cube with its perfect dimension of 120 × 120 × 120. Outside the flood narrative, **tevah** only appears as the word for Moses' basket (Exod 2:3, 5). The genres of both the biblical and the Mesopotamian texts forbid a serious search for archaeological remnants of the ark.

The story of the ark also appears in the Apocrypha and NT. The mother of the seven in 4 Maccabees is compared to the ark of Noah (4 Macc 15:31). In the Gospels, the ark appears in warnings about the coming of the Son of Man (Matt 24:38; Luke 17:27). Hebrews praises Noah's faithfulness in building the ark (11:7).

ED NOORT

ARK OF THE COVENANT [אֲרוֹן ʾaron; κιβωτός kibōtos]. The Hebrew word, which originally designated a box or chest, became primarily associated with a sacred cult object kept in the TABERNACLE or the Temple, indicating the presence of God in the midst of Israel.

A. Terminology

The word ʾaron, translated as *ark*, appears over 200 times in the Bible, and all but a handful of these references are to a boxlike object symbolizing the presence of God in the midst of Israel. The term is used for a coffin (Gen 50:26) and a collection box in the Temple (2 Kgs 12:9, 10; 2 Chr 24:8, 10, 11). Seldom does the term appear without accompanying terminology indicating a relationship to God, and these fuller designations of the ark are often characteristic of particular textual traditions and their attendant understandings of the ark and its significance for Israel. There are twenty-two separate extended titles for the ark, as well as oblique references to the ark, especially in the Psalms, where the term ʾaron is not itself used.

1. Books of Samuel and Chronicles

Nearly a third of all references to the ark are in the books of Samuel. Since the Chronicler uses the books of Samuel as a source, its designations of the ark reflect those used in 1 and 2 Samuel.

The ark is designated eighty-two times in association with the God of Israel, and some of the solitary uses of ark have such a fuller designation as antecedent. Many have regarded the reference in 1 Sam 4:4 (*see* 2 Sam 6:2; 1 Chr 13:6) as the fullest and most ancient name for the ark, "the ark of the covenant of the LORD (Yahweh) of hosts, who is enthroned on the cherubim." Although not as expansive, most other references to the ark in the historical books use some designation relating the ark to God's presence, e.g., "the ark of God," "the ark of Yahweh," "or the ark of the lord of all the

earth." Attempts to treat the designation of the ark of God and the ark of Yahweh as two separate traditions have proved largely unsuccessful, and the two designations seem interchangeable. In the story of the ark's capture by the Philistines the text uses the phrase "the ark of the God of Israel" (1 Sam 5:7, 8 [three times], 10, 11; 6:3) seven times as the Philistine term for the ark while the narrator in the same context calls it the ark of Yahweh and relates it to the power of Yahweh's hand (1 Sam 5:3, 4; 6:1, 2, 11, 15, 18, 19; 7:1).

2. Deuteronomy

The book of Deuteronomy and the editor of the Deuteronomistic History overwhelmingly prefer to use the phrase "ark of the covenant (בְּרִית berith)," sometimes additionally including a form of the divine name, such as "the ark of the covenant of God" or "the ark of the covenant of Yahweh." Apparently the ark is emblematic of the relationship between God and Israel as covenant partners. This association of ark with covenant occurs forty times, including thirty with the divine name.

3. Priestly tradition

The priestly tradition in the Pentateuch, which includes the detailed description of God's instructions for and the fashioning of an elaborate gold-covered ark, refers to this sacred object solely as the "ark of testimony." The term ʿedhuth (עֵדוּת), although usually translated *testimony*, is a synonym in the P tradition for *covenant* as shown in other characteristic P phrases, such as "the tablets of the testimony," whereas other traditions would use *covenant*. Indeed, the NRSV translators have used the English word *covenant* as the preferred translation, noting the term *testimony* only in the footnote, thus obscuring the distinctive P terminology. An example of this can be seen in Exod 25 where the term ʿedhuth is translated as *covenant* rather than *testimony*, both in the designation of the "ark of the testimony" (v. 22) and for the tablets of the *testimony* that are placed into the ark (vv. 16, 21; *see* Exod 27:8; 31:18). The distinctiveness of the P designation as the "ark of the testimony" is almost entirely obscured by the NRSV translators but remains evident in most other modern English translations. Since the P writer also knows the term for covenant (berith), it is unclear what distinction is being made in using the term ʿeduth as its exclusive replacement in reference to ark and tablets.

4. Psalms

The ark is mentioned explicitly outside the Pentateuch and the historical books only twice, in Ps 132:8 and Jer 3:16. However, particularly in the Psalter there may be many allusions to the ark through the use of terms associated with the presence and power of God that the ark represents. Psalm 132:8, in the context of celebrating David's search for the ark, uses the phrase "the ark of your might," thus, other references to "his might" may well be references to the ark. This seems obviously true in Psalm 78:61, which refers to the Philistine capture of "his might" (NRSV *power*) and "his glory." Ps 96:6 refers to God's "might and glory" in the Temple. The term *glory* is used in 1 Sam 4:21-22 to lament the fate of the ark, "The glory has departed from Israel for the ark of God has been captured." Psalm 96:6 and 105:4 (seek Yahweh and his strength) are both quoted in 1 Chr 16:11, 27 as part of a liturgy for the procession of the ark. Thus, many liturgical texts in the Psalms may contain allusions to the ark and its presence and procession in the cultic life of Israel. The processional hymn in Ps 24 speaks of allowing the King of glory to enter. Psalms 47:6 and 68:1 (similar to the Song of the Ark in Num 10:35) may indicate processions of the ark.

It should also be considered that wide use of the terms "before God" or "before Yahweh" are possible references to the ark, particularly when associated with tabernacle or Temple (e.g., Lev 16:1-2; Josh 6:8; Judg 20:26-27; 1 Sam 10:25; 2 Sam 6:4-5, 14, 16, 17, 21; 1 Kgs 8:59, 62-65; 9:25; 2 Kgs 16:14; 1 Chr 1:6; 13:10).

B. The Ark as Cult Object

The ark, under all of its extended names and physical descriptions, is a cultic object of central importance to Israel from the earliest stories of wilderness life through the period of the Temple under the monarchy. Its significance may be described in several ways that overlap and coexist, although some dimensions of meaning may receive greater emphasis in particular periods of Israel's life or in the perspective of Israel's differing literary traditions.

1. Divine presence

In all of its appearances in biblical tradition the ark is associated with divine presence. Israel's god Yahweh was thought to be present wherever the ark was present. In Num 10:33-35 the ark would be taken out to find a resting place for Israel, and the accompanying song begun "Arise, O LORD . . ." for setting out, and "Return, O LORD . . ." for the return. Even Israel's enemies, the Philistines, spoke of the entry of the ark into Israel's camp as the arrival of Israel's gods (1 Sam 4:6-7; *see also* 6:3, 5, 8, 20). Moses approached the ark to speak with the LORD (Num 7:89). The ark in the midst of camp or city, in tabernacle or Temple, meant that God was in the midst of the people.

2. Throne/Footstool

Perhaps the most complete title for the ark appears in 1 Sam 4:4, "the ark of the covenant of the LORD of hosts, who is enthroned on the cherubim." This combines references to Israel's God as both king and warrior. This title is used at SHILOH and again when David brings it to Jerusalem following its period of absence at KIREATH-JEARIM (2 Sam 6:2).

Earlier scholarship suggested that the ark was a portable divine throne, a box surmounted by the winged creatures known as CHERUBIM, that could be carried by poles in procession or to battle. Above these cherubim God was invisibly enthroned. This view is challenged by the account of the placement of the ark in Solomon's Temple in an inner chamber beneath the outstretched wings of cherubim standing 10 cubits high with wings stretched 10 cubits (1 Kgs 6:23-28; 8:6-8). Above these, God was invisibly enthroned and the ark was placed beneath the outstretched wings of the cherubim. Such cherubim thrones are also known elsewhere in the ancient Near East.

If God is enthroned above the cherubim and the ark is placed as a box beneath this throne, then the ark is not God's throne but God's FOOTSTOOL. Indeed the ivories at Megiddo show such boxes at the feet of the enthroned king. El, the chief god of the Canaanite pantheon, is described as having a stool on which his feet are placed (hdm).

Using the same word as El's stool (הֲדֹם hadhom) the ark is referred to as God's footstool. In Ps 132:7, celebrating David's transfer of the ark to Jerusalem, the people are summoned, "Let us enter his dwelling, let us worship at his footstool." David's words in 1 Chr 28:2 are "I had it in my heart to build a house of rest for the ark of the covenant of Yahweh, for the footstool of our God." Psalm 99 celebrates the Lord as king, "enthroned upon the cherubim" (99:1) and calls the people to "extol the LORD our God, worship at his footstool" (99:5).

3. War palladium

The ark of the covenant often played a special role in making God's presence manifest at times of threat from enemies. It would be carried forth as a war palladium to ensure that God's presence as a warrior would make the difference in battle. In Num 10:35 every departure of the ark from camp was to be accompanied by a battle cry, "Arise, O LORD, let your enemies be scattered, and your foes flee before you."

The title of 1 Sam 4:4 for the ark includes reference to the "LORD of hosts," a term more clearly rendered as "LORD of armies." In that story the ark is brought out to the field of battle against the Philistines in the hope that Israel's God would fight for them and give them victory. "Let us bring the ark of the covenant of the LORD here from Shiloh, so that he may come among us and save us from the power of our enemies" (4:3). Even the Philistines were fearful that this would prove to be the case (4:5-9).

This tradition of the ark as war palladium is often treated by scholars as part of an early Israelite HOLY WAR tradition that died out under the monarchy. This association of the ark with war is well attested in Israel's premonarchic traditions. A military expedition against the wishes of Moses in Num 14:43-44 fails because "the LORD will not be with you" and the ark stayed in the camp. The capture of Jericho under Joshua features the ark prominently in the procession around its walls (Josh 6-7). The ark was the place to seek oracles on the course of a military campaign by the tribes of Israel against the tribe of Benjamin (Judg 20:26-27).

4. Association with tent shrine; repository

In biblical references the ark is often associated with a tent shrine. Although the shrine at Shiloh is referred to as a temple (1 Sam 1:9; 3:3), Ps 78:60-61 refers to the capture of the ark by noting, "He abandoned his dwelling at Shiloh, the tent where he dwelt among mortals." In denying David the right to build a temple, Nathan is emphatic in delivering God's word, "I have not lived in a house since the day I brought up the people of Israel from Egypt until this day, but I have been moving about in a tent and a tabernacle" (2 Sam 7:6).

When the Temple is built, Solomon brings both ark and tent of meeting in procession into the sanctuary of the Temple (1 Kgs 8:4; 2 Chr 5:5). Many believe that references indicate a tent sheltering the ark within the Temple, much as the ark in the priestly traditions of the tabernacle also is hidden by veils and coverings, the exact nature of which is difficult to determine (Exod 30:6; 40:3, 21; Num 4:5). Josephus describes the wings of the cherubim as a tent or dome covering the ark (*Ant.* 7.103-4). Second Maccabees 2:4-8 indicates that ark and tent were removed from the Temple in the destruction of Jerusalem, and Heb 9:4 states that the ark stood behind the second curtain in the Temple within a *tent* called the Holy of Holies.

The ark's cultic significance within these holy structures (tent and temple) has much to do with its role as a repository for sacred objects, most notably the tablets of the Law given to Moses on Mount Sinai. Solomon, in dedicating the Temple, announces, "There I have provided a place for the ark, in which is the covenant of the LORD that he made with our ancestors when he brought them out of the land of Egypt" (1 Kgs 8:21; *see* 2 Chr 6:11). This tradition is no doubt the origin of the phrase "ark of the covenant," which is used over forty times in the biblical tradition (priestly references to "ark of the testimony" are used thirteen times). Deuteronomy 10:1-5 tells how Moses made the ark and deposited the tablets given to Moses, emphasized in keeping with Deuteronomstic theology, the importance of the covenant relationship between God and Israel. Later Jewish tradition claimed that the ark also contained a jar of manna and the rod of Aaron (*see* Heb 9:4). Biblical references do not seem to support this claim, stating only that a jar of manna was placed "before the covenant (ʿedhuth)" (Exod 16:34) and that the staff of Aaron was placed "before the covenant (ʿedhuth) as a warning to rebels" (Num 17:10).

C. History and Theology of the Ark

1. The song of the ark

The oldest traditions of the Pentateuch seem to presume an association of the ark with Moses, and its significance as a sign of divine presence. The ancient poetic couplet known as the Song of the Ark in Num 10:35-36 links the ark to the wilderness period under the leadership of Moses. It is sent forth to locate campsites for Israel and to protect them from enemies. The departure of the ark is marked by a cry that begins, "Arise, O LORD" and at its return by "Return, O LORD" There is a virtual identification of Yahweh with the ark. When the ark did not accompany the group that attempted to invade Canaan prematurely, but remained with Moses, their defeat is attributed to the absence of the ark and presumably the presence of Yahweh (Num 14:43-44).

2. Deuteronomistic history

The historical books that make up the Deuteronomistic History from Joshua through 2 Kings contain the largest number of references to the ark. These appear both in apparently older traditions being used by the historian and in the comments of the Deuteronomistic editors.

a. Joshua/Judges. In Josh 3–4 the ark leads Israel into the promised land and represents both the presence and the power of God with them. It is referred to as "the ark of the covenant of the LORD your God" (3:3) and "the ark of the covenant of the LORD of all the earth" (3:11). The waters pile up in a heap when the bearers of the ark enter the Jordan River (3:13; 4:7, 18). This tradition already assumes that the ark is so holy that it can be borne only by priests of the tribe of Levi (3:3, 8, 13, 17; *see also* Deut 10:8-9).

Joshua set up a sanctuary at Gilgal where Israel crossed the Jordan, and it is presumed that the ark was kept there. It figures prominently in the cultic/military processions around Jericho leading to the collapse of its walls and its defeat (Josh 6–7), and the "ark of the covenant of the LORD" is present at the renewal of the covenant before Mount Ebal and Mount Gerizim (Josh 8:30-35).

Israel's sanctuary and the ark are at Bethel when the tribes of Israel consult God over their military action against the tribe of Benjamin. "And the Israelites inquired of the LORD (for the ark of the covenant of God was there in those days . . .)" (Judg 20:27-28).

b. Ark narrative. When the book of 1 Samuel opens, the ark is at Shiloh where the sanctuary is presided over by Eli and his two corrupt sons, and where the prophet Samuel is raised as a boy serving in the sanctuary (1 Sam 3:3). Here an oracle of judgment on the house of Eli is revealed to Samuel that will involve the capture of the ark.

The narrative of 1 Sam 4–6 has long been identified as a unified literary piece, incorporated into the narrative of events leading up to the establishment of kingship in Israel. This Ark Narrative is so named because its central character seems to be the ark itself, or perhaps, more accurately, the presence and power of Yahweh manifested in the ark. None of the human characters introduced before or after the Ark Narrative play a role in the story, except that Eli falls dead when hearing news of the capture of the ark and the death of his sons (4:12-18).

The Ark Narrative tells the story of Philistine aggression against Israelite territory. To meet this threat "the ark of the covenant of the LORD of hosts, who is enthroned on the cherubim" is brought to the field of battle (4:4). This first appearance of the longer title for the ark emphasizes its significance as a war palladium in this battle situation, but appropriately reminds the reader of Yahweh's kingship in a larger narrative leading to the people's demand for an earthly king. Even the Philistines fear that the arrival of the ark means that they will fight against Israel's gods (4:7-8). The battle, however, is a disaster for Israel, and the ark is captured. Eli's sons are killed, and the news causes Eli to fall dead. The ark is carried away into Philistine territory causing Eli's daughter-in-law to proclaim, "The glory has departed from Israel, for the ark of God has been captured" (4:22).

First Samuel 5–6 narrate the adventures of the ark in Philistine territory. There are almost no human characters except for collective voices of the Philistines. The ark is a clear manifestation of Yahweh's presence and the power of Yahweh's *hand*. When the ark is placed before the idol of Dagon, the image of the Philistine god falls face forward and loses his hands. A plague of disease comes upon the Philistine cities, and they finally return the ark to Israelite territory on an oxcart with golden offerings to appease Israel's God. It finally comes to lodge at Kireath-jearim for twenty years in the care of the house of Abinadab and his son Eleazar (6:21–7:2). The single reference to the ark during the time of Saul's kingship in 14:18 is probably a mistake, as indicated by the LXX reading of *ephod* rather than *ark*. First Chronicles 13:3 states that the ark was neglected during Saul's time, and Ps 132 implies that it was lost, since David must launch a search for it in order to bring it to Jerusalem.

c. David brings the ark to Jerusalem. Second Samuel 6 is the account of David's transfer of the ark from Baale-judah (Kireath-jearim, *see* Josh 15:9) to Jerusalem with great ceremony and portrays his own personal participation by dancing before the ark. Some scholars have regarded this as a continuation of the Ark Narrative in 1 Sam 4–6, but this view has diminishing support, and it seems unlikely that these two important stories about the ark were ever joined in a single literary composition. It is clear that this story represents David's recognition of the political importance of joining his fledgling monarchy with the older religious traditions of the Shiloh cult, and the ark is a potent symbol of that older tradition.

This seems both a politically shrewd and religiously meaningful move at the beginning of his kingship. The ark's presence in Jerusalem makes David's capital the political and religious center of the Israelite kingdom. The full Shilonite title for the ark is used, "the ark of God, which is called by the name of the LORD of hosts who is enthroned on the cherubim" (2 Sam 6:2). Its holiness is emphasized by the death of Uzzah, who inadvertently touches the ark when it is about to fall (6:6-7). Overcoming his own fear of such holy power, David finally dances before the ark in a great show of rejoicing and installs it in a tent sanctuary in Jerusalem (6:14-15, 17). The ark seems to have resumed its use as a war palladium under David (2 Sam 11:11; 15:24-29). Indeed, David's transfer of the ark to Jerusalem is preceded by accounts of victories over the Philistines in which David "inquired of the Lord" (5:15, 23). This could mean that David was seeking guidance before the ark even before transferring it to Jerusalem. It has been plausibly suggested that his dance before the ark is reminiscent of processions of the victorious warrior (in this case Yahweh and David).

d. Solomon installs the ark in the Temple. It is Solomon who builds the Temple in Jerusalem, and he installs the ark in its innermost sanctum with solemn procession and cultic ceremony (1 Kgs 8:1-12). He seems to have brought both ark and tent, and the cherubim that the ark is placed under seem less like a part of the ark than a canopy (throne pedestal?) above it. There are no further references to the ark in the books of Kings, although there is much speculation over its fate in the various invasions experienced by Jerusalem. Psalm 132 seems likely to be a part of a liturgy involving the processional of the ark (as also Pss 24, 47, 68). Jeremiah 3:16-17 may imply the continued existence of the ark in this period, even though it condemns over-reliance on such sacred symbols and implies they will not be needed in the future. The Chronicler largely echoes the traditions associated with the ark reflected in the sources he draws upon in the books of Samuel and Kings. There is some additional attention to the role of Levitical priests and other Temple personnel in connection with the ark (1 Chr 15–16) and greater attention given to Solomon's procession of the ark to the Temple.

e. Deuteronomy. Apart from stories about the ark, it is clear that certain traditions have distinctive views of the ark that arise out of particular theological agendas. The book of Deuteronomy seems to limit the meaning of the ark to its function as a receptacle for the tablets of the Law given to Moses. There is no mention of its function as a war palladium, an enthroned invisible Yahweh, the presence of a holy power. In the Deuteronomic account, when God gives Moses a second set of tablets, only then is the building of the ark commissioned (Deut 10:1-5). It is made out of acacia wood with no mention of gold ornamentation or cherubim, and it is the tablets of the covenant that the ark holds that are significant. When Moses makes a copy of the additional laws given to him, it is to be placed beside the ark (31:26). All other references to the ark seem to be incidental, and in every instance it is the ark's function as a simple wooden receptacle for the covenant that is important. This simplified function of the ark may well reflect Deuteronomy's central concern for idolatry, and the desire to remove any object that can be confused with God's own reality as an object of worship.

3. The Priestly narrative

The Priestly tradition of the Pentateuch also has a particular perspective on the ark. This is no doubt affected by the final redaction of the Priestly material in the period during and after the Babylonian exile (587–539 BCE). Presumably the ark is now lost, but the Temple is rebuilt, and Priestly traditions and functions have taken on renewed importance. Lost along with the ark are the tablets of the covenant. These crises affect the way in which the Priestly narrative treats the ark.

On the one hand, the Priestly tradition gives us the most ornate picture of the ark. It is constructed from a heavenly blueprint given by God to Moses for the tabernacle and all its furnishings (Exod 25:10-22). It is built by the master craftsman, Bezalel, from acacia wood, but every part is plated with gold and rich ornamentation (Exod 37:1-15). The cherubim are relegated to decorations on a covering (כַּפֹּרֶת kapporeth) for the ark (Exod 37:6-9). (The NRSV has retained the archaic translation "mercy seat" with *cover* as the alternative in a footnote. It is not a seat of any sort.) The cherubim face each other and their wings are extended over the cover. Absent is any sense of a cherubim throne, or a sign of continuous divine presence. The ark could be a meeting place with God; God would speak with Moses from between the cherubim (Num 7:89), but God's presence is not continuously present there. Although elsewhere in the Bible the ark is connected with God's name 112 times, not once is any form of God's name used with the ark in the Priestly materials.

The ark is the repository of the tablets of the Law (Exod 25:16, 21), and in this sense the Priestly and Deuteronomic traditions are agreed that the ark's primary function is as receptacle for this honored covenant relic. However, the Priestly writer constantly uses the term *testimony* (ʿedhuth) rather than *covenant* (berith) for these tablets. Hence, the Priestly designation is "ark of the testimonies" rather than "ark of the covenant." (The NRSV very unhelpfully translates both of these terms as *covenant*, only indicating in the footnote that the term is *testimony*.)

All of these distinctive features of the Priestly tradition would seem to relate to the crisis of faith brought by the exile. Both ark and tablets were presumably lost. Hence, it was important that the ark not be seen as the actual, enthroned presence of God. It was a meeting place that was lost, but not the enthroned God or the continued presence of God. Likewise, what was lost was not the "covenant," which is eternal, but the "testimonies," which were valued relics, the tablets, but only objects. Covenant continues unabated. A valued receptacle for the tablets given to Moses was lost, but the reality of God's presence is continued and can be accessed in the rebuilt Temple without the ark.

D. Loss of the Ark

1. Uncertainties

No one knows how the ark was lost. Speculation has centered on every hostile incursion that involved the Temple: Shishak's raid in the 10th cent. (1 Kgs 14:25-28); Jehoash's plundering of the Temple after Judah's defeat by Israel (2 Kgs 14:8-14); Manasseh's idolatrous renovation of the Temple (2 Kgs 21:4-6); or Nebuchadnezzar's destruction of the Temple (2 Kgs 25:13-17). The ark is not listed among the furnishings of the Temple taken by Nebuchadnezzar at the time of Babylonian sacking of Jerusalem. The problem is the utter silence on this matter. In Chronicler, Josiah did order that the "holy ark" be placed permanently in the Temple rather than left on poles (2 Chr 35:3), but this tradition is not known in the older Deuteronomistic history.

2. Second Temple and later traditions

An account in 2 Macc 2:4-8 claims that Jeremiah hid the ark, the tent, and other furnishings in a cave on Mount Nebo. Jewish tradition begins with the historian Eupolemus, who echoes this tradition (Eusebius, *Praep. ev.* 9.39). A legend in 2 Bar 6:7 says that an angel descended from heaven and removed the ark and other sacred objects at the time Jerusalem was destroyed. Most of these accounts seem to be ways of avoiding the unthinkable conclusion that the sacred ark was destroyed at the time the Temple and Jerusalem were destroyed by a Babylonian army. This terrible truth is perhaps reflected in 2 Esd 10:20-23 in a lament over the destruction and desecration of the Temple and the ark. Clearly no ark was rebuilt for the Second Temple, perhaps reflecting Jeremiah's contention that such objects were not needed for a renewed future (Jer 3:16). Even Ezekiel's vision of a new Jerusalem and Temple has no place for the ark (Ezek 40–48).

3. NT references

There are two references to the ark in the NT. In Heb 9:1-5 the ark is described as being known under the first covenant. It is ornate and enshrined in the most holy inner chamber of the tabernacle in keeping with the Priestly description, although it is called the "ark of the covenant" rather than the "ark of the testimonies." Most notably it is said to contain the tablets of the law, the jar of manna, and Aaron's rod, whereas the latter two are only placed before the ark in Exod 16:32-34 and Num 17:8-10.

In Rev 11:19 a vision of the eschatological temple includes the "ark of his [God's] covenant." In this final glimpse of the ark in the heavenly kingdom, the ark is once again a sign of God's presence.

Bibliography: A. F. Campbell. *The Ark Narrative (1 Sam 4–6; 2 Sam 6)* (1975); T. E. Fretheim. "The Ark in Deuteronomy." CBQ 30 (1968) 1–14; J. Gutman. "The History of the Ark." ZAW 87 (1971) 22–30. P. D. Miller Jr. and J. J. Roberts. *The Hand of the Lord* (1977). G. von Rad. "The Tent and the Ark." *The Problem of the Hexateuch and Other Essays* (1966) 103–24; C. L. Seow. "The Designation of the Ark in Priestly Theology." HAR 8 (1985) 185–98; C. L. Seow. *Myth, Drama, and the Politics of David's Dance* (1989); M. H. Woudstra. *The Ark of the Covenant From Conquest to Kingship* (1965).

BRUCE C. BIRCH

ARKESAEUS [Ἀρκεσαιος Arkesaios]. Persian governor who sat with and advised King Artaxerxes to replace Queen VASHTI (Add Esth 1:14). *See* ESTHER, ADDITIONS TO.

ARKITE ahr´k*i*t [עַרְקִין 'arqi]. The Arkites are listed among the descendants of Canaan and are likely Phoenician (Gen 10:17; 1 Chr 1:15). These descendants are associated with the Mediterranean town of Arka in northern Lebanon, which later was called Arca Caesarea by the Romans.

ARM [זְרוֹעַ zeroa'; βραχίων brachiōn]. The basic meaning of zeroa' or brachiōn is *arm,* though in the expression "the arm of his hands" (Gen 49:24) it may point at *wrists,* and in the case of animals (e.g., Num 6:19) it should be understood as equivalent to the English word *shoulder.*

The term is widely used in a metaphorical sense as *power* (and at times, *strength*) and is often associated with Yahweh (e.g., Exod 6:6; Deut 4:34; Isa 51:9; Luke 1:51; John 12:38). The well-known expression "outstretched arm" (referring to Yahweh's arm) tends to appear in parallel with expressions such as "mighty hand" (e.g., Deut 26:8; Ezek 20:33) or "mighty power" (Jer 27:5). The divine arm has been imagined as instrumental in bringing Israel out of Egypt (e.g., Deut 4:34; Acts 13:17) as well as in the act of creation (Jer 27:5). Yahweh's *arm* (or *power*) fulfills divine punishment (e.g., Isa 10:4), describes the future kingship of Yahweh (Ezek 20:33), and the conquest of the land (Ps 44:4). People are portrayed as asking Yahweh to be their *arm* in times of sorrow (Isa 33:2). Yahweh's arm is associaed with *holiness* (e.g., Ps 98:1), *glory* (Isa 63:12), and *might* (e.g.,

Ps 89:11). Biblical writers could refer to Yahweh's arm as *walking* beside Moses (Isa 63:12), and as an *object* by which Yahweh has sworn by (Isa 62:8).

Arm meaning *power* (or strength), however, is not exclusively associated with Yahweh. It is also associated with Assyria's arm (Ps 83:8) or Pharaoh's arms (Ezek 30:22), or the arm of a particular house in Israel or individual (1 Sam 2:31). In fact, the Hebrew term *arm* may be used in an adjectival sense, such as "a man of arm," i.e., a powerful/strong man (Job 22:8) and in the mythological "everlasting arms" (or "arms of old") in parallel to "ancient gods" in Deut 33:27, as well as in the use of arms' signifying military forces (e.g., Dan 11:31).

EHUD BEN ZVI

ARMAGEDDON, OT AND NT ahr´muh-ged´uhn [Ἁρμαγεδών Harmagedōn]. Occurs only in Rev 16:16 as the site of an eschatological battle that prepares the way for the millennium.

The term *armageddon* derives from the Hebrew for either "mount of Megiddo" (הַר מְגִדּוֹ har meghiddo) or "city of Megiddo" (עִיר מְגִדּוֹ 'ir meghiddo). "Mount of Megiddo" is preferable on etymological grounds. Several references to Megiddo occur in the OT. The ancient city of MEGIDDO (Josh 12:21; 17:11; Judg 1:27; 1 Kgs 4:12; 9:15, 27; 2 Kgs 9:27; 1 Chr 7:29) sat on a mound in northwestern Palestine not far from Mount Carmel. Megiddo was adjacent to two major trade routes, one of which carried traffic from Egypt to Syria. Beyond Rev 16:16 no extant literature mentions a "mountain of Megiddo."

In Revelation the rulers of the whole world converge upon Armageddon "for battle on the great day of God the Almighty" (Rev 16:14). This battle prepares for the final defeat of the world's imperial powers by Christ and the armies of heaven, leading to Christ's millennial reign (19:11–20:3).

The battle of Armageddon probably alludes to the battle against GOG AND MAGOG in Ezek 38–39, but Revelation does not follow Ezekiel's details. Revelation and Ezekiel both describe a great feast in which birds devour the remains of God's enemies (Ezek 39:4-6, 17-20; Rev 19:17-18). Yet Revelation places the battle of Armageddon before the millennium, reserving a second battle against SATAN, Gog, and Magog for after the millennium (Rev 20:7-10). Perhaps Revelation uses the expression "mountain of Megiddo" to evoke Ezekiel's prophecy concerning God's battle "on the mountains of Israel" (Ezek 38:8; 39:2, 4, 17).

In Revelation Armageddon probably functions as the symbolic, not literal, setting for Christ's victory over the world's empires. Other place names in Revelation, notably *Babylon,* allude to but do not denote actual places. But why locate this great battle at *Armageddon?* Scripture records pitched battles on a "plain of Megiddo" (2 Chr 35:22; Zech 12:11; *see* 2 Kgs 23:29, 30; also *see* "waters of Megiddo," Judg 5:19), and the pharaohs

Thutmose III and Merneptah conducted campaigns in the area. The plain also hosted a permanent military encampment during Roman occupation. Revelation combines eschatological images from Ezekiel with the heritage of war and Roman occupation associated with Megiddo in order to portray Christ's destruction of imperial power. *See* ESCHATOLOGY OF THE NT; MILLENNIUM; REVELATION, BOOK OF.

Bibliography: Eric Cline. *The Battles of Armageddon* (2000); John Day. "The Origin of Armageddon: Revelation 16:16 as an Interpretation of Zechariah 12:11." *Crossing the Boundaries: Essays in Biblical Interpretation in Honour of Michael D. Goulder* (1994) 315–26.

GREG CAREY

ARMENIAN GOSPEL OF THE INFANCY. *See* GOSPEL OF THE INFANCY, ARMENIAN.

ARMENIAN VERSION. *See* VERSIONS, ANCIENT.

ARMLET [אֶצְעָדָה ʾetsʿadhah, צְעָדָה tseʿadhah]. A piece of JEWELRY worn around the upper arm that signified wealth or royalty. ANE artwork depicts armlets that were worn by royalty.

Part of the Midianite booty brought to Moses and Eleazar as an atonement offering included gold *armlets* (Num 31:50). These bangles were listed among the items that Yahweh vowed to confiscate from elite women as part of the punishment for Israel's pride and greed (Isa 3:20). The Amalekite who mercifully killed the dying Saul brought the king's armlet and crown to David (2 Sam 1:10). The crowning of Joash may have involved presenting him with a royal armlet (2 Kgs 11:12), though the Hebrew there is uncertain (הָעֵדוּת haʿedhut; NRSV and NIV have "covenant").

LISA MICHELE WOLFE

ARMONI ahr-mohʹni [אַרְמֹנִי ʾarmoni]. A son of SAUL and his concubine, RIZPAH. He and his brother MEPHIBOSHETH die at the hands of the Gibeonites in order to atone for Saul's bloodguilt (2 Sam 21:8-9). The story of Saul's transgression against the Gibeonites does not appear in 1 Samuel.

ARMOR. *See* WAR, METHODS, TACTICS, WEAPONS OF.

ARMOR OF GOD. The armor of God is a rare feature of the larger biblical tradition of divine warfare (e.g., Exod 14–15; Deut 32–33; Pss 18, 68; Hab 3; for armor, *see* Isa 59:17), widely present in ANE cultures (e.g., ENUMA ELISH; *see* Marduk's armor at 4:35-40, 57-58).

Isaiah 59:17 is the earliest biblical instance of God wearing armor. Yahweh fights against a violent society where no one *intervenes* on behalf of vulnerable victims. Yahweh dons "righteousness/justice as breastplate," a "helmet of salvation," "garments of vengeance," and a "cloak of zeal." Reminiscent of the ideal monarch in Isa 11:5, who wears a belt of justice and fidelity, Isa 59 also anticipates the poem in 63:1-6, where the divine warrior returns from battle with garments drenched in the blood of Bosrah and Edom. Yahweh's armor represents divine intervention on behalf of the victims of violence, which include both human victims (v. 15), and the *virtues* that make social life possible (v. 14).

Centuries later Wisdom of Solomon adapts and expands the Isaianic motif to describe divine vindication of the just (Wis 5:17-20). God puts on *zeal* as his whole armor (πανοπλία panoplia; v. 17), which consists of Isaiah's "breastplate of righteousness" and the helmet, now representing "impartial justice" (κρίσις ἀνυπόκριτος krisis anypokritos; v. 18). Shield (*holiness*; v. 19) and sword (*wrath*; v. 20) complete the ensemble. As in Isaiah, God dresses for battle against the violent victimizers of the vulnerable righteous ones. In both Isaiah and Wisdom of Solomon the nature of this warfare is left to an imagination informed by the narrative traditions of God's acts of liberation and judgment.

The divine armor is radically transformed in the Pauline literature, explicitly bringing human actions into the sphere of God's *warfare*. In 1 Thess 5:8 Paul transfers God's breastplate and helmet onto anxious Thessalonians. Wearing a "breastplate of faith and love" and a "helmet of the hope of salvation" (notice Paul's triad of virtues), believers are summoned to employ the divine armor in resisting the darkness of imperial arrogance ("peace and security"; v. 3). In Eph 6:10-20 believers are to don God's panoply for struggle, not against members of a violent society ("blood and flesh"), but against the diabolical powers that control that society (2:1-3; 6:12). Added to Isaiah's breastplate and helmet are a belt of *truth*, footwear of the "gospel of peace," shield of *faith(fullness)*, and sword of the Spirit, God's word (vv. 14-17). The Pauline view of the church as the body of the messiah who is himself at war with the powers (1 Cor 15:24-26), but who *kills* with his own death on the cross (Eph 2:16), accounts for the transfer of the divine armor to believers. With the emphasis on peace (6:15), the armor becomes, ironically, a metaphor for the battle against war and violence.

Bibliography: Thomas R. Yoder Neufeld. *"Put on the Armour of God"; The Divine Warrior from Isaiah to Ephesians* (1997).

THOMAS R. YODER NEUFELD

ARMOR-BEARER [נֹשֵׂא כֵלִים noseʾ kelim]. The personal attendant(s) of a king or warrior who performed functions related to warfare. The role occurs 21 times in the OT but may have evolved into the position of captain (שָׁלִישׁ shalish). Abimelech (Judg 9:54); Jonathan (1 Sam 14:1-17); Saul (1 Sam 16:21; 31:4-6; 1 Chr 10:4-5); and Joab (2 Sam 18:15; 2 Sam 23:27; 1 Chr 11:39) had armor-bearers. Some texts describe a "young man" (נַעַר na'ar, Judg 9:54; 1 Sam 14:1, 6; 2 Sam 18:15) who has a devoted, personal relationship with his master and fights alongside him (1 Sam 14:12-14; 23:27; 31:4-6), an association that implies a society based upon individual patron-client relationships. Second Samuel 18:15 presents a *group* of servants connected to a particular warrior (compare Neh 4:16).

An armor-bearer performed a variety of functions and should thus be distinguished from a "shield-bearer" (nose' tsinnah), who is portrayed as an expendable assistant (1 Sam 17:7, 41). An armor-bearer could serve as a bodyguard for his master (1 Sam 31:4-6) or as a personal companion for the master on dangerous missions (Judg 9:54; 1 Sam 14:1-17). More frequently, the armor-bearer finishe off enemies that his master had incapacitated. Armor-bearers killed their own masters to spare them disgrace in hopeless situations or when the master was mortally wounded (Judg 9:54; 1 Sam 31:4-6). *See* CAPTAIN; SHIELD-BEARER.

Bibliography: Donald G. Schley. "The shalishim Officers or Special Three-Man Squads?" *VT* 40 (1990) 321–26.

BRAD E. KELLE

ARMORY [אוֹצָר 'otsar, בֵּית הַכְּלִי beth hakkeli, נֶשֶׁק nesheq]. An armory becomes necessary in times of urbanization and growing political and military complexity as the space for the storage and distribution of weapons in times of war or internal crisis (2 Kgs 20:13; Neh 3:19; Isa 39:2; Jer 50:25). Its prerequisites are a source of arms, possibly an arms industry with uniformity in manufacture and style, political and administrative organization, and control over and communication with fortresses and outposts. These conditions applied in the late monarchy, and much of the evidence pertains to this period.

Little attention has been directed to the identification of armories in excavated fortresses in the eastern Mediterranean, but literary evidence persists in Jer 50:25; 2 Kgs 10:2; 20:17; 1 Chr 12:2; Ps 78:9. Samuel warned of the establishment of such centers, and the impressment of sons and daughters to work in them (1 Sam 8:12-13). Rehoboam distributed weapons into armories throughout Benjamin and Judah (2 Chr 11:5-12). *See* ARMOR, FORTRESS; WAR, METHODS, TACTICS, WEAPONS OF.

T. R. HOBBS

ARMS. *See* WAR, METHODS, TACTICS, WEAPONS OF, BRONZE AGE THROUGH PERSIAN PERIOD; WAR, METHODS, TACTICS, WEAPONS OF, HELLENISTIC THROUGH ROMAN PERIODS.

ARMY [צָבָא tsava'; στράτευμα strateuma]. An organized collection of armed men, recruited for large-scale combat. In the OT the term *army* (tsava') is very common. The Greek equivalent, strateuma, is much less common in the NT, although its presence is certainly presupposed.

A. Historical Issues

The biblical story of Israel presents the development of a tribal society into a kingdom, and then into a form of theocracy. From the perspective of military history, there is little in the story that does not accord with what is known of the military organizations and histories of the nations involved, and occurring at the times suggested.

From an anthropological perspective, the Israelite and Judean armies were transformed from those that practiced "primitive" or "pre-state" warfare, into those that conformed to the standards of organization and control in more complex societies. Military anachronisms are few.

B. Archaeological Evidence

Epigraphic monuments, campaign reports, court documents, and administrative records provide the picture of military establishments, dress, and organization in Egypt, Mesopotamia, and Anatolia. Within Israel and Judah sources are more limited. Ostraca from Lachish and Arad, remains of fortresses and weapons, and campaign records filtered through the "biblical" perspective, compose the evidence. This data suggests a premonarchical force, and a monarchical army, designed mainly for defense. Early in the monarchy garrison outposts were established surrounding the territory of Israel and Judah.

It is difficult to identify the distinctive characteristics of Israelite and Judaean soldiers. Akkadian and Egyptian sources offer only rough stereotypes of their enemies in the Levant, with few distinguishing features. In contrast to the details of Sea Peoples in Egyptian sources, "Canaanites" are one-dimensional.

C. Militarization

The transition from "tribal" society to a monarchy, at the end of the Late Bronze Age and the beginning of the Iron Age, precipitated the formation of an organized, standing army. Already by the end of David's reign, a minimal general staff was established, including skilled and competent non-Israelites, and a variety of specialist, possibly mercenary, regiments within the army (2 Sam 8:15-18). Such armies are a burden on society, consuming most of the host society's resources. Access to metals, wood, leather, personnel, food, and a trained staff become priorities. Unable to produce sufficient surplus to meet these needs, the institution must reach beyond its borders. At first Israel exercised control over territory acquired from weaker neighbors (2 Sam 8:13-14). This imperial expansion was limited and eventually reversed. Support for these new political realities is executed through the process of militarization, in which the host society regards the military element as essential to its security and prosperity.

This pattern enabled an army to survive with varying degrees of success throughout the monarchy. As a colony of Persia, then Greece and Rome, the "protection" afforded by the occupying powers obviated the need for an extensive local armed force. An army was revived during the brief period of independence under the Hasmoneans.

D. Organization

In the OT period the army, divided between foot soldiers and horse soldiers, was organized into squads of ten (עֶשֶׂר ʿesher, or five יָד yadh; 2 Kgs 11:7; 25:25), companies of fifty (חֲמִשִׁים khamishim, fifties; 2 Kgs 1:9), battalions of one hundred (מֵאוֹת meʾoth, hundreds; 1 Chr 12:14), regiments of one thousand (אֲלָפִים ʾalafim, thousands; 1 Chr 12:14), and even larger divisions. Regiments with special skills such as archery (1 Chr 5:18), slings (Judg 20:15-16; 2 Kgs 3:25), and sword handling (2 Sam 24:9; 2 Kgs 3:26) were raised. The majority of line troops carried spears and shields. Engineers and sappers (2 Kgs 24:16), and a limited administration were necessary (2 Kgs 25:19).

Cavalry organization is unclear, and their infrequent use by the armies of Israel and Judah suggests that they were formed into independent squadrons for scouting. Chariotry was divided into teams, and probably into squadrons. However, chariotry was an expensive form of warfare, ideal for long-term campaigning. Recent work at Megiddo supports the interpretation that the pillared buildings of Area L served as stables for Ahab's chariot city.

In the *War Scroll* (1QM) army organization is done according to tribe and clan. In this ideal formation light and heavy infantry and cavalry are carefully deployed by their tribal leaders. Slingers, swordsmen, javelin throwers, and spearmen all maneuver on the orders of the priests and the regimental leaders. They are encouraged by trumpets and the rich symbolism of the inscribed banners, weapons, and musical instruments. The image is an ideal one but uses known formations and divisions of forces. An inconclusive debate persists over the pattern of organization, Roman or Hasmonean, in the *War Scroll*.

The army was fed and equipped through a "commissary" department and the support of manufacturing centers for weapons, uniforms, and chariots (1 Sam 17:22; 2 Sam 8:10-18; *see also* 1 Chr 12:40).

Recruiting was done in towns and villages, reflecting the age-old belief that country lads make the best soldiers. Some of the elite city-dwellers would be in training for court positions and roles in local governments, and rarely found themselves in the army, except in positions of command. Soldiers in the OT period were recruited from the age of twenty (Num 1:3). In the idealized army of

the *War Scroll*, the soldiers were between forty and fifty years old. Officers were older (1QM VI–VII). This does not reflect Roman custom, which trained men at a much earlier age, in adolescence, and put them into line when they were over the age of twenty. In times of emergency, all of the able-bodied were recruited into the rebel armies (1 Macc 2:39-68; Josephus, *J.W.* 2.358-97).

In the period of the NT (4 BCE until 125 CE), the Roman provinces in Palestine were dominated, first by local militias raised by Temple and palace, and later by Roman legions stationed in and around the region. The army formed for the first Jewish revolt was based on Roman patterns of organization and fighting skills.

E. Weaponry

Types of WEAPONRY used in preindustrial states changed little over a thousand years. No full taxonomy exists for the identification of types of swords, javelins, shields, bows, and other weapons used in the biblical period. Hand weapons, such as javelins, swords, and daggers were for close-order fighting. Spears were propelled by the human arm. Slingshots were fired through the use of centripetal power, and arrows projected by the elasticity of bowstrings.

Over time, simple, one-piece bows gave way to the composite bow with a range of up to 300 m. Bronze was refined to provide a hard-edged blade capable of inflicting severe cuts. Bronze spear points and arrowheads were designed with barbs and complex shafts to inflict a wound impossible to treat. Preferred hand-held weapons were spears, javelins, and, rarely, daggers, that inflicted serious stab wounds. Swords for slashing were symbols of rank. In close-order combat they were unwieldy and awkward to use.

Siege engines were essential for the kind of warfare that developed in urbanized societies. These nerve centers also housed treasuries and the "civil service" of the invaded territory. They provided essential personnel and intellectual resources for the invaders.

Simple engines, such as large wicker canopies under which sappers undermined city walls, are depicted in ancient reliefs. Towers, ramps, and battering rams were all part of the arsenal of siege warfare, and brief mention is made of them in the Bible. Israel and Judea were more often victim and object of siege warfare than they were its practitioners.

Chariots were uncommon in Israel's army, and were probably restricted to means of royal military transport (2 Kgs 9:21), or for short-lived chariot regiments within the late pre-exilic army (2 Kgs 13:7). Use of chariots, and even cavalry, on unsuitable terrain, or in unstable weather conditions could prove disastrous (Josh 11:4-11; Judg 4:12-16).

F. Leadership

The charismatic warrior-leader of the tribal fighters gave way to tacticians of the structured and organized army. Knowledge of one's troops, and the consequent trust between leader and men (1 Kgs 12:16), was eventually replaced by professionalism in soldiers whose rank increased or decreased within a system. The warrior-king, demanded by the tribal elders (1 Sam 8:20), had given way to the substitute commander-in-chief. Piety no longer was a qualification of leadership. The latter ideal, found in the *War Rule*, is a revival of ancient practice.

G. Army as Metaphor

Armies are organizations dedicated to offensive or defensive warfare, and trained in the skills of death. From a theological perspective, it is therefore disturbing to see the people of God metaphorically perceived not only as a vineyard (Isa 5:1-7), a family (Eph 3:15), a flock of sheep (Ps 79:13), and a house (Heb 3:6) but also as an army (Isa 49:1-7). Frequently in the OT Yahweh is addressed as "The LORD of Hosts (Armies)" (יהוה צְבָאוֹת yhwh tseva'oth), and is also confessed as a "Man of War" (אִישׁ מִלְחָמָה 'ish milkhamah [Exod 15:3]), thus betraying the self-understanding of Yahweh's followers as patterned on a military organization. Beyond this, Christians are encouraged to see the marks of suffering, no longer as symbols belonging to Christ, but as badges of honor, and scars from battle (2 Tim 2:3). Soon the slave-follower of Christ has become the "good soldier" (2 Tim 2:3-4; Phil 2:25; Phlm 2), equipped with the appropriate armor in a spiritual war (Eph 6:10-20; Isa 59:15b-19). The *War Scroll* clearly takes for granted the reality of the metaphor.

The theological implications of the use of this metaphor are profound. Metaphors not only express a vision of reality, but foundational, conceptual metaphors help to shape reality. Are these domestic and military metaphors alternative and competing ways of seeing the community? Or are they consistently to be seen as two sides of the reality of the community's life? Identification as a soldier is open to the appropriation of all the dark aspects of life in an army.

Bibliography: D. Dawson. *The First Armies: Cassell's History of Warfare* (2003); Philip J. King and Lawrence E. Stager. *Life in Biblical Israel* (2001).

T. R. HOBBS

ARNA ahr´nuh. Ancestor of the prophet EZRA (2 Esd 1:2). Named as ZERAHIAH in a parallel list (Ezra 7:4).

ARNAN ahr´nuhn [אַרְנָן 'arnan; Ὀρνα Orna]. Arnan appears only in a list of David's descendants (1 Chr 3:21). The Hebrew construction is awkward while the LXX clarifies the reading but alters the genealogy, leaving it unclear whether Arnan is the son of REPHAIAH and the father of OBADIAH or one of the sons of PELATAIAH.

ARNI ahr´ni [Ἀρνί Arni]. Judah's great-great-grandson (Luke 3:33). Manuscript evidence is divided between Arni and Aram or omits Arni. *See* GENEALOGY, CHRIST.

ARNON ahr´nuhn [אַרְנוֹן 'arnon]. A stream with a sizeable gorge in Transjordan, known today as the Wadi al Mujib. It runs northwest, then westward to the middle shore of the Dead Sea. The Arnon marked the northern boundary of central Moab (Num 21:13), and the southern boundary of Israel's early tribal territory through the late 9th cent. BCE (Josh 12:1; 2 Kgs 10:33). Israel reportedly captured the land north of the Arnon when they conquered the Amorite king Sihon (Num 21:24).

King Mesha constructed a road at the Arnon (Moabite Inscription line 26), likely the King's Highway. *See* KING'S HIGHWAY; MOAB, MOABITES; MOABITE STONE.

LISA MICHELE WOLFE

AROD, ARODITE air´od, air´uh-dit [אֲרוֹד 'arodh, אֲרוֹדִי 'arodhi]. 1. Arod, listed as the sixth of GAD's seven sons (Arodi, Gen 46:16).

2. The clan named for Arod according to Num 26:17.

ARODI air´uh-di [אֲרוֹדִי 'arodhi]. Listed as the sixth of seven sons of GAD who accompanied JACOB to Egypt (Gen 46:16; Arod, Num 26:17).

AROER uh-roh´uhr [עֲרֹעֵר 'aro'er; Ἀρονρ Aroēr]. A place name meaning "crest of a mountain" or "juniper."

1. Aroer on the ARNON, a fortress or a settlement on the northern slope of the Wadi el-Mujib. The biblical river Arnon formed the northern border of Moab. The fortress, on the edge of a canyon (Deut 2:36; 4:48; Josh 12:2; 13:16), gave it a strategic location. Aroer was included in the conquest of the TRANSJORDAN area (Deut 2:36; Josh 13:9). It was settled by Gad though it was assigned to Reuben (Num 32:34; Josh 13:16), and it was the beginning point for David's census in Transjordan (2 Sam 24:5). Aroer was the southern border of the Syrian king Hazael (2 Kgs 10:33).

2. Aroer in the Transjordan, modern Amman (Josh 13:25; Judg 11:33), was on the border between Gad and Ammon.

3. Aroer in the Negev, west of the Jordan (1 Sam 30:28). David gave loot to the elders of Aroer, after he recovered his wives from the Amalekites. Hotham the Aroerite was the father of two of David's mighty men (1 Chr 11:44). In the LXX the Negev place name appears in Josh 15:22. The location of Aroer in the Davidic period remains unknown but might be Tell Esdar.

4. In the OT, Aroer refers to cities of Aroer located near Damascus (Isa 17:2a). The LXX text omits this

reference to Aroer, and modern English translations follow this omission.

DANIEL HAWK

AROM air´uhm [Ἀρόμ Arom]. A family head whose unspecified number of descendants relocated themselves to Jerusalem and Judea after the exile had ended (1 Esd 5:16).

AROMA. See ODOR.

ARPACHSHAD ahr-pak´shad [אַרְפַּכְשַׁד ʾarpakhshadh; Ἀρφαξάδ Arphaxad]. Shem's third son; a grandson of Noah, born two years after the flood (Gen 10:22; 11:10). He appears as ARPHAXAD in the LXX and the Lukan genealogy of Jesus that goes from Joseph back to Adam (Luke 3:36). The meaning of this name is disputed, though it is likely not Semitic. See JUDITH; SHEM.

LISA MICHELE WOLFE

ARPAD ahr´pad [אַרְפָּד ʾarpadh]. One of the great cities of Syria (along with HAMATH, with which it is always linked; DAMASCUS; and CARCHEMISH) (2 Kgs 18:34, 19:1; Isa 10:9, 36:9, 37:13; Jer 49:23). Arpad fell prey to the Assyrian conquests of the 9th and 8th cent. BCE and was conquered by TIGLATH-PILESAR III in 740 BCE. It is identified with modern Tell Rifaat.

SUSAN ACKERMAN

ARPHAXAD ahr-fak´sad [Ἀρφαξάδ Arphaxad]. Noah's grandson and one of Jesus' ancestors in Luke's genealogy (3:23-38). King of Media whom King Nebuchadnezzar defeated and killed (Jdt 1:1-15). See ARPACHSAD.

ARRAY, BATTLE [עָרַךְ ʿarakh]. The organization of opposing armies on the battlefield (Judg 20:30; 2 Sam 10:8-17; Jer 50:9). Diverse forces, composed of infantry, archers, slingers, and minimal cavalry and chariotry, needed to be deployed to the best advantage of their capabilities. Distance weapons, such as slings and bows, were usually placed on the flanks. Shock troops, using swords, thrusting javelins, and clubs were massed in the center. Numbers of troops mattered, and the goal was to break the enemy's line by force. Control of the forces was virtually impossible. See BATTLE; WAR, METHODS, TACTICS, WEAPONS OF.

T. R. HOBBS

ARRAY, HOLY [הַדְרַת קֹדֶשׁ hadhrath qodhesh]. Literally "splendor of holiness," this ambiguous phrase appears in 1 Chr 16:29; 2 Chr 20:21; Pss 29:2; 96:9. It refers either to the condition (i.e., attire) in which one should approach the deity in worship or to the actual theophanic appearance of the deity. The latter interpretation rests largely upon a possible parallel in the Ugaritic Kitra Legend where hdrt (a potentially corrupt hapax legomenon) stands in parallel construction with "dream."

DEREK E. WITTMAN

ARROW. See BOW AND ARROW.

ARSACES ahr´suh-seez [Ἀρσάκης Arsakēs]. The Arsacids were an Iranian royal dynasty that dominated Parthia for almost five centuries from ca. 250 BCE–224 CE. The sixth Arsacid (= Mithradates I; r. 179–139/8 BCE) defeated the Seleucid Demetrius II and imprisoned him (1 Macc 14:1-3). According to Josephus, Mithradates later released Demetrius when Antiochus VII invaded Parthia (Ant. 13.253) in an attempt to forestall the invasion by destabilizing Syria. Mithradates I also figures as one of the recipients of the letter sent by the Roman consul Lucius proclaiming the Roman alliance with Simon Maccabeus (1 Macc 14:2; 15:22). See DEMETRIUS.

J. R. C. COUSLAND

ARSINOE ahr-sin´oh-ee [Ἀρσινόη Arsinoē]. Sister and consort of PTOLEMY IV PHILOPATOR, king of Egypt. She marched with Philopator and his army to meet the Seleucid king Antiochus III in battle at RAPHIA (217 BCE). When the battle began to turn in favor of Antiochus, Arsinoe went among Philopater's troops with her hair disheveled and with weeping and wailing. She prevailed on them to protect their wives and children and promised to give them two minas of gold if they were victorious. Philopator's army rallied to defeat Antiochus (3 Macc 1:1-4).

MARIANNE BLICKENSTAFF

ARSINOUS. Post-apostolic author whose writings were rejected from the Muratorian Canon because he was not an apostle. See MURATORIAN CANON.

ARTAPANUS [Ἀρτάπανος Artapanos]. Hellenistic Jewish writer whose treatment of the Jews was summarized by Alexander Polyhistor in the mid-1st cent. BCE. Polyhistor's On the Jews was in turn used independently by Clement of Alexandria in his Stromateis and Eusebius in his Preparation for the Gospel. Given this process of transmission, none of the three preserved fragments is a verbatim quotation of Artapanus, though they are generally agreed to be a reliable reflection of his ideas.

Artapanus wrote his On the Jews (Judaica) in Egypt during the 3rd or 2nd cent. BCE (ca. 250–100 BCE). The work, which combines elements of popular fiction, propagandistic national history, and apologetics, presents biblical characters as cultural benefactors and thus refutes the pagan slur that Jews had made no significant contributions to human civilization. Abraham (frg. 1) teaches astrology to the Egyptian king; Joseph (frg. 2) benefits the Egyptians through agricultural reforms and by discovering measurements; and Moses (frg. 3) invents boats, devices for construction, implements for drawing water, military weapons, and philosophy. Highly syncretistic in method and strategically euhemeristic in perspective, Artapanus equates Moses with the Greek mythical singer Musaeus, identifies him as the teacher of Orpheus, and says that the Egyptian priests deemed him worthy of divine honor, hailing him as Hermes because of his skill in interpretation (hermēneia). This glorification of Moses, who is presented as startlingly supportive of Egyptian religion and its animal cults, is combined with a concern to defend him against all defamatory charges. Thus, instead of having Moses murder an Egyptian for beating a Hebrew (Exod 2:11-14), Artapanus depicts him as acting in self-defense against a would-be assassin.

Bibliography: J. J. Collins. "Artapanus." *OTP* 2:889–903; C. R. Holladay, ed. *Fragments from Hellenistic Jewish Authors.* Vol. 1: *Historians* (1983) 189–243.

JOHN T. FITZGERALD

ARTAXERXES ahr′tuh-zuhrk′seez [אַרְתַּחְשַׁשְׁתְּא ʾartakhshasteʾ, אַרְתַּחְשַׁסְתְּא ʾartakhshasoteʾ]. The name of three Persian kings. 1. Artaxerxes I Longimanus (465–424 BCE), son of XERXES I. Bishlam, Mithredath, Tabeel, and the rest of their associates sent a letter to Artaxerxes (Ezra 4:7). Ezra 4:8-23 contains a communication in Aramaic from Rehum and Shimshai, Persian officials who identify Jerusalem as a rebellious city and report about the Jewish rebuilding of Jerusalem, resulting in Artaxerxes ordering a halt in the building activities (Ezra 4:21). The Jews finished building the Temple according to the decree of CYRUS, DARIUS, and Artaxerxes (Ezra 6:14). While this last reference is a notorious crux—for chronological reasons since the Temple was dedicated in 516—all of these references are presumably to Artaxerxes I.

It is generally agreed that Nehemiah came to Jerusalem in the 20th year of Artaxerxes I (445 BCE; Neh 2:1). Much more disputed is the date of Ezra's arrival. Ezra came to Jerusalem in the 7th year of an Artaxerxes (Ezra 7:8). If under Artaxerxes I, Ezra came in 458; if under Artaxerxes II, Ezra arrived in 398. The principal argument in favor of Artaxerxes coming to Jerusaleum in 458 is the order suggested by the books of Ezra and Nehemiah.

2. Artaxerxes II Memnon (404–358 BCE). Those who favor a date for Ezra under Artaxerxes II note the mention of a wall (Ezra 9:9), possibly referring to the wall repaired by Nehemiah, and the fact that the high priest in the time of Nehemiah was Eliashib while in the time of Ezra the high priest was Johanan son of Eliashib (Ezra 10:6). None of the arguments is decisive. In any case, Ezra and Nehemiah came to Jerusalem according to the biblical account under the auspices of an Artaxerxes.

If the books of Chronicles were written in the 4th cent., Artaxerxes II would likely have been the contemporary Persian king, but there is no mention of him. Born as Arsaces, the eldest son of Darius II reigned longer than any other Persian king. He faced the revolt of his brother Cyrus the younger. Artaxerxes II reconquered Egypt, which had revolted against Persia in 405.

3. Artaxerxes III Ochus (358–38 BCE). Under Artaxerxes III, Tennes, king of Sidon, revolted ca. 349, but the effect of this revolt on Israel cannot be measured.

The name Artaxerxes may have been claimed by Arses (338–36 BCE), son of Artaxerxes III, and Bessos, who claimed the throne after Alexander's defeat of Persia. *See* EZRA AND NEHEMIAH, BOOK OF; PERSIA, HISTORY AND RELIGION OF.

Bibliography: Pierre Briant. *From Cyrus to Alexander: A History of the Persian Empire I* (2002); Lester L. Grabbe. *Judaism from Cyrus to Hadrian.* Vol. 1: *The Persian and Greek Periods* (1992).

RALPH W. KLEIN

ARTEMAS ahr′tuh-muhs [Ἀρτεμᾶς *Artemas*]. Paul planned to send Artemas, who was a messenger, to signal TITUS to meet him at Nicopolis during the coming winter (Titus 3:12).

ARTEMIDORUS (of EPHESUS). Artemidorus' *Oneirocritica* (mid-2nd cent. CE) is the only surviving "dreambook" from Western antiquity. Written as an apology for the practice of divination generally, Artemidorus' systematic treatment of dream symbols provides insights into Greek culture of the time and established the basis for subsequent dream interpretation in Western practice.

Bibliography: Artemidorus, *Oneirocritica* R. Pack, ed. (1963); R. J. White, trans. *Artemidorus: The Interpretation of Dreams* (1975); L. H. Martin. "Artemidorus: Dream Theory in Late Antiquity." *The Second Century* 8 (1991) 97–108.

LUTHER H. MARTIN

ARTEMIS ahr′tuh-mis [Ἄρτεμις *Artemis*]. In Greek mythology Artemis was the daughter of Zeus and Leto and sister of Apollo (*Theog.* 918-20). Her association with nature, hunting, and sacrifice all suggest, however, that this type of goddess, called by various names in the ancient Mediterranean world, predates the rise of Greek civilization. In her classical form, Artemis was a virgin huntress, the "mistress of the animals" (πότνια θηρῶν *potnia thērōn*) and goddess "of the wild" (ἀγροτέρη *agroterē*) who roamed the mountains and forests with a band of dancing nymphs (*Il.* 21.470-71; *Hymn* 5.16-20; 27.1-22), attesting to her close association with the natural world.

The Greeks developed this connection with nature in divergent ways. At times they emphasized her benevolence as the guardian of animals (*Ag.* 140-43) and children (*Hipp.* 161; *Iph. taur.* 1097). Yet stories surrounding her savage and vengeful behavior were more common. She was the slayer of both animals and humans (*Il.* 21.482-86; *Od.* 15.403-11, 477-79), with the daughters of Niobe, Iphigeneia, and Actaeon being some of her more famous victims (*Il.* 24.602-9; *Ag.* 104-247; *Bach.* 337-40). The cultic rites for Artemis at Brauron likely preserve echoes of human sacrifice, additional testimony of the darker aspects of her nature.

Artemis was especially popular in Asia Minor, which Luke corroborates in his story of the "riot in Ephesus" (Acts 19:23-40). Archaeology has determined that the Ephesians worshiped the "great" Artemis as a fertility goddess rather than as a chaste huntress. *See* DIANA; GREEK RELIGION.

DAVID M. REIS

ARTISAN. *See* CRAFTS.

ARTS. The arts have been instrumental in disseminating the stories and lessons of the Hebrew and Christian scriptures, and also function as media through which scripture is interpreted. Artistic representations of scripture provide windows into how scripture was interpreted by groups of people throughout history.

A. Early Jewish Art
B. Early Christian Art
C. Byzantine Art
D. Romanesque and Gothic Art
E. Italian Renaissance Art
F. High Renaissance
G. Late Renaissance and Mannerism
H. Baroque
I. Nineteenth Century
J. Twentieth Century
Bibliography

A. Early Jewish Art

The Near East in the 3rd cent. CE was a melting pot of faiths, including Judaism, Christianity, Mithraism (*see* MITHRAS, MITHRAISM), MANICHAEISM, GNOSTICISM, and many more. Although they competed, they also influenced one another artistically. The blended style became known as Greco-Oriental. This style can be seen in the Mesopotamian settlement of Dura-Europos (*see* DURA) on the upper Euphrates River in Syria. This was a Roman frontier station that was captured by the Persians under Shapur I around 256 CE and abandoned soon afterwards. Subsequently, it was used as a sanctuary by several religions including Mithraism, Judaism, and Christianity. The murals preserved on the walls of the assembly hall in the house-synagogue depicted scenes from Jewish history. One narrative tells the story of the early life of Moses from Exod 1:8–2:10. The painting

Figure 1: *Finding of the Baby Moses*, from the house-synagogue at Dura-Europos, Syria. 245–56 CE. National Museum, Damascus, Syria.

shows the events of the story unfolding in a continuous narrative that like Hebrew, is read from right to left. In the first scene, Moses' mother sets him afloat in the Nile River in a basket made of reeds to prevent his death when Pharaoh decrees that all Jewish male infants be killed. In the center we see Pharaoh's daughter, who goes to the river to bathe, rescuing Moses from the water. In the final scene she hands the baby to a maidservant (Moses' real mother). The composition blends Roman narrative with the frontal poses, strong outlines and flat colors that are found in Near Eastern Art. Although synagogues did not contain representational sculpture because Jewish law forbade praying to images or idols, paintings and mosaics often decorated the walls and floors.

After the split of the Roman Empire in 395, most Jews lived outside Palestine, in communities in the Middle East, North Africa, and Europe. Their lifestyle and practices set them apart from mainstream communities and the history of Jewish art is fragmented because many homes and synagogues were attacked and burned.

B. Early Christian Art

By the late Middle Ages, the Christian Church was the greatest patron of Western art, but the Christian art produced prior to that shows its modest beginnings. The Roman persecution of Christians created a secretive environment for early Christians until Constantine granted full religious freedom to Christians throughout the Roman Empire in 313.

Christians, like Jews, often met in private homes for worship. Often private patrons also owned cemeteries and funeral basilicas where they allowed the congregations to hold worship, commemorative meals, and funeral rituals. Catacombs were excavated below ground for burial. The first Early Christian art was painted and sculpted for use within these subterranean burial galleries outside Rome. The catacombs consist of narrow passages and small burial chambers lined with rectangular burial spaces. The burial niches were filled with stone sarcophagi and sealed with tile or stone slabs.

The walls and ceiling were painted with stories and symbols of Early Christian culture. The first symbols were simple—a fish, a dove, an anchor, a vine, a lamb, and the sign of the Cross. Each of these was taken from the Bible. The anchor, for example, represented the Christian promise of Salvation: "Which hope we have as an anchor of the soul, both sure and steadfast" (Heb 6:19). The vine comes from John 15:1, "I am the true vine" and is an important part of the Jonah stories so often depicted in the catacombs.

The two most popular visual narratives in the catacombs were the Scenes of Jonah and Christ as the Good Shepherd. The Good Shepherd, Orants and Story of Jonah were painted on a ceiling in the largest of the surviving catacombs dedicated to Saints Peter and Marcellinus. Jonah and the Whale (Jonah 1–2) proved a popular subject to make the association between Jonah's rebirth after three days and the resurrection of Christ after the same period of time. The early Christian artists, as those of other religions, were hesitant of portraying God in human form so as not to be guilty of idolatry. The cross was initially not the desired symbol it now is in 21st cent. culture. Crucifixion was one of the most humiliating forms of execution and was usually reserved for slaves and non-Romans.

Scala/Art Resource, NY

Figure 2: *Christ as a Good Shepherd*. First half of 4th cent. from the Museo Pio Cristiano, Vatican Museums, Vatican State.

The sculpture in Figure 2 is based on the god HERMES, protector of flocks, who carried a ram on his shoulders. The artist makes a significant change from the classical sculptures of this deity by portraying the Christ figure in a natural way as a youthful shepherd rather than an idealized god. References to Christ as the Good Shepherd and to sheep using themes of sacrifice and salvation can be found throughout the NT. Jesus uses the shepherd imagery in his teachings to convey God's love and understanding in Luke 15:5 (parable of the lost sheep being brought back into the fold by Christ) and Matt 18:12-14. John the Baptist describes Jesus as the "the lamb of God, who takes away the sins of the world" (John 1:29). Psalm 23 envisions God as an all-providing Shepherd. The Good Shepherd is depicted not only in freestanding sculpture and catacomb wall frescoes but also in sarcophagus relief sculpture.

Figure 3: Sarcophagus of Junius Bassus. Museum of the Treasury, St. Peter's Basilica, Vatican State.

The Junius Bassus sarcophagus is considered the finest example of extant early Christian sarcophagi. It was made for a Roman prefect who died in 359 CE. The front is divided into ten panels with stories from the OT and NT. In the upper row, are the Sacrifice of Isaac, St. Peter Taken Prisoner, Christ Enthroned between Sts. Peter and Paul, and Christ before Pontius Pilate (two areas). In the lower row are the Misery of Job, the Temptation of Adam and Eve, Christ's Entry into Jerusalem, Daniel in the Lions' Den, and St. Paul Led to His Martyrdom. The Early Christian way of thinking, which stressed the divine Christ rather than the human Christ, is evident in the narratives selected for sculpting in these panels. His suffering and death are barely hinted at in these narratives.

The central sections are devoted to the life of Jesus, and their placement has iconographic significance. Christ is enthroned giving the Law to Sts. Peter and Paul. Below them is Christ's Entry into Jerusalem. Adam and Eve are to the left of the Entry and signify the original sin and guilt redeemed by Christ's death on Earth. The upper left panel showing the Sacrifice of Isaac is an OT prefiguration of Christ's sacrificial death and resurrection. The style of the Junius Bassus sarcophagus is a blending of the classicism of Greek and Roman sculptures seen in deep niches and the Constantinian style found in his arch of the puppet-like figures with oversized heads.

C. Byzantine Art

During the 5th and 6th cent., Italy was invaded by the Visogoths, Vandals, and Ostrogoths. It fell to the Ostrogoths in 476. Rome was sacked twice. Mean-

Figure 4: Emperor Justinian I, Bishop Maximianus, and attendants. Mosaic from the north wall of the apse. San Vitale, Ravenna, Italy.

Vanni/Art Resource, NY

Figure 5: West tympanum with Last Judgment. Gislebertus, first half 12th CE. Cathedral St. Lazare, Autun, France.

while, the eastern Empire and its capital of Constantinople were flourishing. Byzantine power, wealth, and artistic patronage were at a height during the rule of Justinian I (ruled 527–565). In addition to expanding the Byzantine Empire, Justinian reconquered Italy and Sicily from the Ostrogoths and established Ravenna as the administrative center of Byzantine Italy. Justinian initiated or brought to completion major building campaigns, Hagia Sophia in Constantinople and San Vitale in Ravenna, respectively.

San Vitale was dedicated in 547 to the 4th cent. Italian martyr, Saint Vitalis. It is very possible that Justinian and his empress Theodora may never have set foot in San Vitale, but two large mosaic panels place them in a procession down the central aisle in a Eucharistic gift procession. Their position in this location reaffirms their authority in political and religious contexts. Justinian holds the bread that will be transubstantiated into the body of Christ during the Mass. On his left is the archbishop of San Vitale, Maximianus. The mosaic, probably done by an imperial workshop, shows the new style of the day. Figures are tall and flat, with small feet and almond eyes. The mosaic *tesserae*, or cut pieces of colored glass, are richly painted in blue and gold. The figures are held together by a black outline. The *chi* and *rho* (the first two letters of Christ in Greek) are clearly seen on the shield of the soldier in the left side

of the painting. This refers back to Constantine's vision at the Milvian bridge outside Rome of angels who told him that he would conquer by this sign (*chi rho*).

D. Romanesque and Gothic Art

The most popular sculptural scenes of the Romanesque period (1050–1200) were the Last Judgment, OT prophets, and the mission of the Apostles. The pilgrimage churches flourished as worshippers visited. One of the first sculptors whose name comes down to us, Giselbertus, sculpted a *Last Judgment* scene on the west tympanum of Autun Cathedral in France. Christ is shown in a *mandorla* or almond shape. The figures surrounding him are about to be judged by having their souls weighed. Angels stand ready, as do demons, to take the soul to the measured location. This is an especially terrifying scene to the tired and forlorn pilgrim who encounters it as his/her first image in the church.

The greatest Romanesque painting was produced in the scriptoria of northern France, Belgium, and southern England. Medieval manuscripts by the end of this period had regained an appreciation for achievements in antiquity.

The Gothic period is best known for its church architecture and sculpture. The invention of flying buttresses, visible here in Notre Dame, Paris allowed for

Vanni/Art Resource, NY

Figure 6: Notre-Dame. Rear view, from the river. Paris, France.

greater height and greater light in these churches built by the inhabitants of the Medieval cities. Walls of stained glass depicted biblical and extra-biblical narratives in rich colors in this period.

E. Italian Renaissance Art

Although artists still belonged to the guild system at the beginning of the Renaissance, their identities are known and artistic styles recognizable. Major accomplishments occurred in sculpture, painting and architecture. Luca della Robbia (ca. 1400–1482), was given his "big break" in 1431 when he received the commission from the Opera del Duomo (a committee that included artists and theologians) to carve the *Cantoria* or choir

Scala/Art Resource, NY

Figure 7: Cantoria. Marble. Luca Della Robbia, Museo dell' Opera del Duomo, Florence, Italy.

gallery for the cathedral of Florence, S. Maria del Fiore. The gallery was to be placed over the door of the left (North) sacristy in the cathedral or Duomo. After a political crisis and a ban on expenditures from 1428 to 1431, construction on the Florentine cathedral finally resumed with this commission. The historical documents described Luca's *Cantoria* as an organ loft but, given the small choirs and portable organs of the period, it does not exclude singers and possibly other instrumentalists as well from using it. Luca carved a

visual narrative of the verses of Ps 150 in high relief sculpture. This Psalm describes ways to praise God. Luca's composition was a series of four reliefs on each side and one at each end. The individual units depict children dancing and playing various instruments and are divided by pairs of flattened pilasters. The gallery itself is a rectangular shape that resembles a Roman sarcophagus and is supported on acanthus consoles. The entire psalm was incised above and below the figural panels. The frolicking and musical children praise the Lord "with the sound of the trumpet . . . with the psaltery and harp . . . with the timbrel and dance . . .with stringed instruments and organs . . . upon the high sounding cymbals." The children are grouped and posed each in a beautifully balanced and arranged composition. Each panel has its own scene and the ever-popular singing boys. These boys are so realistically portrayed that some are identified as treble and some bass.

Donatello, on the other hand, portrays an actual *Cantoria* he sculpted younger, smaller, energetic boys

Scala/Art Resource, NY

Figure 8: Dancing Putti. Detail from the Cantoria. Donatello, Museo dell'Opera del Duomo, Florence, Italy.

who are more often referred to as *putti* than children. Donatello (ca. 1386–1466), the more famous Florentine sculptor, was in Rome at the time that Luca received the commission. The story goes that Donatello's contract read, "If yours (Donatello's) is as good as della Robbia's then we'll pay you this much . . . if it is better then we'll pay you more." Donatello's *Cantoria* was to be placed over the door of the right (South) sacristy and directly opposite Luca's. Having recently returned from Rome filled with ideas from ancient art, Donatello's *Cantoria* is a composition based in classical art but with new twists and unconventional combinations. Donatello used a type of very sophisticated illusion in his *Cantoria*. He carved the *putti* on two long slabs of marble. They were performing two continuous dances in a circle. All of the *putti* were behind a series of free-standing paired colonnettes that also created more depth to the entire structure. He knew that his *cantoria* would be seen in competition with

Scala/Art Resource, NY

Figure 9: Original Sin and Expulsion from the Garden of Eden. Michelangelo. Sistine Chapel, Vatican Palace, Vatican State.

Luca's, and Donatello wanted to show his excellence at perspective in a relief sculpture context.

Both of the *cantoria* were removed when the musical requirements for a grand-ducal wedding in the 17th cent. rendered them obsolete. The Florentine architect, humanist and writer, Leone Battista Alberti, praised Luca della Robbia alongside far better known artists Brunelleschi, Ghiberti, Donatello, and Masaccio in an introductory note to *Della pittura (On Painting)*. *Della pittura*, written in Latin in 1435 and quickly translated into the vernacular Italian in 1436, was both an instructional manual and a theoretical treatise intended, in part, to educate Florentine artists about the intellectual side of their profession. Alberti later criticized Donatello's *Cantoria* saying that the figures danced and twisted too much.

F. High Renaissance

Michelangelo, who preferred to sculpt rather than to paint, could not decline Pope Julius II della Rovere's "request" to continue the decoration of his private place of worship, the Sistine Chapel. The walls of the chapel, built in the 1480s by Julius' uncle, Pope Sixtus IV, had been adorned with scenes of "the world during

Law," specifically from the lives of the lawgivers Moses and Jesus. Michelangelo painted the ceiling with Genesis-based scenes from the world before Law. An image of the world after Law would complete the theological program when he returned (1534–41) to paint the *Last Judgment* on the altar wall.

The ceiling's nine bays are divided into three triads of images: the creation of the world (Gen 1), the stories of Adam and Eve (Gen 2–3), and the Noah stories (Gen 6–9). *Original Sin and Expulsion from the Garden of Eden* illustrates well the artist's surprising use of landscape in the Adam and Eve images. This is not the green, flowery conception that most of us have of Paradise: here sin is born in a rocky landscape filled with boulders and a twisted tree stump. The left side of the composition shows the moment of temptation as the serpent, wrapped around the thick trunk of the tree of knowledge, passes its fruit to Eve. Adam holds the limb back to allow the pass to be easier. The right side of the image shows the effect of sin: the land is terribly vacant and barren behind the sinful couple and the anguish visible in their faces heightens the drama of their expulsion.

G. Late Renaissance and Mannerism

Michelangelo was called upon a second time to decorate the Sistine chapel. This time he was to paint a fresco of the *Last Judgment* on the entire altar wall. The evaluation of souls is one of the least comfortable scenes for artists to paint and for Christians to reflect upon. The depiction recalls Matt 24:30-31. Michelangelo combines Heaven, Hell, Death and Last Judgment.

According to a contemporary letter written in 1534, Michelangelo was first approached by Pope Clement VII de Medici (1523–34) to replace the current altar fresco in the Sistine Chapel (Perugino's *Assumption of the Virgin*) with a Resurrection scene. This probably referred to a Resurrection of the souls or Last Judgment scene. Clement died later that year and his successor, Pope Paul III Farnese (1534–49),

Scala/Art Resource, NY

Figure 10: The Last Judgment. Michelangelo. Sistine Chapel, Vatican Palace, Vatican State.

took over the project. By that point it is very clear that Michelangelo was to do what would become one of the most famous scenes of the final judging of souls for their eternal placement in heaven or hell. The new altar wall for the Pope's private chapel not only replaced the fresco behind the altar but also the rectangular fresco scenes on either side of the fresco immediately above the altar. Michelangelo's composition takes over almost the entire west wall of the chapel, and most of his figures are over life-size. Traditionally, the Last Judgment was placed on the entrance wall of ecclesiastical buildings.

Michelangelo was influenced by several major paintings that he visited as a child in Florence. These include the medieval *Last Judgment* mosaic in the Baptistery, Orcagna's frescoes in Santa Croce, and Nardo di Cione's *Hell* in Santa Maria Novella. Michelangelo also studied Giotto's *Last Judgment* in the Scrovegni (Arena) Chapel in Padua. Another influence for Michelangelo was Dante's *Inferno*.

The right side of the detail is Hell. Dante's Charon drives the damned from his boat into Hell with an oar. Nude figures are surrounded by snakes, while others seem to be swallowed up in the murky area below. The nude figures in the lower left are being drawn out of their graves. Some are being brought upwards to receive their judgment by Christ. The angels blow their trumpets in the center of the composition.

The beardless Christ is located in the area of the painting that is best lit by the natural light of the chapel windows. Often considered a "damning Christ," he draws up the souls with his left arm and casts down those consigned to Hell with his right arm. Christ's proportions are of the contemporary Mannerist style. Michelangelo's forms, both in proportion and gesture, are characteristic of the style of the day or *La Maniera*. Mary is positioned on the favored side of Christ. Michelangelo's self-portrait is believed to be located in the flayed skin of St. Bartholomew.

Since the completed cleaning and restoration in the 1990s, the composition has been returned to its glorious color and power. The ultramarine blue was recovered in the sky and on various pieces of drapery throughout the colossal painting. The nude figures have now been returned to their original status; they had been covered by Michelangelo's assistant Daniele da Volterra because of intense scrutiny of Roman Catholic art during the Council of Trent (1545–63). The nudity and the stylistic changes were frequent points of discussion by contemporary Christians in the 16th cent. Pietro Aretino is among the first contemporaries of Michelangelo to criticize the fresco for being a display of skill and not a decorous handling of the holy subject. It is interesting to note, though, that engravings of the fresco were published frequently and in multiple copies as early as the 16th cent., and the well documented inquisition of the artist Paolo Veronese (1528–88) on July 28, 1573, quoted the inquisitor as saying that there was nothing that was not "spiritual" about the nudes of Michelangelo's *Last Judgment*.

The Crucifixion is by far the most popular image of suffering in the Christian world—in both Eastern and Western traditions. In 1569, Giovanni Stradano (1523–1605) painted a *Crucifixion* for the church of SS. Annunziata in Florence, Italy. The Council of Trent was completed in 1563 and the Catholic Reformation was responding to the Protestants' criticism. Giovanni Stradano was a Flemish artist who came to Florence to learn Italian art and culture. He followed the current contemporary style, Mannerism, taught by Giorgio Vasari. The renovation of the church was part of a large city project to modernize the major churches of Florence. The chapels were being decorated with narrative paintings to re-emphasize the Catholic church's commitment to teaching Biblical stories through artistic objects.

Stradano, working on panel, chose to not just depict the more popular painted Crucifixion story from John with Mary and John the Beloved in attendance but rather the story of the Good Thief as told in Luke 23:32. Stradano represented the precise moment Jesus is speaking the words "this day you shall be with me in Paradise." Stadano included iconographic elements of Jesus Christ as the New Adam, the Virgin Mary as the New Eve, the Cross as the tree of life with its Eucharistic significance in the body of Christ and finally, the defeated Satan as the dog in chains. This multi-figured composition incorporated the Mannerist characteristics of elongated proportions and contorted body positions with bright yellow and orange drapery colors Stradano's painting teaches forgiveness to a Catholic people who have just watched their Christianity torn by Protestants. The Church who has reformed is also the subject asking for forgiveness at the most foundational level.

H. Baroque

The Baroque style was a period of religious fervor closely linked to the Counter or Catholic Reformation. The most famous expositor of the Baroque was Caravaggio. Caravaggio was poor and indigent for most of his life. Much of what we know about Caravaggio is from police documents that survive in the archives of Rome and Naples. He lived the life of a wanderer. He struggled with his religiosity and Catholicism as well by working for some of the most pious individuals of the 17th cent.

Caravaggio would take a well-known subject and change it in some substantial way. Traditionally, paintings of the Supper at Emmaus show the moment that a bearded Christ breaks the bread and is recognized by his followers. In his *Supper at Emmaus* Caravaggio, an oil painter working in a Catholic Reformatory

Erich Lessing/Art Resource, NY
Figure 11: Supper at Emmaus, Caravaggio, 1601. National Gallery, London.

Roman culture, has chosen a moment earlier in the narrative—the blessing of the bread—for his painting. The change in the iconographic or symbolic nature of the narrative as it relates to contemporary papal culture in this painting has been discussed at length in art historical scholarship. The relevance of that instant of blessing the bread may also be relevant to a discussion of food and hunger.

The dramatic, tenebrist light intensifies the moment of recognition. Caravaggio's table allows for a position for the viewer. We sit next to the unnamed disciple with a bowl of delicately balanced fruit about to fall into our space. Jesus is seen uncharacteristically clean-shaven so as to disguise him from those at table. Caravaggio included all types of people in his paintings. Most scholars believe that he preferred the company of the more indigent of Rome to that of his wealthy patrons. He was in line with the contemporary teaching of Ignatius of Loyola and St. Philip Neri. In this case, both the artist and the viewer hunger for God's food and blessing. Christ is recognized anew in each Eucharistic celebration as the celebrant blesses/consecrates our bread, only for the worshipper to hunger again for His attention and revelation. Caravaggio's followers included the female artist Artemisia Gentileschi and the Spaniard Jusepe Ribera.

The leading sculptor of the Baroque was Gianlorenzo Bernini. He was a man who loved his family and his Church. He was a devout Catholic and was in service to the Popes most of his life. He was a creative genius and a very opinionated person who sometimes fell out of favor with a Pope. When this occurred other enterprising individuals hired him for private commissions. Cardinal Federico Cornaro, a member of one of the most distinguished families of Venice, commissioned Bernini, while Pope Innocent X and Bernini had a dispute. Cornaro asked Bernini to create a family chapel dedicated to the mystic St. Teresa of Avila in the left transept of the Roman church Santa Maria della Vittoria.

Cardinal Cornaro is believed to have had papal ambitions and was looking to have the chapel draw attention to him, which it definitely did. Cornaro was also sympathetic to the Discalced Carmelites, the order founded by Teresa and affiliated with Santa Maria della Vittoria. Four Spanish saints had been canonized in 1622—Isidore of Seville, Ignatius of Loyola, Francis of Xavier, and Teresa of Avila—and all but Teresa had been honored with churches named after them. Teresa did not yet even have a chapel dedicated to her.

The chapel decoration began as an opportunity for two men in need of recognition to achieve it but remains one of the most loved works of Bernini and the most famous reason to know the Cornaro family name. It is a theatre stage-set complete with a sculpted audience (deceased members of the Cornaro family) seated to the right and left of the central sculpture.

Scenes from the life of St. Teresa are painted to look like gilded bronze reliefs in the vault. The ceiling fresco contains clouds, angels and an image of the Holy Spirit that descends into the chapel. The viewer is invited to kneel at the elegant marble balustrade and ponder the writings of St. Teresa.

This is Italian Baroque art at its best—theater, drama, religious meditation—in one visionary experience. Bernini inserted a window glazed with yellow glass above the figures to cast a golden light upon them. St. Teresa is shown experiencing "transverberation" from an angel who, according to her own description of the vision, plunged an arrow with a flaming tip into her heart and entrails again and again.

Scholars have struggled with the idea that Bernini may have intentionally conveyed a sexual parallel to erotic love in this sculpture. In the 18th cent., one scholar remarked, "If that is divine love, I have known it!" Twenty-first-century art historians have tried to defend both Bernini's and Teresa's honor with comments based on formal elements in the composition. Bernini evidently did not intend a lascivious interpretation as he covered Teresa's body with layers of heavy drapery so that only her face, one limp hand, and her feet can be seen. Her unfocused eyes and open mouth convey her absorption in this miraculous experience.

Bernini, like the Medieval monastics studying the erotic language of the Song of Songs, was not embar-

rassed to sculpt a physical love through a language of yearning, of *eros*, which he found appropriate between God and St. Teresa. Bernini heard Teresa's words and incorporated them into an image from his world and his loves—God, wife, family—to result in a woman overtaken by the love of the Holy Spirit of God. Artists of the Renaissance and Baroque were trained to take their inspiration from life and nature and to depict things realistically. Bernini remained focused on Teresa's teachings and the drama of her mystical experience of God rather than view it with the same clouded eyes as Teresa's confessor and theologian of the Inquisition who, after reading her *Meditations on the Song of Songs,* found it evil and ordered that it be burned.

I. Nineteenth Century

In the 19th cent., religious subjects were no longer a major thematic area for artists or patrons. Individual artists choosing to use biblical narratives as inspiration for their art can now be identified. Edward Hicks, a Quaker in Pennsylvania, painted 62 versions of the *Peaceable Kingdom*

Private Collection. Art Resource, NY

Figure 13: The Peaceable Kingdom, Edward Hicks, ca. 1844–45.

Despite the facts that he was not very well known during his lifetime nor was he trained as an artist by today's standards, depictions of *Peaceable Kingdom* can be found today in classrooms, churches, art studios and art history lecture halls. Hicks' versions of *Peaceable Kingdom* illustrate Isa 11:6-9 with pleasing colors for the eye. The paintings clearly symbolize the theme of the biblical narrative for the faithful. What is most difficult about the now famous paintings is the actual request Hicks makes of his audience—peace.

Most versions of the theme have two scenes within the composition. The Philadelphia painting depicts William Penn (Pennsylvania means "Penn's Woods") in 1682 as he signs a treaty with the Leni-Lenape Indians. William Penn was a founder of American Quakerism also known as the Society of Friends. The foreground

Nimatallah /Art Resource, NY

Figure12: Ecstasy of St. Theresa of Avila, Gian Lorenzo Bernini, 1645. Cornaro Chapel, S. Maria della Vittoria, Rome.

Figure 14: The Gates of Hell, Auguste Rodin, conceived 1880–1917; cast 1928 by the founder Alexis Rudier, Paris. Bequest of Jules E. Mastbaum, 1929. Rodin Museum, Philadelphia, Pennsylvania.

contains domestic and wild animals, as well as a child, all sharing a common space to recall the Isaiah passage. Hicks was part of the American Folk art tradition.

Hicks' training as a craftsman corresponded to his religious lifestyle. After the death of his mother when he was a young boy, a devout Quaker family raised him. He learned the techniques of painting and lettering as an apprentice from age 13 to 20. He attempted farming for a time but at the age of 32 he became a Quaker minister. His spiritual beliefs had roots in 18th cent. quietism. Simplicity and self-discipline were a part of his lifestyle. Hicks traveled and spoke at many meetings and saw the divisions between the more Orthodox Quakers from England and the more liberal-minded Quakers in America.

The *Peaceable Kingdom* series began approximately 8 years into his ministry. His "painted sermons" were intended to teach other Quakers with the same intense religious conviction that he held. In later paintings, the animals represented the different factions in the Quaker unrest. The Isaiah text is in the border of the picture. Hicks worked only in oils and preferred simple, brightly colored figures in an organized placement on a flat picture plane. The innocence of a child whose arm hugs the neck of the lion is a powerful statement of peace.

Auguste Rodin was recognized as an exceptional artist during his lifetime. This recognition was based in part on colossal projects dealing with the theme of heaven and hell. Rodin's *Gates of Hell* places its meaning in a confused and multi-figured composition. At the age of 40, this was Rodin's first major commission. Rodin was a contemporary of the French painters Manet and Monet and like the Impressionist paintings, his bronze sculptures reflect light dramatically. Shapes and contours of the forms and figures are reflected in the polished bronze. The *Gates of Hell* were intended as doors commissioned for the entrance to the École des Arts Dècoratifs in Paris in the tradition of the Renaissance master Lorenzo Ghiberti's bronze doors of the Florentine Baptistery. Rodin sketched numerous preparatory drawings that revealed his experimentation with the various figures, their gestures and arrangement. He did not work directly in bronze and, in fact, never finished the *Gates of Hell*. The *Gates* in bronze are made from plaster casts taken directly from Rodin's clay models. The identity or role of each figure in the composition is not immediately apparent. Instead, viewers must dissect the works and be allowed to recall influences such as Baudelaire as they try to make sense of the piece.

A major movement in the 19th cent. was the pre-Raphaelite Brotherhood. William Morris and Edward Burne-Jones were the leaders of the second phase of the pre-Raphaelite movement in England. Both men learned about the work of the Pre-Raphaelite Brotherhood (PRB) while undergraduate students at Oxford University. Morris and Burne-Jones studied the works and artistic philosophies of the founding members William Holman Hunt, John Everett Millais and Dante Gabriel Rossetti. These artists formed the PRB in September 1848 with the hopes of restoring British art to the Italian style of painting practiced before the age of Raphael (1483–1520). Frustrated with the current teaching that they were receiving at the Royal Academy in London, these artists longed for the simplicity of form, pure local color, and scientific perspective found in mainly Florentine painting of the 15th cent. Their first paintings were inscribed with the secret initials 'PRB' and exhibited in 1849.

In 1856 Morris and Burne-Jones met Rossetti. Although inspired by the first generation of PRB members, Morris and Burne-Jones took the brotherhood in a different direction. Instead of the simple, shadowless forms of the 1840s when the artists were inspired by their study of renaissance engravings, the 1850s became a time of naturalism, brilliant colors painted on a white ground. William Morris used a white background in the *Angel Holding a Sun* by. The watercolor and pencil work was a design for a stained glass window. This decorative style was inspired by the poetry of Rossetti and Morris. The form and content maintained a connection to the medieval world. The regal blue and luminous gold paints Morris used are reminiscent of Byzantine mosaics.

Burne-Jones, the leader of late pre-Raphaelism combined his moral imagination with the narrative art of the Renaissance world. Burne-Jones painted *St. George and the Dragon*, a very popular subject in both 15th cent. Florentine painting and sculpture. Donatello, the early Renaissance sculptor discussed above, is but one artist who used the story to demonstrate a new method of relief sculpture on the base of one of the niches of Orsanmichele in Florence. Like Donatello, Burne-Jones pushed the action to the foreground where George shoves the sword into the dragon's mouth.

J. Twentieth Century

During the 20th cent., science and religion combined in artists' renditions of religious stories. The Spaniard Salvador Dali was a Surrealist painter. In the 1950's after the advent of the nuclear weapon, Dali incorporated his own understanding of the science of the atom into his art. Dali, who was raised Catholic, drew from Christian traditions and combined them with his scientific interests. The resulting amalgamation was "Nuclear Mysticism." Dali used his wife Gala as a model for the Madonna in his painting titled *Assumpta Corpuscularia Lapislazulina* (1952). The painting reflects his fascination with atom splitting. The figure of the Madonna is in the process of disappearing. His painting *Christ of Saint John of the Cross* (1951) appears in the midst of her dissipating body. Dali's *Crucifixion* (1954) drew from the classic theme of Christ's sacrifice, while expressing the subject using the hypercubic octahedron. The body of Christ floats away from the cross, and the nails do not appear to pierce his skin.

Artists throughout the centuries found solace, employment and a plethora of subjects from which to choose in the Bible. Their art taught and inspired the literate and illiterate in ways that can only be hypothesized now. For those interested in the history of biblical interpretation, art provides a non-literary entry into the vast range of biblical interpretations. *See* AESTHETICS; CARVING; CHRISTIAN ART; CRAFTS; DESIGN.

Bibliography: Robert B. Kruschwitz, ed. *Christian Reflection: A Series in Faith and Ethics* (2000–2005); H.W. Janson. *History of Art. The Western Tradition.* Rev. 6th ed. (2004); Marilyn Stokstad. *Art. A Brief History* (2000); David G. Wilkins, ed. *The Collins Big Book of Art from Cave Painting to Pop Art* (2005).

HEIDI J. HORNIK

ARUBBOTH uh-ruhb´oth [אֲרֻבּוֹת ʾaruboth]. Mentioned as the city of BEN-HESED, one of the twelve officers of King Solomon (1 Kgs 4:10), Arubboth lies between SHAALBIM and BETH-SHEMESH on one side and DOR on the other. In Josh 12:17 the king of Hepher is associated with the kings of TAPPUAH, APHEK, and SHARON. Using this evidence, most scholars locate Arubboth and the land of HEPHER in the plain of SHARON. Others locate Arubboth in northern Samaria. Various scholars have connected Arubboth to Arbatta of 1 Macc 5:23, Narbata "60 Stadia from Caesarea" of Josephus (*J.W.* 2.291), and/or Nabrakta, "many towns near Sebaste" of *Megillat Ta'anit* (25 Marheshwan). None of these suggestions is well founded, and the data are too sparse for fixing the exact site of Arubboth.

Bibliography: A. Zertal. *Arubboth, Hepher and the Third Solomonic District* (1984); *The Manasseh Hill Country Survey,* III (2000) 327–32.

YOEL ELITZUR

ARUMAH uh-roo´mah [אֲרוּמָה ʾarumah]. The home of Abimelech, Gideon's son by his Shechemite concubine (Judg 8:31). Arumah was Abimelech's home base while he attempted to retain kingship over Shechem (Judg 9:31, 41). The Hebrew of Judg 9:31 reads בְּתָרְמָה bethormah, which may be a corruption of בֵּת אֲרוּמָה beth ʾarumah, "house of Arumah."

It is in the area of Shechem, southeast of Mount Gerazim, in Samaria's northern central hill country. Khirbet ʿUrmah, a Middle Bronze Age and Iron II excavation site in Ephraim, was probably Arumah. *See* ABIMELECH, SHECHEM.

Bibliography: Israel Finkelstein. *The Archaeology of the Israelite Settlement* (1988).

LISA MICHELE WOLFE

ARVAD ahr´vad [אַרְוַד ʾarwad; Ἀράδιος Aradios]. An island city on the northwestern Mediterranean coast, north of Tyre, which is associated with today's Ruad. In the biblical genealogies, Arvadites are a tribe of Canaan (Gen 10:18; 1 Chr 1:16). Arvadites came to Tyre's aid as rowers and guards when Babylon attacked (Ezek 27:8, 11).

Numerous texts from the 14th to 7th cent. BCE mention Arvad. The Amarna Letters indicate that the ships and warriors of Arvad (Arwada) were an ominous force (*see* 105:12, 16, 18, 87). TIGLATH-PILESER I reports journeying in an Arvadite ship (*ANET,* 275), while SENNACHERIB and ASHURBANIPAL (*ANET,* 287, 294-97) list it in regard to their conquests and coalitions. In 1 Macc 15:23, it is called ARADUS.

LISA MICHELE WOLFE

ARZA ahr´zuh [אַרְצָא ʾartsa]. Administrator of Elah's palace at Tirzah. When Elah became drunk, Zimri murdered Elah and succeeded him as king (1 Kgs 16:8-10).

ARZARETH ahr´zuh-reth. The ten tribes of Israel were allegedly deported to Arzareth, a land far beyond the Euphrates River from which they would return in the last days (2 Esd 13:45-46). No such location is known. The name may represent a Latin corruption of ʾerets ʾaheret ("another land") in Deut 29:17.

ASA ay´suh [אָסָא ʾasa]. 1. Son of Abijam (or Abijah) and grandson of Rehoboam, he was the third king of Judah after the division of the united monarchy (1 Kgs 15:8; 1 Chr 14:1). He reigned over Judah forty-one years (1 Kgs 15:10). Asa has the second longest rule among the kings of Judah; only Manasseh reigned longer (2 Kgs 21:1). His mother was Maacah, the daughter of Abishalom (1 Kgs 15:10). Since Maacah also appears as Abijam's mother (1 Kgs 15:2), it is possible that after Abijam's premature death, Maacah continued in her official position as the "queen mother." It is possible that Asa was young when he became a king and that the affairs of the kingdom were being administered by his grandmother (compare 1 Kgs 15:1, 10).

The DEUTERONOMIC HISTORIAN declares that Asa walked in the ways of the Lord as his father David had done (1 Kgs 15:11). Because of Asa's piety and faithfulness to God, he is credited with promoting extensive religious reforms aimed at removing the idolatrous practices from the Temple of the Lord. He cleansed the Temple by removing the male Temple prostitutes and eliminating all the idols that the previous kings had made. He also removed the "abominable image" Maacah had made for Asherah, the fertility goddess of the Canaanites. The image was cut down and burned in the Kidron Valley. He also removed Maacah from her position as "queen mother" because of her devotion to ASHERAH. However, he did not remove the high places, which were the local shrines where Asherah the goddess was worshiped. Asa brought to the Temple gold and silver vessels and other artifacts that he and his father had dedicated to the service of the Lord (1 Kgs 15:9-15).

Sometime during the reign of Asa, Zerah, the Cushite (or Ethiopian), invaded Judah and engaged Asa's army at Mareshah, an outpost that had been fortified by Rehoboam (1 Chr 11:8). The identity of Zerah is debatable. Some identify him with a Cushite general in the Egyptian army. Others identify him and his army with the nomadic people of Cushan (compare Hab 3:7). Zerah's army numbered one million men and three hundred chariots (2 Chr 14:9). This number may reflect the Chronicler's theological ideology that victory against large enemy armies is the work of the Lord. Confronted with a superior army, Asa prayed to the Lord asking for help. In answer to Asa's prayer, the Lord struck the Cushites, giving Asa total victory against his enemies. Asa's army pursued Zerah and his army and seized the plunder.

Encouraged by the oracle of the prophet Azariah, the son of Oded, Asa began implementing religious reforms. Asa removed all the idols and repaired the altar of the Lord. He then called a solemn assembly for all Judah and Benjamin and included people from Ephraim, Manasseh, and Simeon who had joined him in his fight against the Cushites, and the people bound themselves in a covenant to seek the God of their ancestors.

During his reign there was war between Judah and Israel (2 Kgs 15:16). Baasha, king of Israel, fortified Ramah, about five miles north of Jerusalem, to serve as a border fortress and as an attempt at closing the border between Israel and Judah to prevent anyone from entering or leaving. According to the Chronicler, this happened in the 36th year of Asa's reign (2 Chr 16:1, 11), but Baasha was at that time long dead (1 Kgs 15:33); therefore this 36th year must be calculated either from the separation of the kingdoms of Israel and Judah or amended to the 16th year of Asa.

Although the Chronicler says that Asa fortified several cities in Judah and that he had a large army (2 Chr 14:6-8 [Heb. 14:5-7]), Asa was unable to confront Baasha. Confronted with a threat on his northern border, Asa took whatever remained in the royal treasury and sent a gift to Benhadad I of Damascus, asking for help in his struggle against Israel. Threatened with an invasion by the Arameans, Baasha stopped fortifying Ramah and returned to Tirzah, the capital of his kingdom. Benhadad invaded Israel and conquered Ijon, Dan, Abel-beth-maacah, and the store cities of Naphtali. Baasha was forced to stop fortifying Ramah. Asa imposed forced labor upon the citizens of Judah and used the materials found at Ramah to fortify Geba and Mizpah in Benjamin (1 Kgs 15:22), thus moving Judah's border north and creating a buffer zone in order to protect the nation against future invasions.

Asa was criticized by Hanani, the seer, for relying on the army of the king of Aram, instead of relying on the Lord. Hanani told Asa that had he relied on the Lord, he would have had the king of Aram as his vassal. In addition, as a consequence of his unfaithfulness, his kingdom would be involved in wars (2 Chr 16:9). Asa, instead of repenting from his infidelity, was angry and put Hanani in prison and harshly punished some of the people, probably people who sympathized with the prophet (2 Chr 16:7-10).

The Chronicler reports that in the 39th year of his reign, Asa developed a disease in his feet. The Chronicler appears to represent the disease as a punishment for his treatment of the prophet. Again, instead of seeking help from the Lord, Asa relied on physicians (2 Chr 16:12). In the end, however, Asa is commended for serving the Lord all the days of his life (1 Kgs 15:14).

When Asa died, he was buried in a tomb prepared for him in the city of David. The detail about his burial and the great fire made in his memory is evidence that Asa was held in high regard by the people of Judah. Asa appears in the NT in the genealogical list of Jesus' ancestors (Matt 1:7-8). After his death, Asa was succeeded by his son Jehoshaphat.

2. A Levite, son of Elkanah and father of Berechiah. Berechiah was one of the Levites who lived in the villages of the Netophathites after the people returned from Babylon (1 Chr 9:16).

CLAUDE F. MARIOTTINI

ASAHEL as′uh-hel [עֲשָׂהאֵל ʿasah’el; Ἀσαηλ Asaēl]. 1. Brother of JOAB and ABISHAI, and the youngest son of David's sister ZERUIAH (2 Sam 2:18; 1 Chr 2:16). One of the group of "Thirty" (2 Sam 23:24), he was commander of the fourth division of David's army (1 Chr 27:7). Asahel was a swift runner (2 Sam 2:18), who, after the battle at Gibeon, pursued and overtook ABNER, the commander of ISHBOSHETH's army, to kill him. Abner, unwilling to fight with Asahel, asked him to fight someone else. When Asahel refused, with great reluctance and in order to preserve his own life, Abner killed him with the blunt end of his spear (2 Sam 2:18-23). A few years later at Hebron, JOAB killed Abner to avenge Asahel's death (2 Sam 3:26, 27, 32).

2. One of the Levites whom King JEHOSHAPHAT sent throughout Judah to teach the Law of Moses (2 Chr 17:8).

3. One of the Levites appointed by HEZEKIAH to be in charge of contributions given for the support of the Temple (2 Chr 31:13).

4. The father of JONATHAN, one of the few leaders of the postexilic community who opposed Ezra's policy of requiring the men of Judah to send away their foreign wives (Ezra 10:15; 1 Esd 9:14).

CLAUDE F. MARIOTTINI

ASAIAH uh-zay'yuh עֲשָׂיָה ['asayah]. 1. Son of Haggiah (1 Chr 6:30 [Heb. 6:15]) whom David appointed to move the ark from Obed-edom's house to Jerusalem (1 Chr 15:6, 11).

2. Clan leader in the tribe of Simeon who helped drive Ham's descendants from the pastures of Gedor (1 Chr 4:36).

3. One of King Josiah's officials sent to consult the prophetess Huldah concerning the authenticity of the book of the law found in the Temple (2 Kgs 22:12, 14; 2 Chr 34:20).

4. A descendant of Judah who returned to Jerusalem after the captivity (1 Chr 9:5).

CLAUDE F. MARIOTTINI

ASAIAS uh-zay'yuhs [Ἀσαιας Asaias]. Named in 1 Esd 9:32. *See* ISSHIJAH.

ASAPH ay'saf [אָסָף 'asaf; Ασαφ Asaph]. 1. A Levite son of BERECHIAH from the GERSHOM clan (1 Chr 6:39 [Heb. 6:24]; 15:17). Asaph and his descendants became influential MUSICIANS in the religious life of Israel. He was appointed by David to serve with HEMAN and JEDUTHUN as the chief musicians of the Temple, to minister before the ARK OF THE COVENANT, "to invoke, to thank, and to praise the Lord" (1 Chr 16:4-5), and to prophesy with the aid of musical instruments (1 Chr 25:1).

He probably founded a school of singers and musicians who were called "the sons of Asaph" (1 Chr 25:1, 2; 2 Chr 20:14; 29:13) and played a prominent role in the worship and music of the postexilic community (Ezra 2:41; 3:10; Neh 7:44; 11:22). Twelve psalms (Pss 50, 73–83) carry his name in their titles.

2. The father of JOAH, a *recorder* in the court of HEZEKIAH, king of Judah (2 Kgs 18:18, 37; Isa 36:3, 22), perhaps a kind of secretary of state who carried out royal decrees.

3. NEHEMIAH came before King ARTAXERXES and requested that Asaph, "keeper of the king's forests," provide timber for the rebuilding of the Temple (Neh 2:8).

4. The son of ABIJA (Matt 1:7 NRSV) and the father of JEHOSHAPHAT (Matt 1:8 NRSV). According to biblical tradition, Abija was the father of ASA, and Jehoshaphat was Asa's son (1 Chr 3:10; 1 Kgs 22:41). Perhaps Matthew changed Asa to Asaph for theological reasons or was following a manuscript that had Asaph.

CLAUDE F. MARIOTTINI

ASARAMEL uh-sair'uh-mel [ἀσαραμέλ asaramel]. "Court of the people of God" and title for Simon, "the prince of the people of God" (1 Macc 14:28).

ASAREL as'uh-rel [אֲשַׂרְאֵל 'asar'el]. One of Jehallelel's four sons in Judah's list of descendants (1 Chr 4:16).

ASARELAH as'uh-ree'luh [אֲשַׂרְאֵלָה 'asar'elah]. One of ASAPH's four sons whom DAVID designated to prophesy, using musical instruments such as lyres, harps, and cymbals (1 Chr 25:2).

ASCENSION [עָלָה 'alah; ἀναβαίνω anabainō; ἀναλαμβάνω analambanō; ἁρπάζω harpazō]. *Ascension* (lit. "movement upward") is a widespread and diffuse category in the ancient world that describes temporary heavenly journeys by seers (either in ecstasy or physically), ascents of heavenly beings who have made earthly appearances, assumptions of the soul at death, and raptures, i.e., bodily translations into the "beyond" as the conclusion of one's life, without the intervention of death.

   A. Religious and Historical Background
   B. Old Testament and Early Judaism
   C. New Testament
      1. Ascension, resurrection, and heavenly exaltation of Jesus
      2. Ascension as a visible event
      3. Ascension and metaphorical language
   Bibliography

A. Religious and Historical Background

Especially in the Greco-Roman milieu, a person who ascends to the gods (a hero, an emperor, a famous philosopher) becomes a divine being himself. To say that "Romulus has gone to heaven" is materially identical with the statement that "Romulus has become a god," and vice versa: "Romulus has become a god" implies his previous ascent to the world of the gods. However, in a Jewish-monotheistic context, this strong connection between ascension and deification has always been suspect, since it tended to compromise belief in the uniqueness and superiority of Yahweh over creation: "The heavens are the LORD's heavens, but the earth he has given to human beings" (Ps 115:16). For this reason, the notion of ascent takes on a somewhat different dynamics in Jewish and Christian sources.

B. Old Testament and Early Judaism

The brief and somewhat cryptic statement in Gen 5:24 that "Enoch walked with God; then he was no more, because God took him" has been interpreted as Enoch's physical escape from death and his departure to the heavenly realm (Sir 44:16; 49:14; Heb 11:5). His whereabouts both before and after his translation have been elaborated extensively (e.g., *1 En.* 12:1-2; 81:6; 87:3-4; *Jub.* 4:16-26; 1QapGen[ar] 2-5; *2–3 Enoch*).

Of Elijah, a more elaborate and spectacular report of his physical translation to heaven is given in 2 Kgs 2:1-18. When Elijah and Elisha had crossed the Jordan, Elisha saw how "a chariot of fire and horses of fire separated the two of them, and Elijah ascended in a whirlwind into heaven" (2 Kgs 2:11), a fitting end for a prophet whose career was characterized by fire (e.g., 1 Kgs 18:38; 2 Kgs 1:10, 12).

Convictions that Enoch and Elijah were being kept alive somewhere for a future task evolved into speculations about their (eschatological) return to earth. The first contours of what may be called the rapture-preservation paradigm are already found in Mal 3:23-24. In addition to Enoch and Elijah, such pious figures as Moses, Ezra, Baruch, Phinehas, and Melchizedek were believed to have escaped death and to have been translated to heaven, where they wait for a future reentry at the end of times.

C. New Testament

New Testament examples of ascension include the experience of Paul described in 2 Cor 12:1-10, the rapture of the saints at Christ's Parousia in 1 Thess 4:17, and the ascent of the Two Witnesses in Rev 11:12. The large majority of ascension texts, however, refer to the ascension of Jesus.

1. Ascension, resurrection, and heavenly exaltation of Jesus

In a way, all the NT writers presuppose the ascension of Jesus, that is, they are all convinced that, at the end of his earthly life, Jesus was somehow taken up in God's heavenly presence: he did not remain in the realm of death, but he arose from the grave and was with God in heaven. From the very earliest period of christological confession, it was asserted with the words of Ps 110:1 that Jesus was now "seated at the right hand of God," i.e., in a position of authority in the closest proximity to God.

Jesus' session at the right hand is associated with his resurrection from the dead (e.g., Rom 1:3-4; 8:34; Eph 1:20-21, etc.). Consequently, a number of texts picture the resurrection of Jesus as a victorious ascent through the heavenly regions (e.g., Eph 4:8-10; 1 Pet 3:21-22; Heb 4:14). In this complex, the post-resurrection appearances of Jesus are understood as appearances of the already exalted Lord (e.g., Acts 9:3-9; 22:6-11; 26:12-18; 1 Cor 15:8; also Matt 28:18 "All authority in heaven and on earth *has been given* to me"). Psalm 110 was interpreted by early Christians as an explanation of Jesus' promotion to a higher status, and it also stimulated reflection on his present activities in heaven. This is clearly seen in the Epistle to the Hebrews, where Christ's journey to the Father is compared with the high priest's annual entrance into the Holy of Holies and his continual intercession for his people.

In the the Gospel of John, Jesus' ministry culminates in his lifting up (exaltation) at the cross, which is identical with or at least coincides with his glorification.

2. Ascension as a visible event

Generally speaking, the NT writers are more con-

cerned with Jesus' present exalted status in heaven than with the question of how he came to be there. However, the NT contains a few passages that depict Jesus' ascension as a visible event, separate from the resurrection, and observed by eyewitnesses, Luke 24:50-53; Acts 1:9-11; and Mark 16:19 (a 2nd cent. addition influenced by the Gospels and Acts). These texts are part of the larger framework of Jesus' post-resurrection appearances and should be estimated accordingly.

Acts 1:3 implies that the ascension of Jesus occurred after a period of forty days of appearances. However, seen from the perspective of Luke–Acts as a whole, where Jesus' exaltation appears to coincide with his resurrection rather than with his ascension (e.g., Luke 24:26; Acts 2:32-36; 5:31; 13:30-37), the post-resurrection appearances described in the Gospel and Acts are appearances of the already exalted Lord from heaven, rather than manifestations of Jesus in a quasi-earthbound state, risen but not yet exalted. The ascension of Jesus simply rounds off the period of appearances and, in line with early Jewish rapture traditions, serves as a guarantee of his eschatological return (Acts 1:11).

3. Ascension and metaphorical language

Especially since the Enlightenment and the rise of biblical criticism, the ascension has been taken as a stock example of a mythological worldview, a perception of reality that was bound up with the conception of the world as part of a three-tiered universe and hence outdated. In our time, more appreciation is expressed for the significance of myth and metaphor as ways of saying that which cannot be said literally or cannot be reduced to propositional statements. Seen from that perspective, the ascension of Jesus may still be a forceful way of describing a reality that cannot be expressed otherwise. *See* ASCENT; ASCENT TO HEAVEN; CHRISTOLOGY; JESUS CHRIST; RESURRECTION.

Bibliography: M. Himmelfarb. *Ascent to Heaven in Jewish and Christian Apocalypses* (1993); A. W. Zwiep. *The Ascension of the Messiah in Lukan Christology* (1997).

A. W. ZWIEP

ASCENSION OF ISAIAH. See ISAIAH, ASCENSION OF.

ASCENT עָלֹה ʿolah, עָלָה ʿalah; ἀναβαίνω anabainō, ἀνάβασις anabasis, ἄμβασις ambasis]. The basic meaning is movement from a lower to a higher elevation. A path or mountain pass is referred to as an "ascent" (Num 34:4; Josh 15:3; Judg 1:36). Cities were usually built on an elevated location, hence, e.g., Judah "goes up" to Timnah (Gen 38:12), and the way to a city can be an "ascent" (1 Sam 9:11). Perhaps related to this, ʿalah is often used to describe a military attack brought against a city (e.g., Isa 7:1).

Often, a dimension of value is added to this basic meaning, so that one "goes up" to something that is better, holier, or more important, as one "goes up" to a person of high rank, e.g., the people of Israel "go up" to Deborah for judgment (Judg 4:5).

The journey to Canaan from the desert or from Egypt is described as an ascent (e.g., Exod 13:18; 33:1). In both cases, movement is to a higher elevation, but in the biblical traditions, these moves also create a decisive increase in well-being and status. The verb ʿalah is often used to describe the exodus, usually in the causative form with God as the subject, e.g., "This is your God, who brought you up out of Egypt" (Neh 9:18).

A similar sense applies to personal deliverance from danger. One "goes down" into realms of death and illness (*see* DESCENT), so, correspondingly, one "goes up" (more specifically, is "brought up" by God, e.g., Jonah 2:6 [Heb. 2:7]) to healing or safety.

The verb ʿalah is often used in conjunction with sacrifice (e.g., Isa 60:7, where sheep and rams "go up for acceptance on my altar," author's trans.). The choice of this verb may relate to the elevation of the animal on the altar or the ascent of the smoke to God in HEAVEN. The depiction of God dwelling in heaven is also assumed when persons are said to "ascend" to God, e.g., Moses (Exod 24:1) and Elijah (2 Kgs 2:1). The Greek verb **anabainō** (often the LXX translation for ʿalah) is used in the NT to describe Jesus' ASCENSION. Even God is said to "go up" after vanquishing chaos, in the language of divine enthronement (Ps 47:5 [Heb. 47:6]).

Finally, pilgrimages are described as "ascents," both because they involve a journey to a city and a "going up" to God. Thus Saul encounters men who are "going up to God at Bethel" (1 Sam 10:3). The designation of Pss 120–134 as Psalms of Ascent (*see* SONGS OF ASCENT) probably reflects their use during pilgrimages.

WILL SOLL

ASCENT OF HERES. *See* HERES, ASCENT OF.

ASCENT TO HEAVEN. Ascent to heaven emerges as an important mode of communication with God in the APOCALYPTIC literature of the Hellenistic and Roman periods. The prophets of the OT heard God's voice, sometimes gazed upon God's presence (Isa 6, Ezek 1), and occasionally were transported from place to place (Ezek 8:2-3; 11:24; 40:1-2). The only prophet in the OT to ascend to heaven is Elijah, who was taken up in a fiery chariot at the end of his life (2 Kgs 2:11); there is no report on his experience. The first Jewish text to describe an ascent to heaven is the *Book of the Watchers* (*1 En.* 1–36), one of the earliest of the apocalypses, probably composed in the late 3rd cent. BCE. The hero of its story is Enoch, the ante-diluvian patriarch who, according to the biblical account, walked with God and then "was no more, because God took him" (Gen 5:21-24; quotation, v. 24). The details of the passage from Genesis, the only passage in the long genealogy to go beyond the standard notice of age at the birth of the first son and total length of life, hint at its author's knowledge of a larger body of lore about Enoch, perhaps including an ascent to heaven.

Enoch ascends to heaven in the *Book of the Watchers* in order to plead the case of the fallen Watchers, the angels who descended to earth to marry women according to Gen 6:1-4. The Watchers entrust Enoch with this task because of his professional skills: he is identified as a scribe, and thus he knows how to draw up a petition on their behalf. Heaven in the *Book of the Watchers* is clearly understood as a temple. For example, God sits on a throne of cherubim surrounded by a crowd of angelic priests; his seat is the heavenly equivalent of the throne of sculpted cherubim in the holy of holies in the Jerusalem Temple. Enoch's ability to pass through the heavenly temple to stand before God's throne shows that he is not only a scribe but also a priest, for only a priest could traverse the awesome and terrifying precincts of that temple unharmed.

The idea of heaven as temple reflects the belief that heaven is the true abode of the deity. That abode is sometimes imagined as a palace, which befits its glorious inhabitant, and at other times as the heavenly prototype for the god's dwelling place on earth, the temple his devotees build him. During the Second Temple period, there is increasing interest in the heavenly temple in Jewish texts, perhaps because many of its contemporaries saw the Second Temple as an inadequate replacement for the First Temple. Further, many authors of the Second Temple period express distress about the sins of the priests who ran the Temple; the *Book of the Watchers*, for example, appears to criticize the marriage practices of some contemporary priests. For anyone who was anxious about the failings of earthly priests, it was reassuring to remember the existence of the heavenly temple with its angelic priests, which was still functioning properly. Enoch's ascent to heaven also demonstrates the permeability of the boundary between the divine sphere and the human. Enoch is, to be sure, an exceptionally righteous human being. Nonetheless, the fact that he can stand before God in the heavenly temple like the angelic priests surely reflects positively on the status of all humanity.

Following the *Book of the Watchers*, several early Jewish and Christian apocalypses and related works, including *2 Enoch*, *3 Baruch*, the *Testament of Levi*, the *Apocalypse of Zephaniah*, the *Apocalypse of Abraham*, and the *Mart. Ascen. Isa.* 6–11, depict ascents to heaven. These texts are difficult to date, but none is clearly earlier than the 1st cent. CE. *Testament of Levi* and the *Mart. Ascen. Isa.* 6–11 are Christian compositions, though the *Testament of Levi* draws on an earlier Jewish work about Levi in Aramaic, and all of these works reach us only because of their appeal to Christians, who copied and transmitted them.

While the *Book of the Watchers* visualizes a single heaven, the later works picture seven heavens. The only exception is the *Apocalypse of Zephaniah*, which maintains the older picture. In *3 Baruch*, the ascent ends in the fifth heaven not because there are only five heavens in its schema, but because Baruch is not allowed to enter the heavenly temple located above the fifth heaven. The contents of the heavens in the ascent apocalypses include cosmological phenomena (*2 Enoch* and *3 Baruch*) and the fate of souls after death (*Apocalypse of Zephaniah, Mart. Ascen. Isa.* 6–11), as well as the liturgy of the heavenly temple (*2 Enoch, 3 Baruch, Testament of Levi, Apocalypse of Abraham*, and *Mart. Ascen. Isa.* 6–11). All of these subjects appear in the *Book of the Watchers*, though the *Book of the Watchers* treats cosmological phenomena and the fate of souls after death in Enoch's tour to the ends of the earth rather than in the course of his ascent to heaven. The multiple heavens of the later works allow them to integrate these interests into their heroes' ascents. The later works differ considerably among themselves on the contents of the lower heavens, but all place the Lord's throne in the highest heaven. Though most show no particular interest in the earthly temple, all of them understand the divine throne room as a temple, and their treatment of the process of ascent reflects this understanding. The visionary's passage through the heavens to the divine throne is described as a kind of priestly investiture, sometimes involving a garment that permits the visionary access to the precincts of the heavenly temple. Collective eschatology is not a central concern of most of the ascent apocalypses; of the texts mentioned here, only the *Apocalypse of Abraham* contains a symbolic vision of history.

Heavenly ascent has a long afterlife in Jewish and Christian literature. It continues to be a theme of Christian apocalypses through the Middle Ages, and it is a central interest of the early Jewish mystical tradition. *See* ASCENSION; ASCENSION OF ISAIAH; BOOKS REFERRED TO IN THE BIBLE.

Bibliography: Martha Himmelfarb. *Ascent to Heaven in Jewish and Christian Apocalypses* (1993).

MARTHA HIMMELFARB

ASCETICISM [ἄσκησις askēsis]. A modern English rendering of the Greek word askēsis, *asceticism* originally meant to practice, train or exercise (as in athletics), to work or shape (in reference to raw materials), to form or create (by artistic means), to dress (e.g., the body, with clothing or jewelry). From such basic root meanings there have developed, in ancient and modern ethical and moral discourses and religious contexts, connotations of the term that reflect duality, or the conviction that reality is split between the transcendental (things related to the spirit) and mundane (things of the world). *Asceticism*, then, becomes shorthand for a complex range of responses to such a conviction. Things related to the body or to the world are considered inferior spiritual things. Responses to "the world" have generally been described and understood in terms of negatives—proscriptions, renunciations, withdrawals, suffering, pain, humiliation. But such descriptions in isolation belie the simultaneous development and articulation of positives—salvation, enlightenment, liberation, a new subjectivity. Because asceticism is basic to the complex origins of Christianity and is of fundamental importance to ancient Jewish history, critical interpretation of the phenomenon requires sensitivity, nuance, and balancing of the negatives and positives in the engagement of Jewish-Christian texts and practices.

Jewish-Christian biblical traditions include forms of ascetic piety as expressions or reflections of the split nature of reality between spirit and flesh or heaven and earth. In Jewish traditions certain individuals and groups (John the Baptist; the Essene community at Qumran, e.g.) modeled renunciations and disciplined practices—fasting, periodic sexual celibacy for the sake of ritual purity, and the monastic life—as reflection of the call to holiness. Such individuals and groups may have served as models for Christian groups (compare Mark 2:20 and Acts 13:2).

The earliest Christian texts do not include the Greek term that is translated as *asceticism*. (Acts 24:16 is an exception: the NRSV translates the verbal form ἀσκέω askeō as "do my best.") The absence of this one term in the texts does not suggest much, because many different terms in different contexts are used to refer to the phenomenon of asceticism in the earliest Christian texts (compare ἐγκρατεύομαι enkrateuomai, "exercise self-control," in 1 Cor 9:25; *see* also Matt 6:16-18; 1 Cor 7:29-32; 2 Cor 11:27).

The development and elaboration of rationalizations, apologetics, and theologies for asceticism, as well as the explosion of the diverse practices of asceticism, should be associated with later individuals and groups. Yet it is important that no one individual or group be assumed to define or capture asceticism. Montanists, Marcionites, and Manichaeans were as important to the development and modeling of asceticism as were Antony, Athansius, and Origen. Female ascetics—with their cultivation of gender-specific piety—were significant to the development of the phenomenon.

What *asceticism* in all its variety seemed to represent in biblical traditions was an articulation and "performance" of the work needed in order to de-form and re-form the self and the world in light of the conviction of split-ness and fallen-ness.

VINCENT L. WIMBUSH

ASENETH as'uh-nath [אָסְנַת 'asenath; Ασεν-εθ Aseneth]. An Egyptian woman and daughter of Potiphera (פּוֹטִי פֶרַע poti fera' in Heb., Πεντεφρη Pentephrē in LXX), the priest of On (Gen 41:45). Aseneth, whose name likely means "belonging to the goddess Neith," is offered in marriage to Joseph by the Pharaoh following Joseph's installation as the second-in-command. The couple has two sons, Manasseh and Ephraim, before the famine in Egypt begins (Gen 41:50; 46:20).

Aseneth's marriage to Joseph is described in a rather unremarkable way in the Pentateuch, but the issue of exogamy clearly caused some distress among later interpreters. The Hellenistic tale *Joseph and Aseneth* (or, simply, *Aseneth*) retells the story of their meeting, adding elements of romance and conversion, to provide a more proper context for their marriage. In this story, Aseneth is renamed "City of Refuge" following her acts of repentance (including professing Joseph's God and removing improper foods), in essence erasing her pagan past and remaking her into both a suitable spouse for the patriarch and a model for Gentile proselytes. One rabbinic tradition suggests that Aseneth was the child born from the rape of Dinah by Shechem, thus not really an outsider at all, and that she was delivered to the family of Pentephres by an eagle. See JOSEPH AND ASENETH.

Bibliography: Edith McEwan Humphrey. *Joseph and Aseneth* (2000); R. S. Kraemer. *When Aseneth Met Joseph: A Late Antique Tale of the Biblical Patriarch and His Egyptian Wife, Reconsidered* (1998).

JESSICA TINKLENBERG DEVEGA

ASHAMED. *See* SHAME.

ASHAN ay'shuhn [עָשָׁן 'ashan]. Ashan, northwest of BEER-SHEBA, was allotted to the tribe of JUDAH, then to the descendants of SIMEON, whose territory fell within Judah's boundaries (Josh 15:42; 19:7; 1 Chr 4:32). Ashan is also listed among the cities of refuge (1 Chr 6:59). The importance of the list was first administrative and later theological: it designated the land the people identified as their allotment from God.

JOAN COOK

ASHBEL ash'bel [אַשְׁבֵּל 'ashbel; Ασβηλ, Asbēl]. Ashbel appears in lists of descendants of BENJAMIN. Genesis 46:21 lists him as the third of ten sons; Num 26:38 and 1 Chr 8:1 as the second of five. First Chronicles 7:6 names JEDIAEL instead of Ashbel among Benjamin's three sons. The list in Genesis sets the number of Jacob's family who migrated to Egypt at 70 (*see* Gen 46:27, LXX gives the number 75; and Deut 10:22).

JOAN COOK

ASHDOD ash'dod [אַשְׁדּוֹד 'ashdodh]. Biblical Ashdod, a major Bronze and Iron Age tell in the southern coastal plain of Israel, is located 3.5 mi. southeast of the modern Mediterranean town of Ashdod. The ancient site includes a ca. 20-acre acropolis and ca. 70-acre lower city. It is best known in the Bible as a Philistine town. The 1962–1972 excavations at the site were co-sponsored by the Israel Department of Antiquities, the Pittsburgh Theological Seminary, and the Pittsburgh Carnegie Museum under the direction of M. Dothan, D. N. Freedman and J. Swauger. Twenty-three strata, spanning the 17th cent. BCE through 7th cent. CE, were uncovered at the site.

Archaeological excavations on the acropolis revealed a Middle Bronze Age IIC city that was fortified by an earthen glacis, mudbrick city wall, and monumental gate. During the following Late Bronze Age (16th–13th cent. BCE), the city expanded in size to include the lower city. Akkadian texts from Ugarit that mention Ashdod testify to its importance as a producer of textiles and international maritime center during the 14th and 13th cents BCE. Numerous artifacts, including a fragmentary doorpost inscribed with an Egyptian name, and several mudbrick structures similar to those known in Egypt, are indicative of Egyptian imperial influence at Ashdod and generally in southern Canaan during this time. A thick conflagration layer covered Stratum XIV, the last Late Bronze Age settlement. This destruction, dated to the end of the 13th cent., is associated with the arrival of the Philistines.

Ashdod appears numerous times in the Bible, most notably as one of the five Philistine cities mentioned in Josh 13:3, and served as an important non-Israelite center during the 12th–7th cent. BCE. Most of the 12th and 11th cent. Iron Age I occupation attributed to the initial settlement of the Philistines was uncovered on the acropolis. This settlement slowly expanded in size to include the lower city. Ashdod, mentioned as a Philistine town in the Egyptian Onomasticon of Amenope of the 11th cent., was well planned, as evidenced by the excavation of a main street flanked by blocks of structures. Distinctive material culture associated with the arrival of the Philistines includes large quantities of Aegean-style locally produced pottery, a complete ceramic figurine of a seated goddess nicknamed "Ashdoda," and other Aegean-style artifacts that testify to their foreign origins. Two seals, one engraved with signs that resemble the Cypro-Minoan script used in Cyprus and a second bearing incised humans and animals, are the only examples of what may represent early Philistine script.

Biblical Ashdod is infamous as a center for the worship of Dagon. According to 1 Sam 5, the Philistines brought the captured Israelite Ark of the Covenant into the Temple of Dagon, thus causing the statue of Dagon to fall on his face. Following the Ark's arrival, a plague afflicted the residents of Ashdod. Subsequently the Ark was sent to the Gath and later Ekron, where disasters were also inflicted on their inhabitants.

Ashdod continued as a fortified Philistine center in the Iron II period. During the 9th–8th cent. BCE, the city reached is zenith. The most impressive structures were uncovered in the lower city. These include a massive city gate with three chambers and a tower flanking each side of the entryway, an impressive fortification wall, and a fortress. A Stratum VIII temple dating to this period contained numerous cultic objects comprising ceramic zoomorphic figurines, vessels used in libations, and female plaque figurines. Assigned to this period is the city's conquest by King Uzziah of Judah as recorded in 2 Chr 26:6, a claim that modern scholars usually treat as questionable. Approximately 3,000 human skeletons found in the Stratum VIII destruction debris are attributed to Sargon II's capture of the city in 711 BCE, as recorded in his annals and mentioned in Isa 20:1. Three fragments of a cuneiform text originating from a basalt victory stela recovered from Ashdod attest to Assyrian presence at the site.

The Neo-Philistine Strata VII–VI late Iron Age II city continued to be inhabited through the 7th cent. BCE. Noteworthy is the discovery of a well-preserved potters' quarter, complete with kilns and workshops. The Egyptian Pharaoh Psamtik I's 29-year siege of the city, described by the Greek historian Herodotus, is probably responsible for the destruction of the Stratum VII city. The reference to "the remnant of Ashdod" in Jer 25:20 is often interpreted as an allusion to this event. The southern coastal plain, including Ashdod, is incorporated into the Babylonian empire at the end of the 7th cent. BCE, marking the end of Philistine dominance in the region.

Following the return of the exiles from Babylon, Nehemiah (the Persian period governor of Judea in the 5th cent. BCE), condemns Judeans for intermarrying with the Ashdodites (Neh 13:24). Persian period remains on the tell, include a large public building with imported Attic pottery and an ostracon describing a delivery of wine. This Aramaic inscription may reflect the Ashdodite dialect referred to in Neh 13:24.

During the Hellenistic period the name of the city was changed to Azotus. A well-planned classical city and parts of an agora have been uncovered during excavations. Noteworthy finds from this area included altars, a lead plaque depicting a deity with a fish tail, and coins dating to the late 2nd cent. BCE. According to 1 Macc 10:84 and 11:4, Jonathan burned Azotus and destroyed the old temple of Dagon.

The only reference to Ashdod in the NT is in the account of Philip, who after baptizing the Ethiopian eunuch, was carried away by the Spirit and "found himself at Azotus" (Acts 8:40). Following the destruction of the Roman period Stratum III city by Vespasian in 67 CE, the city experienced decline and never fully recovered its former importance.

Bibliography: Moshe Dothan. *Ashdod II-III: The Second and Third Seasons of Excavations (1963, 1965, Soundings in 1967)* (1971); Moshe Dothan. "Ethnicity and Archaeology: Some Observations on the Sea Peoples at Ashdod." *Biblical Archaeology Today, 1990: Proceedings of the Second International Congress on Biblical Archaeology.* A. Biran and J. Aviram, eds. (1993); Moshe Dothan and David Ben-Shlomo. *Ashdod VI: The Excavations of Areas H and K (1968–1969)* (2005); Moshe Dothan and David N. Freedman. *Ashdod I: The First Season of Excavations 1962* (1967); Moshe Dothan Yosef Porath. *Ashdod IV: Excavations of Area M* (1982); Moshe Dothan and Yosef Porath. *Ashdod V: Excavations of Area G. The Fourth–Sixth Seasons of Excavations (1968–1970)* (1993).

ANN E. KILLEBREW

ASHDOD-YAM ash´dod. *See* ASHDOD.

ASHER, ASHERITES ash´uhr [אָשֵׁר ʾasher, אִשְׁרִי ʾasheri, Ἀσήρ Asēr]. 1. The eighth son born to Jacob through his concubine Zilpah. The meaning of the name, "fortunate one," is confirmed by the birth report of the eponymous ancestor (Gen 30:12-13) and the blessed status accorded the tribe in the testamentary benedictions attributed to Moses (Deut 33:24).

2. The ascription of blessing, however, stands in contrast to intimations that the tribe of Asher enjoyed a lesser status than other Israelite tribes, in contrast to the ascription of blessing. In genealogies and tribal lists it is grouped with the three other tribes (Gad, Dan, and Naphtali) that traced descent from Bilhah and Zilpah, Jacob's concubines. Although lists of the sons of Jacob in Genesis generally follow the sequence of birth, tribal lists outside Genesis consistently accord pride of place to the tribes associated with Jacob's wives, the four associated with his concubines being listed last. Other biblical texts reflect a corresponding perspective. Asher, Dan, and Naphtali constitute the rear guard during Israel's wilderness (Num 10:26) and later, joined by Reuben, Gad, and Zebulun, the tribes are appointed to recite curses from Mount Ebal (Deut 27:13). Ezekiel's vision of the New Temple assigns the western gates, on the backside of the Temple, to Gad, Asher, and Naphtali (48:34).

The ambivalent status of Asher may derive from its distinctive geographical and historical situation. According to the description of its tribal allotment (Josh 19:24-31), Asher's territory was bounded on the south by Carmel, encompassed the western slope of the Galilee and the Plain of Acco, and extended into areas controlled by the powerful Phoenician city-states of Tyre and Sidon. In reality, however, the tribe was probably confined to the highlands for most of its existence in the land. A short note reports that the tribe failed to possess the greater part of its inheritance and lived as a minority population within the area of its settlement (Judg 1:31).

As was the case with the other concubine tribes, the territory inhabited by Asher comprised a frontier region, characterized by a mixed population and significant

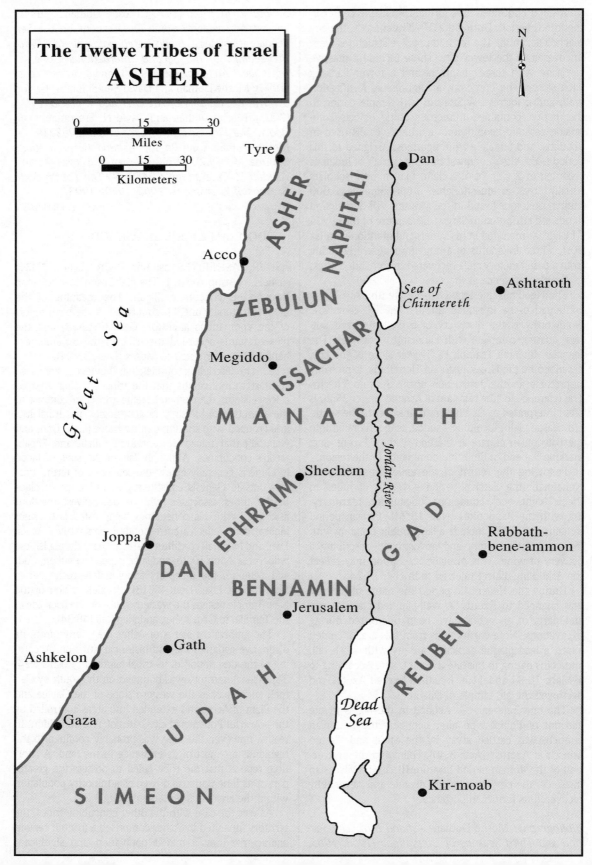

The Twelve Tribes of Israel
ASHER

0   15   30
Miles

0   15   30
Kilometers

N

Great Sea

ASHER

NAPHTALI

Tyre

Dan

Acco

ZEBULUN

Sea of
Chinnereth

Ashtaroth

ISSACHAR

Megiddo

MANASSEH

Jordan River

Shechem

EPHRAIM

DAN

GAD

Joppa

Rabbath-
bene-ammon

BENJAMIN

Jerusalem

Gath

Ashkelon

JUDAH

REUBEN

Gaza

Dead
Sea

SIMEON

Kir-moab

interaction with the neighboring cultures. For this reason, economic and social ties with the maritime PHOENICIANS may have competed with the kinship ties that bound the Asherites to their Israelite kindred farther inland. Asher may often have found itself caught between conflicting commitments, a situation illustrated by two references to the tribe in Judges. In one case, Deborah reproaches Asher for its passivity and refusal to join its Israelite kin in a campaign against the Canaanites, implying that the tribe's maritime interests are to blame (Judg 5:17b). On another occasion, however, the tribe responds readily to Gideon's summons to muster for battle against the Midianites (Judg 6:35) and participates in the pursuit when Gideon prevails (7:23).

Though geographically constrained, the tribe seems to have enjoyed a prosperous existence and a reputation as an agricultural center. The blessing of Jacob mentions Asher's "rich food" (Gen 49:20), and a corresponding blessing by Moses invites the tribe to "dip his foot in oil" (Deut 33:24). The latter reference indicates that olive oil, a prized commodity in the ancient world, constituted a primary source of the tribe's economic wealth and renown. The tribe's fortunes no doubt increased during the reign of David, when virtually the entire territory of its allotment came under Israelite control (2 Sam 24:6-7), and into the early years of Solomon's reign, when the area provisioned the royal court (1 Kgs 4:16). The lowland areas, however, were later ceded back to the king of Tyre in exchange for services rendered in the construction of the Jerusalem Temple (1 Kgs 9:11-14). In any case, Asher was known for providing "royal delicacies" (Gen 49:20b), whether to Israelite or Phoenician kings.

A genealogical listing in 1 Chr 7:30-40 appears to place elements of the tribe well to the south, adjacent to the territories of Ephraim and Benjamin. The Asherite genealogy shares a number of names with the corresponding lists of these tribes (e.g., "Beriah" [1 Chr 7:23; 8:13] and "Heber" [1 Chr 8:17]), and many of the names are associated with sites within the Ephraimite highlands. The form of the genealogy diverges in significant ways from the others associated with Asher and is beset with textual problems. It is, therefore, not clear whether the text refers to an enclave of Asherites that settled south of their kindred, or is instead a literary construction, pieced together by the Chronicler.

Luke specifically reports that the prophetess Anna is a member of the tribe of Asher (Luke 1:36). The designation may reinforce the sense of blessing signified by the name or, if undertones of Asher's peripheral status lingered into the NT period, it may express Luke's care to demonstrate that the gospel extends to those on the periphery of society. See ALLOTMENT; TRIBES, TERRITORIES OF.

Bibliography: Zecharia Kallai. *Historical Geography of the Bible: The Tribal Territories of Israel* (1986).

L. DANIEL HAWK

ASHERAH uh-shihr´uh [אֲשֵׁרָה ’asherah]. Asherah, along with Astarte and Anath, was one of the three great goddesses of the Canaanite pantheon. She was particularly known as a mother goddess, the consort of the high father god El. Thus, in Late Bronze Age texts (ca. 1550–1200 BCE) that come from the Canaanite city-state of Ugarit on the north Levantine coast, the gods of the pantheon are called "the children of Asherah," and Ugaritic texts also speak of the gods as the 70 children of Asherah. A Hittite myth from roughly the same date similarly describes the gods as the "seventy-seven" and "eighty-eight" children of Asherah. Asherah's divine children can further be referred to as her "pride of lions," and, indeed, the lion seems frequently used as an image of Asherah. For example, on several gold and electrum pendants that come from Ugarit and nearby sites and that arguably depict Asherah, the goddess is depicted as nude, facing frontally, and standing atop a lion. Similar gold and electrum pendants depict Asherah with a tree or branch etched in her pubic region, an indication that tree imagery also is frequently used to represent Asherah; the goddess is, in addition, associated with images of snakes. This is probably because both trees—especially deciduous trees—and snakes are potent images of fertility in general and birth in particular, as both periodically shed a part of themselves (skin, leaves) only to be symbolically born anew. In fact, so close is the association of Asherah with snakes that an epithet used of Asherah in a Punic devotional tablet, khwt, may mean "serpent," cognate with terms for "serpent" found in other Semitic languages. Similarly, in biblical Hebrew, terms meaning "terebinth" and "oak" (’elon, ’ellah, ’ellon, and ’allon) seem derived from an epithet used of Asherah at Ugarit, Elath, and thus indicate the close association of Asherah with trees.

Other information from the OT affirms Asherah's close association with serpents and especially trees. In the garden of Eden story, e.g., (Gen 2:4b–3:24), a serpent and two sacred trees are closely associated with Eve, whose epithet "mother of all the living" closely mimics the role of the mother goddess Asherah. Even more significant are the approximately forty times the term ’asherah occurs in the Hebrew, occasionally as the proper name of the Canaanite mother goddess (Judg 3:7; 1 Kgs 15:13; 18:19; 2 Kgs 23:4) but more often as a common noun ("an asherah" or "the asherah"). This asherah seems to have been a religious icon in the shape of a stylized pole or tree: thus the biblical writers can speak of it as being "made" or "built," "stood up," "erected," or even "planted"; if destroyed, it is "burned," "overturned," "broken," "hewn down," "cut down," or even "uprooted." Although there is some debate, a vast majority of biblical scholars quite reasonably presume that this tree like icon represented the Canaanite mother goddess Asherah. The biblical writers condemn the presence of an asherah icon in ancient Israel (and, by implication, the presence of the goddess the icon represents) as foreign and inappropriate in the worship of the Israelite god Yahweh.

Many scholars assume that the viewpoint of the biblical writers represents the typical viewpoint in ancient Israel. Archaeological discoveries made in the late 20th cent., however, have caused other scholars to reconsider the role of Asherah in ancient Israelite religion. Most significant is the evidence from the site of KUNTILLET ʿAJRUD in the northern Sinai. There, archaeologists found a bounty of religious remains dating from the late 9th or early 8th cent. BCE, including three inscriptions that refer to Yahweh in conjunction with his "asherah," meaning, most plausibly, Yahweh in conjunction with an asherah icon and so in conjunction—probably in a consort relationship—with the goddess that icon represented. Iconographic remains from Kuntillet ʿAjrud also suggest Asherah was worshiped alongside Yahweh at the site. One of the inscriptions pairing Yahweh with an asherah/Asherah, e.g., was found on a large store jar or pithos, on which were also found images of a stylized tree and a lion, both of which are arguably to be associated with Asherah.

An 8th cent. BCE inscription from Khirbet el-Qom, seven mi. east-southeast of the city of Lachish, contains language quite similar to the inscriptions from Kuntillet ʿAjrud and thus again seems to suggest at least some ancient Israelites worshiped Asherah as the consort of Yahweh. Scholars have also suggested that a 10th cent. BCE terra cotta stand from the site of TAANACH presents images of Asherah in association with Yahweh. This stand, which rises about 54 cm high, is divided into four registers. The bottommost register shows a naked woman, facing frontally, with her arms extended to touch the heads of two lions. This is most easily interpreted as Asherah, given her known associations with lions. The third register from the bottom, which again shows two flanking lions, but this time with a tree in between, likely refers iconographically to Asherah in her alternate guise as a tree. The other two registers can possibly be interpreted as representations of Yahweh. The second from the bottom is void in the center, with two flanking beasts that are winged: these are two cherubs, and what is arguably between them is Yahweh invisibly enthroned upon these beasts' outstretched wings, just as is described in biblical texts like 1 Sam 4:4 ("Yahweh of Hosts who sits enthroned upon the cherubim"). The top register, which may represent a bull, is often also taken to represent Yahweh in theriomorphic form, given that Yahweh is called אֲבִיר יַעֲקֹב ʾavir yaʿaqov literally the "Bull of Jacob," in Gen 49:24; Ps 132:2; and Isa 49:26; 60:16.

We should further note the literally thousands of terra cotta female figurines of the pillar-base type (meaning a female figurine whose lower body is in the shape of an unmodelled and featureless column and whose upper body is dominated by enormous breasts) that have been found by archaeologists at virtually every ancient Israelite site. These are often taken as representations of Asherah, with the pillar representing the trunk of Asherah's tree and the breasts representing the nurturing attributes of the mother goddess. But the inhabitants of the Israelite sites where these pillar figurines were found were surely devotees of Yahweh. What we see in the pillar figurines, then, is still more evidence that, along with the remains from Kuntillet ʿAjrud, Khirbet el-Qom, and Taanach, suggests that at least some significant portion of the ancient Israelite population worshiped Asherah in conjunction with Yahweh.

To be sure, not all ancient Israelites accepted this sort of worship, and we have already noted that within the biblical text, there is manifold opposition to it. According to Deut 16:21-22, e.g., the Israelites are forbidden to erect an image dedicated to the goddess Asherah as it is one of the things "Yahweh your God hates," and Exod 34:13; Deut 7:5; and 12:3 further command that any asherah icon the Israelites encounter should be hewn down. The books of 1-2 Kings follow suit by lavishing praise upon several kings of Israel's Southern Kingdom of Judah who do just that, in particular kings Asa (1 Kgs 15:13), Hezekiah (2 Kgs 18:3-4), and Josiah (2 Kgs 23:6, 14, and 15). Josiah is also praised for removing the vessels that were used to offer sacrifice to Asherah from the Temple in Jerusalem and for breaking down the houses within the Temple compound in which women wove garments that were draped over the goddess's icon.

Yet the fact that the biblical writers find it necessary to condemn repeatedly Asherah worship, and the fact that kings Asa, Hezekiah, and Josiah are said to have repeatedly destroyed an asherah icon (King Asa in the 9th cent. BCE; King Hezekiah in the 8th cent. BCE; and King Josiah in the 7th cent. BCE) suggests that whatever the opposition of the biblical writers to Asherah worship, many if not most in ancient Israel found devotion to Asherah to be an appropriate part of their devotion to Yahweh. The Asherah icon that Josiah destroyed was said to have stood in Yahweh's Temple in Jerusalem. In addition, sacrifice was offered to the goddess there, and the Temple provided housing—and presumably financial support—for women who were in Asherah's service. Thus it appears that, at least in Josiah's day (ca. 640–609 BCE), there were some associated with the Temple in Jerusalem (priests?) who saw Asherah worship as an appropriate part of the worship of Yahweh.

In Israel's Northern Kingdom, evidence also suggests that many, even among the priestly and prophetic elite, worshiped Asherah side by side with Yahweh. In addition to tearing down the Asherah icon that stood in the Jerusalem Temple in the late 7th cent. BCE, e.g., Josiah is said to have torn down an Asherah icon that stood at the temple dedicated to Yahweh in Bethel (2 Kgs 23:15), which, along with Dan, was one of the two major sacred sites of the Northern Kingdom. The priesthood that served at Bethel seemed to find the presence of Asherah's icon to be a part of their faith. An Asherah icon erected in Samaria during the reign of King Ahab (1 Kgs 16:33) was also allowed to remain standing by the reformer King Jehu (2 Kgs 13:6), even though Jehu, inspired by the prophet Elisha, was generally at pains to remove all non-Yahwistic worship and imagery from the land.

Why might Asherah worship have been accepted by so many in Israel? Most scholars recognize that at least some portions of the people of Israel emerged out of Canaanite culture in ca. 1200 BCE, in the waning years of the Late Bronze Age. Many aspects of ancient Israel's religious language and tradition consequently also had roots in Canaanite culture, especially in Canaanite motifs and traditions concerning the god El that were appropriated by the ancient Israelites and used to describe Yahweh. Indeed, El traditions were so heavily appropriated that at least some ancient Israelites seem to have assumed they should appropriate for Yahweh the traditions concerning El's consort Asherah. For these ancient Israelites, then, Asherah is worshiped as Yahweh's consort; for as Yahweh supplants El as an object of worship, Yahweh lays claim to El's wife.

Asherah worship, moreover, may have been particularly promoted in royal circles, especially in the southern capital city of Jerusalem. The royal ideology of Israel's Southern Kingdom (although not of the Northern) viewed the reigning king as the adopted son (metaphorically) of the father god Yahweh. For those who viewed Asherah as Yahweh's consort, this meant the king was also the adopted son of this mother goddess. Yet while the king's actual biological father was necessarily dead (else the king would not have succeeded to the throne), the king's biological mother may still live. She could thus be easily identified as the human equivalent of the king's divine mother, Asherah, and, in fact, as the goddess's representative on earth, an enormously powerful position for a woman to assume in the otherwise male-dominated traditions of ancient Israelite religion.

Bibliography: Susan Ackerman. "The Queen Mother and the Cult in Ancient Israel." *JBL* 112 (1993) 385–401; John Day. "Asherah in the Hebrew Bible and Northwest Semitic Literature." *JBL* 105 (1986) 385–408; Ruth Hestrin. "The Lachish Ewer and the ʾAsherah." *IEJ* 37 (1987) 212–223; Saul M. Olyan. *Asherah and the Cult of Yahweh in Israel* (1988); Steve A. Wiggins. *A Reassessment of "Asherah": A Study According to Textual Sources of the First Two Millennia BCE* (1993).

SUSAN ACKERMAN

ASHEROTH. *See* ASHERAH.

ASHES [אֵפֶר ʾefer, דֶּשֶׁן deshen, פִּיחַ piakh; σποδός spodos, αἰθάλη aithalē]. ʾEfer is the word most frequently used in the OT to designate the substances remaining after combustion has occurred, whether in domestic ovens, urban conflagrations, or as a result of ritual sacrifices (1 Kgs 20:38; 20:41; 2 Kgs 23:4; Ps 147:16; Job 2:8). Ashes are often mentioned in connection with DUST and SACKCLOTH as signs of MOURNING, GRIEF, and humiliation (2 Sam 13:19; Job 2:8, 12; Isa 61:3; Jer 6:26); the application of ashes to the head and body at times of personal and national crisis, often accompanied by FASTING, indicated penitence (Isa 58:5; Ezek 27:30; Jonah 3:6; Esth 4:1, 4:3; Dan 9:3; Jdt 4:13).

Figuratively, the word *ashes* is used to refer to worthless things or persons (Job 13:12; Isa 44:20); destruction (Ezek 28:18; Mal 3:19; Lam 3:16); and, in combination with DUST, to human mortality (Gen 18:27; Job 30:19; 42:6; Sir 10:9; 17:32). Numbers 19:9-10, 17-19 describe the ashes of the RED HEIFER that was slaughtered outside the camp and burned with its flesh, blood, and dung. When combined with spring water, these ashes produced a "water of lustration" (NRSV, "water for cleansing") that was efficacious in eliminating ritual defilement acquired from contact with or propinquity to a corpse, grave, or a human bone.

Two other words are also generally translated *ashes.* **Deshen** refers to the residue of burned fuel and fat resulting from sacrifice at altars (Lev 1:16; 4:12; 6:10-11; 1 Kgs 13:3, 5) and from burned corpses (Jer 31:40); and **piakh** designates the carbon formed in a kiln (Exod 9:8, 10), said to have been used by Moses to produce boils among the Egyptians. The LXX regularly renders ʾefer and deshen by spodos and piakh by aithalē. Matthew 11:21 and Luke 10:13 refer to donning sackcloth and ashes (spodos) to demonstrate repentance, and Heb 9:13 recalls the purifying ashes (spodos) of the red cow of Num 19.

JUDITH R. BASKIN

ASHHUR ashʹuhr [אַשְׁחוּר ʾashkhur]. Father of seven sons by Helah and Naarah, descendant of Judah, son of Hezron and his wife Abijah, and founder of the town Tekoa (1 Chr 2:24; 4:5-6). The Septuagint names him the son of Caleb and his wife Ephrathah. *Hur* in 1 Chr 2:19 may be an abbreviation of Ashhur.

ASHIMA, ASHIMAH uh-shiʹmuh [אֲשִׁימָא ʾashimaʾ, אֲשִׁמָה ʾashmah]. The god worshiped by the people from HAMATH who lived in SAMARIA after the Assyrian exile of 722 BCE (2 Kgs 17:30). The word is likely an Aramaic form meaning "the Name," thus referring to one of the NW Semitic goddesses ANATH, ASTARTE, or ASHERAH. It could be a deliberate Hebrew corruption of Asherah (אָשָׁם ʾasham, "guilt") in Amos 8:14. *See* NIBHAZ.

STEVEN D. MASON

ASHKELON ashʹkuh-lon [אַשְׁקְלוֹן ʾashqelon; Ἀσκαλων Askalōn]. Biblical Ashkelon is a large semi-circular

150-acre tell facing the Mediterranean Sea next to the modern city of Ashkelon. Its name is closely related to the Northwest Semitic Canaanite root *tql meaning "to weigh," from which the Hebrew word sheqel שֶׁקֶל developed. In classical sources, the city is referred to as Ascalon. Throughout most of its history Ashkelon served as a major maritime seaport. The city was favorably situated above a prehistoric underground river and aquifer that provided abundant fresh water to its inhabitants and permitted the development of extensive agricultural fields in antiquity. One of its most famous agricultural products is a variety of onion that derived its name from Ascalon, the *caepa Ascalonia* (scallion). Ashkelon is best known in the Bible as one of the Philistine Pentapolis cities, a league of five Philistine centers mentioned in Josh 13:3.

From the 1930s until the present, a series of excavations have uncovered cultural remains at Ashkelon and its immediate surroundings, dating from prehistoric through medieval periods. More recent excavations have discovered significant archaeological remains on the tel that span the 4th millennium BCE until its final abandonment and destruction by the Mamluk Sultan Baybars at the end of the Crusader period. The earliest historical mention of the city is in the Egyptian Execration texts dating to the 19th and 18th cents. BCE. During this time, Ashkelon was a major Middle Bronze Age II urban center. Massive fortifications excavated at the northern end of the mound including earthenwork ramparts and a mudbrick gate, complete with an arch, testify to Asheklon's prominence during the first half of the 2nd millennium BCE. At the base of the rampart and along the roadway leading to the gate, a bronze bull measuring 10 cm long and 11 cm high, originally covered with silver, was discovered inside a beehive-shaped ceramic model shrine. These cultic objects probably marked a wayside sanctuary frequented by those entering the city. The bull is well known in Canaanite religious practices, and its image is associated with the gods El and Ba'al and later Yahweh. This Middle Bronze Age city was destroyed in the mid 16th cent. BCE. It is tempting to attribute Ashkelon's devastation to Egyptian campaigns in southern Canaan following Egypt's successful expulsion of the Semitic Hyksos (or foreign rulers) from the Delta region, resulting in its reunification under New Kingdom pharaohs.

Late Bronze Age Ashkelon is mentioned in at least seven clay tablets from the mid-14th cent. el Amarna archive. These letters represent correspondence between the Egyptian Pharaoh Akhenaten and Yidya, the local ruler of city. During the 14th through early 12th cent. BCE, Canaan fell under New Kingdom Egyptian imperial rule and, at times, Ashkelon most likely served as an Egyptian outpost. The city is mentioned in Ramesses II's military campaign to Canaan, carved in relief on the southern outer wall of the temple of Amen-Ra at Karnak. Ashkelon also appears in Merneptah's Israel Stela (ca. 1207 BCE) as one of three Canaanite cities that rebelled against the Egyptians. Thus far Late Bronze Age levels have been reached only in a very small section on the tell. The finds include a series of courtyard surfaces, silos, bread ovens, and a few burials comparable to earlier Hyksos burial customs in the Nile Delta region.

For most of the biblical period, Ashkelon was a major Philistine center. The depiction of Ramesses III's land and sea battles against a coalition of peoples from the sea incised on the walls of his mortuary temple at Medinet Habu mention the *Peleset* who are associated with the biblical Philistines. As a result, scholars have traditionally dated the appearance of the Philistines at Ashkelon and other Pentapolis cities to the first half of the 12th cent. BCE. A century later, Ashkelon is listed in the early 11th cent. Onomasticon of Amenope specifically as a Philistine city.

In the Bible, Ashkelon is infamous as the city where Samson killed thirty men to procure their clothes as a payment for a wager he had lost to the Philistines (Judg 14:10-19). It was also one of the Philistine cities struck by a plague following the Philistine capture of the Ark of the Covenant (1 Sam 6:4, 17). The Iron Age I, 12th and 11th cent. BCE settlement probably covered the entire 150-acre mound, hinted at by the discovery of fortifications dating to this period uncovered on the northern edge of the site. The Philistines' foreign origins are indicated by significant quantities of locally produced, Aegean-style objects including pottery and clay loom weights and other artifacts well known in the Aegean region and Cyprus. The sudden appearance of pig bones associated with Philistine occupation levels serves as an ethnic marker that differentiates them from indigenous Canaanites and Israelites.

Ashkelon's significance as a Philistine center during the Israelite period is alluded to in David's lament following the death of Saul and Jonathan on Mt. Gilboa. To prevent rejoicing by the Philistines, David pled that the news of this event would not be proclaimed in Ashkelon (2 Sam 1:17-30). Excavations reveal that the tell was occupied continuously during the Iron Age II (10th – 7th cent. BCE). Local rulers of Ashkelon appear in Assyrian sources as vassals largely loyal to the Assyrians. However, in the late 8th cent. Sidqa, one of Ashkelon's rulers, formed an alliance with Hezekiah against the Assyrians. Sennacherib's punishment came swiftly during his 701 BCE campaign to Judah and Philistia, resulting in widespread destruction of the region and Sidqa's deportation.

During the final centuries of the Iron Age, Ashkelon was a center for wine production, as testified by the discovery of an architectural complex that included at least three workrooms and the remains of plastered platforms, vats, and basins. The end of Iron Age Ashkelon is marked by its devastation by Nebuchadnezzer in 604 BCE and the exile of the last Philistine king, Aga', an event documented in the Babylonian Chronicle and reflected in the biblical prophecy (Jer 25:20; 47: 5, 7; Amos 1:8; Zeph 2:4, 7; Zech 9:5). Archaeological excavations have uncovered physical evidence of Nebuchadnezzer's campaign and Ashkelon's demise, indicated by the massive destruction of the city, including the ruins of a public marketplace.

During the subsequent Persian period, Ashkelon develops into an impressive Phoenician center. A series of warehouses and large quantities of imported Phoenician and Greek pottery vessels testify to Ashkelon's importance as a major port city. One of the most notable finds is a burial ground for hundreds of individually interred dogs, perhaps related to a local Phoenician cult at the site.

For most of the Hellenistic and Roman periods, classical Ascalon was a flourishing autonomous and free city, briefly threatened by Jonathan the high priest (1 Macc 10:84-87; 11:60). Tradition holds that it was the birthplace of Herod the Great, who rebuilt and enriched the city. Public buildings, including a forum, and private villas dating to the classical period have been uncovered on the mound. In the later Byzantine period, it became a seat of a bishop and a thriving Christian center. Ashkelon remained an important port, especially for the export of wines from the Holy Land. In its final centuries, it was a major early Islamic and Crusader settlement. Following its destruction by the Mamluks in 1270, the mound was abandoned.

Bibliography: Lawrence E. Stager. "When Canaanites and Philistines Ruled Ashkelon." *BAR* 17 (1991) 24–37; 40–43; Lawrence E. Stager. "Why Were Hundreds of Dogs Buried at Ashkelon?" *BAR* 17 (1991) 26–42; Lawrence E. Stager. "Eroticism and Infanticide at Ashkelon." *BAR* 17 (1991) 34–53, 72; Paula Wapnish and Brian Hesse. "Pampered Pooches or Plain Pariahs?" *BA* 56 (1993) 55–80.

ANN E. KILLEBREW

ASHKENAZ ash'kuh-naz [אַשְׁכְּנַז 'ashkenaz]. Gomer's eldest son listed in the Table of Nations (Gen 10:3; 1 Chr 1:6). Ashkenaz represents a geographical area east of the Black Sea, most likely belonging to the Scythians. Jeremiah names them a threat to Babylon (51:27), and HERODOTUS describes the SCYTHIANS attacking the Cimmerians (4:11).

Since at least the 11th cent. CE, the term has referred to Eastern European Jews.

LISA MICHELE WOLFE

ASHNAH ash'nuh [אַשְׁנָה 'ashnah]. 1. A city in the lowlands of JUDAH (Josh 15:33). Although the location is uncertain, Aslin is suggested.

2. A city farther south in the lowlands of Judah (Josh 15:43). Modern Idna between HEBRON and LACHISH is a possible location.

ASHPENAZ ash'puh-naz [אַשְׁפְּנַז 'ashpenaz]. Nebuchadnezzar's official who allowed Daniel and his friends to consume water and vegetables while a part of the royal court (Dan 1:3-4, 7-14, 18).

ASHTAROTH ash'tuh-roth [עַשְׁתָּרֹת 'ashtaroth; Ασταρωθ Astarōth]. In Deut 1:4; Josh 9:10; 12:4; and 13:12, Moses and the Israelites are said to have defeated King Og of Bashan, who reigned in the towns of Ashtaroth and Edrei, as part of their conquests east of the Jordan before the people crossed over the river and took the territory that became the Israelite heartland. Subsequently, in Josh 13:31, Ashtaroth, along with Edrei, is said to have been assigned to the Machirite clans of the tribe of Manasseh as part of their tribal inheritance. Then, in 1 Chr 6:71 (in OT 6:56), Ashtaroth is said to have been given to the Gershomites as part of the special allotments given throughout Israel to these and other members of the priestly tribe of Levi, who otherwise were landless. This same tradition seems reflected in Josh 21:27, although there the city is called by the variant name Beeshterah. The city Ashtaroth is probably to be identified as well with Ashteroth, one of two paired cities, Ashteroth-Karnaim, mentioned in Gen 14:5. This is particularly indicated in Deut 3:11 and Josh 12:4, where King Og of Ashtaroth is described as one of the last of the Rephaim, who are the people Gen 14:5 locates at Ashteroth-Karnaim. The designation of one of David's mighty men, Uzzia, as an Ashterathite in 1 Chr 11:44 also seems meant to indicate this man came from Ashtaroth/Ashteroth.

Ashtaroth is identified with modern Tell Ashtarah, which lies about 35 km east of the Sea of Galilee, in ancient Bashan/modern Syria, just north of the Wadi Yarmuk. The name *Ashtarah*, instead of *Ashtaroth* or *Ashteroth*, is undoubtedly the more authentic, as is indicated by the rendering of the city's name in the 14th cent. BCE letters from Egyptian el-Amarna as 'ash-tare (El Amarna Letters 197:10; 256:21) and in later Assyrian texts as as-tar-tu. The appellation is derived from the name of one of the great goddesses of the Canaanite pantheon, Astarte. The biblical writers have deliberately manipulated this term for theological reasons, imposing upon it the vowels of the word **bosheth**, "shame."

The location of Ashtaroth is strategically important, as the city lay on the great KING'S HIGHWAY that ran the length of the eastern Jordan Valley and served as a major trade route between the Arabian peninsula and other points south and the major Syrian cities of the north, with access beyond to Mesopotamia. Moreover, another major highway running east-west from the Jezreel Valley intersected with the King's Highway at Ashtaroth. The site should thus have been a real prize for the Israelite clans to which it is said to have been allotted, although whether the Israelites actually held Ashtaroth except for very short periods—most important, when it was taken by Jeroboam II of Israel in the first half of the 8th cent. BCE (see Amos 6:13-14)—is dubious. Certainly Jeroboam's claim on the city was short lived, as in 732 BCE it fell to the Assyrian king TIGLATH-PILESER III as part of the massive conquests undertaken by his empire.

SUSAN ACKERMAN

ASHTERATHITE ash'tuh-ruh-th*i*t [עֶשְׁתֵּרָתִי 'ashterathi]. A resident of Ashtaroth (1 Chr 11:44). *See* ASHTAROTH.

ASHTEROTH-KARNAIM ash'tuh-roth-kahr-nay'im [עַשְׁתְּרֹת קַרְנַיִם 'ashteroth qarnayim]. In Gen 14:5, King Chedorlaomer of Elam and three allies defeated a group called the Rephaim in a place called Ashteroth-Karnaim. Ashteroth-Karnaim is probably identical to the city Ashtaroth mentioned in Deut 1:1; Josh 9:10; 12:4; 13:10, 31; and 1 Chr 6:71, as particularly indicated in Deut 3:11 and Josh 12:4, where King Og of Ashtaroth is identified as one of the last descendants of the Rephaim. Some, however, identify Ashteroth-Karnaim with the city Karnaim mentioned in Amos 6:13. The two sites were quite near each other, both lying about 35 km east of the Sea of Galilee, in ancient Bashan/ modern Syria. Ashteroth/Ashtaroth is specifically identified with modern Tell Ashtarah, and Karnaim with modern Sheikh Sa'ad, which is located 4 km to the northeast. The name Ashteroth/Ashtaroth is derived from the name Astarte ('ashtart), who was one of the three great Canaanite goddesses, although the biblical writers have imposed upon the term the vowels of the word bosheth (בֹּשֶׁת, "shame") for theological reasons. The name Karnaim (qarnayim) means "two horns." The composite name Ashteroth-Karnaim does not refer to a cult of a two-horned Astarte but only indicates the close proximity of Ashteroth/Ashtaroth and Karnaim.

SUSAN ACKERMAN

ASHURBANIPAL, ASSURBANIPAL ash'uhr-ban'uh-puhl. During the reign (668–627 BCE) of Ashurbanipal, the last great Assyrian king, Assyria reached the zenith of its power, expanding its territory from Egypt to Elam. Assyria, however, began to disintegrate toward the end of his reign. It is somewhat ironic that the end of his reign is obscure due to the lack of references and records after 639 BCE, since he is credited with building one of the most extensive libraries in antiquity.

A. His Campaigns

Ashurbanipal's father, Esarhaddon, died on his way to Egypt to quell a rebellion incited by Tirhakah, king of Kush. As soon as Ashurbanipal took the throne, he sent his army to Egypt and defeated Tirhakah in Memphis in 667 BCE, but Tirhakah was able to escape to Thebes. When Tandamane, nephew of Tirhakah, was threatening to invade Memphis, Ashurbanipal sent his army to Egypt for the second time in 663 BCE. His army defeated Tandamane and finally conquered Thebes as

well. Ashurbanipal's third campaign was conducted against Tyre in 662 BCE, most likely because Ba'al, king of Tyre, sided with Tandamane. Ba'al quickly surrendered when his city came under siege, but Ashurbanipal allowed him to keep his kingship. Egypt became independent again under Psammeticus about 655 BCE, but there was no sign of hostility between Egypt and Assyria during Assyria's final years. In 652 BCE, Ashurbanipal faced his toughest challenge during his long reign. His brother Shamash-shum-ukin, who had been appointed ruler of Babylonia by Esarhaddon, revolted against him with the support of the Chaldeans, the Elamites, and the Arabs. It was a long and bitter war that ended in Ashurbanipal's victory in 648 BCE. There is a tradition in 2 Chr 33:10-13 that suggests that Manasseh was taken captive to Babylon; perhaps Manasseh took the side of Shamash-shum-ukin during this war but was forgiven by Ashurbanipal. Ashurbanipal continued punitive campaigns against Elam until he sacked its capital Susa ca. 640 BCE. He also campaigned against some of the northern Arabian tribes around 644–643 BCE.

B. His Library

Besides his many military campaigns, Ashurbanipal is most notable for his library in Nineveh. He boasted that he could read and write the cuneiform script and pursued his cultural interests with passion. He employed many scribes to collect, revise, compile, and edit thousands of texts brought together in his library. The library showed some subject arrangement and some type of catalog system. A large collection of cuneiform tablets has been recovered in good condition from this library because apparently the Medes who invaded Nineveh in 612 BCE pushed in the walls of the building without removing the tablets. Of no use to the invaders, the contents of the library survived to become a major source of knowledge about history and culture of the ANE.

Bibliography: G. Frame. *Rulers of Babylonia: From the Second Dynasty of Isin to the End of Assyrian Domination (1157–612 BC).* RIMB, Vol. 2 (1995); A. K. Grayson. "The Chronology of the Reign of Ashurbanipal." *ZA* 70 (1981) 227–45; D. D. Leckenbill. *Ancient Records of Assyria and Babylonia* (1924); J. Oates. "Assyrian Chronology, 631–612 B.C." *Iraq* 27 (1965) 135–59; A. Spalinger. "Assurbanipal and Egypt: A Source Study." *JAOS* 94 (1974) 316–28.

URIAH KIM

ASHURITES ash'uh-r*i*ts [אֲשׁוּרִי 'ashuri]. A people over whom ISHBOSHETH reigned (2 Sam 2:9). Since "Ashurites" is another name for "Assyrians" who lived later, it should probably be read ASHERITES as in Judg 1:32, a tribe who allowed the Canaanites to live among them. The Vulgate refers to them as Geshurites.

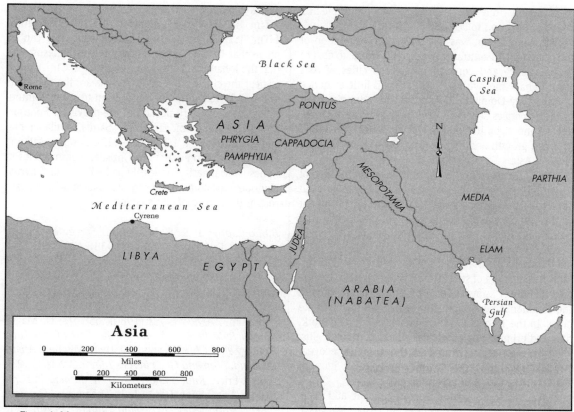

Figure 1: Map of Asia.

ASHVATH ash´vath [עַשְׁוָת ʿashwath]. One of Japhet's three sons and a descendant of Asher born to Jacob and Leah's servant Zilpah (1 Chr 7:33).

ASIA ay´zhuh [Ἀσία Asia]. In the time of Paul, the Roman province of Asia was bounded on the north by Bithynia and Pontus, on the south by Lycia and Pamphylia and on the east by Galatia.

In 133 BCE Attalus III of Pergamum bequeathed his kingdom, and thus supremacy over western Asia Minor, to the Roman people; Manius Aquillius created the province of Asia between 129 and 126 BCE. The rise of the power of Pontus under the leadership of Mithridates VI from around 110 BCE had far-reaching consequences for Asia. Mithridates was a direct challenge to Roman control of Asia and the conflict between the two powers involved all the peoples between the Euphrates and the Aegean. The first war between Rome and Mithridates lasted from 89 to 84 BCE; Mithridates was eventually defeated and agreed to the terms of the peace laid down by Sulla.

After his defeat of Pompey, Julius Caesar's general policy in Asia was considerate, and he granted favors and privileges to the cities, which evoked widespread gratitude. Faced with the general economic distress of the province, caused in particular by the exactions of Pompey, Brutus, Cassius, and Antony, Augustus (the name he took in place of Octavian in 27 BCE) aimed to rebuild a vigorous city life. He also elevated Ephesus to the status of the capital of the province of Asia, in place of Pergamum. Augustus continued and extended reforms of the tax system instituted by Caesar, reforms that did much to increase the prosperity of the cities. He also stimulated urban development in the province and throughout his long reign, which ended in 14 CE, he generally adopted policies that were beneficial for the cities of Asia. The importance of Augustus in the eyes of the people of Asia is shown by the development of the Imperial cult in Asia from 29 BCE. The cult subsequently flourished in the province.

In the provinces of the East, including Asia, Tiberius' government was generally beneficial and he attempted to prevent extortion and cruelty, and to maintain law and order. Asia was little affected by Caligula's grandiose ideas and desire to play the part of an Oriental ruler, and Claudius' policies generally promoted the welfare of the province. For example, he aided cities that had been affected by some sort of disaster, gave various benefits to other cities, and took steps to ensure proconsuls discharged their duties and did not practice extortion. Nero continued the bureaucratic methods of Claudius, including allowing imperial procurators to have increased power; he also adopted measures for the benefit of the province. His seizure of works of art from the cities of Greece and Asia greatly damaged what popularity Nero had in these regions, but overall the East was little affected by his cruelty and folly.

Vespasian's reign was marked by a continuation of the trend toward centralization and his efforts to ensure the allegiance and contentment of the cities of Asia seem to have met with success. There is little evidence of cruelty by Domitian in Asia, and his administration of the provinces seems to have been marked by intelligence and vigor. In fact, the Flavian period was a time of urban growth and architectural development in the cities of Asia.

Thus, the peace in Asia that began with the reign of Augustus lasted throughout the 1st cent. CE, and indeed continued throughout the 2nd cent. The establishment of the *Pax Romana*, and the spirit of confidence that peace engendered, along with improvements throughout the empire, made it possible for the extensive natural resources of Asia to be greatly developed and this introduced an era of stability and prosperity, such as the area had never known. This becomes most apparent in the commencement of building work undertaken in the cities. In the 1st cent. CE the increase in building work, financed primarily by municipal funds and private gifts, gives the impression that a gradual and sound recovery had taken place, a recovery that laid the foundation for the wide expansion of urban life and culture.

There were also some very significant and well-established Jewish communities in Asia. We have evidence that at least some of these communities were involved in the life of their cities, and they clearly had an impact on the development of early Christianity in the province.

In the NT, *Asia* can designate a continent that is distinct from Europe (*see* Strabo, *Geogr.* 2.5.24, 31; 7.4.5), or it can be used with the adjective "Minor" of the western peninsula of modern Turkey. Neither usage is found in the Bible. In the Apocrypha, *Asia* is used to describe the Seleucid Kingdom, and the ruler of this kingdom is called "the king of Asia" (1 Macc 8:6; 2 Macc 3:3; compare 1 Macc 11:13; 12:39; 13:32). *Asia* is most often used in the NT with the meaning of the Roman province. (For example, see Acts 19:10, 26-27; 27:2; Rom 16:5; 1 Cor 16:19; 2 Cor 1:8; 1 Pet 1:1.) In Acts 2:9-10, *Asia* is used to refer to a portion of the province, as is shown by the inclusion in the list of Phrygia, which was part of the province of Asia.

According to the Acts of the Apostles, Paul was active in the province of Asia (Acts 13:1–16:10; 18:19–19:41; 20:6-38). The NT Letters of Colossians, Philemon, and Ephesians give us information about Christian communities in Asia, although in the case of Ephesians, the location of the original recipient is debated since there is general agreement that the phrase ἐν Ἐφέσῳ en Ephesō found in some manuscripts at Eph 1:1 was not part of the original text. Believers in Asia are mentioned in a number of other

NT documents (Rom 16:5; 1 Cor 16:19; 2 Cor 1:8; 2 Tim 1:15; 1 Pet 1:1; compare 1 Cor 15:32; 16:8; 1 Tim 1:3; 2 Tim 1:18; 4:12). A strong case can be made that John's Gospel was written in Ephesus, and that the Johannine Letters were written to Christians in or near the city. Communities in Asia are the recipients of John's Revelation; this was written to seven communities in the western portion of the province: Ephesus, Smyrna, Pergamum, Thyatira, Sardis, Philadelphia, and Laodicea (Rev 1:11; 2:1–3:22). Around 110 CE, Ignatius also wrote letters to Christian communities in Ephesus, Magnesia, Tralles, Philadelphia, and Smyrna. Undoubtedly, communities in Asia played an important role in the spread of Christianity.

Bibliography: T. R. S. Broughton. *Survey of Ancient Rome.* T. Frank, ed. Vol 4. (1938) 499–918; S. J. Friesen. *Twice Neokoros. Ephesus, Asia and the Cult of the Flavian Imperial Family* (1993); S.J. Friesen. *Imperial Cults and the Apocalypse of John* (2001); A. D. Macro. "The Cities of Asia Minor under the Roman Imperium." *ANRW* II 7.2 (1980), 658–97; D. Magie. *Roman Rule in Asia Minor to the End of the Third Century after Christ.* 2 vols. (1950); S. Mitchell. *Anatolia. Land, Men and Gods in Asia Minor.* 2 vols. (1993); S. R. F. Price. *Rituals and Power. The Roman Imperial Cult in Asia Minor* (1984); L. L. Thompson. *The Book of Revelation: Apocalypse and Empire* (1990); P. R. Trebilco. *Jewish Communities in Asia Minor.* SNTSMS 69 (1991); P. R. Trebilco. "Asia." *The Book of Acts in its Greco-Roman Setting.* D. W. J. Gill and C. Gempf, eds. (1994) 291–362.

PAUL TREBILCO

ASIAN AMERICAN INTERPRETATION. Rather than being defined as a single method or approach, Asian American biblical interpretation is a particular discourse that has evolved in response and relationship to the multicultural reality of contemporary Asian North America. This discourse involves critical reflection on the various social and political dynamics that shape the Asian North American experience and represents the work of a broad cross-section of scholars working in the United States and Canada who have racial and ethnic identities connected to the histories and cultures of East, Southeast. and South Asia, and the Pacific Islands. In some cases, such ties are direct and immediate. In others, they are less direct and quite complex, negotiated in the context of transgenerational Asian North American communities, multiracial or hapa identities, or international and cross-cultural adoption. Thus, the designation "Asian American" refers not to a single group or culture, but to the experience of living in North America in the midst of a particular collection of racial/ethnic minority communities. In keeping with such diversity, Asian American biblical interpretation aims to reflect and interrogate the ways in which social location, culture, and identity affect how the Bible is read and appropriated, and how the field of biblical studies is constructed and taught.

Since the late 20th cent., Asian American biblical interpretation has developed primarily along three trajectories of biblical criticism: cultural hermeneutics, cultural studies, and postcolonial biblical interpretation (Foskett and Kuan 2006). Each emphasizes a particular set of concerns, none of which is entirely exclusive of those addressed by the other approaches.

A. Cultural Hermeneutics

Drawing on the work of those who were formally reading the Bible in the contexts of East, Southeast, and South Asian cultures and religious traditions in the 1970s and 1980s, Asian biblical students and scholars in North America began addressing the hermeneutical concerns and principles that eventually coalesced as Asian American biblical interpretation. Asian American cultural hermeneutics is also directly related to the work of Asian Americans in theological studies. Representing fields as diverse as congregational studies, historical studies, sociology, literary studies, pastoral care, Christian education, and constructive theology, scholars have plumbed the particular and complex contexts that have shaped Asian American lives, communities, and theologies. Such work has enriched the discourses that constitute Asian American biblical interpretation.

Two ways of reading the Bible have been at the forefront of Asian North American cultural hermeneutics. The first approach generally draws on categories, concepts, and experiences rooted in Asian American traditions, cultural practices, and social contexts to illumine passages, themes, and concepts in the Bible. The second approach parallels the work of cross-textual and dialogical Asian biblical interpretation. Here interpreters engage biblical texts and traditions in the context of Asian North American cultural and religious pluralism. They place nonbiblical texts and traditions in mutual conversation with the Bible. In short, this mode of reading regards the Bible as a central, if not exclusive, sacred text.

B. Cultural Studies

Asian American interpretation has also been practiced as a form of cultural studies. In this approach, Asian North American scholars have adapted liberationist perspectives articulated by Asian biblical scholars advocating for the politically, socially, and economically oppressed in India, Korea, and the Philippines in the 1970s and 1980s. Here liberationist agendas merge with the aims and practices of ethnic studies, feminist hermeneutics, and the analysis of gender, race, and class. The result is a complex discourse that focuses on the construction of identity, race/ethnicity, gender, and class either "in" the biblical text or "in the act of reading the text."

Recent work in Asian American interpretation underscores the sometimes reciprocal and complex questions that emerge when the concerns of Asian American studies are brought to bear on biblical interpretation (Liew). Interpreters have shown that Asian American identity and experience function not only as a position from which to engage the Bible but also as a construct that has itself been formed and renegotiated in the act of reading the Bible. In this regard, Asian American biblical interpretation has established a place for itself not only in biblical studies but in the field of Asian American studies as well.

C. Postcolonial Readings

As postcolonial readings of the Bible have emerged in Asian biblical interpretation and theology (Sugirtharajah) and in North American scholarship, postcolonial hermeneutics has also found a place in Asian American readings of the Bible. Following the lead of scholars who have argued for the connection between diasporic interpretation and postcolonial studies, Asian American interpreters have examined the Asian diaspora as a context for reading the Bible. Others have drawn on the work of postcolonial theorists to plead for the further integration of notions of hybridity and heterogeneity in Asian American studies and in Asian American readings of the Bible. Such readers have put postcolonial theory to use in shaping Asian American biblical interpretation as an expression of both cultural hermeneutics and cultural studies.

Asian American biblical interpretation is surely a multivocal discourse whose participants include scholars working at the intersection of biblical studies, theology, and Asian American studies, as well as clergy and laity. Like African American and Latino/a biblical hermeneutics, it brings together a constellation of questions and concerns that illustrate not only the continuing significance of the Bible and biblical tradition in North America but also the multiculturalism of the North American context.

Bibliography: Mary Foskett and Jeffrey K. Kuan. *Ways of Being, Ways of Reading: Asian American Biblical Interpretation* (2006); Chan-Hie Kim. "Reading the Bible as Asian Americans." *NIB.* Vol. 1 (1994); Pui-Lan Kwok. "Discovering the Bible in the Nonbiblical World." *Semeia* 47 (1989); Archie C. C. Lee. "Cross-Textual Interpretation and Its Implications for Biblical Studies," in *Teaching the Bible: Discourses and Politics of Biblical Pedagogy*, ed. Fernando F. Segovia and Mary Ann Tolbert (1998); Tat-siong Benny Liew and Vincent L. Wimbush, eds. *Encountering Texts, Encountering Communities: A Symposium on African and Asian American Engagements with the Bible.* *Union Seminary Quarterly Review* 56 (2002); Tat-siong Benny Liew, ed. *The Bible in Asian America.* Gale Yee, ed. *Semeia* 90–91 (2002); Fumitaka Matsuoka and

Eleazar S. Fernandez, eds. *Realizing the America of Our Hearts: Theological Voices of Asian Americans* (2003); Fernando F. Segovia and Mary Ann Tolbert. *Reading from This Place.* Vol. 1, *Social Location and Biblical Interpretation in the United States* (1995); R. S. Sugirtharajah. *Postcolonial Reconfigurations: An Alternative Way of Reading the Bible and Doing Theology* (2003); Gale A. Yee. *Poor Banished Children of Eve: Woman as Evil in the Hebrew Bible* (2003).

MARY FOSKETT

ASIAN INTERPRETATION. The term *Asian* is used, as a matter of convenience, to set a geographical boundary. However, the term is admittedly too broad to reflect the complexity of biblical interpretation in Asia, which has complex racial, linguistic, political, social, and ideological identities.

Generally speaking, Asian interpretations of the Bible take seriously the text and the interpreter. The reader examines 1) the semantic domain of the biblical texts and the traditional theology that was shaped by Western traditions. The reader then 2) compares and contrasts the composite horizons of the Asian context(s) with the presuppositions of the interpreters. To miss either *1* or *2* is to drift from the intent of an Asian biblical interpretation.

Asian interpretations of the Bible can be grouped broadly into camps that are interrelated to one another:

A. Indigenous Interpretation

The task of Bible translation is a first step toward indigenous interpretation. Other steps include the translation of Western Christian classics (e.g., the work of the Institute of Sino-Christian Studies and Liu Xiao-feng), and the teaching of biblical languages in the native tongues of the people (rather than Latin and English).

Translation is always interpretation. Some translators are more literal than others, when striving for literal word for word equivalence. But most translators who take seriously the context of the reader are attempting to express biblical concepts and narratives in the dynamic words and idioms of the target language.

The use of Asian texts and resources in indigenous interpretation is prominent. Many Asians explore the intertextual relationship between the biblical texts and the Asian texts. For example, one could identify the affinity between Christian faith and the Mahayana texts; or use Yin-yang philosophical texts, *I Ching*, to express the Trinity; or link the book of Job with the Hindu text, *Bhagavadgita*; or employ Confucian texts to Paul's ethical teaching.

B. Contextual Interpretations

In order to take the composite horizons of Asia seriously—which consist of hybrid people-groups, diverse cultures, pluralistic religions, and regional issues— Asian interpretations address the various regional distinctions in the following examples: animism and Christian pneumatology in Indonesia, or Japanese womanist reading of Mark, or Chinese women trapped in Confucian society.

C. Global Biblical Interpretation in Asia

Not all interpretations offered by Asian exegetes are considered Asian interpretation. Besides writing in their own languages, many Bible commentaries in Asia are dominated in form and content by Western interpretation, so much so that these Asian interpretations have nothing to do with contexts, experiences, and the thought of Asia. A few Asian biblical scholars even prefer to write in foreign languages.

The issue is not whether Western interpretation is inferior or whether Asians can read the Bible as critically as any Westerner. The strategy instead concerns incarnational interpretation in a global village. Since reading is always contextual, Asian interpretations are distinctive in their engagement with Asian soil, sources, and lived experience. Analogous to the Hellenization process that changed the Jewish world and shaped the Roman culture in antiquity, modern globalization of our day has brought about global interpretations that, on one hand, differentiate contextual readings, and, on the other hand, integrate contextual readings into a constructive dialogue. The *Global Bible Commentary* provides examples of global interpretations. Another helpful resource is *Navigating Romans through Cultures.* Cross-cultural and intertextual readings of many Asian scholars, especially those who are trained in the West, are heading in the direction of Asian global interpretation. Global interpretation protects the universal church against the aberrations of Asian interpretations, *and* it protects Asian interpretations against aberrations of Christian interpretations in the West. Insofar as the global interpretation brings the best of the Asian tradition/wisdom into the Bible, it will help compensate for the biases of a Western-dominated, limited interpretation of the Bible.

Bibliography: John C. England et al., eds. *Asian Christian Theologies: A Research Guide to Authors, Movements, Sources* (2002–2004); Ken Gnanakan, ed. *Biblical Theology in Asia* (1995); Daniel Patte, et al. *Global Bible Commentary* (2004); Bong Rin Ro and Ruth Eshenaur. *The Bible and Theology in Asian Contexts* (1984); Choan-Seng Song. *Theology from the Womb of Asia* (1986); R. S. Sugirtharajah. *The Bible and the Third World* (2001).

KHIOK-KHNG (K.K.) YEO

ASIARCH ay´zhee-ahrk [Ἀσιάρχης Asiarchēs]. The title given to an elected or appointed official of high rank, typically drawn from the leading families, who served a limited term performing various public services including festivals for cities in the Roman province of

Asia. It is unclear whether an asiarch's function was primarily municipal or associated with provincial matters, including imperial cult worship. The debate centers on whether the designations asiarch and "high priest" (ἀρχιερεύς archiereus) were interchangeable. Identifying the function of the office is made difficult by the likelihood that it changed over time. In addition to Acts 19:31, where Ephesian asiarchs are portrayed as sympathetic to Paul and urge him to avoid the riot incited at the theater, the term appears in a handful of literary sources, on bronze coins, and in numerous inscriptions from Asia Minor, most of which date from the 2nd to 3rd cent. CE. The reference to Paul's friendship with Ephesian asiarchs in Acts 19 is controversial in that there is nothing to suggest that there were multiple officeholders at any one time. Perhaps more important, however, Paul's good standing with high-ranking officials seems designed to distance Paul from any association with the potentially illegal activity of the rioters.

Bibliograpy: Steven J. Friesen. "Asiarchs." *Zeitschrift für Papyrologie und Epigraphik* 126 (1999) 275–90.

RUBÉN RENÉ DUPERTUIS

ASIBIAS as´uh-bi´uhs [Ἀσιβίας Asibias]. Apocryphal form of HASHABIAH (1 Esd 9:26). *See* HASHABIAH.

ASIEL as´ee-uhl [עֲשִׂיאֵל 'asi'el; Ἀσιήλ Asiēl]. 1. Father of Seraiah, great-grandfather of Jehu, a Simeon chief who sought pasture land in Gedor (1 Chr 4:35).

2. An ancestor of TOBIT and member of the tribe of Napthali (Tob 1:1).

3. Scribes who copied books dictated by EZRA (2 Esd 14:24).

ASK, REQUEST [שָׁאַל sha'al, בָּעָה ba'ah, בָּקַר baqar, בָּקַשׁ baqash, דָּרַשׁ darash; αἰτέω aiteō, ἐρωτάω erōtaō, ἐπερωτάω eperōtaō, δέομαι deomai, ζητέω zēteō, πυνθάνομαι pynthanomai]. The Hebrew word most frequently translated *ask* is sha'al. It is used when posing a question, requesting something of material value, or appealing to God (or to an oracular device or to a prophet) for counsel in times of crisis. Other Hebrew words translated "ask" or "request" are ba'ah (Isa 21:12), baqar (Ps 27:4), baqash (Esth 2:15), and darash (Ezra 20:40).

Posing a question may serve as a springboard to a crucial development in a narrative. Sha'al is used when Judah's friend Hirah inquires about the "temple prostitute," his mistaken identification of Tamar, Judah's maltreated daughter-in-law (Gen 38:21). Sisera asks for water after his campaign against Israel, unmindful of Jael's designs to assist in Israel's victory (Judg 5:25), and Bathsheba asks Solomon to give Abishag to Adonijah for a wife, thus establishing the latter's claim to the throne (1 Kgs 2:20, 22), only to be rebuffed by her son.

Individuals frequently ask God for victory in battle, help in a crisis, or evidence of trust and faith. David inquires of the LORD regarding imminent battles (1 Sam 23:4; 30:8); Isaiah tells Ahaz to ask for a sign when the king faces threats from the Syro-Ephraimite alliance (Isa 7:11). The psalmist celebrates the compassion and patience of God who responded to the Israelites' request for meat by sending quails (Ps 105:40) and encourages the people to petition God (literally, "ask") "for the peace of Jerusalem" (Ps 122:6).

Posing a request to God guarantees neither response nor victory. In contrast to David, who receives many replies from God, Saul is repeatedly rejected by God, who "did not answer him, not by dreams, or by Urim, or by prophets" (1 Sam 28:6). When the Israelites are poised to fight against one of their own tribes, Benjamin, they ask God if they should proceed. Although God answers affirmatively, they nonetheless are defeated, emphasizing the total disintegration of the tribal system (Judg 20:27).

Various texts illustrate that *not requesting* of God or petitioning other deities may be disastrous or may illustrate lack of faith. Joshua is duped by the Gibeonites because he does not "ask direction from the LORD" (Josh 9:14). Saul neglects to seek God's counsel, turning instead to a medium (1 Chr 10:13). God warns the Israelites not to appeal to the gods of the nations (Deut 18:11), as divination was associated with manipulation of the transcendent (Judg 18:5) and the avoidance of God's will. God laments when the people engage in such practices (Hos 4:12) or when their requests are without accompanying righteous practice (Isa 58:2).

In the NT, the words most commonly translated *ask* or *request* are aiteō (Matt 5:42), erōtaō (John 9:2), eperōtaō (John 18:7), deomai (Acts 21:39), zēteō (1 Cor 1:22), and pynthanomai (Luke 15:26). They are used to indicate the posing of questions, the making of demands, or an inquiry about someone. In addition, they may signal a faith stance (John 16:24, 26) or indicate prayer (Luke 22:32; John 14:16; 1 Thess 3:10).

SHARON PACE

ASMAR, TELL. A large site ca. 50 km northeast of Baghdad, identified with ancient Eshnunna, excavated by H. Frankfort (1930–1936) and by R. McC. Adams (1957–1958), revealing occupation levels from the late 4th millennium BCE. Its most important period may have been from the late 3rd to the early 2nd millennium BCE as a provincial capital in the Third Dynasty of UR. Significant remains from this period include the Shu-Sin temple to the dynasty's deified fourth king. In the ensuing Isin-Larsa period, Eshnunna was the capital of an independent and powerful city-state, but was conquered by HAMMURABI (1792–1750 BCE) in the subsequent Old Babylonian period.

RALPH K. HAWKINS

ASMODEUS az´moh-dee´uhs [Ασμοδαῖος Asmodaios]. In Tobit, a wicked demon who kills each of Sarah's seven husbands in the bridal chamber (Tob 3:8; 6:14). According to some manuscripts jealousy motivates Asmodeus. The angel Raphael instructs Tobit's son Tobias to burn tissues of fish liver and heart, an odor that drives the demon all the way from Media to Egypt. Raphael binds Asmodeus there, enabling Tobias to marry Sarah.

Asmodeus traditions also appear in *T. Sol.* 5 and may relate to the Sadducees' challenge to Jesus concerning the resurrection (Mark 12:18-27). *See* SOLOMON, TESTAMENT OF; TOBIT.

GREG CAREY

ASNAH as´nuh [אַסְנָה ʾasnah, Ἀσανα Asana]. A family head whose descendants returned to Jerusalem after the exile (Ezra 2:50; 1 Esd 5:31). Absent in list in Neh 7:52.

ASP [פֶּתֶן pethen; ἀσπίς aspis]. The translation for Hebrew pethen and Greek aspis in Isa 11:8. These words can also be rendered in the NRSV as viper, serpent, cobra, or adder. Many suggest that the pethen is a cobra, in part because a pethen is described as "deaf" (Ps 58:4), which characterizes the Egyptian cobra (naja haje) as it has no visible hearing organ. Thus, it was unresponsive to the music of the snake charmer (Ps 58:5), making it all the more dangerous. The cobra also features a flattened head and a hood, which expands prior to striking its prey. Its venom disrupts the functioning of the nervous system and is lethal—sometimes in as little as thirty minutes—if untreated. Regardless of its exact identification, the asp is a symbol of harmful poison. It appears in various figures of speech. The wine of the enemy is the "cruel venom of asps" (Deut 32:33). The food of the wicked—their excess riches—turns to the venom of asps in their stomachs, causing them to vomit their wealth (Job 20:14-16). God employs the asp to destroy the wicked (Sir 39:30); but God protects the righteous from its poison (Ps 91:13). Sinners are recalcitrant like the hearing-impaired asp (Ps 58:4-5). In the prophetic vision of utopia, the young child will play over the holes of the deleterious snake without fear (Isa 11:8). The venom of asps is also associated with the deceitful speech of humans bound by sin (Rom 3:13; compare Ps 140:3).

MARK RONCACE

ASPATHA as-pay´thuh [אַסְפָּתָא ʾaspathaʾ]. One of Haman's sons, all killed and hung on the gallows (Esth 9:7). *See* HAMAN.

ASPHAR as´fahr [Ἀσφάρ Asphar]. A pool in the Tekoa wilderness where Jonathan Maccabeus and Simon Maccabeus camped after escaping from Bachides' murder plot (1 Macc 9:33).

ASPHARASUS as-fair´uh-suhs [Ασφαρασος Aspharasos]. One of the exiles whom King Darius allowed to return with Zerubbabel (1 Esdr 5:8), among a list somewhat different than in Ezra 2:2.

ASRIEL as´ree-uhl [אַשְׂרִיאֵל ʾasriʾel]. One possible meaning of the name is "God is joined." Asriel, a son of GILEAD and an Aramean concubine, was a descendant of MANASSEH listed in Moses' second census taken in the wilderness (Num 26:31). He was also Moses' captain in the wilderness (Num 26:3). Along with other sons of Gilead, Asriel received land to maintain the tribe (Josh 17:2). Some readings have listed Asriel as a son of Manasseh.

MEREDITH BURK HAMMONS

ASS. The ass, or DONKEY [חֲמוֹר khamor] was the main beast of burden used in biblical times. It had a very versatile and distinguished role. The Hebrew Bible contains several terms to distinguish gender and age by using ʾathon (אָתוֹן) and ʾayir (עַיִר) for she-ass and young ass, respectively. The domesticated ass (*Equus asinus*) is the descendant of the wild ass (*Equus africanus*), which was once widespread over the whole of Saharan Africa and most probably also in Arabia. Of all domestic animals, the African ass is second only to the camel in performance under desert conditions, in its ability to graze on desert scrub (Gen 36:24), and its power to go for long distances without drinking. Although the domestic donkey is slower than the horse, being descended from the wild ass of the hot deserts of Africa and Arabia made it immune to the harsh climate of the Near Eastern environment.

It seems that the original reason for domesticating the wild ass was the consumption of its flesh and milk; however, it is most likely that the donkey became a favorite because of its ability to carry heavy loads before the invention of the wheel and the introduction of the wagon.

Even when horse riding became preferred because of its greater speed, donkey riding did not cease completely. Because of its anatomy, namely low withers and low carriage of the head and neck, the only way to ride a donkey for any length of time is to sit well back on the loins. However, even then the rider will be jolted by the shocks of the moving legs if going at any speed. Thus, the donkey is quite unsuitable for riding at speed, and this would have precluded its use as a mount in hunting or battle. In spite of the horse's popularity in eastern Asia and Europe, during the Iron Age the domestic donkey remained the common means of transport throughout Egypt and Western Asia.

In Israelite society, donkeys (and oxen) seem to have been the most common, and important, animals since they, and not horses or camels, are the ones enumerated among the prized possessions not to be coveted: "Do not lust after your neighbor's wife; do not covet your neighbor's household, his land, his slave, his slave-girl, his ox, his donkey, or anything that belongs to him" (Deut 5:21). Having a donkey was considered basic (Deut 22:3), thus it was important to take care of it, have it well fed (Isa 30:24), and let it rest along with all other employees and animals (Deut 5:14). The importance of this animal is demonstrated also by the fact that as part of the rules for the renewal of the covenant, an instruction is given to redeem its firstling with a lamb (Exod 34:20).

The donkey provided transportation for people (Gen 22:3; Exod 4:20) and was used as a pack animal (Gen 42:27; 44). This is well illustrated in Egyptian as well as Mesopotamian art. In a wall painting in a tomb at Beni Hassan in Egypt (19th century BCE), white donkeys are depicted being led by Semites migrating into Egypt. One donkey is laden with smelting equipment and the other carries two children (ANET, fig. 3). On a relief from Nineveh, Ashurbanipal (668-633 BCE) depicts prisoners taken from a captured Egyptian city, among whom are two children riding on a donkey covered with a blanket-saddle (ANET, fig. 10). While it was employed in basic agricultural tasks such as plowing (Deut 22:10) and threshing (ANET, fig. 89), the donkey was used also as a riding animal for people of high standing, women (Josh 15:18 = Judg 1:14; 1 Sam 25:20) as well as men (2 Sam 17:23; 1 Kgs 2:40), even royalty (2 Sam 19:27). David had a special overseer, Jehdeiah the Meronothite, in charge of the donkeys (1 Chr 27:30). Riding a donkey took some preparation (2 Sam 19:27; 1 Kgs 13:13, 23), such as putting on a headgear or a bridle (methegh, Prov 26:3). However, it seems that the female of the white variety was preferred for riding, as alluded to in Judges 5:10. Other instances where riding she-asses is specifically mentioned are those describing Balaam the Seer (Num 22) and the Shunamite woman (2 Kgs 4:24). It seems that young donkeys in large numbers were also considered a status symbol (Judg 10:4).

The value of the donkey is well documented in Egyptian and Assyrian reports of donkeys being taken as booty or given as tribute. *See* ANIMALS OF THE BIBLE.

Bibliography: O. Borowski. *Every Living Thing: Daily Use of Animals in Ancient Israel* (1998); J. B. Pritchard. *Ancient Near Eastern Texts Relating to the Old Testament* (1969).

ODED BOROWSKI

ASSAPHIOTH [Ασσαφιωθ Assaphiōth]. The ancestral head of a family of Temple servants for SOLOMON (1 Esd 5:33) in a list somewhat different from Ezra 2:55.

ASSASSIN. The Bible contains numerous examples of politically motivated murders of important figures. Such assassinations include those of Eglon, the king

of Moab, by Ehud (Judg 3:15-22); of Abner, David's adversary, by Joab, the commander-in-chief of David's army (2 Sam 3:27); of Ishbaal, Saul's son, by the sons of Rimmon (2 Sam 4:5-7); of Amnon, David's son, by Absalom's servants (2 Sam 13:28, 29); of Amasa, commander of the army under both Absalom and David, by Joab (2 Sam 20:9, 10); of Joash, king of Judah, by his servants (2 Kgs 12:20); of Zechariah, king of Israel, by Shallum in a coup (2 Kgs 15:8-10); and of Shallum, by Menahem in a further coup (2 Kgs 15:13-14), among others. In Esth 2:21 (*see* 6:2), King Ahasuerus (Xerxes) of Persia is the subject of a foiled assassination attempt whose discovery by Mordecai plays an important part in the subsequent salvation of the Jews.

While such murders are a fairly common aspect of the succession of rulers and the rise and fall of dynasties in biblical history, it is important to note David's revulsion at the assassination of his rival Ishbaal in 2 Sam 4:9-12. There also would seem to be no link between these political killings and the tradition of holy violence associated with the Aaronite priest Phinehas in such passages as Num 25:1-13; Ps 106:28-31; Sir 45:23-24; 1 Macc 2:26, and 54. However, it is possible that some such link was indeed asserted by certain groups in the 1st cent. CE. In his description of the various factions whose actions contributed in one way or another to the Judean war (66–70 CE), Flavius Josephus refers to a band of radical anti-Roman assassins whose use of curved knives concealed under their clothing earned them the title of *sicarii* or "dagger men" (what they called themselves, if anything, is not known). It is important to distinguish clearly between this group and other revolutionary groups such as the so-called Zealots, who featured in the final stages of the Judean war. We first learn of the *sicarii* in *J.W.* 2.254–257 where Josephus describes the panic caused in the time of Felix (52–60 CE) by their tactic of mingling with crowds on festival days and murdering their political enemies (often Jews sympathetic to Rome) in broad daylight. They also resorted to kidnapping (*Ant.* 20.208–210). In Acts 21:38 Paul is mistakenly identified as "the Egyptian who recently stirred up a revolt and led the four thousand assassins out into the wilderness." While Josephus informs us about this "Egyptian" (*J.W.* 2.261; *Ant.* 20.167–169) he does not refer to him as one of the *sicarii*. Further, although Josephus brands these men as "bandits," they apparently shared the revolutionary ideology of the so-called "Fourth Philosophy," whose violent resistance to the Roman take over of Judea in 6 CE had been inspired by a religious desire to be ruled by God alone (*J.W.* 2.118; *Ant.* 18.23; *see* Acts 5:37). Josephus states that in all other respects they were just like the Pharisees (*Ant.* 18.23; but see *J.W.* 2.118). Two leaders of the *sicarii* at the time of the Jewish revolt, Menahem and Eleazer ben Jair, were relatives of Judas the Galilean, the original leader of the Fourth

Philosophy, suggesting that leadership of the group was hereditary. Menahem, who was murdered by an opposing faction in Jerusalem during the early stages of the war, seems to have had messianic pretensions (*J.W.* 2.443), while Eleazer was forced to flee with his *sicarii* to the mountain stronghold of Masada (*J.W.* 2.447). It was here that resistance to the Romans finally ended in 74 CE (*J.W.* 7.389–401).

The English word *assassin* is a consequence of the Crusader attempts to conquer the Holy Lands, and it came into use via French and Italian words that referred to the secretive and deadly 11th cent. CE Islamic order of khashashin. *See* JEWISH WARS; PHARISEE, ZEALOT.

PAUL SPILSBURY

ASSEMBLE [קָהַל qahal, קָבַץ qavats, אָסַף ʾasaf, עֵדָה ʿedhah, כָּנַס kanas; συνάγω synagō, συνέρχομαι synerchomai, ἐκκλησιάζω ekklēsiazō]. Most worthy of note is the Hebrew verb קָהַל qahal, used always for people, never for animals or things. The meaning can be neutral, as in their gathering around Aaron (Exod 32:1), often with the congregation, ʿedhah or qahal, as subject (Lev 8:3, 4; Num 10:7; 20:10; Judg 20:1), or as an activity of the entire people (Jer 26:9; 2 Chr 20:26). The act of assembling may be hostile, as in Num16:3; 17:7; and 20:2 where the people assemble against Moses and Aaron, or defensive as in Esth 8:11 and 9:15-18 where the Jews assemble to defend themselves in the face of the impending pogrom by the Persians. In the LXX this Hebrew root is most often rendered with the Greek ekklēsiazō In the NT ἐκκλησία ekklesia is the common term for an assembly. *See* CHURCH, IDEA OF THE; COMMUNITY; SYNAGOGUE.

JOHANNA VAN WIJK-BOS

ASSEMBLY. *See* ASSEMBLE; CONGREGATION.

ASSEMBLY, DIVINE. *See* DIVINE ASSEMBLY.

ASSEMBLY, GREAT. *See* GREAT ASSEMBLY.

ASSHUR ashur [אַשּׁוּר ʾashur]. 1. Shem's second son (Gen 10:22) is the eponymous ancestor of Assyria.

2. A place located in modern Iraq, the ancient city of Asshur grew first into a nation and then into the Assyrian empire. *See* ASSYRIA AND BABYLONIA.

3. The patron god of Assyria does not appear in the Bible except as a theophoric element in the name Esarhaddon (Ezra 4:2). *See* GODS AND GODDESSES.

SUSANNA W. SOUTHARD

ASSHURIM ash'uh-rim [אַשּׁוּרִם ʾashurim]. 1. Abraham and his wife Keturah's great grandson.

2. Tribe who descended from Abraham, Jokshan, and Dedan, residing south of Palestine (Gen 25:1-3).

3. Residents of southern Arabia (Ezek 27:23).

ASSIR as'uhr [אַסִּיר ʾassir]. 1. A Levite son of KORAH of a KOHATHITE clan. He was the brother of ELKANAH (Exod 6:24; 1 Chr 6:22 [Heb. 6:7]).

2. A Levite from the Kohathites, the son of ABIASAPH (1 Chr 6:23 [Heb. 6:8]) and the father of TAHATH (1 Chr 6:37 [Heb. 6:22]).

CLAUDE F. MARIOTTINI

ASSOCIATIONS, COLLEGIA, CLUBS. The term *associations* and its cognates (e.g., *clubs*, *guilds*, the Latin *collegia*), are used by modern scholars to refer to a large number of chronologically and geographically diverse groups of people in antiquity. These relatively small groups of men and/or women with a common interest or connection met regularly for social and religious interaction. Evidence for associations, found primarily in inscriptions and papyri, begins as early as the 5th cent. BCE and continues well into the 4th cent. CE. The activities of a particular association are most often revealed through its honorific inscriptions and community regulations. These regulations detail such features as membership, behavioral and leadership requirements pertaining to meetings, banquets, and rituals, and the penalties exacted for transgressing group norms (e.g., fines, floggings, and expulsions).

Associations have provided important contextual information for the biblical world. For example, the Semitic cult meal, the marzeakh, has been shown to be similar in form to association banquets from the same time period, and the community regulations found among the Dead Sea Scrolls share features with association regulations. Most biblical scholarship, however, focuses on the Greco-Roman associations, particularly how they help inform the social contexts of early Christianity and formative Judaism.

Scholarly attempts at classifying associations tend toward a number of categories: professional guilds, cultic groups, domestic groups, ethnic associations, and burial societies. It was among this latter category of "funerary associations" that scholars in the late 19th and early 20th cent. placed the Christian groups, focusing primarily on their internal structure and their legal status. Although this specific categorization has been successfully challenged in the late 20th cent., recent work continues to investigate how understanding the internal structure and external relationships of the associations can inform our understanding of Christian communities and synagogues.

Inscriptions and papyri recording the life of associations reveal that these communities faced many of the challenges reflected in the texts of the NT. Although they aspired toward an egalitarian community, sometimes even calling one another "brother," in practice, a hierarchy remained in place, often with the social elites occupying positions of power. While leaders were honored for their activities (compare 1 Thess 5:12-13), factionalism did occur (compare 1 Cor 1:10-12). Money played a part in association membership—the income and expenditures being noted and sometimes disputed (2 Cor 8-9; Phil 4:15-18). Meals were shared regularly but conflicts could flare up during these social or cultic times (compare 1 Cor 11:17-22). We even find regulations prohibiting the taking of another association member to court. Like the Pauline communities, the associations were locally based but could have a loose network of connections with similar groups in other places. One even finds some overlap in the use of nomenclature such as "church" (ἐκκλησία ekklēsia) and "synagogue" (συναγωγή synagōgē) and leadership titles such as "bishop" (ἐπίσκοπος episkopos), "deacon" (διάκονος diakonos), and "elder" (πρεσβύτερος presbyteros).

Bibliography: Richard S. Ascough. *Paul's Macedonian Associations: The Social Context of Philippians and 1 Thessalonians.* WUNT II/161 (2003); Philip A. Harland. *Associations, Synagogues, and Congregations: Claiming a Place in Ancient Mediterranean Society* (2003).

RICHARD S. ASCOUGH

ASSOS as´os [Ἄσσος Assos]. A well fortified coastal city in the Roman province of Asia, north of the island of Lesbos in the Troad. Paul met his companions in Assos after they left TROAS separately by land and sea on their way to MILETUS (Acts 20:13-14). In the 4th cent. BCE it was the home of a philosophical school where Aristotle taught and the birthplace of Cleanthes, a Stoic philosopher. Assos was occupied by the 9th cent. BCE by Carians then colonized by Aeolians in the 8th to 7th cent.. After being ruled by Lydians and Persians (6th to early 5th cent. BCE), it became independent, joining the Delian League at the end of the Persian Wars. In the mid–4th cent., its ruler Hermias briefly established Assos as a prominent cultural center. After being dominated by the Seleucids and Pergamon, Assos became part of the Roman Empire in 133 BCE.

Archaeological remains from the 6th cent. BCE include a Doric temple of Athena. The acropolis and lower city were both fortified with massive walls that date to the 4th cent. BCE. There are two small, fortified harbors along with the remains of a gymnasium, theater, and agora that date to the Hellenistic and Roman periods.

MILTON MORELAND

ASSUMPTION OF MOSES. *See* MOSES, ASSUMPTION OF.

ASSURANCE [בֶּטַח betakh; πληραφορία plēraphoria, πίστις pistis]. Familiar English translations use "assurance" to represent four Hebrew and four Greek words. While each of these words supplies its own nuance, they share in common the ideas of security, confidence and certainty, thus giving "assurance" the sense of the cer-

tainty that God is faithful and what God has promised. "Assurance" is that essential aspect of the life of faith that allows believers to respond to God and act in full confidence, without fear or apprehension, and with firm certainty that God will supply the meaning and the conclusion to acts of faith according to divine purposes. The Scriptures make clear that such confident assurance finds its source in the character of God. Therefore, the believer can have assurance in the life of faith (Rom 4:19-22; 2 Cor 5:5-8); access to God (Eph 3:11-12; Heb 10:19-23); and salvation (2 Tim 1:12; Rom 8:28-31).

GARY COLLEDGE

ASSURBANIPAL. *See* ASHURBANIPAL, ASSURBANIPAL.

ASSYRIA AND BABYLONIA uh-sihr´ee-uh, bab´uh-loh´nee-uh [אַשּׁוּר ʾashur; Ασσυριοι Assyrioi; בָּבֶל bavel; Βαβυλων Babylōn]. Two Mesopotamian kingdoms, both named after their capital cities, that exercised a profound cultural influence on Israel while destroying its political independence.

  A. Geography
  B. History
    1. From Sumer to the empire of Akkad
    2. The Neo-Sumerian revival
    3. The rise of Assyria and Babylon
    4. The Hittite invasion and the rise of the Kassites and Hurrians
    5. The era of international diplomacy and the reemergence of Assyria
    6. The decline of the great powers and the fall of the Kassites
    7. Nebuchadnezzar I and the Babylonian revival
    8. Tiglath-pileser I and the Assyrian revival
    9. Aramean incursions and Assyrian and Babylonian decline
    10. The emergence of the Neo-Assyrian empire
      a. Ashur-nasir-apli II and Shalmaneser III
      b. Shamshi-Adad V to Ashur-nirari V
      c. Tiglath-pileser III
      d. Shalmaneser V
      e. Sargon II
      f. Sennacherib
      g. Esarhaddon
      h. Ashurbanipal
    11. The end of Assyria and the rise of the Neo-Babylonian/Chaldean empire
      a. Nebuchadnezzar II
      b. Awil-Marduk and Neriglissar
      c. Labashi-Marduk and Nabonidus
  C. Religion
  D. Government
  E. Art
  Bibliography

A. Geography

Both kingdoms were located in what is now Iraq. Babylon traditionally controlled the southern area from the Persian Gulf through central Iraq, where the Tigris and Euphrates rivers come in closest proximity, and then up the Tigris toward the lower Zab River. Babylon also tried to control the area up the Euphrates, but their control seldom extended beyond Idu (Hit), the area between Hindanu and Idu, and sometimes south of that point, often being independent of both Babylon and Assyria. Assyria's original homeland was along the Tigris north of the lower Zab and along the lower Zab to the east, though it was soon extended along the Tigris and the streams that fed it north of the upper Zab, and extending west toward the Jebel Sinjar. The border between Assyria and Babylon was constantly changing, however, the area south of the lower Zab and along the streams that fed the Radanu and the Turna being often contested. Moreover, in times of imperial expansion each state controlled vastly more territory than their original homelands.

To some extent the imperial expansion of both states was influenced by the geographical limitations of their homelands. The area between the lower courses of the Euphrates and Tigris and the Persian Gulf, often referred to as the Sealand, was covered with vast reed marshes with interspersed areas of dry land. It was a paradise for fishing and hunting, provided a limitless supply of reeds, supported limited agriculture, and was difficult for a central authority to control because of the infinite number of hideouts it provided. Yet whoever controlled this area controlled the main trade route to the Persian Gulf. Upstream along the lower Euphrates the cultivation of date palms was a major activity, and farther north in central and northern Babylonia, along with date palms and vegetables, barley was a major crop, and sheep and goats were raised in the steppe and allowed to graze in the fields at the appropriate times of the year. Agriculture in Babylonia, particularly in the south, but even in northern Babylonia, was heavily dependent on irrigation, and because of poor drainage there was a recurring problem of the soil becoming too saline. Without strong central authority to regulate the flow of water in the canals throughout the region, the productivity of the land would quickly decline, bringing famine in its wake—a common phenomenon in periods of political disorder in the region. Up the Tigris in Assyrian territory rainfall was higher, irrigation, though practiced, was not as important, and salinization was not as big a problem, since the higher elevation provided better drainage, and along with barley and domestic animals, fruit trees were raised and beekeeping was practiced.

Neither territory, however, was blessed with forests for lumber, minerals, or precious stones. All these

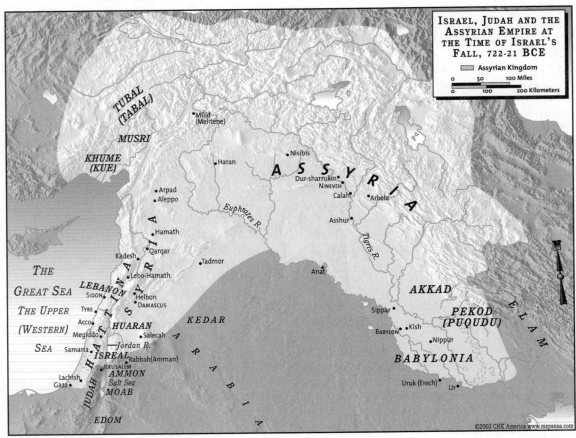

Figure 1: Map of the Assyrian Empire.

products had to be acquired by trade or conquest, and the desire to keep the trade routes open was a major force driving imperial expansion. In Assyria fear of invasion also played a major role in the impetus for expansion. Babylonia was at least partially protected by the natural boundaries of the Euphrates and the Tigris. Its northern border was defensible, and it was protected on the south by the Persian Gulf and the forbidding marshes. Assyria, however, lacked such natural protective boundaries and was open to attack from all sides. The mountains to its north and east were the home of tribesmen who constituted a constant threat to Assyria's heartland, Mount Kashiyari (Tur Abdin) to the northwest was another source of concern, and the large populations that were always supported by the fertile valleys of the streams that fed the upper Habur below Mount Kashiyari due west of Assyria, was a third source of concern. In its initial stages, Assyrian expansion was aimed at keeping the mountain folk in the mountains, making all of Mount Kashiyari subject to Assyria, and in preventing a strong hostile state from emerging again in the upper Habur region.

B. History

1. From Sumer to the empire of Akkad

Neither Assyria nor Babylonia represented the earli-

est culture in this region. Babylon became an important city only in the early 2nd millennium BCE, and Assyria did not become a significant political power until the second half of the 2nd millennium. In the 3rd millennium the center of culture and power was farther south. Along the lower Euphrates in the far south lay the southern cities of Uruk (biblical Erech), Larsa, Ur, and Eridu. In the central area, but still well south of Babylon, were the cities of Nippur, Isin, Adab, and Shuruppak, and farther east, Umma and Lagash. In the north, in the general area of Babylon, lay Kish, Cuth (Cutha/Cuthah), Sippar, and Akkad (or Agade, biblical Accad). Though never the dominant political power, Nippur, the city of the storm-god Enlil, appears to have been an important religious center for the whole region.

In the 3rd millennium sources the central and southern areas were known as the land of SUMER (biblical Shinar), and the northern area as the land of Akkad. The population in the central and southern cities spoke Sumerian, a non-Semitic language, but in the north Akkadian, a Semitic language, seems to have been increasingly dominant. This process was accelerated when SARGON I (2350–2294 BCE), having taken the throne of Akkad, defeated a coalition of the southern cities and imposed his imperial control

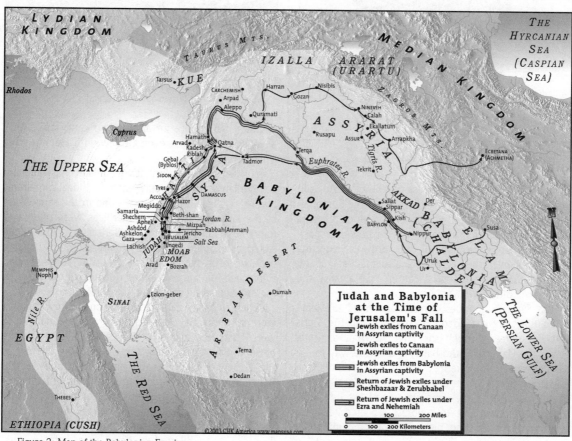

Figure 2: Map of the Babylonian Empire.

over all of Akkad and Sumer. He tried to legitimate his rule by appealing to southern religious sensibilities. He appointed his daughter, who bore the Sumerian name, Enheduanna, as priestess of An in Uruk, and she composed a poem in Sumerian about the marriage of

Scala/Art Resource, NY
Figure 3: Head of Sargon; Iraq Museum, Baghdad.

Inanna-Annunitum, city goddess of Akkad, to An, god of heaven, city god of Uruk, and head of the Sumerian pantheon. The poem functioned as politico-religious justification for Sargon's rise to imperial power, respecting the religious traditions of the south, yet asserting his control over the region. He also maintained and repaired the southern cultic centers, particularly the important cultic center at Nippur.

But Sargon's conquests were not limited to Akkad and Sumer. He extended his conquests up the Tigris and Euphrates, through the later Assyrian territory, across the Habur and the Balih, and all the way to the Mediterranean, conquering, among many others, the important north Syrian city of Ebla (Tel-Mardikh). He even crossed over the Amanus Mountains into Anatolia. Sargon was able to suppress repeated southern attempts at revolt, and his successors, including the illustrious Naram-Sin (2270–2233 BCE), were able to

Erich Lessing/Art Resource, NY
Figure 4: Stele of Naram-Sin; Louvre, Paris.

maintain his empire for almost two cent. (ca. 2350–2150 BCE). There was even a treaty with Elam in what is now Iran.

This empire was formative for later Assyrian and Babylonian culture. It represented the ideal monarchy. Statues of the Akkadian kings stood in the sanctuaries of the large urban centers, sacrifices were offered to them, some later kings made pilgrimage to Akkad, the Assyrians adopted the titulary of the Sargonic kings, on occasion even naming themselves after the Akkadian rulers, and the late Babylonian rulers were interested in the archaeological remains of the Akkadian period.

The exploits of Sargon and Naram-Sin, in particular, were so impressive that a number of legendary texts were composed about them already in their lifetime or soon afterward. These texts were very popular in the ancient Near East, and not only in Assyria and Babylonia. There were Hittite translations of some of these texts, and a copy of one of the Akkadian texts has been found as far afield as Amarna in Egypt. It is likely that this literary tradition was known in Israel as well. The Israelite tradition of the baby Moses being rescued from a reed basket on the river bears a remarkable resemblance to a similar tradition about the baby Sargon. Motifs from the legend about Naram-Sin and the Enemy Hordes are also attested in Israelite sources.

2. The Neo-Sumerian revival

Eventually, however, the empire collapsed under attack from the mountain people known as the Gutians, and the center of political power shifted farther south again, where there was a Sumerian renaissance. The famous temple builder, Gudea of Lagash, and Utuhegal of Uruk, who defeated the Gutians, date from this period, but it was Ur, under the powerful kings of the Ur III dynasty (ca. 2050–1950 BCE), who reestablished the empire of Sumer and Akkad. Though their conquests may not have been as extensive as those of the kings of Akkad, they controlled most of Mesopotamia, including Assyria and the middle Euphrates region, where they had a governor installed at Mari.

During the Ur III period there was a growing influx of tribal groups into Mesopotamia from the bordering steppe country. These newcomers, who were known, among other designations, as Amorites, or Westerners, spoke a west Semitic language distinct from Akkadian. They began to put pressure on the settled country around the urban centers, and the rulers of Ur responded to this pressure by building a wall to keep the Amorites out. Over the long term this wall was not successful. The infiltration continued, and the disruptions to trade and agriculture caused by the tribal groups eventually weakened Ur until it was unable to mount a successful defense against an Elamite attack.

With the fall of Ur, the power shifted farther north. Larsa, upstream on the Euphrates, and Isin, even farther north in the central plain not far from Nippur vied for control of the remnants of Ur's empire, hence the designation of this period as the Isin-Larsa era (1950–1800 BCE). Neither dynasty, however, was able to regain a lasting control over the territories north of central Babylonia. With the fall of Ur III, the rulers of Ashur appear to have become independent of southern control.

3. The rise of Assyria and Babylon

During the Isin-Larsa period traders from Ashur engaged in intensive trade with cities in central Anatolia. The Assyrian traders with their donkey caravans made the long trip from Ashur to Kultepe (ancient Kanish), Boghazkoi (ancient Khattusha), and Alishar (ancient Ankuwa?), carrying textiles from Assyria and tin from farther east, which they sold in Anatolia for gold, silver, and other metals. Similar trade may have been carried out under the rulers of Akkad, supported by imperial power, but Assyria during the Isin-Larsa period does not seem to have had any political control over Anatolia. This trade, attested by a large corpus of Old Assyrian correspondence found in the Anatolian

sites, appears to have been the result of mutual economic agreements, not military conquest or political domination, and both the Assyrian merchants and the Anatolian rulers and traders seem to have profited from the trade.

Eventually the trade seems to have been disrupted by political shifts in Anatolia itself, where the Hittites were emerging as a major power, and by conflict in the Assyrian heartland. By 1800 BCE, numerous Amorite dynasties had seized power in the urban centers of northern Babylonia, along the Euphrates, east of the Tigris, in the valleys of the upper Habur and Balih rivers, and in northern Syria in places like Qatna and Aleppo. Under the rulers of its 1st dynasty, Babylon first comes to prominence in this period, but early in this period, Eshnunna to the northeast on the Diyala River was the more powerful kingdom. It was able to gain control of Assyria for a short period, before Shamshi-Adad I, an Amorite interloper, perhaps originally from Terqa on the middle Euphrates, after a brief sojourn in Babylonia, marched up the Tigris and seized the throne of Assyria. He did not rule from Ashur, however. His original capital was Ekallatum in the Assyrian heartland where he installed his oldest son, the crown prince Ishme-Dagan as ruler. Shamshi-Adad, meanwhile, continued to extend his control through Assyria, west across the upper valleys of the Habur and the Balih, and then downstream through the middle Euphrates region. At Mari on the middle Euphrates, where he had driven out another Amorite dynasty, he installed his younger son, Yasmah-Adad. For his own capital he chose Shubat-Enlil along the upper Habur, from where he could keep an eye on his whole realm.

Shamshi-Adad I controlled a major area of upper Mesopotamia and on occasion campaigned as far as the Mediterranean, but strong rivals limited farther expansion. To the west lay the powerful kingdom of Yamhad with its capital at Aleppo. To the southwest was Qatna. To the southeast lay the still powerful kingdom of Eshnunna, and to the south was the growing kingdom of Babylon, engaged at the moment in a fierce struggle with the contending kingdoms of Isin and Larsa. Farther east Elam was still a threat. In addition to these great kingdoms, whose rulers were constantly trying to woo one another's vassal kings away from their present overlord, there was also a threat from the stateless tribal groups who continued to move into Mesopotamia from the steppe. Keeping in check these semi-nomadic Amorites, among whom the ancestors of Israel are probably to be counted, was a constant concern. Finally, in the mountains to the north and east of Assyria were mountain tribes who posed a recurring threat to the security of Shamshi-Adad's realm.

Once the father had died, the sons of Shamshi-Adad were no longer able to hold the realm together. With the support of Aleppo, Zimri-Lim of the preceding Mari dynasty drove out Yasmah-Adad and reclaimed his ancestral throne. Ishme-Dagan was caught in a struggle with Mari and its supporters to the west, Eshnunna to the east, and Babylon to the south. Larsa, under Rim-Sin, had finally defeated Isin, but shortly afterward, the vigorous Hammurabi of Babylon defeated Larsa, thus bringing southern Mesopotamia under Babylon's control. Following a period of rapidly switching alliances, treachery, and deceit, Hammurabi finally gained the upper hand over all his immediate rivals and erstwhile allies. Eshnunna, Assyria, and finally Mari fell to the victorious Babylonians. West of the Euphrates Aleppo still headed a powerful state, but Hammurabi controlled Babylonia and Assyria, including the Habur, the Balih, and the middle Euphrates.

Art Resource, NY Réunion des Musées Nationaux
Figure 5: Head of Hammurabi; Louvre, Paris.

4. The Hittite invasion and the rise of the Kassites and Hurrians

Hammurabi's empire did not long survive Hammurabi, however. Under Samsu-iluna, his son and successor, most of the empire was lost. Assyria, where a native Assyrian dynastry reestablished itself in Ashur, remained a nominal vassal of Babylon, but Babylon's control over Assyria was probably very loose at best. The southern part of Babylonia was lost to the dynasty of the Sealand, across the Tigris another Rim-Sin set up a rival state in Yamutbal, the ancestral homeland of the last Larsa dynasty, and on the middle Euphra-

tes at Terqa, the independent kingdom of Hana was established. The first rulers at Terqa bore Amorite type names, but there is some evidence that this area was taken over by the Kassite dynasty that eventually seized control of Babylon itself.

It was the Hittites in faraway Anatolia, however, who ended the first dynasty of Babylon. Hattushilis I (ca. 1650–1620 BCE) and his adopted son, Mursilis I (ca. 1620–1595 BCE), of the Hittite Old Kingdom, campaigned against the kingdom of Yamhad. Once Urshu, Carchemish, and the other great cities along the way had been conquered or neutralized, the way was open to Babylon. Some agreement with the kingdom of Hana was apparently reached, and Mursilis' Hittite army marched down the Euphrates and sacked Babylon, ending the reign of Samsu-ditana (1625–1595 BCE) and with him the 1st dynasty of Babylon. The Hittites were unable to capitalize on their victory, however, since revolt at home while Mursilis was on this campaign threw the Hittite Empire into chaos.

With the collapse of Yamhad, Babylon, and the Hittite Empire, the whole Near East fell into a dark age of almost a hundred years. Because of the lack of contemporary sources for this period, the historical gap must be filled in from later sources. The Sealand was the first to benefit from the fall of Babylon. Gulkishar, the sixth king of this dynasty, apparently gained control of northern Babylonia and Babylon itself, which was sufficient to have the Sealand dynasty included in the Babylonian king list, but the Sealand's hold over northern Babylonia was short lived. The non-Semitic Kassites, probably originally from the mountains to the northeast of Babylon, but who had established themselves in the kingdom of Hana, moved down the Euphrates and captured Babylon, which they controlled for about four cent., until ca. 1159 BCE. They also recaptured the south from the Sealand. Their administrative center, however, lay farther north between the Tigris and Euphrates, where the two rivers came closest together, at a city eventually named Dur-Kurigalzu, "Fortress of Kurigalzu," after the Kassite king Kurigalzu I (ca. 1400 BCE). Thus the Kassites controlled all of Babylonia, which came to be known by the Kassite name Karduniash, as well as stretches of the middle Euphrates during most of the cent. of generally peaceful Kassite rule.

Though they introduced their own gods into the Sumero-Akkadian pantheon and gave their country a Kassite name, the Kassites rulers quickly adapted themselves to the land and people they ruled. They continued the traditional use of Akkadian and Sumerian for their inscriptions, so much so, in fact, that only traces of their own Kassite language have been preserved in the sources. There were significant cultural changes however. The boundary stones they introduced to mark land boundaries, the *kudurru* stones, were decorated by a wealth of divine symbols, and the texts inscribed on them point to a quasi-feudal system where tax-free land was distributed to loyal servants of the king in reward for past services rendered.

While the Kassites profited from the Hittite sack of Babylon, and moved in to fill the vacuum left by the collapse of the 1st Babylonian dynasty, the Assyrians had no such luck. Instead, another new, non-Semitic, population group, the Hurrians, moved into the upper Habur region and quickly became a rival to the Hittites, the Kassites, and even the Egyptians. They had been present in the mountains already in the time of the kings of Akkad and had increased in number during the Old Babylonian period, infiltrating into northern Syria, the upper Habur region, and eastern Assyria; but the powerful kingdom of Yamhad centered on Aleppo had blocked more serious Hurrian expansion into north Syria, and Babylon had limited Hurrian expansion into Mesopotamia. When the Hittite kings Hattusilis I and Mursilis battered Yamhad and eventually sacked Babylon, the collapse of those buffers opened the way for rapid Hurrian expansion into the whole area. The Hurrians established a number of states, the most important being the kingdom of Mitanni with its capital, Washukkani, somewhere in the valleys of the upper Habur. With an Indo-Aryan elite and a primarily Hurrian population, they revolutionized warfare with their use of horses and light chariotry. Soon their control had spread across the Euphrates and northern Syria into Cilicia (Kizzuwatna). Assyria was reduced to the status of a vassal of the expanding Mitanni. With its Amorite vassals and allies the influence of Mitanni was felt as far south as Palestine, where Mitanni and its allies were perceived by the Egyptians as a continuing threat to their security.

Semitic invaders referred to by the Egyptians as the Hyksos, "the rulers of foreign lands," had ruled Egypt from Avaris (later Tanis) in the delta for about a cent. (ca. 1670–1570 BCE) before Ahmoses captured Avaris and succeeded in driving the Hyksos out of Egypt. But the early Egyptian rulers of the 18th dynasty were not satisfied with regaining control of Egypt. They wanted to create a sufficient geographical buffer to prevent any future invasion of Egypt. So they embarked on a period of imperial campaigns against the states in Palestine and Syria, penetrating as far as the Euphrates under Thutmose I (ca. 1512–1500 BCE) and again under Thutmose III (ca. 1490–1436 BCE), and as far as the Orontes under Amenophis II (ca. 1438–1412 BCE). This put Egypt in direct conflict with Mitanni, the major ally and in some cases suzerain over the threatened Palestinian and Syrian states.

5. The era of international diplomacy and the reemergence of Assyria

Egypt's earlier successes could not be sustained, however, and by the end of Amenophis II's reign a certain balance of power had been obtained. Egypt main-

tained her control of Palestine and the Lebanon, but Syria north of the Lebanon remained under Mitanni's hegemony. The Hittite kingdom was reviving, however, and was beginning to challenge Mitanni's control of north Syria. During this period of equilibrium, international diplomacy thrived, as the Egyptian archive of cuneiform correspondence found at El Amarna, supplemented by the Hittite archives at Boghazkoy, demonstrate. The major players were Egypt, the Hittites, Mitanni, and Kassite Babylon. They corresponded with one another in Akkadian, the diplomatic language of the day, as relatively equal great powers, though Egypt clearly regarded itself as superior. They arranged dynastic marriages, trade arrangements, often portrayed as mutual gifts between the royal courts, and even cultural missions. Egyptian gold was in great demand in Mitanni and Babylon, and the Asiatic states sent jewelry, clothing, horses, chariot fittings, and the like in return. While Mitanni still controlled Assyria, the goddess Shaushka of Nineveh (Assyrian Ishtar) made a couple of state trips to Egypt (her statue was sent to Egypt with accompanying priestly caretakers and state officials), and Egyptian physicians were highly prized by the Hittites.

This equilibrium was shattered when Shuppiluliuma (ca. 1375–1335 BCE) came to the Hittite throne and challenged both Mitanni hegemony in north Syria and Egyptian hegemony in the Lebanon. After losing its territory west of the Euphrates to Shuppiluliuma, Tushratta of Mitanni was murdered, and the kingdom was split between rival claimants to the throne. The Hittites backed Kurtiwaza (or Mattiwaza—the correct reading is still debated), a son of Tushratta who had sought asylum at the Hittite court, and eventually established him in a much reduced Mitanni east of the Euphrates. In the meantime, however, Assyria had asserted its independence and together with Alshe to the northwest plundered much of what had been the heartland of Mitanni in the Habur region. This success emboldened Ashur-uballit I (1365–1330 BCE) of Assyria to write to Egypt as an equal, much to the chagrin of Burnaburiash, the Kassite ruler of Babylon. Burnaburiash complained to Egypt that Assyria was his vassal and that it was therefore inappropriate for Egypt to accept an embassy from Assyria without Babylonian approval. The Hittites were also disturbed by Assyria's expansion and supported what was left of Mitanni, now called Hanigalbat, as a buffer east of the Euphrates against the Assyrians. The struggle with Egypt for control of north Syria and the Lebanon, however, prevented Shuppiluliuma from dealing more effectively with Assyria, and following Shuppiluliuma, the Hittites were weakened by a prolonged plague in Hatti, reflected in the famous plague prayers of Mursilis II (1334–1306 BCE).

This gave Assyria the opportunity to secure its southern border with Babylon. One of Ashur-uballit's daughters had married Burnaburiash of Babylon, probably when Assyria had accepted vassalage to Babylon as a counterweight to Mitanni early in Tushratta's war with Suppiluliuma. Later in the reign of Ashur-uballit, Kara-hardash, the son of Burnaburiash and Ashur-uballit's daughter, took the Kassite throne, but his Kassite troops rebelled, killed Karahardash, and installed Nazibugash as king. Ashur-uballit used his grandson's murder as an excuse to intervene in Babylonian affairs. He marched into Babylon, killed Nazibugash, and replaced him with Kurigalzu II, a younger son of Burnaburiash, thereby clearly elevating Assyria to the senior partner in the alliance between Assyria and Babylon. Neither Kurigalzu II nor his successor Nazi-maruttash was able to reverse the Assyrian dominance. Despite border conflicts, the Assyrians under Enlil-nirari (1329–1320 BCE), Arik-den-ili (1319–1308 BCE), and Adad-nirari I (1307–1275 BCE) continued to hold the upper hand. Hittite power revived under Muwattalis, Urhi-Teshub, and Hattusilis III, but their renewed conflict with the 19th Egyptian dynasty prevented them from providing sufficient support to Hanigalbat, their buffer against Assyria east of the Euphrates. Adad-nirari I took advantage of that distraction to conquer Hanigalbat and extend Assyrian control as far west as the Euphrates. Urhi-Teshub of Hatti grudgingly acknowledged Assyria's status as a great power, and under Hattusilis III diplomatic relations between the two states improved, though Hattusilis also attempted to cultivate diplomatic relations with Kassite Babylon, probably as a counterweight to Assyria should hostility between Hatti and Assyria resume. Hittite messengers regularly passed through Assyrian-controlled territory to reach the Kassite court, and Hattusilis maintained good relations with Kadashman-Turgu, Nazi-maruttash's successor. When Kadashman-Turgu died, however, Hattusilis' message of support for his son Kadashman-Enlil was received with great suspicion and hostility, much as David's message of condolence to Hanun of Ammon at the death of his father Nahash was received (2 Sam 10:1-5). The Babylonian court regarded Hattusilis' message as arrogant Hittite meddling in Babylonian affairs, and consequently the new Babylonian king was less than enthusiastic about sending regular messengers to the Hittite king. One excuse the Babylonian king apparently made for the interruption of his international correspondence was the threat from the Ahlamu Arameans. They appear to have represented the first wave of a growing influx of Aramean tribesmen from the steppe into North Syria, upper Mesopotamia, and Babylon.

Sometime toward the end of Adad-nirari's reign or early in the reign of his son Shalmaneser I (1275–1246 BCE) hostilities between Assyria and Hatti did resume. Shattuara II of Hanigalbat with the support of the Hittites and their Aramean allies, the Ahlamu, rebelled. At the beginning of his reign Shalmaneser was faced with a number of rebellions, but having secured his border on the mountains to the north, he turned west

against Hanigalbat and succeeded in recapturing the territory previously captured by Adad-nirari. He also begins the calculated terror tactics so characteristic of the later Assyrian military campaigns. He claims to have captured and blinded 14,400 of the enemy combatants. Similar blinding of captive combatants is later attested for Ashur-bel-kala and Ashur-nasir-apli II. One may compare the biblical account of the Ammonite practice of blinding one eye of defeated enemy (1 Sam 11:1-2 with additional material in 4QSam^a).

The renewed hostility between Hatti and Assyria led Hatti to push for an economic blockade against Assyria. When the Assyrians under Shalmaneser I attempted to set up trading relations with Canaan, the Hittite king Tudhaliya IV (1250–1220 BCE) pressured his Syrian vassals to prevent it. Tudhaliya's treaty with his vassal Shaushga-muwa of Amurru (the northern Lebanon region), specifically prohibits Shaushga-muwa from sending merchants to Assyria or allowing Assyrian merchants to visit or pass through Shaushga-muwa's territory. Any who attempted to do so were to be arrested and sent as prisoners to the Hittite court.

Nonetheless, by the end of Shalmaneser's reign, Tudhaliya was again in correspondence with the Assyrian court. When Assyrian messengers brought him news that Shalmaneser I had died, and that his son Tukulti-Ninurta I had succeeded to the throne, the Hittite monarch wrote not only to the new Assyrian king, but to Babu-ahu-iddina, a high official in the courts of Adad-nirari I, Shalmaneser I, and now Tukulti-Ninurta I, and who, therefore, was presumably already well known to the Hittite diplomats. It was clearly expected that great kings send diplomatic greetings and appropriate presents at the accession of other great kings as numerous complaints in the correspondence of this period make clear. Like Hattusilis III's earlier advice to the new Babylonian king Kadashman-Enlil II, however, Tudhaliya IV's advice to the young Tukulti-Ninurta I to begin his military career only against enemies that he outnumbered three or four to one appears to be condescending and perhaps self-serving. Tudhaliya could not have been very pleased at the prospect of the young Assyrian king resuming the successful military campaigning that had marked the early years of his father, Shalmaneser I.

Apparently Tukulti-Ninurta I (1245–1209 BCE) ignored the Hittite advice and renewed the attempt at Assyrian expansion. He subdued the Gutian Mountain tribes to the north and west of Assyria along the upper reaches of the Euphrates. He resubdued Katmuhu, and then conquered the rest of the Mount Kashiyari region. From there he moved into Nairi, the valleys north and west of Mount Kashiyari, loosely controlled at that time by Alzu, and defeated and subjugated its people as far west as the mountainous territory of Amadani on the upper reaches of the Euphrates. He claims in some of his later inscriptions to have uprooted 28,800

Hittites from beyond the Euphrates and resettled them in Assyrian territory, but when, where, and even if this actually happened is difficult to establish. It is clear, however, that the Hittites were too busy with the threat to their west to mount an effective response to Assyrian expansion.

The Hittites may have attempted to enlist Babylonian support against Assyria. Kashtiliashu IV (1249–1242 BCE), whom the Assyrians regarded as a vassal, was caught in breach of treaty when his messengers were seized bearing letters that suggested he was planning a revolt. Despite Assyrian attempts to resolve the issue diplomatically, Kashtiliashu refused, and Tukulti-Ninurta invaded Babylonian territory. After a long, debilitating campaign, a decisive battle was finally fought, and the Assyrians routed the Babylonians and captured Kashtiliashu. Tukulti-Ninurta took him captive back to Assyria along with other Babylonians and the plundered treasures of Babylon, including tablet collections, cultic objects, and, most significant of all, the statue of the Babylonian god Marduk. This overwhelming victory brought the whole Babylonian realm, including all of lower Mesopotamia and the island of Dilmun (Bahrain) under Tukulti-Ninurta's control, and through his appointed officials he ruled Babylon for seven years.

His greatest success, however, may have been Tukulti-Ninurta's undoing. Culturally, Babylon was more advanced than Assyria, and Tukulti-Ninurta may have become too enamored of the Babylonian culture and cult to please the nobles and priests of Assyria. Many of the Babylonians Tukulti-Ninurta brought to Assyria seem to have been supported by the Assyrian state, and some of them, including the former Kassite king, who was his distant relative, may have become influential members of Tukulti-Ninurta's court. A certain Kashtiliashu, perhaps the same person, is known to have held the *limmu* office during Tukulti-Ninurta's reign. The statue of Marduk remained in Assyria for about a century where it was treated with respect and apparently a growing veneration, a development that may not have pleased the priests of Asshur. Moreover, Tukulti-Ninurta was unable to silence such dissatisfaction by continuing military successes. The Elamites under Kiten-Hutran twice invaded Babylonia, and Tukulti-Ninurta apparently did nothing to support his southern vassals. His earlier conquest of Babylon appears to have exhausted his military, and when, seven years later, the Babylonians revolted and put Kashtiliashu's son, Adad-shuma-usur, on the throne of Babylon, Tukulti-Ninurta was unable or unwilling to suppress the revolt. This marked a major loss of territory and income to Tukulti-Ninurta and must have seriously diminished his earlier prestige as a great military leader. The latter part of his reign does not seem to have been enhanced by any major military successes. His later years were spent primarily in building activi-

ties, as he became progressively more isolated from the population and nobility of Assyria. This growing self-isolation culminated in his construction of the city, Kar-Tukulti-Ninurta, that he built for himself and his god on the other side of the Tigris from Ashur. To judge from his Psalm to Ashur, he also became increasingly paranoiac, convinced that the whole world was hostile to and plotting against his beneficient rule, his god, his city, and the whole land of Assyria. One should note that the portrayal of the other nations in this psalm resembles in many respects the biblical Zion Tradition's portrayal of hostile vassal kings plotting to attack Jerusalem. Eventually Tukulti-Ninurta's lack of continuing military success, the expense of his building projects, and his isolation led to an internal revolt. His son Ashur-nasir-apli and the Assyrian nobility removed Tukulti-Ninurta from the throne, locked him up, and eventually murdered him.

6. The decline of the great powers and the fall of the Kassites

The death of Tukulti-Ninurta marked a period of decline for Assyria that corresponded to a general decline of all the great powers of the earlier period. To the W the Hittite Empire collapsed under the attack of the Sea Peoples, and its collapse set in motion a tide of refugees from Hatti into north Syria, further destabilizing that region. The collapse of Hittite authority also opened the way for a flood of ARAMEAN movement into central and north Syria and across the Euphrates into the former Assyrian territories and down the Euphrates into Babylonia. Egypt survived, but its control of Palestine grew progressively weaker, and it was during this period of the decline or collapse of the great powers that saw the beginnings of the Israelite state and the formation of Aramean or Neo-Hittite states from southern Syria all the way through northern Syria along the upper reaches of the Euphrates.

In Assyria a struggle between different heirs of Tukulti-Ninurta led to a total reversal of the status of Assyria and Babylon. Adad-shum-usur of Babylon (1221–1192 BCE) wrote an insulting and condescending letter to Adad-nirari III of Assyria (1202–1197 BCE), and soon after Enlil-kudur-usur seized the throne of Assyria in a coup, Adad-shum-usur defeated him, and his own Assyrian countrymen turned Enlil-kudur-usur over to the Babylonian king. Adad-shum-usur was probably instrumental in installing Ninurta-apil-ekur (1191–1179 BCE) as king of Ashur. Sometime during this period of Kassite ascendancy over Ashur, which apparently continued through the reign of Merodach-baladan I (1176–1164 BCE), the statue of Marduk was returned from Assyria to Babylon. After Merodach-baladan I, however, renewed Elamite incursions into Babylonia dramatically weakened the Kassite state. Shutruk-Nahhunte conquered Babylonia and deposed its ruler Zababa-shum-iddin, and then Shutruk-Nahhunte's son

Kudur-Nahhunte defeated Enlil-nadin-ahhe, the last Kassite ruler, deported many Babylonians to Elam, and removed the statue of Marduk to Elam.

7. Nebuchadnezzar I and the Babylonian revival

In Babylonia the Kassite dynasty was replaced by the 2nd dynasty of Isin, but the first rulers of the Isin dynasty remained under strong Elamite pressure. Despite the long rule of Ashur-Dan I in Assyria (1178–1133 BCE), Assyria also remained relatively weak. At his death there was a struggle for the throne of Assyria, and the Babylonians under Ninurta-nadin-shumi (1132–1127 BCE) granted asylum to Ninurta-tukulti-Ashur, one of the claimants to the Assyrian throne. The Babylonians campaigned deeply enough into Assyria that Ashur-resh-ishi I of Assyria had to move defensive troops into the Arbail area. In the meantime, the very vigorous Nebuchadnezzar I came to the throne of Babylon (1126–1105 BCE). He had a peace treaty with Ashur-resh-ishi I, but early in his reign their relations soured. Either Nebuchadnezzar I, or perhaps his predecessor Ninurta-nadin-shumi, wrote a disparaging letter to the Assyrian king threatening to restore Ninurta-tukulti-Ashur to the throne of Assyria if his demands were not met. This threatening diplomacy apparently didn't work, and Nebuchadnezzar twice attacked Assyrian border forts, though Ashur-resh-ishi I successfully repelled these attacks. Nebuchadnezzar was more successful on his southern and eastern front. In a major campaign against Elam he defeated Hulteludish and restored the statue of Marduk to Babylon. This was apparently the occasion for the composition of the so-called Marduk Prophecy in which Marduk explains the removal of his statue to Hatti, Assyria, and Elam as trips that the god himself had initiated. The trips to Hatti and Assyria were far enough in the past to be portrayed as relatively benign trips, but the more recent trip to Elam was portrayed as due to Marduk's anger at his own people. Nonetheless, the period of Marduk's anger passed, and he prophesies that a new king of Babylon (Nebuchadnezzar I) will arise to bring him back to Babylon and restore the ancient cultic rites of Babylonia. Whether a genuine prophecy written just prior to Nebuchadnezzar's Elamite campaign to encourage the king or a prophecy *ex eventu* to celebrate Nebuchadnezzar's success and secure cultic privileges, the text clearly envisions the Elamite campaign of Nebuchadnezzar I.

8. Tiglath-pileser I and the Assyrian revival

Babylon's preeminence over Assyria was not destined to last. Nebuchadnezzar I's successor, Enlil-nadin-apli (1104–1101 BCE), attempted to conquer Ashur, but in his absence his uncle Marduk-nadin-ahhe and the nobles rebelled against him, and when he returned home, they killed him. Marduk-nadin-ahhe (1100–1083 BCE) replaced him, and early in his reign he had some successes against Assyria. Perhaps while

the new Assyrian king Tiglath-Pileser I (1115–1077 BCE) was on campaign elsewhere, the Babylonian king raided Assyria, plundered the city of Ekallate north of Ashur, carrying away the divine statues of Adad and Shala. He defeated the Assyrians in a border engagement in his ninth year, and his government remained intact as late as his thirteenth year. He controlled Ur in the south, as far as the lower Zab in the northeast, and up the Euphrates as far as Rapiqu. Even the tribal regions between the Radanu and the lower Zab were under his control early in his reign. But Tiglath-Pileser I gradually put an end to Babylon's dominance. His first five years of rule were marked by many successful military campaigns. During this period he claims to have conquered forty-two lands and their rulers, apart from many other campaigns that he did not bother to include in his accounts. These campaigns included two against Katmuhu before he succeeded in adding this territory to Assyria. He also campaigned against the various mountain tribes in an arch from the lower Zab in the east to Melidi in the far northwest. There was a major campaign against the Qumeni just to the northwest of Assyria and three campaigns against the Nairi in the territory north of Mount Kashiyari and as far west as the Euphrates, which he crossed to take tribute from Melidi. He also conquered the land of Ishua on the Euphrates north of Carchemish. Another campaign against the Ahlamu-Arameans took him up the Euphrates from Suhu to Carchemish, and at some point across the Euphrates to attack settlements in the Jebel Bishri. The following year saw additional campaigning, and three of those campaigns, all of which seem to have occurred after his tenth regnal year, are of particular interest. In one campaign Tiglath-Pileser marched to Mount Lebanon and took tribute from the lands of Byblos, Sidon, and Tyre. The tribute included a crocodile and a large monkey. While in the region, Tiglath-Pileser also took a boat ride on the Mediterranean and during the ride managed to kill a whale. Upon his return from Amurru, he imposed tribute on Ini-Teshub, the king of Hatti, presumably situated in Carchemish, though his capital city is not mentioned in the text. Tiglath-Pileser claims to have crossed the Euphrates some twenty-eight times in pursuit of the Ahlamu-Arameans and to have defeated them from Mount Lebanon to the city Tadmor in the desert, and from Anat of Suhu on the Euphrates downstream as far as Rapiqu on the Babylonian border. His final two campaigns were against Babylonia, apparently in a delayed response to the earlier Babylonian attacks against his territory. In his first Babylonian campaign in the lower Zab region Tiglath-Pileser had only limited success, but in his second campaign he outflanked the border fortifications, defeated the Babylonian chariotry, and penetrated into central Babylonia. He captured the major Babylonian cities, including Babylon, where he burned the palace of Marduk-nadin-ahhe, but he withdrew without recovering the statues of Adad and Shala.

This Babylonian defeat and a famine that occurred soon afterward led to a massive incursion of Arameans into Babylonia, and Marduk-nadin-ahhe simply disappeared, but the Babylonian campaign was also the highwater mark of Tiglath-pileser's military success. Despite his claims of victory, Tiglath-Pileser's campaigns against the Ahlamu-Arameans appear to have been largely defensive in nature—chasing them from Assyrian territory and then punishing them by raiding their encampments, sometimes far into the desert. The success of these punitive expeditions seems to have been quite ephemeral, however. As soon as the Assyrian army returned home, the Ahlamu-Arameans again pushed into Assyrian territory. The famine in the latter part of Tiglath-Pileser's reign seems to have given even more impetus to Aramean incursions into Assyria as well as into Babylonia. Eventually the Arameans thrust into the very heartland of Assyria, causing widespread distress and panic even in Ashur and Nineveh. An Assyrian chronicle fragment suggests that the Aramean invasion was so threatening that Tiglath-pileser was forced to retreat from Assyria proper to the outlying region of Katmuhu.

Assyria's revival in the early part of Tiglath-Pileser's reign was accompanied not only by significant building activity on the part of the king, but by other cultural developments as well. There was a great deal of scribal activity in collecting, copying, and editing cuneiform libraries, and there appears to have been significant Babylonian influence in this process. Palace edicts, Middle Assyrian laws, and Assyrian chronicles were among the wide variety of texts collected and edited during this period. Tiglath-Pileser's scribes also produced the first real Assyrian annals, since they narrate military events in chronological order, clearly distinguishing one year's campaign from the next. Tiglath-Pileser also introduces a number of new themes to those earlier themes characterizing the typical behavior of Assyrian kings, and these new themes are taken up by a number of the following kings. These include: "the king's concern for the reconstruction and prosperity of his land and people; the addition of new lands and people to Assyria; the expansion of cultivated land; the importation and planting of exotic trees; the gathering of flocks and herds of wild animals which are brought to Assyria; the hunting and killing of wild animals; and the increase in the number of chariots and horses" (RIMA 2, 6). It is interesting that these themes are introduced at the end of the 12th cent., only a little over a cent. prior to the time of Solomon, because despite the general lack of interest in such matters by the religiously oriented DEUTERONOMISTIC HISTORIAN, traces of similar motifs may still be found in the description of Solomon's reign. The increase of the population and extent of Solomon's rule are stressed (1 Kgs 4:20; 5:5 [Eng 4:25]) as is the multitude of his horses and chariots (1 Kgs 5:6 [Eng 4:26]; 1 Kgs 10:26).

The importation and planting of exotic trees is perhaps alluded to by the statement that Solomon made cedars as numerous in Jerusalem as the sycamores of the Shepelah (1 Kgs 10:27) and by the note that Solomon spoke about various trees and animals (1 Kgs 5:13 [Eng 1 Kgs 4:33]). Solomon clearly imported exotic animals into the country (1 Kgs 10:22), and the list of his daily provisions, which include deer, gazelles, and roebucks, suggest that he may have kept herds of these animals to supply his table (1 Kgs 5:3 [Eng 4:23]). In other words, Solomon in his reign mimicked the practices of the great kings of the period just preceding him.

9. Aramean incursions and Assyrian and Babylonian decline

Assyria's decline at the end of Tiglath-pileser I's reign continued during the reign of his successor Ashared-apil-ekur (1075–1074 BCE), and was only temporarily reversed in the early years of Ashur-bel-kala (1073–1056 BCE). While the Arameans continued to pour into Babylon, the new Babylonian king, Marduk-shapik-zeri (1082–1070 BCE), was able to defeat their sheikhs and begin rebuilding the fortifications of Babylon. Toward the end of his reign he made a peace treaty with Ashur-bel-kala, but died shortly afterward. Ashur-bel-kala then intervened in Babylon, appointed Adad-apla-iddina (1069–1048 BCE), a commoner, as king of Babylon, and married the daughter of Adad-apla-iddina, thus effectively uniting Assyria and Babylon. Ashur-bel-kala successfully campaigned in the mountains of Urartu, but his main enemy was the Arameans. He went on numerous campaigns against them, in the Tur-Abdin region, along the Habur and Balih, to Carchemish, against Mari and the land of Suhu, and, if one may believe his claims, as far afield as Mount Lebanon and Tadmor in the wilderness, and down the Euphrates from Anat to Rapiqu. There is a certain imitation of his father Tiglath-pileser I here, both in the way he describes the extent of his campaigns against the Arameans and especially in his claim that he made a fishing expedition off the coast of Arvad in the course of which he killed a whale. Yet despite any successes he may have had against the Arameans early in his reign, by the end of his reign the Arameans were occupying much of the land earlier claimed by Assyria. He was followed by eight Assyrian kings who left very few inscriptions: Eriba-Adad II (1055–1054 BCE), Shamshi-Adad IV (1053–1050 BCE), Ashurnasirpal I (1049–1031 BCE), Shalmaneser II (1030–1019 BCE), Ashur-nirari IV (1018–1013 BCE), Ashur-rabi II (1012–972 BCE), Ashur-resha-ishi II (971–967 BCE), and Tiglath-pileser II (966–935 BCE). Ashur-resha-ishi II had a vassal in the upper Habur region, but all the other evidence suggests that the Arameans had largely restricted Assyria to its homeland during this extended period that overlaps with the formation of the Israelite state under the reigns of Saul, David, and Solomon.

Meanwhile Babylon was faring no better. Arameans and a usurper rebelled against Adad-apla-iddina and desecrated the sanctuaries of the land, destroying the urban centers of Akkad, Der, Nippur, Sippar, and Dur-Kurigalzu. The Suteans also attacked and plundered Sumer and Akkad. Apparently Adad-apla-iddina was able to regain control and restore the cult of the gods, but little is known of his three successors, and the Isin dynasty came to an end in weakness around 1027 BCE. It was succeeded by three kings of the 2nd Sealand dynasty. During the reign of the first, Simbar-Shipak (1026–1009 BCE), the Assyrians returned the throne of Enlil made by Nebuchadnezzar I that the Arameans and Suteans had carried off in the time of Adad-apla-iddina. Simbar-Shipak was killed in a rebellion, however, and his two successors had very brief reigns marked by famine and Aramean incursions. The Sealand dynasty was followed by three kings of the Bazi dynasty about whom relatively little is known (1005–986 BCE). This dynasty was followed by the six-year rule of the single member of the Elamite dynasty (985–980 BCE). Nabu-mukin-apli then came to the throne of Babylon (979–944 BCE), but the Arameans continually disrupted normal life in Babylonia between his seventh and twenty-fourth years, and little is known of his immediate successors Ninurta-kudurri-usur and Mar-biti-ahhe-iddina.

10. The emergence of the Neo-Assyrian Empire

Ashur-dan II (934–912 BCE) began Assyria's long resurgence, and his reign marks the beginning of the Neo-Assyrian Empire. In his accession year he was under attack by an Aramean force, but having successfully repelled the attack, he began recapturing and resettling areas that had been abandoned by the Assyrians. He also reasserted Assyrian control over Katmuhu. By providing security within the Assyrian homeland and building up resources within Assyria proper, he set the stage for further expansion under his successors.

Adad-nirari II (911–891 BCE), in a very active reign, extended the successes of his predecessor, though on the southern front with Babylon his results were mixed. Early in his reign he defeated Shamash-mudammiq of Babylon at the foot of the Jebel Hamrin as far as the Diyala, and he was able to restore the cities of Arrapha and Lubdu to Assyria as well as to add territory between the lower Zab and the Radanu to Assyria. He also took Idu (Hit) and Zaqqu on the Euphrates away from Babylon and made them Assyrian border fortresses again. Later in his reign, probably during his campaigning against the Arameans, he fought against Shamash-mudammiq's successor, Nabu-shuma-ukin I, and this time, perhaps because of his troop commitments in the west, he was less successful. According to the pro-Assyrian Synchronistic Chronicle, Adad-Nirari defeated Nabu-shuma-ukin I, took much booty, and then exchanged daughters in a treaty that established the boundaries between the states, but since the new borders restored Babylonian territory in the northeast to Babylon, the Assyrians may actually have lost this battle and been forced to deal with the Babylonians as equals.

Adad-Nirari's campaigns to the north and west were more successful. He campaigned against the mountain tribes to the east and north of Assyria, maintained control of Katmuhu, and successfully attacked the Nairi lands as far west as Alzu. His campaigns against the Arameans along the Habur River in the years 901–894 BCE are particularly instructive. In 901 BCE he began his expansion into this area south of Mount Kashiyari with an attack on Nisibin, the site of his main opponent, Nur-Adad, the Temannite. The city did not fall, but Adad-nirari's troops controlled the countryside. He campaigned there again in 900 and 899 BCE, when he captured Huzirina, a city farther west than Nisibin. This produced tribute from Bit-Adini on the Euphrates, and Assyrian campaigns continued in the upper Habur region in 898, 897, and 896 BCE. Finally in 896 BCE, Nisibin fell, and Nur-Adad was brought back to Assyria. The rest of that year, 895 BCE, and the beginning of 894 BCE were spent in campaigning in the northern mountains, but later in 894 BCE Adad-nirari capitalized on his conquest of Nisibin. In a show of force he marched as far west as Guzana, where he received tribute from Bit-bahiani, and then he marched down the Habur, receiving tribute along the way. Reaching the Euphrates, he turned south, taking tribute throughout the land of Laqu from Sirqu (ancient Terqa) as far south as Hindanu. The persistent pressure on the strongest Aramean state in the Habur region eventually caused it to collapse, and its fall persuaded other states to try to buy off the Assyrians with tribute. Because the Aramean states were unwilling or unable to unite against Assyria as their common enemy, Assyria was able to begin picking them off one by one. And as Assyria incorporated more territory, people, and resources under its rule, it grew progressively stronger and capable of further extending its conquests.

Tukulti-Ninurta II (890–884 BCE) continued the constant campaigning of his predecessor and was able to maintain the stability of Assyria's empire, though he did not succeed in adding much territory to it. He campaigned across Mount Kashiyari into the Nairi lands, and he also campaigned against the Arameans and Lullu in the mountains to the east of Assyria, driving them across the lower Zab. In 885 BCE he marched south through the desert to attack settlements on the Tigris north of the border with Babylon. Then he moved through Babylonian territory from Dur-Kurigalzu to Sippar of Shamash, before turning north to march up the Euphrates in a show of force to hunt and collect tribute. His movement through Babylonian territory was not marked by any battles or any collection of tribute, so it was probably not a hostile act, but permitted by the peace treaty between the two states. He collected no tribute until he reached Anat, where Ili-ibnu, the governor of Suhi, furnished him very rich tribute. The Assyrian king then continued up the Euphrates, but did not receive tribute again until reaching Hindanu, and then again from different chieftains at several sites in the territory of Laqe. Eventually he turned up the Habur, then followed the Habur upstream to Nisibin, taking tribute all the way. Eventually he turned west to Huzirina, crossing the Jezirah to attack and subdue some settlements on the upper Balih, before returning home.

Meanwhile in Babylon Nabu-apla-iddina (887–855 BCE) maintained the Babylonian borders and a powerful state, having stopped the Sutian incursions into Babylonia. It may be in his time of security that the Erra epic was composed, looking back on the earlier troubled time. He seems to have encouraged Suhi, Assyria's vassal on the Euphrates just north of the Babylonian border to revolt. In 882 BCE, Ibni-ilu, the governor of Suhi, who had paid tribute to Tukulti-Ninurta in 885 BCE, had to flee to Assyria. In 878 BCE, Kudurru, the new governor of Suhi, aided by the Babylonians, refused tribute to Ashur-nasir-apli II, and a battle was fought at Suru, but though the Assyrians claimed a great victory, they could move no farther south, and shortly afterward the whole region revolted against Assyria.

a. Ashur-nasir-apli II and Shalmaneser III. The twenty-five year reign of Ashur-nasir-apli II (883–859 BCE), son of Tukulti-Ninurta II, was marked by constant warfare and frightful Assyrian atrocities. On his southern and eastern fronts Nabu-apla-iddina of Babylon was too strong for Assyria to expand significantly in that direction, and despite his grandiose claims, Ashur-nasir-apli actually lost Suhi and parts of Laqe on the Euphrates. He was faced with constant rebellions in Mount Kashiyari, Nairi, and Zamua on his northeastern border, and he repeatedly put them down with horrendous violence. He burned captives alive, including adolescent children, blinded and cut off the arms of captured soldiers, made piles of decapitated heads at the gates of cities, and opponents who particularly enraged him he flayed and hung their skins on city walls. Such frightfulness did not create genuine loyalty among his frightened vassals as the numerous rebellions indicate. Nonetheless, his relentless military campaigning, including several campaigns against Bit-Adini (Beth-eden of Amos 1:5), enabled Ashur-nasir-apli II to exact tribute from most of the states on the Habur and Balih, and even across the Euphrates at Carchemish, and down into northern Syria. In 875 BCE, having taken tribute, hostages, and supplementary troops from Sangara of Carchemish, he marched into the territory of Lubarna, the ruler of Patinu on the Orontes River, taking tribute from him, marrying into his family, and even expropriating one of his fortress cities where he settled Assyrians. He took tribute from Bit-Gusi more inland,

and he plundered the land of Luhutu. He then moved on to the Mediterranean where he received tribute from Tyre, Sidon, Byblos, Mahallatu, Maizu, Kaizu, Amurru, and the city Arvad. He also climbed the Amanus to cut down logs for his building program in Assyria, where he was building a new capital at Calah between Ashur and Nineveh. Despite his portrayal of this sweep to the Mediterranean as a military campaign, there remain serious questions how much of it was actually military and how much of it actually involved reciprocal trading to acquire the goods he needed for work on his temples and palaces in Calah. He claims to have settled people of Suhu, Laqu, Sirqu, Zamua, Bit-Adini, Hatti, and Patina in Calah, but how many of these were actually exiles, and how many were hired craftsmen or traders remains a question. Ashur-nasir-apli created a large zoo in Calah with herds of wild bulls, elephants, lions, ostriches, monkeys, wild asses, deer, ayalu-deer, female bears, panthers, and other beasts of the mountains and plains. He also created a pleasure garden with exotic plants and trees from the territories he crossed over. At the dedication of his palace he held a huge banquet for some 47,074 men and women from all parts of his land, 5,000 dignitaries and envoys from the lands Suhu, Hindanu, Patinu, Hatti, Tyre, Sidon, Gurgummu, Melid, Hubushku, Gilzanu, Kummu, and Musasiru, 16,000 people of Calah, and 1,500 palace functionaries—altogether 69,574 people for a ten-day banquet with food, drink, bathing, and anointing. One may think of Solomon's festival at the dedication of his Temple as a analogy (1 Kgs 8:65-66), and one may compare the list of supplies for Ashur-nasir-apli's banquet to the far more modest list of Solomon's daily provisions (2 Kgs 4:22-23).

Ashur-nasir-apli II's western campaign into northern Syria must have alarmed all the states of northern Syria, because when his son, SHALMANESER III (858–824 BCE), came to the throne, they had created a coalition to block further Assyrian expansion in the west. In 858 BCE, when he crossed the Euphrates, a coalition of Sam'al, Patina, Bit-Adini, Carchemish, Que (Cilicia), and other allies tried to block his way, but Shalmaneser was able to scatter their forces and move into Patina. The next year he was able to break up the coalition, and having isolated Bit-Adini, by concentrated campaigns in 856 and 857 BCE, he was finally able to destroy the remnants of that state on the Euphrates. The fate of the north Syrian states in these few years set off alarm bells farther south in central and southern Syria, and when Shalmaneser approached the cities of Irhulene of Hamath in 853 BCE, he was blocked by a coalition of twelve kings and their combined forces—1,200 chariots, 1,200 cavalry, and 20,000 infantry of Hadadezer of Damascus; 700 chariots, 700 cavalry, and 10,000 infantry of Irhulene of Hamath; 2,000 chariots and 10,000 infantry of Ahab of Israel; 500 infantry from Byblos; 1,000 infantry from

Egypt; 10 chariots and 10,000 infantry from Irqanate; 200 infantry of Matinu-baal of Arvad; 200 infantry from Usanate; 30 chariots and ?000 infantry of Adon-Baal of Shianu; 1,000 camels of Gindibu the Arab; ?00 infantry of Ba'asa, the man of Bit-Ruhubi, the Ammonite. It is clear from the numbers that Ahab was a major partner in this coalition. The battle was fought at Qarqar in the Orontes River valley, and Shalmaneser claimed a great victory, though his advance farther south seems to have been stopped.

In the meantime Marduk-zakir-shumi I (854–819 BCE) had come to the throne of Babylon, but his brother Marduk-bel-usati rebelled against him, and the Diyala region and the tribal lands near the Persian Gulf supported this younger brother. Markuk-zakir-shumi I called on Shalmaneser III for help, and in 851 and 850 BCE, Shalmaneser campaigned in Babylonia, finally capturing and executing Marduk-bel-usati and his soldiers. While in Babylonia he offered sacrifices in Cuth, Babylon, and Borsipa, and hosted a big banquet for the people of Babylon and Borsippa. He also campaigned in the south of Babylonia against the Chaldeans.

In 849 BCE, Shalmaneser again crossed the Euphrates, where he destroyed a number of the cities of Sangara of Carchemish; moving on to the southeast of Aleppo, he was attacked by the same coalition he had supposedly defeated in 853 BCE, this time farther north than Qarqar. In 848 BCE, he again fought against the coalition, capturing some of the cities of Irhulene. The next two years he was occupied closer to home, but in 845 BCE, he crossed the Euphrates with 120,000 troops to meet the Syrian coalition. The Assyrians claimed a great victory, but the text does not say where, nor does it record any conquests, so there is serious suspicion that the Assyrians were defeated.

In 844–842 BCE, he was involved in areas to the east, north, and northwest of Assryia, but in 841 BCE he again crossed the Euphrates to attack the coalition. Unfortunately the death of a number of the coalition leaders had left the coalition in shambles. Hadad-ezer of Damascus, who had fallen ill, was murdered and succeeded by his servant HAZAEL. Ahab of Israel had also died, and sometime after Hazael's coup in Damascus, Jehu led a similarly successful, but extremely bloody coup against Ahab's son Joram in Israel. Without the ties to the old leaders, many of the earlier coalition members opted out, including Hamath and many of the coastal states, and it is not clear whether even Israel remained involved. Shalmaneser defeated Hazael at Mount Saniru before Mount Lebanon and chased him and the remnants of his army to Damascus. Shalmaneser was unable to capture Damascus, but he kept Hazael penned up there while the Assyrian army marched through Hazael's territory razing and destroying. Shalmaneser then crossed through Israelite and Phoenician territory to the coast, where he received tribute from Tyre, Sidon, and Jehu of Israel.

Erich Lessing/Art Resource, NY
Figure 6: Jehu paying tribute to Shalmaneser; British Museum, London.

In 840–839 BCE, Shalmaneser was occupied in north Syria and in a major campaign against Que (Cilicia), but in 838 BCE, he again moved west against Hazael of Damascus. He captured a number of Hazael's cities and then moved on to take tribute from Tyre, Sidon, and Byblos. He may have penetrated as far south as the Egyptian border. Between 837–832 BCE, he campaigned against Que, Tabal (Cappadocia), Urartu, and Namri to the east, taking tribute as far east as from tribal leaders of Parsua (Persia). In 831 BCE, when he learned of a revolt in Patinu, he sent his field marshal Dayyan-Ashur to suppress it, and when the people submitted, handing over the guilty ringleaders, he set up a colossal statue of Shalmaneser III in Kinalua (Kullani, biblical Calneh [Amos 6:2] or Calno [Isa 10:9]), the capital of Patinu. Though the king no longer went on campaign, the years 830–828 BCE saw further campaigns to the east and north of Assyria, but then things fell apart.

b. Shamshi-Adad V to Ashur-nirari V. Revolt broke out in Assyria in 827 BCE and continued until 820 BCE. The revolt was apparently instigated by one of Shalmaneser's sons, a certain Ashur-da'in-apla, and Shamshi-Adad V (823–811 BCE), who succeeded his father, had great difficulty putting the revolt down. He apparently needed the help of the Babylonian king Marduk-zakir-shumi I, since the treaty between Shamshi-Adad V and Marduk-zakir-shumi I clearly puts the Assyrians in the more dependent position. (It was probably during this period of internal confusion in Assyria that Hazael of Damascus regained his strength, eventually campaigning far into northern Syria, at one point even crossing the Euphrates.) Gradually, however, Assyria regained its dominance over Babylon. The years 819–816 BCE were spent campaigning in the northeast, reaching as far as the territory of the Medes. But in 814 BCE, Shamshi-Adad invaded Babylonia's eastern territories, testing Marduk-balassu-iqbi (818–813 BCE), Marduk-zakir-shumi I's successor. After initial Assyrian successes a combined force of Babylonians, Chaldeans, Elamites, and Arameans turned Shamshi-Adad V back, but in his second Babylonian campaign in 813 BCE, Shamshi-Adad captured Marduk-balassu-iqbi and took him to Assyria, where he flayed him in Nineveh. Shamshi-Adad returned to Babylon in 812–811 BCE, capturing Baba-aha-iddina (812 BCE), Marduk-balassu-iqbi's successor. He plundered the eastern territories of Babylonia, carrying off many gods and taking tribute from CHALDEA, but he appears to have shown more respect to the central Babylonian cities of Cuth, Babylon, and Borsippa, where he made sacrifices.

Adad-nirari III (810–783 BCE) succeeded his father Shamshi-Adad, but in many ways he was overshadowed by other Assyrian figures of the time, since he was still a minor when he succeeded his father. For four years the influential queen mother, Sammuramat, the famous Semiramis of Greek legend, ruled in his name, and the field marshal, Shamshi-ilu, ruled almost independently in Til-Barsip on the Euphrates, the westernmost area of the empire still under firm Assyrian control. In his first few years Adad-nirari was primarily occupied on his eastern borders, though in 808 BCE he did succeed in recapturing the important province of Guzanu. In 805 BCE, however, he subdued the king of Arpad and eight kings allied with him west of the Euphrates, and according to the Eponym List further western campaigns were carried out to Hazazu in 804 BCE, to Baʾalu in 803 BCE, and to the sea in 802 BCE. At some point during these years of regaining control of the western provinces that had been lost at the end of Shalmaneser III's reign, Adad-nirari III and Shamshi-ilu the field marshal established the border between Hamath and the king of Arpad, and Adad-nirari III and Sammuramat drew up the boundary between Kummuh and Gugum farther to the north. The Eponym list suggests a large number of other military campaigns, most of them on Assyria's eastern borders, but there are no annals to give detailed accounts of these campaigns. At some point Shamshi-ilu led a successful campaign against Urartu that he commemorated on a stela set up in his own name in Til-Barsip, the old capital of Bit-Adini, but this may have been under Shalmaneser IV. The Eponym List records a campaign to Mansuate in 796 BCE, and it was probably during this campaign that Adad-nirari confined the ruler of Damascus to the city and took tribute from him, and that was probably the same year he took tribute from Joash of Samaria. Whether his tribute from Tyre and Sidon is to be attributed to the same year, or whether it should be connected to the campaigns of 803–802 BCE is less clear. Adad-nirari's scribes may have conflated several campaigns in the inscriptions recording his success in the west.

Urartu to the north of Assyria had become the main threat when Shalmaneser IV (782–773 BCE) succeeded his father, Adad-nirari III. He waged a number of campaigns against Urartu, but they all seem to have been defensive in nature. In 773 BCE, Shamsi-ilu, the field marshal, led a campaign against Damascus, took tribute from its ruler Hadiyani, and on his return set up a boundary stone for the king of Kummuh. Another Assyrian official, Bel-Harran-beli-usur, the palace herald of the king of Assyria, founded a new city in the desert on the Wadi Tharthar and named it Dur-Bel-Harran-beli-usur after himself. Such independence on the part of Assyrian officials indicates the degree to which the Assyrian monarchs were losing centralized control during this period.

Ashur-dan III (772–755 BCE) followed his brother Shalmaneser IV to the throne, but though he ruled eighteen years, he left almost no inscriptions. According to the Eponym List there were campaigns to Hatarikka (biblical Hadrach) in north Syria in 772, 765, and 755 BCE, to eastern Babylonia in 771, 769, and 767 BCE, and to MEDIA in 766 BCE, but more significant are the references to plague in 765 and 759 BCE, and revolt in the capital in 763–762 BCE, revolt in Arrapha in 761–760 BCE, and revolt in Guzana in 759 BCE, though Guzana may have been recaptured in 758 BCE, when peace was restored in the land. Nonetheless, it is clear that Ashur-dan III had to struggle just to hold Assyria together.

In the meantime Babylon had fallen into a period of anarchy and chaos that allowed Aramean tribesmen to ravage the countryside. It was not until the reign of Eriba-Marduk (769–761 BCE) that things begin to return to normal. He killed or drove off the Arameans who had taken the fields of Babylon and Borsippa and returned the land to the citizens of those cities. This reprieve was short-lived, however. He was replaced by Nabu-shuma-ishkun (760–748 BCE), a member of the Bit-Dakkuru tribe. A literary text attributes a large number of crimes to him. He apparently favored the Chaldeans and Arameans at the expense of the older population of the land, and he offended their religious sensibilities by installing the gods of the Sealand, the Chaldeans, and the Arameans in Esagil. There was also renewed and bloody conflict between the various population groups over the fields of Borsippa.

In Assyria Ashur-nirari V (754–745 BCE) succeeded his father, but his ten-year reign was marked by little success. His campaign to Arpad in 754 BCE probably led to his treaty with Mati-ilu of Arpad that is preserved in a fragmentary copy, but he apparently remained in Assyria for the rest of his reign except for campaigns to Namri in 749 and 748 BCE. Sardur II of Urartu claims to have defeated him, and Ashur-nirari left almost no inscriptions. In 746 BCE, revolt broke out in Calah, and in 745 BCE, his son Tiglath-Pileser III seized the throne.

c. **Tiglath-pileser III.** With TIGLATH-PILESER III a new era of Assyrian expansion began. At the beginning of his reign Urartu was threatening Assyria's existence. With its allies in north Syria Urartu was positioning itself to block Assyria's trade to the west, and with its allies to the east and the unruly Chaldeans and Arameans in Babylonia, Assyria's trade routes to the east and the Persian Gulf were threatened. Tiglath-Pileser III systematically began to dismantle these multiple threats. In the course of his reign he reorganized the Assyrian government to ensure far stronger centralized control, limiting the power and military resources of provincial governors by a series of checks and balances in which military and political officials kept tabs on one another. Militarily he first moved to secure his eastern and southern borders. In 745 BCE he subdued the Aramean tribes from Dur-Kurigalzu and Sippar of Shamash to the Uqnu River by the shores of the Persian Gulf and appointed governors over them, thus becoming the nominal overlord of Nabonassar of Babylon (747–734 BCE). The following year he campaigned against Namri to the east, and then in 743 BCE he turned west. Under Urartian encouragement Mati-ilu of Arpad had broken his treaty with Assyria, and Sarduri of Urartu, Sulumal of Melid, and Tarhularu of Gurgum came to his aid. Tiglath-pileser defeated the Urartians, put Arpad under siege, and ravaged Gurgum, forcing Tarhularu to submit. Arpad held out for three years, but fell to the Assyrians in 740 BCE. With its fall a number of other north Syrian states apparently swore loyalty to Tiglath-pileser, including Tutammu the king of Unqi (formerly Patina). But in 739 BCE, while Tiglath-pileser was fighting northwest of Nineveh in the plain before the Zagros against the Ahlameans and their Urartian supporters, a certain Azriyau organized a coalition against the Assyrians which included nineteen provinces of Hamath. Tutammu of Unqi apparently joined the coalition, breaking his treaty with Assyria, and in 738 BCE Tiglath-pileser retaliated. He captured Tutammu's royal city Kullani/Kinalia (biblical Calno/Calneh), deported its population, stripping them of their possessions, executed Tutammu, subdued all of Unqi, and turned it into an Assyrian province. He also annexed the nineteen rebellious provinces of Hamath to Assyria. The fall of Arpad and Kullani made a profound impression on the inhabitants of Israel and Judah, as the prophets Amos (6:2) and Isaiah (10:9) both attest, and it may be that the Azriyau who organized this unsuccessful anti-Assyrian coalition was none other than Azariah/Uzziah of Judah who probably died in 738 BCE, the same year Kullani fell. In response to the coalition's defeat most of the states of north, central, and southern Syria and the Phoenician coast hastened to pay tribute to Tiglath-pileser III, including Rezin of Damascus and Menahem of Samaria. Tiglath-pileser III then turned back to his northeastern border, where he campaigned in 737 and 736 BCE, and to his northern border with Urartu where he campaigned in 735 BCE.

While Tiglath-pileser III was thus occupied on his eastern and northern borders, REZIN of Damascus used the opportunity to try to create another anti-Assyrian league. He was joined by Israel under Pekah, the son of Remaliah, who had assassinated Pekahiah, Menahem's son, and the Phoenicians, the Philistines, and Samsi, queen of the Arabs, also seem to have joined the league. Egyptian support may have been expected as well. Judah, however, under first Jotham, and then at his death in 735 BCE, under Ahaz, refused to join. Rezin and Pekah tried to force the issue by a surprise attack on Jerusalem, hoping to quickly isolate the city, breach its wall, and remove Ahaz as king of Judah, replacing him with a more agreeable figure, perhaps the son of Ittobaal of Tyre. The surprise attack failed, however, and the coalition had no time for a prolonged siege of Jerusalem, since they had to move their forces north to meet the expected Assyrian response. At some point in this process Ahaz sent messengers to Tiglath-pileser, submitting to him and asking for his help against Damascus and Israel. Tiglath-pileser was happy to comply. In 734 BCE, Tiglath-pileser marched through Phoenicia and Philistia, taking Gaza and effectively blocking any chance for significant Egyptian assistance to his enemies. Hiram of Tyre submitted, and Hanunu of Gaza, who had fled to Egypt, soon returned and became an Assyrian vassal. In 733 BCE, the Assyrians moved against Damascus and Israel, ravaging both territories. Their Arab allies were defeated and submitted to Assyria, leaving besieged Damascus totally isolated. It fell in 732 BCE, and Samaria was only spared because Hoshea murdered Pekah, pledged allegiance to Assyria, and was confirmed as king in Samaria to rule over a vastly reduced realm. The Galilee, Transjordan, and the coastal area south of Mount Carmel were stripped from Israel and turned into Assyrian provinces. Having subdued the west, Tiglath-pileser then turned back to Babylon in 731 BCE.

Nabonassar had been followed by Nabu-nadin-zeri (733–732 BCE), but he was deposed in a revolt led by Nabu-shuma-ukin II (732 BCE), and he, in turn, was replaced by Nabu-mukin-zeri (731–729 BCE) of the Amukanu tribe. Babylonia was seriously splintered, and even the rival Chaldean tribes did not join in a common front against Assyria. Tiglath-pileser simply crushed them one by one, Bit-shilani, Bit-Sha'alli, and Bit-Amukanni, though Nabu-mukin-zeri appears to have escaped and continued to control parts of southern Babylonia for a couple of years. In contrast, Balasu of Bit-Dakkuri and Merodach-baladan of Bit-Yakin, the king of the Sealand, avoided the fate of the other Chaldean tribes by submitting and paying tribute before the Assyrians could attack them.

Having subdued Babylonia, Tiglath-pileser III was installed as king of Babylon, took the hand of Bel in the celebration of the Babylonian NEW YEAR like any legitimate Babylonian king, and ruled over Babylon for two years (728–727 BCE), being listed in the Babylonian king list as Pulu (biblical Pul [2 Kgs 15:19]). When Tiglath-pileser died in 727, Assyria controlled an empire that stretched from the Persian Gulf to the borders of Egypt, including major portions of Cilicia and Anatolia as well.

d. Shalmaneser V. While Egypt had sent a minor contingent to support the anti-Assyrian coalition in the mid-9th cent., Assyria's expanded empire was now a direct threat to Egypt, and Egypt began serious efforts to provoke revolt in Palestine and southern Syria. Shalmaneser V (726–722 BCE), who succeeded Tiglath-pileser on the throne of both Assyria and Babylon (under the throne name Ululai), caught Hoshea of Samaria withholding his tribute and corresponding with the Egyptian king So, probably Osorkon IV of Tanis. Shalmaneser moved very quickly, apparently before preparations for a more general revolt could be completed, imprisoning Hoshea and putting Samaria under siege. Samaria fell in 722 BCE after a three-year siege, apparently without any Egyptian aid materializing, and Shalmaneser V deported the Israelite population to the province of Guzanu (biblical Gozan) on the Habur and to the territory of the Median tribes on Assyria's northeastern frontier.

e. Sargon II. SARGON II (721–705 BCE), who succeeded Shalmaneser V in an irregular fashion, also claims to have captured Samaria, but his claims for his successes in his accession year and his first regnal year appear increasingly dubious. His accession was greeted with revolt in both Babylon and in the west. In 721 BCE, MERODACH-BALADAN II, the former vassal of both Tiglath-pileser III and Shalmaneser V, seized Babylon and claimed kingship over Babylonia (721–710 BCE). By clever diplomacy he had become the foremost Chaldean leader, won the support of the Aramean tribes in eastern Babylonia, and had arranged an anti-Assyrian treaty with Elam. Sargon II tried to respond to the revolt by marching down the Tigris and invading Babylonia from the east, the strategy that had worked for Tiglath-pileser III, but Sargon's maneuver was blocked by the Elamites at Der, and Sargon had to retreat, leaving Merodach-baladan to rule over Babylonia for eleven years. Chaldean rule was not popular in the great cities of Babylonia, where the economic hardships caused by the loss of trade and the extortions of the tribesmen in the countryside tended to make the city populations pro-Assyrian, but for the moment Sargon could not exploit this weakness within Babylonia. He was also faced with a major rebellion in the west led by Ilubi'di of Hamat. Arpad in north Syria, the cities along the Mediterranean coast as far north as Simirra, the inland states from Damascus to Samaria, and the Philistines, including Hanun of Gaza, all joined in the revolt. Only Ahaz of Judah appears to have remained loyal, and even he would have been unable to send his yearly tribute, since all the territories between Judah and Assyria had joined in the revolt. In 720 BCE, after defeating the coalition near Qarqar, Sargon proceeded to capture all the rebelling cities and plunder and

deport their inhabitants. An Egyptian army came to the aid of Hanun of Gaza, but Sargon defeated the Egyptians near Rapihu, captured Hanun, and destroyed Rapihu, deporting its population. It may have been in the aftermath of this victory that Sargon tried to open up a trade emporium with Egypt.

The other major threat to Assyria was from Urartu to the north, which kept trying to stir up revolt against Assyria all along its northern frontier. Sargon was engaged somewhere in this broad area every year from 719–711 BCE. In 717 BCE, he removed the rebellious ruler of Carchemish, deported its population, and resettled it with Assyrians. In 714 BCE, in his famous eighth campaign that he describes quite poetically and in detail in a letter to the god Ashur, Sargon II marched deep into Urartu and inflicted a crippling defeat on this enemy. While major parts of the Assyrian army were thus engaged in the north, other units were occasionally engaged along the border with Egypt. In 715 BCE, an Assyrian army operated against various Arab tribes east and south of Palestine, and even the Egyptian pharaoh sent gifts to Sargon. It was probably in the same year that Sargon removed Azuri, the ruler of Ashdod whom he had caught sending letters to the surrounding states trying to get them to join a revolt against Assyria. Sargon replaced him with his brother Ahimeti, but the people of Ashdod could not stand Ahimeti. Within a year, clearly after the Assyrian troops had withdrawn from the area, the Ashdodites chased Ahimeti out of town, replacing him with a commoner known as Yadna or Yamani. Though this is disputed, the names could be interpreted as alternate nicknames given to him by the Philistines referring to his place of origin or ethnicity—the Cypriot/Greek. The names do not have the gentilic endings expected in Akkadian, but the names were not given him by the Assyrians, who probably just preserved the Philistine nicknames as proper names. In any case, Yadna/Yamani, like Azuri, began sending messengers to the surrounding states, including HEZEKIAH of Judah, trying to get them to join in a revolt against Assyria, and promising them Egyptian and Nubian support. (Most English translations render the Akkadian and Hebrew terms for NUBIA as ETHIOPIA, but the area designated by these terms corresponds to modern Sudan, not modern Ethiopia, which is too far east.) By this time the Nubians had imposed their rule over the Egyptian dynasts of the delta region, and Nubia was the real power in Egypt. Isaiah opposed the alliance with Ashdod and its Egyptian and Nubian backers, and he demonstrated publicly against it in Jerusalem, repeatedly parading in the nude in front of the palace where the foreign diplomats were periodically meeting with Hezekiah's court (Isa 20). Hezekiah apparently held back, and in 711 Sargon sent his field marshal to put down the revolt in Ashdod. Yamani fled, apparently receiving asylum from the Nubian pharaoh Shabako on the Egyptian-Nubian border, but Ashdod and the surrounding cities that supported the revolt against Assyria did not fare so well. Sargon's field marshal besieged, captured, and plundered them, deported their population, and then resettled the cities with captives from the eastern part of Sargon's empire. No Egyptian or Nubian force came to the aid of Ashdod, though Shabako's granting asylum to Yamani suggests that Nubia was still behaving as an enemy of Assyria. Four years later in 707 BCE, Shabataka, Shabako's successor, extradited Yamani to Assyria, but again, this does not necessarily indicate either Nubia's submission to Assyria nor a long-term desire for peace. Yamani had outlived his usefulness as an exile, and his extradition seems to have been no more than a ploy to gain time and useful intelligence as Nubia prepared for further intervention in Palestine.

In the meantime Sargon had regained control of Babylonia. In 710 BCE, he marched down east of the Tigris and breached the defensive line Merodach-baladan had set up. No Elamite army blocked the Assyrian advance, and this forced the Chaldean army to move south to confront the threat. Although the Chaldeans took hostages from the Babylonian cities on their way south, this Chaldean withdrawal allowed the major cities of Babylonia to open their gates to the Assyrian forces, and Sargon was crowned king of Babylon (710–705 BCE). Sargon continued campaigning in Babylonia against the Chaldean tribes through 707 BCE, finally forcing Merodach-baladan to submit, release all his Babylonian hostages, and pay very heavy tribute, but Merodach-baladan's life was spared, and he remained the leader of the Bit-Yakin tribe. Sargon also captured border areas of Elam and installed Nabu-damiq-ilani in a fortress there to block any Elamite counterattack. The king of Dilmun (Bahrain), impressed by Sargon's successes, sent tribute to Sargon. In the meantime Sargon's governor in Que campaigned against the famous Midas of Mushku, compelling him to pay tribute to Sargon. Sargon's troops also put down a revolt in Cyprus that Sargon had subdued in an earlier campaign. Unfortunately, Sargon's campaigns against Urartu and Mushku weakened both states so that they no longer served as an adequate buffer against the Cimmerians, who, having defeated Argisti of Urartu, now appeared in Assyrian territory. Sargon, after years of building, had dedicated his new capital of Dur-Sharrukin (Fortress of Sargon) north of Calah, but he personally took up the campaign against this new threat in the mountains northwest of Assyria proper. Sometime in 705 BCE, while campaigning in these mountains, Sargon and the elite troops that served as his personal bodyguard were ambushed and wiped out in a defeat so thorough that Sargon's body was never recovered for proper burial. Isaiah celebrated this event with a mock elegy (Isa 14:4-23), and SENNACHERIB (704–681 BCE), Sargon's successor, took omens to learn the reasons for this shocking display of divine anger and made offerings to appease the Assyrian gods. He also abandoned Sargon's new city, Dur-Sharrukin, either closing the buildings or leaving them unfinished, eventually moving his capital to Nineveh.

f. Sennacherib. Sargon's surprising defeat and unexpected death led to plans for revolt in both Babylon and Palestine, and by 703 BCE both areas were in open revolt. Sennacherib was acknowledged as king of Babylon for two years (704–703 BCE), but for some reason a native Babylonian, Marduk-zakir-shumi II, was installed, presumably as an Assyrian vassal, at the the New Year's festival of 703 BCE. Merodach-baladan II, who had the support of the Chaldean and Aramean tribes, the promise of Elamite assistence, and was courting the support of Hezekiah and other western vassals of Assyria, moved quickly, and within a month he had removed Marduk-zakir-shumi and taken the throne of Babylon for himself. Merodach-baladan placed an advanced body of Elamite troops at Cuth to halt the Assyrian advance, while his main forces were stationed at Kish. Sennacherib, however, blocked the movement of reinforcements from Kish with an advanced body of his troops, while his main army captured Cuth by storm. He then moved on to Kish and scattered the Babylonian forces there. The Babylonian cities greeted Sennacherib as a deliverer, and Sennacherib moved on to pacify and destroy the fortifications in the Chaldean areas of southern Babylonian. Chaldea was put under the rule of Assyrian officials, and northern Babylonia was put under the rule of a native Babylonian, Bel-ibni (702–700 BCE).

Sennacherib then moved against the west, marching down the Phoenician coast and through Philistia, destroying Judah's weaker allies, thus isolating Judah and at the same time effectively blocking Egyptian aid to Hezekiah. Sennacherib then began to systematically destroy the Judean fortresses that controlled the access roads leading up from the coastal plain to Jerusalem, Hezekiah's capital. An army of Nubian and Egyptian troops did appear in the coastal plain, but in an initial engagement Sennacherib's troops succeeded in repulsing the Nubian/Egyptian attack. At this point the situation becomes murky. Sennacherib claims to have taken forty-six of Hezekiah's walled cities and to have shut Hezekiah up in Jerusalem like a bird in a cage. Both the Assyrian and the biblical records also indicate that Hezekiah eventually paid a very heavy tribute to Sennacherib. Yet it is clear from both accounts that Sennacherib did not capture Jerusalem, and that the tribute was sent to Assyria only after Sennacherib had returned home. This and other details of the biblical account that do not fit well in 701 BCE have led some scholars to posit two different campaigns of Sennacherib against Jerusalem, one in 701 BCE and another in 689 or 688 BCE after Sennacherib's final destruction of Babylon. Other scholars have suggested that the Egyptian/Nubian army did not retreat to Egypt after its initial defeat but regrouped and remained a threat, and that Sennacherib was worried that his army, perhaps weakened by plague after prolonged siege operations, was not capable of sustaining the siege of Jerusalem as long as it would take to capture the city. Sennacherib made far more of his successful conquest of Lachish,

Erich Lessing / Art Resource, NY

Figure 7: Seige of Lachish illustrated in a relief from the palace of Sennacherib at Nineveh; British Museum, London.

one of Hezekiah's important outlying fortress cities, than he did of his attack on Jerusalem, and in Judah the failure of Sennacherib to capture Jerusalem was celebrated as a great deliverance of Jerusalem wrought by Yahweh, the god of Israel.

Sennacherib may also have been worried about the deteriorating situation in Babylon. Once the main Assyrian army left Babylon and marched west, Merodach-baladan again stirred up his Aramean, Chaldean, and Elamite allies, and Bel-ibni did not have strong enough forces to effectively control the area. In 700 BCE, the Assyrian army had to again move through Chaldean territory and even cross the border into Elam in order to pacify southern Babylonian. Sennacherib removed the unfortunate Bel-ibni and replaced him with one of Sennacherib's own sons, Ashur-nadin-shumi (699–694 BCE). Merodach-baladan II died soon afterward, but Ashur-nadin-shumi was still faced with rebellious clans of the Bit-Yakin tribe, supported by Elam. Assyria decided to deal with this threat by invading Elam, and for this purpose Sennacherib had a fleet of ships constructed in Nineveh and sailed down the Tigris by Tyrian, Sidonian, and Cypriot sailors, then transferred by canal to the Euphrates, and then down

the Euphrates to the Persian Gulf. There Assyrian troops embarked on them, sailed across the Gulf, and attacked the Elamite homeland. Elam's response was quite energetic. An Elamite army crossed the border, marched up the Tigris, and attacked into central and northern Babylonia while the main Assyrian army was still in the south. The Elamite king captured Ashur-nadin-shumi at Sippar and set up as king of Babylon in his place a native Babylonian named Nergal-usheshib (693 BCE). The Assyrian army, returning from the south, met Nergal-usheshib at Nippur and defeated him, but they made no move on the city of Babylon, and another Chaldean leader, Mushezib-Marduk (692–689 BCE), installed himself as king there. After regrouping and refitting, in 692 BCE the Assyrian army marched down the Tigris to attack Elam from the province of Der, but Assyria was not able to hold its advantage. Mushezib-Marduk had to flee to Elam, but he returned with an army and seized Babylon, and the king of Elam came to his support with a large Elamite army, augmented by Aramean and Chaldeans. This large force marched up the Tigris into the province of Arrapkha and met the Assyrian army at Halule on the Diyala, where a horrendously bloody battle was fought in 691 BCE. Though Sennacherib claimed victory, his losses were far too high to follow up until 689 BCE, when internal problems in Elam prevented further Elamite assistance to Mushezib-Marduk. By this time Sennacherib, who had never been a particular admirer of Babylon or its god MARDUK, was totally fed up with Babylon and the never-ending difficulties that seemed to be associated with the city. Mushezib-Marduk's Chaldeans and their Aramean and Arab allies took refuge in Babylon, where Sennacherib besieged them for nine months, until famine and disease debilitated the city's defenders. When the city finally fell, Sennacherib had his soldiers sack the city. The statue of Marduk was taken to Assyria, and many of the images of the other gods were smashed in their temples. Sennacherib was so intent on wiping out the memory of Babylon, he had his soldiers divert the waters of the canals so that they would wash away the foundation trenches of the temples to ensure that the temples could never be rebuilt. Such behavior was normally regarded as sacrilege even in Assyria, where there were many devotees of Marduk and the Babylonian gods, but Sennacherib provided theological justification for his actions by a curious theological text in which Marduk is put on trial by a divine court headed by Ashur and condemned to death for rebellion against the divine assembly.

Following the destruction of Babylon in 689 BCE, there were campaigns against the Arab allies of Babylon deep into the desert, against the oasis of Adummatu/ Dumah and perhaps other encampments, but Sennacherib's annals either end or are not extant beyond 689 or 688 BCE, so there is no extant evidence of any significant campaigning after that point. Sennacherib's final years appear to have been spent in building activities and enjoying the fruits of empire. In 681 BCE, he was murdered by some of his sons in a palace coup. Second Kings 19:32 identifies two culprits and the site of the murder, but the Hebrew tradition garbles the Assyrian names. Adramelech has been plausibly equated with Sennacherib's son, Arda-mulishi, but Sharezer is otherwise unknown, and the divine name NISROCH is garbled beyond recognition.

g. Esarhaddon. Sennacherib had chosen his son ESARHADDON as his successor and had put him in charge of Babylonia after the destruction of Babylon in 689 BCE, but Esarhaddon's rivals had succeeded in alienating the two in the intervening years. Esarhaddon was apparently campaigning in the northwest of the empire when his father was murdered, and as the ringleaders of the coup squabbled among themselves, he marched on the capital. The main Assyrian army was prepared to resist him in the Nisibin area, but some units switched sides, and Esarhaddon's army kept growing as he approached the capital. The rebellious sons fled and sought refuge in Urartu (Armenia), Esarhaddon was installed as king (680–669 BCE), and he proceeded to purge the army of his opponents. This period of unrest gave the chief of the Bit-Yakin tribe an opportunity to revolt, but once things in Assyria were settled, Esarhaddon marched down the Tigris and subdued the rebellious tribes. The ringleader fled to Elam, but the Elamites, who had changed their foreign policy, simply executed him. In the northwest, in former Urartian areas, the Scythians had moved in, and in the provinces of Hilakku and Tabal, the Cimmerians were causing trouble. The Assyrian governors had some success against them in 679 BCE, but the pressure kept building, and by the end of Esarhaddon's reign, Hilakku and Tabal were lost to Assyria. In the west he put down a revolt of the king of Sidon and another ruler of maritime cities on the north Syrian coast, executing both offenders. He also installed his candidate as leader of the Arab tribes in the western desert controlling the desert approaches to Egypt. In Babylon Esarhaddon took a conciliatory approach in contrast to his father, and throughout his reign the rebuilding of Babylon and its temples progressed. Esarhaddon had intended to restore the statue of Marduk to his rebuilt temple in Babylon with great pomp and ceremony, and he actually had an inscription written up describing the return, but Esarhaddon died before the event took place, and later Ashurbanipal, his son, simply used the same inscription to describe his return of the statue to Babylon. The pro-Babylonian policy was successful, and by 676 BCE Esarhaddon was using Babylon as a base to campaign deep into Media and Persia. In 672 BCE, the Median vassals, and presumably all the other Assyrian vassals, were forced to sign treaties to support the accession of Esarhaddon's two sons whom Esarhaddon had chosen as his successors. Ashurbanipal was to succeed him to the throne of Assyria, and Shamash-shum-ukin

was to succeed him to the throne of Babylon. In the meantime, Esarhaddon had decided to invade Egypt to put an end to the Nubian king Taharqa's (Tirhakah, 2 Kgs 19:8) attempts to stir up trouble in Phoenicia and Palestine. In 671 BCE, Esarhaddon invaded Egypt, defeated Taharqa, and captured Memphis. Once the Assyrian army withdrew, however, Taharqa returned, recaptured Memphis, and forced some of the princes of lower Egypt to renounce their allegiance to Esarhaddon. In 669 BCE, Esarhaddon set out on another campaign against Egypt, but he died on the way, and the campaign was temporarily postponed.

h. Ashurbanipal. The succession of both ASHURBANIPAL (668–626 BCE) and Shamash-shum-ukin (668–648 BCE) went smoothly, but the succession and other matters, including negotiations with Tyre, delayed the campaign against Egypt, allowing Taharqa to consolidate his control of Egypt. Finally in 667 BCE, a large Assyrian army, including contingents from its vassals in Syria and Palestine, marched into Egypt, and Memphis was recaptured. After the main Assyrian army withdrew from Egypt, the native rulers rebelled, but the Assyrian garrisons put the rebellion down, and the ringleaders were taken to Nineveh, treated with clemency, and then returned to their posts in Egypt. In 664 BCE, after the death of Taharqa, the Nubian dynasty under Tanuatamun again tried to regain control of lower Egypt, marching as far north as Memphis, where he defeated the Egyptian princes loyal to Assyria. Ashurbanipal quickly responded, however. An Assyrian army marched into Egypt in 663 BCE, Tanuatamun fled, and the Assyrians marched all the way to Thebes, besieging and capturing this ancient capital. In the northwest Gyges of Lydia, who was under pressure from the Cimmerians, sought and received Assyrian support, and was able to defeat the Cimmerians. Within a few years, however, Lydia had allied itself with Egypt, and Gyges supported Psammeticus, the prince of Sais and new Egyptian ruler, when he expelled the Assyrian garrisons between 658–651 BCE. Assyrian support for Gyges ceased, and in 652 BCE Gyges fell to a new Cimmerian onslaught.

In the meantime, despite a lot of friction between Ashurbanipal and his brother Shamash-shum-ukin caused by Assyrian officials' refusal to treat the Babylonian ruler as Ashurbanipal's equal co-ruler, their cooperation was sufficient to carry out a successful war against Elam, which Assyria conquered, installing a supposedly pro-Assyrian Elamite as vassal king there. Shamash-shum-ukin warned against the choice, but his advice was dismissed, and the new Elamite ruler soon began to ally himself with the Chaldean tribes. The tribesmen had considerable support in central Babylonia, and eventually Shamash-shum-ukin joined the rebels, who were also supported by the desert Arabs and encouraged by Psammeticus of Egypt. War broke out in 652 BCE, when an Elamite army moved against northern Babylonia, and Shamash-shum-ukin attacked the Assyrian garrisons in the great Babylonian cities. The Assyrians defeated the Elamite army, and a coup in Elam prevented new Elamite forces from taking the field. In the meantime the Assyrians seized control of southern Babylonia isolating Shamash-shum-ukin in Borsippa and Babylon, which the Assyrians put under siege. In 650 BCE, an Arab attempt to relieve the siege failed, and the situation in Elam continued to deteriorate. With no further support, famine that had reduced the defenders of Borsippa and Babylon to cannibalism finally forced the cities to surrender in 648 BCE. Shamash-shum-ukin burned himself to avoid the desecration of his body, his palace was sacked, and any surviving rebel leaders were hunted down, butchered, and fed to the scavengers. Ashurbanipal took the throne of Babylon for a year (647 BCE), but then he turned it over to a vassal king named Kandalanu for the rest of his reign (646–626 BCE). In 648 BCE, the Assyrians invaded Elam again, but it remained a base of support for rebellious Chaldean tribesmen, so from 642–639 BCE the Assyrian army marched through all of Elam, devastating and plundering all its cities. Then in campaigns against the Arab tribes between 641 and 639 BCE, Ashurbanipal pacified the Arabs. At this point Ashurbanipal's annals cease.

Though Ashurbanipal had removed the Elamites as a threat and had temporarily subdued the Chaldeans and the Arabs, the Assyrian Empire was on very shaky ground. In the west Egypt had gained its independence, and all of Palestine and Syria was ripe for rebellion. In the north and northwest, the collapse of Urartu had allowed new groups to move into those areas, and Assyria was no longer able to hold its outlying provinces. In the northeast the Medes, once Assyria's vassals, were consolidating into a very strong state and were no longer subservient to Assyria. It was the end of an era; the old age was passing away. In this political context, Ashurbanipal's collection of the cuneiform literary deposit of the past in his vast library seems part of a larger cultural fascination with the past in view of a very uncertain future.

11. The end of Assyria and the rise of the Neo-Babylonian/Chaldean Empire

Because of a lack of records, the end of Ashurbanipal's reign is obscure. There was a struggle for the throne of Assyria, probably beginning even before Ashurbanipal's death. By 628 BCE, Josiah in Judah had clearly thrown off the Assyrian yoke, and by 626 BCE, NABOPOLASSAR, the Chaldean, had seized the throne of Babylon (626–605 BCE). There was see-saw warfare between Nabopolassar and the Assyrian army for ten years, during which time Egypt sent troops to the aid of Assyria, but the fighting gradually moved northward into Assyrian territory. In 615 BCE, the Babylonians attacked Ashur, but were repulsed, but later in the

same year the Medes, who had allied themselves with the Babylonians, captured and destroyed Ashur. Then in 612 BCE, a combined army of MEDES and Babylonians besieged Nineveh, took and destroyed the city, and killed the Assyrian king Sin-sharra-ishkun, an event celebrated in the book of Nahum. Ashur-uballit II took the throne of Assyria, or what remained of Assyria, in Harran, but in 610 BCE, a combined army of Medes and Babylonians captured Harran and drove the Assyrians and their Egyptian allies across the Euphrates. In 609 BCE, the Assyrians with the aid of another large Egyptian army crossed the river and tried to retake Harran, but failed. It was Josiah's attempt to block or delay the march of this Egyptian army at Megiddo that led to the death of the Judean king and Egypt's reduction of Judah to an Egyptian vassal (2 Kgs 23:29-34). For the next couple of years the Babylonians systematically dismantled Assyrian support in the Urartu region, and then the fighting shifted to the Euphrates where Egypt was now Babylon's main enemy, the Assyrians having been effectively annihilated as a coherent fighting force.

a. Nebuchadnezzar II. In 605 BCE, the Babylonian crown prince, Nebuchadnezzar II, led the Babylonian army in an attack on Carchemish across the Euphrates, and inflicted a major defeat on the Egyptians, an event celebrated in Jer 46. The remnants of the Egyptian army fled south, but the swift Babylonians overtook them at Hamath and wiped out what remained of the Egyptian army. The victorious Babylonians conquered all of the territory of Hamath, and a march farther south was delayed only by the news that Nabopolassar had died. To forestall any question about the succession, Nebuchadnezzar II rushed back to Babylon and was installed as king (604–562 BCE). He then returned to his campaigning in Syria. In 604 BCE, Nebuchadnezzar sacked Ashkelon in Philistia, and in that same year Jehoiakim of Judah, who had been an Egyptian vassal, switched sides and became an unwilling vassal of Babylon. The campaigning in Syria-Palestine continued during the next three years, and in 601 BCE, the Babylonians fought a bloody battle with Egypt on the Egyptian border. Both sides suffered severe losses, and in 600 BCE, Nebuchadnezzar II stayed home to refit his army. Misreading these two events, Jehoiakim broke his treaty with Babylon and rebelled, apparently counting on Egyptian help that did not materialize. While his main forces were campaigning against the Arabs, Nebuchadnezzar sent Chaldean and Aramean raiding parties against Judah, and bands of Ammonites, Moabites, and Edomites also harassed Judah, but in 598 BCE, the main Chaldean army attacked Judah and besieged Jerusalem. Jehoiakim died, and his son Jehoiachin surrendered within three months, on either March 15 or 16, 597 BCE. Jehoiachin, most of the Judean court, and much of the country's elite were deported to Babylon, and the brother of Jehoiakim, Zedekiah, was appointed to rule as vassal king over Judah.

Despite a revolt at home in 594 BCE, Nebuchadnezzar II remained in firm control of Palestine until Hophra (Apries) of Egypt invaded Palestine and Phoenicia and persuaded Zedekiah to revolt against Babylon. In 587 or 586 BCE, Nebuchadnezzar took and destroyed Jerusalem, captured Zedekiah, executed Zedekiah's sons in Zedekiah's presence, and then blinded Zedekiah. Unlike the Assyrians, who tended to resettle depopulated areas with captives from other parts of their empire, the Babylonians seemed happy to leave Judah as largely uninhabited ruins, though Nebuchadnezzar did appoint Gedaliah as governor over the remnant of the Judean population. When Gedaliah was murdered shortly afterward by disgruntled Judean soldiers, however, much of the remaining Judean population fled to Egypt fearing further Babylonian retaliation. In the meantime, the Babylonians subdued the other rebel cities, and put the port city of Tyre under siege. The siege lasted for at least thirteen years, ending in 571 BCE, but according to Ezekiel, who had repeatedly prophesied that Nebuchadnezzar would capture and plunder Tyre, the end of the siege clearly did not fulfill his earlier prophetic words (Ezek 29:17-20). Tyre was not plundered, and the city retained its commercial importance. Our records are spotty for the end of Nebuchadnezzar's reign, but there was an attempted invasion of Egypt that appears to have had only limited success. Though Nebuchadnezzar maintained good relations with the Medes, their control of the northern and eastern trade routes made it essential for Babylon to maintain control of the Mediterranean Sea trade and the trade routes out of Arabia, which explains Babylon's ongoing conflict with Egypt, to whom the trade with Phoenicia and the Arabs was also economically important. While Nebuchadnezzar II was occupied in Syria, the Medes under Cyaxares had extended their conquests west through all of Urartu until they encountered the kingdom of Lydia in Asia Minor. In 585 BCE, NABONIDUS, an official of Nebuchadnezzar, had negotiated a treaty marking the border between Lydia and the Medes, but neither this treaty nor the friendship between Babylon and the Medes were destined to last.

b. Awil-Marduk and Neriglissar. Nebuchadnezzar II's son, Awil-Marduk (see EVIL-MERODACH) succeeded him (561–560 BCE), but his reign was very short. He released Jehoiachin of Judah from prison and treated him with favor (2 Kgs 25:27; Jer 52:31), but little more is known of this king, who was killed in a revolt. Neriglissar, (see NERGAL-SHAREZER) son-in-law of Nebuchadnezzar II, probably identical with the RAB-MAG official present at the capture of Jerusalem under Zedekiah (Jer 39:3), seized the throne (559–556 BCE). In his third year, in response to an attack on Syria, he undertook a major campaign across the Taurus Mountains as far as the border with Lydia, but despite initial successes, Neriglissar was unable to capture his main opponent, and he returned home and died shortly afterward.

c. Labashi-Marduk and Nabonidus. His son Labashi-Marduk assumed the throne briefly, but was quickly removed by the chief state officials, who installed the experienced royal official NABONIDUS as king (555–538 BCE). This was the same Nabonidus who had negotiated the Median-Lydian treaty under Nebuchadnezzar II. Despite his inclusion in the Babylonian king list as a member of the Chaldean dynasty, he was neither Chaldean nor a native Babylonian. He was originally from Harran, where his mother, who was perhaps of the royal Assyrian family, was an important high priestess of the moon god Sin. As an outsider and a zealous devotee of the moon god, which Nabonidus may have seen as a religious way to unite the disparate populations of his empire, the new king soon alienated himself from the priests of Marduk in Babylon, and hostility between the king and the religious elite in Babylon simmered during much of his reign. In his first year he campaigned across the Taurus, but in his second year he was in Hamath, and by his third year he had begun campaigning against the Arabs of the desert east of Syria-Palestine. In 550 BCE, Cyrus of Persia, perhaps as an ally of Nabonidus, defeated Astyages of the Medes and assumed rule over the Medes and Persians. In the meantime Nabonidus spent some ten years (549–540 BCE), in the desert oasis of Tema, not returning to Babylon even to celebrate the important Babylonian New Year's festival that called for the public participation of the king in taking the hand of Bel. The crown prince, Bel-shar-usur (the Belshazzar of Dan 5), served as Nabonidus' governor in Babylon, but the yearly ritual did not take place in the absence of the king, and thus the king's absence was deeply resented by the Babylonians. Nabonidus' stay in the desert may have been to secure the Arabian trade routes as an economic counterbalance to the loss of all the northern and eastern routes to Persia, but to many of Nabonidus' Babylonian contemporaries, the king's peculiar sojourn in the desert was yet another sign of Nabonidus' sinfulness and perhaps even insanity. This tradition, found in some of the anti-Nabonidus pro-Persian propaganda from the end of Nabonidus' reign, was picked up by the author of Daniel and transferred to the better known Nebuchadnezzar (Dan 4:28-37), though a fragmentary text from Qumran still identifies the crazy king as Nabonidus. By 547 BCE, Cyrus had conquered Lydia and was a growing threat to Babylon. Nabonidus finally returned to Babylon in 540 BCE, but given the hostility toward Nabonidus in Babylon, it was too late to stave off the Persians. In 539 BCE, Cyrus forced a crossing of the Tigris at Opis, the defeated Babylonians withdrew, and Cyrus captured Sippar without a fight. Two days later one of Cyrus' commanders entered Babylon without a fight, and eventually Nabonidus was captured in Babylon. Within weeks Cyrus entered Babylon triumphantly. The Babylonians greeted him as a deliverer, and Cyrus treated them with great sensitivity. Nabonidus had gathered the gods of the country into Babylon to prevent them from falling into the hands of Cyrus, but now Cyrus restored them to their appropriate cultic sites, and he allowed the cultus, especially in Babylon, but probably in the rest of the country as well, to proceed as normal, endearing himself to the Babylonians. With Cyrus' victory and the imposition of Persian rule, the independent history of Babylonia and Assyria came to an end.

C. Religion

Just as the melding of Sumerian and Akkadian culture in the last half of the 3rd millennium BCE set the stage for the preservation of Sumerian and dialectal developments of Akkadian as the official languages of both Assyria and Babylonia despite the influx of Amorites, Hurrians, Kassites, and Arameans, all of whom spoke different languages, so the melding of Sumerian and Akkadian culture in that formative period continued to dominate the shape of Assyrian and Babylonian religion to the very end of the history of these two states. Amorite, Hurrian, Kassite, and Aramean gods might be introduced to the Sumero-Akkadian pantheon in a limited fashion, but for the most part, the continuity in the cultus of these two states from the earliest period to the latest is more striking than any discontinuity.

In the earliest recoverable expressions of Mesopotamian religious piety, it seems clear that the Mesopotamians experienced the numinous as the mysterious powers in nature—plants, water, wind, rain, sun, moon, stars, etc.—and because these powers were multiple, they believed in many gods. At first the deity was identified with the phenomenon in which it was experienced, but as the deities were progressively anthropomorphized, the secondary human form tended to become hostile to the earlier nonhuman form in which the power was encountered. Thus Enki/Ea, originally identical with the apsu, the sweet subterranean waters that rise in springs, sweet-water lagoons, and the like, defeats the apsu, his enemy, in the Babylonian creation epic, and makes his home in this captive enemy. This movement to the human form, sometimes with the earlier nonhuman form remaining as a symbolic representation of the deity, sometimes as a symbol of the enemy overcome by the deity, went hand in hand with the organization of the divine world into a political framework like that which characterized human society. The numerous gods and goddesses of the Mesopotamian world were assigned spouses and children, they became patron deities of particular cities, and eventually, as kingship developed in human society, they were given a hierarchical ranking, which fluctuated in part, based on the rise and fall in political prominence of the cities of which they were the patron deities.

In the period of the Sumerian-Akkadian synthesis, when the gods were seen as functioning as a divine council under the leadership of three high gods, a few of the more important deities were the following:

Nature	Function	Sumerian Name	Akkadian Name
Sky	Titular head of assembly	An	Anu
Storm god	Executive of assembly	Enlil	Enlil
Sweet water	Counselor of assembly	Enki	Ea
Venus Goddess of love and war		Inanna	Ishtar
Moon		Nanna	Sin
Sun	God of justice	Utu	Shamash
Storm god		Ishkur	Adad

Among other prominent deities one should also mention DAGAN, the important grain god of the middle Euphrates region; NERGAL, king of the underworld and city god of Cuth; MARDUK of Babylon; Ashur, who shared the same name as his city and may have originated as the deified city; Nabu (biblical Nebo), city god of Borsipa; and Ninurta, a Sumerian storm god popular among the Assyrians and common in their royal names.

The tradition developed quite early that the divine assembly would elect a particular deity to kingship over the gods for a period of time, during which time his or her patron city and its king would exercise rule over Sumer and Akkad. This motif is given very clear expression in the prologue to the Old Babylonian Code of HAMMURABI, where the high gods choose Marduk, Babylon, and Hammurabi to rule. Once the assembly had voted to move the kingship, however, there was nothing the god and goddess of the former imperial city could do to save their city. We read of the moon god's vain lament over the judgment announced on his city Ur, the doomed capital of the Ur III empire, and of the divine council's announcement of the day of judgment on Tishpak and his city Eshnunna in the Old Babylonian period. In the ENUMA ELISH, the Babylonian Creation Epic, Marduk is assigned permanent kingship over the gods, but this seems to be a later development, and in Assyria that role was normally assigned to Ashur, not Marduk.

There were hundreds more gods and goddesses than the few mentioned here, many of whom significantly overlapped with one another. In the course of time, some gods or goddesses of similar nature tended to merge into a single divine figure with varying names; but the opposite also happened, sometimes the epithet of a particular deity split off from that original deity and became an entirely separate deity. Moreover, local manifestations of a particular deity sometimes became so distinct that they were treated as separate deities. Thus the Ishtar of Arbela and the Ishtar of Nineveh are treated as distinct goddesses, just as one may suspect that the Yahweh of Samaria and the Yahweh of Teman were seen as separate figures in Israel. Mesopotamian theologians made long lists of their many gods, sometimes arranging them into family groups, in an attempt to bring order to this chaos of multiplicity, and in the later periods there were some attempts to reduce this multiplicity by seeing many of the gods as simply separate manifestations of particular aspects of a single high god.

In this hierarchical world of multiple divine figures, often with rival agendas, it was important for a human supplicant to have influential intercessors. By the early 2nd millennium the notion of a personal god and goddess, who would intercede with the other gods on behalf of their human client, was well established. And, if one had reason to suspect that one's personal god and goddess was angry, one could pray to other deities to intercede with one's personal god and goddess. Both motifs are well attested in the prayers and hymns the Mesopotamians addressed to their gods.

The public religious life of the Mesopotamian communities focused on the temples. The structure of important temples normally included a ziggurat, a tall pyramid-shaped tower, and one such in Babylon lies behind the biblical story of the tower of Babel. The statues of the temple's patron god and goddess as well as lesser divine functionaries were housed in niches in the temple, and they were cared for in the elaborate daily ritual overseen by the priests, though the building and financial upkeep of the temple and its rituals depended heavily on royal largess. While the Mesopotamians did not see the deities as restricted to their images, the deity was present in the image, so that the deity went where its image went, and the absence of the image, as when captured in war, could signify the deity's abandonment of his or her people. Individuals with particular concerns could apparently, at least in some periods, visit the temple "to see the face of the deity," that is, to present their concerns before the image of the deity, but it was probably at the great yearly festivals when the images were carried in processions that the general public had the most exposure to the major divine statues. Much of an average individual's everyday piety was probably exercised before the smaller images of one's personal deities kept in one's own home.

Since success in all human endeavors depended on the will of the gods, it was important to discern that will, to avoid angering the gods, and, if one had offended them, to find a means of overcoming that alienation. Before any important endeavor, the religious person sought to determine whether the gods would grant success to that endeavor. Prophecy is well attested in the Old Babylonian period and again in the Neo-Assyrian period, but the dominant method for discerning the divine will in Mesopotamia was by various types of DIVINATION, the most important being the inspection of the entrails of a sacrificial animal. One typically phrased the question to be answered to the deity in a way that the answer would be

unambiguous and not misleading—unintentional ambiguity on the part of either the supplicant or the deity could be catastrophic, so much so that the officiant prayed that the deity would respond according to client's intent, not, should the priest garble the question, according to what the priest actually said. The priest also implored the deity to ignore any deficiency in the ritual or its participants that might anger the deity and to put a true answer in the sacrificial animal—the possibility that an angry god might lie was frighteningly real. Then one examined the entrails of the animal in a well-established way to see what the answer was. The answer could be yes, no, or unclear. Whatever the answer, one would check it at least once and sometimes more, by repeating the process. The worst possible outcome was an unclear response, since that indicated that the deities, who were probably angry for some reason, were refusing to respond to the supplicant's query, leaving the inquirer in the quandary of either delaying any action until the gods responded, or of impiously and rashly acting without divine approval. If the omens indicated bad news, there were also elaborate rituals to ward off the threatened evil.

D. Government

In the hierarchical world of ancient Mesopotamia, the king stood between the gods and ordinary mortals, and in the Old Akkadian through the early Isin-Larsa periods, some prominent kings were even given a qualified deification. In contrast to Israel, Mesopotamia preserved little notion that kingship was a historical development. According to the Sumerian King List, kingship with all of its attributes intact was lowered from heaven by the gods. In both Babylon and Assyria, the human king was chosen by the gods and served at their pleasure, though kingship was normally hereditary, passing from father to son. Nonetheless, the enthronement ceremonies in both states, but particularly in Assyria, reminded the human king that the real king was the god. In Assyria this view was so dominant that apart from Shamshi-Adad I, Assyrian rulers until the time of Ashur-uballit I referred to themselves as priests of Ashur and did not use the term king in their titulary.

Beneath the king were a group of very high officials, all of whom, despite their titles, often functioned as military leaders. Four are mentioned in the Bible: the ta/urtanu commander-in-chief or field marshal (originally "second in command" [TARTAN, 2 Kgs 18:17; Isa 20:1]), the rav shaqe, the rav saris (RABSARIS, originally "chief eunuch"), and the rav mugi (RABMAG [Jer 39:3]). Other top officials included the chamberlain, chief vizier, palace herald, and the governors of important provinces. In the Assyrian Empire top officials like the field marshal might also hold governorships over important provinces and, until Tiglath-pileser III's reorganization of the government, they could, on occasion, amass enough power to rival or threaten the king. Beneath the provincial governors, there was a host of other military officials, local magistrates, judges, tax collectors, and other minor functionaries. One should also mention the clergy, since high priestly officials could occasionally acquire significant political influence.

The king's three main roles were to provide security for the state by his military and diplomatic leadership, to support and maintain the state cults, and to secure economic well-being and a just order for his citizens. Each of these tasks often called for massive building projects—fortifications, palaces, temples, aqueducts, etc., so any successful king tended to leave inscriptions about his building activities.

E. Art

Most of the significant art of ancient Mesopotamia was done in the service of the gods or of the king and his high officials, since they controlled the wealth. The miniature art of the engraved cylinder seals probably extended to the general public, as did the thousands of small figurines, prophylactic plaques, crude toylike models of chariots, horses, and the like, and the occasional impressively realistic small stone carvings of animals or birds, sometimes used as weights for business, but little of this more popular art has more than antiquarian interest. There is very fine decorated pottery from the pre-historic periods, but such pottery is lacking for the later periods, when the fine vessels of the rich were made of stone, ivory, or precious metals, and pottery was used only for mundane purposes. Even most of the common JEWELRY seems mundane and dull to modern sensibilities.

The monumental ARCHITECTURE of the temples and palaces offered more opportunity for serious artistic expression. In Babylonia one can trace a development from the brightly colored cone mosaics that decorated the pillars of early Sumerian temples to the Neo-Babylonian glazed, enameled-brick decorations, the best known example of the latter being the magnificent Ishtar-gate of Babylon, reconstructed in the Pergamon Museum in Berlin. In Assyria one may trace a development from the cartoonlike panels of the royal standard of Ur, through the early Sumerian votive tablets, to the storytelling reliefs on victory stelae such as Eannatum of Lagash's "stela of the vultures" and Naram-Sin's Old Akkadian victory stela, down to the multiple panels of reliefs on Ashur-nasir-apli II's White Obelisk and Shalmaneser III's Black Obelisk, both now in the British Museum. Similar multiple-panel relief work done in bronze is beautifully illustrated by Shalmaneser III's bronze gates from Balawat, also now in the British Museum. This development reaches its most mature form in the mural reliefs on stone panels arranged in a storytelling sequence that decorated the hallways leading to the throne rooms in the palaces of Tiglath-pileser III, Sargon II, Sennacherib, and Ashurbanipal. The scenes portray life in camp, preparation for battle, battle and its aftermath, and royal hunts with such close attention to detail that these reliefs are invaluable to the historian. From Sennacherib's portrayal of the siege of Lachish, e.g., archaeologists were able to identify the actual siege

ramp at the site. Artistically, however, it is the portrayal of the animals in these reliefs that is the most impressive—war horses, camels, hunting dogs, dying lions, fleeing wild horses, gazelle herds, and deer being chased into a trap are all portrayed with a moving realism.

Painted murals were also used in temples and palaces, though few survive, since when buildings collapsed, such paintings were normally lost. But there are a few notable exceptions. The earliest is from the temple at Tell Uqair in the late 3rd millennium BCE, followed by the wall paintings from Mari in the early second millennium. From the mid 2nd millennium there are Kassite examples at Aqar-quf, and from the Assyrian period there are examples from Nimrud, Til-Barsip, and Khorsabad. One can probably also assume that intricately designed carpets were widely used in the palaces of the Mesopotamian elite, though again due to the problems of preservation, little trace has been found of them. Nevertheless, some sense of their appearance is provided by the limestone slabs carved to resemble carpets often found in the doorways of Assyrian palaces.

Sculpture in the round, portraying animals or humans, is attested from the Protoliterate period onward. The early statues of humans tend to be more geometrical than naturalistic, but the famous ram in the bush from the royal tombs of Ur is impressive both for its beauty and its naturalism.

Erich Lessing / Art Resource, NY

Figure 8: Ram with blossoming bush from the Great Death-pit at Ur; British Museum, London.

Perhaps the most striking art work of the Old Akkadian period, at least to modern sensibilities, is the marvelous bronze head of Sargon the Great, deformed though it is by the gouging out of the inlaid eyes of precious stone or gold. The well-known statues of Gudea in the immediately following period are noteworthy, and there are a number of statues of local rulers or deities from Ashur, Mari, and other cities during the Isin-Larsa period. Perhaps the most impressive is the statue of a fertility goddess holding a vase. Running through the statue and the vase is a channel that was originally connected to a water source so that the vase overflowed with water. There are a number of representations of Hammurabi, the head in black granite being particularly impressive. The most distinctive art of the Kassite period are the curious religious symbols cut in relief on the kudurru or boundary stones. Assyrian sculpture begins to appear with the rise of Assyrian power from the 14th cent. There are statues in the round of both gods and human rulers, but while naturalistic, they are not particularly lifelike. More impressive and well known to modern museum goers are the gigantic winged human-headed bulls and lions that served as protective deities at the entrances to palaces and temples.

As examples of nonmonumental art, one should note the large collection of beautifully carved ivories from 8th cent. Nimrud, though it is likely that most of this work was done by Syrian rather than native Assyrian craftsmen. Much of the metal work of Mesopotamia has been lost because of the reuse of the metals, but there are metal weights in the shape of animals, and decorated metal containers of various sorts, as well as artistically shaped metal gear associated with chariots and cavalry horses. From the portrayal of the Assyrian cavalry horses and chariotry in the reliefs, one can also get some notion of the artistry in metal, leather, and fabric that went into outfitting the often elaborate caparisons for these war horses. Finally, the recently discovered gold jewelry from the tombs of members of the royal family at Nimrud shows how intricate and beautiful fine Assyrian jewelry could be, even for modern sensibilities. *See* ABIB, TEL; AMOS, BOOK OF; ASSYRIAN TEXTS; EXILE; HOSEA, BOOK OF; ISAIAH, BOOK OF; JEROBOAM II; NEBUZARADAN; OSNAPPAR; PEKOD.

Bibliography: A. K. Grayson. *Assyrian and Babylonian Chronicles* (1975); Thorkild Jacobsen. *The Treasures of Darkness: A History of Mesopotamian Religion* (1976); Joan Oates and David Oates. *Nimrud: An Assyrian Imperial City Revealed* (2001); H. W. F. Saggs. *The Might That Was Assyria* (1984); H. W. F. Saggs. *The Greatness That Was Babylon: A Survey of the Ancient Civilization of the Tigris-Euphrates Valley* (1988); Joan Goodnick Westenholtz. *Legends of the Kings of Akkade: The Texts.* Vol. 7. *Mesopotamian Civilizations*, ed. J. S. Cooper (1997).

J. J. M. ROBERTS

ASSYRIAN TEXTS uh-sihr´ee-uhn. Among the richest sources of light on the world and the text of the OT are the vast collections of cuneiform texts recovered from excavations in ancient Assyria and the smaller body of monumental inscriptions discovered in foreign regions where Assyrian kings had set them up to celebrate their conquests.

The Assyrian king lists, the eponym lists, the chronicles, and the annals are among our main sources, not only for Assyrian history but also for putting the history of Israel in a firm chronological framework. The Assyrians named each year after a high official, chosen as the eponym (Assyrian limmu), and they kept lists of these officials, which are complete from 910 until 649 BCE. The reference to a solar eclipse in two of these lists for the year 763 BCE enables scholars to connect the Assyrian chronological framework to modern chronology, and the existence of several synchronisms between the Bible and Assyrian sources makes it possible to tie biblical chronology into the same absolute chronology. Moreover, the existence of overlapping Assyrian and biblical accounts of the same events, such as SARGON's conquest of Ashdod or SENNACHERIB's siege of Jerusalem, to mention only two, provide the evidence for much more reliable reconstructions of Israelite history than would be possible from either the biblical or Assyrian sources when taken alone. Important historiographical information may also be found in many of the letters to or from the Assyrian court, as well as in the records of oracular responses to divination queries posed to the gods by the Assyrian king when planning military or diplomatic actions.

The middle Assyrian lawcode, like the earlier Sumerian codes and the Babylonian codes of Eshnunna and Hammurabi, provides useful comparative material for putting the OT legal material in context. More unique are the very fragmentary harem edicts issued by a number of Assyrian kings. For a glimpse into the restrictions, struggles, and controversies associated with life in the royal harem there is nothing equivalent among our ancient sources. Neo-Assyrian political treaties, when compared to the earlier Old Babylonian and Hittite treaties, enable one to trace the development of international treaties over a considerable period of time and to locate Israelite covenantal theology in its appropriate typological sequence. One of the best commentaries on the Assyrian understanding of the theology of the political treaty is provided by the Tukulti-Ninurta epic's account of the struggle between this Assyrian king and his Babylonian rival, Kashtiliashu.

There are a number of distinctly Assyrian hymns, prayers, prophecies, and divination texts, as well as a distinctly anti-Babylonian revision of the Babylonian creation account, the ENUMA ELISH. But perhaps more significantly, the Assyrians were also preservers of the Babylonian literature to which they were culturally deeply indebted. Thus there are Neo-Assyrian copies of most of the important Babylonian literature. Were it not for the late Assyrian king, ASHURBANIPAL (668–629? BCE), and his great library at NINEVEH, our knowledge of Babylonian literature would be immensely poorer.

J. J. M. ROBERTS

ASSYRIANS. *See* ASSYRIA AND BABYLONIA.

ASTARTE as-tahr′tee [Ἀστάρτη Astartē]. Astarte is the Greek form of the name Ashtarth (עַשְׁתָּרְתְּ ʿashtarth), who, along with ASHERAH and ANATH, was one of the three great goddesses of the Canaanite pantheon. In Canaanite religion, Astarte was a deity associated, first, with love and fertility: in a Late Bronze Age text (ca. 1550–1200 BCE) that comes from the Canaanite city-state of Ugarit on the north Levantine coast, e.g., she plays the role of the divine courtesan who is enthroned beside the high god of the Canaanite pantheon, El, at a banquet of the gods (El's consort, the mother of the gods, Asherah, is notably absent). The Papyrus Harris, an Egyptian text from roughly the same period, also speaks to Astarte's role as a goddess of love and fertility (although not of marriage and motherhood) by describing her as one of "the great goddesses who conceive but do not bear." Astarte's identification as a goddess of love and fertility continues into the 1st millennium BCE, as is indicated both in biblical Hebrew, in which the noun עַשְׁתָּרוֹת ʿashteroth, derived from the divine name Ashtart/Astarte, means "increase" or "progeny" (Deut 7:13; 28:4, 18, 51), and also in mid- to late 1st millennium extrabiblical texts in which Astarte is identified with the Greek goddess of sexual love, Aphrodite.

Astarte and Aphrodite are in addition both associated with the heavens. Thus both are associated with the Morning and Evening Star, Venus; Astarte is called the "Lady of Heaven" in 2nd millennium BCE Egyptian texts and "Astarte of the Highest Heavens" in a 1st millennium BCE text from Phoenicia. Indeed, Astarte's sacred precinct in the Phoenician city of Sidon, which was particularly associated with her worship, was known as "the highest heavens," and in her iconography, Astarte can be represented by a star. This tradition persists even into the 2nd cent. CE Roman grammarian Herodian's description of Astarte as "Queen of the Stars." Astarte is called "Queen" also in a 5th cent. BCE inscription from Kition, Cyprus; and a later source that may date back to roughly the same period similarly describes her queenly role by noting that she wears on her head a bull's head as an emblem of royalty.

Astarte is furthermore associated with war in both 2nd millennium and 1st millennium BCE materials. Egyptian representations of the goddess show her on horseback and carrying shield and spear, and she is also described in Egyptian texts as a mighty charioteer and even compared to part of a war chariot. She is, moreover, described in Egyptian materials as "Lady of Combat" and "Lady of the Chariot." In Ugaritic literature, Astarte is often paired with Anath, who is also a war goddess. Astarte and Anath are also both closely associated with the warrior god Baal in Ugaritic myth, so much so that Astarte can even be called by the epithet "Name of Baal," which means, more idiomatically, "Named with Baal" or "Baal's Other Self."

Astarte's associations with war may be further indicated in 1 Sam 31:10, in which the armor of the dead king Saul is taken by the Philistines to the temple of Astarte. Yet as this 1 Sam 31:10 text that associates Astarte with Philistine religion suggests, the worship of Astarte is something the biblical writers unanimously perceive as foreign; therefore they unanimously condemn worship of the goddess. Thus, in Judg 2:13-14 and 10:6-7, the people are castigated for worshiping the "Baals and the Astartes," who are described as the gods of Aram, Sidon, Moab, Ammon, and the Philistines, and in 1 Kgs 11:5 (*see also* 1 Kgs 11:33 and 2 Kgs 23:13), King Solomon is condemned for introducing the worship of Astarte, the goddess of Sidon, into Israel under the influence of his foreign wives. Likewise, in Jer 7:16-20; 44:15-19, 25, the late 7th and early 6th cent. BCE prophet Jeremiah condemns a group of Israelites for worshiping a goddess called the "QUEEN OF HEAVEN," who seems to represent a syncretistic deity who incorporates aspects of both Canaanite Astarte and Mesopotamian Ishtar. Still, in Jer 44:15-19, 25, the Queen of Heaven's devotees—especially her women devotees—vehemently repudiate Jeremiah's censure, arguing that they have found the worship of this Astarte-like goddess to be efficacious in protecting them from famine and enemy armies (this because of Astarte's—and also Ishtar's—associations with fertility and with war). They go on to claim this worship was efficacious in a way the worship of the Israelite God Yahweh was not (since Yahweh had failed to protect them during the Babylonian destruction of Jerusalem in 586 BCE). Thus, despite the biblical writers' conviction that the people of ancient Israel should worship Yahweh alone, we see here evidence that at least some of the Israelites conceived of their religious devotions differently. Women, especially, may have devoted themselves to the Queen of Heaven rather than or alongside of Yahweh because the religious observances associated with her worship (especially home-based rituals of burning incense, pouring out libations, and baking offering cakes) could have afforded them opportunities for religious expression. These opportunities had always been scarce in the male-dominated worship of Yahweh, and they may have become increasingly rare in the aftermath of King Josiah's religious reforms of the late 6th cent. BCE (2 Kgs 23:4-25).

Bibliography: Susan Ackerman. *Under Every Green Tree: Popular Religion in Sixth-Century Judah* (1992); Stephanie L. Budin. "A Reconsideration of the

Aphrodite-Ashtart Syncretism." *Numen* 51 (2004) 95–145; Judith M. Hadley. "The Fertility of the Flock: The De-personalization of Astarte in the Old Testament." *On Reading Prophetic Texts: Gender–Specific and Related Studies in Memory of Fokkelien van Dijk-Hemmes* (1996).

SUSAN ACKERMAN

ASTONISHMENT, AMAZEMENT. The language of astonishment and amazement, of wonder and awe, depicts the human reaction to God's mighty acts throughout Scripture. The expression of surprise—sometimes bewilderment—usually accompanied by fear and ultimately by faith, comes to characterize the experience of the divine. Preexisting expectations are challenged and new dimensions of faith are provoked. There is a considerable semantic range of terms that contribute to this multidimensional concept. In Hebrew תָּמַהּ tamah, to be astounded or astonished (qal), extends to being stunned or numb, and thus (in hitp) to gazing at each other. The related noun תִּמָּהוֹן timmahon describes confusion (of mind/heart, as in Deut 28:28). And פֶּלֶא pele', to be extraordinary, wonderful (niphal), describes the reaction evoked by God's acts of salvation (common in the Psalms). The key Greek term used to translate this wonder is θαυμάζω thaumazō, usually in the sense of marvel and admiration. The aspect of astonishment involving shock and confusion is found in ἔκστασις ekstasis (literally "put out of place," leading to the English word *ecstasy*).

When Jacob awakes from the dream that newly assures him of God's presence and promise, he exclaims "how *awesome* is this place!" (Gen 28:12-17). When the prophets relate the day of God's judgment, they describe how all will be *stunned* or *astounded* (Isa 29:9; Jer 4:9; Hab 1:5). When Simeon declares the newborn Christ "the light of revelation to Gentiles and glory to Israel," his parents are *amazed* (Luke 2:33). When Jesus heals a boy with a demon, all are "*astounded* at the greatness of God" (Luke 9:43). When Peter finds only linen cloths in the tomb where Jesus was laid, he is *amazed* (Luke 24:12). At the day of Pentecost when the assembled crowds find themselves speaking in many languages concerning God's deeds of power, all are *amazed* and *astonished* (Acts 2:7, 12).

In both OT and NT, people are described as astounded (תָּמַהּ tamah; θαυμάζω thaumazō)—stunned, shocked, amazed—at the greatness of God and the signs (אוֹת 'oth; σημεῖον sēmeion) of God's work, whether this is the work of judgment or salvation (OT: Job 26:11; Ps 48:5; Isa 29:9; Jer 4:9; NT: Matt 8:27; 15:31; 22:22; Acts 8:13; 9:21; 12:16; 13:41). Yet the language is particularly clustered in hymnic literature of the OT and throughout the Gospels and Acts of the Apostles in the NT. Whereas, e.g., the notion of wonder (pele') is largely absent in narrative sections of the Pentateuch (except Exod 3:20; 34:10)—where the

signs ('oth) of God are plentiful and the actual events of salvation described—it is common in the Psalms where the effects of these acts are explored with reference to experience (e.g., Pss 78:4; 145:4-7). God's mighty acts intend an active response: astonishment does not simply describe the numbing moment of shock but also the regular pattern of praise. The Psalms rehearse God's mighty acts and they also prescribe the people's response. God's wonders are for extolling, remembering, pondering, and proclaiming. From Jacob to Simeon to Peter, we may note this outcome to their experience of God.

These biblical paradigms of astonishment are instructive. Whether the act of God comes as spontaneous surprise or long-expected fulfillment, it is received as an act of undeserved grace. It brings about a rupture of conventions and categories and, thus, a time of bewilderment and redefinition. Fear is the common reaction—the fear of personal inadequacy, the loss of control followed by, more important, the fear of God. This fear—the recognition of God's might and majesty—is the underpinning for faith. God's creatures are newly aware of the presence and providence of their Creator. This fear is the counter to complacency: it brings God's faithful people to wonder and keep on wondering at the greatness of their God. Buber called it "abiding astonishment." For Christians it encapsulates what is the appropriate, continual response to God's resurrection of Christ.

Bibliography: W. Brueggemann. *Abiding Astonishment* (1991); M. Buber. *Moses* (1946 [1988]) 75–76.

JO BAILEY WELLS

ASTROLOGER(S). *See* ASTRONOMY, ASTROLOGY; MAGI; STAR OF BETHLEHEM.

ASTRONOMICAL BOOK. *See* ENOCH, FIRST BOOK OF.

ASTRONOMICAL DIARIES. Daily records of the observed or predicted positions of the moon and of the planets, observed or predicted lunar or solar eclipses, meteors or comets, weather conditions, commodity prices, river levels, and unusual happenings such as plagues and important local political events (e.g., ANTIOCHUS IV's religious policy) compiled beginning with Babylonian king **Nabu-natsir** (747–734 BCE) and still being produced as of 61 BCE.

Bibliography: A. Sachs and H. Hunger. *Astronomical Diaries* (1988–96).

JOANN SCURLOCK

ASTRONOMY, ASTROLOGY. Well into the 18th cent. CE, astronomy and astrology equally referred to the study of the sky, its inhabitants, and their impact upon people on the land below. In the biblical periods, while peasants read the sky as a seasonal, agricultural calendar, city experts (priests, scribes) read the regularities of the sky to set festal calendars and observe predictable social events (horoscopes) concerning societies, cities, and royalty (there were no horoscopes for individuals apart from royalty). These city experts, priests, and scribes were the astronomers/astrologers of the day in Mesopotamia and elsewhere in the circum-Mediterranean.

These astronomers/astrologers read the sky in terms of Sumero-Babylonian constellational names and patterns, notably the sexagesimal system that marked off the circle of the sky to situate star sets. Of common interest was the constellational pathway of the sun that marked an annual orbit through a 360 degree circle with a constellation marking off every 30 degrees. This was the zodiac with its twelve constellations led by Aries, the Ram or Lamb of the sky, created before all other constellations and marker of the new year. The sky and land constituted a single social arena in which humans and celestial entities readily interacted. In Hellenism, stars were living entities, and the earth was a round body encapsulated by the sky, with deities resident in and beyond the vault of the sky.

According to Mesopotamian lore, access to a deity's real home in his/her celestial temple and its attendant city required passing through the opening in the firmament that led to the other side of the vault of the sky. This opening was to be found directly over the deity's earthly temple. In ancient Israel also, God's "holy habitation," his "dwelling place," is in the sky (Deut 26:15; 1 Kgs 8:43). The prophet Micaiah "saw the LORD sitting on his throne, and all the host of heaven standing on his right hand and on his left" (1 Kgs 22:19). God's holy temple, his throne, is in the sky (Ps 11:4) although he does have a house below in Jerusalem (2 Chr 36:23). In Acts, the sky opens above Jerusalem to allow the resurrected Jesus to ascend to God (Acts 1:2-9). The seer of Revelation passed through this opening (Rev 4:1). The celestial Jerusalem descends through this opening ultimately to come to rest where the earthly Jerusalem is located (Rev 21:2-10).

In events surrounding Jesus' birth, one of God's sky servants, "the angel of the Lord," descends from the sky to do God's bidding (Matt 2:13; Luke 1:11, 26; 2:9) while a huge cluster of sky servants appear to shepherds. The ancients knew that earthquakes were caused by celestial phenomena (see Dio Cassius, Roman History 68.24–25). Thus we learn of such sky-caused earthquakes occurring at Jesus' death (Matt 27:54) and resurrection (Matt 28:2, ascribed to the angel of the Lord). Comets always portended political turmoil, hence Jerusalem (Herod) hearing of such a star from Persian Magi would be quite troubled (see Matt 2:2-10).

Other sky lore in the Jesus story includes: the nickname, "sons of thunder" (thunder readers/controllers) given by Jesus to James and John, sons of Zebedee (Mark 3:17); talk of "fire from the sky" or "casting fire on the land" (Luke 9:54; 12:49); Jesus' seeing Satan falling from the sky like lightning (Luke 10:18; see Rev 12), and God's sky servants at Jesus' tomb looking like lightning to humans, a sign of their origin (Matt 28:3, see Ezek 1:13-14; Dan 10:6).

In the synoptic tradition, seeking "signs from the sky" or in the sky as well as reading the sky for signs of the times were quite the matter of course (Matt 16:2; Mark 8:11; Luke 11:16). Furthermore, Jesus referred to a celestial "Son of Man," to appear as lightning (God's arrows, Ps 144:6; Zech 9:14) for the purpose of judgment (Matt 24:27; Luke 17:24). Jesus' final discourse is replete with astronomical vocabulary (Matt 24:29; Mark 13:24-25; Luke 21:9-12a, 25-26; so also the prophets (Ezek 1; 10; Dan 7; 10:4-9; all of Enoch and Rev 4–21; the entities seen by John are largely constelled stars).

The emergence of the theocracy proclaimed by Jesus would be signaled by celestial and social indicators directed to Israel as befits the intervention of the God of Israel (e.g., its denouement: Matt 24:29-31). This was such common knowledge that even those Jesus group members expecting the coming of the Lord knew that "the signs of truth will appear: first the sign of an opening in the sky, then the sign of the sound of the trumpet, and thirdly the resurrection of the dead . . ." (Did. 16:6).

Bibliography: August Bouché-Leclerq. *L'Astrologie grecque* (1979); Frederic H. Cramer. *Astrology in Roman Law and Politics. Memoirs of the American Philosophical Society.* Vol. 37 (1954); Bruce J. Malina. *On the Genre and Message of Revelation: Star Visions and Sky Journeys* (1995).

BRUCE J. MALINA

ASTYAGES as-ti´uh-jeez [Akkadian **Istumegu**; Ἀστυάγης *Astyagēs*]. The fourth and last king of Media who ruled from 584 BCE until 550 BCE. The empire he inherited from his father, Cyaraxes, included Assyria and Persia and equaled the power of the Babylonian Empire under Nebuchadnezzar. The Median Empire ended when Astyages was defeated by Cyrus II of Persia. According to the *Chronicle of Nabonidus*, the army of Astyages revolted and delivered him in fetters to Cyrus. There is little other historically reliable information on his reign. The claim by Ctesias that Cyrus married Astyages' daughter, Amytis, may also be correct.

PAMELA J. MILNE

ASUR ay´suhr [Ἀσουρ *Asour*]. Family head whose descendants were among the 372 Temple servants who returned after the exile (1 Esd 5:31). Excluded in Ezra 2:51 and Neh 7:53.

ASYLUM. *See* REFUGE.

ASYNCRITUS uh-sin´kri-tuhs [Ἀσύγκριτος *Asynkritos*]. A Christian who returned to Rome after the rescinding of the Edict of Claudius or someone Paul addressed in a letter fragment added to Romans (Rom 16:14).

ATAD ay′tad [אָטָד ʾaṭadh; Ἀταδ Atad]. Goren ha-Atad, also translated as "the threshing floor of Atad," became a seven-day mourning site for Joseph and his family as they transported Jacob's body from Egypt to Hebron for burial (Gen 50:10-11). The word ʾatad means *thorns*. According to the biblical text, the Canaanites gave the place another name: ABEL-MIZRAIM, "the mourning of Egypt," although the phrase more likely means "the meadow of Egypt." Beth Agla/Beth Hoglah between Jericho and the Dead Sea could be Atad's location, based on a mosaic map of the 6th cent. CE found at Medeba.

SUSANNA W. SOUTHARD

ATARAH at′uh-ruh [עֲטָרָה ʿatara]. "Crown" or "wreath." Jerahmeel's second wife and Onam's mother in the list of Judah's descendants (1 Chr 2:26).

ATARGATIS uh-tahr′guh-tis atargatis [Ἀτάργατις Atargatis]. While not mentioned in the Bible, Atargatis was a well-known goddess in Syria, Palestine, and beyond in the Hellenistic period. Her name is Semitic, a juxtaposition of the old Canaanite deities ASTARTE and ANATH. The god HADAD was her consort. The Greeks knew her as *Derceto* and *Dea Syria*. In the 2nd cent. CE, Lucian of Samosata composed *De Syria Dea*, describing and satirizing the goddess and her cult. The Atargateion, a temple of Atargatis, located near Carnaim in the region of Gilead is mentioned in 2 Macc 12:18-29 as the site where JUDAS THE MACCABEE killed 25,000 people. The center of her cult was located at Hierapolis in Syria with abundant inscriptional evidence and pictorial representations.

WILLIAM R. BROOKMAN

ATAROTH at′uh-roth′ [עֲטָרֹת ʾataroth]. 1. Located east of the Dead Sea, south of Mount Nebo, and north of the Arnon River; likely the Iron Era site Khirbet Atarus. Num 21:21-24 and 32:33 identify it as part of the Amorite land that Israel captured from King Sihon. The Gadites and Reubenites requested Ataroth for the purpose of raising cattle (Num 32:3). When it was granted to them, the Gadites rebuilt the area (Num 32:34). In the Mesha Stele, King Mesha of Moab recounts his destruction and resettlement of Ataroth (lines 10–14).

2. Elsewhere, Josh 16:2, 7 describe Ataroth as part of the Archites' land, on the eastern border of Ephraim's tribal territory, to the west of the Jordan in the hill country. *See* MOABITE STONE.

LISA MICHELE WOLFE

ATAROTH-ADDAR at′uh-roth-ad′uhr [עֲטָרוֹת אַדָּר ʾatroth ʾaddar]. A town that, according to Josh 16:5 and 18:13, lay on the border between Ephraim (to the

north) and Benjamin (to the south). It is probably the same as the Ataroth mentioned in Josh 16:2, a town previously said to belong to the Archites, a group otherwise known only as the people of David's loyal retainer Hushai (2 Sam 15–17). The Ataroth mentioned in Josh 16:7 is a different site, located in the western Jordan Valley, opposite the point where the river Jabbok flows into the Jordan. The Ataroth of Num 32:3 and 32:34 is another town still that lies east of the Dead Sea in Moab, about 8 mi. NW of Moabite Dibon. It is to be identified with modern Khirbat ʾAtarus. So many sites are named Ataroth because the word means "crowns," designating a town built on a hilltop or similar height. Addar means "majestic" or "noble."

SUSAN ACKERMAN

ATER ay′tuhr [אָטֵר ʾater; Ατηρ Atēr]. 1. A family—Babylonian name Ater; Hebrew name Hezekiah—who returned with ZERUBBABEL from exile (Ezra 2:16 = Neh 7:21 = 1 Esd 5:15).

2. A family of gatekeeper returnees (Ezra 2:42 = Neh 7:45 = 1 Esd 5:28).

3. A person who signed a postexilic covenant (Neh 10:17).

ATHACH ay′thak [עֲתָךְ ʿathakh]. Town in Judah whose people shared in the spoil recovered in David's battle against the Amalekites (1 Sam 30:30). Possibly ר (r) was mistaken for ך (kh) and the town is Ether [עֶתֶר ʿether]. *See* ETHER.

ATHAIAH uh-thay′yuh [עֲתָיָה ʿathayah]. Son of UZZI-AH and descendant of JUDAH through PEREZ, Athaiah appears in Nehemiah's list of postexilic inhabitants of Jerusalem (Neh 11:4). Some scholars identify Athaiah as UTHAI from the parallel list in 1 Chr 9:4. However, this is improbable because the two genealogies differ completely.

ATHALIAH ath′uh-li′uh [עֲתַלְיָה ʿathalyah] This personal name, which includes the divine element (יה yh), may be interpreted to mean "Yahweh is sovereign." 1. The daughter of an Israelite king (either OMRI or AHAB), the wife of the Judahite king JEHORAM, the mother of King AHAZIAH of Judah, and the sole ruler of Judah for more than six years. She is presented as contaminating Judah's allegiance to Yahweh and disrupting the Davidic succession. Her negative influence is hinted at in the REGNAL NOTICE of Jehoram, son of King JEHOSHAPHAT of Judah, who is accused of having "walked in the way of the kings of Israel, as the house of Ahab had done, for the daughter of Ahab was his wife" (2 Kgs 8:18). Regnal notices typically mention the mother; this is the only mention of a wife. Athaliah and her northern heritage are directly named in the regnal notice of her son Ahaziah (2 Kgs 8:26). The notices insinuate that Athaliah bears responsibility for the unfaithfulness of the Judean monarchy, though no details of Judah's apostasy or Athaliah's actions are specifically mentioned.

The inconsistencies in the regnal notices in this section of 2 Kgs and in the parallel notices in 2 Chr 21:3-6 and 22:1-4 make it difficult to determine whether Athaliah was the child of Omri or of Ahab. (No connection is made between Athaliah and JEZEBEL.) The NRSV interprets "daughter of Omri" (2 Kgs 8:26) broadly, calling her Omri's "granddaughter." Since Jehoram's wife is not named in his regnal notice (2 Kgs 8:18), some scholars suggest another "daughter of Ahab" might have been married to Jehoram. Athaliah's is the only name mentioned, however.

No reasons for her marriage into the Judean royal family are supplied, though it likely solidified relations between Judah and Israel. The regnal notices suggest it also reshaped the southern kingdom "in the way of the house of Ahab, doing what was evil in the sight of the LORD." The house of Ahab was wiped out by JEHU in a bloody coup. King Ahaziah of Judah, in the northern kingdom at the time, was also killed, as were 42 of Ahaziah's relatives (2 Kgs 9:27; 10:13-14). If the marriage of Athaliah provided security for Judah, Jehu's coup ended that security.

After the death of her son, Athaliah "set about to destroy all the royal family." It is not clear why she chose to do this. Though other kings removed family members when they sensed a challenge (e.g., SOLOMON had ADONIJAH killed in 1 Kgs 2:23-25), no challenge to Athaliah is mentioned. No purpose for the purge is apparent. Since the Hebrew uses the expression "seed of the kingdom" (2 Kgs 11:1), Athaliah appears focused on the male heirs of the Davidic line. The irony is that it is a daughter—JEHOSHEBA, Ahaziah's sister—who preserves the dynasty by rescuing Ahaziah's son, JOASH, and hiding him with her for six years.

For six years "Athaliah reigned over the land" (2 Kgs 11:3; ca. 842–837). No description of her reign is provided and there is no regnal notice to assess her rule or link her in the sequence of kings of Judah. Thus we are not told whether she, as daughter of a northern ruler, "walked in the way of the kings of Israel." At the same time, the text does not grant her a place in the Davidic dynasty, implying that Athaliah's reign stands outside the dynastic lineage of David. The priest JEHOIADA (identified as Jehosheba's husband in 2 Chr 22:11) reestablishes the line by bringing Joash out of hiding. Though Athaliah did not appear to notice the child was missing when she was destroying heirs, she recognizes the seven year old Joash as he is acclaimed king in the temple. Athaliah is put to death at the palace. The depiction of Athaliah as a ruthless usurper acting alone deflects attention away from Judah's apparent acceptance of northern influence and the interruption in the Davidic dynastic chain.

Athaliah's death is followed by the destruction of the house of BAAL and the killing of the Baal priest MATTAN. This is far less dramatic than Jehu's anti-Baal purge. Though Athaliah's northern lineage and the death of Mattan insinuate Athaliah's involvement in the Baal cult, no direct connection is made. Even 2 Chr 24:7, which calls Athaliah "that wicked woman," blames her children for using "the dedicated things of the house of the LORD for the Baals." The biblical view of Athaliah is clearly negative though the evidence is implied rather than supplied.

2. A son of Jeroham, in a census list of the Benjaminite families in Jerusalem (1 Chr 8: 26).

3. Father of Jeshaiah, who was among the returnees from Babylon with Ezra (Ezra 8: 7).

ELNA K. SOLVANG

ATHANASIUS. Bishop of Alexandria from 328 to 373 CE, Athanasius is remembered largely for his biblical and theological arguments for Nicene Trinitarianism, with regard to Christ first and foremost (against the Arians) but also regarding the Holy Spirit. He was not a learned philologist and exegete in the tradition of Origen and Eusebius, and did not write commentaries, but his interpretive strategies and conclusions decisively shaped the development of Christian doctrine. Establishing the eternal, divine preexistence of the Word on the basis of paradigmatic texts from John and other NT books, he applied verses speaking of a temporal beginning specifically to the incarnation. His constant and variegated recourse to Scripture richly illustrates the centrality of the Bible in early Christian apologetic, doctrinal, polemical, and pastoral discourse. His *Festal Letter 39* for the year 367 CE, which includes the earliest extant listing of the NT as we have it, upholds a sharply defined two-testament biblical canon as a bulwark against idiosyncratic teachers and esoteric writings. *See* CANON; JESUS CHRIST; TRINITY.

Bibliography: David B. Brakke. "Canon Formation and Social Conflict in Fourth-Century Egypt: Athanasius of Alexandria's Thirty-ninth Festal Letter." *HTR* 87 (1994) 395–419; James D. Ernest. *The Bible in Athanasius of Alexandria.* BAC 2 (2004).

JAMES D. ERNEST

ATHARIM ath´uh-rim (אֲתָרִים ʾatharim, Ἀθαριν, atharin). A place through which the Israelites enter the NEGEB. Their presence on the route causes the king of ARAD to take up arms (Num 21:1). "The way of the trails" is a preferable translation of the Masoretic Text over KJV (which follows the Targum).

ATHBASH ath´bash [אתבשׁ ʾathbash]. A cryptographic code system known as a substitution cipher used three times in the book of Jeremiah. The principle is that of substituting the initial letter of the Hebrew ALPHABET (*aleph*) with that of the last letter (*tav*), and vice versa. The second letter of the alphabet (*beth*) is replaced by the letter second from the end of the alphabet (*shin*) (thus the term *athbash*), and so on throughout the sequence of all the letters. In Jer 51:1, lev qamay is athbash for kaseddim (Chaldees, Chaldea), and in Jer 25:26 and 51:41, sheshak (Sheshach) is athbash for bavel (Babel).

WILLIAM R. BROOKMAN

ATHEISM. Atheism is the denial of the existence of God. It is, ironically, a phenomenon that receives its meaning from that which it rejects—God.

Both the OT and NT are written from the perspective of faith in God, and in the documents that comprise these collections, the existence of God is not questioned. These writings contain no philosophical arguments for or against the existence of the Divine. The writings in both Testaments understand God's presence to be integral to life on earth. Rather than discussion about the existence of God, the biblical text is concerned about the worship of and devotion to the true God. The contest is not between God and atheism, but, rather, between God and gods. This is true for both the ancient Hebrews and for early Christians.

The book of Exodus contains the command not to worship other gods (Exod 34:14) and the warning that sacrifice to other gods will lead to destruction (Exod 22:20). Elsewhere in the OT, always with a tone of chastisement or disapproval, are accounts of strange gods, of gods of foreigners, of gods of silver and gold, of making offerings to other gods, of walking after other gods, and of worshiping other gods. In each of these instances it is clear that for the ancient Hebrews the issue was belief in a false god, but not lack of belief.

Ironically, Christians were called "atheists" by their Roman contemporaries, since Christian religious belief and practice were not consistent with traditional Roman religion, and Christians did not worship gods of the Roman pantheon. *See* BELIEF; FAITH.

MARIAN BERKY

ATHENAEUS. Athenaeus (ca. 200 CE) of Naucratis wrote *The Deipnosophists*, a fictional depiction of a banquet attended by lawyers, poets, doctors, musicians, philosophers, and other intellectuals. His book, an important source of information about dining customs, includes the names of hundreds of ancient writers and their works.

MARK A. CHANCEY

ATHENOBIUS ath´uh-noh´bee-us [Ἀθηνόβιος Athēno-bios]. Antiochus VII Sidete's "friend" who, on his behalf, demanded that Simon Maccabeus return the cities and the money that he had acquired outside Judea or make monetary restitution for both (1 Macc 15:28-36).

ATHENS ath´inz [Ἀθῆναι Athēnai]. The city of Athens and its immediate territory of Attica lie at the south end of the mainland of GREECE. To the north lay Boiotia, and to the west the Megarid and the isthmus of CORINTH. Athens is surrounded by a series of mountains: Parnes to the north, Pendeli to the east, and Hymettos to the south. The main harbor of the city of Athens was the Piraeus, which gave access to the Saronic Gulf and the AEGEAN. Just offshore was the island of Salamis. The Piraeus had been linked to the city of Athens by "Long Walls" constructed in the mid-5th cent. BCE though these were dismantled at the end of the Peloponnesian War (404 BCE).

Athens had been linked with the foundation of democracy at the end of the 6th cent. BCE. Roman visitors to the city were interested in the visible remains of the political buildings as well as its rich cultural past; this is reflected in the writing of the Roman travel-writer PAUSANIAS (2nd cent. CE). Among the buildings he noted in the heart of the city was the Royal Stoa (where one of the chief magistrates or archons resided, and where the laws of Athens were displayed), the bouleuterion (building to house the council of 500), and the circular tholos (in which the presiding tribe met). In the same area was the "Painted Stoa", an open-fronted colonnade inside which were displayed panel paintings depicting the Athenian defeat of the Persian force that landed at Marathon in 490 BCE.

Athens was one of many former independent cities in the province of Achaia that had its focus at the Roman colony of CORINTH. Athens made the mistake of celebrating the assassination of Julius Caesar in 44 BCE by erecting a new statue group of the tyrannicides representing Brutus and Cassius in the area of the agora. This was placed next to two pairs of statues— one dating from the late 6th cent. BCE that had been removed by the Persians in 480 BCE and then returned following ALEXANDER THE GREAT's conquests, and a replacement group of the 470s—showing Harmodios and Aristogeiton whose attacks on the tyrants in the late 6th cent. BCE brought about the establishment of the democracy; the statues were celebrated enough to be copied by Roman artists and a copyist factory with molds of the group has been found in a Roman workshop in the Bay of Naples. Such a blatant show of support for the Republic brought Athens mistrust as Augustus, the adopted son of Julius Caesar, came to power (*see* AUGUSTUS; CAESAR, JULIUS).

Paul arrived in Athens by sea from Macedonia, presumably arriving at the Piraeus (*see* PAUL, THE APOSTLE). According to the book of Acts, the city itself was "full of idols" (17:16). This reflects the way the city was dominated by the acropolis, which contained a number of sanctuaries, but most notably the Parthenon, the main temple to Athena, the patron deity of the city

David W. J. Gill

Figure 1: The Parthenon.

Next to it, and clearly visible on the skyline, was the circular temple of Roma and Augustus, a reminder of the imperial cult. Access to the acropolis had been improved during the reign of Claudius by the construction of a new set of stairs. Other cults in the city included the Theseion, a hero shrine to Theseus who was said to have unified Attica. Theseus's "bones" had been returned to the city in the 470s BCE and placed in a special tomb on the slopes of the Acropolis decorated with paintings showing scenes from the life of the hero. Among the cults that Paul had noted was an altar dedicated to an "Unknown god" (Acts 17:23).

Athens was dominated by colossal statues of the gods. One of the most prominent was the bronze statue of Athena Promachos ("fighting") dating probably from the 430s BCE. This was placed at the west end of the Acropolis and it was said that the tip of the spear could be seen glinting in the sunlight as ships came round Cape Sounion in the southern part of Attica. More impressive was the colossal statue of Athena Parthenos that was displayed inside the Parthenon. This statue, made during the 430s, was constructed from gold and ivory. The shield of Athena was decorated with scenes of the female warriors, the Amazons, attacking the city of Athens; this was known to have been a popular scene in the Roman period as a series of marble reliefs quoting elements of the shield were discovered in the harbor of the Piraeus, presumably on the way to being shipped to Italy. Both statues were the creations of the celebrated Athenian sculptor Pheidias.

Paul seems to have been attracted to the main public space of the city, the AGORA ("market-place", Acts 17:17). This was surrounded by open colonnades or stoas; the philosophical group the Stoics (*see* Acts 17:18) gained their title from debating in such structures. At the east side of the agora was the Stoa of Attalos—now reconstructed by the American School of Classical Studies at Athens—which was a benefaction to the city by one of the kings of Pergamon in north-west Anatolia. The open space of the agora had attracted two Roman imperial benefactions. During the reign of Augustus a temple of Ares was erected in the middle of the agora almost certainly to house the imperial cult; the temple itself had been constructed in the mid-5th cent. BCE and had been transplanted from one of the towns outside Athens. A second building was constructed probably soon after 15 BCE when Agrippa, the son-in-law of Augustus, visited the city. This was a large concert hall, or odeion, seating around 1,000 people. To the east of the agora, but connected by a colonnaded street, was the market of Caesar and Augustus; an inscription from the entrance connecting the two areas carried an inscription dating the project to 11–9 BCE.

Paul himself was brought before the AREOPAGOS (Acts 17:19), one of the historic courts of the city which can be traced back to the 7th cent. BCE. It originally met on the hill of Ares to the south of the agora and to the north-west of the acropolis, though by the Roman period it may have met elsewhere in the city. One of its

David W. J. Gill
Figure 2: Agora.

members, Dionysos, became a member of the fledgling church that Paul established (Acts 17:34). One change to the cultural life of the city was the apparent conversion, perhaps in the 1st cent. CE, of the theater of Dionysos to a location for gladiatorial shows.

Bibliography: J. M. Camp II. *The Athenian Agora: Excavations in the Heart of Classical Athens* (1986); J.M. Camp II. *The Archaeology of Athens* (2001); D. W. J. Gill. "Achaia." *The Book of Acts In its Graeco-Roman Setting* (1994) 433–53; M. C. Hoff and S. I. Rotroff, eds. *The Romanization of Athens: Proceedings of an International Conference Held at Lincoln, Nebraska, April 1996* (1997); J. M. Hurwit. *The Athenian Acropolis: History, Mythology, and Archaeology from the Neolithic Era to the Present* (1999); L. Parlama and N. C. Stampolidis. *Athens: The City Beneath the City. Antiquities from the Metropolitan Railway Excavations* (2000); T. L. Shear Jr. "Athens: From City-State to Provincial Town." *Hesperia 50* (1981) 356–77; H. A. Thompson and R. E. Wycherley. *The Agora of Athens.* Athenian Agora. Vol. 14 (1972); J. Travlos. *Pictorial Dictionary of Ancient Athens* (1971).

DAVID W. J. GILL

ATHLAI ath´li [עַתְלָי 'athlay]. Descendant of Bebai who dismissed his foreign wife as Ezra instructed God's covenant required him (Ezra 10:28; not in 1 Esd 9:29).

ATHLETICS. Athletic competitions were an important part of Greek and Roman culture and were often held in conjunction with festivals. Greek sports included the pentathlon; foot, horse, and chariot racing; wrestling; boxing; and the *pankration.* The Romans were especially fond of chariot racing, and they introduced gladiatorial sports. Throughout the Greco-Roman world, sizable cities often had sports-related architecture such as gymnasia, hippodromes, stadiums, and amphitheaters. Athletic terms appearing in the Bible include running (1 Cor 9:24-26; Gal 2:2; 5:7; Phil 2:16; 3:12-15; 2 Tim 4:7-8); boxing (1 Cor 9:26-27; 2 Tim 4:7); the victor's crown, which was a wreath (1 Cor 9:25); physical training (1 Tim 4:8); games (2 Macc 4:18-20); gymnasium (1 Macc 1:14; 2 Macc 4:9); and wrestling and discus throwing (2 Macc 4:13-15). *See* also FESTIVALS, GRECO-ROMAN; RACE (SPORT).

Bibliography: David Matz. *Greek and Roman Sport: A Dictionary of Athletes and Events from the Eighth Century BC to the Third Century AD* (1991); Z. Weiss. "Adopting a Novelty: The Jews and the Roman Games in Palestine." *The Roman and Byzantine Near East.* Vol. 2: *Journal of Roman Archaeology* (1999) 23–50.

MARK A. CHANCEY

ATONEMENT. "Atonement" derives from the combination "at + one + ment" in Middle English, where it carried the sense of reconciliation. In doctrinal statements in the Christian tradition, it typically denotes

Jesus' sacrifice on the cross: "Christ's death for us." In the biblical materials, however, the concept of "atonement" refers more broadly to various means by which particular persons (or humanity) are restored to right relationship with God.

A. Atonement in the OT
B. The Atoning Death of Jesus in the NT
Bibliography

A. Atonement in the OT

In the OT, the concept of atonement (*see* the term כֹּפֶר kofer, used 121 times in the OT, translated consistently in the LXX as ἱλάσκομαι, hilaskomai) is the resolution of estrangement between two parties whose relationship has been interrupted or broken by sin or other infraction, and is generally tied to the rites of sacrifice and mediation. In divine-human relations, God is the source of atonement, even in those texts where God provides means for achieving atonement. God atones for both land and people (Deut 32:43), forgives (Jer 18:23), and arranges a sacrificial system through which God mediates atonement.

Since early in the 20th cent., debate has swirled around whether the work of atonement centered on EXPIATION (God's freeing and cleansing people from the onus and blemish of sin) or on PROPITIATION (sacrifice as a means of averting God's wrath). Against the claim that Israel had no notion of propitiation, some have emphasized the need in atonement to assuage God's wrath in the face of human sin. The linguistic evidence related to the use of kofer in the OT prioritizes a definition of atonement as "to wipe away" or "to cleanse," though not exclusively so. However one decides the linguistic issue, it is crucial that the wrath of the God of Israel not be confused with the retributive, begrudging, and capricious dispositions of the Greek and Roman gods, to whom sacrifices were offered in order both to placate the deities and to solicit their favor. The God of Israel is "slow to anger and abounding in steadfast love" (e.g., Exod 34:6; Num 14:18); "wrath" is less a divine property or attribute of God's affect, more the divine response to human unfaithfulness. Atoning sacrifice, then, is oriented toward addressing human sin rather than achieving a transformation in God's self or in God's disposition toward humanity.

It remains true, however unfortunate for contemporary readers, that biblical texts concerning sacrifice never unveil the inner logic of these ritual acts. How to perform the rite is given careful attention, and it is evident that sacrificial rites are effective in restoring right relations with God. How this is so is less clear. Perhaps their meaning was so obvious to those who practiced them that commentary was unnecessary. Contemporary scholars are not all of one mind. Thus, to cite three major lines of inquiry, Milgrom interprets atonement as redemption through the substitution of an animal for a human being (Lev 16) or, in a few cases, as purification of the sanctuary and, by extension, of the community of God's people (e.g., Lev 15:31; 16:19); Janowski emphasizes the redemption of forfeited life through a MEDIATOR, whose substitution effects forgiveness (e.g., Exod 32:30, 32), and atonement through the symbolic offering of oneself in the offering of sacrifice (Lev 4:31; Ezek 40–48).

The variety of sacrifices—burnt offering, peace offering, sin offering—and general regulations for how to perform them are found in Lev 1–7, though related rituals are found throughout the Pentateuch. The "sin" (or "purification") and "guilt" (or "restitution") offerings of Lev 4–5 bring the dynamic relationship between God and humanity into focus. By means of an unblemished sacrifice, the sacrifice of purification addresses the blemish or stain resulting from specified actions. The offering of restitution addresses the condition of human indebtedness resulting from those acts. Both offerings are effective without reference to whether a person's infraction was willful or even known. In the "purification offering" (Lev 4:1–6:7; 6:24–7:10), the unblemished animal is presented to Yahweh as a sin offering, the priest lays his hand on the head of the bull before it is slaughtered, the blood is smeared or sprinkled on the altar, and the fat is removed and burnt upon the altar. In the sacrifice offered annually on the Day of Atonement (Lev 16), the high priest presents a bull as a sin offering for himself and his kin, sprinkling the blood upon the mercy seat. After this, he slaughters the goat of the sin offering, making atonement for the holy place, on account of the sins of Israel. Then, he presents a second goat, lays his hands upon it, confesses the sins of the whole people over it, and sends it away into the wilderness. According to Lev 16:22, "the goat shall bear on itself all their iniquities to a barren region; and the goat shall be set free in the wilderness"—a symbol of the eradication of the uncleanness and guilt of sin from the community.

The essential ingredients of the process of atonement are sketched in Lev 19:22: "And the priest shall make atonement for him with the ram of guilt offering before the LORD for his sin that he committed; and the sin he committed shall be forgiven him." Human sin has resulted in broken relations between the sinner and God. It is this broken relationship (and not divine anger) that must be addressed, and both mediation and substitution are necessary in the process of making atonement. Thus, the priest (as mediator) resolves this tension through a sacrifice, which is provided by the sinner (as a substitute) but offered at the hands of the priest. As is often the case, the location of this sacrifice is noted: "before the LORD"—that is, in the Temple, the house of the Lord.

Basic, first, is the opposition of life and death—with death a great evil to be avoided, and with everything related to death (whether the corpse itself, or bloody discharge or disease) rendering people unclean and unfit to worship God. Second, in the sacrifice, the notion of "identification" or "representation" seems pivotal. By laying hands on the beast's head in the ritual of sacrifice, sinners identified themselves with the beast, indicating that the beast now represented sinners in their sin. The same might be said for the rituals involving blood, the sprinkling or smearing of the animal's blood on the people on whose behalf the sacrifice is made (e.g., Exod 24:8; 29:10, 15, 19-20; Lev 3:2, 8, 13; 14:14). In a signal text, Lev 17:11-14, the shedding of blood—regarded as the substance of life, and therefore sacred to God—signifies the offering of the lives of those for whom the sacrifice is made.

In God's economy, Israelites were thus to do to their animals what they were not allowed to do to their children or themselves; animal life substitutes for human life, and this had efficacy in the restoration of right relations with God. This is not to say, however, that sacrifice could be seen as a way of inducing God to grant forgiveness. Such prophetic voices as Isaiah (1:10-17), Hosea (e.g., 8:13), and Micah (6:6-7) amply attest the priority of contriteness and repentance, the offering of one's life in worship and service, in the offering of the sacrificial animal.

B. The Atoning Death of Jesus in the NT

From Roman or Jewish perspectives, the crucifixion of Jesus was so ignominious a culmination of Jesus' life that its interpretation among his earliest followers was crucial. Representing such difficulties, Paul writes that proclamation of "Christ crucified" is "a stumbling block to Jews and foolishness to Gentiles" (1 Cor 1:23). According to the Gospels, Jesus himself was remembered not only to have anticipated his heinous death but already to have begun the process of interpretation.

In a prominent mission statement, the Gospels of Matthew and Mark report Jesus' words, "The Son of Man came not to be served but to serve, and to give his life a ransom for many" (Matt 20:28; Mark 10:45); in the context of instructing his followers to devote their lives to the service of others, Jesus thus reveals the purpose of his own, even to the point that he will embrace death on behalf of others. Similarly, in the celebrated words of the Last Supper, the Gospels report how Jesus interpreted his imminent death in sacrificial terms: "This is my blood of the covenant, which is poured out for many" (Mark 14:24; Matt 26:28 adds: "for the forgiveness of sins").

According to the Gospels, Jesus thus draws on a plethora of images from the OT by way of communicating the saving significance of his death. With echoes from Isa 52:13–53:12, the phrase "for many" unavoidably signals the vicarious nature of Jesus' death on behalf of humanity. Interpreters often take Jesus' reference to "RANSOM" (λύτρον lytron) in its usual

sense in Greek literature, where it pertains to the "price of release" of a slave or prisoner of war. In the OT, the connection between "ransom" and "atonement" is more straightforward (e.g., Exod 21:30), but when the Lord is named as the one who ransoms (e.g., Exod 30:12, 16; Ps 49:15; Hos 13:14) there is no hint that actual payment is involved. Rather, God ransoms by liberating (λυτρόομαι, lytroomai) the people from Egypt (Exod 6:6; 16:13), a claim echoed in Luke 1:68; 2:38; 24:21. Similarly, the sayings at the Last Supper trade on images and language from Israel's covenant sacrifice (Exod 24:8), the restoration of Israel that signals the end of exile (Zech 9:9-11), and the hope of covenant renewal (Jer 31:31-33). In these myriad ways, Jesus' death marked the long-awaited restoration of God's people, Jew and Gentile. In his exposition of his own death, Jesus pushed back into Israel's history and embraced fully Israel's hope of redemption. The new exodus, God's decisive act of deliverance, was inaugurated in Jesus' mission, the climax of which is his death on the cross.

Within the Passion Narratives of the Gospels, multiple plotlines converge in the crucifixion of Jesus. At some points, Jesus' execution appears to be the work of his enemies, whose calls for his crucifixion carry the day. At other points, God's will is apparently expressed in the cross: "For the Son of Man is going as it has been determined" (Luke 22:22); "Father, if you are willing, remove this cup from me; yet, not my will but yours be done" (Luke 22:42). At still others, Jesus' own will is expressed in the cross; this is implicit, e.g., in Jesus' lack of resistance at his capture and silence before his accusers. This same pattern is repeated otherwise in the NT, with both God and Jesus portrayed as the subject of Jesus' atoning death. Neither in the Gospels nor otherwise in the NT, however, do we find story lines portraying God as the subject and Jesus as the object (i.e., God punishing Jesus in his death) or Jesus as the subject and God as the object (i.e., Jesus giving up his life to appease God).

We do find, as we turn to the pages of the NT more broadly, a generous menu of choices for making sense of Jesus' atoning death. Indeed, the NT writers seem never to tire of generating new models for communicating the saving importance of the cross. Taken as a whole, however, these images tend to congregate around five spheres of public life in antiquity: the court of law (e.g., justification), the world of commerce (e.g., redemption), personal relationships (e.g., reconciliation), worship (e.g., sacrifice), and the battleground (e.g., triumph over evil). An expansive terminology attests this variety. With regard to images of sacrifice, e.g., Paul and John refer to Jesus as the "Passover lamb" (1 Cor 5:7) and "the lamb of God who takes away the sins of the world" (John 1:29; Rev 5:6); language regarding the handing over of Jesus can hark back to the binding of Isaac (i.e., the Akedah; Rom

8:32); 1 Pet observes how Jesus "bore our sins in his body on the tree" (2:24); and Jesus' death is portrayed as "blood of the covenant" (Mark 14:24) and as "first fruits" (1 Cor 15:20, 23; Deut 16). Another example: although the language of "reconciliation" is rare in the NT (καταλάσσω, katalassō; 2 Cor 5:18-20; Eph 2:16; Col 1:20, 22), the concept inhabits other texts as well, including references to "peace" (e.g., Eph 2:14-18) and the many acts (e.g., Rom 16:16), pleas (Philemon), and testimonies (e.g., Acts 15:8-9; Gal 3:26-29) of reconciliation that occupy the pages of the NT. In these ways, the NT writers draw on the life-worlds of their audiences while at the same time working to induct them into the world of the OT and the ways of Israel's God.

Nor is the variety of NT images of atonement simply a function of the different writers of its books. Paul himself can write of substitution, representation, sacrifice, justification, forgiveness, reconciliation, triumph over the powers, and redemption. John can speak of illumination as well as sacrifice. Although in Hebrews the notion of sacrifice is paramount, Jesus is presented as both the perfect high priest and the perfect sacrificial victim. First Peter speaks of Jesus' death as a ransom and sacrifice, while the book of Revelation presents Jesus' death in terms of military triumph and redemption. This variety might appropriately lead us to the conclusion that the significance of Jesus' death could not be represented without remainder by any one concept or theory or metaphor. This is due first to the universal profundity of Jesus' death as saving event, and then to the variety of contexts within which Jesus' death required explication and to the variety of ways in which the human situation can be understood.

Within this variety we can discern common threads. First, each image of the atonement presumes a portrait of the human situation, of human need. We find in the NT an abundance of terms and phrases for conceiving the condition that characterizes human existence apart from God: slavery, hard-heartedness, lostness, friendship with the world, blindness, ungodliness, wickedness, unrighteousness, living according to the sinful nature, the reprobate mind, the darkened heart, lacking worship, enemies of God, dead in one's trespasses and sins, children of (the first) Adam, lacking the glory of God, and more. How one articulates the saving significance of Jesus' death is tied to one's conception of the human situation. People who are blind need illumination. Slaves need liberation. The lost need to be found.

Second, the message of atonement is all encompassing. That is, it cannot be reduced to one group of people, to one individual, nor to some aspect of the human person. What happened on the cross had universal significance: for Jew and Gentile, for slave and free, for male and female. The work of Christ on the cross has as its object even the cosmos, giving rise to images of new creation (2 Cor 5:17) and all-encompassing reconciliation (Col 1:15-20). The atonement is not narrowly focused on the individual's relationship to God, but involves persons in their relationships to others, both neighbor and enemy, and to the world. The cross is less about a transaction after which persons are no longer guilty, more about salvation as a call to reflect in day-to-day life the quality of life, oriented to the other, on exhibition in Jesus' death on behalf of others. Inherent within atonement theology is an ethics of service. Atonement is a divine gift, but it summons and enables human response.

Finally, in the restoration of broken relationships, God's initiative is paramount. Two Pauline texts provide important orientation to this central theological concern of the NT witness to Jesus' atoning death. Romans 5:1-11 states that the death of Christ is the ultimate expression of the love of God: "But God demonstrates his love for us in that while we were still sinners Christ died for us." This affirmation entails four claims. First, the love of God has no human parallels by which to comprehend it; God's love is immeasurable. Second, God's love is prevenient; it precedes and is in no way dependent on human activity or response. Third, Paul's audience can be certain that their suffering has significance because the suffering of Christ has proved so meaningful. Through his death "we have been justified," "saved," "reconciled." In the midst of our impotence, Christ took on the measure of our powerlessness and died in our place. As a result of his death, we share in his life, and we find that our own suffering has significance in relation to his. Fourth, we are told that *God* demonstrates his love by means of what *Christ* did. We might have anticipated that God's love would be revealed in God's own deed, and this would certainly have been the case were Paul sketching an atonement theology oriented toward the role of the cross in assuaging divine wrath. Instead, Paul asserts the oneness of the purpose and activity of God and God's Son in the cross.

As the apostle puts it elsewhere, "in Christ God was reconciling the world to himself" (2 Cor 5:19). In this further passage where descriptive terms for the saving effects of Jesus' death congregate (2 Cor 5:14–6:12: substitution, representation, sacrifice, justification, forgiveness, and new creation), Paul carefully shows how the work of God and of Christ are one. What is more, Paul does not speak of any need for mutual reconciliation. "The world" is estranged from God and needs to be brought back into relationship with God, but we find no hint that God is estranged from "the world." For this reason, Paul has no need to show how God can be appeased, or how God might come to extend his love again. Rather, Paul affirms that God's love always has the upper hand in divine-human relations, and that the work of Christ had as its effect the bringing of "the world" back to God. *See* RECONCILE, RECONCILIATION; SACRIFICES AND OFFERINGS.

Bibliography: Mark D. Baker, Mark D. Green, and Joel B. Green. *Recovering the Scandal of the Cross: Atonement in NT and Contemporary Contexts* (2000); Roger T. Beckwith and Martin J. Selman, eds. *Sacrifice in the Bible* (1995); John Driver. *Understanding the Atonement for the Mission of the Church* (1986); John Goldingay, ed. *Atonement Today* (1995); Michael J. Gorman. *Cruciformity: Paul's Narrative Spirituality of the Cross* (2001); Martin Hengel. *The Atonement: The Origins of the Doctrine in the NT* (1981); Morna D. Hooker. *Not Ashamed of the Gospel: NT Interpretations of the Death of Christ* (1994); Jacob Milgrom. *Studies in Cultic Theology and Terminology* (1983); Jacob Milgrom. *Leviticus.* 3 vols. AB (1991–2001); Anthony J. Tambasco. *A Theology of Atonement and Paul's Vision of Christianity* (1991).

JOEL B. GREEN

ATONEMENT, DAY OF. *See* DAY OF ATONEMENT.

ATRAHASIS MYTH. Atrahasis is an earlier Babylonian counterpart of the biblical Noah. Of the surviving Mesopotamian flood accounts, the Atrahasis Myth is most relevant to studies of the corresponding biblical narrative (Gen 6–9) because it sets the flood in a similar context of human creation-destruction-repopulation. *See* GILGAMESH, EPIC OF.

SUSANNA W. SOUTHARD

ATROTH-BETH-JOAB at′roth-beth-joh′ab [בֵּית יוֹאָב עַטְרוֹת, ʿatroth beth yoʾav]. Located somewhere near BETHLEHEM in Judah, Atroth-Beth-Joab is a town included in HUR's genealogy (1 Chr 2:54). The name translates as "crowns of the house of Joab." The KJV has "Ataroth, the house of Joab."

ATROTH-SHOPHAN at′roth-shoh′fan [עַטְרוֹת שׁוֹפָן, ʿatroth shofan]. GADITES rebuilt the town of Atroth-Shophan east of the Jordan River after it was taken from the Amorite king SIHON (Num 32:35). The name is probably related to nearby ATAROTH. The exact location is unknown. KJV translates Atroth and Shophan as two separate towns.

ATTAI at′i [עַתַּי ʿattay]. 1. A member of Judah's tribe who was the son of Egyptian slave Jarha by Sheshan's daughter and was the father of Nathan (1 Chr 2:35-36).

2. A Gaddite warrior who went over to David's side against Saul at the battle of Ziklag (1 Chr 12:11).

3. King REHOBOAM's son by his wife Maachah, who was favored by Rehoboam and also Solomon's grandson (2 Chr 11:20).

MEREDITH HAMMONS

ATTALIA at′uh-li′uh [Ἀτταλεία Attaleia] A city on the SW coast of Asia Minor (36 50′N; 30 46′E) on the Catarrhactes (Aksu) River, founded by ATTALUS II of PERGAMUM (159–138 BCE) that became the main harbor for the region of PAMPHYLIA. AUGUSTUS settled veterans in the city and it became a Roman colony in the 3rd cent. CE. The Apostle Paul passed through Attalia at the end of his first missionary journey (Acts 14:25). The modern city of Antalya has significant archaeological remains including a triumphal triple gate built during the reign of HADRIAN (117–138 CE).

ADAM L. PORTER

ATTALUS at′uh-luhs [Ἄτταλος Attalos]. The name of three kings of Pergamon. Attalus II Philadelphus (159–138 BCE) promoted the Syrian pretender Alexander Balas (*Diod. Sic.* 31.32a) and is also a recipient of the letter sent by the Roman consul Lucius proclaiming the Roman alliance with Simon Maccabeus (1 Macc 15:22).

J. R. C. COUSLAND

ATTHARATES ath′uh-ray′teez [Ἀτταρατης Attaratēs, Ἀθαρατης Attharatēs]. In Codex ALEXANDRINUS, the governor who exhorted the returning exiles to celebrate (1 Esd 9:49-53). Corruption of title "tirshatha."

ATTHARIAS ath′uh-ri′uhs [Ἀθαριας Attharias]. Title in 1 Esd 5:40 for Nehemiah or for the Persian governor who joined NEHEMIAH.

AUGURY [נַחַשׁ nachash]. A term that refers to several forms of DIVINATION including hydromancy or lecanomancy (Gen 44:5), speech omens (1 Kgs 20:32-33), and the search for OMENS through the observation of natural phenomena (Num 24:1), such as the wind's rustling in a tree (suggested by Judg 9:37).

ANN L. FRITSCHEL

AUGUSTAN COHORT [σπεῖρα Σεβαστός speira Sebastos]. Acts 27:1 refers to the Augustan Cohort (*Cohors Augusta*, often an honorary title). The soldiers named in Acts 27:42 are probably part of this cohort. A COHORT, an auxiliary unit that usually ranged from 500 to 1,000 soldiers, was an innovation of Augustus. Similar to a LEGION, it was much smaller and consisted primarily of noncitizens, with the promise of citizenship serving as the chief means of recruitment. Roman citizens would have served as CENTURIONs in the cohort. Acts likely refers specifically to the Augustan Cohort I based in Syria during the 1st cent. CE, consisting largely of Syrian soldiers and possibly Samaritans and Jews, and serving Agrippa II. Based upon inscriptional evidence, the cohort was likely stationed in the Hauran Mountains near the present-day border of Jordan and Syria. While it may have been unusual for this cohort to be involved in escorting imperial prisoners to Rome, HEROD likely had some of the cohort with him at the trial of Paul in Caesarea (Acts 26), making it natural for them to escort Paul, particularly since the centurion, Julius, was a Roman citizen.

Bibliography: F. J. Foakes-Jackson and K. Lake. *The Beginnings of Christianity.* Vol. 5 (1979); Michael Grant. *The Armies of the Caesars* (1974); M. P. Speidel. "The Roman Army under the Procurators: The Italian and the Augustan Cohort in the Acts of the Apostles." *AncSoc* 13–14 (1982–83) 233–40.

KENNETH D. LITWAK

AUGUSTINE Augustine of Hippo (354–430) stands preeminent among the scriptural interpreters of the Western church. He was preeminent among his contemporaries in Late Antiquity for his pastoral commitment as an exegete. He was preeminent in his influence at phase after phase of movements of reform and renewal over a millennium and a half after his death in 430 as the invading Vandals besieged the small coastal town of Hippo where he had been bishop for nearly thirty-five years.

From his somewhat tentative quotation of Scripture in the early dialogues (386–387), Augustine quickly moved to robust attacks on the Manichees in the frame of allegorical interpretations of Genesis. This was followed by an intense self-imposed biblical apprenticeship after his ordination to the priesthood (391) with commentaries on the Psalms and select Gospel passages. The *83 Questions*, written at the same period, a collection of inquiries into problematic scriptural texts, is a witness to his growing concentration on the Pauline Epistles, leading to an aborted commentary on Romans and the justly famous replies to the Milanese priest, Simplician, esp. on Rom 9, in which the newly consecrated bishop begins to elaborate his theology of grace.

By the end of the first decade of his episcopacy, Augustine was ready to embark on his masterpiece of biblical hermeneutics, *De doctrina Christiana*. Abruptly interrupting this work in Book III 25.35 in the middle of an intricate discussion of ambiguous elements of scripture, Augustine plunged into a work of a very different genre, the *Confessions*. Its strong focus was the role of Scriptures in his own spiritual life and that of the church community. His extraordinary persistence in grappling with the challenge of Scripture within the life of the church was once more demonstrated in the opening years of the 5th cent. as he tackled the *Literal Meaning of Genesis* (401–415). The Bible is omnipresent throughout his immense literary output in the next three decades, with hundreds of sermons, letters, and apologetic works against Manichees, Donatists, and Pelagians, as well as in his monumental theological works, *City of God* and *On the Trinity*. These works reveal a man who knows the Scriptures by heart. Indeed, what characterizes Augustine as a biblical interpreter is the fusion of an exuberant ministry as preacher, writer, and controversialist, together with an intense introspection into the transformative dynamics of God's word so powerfully evident throughout the *Confessions*.

Augustine's approach to Scripture is ruled by a theological perspective in which the Incarnate Word and the word of Scripture are indissolubly linked. The humility of the Incarnate Word is mirrored in the humble word of Scripture, whose riches are hidden from the proud. Capitalizing on his own rhetorical training, and attentive to his predecessors like Ambrose of Milan and Tyconius of Carthage, Augustine charted a new course for biblical scholars with his insights into the theory of signs and his nuanced understanding of Scripture as a conversation between divinity and humanity.

Bibliography: P. Bright, ed. *Augustine and the Bible* (1997). C. Kannengiesser. "Augustine." *Handbook of Patristic Exegesis* (2004) 1149–1233.

PAMELA BRIGHT

AUGUSTUS aw-guhs´tuhs [Αὐγοῦστος Augoustos]. Although mentioned only once in the NT (Luke 2:1), Caesar Augustus (b. Sept. 9, 63 BCE–d. Aug. 19, 14 CE) shaped the structures, values, and practices of the imperial world that the followers of Jesus negotiated on a daily basis.

Augustus was the name given to the Roman emperor Octavian. Octavian's father, Gaius Octavius (d. 59 BCE), was a senator, and governor of Macedonia in 61 BCE. Octavian's mother, Atia, was a niece of JULIUS CAESAR. The childless Julius Caesar adopted his great-nephew Octavian, making him principal heir and recipient of three-quarters of Caesar's estate.

After Caesar's murder (March 15, 44 BCE), Octavian emerged as leader of Caesar's friends and veterans. Conflict with Mark Antony was eased in late 43 by a triumvirate with Antony and Lepidus that centered on avenging Caesar's murder and securing their own power. They divided the empire threefold and proscribed opponents, decimating the senatorial ranks, seizing property, and raising taxes to fund an army that defeated assassins Brutus and Cassius at Philippi in 42 BCE. Though the triumvirate was renewed (37 BCE), Lepidus moved unsuccessfully against Octavian in 35 BCE and resigned. While Octavian's power rose in Italy and the west, Antony struggled. He was alienated from his wife, Octavia—Octavian's sister—and defeated in the east by Parthia. Antony appealed for help to his lover, the Egyptian Cleopatra. In the ensuing battles of Actium in 31 BCE and Alexandria in 30 BCE, Octavian defeated Antony, who committed suicide.

The victory ended decades of civil strife. At the time, there was widespread pessimism, weariness with war, and a sense that belief in the gods and ancestral values was dissolving. Rome's political and cultural identity seemed lost. Octavian was to effect a profound transformation. He set about restoring the republic (in name at least) as a monarchy and reviving cultural identity. He reversed the widespread neglect of gods and temples. He replaced Rome's divisiveness and self-destruction with order and a renewed sense of mission to rule the world. Public festivals, including religious observances, secured Roman identity and prestige. Veneration for a ruler chosen by the gods—Octavian—replaced factional commitments to power-grasping generals.

Octavian effected the transformation through adroit appeals to political precedents, strategic alliances with a dependent senate, patronage, control of the legions, wealth, and visual imagery that identified Octavian with Rome's special identity. He avoided outward trappings of monarchy, disrespect for republican structures, and ostentation that alienated members of the elite—mistakes Julius Caesar had made.

Celebrations of his victory at Actium—prayers, sacrifices, holidays, shrines, temples, a triumph, loyalty oaths—not only identified Octavian as the bringer of peace and unity—but also defined him as chosen by the gods. In 28–27 BCE he returned emergency powers that had been granted the emperor to the senate as the decision-making body. Legally and politically, the republic, or a form of it, seemed to be restored.

But in actuality, Octavian maintained considerable power. He remained as consul. The senate could not introduce legislation. He maintained the loyalty of veterans and clients. Many in the senate, including those from Italy and the provinces, owed him their positions. The senate's indebtedness to Octavian was signaled by honoring him with the name "Augustus" ("Illustrious One"). Because of continuing unrest in the provinces and threats from Parthia, Augustus retained responsibility for some of the provinces. Thus he gained considerable territory, legions, and a source of wealth through taxation.

Augustus remained a permanent consul until 23 BCE. At that point, he became tribune with unlimited power in Rome, and received power over all governors (*imperium maius*). He traveled extensively in the provinces and in 23 BCE acted decisively against a conspiracy. In 19 BCE his power in the provinces was extended to Italy and Rome so that Augustus became consul for life. He was the *princeps* with extraordinary powers. No one could be elected without his endorsement. In 19–18 BCE, he reduced the size of the senate to about 600, increased the minimal required wealth to a million sesterces, and decreased the length of consulships from a year to six months. This move increased senatorial prestige but reduced effective power.

In 18 BCE he instituted the *Ludi Saeculares* ("Secular Games") to celebrate the beginning of a golden age, defined by his accomplishments, further identifying himself with Rome's destiny and well-being. In accord with the themes of fertility and abundance, he rewarded members of the patrician class who had more than three children, and legislated against adultery. In 12 BCE when Lepidus died, he became *pontifex maximus*, again associating himself with the gods as protectors of Rome. In 2 BCE, he received the title *pater patriae*,

father of the fatherland, in recognition of his wise provision for Rome's well-being.

Five further dimensions of his transformation of the Roman world should be noted. Military acumen enabled Octavian's rise and ended civil wars. First, after Actium he united the armies previously committed to individual leaders, reduced the number of legions, maintained a standing army supported by taxes, custom duties, tributes, and war booty, discharged veterans with a cash bounty, established colonies in the provinces, and exercised patronage by appointing military commanders.

Second, he expanded the empire, adding territory in Spain, Germania around the Danube and Rhine, Egypt, and Asia Minor. His victories presented Augustus as guarantor of Rome's order blessed by the gods. The senate built the *Ara Pacis Augustae* to honor his victories in Spain and Gaul (13–9 BCE). Three times he closed the Shrine of Janus Quirinus to indicate the end of war. *Pax Augustae*—Augustan Peace—was built on military power, conquest, territorial domination, and a dependent senate.

Third, he addressed social problems in Rome such as water supply (12 BCE), food supply (8 CE), and civic order (permanent fire brigade [6 CE]) and police force). Throughout the provinces he ensured political and military control with extensive road construction, and appointed officials for tax collection.

Fourth, he rebuilt Rome, including the temple of Mars Ultor (the Avenger), the senate house, and eighty-two other temples. Numerous statues of the emperor were erected throughout the city. Thus he presented himself as a second Romulus in building the city, and ensured his ubiquitous presence in public spaces.

And fiinally, he provided a successor to prevent civil strife and to maintain his legacy of power. Having only one daughter, Julia, and no son, he made several efforts to settle the succession on adopted relatives but death intervened. Finally, he chose his stepson Tiberius who assumed power on Augustus's death in 14 CE.

Augustus's official "image" was of the savior and rebuilder of Rome and its empire. He had restored the republic, established monarchy, ended civil war, refurbished Rome, expanded its territory, elevated the provinces, and ensured a peaceful succession (Tacitus, *Ann.* 1.ix). Tacitus had opponents criticize him for deception, cruelty, duplicity, craving power and glory, and establishing peace by bloodshed (*Ann.* 1.x). For the empire's poor, the vast majority of its population, he was a brutal and highly efficient ruler who secured Roman elite interests, exacted taxation, seized land, and ensured the subordination of millions. The political system he constructed continued for centuries and constituted the world that early Christians and NT writers negotiated daily. *See* EMPEROR; ROMAN EMPIRE

Bibliography: W. Carter. *The New Testament: Negotiating the Roman Imperial World: An Essential Guide* (2006); W. Eck. *Augustus* (2003); K. Garlinksy. *Augustan Culture: An Interpretive Introduction* (1996); K. A. Raaflaub and M. Toher. *Between Republic and Empire: Interpretations of Augustus and His Principate* (1990); P. Zanker. *The Power of Images in the Age of Augustus* (1990).

WARREN CARTER

AURANUS aw-ray´nuhs [Ἀυρανός *Auranos*]. Leader, appointed by Lysimachus, over 3,000 men to quell an uprising of the Jews in Jerusalem (2 Macc 4:40).

AURELIUS, MARCUS. Marcus Aurelius (121–80 CE), adopted son of Antoninus Pius, was emperor of Rome from 161–80 CE, serving jointly with Lucius Verus for eight years (161–69 CE). He devoted considerable effort to combating enemies on the frontiers, such as the Parthians in the east and Germanic tribes in the north. He supported the persecution of Christians, and Justin Martyr and the widow Felicitas died during his reign. Nonetheless, many ancient writers regarded him as a wise and benevolent ruler. His book, *The Meditations*, is an important source of information about 2nd cent. Stoicism.

MARK A. CHANCEY

AUTHOR OF LIFE [ἀρχηγόν τῆς ζωῆς *archēgon tēs zōēs*]. Peter's title for Jesus (Acts 3:15) follows the healing of the lame man at Solomon's portico, reminding witnesses that Jesus' name is the source of healing. The power of Jesus' divine name evokes OT references to God's protection and deliverance (Pss 20:1-7; 44:4-8; 54:1-7).

HEIDI GEIB

AUTHORITIES, CITY [ἀγορανόμος *agoranomos*, ἄρχοντες *archontes*, βουλή *boulē*, γερουσία *gerousia*, γραμματεύς *grammateus*, πρῶτοι *prōtoi*, στρατηγοί *stratēgoi*]. City governments in the Greco-Roman period were organized (to varying degrees) according to either the Hellenistic or Roman model. A Hellenistic city, or polis (πόλις), was governed by a boulē, or council, elected by the ekklēsia (ἐκκλησία), or assembly of citizens. Some cities also had a gerousia, or council of elders. The titles of individual officials varied widely; frequently attested terms for the more important include prōtoi (Acts 13:50; 28:7), archontes, and stratēgoi. Lesser officials included the agoranomos, or market overseer, and grammateus, a secretary or scribe (Acts 19:35). A Roman-style city had two chief magistrates, the *duoviri*, and a *curia*, or city council, elected by the citizens. Other officials, *aediles* and *quaestores*, oversaw the city's day-to-day administration, such as the proper functioning of temples and civic buildings, the maintenance of roads, the protection of the water system, the distribution of corn, and the protection

of public safety. The officials at the Roman colony of Philippi, called stratēgoi in Acts (16:20, 22, 35, 36, 38), were probably *aediles*.

Bibliography: Helmut Koester. *History, Culture, and Religion in the Hellenistic Age* (1995).

MARK A. CHANCEY

AUTHORITY [מֶמְשָׁלָה *memshalah*; שָׁלְטָן *sholtan*; ἐξουσία *exousia*]. Within the biblical texts, authority designates primarily 1) the earthly or heavenly ruler who exercises power over others, 2) the power that such a ruler exercises, or 3) the realm over which such a ruler governs. Authority likewise designates 4) the human prerogative to take a given action.

In the OT authority is associated with God (Ps 103:22; Dan 6:27), earthly kings (1 Kgs 9:19; 2 Kgs 20:13; Isa 39:2; Jer 34:1), and the visionary figures of Daniel (Dan 7:6, 12, 14, 26, 27). But God's authority contrasts starkly with that of humans. While God's authority lasts "throughout all generations" (Ps 145:13) and "has no end" (Dan 6:26), human authority is "given" by God (Dan 7:6, 14, 27) and will likewise be "taken away," "consumed," and "totally destroyed" by God (Dan 7:26).

NT usage broadly parallels OT usage. Here ultimate authority belongs to God (Luke 12:5; Acts 1:7; Rom 9:21; Jude 24-25; Rev 16:9), the source of "all authority" (Matt 28:18). But God grants provisional authority to Satan and satanic powers (Luke 4:6; Rev. 6:8; 9:3; 13:5, 7; 17:12) as well as to human rulers (John 19:11; Rom 13:1, 2; Rev 17:12).

Accordingly, in the NT, authority is associated with Satan (Luke 4:5-6; Acts 26:18; Rev 13:2 compare 12:9), with earthly and/or heavenly rulers as a group (Luke 22:25; Rom 13:1, 3; 1 Cor 15:24; Eph 1:21; 3:10; 6:12; Col 1:13, 16; 2:10, 15; Titus 3:1; 1 Pet 3:22), and with specific rulers such as Herod (Luke 23:7), Pilate (John 19:10), and the chief priests (Acts 9:14; 26:10). In Revelation, authority to enact the judgment of God is associated with "Death and Hades" (6:8), locusts (9:3, 10), horses (9:19), the beasts from sea and land (13:5, 7, 11). But all such authority is merely temporary, since God has already "disarmed" these powers, "made an example" of them, and "triumphed" over them through the death of Christ (Col 2:15). Ultimately, God will "bring [the authorities] to nothing" (1 Cor 15:24) and "subject" them to Jesus Christ (1 Pet 3:22).

A prominent new focus within the NT relates to the authority that God grants to Jesus (Matt 9:8; Mark 11:28; John 5:27; 10:17-18; 17:2; Rev. 2:28; 12:10). Here Jesus exhibits authority to teach (Mark 1:22; Luke 4:32; Mark 11:28, 29, 33), heal (Matt 10:1// Luke 9:1), cast out demons/unclean spirits (Mark 1:27; 3:15; 6:7), forgive sins (Mark 2:10; Matt 9:8), grant eternal life (John 17:2), "lay down [his life] and . . . take it up again" (John 10:18).

Jesus, likewise, gives authority to his followers "to become children of God" (John 1:12), "to build up and not tear down" (2 Cor 10:8; 13:10), and ultimately "to rule . . . over the nations" (Rev 2:26-27). Accordingly Paul speaks repeatedly of his own authority as an apostle (1 Cor 9:5, 12, 18; 2 Cor 10:18; 13:10; 2 Thess 3:7-9) and of the authority of believers vis-à-vis the ethical decisions that they face (1 Cor 6:12; 7:4, 34; 8:9; 11:10).

DOROTHY JEAN WEAVER

AUTHORITY OF SCRIPTURE. Traditionally the church has understood the authority of the Bible as in some sense the definitive, mediated authority of God. (For early Jewish views of authority, *see* CANON OF THE OT.)

A typical 1st century view had "Moses and the prophets" speaking the oracles of God to the people of Israel (*see* Luke 16:19-31). While these messengers were understood to be fallible, the words God gave them were considered infallible. They were subject to human discernment but not criticism (*see* Deut 18:15-22).

In the Gospels Jesus treats the Law, the Prophets, and the Writings as divinely authorized, even while interpreting them unconventionally and adding words according to his own authority (*see* Matt 5–7; Luke 4:14-30; 24:13-49). Jesus' dominical approach transforms the Scriptures of Israel into what the later Church would call the OT, and authorizes new testimony concerning his life and legacy, the most trusted of which the later church would compile as the NT.

The earliest Christian writings describe the speech of the apostolic church as divinely authorized (1 Thes 1:2-10; 4:1-8; 5:19-20). This respect for apostolic discourse persists throughout the NT and subapostolic eras (2 Pet 1:12-21; *Did.* 11; *1 Clem.* 47:3) and characterizes the patristic Church's attitude toward the emerging canon of the two Testaments (*see* CANON OF THE NT; CANON OF THE OT).

In both the patristic east and west the Bible was taken as a source par excellence of sanctifying knowledge of the holy God who originated it and of the holy life that abides in God (for instance, in Athanasius's *On the Incarnation of the Word* and Augustine's *On Christian Doctrine*). The medieval eras of Roman Catholicism and Eastern Orthodoxy develop this axiom that the living God is available in the performance and study of the Scriptures.

The early church believed that its Bible faithfully embodied the apostolic traditions of Jesus. The Bible's apostolicity and the church's apostolicity were one. When faced with alternative visions of Christian authority such as Marcionism, Montanism, and Gnosticism, the apostolic churches of the Roman Empire drew on the interconnectedness and coherence of their holy writings, heritage, and ongoing work to delineate their canon, develop the catholic rules of faith they would use to interpret the Scriptures, and define the authority of the catholic episcopate (for instance, in Irenaeus' *Against Heresies* and Basil the Great's *On the Holy Spirit*).

Four centuries of discussion and debate produced an ecumenical consensus of respect for the underlying unity of holy Scripture and holy tradition. Notably, this consensus prevailed despite stalemated dogmatic disagreements, permanent schisms, and even failure to agree on the boundaries of either the OT canon (*see* APOCRYPHA, DEUTEROCANONICAL) or the NT canon (in the case of the Armenian, Coptic, Ethiopic, and Nestorian New Testaments, each of which differs from the dominant standard in a minor way of its own).

As the European Reformations tested that consensus about the unity of Scripture and tradition in an unprecedented way in the West, two convictions on the authority of Scripture dominated. Catholics located the authority of Scripture within the broader authority of the church, to which God entrusted it. Protestants located the divine authority of Scripture above and prior to the derivative and fallible authority of the church. Protestants nevertheless granted that the church had borne Scripture, and the church successfully discerned its canonicity in the apostolic era, and must still keep it obediently if it is not to distort its good news. For Protestants, authoritative "Scripture" was in some sense over and against authoritative "Tradition." The former was the church's "norming norm" (*norma normans*), the latter its "normed norm" (*norma normata*).

Protestant positions further fragmented into moderate camps such as Lutherans and Anglicans that held tradition valid insofar as it conforms to Holy Scripture. Radical camps of Calvinists and "Anabaptists" held tradition valid only insofar as it derives from Holy Scripture. The former groups recognized a subordinate but supplemental authority of traditions other than Scripture, whereas the latter recognized only Scripture as ecclesiastically authoritative for Christians. These two camps resembled a subtler division in Tridentine Catholicism, in which many contended that Scripture and tradition are two complementary sources of divine authority, but some contended that they are one source in two distinct forms. Eastern Orthodoxy tended to prefer that they are one source in two distinct forms. Common to all these visions was the classical patristic conviction that Scripture's authority is the Triune God and its content the revelation of that God and God's gospel.

A new view on the authority of Scripture arose during the Enlightenment. Skeptics and apologists alike came to see the Bible's authority as derivative of and conditional upon its historical, scientific, or existential accuracy. Whether critics defended or problematized the validity of the Scriptures, their arguments often shifted the burden of proof onto the Bible itself and moved the criteria of authority to other epistemological grounds than the Bible's place in the apostolic faith. This could be a natural theological development, honoring, for instance, the Lutheran teaching that the locus of the Bible's authority is the divine Law and gospel that lie within it. Or it could work against the prior tradition, substituting human experience or method for divine agency as Catholics or Calvinists understood it. This modern view further divided Christians into new and very influential camps of historicists, spiritualists, experientialists, fundamentalists, pragmatists, liberationists, and outright skeptics. Each of these camps has contended for variations of its own vision of how divine authority is or is not mediated to and through the Bible.

The modern debate has yet to conclude. However, the apostolic and patristic consensus that the Bible is a definitive and basically unproblematic divine authority for the church has made something of a comeback in both Protestant and Catholic circles, and has never seriously faded in Orthodox circles. Protestant postliberals such as Karl Barth, Catholic advocates of *ressourcement* such as Henri de Lubac, and assorted evangelical traditionalists and postmodernists are fueling a resurgence of the classical view. *See* APOCRYPHA; ATHANASIUS; AUGUSTINE; CANON OF THE NT; CANON OF THE OT; DEUTEROCANONICAL; GNOSTICISM; IRENAEUS.

Bibliography: William J. Abraham. *Canon and Criterion in Christian Theology* (1998). Hans Frei. *The Eclipse of Biblical Narrative* (1974); Henri de Lubac. *Scripture in the Tradition* (2000); Nancey Murphy. *Beyond Liberalism and Fundamentalism: How Modern and Postmodern Philosophy Set the Theological Agenda* (1996); John Webster. *Holy Scripture: A Dogmatic Sketch* (2003); Robert L. Wilken. *The Spirit of Early Christian Thought: Seeking the Face of God* (2003); Telford Work. *Living and Active: Scripture in the Economy of Salvation* (2002); Frances M. Young. *Biblical Exegesis and the Formation of Christian Culture* (2002).

TELFORD WORK

AUTHORIZED VERSIONS. A term that refers to translated biblical texts approved for use by authoritative bodies or offices. Early authorized versions include the Great Bible (1539) used by Protestants and the Douay-Rheims Bible (1609) used by Catholics. The King James Bible (1611) is also known as the Authorized Version. Official updates of the AV include the Revised Version (1885) and the American Standard Version (1901). *See* VERSIONS, ENGLISH.

AUTHORSHIP, NT. The attempt to identify the historical author of individual NT documents presents a difficult—at times vexed—problem. In some cases, where no author is named in the document, one is forced to rely on ancient traditions of varying reliability. In other cases, where an author is named but the document differs from other documents bearing the same author's name, or the content of the document militates against the claimed authorship, a variety of evidence—linguistic, cultural, historic—is brought into play.

The fact that some documents are anonymous—e.g., the Gospels, Acts, Hebrews, 1 John—indicates that some authors at least did not think their identity was necessary for the document to be regarded as reliable. It also indicates that knowledge of the author's identity was not considered necessary for a document to be included in the canonical list developed by the church during the first four cent. of its existence. That the content, not the reputed author, was decisive in determining the value of a given document is attested by the case of Serapion, bishop of Antioch in the late 2nd cent., and a document called the Gospel of Peter. When the bishop was asked by some Christians if they could use the document, presumably in worship, he readily assented, on the supposition that the Apostle Peter had written it. When he later determined that its content had docetic elements, he counseled against its use by his churches (*see* Eusebius, *Hist. eccl.*, 6.12.2-6), since such content clearly was not of apostolic origin. In this instance, content was determinative, not the reputed author. Since that is the case, determination of the actual historical author is not decisive for determining the canonical value of a given NT document.

To determine the historical authorship of a NT document, a variety of evidence is used:

1) **Language and style.** The quality of the Greek in which the document is written, and the style of its composition, including rhetorical devices used in literature of the 1st cent., give clues to the educational level of the author, and hence aids in determining who the author might be. Again, if more than one document bears the same name, a comparison of language and style can show whether or not the same author is likely to be responsible for all documents bearing that name.

2) **Content.** The thought world reflected in the document's prose—that of the OT, of the Qumran writings, of Greco-Roman vocabulary, whether reflecting various official or mystery religions, or secular philosophies such as Stoicism, Platonism, Epicureanism, or the like—provides clues to the time when the document was composed, and thus the possibility of the authorship of a given writing. The more adaptation to the secular thought world appears to be present, the later the document is likely to be, since the need for such adaptation grew as the number of Christians grew and made themselves felt within their surrounding cultures. The relationship of the document's content to

the content of other Christian writings can also help in suggesting whom the author might be.

3) Historical situation. Reference to events that occurred during the first two centuries CE can help to place a possible author relative to the time that author is known to have lived. References to advanced church governance, which presumably developed as the church grew, will also help in determining the time of the writing and thus the author. As the church expanded, a secular culture increasingly aware of it began to question, and in some cases forbid, Christian practices; references to persecutions may thus also provide a clue to when the document was written, and hence by whom.

Such evidence is used to help determine which of three possibilities for authorship apply to various NT writings: anonymous, genuine, or pseudonymous.

4) Anonymous (no author named). None of the Gospels contains within its text the name of its author; names currently appended are due to early traditions, linking each to an apostle (Matthew, John) or a close follower of one (Peter for Mark, Paul for Luke). Similarly Acts, clearly by the same author as Luke, remains anonymous in its text. Among the epistles, Hebrews and 1 John give no hint of authorship, and 2–3 John claim an otherwise unidentified "Elder" as their author.

5) Genuine (written by the named author). The majority of the named documents in the NT bear the name Paul, of which seven are generally acknowledged as having been written by him (Romans, 1–2 Corinthians, Galatians, Philippians, 1 Thessalonians, Philemon). The Pauline authorship of the remainder are more (Ephesians, 1–2 Timothy, Titus), or less (2 Thessalonians, Colossians) disputed, on the basis of the criteria listed above. The eponymous authorship of the epistles of James, 1–2 Peter, and Jude are also questioned in many quarters.

6) Pseudonymous (not written by the person named in the document as author). This was a far more wide-spread practice in the world of the NT than in our contemporary world, and carried less moral opprobrium. Students who expounded ideas of their teacher were obliged to attribute those ideas not to themselves but to their teacher, including letters and tracts. Followers of Pythagoras routinely attributed their works to their master, and the rhetorical work *Ad Herrenium* warns against using the intellectual labors of others to gain fame for oneself. Rabbis routinely handed on traditions in the originator's name, and Tertullian affirmed that what disciples published should be regarded as their master's work (*Marc.* 4.5). It would therefore not be surprising if the same practice were followed by

authors of NT writings as well. Members of the circle who revered Paul or Peter, e.g., who expounded ideas gained from their teacher, would attribute those writings to the apostles rather than themselves (e.g., 1–2 Timothy, Titus for Paul, 1–2 Peter for Peter). Moral indignation was directed at those who wrote false doctrine, rather than at those who wrote sound doctrine in their masters' names.

PAUL J. ACHTEMEIER

AUTHORSHIP, OT. In both Jewish and Christian tradition, many books of the OT have been attributed to authors known from the biblical text. The PENTATEUCH (Genesis, Exodus, Leviticus, Numbers, Deuteronomy) is traditionally described as the book of Moses. So persistent is the tradition that Moses wrote these books—even though the Bible does not say so—that many scholars through the ages have discussed the fact that Deut 34 records his death: The normal solution has been to say that these verses were added by Joshua. In Jewish tradition the book of Joshua was written by that figure, Judges and Samuel by Samuel, and Kings by Jeremiah, who also wrote Lamentations. All the OT Wisdom books (Proverbs, Ecclesiastes, Song of Songs) were attributed to Solomon, except for Job, which some rabbis thought was written by Moses. David wrote the Psalms, and each of the prophets wrote the books appearing under their names.

The OT itself is much more reticent about authorship. The Pentateuch is anonymous, only certain specific sections being attributed to the work of Moses (e.g., Deut 27:3). The historical books from Joshua to Kings likewise have no attribution of authorship. The Proverbs are said to be "of Solomon," but this is not necessarily an ascription of authorship, any more than is the description of the Psalms as "of David": within the texts themselves other authors are named, e.g., the "men of Hezekiah" (Prov 25:1) and even Moses (Ps 90). Nothing at all is said in the OT about the authorship of most books. Only the prophetic writings are mostly headed with a claim that they represent the "words" or "visions" of the particular prophet whose name they bear.

Critical biblical scholarship has noted the comparative paucity of direct evidence for authorship within the OT text, and has, on the whole, developed its theories about the origins of the books without treating such ascriptions of authorship as necessarily significant. The earliest victim of critical work on the text was the traditional (though, as we have seen, not biblical) claim that Moses wrote the Pentateuch. One of the earliest critical students of the Pentateuch, Jean Astruc (1753), analyzed Genesis into a series of "sources" that he thought Moses had used in compiling the finished work, but subsequent scholars became convinced that the compilation of these sources could owe nothing to Moses at all, but derived from a later age. Both the sources themselves, and the "redactor(s)" who wove them together, were essentially anonymous figures: we could sometimes give them a rough date, but naming them was impossible. The Pentateuchal sources were assigned sigla (J, E, D, and P), and the redactor was sometimes referred to as R. But beyond saying that such writers must have been learned scribes, scholars found it impossible to say anything about them as personalities.

Other OT books are even more clearly anonymous productions. The Proverbs may well go back into remote antiquity as folk sayings. Those who collected them together (perhaps indeed at the royal court, hence the ascription to "Solomon") are essentially unknown to us, and the collections probably passed through many stages before arriving at the books we now have. Similar things might be said about the Psalms, which are now recognized as texts that were intended for endless reuse, and to which new compositions were added from time to time.

It is only in the collections of the prophetic books that most scholars still detect some material that genuinely goes back to the prophet to whom it is attributed, and even here we must reckon with a long development in which many anonymous oracles were added to—and came to share in the prestige of—the words of the original prophet. The book of Isaiah, e.g., is probably the product of several centuries of supplementation and addition. Some think there was a continuing "school" of Isaiah, from which all the material derives, but others believe that the attribution to Isaiah is in some cases more or less arbitrary.

In sum, "authorship" is a category hardly used by most biblical critics. See DOCUMENTARY HYPOTHESIS; SOURCE CRITICISM; TRADITION HISTORY.

JOHN BARTON

AUTONOMY. Perhaps nothing stands farther removed from the biblical construction of subjectivity, or personal identity, than the modern notion of autonomy. Biblical Hebrew has no equivalent word, and the Greek word autonomia, from which the modern English term comes, is lacking in the NT. What really sets the Bible and modernity apart on this issue is the absence in the Bible of anything comparable to the modern insistence on a self-legislating subject, independent of anything outside itself as a source of knowledge or moral value. The demands of traditional societies—especially communal survival—foster the cultivation of attitudes and orientations typically contrary to cherished modernist ideals.

Among the orientations running contrary to modernity is the recurrent subordination of individual to communal goals and aspirations. This does not mean, as once was maintained, that ancient Israel lacked any concept of individuality or disdained all forms of personal autonomy and initiative. The distinction lies in how these common human values, to the extent that they represent variable "solutions" to basic human problems, are ranked or preferred. A comparison of biblical Israel and the modern West reveals not an absolute dichotomy between them with regard to personal autonomy but rather something in between. Just as modernity's preference for individual goals over those of collateral or lineal groups (employer versus family) does not allow one to totally disregard another's interests, so in the Bible individuals can have personal hopes or dreams.

That said, if moderns locate authenticity in the rejection of every form of heteronomy, characteristically the Bible proposes with equal insistence something akin to it in its ubiquitous promotion of the virtue of obedience. This is, first of all, the obedience the son owes to his father and mother (Deut 21:18-21; Prov 1:8), where the very heteronomy of that obedience is touted as a kind of educational ideal by the sages (e.g., Prov 13:24). Wisdom does not come to those who search for the truth through self-discovery and individual experimentation but to those who are careful to heed the voice of instruction from "without" in the form of the authoritative tradition. This ideal is also evident in the religious sphere, where, as Deuteronomy puts it, Israel's scrupulous obedience to the commandments will define Israel's righteousness before the LORD and the very essence of covenant fidelity (Exod 19:5). What warrants this obedience to the covenant's stipulations is not its rationality or the pragmatic benefits it brings (as in modernity), but like the natural claim of parents, the authority of the LORD as Israel's only God. The distance separating this kind of personal fidelity from modern liberal creeds is epitomized nowhere better than in the portrayal of Abraham as the ideal of obedience in Gen 22, or in the obedience of the son Jesus, who prays, "not what I want, but what you want" (Mark 14:36). What matters is that the LORD has commanded it.

Ironically, this is even the viewpoint of Israel's sages, where the traditional esteem for understanding and its ability to master a situation is juxtaposed to trust in the LORD, who alone has moral competence to legislate for humanity (see Prov 3:7). The effort to decide for oneself is bound to end in moral failure (see Prov 14:12). Hope for humanity lies in a more radical form of "heteronomy," when God will remove its old heart and replace it with a new one. God's own spirit in people will guarantee their obedience (Ezek 36:25-27; Jer 31:31-34). Where for moderns, "freedom" is the ground of morality, here morality turns on overcoming the "autonomy" of the moral agent as a knower and a doer, without diminishing humanity's responsibility. Adam and Eve's sin (Gen 2:4b–3:24) becomes paradigmatic of human guilt more generally because, in choosing an autonomous "knowing" over dependence upon God, they are guilty of what the OT elsewhere calls "pride" and sees as lying at the root of all sin (Prov 16:18; Amos 6:8; Isa 2:6-22; Zeph 3:11-13; Ezek 28:11-19). Text after text in the OT makes the point that human autonomy, with its allied notions of arrogance and self-sufficiency ("by the power of my hand I have done it"), not only are the essence of pride, but as such constitute, implicitly, a rejection of God's sovereignty (Deut 8:11-18; Isa 10:12-15; Ps 12:4-5). The horizon against which human action takes place always turns on the issue of loyalty, not personal autonomy—the question is not whether one will be ruled by another, but only whom one will serve. *See* ANTHROPOLOGY, OT THEOLOGICAL.

ROBERT A. DIVITO

AVARAN av'uh-ran [Αυαραν Auaran]. An appellation with uncertain meaning for Eleazar, Judas Maccabeus's brother, who died while heroically killing King Antiochus IV's elephant (1 Macc 2:5; 6:43-46).

AVE MARIA [Lat., Hail Mary]. A well-known prayer based on the words with which the angel GABRIEL (Luke 1:28) and ELIZABETH (Luke 1:42) greet Mary, the mother of Jesus.

The evolution of the prayer occurred over several centuries. Ancient juxtaposition of the Lukan texts is evidenced in the East by the 5th cent. CE Syrian Liturgy of Saint James and Coptic Liturgy of Saint Mark. Liturgical use of the Ave Maria in the West is dated to the 7th cent., serving first as an Offertory antiphon for the Feast of the Annunciation and gradually being included in other masses honoring the Virgin Mary. Its devotional use in the West is known from homilies and commentary on the prayer dating as early as the 11th and 12th cent. The prayer later became a staple of Catholic devotion in the Roman Breviary of 1568 and as part of the Divine Office (Liturgy of the Hours). The prayer also remained familiar to Roman Catholics through the practice of praying the Rosary. Although the prayer was eventually omitted from the Divine Office (Liturgy of the Hours) in 1955, the Second Vatican Council recognized the Little Office of the Blessed Virgin as part of the public liturgy. The Ave Maria is well known by musical audiences through the works of Franz Schubert and Charles Gounod.

Bibliography: Nicholas Ayo. *The Hail Mary: A Verbal Icon of Mary* (1994). H. Thurston. "The Origins of the Hail Mary." *Familiar Prayers: Their Origin and History* (1953).

MARY FOSKETT

AVEN ay'ven (אָוֶן 'awen). Hebrew word often translated "wickedness." As a place name (Hos 10:8) it also appears as ON (Ezek 30:17) or in a compound as BETHAVEN (Josh 7:2). The LXX identifies a city as Heliopolis (אֹון 'on) that the MT knows as Aven (Ezek 30:17). *See* AVEN VALLEY.

AVEN VALLEY ay'ven (בִּקְעַת־אָוֶן biq'ath 'awen). One of the places mentioned in AMOS' oracle against ARAM (Amos 1:5), the name could be translated as "valley of wickedness." Proposals for its location include the Beqah Valley in modern Lebanon and the Suweinit-Qelt Valley, north-northeast of Jerusalem. *See* AVEN.

AVENGE [נָקַם naqam; ἐκδικέω ekdikeō]. *Avenge* means to inflict deserved or appropriate punishment on a perpetrator of wrongs to oneself or others. The corresponding noun is *vengeance*, though that word can also denote *revenge*, malicious retaliation to repay some wrong. This family of words overlaps with *retribution*, and with such colloquial expressions as "get even" and "even the score."

The Hebrew root nqm denotes both the positive *avenge* (e.g., Josh 10:12-13; Jer 15:15) and the negative *revenge* (e.g., Ezek 25:12; Ps 8:2 [3]; Lam 3:60).

"Avenger (goel) of the blood" is a special case: goel (elsewhere translated *redeemer*) designates a member of the extended family to preserve or restore family property, honor, or lineage, while *blood* suggests that avenging the murder will restore honor or even strength to the family.

Some other Hebrew words can be synonyms, though none is restricted in meaning to vengeance or retribution: slm and gml can mean *repay, recompense*, or *requite*, while pqd and sub can describe how an evil deed will redound to the doer.

According to the Genesis narrative, vengeance is introduced to the human community by the Lord to protect the guilty fugitive, Cain (Gen 4:15). Note that the Lord renders judgment against Cain before the term *vengeance* is introduced; indeed, strict justice would have required Cain's life—a regimen not introduced until the covenant with Noah (Gen 9:1-16). In Cain's case, punishment is wandering "away from the presence of the Lord" (4:16). His mark tells those who meet him that he is protected by divine vengeance. One of his descendants, Lamech, transformed the divine threat of vengeance into the revenge of the injured (4:24).

While the word *avenge* is not used in Gen 9:5-6, the idea of retribution for killing a human is. Since all humans are created in the image of God, all are under the protection of God's law of retaliation—life for life—for murder. Human agents will impose capital punishment under the divine mandate. This text does not speak of a particular legal process; with the interposition of judges or other authorities who are neither victims, nor their surrogates, the concept of vengeance becomes less than pertinent.

With the exception of AVENGER OF BLOOD, the terminology of vengeance is rare in the legal codes of the Pentateuch. It is used only once in the Covenant Code, in Exod 21:20, specifying that a slave owner who kills a slave will be punished. By the logic of the *lex talionis*, the punishment should be death, but the substitute wording sounds as though something less severe will be exacted.

In Lev 19:18, the commandment to love a fellow Israelite is coupled with a prohibition of "taking vengeance or bearing a grudge" against anyone. This negative use of nqm indicates that the legal community aims to suppress hostility among members. This effort was not entirely successful, for supplicants besought the Lord to avenge them against enemies (Judg 16:28; Jer 11:20; 15:15; 20:12; Ps 79:10). If the supplicant relies upon God to avenge, it at least eliminates the impulse to do it oneself (1 Sam 24:12).

God's vengeance is mentioned in the table of curses at the end of the Holiness Code (Lev 26:25). This will be exacted against God's own people for breach of the covenant. The same idea appears in several prophecies of judgment against the people of God (Isa 1:24; Jer 5:9; 29; Ezek 24:8). The term may point to extralegal retaliation necessitated by the breakdown of the legal order.

Although God can take vengeance on his own people, it is much more natural and common to find the expression for military action against enemies of the nation (e.g., Num 31:3; Deut 32:35; Isa 34:8; 59:17; Jer 50:15; 51:6; Ezek 25:14). It is fairly common to pair "vengeance" against enemies with "vindication" of Israel (e.g., Deut 32:35-36). This theological usage is paralleled by usage for the nation's ruler taking vengeance against his (and the people's) enemies (e.g., 1 Sam 14:24; 2 Sam 4:8; Ps 18:48).

The NT, like Lev 19:20, condemns individuals avenging themselves. Jesus said not to resist an evildoer, but to love one's enemies (Matt 5:38-42; 6:5). Paul exhorts his people not to repay anyone evil for evil and never to avenge themselves, but to treat enemies well and allow for God's wrath instead (Rom 12:17-21). Paul is willing to promise that God will avenge those who have been wronged by others in the community (1 Thess 4:6). In an apocalyptic vision, John the Seer promises vengeance for all those who have been martyred (Rev 6:10; 19:2). *See* REDEEM, REDEEMER; VENGEANCE.

DALE PATRICK

AVENGER OF BLOOD גֹּאֵל הַדָּם go'el haddam]. "Avenger of the Blood" is a rough effort to render the Hebrew go'el haddam. In this expression, *blood* means killing, probably because the most common ways of killing in that period involved significant loss of blood.

Avenger translates a word (go'el) whose primary meaning deals with restoration or redemption (*see* REDEEM, REDEEMER). It was used of someone acting in the interests of the family to free another from slavery, to purchase land to keep it within the family, even to perform the duty of a Levirate, as well as of someone who pursues and executes the killer of a family member. Thus, by analogy, when a family member is killed, his or her loss can somehow be restored or compensated by the death of the killer (*see* BLOODGUILT; CRIMES AND PUNISHMENTS).

The full expression is found mostly in laws governing murder and asylum (Num 35:19, 21, 24, 27; Deut 19:6, 12; Josh 20:3, 5, 9, and once in a narrative, 2 Sam 14:11). It is one of the few traces of a self-help system of retribution remaining in biblical law. According to Exod 21:12-14, a killer could take sanctuary at an altar and a court would hear the case to decide whether he had killed intentionally or accidentally. The distinction is made anecdotally in Exod 21:13-14; Num 25:16-18; Deut 19:4-5, 11; and Josh 20:3. If the asylum-seeker is found guilty of murder, the avenger of the blood becomes executioner.

Courts, not the avenger, decide the fate of the accused. Thereby, family feuds are avoided. Courts are responsible to protect the innocent as well as to purify the land of bloodguilt (*see* Deut 19:10, 13). Only the guilty is executed, not other family members in addition to him (Deut 24:16) or in his place (Num 25:31).

According to Num 35; Deut 19; and Josh 20, whole cities are to be established as places of asylum, but the passages do not say whether the murder trial takes place in the city of asylum or the city in which the killing occurred (*see* CITY OF REFUGE).

The narratives of blood vengeance have features that distinguish them from regular legal practice. Second Sam 21 has David imposing the death penalty against Saul's sons in violation of Deut 24:16; this may have masked the elimination of potential rivals (notice the curse against David in 2 Sam 16:7-8). Cases involving killing on the battlefield (Judg 8:18-21; 2 Sam 8:27, 30) are probably extralegal vendettas. Second Sam 14:8-11, which purports to deal with regular law, involves an irregular royal intervention requiring the supplicant to bear guilt.

While God can be named a go'el, redeemer, and can take vengeance on humans, God is never called "avenger of the blood" (but note Ps 9:12). Perhaps the expression was too specific or too anthropomorphic to apply metaphorically to God.

It would be a mistake to associate the "blood" of our expression with the use of blood in sacrifice. Human blood is never used ritually. It is the execution of the capital offender that "purges the guilt of innocent blood from Israel" (Deut 19:13; 13:5; 17:7; 19:19; 21:9, 21; 22:22, 24; 24:7).

DALE PATRICK

AVESTA. The collection of the ancient texts of the Zoroastrians, orally composed ca. 1500–500 BCE and orally transmitted in fixed form until they were written down ca. 600 CE in a newly devised alphabet. Their language is old Iranian and closely related to Old Indic. The manuscripts are from the 13th to 19th cent.

The geographical horizon of the texts goes from Chorasmia, south of the Aral Sea, to the Helmand River in southern Afghanistan. The texts contain no other historical information, but they were known in western Iran under the Achaemenids (550–330 BCE), and Avestan ideas must have been widespread in the Near East at the time.

Among the texts are the *Yasna* (sacrifice), which accompanies the morning ritual (*yasna*) and the *Yashts* (sacrificial texts), hymns to individual deities. The *Videvdad* ("rules about how to discard the bad old gods") contains the story of how AHURA MAZDA established the lands only to have Angra Manyu produce evil things in them (ch. 1); the story about Yima, first king, and the flood (ch. 2); and the stories of how Zarathustra chased the daēwas and Angra Manyu back to Hell and of the fate the soul after death (ch. 19).

In some manuscripts, the Avestan texts are accompanied by a Pahlavi translation from the Sasanian period (224–651 CE), the *zand* (zend), hence the terms Avesta and Zand or Zand-Avesta. The originally oral *zand* tradition of legal texts, e.g., the *Videvdad*, was probably known to the Jewish community in Babylon.

Bibliography: J. Kellens. "Avesta." Vol. 3. *Encyclopædia Iranica*. E. Yarshater, ed. (1988) 35–44; P. O. Skjærvø. "The Achaemenids and the *Avesta*." *Birth of the Persian Empire: Volume 1. The Idea of Iran*. V. S. Curti and S. Stewart, eds. (2005).

AVITH ay′vith [עֲוִית ʿawith]. In Gen 36:35 and 1 Chr 1:46, Avith appears as the royal residence of the Edomite king HADAD, son of BEDAD, credited with defeating the MIDIANITES in MOAB. The LXX has alternately, Γεθθαιμ Geththaim. Some scholars associate Avith with the Aramaic name ghuwaith.

AVIV, TEL. *See* ABIB, TEL.

AVOT, KHIRBET. Khirbet Avot is a small site covering about 2 acres in eastern upper Galilee about 7 km west-southwest of Tel Qedesh and 12 km northwest of Tel Hazor. It sits on top of a hill near seasonal springs.

The site was settled during Early Bronze II then abandoned. Apart from a single possible Middle Bronze burial, the site remained abandoned until Iron I. The Iron I settlement has several broad-room buildings linked in a pattern that suggests a circular- or elliptical-shaped village. Pottery from the site shows a close connection with other northern Galilee pottery and even with Tyre. The remains suggest a lengthy Iron I settlement period interspersed with interruptions. After Iron I the site was again abandoned until the Persian period.

Khirbet Avot is one of a group of villages settled in Iron I either on new sites or after lengthy periods of abandonment. This site, along with other Iron I settle-ments in the area, is usually identified as part of the territory of Naphtali (Josh 19:32-39).

JOEL F. DRINKARD, JR.

AVVA av′uh [עַוָּה ʿawwah; עַוָּא ʿawwaʾ]. One of the towns from which the Assyrian King Sargon moved its inhabitants to repopulate the cities of Samaria after the Israelite deportation (2 Kgs 17:24).

AVVIM, AVVITES av′im [עַוִּים ʿawwim, עַוִּים ʿawwiyim]. 1. A people living near GAZA until the CAPHTORIM destroyed them, and whose land Joshua's campaigns did not take (Deut 2:23; Josh 13:3). The LXX identifies them with the HIVITES.

2. A people deported to SAMARIA by the Assyrians (2 Kgs 17:31).

AWAKE [עוּר ʿur; γρηγορέω grēgoreō]. To rouse from sleep or from lethargy to alertness or action. *Awake* is frequently used in the OT to rally attention: When Sisera's army is defeated, the people sing, "Awake, awake, Deborah! Awake, utter a song!" (Judg 5:12). The psalmist and prophet ask God to *awake* and take action on the people's behalf (Pss 7:6; 44:23; 59:5; Isa 51:9; 52:1). To *awake* also refers to emotional states: The soul *awakes* in joy and praise (Pss 57:8; 108:1); love is *awakened*, as passion kindles between lovers (Song 2:7; 3:5; 5:2; 8:4).

Awake means to restore someone to a conscious state, whether from sleep (1 Sam 26:12; Ps 102:7) or death (Job 14:10-12; Dan 12:2). Sleep is a metaphor for death, as when one "sleeps with one's ancestors" (e.g., 1 Kgs 2:10; 11:43; 14:31); therefore, to be *awake* is to live. Sometimes the line is blurred between sleep and death, when those who have died are awakened (1 Kgs 17:17-24; 2 Kgs 4:32-36; Matt 9:18, 23-24). Paul says that those who "sleep" will be the first fruits of the resurrection (1 Cor 15:20) as they awaken to new life.

Awake often describes a state of spiritual readiness and preparation. Jesus asks his disciples to stay *awake* with him in Gethsemane as he agonizes before his arrest. The disciples fall asleep literally and figuratively; they do not keep vigile with him and then disown him when he is arrested (Matt 26:40-41; Mark 14:34-38). Parables of the kingdom of heaven exhort listeners to "stay *awake*," to be prepared at any moment for the *parousia*, because they do not know the day and hour of Christ's return (e.g., Matt 24:42-51; 25:1-30; Mark 13:35-37).

MARIANNE BLICKENSTAFF

AWE [יִרְאָה yir′ah, מָגוֹר maghor]. Described theologically as *mysterium tremendum*, awe is a biblical posture in the presence of God or great leaders. The root yrʾ underlies both Jacob's fright and the awesomeness of the place in his dream encounter with God (Gen 28:17). Other examples include Pss 5:7 and 33:8. *See* FEAR.

SUSANNA W. SOUTHARD

AWL [מַרְצֵעַ martseʿa]. A boring piece lodged in a slave's ear as a symbol of permanent slave status (Exod 21:6; Deut 15:17). The piercing ceremony occurs after a slave declares a love for his or her master and a desire to remain in the household. Ear piercing also occurs in Middle Assyrian laws (ca. 1076 BCE, Assur) as a punitive measure not reserved only for slaves.

STEVE COOK

AWNING [מְכַסֶּה mekhasseh; περιβόλαιον peribolaion]. Common translation of mekhasseh that comes from the root khsh, "to cover." Ezekiel uses it in an extended metaphor portraying Tyre as a royal ship (Ezek 27:7). The awning perhaps serves to shelter passengers from the sun's rays. Scholars often note that the place of origin of the awning's blue and purple cloth, Elishah, is probably modern-day Cyprus or some part of that island. Also, scholars often note the similarity between mekhasseh and מִכְסֶה (mikhseh) used of Noah's ark (Gen 8:13) and the tabernacle (Exod 26:14; 35:11; 36:19; 39:34; 40:19; Num 3:25). *See* TABERNACLE.

STEVE COOK

AX [גַּרְזֶן garzen, קַרְדֹּם qardom; ἀξίνη axinē]. While axes were standard equipment as weapons of war for the Egyptian and Mesopotamian armies, they are seldom mentioned in the biblical text as anything other than a common implement for clearing trees (Deut 20:19; Matt 3:10), trimming branches (Judg 9:48), or cutting down a trellis of vines (Ps 74:5), in keeping with the material culture of ancient Israel that was primarily agriculturally based. Certainly, farmers took up their tools to defend themselves, but that is seldom the function assigned to the ax in the description of Israelite warfare. More often the SWORD, the SLING, the spear, and the BOW AND ARROW are used by the Israelite troops. Further, in the premonarchic period, although they owned a variety of farm implements, the Israelites lacked blacksmithing skills and were forced to take their axes, MATTOCKs, and PLOW blades to the Philistines for sharpening (1 Sam 13:20-21). Even when David conquered the Ammonite cities of Transjordan, the text only mentions the use of an ax as part of the reconstruction process (probably as a chisel as in 1 Kgs 6:7) of the destroyed city of Rabbah (2 Sam 12:31 uses maghzerah מַגְזֵרָה for iron *ax*, while the parallel text in 1 Chr 20:3 uses the similar sounding megherah מְגֵרָה). In later periods (9th cent.), an iron ax blade would have been an expensive tool, one that might be loaned out or shared by a village community, a loss that could precipitate dire financial consequences. This helps to explain the gratitude of the men when Elisha caused an iron ax head (barzel בַּרְזֶל) that had flown off its handle (compare a similar incident in Deut 19:5) to float to the surface of the

Jordan River (2 Kgs 6:5). In its juxtaposition with the saw (massor מַשּׂוֹר), the ax, even within a prophetic metaphor for Assyria's role as the tool of God's wrath in punishing Israel, is merely an everyday implement, not a standard weapon (Isa 10:15). It is only in the context of the military activities of foreign armies that the ax is wielded to mow down the enemy like trees or to smash towers in the midst of a siege (Jer 46:22; Ezek 26:9). *See* HAMMER; TOOLS; WEAPONS AND IMPLEMENTS OF WAR.

VICTOR H. MATTHEWS

AXLE. *See* WHEEL.

ʿAYIN iʾyin [ע ʿ]. The 16th letter of the Hebrew alphabet, which derives from the original Semitic word, *ʿayn-, eye*. *See* ALPHABET.

AYYAH ahʾyuh [עַיָּה ʿayyah]. A town belonging to the northern tribe Ephraim (1 Chr 7:28). The similarity of the name to Ai (עַי ʿay) may mean that Ayyah is Ai (et-Tell) or Khirbet Haiyan. The mention of AIJA in Neh 11:31 may be a reference to this same Ayyah.

AZAEL ayʾzay-uhl [Ἀζαηλος azaēlos]. Descendant of EZORA who divorced his foreign wife and put aside their children during Ezra's reform (1 Esd 9:34). The corresponding list in Ezra 10 omits the descendants of Ezora.

AZALIAH azʾuh-liʾuh (אֲצַלְיָהוּ ʾatsalyahu). "Yahu has set apart." Meshullam's son, mentioned primarily to identify his son Shaphan, whose reading of the Law motivated Josiah's reforms to set the people apart from pagan cults (2 Kgs 22:3; 2 Chr 34:8).

AZANIAH azʾuh-niʾuh [אֲזַנְיָה ʾazanyah]. A Levite whose son Jeshua placed his name on the sealed covenant document (Neh 10:9).

AZAREL azʾuh-rel [עֲזַרְאֵל ʿazarʾel; Ἀζαραηλ Azaraēl]. 1. One of the Benjamites who joined David at Ziklag (1 Chr 12:6).

2. A Levite son of Heman and head of the eleventh division of Temple musicians (1 Chr 25:18).

3. Son of Jeroham and a leader of the tribe of Dan who entered David's service (1 Chr 27:22).

4. One of the descendants of Binnui, who divorced his Gentile wife as part of the religious reform after the Babylonian exile (Ezra 10:41).

5. Son of Ahzai and father of Amashai, one of 128 mighty warriors of the priests who served in the Temple under Zabdiel's leadership (Neh 11:13).

6. A priest appointed trumpeter at the dedication of the walls of Jerusalem (Neh 12:36), perhaps the same priest as in number 5 above.

CLAUDE F. MARIOTTINI

AZARIAH az´uh-rī´uh [עֲזַרְיָה ʿazaryah, עֲזַרְיָהוּ ʿazaryahu]. Azariah is the name of numerous individuals in the OT. The name means "Yahweh has helped." The majority of these individuals are found in the books of Chronicles, Ezra and Nehemiah, and many are associated with the priestly and Levitical families.

1. Azariah, son of Zadok, served in the court of Solomon as the high priest (1 Kgs 4:2). That he is listed first among Solomon's officials indicates that Azariah's high priestly role was of great significance.

2. Azariah, son of Nathan, is another official in Solomon's administration (1 Kgs 4:5). He oversaw the 12 prefects responsible for providing monthly provisions to the palace (1 Kgs 4:7-19).

3. The son of Amaziah and Jecoliah, Azariah was the king of Judah in the first half of the 8th cent. BCE (2 Kgs 15:1-2). He is also referred to as UZZIAH (2 Kgs 15:13).

4. A descendant of Judah, son of Jacob through the lineage of Tamar (Judah's daughter-in-law (Gen 38) in the genealogical lists of Chronicles (1 Chr 2:8).

5. Another more distant descendant of Judah in the same genealogical list (1 Chr 2:38-39), whose father was Jehu and whose son was Helez.

6. Azariah, son of Ahimaaz, was a Levite and a descendant of Aaron (1 Chr 6:9 [Heb. 5:35]).

7. Azariah, son of Johanan (and father of Amariah), was a grandson of Azariah (6 above). This is probably the same Azariah of Ezra 7:3, although here his father's name is given as Meraioth. The discrepancy can partly be explained by the number of Azariahs and Amariahs in the Chronicles text. The Chronicler identifies him a priest during Solomon's time (1 Chr 6:10 [=Heb. 5:36]). Whether or not this was the same Azariah the high priest in 1 Kgs 4:2 (see 1 above) is uncertain because of the different patronym.

8. Azariah, son of Hilkiah, was another descendant of Levi through the Aaronid lineage (1 Chr 6:13 [Heb. 5:39]). Being the father of Seraiah, he was also the grandfather of Ezra (Ezra 7:1).

9. Azariah, son of Zephaniah, was the ancestor of Heman, a Kohathite Temple singer during the time of David and Solomon (1 Chr 6:36 [Heb. 6:21]).

10. Among the first returnees from exile was Azariah son of Hilkiah, identified as the chief officer of the Temple among the priests (1 Chr 9:11). His patronym is five generations long, perhaps pointing to the importance of his family lineage.

11. Azariah, son of Oded, is identified as a prophet who encouraged Asa king of Judah to pursue religious reforms (2 Chr 15:1-7). According to the Chronicler, as a result of Asa's successful reforms, Judah enjoyed a period of peace.

12–13. Two sons of Jehoshaphat, king of Judah, by the same name (2 Chr 21:2). In Hebrew, one is listed as ʿazaryah and the other as ʿazaryahu. They were killed by Jehoram, their brother, when he succeeded their father to the throne (2 Chr 21:3-4).

14–15. Azariah, son of Jehoram, and Azariah, son of Oded, were two of the commanders of hundreds who assisted Jehoida in revolting against and deposing Queen Athaliah of Judah and installing Joash in her stead (2 Chr 23:1).

16. Azariah is identified as the chief priest who led eighty other priests in preventing King Uzziah from making an incense offering on the incense altar of the Temple (2 Chr 26:17, 20). The tension between a priest and a king in the cultic role is one that can be found elsewhere in Samuel and Kings.

17. Azariah, son of Johanan, was one of the Ephraimite chiefs who stood with the prophet Oded in preventing the army of Israel from bringing Judahite captives into Samaria following Pekah's defeat of Ahaz (2 Chr 28:12).

18–19. Two Levites who participated in the cleansing of the Temple under King Hezekiah (2 Chr 29:12). The first, identified as the father of Joel, was a descendant of Kohath, and the second, the son of Jehallelel, hailed from the family of Merari.

20. The chief priest and chief officer of the Temple during Hezekiah's reign (2 Chr 31:10, 13).

21. Azariah, son of Maaseiah, was one of those who repaired the section of the wall of Jerusalem next to his house (Neh 3:23-24).

22. One of the leaders of the exiles who returned to Judah from Babylon under the leadership of Zerubbabel (Neh 7:7).

23. A Levite who assisted the people in understanding the Torah read by Ezra (Neh 8:7).

24. One of the priests who set his seal on the covenant that the returnees from exile made to bind themselves to the commandments of Yahweh (Neh 10:2 [Heb. 10:3]).

25. A leader who took part in the dedication of the wall of Jerusalem (Neh 12:33). It is uncertain whether or not he is the same Azariah who repaired a section of the wall of Jerusalem (see 21 above).

26. Azariah son of Hoshaiah was one of two men who rejected Jeremiah's prophetic message not to go down to Egypt after the destruction of Jerusalem (Jer 43:2). Instead, they forcibly took a group of people from Judah, including Jeremiah and Baruch, to Egypt.

27. One of the three friends of Daniel, whose was given the Chaldean name Abednego (Dan 1:6-7, 11, 19; 2:17). Together with Daniel, Hananiah, and Mishael, he consumed only vegetables and water rather than defile himself by eating royal food. Threatened with the fiery furnace for refusing to worship the golden image that the king made, he and his friends stood firmed (Dan 3). In the LXX tradition, Azariah is attributed with a prayer. See AZARIAH, PRAYER OF; DANIEL, ADDITIONS TO.

JEFFREY KUAN

AZARIAH, PRAYER OF az´uh-ri´uh. A communal confession of Israel's sinfulness (*see* Dan 9:4-19; Ezra 9:6-15; Neh 9:6-37; Bar 1:15-3:8). The prayer appears in Greek texts of Dan 3 (between vv. 23 and 24) in Codex Chisianusand in Theodotion (*see* SEPTUAGINT). The prayer is divided into two parts (3:26-37 and 38-45): a contrast between God (3:26-38) and the community (3:29-37) in the first, and a description of the people's needs (3:38) and desire to worship and obey (3:39-41), concluding with a plea for divine help (3:42-45) in the second.

Arguments that this was an independent prayer of national lament (*see* Pss 44, 74, 79, 80) link to studies that revert the text to Hebrew. This insertion is part of the Greek translator's effort to preserve independent spiritual traditions. The redactor saw that AZARIAH ("The Lord has helped") manifested his name by inserting the prayer. The three youths are witnesses to Israel's fidelity to the commandments (Dan 1:8-16) but, like the martyrs of 2 Macc 6–7, they identify themselves with their compatriot's burden of disobedience and sin. As the entire community prayed in the confession of sins on the DAY OF ATONEMENT, these youths pleaded for the restoration of Temple worship after God had forgiven Israel's infidelities for the sake of the divine Name and for the patriarchs. This prayer follows the pattern of traditions of martyrs who express solidarity with the sinful Israelites and who offer themselves as vicarious victims for the entire community (*see* Dan 9:4-19).

Bibliography: Carey A. Moore. *Daniel, Esther and Jeremiah: The Additions* (1977) 39–61.

LAWRENCE FRIZZELL

AZARIAS az´uh-ri´uhs [Ἀζαρίας Azarias]. Greek form of Hebrew name Azariah. Angel Raphael's assumed name (Tob 5:13; 6:7, 14; 7:9; 9:2).

AZARU az´uh-roo [Ἀζουρος Azouros, Ἀζαρος Azaros]. According to 1 Esd 5:15, 432 of his descendants returned from exile in Babylon to Jerusalem and Judea. For a similar list, see Neh 10:17-18.

AZAZ ay´zaz [עֲזָז ʿazaz]. Bela's father in Reuben's (i.e., Judah's) genealogy (1 Chr 5:8).

AZAZEL uh-zay´zuhl [עֲזָאזֵל ʿazaʾzel]. 1. The goat used in DAY OF ATONEMENT rituals (Lev 16:8, 10, 26). Azazel could mean *scapegoat* or indicate the animal's destination (a *sharp* or *rugged* place).

2. A demon named Azazel, leader of angels who corrupt humankind, is bound and buried under sharp rocks in the desert (*1 En.* 8:1-4; 10:4-6). *See* EXPIATION; SACRIFICE AND OFFERINGS.

AZAZIAH az´uh-zi´uh [עֲזַזְיָהוּ ʿazazyahu]. The name means "Yahweh is strong." 1. A Levite who played the

lyre as the ARK OF THE COVENANT entered Jerusalem (1 Chr 15:21).

2. The father of Hoshea, Ephraimite chief officer under King David (1 Chr 27:20).

3. A Temple overseer during HEZEKIAH's reign (2 Chr 31:13).

AZBUK az´buhk [עַזְבּוּק ʿazbuq]. Nehemiah's father who ruled part of Bethur and helped rebuild the Jerusalem wall after the exile (Neh 3:16). A non-Israelite name.

AZEKAH uh-zee´kuh [עֲזֵקָה ʿazeqah]. A city of Judah, located in the foothills of SHEPHELAH) between the coastal plain and the central hill country (Josh 15:35; Neh 11:30). Identified with modern Tell Zakariya, Azekah served as a Judean border fortress, which—along with its counterpart Socoh—guarded the Valley of Elah (the modern Wadi es-Sunt) one of the three major ancient roads into the Judean highlands. The military significance of the city is suggested by biblical and extra-biblical evidence. The Israelites' battle against the five Amorite kings at GIBEON ends at Azekah (Josh 10:10-11). The military encounter between Israel and the Philistines in which David and Goliath duel takes place in the Valley of Elah, between Socoh and Azekah (1 Sam 17:1-2). Rehoboam later fortified Azekah (2 Chr 11:9). Azekah is listed as one of the remaining fortified cities of Judah against which the Babylonian army encamped (Jer 34:7), a notice substantiated by Lachish Letter IV. That ostracon, presumably written by the commander of a Judean outpost, relates to his superior at Lachish that "we cannot see (the signals of) Azekah," indicating the destruction of that city. *See* ELAH, VALLEY OF.

JEREMY M. HUTTON

AZEL ay´zuhl [אָצֵל ʾatsel]. Father of six sons, Eleasah's son, and a descendant of Saul's son Jonathan, mentioned in the list of Benjamin's descendants (1 Chr 8:37-38; 9:43-44).

AZETAS uh-zee´tuhs [Ἀζητάς Azētas]. A family head mentioned with Kilan whose descendants returned from the exile (1 Esd 5:15). Absent from lists in Ezra 2:16 and Neh 7:21.

AZGAD az´gad [עַזְגָּד ʿazgadh; Ἀσγαδ asgad]. A name meaning "Gad is mighty," Azgad's descendants are among returnees to Jerusalem with ZERUBBABEL (Ezra 2:12//Neh 7:17; 1 Esd 5:13) or with EZRA (Ezra 8:12; 1 Esd 8:38 [Ἀσγαθ Asgath]). Azgad also appears among those signing a sealed commitment to the Law (Neh 10:15).

AZIEL ay´zee-uhl [עֲזִיאֵל ʿaziʾel]. A Levite harp player who performed for the procession of the ark to Jerusalem (1 Chr 15:20). *See* JAAZIEL.

AZIZA uh-zi´zuh [עֲזִיזָא ‘aziza’]. One of Zattu’s six sons who sent away his foreign wife and their children following Ezra’s instructions concerning the people of the land (Ezra 10:27). *See* SARDEUS.

AZMAVETH az´muh-veth [עַזְמָוֶת ‘azmaweth]. 1. A warrior from BAHURIM, one of David’s mighty men known as the “Thirty” (2 Sam 23:31; 1 Chr 11:33), and father of JEZIEL and PELET (1 Chr 12:3).

2. The second of the three sons of JEHOADDAH (1 Chr 8:36), a descendant of King Saul through JONATHAN.

3. The son of ADIEL and overseer of David’s royal treasury (1 Chr 27:25).

4. Levitical singers from this Benjaminite village, also known as BETH-AZMAVETH (Neh 7:28), participated in the dedication of Jerusalem’s walls (Neh 12:29). Forty-two descendants of Azmaveth were among those who returned with ZERUBBABEL from Babylonian captivity (Ezra 2:24).

CLAUDE F. MARIOTTINI

AZMON az´mon [עַצְמוֹן ‘atsmon; Ασεμωνα Asemōna]. A town in the area of Canaan’s southern boundary (Num 34:4-5). Joshua 15:4 mentions the town as being within the southern extent of Judah’s tribal allotment. The place has been identified as Ain Qoseimeh and as Ain Muweilih.

AZNOTH-TABOR az´noth-tay´buhr [אַזְנוֹת תָּבוֹר ’aznot tavor]. Landmark, perhaps a town, that forms the western boundary of the land allotted to the Naphtali tribe (Josh 19:34).

AZOR ay´zor [Αζώρ Azōr]. The only biblical reference to Azor, son of ELIAKIM and father of ZADOK, is in Matthew’s genealogy of Jesus (Matt 1:13-14).

AZOR, TEL ay´zor. Tel Azor is located approximately 6 km southeast of Jaffa. It is usually identified with Azor named in the LXX in place of the Hebrew word *Jehud* in Josh 19:45. The site is also named in an Assyrian inscription as one of the cities of the king of ASHKELON conquered by SENNACHARIB.

Explorations at Azor have focused on the cemetery, with burials from the Chalcolithic period through the Iron Age. The remains of a Crusader castle (Chateau des Plains) occupy the top of the tell.

The Chalcolithic burials are marked by rock-cut tombs and ossuaries. The ossuaries are often decorated with geometric or zoomorphic designs. Two Early Bronze I burial caves contained secondary burials, burial offerings, jewelry, and weapons. Late Bronze and Iron I burials contained human and animals buried side by side.

Numerous Iron Age burials are of five distinct types: pit burials with individual burials, burials in large stone jars broken and joined at the shoulders, burials in coffins of unfired bricks, cremation—the charred skeletal remains in a large stone jar, and communal burials presumably of several generations of a family. Much of the pottery in these burials is Philistine and Cypriot-Phoenician.

JOEL F. DRINKARD, JR.

AZOTUS, MOUNT uh-zoh´tuhs [ὄρος Αζωτος horios Azōtos]. Mount Ashdod (1 Macc 14:34; Acts 8:40). *See* ASHDOD.

AZRIEL az´ree-uhl [עַזְרִיאֵל ‘azri’el]. 1. Head of a Manassehite family in Transjordan (1 Chr 5:24).

2. Father of Jerimoth, chief of the tribe of Naphtali under King David (1 Chr 27:19).

3. Father of Seraiah, one of those sent by King Jehoiakim to arrest Jeremiah and Baruch (Jer 36:26).

AZRIKAM az´ri-kuhm [עַזְרִיקָם ‘azriqam]. 1. A Benjaminite and the first of the six sons of Azel, a descendant of King Saul’s son Jonathan (1 Chr 8:38; 9:44).

2. An officer in charge of Ahaz’s palace, killed by ZICHRI, “a mighty warrior of Ephraim,” who served in the army of PEKAH, king of Israel, when the Northern Kingdom attacked Judah (2 Chr 28:7).

3. A Levite from the clan of Merari, he was the son of Hashabiah and father of Hasshub and grandfather of SHEMAIAH, who was one of the Levites in charge of the outside work of the Temple after the exile (1 Chr 9:14; Neh 11:15).

4. The last named of the three sons of Neariah and a descendant of ZERUBBABEL and David (1 Chr 3:23).

CLAUDE F. MARIOTTINI

AZUBAH uh-zoo´buh [עֲזוּבָה ‘azuvah]. 1. The mother of King Jehoshaphat and daughter of Shilhi (1 Kgs 22:42; 2 Chr 20:31).

2. Caleb’s first wife who bore him three sons (1 Chr 2:18-19).

AZZAN az´uhn [עַזָּן ‘azzan]. Moses appointed PALTIEL, son of Azzan, to represent ISSACHAR among the leaders who helped allot land to the tribes (Num 34:26). The name *Azzan* means “(the deity) has shown strength.”

AZZUR az´uhr [עַזּוּר ‘azzur]. 1. One of the names written on a sealed commitment to the Law (Neh 10:17).

2. Father of JEREMIAH’s rival HANANIAH (Jer 28:1).

3. Father of JAAZANIAH whom Ezekiel, in a vision, sees among a group of twenty-five men (Ezek 11:1).

Bb

B. Letter symbolizing the 4th cent. manuscript Codex Vaticanus. *See* VATICANUS, CODEX.

BAAL I. *See* BAAL, KING OF TYRE.

BAAL II. *See* BAAL, KING OF TYRE.

BAAL bay´uhl, bah´ahl [בַּעַל baʿal]. In the OT the word baʿal occurs both as a noun meaning "lord, master, husband," and as the proper name of a deity. Used in the second sense, Baal is the pagan god most frequently mentioned in the Bible and the archetypical rival of Yahweh; the classic indictment of the Israelites says that, instead of serving Yahweh, they "went after" or "whored after" Baal or the Baals (Deut 4:3; Judg 8:33; 1 Kgs 18:18; Jer 2:23; 9:13).

Because of the regular occurrence of the plural "Baals" (Judg 2:11; 3:7; 8:33; 10:6, 10; 1 Sam 7:4; 12:10; 1 Kgs 18:18; Jer 2:23; 9:13; Hos 2:13, 16-17; 11:2; 2 Chr 17:3; 24:7; 28:2; 33:3; 34:4), it has long been held by biblical scholars that Baal was not a divine personality in his own right but a designation of an otherwise unspecified local divinity. However, the discovery of the cuneiform tablets from Ras Shamra (ancient UGARIT) has furnished compelling evidence that Baal was a major figure in the mythology and the cult of the ancient Syrians. The main sources for determining the profile of Baal are the Ugaritic texts that constitute the so-called Baal Cycle. They corroborate and expand the other data on Baal, both biblical and extrabiblical.

The first issue that the Ugaritic texts resolve concerns the identity of Baal. In view of the regular occurrence of the parallelism between Haddu and Baal, the proper name of the god is actually Haddu (*see* HADAD), Baal being a traditional epithet used as another name of the deity. The identity between Haddu and Baal helps to explain the frequent occurrence of Haddu in the theophoric names of the Ugaritic kings while Baal was the patron deity of the dynasty and the leading god of Ugarit. Ancient Near Eastern parallels for this use of an epithet as proper name are BEL (for the Babylonian god MARDUK) and Adonay (for Yahweh; *see* ADONAI, ADONAY). The custom to treat Baal as a divine name has an old pedigree: Baal occurs as a divine name in god-lists from Abu-Salabikh (ca. 2600 BCE), in the Ebla texts (ca. 2300 BCE), and as a theophoric element in Amorite names of the Old Babylonian period (ca. 1750 BCE).

Once it has been established that in the Ugaritic mythology Baal and Haddu are two names for a single deity, a follow-up question concerns the relation between the one Baal and his various names and local manifestations. A look at an Ugaritic list of gods shows that at least seven Baal-gods received sacrifice in the official cult (Pardee 2002, 12–16). Something similar holds for Haddu. Different cities and different populations worshiped their own particular Haddu (or Adda, HADAD, etc.). Such diversity in the worship of the god does not imply that each local Baal or Haddu had its own mythology, however. Though differentiated by local identity, they all partake of a common stock of mythological motifs. In other words, the tale of the Ugaritic Baal cycle is valid for Haddu of Aleppo, Hadad-Rimmon of the Arameans, and the Canaanite deity Baal known from the Bible.

Baal is fundamentally a storm-god. That is why Baal carries the epithet "Rider of the Clouds" and the iconography depicts him as a man of huge dimensions, brandishing a club of thunder in his one hand and a spear of lightning in the other. As a storm-god, Baal has two faces. He can be a terrible power of devastation as he wrecks ships at sea and cuts down trees in the forest, but he is also a beneficial god who rains on arid plains and gives fertility to the fields. The myths about Baal have their background in the natural phenomena associated with the storm. The battle between Baal and Yam ("Sea") is informed by the experience of sailors in foul weather, and the battle against Mot ("Death") takes its cue from the succession of spring fertility (Baal), the withering summer season (Mot), and the rainy season in fall (Baal).

The Ugaritic texts known as the Baal Cycle (Smith 1997) have a narrative plot that consists of three episodes. The first episode tells about the battle for kingship between Baal and Yam. Yam takes the initiative by sending his messengers to the assembly of the gods demanding that they acknowledge his claim to kingship. The message is addressed first of all to El, the father of the gods and the president of the assembly. El complies with the wish of Yam and orders Kothar the craftsman to start building a palace. All the gods seem to accept Yam's superiority—all except Baal. Baal refuses to honor Yam's claim to kingship and engages a battle. After a first undecided round, Kothar fashions two weapons, one called Yagarrish ("He chases"), the other Ayyamarri ("He expels all"). These weapons prove to be the key to Baal's victory. He defeats Yam and seizes kingship in his stead. In the words of the poem, "Yam is truly dead, and Baal rules as king."

The second episode of the cycle is devoted to the building of a palace for Baal. Since El as the head of the pantheon has to grant permission to build, ANATH goes to him to plead in favor of Baal. When she is unsuccessful, she persuades the wife of El and mother of the gods, Athirat (known in the OT under the name of ASHERAH), to intercede with El on behalf of Baal. In the end, El gives in to the entreaties of his consort and orders Kothar to begin building a royal palace for Baal. One particular feature of the palace is a point of discussion between Baal and Kothar, in which Kothar insists on installing a window, that Baal adamantly refuses. When the palace is finished and Baal hosts a housewarming party for his brothers the gods, he changes his mind about the window and orders its construction. The aperture makes the inhabitants of the palace more vulnerable to intruders, but it also creates a way for the blessings of Baal to reach the earth; without this "rift in the clouds" there would be no rainfall.

The third and final episode of the Baal Cycle concerns his troubles with MOT ("Death"). At the inauguration feast of his palace, Baal sends word to Mot informing him that Baal's rule is now official. Mot challenges him to a contest, boasting that he will swallow Baal alive. Frightened by this threat, Baal proclaims his submission to Mot, who then orders Baal to make his way to the underworld, meaning that he is to join the dead. Baal obeys and disappears, to the consternation of El who, at the announcement of Baal's death, performs the proper rites of mourning. After the burial of Baal, the gods seek to replace him with Athtar who evidently is not up to the task as Baal's throne proves to be too large for him. Wild with grief for her lost lover, Anath seizes Mot and turns him into bits and pieces; "with a sieve she winnows him, with a fire she burns him, with millstones she grinds him, in a field she sows him." The annihilation of Mot means the return of Baal, though as the god of death Mot cannot die. In the end, however, he is forced to accept Baal's kingship; the extent of his own rule is limited by the superior rule of Baal.

The three episodes from the Baal Cycle seem only loosely connected. Independently from one another, the motif of the battle with Yam and the battle with Mot have counterparts in other parts of the ancient Near East in connection with gods of the same type as the Ugaritic Baal. The earliest reference to the battle against Yam comes from the Mari archives (ca. 1750 BCE). In a prophetic letter to King Zimrilim, Addu of Aleppo reminds the ruler that at his enthronement the god gave him the weapons with which he slew Tiamtum ("Sea"). According to oblique references in the Ugaritic texts, the battle against Yam also involved the slaying of the sea-monsters Litan and Tunnan. These mythological feats are ascribed to Yahweh in Pss 74:12-17; 89:10-15; Isa 27:1. The biblical references show that the traditional motif remained popular until the Persian and, perhaps, the Hellenistic Period. It has been speculated that the tale of the battle between Marduk and Tiamat, described in ENUMA ELISH, is borrowed from the Baal mythology as well.

The conflict between Baal and Mot is a mythological expression of the seasonal succession and its impact on the agricultural cycle. The period of intense summer heat is conceived as a time of death; the soil is parched and all fertility seems gone. In the language of mythology, this is the time of Baal's disappearance. The absent deity is either gone on a journey or, in the worst scenario, he is dead. The contest at Mount Carmel between Baal and Yahweh, represented by the Baal prophets on the one hand and Elijah on the other, should be understood against this mythological background (1 Kgs 18:20-46). The confrontation takes place in the third year of a great drought (1 Kgs 18:1; compare 17:1); the land yearns for rain. According to the tenets of the Baal mythology, the god has to come back from the underworld to terminate the reign of Mot. Elijah refers to the god's absence by suggesting that he is "on a journey or perhaps asleep" (1 Kgs 18:27). Since shouts, sacrifice, and self-mutilation fail to wake Baal from his sleep, he proves powerless in the day of need. The story demonstrates that rain is a gift from the one God "who neither slumbers nor sleeps" (Ps 121:4).

Baal's journey to and from the netherworld shows that he belongs to the category of "dying and rising gods." In the mythological reality, Baal really dies; he has not merely vanished. Another Ugaritic myth says that he dies from the attack of beasts while hunting (*KTU* 1.12). That motif has a distant echo in the myth about Adonis being killed by a boar but resurrecting to life (Lucian, *Syr. d.* 6; Ribichini 1995). The Amorite tribal name Yamutbal (variant: Emutbal), "Baal has died," is witness to the antiquity of the tradition. In the 5th cent. BCE, the prophet Zechariah refers to "the mourning for Hadad-Rimmon in the plain of Jezreel" (Zech 12:11), which shows that the ritual for the dying storm-god was still being celebrated or at least remembered at the time. The death of Baal at the onset of summer is followed by his resurrection in autumn. It stands to reason that the new year festival in autumn would ritually celebrate the god's return, but our knowledge of the festival is too limited to be certain about the matter).

The Baal mythology has influenced the biblical conception of Yahweh in two ways. In some respects the writers of the Bible emphasize the difference between Baal and Yahweh. The narrative of the contest at Mount Carmel is an example because the author implies that Yahweh, unlike Baal, does not sleep or go on a journey. The author of Hab 1:12 is even more outspoken, assuming the original text says that Yahweh "does not die." In other respects, however, Yahweh has been given traits that originally belonged to Baal. Rain and fertility are his gifts to the Israelites, as Hosea insists. More striking even is the transfer of such motifs as the victory over

Yam and Leviathan (Ps 74:12-17; Isa 27:1) and the claim to kingship from Baal to Yahweh. The takeover of Baal mythology for the greater glory of Yahweh also takes the form of literary borrowing: both Pss 20, 29 go back to Canaanite hymns to the storm-god.

Some modern authors consider the correspondences between Yahweh and Baal too striking to be the result of a mere transfer. In their view, the similarities between the two gods are due in large part to the fact that Yahweh, just like Baal, is in essence a storm-god. However, the evidence does not appear to support this interpretation. The one Canaanite deity with whom Yahweh has a relationship of near identity is not Baal, but El. The divine pair El and Athirat from the Ugaritic texts is matched by the pair of Yahweh and Asherah, both in the inscriptions from KUNTILLET ʿAJRUD and Khirbet el-Qom (see QOM, KHIRBET EL) and in several Bible passages. Like El, Yahweh presides over the divine council. In the Bible, El is no rival to Yahweh because El is understood as a different name for Yahweh (see GOD, NAMES OF). The transfer of Baal mythology to Yahweh does not follow from a unity of character, then, but from the claim that the one God of Israel holds all the powers divided over various gods in a polytheistic context. See BAAL, PLACE; BAAL-ATH; BAALATH-BEER; BAAL-BERITH; BAALE-JUDAH BAAL-GAD; BAAL-HADAD; BAAL-HAMON; BAAL-HANAN; BAAL-HAZOR; BAAL-HERMON; BAAL-MAL-AGE; BAAL-MEON; BAAL-PEOR; BAAL-PERAZIM; BAALS; BAAL-SHALISHAH; BAAL-SHAMEM; BAAL-TAMAR; BAAL-ZEBUB; BAAL-ZEPHON.

Bibliography: Alberto R. W. Green. *The Storm-God in the Ancient Near East* (2003); Thorkild Jacobsen. "The Battle between Marduk and Tiamat." *AOS* (1968) 104–108; Tryggve N. D. Mettinger. *The Riddle of Resurrection: "Dying and Rising Gods" in the Ancient Near East* (2001); Johannes C. de Moor. *New Year with Canaanites and Israelites* (1972); Johannes C. de Moor. *The Seasonal Pattern in the Ugaritic Myth of Baʿlu According to the Version of Ilimilku* (1971); Charles F. Nims and Richard C. Steiner. "A Paganized Version of Psalm 20:2-6 from the Aramaic Text in Demotic Script." *AOS* (1983) 261–74; Dennis Pardee. *Ritual and Cult at Ugarit* (2002); Mark S. Smith. "The Baal Cycle." *Ugaritic Narrative Poetry.* Simon B. Parker, ed. (1997) 81–180; Simon B. Parker. *The Ugaritic Baʿal Cycle, Volume 1: Introduction with Text, Translation and Commentary of KTU 1.1–1.2.* VTS vp 55 (1994); Giovanni Pettinato. "Pre-Ugaritic Documentation of Baʿal." Gary Rendsburg, et al., eds. *The Bible World: Essays in Honor of Cyrus H. Gordon* (1980) 203–09; Sergio Ribichini. "Adonis." *DDD* (1995) 12–17.

KAREL VAN DER TOORN

BAAL, KING OF TYRE. Two kings of Tyre who carry the name "Baal," an abbreviated form of a theophoric personal name of the type Mattan-Baal or Baal-milku. 1. Baal I was King of Tyre during the reigns of the Assyrian kings Esarhaddon (680–69 BCE.) and Assurbanipal (668–27 BCE.). In 677 Esarhaddon defeated Sidon and gave Baal the cities of Marubbu and Sarepta (ZAREPHAT) that had belonged to Sidon. The treaty between Esarhaddon and Baal obliges the Tyrian king to strict political loyalty to his Assyrian overlord; however, Baal apparently was able to maintain a certain measure of independence while officially a vassal of Esarhaddon and Assurbanipal.

2. Baal II [Βααλ Baal] is mentioned by Josephus (*C. Ap.* 1.156) as a contemporary of Nebuchadnezzar II (604–562 BCE). He is the successor of Ittobaal III.

Bibliography: H. Jacob Katzenstein. *The History of Tyre from the Beginning of the Second Millennium B.C.E. until the Fall of the Babylonian Empire in 538 B.C.E.* (1973).

KAREL VAN DER TOORN

BAAL, PERSON bayʿuhl [בַּעַל baʿal]. 1. A man listed in the Reubenite genealogy (1 Chr 5:5-6) as a contemporary of the Assyrian king TIGLATH-PILESER III (744–27 BCE).

2. A Benjaminite who was the brother of KISH, Saul's father. He was from Gibeon (1 Chr 8:30; 9:36).

KAREL VAN DER TOORN

BAAL, PLACE. *See* BAALATH-BEER.

BAALS bayʿuhl [בַּעַל baʿal, בְּעָלִים beʿalim]. The prophets of the OT frequently accuse the Israelites of going after the Baals (Judg 2:11; 3:7; 8:33; 10:6, 10; 1 Sam 7:4; 12:10; 1 Kgs 18:18; Jer 2:23; 9:13; Hos 2:13, 17; 11:2; 2 Chr 17:3; 24:7; 28:2; 33:3; 34:4). Since the word baʿal occurs both as a noun denoting "lord, master, husband" and as the name of the Syrian storm-god, the plural allows two different interpretations. The prophets might be implying that their audience was worshiping anonymous local deities or that they were devotees of the Syrian god Baal in one or the other of his local manifestations. The use of the definite article (habbeʿalim) might be taken to favor the first understanding; the popularity of the god Baal in the milieu of the early Israelites militates in favor of the second. In order to reach a verdict on the matter we must first look at the kind of plurality that is implied in the expression "to go after the Baals."

The veneration of locally differentiated Baals has left its imprint on the toponymics of ancient Israel. In the Bible there are a score of place-names that contain the element baʿal: Baal-Gad, Baal-Hammon, Baal-Hazor, Baal-Hermon, Baal-Judah, Baal-meon, Baal-Perazim, Baal-Shalisha, and Baal-Tamar. The element baʿal in these names stands for a deity. The optional variant Beth-baal-meon (Josh 13:17; *KAI* 181:30) for Baal-meon

(Num 32:38; 1 Chr 5:8; *KAI* 181:9) implies that the Baal-toponyms refer to a sanctuary ("house") for a local god Baal. The alternation between Beth-peor (Josh 13:20) and Baal-peor leads to the same conclusion.

The extrabiblical comparative evidence of compounded Baal names exhibits two types. The most common compound contains as its second element the name of a mountain or a city; examples include Baal-Zaphon, Baal-Carmel, Baal-Lebanon (b'l lbnn, *KAI* 31:1-2), Baal-Tabor, and Baal-of-Sidon (*KAI* 14:18). The second type is compounded with a field of action, an attribute, or a habitat; examples include Baal-marqod ("Lord of the Dance"), Baal-marpe' ("Lord of Healing"), b'l smdh ("Baal of the Club," *KAI* 24), and BAAL-SHAMEM ("Lord of the Heavens"); a biblical example is BAAL-BERITH ("Lord of the Covenant"). Names in which the element ba'al is compounded with the name of a family or a clan are notoriously absent from the evidence. The god Rakib-El is called the ba'al of the royal family of Sam'al (*KAI* 24:16; 215:22), but that relationship has not yielded a compounded Baal name.

Considering the comparative evidence, as well as the fact that the majority of the biblical Baal toponyms is compounded with a geographical name, prudence counsels us to interpret the biblical Baal toponyms primarily as references to Baals differentiated by the locality where they are believed to dwell. The point is not superfluous, as it has been argued that the second element of the biblical Baal toponyms is usually the name of a family or a clan (Rosen 1988). While this is certainly a possibility deserving serious consideration, there is no unambiguous evidence to support it. Oftentimes a name could refer to either a clan or a topographical area; faced with a choice between the two, we should probably interpret the name as a topographical indication. On the assumption that we are dealing with localized Baals, there is good reason to take the name Baal in the compounded Baal toponyms of the Bible as the proper name of the Syrian storm-god.

For many modern students of ancient religion it is not clear why one particular member of the West-Semitic pantheon should be worshiped at different localities under different names as though he were not a single god but a family of gods. Before we attempt to interpret the phenomenon of plurality of one divine persona, we must acknowledge that the worshipers of the time were well aware of the plurality. In the official cult at Ugarit, there were seven Baal gods who received sacrifice (Pardee 2002). Those who compiled the list were familiar with the mythology of Baal, and knew that the name stood for a single figure in the official mythology; in the cultic reality, however, they had to distinguish a plurality of Baal figures.

An obvious parallel from modern times to the pluriformity of a single god is the veneration of the Holy Virgin. Though worshipers know that there is only one Mary, Mother of Jesus, they distinguish her different local manifestations. A crucial element in the differentiation is the physical representation of the Holy Virgin through her image; the images are obviously different; and since worshipers address their devotion not to an abstract heavenly figure but to the Virgin as they know her from her image, the local form of the Virgin matters greatly. A similar mechanism was operating in antiquity: the plurality of Baals was a fact of the cult; though a single figure in mythology, Baal had as many cultic manifestations as he had images, all of which were entitled to offerings.

Bibliography: Dennis Pardee. *Ritual and Cult at Ugarit* (2002); Baruch Rosen. "Early Israelite Cult Centres in the Hill Country." *VT* 38 (1988) 114–17.

KAREL VAN DER TOORN

BAALAH bay′uh-luh [בַּעֲלָה ba'alah]. The term, associated with several places in Judah, means "Lady" or "Mistress"; the identity of the deity is unknown.
1. A location, also known as KIRIATH-JEARIM, along the boundary of Judah's tribal territory (Josh 15:9; 1 Chr 13:6).
2. A town located in the southern part of Judah (Josh 15:29). In the list of Simeonite towns in Judah, it is called BALAH (Josh 19:3; 1 Chr 4:29, BILHAH).
3. A mountain mentioned in the list of locations along Judah's tribal boundary (Josh 15:11).

KAREL VAN DER TOORN

BAALATH bay′uh-lath [בַּעֲלָת ba'alath]. A place located in DAN (Josh 19:44). It appears in lists of Solomon's construction projects (1 Kgs 9:17-18; 2 Chr 8:5-6). The term is common in West Semitic languages as the name of a goddess. The occurrence of Baalath as a place name attests to the spread of the cult of the goddess. The term means "Lady" or "Mistress," and is the counterpart of ba'al, *Lord.* The identity of Baalath is disputed and probably varies depending on context. We do not know for certain with which particular goddess the Israelites identified her, though on the whole the goddess ANATH, the "sister" of BAAL, is the most likely candidate.

KAREL VAN DER TOORN

BAALATH-BEER bay′uh-lath-bee′uhr [בַּעֲלַת בְּאֵר ba'alath be'er]. "Mistress of the Source." A town marking the border of the tribal territory of Simeon (Josh 19:8). It is called Baal in 1 Chr 4:24-33. It is generally assumed that these are the same. The "Mistress" of the source is the goddess BAALATH. The actual name of the goddess is presumably ANATH. The later name *Baal* is best explained as the result of a corruption.

KAREL VAN DER TOORN

BAALBEK. The ancient city of Heliopolis is located near the modern Baalbek and lies between Mount

Lebanon and the ANTILEBANON mountain range. There was a Hellenistic settlement at the site controlled by the Itureans as part of the kingdom of Chalcis. In 15 BCE Heliopolis formed part of the territory of the Roman colony established on the coast at Beirut; at the end of the 2nd cent. CE, as part of the emperor Septimius Severus' reforms of Syria, Heliopolis became a colony in its own right, Colonia Iulia Augusta Felix Heliopolis.

Kevin Butcher
Figure 1: Temple of Jupiter.

Heliopolis was important as a cult centre of Zeus, the equivalent of the Roman deity Jupiter. The sanctuary was remodelled on a grand scale in the 2nd cent. CE and covered much of the earlier Hellenistic temple two blocks for the podium have been found in nearby quarries each weighing well over 1,000 tons. The corner columns, each cut from a single block of limestone each weighed some 130 tons. The temple features on coins of Heliopolis minted in the late 2nd cent. and in the 3rd cent. CE. At Baalbek, Jupiter is often associated with the Roman deities Venus and Mercury. Other temples were constructed at the site, such as 'the temple of Bacchus,' though the precise dedication is not known.

Bibliography: Kevin Butcher. *Roman Syria and the Near East* (2003); Fergus Millar. *The Roman Near East, 31 BC–AD 337* (1993); Friedrich Ragette. *Baalbek* (1980).

DAVID W. J. GILL

BAAL-BERITH bay'uhl-bi-rith' [בַּעַל בְּרִית ba'al berith]. A deity worshiped in Israel during the time of the judges, particularly in the region of Shechem. The name occurs once in reference to the Israelite's worship of this deity after the death of Gideon (Judg 8:33), and once in reference to the deity's temple in Shechem (Judg 9:4).

In ancient Israel and Canaan, divine names functioned differently from how modern readers might expect. The main gods (Canaanite El or Baal, or Israelite Yahweh, for example) could be worshiped in unique ways in particular locations, perhaps even becoming fragmented into different local "manifestations." Baal-Berith at Shechem was probably a local version of a larger divine reality.

The name is an epithet (a kind of formalized nickname) that means "Lord of the Covenant," and technically could be a title for any deity, including Yahweh. A deity named EL-BERITH ("God of the Covenant") is mentioned in Judg 9:46, and it is unclear whether these titles refer to the same or different deities, or who those Gods might be. One strong possibility is that both titles refer to the Canaanite "high God" El and that over time they came to be identified with the Israelite God, Yahweh. In this view, the cult of Baal-Berith at Shechem was part of the legitimate origins of the worship of Yahweh in Israel, and only later was remembered as an unorthodox religious practice.

BRYAN D. BIBB

BAAL CYCLE. *See* BAAL.

BAALE-JUDAH bay'uh-lee-joo'duh [בַּעֲלֵי יְהוּדָה ba'ale yehudhah]. Location of the ark of God before being moved to Obed-edom and then Jerusalem (2 Sam 6:2). Same as KIRIATH-JEARIM (2 Sam 6:21).

BAAL-GAD bay'uhl-gad' [בַּעַל גָּד ba'al gadh]. A location in the BAQAH VALLEY at the foot of Mount Hermon (Josh 11:17; 12:7; 13:5). Since Baal was the god of Mount Hermon (*see* Judg 3:3), the name Baalgad presumably refers to BAAL the deity. The Hebrew word gadh means *fortune*. Gad is likely a reference to Baal in his capacity as patron deity of (the family of) Gad, not Gad the tribe.

KAREL VAN DER TOORN

BAAL-HADAD. *See* BAAL; HADAD.

BAAL-HAMON bay'uhl-hay'muhn [בַּעַל הָמוֹן ba'al hamon]. The location of a vineyard of King Solomon in Song 8:11 cannot be satisfactorily identified. It is a possible namesake of Balamon known from Jdt 8:3, but since Balamon is located in the vicinity of Dothan, Baal-hamon and Balamon are presumably two different localities. The meaning of the term ba'al hamon is "lord of plenty," hence "owner of wealth."

KAREL VAN DER TOORN

BAAL-HANAN [בַּעַל חָנָן ba'al khanan]. A personal name meaning "Baal has shown mercy." The name Baal-hanan is theophoric, and the god referred to is the Syrian storm-god BAAL. 1. An Edomite ruler (Gen 36:38-39; 1 Chr 1:49-50).

2. An official of King David (1 Chr 27:28).

3. The ruler of the Phoenician city of Arvad mentioned on the Assurbanipal Prism.

KAREL VAN DER TOORN

BAAL-HAZOR bay'uhl-hay'zor [בַּעַל חָצוֹר ba'al khatsor]. A locality near Ephraim (2 Sam 13:23) commonly identified with Jebel el-'Atsur, the highest top of Mount Ephraim. If Hazor is the name of the mountain peak, BAAL is the Syrian storm-god, and the town owes its name to the veneration of Baal as Lord of the mountain. Hazor (khatsor) probably means "enclosure, cattle pen."

KAREL VAN DER TOORN

BAAL-HERMON bay'uhl-huhr'muhn [בַּעַל חֶרְמוֹן ba'al khermon]. A mountain at the border of the hill country of Lebanon (Judg 3:3) mentioned as part of the territory of the tribe of Manasseh (1 Chr 5:23). Baal-Hermon combines the name of a deity with the name of Mount Hermon. Since Mount Hermon is identified as Jebel esh-Shaikh, the southern peak of the Anti-Lebanon, Baal-Hermon was presumably one of the peaks on the eastern slopes of Mount Hermon. See BAAL; BAALS; HERMON, MOUNT.

KAREL VAN DER TOORN

BAALIS bay'uh-lis [בַּעֲלִים ba'alis]. A 6th cent. BCE Ammonite king (Jer 40:14). The Hebrew spelling of his name is incomprehensible; it contains the name Baal, but it lacks an appropriate predicate. It could either be an abbreviated form of the official name used as a pet name, or a corruption due to dialectal differences between Ammonite and Judahite. The 1984 discovery of a seal impression containing the name Baal-Yisha 'at Tall al-'Umayri is evidence in favor of the second possibility. The LXX (Jer 47:14) reads the name Baalis as Belisa. There is reason, then, to understand Baalis as a corruption of Baal-Yisha'; whether the Baal-Yisha' of the seal is identical with Baalis is another matter. See 'UMAYRI, TALL AL.

Bibliography: Larry G. Herr. "The Servant of Baalis." *BA* 48 (1985) 169–72.

KAREL VAN DER TOORN

BAALISM. *See* BAAL.

BAAL-MALAGE [ᵈ ba-al-ma-la-ge-e]. The treaty between the Assyrian king Esarhaddon and Baal of Tyre mentions Baal-malage alongside Baal-shamem and Baal-zaphon as native Tyrian deities that will punish the Tyrians should they rebel against the Assyrian king.

BAAL-MEON bay'uhl-mee'on [בַּעַל מְעוֹן ba'al me'on]. A place in Moab (Num 32:38; Ezek 25:9; 1 Chr 5:8) also known under the names Bethbaal-meon (Josh 13:17), Beth-meon (Jer 48:23), and Beon (Num 32:3). It appears on the MOABITE STONE and Samaria Ostracon 27. Usually identified with Khirbet Ma'in (8 km SW of Madaba), Baal-meon was an Israelite city conquered by the Moabites.

BAAL refers to the Syrian god, and *meon* means "dwelling-place." It presumably refers to a settlement with a local Baal cult that gave the town its name.

KAREL VAN DER TOORN

BAAL-PEOR bay'uhl-pee'or [בַּעַל פְּעוֹר ba'al pe'or]. Baal-peor is both a toponym (Hos 9:10) and the name of a deity (Num 25:3-5). According to Num 25:1-9, the people of Israel participated in the sacrificial cult of Baal-peor at the invitation of the Moabite women. The event took place at Shittim in the plains of Moab northeast of the Dead Sea. The biblical information on Baal-peor is limited; it is said that he was the god of Moabite women (Num 25:2); that his cult included a sacrificial meal in honor of the dead (Num 25:2; Ps 106:28); and it is intimated that his worship had aspects of sexual debauchery (Num 25:1, 6-8). According to Num 31:16, it was BALAAM, the man of nocturnal visions (Num 24:3-4), who had incited the Moabite women to invite the Israelite men to join them in the festivities for Baal-peor. Other texts do not make the connection between Balaam and Baal-peor.

Some link the name Peor to the Hebrew verb p'r (פער, "to open wide") and suggest that it refers to the mouth of the netherworld (Spronk 1986, 231–33). On this interpretation, Baal-peor is the Lord of the entrance of the netherworld. While it is clear from Ps 106:28 that the cult of Baal-peor is associated with the worship of the dead, there is no firm basis for relating the nature of the deity to the supposed meaning of "peor." On the assumption that the Syrian storm-god BAAL is also a god with power over the underworld, Baal-peor can then be taken as a local manifestation of the god.

It is clear from Num 23:28 that Peor is the name of a mountain. Used as a toponym, Baal-peor is a variant of Beth-peor (Deut 3:29; 4:46; 34:6; Josh 13:20), which suggests that the full name of the place, unattested in the OT, would have been Beth-baal-peor. It may have been identical with the BAMOTH-BAAL. The burial of Moses at Beth-peor (Deut 34:6) could be significant of the chthonic associations of Baal-peor.

Bibliography: Klaas Spronk. *Beatific Afterlife in Ancient Israel and in the Ancient Near East* (1986).

KAREL VAN DER TOORN

BAAL-PERAZIM bay'uhl-pi-ray'zim [בַּעַל פְּרָצִים ba'al peratsim]. A location south of Jerusalem remembered for David's victory over the Philistines (2 Sam 5:18-20;

1 Chr 14:9-11). The name of the place is associated with the verb parats (פָּרַץ "to break through"). This etymology is unlikely. Perazim is the name of a mountain between Jerusalem and Bethlehem (Isa 28:21). The element ba'al is best understood as the proper name of the Syrian storm-god, here compounded with the name of a mountain. A connection with Perez the ancestor of David is unlikely.

KAREL VAN DER TOORN

BAALSAMUS bay'uhl-say'muhs [Βααλσαμος Baalsamos]. In 1 Esd 9:43, someone who assisted Ezra in the public reading of the book of the law (MAASEIAH in Neh 8:4).

BAAL-SHALISHAH bay'uhl-shal'uh-shuh בַּעַל שָׁלִשָׁה a'al shalishah]. A town, most likely located in the Jordan Valley or on the slopes opposite Gilgal, from which a man came to meet Elisha (2 Kgs 4:42). The name is connected to "the land of SHALISHAH" (1 Sam 9:4) that Saul passed through searching for his father's donkeys.

The first part of the name most likely refers to the Syrian storm-god. The second element is problematic; it could be a personal name (1 Chr 7:35, 37), referring to the cult of Baal as patron deity of the Shalishah clan. Alternatively, it is possible that the element Shalishah refers to a topographical feature.

KAREL VAN DER TOORN

BAAL-SHAMAYIM. *See* BAAL-SHAMEM.

BAAL-SHAMEM [בעל שמם b'l shmm; Aram. שְׁמִן־ בְּעַל b'l shmyn]. A name meaning "Lord of Heaven" (Augustine, *Quaest. Hept.* 7.16: dominus coeli). The name does not appear in the OT. One of the earliest references to Baal-shamem occurs in a bilingual inscription from Karatepe, from which we learn that Baal-shamem is originally a storm-god. Baal-shamem could be another designation of the Syrian storm-god BAAL. In the course of the first millennium BCE, Baal-shamem developed into a supreme god distinct from the Syrian storm-god. In the Hellenistic period Baal-shamem is identified with Zeus (or Zeus Hypsistos) and associated with the sun (*see* especially Philo of Byblos in Eusebius, *Praep. ev.* 1.10, 7). The Seleucid kings identified the god with Zeus Olympios.

The postexilic custom of referring to Yahweh as "the God of Heaven" is not unrelated to the cult of Baal-shamem in that period. The emergence of this designation in reference to the God of the Jews fits in with the tendency in the Persian and Hellenistic periods to focus religious worship on a single supreme deity located in heaven.

Baal-shamem may be alluded to in the Book of Daniel, which refers to the "appalling abomination" (שִׁקּוּצִים מְשֹׁמֵם shiqqutsim meshomem) present in

the Jerusalem temple (Dan 9:27; 11:31; 12:11). It is possible that this alludes to a Zeus image installed in the Jerusalem temple by Antiochus IV; if so, it would reflect a religious policy in which the authorities made an attempt to fuse the god of the Jews and the principal god of the Greek civilization.

KAREL VAN DER TOORN

BAAL-TAMAR bay'uhl-tay'mahr [בַּעַל תָּמָר ba'al tamar]. The place of the Israelites' victory over the Benjaminites. The site is located between Gibeah and Bethel (Judg 20:33). The name preserves the memory of a cult place dedicated to the Syrian storm-god BAAL. *Tamar* might be the designation of the date palm or the personal name of a woman, perhaps in her capacity as ancestress of a clan.

KAREL VAN DER TOORN

BAAL-ZEBUB bah'uhl-zee'buhb, [בַּעַל זְבוּב ba'al zevuv]. According to the account of 2 Kgs 1, the Israelite King Ahaziah sent messengers to consult "Baal-zebub, the god of Ekron" concerning whether or not he would recover from a wound due to a fall. Discussions concerning the identity of the deity focus on the second element of his name. Scholars are divided as to whether ba'al zevuv is the original name; many hold that zevuv is a deliberate distortion of zavul, "prince." If the second interpretation is correct, the god Baal-zebub would be the same as the Syrian storm-god Baal, who, in the Ugaritic texts, frequently carries the epithet zbl, "prince."

Those who take the view that Baal-zebub is the real name of the deity can point to the Septuagint rendering Βααλ μυια baal myia, i.e., "Baal of the fly." The Hebrew word zevuv does indeed mean "fly" or "flies" as a collectivity; one may compare Ugaritic dbb and Akkadian zubbu. A deity might be called "Lord of the Flies" despite the fact that flies are associated with illness because sculpted flies could have had an apotropaic function. An ingenious solution to the riddle suggests that the flies in question were ornamental flies applied to the statue of the god, analogous to the Mesopotamian goddess Belet-ili who had a fly necklace (*see CAD Z* 155). On this view, Baal-zebub was "a Baal figure with some kind of fly ornament that signifies the apotropaic and healing function of the deity" (Tangberg 1992). The principal objection against the interpretations on the basis of the name Baal-zebub, however, is the fact that this name does not occur outside the OT; its closest analogue is the Mesopotamian "Goddess of the Honeybees" (Ińtar ńa nubtim in Mari texts, dNIN.NIM.DU6.GA in Sumerian texts from the Third Dynasty of Ur). Since we know that the Hebrew scribes did use dysphemism to avoid the name of pagan deities (such as בֹּשֶׁת bosheth, "shame," instead of ba'al), zevuv is still most plausibly explained as a derisive alteration of the real name.

Even before the Ugaritic texts made us familiar with the expression zbl b'l ar', "Prince Baal of the Earth," some biblical scholars already suggested that the actual name of the god of Ekron was Baal-zebul, mainly on the basis of the occurrence of BEELZEBUL in the NT. They could refer to the Hebrew word zevul, "lofty abode," which goes back to the same root as Ugaritic zbl, "prince." In the expression zbl b'l ar', the word ar', "earth," stands for the underworld (Dietrich & Loretz 1980). In other words, the title presents the Syrian storm-god Baal in his capacity as lord of the underworld. From the Baal mythology as it has been preserved in the Ugaritic Baal Cycle we do know that Baal had power over MOT ("Death"). Ritual texts present him as a healer who can save his devotees from death by curing their disease.

A sober assessment of the available evidence leads to the conclusion that Baal-zebub, the god of Ekron, is, in fact, the Syrian storm-god who had power to revitalize the sick. The fact that the Philistine population of Ekron had adopted this Syrian deity is no cause for surprise; the popularity of Dagan among the Philistines shows that the Philistine settlers took over the pantheon of the Phoenicians and the Syrians as their own.

Bibliography: Manfried Dietrich and Oswald Loretz. "Die Ba'al-Titel b'l ar' and aliy qrdm." *UF* 12 (1980) 391–93; Arvid Tangberg. "A Note on Ba'al-Zebub in 2 Kgs 1:2, 3, 6, 16." *SJOT* 6 (1992) 293–96.

KAREL VAN DER TOORN

BAAL-ZEPHON bah'uhl-zee'fon [צְפֹן בַּעַל ba'al tsephon]. In the OT, Baal-zephon occurs as the name of a place in the Egyptian delta (Exod 14:2, 9; Num 33:7). The location is unknown.

The name Baal-Zephon is not Egyptian but West-Semitic, meaning "Baal of Mount Zaphon." Mount Zaphon is Jebel el-Aqra', 40 km north of Ugarit, known in Hittite and Akkadian as Khazi and in Greek as Kasios (hence Zeus Kasios). In the Ugaritic mythology, Mount Zaphon is the abode of the divine council. As the king of the gods, Baal naturally has his palace there too. Baal-zaphon is none other, then, than the Ugaritic Baal, the Syrian storm-god also known as Haddu or HADAD. The popularity of his cult was such that it also gave its name to a Phoenician settlement in the Nile delta.

Though Baal-zaphon is an allomorph of BAAL, cult lists will often distinguish Baal-zaphon from other incarnations of Baal. This multiplicity of BAALS has to do with the cultic reality of different statues of Baal, each of which had its own name and temple. Dedications to Baal-zaphon make it clear that his worshipers venerated him particularly as a patron god of navigation; votive anchors were a usual offering to the god. The link between Baal-zaphon and navigation explains the popularity of his worship among Phoenician sailors and, thus, the spread of his cult.

Although navigation was alien to the Israelites, the mythology surrounding Mount Zaphon has left traces in the OT. When Ps 48 speaks about the "holy mountain" of God, it calls Mount Zion "the summit of Zaphon" (יַרְכְּתֵי צָפוֹן yarkethe tsafon, Ps 48:3). The psalm offers an instance of borrowing from Ugaritic mythology for the greater glory of the God of Israel. In Ps 20:3, on the other hand, the Hebrew scribe who adapted the Phoenician hymn substituted "Zion" for "Zaphon" (Nims & Steiner 1983). There is no ground for speculating that the exodus from Egypt was originally ascribed to Baal-zaphon, and only secondarily to Yahweh.

Bibliography: William Foxwell Albright. "Baal Zephon." *Festschrift Alfred Bertholet zum 80. Geburtstag* (1950) 1–14; Otto Eissfeldt. *Baal Zaphon, Zeus Kasios und der Durchzug der Israeliten durchs Meer* (1932); Charles F. Nims and Richard C. Steiner. "A Paganized Version of Psalm 20:2-6 from the Aramaic Text in Demotic Script." *JAOS* 103 (1983) 261–74.

KAREL VAN DER TOORN

BAANA bay'uh-nuh [בַּעֲנָא ba'ana']. The meaning of Baana could be derived from ben 'anah (בֶּן עָנָה, "son of distress") or from ba'al 'anah (בַּעַל עָנָה, "Baal has answered"). 1. The son of Ahilud, one of Solomon's twelve prefects responsible for supplying provisions for the palace one month of each year. He represented the regions Taanach, Megiddo, and Beth-shean (1 Kgs 4:12).

2. The son of HUSHAI, another prefect of Solomon, responsible for the regions Asher and Bealoth (1 Kgs 4:16).

3. The father of ZADOK, one of those who repaired a portion of Jerusalem's walls during the days of Nehemiah (Neh 3:4).

GNANA ROBINSON

BAANAH bay'uh-nuh [בַּעֲנָה ba'anah]. A variant of BAANA. 1. One of the two sons of RIMMON, the Benjaminite. He and his brother Rechab were captains of Saul's son Ishbosheth's raiding bands. They murdered Ishbosheth and brought his head to David, thinking that they would be rewarded but, to their great disappointment, David ordered their hands and feet to be cut off and their mutilated bodies to be hanged as a public warning against regicide (2 Sam 4:2-12).

2. The father of Heleb ("Heled" in 1 Chr 11:30) from Netophah, one of the Thirty mighty men of David (2 Sam 23:29).

3. One of the leaders who returned from Babylonian exile with Zerubbabel (Ezra 2:2; Neh 7:7). He could be Baana #3 (1 Esd 5:8).

4. One of the leaders who, with Nehemiah the governor, set his seal on the firm covenant to observe the law of Moses, perhaps the same person who returned from the exile.

GNANA ROBINSON

BAARA bay´uh-ruh [בַּעֲרָא ba'ara']. In Benjamin's genealogy, a wife whom Shaharaim dismissed, perhaps a Moabite, who apparently bore him no children (1 Chr 8:8-11). It is not mentioned whether she returned to her family.

BAASEIAH bay´uh-see´yuh [בַּעֲשֵׂיָה ba'aseah]. A Levite descendant of the Koharthites and an ancestor of ASAPH, who served in the Temple by singing (1 Chr 6:25). See MAASEIAH.

BAASHA bay´uh-shuh [בַּעְשָׁא ba'sha'] The third king of Israel after its sucession from Davidic rule in Jerusalem (ca. 902–886 BCE). Of the tribe of Issachar, Baasha performed the first in a series of coups d'état*s* in Israel when he overthrew NADAB, son of Jeroboam I of Ephraim, while the latter lay siege to the Philistine city of GIBBETHON (1 Kgs 15:27-28). Baasha, in a prolonged military dispute with King ASA of Judah (1 Kgs 15:16, but contrast 2 Chr 16:1, which implies a dispute of short duration toward the end of Asa's long rule), attempted to move Israel's border to within 9 km of Jerusalem by fortifying RAMAH. Asa outmaneuvered him by bribing BENHADAD of Damascus to attack Israel from the north. With Baasha's attention diverted in this way, Asa returned the border northward by fortifying Geba and Mizpah (1 Kgs 15:22; compare Jer 41:9).

Bibliography: D. Elgavish. "Objective of Baasha's War against Asa." *Studies in Historical Geography and Biblical Historiography.* G. Galil and M. Weinfeld, eds. (2000)141–49.

WESLEY IRWIN TOEWS

BABA BATHRA. A tractate of the MISHNAH, paralleled in the TOSEFTA, relating to property, sales, bequests, and contracts. Baba Bathra (literally, the "last gate") is the final third of Mishnaic material on torts. There is Palestinian and Babylonian TALMUD commentary on this tractate.

BABA METSI'A. A tractate of the MISHNAH, paralleled in the TOSEFTA, relating to possession, guardianship, usury, and hire. Baba Metsi'a (literally, the "middle gate") is the second third of Mishnaic material on torts. There is Palestinian and Babylonian TALMUD commentary on this tractate.

BABA QAMA. A tractate of the MISHNAH, paralleled in the TOSEFTA, relating to injuries, public and private domain, and restitution. Baba Qama (literally, the "first gate") is the initial third of Mishnaic material on torts. There is Palestinian and Babylonian TALMUD commentary on this tractate.

BABATHA. A Jewish woman, who resided in Maoza, south of the DEAD SEA, at the turn of the 2nd cent. She perished in the wake of the Bar Kochba revolt (135 CE; *see* BAR KOCHBA, SIMON). All the information about this woman is derived from her document archive, which was discovered in a cave in the Judean Desert, where she found refuge after the failure of the revolt. From the archive we learn that she came from a wealthy family who migrated from EN-GEDI to Maoza. They owned date groves, which Babatha inherited. Yet it is also clear that she was illiterate. She was married and widowed twice between 120 and 130 CE. Her first marriage (ended before 124 CE) left her a widow and mother to a son. Some of the papers in her archive document her struggle to obtain the guardianship of her son, a struggle that ultimately failed. Her second marriage (127 CE) was to a man from En-Gedi who was already married to another woman, and who was substantially poorer than Babatha, since he borrowed money from her in order to dower his grown daughter from his other marriage. He did not live long after this marriage, and his death brought about an ugly struggle over his inheritance between his two wives.

The Babatha archive is an important resource for Jewish women and the Jewish family's legal and social history. It shows some of the possibilities that were available to women in marriage practices, property ownership, inheritance, and education, according to, and in contradiction of typical LAW IN EARLY JUDAISM, which is recorded in RABBINIC LITERATURE. *See* FAMILY; MARRIAGE; MANUSCRIPTS FROM THE JUDEAN DESERT; WOMEN IN THE NT; WOMEN IN THE OT.

TAL ILAN

BAB-EDH-DHRA'. An Early Bronze Age (3300–2200 BCE) site located in the southeastern Dead Sea plain region. The site overlooks the Lisan peninsula of the Dead Sea. It is comprised of a 12-acre walled town and a 30-acre cemetery. Excavations by Lapp from 1965–1967 and the Expedition to the Dead Sea Plain (EDSP) from 1975–1981 have delineated the history of the walled town site, which was occupied from 3150 BCE to 2200 BCE and shared the cultural traits of the well-known Early Bronze Age town culture of the Southern Levant. In the cemetery, four different types of burial patterns were traced, including two types of shaft tombs, and round and rectangular burial houses. The tomb types correspond to the major phases of the town site.

Bab-edh-Dhra' has often been associated with the "cities of the plains" (Gen 13:12; 19:29). After a 1924 survey in the region dated the ruins of Bab-edh-Dhra' as the only 3rd millennium BCE site in the region, W. F. Albright speculated that the ruins may have been a sanctuary for the "cities of the plains," which probably were located under the continually rising waters of the southern basin of the Dead Sea. This theory became a widely accepted hypothesis. More recent studies have demonstrated that the level of the Dead Sea is dependent on rainfall in the highlands and was much higher during the humid climate of the Early Bronze Age. The higher level would eliminate the southern basin as a location for the cities of the plains. The discovery of Numeira, a second Early Bronze Age II walled town site nearby has prompted many to relate the two sites to the biblical traditions about Sodom and Gomorrah (Gen 18–19). *See* SODOM.

Bibliography: W. E. Rast and R. T. Schaub. *Bâbedh-Dhrâʾ: Excavations at the Town Site (1975–1981)* (2003).

R. THOMAS SCHAUB

BABEL bay´buhl [בָּבֶל *bavel*]. Genesis 11:1-9 records the OT's version of how Babylon received its name. The inhabitants of the earth/land (אֶרֶץ *ʾerets* can mean both) all speaking one language, come together in a plain in SHINAR to build a city whose showpiece is a tower reaching heavenward/skyward (vv. 1-4). For whatever reason, Yahweh, upon inspection, is dismayed. Yahweh takes the action necessary to abort this real estate project (vv. 5-9).

Yahweh confuses the common language (בָּלַל *balal* vv. 7, 9), thus ending the possibility of verbal communication among the builders, and then scatters them well beyond the borders of Shinar. One might translate v. 9 as, "For that reason its name was called Babel (*bavel*), for there Yahweh made a babble of/babbled (*balal*) the language of the whole earth/land."

Clearly, v. 9 does not supply a literal etymology of Babylon. If it did, the name of the city would be *Balalon*, not *Babylon*. The name of this megacity in Akkadian is Bab-ilu (Sumerian Ka-dinger), "gate of the god (Marduk)." In later Neobabylonian it was identified as Bab-ilani, "gate of the gods," the source of the spelling "Babylon." The interpretation of the famed metropolis as *Confusionville* or *Babbleburg* would have come as a complete surprise or shock to the residents of Babylon.

The Hebrew verb *confuse* (*balal*) is most often a technical term in cookery where it refers to the mixing up of food products. Hence, in certain offerings to God, oil is mixed (*balal*) with flour in order to moisten the flour (Exod 29:2; Lev 2:4, 5; 7:10, 12; 9:4; 14:21; 23:13; Num 7:13). Apart from Gen 11:7 and 9, the only other time **balal** appears in a context unrelated to food is Hos 7:8*a*, "Ephraim mixes with/is mixed up with the nations."

There are two problems of interpretation related to the Babel story. The first is that 11:1-9 gives the impression that *Babylon* as a name emerges first in conjunction with this incident. Yet, Gen 10:8-10 suggests a Babylon in existence before Gen 11. If one reads chs. 10 and 11 linearly then there is indeed confusion in the OT about when all this confusion started. But if 11:1-9 is understood as a kind of flashback, then the apparent discontinuity disappears.

The second issue in the Babel story focuses on meaning. Is Babel God's punishment on humanity's pride for trying to breach the barrier between God and humankind, between heaven and earth? Or, is Babel God's nudging and reorienting of the occupants away from their preoccupation with security to the role of earth/land fillers (Gen 1:27)? Are the Babelians punished by God or pushed by God? Both readings are possible.

VICTOR P. HAMILTON

BABES, BABIES, BABY. *See* BIRTH; CHILD, CHILDREN.

BABOON [תֻּכִּיִּים *tukkiyyim*]. One type of animal brought to Solomon (1 Kgs 10:22; 2 Chr 9:21). *See* ANIMALS OF THE BIBLE; PEACOCK.

BABYLON, OT bab´uh-luhn [בָּבֶל *bavel*]. City in southern Mesopotamia, located on a branch of the Euphrates (latitude 32°33' N, longitude 44°26' E), 59 mi. (90 km) southwest of Baghdad. Babylon rose to prominence early in the 2nd millennium BCE, as the region experienced significant sociopolitical changes, and became the capital of important political entities throughout various periods of ancient Near Eastern history, playing a significant role in Israelite history and ideology. The name *Babylon*, and several ideas associated with it, were transported to the West by means of the OT, and subsequently the NT and classical authors.

    A. The Name "Babylon"
    B. Archaeological Data
    C. Political History
    D. Babylon and the OT
    Bibliography

A. The Name "Babylon"

Babylon went by a variety of names in antiquity. The earliest form of the toponym appears to have been *babil(a)*, which has neither Sumerian nor Akkadian origin, and so perhaps derives ultimately from the population inhabiting Mesopotamia before the Sumerians, the so-called proto-Euphratean population. Although the meaning of this early name for the city is long since lost to antiquity, it appears to have given rise to an Akkadian form, created through popular etymology, *bab-ilim*, "Gate of God," and a Sumerian equivalent, *ka-dingirra*, also meaning "Gate of God." It is impossible to be certain which is derivative of the other, but it is more likely that the Akkadian was created by wordplay on the older *babil(a)*, and preceded the Sumerian equivalent. The later plural Akkadian form, *bab-ilani*, "Gate of the Gods," became *babulon* in Greek, resulting in the modern name "Babylon." Several literary names for the city, such as **tintirki**, probably became popular in the

12th cent. BCE. The toponym was eventually used to designate the greater region of southern Mesopotamia, or "Babylonia," in what is today southern Iraq, Kuwait, and parts of western Iran.

B. Archaeological Data

Babylon was located in Mesopotamia, the site of the world's first urban civilization. Many features converged to make urbanization possible, but primary among them was access to the slow-moving water of the Euphrates, and to a lesser extent the Tigris, which makes the alluvial plain of southern Mesopotamia easily irrigable. Urbanization took place in this region in the late 4th and early 3rd millennia BCE. The Euphrates did not flow through a single channel at this time but through several branches along which the most important cities were established. Babylon itself was located along the Araḫtum-branch, which in later texts is identified with the Euphrates itself. We have no textual witness to the city's existence prior to the middle of the 3rd millennium BCE, at which time it had little political significance. Potsherds have been reported from the surface of the site from the mid-third millennium BCE.

After centuries of unscientific travelers and researchers visiting the site, scholarly excavations were conducted from 1899 to 1917 by the Deutsche Orientgesellschaft under the direction of Robert Koldewey. The work of the Germans, and subsequent excavations of the city in the 20th cent. were largely limited to the Neo-Babylonian levels because of the rise of ground water, and it has not been possible to do much with deeper and earlier strata. The Neo-Babylonian city yielded a strongly fortified inner and outer circuit of walls made of baked bricks. The outer wall included Nebuchadnezzar's summer palace on the northern part of the mound. Herodotus remarked on the unusual thickness of these magnificent walls, which were entered by eight gates, each named after a god. One particular city gate, the famed Ishtar Gate, was spectacularly decorated in blue enameled bricks, serving as a background for alternating red and white dragons symbolizing MARDUK, god of Babylon, and bulls, symbolic of Adad. The city center was formed by the temple precinct Esagila, containing the cult rooms of Marduk, his wife, and other gods and goddesses. Religious structures had a square or rectangular courtyard, with a lopsided room to the side through a central entrance followed by a second room, in which stood a podium as the base of the divine statue. Situated just to the north of Esagila was the most famous architectural achievement of ancient Babylon, the temple-tower Etemenanki ("house of the foundation of heaven and earth"), the seven-staged brick "tower of BABEL," which had been sought for centuries. German excavators in 1913 uncovered the building's remains, which had been torn down in the time of Alexander the Great. Unfortunately little was left of the monument because of the ancient practice of reusing mud bricks for building materials.

The city contained a number of royal palaces. Nebuchadnezzar built a magnificent new palace late in his reign, the ruins of which contained a museum in which he housed a large collection of "antiquities," including monumental pieces from across northern Mesopotamia and Syria-Palestine, revealing the king's interest in archaeology and history. Family dwellings in Babylon's domestic quarter were complex buildings with a large courtyard, entered through a reception room. Outer rooms surrounded the whole courtyard and included annexes and other buildings surrounding the foyer. The ceramic and pottery remains illustrate daily life, as well as thousands of commercial and legal inscriptions on clay tablets. The city's enduring literary legacy is illustrated by the discovery of cuneiform astronomical inscriptions dating late in Babylon's history (approximately 75 CE).

C. Political History

The history of ancient southern Mesopotamia may be periodized according to intermittent empires built with the city of Babylon at their center. The first of these periods is marked by the arrival of the AMORITES into central and southern Mesopotamia. Their appearance constitutes a turning point in ancient history at the turn of the 2nd millennium BCE, when Amorite city-states began to supplant the older Sumero-Akkadian culture of the previous millennium. The first dynasty of Babylon was established by Amorites in the 19th cent. BCE and rose to prominence under its 6th ruler, HAMMU-RABI (1792–1750 BCE). At this time, the city of Babylon rose from relative obscurity to become the political center of the country, and then an empire extending for the first time beyond southern Mesopotamia into the northwestern bend of the Euphrates River. This period of Babylon's history as the capital of an empire is known as the Old Babylonian period (2003–1595 BCE).

Near the end of the Old Babylonian period, the role of the Amorites began to wane, and Kassite rulers took up governance of Babylonia for several centuries in what is most conveniently called the Middle Babylonian Period (1595–1155 BCE). During these centuries, the Kassites were only one of numerous ethnolinguistic groups in Babylonia, but they were ready and able to fill the power vacuum created by the collapse of the Old Babylonian dynasty. Kassite nationalism, with a relatively stable economy and political rule, resulted in the elevation of Babylonian culture and prestige across the ancient world in an age of internationalism.

Due to the successes of the Kassite rulers, Babylon came to be venerated as an ancient holy city, an important symbol of power and legitimacy for rulers hoping to dominate the ancient world. During the opening centuries of the 1st millennium, control of the city became the objective of Assyrian kings to the north, who considered Babylon to be the cultural capital of all Mesopotamia. Eventually, a dynasty of native Babylonians (perhaps Chaldeans ethnically) defeated the Assyrians and restored Babylon to a brief period of renewed grandeur. During the 7th and 6th cent. BCE, Babylon rose again to premier international status and enjoyed a spectacular period of strength and prosperity. Although this Neo-Babylonian Empire (625–539 BCE) may be perceived as a mere interlude between the Assyrians and Persians, the grandeur of the empire, especially under NEBUCHADNEZZAR II, and its legacy in the biblical and classical sources, left an indelible mark on subsequent history, making this one of the most important and interesting periods of ancient Babylonian history. With the rise of CYRUS, Babylon became a province in the Persian Empire and was eventually taken by Alexander the Great and his successors. During the Hellenistic period, Babylon lost its political supremacy to Seleucia on the Tigris. But throughout its history, even including periods of political weakness, Babylon was significant as a cultural and religious center, whose influence reached across the ancient Near East to the West in Greco-Roman times and came to symbolize all of Eastern culture.

D. Babylon and the OT

The OT contains nearly 300 references to Babylon, the region of Babylonia, or its inhabitants, as well as 89 references to the ethnically precise term "Chaldea/n/s." Because of its international and cultural significance, and its role later in destroying Jerusalem and deporting large portions of its citizens, Babylon came to carry theological significance in the Bible even beyond its obvious historical importance. The city itself came to symbolize ungodly power.

The first references to Babylon in the Bible, and the only ones in the Pentateuch, are found near the conclusion of the Primeval History in the term *Babel* (Gen 10:10; 11:9). The Tower of BABEL episode (Gen 11:1-9) serves as the literary climax of the Primeval History, and traces the vitiating consequences of sin in humankind (Gen 3–11). The tower is to be identified with a Mesopotamian ziggurat, or stepped pyramid, which developed in the early stages of Mesopotamian urbanization. Perhaps because of Babylon's role later in Israel's history or simply because of its cultural significance more generally, the city came to symbolize for the Israelites the worst kind of idolatry, degrading the divine in pagan polytheism. The Tower of Babel narrative concludes in an ironic wordplay. Although Akkadian speakers understood the name of the city as "gate of God," the Israelites knew better. God turned humankind's gate of heaven into confusion: "Therefore it was called Babel [bavel], because there the Lord confused [balal] the language of all the earth" (11:9). In this derogatory interpretation of the city's name, Babylon represents humanity's unified rebellion against God and is therefore marked by confusion, turning the "gate of heaven" into "confusion of speech."

Babylon's historical significance is obvious by the many references in the OT historical books to events in which Babylon plays a central role. Names of specific Babylonians (such as Merodach-baladan, Nebuchadnezzar, Evil-merodach, Nebuzaradan, etc.) were once only dimly known through the classical sources, but are now attested in native Babylonian sources and shed considerable light on our understanding of the biblical narratives. Beyond such specifics, the retrieval of native Babylonian sources since the 19th cent. has made it possible to reconstruct, in part, the history of ancient Babylon, giving insight into the general history of this city mentioned so frequently in the historical books.

In addition to these historical connections between Babylon and Israel—and indeed, partly because of these connections—Babylon also plays an important theological and ideological role in the OT. Especially notable in this regard is the pejorative tone adopted so frequently by Israelite prophets when referring to Babylon, a nation used as an instrument of divine wrath against Israel, which destroyed Jerusalem and deported large portions of its citizens. Thus Babylon is referred to by the ancient literary cipher known as ATHBASH, in which "Sheshach" is a cryptogram for "Babylon" in contexts of rebellion and horror, and "Leb-qamai" stands for "Chaldea" (Jer 25:26; 51:1, 41; respectively). Babylonian religion and imperialism come under especially sharp attack in the Hebrew prophetic literature. From the perspective of the Israelite prophet, Babylon may be compared to SHEOL, for just as Sheol's appetite for the dead is insatiable, so is the greed of the Babylonian empire for other nations (Hab 2:5). In Jeremiah, Babylonia is cryptically denoted when Yahweh warns that disaster will break forth "out of the north" (1:14; 6:1, 22-23). The downfall of the king of Babylon is celebrated in Isa 14:4-23 in terms that came to symbolize the destruction of any hostile enemy of God. In Second Isaiah, Babylon is a symbol of the evil oppressor. The role of Babylon in Dan 1–5 is that of a ferocious human empire capable of many atrocities, yet vulnerable and ultimately doomed because of God's opposition. Belshazzar's writing on the wall illustrates the outcome of obstinate royal opposition to God's will (Dan 5). In many poetic passages, Babylon came to represent the place of exile and alienation: "By the river of Babylon—there we sat down and there we wept" (Ps 137:1).

Once Babylon became a literary and ideological type for the ungodly city, other prophetic warnings and judgments concerning wicked cities were applied to it. So, e.g., Tyre is compared to a prostitute in Isa 23:15-18, as is Nineveh in Nah 3:4-5. The NT's image of Babylon as the "mother of whores"—undoubtedly a cipher for Rome (Rev 17:5)—is drawn from such OT associations. *See* ASSYRIA AND BABYLONIA; BABEL;

EVIL-MERODACH; MERODACH-BALADAN; MESO-POTAMIA; NEBUCHADNEZZAR; NEBUZARADAN.

Bibliography: Bill T. Arnold. *Who Were the Babylonians?* (2004); Ignace J. Gelb. "The Name of Babylon." *Journal of the Institute of Asian Studies* 1 (1955) 1–4; Andrew R. George. *Babylonian Topographical Texts* (1992); Evelyn Klengel-Brandt. "Babylon." OEANE 1:251–56; C. B. F. Walker. *Cuneiform* (1987).

BILL T. ARNOLD

BABYLON, NT bab´uh-luhn [Βαβυλῶνος Babylōnos]. The word *Babylon* occurs a dozen times in the NT: four times in Matthew's genealogy of Jesus, once in Acts, once in 1 Peter, and six times in Revelation. These texts allude to Babylon's interventions in Israel's history, but they do so for different reasons. Matthew and Acts refer to the Babylonian exile as a way of understanding Jesus in relation to Israel's history, while 1 Peter and Revelation use Babylon as a symbol for Rome.

In Matthew's genealogy the references to Babylon help organize the lineage of Jesus into three historical periods: Abraham to David, David to the Babylonian exile, and the exile to Jesus the messiah (Matt 1:11, 12, 17). The Babylonian EXILE began in the early 6ᵗʰ cent. BCE and marked the end of Israel's Davidic monarchy that ruled from Jerusalem. In the context of Matthew's genealogy, the references to Babylon are part of a strategy that defines Jesus' place in Israel's history: Jesus is described as the messiah, the culmination of Israel's history in the lineage and heritage of David.

Acts mentions Babylon once, in passing, in a speech by Stephen before Jewish leaders in Jerusalem (Acts 7). The purpose of the speech is to demonstrate that the rejection of Jesus by most Jews was part of a pattern of Israel's resistance to God's will. In the speech, Stephen argues that an example of this resistance was the Hebrews' opposition to Moses in the wilderness. Their opposition to Moses caused God to turn away from them and to punish them later with exile. To make this point, the author of Acts quotes Amos 5:25-27, but makes a change. Instead of quoting the promise of God as, "I will take you into exile beyond Damascus" (Amos 5:27), the author writes, "I will remove you beyond Babylon" (7:43). The shift from Damascus to Babylon in the citation of Amos emphasizes the theme of Babylon as a place of exile and punishment for disobedience. The speech then concludes with hostile condemnation of the Jewish leaders for again resisting God's will by rejecting Jesus.

First Peter also mentions Babylon once, but here the term is a political metaphor for Roman rule. There is some dispute about the meaning of the reference, which occurs near the end of the letter in the phrase, "She who is in Babylon, chosen together with you, sends you greetings" (1 Pet 5:13*a*). Most scholars conclude that Babylon serves here as an allusion to the city of Rome, which would mean that the greetings come from the church in Rome. The connection of Rome with Babylon made sense for two reasons. First, both Babylon and Rome had besieged Jerusalem and had destroyed the Temple there (*see* TEMPLE, JERUSALEM). Second, both cities were the centers of oppressive imperialism that dominated the Jewish homeland and the diaspora communities. The author's use of this metaphor in 1 Peter implies a political awareness that the churches lived under Roman domination as exiles and outsiders (1:1, 17; 2:11).

Half of the NT references to Babylon come in the book of Revelation, where the term also serves as a metaphor for Rome. Revelation's attitude toward the Roman Empire is summarized in Rev 14:8 when an angel proclaims, "Fallen, fallen is Babylon the great! She has made all nations drink of the wine of the wrath of her fornication." The connection between Babylon and Rome is made explicit in the vision of ch. 17, in which a woman sits on a seven-headed beast. Written on the woman's head is, "Babylon the great, mother of whores and of earth's abominations" (17:5). An angel interprets the vision to John and explains that the seven heads of the beast who carries the woman stand for seven hills and for seven rulers. When Revelation first circulated in the late 1ˢᵗ cent. CE, this would have been a clear allusion to Rome's topography and imperial domination.

Revelation 18 follows with another vision containing judgment oracles, laments, and taunts about the destruction of Babylon/Rome. The reasons for Rome's judgment include economic exploitation of the realm (18:3, 19), arrogance (18:7), a lifestyle of wanton luxury (18:9-14), deception of the whole world (18:23), and violence against all people (18:24). The saints, the apostles, the prophets, and the heavenly multitudes rejoice at the destruction of Roman imperialism, for God's judgments are true and just (18:20; 19:1-3).

Thus the NT traditions treat Babylon as a significant marker in the history of Israel and as a metaphor for the experiences of the churches in the Roman Empire.

Matthew and Acts both use the memory of Babylon to explain Jesus' connection to Israel's history. While Matthew focuses on the Babylonian exile to describe Jesus as the Davidic messiah, Acts cites the Babylonian exile as an example of Israel's resistance to God's work that is parallel to Israel's rejection of Jesus. First Peter and Revelation, on the other hand, use the memory of Babylonian destruction and domination to describe the oppressive political context of the churches in the Roman Empire.

STEVEN FRIESEN

BABYLONIA. *See* ASSYRIA AND BABYLONIA.

BABYLONIAN JOB. *See* I WILL PRAISE THE LORD OF WISDOM.

BABYLONIAN JUDAISM bab´uh-loh´nee-uhn. Many inhabitants of Judah were deported to Babylonia when Nebuchadnezzar conquered Judah in 587/586 BCE. Following the Persian occupation of Babylonia, Cyrus permitted the deportees to return, yet many remained. Rabbinic Judaism emerged during the Sassanian Empire (ca. 220 CE). The community was organized under the leadership of an exilarch. Talmudic academies for study of the MISHNAH arose in centers such as Sura and Pumbeditha (*see* TALMUD), which persisted into the 11th cent. CE. Jews continued to live in Babylonia (Iraq) through the 20th cent. *See* DIASPORA.

Bibliography: Jacob Neusner. *A History of the Jews of Babylonia.* 5 vols. (1965–1970).

BURTON L. VISOTZKY

BABYLONIAN TEXTS. Texts written in CUNEIFORM script that were composed in the southern dialect of the AKKADIAN language and rediscovered only in the modern era in Iraq (ancient Mesopotamia). The Babylonian dialect, along with its northern counterpart, Assyrian, emerged sometime near the turn of the 2nd millennium as a geographically situated dialect that can be distinguished from Assyrian on the basis of phonological, morphological, and lexical variations. Babylonian texts are attested across a wide chronological expanse extending from the 20th cent. BCE down to the 1st cent. CE (1900 BCE–100 CE).

The earliest stage of this is represented by texts composed in the Old Babylonian language (1900–1500 BCE); the best studied being those from the court of King HAMMURABI. Texts include letters, law codes, contracts, economic dockets, omens, royal inscriptions, lexical lists, scholarly works such as mathematical, medical, and grammatical texts, and literary works such as hymns, prayers, and mythological works (compare the epics of GILGAMESH and ATRAHASIS).

The next stage of the Babylonian dialect of Akkadian is designated Middle Babylonian (1500–1000 BCE). Letters, legal and economic texts, royal inscriptions and boundary stones (or kudurrus) have been recovered. The Babylonian language, in its "Old" and "Middle" stages, functioned as a lingua franca throughout the Near East, and as many texts recovered from outside Mesopotamia proper indicate, at least the written form of the language was not restricted to Babylonia or southern Mesopotamia itself (from modern Baghdad south to the Persian Gulf).

The next stage of the language, Neo-Babylonian (1000–600 BCE), is attested by a large number of non-literary texts as well as a few literary texts. It was followed by Late Babylonian, the language's final stage that extended from the 7th cent. into the Hellenistic period, or specifically the 1st cent. of the Common Era. Both of these stages of the Babylonian dialect are represented in numerous texts containing letters and administrative records.

Building upon Old Babylonian, or perhaps what was viewed as the classical form of the language, another literary dialect called Standard Babylonian was also employed (1400–300 BCE). It illustrates consistent grammatical and lexical characteristics reflective of a traditional poetic style and a distinctive set of linguistic elements that spanned more than a thousand years. Whether or not Standard Babylonian constituted an attempt to preserve an inherited or canonical corpus of older literary works remains a point of discussion. Texts composed in Standard Babylonian, primarily a literary, nonspoken dialect of the language include such works as ENUMA ELISH and various royal inscriptions.

Bibliography: B. R. Foster. *Before the Muses* (2005).

BRIAN B. SCHMIDT

BABYLONIAN THEODICY. The theme of the righteous sufferer wrestling with the universal problem of suffering in a cosmic order ordained by the gods is found in Sumerian and Akkadian literature as a monologue or dialogue between a sufferer and his god or a pious friend, often framed by a narrative introducing the sufferer and his condition. In the Sumerian text the sufferer speculates about the origin of sin and feels his guilt. Later texts feature complaints about the remoteness of the gods and the randomness of divine anger. The sufferer's outcast status, sickness, and depression are thought to be the result of Marduk's anger and the departure of the sufferer's personal god. This disruption of the divine-human relationship results in the confusion of omens, rendering exorcists and diviners ineffective. The status of the sufferer is compared to one who has committed cultic offenses. Mercy and restoration to good health are granted solely by Marduk in the texts dating from the first millennium BCE. The literary device of declaring sins publicly at the city gate or passing through Temple gates might be used to illustrate the return to divine favor.

The specific text referred to as The Babylonian Theodicy, much like the book of Job, is cast into the form of a dialogue between the sufferer and his friend in a strophic structure. Most interesting are the statements that correct cultic behavior does not prevent suffering, that social disorder is created by the gods, and that the gods' ways are unfathomable. *See* DIALOGUE OF PESSIMISM; I WILL PRAISE THE LORD OF WISDOM; JOB, BOOK OF.

Bibliography: W. W. Hallo, ed. *The Context of Scripture* I (1997); S. N. Kramer. "Man and His God." in *Wisdom in Israel and in the Ancient Near East* (1955); G. L. Mattingly, et al. *The Bible in the Light of Cuneiform Literature. Scripture in Context* III (1990); W. L. Moran. "The Babylonian Job." *The Most Magic Word.* R. S. Hendel, ed. *CBQMS* 35 (2002).

BEATE PONGRATZ-LEISTEN

BACA, VALLEY OF bay´kuh [בְּכָא bakha']. The valley of Baca may be an unknown geographical location that pilgrims to the Jerusalem Temple passed through, or a symbolic expression of the pilgrims' sorrow turned to joy along the way (Ps 84:6). Baca means either "weeping" (LXX translation of Ps 84:6) or "BALSAM" (2 Sam 5:24). The notion of "weeping" or "dripping" may refer to a gum-exuding tree. Whether literal, symbolic, or a play on words, the phrase in Ps 84:6 represents a joyful transformation. The valley of Baca does not refer to Mecca, as some have claimed.

SUSANNA W. SOUTHARD

BACCHIDES bak´uh-deez [Βακχίδης Bakchidēs]. Bacchides was a general and friend of the Syrian king DEMETRIUS I (Soter), as well as the governor of the Seleucid territories that were either west of the Euphrates or in Mesopotamia (1 Macc 7:8-20; Josephus, *Ant.* 12.389–434). In 162 BCE, at the beginning of the Maccabean revolt led by Judas Maccabeus, Bacchides was sent to install ALCIMUS as high priest and to punish the rebels. Bacchides and Alcimus appeared to the Jews in a conciliatory manner. As a result, the HASIDIM among the Jews trusted that a high priest would not harm them, but Bacchides instead killed 60 of them and placed Alcimus in charge of the country. In 160 BCE, after having been sent a second time to Judaea with 20,000 soldiers and 2,000 horsemen, Bacchides defeated the Maccabean army, which numbered only 3,000, and killed its leader Judas (1 Macc 9:1-24). Bacchides then put the Hellenists in charge of the country, while he continued to chase Judas's brother, Jonathan, and his army purposely on the Sabbath, without, however, besieging them (1 Macc 9:25-49). Bacchides built many strongholds in Judea during a period of relative peace. Alcimus died in 159 BCE, and Bacchides left the country. In 157 BCE, he returned for a third unsuccessful effort to besiege the Maccabees. This eventually resulted in a peace treaty, with Bacchides going back to Syria and Jonathan and Simon ending the war and destroying the Hellenists or "ungodly ones" in Israel (1 Macc 9:50-73).

GERBERN S. OEGEMA

BACCHUS. *See* DIONYSUS.

BACENOR buh-see´nor [Βακήνωρ Bakēnōr]. Officer in Judas Maccabeus's army over the soldier Dositheus who attempted to capture GORGIAS, the governor of Idumea (2 Macc 12:35). His soldiers may be the Toubiani (2 Macc 12:17). *See* TOB.

BACKSLIDING. *See* APOSTASY.

BAD, TO BE [רַע ra', רָשַׁע rasha'; πονηρός ponēros, πονηρία ponēria, κακός kakos, κακία kakia, σαπρος sapros]. In Hebrew and Greek usage the ascription *bad* frequently signifies a negative evaluation in light of given aesthetic norms or standards of practicality, usefulness, or well-being. *Bad* can be a moral evaluation and signifies a failure on the part of individuals and groups to act according to accepted behavioral norms, ethical or legal standards, or covenantal obligations. *Bad* is neglect of the God of Israel. In addition, it is used of actions that have the effect of hindering, harming, or severing proper relationships to other persons or principles.

Bad can mean *worthless* (Lev 27:10, 12; Num 24:13; Jer 24:2; 29:17; Matt 6:23; 7:17), or potentially or actually *harmful, painful,* or *injurious* to a person, a thing, or to one's reputation (Gen 26:29; Deut 22:15; Josh 23:15; Neh 6:13; Rev 16:2). It can be *unseemly* or *repugnant* in appearance, character, or form (Gen 41:3; Exod 7:18; Isa 50:2). *Bad* can also be *troubling* or *distressing* (Josh 23:15; Jer 49:23; Ps 94:13).

Moral evaluations equate *bad* with *evil* (Matt 24:48; Phil 3:2; Rev 2:2) and imply a capacity, tendency, or an intent to be harmful or damaging to persons, objects, or relationships (Deut 17:5; 1 Sam 2:23; 1 Kgs 16:7; Ezek 20:44; 30:12). *Bad* can indicate guilt when a legal code is violated (Ps 109:7). When the focus is a person or a group's covenant unfaithfulness, *bad* means *wicked, unrighteous,* or *sinful* (2 Sam 4:11; 2 Kgs 17:11; Mark 8:11; Luke 11:29).

JEFFREY B. GIBSON

BADGER. *See* ROCK BADGER.

BAEAN bee´uhn [Βαιάν Baian]. The expression "sons of Baean" probably refers to a gentile clan or tribe connected with the name *Baean,* a city or an area with fortified towers surrounding Judah in the time of the Maccabees. They had joined the Idumeans in killing the Jews when they tried to rebuild their Temple after the Maccabean Revolt in 167–64 BCE, but were destroyed by Judas Maccabeus (1 Macc 5:1-5; 2 Macc 10:15-23). This unknown tribe may also have been intended in Num 32:3, and Josh 15:6; 18:17 under the names of "BEON" and "Bohan."

GERBERN S. OEGEMA

BAG, BAGGAGE [חָרִיט kharit, כִּים kis, כְּלִי keli, צְרוֹר tseror, שַׂק saq; βαλλάντιον ballantion, θυλάκιον thylakion, πήρα pēra]. The word *bag* refers to several flexible fabric or leather containers of varying sizes. Bags have four main uses in the Bible: to contain grain (Gen 42:25); to hold money (Gen 42:35), which references a bag inside a bag; to contain weights (Deut 25:13); and hold supplies in baggage (1 Sam 10:22).

The term *bag* translates several Hebrew words: saq, a sack (Gen 42:25); tseror, which refers to something bound up like a parcel or pouch (Gen 42:35), although it is used in parallel with saq; also kheli, which has a wide range of meanings including a container or a load, like baggage (Gen 43:11); kis, a bag (Deut 25:13) or a purse (Isa 46:6); and kharit, a bag or purse

(2 Kgs 5:23). The meanings range from a word for a woman's purse to a generic "item."

The NT Greek words translated bag include pēra, a leather pouch, bag, or purse for money (Matt 10:10); and ballantion, a bag or money purse (Luke 10:4). The Apocrypha uses thylakion, a small bag (Tob 9:5).

KENNETH D. LITWAK

BAGOAS buh-goh´uhs [Βαγώας Bagōas]. Holoferne's personal steward, a EUNUCH, who delivered HOLOFERNE's dinner invitation to JUDITH, and was first to find him beheaded the next morning (Jdt 12:11; 14:14-18).

BAHARUM buh-hair´uhm [בַּחֲרוּמִי baharumi]. Town of origin of AZMAVETH, one of David's warriors (1 Chr 11:33), although Azmaveth's town is named BAHURIM in 2 Sam 23:31.

BAHURIM buh-hyoor´im [בַּחֻרִים bakhurim]. A Benjaminite village near Jerusalem, Bahurim may correspond to modern Ras et-Tmim or Khirbet Ibqe'dan. MICHAL's husband PALTIEL followed her weeping as far as Bahurim when she returned to King DAVID (2 Sam 3:16). Bahurim was also the residence of SHIMEI son of GERA, who cast stones at David and later begged for mercy (2 Sam 16:5; 19:16; 1 Kgs 2:8). JONATHAN and AHIMAAZ also hid in Bahurim (2 Sam 17:18). AZMAVETH, a member of David's guard, was probably from Bahurim (2 Sam 23:31; 1 Chr 11:33).

SUSANNA W. SOUTHARD

BAITERUS bi´tuh-ruhs [Βαιτηροῦς Baitērous]. A family head whose descendants returning from the exile numbered 3,005 (1 Esd 5:17). Absent from lists in Ezra 2:3-35 and Neh 7:8-38.

BAKBAKKAR bak-bak´uhr [בַּקְבַּקַּר baqbaqqar]. A Levite descendant of ASAPH living in Jerusalem after the exile had ended (1 Chr 9:15). Absent from the parallel list in Neh 11:16.

BAKBUK bak´buhk [בַּקְבּוּק baqbuq]. A family head whose descendants were of the Nethinim, Temple servants, who returned to Jerusalem after the exile (Ezra 2:51; Neh 7:53). See NETHINIM.

BAKBUKIAH bak´buh-ki´uh [בַּקְבֻּקְיָה baqbuqyah]. A Levite who led prayer (Neh 11:17), stood opposite the Levites in charge of the songs (Neh 12:9), and guarded the storehouses (Neh 12:25). The name does not appear in the LXX in any of these cases. See BUKKIAH, MATTANIAH.

BAKE [אָפָה 'afah]. Baking bread and cakes was one of the most important food-preparation activities undertaken in the Israelite household on a daily basis (Gen 19:3; Lev 26:26; 1 Sam 8:13; 2 Sam 13:8; 1 Kgs 17:12-

13; Isa 44:15; Hos 7:4), even after commercial bakeries were established in larger towns such as Jerusalem (Jer 37:21). Bread was literally the "staff of life" for the ancient Israelites; along with other foods made from wheat, barley, and other grains, bread was the primary source of carbohydrate in the Iron Age diet.

Several hundred types of breads and pastries have been documented in ancient Near Eastern literature, and it is likely that the Israelite repertoire included many different varieties of baked goods. The simplest form of flat bread was made by kneading and baking dough, which consisted of flour, water, and perhaps salt. This unleavened bread was prepared when baking was done in haste (Exod 12:39), when ritual demanded it (Exod 13:6-7; Lev 2:5; 23:4-6), and on other occasions (Gen 19:3). Leavened bread and cakes—baked with the additives oil, honey, date syrup, and a variety of herbs and spices—were also common. Bread was usually baked in an oven (Lev 2:4), but it could also be baked on a ceramic or iron griddle set on stones over a fire pit (Lev 2:5; 7:9; Ezek 4:3) or directly on a hot stone in ashes (1 Kgs 19:6). Women are most closely associated with the preparation and baking of bread for daily consumption at the household level. This may explain the dearth of references to cooking and baking in the OT.

Baking bread was also required for sacred meals (Lev 24:5), as in references to baking and cooking facilities in the Temple in Jerusalem (Ezek 46:20, 23-24). In this context, the baking of wheat bread was carried out by priests. In contrast, all family members participated in preparing cakes for the QUEEN OF HEAVEN in Jerusalem and other towns in Judah (Jer 7:18), although it was women who are specifically credited with baking the cakes in the image of this deity (Jer 44:19).

Ethnographic evidence suggests that in small-scale agricultural societies, women were the primary food producers at the household level, and the biblical references support this. Women were occupied up to several hours per day with the grueling task of preparing grains and baking bread for the family, in addition to their other cooking tasks (see COOKING AND COOKING UTENSILS). Israelite women controlled the technology of bread production in the household and the feeding of family members, and they gained power and prestige in their families and communities as a result. However, public bakeries functioned on Bakers' Street in Jerusalem (Jer 37:21) as well as in other towns in Judah by the late pre-exilic period, and we can assume that men did the baking in these establishments. Women would have remained the primary bakers in their own households throughout the biblical period, however.

Identifying the archaeological remains of bread production and baking is difficult because the activities involved in transforming grains into bread are complex and involve a number of specialized tools and equipment. Although the remains of a variety of tools used in the production of bread have been identified in Egypt (including sieves, winnowing baskets, ground stone tools, wooden equipment, brushes, etc.), the Levantine climate does not support the preservation of most of these items. Archaeological correlates for bread production in ancient Israel are usually limited to the ground stone tools used to process the grains and the ovens in which the final product was baked.

Many examples of these artifacts and installations are known from Iron Age Israel. Ground stone artifacts, especially the upper handstone (pelakh rekev) and lower grinding slab (pelakh takhti), are found in large numbers in Iron Age sites, and many of these tools can be directly connected to household food production. Open hearths and dome-shaped clay ovens (tannur) are often found in the courtyard of the family compound, although several families could also share ovens. These baking installations were fueled by cakes of animal dung mixed with straw or with a fire made of wood, the leftovers from olive pressing, and other combustible materials. When a hearth was used, bread was baked on a layer of stones or on a griddle set on stones; in the tannur, bread was placed directly on the hot interior walls. *See* BREAD.

Bibliography: Robert I. Curtis. *Ancient Food Technology* (2001); Philip J. King and Lawrence E. Stager. *Life in Biblical Israel* (2001); Carol Meyers. "Having Their Space and Eating There Too: Bread Production and Female Power in Ancient Israelite Households." *Nashim* 5 (2002) 14–44.

JENNIE EBELING

BAKERS' STREET חוּץ הָאֹפִים khuts ha'ofim]. ZEDEKIAH improved JEREMIAH's prison isolation, putting him in the courtyard of the jail and ordering that he be brought the daily minimum ration for a prisoner, a low-quality, blackish, rounded type of coarse BREAD "from the bakers' street" (Jer 37:21). Cities favored that the craftsmen group themselves in sectors. In Jerusalem, as in Damascus and Samaria (1 Kgs 20:34), STREETs were arranged such that commercial premises were part of the craftsman's HOUSE. Jerusalem's bakers' street was probably located in the northwest of the city, near the TOWER OF THE OVENS (Neh 3:11; 12:38). *See* ARCHITECTURE, OT.

JORGE TORREBLANCA

BALAAM bay'luhm בִּלְעָם bil'am; Βαλαάμ Balaam]. Balaam is a non-Israelite prophet or seer featured in Num 22–24 as the one who blessed Israel in defiance of King BALAK of Moab who had hired him to curse Israel (*see* MOAB, MOABITES). Balaam is evaluated both positively and negatively in the Bible itself and in the history of biblical interpretation. On one hand, Num 22–24 portrays Balaam in a largely positive light. Even though he is a foreign prophet, Balaam ended

up obeying Israel's God rather than the Moabite king by blessing Israel in four separate oracles. The prophet Micah affirmed the way Balaam turned back the evil scheme of King BALAK of Moab who had hired Balaam to curse Israel (Mic 6:5). On the other hand, some texts portray Balaam quite negatively. Deuteronomy 23:3-6 prohibited Moabites and Ammonites from ever entering the assembly of God's people because of their association with the prophet Balaam. Balaam was killed later in Numbers as punishment for having led the Midianite women to lure Israel astray in the worship of a false god named BAAL-PEOR (Num 25; 31:8, 16; Josh 13:21-22). Other texts assume Balaam actually tried to curse Israel but was prevented from doing so by God (Josh 24:9-10; Neh 13:2). NT references to Balaam are uniformly negative, portraying him as a prototype of false prophets and teachers in the NT period (2 Pet 2:15; Jude 11; Rev 2:14).

Archaeologists have discovered texts printed on plaster panels in a non-Israelite temple at Deir 'Alla in modern day Jordan that contain the name Balaam (*see* DEIR 'ALLA, TEXTS). The 8th cent. BCE inscription tells of Balaam receiving a nighttime vision from a council or assembly of gods called the "shaddai" gods. Interestingly, the Hebrew phrase "EL SHADDAI" (trans. as "God Almighty" or "God of the Mountain") also occurs as a title for God in the biblical oracles of Balaam (Num 24:4, 16). In the Deir 'Alla inscription, the gods inform Balaam that a drought is imminent and the order of nature is about to be thrown into chaos. Balaam prays to the gods to reverse their decision in order to avoid the disaster. The existence of this non-biblical tradition about this legendary prophet from the TRANSJORDAN area around Moab, the setting for the biblical story of Balaam, suggests that these texts likely drew from a common Balaam tradition associated with the Transjordan.

The major biblical tradition concerning Balaam is Num 22–24. These chapters divide into three large sections: 1) Num 22:1-40—Balaam's three encounters with God as the Moabite King Balak hires Balaam to curse Israel; 2) Num 22:41–24:13—Balak's three attempts to curse Israel foiled by Balaam's three blessings of Israel; and 3) Num 24:14-25—Balaam's fourth climactic oracle of blessing for a distant future beyond the present generation of Israelites. The Balaam cycle is a carefully crafted story with recurring cycles of three scenes or episodes built into its narrative structure. The repeated theme of "seeing" or "not seeing" appears throughout both the narrative scenes and the oracles of Balaam.

Numbers 22:1-40 opens the cycle with King Balak of Moab in "great dread" of the Israelites upon their arrival at the boundary of the promised land of Canaan after they had wandered through the wilderness 40 years after leaving Egypt. King Balak sent a team of officials to hire a professional prophet or seer named

Balaam to deliver a powerful curse against Israel. However, Balaam reminded the officials that he can only speak and do what the Lord tells him (Num 22:8). Over the course of three encounters between Balaam and God, God first told Balaam not to go with the officials, but then in a second encounter God reverses this instruction and tells Balaam to go with the officials. Balaam obeys God and begins his trip on his DONKEY. Unexpectedly, however, God stands in the road as a threatening ANGEL and blocks the obedient Balaam and his donkey on their way to King Balak. Ironically, the donkey is able to see the angel with the drawn sword while the hired religious specialist Balaam is unable to see the angel standing before them. Three times the donkey tried to avoid or stop before encountering the terrifying angel, and each time Balaam beat the donkey because Balaam did not realize the reason for its behavior. In the last instance, "the LORD opened the mouth of the donkey" and the donkey complained to Balaam that he was only trying to protect him (Num 22:28-30). This motif of a talking animal lends a fable quality to the narrative. Finally "the LORD opened the eyes of Balaam, and he saw the angel of the LORD" (Num 22:31). The enigmatic episode of God attacking an obedient messenger going on a journey that had been commanded by God occurs in other OT narratives (Moses in Exod 4:24-26; Jacob in Gen 32:22-32). In the end, however, God allows Balaam to proceed on his journey to visit King Balak.

Num 22:41–24:13 relates three attempts by King Balak to have Balaam curse Israel, but his attempts failed in each case because Balaam ended up blessing rather than cursing the Israelites. Each of the three attempts or episodes includes a similar set of elements: ascending a high place or mountain, building an altar and offering sacrifices, Balaam's consultation with God, Balaam's deliverance of an oracle of blessing, Balak's increasing anger, and Balaam's final response each time that "Whatever the LORD says, that is what I must do" (Num 23:26).

Numbers 24:14-25 is the fourth and climactic oracle spoken by Balaam. Its four pronouncements set it apart from the three-part repetitive structure of the previous three oracles. Balaam simply proclaimed the fourth oracle of blessing directly upon Israel without any altars, sacrifices or consultation with God. The four oracles in Num 23–24 display a meaningful progression in the use of the imagery of "rising" and "falling down" around the topic of kingship, both human and divine. The first oracle makes no mention of kingship at all with Balaam as the one who is lifted up high on a hill (Num 23:9). The second oracle portrays the people of Israel as "rising up like a lioness," and the only kingship that is mentioned is the kingship of God (Num 23:21, 24). In the third oracle, Balaam "falls down" before the vision of the Almighty, and God is portrayed as a crouching LION ready to rise up (Num 24:4, 9). The third oracle speaks of Israel's king as high and exalted, but it is not clear whether the king who is exalted is God or a human king (Num 24:7). The fourth and climactic oracle translates the previous heavenly visions into earthly realities, including a vision of a human king arising out of Israel sometime in the distant future: "I see him, but not now; I behold him, but not near—a star shall come out of Jacob, and a scepter shall rise out of Israel" (Num 24:17). Many scholars understand this future royal figure as pointing to King DAVID who defeated Moab and Ammon (2 Sam 8:2, 11-14; see AMMON, AMMONITES). This hope of a Davidic king gets extended to a future hope for a MESSIAH who would usher in God's kingdom in a new apocalyptic age (Dan 7; Rev 2:26-28). The image of the star and its association with the coming messiah is associated with the star over Bethlehem, a sign that the messiah had been born (Matt 2:1-10; see STAR OF BETHLEHEM). Thus, the significance of Balaam and his oracles extends far beyond the boundaries of the book of Numbers into both the OT and NT and beyond. See BLESSINGS AND CURSINGS; PROPHECY.

DENNIS T. OLSON

BALADAN bal′uh-duhn [בַּלְאֲדָן bal’adhan]. Father of the Babylonian king MERODACH-BALADAN (i.e., Marduk-apaliddina) whose envoys King HEZEKIAH allowed to tour all his storehouses (2 Kgs 20:12).

BALAH bay′lah [בָּלָה balah]. In Josh 19:3, the tribe of SIMEON receives the NEGEV town of Balah inside Judah's territory as an allotment. The text implies a location south and east of BEER-SHEBA. Scholars also identify Balah with BAALAH (Josh 15:29) and BILHAH (1 Chr 4:29).

BALAH, DEIR EL bay′luh. Situated approximately 8 mi. (13 km) southwest of Gaza, on what was known as the "Way of Horus," which was the coastal route between Egypt and Canaan. Cultural remains from the site were known and documented well before archaeologists arrived.

The most notable genre of artifact yielded by the site was a late Bronze Age assemblage of locally made clay anthropoid coffins; the four actually excavated each contained multiple skeletons and an impressive cache of grave goods. Fifteen archaeological campaigns to the site (1972–1982) documented nine strata ranging from mid-14th cent. BCE to 4th cent. CE. Among the more historically significant strata were IX through IV—all Egyptian. The earliest (IX), an administrative center, dated to the Amarna Age and Akhenaten (1379–62 BCE), has contributed to a reexamination of the view that, during the kingship of AKHENATEN, Egypt demonstrated little or no interest in Canaanite matters. A Stratum VII fortress reflected clear similarities to portrayals of fortresses in reliefs at Karnak, dated to the time of Seti I (1318–04 BCE). Three successive strata (VI–IV) were stratigraphically dated to the reign of Ramesses II (1304–1237 BCE).

That Deir el-Balah was perhaps the northeasternmost New Kingdom Egyptian outpost on the southern Canaan border was demonstrated by a variety of cultural remains traced to the site prior to excavation and recovered from the site during excavation. Egyptian scarabs, seals, jewelry items, bronze mirrors, bowls, jars and wine sets, ushabti figurines, pieces of blue frit and carnelian (both fragments of the Egyptian flail or scepter) and funerary stelae bearing hieroglyphic inscriptions all reflected the work of Egyptian artisans. Also included among the various ceramic assemblages were Mycenaean and Cypriot vessels.

The discovery of several kilns coupled with chemical analysis of the clay coffins confirm the manufacturing of the anthropoid coffins at the site, as well as most of the other excavated pottery forms. Iconographic parallels between the lids of the anthropoid coffins and various images and techniques from New Kingdom Egypt, the portrayal of various Egyptian deities in different media, the rich, collective representation of Egyptian artistic motifs and symbols, as well as the site's strategic location come together to support the conclusion that Deir el-Balah was an important late 14th cent. to 13th cent. BCE Egyptian outpost on Canaan's southern border.

JOHN I. LAWLOR

BALAK bay´lak [בָּלָק balaq; Βαλακ Balak]. "Devastator." King of MOAB, son of ZIPPOR. Fearing the Israelites, Balak sends for BALAAM, the seer, to curse the Israelites. Balaam curses the Moabites instead (Num 22–24). References to Balak also appear in Josh 24:9; Judg 11:25; Mic 6:5; and Rev 2:14.

HEATHER R. MCMURRAY

BALAMON bal´uh-muhn [Βαλαμων Balamōn]. A town in Samaria. In a field between this town and Dothan, Judith's husband, Manasseh, was buried (Jdt 8:3). See BELMAIN.

BALANCES [מֹאזְנַיִם mo'znayim]. Balances were necessary in the world before coinage for each transaction in precious metals (especially silver and gold), since the sole way of determining their value was by weight. Throughout the Bronze and Iron ages, balances were constructed of two pans, suspended by cords from a horizontal beam. The beam was suspended from its middle and either held by hand (in small balances or hand balances), or mounted on a vertical beam (in large balances). Both these types are shown in Egyptian representations, where one often finds a scene of weighing the heart of the deceased as judgment on his afterlife. Some Egyptian balance beams were hollow, with cords passing inside, while a tonguelike arm fixed at a right angle to the

beam pointed vertically when the desired equilibrium was reached. Archaeological evidence for balances includes mainly bronze pans (discovered at Ashdod, Ashkelon, Ekron, Tell Jerishe, etc.; the earliest pans from Israel date to the Middle Bronze Age). Rarely, other parts survived, such as a bone beam from 8th cent. BCE Lachish. Remains of wood between pans from Megiddo tomb 912A indicate a wooden beam in origin. One unprovenanced Judahite four-shekel weight carries an engraving of a man holding hand balances. Such balances are also seen in an Iron Age relief from Marash in Syria. Graduated scales using leverage were a later invention, from around the 4th cent. BCE.

The OT does not detail the process of weighing but stresses its moral aspect. This is expressed by the terms *falsified balances* and *wicked balances* as opposed to *just balances* and *even balances* (e.g., Amos 8:5; Ezek 45:10; Hosh 12:8; Prov 11:1, Job 31:6). It indicates that balances were used for fraud, e.g., by suspending the beam not from its exact middle. The term פֶּלֶס peles (Isa 40:12, translated as "scales") perhaps also denotes balances, or the indicator arm. Some details about weighing appear in Jer 32:9-10. Jeremiah bought a field for seventeen shekels; weighing comprised part of the payment and the author stressed it twice, in order not to leave any doubt about the legality of the act. On the other hand, weighing Absalom's hair (2 Sam 14:26) only comes to prepare the readers for Absalom's death, since the heavy weight signifies long hair; but this is an exception, as hair was not usually weighed.

The biblical expression שַׁחַק מֹאזְנַיִם shaqakh m'oznayim (Isa 40:15) was often explained by the context as "dust of the scales." In fact, it is a technical term, identical to shiqu(m) in Mesopotamia—a small amount of weight, negligible because it does not tip the scales. Such a small amount could not be measured by ancient balances, whose margins of error hovered around 1–3 percent. Documents from Mari (18th cent. BCE) show that various methods of weighing were used. One common method (additive weighing) was to put the object for weighing on one pan and weights on the other, adding smaller weights until equilibrium. Sometimes, a weight heavier than the object was placed against it, and then smaller weights were added on the pan of the object. If irregular pieces of silver ("hacksilber") were weighed, one could also "chip" flakes from such pieces (or add such flakes) until equilibrium.

Weighing by balances as a daily procedure was cumbersome. This explains why it was gradually replaced by coinage (starting in the 5th cent. BCE). As a result, balances and weights were less of an issue by the time of the NT. See WEIGHTS AND MEASURES.

RAZ KLETTER

BALAS, ALEXANDER. See ALEXANDER BALAS, EPIPHANES.

BALBAIM bal-bay′im [Βελβαιμ Belbaim]. Uniden-tifed place that marked the boundary of the camp of HOLOFERNES and his army before they advanced to Bethulia (Jdt 7:3). *See* BELMAIN.

BALD LOCUST. *See* LOCUSTS.

BALDNESS [גִּבֵּחַ gibbeakh, קָרַח qarakh]. Head hair loss (baldness) can be natural (gibbeakh "baldness of the forehead") as in Lev 13:40-41 or intentional (qarakh "baldness of the head"), e.g., as a sign of mourning mentioned likely without approval by the prophets (Isa 22:12), but forbidden to priests (Num 21:5) and Israelites as well (Deut 14:1); or signaling the end of a NAZARITE VOW (Num 6:18). Natural baldness does not render one unclean unless associated with a skin problem (Lev 13:42-44). Like hair, baldness—especially intentional—is a multivocal symbol with many poten-tial meanings.

The physical body is often used to play out culturally shared beliefs about social events. Thus a prophet's hair can stand for the people of Jerusalem, cut down by the sword and thrown to the wind (Ezek 5). Shaving the hair can symbolize castration, physically irreversible yet symbolically reparable since hair can grow back (Isa 7:20). Specific parts may have multiple representations. Head and facial hair is hair, but it may also represent sex organs (2 Sam 10:4). Thus the boys who taunted Elisha as "bald-head" may have been challenging his masculinity (2 Kgs 2:23-24). That would explain Elisha's cursing them, and God's sending a bear to kill forty-two of them for disrespecting a prophet. By the same token, when Hanun the Ammonite shaved off half the face hair and exposed the genitals of David's envoys (2 Sam 10:4), David responded by killing them (2 Sam 11:1). In the Samson Saga (*see* Judg 13:25; 14:6, 19; 15:14), hair represents Samson's strength that is provided by the spirit of the LORD. Samson loses his strength when his hair is cut (Judg 16:19-20). *See* HAIR, HAIRS.

JOHN J. PILCH

BALL [דּוּר dur]. Used metaphorically in Isaiah's address to Shebna, King Hezekiah's servant. Predict-ing Shebna's dismissal into exile into Assyria, Isaiah claimed that God would hurl him round and round like a ball (Isa 22:18). In Isa 29:18 the same Hebrew word is translated "round about."

BALM [צְרִי tsiri]. Balm is a nonspecific term for a variety of medicinal and aromatic mixtures made from olive oil and various resins. Many of these resins were extracted from trees and scrubs found in the semiarid regions of Transjordan, Arabia, and southern Egypt, and this might explain their presence among the goods traded by the Ishmaelites, who were carrying gum, resins, and balm from Gilead to Egypt (Gen 37:25). A further sign of the popularity of such remedies is found in the trading manifests of goods exchanged throughout the ANE (Gen 43:11; Ezek 27:17). Evidence of the processing of healing resins also has been found at En-Gedi. Since physicians were virtually nonexistent in the villages and towns of ancient Israel, herbal medicine, combined with consultation with Levitical priests (Lev 13:2-3) or prophets (2 Kgs 5:3-6), sacrifices, purges, prayers (Ps 41:3), and the admonition to maintain a "cheerful heart" (Prov 17:22) would have been the most common practices. The region of Gilead in the central Transjordan area (from the Arnon River north to Bashan) is associated with a particularly efficacious balm. Among the candidates for this "balm of Gilead" (Jer 8:22; 46:11) are the Pink Rock Rose (*Cistus inca-nus creticus*) an evergreen subshrub, a small tree or large shrub (*Commiphora opobalsamum)*, common around the Red Sea, and *Balanites aegyptiaca*, a small or medium-sized tree 3.5–5.5 m high with recurved spiny branches and fleshy succulent leaves. Its bark, fruit, roots, and gum have been used medicinally for a variety of ailments. Even so, there is no assurance given that any "balm" will heal a wound. Its application is prescribed as one possible step in the healing process that would also, necessarily, include divine aid (Jer 51:8). *See* GILEAD, BALM OF; PERFUME.

VICTOR H. MATTHEWS

BALSAM [בְּכָאִים bikha′im]. The assonance with the word for spice (בֹּשֶׂם bosem) may be the basis for tying this to BALM (צְרִי tsiri) in the NEB translation of Ezek 27:17. During a campaign against the Philistines in the Valley of Rephaim (southwest of Jerusalem), David is commanded to approach the enemy from the rear near a stand of "balsam trees" (2 Sam 5:23-24// 1 Chr 14:14-15). It is not clear which species of tree or shrub is meant, with mulberry and mastic terebinth suggested. Lack of the definite article in 2 Sam 5:23 suggests that the reference is a place name, Bachaim, with an associated ASHERAH grove. The command to wait until he hears "the sound of marching in the tops of the balsam trees" (2 Sam 5:24) could then be a part of a divinatory ritual in which God indicates the moment for the attack.

VICTOR H. MATTHEWS

BALTHASAR bal-thaz′uhr [Βααλτασάρ Baaltasar]. The name provided in church traditions for one of the MAGI (Matt 2:1-12). *See* MELKON.

BAMAH bay′muh [בָּמָה bamah, בָּמוֹת bamoth]. Although it is sometimes a place name (Ezek 20:29; Num 21:19, 20), **bamah** is most often translated "HIGH PLACE," referring to a cult site. It can also refer to height(s) in general (Mic 3:12 = Jer 26:18; Ezek 36:2) and particularly the site of battle advantage (2 Sam 1:19, 25). Hence, as a metaphor of dominance Yahweh is pictured astride the heights (Amos 4:13; Mic 1:3; Job 9:8), and Babylon's pretensions drive it to strive for the same "cloudy heights" (Isa 14:14). God exalts Israel to the same loftiness (Deut 32:13; Ps 18:33; 2 Sam 2:34; Hab 3:19; Isa 58:14). *See* BAMOTH-BAAL.

ROBERT B. COOTE

BAMOTH-BAAL bay′moth-bay′uhl [בָּמוֹת־בַּעַל bamoth-ba‘al; Βαμωθβααλ Bamōthbaal]. A town on the plateau east of the Jordan near Mount Nebo, exact site uncertain, serving as a stopping place on the Israelite trek from Egypt (Num 21:19, 20; 22:41). A few have interpreted it as simply a sanctuary site, literally, "the heights of Baal" (note the act of sacrifice, Num 23:1-12). Bamoth (Josh 13:17) and Beth-Bamoth in the Moabite stone, line 27, probably refer to the same place. *See* NEBO, MOUNT.

ROBERT B. COOTE

BAN ban [חֵרֶם kherem]. Kherem ("devoted thing," "devoted to destruction") is a category or status encompassing things or people consecrated irrevocably into God's ownership and unavailable for secular use. Leviticus 27:21, 28-29 applies this status to fields, animals, and enslaved people as a result of voluntary dedication. Things that were kherem became Priestly property according to Num 18:14 and Ezek 44:17. People who were kherem were put to death (Exod 22:19 [E 20]; Lev 27:29).

The ban appears most often in the context of warfare (Josh 6–8, 10–11; *see* HOLY WAR). At least some of the booty secured in holy war belonged to the LORD and became herem. Such booty had to be isolated or more often destroyed (*see* EXTERMINATE and DESTROY, UTTERLY). Because they were valuable as slaves, enemy populations routinely fell under the ban and were to be killed (Deut 20:16-17). However, material booty and cattle did not always come under the ban (Deut 2:34-35; 3:6-7; Josh 8:2, 26-27; 11:14). The story of Achan shows that the danger of being kherem could be transferred (Josh 6:18; also Deut 7:26).

Deuteronomy utilized the concept of the ban to demand the elimination of foreign religious elements (Deut 7:2, 26; 13:16, 18 [E 17, 19]). Prophets used it to threaten a reverse holy war directed against Israel (Isa 43:28; Jer 25:9; Mal 3:24) and to promise future divine action against Israel's enemies (Jer 50:21, 26; 51:3; Mic 4:13).

Bibliography: Philip D. Stern. *The Biblical Herem.* BJS 211 (1991).

RICHARD D. NELSON

BAND [חַיִל khayil, גְּדוּד gedhudh, שָׂפָה safah; σπεί-ρω speirō, σπεῖρα speira]. 1. Group of people assembled for a common purpose. A gathering of people such as prophets (khayil 1 Sam 10:5, 10), or shepherds (Isa 31:4), or revelers (Jer 15:17; compare REMNANT). A

group of soldiers (Ezra 8:22; speira Matt 27:27; Act 10:1); a marauding group of men (2 Kgs 13:21) or deadly messengers (Ps 78:49); an encampment of Philistines (2 Sam 23:13); Rezon becoming captain over a band (1 Kgs 11:24), or David making Amasai and his men captains over a band (1 Chr 12:19).

2. Binding of a person physically, with swaddling bands (speirō Luke 2:7, 12), or with a chord, rope, or with shackles (gedhudh, Judg 15:13, 14; 16:11; Job 39:10; Ezek 3:25; 4:8). Or binding metaphorically, referring to oppression or bondage; e.g., God breaking the bands of the yoke or wickedness (Lev 26:13; Isa 56:6; Ezek 30:18; 34:27).

3. Pertaining to, or part of, a garment. A SASH, of fine workmanship, made of gold, blue, purple, and crimson yarns and twisted linen (safah Exod 39:5), which was worn in conjunction with the EPHOD, a priestly garment (Exod 28:8, 27-28; 29:5; 39:20; 39:21; Lev 8:7). The binding around the hole of a robe, which keeps the hole from fraying (Exod 39:23).

JILL L. BAKER

BAND, DECORATION [חָשׁוּק khashuq]. This is a decorative element in the Priestly description of the Tabernacle construction in Exod 27, 36, and 38, which has been understood as metal bands that connected the PILLARs of the TABERNACLE to each other. They are described as being overlaid with gold in some instances and silver in others (e.g., Exod 36:38; 38:10-19). The word is related to the verb חָשַׁק (khashaq), which means "to be attached to, to cleave to," and is typically used of affectionate attachment. While some have thought these bands were that upon which the curtains were hung, most modern translations consider these the silver and gold bands that constitute part of the pillars of the Tabernacle, below the capitals. A related term, חִשּׁוּק (khishuq), used in the plural form in 1 Kgs 7:33 is translated "their spokes," and may refer to the parts of the wheels that bind them together.

C. MARK MCCORMICK

BANDAGE [אֲפֵר ’afer, חָבַשׁ havash, רָכַךְ rakhakh; καταδέω katadeō]. The OT contains both the nouns for a covering or bandage, ’afer (1 Kgs 20:38, 41; Ezek 30:21), and verbs for bandaging or treating physical wounds, primarily havash, which means to bind, or bind up (Job 5:18; Isa 1:6; Ezek 30:21; 34:16 and figuratively in Isa 30:26; 61:1; Ezek 34:4; Hos 6:1 in par. with רָפָא, rafa’ healing). Rakhakh is used for softening wounds with oil before bandaging (Isa 1:6). In the NT, katadeō means to bind a bandage on someone's wound, as in Luke 10:34. *See* HEALING.

KENNETH D. LITWAK

BANDITRY [בָּזַז bazaz, גָּזַל gazal, פָּרִיץ parits, שָׁסָה shasah; λῃστής lēstēs]. Properly speaking, *banditry* refers to the activity of outlaws or brigands, often operating in armed companies outside of the "legitimate" state's institutions. Armed robbery is a major but not the only activity of bandits. Groups of bandits may actually administer quasi-governmental institutions, including policing functions, economic redistribution, protection from external threats, influence peddling, and the like, in the absence of a powerful legitimate state. Very much like terrorists (*see* TERRORISM), bandits challenge the state's monopoly on certain types of violence. A state is a robber-band that has been recognized as legitimate by other states; a robber-band is an unrecognized state or one that operates within territory claimed by another state. Just like legitimate states, the popularity and policies of bandits are variable. Instances of banditry may serve as a barometer for the extent to which a given state is successful in its control and penetration of a particular region.

The OT refers to banditry and various types of robbery both literally and as a metaphor for rapacious political practices (e.g., Lev 19:13; Job 20:19; Ezek 22:29). The terminology of robbery is also used to foretell misfortunes and instability, or to describe moral corruption (e.g., Jer 7:11; Ezek 7:22; 39:10). Descriptions of actual banditry also appear in the OT, albeit without being identified with any single technical term. The most remarkable case is that of DAVID, who is represented as a bandit-chief during the monarchy of Saul in 1 Sam 23–27. David appears in this material as the chief of a roving band of marauders who are operating at odds with, and within territory claimed by, the legitimate Israelite state under Saul.

In the NT, lēstēs appears as a technical term referring to bandits. Incidences of banditry under Roman rule were very widespread in Judea and elsewhere. In the synoptic Gospels, Jesus characterizes the Temple as illegitimate, by describing it as a den of robbers (Matt 21:13; Mark 11:17; Luke 19:46), quoting from Jer 7:11. It is bandits who leave a traveler for dead in the parable of the good Samaritan (Luke 10:30, 36); bandits who threaten the sheep whom the good shepherd protects (John 10:1, 8); and bandits who threaten Paul during his travels in 2 Cor 11:26. The Passion Narratives of all four canonical Gospels contain references to bandits. In the Gospel of John, BARABBAS is described as a bandit (18:40). Jesus is handled like a bandit at his arrest (Matt 26:55; Mark 14:48; Luke 22:52), and his death by CRUCIFIXION underscores this treatment. The two men who were crucified alongside Jesus were bandits (Matt 27:38; Mark 15:27). These references appear to stress Jesus' innocent degradation, and the unjust and ironic reduction of his social status to a point where he is treated as less valuable than even a bandit.

WILLIAM E. ARNAL

BANDS, MAGIC [כְּסָתוֹת kesathoth, כֶּסֶת keseth, cushion; Akkad. kasu, to bind; kasitu, binding magic;

προσκεφάλιον proskephalion]. Described in Ezek 13:18, 20, 21, par. to Mesopotamian incantation texts, which suggest that these objects were used either for NECROMANCY, DIVINATION, sorcery, childbirth, or HEALING rituals. Binding magic continued to be important in the ancient Mediterranean world. *See* BIRTH; MAGIC, MAGICIAN.

ANN L. FRITSCHEL

BANGLES. *See* JEWELRY.

BANI bay´ni [בָּנִי bani; Βανι Bani, Βαανι Baani]. A name similar to BUNNI and BINNUI, all of which are easily confused. The Hebrew can also be understood as the term "son of," so that in a number of places the LXX chooses that meaning rather than the name Bani (e.g., 2 Sam 23:36). 1. A Gadite, one of David's "Thirty" heroes (2 Sam 23:36).

2. The son of Shemer, a descendant of Merrari, the son of LEVI, and one of the ancestors of Ethan the son of Kishi (1 Chr 6:46).

3. One of the sons of PEREZ the son of JUDAH (1 Chr 9:4), one of the ancestors of Uthai the son of Ammihud, who was in Jerusalem in Nehemiah's time.

4. A postexilic family group. In some cases the text reads "Binnui":

   a. Among those who returned to Judah with Zerubbabbel after the exile (Ezra 2:10; 1 Esd 5:12; Neh 7:15).

   b. Among those who married foreign women (Ezra 10:29, 34, 38; 1 Esd 9:30, 34).

   c. Returnees from Babylonia to Judah with Ezra (Ezra 8:10).

   d. Among those who sealed Ezra's covenant (Neh 10:13-15).

   e. Among those who assisted Ezra in organizing the people and instructing them in the book of the law (Neh 8:7).

   f. The ancestor/family line of Uzzi, overseer of the Jerusalem Levites of the order of Asaph (Neh 11:22).

   g. The ancestor/family line of Rehum, a Levite who contributed for repairing a section of the Jerusalem wall (Neh 3:17).

   h. A Levite (group or individual) who took part in the Feast of the Tabernacles at the time of Ezra (Neh 9:4-5).

O. LIPSCHITS AND O. SERGEY

BANISHMENT [שָׁרֹשִׁי sheroshi, גְּרוּשָׁה gerushah]. Banishment is forcing a person, a family, or a group of people to be separated from the CONGREGATION, usually as a result of a punishment, which may also include confiscation of property and possessions (Ezra 10:8). Biblical law never prescribed banishment as a legal penalty, since the effect of leaving the house, the land, and the congregation was for the Israelites a way of being cut off from Yahweh (Hos 9:3-5; Gen 4:14; Ezek 11:15) and perhaps even being forced to worship idols (Deut 4:27-28; 1 Sam 26:19; Jer 16:13). It is a form of EXCOMMUNICATION.

Because in this sense it is never a legal prescription, banishment was not prescribed for someone who committed a crime, such as murder. But in, effect, an accused murderer was banished from family and homeland and often sought asylum in a designated CITY OF REFUGE.

Ezra 10:8 may be understood as a threat of banishment, and this penalty appears probably also in Ezra 7:26 by the Aramaic, lishroshu, which probably means "rooting out," with the meaning of "exclusion from the community." There is no reason to translate this verb as "flogging," as suggested by some scholars.

Various Hebrew and Greek terms carry the sense of banishment, as when the NRSV says that Solomon banished Abiathar from the priesthood (1 Kgs 2:27), Yahweh declined to banish Aram (2 Kgs 13:23), Yahweh banished Israel (2 Kgs 17:20), the banishment effected by the Babylonian exile (Jer 46:28), the removal, "banishment," of gladness from the land (Isa 24:11). It can also be used to describe living in exile (2 Macc 10:15).

Although "BAN" and related English terms have sometimes been used to translate and describe the Hebrew kherem (חֵרֶם), the Hebrew concept of "devoted things" is quite different than simply things that are banned as described here. *See* ANATHEMA; DEVOTED.

O. LIPSCHITS AND O. SERGEY

BANK [שָׂפָה safah; κρημνός krēmnos]. The edge of a river or sea where the water meets the dry land. In the cosmology of the OT, water and land were two different realms, separated by God during creation (Gen 1:9-10). A bank therefore formed the boundary between two domains. This may explain why animals that live along the edge of the water, such as storks and herons, are considered unclean (Lev 11:19; Deut 14:18). Visions, dreams, and divine encounters involve banks: Pharaoh's dream (Gen 41:1-4), two of Daniel's visions (Dan 10:2; 12:5-13), Jesus' teaching by the sea (Matt 8:32), the disciples recognizing the risen Jesus (John 21:4-14), and scenes in Revelation (Rev 10:1-11, 12:18–13:10).

KEVIN A. WILSON

BANKING. The simple economy of agrarian Israel did not need banks comparable to those in Mesopotamia where royal palaces and especially temples loaned money at interest for building projects, canal construction, mortgages, business enterprises, and foreign trade. According to the OT, money should be loaned interest free to help poor Israelites. For safekeeping, Israelites buried money in the ground or gave it to neighbors (Exod 22:7). The Temple stored national wealth (1 Kgs 14:26), and commerce was a royal function (1 Kgs 10:14-29; 2 Chr 20:35-37). Only after the Babylonian exile did Jews become familiar with banking practices. In the NT the word for banking comes from the word *table* (τράπεζα trapeza, Luke 19:23), because foreign and Jewish currencies were exchanged upon a table. In the Temple precincts, diaspora Jews traded foreign currency for the Jewish Temple shekel to buy sacrificial animals or to make donations (Matt 21:12; Mark 11:15; John 2:14-15). *See* DEBT; MONEY-CHANGER; TRADE AND COMMERCE.

ROBERT GNUSE

BANNAS ban´uhs [Βάννος Bannos]. One of the ancestors of the seventy-four Levites who returned with Zerubbabel to Jerusalem (1 Esd 5:26), but not included in Ezra 2:40.

BANNER [נֵס ges]. With the advent of urbanization in the ancient world, warfare increased in complexity. An order of battle with divisions of arms such as shock troops, archers, slingers; a mixture of types of troops such as cavalry, infantry, and chariotry; and occasional regional divisions demanded greater organization and control. It is possible that in ancient Israel, as in other contemporary armies, uniforms depicting different troops were used. But by far the most common method of identification for troops on the march or in combat was the battle standard, or banner.

Pharaoh Narmer's battle mace (ca. 3000 BCE) depicts a victory celebration in which banners are paraded before the enthroned victor. The 5th cent. BCE Persian army also used banners to identify the location of the king and his commanders during battle. At Qadesh, Pharaoh Ramses divided his chariot force into four geographical divisions identified by their regional gods.

The OT mentions a variety of uses for such banners. They serve as rallying points in battle (Ps 60:4; Isa 11:10, 12; possibly Zech 9:16). They signal advancing danger or the beginning of a battle or siege (Jer 4:6; Isa 18:3; Jer 51:12, 27; also used metaphorically in Num 26:10).

Once engaged, an army is recognizable so long as its standards remain (Jer 4:21), and after victory banners are raised over a conquered foe (Ps 20:5; Isa 62:10). Lone and abandoned banners provide a poignant image of defeat (Isa 30:17; 31:9). In the OT, the common site of an invading army on the march with banners unfurled created terror among the resident population (Song 6:4; Isa 5:26).

The raising of a banner over an endangered fortress could have been both a warning to others in a chain and a sign of encouragement. In Lachish Letter IV line 11, the "coded signals" or "signs" of Azekah are no longer visible from Lachish, suggesting that Azekah had fallen (Jer 34:7). The use of such signals was common in Roman fortress chains.

In Num 1–2, the tribal armies of Israel are arranged in camp according to the tribe and clan. These standards constitute the camp colors of Israel's ancient army and ensure a secure battle order.

Persian, Greek, Maccabean, and Roman armies used banners in this way as a means of identification of various troop types and regiments in camp and in battle. One or all of these military traditions provide the background for the common use of banners in the description of the army of the Sons of Light in the War Scroll from Qumran (1 QM). The divisions of this apocalyptic army (the congregation) into divisions, tribes, thousands, hundreds, fifties, and tens is delineated by numerous banners upon which are the names of units and leaders. As they approach for battle, engage in battle, then withdraw after victory, slogans are written on the banners.

The banners themselves vary in size from 21 ft. (ca. 7 m) for the largest banner of the whole congregation to 10.5 ft. (ca. 3.5 m) for the smallest for the unit of 10 soldiers. It is clear in this configuration that the banners not only serve as rallying points for the army, and for maintaining order, but also as a means of propaganda.

The proprietary function of banners is used in an entirely different manner in Song 2:4. At the banquet for the two lovers, the insignia on the banner testifies to tenderness, not violence. *See* ARMY; ARRAY, BATTLE; DEAD SEA SCROLLS; STANDARD.

T. R. HOBBS

BANQUET [מִשְׁתֶּה misteh; δεῖπνον deipnon]. Banquets were important events that were used to mark important social and religious occasions throughout the historical periods and cultural contexts referenced by the Bible. The reclining banquet was most common from ca. the 8th cent. BCE to the early medieval period CE. Diners reclined on couches and enjoyed a luxurious repast while being attended to by servants (pictured negatively in Amos 6:4-6; *see* Plato's *Symposium* for the Greek archetype). The custom appears to have arisen in the ancient Near East, but was quickly adopted by the Greeks (ca. 6th cent. BCE) and later by the Romans and came to dominate throughout the Greco-Roman world. In the NT, Jesus is always pictured as reclining at meals (e.g., Mark 4:15; 6:39; 8:6; 14:18). Prior to the adoption of the custom of reclining, there are references to sitting at a banquet as the common posture in the ancient Mediterranean world. *See* FEASTS AND FASTS; FOOD; MEALS; WINE.

DENNIS E. SMITH

BANQUET HALL [בֵּית־מִשְׁתֶּה beth mishteh]. A banquet hall was a chamber containing couches and tables for a reclining meal (Esth 7:8; Amos 6:4-7; also Jer 16:5-8). In the Greco-Roman world, dining rooms for

reclining banquets were found at pagan temples (1 Cor 8:10) and other locations including private homes (Mark 2:15). *See* COUCH; TABLE FELLOWSHIP.

DENNIS E. SMITH

BAPTISM [βάπτισμα baptisma, βαπτισμός baptismos, βάπτισις baptisis]. Baptism is a rite of immersion in water. The equivalent Hebrew word to Greek baptisma (Matt 3:7; Rom 6:4 et al.), baptismos (*Ant.* 18:117; Heb 6:2; 9:10; Col 2:12) or baptisis (*Ant.* 18:117), is טְבִילָהּ tavalyahu, which in Rabbinic literature refers to full immersion in water and proselyte baptism. The word רַחְצָה rakhtsah (used of the dipping of sheep in Song 4:2; 6:6), may have functioned as an earlier equivalent, since the verb רָחַץ rakhats, "wash," is used of ritual bathing (Lev 14:8).

A. Immersion in the OT and Second Temple Judaism
  1. Immersions in biblical law
  2. Immersions in Second Temple Judaism
    a. Proselyte baptism
    b. Other immersions
    c. Efficacy
    d. Pools
B. John the Baptist's Immersion
  1. Meaning
  2. Process
C. The Baptism of Jesus by John
D. Baptism in the NT Church
  1. The Fourth Gospel
  2. The synoptic Gospels
  3. The Acts of the Apostles
  4. Philip and the Ethiopian Eunuch
  5. "In the name of Jesus"
  6. John's baptism
  7. Meaning
  8. Process
Bibliography

A. Immersion in the OT and Second Temple Judaism

Among various schools of thought in ancient Judaism there was an interest in defining and preserving the laws of ritual purity. Israelites are "to distinguish between the holy and the common, and between the unclean and the clean" (Lev 10:10).

1. Immersions in biblical law

Many things could render a body ritually unclean: e.g., contact with a corpse (Num 19:10-13; Lev 11), skin diseases (Lev 13), and bodily discharges (Lev 15). Immersion in water was used to rid the body of ritual impurity after someone had a contagious skin disease (Lev 14:8-9), a genital discharge (Lev 15:13), contact with a corpse (Lev 22:4-6; Num 31:23-24), or a seminal emission (Deut 23:11; Lev 15:16). It was required when a person had eaten an animal that died a natural death or been savaged (Lev 17:15); touched the body, bed, or chair of someone with a genital discharge or sat on his chair (Lev 15:6-8, 11-12); been spat on by such a person (Lev 15:8); carried anything under him (Lev. 15:10); or touched the bed or seat of a menstruant (Lev 15:21-22; 25-27). By implication one would probably also have immersed after touching, picking up, or eating a carcass of an unclean animal (Lev 11:24-28, 31, 39-40). Along with immersion, various types of sprinklings, sacrifices, and the passage of time could be required before ritual purity was reestablished. Ritual purity was a requirement for those entering the Temple (Lev 15:31; *J.W.* 5:227) and for the eating of sacrificed animals (Lev 8:19-21). The unclean, like the uncircumcised, were considered repugnant to God (Lev 11:43; Ezek 36:24-29*a*). In Isa 52:1, "the uncircumcised and the unclean" shall no longer enter Jerusalem when God acts in judgment. People are advised to "depart, depart, go out from there! Touch no unclean thing; go out from the midst of it, purify yourselves, you who carry the vessels of the LORD" (Isa 52:11).

2. Immersions in Second Temple Judaism

a. Proselyte baptism. When people converted from paganism to Judaism there was an initial immersion, known as proselyte baptism, designed to rid the body of ritual uncleanness (*b. Yebam* 46*a*–48*b*; *b. Gerim* 60*a*–61*b*). Gentiles were unclean and needed to be purified at the point of their entrance to Israel (*J.W.* 2:150; *Ant.* 14:285; 18:93-4; *t. Yoma* 4:20; *t. Pesah* 7:13, and *see* Acts 10:28; John 18:28). Up until this point they were not allowed into the Temple proper on account of their uncleanness (*m. Kelim* 1:8; 1 Macc 9:34; Philo, *Legat.* 212; *Ant.* 12:145f.; *t. Yoma* 4:20). It was noted that one "who has become a proselyte is like a child newly born" (*b. Yebam* 48*b*), because of his/her new participation in the community of Israel, with resulting new legal status (*m. Yebam* 11:2; *m. Hul.* 10:4). In most cases self-immersion was the norm, but the feeble or very young would be immersed by another.

b. Other immersions. Apart from what is prescribed in biblical law, Jews could use immersions in rituals of repentance and pleading forgiveness from God (*T. Levi* 2:3B1-2; the *Sibylline Oracles* 4:162-70). In the *Apoc. Mos.* 29:6-13, Adam and Eve stand in the river Jordan for forty (or thirty-four) days in order to beg God for forgiveness. Certain schools of thought adopted a more stringent line in terms of ritual purity, most famously the Pharisees and the Essenes, who would take frequent purificatory baths, and also solitary ascetics like Bannus (Josephus, *Life* 10).

c. Efficacy. In the RULE OF THE COMMUNITY (1QS) of the Dead Sea Scrolls, most likely composed by ESSENES, we find a view that immersions are ineffective if someone is sinful or outside the community: "he shall . . . not be purified by waters for impurity or

be made holy by seas and rivers or be purified by any water for (ritual) washing. Unclean, unclean will he be all the days he despises the precepts of God, up until he receives instruction in the community of his counsel" (1QS3:3-6, and *see* 1QS5:13-15). After "the humble submission of his soul to all the precepts of God his body will be purified when sprinkled with waters for impurity and made holy with waters for cleansing" (1QS3:6-9). This understanding is probably derived from Isa 1:12-20, where God tells the Israelites that nothing they do in terms of ritual is of any value without righteousness, justice, and obedience to the law.

d. Pools. Ritual immersion could take place in different bodies of water. Such water was rated for its efficacy in six grades in ascending order of quality (*m. Miqw.* 1:1-8): 1) ponds, cisterns, ditch-water, cave pools, rain-pools, or any collection of water less than 40 seahs; 2) rain-pools while it is still raining; 3) a pool containing more than 40 seahs; 4) a type of well; 5) smitten water that was salty or hot; 6) "living water" found in rivers, lakes, or springs. Certain types of ritual impurity could only be removed by immersion in living water (e.g., Lev 14:5-6, 50-52; 15:13; Num 19:17; Deut 21:4). In the first centuries CE a special type of pool, called miqvaoth, was constructed. These were pools containing more than 40 seahs (ca. 500 L) of largely rainwater. Such miqvaot have been found in numerous archaeological excavations in Israel.

B. John the Baptist's Immersion

John's action in baptizing people gave him the epithet "the Immerser," or "the Baptizer" (ὁ βαπτιστής ho Baptistēs, e.g., Matt 16:14 = Mark 8:28 = Luke 9:19; or βαπτίζων Baptizōn or Mark 1:4; 6:14, 24).

1. Meaning

John announced "a baptism of repentance for the forgiveness of sins" (Mark 1:4) or, as Josephus put it, the immersion would be acceptable to God—and thereby effective, "if it was . . . a purification of the body, now that the soul had been cleansed already by righteousness" (*Ant.* 18:116). John immersed people in the river Jordan and other places nearby where there was natural water, which may indicate a wish to use the highest grade of water for immersion. As in the Community Rule, John required baptizands—those coming for baptism—to be repentant of past misdeeds prior to immersion, and additionally baptism was not to be undertaken without a person *first* "bearing good fruit" worthy of repentance (Luke 3:7-8, and *see* Matt 3:7-8), meaning good deeds (Luke 3:10-14). Josephus states that John's baptism was an immersion following prior inner cleansing of the soul (*Ant.* 18:117), which equates to the gospels' emphasis on forgiveness of sins. This necessity for repentance and forgiveness of sins (inward cleansing) in order to make ritual immersion (outer cleansing) effective would have distinguished

John's baptism from other kinds of immersion practiced by 1st cent. Jews. The priority of inner cleansing is endorsed implicitly by Jesus in Matt 23:25-26 (modified in Luke 11:39-41), where Jesus criticizes the Pharisees' practice of bodily ablutions, when they do not necessarily consider whether the inside of the person is "clean."

The synoptic Gospels present John's baptism as an eschatological action in that it prepared people for the imminent arrival of the one to come, who would be the agent of divine judgment. He would separate out those who were forgiven, cleansed, and righteous from those who were not. The former group would receive the Holy Spirit and the latter group burn in unquenchable fire (e.g., Matt 3: 11; Mark 1:8; Luke 3: 16; John 1: 33).

2. Process

John actively baptized another person (Mark 1:8a). Elsewhere in Second Temple Judaism only the feeble and young are baptized by another person, otherwise self-immersion was normative. The meaning of John's active immersion of another person remains unclear.

It is unlikely that baptizands were naked, since public nakedness was shameful in Second Temple Judaism. Essene men wore a loincloth, and women wore a wrap (J.W. 2:161). In the Mishnah there is the view that certain garments would "interpose" and cause the immersion to be rendered ineffective, namely wool or flax (linen), though cotton or hair cloth is not mentioned and Rabbi Judah apparently stated alternatively that those made of wool and those of hair do not interpose, because the water enters into them (m. Miqw. 9:1). It states also that "he who kept hold on a man or on utensils and immersed them—they are unclean" unless "he rinsed his hand in the water" beforehand or else the immerser should "loose his hold on them so that the water may come into them" (m. Miqw. 8:5).

C. The Baptism of Jesus by John

Jesus' baptism by John is reported in the synoptic Gospels (Mark 1:9-11 and par.) and implied in John's Gospel (John 1:32-4). However, discomfort about the baptism of Jesus is found already in Matthew (3:14-15) where Jesus comes forward to be immersed but John tries to prevent him saying, "I need to be baptized by you, and do you come to me?" Jesus calmly reassures him, "Let it be so now; for it is proper for us in this way to fulfill all righteousness." Christian writers of the 2nd cent. were likewise uncomfortable. Ignatius of Antioch stated that Jesus was immersed not so that the water would purify him, but so that he might "purify the water" (Eph 18:2). Justin Martyr could explain that Jesus was baptized "solely for the sake of humanity" (Dial. 88). In the Gospel of the Ebionites, immediately after Jesus' baptism, John asks Jesus to baptize him (Epiphanius, Pan. 30:13:7-8). In the Gospel of the

Hebrews (Jerome, Pelag. 3:2), Jesus mother and brothers urge him to go to John for baptism but Jesus says there is no need because he is sinless.

Jesus' baptism by John culminates in the descent of the Spirit upon him. In Mark 1:9-11, the reference to heavens opening indicates a visionary experience, as in Stephen's vision of Acts 7:56 or Peter's vision of Acts 10:11 (Rev 4:1; John 1:51). Jesus "saw" the Spirit descending. His vision takes place "immediately" as he comes up out of the water. Luke detaches the visionary experience from the baptism and places it at a time when Jesus is in prayer afterward (Luke 3:21-22). The motif of Jesus in prayer is especially dear to Luke (5:16; 9:18, 28–29). Luke also adds that the Spirit was "in bodily form" like a dove. In Matt 3:16-17, while Jesus still sees this descent of the Spirit, the voice makes a public announcement presumably heard by those around Jesus as well. In the Fourth Gospel, the whole visionary experience belongs to John the Baptist, who claims that he has seen the Spirit descending as a dove out of heaven and remain on Jesus (John 1:32-23).

D. Baptism in the NT church

1. The Fourth Gospel

In between the baptism begun by John and the widespread use of baptism within the early church there is the intermediate period of Jesus' ministry, in which a form of baptism similar to that initiated by John may have been practiced. Only John 3:22 and 4:1-3 mention baptism in connection with Jesus' ministry: "After this Jesus and his disciples went into the Judean countryside, and he spent some time there with them and baptized" (3:22) and "when Jesus learned that the Pharisees had heard, 'Jesus is making and baptizing more disciples than John'. . . . he left Judea and started back to Galilee" (4:1-3). In 4:2 an editorial comment denies that Jesus himself baptized people. John 3:5 affirms the necessity of birth through water and the Spirit, which is traditionally considered a reference to Christian baptism. However, in Johannine language those born of the Spirit of God are defined as those who believe in Jesus as Christ and Son of God (John 1:12-13; 1 John 5:1), while birth through water here is defined as "what is born of human nature."

2. The synoptic Gospels

In the synoptic Gospels a baptizing mission by Jesus or his disciples is not explicitly mentioned. The popular belief that Jesus was in fact John risen from the dead (Mark 6:16 = Luke 9:9) may imply that Jesus' mission was very similar to that of John, who was distinguished by his baptism (Mark 6:14; Luke 9:7). The risen Lord authorizes baptism by the disciples in Matt 28:16-20 and in the long ending to Mark's Gospel (2nd cent. CE). In Mark 16:16 Jesus instructs his disciples that those who believe and are baptized will be saved. However, the long ending, Mark 16:9-20 is not found in the oldest manuscripts and is widely believed to be a later addition to the Gospel. The only 1st cent. witness to this tradition remains Matt 28:19.

As noted above, Jesus expressed the belief that inner purity of the heart in terms of moral action was necessary prior to external purifications (Matt 23:25-26). While Mark interpreted this tradition to mean that Jesus had invalidated the entire Jewish purity system for Gentile-Christian communities (so Mark 7:19b), a complete rejection of the purity system by Jesus himself does not fit well with the conflicts between Jewish- and Gentile-Christians in the 1st cent. (Gal 2; Acts 15). Jewish-Christians continued to observe Mosaic law. Jesus' statements in Mark 7:15-23 may mean no more than that Jesus advocated the importance of internal, moral purity (Matt 23:25-26), and did not support certain specialized practices of immersion advocated by the Pharisees (see Mark 7:1-4), which he brands "human traditions" (Mark 7:8), since they are not found in Mosaic law.

3. The Acts of the Apostles

In Acts it is stated that the replacement for Judas among the twelve apostles should be, like the others, someone who was with Jesus "beginning from the baptism of John" (Acts 1:22), which implies that they had been with Jesus at the Jordan. Only the Fourth Gospel explicitly links any of Jesus' initial disciples with John the Baptist (John 1–2). Luke–Acts assumed that everyone in the Upper Room for Pentecost had already been baptized in water. After the pouring out of the Spirit as described in Acts 2 we have the foundation for baptism in the church that unlike Jewish purification rites or the Baptist's ritual, conveyed the Spirit along with immersion in water. Pentecost fulfills John's prediction that the one who comes after him will baptize with the Holy Spirit (Mark 1: 8; Luke 3:16; Matt. 3:11; John 1:33; Acts 1:4-5). After Pentecost, the apostles immediately go out and baptize those who accept their message (Acts 2:41).

4. Philip and the Ethiopian Eunuch

As portrayed in Acts, the diakonos ("assistant") Philip baptized people "in the name of the Lord Jesus" (Acts 8:16), but his immersions did not involve the baptism of the Holy Spirit. Peter and John came to Samaria in his wake to impart the Spirit by means of the laying on of hands (Acts 8:17, and see 19:6). This water-only baptism appears to be the intermediate kind of baptism, which was not immediately rendered universally redundant after the Pentecost event. In the story of the immersion of the Ethiopian eunuch (Acts 8:26-39), who was a proselyte that had just come from worshiping at the Temple in Jerusalem, Philip and the Ethiopian go down into some kind of natural pool of water together, whereby "Philip baptized him" (Acts 8:38).

5. "In the name of Jesus"

Elsewhere in Acts and in the epistles baptism occurs "in the name of [the Lord] Jesus [Christ]" (Acts 8:16; 10:48; 19:5; 1 Cor 6:11) "for the forgiveness of your sins," so Acts 2:38. Many complex theories have been offered for the origin of the phrase. The simplest explanation for the emergence of this probably Aramaic circumlocution traces it to accounts of Jesus' ministry. The apostles cast out demons and heal "in the name of Jesus," or "by Jesus' authority" (Luke 10:17, see 9:1-2). In Luke 21:8 Jesus warns that many will come "in my name," which would mean "as if authorized by me (Jesus)." In Acts 3:16 people are accepted on the basis of faith "in my name," here "in my authority [as Messiah]" (and see John 1:12). Paul can ask ironically if anyone was baptized "in the name of Paul" in 1 Cor 1:13, adding, "I thank God that I baptized none of you except Crispus and Gaius, so that no one should say you were baptized in my name," which shows that there was potentially some confusion about the authority of baptism if the baptizer did not make it very clear that the baptism was in the name of Jesus.

6. John's baptism

In Acts 19:1-7, Paul discovers in Ephesus about twelve people, identified as "some disciples" who were "believers" (19:1-2), and immersed "into John's baptism." They had either not heard of a "Holy Spirit" or believed (on the basis of some manuscripts) that "anyone received a Holy Spirit"; in other words, they were apparently unaware of the imparting of the Holy Spirit at Christian baptism. The disciples appear to be connected with APOLLOS, who was also "trusting only in the immersion of John" (Acts 18:25, author's trans.). Apollos was a learned Alexandrian Jew "instructed in the Way of the Lord" who "taught accurately the things concerning Jesus." Paul rebaptizes the twelve disciples "in the name of the Lord Jesus," and they receive the Holy Spirit, through the laying on of Paul's hands (Acts 19:6). According to Paul, John always meant to indicate that the one coming after him was Jesus (Acts 19:4). While it is common to see these people as disciples of John the Baptist, the story actually indicates that there were disciples of Jesus who had only been baptized with the type of water baptism heralded by John as with the disciples of Acts 2. Rather than simply laying on hands to impart the Spirit, in their case Paul rebaptizes "in the name of Jesus" and then imparts the Spirit.

7. Meaning

Hebrews 6:2 mentions the fundamental teachings about Christ involving "repentance from dead works and faith toward God, instruction about baptisms, laying on of hands, resurrection of the dead, and eternal judgment." Hebrews 10:22 mentions that the faithful have "hearts sprinkled from an evil conscience, and our bodies washed with pure water." This phrase suggests that John's theology of baptism had been adapted within the Jewish-Christian church(es): the inner being—the heart—is cleansed (remission of sins) and then the body is purified.

In 1 John 5:6 Jesus comes "by water and blood," possibly indicating both Jesus' baptism by John and the metaphorical baptism of his death, predicted by Jesus in Mark 10:38-39; Luke 12:50. The notion that Jesus' death was in some way a baptism passed into Pauline thought. For Paul and his school, baptism was a way of dying to sin and becoming part of the one spiritual body of Jesus Christ (Rom 6:3-11; 1 Cor 12:12-13; 2 Cor 1:21-22; 5:17; Gal 3:26-47; 6:15; Eph 1:14; 4:4-5; Col 2:10-14; Titus 3:5-7), which was also the Christian community. Gentile converts might have understood this motif as comparable to the initiation rituals of Hellenistic mystery cults (of Eleusis, Isis and Serapis, Mithras, Orpheus, Dionysus/Bacchus, and so on). Paul used the formula "in the name of Jesus" ("by the authority of Jesus"), but at times the phrase is shortened, so that one is baptized "into Christ [Jesus]" (Gal 3:27; Rom 6:3). Baptism involved an acceptance of the commandments of the one under whose authority people are baptized, so that the Israelites were "baptized into [the name of] Moses in the cloud and the sea" (1 Cor 10:1-2).

For Paul, one is buried with Christ in the water and raised from the dead upon coming up, when, with the imparting of the Spirit, one is a new creation (Gal 6:15; Rom 6:4; 7:6; 2 Cor 5:17; Eph 2:10, 15; 4:24; Col 3:10; Titus 3:5-7) "in Christ." As such, normal societal divisions no longer existed: "There is no longer Jew nor Greek, there is no longer slave or free, there is no longer male and female; for all of you are one in Christ Jesus" (Gal 3:28, and *see* 1 Cor 12:13). Paul saw Christians as having a spiritual seal or mark (2 Cor 1:21-22; Eph 1:13-14, 4:30) by means of the imparting of the Spirit. Thus Christian water-and-Spirit baptism replaces the mark of Jewish circumcision, a notion we find also in early extracanonical Christian literature (e.g., *2 Clem.* 6:9; 7:6; 8:6; *Barn.* 9:6; 11:11).

In Acts 22:16 there is an understanding of baptism as being about washing away of sins, a conception placed in the mouth of Ananias, who baptized Paul. Paul might have understood baptism also as a kind of washing from sin: "but you were washed, but you were sanctified, but you were rendered righteous, in the name of the Lord Jesus Christ and the in Spirit of our God" (1 Cor 6:11), though elsewhere Paul (or his school) can use the imagery of washing in terms of the common ritual or prenuptial washing of the bride, so that the Church—as the bride of Christ—is prenuptially washed by the word of God (Eph 5:25-7).

An austere position allowed for no secondary repentance after baptism. Hebrews 6:4-8 states that it is impossible to restore again to repentance those

Christians who have once been enlightened, shared in the Holy Spirit, and then fallen away.

Toward the end of the 1st cent. we find in 1 Pet 3:21 an argument against viewing baptism as being connected with ordinary bathing: "baptism . . . now saves you—not as a removal of dirt from the body, but as an appeal to God for a good conscience, through the resurrection of Jesus." As with Pauline texts, no mention is made of ritual impurity in this passage, which is intended for a Gentile audience. By the mid 2nd cent. Justin Martyr, a Palestinian Gentile, indicated that baptizands would pray and entreat God with fasting for the remission of sins beforehand, and then be brought to the water to be "regenerated." Baptism was an "illumination"; the means of being born again (interpreting John 3:5), and of having sin remitted.

On the other hand, until at least the 4th cent. certain Jewish-Christian groups continued to practice immersion of repentance for forgiveness of sins (e.g., the Elchasaites, so Hippolytus, *Haer.* 9:13:4) or the usual Jewish ritual immersions (e.g., the Ebionites, so Epiphanius, *Pan.* 28:6:4-5; 30:16:1), claiming that Peter likewise maintained such practices (*Pan.* 30:15:3).

8. Process

Nowhere is the process of baptism explained clearly in the NT. It seems, however, that while originally baptism was "in the name of [the Lord] Jesus [Christ]," the Trinitarian formula of baptism "in the name of the Father, the Son and the Holy Spirit" soon became standard, since we find it already in Matt 28:20 (ca. 80 CE). Likewise, in the *Didache*, one is "baptized into the name of the Father, the Son and the Holy Spirit" (*Did.* 7:1), as in Justin's *1 Apol.* 61.

While the imparting of the Spirit through the laying on of hands was understood to follow baptism, on one occasion this sequence is inverted: in the case of Cornelius and his household who were "speaking with tongues and exalting God" without being baptized (or receiving the laying on of hands to impart the Spirit). Peter feels then compelled to baptize them in the name of Jesus Christ immediately afterward (Acts 10:44-48; 11:15). This was the exception that proved the rule.

The *Didache* specifies baptism should take place in living water (of a river, lake, sea, or spring). If there is no such water then other water is permitted, and if no cold water, then warm is all right, and if neither of these is available then water is to be poured over the head three times into the threefold name (*Did.* 7:1-4). As noted above, Philip's baptism of the eunuch took place in "some water" near the road, clearly a natural spring, cistern, or cave pool (Acts 8:36, 38). The baptism of Lydia and her household is probably in a river (Acts 16:13, 15). In Titus 3:5-7 the Spirit is described as being "poured out" over Christian believers (*see* Joel 3:1-5), presumably as water was poured out in types of baptism (*see* Acts 10:44-48; 11:15).

In the *Apostolic Tradition* of Hippolytus (ca. 215 CE), the water in the baptismal font was to be "flowing" or else water was to be poured over it (*Trad. ap.* 21). The house-church at Dura Europos in Mesopotamia, ca. 230, contains a font that would have permitted the baptizand to kneel within it, while water was poured over his or her head. In the Lateran baptistery in Rome, a jet of water would have gushed into the font, so that the baptizand could be immersed by standing in the flow. In the case of such a form of baptism, one is necessarily "immersed" by someone who actually does the pouring of the water over the body. John the Baptist is often depicted in early Christian art as baptizing Jesus in the Jordan by pouring water over his head.

Acts mentions whole households being baptized (Acts 10:44-48; 16:13-15; 16:31-33; 18:8) and may indicate that infants were included. Likewise, the saying of Jesus: "whoever receives one such child in my name receives me" (Mark 9:37 and par.) may be interpreted to mean that even small children could be baptized (and *see* Eph 6:1). Tertullian, ca. 200, argued against infant baptism, but never stated it was not a traditional practice (*Bapt.* 18).

In the early church the baptized were naked (*see Trad. ap.* 21:9-11; *Didascalia Apostolorum* 16 [3:12]; Cyril, *Cat.* 20:2; Apostolic Constitutions 3:16). This required the separation of men and women. In the *Didascalia Apostolorum* deaconesses assist women, but it is the bishop who does the "real" baptizing, which involved the pronouncing of the Trinitarian formula and the imparting of the Spirit after the actual immersion (*Trad. ap.* 22:1-6; *Didascalia Apostolorum* 16 (3:12). A deacon or deaconess was required to strip the baptizand and anoint him or her with oil (of exorcism) prior to baptism. The deacon(ess) would go down into the water with the baptizand. The presbyter (priest) would anoint them with the oil of thanksgiving after the baptism. The baptizand then put on white clothes and was led into the assembly of the faithful (*Trad. ap.* 21:19-20).

Overall, baptism developed new meanings as it passed from its origins in the ritual purity practices of Judaism and specifically John's immersion of repentance for the remission of sins, to a period in which Jesus or his disciples were baptizing, to a Jewish-Christian rite of baptism in water and Spirit, to a Gentile-Christian ritual of regeneration strongly influenced by Paul and his school. New meanings appeared in different stages of this development, among different communities, resulting finally in established patterns of Christian baptismal rites in the 2nd to 3rd cent. *See* BATHING; CLEAN AND UNCLEAN; MIQVAH, MIQVAOTH; RULE OF THE COMMUNITY.

Bibliography: G. R. Beasley-Murray. *Baptism in the New Testament* (1962); E. J. Christiansen. "Women and Baptism." *Studia Theologica* 35 (1981) 1-8; O. Cullman. *Baptism in the New Testament* (1950); J. Jeremias. *Infant Baptism in the First Four Centuries* (1960); G. W. H. Lampe. *The Seal of the Spirit* (1951); P. Larere. *Baptism in Water and Baptism in the Spirit* (1993); J. Klawans. *Impurity and Sin in Ancient Israel* (2000); J. Neusner. *The Idea of Purity in Ancient Judaism* (1973); C. E. Pocknee. "The Archaeology of Baptism." *Theology* 74 (1971) 309–11; R. Schnackenburg. *Baptism in the Thought of St. Paul* (1964); J. E. Taylor. *The Immerser: John the Baptist within Second Temple Judaism* (1997); G. Wagner. *Pauline Baptism and the Pagan Mysteries* (1967); R. Webb. *John the Baptizer and Prophet* (1991).

JOAN E. TAYLOR

BAPTIST, JOHN THE. *See* JOHN THE BAPTIST.

BAPTIZE [βαπτίζω baptizō]. A term used in the LXX for self-immersion (2 Kgs 5:14; Jdt 12:7; Sir 31:30). In the NT, baptizō means "baptize" or "immerse" in relation to the BAPTISM of John, Jesus and his disciples, Jewish ritual immersion (Luke 11:38; Mark 7:4), and of the Holy Spirit (Mark 1:8 *et al.*). *See* BAPTISM; JOHN THE BAPTIST.

BAQAH VALLEY. An area 15 km northwest of modern Amman, Jordan, its name derives from בִּקְעָה biq'ah, "valley." With its plentiful resources (soil, springs, clay) and central location (probably on the KING'S HIGHWAY), humans have inhabited the valley almost without interruption since late Middle Paleolithic times (ca. 50,000 years ago). Excavations of Late Bronze Age and Iron Age sites provide information important for discussions about the appearance of the Israelites in history. *See* JORDAN.

STEVE COOK

BAR [בְּרִיחַ beriakh, מוֹטָה motah]. A long, narrow piece of wood or metal used for several purposes. As part of the structure of the tabernacle, a beriakh was made of acacia wood. Five such bars formed the framework of each side of the tabernacle; they were covered with gold and supported by gold rings (Exod 26:26-29; 36:31-33). The Merarites were charged with caring for this portion of the tabernacle (Num 3:36; 4:31).

The same Hebrew word for bar indicates the means of locking a gate. The huge doors in a city wall would be secured with a sturdy beam fastened horizontally across the inside of the gate. As such, "bar" often appears as part of a phrase or in parallel with "gate" or "door" (Judg 16:3; Pss 107:16, 147:13; Isa 45:2; Jer 49:31; Lam 2:9; Ezek 38:11; Amos 1:5). In Nah 3:13, the bar to the gate was apparently made of wood, but elsewhere it was bronze (1 Kgs 4:13) or iron (Ps 107:16; Isa 45:2). "Double gates and bars" serve to illustrate the heavy fortification of King Og of Bashan's territory (Deut 3:5), and Keilah, where David hid from

Saul (1 Sam 23:7). Poets use "bar" metaphorically to describe the boundary-keeping mechanisms of creation, such as the "bars" of the "land" (Jonah 2:6), and the "bars and doors" that restrain the sea (Job 38:10).

Part of a yoke included a "bar" (**motah**), which could be made of either wood or iron (Jer 28:13). The biblical text uses the "bar" part of a yoke metaphorically to describe Israel's oppression (Jer 27:2), or its release from such (Lev 26:13; Isa 9:4; Ezek 34:27).

According to NRSV, Achan sinfully took a "bar of gold" worth 50 shekels as part of the booty from the raid on Jericho (Josh 7:21, 24). This translation is a bit misleading, as it was probably more like a lump of gold. The Hebrew literally calls it a "tongue of gold" (לָשׁוֹן lashon); NIV translates this "wedge of gold." *See* DOOR; GATE; METALLURGY; TABERNACLE; YOKE.

LISA MICHELE WOLFE

BARABBAS buh-rab´uhs [Βαραββᾶς *Barabbas*]. This enigmatic character appears in Jesus' Roman trial in all four Gospels: Pilate offers to release one prisoner as part of a Passover amnesty to which the Jewish crowd, stirred up by the chief priests, choose Barabbas rather than Jesus.

Historically, we know very little about Barabbas. The Gospels are our only sources of information, but they are inconsistent and shaped by the evangelists' attempts to blame Jesus' Jewish opponents for his death. Mark 15:7 ambiguously states that Barabbas was "among the rebels in prison, who had committed murder in the insurrection"; Matt 27:16 simply calls him "a notorious prisoner"; and Luke 23:19 heightens his insurrectionary activity, implicating him in an uprising and murder. Finally, John 18:40 describes him as a λῃστής *lēstēs*, a brigand or political activist. Attempts have been made to link this uprising to those mentioned by Josephus (*J.W.* 2.175-77; *Ant.* 18.60-63), Philo (*Legat.* 299-305), or Luke 13:1, though without success. Whether Barabbas was awaiting trial or had already been sentenced is not clear.

The derivation of the Aramaic patronym *Barabbas* is uncertain: it probably comes from the unusual *Bar Abba*, son of Abba; or perhaps, following the variant Bar Rabba(n), son of a/the Teacher. A number of manuscripts of Matthew give his first name as Jesus, a reading that may be historical. Origen's remark—that no sinner throughout the Scriptures bore the name of Jesus—provides the reason for the name's suppression. The suggestion that Barabbas meant "son of the Father," and was an alternative name for Jesus of Nazareth, has not won wide acceptance.

A complicating factor is that there is no firm evidence for a Passover amnesty in 1st cent. Judea. The evangelists are unclear about the details: John thinks it was a Jewish custom; Matthew and Mark link it to the Roman governor. Perhaps Barabbas was tried on the same day as Jesus but was released, either because the charges were found to be groundless, or as an isolated act of clemency. Christian tradition, reflecting on the injustice of Barabbas' release and Jesus' crucifixion, provided the link between the two men. *See* BANDITRY; PASSION NARRATIVES; PILATE, PONTIUS; TRIAL OF JESUS.

Bibliography: H. K. Bond. *Pontius Pilate in History and Interpretation* (1998); P. Winter. *On the Trial of Jesus.* 2nd ed. (1974).

HELEN K. BOND

BARACHEL bair´uh-kuhl [בָּרַכְאֵל *barakh´el*]. A Buzite, father of Elihu, whose four speeches postponed God's response to Job's challenge (Job 32:2, 6).

BARACHIAH bair´uh-k*i*´uh [βαραχίας *Barachias*]. Father of Zechariah in Matt 23:35. Spelled Berechiah in Zech 1:1. Also called Jehoida (2 Chr 24:20-22) and Jeberechiah (Isa 8:2). *See* BERECHIAH.

BARAITA. An Aram. word derived from the noun **bar** (בַּר bar, "field, outer part"). **Baraita** functions as a technical term in the Babylonian Talmud to designate a Tannaitic tradition, which is not included in the MISHNAH. *See* RABBINIC INTERPRETATION; TANNA, TANNAIM.

MAYER I. GRUBER

BARAK bair´ak [בָּרָק *baraq*; Βάρκας *Barkas*]. The son of Abinoam from Kedesh in Naphtali (Judg 4). Barak was called by DEBORAH to follow the order of Yahweh to raise 10,000 men from the tribes Naphtali and Zebulun in order to lead them to war against SISERA, supreme commander of the Canaanite forces suppressing Israel. Despite Yahweh's assurance that Sisera would be delivered into Barak's hands, Barak was only willing to obey if Deborah confirmed her faith in the promised victory by attending the campaign. Deborah assented, restricting Barak's prospect of honor because of his unwillingness to trust God on his own: The glory to vanquish Sisera would not be Barak's but a woman's. Assured, Barak complied with the order of Yahweh: Accompanied by Deborah he summoned the requested forces and led them by foot to Kedesh and up to Mount Tabor. Sisera, recognizing the Israelite concentration of forces as a rebellion against the Canaanite supremacy, gathered his chariots and army at the river Kishon. Barak followed the instructions of Deborah and lead his poorly armed troops down into battle with the heavily armed Canaanites and won because of the actions of Yahweh, who put Sisera and his army into flight. Sisera, abandoning his chariot, fled on foot. Barak pursued him to find him murdered by JAEL in her tent. Deborah's song (Judg 5)—sung by Deborah and Barak—is a poetical depiction of Israel's victory from a slightly different angle. Hebrews 11:32-34 mentions Barak among the ancestors who were commended for their faith.

SUSANNE OTTO

BARAM, KEFAR. An ancient village in Upper Galilee, 2 km from the modern Israel-Lebanon border. The importance of the site stems from an extant façade of a large 3rd cent. CE synagogue. A second, smaller synagogue is also known to have been located near the ancient village, though remains from that building are no longer extant. The site is virtually unknown from ancient literature. The synagogue façade was noted by medieval pilgrims who referred to the beautifully preserved ruins in travel itineraries. Dedicatory Hebrew inscriptions from both synagogues have been preserved.

The ancient village was located to the northwest of Gush Halav, Nabratein, and Meiron. Synagogues from the late Roman and early Byzantine periods are well known from this area of Galilee. The style of the large synagogue at Bar'am is similar to the synagogues near the Sea of Galilee at Capernaum and Chorazin. The synagogues at Bar'am had three south-facing entrances, and contained elaborate designs including winged Victories, the head of a lion, rope patterns, and laurel leaves. In the 3rd and 4th cent., unlike other parts of the Roman Empire that experienced a decline in the construction of monumental buildings, Galilee had a significant expansion of Jewish public spaces. The extensive number of synagogues from this period testifies to the large number of Jews who continued to occupy villages in the region throughout the Roman period. *See* CAPERNAUM; CHORAZIN; SYNAGOGUE.

MILTON MORELAND

BARBARIAN bahr-bair´ee-uhn [βάρβαρος barbaros]. Barbaros is the Greek transcription of an onomatopoetic Sanskrit word (*barbera-s*), meaning babbling, one who speaks in an unintelligible way. Paul uses the term in this manner to describe people who are speaking foreign languages (1 Cor 14:11). The term sometimes simply meant "foreigner" (*see* Ps 114:1; Acts 28:2, 4).

The Greeks (e.g., Herodotus) applied the term *barbaros* to everything that was not Greek, initially with no offensive meaning. After the Persian War, the term acquired a derogatory nuance for the Greeks, who called the Persian invaders *barbarians*. The term became a synonym for wild, cruel, and uncivilized people (2 Macc 2:21; 4:25; 10:4). Paul, e.g., acknowledges debt to both "Greek and barbarian," who are contrasted with "wise and ignorant" persons (Rom 1:14).

The phrase, "Greeks and barbarians," meaning the whole of humanity, is a Greek equivalent to the Hebrew "Israel and the nations." Philo and Josephus applied the term to non-Jews. In Roman times, the word labeled all those who were not Greco-Roman, that is, those who were "others."

The Roman army recruited people that they regard-ed as barbarians, especially Goths, to protect the northern frontiers of the empire. Romans respected and also feared them for their courage in the battlefield. Despite their fierceness in battle, the Goths were civilized people who lived mostly in peace. Their lifestyle was simple and harsh, especially for those living in very cold climates. They married for life; were monogamous and faithful to their mates; cherished their children and raised them with a firm but kindhearted discipline. Women were influential among them and could even be warriors, like the queen Boadicea. Tacitus (1st cent. CE) provided a mostly favorable description of the "barbarians" in his *Germania*.

As an echo of Paul's words in Gal 3:28, the letter to the Colossians attempts to reconcile perceived differences: "there is no longer Greek and Jew, circumcised and uncircumcised, barbarian, Scythian, slave, or free; but Christ is all in all" (Col 3:11).

CRISTINA CONTI

BARBER [גַּלָּב gallav]. *Barber* appears only once in the Bible, when Ezekiel was commanded to use a sharp sword as a "barber's razor" to be "passed over" the hair of his head and beard (Ezek 5:1).

Little is known of barbering as a trade, although Hebrew men trimmed their hair periodically. ABSALOM reportedly cut his hair annually (2 Sam 14:26). Paul "had his hair cut" at the completion of a NAZIRITE vow (Acts 18:18). Men shaved their beards only in special circumstances (Lev 13:29-30; 14:9). Both hair and beard were trimmed with a sharp knife. *See* BEARD; HAIR.

TONY W. CARTLEDGE

BARIAH buh-ri´uh [בְּרִיחַ bariakh]. Son of Shemiah, whose ancestry can be dated back to Zerubbabel and King David (1 Chr 3:22).

BAR-JESUS bahr-jee´zuhs [Βαριησοῦ Bariēsou]. A Jewish "false prophet" and magician, also known as ELYMAS, who served procounsul Sergius Paulus (Acts 13:6-11). Bar-Jesus' opposition to Paul and Barnabas resulted in Paul inflicting blindness upon him, demonstrating Paul's power and authority in the Holy Spirit at the beginning of his first missionary trip.

ANN L. FRITSCHEL

BAR JONAH, BARJONA *See* JONAH, BAR; PETER.

BAR KOCHBA, SIMON. Leader of the Jewish revolt against Rome in the years 132–35 CE. The name Bar Kochba, emanating from the Aramaic "star" (related to כּוֹכָב kokhav), is found only in the writings of the church father EUSEBIUS, who explains the title as deriving from the belief in the man's messianic role. His association with a star is also suggested in the Jerusalem Talmud, where his name is connected to a verse mentioning the redeemer of Israel (Num 24:17). These two pieces of evidence indicate that his leadership was associated with messianic aspirations for the redemption of Israel. However, in the Jerusalem TALMUD, the man is named Bar Koziba, which means "liar" and may indicate that when the revolt he headed failed, his epithet was altered accordingly. We also know the name of this man from letters written on papyri, which he had issued and that were preserved in caves in the Judean desert. In those documents he is designated Simon Bar Kosba "Prince (Nasi) of Israel," and this was probably the name by which he was known in his lifetime. The name *Simon*, together with the same title, also appears on coins that his administration issued. These coins mention the "freedom of Israel" and Jerusalem, and also allude to the same hopes of redemption. Whether Jerusalem ever came under his jurisprudence during the revolt is an open question.

From the Judean desert letters it transpires that Bar Kochba was a hot-tempered general. This image is also conveyed by stories told about him in the Jerusalem Talmud. Little is known about the Bar Kochba revolt, aside from the fact that it was formidable, and engaged many Roman legions. It was crushed by the Romans in 135 CE, in a last–stand at the town of Beitar. Bar Kochba was probably killed in the fighting. *See* JEWISH WARS.

TAL ILAN

BARKOS bahr´kos [בַּרְקוֹס barqos]. A family head whose descendants were among the 392 Temple servants, called the NETHINIM, who returned to Jerusalem after the exile (Ezra 2:53; Neh 7:55).

BAR KOSIBA, KOZIBA. *See* BAR KOCHBA, SIMON.

BARLEY [שְׂעֹרָה se'orah; κριθή krithē]. A crucial part of the ancient farmer's pantry, though it takes a back seat to the WHEAT that the biblical record frequently pairs with it (e.g., Deut 8:8; Ezek 4:9; Joel 1:4; and Job 31:40). Barley finds little favor in the sacrificial system where it appears once (Num 5:15), costs one-third the price of wheat (Rev 6:6), and feeds the horses (1 Kgs 4:28). Barley's secondary importance reflects its relative yield and dietary contribution. Barley provides about 15 percent less protein than wheat, and its yield amounts to ca. two-thirds that of wheat. Barley is important because it tolerates higher degrees of salinity and alkalinity and will grow well in nutrient-poor soil, under more arid conditions. Sowing barley expands the amount of arable land brought into cultivation and provides a hedge against a failure of the wheat crop due to adverse environmental circumstances.

Barley matures more quickly than wheat. Preceding the ripening of wheat by about four weeks (Gezer calendar, line 4, and Exod 9:32), the early summer harvest of barley does not compete for labor needed to bring in the wheat. Processing the most commonly grown barley for food preparation involves an additional and time-consuming task: processors must remove the hulls by pounding the moistened kernels. Dehulled barley supplies the basic ingredient to cooks, bakers, and brewers for their porridge, bread, and beer.

The barley harvest provides the setting for the book of Ruth, where the harvest proceeds—like that of wheat—through communal labor. Ruth's widowhood ends during the barley harvest, and Judith's begins at that time (Judg 8:2). Jesus feeds the 5,000 with barley loaves (John 6), an act reminiscent of 2 Kgs 4:42-44.

DAVID HOPKINS

BARN [מְגוּרָה meghurah, אָסָם 'asam; ἀποθήκη apothēkē]. A building for storing seed, grain, and goods (Hag 2:19; Matt 13:30; Luke 12:18). Metaphorically, a full barn symbolizes prosperity (Deut 28:8; Prov 3:10) and security; an empty barn indicates poverty and vulnerability; but Jesus overturns this assumption (Luke 12:18-21). *See* AGRICULTURE; FOOD; GRANARY; STOREHOUSE.

BARNABAS bahr´nuh-buhs [Βαρναβᾶς Barnabas]. Also named Joseph, a prominent apostle and associate of Paul in Antioch of Syria, Cyprus, and Asia Minor.

A. Barnabas in the Letters of Paul

In Gal 2:1-10, Paul describes the conference he and Barnabas had in Jerusalem with apostles James, Peter, and John. The parties agreed to support distinctive gospel missions—Peter's to Jews and Paul's to Gentiles—and not to require circumcision for the Gentiles (2:7-8). The three Jerusalem "pillars" extended "the right hand of fellowship" to Paul and Barnabas as an endorsement of their work (2:9).

Some time later, however, tension erupted in Antioch, pitting Paul not only against Peter (Cephas) but against Barnabas also (Gal 2:11-14). Jews and Gentiles had been accustomed to eating together in the Antioch congregation, but when "certain people from James" arrived from Jerusalem, Peter, Barnabas, and "other Jews" dined at a separate table. Paul publicly rebuked Peter for his segregation and seemed especially surprised that "*even* Barnabas was led astray by their hypocrisy" (2:13).

Despite Paul's agitation in Galatians over this incident, the rift with Barnabas was apparently not permanent. In 1 Cor 9:6 Paul cites Barnabas as an apostolic partner who, like Paul, worked to support himself and offer the gospel "free of charge"; and in Col 4:10, Paul sends greetings from "Mark the cousin of Barnabas" and exhorts the audience to welcome him.

B. Barnabas in the Book of Acts

In addition to reporting Barnabas's association with Saul/Paul, the book of Acts also sketches aspects of his earlier, independent career. As a member of the Israelite tribe of Levi and a native of the island of Cyprus, Barnabas (originally named Joseph) migrated to Jerusalem at some point in his life and affiliated with the early Christian community (whether he had met and/or followed the earthly Jesus is unknown). The Jerusalem apostles gave him the "Barnabas" sobriquet, which Luke, drawing on an uncertain etymology, translates as "son of encouragement," befitting his ministry in Acts. Barnabas initially boosts the church's resources by selling a field he owned and laying the proceeds at the apostles' feet (4:36-37). His piety and generosity stand in contrast to the dishonest conduct of Ananias and Sapphira in 5:1-11.

Barnabas first encounters Saul in Jerusalem after Saul's dramatic transformation on the Damascus road and commission to carry the gospel to the Gentiles. True to his reputation as an encourager, Barnabas takes Saul under his wing and commends him to the disciples in Jerusalem, who were wary about taking in a notorious persecutor of the church (9:26-27). The church accepts Saul at Barnabas's behest. However, as Saul begins to preach in the city, violent opposition erupts from certain Greek-speaking Jews (Hellenists), compelling the disciples to dispatch him home to Tarsus (9:29).

Meanwhile, the Jerusalem congregation sends Barnabas to assist the thriving new community of believers in Antioch of Syria, comprised of both Jews and Gentiles. This assignment of the Cypriot Barnabas coincides with the identity of "some men of Cyprus" who first evangelized the Gentiles in Antioch (11:20-21). Barnabas becomes a major leader in the multiethnic Antiochene church and eventually recruits Saul from Tarsus to help instruct the new disciples, called "Christians" for the first time (11:25-26). Barnabas functions as senior tutor for both the church and Saul, as the roster of prophets and teachers in 13:1 suggests—ranking Barnabas first and Saul last.

After at least a year of ministry in Antioch (11:26), the church sets Barnabas and Saul apart for missionary service in the region. The pair first sails to Cyprus, Barnabas's home turf. Barnabas continues to be cited before Saul (13:7), although Saul asserts himself in a confrontation with Bar-Jesus the magician, impresses the island's proconsul and inspires him to believe in Christ, and henceforth is called Paul in Acts (13:9-12). Paul increasingly assumes more leadership as the mission cycles through Antioch of Pisidia, Iconium, Lystra, and Derbe, before returning to Antioch of Syria. But Barnabas is by no means reduced to Paul's sidekick. In the incident at Lystra, despite Paul's feat of healing a crippled man, the pagan crowd touts Barnabas as the supreme "Zeus" (they call Paul "Hermes" for his rhetorical skill; 14:8-13), and the narrator mentions Barnabas before Paul as "apostles" (14:14).

In Luke's account of the Jerusalem conference in Acts 15, corresponding to Gal 2:1-10, "Barnabas and Paul" (note the order) recount everything "that God had done through them among the Gentiles" (Acts 15:12) and receive unanimous support from Peter, James, and "the whole church" for their circumcision-free mission to non-Jews. Thereafter, while reporting further ministry for "Paul and Barnabas" (Paul back in first position) in Syrian Antioch (15:35), Luke nowhere alludes to the crisis over TABLE FELLOWSHIP aired in Gal 2:11-14. However, Acts does reveal a split between the two, albeit over a personal rather than social dispute. Barnabas wants to take John Mark with them on a second missionary journey, even though Mark had abandoned them on the first trek. Paul will have none it, and "the disagreement became so sharp that they parted company." Barnabas heads to Cyprus with Mark, while Paul selects a new partner, Silas (15:36-40). Barnabas makes no further appearance in Acts, as Paul dominates the final chapters.

C. Barnabas in Post-NT Traditions

Speculation about Barnabas persisted for centuries beyond the NT era. Among the church fathers, Tertullian attributed the anonymous canonical book of Hebrews to Barnabas, and Clement of Alexandria credited him with the so-called *Epistle of Barnabas*, written, however, in the 2nd cent., well after Barnabas's time. Later sources further embellish Barnabas's career, identifying him, variously, as one of the seventy-(two) disciples commissioned by Jesus in Luke 10:1, the founder of the church at Rome, and the chief apostle to Cyprus, where he was martyred and buried. *See* BARNABAS, ACTS OF; BARNABAS, EPISTLE OF.

Bibliography: B. Kollmann. *Joseph Barnabas: His Life and Legacy* (2004); M. Öhler. *Barnabas: Die historische Person und ihre Rezeption in der Apostelgeschichte* (2003).

F. SCOTT SPENCER

BARNABAS, ACTS OF. Formally titled *Acts and Martyrdom of Saint Barnabas the Apostle*, this late 5th cent. apocryphal work, putatively penned by John Mark, depends heavily on the canonical Acts, but elaborates on the second missionary journey of Barnabas and Mark to Cyprus, referenced in Acts 15:39. The story ends with Barnabas's execution in the Cypriot capital, Salamis, and the burial of his ashes along with a copy of Matthew's Gospel. As venerated apostle and martyr, Barnabas and his gravesite certify the authority of the church at Cyprus and its independence from Antioch.

F. SCOTT SPENCER

BARNABAS, EPISTLE OF. The Epistle of Barnabas is an anonymous Christian writing of the late 1st or early 2nd cent. that offers an unsparing critique of the Jewish people and warns its audience against becoming like "those people." Chapters 1–16 are dominated by anti-Jewish polemic, while chs. 17–21 offer ethical teaching on "the way of life" and the "way of death." The writing has been known under its current title since the late 2nd cent. CE, but its attribution to Barnabas (the coworker of Paul) cannot be taken at face value. Its time and place of origin remain disputed.

According to the author, the Jewish people have completely misunderstood their own law. In such matters as sacrifice, fasting, circumcision, dietary laws, Sabbath observance, and the Temple, the true intention of God's command is spiritual, not literal. Thus, e.g., a sacrifice pleasing to God is a penitent and grateful heart (2:10), circumcision is a matter of ears that hear and hearts that obey (9:1-4), and the dietary laws are moral allegories about the company one keeps (10:1-12). In making such arguments, the author relies on a combination of allegorical interpretation and selective citation of OT prophetic texts (e.g., Isa 1:11-13; 58:4-10; Jer 4:4; 7:22-23).

The author goes so far as to say that Israel lost its covenant forever as a result of the golden-calf incident (4:6-8) or, perhaps, never quite received it (14:1-4). Whether this assertion is meant to be taken at face value is questionable, since the author presupposes later moments in Israel's history at other points in the epistle. The author also emphasizes Israel's rejection of Jesus as the climactic moment in a long history of disobedience (5:11; 8:1-2; 14:5). The author writes after the destruction of the Temple in 70 CE (16:4-5) and views the Jewish people as having completely forfeited their status as God's covenant people (13:1-7). The audience is repeatedly warned against becoming like "those people" (2:9; 3:6; 4:6; 8:7; 10:12; 13:1, 3; 14:5).

Scholars disagree over the purpose of the writing. Many see it as a polemical document whose primary concern is to dissuade Gentile Christians from adopting Jewish ritual observances. Others have interpreted it as a warning to Christians that possession of the covenant and status as God's people can be lost if they fail to live up to it. Still others have regarded the writing as an academic exercise whose primary purpose is to instruct Christians in how they ought to read the OT. *See* ALLEGORY; ANTI-JUDAISM; APOSTOLIC FATHERS; DIDACHE.

Bibliography: Reidar Hvalvik. *The Struggle for Scripture and Covenant: The Purpose of the Epistle of Barnabas and Jewish-Christian Competition in the Second Century* (1996); James Carleton Paget. *The Epistle of Barnabas: Outlook and Background* (1994); James N. Rhodes. *The Epistle of Barnabas and the Deuteronomic Tradition: Polemics, Paraenesis, and the Legacy of the Golden-Calf Incident* (2004).

JAMES N. RHODES

BARODIS buh-roh´dis [βαρωδις Barōdis]. A family head whose descendants were among the 372 Temple servants, called the NETHINIM, who returned after the exile (1 Esd 5:34; not found in Ezra 2:57; Neh 7:59).

BARREN, BARRENNESS [עָקָר 'aqar; στεῖρα steira]. Barrenness describes a woman who is physically unable to bear children. The case of Eve—the first woman and "mother of all living" (Gen 3:20)—establishes the connection between a woman's self-identity and child-bearing. The patriarchal nature of the society meant that a husband placed a very high value in his wife's ability to provide children. From a financial perspective, barren women faced more risks than other women as they grew older, because older women naturally looked to sons to protect and provide for them. For these reasons, barrenness was considered one of the most lamentable conditions a woman could experience; the barren woman was the antithesis of the joyful woman (Isa 54:1; Luke 23:29; Gal 4:27). Barrenness—like famine, drought, and disease—was typically viewed as a sign of divine disapproval. Conversely, the absence of barrenness was a manifestation of divine blessing (Exod 23:25-26; Deut 7:14).

Every culture has its own strategies for providing for offspring to preserve the family line in the face of infertility. In Israel, strategies may have included designation of a male servant as heir (Gen 15:2; compare the intimate connection between inheritance and family name in Num 27, 36) and sexual relations between the male head of household and the maidservant of the infertile wife (Gen 16; 30). Similar practices are attested in the ancient Near East.

In the Bible, however, the central focus of narratives about infertility is on God's control of conception. The many stories of barren women among Israel's matriarchs and other heroines of the Bible typically develop from occasions for pity (and/or derision) to opportunities for praise. Sarah, Rebekah, Rachel, the mother of Samson, Hannah, and Elizabeth each endured extended times when they were barren because the Lord had "closed the womb" of each woman. The people around them probably concluded that their barrenness was a sign of divine judgment; and the sadness and even desperation of these women is apparent in the narratives. Sarah offers her maidservant Hagar to her husband (Gen 11:30; Heb 11:11); Rebekah's husband, Isaac, prays that her barrenness be removed (Gen 25:21); Rachel's husband, Jacob, angrily says that the problem is with God, not with himself (Gen 29:31); Manoah, Samson's father, has to be convinced that God has promised to end his wife's barrenness (Judg 13:2-3); Hannah, taunted by her cowife, prays fervently for relief; Elizabeth speaks of the "disgrace" she endured (Luke 1:36). In the end, however, each situation turns out instead to be an occasion when God demonstrates power over life (and, by extension, over the life of Israel as God's people) by giving each one a child (1 Sam 2:5; Ps 113:9). The reporting of such developments might also be intended to illustrate divine compassion for those whom the culture tended to ignore and despise, thereby setting an example for God's people to emulate in their dealings with those they tended to ignore and despise.

TIMOTHY WILLIS

BARSABBAS bahr-sab´uhs [Βαρσαββᾶς Barsabbas]. A patronymic ("Son of the Elder" or perhaps "Son of the Sabbath") identifying two characters in Acts. 1. Joseph (also called Justus)—one of two men nominated to replace Judas Iscariot among the apostles (Acts 1:23).

2. Judas—distinguished as a leader and prophet among the Jerusalem fellowship. One of a group sent to announce the church's decisions concerning Gentile believers (Acts 15:22-33).

MATTHEW L. SKINNER

BARTACUS bahr´tuh-kuhs [Βαρτάκος Bartakos]. Father of King Darius' concubine named Apame, to whom the young man Zerubbabel refers (1 Esd 4:29).

BARTHOLOMEW bahr-thol´uh-my*oo* [Βαρθολομαῖος Bartholomaios]. Bartholomaios is the transliteration of the Aramaic, patronymic **bar Talmai**, "son of Talmai (or Ptolemy)." Talmai is the name of two non-Hebrew personalities: a gigantic descendant of the Canaanite Anak (Num 13:22; Josh 15:14; Judg 1:10), and the son of Ammihud, king of Geshur and David's father-in-law (2 Sam 3:3; 13:37; 1 Chr 3:2). In spite of the phonetic differences, Talmai—probably pronounced Tolmai—was used as the Hebrew or Aramaic equivalent for the Greek Ptolemy, the dynastic name of the kings of Hellenistic Egypt (*Meg.* 9*a*). Different forms of this name are rare in Second Temple and Early Rabbinic Jewish onomastics. Thus, e.g., even though Josephus mentions three men called Tholemaios—a Syrian leader (*A.J.* 14.8.1), a general of Herod the Great (*B.J.* 1.314-315), and a "robber" executed under Cuspius Fadus's procuratorship, in 44–46 CE (*Ant.* 20.1-9)—only the latter could have been of Jewish descent. Therefore, it seems reasonable to assume that if a Jewish boy was called Bartholomew, it was for social or family reasons; perhaps because an ancestor was of Syrian origins or had been a slave, an official, or a client of the Egyptian king.

In the synoptic Gospels (Matt 10:3; Mark 3:18; Luke 6:14) and Acts (Acts 1:13) Bartholomew is one of the TWELVE, associated either with PHILIP or MATTHEW. Bartholomew is never mentioned in the Gospel of John. Different harmonizing solutions have been proposed to explain the inconsistency. From the 9th cent. onward, Bartholomew is usually identified with NATHANAEL of Cana (John 21:2), a friend of Philip of Bethsaida and one of the first followers of Jesus (John 1:43-51, as

well as the Berlin Papyrus 11710). This identification is already presupposed by the authors of the *Gospel of Bartholomew* and the *Book of the Resurrection of Christ by Bartholomew, the Apostle*. However, in other apocryphal texts (*Ep. Apos.* 2; *Didascalia Apostolorum* 3; *Book of the Cock* 3:13) Bartholomew and Nathanael are kept distinct, and the latter is considered to be identical with John the son of Alphaeus or Simon the Zealot. Needless to say, there is little ground for any of these identifications.

Later texts and traditions do not lift the veil of mystery that surrounds the historical Bartholomew. His connection with Philip is confirmed in the encratitic *Acts of Philip*, written in the second half of the 4th cent. Here the Savior sends Bartholomew and John to help Philip and his sister Mariamne (i.e., Mary of Magdala) in the Phrygian town of Opheorymos (*Acts Phil.* 8:3-4). However, Bartholomew's missionary destination is Lycaonia (*Acts Phil.* 8:1; *Mart. Phil.* 36; 42), where he will be crucified (*Mart. Phil.* 31). Other legends link him with Matthew. According to Eusebius, Bartholomew had preceded Pantaenus in India, leaving the Indians a copy of the Gospel of Matthew that was written "in Hebrew letters" (*Hist. Eccl.* 5.10.2-3). The term *India* is geographically imprecise and could designate the Horn of Africa, South Arabia, or the Indian subcontinent. Furthermore, as a rule, India is the missionary field of the apostle Thomas. According to other traditions, Bartholomew evangelized either the Bosphorus, or Armenia, or the Egyptian oasis of al-Bahnasah before dying in such regions as a martyr.

Bibliography: István Czachesz. *Commission Narratives: A Comparative Study of the Canonical and Apocryphal Acts* (2005); Charles E. Hill. "The Identity of John's Nathanael." *JSNT* 67 (1997) 45–61; John P. Meier. *A Marginal Jew: Rethinking the Historical Jesus, vol. 3: Companions and Competitors* (2001); Lourens P. van den Bosch. "India and the Apostolate of St. Thomas." *The Apocryphal Acts of Thomas.* Jan N. Bremmer, ed. (2001) 125–48.

PIERLUIGI PIOVANELLI

BARTHOLOMEW THE APOSTLE, THE BOOK OF THE RESURRECTION OF CHRIST BY. The *Book of the Resurrection of Christ by Bartholomew, the Apostle* is a composite Coptic text extant in three fragmentary manuscripts. It can be considered as a narrative and homiletic development of the resurrection story found in John 20. To this we can add that it seems to rewrite some passages of the *Gospel [Questions] of Bartholomew* and the *Acts of Thomas*. Newman also detects, in the episode of the empty tomb, some clues that point out the existence of a polemical debate with Judaism. The *Book of the Resurrection of Christ by Bartholomew, the Apostle* was probably written after the council of Ephesus (held in 431 CE) and before the 9th cent.

The beginning of the text is actually missing in the main manuscript and is difficult to reconstruct from the fragments of the other two codices. After a dialogue between Death and Jesus (4:2-15) and his descent into Hades (5:1–7:5), on Sunday morning, the holy women go to the tomb (8:1). There they meet Philogenes the gardener, an unknown character who is probably to be identified with Bartholomew, "the Italian, the gardener, the greengrocer" (17:3; in John 1:48-50 Jesus sees Nathanael "under the fig tree"). Philogenes tells Mary the mother that he is not responsible for the disappearance of Jesus' body, but God has raised him in the middle of the night (8:2-6). Then the Savior appears to his mother, who calls him "Rabboni" and asks to be blessed by him because she is not allowed to touch him (9:1–10:7). Bartholomew witnesses the entire scene and Jesus' glorious ascension to heaven (12:1–13:11). Adam and Eve are also summoned before God and restored to their pristine condition (14:1–16:14). Later on, the Father sends the Son down into Galilee to console the apostles and Mary (20:1-14). Only Thomas (also called Didymos) was not with them, for he had heard that his son Siophanes was dead in their hometown. Thomas resurrects him in the name of Jesus Christ, and the young man tells him of his tour of heaven and paradise (21:1–22:12). When Thomas meets up with the other apostles again on the Mount of Olives, he refuses to believe that Jesus has appeared to them. Jesus himself has to encourage Thomas to touch his wounds and believe (23:1–24:6). After Jesus' ascension to heaven, at the moment of the celebration of the eucharistic sacrifice, the apostles experience a final mystical vision, which reveals to them "the glory of his body and his divine blood" (25:1-5).

Bibliography: Jean-Daniel Kaestli and Pierre Chérix. *L'évangile de Barthélemy d'après deux écrits apocryphes: II. Livre de la Résurrection de Jésus-Christ par l'apôtre Barthélemy* (1993); Enzo Lucchesi. "Feuillets coptes non identifiés du prétendu *Évangile de Barthélemy.*" *VC* 51 (1997) 273–75; Hillel L. Newman. "The Death of Jesus in the *Toledot Yeshu* Literature." *JTS* 50 (1999) 59–79; Matthias Westerhoff. *Auferstehung und Jenseits im koptischen "Buch der Auferstehung Jesu Christi, unseres Herrn"* (1999).

PIERLUIGI PIOVANELLI

BARTHOLOMEW, GOSPEL [QUESTIONS] OF. Bartholomew is the protagonist of both the *Gospel [Questions] of Bartholomew* and the *Book of the Resurrection of Christ by Bartholomew, the Apostle.* In these writings he is the only witness of the metaphysical activities that occurred during Jesus' passion, as if he were the apostle to whom Jesus promised that he would see "greater things than these" (i.e., Nathanael in John 1:50-51). Therefore, Bartholomew becomes the privileged interlocutor of the resurrected Savior and

his mother Mary, a role perhaps indirectly criticized by Augustine (*Tract. Ev. Jo.* 7.17).

According to the *Gospel of Bartholomew*, at the moment of the crucifixion the apostle saw the angels descending from heaven and worshiping Jesus, who suddenly disappeared from the cross (1:6-7). When Bartholomew questions Jesus, the risen Lord tells of his descent into Hades and the harrowing of Hell (1:9-20). Later Bartholomew asks Mary about the circumstances of Jesus' conception (2:1-4). Mary begins to tell them how God appeared to her in the Temple and announced that she would conceive his son, when Jesus interrupts her before the world is destroyed by fire coming from her mouth (2:15-22).

Finally, Bartholomew asks Jesus to see Beliar, the adversary of humankind, who is compelled to reveal his own name: Satanael, shortened to Satan after his rebellion against God (4:7-48). Bartholomew is told that Satanael's refusal to pay homage to Adam provoked his expulsion from heaven, but the devil was able to take his revenge by seducing Eve. In order to do so, he contaminated the source of the rivers of paradise with the sweat of his breast and armpits, and when Eve drank that water, she got infected with desire (4:52-60). The *Gospel of Bartholomew* ends with a warning not to entrust these secrets to the unworthy (4:66-68) and three questions about the grievous sin, the sin against the Holy Spirit, and the sin of the flesh (5:1-9).

This text, probably written toward the end of the 4th cent. (when Jerome mentioned it in his *Commentary on Matthew*), is only extant in a few Greek, Latin, and Slavonic manuscripts. Some quotations and allusions in the *Book of the Mystery of Heaven and Earth* and in a *Homily on the Annunciation of Gabriel to Mary* point to the existence of an Ethiopic version of the *Gospel of Bartholomew*. The authors of Egyptian magic texts were well acquainted with the episode of the poisoning of Eve. Moreover, the *Gospel of Bartholomew* was one of the sources of the *Book of the Resurrection of Christ by Bartholomew, the Apostle*, written in Coptic between the 5th and 9th cent. In the Byzantine world, Epiphanius the monk seems to refer to the *Gospel of Bartholomew* in his *Life of the Virgin* (late 8th or early 9th cent.), while in the Latin West, it was ultimately rejected as an apocryphal text by the author of the *Decretum Gelasianum* (beginning of the 6th cent.).

Bibliography: Jean-Daniel Kaestli. "Où en est l'étude de *l'Évangile de Barthélemy?*" *RB* 95 (1988) 5–33. Jean-Daniel Kaestli and Pierre Cherix, *L'évangile de Barthélemy d'après deux écrits apocryphes: I. Questions de Barthélemy* (1993); Jacques van der Vliet. "Satan's Fall in Coptic Magic." *Ancient Magic and Ritual Power*. Marvin W. Meyer and Paul A. Mirecki (1995) 401–18.

PIERLUIGI PIOVANELLI

BARTIMAEUS bahr´tuh-mee´uhs [Βαρτιμαῖος Bartimaios]. "Son of Timaeus." A blind beggar healed by Jesus as the latter exits Jericho (Mark 10:46-52). Thereafter, Bartimaeus follows Jesus, presumably into Jerusalem. Similar stories are found in Matt 20:29-34, which mentions two anonymous blind men healed upon leaving Jericho, and in Luke 18:35-43, wherein Jesus heals one blind man upon entering Jericho. All these narratives may serve to contrast the obstructive role of the blind in David's conquest of Jerusalem (2 Sam 5:6-8). *See* BLINDNESS; DISEASE.

HECTOR AVALOS

BARUCH bair´uhk [בָּרוּךְ barukh]. "Blessed." The son of Neriah was JEREMIAH's scribe and a member of a prominent Judean family. Baruch appears only in the book of Jeremiah (32:12-16; 36; 43:1-7; 45). He served Jeremiah by performing standard scribal duties: certifying land transactions, writing down the prophet's words, and presenting Jeremiah's divine oracles to the people and the royal court. Some scholars conclude from the narratives about Baruch's scribal activity that he was the editor of some portions of the book of Jeremiah. While this cannot be confirmed, it seems likely that someone with Baruch's scribal skills would have made compiling Jeremiah's speeches a priority. Outside of the OT, the image of Baruch developed significantly in the religious imagination of ancient Jews and Christians. There are many extrabiblical traditions about Baruch in the Jewish and Christian books attributed to him (*see* PSEUDEPIGRAPHA). These materials portray Baruch as a sage and seer as well as Jeremiah's prophetic successor. He was imaged as one who speaks with God, receives divine revelations, comforts his people, and ascends to heaven.

A *bulla* (clay seal impression) exists bearing the inscription (*see* WRITING AND WRITING MATERIALS) "belonging to Berekyahu, son of Neriyahu, the scribe." The names Berekyahu and Neriyahu are long forms of the names Baruch and Neriah. Although the forms of the letters on this *bulla* appear to date to the 6th cent. BCE, since the true archaeological provenance of this artifact is unclear, it is uncertain that this *bulla* is authentic.

Bibliography: J. E. Wright. *Baruch ben Neriah: From Biblical Scribe to Apocalyptic Seer* (2003).

J. EDWARD WRIGHT

BARUCH, BOOK OF [Βαρούχ Barouch]. This apocryphal text is attributed to Baruch, the son of Neriah and secretary to JEREMIAH, although most scholars think the book was written not in the purported time of the Babylonian exile but sometime during the 2nd cent. BCE. The book nonetheless explores the theme of exile, defined as the consequence of disobeying God's law (4:12), and clearly elaborated in the book's four parts.

An introduction (1:1-14) is followed by a public prayer of penitence (1:15–3:8). After the prayer concludes by highlighting Mosaic law and the obedience it elicits, the third section (3:9–4:4) follows in the form of a poem that compares the Mosaic law to wisdom, an association not uncommon in the period of the Second Temple (Ps 1:1-2; Sir 24:23-29). The fourth section (4:5–5:9) is a prophetic address signaling the restoration of exiles to Jerusalem as a result of their repentance.

Although an original Hebrew version once might have existed, the earliest extant text of Baruch is in Greek. Baruch appeared in the LXX between the books of Jeremiah and Lamentations, and this Greek translation became the basis for later versions. No copies of Baruch were found among the Dead Sea Scrolls, although there was a Greek fragment of the LETTER OF JEREMIAH (7Q2), a deuterocanonical text that has been appended to Baruch since the 4th cent. CE, as well as multiple copies of the APOCRYPHON OF JEREMIAH, an apocalypse with marked parallels to the book of Baruch, such as the introductory setting at the royal court in exile.

In dating the text, the consensus is that the Greek period (332–63 BCE) is the most likely setting for the book, and that the 2nd cent. is the most plausible time of Baruch's composition. The hypothesis that Baruch was written in 163–162 BCE when a portion of Jerusalem's Jews had reached détente with their Seleucid overlords and were urging their coreligionists to do the same remains influential among scholars.

For readers of the OT, a striking feature of Baruch is its echoing diverse books of scripture. The final section, a prophetic address, draws upon the language and thought of Deutero-Isaiah as well as DEUTERONOMY, LAMENTATIONS, and the PSALMS OF SOLOMON. The wisdom poem in the third section echoes PROVERBS, JOB, BEN SIRA, and again Deuteronomy. Baruch's second section, the penitential prayer, borrows copiously from Lev 26, from Deut 4; 28, and 30; from 1 Kgs 8, and from Jer 24 and 32. The most significant confluence is between Baruch's prayer and the penitential prayer in Dan 9:4-19, with the following parallels: Dan 9:5-8 and Bar 1:15-17; Dan 9:10 and Bar 1:21; Dan 9:12-13 and Bar 2:1-4; 3:8; Dan 9:15 and Bar 2:11; Dan 9:17 and Bar 2:14. Scholars have generally thought that Daniel's prayer serves as the basis for that of Baruch, although the issue is still debated.

Citing Baruch's assumed dependence on DANIEL and other texts, certain scholars have judged the book to be derivative and artless. In this vein, critics have also cited stylistic and thematic inconsistencies that are said to detract from Baruch's literary and theological integrity. Recently, however, attention has been drawn to formal literary features of Baruch that impart unity as they bring forth more complex and nuanced points of theology. This recent work has focused on the prayer in 1:15–3:8. As the prayer subdivides into a confession

(1:15–2:10) and a supplication (2:11–3:8), a chiastic structure in 1:18–2:10 underscores the people refusing the words of the prophets, and another in 2:11–3:8 highlights prophecy's fulfillment (2:24-26). There is as well a highly compressed chiasm in 1:18-19 that situates the salvific work of God, as it were, between mentions of the people's disobedience. Subtle exegesis has discerned that subsections of Baruch's prayer work in tandem to establish thematic parallels. For example, the theme of Jerusalem worship is developed in a series of inverse correspondences between the supplications of the Israelites in exile (2:12-18) and the supplications addressed to the Jews in Jerusalem (1:10-13).

Arguably, the prayer's literary and theological crux is found in 2:12, where those praying confess: "We have sinned, we have been ungodly, we have done wrong, O Lord our God, against all your ordinances." These conjoined expressions of sin, iniquity, and transgression are well attested in the penitential prayers of this period, and the precise meanings of these terms in a given text must ultimately be adduced through context as well as other, more specific penitential expressions elsewhere in the text. In the case of Baruch, the terminology in 2:12 reflects that view that *all* of Judah's inhabitants (1:15-16) have defied the divine law given to Moses and reiterated by the prophets (1:18; 4:12). The defiance has resulted in exile, and restoration of the divine-human covenant is possible only through repentance and renewed obedience (2:30-35). The book of Baruch portrays a God who succors sinners with a gratuitous mercy that unfolds in a series of decisive events: punishment through exile, change of the human heart, and onset of restoration.

Bibliography: Devorah Dimant. *Qumran Cave 4, XXI: Parabiblical Texts, Part 4, Pseudo-Prophetic Texts*. DJD 30 (2001); Jonathan Goldstein. "The Apocryphal Book of 1 Baruch." *PAAJR* 46–47 (1979–1980) 179–99; Anthony J. Saldarini. *The Book of Baruch: Introduction, Commentary and Reflections. NIB* 6 (2001).

RICHARD J. BAUTCH

BARUCH, SECOND BOOK OF (SYRIAC). The Second Book of Baruch is one of the several early Jewish and Christian texts attributed to Baruch ben Neriah, the prophet Jeremiah's scribe. Pseudepigraphy—attributing the authorship of a text to a famous person from antiquity—enabled the actual author(s) to gain wider acceptance of their work. The text of 2 Baruch has been preserved only in Syriac and a few fragments in Greek. Second Baruch was composed in Hebrew or Aramaic, translated into Greek, and then translated from Greek into Syriac. This complicated process is due to the fact that many widely circulated Jewish extrabiblical texts came to be highly esteemed also by Christian communities who translated them into their native languages for use in their churches. As a result,

while the original Hebrew or Greek texts themselves have been lost, their contents have been preserved by these translations.

The narrative setting of 2 Baruch, as with all Baruch literature, is the Babylonian destruction of the Jerusalem Temple in 586 BCE. This, however, is only a fictive setting. It seems clear that the text was actually composed after the Roman destruction of the Jerusalem Temple in 70 CE. A key to the possible date of this text arises from the observation that the author of 2 Baruch may have used the seven-vision structure of 4 Ezra (*see* EZRA, FOURTH) as a model for this text. If so, then this would date the composition of 2 Baruch to a time no earlier than 4 Ezra, namely the early 2nd cent. CE. Beyond that, no precise date of composition can be identified for 2 Baruch.

Second Baruch is an apocalypse (*see* APOCALYPSE), a genre of literature in which God reveals to humans unknowable information that has either an eschatological or otherworldly focus and that intends to influence human beliefs and behaviors. The most familiar, although not the most representative examples of this genre, are the books of Daniel in the OT and Revelation in the NT. As an apocalypse, therefore, 2 Baruch narrates a divine revelation to Baruch that contains cosmic or chronological secrets that are otherwise unknowable to humans. God reveals this secret information to Baruch, and Baruch in turn records it in his book for the benefit of his coreligionists and ultimately for all humanity.

There are several passages in this text that recount the interactions between Baruch and the people. These passages suggest that Baruch was viewed as a divinely sent, inspired leader and biblical interpreter. This text may reflect, therefore, the attitudes of a community toward its leader(s), whose teachings give their lives meaning. In this way the text reinforces the authority of the author of this text who presents himself as Baruch or at least as a transmitter of inspired teachings that may have come from Baruch.

Second Baruch appears to be a mixed collection of diverse literary forms: visions, prayers, fasts, disputes with God, and laments. This complex structure led past generations of scholars to conclude that the book is a composite of several different sources (*see* SOURCE CRITICISM). More recent scholarship on apocalyptic literature finds this complexity an inherent quality of the genre. Thus, the book is largely a unified composition and not a mosaic of diverse sources. The overall structure of the book has seven movements, which in various ways reveal some of the secrets of the cosmos and of human history and destiny. Second Baruch consists of visions in which Baruch and God debate issues centering on the question of theodicy: how can God be just if the wicked prosper and the righteous suffer at the hands of the wicked? The overall goal of this apocalypse is to promote obedience to God's commandments as the way to endure and transcend the turmoil of the day. Second Baruch maintains that Jews can thrive in spite of the destruction of the Jerusalem Temple only if they remain obedient to the commandments in the TORAH, that is, if they continue to follow traditional Jewish teachings. This book, therefore, served as an influential theological treatise moving people from a religion centered on the Temple cultus in Jerusalem to one focused on Torah-obedience everywhere.

Bibliography: A. F. J. Klijn. "2 (Syriac Apocalypse of) Baruch." Vol. 1. *The Old Testament Pseudepigrapha.* J. H. Charlesworth, ed. (1983) 615–52; F. J. Murphy. *The Structure and Meaning of Second Baruch* (1985); G. B. Sayler. *Have the Promises Failed? A Literary Analysis of 2 Baruch* (1984); M. F. Whitters. *The Epistle of Second Baruch: A Study in Form and Message* (2003); J. E. Wright. "The Social Setting of the Syriac Apocalypse of Baruch." *JSP* 16 (1997) 83–98.

J. EDWARD WRIGHT

BARUCH, THIRD BOOK OF (GREEK). Like the other Baruch pseudepigrapha, Third Baruch's narrative setting is the Babylonian destruction of Jerusalem in 586 BCE, but, as all scholars would admit, it was actually composed in the Roman period. The author uses the Babylonian setting as a symbol of the events that took place with the Roman conquest of Judea in 70 CE. Identifying the precise date for the composition of this book has proved difficult, but scholarly consensus currently prefers to date it to the 2nd or 3rd cent. CE.

Third Baruch is an apocalypse (*see* APOCALYPSE) that is structured around a tour of the heavens. The text opens with Baruch lamenting the devastation of Jerusalem and then recounts Baruch's ascent through five heavens and his return to earth. This tour of the heavens comes in response to Baruch's prayer to understand the reason for Jerusalem's destruction. God sent the angel Phamael to lead Baruch on his tour through the heavens. During this tour Baruch learned secrets about the workings of the cosmos and about God's control of history. Rather than simply overwhelming him, what Baruch learned during his ascent into the heavens actually comforted him and helped him make sense of the seemingly senseless destruction of Jerusalem at the hands of the Babylonians (i.e., the Romans). During his ascent he asked questions about what he saw and his concerns with theodicy. He learned that although the present state of affairs looks hopeless, God still remains in control of the cosmos and history and that he always listens to the prayers of the righteous.

The five-heaven structure of Baruch's ascent journey has led some scholars to propose that this structure results from an abbreviation of what was an original account with a more traditional seven-heaven structure. It seems likely, however, that the story is not abbreviated since by the end of his tour through the

heavens Baruch has had all of his initial questions and concerns addressed: he saw firsthand that God remains in control of history and daily attends to human prayers. Thus, since Baruch's concerns and questions were ultimately resolved, it does not appear necessary that the five-heaven structure is the result of abbreviation. Astronomical knowledge in antiquity was not uniform, and there were many different models for the structure of the cosmos. Third Baruch may simply attest a five-heaven model. On the other hand, Third Baruch may, in fact, assume the common but not universal seven-heaven model. If so, the fact that Baruch ascended only to the fifth heaven may indicate that the author did not think it appropriate for humans to ascend into God's presence in the highest heaven. This understanding of the five-heaven structure in Third Baruch does not assume that the text has been abbreviated but that this author thought it somehow theologically inappropriate for a human who was to return to earth to stand in the presence of the holy God in the highest and purest heaven.

Although ascent to heaven was not a feature of ancient Israelite piety, during the course of the Persian and Greco-Roman eras this belief became very popular in the Near East and Mediterranean Basin and also became a hallmark of many Jewish and Christian apocalypses. One feature that they all have in common is that while in the other realm the seer is granted insight into the mysteries of the cosmos, of history, and of the future. This knowledge serves as a powerful religious tool in persuading people to adopt beliefs and behaviors that will both please God and empower them to face life's trials and tribulations. Baruch learned many things about the functioning of the cosmos, the history of humanity, and the cultic activities going on in heaven, but the most important thing for him was learning that God and the angels daily attend to human prayers and are working on behalf of the righteous. This knowledge comforts Baruch in his agony over the sufferings of Jerusalem, and in turn, it is meant to comfort the readers as they face the anxieties of their lives. *See* BARUCH, BOOK OF; BARUCH, FOURTH BOOK OF PARALEIPOMENON JEREMIAH; BARUCH, SECOND BOOK OF (SYRIAC).

Bibliography: H. E. Gaylord. "3 (Greek Apocalypse of) Baruch. Vol. 1. *The Old Testament Pseudepigrapha.* J. H. Charlesworth, ed. (1983) 653–79; D. C. Harlow. *The Greek Apocalypse of Baruch (3 Baruch) in Hellenistic Judaism and Early Christianity* (1996); M. Himmelfarb. *Ascent to Heaven in Jewish and Christian Apocalypses* (1993); M. E. Stone, ed., *Jewish Writings of the Second Temple Period* (1984); J. D. Tabor. *Things Unutterable: Paul's Ascent to Paradise in its Greco-Roman, Judaic, and Early Christian Contexts* (1986).

J. EDWARD WRIGHT

BARUCH, FOURTH BOOK OF (PARALEIPOMENA OF JEREMIAH) bair´uhk. Fourth Baruch, also known as the *Paraleipomena of Jeremiah* (things omitted from [the book of] Jeremiah), intends to complete the story of Jeremiah's life by recounting what the Bible omitted about the prophet's career and death. Although Jer 43–44 states that Jeremiah and Baruch were forcibly taken to Egypt by their compatriots, *Paraleipomena of Jeremiah* preserves another tradition regarding the fate of these two leaders: the Babylonians took Jeremiah to Babylon while Baruch remained in Jerusalem where he assumed a communal leadership position.

After the divinely ordained Babylonian destruction of Jerusalem in 586 BCE, Baruch entered a tomb where he wept over the fall of the city and received revelations from angels (4:11-12). God spared Baruch's friend Abimelech (also known as Ebed-Melech; compare Jer 38:7-12; 39:15-18) from witnessing the destruction of Jerusalem and the exile of its inhabitants by causing him to sleep for sixty-six years in the "field of Agrippa" outside of the city. After awaking from his sleep, Abimelech found Baruch still grieving in the tomb (6:1). Thus, it appears that while Abimelech was sleeping for sixty-six years, Baruch was praying and learning from the angels. Baruch greeted his friend, and the two immediately prayed for guidance about what to do next. The answer came when an angel told Baruch of God's plan to return the exiles to Jerusalem (6:11-17). Baruch wrote a letter informing Jeremiah about this revelation, and God miraculously provided an eagle to carry it from Jerusalem to Babylon (6:18–7:23). Upon learning of the news of the exiles' imminent return to Jerusalem, Jeremiah wrote his own letter and sent it back to Baruch via the eagle. Jeremiah eventually led the exiles back to Judah, but before entering Jerusalem he and Baruch prevented the exiles from bringing their foreign spouses with them, thereby attempting to preserve the city's Jewish character. Chapter 9 of the book narrates Jeremiah's final speech to the people in which he predicts the life of Jesus. The people responded in anger and killed Jeremiah because of this sermon. The book closes with the death and burial of Jeremiah.

The *Paraleipomena of Jeremiah* is an originally Jewish text that has been Christianized. These revisions are especially evident in the Christian elements in Jeremiah's predictions about the life of Jesus in ch. 9. Dating many early Jewish and Christian APOCRYPHA and PSEUDEPIGRAPHA has proved difficult. *Paraleipomena of Jeremiah* refers to the destruction of Jerusalem, but the question is "which destruction?" This text uses the Babylonian destruction in 586 BCE as a symbol for the Roman destruction of Jerusalem in 70 CE. The Roman date is made certain by the reference to the "field of Agrippa" (3:14), referring to the estate of Agrippa I who reigned from 37–44 CE. Adding Abimelech's sixty-six-year sleep after the destruction to

the 70 CE date suggests that this text was composed in the early part of the 2nd cent. CE.

Although Baruch plays a significant role in the *Paraleipomena of Jeremiah*, Jeremiah remains the central figure, a role clearly dependent on his biblical background as a prophet. Nonetheless, in *Paraleipomena of Jeremiah* Baruch does assume a leadership role. This suggests that at least some people viewed Baruch as Jeremiah's successor as both a community leader and a recipient of divine revelations. It is also noteworthy that the *Paraleipomena of Jeremiah* is known by two titles: the Greek manuscripts entitle it the "Paraleipomena of Jeremiah," while the Ethiopic manuscript entitles it "The Rest of the Words of Baruch." These two titles indicate that there were two perspectives on who was the central figure of this text. In the *Paraleipomena of Jeremiah* Baruch appears as a leader of the people who functions as Jeremiah's replacement while the prophet is in Babylon ministering to the exiles. No longer just a scribe, Baruch appears as a leader of the people who prays for and comforts his people, maintains Jewish traditions, and receives divine revelations. The Christianized version of this book further transforms Baruch into a prophet who learned well in advance of the life of Jesus of Nazareth.

Bibliography: J. R. Harris. *The Rest of the Words of Baruch* (1889); G. W. E. Nickelsburg. "Stories of Biblical and Early Post-Biblical Times." *Jewish Writings of the Second Temple Period*. Vol. 2, ed. M. E. Stone (1984) 413–25; *Paraleipomena Jeremiou*. R. A. Kraft and A. E. Purintun, ed. (1972); S. E. Robinson. "4 Baruch." *The Old Testament Pseudepigrapha*, vol. 2, ed. J. H. Charlesworth (1985) 413–25.

J. EDWARD WRIGHT

BARZILLAI bahr-zil´*i* [בַּרְזִלַּי *Barzillay*]. 1. A Meholathite whose son, Adriel, married either MERAB (1 Sam 18:19) or MICHAL (some Hebrew and Greek manuscripts, 2 Sam 21:8).

2. A Gileadite from Rogelim who gave David provisions in Mahanaim after Absalom's revolt (2 Sam 17:27; 19:31-40). David ordered Solomon to take care of Barzillai's sons (1 Kgs 2:7).

3. A priest who took the name of his father-in-law, Barzillai the Gileadite. His descendants could not prove their priestly lineage (Ezra 2:61; Neh 7:63). According to 1 Esd 5:38, the priest's name was JADDUS, husband of Barzillai's daughter, AGIA.

HEATHER R. MCMURRAY

BASEMATH bas´uh-math [בָּשְׂמַת *basemath*]. 1. ESAU's wife. Esau's genealogy identifies her as the daughter of ISHMAEL, the sister of Nebaioth (Gen 36:3), and the mother of Reuel and several clans (Gen 36:13, 17). In the Esau story, however, Basemath is the daughter of ELON the Hittite (Gen 26:34; Esau's wife ADAH is given this ancestry in the genealogy). Ishmael's daughter in the narrative is Mahalath (Gen 28:9), who is omitted in the genealogy. In fact, of Esau's three wives, only Basemath is listed in both the story and the genealogy, with a different ancestry in each, attesting to the fluidity of the tradition.

2. A daughter of SOLOMON, who was married to AHIMAAZ, Solomon's official over the district of NAPHTALI (1 Kgs 4:15).

RONALD A. SIMKINS

BASHAN bay'shuhn [בָּשָׁן bashan]. Bashan (Batanae in the Roman world, today roughly corresponding with the Golan Heights) is a region that rests generally north of the Yarmuk River, south of Mount Hermon, and east of the SEA OF GALILEE until reaching the desert and the basalt lava beds of the northwest Arabian Desert. An important agricultural center, Bashan runs about 20 mi. (30 km) east to west, and about 40 mi. (65 km) north to south. After rising about 2,600 ft. out of the Galilee basin, Bashan is a flat region of rich, fertile soil, whose 20–24 in. of annual rainfall supports forests and grasslands, making it famous in the ancient world for its livestock and trees.

Bashan appears early in the historical traditions, which hold that Moses and the wandering Israelites defeated OG of Bashan, along with SIHON of the Amorites, prior to crossing the JORDAN (Num 21:33-35; Deut 1:4; 3:1-11; 4:47; 29:6; Josh 9:10). In these texts, Og was presented in legendary fashion, being a giant and the last of the REPHAIM (Deut 3:11; see Gen 14:5). This territory was then given by Moses to the half-tribe of MANASSEH (Deut 3:13-14; Josh 13:29-31; 1 Chr 5:11-17), portions of which were also given to the daughters of ZELOPHEHAD by JOSHUA, according to Moses' commands (Josh 17:1-6). Bashan also contained GOLAN, as both a city of refuge (Deut 4:43; Josh 20:8) and a Levitical city (Josh 21:6, 27; 1 Chr 6:47, 56). According to 1 Kgs 4:13, 19, SOLOMON made Bashan one of his twelve administrative districts. In the mid-9th cent. BCE, JEHU lost this strip of rich land to HAZAEL of ARAM (i.e., Syria; 2 Kgs 10:33).

As a fertile agricultural region, Bashan plays an important rhetorical role in prophetic and poetic texts. The oaks of Bashan can symbolize haughtiness (Isa 2:13) or provide fine building material for TYRE's ships (Ezek 27:6). Often, the cattle produced in Bashan appear in the literature, drawing upon the region's famous beef industry. MICAH cites Bashan as a garden for grazing cattle, pleading with God to lead the people of Israel to such a lush place (Mic 7:14). In a famous taunt, AMOS mocks the inhabitants of SAMARIA as being "cows of Bashan," playing upon their wealth and power (Amos 4:1). In JEREMIAH, Bashan represents simply a prosperous land (Jer 22:20; 50:19).

JOHN T. STRONG

BASHMURIC VERSION. See VERSION, BASHMURIC.

BASIL. Basil was born into a wealthy Christian family in about 330 CE at Caesarea in Cappadocia and was trained in rhetoric in Constantinople and Athens. He became attracted to ascetic life when he returned to Caesarea, but soon after his ordination entered the christological debates of his time at the request of his bishop, EUSEBIUS. He became bishop of Caesara ca. 370 CE and died ca. 379 CE. Basil quotes Scripture copiously in his works, using it to nurture and validate arguments in his theological treatises to attempt to clarify, against the Arians, the meaning of the term *consubstantial* (*homoousios*) used in the Nicene Creed (*contra Eunomium*), and to promote the divinity of the Holy Spirit (*de Spiritu Sancto ad Amphilocium*). In the front of an edition of his monastic rules, Basil explains that the study of Scripture is the best way to discern one's duty. Accordingly, his ascetic works cite Scripture abundantly, often without further comment, in answer to questions asked by monks about how to conduct their lives. In his homiletical works, Basil progressively moves away from allegorical interpretation in favor of a more literal approach.

Bibliography: Jean-François Racine. *The Text of Matthew in the Writings of Basil of Caesarea* (2004).

JEAN-FRANÇOIS RACINE

BASILIDES, GOSPEL OF. Basilides was a gnostic thinker active in Alexandria between 120–140 CE and known for his elaborate mythological teachings. IRENAEUS, HIPPOLYTUS, and CLEMENT OF ALEXANDRIA are early witnesses for his system of thought, but they unfortunately disagree on fundamental issues. ORIGEN notes that Basilides composed a gospel under his name, but evidence of its contents is scant and based exclusively upon patristic references to his *Exegetika*, a twenty-four vol. commentary on "the gospel" (Eusebius, *Hist. Eccl.* 4.7.7; precisely which gospel remains uncertain). While some scholars have contended that Basilides' gospel, like Marcion's, was a redacted form of Luke, patristic sources suggest that it incorporated material unique to both Matthew (19:11-12) and Luke (16:19-31). It is possible, then, that the gospel was a harmony of the canonical texts and thus another witness to a literary phenomenon known through JUSTIN MARTYR and Tatian. See APOCRYPHA, NT; GNOSTICISM.

DAVID M. REIS

BASIN [כִּיּוֹר kiyyor; λουτήρ loutēr, νιπτήρ niptēr]. The Bible uses a number of words to denote a vessel for holding liquid. A basin was generally used either for the washing of the hands or feet (Exod 30:18-19; 2 Chr 4:6; John 13:5). The Molten Sea (located outside Solomon's Temple) was a very large basin used for priestly washing. *See* BOWLS; MOLTEN SEA; POTTERY; SACRIFICE AND OFFERINGS; SEA.

JOSEPH CATHEY

BASKAMA bas´kuh-muh [Βασκαμα, *Baskama*]. Referred to as Baska in Josephus (*Ant.* 13.210), this site in GILEAD is mentioned in the story of TRYPHO and JONATHAN THE MACCABEE (1 Macc 13:23). Trypho, a former general of ALEXANDER BALAS who helped put ANTIO-CHUS VI on the throne, intending to take the throne for himself, saw Jonathan as an obstacle because the latter supported Antiochus. He captured Jonathan by trickery and eventually executed him in Baskama. The precise location has not been identified, although it has been associated with sites northeast of the Sea of Galilee such as Tell el-Bazuk.

LESTER L. GRABBE

BASKET [סַל *sal*, טֶנֶא *tene'*, כְּלוּב *keluv*, דּוּד *dudh*, תֵּבָה *tevah*; κόφινος *kophinos*, σπυρίς *spuris*, σαργά-νη *sarganē*, μόδιος *modios*]. A container for conveying and storing dry items made in various designs and sizes from various materials.

Hebrew words sal (Gen 40:16-18; Exod 29:3, 23, 32; Lev 8:2, 26, 31; Num 6:15, 17, 19; Judg 6:19) and tene' (Deut 26:2, 4; 28:5, 17) indicate baskets for cakes, bread, produce, and meat. Keluv (Amos 8:1-2) and dud (2 Kgs 10:7; Ps 81:6/7; Jer 24:1-2) also denote baskets. The term tevah (box) is translated as baby Moses' basket (Exod 2; trans. as the ARK OF NOAH, Gen 6–9).

Gospel authors consistently distinguish between two kinds, a kophinos in the feeding of the 5,000 (Matt 14:20; Mark 6:43; Luke 9:17; John 6:13), and a spuris in the feeding of the 4,000 (Matt 15:37; 16:10; Mark 8:8, 20). Saul's escape from Damascus in a spuris (Acts 9:25) implies that such baskets could hold a substantial volume (compare Paul's description of his escape in a braided hamper [sarganē], in 2 Cor 11:33). A modios (Matt 5:15; Mark 4:21; possibly Luke 11:33) was a container that measured approximately one peck.

MATTHEW L. SKINNER

BAT [עֲטַלֵּף *'atallef*]. There are several species of bats in the Levant, some of which are possibly mentioned in the OT. Most bats eat insects, while one species is known to consume fruit. The latter is the *Rousettus aegyptiacus* also know as *Cynonycteris aegyptiaca*, commonly referred to as the "flying fox." The term 'atallefim) men-tioned in Isa 2:20 is considered to be a reference to bats. Some scholars suggest that the חֲפֹר פֵּרוֹת *khappor peroth* of the same verse and "the little foxes, that ruin the vineyard" in Song 2:15 are references to the flying fox. *See* ANIMALS OF THE BIBLE.

Bibliography: Oded Borowski. *Agriculture in Iron Age Israel* (2002).

ODED BOROWSKI

BATASHI, TELL EL. *See* TIMNAH.

BATASHI, TULEILAT EL. Often associated with the city of TIMNAH (Judg 14). The Tuleilat el-Batashi are two small mounds (ca. 1,300 square meters and 650 square meters) on the Nahal Soreq, close to BETH SHEMESH (Josh 15:10). Intermittent occupation dates to the Jericho IX and Yarmoukian Pottery Neolithic (ca. 6,350–5,800 BCE), the Wadi Rabah period (ca. 5,500–4,300 BCE), and the Early and Middle Bronze ages.

Bibliography: Jacob Kaplan. "Excavations at Teluliot Batashi, Nahal Soreq." *ErIsr* 5 (1958) 9–24; E. Stern, A. Lewinson-Gilboa and J. Aviram, eds. "Batash, Teluli-yot." *NEAEHL* (1993) 158.

GARY ROLLEFSON

BATH bath [בַּת *bath*]. A volume measure of liquid, equal to the dry measure EPHA (Ezek 45:11, 14). There were various estimations for the Bath. An estimation of ca. 21-23 L for the bath is based on an upper part of a jar from 8th cent. BCE Lachish. It is strengthened by one entire 7th cent. BCE jar, also from Lachish, inscribed "one b[ath]," with a capacity of ca. 21 L (*TA* 5.87; Lach-ish IV:2114). *See* WEIGHTS AND MEASURES.

RAZ KLETTER

BATHING [רָחַץ *rakhats*; βαπτίζω *baptizō*; λούω *louō*; νίπτω *niptō*; πλύνω *plunō*]. The most common term for bathing and washing in the OT is rakhats. Closely related roots are: כבס *khvs*, "launder" (Lev 14:8); דוח *dhwh*, "rinse"; טהר *thr*, "purify"; שׁטף *shtf*, "rinse"; טבל *tvl*, "dip"; זכך *zkhkh*, "cleanse," קדשׁ *qdhsh*, "sanctify." In the LXX and the NT the terms used are baptizō, "dip, immerse"; louō, "bathe"; niptō, "wash a part of the body"; plunō, "launder."

Bathing in the Bible is performed for various reasons: simple hygiene, as in the case of Pharaoh's daughter (Exod 2:5) or the cleaning of a newborn (Ezek 16:4; soap was extracted from both vegetable and mineral alkali); refreshment and relaxation (2 Sam 11:8; Ezek 23:40; Song 4:2; 5:3; Ruth 3:3); hospitality shown toward guests by washing their feet (Gen 18:4; Judg 19:21; John 13:5; note the wash basins found in the guest house at Tell Beit Mirsim); and after an experience of strong emotion (Gen 43:31; 2 Sam 12:20).

Most instances of bathing occur in connection with ritual purification. Ritual purity was not a matter of hygiene but of HOLINESS. For Yahweh to be present in Israel, certain purity laws had to be followed. Bathing and other rites were required after various impure condi-tions, including corpse contamination, scale disease, and sexual discharges (*see* CLEAN AND UNCLEAN). These rituals marked Israel as distinctive and reinforced the principle that Yahweh was the author of purity and life.

Priests were most subject to bathing. They washed hands and feet before and after entering the sanctuary or officiating at the altar (Exod 30:19). There was apparently a curtained enclosure in the sanctuary court for priests to bathe in (*m. Yoma* 3:4). Other holy items were washed as well in the bronze pool, or "sea," in the Temple court (2 Chr 4:6).

In poetic texts, washing is often a metaphor for forgiveness of sin. The penitent psalmist writes, "wash me and I will be whiter than snow" (Ps 51:7 [Heb. 51:9]). Handwashing too can symbolize innocence (Deut 21:6-7; Ps 26:6; Matt 27:24). Bathing then not only cleanses physical and ritual impurity but also symbolizes the purity of heart that God expects. (For other poetic usages, *see* Gen 49:11; Job 29:6; Ps 58:10 [Heb. 58:11].)

In Hellenistic times, public bathing was introduced. Elaborate baths were constructed in palaces, gymnasia, and in public places. Health resorts were built at the hot springs of Tiberias in Galilee and at Calirrhoe by the Dead Sea (*Ant.* 17.6.5; 18.2.3). The pool of Bethesda was a public pool where the sick congregated hoping for a cure (John 5:7).

New Testament authors refer to the Jewish rites of purification (Luke 11:38; Acts 21:26), but are more interested in the figurative washing away of sins and the rite of Christian BAPTISM (Heb 10:22). Baptism signifies the purity of heart received through Christ and the new Christian's acceptance into the holy community (Acts 22:16; Titus 3:5).

Ritual bathing grows in importance in postbiblical Judaism. Essenes bathed before meals (*J.W.* 2.8.5). The community at Qumran, where a large number of cisterns and ritual baths have been found, required bathing for ritual as well as moral purity (1QS 3:4-5). Rabbinic literature gives specifications for the construction and operation of a ritual bath. *See* MIQVAH.

HANNAH K. HARRINGTON

BATH-RABBIM bath-rab′im [בַּת־רַבִּים *bath rabim*]. A gate beside the pools of HESHBON (Song 7:4) on the eastern side of the Jordan in the central plain. Excavations have not found a gate but did discover a reservoir of the 9th–8th cent. BCE, perhaps the basis for the metaphor for beautiful eyes in the song.

BATHSHEBA bath-shee′buh [בַּת־שֶׁבַע *bath sheva*ʿ]. Wife of Uriah and later of David; mother of Solomon. Listed as "the wife of Uriah" in the genealogy in Matt 1:6. Bathsheba is identified in 2 Sam 11:3 as the daughter of Eliam (Ammiel in 1 Chr 3:5) and wife of URIAH the Hittite, who served in David's army. The dual designation suggests prominence. Her father may be the Eliam son of Ahithophel, one of the "Thirty," David's elite corps (2 Sam 23:34). It is a mystery why DAVID, knowing her identity, would take Bathsheba and sleep with her. Bathsheba's actions are limited to bathing, coming when David sends messengers, returning to her house, being pregnant and sending

word to David. Bathsheba speaks only once—indirectly—in her message: "I am pregnant" (2 Sam 11:5).

Bathsheba is described as "very beautiful" (2 Sam 11:2). Commentators have often viewed her as powerfully seductive. Second Samuel 11, however, focuses not on Bathsheba but on David's abuse of royal power (*see* KING, KINGSHIP). The opening verse notes that although it is "the time when kings go out to battle" David remains in Jerusalem. David's summoning and sleeping with Bathsheba and subsequently arranging for Uriah's death follow the pattern of failing to do what kings are supposed to do. David's desperate efforts to cover his adultery leave Bathsheba a grieving widow (2 Sam 11:26). Later David sends again for Bathsheba to take her for his wife. Bathsheba not only suffers the loss of her husband, but Yahweh strikes dead the child of the adulterous union (2 Sam 12:14-19; *see* ADULTERY). David and Bathsheba conceive another child, SOLOMON, also named Jedidiah (= beloved of Yahweh; 2 Sam 12:24).

In contrast to 2 Sam 11 where Bathsheba is wrapped in silence, in 1 Kgs 1–2 Bathsheba is vocal and active in events that secure Solomon's accession to the throne over his older half-brother ADONIJAH. The identification of Adonijah as "son of Haggith" (1 Kgs 1:5) and Bathsheba's interventions as "Solomon's mother" (1 Kgs 1:11) hint at the complexity of dynastic households and the legitimate political role of royal mothers in securing a future for their sons and themselves (*see* QUEEN). When Adonijah hosts a feast to celebrate what by the rules of primogeniture would be his legitimate and imminent succession to the throne, Bathsheba and the prophet NATHAN intervene. Though Nathan initiates the intervention and instructs Bathsheba what to ask David, she constructs her own argument. They each appear before David to question why Adonijah has become king. Bathsheba reminds David that he swore to her that Solomon would be king (1 Kgs 1:17). Since David is old and there is no prior mention of this pledge, the appeal to David's memory by persons excluded from Adonijah's celebration is highly suspicious. But the narrative also casts suspicion on Adonijah, whose succession claim is introduced in the same words used for Absalom's coup (1 Kgs 1:5-6; *see* ABSALOM). David swears to Bathsheba that he had made a vow and then instructs Nathan to anoint Solomon as king.

In 1 Kgs 2:13-25 Bathsheba mediates Adonijah's appeal to Solomon for permission to marry ABISHAG the Shunammite. To mediate a request for a royal favor is a legitimate function in a dynastic household; this request, however, directly challenges Solomon's kingship if Abishag is understood as one of David's wives (compare David's challenge in 2 Sam 3:14 and David's possession of Saul's wives in 2 Sam 12:8). Abishag is the "very beautiful" young woman selected by David's servants in his old age to lie in his bosom and keep him warm (1 Kgs 1:2), although the text denies any sexual involvement (1 Kgs 1:4) and describes her service as steward (סֹכֶנֶת sokheneth, 1 Kgs 1:4; compare a male steward in Isa 22:15) and royal SERVANT (מְשָׁרֵת mesharath, 1 Kgs 1:4, 15; compare 2 Sam 13:17). Abishag is present when Bath-sheba intercedes for Solomon (1 Kgs 1:15). The text does not report Bathsheba's motives or foreknowledge of how Solomon would react to Adonijah's request to marry someone close to David's affairs who had witnessed Bathsheba and Nathan's appeal to David on his behalf. Bathsheba has either underestimated Solomon's violent response to this request (1 Kgs 2:22), or she has cleverly supplied him an excuse for Adonijah's permanent removal.

Bathsheba is among five women included in the Gospel of Matthew's genealogy of Jesus, all of whom are listed by their own names, except for Bathsheba, who is identified as "the wife of Uriah" (Matt 1:6). By using the language of 2 Sam 11:3, 26; 12:10 and 15, the genealogy indirectly recalls the story of David's abuse of power and Bathsheba's vulnerability.

Bibliography: Elna K. Solvang. *A Woman's Place is in the House: Royal Women and Their Involvement in the House of David* (2003).

ELNA K. SOLVANG

BATH-SHUA bath-shoo′uh [בַּת־שׁוּעַ bath shua‛] "Daughter of SHUA." 1. Canaanite wife of the patriarch JUDAH and mother of his sons ER, ONAN, and SHELAH (1 Chr 2:3).

2. Daughter of AMMIEL, wife of DAVID, and mother of SOLOMON (1 Chr 3:7). The LXX and Vulgate have BATHSHEBA in this verse.

BATTALION. A modern term (ca. 1700) that describes a numerically mid-range group of soldiers with a variety of skills, deployed independently in combat.

Such independent units were rare in antiquity. The biblical equivalent would be the "hundred," over which a competent officer would be placed (Deut 1:15). In NT times the Roman century would be the most approximate unit, although the century rarely fought independently.

T. R. HOBBS

BATTERING RAM [כַּר kar, קְבֹל qevol; βελόστασις belostasis]. A war implement used to breach gates, walls, and fortifications. Originally soldiers crashed tree trunks against city gates, but vulnerability to counterattacks and improved fortifications gave rise to battering rams mounted on massive four-wheeled carriages, surrounded with armor and topped with archers' towers. Either as the nosecone of the carriage or suspended from the roof of the structure, this metal-tipped ram in concert with other weaponry and tactics (Ezek 4:2;

21:22; 26:9; Isa 22:5) could decide the outcome of battles. Israel employed them in Joab's siege of Abel of Beth-maacah (2 Sam 20:15). Battering rams are described at 18th cent. MARI, on the upper Euphrates. However, it took another millennium to perfect their design and implementation, best exemplified by the 9th and 8th cent. Neo-Assyrian military of SHALMANESER III (858–824 BCE) and TIGLATH-PILESER III (745–727 BCE). *See* WAR, METHODS, TACTICS, WEAPONS OF.

MARK J. H. FRETZ

BATTLE [מִלְחָמָה milkhamah; πόλεμος polemos]. The violent confrontation of two large and opposing armies at a specific location in the course of extended hostilities. In biblical times pitched battles involved the clash of armies composed of light and heavy infantry, and archers, with occasional use of slingers, chariotry, and cavalry. Limited communication eliminated control of battles beyond the opening charge.

When one line broke and ran (2 Kgs 14:11-12), discarding their heavy weapons and armor, heavy casualties resulted (Ps 18:37-42). Decisive battles often affected the outcome of a war, giving victory and control to one army over another and its territory. In biblical and related literature, the final encounter between good and evil is seen as a pitched battle. *See* ARRAY, BATTLE; BATTLE; WARFARE.

T. R. HOBBS

BATTLEMENTS [טִירָה tirah, פִּנָּה pinnah; γωνία gōnia, ἔπαλξις epalxis]. Fortification, enclosure, or corner tower constructed atop city walls, especially casemate style—double walls connected by internal partition walls—to provide protection and a platform for observation and counterattacking (Zeph 1:16; 3:6). Figurative battlements appear in Song 8:9; Tob 13:16; and Sir 9:13. *See* CAMP.

MARK J. H. FRETZ

BAVVAI bav′i [בַּוַּי bawway]. A Levite, Henadad's son, who participated in rebuilding the wall of Jerusalem after the exile (Neh 3:18). The name may be a corruption of Bani [בָּנִי]. *See* BINNUI.

BAY. *See* HARBOR; SEACOAST.

BAZAAR [חוּץ khuts]. The town streets designated for merchants' businesses separate from streets with residential houses. Ben-hadad allowed bazaars to be established in Damascus (1 Kgs 20:34).

BAZLITH baz′lith [בַּצְלִית batslith, בַּצְלוּת batsluth; Βασαλωθ Basalōth]. The founder of a family group included among the NETHINIM (probably families of non-Israelite origin, as may be deduced from their names listed in Ezra 2:43-55; Neh 7:46-57; 1 Esd 5:31) who returned to Judah from the exile (Neh 7:54).

BAZLUTH. See BAZLITH.

BDELLIUM [בְּדֹלַח bedholakh; ἄνθραξ anthrax]. A product or resource of the land of Havilah, a region watered by a branch of Eden's river (Gen 2:12). The word's etymology is uncertain. It may have come into Hebrew as a loan word. Some scholars have associated BDELLIUM with a fragrant, yellow, tree resin from Arabia, Assyria, Mesopotamia, or India. Its possible use as a perfume or spice could explain its value, as is the case with AMBER.

ELIZABETH E. PLATT

BEADS, BEADWORK. See JEWELRY.

BEALIAH bee´uh-li´uh [בְּעַלְיָה ba'alyah]. One of the mighty Benjaminite warriors who fought with King David at Ziklag (1 Chr 12:5).

BEALOTH bee´uh-loth [בְּעָלוֹת be'aloth]. 1. A town in the NEGEB included among Judah's tribal allotment in land conquered by Joshua (Josh 15:24).

2. A western GALILEE town in Solomon's 9th administrative district (1 Kgs 4:16). The word is a feminine, plural form of ba'al ("owner," "lord"). See BAALATH-BEER.

BEAM [קָרָה qarah, קוֹרָה qorah, כְּרֻתוֹת keruthoth; ἱμάντωσις himantōsis]. Wooden beams, the most prized made of cedar, were in the roof of the Temple (1 Kgs 6:9, 36; 2 Chr 3:7), royal palace (1 Kgs 7:12), and other public (2 Chr 34:11; Ep Jer 6:20) and private buildings (Song 1:17; Ezra 6:11), city gates and walls (Neh 2:8; 3:3, 6), and God's chambers (Ps 104:3). Beams function as a symbol of unshakable resolve (Sir 22:16), or in the case of "weaver's beam" as a simile for a weapon wielded by a mighty warrior (1 Sam 17:7; 2 Sam 21:19; 1 Chr 11:23; 20:5). See ARCHITECTURE.

GARY GILBERT

BEANS [פּוֹל pol]. The broad bean (Vicia faba) is a leguminous, annual plant with pods containing edible seeds. David and his troops were given beans and other supplies by a former enemy, Machir (possibly reciprocating a previous kindness by David), and Barzillai, illustrating that food exchange can resolve conflict and reinforce relationships (2 Sam 17:28). Ezekiel made bread from beans and other scarce FOOD to represent difficult conditions during the siege of Jerusalem and the exile (Ezek 4:9). Beans were a versatile and hardy plant that sustained persons in times of war, scarcity, and poverty. See PLANTS OF THE BIBLE.

JAMES P. GRIMSHAW

BEAR [דֹּב dov]. The Syrian brown bear (Ursus syriacus) was quite common in Palestine during biblical times. The OT contains several references to bears. The bear is described as a prowling animal (Prov 28:15) with a distinct growl (Isa 59:11), lying in wait for its prey (Lam 3:10), and chasing it until it is caught (Amos 5:19). Bears were considered dangerous, especially those who lost their young (דֹּב שַׁכּוּל dov shakkul, 2 Sam 17:8; Hos 13:8; Prov 17:12). As a shepherd, David had to fight away a bear (as well as a lion) to protect his herd (1 Sam 17:34-37). One incident involving bears is vividly described in 2 Kgs 2. After receiving the prophetic leadership from Elijah, ELISHA stayed in Jericho where he performed some miracles. A group of boys taunts Elisha for his bald head, and he curses them, causing 42 of the boys to be mauled by she bears (2 Kgs 2:23-24). Isaiah mentions the bear grazing and living in harmony with the cow as a picture of peaceful coexistence in the End of Days (Isa 11:7).

Bears were not as visible as other animals since in ancient Near Eastern art they were seldom depicted. The Syrian bear did not become extinct. Sightings of bears were reported near Tiberias, near Beth-shan, in the Golan and the Hermon during the mid-19th and early 20th cent. (Borowski 1998, 201–03). See ANIMALS OF THE BIBLE.

Bibliography: Oded Borowski. *Every Living Thing: Daily Use of Animals in Ancient Israel* (1998).

ODED BOROWSKI

BEARD [זָקָן zaqan; πώγων pōgōn, φάρυγξ pharygx]. Israelite men typically wore beards, depicted in Egyptian and Mesopotamian art as curly, but not unkempt. In Israel, the beard was a symbol of manhood, to be shaved only in purification rites, such as those relating to skin diseases (Lev 13:29-30; 14:9).

Priests were to let their beards grow without shaving the edges (Lev 19:27; 21:5), though other Israelites apparently trimmed their beards (2 Sam 19:24). David uncharacteristically drooled on his beard to feign madness (1 Sam 21:13), while the psalmist exulted in the image of oil running down Aaron's beard (Ps 133:2). Joab's actions in murdering Amasa suggest that beards were typically long enough to be grasped by others as a sign of affection (2 Sam 20:9).

The absence of a beard through shaving or plucking would draw special attention. Thus, Ezra pulled hair from his head and beard to express shock and mourning (Ezra 9:3), and Isaiah predicted a time of mourning when heads and beards would be shaved (Isa 15:2, 41:5; 1 Esd 8:71; Ep Jer 1:31).

The forceful shaving of another's beard was a means of shaming. When Hanun cut off half of the beards and garments of David's envoys (1 Sam 10:4-5; 1 Chr 19:5), the resulting embarrassment sparked an international incident.

Shame through shaving also appears as an image of judgment in Isa 7:20, where Isaiah predicts that

Yahweh will "hire" an Assyrian razor to shave the head, feet, and beards of the Israelites. More pointedly, Ezekiel shaved his head and beard, using the hair as a sign of judgment (Ezek 5:1). But, Isaiah prophesied of one who would willingly submit his cheeks to "those who pull out the beard" (Isa 50:6). *See* HAIR.

TONY W. CARTLEDGE

BEAST [חַיָּה khayya; Aram. חֵיוָא khewa', חֵיוָה khewah; θηρίον thērion]. The Hebrew and Aramaic words translated as *beast* are related to the verbs חָיָה khayah (Heb.) and חֲיָא khaya' (Aram.) which mean "to live." The KJV uses the word *beast/s* 337 times. The NRSV (including the Apocrypha) uses it only 73 times. What happened? In the 4 cent. separating the two translations, the Hebrew, Aramaic, and Greek texts have not changed. English usage, however, has. People do not saddle up their "beasts" anymore. Most of the wild "beasts" and the clean, unclean, and sacrificial "beasts" are simply "animals" now. In the NRSV, 70 percent of the occurrences of the term *beast* are connected with the ghastly monsters that figure in the visions of Dan 7 and Rev 11–20.

1. Four apocalyptic beasts (Daniel 7). Daniel's first apocalyptic vision (*see* APOCALYPTICISM) features a sequence of four "beasts" (חֵיוָן khewan), each more terrible than its predecessor. Three of them are described with the recognizable animalian features respectively of lion, bear, and leopard (7:4-6). The 4th beast resembled no earthly creature, but "it had great iron teeth" and ten horns (7:7). In time it sprouted an 11th horn complete with human eyes and an arrogant mouth (7:8).

Once Daniel's angelic interlocutor identifies the beasts as four kings (7:17), their features and their sequence take on historical significance. Only about the 4th beast, however, and especially about its little horn, does the angel offer any detailed information (7:19-27). Its execution and cremation by God (7:11) occur at the end of the present age, at which time an "everlasting dominion" (7:14, 27) is given to "one like a human being [= son of man] coming with the clouds of heaven" (7:13) whom the angel identifies as "the holy ones of the Most High" (7:18, 27). Students of Daniel debate the identities of the historical nations and personages symbolized by these figures, but many believe that the four regimes alluded to are the Babylonian (lion), Median (bear), Persian (leopard), and the empire of Alexander the Great and his successors; that the little horn is Antiochus IV Epiphanes, the Greco-Syrian tyrant of Antioch 175–163 BCE, during whose reign observant Jews were persecuted and the Temple desecrated; and that the "holy ones" are the "saints" (חֲסִדִים khasidhim) who remained Torah-true and who gave us the book of Daniel.

2. Two apocalyptic beasts (Rev 13). In Rev 13 the author introduces first of all "a beast rising out of the sea, having ten horns and seven heads" (13:1). The description fits the many-headed OT sea serpent Leviathan (e.g., Ps 74:14), though that monster is better anchored in the ancestry of "the great red dragon" of Rev 12. However, the description goes on to reveal that the new beast is a composite of the four beasts of Dan 7 (13:2; compare Dan 7:4-6). Like the mouth on the little horn of Dan 7:8, 11, 20, this monster's mouth utters "haughty and blasphemous words" (13:5). This beast is given authority by the dragon (identified with SATAN in 12:9; 20:2). One of its seven heads receives a mortal wound, but it recovers from the injury (13:3). Worship of this beast is nearly universal except by those already listed in the eternal "book of life of the Lamb" (13:8).

This terrible ruling beast is supported by a 2nd one that rises out of the earth, not the sea (13:11). As agent of the 1st beast, it forces human beings to worship its master (13:15). Whether by tattoo or branding, its "mark" (666, perhaps a numeric equivalent of its name) is placed on the right hand or forehead of small and great, rich and poor alike (13:16-18). During the ensuing chapters of Revelation, this 2nd beast mutates into a "false prophet."

As in the case of Dan 7, readers have long recognized that these beasts represent historical epochs and individuals. The composite beast of Rev 13 is a figure for Imperial Rome and its emperors, who wielded on earth the power of the dragon/Satan. The head that received a mortal wound may refer to Nero, who committed suicide in 68 CE, but was widely believed to have returned from the dead. The 2nd beast or false prophet is the Roman priesthood that promoted the cult of emperor worship. The fact that it "spoke like a dragon" (13:11) identifies its words, too, with Satan. These three foul figures—dragon, beast, and false prophet—appear together in 16:13 as a kind of unholy trinity. *See* BEHEMOTH; DANIEL, BOOK OF; LEVIATHAN; REVELATION, BOOK OF.

W. SIBLEY TOWNER

BEATEN [כָּתַת kathath, נָכָה nakhah, נָגַף naghaf; δέρω derō, κολαφίζω kolaphizō, ῥαβδίζω rabdizō]. The terms translated *beaten* in the NRSV appear primarily in situations of physical violence. Four pentateuchal texts use the term nakhah. In Exod 5:14, the Israelite supervisors are beaten by their taskmasters; in Exod 5:16, the supervisors complain to the Pharaoh about their beating. Two legal texts discuss being beaten: in Exod 22:2, if a thief is caught and beaten to death, one does not incur bloodguilt; and in Deut 25:2, nakhah is used to designate both the one who deserves "scourging" and the punishment itself.

Three Hebrew words are translated *beaten* in descriptions of military defeat: Josh 8:15 uses the term nagha' (it should probably read naghaf); 2 Sam 2:17 uses naghaf, which is otherwise always translated "defeated" or "routed;" and Jer 46:5 envisions the warriors of Judah "beaten down" (kathath). This term has the connotation of crushing, and is also used in Mic 1:7 to describe the fate of the images in Jerusalem: they shall be "beaten to pieces."

In the NT, three terms are translated "beaten." The first, derō is used to signify general beatings in Mark 13:9 and Acts 16:37. The second, rabdizō, designates being beaten by rods in Acts 16:22; 2 Cor 11:25. The final term, kolaphizō, connotes striking, usually with the fists, and occurs in 1 Cor 4:11 and 1 Pet 2:20.

MARY SHIELDS

BEATEN GOLD זָהָב שָׁחוּט zahav shakhut]. Describes the material that Solomon uses to make large and smaller shields for the House of the Forest of Lebanon (1 Kgs 10:16, 17; 2 Chr 9:15, 16). The gold represents a portion of the wealth that Solomon acquired from outside sources.

BEATEN OIL שֶׁמֶן כָּתִית shemen kathith]. Phrase that describes a particularly fine oil that is to be mixed with flour for use in daily burnt offerings (Exod 29:40; Num 28:5). Oil of this quality is also appropriately used for secular purposes. For example, on a list in 1 Kgs 5:11 [Heb. 5:25] beaten oil for human consumption appears as a trade commodity. Identical phrases in Exod 27:20 and Lev 24:2 specify the type of oil—(pure beaten) olive oil—that is to be supplied for the perpetually burning lamps in the tent of meeting. Other references to beaten oil do not specify the type of oil that is to be used.

WILMA ANN BAILEY

BEATEN SILVER כֶּסֶף מְרֻקָּע kesef meruqqaʿ]. Appearing solely in Jer 10:9, beaten silver is a material used in the production of idols (probably as a veneer). The emphasis is on the ordinariness of this product, a commodity of trade with neighboring Tarshish. It has no supernatural qualities.

BEATITUDES bee-at´uh-ty oo d [μακάριος makarios]. This literary form in the biblical material declares God's favor on present circumstances, actions, or practices, and/or God's future reversal or transformation of or salvation from present oppressive circumstances. Beatitudes also often express an implicit imperative or exhortation for humans to live consistently with God's justice. The most well-known "beatitudes" occur at the beginning on the Sermon of the Mount (Matt 5:3-12; Luke 6:20b-21).

Terminology: The term *beatitude* derives from the Latin *beatitudo*; the cognate adjectival form *beatus* commonly constitutes the opening term *blessed* (אַשְׁרֵי ʾashre). Beatitudes are also known as makarisms from the equivalent Greek term makarios. The term makarios often designates blessings on humans in contrast with vocabulary commonly used to introduce blessings directed to God (בָּרַךְ barakh; εὐλογητός eulogētos; e.g., contrast Tob 13:1 and 14). English translations of ʾashre/makarios vary ("Happy," "Blessed," "Fortunate"). Perhaps the term is best rendered by a phrase expressing the central theological perspective, "God is pleased when . . ." or "God's favor or approval rests on the ones who . . ."

Distribution: Beatitudes in various forms occur in Egyptian and classical Greek literature. In Jewish literature, beatitudes appear in the OT, Apocrypha, and Pseudepigrapha. They occur throughout the NT and in non-canonical Christian literature.

Old Testament. Of the more than forty beatitudes, twenty-five appear in Psalms and ten in wisdom literature (Job 5:17; Prov 3:13; 8:32, 34; 14:21; 16:20b; 20:7; 28:14; 29:18b; Eccl 10:17). The rest appear in "historical" and prophetic writings (Deut 33:29; 1 Kgs 10:8; Isa 30:18; 32:20; 56:2; Dan 12:12).

The form varies, though dominant is ʾashre ("Blessed") with noun/pronoun and/or participle designating the subject, with a clause, of varying length, describing the qualities or circumstances of blessing. Third-person forms occur more than second-person; plurals (emphasizing communal values and practices) are more common than singulars. A subsequent clause can elaborate the basis for the blessing.

At the heart of being blessed is the recognition of God as God (Pss 33:12; 144:15b). Those who focus their lives on God and value covenant relationship with God are declared blessed. They take refuge in (Pss 2:12; 34:8b), trust (Pss 40:4; 84:12b; Prov 16:20b), fear (Pss 112:1; 128:1; Prov 28:14), find strength in (Ps 84:5), and are disciplined and taught by the Lord (Ps 94:12) who is their helper and hope (Ps 146:5). Often these qualities of a faithful and blessed life are elaborated in the verses surrounding the beatitude.

Consistent with this focus on relationship with God, commitment to the way of life revealed in Torah is blessed. The faithful delight in it (Ps 1:1-2), walk or live it (Ps 119:1; Prov 29:18b) with integrity (Prov 20:7), and seek God in living the teaching (Ps 119:2). Specifically, the blessed do justice, keep Sabbath, and refrain from evil (Isa 56:21), being merciful to the poor (Ps 41:1; Prov 14:21), and doing righteousness (Ps 106:3). Similarly, those who encounter wisdom, the manifestation of God's purposes and presence, are blessed (Prov 3:13; 8:32, 34), as are Temple worshipers (Pss 65:4; 84:4; 89:15).

The blessed encounter God's saving presence in various ways. God intervenes to save people from sins (Ps 32:1-2), and in battle from enemies (Deut 33:29; Isa 30:18). Those who revenge the Babylonians are blessed (Ps 137:8-9). The blessed participate in a transformed creation (Isa 32:20), enjoy posterity (Ps 127:5), deliverance from enemies, abundant food, and national security (Ps 144:7-15). They are blessed in persevering oppression while awaiting God's salvific intervention (Dan 12:12).

Apocrypha: The writings of the Apocrypha contain fifteen beatitudes introduced by forms of makarios, predominantly in Wisdom literature, especially Sirach. The masculine singular dominates, though some masculine plural and feminine singular forms appear. A noun or substantive participle follows; often a further clause (especially relative) describes the circumstances of blessing. Tobit 13:14 includes a sequence of three beatitudes and a contrast with curses in 13:12.

These beatitudes continue the emphasis on faithful relationship with God. Tobit's prayer celebrating God's covenant relationship with Israel blesses those who love Jerusalem, rejoice in its peace, and grieve its distress (Tob 13:14). Sirach 14:20 blesses the one who meditates on wisdom, and 48:11 blesses those who saw Elijah. Wisdom of Solomon blesses the barren woman and the eunuch who have not sinned (3:13).

The remaining blessings concern appropriate societal and domestic interactions, especially those of the righteous man in a patriarchal society. Control of one's speech and protection from the destructive speech of others (Sir 14:1-2; 28:19), a compliant wife (26:1), good friends, wealth without greed, and those not serving an inferior are blessed (25:8-9; 31:8). The beatitudes' implicit exhortations uphold honorable societal living. The book closes by blessing those who live its teaching as evidence of fearing the Lord (50:28).

Pseudepigrapha: Beatitudes continue to affirm central values and practices for life lived in pleasing relationship with God. Psalms of Solomon blesses those who have "moderate sufficiency" but not excessive (sinful) wealth (5:16), and those whom God disciplines (10:1). *Second Enoch* blesses those who serve God, aid the poor, speak truth, show compassion, understand God's ways, and live the teaching (the nine beatitudes of *2 En.* 42:6-14; 44:4; 48:9). *Second Enoch* 52 alternates seven beatitudes with curses or woes to emphasize praise for God, respect for the tradition, and peace making. *Second Baruch* 10:6-7 blesses those who have not seen the destruction of Jerusalem by Babylon/Rome. Especially prominent in apocalyptic texts within this collection are beatitudes that proclaim God's eschatological vindication of the suffering righteous and judgment on the sinners (*1 En.* 103:5). Positing various end-time scenarios, they bless the righteous who have endured oppressive injustice to find God's salvation (*Pss. Sol.* 4:23; 6:1; 17:44; 18:6 involving a messiah; *1 En.* 58:2; 81:4; 82:4; 99:10; *2 En.* 66:7).

Christian Writings: Thirty of the forty-four NT beatitudes appear in three gospels with fifteen in Luke, thirteen in Matthew, two in John, and none in Mark. Revelation employs seven beatitudes. The remaining seven appear in Romans, James, and 1 Peter. As with the literature discussed above, NT beatitudes take vari-

ous forms. In noncanonical Christian literature, beatitudes appear, e.g., in the *Gospel of Thomas* (13x; *Gos. Thom.* 1, 7, 18, 19, 49, 58, 68–69, 79, 103). Seven of these have some connection with the synoptic gospels. They are evident in various Apocryphal Acts such as the *Acts of Paul and Thecla*. In sections 5–6, e.g., Paul announces a series of thirteen beatitudes introduced as "the word of God concerning self-control (or the life of chastity) and the resurrection."

The beatitudes in the canonical Gospels (exempting temporarily Matt 5 and Luke 6) affirm commitment to Jesus (Luke 7:23; 10:23; 11:27, 28; Matt 11:6; 13:16), specific acts of discipleship (Luke 1:45; Matt 16:17), obedience and belief (John 13:17; 20:29), and preparedness for Jesus' return to establish God's empire (Luke 12:37, 38, 43; 14:14, 15; 23:29; Matt 24:46). Revelation blesses those who read and observe the writing's teaching (1:3; 22:7). Its five other beatitudes bless those who participate in the final establishment of God's purposes at Jesus' return in the resurrection (14:13; 16:15; 19:9; 20:6; 22:14). Paul, quoting Ps 32:1-2, blesses those forgiven and against whom God does not reckon sin (Rom 4:7, 8) and those who live faithfully (14:22*b*). James blesses those who endure temptation (1:12) and do the law (1:25). First Peter declares blessed those who suffer righteously for the name of Christ (3:14; 4:14).

The most well-known beatitudes occur in a sequence of nine at the beginning of the Sermon on the Mount (Matt 5:3-12). These beatitudes exhibit formal features evident in the tradition. The opening makarioi is plural and is followed by either a substantive adjectival or participle phrase, with a subsequent clause ("for") announcing future eschatological reversal (comfort for the mourning) or reward (the merciful obtain mercy). Luke's Sermon on the Plain begins with a sequence of four beatitudes (6:20*b*-23). Three parallel Matthew's beatitudes though they use the second-person "you" not Matthew's dominant third-person (except 5:11). Luke follows them with four curses (6:24-26).

Scholars have long debated the origin and relationship of the two sequences. One theory posits three beatitudes of eschatological reversal deriving from Jesus influenced by Isa 61 (the poor; who mourn; who hunger). Q adds the beatitude on persecution (Luke 6:22-23; Matt 5:11-12; *see* Q, QUELLE). Subsequently, Q is expanded in two forms to add Luke's woes and Matthew's beatitudes on the meek, merciful, pure in heart, and peacemakers. The gospel redactors complete the process, with Matthew adding, e.g., another beatitude on persecution (5:10).

Equally debated are the meanings of these beatitudes. The eschatological quality of the declarations in reversing current circumstances, notably in the future tenses of the second clauses, has been widely recognized. God's empire will bring a transformation of present circumstances and establishment of God's justice. The beatitudes also exhort behaviors in accord with God's justice. Interpreters have claimed that Matthew spiritualizes the beatitudes. Such a claim, though, is unconvincing given the echoes of Isa 61, the evoking of Ps 37 in Matt 5:5, and Jesus' healing of the crowds in 4:23-25. The Matthean beatitudes reflect the way Jesus reverses the physical brokenness (that results from imperial structures) to display God's life-giving empire (4:17) and to anticipate its final establishment (Matt 11:2-6).

Bibliography: Hans Dieter Betz. *The Sermon on the Mount* (1995) 91–153, 571–89; Warren Carter. *Matthew and the Margins* (2000) 128–37.

WARREN CARTER

BEAUTIFUL GATE [ἡ θύρα ἡ λεγομένη ὡραία hē thyra hē legomenē hōraia]. Gate of Herod's Temple courts where Peter and John healed a lame man (Acts 3:2, 10). No other ancient source mentions a gate by this name, but Josephus describes two good candidates: one very large and richly appointed, apparently standing between the Court of Women and the Court of the Israelites (*J.W.* 5.204, possibly the Nicanor Gate), and another more likely one, whose Corinthian bronze plating caused it to excel those plated in silver and gold leading into the eastern cloisters of the Court of Women (*J.W.* 5.201). *See* GATE; NICANOR GATE; TEMPLES, HEROD'S.

JAMES RILEY STRANGE

BEAUTY. Beauty (and aesthetics more generally) has been a central topic in Western philosophical thought for thousands of years, and yet it has been little studied by biblical scholars. There can be no doubt that ancient Israelites and Judahites, like other ancient and traditional peoples, had a rich and vibrant aesthetic sensibility. This much, at least, is suggested by even the most cursory of looks at the various terms derived from the Hebrew root יָפָה yph, which are routinely translated in English as "beauty, " "beautiful, " or "to be beautiful." These nominals and verbs appear to privilege the perception of attractiveness or pleasingness in the visual domain, especially when applied to persons. Both men (Gen 39:6; 1 Sam 16:12; 2 Sam 14:25; Song 1:16) and women (Gen 12:11; 29:19; 2 Sam 13:1; Song 1:15; Esth 1:11) are perceived as having good "looks" (מַרְאֶה mar'eh) or an attractive "form" (תֹּאַר to'ar). Ascertaining more specifically what criteria elicit this perception of "beauty" on the part of the biblical writers requires detailed study. But here, too, preliminary impressions may be registered for illustrative purposes. Among the visual stimuli associated with the various biblical characters judged "beautiful" (yph) are long, thick, dark hair (2 Sam 14:25-26; compare 18:9; Song 4:1), the ruddiness and translucence of a healthy and strong appearance (1 Sam 16:12; 17:42;

Song 5:10; compare Lam 4:7; note the Shulammite's countercultural stance in Song 1:5: "I am black and beautiful"), striking eyes (Gen 29:17; 1 Sam 16:12; Prov 6:25; Song 4:1), and personal adornment—dress, jewelry, cosmetics (Jer 4:30; 10:4; Ezek 16:3; Song 5:14; 7:2). Other than persons are occasionally held as "beautiful" (yph), such as cows (Gen 41:2; Jer 46:20), trees or plants (Jer 11:16; Ezek 31:3, 7, 9), and Mount Zion (Ps 48:3), and other sensorial domains sometimes engaged—grace (Ps 45:3; compare Esth 2:17), voice (Ezek 33:32), taste (Eccl 5:17). And though Yahweh is never characterized with yph in the OT, any number of other terms are used positively to register an aesthetic appreciation of (or by) the deity, e.g., נֹעַם no'am "pleasantness" (Pss 27:4; 90:11; "beauty" NRSV), נָעִים na'im "pleasant" (Pss 135:3; 147:1), צְבִי tsevi "beauty" (Isa 28:5), פָּאַר pe'or "beautified" or "glorified" (Isa 49:3), כָּבֹד kavodh "glory" (Ps 19:2), הָדָר hadhar "honor" or "glory" (Ps 104:1; 1 Chr 16:27), חָמַד khamadh "to desire" (Ps 68:17), חָפֵץ khafets "delight" (Isa 42:21; Pss 16:3; 18:20; 73:25; 112:1; Job 22:3). Even this short list of terms for beauty used with reference to Yahweh shows that Israel's aesthetic vocabulary is robust.

The bride of the deity, Jerusalem, is as beautiful as her consort in Ezek 16. She wears beautiful clothing and her ornaments are pleasing. Similarly, decoration of various sorts and qualities, including clothing and jewelry but also temples and palaces, cult vessels, ceremonial furniture, and the like, were valued for aesthetic attribute in ancient Mesopotamia. The high estimate placed on the quality of being adorned is consistent with what one finds in the ethnographic literature on non-Western aesthetics more generally.

Apparently, Western and non-Western perceptions of aesthetic value will not always be in direct alignment. The body of literature that is emerging from ethnographic studies provides an important resource for thinking through the field's traditional, tight focus on beauty and its central preoccupation with visual phenomena. First, all sensorial experiences—including olfactory, tactile, and gustatory experiences, as well as experiences of movement—are amenable to aesthetic perception and valuation; beauty is not merely the visual and auditory phenomena historically privileged in the West. Indeed, it is often the case that the very nomenclature utilized to communicate aesthetic preference will derive from these other sensorial domains, such as with words for "sweetness" in some cultures (compare Judg 9:11; Song 5:16). Second, there is a growing awareness from a cross-cultural perspective that the realms of aesthetic appreciation and valuation are potentially multiple and varied, not to be restricted solely to the graphic and plastic arts of Western preference. The latter preoccupation may account, at least in part, for the lack of scholarly attention to aesthetics in biblical studies—after all, the representational remains from ancient Judah and Israel are meager and poor. There is reason to broaden aesthetic inquiry into other realms, such as music, dance, and literature. Von Rad identifies literature in particular as one of the chief domains of Israelite aesthetic interest (Pss 19:15; 45:2; Prov 15:26; 16:24). It is possible to argue also that aesthetic perception is critical to the happiness of our everyday lived experience, and thus the kinds of human activities and products that may be imbued with aesthetic value for any culture is potentially limitless. Third, there are categories in addition to beauty (or its equivalent), such as the ugly and the comic, that result in feelings of aesthetic appreciation. Fourth, there is a growing convergence in the literature on the kinds of criteria for assessing aesthetic value and perception that have broad cross-cultural validity. These would include estimates of skill, symmetry and balance, clarity, smoothness and brightness, youthfulness and novelty, and fineness. Finally, aesthetics is not always conceptualized as a separable cognitive and experiential domain. Often aesthetic sensibilities bleed over into and get mixed up with other sensibilities. In fact, this particular mix of qualities is very old, as shown by the ancient Hebrew טוב tov "good," which, like the Akkadian damqu (*CAD* D, 68*b*-73*b*), carries both aesthetic (Gen 1:31; 2 Sam 11:2; Ps 133:1; Esth 2:7) and ethical (Deut 1:39; Hos 8:3; Mic 6:8) meanings. One of the characteristics of Israel's aesthetic sensibility is precisely this tendency for the language of beauty to be associated more generally with the social phenomenon of value.

In sum, ancient Israel was well acquainted with the reality of beauty, both appreciatively and critically.

Bibliography: R. Anderson. *Calliope's Sisters: A Comparative Study of Philosophies of Art* (1990); F. Boas. *Primitive Art* (1927); J. Dewey. *Art as Experience* (1934); F. W. Dobbs-Allsopp. "The Delight of Beauty and Song 4:1-7." *Int.* 59 (2005) 260–77; W. A. Dyrness. "Aesthetics in the Old Testament: Beauty in Context." *JETS* 28 (1985) 421–32; L. Ferretter. "The Power and the Glory: The Aesthetics of the Hebrew Bible." *Literature & Theology* 18 (2004) 123–38; C. W. Reines. "Beauty in the Bible and the Talmud." *Judaism* 24 (1975) 100–07; E. Scarry. *On Beauty and Being Just* (1999); W. Van Damme. *Beauty in Context: Towards an Anthropological Approach to Aesthetics* (1996); G. von Rad. *Old Testament Theology*, Vol. I (1962); I. Winter. "Aesthetics in Ancient Mesopotamian Art." *CANE*, IV. 2569–80.

F. W. DOBBS-ALLSOPP

BEBAI bee'bi [בֵּבַי bevay; Βηβαι Bēbai]. 1. The ancestor of 623 exiles who returns with Zerubbabel from the exile (Ezra 2:11; 1 Esd 5:13; Neh 7:16 instead indicates 628). Other decendants return with Ezra (Ezra 8:11; 1 Esd 8:37). Some of Bebai's descendants appear

in the list of men who dismiss their foreign wives (Ezra 10:28; 1 Esd 9:29).

2. One of the leaders of the people who sets his seal to an agreement to observe the Torah (Neh 10:15 [Heb. 10:16]).

3. A unidentified location listed in some manuscripts of the book of Judith (*see* NRSV footnote for 15:4). As the story is a fictional account that incorporates numerous otherwise unknown geographical locations, here Bebai is most probably a manufactured name utilized by the book's author to help lend an air of authenticity to the events it describes.

LINDA DAY

BECHER bee'kuhr [בֶּכֶר bekher; Βαχιρ Bachir]. The father of Zemirah, Joash, Eliezer, Elioenai, Omri, Jeremoth, Abijah, Anathoth, and Alemeth (1 Chr 7:8). Two genealogies place Becher as the second son of BENJAMIN (Gen 46:21; 1 Chr 7:6), but he is replaced by ASHBEL in other genealogies (Num 26:38; 1 Chr 8:1). Further, the MT of Num 26:35 identifies Becher as the second son of EPHRAIM, but he is omitted in the LXX, and 1 Chr 7:20 lists BERED as the second son of Ephraim. Perhaps the geographical proximity of Benjamin and Ephraim led to such confusion.

RONALD A. SIMKINS

BECORATH bi-kor'ath [בְּכוֹרַת bekhorath]. A Benjaminite ancestor of Saul, Israel's first king. Zeror's father and Aphiah's son (1 Sam 9:1).

BECTILETH bek'tuh-leth [Βεκτιλεθ Bektileth]. The plain of Bectileth, near Cilicia in southeast Asia Minor, a stop on the Assyrian military campaign in Judith (Jdt 2:21). Its location roughly 300 miles west of Nineveh, a distance that the army traverses in a mere three days, is logistically impossible, suggesting that the reference is one of the many fictional and satirical details in the story. Some have proposed a connection with the Beqʿah Valley or with Bakatailloi in Syria.

LINDA DAY

BED [מִשְׁכָּב mishkav, מִטָּה mittah, עֶרֶשׂ ʿeres; κλίνη klinē, κοίτη koitē]. The bed, couch, or litter function as both physical objects as well as metaphors for a person's state of being. The bed can be a piece of furniture designed for repose, a haven where the body and the mind can be refreshed with sleep or quiet meditation (Ps 4:4; Job 7:13). It can also be an intimate, even secret place where plots may be conceived (Ps 36:4), wicked deeds devised (Mic 2:1), or days idled away by the lazy (Prov 26:14). The injured and the sick are confined to their beds by their infirmities and pain, and thus removed from society and their normal activities (Job 33:19; Matt 8:14), and those who will not recover find the bed their final home (Gen 49:33; 2 Kgs 1:4). A return to health or a restoration of vigor is described as arising from one's bed (Matt 9:2; Acts 9:34). Perfumed and decorated beds or couches are associated with celebrations or banquets (Ps 149:5; Esth 1:6), and with the sanctity of marriage (Heb 13:4). Conversely, the bed is the place where adulterous acts may occur (Prov 7:17) and, metaphorically, where the unfaithful commit idolatrous devotions (Isa 57:7-8). On a larger scale, the bed can represent the wealth of a household (Og's iron bed in Deut 3:11 and the beds of ivory in Amos 6:4), the sexual rights of the head of a household (see Reuben's "defiling" Jacob's bed by laying with his concubine in Gen 49:4), and also functions as evidence of injustice when the last vestiges of a man's property, literally his bed, are taken from under him (Prov 22:27). In the NTperiod, at least, the whole family is said to sleep together in a bed (Luke 11:7) and that it stood above the floor (Luke 8:16). In biblical narrative, a bed can serve as a prop signifying a shift in the action (see David's arising from his bed and viewing of Bathsheba in 2 Sam 11:2) or as a moment of transition between scenes (see Ahab's sulking on his bed after Naboth's refusal to sell his vineyard in 1 Kgs 21:4 and the friends carrying a paralyzed man on his bed to see Jesus in Matt 9:2). Beds and couches also function as the site of political acts. For example, Ishbaal is murdered "on his bed" (2 Sam 4:11), David reacts to Solomon's accession to the throne by bowing and worshiping on his bed (1 Kgs 1:47), and the wounded Joash is slain "on his bed" (2 Chr 24:25). Finally, both power and defilement are attached to the places where persons lay down. Thus the power associated with a prophet's bed is evidenced in the Shunamite's attempt to heal her son by placing him on Elisha's bed (2 Kgs 4:20). As by association, the Holiness Code decrees that a man's seminal discharge makes both him and his bed ritually impure (Lev 15:4), and this is also true for a menstruating woman (Lev 15:21). See CHAMBER; COUCH; CUSHION; FURNITURE; HOUSE; LITTER.

VICTOR H. MATTHEWS

BED, GARDEN [עֲרוּגָה 'arughah; πρασιά prasia]. A plot for growing plants (Song 5:13; 6:2). Used figuratively as cheeks (Song 5:13), a place for depositing instruction (Sir 24:31), and a home (Ezek 17:7).

BEDAD bee'dad [בְּדַד bedhadh]. Father of Hadad, an Edomite king or chief (Gen 36:35; 1 Chr 1:46).

BEDAN bee'dan [בְּדָן bedhan]. 1. The son of ULAM of the tribe of MANASSEH, of whom nothing else is known (1 Chr 7:17).
2. In the MT of 1 Sam 12:11, an otherwise unknown Israelite leader mentioned alongside JERUBBAAL (GIDEON), JEPHTHAH, and either SAMSON (LXX) or SAMUEL (MT).

BEDEIAH bi-dee'yah [בְּדְיָה bedheyah]. Perhaps an abbreviation of "servant of Yahu" (עֲבַדְיָה 'ovadhyah). One of Bani's descendants who sent his foreign wife and their children away as Ezra instructed (Ezra 10:37; 1 Esd 9:34).

BEE [דְּבוֹרָה devorah BEDOVIN. Unlike HONEY, a frequent biblical symbol, the bee (Apis mellifera syriaca) has only four citations (Deut 1:44; Judg 14:8; Ps 118:12; Isa 7:18), usually referring to Israel's enemies. The carcass-inhabiting bees in Judg 14:8 may refer to a different species, Chalicodoma. See INSECTS OF THE BIBLE.

BEELIADA bee'uh-li'uh-duh [בְּעֶלְיָדָע be'elyadha']. One of the thirteen sons of David born in Jerusalem (1 Chr 14:7). His name appears as ELIADA in the parallel lists (2 Sam 5:16; 1 Chr 3:8), perhaps indicating a tendency to remove references to the foreign deity BAAL in Israelite names.

BEELZEBUL bee-el'zi-buhl [βεελζεβούλ Beelzeboul]. Jesus' opponents refer to him, and also to the ruler or prince of demons, as "Beelzebul" (Matt 10:25; 12:24, 27; Mark 3:22; Luke 11:15, 18, 19), with the claim that Beelzebul was his means of exorcising demons. Beelzebub is the commonly known KJV translation, and it is found in Symmachus' Greek manuscript and the Vulgate (See BAAL-ZEBUB).

Unknown outside biblical texts, the Hebrew ba'al-zevuv is a rival of Yahweh and the representation of Baal in the Philistine city Ekron. Ahaziah inquired of this god whether he would recover from an injury (2 Kgs 1:2, 3, 6, 16). Ba'al-zevuv literally means "Baal of the flies," as zevuv is the collective noun for flies (Eccl 10:1). The Hebrew zbl ("exalted," 1 Kgs 8:13 = 2 Chr 6:2) and the Ugaritic epithet zbl ("prince," KTU 1:2i:38, 43; 1:6:i:42) for Baal indicate that ba'al-zevuv is probably a term of ridicule, perhaps alluding to the negative connotation of flies (Isa 7:18) or the association of flies with demons or other gods. The LXX maintains the translation as "Baal of the fly" (βααλ μυῖαν baal muian) and Josephus uses the term "fly god" (θεόν μυῖαν theon muian, Ant. 9:19) in retelling Ahaziah's story.

Other meanings of the title ba'al-zevuv that have been suggested are less likely. 1) The interpretation that this god drives away flies can be maintained, against the majority view, only if dbbm is translated flies instead of demons in a Ugaritic incantation (KTU 1:169:1). 2) That the god provided oracles through the buzzing of flies is not supported by any Semitic evidence. 3) If the god's name is analogous to "Nintu with the flies," it could mean "Baal (statue) with fly (ornament)." However, no such epithet for Baal is known. 4) The comparison of zevuv with dbb (flame) to yield "Baal of the Flame" is unsuccessful, for no such deity is attested. 5) There are no Semitic examples of flies as symbols of death and disease.

The much less common form **beelzevul** is attested as a Punic personal name (b'l 'zbl) from 2nd cent. BCE Sardinia and by the remarkable appearance in the NT of Beelzeboul (from Aram. be'el, "master"). Beelzeboul ("Baal-Prince") was used derisively for the prince of demons, for Satan, and pejoritively of Jesus' exorcistic authority, probably because pagan gods were considered demons (Deut 32:17; Pss 95:5 (LXX); 106 (LXX 105):37; Bar 4:7; 1 Cor 10:20; Rev 9:20) and because the god Baal was associated with exorcism (*KTU* 1:169). Further, since Matt 10:25 juxtaposes "master of the house"—that is, Jesus, the leader of his disciples (10:24)—with "Beelzeboul," and because in late Hebrew zevul meant residence, especially the temple and also heaven as the dwelling place of God (1Q28 10:3; 1Q33 12:1, 2; *b. Hag.* 12b), this term conveyed the idea that Satan was leader or head of a household of demons (Mark 3:22-27).

Alternative suggestions for how Beelzeboul could have become a designation for the prince of demons are less likely. The Greek zeboul is not likely to be a substitute for the Aram. zivul, "dung," because there is no such Aramaic word meaning dung. Zivul could suggest the word zivukha' ("sacrifice"). However, the resulting "lord of sacrifice" does not explain its use for Satan. Alternatively, Beelzeboul could derive from the Aramaic be'el devava' ("enemy"). However, the spelling is enough different from Beelzeboul to make this interpretation problematic. *See* DEMON; SATAN.

Bibliography: J. Day. *Yahweh and the Gods and Goddesses of Canaan* (2002) 77–81; L. Gaston. "Beelzebul." *TZ* 18 (1962) 247–55; H. Gese, M. Höfner, and K. Rudolph. *Die Religionen Altsyriens, Altarabiens und der Mandäer* (1970) 122, 212.

GRAHAM H. TWELFTREE

BEER bee′uhr [בְּאֵר be'er]. The Hebrew word for *well* (Gen 26:15-32). During the Israelites' wilderness wandering, after they left Moab and traveled along the Arnon River they came to a place called "Beer" (Num 21:16), and they celebrated it as Yahweh's gift to Israel (21:17-18). Its precise location remains unknown. JOTHAM fled to Beer from his brother Abimelech's rampage against all of Jerubaal's sons (Judg 9:21). Some associate this place with el-Bireh, south of the Sea of Galilee, and north of the Jezreel Valley. *See* BEEROTH.

LISA MICHELE WOLFE

BEERA bee′uh-ruh [בְּאֵרָא be'era']. Zophah's eleventh son and a descendant of Asher (1 Chr 7:37).

BEERAH bee′uh-ruh [בְּאֵרָה be'erah]. A chieftain and a son of Reuben. He was taken into exile by Tilgath-Pilneser of Assyria (1 Chr 5:6).

BEER-ELIM bee′uhr-ee′lim [בְּאֵר אֵילִים be'er 'elim]. "Well of chiefs" or "terebinth." A city in Moab (Isa 15:8). Possibly the same as BEER (Num 21:16). *See* BEER.

BEERI bee′uhr-*i* [בְּאֵרִי be'eri]. 1. The father of Esau's wife, Judith, a Hittite (Gen 26:34) in the land of Canaan, thus indicating that Esau violated the prohibition against marrying Canaanites.

2. The name of the father of the prophet Hosea (Hos 1:1). The name possibly means "little spring" or "my well."

VALERIE BRIDGEMAN-DAVIS

BEER-LAHAI-ROI bee′uhr-luh-h*i*′roi [בְּאֵר לַחַי רֹאִי be'er lakhay ro'i]. The spring where Sarai's slave, Hagar, "saw" God (Gen 16:14). Its name, "The Spring of the Living One (who) Sees Me," came from Hagar's encounter with El-Roi (The God Who Sees Me). Hagar was the first person in the biblical text to identify God with a name. The well was located in an oasis somewhere in the wilderness of Kadesh Barnea, near Bered, a place-name only found in this story. In Gen 24:62, the name refers to a town or village attached to a well. After Abraham died, the epic story says that Isaac settled at Beer-Lahai-Roi (Gen 25:11).

VALERIE BRIDGEMAN-DAVIS

BEEROTH bee′uh-roth [בְּאֵרוֹת be'eroth]. Beeroth, whose name means "wells," was one of several HIVITE towns in the territory of Benjamin. By pretending they had traveled from a far distance, Beerothites made peace with Joshua and were thus spared, but were later forced to cut wood and carry water for Israel's worship (Josh 9:17-27).

King Saul, a Benjaminite, attempted to purge the territory of Benjamin of its non-Israelite population, and his attack on GIBEON undoubtedly included Beeroth (2 Sam 21:2, 5) whose inhabitants fled to GITTAIM where they then settled (2 Sam 4:3). Two Beerothites, sons of Rimmon, Recab and Baanah, later assassinated Saul's son ISHBOSHETH (ISHBAAL) (2 Sam 4:2-7). Another Beerothite, NAHARAI (2 Sam 23:37; 1 Chr 11:39), joined David's mighty men as JOAB's armor-bearer. Eventually Beerothites became a part of Israel and resettled Beeroth after the Babylonian exile (Ezra 2:25; Neh 7:29).

Beeroth's location remains a mystery. Eusebius refers to a village of his day named Beeroth, that is the same as the OT town Nicopolis (Emmaus) (*Onomasticon* 48:9-10), west of Jerusalem near Kiriath-jearim, or "under Gibeon." He places Beeroth near the 7th milestone on the road from Jerusalem near el-Jib, northwest of Jerusalem. In his Latin translation of the *Onomasticon* (49:8-9) Jerome mentions Neapolis instead of Nicopolis as the destination and places Beeroth between Ramah and el-Bireh, north of Jerusalem. A number of other sites have been proposed, such as Nebi-Samwil. The most likely site of the OT town remains el-Bireh.

Bibliography: Y. Aharoni. *The Land of the Bible, A Historical Geography.* Rev. ed. (1979); Y. Aharoni and M. Avi-Yonah. *The Macmillan Bible Atlas.* Rev. ed. (1993); R. G. Boling and G. E. Wright. *Joshua.* AB 6. New York (1982).

J. GORDON HARRIS

BEEROTH-BENE-JAAKAN bee´uh-roth-ben´i-jay´uh-kuhn [בְּאֵרֹת בְּנֵי־יַעֲקָן, be'eroth bene-ya'aqan]. The Israelites depart from this area in the northeastern part of the Sinai for MOSERAH where AARON dies (Deut 10:6). The name literally means "the wells of the children of Jaakan," although some have suggested that Jaakan should be read Aqan (Gen 36:27). According to Num 33:31, the Israelites also traveled from MOSERAH to a place named simply Bene-jaakan.

STEVE COOK

BEER-RESISIM. Middle Bronze Age I settlement in the Negev where people subsisted on a mixed economy of grazing, farming, and trading of copper and other goods.

BEER-SHEBA bee´uhr-shee´buh [בְּאֵר שֶׁבַע be'er sheva']. The city of Beer-sheba, part of the territorial inheritance of Simeon, is described in the Bible as the southern-most city of the land of Israel. In the 20th cent. it was identified with Tel Beer-sheba, located at the intersection of Wadi el-Khalil and Wadi es Seba', near the modern city of Be'er Sheva. Interesting features include a 20 m well (date disputed), underground storage pits from the 12th–11th cent. BCE, an enclosed settlement of the 11th cent. BCE, and a 10th cent. BCE fortified city of nearly three acres. (*See* SEBA, TEL ES.)

In the Bible, the name of the city itself, which can mean either "well of seven" or "well of the oath," is explained by two narratives, both of which underscore the potential danger for the patriarchs when negotiating in a new land. In one, Abraham is challenged by duplicitous Philistine servants, even though he had legitimately negotiated for water rights. Abraham's own insistence and savvy, however, protect him as he offers seven (sheva') lambs to Abimelech, and the two swear (nishbe'u) a binding oath before the powerful king's army commander, Phicol (Gen 21:30-33). A similar account is repeated in the next generation, as Isaac must renegotiate the settlement with the same king and commander. This time, Isaac's servants dug their own well (be'er), solidifying Isaac's rightful claim (Gen 26:33).

Beer-sheba is portrayed as the spiritual and physical home of the patriarchs in additional ways. Abraham is said to live there after God tested him with Isaac (Gen 22:19). It served as Jacob's home before he departed to Haran to flee Esau's murderous revenge (Gen 28:10). Although the narratives of Genesis do not specify that God saved the patriarchs from these ominous situations, their successful escapes and negotiations underscore the hidden hand of the inscrutable God who repeatedly rescues them and to whom they respond in worship. Abraham "calls upon the name of the LORD, the Everlasting God [El Olam]" in Beer-sheba and planted a tamarisk tree, perhaps to mark the cultic center (Gen 21:33). Isaac receives a reassurance of promise and blessing from God at Beer-sheba, to which he responds by building an altar (Gen 26:23-25). Similarly, Jacob offers sacrifices to the God of Abraham before he continues to Egypt where he and his family escape famine (Gen 46:1, 6).

In addition to the city, the wilderness of Beer-sheba becomes a locus where the divine presence may be encountered. In Beer-sheba's vicinity Hagar wandered with Ishmael before God intervened to save their lives (Gen 21:14). In later generations, the prophet Elijah first stops in Beer-sheba when he escapes Jezebel's plan to have him killed. There, Elijah is protected by an angel before he continues his journey to Mount Horeb, where he witnesses a theophany (1 Kgs 19:1-18).

Beer-sheba was well known as the southernmost outpost of Judah, as it forms a merism with Dan, referring to the entirety of the land of Israel (Judg 20:1; 1 Sam 3:20; 2 Sam 3:10). Samuel's sons are identified as being judges there, pointing to Beer-sheba's importance as an administrative center (1 Sam 8:2). Perhaps it was the association of Beer-sheba as the place where the patriarchs offered sacrifice that led to its reputation as a cultic center. Individuals apparently made pilgrimage feasts to Beer-sheba, but by the time of Amos (8th cent. BCE), it already had the reputation as being dominated by foreign worship practices (Amos 5:5). Because of the associated idolatry, Amos condemns individuals who worship at Beer-sheba as those who abandon their obligations to God (Amos 8:14).

SHARON PACE

BEESHTERAH bee-esh´tuh-ruh [בְּעֶשְׁתְּרָה be'eshterah]. One of the Transjordanian Levitical cities located in the tribal territory assigned to MANASSEH (Josh 21:27). In the parallel of 1 Chr 6:71 [Heb. 6:56] the city is called ASHTAROTH, which reflects its probable relationship to the goddess ASHTARTE.

BEGGAR. *See* ALMS, ALMSGIVING.

BEGINNING AND END. *See* ALPHA AND OMEGA.

BEGOTTEN. *See* GOD's ONLY SON.

BEHEADING. *See* CRIMES AND PUNISHMENT (OT AND NT).

BEHEMOTH bi-hee´muhht [בְּהֵמוֹת behemoth]. Although the term behemah (בְּהֵמָה), beast, cattle occurs frequently in the OT, only once, in one of its rare plural occurrences, is it clearly a proper name (Job 40:15), which has become a synonym for huge in modern English.

The Behemoth of Job is related to ancient Near Eastern myth. However, the plain meaning of this text establishes that, like Job himself, Behemoth is one of God's beloved creatures (40:15): herbivorous (v. 15) with immense physical strength and sexual potency (vv. 16-17), enjoying primacy among God's creative acts (v. 19), and exhibiting a gentle quality, quietly living near playful animals (v. 20) in the reeds and "willows of the wadi." These features have led many to identify Behemoth as a HIPPOPOTAMUS.

Given that Yahweh's speeches in Job 38–41 evoke the created order and its beloved creatures, perhaps this text does indeed celebrate the most extreme of the living animals. Later on, however, Behemoth regains its mythic dimensions. In 2 Esd 6:49-52, Behemoth and LEVIATHAN are identified as the unnamed "great sea monsters" that God created on the 5th day (Gen 1:21). In 1 En. 60:7-19, Behemoth is located in a desert, "east of the garden of Eden." Primeval myth is linked with end-time myth in 2 Bar. 29:4, and in the rabbinic tradition, where the two monsters become food for the righteous in the world to come. See BEAST; LEVIATHAN; WILD BEAST.

W. SIBLEY TOWNER

BEHOLD, TO [שׁוּר shur, רָאָה ra'ah, חָזָה khazah, נָבַט navat; εἶδος eidos]. Verbs for beholding relate to gazing at something—looking at it intently. "To behold" would be a long look compared with its opposite, a quick glance. The Hebrew verbs rendered "behold" include shur, which means "to behold," "regard," "gaze," or "observe" (Num 23:9, where it is used in parallel with ra'ah; 24:17); ra'ah, which can mean to "look at," "behold," or "inspect" (Job 19:27; Pss 37:37; 84:9; 97:6; Isa 33:17; Jer 2:31; Lam 1:18) in the Qal stem, "appear," or "behold" (Ps 42:2) in the Niphal, and "behold," "show," or "exhibit" (Esth 1:11) in the Hiphil; khazah, which means "to see," "behold," or "look on intensely" (Job 23:9; Pss 11:7; 17:15; 27:4; 46:8); navat, which means to "look upon, or "behold," in the hiphil stem (Ps 119:18). In some cases, words for beholding may be used in parallel with verbs for simply "seeing." For example, "behold" seems equivalent to "see" in Hab 1:13: "Your eyes are too pure to behold evil." The NRSV renders the dative noun τῇ ὄψει (tē opsei) "to behold" (Jdt 8:7), εἶδος (eidos) as "to behold" in Sir 43:1. No Greek words in the NT are rendered "behold" in the NRSV.

KENNETH D. LITWAK

BEIT MIRSIM, TELL. See MIRSIM, TELL BEIT.

BEIT RAS. See RAS, BEIT.

BEITIN, TELL. See BETHEL, SHRINE.

BEKA bee´kuh [בֶּקַע beqa']. A measure of weight, half-Shekel (approx. 6g), mentioned twice in the Bible in relation to the "shekel of the sanctuary" (Gen 24:22; Exod 38:26). The noun (beqa') means "split." Thirty inscribed beqa' weights are known from Iron Age Judah. See WEIGHTS AND MEASURES.

RAZ KLETTER

BEL bel [בֵּל bel]. "Lord," an alternative name for Akkadian heads of pantheon, especially ENLIL of Nippur and MARDUK of Babylon, derived from the Akkadian noun belu, "lord," and equivalent to West Semitic ba'al. The Babylonian god Marduk is the Bel of Isa 46:1; Jer 50:2; 51:44 and the story of BEL AND THE DRAGON, which parodies the Babylonian custom of offering gods enormous amounts of prepared food whose "leftovers" were eaten by temple personnel. The beast exploded in the story is Marduk's characteristic animal, the mushushu-dragon. In the ENUMA ELISH myth, Marduk is elected king of the gods as his price for slaying the primoridal sea monster Tiamat. Using the winds as weapons, he is victorious and creates the heavens and the earth from Tiamat's lifeless corpse. These heroic deeds link Marduk to Ba'al of Ugaritic mythology and the defeat of Rahab and Yam. See BAAL.

JOANN SCURLOCK

BEL AND THE DRAGON [Βὴλ καὶ Δράκων Bēl kai Drakōn]. Two short stories, in the SEPTUAGINT (Dan 14) and THEODOTION (Dan 13), are part of a tradition about Daniel (see DANIEL, ADDITIONS TO; DANIEL, BOOK OF). Perhaps the account of how Daniel exposes the false god Bel (from בַּעַל ba'al, meaning "Lord") and destroys the snakelike idol of Bel worshiped by the Babylonians was stimulated by Jer 51:34-35, 44 (see BAAL). Both stories present a polemic against IDOLATRY.

Daniel discounts the claim that the statue of Bel is a living god that consumes vast quantities of food. To prove to the king of Babylon (Xerxes I [r. 486–465 BCE]) that the priests and their families, and not the false god, were the ones devouring the food set before the idol, Daniel spread ashes on the floor of the temple of Bel, and the temple was sealed for the night. The next morning, the footprints on the floor proved that the priests had a secret passage into the temple. The king had the priests killed and the statue of Bel and the temple destroyed (13:22).

Next, Daniel burst open a statue of a drakōn ("snake," not dragon) whom the Babylonians worshiped as a living deity (13:23-30) by "feeding" it an inedible concoction (see SNAKE). The Babylonians, protesting that the king had become a Jew (13:28), threatened him, and he handed Daniel to them. Daniel was thrown to the lions (13:31-32), just as in Dan 6:11-25. Not only did the lions not eat Daniel, but after a week, an ANGEL (Dan 6:23) whisked Habakkuk from Judea to Babylon with a meal for him to eat (13:33-38). When the king discovered that Daniel was alive and unharmed, he expresses faith in the one God (13:41; Dan 6:26-28).

The purpose of these stories was to confirm Jewish faith for a general audience (Wis 13:1-19), and perhaps they served as a polemic against Egyptian worship of serpents.

Bibliography: Otto Kaiser. *The Old Testament Apocrypha: An Introduction* (2004) 48–53; Carey A. Moore. *Daniel, Esther and Jeremiah: The Additions* AB 44 (1977) 117–49.

LAWRENCE E. FRIZZELL

BELA bee'luh [בֶּלַע *belaʿ*; Βαλα **Bala**]. 1. The first son of BENJAMIN, who is consistently listed as such in all the genealogies of Benjamin (Gen 46:21; Num 26:38; 1 Chr 7:6; 8:1), despite the fluidity of Benjaminite genealogies.

2. The son of Beor, the 1st king to reign in Edom (Gen 36:32). Because of his patronymic, the Targum identified Bela with Balaam, "son of Beor." The LXX instead identified him with Balak, king of Moab.

3. The son of Azaz, a Reubenite, who lived in Aroer, the southernmost region of the territory of Reuben (1 Chr 5:8-9).

4. Another name for ZOAR, one of five allied cities in the Dead Sea region that fought against an eastern coalition of four kings (Gen 14:2). Because, unlike the other cities, no king is listed for Bela, some scholars suggest the text originally read, "Bela, king of Zoar." *See* SODOM.

RONALD A. SIMKINS

BELIAL bee'lee-uhl [בְּלִיַּעַל *beliyaʿal*]. This term, also written as Beliar, is used as a name for Satan. Its basic meaning is "worthlessness" or "wickedness." In the OT the word describes idolatrous and immoral people, who oppose God, plot evil, and bear false witness (Deut 13:13 [Heb. 13:14]; Judg 19:22; Prov 19:28; Nah 1:11). When used for a form of power, the term indicates death and destruction (2 Sam 22:5; Ps 18:4 [Heb. 18:5]).

The Dead Sea Scrolls identify Belial as an evil angel of darkness. God created Belial and allows him dominion in the present age, where he draws people into apostasy and immorality (1QM XIII, 10-12; CD IV, 12-19). The righteous must, therefore, resist Belial each day, knowing that yielding to him sets a person against God, and that God will eventually send Belial to punish the faithless (1QS X, 21; CD VIII, 1-3). Under Belial's power are the angels of destruction and the people known as sons of darkness, who oppose the ways of God and follow the paths of wickedness. Belial's domin-

ion will end when the sons of light, with angelic help, subject Belial's army to eternal destruction (1QM I, 1-5; XVIII, 1-3; 11QMelch II, 12-13).

Similar perspectives appear in other Jewish and early Christian texts. Belial is the prince of deceit, who uses evil spirits to lure people into sin and accuses people before God (*T. Benj.* 3:3-4; *Jub.* 1:20). Yielding to sinful impulses brings people close to Belial. Therefore, the righteous are to reject Belial, evil, darkness, and impurity by holding fast to the law of God (*T. Sim.* 5:3; *T. Levi* 19:1). Some see Belial at work in David's affair with Bathsheba and the apostasy of King Manasseh (*Liv. Pro.* 17:2; *Mart. Ascen. Isa.* 2:4). Others say that at the end of the age Belial will come from the line of Augustus to lead people astray (*Sib. Or.* 3:63-74). Since Belial is the angel of iniquity, who rules this world (*Mart. Ascen. Isa.* 2:4), the struggle against him will continue until God and his hosts bind Belial and cast him into eternal fire. Only then will people be free from his influence (*T. Levi* 18:12; *T. Jud.* 25:3; *T. Zeb.* 9:8; *T. Dan* 5:10-11).

In the NT, Beliar is mentioned only in 2 Cor 6:15, where the name is a synonym for Satan. The context is an exhortation to holiness: On one side are Beliar, lawlessness, darkness, unbelievers, and idolatry. On the other side are Christ, righteousness, light, believers, and the community of faith, which is the "temple" of God. Echoing traditions about Belial, the passage calls Christians to resist evil and maintain their distinctive identity as God's people. *See* ANTICHRIST; SATAN.

CRAIG R. KOESTER

BELIAR. *See* ANGEL; ANGELIC HOST; ARCHANGEL; BELIAL.

BELIEF [πίστις **pistis**]. The word *belief* occurs only once in the NRSV Bible, in Paul's 2nd letter to the Thessalonians, where he exhorts them to be thankful because they have been chosen "as the first fruits for salvation through sanctification by the Spirit and through belief in the truth (2 Thess 2:13). More often translated as "faith," belief is a theme in every book of the Bible.

In the OT belief is grounded in God's trustworthiness. God's fidelity to divine promises and to the covenant (Deut 7:9; 32:4; Pss 36:5; 40:11) makes belief on the part of human beings possible. One can believe and trust God because God is faithful.

In the NT, Paul's response to the jailor in Philippi who asks what he must do to be saved is paradigmatic: "Believe in the Lord Jesus and you and your household will be saved" (Acts 16:30-31). Belief is not only intellectual assent, but it is commitment to God and the person of Jesus. It is not a single act, but continues to grow (2 Cor 10:15). It is evident in loving deeds (1 John 3:29; Gal 5:6). Belief is "the assurance of things hoped for, the conviction of things not seen" (Heb 11:1).

BARBARA E. REID

BELL [פַּעֲמֹן pa'amon, מְצִלּוֹת metsilloth]. The HIGH PRIEST wore bells attached to the lower hem of his long, blue "robe of the EPHOD" (Exod 28:31-35; 39:25-26), which provided a visual and aural confirmation of the priest's ritual significance. Evidently, they functioned to protect the High Priest as he entered the ritually dangerous HOLY OF HOLIES, "so that he may not die" (v. 35). As part of his vision of ritual purity in the restored community, the prophet Zechariah says that horses will have bells inscribed, "Holy to the Lord," a designation previously limited to sanctuary items (Zech 14:20). *See* MUSICAL INSTRUMENTS.

BRYAN D. BIBB

BELLOWS [מַפֻּחַ mappuakh; φυσητήρ physētēr]. Bellows are only mentioned in the OT in Jer 6:29 metaphorically, and then in 4 Macc 8:13 as a means of torture. Bellows were used in the smelting and working of copper and bronze in Mesopotamia from the 3rd millennium onward. The oldest depiction of the use of bellows in metalworking comes from the tomb of Rekhmire, ca. 1450 BCE. These bellows were used by standing on them, and pulling them up with ropes.

Archaeological evidence of the use of bellows are remains of blow-pipes (tuyeres), found on many sites in the southern Levant. The earliest example is Timna, an Egyptian mining center dated to the Late Bronze Age. The largest collection of tuyeres comes from the site of Tell el-Hammeh in the Zerqa Valley in Jordan, where they were used in the 9th cent. BCE iron-smelting industry.

EVELINE J. VAN DER STEEN

BELMAIN bel'mayn [Βελμαιν Belmain]. One of several Judean cities notified about the advance of HOLOFERNES' Assyrian army (Jdt 4:4). There are various spellings of this place name among Greek and Syriac manuscripts. Additionally, cities mentioned in Jdt 7:3 (Balbaim) and 8:3 (Balamon) could be the same as Belmain. One proposal for its location is Abel-maim, about 13 mi. south of Scythopolis. *See* BILEAM; IBLEAM.

STEVE COOK

BEL-MARDUK. *See* BEL; MARDUK.

BELNUUS bel'noo-uhs [Βάλνουος Balnouos]. A postexilic Jew, descendant of Addi, according to 1 Esd 9:31 (compare Ezra 10:31). *See* BINNUI.

BELOVED [דּוֹד dodh, אָהֵב 'ahev, יָחַד yakhadh; ἀγαπητός agapētos]. In the OT, *Beloved* may describe a sexual partner (דּוֹדִי dodhi in Song 1:13 and throughout, where both lovers celebrate the beauty of the beloved). The intensity and exclusivity of such love colors references to Israel as God's beloved (e.g., Jer 12:7, "I have given the beloved [yedhidhuth] of my heart

into the hands of her enemies"; compare Jer 11:15). Some psalms (60:5; 108:6; 127:2) emphasize God's protection of and provision for the beloved. *Beloved* (from yakhadh) may designate an only or favored child (Gen 22:2, 12; LXX has agapētos; compare Judg 11:34; Amos 8:10). LXX uses agapētos also for words from חָמַד (khamadh "desire, delight") in, e.g., Dan 9:23; 10:11, 19.

In the synoptic Gospels *beloved* refers exclusively to the huios agapētos, the beloved son, recalling Jewish interpretations of Gen 22 in which the binding of Isaac represents the perfect obedience of the beloved son (Matt 3:17; 12:18 and parallels; compare 2 Pet 1:17). (*See also* Matt 17:5 and parallels). Agapētos is absent from the Gospel of John, although the unnamed disciple "whom Jesus loved" plays a prominent role. In Acts and the Epistles, Christians are members of a fictive family beloved by God (e.g., Rom 1:17). Thus, individuals are beloved brothers, sisters, or children (e.g., Paul and Barnabas, Acts 15:25; Timothy, 1 Cor 4:17), and Paul emphasizes love as the basis for his instructions (e.g., 1 Cor 4:14; 2 Cor 5:19). *Beloved* appears frequently in exhortation (Rom 12:19; 1 Cor 10:14; Phil 4:1; Heb 6:9; 1 Pet 2:11). Christians as God's beloved people are called to love others (1 John 4:7, 11). *See* BELOVED DISCIPLE; BROTHER, BROTHERHOOD; BROTHERLY LOVE; CHRIST; CHURCH, IDEA OF; LOVE IN THE NT; LOVE IN THE OT; SON OF GOD.

JUDITH ANNE JONES

BELOVED DISCIPLE. "Beloved Disciple" is an abbreviated form of "the disciple whom Jesus loved" (ὁ μαθητὴς ἐκεῖνος ὅν ἠγάπα ὁ Ἰησοῦς ho mathētēs ekeinos hon ēgapa ho Iēsous), a phrase that appears in some form five times in John (13:23; 19:26; 20:2; 21:7, 20). In spite of the Evangelist's reticence to further identify this figure, there has been endless speculation regarding the Beloved Disciple's possible historical identity and/or narrative function in the Gospel. A few scholars have even proposed Mary Magdalene as the disciple in question. There is no consensus as to a historical individual behind the epithet, with some exegetes insisting that the figure is purely symbolic. Nor is there a clear sense as to what role the character plays in the narrative, though "ideal disciple" has been a strong candidate. What follows is a brief analysis of the textual evidence, followed by a discussion of the historical vs. literary approach to interpreting the Beloved Disciple.

One should be wary of assuming too much about this puzzling figure. As is often the case, interpretive enigmas tend to accrue ever more material as potential data. In this instance, any unidentified disciple in the Gospel has become fair game to be included in the discussion. For example, the unidentified disciple in John 1:35-40 and the unnamed disciple who accompanies Peter in 18:15-16 have both been read as additional appearances of the Beloved Disciple, as has the reference to an eyewitness in 19:35. Although especially in the latter case, there may be good reasons for this identification (*see* 21:24), in every case an argument can be made to the contrary. For instance, the reference to an unidentified eyewitness in 19:35, which does not even mention a disciple, may refer to the soldier at the cross, and thus parallel the witness of the synoptic centurion (Mark 15:39; Matt 27:54; Luke 23:47). In short, none of the unidentified figures mentioned above can be used with certainty as evidence for the Beloved Disciple's identity or role in the narrative.

Even when there is explicit mention of the "disciple whom Jesus loved," understanding this figure remains difficult. Based on the reference to the disciple testifying and writing about "these things" (21:24), ancient writers typically associated the traditional author of the Gospel, John the son of Zebedee, with the Beloved Disciple. However, few scholars would make this connection now. Even those who still see a link between John and the gospel traditions suggest that the Beloved Disciple cannot simply be identified as John, nor as the writer, since 21:24 makes clear that there are others involved in the composition of the Gospel. Instead, the Beloved Disciple is viewed by some as a transmitter of the tradition that originated with the son of Zebedee.

Beyond the traditional approach, there have been multiple suggestions regarding the Beloved Disciple's identity. Possible candidates proposed include Lazarus, Andrew, Philip, Nathanael, Thomas, the rich young ruler, and even Judas Iscariot. The far-ranging list suggests that there is no evidence upon which to reach a conclusion. If the Beloved Disciple was an actual person, all that seems certain is that he was an esteemed figure in the memories of those responsible for the final edition of the Gospel. Moreover, the scenes in which he appears with Peter suggest an interest in legitimating the authority of the tradition stemming from the Beloved Disciple, alongside the Petrine tradition (13:23-25; 20:1-10; 21:7, 20-22).

While not ruling out the possibility of a historical person behind the Beloved Disciple, another approach focuses on the disciple's literary or symbolic aspects. From this perspective, Beloved Disciple is viewed as a representative figure, typically an "ideal disciple" who epitomizes the intimate devotion to Jesus that all followers should have. Yet, there are questions regarding this interpretation as well. The disciple's appearances in ch. 13 and 20 highlight the problem. Certainly, in 13:23-25 the intimate relationship between Jesus and the disciple is emphasized. The disciple reclines "in the bosom" of Jesus (ἐν τῷ κόλπῳ τοῦ Ἰησοῦ en tō kolpō tou Iēsou) just as Jesus is in the bosom of the Father (εἰς τὸν κόλπον τοῦ πατρός eis ton kolpon tou patros, 1:18). The disciple also has access to Jesus that Peter does not have. Still, in spite of his intimate presence with Jesus, the Beloved Disciple is strangely absent from the events of the narrative. Though he gains information, there is no mention of communication with the other disciples, and no insight gained by anyone around the table (13:28). A similarly perplexing occurrence is found in 20:8-10. Although the Beloved Disciple "sees and believes" upon entering the empty tomb, the object of his belief is not clear. Neither Peter nor the Beloved Disciple understand the Scripture. Both simply return home.

Individually, such stories do not represent a picture of ideal discipleship, since one would expect an ideal disciple to be more active—to demonstrate more understanding and to witness more readily. If the Beloved Disciple is "ideal," he is not so in any single appearance, but only as a composite picture. The Beloved Disciple appears to epitomize different aspects of discipleship in different scenes. John 13 features intimacy with Jesus, as does the appearance at the foot of the cross. In 20:1-10, the Beloved Disciple acts as an eyewitness, confirming Mary's report of the empty tomb. John 21 features recognition of the risen Lord, and again, the role of witnessing.

Finally, if the Beloved Disciple was known to those responsible for the Gospel's final composition, his identity was left undisclosed. Instead, the Beloved Disciple is one of several anonymous characters to populate the Gospel (e.g., the Samaritan woman, the man born blind, the mother of Jesus). Thus, the contemporary reader would do well to honor the anonymity of the character and focus instead on the characteristics mentioned above. And although this figure is known as "the disciple whom Jesus loved," the Evangelist makes clear that as such, he is not alone. Before the epithet appears in the Gospel, the narrator makes clear that Jesus loved "his own" in the world and loved them to the utmost (τέλος telos, 13:1). See JOHN, GOSPEL OF.

Bibliography: James H. Charlesworth. *The Beloved Disciple: Whose Witness Validates the Gospel of John?* (1995).

COLLEEN M. CONWAY

BEL-SHAR-USUR. *See* BELSHAZZAR.

BELSHAZZAR bel-shaz´uhr בֵּלְשַׁאצַּר belsha'tsar, בֵּל אֲשַׁצַּר bel'shatsar; Akkad. Bel-shar-usur ("Bel protect the king"); Βαλτασάρ Baltasar]. In Dan 5:2, 11, 13, 18, 22 and Bar 1:11-12, Belshazzar is the son of the Neo-Babylonian king Nebuchadnezzar, but cuneiform documents and inscriptions state that Belshazzar was the son of the last Neo-Babylonian ruler, Nabonidus. The authors of Daniel and Baruch either used the term *father* to mean "predecessor," were mistaken about Belshazzar's parent, or used material associated with Nabonidus to create a negative impression of Nebuchadnezzar.

MARSHALL JOHNSON

BELT [אֵזוֹר 'ezor, חֲגוֹר khaghor; ζώνη zōnē, παραζώνη parazōnē]. A belt gathered the two flaps of the normally sleeveless undergarment or tunic around the body. It was a long, narrow, multifold strip of cloth, normally made of wool that both men and women wore. The 'ezor (Jer 13:1-11) was commonly linen. The khaghor, often translated "GIRDLE" or "LOIN-CLOTH," can mean a soldier's belt (1 Sam 18:4).

In NT times, the belt could be folded and used as a purse. John the Baptist wore a garment around his waist of camel's hair, and a leather belt, rather than a leather loincloth. (Matt 3:4; Mark 1:6). *See* CLOTH, CLOTHES; WAR, METHODS, TACTICS, WEAPONS OF.

GILDAS HAMEL

BELTESHAZZAR bel´ti-shaz´uhr [בֵּלְטְשַׁאצַּר belte-sha'tsar, Βαλτασαρ, Baltasar]. The Babylonian court name given DANIEL by NEBUCHADNEZZAR (Dan 1:7). The name could mean "protect the life of the king" or "protect his life." The LXX renders the name Baltasar, the same as that of the king in Dan 5. *See* SHADRACH, MESHACH, ABEDNEGO.

BELTETHMUS bel-teth´muhs [Βεέλτεθμος Beeltethmos]. A Persian officer in Judah (1 Esd 2:16, 25). Rather than a proper name, it may be a title for a chancellor or royal deputy as in Ezra 4:8, 9, 17 (βααλταμ Baaltam), perhaps a corruption of the Aramaic (בְּעֵל טְעֵם be'el te'em), meaning "advice" or "order."

BEN-ABINADAB ben´uh-bin´uh-dab [בֶּן־אֲבִינָדָב ben 'avinadhav] "Son of Abinadab" or "son of a noble father." One of Solomon's twelve governors, each of whom "provided food for the king and his household" one month in a year (1 Kgs 4:7-19). He was in charge of Naphath-dor, the coastal area around the port city of Dor, in the northern part of the plain of Sharon. Ben-Abinadab was married to Solomon's daughter, Taphath (1 Kgs 4:11).

BENAIAH bi-nay´yuh [בְּנָיָהוּ benayahu, בְּנָיָה benayah]. "Yahu has built" or "Yahu has made (a child)." 1. A military leader during David's reign who ultimately came to be army commander during Solomon's reign. The son of the priest (1 Chr 27:5) Jehoiada of Kabzeel (2 Sam 23:20), a town of unknown location, but probably in southern Judah near Edom (Josh 15:21), Benaiah gained prominence during the latter part of David's reign as the commander of "the Cherethites and the Pelethites," usually understood as mercenary Cretans and Philistines (1 Sam 8:18; 20:23; 1 Chr 18:17; *see* CHERETHITES AND PELETHITES). He became a member of David's elite warriors, "The Thirty," but not of the inner circle, "The Three" (2 Sam 23:23). If Benaiah's son Jehoiada succeeded Ahithophel as David's counselor (1 Chr 27:34), then Benaiah would

have been a mature, experienced military man before Solomon's reign.

In the list of David's heroes in 2 Sam 23:8-39 (1 Chr 11:22-25), Benaiah's exploits are placed between comments on two brothers of Joab, David's army general (vv. 18, 24). The fact that Benaiah fought Moabites (the Hebrew behind "two sons of Ariel of Moab" in v. 20 is obscure) and an Egyptian rather than Philistines (the only enemy specified elsewhere in the list) indicates that he came to prominence only after David had secured his kingdom. The references to the killing of a lion in a pit on a snowy day (v. 20) and to the killing of a "handsome" Egyptian with a mighty spear (v. 21) are traditional motifs in ancient Near Eastern hero stories.

When Solomon's older brother Adonijah claimed the right to succeed David, Solomon commanded Benaiah to assassinate Adonijah and his supporters, Joab and Shimei (1 Kgs 2). After these political murders, Benaiah became army general (1 Kgs 4:4) and "the kingdom was established in the hand of Solomon" (1 Kgs 2:46).

2. A warrior from Pirathon in the area of Ephraim, a member of David's elite military group "the Thirty" (1 Sam 23:30; 1 Chr 11:31). He led the army division that served in the 11th month (1 Chr 27:14).

3. A Simeonite clan leader who was among those who secured pasture land by conquering the Meunim near Gedor in the central hills of Judah at the time of King Hezekiah (1 Chr 4:34-41).

4. One of the Levites who played the upper-register harp (Alamoth) at the installing of the ark of Yahweh in Jerusalem (1 Chr 15:18, 20). *See* MUSIC.

5. A "Levite of the sons of Asaph, grandfather of Jahaziel, who, possessed by the spirit of Yahweh, roused King Jehoshaphat and Judah to prevail over a coalition of Ammonites, Moabites, and Edomites (2 Chr 20:14).

6. A priest among those who blew trumpets to herald the bringing of the ark to Jerusalem (1 Chr 15:24). David appointed him and Jahaziel to blow trumpets regularly before the ark of the covenant of God (1 Chr 16:6). *See* MUSIC.

7. One of the Levites who assisted Conaniah in collecting and storing tithes and contributions brought to the Temple in Jerusalem at the time of King Hezekiah (2 Chr 31:13).

8. Father of Pelatiah, an official in Jerusalem whose advice with respect to the threat from Babylon was opposed by Ezekiel. While Ezekiel castigated Pelatiah and his associates for their violence, Pelatiah died (Ezek 11:1, 13).

9. A descendant of Parosh forced by Ezra to put away his foreign wife (Ezra 10:25; 1 Esd 9:26).

10. A descendant of Pahath-moab forced by Ezra to put away his foreign wife (Ezra 10:30).

11. A descendant of Bani forced by Ezra to put away his foreign wife (Ezra 10:35).

12. A descendant of Nebo forced by Ezra to put away his foreign wife (Ezra 10:32; 1 Esd 9:36).

Bibliography: Alexander Zeron. "Der Platz Benajahus in der Heldenliste Davids (2 Sam 23:20-23)." *ZAW* 90 (1978) 20–28.

MARSHALL JOHNSON

BEN-AMMI ben-am′*i* [בְּנִי־עַמּוֹן bene ʿammon]. "Son of my people; son of my kin." The name Lot's younger daughter gave to her son who was born from her incestuous encounter with her father after the destruction of Sodom and Gomorrah (Gen 19:38). This child is the ancestor of the Ammonites, perennial adversaries of the ancient Israelites.

VALERIE BRIDGEMAN-DAVIS

BEN-DEKER ben-dee′kuhr [בֶּן־דֶּקֶר ben-deqer]. The "Son of Deker" is one of twelve prefects over Solomon's districts of Israel (1 Kgs 4:9). Ben-Deker's district comprises a small territory in the SHEPHELAH within the allotment of DAN.

BEN DOSA, HANINAH. *See* HANINAH BEN-DOSA.

BENE-BERAK been′ee-bihr′ak [בְּנֵי בְרַק bene veraq]. A city in the southern location of the area allotted to the tribe of Dan (Josh 19:45).

BENEDICTION [בְּרָכָה berakhah; εὐλογία eulogia]. The English term reflects the Latin *benedictio*, literally "a pronouncement of weal," which in the Vulgate regularly renders berakhah and eulogia (e.g., Exod 32:29; Prov 10:6; Isa 65:8; Sir 3:8; Gal 3:14; Rev 5:13). Although basically a synonym of "blessing," benediction is most often used to designate liturgical invocations for bestowal of divine favor upon worshipers; and, especially in Jewish prayers, formulaic ascriptions of praise to God for benefactions received.

1. The most familiar example of a liturgical benediction is the priestly blessing in Num 6:24-26 (compare Lev 9:22; Sir 50:20-21; and *see also*, e.g., *m. Ber.* 5.4; *m. Meg.* 4.10; *m. Tamid* 5.1). Also often identified as benedictions are the petitions for blessing found in the conclusions of many NT epistles (e.g., Rom 15:13; 1 Cor 16:23; 1 Pet 5:14).

2. Doxological benedictions of God are a feature of Jewish prayer, as exemplified by the "Eighteen [Benedictions]" (*Shemoneh Esreh*) that follow major petitions in the daily synagogue service (the ʿAmidah; e.g., *m.* Taʿan. 2.2). Scriptural examples of such petitions are the doxologies that conclude major parts of the Psalter (41:13 [Heb. 41:14]; 72:18-19; 89:52 [Heb. 89:53]; 106:48) and introductory praises in several NT epistles (Eph 1:3; 2 Cor 1:3; 1 Pet 1:3). *See* BLESS; BLESSINGS AND CURSINGS.

S. DEAN MCBRIDE

BENEDICTUS. The Latin word for *blessed*. Benedictus is the traditional title for the hymn of Zechariah in Luke 1:68-79, the second of three hymns in Luke's infancy narrative. After naming the infant John, Zechariah's mute tongue is released, and he responds with a hymn of praise that begins, "Blessed be the Lord God of Israel." There is a long history of the use of the Benedictus in Christian liturgy.

The Benedictus follows a traditional form by beginning with a statement of praise, followed by recital of the benefits of God that provide reasons for this praise. This recital is interrupted in vv. 76-77 by direct address to the infant John, announcing his future prophetic role. Most of the hymn, however, celebrates God's salvation for Israel through the coming of the promised Davidic Messiah.

There is scholarly debate about the origin of the Benedictus. Some scholars maintain that the Benedictus originated among followers of John the Baptist or in early Jewish Christianity and reflects the thinking of one of these groups. It is true that the Benedictus celebrates salvation for the Jewish people, including political salvation. Nevertheless, it fits well in the Lukan infancy narrative, for it combines previous themes concerning the role of John the Baptist (Luke 1:16-17), the coming of the promised Davidic Messiah (1:32-33), and the fulfillment of the promise to Abraham (1:54-55). *See* HYMNS; MAGNIFICAT.

Bibliography: Raymond E. Brown. *The Birth of the Messiah* (1993).

ROBERT C. TANNEHILL

BENEFACTOR [εὐεργέτης euergetēs]. Conferral of benefits was standard expectation in Mediterranean society. Numerous inscriptions found in many areas of the ancient Mediterranean world attest an unwritten contract between public servants and their beneficiaries. In response to uncommon generosity communities were expected to acknowledge their benefactors publicly, especially by erecting chiseled prominently positioned monuments and bestowing awards that might include front-seating at public events, freedom from levies, or maintenance upon arrival in the host city.

Construction or upkeep of public buildings, as well as underwriting or production of a variety of civic and cultural events, such as dramatic performances and games, invited frequent recognition in civic decrees. The most common form of laudation includes a "whereas" extolling the virtue and performance of honorees. This is followed by a "be it resolved," specifying appropriate awards.

Through such recognition benefactors hoped to secure immortality. Poets had long assumed the task of rescuing mortals from oblivion. HOMER set the pace, and a trend toward extension of recognition for "exceptional merit" (ἀρετή aretē) developed in Pindar's praise of illustrious athletes. In the course of time, formal recognition of beneficence immortalized physicians, veterinarians, and musicians, to cite only a few. Even self-praise did not raise eyebrows.

The term euergetēs underlies the rendering "benefactor" in most translations of Luke 22:25, the only NT use of the noun. The abstract euergesia (εὐεργεσία, beneficence) appears in Acts 4:9; 1 Tim 6:2; and the verb euergeteō (εὐεργετέω, "confer a benefit") in Acts 10:38, acknowledging Jesus' beneficence. From positive usage of the cognates in Acts, it seems clear that in Luke 22:25 the caution, "you shall not be so," refers to the behavior of officials who enjoyed being called benefactors but nullified the claim by their oppressive regimes. In biblical usage the positive perspective is confirmed by LXX use of the euerge-field in renderings of Ps 12:6 [Heb. 13:6]; 114:7 [Heb. 116:7]; and 56:2 [Heb. 57:2]; in reference to God's conduct. Hebrew references to beneficence thereby moved into the public Greco-Roman square.

Although the rendering *benefactor* serves as a convenient gloss for the term euergetēs, expression of the concept is by no means limited to the noun. Since some public figures or leaders might promise much but deliver little, a phrase such as "capable in deed as well as word" (Luke 24:19) would immediately signal description of a true benefactor. In Rom 15:16 Paul terms himself a "public servant (λειτουργός leitourgos) of Jesus Christ for the nations." That he views himself as a benefactor can be inferred from the phrase "word and deed" (v. 18) as prelude to his boast about his accomplishments in a vast geographical area. This self-adulation climaxes with a statement about his "building" contribution. Of special significance is Paul's use of the term philotimeomai (φιλοτιμέομαι, "love honor" = "be eager"). This verb, as well as the cognate noun philotimia (φιλοτιμία, "love of honor"), appears frequently in documents honoring benefactors for their total dedication to the public interest. In short, implies Paul, no one can lay claim to greater beneficence. The theme of beneficence in reference to God, with consideration of appropriate response, leaps out in Rom 2:1-11. In a dramatic account, Luke 7:2-10, two benefactors, Jesus and an unnamed centurion, merit accolades.

Bibliography: Frederick W. Danker. *Benefactor* (1982); Holland Hendrix. "Benefactor/Patronage Networks in the Urban Environment: Evidence from Thessalonica." *Semeia* 56 (1992) 39–58.

FREDERICK W. DANKER

BENE-JAAKAN ben´ee-jay´uh-kuhn [בְּנֵי יַעֲקָן bene ya'aqan]. Between the Wilderness of Sinai and the Reed Sea (Num 33:31-32). In Deuteronomy it is located near the site of Aaron's death (10:6).

BEN ELEAZAR, RABBI SIMON. *See* SIMON BEN ELEAZAR.

BEN-GEBER ben-gee´buhr [בֶּן־גֶּבֶר ben gever]. Ben-Geber governed RAMOTH-GILEAD, the sixth of Solomon's twelve regional districts (1 Kgs 4:13), each of which supplied royal court provisions one month a year (1 Kgs 4:7). Ben-Geber was probably the same as GEBER son of URI over the land of GILEAD (1 Kgs 4:19).

SUSANNA W. SOUTHARD

BEN-HADAD ben-hay´dad [בֶּן־הֲדַד ben hadhadh]. The Hebrew form of the Aram. name "Bar-Hadad," meaning "son of (the god) Hadad." In the OT, the name appears as a general dynastic reference to Aram-Damascus in Jer 49:27 and Amos 1:4, but elsewhere designates at least two individual Aramean kings (*see* ARAM, ARAMEANS). In extrabiblical Aramaic texts, the name appears in reference to individual kings in the Zakkur Stela (late 9th or early 8th cent. BCE) and the Melqart Stela (early 8th cent. BCE). There is great difficulty in correlating the various Ben-Hadads with specific kings and formulating a clear sequence of their accession. Yet the figure of an Aramean king named Ben-Hadad plays a large literary and theological role within the OT.

A. The Historical Kings of Aram-Damascus

Biblical and extrabiblical texts yield seven uses of the name Ben-Hadad (Zakkur Stela; Melqart Stela; 1 Kgs 15; 20; 2 Kgs 6; 8; 13). Only two individuals named Ben-Hadad are clearly identified by their patronym in the OT: 1) Ben-Hadad, son of Tab-Rimmon (1 Kgs 15:16-21), and 2) Ben-Hadad, son of Hazael (2 Kgs 13). Ben-Hadad, son of Tab-Rimmon and often designated Ben-Hadad I, is the earliest Ben-Hadad in the OT. The text identifies him as the king of Aram-Damascus during the reigns of Baasha of Israel and Asa of Judah (ca. 900 BCE). Asa convinced Ben-Hadad I to break an alliance with Baasha and attack Israel from the north. As a result, Ben-Hadad I conquered some northern Israelite territories (1 Kgs 15:20). The biblical texts provide the only sources for these events, but archaeological data from Tell al-Qadi (perhaps Dan) may attest to the conquest.

The next appearance of a king named Ben-Hadad occurs in the stories of AHAB (868–54 BCE), specifically in the context of three battles between Israel and Aram in 1 Kgs 20 and 22. Second Kings 6:24–7:20 then relates a battle with a Ben-Hadad placed in the time of Ahab's son, Jehoram. These chapters depict Israel and Aram as enemies, Ahab as a weak vassal to Ben-Hadad, and the Israelite military as small (1 Kgs 20:15, 27). Assyrian royal inscriptions, however, present a different picture of both Israel's status and its relationship with Aram during this period. The Monolith Inscription (*COS* 2.113A:261–264) of Shalmaneser III identifies the king of Aram-Damascus during Ahab's time as Hadadezer (Adad-idri) not Ben-Hadad. It also describes

Shalmaneser's encounter in 853–852 BCE with a south Syrian-Palestinian coalition that featured a partnership between Hadadezer and Ahab. Moreover, Shalmaneser credits Ahab with a powerful military force in 853 BCE, including 2,000 chariots, a chariot force equal to Assyria's.

Interpreters have suggested a number of solutions for these discrepancies, some depending on the Melqart Stela. Some have argued convincingly that the Ben-Hadad of the Melqart Stela was not a king of Damascus but of some other northern Aramean territory. Hence, other interpreters identify the Ben-Hadad in 1 Kgs 20 and 22 with Hadadezer in the Assyrian inscriptions and assume that relations between Israel and Aram oscillated during the time of Omri and Ahab. In order to avoid the unusual occurrence of two successive kings with the same name (Ben-Hadad, son of Tab-Rimmon and Ben-Hadad = Hadadezer), this view posited that Ben-Hadad is a royal title. Elsewhere in biblical and extrabiblical texts, however, Ben-Hadad appears consistently as a personal name (1 Kgs 15:18; 2 Kgs 13:3, 24).

Several facets of 1 Kgs 20 and 22 do not fit the historical circumstances of Ahab's reign. For example, 1 Kgs 20:34 has the Aramean king mention cities that his father took from the Israelite king's father, yet evidence like the Mesha Stela renders it unlikely that Omri was in such a weakened state. On the contrary, the hostility between Israel and Aram and Israel's relative weakness in 1 Kgs 20 and 22 fit with what is known of the Jehu dynasty. The fact that the name "Ahab" appears only three times in 1 Kgs 20 and once in 1 Kgs 22, which most often refer only to "the king of Israel," makes the identification with Ahab seem secondary. Hence, the majority of interpreters conclude that the three battles in 1 Kgs 20 and 22 have been editorially placed in the era of Ahab for theological reasons but actually refer to events that occurred during the later, weaker Jehu dynasty. The Ben-Hadad in these texts thus refers historically to the son of Hazael mentioned later in 2 Kgs 13, and the three battles may be duplicates of the three battles in 2 Kgs 13 in which Joash (or possibly Jehoahaz) threw off "Ben-Hadad" at the same location of Aphek.

The next mention of a Ben-Hadad occurs in the ELISHA stories in 2 Kgs 8. Verses 7-15 tell the story of the sickness and death of an Aramean king named Ben-Hadad and the immediate succession of Hazael, who may be pictured as murdering Ben-Hadad. An Ashur statue inscription of Shalmaneser III, however, indicates that Hazael usurped the throne of Damascus immediately upon the death of Hadadezer (COS 2.113G). Those interpreters who identify the Ben-Hadad in 1 Kgs 20 and 22 as Hadadezer thus see little problem here. Yet some interpreters take 2 Kgs 8 to indicate that there was another Ben-Hadad who reigned briefly in Damascus after Hadadezer and before Hazael and

that the Assyrian text telescopes these events because Assyria had no dealings with this short-term ruler. There is enough time between the Assyrian texts' last mention of Hadadezer as king in 845 BCE and first mention of Hazael as king in 841 BCE for a brief reign. Some readings of the Melqart Stela have likewise suggested it should be rendered "Ben-Hadad son of Ezer" and taken as a reference to this otherwise unknown Aramean king. In light of Shalmaneser's inscription, however, it is perhaps more likely that the name "Ben-Hadad" was later added incorrectly to 2 Kgs 8 after the stories about a Ben-Hadad in 1 Kgs 20 and 22 had become linked with Ahab.

The final individual Ben-Hadad mentioned in the OT is the son of Hazael in 2 Kgs 13. Hazael's reign (ca. 841–805 BCE) overlapped a period of Assyrian weakness, was the highpoint of Aram-Damscus's power, and resulted in an empire that controlled most of Syria-Palestine. Although the date of Hazael's death is uncertain, 2 Kgs 13:22-24 connects it with the death of Jehoahaz of Israel and thus places Ben-Hadad's accession in the general timeframe of a resurgence of Assyria under Adad-nirari III (ca. 805 BCE). Perhaps as early as 803 or as late as 796 BCE, the Assyrians besieged Damascus and collected tribute from Ben-Hadad, who is designated as mari', "lord," in Assyrian texts (COS 2.114E:274-275). The Zakkur Stela also records that this Ben-Hadad unsuccessfully led a coalition of kings against Zakkur, king of Hamath and Lush, a coalition likely defeated by Assyrian intervention.

Before or after these confrontations, 2 Kgs 13 tells of three battles in which Israel defeated Ben-Hadad, son of Hazael, although scholars debate whether Jehoahaz or Joash should be credited with these victories (compare the battles in 1 Kgs 20; 22). There are no available sources that indicate how long Ben-Hadad ruled or what happened in the latter part of his reign, but it does not appear that he was able to maintain the expanded territories that Hazael had acquired.

Based on the above evidence, some interpreters have identified as many as four Ben-Hadads: Ben-Hadad, son of Tab-Rimmon (1 Kgs 15); Ben Hadad, i.e., Hadadezer (1 Kgs 20); Ben-Hadad, son of Hadadezer (2 Kgs 8); Ben-Hadad, son of Hazael (2 Kgs 13). Yet if 1 Kgs 20 and 22 belong to the period of the Jehu dynasty and if 2 Kgs 8 misidentifies Hazael's predecessor, then the evidence most clearly points to only two Ben-Hadads: Ben-Hadad, son of Tab-Rimmon (1 Kgs 15) and Ben-Hadad, son of Hazael (1 Kgs 20; 22; 2 Kgs 6; 13).

B. The Literary and Theological Function of "Ben-Hadad"

Regardless of the historical identifications, the character Ben-Hadad serves a particular literary and theological function in the OT. Indeed, the historical and redactional complexities of texts like 1 Kgs 20 and 22 and 2 Kgs 6 and 8 suggest that the primary function of those stories is theological and that Ben-Hadad came to represent the eponymous father of Aram-Damascus in Israelite and Judean memory. In general, the figure of Ben-Hadad regularly fulfills the role of an instrument of God's punishment against Israel or an object lesson of God's punishment against unjust nations. For example, the use of "Ben-Hadad" as a general dynastic reference to the Aramean royal house in Jer 49:27 and Amos 1:4 presents that house as an object of God's judgment on injustice.

More specifically, the OT Ben-Hadads often function within the Elijah and Elisha stories as symbols that provide theological evaluations of the Omride and Jehu dynasties. The stories particularly highlight Ahab's unfaithfulness and use the character of Ben-Hadad to serve as an instrument of punishment or a sign of favor from God. This literary function may explain why the later historical battles with Ben-Hadad son of Hazael were relocated into the time of Ahab and Jehoram. It may also explain why 2 Kgs 8 incorrectly identifies the Aramean king in the time of Elisha and Hazael as Ben-Hadad, since that name had come to represent the instrument of punishment on Ahab. Consequently, victory over the figure of Ben-Hadad in 2 Kgs 13 represents a sign of the return of God's favor to Israel. *See* ARAM, ARAMEANS.

Bibliography: P. E. Dion. *Les Araméens à l'âge du fer: Histoire politique et structures sociales* (1997); E. Lipiński. *The Aramaeans: Their Ancient History, Culture, Religion* (2000); J. M. Miller. "The Elisha Cycle and the Accounts of the Omride Wars." *JBL* 85 (1966) 441–454; W. Pitard. *Ancient Damascus: A Historical Study of the Syrian City-State from the Earliest Times until Its Fall to the Assyrians in 732 B.C.E.* (1987); G. Reinhold. "The Bir-Hadad Stele and the Biblical Kings of Aram." *AUSS* 24 (1986) 115–126.

BRAD E. KELLE

BEN-HAIL ben-hay´uhl [בֶּן־חַיִל *ben khayil*]. "Son of might." Jehoshaphat's officer commissioned to teach the Judeans the book of the law (2 Chr 17:7).

BEN-HANAN ben-hay´nuhn [בֶּן־חָנָן *ben khanan*]. Son of Shimon and a descendant of Judah (1 Chr 4:20).

BEN HANNANIAH, RABBI JOSHUA. *See* JOSHUA BEN HANNANIAH.

BEN-HESED ben-hee´sed [בֶּן־חֶסֶד *ben khesedh*]. Of Solomon's twelve regional administrators, Ben-Hesed governed the third district, including ARUBBOTH, SOCOH, and HEPHER in West Manasseh (1 Kgs 4:10). Each district supplied royal court provisions one month a year (1 Kgs 4:7).

BEN-HINNOM ben-hin´uhm. *See* HINNOM, VALLEY OF.

BEN-HUR ben-huhr´ [בֶּן־חוּר *ben khur*]. Literally "son of Chur." One of Solomon's twelve officers who each provided Solomon and his household food for one month of the year (1 Kgs 4:8).

BEN HYRCANUS, RABBI ELIEZER. *See* ELIEZER BEN HYRCANUS.

BENINU bi-n*i*´ nyoo [בְּנִינוּ *beninu*]. A Levitical signatory of the covenant renewal under Ezra. The name means "our son" (Neh 10:13 [Heb. 10:14]).

BENJAMIN GATE [שַׁעַר בִּנְיָמִן *sha'ar binyamin*]. Probably located in the northeast part of the land of Benjamin (Jer 37:13; 38:7; Zech 14:10), it may correspond to the post-exilic MUSTER/INSPECTION GATE or SHEEP GATE (Neh 3:31, 32). The Upper Benjamin Gate of Jeremiah's confinement (Jer 20:2) may be at the Temple courts.

BENJAMIN, BENJAMINITES [בִּנְיָמִן, בִּנְיָמִין *binyamin*, בֶּן־יְמִינִי *ben-yamini*; Βενιαμίν *Beniamin*]. 1. The youngest son of Jacob and the eponymous ancestor of the Israelite tribe that occupied the highland region between Ephraim and Judah.

The name *Benjamin* means "son of the right hand" or "son of the south." (Israel's primary directional orientation was to the east.) Since the right hand was associated with goodness or favor, some have suggested that the name should be understood as "fortunate son." This view finds support in the birth narrative of Benjamin (Gen 35:18), where Jacob confers the name to counter the one Rachel gives the child as she breathes her last: "Ben-Oni" ("son of my anguish"). It is more likely, however, that the name derives from tribal Benjamin's location to the south of Ephraim, the tribe that dominated the central highlands. Tribal lists and traditions attest to a close relationship between the two tribes, suggesting that the designation "son of the south," or even "southerner," identifies Benjamin with reference to its geographical identity vis-à-vis Ephraim.

The Joseph novella accentuates Benjamin's role as a means of negotiating the tribe's relationship with Ephraim and Manasseh (the "Joseph" tribes) and Judah. Joseph and Benjamin are the only two sons born to Jacob through Rachel, his favorite wife, and are so listed in tribal genealogies (Gen 35:24; 46:19-22). The novella makes a point of relating the strong affection that Joseph feels for Benjamin. When he learns that Benjamin remains with Jacob in Canaan, Joseph demands that his brothers bring the child to him when they return to Egypt to release Simeon and trade for food (42:18-20, 29-34). Benjamin's appearance with his brothers, on their return, precipitates a dramatic scene that climaxes when Joseph pronounces a blessing over "his mother's son" and then, overcome by emotion, rushes out of the room in order to weep in a private chamber. During the following meal, Joseph gives Benjamin five times the portions from his table that he gives to his other brothers (43:16, 26-34). Later, when Joseph reveals his identity, he makes specific reference to his younger brother and falls on his neck weeping (45:12-14). When the brothers leave once again to bring Jacob down to the Egypt, Joseph gives Benjamin five sets of clothing and 300 shekels of silver (45:22).

Judah, for his part, plays the role of middle-man and rescuer. He makes possible the meeting between Joseph and Benjamin by convincing his father to allow the child to go to Egypt when the famine intensifies; he overcomes his father's determination to keep Benjamin in Canaan by offering himself as surety in place of the boy (42:35-43:15). On the brothers' departure from Egypt, Judah makes a corresponding offer to Joseph. When Joseph threatens to enslave Benjamin (after his men have "found" his personal cup in the younger brother's sack), Judah offers himself as a slave in his place, adding that he cannot bear to face his father's grief at the loss of Benjamin (44:18-34). The gesture proves too much for Joseph and precipitates the disclosure of his identity (45:1) and, ultimately, his provision of refuge in Egypt for the entire house of Jacob. The novella, in sum, portrays the relationship between Benjamin and Joseph in terms of close kinship, but that between Benjamin and Judah in terms of deliverance. The story thus echoes a historical reality in which Benjamin enjoyed a close relationship with Ephraim during the tribal period but was subsumed by Judah after the nation split into two kingdoms.

2. The son of Bilhan and great-grandson of the patriarch Benjamin, according to a late genealogical list (1 Chr 7:10). As the names in the list also represent tribal divisions, the name represents an oddity: a segment of the tribe that identified itself by the tribal name.

3. One of the many Israelite males on a list of those who pledged to put away their foreign wives and bring a guilt offering in response to Ezra's proclamation that the Israelites had broken faith with God through inter-marriage with foreigners (Ezra 10:32).

4. An official of Judah, who participated in the dedication of the walls of Jerusalem during the time of Nehemiah (Neh 12:34). He is probably the same individual who is reported to have labored to repair a section of the wall (Neh 3:23).

5. The tribe of Benjamin takes its name from the son of Jacob (see 1 above). Attempts have been made to connect the tribe's origins with the **banu yamin**, a nomadic people mentioned in documents from the archives of Zimri-Lin, a king of Mari who reigned in the last decades of the 18th cent. BCE. A vast span of time, however, separates these references from the early period of Israel's occupation of Canaan, making any direct connection highly unlikely.

Although a minor tribe in terms of population and territory, Benjamin plays a prominent role in Israel's history and literature. The Book of Joshua elaborates the campaigns waged against cities within Benjamin (Josh 2:1-10:15) but offers only brief summations of those that occurred elsewhere in the land. Ehud, the first judge whose exploits are elaborated in detail, is a Benjaminite (Judg 3:12-30), and Benjamin is at the center of the outrageous events of rape, murder, and internecine war that conclude Judges (Judg 19-21). The tribe also figures significantly in the rise of the Israelite monarchy. A Benjaminite (Saul) becomes Israel's first king, another (Abner), facilitates the transference of the kingdom to David after Saul's death, and a third (Sheba) leads an insurrection against David.

A. Tribal Period

Benjamin inhabited a small region north of Jerusalem, wedged between the territories of Ephraim and Judah. Its territory was transected by two major routes into the highlands, one from the coast through the Valley of Aijalon (also called the Ascent of Beth-horon) and the other from Jericho toward Gibeah and Michmash, in one direction, and toward Jerusalem in another. As was the case with its neighbors to the north and south, the Jordan River marked the eastern boundary of its settlement, although a close relationship with the inhabitants of Jabesh-gilead is suggested by a number of texts (Judg 21:8-14; 1 Sam 11:1-11; 31:12-13). The western part of its possession was dominated by the city of Gibeon and its dependencies, which enjoyed a peace treaty with Israel and remained a Canaanite enclave throughout the period (Josh 9:1–10:15). Benjaminite land extended northward to Bethel which, although appearing in a list of Benjamin's cities (Josh 18:22), was an Ephraimite possession from the beginning (Judg 1:22-25). A corresponding situation obtained to the south, where tribal lands reached toward, but never included Jerusalem, which although listed among the cities of Benjamin was eventually taken by David and incorporated into the territory of Judah (Josh 18:28; 15:63; 2 Sam. 5:4-8).

The heart of Benjamin's land therefore comprised a relatively small but strategically important area to the north and northwest of Jerusalem. Its situation between Bethel and Jerusalem, the two major shrines of the monarchical period, may explain a cryptic blessing preserved in the Blessing of Moses, which describes the High God resting with and surrounding Benjamin, and settling between his shoulders (Deut 33:12). Later rabbinic tradition followed this line and viewed the blessing as a reference to Jerusalem's assignment to the allotment of Benjamin (Josh 18:28).

Benjamin seems to have been closely aligned with Ephraim, and to a lesser extent Manasseh, during this period. The tribes are grouped together in both Priestly and Deuteronomic texts (Num 1:10-11, 32-36; 2:18-24; 7:48-65; 10:21-24; 13:8-9; 26:28-41; Deut 27:12). This is also the case in the ancient "Song of Deborah,"

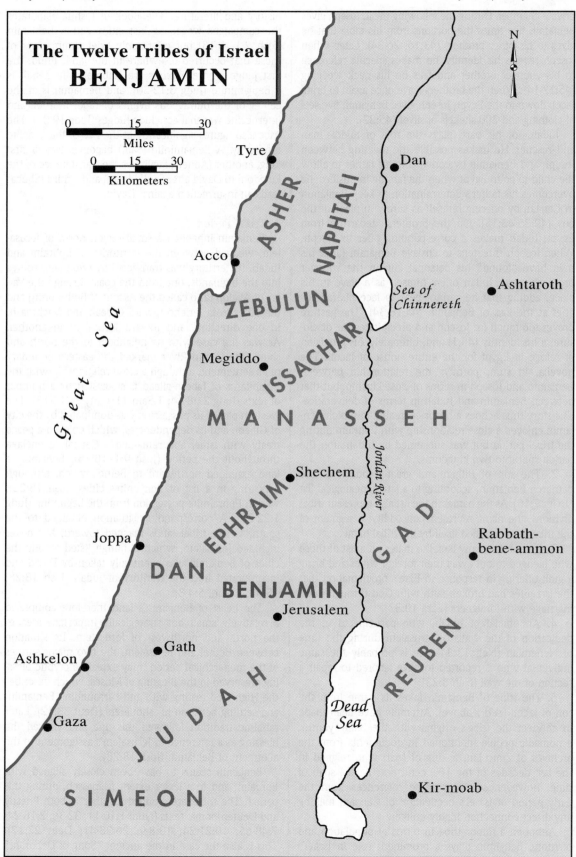

The Twelve Tribes of Israel
BENJAMIN

0 15 30
Miles

0 15 30
Kilometers

N

ASHER

NAPHTALI

Tyre

Dan

Acco

Great Sea

ZEBULUN

Sea of
Chinnereth

Ashtaroth

Megiddo

ISSACHAR

MANASSEH

Shechem

Jordan River

EPHRAIM

GAD

Joppa

Rabbath-
bene-ammon

DAN

BENJAMIN

Jerusalem

REUBEN

Ashkelon

Gath

*Dead
Sea*

Gaza

JUDAH

SIMEON

Kir-moab

which reports that Ephraimites followed Benjaminites in response to Deborah's call to wage war against the Sisera (Judg 5:14). The two tribes also fight together when Ehud musters troops in the Ephraimite highlands and leads them against the Moabites (Judg 3:26-30). Strong ties are also implied by traditions that report conquests within Benjamin's territory under the leadership of Joshua, the Ephraimite chieftain who led Israel to victory over the peoples of the land (Josh 6:1-10:15). It is likely as well that both tribes shared the sanctuary of Gilgal, one of the most significant sanctuaries in the tribal period, which was located near the Jordan at the intersection of Ephraimite and Benjaminite territories.

Biblical texts depict an aggressive, cunning, and fiercely independent tribe, one that could be dangerous even to friends. A poetic fragment probably deriving from this period calls Benjamin "a ravenous wolf" that devours its prey by morning and divides the spoil in the evening (Gen 49:27), no doubt a reference to raids against caravans that traversed the roads winding through its territory. A more illuminating portrait is preserved in the latter chapters of Judges, where Benjamin ignites intertribal warfare when it refuses to hand over men who gang-raped the concubine of a Levite traveler staying the night in Gibeah (Judg 19-21). The atrocity unites Israel against the Benjaminites who, even when faced by the assembled might of all the tribes, decide to fight rather than submit one of their own to judgment. Despite being overwhelmingly outnumbered (400,000 to 26,000) the tribe successfully repels two attacks, and the Israelites prevail a third time only by subterfuge (20:1-48). During the account, the writer specifically mentions the Benjaminites' reputation as marksmen, remarking of a contingent of slingers that "every one could sling a stone at a hair, and not miss" (v. 16). The affair so decimates the tribe and its cities that the surviving men can only acquire new wives by receiving women who have been taken as plunder from Jabesh-gilead and by kidnapping young women as they dance during a festival at Shiloh (21:1-24).

B. Monarchy

Saul, Israel's first king, was a Benjaminite who was selected and anointed by Samuel, an Ephraimite judge and priest (1 Sam 1:1-28; 9:1-2). Benjamin's strategic location in Israel, as well as its reputation for prowess in war, made Saul a politically expedient choice, despite his protests to the contrary (1 Sam 9:21). After Samuel anointed him, Saul successfully united all the Israelite tribes and led them to victory when the Ammonites threaten Jabesh-gilead (11:1-11). A Philistine attempt to dominate the Benjaminite hill country led to an uprising initiated when Saul's son Jonathan attacked a garrison at Michmash, a location overlooking the Wadi es-Suweinit in the tribal heartland. Here as well, Saul won a decisive, if not final victory over the Philistines and was able to expel them from the entire region. Additional campaigns led to victories against the Moabites, Edomites, and the kings of Zobah (1 Sam 14:1-48). Internally, Saul attempted to expand Benjaminite settlement westward by annihilating the Gibeonites (2 Sam 21:1-2).

With the deaths of Saul and Jonathan, the Benjaminites rallied to Ishbaal, Saul's surviving son, and therefore found themselves at odds with David and the tribe of Judah. The two tribes clashed at the pool of Gibeon, with the result that the Benjaminites were soundly defeated (2 Sam 2:12-32). Benjamin, however, continued to exert considerable influence over the rest of the Israelite tribes. A measure of this influence can be detected in Abner's role in bringing the rest of the tribes over to David. Abner, Ishbaal's general and kinsman, was the real power behind the throne (2 Sam 2:8-9). After promising to swing Israel's support from Ishbaal to David, a message from Abner to the elders of Israel and a direct meeting with the Benjaminites were sufficient to redirect the tribes' loyalties (2 Sam. 3:6-21). Benjaminites, in fact, sealed the transfer; Ishbaal was assassinated by the two captains of his raiding parties (4:1-12). The tribe, nevertheless, remained restive under the reign of David, a situation alluded to by David's harassment by Shimei (2 Sam 16:11; 19:16-23). It is by no means insignificant that Sheba, a Benjaminite, was able to rally the Israelites against David late in his reign and mount the most serious insurrection David faced during his kingship (2 Sam 20:1-22).

Benjamin constituted its own district when Solomon reorganized his kingdom for the purpose of taxation (1 Kgs 4:18), and Gibeon served as Israel's primary site for sacrifice in the early years of his reign (2 Kgs 3:4-5). These circumstances suggest efforts to constrain the tribe's unruliness, either by force or by currying favor. Whatever the case, Benjamin's tradition alignment with Ephraim had given way to a new alignment with Judah by the time Rehoboam assumed the throne. Although an editorial comment declares that "there was no one who followed the house of David, except the tribe of Judah alone" (1 Kgs 12:20), the following narrative reports that the tribe of Benjamin joined the tribe of Judah in mustering to fight against Jeroboam and the rebellious northern tribes (1 Kgs 12:21, 22). However it happened, the incorporation of Benjamin was essential to the survival of Judah, as it constituted a buffer zone between Jerusalem and the Northern Kingdom.

With the division of Israel into two kingdoms, most of Benjamin was thus absorbed into the kingdom of Judah. Only the northeast quadrant (in the vicinity of Jericho) seems to have been held by the Northern Kingdom; the rebuilding of Jericho is associated with the reign of the Israelite king Ahab (1 Kgs 16:34). The region was contested during the early years of the divided monarchy. Rehoboam was initially able to take the towns of Bethel, Jeshanah, and Ephron (2 Chr 13:19), but these were recovered by Baasha, who pushed far into Benjaminite territory and fortified Ramah (1 Kgs 15:17). Asa, in turn, was able to revive an alliance with Ben-Hadad of Damascus (through a large payment of gold and silver), which forced Baasha to abandon his fortifications. Asa then fortified Geba to the east and Mizpah to the north, thereby securing the main roads to Jerusalem (1 Kgs 15:18-22). Benjamin thereafter remained a contested area throughout the period of the divided monarchy, a situation attested by Hosea's warnings to the land during the Syro-Ephraimite War (Hos 5:8).

The description of Benjamin's allotment (Josh 18:11-28) reflects the delineation of tribal lands at various points during the Judahite monarchy. The boundary descriptions and city lists closely correspond to those that define Judah (Josh 15:1-63), indicating that an editor has artificially separated materials that originally shared a close literary relationship. The specificity and tight organization of the materials suggest that the source documents derive from an administrative context that viewed Benjamin as part of the Kingdom of Judah and defined its territory accordingly. The description of Benjamin's territory in the Masoretic Text shows signs of a complex editorial process. The delineation of its northern boundary extends just south of Bethel (v. 13), whereas the city list includes cities (notably Bethel) that presume possession of territory farther north into the Ephraimite highlands (vv. 21-22). The city lists comprise two districts (vv. 21-24 and vv. 25-28) but do not include key cities located in the tribal heartland (e.g., Gibeah, Nob, and Anathoth). The lists follow the form of the Judahite city lists, which are organized into eleven districts. Given this scheme, it is likely that the cities in vv. 25-28 constituted a twelfth (Benjaminite) district within the Judahite source document, while those in vv. 21-24 comprise an additional district added when Judah's territory expanded northward during the reign of Josiah (2 Kgs 23:15-20). The boundary lists, in sum, derive from and delineate Benjamin's territory during the early phase of the Judahite monarchy, while the city lists reflect its status during the time of Josiah.

Benjamin seems to have escaped the depredations suffered by Judah when Nebuchadrezzar destroyed Jerusalem and devastated the land in 587 BCE, and many of its towns continued to flourish during the exilic period. Some have explained this situation by suggesting that Benjaminite circles opposed the seditious policies of Zedekiah that brought on the Babylonian invasion, the putative link being the preaching of Jeremiah, who hailed from Anathoth (Jer 1:1) and who was arrested on charges of defecting to the Chaldeans (Jer 37:11-21). It is significant, in this regard, that the Chaldeans established Mizpah in Benjamin as the administrative center of the region after exiling the populace of Jerusalem and Judah (2 Kgs 25:22-23; Jer 40:6-12).

C. After the Exile

Benjamin was folded into the Persian province of Yehud (Judah) following the exile, yet retained its tribal identity. Literature of the period characteristically speaks of "Judah and Benjamin" as a single unit (2 Chr 11:1, 3, 10, 12, 23; 14:8; 15:2, 8-9; 17:17; 31:1; 34:9; Ezra 1:5; 4:1; 10:9; Neh 11:36). Benjaminites therefore, participated significantly in rebuilding and restoration efforts and held important positions in the governance of Jerusalem (Neh 11:7-9). The mass of genealogical material and special attention accorded to Benjamin in Chronicles demonstrates an impulse to maintain the tribe's identity in its own right (1 Chr 7:6-12; 8:1-40; 9:3, 7-9; 12:2-7, 16-18, 29; 21:6; 2 Chr 14:8). As was the case prior to the exile, Benjaminite territory seems to have suffered from antagonism between north and south. Excavations have revealed destruction layers dated to the early 5th cent. BCE at Benjaminite towns (Bethel, Gibeon, Gibeah); these may indicate a period of intense conflict between Jerusalem and Samaria. Benjaminite identity evidently remained strong through the Hellenistic period and into the Roman era. The apostle Paul made a point of defining himself as "a descendant of Abraham and a member of the tribe of Benjamin" (Rom 11:1), an attribute he considered a matter worthy of boasting (Phil 3:5). *See* TRIBES, TERRITORIES OF.

Bibliography: Z. Kallai. *Historical Geography of the Bible* (1986); Y. Levin. "Joseph, Judah and the "Benjamin Conundrum." *ZAW* 116 (2004) 223–41

L. DANIEL HAWK

BEN LEVI, RABBI YOSHUA. *See* YOSHUA BEN LEVI.

BENO bee′noh [בְּנוֹ *beno*]. Either the Levite son of Jaaziah, or the term should be translated "his son" (1 Chr 24:26, 27).

BEN-ONI ben-oh′ni [בֶּן־אוֹנִי *ben 'oni*]. Rachel's name for Benjamin, which she gave him as she died in childbirth (Gen 35:18). It means, "son of my sorrow." *See* BENJAMIN, BENJAMINITES.

BEN SIRA. *See* SIRACH.

BEN ZAKKAI, RABBI JOHANAN. *See* JOHANAN BEN ZAKKAI.

BEN-ZOHETH ben-zoh′heth [בֶּן־זוֹחֵת *ben zoheth*]. A Judahite, son of Ishi, or the term should be translated "and the son of Zohith" (1 Chr 4:20).

BEON bee′on [בְּעֹן *be'on*]. A town or pastoral region in northern Moab sought as territory by the Gadites and Reubenites (Num 32:3).

BEOR bee'or [בְּעוֹר be'or; Βεωρ Beōr]. "A burning, a torch." 1. Father of BALAAM, who was summoned by the king of Moab to curse the Israelites (Num 22:5; 31:8; Deut 23:5; Josh 13:22; 24:9; Mic 6:5; 2 Pet 2:15).

2. Father of the Edomite king BELA (Gen 36:32; 1 Chr 1:43).

BERA bihr'uh [בֶּרַע bera']. King of Sodom who rebelled against Chedorlaomer but was defeated; Abram's nephew Lot was among the captured (Gen 14).

BERACAH ber'uh-kuh [בְּרָכָה berakhah]. One of David's band of insurgent archers from Saul's tribe, Benjamin (1 Chr 12:3). The name means *blessing*.

BERACAH, VALLEY OF ber'uh-kuh [עֵמֶק בְּרָכָה 'emeq berakhah]. The name means "valley of blessing, praise," a pun on the root brk, signifying the place where the JUDAHITES praised (berakhu) God for delivering them from their enemies (2 Chr 20:26). The MOABITES and their allies had marched against Judah from EN-GEDI, up the Ascent of Ziz, but were routed in the wilderness of TEKOA (2 Chr 20). Beracah could also be a double entendre on the word brekhah (pool), indicating the existence of a nearby spring. Its location has variously been identified as Wadi el-Arrub, Khirbet Bereikut, and the valley of el-Baq'ah.

FOOK KONG WONG

BERAIAH bi-ray'yuh [בְּרָאיָה bera'yah]. One of the nine sons of SHIMEI of the tribe of BENJAMIN (1 Chr 8:21). The genealogical account illustrates the tribe's rise to prominence in preexilic Jerusalem.

BERAKHOT [בְּרָכֹת berakhoth]. "Blessings." The best known blessing in Scriptures is the priestly BENEDICTION, Num 6:24-26, a trifold blessing that, to this day, is recited by priests over the congregation. A tractate of the MISHNAH is entitled *Berakhot* and deals with the daily liturgy of Jewish worship. In general, a Jewish blessing begins with the words, "Blessed are You, Lord our God, ruler of the universe . . ." Such blessings are recited when one performs a commandment (e.g., eating matsah), and before enjoying something of God's creation, be it food, the beauties of nature, and so on.

JUDITH Z. ABRAMS

BEREA bi-ree'uh [Βερεα Berea]. A town north of Jerusalem where Bacchides and Alcimus camped with their soldiers after they had beseiged Jerusalem (1 Macc 9:4). Judas' forces were located at Elasa (1 Macc 9:5). Judas fell in battle and was buried in Modein by his brothers Jonathan and Simon.

BERECHIAH ber'uh-ki'uh [בֶּרֶכְיָה berekhyah; Βαραχ– ιας Barachias]. 1. Son of ZERUBBABEL (1 Chr 3:20).

2. ASAPH's father (1 Chr 6:39 [Heb. 6:24]; 15:17).

3. Gatekeeper of the ark during David's reign (1 Chr 15:23), possibly the same as above.

4. ASA's son (1 Chr 9:16).

5. MESHILLEMOTH's son and an Ephraimite chief (2 Chr 28:12).

6. Father of MESHEZABEL and son of MESHULLAM (Neh 3:4, 30) whose granddaughter married the son of TOBIAH the Ammonite (Neh 6:18).

7. Son of IDDO and father of ZECHARIAH (Zech 1:1, 7). However, Iddo is Zechariah's father in Ezra 5:1; 6:14; Neh 12:16. The Zechariah, son of BARACHIAH, mentioned by Jesus (Matt 23:35) further complicates the issue of identity (*see* Isa 8:2 and 2 Chr 24:20-22).

STEVEN JAMES SCHWEITZER

BERED bihr'ed [בֶּרֶד beredh]. 1. A grandson of EPHRAIM, younger son of JOSEPH (1 Chr 7:20). The name BECHER appears in a parallel register (Num 26:35-36). However, it lists Becher as a son of Ephraim.

2. The well of Beer-lahai-roi was supposedly located between Kadesh and Bered (Gen 16:14). Bered has been variously identified as Jebel umm el-Bared, Way of Shur, and el-Khalasa, respectively southeast, north, and northeast of Kadesh.

FOOK KONG WONG

BERENICE. *See* BERNICE.

BERI bihr'i [בֵּרִי beri]. This name occurs only once (1 Chr 7:36), identifying Beri as the fourth of the eleven sons of ZOPHAH of the tribe of Asher. It is not mentioned in the par. genealogies (Gen 46:17-18; Num 26:44-47). This name is etymologically unrelated to the Beriites mentioned in Num 26:44.

FOOK KONG WONG

BERIAH, BERIITES bi-ri'uh, bi-ri'ts [בְּרִיעָה beri'ah, בְּרִיעִי beri'i]. 1. The fourth son of ASHER (Gen 46:17; 1 Chr 7:30, 31) and the eponymous ancestor of the Beriites (Num 26:44).

2. The Asherite Beriah's descendants (Num 26:44).

3. A son of EPHRAIM, so named because "evil (בְּרָעָה bera'ah) has befallen his house" (1 Chr 7:23).

4. A son of ELPAAL (1 Chr 8:12-13) or EBER.

5. Fourth son of SHIMEI, a Levite (1 Chr 23:10).

Bibliography: Sara Japhet. *1 & 2 Chronicles: A Commentary* (1993).

FOOK KONG WONG

BERLIN GNOSTIC CODEX. Papyrus-bound codex, dating to the 5th cent. CE, found in 1896 in Akhmim, Egypt, and housed in Berlin (Codex Berolinensis Gnosticus 8502). The single-quire Coptic codex is one of the most important witnesses to Gnosticism, containing two sections of a fragmentary *Gospel According to*

Mary, the *Apocryphon of John*, the *Wisdom of Jesus Christ*, and the *Acts of Peter*.

PETER ARZT-GRABNER

BERNICE buhr-nees´ [Βερνίκη Bernikē, Βερενίκη Berenikē]. Born in 28/29 CE, the oldest daughter of Agrippa I, Julia Bernice was both a member of the Jewish royal family and a Roman citizen. As a teenager, she married Marcus, son of Alexander the alabarch (and nephew of PHILO OF ALEXANDRIA). When he died soon afterward, she married her father's brother, Herod king of Chalcis to whom she bore two sons. Herod died in 48, leaving Bernice an extremely wealthy young widow; she (and presumably her sons) went to live with her unmarried brother, Agrippa II, who had now inherited Chalcis. Their relationship led to scurrilous (and probably groundless) rumors of incest. Perhaps in an effort to stifle these slanders, Bernice married Polemo of Cilicia in 63, though the marriage quickly ended in divorce, and she returned to her brother's court where she once again took her place at his side. The two royals greeted Festus in Caesarea when he arrived as procurator of Judea in 60 CE. They listened to Paul's defense, and Agrippa pronounced him innocent on the same occasion (Acts 25:14–26:32). Both later remained loyal to Rome and tried to prevent the outbreak of revolt in 66, Bernice jeopardizing her own life (Josephus, *J.W.* 2.309-14). Soon afterward, Bernice began an affair with TITUS and followed him to Rome in 75, openly living with him as his wife. She helped to finance the Flavian rise to power and probably expected to be rewarded with marriage. If so, she was to be disappointed. Bernice was unpopular, and Titus, on his accession in 79, seems reluctantly to have sent her back to Palestine. Nothing is recorded of her death.

Bibliography: N. Kokkinos. *The Herodian Dynasty* (1998); G. H. Macurdy. "Julia Berenice." *AJPhil* 56 (1935) 246–53.

HELEN K. BOND

BEROEA bi-ree´uh [Βέροια Beroia, Βέρροια Berroia]. 1. Modern Verria, a city in southwestern Macedonia on the river Astraeus "at the roots of Mount Bermius" (Strabo 7, frg. 26). First to surrender to the Romans after their victory at Pydna (168 BCE), it became the seat of the Macedonian koinon ("commonality") and provincial center of the imperial cult. "A large and populous city" (Lucian, *Asin.* 34), it was "off the beaten path" (Cicero, *Pis.* 36)—i.e., the Via Egnatia to Rome—though en route to ATHENS. Paul and Silas fled to Berea, 80 km/50 mi. southwest of THESSALONICA, to escape Jewish agitators (Acts 17:10, 13). Berean Jews were "more receptive" but also more exacting in their verification of Paul's message from the Scriptures (17:11). Paul's colleague, Sopater, was a Berean (20:4).

2. Aleppo in northern Syria, made into a Macedonian city by Seleucus Nicator between 381 and 281 BCE. Menelaus, the renegade high priest, was executed there at the order of Antiochus Eupator by being hurled into a tower of ashes (2 Macc 13:1-8; Josephus, *Ant.* 12.385).

KEVIN L. ANDERSON

BEROSSUS [Βηρωσσος Bērōsos]. The Babylonian priest, astronomer, and historiographer, Berossus, composed an ambitious history of Babylon, beginning with its ancient cosmogonies and extending to his own time. His *History of Babylonia* (ca. 290 BCE) is lost. Nevertheless, fragments survive in other writers, including ALEXANDER POLYHISTOR, JOSEPHUS, and EUSEBIUS. For example, Berossus' report that Sennacherib lifted the Assyrian siege upon Jerusalem due to a plague is found in Josephus (*Ant.* 10.21-23; *see* 2 Kgs 19:35-36). The mythological portions of the *History* not only preserve a retelling of the same basic story found in the ENUMA ELISH but they also reflect an allegorical or naturalistic interpretation of such myths (although perhaps attributable to later editors). Berossus aspired to preserve the history of Babylon in the style of Greek narrative history, an accomplishment paralleled by the work of his later Egyptian contemporary Manetho. In this process, he probably employed temple archives, mythological writings, and king-lists. The range of his narrative, extending from creation through deluge into contemporary history, can be compared to Josephus' *Jewish Antiquities* and portions of the OT.

Bibliography: Gerald P. Verbrugghe and John M. Wickersham. *Berossos and Manetho Introduced and Translated: Native Traditions in Ancient Mesopotamia and Egypt* (2001).

CASEY D. ELLEDGE

BEROTHAH bi-roh´thuh [בְּרוֹתָה berothah]. A town mentioned along with Hamath and Damascus as marking Israel's northern boundary in Ezekiel's vision (Ezek 47:16). Sometimes identified with Beirut. Probably the same as BEROTHAI.

BEROTHAI bi-roh´thi [בְּרֹתַי berothay]. Following successful battles against neighboring areas, David takes bronze from Berothai and BETAH, towns of King HADADEZER of ZOBAH in the Biqaʿ Valley of modern Lebanon, as spoils of victory (2 Sam 8:8). This city may be the same as BEROTHAH.

BERRY [גַּרְגַּר garger]. Berries are only mentioned explicitly in Isa 17:6. Although the NRSV translates this term as *berries*, it more likely refers to ripe olives. Other plants mentioned in the OT and NT bore berries. These may include blackberries, juniper, mulberries, and capers. *See* OLIVE, OLIVE TREE.

BERYL [תַּרְשִׁישׁ tarshish; βήρυλλος bēryllos]. The tenth stone in the high priest's BREASTPIECE (Exod 28:20; 39:13; of royalty see Ezek 28:13). The man in Daniel's vision whose "body was like BERYL" (Dan 10:6) suggests that BERYL was used metaphorically to describe things that take on the brightness of a shining precious stone. The chariot's shining wheels in Ezekiel are of BERYL (Ezek 1:16; 10:9). The eighth stone in the wall's foundations of the New Jerusalem is bēryllos (Rev 21:20). The Hebrew term is possibly related to the port of Tarshish (e.g., 1 Kgs 10:22). BERYL, a member of the hexagonal crystal mineral group that includes EMERALD, has a variety of colors with light green to bluish-green being prominent.

ELIZABETH E. PLATT

BESAI bee′si [בֵּסָי besay]. A family head whose descendants were among the Temple servants, called the Nethinim, who returned after the exile (Ezra 2:49; Neh 7:52).

BESCASPASMYS bes′kuhs-paz′muhs [Βεσκασπασμυς Beskaspasmys]. Descendant of Addi who dismissed his foreign wife as Ezra instructed God's covenant required him (1 Esd 9:31). See MATTANIAH.

BESODEIAH bes′uh-dee′yah [בְּסוֹדְיָה besodheyah]. Father of Meshullam who joined Joiada in the repairing of the Old Gate when they returned to Jerusalem after the exile (Neh 3:6).

BESOR, WADI bee′sor, wah′dee [נַחַל הַבְּשׂוֹר nakhal habbesor]. A major wadi David crossed in pursuit of the Amalekites who had plundered and burned ZIKLAG (1 Sam 30:9, 10, 21). The Wadi Besor, also known as the Wadi Gaza or Wadi Shallaleh, enters the Mediterranean approximately 5 mi. south of Gaza. It was one of two major wadis of the western Negev. The Besor extended eastward from the Mediterranean Sea to Beer-Sheba and beyond to its origin near Arad. The large area for which it provided drainage, combined with the flooding that occurred during the rainy season, created an extremely large wadi bed reaching a width of some 150 m. The strategic location and the economic significance of the region are attested in towns located along the Besor including Tell el-Ajjul, Tell Jemmeh, Tell el-Farah (south), Beer-Sheba, and Arad. In spite of the limited rainfall of 10 to 12 inches annually and the threat of crop failure, the region was often quite successful in the production of cereal crops like wheat and barley. Consequently, the region of the Besor witnessed many conflicts not only between local groups but also on the international level between world powers including the Egyptians, the Assyrians, and the Babylonians.

LAMOINE F. DEVRIES

BESSUS. See ARTAXERXES.

BESTIALITY. In contemporary usage, bestiality primarily refers to sexual acts between human beings and animals. However, older usages include "the instinct of beasts" and the "beast signs" in astrology (see ASTRONOMY, ASTROLOGY). The term zoosexuality has been used to refer specifically to sex between human beings and other animals. Zoophilia may refer to affections for and relations with animals that are not sexual. Four texts in the Bible that refer to bestiality, Exod 22:19; Lev 18:23; 20:15-16; and Deut 27:21, have been and continue to be used by Jewish, Christian, and Muslim commentators to condemn and outlaw bestiality. In these texts, bestiality is a "defilement" and "perversion" (Lev 18:23), and the punishment is death (Exod 22:19; Lev 20:15-16; see CLEAN AND UNCLEAN).

A few things are worth noting. First, both male and female human beings are addressed in the two Leviticus passages. Since the vast majority of laws in the OT address men only, the prohibition for women and men is significant. Second, the context of the prohibitions is important. In Exod 22:19, the prohibition of bestiality is preceded by the commandment to kill sorceresses, and it is followed by a ban on sacrificing to other gods. The immediate context concerns religious practice. In Lev 18:23, bestiality is included in a curious collection at the conclusion of a long passage on the incest taboo (Lev 18:6-18; see INCEST). That ending collection has laws against sex with a woman during her period, sex with a neighbor's wife, devoting one's children in the fire to Molech, a ban on male-to-male sex, and finally on bestiality. In Lev 20:15-16 and Deut 27:21, the curse on bestiality is surrounded by incest taboos. This suggests that we have a massively different sexual economy in which sex with animals, the same sex, and extended relatives are on the same par—all in terms of the shame or honor of the man in question (see HOMOSEXUALITY; HONOR; SHAME). Hence the laws on bestiality are located within the incest taboos and laws forbidding male-to-male sex. On the one hand this means that animals were on the same level, sexually, as a man's extended family or tribe and his fellow males. All were sexually forbidden. But it also means that men were the only ones considered by the law to be responsible beings, and as such, they were equally responsible for their dependents, be they wives, children, or animals.

Finally, the religious context of Exod 22:19 points to another issue. Laws are usually made to deal with certain practices that require policing. The religious context of Exod 22:19 suggests the importance of animals in religions from which the writers of these laws wanted to distance themselves, especially animal representations of deities, fertility rites, and mythology in which animal figures were important. Bestiality is therefore as much a religious as a social and moral question. *See* ANIMALS OF THE BIBLE; SEX, SEXUALITY; SEXUAL ABUSE.

ROLAND BOER

BET [ב v]. The second letter of the Hebrew alphabet, which derives from the Semitic name *bayt-*, meaning "house." *See* ALPHABET.

BETA [β B b]. The second letter in the Greek alphabet, which derives from the Phoenician *bet. See* ALPHABET.

BETAH bee´tuh [בֶּטַח betakh]. One of the towns in King Hadadezer's kingdom from which King David took bronze after defeating him (2 Sam 18:8). *See* TIBHATH.

BETEN bee´tuhn [בֶּטֶן beten]. Town situated within the land Joshua gave to the Asher tribe (Josh 19:25), when he apportioned the remaining territories. *See* ASHER, ASHERITES.

BETHABARA beth-ab´uh-ruh [Βηθαβαρά Bēthabara]. Location of John's baptismal activities beyond the Jordan (John 1:28), according to some inferior manuscripts. Although the KJV accepts Bethabara, the better attested reading, BETHANY, has been accepted in recent translations. May be the same as BETH-BARAH or BETH-NIMRAH.

BETH-ANATH beth-ay´nath [בֵּית־עֲנָת beth ʿanath]. A town Joshua allotted to the Naphtalites (Josh 19:38). Its Canaanite inhabitants became forced labor (Judg 1:33). Perhaps located east of Acco. *See* NAPHTALI, NAPHTALITES.

BETH-ANOTH beth-ay´noth [בֵּית־עֲנוֹת beth ʿanoth]. A town with its villages that had been allocated to the Judah tribe (Josh 15:59). Located southwest of Jerusalem. Perhaps modern Khirbet ʿAinun. *See* JUDAH, JUDAHITES.

BETHANY beth´uh-nee [Βηθανία Bēthania, Βατάνη Batanē, Βαιτάνη Baitanē]. The ministries of Jesus and John the Baptist are associated with two places named Bethany.

1. Bethany near Jerusalem appears several times in the NT

A common opinion connects Bethany to Ananiah (Neh 11:32). If true, this connection might explain the name *Bethany* as a derivation from Beth Ananiah, or "house of Ananiah." Different manuscripts of Judith refer to a town named **Batanē** or **Baitanē** (1:9). Some translations render this as Bethany (NRSV, NAB, NJB) and others Betane, but this town is most likely south of Jerusalem, and not the town in the NT.

Bethany was on the Mount of Olives (Mark 11:1), fifteen stadia (1.75 mi.) from Jerusalem (John 11:18). Today, on the eastern side of the Mount of Olives, almost 2 mi. from Jerusalem, sits modern Bethany, whose Arabic name is el-Azariyeh, a derivation from the Greek **Lazarion**, "the place of Lazarus," by which the site was known to Eusebius in the 4th cent. CE. Jesus raised Lazarus from the dead in Bethany (John 11:1-44). Proximity to Jerusalem makes Bethany Jesus' last stop on his way to Jerusalem to die (Mark 11:1; Luke 19:29). His arrival there signals geographically that he nears the passion. Pilgrims regularly remained outside of Jerusalem, due to overcrowding, and so it is not unusual that during Passover week Jesus returns to Bethany following his triumphal entry into Jerusalem (Mark 11:11; Matt 21:17). Jesus spends Passover week in Bethany also in John, but goes there only prior to the triumphal entry. After raising Lazarus (John 11:1-44), Jesus returns to Bethany six days before the Passover to be with Lazarus, Mary, and Martha (John 12:1-2). During Passover week, Jesus is anointed while dining in Bethany (Matt 26:6-13; Mark 14:3-9; Luke 7:36-50; John 12:3-8). Luke associates the ascension of Jesus with Bethany (24:50-51). Excavations have unearthed churches clustered around the tomb of Lazarus. Nearby, excavators discovered houses and other signs of habitation in the town of Bethany, occupied from the 6th/5th cent. BCE to the 14th cent. CE, with artifacts from the 1st cent. CE.

2. The Gospel of John refers to the place where John the Baptist conducted his ministry as "Bethany beyond the Jordan" (1:28).

Origen, in the 3rd cent., could not find a Bethany east of the Jordan River, but local tradition maintained that John baptized in BETHABARA. Consequently, Origen replaced Bethany in his text with Bethabara. Scholars follow broad manuscript support in generally assuming that Bethany was the original reading, but Origen's industry introduced Bethabara and the related variants Bethebara and Betharaba (by metathesis) into the manuscript tradition. What this circumstance demonstrates is that even in Origen's time, "Bethany beyond the Jordan" was not readily locatable. The modern era found it equally difficult, but hypotheses have flourished. Some believed the changing course of the Jordan obscured the site altogether. Some accepted Origen's alteration as the original reading. Others argued that Bethany designates not a town but the region of Batanea. But now, excavators at Wadi el-Harrar, east of the Jordan and north of the Dead Sea, believe the elusive site lies there. Excavations from 1996–2002 indicate ancient and medieval habitation beginning in the 2nd cent. BCE. Stone jars characteristic of 1st cent. Jewish communities survive. Also discovered were several churches, including one matching Byzantine descriptions of the 4th cent. Church of St. John the

Baptist built by Constantine's mother Helen. Consequently, excavators cite the Byzantine identification of the site as proof that it is "Bethany beyond the Jordan."

Bibliography: Rami Khouri. "Where John Baptized: Bethany beyond the Jordan." *BAR* (January/February 2005) 35–43; S. J. Saller. *Excavations at Bethany (1949–1953)* (1957).

GEORGE L. PARSENIOS

BETHANY BEYOND THE JORDAN. *See* BETHABARA.

BETH-ARABAH beth-air'uh-buh [בֵּית הָעֲרָבָה beth ha'aravah]. One of the towns marking the border between the allotments of Benjamin and Judah (Josh 15:6; 18:18). It is listed as one of Judah's towns (Josh 15:61) and as one of Benjamin's (Josh 18:22), hinting that it may have been so at different times.

BETH-ARBEL beth-ahr'buhl [בֵּית אַרְבֵּאל beth 'arve'l]. A town whose destruction by SHALMAN must have been notorious for its level of brutality (Hos 10:14), serving as an analogy to the coming catastrophe upon BETHEL for the Israelites' failure to seek the Lord. Several ancient locations share the name *Arbela* and may qualify for the geographic reference in Hos 10. One is located in the TRANSJORDAN and another in GALILEE.

STEVEN D. MASON

BETH-ASHBEA beth-ash'bee-uh [בֵּית אַשְׁבֵּעַ beth 'ashbea']. A Judean town probably located in the SHEPHELAH and the residence of some families who were linen workers (1 Chr 4:21).

BETHASMOTH. *See* AZMAVETH.

BETH-AVEN beth-ay'vuhn [בֵּית אָוֶן beth 'awen]. Perhaps an older name for the town AI. Otherwise, its precise location is unknown. Joshua 7:2 locates it east of Bethel and near Ai, particularly in the wilderness on Benjamin's border (Josh 18:12). But 1 Sam 13:5 and 14:23 situate it west of Michmash, where Saul and the Philistines battled. Hosea (4:15; 5:8; 10:5) uses it figuratively to condemn Bethel of idolatry since it literally means "house of wickedness." *See* BENJAMIN, BENJAMINITES.

EMILY CHENEY

BETH-AZMAVETH beth-az'muh-veth [בֵּית־עַזְמָוֶת beth 'azmaveth]. Named in Neh 7:28. *See* AZMAVETH.

BETH-BAAL-MEON beth-bay'uhl-mee'on [בַּעַל מְעוֹן בֵּית beth ba'al me'on]. Town in northern Moab (Josh 13:17). *See* BAAL-MEON; MOAB, MOABITES.

BETH-BARAH bet-bair'uh [בֵּית־בָּרָה beth barah]. A town near the Jordan River, between its valley and the Esdraelon Plain. The town marked one of the boundaries of the area that the Ephraemites, led by Gideon, took from the Midianites (Judg 7:24). John the Baptist may have baptized the crowds here. *See* MIDIAN.

BETHBASI beth-bay'si [Βαιθβασι Baithbasi]. A village located southeast of Bethlehem, about 3 mi. northeast of Tekoa (modern Khirbet Beit Bassi), to which Jonathan, Simon, and followers retreated from Bacchides (1 Macc 9:62).

Bibliography: Jonathan A. Goldstein. *1 Maccabees. AB* 41 (1984).

PAUL L. REDDITT

BETH-BIRI beth-bihr'i [בֵּית בִּרְאִין beth bir'i]. A town belonging to the tribe of Simeon prior to the time of David (1 Chr 4:31). *See* BETH-LEBAOTH; SIMEON, SIMEONITES.

PAUL L. REDDITT

BETH-CAR beth-kahr' [בֵּית כָּר bethkar]. An unknown site located presumably between Mizpah and Philistine territory, where Samuel's army defeated the Philistines (1 Sam 4:11).

PAUL L. REDDITT

BETH-DAGON beth-day'gon [בֵּית דָּגֹן beth dagnon, Βηθδαγων Bēthdagōn]. "House of Dagon." 1. A village listed as part of Judah's inheritance of uncertain location but in the SHEPHELAH since it is associated with lowland cities (LACHISH, AZEKAH, and ACHZIB, Josh 15:41).

2. A village of uncertain location belonging to the tribe of ASHER in northern Israel east of CARMEL (Josh 19:27).

3. Common name for a temple to the PHILISTINE god DAGON, such as at AZOTUS (1 Macc 10:83), ASHDOD (1 Sam 5:2), and other places (1 Chr 10:10), often translated as "house of Dagon" (1 Sam 5:2, 5).

TERRY W. EDDINGER

BETH-DIBLATHAIM beth'dib-luh-thay'im [דִּבְלָתָיִם בֵּית beth divlathayim]. Among the named towns in JEREMIAH's oracle against MOAB (Jer 48:22) it is also mentioned on the MOABITE STONE as one of the towns King MESHA rebuilt. AMON-DIBLATHAIM, named in the wilderness wanderings (Num 33:46-47), may be the same place or perhaps nearby.

BETH-EDEN beth-ee'duhn [בֵּית עֶדֶן beth 'edhen]. "House of EDEN." An ancient Aramean kingdom in MESOPOTAMIA, located on both sides of the EUPHRATES south of Carchemis, recognized as the Ashata in the Amarna Period. The kingdom was probably founded in the 10th cent. BCE and its capital, Barsib, was conquered by the Assyrians under SHALMANESER III in 856 BCE. Words of God through Amos condemn the ruler (scepter) of Beth-Eden (Amos 1:5).

CHANNA COHEN STUART

BETH-EGLAIM beth-eg'lay-im [בֵּית אֶגְלַיִם beth 'eghlayim]. A town not mentioned in the Bible (unless it is ENEGLAIM, Ezek 47:10) but noted by Eusebius (*Onomast.* 48.19) as being located 8 mi. from Gaza, Beth-Eglaim is usually associated with the archaeological site of Tell el-'Ajjul on the coast southwest of Gaza. The identification is made not only on the basis of the location given by Eusebius but also by comparison of the meanings of the place names. Beth-Eglaim means "house (or temple) of the two calves," while Tell el-'Ajjul means "hill of the calf." This identification is not universally accepted, and others have identified Tell el-'Ajjul as Sharuhen.

Tell el-'Ajjul became an important city during the Middle Bronze Age, its expansion associated with the HYKSOS period in Egypt. The Hyksos maintained close relations with Canaan, and Tell el-'Ajjul's location on the main route between the two areas would have made it important for trade. The fact that it also served as a port would have added to both its strategic and economic importance. Excavations from this period have revealed the great wealth of the city, including a succession of palaces. The city was taken over by the Egyptians when the Hyksos were expelled from Egypt, and it became one of the main administrative centers for the Egyptian Empire in Palestine. After the decline of the Egyptian Empire at the end of the Late Bronze Age, Tell el-'Ajjul was almost completely abandoned, with Gaza becoming the most important city in the area.

KEVIN A. WILSON

BETH-EKED beth-ee'kid [בֵּית־עֵקֶד beth 'eqedh]. Traveling through Beth-eked of the Shepherds on his way from JEZREEL to SAMARIA, JEHU and his forces slaughtered forty-two relatives of King AHAZIAH of Judah at a nearby pit (2 Kgs 10:12-14). The location is unknown, but often associated with Beit Qad, 3 mi. north of Jenin. The name *Beth-eked* can be translated as "house of binding," "house of shearing" (KJV), or "house of meeting" (Targum).

SUSANNA W. SOUTHARD

BETHEL, DEITY beth'uhl [בֵּית־אֵל beth 'el]. A West Semitic deity attested first in 7th cent. BCE treaty texts, mentioning the god Bayt'il with 'Anat-Bayt'il (SAA II, text 5, col. Iv, line 6; text 6, line 467), a consort or hypostasis of Bayt-'il. The god appears in Elephantine documents and as a divine element in numerous names from the 7th cent. onward: "Bethel is my light," "Bethel Has Given," "Bethel is My Shepherd," "Bethel Saved

Me," "Bethel is Mighty," and so on. The Bible attests a theophorous Bethel name in Zech 7:2.

It is likely that Bethel in Jer 48:13 refers to a deity, as its parallelism with CHEMOSH, the Moabite god, suggests. Less compelling are proposals to identify the deity in Gen 31:13; 35:7; Amos 3:4; 5:5; and Hos 4:14; 10:15.

The origin of the name is uncertain. It is perhaps abbreviated from the longer 'el beth 'el "god of the divine sanctuary" (Gen 35:7). Bethel worship seems to have generated mythologies about the deity's origins. Thus, the *Phoenician History* of Sanchuniathon, as told by Philo of Byblos (116–64 BCE)—whom Eusebius of Caesarea (ca. 250–340 CE) quotes—suggests that heaven and earth brought forth Baityl and others (*Praep. ev.* 1, 10, 16), later positing that heaven contrived **baitylia** ("enlivened stones"), referring apparently to meteors.

Bibliography: J. P. Hyatt. "The Deity Bethel in the Old Testament." *JAOS* 59 (1939) 81–98; S. Ribichini. "Baetyl." *DDD* (1995) 157–59; W. Röllig. "Bethel." *DDD* (1995) 173–75; K. van der Toorn. "Anat-Yahu, Some Other Deities, and the Jews of Elephantine." *Numen* 39 (1992) 80–101; S. P. Vleeming and J. W. Weselius. "Bethel the Saviour." *JEOL* 28 (1983/84) 110–40.

C. L. SEOW

BETHEL, SHRINE beth'uhl [בֵּית־אֵל beth 'el "house of El/God"]. The name means "house of El/God." The name of two places mentioned in the OT: a town in Benjamin and Ephraim, mentioned more often than any place except Jerusalem, and a town in Judah (1 Sam 30:27, possibly the same as Bethul, Josh 19:4; and Bethuel, 1 Chr 4:30), exact location unknown. This article concerns the first Bethel.

A. Name and Location
B. Archaeology
C. References to Bethel in the Biblical Period
  1. Early Israel
    a. Cult sites
    b. Priestly houses
  2. Davidic Israel
    a. David's dual priesthood
    b. The Davidic history of early Israel (J)
    c. Solomon and the supremacy of the
      Aaronids
  3. Conflicts of the Israelite monarchies
    a. Jeroboam I and the cults of Bethel and
      Dan
    b. The Israelite history of Israel (E)
    c. Bethel rites and the tithe
    d. The golden calf (Exod 32) and Bethel
  4. The house of David under Assyrian and
    Babylonian control
    a. Hezekiah's reform
    b. Bethel in the Deuteronomistic History

A. Name and Location

In origin the name probably designated a shrine of the Canaanite patriarchal deity El. In the OT, El is nearly always a generic designation for Yahweh, making Bethel nothing less than "the temple of God." Bethel is said to have been named *Luz* before being renamed by Jacob (Gen 28:19; 35:6 and elsewhere). It was also named El-bethel, "God of Bethel" (Gen 35:7), and was sometimes referred to as beth ʾawen, "house of evil," a derogatory pun (e.g., Josh 7:2; 1 Sam 13:5; Hos 4:15; *see also* Amos 5:5, BETH-AVEN).

Bethel was located on the main ridge road between Hebron and Shechem, about 10 mi. north of Jerusalem and near the border between the tribal territories of Benjamin and Ephraim as described in Joshua. Its long-standing importance stemmed from its relative altitude, abundance of nearby springs, proximity to north-south and east-west crossroads in central Palestine, and position between the Judean plateau to the south and the Ephraimite hills to the north. As a frontier town, Bethel is said in one place to belong to Benjamin (Josh 18:22) and in another to Ephraim (Judg 1:22). It appears to have changed hands under the kings of Israel and Judah—taken from Israel by Abijah (2 Chr 13:19) and returned to Israel by Baasha (1 Kgs 15:17).

B. Archaeology

The identification of Bethel with the village Beitin in 1838 was among the earliest archaeological identifications in modern times. Further excavations in 1934, 1954, 1957, and 1960, indicate that ancient Bethel was a nearly continuous settlement, marked by occasional destruction, from at least the Middle Bronze Age to the Byzantine period. In the Early Iron Age, four distinct settlement phases have been detected, separated by destruction layers most recently dated approximately to 1175, 1100, and 1050 BCE. Each phase exhibits a poorer culture than its predecessor, until the last. Bethel survived a spate of destruction that swept its neighborhood about 1000 BCE. The reason for this destruction and Bethel's survival is unknown. Debate continues over whether Bethel may have been abandoned during the late 6th cent. and early 5th cent. BCE; however, the resurgence of Benjamin in the early Persian period included the renewal of Bethel (Zech 7:2; Ezra 2:28; Neh 7:32; 11:31), which flourished until the Muslim invasion in the 6th cent. CE.

The excavators of Bethel believed its archaeology confirmed the biblical description of the conquest of Canaan: a wealthy Late Bronze Age Canaanite city was destroyed and at once resettled by poorer Israelites. However, the Bible mentions no such destruction (Judg 1:22-25), and so far no other excavated site in Palestine has shown the same sequence. Thus the initial interpretation of the first phase of Iron I settlement at Bethel has generally been discarded.

C. References to Bethel in the Biblical Period

1. Early Israel

a. Cult sites. Bethel never stood alone among the cult shrines of Israel, and its relationship with other cult sites was important for its treatment in the Bible. These included Shiloh (10 mi. north of Bethel), Gilgal (somewhere not far below Bethel, but contrast 2 Kgs 2:1-2), Shechem (in the early Israelite heartland), and Dan and Beersheba (near northern and southern limits of Israelite settlement). At each shrine, resident priests served as guardians and officiated at rites, which included sacrifice, libation, incubation, votive offering, intermediation, and adjudication. Each shrine probably served also as a depository for produce and valuables.

b. Priestly houses. Several early Israelite priests had Egyptian names, including Moses and Aaron. They were the eponymous ancestors of the two main priestly houses during the OT period, the Mushids and Aaronids. Research indicates that early on Mushids controlled Shiloh, Dan, and possibly Gilgal, and Aaronids probably Bethel and Hebron and possibly Beersheba. Whether the ostensible division between north and south predated the reign of Solomon, when the Aaronids became dominant in Jerusalem, is uncertain. Throughout the biblical period, the houses were at times in conflict with each other—and probably within each as well, despite the lack of clear evidence.

Shiloh was destroyed around 1050 BCE but retained influence. Sanction for the first four Israelite dynasties, by Samuel and Ahijah, came from Shiloh. Its relocated priesthood, however, came under pressure from Saul. Saul established an Israelite monarchy centered in Benjamin, which, with Shiloh's absence, gave Bethel a new primacy. Samuel's circuit included Bethel and Gilgal.

2. Davidic Israel

a. David's dual priesthood. David usurped the house of Saul and made Jerusalem a new Israelite cult center. There David established a dual Mushid and Aaronid priesthood. The Mushid priest Abiathar, descended from Shiloh, represented tribal Israel, whose palladium, the ark, David took over; the Aaronid priest Zadok, brought from Hebron rather than Bethel, represented David's household and its Judahite ties.

b. The Davidic history of early Israel (J). The date of J is uncertain, but it probably originated during the short time the house of David ruled all Israel because of the following characteristics: the Yahwistic narratives reflect the standpoint of the house of David; they focus on the idea of tribal Israel; the texts share similarities with 1–2 Samuel; the Yahwistic texts treat Egypt as the arch threat, and the texts function to authenticate Bethel. J's main features affirm both the Mushids and the Aaronids. The Mushid founder, Moses, heads delivered Israel. Shiloh, however, does not appear; Bethel, probably Aaronid, is presented as the geographical and cult center of early Israel. The Davidic monarchy was happy to confirm Bethel as a new center of Israel, farther south than Shechem or Shiloh. In J, both Abram and Jacob (Israel) are founders of Bethel.

Bethel marks the center of God's land grant to Abram and Israel, as well as the shrine founded by the eponymous ancestor to verify the grant. When Abram first arrives in Canaan, he erects two altars to Yahweh (Gen 12:7-8). The first is at Shechem, where Yahweh announces, "To your descendants I will grant this land." Shechem later becomes the burial place of Joseph, the father of Ephraim and Manasseh. The second altar is near Bethel. There Abram invokes Yahweh as his land-granting patron. After a journey to Egypt foreshadowing Israel's later delivery (Gen 12:10-20), Abram returns to the altar near Bethel and again invokes Yahweh. Yahweh reappears to confirm the land grant and to define it with this altar as its center: "Look from here in all directions—all the land you see I will grant to you and your descendants forever" (Gen 13:3-17). Abram's shrine is said to be not at Bethel but nearby, between Bethel and Ai (Gen 12:8; 13:3-4). Abram is not the founder of Bethel itself. That honor belongs to Jacob, the father of all Israel. Fleeing Esau, Jacob finds himself at "the place/shrine" (Gen 28:11; NRSV, "a certain place"). As he is just about to fall asleep, Yahweh appears and repeats the land grant: "The land you are lying on I will grant to you and your descendants." Jacob recognizes what neither he nor anyone else had hitherto known, that Yahweh is also "at this place," not just Abram's nearby altar (28:16). Hence he renames the site "the house of God" and builds an altar there, reestablishing the cultic and cosmic center of the territorial dominion of tribal Israel under Israel's god Yahweh—now resident in Jerusalem. *See* J, YAHWIST.

c. Solomon and the supremacy of the Aaronids. Solomon succeeded David in what was partly an Aaronid coup. The Mushid faction headed by Abiathar was ejected, and the Aaronid faction headed by Zadok became henceforth the priesthood of the house of David in Jerusalem. (The tradition of Aaron did not become a part of the Davidic history of early Israel until much later, through the P strand; *see* P, Priestly.)

3. Conflicts of the Israelite monarchies
a. Jeroboam I and the cults of Bethel and Dan. The house of David was usurped by Jeroboam I, backed by a prophet from Shiloh, but survived as a rump kingdom. In reconstituting the kingdom of Israel, Jeroboam reestablished Dan and Bethel as border cults at the northern and southern extremities of his territory. Many argue that he created his own dual priesthood, Mushids at Dan (Judg 18:30-31) and Aaronids at Bethel (*see* Judg 20:26-28). Others interpret the expression

in 1 Kgs 12:31—he "appointed priests from among all the people [compare 2 Kgs 17:32], who were not Levites"—to mean that he appointed a new priesthood unrelated to the traditional priestly families, excluding Aaronids from Bethel, perhaps because Aaronids had become the sole priesthood of the house of David.

b. The Israelite history of Israel (E). The E strand, which may go back as early as Jeroboam, reflects a non-Davidic Israelite standpoint. Even more than J, E highlights the role of Moses. E underscores the importance of multiple cult sites (at least nine) but places greatest emphasis on Bethel and Horeb. This matches J's emphasis on Bethel and Sinai, but now with a marked anti-Davidic implication. *See* E, ELOHIST.

c. Bethel rites and the tithe. In J, Jacob stops at Bethel on his way to Haran. In E, Jacob stops at Bethel both on his way to Haran and on his way back (Gen 35:1-8), framing the birth of the sons of Israel who will inherit the land centered there. In E, the temple character of the site is enlarged (Gen 28:11-22): God appears to Jacob in a dream positioned above a palatial stairway (NRSV note), on which court servants ascend and descend. The cultic themes of E are epitomized in E's additions to J's account of the founding of Bethel. These include incubation, a vow, and erecting a standing stone and anointing it with oil.

The tithe vowed by Jacob at Bethel (compare Amos 4:4) was more than a religious contribution. In the time of the Israelite monarchies, Bethel was a monarchic shrine (compare Amos 7:13), and its tithe was a tax in kind. A small portion of the tax went toward the upkeep of the shrine. Much the greater part was added to the monarchic store of commodities for provisioning workers impressed for agriculture and building projects, and for export in return for metallic wealth, military materiel, and luxury goods. In a monarchic context, the tithe belonged to the "ways of the king" described by Samuel (1 Sam 8:15-18). *See* TITHE.

d. The golden calf (Exod 32) and Bethel. The identity of the monarchic priesthood of Bethel, though uncertain, bears on the interpretation of the story of Aaron and the calf made from golden earrings in Exod 32. This story shares language with the Deuteronomistic account of Jeroboam's refounding of Dan and Bethel—"these are your gods . . ." (Exod 32:4, 8; 1 Kgs 12:28)—linking Aaron with Jeroboam and showing a disapproval of both. This disapproval is amplified by E's story of Jacob's return to Bethel: Jacob ordered his people to purify themselves by removing their earrings before arriving at Bethel (Gen 35:1-7). If under Jeroboam I or his successors the priests of Bethel were Aaronids, then the story of Aaron and his calf was a critique of the Bethel cult. The story might have originated, as some have thought, in Jerusalem, whose polemic against Bethel is evident in several places in the Prophets. Others find this unlikely: why would Aaronids in Jerusalem denigrate their founder, even if he was connected with Bethel? Perhaps, therefore, the story is non-Davidic, and indeed a part of E. In this view, E is traced to Mushids descended from Shiloh, and the story of the calf is seen as an attack against either the Aaronids of Bethel or Jeroboam's nouveau priests of Bethel. However, since it is more likely that E was written for rather than against Jeroboam, perhaps the story, which otherwise does not show an E coloring, comes from a non-Aaronid Jerusalemite source, namely the Mushid priests of Josiah's reform who traced their heritage to Shiloh. See GOLDEN CALF.

4. The house of David under Assyrian and Babylonian control

a. Hezekiah's reform. When Samaria, the Israelite monarchic capital, fell to the Assyrians, the succession of non-Davidic dynasties came to an end. According to 2 Kgs 17:24-28, the cult of Bethel resumed with Assyrian support, an indication that despite two centuries of monarchic control the cult still played a popular role. (The story that the cult was restarted to relieve a plague of lions has an ironic connection with 1 Kgs 13.)

Hezekiah formed an anti-Assyrian alliance and launched a reform that made Jerusalem the sole cult center of a newly constituted Israel throughout the territory once ruled by David. Despite the Aaronid ascendancy in Jerusalem, Hezekiah's legitimating history of Davidic sovereignty over a unified Israel, the forerunner of the Deuteronomistic History, continued the Davidic tradition of crediting Moses with the revelation of divine law, and it placed the ark originally in Shiloh. Hezekiah took in Mushid Levites but jettisoned Moses' bronze serpent from the Temple. See HEZEKIAH. Hezekiah's rebellion and reform failed. However, Jerusalem survived the Assyrian siege of 701 BCE, and for the next century hostility to Bethel was a stock corollary of Davidic acclaim for Jerusalem. This hostility is evident in both the Former and Latter Prophets.

b. Bethel in the Deuteronomistic History. Josiah's reform in 622 BCE apparently owed much to a priestly family with ties through Anathoth to the old Mushids of Shiloh. See DEUTERONOMISTIC REFORM; JOSIAH. The Deuteronomistic History acquired its present form mainly in support of Josiah's reform. See DEUTERONOMISTIC HISTORY. Jerusalem opposition to Bethel, whose reinstated altar epitomizes the secession of Israel from Jerusalem, is axiomatic for Josiah's history. At the moment Jeroboam inaugurates the altar at Bethel, a "man of God" from Judah arrives to announce that a Davidic son was to appear, named Josiah, who would desecrate the altar, a prediction sealed when the altar is torn down in Jeroboam's presence (1 Kgs 12:33–13:5). The history reaches its climax centuries later, when Josiah tears down the high place and altar at Bethel and crushes them to dust, just as Moses, according to the same history, did to the golden calf (2 Kgs 23:15;

Deut 9:21), and desecrates what is left of the altar (2 Kgs 23:16-18).

The opposition of Jerusalem and Bethel is prefigured in Judg 1, the Deuteronomistic summary of Israel's failure to complete the conquest of Canaan. There the success of Judah is framed by references to Jerusalem (vv. 4-8, 21). The failure of the rest of Israel is framed by references to Bethel and Dan (vv. 22-26, 34) and capped by a story (Judg 2:1-5) in which a messenger of Yahweh from Gilgal appears to "all Israel" at Bochim ("weepers") and faults them for failing to "tear down their altars." At this the people weep, giving the place its appellation. Bochim was probably Bethel, as indicated by the LXX of Judg 2:1 and par. in Judg 20:23, 26; 21:2 (also Gen 35:8; Hos 12:4). See BOCHIM.

References to Bethel in 2 Kgs 2:2 and 2:23-24 do not involve a contrast with Jerusalem, since they belong to a source used by the Deuteronomistic History uninterested in this contrast. The contrast is, however, implied in an insertion made by the Deuteronomistic historian into the same source: 2 Kgs 10:29.

c. Bethel in the Latter Prophets. In Hos 4:15, Yahweh forbids pilgrimages to Beth-Awen. The significance of Bethel in Hos 5:8 ("shout in Beth-Awen")—part of a passage with many obscurities—is unclear. It belongs, though, to a larger passage that climaxes with a theophany (6:3-6) in which Yahweh persists in rebuking Israelites for substituting rites for rights. Here a theophany associated with Bethel (and other sites) replicates not only Yahweh's original appearance to Jacob/Israel at Bethel, but also especially the Deuteronomistic motif of weeping in repentance at Bethel.

The opposition of Jerusalem and Bethel is fundamental to the book of Amos. Its exordium declares, "Yahweh roars from Zion and shouts aloud from Zion" (1:2). Yahweh "roars" his denunciation of the cult of Bethel (4:4; 5:4-5). These decrees belong to a set of oracles that climax, as in Hosea, with the assertion that Yahweh demands justice before ceremony. The prophet Amos arrives in the Israelite royal sanctuary at Bethel, where he receives five visions and denounces the cult (7:1–9:1). Outraged, the priest of Bethel silences him. Ironically, the priest's order for Amos to leave Bethel precipitates the vision of the end (7:10–8:3). The end arrives when Yahweh appears next to the altar at Bethel, to destroy the shrine and annihilate its devotees (9:1-6), in favor of the house of David (9:11).

5. The Persian Period

Josiah's reform failed and the Aaronids of Jerusalem reasserted themselves. The Aaronids are featured in P, whose incorporation into the Hexateuch forms its last major revision. Bethel plays only a minor role in P (compare Gen 35:9-15). Not surprisingly, Bethel does not figure at all in the central P account of the tabernacle and its rites. By the Persian Period, Bethel had ceased to play a significant cultic role.

D. Allusion to the Name Bethel in John 1

The name Bethel does not occur in the NT. However, it is alluded to in John 1:51, where Jesus is symbolically identified, through reference to Gen 28:12, as "Bethel," i.e., the true "house of God" in place of the Temple, a motif developed later in the Gospel.

ROBERT COOTE

BETH-EMEK beth-ee'mik [בֵּית הָעֵמֶק beth ha'emeq]. Town northeast of ACCO in the northern part of the land that Joshua allotted to the ASHER tribe.

BETHER bee'thuhr [בֶּתֶר bether; Βαιθηρ Baithēr]. Bether, a town in the hill country of Judea about seven mi. southwest of Jerusalem, was included in a list of cities allotted to Judah (Josh 15:59 LXX; MT omits the list due to a scribal error). Song of Songs 2:17 mentions "the hills of Bether" (KJV, translated "cleft mountains" in NRSV). Bether is the place where Bar-Kokhba and his forces made their ill-fated last stand against the Romans ending the Second Jewish Revolt (132–35 CE). The remains of the fortress, at a site known today as Khirbet el-Yahudi located near the modern town of Bittar, can still be seen, surrounded on three sides by a steep canyon and on the fourth by a deep moat.

JOSEPH L. TRAFTON

BETHESDA buh-thez'duh [Βηθεσδά Bēthesda]. "Sheep Pools," "The House of Lovingkindness." In Jerusalem at the end of the second Temple period, located north of the Temple compound, this pair of large pools with five colonnades is probably the Probatica mentioned in John 5:2 and in the Copper Scroll (Column 11, line 57, there called Beit Eshdatain, probably "The House of Spontaneous Shaking.") This word, used very rarely in Jewish sources, is used in the Aram. translation (Targum) on Isa 7:2, "And his heart was moved, and the heart of his people, as the trees of the forest *are moved* with the wind." Excavations have revealed that a health rite took place there during the Roman period. The lower of the two pools was probably used for washing sheep, which were then sold for sacrifices at the nearby Temple. Bethesda continues to survive as a symbol of healing to this day, most notably, in a fountain in Central Park, New York City, where the angel of Bethesda is placed above the fountain in its center. *See* HEALING; JERUSALEM; WATER.

JUDITH Z. ABRAMS

BETH-EZEL beth-ee'zuhl [בֵּית הָאֵצֶל beth ha'etsel]. A town in the SHEFELAH whose name means "House of Withholding" and forms a pun on the verb "shall remove/withhold" (Mic 1:11).

BETH GADER beth-gay'duhr [בֵּית־גָּדֵר beth gadher]. Town, "house of the wall," founded by HAREPH (1 Chr 2:51). Its specific location in Judah is unknown. *See* GEDER.

BETH-GAMUL beth-gay'muhl [בֵּית־גָּמוּל beth gamul]. A town in the tableland of Moab (Jer 48:21, 22-24), probably located east of Dibon and possibly the same as Umm el-Jamal or Jemeil.

BETH-GILGAL beth-gil'gal [בֵּית הַגִּלְגָּל beth haggilgal]. Town whose precise site is unknown. According to Neh 12:29, it was located near Jerusalem. Some Levite singers lived there.

BETH-HACCHEREM beth-hak'uh-rem [בֵּית הַכָּרֶם beth hakkarem]. Beth-Haccherem, meaning "the place of the vineyard," is mentioned in Jer 6:1 as the location of a fire beacon. Later it appears as one of five districts, or district capitals, of the province of Judah, ruled by MALCHIJAH, son of Rechab, during the Persian Period (Neh 3:14).

Both 3QInv (3Q15) and 1QapGen mention a Beth-haccherem in conjunction with the King's Valley, the location of Absalom's tomb (2 Sam 18:18). Some scholars have proposed that Καρεμ (Karem), a LXX addition to the list in Josh 15:59, may be Beth-haccherem.

Some have suggested that 'Ain Karim, approximately 6.5 km west of Jerusalem, preserved the name of the ancient site. The most recent proposal for Beth-haccherem is Ramat Rahel, approximately 4 km south of Jerusalem, a location ideal for a fire signal station and easily harmonized with the ancient sources.

RANDALL W. YOUNKER

BETH-HAGGAN beth-hag'uhn [בֵּית הַגָּן beth haggān]. "House of the garden." Town toward which Jehu pursued King Aziah (2 Kgs 9:27). Located in Issachar's territory but allotted to the Levites. Same as EN GANNIM (Josh 19:2; 21:29) and modern Jenin.

BETH-HARAM beth-hair'uhm [בֵּית הָרָם beth haram, בֵּית הָרָן beth haran; Βαιθαραμ Baitharam, Βαιθαραν Baitharan)]. A GADITE town in the Rift Valley east of the JORDAN RIVER, northeast of the DEAD SEA (Num 32:36; Josh 13:27). When captured by ALEXANDER JANNAEUS in the early 1st cent. BCE, it was known by its Aram. variant, Bethramtha. Josephus reports (*Ant.* 18:26.8) HEROD ANTIPAS fortified the city with a wall and changed its name to Julias in honor of the wife of Augustus, Livia Drusa/Drusilla. The name *Livias* gained currency in contemporary writings, although Eusebius notes (*Onom.* 219/48:13) the locals still called it by its Aram. name.

KENT BRAMLETT

BETH-HARAN. *See* BETH-HARAM.

BETH-HOGLAH beth-hog'luh [בֵּית חָגְלָה beth khoglah]. "Partridge house." A town in the territory of BENJAMIN, bordering Judah (Josh 15:6; 18:19, 21) and located near a spring west of the Jordan, southeast of

Jericho. Its ruins are visible near the modern village of ʿAin Hajala on the West Bank.

BETH-HORON beth-horʹuhn [בֵּית חוֹרֹן‎ bet khoron]. A Levitical twin city, including Lower Beth-horon and Upper Beth-horon (identified with the modern villages of Beit ʿUr et-Tahta and Beit ʿUr el-Fauqa, respectively), assigned in Josh 21:22 and 1 Chr 6:68 [Heb. 6:53] to Ephraim on its border with Benjamin (Josh 16:3, 5; 18:13-14). The Chronicler says Beth-horon was built by SHEERAH, the daughter of Beriah, a son of Ephraim (1 Chr 7:24).

Its strategic location in the western hill country in the valley of AIJALON, along the major route from the coastal plain through the hill country and on to JERICHO and RAMMOTH-AMMON, is surely why it is mentioned during the Conquest on "the day the sun stood still" (Josh 10:10-13) and during Saul's battles with the Philistines (1 Sam 13:18). Solomon fortified it (1 Kgs 9:17; 2 Chr 8:5), and during AMAZIAH's reign it was attacked by disgruntled Israelite soldiers (2 Chr 25:13).

Beth-horon plays a predominant role in the Maccabean Revolt (1 Macc 3:16, 24; 7:39) and was subsequently fortified by the Syrian general, BACCHIDES (1 Macc 9:50). In *Jub.* 34:4 the king of Beth-horon is part of a Canaanite coalition that attacks Jacob, and in Jdt 4:4 it is part of the Jewish structure defending Jerusalem against HOLOFERNES.

LAMONTTE M. LUKER

BETH-JESHIMOTH beth-jeshʹuh-moth [בֵּית הַיְשִׁמֹת‎ beth hayshimoth]. One of the final dwelling sites of the Israelites before crossing the JORDAN RIVER into CANAAN. Identified in four verses (Num 33:49; Josh 12:3; 13:20; Ezek 25:9) it is located in the ARABAH on the eastern side of the Jordan River. The text locates Beth-Jeshimoth within the inheritance given to the tribe of REUBEN, but consistently located in what was understood as the territory of MOAB.

MICHAEL OBLATH

BETH-LE-APHRAH bethʹli-afʹruh [בֵּית לְעַפְרָה‎ beth leʿafrah]. A town in the SHEFELAH whose name puns with "dust" (עָפָר‎ ʿafar, Mic 1:10*b*), referring to the custom of lamenting in dust and ashes.

BETH-LEBAOTH bethʹli-bay'oth [בֵּית לְבָאוֹת‎ beth levaʾoth]. "House of lionesses." A town among the allotment to SIMEON in Josh 19:6 and lies within the bounds of Judah's territory in the NEGEV. Joshua 15:32 names this town simply "Lebaoth," while 1 Chr 4:31 seems to refer to it as "BETH-BIRI."

BETHLEHEM bethʹli-hem [בֵּית לֶחֶם‎ beth lekhem; Βηθλεεμ bēthleem]. "House of bread." 1. A city in Judah 10 km south of Jerusalem, located on a spur running east from the watershed. It may be the Bit-Lahmi mentioned in the 14th cent. BCE Amarna Letter, n. 290 as "a town of the land of Jerusalem." The ancient site is on the hilltop east of the Church of the Nativity. Manger Square is a filled-in valley, which originally separated the city from the hill to the west on which the modern town is built. The adjoining valleys are fertile, but quickly give way to the desert where shepherds roam with their flocks.

Prehistoric people first occupied Bethlehem, but it enters our history as the setting for the book of Ruth and as the birthplace of Ruth and Boaz's descendent, David (ca. 1000 BCE). Samuel anointed David king in Bethlehem (1 Sam 16:1-13), and David made his home there (1 Sam 17:12, 15; 20:6, 28). The Philistines put a garrison in Bethlehem (2 Sam 23:14-16; 1 Chr 11:16-18) that remained until David established his capital in Jerusalem. David's grandson Rehoboam fortified Bethlehem (2 Chr 11:6). No traces of the wall have been found, but the excavations have not been complete or systematic.

Bethlehem, though only a small village, became central to the messianic hope as the birthplace of a ruler of Israel (Mic 5:2). Of the inhabitants deported to Babylon in 586 BCE, between one and two hundred returned to Bethlehem in 538 BCE (Neh 7:26; Ezra 2:21).

Joseph and Mary were natives of Bethlehem, where they had a "house," according to Matthew (Matt 2:11). Luke concurs that Jesus was born in Bethlehem, the "city of David" (Luke 2:4-7); thus some scholars argue that the Gospel's attempt to link Jesus to a messianic role by emphasizing that his birthplace is Bethlehem. It is more likely, however, that Jesus' birth in Bethlehem was an embarrassment to the early Christians, because he did not act like a Davidic Messiah. According to the 1st cent. BCE, *Psalms of Solomon*, the Davidic Messiah would expel foreigners (e.g., the Romans) and brutally purify the Jewish people of sinners (*Ps. Sol.* 17). Jesus' complete lack of a political agenda of this nature makes the invention of Bethlehem as his birthplace rather improbable.

Justin (*Dial.* 78) and Origen (*Cel.* 1.51) in the 2nd and 3rd cent. each report that they saw a cave described as Jesus' birthplace. The silence of the Gospels on this point betrays a strong local tradition, which did not waver even when the cave was taken over by a pagan cult not long after 135 CE and thus became inaccessible for 180 years (Jerome, Letter 58). Many houses in the area still use adjacent caves for stables and storage. The cave complex beneath the Church of the Nativity was in the northwest corner of ancient Bethlehem, and excavations have revealed evidence of use in the 1st cent. BCE and CE.

The empress Helena ordered the construction of the first church (Eusebius, *Vit. Const.* 3.43), in 339 CE. An octagon was built above the cave, which could be seen through a large circular hole in the floor. Architecturally it served as a pilgrimage shrine, in a similar manner as the rotunda erected above and around the tomb of Christ. Another similarity to the Holy Sepulchre was the five-aisle basilica to the west with an atrium. St. Jerome produced most of his extraordinary output of biblical interpretation in a monastery on the north side of the church between 385 and 420.

Todd Bolen/Bible Places

Figure 1: Church of Nativity, Cave of Birth.

This complex was destroyed in the Samaritan uprising of 529. In his rebuilding Justinian (527–65) replaced the octagon with a triapsidal sanctuary and enlarged the basilica by one bay and a narthex. This edifice survives to the present day. It escaped destruction by the Persians in 614, because they found on the facade a mosaic of the MAGI in dress that was familiar to them.

2. A town in Zebulun (Josh 19:15; Judg 12:8-10).

3. A town in Ephraim where Ibzan, a judge of Israel, lived (Judg 12:8, 10).

4. A descendant of Caleb (1 Chr 2:51, 54; 4:4). *See* DAVID; JEROME; MESSIAH.

JEROME MURPHY-O'CONNOR

BETH-LOMON beth-loh´muhn [βαιθλωμων Baith-lōmōn]. Ancestor of 123 descendants who returned to Jerusalem and Judea when CYRUS ended the Babylonian EXILE (1 Esd 5:17).

BETH-MAACAH beth-may´uh-kuh [בֵּית מַעֲכָה beth ma'akhah]. A clan or territory that later became part of the town name ABEL OF BETH-MAACAH (2 Sam 20:14-15). (*See* ABEL-BETH-MAACAH.)

BETH-MARCABOTH beth-mahr´kuh-both [הַמַּרְכָּבוֹת בֵּית beth hammarkavoth]. A town in the tribal allotment for SIMEON (Josh 19:5) in the south central area of Judah, it is also listed as one of the towns inhabited by the families of SHIMEI and his brothers, sons of MISHMA and grandsons of Simeon (1 Chr 4:31).

BETH-MEON beth-mee´on [בֵּית מְעוֹן beth me'on]. A town in Moab located east of the Jordan (Jer 48:23) and mentioned on the Moabite Stone. Usually called BAAL-MEON.

BETH-MILLO beth-mil´oh [בֵּית מִלּוֹא beth millo']. An administrative center and residence of the king for Shechem (Judg 9:6, 20) and Jerusalem (2 Kgs 12:21).

BETH-NIMRAH, NIMRAH beth-nim´ruh, nim´ruh [בֵּת־נִמְרָה]. "House of leopard." A city in the eastern Jordan Valley, conquered from Sihon, given to the tribe of Gad and built by them (Num 32:3, 36; Josh 13:27). Mentioned as a living place by Josephus (Βηθεvvαμρις Bēthennamris), Eusebius, and Jerome (Βηθvαμαρις, Bēthnamaris) as well as rabbinical sources (e.g., נמרן nmrn). Both Eusebius and the rabbis noted the change from biblical Nimrah to contemporary Nimrin.

The site is identified with Tall Nimrin, 16 km northeast of Jericho. According to excavations during the 1990s, contrary to an earlier survey, the site was occupied continuously from aproximately 2000 BCE to the present. *See* LEOPARD; NIMRIM, THE WATERS OF.

Bibliography: Burton MacDonald. *East of the Jordan: Territories and Sites of the Hebrew Scriptures* (2000) 114–15.

YOEL ELITZUR

BETH-PAZZEZ beth-paz´iz [בֵּית פַּצֵּץ beth patsets]. A town, "House of Shattering," in the territory of the tribe of Issachar, probably east of Mount Tabor (Josh 19:21).

BETH-PELET beth-pee´lit [בֵּית־פָּלֶט beth palet]. Means "house of escape" (or "deliverance"). A town located in southern Judah near Edom and allocated by Joshua to Judah's tribe (Josh 15:27). Also, one of the towns where the returning exiles resettled (Neh 11:26). Possibly located southeast of Beer-sheba. According to Flinders Petrie's excavation, Tell el-Far'ah is the site of Beth Pelet; but the tell is more likely Sharuhen. *See* PALTITE, THE.

BETH-PEOR beth-pee´or [בֵּית פְּעוֹר beth pe'or]. "House of Peor," a Transjordanian site referenced only four times in the OT. The precise location is undetermined, but scholarly suggestions focus on the area NE of PISGAH in the direction of Heshbon. Deuteronomy 3:29 and 4:46 place Israel "in the valley opposite Beth-Peor" prior to entrance into Canaan, while Deut 34:6 locates Beth-Peor "in the land of MOAB" when referencing the burial place of Moses. Joshua 13:15-23 outlines the tribal territory of Reuben, and seems to locate Beth-Peor near the "slopes of Pisgah" (13:20).

JOHN I. LAWLOR

BETHPHAGE beth´fuh-jee [Βηθφαγή Bēthphagē]. A small village outside Jerusalem at the MOUNT OF OLIVES, Bethphage is mentioned in the "triumphal entry" stories (Matthew, Mark, and Luke) when Jesus sends two disciples into a village to find a donkey. The name, Bethphage, probably refers to the Aram. name for a type of fig that never appears to be ripe. According to Mark 11:1-2, Jesus was near the villages of Bethphage and BETHANY when he requested a donkey. Matthew 21:1-2 says he was in Bethphage at the time he sought a donkey and a colt.

The exact site of ancient Bethphage is unknown. Examining Mark's story, Bethphage must have been located above the KIDRON VALLEY, just east of Jerusalem. Mark (followed by Luke 19:29) has Jesus coming from Jericho toward Jerusalem and lists Bethphage before Bethany in his story. The ancient road from Jericho to Jerusalem crossed the ridge between Mount Scopus and the Mount of Olives. Thus some have suggested that the modern village of Abu Dis (southeast of Bethany) may have been the location of Bethphage. The ancient site of Bethany is known to be the modern village of el-ʿAzariyeh whose Arabic name still preserves the Greek name Lazarion (the place of LAZARUS). Others have suggested that the modern village of Kefar et-Tur (northwest of Bethany on the Mount of Olives) is nearer to the original site. Neither location has extensive evidence of being an Early Roman village.

Additional clues to Bethphage's location may be found in the Mishnah and early Church Fathers. In the Mishnah the walls of a village called Beth Page are said to be the outer limit of Jerusalem. Pilgrims are described as those visitors who traveled to Jerusalem from beyond the limits of this village. Jerome noted that Paul visited Bethany and Bethphage, and he implied that the villages were located on a hill above Jericho. Epiphanius (8th cent.) believed that Jesus' journey to Jerusalem on the donkey began 1,000 paces from the Church of the Ascension.

The Franciscan Chapel of Bethphage is the modern starting point for the Palm Sunday Procession. A painted stone from the Crusader period found in 1877 was believed to be the stone used by Jesus to mount the donkey. The stone is enshrined in a chapel built in 1883 on the site of the discovery, whose location most closely agrees with the description of Epiphanius, a half-mile east of the Mount of Olives.

MILTON MORELAND

BETH-RAPHA beth-raye´afuh [בֵּית רָפָא beth rafaʾ]. Son of ESHTON in Judah's genealogy (1 Chr 4:12), but because of the clear construct form with beth, it may well be the name of a clan or a place.

BETH-REHOB beth-ree´hob [בֵּית־רְחוֹב beth rekhov]. A town or region in Syria north of Dan and south of Hamath, also called "Rehob near Lebo-hamath," the northernmost sojourn of the spies sent by Moses (Num 13:21). Ammonites hired Syrian mercenaries from Beth-rehob and ZOBAH to battle King David (2 Sam 10:6-19). The Syrian King HADADEZER (vv. 16, 19) is called "son of Rehob of Zobah" (2 Sam 8:3, 12). The tribe of Dan captured LAISH "in the valley that belongs to Beth-rehob" (Judg 18:28).

LAMONTTE M. LUKER

BETH-SAIDA beth-say´uh-duh [βηθσαϊδά bēthsaida]. Bethsaida is a regular site of Jesus' ministry. Bethsaida and CHORAZIN share the eschatological condemnation: "Woe to you, Chorazin, woe to you, Bethsaida" (Matt 11:21; Luke 10:13). Bethsaida is the initial objective of Jesus' journey in Mark 6:45, although his boat eventually lands in the region of Gennesaret (6:52). The healing of the blind man in Mark 8:22-26 occurs in Bethsaida, and Luke places the feeding of the 5,000 in Bethsaida (9:10). According to John 1:44, Philip, Andrew, and Peter come from Bethsaida, which is later in John called Bethsaida "in Galilee" (12:21).

Several sites north of the Sea of Galilee might be the biblical Bethsaida, especially et-Tell, el-Araj, and el-Mesadiyeh. Excavations at et-Tell since 1987 suggest to excavators that et-Tell is Bethsaida. This belief rests on the coordination of archaeological finds with Josephus' testimony. Josephus reports that the Tetrarch Philip expanded Bethsaida in size and dignity to the rank of a city (polis), and named it Julias in honor of Julia, the daughter of Augustus (Ant. 18.28). Numismatic evidence, it must be said, proves that Josephus was wrong about the real honoree. Philip honored Livia, the wife of Augustus. Livia took the name Julia Augusta after Augustus' death, often being called simply Julia. The significance of correcting Josephus will be seen below.

Josephus' comment still has value, however, as the lone association in ancient literature between biblical Bethsaida and Philip's city Julias. Josephus' further descriptions of Julias seem to describe et-Tell. Among other comments, Josephus claims that the Jordan flows into the Sea of Galilee only after it passes Julias (J.W. 3.515). Thus, Julias does not sit on the shore of the Sea of Galilee, undermining the possibility that either el-Araj or el-Masadiyeh could be Julias. Both are coastal sites, while et-Tell, 2 mi. north of the Sea of Galilee, east of the Jordan, is more reasonably understood as Julias. If et-Tell is Julias, is et-Tell also the biblical town Bethsaida? The excavators believe it is.

While several factors weaken the association of Julias with the biblical Bethsaida, each objection can be answered. For instance, John 12:21, as was noted, refers to "Bethsaida in Galilee," even though et-Tell is not in 1st cent. CE Galilee. In the 2nd cent., however, Ptolemy Claudius refers to Julias as a part of Galilee (Strabo, Geogr. 5.16.4). It is possible that the Fourth Gospel, the latest of the canonical Gospels, reflects a similar understanding that places Bethsaida in Galilee.

Or, there were two Bethsaidas: one at et-Tell; and a "Bethsaida in Galilee" at el-Araj. Additionally, the evangelists never call Bethsaida by the name of Julias, suggesting that the biblical Bethsaida is not Julias. Such an objection rests on the belief, however, that Philip renamed Bethsaida to honor Augustus' daughter Julia. She was banned in 2 CE, so any honor accorded to her must have been earlier than that year. As noted above, however, another Julia was honored in the renaming, and the change reasonably happened in around 30 CE. The excavators suppose that this date is a legitimate approximation of the date of Jesus' death. Throughout Jesus' life, therefore, the town was Bethsaida, and the Gospels reflect this fact. Moreover, the later Gospels recognize that Bethsaida was a polis (Luke 9:10; John 1:44), and no longer a village (kōmē), as at Mark 8:23, 26. This distinction implies basic awareness of the change in civic status under Philip. To some, if Bethsaida means "house of the fisher," it must lie on the sea. Bethsaida could, however, be translated "house of the hunter." On the other hand, et-Tell contains fishing implements.

Certain manuscripts (B, Ψ, W) record the site in John 5:2 as Bethsaida. Scholars reject this evidence, however, favoring either Beth-zatha or Bethesda as the correct reading.

Bibliography: Rami Arav and Richard Freund. *Bethsaida, A City by the Shore of the Sea of Galilee.* 3 vols. (1995–2004); Heinz-Wolfgang Kuhn and Rami Arav. "The Bethsaida Excavations: Historical and Archaeological Approaches." *The Future of Early Christianity: Essays in Honor of Helmut Koester.* Birger A. Pearson, ed. (1991) 77–106; Bargil Pixner. "Searching for the New Testament Site of Bethsaida." *BA* 48 (1985) 207–16.

GEORGE L. PARSENIOS

BETH-SHAN beth-shan´ [בֵּית שְׁאָן beth she'an]. Beth-shan, the "house of rest," lies 15 mi. south of the Sea of Galilee in the fertile Beth-shan Valley. The site is situated along an ancient international road system that connects Transjordan with the Mediterranean Sea at the strategic crossroads where the Jordan and Jezreel valleys meet. In the OT, Beth-shan is located on Tell el-Husn ("the mound of the fortress"), a 10-acre mound on the southern bank of the Harod River. During the later Hellenistic, Roman, and Byzantine periods, Beth-shan was renamed Nysa Scythopolis (*see* SCYTHOPOLIS) and expanded into the valley beyond Tell el-Husn's boundaries reaching a maximum size of 320 acres. Following the Arab conquest of Scythopolis in 636 CE, its inhabitants renamed the site Beisan and thus preserved its original ancient Semitic name.

Excavations on the tel revealed eighteen levels of occupation dating from prehistoric through early Islamic periods, the largest group of Egyptian New Kingdom monuments ever discovered in the Land of

Todd Bolen/Bible Places

Figure 1: Aerial view from southeast showing Tell el-Husn to the right and Scythopolis to the left.

Israel, and sections of the 11th and 10th cent. BCE city contemporary with the period of the united monarchy of Saul, David, and Solomon.

1. Pre-Israelite Beth-shan

Fifth and 4th millennia BCE prehistoric remains dating to the Neolithic and Chalcolithic periods were recovered from the lowest levels of the tel. The earliest city at Beth-shan was established by the end of the 4th millennium. An impressive public structure that probably served as a central storage facility discovered on the tel parallels similar developments at other sites in the region and provides evidence for the rise of urban society at this time in the Beth-shan Valley.

Following several centuries when the mound was unoccupied, an unfortified town was reestablished in the 17th cent. BCE. The site played an important role during the 14th–mid-12th cent. BCE when Beth-shan became a major New Kingdom Egyptian stronghold. The earliest historical sources mentioning Beth-shan date to this period of Egyptian imperial rule in Canaan. The site is recorded in Thutmoses III's list of Canaanite cities appearing in the Temple of Amon at Karnak and is mentioned once in the 14th cent. BCE Amarna Letters. During the 19th Dynasty, Beth-shan is included in the topographical lists of Seti I and Ramesses II and in Papyrus Anastasi I from the time of Ramesses II. Archaeological remains from Levels IX–VI (Lower), dating to the 15th–mid-12th cent. BCE, are contemporary with these texts. Excavations have uncovered temples, governors' residencies, and a residential area for soldiers and Egyptian officials stationed at the site. Finds that attest to Egyptian presence at the site include three basalt stelae dating to the reigns of Seti I and Ramesses II, a larger than life-size statue of Ramesses III, and a rich assemblage of Egyptian-style pottery produced at the site. The text on one of the stelae, erected during the reign of Seti I, describes a rebellion in the northern Jordan Valley that was quelled by Egyptian forces, specifically mentioning the cities of Pella, Rehov, and Beth-shan among others. A second stela records Egyptian military reprisals against raiders, including the ʿapiru that some scholars have identified as comprising an element of the early Israelites. Most noteworthy are a series of temples constructed near the center of the mound spanning the century preceding the appearance of the Israelites. This area continued to be used as a sacred area well into the 11th cent. BCE.

In a cemetery to the north of the mound, fragments of more than fifty anthropoid clay coffins were recovered. These coffins are contemporary with the 19th and early 20th Dynasty Egyptian settlement of Levels VII–VI (Lower). Although initially associated with the Philistines due to the appearance of a decorative motif in clay resembling a feathered headdress applied to three of the coffin lids, the discovery of additional coffins at other New Kingdom Egyptian strongholds

Todd Bolen/Bible Places
Figure 2: Egyptian residence, Building 1500

in Canaan and similar burial customs in Egypt prove conclusively that they are a result of Egyptian presence and influence. Excavations on both the mound and the adjacent cemetery, considered together with the textual evidence, provide indisputable evidence that Beth-shan served as an Egyptian garrison site during the period preceding the emergence of biblical Israel.

2. Biblical Beth-shan

In the books of Joshua and Judges, Beth-shan and the surrounding towns are described as belonging to the territory of Issachar but were assigned to the tribe of Manasseh, who failed to drive out the Canaanite inhabitants of Beth-shan (Josh 17:11-12; Judg 1:27). The Israelites' lack of success was attributed to the determination of the Canaanites who had "iron chariots" (Josh 17:16). Following the destruction of the last Egyptian settlement at Beth-shan sometime in the mid-12th cent. BCE and coinciding with the period of the Judges, the archaeological remains from Level VI (Upper) indicate an indigenous Canaanite population inhabited the city.

Biblical Beth-shan is best known as the location where the bodies of Saul and his sons were impaled and their armor placed in the temple of Ashtaroth following their defeat by the Philistines during the battle waged on Mount Gilboa (1 Sam 31; 1 Chr 10). The men of Jabesh-Gilead later rescued the bodies and buried them under a tamarisk tree (1 Sam 31:11-13; 2 Sam 21:12). Of special interest are two public buildings found above the Late Bronze Age temples identified as "twin temples." A rich assemblage of multi-tiered pottery cult stands decorated with human figures, animals or snakes, and other cultic vessels found inside these buildings strengthens their identification as temples. It is tempting to associate these two structures, recently reattributed to 11th cent. Level VI (Upper), with "the House of Ashtoreth" (1 Sam 31:10) and "the House of Dagon" (1 Chr 10:10), where the defeated Saul's armor was displayed. However, there is no clear archaeological evidence for this association. Although this event suggests that Beth-shan was under Philistine control, the finds from this period are Canaanite in style, and Level VI (Upper) contains no traces of Philistine material culture. Thus, at best, the biblical account of Saul's defeat at the hands of the Philistines is probably based on a historical event in which the Philistine forces participated in a military campaign in the Beth-shan region but never occupied the site. The 11th cent. town was destroyed by conflagration.

Beth-shan is also mentioned as a city in the fifth district established by King Solomon (1 Kgs 4:12). Excavators have suggested a 10th cent. BCE date to several structures attributed to Level V. In one impressive building located on the southeastern corner of the tel, vessels typical of the 10th cent. were found. The destruction of this structure by a violent conflagration is assigned to Shishak (ca. 918 BCE), a pharaoh of the 22nd Dynasty who conducted a campaign to Israel shortly after Solomon's death. This attribution is based on the appearance of Beth-shan as one of the conquered cities in Shishak's list at Karnak. An additional reference to Beth-shan in 1 Chr 7:29 claims the descendants of Joseph lived in the region. The town remained a thriving center through the 8th cent. BCE when Beth-shan was once again destroyed, apparently as a result of the Assyrian conquest of the northern part of Israel during the reign of Tiglath-Pileser III (732 BCE).

The site was sparsely settled until the Hellenistic period when the city witnessed a population increase with the focus of the site moving off the mound and into the valley. During the Roman and Byzantine periods, a pagan temple and later a church and residential area were constructed on the summit. The mound was sporadically occupied during the Islamic and Crusader periods.

Bibliography: Frances W. James. *The Iron Age at Beth-Shan: A Study of Levels VI–IV* (1966); Frances W. James and Patrick E. McGovern. *The Late Bronze Egyptian Garrison at Beth Shean: A Study of Levels VII and VIII* (1993); Amihai Mazar. "Four Thousand Years of History at Tel Beth-Shean: An Account of the Renewed Excavations." *BA* 60 (1997) 62–76; Eliezer Oren. *The Northern Cemetery of Beth-Shan* (1973).

ANN E. KILLEBREW

BETH-SHEAN. *See* BETH-SHAN.

BETH-SHEARIM. Southern Galilean town, first known as Besara. *See* BURIALS.

BETH-SHEMESH beth-sheh′mish [בֵּית־שֶׁמֶשׁ *beth shemesh*]. "House (shrine) of the sun." 1. City in the NE Shephelah that was located in the Sorek Valley to the west of Jerusalem on the border with Philistia. Joshua 19:41 lists Beth-Shemesh as part of the Danite inheritance and describes the town as one of those located along the Sorek Valley as it comes out of the Judean hill country (Zorah, Eshtaol, and Ir-shemesh = Beth-Shemesh). On the other hand, a Levitical list of cities found in Josh 21:16 includes Beth-Shemesh as part of Judah. It has been traditional for scholars to reconcile this discrepancy by arguing for the identification of Beth-Shemesh with a town called "Har-heres" in Judg 1:35—a town that remained under Canaanite rule and was not occupied by the Danites. However, this resolution is problematic. A comparison of town lists from the LXX and geographical analysis of the area indicates that Har-heres likely refers to the hill country near the Aijalon Valley. The most probable resolution of the discrepancy is that the Levitical town lists in Josh 21 date to the days of Solomon when Judahites began to settle in towns that had originally been part of the Danite inheritance. After the division of the kingdoms, Beth-Shemesh thus remained part of Judah, and it is listed with other areas of Judah as part of Solomon's second administrative district (1 Kgs 4:9).

The site of biblical Beth-Shemesh has been identified with Tell er-Rumeilah near the modern city of Beth-Shemesh. Occupation at the site occurred from the Early Bronze Age IV through the Iron Age II. Archaeological data reveal that Beth-Shemesh was a significant town during the biblical period from the Late Bronze Age through much of the Iron II Age (until ca. 701 BCE). The Late Bronze Age town (Str. IV) was prosperous and revealed signs of literacy as well as a jewelry hoard. The Str. III town (Iron Age I) was an unplanned collection of houses, but there is evidence of widespread settlement with Philistine influence. These data correspond with the biblical picture, where Beth-Shemesh is the first place in Judah that the ARK OF THE COVENANT travels when it is returned from Philistia (*see* 1 Sam 6:9-15).

Excavations revealed that the 10th cent. BCE town was significant and had fortifications. These data confirm the biblical picture that David and Solomon established fortified strongholds along the border, and are also consistent with arguments that Judahites began to settle in Beth-Shemesh during the 10th cent. The town continued to play an important role until 701 BCE when Sennacherib destroyed it. According to 2 Kgs 14:11, this town was the location of Amaziah of Judah's defeat by the Israelite king Jehoash. There is much evidence from the end of the 8th cent. BCE that Beth-Shemesh played a large role in Hezekiah's buildup of the kingdom. In addition to large buildings and a large gate complex, there are many installations that were used for wine and/or olive oil production. Throughout the Iron Age II the town also boasted a huge water cistern system. Of particular note are seal impressions that represent at least seven different officials. The presence of these seal impressions indicates that Beth-Shemesh was an important administrative center for Hezekiah. After Sennacherib's destruction, there was only limited settlement during the 7th and early 6th cent. BCE, and then an occupation gap until the Hellenistic period.

2. Town in Issachar (Josh 19:22) located to the south of the Sea of Galilee near the Jordan River north of Jarmuth and south of Jabneel.

3. Town in Naphtali (Josh 19:38) that Judg 1:33 describes as still occupied by the Canaanites. Also mentioned in the late execration (Egyptian) texts from the Middle Bronze Age.

4. A town in Egypt mentioned in the MT of Jer 43:13, but the LXX of Jer 50:13 has the Greek equivalent of Heliopolis.

Bibliography: S. Bunimovitz and Z. Lederman. "Beth-Shemesh." *NEAEHL* 1 (1993) 249–53; S. Bunimovitz and Z. Lederman. "The Iron Age Fortifications of Tel Beth Shemesh: A 1990–2000 Perspective." *IEJ* 51 (2001) 121–47; B. Mazar. "The Cities of the Territory of Dan." *IEJ* 10 (1960) 65–77; A. F. Rainey and R. S. Notley. *The Sacred Bridge* (2006); A. G. Vaughn. *Theology, History, and Archaeology in the Chronicler's Account of Hezekiah* (1999).

ANDREW C. VAUGHN

BETH-SHITTAH beth-shit´uh [בֵּית הַשִּׁטָּה beth hashittah]. "House of the acacia." This is the town where the Midianites fled after Gideon and the Israelites defeated them (Judg 7:22). Its precise location is unknown, but it was likely across the Jordan from Abel-Meholah and near Tell Sleihat. Sometimes it is identified as the modern-day village of Shutta.

EMILY CHENEY

BETH-TAPPUAH beth-tap´yoo-uh [בֵּית־תַּפּוּחַ beth tappuakh]. Listed with Hebron among the towns of Judah in the central hill country (Josh 15:53), Beth-tappuah likely is, or is very near, the modern village of Taffuh, just west of Hebron in the West Bank. The name means "house of the APPLE," though the translation *apple* is problematic.

BETH-TOGARMAH beth´toh-gahr´muh [בֵּית תּוֹגַרְמָה beth togharmah]. Place equivalent to Togarmah (Ezek 27:14; 38:6). *See* TOGARMAH.

BETHUEL bi-thy*oo*´uhl [בְּתוּאֵל bethu'el]. This name is of uncertain meaning. 1. Bethuel was the son of NAHOR, Abraham's brother (Gen 22:20-23). He was called an Aramean of PADDAN-ARAM (Gen 25:20) and was the father of LABAN and REBEKAH (Gen 24:24; 28:5). His lack of participation in Rebekah's betrothal suggests that he was either dead or incapacitated in some manner.

2. Bethuel the town was located in the south of Judah (1 Chr 4:30). In the par. list of Joshua 19:4, the name appears as BETHUL (בְּתוּל bethul).

FOOK KONG WONG

BETHULIA bi-th*oo*´lee-uh [Βαιτούλια Baitoulia, Βαιτυλουά Baityloua]. The hometown of the book of Judith's namesake and heroine. The location of Bethulia is north of Jerusalem in the Samarian hill country, near Dothan. According to the narrative, it is a strategic hill town at the head of a commanding mountain pass (Jdt 7:12-13). The city is mentioned twenty times in the book of Judith but appears nowhere else in biblical literature. Modern scholarly attempts to identify the city based on archaeological evidence have been in vain. Given the heavily ironic and figurative cadences of the book, the name of the town is likely meant as a play on the Hebrew word for young woman, בְּתוּלָה bethulah, and the town did not in fact exist. Its geographic location on the site of biblical Shechem may also be a means of laying claim to the temple site of the Samaritans, whom the 2nd cent. BCE Palestinian Jews viewed as rivals. *See* JUDITH, BOOK OF.

JUDITH H. NEWMAN

BETH-YERAH. Town located at the southwestern end of the Sea of Galilee and identified with Philoteria and Sennabris. Excavations uncovered a granary, a synagogue, and a Roman bath. The site is known from its association with a type of pottery known as Khirbet Kerak Ware. *See* KERAK WARE, KHIRBET.

BETH-ZAITH beth-zay´ith [Βηθζαίθ Bēthzaith]. Location of BACCHIDES' camp after his withdrawal from Jerusalem during an attempt to suppress the revolt of JUDAS (1 Macc 7:19). It is perhaps modern-day Beit Zeita located north of Jerusalem. *See* ALCIMUS.

BETH-ZATHA beth-zaye´athuh [βηθζαθά bēthzatha]. Reliable manuscripts (א, D) locate Jesus' healing in John 5:2 at Beth-zatha ("house of olives"), a place otherwise unknown. Other manuscripts have BETH-SAIDA, Belzetha, and BETHESDA. *Beth-zatha* and the variant *Belzetha* evoke Jerusalem's Bezetha region. Bethsaida has better manuscript support but represents scribal confusion with the site near the Sea of Galilee. Recent commentators accept Bethesda, poorly attested (but in A), because the Qumran copper scroll (3Q15 11 XII–XIII) mentions a site near the Temple named Beth-esdatayin, in the singular Beth-esda, "house of the flowing." A pool excavated near the Temple has five colonnades, as in John 5:2-9.

GEORGE L. PARSENIOS

BETH-ZECHARIAH beth-zek´uh-ri´uh [Βαιθζαχαρια Baithzacharia]. A location near Jerusalem identified in 1 Macc 6:32-33 as the site of a battle between Judas's army and a large Seleucid force (including 32 elephants), soon after ANTIOCHUS IV's death. Judas' brother Eleazar died when an elephant that he had single-handedly killed collapsed on him (1 Macc 6:43-46). The Jewish fighters fled from this overpowering force, and after some further fighting agreed to a temporary cease-fire.

BRYAN D. BIBB

BETH-ZUR beth-zuhr′ [צוּר בֵּית beth tsur: Βαιθσουρ Baithsour]. A fortress city located 20 mi. south of Jerusalem (2 Macc 11:5) on the road to HEBRON. Its Arabic name is Khirbet et-Tubeiqeh.

Three biblical texts pertaining to the periods of Israel's settlement and early monarchy refer to Beth-zur. Beth-zur was included within Judah's allotment (Josh 15:58). Beth-zur occurs in the genealogy of Caleb (1 Chr 2:45), suggesting that the Calebite clan settled or expanded into the named cities. REHOBOAM fortified Beth-zur and fourteen other cities for the defense of Judah (2 Chr 11:5-12). Some scholars argue that the first and third of these texts reflect administrative or strategic realities of later periods rather than those of the periods within which they have been set by the biblical narrative.

O. R. Sellers' archaeological campaigns have outlined Beth-zur's occupation through the pertinent history. Numismatic evidence attests to a thriving center at Beth-zur during the Hellenistic period. Indeed, 1–2 Maccabees mention Beth-zur frequently within their accounts of the Maccabean wars. Judas Maccabeus successfully defended Beth-zur against Lysias (1 Macc 4:29-35), then garrisoned and fortified it (1 Macc 4:61). A second Seleucid assault at Beth-zur followed (1 Macc 6:31, 49-50), and for a time the site remained under Seleucid control and was refortified by Bacchides (1 Macc 9:52). Finally, Simon recaptured it for Judah (1 Macc 11:65-66; 14:7, 33).

Bibliography: A. Alt. "Judas Gaue unter Josia." *PJ* 21 (1925) 100–16; V. Fritz. "The 'List of Rehoboam's Fortresses' in 2 Chr 11:5-12—A Document from the Time of Josiah." *EI* 15:46–53; N. Na'aman. "Hezekiah's Fortified Cities and the LMLK Stamps." *BASOR* 261 (1986) 5–21; O. R. Sellers. *The Citadel of Beth-zur* (1933); O. R. Sellers, R. W. Funk, J. L. McKenzie, P. Lapp, and N. Lapp. *The 1957 Excavation at Beth-zur* (1968).

WESLEY IRWIN TOEWS

BETOLIO [Βαιτολιω Baitoliō]. The ancestral head of fifty-two who returned with their leaders, wives, children, and servants to Jerusalem after the EXILE (1 Esd 5:21).

BETOMASTHAIM bet′uh-mas-thay′im [Βαιτομασ-θαιμ Baitomasthaim]. A town mentioned twice in the book of Judith (Jdt 4:6; 15:4), although once with the variant spelling BETOMESTHAIM, described as close to BETHULIA in the Samarian hill country. Its residents took part in the culminating attack against the retreating Assyrian army (Jdt 15:4). Neither name appears in other biblical books, and most scholars understand the town as a fictive creation of the author. *See* JUDITH, BOOK OF.

JUDITH H. NEWMAN

BETONIM. bet′uh-nim [בְּטֹנִים betonim]. A city east of the Jordan in the northern part of the allocation to the tribe of GAD (Josh 13:26).

BETRAYAL. To abuse the trust of someone through deceit, subterfuge, cheating, or the changing of one's loyalty from one person to another, such as marital infidelity or other forms of treachery that take advantage of trust.

Several Hebrew and Greek words express this concept. The Hebrew רָמָה ramah can be translated to describe deception in cases that involve deliberately misleading someone through the use of disguise (Gen 29:25; 1 Sam 19:17; 28:12), promising to do something and then not doing so (2 Sam 19:26), deceitful speech in general (Josh 9:22; Prov 26:19), or in the more specific sense of "betrayal"—gaining someone's trust in order to harm that person (1 Chr 12:17).

For the general sense of deceiving or misleading, the NT uses παραλογίζομαι paralogizomai (Col 2:4; Jas 1:22). The more specific and negative idea of a betrayer or traitor who hurts those who have trusted him or her is expressed by the noun προδότης prodotēs (Luke 6:16; Acts 7:52; 2 Tim 3:4). Finally, there is the ambiguous term παραδίδωμι paradidomi, which most often has a neutral meaning of "to hand over" or "to pass on" someone or something to someone else (e.g., Matt 5:25; 11:27; Mark 4:29; 7:13; Luke 1:2; 4:6; John 19:30; Acts 6:14; 14:26; 1 Cor 11:2; Gal 2:20). In the noun form, παράδοσις paradosis, it is, in fact, predominantly positive, meaning "that which is handed on (in writing or speech)," i.e., "tradition" (e.g., Matt 15:2; 1 Cor 11:2; Gal 1:14; 2 Thess 2:15).

Of course, there are numerous biblical passages that do not use this specific vocabulary, but can, nonetheless, be described as stories of betrayal because of what takes place in the action of these stories. CAIN betrays ABEL (Gen 4), JACOB betrays and is betrayed by his uncle LABAN several times (Gen 29–31), DELILAH betrays SAMPSON (Judg 16), DAVID betrays URIAH (2 Sam 11), and ABSALOM betrays David (2 Sam 15), just to name some of the most prominent biblical examples. The most famous biblical example of "betrayal" is, in fact, the most ambiguous in terms of vocabulary, and can only be inferred from context. Except at Luke 6:16, the Gospels always refer to the act of JUDAS ISCARIOT with the verb paradidōmi, only noting that he "handed over" Jesus to the authorities (Matt 10:4, 21; 17:22; 20:18; 24:10; 26:15, 16, 21, 23, 24, 45, 46, 48; 27:3, 4; Mark 3:19; 13:12; 14:10, 11, 18, 21, 41, 42, 44; Luke 21:16; 22:4, 6, 21, 22, 48; John 6:64, 71; 12:4; 13:2, 11, 21; 18:2, 5; 21:20).

But if one "hands over" Jesus to his enemies, who then proceed to have him killed, this does not seem neutral, but an act of betrayal. The Gospels signal this condemning evaluation in several significant ways: they record Jesus as pronouncing a terrible judgment on the one who "hands him over" (Matt 26:24; Mark 14:21; Luke 22:22), they contrast Judas' actions with the love of the anointing woman (Matt 26:6-16; Mark 14:3-11; John 12:1-8) and with the tearful repentance of Peter (Matt 26:75; Mark 14:72; Luke 22:62), and they claim that Judas acted under Satan's influence (Luke 22:3; John 13:27). They also allude to or quote Ps 41:9 in reference to Judas, interpreting his act as equivalent to "lift[ing] his heel against me" (Mark 14:18; John 13:18), which seems to be a sign of disrespect and contempt. Whatever the historical facts, and whatever the subsequent Gnostic interpretation (as in the GOSPEL OF JUDAS), the canonical Gospels present Judas' act as one of betrayal.

KIM PAFFENROTH

BETROTHAL. The legally binding marital stage lasting from the acceptance of a marital relationship until the BRIDE moved into her husband's household. Severance of a betrothal required a CERTIFICATE OF DIVORCE (e.g., Matt 1:18-19). *See* BRIDEGROOM; MARRIAGE.

BEULAH by*oo*ʹluh [בְּעוּלָה be'ulah]. This is a figurative name for Zion representing the future prosperity of JERUSALEM. The name be'ulah, a form of the verb ba'al (בָּעַל) which often means "to marry," occurs in Isa 54:1 and 62:4 and is translated *married* by most English versions. The NIV and KJV probably chose to use "Beulah" in Isa 62:4 because the verse also promises that Jerusalem will be called HEPHZIBAH, which is a proper name in 2 Kgs 21:1 for the mother of MANASSEH. Both titles represent an ancient woman's ideal state—married and able to bear children.

STEVEN D. MASON

BEVELED WORK [מַעֲשֵׂה מוֹרָד ma'aseh moradh]. Literally a "work of descent," used to describe the wreath ornamentation on the ten large, bronze stands built for lavers in the Temple (1 Kgs 7:29). The word morad comes from the Hebrew root ירד yrd, "to go down."

BEWITCH [βασκαίνω baskainō]. To sway toward evil though the eye, magic, or rhetorical arguments. Paul rhetorically writes about his opponents' arguments and magical influence upon the Galatians (Gal 3:1). *See* AMULETS; DIVINATION; ENCHANTER.

BEYOND THE JORDAN [עֵבֶר הַיַּרְדֵּן 'ever hay-yarden]. A general term for the mountain ranges and valleys east of the river Jordan, the fertile hill country of MOAB ranging from the tablelands of Madeba extend-

ing to the ZERED River, southwest of the DEAD SEA (Deut 1:5), with the land of MANASSEH in the north, the land of GAD and the land of REUBEN to the south (Josh 13). *See* BETHABARA; JORDAN RIVER.

CHANNA COHEN STUART

BEYOND THE RIVER [עֵבֶר הַנָּהָר 'ever hannahar]. In the OT, the NILE is called יְאֹר (ye'or), and rivers in Israel are not called nahar. The EUPHRATES, however, is often referred to as "the river" (Gen 31:21) or "the great river" (Deut 1:7). Therefore, the term "beyond the river" takes its reference from the Euphrates and could refer to the area east (1 Kgs 14:15) or west (Ezra 4:10) of the river depending on the location of the speaker. As reflected in Ezra, the term designated a satrapy that included Syria-Palestine during the Persian period.

FOOK KONG WONG

BEZA, THEODORE. French Protestant theologian (1519–1605) who, after his education in France, immigrated to Switzerland (1548), taught Greek in Lausanne and then Geneva, where he became rector of the academy and Calvin's successor. Beza edited five editions of the NT and coedited the Geneva Bible (1588, preface).

BEZAE, CODEX. The Codex Bezae Cantabrigiensis is a bilingual codex written in the 5th cent. CE, obviously by a Latin-speaking scribe. Its origin is still discussed (Egypt, France, southern Italy). The name of the codex is connected with Theodore Beza, who used this manuscript for his critical editons of the NT, and to the University of Cambridge, which obtained it as a gift from Beza in 1581 and is still in possession of it. The verso (left side) is in Greek, depending on a very ancient type of text; it is the most important witness of the so-called "Western Text" and represents the most interesting manuscript of all, because of its peculiar readings. The recto (right side) is in Latin, an independent translation of the Greek and, therefore, representing neither the Vulgate nor the Old Latin tradition.

The codex contains (with several lacunae) the canonical Gospels (in the Western order Matthew, John, Luke, Mark), 3 John 11–15 (in Latin only), and Acts. *See* BEZA, THEODORE; TEXT, NT; VERSIONS, ANCIENT.

Bibliography: David C. Parker. *Codex Bezae: An Early Christian Manuscript and its Text* (1992).

PETER ARZT-GRABNER

BEZAI beeʹzi [בֵּצָי betsay; Βησι Bēsi, Βασσαι Bassai, Βεσι, Besi, Βασου, Basou]. 1. One of those who sealed Ezra's covenant (Neh 10:18).

2. A family group of 323 members (Ezra 2:17; 1 Esd 5:16) or 324 (Neh 7:23) that returned to Judah with Zerubbabel after the exile.

BEZALEL bez´uh-lel [בְּצַלְאֵל betsal'el]. Probably means, "In the shadow of El." 1. Son of URI, a Judahite, a skilled artisan endowed with the spirit of God (Exod 31:2). He and OHOLIAB were responsible for constructing the ARK OF THE COVENANT, the TABERNACLE, and all its furnishings (Exod 31).

2. A son of PAHATH-MOAB (Ezra 10:30), one of the returnees who had to divorce their foreign wives and send away their children.

FOOK KONG WONG

BEZEK bee´zik [בֶּזֶק bezekh]. 1. Saul mustered his troops at Bezek before his successful defense of JABESH-GILEAD from the AMMONITES led by NAHASH (1 Sam 11:8). This Bezek is often identified with Khirbet Ibzek, north of SHECHEM.

2. In Judg 1:4-5, Bezek refers to a place and (1:5-7) to a person, ADONI-BEZEK (master/lord of Bezek), who was defeated, along with the CANAANITES and the PERIZZITES, by the tribes of JUDAH and SIMEON. The Bezek of Judg 1:4-7 is thought to be Khirbet Bezka, north of Jerusalem. There is some argument, however, for the existence of only one Bezek (Khirbet Ibzek).

LINDA S. SCHEARING

BEZER bee´zuhr [בֶּצֶר betser]. The Asherite Zophah's son (1 Chr 7:37). Also a city of refuge in Reubenite territory (Deut 4:43; Josh 20:8), rebuilt by King Mesha. *See* MOABITE STONE.

BIBLE TRANSLATION THEORY. In the last half of the 20th cent., several models for Bible translation emerged, which resulted in a very large number of new BIBLE VERSIONS, especially in English. These models are often arranged on a continuum, from more literal to more dynamic.

1. Literal

The translation is characterized by high dependence upon the (Hebrew, Aramaic, or Greek) source text. Clear examples are the *Authorized Version* and *Die Schrift verdeutscht von Martin Buber gemeinsam mit Franz Rosenzweig*. Other translations that fit this category are the *Revised Standard Version*, *New Revised Standard Version*, and the *New International Version* (NIV), though they are more adequate in terms of the grammar of the target language as well.

The more literal correspondence with ancient forms of speech can bring the reader closer to the source text, at the risk of overemphasizing the foreignness and inherent otherness of the Bible. In the case of the *Authorized Version* this translation approach led to a deep appreciation of English literary qualities. In the German work of Buber and Rosenzweig the consistent translation of key terms prevented a loss of thematic connections in the texts of the Bible. While some scholars are optimistic that this approach to translation can

and should respect the word order in the Hebrew sentence, others caution that maintaining the same word order in the target language may emphasize the wrong word. This approach cannot fully take into account the rules and implications of sentence structure and word order in the target language, which often does not match the language rules of the source text.

2. Dynamic

The translation serves as a substitute for the source text. A clear example is the *Good News Bible*. Dynamic (or "functional") equivalence translations are intended to have the same impact on readers in a target language that the original text produced in the source language. The informational content of the source text has, it is claimed, been re-expressed in forms that are natural—"the closest natural equivalent"—to well-constructed texts in the target language. The naturalness of the target language brings the reader closer to the information and message contained in the source text, but it also risks domesticating the source text in ways that cause readers to lose sight of the fact that they are reading a translation. Functional equivalence has often led to nonmetaphorical renderings and to the adaptation or explication of cultural information, which is not present in the source text. However, as *La Bible en Français courant* illustrates, this translation method is able to pay attention to imagery and metaphors in text and translation.

A functional approach to translation is based on optimism about establishing the informational content of the source text and the intention of its authors. It sometimes tends to underestimate the historical distance and cultural differences between the original text and its original recipients, on the one hand, and contemporary translators and readers on the other. Readers will make sense of a translation in line with what they already know from their own culture, experience, and conceptual world. And if implicit information—what was probably still clear to the original recipients—is made explicit, this leads to more redundancy and to changes in emphasis of the translated text. Rather than embed additional interpretation into the text, footnotes can help to bridge the cultural gap more successfully.

Within the functional equivalent approach there is a growing sensibility of style and literary equivalence. The structure and the function of literary texts, even their formatting, may vary from culture to culture. The Dutch *Nieuwe Bijbelvertaling* (2004) focuses not only on the source text's information content but also on the differences in language levels, registers, genres, styles, and other characteristics that mark the actual source texts. Moreover, this approach seeks to render these features in ways that are appropriate in texts in the target language, and so to bring out differences between natural and marked manners of speaking. Thus, while this translation does not preserve the forms of the source language, it does—not always literally—render those features in the biblical text in question.

3. Segmented

As publishers and special-interest groups multiplied, new translations emerged for distinct audiences: No single translation can meet the needs of an entire community. A translation is intended to target a specific social-cultural function (*skopos*) and should anticipate readers' perceptions. It aims at a specific readership or, like the *Contemporary English Version*, at a listening audience in the target culture. It yields a product conforming to specific expectations and norms of acceptability in, say, church traditions (*Revised English Bible*; NIV) or literary circles. (The expectations and norms do not necessarily imply that the whole translation should correspond in form to the source text, but segmenting and targeting often involves a consistent rendering of what are considered key terms and key phrases in a particular text, book, or even in the whole Bible.) To come up to literary expectations on the part of a particular segment of readers, the translation may be rendered in polished style, even where the style of the source text is not polished and would warrant a translation in more common language. For a translation to be accepted, adaptation to the existing terminology of the liturgy in a particular church tradition may also be considered necessary. Although they are mediators, translators are not always free agents, and are often expected to have the same theological view of Scripture that the intended readership is anticipated to have.

Skopos theory analyzes how conditions of acceptability influence the translation process, determining which aspects of the source text receive priority, e.g., which key terms and phrases have actually been selected for consistent rendering, or which elements expressing cultural information have actually been retained literally. Norms such as adequacy (as compared to the source text), acceptability, and indeed the translator's own theology and/or ideological tendencies are already at work in the translation process, which is always an act of interpretation. Ideological tendencies include feminism, "anti-anti-Judaism" (when translating Isaiah or John), an individualist understanding of personhood, as well as attempts (occasionally in the NIV) to harmonize contradictions and to reduce mythological motifs. Such norms can change over time and across cultures. While Bible translations are to be assessed in accordance with their norms, the need for an ethics of Bible translation is increasingly felt as well. *See* BIBLE VERSIONS; VERSIONS, ANCIENT; VERSIONS, CATHOLIC; VERSIONS, ENGLISH; VERSIONS, GREEK.

Bibliography: R. Alter. *Genesis: Translation and Commentary* (1996); M. Buber and F. Rosenzweig. *Die Schrift und ihre Verdeutschung* (1936); E. A. Gutt. *Translation and Relevance: Cognition and Context*

(1991); B. Hatim and I. Mason. *The Translator as Communicator* (1997); E. A. Nida and C. Taber. *The Theory and Practice of Translation* (1969); E. A. Nida and J. de Waard. *From One Language to Another: Functional Equivalence in Bible Translating* (1986); W. A. Smalley. *Translation as Mission: Bible Translation in the Modern Missionary Movement* (1991); G. Toury. *Descriptive Translation Studies and Beyond* (1995); T. Wilt, ed. *Bible Translation: Frames of Reference* (2003).

L. J. DE REGT

BIBLE, BISHOP'S. *See* BISHOP'S BIBLE.

BIBLE, VERSIONS. *See* VERSIONS, BIBLE.

BIBLICAL AUTHORITY. *See* AUTHORITY OF SCRIPTURE.

BIBLICAL CRITICISM. By the phrase "biblical criticism" we understand the reading and appreciation of the Jewish and Christian Scriptures that does so with a firm use of human reason, however much believers would wish to claim the aid of the Holy Spirit to guide them. In that sense the word *criticism* is nonprejudicial; it does not suggest a negative or destructive approach but rather connotes the idea of evaluation. Many who read the Scriptures with the mind as well as the heart confess that it is a liberating experience. They appeal to the directive of Jesus in the Fourth Gospel, "Search the Scriptures . . . they bear witness to me" (John 5:39, if that is the correct meaning of that text). Or perhaps more tellingly, the same Jesus commanded that his followers should "love the Lord your God with . . . all your mind" (Mark 12:30, appealing to Deut 6:4 but adding the word *mind*).

A. History

In a sense the OT contain examples of this critical process already at work. Israel's history, as recorded in 1–2 Kings, is given a fresh nuance by way of critique in the books of 1–2 Chronicles. The praise given to King Jehu for wiping out false gods and their followers (2 Kgs 10:28-30) is reversed by Hosea (1:4-5) on account of his cruelty. In the synoptic Gospels, the teaching of Jesus recorded by Mark (assuming it was the first of the three gospels to be written) is subjected to the later evangelists' reworking, as we can see in the "Sign of Jonah" paragraph. In Mark 8:11-13 the desire for a sign is refused; in the corresponding version of the story in Matthew 12:39 = Luke 11:29, the "sign" is that of Jonah, expanded in Matt 16:4. And even then, in the Mathew–Luke expansions the sign is variously interpreted, either of Jonah–Jesus' burial and resurrection in Matt 12:40 or of Jonah's preaching in Luke 11:30-32. To make sense of how Scripture records various events involves the use of our mind, whatever we may wish to say and believe about the Bible's inspiration and authority.

The historian Josephus, who was influenced by Greco-Roman culture, wrote a record of Jewish history. The later rabbis sought to harmonize the various stories in the OT. The long record of biblical interpreters, starting with Origen, who was the first to seek to account for the different translations, notably in Hebrew and Greek, and to draw conclusions there from, bears witness to the activity of minds applied to Scripture. In a famous example, Origen noted that the style of Hebrews was different from that of Paul's letters, and so he queried, "Who wrote Hebrews, only God knows."

Eusebius, the first church historian, and Jerome, the profound Bible student, offered insights on the phenomena of the Jewish and Christian Scriptures by recognizing the fact that readers must use their God-given intelligence. Augustine, the bishop of North Africa, applied his knowledge of early science to the account in Gen 1 by noting the difficulty that light was created before the sun (Gen 1:3, 16). He noted that when the accounts of Jesus' miracles are compared (say, Matt 8:28-34//Luke 8:26-39 with Mark 5:1-20) the length of Mark's version is considerably longer, though Augustine persisted in believing that, in the main, Mark followed in Matthew's footsteps and shortened his work.

Yet it was the Enlightenment in Europe that saw the greatest shift in the way the Scriptures were read and understood. Up to this point, around the year 1760 CE, the Bible was held to be unique and committed to the church as its sacred and inviolate documents, to be believed without question.

With the Enlightenment, authorship of the various biblical books was challenged, and parts of the Scriptures were assigned to multiple sources. This was the heyday of literary analysis and a tracing of a line of development from primitive Israelite religion, with par. from the ancient Near Eastern worldview, to an exalting of what were deemed superior ethical norms in the Hebrew prophets and Wisdom writers. Similarly, in the NT, the Gospels were analyzed according to their literary genre (*see* FORM CRITICISM) and assigned a setting not in the life of Jesus but in the situations of the early church (life-setting, *Sitz im Leben*). Paul's authorship of Ephesians, 2 Thessalonians, and the Pastorals was questioned. The miraculous elements in the OT saga and the Gospels were placed in doubt as recourse was made to ancient par. in myth and contemporary wonderworkers.

Perhaps more significantly, a wedge was placed between the two parts of the church's Bible. Formerly the so-called OT of the Hebrew Scriptures was valued as a preparation for the Christian gospel and the events of the life of Jesus. Now the OT came to be regarded in its own light and appreciated as the record of the Jewish faith-community across the centuries. This led to a dialogue between synagogue and church that was muted during the Reformation period.

B. Trends and Prospects

The second half of the 20th cent. saw some innovative trends and approaches, such as rhetorical criticism and the subsequent "effect" of the text on later generations, coming to the fore. Less confidence was felt about so-called "assured results" that students and scholars came to regard as settled. For instance, the elaborate source-analysis of the Pentateuch came under fresh appraisal, as did the solutions to the Synoptic Problem. The latter involved such questions as the priority of Mark's Gospel and the detection of a "sayings-collection" of Jesus' words found in Matthew and Luke, called "Q." Perhaps more significantly was the matter of the historicity of the "ancestor stories" in Genesis and the questioning of a confident attempt made in the 19th cent. to reconstruct a life of Jesus from the four Gospels. These are but two examples of the way biblical criticism showed itself to be an ongoing enterprise. *See* AFRICAN INTERPRETATION; AFROCENTRIC INTERPRETATION; ASIAN AND ASIAN AMERICAN INTERPRETATION; BIBLE TRANSLATION THEORY; BIBLICAL INTERPRETATION, HISTORY OF; CANONICAL CRITICISM; CROSS-CULTURAL INTERPRETATION; CULTURAL HERMENEUTICS; CULTURAL STUDIES; FEMINIST INTERPRETATION; FOLKLORE IN INTERPRETATION; FORM CRITICISM, NT; FORM CRITICISM, OT; GAY INTERPRETATION; GENDER STUDIES; HISTORIOGRAPHY AND HISTORICISM; HOLOCAUST AND BIBLICAL INTERPRETATION; IDEOLOGICAL CRITICISM; INTERTEXTUALITY; JEWISH BIBLICAL INTERPRETATION; LATINO/LATINA INTERPRETATION; LESBIAN INTERPRETATION; LIBERATION THEOLOGY; LITERARY INTERPRETATION, NT; LITERARY INTERPRETATION, OT; METAPHOR IN THEOLOGY; MUJERISTA INTERPRETATION; MYTH IN THE NT; MYTH IN THE OT; NARRATIVE CRITICISM; POSTCOLONIAL BIBLICAL INTERPRETATION; POSTMODERN BIBLICAL INTERPRETATION; PSYCHOLOGY AND BIBLICAL STUDIES; RABBINIC INTERPRETATION; READER RESPONSE CRITICISM; REDACTION CRITICISM, NT; REDACTION CRITICISM, OT; RHETORICAL CRITICISM, NT; RHETORICAL CRITICISM, OT; SEMIOTICS; SOCIAL SCIENTIFIC CRITICISM, NT; SOCIAL SCIENTIFIC CRITICISM, OT; SOURCE CRITICISM; STRUCTURALISM AND DECONSTRUCTION; TEXT CRITICISM, NT; TEXT CRITICISM, OT; THEOLOGICAL HERMENEUTICS; THEOLOGY, NT; THEOLOGY, OT; TRADITION HISTORY; WOMANIST INTERPRETATION.

Bibliography: C. W. Dugmore, ed. *The Interpretation of the Bible* (1944); John Hayes, ed. *Dictionary of Biblical Interpretation* (1999). William Yarchin. *History of Biblical Interpretation: A Reader* (2004).

RALPH P. MARTIN

BIBLICAL INTERPRETATION, HISTORY OF.

A. Inner-Biblical Interpretation

The interpretation of biblical materials is already found within the Bible itself. This inner-biblical interpretation can be seen in the OT where texts are sometimes supplied with explanatory glosses (*see* Judg 1:10), reapplied (compare Dan 9:1-2; 24-27 with Jer 25:11-12; 29:10), or reinterpreted (compare Exod 21:11 with Deut 15:12-18). One can argue, perhaps correctly, that 1–2 Chronicles is a rewrite of material in 1 Samuel—2 Kings and that Deuteronomy 12–26 reformulates laws found in Exodus 21–23. Often later texts interacted with earlier texts through allusion but without direct quotation. This intertextuality can be seen in Isaiah 40–55's dialogue with materials in Isaiah 1–33 and the Book of Lamentations.

New Testament writers made extensive use of OT texts, quoting or alluding to hundreds of passages. Such texts could be used to indicate an occurrence as a fulfillment of prophecy, to buttress an argument, to claim Christ and the church as the real subject of much of the OT, and so forth. Luke 24:44-49 illustrates that the early followers of Jesus saw their christological reading of the Jewish scriptures as authorized by him.

Christians could deny the straightforward reference of an OT text in order to relate the text to new realities. For example, according to Paul, the reference to not muzzling an ox (Deut 25:4) does not really have to do with oxen but with whether Christians should receive payment for their services (1 Cor 9:3-10).

Old Testament "prophecies" could be interpreted by Christians not only with reference to the first coming of Christ but also to the parousia or second coming; the SON OF MAN saying in Dan 7:13-14 was frequently used this way in teachings attributed to Jesus.

Paul introduced terminology into his discussion of the OT that was greatly to influence later Christian interpretation. In places, he speaks of OT events as types or allegories (1 Cor 10:6, 11; Gal 4:21-26). Earlier events are viewed as types paralleling present realities and the account of these "were written down to instruct us" (1 Cor 10:11). In Gal 4:21-26, Hagar and Sarah are taken as allegories of the Jewish and Christian covenants or the present and heavenly Jerusalems. The obvious referent of the OT text is seen to contain a deeper, hidden reference (*see* ALLEGORY).

Paul also spoke of the letter that kills and the Spirit that makes alive (2 Cor 3:6; compare Rom 7:6).

Although Paul here does not necessarily have reference to a two-fold sense in a text, he nonetheless used terminology that could be so interpreted.

B. Early Judaism and Christianity

In the Second Temple period (586 BCE–70 CE), a number of forms of biblical interpretation developed: commentary that worked through the text consecutively (some of the writings of PHILO [ca. 20 BCE–50 CE] and the *pesharim* from QUMRAN), commentaries written on problematic texts (such as Philo's *Questions on Genesis*), texts that rewrote portions of the Bible (such as the *Book of Jubilees* covering Genesis and the early part of Exodus), works that tended to reformulate and codify biblical laws (the *Temple Scroll* from Qumran, based on Deuteronomy), and anthologies which brought together passages from various books (*see* 4QFlorilegium from Qumran). Other writings, such as *1 Enoch* and the *Damascus Document* utilized scripture as proof texts for their conclusions. Alongside such written texts, there developed an oral torah (*see* ORAL LAW, ORAL TORAH) which offered interpretation and application of the biblical laws (later calculated at 613). Much of this material was later codified in the MISHNAH (ca. 200 CE). Jewish interpretation can also be seen in the early Aramaic (Targum) and Greek translations of the text (*see* SAYINGS OF THE FATHERS; SEPTUAGINT; TARGUMS; VERSIONS, ANCIENT).

In this material, one finds a variety of approaches ranging from Philo's allegorization, which fused biblical materials with the philosophy of Plato, to the Qumran community, which saw its own history and beliefs as the key to understanding the code in which the Jewish scripture had been written. Sectarian groups–Pharisees, Sadducees, Samaritans, Essenes–developed their own individual approaches.

With the rise of rabbinic Judaism (after 70 CE), religious diversity within Judaism subsided. The results of biblical interpretation of the Torah assumed authority alongside the text. The following quotes reflect the rabbis' views toward interpretation: "Turn Torah over and over again, for everything is in it. Reflect upon it. Grow old and worn in it, and do not stir from it, for you have no better rule than it" (*m. Abot* 5:22); and "no verse can ever lose its plain sense (*peshat*)" (*b. Shabbat* 63a). The rabbis, even though they considered their scripture to be a unity that contained nothing unimportant, argued that the text was polysemic and that a verse could have as many as seventy faces (Numbers Rabbah 13:15-16), so long as the interpretation fell within the borders of orthodox belief and the Oral Torah (*see* RABBINIC INTERPRETATION; TALMUD).

Teaching/study and preaching in synagogues and schools led to the production of various midrashim on scripture. In works such as the *Mekhilta* of Rabbi Ishmael on Exodus, the *Sifra* on Leviticus, the *Sifre* on Numbers and Deuteronomy, and *Midrash Rabbah* on the torah and the five megilloth, one sees true commentary work that argues a case, offers divergent opinions, and sometimes leaves an issue or interpretation open. These commentaries contain both legal type material (*halaka*) and homiletical/narrative material (*aggada*). The former was intended to establish and aid in keeping the legal requirements while the latter was inspirational and edifying.

Early Christian interpretation, already reflected in the NT, drew upon both Jewish and Hellenistic exegetical techniques. The Greeks possessed a long tradition of reading Homer both grammatically and allegorically (*see* GREEK RELIGION AND PHILOSOPHY; HELLENISM). Early Christian interpreters picked up on Paul's terminology and read the OT looking for types and allegories about Christ and the church. The apostolic writings, like the letters of Barnabas and 1 Clement, used typological exegesis, as did Justin Martyr (ca. 100–ca. 165) and Melito of Sardis (late 2nd cent.). In his *Dialogue with Trypho the Jew*, Justin sought to demonstrate the truth of Christianity over against Judaism on the basis of proof from prophecy (*see* APOSTOLIC FATHERS).

Mainstream Christianity also sought to define itself and "authentic" biblical interpretation over against fellow groups such as the Gnostics, Marcionites, and Montanists (*see* GNOSTICISM; MARCION, MARCIONISM; MONTANUS, MONTANISM). In response to such threats, church leaders argued that scriptural interpretation is a prerogative of the church and must be in agreement with accepted, traditional teaching (the rule of faith) and under supervision of episcopal authority (*see* esp. Irenaeus [ca. 130–ca. 200] *Against Heresies*). (*See* HERESY; IRENAEUS).

The first major Christian treatise on biblical interpretation is found in book 4 of *On First Principles* by ORIGEN (ca. 185-ca. 254). Origen advocated a multilevel reading of the scriptures, although at times he vigorously defended the literal reading where others resorted to allegory. He argued that scripture has a body, soul, and spirit, a literal and a twofold spiritual sense. Some texts he argued contain no literal sense because their statements are absurd. Difficulties in the text have been placed there to challenge the interpreter. The spiritual meaning is intended to be appropriated by Christians as an aid in their growth toward the heavenly world. Exegetes influenced by Origen (such as GREGORY OF NYSSA [ca. 335–395] and Didymus the Blind [d. 398]), the so-called "school of ALEXANDRIA," laid great weight on the spiritual and allegorical reading of the text. In contrast to this Alexandrian school, exegetes in the region of ANTIOCH were advocates of a more literal reading of the Bible, probably being influenced by Jewish exegesis, Aristotelian philosophy, and conservative Hellenistic grammarians. The most significant members of this school were Diodore of Tarsus (d. ca. 394) and Theodore of Mopsuestia (ca. 350–428). They

argued that allegorical interpretation was without controls and emptied history of meaning. The Antiochians argued for what they called *theoria*, which appears to have been spiritual truths that did not abrogate history, and they greatly limited the number of messianic texts in the OT.

The two most influential early Christian interpreters were JEROME (347–420) and AUGUSTINE (354–430). Both stood somewhat midway between the Alexandrians and the Antiochians. Both produced many commentaries. Jerome mastered Hebrew with the help of Jewish instructors and went back to the Hebrew to produce his translation of the OT, which came to be called the VULGATE. Augustine's *On Christian Doctrine* contains his fullest statements on biblical interpretation. He argued that the arts and other aids must be applied in the study of scripture and that one should know the original languages (though he did not). For Augustine the primary purpose of scriptures was to teach love, and if the literal sense of a text was not edifying, then it must be taken nonliterally. Augustine's works, even his "literal commentary" on Genesis, are filled with allegory.

Early Christian exegetes bequeathed to the Middle Ages the view that scriptures were a multilayered embodiment of all truth, that is, scripture possessed multiple, generally four, meanings in each passage. The nomenclature used–literal/historical, allegorical, tropological, and anagogic–was formulated by John Cassian (ca. 360–435 CE) in his *Conferences* (14:8). This fourfold interpretation, the *Quadriga*, was later summarized in the following poem: "The letter teaches what happened; allegory what to believe; morality how to behave; anagogy what to hope for."

C. The Medieval Period

In the early Middle Ages, Judaism and Christianity shared somewhat similar approaches to biblical interpretation. This was the period which witnessed the compilation and veneration of the work of past traditional interpreters.

By the 6th cent., the Jerusalem and Babylonian Talmuds had been collected, containing much of the Mishnah and commentary thereon, called the *gemara*, which among other things sought to expound the biblical basis for mishnaic regulations. The great Midrashim were compiled. The Tiberian Masoretes produced a vocalized and accented version of the Hebrew Bible, preserving the traditional form and pronunciation of the text along with interpretive notations about unusual terms, notes, and word and letter calculations as aids in copying the text (the so-called Masora). *See* MASORA; MASORETES.

Western Christians assigned sanctity to the interpretation of the venerable fathers, especially Ambrose (ca. 340–397), Augustine, Jerome, and Gregory the Great (540–604), declared to be the four great doctors of the

Latin church by the Venerable Bede (ca. 673–735). Their, and to a lesser extent others', interpretations were preserved in the *catenas* ("chains") of tradition on the text and in commentaries which might contain some originality but consisted primarily of compilation, summation, clarification, and harmonization of patristic sources. In addition, there developed the practice of glossing texts between the lines and along the margins, generally consisting of explanatory material drawn from the fathers. (This glossing reached its apex in the great multivolumed *Glossa ordinaria* of the twelfth century, long in use and first printed in 1480).

Both religions assigned authority to both the biblical text and the classic interpretations. In Judaism, talmudic teachings and studies would take their place alongside and sometimes overshadow the Bible. Veneration of the ancient fathers became so standard in Christianity that Hugh of St. Victor (1096–1141), in his *Didascalion*, could place early church documents among the canonical holy scriptures.

In the 8th cent., a Jewish sect called the Karaites ("scripturalists") arose. This "back-to-the-Bible" group with its emphasis on *sola scriptura* argued that the Bible should be read directly and interpreted without utilizing the lens of rabbinic authorities. Blossoming in Jerusalem in the 10th cent., this group was probably influenced by Islamic thought which had absorbed much Aristotelian philosophy with its emphasis on reason rather than faith. In addition, Arabic study placed a strong emphasis on grammar and grammatical analysis of texts.

Saadya Gaon (882–942), the greatest Jewish scholar of the first millennium, responded to the Karaites and defended the use of rabbinic materials as well as reason in understanding scripture. His commentaries, lexicon, treatises, and Arabic translations of the Hebrew Bible were marked with philosophical sensitivity and the first use of scholarly philology.

Three centers of Jewish biblical scholarship flourished between the 10th and 13th cent.: in Islamic Spain, in Provence in southeastern France, and in northern France. The most influential of the Spanish Jews was Abraham IBN EZRA (1089–1164) who, although a sophisticated philosopher, produced commentaries that focused almost entirely on the analysis of the *peshat* (plain/straightforward) sense of the text. In Provence, the Kimhi family developed *peshat* interpretation although not so stringently as that of Ibn Ezra. David (1160–1235) was its most influential member. In northern France, pride of place belonged to RASHI (1040–1105) who was a firm practitioner of the *peshat* method but did not hesitate to incorporate midrashic materials as long as they did not contradict his *peshat* interpretation. The ethical and homiletic dimension of his scholarship has made Rashi the most famous and influential exegete in Jewish history.

Beginning in the 12th cent., new developments began to appear in Christian exegesis as well. These included a renewed emphasis on the literal sense of the text, a recognition but not a realization of the widespread need to learn the original languages of the Bible, the appearance of the complete Bible in a portable and unglossed form, and various tools and aids for the use of the Bible.

The causes motivating these developments were numerous: greater contact between Jews and Christians brought together in urban settings, the increased development of cathedral schools and the founding of universities where the Bible was taught as an academic subject, the separation of extensive theological discussion and disputation from commentary and the utilization of these in the creation of theological sentences arranged topically, the use of Aristotelian logic and dialectic with a stress on the univocality of language, the greater role of preaching with the founding of the Dominican and Franciscan orders, and a certain weariness with extravagant allegory. A few examples will illustrate these developments.

Scholars associated with the Abbey of St. Victor in Paris (esp., Hugh, Godfrey, and Andrew) stressed the importance of the literal sense of scripture and were in close contact with Jews and Jewish interpretation. Andrew (d. 1175), e.g., could discuss Isa 7:14 without reference to Mary and the birth of Jesus.

By assigning four senses to a text, one could read almost any doctrine into any text. Alain of Lille (1120–1202) could speak of the Bible as a "nose of wax," that is something that could be shaped and fitted to one's belief. Thomas Aquinas (ca. 1225–74) argued that theological truths should be drawn only from the literal sense of a passage, appealing to Augustine's *Letter to Vincent* where the latter declared that "nothing necessary for the faith is contained under the spiritual sense which scripture does not convey elsewhere through the literal sense" (*Summa Theologiae* Ia.1, 9–10).

New tools and aides for Bible study were produced in the 13th cent.: books of *distinctions* listed various theological terms with supporting and illustrative biblical texts, and a verbal concordance. These tools aided in locating information in the Bible using the chapter divisions attributed to Stephen Langton (d. 1228), with chapters divided into lettered (a-g) sections. (Our verse division and enumeration is derived from Robert Estienne's 1555 Latin edition of the Bible.) The *Historia scholastic* of Peter Comestor (d. ca. 1179), a history of the world from creation to the end of the book of Acts, also became popular, providing a reference for contextualizing biblical events. The apex of late medieval interpretation is found in the literal commentary by Nicholas of Lyra (ca. 1270–1349) who drew widely from Jewish sources and knew Hebrew.

D. The Renaissance

Humanists in the 15th cent., decades before the Reformation, made radical moves in biblical study. Interest in Hebrew (taught by rabbis) and Greek (stimulated by the migration of Easterners to the west after the fall of Constantinople in 1453) flourished. Lorenzo Valla (1407–57) began collation of the Vulgate NT with Greek manuscripts. The invention of the movable type printing press in the early 1450s made the production of books and Bibles cheaper, more rapid, and with identical content. Polyglot texts with Greek, Hebrew, Aramaic, and Latin versions of biblical texts were published. Conrad Pellican (1478–1556) and Johannes Reuchlin (1455–1522) published Hebrew grammars (1503/4, 1506). Erasmus (1446/9–1536), whose shadow fell across the entire European world of learning, published an edition of the Greek NT with an independent Latin translation. The general Renaissance nostalgia for the past, the drive to return to the sources (*ad fontes*), and the desire to encounter ancient texts without the compilation of encrusting traditions, all became characteristic of biblical interpretation.

E. Protestant Reformation and Catholic Response

The reformers gladly welcomed the new "sacred philology" and took advantage of the printed word to disseminate their view. Certain positions were shared by practically all Protestants. 1) The church had drastically gone wrong at some point in its earlier history and departed from the original purity of the church reflected in the NT. Although Protestants differed as to when this deviation from the true path had occurred, they were unanimously agreed that the Bible, properly understood, was the primary instrument for reforming the church and for returning it to its original purity. 2) Theology and the church's institutional life should be based on the principle of *sola scriptura*. 3) The authoritative form of the Bible should be the Hebrew and Greek, with translations in the vernacular to be based on the original languages. 4) The canon of the OT should contain only the books found in the Hebrew Bible. The first defense of this Protestant canon was published by Andreas Bodenstein (Karlstadt, ca. 1480–1541) in 1520. 5) People should have the right to read and interpret the Bible on their own. The individual's prerogative to interpret scripture was often played off against the authority of the pope and church councils. 6) Most protestant reformers denied the multilevel reading of scripture and emphasized the literal sense, but the latter they generally understood as having a more Christological and ecclesiological dimension than would later be the case. 7) The individual reader of the scriptures should personally encounter and engage the scriptures in an existential manner, being directed by the Holy Spirit who had inspired the biblical writings in their original encodement. 8) The central doctrine of the Christian faith and the central thrust of the biblical materials were understood as "justification by faith" through the gracious act of God in Jesus Christ. Thus Luther (1483–1546) distinguished among biblical writings, depending upon how much emphasis a certain work placed on Christology and justification by faith. For Luther, there was clearly "a canon within the canon" with Romans, Galatians, and the Gospel of John being the most favored NT books (*see* CANON).

Catholics responded to these positions with a number of arguments. 1) To allow the individual (Luther's everyman or his German plowman) freedom to interpret the Bible was absurd when the great reformers could not themselves agree on how to read a text (such as Matt 26:26) and would lead to a widespread fragmentation of the Christian church. 2) To turn one's back on the classical interpretation and to adhere to a doctrine of *sola scriptura* was futile since the scriptures were so unclear. 3) Before the NT was written, there was only the church and tradition; the church created the Bible, not the Bible the church. (The gradual and grudging recognition and acceptance of this view characterized Protestant scholarship for centuries.)

The fourth session of the Catholic Council of Trent (8 April 1546) took several positions countering some Protestant views on the Bible and its interpretation. 1) The longer canon, including what the Protestants following Jerome called "the apocrypha," was declared the canon of the Bible. 2) Both written books (the Bible) and unwritten traditions were declared revelatory of Christian truths and rules. 3) The church, not individuals, was declared the judge of the true sense and meaning of the scriptures. 4) The Latin Vulgate (not Hebrew and Greek texts) was declared the official version of the Bible for use in public lectures, dispositions, and exposition. 5) Work on theological and biblical subjects would have to be approved by the church before publication. Catholic and Protestant positions eventually hardened into controversy, rigid orthodoxy, and even warfare.

F. Seventeenth-Nineteenth Centuries

In many respects, the 17th cent., especially the years 1640–80, represents the watershed in the interpretation of the Bible. Already in the 16th cent., authors took note of the existence of skeptics who challenged Christians' high views about the Bible and questioned its contents. These skeptics cast their shadow but, due to censorship and cultural conditions, left no substance in the world of scholarship. In the seventeenth century, matters were different. Scientific discovery, world exploration, philosophical questioning of all claims to absoluteness, desire for a society where one would think what one wanted and say what one thought, and a growing confidence in the "inner light" and reason all led to new perspectives on the Bible and an erosion of its authority on many matters historical, cultural, and philosophical. Among the contributors to this reassessment were: Hugo Grotius (1583–1645), Thomas Hobbes (1588–1679), Isaac de la Peyrére (ca. 1596–1676), Baruch

Spinoza (1632–77), and many Deists, Unitarians, Quakers, and radical social groups.

By the end of the 17th cent., the historical-critical method (the quest for the *sensus historicus*) was reasonably well developed (though not necessarily widely accepted), resting on the following presumptions. 1) The Bible is a book of antiquity separated from the present both chronologically and conceptually. 2) The Bible should be studied and read like any other book, that is, in a straightforward fashion. Individual books or groupings of books must be read on their own, not filtered through the Bible as a whole or church/ synagogue tradition. 3) A biblical text is the product of a human author(s) living in a particular time and place. 4) The form and content of a text reflect and are intelligible only in light of the author's conceptions, intentions, and beliefs, which are conditioned by the time and context of the original writer's and readers' environment and thought world. 5) The authenticity and validity of the Bible or a biblical text depend, in no small measure, on how they and their content measure up to the canons of human thought and reason. 6) The causes and nature of events in the Bible must be understood in terms of historical analogy, what was possible then is possible now and vice versa (the latter perspective was more hinted at then openly declared).

A rearguard action sought (and still does) to counter these conclusions and reaffirm and support, at least in principle, the classical and traditional views of the Bible. Among these were the British Latitudinarians, physico-theologians, and orthodox of various stripes.

The 18th cent. witnessed two major new developments. On the one hand, the Bible and its contents became the object of outright ridicule and derision. For Voltaire (1694–1778), Thomas Paine (1737–1809), the French Encyclopedists, and others, the Bible was a collection of superstitions, incongruities, primitive mentality, and priestcraft.

On the other hand, scholarly discussion and study of the Bible, utilizing new approaches and methodologies, moved into academic circles and became a part of university professional work. In this context, one must understand the flowering of biblical criticism in the late 18th cent. not only as the continuation of the mainstream of philological, textual, and historical criticism which had begun in the Renaissance but also as a major apologetic activity aimed at offering more reasonable discussion of the Bible and explanations of its problems than that of its despisers. The so-called historical-critical method, generally traced to the eighteenth century, is frequently presented as an attempt to undercut the Bible's authority, to bring it into line with modern thought, and to free biblical study from dogmatic dominance. In some respects, just the opposite is probably a more accurate description. The practitioners of the method were primarily Protestant scholars; they were not anti-biblical although their work was frequently anti-Catholic and anti-Jewish and often at variance with traditional Christianity.

The basic staple of biblical interpretation, the general introduction which surveys the problems and approaches to every book in the Bible, made its appearance in the latter half of the 18th cent. The basic issues in biblical research became the nature and origin of the Pentateuch, the authenticity of many other books (such as Isaiah), the origin and relationship of the four gospels (the SYNOPTIC PROBLEM), and the quest for the historical Jesus and how this historical figure relates to the four portraits in the gospels.

By about 1835, after consideration of diverse alternatives, conclusions that continue to dominate academic study of the Bible had been formulated, at least in principles. 1) The Pentateuch was assumed to have been composed by the combination of several, generally four, different sources (*see* DOCUMENTARY HYPOTHESIS; D, DEUTERONOMIC, DEUTERONOMISTIC; E, ELOHIST; J, YAHWIST; P, PRIESTLY WRITERS; SOURCE CRITICISM; TRADITION HISTORY, OT). In the lectures of Eduard Reuss in 1833 and in works published by Wilhelm Vatke and J. F. L. George in 1835, the priestly stratum ("P") of material was considered the most recent. 2) The theory that Mark was not dependent upon Matthew and/or Luke but was the first gospel written and was utilized by the other two Synoptics had found expression. In 1783 J. B. Koppe expounded the theory that Mark was not the epitomizer of Matthew and, in 1786, G. C. Storr argued for the priority of Mark (*see* SYNOPTIC PROBLEM). 3) As early as 1801, Herbert Marsh proposed that the gospel writers had used a no longer extant source, which has come to be called "Q." *See* Q, QUELLE. 4) The Gospel of John (and associated Johannine letters) moved into a separate research field with little connection to synoptic study. In 1792 Edward Evanson), an Englishman, , was the first major critic of the authenticity of John, which he placed, along with Matthew and Mark, in the second century. 5) The attempt to use the gospel materials to reconstruct a HISTORICAL JESUS noticeably different from the biblical portraits progressed apace. At his death, the deist H. S. Reimarus (1694–1768) left behind a manuscript, later partially published by G. E. Lessing (1729–81), that presented a rather human Jesus and depicted early Christians and the gospel writers as fraudulent connivers (already anticipated by the English deist Peter Annet [1693–1769]). The life of Jesus published by D. F. Strauss in 1835 with its radical reinterpretation produced a shadow that fell across most subsequent gospel and Jesus research. 6) The authenticity of the pastoral epistles was systematically challenged by F. C. Baur in 1835 as part of his depiction of early Christianity as comprised of Petrine and Pauline parties (again a view anticipated by English deists). 7) Analysis of non-pentateuchal books in the OT challenged the authenticity of some materials and analyzed the books into various sources. The idea of a Second Isaiah (chs. 40 and following) was first proposed in modern times by Koppe in 1780. 8) Given the dominance of a historical consciousness in the nineteenth century, effort was made to produce a history of Israel comparable to those written on ancient Greece and Rome. One of the first published was written by H. H. Milman in 1829. W. M. L. de Wette had argued in 1806–07 that the Hebrew Bible did not provide the material necessary for writing a history of Israel.

In the second half of the 19th cent., scholars continued to explore the issues just noticed, supporting, opposing, and modifying them, often giving proposed solutions their classical formulations. These further developments deserve notice.

1. The decipherment of Egyptian hieroglyphics (*see* HIEROGLYPH), by Champollion (1790–1832) utilizing the ROSETTA STONE discovered in 1799, and of Akkadian CUNEIFORM in mid-century made available two vast worlds of literature. What had previously been known of these cultures from the Bible and classical sources had been used earlier by numerous interpreters; but now primary sources of multiple types became available for study and for supplementation of and comparison with the Bible. In 1875, e.g., George Smith published his *The Chaldean Account of Genesis*. These texts would elucidate the Bible in innumerable ways. In addition, previously known early non-biblical texts produced in Jewish and Christian communities were reedited and absorbed into biblical study especially in the history-of-religion school (*Religionsgeschichtliche Schule*) in Germany. Religion was considered in this movement as a historical phenomenon understandable only in light of its origins and roots. Comparative religious phenomena and literature, not doctrinal concepts, must be utilized in interpretation.

2. Archaeological excavations throughout the Near East exposed the nature of ancient life in many ways. The *realia* of ancient times and the history of cities and cultures could be recovered and used in interpreting the Bible. *See* ARCHAEOLOGY.

3. The end of the century witnessed a concern with the communal life and sociology of the ancients and how biblical materials (both oral and written) might have been employed in such cultures. This led to an interest in the pre-written or oral forms and usage of biblical materials. One of the pioneers in this work was Herman Gunkel (1862–1932). Many scholars had spoken about some of these matters before, even hypothesizing an oral gospel behind the Synoptics, but Gunkel and others sought to give methodological shape to such study which came to be called form-criticism and tradition-history. A similar concern with genres had already been characteristic of the "Bible as literature" movement. *See* FORM CRITICISM, OT.

With these developments, a multilayered reading of the Bible, as in the early church and synagogue, often became a factor in the academic field. Now the fourfold reading, especially in the Pentateuch and the Synoptics, elucidated a passage in terms of its preliterate oral form, as part of an isolated source or cycle of tradition, as a component within a larger document, and as a text within the Bible as a whole.

G. Twentieth Century

In the 20th cent., the main lines of research, designated the historical-critical approach, continued unabated. Albert Schweitzer in his quest for the historical Jesus (1906, Eng. trans. 1910) hoped to put to rest the effort but succeeded instead in writing yet another life of Jesus. Both liberals and conservatives have continued to pursue the task. For convenience's sake, the quest has been divided into three phases: the old, the new (from the mid 1950s, in the wake of Bultmann's work with a focus on the movement from Jesus the preacher to the preached Jesus), and the third from the 1990s drawing upon the social sciences and Q research (*see* HISTORICAL JESUS; JESUS CHRIST).

The 1920s, influenced in no small part by the theology of Karl Barth (1886–1968), saw the rebirth of biblical theology after some years of dormancy. Much of the work was philologically oriented. OT theology was heavily influenced by covenant perspectives reintroduced into biblical study by Max Weber (1864–1920) and also by an emphasis on *Heilsgeschichte* (Salvation History).

Four previously unknown collections of texts were absorbed into Biblical study: the AMARNA LETTERS from 14th cent. BCE Egypt; the Ugaritic texts from Syria, also dated to the 14th cent.; the NAG HAMMADI codices from Egypt, dated to the early cent. of the church; and the QUMRAN texts (DEAD SEA SCROLLS) from the 2nd cent. BCE to 1st cent. CE.

Two main schools dealing with the history and religion of ancient Israel competed with one another in the mid-decades of the century. W. F. Albright (1891–1971) and his students stressed the roles of archaeology and empiricist approaches to historical reconstruction while Albrecht Alt (1883–1856) and his students focused on geographico-historical concerns and the history of tradition.

A major controversy, beginning in the 1940s, was triggered by the program of demythologization of the NT by Rudolf Bultmann (1884–1976). Bultmann was heavily influenced by form-criticism and the desire to translate NT thought into modern, primarily existentialist, categories. *See* FORM CRITICISM, NT.

Beginning in mid-century biblical interpretation became an inter-confessional enterprise. Gradually Jewish scholarship had moved into the mainstream and then blossomed after the creation of the state of Israel. Pope Pius XII's encyclical *Divino Afflante Spiritu*

(30 September 1943) granted much of what earlier Catholic Modernists had wanted but were denied. The Second Vatican Council (1962–1965) extended the freedom of inquiry. Although still present in society worldwide, the fundamentalist movement which peaked in the early decades of the century modified somewhat so that many conservative evangelicals came to participate, at least methodologically, in the mainstream of scholarship.

The 20th cent. witnessed an enormous increase in the publication of biblical studies. New translations of the Bible became almost epidemic. Prior to 1950, few commentaries on the Bible were available whereas today the available commentary series are numerous and almost overwhelming.

New approaches to biblical study increased during the course of the century as did weariness with the historical-critical methodology. The social sciences and literary study were drawn upon for new perspectives and methodologies. The routine theological and academic approaches came to be considered by many as elitist and Euro-centric. A more pluralistic perspective arose, reflecting similar interests to those in culture in general. Numerous voices from the "margins" made significant impact on biblical interpretation: feminist, Afro-American, third world, liberation, post-colonial, and other readings of the scripture became common and recognized as legitimate disciplines. See BIBLICAL CRITICISM; AFRICAN INTERPRETATION; AFRO-CENTRIC INTERPRETATION; ASIAN AMERICAN INTERPRETATION; ASIAN INTERPRETATION; BIBLE TRANSLATION THEORY; CANONICAL CRITICISM; CROSS-CULTURAL INTERPRETATION; CULTURAL HERMENEUTICS; CULTURAL STUDIES; FEMINIST INTERPRETATION; FOLKLORE IN INTERPRETATION; FORM CRITICISM, NT; FORM CRITICISM, OT; GAY INTERPRETATION; GENDER STUDIES; HISTORY AND HISTORIOGRAPHY; HOLOCAUST AND BIBLICAL INTERPRETATION; IDEOLOGICAL CRITICISM; INTERTEXTUALITY; JEWISH BIBLICAL INTERPRETATION; LATINO/LATINA INTERPRETATION; LESBIAN INTERPRETATION; LIBERATION THEOLOGY; LITERARY INTERPRETATION, NT; LITERARY INTERPRETATION, OT; METAPHOR IN THEOLOGY; MUJERISTA INTERPRETATION; MYSTICAL BIBLICAL INTERPRETATION; MYTHOLOGY IN BIBLICAL INTERPRETATION; NARRATIVE CRITICISM; POSTCOLONIAL BIBLICAL INTERPRETATION; POSTMODERN BIBLICAL INTERPRETATION; PSYCHOLOGY AND BIBLICAL STUDIES; QUEER THEORY; RABBINIC INTERPRETATION; READER RESPONSE CRITICISM; REDACTION CRITICISM, NT; REDACTION CRITICISM, OT; RHETORICAL CRITICISM, NT; RHETORICAL CRITICISM, OT; SEMIOTICS; SOCIAL SCIENTIFIC CRITICISM, NT; SOCIAL SCIENTIFIC CRITICISM, OT; SOURCE CRITICISM; STRUCTURALISM AND DECONSTRUCTION; TEXT CRITICISM, NT; TEXT CRITICISM, OT; THEOLOGICAL HERMENEUTICS; THEOLOGY, NT; THEOLOGY, OT; TRADITION HISTORY; WOMANIST INTERPRETATION.

Bibliography: P. R. Ackroyd et al, eds. *The Cambridge History of the Bible* (3 vols., 1963–1970); William Baird. *History of New Testament Research* (3 vols., 1992–); Gerald Bray. *Biblical Interpretation: Past and Present* (1996); R. J. Coggins and J. L. Houlden, eds. *A Dictionary of Biblical Interpretation* (1990); R. M. Grant and David Tracy, *A Short History of the Interpretation of the Bible.* 2nd ed. (1984); W. W. Hallo and K. L. Younger, ed. *The Context of Scripture*, 3 vols. (1997–2002); Christopher de Hamel, *The Book: A History of the Bible* (2001); R. A. Harrisville and Walter Sundberg. *The Bible in Modern Culture*, 2nd ed. (2002); A. J. Hauser and D. F. Watson, eds. *A History of Biblical Interpretation.* 3 vols. (2003–); J. H. Hayes, ed. *Dictionary of Biblical Interpretation* (2 vols., 1999); Christopher Hill, *The English Bible and the Seventeenth-Century Revolution* (1993); W. G. Kümmel. *The New Testament: The History of the Investigation of Its Problems* (1973); J. D. McAuliffe et al., ed. *With Reverence for the Word: Medieval Scriptural Exegesis in Judaism, Christianity, and Islam* (2003); D. K. McKim, ed. *Dictionary of Major Biblical Interpreters* (2007); S. M. Miller and R. V. Huber, *The Bible: A History: The Making and Impact of the Bible* (2003); Robert Morgan. *The Interpretation of the Bible* (1988); M. J. Mulder, ed. *Mikra: Text, Translation, Reading, and Interpretation of the Hebrew Bible in Ancient Judaism and Early Christianity* (1988); H. O. Old. *The Reading and Preaching of the Scriptures in the Worship of the Christian Church.* 6 vols. (1998–); Jaroslav Pelikan. *Whose Bible Is It? A History of the Scriptures through the Ages* (2005); John Rogerson. *Old Testament Criticism in the Nineteenth Century: England and Germany* (1984); John Rogerson, ed. *The Oxford Illustrated History of the Bible* (2001); John Rogerson et al., eds. *The History of Christian Theology. Volume 2: The Study and Use of the Bible* (1988); Magne Sæbø, ed. *Hebrew Bible / Old Testament: The History of Its Interpretation* (3 vols. in 5, 1996–); John Sandys-Wunsch. *What Have They Done to the Bible? A History of Modern Biblical Interpretation* (2005); S. M. Wylen. *The Seventy Faces of Torah: The Jewish Way of Reading the Sacred Scriptures* (2005); William Yarkin. *History of Biblical Interpretation: A Reader* (2004).

JOHN HAYES

BIBLICAL SPIRITUALITY. *See* SPIRITUALITY.

BIBLICAL THEOLOGY. Biblical theology is a constructive theological engagement with the Bible that seeks to provide greater conceptual articulation, coherence, or development of the Bible's texts, ideas, metaphors, stories, and poetry involving God, humans, and the world in dialogue with various methods, contexts, and historic theological traditions. For Christians, biblical theology typically refers to constructive theological work that includes both the OT and NT as opposed to strictly OT theology or NT theology. Some biblical theologians work in deliberate isolation from postbiblical Christian traditions, systematic theology, or church doctrine. Others pursue biblical theology through intentional conversation and engagement with doctrinal or systematic theology. For those in the Jewish tradition, biblical theology typically refers to theological reflection focused on biblical texts in the Tanakh or Hebrew Bible (roughly equivalent to the Christian OT but with important differences in canonical order and interpretive framework). Jewish scholars generally engage biblical theology in dialogue with the long and rich tradition of Jewish rabbinic commentary and legal-ethical teaching that extends from ancient and medieval times to the present.

A. Brief History of Biblical Theology

1. Before J. P. Gabler

Biblical theology understood broadly as constructive theological engagement with scriptural traditions began already in the Bible itself with inner biblical interpretation of older traditions within the OT and with the NT's christological appropriation of OT texts and traditions. Ancient and medieval postbiblical interpretation and commentary on the Bible, both Jewish and Christian, assumed that Scripture was the word of God. Scholars interpreted the Bible through various methods such as rabbinic MIDRASH or Christian ALLEGORY or the "literal" sense of Scripture. In the Christian tradition, the creeds and traditions of the church often provided rules of faith that guided theological interpretation of the Bible. Christian teaching and preaching of the Bible assumed an essential inner-unity and harmony between the two Testaments in their witness to the one God of Jesus Christ. In the 16th cent., Christian Reformers, such as Martin Luther and John Calvin, sought to recover again the "plain" or "literal" sense of Scripture by translating and interpreting the Bible from the original Greek of the NT and Hebrew of the OT. Luther wrote a *Large Catechism* and *Small Catechism* as summaries of the theology of the Bible as theological guides for reading. Calvin wrote *The Institutes of the Christian Religion* as an ordered and systematic account of Biblical Theology. The label *biblical theology* appears for the first time in the 16th cent. Through most of this period from the ancient period through the 16th cent., the study of the Bible and the study of theology were integrated with each other. The predominant aim of the theological interpretation of Scripture was a practical one: to form and shape the beliefs, attitudes, habits, and practices of communities of faith, their leaders, and their members.

2. J. P. Gabler (1787)

The emergence of an independent discipline of biblical theology that was consciously distinct from Christian dogmatic theology is often traced to Johann Philipp Gabler's inaugural address of 1787 at the German university at Altdorf. Gabler distinguished "a true biblical theology" as a historical account of what different biblical authors "thought about divine things" from "a pure biblical theology" that sifted out from all these biblical concepts those lasting truths of the Bible that are valid for all time from the beliefs that were historically conditioned and time-bound. These "pure" and enduring biblical concepts could then be passed on to dogmatic theologians who would use them in their own historically conditioned and philosophically shaped theological constructions. Others before Gabler had begun to argue for separating a historical study of Scripture as a set of historically conditioned human words from the dogmatic work of theologizing from biblical texts. But it was Gabler who most clearly set a new course for separating the discipline of biblical theology from the work of dogmatic theology. Gabler's presupposition that human reason could successfully separate out timeless, universal truths from the Bible's otherwise historically conditioned teachings was itself a time-conditioned product of the 17th cent. Enlightenment and its trust in human reason as a reliable arbiter of universal truth.

Gabler never attempted to realize his program; he simply laid the groundwork. The first half of Gabler's program—"true" biblical theology as a historical investigation of different theologies and ideas of the varied traditions of the OT and NT—became the dominant mode of constructing "biblical theology" for much of the modern period. The second half of his program—seeking "pure" biblical theology as timeless and universal truths—became less dominant. However, various scholars continued to isolate certain concepts or periods in the history of biblical traditions as more enduring and central than others in conjunction with diverse philosophical positions (Kant; Hegel).

3. The separation of OT and NT theology and attempts at reintegration

One important effect of the strongly historicist approach to analyzing the traditions of the Bible was the separation of OT theology from NT theology as two quite distinctive enterprises. G. L. Bauer's two-volume *Biblical Theology* (1796, 1802) was the first to separate OT theology and NT theology. More and more, the perceived discontinuities between the theologies of the OT and NT made any clear or compelling accounts of their theological unity increasingly difficult. Nevertheless, various strategies were employed for presenting a more comprehensive view of the theology of the Bible. Thus, Walther Eichrodt's two volumes of OT theology sought to link the conceptual center of OT theology—God's covenantal relation with Israel, humanity, and the world—with the NT theme of the kingdom of God. The work of Gerhard von Rad and Hartmut Gese sought to trace lines of interconnection through continuing streams of traditions that ran from the OT to the NT. The so-called Biblical Theology Movement (1945–1961) among some American Protestant scholars sought to tie together history and revelation. They believed that the central biblical confession that God acts in history could be confirmed through critical, historical, and archaeological investigation. They also argued that historical-critical study of biblical words and concepts confirmed a contrast on key theological ideas between a unique Hebrew worldview and a more nonbiblical Greek worldview. Both of these assumptions were severely criticized for a naive understanding of history and its relationship to the agency of God, and for a misuse of semantics and word studies.

4. Recent developments

Holistic theological interpretation of the Bible floundered for some decades after the demise of the Biblical Theology Movement. However, biblical theology has emerged again as a thriving enterprise, albeit with many challenges and considerable diversity of approaches. This emergence is due in part to the postmodern awareness that all human knowing is contextual, provisional, freighted with presupposition, and dependent in part on prior traditions (whether religious or academic). The historical study of the Bible and its traditions is no longer the sole or dominant method in biblical theology, although it remains essential for the necessary task of meaningfully translating an ancient text of Hebrew or Greek signs into a modern language. Confessional religious interpretation, whether Jewish or Christian, has increasingly become a more accepted conversation partner in developing biblical theology, although others still resist this move. A number of varied interpretive methods (literary, narrative, sociological, ideological, cultural-linguistic, liberationist, canonical) and interpretive orientations (an emphasis on the reader and the social locations of gender, race, class, and experiences of global colonialism) have also reshaped the landscape of biblical interpretation, including biblical theology. Historical-critical study of the Bible remains important and necessary, but it now must find its place in a much more complex interpretive environment.

Some of the most significant challenges that face interpreters in relating the Bible and theological interpretation include the wide diversity of biblical traditions, the descriptive versus prescriptive character of biblical theology, the nature of the relationship of the Bible and systematic theology, and ethical and theological concerns about the use and abuse of some biblical texts and images (e.g., patriarchy, hierarchies of power, violence, or holy war).

B. The Variety of Proposals for Ongoing Work in Biblical Theology

The arena of biblical theology remains a highly contested domain. A number of varied proposals for renewing or redirecting biblical theology that try to address some of the challenges outlined above have been offered. The following examples illustrate the spectrum of views.

1. Biblical theology as descriptive exegetical studies

Some scholars advise against any attempts to make biblical theology into an interdisciplinary arena for Bible and theology (James Barr and Krister Stendahl). They argue that biblical scholars should confine themselves to projects of limited, descriptive biblical exegesis, since that is their area of expertise; they are not trained to do prescriptive, systematic, or dogmatic theology. Prescriptive theological judgments, they argue, inevitably import dogmatic arguments into what should be a more objective, descriptive task of exegesis. Biblical theologians should simply concentrate on the descriptive enterprise of studying what ancient biblical writers, redactors, and audiences thought about God, humans, and the world. Biblical theology is best done not in large comprehensive volumes of biblical theology that set up unrealistic expectations of comprehensiveness but in individual and focused critical studies of particular themes, aspects, or texts. Such limited studies recognize their provisional character as descriptive probes into what some ancient text or set of texts meant in their original ancient settings. Modern appropriation of the Bible should involve, as a first stage, sinking ourselves into the past meaning of the biblical text, allowing it to interpret and criticize our modern thoughts, traditions, and assumptions. Proponents of this view acknowledge that the goal of objectivity and independence from presuppositions will always be elusive and imperfect. But it should remain a goal nonetheless, insofar as the data and evidence associated with given biblical texts allow. The results of such descriptive exegetical work can be handed on as data for trained theologians and ethicists to use, as they bring an array of other resources into dialogue with the Bible.

2. A canonical biblical theology

The canonical approach to biblical theology pays primary attention to how biblical texts have been theologically edited and shaped over generations so that they continue to address future generations of communities of faith with the living word of God (Brevard Childs). A biblical theologian ought to begin by first examining the "discrete witness of the OT" and the "discrete witness of the NT" in order to avoid a premature collapse of the OT into the NT. The distinctive and multiple voices of both the OT and NT should then be brought into sustained dialogue and argument with each other and with diverse contemporary theologians around a number of topics that are shared with Christian systematic or dogmatic theology. However, the distinctiveness of the biblical witness should be maintained. Canonical interpreters recognize the ongoing need for Christian communities of faith in diverse global contexts to reformulate their theologies in fresh ways to address varied contemporary and contextual arenas.

Historical-critical insights are used to the extent that they aid in discerning the theological and hermeneutical shaping of biblical texts. While some past biblical theologies have proposed a single overarching biblical theme as an abstract and timeless theological "center" of the Bible, a canonical approach urges a recognition of the diversity of theological witnesses within the Bible. All theological appropriation of the Bible is time-bound and provisional, ultimately subject to the divine subject, to which Scripture has borne witness in many and varied ways over centuries of time.

3. A christocentric biblical theology

Another Christian approach to biblical theology argues for an interdisciplinary study of the Bible and Christian theology together with the unifying center as Jesus Christ (Francis Watson). Even the OT should be interpreted christocentrically but not christomonistically. While it is acknowledged that nothing in the OT speaks directly of Jesus (christomonism), all the diverse witnesses and themes of the OT (creation, exodus, command, promise, kingship, priesthood, prophecy) should somehow be brought into relationship with the center who is Christ (christocentrism). Such a view would reject a canonical approach that includes the "distinct witness of the OT" on its own terms as one step along the way toward a Christian biblical theology. For Christians, according to this perspective, there is no distinct witness of the OT apart from its function as preparation for Jesus and its relationship to the Christ-event.

4. Contextualized biblical theologies: gender, race, class, and postcolonial perspectives

Increasingly significant voices in biblical theology are emerging from diverse social, political, and global locations, in which matters of gender, race, class, and postcolonial location affect theological interpretation of the Bible (Phyllis Trible and R. S. Sugirtharajah). Feminist, mujerista, womanist, liberationist, and postcolonial interpreters study biblical texts with widely diverse methods (literary, sociological, rhetorical, deconstructionist). Studies of discrete biblical texts or themes or images from these contextualized perspectives tend to share some common elements in spite of their diversity. They often emphasize real-world contexts and communities, and the realities of suffering, injustice, and oppression are clearly in view. The results of biblical-theological interpretation are often prescriptive with meanings or implications that are readily applicable to contemporary society, politics, community dynamics, and individual beliefs and actions. Such contextualized biblical theologies argue that biblical-theological interpretation is always shaped to some degree by the contextual dynamics of power and ideology, whether at the level of the biblical text itself or in historical or contemporary readers of biblical texts. Biblical theology conceived in this mode would urge interpreters to be intentional and self-reflective about their own social, political, and religious locations, and the influence that such contexts may play in interpretation. Issues of ethics, justice, and power are inevitably entangled in biblical-theological work.

5. Jewish biblical theology

Some Jewish biblical scholars have criticized past efforts in biblical theology as heavily biased by Christian and Protestant assumptions of theology, canon, and history (John Levenson, Benjamin Sommer, and Tikva-Frymer-Kensky). The Jewish tradition reveres as authoritative not only the Bible or written Torah but also a long tradition of commentary called ORAL TORAH (Mishnah, Talmud, ancient and medieval rabbinic commentary, modern scholarship). Thus, some speak not of a Jewish biblical theology but simply a Jewish theology that encompasses both Scripture and tradition. Others, however, would affirm a proper role for Jewish biblical theology as an exploration focused on the theology of the traditions, authors, and redactors of the Jewish Scriptures that may or may not always agree with postbiblical Jewish tradition and commentary. A recurring feature of those engaged in Jewish biblical theology is a resistance to harmonizing the diverse voices of the Bible into one central theme or coherent system. Instead, they affirm the frequent presence of diverse and opposing theological perspectives coexisting in the same Bible, the same biblical book, and even in the same individual biblical text. This juxtaposition of diverse theological voices in dialogue together is a feature not only of the Bible but of Jewish tradition in general, where opposing viewpoints or judgments are often allowed to stand together. This paradigm of dialogical coexistence of opposing theological perspectives also finds resonance in the work of the Russian literary theorist, Mikhail Bakhtin, whose work has also informed Christian biblical theologians.

C. Conclusion

Biblical theology as constructive theological engagement with the Bible remains a vital part of the field of biblical studies. The future of biblical theology will be enhanced if it maintains a healthy combination of methods and perspectives: 1) a scholarly rigor disciplined by the detailed exegesis of biblical texts; 2) a creative and imaginative engagement with the rich collection of metaphors, laws, narratives, and poetry of the Bible; 3) an openness to hearing the diverse voices of the Bible itself as well as readers both past and present; 4) a practical concern for the implications of biblical theology for the actual living out of faith in communities and the world today; and 5) a commitment to seeking truth and knowledge of God along with an appropriate humility and awareness of the boundaries and limits of human knowing. Biblical theology will always be provisional, contextual, and partial insofar as its infinite subject, God, defies any finite human system of comprehending God in all fullness. Scripture itself testifies that its own rich witness is partial, even if also sufficient to sustain communities of faith. Moses saw only the backside of God and not God's face (Exod 33:18-23; see Deut 29:29). The apostle Paul affirmed that we see now "in a mirror, dimly, but then we will see face to face" (1 Cor 13:12). See BIBLICAL CRITICISM; BIBLICAL INTERPRETATION, HISTORY OF; GOD, METAPHORS FOR; HISTORICISM; HISTORIOGRAPHY AND HISTORICISM; JESUS, METAPHORS FOR; LIBERATION THEOLOGY; METAPHOR IN THEOLOGY; THEOLOGY, NT; THEOLOGY, OT; THEOLOGICAL HERMENEUTICS.

Bibliography: James Barr. *The Concept of Biblical Theology* (1999); Craig Bartholomew et al., ed. *Out of Egypt: Biblical Theology and Biblical Interpretation* (2004); Alice Bellis, Alice Ogden, and Joel Kaminsky, ed. *Jews, Christians, and the Theology of the Hebrew Scriptures* (2000); Brevard Childs. *Biblical Theology of the Old and New Testaments, Theological Reflection on the Christian Bible* (1992); Julianna Claassens. "Biblical Theology as Dialogue: Continuing the Conversation with Mikhail Bakhtin and Biblical Theology." *JBL* 122 (2003) 127–44; Leo Perdue. *Reconstructing Old Testament Theology, after the Collapse of History* (2005); J. Sandys-Wunsch and L. Eldredge. "J. P. Gabler and the Distinction between Biblical Dogmatic Theology." *SJT* 33 (1980) 133–158; R. S. Sugirtharajah. *Post-Colonial Criticism and Biblical Interpretation* (2002); Phyllis Trible. "Overtures to a Feminist Biblical Theology." Ben Ollenburger, ed. *Old Testament Theology,*

Flowering and Future (2004), 399–408; Francis Watson. *Text, Church, and World, Biblical Interpretation in Theological Perspective* (1994); Francis Watson. *Text and Truth, Redefining Biblical Theology* (1997).

DENNIS T. OLSON

BICHRI bik´ri [בִּכְרִי bikhri]. Known in the OT only as the father of SHEBA (2 Sam 20:1-22) he is a Benjaminite whose name is related to that of a tribe of Bichrites loyal to SAUL instead of DAVID (2 Sam 20:14).

BIDKAR [בִּדְקַר bidhqar]. King Jehu's aide who threw Joram's dead body on Naboth's ground to fulfill God's oracle (2 Kgs 9:25).

BIER [מִטָּה mittah; σορός soros]. A stretcher (from נָטָה natah, "to stretch") used for carrying a deceased human body in a funeral procession (2 Sam 3:31; Luke 7:14). Soros can mean "coffin" but in Luke a bier/stretcher is clearly implied, since the resuscitated youth "sits up" in v. 15. In both biblical stories, reference to the bier reinforces the depiction of a funeral procession and heightens the pathos of the narrative.

BYRON MCCANE

BIGAMY. *See* MARRIAGE, NT; MARRIAGE. OT.

BIGTHA big´thuh [בִּגְתָא bightha´]. An attendant among King Ahsuerus' seven enuchs who were requested to bring him Queen Vashti (Esth 1:10). Possibly same as BIGTHAN.

BIGTHAN big´thuhn [בִּגְתָן bighthan]. One of King Ahasuerus' eunuchs. With Teresh he guarded the king. After Mordecai revealed their plot to kill King Ahasuerus, the king had them both executed (Esth 2:21; 6:2). Probably same as Bigtha. *See* BIGTHA.

BIGVAI big´vi [בִּגְוַי bighway; Βαγουι Bagoui, Βαγοι Bagoi, Βαγο Bago]. 1. One of the Jewish leaders who returned to Judah with Zerubbabel (Ezra 2:2; Neh 7:7). Another seventy-two males of this family returned with Ezra (Ezra 8:14; 1 Esd 8:40).

2. One who sealed Ezra's covenant (Neh 10:16-17).

BILDAD bil´dad [בִּלְדַּד bildadh]. Bildad the Shuhite, ELIPHAZ, and ZOPHAR are friends who gather to offer JOB dialogue in three cycles in the central poetic portion of the book. Bildad's speeches (Job 8; 18; 25) often support the view that the wicked, not the righteous, suffer. *See* SHUAH.

BILEAM bil´ee-uhm [בִּלְעָם bil'am]. A town within Manasseh's allotted section that was reassigned along with its pasture lands to some of the Kohathites (1 Chr 6:55). Joshua 17:11 lists IBLEAM instead.

BILGAH bil'guh [בִּלְגָּה bilgah]. Aaronite designated head of the fifteenth division of priests by David (1 Chr 24:14). A priest who returned with Zerubbabel (Neh 12:5, 18).

BILGAI bil'gi [בִּלְגַּי bilgay]. Mentioned as one of the priests who placed his name on the sealed covenant document (Neh 10:9). Probably same as BILGAH.

BILHAH bil'huh [בִּלְהָה bilhah]. Bilhah, LABAN's servant given to RACHEL at her marriage to JACOB (Gen 29:29), bore Jacob two sons, DAN and NAPHTALI at Rachel's behest. Bilhah is later mentioned as having sexual relations with REUBEN, disqualifying him from his inheritance as Jacob's firstborn son (Gen 35:22; 49:4).

JESSICA TINKLENBERG DeVEGA

BILHAN bil'han [בִּלְהָן bilhan]. 1. Eldest son of Ezer, the Horite, a subbranch of Edomites (Gen 36:27).

2. Eldest son of Jediael, a Benjaminite (1 Chr 7:10). This list differs significantly from par. lists (Gen 46; Num 26; 1 Chr 8) and may not be original.

FOOK KONG WONG

BILL OF DIVORCE. *See* CERTIFICATE OF DIVORCE; DIVORCE; MARRIAGE.

BILSHAN bil'shan [בִּלְשָׁן bilshan; Βαλασαν Balasan, Βαλσαν Balsan]. "Inquirer." One of the leaders of the Jews who returned to Judah with ZERUBBABEL after the exile (Ezra 2:2; Neh 7:7; 1 Esd 5:8).

BIMHAL bim'hal [בִּמְהָל bimhal]. This name occurs only once (1 Chr 7:33) and may be a shortened form of בֶּן־מָהָל (ben mahal), "son of circumcision." He is listed as a son of JAPHLET of the tribe of ASHER, head of his ancestral house, and a mighty warrior.

BINDING AND LOOSING [קָשַׁר qashar; פָּתַח pathakh; δέω deō, λύω lyō]. A variety of Hebrew and Greek terms are used for "binding" and "loosing," concepts that appear in many religions with various meanings. These terms and related concepts are found separately in many biblical contexts, e.g., Deut 6:8; Judg 16:6; Isa 61:1; Tob 7:11; 8:3; Acts 22:30; Rom 7:1; and Rev 1:5. Such terms are used together, e.g., in Job 38:31; 39:5-6 (God's cosmic power and care for wildlife), Mark 11:2-5 (untying a tied colt), and 1 Cor 7:27 (marriage ties).

The most problematic texts combining the terms are Matt 16:19 and 18:18. Traditional Catholicism understands that Jesus here founded the church with Peter as its first head, in effect, its first pope. Interpreters citing rabbinic usages propose that the terms refer to the authority to release people from vows, or to declare actions either forbidden or permitted. Other interpreters suggest a further range of possibilities, e.g., that Jesus authorized Peter, then a larger group of disciples, to rule on matters of doctrine and discipline, to interpret Scripture, to condemn or excommunicate sinners or grant forgiveness, or to bind Satan (or demons) and free their victims. Many interpreters attribute both texts to the post-Easter, Matthean church as an attempt to legitimate its emerging leadership.

Bibliography: Herbert W. Basser. "Derrett's 'Binding' Reopened." *JBL* 104 (1985) 297–300; 743–45. J. Duncan and M. Derrett. "*Binding and Loosing* (Matt 16:19, 18:18; John 20:23)." *JBL* 102 (1983) 112–17; David Ekem. "Another Look at the Translation of Matthew 16:19." *BT* 55 (2004) 119–24; Richard H. Hiers. "'Binding' and 'Loosing': The Matthean Authorizations." *JBL* 104 (1985) 233–50.

RICHARD H. HIERS

BINDING OF ISAAC [יַעֲקֹד אֶת־יִצְחָק ya'aqodh 'eth yitskhaq]. Also called the AKEDAH, especially in the Jewish tradition, this phrase refers to Abraham "binding" (ya'aqodh) his son Isaac in preparation for offering him as a sacrifice (Gen 22:9), or to the entire story. *See* ABRAHAM, OT.

TERENCE E. FRETHEIM

BINEA bin'ee-uh [בִּנְעָא bin'a']. A Benjaminite descendant of King Saul. He is Moza's son and the father of Raphah (or Raphaiah), Eleasah, and Azel (1 Chr 8:37; 9:43).

BINNUI bin'yoo-i [בִּנּוּי binnuy]. Name borne by a person and a clan-group in the post-exilic period. The person known as Binnui appears as one of the citizens helping to build the wall of Jerusalem under Nehemiah's direction (Neh 3:24). In Neh 10:10 he is identified as a Levite, as is the case in Neh 12:8. His son Noadiah appears among a list at Ezra 8:33. The name also appears to designate a clan or family group in a list of such groups at Ezra 10:30. It also appears at 10:38, though there is some textual evidence for another name, "Bani." The group also appears in a listing at Neh 7:15.

KENNETH G. HOGLUND

BIOGRAPHY. Traditionally, the Gospels were read as "the story of Jesus." In the 19th cent., biographies took up the historical challenge of explaining their subjects through an account of their upbringing, psychological development and so forth, and of setting their activities in a wider historical context. Because these features are missing in the Gospels, scholars denied that the Gospels were biographies, instead, they were treated as folk literature, collections of short anecdotes and sayings that had been handed down orally (Bultmann 1972). The scholarly consensus through most of the 20th cent. held that the Gospels were *sui generis*, of a unique genre.

Form-critical analysis concentrated on individual passages and their setting in the life of the early church, while redaction-critical studies attempted to reconstruct the evangelist's community from his theological emphases. During the 1980s, the application of literary-critical methods to the Gospels showed the evangelists to be self-conscious writers, capable of considerable narrative skill. This development revived the question of Gospel genre.

Obsession with "personality" is a feature of modern biography. The ancients were interested in a person's character as displayed in great deeds, words, and public life. The word *biography* itself does not appear until the 9th cent. Ancient "lives" (*bioi* in Greek or *vitae* in Latin) were relatively short prose narratives, 10,000–20,000 words in length, about the length of a typical scroll. Unlike modern biographies, they do not cover the whole life in detail. Lives may begin with mention of the person's ancestry or city and birth, but then the narrative jumps to their debut in public life. While lives of generals or statesmen are more chronologically ordered, accounts of philosophers or writers are arranged topically, but both sorts usually cover the subject's death in great detail as evidence of true character. Verbal analysis reveals that the hero of ancient biographies is the subject of a quarter to a third of the verbs, while another 15 percent to 30 percent occur in reports of their sayings or speeches.

The Gospels are of similar length, composition, and structure to that of ancient lives. The concentration on Jesus' public ministry from his baptism to his death, and on his great deeds and words is also not very different, and the amount of space given to the last week of Jesus' life—his death and resurrection—are comparable to other ancient biographies. About half of the verbs in the Gospels either have Jesus as subject or are spoken by him. These marked similarities of form and content show that the Gospels share the main generic features of ancient biography and must be interpreted accordingly.

Such a biographical focus upon Jesus must affect the way the Gospels are read, taught, and preached. No similar accounts were compiled for rabbis from that period, such as Hillel or Shammai, despite the many individual anecdotes about their teaching and activities. This is because rabbinic material is primarily focused upon the Torah, the Law, while the biographical genre of the Gospels makes an explicit theological claim about the centrality of the person of Jesus, in whose life, death, and resurrection God is revealed. Therefore, every passage must be interpreted in the light of each evangelist's narrative and theological understanding of Jesus. The four separate accounts of Jesus' life within the NT allow for a plurality of interpretations as each writer seeks to tell the story of the one Jesus afresh for his audience. *See* BIBLICAL INTERPRETATION, HISTORY OF; GENRE; JESUS CHRIST; JOHN, GOSPEL OF; LUKE, GOSPEL OF; MARK, GOSPEL OF; MATTHEW, GOSPEL OF.

Bibliography: David E. Aune. *The Westminster Dictionary of New Testament and Early Christian Literature and Rhetoric* (2003); Rudolf Bultmann. *The History of the Synoptic Tradition*, rev. ed. with supplement (1972). Richard A. Burridge. *What Are the Gospels? A Comparison with Graeco-Roman Biography*, rev. ed. (2004); Richard A. Burridge. *Four Gospels, One Jesus? A Symbolic Reading* (2005); Charles H. Talbert. *What Is a Gospel? The Genre of the Canonical Gospels* (1977).

RICHARD A. BURRIDGE

BIRD OF PREY [עַיִט 'ayit]. One of the prime characteristics of the fauna of Israel/Palestine is its vast abundance of birds of prey (eagles, vultures, hawks, falcons, etc). This was evidently the case in biblical times, as well. Probably due to their frequent contact with carcasses, all large carrion eaters among the birds were considered ritually unclean, and hence inedible (Lev 11:13-19; Deut 14:12-18). The fact that the word 'ayit (lit. "screamer") is missing from the texts listing various unclean birds corroborates the hypothesis that this term does not denote any particular species. Rather, it is used as a generic term, to be translated "bird of prey." In the OT, 'ayit birds are commonly associated with the notion of untimely death, without the opportunity of a proper burial (Isa 18:6; Ezek 39:4). Their appearance could probably sometimes be regarded as a bad omen (Gen 15:11). However, soaring majestically in the sky, and then suddenly swooping down on their victims, birds of prey also provided apt metaphors for conquerors and their armies. In Isa 46:11, the Persian general Cyrus is thus depicted as "a bird of prey from the east." *See* BIRDS OF THE BIBLE; EAGLE; FALCON; NIGHTHAWK; VULTURE.

GÖRAN EIDEVALL

BIRDS OF THE BIBLE [עוֹף 'of; τετεινά teteina]. The bird-life of present-day Israel and Palestine is rich and varied. Migratory birds pass through the area in vast flocks. Ornithologists come as pilgrims to admire the sight of thousands of large raptorial birds passing by, on their way to their winter homes in Africa. By taking this route in daytime, large birds are able to ride on warm currents of air. Some birds of prey, like griffon vultures and eagles, are permanent residents in the land. Herons, grebes, and other sea birds can be spotted at the Sea of Galilee. In the second half of the 19th cent. CE, extensive explorations of the Palestinian fauna were performed by Tristram. According to his report, at least 348 different bird species were dwelling in the area, either permanently or periodically (Tristram 1884). Recent estimations suggest that the correct figure is approximately 400 (Bodenheimer lists 413 species). If a survey like Tristram's had been made during the biblical period, it would probably have yielded a similar result. Some changes have nevertheless taken place. Thus the ostrich appears to have been rather common during the biblical period. By the 19th cent., it had become a rarity. Now it has disappeared from the area altogether. Although some birds have left the scene and others arrived, we may safely assume that the diversity of the biblical period roughly corresponded to the present situation. Only a small amount of these 300–400 kinds of birds are mentioned by name in the Bible. Still, despite the fact that the biblical writers usually had quite other purposes than ornithological instruction in mind, some passages contain accurate observations concerning the life of various birds. For instance, the reader learns about different nesting habits—in trees (Ezek 31:6), by rivers and streams (Ps 104:12), or on mountain tops (Jer 49:16)—and about the migratory habits of some species (Song 2:12; Jer 8:7).

A. Birds in Biblical Palestine

1. Terminology and classification

a. Generic terms in the Bible. Biblical terminology does not always correspond to the classifications of modern zoology. In the OT, the Hebrew word ʿof is used as a generic term, to designate all birds—or, to be more precise: all flying creatures, at times even including insects. The related verb ʿuf עוּף means "to fly." Thus it is hardly surprising that the bat is listed among the unclean "birds" (Lev 11:19; Deut 14:18). The term tsippor צִפּוֹר can denote a variety of small birds (but perhaps primarily those belonging to the passerines). In some cases, however, this term seems to carry an even broader sense, covering all kinds of birds (Deut 22:6; Ps 8:8; Ezek 39:17). In addition to these generic terms, one finds more than 30 Hebrew bird names in the OT. In several cases, though, the exact reference cannot be determined. In fact, identifying the birds mentioned in passages is one of the most vexed problems confronting

Bible translators. The difficulties involved are manifold. One and the same term can denote one species or another, depending on the context, and sometimes a whole family of birds. In several cases, the exact meaning was not known by the ancient translators. In the NT, the most frequent generic term is peteinon πετεινόν, with the basic sense of "winged creature." While the word orneon ὄρνεον is also used to designate all kinds of birds, ornis ὄρνις is only used in the specialized sense "hen" (Matt 23:37; Luke 13:34).

b. Birds of prey. In the biblical texts, the Hebrew word ʿayit עַיִט should probably be treated as a generic term for the entire group of large BIRDS OF PREY (the families of *falconidae* and *vulturidae*). This hypothesis is consonant both with the actual usage of the word ʿayit, and with the observation that it is conspicuously absent in the passages where various kinds of unclean birds are listed. In modern usage, though, ʿayit means "eagle." In the biblical texts, another Hebrew word, nesher נֶשֶׁר, is usually translated "eagle." Presumably due to the contrasting associations evoked by eagles and vultures in Western culture, this translator's preference persists also in recent versions, such as the NRSV, despite an emerging scholarly consensus that nesher in most cases refers not to the eagle but to the majestic griffon vulture (*Gyps fulvus*). The clearest example is Mic 1:16, a passage which alludes to the baldness of the nesher (*see* VULTURE). Another word, nets נֵץ, is apparently used as a general designation for hawks of all kinds (Lev 11:16; Deut 14:15; Job 39:26). Tristram recorded as many as 37 different species of raptorial birds, including the Lämmergeier (*Gypaëtus barbatus*, possibly to be identified with the peres פֶּרֶס, mentioned in Lev 11:13), the Egyptian eagle (*Neophron percnopterus*), and several kinds of falcons and kites. All birds of prey were considered ritually unclean.

c. Owls. It is extremely difficult to identify the owls mentioned in the OT. Tristram registered eight species of owls (*strigidae*). Some of these are probably mentioned in the bird lists in Lev 11 and Deut 14. It is possible that Hebrew kos כּוֹס, occurring in Lev 11:17, Deut 14:16 and Ps 102:6 (= Heb 102:7), designates the little owl (*Athene noctua glaux*), one of the most common species in the area. Alternatively, it refers to the tawny owl (*Syrnium aluco*). It is hard to be more specific, without resorting to sheer speculations. Scholars have, for instance, suggested that takhmas תַּחְמָס in Lev 11:16 might refer to the barn owl (*Strix flammea* or *Tyto alba*) or to the goatsucker, whereas NRSV has opted for the nighthawk. Further, it is possible that the Hebrew word yanshuf יַנְשׁוּף in Lev 11:17 and Isa 34:11 denotes the screech owl. The yanshuf was taken to be the ibis by the ancient versions (LXX and Vulgate), but this term is usually (and perhaps wisely) nowadays rendered with "great owl," or just "owl." In Isa 34:11-14, it is not certain whether some words refer to owls or to some other creatures associated with ruins and desolate places. Thus, the word qippodh קִפּוֹד in 34:11, which is usually translated "hedgehog" (NRSV), might designate the bittern or some kind of owl. Further, qippoz קִפּוֹז in 34:15 has been identified both as the arrow snake and as the Scops owl (Tristram). According to a likely interpretation of Isa 34:14, Edom is said to be haunted by a demon named Lilith ("night ghost"). However, some scholars prefer taking lilith לִילִית as referring to an owl.

d. Passerines. The Hebrew term tsippor is used as a designation for all small birds. Presumably onomatopoeic in origin ("chirper"), this word is primarily connected with numerous passerine birds (Tristram registered 161 different species). In some passages, e.g., Ps 84:3 [Heb. 84:4] and Prov 26:2, where it stands together with the swallow (deror דְּרוֹר), tsippor may refer specifically to the common house sparrow (*Passer domesticus*). Note the similarity in sound between tsippor and *sparrow*. However, in a passage like Isa 31:5, the reference is arguably to larger birds (perhaps birds of prey?), hovering over their young. In Lev 11:15 and Deut 14:14, the term 'orev עֹרֵב, which is usually translated "raven," probably designates the entire family of *corvidae*, including several kinds of ravens, jackdaws and crows.

e. Water birds. Herons, bitterns, pelicans, cormorants, and several other birds belonging to the family of *steganopodes* can be seen at the Sea of Galilee. Towards the end of the bird lists in Lev 11 and Deuteronomy, one probably finds a number of water birds. However, their identification is a complicated matter. It is often assumed that 'anafah אֲנָפָה in Lev 11:19 is used as a designation for all kinds of herons, and that shalakh שָׁלָךְ in Lev 11:17 denotes the cormorant (*Phalacrocrorax carbo*). However, Driver has argued that shalakh signifies the fisher owl (*Ketupa indus*), whereas 'anafah stands for the cormorant.

f. Gallinaceous birds and doves. Among the gallinaceous birds, the ancient Israelites were probably well acquainted with the partridge קֹרֵא qore' (Jer 17:11) and the quail selaw שְׂלָו (Exod 16:13). Several kinds of pigeons or doves (*columbae*) are found in Palestine. In the OT the Hebrew word יוֹנָה yonah denotes the rock dove (*Columbia livia*), while תּוֹר tor signifies all kinds of turtle doves.

2. Religious and economic perspectives

a. Clean and unclean birds. Most importantly, all birds were divided into two categories: the CLEAN AND UNCLEAN. The underlying principles behind this division are not entirely transparent, but it is clear that a ritual concept of purity is involved. Contact with carcasses was regarded as contaminating (Lev 11:39-40). Hence, all carrion-eating birds were taboo. The unclean birds listed in the virtually identical passages of Lev 11:13-19 and Deut 14:12-18 can all be termed "birds of prey" (in a wide sense), since they feed either on live prey (fish, in several cases) or on carcasses. It is safe to conclude that also raptorial birds not mentioned in these lists belonged to the unclean category. It is stated in the Mishnah that "any bird that seizes food in its claw is unclean" (*m. Hul.* 3:6). Although it does not necessarily follow that all non-raptorial birds belonged to the clean category, we know that at least all passerines, partridges and pigeons were considered clean. However, only doves and pigeons seem to have been accepted as sacrificial animals (Lev 1:14; *see also* Gen 15:9). Pigeons and turtledoves were the offerings of the poor, who could not afford to bring a lamb for the ritual (Lev 5:7; 12:6; *see also* Luke 2:24).

b. Birds in the household economy. All kinds of clean birds were edible, at least in principle (Deut 14:11, 20). But in practice, what role did birds play in the household economy during the biblical period? Eggs from wild birds were apparently collected and cooked (Deut 22:6; Isa 10:14). Pigeons were raised at home or in dovecots (Isa 60:8; *see also m. Sabb.* 24:3), in order to be cooked for dinner or sacrificed in the Temple. In the Hellenestic period, doves and pigeons were raised industrially, in large underground *columbaria*. Small birds, such as sparrows and partridges, were caught, sold, and eaten (after removing the blood, *see* Lev 17:13). Some information about the methods used by the fowlers, involving a variety of traps and nets, can be gathered from the bird-hunting imagery used in a number of poetic and prophetic passages (Job 18:8-10; Ps 124:7; Prov 1:17; 6:5; Jer 5:26-27; Hos 7:12; Amos 3:5). The custom of raising domestic FOWL was introduced rather late, but in the NT period it had become important for many households.

B. Birds in the Texts of the Bible

1. The OT

a. Narrative texts. A couple of birds have prominent roles in the story of the FLOOD. In accordance with the custom of ancient navigators, Noah sends out birds as scouts. First, he releases a raven, and then a dove, the latter returning with an olive branch (Gen 8:6-12). Utnapishtim sends out a similar set of birds in the Babylonian version of this story, as recorded in the *Gilgamesh* epic (*ANET*, 94–95), albeit in reverse order: dove, swallow, raven. Otherwise, birds are not granted important roles in the narratives of the OT. Clean birds are caught and eaten. In one famous episode during the desert wandering, the Israelites are saved from starvation by the arrival of innumerable delicious quails (Exod 16). Raptorial birds are often mentioned in the context of untimely death. The destiny of those who were executed or killed at the battle field, and who were not allowed to be buried properly, was to be eaten by birds and other animals (Gen 40:19; 1 Sam 17:44, 46). This motif was a common ingredient in curses (Deut 28:26; 1 Kgs 14:11; 16:4; 21:24).

b. Poetic and prophetic texts. Bird metaphors are relatively frequent in the poetic parts of the OT. Generally speaking, large birds, and especially birds of prey, are associated with strength and power, whereas small birds who were hunted by larger birds as well as by fowlers tend to be associated with notions of weakness and vulnerability (*see* Ps 102:7 [Heb. 102:8]; Prov 7:23; Hos 7:11-12). Hence, in Lamentations, the persecuted speaker can depict himself (embodying the nation?) as a hunted bird (Lam 3:52). Using an equally apt metaphor, the prophets could picture an approaching enemy army as an attacking eagle or vulture (Jer 48:40; Hos 8:1). God is sometimes depicted as a large bird of prey, caring for the Israelites like a **nesher** (vulture or eagle) cares for its young (Deut 32:11), carrying them on its wings (Exod 19:4). A recurring motif in the Psalms, to seek shelter "in the shadow of your wings" (e.g., Ps 57:1 [Heb. 57:2]; 63:7 [Heb. 63:8]) would seem to imply that God is pictured as a mother bird. In several cases, the thrust of a metaphor appears to be based upon the characteristic habits of the bird in question. Thus, the owl, a howling creature of the night, was associated with mourning (Ps 102:6 [Heb. 102:7]). Doves were also closely connected with lamenting, because of their allegedly moaning sounds (Isa 38:14; 59:11). In addition, the dove was associated with love (Song 1:15; 4:1; 5:2, etc.) and with swiftness (Hos 11:11). Flying away, like a bird on its wings, is used as a powerful metaphor for freedom in the Psalms (Ps 55:6 [Heb. 55:7]; 124:7). In the oracles against foreign nations in the prophetic literature, finally, a recurring motif describes a city laid in ruins as the abode of owls, ravens, ostriches, and other birds (Isa 13:21; 34:11-15; Zeph 2:14).

2. The NT

Birds appear in rather prominent roles in a couple of stories about Jesus from Nazareth and his disciples. All four evangelists recount that the Spirit descended upon Jesus in the guise of a dove (Matt 3:16; Mark 1:10; Luke 3:22; John 1:32). According to the Synoptic Gospels, this took place at his baptism. In another famous episode, Peter's threefold denial is accompanied by the crowing of a cock (Mark 14:30-31, 66-72). When it comes to the teachings of Jesus, one should first of all notice that in the Sermon on the Mount he invites his audience to observe the birds in the sky (Matt 6:26). According to the Lucan version of this exhortation, birds of a certain species are to be studied, namely the ravens (Luke 12:24). At any rate, the point seems to be that one can learn something important about divine grace and providence through ornithological observations. Another saying focuses on the small, seemingly insignificant sparrows: sold for a penny each, yet not forgotten by their creator (Matt 10:29; Luke 12:6-7). However, Jesus apparently takes for granted that human beings are far more valuable than birds (Matt

6:26). Further, a few references to birds are found in the parables (Mark 4:4 = Matt 13:4; Mark 4:32 = Matt 13:32). In a creative adaptation of a metaphorical motif known from the Psalms, finally, Jesus likened himself to a hen gathering the chicks under her wings (Matt 23:37; Luke 13:34). *See* ANIMALS OF THE BIBLE; BIRD OF PREY; BROOD; BUZZARD; CLEAN AND UNCLEAN; COCK; CORMORANT; CRANE; CROW; DOVE; EAGLE; FALCON; FOWL; NEST; NIGHTHAWK; OSPREY; OSTRICH; OWL; PARTRIDGE; PELICAN; PIGEON; QUAIL; RAVEN; SEA GULL; SPARROW; STORK; SWAN; TURTLEDOVE; VULTURE; WATER HEN; WING.

Bibliography: Fritz Bodenheimer. *Animal Life in Palestine* (1953); G. R. Driver. "Birds in the Old Testament: I. Birds in Law." *PEQ* (1955) 5–20; G. R. Driver. "Birds in the Old Testament: II. Birds in Life." *PEQ* (1955) 129–140; Göran Eidevall. "Lions and Birds as Literature: Some Notes on Isaiah 31 and Hosea 11." *SJOT* 7 (1993) 78–87; J. Feliks. *The Animal World of the Bible* (1962); Alice Parmelee. *All the Birds of the Bible: Their Stories, Identification, and Meaning* (1959); Henry B. Tristram. *The Fauna and Flora of Palestine.* The Survey of Western Palestine (1884) 30–139.

GÖRAN EIDEVALL

BIRKET EL-HAMRA. *See* SILOAM.

BIRSHA bihr′shuh [בִּרְשַׁע *birsha*ʿ]. King of the city of Gomorrah against whom the kings of Shinar, Ellasar, Elam, and Goiim waged war (Gen 14:2, 8, 10-11).

BIRTH [יָלַד *yaladh*; γεννάω *gennaō*]. Biblical tradition celebrates the birth of children as a sign of great blessing (Ruth 4:14; Luke 1:14, 57-58), and Genesis casts reproduction as central to the human vocation (Gen 1:28). Divine control of reproduction is illustrated by texts that speak of God opening (Gen 29:31; 30:22) or closing the womb (1 Sam 1:5-6), or giving (Ruth 4:13) or taking away (Hos 9:14) pregnancy.

Early Jewish, Greek, and Roman sources lend witness to ancient views of conception which held that coital position and the disposition of sexual partners during intercourse could directly affect the appearance and demeanor of the child they conceived. In keeping with the Sumerian and Babylonian metaphor of the fecund female as a ploughed or tilled field, biblical tradition emphasizes female infertility, characterizing both non-producing fields and childless women as barren (Sir 26:20-21). Although contraception is absent from the Bible, Rabbinic interpretation refers to Onan (Gen 38:9) "threshing inside and winnowing outside," and applies the same phrase to allow for the practice of *coitus interruptus* in cases of intercourse involving a female minor, pregnant woman, or nursing mother.

While the ancients regarded nine months' gestation as the norm, comments regarding atypical cases are also extant. In the case of premature birth, infants born at seven months were generally considered more vital than those born at eight. The Babylonian Diagnostic Handbook and inscriptions at the Temple of Asclepios in Epidaurus allude to the phenomenon of the "sleeping fetus" and delayed birth.

The difficulty and pain of labor and delivery is well attested in the biblical texts (*see* the etiological story involving EVE in Gen 3:16). Stories recounting the difficult birth of Esau and Jacob (Gen 25: 21-26) and the death of Rachel giving birth to Benjamin (Gen 35:16-20), as well as numerous birthing metaphors (2 Kgs 19:3; Isa 26:17-18; Hos 13:13; Mic 4:9-10; John 16:21; Rev 12:2), demonstrate the risks and dangers that the biblical writers associated with childbirth. Untimely births (Eccl 6:3-5; Ps 58:8) and miscarriages (Hos 9:14) are recounted and sometimes taken as a sign of divine judgment. John 3:3-7 alludes to the water and blood associated with childbirth to speak metaphorically of spiritual rebirth.

Not surprisingly, the use of herbs, amulets, and incantations to sustain pregnancy and ease birth was common. Midwives assisted women in labor and delivery (Exod 1:15-21). Stol argues that whereas the birthstool was widely used by the ancients, Egyptian hymns and incantations as well as Exod 1:16 refer instead to a pair of stones or bricks upon which women would squat to give birth. Following birth, the NAVEL CORD was cut and the newborn was cleansed, rubbed with salt and swathed in bands (Ezek 16:4). In the Roman era, infants were swaddled (Luke 2:7). *See* BARREN, BARRENNESS; CHILD, CHILDREN; MIDWIFE.

Bibliography: M. Stol. *Birth in Babylonia and the Bible: Its Mediterranean Setting* (2000).

                                                                    MARY FOSKETT

BIRTH OF MARY, GOSPEL OF THE. *See* MARY, GOSPEL OF THE BIRTH OF.

BIRTH, NEW. *See* NEW BIRTH.

BIRTH, VIRGIN. *See* VIRGIN BIRTH.

BIRTHRIGHT [בְּכֹרָה bekhorah; πρωτοτόκια *prōtotokia*]. The special privilege assigned to the first-born of any father. This meant, in the first place, that he inherited two portions, that is, double the portions for the other males. (Females inherited only when there were no males.) *See* Deut 21:15-17; on females, Num 27:1-11.

The right of the firstborn also meant leadership among the brothers after the death of the father. The birthright could be forfeited, as in the case of Reuben, the firstborn of Jacob, who slept with Bilhah, a concubine of his father (Gen 35:22). The birthright was yielded to Joseph, according to 1 Chr 5:1-2. Joseph was not the second of Jacob, but the first of Rachel,

the favorite among Jacob's wives (Gen 30:22-23), a replacement that was irregular. It reflects the realities of the respective tribes in Israel, not the legal prescriptions about the birthright.

                                                                    JORGE PIXLEY

BIRTHSTOOL [רַהַט rahat]. A seat on which a woman labored to give birth, with the assistance of midwives (Exod 2:16). *See* BIRTH; MIDWIFE; PUAH; SHIPHRAH.

BIRZAITH bihr-zay'ith [בִּרְזוֹת birzawith, בִּרְזָיִת birzayith]. The name in 1 Chr 7:31 probably means "well of olive" but does not appear in the par. genealogies in Gen 46:17 and Num 26:44-47. Formulas like "father of Bethlehem" and "father of Kiriath-jearim" (2 Chr 2:50-55) support interpreting Birzaith in "father of Birzaith" as a town and identifying it with the modern town of Birzeith near Tyre. If Birzaith was a person, he was the son of MALCHIEL, an Asherite. *See* ASHER.

                                                                    FOOK KONG WONG

BISHLAM bish'luhm [בִּשְׁלָם bishlam]. Possibly the title of a Persian official (Ezra 4:7). In the Vulgate and in 1 Esd 2:16, Bishlam is understood to be a proper name, although it is otherwise unattested. Some have tried to understand this as a form of qualifier, "in accord with," although the word order would not support this. Others have suggested a textual problem obscured the original reading "biyerushalayim," or "concerning the matter of Jerusalem."

                                                                    KENNETH G. HOGLUND

BISHOP [ἐπίσκοπος *episkopos*]. The term designates a person who exercises a function of oversight; within the NT an individual oversees a community of believers. In the Hellenistic Greek, the term was used of both men and women who exercised a variety of oversight functions in different spheres of human activity. One of the earliest uses employs the term *episkopos* to describe those responsible for watching over a ship's cargo (Homer, *Od.* 8.163). Sophocles (5th cent. BCE) used the term for guardians or supervisors, as did Plato (*Leg.* 8.849*a*). Aristophanes (4th–5th cent. BCE) employed "overseer" for an official sent to serve as an administrator in a subject state (*Av.* 1022-1023; *see* 1 Macc 1:51). Plato's usage reflects the many contexts in which the term could be used.

Plato mentions women who served as overseers or mentors of young married couples (*Leg.* 6 [784*a*]), women who functioned as overseers during athletic events, and women who fed children, and those who were nannies or baby-sitters (*Leg.* 7 [795*d*]). The term *episkopos* is masculine in form. Nonetheless, Plato used the term in its masculine form when speaking of women who exercised any of these forms of oversight.

The function of oversight was designated by the noun ἐπισκοπή episkopē), a term that is closely related to "overseer." Reprising an expression that occurred in Jeremiah's oracle against Jerusalem (Jer 6:15 [LXX]), Luke 19:44 and 1 Pet 2:12 use the term *oversight* to describe the oversight that God will exercise on the day of judgment. Hence, the NRSV translates episkopē as visitation. The day of divine "oversight" is the day of judgment.

The LXX often uses episkopē to render the Hebrew פְּקֻדָּה pequdah, a word that means "commission" or "office." The word is used in this sense in Ps 109:8, "may another seize his position," a passage that Luke uses to describe Peter's decision that another person should be chosen to take Judas' place among the Twelve: "Let another take his position as overseer" (Acts 1:20 [NRSV]). Probably some few years after the composition of Acts, 1 Timothy also used episkopos to describe a function within the early church: "whoever aspires to the office of bishop desires a noble task" (1 Tim 3:1 [NRSV, NAB]). Other translators are hesitant to use "bishop" in the their own renditions of 1 Tim 3:1 since "bishop" had not yet acquired the technical meaning that it would have in the later church. Thus, the NIV renders the epistle's phrase, "sets his heart on being an overseer," while the NJB offers "want to be a presiding elder" and the REB, "aspire to leadership." The oldest NT text to speak about the overseer/bishop is the greeting of Paul's Letter to the Philippians, which is addressed "to all the saints in Christ Jesus who are in Philippi, with the bishops and deacons" (Phil 1:1). The letter does not further specify whom these persons were nor what function they may have exercised. Luke's version of Paul's farewell address to the elders of the church at Ephesus urges them to "keep watch over yourselves and over all the flock, to which the Holy Spirit has made you overseers (episkopous), to shepherd the church of God" (Acts 20:28). Combined with Phil 1:1, Acts 20:28 suggests that the overseer was a feature of the Pauline churches, even though it is not mentioned in the various lists of charisms in 1 Cor 12.

A singular reference to the overseer/bishop, linked with that of the shepherd, is to be found in 1 Pet 2:25. There, in language that seems to be derived from Ezek 34:4-16, the Petrine author describes Christ as "the shepherd and guardian (episkopon) of our souls." The image of Christ as shepherd is common in the NT (John 10:11-18; 1 Pet 5:4; and the parable of the lost sheep, Matt 18:12-14; Luke 15:3-7; *Gos. Thom.* 107) but the doubled image of Christ as shepherd and overseer is unique within the NT. First Peter 2:25 refers to Christ gathering and then watching over those who had been estranged from God prior to their conversion.

An image of a shepherd gathering and bringing back straying sheep similar to the image of 1 Pet 2:25 and reflecting Ezek 34 is found in the Damascus Document where it is used in reference to the overseer (mevaqqer, CD 13:7-19). Fragments of the Damascus Document were found among the Dead Sea Scrolls. These Qumran fragments do not mention the overseer, but he is mentioned in the Rule of the Community (1QS6 xii-xx). The overseer had teaching, financial, and disciplinary responsibilities as well as responsibility for the introduction of new members into the community (*see* CD 13:7-19; 1QS 6 xii-xx; CD 13 vii-xix; 14 xi-xiii; 15: viii, xiv).

Later 1 Peter uses the same doubled image to describe the functions of the elders of the church: "I exhort the elders among you to tend the flock of God that is in your charge, exercising the oversight (episkopountes), not under compulsion but willingly, as God would have you do it—not for sordid gain but eagerly" (1 Pet 5:1-2). The passage indicates that elders are to fulfill their function of oversight by the strength of their example rather than by the exercise of raw power (1 Pet 5:3; *see* Luke 22:24-27). Linking the function of oversight with that of shepherd in both 1 Pet 2:25 and 5:2 and suggesting that it is the chief shepherd who will award the crown of glory (1 Pet 5:4), the author of 1 Peter suggests that overseers are to pattern their exercise of oversight after the model of Christ, who is the chief shepherd. Moreover, their ministry within the church is to be seen in continuity with leadership within Israel, so aptly described in the shepherd imagery of Ezek 34.

The linkage between shepherding and overseeing in the exhortations addressed to elders (Acts 20:17-18; 1 Pet 5:1) suggest that *elder* and *overseer* apply to one and the same person. *Elder* denotes a personal qualification of someone who fulfills a function of oversight within a church. Titus 1:5-9 makes a similar point in describing elders who are appointed to a function of oversight within various towns.

Titus 1:7 describes the bishop/overseer as God's steward. This description reflects the household structure of the churches for which the Pastoral Epistles were intended. Within the Greco-Roman household, the steward (οἰκονόμος oikonomos), generally a slave, was the household manager. His responsibilities included oversight over the master's other household slaves and the coordination of their activities. In some respects his duties were akin to a modern-day chief of staff, with all the power and responsibility that that position entails. Since the Pastoral Epistles describe the church as God's house or household (1 Tim 3:15), the bishop/overseer as the steward of God was considered to have a role similar to that of the chief slave within the Greco-Roman household; subordinate to the master, he supervised the other slaves.

Specific to the role of the Christian bishop/overseer was the responsibility to preach sound doctrine and to confront error (Titus 1:9). "Sound doctrine" was the cipher that the communities to which the

Pastoral Epistles were directed used to describe a correct understanding of the faith that led to appropriate behavior. Titus stipulates that the overseer must "have a firm grasp of the word that is trustworthy in accordance with the teaching" (Titus 1:9) in order to fulfill his ministry of the word. He must fully share in and understand what the community believes. Similarly, 1 Tim 3:6 stipulates that the bishop/overseer not be a neophyte in the faith lest he "be puffed up with conceit and fall into the condemnation of the devil." These two ways of explaining the mature faith that is required of the overseer may well clarify why it is that the overseer was an elder in the faith community.

Both Titus and 1 Timothy describe the other qualifications of the bishop/overseer in a catalog of virtues; 1 Timothy mentions eleven virtues (1 Tim 3:2-4), Titus, twelve virtues (Titus 1:7-8), to which should be added the five required of the elder (Titus 1:6). In the Greco-Roman world such catalogs were used for their cumulative effect rather than for the individual vices that they contained. Thus, the expectation is that the overseer/bishop be a good man. First Timothy underscores this notion by emphasizing that the overseer should enjoy a good reputation, even outside the faith community: "He must be well thought of by outsiders, so that he may not fall into disgrace and the snare of the devil" (1 Tim 3:7).

Among the qualities of the overseer in both 1 Timothy and Titus are that they be good family men, faithful to their wives and raising their children well. The overseer's qualities in 1 Timothy emphasize that the overseer should be a person who has managed his own household well; otherwise, he will not be capable of managing the household that is the church of God (1 Tim 3:5).

First Timothy 3:1-8 is the first panel of a diptych; the other panel consists of a list of qualifications of the helper/deacon (1 Tim 3:8-13). This pairing of overseer/helper (bishop/deacon) reflects the mention of overseer and helper in Phil 1:1. It indicates a structure of a two-role leadership function in the early Pauline churches. This pairing of bishops and deacons recurs in 1 Clement, where it is said that the apostles, having preached in the country and in towns, "appointed their first fruits, when they had tested them by the spirit, to be bishops and deacons for the future believers" (1 Clem. 42:4), noting that the apostles gave these offices their permanent character and set down guidelines for succession in these offices (1 Clem. 44:2-3). The Didachist urges his community to choose true and approved men as bishops and deacons (Did. 15:1).

In his letters, Ignatius of Antioch (d. ca. 117 CE) wrote at length about the function of the bishop in the churches to which he wrote. By this time, at least in those churches, the episcopacy was an office with clearly defined responsibilities. One of his seven letters is addressed to Polycarp, the "bishop" of Smyrna (Ignatius Pol.). Other bishops named by Ignatius are Onesimus (Ignatius Eph. 1:3), Damas (Ignatius Magn. 2:1), and Polybius (Ignatius Trall. 2:2).

While Ignatius often links the office of bishop with that of the deacon, he more commonly associates one bishop with deacons and a college of elders, the presbytery (Ignatius Magn. 6:1; 13:1; Ignatius Trall. 2:2-3; 3:1; 7:2; Ignatius Phld. 4:1; 10:2; Ignatius Smyrn. 8:1; 12:2; Ignatius Pol. 6:1). The bishop, together with the presbytery and deacons, is key to the unity of the church. Without these three, "nothing can be called a church" (Ignatius Trall. 3:1). Echoing Titus, Ignatius says that bishops are appointed in every quarter (Ignatius Eph. 3:2), suggesting that their responsibility is that of stewardship (Ignatius Eph. 6:1). Ignatius urges obedience to the bishop (Ignatius Eph. 5:3; Ignatius Magn. 3:1; 13:2; Ignatius Trall. 2:1; 13:2; Ignatius Smyrn. 8:1; Ignatius Pol. 6:1) for believers should respect the bishop "as the Lord himself" (Ignatius Eph. 6:1; see Ignatius Trall. 3:1). When marrying, men and women should do so with the consent of the bishop (Ignatius Pol. 5:2); the bishop is to be the guardian of widows (Ignatius Pol. 4:1). Without the bishop nothing is to be done (Ignatius Magn. 7:1; Ignatius Trall. 2:2; Ignatius Phld. 7:2; Ignatius Pol. 4:1), especially baptism and eucharist (Ignatius Smyrn. 8:1). See APOSTLE; CLEMENT, EPISTLE OF; DIDACHE; ELDER IN NT; IGNATIUS, EPISTLES OF; MINISTRY, CHRISTIAN.

Bibliography: P. J. Achetemeir. *1 Peter* (1996); R. F. Collins. *I and II Timothy and Titus* (2002); W. R. Schoedel. *Ignatius of Antioch* (1985); F. A. Sullivan. *From Apostles to Bishops* (2001); B. E. Thiering. "Mebaqqer and Episkopos in the Light of the Temple Scrolls." *JBL* 100 (1981) 59–74.

RAYMOND F. COLLINS

BISHOP'S BIBLE. A revision of the Great Bible (1539–40), initiated by the archbishop Matthew Parker and mandated for use in every church in England in 1568. It never became as popular in England as the Geneva Bible.

BIT [מֶתֶג metheg; χαλινός chalinos]. The empty space between a horse's incisor and molar teeth provides a place for a bit connected by cheek pieces on each side of the mouth to the reins. Pressure exerted through the reins influences the HORSE to turn or stop, thus providing some control. The use of bronze or iron bits (ca. 1300 BCE) thus revolutionized warfare (Ps 32:9; Jas 3:3). Some Iron Age biblical references to the use of bits with horses also reference the nose ring, perhaps still in use on donkeys (2 Kgs 19:28; Isa 37:29).

Bibliography: Robert Drews. *Early Riders: The Beginnings of Mounted Warfare in Asia and Europe* (2004).

DEBORAH CANTRELL

BITHIAH bith´ee-uh [בִּתְיָה bithyah]. Pharaoh's daughter; mother of Miriam, Shammai, and Ishbah; and wife of Mered, a descendant of Judah (1 Chr 4:18).

BITHYNIA bi-thin´ee-uh [Βιθυνία Bithynia]. A coastal province located in the northwest corner of Asia Minor, Bithynia was named for one of the Thracian tribes who settled there, subduing some of the native tribes, before the 8th cent. BCE. The area was transferred from Lydian to Persian control in 546 BCE but ruled itself independently during Hellenistic times. Its last king, Nicomedes III, willed Bithynia to the Roman government, and the region became a Roman province in 74 BCE. POMPEY joined it with Pontus in 65–63 BCE; soon its major city, Nicomedia, became the residence of the governors (proconsuls). The borders of this fertile area extended from Parthenius on the east to the Rhyndacus River on the west, from the Black (Euxine) Sea on the north to Galatia and Phrygia to the south (ca. 18,000 sq. mi.). By the Roman era, its most important cities were Nicomedia and Nicaea, followed by Chalcedon and Prusa. The most notable geographical landmark is the "Mysian" Olympus, which rises to 7,600 ft. The agricultural fertility of the plains along the Black Sea and the lower course of the Sangarius River was well attested in antiquity, while other mainstays of the regional economy were fishing and ship building.

Paul planned to enter Bithynia, probably to reach Nicaea and/or Nicomedia in the western portion of the province, but he felt compelled to travel to Troas instead (Acts 16:7). Nonetheless, 1 Peter bears witness to a 1st cent. Christian community there, since Bithynia is one of the five provinces to which the letter is addressed (1:1). Primarily because of its troubling financial irregularities, PLINY the Younger was appointed special commissioner of the province in 111 CE. By the time of Pliny's letter to TRAJAN in 112 CE (Letter 96), Christians were numerous enough even in the rural areas to cause Pliny concern. The pagan temples and the sacrificial cult they served were, according to Pliny, in radical decline due to the growing number of Christians, and the potential task of prosecuting those in the movement was an undertaking large enough to merit the advice of the emperor. Trajan's advice to prosecute those who were denounced directly to the government as Christians and who also refused to deny or repent from it did not ultimately curb the growth of the new religion in Bithynia. Nicaea hosted Christianity's initial ecumenical council (325 CE), and Chalcedon hosted the critical ecumenical council of 451.

PAMELA HEDRICK

BITTER [מרר marar; πικραίνω pikrainō]. Describes undesirable feelings, taste, morals, and motivation; it even becomes a personal and place name. It labels attitudes analogous to the flavor it describes. The quintessential example of this is the bitter herbs used in the Passover ritual (Exod 12:8; Num 9:11) as a reminder of the feelings and experience of slavery (Exod 1:14). Other places where *bitter* refers to taste include Rev 8:11; 10:9-10.

In an etiological story, Israel wandered to a desert location named *Marah*, or *bitter*. Its exact location is unknown, but it may have been along the eastern side of the Gulf of Suez in the Sinai desert. Not coincidentally, the water there tasted *bitter*, but when Moses tossed some wood into the water upon God's guidance, it became *sweet* (מָתֹק mathoq Exod 15:22-25*a*).

In Numbers, "the water of bitterness" (מֵי הַמָּרִים me hammarim, 5:18, 19, 23, 24) determined the guilt or innocence of a woman accused of adultery. In that case, *bitter* referred to the painful outcome of the ritual for the condemned, and probably to the taste of the potion (*see* WATER OF BITTERNESS).

Bitter is a theme in the book of Ruth even though it only appears there three times. Naomi, whose name means *pleasant*, feels that her life has become *bitter* due to Yahweh's treatment of her (1:13), therefore she renames herself *Bitter* (1:20, מָרָא mara᾿). Others whose lives are described as *bitter* on account of God include Job (27:2), and the collective people of Israel (Lam 3:5); conversely, in Ps 106:33 Israel's complaining caused God's spirit to be *bitter*. In some places, *bitter* is analogous to evil or sin (Isa 5:20; Jer 2:9; Hos 12:14 [Heb. 12:15]; Jas 3:14). Fittingly, various forms of this word appear in the midst of complaint and condemnation (Job 3:20; 13:26; Jer 6:26; 31:15; Ezek 21:6; Amos 8:10).

LISA MICHELE WOLFE

BITTER HERBS [מְרֹרִים merorim]. The term merorim, normally rendered "bitter herbs," occurs in three biblical passages. Two of the passages, both belonging to the Priestly strand of the Pentateuch, deal with the foods to be eaten at PASSOVER. Exodus 12:8 says, "They shall eat the lamb that same night; they shall eat it roasted over the fire with unleavened bread and bitter herbs." The rules for eating the meal at the second Passover, one month after the first, again require consuming the meat together with unleavened bread and bitter herbs (Num 9:11). Apart from these two verses, the word is found only in Lam 3:15 where the poet laments: "He has filled me with bitterness [merorim], he has sated me with WORMWOOD" (*see also* 1QS 4 xiii; 1QpHab 9 xi).

The fact that the term dictated a part of the PASSOVER menu made it important to define exactly what these bitter herbs might be. According to *m. Pesaḥ* 2:6, one may fulfill the Passover requirement for bitter herbs by eating "lettuce, chicory, pepperwort, snakeroot, and dandelion [maror]"; these may be combined, with the minimal amount to be eaten defined as "an olive's bulk." The identity of these plants and related issues receive further discussion in the talmuds (*b. Pesah.* 39a-b; *see also y. Pesah.* 2.6, 29c). The Mishnah also supplies a reason for the command to eat bitter herbs—because the Egyptians had embittered their lives (*m. Pesah.* 10:5; *see* Exod 1:14). *See* PLANTS OF THE BIBLE; THISTLES.

JAMES C. VANDERKAM

BITTERNESS. *See* BITTER.

BITUMEN [חֵמָר khemar]. The NRSV uses this term to translate the Hebrew **khemar.** Other versions use the word *pitch* or *tar.* The first appearance of the word in the Bible is when the peoples of the earth migrated from the east to the plain of Shinar and settled there. They burned bricks for construction blocks and gathered bitumen to use as mortar to hold them together and cover them (Gen 11:3).

The story of the battle between Chedorlaomer king of Elam and the kings of Canaan in Gen 14 does not appear to reflect actual events, but it does suggest that the source of bitumen in the land of Canaan was the Dead Sea region. According to Gen 14:10, there were "pits of bitumen" in the Valley of Siddim by the Dead Sea.

The third and last time the word appears in both the OT and the NRSV translation is Exod 2:3. Here Moses' mother is said to have made a cradle of papyrus and plastered it with bitumen to make it waterproof in order to set it among the reeds where the daughter of Pharaoh came to bathe.

JORGE PIXLEY

BIZIOTHIAH biz´ee-oh-th*i*´uh [בִּזְיוֹתְיָה bizyothyah]. A town near Edom's boundary that lay within the territory assigned to Judah. Possibly the text is corrupt and the Hebrew needs to be read as "and her daughters" to refer to nearby villages (Josh 15:28).

BIZTHA [בִּזְתָא bizzetha']. An attendant among King Ahasuerus' seven eunuchs who was requested to bring him Queen Vashti (Esth 1:10).

BLACK [שָׁחֹר shakhor, קֵדָר qedhar, חוּם khum, חֹשֶׁךְ khoshek; μέλας melas]. The color *black* describes human hair (Lev 13:37; Song 5:11; Matt 5:36), the color of goats (Gen. 30:32-40), horses (Zech 6:2; Rev 6:5), and ink (2 Cor 3:3; 2 John 12). Though occasionally employed metaphorically to describe gloom or mourning (Job 3:5; Isa 50:3; Joel 2:2), *black* expresses a range from positive to negative sentiment. For example, shakhor is used in Song 1:5 to affirm the beauty of a desired woman in the phrase "I am black (i.e., "sun-darkened") and beautiful" (1:15), while Lam 4:8

uses the same term to suggest that the sun has aversely diminished the appearance of formerly "brownish-red" complexioned princes. It should be emphasized that the concept of racial blackness was alien to the biblical authors, and that no terms for "blackness" are ever used to describe an ethnic group. Even the famous dark skin of the Cushites was never explicitly deemed "black."

RODNEY S. SADLER, JR.

BLASPHEMY. In the OT, blasphemy renders a series of four distinct Hebrew terms that mean to revile, curse, slander, reproach, or despise someone. In most cases, blasphemy involves speech, of which God is the object. Blasphemy, something said in disrespect against God, was strictly prohibited (Exod 22:27; Lev 24:10-23; 1 Kgs 21:13; 2 Kgs 19:3; Isa 37:3; Job 2:9-10). Sometimes actions can also be called blasphemy, as in the building of the golden calf (Neh 9:18, 26).

In the NT, blasphemy is most often seen in verbal remarks. Jesus taught that blasphemy against the Spirit, by claiming that his work is from the devil, is an unforgivable sin (Mark 3:29; compare Matt 12:31). Jesus is charged by his opponents with blaspheming when taking the divine prerogative of forgiving sins, an act that is seen as an imposition on God's unique glory and authority (Mark 2:7; compare Luke 7:37-50). In John 10:33, Jesus is again charged with blasphemy when it is believed that he compares himself and his work too closely with God.

By far the most important texts pertaining to blasphemy pertain to the Jewish leadership's examination of Jesus (Matt 26:65; Mark 14:64). Jesus is accused of blasphemy when he claims that as the Son of Man he will sit at God's right hand, exercising judgment and authority. While Jesus claimed the right to be exalted by God's side, the leadership read this claim as an offense against the unique glory of God. The implicit claim to one day judge the Jewish leadership could also be seen as blasphemous on the basis of Exod 22:27.

However, this reading of Exod 22:27 is disputed in the Mishnah (*Sanh.* 7.5; compare *Sanh.* 6.4), wherein blasphemy requires that the name of God be used. Yet there are examples in Judaism of cultural blasphemy, where the use of the name is not required (*Num. Rab* 10.2; *Ant.* 6.183; 10.233, 242; 2 Kgs 18–19; Philo, *Dreams* 2.130–31). Since the examination of Jesus by the Jewish leadership was not a formal trial but merely a gathering of evidence for Rome, the mishnaic standard was not required.

DARRELL L. BOCK

BLAST OF TRUMPET OR DIVINE BREATH. *Blast* translates several Hebrew and Greek words and concepts most often referring to the divine breath or the blowing of trumpets, portending direct divine judgment or action. **Ruakh** (רוּחַ), "breath" occurs in Exod

15:8, when the breath of God's nostrils parts the sea (Isa 27:8; Hos 13:15). In Job 4:9 God's neshamah (נְשָׁמָה "ordinary breathing") annihilates the wicked. Some passages, such as Ps 18:15, combine these concepts. Mashakh (מָשַׁךְ), the drawing out of a prolonged sound, describes the sound of a trumpet in Exod 19:13, while in that immediate context (19:16, 19) qol (קוֹל), "sound" indicates the same thing. For trumpets sounding during a holy assembly, Lev 23:24 employs teruʿah (תְּרוּעָה), a word Zeph 1:16 uses with reference to God's destructive breath.

In the LXX phōnē (φωνή) "sound," "voice" translates the sound of a trumpet, a usage we find in Rev 8:3. The sounding of trumpets marks diverse eschatological signs in the NT (e.g., Matt 24:31; 1 Cor 15:52; 1 Thess 4:16).

GREG CAREY

BLASTUS blas'tus [Βλάστος Blastos]. Blastus was a chamberlain who controlled access to HEROD AGRIPPA I's private quarters (Acts 12:20). Delegates from TYRE and SIDON, seeking the resumption of food shipments to the region, persuaded Blastus, perhaps through a bribe, to arrange an audience with Agrippa. Nothing else is known about this royal attendant.

HEIDI S. GEIB

BLEACH [לָבֵן laven; λευκαίω leukaiō]. Making white, esp. in the sense of ethically becoming pure (Isa 1:18; Dan 11:35; 12:7). Also used metaphorically for the cleansing effect of Jesus' sacrificial blood (Rev 7:14) and for displaying his glory (Mark 9:3).

BLEMISH. See SACRIFICES AND OFFERINGS.

BLESS [בָּרַךְ barakh; εὐλογέω eulogeō]. Barakh has several meanings: "bless," "be strong," and "kneel." In both the OT (LXX) and the NT, barakh is usually represented by eulogeō ("eulogize, bless") but rarely also by ἐπεύχομαι epeuchomai "entreat, pronounce (a blessing)" (Deut 10:8; 1 Chr 23:13) and αἰνέω aineō "praise" (Ps 100:4 [LXX 99:4]). Words and ritual acts associated with "blessing" are the primary means by which divine favor is invoked, distributed, acknowledged, and lauded in biblical and kindred Israelite, Jewish, and Christian traditions. Ancient Israel shared with other cultures in its Near Eastern environment basic notions of how divine providence operates in both the natural world and history, and of how essential endowments for the continuation and enhancement of life—especially progeny, prosperity, health, longevity, security, and peace (e.g., Gen 24:35-36; Deut 7:12-16; Ps 128:5-6; Ezek 34:26-29)—are sought and celebrated through prayers, hymns, and other rites of worship (see WORSHIP, NT CHRISTIAN; WORSHIP, OT). Of course, biblical sources insist that "all blessings flow" from a single sublime source, "God" the creator

and sole sustainer of cosmic order, who is programmatically identified as "the LORD" (Yahweh), Israel's only divine sovereign. God's benefactions, together with human petitions for them, and ardent praise of God for blessings received are reciprocal actions in the biblical economy of divine providence (see PRAISE; PRAYER; PROVIDENCE).

A. Principal Formulations

God's words of blessing are transactional or performative in character, effectuating what they describe. They can be issued as decrees, using imperative verb forms addressed directly to human beings and other created entities (e.g., Gen 1:22, 28; 9:1). More often divine blessings are articulated as promises, using subjunctive and future-indicative forms, which make their implementation conditional upon faithful human observance of divine commands (e.g., Gen 12:1-3; 26:3; Lev 26:3-13; Deut 28:1-2). Human agency usually "blesses" persons and things by invoking the Lord's name or an epithet. A blessing may be pronounced to solicit divine favor, as in the Aaronic benediction (Num 6:24-26; see also, e.g., 1 Sam 2:20; Ps 134:3; Rom 15:5; 2 Thess 3:16). To "bless" the deity means to offer to God praise and homage (e.g., 1 Chr 29:10; Pss 34:1 [Heb. 34:2]; 63:3-4 [Heb. 63:4-5]; Dan 4:34). Specific blessings, as well as declarations of praise, are typically introduced using the formulas "blessed/lauded be" (בָּרוּךְ barukh) and "blessed/lauded (may) you be" (בָּרוּךְ אַתָּה barukh ʾattah); Greek equivalents generally distinguish between a human subject (using εὐλογημένος eulogēmenos "one who is blessed," e.g., LXX Deut 28:3; Matt 21:9; John 12:13) and the deity as subject (εὐλογητός eulogētos "blessed," e.g., 1 Macc 4:30; Luke 1:68; Eph 1:3).

B. Contexts and Functions

Petitions for and pronouncements of divine blessing and responsive benedictory praises of God are constant features of worship at the Jerusalem Temple as portrayed in biblical sources (e.g., 1 Kgs 8:14-66; 1 Chr 16; Pss 24:3-5; 100; 115:12-18; 118:26; 128; 134:3; Sir 50:18-21). But acts of blessing also figure importantly in other spheres of life, on both special and everyday occasions. Patriarchal testamentary bequests and prognostications are identified as performative blessings that once uttered cannot be revoked, at least by human agency (see esp. Gen 27:1-40; 48:1–49:28; Deut 33; Luke 24:50-53). Blessings are regularly given in homage and exchanged as salutations (e.g., Gen 47:7-10; Ruth 2:4; 1 Sam 13:10; 2 Kgs 4:29). They are offered in praise of God, the provider, before and after meals (compare Deut 8:10 with, e.g., Matt 14:19; Mark 6:41; 8:6-7; Luke 9:16; 24:10; Acts 27:35; and m. Ber. 6). The benedictions prescribed for the Passover celebration are developed in early Christian worship into the eucharistic liturgy (e.g., Matt 26:26; Mark

14:22; Luke 22:19; 1 Cor 10:16; 11:24; *Did.* 9–10). *See* BENEDICTION; BLESSINGS AND CURSINGS; CURSE; DOXOLOGY.

Bibliography: C. W. Mitchell. *The Meaning of* BRK *"To Bless" in the Old Testament* (1987); W. S. Towner. "'Blessed Be YHWH' and 'Blessed Art Thou, YHWH': The Modulation of a Biblical Formula." *CBQ* 30 (1968) 386–399; C. Westermann. *Blessing in the Bible and the Life of the Church* (1978).

S. DEAN MCBRIDE

BLESSINGS AND CURSINGS. The general concepts may be represented as inclusive antonyms in biblical Hebrew by the feminine plural nouns בְּרָכוֹת berakhoth and קְלָלוֹת qelaloth (LXX εὐλογίαι eulogiai and κατάραι katarai, Deut 28:2, 15, 45); and, similarly, by the feminine singular forms of these same nouns, used as collectives: "blessing and cursing/curse" בְּרָכָה וּקְלָלָה berakhah uqelalah (LXX εὐλογίαν καὶ κατάραν eulogian kai kataran, Deut 11:26; compare Gen 27:12; Deut 11:27-29; 23:4 [Heb. 23:5]; 30:1, 19; Josh 8:34; Ps 109:17; Zech 8:13; Sir 3:8-9; James 3:9-10). These antipodal categories, which are also commonly identified as "benedictions and maledictions," together comprise the verbal instruments that biblical and other ancient sources attest as invocations respectively of the positive and negative dispositions of divine providence. The terms may refer to the invocatory rites and words themselves; and, interpreted as efficacious performative utterances, they may also denote the salutary or baneful results these actions are supposed to produce (e.g., Gen 27:12; Num 22:6; Ps 109:17-18; Jer 24:9; 44:22). Their use and significance are constant rather than occasional in biblical perspectives, relevant wherever and whenever the effects of divine sovereignty are experienced in the natural order and the circumstances of human existence.

A. Overview
B. Characteristic Vocabulary and Formulations
  1. Blessings
  2. Cursings
C. Principal Settings and Functions
  1. Cult and worship
  2. Covenantal sanctions
  3. The two ways
Bibliography

A. Overview

Blessings/benedictions are pronouncements that variously solicit, distribute, and celebrate well-being. When blessings are actualized through divine agency, they yield benefits such as fecundity, security, health, peace, and happiness (e.g., Gen 26:12-14; 28:3-4; Num 6:22-27; Deut 7:12-16; Ps 5:11-12 [Heb. 5:12-13]; Sir 50:22-24). Blessing of the deity, especially in hymns and prayers, is an act of worship that returns praise to the one who has bestowed particular benefactions (e.g., Gen 24:26-27; Exod 18:10; Ps 28:6; 66:20; Luke 1:68-75). Conversely, *cursings/curses/maledictions* (also referred to as *imprecations*) are pronouncements that intend to restrain, punish, or inflict injury on specified targets (e.g., Gen 3:14; Deut 29:19-28 [Heb. 29:18-27]; Ps 137:5-6; Jer 20:14-18). Because acts of cursing trade in calamity, they may threaten the natural realm as well as endanger both personal and communal well being (e.g., Gen 4:11-12; Deut 28:15-19; Isa 24:6; Jer 20:14-18; Job 3:1-10). Accordingly, biblical legislation treats cursing as a capital offense, akin to sacrilege, if it is directed against the primary guarantors of social order—either of one's parents, or a political leader, or the deity (Exod 21:17; 22:28 [Heb. 22:27]; Lev 20:9; compare 24:11-23; 2 Sam 16:10; 19:21; 1 Kgs 2:8-9; 21:10, 13; Prov 20:20; 30:11; Eccl 10:20; Sir 3:16).

In broad scope, these conceptual counterparts correlate with the range of cosmic powers under divine control that either create, restore, enhance, and safeguard life or result in misfortune, destruction, and death. Mesopotamian polytheistic traditions often identify such powers as specialties distributed among particular deities in a pantheon (e.g., Laws of Hammurabi, epilogue [xlix 18n-li 91]; "Vassal-Treaties of Esarhaddon," 414-471). Biblical sources, on the other hand, regularly ascribe forces of both good and evil to Yahweh alone, whose comprehensive sovereignty they are supposed to reveal and implement (*See*, e.g., Deut 32:39; 1 Sam 2:6-8; Isa 43:11-13; 45:5-7; Hos 6:1-2; Job 1:21; 2:9; Prov 11:19; 14:27; Tob 13:2; Wis 16:13; Sir 33:10-13). This poses acute issues for biblical reflections on theodicy: Are manifestations of blessing in human affairs sufficient evidence of an intact, favorable relationship between those who experience them and the LORD? Is ostensible cursedness necessarily demonstrative of estrangement from the deity or indicative of the LORD's discriminative retribution against wrong-doers? (*See*, e.g., Num 23:11-12, 25-26; Deut 29:19-28; Job 4:7-9; 5:17-27; Ps 37:22-26; Eccl 6:1-6; 9:1-12; Ezek 18:1-24; Gal 3:6-14.)

B. Characteristic Vocabulary and Formulations

The terminology, idioms, and types of "blessings and cursings" exhibited in biblical and related early Jewish and Christian sources are quite varied, as are the social settings and functions they represent. Syntactical options include articulation as conditional promises and threats, featuring subjunctive and future-indicative verb forms (e.g., Lev 26:3-26; Deut 11:13-17; Ps 137:5-6; Rev 22:18-19) as well as positive and negative wishes and requests, with precative and imperative diction (Gen 9:27; 27:28-29; 2 Sam 3:29; Ezra 6:12; Mark 11:14; Heb 13:20-21). The principal expressions, however, are formulaic.

1. Blessings

Although many other verbal roots are also used to describe divine favor and benevolence (e.g., חָנַן khnn ["to show favor, be gracious to"], יָטַב ytb ["to treat well, benefit"], רָצָה rtsh ["to be pleased with"], שָׂכַל skhl ["to prosper, make successful"]), lexical derivatives of the West Semitic root בָּרַךְ brk supply the focused, operational Hebrew terminology of "blessing." In addition to the feminine noun with this basic sense (sing. berakhah, pl. berakhoth), such terminology includes verbal constructions that describe petitions for and results of blessing, whether initiated directly by the deity (e.g., Gen 1:22, 28: 2:3; 12:2; Exod 20:11, 24; Job 1:10; Isa 51:2) or by human beings, clergy in particular, either expressly or implicitly invoking divine agency (e.g., Gen 14:19; Num 6:22-27; Deut 10:8; 2 Sam 6:18; Ps 129:8; 134:3; Sir 50:20-21). Inflected forms, such as בָּרוּךְ barukh ("blessed [be]") commonly introduce benedictory pronouncements (e.g., Deut 28:3-6; 1 Sam 25:32-33; 1 Kgs 10:9; Ps 68:19 [Heb. 68:20]; 115:14-15). These Hebrew forms of brk are usually represented in the LXX and the NT by εὐλογέω eulogeō, "to eulogize, laud, bless" (see also, e.g., Tob 3:11; Sir 45:15; Luke 6:28; Rom 12:14).

The denominative verb אָשַׁר 'ashar ("to declare happy," e.g., Gen 30:13; Ps 72:17; Prov 31:28; Mal 3:12 [regularly rendered in the LXX by forms of the verb μακαρίζω makarizō]) and, most often, the fixed nominal אַשְׁרֵי 'ashre ("happy, fortunate," e.g., Deut 33:29; 1 Kgs 10:8; Job 5:17; Ps 1:1; Isa 56:2 [LXX μακάριος makarios]) are used to acknowledge the sense of personal well being that results from divine blessing (compare Ps 41:1-3; 128:1-4; 144:12-15). Makarios is developed and extensively attested in later Jewish and NT literature in the form of beatitudes (i.e., declarations of blessedness), also identified as makarisms: e.g., Sir 14:1-2; 25:8-9; Matt 5:3-11; Luke 6:20-22; James 1:12; Rev 22:7, 14 (see BEATITUDES; BLESS).

2. Cursings

Derivatives of several roots, with overlapping semantic horizons, provide the primary Hebrew antonyms of terms for blessing and blessedness. In large measure, the corresponding terminology in the Greek NT follows the precedents set by the LXX translators.

Juridical and cultic practices of adjuration—i.e., binding oneself or another to the truthfulness of a testimony or to the keeping of a solemn promise by means of an oath that invokes a curse as conditional penalty— are expressed by the verb אָלָה 'alah: e.g., Judg 17:2; 1 Kgs 8:31; Hos 4:2; 104. (These occurrences are usually rendered in the LXX by forms of ἀράομαι araomai, "adjure, invoke a curse." This sense is expressed using the verb ἀναθεματίζω anathematizō, anathematize, in Mark 14:71; Acts 23:12, 14.) The cognate feminine noun (sing. אָלָה 'alah, pl. אָלוֹת 'aloth may connote either an "imprecatory oath, adjuration" (e.g., Gen 24:41; Lev 5:1; Num 5:21; 1 Kgs 8:31; Neh 10:29 [Heb. 10:30]) or the state of accursedness, execration that results when the penalty is actualized (e.g., Num 5:27; Jer 29:18; Zech 5:3; Dan 9:11; compare Bar 1:20; 3:8). Such imprecatory oaths are sometimes specifically associated with covenants and loyalty-oaths (e.g., Gen 26:28; Deut 29:20-21 [Heb. 29:19-20]; Isa 24:5-6; Ezek 17:18-19).

Verb-forms of אָרַר 'rr ("to execrate, pronounce accursed," e.g., Gen 5:29; 12:3; Num 22:12; Judg 5:23 [usually καταράομαι kataraomai in the LXX; compare also, e.g., Sir 23:14; Matt 5:44; Rom 12:14; James 3:9]) and the cognate feminine noun מְאֵרָה me'erah ("curse, calamity," e.g., Deut 28:20; Mal 2:2; 3:9 [LXX κατάρα katara]) refer to specific acts of execration and their results. Inflected forms of אָרוּר 'arur, accursed [be] [LXX ἐπικατάρατος epikataratos]) characteristically introduce maledictions that parallel formulaic barukh-pronouncements (e.g., Gen 3:14, 17; 9:25; Deut 27:15-26; 28:16-19; Judg 21:18; Jer 17:5; Mal 1:14; compare Tob 13:12).

The verbal range of קָלַל qll (Gen 12:3; Lev 19:14; Judg 9:27; Ps 62:4 [Heb. 62:5]; 109:28) includes contemptuous and disrespectful words and actions as well as imprecatory speech per se. (The distinction is recognized in the LXX, which uses forms of καταράομαι kataraomai, "utter a curse," to render many occurrences of the Hebrew verb but represents others with forms of κακαλογέω kakalogeō "revile, speak evil of" [Exod 21:16; 22:27; Prov 20:9; 2 Sam 3:13; compare Matt 15:4; Mark 7:10]). Cursing is, however, the appropriate contextual sense of the noun (sing. qelalah, pl. qelaloth, e.g., Judg 9:57; Prov 27:14; Jer 29:22; compare Sir 41:9-10; Heb 6:8).

Less often attested, but clearly belonging to the same semantic range as the above, are the Hebrew roots זָעַם z'm ("to denounce, damn," e.g., Num 23:7-8; Prov 24:24; 4QBer[a] frg. 7 1.1) and קָבַב qbb ("to utter a curse [against]," e.g., Num 22:11; 23:8, 13, 35; Lev 24:11; Job 5:2; Prov 11:26).

The various expressions of grief, warnings and threats, and other "woe-sayings" in OT literature introduced by the Hebrew interjections אוֹי 'oy and הוֹי hoy do not seem to belong to a distinct genre or genres of speech that can be coherently related to cursings, in spite of occasional overlaps of theme (compare respectively, e.g., Num 21:29-30; Isa 3:9, 11; Jer 4:13; Ezek 24:6-13; Hos 7:13; Zech 11:17 and Isa 5:8-24; 45:9-10; Jer 22:18-19; Hab 2:6-19). In the NT, however, formulaic "woe-sayings" (also introduced by οὐαί ouai) do appear to function as denunciations that are quasi-curses (e.g., Matt 11:21; 23:13-36; Luke 21:23-24; compare Sir 2:12-14); in Luke 6:24-26 "woe-sayings" are conspicuous as negative counterparts to "beatitudes."

C. Principal Settings and Functions

Biblical literature portrays blessings and cursings as substantive and pervasive features of applied theology. The chief concepts and practices, though deeply rooted in the broad cultural environment of the ancient Near East, are represented as governed by two theological axioms: (1) The LORD, ancient Israel's tutelary deity, is creator and sustainer of cosmic order as well as preeminent sovereign over the world of human nations within which Israel's discrete identity emerges and continues to develop (e.g., Exod 19:3-6; Deut 4:32-39; Ps 47; 67; 97; Isa 40:21-31; Sir 24; Acts 17:22-31). (2) While the LORD's exercise of sovereignty is not always transparent and cannot be coerced, it is supposed to be both characteristically generous and sufficiently discriminating to take account of and to respond appropriately to human needs, behavior, attitudes, and petitions (e.g., Gen 18:17-32; Num 23:7-12; Deut 4:25-31; Isa 55:6-13; 65; Sir 2; Matt 20:1-16; Rom 1:18–2:16). Blessings and cursings are means of invoking these interrelated aspects of the LORD's providence in order to achieve specific ends.

1. Cult and Worship

The essential act of ancient Israelite and later Jewish and Christian worship is praise of God, giving homage to the one whose profound benevolence makes possible life in general and sustains the community of the faithful in particular (e.g., Ps 100; 117; Tob 13). Fertile land, fructifying rains, and the bounties they produce are perennial divine gifts acknowledged in hymnic praises, petitionary prayers, and celebratory rites (e.g., Deut 11:10-15; 12:7; Ps 65:9-13; 104:10-30; Isa 30:23-25). The official Yahwistic cultus, eventually centered at the Jerusalem temple and idealized in the tabernacle traditions of the Pentateuch, sought to assure the constancy of these and other blessings of the LORD (e.g., Exod 20:24; 39:32-43; Lev 9:22-24; Num 6:22-27; Ps 128). Also understood to be of critical importance for the well being of the worshiping community and its individual members were cultic means to identify, preempt, and either execrate or expiate anything that threatened adversity. Such means included imprecatory oaths that invoked divine assistance in distinguishing between innocent and guilty parties (e.g., Num 5:11-31; Deut 29:18-21 [Heb. 29:17-20]; 1 Kgs 8:31-32); other forms of cursing were deployed against the plots and assaults of both personal and national enemies (e.g., Pss 54–56; 79; 83; 109; 129; compare Luke 6:27-31). In brief, cultic institutions functioned to maximize the actualization of blessings and to minimize, thwart, or redirect the injurious effects of cursings.

2. Covenantal Sanctions

Blessings and, especially, cursings are widely attested in ancient Near Eastern epigraphs and other sources as formal devices to safeguard tombs, boundary markers, stelas and building inscriptions as well as royal decrees, testaments, and various types of treaties and contractual arrangements. (For representative texts, see ANET[3] 178-180, 199-206, 531-541, 653-662.) In such contexts blessings are relatively rare; they seek to persuade, invoking divine favor as reward for desirable and expected behaviors (e.g., "Treaty between Mursilis and Duppi-Tessub of Amurru," 21 [ANET[3] 205]; Laws of Hammurabi, xlix 1-17 [ANET[3] 178]). Cursings are much more commonly and elaborately employed as sanctions; they are punitive in intent, threatening retribution by divine forces for acts such as textual defacement, removal of monuments, and non-compliance with the terms of agreements and decrees (e.g., Inscription of Kilamuwa [ANET[3] 654]; "Treaty of Esarhaddon with Baal of Tyre," iv [ANET[3] 534]; compare Ezra 6:12). The chief biblical examples of such sanctions, in Lev 26 and Deut 28, pertain to the exclusive suzerainty of the LORD in covenantal relationship with Israel. In each case, a presentation of conditional blessings to reward faithful observance of the covenant's terms (Lev 26:3-13; Deut 28:1-14) is followed by a longer recitation of conditional curses to punish disobedience (Lev 26:14-39; Deut 28:15-68). Also noteworthy is the liturgy of cursing described in Deut 27:11-26, which is in effect an enacted loyalty-oath against secret violations of laws promulgated through Moses: after each of twelve curses proclaimed by the Levites, the assembled people respond "Amen!" (compare 1QS cols. 1-2).

3. The Two Ways

In Deut 30 especially, a more abstract theological significance is attributed to the polarized sanctions of blessing and cursing (compare 11:26-30; 27:12-13). They are described first as sequential eras of covenantal history, to emphasize the promise that genuine repentance, even under conditions of curse in exile, would bring another reversal of fortunes, with a return to Israel's homeland and a renewal of blessing (vv. 1-10; compare Deut 4:25-31; Lev 26:40-45; Bar 1:20; 3:8). Then, in Deut 30:15-20, the contrast between blessing and cursing is identified as emblematic of the existential choice Israel must make between "life and [what is] good," which is equated with strict fidelity to the covenantal laws, and "death and [what is] evil," characterized by apostasy and exile (compare Jer 17:5-8; 21:8-10; Am 5:14-15). These stark options correlate with the dualism that is variously developed in later Jewish and Christian ethical discourses on the "two ways," the paths of righteousness and wickedness respectively, and eschatological judgment (Pss 1; 112; Prov 1–3; Matt 25:31-46; Rom 5–8; 1 John 5:18-21; 4Q473; Did. 1.1–6.3). See BEATITUDES; BENEDICTION; BLESS; COVENANT, OT AND NT; CURSE; OATHS; WOE.

Bibliography: N. Weeks. *Admonition and Curse: The Ancient Near Eastern Treaty/Covenant Form as* *a Problem in Inter-Cultural Relationships* (2004); K. N. Grüneberg. *Abraham, Blessing and the Nations: A Philological and Exegetical Study of Genesis 12:3 in its Narrative Context* (2003).

S. DEAN MCBRIDE

BLESSINGS, APPENDIX B TO 1QS. *See* DEAD SEA SCROLLS.

BLIGHT [שִׁדָּפוֹן shiddafon]. Refers in Hebrew to scorching, the effect of the east wind, the *sirocco*, from the desert that occasionally strikes Palestine. In Deut 28:22 blight is listed among the curses to befall Israel if it does not keep the laws. In Solomon's prayer it is a motive for prayer at the Temple that will get Yahweh's response (1 Kgs 8:37; 2 Chr 6:28). In Amos 4:9 and in Hag 2:17 it is a punishment sent by God in the hope of eliciting conversion.

JORGE PIXLEY

BLINDNESS [עִוֵּר 'iwwer; τυφλός typhlos]. Words from the Hebrew root 'iwwer (twenty-six times in the OT) and the Greek tuphlos (fifty-two times in the NT) connote a loss or lack of sight that was considered total and permanent. The OT and the NT also use other words to describe both physical and metaphorical sight-lessness of varying degrees, but English translations render all senses with the word *blind*.

No single named individual in the OT is called blind, not even Samson (Judg 16:21) or King Zedekiah (2 Kgs 25:7) whose eyes were gouged out. Isaac (Gen 27:1) and Jacob (Gen 48:10) suffered some degree of visual impairment related to age, as did the priest Eli (1 Sam 3:1) and the prophet Ahijah (1 Kgs 14:4). Temporary blindness was also known (Gen 19:11; 2 Kgs 6:18). According to biblical legislation, blind priests are blemished but not impure or unclean (Lev 21:17-24). They may not offer sacrifice, but they can partake of it. The OT makes no mention of treatment for eye diseases, yet legislation does manifest humanitarian concern for sightless people (Lev 19:14). Blindness emerges as impurity in Qumran texts (1QSa 2 iii-x). Although blind people could not join the Qumran community, members who became blind could remain. Like other ancient Near Eastern peoples, ancient Israelites believed only God could restore sight to the blind.

In Hellenistic Judaism, Tobit is explicitly called blind (but only in Sinaiticus) and the biblical tale about him and his family reflects the growing interest in therapeutic treatment of eye diseases in this period. It has been suggested that his condition is leukoma, a dense, white opacity in the cornea caused by bird droppings. It was the angel Raphael ("God heals") who instructed Tobit to use fish-gall for his problem, yet in final analysis God (Tob 11:14-17) or God's agent, Raphael (Tob 3:17; 12:14), gets credit for Tobit's recovery of sight.

Among ancient writings, the NT uses the **tuph** word-group and its derivatives far more frequently than any other body of literature. Forty-six of the fifty-two occurrences appear in the Gospel accounts of Jesus' healing activity. Three distinct stories relate how Jesus restored sight to a particular person. The story of the blind man outside Bethsaida (Mark 8:22-26) has no parallels but is similar to the healing of a deaf man with a speech impediment (Mark 7:31-37). The story of the blind Bartimaeus at Jericho (Mark 10:46-52) is the oldest version and the basis for parallels in Matt (9:27-31; 20:29-34) and Luke (18:34-53).

The story about Jesus' encounter with a man born blind (John 9) is unique in ancient literature in that it claims that a human person and not a god restored his sight. The only similar story is reported by Pausanias (*Descr.* 4:10-13; 2nd cent. CE). A certain Ophineus, a Messenian seer blind from birth, experienced a violent pain in his head one day and received his sight. Not long after, however, he lost his sight again. Contemporary attempts at understanding the condition of the man born blind tend to adopt the perspective of Western science. For example, one interpretation hypothesizes that the man in John 9 was born with cataracts caused by maternal rubella. Perhaps he was not totally sightless. Jesus applied pressure to the eye. The man could now see, though with blurred vision, because Jesus' pressure on the eye removed the lens from the refractive ocular pathway. Although such interpretations are interesting to modern readers, it is preferable to ask how the ancient Israelites understand blindness. What would restoration of sight (even blurred vision, without corrective lenses) mean to them?

According to Genesis, in the beginning there was only darkness (Gen 1:2). Darkness was a positive entity existing in its own right, not the absence of light, since light was not yet created. Moreover, darkness had no dependent relationship upon any source. This concept so plainly set out in Genesis is fundamental to understanding human blindness and its significance in the ancient Israelite world. God created light (Gen 1:3), also a positive entity existing in its own right. Light was not dependent on any source such as the sun, moon, or stars, since these did not yet exist. God would create them on the fourth day (Gen 1:14-19). In this scheme of things, the appearance of light in the morning is properly called dawn and not sunrise. By the same token, the appearance of darkness in the evening is dusk and not sunset. Thus, day and night are simply the structured framework in which the sun, moon, and stars will operate when they are created.

The first human being was animated by God's living breath (the breath of life, Gen 2:7) and endowed with "living light" (the light of life) that differs from the light of the sky. "God indeed does all these things, twice, three times with mortals, to bring back their souls from the Pit to be lighted with the living light (the light of life) (Job 33:29-30; compare Ps 56:13; John 8:12). Because they possess this living light, human beings are alive and can see.

How did the ancients understand vision? The Greeks believed that sight occurs due to fire emanating from the eyes. Empedocles (495–435 BCE; "On Nature") explained that Aphrodite created the human eye as a kind of lamp. The eternal fire was wrapped in membranes that let the firelight shine through the pupil of the eye to facilitate vision. Aristotle observed: "Sight (is made) from fire and hearing from air" (*Problems* 31, 960a). "[V]ision is fire" (959*b*). The Israelite tradition located the living light in the heart. According to this tradition, the human person consists of three mutually interpenetrating yet distinguishable zones that served as the vehicles for interacting with other persons and things in the human environment: heart-eyes, the zone of emotion fused with thought; mouth-ears, the zone of expressive speech; and hands-feet, the zone of purposeful action. The heart-eyes zone relates to blindness. In this scheme of things, darkness emanates from the eyes of sightless persons because their hearts are presumably full of darkness. Similarly, harm emanates from the "evil eye" of the envious-hearted person (Mark 7:21-22, "evil eye" is commonly translated as envy).

The parable about the eye as lamp of the body told by Matthew's Jesus (6:22-23) reflects this understanding: one whose eye is not sound is blind (*see* 1 John 2:9-11). In the Semitic idiom "to be blind" means "to be hardened, inflexible, adamant in one's position" (*see* Isa 6:10). This kind of obstinate refusal to see, to remain blind, will have serious consequences (*see* Matt 15:14; 23:16-27). Such figurative blindness was as serious as physical blindness in the ancient world.

Continuing with this line of thinking, consider again the man born blind (John 9). At the very outset Jesus implies that the man's heart is not full of darkness. Neither he nor his parents have been punished by God for their sins. In fact, Jesus denies the association of sin and physical infirmity in this instance (9:3, 41). That this man is alive at all is a marvel since congenitally blind infants were most often exposed. Jesus, however, was confident that he could help the man to regain his sight, and he did. According to the logic of John 9, this recovery of sight is correlated with faith and manifest as perception into Jesus' true identity. Jesus' remedy for the blind man's condition was rooted in a process of symbolic healing to which the cultural understanding of blindness admirably lends itself. *See* DISEASE; HEALTH CARE; HEALING; MEDICINE; SUFFERING AND EVIL.

Bibliography: J. Keir Howard. *Disease and Healing in the New Testament: An Analysis and Interpretation* (2001); John J. Pilch. *Healing in the New Testament: Insights from Medical and Mediterranean Anthropology* (2000).

JOHN J. PILCH

BLOOD. *See* BLOODGUILT; BLOOD, FLOW OF; CLEAN AND UNCLEAN; SACRIFICES AND OFFERINGS.

BLOOD OF JESUS. *See* ATONEMENT; CRUCIFIXION.

BLOOD, AVENGER OF. *See* AVENGER OF BLOOD.

BLOOD, FIELD OF. *See* FIELD OF BLOOD.

BLOOD, FLOW OF. *See* FLOW OF BLOOD.

BLOODGUILT. "Bloodguilt" was coined by early Bible translators to translate the Hebrew word דָּם dam, *blood*, when it meant "responsibility for felonious homicide."

Dam bears an amazing range of meanings in biblical Hebrew. Because the body fluid was thought to bear the life of the animal or human, the consumption of blood was forbidden (e.g., Gen 9:3-4; Lev 17:10-11, 14; Deut 12:15-16, 23-24). Sacrificial blood appears once for covenant kinship (Exod 24:6, 8) and was regularly used to cleanse the altar and sanctuary of the residue of sin (Lev 16:14, 15-16, 18-19; 17:6, 11). Human blood plays no ritual role in the Bible.

In criminal law the flow of blood often associated with violent death came to stand for murder. Blood is often said to be "shed" or "spilt." If the situation was not a battle and the victim did not deserve to die, the death would be a case of "innocent blood," and the killing would be a case of homicide (Gen 9:6; 37:22; Num 35:33; Deut 21:7; 1 Sam 25:31; Ps 79:3; Ezek 16:38; etc.). **Dam** can also mean guilt for murder, hence "bloodguilt" (Num 35:33; Deut 17:18; 19:10; 21:8; 22:8; Judg 9:24; 1 Sam 25:26, 33; Hos 1:4; 4:2; 12:15; Prov 28:17). Expressions like "his blood be upon him" or "upon his head" (Lev 20:9, 11, 12, 13, 16, 27, etc.) are designed to attach guilt for an execution to the wrongdoers rather than the executioners. Finally, there are various ways God is said to requite a murder, e.g., seek "a reckoning for his blood" (Gen 42:22) or "require his blood" (2 Sam 4:11; Ezek 3:18, 20; 33:8, etc.).

The intentional use of deadly force (Num 35:16-18; Deut 19:5, 11) brings guilt on the assailant. It is this for which "bloodguilt" was coined by translators. Since the guilt is for taking a life, the guilty party must be put to death. The substitution of a ransom is strictly forbidden (Num 35:31-32) for felonious homicide, though it is allowed for negligent homicide (Exod 21:30).

Serious effort has been expended to distinguish acts that incur guilt from those that do not. Killing during war is not murder; even lethal acts of self-defense are justified (Exod 22:2 [Heb. 22:1]). Provisions in three legal codes differentiate accidental from felonious homicide and provide for the protection of accidental killers from vengeance (Exod 21:12-14; Num 35:11, 16-25; Deut

19:1-13). A number of cases involving death or injury are given special consideration within these parameters, e.g., killing a slave by beating (Exod 21:20-21) and causing a miscarriage during a brawl (Exod 21:22-25).

Some of the most notorious cases of murder in the OT involve killing by proxy. After David impregnated Uriah's wife, he engineered Uriah's death. Joab did the dirty work for him (2 Sam 11:14, 18-25). Nathan easily identified David's crimes: "You have smitten Uriah the Hittite with the sword" (2 Sam 12:9).

When Jezebel engineered Naboth's judicial murder in Ahab's name, Ahab was charged with murder (1 Kgs 21:8-19). Although this murder is by proxy and had the semblance of legality, Elijah could enunciate the Lord's verdict on Ahab.

Bloodguilt adheres not only to the killer but also to the people and its land and thus is an intensely communal matter. The prayer accompanying the ritual purging the community of guilt for an unsolved murder (Deut 21:1-9) reads, "'Our hands did not shed this blood, nor were we witnesses to it. Absolve, O LORD, your people Israel, whom you redeemed; do not let the guilt of innocent blood remain in the midst of your people Israel.' Then they will be absolved of bloodguilt" (Deut 21:7-8). Numbers 35 articulates a similar concept of communal guilt: "blood pollutes the land, and no expiation can be made for the land . . . except by the blood of the one who shed it" (35:33).

The NT has few occasions to use "blood" in the sense of "guilty of murder." Matthew is the only Gospel to use the expression: when Pilate washes his hands (27:24); when the crowd says, "His blood be on us and on our children!" (27:25); and when Judas repents (27:4). The absence of the wording in the other Gospels suggests the scene is formulated to recall OT usage. *See* CLEAN AND UNCLEAN; CRIMES AND PUNISHMENTS; LAW IN THE OT; LEX TALIONIS.

DALE PATRICK

BLUE [תְּכֵלֶת tekheleth; ὑάκινθος huakinthos]. A color term that translates the Hebrew tekheleth. The exact shade is unknown, but it is often thought to be a bluish purple. All the uses of blue in the OT refer to dyed yarn or fabric. The primary use of the term *blue* is in connection with PURPLE and CRIMSON. Throughout the description of the tabernacle in Exodus the terms appear in this order: blue, purple, crimson. These three terms describe the textiles for the tabernacle and the priestly vestments. The colors are most often used with the terms "fine LINEN" or "fine twisted Linen." In every use, blue describes a precious item. The color indicates honor or wealth. The association with priestly garments and the blue cord of Num 15:39 suggests that the color may have represented holiness as well.

When used alone, the color blue describes the cord that binds the EPHOD to the BREASTPIECE of the priest's vestments (Exod 28:28) and the cord that binds the rosette to the TURBAN of the priest. Blue was the color of the priestly robe worn beneath the ephod (Exod 23:31). The curtains of the tabernacle have blue loops, which hold the curtains to one another with golden clasps (Exod 26:4; 36:11). When breaking camp blue cloths cover the ARK OF THE COVENANT, the table of the BREAD OF THE PRESENCE, the LAMPSTAND, the golden altar, and the utensils of the service (Num 4:6-7, 9, 11-12). The blue cord on the corners of the fringe of their garments reminds the Israelites to be faithful to the commandments (Num 15:39). Blue is the color of Mordecai's garments in Esth 8:15, as well as warriors garments in Ezek 23:6 and garments of trade in Ezek 27:24. It was the color of a ship's awning in Ezek 27:7. The blue and purple cloth is among the valuable items seized by Judas (1 Macc 4:23).

Blue dye may have been produced by a variety of *murex* mollusks similar to those used in the production of purple dye. The process of producing dyes from *murex* mollusks is a lengthy and difficult process. Hence purple- and blue- dyed fabrics were prized and reflected the wealth and status of the wearer. However, textiles found at the Cave of Letters, dating to the Bar Kokhba revolt of 132 CE were found to be dyed with indigo, a plant dye. Since indigo dyes were used in Egypt and elsewhere in the ANE they may have been used in the production of some of the blue fabrics mentioned in Scripture. *See* COLORS.

Bibliography: Athalya Brenner. *Colour Terms in the Old Testament* (1982); Benjamin Goodnick. "The Tassel and the Blue Cord." *JBQ* 21 (1993) 99–108; M. Saltzman. "Has Authentic Tĕkēlet Been Identified?" *BASOR* 269 (1987) 81–84; Irving Ziderman. "First Identification of Authentic Tĕkēlet." *BASOR* 265 (1990) 25–33.

MARY P. BOYD

BOANERGES [Βοανηργές Boanerges]. A Hebrew or Aram. term of uncertain etymology ascribed to JAMES and JOHN by Jesus (Mark 3:17). The narrator renders the word into Greek as "sons of thunder," suggesting that they either spoke boldly and vigorously, experienced a sudden awakening, or perhaps even survived a lightning strike.

JAMES A. METZGER

BOARD. *See* BUILD; SHIPS AND SAILING IN THE NT; WOOD.

BOAST [בַּד badh, גָּדַל gadhal, גֹּדֶל godhel, הָלַל halal; γαυρόω gauroō, κατακαυχάομαι katakauchaomai, καυχάομαι kauchaomai, καύχημα kauchēma, καύχησις kauchēsis, κόμπος kompos, μεγαλορήμων megalorēmōn]. A boast is a verbal expression that usually conveys arrogant presumption about what will occur or has occurred solely through human efforts, especially through victory in battle, and so is devoid of God's purposes and influence. This arrogant way of speaking is often depicted as characteristic of foreign peoples such as the Moabites and the Ammonites (Isa 16:6; Jer 48:30; 49:4; Zeph 2:8, 10) and of foreign leaders such as the Aramean king Ben-hadad (1 Kgs 20:11), an unnamed Assyrian king (Isa 10:12), the Assyrian general Holofernes (Judg 6:17), the governor Nicanor (2 Macc 15:6), King Ptolemy Philopator (3 Macc 3:11), the Egyptian Pharaoh (3 Macc 6:4), and the Assyrian king Sennacherib (3 Macc 6:5). In the Psalms and Wisdom literature, boasting is an activity of wicked, deceitful, rich people who rely on their wealth (Pss 5:5; 10:3; 12:3; 49:6; 75:4) and brag about their possessions, such as horses and chariots, instead of about God (Pss 20:7; 34:2; 44:8).

Paul can positively boast of his weaknesses and suffering (2 Cor 11:23–12:13), his ministry (2 Cor 1:14), and his congregations (2 Cor 1:14; 7:14; 8:24; 9:2-3; 1 Thess 2:19), only because in each case he claims that God's purposeful activity and the lordship of Christ lie at the heart of them. Primarily, Paul holds the view that he and his letter recipients ought to boast only about what Christ has done, not about what they have done (Rom 11:18) or about what he or any other leader has accomplished (1 Cor 1:31; 3:21-22; 2 Cor 1:12; 10:17). See PRIDE.

EMILY CHENEY

BOAT [πλοῖον ploion, σκάφη skaphē]. Boats were a small vessels powered either by rowing or small sails and used in smaller lakes and rivers, generally for fishing or local transportation. Jesus and the disciples were regularly associated with boats, and Jesus even used one as a platform for speaking to a crowd (Mark 4:1). The smallness of boats highlights Sirach's claim that hypocrites are tossed about "like a boat in a storm" (Sir 33:2). An even smaller type of boat was the skiff towed by larger sea-faring vessels, which plays a minor role in the story of Paul's shipwreck in Acts 27. See SHIPS AND SAILING.

BRYAN D. BIBB

BOAZ [בֹּעַז bo'az; Βόες Boes]. Boaz is a kinsman of Naomi's dead husband, Elimelech (Ruth 2:1). He "redeems" (rescues) Naomi and her widowed daughter-in-law RUTH from poverty by marrying Ruth. Thus, Naomi can claim Ruth's child, OBED, as her dead husband's heir keeping the family "name" and the family's property rights "alive" (see Lev 25).

The name Boaz means "in Him (is) Strength" and although the NRSV calls him "a prominent rich man," the Hebrew and the Greek (גִּבּוֹר חַיִל gibor khayil; δυνατός dynatos) basically mean "powerful." Since Obed becomes the grandfather of DAVID (Ruth 4:21; 1 Chr 2:11-12), Boaz is named as an ancestor of Jesus (Matt 1:5 [boes]; Luke 3:32).

KATHLEEN A. FARMER

BOCHERU [בְּכְרוּ bokheru]. One of Azel's six sons and a descendant of Saul, Israel's first king from the tribe of Benjamin (1 Chr 8:38; 9:44).

BOCHIM [בֹּכִים bokhim]. "Weepers." Place west of the Jordan above Gilgal where the Israelites wept after the angel of the Lord reprimanded them for breaking God's command (Judg 2:1-5).

BODMER PAPYRI. Collection of Greek and Coptic manuscripts from an ancient scriptorium situated at Pabau in the Panopolite nome in Egypt, and in 1956 acquired by Martin Bodmer (1899–1971). Most of them are housed in the Bibliotheca Bodmeriana in Geneva. The codices and rolls, dated from the 2nd to the 4th/5th cent., contain texts of the OT and NT, ancient Greek, and early Christian literature. The most important of them are P. Bodmer IV, XXV, and XXVI containing three plays of Menander (Dyskolos, Samia, Aspis), and P. Bodmer II with an almost complete version of the Gospel of John dating to ca. 200 CE.

Bibliography: *Bibliotheca Bodmeriana: The Collection of the Bodmer Papyri.* 10 vols. (2000).

PETER ARZT-GRABNER

BODY [גְּוִיָּה gewiyyah, בָּשָׂר basar; σῶμα sōma, σάρξ sarx, σκῆνος skēnos]. The OT primarily uses two terms to refer to the body: gewiyya—for human or animal corpses (e.g., Judg 14:8-9; 1 Sam 31:10, 12; Ps 110:6; Nah 3:3) as well as bodies, whether human (Gen 47:18; Neh 9:37) or heavenly (Ezek 1:11, 23; Dan 10:6); and basar, frequently with reference to body or "human being," though with a basic sense of *flesh*. In the LXX, sōma is sometimes used to translate both Hebrew words. Sōma is the predominate term for *body* in the NT, though other words are possible, especially sarx, *flesh*—e.g., 1 Tim 3:16; 1 Pet 3:18, with reference to "life in this world"), but also skēnos, *tent*—e.g., 2 Cor 5:1, with reference to the temporality of earthly life).

    A. Body in the OT
    B. Body in the NT
        1. Anthropology
        2. Ecclesiology
        3. Eschatology
    Bibliography

A. Body in the OT
    When used of a living person in the OT, gewiyyah refers to a human being (and not to a part of a person), and especially to people in distress. In the context of famine, e.g., a man appeals to Joseph, saying, "There is nothing left . . . but our bodies and our lands" (Gen 47:18).

More generally, *body* refers to the form of the human being in his or her entirety. The dualism of body and soul, familiar in certain Greek circles, has little basis in the OT, where people are souls (rather than have them) and are bodies (rather than possess them). Embodiedness draws attention to the creaturely status of human beings, as well as to their transitoriness. As bodily creatures, humans are intrinsically related to the material world in which they live, which, then, provides the context for their relatedness to both non-human and human creatures and for ethical comportment. As bodily creatures, humans experience a range of vulnerabilities—e.g., to their own desires and hungers, to abuse at the hands of other humans, to the elements, to disease, and to death; bodily existence thus underscores the invariability of human dependence on God and the necessity of human interdependence within the human family and with the natural world.

Insights from cultural anthropology since the mid-20th cent. have expanded our appreciation of the significance of the body in religious and social life. This includes attention to temporary transformations of the body (e.g., letting one's hair grow as part of the Nazirite vow, Num 6:5) as well as permanent ones (e.g., circumcision as a sign of the covenant, Gen 17:11), refraining from food (e.g., Neh 9:1), donning particular clothing (e.g., sackcloth, Gen 37:34; or fine linen and purple, Prov 31:22). These body-related practices are communicative performances that, e.g., broadcast or solidify kinship bonds, signal status transformations, or mark one's social standing.

The body is not only the site of such social representations but also serves as a mirror for society or as a model for bounded systems like religious communities. For Israel, boundaries were needed to ensure the integrity of the person and of the group, with the primary socio-religious boundary being that which prevented an impure person or object from entering sacred space. Contaminants could take myriad forms—e.g., a bodily discharge, a physical defect, or other such symbols that cross the boundary from life to death. For making sense of the often puzzling laws regulating food, sex, skin diseases, and bodily discharges (Lev 11–15, 18), these insights are especially important, since they demonstrate how polluting the body threatens the purity or holiness of the community. Accordingly, holiness, that gift and charge from Yahweh to Israel, was woven into the fabric of daily, bodily routine.

B. Body in the NT

The significance of the body in the NT writings reflects to varying degrees the confluence of perspectives from the Hebrew Bible and from Greco-Roman philosophical, religious, and medical traditions. Although many presume a body-soul dualism among the Greeks and Romans—and, thus in the world of the NT writers—"Greek thought" cannot be reduced to a single viewpoint (*see* GREEK RELIGION AND PHILOSOPHY). For Aristotle, e.g., the soul is that in virtue of which an organism is alive (*On the Soul* 2.1 §§412a–413a10). For him, the *soul* was not immaterial; even if *soul* is not the same thing as body, neither is it nonmatter but can still occupy space. Even Plato thought that the soul was constructed from elements of the world, though he famously argued for a distinction between body and soul. Within Epicureanism, mind and spirit were understood to be corporeal because they act on the body, and all entities that either act or are acted upon are bodies by definition. Borrowing in part from Aristotle, Stoicism taught that everything that exists is corporeal; accordingly, only non-existent "somethings" (like imagined things) could be incorporeal. Ancient medical writers emphasized the inseparability of the internal processes of the body (what we today call "psychology") and its external aspects ("physiology"); any differentiation between inner and outer was fluid and permeable. We can summarize the belief cluster shared by most philosophers and physicians of the Hellenistic period by noting that the *soul* is corporeal and generated with the *body*; it neither exists before the body nor is separable from it after the body's demise. What happens after we die? Cicero summarizes the two primary, competing views: either body and soul are annihilated at death or the soul separates from the body (*Tusculan Disputations* 1.11.23-24).

For students of the NT, *body* has particular significance along three lines: humanity (anthropology), the church (ecclesiology), and the afterlife (eschatology).

1. Anthropology

Following in the well-worn path of the OT, NT writers largely adopt a view of the body as "the person," not a part of a person. To be sure, some texts are more ambiguous and continue to be debated—e.g., Matt 10:28; 2 Cor 5:1-10. More pervasive though is the assumption that God's salvific intervention in Christ is concerned with the restoration of humans, as whole persons, and with the human family. There is no more profound representation of this than the "enfleshment" of the divine Logos, the INCARNATION (John 1:14). Not surprisingly, then, the Gospels chronicle Jesus' ministry of healing so that physical needs are correlated with spiritual needs, and spiritual needs are bundled with social needs—or, better, where spiritual, social, and physical needs are simply regarded as human needs. Thus, e.g., cleansing a leper allows him new access to God and to the community of God's people (Matt 8:1-4; *see* Lev 13-14), healing a paralytic is tantamount to forgiving his sins (Matt 9:2-8), extending the grace of God to toll collectors and sinners exhibits the work of a physician (Matt 9:9-13), and, as throughout the biblical tradition, recovery of sight serves too as a metaphor for the insight of faith (Matt 9:27-31).

2. Ecclesiology

Using a number of parallel expressions, Paul refers to the church as the body of Christ more than 20 times (e.g., Rom 7:4; 1 Cor 10:16-17; 12:13). The use of the term *body* in reference to an assembly would not have been unusual, but Paul's usage moves further, to assert the essential unity of believers—who partake of the one eucharistic loaf and cup (1 Cor 10:16-17) and one baptism (1 Cor 12:13; Eph 4:4-6); to emphasize diversity of membership instead of ethnic identity or social status (e.g., 1 Cor 12:13); to prioritize the needs of the organic whole over the desires of its individual members (Rom 12; 1 Cor 6); to validate mutuality in the context of diversity of gifts within the church (1 Cor 12); and to call believers to cruciform servanthood by setting before them the exemplar of Christ who gave himself "for you" (1 Cor 11:17-34).

3. Eschatology

What of the AFTERLIFE? Although "immortality of the soul" is popular in Christian tradition, NT writers actually promote instead the "resurrection of the body." With regard to the nature of post-resurrection corporeality, two examples will suffice. First, the disciples in Luke's Gospel regard Jesus as a *ghost* or *spirit* (πνεῦμα, pneuma—probably referring in this case to a ghostly apparition or the disembodied residue of a dead person, 24:37), but their analysis is flatly contradicted by Jesus. He grounds the continuity of his identity, first, in his materiality, his physicality, in the constitution of flesh and density of bones: "Look at my hands and my feet; see that it is I myself. Touch me and see . . ." (Luke 24:39). Then, requesting something to eat and consuming broiled fish in the presence of his disciples (24:41-43), he demonstrates that he is no angelic being (*see* Tob 12:15, 19).

Second, in 1 Cor 15, Paul defended belief in the future resurrection by appeal to what had already become Christian tradition (vv. 1-11), observing that a denial of the future resurrection was tantamount to denying the resurrection of Christ (vv. 12-34), and sketching how one might plausibly conceive of the resurrection of the dead (vv. 35-58). His central affirmation concerns the import of the *body* (sōma) to human existence and identity, and, then, of God's provision of a body well-suited to the form of existence envisioned. Thus, Paul distinguishes between two sorts of bodily existence, the σῶμα ψυχικόν (sōma psychikon) and the σῶμα πνευματικόν (sōma pneumatikon). The first expression is drawn from Gen 2:7, which has it that Adam was created a living psychē (note that Adam thus is a psychē, and does not have a psychē); hence, the first Adam was an "ensouled body." However, since this body is subject to death and decay, it is ill-suited for eternal life with God. What is needed is a different form of existence, and this is given to us by the last Adam, Christ, (*see* SECOND ADAM). Hence, the sōma

psychikon (or ensouled body) is a body for this age, but the sōma pneumatikon (or "enspirited body") for the age to come. Working within the categories of the natural science of his day, Paul thus thinks of pneuma (usually translated as *breath* or *spirit*) as a kind of *stuff*, and, working within those categories, the apostle speaks of the afterlife using the cognate term pneuma tikos, "pertaining to the spirit," by way of identifying the substance of the resurrection body (1 Cor 15:44, 46). Paul portrays the afterlife in astral terms (compare Dan 12:1-3), with the resurrection body made up of the same matter of which the stars are made—that is, quintessence, that fifth and highest element of the universe, beyond air, earth, fire, and water. In this way, Paul affirms a profound continuity between life in this world and life everlasting with God, a continuity whose form is bodily existence. Paul does not write of immortality of the soul, nor does he urge belief in the resuscitation of dead bodies that might serve as receptacles for souls that had escaped the body in death. Rather, he sets before his audience the promise of the transformation of their bodies into glorified bodies. As with the incarnation, then, so with the eschaton, we find profound significance allotted to embodied existence. *See* CLEAN AND UNCLEAN; RESURRECTION.

Bibliography: Howard Eilberg-Schwartz. *The Savage in Judaism: An Anthropology of Israelite Religion and Ancient Judaism* (1990); Dale B. Martin. *The Corinthian Body* (1995); Graham J. Warne. *Hebrew Perspectives on the Human Person in the Hellenistic Era: Philo and Paul* (1995); Joel B. Green. "Restoring the Human Person: New Testament Voices for a Wholistic and Social Anthropology." *Neuroscience and the Person*, ed. Robert John Russell, et al. *Scientific Perspectives on Divine Action* 4 (1999) 3–22; John P. Wright and Paul Potter, eds. *Psyche and Soma: Physicians and Metaphysicians on the Mind-Body Problem from Antiquity to Enlightenment* (2000).

JOEL B. GREEN

BODY OF CHRIST. *See* CHRIST, BODY OF.

BODYGUARD [טַבָּח tabbakh]. An individual or group charged with the protection of another, particularly of a king. The most common term, tabbakh, also means *slaughterer* (and sometimes *cook*), and is found in reference to Potiphar (שַׂר הַטַּבָּחִים sar hattabbakhim, chief of the guard; Gen 37:36 and 39:1); the prison guard over Joseph (Gen 40:3-4; 41:10-12); and NEBUZARADAN, bodyguard of King Nebuchadnezzar (2 Kgs 25:8; Jer 52:12). David's chief bodyguard, ACHISH, is literally "keeper of my head" in 1 Sam 28:2. The NRSV also interprets "obedient ones" as *bodyguard*, referring to the group of David's followers led by Benaiah (2 Sam 23:23 and 1 Chr 11:25). *See* GUARD; KING, KINGSHIP.

JESSICA TINKLENBERG DEVEGA

BOHAIRIC VERSION. *See* VERSIONS, COPTIC.

BOHAN, STONE OF boh'han [אֶבֶן בֹּהַן 'even bohan]. A marker on the boundary between JUDAH and BEN-JAMIN, it was probably a topographical feature in the shape of a thumb, the literal meaning of bohan (Josh 15:6; 18:17). Bohan, the son of REUBEN, is mentioned nowhere else.

BOIL [שְׁחִין shekhin; ἕλκος helkos]. Medically, a boil is a painful pus-filled bump under the skin. Semitic cognates suggest *inflammation* is meant in the OT. *Sores* suit the Greek. A [weeping] boil renders one impure, with devastating consequences (Lev 13:18-20).

JOHN J. PILCH

BOLDNESS, CONFIDENCE IN FAITH [מִבְטָח mivtakh; παρρησία parrēsia; θαρρέω tharreō]. Biblical ideas about bold faith are often, but not uniformly, expressed by the specific terms listed above. In the Greek tradition parrēsia was particularly associated with free, frank speaking. The Biblical concept implies a steady reliance on God that may show itself in fearless words or actions.

Various OT texts advocate placing confidence in God rather than in human beings (e.g., Pss 27:1-3; 62:5-12; 118:6-9; Prov 3:26; 14:26; Isa 12:2; 30:15-16). The patriarchs and matriarchs in Genesis often acted boldly to divine promises. The Israelites under Moses left Egypt "boldly" (Exod 14:8). Soldiers in Israel's holy wars were taught to be confident of victory because God was with them (Deut 20:3-4; 31:6-7, 23; Josh 1:5-9; 1 Sam 17:45-47; Jdt 14:13; 16:10; 1 Macc 4:35; 2 Macc 15:7, 11). The Hebrew prophets typically spoke bravely despite opposition. Sir 49:10 says that the twelve prophets gave Israel "confident hope." Some relatively late texts mention bold confidence in relation to eschatological rewards (Wis 5:1; 2 Esd 7:98). On the other hand, profound faith raised searching questions about God's justice (e.g., Gen 18:22-33; Exod 32:11-13; Job 23; Jer 12:1-4; Hab 1).

In the NT confidence in God is bound up with faith in Jesus as the Christ (Eph 3:11-12). Jesus' own boldness as a witness to divine truth is stressed in all the gospels, particularly John (e.g., Mark 8:32; John 18:20). In some passages Jesus teaches about the limitless power accessible to those who have faith without doubting (Mark 9:23-29; Matt 21:21-22; compare Jas 1:5-8). Jesus' disciples are often portrayed as having doubts, especially before his resurrection (e.g., Matt 14:22-33). After that event, however, the apostles and their colleagues proclaimed God's message boldly (Acts 4:13, 29, 31; 8:28; 18:25-26; 28:30-31), and their boldness is attributed to God (2 Cor 3:4–5:10; 1 Thess 2:2; compare John 16:25-33).

Women, as well as men, showed bold faith. Mary accepted and celebrated Gabriel's announcement (Luke 1:38, 46-55). Women risked disapproval to seek Jesus' healing or blessing (Mark 5:25-34; 7:24-30; Luke 7:36-50), several stayed near his cross (Matt 27:55-56), and some in the early church risked death for their faith (e.g., Rom 16:3-4).

Paul contrasted sound confidence with "boasting in the flesh" (Phil 3:3-11) and described Abraham as a model of indomitable trust (Rom 4:18-22). He stressed the importance of confidence in the face of opposition or persecution (Phil 1:12-20; compare Col 4:3-4; Eph 6:18-20). Yet he recognized that believers may sincerely disagree on some issues; in such cases he counseled love, tolerance, and action in line with individual convictions (Rom 14:5, 23; 1 Cor 8).

The author of Hebrews stressed that Christians must stay sure of their salvation (Heb 3:6; 10:35), recalling the anchor of their confidence in Jesus' death and exaltation (Heb 4:14-16; 6:19-20; 10:19-22; 12:1-2). Heb 11 also urges church members to draw inspiration from many examplars of bold faith in the OT. The writer of 1 John argued that loving belief in Jesus supports prayer and provides confidence for the day of judgment (1 John 2:28; 3:21; 4:17; 5:14).

DAVID HAY

BOLT. *See* LOCK; THUNDER AND LIGHTNING.

BOND [מוֹסֵר moser, אִסָּר 'issar, מְסֹרֶת masoreth; δεσμός desmos, δέσμιος desmios, ἅλυσις halysis, σύνδεσμος syndesmos]. An idea represented by a variety of Hebrew and Greek terms referring to either physical (chains, shackles) or metaphorical (oppression, restriction) restraints as well as special unifying connections or oaths, often legal or covenantal obligations.

At least three Hebrew terms are used in the OT. **Moser**, the most frequent term for "bond," can refer to either restraining devices (Judg 15:14; Job 39:5; Ps 107:14), or the act of restraining or oppressing (Ps 116:16; Isa 52:2; Jer 30:8), or a pledge or oath (Jer 2:20; 5:5; 30:8). **'Issar** indicates the binding nature of pledges or oaths (Num 30:3). **Masoreth**, found only in Ezek 20:37, refers to covenantal obligations.

At least four Greek terms are used in the NT. **Des-mos** refers to physical chains (Luke 8:29; Acts 26:29; Col 4:18; 2 Tim 2:9) or to a state of bondage/imprisonment (Luke 13:16; Acts 20:23; 23:29). **Desmios** indicates someone who is kept in chains as a prisoner (Matt 27:15; Mark 15:6). **Halysis** refers to chains meant to restrict one's movements (Mark 5:3; Luke 8:29). **Syndesmos** occurs in contexts that refer to something that connects or unifies (Eph 4:3; Col 2:19; 3:14). *See* BONDS, BONDAGE.

LINDA SCHEARING

BONDS, BONDAGE. *See* SLAVERY.

BONE [עֶצֶם 'etsem; ὀστέον osteon]. Anatomically, the human skeleton at birth has 350 bones. By adulthood the number is 206 because some bones fuse together. Of these, the Bible mentions only a few: the skull (Judg 9:53), jaw (Isa 30:28), rib (Gen 2:21-22), hip (Gen 32:25), and legs (John 19:31-33). When biblical authors understood bones literally, it was from a folk medical perspective. Bones felt fever (Job 30:30) and pain (Job 30:17). Dry bones were dead (Ezek 37:3-4); figuratively they describe a dispirited personality (Prov 17:22). A noteworthy figurative meaning is the combination "flesh and bone" to signify the whole human body, a status allowing a person to establish relationships with others. Thus, that phrase points to close kinship (Judg 9:2; 1 Sam 5:1; 19:12; Luke 24:39).

JOHN J. PILCH

BOOK [סֵפֶר sefer, βιβλίον biblion]. In antiquity a book generally took the form of scrolls that had been attached end to end. In the Roman period, wooden tablets, which had been laced together, also came into use. Known as a *codex*, this proved to be easier to use than unrolling a long scroll. By the early Christian era, sheets of papyrus or leather parchment emerged to replace the wooden tablets. Such papyri and parchments were bound together, making a collection of writings much lighter and more manageable. Most of the early Christian documents that survive from the 2nd and 3rd cent. were constructed in the form of a codex.

In the OT, the semantic range of sefer is broad. As stated by Solomon (Eccl 12:12), there does not seem to be any end to the making of books, and the content of what was labeled as a book varied considerably. The Hebrew term is a cognate from the Akkadian sipru, which may be regarded as any sort of written document, and it is best to think of the Hebrew term in that respect. In Gen 5:1 and Neh 7:5, a genealogical record is a book. Royal archives are called "the book of records, the annals" in Esth 6:2. The term can also designate a letter (Jer 29:1), a legal document (Deut 44:1), a collection of laws (Deut 28:1; Josh 1:8), or a royal decree (Esth 8:10). The OT also mentions a number of books that are not extant but were clearly utilized as sources in the composition of the canonical texts. (*See* BOOKS REFERRED TO IN THE BIBLE.) These include the Book of Jashar (Josh 10:13; 2 Sam 1:18), the Book of the Wars of the LORD (Num 21:14), the Book of the Acts of Solomon (1 Kgs 11:41), the Book of the Chronicles of the Kings of Israel (1 Kgs 14:19; 15:31; 2 Kgs 10:34), The Book of the Chronicles of the Kings of Judah (1 Kgs 14:29; 15:7; 2 Kgs 8:3), the Book of the Kings of Israel (1 Chr 9:1; 2 Chr 20:34), the Book of the Kings of Israel in Judah (2 Chr 27:7; 35:27), the Book of the Kings of Judah and Israel (2 Chr 16:11; 25:26).

In the NT, the term **biblion** is used to refer to any scroll or book. Eventually, the plural **ta biblia** was used by Greek-speaking Christians to refer to the entire collection of books that became the OT and NT, and the word *Bible* ultimately derives from this term. When Paul asked Timothy (2 Tim 14:13) to bring him books and parchments, he used **ta biblia** and the term **mem-branas**, which is borrowed from Latin and can only have the meaning of parchment made from animal skin. There is disagreement whether these two terms are synonymously used to refer to Scriptures in this context. *See* CODEX; PAPYRUS; SCRIBES; SCROLLS; WRITING AND WRITING MATERIALS.

BUZZ BROOKMAN

BOOK OF JASHAR. *See* JASHAR, BOOK OF.

BOOK OF LIFE. *See* LIFE, BOOK OF.

BOOK OF REMEMBRANCE. *See* BOOKS REFERRED TO IN THE BIBLE.

BOOK OF THE ACTS OF SOLOMON. *See* BOOKS REFERRED TO IN THE BIBLE.

BOOK OF THE ANNALS OF THE KINGS OF ISRAEL. *See* BOOKS REFERRED TO IN THE BIBLE.

BOOK OF THE COVENANT. *See* COVENANT, BOOK OF THE.

BOOK OF THE DEAD. A compendium of Egyptian incantations, hymnic interludes, magic spells, and pictorial vignettes of mythic action needed for a mummy's successful reanimation in the afterlife. While originating as Old Kingdom pyramid texts, by the Middle Kingdom texts were inscribed inside coffins. By the New Kingdom the spells and illustrations were made into a specially commissioned or ready-made scroll used in elite and nonroyal burials. The most lavish example is the 78 ft.-long Papyrus of Ani, now in the British Museum.

In the mythology of HELIOPOLIS, the Sun God Amon-Re regenerated nightly; this imagery later merged with the cult of OSIRIS, God-King of the Dead, who was revived by his wife, Isis. This cult was associated with the lucrative funerary industry at Abydos, run by the Theban scribal bureaucracy. The *Book of the Dead* helped the deceased to make the perilous journey after death to the Field of Offerings, providing special information, helpful pictures, and incantations. The high point occurs in ch. 125, "The Negative Oath of Innocence," where the deceased's heart, witness to all deeds performed, is weighed on a scale against the goddess Ma'at (represented by a feather). Like "Lady Wisdom" of Prov 8, Ma'at stands for cosmic order and human justice. During the ceremony, mummies recited lengthy descriptions of all the sins they had *not* committed. The scribal god Thoth recorded the verdict: the successful deceased merged with Osiris, living again bodily and forever. The hybrid monster, Ammit, ate the hearts of the wicked, representing final annihilation of the human person.

Overtones of the Egyptian scribal ethics in the *Book of the Dead* are found in Wisdom literature, particularly Proverbs and Job. Proverbs 16:11; 17:3; 20:9-10; and 24:10-12 directly reference the visual imagery and content of the scene of judgment of the heart, but now it is the Lord who performs all the roles. The same appears in Psalms (62:8-10) and Daniel (5:27); and in Rev 6, one of the four horsemen carries a set of scales. Job's ritual oath of innocence in ch. 31 follows a pattern similar to the Egyptian Negative Confession, and is notable for its use of the full curse formula, whose grisly predictions are reminiscent of the *Book of the Dead*'s colorful (and often enigmatic) rhetoric. *See* HEART; JUDGMENT; SOPHIA.

Bibliography: Raymond Faulkner, trans. *The Egyptian Book of the Dead: The Book of Going Forth by Day* 2nd, rev. ed. 1998; Erik Hornung. *The Ancient Egyptian Books of the Afterlife*. David Lorton, trans. (1998).

CAROLE R. FONTAINE

BOOK OF THE KINGS OF ISRAEL. *See* BOOKS REFERRED TO IN THE BIBLE.

BOOK OF THE KINGS OF JUDAH AND ISRAEL. *See* BOOKS REFERRED TO IN THE BIBLE.

BOOK OF THE LAW. *See* BOOKS REFERRED TO IN THE BIBLE.

BOOK OF THE TWELVE. The "Book of the Twelve" denotes the collection of books from Hosea to Malachi that comprise the fourth "book" of the Latter Prophets (Isaiah, Jeremiah, Ezekiel, and the Twelve) in the Nevi'im (Prophets). The English names given to this corpus include the Minor Prophets, the Twelve, the Twelve Prophets, and the Book of the Twelve. These names reflect ancient traditions that these writings were transmitted on a single scroll and counted as a single unit.

A. Ancient Evidence

Sirach 49:10 associates the "bones of the twelve prophets" with hope for Israel in a hymn that blends references to kings and canonical prophets (Isa 48:20; Jer 49:6; and Ezek 49:8). Manuscript fragments from Qumran and the Judean Desert dating from 150 BCE to 135 CE include *4 Ezra* 14 and Josephus (*Ag. Ap.* 1.38-40); each lists the number of books in the OT canon. The two numbers do not agree, but clearly both

count the Book of the Twelve as a single entity. The Babylonian Talmud (*B. Bat.* 13b–15a) treats the Twelve corporately. Jerome's introduction to the Book of the Twelve in the Vulgate states, "The Twelve Prophets are one book," and advocates a chronological hermeneutic for interpreting the prophets.

The LXX both confirms the common transmission of the Book of the Twelve and complicates its interpretation. The twelve writings always appear together in the LXX, confirming that they were treated as a group. However, the MT and LXX present two different orders for the first six writings.

B. Unifying Elements

Most models for interpreting these traditions agree upon three unifying elements: chronological structure, recurring themes, and intertextual associations.

1. Chronological structure

Hosea, Amos, and Micah begin with superscriptions that intertwine references to five 8th cent. kings of Judah (Uzziah, Jotham, Ahaz, Hezekiah) and Israel (Jeroboam). Zephaniah 1:1 is set during the reign of Josiah. Haggai (1:1, 15; 2:1, 10, 20) overlaps Zechariah (1:1, 7; 7:1) in the early Persian period. This chronological arrangement pivots around the destruction of Jerusalem that is anticipated in Zephaniah, but has already occurred in Haggai-Malachi.

2. Recurring themes

A number of recurring themes add cohesion to the Book of the Twelve, including the day(s) of Yahweh, the infertility/fertility of the land, and ongoing discussion of the theodicy problem that draws upon Exod 34:6-7. The "day of Yahweh" (and related terms) is a prominent characteristic of the corpus, one that anticipates the destruction of Israel and/or Judah in Hosea–Zephaniah, and future retribution against the nations who abused Judah, especially *after* Jerusalem's restoration (*see* Joel 4; Obad 15–21; Nah 1:2-8; Zeph 3:8-20; Zech 12–14).

A cluster of images depict the infertility and fertility of the land, portraying God's judgment in agricultural terms (Hos 2:8-9, 12; Joel 1–2; Amos 4:9; Hab 3:17) in the pre-exilic section of the Twelve. These images change to promises in the post-exilic portion with the reconstruction of the Temple (Hag 2:17, 19; Zech 8:9-12; Mal 3:8-11). Several passages also use locust imagery to depict foreign nations devouring the land (Joel 1–2; Nah 3:15; Hab 1:8-9; Mal 3:11; Amos 4:9; 7:1).

A number of texts in Hosea–Zephaniah (Joel 2:13; Jonah 4:2; Nah 1:3; and Mic 7:18-19) explore theodicy by drawing upon variations of Exod 34:6-7 and underscoring the theological crisis created by Jerusalem's destruction.

3. Catchwords and intertextuality

Hosea ends and Joel begins with extended calls to repentance. Joel 4:16, 18 contains parallels to the beginning and end of Amos (1:2; 9:13). Amos 9:12 summarizes the message of Obadiah, and Amos 9:2 and Obad 4 share an unusual phrase ("from there I will bring them/you down"). The semi-acrostic poem that begins Nahum (1:2-8) contains catchwords from Mic 7 in those places interrupting the acrostic pattern, and exhibits similar perspectives to Habakkuk.

C. Placement of the Undated Writings

The function of the six undated writings within the corpus is complex. Joel and Obadiah have thematic connections to their immediate and larger literary settings. Joel adapts language and forms from Hosea on one end and Amos on the other. Joel serves as the "literary anchor," meaning that it reflects significantly upon the Twelve's recurring themes. Obadiah imitates the structure and language of Amos 9 to show that the fate of Edom (Israel's brother) parallels the fate of the northern kingdom, yet Obadiah's prediction of Edom's destruction is presumed in Mal 1:4.

Jonah precedes Micah and Nahum in the MT. because 2 Kgs 14:25 places Jonah in the reign of Jeroboam II (see Amos 1:1; Mic 1:1). Since Jonah portrays Assyria's repentance, it creates a bookend around Micah with Nahum, where Nineveh's destruction is described.

Nahum and Habakkuk deal with God's plans for the Assyrians and Babylonians, respectively. Nahum and Habakkuk thus transition from Micah (which presupposes an Assyrian threat [5:5-6], yet anticipates the coming of the Babylonians [see 4:10], not unlike Isaiah 36–39) and Zephaniah (whose Josianic setting [1:1] and anticipation of Jerusalem's destruction by Babylon does the same [see 1:7-18; 2:13]). Zephaniah 3:8-20 also expands the judgment to the nations (3:8) to remove Jerusalem's oppressors and return its exiles (3:19-20) following a purifying judgment on Yahweh's people (3:11-13), actions that Jerusalem should see as positive (3:14-18). Haggai 1 then presupposes the exiles have returned.

Reference to the Persian governor (1:8) and the presumption of a functioning Temple explain Malachi's position after Zechariah, where Temple construction is ongoing. The end of Malachi also alludes to the Torah and the beginning of the Nevi'im.

D. Hypotheses About the Formative Stages

The Book of the Twelve is a complex unit that did not result from a single editorial decision to incorporate these twelve writings. Hosea, Amos, Micah, and Zephaniah show signs of protracted common transmission. Hosea and Micah alternate judgment and salvation for Israel and Judah, respectively. Amos and Zephaniah exhibit a core message of judgment against the same

entities, though each ends with eschatological promises. Nahum and Habakkuk, though the timing of their incorporation is debated, presuppose this message of impending doom for Judah and Jerusalem with the announcement of Assyria's imminent demise (Nahum) followed by Yahweh's use of Babylon to punish Judah (Habakkuk). Haggai and Zechariah have long been the subject regarding theories of common editorial tradents. Joel, Obadiah, and perhaps Malachi may have compiled preexisting speeches specifically for their current locations in the Book of the Twelve. Disagreements exist regarding the extent to which Malachi was involved with Haggai–Zechariah, and when Zech 9–14 was incorporated. Still, the similar superscriptions in Zech 9:1; 12:1; and Mal 1:1 suggest awareness of the larger context. Jonah was probably the last complete writing to enter the Twelve. With its prophetic antihero and openness to foreign nations, Jonah stands outside the theological mainstream of the Book of the Twelve.

Bibliography: Paul R. House. *The Unity of the Twelve* (1990); Paul R. House and James W. Watts, ed. *Forming Prophetic Literature: Essays on Isaiah and the Twelve in Honour of John D. W. Watts* (1996); Barry Alan Jones. *The Formation of the Book of the Twelve: A Study in Text and Canon* (1995). James Dominic Nogalski. *Literary Precursors to the Book of the Twelve* (1993); James Dominic Nogalski. *Redactional Processes in the Book of the Twelve* (1993); James Dominic Nogalski and Marvin A. Sweeney, ed. *Reading and Hearing the Book of the Twelve* (2000); Paul L. Redditt and Aaron Schart, ed. *Thematic Threads in the Book of the Twelve* (2003).

JAMES D. NOGALSKI

BOOK OF THE WARS OF THE LORD. *See* BOOKS REFERRED TO IN THE BIBLE.

BOOK OF THE WATCHERS. *See* WATCHERS, BOOK OF THE.

BOOKS REFERRED TO IN THE BIBLE. Among the many written documents or "books" mentioned in the Bible, some are cited as sources, others are attributed to biblical figures, and still others are said to be of divine authorship.

In Numbers, "the Book of the Wars of the LORD" is cited as a source for a brief piece of poetry (21:14). The title and quotation imply a poetic anthology celebrating Israel's military successes and Yahweh's fighting on Israel's behalf.

"The Book of Jashar" is identified as the source of David's lamentation over Saul and Jonathan (2 Sam 1:18) and of several additional lines of poetry (Josh 10:12-13). Judging by these citations, it appears to have been a poetic anthology. *See* JASHAR, BOOK OF.

First Kings names "the Book of the Acts of Solomon" as a document containing a fuller treatment of Solomon's reign (11:41). If it was an account of "all that he did" (v. 41), it may have been similar to extant royal annals and chronicles from Assyria and Babylonia; or it may have contained material similar to the lists of Solomon's officials (4:2-6), administrative districts (4:7-19), and building activities (9:15-19). If it included "his wisdom" as well (11:41), it may have been more biographical, even hagiographical, as the narrative material in 3:4-13, 16-28; 4:29-34; and 10:1-10. This reference is possibly a literary artifice invented to supply Solomon with a summary comparable to later monarchs.

First and Second Kings cite "the Book of the Annals of the Kings of Israel" as containing additional information concerning the reigns of eighteen of Israel's twenty kings (1 Kgs 14:19; 15:31; 16:5, 14, 20, 27; 22:39; 2 Kgs 1:18; 10:34; 13:8,12; 14:15, 28; 15:11, 15, 21, 26, 31). This citation is lacking only for Jehoram (assassinated by Jehu), and for Israel's last king, Hoshea (deposed and exiled to Assyria by Sargon I). Similarly, "the Book of the Annals of the Kings of Judah" is referred to in the concluding summaries of the reigns of fifteen of the twenty Judean monarchs (1 Kgs 14:29; 15:7, 23; 22:45; 2 Kgs 8:23; 12:19; 14:18; 15:6, 36; 16:19; 20:20; 21:17, 25; 23:28; 24:5). The exceptions are Ahaziah (assassinated by Jehu), his mother Athaliah, and three of Judah's last four kings—Jehoahaz (deposed and exiled by Pharaoh Necho), Jehoiachin, and Zedekiah (both deposed and exiled by the Babylonian Nebuchadnezzar). If these titles are not simply literary allusions to an internationally assumed court archives tradition (*see* examples in Ezra and Esther below), the fuller accounts may have been court records or royal annals, or they could have been excerpted from such materials. *See* KINGS, FIRST AND SECOND BOOK OF.

First and Second Chronicles cite entirely different documents. Some are associated with kings: "the Book of the Kings of Israel" (1 Chr 9:1; 2 Chr 20:34), "the Book of the Kings of Israel and Judah" (2 Chr 27:7; 35:27; 36:8), "the Book of the Kings of Judah and Israel" (2 Chr 16:11; 25:26; 28:26; 32:32), and "the Commentary on the Book of Kings" (2 Chr 24:27). Others refer to writings of prophets and seers: Samuel, Nathan, and Gad (1 Chr 29:29); Nathan, Ahijah, and Iddo (2 Chr 9:29); Shemaiah and Iddo (2 Chr 12:15); Iddo (2 Chr 13:22); Isaiah (2 Chr 26:22); and "the seers" (33:19). With only three exceptions, these documents are always mentioned at junctures where 1 and 2 Kings cite sources by different names (the exceptions are the genealogical registry in 1 Chr 9:1, lacking in Kings; 1 Chr 29:29, where Kings mentions no fuller account for David; and 2 Chr 35:26-27, one of several divergences from the treatment of Josiah in 2 Kings). These books are cited only for kings who meet with the Chronicler's approval; and when the annals cited

in Kings refer only to "kings of Judah," the document named in Chronicles always includes "Israel" also. Finally, the writings associated with prophets are never referred to as "books." These "sources" in Chronicles appear to be adaptations of the titles cited in Kings and allusions to the prophetic content of Kings. *See* CHRONICLES, FIRST AND SECOND BOOK OF.

Ezra mentions "the book of the annals of your ancestors" (4:15), an allusion to state records or royal archives assumed to be available to the Persian king Artaxerxes.

Nehemiah refers to "the Book of the Annals" in a list of Levite heads of houses (12:23), as well as to "the book of the genealogy of those who were the first to come back" (7:5). The former is fragmentary and difficult to assess. The latter is widely considered to represent a contemporary list or compilation of lists incorporated into Neh 7 and Ezra 2. *See* NEHEMIAH, BOOK OF.

Esther mentions "the book of the annals" associated with the royal court (2:23) and "the book of records, the annals" (6:1), and later alludes generically to "the annals of the kings of Media and Persia" (10:2).

New Testament books frequently contain quotations from books of the OT, but references to books by name are quite rare. Luke 3:4 cites "the book of the words of the prophet Isaiah," and Luke 4:17 introduces another quotation with "the scroll of the prophet Isaiah." Luke 20:42 refers to "the book of Psalms," as does Acts 1:20. Acts 7:42 refers to "the book of the prophets" to introduce material from Amos, a reflection of the fact that the twelve so-called "minor prophets" were collected on a single scroll. In a quotation from Deut 27:26, Gal 3:10 transposes "this law" in the verse it is quoting into "the book of the law." *See* BOOK OF THE LAW.

The biblical figure most frequently associated with writing books is Moses. Moses is said to have documented "in a book" the divine judgment on Amalek (Exod 17:14) and to have written down the "book of the covenant" at Yahweh's dictation (Exod 24:3-7). In Deut 31:24, Moses is described as "writing down in a book the words of this law." Subsequent references to "the book of the law of Moses" allude to or quote Deuteronomy (Josh 8:31; 23:6; 2 Kgs 14:6) and Leviticus (Neh 8:1). References to "the book of Moses" reflect Deuteronomy (2 Chr 25:4; 35:12), Leviticus (Ezra 6:18; Neh 13:1), and Numbers (Neh 13:1-2). In Mark 12:26, "the book of Moses" introduces a quotation from Exodus. *See* COVENANT, BOOK OF THE; DEUTERONOMY, BOOK OF.

Other writers include Israelites sent by Joshua to "write a description" of the land "in a book" (Josh 18:8-9); Joshua, who wrote words "in the book of the law of God" (Josh 24:26); Samuel, who wrote "in a book" the "rights and duties of kingship" (1 Sam 10:25); and Isaiah, who was instructed to "write on a tablet . . . inscribe in a book" his sayings (30:8; *see also* 8:1).

The prophetic witness as written material is featured prominently for the first time in Jeremiah (25:13; 30:2; 36:1-32; 45:1; 51:60). The reference in Luke 20:42 to "the book of Psalms" also cites David as its author.

Beyond human authorship is a variously conceived "book of the LORD" (Isa 34:16), "book of remembrance" (Mal 3:16), "book of the living" (Ps 69:28), or "book of life" (Phil 4:3; Rev 3:5; 13:8; 17:8; 20:12, 15) in which names and/or deeds of people were written (or not). Allusions to this heavenly book appear in Exod 32:32-33; Isa 4:3; 65:6; Ps 40:7; 56:8; 87:6; 139:16; Dan 7:10; 12:1; Luke 10:20; and Rev 21:27. See BOOK.

Bibliography: B. O. Long. *1-2 Kings* FOTL 9 (1984); H. G. M. Williamson. *1-2 Chronicles* (1982).

JEFFREY S. ROGERS

BOOT [נַעַל na'al, סְאוֹן se'on]. The Bible seems to make no distinction between different types of shoes, boots, or sandals. Some biblical references may well indicate barred or closed shoes in war-related verses (1 Kgs 2:5; Deut 33:25). On the LACHISH inscriptions, the Israelites seem to have been barefooted or wearing open shoes (i.e., sandals) while the Assyrians seem to wear a closed type of shoe (i.e., boot) as a part of their war clothing. See CLOTH, CLOTHES; WAR, METHODS, TACTICS, WEAPONS OF.

CHANNA COHEN STUART

BOOTH [סֻכָּה sukkah]. A temporary building set up in the fields during harvest time; also the name of a harvest holiday celebrated in the autumn. These booths are to remind the Israelites that they dwelled in booths as they traveled from Egypt to the land of Israel (Lev 23:42-43). The holiday is still celebrated to this day with those observing it most rigorously by sleeping and eating in the booths. The holiday lasts for seven days with a festival day at the beginning and the end of the week. During the Second Temple period it concluded with the Water Drawing Ceremony. See BOOTHS, FEAST OF; PAVILION; TABERNACLE.

JUDITH Z. ABRAMS

BOOTHS, FEAST-FESTIVAL OF [חַג הַסֻּכּוֹת hagh hassukkoth]. Each major festival in the OT represents a week of HARVEST in the spring, in the summer, and in the autumn. Spring brings early grain, especially barley, and is also time to move the flocks on from one pasture to another. Summer sees the larger grain-harvest of wheat. Autumn is the last time of gathering for the cycle, and the grapes and olives and nuts of that season make it the most joyous time of all.

A. The Cycle of Festivals
The CALENDAR of ancient Israel developed profoundly theological explanations of the following recurring festivals. Passover was associated with the exodus from Egypt, Weeks or Pentecost with the solemnization of the covenant, and Booths (or Tabernacles, as it is also known) with the sojourn in the wilderness. Nonetheless, the primacy of agricultural practice and experience should be recollected throughout, if one is to appreciate the sense of the calendar and the genuine joy and enjoyment involved in the festivals. The fundamental importance of the three great agricultural festivals is signaled by the requirement that every male of Israel appear before the Lord every year at these times (Exod 23:14-17; 34:23; Deut 16:16-17). That is, of course, an idealized expectation, but it enables us to appreciate how deeply felt was the connection between the rhythm of the fields and the rhythm of God's choice of Israel. It could be felt in city, town, and country, wherever the biblical calendar was known.

The greater and richer the harvest, the more intense and cooperative the work of any agricultural commune must be. That demanded a social structure at the local scale, and the hard labor of harvesting was basically undertaken by the Israelites themselves: slavery does not appear to have been a major institution until the monarchy, and even then had more to do with building and service for the king than with agriculture. A primary motivation in this communal work was the urgency of harvest. Once ripe, a crop must be taken in quickly, with as little waste and damage as possible, if the full benefit is to be enjoyed. One way to enjoy the crop is to share some of it (indeed, a great deal of it) at the time of harvest itself. That celebration leads naturally to SACRIFICE, a moment when Israel gathers with Israel's God to consume with pleasure and generosity what God permits to be produced on God's land.

B. Sukkoth (Huts or Booths or Tabernacles) in Ancient Israel and Early Judaism
The last of the three great festivals, and the greatest in terms of the value and quantity of the crops involved, is Sukkoth, meaning Booths or Tabernacles. Actually, the term sukkah can also mean "thicket," such as an animal might lurk in. The point is to refer to a rough, natural shelter of plaited branches that would permit the celebrants to lodge in the fields. Grapes and olives were taken in at this time; they require particular care in handling and storage, and sometimes it was prudent to remain overnight near enough to protect the ripened yield. Camping in the fields was a wise practice. Sukkoth, in its material and social dimensions, was a feast of particular joy, and the principal festival of ancient Israel (and may indeed pre-date Israel; see Judg 9:27). It could be simply referred to as the "Feast of the Lord," without further specification (see Lev 23:39; Judg 21:19), in view of its prominence. In the OT Sukkoth is clearly marked as the principal festival of the year.

As in the cases of Passover and of Weeks, the festival was also associated with the formation of Israel, and the sukkoth were held to be reminiscent of the people's period in the wilderness. But that was a later development, reflected from the time of the Priestly source (see Lev 23:39-43), which also specified the greatest amount of sacrifice for Sukkoth among all the festivals (see Num 29). Deuteronomy also would have the three great festivals—Passover, Weeks, and Sukkoth—conceived as feasts of pilgrimage (Deut 16:16-17) that involve travel to the central sanctuary in Jerusalem, although they were in origin (and probably remained in practice as well, under various forms) local, festal celebrations. Because the correspondence to harvest endured, embedded in the timing of feasts, villages celebrated Sukkoth while offerings in the Temple marked the participation of Israel as a whole.

The success of the Deuteronomic calendar corresponds to the emergence of the canon, and results in the agricultural year becoming the covenantal year: the cycle of exodus, Sinai, and wilderness was superimposed on the cycle of barley, wheat, and grapes, and the Temple (the only place where sacrifice could be offered) became the focus of all three festivals. But it is noteworthy that of the three major feasts of Judaism, Sukkoth has survived best in the Rabbinic revision of practice that followed the destruction of the Temple. Sacrifice, of course, is not involved, but the construction of the sukkah and associated practices of festivity make this the most joyous occasion of the Jewish year (see the tractate Sukkah in the Mishnah).

Yet in ancient Israel, whether on the agricultural or the covenantal explanation, sacrifice was central to all the festivals, and sacrifice on a monumental scale. It is not surprising that Sukkoth is marked as the greatest sacrifice in terms of the quantity and value of offerings, because it came at the time of year when the disposable wealth of produce was at its height. The underlying dynamic of sacrifice is that when Israel enjoys the produce of God's land with God, according to the preparation and timing and consumption that God desires, Israel is blessed. Sacrifice is a feast of holy consumption that carries in itself the promise of further enjoyment. Penance may of course be involved in sacrifice, but most of the sacrifices of Israel—the festival sacrifices above all—are emphatically understood as occasions of communal, festal joy. For that reason, the Temple itself is a house of joy, and its dedication is crucial. In this context, it is vital to note that, even before it was associated with the period in the wilderness, Sukkoth was associated with the time that the Temple was dedicated by Solomon (see 1 Kgs 8:2).

Tishri (during which Sukkoth occurs) is the seventh month, and the Temple's dedication then made Sukkoth the time when, in a Sabbath year, the Torah would be read out (so Deut 31:9-13). That is the basis of the later Rabbinic celebration of Simkhat Torah ("joy of the law") that closes Sukkoth. The number seven, of course, is basic to the entire calendar that coordinates the feasts, each of which was to last a week. (Although that is not specified in the case of Weeks, both its status as a festal convocation [Lev 23:21] and its name make that probable.) The weeks of the year mark out the quarters of the lunar month, and each week ends with the Sabbath that is itself a regular feast. (The timing of each major feast in the middle of its month corresponds to the full moon, as is appropriate for a feast of harvest.) The Sabbath year and the jubilee year (the Sabbath of Sabbaths) fit into the scheme that makes seven a basic unit of measurement. So there is a sense in which Tishri marks the NEW YEAR, as well as Abib (see Exod 12:2; 13:4, later called Nisan and the tractate ROSH HASHANAH 1:1 in the Mishnah), the month of the Passover. When the book of Zechariah envisages the establishment of worship for all the nations in Jerusalem in a new, eschatological dispensation, it is natural that the feast concerned should be Sukkoth (Zech 14:16-21): the climactic feast of the year becomes the climactic feast of all history.

C. Tabernacles in the NT

The most distinctive appropriation of a Judaic festival within the church was occasioned by Passover. Although the Gospel of John presents Jesus' death as at the time the paschal lambs were slain (John 19:14, 31), the synoptic Gospels imagine that the LAST SUPPER was a Seder, the meal of Passover (Matt 26:17-29; Mark 14:12-16; Luke 22:7-13). There are several reasons why scholars tend to favor the Johannine chronology. No mention is made in the synoptic accounts of the supper of the lamb (much less its selection and preparation days before), the bitter herbs, the unleavened bread, or the exodus from Egypt, all of which are prescribed in Exod 12. Moreover, the cultic authorities are presented as solemnly deciding to act in the case of Jesus before the feast itself (Matt 26:3-5; Mark 14:1-2). It seems clear that Jesus died near the time of Passover (having entered Jerusalem at or near Sukkoth), and that this timing then became coordinated with the Passover itself within the practice of the church, because the disciples experienced his resurrection during the paschal season.

The attempt to cram all the events leading up to Jesus' death into a single, holy week is problematic, and the thesis (which some scholars have derived from the synoptic Gospels) that Jesus' public activity lasted only one year, culminating in his final Passover, is quite unrealistic. The liturgical power of the Passover feast—which became the principal festival of Christianity as a result of the timing of Jesus' resurrection, even while the Temple still stood, when Sukkoth was the principal festival of Judaism—has resulted in the misimpression that Passover was the only feast that mattered greatly to Jews or Christians. The dominance of Passover in the NT is primarily a function of how the Pascha (as Christians called the Passover in Greek, reflecting the Aram. pronunciation) emerged as the main Christian feast.

D. The Tabernacles of Jesus

Jesus' entry into Jerusalem is likely to have occurred well before the time of his death in the spring prior to Passover. His procession at or near the time of Sukkoth would help to explain the text of the Gospels. The leafy branches to be used within the procession of Sukkoth—bound as what the Mishnah calls lulavim, consisting of myrtle, willow, and palm, waved about with lemons—are an important symbol within the scene as presented in the Gospels (see Sukkah 3:1–4:5 [and the related provision for the booths in Neh 8:14-16], together with Matt 21:8; Mark 11:8; John 12:13). In the cry "Hosanna" (meaning "save us" [Matt 21:9; Mark 11:9; John 12:13]) a characteristic element of the Sukkoth celebration comes to expression (see Sukkah 3:9; 4:5).

Procession to the Temple, lulavim in hand, was a requirement of this feast, even on the Sabbath, because that was an intrinsic part of the festivity (Sukkah 4:4). There was a vigorous, sometimes even violent strain in all this. The same passage of the Mishnah relates that attendants used to scatter lulavim for people to collect as they would, but that led to people fighting over them and even hitting one another with lulavim, until that practice was stopped.

When Simon Maccabeus entered Jerusalem, he enjoyed a similar triumph (see 1 Macc 13:51), so it is clear that the tenor of Sukkoth was not limited to the feast itself. But Jesus' entry is marked as a religious occasion, not only by the cries of "Hosanna," but by the usage of material from the Hallel, a string of psalms (Pss 113–118) that were sung all through Sukkoth. Psalm 118:25-26 is actually cited as the crowd's song (Matt 21:9; Mark 11:9; Luke 19:38; John 12:13), and it is specified in the Mishnah as a portion of the Hallel, which is to be sung (see Sukkah 4:5).

The connections between Jesus' entry and Sukkoth go much deeper. They include the formative impact of the book of Zechariah on the Gospels' accounts, because Zechariah was targeted on the feast of Sukkoth. The Tg. Zech. 14 predicts that God's kingdom will be manifested over the entire earth when the offerings of Sukkoth are presented both by Israelites and non-Jews at the Temple. It further predicts that these worshipers will prepare and offer their sacrifices themselves without intermediaries. The last words of the book promise that "there shall never again be a trader in the sanctuary of the Lord of hosts at that time" (Tg. Zech. 14:21). The thrust of the targumic prophecy brought on the dramatic confrontation that Jesus provoked in the Temple.

The Targum emphasized the coming transformation of worship in the Temple as well as the ultimate vindication of Israel that would give the people of God back their land. Jesus himself had been pushed out of Galilee by Antipas (see Luke 13:31-33), just as the Israelites had been displaced from control of their own territory by the Romans. Zechariah's vision of a Sukkoth that restored the land to Israel and the Temple to the sacrifice God desired was a fundamental part of Jesus' motivation during his last weeks in Jerusalem. The Romans would be banished and Zion's gates opened to all who would join with Israel there in worship (Tg. Zech. 14:9): "And the Kingdom of the LORD shall be revealed upon all the inhabitants of the earth; at that time they shall serve before the LORD with one accord, for his name is established in the world; there is none apart from him." The Targum not only specifies that Zechariah's vision is of the kingdom, it also spells out, in a way the Hebrew text does, the immediate impact of that kingdom upon all of humanity.

The focus of Jesus' action on the Temple, in his occupation of the outer court as a protest and enactment of the kind of purity he demanded there (Matt 21:12-13; Mark 11:15-17; Luke 19:45-46; John 2:14-17), comports well with the pivotal place of the Temple at the close of the book of Zechariah. Even Jesus' appropriation of property—the foal that he rides into the city (Matt 21:1-7; Mark 11:1-7; Luke 19:29-35)—is an enactment of Zechariah's prophecy. The book itself claims that the very horses in Jerusalem will be marked ornamentally with the words "holy to the LORD" (Zech 14:20), and Zech 9:9 presents the messianic king as riding on a colt. For a royal figure, garments might well be strewn in the way (2 Kgs 9:13). That was all the more natural at Sukkoth in the case of Jesus, the son of David (see Matt 21:7-9; Mark 11:7-10; Luke 19:35-38).

At the time of Sukkoth, even priestly garments were turned into wicks for illumination, and flaming torches accompanied the song and dance of the procession (Sukkah 5:3-4). What were a few more garments tossed about in such a mêlée? All this festivity was appropriate because this messiah made known the identity of the Lord as king, and in the Targum that is taken to refer to the revelation of the kingdom of God (Tg. Zech. 14:9; see Mark 11:10; Luke 19:38; John 12:13). In all of this, the deep connection to an eschatological understanding of Sukkoth is evident.

The same connection is evident in the vision that marks the beginning of Jesus' journey to Jerusalem, the transfiguration. Peter, in all accounts of the transfiguration (Matt 16:28–17:13; Mark 9:1-13; Luke 9:28-36), proposed to build huts or sukkoth at the place of the vision for Jesus and Moses and Elijah, and this marks both the timing and the significance of the transfiguration of the vision of Peter, James, and John.

Mark's Gospel presents Peter's offer as a witless suggestion (Mark 9:5-6). That typifies what frequently happened during the formation of the Gospels. When the significance of Judaic symbolism was forgotten, that was attributed to the ineptitude of the apostles, because of the lack of Jewish cultural knowledge among those transmitting the traditions. In the present case, the sukkoth Peter referred to reflects both the great feast that was coming and the wisdom that Jesus, like Moses and Elijah, represented the hope that the divine would commune with Israel in the makeshift huts Peter would build for these great prophets.

The transfiguration represents the mature development of Jesus' spirituality; he was able not only to articulate his own vision but to initiate others into its richness. His disciples now saw him as a living presence in the pantheon of Israel's patriarchs and prophets around God's throne. Zechariah prophesied that at the feast of Sukkoth the Temple would become the definitive tabernacle, the place where Israel would be regenerated, and the visionary world Peter glimpsed on the mountain would take on flesh and blood. Sacrifice in the Temple would become a universal feast with God, open to all peoples who accepted the truth that was to be initially revealed in Israel alone. Jesus embraced that prophecy, made it his own, and conveyed it to his followers.

Bibliography: Abraham P. Bloch. *The Biblical and Historical Background of the Jewish Holy Days* (1978); Bruce Chilton. *Redeeming Time: The Wisdom of Ancient Jewish and Christian Festal Calendars* (2002); T. W. Manson. "The Cleansing of the Temple." *BJRL* 33 (1951) 271–82; A. Allan McArthur. *The Evolution of the Christian Year* (1953); J. L. Rubenstein. "Sukkot, Eschatology and Zechariah 14." *RB* 103 (1996) 161–95; Thomas J. Talley. *The Origins of the Liturgical Year* (1991); Hakan Ulfgard. *The Story of Sukkot: The Setting, Shaping, and Sequel of the Biblical Feast of Tabernacles* (1998).

BRUCE CHILTON

BOOTY [בַּז baz, שָׁלָל shalal; προνομή pronomē, σκῦλον skulon]. Objects or people taken by victorious armies as their reward for a successful campaign. The taking of booty is a central theme in the Israelite conquest narratives (*see* Josh 11:14). The two Hebrew terms appear memorably in the name of one of Isaiah's "sign children," Maher-Shalal-Hash-Baz, which means, "the spoil speeds, the prey hastens" (Isa 8:3). *See* BAN; SLAVERY; SPOILS OF WAR.

BRYAN D. BIBB

BOR-ASHAN. *See* ASHAN.

BORITH bor'ith. Bukki in 1 Esd 8:2. *See* BUKKI.

BORN AGAIN. *See* NEW BIRTH.

BORN, TO BE. *See* ABORTION; BIRTH; NEW BIRTH.

BORROW, LEND [עָבַט 'avat; δανίζω danizō]. Objects, food, or money could be borrowed, and repayment was expected. Old Testament guidelines provided for the restitution of borrowed property that was damaged while on loan (Exod 22:14-15). Loans were viewed as a form of charity (Sir 29:1-20), and thus interest with the repayment was condemned (Exod 22:25; Lev 25:36-37; Deut 23:19), except for loans extended to foreigners within Israel, who were most likely merchants who could afford such repayment (Deut 23:20). By contrast, in Mesopotamia interest on money was 20 percent, and on produce 33 percent. In addition, loans or debts in Israel were to be released every seven years according to Deut 15:1-11, and external historical evidence indicates that Jews faithfully attempted to keep this guideline. Jesus did not condemn loans because commercialism had developed by his day (Luke 16:1-8), but he encouraged lenders to be fair (Luke 6:30). Hellenistic interest rates could fluctuate from 10 percent to 30 percent, depending on economic stability. *See* DEBT, DEBTOR; DEPOSIT.

ROBERT GNUSE

BOSOR bohsor [Βοσορ Bosor]. 1. A city in GILEAD where JUDAS MACCABEUS rescued besieged Jews (1 Macc 5:26, 36). Located 40 mi. east of the SEA OF GALILEE it is likely the site of modern Bosra al Harir.

2. A scribal error for BEOR in 2 Pet 2:15.

BOTTLE. A word regularly used to describe various containers. "Bottle" is used figuratively by the NRSV when Ps 33:7 states that God has "gathered the waters of the sea as in a bottle." *See* also the reference of God gathering the psalmist's tears in God's bottle (Ps 56:8).

L. JULIANA M. CLAASSENS

BOTTOMLESS PIT [ἄβυσσος abyssos]. Transcendent abode of demons, beasts, and their king ABADDON (Rev 9:1-2, 11; 11:7; 17:8; 20:1) and of the dead. *See* ABYSS.

BOUGAEAN boo-gee'uhn [Βουγαῖος Bougaios]. Used in the LXX to identify HAMAN (Esth 3:1), perhaps as an updated equivalent of the Hebrew "AGAGITE," both terms apparently designating peoples hostile to Israel. "Bougaean" may mean something like "barbarian," comparable perhaps to "Macedonian" in Esth 9:24, an ethnic group with a belligerent and hateful reputation.

NICOLE WILKINSON DURAN

BOUNDARIES, TRIBAL [גְּבוּל gevul]. Joshua 15–19 describes tribal allotments west of the Jordan. Depictions combine town lists and boundary lines. Overlaps in the boundary descriptions (e.g., 15:5b-11 and 18:15-19) show that a static list of border points (towns, geographical features) has been enhanced by the verbs "goes," "goes up," "goes down," "passes along," and "turns." Although boundaries usually run in a single direction, they sometimes extend in two successive segments from a middle point (16:6-8; 19:10-12). Increased complexity and detail indicate disputed areas (15:8; 18:16 and 16:6-8; 17:7-9). The Stone of Bohan (15:6; 18:17) suggests a natural or artificial marker stone. *See* BOUNDARY STONES; TRIBES, TERRITORIES OF.

RICHARD D. NELSON

BOUNDARY STONE [גְּבוּל *gevul*]. Stone markers indicated the extent of privately owned fields and separated tribes. Israel's legal and wisdom traditions regarded the displacement of such landmarks as a reprehensible crime (Deut 19:14; 27:17; Prov 22:28; compare Hos 5:10). Land grabs could be affected by surreptitiously relocating a landmark, but more likely tactics would be economic pressure against the poor (Isa 5:8; Mic 2:2) and legal chicanery (1 Kgs 21), making widows and orphans classic victims (Prov 15:25; 23:10). The Stone of Bohan designated part of the border between Judah and Benjamin (Josh 15:6; 18:17). *See* LANDMARK.

RICHARD D. NELSON

BOW. *See* RAINBOW.

BOW AND ARROW [קֶשֶׁת *qesheth*; τόξος *toxos*; חֵץ *khets*, חִצִּי *khetse*, רֶשֶׁף *reshef*]. A bow is a strong, flexible, narrow piece of material, bent to form an arc, with a cord secured to both ends of the arc, from which the user shoots projectiles (arrows) consisting of 1) a light-weight, straight shaft made of reed or a strip of wood, 2) a stone, bone, or metal tip, and 3) a feathered tail. This weapon first appeared ca. 10000 BCE, and most forms of the bow were developed already by 8500–4300 BCE, even the composite bow—constructed by fusing several materials together to strengthen and increase tension.

Bows and arrows were used for hunting, target practice, and as military weaponry. They enabled archers to maim or kill, to set a city or ship on fire, or to send messages, from a distance. Lightweight, relatively compact, quickly ready to fire, very mobile, and accurate from great distances, the bow could deliver a constant barrage of lethal force on an enemy, whether from a phalanx on the field of battle, from behind fortifications, or from moving chariots. (*See* WAR AND IMPLEMENTS OF WAR.) ARCHERS carry quantities of arrows (ca. 25–30 arrows) in QUIVERS. Military annals and records of supplies from Egypt to Assyria to Greece include large quantities of bows and arrows, and even the Ugaritic goddess Anat desired them (*see* the Ugaritic story of Aqhat).

Bows were of the simple convex short or long variety—used by chariot and infantry archers, respectively—or the powerful composite bow (known from Mari as [Akkadian] tilpanu). Arrows came in various shapes and were made of materials tailored to specific uses: long or short range, darts, to pierce armor, carry flame, to act as a whistle. Arrowheads were made of flint, stone (e.g., obsidian), metal, and later of lead. Numerous designs of the points (tapered, notched, oval) and tails (tanged, winged, and notched) were created using different knapping techniques.

In the Bible a twisted bow figuratively signifies untrustworthiness or treachery (Ps 78:57; Jer 9:3; Hos 7:16), breaking the bow, the end of war, peace, or defeat (Ps 46:9; Jer 51:56; Hos 1:5); and setting it in the sky after the deluge (Gen 9:13-16) is God's promise never again to make war on humanity. Arrows are also equated with lightning bolts (2 Sam 22:15 // Pss 7:12–13; 18:14; 144:6; Hab 3:11; Zech 9:14). More literally, bow and arrow imagery was used to evoke fear or convey judgment (Num 24:8; Deut 32:23, 42; Isa 5:28; 13:18; Jer 6:23) and to describe their use (1 Kgs 22:34; 2 Kgs 9:24; 1 Chr 5:18; 12:2; 2 Chr 14:8; 17:17; 18:33; 26:14; Neh 4:13, 16). Arrows are also used for purposes of divination (Ezek 21:21) and prophecy (2 Kgs 13:15-19). *See* WAR, METHODS, TACTS, WEAPONS OF.

MARK J. H. FRETZ

BOW DOWN, TO [שָׁחָה *shakhah*; προσκυνέω *proskuneō*]. The verb usually translated "to bow down" can also be rendered "to prostrate oneself," "to make obeisance," "to bend low," and, most significantly, "to worship" (as in bowing down before) Yahweh, or even some other god, on occasions of prayer or sacrifice. Bowing down involves falling to one's knees with the forehead touching the earth, as is indicated in biblical texts (e.g., Gen 19:1) and artistic representations (e.g., the scene of Israel's King Jehu of Israel bowed down before his Assyrian overlords on the "Black Obelisk" of SHALMANESER III). Typically, as on the "Black Obelisk," one prostrates oneself before another of higher rank: the vanquished before a conqueror, a subject before a king, a woman before a man, a worshiper before God. In some texts, this becomes a source of tension: Joseph's brothers resent his prediction that they will bow down to him and thus acknowledge him as their superior (Gen 37:5-11), and the Jew Mordecai refuses to bow in submission before the Persian king's minister Haman (Esth 3:2).

In the NT, references to bowing down and the related acts of making obeisance and worshiping most frequently describe Jesus' followers bowing before him to pay him homage (Matt 2:2, 11; Mark 5:6; 7:5) or worshipers bowing before God, or some other deity—even the beasts of Revelation—to worship (John 4:23; Rom 11:4; 14:11; Rev 13:4, 12). As in Hebrew tradition, the act involves prostration (Luke 5:12; Rev 7:11).

SUSAN ACKERMAN

BOWELS [מֵעֶה *me'eh*; κοιλία *koilia*, σπλάγχνον *splanchnon*]. Among several terms that refer either to specific body parts or to internal organs in general (Num 5:22; 2 Chr 21:15; Acts 1:18; 2 Macc 9:5-6). The same terms are variously translated as ENTRAILS, inmost parts, HEART, and BODY.

BOWL [קְעָרָה qeʿarah, קְעָרֹת qeʿaroth; φιάλη phialē]. Several Hebrew and Greek terms are used for such VESSELS made of POTTERY, wood, or stone, depending upon their religious or household context. Archaeology and biblical texts indicate that bowls were used extensively for a variety of purposes in the biblical period. See BASIN; PLATE, PLATTER.

CHANNA STUART

BOX [אַרְגַּז ʾarghaz, פַּך pakh, ἀλάβαστρον alabastron]. Receptacle for objects, often holy, such as the Ten Commandments (Deut 10:5; 1 Kgs 8:9), and Scripture (Matt 23:5). See FLASK; MONEY BOX; PERFUME; POTTERY; VESSELS.

BOZEZ boh´ziz [בּוֹצֵץ botsets]. Name of one of two rocky crags between which Jonathan and his armor bearer passed to reach the Philistine garrison (1 Sam 14:4). Located between Geba (Saul's camp) and Michmash (the Philistine's camp).

BOZKATH boz´kath [בָּצְקַת botsqath]. 1. A town in the SHEPHELAH included among JUDAH's tribal allotment in the land conquered by Joshua (Josh 15:39).

2. Home of King JOSIAH's maternal grandfather ADAIAH (2 Kgs 22:1).

BOZRAH boz´ruh [בָּצְרָה botsrah; Βοσορρα Bosorra]. The Hebrew word botsrah means "enclosure" or "fortified place" and may refer to the defensive features of the three cities that bear the name. 1. A city in MOAB, probably the same as BEZER, a Reubenite city of refuge (Jer 48:24).

2. An important city in northern EDOM, identified with the modern Busayra/Buseirah in southern Jordan. In prophetic oracles, Bozrah is a symbol for all of Edom (Isa 34:6; 63:1; Jer 49:13, 22; Amos 1:12; the KJV translation "Bozrah" in Mic 2:12 is better understood as "pen" or "fold"). While Bozrah is mentioned as the home of King JOBAB in Edomite king lists (Gen 36:3; 1 Chr 1:44), archaeological evidence suggests that Bozrah was not a major city until at least the 8th cent. BCE.

3. A city in the BASHAN, identified as present-day Busra ash-Sham in southern Syria. Judas Maccabeus captured the city, which is mentioned in a list of cities by Tutmose III and in the Amarna Letters, in the 2nd cent. BCE (1 Macc 5:26, 28). Bozrah was an important city in the Nabatean Empire. After the annexation of Nabatea in 106 CE by the general of Trajan, Cornelius Palma, Bozrah became the capital of the Roman province Arabia Petraea. Under the Romans, it was named Nova Trajana Bostra, became the garrison for the Legion III Cyrenaica, and gained status as a metropolis. Bozrah flourished, served as a major intersection for caravan routes, and Muhammed visited the city in the early 7th cent. CE. The city is a rich archaeological site with a well-preserved Roman amphitheater and ruins from Roman, Byzantine, and Muslim periods.

NYASHA JUNIOR

BRACELET. See JEWELRY.

BRAID [πλέγμα plegma, ἐμπλοκή emplokē]. Elaborate, fashionable plaiting of hair that is considered ostentatious and immodest for Christian women (1 Tim 2:9; 1 Pet 3:3).

BRAMBLE [אָטָד ʾatadh, βάτος batos]. The term used to describe a spiky shrub of entwined vines. The most likely species referred to is the European boxthorn (Lycium europaeum). In Judg 9:14 the bramble is used as a metaphor for the lowest in society in contrast to the olive tree, fig tree, and grapevine. Bramble in Luke 6:44 is a metaphor for the inherent nature of individuals saying that the bramble ("a bad tree") will not bear good fruit.

DAVID LIPOVITCH

BRANCH [צֶמַח tsemakh]. "Branch" describes an heir or descendant of the Davidic king; חֹטֶר khoter (shoot) and נֵצֶר netser (twig, offshoot) are related terms in Isa 11:1. In Jer 23:5, an oracle of Yahweh announces the raising up for David of a צֶמַח צַדִּיק tsemakh tsaddiq, that can be translated "righteous branch" or, better, "legitimate branch," that is, a legitimate heir to the Davidic throne. A 3rd cent. Phoenician inscription uses the same words to refer to a legitimate royal heir, and a 5th cent. Phoenician inscription mentions a בן צדק bn tsdq or "legitimate son." The term in Jer 23:5 may be a pun on the word Zedekiah, the puppet king installed by Nebuchadnezzar. Jeremiah states that the future "legitimate branch" will act wisely and perform justice and righteousness in the land, again in sharp distinction to Zedekiah. The branch is given the name יְהוָה צִדְקֵנוּ YHWH tsidhqenu "Yahweh is our righteousness" or, better, "Yahweh is the source of our vindication" that may be an ironic pun on the name Zedekiah.

In a secondary passage, Jer 33:14-16 (all of vv. 14-26 are lacking in the LXX), a divine oracle announces a Davidic צֶמַח צְדָקָה tsemakh tsedhaqah ("branch of righteousness" or "legitimate branch"). The territory to be ruled by the branch is described as Judah and Jerusalem (Jer 33:16) instead of Judah and Israel (Jer 23:6), and the new name ("Yahweh is the source of our vindication") is given to the city of Jerusalem instead of to the branch himself.

The term occurs twice in the post-exilic prophet Zedekiah in passages whose meaning is debated. After the high priest Joshua has been ritually purified and confirmed in his office, the angel of Yahweh announces, "I am going to bring my servant the branch" (Zech 3:8). While Zerubbabel, whose name means "seed of Babylon," participates with Joshua in building the Second Temple, this promise may refer to a future time when kingship will be reestablished without identifying Zerubbabel as that future royal figure. A divine oracle in Zech 6:12 designates a person, presumably Zerubbabel, as the branch who is to build the Temple of Yahweh. The prophet Zechariah is instructed to make crowns and set one of them on the head of Joshua son of Jehozadak (v. 11) and store the second one as a memorial in the house of Yahweh, apparently for the king of the future (6:14). *Biblia Hebraica Stuttgartensia* suggests emending *crowns* to *crown* in v. 11 and changing "Joshua son of Jehozadak" to "Zerubbabel son of Shealtiel." These changes are based on the assumption that Zerubbabel was deposed by the Persians for aspiring to be king, leading to subsequent editing of the text. An apparently secondary paragraph in Zech 4:6-10*a* gives pride of place to Zerubbabel while the rest of the context (4:1-4) outlines the diarchic joint rule of Joshua and Zerubbabel.

Several references in the Dead Sea Scrolls indicate that the term *branch* had become a messianic title. The messiah is referred to as "the branch of David" (דויד צמח tsmkh dwyd) in 4Q174 1 xi and as "the messiah of righteousness ... the branch of David" (tsmkh dwyd) in 4Q252 5 iii-iv. *See* MESSIAH, JEWISH; PALM TREE; VINE.

Bibliography: Carol L. Meyers and Eric M. Meyers. *Haggai, Zechariah 1–8.* AB 25B (1987).

RALPH W. KLEIN

BRAND. *See* FIREBRAND.

BRAND, CAMEL. *See* WASM.

BRAZIER [אָח ʾakh]. A portable fire-pot used for indoor heating during the cold months. Used when King Jehoiakim burned Jeremiah's scroll (Jer 36:22-23).

BREACH [פֶּרֶץ perets]. Most commonly in the Bible, a break or breaks an army makes in the walls of a city, through which the army intends to enter and conquer. *Breach*, both as verb and noun, can occasionally refer to the forging of other types of openings and to the openings themselves, e.g., the opening of a mine shaft in Job 28:4 or the breaking down of the walls surrounding a vineyard in Isa 5:5 and Ps 80:12 [Heb. 80:13]. These openings, moreover, can be forged not only from the outside in an attempt to get into an enclosed space but also from inside an enclosed space in order to escape its confines. Most famously, in Gen 38:29, one of Tamar's twin sons thrusts himself past his brother

and out of the womb: thus he is called **perets** (Perez), which means "breach" in Hebrew. This same Hebrew term can be used metaphorically to speak of those who "break out" against the law (i.e., outlaws or criminals) and still other sorts of breaking out, e.g., God's wrath breaking out against evildoers or the rapid population growth of the Israelites in Egypt—although this linguistic affinity is typically obscured in English translations. Conversely, the linguistic affinity English translations suggest between the core meaning of breach—to break through a wall—and the idiom "breach of faith" (Josh 22:22) is not reflected in Hebrew.

SUSAN ACKERMAN

BREAD [לֶחֶם lekhem; ἄρτος artos]. The Hebrew word for bread (lekhem) means in the first instance bread made from cereals, but can also refer to food in general [*see also* the alternative terms for bread, i.e., "cakes" (עֻגָה ʾughah) in Gen 18:6 and "unleavened wafers" (מַצָּה matsah) in Exod 29:2 and Lev 2:4. The Greek word for bread (artos) is used to describe the bread (leavened or unleavened) that formed the daily sustenance of most people.

A. Bread as the Food of Subsistence

In the biblical world, bread constituted for most people the food of subsistence. Rich and poor, urban and rural, at home and while traveling, bread, in conjunction with cereal in other forms, formed the primary component of people's daily diet. Bread was eaten at every meal, accompanied by smaller amounts of vegetables and fruits, oil and salt (meat was considered a luxury item and seldom eaten by most). It is thus no wonder that the word for bread is often used to describe food in general (e.g., Deut 10:18; Ps 136:25; Jer 52:6).

The nature and quality of bread varied greatly. Bread was most often made from barley or wheat milled into flour, and could be leavened or unleavened. Wheat, which frequently had to be imported, was more expensive than the hardier barley that grew well in all kinds of soil and was less dependent on rain than wheat. Thus, bread made from fine wheat flour, which was sifted multiple times, coarse barley bread or cakes, or no bread at all served as an indication of the socioeconomic standing of the individual as well as the society at large.

The art of baking bread belonged throughout the ages to women. Jeremiah 7:18 refers to the division of labor with regard to the baking of bread when it is said that the children gather wood, the fathers kindle the fire, and the women kneaded the dough (*see also* the examples of Sarah in Gen 18:5 and Tamar in 2 Sam 13:8). Then again, the reference to a "bakers' street" in Jer 37:21 attests to the professional development of the art of baking bread.

B. Bread in the Biblical Traditions

In the biblical traditions, bread, in addition to water and clothing, is considered to be one of the basic human needs to sustain life (Ps 104:15; Sir 39:26). Bread as the sustenance necessary for daily living finds its way into virtually every aspect of the OT literature. For instance, bread is included in practically every list of provisions, constituting together with parched grain, raisins and figs, summer fruit, wine, and occasionally a small quantity of meat (1 Sam 17:17; 25:18; 2 Sam 6:19; 16:1) an essential part of people's daily sustenance.

Bread presumed such basic agricultural activities as having a land to plant crops, the ability to sow, harvest, winnow, and mill. For landless people, these basic activities were not taken for granted. The promised land is described as a land where Israelites may eat bread without scarcity (Deut 8:9); where they would be able to ensure their daily bread by tilling the land.

For much of Israel's history, though, Israel was a people on the move without the means to plant a wheat or barley crop to ensure their daily bread. Yet bread plays a central role even in the wilderness narratives. In the wilderness, Israel's daily bread is called *manna*—a fine flaky substance that was baked into bread.

In the OT, bread is meant to be shared. In Exod 2:20, the expression "to break bread" is used to describe this ethos of hospitality. This notion is depicted in the classic story in Gen 18 where Abraham and Sarah provide an elaborate feast to the heavenly visitors that includes round, flat loaves made from three measures of choice flour, a roasted calf, curds, and milk—much more than the "morsel" of bread Abraham promised his guests (Gen 18:5).

The importance of bread is especially evident during a time of war or famine where there is a lack of bread. For instance, in Lam 1:11, we see the extreme desperation when people are searching in vain for bread, trading their treasures for a scrap of bread (also Lam 4:4; 2 Kgs 25:3).

Bread also had its place in religious observances. This is evidenced in the Festival of Unleavened Bread, during which time people were not allowed to eat leavened bread. During this weeklong yearly ritual, Israel was reminded of the exodus out of Egypt where their ancestors had to eat unleavened bread, having no time for the bread to rise (Deut 16:3). Another example comes from Lev 23:17, where Israel is instructed to bring two loaves of bread made of the choicest flour as a token of thanksgiving for the harvest that God has blessed. In both these instances, bread serves as a symbolic device, pointing beyond the food to the experience of God's action in their lives. This is also true in the case of the bread of presence that served as a concrete symbol of God's presence in the Temple (Num 4:7; 1 Sam 21:6; 1 Kgs 7:48).

Finally, bread took an expanded place in everyday speech when this basic element of sustenance became used in figurative expressions. For instance, the word *bread* is used in conjunction with a number of nouns, e.g., "bread of adversity" (Isa 30:20), "bread of tears (Ps 80:5), "bread of anxious toil" (Ps 127:2), and "bread of wickedness" (Prov 4:17). In all of these instances, the connotations of eating bread on a daily basis became a way to describe a reality where adversity or tears or anxious toil have become a part of the subject's life as much as bread ingested daily.

Also in the NT, bread plays a key role. The narratives telling the story of Jesus multiplying the fish and loaves of bread (Luke 9:10-17; Mark 6:35-44; Matt 14:15-21; John 6:5-15) employ this basic connotation of bread when it shows how Jesus provided in people's most basic need for food.

The notion of eating bread together becomes a leading theme in the NT, as much of Jesus' teaching occurs during meals that are often characterized as breaking bread together (Luke 24:35; Acts 2:42, 46; 20:7, 11; 27:35). Also Jesus' teaching is marked by references to bread, e.g., the parable of the woman baking bread as illustration of the kingdom of God (Matt 13:33; Luke 13:21).

The significance of bread in the NT is most evident in the role it plays in the eucharist. During the Passover, Jesus gave new meaning to the symbol of bread, building on the life-giving qualities of bread as well as the ability of bread to evoke God's saving and sustaining action in Israel's life (Luke 22:17-20 and the par. passages in Matt 26:26-29 and Mark 14:22-25).

C. Theological Significance of Bread

Bread became part of Israel's theological discourse, serving as an important symbol with a wide range of associations and meanings that spans both the Testaments, as well as the postbiblical literature.

Accordingly, bread points beyond its material substance to Israel's experience of God as the provider of food. For example, in Exod 16, the manna or "bread from heaven" ("bread of angels" in Ps 78:25) is regarded as a sure sign of God's presence in the wilderness. Also in Ps 104:14, God is praised for bringing forth bread from the earth. This testimony is based on the belief that God is the one who enables a good harvest, who sends the rain, and who provides for a time of security and prosperity so that people can engage in the activities that bring forth bread: planting, harvesting, winnowing, and baking.

Israel's belief in God as the one who provides their daily bread indicates a deep trust that God will continue to provide in their daily needs. Something of this understanding is reflected in the bread petition of the Lord's Prayer (Luke 11:3): "Give us each day our daily bread," expressing the belief that God will provide a trust that has to be renewed daily.

Key to Israel's understanding of God as the provider of bread is the fact that God provides bread to the poor, hungry, widows, orphans, and foreigners (Ps 146:7; Deut 10:18). The notion that all should have bread to eat is also at the heart of the manna narrative where everyone receives enough bread to eat and lacks nothing (Exod 16:18). The NT narratives of the multiplication of the bread build on these themes, when through Jesus, God provides abundantly to all who are hungry.

Bread also becomes an important symbol of the eschatological era. Both Rabbinic and early Christian texts deemed bread to be part of the abundance of food that God will provide in the end times. So one sees in 2 Bar. 29:8 that in the last days, a treasury of manna will come down from heaven (see also the images of miraculously yielding grain and even bread trees in Gen. Rab. 15.7 and Ber. 38a-b). In light of the central role that bread played in every aspect of Israel's theological literature, it is not surprising that the daily and satisfying substance of bread would form the basis of a rabbinic vision of the end time.

In a further development, bread is understood not only to denote physical food, but comes to signify teaching or learning. This idea appears already in Deut 8:3 where bread is connected to the word of God—a perspective that becomes even more evident in post-biblical literature (Pesiq. Rab Kah. 12; Gen. Rab. 70:5; Num. Rab. 8:9). In these texts bread comes to signify the word of God by which God teaches God's children. In Prov 9:5 this connection is elaborated when Woman Wisdom invites her audience to come eat from the bread she provides (see also Sir 15:2-3 where Wisdom will provide "the bread of learning"). Bread as basic sustenance is used to express the view that learning is as necessary for life as bread and water. Moreover, to eat the bread that Wisdom offers means that one truly embraces God's word, wisdom, or law as one's own.

These themes form the inspiration for the NT appropriation of the theological significance of bread. In John 6, Jesus calls himself the Bread of Life. For John, the life-giving nature of bread becomes a symbol of Jesus who not only provides bread, but also becomes the very substance that gives eternal life to those who ingest it (John 6:51). The act of eating bread is once again an apt metaphor to describe the active participation of the human in accepting and internalizing Jesus' words that are essential for life.

The remarkable legacy of bread is that the everyday substance of bread became interwoven with the liturgical practices of the church. Every time believers eat a piece of bread during the eucharist, they look beyond the bread to the theological traditions that are evoked by bread. It is significant that in the account of the disciples on their way to Emmaus, it is in the act of breaking the bread that they encounter the risen Christ, once more building on the OT theme of bread as symbol of God's presence. See BREAD OF PRESENCE; CEREAL OFFERING; DOUGH; EUCHARIST; KNEAD; LEAVEN; LORD'S PRAYER; LORD'S SUPPER; OVEN; WAFERS.

Bibliography: L. Juliana M. Claassens. The God Who Provides: Biblical Images of Divine Nourishment (2004); Philip J. King and Lawrence E. Stager. Life in Biblical Israel (2001); Jane Webster. Ingesting Jesus: Eating and Drinking in the Gospel of John (2003); John Wilkins, et. al., eds. Food in Antiquity (1995).

L. JULIANA M. CLAASSENS

BREAD OF PRESENCE. לֶחֶם הַפָּנִים [lekhem happanim]. Sometimes translated as showbread (in Exod 35:13; 1 Kgs 7:48), the Bread of Presence refers to the two stacks of six unleavened breads (symbolizing the twelve tribes of Israel) that were weekly placed by the high priest on the golden table in the Temple in the vicinity of the tabernacle (also referred to as הַמַּעֲרֶכֶת לֶחֶם lekhem hammaʿarakheth "the arranged bread" in 1 Chr 9:32, or the "regular" or "continual bread" לֶחֶם הַתָּמִיד lekhem hattamidh in Num 4:7). Aside from its rich symbolic significance (see below), the Bread of Presence served the secondary function of providing for the priests; after being replaced on the Sabbath, the holy bread was given to the priests to eat in a sacred place (Lev 24:5-9).

The Bread of Presence should be understood together with the rituals of the golden, seven-branched lampstand that was set alight every evening, as well as the incense that was burned on a golden incense burner on the Sabbath at the changing of the Bread of Presence (Lev 24:1-9; Exod 25:23-39; 30:1-10). These rituals, together with the tabernacle, symbolically created the sacred space for God to dwell among God's people. Placing the bread, light, and incense in the presence of God sanctified these ordinary substances. Moreover, to this day, the sensory experiences of light, aroma, and food continue to be a central aspect of the religious expression of many denominations (compare especially the Catholic and Eastern Orthodox traditions).

The significance of the Bread of Presence is clear from the fact that it is frequently cited in the Chronicler's history (2 Chr 2:3 [Heb. 2:4]; 13:11; 29:18; Neh 10:33 [Heb. 10:34]), in addition to being mentioned by Josephus (Ant. 3.139–143; 3.255–257. Compare also the Arch of Titus in Rome that shows the golden table and the golden lampstand being carried away after Titus' triumph over Jerusalem in 70 CE).

Scholars are divided over whether the Bread of Presence served as a way to feed the deity. The ritual of placing bread in the sanctuary is attested among Israel's neighbors such as the Egyptians, Hittites, and Babylonians, which shows concern for the daily care and provision for the gods. Some scholars, however, see Israel's ritual of the Bread of Presence to be markedly different from its neighboring cultures, citing as evidence the fact that the Bread of Presence did not constitute a daily offering but rather occurred once a week, thereby challenging the notion that God is dependent on the daily provision of food (compare Ps 50:12-13).

Regardless of the origin of this ritual, we see Israel's distinctive theological formulation of the Bread of Presence with regard to its connection with the Sabbath, creation, and the covenant. As God rested at the end of the creation week, so God enjoys the incense of the bread offering on the day of rest. Moreover, Lev 24 emphasizes the continual nature of the Bread of Presence (compare the repetition of the terms תָּמִיד tamidh "regularly" and עוֹלָם 'olam "forever"). So, the Bread of Presence serves as a reminder of the eternal covenant between God and Israel (בְּרִית עוֹלָם berith 'olam in Lev 24:8), hence functioning as a symbol of God's enduring presence with God's people and God's promise to provide for Israel throughout its journey from the wilderness to the promised land, and forevermore. Moreover, the Bread of Presence denotes the eternal statute (חֻקַּת עוֹלָם khuqqath 'olam in Lev 24:3), i.e., the covenant obligation according to which Israel promises to regularly supply the oil, incense, and bread for Temple worship.

It is significant that the Bread of Presence is not a fixed relic, but is constantly reinterpreted in new contexts. For example, 1 Sam 21:3-6 recounts how David and his men are saved by the Bread of Presence. In an interesting play on the words *holy* (קֹדֶשׁ qodhesh) and *ordinary* (חֹל khol), David "breaks" the ritual associated with the Bread of Presence by allowing nonpriests to eat the sacred bread. This account is picked up in the Gospel writers' account of Jesus' confrontation with the Pharisees with regard to the disciples picking grain on the Sabbath (Matt 12:1-4; Mark 2:23-26; Luke 6:1-4). In support of the belief that human need is more important than ritual observance, Jesus cites the example of David, who, in need of food, ate the Bread of Presence. Both these texts offer an example of an inner-biblical conversation that argues against a narrow understanding of holiness; both David and Jesus are portrayed as overturning traditional conceptions of what is sacred. *See* SACRIFICE AND OFFERINGS; UNLEAVENED BREAD; WORSHIP IN THE OT.

Bibliography: Roy Gane. "'Bread of Presence' and the Creator-in-Residence." *VT* 42 (1992) 179–203; Jacob Milgrom. *Leviticus: A Book of Ritual and Ethics* (2004).

L. JULIANA M. CLAASSENS

BREAK, TO [κλάω klaō]. An expression used in the NT in reference to bread to describe the act of sharing a meal. For instance, in the food miracles, Jesus would take the loaves, give thanks, break, and then hand them to the disciples to share with the people (Mark 6:41; 14:22; Luke 9:16; Matt 14:19; 15:36).

In the early church, the communal meals became known by the ritual "to break bread" (e.g., Acts 2:42, 46; 20:7, 11). This expression also became synonymous with the Eucharist or Lord's Supper. For example,

in 1 Cor 10:16, Paul asks: "The bread we break, is it not sharing the body of Christ?" Thus, the act of breaking the bread serves as a symbol of Jesus' body broken on the cross. In this ritual, the participants are called to remember the crucified and resurrected Christ (compare also Jesus breaking the bread at the Last Supper in Mark 14:22; Matt 26:26; Luke 22:19).

In the gospel traditions, the act of breaking bread functioned as an important symbol of crossing boundaries. Jesus' ministry is exemplified by with whom Jesus chose to break bread, often the outcasts of society. The act of breaking bread, moreover, stands for sharing. It nourishes the recipients, but also inspires them to go out and share bread with others. Finally, the act of breaking *one* bread, and all partaking from the same loaf, points to the union that is to exist between all the members of the community. *See* BREAD; EUCHARIST; LORD'S SUPPER.

L. JULIANA M. CLAASSENS

BREAKFAST [ἀριστάω aristaō]. The Greek can be translated as breakfast (John 21:12, 15), lunch (Luke 14:12), or an unspecified MEAL (Matt 22:4; Luke 11:37-38). The breakfast in John 21 signals a new beginning for the community by recalling the creation story. The light dawns, the sea is filled with fish, and the disciples move to dry land (John 21:4, 6, 8-9; Gen 1:3, 20-21, 9). Jesus, as host, gives FISH and BREAD to the disciples. The disciples also contribute fish, and Jesus commands Peter to "feed my sheep." The disciples will continue Jesus' work of providing abundance for the future faith community.

Bibliography: Jane S. Webster. *Ingesting Jesus: Eating and Drinking in the Gospel of John* (2003).

JAMES P. GRIMSHAW

BREAST [שַׁד shadh, חֵיק kheq, שֹׁד shodh, מֵעֶה me'eh, חָזֶה khazeh; κόλπος kolpos, στῆθος stēthos]. There is no more intimate image than that of a child at its mother's breast. This image appears in the Bible to signify the care of animal (shadh, Lam 4:3) and human mothers for their young (kheq, 1 Kgs 3:20; shodh, Job 24:9), as well as God's providence and protection (shodh, Ps 22:9). Isaiah invites Israel to rejoice and to "nurse and be satisfied" from the "consoling breast" of Jerusalem (shodh, 66:11), a metaphor for the contentment, peace, and security it offers the post-exilic community.

The breast is symbolic of the seat of the inner life, and so the psalmist laments, "my heart is like wax; it melts within my breast" (me'eh, 22:14). Siblings who share their mother's breast have strong bonds of affection for one another, as is evident in the exclamation of the bride-to-be in the Song of Songs, "O that you were like a brother to me, who nursed at my mother's breast!" (shadh, 8:1).

Prescriptions for sacrificial offerings involve the breast of an animal (khazeh, Lev 7:30-34; 10:14-15; Num 18:18). The breast of a ram is designated for the ordination of priests (khazeh, Exod 29:26, 27; Lev 8:29) and for the rite of consecration for nazirites (khazeh, Num 6:20).

To strike one's breast (stethos) is a gesture signifying grief, sorrow, or contrition, as with the toll collector in the Temple (Luke 18:13) and the crowd who witnessed Jesus' crucifixion (Luke 23:48).

An expression of intimacy between Jesus and the Beloved Disciple is that the latter reclines against Jesus' breast (kolpos) at the Last Supper (John 13:23). So too, Jesus is "close to the Father's heart," literally, "in the breast (kolpos) of the Father" (John 1:18). In Luke's parable of the rich man and Lazarus, after his death Lazarus rests in the bosom (kolpos) of Abraham (16:23), indicating his close association with his ancestor in faith.

BARBARA E. REID

BREASTPIECE [חֹשֶׁן khoshen]. The breastpiece was a bag woven from gold, purple, blue, and crimson threads worn by the high priest over his EPHOD (Exod 28:5-30; 39:8-21). Adorned with precious stones arranged in four rows of three each, corresponding to the tribes of Israel, and attached to the ephod at the waist and shoulders by golden rings and blue and gold cords, it held the URIM AND THUMMIM used by the high priest for divination.

ROBERT KUGLER

BREASTPLATE [שִׁרְיוֹן shiryon; θώραξ thōrax]. Chest armor made of leather, metal, or a combination of the two, used throughout the Near East as early as the 3rd millennium BCE (1 Kgs 22:34; 2 Chr 18:33). The breastplate evolved into a two-piece cuirass, which protected the back. The Romans wore the molded metal cuirass.

God puts on righteousness like a breastplate (Isa 59:17; echoed in Wis 5:18). Paul adapts the theme to represent the spiritual warfare waged by Christians (Eph 6:14; 1 Thess 5:8). Both cavalry and apocalyptic locusts appear wearing breastplates (Rev 9:9, 17). See BREASTPIECE; WAR, METHODS, TACTICS, WEAPONS OF.

MARK J. H. FRETZ

BREATH. A variety of Hebrew and Greek words behind the English noun breath and the verb breathe contain a wide range of meanings, both figurative and literal.

The divine activities of judgment and creation are described in terms of breath. For example, two Hebrew terms, נְשָׁמָה neshamah (blast/breath) and רוּחַ ruakh (breath/spirit), occur in close proximity in 2 Sam 22:16: ". . . at the blast of breath from his nostrils," when expressing in anthropopathic terms the anger of Yahweh in judgment.

In the synonymous parallelism of Job 33:4 these terms are used interchangeably: "The Spirit [ruakh] of God has made me; the breath [neshamah] of Shaddai gives me life" (author's translation). Genesis 2:7 has a different verb for "breathe" to express the same idea: "he [the Lord God] breathed [נָפַח nafakh; ἐμφυσάω emphusaō] into his [i.e., Adam's] nostrils the breath [neshamah; πνοή pnoē] of life" (author's translation). Themes of wind, breath, spirit, and new creation occur in Ezek 37:9 (see also Ps 104:29-30; Wis 15:11; Philo, Creation 135; and Gen. Rab. 14:8).

The NT uses the OT concept that God's Spirit (πνεῦμα pneuma) gives life (e.g., Matt 1:18; 3:11; Luke 1:15-47; Rom 8:11). The Holy Spirit manifests as a breath, wind, or spirit (pnoē, pneuma) at the creation of the church at Pentecost (Acts 2:2-4). John is the only writer to overtly symbolize the act of breathing when Jesus "breathes" (emphusaō) on the disciples (John 20:22). This act recapitulates John's theology of being born "from above" (ἄνωθεν anōthen, John 3:3) and echoes "he breathed" (emphusaō) in Gen 2:7, its first occurrence, connecting Jesus and the new creation with God and the first creation. As God created life in Gen 2:7, in the same way Jesus creates eternal life by breathing on his disciples after he is raised from the dead. See HOLY SPIRIT; SPIRIT.

BEN C. AKER

BREATHE [פּוּחַ puakh, נָפַח nafakh, נָפַשׁ nafash; ἐμπνέω empneō]. Even though the people of the biblical world did not know the precise physiology of respiration, breathing was understood as one of the fundamental components of life, and the noun "breath" is sometimes synonymous with "life" or "soul." When God creates the earth-creature in Gen 2:7, God forms the body, then breathes life into the body to animate it. "To breathe" can also be used figuratively. For example, in the Song of Songs, the day breathes, which means that the air is growing cooler (2:17; 4:6). Sometimes God breathes hot, which means God is angry (compare Ezek 21:31[Heb. 21:36]). Saul also breathed "threats and murder" (Acts 9:1) in his anger. Another NT use of the verb occurs in John 20:22 where the resurrected Jesus breathes the Holy Spirit onto his disciples. See BREATH; SOUL.

JENNIFER L. KOOSED

BRETHREN. See BROTHER, BROTHERHOOD.

BRIBE, BRIBERY [שֹׁחַד shokadh]. The word bribe comes from the Hebrew word for gift, which is what a bribe actually was, a "gift" designed to influence someone's behavior. In some instances a "gift" was a strategic act to influence positively a more powerful person's disposition; in other instances, a "gift" given to a judge to influence a courtroom decision could be seen as highly immoral. Such immoral bribery is recalled of

Samuel's sons (1 Sam 8:3) and is condemned in general elsewhere (Job 15:34; Ps 26:10; Isa 1:23; 33:15; Ezek 22:12; Amos 5:12; Mic 3:11; 7:3). Because judges in the ancient world often were paid by the litigants, such payments could become virtual bribes, especially if only the affluent litigant could pay. Since, so often, the purpose of the bribe was to pervert judgment (1 Sam 8:3; Prov 17:23; Isa 5:23), ultimately it was prohibited in the law codes (Exod 23:8; Deut 16:19; 27:25). Only occasionally the "bribe" or "gift" was seen as accomplishing something positive—gaining advancement (Prov 18:16) or averting anger from others (Prov 21:14). *See* DEBT, DEBTOR; MONEY, COINS.

ROBERT GNUSE

BRICK [לְבֵנָה levenah]. One of the three primary building materials in the ANE, along with wood and stone. Brick usage is ubiquitous across the ANE even in regions where stone is readily available. Bricks were lighter than stone, and required less labor for large structures. Almost any combination of sand, silt, and clay mixed with binders can be used to produce bricks. Most bricks were sun-dried and produced a durable building material. Although kiln-fired bricks were much more durable, they were also more costly to produce, and were reserved primarily for special uses such as monumental structures. Evidence of sun-dried brick construction dates as early as Pre-pottery Neolithic at Jericho (ca. 8000–7000 BCE) where houses with mud-brick walls were constructed. These earliest bricks were handmade; from at least the Early Bronze Age (ca. 3200–2200 BCE), molds were used to make bricks of uniform size and thickness. From Mesopotamia, glazed bricks were used along processional ways such as the Ishtar Gate in Babylon.

In two pentateuchal narratives bricks play a significant role. In the Tower of Babel narrative, the inhabitants of Shinar made bricks for their city and tower, specifically "burned bricks," kiln-fired bricks (Gen 11:3). The narrator is apparently more familiar with construction using stone and mortar, for he states "they had brick for stone, and bitumen for mortar" (Gen 11:3). The construction described does indicate an awareness of Mesopotamian building practices.

The narrative of Exod 1 and 5 describes the plight of the Hebrews in Egypt. As part of their harsh labor, they were forced to make bricks for Pharaoh's building projects. The same words for brick and mortar are used as in the Gen 11 narrative. Here, however, the bricks are sun-dried bricks; no mention is made of firing them. There is the added mention of straw being used as a binder. Binders were added to the clay/silt to strengthen the bricks and prevent them from cracking as they dried. An Egyptian painting from the 18th dynasty tomb of the vizier/governor Rekhmire (ca. 1479–1425 BCE) depicts construction workers and brick makers digging the clay, making bricks in molds, carrying the bricks to

a building site, and then laying the bricks in courses. These paintings, as well as remains from numerous excavations in Egypt, show that bricks were a primary component of house construction at this time.

A text from Isaiah suggests that brick was considered an inferior building material as compared to stone. In Isa 9:9, the arrogant people of Israel say in response to God's judgment on them: "The bricks have fallen, but we will (re)build with dressed stones; the sycamores have been cut down, but we will put cedars in their place." The former structures had been built of bricks and had been destroyed in God's judgment. Rather than letting this judgment lead them to repentance, the people say they will rebuild with finely hewn stone. In place of inferior sycamore beams or posts, they will use prized cedar (of Lebanon). The oracle continues with further judgment against Israel.

Bibliography: P. R. S. Moorey. *Ancient Mesopotamian Materials and Industries: The Archaeological Evidence* (1994).

JOEL F. DRINKARD JR.

BRIDAL CHAMBER. *See* BRIDE; BRIDEGROOM.

BRIDAL JEWELRY. *See* JEWELRY.

BRIDE [כַּלָּה kalah; νύμφη nymphē]. A *bride* is a woman betrothed to marry, a woman celebrating her wedding, or a newly married woman. BETROTHAL was a legally binding contract joining a couple in MARRIAGE before they actually lived together (e.g., Matt 1:18-19).

The betrothals of Rebekah (Gen 24:1-67), Leah and Rachel (Gen 29:1-30), Ruth (Ruth 3–4), and Sarah (Tob 7:11-14) illustrate the care families took to find an appropriate match within certain family boundaries. Disapproval of a bride led to family unrest (e.g., Esau's brides [Gen 26:34-35], Moses' Cushite wife [Num 12:1], and Samson's first bride [Judg 14:1-3]).

The bride's love and devotion were idealized and prized (Jer 2:2; Song 3:6-11). That the BRIDEGROOM sometimes calls his bride "my sister" may indicate that the couple's relationship was, ideally, as close and as loyally familial as a sister's and brother's (Song 4:9, 10, 12; 5:1, 2; Tob 7:11). Paul uses the metaphor of a couple's devotion to identify the church as the BRIDE OF CHRIST (2 Cor 11:2; John 3:29).

Brides traditionally were associated with great joy (Isa 62:5; Jer 7:34; 16:9; 25:10; 33:11), beauty, and love (Song 4:8-12; 5:1). A vision of the New Jerusalem descending as a bride adorned for her husband, the Lamb, represents the joy and celebration of a new creation (Rev 19:7-9; 21:2).

The absence of the bride characterizes divine judgment, when joy turns to sorrow and "the voice of the bridegroom and bride will be heard no more" (Jer

7:34; 16:9; 25:10; Joel 2:16; Bar 2:23). The prophet Jeremiah says that the people are like a once-faithful bride who has turned to adultery when they forsake Yahweh (Jer 2:2; 3:1-10).

Few details are known about betrothal and weddings in biblical times. Evidence suggests that the bridegroom or his family negotiated with the bride's family and exchanged gifts or a bride price (e.g., Gen 24:53; 29:15-20; Exod 22:16, 17; Tob 6:11-13). The bride processed with her family to meet the bridegroom and his family (1 Macc 9:37-39). Descriptions of the bride's ornaments and jewelry (Isa 49:18; 61:10; Jer 2:32) and expensive myrrh (Song 1:13; 3:6; 4:6, 14; 5:1, 5, 13; 3 Macc 4:6) reflect the great worth and beauty of the bride and suggest the cultural importance of the wedding itself.

The book of Tobit offers the most detailed account of a wedding: the bride and bridegroom join hands, there is a pronouncement of marriage, and a written marriage contract is drawn up (Tob 7:11-13). The wedding feast lasts for seven days (Tob 8:19; 11:18; John 2:1-10). The couple enters a wedding CANOPY (*see* Ps 19:5; Joel 2:16) and retires to a bridal chamber (Tob 7:15-16; 3 Macc 1:19). *See* FAMILY.

MARIANNE BLICKENSTAFF

BRIDE OF CHRIST [γυνή gynē, νύμφη nymphē].
A metaphor for the church (*see* CHURCH, IDEA OF THE). Paul promises the Corinthian community in marriage as a virgin (παρθένος parthenos) presented to Christ (2 Cor 11:2). Revelation announces the wedding of the church as bride (gynē, nymphē) to the Lamb (Rev 19:7; 21:2, 9; 22:17). Deuteropauline tradition likens the relationship of husband and wife (gynē) to that of Christ and the church (Eph 5:23-25). *See* also *Odes Sol.* 3; 42; Tertullian, *Mon.* 5; *Fug.* 15; Origen, *Comm. Matt.* 14; *Herm. Vis.* 3; and *2 Clem.* 15.

The metaphor "bride of Christ" borrows from an OT tradition describing Israel as bride or wife of Yahweh (e.g., Isa 54:5-8; 62:4-5; Ezek 16:8-14; Hos 2:19-20). Psalm 45 and Song of Songs frequently are interpreted as wedding songs depicting the mystical love between the deity and Israel; later church tradition places Christ in the role of bridegroom and the church in the role of bride (e.g., St. John of the Cross). In some Christian traditions, women who join religious orders indicate their devotion to the church by symbolically becoming "brides of Christ" upon taking their vows.

MARIANNE BLICKENSTAFF

BRIDEGROOM [חָתָן khathan; νυμφίος nymphios, γαμβρός gambros].
Bridegroom refers variously to: 1) a man betrothed but not yet married, 2) a man celebrating his wedding feast, 3) a husband, already married. The Hebrew khathan is translated into Greek as both nymphios (usually meaning *bridegroom*) and gambros (usually meaning *son-in-law*). This seeming ambiguity illustrates that betrothal was a legally binding contract even before a couple lived together as husband and wife (e.g., Matt 1:18-19).

A bridegroom was traditionally associated with joy, celebration, and feasting (Ps 19:5; Isa 61:10; 62:5). Jesus performed the first of his signs at a wedding by turning water to wine, and the wedding guests questioned the bridegroom about the excellent quality of the wine (John 2:1-11). The bridegroom's absence characterizes divine judgment, when joy turns to sorrow and "the voice of the bridegroom and bride will be heard no more" (Jer 7:34; 16:9; 25:10; Joel 2:16; Bar 2:23).

Little is known about weddings or the role of the bridegroom in biblical times. Some texts mention negotiations with the bride's family (Tob 6:11-13) and the exchange of gifts or a bride price (e.g., Gen 24:53; 29:15-20), and the procession of the bride's family to meet the bridegroom (1 Macc 9:37-39). The book of Tobit describes the pronouncement over the couple as husband and wife and a written marriage contract (7:12-14; *see* BABATHA; CERTIFICATE OF DIVORCE). Bridegrooms are described as wearing a garland (Isa 61:10; 3 Macc 4:8), entering a wedding canopy (e.g., Ps 19:5; Joel 2:16), celebrating the wedding feast (Tob 8:19; 11:18; Matt 22:2-12; John 2:1-11), and entering a bridal chamber with the bride (Tob 7:15-16).

While several men become betrothed and thus fulfill the role of bridegroom (e.g., Isaac [Gen 24:1-67]; Jacob [Gen 29:1-30]; Moses [Exod 2:16-21]; Boaz [Ruth 3–4]; and Joseph [Matt 1:18-19]), men who actually bear the designation *bridegroom* (khathan, nymphios, or gambros) are few in number. Counterintuitively, they are associated with violence, either as victims or as perpetrators, and most are separated from or abandon their brides. Among them are Lot's sons-in-law (Gen 19:12, 14); Moses, the "bridegroom of blood," (Exod 4:25-26); Samson (Judg 15:6); a Levite from Ephraim who dismembers his concubine (Judg 19:5); and David (1 Sam 18:18; 22:14).

Jesus calls himself a *bridegroom* (nymphios, Matt 9:15; Mark 2:19-20; Luke 5:34-35; John 3:29; *Gos. Thom.* 104), even though, by tradition, he was never married. The synoptic Gospels and *Gos. Thom.* do not mention a bride but instead apply to Jesus the prophets' wedding imagery illustrating sorrow in the coming judgment, when Jesus the bridegroom will be "taken away," and his followers will mourn and fast.

Paul identifies the church as the BRIDE OF CHRIST (2 Cor 11:2, a theme reiterated in Eph 5:25-32; possibly in John 3:29; and in Rev 19:7-9; 21:2). This marriage imagery reflects the theme of God's people as wife or bride (Isa 54:5-6; Jer 3:1-14; Ezek 16:1-63; Hos 2:19-20) and places Jesus in the deity's role as husband or bridegroom to a people. Bridal imagery describing the relationship of the soul to a redeeming bridegroom appears in later Gnostic writings, especially in the *Exegesis of the Soul* and *Gospel of Philip. See* BETROTHAL; BRIDE; FAMILY; MARRIAGE.

MARIANNE BLICKENSTAFF

BRIDESMAIDS [παρθένοι parthenoi]. The term *bridesmaids* ("virgins") occurs only in Matt 25:1-13, where the NRSV describes ten virgins as *bridesmaids* who go out to meet the BRIDEGROOM. Many interpreters think the ten virgins represent the church (*see* BRIDE OF CHRIST) and view this parable as an allegory of the delayed PAROUSIA. Not all members of the church will be prepared to enter the Kingdom of Heaven when Christ returns; only the "wise" bridesmaids, who have brought enough oil for their lamps, will enter the wedding feast. Some interpreters are dismayed that the "wise" bridesmaids will not share their oil with the "foolish," in direct contrast to earlier exhortations to give to those in need (Matt 5:42). *See* LAMPS, NT; OIL; PARABLE; VIRGIN.

MARIANNE BLICKENSTAFF

BRIDLE. *See* BIT.

BRIER [סַלּוֹן sillon, חֵדֶק khedheq, שַׁיִת shayith, שָׁמִיר shamir, סִרְפַּד sirpadh; ἄκανθα akantha, κόνυζα konuza, σκόλοφ skoloph]. The translation of several Hebrew terms describing vegetation of little or no value. *Briers* describes Israel's enemies (Ezek 28:24). In Mic 7:4 and Isa 5:6; 7:23-25; 55:13, *brier* describes the people, the land, and their lack of worth.

DAVID LIPOVITCH

BRING A MESSAGE. *See* MESSAGE.

BROAD PLACE [מֶרְחָב merkhav, רָחַב rakhav, πλατυσμός platysmos]. Old Testament poets often portrayed ANXIETY as being surrounded or constrained by threatening forces (e.g., Ps 22:12-13, 16-18). God responds, delivering the endangered one to a "broad place," where clear vistas afford protection and safety (2 Sam 22:20; Job 36:16; Pss 18:19; 31:8; 118:5).

BROAD WALL [הַחוֹמָה הָרְחָבָה hakhomah harekhavah]. The name refers to a west or northwest section of the JERUSALEM wall that was "abandoned" or not repaired in the post-exilic restoration because it was still standing (Neh 3:8; 12:38). Stones from existing houses were used to fortify it (Isa 22:10). Archaeological digs by N. Avigad uncovered a 23 ft.-wide wall, perhaps this Broad Wall, that he thinks was part of one encircling the Western Hill built by HEZEKIAH to withstand the battering rams of SENNACHERIB's invasion.

Bibliography: N. Avigad. "Excavations in the Jewish Quarter of the Old City of Jerusalem." *IEJ* 20 (1969/1970) 1–8, 129–40, and *IEJ* 22 (1971) 193–200.

FOOK KONG WONG

BRONZE [נְחֹשֶׁת nekhosheth]. An alloy of copper and tin. During the OT period copper was mined in the East Wadi Arabah (*see* COPPER) by the Edomites. The origins of the tin used to make bronze are still a matter of debate, but it probably came from Anatolia.

The Hebrew word **nekhosheth** means "copper" but in the Bible it is generally translated as "bronze," because it mostly refers to the objects made of the metal. Analysis of metal remains from archaeological sites in Israel and Jordan shows that in the biblical period copper was almost always used in the form of bronze. Most of the furniture used in both the tabernacle and later in the Temple in Jerusalem was made of bronze, because, even though it was less valuable than gold or silver, it was stronger and better suited for construction purposes. Archaeological sites in Israel and Jordan have revealed many remains of bronze objects. Among them are WEAPONS (daggers, arrowheads, spearheads) and armory (rings and small pierced discs belonging to coats of mail, or fragments of bronze plates belonging to shields) that illustrate the arms worn by Saul and Goliath (1 Sam 17:5, 6; 1 Sam 17:38-39), personal ornaments (beads, earrings, bracelets, fibulae, and the like), and household items (cups and wine-sets), agricultural tools (axes, parts of possible ploughs), and religious or ritual objects. The production of small bronze ornaments and household items was a cottage industry in Israel and Transjordan as well as in Philistia. On many sites, such as Tell Acco, Qasile, Tell Masos, and Tell Dan, remains of bronze production were found, such as small furnaces, tuyeres (blow-pipes), and crucibles, as well as moulds for casting jewelry. These objects were made by remelting scrap bronze, of which hoards have also been found. It can be assumed that most of the bronze that was in use at any one time in this period has been remelted, so that much more bronze was in actual use than has been found in archaeological contexts.

Large bronze objects, such as the pillars and the capitals, and the various vessels mentioned in 1 Kgs 7 that were made by Hiram of Tyrus for the Temple of Solomon, were the work of professional bronzesmiths. These objects were made in the plain between Succoth and Zarethan, east of the Jordan. The identification of this plain is not certain, but the excavations at the site of Deir Alla in the East Jordan Valley have revealed the presence of very large installations, which were most likely used for the production of very large bronze objects. The excavator, Franken, has suggested that the presence of a special type of clay in this region, which was suitable for the creation of large moulds, was the reason why these objects were produced here. The installations date to the 12th cent. BCE, two centuries before the date of the building of the Temple, and they can therefore not be related directly to the Temple furniture, but it is likely that "the plain of Succoth and Zarethan" was the reputed production center for large bronze objects, and this reputation was transferred into the biblical account.

Bronze is a relatively strong alloy, and therefore continued to be used for the production of weapons and armory, long after iron came into use (1 Sam 17; 2 Sam 22:35; 1 Kgs 4:13; 14:27). It is often mentioned—sometimes together with iron—as a symbol of strength (Deut 33:25; Job 20:24; Jer 1:18). Bronze and iron weapons remained in use side by side until the end of the Persian period.

JEWELRY mentioned in the Bible is almost invariably made from gold. However, archaeological evidence shows that most of the jewelry, such as rings, earrings, bracelets, and other ornaments, was made of bronze. Bronze played an important role in religion and ritual. Most of the furniture used in both the tabernacle and the Temple was either made of bronze (Exod 27; 35; 1 Kgs 7), or made of wood and plated with bronze.

A bronze bull, 18 cm in length, was found on a height in the northern Samaria hills, the heartland of early Israelite settlement, and dated to the Early Iron Age (1200–1000 BCE). It may have played a role in the religious practices of the earliest Israelite settlers, although it was probably made in a Canaanite workshop. The story of the golden calf (Exod 32) may have its origin in these cult practices. The serpent that Moses made to save the Israelites from the plague of snakes was made of bronze (Num 21:8-9).

EVELINE J. VAN DER STEEN

BRONZE SEA. *See* SEA, MOLTEN.

BRONZE SERPENT. *See* NEHUSHTAN; SERPENT, BRONZE.

BROOCH. *See* JEWELRY.

BROOD. *See* BIRDS OF THE BIBLE; COCK; VIPER.

BROOK [נַחַל nakhal; χειμάρρους cheimarrous]. A small stream that only has water after rains and is dry most of the year. In Ar., known today as a *wadi*. In one of his laments, Jeremiah calls God "a deceitful brook," a reference to the lack of water in dry times (Jer 15:18). In 2 Sam 17:15-20 a brook is a barrier that Absalom's servants do not cross. In Jdt 2:24 Holofernes and his army follow the brook Abron from the Euphrates to the sea, apparently the Mediterranean.

JORGE PIXLEY

BROOM [רֹתֶם rothem]. The broom tree (*Retama raetam*) is a bush native to the desert and hill country of Israel and its neighbors. Its branches are used in the manufacture of brooms. The term is used to translate the Hebrew rothem. In 1 Kgs 19:4-5, a broom tree was the site of Elijah's request to die and his subsequent visitation by an angel. Job 30:4 describes the use of the roots of this plant as fuel by desperate individuals

shunned by society. In Ps 120:4 the coals produced by burning the wood of this tree are used in parallel with a warrior's sharp arrows as the punishment for the deceitful. In Isa 14:23 the fate of Babylon is described as being swept by the Lord of Hosts with the broom (מַטְאֲטֵא mat᾽ate᾽) of destruction.

DAVID LIPOVITCH

BROTH [מָרָק maraq]. Liquid prepared by stewing meat in water. Gideon served this substance along with bread and meat to God's messenger (Judg 6:19-20). In response to the messenger's instruction, Gideon poured out the broth as libation offering. *See also* the negative use of "broth of abominable things" (Isa 65:4). *See* FOOD; MEALS.

L. JULIANA M. CLAASSENS

BROTHER, BROTHERHOOD [אָח akh; ἀδελφός adelphos, ἀδελφότης adelphotēs]. Siblings (brothers and sisters [אָחוֹת akhoth, ἀδελφαί adelphai]) had important functions within antiquity's family systems. Central sibling obligations were to strive for harmony, to offer mutual social and practical support, and to defend family interests, such as honor and finances; *see* FAMILY and SISTER.

In the OT period with its nomadic (early) and agrarian (later) ways of life, siblings formed part of patriarchal family structures that aimed at keeping family property—whether flocks or farms—undivided. Given the high rate of childhood mortality, having many children was considered an assurance for the future and a blessing. Firstborn sons/brothers were sometimes allotted double inheritance, although practices varied greatly. Daughters/sisters were usually attended to by dowries, which could be of considerable size. *See* FIRSTBORN; INHERITANCE. Brothers were mutually responsible for securing succession, if necessary by marrying a brother's widow (Gen 38; Deut 25:5-10); *see* LEVIRATE MARRIAGE. The preeminence often given to younger siblings in the OT may recognize that Israel as God's chosen people is least among the nations, or it could represent altruistic regard for vulnerable groups.

Siblings have central roles in the OT and the Apocrypha: Cain and Abel (Gen 4:1-16), Esau and Jacob (Gen 25:19–35:29), Rachel and Leah (Gen 29–30), Joseph and his brothers (Gen 37–50), Moses, Miriam, and Aaron (Exod 1–7; 15:20-21), and the Maccabean brothers (4 Macc 8:1–14:10).

Siblings should nourish close relations (Prov 18:24), be in agreement (Ps 133:1; Prov 17:17), and love one another (Lev 19:16-17); *see* BROTHERLY LOVE. However, reality often differed from ideals: the OT describes tensions (Ps 50:20; Jer 9:4) and cases of serious conflict (Gen 4:8; 37:20). The winners were not always those deserving victory (Gen 27–28); yet, the OT portrays God as high-minded even toward evildoers (Gen 4:15).

Sibling terms were also used figuratively, of fellow Israelites (Deut 15:11-12; Ps 22:23), colleagues (Num 8:23-26; 2 Chr 29:34), political allies (1 Kgs 9:13; Amos 1:9; 1 Macc 12:6-7), friends (2 Sam 1:26), and lovers (Song 4:9-10). Members of Qumran called one another brothers (1QS VI 8 viii-x). Israel could be depicted as a family or a siblingship (brotherhood) with God as father (Hos 2; Mal 2:10); however, the OT does not develop on siblingship as a concept, except perhaps in Zech 11:14.

Scholars have devoted more attention to sibling relationships in the Greco-Roman period than in the earlier centuries. With the increasing trend toward urbanization, in Greco-Roman antiquity sibling groups appear to have become smaller, consisting of two to three persons. Usually, brothers and sisters inherited on an equal footing, and primogeniture was not practiced. Since parents often died before all their children were adults, siblingship was the longest familial relationship. Aristotle characterizes the relationship between brothers as the primary example of friendship (*Eth. nic.* viii, 12; 1161b-1162a). Siblingship (ἀδελφότης adelphotēs) continued to be a key topic for ancient moralists (*see*, e.g., Plutarch's "On Brotherly Love").

The basic characteristics of OT siblingship recur in the NT. In particular, siblings were expected to display emotional closeness, leniency, and forgiveness. Sibling relations did not imply equality of gender and status, but unity despite differences, with the obligation of the stronger and the weaker to mutual support. As in OT times, conflict occurred, particularly between brothers, often manifesting itself in quarrels over inheritance (Luke 12:13-15). The prominence of sibling groups in the NT shows the importance of family relations for the spread of the gospel: Peter and Andrew (Mark 1:16 par.), James and John (Mark 1:19 par.), Martha, Mary, and Lazarus (John 11:1-44). Siblings also occur in Jesus' parables: the Two Sons (Matt 21:28-32), the Prodigal and His Brother (Luke 15:11-32). Jesus is depicted as having brothers and sisters (Mark 3:31; John 7:3; Acts 1:14); *see* JESUS, BROTHERS AND SISTERS OF. He also refers to sibling relations on other occasions, particularly in cases of family disruption (Mark 13:12 par.).

Characteristic of the NT is its figurative use of sibling vocabulary, which by far outnumbers sociobiological references. Such uses also occur between members of philosophical groups (Stoics, Epicureans), mystery cults (the Mithras and Isis/Osiris cults), and voluntary associations (professional groups, burial societies). However, the frequency and intensity of such language in the NT exceed what is known from other sources. Christian usage is likely to be rooted partly in Jesus' reference to followers as his siblings (Mark 3:31-35; 10:28-31), partly in other figurative usage, especially of the OT.

The NT employs ἀδελφοί adelphoi figuratively of males and females alike, and Christian women are spoken of as sisters in a matter-of-fact way (Rom 16:1; 1 Cor 9:5; Phlm 2; Jas 2:15); *see* SISTER.

Figurative usage is employed throughout the NT. However, two different trajectories emerge; in one, Christian siblingship is central, in the other it is less prominent:

1. Paul is a primary example of the first type. He consistently addresses Christians as siblings whether they are his co-workers or simply church members. Paul describes Christ as "firstborn among many siblings" (Rom 8:29). Siblingship implies putting Christian love into practice (Rom 12:9-13; 1 Thess 4:9-12), welcoming weaker believers (Rom 14:1–15:13; 1 Cor 8:1–11:1), not condemning or taking one's Christian siblings to court (1 Cor 6:1-11), and treating those who are social inferiors as siblings (Phlm 15-16). Siblingship also serves as a boundary marker to designate some as deviant Christians: the "false siblings" (NRSV: "false believers") of Gal 2:4; 2 Cor 11:26 are the only examples of the term ψευδάδελφος pseudadelphos in Greek literature.

The idea of Christian siblingship is also firmly established in Q (6:41-42; 17:3-4) and is developed further in Matthew (5:21-26; 18:15-17, 21-22, 35). Matthew is the first to speak explicitly of a spiritual family with God as father and Christians as children/siblings (23:8-10). Siblingship, signaled by adelphotēs, philadelphia, is a key Christian virtue in 1 Pet (1:22; 2:17; 3:8; 5:9), 2 Pet (1:7), and Heb (13:1). Hebrews also speaks of Christians as siblings of Christ (Heb 2:11-18). James (1:9-10; 2:14-16; 4:11-12) and 1 John (2:9-11; 3:10-17) emphasize siblingship as an obligation to social responsibility and mutual love, loving God being inseparable from loving one's Christian siblings (1 John 3:10).

Within this trajectory, Christian fellowship appears to be modeled on sociobiological siblingship, reflecting ideas and ideals associated with it. In these writings, Christian siblingship is seen partly in analogy with (Paul) and partly in tension with a Christian's ties to biological family (Q, Matthew). Figurative usage is applied exclusively to other Christians (except for Rom 9:3, Jews).

2. Christian siblingship has a well-established, yet less pronounced place in other NT writings. Mark does not directly speak of Christians as siblings, though it may be implicit in 3:31-35; 10:28-31. Luke takes Christian siblingship for granted (22:32), but does—unlike Matthew—not develop on it in the special material, and seems to tone it down in its Q material (Luke 6:33 vs. Matt 5:47; Luke 17:3-4 vs. Matt 18:15). Luke also employs it with a more universal slant, as referring to one's neighbor in general (6:27-36). In Acts, sibling terminology occurs frequently: the scope is broadened so as to include Christians (1:15-16), Jews (2:29; 7:2), and maybe Gentiles (17:16-34, esp. 28-29). Thus, Luke–Acts' use of siblingship ideas serves to stress the

continuity between Israel and the church as the people of God.

The Gospel of John very seldom refers to Christian siblingship (20:17; 21:23); instead, it focuses on the idea of Christian friendship (15:13-15). Also the deuteropauline and the Pastoral Epistles employ sibling vocabulary sparingly. The letters reflect a process of accommodation to traditional family hierarchies, which makes the concept of a siblingship that erases other distinctions between Christians more problematic. This is seen in 1 Tim 6:2, in which slaves are exhorted not to use their status as Christian siblings as a pretext for disrespect toward their masters. Within this second trajectory, the idea of siblingship is employed with less creativity theologically and rhetorically.

The NT focus on Christian siblingship puts it at the heart of early Christian ecclesiology. However, the variation in usage is also likely to mirror differences in the understanding of Christian relations internally and toward outsiders. *See* CHURCH, IDEA OF.

Bibliography: Reidar Aasgaard. *"My Beloved Brothers and Sisters!" Christian Siblingship in Paul* (2004); Reidar Aasgaard. "Brothers and Sisters in the Faith: Christian Siblingship as an Ecclesiological Mirror in the First Two Centuries." Jostein Ådna, ed. *The Church Takes Shape* (2005) 285–315; Frederick E. Greenspahn. *When Brothers Dwell Together: The Preeminence of Younger Siblings in the Hebrew Bible* (1994); David G. Horrell. "From ἀδελφοί to οἶκος θεοῦ: Social Transformation in Pauline Christianity." *JBL* 120 (2001) 293–311; Carolyn Osiek and David Balch. *Families in the New Testament World* (1997); Leo G. Perdue et al. *Families in Ancient Israel* (1997).

REIDAR AASGAARD

BROTHERLY LOVE [φιλαδελφία philadelphia]. In the OT, brotherly love was an important value, involving not only emotional but also social and financial aspects: brothers should secure the harmony, honor, and economical interests of their family. Despite obvious tensions between ideal and reality, there are moving stories about brotherly love, e.g., of Joseph (Gen 37–50) and of the Maccabean brothers (4 Macc 8:1–14:10). In a figurative sense, brotherly love could be shown toward fellow Israelites (Lev 19:17-18), and even extend to resident aliens (Deut 10:17-19).

In the NT (particularly Matthew, Paul, James, 1–2 Peter, and 1 John), brotherly love is a fixed ideal, signaled by philadelphia (Rom 12:10; 1 Thess 4:9; Heb 13:1; 1 Pet 1:22; 2 Pet 1:7), φιλάδελφος philadelphos (1 Pet 3:8), and philadelphia (1 Pet 2:17; 5:9), terms otherwise rare within Greek literature. In the NT, philadelphia is used only figuratively, mainly of intra-Christian relationships (Rom 12:9-13; 1 Thess 4:9-12), and very occasionally of other relationships (Matt 25:40). While reflecting OT usage, it also utilizes

Greco-Roman notions of brotherliness, such as forgiving, unity in diversity, and mutual responsibility.

The specific rights and obligations associated with philadelphia make it a central concept within NT ethics and ecclesiology. *See* BROTHER; CHURCH, IDEA OF; LOVE IN THE NT.

REIDAR AASGAARD

BROTHERS OF THE LORD. *See* JESUS, BROTHERS AND SISTERS OF.

BROWN. *See* COLORS.

BRUCIANUS, CODEX. This Coptic Codex, also called "The Books of Jeû," was written in Upper Egypt in the 6th cent. CE. It is a very important witness to Gnosticism. It contains a unique presentation of Valentinian Gnosticism; an exposition of the mysticism of the Greek alphabet, analogue to the Hebrew Sepher Yetzirah; and a sort of magical book.

PETER ARZT-GRABNER

BUCKET [דְּלִי deli; κάδος kados, ἄντλημα antlēma; Lat. vas]. A container, often leather, used to draw water from cisterns and wells (John 4:11). The water it holds is used metaphorically to emphasize the prosperity of Israel (Num 24:7) and the insignificance of other nations (Isa 40:15; 2 Esd 6:56).

BUCKLE. *See* JEWELRY.

BUGATHAN. *See* BIGTHAN.

BUGLE. *See* TRUMPET.

BUILD [בָּנָה banah; οἰκοδομέω oikodomeō]. The root of the Hebrew verb בָּנָה is related to bny. It occurs in all Semitic languages except for Ethiopic. Its basic meaning is "to build" with derived meanings such as "to rebuild," "to fortify," and "to establish." Nouns derived from this root include בִּנְיָה (binyah) building, בִּנְיָן (binyan) structure, מִבְנֶה (mivneh) structure, and תַּבְנִית (tavnith) construction, pattern.

The subject of the verb can be God (Gen 2:22; Ps 127:1), humans (1 Kgs 18:32), or an abstract idea (Prov 9:1). The object of the verb includes cities (Judg 18:28), houses (Deut 8:12), altars (Exod 17:15), high places (1 Kgs 14:23), and the Temple in Jerusalem (1 Chr 22:9-10; Hag 1:2, 8). Stones were the most popular building materials in the hill country. Ashlar masonry was used in the building of temples, city gates, and royal residences. Mud bricks, made from a mixture of chopped straw, clay, and sand, were used in the coastal plain and the valleys. Timbers were used primarily for roof beams, window frames, and doors.

The verb also has, by extension, figurative meanings. Rachel and Leah together build the house of Israel

(Ruth 4:11), and a man has the obligation to build up the family of his deceased relative (Deut 25:9). God, in turn, builds (i.e., establishes) the Davidic dynasty (2 Sam 7:5-16), nations (Jer 31:4), and steadfast love with his people (Ps 89:2). Theologically, God is the ultimate builder behind every kind of building activity. Without God's blessing the builder labors in vain (Ps 127:1), and no one can rebuild what Yahweh tears down (Job 12:14). The wise person is one who can discern the appropriate time, determined by God, to build up or to tear down (Eccl 3:3). God's restoration of Israel is also expressed in terms of rebuilding it (Jer 24:4-7), its houses and cities (Ezek 36:33-36), and the Davidic dynasty (Amos 9:11).

The Greek word most commonly used to translate banah in the LXX is oikodomeō. It is used literally and figuratively in biblical and extrabiblical texts. In the NT, it refers to the building of the Temple in Jerusalem (John 2:20), tombs of the prophets (Luke 11:47-48), barns (Luke 12:18), and towers (Luke 14:28). Believers are exhorted figuratively to encourage and build up one another (1 Thess 5:11; Rom 15:2). Likewise, the exercise of spiritual gifts should be for the building up (i.e., edification) of one another (1 Cor 14:26). This word is also used of the establishment and building up of local churches (1 Cor 3:10-15).

A divine subject is implied from the context in some instances (Acts 9:31) and clearly stated in other instances (Acts 20:32). This word also has a messianic connotation in the NT. Jesus will build a faith community that can withstand the power of death (Matt 16:18). His resurrection is compared with the rebuilding of the Temple (Mark 14:58; John 19-22). See ARCHITECTURE, NT; ARCHITECTURE, OT; CORNERSTONE; WALLS.

Bibliography: Philip King and Lawrence Stager. *Life in Biblical Israel* (2001) 21–28.

FOOK KONG WONG

BUKKI buhk'*i* [בֻּקִּי buqqi]. Probably a shortened form of BUKKIAH. 1. Representing the tribe of Dan, Bukki was one of the twelve delegates who divided up the promised land among the tribes (Num 34:22).

2. Son of ABISHUA, an Aaronite (1 Chr 6:5). *See* BORITH; PRIESTS AND LEVITES.

FOOK KONG WONG

BUKKIAH buh-k*i*'uh [בֻּקִּיָּהוּ buqqiyyahu]. His name may mean "proved of Yahweh." One of the sons of HEMAN who was commissioned by DAVID to prophesy with musical instruments (1 Chr 25:4). He was the leader of the sixth division of musicians (1 Chr 25:13).

BUL [בּוּל bul]. The eighth Hebrew month (October–November), later known as MARCHESHVAN. Month when construction of the Temple was completed (1 Kgs 6:38). *See* CALENDAR.

BULL [שׁוֹר shor, אַבִּיר 'abbir, פַּר par, calf עֵגֶל 'eghel]. The offering of bulls as SACRIFICES AND OFFERINGS or as gifts was a central part of Israelite worship. The intention of the donor, either the individual or the people of Israel, was to achieve a state of purity leading to one of holiness and nearness to God. Leviticus 19:1-18 defines the relationship between the divine injunction to be holy, the people's offering of well-being (זֶבַח שְׁלָמִים zevakh shelamim) and personal acts of justice and compassion required of all. The Israelites were enjoined to offer these gifts exclusively to the God of Israel.

Bulls were considered the pride of the herd in the Israelite sacrificial system. They were offered at the dedication of the tabernacle (shor Num 7:3), the consecrations of the priests (par Exod 29:10-15) and the Levites (par Num 8:8), on the New Year (par Num 29:2) and the Day of Atonement (par Num 29:8,9) and the three pilgrim FESTIVALS (Passover, Num 28:19; Weeks, Num 28:26-31, esp. v 27; Booths, 29:1-38). The sacrifice of a bull also accompanied the admission of sins by a king and the sin offering of the high priest as he prepares the scapegoats on the Day of Atonement (par Lev16:11). Bull sacrifices were offered at the Tent of Meeting and administered by the priests (shor Lev 4:10, 7:23; par Ps. 50:9; 'abbir Ps 50:13; 51:19.)

Without becoming necessarily syncretistic or idolatrous, the Israelites used bulls as poetic symbols of power. The abundance of cattle attributed to Abraham was intended to reflect his wealth and power (Gen 13:2). In Jacob's blessing of Joseph, God is called 'avir ya'akov, the "Mighty One of Jacob" (*see* Gen 49:24, also Isa. 10:13 where 'abbir, a wild bull, is used to describe the king of Assyria). Bulls (par) characterize Gideon (Judg 6:25). Bulls (par) are part of the gifts of Hannah (1 Sam 1:24), Elijah's test of Ba'al (1 Kgs 18:23), and Job's rewards (Job 42:8). Joseph is likened to "a firstling bull (shor) in his majesty" (Deut 33:17).

Bulls held a special place in worship in Jerusalem: 22,000 cattle were sacrificed at the dedication of the temple of Solomon (1 Kgs 8:63, 64). The bronze bowl, called the Sea, created by Hiram of Tyre for the Temple, rested on a pedestal of twelve bronze bulls (1 Kgs 7:25; 2 Kgs 16:17). The Babylonians removed the bowl, but not the bull icons, from the Temple in 597 BCE (Jer 52:20; 2 Kgs 24:13).

Yet the danger of syncretism was present, because the religion of Israel's Canaanite neighbors included bull cults dedicated to the chief god of the Canaanite pantheon, El, and his son Ba'al representing virility, fertility, the weather, and war. The prophets chose to denounce the use of bull icons in the Northern Kingdom as marks of apostasy (Amos 4:4, 5:5, 7:9; Hos 2:18, 8:4-6, 10:5, 12:11, 13:2). Archaeologists have discovered a major sanctuary complex at Tel Dan, where 1 Kgs 12:28-29 reports that King Jeroboam set up a golden calf. The site was built in the 10th and expanded in the 8th and 7th cent. by Jeroboam, Ahab, and Jeroboam II, whose reigns were under consistent prophetic attack for worshiping foreign gods.

Later biblical texts repeat the warnings not to follow the practices of the Egyptians and the Canaanites (Lev 18:1-5, Ps106:19-20). Bulls continued to be labeled as the symbols of Israel's historic enemies (par Ps 22:12-13). Yet, echoes of the ancient gods of Canaan remain in Ps 29:6 ('eghel) a hymn of glory to the God of Israel (compare Ps 50:13 with 51:19). In the vision of Ezek 1:10, one of the four winged creatures has the face of a human in front and the face of a bull in back (see also Ezek 39:18, the defeat of Gog's army). See ANIMALS OF THE BIBLE; CALF, GOLDEN; SACRIFICES AND OFFERINGS.

Bibliography: Samuel E. Balentine. *Leviticus. IBC* (2002); Avraham Biran. *Biblical Dan* (1994); Michael Coogen. "God on a Bull at Hazor." Yigael Yadin. *Hazor.* 4 vols. (1958-1964), II-IV, Plates 324; Jacob Milgrom. *Leviticus 23–27* AB 3B (1964).

LEIVY SMOLAR

BULRUSH [אַגְמֹן 'aghmon]. The translation of the Hebrew word 'aghmon in Isa 58:5. The bulrush or papyrus (*Cyperus papyrus*) grows in swamps and was used in the manufacture of basketry and boats. The root אגם ('gm) is shared by the Hebrew word for marsh (אֲגַם 'agham), and the term 'aghmon may simply refer to marsh plants in general. In Isa 58:5, the bulrush is used to parallel the bowing of a person's head in humility.

DAVID LIPOVITCH

BULWARK [אָשְׁיָה 'oshyah, חֵל khel, עֹז 'oz; ἑδ-ραίωμα hedraioma, φυλακή phylake]. The translation of several Hebrew and Greek words related to fortifications (towers, pillars, and foundations), strength, and security.

Several Hebrew terms carry significance for this word: 'oshyah (for the destruction of Babylon, Jer 50:15; "towers" NIV, "pillars" NASB, "foundations" KJV), 'oz (for the words of children, Ps 8:2; elsewhere translated "strength" NASB, KJV; "praise" NIV), khel (as a metaphor for victory, Isa 26:1; "ramparts" NIV, NASB. In 4 Macc 13:13, the body is a guard (phylake) for the law. In the NT, hedraioma is used in 1 Tim 3:15 figuratively presenting the church as the pillar, ground, or foundation of the truth.

The general meaning of this term is a literal form of defensive structure, wall, or obstruction designed to represent and provide strength and security. The strongholds of the OT world provided protection from violence seen prevalent in the biblical text and in his-

tory. The Hebrew text carries a figurative meaning as in Ps 8:2 and Isa 26:1. The figurative imagery in 1 Tim 3:15 reflects the root that forms hedraioma, hedra (ἕδρα), which literally means "bench or base." The church universal is to be the benchmark for the establishment of truth within society. Likewise, truth is the foundation for security within the church. *See* WEAPONS AND IMPLEMENTS OF WAR.

MICHAEL G. VANZANT

BUNAH by*oo*'nuh [בּוּנָה bunah]. The Judahite Jerah-meel's second son (1 Chr 2:25). *See* JUDAH.

BUNNI buhn'*i* [בֻּנִּי bunni]. 1. A Levite who heard Ezra's reading of the Law (Neh 9:4).

2. A chief of the people who made a covenant with EZRA and others to observe the Mosaic Laws (Neh 10:15).

3. The levitical ancestor of SHEMAIAH who agreed to live in Jerusalem (Neh 11:15).

BURDEN [מַשָּׂא massa'; φορτίον phortion, βάρος baros]. Used in both the OT and NT in the literal sense of a weight or load to be borne, *burden* is regularly used in a figurative sense in the OT to refer to 1) sins and iniquity, 2) external oppression, 3) cares and strife, or 4) responsibilities and tasks of daily life. The most common Hebrew word for "burden" in the OT, massa', is also rendered "oracle" (e.g., Isa 13–23; Jer 23; 2 Kgs 9:25). Of the words rendered *burden* in the NT, two are most common. Phortion (Matt 11:30; 23:4; Luke 11:46) refers to characteristic religious requirements, while its single occurrence in Paul (Gal 6:5) refers to personal moral responsibility. Baros, too, refers to personal moral responsibilities (Acts 15:28), but also to work load (Matt 20:12) and the weight of daily trials and difficulty (Gal 6:2). *See* LIFT, TO OR TO BEAR; PERSEVERANCE.

GARY COLLEDGE

BURIAL [קְבֻרָה qevurah; ταφή taphe]. The placement of a deceased human body in a tomb or in the earth. Public ritual deposition of the dead is a characteristic of every known human society. The world has yet to see a human society that can willingly let its dead lie where they fall.

The OT depicts burial practices that cohere well with the archaeological evidence from the Iron Age (1200–587 BCE). The prevailing custom in the ANE, going back to the Middle Bronze Age (2000–1500 BCE), was burial in caves by extended family groups. Second-ary burial—i.e., reburial of human bones after the flesh of the body has decayed—was common. Later, during the Iron Age, the Israelite "bench" tomb emerged as the most common form of tomb architecture. In these square (or slightly rectangular) underground chambers, typically about 8 ft. on a side, a waist-high bench ran along three sides of the tomb. The side in which the entrance was situated usually did not have a bench. At the time of death, bodies were laid on the benches, and after decomposition was complete, the bones were gathered into a repository hollowed out beneath one of the benches. Over time, this repository came to hold all the bones of family members long dead, and when an individual's bones were placed therein, that individual was dissolved into the collective ancestral heap. The familiar biblical expression "to sleep and to be gathered to one's fathers" (2 Kgs 22:20, *et al.*) vividly captures the contours of this Israelite custom.

Ancient Israelite ideas about the afterlife cohered with these burial practices. The OT calls the domain of the dead *Sheol*, describing it as a dark and shadowy realm beneath the earth—not unlike an Iron Age "bench" tomb—in which the dead experienced few joys or pleasures. Israelite customs of mourning are also evident in some biblical texts: Job's "comforters" sit with him for the first seven days, a practice that survives in Judaism to this day.

The conquest of Syro-Palestine by Persians, Greeks, and Romans introduced changes in burial practices, but the tradition of multiple burial in underground chambers persisted. Cist graves—i.e., individual graves lined with stone slabs—appeared when the exiles returned from Babylon in the 6th cent. BCE and again during the Roman occupation. Wooden coffins and stone sarcophagi were used during the Hellenistic and Roman periods, but burial by extended family groups in underground tombs was still typical. Tomb architecture, however, was significantly modified. A typical tomb from the Roman period was square (or slightly rectangular), about 8 to 10 ft. on a side, but now, instead of benches around three sides, niche were carved directly into the walls of the tomb. Two types of Greco-Roman niches proliferated in Syro-Palestine during the Roman period (37 BCE–367 CE): the *arcosolium*, a broad, arch-shaped niched carved along the wall of the cave, in which a body could be laid parallel to the wall, and the *loculus*, a deep narrow slot carved perpendicular to the wall of the tomb, large enough to hold one body. Secondary burial also continued. The saying of Jesus in Matt 8:21-22 and Luke 9:59-60 presupposes secondary burial: the would-be disciple asks for time to gather his father's bones, but Jesus denies the request. In *loculus* tombs from the Early Roman period around Jerusalem, ossuaries (i.e., limestone boxes large enough to hold the bones of one or two adults) were used for bone gathering. The inscription on the so-called "James" OSSUARY is a modern forgery, but the artifact itself is a typical specimen.

It was once thought that secondary burial in ossuaries was motivated by belief in resurrection of the body, but the literary sources that make that claim (the 4th and 5th cent. CE *Talmudim*, e.g.) are too late to furnish evidence for Jewish burial practices in the 1st cent. CE. Early Jewish customs of mourning are evident in the NT, however, particularly in John 11, where Mary and Martha are joined by friends and relatives at their home for several days of mourning for their deceased brother.

The pattern of burial practices in the urban Roman world of Paul and his congregations was significantly different from that of the OT and the world of Jesus. In cities of the Roman Empire during the 1st cent. CE, secondary burial was unknown, and bodies were commonly placed in tombs that were built above ground, not underground. These tombs typically included many features of a Roman house—a front door, windows, a pediment, frescoes, and other interior decorations—and they were usually located along the main roads leading into the city. In the Latin West, cremation was widely practiced: the body of the deceased was burned, and the ashes were collected in an urn and placed within a tomb that belonged either to a family or to a *collegium*, i.e., a voluntary association that provided burial services for its members. Some tombs held large numbers of urns: at Ostia and Isola Sacra, e.g., some tombs held dozens of cremations. Romans also feasted with their dead on regularly scheduled occasions. These meals were called *refrigeria* because they were believed to be "refreshing" to both the living and the dead. In the Greek East, by contrast, inhumation was the most common form of burial: bodies were typically placed in niches, usually of the *arcosolium* type.

During the second half of the 2nd cent. CE, the dominant burial practice in the Latin West changed from cremation to inhumation. The reasons for this change are unclear, but when the aristocracy in Rome made the change, the rest of the empire rapidly followed. Since burial by inhumation uses up considerably more space than cremation, crowding soon became an issue. In the late 2nd cent. CE, catacombs were developed as a solution to this problem: Romans began to build their burial places underground, laying their dead in niches carved into the walls of labyrinthine underground passageways. The presence of Christians in the catacombs of Rome can be documented in the early 3rd cent. CE, but contrary to popular imagination, the catacombs were never used by Christians as a refuge from persecution. *See* BIER; EMBALMING; IMMORTALITY; MOURNING; OSSUARIES; RACHEL'S TOMB; RESURRECTION; SHEOL; TOMB; TOMB OF THE KINGS.

Bibliography: E. Bloch-Smith. *Judahite Burial Practices and Beliefs about the Dead* (1992); B. R. McCane. *Roll Back the Stone: Death and Burial in the World of Jesus* (2003); I. Morris. *Death Ritual and Social Structure in Classical Antiquity* (1992); J. M. C. Toynbee. *Death and Burial in the Roman World* (1971).

BYRON MCCANE

BURNING שָׂרַף saraf, בָּעַר ba'ar, יְצַת yitsath; καίω kaiō]. As a verb, "burning" (saraf) describes destruction (Josh 11:13) or sacrifice (Num 19:6); only two usages are non-destructive (Gen 11:3, Isa 44:16). As a noun it describes the "fiery dragons" (Num 21:8) and the SERAPHIM. Ba'ar describes the "burning bush" (Exod 3:2; *See* BUSH, BURNING); the hearts of individuals (Hos 7:6); the Lord's burning anger (Isa 30:7). Yitsath describes a destructive event (Jer 51:58) or the burning of God's wrath (compare חָרָה kharah). In the NT, "burning" (kaiō) describes lamps (Matt 5:15), fiery destruction (Matt 3:12; Rev 18:18) or the inner burnings of the soul ("lust," Rom 1:27; "hearts," Luke 24:32). *See* SACRIFICES AND OFFERINGS.

ARCHIE WRIGHT

BURNING BUSH. *See* BUSH, BURNING.

BURNT OFFERING. *See* FIRE; SACRIFICES AND OFFERINGS.

BURY. *See* BURIAL.

BUSEIRAH. *See* BOZRAH.

BUSH, BURNING לַבַּת־סְנֶה labbath seneh; βάτος καίεται πυρί batos kaietai pyri]. Moses sees a burning bush that is not destroyed by the fire (Exod 3:2-4; *see also* Deut 33:16]). In the NT the bush is mentioned in Mark 12:26 and Luke 20:37. Stephen mentions it in his sermon where Moses appears as a deliverer rejected by his people (Acts 7:30, 35; *see* Exod 2:14). The bush is located in Horeb at the site of future worship, covenant making, and revelation of law. Sinai (סִינַי sinay), the location were God reveals the law, may be related to this word for "thorn-bush" (seneh).

Some readers crave a physical explanation for the phenomenon: e.g., the color of the foliage or the rays of the sun striking the branches; however, the significance of the bush lies in its symbolism. A variety of interpretations have been offered. According to one reading, Exod 3:2*a* may be understood: "The angel . . . appeared . . . as a flame of fire . . ." Here the fire could represent the guidance, revelation, and presence of God, a connection that runs through Exodus (e.g., 13:21; 19:18; 40:38). Another reading of Exod 3:2*a* is, "The angel . . . appeared . . . in a flame of fire . . ." For some readers the bush is Israel; the fire represents the Egyptian persecution. Nonetheless, God is present to protect the people from being consumed. Persecuted branches of both Judaism and Christianity have chosen the burning bush as their emblem. *See* BURNING.

Bibliography: Cornelis Houtman. *Exodus.* Historical Commentary on the Old Testament (1993) 335–45;

Etan Levine. *The Burning Bush: Jewish Symbolism and Mysticism* (1981).

WILLIAM JOHNSTONE

BUSHEL [μόδιος modios]. Translated "bushel," modios designates a vessel large enough to cover a lamp and conceal its light (Matt 5:15; Mark 4:21; Luke 11:33 RSV). It should not be thought of in these contexts first as a unit of measure, but as a measuring vessel or domestic utensil. As a unit of measure, modios was equivalent to approximately 8 quarts (1 peck) dry measure, substantially smaller than today's bushel. *See* WEIGHTS AND MEASURES.

GARY COLLEDGE

BUZ buhz [בּוּז buz]. 1. Son of MILCAH and NAHOR, Abraham's brother (Gen 22:21).
2. A family listed among the clans of Gad during the divided kingdoms (1 Chr 5:14). Job's friend, ELIHU, was a BUZITE (Job 32:2).
3. A nation-state upon whom Jeremiah prophesied God's wrath (Jer 25:23).

BUZI byoo'zi [בּוּזִי buzi]. Father of the priest and prophet Ezekiel (Ezek 1:3).

BUZITE byoo'zit [בּוּזִי buzi]. Someone from Buz (Jer 25). An appellation for Barachel, the father of Elihu, to identify him with the Buz territory (Job 32:2, 6). *See* DEDAN; TEMA.

BUZZARD [דַּיָּה dayyah, דָּאָה da'ah]. An unclean bird of prey whose diet probably included carrion (Lev 11:14; Deut 14:13). Isaiah described EDOM as the abode of buzzards because buzzards symbolized the destruction prophesied against this land (Isa 34:15). Since its identification is uncertain, one should be cautious in equating dayyah with the American turkey buzzard (a bald vulture) or the European buzzard (a hawk). *See* BIRDS OF THE BIBLE.

JOEL M. LEMON

BYBLOS bib'los [βύβλος Byblos]. "Papyrus" or "book." Greek name for the Phoenician seaport Gebal (Ezek 27:9). *See* GEBAL.

BYWORD [מִלָּה millah, מָשָׁל meshol, שְׁנִינָה sheninah; διήγημα diēgēma, θρύλημα thrylēma]. An Old English translation of the Latin *proverbium*, a byword is a PROVERB or maxim. To become a byword was a terrible fate, meaning that one's life would be a cautionary tale, warning others how to avoid the same pitiable situation (e.g., Deut 28:37).

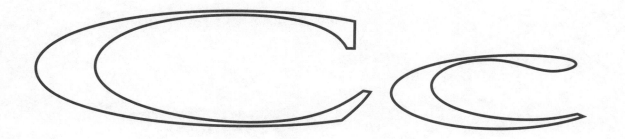

CABBON kab´uhn [כַּבּוֹן kabbon]. One of sixteen towns that comprised part of Judah's districts, located in the Lowland (SHEPHELAH) in southwest Palestine (Josh 15:40).

CABUL kay´buhl [כָּבוּל kavul]. A territory within the tribal boundaries of Asher (Josh 19:27). Although at one point in history this land belonged to Israel, it later came under the control of the Phoenician states. This transfer is explained in 1 Kgs 9:10-14, which depicts Solomon giving twenty cities in the land of Cabul as a gift to King Hiram of Tyre, who had supplied Solomon with lumber for his palace and the Temple in Jerusalem. Hiram did not like the cities and named them Cabul, a disparaging etiology drawn from the Hebrew כְּ־בָל (ke-val), meaning "like nothing" (1 Kgs 9:12-13). It is possible, however, that the original name of the region came from גְּבוּל (gevul), meaning "border," as the ב (v) and ג (g) interchange is quite common. The name of the region is preserved in the modern village of Kabul, 9 mi. southeast of Acco. See ASHER.

KEVIN A. WILSON

CAESAR see´zuhr [Καῖσαρ Kaisar]. Originally the cognomen (personal name) of the Roman dictator Gaius Iulius, who was murdered in 44 BCE. Caesar was taken up as the family name of his adopted heir Octavian (Augustus) and thereafter came to designate each successive Roman emperor. Caesar (NRSV translates emperor) appears in the NT, particularly the Gospels and Acts, often in contrast to or as an analogue to the rule of God or Jesus (e.g., Matt 22:17-21). Emperors established laws, judged cases, functioned as the final court of appeals, and served as the high priest of the Augustan system of Roman religion.

STEVEN ROBERT MATTHIES

CAESAR, APPEALS TO. See APPEALS TO CAESAR BY PAUL.

CAESAR, JULIUS see´zuhr, joo´lee-uhs [Lat. Gaius Iulius Caesar]. Gaius Julius Caesar (100–44 BCE) was a politician, general, and (according to law and popular devotion) deity. Caesar's solution to the collapse of Rome's republican government in bloody civil war was military dictatorship based on his own divinity. Derived from an ancient patrician family, he had very early proclaimed descent from gods and kings along both maternal and (especially) paternal lines, tracing his lineage

to the legendary Iulus, descendant of Venus through Aeneas. Before his assassination, Caesar had himself become the god Divus Iulius. In 42 BCE, the senate confirmed this by solemn and legal decree, responding to widespread and deeply held popular conviction (see EMPEROR WORSHIP).

Caesar's divine honors rested on the successes of an earthly career, combining shrewd politics, military command, and bribery. Lavish spending, e.g., helped secure his election as chief priest (63 BCE). More crucial was the reconciliation Caesar effected between Pompey and Crassus. The resulting political alliance of these three (the so-called "first triumvirate") was powerful enough to subvert the balance of the constitutional government. Waging an aggressive war of conquest against Gaul (58–50 BCE), Caesar flooded Roman markets with slaves, acquired fabulous wealth, dispensed many political favors, and won the fierce devotion of his soldiers. Upon the death of Crassus in 53 and his victory over Pompeian forces in the ensuing civil war (49–46 BCE), Caesar, as dictator, enacted his most lasting legacies (45 BCE): reformation of the calendar and establishment of the cult of the military dictator. After his assassination, Caesar's great-nephew and adopted son, Gaius Octavius, soon styled himself the "son of god" (Divi filius). Later, "the Blessed One," more commonly known as AUGUSTUS (a name the senate conferred), was able to put Caesar's institutions into efficient, effective, and more permanent practice.

Bibliography: Matthias Gelzer. *Caesar: Politician and Statesman.* (1968); Christian Meier. *Caesar: a Biography* (1982); Stefan Weinstock. *DIVUS JULIUS* (1971); Zwi Yavetz. *Julius Caesar and Jis Public Image* (1983).

HANS-FRIEDRICH MUELLER

CAESAR'S HOUSEHOLD [Καίσαρος οἰκία Kaisaros oikia]. Composed primarily of slaves and freedpersons of the imperial household. The familia Caesaris numbered in the thousands, spread throughout the Roman Empire. One branch focused on domestic service to the emperor's family and managed imperial establishments and estates. The other branch was employed in a wide range of administrative posts, some powerful, in the civil service. Perhaps Christians were among the familia Caesaris, since Paul sends the Philippians greetings from "those of Caesar's household" (Phil 4:22). See HOUSEHOLD, HOUSEHOLDER; PHILIPPIANS, LETTER TO THE; ROMAN EMPIRE.

RICHARD S. ASCOUGH

CAESAREA MARITIMA sees´uh-ree´uh [Καισάρεια Kaisareia]. Midway between Haifa and Tel Aviv stands the remains of a port city built by HEROD THE GREAT. The city became the political center of the Roman and Byzantine province called *Palestina Prima.* The fifteen biblical references to the city all occur in the book of Acts. Caesarea also became the center of ecclesiastical administration during the Byzantine Period, eclipsing even Jerusalem until the latter was designated as a patriarchate in the 6th cent.

the Romans deposed Archelaus because of ineffectual leadership. They chose to rule Judea directly through a prefect who resided in Caesarea. While Pontius Pilate was the prefect of Judea, he dedicated a temple to Tiberias at Caesarea. An inscription to this effect was found during the excavation of the theater.

There were serious tensions between the Jewish and Gentile citizens of Caesarea. In 66 CE, the desecration of a synagogue led to a riot by the city's Jews. This led to a massacre of most of the city's Jewish

Todd Bolen/Bible Places

Figure 1: Caesarea Maritima, ancient harbor area from northwest

The site was an anchorage along the Mediterranean coast. Known as Straton's Tower, it was a Sidonian possession that served shipping traffic between Egypt and Phoenicia. Built in the 4th cent. BCE, STRATON'S TOWER was acquired by Alexander Yannai in 100 BCE. This led to Jewish settlement in the area. Pompey ended Jewish rule there in 63 BCE, but thirty years later Augustus gave Straton's Tower to Herod the Great. Herod decided to build a city with a substantial port to replace the ancient anchorage.

The construction of the city took place between 22 and 9 BCE. It was designed to be a typical Hellenistic polis with a theater, amphitheater, agora, a royal palace, a temple dedicated to the emperor, and streets arranged on a grid pattern. Among the city's more important engineering achievements were its artificial harbor, aqueduct, and sewer system, which was flushed clean by the tides. The city was administered by a council and magistrates, who were subject to a military commander appointed by Herod. The Greek-speaking population swelled under encouragement from Herod, who saw the new city as a balance to ancient and Jewish Jerusalem. He named his city Caesarea to honor his patron Augustus Caesar. The name Caesarea Maritima, which is used today for Herod's city, was unknown in antiquity.

Herod's will named his son Archelaus as ruler of Judea in whose territory Caesarea was located. In 6 BCE,

population. The anti-Roman uprising of 66 BCE, and the slaughter that followed, precipitated a rebellion. During the revolt, Caesarea became the principal support base for Vespasian's army. After becoming emperor, Vespasian refounded the city as a Roman colony. It was the primary center of Roman culture in the region. Hadrian visited the city in 130 CE and probably had the city's hippodrome built then.

Caesarea played a significant role in the development of early Christianity. Philip, one of the Seven, came from Jerusalem to evangelize the city (Acts 8:40). Cornelius, the first Gentile convert, was a centurion stationed at Caesarea. Peter came from Jerusalem to baptize him (Acts 10). Cornelius' conversion initiated the process that transformed Christianity from a type of messianic Judaism into a world religion with an identity distinct from Judaism. Paul passed through the city several times (e.g., Acts 9:30; 18:22; 21:8). He was imprisoned there for two years before being sent to Rome for trial (Acts 23–26).

During the Byzantine period, strained relations between the city's Christian rulers and the city's Jewish and Samaritan citizens resulted in two revolts against Byzantine rule. The end of Byzantine power in Palestine, achieved by Omar and his Arab army, led to Caesarea's demise. Most of the population left the city, and its harbor silted up. The Crusaders came to

Figure 2: Caesarea Maritima, Aerial View of Aqueduct

Caesarea's environs in the 12th cent. Louis IX of France built a fortress there in 1251. The Mamlukes destroyed the fortress in 1291, and Caesarea was then unoccupied until the modern period.

Caesarea's historical importance and monumental structures have attracted exploration and excavation since the 19th cent. Full-scale excavation has been in progress for almost fifty years, revealing structures from the Hellenistic to the Crusader Periods. The site has played an important role in the development of underwater archaeology since Herod's port is now submerged beneath the Mediterranean.

Bibliography: Kenneth G. Holum, et al., *King Herod's Dream: Caesarea on the Sea* (1989); Avner Raban and Kenneth G. Holum, ed. *Caesarea Maritima: A Retrospective after Two Millennia* (1996).

LESLIE J. HOPPE

CAESAREA PHILIPPI ses´uh-ree´uh-fil-ip´*i* [Καισαρείας τῆς Φιλίππου Kaisareias tēs Philippou]. Caesarea Philippi is mentioned twice in the NT: Matt 16:13 and Mark 8:27. Both texts identify the place as the setting for Peter's confession of Jesus as the Messiah. Today the site is known as Banias, an Arabic word derived from the Greek Panias. The site is 33 mi. north of the Sea of Galilee at the southwestern extremity of Mount Hermon. The Hermon River, one of the sources of the Jordan, emerges from a prominent cave at the site.

Panias was a cult center in the Seleucid period. The

Figure 1: Caesarea Philippi, Cave of Pan, Sacred Area

Greeks built a shrine here to the god Pan, the god of woodlands and caves. Caesar Augustus gave Panias to Herod the Great in 20 BCE. In gratitude, HEROD built a temple to Augustus near the cave. Following Herod's death, Augustus confirmed his son Philip as tetrarch of the region that Luke called Ituraea and Trachonitis (*see* Luke 3:1), which included Panias. To express his thanks to the emperor, Philip built a polis at Panias, which he renamed "Caesarea." The polis became known as "Caesarea Philippi" to differentiate it from the Caesarea built along the Mediterranean coast by Herod the Great.

AGRIPPA II, the last Jewish king to rule the region, enlarged the city and named it "Neronias" in honor of Nero (ca. 53 CE). The name by which the town was usually known, however, was Caesarea Panias. In 70 CE the Romans celebrated games at Caesarea Philippi to mark Titus' capture of Jerusalem and the end of the First Revolt. In the Late Roman and Byzantine periods, "Caesarea" dropped out of the town's name and it became simply "Panias." Christianity was well established in the region by the 4th cent., since the bishop of Panias attended the COUNCIL OF NICEA. During the medieval period both Arabs and the Crusaders fortified the area, but by the end of the 13th cent., the fortunes of Panias declined and just a few poor Arabs and Druze lived there.

A series of archaeological surveys of the Banias region began in 1967. From 1985, full-scale excavations have focused on the sanctuary of Pan and associated temples from the Greek and Roman periods, the palace of Herod Philip, the town itself, and medieval fortifications.

Bibliography: John F. Wilson. *Rediscovering Caesarea Philippi: The Ancient City of Pan* (2001).

LESLIE J. HOPPE

CAGE [סֹגַר saghar, סוּגַר sughar; γαλεάγρα galeagra]. Indicates an enclosure that usually contained birds or animals within bars. Stocks or human cages were commonly used for captives by the brutal conquerors of the *ANE*. In Ezek 19:9 the word usually translated *cage* can also mean a wooden or iron neck-stock. In the passage a roaring lion (Jehoiachin) was pulled into a cage with pruning hooks, or put into a neck-stock, and taken to Babylon. Jeremiah 5:27 (כְּלוּב keluv) carries the idea of a "basket," while in Rev 18:2 "prison" (Φυλακή phulakē) is understood, though NRSV translates as a *haunt*). The KJV translates the word as "cage" in all three instances. The failed siege of Jerusalem (ca. 701 BCE) by Sennacherib of Assyria (2 Kgs 18–19) is described in Sennacherib's Annals as leaving Hezekiah trapped in Jerusalem like a "bird in a cage (Akkadian šigaru)."

MICHAEL G. VANZANT

CAIAPHAS kay´uh-fuhs [Καϊάφας Kaiaphas]. Probably from קייפא qyyf']. Joseph Caiaphas was the Jew-

ish high priest who interrogated Jesus and handed him over to Pilate. Each of the Gospel accounts presents Caiaphas in a differing light.

Mark's Gospel refers to him simply as "the high priest" (Mark 14:53, 60, 61, 63) and presents him as the convenor of a kangaroo court intent on putting Jesus to death. The court meets at night. False witnesses fail to agree. Jesus is condemned for blasphemy by nothing more than his own testimony. Finally, members of the court ridicule him (Mark 14:53, 55-65). Matthew follows his Markan source closely, although he adds Caiaphas' name, both in the preliminary meeting of the chief priests (Matt 26:3-5) and in the Jewish proceedings against Jesus (26:57).

In Luke's presentation, however, the Jewish trial is condensed and has the air of a preliminary investigation. The high priest is not singled out, and the gathered assembly simply question Jesus regarding his messianic identity before passing him to Pilate (Luke 23:66-71). This evangelist waits until the trials of apostles in the opening chapters of Acts before introducing the high priest into the narrative (Acts 4:5-22; 5:17-40; 7:8-60; 9:1). Luke knew Caiaphas' name, although Luke 3:2 and Acts 4:6 suggest that he may have assumed that Annas, a former high priest, still occupied the office.

John's Gospel is different again. Caiaphas appears at a council meeting, which has gathered to try Jesus in his absence (11:47-53). He is introduced as "high priest that year" (11:49, presumably "that fateful year"); and suggests that "it is expedient for you that one man should die for the people, and that the whole nation should not perish" (11:50; *see* 18:14). John suggests that this prophetic insight is due to his role as high priest, a role that was often believed to endow its incumbent with prophetic insight (11:51). Although Caiaphas is referred to several times throughout the Passion Narrative, the high priest (who questions Jesus about "his disciples and his teaching" in 18:19-23) seems to be Annas; the meeting between Caiaphas and Jesus is passed over in silence (18:24, 28).

All four Gospels were written in the late 1st cent. at a time when relations between Christian groups and local synagogues were strained. All reflect a degree of tension, hurt, and hostility in their depictions of Jesus' Jewish opponents, and each evangelist had his own particular theological agenda: Mark wanted to highlight God's rejection of the Jewish Temple and its leadership; Matthew and particularly John, two strongly Jewish Gospels, may have been interested in presenting Jesus as the "true" high priest; and Luke wanted to draw parallels between the death of Jesus and that of Stephen, and to contrast the apostolic leaders of "new Israel" with the degenerate chief priestly leaders of old. It is clear, then, that the Gospels cannot be used uncritically for an evaluation of the historical Caiaphas.

Unfortunately, our sources for Caiaphas' life are fairly meager and we must be content with only a general outline. According to Josephus, Caiaphas was appointed high priest by the Roman prefect Gratus in ca. 18 CE (*Ant.* 18.35). He came from an aristocratic, priestly (possibly high priestly) family that, according to rabbinic tradition, was associated with the village of Beth Meqoshesh (*t. Yebam.* 1.10). Attempts to find clues to his family's origins from their nickname "Caiaphas" are highly speculative. His native language would have been Aram., but—similar to other aristocrats of his day—he would have been proficient in Greek and he would have made his home in Jerusalem's wealthy and fashionable Upper City.

The nature of the high priesthood underwent a number of changes prior to Caiaphas' accession. Herod I had kept a tight control over the office, sharing it amongst a number of Diaspora families (particularly that of Boethus) and keeping the high priestly vestments under his own control in the Antonia Fortress. Rome, however, took a less intrusive approach: Herod's innovations were gradually eroded and Jewish authorities were given greater autonomy over religious affairs. In the first phase of Roman rule (6–41 CE), the high priesthood was almost exclusively in the hands of the family of Ananus, son of Sethi (the Annas of the NT). According to John 18:13, Caiaphas married Annas' daughter, a liaison that must significantly have helped his advancement. The whole family, including Caiaphas, were probably Sadducees—the small yet prestigious aristocratic priestly group that was particularly concerned with the Temple and its cult (*Ant.* 20.199; Acts 4:1; 5:17).

As high priest, Caiaphas was the supreme cultic official in the Jerusalem Temple, the mediator between Israel and its God, and the only man able to enter the holy of holies once a year and atone for the people's sin. He was the figurehead of the Jewish faith, and he ensured that a delicate compromise was maintained, by which Rome allowed the vast Temple complex to run unhindered. He was the natural spokesman for the Jewish nobility and might well engage in politics, especially when issues about the Temple were concerned. Whether a fixed council known as the Sanhedrin existed in the 1st cent. is debatable; more likely, decisions were reached through ad hoc meetings of chief priests and aristocrats as Josephus suggests.

Caiaphas clearly worked well with Gratus' successor, Pontius Pilate (prefect from 26–37 CE). Josephus records only a handful of incidents from this period, and all seem to have occurred at feasts when Caiaphas would have been otherwise engaged. The execution of Jesus of Nazareth shows the two men working together; presumably both men were equally anxious to avoid a disturbance in Jerusalem at Passover. Historically, John's suggestion that the chief priests feared for the Temple may be close to the truth; the last thing Caiaphas wanted was for Jesus to cause an uprising, to have Roman troops intervene, and the feast disrupted.

The incident in the Temple (Mark 11:15-17 and par.) may well have sealed his fate (Mark 11:18).

Caiaphas and other Jewish aristocrats are often accused of being collaborators, quislings, or puppets of the Roman regime. There is no evidence, however, that they were particularly pro-Roman. It was in everyone's interests for taxes to be paid and rebellions quashed: Jewish interests were safeguarded through diplomacy and compromise, not violence and bloodshed. Not everyone went along with their approach: some despised any kind of compromise and urged confrontation; and many had harsh things to say about their leadership. Nor is there any evidence that Annas and his family had a monopoly on the sale of sacrificial animals in the Temple, or that they ran a vendetta against the followers of Jesus (Luke is doubtless exaggerating this hostility in the first half of Acts for rhetorical reasons).

The longest serving high priest of the 1st cent. CE, Caiaphas was deposed in 37, shortly after Pilate, by the Syrian legate Vitellius (*Ant.* 18.95). We hear no more about him, although a tomb found to the south of Jerusalem in 1990 may have been his final resting place. *See* ANNAS; PILATE; SANHEDRIN; TRIAL OF JESUS.

Bibliography: H. K. Bond. *Caiaphas: Friend of Rome and Judge of Jesus?* (2004); J. C. Vanderkam. *From Joshua to Caiaphas: High Priests after the Exile* (2004).

HELEN K. BOND

CAIN קַיִן qayin; Καΐν Kain]. The name Cain (Qayin) is connected to קָנָה qanah ("aquire," or "create"). In Eve's words of Gen 4:1, "I have created (qaniti) a child with the help of the LORD" (author's translation; compare Gen 14:19). The story of Cain and ABEL (Gen 4:1-16) tells of the rivalry between the first human brothers, sons of ADAM and EVE. The story is an integral part of the Yahwistic primeval narrative (*see* YAHWIST). The sequence of sin-investigation-punishment is shared with the Paradise story (e.g., Gen 3:9//4:9; 3:13//4:10; 3:17//4:11). It should, therefore, be understood in terms of a primeval individual narrative rather than in ethnological or occupational group terms (such as nomads versus sedentary settlers, shepherds versus farmers, or Kainite tribes versus other tribes). The different occupation of each (Cain is a farmer, and Abel is a shepherd) depicts the two major human activities in biblical times. The story relates how each brother brings offering to God. Although Abel brought "the firstlings of his flock and their fat portions," while Cain offered just "fruits of the soil," this distinction is not explicitly stated as the reason for God's preference for Abel's offering (the explanation given by traditional [e.g., Heb 11:4] and modern commentators).

Cain's distress over the rejection of his offering (Gen 4:5) is understandable on the human level, for being the firstborn he may have expected to be preferred over his younger brother. The divine intervention in Gen 4:6-7 explains, however, that such expectations are irrelevant to his fundamental obligation to master the tendency to sin. The permanent presence of sin, and the choice between succumbing to it or not, are expressed by the metaphor of a crouching predator: "Sin is lurking at the door" (Gen 4:7). The fact that the divine warning comes before the crime, and that Cain ignores it, establishes his intention to commit it. Also, that he kills his brother "in the field" (Gen 4:8), outside the inhabited region, and that he later denies the deed (Gen 4:9), suggest that the murder was premeditated. The curse laid upon Cain to wander without being able to till the soil resonates with the curse upon Adam (Gen 3:17). The bond between the soil and Cain is severed, as are his links with home and family. The story is not concerned with the legal aspect of the murder, but with its outcome. The protective sign given to Cain (4:15) may be understood as a symbolic deterrent against another murder. Cain's violent character is reflected in his offspring (Gen 4:22-24). Cain became emblematic for those who murder (compare Wis 10:3; *Jub* 4:5). His denial, "Am I my brother's keeper?" (Gen 4:9), became a dictum for denial of an improper action already committed. In the NT, Cain stands for the murderer par excellence (1 John 3:12).

DEVORAH DIMANT

CAINAN kay'nuhn [Καϊνάμ Kainam, Καιναν kainan]. Noah's great-grandson; an ancestor of Jesus (Luke 3:36, LXX of Gen 10:24; 11:12).

CAIRO GENIZAH. *See* GENIZAH.

CAKE. *See* BREAD.

CALAH kay'luh [כָּלַח kalakh; Χαλαχ Chalach]. Mentioned in Gen 10:11-12 as one of the cities built by NIMROD (hence the modern name Nimrud), situated on the Tigris River about 35 km downstream from NINEVEH. Ancient Calah was the Assyrian capital for Assurnasirpal II (88–859 BCE) and until late in the reign of Sargon II (721–705 BCE). Buildings excavated at the site include the ziggurat of the chief god of the city, Ninurta, and the Nabu temple containing a double set of cellae for the celebration of the AKITU (new year's) festival of Nabu and his wife Tasmetum, as well as an important tablet library. The public rooms of the North West Palace were lined with orthostats of Assurnasirpal II, showing war and tribute scenes. The harem contained the intact tombs of several queens of Assyria, yielding gold diadems, gold earrings, armlets and anklets, cups and bowls, rock crystal vessels, and the remains of richly embroidered linen sewn with gold rosettes. The arsenal had private rooms decorated with tile panels, the first attested use of lead glaze and tin oxide pigments. It was used to store war booty including ivory panels in Assyrian, Syro-Hittite, and Syro-Egyptian style. Parts of the archives of its male and female administrators and of the provincial governor survive. The Babylonians and their Median allies destroyed the city in 614–12 BCE, massacred the inhabitants and, chaining the hands of over 180 young men, threw them into the palace wells to drown.

Bibliography: J. Oates and D. Oates. *Nimrud* (2001).

JOANN SCURLOCK

CALAMOLALUS kal'uh-mol'uh-luhs [Καλαμωλάλος Kalamōlalos, LXX[A]; Καλαμωκάλος Kalamōkalos, LXX[B]]. Along with Ono, his 725 descendants were among the exiles returning from Babylon (1 Esd 5:22). The name may be a corruption from combing LOD and HADID (Ezra 2:33; Neh 7:37).

CALAMUS kal'uh-muhs [קָנֶה qaneh]. *Acorus calamus* was brought from Asia as a perfume. *See* PLANTS OF THE BIBLE; SPICE; SWEET CANE.

VICTOR H. MATTHEWS

CALCOL kal'kol [כַּלְכֹּל kalkol]. Son of ZERAH and grandson of TAMAR and JUDAH, Calcol belonged to a guild of musicians known as "the children of MAHOL," whom Solomon is said to have exceeded in wisdom (1 Chr 2:6; 1 Kgs 4:31 = Heb 5:11).

CALDRON [קַלַּחַת qallakhath, סִיר sir; λέβης lebēs]. Pot for boiling meat offerings or human body parts (1 Sam 2:14; 2 Chr 35:13; 2 Macc 7:3). *See* POTTERY.

CALEB, CALEBITES kay'luhb [כָּלֵב kalev; Χαλεβ Chaleb]. 1. Caleb, the son of Jephunneh, is one of the spies sent to evaluate whether Israel could take the "promised land" from the Canaanites (*see* CANAAN; CONQUEST). He is listed among the Judean delegation to this task (Num 13:6); however, he and his brother Othniel are said to be "Kenizzite" (Num 32:12, Josh 14:6, Judg 3:9-11), descendants of Kenaz, the grandson of Esau (Gen 36:15), and thus Edomite. This suggests that Caleb was not originally a Hebrew but had joined with the Israelite community at some point, perhaps not long before he appears in the narrative as one of the spies. Being an Edomite, someone who knew the local terrain and language, would make him an excellent choice to be a spy among the Canaanites. He also has the zeal of a convert, as shown in his optimistic support for the invasion (Num 13:30). In fact, only he and Joshua have the courage and faith to recommend Israelite military action (Num 14:6-9). He is rewarded for his faith by God, who promises to give him an inheritance in the land that he had scouted for the Israelites (Num 14:24).

This narrative clearly offers an explanation for the continued existence of the Calebite clan, who maintained their sense of separateness even while living in southern Judah. After the successful conquest of the land, Caleb comes to Joshua to remind him of God's promise and to ask for his share of the land (Josh 14:6-14). Thus, the narrator reports that he was given HEBRON, and that the Calebites possess that city "to this day" (v. 14). Other texts, however, indicate that Caleb controlled the villages around Hebron, while the city itself was given to the Levite descendants of Aaron (Josh 21:9-12; 1 Chr 6:54-56). This must reflect a change in the tradition to accommodate the relatively late special status given to the Levites.

Later in the narrative, Caleb offers to give his daughter Achsah as wife to anyone who could subdue Kiriath-Sepher (Debir), and the successful champion ends up being his brother Othniel. In the process, Caleb grants his daughter "the upper springs and lower springs" in the southern desert, which indicates the extension of Calebite territory into the Negeb (Josh 15:14-19; Judg 1:11-15). This resonates with the report of an Egyptian mercenary soldier in 1 Sam 30:14, who distinguishes between one part of the Negeb "which belongs to Judah" and one called the "Negeb of Caleb." It is interesting to note that David (whose reign begins in Hebron) marries the daughter of Nabal, a man described as "surly and mean; he was a Calebite" (1 Sam 25:3).

2. The name also belongs to Caleb the son of Hezron in the line of Perez, Judah's son by his daugher-in-law Tamar (1 Chr 2:18-20). This Caleb has no historical significance other than the fact that he becomes the great-grandfather of Bezalel, the artisan placed in charge of building the tabernacle in Exod 31:2. The fact that Caleb's father Hezron died in a place called CALEB-EPHRATHAH (Ephrath also being the name of Caleb's wife) suggests that this whole line is associated with the Calebite clan, thus providing another explanation for the origins of the Calebites. A variant spelling of his name occurs in 1 Chr 2:9 (כְּלוּבָי keluvay). Also, the Hebrew text of 1 Chr 2:50 refers to a supposed "Caleb, son of Hur," but we should interpret "Caleb" here to summarize the previous genealogy and therefore "son of Hur" to begin a new list.

The term Caleb itself means "dog," which raises the question of why one would choose this name for a son. In the ancient world, dogs are often mentioned in negative terms as lowly animals with little honor or reason, but some texts use dogs as a metaphor for humility and faithfulness (see DOG). In 2 Kgs 8:13, Elisha tells Hazael, the prince of Aram, that he will achieve great military victories over Israel, and Hazael demurs by referring to himself as "a mere dog." This response shows his sense of subordination to his father the king. In this context, the name Caleb could be used as part of a theophoric name, meaning "faithful servant" or the like.

Bibliography: José M. Galán. "What is He, the Dog?" *UF* 25 (1993) 173–80; Gary N. Knoppers. "Hierodules, Priests, or Janitors? The Levites in Chronicles and the History of Israelite Priesthood." *JBL* 118 (1999) 49–72.

BRYAN D. BIBB

CALEB-EPHRATHAH kay´luhb-ef´ruh-thuh [אֶפְרָתָה כָּלֵב kalev ʾefrathah]. Town in GILEAD where Hezron died. The LXX reads that Caleb came to Ephrathah after Hezron's death (1 Chr 2:24).

CALENDAR. A calendar is a system for reckoning time and, in a derived sense, a list of days and months. For the periods reflected in the OT, we have no full description of a system for days, months, and years in which writers define when the units began and how long they lasted. Instead of comprehensive calendrical accounts, there are lists of key dates and indications regarding days, months, years, and occasionally larger units involving several or many years. Some extrabiblical texts, most notably *1 En.* 72–82, *Jubilees*, and a series of the Dead Sea Scrolls, supply something more nearly akin to a full calendar.

    A. Old Testament
      1. Preliminaries
      2. Months
        a. Canaanite names
        b. Ordinal names
        c. Babylonian names
        d. Implications for the year
    B. Other Literature
      1. Literary texts
      2. Aramaic papyri
      3. Other Greek sources
      4. Another tradition
        a. *1 Enoch* 72–82
        b. *Jubilees*
        c. Dead Sea Scrolls
        d. New Testament
    Bibliography

A. Old Testament

The texts included in the OT come from a wide range of dates and give evidence for different periods, with details from more than one way of reckoning time. No surviving text has the primary purpose of conveying information about an annual or monthly calendar. Rather, the hints about the ways in which time was calculated tend to occur as short notices in literary contexts or in lists of festivals.

1. Preliminaries

Genesis 1 establishes a fundamental point about the heavenly bodies whose movements allow the observer to measure time. "And God said, 'Let there be lights in the dome of the sky to separate the day from the night; and let them be for signs and for seasons and for days and for years, and let them be lights in the dome of the sky to give light upon the earth.' And it was so. God made the two great lights—the greater light to rule the day and the lesser light to rule the night—and the stars" (Gen 1:14-16). These words strictly subordinate the luminaries to the Creator God who assigns them calendaric functions. They are not divine beings, only created entities.

Both in the Bible and outside there is evidence for an agricultural way of designating the seasons. The Gezer Calendar (written in Hebrew in the 10th cent. BCE) reads: "Two months of ingathering. Two months of sowing (cereals). Two months of late planting (of legumes and vegetables). A month of harvesting barley. A month of harvesting (wheat) and measuring (grain). Two months of (summer) pruning. A month of (ingathering) summer fruit." Similar language appears in two lists enumerating the three Israelite pilgrimage festivals (Exod 23:15-16; 34:18, 22). Both relate the Festival of Unleavened Bread to the month ABIB, but they designate the other two holidays as the Festival of Harvest (of wheat in 34:22, where it is also called the Festival of Weeks) and the Festival of Ingathering at the end (23:16) or turn (34:22) of the year. A related festival list appears in Deut 16:1-17. It too includes the three pilgrimage festivals and adds that the first (UNLEAVENED BREAD) and the third (BOOTHS) last seven days and that the middle holiday (Weeks) was to fall "seven weeks from the time the sickle is first put to the standing grain" (v. 9). None of these festivals receives a date here, but all must be kept at "the place which the Lord your God will choose as a dwelling for his name" (e.g., v. 6). The passage associates Weeks and Booths with harvest seasons.

2. Months

A basic unit of time, defined by the lunar cycle, is the month. While the approximate length of a month could be determined by simple observation, the sources offer evidence of three ways for naming them and some conflicting indications about which month was thought to be the first in the year. The first and third sets of names play a part only in particular contexts, while the second enjoys the widest attestation.

a. Canaanite names. There are four unusual month names, one of which is related to a single festival and three of which appear only in the account in 1 Kgs 6 and 8 about the building of Solomon's Temple. The one that does not figure in 1 Kgs is the month name *Abib*, which is mentioned in three places in the book of Exodus (13:4; 23:15; and 34:18) and once in the book of Deuteronomy (16:1). All of these passages deal with the exodus and Festival of Unleavened Bread. Abib is never explicitly called the first month of the year, but its association with the exodus from Egypt and the meaning of the word (uncut ear of barley, etc.) place it in the spring.

The other three unusual month names date events in 1 Kgs 6 and 8. First Kings 6:1 assigns the beginning of the Temple building project to "the four hundred eightieth year after the Israelites came out of Egypt, in the fourth year of Solomon's reign over Israel, in the month of ZIV, which is the second month." The same date is recorded in 6:37. The word *Ziv* as a month name has not been identified in other texts, either in the Bible or elsewhere. As it is called the second month and the spring would be the preferred time to begin a large project, Ziv would have been a spring month. The fact that it is glossed as the second month suggests that when 1 Kgs 6:1 was written, the name may not have been familiar. When it came time to bring the ARK OF THE COVENANT into the new structure, "[a]ll the people of Israel assembled to King Solomon at the festival in the month ETHANIM, which is the seventh month" (8:2). Ethanim is attested in Phoenician as a month name (*see KAI* 37 A 1, 2; 41.4 [inscriptions from Kition and Tamassos]. Then, 1 Kgs 6:38 dates completion of the temple to "the eleventh year, in the month of BUL, which is the eighth month." This month is also mentioned in Phoenician inscriptions (*KAI* 14.1; 32.1; 38.2 [from Sidon, Cyprus, and Idalion]). Whether one may conclude from such sparse evidence that at some time Israelites used a full roster of Canaanite month names is debatable, and the fact that all four of them figure only in very specific contexts increases the uncertainty. The par. passages in 2 Chronicles lack these names, leaving only ordinal designations for months (2 Chr 3:2; 5:3).

b. Ordinal names. Many passages in the OT designate months as first, second, etc. The ordinals from first (e.g., Gen 8:13) to twelfth (Esth 9:1, etc.) are attested, with no indication that a thirteenth month was ever intercalated. In some cases, as with the Canaanite month names in 1 Kgs 6 and 8, the ordinal designations accompany month names. The works with this method of designating months include the Pentateuch, narrative works such as 1–2 Kings, 1–2 Chronicles, Ezra, Nehemiah, and Esther, prophetic books like Jeremiah, Ezekiel, Haggai, and Zechariah (besides dating the prophet's visions [1:1, 7; 7:1], it speaks of fasts in the fourth, fifth, seventh, and tenth months [7:3-4; 8:19]), and the apocalyptic book of Daniel (one instance, 10:4).

Writers often employed ordinal month names to define the times for celebrating festivals. There are verses that assign Unleavened Bread to the month Abib (*see* above), but in the full, more precise rosters of holidays the ordinal designations prevail. There are two such lists—Lev 23 ("the appointed festivals of the Lord" [v. 1]) and Num 28–29 (the offerings to be brought on the holidays). The former passage is a part of the HOLINESS CODE, the latter of the priestly document. The calendrical data from the two, supplemented from other passages, may be summarized as follows:

Both begin with the SABBATH day, but Num 28:3-8 calls for two daily sacrifices and 28:11-15 adds a special offering for the first day of each month.

Month 1, day 14	Passover	Exod 12:2 identifies the month of the exodus and thus of Passover as the first in the year; each Israelite family was to select the lamb for Passover on 1/10 [12:3] and slaughter it at twilight on 1/14 [12:6]; Num 9:1-5
Month 1, days 15-21	Festival of Unleavened Bread	See also Exod 12:15-20.
Month 1, day ?	Day after the Sabbath for offering the sheaf of the first fruits of the harvest	Lev 23, not Num 28, mentions the ritual, with no date specified
Month 3, day ?	Festival of Weeks on day fifty after the sheaf offering	Calculated as seven complete weeks and one day later, but neither text mentions a specific date, only that it occurs on the fiftieth day after another undated event
Month 7, day ?	Day of a "holy convocation commemorated with trumpet blasts"	Lev 23:24
Month 7, day 10	Day of Atonement	See Leviticus 16 for the full rituals of the day; see also Exod 30:10
Month 7, days 15-21	Festival of Booths	With an eighth day added

The list of ordinal months begins in the spring of the year and mentions no festivals after the seventh month—a month particularly rich in holidays. The two seven-day festivals—the Festival of Unleavened Bread and the Festival of Booths—are separated by exactly one-half year. Both are also extended by one day: Unleavened Bread is associated with the previous day, Passover; Booths has a supplementary eighth day. Unlike these two pilgrimage festivals (so described in Exod 23:14-17 and 34:18-24), the third holiday—the Festival of Weeks—lasts one day and receives no fixed date. This omission later occasioned disagreements about when one was to celebrate the festival.

Other scriptural passages that designate months by ordinals add to the roster of holidays. Numbers 9:6-13 legislates a second Passover for those who were impure due to contact with a corpse or were away on 1/14 and thus could not celebrate the Passover at its stipulated time. The second Passover falls on 2/14, exactly one month after the first. The book of Ezekiel, in the vision of the new Jerusalem and Temple (Ezek 40–48), supplies a shorter list of holidays that partially overlaps with the one above (45:18-25).

Month 1, day 1	Sacrifice a bull with whose blood the priest will cleanse the Temple
Month 1, day 7	The same sacrifice as on 1/1, this one to atone for the Temple because of "anyone who has sinned through error or ignorance" [v. 20]
Month 1, day 14	Passover sacrifice
Month 7, days 15–21	Seven-day festival

Festival lists are not the only passages in which one meets the ordinal months. The rather full chronology of the flood, from the Priestly editor in Genesis (see DOCUMENTARY HYPOTHESIS) employs numbered months as well and illustrates their use in a narrative context (see 2 Kgs 25 as another example).

Month 2, day 17 (Greek 2/27)	Year 600 of Noah's life	Flood begins and Noah and enter the ark (7:11, 13); waters rise for 150 days (7:24; 8:3)
Month 7/day 17 (Greek 7/27)		Ark rests on mountains of Ararat (8:4)
Month 10, day 1 (Greek 11/1)		Tops of mountains visible (8:5)
Month 1, day 1	Year 601 of Noah's life	Waters dried up from the earth (8:13)
Month 2, day 27		Earth dry (8:14)

c. **Babylonian names.** Once contact between Babylon and the Judeans became direct and sustained in the exilic period and with Persia in postexilic times, Judeans began using the names that their overlords gave to the months. This fact is acknowledged in the Talmud (y. Roš. Haš. 1.56d): "They carried the names of the months back with them from Babylonia." The books that employ these names are Ezra, Nehemiah, Esther, and Zechariah, each of which dates from the postexilic period. In some cases where a writer uses a Babylonian month name, an ordinal is attached to it in explanation (Esth 2:16; 3:7, 13; 8:9, 8:12; 9:1; Zech 1:7; 7:1). Only five months with such names occur in the OT, but the complete list is amply attested in cuneiform and later Jewish sources.

Babylonian names	Hebrew names
Nisannu	NISAN (Neh 2:1; Esth 3:7)
Aiaru	
Simanu	SIVAN (Esth 8:9)
Duzu	
Abu	
Ululu	ELUL (Neh 6:15)
Tashritu	
Arahsamnu	
Kislimu	CHISLEV (Neh 1:1; Zech 7:1)
Tebetu	TEBET (Esth 2:16)
Shabatu	SHEBAT (Zech 1:7)
Addaru	ADAR (Ezra 6:15; Esth 3:7, 13; 8:12; 9:1, 15, 17, 19, 21)

The Mesopotamian system from which these names derive views the spring as the beginning of the year, and that is clearly the order followed in the OT. The relatively frequent mention of the twelfth month, Adar, in the book of Esther is due to the fact that the days on which the Jews defended themselves against their enemies were the thirteenth and fourteenth of this month. That successful defense is presented as the basis for the Festival of PURIM that, according to Esth 9:21, 27 is celebrated on Adar 14–15 (only the fourteenth day for the Jews living in unwalled towns [9:19]).

d. Implications for the year. In all three arrangements (Canaanite, ordinal, and Babylonian) for naming the months, the year begins in the spring. Exodus 12:2, in the context of the departure from Egypt and the Passover, is explicit about this: "This month shall mark for you the beginning of the months; it shall be the first month of the year for you." There are, however, a few indications that a time in the autumn was considered the end of a year. Regarding the Festival of Booths, Exod 23:16 says it is "the festival of ingathering at the end of the year when you gather in from the field the fruit of your labor." The par. in Exod 34:22 refers to this time as "the turn of the year." Furthermore, Lev 25:9 says that the year of jubilee begins on 7/10, the Day of Atonement. At least this special year, then, begins in the autumn. No autumnal month, however, is ever called the first month. It could be that the slender evidence that has survived points to different inceptions of the year, depending on the subject under consideration. This is the solution expressed much later (ca. 200 CE) in *m. Roš. Haš.* 1.1, where four new year days are distinguished, including Nisan 1 for kings and festivals and TISHRI (seventh month) 1 for the regnal years of foreign kings, years of release, and JUBILEE years.

The chronology of the flood (by the Priestly editor) conveys some information about the length of a month and perhaps also of the year. The span of time when the waters rise—from 2/17 to 7/17—is said to be 150 days, implying that each month has thirty days. In the MT, the flood lasts from 2/17 in one year to 2/27 in the next. In the LXX version, it is from 2/27 until 2/27. It appears that the deluge lasts one year, and one suggestion is that the dates in the MT assume a lunar year of 354 days with the extra eleven days extending the flood to a full solar year of 365 days.

B. Other Literature

Jewish writings outside the OT offer a wider range of names for months.

1. Literary texts

The Greek translation of Esther, which adds six sections to the Hebrew version, uses Babylonian names in the extra sections (e.g., Addition A [11:2] has Nisan, Addition B [= 13:6] has Adar) and employs them and the ordinals where it translates the Hebrew version

(e.g., 3:12; 8:9 [Nisan for MT's Sivan]). The book of Judith has just one month date (1/22 [2:1]), as does Baruch (Sivan 10 [1:8]). The books of Maccabees express more dates and use both ordinal and Babylonian month names. A special contribution they make is to introduce the Festival of HANUKKAH (eight days beginning on Chislev 25), which celebrates the purification of the Temple in 165 BCE after it was defiled.

1 Maccabees	
1:54	Chislev 15
4:52, 59	Chislev (= ninth month) 25 (beginning of the eight days of Hanukkah)
7:43, 49	Adar 13 (festival marking victory of Nicanor)
9:3	First month of Seleucid year 152
9:54	Second month of Seleucid year 153
10:21	Seventh month of Seleucid year 160 (Festival of Booths)
13:51	2/23 in Seleucid year 171 defeat of the citadel, to be celebrated annually (v. 52)
14:27	Elul 18 in Seleucid year 172 a great assembly honors Simon
16	Shebat (eleventh month) in Seleucid year 177 Simon murdered
2 Maccabees	
1:9	Festival of Booths in Chislev (= Hanukkah)
1:18	Chislev 25
10:5	Chislev 25 (eight-day festival [v. 26])
11:21	Lysias's letter dated to the (unattested) Hellenistic month Dioscorinthius 24
11:33	King Antiochus's letter dated to the Hellenistic month Xanthicus 15
11:38	Roman letter dated to the Hellenistic month Xanthicus 15
15:36	12/13 (Adar) is Nicanor Day, the day before Mordecai's Day (= 12/14 or Purim)

First Esdras, which includes the end of 2 Chronicles and parts of Ezra and Nehemiah, reproduces the dates of its source texts but adds two references: 5:6 calls Nisan the first month, and 5:57 speaks of the new moon of the second month. *Joseph and Aseneth* refers to months by ordinals (1:1 [second month], 2 [fourth month]; 3:1 [fourth month]; 22:2 [second month]).

2. Aramaic papyri

A different kind of evidence comes from legal documents relating to Jewish and Samarian people. The earliest examples are the Aram. papyri from Egypt, especially from the Jewish military unit stationed at Elephantine near Syene. Among the documents by or about Jews (dating from the later 5th to the 4th cent. BCE) are several that use date formulas. There appears to have been no distinctively Jewish calendar used by Jews in Egypt at this time; they employed names familiar in their area. Among the texts, there are examples of three forms for dates. In some, only Egyptian month names appear, in some only Babylonian names (e.g.,

Nisan), and in some both kinds figure in the formula, with the Babylonian name coming first. The familiar "Passover Papyrus" from Elephantine, written by a Jew, Hananiah, to the Jewish garrison, mentions the month Nisan as the one in which the festival days occur.

The Samaria Papyri (4th cent. BCE) found at Wadi ed-Daliyeh are contracts and therefore bear dates. The preserved examples use the Babylonian month names. Attested instances are Adar (WDSP 1.1; 7.19), Tebet (only the last letter survives, 2.12), and Shebat (3.11; 6.1).

3. Other Greek sources

The Hellenistic month names attached to the letters sent by non-Jews in 2 Macc 11 illustrate a phenomenon that became widespread. Jewish writers adopted month names from foreign literary sources or correlated them with Hebrew names so that their wider audiences would understand them. For example, the writer of 3 Maccabees uses the two Egyptian month names *Pachon* and *Epeiph* to date events that befell Jews in Egypt without giving their Hebrew or Greek equivalents (6:38). Josephus wrote for an international audience and made allowance for it by explaining scriptural dates. For example, in the instructions regarding Passover, he reports that the sacrificial lamb was to be prepared on "the tenth of the month Xanthicus over against the fourteenth day (this is the month called by the Egyptians Pharmuthi, by the Hebrews Nisan, and by the Macedonians termed Xanthicus)" (*A.J.* 2.311 [LCL]; *see* 2.318 where Xanthicus alone appears). He also uses ordinals for months but regularly explains through other names which month he means. He does this in his biblical paraphrase as in the example quoted above and elsewhere.

4. Another tradition

A large amount of information comes to light in a series of Jewish texts that appear to belong to a single tradition. *First Enoch* 72–82 (the Astronomical Book), *Jubilees*, and several of the Dead Sea Scrolls contain data about solar and lunar calendars and evidence about Jewish disputes regarding them.

a. *First Enoch* 72–82 (preserved in Ethiopic) is a greatly modified remnant of a much larger work composed in Aram. in perhaps the 3rd cent. BCE. J. T. Milik identified four fragmentarily preserved Qumran scrolls (4Q208-11) as witnesses to this earlier Astronomical Book. Two of these (4Q208-9) are important for calendar reasons. They set forth in detail a scheme for how much of the moon's surface is illuminated each day of a month (always called first, second, etc.); it is not clear whether, in the original text, the catalog of illuminated/unilluminated portions continued for a few months, an entire year, or more. The scheme divides the lunar surface into fourteen parts, one more of which is illuminated each night as it moves from new moon to full moon, and one more is darkened each night in the waning period. The pattern calls for alternating months of thirty and twenty-nine days, with a year lasting 354 days. Though the Aram. copies have preserved no part of it, *1 En.* 72 describes a solar year of 364 days. The text pictures the sun rising along six equal segments of the eastern horizon (called gates) and setting in six corresponding gates in the west. Beneath the Enochic solar year lies a much older calendar well attested in cuneiform sources; in it a year consists of twelve months of thirty days each. To this schematic pattern, the Enochic tradition adds four extra days— two at the equinoxes and two at the solstices (3/31, 6/31, 9/31, and 12/31)—yielding a year of 364 days. The writer criticizes those who do not include the extra four days in the year. All of the astronomical information disclosed to Enoch is, the book claims, a revelation from the great angel Uriel. The book does not deal with the Sabbath or the scriptural festivals, but it mentions four seasons of ninety-one days each.

b. *Jubilees.* It may be that a solar year of 364 days underlies the Aram. Levi Document (the dates on which patriarchs such as Judah and Levi are born suggest this), but the most explicit heir and corrector of Enoch is the author of the book of *Jubilees* (ca. 160–150 BCE). Some fifteen fragmentary copies of the book, all written in Hebrew, have surfaced in the Qumran caves. The writer or the tradition he represents also attributed calendrical revelations to Enoch (4:17, 18, 21) and exploited the sabbatical potential in the Enochic solar system. The book's fullest statement about the annual calendar comes, however, in connection with the story of the flood. For it, the dates in the book (months are always expressed as ordinals) agree with the ones in the Hebrew Genesis, but as the author elaborates on the covenant made with Noah, he explains special features of the system.

- 1/1, 4/1, 7/1, and 10/1 divide the seasons, each of which has exactly thirteen weeks (ninety-one days), and commemorate events during the flood (6:23-29)
- Fifty-two weeks exactly in a year (6:30)
- 364 days in a year (6:32)

The point on which the writer takes issue with the *Astronomical Book of Enoch* is the place of the moon in measuring time. For *Jubilees* it has no role. The nations observe the moon that completes the year ten days too soon (354 days against 364 days); in this way they confuse secular and sacred times, both of which flow in an unchanging rhythm in the 364-day year (6:35-37).

In line with its practice of antedating Mosaic legislation to the time of the patriarchs, *Jubilees* has the patriarchs celebrate festivals on their correct dates (Unleavened Bread, 18:18-19; the Day of Atonement, 34:17-19; Booths, 16:20-31). The most important of them was the Festival of WEEKS—a holiday that is relatively unimportant in the Scriptures. The covenant that binds God and the people is identified with the Festival of Weeks and enhances its importance. *Jubilees* is the first text to offer a fixed date for the Festival of Weeks. God made the covenant with Noah in the third month (6:17, 19, 32-38), the very month for the covenant at Mount Sinai centuries later (Exod 19:1; Jub 1:1). The book dates both renewals made with Abra(ha)m to the Festival of Weeks, which falls in the middle of the third month (14:10, 18, 20 for the Gen 15 covenant; 15:1 for the Gen 17 covenant). From 44:1-6, where Jacob observes the festival, one can calculate that the date is 3/15.

c. Dead Sea Scrolls. The texts from Qumran agree about the 364-day year with the *Astronomical Book of Enoch* and *Jubilees* but follow the Enoch text, not *Jubilees*, in accepting a 354-day lunar year. A number of texts, which are not exclusively calendrical, make calendrical statements. For example, David's Compositions, one of the extra units in the first Psalms scroll from cave 11, says: "And he wrote 3,600 psalms; and songs to sing before the altar over the while-burnt **tamidh** offering every day, for all the days of the year, 364; and for the **qorban** of the Sabbaths, 52 songs" (XXVII, 4-7 [Sanders, DJD 4, 92]). 4Q252 (4QCommentary on Genesis A) joins David's Compositions in documenting the 364-day year and does so in its chronology of the flood (I, 1–II, 5). It begins on 2/17 (I, 4) and ends on 2/17 the next year (II, 1-2) "at the end of a complete year of three hundred sixty-four days." (II, 2-3 [Brooke, DJD 22, 199]). The writer also notes the day of the week on which the events during the flood occurred (the days are numbered, not named). All of the dates presuppose the 364-day arrangement of *1 En.* 72–82 and Jubilees.

Other texts, especially the Commentary on Habakkuk, show that a calendrical dispute pitted the scrolls group against their fellow Jews. As 1QpHab XI, 4–8 makes clear, the TEACHER OF RIGHTEOUSNESS, an early leader, and his followers observed the DAY OF ATONEMENT at a different time than their opponent the Wicked Priest who may have been the high priest.

The TEMPLE SCROLL offers a full list of festivals, using the 364-day year and numbered months for dating them. The list in cols. XIII–XXIX follows the one in Num 28–29 but amplifies it with several other holidays, which are also mentioned in other scrolls. The new holy times are:

Month 1, days 1–7?	Days of consecration of priests
Month 5, day 3	Festival of New Wine (date inferred)
Month 6, day 22	Festival of New Oil (date inferred)
Month 6, days 23–29?	Festival of the Wood Offering (*see* Neh 10:35-38)

The text dates the New Wine festival fifty days after the Festival of Weeks, and the New Oil festival

fifty days after New Wine. These, with the waving of the sheaf and the Festival of Weeks (also separated by fifty days), are presented as first-fruits holidays. Neither the Temple Scroll nor any other text found at Qumran mentions the festivals of Purim or Hanukkah.

The specifically calendaric works are 4Q317 (Phases of the Moon), 319 (Otot), 320-30, 334, 337, and 394 1-2 (also called 4Q327). In the edition of these texts in DJD 21, S. Talmon classifies them under four headings (DJD 21).

First, calendrical documents include lists of specific kinds of information, e.g., the months and how many days are in each one (6Q17) or the Sabbaths and festivals (4Q326, 4Q394 1-2).

Second, Mishmarot (watches) registers the list of twenty-four priestly families (1 Chr 24:1-19) that rotated duty at the Temple, with one group serving one week when it was relieved by the next watch on the list. The names of these groups identify the weeks when they serve, in effect naming weeks just as one names months. Because there were twenty-four groups, each year every group would serve twice (24 × 2 = 48 weeks) with four serving a third time to complete the fifty-two weeks. As the system would return to its starting point after six years, once each of the twenty-four had had opportunity to serve three times in a year, there are Mishmarot lists that cover six years. Apparently the compilers of these lists extrapolated backward which priestly group would have been serving and when every year all the way back to the time of creation (e.g., 4Q320 1). Some texts (e.g., 4Q329) simply list the groups; others indicate which group served at key times such as beginnings of years and months (319 7; 328-29). The examples that correlate festivals and the priestly watch that would be serving on them allow one to calculate precise dates for holidays such as waving the sheaf (1/26) and Weeks (3/15; *see* 320 4 iii-vi; 321 4-7).

Third, there are mixed types. An especially interesting sort are the texts that align dates in a solar month, the priestly group on duty, and two dates in the lunar month (called הקוד] hqwd and X; 4Q320, 321, 321a). It appears now, in light of new evidence from cuneiform texts, that hqwd refers to the day after the full moon, and the X date (which lacks a name) is at the time of total lunar eclipse.

A final type is represented by the fragmentary Otot (= "signs") text (4Q319), which records a number of signs occurring regularly within six forty-nine-year units (jubilees), that is, a 294-year period. The signs may mark times when intercalations occurred, but there is no proof of this.

d. New Testament. The Christian writers supply little information about calendars. There are references to the Jewish festivals, but their dates receive no attention. The Passover figures prominently in the Passion Narratives in the Gospels (also Luke 2:41-42; John

2:13, 23; 4:45; 6:4; 11:55; Acts 12:3-4; Heb 11:28), and in the Gospel of John, Jesus and his disciples celebrate several of the festivals (e.g., Booths, 7:1-14, 37), including Hanukkah (the Festival of the Dedication, 10:22). PENTECOST (the Festival of Weeks) is the occasion for the pouring out of the Spirit in Acts 2. Acts 20:6 mentions the "days of Unleavened Bread" and v. 16 reports that Paul "was eager to be in Jerusalem, if possible, on the day of Pentecost." "The Fast" in 27:9 is the Day of Atonement (see also Heb 9:7), mentioned here to indicate how late it was in the season for sailing. But the holidays are not dated, nor are matters such as the length of the months and years considered. See ATONEMENT, DAY OF; BOOTHS, FEAST-FESTIVAL OF; FEAST OF WEEKS; FEASTS AND FESTIVALS; PASSOVER AND FEAST OF UNLEAVENED BREAD.

Bibliography: F. Dobbs-Allsopp, J. Roberts, L. Seow, and R. Whitaker. *Hebrew Inscriptions: Texts from the Biblical Period of the Monarchy with Concordance* (2005); J. van Goudoever. *Biblical Calendars* (1959, 1961 2nd ed.); S. Talmon, J. Ben-Dov, and U. Glessmer. *Qumran Cave 4 XVI Calendrical Texts* (2001); J. VanderKam. *Calendars in the Dead Sea Scrolls: Measuring Time* (1998).

JAMES C. VANDERKAM

CALF [עֵגֶל ʿeghel]. Young calves were considered a culinary delicacy and were prepared for special meals. According to the biblical story, when the three guests came to Abraham to announce the imminent birth of Isaac, he offered them a meal including a young calf (בֶּן־בָּקָר ben baqar), fresh milk, and baked goods (Gen 18:6-8). Calves, specially selected for fattening (ʾeghel marbeq; Jer 46:21; Amos 6:4), were served on particular occasions, as mentioned when Saul visited the spiritualist woman at En-Dor (1 Sam 28:24). Young calves were also considered choice animals for sacrifice (Lev 9:2; 16:3; Num 7). In several instances, the calf is used as a symbol of peaceful conditions (Isa 27:10) and coexistence: "And the wolf shall dwell with the lamb, and the leopard shall lie down with the kid; and the calf and the young lion and the fatling together; and a little child shall lead them" (Isa 11:6). On the other hand, the behavior of this young animal is used as a metaphor for misbehavior (Jer 31:18).

Canaanite religion used the bull and calf as symbols of divinity, and this influenced Israelite religion. The story of the golden calf (Exod 32) is one expression of this influence. Another example is the erection of calves by Jeroboam in Dan and Bethel (1 Kgs 12:28-29). This particular event reverberates in 2 Kgs 10:29 and 17:16. In reality, the bronze bull statuette from the bull site in the Samaria hill country is a remnant of such cultic use of the bull in early Israelite religion. A. Mazar, the excavator, suggests that "the figurine was probably used by Israelite settlers in this region of the northern Samarian hills." See BAAL; CALF, GOLDEN; HEIFER.

Bibliography: A. Mazar. *Archaeology of the Land of the Bible: 10,000–586 BCE* (1990).

ODED BOROWSKI

CALF, GOLDEN [עֵגֶל זָהָב ʿeghel zahav]. Traditional interpreters have long considered the episode as a sign of the Israelites' betrayal of the covenant. Scholars now note that the biblical texts associated with the story of the golden calf (Exod 32; Deut 9; 1 Kgs 11–12; Hosea; and postexilic comments) reflect diverse political and religious interests in the cent. following the division of Solomon's kingdom (ca. 920 BCE).

Ancient Near Eastern bull and calf icons, made of wood inlaid or entirely of gold, were used as symbols of fertility or war. Bull icons were dedicated to El, the chief god of the Canaanite pantheon. Icons were also used as pedestals, with a god astride them or with no god visible (see BULLS). Thus, some scholars suggest that the Israelites portrayed in Exod 32 were not idolaters and did not intend to replace Yahweh as God.

A. Exodus 32

While Moses remains the commanding figure in Exod 32, the variations in the story are illustrated in the treatments of Aaron. Verses 1-6 describe the Israelites at the base of Sinai complaining to Aaron that Moses, now absent for forty days and nights, has abandoned them. Aaron has the people gather their gold and jewels and casts them into a fire. The people hail the calf with the words, "This is your God, O Israel, who brought you out of the land of Egypt." Aaron builds an altar and proclaims "a feast to the Lord." The people then "eat, drink and rejoice." Moses, informed by God of the situation, intercedes for the people, and then descends from the mountain carrying the "Tablets of the Covenant" (15) (see TEN COMMANDMENTS). When he sees the Israelites rejoicing around the calf, he smashes the tablets, burns and pulverizes the statue of calf, throws the dust into the water, and forces the Israelites to drink it (19, 20).

Moses accuses Aaron but assumes Aaron acted under duress. "What did this people do to you that you brought a great sin upon them?" (21). Aaron accuses the Israelites and defends himself, "I threw it [the gold] into the fire and out came this calf" (24; compare v. 35: "the calf . . . that Aaron made"). Moses then calls for those loyal to God to follow him. When the Levites volunteer, Moses consecrates them and orders them to kill the rebellious people (26–29). Scholars suggest the elevation of the Levites by Moses reflects a historic competitiveness between the priestly families of Moses and Aaron (compare Exod 29; Judg 18:30; 2 Sam 8:15).

Moses then confronts the Israelites with their great sin, intercedes again with God, this time placing his own life in peril (32:33). God agrees to punish only the guilty, tells Moses that a messenger (or angel) will "walk before" the people (compare vv. 34 and 1; 33:12-14), and inflicts a plague on them (35).

B. First Kings 11–22

Most scholars agree that many linkages exist between Exod 32 and 1 Kgs 11–12. In 1 Kgs 11–12, the story of JEROBOAM and the golden calves of BETHEL and DAN is part of the royal saga of ancient Israel, closely edited by the DEUTERONOMIC HISTORIAN (DH), in which God rewards and punishes monarchs for keeping or betraying the covenant. According to DH, Jeroboam acts initially as God's instrument to punish Solomon for worshiping foreign gods, when he leads a rebellion of the dissident northern tribes.

Once the rebellion succeeds, King Jeroboam fortifies his borders against Judah and formalizes his role as a sacral king. He places a golden calf in each of two historic and strategic shrines in Dan and Bethel (1 Kgs 12:25-28; Gen 28:22) and proclaims "You have gone up to Jerusalem long enough. Here are your gods, O Israel, who brought you up out of the land of Egypt" (1 Kgs 12:28). He bypasses the Levites, appoints his own priests, and proclaims a "festival to the Lord" on a date different from the festival date in Jerusalem. To DH, these are the sins of Jeroboam (1 Kgs 12:30; 13:33-34).

C. Hosea

The 8th cent. prophet Hosea denounces the northern kingdom, the worship of calves at Samaria (10:5), Gilead (12:11) and Bethel, called here Bethaven, the house of sin (4:15; 5:8; 10:5; Bethel and Gilgal, Amos 4:4; 5:5; Hos 12:11). In his words of compassion, Hosea recalls how Jacob discovered God at Bethel and yearns for Samaria to ask God: "Forgive all iniquity and accept that which is good; so we will render instead of bullocks the offering of our lips (14:2; author's translation).

D. Deuteronomy 9

Scholars generally agree that Deut 9:7-21, Moses' retelling of the story of the golden calf in the wilderness, emerged from the religious reforms of the royal court of the southern kingdom of Judah (ca. 620 BCE). Moses harshly reminds the new generation of Israelites of the terms of the covenant to worship the God of Israel exclusively. Moses reveals that at Sinai only Moses' fervent intercession had saved the people. God had been prepared to destroy the Israelites and Aaron as well. The justifications by Aaron and the role of the Levites that appear in Exod 32 are absent in Deuteronomy.

E. Postexilic perspectives

The unified post-exilic priesthood of Jerusalem rejected the worship of the calves while allowing Aaron to justify his role in Exod 32. The Levites and the sons of Aaron are both portrayed as exiles of Jeroboam who find refuge in Jerusalem (2 Chr 11:15; 13:8-12).

Nehemiah 9:18-21 and Ps 106 contain the broadest interpretation of the golden calf episode as a story illustrating human and divine rejection, intercession and atonement, and divine mercy. *See* BAAL; CALF; IDOLATRY.

Bibliography: M. Aberbach and L. Smolar. "Aaron, Jeroboam and the Golden Calves." *JBL* 86 (1967) 129–40; David Frankel. "The Destruction of the Golden Calf: A New Solution." *VT* 443 (1994) 330–31. Baruch Halpern. "Levitic Participation in the Reform Cult of Jeroboam." *JBL* 95 (1976) 31–40; J. Gerald Janzen. "The Character of the Golden Calf and Its Cult in Exodus 32." *CBQ* 52 (1990) 597–607; Nicholas Wyatt. "Of Calves and Kings: the Canaanite Dimension in the Religion of Israel." *Scandinavian Journal of the Old Testament* 6:1 (1992) 68–91.

LEIVY SMOLAR

CALIGULA kuh-lig′yuh-luh. Caligula (Gaius Iulius Caesar Germanicus, 12–41 CE, r. 37–41) became EMPEROR chiefly through a process of elimination. His father, brothers, and other close relatives were executed, compelled to commit suicide, or died under suspicious circumstances, all at the behest, real or perceived, of his predecessor, the emperor Tiberius, and his associates.

Despite his youth and relative inexperience in public life, Caligula's accession was received enthusiastically, largely due to the popularity of his father, Germanicus. Caligula enhanced this goodwill through modest and deferential behavior in the first months of his reign, but after a near-fatal illness in October of 37, abruptly raising the question of who might succeed him, his approach to ruling became more aggressive as he eliminated potential rivals and clashed openly with the Senate.

Such behaviors characterized the remainder of Caligula's reign and prompted a severely negative evaluation by the ancient literary tradition. The particular challenge that such sources pose for the modern interpreter is that they depict Caligula as insane, making it difficult to make sense of his actions.

Unlike Tiberius, Caligula tended to disfavor the aristocracy (above all the Senate) while appealing directly to the people, whose support he cultivated through lavish expenditures. This fact does not by itself render easy the explanation for many of Caligula's actions, however. For example, Caligula's introduction of a tax on prostitutes can best be understood in terms of his desire to increase state revenue. But reports that he installed a brothel in the imperial palace and an alleged plan to nominate his favorite horse for the consulship remain difficult to explain. Troubled relations with his

Jewish subjects raise even more questions. A modern consensus on Caligula and his reign is unlikely.

Bibliography: A. A. Barrett. *Caligula: The Corruption of Power* (1989); T. A. J. McGinn. "Caligula's Brothel on the Palatine." ECM/CV n.s. 17 (1998) 95–107.

THOMAS A. J. MCGINN

CALL, CALLING, CALL STORIES [קָרָא qaraʾ; καλέω kaleō, κλῆσις klēsis]. A call is an invitation or summons by God to fulfill a mission or particular function. In the Bible a call is often presented in the form of a narrative. In the OT the term qaraʾ is not restricted to one event or person, but used in many different ways, including naming, calling a nation into relationship with God, an invitation, and as a divine call to mission.

Numerous OT call narratives emphasize a divine encounter and commission as key aspects of the narrative; e.g., Abraham (Gen 12:1-9), Moses (Exod 3:1-21), Samuel (1 Sam 3:1-18), Hosea (Hos 1–3), Isaiah (Isa 6:1-8), Jeremiah (Jer 1:1-19), Ezekiel (Ezek 2:1-10), Gideon (Judg 6). Six basic parts of these call stories, according to Habel, include: divine confrontation, introductory word, commission, objection, reassurance, and sign.

New Testament call stories also may refer to an invitation to relationship with God as well as a summons to a specific function or mission. Most prominent are the carefully crafted narratives about Paul (Acts 9, 22, 26). However, there are many others: John the Baptist (Luke 1:5-20; Mark 1:2-8), Jesus (Mark 1:9-13; Matt 3:13-17), the Twelve (Mark 1:14-20;2:13-14; Matt 4:18-22; John 1:43-51), Timothy (1 Tim 6:11-12), and Priscilla and Aquila (Acts 18:18-28). These other stories have not received the same attention as those of the prophets and Paul because their narrative presentation is not as self-evidently structured.

Paul's call, both in Acts and at various points in letters that bear his name, has been the object of great scrutiny. One major debate addresses the continuity between Paul's pre-conversion Judaism and his *conversion* to Christianity. In fact, it is the term conversion that is at the center of the controversy. It is argued that the narratives in Acts are call stories, like those of the prophets. It is our Western introspective reading of Paul through the eyes of Martin Luther, rather than through Paul's Judaic background, that characterizes them otherwise. It is notable that Paul's call narrative contains features similar to the prophetic call genre.

While the understanding of call and call narratives has undergone change in the history of biblical interpretation, what has not changed is that all those who are called into relationship with God are called into a life of service to the one who calls; functions may differ, but the goal is the same.

Bibliography: William Baird. "Vision, Revelation and Ministry: Reflections on 2 Cor. 12:1-5 and Gal. 1:11-17."

JBL 104 (1985) 651–662; Norman Habel. "The Form and Significance of the Call Narratives." ZAW 77 (1965) 297–323; William H. Myers. God's Yes Was Louder than My No (1994).

WILLIAM H. MYERS

CALLISTHENES kuh-lis´thuh-neez [Καλλιθένης Kallisthenēs]. 1. An historian who accompanied Alexander the Great and recorded his conquests, but was said to have been executed by Alexander ca. 329 BCE. *See* PSEUDO-CALLISTHENES.

2. A man, otherwise unknown, burned by Judas Maccabeus's men for having burned the "sacred gates," presumably of the Temple (2 Macc 8:33). *See* JUDAS MACCABEUS; NICANOR.

LESTER L. GRABBE

CALNEH, CALNO kal´neh, kal´noh [כַּלְנֵה kalneh, כַּלְנוֹ kalno]. Mentioned in Isa 10:9 alongside CARCHEMISH, HAMATH, ARPAD, and DAMASCUS (and with Hamath in Amos 6:2), Calno/Kullania is probably the same as the neo-Hittite state of Unqi/Pattina whose capital was Kinalua. While paying tribute to Ashurnassirpal II (883–859 BC), Unqians were among the guests at the dedicatory banquet for his new capital of CALAH. In not joining the Qarqar coalition that included AHAB of Israel, JEHOSHAPHAT of Judah, and BEN-HADAD of Damascus against SHALMANESER III (858–824 BCE), Unqi made its own bid for independence in 831 BCE under the usurper Tsurri, whom the Assyrian turtan Dayyan-Ashur drove from Kinalua and replaced with a more pliant ruler. Unqi revolted for the last time against TIGLATH-PILESAR III (744–727 BCE). When added to the Assyrian Empire in 738 BCE, Calneh became the seat of a provincial governor.

JOANN SCURLOCK

CALVARY kal´vuh-ree [Lat. *Calvariae*]. Vulgate translation for κρανίον kranion, *skull*, the place of Jesus' crucifixion. *See* GOLGOTHA.

CAMBYSES kam-bi´seez [Καμβύσης Kambysēs]. The son of CYRUS the Great and the second emperor of the Persian Empire (530–522 BCE), Cambyses' main achievement was the conquest of Egypt, commencing in 525 after several years of preparation. It seems that Cambyses was quite respectful of the Egyptian cults, despite a negative tradition that he committed sacrilege. In 522 a revolt against Cambyses took place in Persepolis, led by an individual claiming to be Cambyses' brother Bardya (Greek: Smerdis). Cambyses immediately began the march back to PERSIA but died on the way. He does not appear to be mentioned in the Bible.

LESTER L. GRABBE

CAMEL [גָּמָל gamal]. The camel comes in two varieties, the one-humped camel or dromedary (*Camelus dromedarius*), and the two-humped camel or Bactrian (*Camelus bactrianus*). The exact time and place of and the purpose for the domestication of the camel are still being debated. Some argue that the camel was domesticated some time during the 3rd millennium BCE, but it did not reach northwest Arabia and Syria-Palestine before the end of the 2nd millennium. Others claim that the camel was originally domesticated in southern Arabia for the use of its milk and from there was introduced at around 2500–1500 BCE into Somalia and Socotra. Some propose that the camel was first domesticated for use as a pack animal, and only later did certain societies learn to use its other by-products and services. Some propose that the dromedary, which is better adapted to hot climates than the Bactrian camel, was developed in Arabia from the two-humped camel especially to withstand heat, as a result of the rise of the overland incense trade developed by Semites around 2000 BCE. The overland trade is reflected in the Joseph story: "Then they [Joseph's brothers] sat down to eat; and looking up they saw a caravan of Ishmaelites coming from Gilead, with their camels carrying gum, balm, and resin, on their way to carry it down to Egypt" (Gen 37:25).

Textual references to the camel and finds of skeletal remains in the Near East dated to before the end of the 2nd millennium BCE are rare. This led W. F. Albright to conclude that the camel could not have been domesticated before the end of the 12th cent. BCE and that references to camels in Genesis and Exodus are anachronistic (Albright 1949, 207). Albright maintained that the camel's early appearance in Bible stories in Gen 12:14-16; 24:10-67; 31:17-35; 37:25 is out of place. Accordingly, its first appearance in the Bible at the proper historical time is during the period of the settlement of Canaan, as described in Gideon's encounter with the Midianites in Judg 6–7.

Close examination of the domestication process and the evolution of relatively late implements indicates that the camel was actually domesticated long before the year 1100 BCE in southern Arabia, rather than in its northern regions, until the period suggested by Albright (Bulliet 1975, 36–38). Evidence from the Near East shows camel domestication and use, although not widespread, in 2500–1400 BCE. It is quite possible that local tribes in the area owned a few of the animals, perhaps as articles of prestige, without being heavily involved in breeding them. Thus, the presence of camels in the patriarchal stories can be defended, and the story can be treated as primary evidence of camel use, without disputing Albright's contention that camel-breeding nomads did not exist in Syria and northern Arabia until later (Bulliet 1975, 54–67).

The camel's anatomy requires a special harness with straps, known as a withers-strap, that goes between or around the humps or is supported by a saddle over one hump (Gen 31:34). As a pack animal, the camel was used in many Near Eastern communities. This is reflected in the traditions assigning the camel to the Ishmaelites (Gen 37:25) and the Amalekites (Judg 6:5; 1 Sam 15:3).

As a herd animal, the camel became known in Syria-Palestine only after control of the incense trade had passed to the Semites, who then had a good use for the camels as pack and riding animals (Gen 24; 31:34), rather than entirely subsistence related (2 Kgs 8:9). However, its by-products continued to be used, especially its dung and hair, which, together with black wool, was used for weaving tents and nets.

In addition to riding (Isa 21:7), camels were given as royal presents, as when Ben-Hadad gave to Elisha forty loaded camels (2 Kgs 8:9). The Bible records that David had large herds of camels under the charge of an individual from Arabia (1 Chr 27:30).

Like other domesticated animals, the camel was susceptible to diseases, as mentioned in Zech 14:15, "And a plague like this plague shall fall on the horses, the mules, the camels, the donkeys." Whether the camel was domesticated first for its milk or meat, there is a clear prohibition against consuming its meat (Lev 11:4; Deut 14:7), but nothing is said about drinking its milk.

The presence of the camel in Iron Age II Palestine is well substantiated. SENNACHERIB (704–681 BCE) makes the following claim after his campaign in Judah: "I drove out (of them) 200,150 people, young and old, male and female, horses, mules, donkeys, camels, big and small cattle beyond counting and considered them booty" (Pritchard 1969, 288). That the Judeans had camels is illustrated on a relief, which shows Judean refugees from Lachish leaving the besieged city with a loaded camel. The zooarchaeological record indeed verifies the presence of this animal at the site during Sennacherib's time.

Assyrian and later military campaigns against Egypt can be traced in the zooarchaeological record. About 500 dromedary bones were found at Tell Jemmeh, the majority of which belong to the Assyrian (675–600 BCE) and neo-Babylonian/Persian (ca. 600–332 BCE) periods. However, they represent only a very small proportion of the faunal remains: only 25 percent of the Assyrian faunal sample, and 35–47 percent of the neo-Babylonian/Persian sample. It has been suggested that the camels were assembled at the site as part of the Assyrian military campaigns against Egypt. The camels were used for travel in the northern Sinai from Tell Jemmeh to Egypt. One such example is recorded by Esarhadon (680–669 BCE). In his tenth campaign, when crossing the Sinai from Raphiah he "put [water bottles] . . . upon the camels which all the kings of Arabia had brought" (Pritchard 1969, 292). *See* ANIMALS OF THE BIBLE.

Bibliography: William F. Albright. *The Archaeology of Palestine* (1949); Oded Borowski. *Every Living Thing: Daily Use of Animals in Ancient Israel* (1998); R. W. Bulliet. *The Camel and the Wheel* (1975); J. B. Pritchard. *Ancient Near Eastern Texts Relating to the Old Testament* (1969).

ODED BOROWSKI

CAMEL BRAND. *See* WASM.

CAMEL'S HAIR [τριχῶν καμήλου trichōn kamēlou].

John the baptizer "was clothed with camel's hair, and had a leather girdle around his waist" (Mark 1:6; Matt 3:4), probably an allusion to Elijah (2 Kgs 1:8). The prophets' "hairy mantel" (Zech 13:4) is probably related to Elijah's dress. Camel's hair was used for making coats and tents and was also worn as a sign of mourning. Jesus contrasted John the baptizer's camel's hair clothing with the "soft garments" worn by those who live in kings' houses (Matt 11:8; Luke 7:25).

Bibliography: P. Joüon. "Le costume d'Élie et celui de Jean Baptiste: Étude Lexicographique." *Bib* 16 (1935) 74–81.

CRAIG A. EVANS

CAMEL'S THORN [ἀσπάλαθος aspalathos]. Camel's

thorn, a low-lying shrub, is mentioned in the "Praise of Wisdom" in Sir 24:15. An extract from this bush was part of a perfume ointment used for anointing in the Temple (Exod 30:22-38). This extract is also a referent for ancient "manna." By listing such a term in Sir 24, the sapiential author is explicitly linking Wisdom with priestly activities. *See* PERFUME.

SAMUEL L. ADAMS

CAMP [חָנָה khanah, מַחֲנֶה makhaneh; παρεμβολή

parembolē, στρατοπεδεύω stratopedeuō]. A temporary place of residence for a group of people; the act of setting up such a dwelling; a band of people. The term in the Pentateuch frequently refers to Israel's wilderness dwelling, and the process of settling and resettling that residence (Exod 14:2; 19:16-17). The placement of the tabernacle in relation to the camp varies among the pentateuchal writers (Exod 33:7; Num 1:50–2:2). Of great concern was keeping that which was "unclean" out of the "camp" (Lev 13:46; Num 5:2-3; 12:14; Deut 23:10-14), therefore, purification took place outside the "camp" (Lev 16:26-28; Num 19:7-9). Hebrews draws on such legislation to explain Jesus' death outside of Jerusalem, and in turn directs his followers outside the parembolē (13:11-13).

Camp also indicates non-Israelite settlements, particularly those of armies. The Ammonites (1 Sam 11:11) and Philistines (1 Sam 13:17) resided in *camps*; Judith encountered Holofernes at the Assyrians' *camp*; the conflict in 1 Macc takes place between the *camp* of Judas Maccabeus (1 Macc 4:5) and that of the Gentiles (1 Macc 4:7); and Paul was imprisoned in the Roman army's **parembolē**, or *barracks* (Acts 21:34).

At times *mahaneh* refers to a group of people, for instance the tribes of Israel, or *encampments*, which were broken into *companies* (Num 2, צָבָא tsava'). A military camp also can indicate not only the dwelling of the troops, but the *army* itself (1 Sam 17:1, 46). *See* MILITARY; TABERNACLE; UNCLEAN.

LISA MICHELE WOLFE

CANA kay'nuh [קָנֶה qaneh; Κανά Kana]. The name

for this Galilean village probably comes from the Hebrew 'qaneh', which means reed. In the NT, Cana is mentioned only in the Gospel of John (2:1-11; 4:46; 21:2). Josephus mentions living in Cana during his stay in Galilee (*Life*, 86). Beyond these references, the location of Cana of Galilee is uncertain. Ancient pilgrim literature mentions primarily two locations as veneration sites. One of these, Kefr Kenna, is just 4 mi. from Nazareth and on the road to Capernaum and Bethsaida. This location suggests the site arose as a conveniently accessible location for pilgrims. On the other hand, the other site, Khirbet Qana, is 8 mi. northwest of Nazareth on the north side of the Bet Netofa Valley. This identification better fits the account of Josephus, which situates Cana near the Plain of Asochis (Josephus, *Life*, 208). Moreover, since 1998, the University of Puget Sound has conducted an archaeological excavation at Khirbet Qana and initial results confirm the site's identification as Cana of Galilee. The excavation has revealed an active settlement at the location from the Hellenistic though the early Arab periods. Especially notable is a cave that matches the description of a veneration cave in pilgrim accounts of Cana.

Unfortunately, identifying the probable historical site of Cana does not make the story of Jesus' sign at the wedding in Cana easier to interpret. Indeed, while 19th cent. explorers were busy trying to locate the historical Cana, 19th cent. biblical critics were troubled by the "vulgarity" of the account of Jesus' activity there. To them, the story of the wedding at Cana, especially the steward's comment after tasting the good wine (John 2:10) implied both that Jesus was keeping company with drunken guests, and that he had contributed to a celebration more appropriate to the wine god, Bacchus, than the God of Israel! The miracle did not seem edifying.

Recent interpretation has moved away from this moralistic focus to consider the story's symbolic potential. Given the introduction of the Word as sharing in the creation with God (1:1-4), this first sign becomes a manifestation of Jesus' ongoing creative activity. In the prologue, the glory of the Word is revealed as "full of grace and truth" (1:14). So too, at this wedding feast, Jesus' glory is revealed—symbolized by abundant wine that fills the jars to the brim. When Jesus returns to

Cana, the recollection of this sign sets the scene for his second sign—healing the son of a Gentile officer (4:46). Here again, an act of grace evokes belief in Jesus, this time on the part of a whole Gentile household (4:53-54). Thus, in the Gospel of John, the narrator carefully locates the first two "signs" of Jesus as Cana, even though the sick boy was at Capernaum. As a result, in the Johannine tradition, Cana emerges as the initial locus of Jesus' earthly ministry, in contrast to the focus on Capernaum in the synoptic tradition.

Bibliography: Peter Richardson. "What Has Cana to Do with Capernaum?" *NTS* 48 (2002) 314–331.

COLLEEN M. CONWAY

CANAAN, CANAANITES kay'uh-nuhn [כְּנַעַן; kena'an; Χανααν Chanaan]. 1. Ham's son and the grandson of Noah (Gen 9:18-27; 10:6). He is the eponymous ancestor of the Canaanite people. Noah curses Canaan to be literally "a slave of slaves" among his kin (Gen 9:22, 25-27).

2. A noun for "trader" or merchant (e.g., Hos 12:8; Prov 31:24; Job 40:30). The association of commerce with Canaanites continues with the mercantile power of the Phoenicians in the Iron Age.

3. In the Bible there are numerous references to the land of Canaan and to its inhabitants. One finds equivalents to both terms in extrabiblical sources. *Canaan* and *Canaanite* were terms still used in the NT (Acts 7:11; 13:19). The last named reference employs a traditional phrase, the "seven nations" or peoples of Canaan, drawing on earlier texts such as Deut 7:1 to describe the pre-Israelite inhabitants of the land. As a geographical term, Canaan refers to the eastern Mediterranean coastal area approximating the modern states of Lebanon and Israel (inclusive of the disputed territories), and parts of Syria such as its southern coast and lower reaches of the Orontes Valley. Hebrew is a "language of Canaan" (Isa 19:18), one of what scholars now refer to as Semitic languages.

In the OT, Canaan is depicted as both the land of promise and the location of a corrupting culture. Thus, Canaan is associated with blessing and danger.

A. Canaan and the Land of Promise in the Bible
B. Canaan(ites) in Ancient Near Eastern Texts
C. Canaanite Religions in the OT and in
   Modern Analysis
   1. Canaanite deities
   2. Canaanite polytheism and culture
D. Israel in and of Canaan
Bibliography

A. Canaan and the Land of Promise in the Bible
According to Gen 12:1-3, Israel's ancestors were promised a land, descendants to occupy it, and blessings through them for the families of the earth. These promises, which begin with the command to Abram and Sarah to leave their country and to go to "the land that I (= God) will show you" (12:1), are a central theme in the Pentateuch. This "land" can be described in various ways in pentateuchal texts. On occasion the land is referred to by its various non-Israelite inhabitants. Among the inhabitants are the Hittites, Girgashites, Jebusites, Horites, Amorites, Hivites, Perizzites, Amalekites, Geshurites, Maacathites, Kenites, Kenizzites, Kadmonites, Philistines, Rephaim, Anakim/Anakites, Caphtorim, and Horim. As noted previously, one tradition describes Canaan as inhabited by seven nations before the emergence of Israel, but that number is a representative one rather than exhaustive. Some of these population groups of Canaan are mentioned in extrabiblical texts and some are not. The Philistines, e.g., are known from Egyptian texts as one of the "Sea Peoples" who are coming into the eastern Mediterranean region in the time of Ramesses III in the early 12th cent. BCE. The Hittites and the Amorites, likewise, are broad ethnic/cultural terms known from extrabiblical texts. The majority of the names listed above, however, are preserved solely in the OT. Moreover, from the perspective of the biblical writers, some of these population groups were present in their day and others were known only from tradition. In the latter category come the Rephaim. A late comment like Gen 12:6b, "at that time the Canaanites were in the land," reflects a perspective far removed in time from that of the ancestral period. The books of Joshua and Judges portray Israel's occupation of and progressive settlement in the promised land. Casual readers may infer from certain claims in Joshua that much of the pre-Israelite population of Canaan was destroyed, but the books of Judges and 1–2 Samuel make it clear that such was not the case.

Geographic descriptions of the land Canaan are general and overlapping, like many of the references to the inhabitants of the land. In Gen 15:17-21, the land promised to Abraham's descendants extends from the River of Egypt (probably the modern Wadi el Arish) to the Euphrates River. Canaanites are but one of ten population groups listed in this passage, and the land of promise is not described explicitly as Canaan. One should not assume, therefore, that the land of Canaan is synonymous with the vast region succinctly described in 15:18b-21, although a significant part of it could be referred to as Canaan. The territory described would be that also attributed to the rule of David and Solomon (1 Kgs 4:20-21).

The victory song of Moses and Miriam contains a reference to the "melting" in fear of "all the inhabitants of Canaan" (Exod 15:15). Since those inhabitants are mentioned in context with the Philistines, Edom, and Moab, perhaps they are a catchall term for those inhabitants not included among the other three peoples. Edom and Moab are not part of the land of Canaan in other biblical texts, although they are linked in story and genealogy with Israel's ancestors (Gen 19:30-38; *see* below).

According to the Table of Nations, "Canaan" is the son of Ham (10:6). That the land of Canaan derives from his name is not stated explicitly, but it is implied in what else is narrated about Canaan's descendants. Sidon is the firstborn son of Canaan as well as a city in the territory of Canaan. Moreover, several of the descendants of Canaan are population groups elsewhere associated with Canaan (10:15-19). Sidon was a prominent city on the east coast of the Mediterranean in the 2nd millennium BCE, and became a well-known Phoenician city-state in Iron Age II, where its fortunes were sometimes linked with Tyre to its south. *Sidonian* was also a recognized term in Iron Age II for "Phoenician" or for inhabitants of the Syrian-Lebanese coastal territory.

B. Canaan(ites) in Ancient Near Eastern Texts

Egypt had political control of much of the land of Canaan at various points in the Middle and Late Kingdoms of the 2nd millennium BCE. For example, Egyptian diplomatic correspondence from the Late Bronze Age (ca. 1550–1200 BCE) preserves several references to the land of Canaan and its inhabitants. In the so-called TELL EL AMARNA tablets one finds references to the "land[s] of Canaan" (EA 8:15-17, 25; 14:II, 26; 30:1; 110:49; 131:61; 148:47; 151:50), the "province of Canaan" (EA 36:15), "cities of Canaan" (EA 137:76), "kings/rulers in Canaan" (EA 30:1; 109:46; 367:8), and "Canaanites" (EA 9:19). The correspondence cited comes from Alashia (probably Cyprus), Babylon, Byblos, Egypt, and Tyre, demonstrating wide acquaintance with the terminology.

In this same correspondence there are references to a social class or group of people known as the HABIRU who are mobile, unruly, and causing trouble. Some scholars have interpreted the term as a cognate form to the term *Hebrew*. Note, e.g., that Abram is called "the Hebrew" (Gen 14:13) in his dealings with other inhabitants of the land. Scholars have even interpreted some of the references to the Habiru in the Tell el Amarna correspondence as indications of the emerging Israelite tribes in Canaan, but this seems unlikely. Indeed, the linguistic equation between Habiru and Hebrew is problematic.

In Egyptian usage, neither Canaan nor Canaanite would be exclusive terms for the land and inhabitants. As with the biblical writers, several overlapping terms can be used for the geography and peoples of Canaan. For example, toward the end of the famous stele celebrating the conquests of Pharaoh Merneptah (ca. 1210 BCE), there is a reference to Egyptian victories over Hatti, Canaan, Ashkelon, Gezer, Yenoam, Israel and Hurru. Hatti, Canaan, and Hurru are general toponyms, and while they are not synonyms, they can sometimes

be used interchangeably. *Hatti* is related to the word for Hittites and reflects their presence and influence in Syria in the Late Bronze Age. Hurru is a typical Egyptian term for greater Syria. Ashkelon, Gezer, and Yenoam are cities of Hurru/Canaan. The name *Israel* is marked with the indicator for a people rather than for land or city.

From the 2nd cent. BCE (Hellenistic Period) some coins minted in Beirut refer to that city as "in Canaan." The language is Phoenician. Some coins with Greek inscriptions from Beirut use an abbreviation for its location (Φ PH), which very likely stands for Phoenicia. This numismatic data indicate a link between the older Semitic term *Canaan* and one of its successor terms, *Phoenicia*. The Phoenicians of the Iron Age and later are one continuation of the broader Canaanite culture of the Middle and Late Bronze ages. The accounts of conflicts in Israel during the Omride Dynasty (9th cent. BCE, during the time of Elijah and Elisha) in 1–2 Kings are one reflection of the emerging mercantile economy of the Phoenician city-states. Stated differently, the tensions between Israel and the Phoenician cults of Baal are a continuation of the polarity between Israel and Canaan depicted in the Pentateuch, Joshua and Judges.

C. Canaanite Religions in the OT and in Modern Analysis

A single religion for the Canaanites is not assumed by the biblical writers, nor should it be by modern readers. There were various religious cults just as there were various population groups in the land. The term *Canaanite Religion* is simply a modern category in which to place the variety of cults and beliefs of the region.

The biblical writers offer strong criticism of the religious practices of Canaan. In Deuteronomy, e.g., both the people and the worship centers of Canaan are to be rejected categorically by the Israelites coming into the land (Deut 7:1-6; 12:2-7). Several characteristics of public worship in Canaan are noted in the instructions to destroy the Canaanite shrines rather than adapting them for Israelite worship. Shrines can be set on hills and associated with trees. The succinct descriptions imply an open-air format as the most common type. No temples (i.e., houses for deities) are mentioned in the two lists, but they did exist at the larger worship centers, as archaeological research has made abundantly clear. For example, multiple temples dating to the Late Bronze Age have been discovered at HAZOR and BETH SHAN, representing Canaanite religious practices under the political oversight of Egypt. No deities are named either in the brief Deuteronomic instructions, but they are represented by the images associated with the shrines. There are explicit references to altars, standing stone/pillars, wooden poles, and images of deities, all of which should be destroyed. Not all of the rituals and symbolic functions associated with these cultic imple-ments are known. Even common ritual practices such as animal sacrifice on a large open-air altar may represent significantly different meanings for participants. Smaller altars could be used for the burning of incense, itself a sacrificial act that became very popular in the Iron Age. The standing stones are more obscure in meaning; suggestions range from phallic symbols to pedestals for deities. The wooden poles (אֲשֵׁרִים ’asherim) are also difficult to explain fully as cultic objects. They may represent fertility due to their origin from a green tree. They may also represent a goddess, ASHERAH, perhaps a mother-goddess figure. The evidence for this in the OT is ambiguous, but Iron Age inscriptions from Kuntillat Ajrud and Khirbet el Qom, which mention Asherah, have been taken by some as a reference to a goddess and even as the consort of Yahweh.

Instead of multiple sanctuaries for animal sacrifice, Deuteronomy urges one site, a place from among all the tribes where the Lord would "put his name there" (12:5, 14, 21). That site is not named, but after the construction of an Israelite TEMPLE in Jerusalem, the Lord's "choice" was commonly identified with that city (1 Kgs 8:20; Ps 78:67-72; 132). A Phoenician king, Hiram from Tyre, assisted in the construction of the Israelite Temple in Jerusalem (1 Kgs 5:1-12). The description of its floor plan and cultic implements in 1 Kgs 6–7 have analogies elsewhere in the Middle East in tripartite, long-room temples. The closest par. currently known come from northern Syria (Tell Tayanat, Ain Dara). Similar things can be said for the basic categories of sacrifice carried out at the Temple. Some of the terms used in the OT have cognates in extrabiblical texts.

1. Canaanite deities

There are several Canaanite deities mentioned in the OT. A common reference for them is literally "other gods," a phrase that communicates very little about them. In a retrospective summary, an author states that upon entering Canaan the Israelites abandoned the Lord their God and "followed other gods from the gods of the peoples around them" (Judg 2:12). In con-text, the author also mentions the BAALs in the plural (בְּעָלִים ba‘alim), Baal in the singular, and the Astartes in the plural (2:11-13). The use of the plural refer-ences likely functions as general categories, and taken together they mean something like gods and goddesses (1 Sam 7:4). *Baal* is a common term, meaning owner or master, and several deities, including those who had other names or titles, could be referred to as Baal (Num 25:1-5; 2 Kgs 1:2-4). Phoenician and Punic inscrip-tions from the Iron Age demonstrate the popularity of the term for both gods and goddesses. Some Israelites referred to Yahweh as Baal (Hos 2:16), although the prophet Hosea and other biblical writers rejected the term as inappropriate for Israel's God.

ASTARTE is a particular goddess. She is referred to as the God of the Sidonians (= a Phoenician deity, 1 Kgs 11:5). As might be expected, Iron Age Phoeni-cian inscriptions refer to her. A shrine was built for her by Solomon on a hill east of the Temple area in Jerusa-lem; and later it was destroyed by King Josiah (2 Kgs 23:13). Astarte may also have been the consort of one or more of the Baals in the various Canaanite cults.

The book of Genesis preserves terminology used for deities in Canaan. Abram, e.g., meets the priest-king of Salem, who blesses Abram by "God most high, creator of heaven and earth" (14:19-20). This is generic termi-nology for a high deity in Canaan. Similar terminology appears in Iron Age inscriptions. The biblical writer has Abram reply by reference to "Yahweh [= LORD in most English translations], God Most High, creator of heaven and earth" (14:22). That reply adopts the generic terminology for a high deity and applies it to the God of Israel. Something similar takes place with the phrase אֵל שַׁדַּי ’el shadday, often translated as "God Almighty" (Gen 17:1). It is another phrase for a high deity, recognizable in Canaan, which is applied to Yahweh, the God of Israel.

Thus, in comparing various terminologies for deities in the OT, one finds a two-pronged approach at work. On the one hand, some terminology for deity common in Canaan is also employed by Israel to refer to Yahweh the God of Israel. On the other hand, other common terminology (e.g., Baal) is rejected for application to Yahweh. Both phenomena are to be expected. Most religions based on claims of particularity or uniqueness nevertheless have elements in common with their broader context.

2. Canaanite polytheism and culture

Polytheism was the primary religious pattern in Canaan. Thus the various biblical injunctions against polytheism and for the exclusive worship of Yahweh set Israel apart in the Canaanite context. The same thing can be said about the prohibition against the making of graven images for deities in Israel (Exod 20:4-6), since archaeological investigation demonstrates the avail-ability and even prominence of images for the divine in Canaan. Some of the commands against the worship of other deities, however, tacitly assume their reality and presuppose their appeal. This seems to be the context of the second commandment in the Decalogue, where Israel is asked to "have no other deities besides/before" Yahweh (Exod 20:3). There is frank acknowledgment elsewhere that Israel's ancestors worshiped other gods (Josh 24:2, 15), and the repeated polemic against the worship of other gods among the biblical writers strong-ly implies that at least some Israelites found polytheism a more satisfactory option. Modern scholars are divided over the frequency of polytheism in Israel, especially in the premonarchical and monarchical periods.

There was once a strong tendency among scholars to conclude that Canaanite religion was heavily influenced by fertility concerns and thus sexually charged and immoral. This assumption takes polemical references in the OT as blanket descriptions of Israel's opponents and tends to universalize from the occasional text or scattered remains of material culture that are attributed to the Canaanites. Among many current scholars, however, the tendency is in the other direction, namely, to deny such things as sacred prostitution or other sexual rites as a part of Canaanite religion. The degree to which concerns for fertility also influenced various Canaanite cultic practices is a complex question, for which there are no easy answers.

The rejection of Canaanite culture and religion in the Bible, while widespread and polemical, is not absolute. One sees this dynamic in the ancestral stories of Genesis. On the one hand, Abraham sends his servant to relatives in north Syria in order to procure a wife for his son Isaac because he did not want his son to marry a Canaanite woman (Gen 24:1-67). Isaac's wife, Rebecca, complains about the local Hittite women and seeks a wife for her son, Jacob, from her relatives rather than from the Canaanites (Gen 27:46–28:5). On the other hand, Abraham married Keturah after the death of Sarah (Gen 25:1-6), and Judah, one of the sons of Jacob, married a Canaanite woman (Gen 38:2). Keturah is not described as a Canaanite, but is one of the inhabitants of the land. Their descendants are associated with the peoples to the east of Canaan, who live in the wilderness areas and the fringes of sedentary culture.

Kinship is an important marker of social relations in the ancient Near East, and its influence on defining the land of Canaan and its various inhabitants should not be overlooked. Claims of kinship serve to explain political alliances, settlement patterns, and cultural profiles. Some of these things approximate what modern people understand by ethnicity, but in spite of the familial language, they do not define racial identity. The Israelites are linked with the Arameans and Syria through Laban and Nahor (Gen 22:20-24; 25:20; compare 11:27 and Deut 26:5), with the Edomites through Esau (Gen 36:1), and with the Moabites and Ammonites through Lot (Gen 19:30-38). All but the Arameans are peoples located east of the main tribal settlements of Israel in Canaan. In the Iron Age Ammon, Moab, and Edom became nation-states. The Moabites had a patron deity named Chemosh, and the Ammonites had a deity known as Milcom. The same may be true of the Edomites and their worship of a deity named Qos or Qaus, but less is known about them. Some scholars, therefore, have proposed that the Moabite and Ammonite states in Iron Age II practiced monolatry, giving marked preference for their patron deity in distinction to other options that would have been recognized but subsumed in the official state cult. It has been suggested that the more exclusive preference for Yahweh among the Israelite tribes has a partial analogy in the type of tribal monolatry practiced in Ammon and Moab on the fringes of Canaan.

D. Israel in and of Canaan

With a dominant tone of rejection, the biblical writers make a fundamental distinction between Israel and the Canaanites. As stated succinctly in Lev 18:3, Israel is not to be like the Egyptians, from the land where it once lived, or like the Canaanites, in the land where it would go to live. Even if scholars question the historical reliability of the story behind this distinction, one can grasp the self-understanding it represents. It broadly influences instruction in the Pentateuch and underlies much of the prophetic critique. In current scholarship there is broad agreement that the people called Israel, who emerge in Canaan at some point in the early Iron Age (if not earlier), should be considered as one subset of Canaanite culture. For some scholars this means that Israel's historical origins are literally in Canaan, and the ancestral accounts of an outsider status reflect an ideological stance rather than historical memory. For virtually all scholars Israel's self-proclaimed particularity should be set in a larger Canaanite cultural continuum. Indeed, Israel could hardly be anything else than Canaanite, culturally speaking, regardless of its particular antecedents and the uniqueness of its religious claims.

Along with the claims of original outsider status, there are voices that acknowledge the Canaanite connection with Israel's identity. Ezekiel, e.g., portrays Jerusalem's origins in parabolic form as Canaanite: "your birth was in the land of the Canaanites; your father was an Amorite and your mother a Hittite" (16:3). Of course, Jerusalem was a city of Canaan, and had been in existence for centuries before it fell finally to David (2 Sam 5). Its emergence as the capital of Israel and Judah did not erase its heritage. Thus, for Israelites, Canaan was more than a land of promise: Its geography and culture also served to define Israel.

Bibliography: Othmar Keel and Christoph Uehlinger. *Gods, Goddesses, and Images of God in Ancient Israel.* Allan W. Mahnke, trans. (1996); N. P. Lemche. *The Canaanites and Their Land* (1991); A. F. Rainey. "Who Is a Canaanite? A Review of the Textual Evidence." BASOR 304 (1996) 1–15; Mark S. Smith. *The Origins of Biblical Monotheism: Israel's Polytheistic Background and the Ugaritic Texts* (2001); Mark S. Smith. *The Early History of God. Yahweh and Other Deities in Ancient Israel* (2002).

J. ANDREW DEARMAN

CANAAN, CONQUEST OF. *See* ISRAEL, HISTORY OF.

CANAL. The eastern frontier canal and the fortresses along its banks guarded the Egyptian end of the ancient north Sinai road. The Bible preserves a reference to a canal in the place name, PI-HAHIROTH, lit. "mouth of the canal(s)," a stop on the exodus route near MIGDOL (Exod 14:2, 9; Num 33:7-8). *See* EGYPT.

CANANAEAN kay´nuh-nee´uhn [Κανanalος Kananaios]. Derived from קָנָא qana', "be zealous." An appellation for Jesus' disciple Simon (Matt 10:4; Mark 3:18) that differentiates him from Simon Peter and indicates his affiliation with the Zealots. In Luke 6:15 and Acts 1:13, the equivalent appellation "Zealot" (ζηλωτής zēlōtēs) is used for Simon. *See* ZEALOT.

CANDACE kan-duh´see [Κανδακή Kandakē]. Candace is not a proper name but the hereditary royal title for the Ethiopian queen mother. Bion of Soli's writings (2nd cent. BCE) identify the Ethiopian queen mother as the **Kandakē**. Her position of political and economic power made her the *de facto* ruler of ancient ETHIOPIA (a Sudanese region along the Nile known as Meröe) while her son was regarded as the divine spiritual head of the nation. In the NT, the Candace is the employer of the Ethiopian eunuch treasurer converted by Philip (Acts 8:26-40). The identity of this Candace cannot be determined.

HEIDI S. GEIB

CANE [קָנֶה qaneh]. An aromatic grass or reed often associated with **bosem** בֹּשֶׂם, a fragrant or SWEET CANE. The most likely choice for this wetland reed is the *Acorus calamus* (*Araceae*), native to the marshlands of Persia and India. The rhizome, which is dried for transport, has a very sweet, lingering aroma suitable as an ingredient in concocting perfumes. This may explain its inclusion in the recipe for the sacred anointing oil (Exod 30:23). The market for this exotic plant is also demonstrated in its listing among the items that formed the international luxury trade that are suitable for sacrificial offering (Jer 6:20; Ezek 27:19). The poetic reference to CALAMUS or "sweet cane" in Song 4:10's depiction of a pleasure garden includes it among the choicest, most fragrant plants known to the author and his audience. *See* PLANTS OF THE BIBLE.

VICTOR H. MATTHEWS

CANNEH kan´uh [כַּנֶּה kanneh]. A geographical reference (probably a city name) mentioned only in Ezek 27:23, often understood as a variant of CALNEH. This passage in Ezekiel may well have come from an independent list of trading commodities and their sources, lending plausibility to those who suggest that Canneh (Akkadian **Kannu'**) was located in Upper Mesopotamia near HARAN and (Beth-)EDEN, on one of the great trade routes from Assyria to Syria. Calneh, however, is probably to be located closer to CARCHEMISH to the west. Assyrian sources attest a royal highway in the region, thus facilitating Canneh's robust development

as a center of trade. The Targum identifies Canneh as the city of Nisibis, a prominent Assyrian city farther to the east.

WILLIAM BARNES

CANON OF THE NEW TESTAMENT. The common designation for the Scriptures that comprise the second part of the Christian Bible, the New Testament (NT). When using the reference "NT canon," scholars generally refer to those twenty-seven early Christian books that were selected by the church for inclusion in the Christian Bible. The primary canonical issues that have led to considerable scholarly debate in recent years include the definition of Scripture and how canon is distinguished from it (*see* § A and B), the time and location of the acceptance of Christian writings as *Scripture* (§ C), the social factors that gave rise to a biblical canon for the church, and the criteria used in the selection process (§ D and E).

The study of canon formation is made more complex by that fact that the early church left no traditions behind to describe the processes that led to the identification and selection of the Christian Scriptures that were included in its Bible. The following discussion will focus largely on these issues that helped shape the contours of the NT canon of Scriptures.

A. Scripture in Early Christianity
B. Prophecy, Spirit, and Scripture
C. The Origins of a NT Canon
   1. Jesus and the NT Canon
   2. The OT of the early church
   3. Terms for canon and uses in antiquity
   4. A fixed scripture canon
D. The Emergence of An Old and
   New Testament
   1. Closing of the biblical canon
   2. The role of heresy
   3. Theological factors
   4. Historical factors
   5. Criteria for selection
      a. Apostolicity
      b. Orthodoxy
      c. Antiquity
      d. Use
   6. Collections of early Christian writings
E. Problems in the Formation of the NT Canon
   1. Decanonization
   2. Issues related to translation
   3. Issues related to the text of scripture
   4. Closure of the NT canon
F. Summary
Bibliography

A. Scripture in Early Christianity
   When the early church began, the notion of Scripture—that is, the belief that some writings reflected the

identity and will of God—was already well established among both Jews and Christians. The earliest Christians already accepted as Scripture many sacred writings that later comprised their OT Scriptures.

The notion of Scripture developed from a widespread belief in the existence of a "heavenly book" that contains both divine knowledge and decrees from God. The content of this heavenly book generally included wisdom, destinies (or laws), a book of works, and a book of life. This notion goes back to ancient Mesopotamia and Egypt where the heavenly book not only indicated the future plans of God but also the destinies of human beings. This is similar to the Jewish Scriptures when Moses pleads with God to forgive the Israelites for their sin: "But now if you will only forgive their sin—but if not, blot me out of the book that you have written." But the Lord said to Moses: "Whoever has sinned against me I will blot out of my book" (Exod 32:32-33). Likewise, the psalmist puts his future in the future plans of God: "Your eyes beheld my unformed substance. In your book were written all the days that were formed for me, when none of them as yet existed" (Ps 139:15-16).

In the NT, Paul speaks of God having a "book of life" in which the names of his colleagues in ministry are found (Phil 4:3). In the last book of the NT, all people are brought before the great white throne of God at the end of the ages and books were opened and "anyone whose name was not found written in the book of life was thrown into the lake of fire" (Rev 20:12, 15).

Belief in such divine books gave rise to the notion that the repository of divine knowledge and heavenly decrees are contained in an earthly divine book. Among the ancient Israelites, and long before the notion of a Bible existed, the Law was believed to have come directly from God. They believed that Moses proclaimed the words and ordinances of God (Exod 24:3) and that he was commissioned by God to write them down (Exod 34:4, 27). They also believed that God was the primary writer of the TEN COMMANDMENTS (Exod 34:1; Deut 4:13; 10:4). In time the Jews came to believe that the laws of God were written down and preserved in sacred writings. This belief played a pivotal role in the development of their notion of a revealed and authoritative Scripture.

By no later than the mid 2nd cent. BCE, *Scripture* became the common term to identify the Jewish sacred writings that now comprise the OT. Many other writings that were initially included in sacred collections were eventually excluded from the OT in the late 1st and early 2nd cent. The final fixing of the Hebrew Bible had not yet taken place when Palestinian Judaism directly and regularly influenced early Christianity, namely before 62–135 CE. Before the Christians separated from Judaism, many other books, often referred to as apocryphal and pseudepigraphal writings, were widely accepted as sacred Scripture by various sects of Jews.

While the notion of sacred writings is quite early in the history of Judaism (Deut 4:2), the designation "Scripture" is surprisingly rather late. The earliest known source that uses the term *Scripture* or *writing* (Greek = γραφή graphē; Lat. = *scriptura*) in its absolute sense, appears to be the legendary *Letter of Aristeas* (2nd cent. BCE) in which the author states: "We are exhorted through scripture also by the one who says thus, 'thou shalt remember the Lord, who did great and wonderful deeds in thee'" (*Ep. Arist.* 155). The author later clarifies the importance of the law of God (the Pentateuch), claiming that all of the laws have been made with righteousness in view and "that no ordinances have been made in scripture without purpose or fancifully, but to the intent that through the whole of our lives we may also practice justice to all mankind in our acts, remembering the all-sovereign God" (*Ep. Arist.* 168). These two examples do not define or defend the Scripture, but simply use it as a designation for sacred writings, and they assume that the readers will understand it in the same way. This, of course, suggests that its meaning is *prior* to the writing of the *Letter of Aristeas* and earlier than our current information shows.

Writing something down was often seen as a mark of revelation as in the case where God wrote down the law (Exod 24:12; 31:18; 32:15, 32; 34:1; Deut 4:13; 9:10). Moses wrote down the commandments of God (Exod 24:4; 34:27) and later the king of the nation was instructed to preserve the law by having it copied or reproduced (Deut 17:18). The act of writing down or copying the law of God was viewed as an act that declares the will of God.

The origin of this notion of Scripture among the Jews, of course, is traced to the biblical writers who spoke of the divine status of the words of God that were to be read and etched on doorposts (Deut 6:6-9). There are no references to the technical term *scriptures* in the OT itself, even though the notion of sacred writings did exist certainly during the penning of Deuteronomy. The presence and respect for sacred Scripture is more rarely frequent before the reforms of Josiah in 621 BCE, but there are frequent references in 1–2 Kings and 1–2 Chronicles that cite the failure of the Jews to keep the law of Moses or the law of God (1 Kgs 2:3; 2 Kgs 10:31; 14:6; 17:13; 19:26-28; 21:8; 22:3-13; 23:24-25; 1 Chr 16:40; 22:12; 2 Chr 6:16; 30:16; 35:26; Ezra 3:2; 7:6; Neh 8:1; Jer 2:8; 5:4-5; 44:10; Dan 9:11, 13). Before then, however, there are only a few references to observing the law of God (Hos 4:6; Amos 2:4).

Paul reflects the normative status of the Scriptures in his day and claims that they were written for his readers' benefit. Citing the story of Abraham's faith and God's promise, he writes: "Therefore his faith 'was reckoned to him as righteousness.' Now the words, 'it was reckoned to him,' were written not for his sake alone, but for ours also" (Rom 4:22-24a). He adds to this the purpose of the Scriptures, namely that "whatever was written in former days was written for our instruction" (Rom 15:4). After citing Deut 25:4, he claims that "it was indeed written for our sake, for whoever plows should plow in hope and whoever threshes should thresh in hope of a share in the crop" (1 Cor 9:10). Finally, after citing the fate of those mentioned in the Scriptures who grumbled and were destroyed, he writes: "These things happened to them to serve as an example, and they were written down to instruct us, on whom the ends of the ages have come" (1 Cor 10:11). In these examples, Paul claims that the Scriptures were not only for the past generations, but for the current one as well. The essence of or nature of Scriptures is that they are relevant, authoritative, and without respect of time. That is, they are adaptable to new circumstances.

One of the closest parallels to sacred writings outside of the biblical literature is probably Homer's *Iliad* and *Odyssey*. Heraclitus (ca. 1 BCE–1 CE), for instance, observes that children were trained in the writings of Homer and that they were to occupy their life to the end of their days (Heraclitus, *All.* I.2).

The Greek noun graphē ("writing") is used fifty-one times in the NT to refer to sacred Scripture (Mark 12:10; Luke 4:21; 22:37; John 2:22; 7:38; 42; 10:35; 13:18; 17:12; 19:24, 28, 36, 37; 20:9; Acts 1:16; 8:32, 35; Rom 4:2; 9:17; 10:11; 11:2; 2 Cor 4:13; Gal 3:8, 22; 4:30; 1 Tim 4:13; 5:18; 2 Tim 3:16; Jas 2:8, 23; 4:5; 1 Pet 2:6; 2 Pet 1:20). The plural form of "Scripture," "the Scriptures" (ταῖς γραφαῖς tais graphais) is found in Matt 21:42; 22:29; 26:54, 56; Mark 12:24; 14:49; Luke 24:27, 32, 45; John 5:39; Acts 17:2, 11; 18:24, 28; Rom 1:2; 15:4; 1 Cor 15:3, 4; 2 Pet 3:16. The verb "I write" (γράφω graphō) is sometimes used of the simple act of writing with no special connotations, but is often used in the absolute sense of sacred writings. In the perfect passive form of the verb, namely "it is written" (γέγραπται gegraptai), the verb most often refers to sacred Scripture. This word is used some sixty-five times in the NT in reference to Israel's and the church's sacred Scriptures (e.g., Matt 4:4-10; Luke 4:8; 19:46; 1 Cor 9:9). Frequently, the words "it is written" or "*just as* it is written" (καθὼς γέγραπται kathōs gegraptai) precede the quoting of a Scripture passage (Mark 1:2; Luke 2:23; Acts 7:42; and 15:15). The term *just as* occurs frequently in the NT and some 16 times in Romans alone (1:17; 2:24; 3:4, 10; 4:17; 8:36; 9:13, 33; 10:15; 11:8, 26; 12:19; 14:11; 15:3, 9, 21). Whether "it is written" or "just as it is written" is employed, both designations refer to the OT sacred Scriptures of Israel and the church. While it is often unclear which Scriptures are in view, there is little question that the Jewish Scriptures were believed to have a divine origin and functioned authoritatively for both synagogue and church. References to unknown scriptures (John 7:38 and Jas 4:5; *see also* 1 Cor 2:9; 9:10; Eph 5:14 and Luke 11:49) reflect the uncertainty in the 1st cent. over the scope of the Scripture collection.

In the time of Jesus, the term *Scripture* usually referred to the Law or to the Law and the Prophets, but on one occasion it also referred to the "psalms" (Luke 24:44). This reflects the incompleteness of the OT canon in the 1st cent. While the notion of Scripture was clearly present in the early Christian community, the adoption of new Christian Scriptures and the limits of the OT canon were not. Such decisions took centuries and are rooted in the Christian notion that the age of the Spirit had come upon the followers of Jesus.

B. Prophecy, Spirit, and Scripture

The origin of a Christian Scripture is rooted in the belief that the Holy Spirit had come upon the followers of Jesus. Prior to the emergence of the Christians, there was an ancient Jewish belief that prophecy and the presence of the spirit had vanished in Israel (1 Macc 14:40-41). That belief gave rise to the notion among some Jewish teachers that only writings produced during the time of the spirit-inspired prophets (Moses to Ezra) were acknowledged as sacred Scripture, and all writings after that did not belong in the Jewish Scriptures (Josephus, *Ag. Ap.* 1.43-44). This view did not reflect the views of some Jews who believed that the Spirit of God was active in their own community as well as in their writings. In the Essene sect, e.g., the author of the RULE OF THE COMMUNITY declares to the QUMRAN residents that anyone who spurns the decrees of the community also rejects the decrees of God, without allowing himself to be taught by the community counsel and concludes "for, by the spirit of the true counsel concerning paths of man, all his sins are atoned so that he can look at the life of life" (1QS 3.6-8) and later adds that "these are the counsels of the spirit for the sons of truth in the world" (1QS 4.6). The residents at Qumran believed that the presence and power of the Holy Spirit were active in their community and teachings. For example, one Essene writer calls upon God saying: "You [God] have graciously granted us Your Holy Spirit. Take pity on us" (4Q506 131-132 XI; *see also* CD 7:4; 1QS III, 7; 1QS IV, 21; 1QSb II, 22 and II, 24; 4Q213a I, 14; 4Q287, 13; 4Q416 2 II, 25; 4Q418 VIII, 6; 4Q509 97-98 I, 9).

The early Christians also believed that the Holy Spirit was still active in their midst, and that belief stands behind their production and eventual recognition of the NT Scriptures. Christians taught that the outpouring of the Holy Spirit came as a result of the activity of Jesus (John 7:39; 20:22; Luke 24:49; Acts 1:8; 2:17-18), and they recognized that the gift of prophecy in their churches (Rom 12:6; 1 Cor 12:29; 14:1, 3-5; compare Acts 21:4, 10-11). Paul believed that he had spoken by the Spirit when he wrote his letter to the Corinthians (1 Cor 7:40). The same is true for many early church writers. Clement of Rome, for instance, recognized that Paul wrote 1 Corinthians "with true inspiration" (*1 Clem.* 47.3), but adds that his own epistle was "written by us through the Holy Spirit" (63.2). The author of *2 Clem.* introduces *1 Clem.* 23.3 with the words, "for the prophetic word also says" (*2 Clem.* 11.2).

The early church father, Ignatius (ca. 115–117 CE), claiming that he spoke in the power of the spirit, wrote: "I spoke with a great voice—with God's own voice" and responded to those who accused him of saying this because he had previous knowledge of a situation, saying that "the Spirit was preaching and saying this" (*Ign. Phld.* 7.1*b*-2). The Montanists of the late 2nd cent. argued that the prophetic voice was still alive in the church and they produced many writings that they believed were prompted by the spirit. Their argument was so persuasive that even Tertullian (ca. 200), the great church father and teacher, joined their ranks. Justifying additional sacred books, he argued:

> It is mere prejudice to heed and value only past demonstrations of power and grace. Those people who condemn the one power of the one Holy spirit in accordance with chronological eras should beware. It is the recent instances to which far higher respect ought to be paid; for they already belong to the time of the End, and are to be prized as a superabundant increase of grace, which god, in accordance with the testimony of scripture, has destined for precisely this period of time. (*Intro. to Passio Perpetuae* 1.1-2).

In the first five centuries of the church, the inspiration of and being filled with the Spirit (essentially the same activity) are attributed to everyone who speaks or writes the truth of the gospel. The only time when something said or written was not considered inspired was when one spoke "heresy," that is, something contrary to the truth of God. Bishop Serapion (ca. 200 CE) rejected the Gospel of Peter, and attributed it to "some hole of heresy" that is, contrary to the truth of God (Eusebius, *Hist. eccl.* 6.12.4). He also rejected "pseudepigraphal" writings, that is, "writings that falsely bear their [apostles] names" (Eusebius, *Hist. eccl.* 6.12.2-3). The early Christians believed that the power of the Spirit was active in their midst and prophetic words were an essential component of their religious experience. Inspiration, at that time, was not limited to sacred writings, but included all speech led or prompted by the Spirit. Inspiration was a corollary to the recognition of the canonization of a book. Unlike many of the Pharisees, the primary sect of Judaism that survived the 1st cent. CE, the Christians did not believe that prophecy had ceased, and they continued to produce writings that they believed were inspired of God (2 Pet 3:15).

The practice of calling *Christian* writings "Scripture" came near the end of the 2nd cent. and that practice was neither automatic, universal, or instantaneous. Some of the early Christian writings, e.g., the Gospels, were widely received as authoritative sources of understanding who Jesus was and what he did almost from the beginning of the church, but they were not called "Scripture" until much later. Several NT writings were widely circulated and cited in the late 1st and early 2nd cent. churches, but their scriptural status had not yet been declared.

C. The Origins of a NT Canon
1. Jesus and the NT canon

The NT Scriptures had their origin in a story that gave identity, hope, and clarity of mission to the early Christians. That story is inextricably bound to the early church's belief in God's activity in Jesus of Nazareth, whom the early Christians accepted as their promised messiah, who was raised from the dead, and who delivers them from their sins and offers them hope (Rom 5:8-9; 10:9-10; 1 Cor 15:3-11; Eph 1:3-14). Their faith in Jesus as the Lord lies at the heart of the origins of the NT canon of Scripture. In the broadest definition of canon, namely a normative guide or authority, the earliest "canon" of the church was Jesus, that is, his life, teachings, and fate were all central to his followers and pivotal in their worship and mission. His story is what first gathered the Christian community together after his death and resurrection, and gave rise to its written traditions that were eventually identified as a fixed collection of Scriptures called the "New Testament" and read alongside its first Scriptures (the OT). This story of and about Jesus was first told in preaching (Acts 2:17-36) and teaching (1 Cor 15:3-8), and in time both the story and its implications for humanity were expanded and expressed in a variety of written forms (epistles, gospels, history, apocalyptic, and sermon). These writings formed what eventually became the NT biblical canon.

2. The OT canon of the early church

The earliest Christians also accepted the normative status of the OT writings along with an indeterminate collection of other noncanonical writings commonly designated apocryphal and pseudepigraphal writings. They rooted Jesus' life, ministry, and fate in their Jewish Scriptures. In the NT, Christians cited the OT writings largely, but not exclusively, in a prophetic manner contending that Jesus is the fulfillment of the prophecies of the OT Scriptures (e.g., Matt 1:23; 2:6, 13-15, 16-18; 1 Cor 15:3-5). They did not speak of a closed or fixed collection of NT or Christian Scriptures before the 4th cent. CE.

3. Terms for canon and uses in antiquity

The familiar ancient word *canon* (κανών kanōn, derived from κάννη kannē) and perhaps a loan word that has a par. in the Hebrew term קָנֶה qaneh, initially referred to a "measuring rod" or "measuring stick" (*see* Ezek 40:5). In time, it came to refer to guides or standards to follow in a variety of areas, whether in art, architecture, music, philosophy, or rhetoric. The word likely originated in Semitic languages of Sumerian origin and may be related to the Babylonian/Assyrian word **kannu**. Among the Greeks, the word came to refer to a standard or norm by which all things are judged or evaluated, whether the perfect form to follow in architecture or the infallible criterion (κριτή ριον kritērion) by which things are measured.

In the NT, **kanōn** (canon) is only found in Paul's letters where it speaks of guidelines established by God, the limits of Paul's ministry, and the boundaries of another's ministry (2 Cor 10:13, 15, 16). It is used once as the standard or norm of true Christianity (Gal 6:16). Later, Clement of Rome (ca. 90 CE) uses it in reference to the church's revealed truth when he encourages the church to "put aside empty and vain cares, and let us come to the glorious and venerable *rule of our tradition*" (*1 Clem* 7:2). Similarly, in Irenaeus *canon* refers to the essence or core of Christian doctrine saying that a true believer retains "unchangeable in his heart the *rule of the truth* which he received by means of baptism" (*Haer.* 1.9.4, ANF).

The ancient Alexandrians collected many volumes in their famous library in Egypt, and they produced something like lists of writers, called **pinakes** ("indexes"), whose Greek was used as a model for other writers. This was similar to Cicero's Lat. term *classes* (*classici*) and Quintilian's Latin word *ordo*. Indeed the very word *classic*, when applied to the ancient writers, suggests writers who were among those who had reached a certain standard of writing for others to imitate. The grammarians at the great library of Alexandria sought to preserve an accurate and faithful text of the classics in literature and provided lists or indexes (**pinakes**) that included the most commonly recognized ancient writers. Among them are Homer, Euripides, Menander, Demosthenes, and later Hesiod, Pindar, Sappho, Aeschylus, Sophocles, Aristophanes, Herodotus, Thucydides, and Aesop. In antiquity, one who wrote well is one who did not move far from these sources as models or examples to follow, whether in subject matter, style, or grammar. Those who ignored the classics when they wrote were largely ignored themselves or severely criticized. Not everything written in the ancient world was placed in that collection, but those that were included were copied with great care by those who were selected and trained to preserve the accuracy of their texts as well as order them for identification and location. The Greek grammarians at Alexandria selected Homer, the author of the *Iliad* and the *Odessey*, along with Hesiod, author of *Theogony* and *Erga* as the "standards" of epic poetry, and Pindar, Bacchylides, Sappho, Anacreon, Stesichorus, Simonides, Ibycus, Alcaeus, and Alcman became the nine standard lyric poets. Although the order differed in the various epigrams that listed these works, the names that comprised them were generally the same. It was a standard list.

The notion of a fixed biblical canon comprised of standard sacred writings that eventually emerged in both the Jewish and Christian communities may have been influenced by the Alexandrian standards or pinakes, and they are the only known par. to a fixed collection of revered writings in the ancient world. However, such thinking was not an initial part of the Jewish milieu in which the church was born. The development of a biblical canon, to which no book could be added or taken away, was a later development in the church, long after the production of those writings that eventually gained canonical status. The canonical process began with widespread use of Christian writings alongside of the OT Scriptures in the churches, and it took place in a culture with many kinds of canons or guides.

The Gospels and some of the writings of Paul received favorable reception in churches in the 1st and 2nd cent., but the widespread practice of identifying them as "Scripture" and by author was a later practice that was not common among the early Christians until the end of the 2nd cent. Clement of Rome shows awareness of the language of 1 Cor 15:23 and 1 Cor 12:21 in *1 Clem.* 37.3-4, but he makes no mention of Paul as the author even though he knew it as he demonstrates in *1 Clem.* 47:1-3. Early in the 2nd cent., the Gospel of Matthew was frequently cited in churches, but not by its author. It was cited as sayings of Jesus, its primary subject, rather than by its author. For example, Clement of Rome frequently shows awareness of and dependence upon Matthew, but he does not cite the Gospel by name (compare, for instance, *1 Clem.* 16.17 with Matt 11:29; *1 Clem.* 24:5 with Matt 13:3-9; and *1 Clem.* 46.8 with Matt 18:6 and 26:24. In the case of the Epistle of Barnabas, compare *Barn.* 4.14 with Matt 22:14; *Barn.* 5.8 with Matt 9:13; *Barn.* 7.9 with Matt 27:28. In the writings of Ignatius, compare *Ign. Smyrn.* 1.1 with Matt 3:15; and *Ign. Phld.* 3.1 with Matt 15:13. In the case of *2 Clement*, compare *2 Clem.* 3.2 with Matt 10:32; *2 Clem.* 4.2 with Matt 7:21; and *2 Clem.* 6.2 with Matt 16:26. In Polycarp's *To the Philippians,* compare *Pol. Phil.* 2.3 with Matt 5:3 and 5:10; *Pol. Phil.* 12.3 with Matt 5:16, 44, 48. In the *Martyrdom of Polycarp*, compare *Mart. Pol.* 4 with Matt 10:23; *Mart. Pol.* 6.2 with Matt 10:36 and 27:5; *Mart. Pol.* 7.1 with Matt 26:55 and 6:10; *Mart. Pol.* 8:1 with Matt 21:7; *Mart. Pol.* 11.2 with Matt 25:46; and *Mart. Pol.* 14.2 with Matt 20:22-23).

It is not clear which *Christian* writings were acknowledged as Scripture by the early church in its first two cent. There is no doubt that the canonical Gospels, and several of the letters of Paul, were cited regularly in the Christian community and in a scriptural-like manner, that is, authoritatively. There are no early traditions, however, that clearly identify who or when Christians regarded the NT writings as Scripture. When *some* church leaders began to refer to Christian writings, all of them did not cite the same writings nor did they do so at the same time. The first clear listing of Christian Scriptures as sacred Scripture comes in the 4th cent. in the writings of Eusebius (*Hist. eccl.* 3.25). From use or citation to sacred Scripture and canon took almost three cent. for most Christians. It is appropriate therefore to speak of a long process of canonization.

4. A fixed scripture canon

The understanding of a *fixed* collection of sacred books to which others may not be added is neither discussed nor clearly traceable in Jewish traditions, much before the end of the 1st cent. CE and much later in Christian traditions. The first known selection of Christian writings for liturgical and catechetical purposes in the church appears to have come from Marcion (ca. 140 CE), but his aim was not so much to put together a closed biblical canon of Christian Scriptures as it was to sever the church from its Jewish roots. Marcion selected ten letters of Paul and an edited edition of the Gospel of Luke for use in his churches. As Tertullian wrote, Marcion "expressly and openly used the knife, not the pen, since he made such an excision of the Scriptures as suited his own subject matter" (Tertullian, *Praescr.* 38.7, ANF). He used only what furthered his purposes and he expunged what did not, including the OT Scriptures and the NT writings that Marcion believed had a Jewish bias. His followers, however, did not consider Marcion's collection a closed biblical canon and freely cited other NT literature, including the Gospel of Matthew. Contrary to Adolf von Harnack, who earlier argued that Marcion created the first NT biblical canon—and the early Christians responded by producing a larger biblical canon, a theory that is still advanced by some scholars today—Marcion's followers did not interpret his actions that way and felt free to include other Christian writings in their worship and catechetical instruction.

The first clearly closed collection of Christian Scriptures comes from Irenaeus (ca. 170–80 CE) who argued that there could only be four Gospels (Matthew, Mark, Luke, and John). The fact that he argued so strenuously and unconvincingly for four Gospels only (*Haer.* 3.11.8-9; 3.1.1) suggests that his views were not universally acknowledged at the end of the 2nd cent.

> It is not possible that the gospels can be either more or fewer in number than they are. For since there are four zones of the world in which we live, and four principal winds, while the church is scattered throughout all the world and while the "pillar and ground" of the church is the Gospel and the spirit of life, it is fitting, therefore, that she should have four pillars, breathing out immortality on every side, and vivifying men afresh. (*Haer.* 3.11.8-9)

There is evidence that other gospels continued to be read in churches during and well beyond his lifetime. Tatian (ca. 170–80), for instance, produced a harmonized version of the Gospels commonly called the *Diatessaron* (lit. "through-four"), but originally called *The*

Gospel of the Mixed. In it Tatian used not only the four canonical Gospels but also the Gospel of Peter and other Christian writings as well. Like Clement of Alexandria (ca. 170–80), Tatian used more than the four canonical Gospels in his work. Tertullian (ca. 200), on the other hand, minimized the value of Luke's Gospel and chided Marcion for using it because it was written not by an "apostolic man," that is, "not a master, but a disciple, and so inferior to a master" (*Marc.* 4.2.5).

Unlike Irenaeus's defense of the four canonical Gospels, Eusebius (ca. 320–30) simply introduces them as the "holy tetrad of the Gospels" without any defense (*Hist. eccl.* 3.25.1). This suggests that by the 4th cent. the canonical Gospels were well entrenched, but that was not the case at the end of the 2nd cent. when Irenaeus defended his selection of four Gospels. Similarly, when the Muratorian Fragment (ca. 350–75) lists the Gospels (lines 1–33), there is no defense of their inclusion, but only a summary of their contents. Like Eusebius, he acknowledges them and assumes that their number was already fixed and widely acknowledged in his generation.

As was true in the earlier Jewish tradition, the 2nd and 3rd cent. CE saw the production of many pseudonymous Christian writings attributed to apostles, including gospels, acts, letters, and apocalypses that continued to be read in some churches for several centuries. Some Christian writings were read in several churches early on (Col 3:16, and by implication, also 2 Pet 3:15-16). No later than the mid-2nd cent., some of the Gospels were being read alongside of and sometimes instead of the "Prophets" (the OT). Justin Martyr (ca. 150–160) describes the use of Scripture in a Christian worship service thus: "And on the day called Sunday there is a meeting in one place of those who live in cities or the country, and the memoirs of the apostles [the Gospels] or the writings of the prophets are read as long as time permits" (*1 Apol.* 67).

The use of NT writings in churches for catechetical and missional purposes was widespread in the 2nd cent., but they were not generally called "Scripture" until the end of that century. Their scriptural status was only gradually recognized after widespread use. All of the Christian Scriptures, however, were not universally nor simultaneously acknowledged as sacred Scripture by all of the Christians. The absence of early Christian references to several NT writings suggests this. For example, the earliest reference to the PASTORAL LETTERS is in the early 3rd cent., while the Gospels and the majority of Paul's writings were cited and copied in the 2nd cent. There are also very few references to several of the General or CATHOLIC EPISTLES in the 2nd cent., such as 2 or 3 John and Jude.

D. The Emergence of an Old and New Testament

When the church began, the notion of an Old or New Testament referring to the two parts of the Christian Bible was not yet a part of *lingua franca* of the Christian community. The term *testament* is found in both the OT and NT and in both Testaments it is used to describe the covenantal relationship that God made with the people of God (Gen 15:18; 17:2-13). The "old" covenant referred to a relationship between God and the people of God based on the giving and keeping of the Law. The children of Israel broke that Law (Ezek 16:8-15; 44:7) and so God made a "new" covenant with Israel that brought forgiveness of sins and established a new relationship with God (Jer 31:31-34; 32:40; Ezek 37:26). In the NT writings, the "new" covenant, or new relationship between God and the people of God, is initiated in the death of Jesus (*see* Luke 22:20, compare Mark 14:24 and Matt 26:28, which do not use the word *new*).

The labels "Old Testament" and "New Testament," as references to bodies of sacred literature, are not found in the Christian community until the end of the 2nd cent. CE in the writings of Melito, Irenaeus, and Tertullian. It is therefore premature to speak of an "Old" or "New Testament" canon in the initial stages of the church's development.

Irenaeus was apparently the first to use these terms to distinguish the two parts of the church's Scriptures. He writes,

Inasmuch, then, as in both Testaments there is the same righteousness of God [displayed] when God takes vengeance, in the one case indeed typically, temporarily, and more moderately; but in the other, really, enduringly, and more rigidly . . . For as, in the New Testament, that faith of men [to be placed] in God has been increased, receiving in addition [to what was already revealed] the Son of God, that man too might be a partaker of God." (*Haer.* 4.28.1-2, *ANF*)

Likewise, Melito, bishop of Sardis (ca. 170-180), speaks of "the books of the old covenant [or "testament"] [ta tēs palaias diathēkēs graphōn]." These words are preserved in the 4th cent. (Eusebius, *Hist.eccl.* 4.26.13), but we also find a similar reference in Tertullian (ca. 200) who states, "If I fail in resolving this article (of our faith) by passages which may admit of dispute out of the Old Testament, I will take out of the New Testament a confirmation of our view" (*Adv. Prax.* 15, *ANF*). *See also*, Clement of Alexandria, *Strom.* 15.5.85, and Origen, *Princ.* 4.11.

In Alexandria, Origen (ca. 220) argued that his teachings were "found both in the *so-called Old Testament* and in the *so-called New*" (*Comm. Jo.* 5.4; compare 10.28 and *Princ.* 4.11; emphasis added). While these terms emerged in the 2nd cent., they still had to be explained to the churches in the 3rd and 4th cent. Eusebius (ca. 325 CE), describes Josephus' canon of Scripture thus: "He gives the number of the canonical scriptures of the *so-called Old Testament*, and showed as follows

which are undisputed among the Hebrews as belonging to ancient tradition" (*Hist. eccl.* 3.9.5, LCL). Later, while speaking of Christian writings widely accepted as Scripture in the churches, Eusebius writes: "At this point it seems reasonable to summarize *the writings of the New Testament* which have been quoted" (*Hist. eccl.* 3.25.1, LCL, emphasis added). These distinctions were used by some of the church fathers in the late 2nd cent., but they were not generally employed until the middle to the late fourth century. In canon 59 of the Synod of Laodicea (ca. 360), for instance, we read, "[It is decreed] that private psalms should not be read in the church, *neither uncanonized books, but only the canonical [books] of the New and Old Testament.*"

The notion of "old" in antiquity did not mean the same as it often does today, namely, outdated or irrelevant. In antiquity, *old* often meant reliable and trustworthy. Whatever was new, religiously speaking, was unworthy of serious consideration. Indeed, having roots in antiquity was critically important for the mission of the early church, and it added credibility to its message. The majority of churches in the 2nd cent. condemned Marcion's attempt to sever the church's relations with its Jewish historical roots and its scriptural tradition. Consequently, he was excommunicated from the church. The marvel for the church then was not that it had accepted something *old* but rather something *new*!

1. Closing the biblical canon

The limits of the Old and New Testaments that defined the faith and mission of the Christians were largely fixed by the middle to late 4th cent. even though questions about some books inside or on the borders of those collections continued for a while longer. Despite the complex and often unknown circumstances that led to the closing of the biblical canon, the available evidence allows some conclusions to be formed.

2. The role of heresy

Some scholars contend that the 2nd cent. church responded to well-known heresies that produced and promoted their own divergent literature by establishing a Christian biblical canon. Marcionism, Gnosticism, and the Montanists posed serious challenges to the larger church in the 2nd cent., and all three so-called heresies produced literature that supported their theological positions. Marcion edited the Gospel of Luke and the letters of Paul for his own advantage, but did not produce a closed canon of Scriptures. The Gnostics produced large amounts of literature that challenged the common views of the church on the humanity of Jesus, and they reserved the highest levels of salvation to those who had acquired a special esoteric knowledge of the will and plan of God. Many of them welcomed many parts of the OT and NT Scriptures, but they also produced other literature that the church later condemned as heretical.

The Montanists, on the other hand, were a charismatic community that emphasized the presence of continuing prophecy in their community, much of which was written down but evidently later destroyed. None of their writings survive. They did not produce a fixed collection of Christian Scriptures, however, and the greater church did not respond to their literary activity by producing one.

It is alleged that in each of these cases, the church responded by producing a fixed collection of Christian writings that could be read in the churches, but rather than establishing biblical canon of Scriptures, the early church fathers produced a "canon of faith," that is, a *regula fidei*, that set forth the basic beliefs of the church. The argument of the 2nd cent. was that the apostles had handed on to the leaders of the churches, the bishops, the truth of the Gospel, and that this truth contradicted the heretical claims of the heretical groups of the 2nd cent. After listing the succession of bishops in the church, Irenaeus claims:

> In this order, and by this succession, the ecclesiastical tradition from the apostles and the preaching of the truth have come down to us. And this is the most abundant proof that there is one and the same vivifying faith, which has been preserved in the Church from the apostles until now, and handed down in truth. (*Haer.* 3.3.3)

For Irenaeus, the rule of faith preserved the church from the error that was set forth in the heretical writings of the 2nd cent. Most of the beliefs in this *regula fidei*, or rule of faith, focused on the identity and work of Jesus and was summarized in early form approximating the Apostles' Creed that is still commonly cited in Christian worship. There is no evidence that the church set forth a fixed list of NT Scriptures to address the concerns of heresy in the 2nd cent.

3. Theological factors

The factors that shaped the contours of Scripture collections were theological, social or historical, and practical. In the first instance, there was a *theological* perspective among the Jews that with the cessation of prophets following Ezra, the production of divine literature ceased. The Christians, however, did not accept that belief, but rather believed that they lived in the age of the Spirit and the gift of prophecy had not ceased. They not only acknowledged as Scripture those writings that they received from the Jews (the OT writings that were initially less precisely defined than they later became), they also believed that a new day of the Spirit had arrived and that new prophetic writings were needed for their community of faith. The boundaries of these Scriptures were also largely framed by a commonly accepted body of beliefs about Jesus that circulated in the early Christian churches and by the specific needs of the emerging church.

4. Historical factors

The historical factors that led the church to finalize its sacred collections included the empire-wide Roman persecutions of the church during the Decian (ca. 250–51) and Diocletian (ca. 303–313) empires. In the Diocletian persecution, Christians were required under the threat of death to turn over their sacred writings to the authorities to be burned (see examples of this in Eusebius, *Hist. eccl.* 8.5-6 and *Gesta apud Zenophilum in Corpus Scriptorum Ecclesiasticorum Latinorum* 26. These acts of violence forced Christians to decide which literature was sacred, and consequently could not be turned over to the authorities, and which literature could be turned over to the authorities in good conscience. Those Christians who turned over the sacred texts were called *traditors* ("traitors") and those who suffered the loss of life to protect their Scriptures were called *confessors* or martyrs.

Another important contributing factor was Constantine's (ca. 314–340) push for religious conformity within the Christian communities under the threat of banishment for those who did not comply. These factors do not appear to have influenced the scope of the Jewish biblical canon.

A more *practical* historical factor, that surely influenced many churches, was Constantine's request of Eusebius to produce fifty copies of the church's Scriptures to be used in the churches of the New Rome, Constantinople, the new capital of the Roman Empire. The contents of these volumes likely had a significant influence on many in the church in the vicinity of Constantinople (Greece and Asia Minor) and even farther away.

Another practical matter had to do with the actual size of books in the late 4th cent. Prior to the late 4th cent., the size of books was not large enough to include all of the sacred writings that are currently in the Christian Bible. Before then, churches and synagogues often had unbound collections of books. By the 4th cent., the codex had developed to the point where it could include all of the current books in the Christian Bible, both Old and New Testaments. It may also be that the codex was limited enough so that some books on the margins could not be included and that may also have affected the final size of the Christian Bible.

5. Criteria for selection

The criteria that were generally employed to identify and select those writings that were finally included in the NT canon include:

a. Apostolicity. That is, if a writing was believed to have been written by an apostle, it was accepted. This is implied in the way that the church dealt with heretical documents put forth in the name of an apostle (*Hist. eccl.* 3.25.6). Eusebius cites Bishop Serapion (ca. 200) saying to his churches: "For our part, brethren, we receive both Peter and the other apostles as Christ, but the writings which falsely bear their names we reject, as men of experience, knowing that such were not handed down to us" (*Hist. eccl.* 6.12.3).

b. Orthodoxy. That is, if a writing agreed with the generally accepted "canon of faith" (*regula fidei* or orthodoxy), it was also seriously considered. According to Irenaeus, who focused on the truth committed to the apostles, nothing could be accepted in the churches that denied the faith that had been handed down from the apostles to the bishops of the church (*Haer.* 3.3.2-3). Eusebius also made the point that Serapion rejected the *Gospel of Peter* based on its heretical substance (*Hist. eccl.* 6.12.1-6). His initial assumption that it was written by the Apostle Peter was changed following his reading and assessing the document.

c. Antiquity. If the writing was from the generation of the apostles, it had greater possibilities for inclusion in the Scripture canon. Notice how the author of the *Muratorian Fragment* rejected reading Hermas in the church because it was written "recently in our times" rather than in the generation of the apostles:

> But Hermas wrote the Shepherd very recently in our times in the city of Rome while bishop Pius, his brother, was occupying the [episcopal] chair of the church of the city of Rome. And therefore it ought to be read, but it cannot be read publicly to the people in church either among the prophets, whose number is complete, or among the apostles, for it is after [their] time (*MF*, lines 73-80, trans. by Metzger, 307).

d. Use. A writing was more likely to be included if it found wide acceptance and use in the churches. This criterion seems to have weighed heavily in Eusebius' lists since he describes the writings as "recognized," or disputed," or "spurious" and therefore rejected (*Hist. eccl.* 3.25.1-7). For Eusebius, those books that were recognized and accepted in the larger churches were more likely to be included in the NT canon. He acknowledges that the Gospel of John and 1 John "[have] been accepted without controversy by ancients and moderns alike" but indicated that there was dispute over 2–3 John and Revelation among the "ancients" (*Hist. eccl.* 3.14.17-18).

These criteria are not found in all ancient writers who discuss the normativity of the Scriptures, and there are no documents that state that all of these specific criteria were employed in each case in the canonical process. Rather, it appears that one or more of these criteria tipped the scales in favor of inclusion, but all of the NT writings cannot be accounted for on the basis of these criteria. It is not clear why some Christian writings were excluded (e.g., *Didache*, *Hermas*, *1 Clement*), and why some were included (Mark, Luke, the Pastoral Letters, 2 Peter). The most important criterion appears to have been

church use, namely that many churches, especially the influential ones, found the writings that made it into the NT canon were quite useful in their worship, teaching, and mission. The NT writings continued to be valued in the churches and were included in the NT canon because they able to address the current religious needs and issues facing the churches. Also, the corpus of writings was received in the churches because they continued to offer life and hope in the variety of circumstances that the church experienced, that is, they were adaptable to the contemporary issues facing the church.

6. Collections of early Christian writings

The collecting and circulating of Christian Scriptures was an initial step in the canonization process. When Christians began to make lists or catalogs of sacred Christian writings that were accepted as Scripture in the churches, the formal recognition of a *fixed* list or collection of canonical Scriptures was not far behind. In the 4th cent., Eusebius was the first to produce a list of those books that had obtained a canonical (endiathēkou, or "encovenanted") status in the churches (*Hist. eccl.* 6.14.1). Elsewhere he writes:

> At this point it seems reasonable to summarize the writings of the New Testament which have been quoted. In the first place should be put the holy tetrad of the Gospels. To them follows the writing of the Acts of the Apostles. After this should be reckoned the epistles of Paul. Following them the Epistle of John called the first, and in the same way should be recognized the Epistle of Peter. In addition to these should be put, if it seem desirable, the Revelation of John, the arguments concerning which we will expound at the proper time. These belong to the Recognized [*homologoumenois*] Books. (*Hist. eccl.* 3.25.1-3, LCL)

Sacred writings were generally acknowledged as Scripture first through use in local churches, then by local gatherings of churches, and finally by councils of churches. Some sixteeen known lists or catalogs of NT Scriptures, dating from the 4th to the 6th cent., include most of the books of the NT. Several major manuscripts from that period also identify most of the literature that comprises the current NT canon, but they include as well several other books that were eventually excluded from the church's biblical canon. The contents of each list or catalogue vary with the others in terms of the books listed and their order or sequence in listing the books. Often the Catholic Epistles follow Acts rather than the letters of Paul, and often some of the Catholic Epistles are missing and some non-canonical writings are included. These lists include:

List	Source	Date
1. Eusebius	*Hist. eccl.* 3.25.1-7	ca. 303–325, from Palestine/ western Syria
2. Catalog in Codex Claromontanus		ca. 303–367
3. Cyril of Jerusalem	*Catech.* 4.33	ca. 350, from Palestine
4. Muratorian Fragment		ca. 350–375, from the east
5. Athanasius	*Ep. Fest.* 39	ca. 367, from Alexandria/ Egypt
6. Mommsen Catalog		ca. 365–390, from northern Africa
7. Epiphanius	*Pan.* 76:5	ca. 374–377, from Palestine/ western Syria
8. Apostolic Canon 85		ca. 380, from Palestine/ western Syria
9. Gregory of Nazianzus	*Carm.* 12.31	ca. 383–390, from Asia Minor
10. African Canons		ca. 393–419, from Northern Africa
11. Jerome	*Ep.* 53	ca. 394, from Palestine
12. Augustine	*Doctr. Chr.* 2.8.12	ca. 396–397, from northern Africa
13. Amphilochius	*Iambi ad Seleucum* 289–319	ca. 396, from Asia Minor
14. Rufinus	*Sym.* 36	ca. 400, from Rome/Italy
15. Pope Innocent	*Ad Exsuper. Tol.*	ca. 405, from Rome/Italy
16. Syrian Catalog of St. Catherine's		ca. 400 CE, from eastern Syria

The major manuscripts noted above include but are not limited to the following:

Codex Vaticanus (ca. 331–350, from Alexandria/ Egypt)
Codex Sinaiticus (ca. 331–350, from Alexandria/ Egypt)
Codex Alexandrinus (ca. 425, from Asia Minor)
Syriac Peshitta (ca. 400, from eastern Syria)

It is instructive that these manuscripts both included books that did not finally become a part of the NT and excluded books that did. This will be noted more specifically below. These codices, which were collections of sacred Scriptures for the churches that produced them, reflect the status of the Christian Scriptures for those churches.

E. Problems in the Formation of the NT Canon

1. Decanonization

There are a number of books that were initially included among the manuscripts of various Christian communities and cited as Scripture in the early church fathers but were later rejected by the church. Church councils of the 4th and 5th cent. did not settle such matters, as some have supposed. For several cent. after that period, various noncanonical books appear in collections of NT books without any discernible means of differentiating between them. For example, *Codex Sinaiticus* (a middle to late 4th cent. biblical manuscript) includes the *Epistle of Barnabas* and the *Shepherd of Hermas*. *Codex Alexandrinus* (5th cent.) includes in its NT collection *1–2 Clement* and the *Psalms of Solomon*. *Codex Claromantanus* (5th cent.) includes *Hermas*, the *Acts of Paul*, and the *Apocalypse of Peter*, but omits Philemon, 1–2 Thessalonians, and Hebrews from its NT collection. For whatever reasons, *Codex Vaticanus* omits 1–2 Timothy, Titus, and Revelation, though producers of the codex or book likely intended the latter to be included. This variety of books in the early manuscripts suggests that the early church was not uniform in its adoption of a closed biblical canon for a longer period than was originally thought. Eventually, books that no longer addressed the needs and concerns of the emerging church were left out of the sacred collections.

2. Issues related to translation

Remarkably, the early Christians were not much concerned with the translation of the Christian Scriptures. No community of Christians believed that its translation was inferior to another community's translation. Those who used the Old Latin or Syriac Peshitta translations, e.g., did not believe that their translation was less inspired than Hebrew OT or the Greek NT. This matter has become a problem for some Christians who believe that inspiration is located in the original languages of the biblical text as well as the original text that the writers produced, but no such arguments were made in antiquity. While the church came close to adopting the Greek Bible as its Scriptures, as well as the Lat. Vulg. at a later time, it did not reject the need for other translations of the Christian Scriptures. Concern over which books were included and whether to admit or reject certain writings became concerns for the church in the 4th cent. and following, but not which translation was normative. In the 2nd cent. and later, a number of translations of some Christian Scriptures were produced, but there was no suggestion that this was inappropriate or that the Spirit was present in or able to use the Greek, Lat., or Hebrew versions of the Christian Scriptures.

3. Issues related to the text of scripture

Similarly, and somewhat surprisingly, there apparently was little concern in the early church for the *text* of the Scriptures that the Christians adopted. Textual scholars are well aware of the considerable differences in the variety of biblical manuscripts that have survived antiquity, but until the time of Erasmus in the early 16th cent. there was little concern expressed over this problem in the church. Textual critical scholars who compare various biblical manuscripts today are very much aware that there are no two biblical manuscripts exactly alike, and yet all of them functioned as Scripture in the communities that reproduced and used them. Some deliberate changes were made to the text of the Scriptures in many of these manuscripts, and many accidental errors or changes were also made. The exact meaning of the biblical text is significantly affected by these changes, but there is little attention given to them throughout most of the history of the biblical text. It was also common in the first two centuries for Christian copiers to correct perceived errors in the biblical manuscripts that they were reproducing. The presence of many such changes in the biblical text may also indicate that at an early stage of the church's development, the biblical manuscripts were not yet acknowledged as divine Scripture and so those changes were not considered a significant matter.

Some errors in early manuscripts were common because the earliest copiers were less professional and probably volunteered their labor in the church. By the mid-4th cent., more professional copiers were used in preparing biblical manuscripts and there is more consistency in the later copies of the NT Scriptures. A simple comparison of the earlier biblical papyri manuscripts of the 2nd and 3rd cent. with the later more professionally produced biblical codices of the 4th and 5th cent. demonstrates this point. The Christian scribes or copiers were not as careful in reproducing their biblical texts as were the Jews who attempted to produce exact and carefully prepared copies of their Scriptures. The papyri manuscripts of the first three cent. show uneven columns, misspelled words, corrections to the text, and other changes, including making theological changes in the biblical text.

The ancient Christians were not so much concerned with the *text* of their Scriptures as they were with the specific books that made up their NT collection. This is also true for their OT collections. There is considerable variety not only in the books that were accepted but also the text of those books. There are no two ancient biblical manuscripts exactly alike before the invention of the printing press. One of the oldest complete Bibles that has survived antiquity, *Codex Vaticanus*, lists more books than are in the current Protestant OT, and fewer than are in the current NT canon. There is little uniformity in which books were accepted as sacred among the Christians for many cent., and that precipitated decisions made at the Council of Trent in 1546.

4. Closure of the NT canon

Closure is both a historical and a theological issue. Historically, one may ask on what basis the NT canon was closed, even if it is essentially the same in most Christian churches? Is the biblical canon of Scriptures still open? When did it close and by what authority? There were a number of church councils, beginning

at the end of the 4th cent., that dealt with the closure of the biblical canon, but it was settled for most Christians at the Council of Trent in 1546. Even then, some debate continued over the inclusion of some books of the biblical canon (e.g., Revelation, James, Hebrews). The biblical canon is closed for the majority of Christians, even if the collections espoused are not the same in all churches. The Roman Catholic, the Eastern Orthodox, and the Protestant churches continue to be at variance in regard to a few of the books each recognizes as Scripture. The church has not claimed that the age of the Spirit is over, and there are no clear theological reasons for saying that the biblical canon is complete. As recently as the time of the Reformation, Luther wanted to dismiss James, Hebrews, Jude, and Revelation. Although historically the biblical record appears to be complete and unchangeable, debate over this issue has resumed in recent times. Some biblical scholars argue for increasing or decreasing the current biblical canon. Adding to the problem, most lectionaries do not include and make use of all of the books of the current biblical canon, and clergy, whether followers of a lectionary or when working with a private agenda, have been known to ignore large parts of the current biblical canon in their preaching and teaching in the churches. Many scholars speak about a "canon within the canon" to described this practice of selectivity, which seems very widespread.

F. Summary

The grounds for the early church accepting of new Scriptures are rooted in its fundamental belief that God has acted decisively in the activity and fate of Jesus. From the beginning, the church recognized the value of those writings that told of Jesus' life, teachings, death, and resurrection (the Gospels). They were frequently used in the church and even cited authoritatively because they contained the words of Jesus, the Lord of the church. By the middle of the 2nd cent. they gained a special recognition as "memoirs of the apostles" (Justin, *1 Apol.* 67). Their authority was not in who wrote them, but rather in what they said about Jesus. The obvious value of the continuation of the story of the mission of Jesus in the church (Acts) and the call of Christians to faithful living and obedience to the mission of Jesus (the epistles) was also acknowledged and received early on in churches.

This recognition, coupled with the church's belief that its writers were acting in the power of the Spirit, easily moved the church to collect and circulate these writings in its churches. Their usefulness in the church's life, worship, instruction, mission, and apology was obvious, particularly in regard to the Gospels (especially Matthew) and Epistles, and they circulated widely among the Christians in the 1st and 2nd cent. When the churches began to read Christian writings alongside the OT scriptures in their worship, the process of scriptural recognition and canonization was in process, though the completion of that process was not complete for most Christians until the 4th and 5th cent.

The canonization of the NT writings, that is, the processes that led to the recognition and adoption of the church's *Christian* Scriptures, essentially took place in five stages of development beginning in the 1st cent. CE and largely concluding in the middle to late 4th cent. While the matter was not completely settled for all churches then, or even subsequently, there was widespread agreement on the broad contents of the biblical canon. These five stages include: 1) the acknowledgment of Jesus as the central authority figure for Christian faith; 2) the recognition of the value of Christian writings for preaching and catechetical instruction that reflected the teachings, activity, death and resurrection of Jesus (Gospels), as well as the literature that reflected the continuing mission of Jesus in the world (the rest of NT literature); (3) the rise of the NT writings to the status of Scripture (2nd cent. and later); 4) the conscious groupings of this literature into closed collections—e.g., the four Gospels and the epistles of Paul (2nd and 3rd cent.); and (5) the formation of a *closed* list of Christian Scriptures by the early to mid 4th cent. CE, to which nothing could be added or deleted.

The acceptance of those NT writings that faithfully told the church's story began in the 1st cent. and was largely determined in the 4th cent. At almost the same time, the Scriptures of the OT Scriptures were also moving toward stabilization in the Christian community. Historically, the greater church has never fully agreed on all of the writings in its biblical canon, especially regarding its OT Scriptures, but to some extent also in regard to its NT Scriptures.

Some writings were acknowledged as authoritative documents almost from the earliest use in the churches, as in the case of the Gospel of Matthew. In the first third of the 4th cent., Eusebius tells of considerable uncertainty over several "disputed" (*antilegomena*) books of the NT, namely James, Jude, 2 Peter, 2–3 John but also Hebrews and Revelation (*Hist. eccl.* 3.25.4-5). By the end of the 4th cent., however, his "doubtful" list eventually was more widely accepted, but not without considerable hesitation, especially in the cases of Hebrews, James, Jude, and Revelation.

The literature that survived in the religious communities of both Judaism and early Christianity was that which was believed by those communities to have continuing validity for their faith, identity, conduct, and mission, and was adaptable to new circumstances. For the Jews and the Christians, something more than the OT Scriptures seemed necessary to meet their needs. The Jews saw the value of codifying the oral traditions, which became known as the "oral Torah," and calling it the MISHNAH. They then added this literature to their sacred traditions, though they did not call these oral traditions "Scripture" or include them in their Hebrew Bible.

Both Jews and Christians saw the value of the biblical writings in their worship, instruction, and mission. The Christians developed and passed on in the churches a NT collection of Scriptures that they received as inspired Scripture on par with their OT Scriptures. Like the Jews, they too produced commentaries on their own Scriptures and also translations because they saw the working of God in this literature through its adaptability in the changing circumstances of the church. Some of the literature did not survive that test and was removed from sacred collections. In time, those collections became inviolable, that is, canon, even though the church never fully agreed on the specific books, translations, or texts that comprised it. *See* CANON OF THE OLD TESTAMENT.

Bibliography: J.-M. Auwers and H. J. De Jonge, eds. *The Biblical Canons* (2003); J. Barton. *Holy Writings, Sacred Text: The Canon in Early Christianity* (1997); F. F. Bruce. *The Canon of Scripture* (1988); J. K. Elliott, ed. *The Apocryphal New Testament: A Collection of Apocryphal Christian Literature in English Translation Based on M. R. James* (1993); Harry Y. Gamble. *Books and Readers in the Early Church: A History of Early Christian Texts* (1995); Harry Y. Gamble. "The New Testament Canon: Recent Research and the Status Quaestionis." L. M. McDonald and J. A. Sanders, eds. *The Canon Debate* (2002); William A. Graham. *Beyond the Written Word: Oral Aspects of Scripture in the History of Religion* (1987); F. W. Grosheide, ed. *Some Early Lists of the Books of the New Testament. Vol. 1, Textus Minores* (1948); Geoffrey M. Hahneman. *The Muratorian Fragment and the Development of the Canon* (1992); Martin Hengel. *The Septuagint as Christian Scripture: Its Prehistory and the Problem of Its Canon*, trans. M. Biddle (2002); A. van der Kooij and K. Van der Toorn, ed. *Canonization and Decanonization. Papers Presented to the International Conference of the Leiden Institute for the Study of Religions* (1998); Lee Martin McDonald. *The Formation of the Christian Biblical Canon.* 3rd ed. (2005); Lee Martin McDonald. "The Gospels in Early Christianity: Their Origin, Use, and Authority." S. E. Porter, ed. *Reading the Gospels Today* (2004) 150–78; Bruce Metzger. *The Canon of the New Testament: Its Origin, Development, and Significance* (1987); L. V. Rutgers, P. W. van der Horst, H. W. Havelaar, L. Teugels, ed. *The Use of Sacred Books in the Ancient World* (1998); James A. Sanders. *From Sacred Story to Sacred Text* (1987); Wilhelm Schneemelcher, ed. *New Testament Apocrypha. 2 Volumes.* Rev. Ed. (1991/1992); Albert C. Sundberg. "The Septuagint: the Bible of Hellenistic Judaism." *The Canon Debate* (2002) 68–90; Eugene C. Ulrich. "The Notion and Definition of Canon." *The Canon Debate* (2002) 21–35.

LEE MARTIN MCDONALD

CANON OF THE OLD TESTAMENT. The OT canon was and remains the official collection of the holy scriptures of Judaism, and it is also the first part of the Christian Bible. Jewish tradition divides its canon into twenty-four books and arranges them in three divisions: the Law, the Prophets, and the Writings. The Christian OT in the Protestant tradition has the same content, but is divided into thirty-nine books and is arranged in a different way that concludes with the prophetic books. Other Christian traditions (Roman Catholic, Orthodox) include also the APOCRYPHA (deuterocanonical writings) in their canon of the OT.

The second half of the 20th cent. marked a turn in the conceptions of the history of the OT canon. This shift is due to 1) the knowledge of new manuscript materials from Qumran, both biblical and parabiblical; 2) a reassessment of apocryphal and pseudepigraphic literature; 3) new insights into the nature of oral tradition; and 4) a developing recognition of variety in the religious thought and social organization in early Judaism. Research now looks far beyond the study of old canonical lists and the frequency, context, and purpose of biblical quotations contained in rabbinic writings or in Christian sources. To study the history of the OT canon it is now necessary to consider the information offered by the manuscripts themselves, the process of editing and transmitting biblical texts, early Jewish exegesis, and also the history of Jewish and Christian literature beyond their respective canonical texts. The renewed interest in the Bible as canon, or what makes an ancient text function as sacred Scripture, also is influenced by comparatively new postmodern or postcritical perspectives on literature, history, and religion.

This article deals with introductory questions, the canonization process, the structure of the canon, the authority of the canonical books, the closing of the Hebrew canon, and the constitution of the OT Christian canon, focusing mainly on the formative phase during the Hellenistic and Qumran period (the 2nd cent. BCE and the 1st cent. CE).

A. Definition and Terminology
B. Comparative Context
  1. Sacred book and canonical book
  2. Precedents in the ancient Near East
  3. Classical books and canonical books
  4. The canons of the Hebrew Bible/OT in Judaism and Christianity
  5. Questions and proposals concerning the Hebrew Bible/OT canon
  6. Formation of the canon of biblical books
    a. Moving beyond the traditional theory on history of canon
    b. The correlation between the canonical process and the growth of the literature involved
    c. The dead sea scrolls and the canon of scripture in the Second Temple period
    d. The developing text of the Hebrew Bible/OT
  7. The closing of the canon in Judaism after 70 CE
  8. Criteria of canonicity
  9. A tripartite or bipartite grouping of scripture
  10. The authority of the canonical books
  11. Canonical and noncanonical
  12. The Christian canon of the OT
  13. Canonical hermeneutics
Bibliography

A. Definition and terminology

The Greek κανών (kanōn) is generally related to Greek kanna or kannē, meaning "pole/reed," and this in turn to Hebrew קָנֶה qaneh, Ugaritic qn, Akkadian qanu, and thence perhaps ultimately to Sumerian. Its basic meaning is "reed"; extended meanings in classical Greek are "norm" and "list." The term canon came to have a twofold meaning in later Christian tradition: "norm" for the church, and "list" of sacred writings of the OT and NT. The Hebrew language does not have any expression that equals "canon," although the absence of a technical term does not necessarily prove the absence of a concept. Canon may be defined as the closed list of textually fixed or at least stable literary works accepted retrospectively by a group as authoritative and binding for religious practice and doctrine. It defines a fixed corpus of literature to which nothing can be added, and from which nothing can be removed.

The use of the word canon in connection with the Bible is post-biblical and Christian, although the idea originates in Judaism. Galatians 6:16 states that Christians are to live by a single kanōn, or normative rule of life. The religious connotation of the term probably goes back no farther than the 4th cent. BCE. It has long been fashionable to apply it similarly to the Hebrew Bible, but religious reverence for the biblical text was a postbiblical phenomenon and slow to emerge even in the rabbinic period. Rabbinic discussions concerning the canonical character of certain biblical books, such as Song of Songs and Ecclesiastes or Qoheleth, turn on the expression "defile the hands." It is often supposed that books that were said to "defile the hands" were considered as canonical, whereas books to which this expression was not applied were excluded from the biblical canon. However, the expression "defile the hands" may have no more significance than a reference to the ritual purification to be performed after having used books and before starting any other secular activity. The disputes over Esther, Ecclesiastes, and the Song of Songs were more theoretical or academic than real, and in any case were all settled in favor of their inclusion.

The term canon implies a distinction between inspired and noninspired books that applies differently to canonical and noncanonical books and in Judaism to the Written Law and the Oral Law. This distinction is very difficult to apply in the case of books such as Sirach, Tobit, Wisdom, *Enoch*, *Jubilees*, and some Qumran writings. In Judaism "a canonical book is a book accepted by Jews as authoritative for religious practice and/or doctrine, and whose authority is binding upon the Jewish people for all generations". In the rabbinic view, all divinely inspired literature is canonical—the Written Law, or TORAH—but not all canonical literature is inspired—the ORAL LAW, ORAL TORAH. Within the canon of inspired texts, the rabbis distinguished degrees of canonicity, with the Pentateuch having more authority than the Prophets or Writings. In post-talmudic (medieval) times, the Prophets were in turn assigned a higher degree of authority than the Writings.

The term *canon*, as a list that implies "a task, not only of collecting, but also of sifting and rejecting", belongs to the "normative" Judaism or Christianity of the 3rd to 4th cent. CE. Reports in the rabbinic literature, concerning the composition of the closed canon for the Jewish Bible, show that exclusion rather than inclusion marked the closing of the collection. Therefore, the term *scripture(s)*, instead of *Bible* or biblical *canon*, seems more fitting for collections of sacred books in the Second Temple period. In this period certain works were long since established and acknowledged as possessing authoritative status as sacred Scripture. But that certain books exercised such "scriptural status" does not mean that there was a canon yet. There is no evidence in the Qumran scrolls (or in wider Judaism prior to the fall of the Temple in 70 CE), of a considered, inclusive-and-exclusive list.

Canonicity refers to books but not to a particular form or textual version of a book. It is the book of Jeremiah, e.g., that is canonical, not a particular textual form—LXX vs. MT—of the book. In the traditional terminology there were authorized texts and canonical books.

The "post-Scriptural scriptures" of Judaism are the so-called APOCRYPHA, which are Jewish in origin but not part of the Jewish canon of the TANAKH. The term *apocrypha* means "hidden" or "secret" and refers to books given to the wise among the people but "hidden" from others. These are Tobit, Judith, 1–2 Maccabees, the Wisdom of Solomon, Ecclesiasticus (also known as Sirach, or the Wisdom of Jesus ben Sira), and Baruch (of which ch. 6 is known as the Epistle of Jeremiah), as well as "additions" or longer endings to Esther (in eight sections) and to Daniel (in three sections: the Prayer of Azariah and Song of the Three Young Men; Susanna; and Bel and the Dragon). These additional books are sometimes called Deuterocanonicals, in opposition to the "Protocanonical" or uncontested books contained in the HB. They have played a far more important role in Christian history than in Jewish history (*see* APOCRYPHA, DEUTEROCANONICAL).

The term PSEUDEPIGRAPHA refers to Jewish and Christian writings dating from the last centuries BCE to the first centuries CE, which did not become part of the canon, Jewish or Christian. Jewish tradition refers to this literature, Apocrypha and Pseudepigrapha, as "exterior books." From the earlier notion of the Pseudepigrapha as simply denoting ancient Jewish works that were known to us prior to the discovery of the Dead Sea Scrolls, there is an increasing tendency to view Pseudepigrapha as a literary genre or group of falsely attributed writings, and accordingly to include among these material documents found in Cave 4 at Qumran, such as *Pseudo-Daniel* or *Pseudo-Ezekiel*.

The term *parabiblical* is applied to new Qumran writings closely related to biblical texts or themes and more specifically to anthological or periphrastic texts, such as a *Reworked Pentateuch* in the frontier between the biblical and the nonbiblical text, as well as to rewritings or developments on biblical books such as the *Genesis Aprocryphon*.

B. Comparative Context

1. Sacred book and canonical book

The so-called great or universal religions—those that at some point surpassed the limits of an ethnicity or of a reduced geographical space—came to be so through the availability of sacred books, which constituted their basic foundation. Such is the case of the paradigmatic "religions of the Book," monotheistic or Abrahamic, born from the Bible: the Hebrew *Tanakh*, the Christian *Bible*, and the Islamic *Quran*. The concept of sacred book can be also applied to the Hindu *Vedas*, to the pâli canon of Buddhism, and to the *Avesta* of Iranian religion. The founders of important religious traditions, like Hermes, Pythagoras, or Zarathustra, received from heaven, according to their respective traditions, a book that guaranteed their status as messengers of the deity. All these religious traditions developed in a greater or smaller measure, a *canon* of Scriptures that were considered sacred, and whose constitution implies a defined *code* of relationships between the sacred and the profane, the pure and the impure, the ritual and the literary, the canonical and the apocryphal, divine inspiration and profane—or borrowed from neighboring religions—inspirational sources. The idea of "sacred Scripture" entails the view that all its elements, even the most material, are invested with a sacred character. If a book is sacred, so is the language, the type of script, even the style in which it is written. The mere thought that a text could be inspired by God and so possess sacred character determines the kind of interpretation to apply, which is very different when a work is profane.

2. Precedents in the ancient Near East

In the ancient Near East there was already some idea of "canonicity," applicable to texts that supposedly had been sent from heaven, were transmitted with compunctious, scrupulous fidelity, were kept in sacred places, and contained promises for those who made a good use of them and curses for those who destroyed or did not respect them. From this perspective, the concept of canonicity stays together with the process of formation of the OT from the very beginning. The biblical authors accepted the idea of having God communicate with humankind not only through prophets, oracles, and dreams but also through written messages that God seemingly wrote (compare Exod 24:12; 31:28; 32:32-33; 1 Chr 28:19; Dan 5:24).

Mesopotamia and Egypt each developed a canon of works that were considered sacred and hence repeatedly copied, translated, and imitated in the scribal schools attached to temple or palace. An empirical model of the transmission of canon can be offered by the "canonization" of the literary Mesopotamian texts—namely their textual standardization and beginning of their exclusively written transmission—in the Late Bronze Age, the intervening period between the formative Old Babylonian and the normative Neo-Assyrian Period. Mesopotamian classical texts were stabilized some time before the 11th cent. BCE in a form that lasted for over a millennium. The techniques of standardization characterize also the Jewish canon, such as the arrangement of poetry in verses or lines, glosses identifying variant readings, colophons, and catalogs. The Gilgamesh Epic provides us with an unrivaled illustration not only of the final fixation of a traditional text but also of the evolution of such a text from its Sumerian beginnings. Besides the neo-Assyrian standard or "canonical texts" there were also texts known as "extraneous," which were as well collected, organized, and transmitted as those texts that were described as "good." The extraneous texts may have been less authoritative than "good texts," but they were deemed worthy of preservation and incorporation into a kind of canon of Akkadian literature, which was defined by the mainstream scribal curriculum through the ages.

3. Classical books and canonical books

The "classical" texts of the Greeks have a very different character from those of the Hebrew and Christian sacred Scriptures. However, a certain parallelism can be established between the canon of biblical books and the Alexandrian canon of Greek poets, i.e., the lists (pinakes) of select (egkrithentes) or first-class (classici) authors drawn up in the Library and Museum of Alexandria from the beginning of the 3rd cent. BCE: the classics include the epic authors (Homer and Hesiod), the tragic poets (Aeschylus, Sophocles, and Euripides), the lyric poets, the prose writers, including the historians, and finally the orators. The criteria for selection of "classics" were fundamentally literary and aesthetic. The canon of Greek "classical" authors, which was established by the Alexandrian philologists, was a prec-

edent or a parallel phenomenon that inspired the rabbinic efforts at canonization (Moses, the Prophets, and the Writings considered sometimes as the counterparts of Homer, Hesiod, and the Tragic Poets). The influence of the School of Alexandria is evident in the rules and techniques of rabbinic exegesis practiced already before the rabbinic period. Both traditions, Greek and Jewish, ultimately derive from a Mesopotamian precedent.

The canonical books of the Hebrew Bible, like classical works of the Greek and Latin world, were fundamentally models to be imitated (mimesis), and not only models to be commented upon and interpreted. The Scripture, even before becoming canon, has as a main feature the capacity of generating new literature, denominated parabiblical, apocryphal, or pseudepigraphic.

The Bible passed into the West as a religious book, and only secondarily as a classical book. In approximately 400–420 CE, Macrobius established the corpus or canon of the great writers of antiquity. Circa 427, Augustine inserted this pagan corpus after the canon of Christian Scripture in his *De doctrina christiana*. A year before (in 426), the canon of laws was formed, published by Theodosius II in 438. These various compilations and canons were attempts for coexistence between classical paideia, Roman law, and Jewish-Christian tradition. The relationship between the Bible and the classics took shape in the tension often described as "Athens vs. Jerusalem." Much of Western identity, and the richness of its moral and intellectual reflection, derives from the interaction between these two great traditions.

4. The canons of the Hebew Bible/OT in Judaism and Christianity

The Jewish *Tanakh*, acronym of the first letters of the Hebrew titles of its three parts (Torah; Nebi'im; Kethubim) counts twenty-four books, arranged as follows: The Pentateuch or Five Books of Moses (5 books), the Prophets (8), and the Writings (11). First and Second Samuel, 1–2 Kings, the Book of the 12 Minor Prophets, Ezra and Nehemiah, and 1–2 Chronicles are each counted as single books. In the medieval period, these twenty-four books were arranged somewhat differently, with Samuel, Kings, and Chronicles each counted as two books; with Ezra and Nehemiah each counted as a separate book; and with the Song of Songs, Ruth, Lamentations, Ecclesiastes, and Esther counted as a single collection (the Five Scrolls).

Christians are accustomed to speak of "the Old Testament" and "the New Testament." In an effort to avoid the connotations of "the superseded" or "the updated" that may be carried by the terms "old" and "new," an alternative nomenclature of "First Testament" has been proposed. This term is commended by its use in Heb 8:7; 9:15-18 and LXX Lev 26:45, although in both passages it does not refer to a body of

Jewish sacred literature. The question of terminology remains under discussion in Jewish-Christian dialogue, and for this article the traditional terminology will continue to be used.

The Christian canons of the OT place the books after the Pentateuch in three different groups: the Historical Books, Poetry or Wisdom, and the Prophets. The HB culminates in Ezra–Nehemiah and Chronicles with the people's return to the land of Israel after the exile. In contrast, the OT of the Christian Bible(s) ends with the prophecies of judgment and the promise of the messianic age, thus moving toward a NT. This structure could have Jewish precedents in the closing of "the Law and the Prophets," with the books of Isaiah and Minor Prophets as attested by Bava Batra 14*b*. This order of books may correspond to that of the list known by Judas Maccabaeus around 164 BCE.

The Protestant canon of thirty-nine books contains precisely the same writings as the Jewish canon. Roman Catholic Bibles contain an additional seven books, the "Apocrypha" or "Deuterocanonicals," for a total of forty-six: Tobit, Judith, Additions to Esther, Wisdom of Solomon, Ecclesiasticus (Sirach), Letter of Jeremiah, Additions to Daniel, 1–2 Maccabees. Greek Orthodox Bibles include all the writings found in the Catholic canon, plus an additional three books for a total of forty-nine (1 Esdras, 3 Maccabees, and the Prayer of Manasseh), as well as a longer ending to the Psalter (Psalm 151). In this tradition, 1–2 Samuel and 1–2 Kings are known as 1–4 Kingdoms, 1–2 Chronicles as 1–2 Paraleipomena, and Ezra–Nehemiah together as 2 Esdras. The Slavonic Orthodox Church also includes 2 Esdras (called 4 Ezra in the Lat. Vulg.), while the Ethiopian Church apparently recognizes *1 Enoch* and *Jubilees* as part of the OT. The varying forms of Christianity have varying canons, from the minimalist Syrian to the maximalist Ethiopian.

5. Questions and proposals concerning the Hebrew Bible/OT canon

The question of canon contains many other questions and, especially, one connected with identity or identity awareness of the cultural or religious group that refers itself to that stricture or code. A canon is the expression of the collective memory of a culture or religion, of how it has constructed its past and its history, its tradition, and the constantly renewed interpretation of its own identity. The canons of Jewish and Christian sacred Scriptures defined their respective identities against the surrounding pagan world. The process of constituting the Jewish biblical canon answered to a purpose of identity and of internal integration of Judaism. In contrast to the critical historicist idea that canons are simply ideological banners for social groups that propose them as forms of self-definition, the "traditional idea of a high canon" is an assertion of value and a means of constituting a community of interpretation.

The canon establishes which books are considered revealed or inspired, thus marking the path through which the central trend of a religion runs, be it Jewish, Christian, or Islamic, or one of their confessions, such as Catholic, Protestant, or Orthodox in the case of Christianity. The apocryphal or extra-canonical elements lack normative value and at times overflow the margins through which the central trend moves. They belong, nevertheless, to the same tradition, be it Jewish or Christian, and they contribute to the enrichment of both identities. The formative process of the Hebrew and Christian canons moves in parallel to that of Judaism and Christianity; thus the history of their respective canons is also the history of the religions themselves.

The subject of canon incorporates numerous topics, including 1) when and how the biblical books were formed; 2) when and how the collections of books which compose the Bible were edited; 3) which urges precipitated the constitution of this canon (political, religious, and cultural); 4) in what sense the literary structure of the canon orients biblical interpretation; 5) what relationship can be established between biblical and apocryphal literature and the different social and religious groups (not books) that constituted Judaism in the Hellenistic era. The study of canon also asks in what measure canon-established orthodoxy precedes heterodoxy, or the latter precedes or runs parallel to the former, and which are the basic points of coincidence and divergence in the shaping of the biblical canon that contributed to Judaism and Christianity, following "diverging" or rather parallel paths.

The discussion of these topics is to be carried out in a wide perspective that includes a shift from the national literature of Israel to the sacred Scripture of Judaism, from a religion that was Temple-based to one that was text-based, from a variety of editions and texts to the fixing of a single text for each book, from a dynamic revelation to the literal exegesis, and from individual scrolls for individual books to the codex that could contain the totality of OT and NT Scriptures, opening thus the possibility of a single volume, with the idea of a unitary canon.

The concept of canon is circumscribed by definition to the idea of a closed list of books, with the exclusion of others. Thus one should not speak of "canon" but of "scripture" to make reference to the books that during the Second Temple period progressively received a degree of religious "authority," which made them candidates to be included in the final list of canonical books. From this point of view, Christianity did not know a consensual and final list of authorized books of the OT until the 4th cent. CE. In Judaism as well, only at about the same date is there a clear mention of such a list of books deemed as canonical, although doubtlessly there was already in previous centuries the idea that certain sacred and authorized books were the reference point for Jewish faith and practice. The lack of precision in the terminology affects the actual discussion concerning the Hebrew Bible/OT canon, as some scholars acknowledge that the Pharisees' canon was already well fixed in the mid 2nd cent. BCE, while others suppose that at the start of the Christian period, in both Palestine and Alexandria, the canon as yet had no exact limits.

6. Formation of the canon of biblical books

If the final list of canonical books is important, equally important is the historical process through which some particular books came to acquire sacred character and recognition of authoritative value. This process spans several centuries. To it contributed numerous factors of literary, social, and religious character. Before the ultimate establishment of a canon the idea of canon does not exist; it takes shape as the canon is constituted.

a. Moving beyond the traditional theory on history of canon. The traditional understanding, introduced into modern scholarship by H. E. Ryle and F. Buhl at the beginning of the 20th cent., about the formation of canon is outdated. The traditional view proposed that the diachronic formation of the Jewish canon occurred in three successive stages, which correspond to the three parts of its synchronic structure: The books of Scripture contained in the "Law" were rendered canonical under Ezra sometime in the mid 5th cent. BCE, prior to a schism between Jews and Samaritans in 432 BCE; accordingly, the Samaritans never acknowledged the sacred character of the prophetic books. The "Prophets" achieved their canonicity by the end of the 3rd cent. BCE, prior to the composition in approximately 180 BCE of the extra-canonical book of Ecclesiasticus or Sirach. The Writings received final approval and canonical standing by 100 CE, perhaps at a rabbinical "council" held in Jamnia/Yabneh ca. 90 CE, where the canon was decisively closed with the exclusion of the apocryphal or "external" books.

However, since the 1970s scholars have challenged several aspects of this hypothesis. First, they argue that the formation of the canon of prophetic books should not be connected with the Samaritan schism, as if the Samaritans had never acknowledged the sacred character of the prophetic books because this collection had entered the canon after the Samaritan schism; and this schism in any case did not take place so early as previously thought, but rather well into Hellenistic times. Second, it is now recognized that the so-called Yabneh "Council" was not a council in the sense of later church councils; the decisions that were taken there did not have coercing force, nor were they referred to the totality of the canon, but rather to the sacred character of the book of Qohelet, and possibly also of Song of Songs.

For a long time it was thought that in addition to the Palestinian rabbinic canon there existed a second canon circulating in the Jewish diaspora. Christianity had assumed this wider canon, which was the basis for the selection of books included in the later SEPTUAGINT (hereafter LXX) codices, before the shorter rabbinic canon was first established ca. 90 CE. This theory is also challenged by more recent studies. The traditional theory was based on the fact that the codices of the LXX contained several apocryphal books. However, the great Greek codices of the 5th cent. CE were very much longer than codices in previous centuries and they are all of Christian origin, for from the 2nd cent. CE onward, the Jews ceased to use the LXX version, which they replaced with Jewish recensions of this version by Aquila, Symmachus, and Theodotion. In fact, Greek codices reflect the situation of the 4th and 5th cent. CE, which is not comparable with that of previous centuries, particularly of the 1st cent. CE. The theory of the Alexandrian canon had two other props that have also collapsed. The first was that Hellenistic Judaism and Palestinian Judaism were both different and remote from each other. The second was that the apocryphal books were mostly composed in Greek on Egyptian soil. There is therefore no evidence of the existence of a canon of scriptures in Alexandria in the two cent. BCE and the 1st cent. CE, which are different from the Palestinian proto-Rabbinic canon.

b. The correlation between the canonical process and the growth of the literature involved. The process of recognition of the authority of the Scriptures runs in par. with the literary growth and progressive fixing of the text of the books that were candidates to be acknowledged as authoritative Scripture and to be integrated into a closed canon.

Certain expressions of the Hebrew Bible seem to indicate who the transmitters were who contributed to the formation of the Scriptures in either its bipartite (The Law and the Prophets) or tripartite form (The Law, the Prophets, and the Writings). Priests and prophets occur frequently, as parallel terms, representing law and prophecy (Jer 5:31). Priests, prophets, and wise men may equally represent the future tripartite structure of the canon (Jer 8:8-10; 18:18; Ezek 7:26). The temporary disappearance of the priesthood during the exile and the complete disappearance of prophecy later helped to give the wise man more independence to the extent that the sages took over the prophetic claim to mediate revelation, leading to the rabbinic statement that prophecy has been taken from the prophets and given to the sages. It was by virtue of such a claim that the biblical canon came to be expanded to cover a miscellaneous body of writings, over and above the Law and the Prophets.

The history of the formation of the Bible and of the biblical canon runs in parallel with the history of Temple and priesthood, and also with the formation of a text-centered religious community. Both histories can be traced back to the moment in 622/21 BCE, in which priests find in the Jerusalem Temple the book that Josiah proclaims as fundamental Law for the people of Israel (2 Kgs 22–33). The earliest emergence of text-centeredness is dated to Josiah's reform, when the cultic worship outside the Temple of Jerusalem was destroyed and the reading of the Torah took the place of sacrificial worship in communities outside of Jerusalem and Temple. Second Maccabees 1:18–2:18 establishes a parallelism between the fate of the Temple and of the sacred book in the moments of Ezra's restoration and of the Maccabees' restoration. In the context of the festivities of the purification of the Temple it is said that "(Nehemiah) founded a library and collected the books about the kings and prophets, and the writings of David, and letters of kings about votive offerings. In the same way Judas also collected all the books that had been lost on account of the war that had come upon us" (2 Macc 2:13-14). Similarly, in the thirtieth year after the destruction of the Temple by Nebuchadnezzar, a cryptical reference to the destruction of the Second Temple in 70 CE, 4 Esdras (14:1-48) recounts how an angel commissions Ezra to produce ninety-four books, namely twenty-four canonical books and seventy esoteric books that will remain hidden.

The formation of the Pentateuch was the most meaningful measure initiated by the majority faction of Judaism, which was ready to accept Persian rule, which, in its turn, sanctioned the Jewish laws and customs that were expressed in those texts. This happened probably in the middle of the 5th cent., as Nehemiah's mission (ca. 444–32 BCE) supposed that the deuteronomic and priestly texts of the Pentateuch already enjoyed the status of recognized norms. The passage Ezra 7:26 does not constitute a royal authorization of Jewish Law, but it rather presupposes it.

Inasmuch as in the Persian period there were laws not collected in the Pentateuch, and in some circles they were considered as having the value of the Torah given at Sinai, it is necessary to establish a difference between Torah and Pentateuch, because the latter did not represent the only and complete Torah rooted in the Sinai revelation. In Persian times Torah variants could still be considered. Some circles could keep for some time traditions that were not incorporated into the form that the Torah has within the Pentateuch. The Temple Scroll found at Qumran suggests the existence of alternative or complementary Torah books in relationship with the Torah (Pentateuch) of today (*see* below).

The insertion of Deuteronomy between the books of Numbers and Joshua determined the constitution of two great collections: the Torah or Pentateuch and that of Prophets, which are subdivided into Former (the historiographical collection of Joshua–Judges–Samuel–Kings) and Latter (Isaiah–12 Prophets–Jeremiah–Ezekiel, or afterward Isaiah–Jeremiah–Ezekiel–12 Prophets). To this second collection belonged some books that are now in the Writings. Such was perhaps in the earlier times the case of the Psalter, attributed to King David, who was considered a prophet like Samuel, supposed author of the books with his name. The Qumran PESHARIM comment only on prophetic texts and Psalms, which suggests the attribution of prophetic value to the Psalter. The headings of the Psalms, with their references "to David" (לְדָוִד ledawidh) and to events from David's life and of the times of the monarchy and exile, are a hint of how the first collections of Psalms were initially related to the collection of Former Prophets. The historical books also contain Psalms (2 Sam 22 = Ps 18; 1 Chr 16:8-36 = 105:1-15; 2 Chr 6:41-42 = Ps 132:8-10). The dividing line between prophetic books and Writings was not sharply defined, as the different distribution of books in the Greek Bible indicates. The book of Psalms is placed in the borderline between the prophetic books and the Writings, finally leaning toward the latter.

Throughout the process of canonization, which occurs over many centuries, redactors or editors appear to be engaged in illuminating the authority of a particular biblical book or collection of books. First, the theologized transformations of final editions of the biblical books brought about a more elevated perception of their scriptural status—as, e.g., with the addition of Prov 1–9 to the more pedestrian earlier edition, and with the postscript of Esth 9:18-32, with its Purim connection. Second, the appendices in Deut 34:10-12 and Mal 3:22-24 [4:4-6] initially functioned as examples of a progressive scripture-conscious redaction: Deut 34:10-12 functions primarily to describe Moses as a prophet, and thus complete the book of Deuteronomy and the Torah; on the other hand, Mal 3:22-24, coming at the end of the book of the Minor Prophets, and eventually at the end of the entire prophetic corpus, reminds its readers of the essential relation between the Prophets and the Law. Third, the end of the prophetic collection has been successively shaped to provide a series of expanding canonical inclusios: Zech 11 matching Hos 1 (for the Minor Prophets), Zech 14 matching Isa 2 and 66 (for the Latter Prophets), and Mal 3:22-24 matching Jos 1:2, 7 (for the Prophets). Fourth, the epilogue of Eccl 12:9-14, which refers to the "making of many books," becomes a "point of crystallization" in the formation process of the Scriptures. Fifth, the books of Chronicles interpret Israel's history in relation to a body of authoritative Scripture; these books indicate an awareness of Scripture beyond the Pentateuch and even beyond the Former Prophets. Sixth, and as a final example of inner-biblical awareness of an emerging Scripture, the books in the collection of Writings presuppose the written tradition of the Law and the Prophets, to which they make frequent reference and allusion.

c. The Dead Sea Scrolls and the canon of Scripture in the Second Temple period. The Qumran scrolls give us a glimpse into the time between the two points when much of the "biblical" literature was written and when it was formally recognized in a canon of Scripture. In this intermediate period this literature was edited (many of the books in different editions), translated, interpreted, and recognized as authoritative sacred Scripture.

The Dead Sea caves have yielded fragmentary copies of all the books of the Hebrew Bible except Esther. From the Apocrypha or deuterocanonical books we have Tobit, Sirach, and the Letter of Jeremiah in Greek. Representing the Pseudepigrapha are *1 Enoch*, *Jubilees*, and texts related to the *Testament of Levi* and the *Testament of Naphtali*.

The evidence at Qumran relating to the developing Jewish canon is ambiguous. The caves have yielded no codices to indicate an order of books, nor is it clear in what sense the preserved texts of the Aprocrypha and Pseudepigrapha may have been authoritative. Nonetheless, the large number of manuscripts of the *Jubilees* Torah and the Astronomical Book and prophetic parts of *1 Enoch* indicate that these works had some kind of authoritative status at some point in the history of the Qumran community and its antecedents. That these texts had some sort of scriptural status seems indicated by the commentaries on the story of the watchers (4Q180–181) and perhaps the *Apocalypse of Weeks* (4Q247). CD 16:2-4 cites *Jubilees* as authoritative.

The Qumran Essenes believed that prophetic inspiration had not ceased with the death of the last prophet, Malachi, in the Persian period. New books could offer new credentials of prophetic legitimacy (*1 En.* 81:2; 103:2-3). The members of the Qumran community conceived of themselves as living in the biblical age, and Qumran literature evinces an open-ended biblical canon. Before canonical decisions were made, the Temple Scroll and Jubilees could have fallen under the rubric of Torah, representing a continuum with Genesis–Deuteronomy in the rewriting of pentateuchal sources.

For the Qumran community the Temple Scroll, conceived as an expanded form of the Torah, could be as authoritative as the Five Books of Moses. Some facts suggest that the Essene community of Qumran accorded this book "quasi-canonical" or scriptural status. The number of copies and the great size of the scroll 11QTemple[a] may suggest a special status. The Temple Scroll replaces the references to Yahweh in the third person with direct speech in the first person. Even laws that have no equivalent at all in the Pentateuch and are only transmitted by the Temple Scroll are placed in Yahweh's own mouth. In the nonbiblical sectarian manuscripts from Qumran in square script, the TETRAGRAMMATON is often written in paleo-Hebrew characters. However, in biblical manuscripts written in the square script, the tetragrammaton is regularly written in the same square script as the rest of the text. This is the system followed in the Temple Scroll, which seems

to indicate that this text was considered by the Qumran Essenes as a scriptural or authoritative book.

The Psalter was not yet closed for all Judaism in the 1st cent. BCE. Some of the Psalters found at Qumran show that the last third of Psalms was the section with the greatest textual fluidity. Three manuscripts (4QPs[f] = 4Q88, 11QPs[a-b] = 11Q5-6) include apocryphal Psalms, some of them known from the Greek Psalter (Ps 151) or the Syriac Psalter (Pss 151, 154, and 155). Some scholars view these Qumran Psalters as biblical or "canonical," which suggests that the number and sequence of the canonical psalms had not yet been definitively established in the Qumran period. Other scholars, however, view these scrolls as a secondary compilation for liturgical use or as library editions.

Most of the Qumran biblical scrolls are evidently the product of general Judaism, not merely idiosyncratic of the group at Qumran. Just as there was a plurality of Jewish groups during this time, there seems to have been a plurality in conceptions of Scripture. The evidence from Sirach (Sir 38:34–39:1 and 44–49) and from Qumran warns us to be cautious in our views about what may have been included in the category of authoritative "Scripture" near the turn of the era and what was already excluded.

d. The developing text of the Hebrew Bible/OT. The tendency to produce a standardized text of a book, with a fixed arrangement of its literary units, as well as an established sequence in which the books were to be read, manifests an increasing recognition of the scriptural status and, ultimately, of the canonicity of the given books. The biblical manuscripts from Qumran confirm the antiquity of the consonantal text of the Masoretic tradition, discernible especially in the remarkable proximity of Genesis[b] (4Q2) and in the long text of Isaiah[b] (1Q8) to the medieval texts. The Qumran biblical scrolls testify also to the existence of a degree of textual pluralism in the centuries just before the turn of the era. The pre-Samaritan Qumran texts (4QpaleoExod[m], 4QExod-Lev[f], 4QNum[bb], and secondarily 4QDeut[n] and possibly Lev[d]) reflect the characteristic features of the Samaritan Pentateuch, with the exception of the latter's ideological readings, although they occasionally deviate from it. A few Qumran texts are very close to the presumed Hebrew source of the LXX, such as 4QJerb[d] with regard to both the arrangement of the verses and their shorter text and in a lesser extent 4QLev[d], 4QDeut[q], 4QSam[a], 4QNum[bb], and 4QExod[b]. Many Qumran texts are not exclusively close to either the Masoretic text, the Samaritan Pentateuch, or the LXX. These texts may contain (groups of) readings that diverge significantly from the other texts, such as 4QJosh[a] and 4QJudg[a], or represent liturgical or excerpted text, such as 4QExod[d] and 4QDeut[jn] (Tov, 2001; *see also* MASORETES). The Psalm texts, particularly 11QPs[a], are liturgical texts or represent a different edition of the book of Psalms according to two opposing opinions. Qumran has provided manuscript evidence documenting two or more literary editions of some of the biblical books. Qumran has provided manuscript evidence documenting two or more literary editions of some of the biblical books. These editions vary from each other by a different arrangement of the literary units (4QJosh[a], 4QJer[b]) and/or longer or shorter omissions and additions (such as the intentionally expanded version of Exodus in 4QpaleoExod[m], or 4QJudg[a] which lacks 6:7-10 considered as a redactional passage inserted into the Gideon story). In the 3rd cent. BCE, the Hebrew text underlying the LXX had authority/status as the text of the Temple circles (e.g., the Torah was translated into *Greek* by wise men sent from Jerusalem by the high priest Eleazar; *see* ARISTEAS, LETTER OF). Later, especially from the Maccabean times onward, this textual tradition gave way to the proto-Masoretic text. At the turn of the era, the text of many of the biblical writings was not finally fixed, and scribal and exegetical practice allowed a great deal of interpretative freedom. But the Qumran manuscripts show the progressive hegemony of the text that is close to the MT.

From the Mishnaic period onward (2nd cent. CE), Judaism established the canon and fixed the Masoretic Hebrew text of its books, even though different reading traditions endured. In this period, Christianity transmitted as the authorized text of its canonical books the text of the ancient Greek translators, known under the generic name of "version of the Seventy," strictly speaking only applicable to the Greek version of the Pentateuch. For centuries, polemics between Jews and Christians revolved around this diversity of authorized texts and the number of canonical books. Biblical manuscripts from Qumran have demonstrated that the texts of the Greek Bible transmitted by the Christians are based in Hebrew texts from before the advent of Christianity. Therefore, those polemics have lost their substantial motivation, since authorized texts transmitted by Jews and Christians go back to previous textual traditions that were established before Jews and Christians made their decisions. Traditional terminology has reflected this historical situation by assigning the term "canonical" to books and the term "traditional" or "authorized" to the different texts of the same canonical book.

In a canonical perspective such as that represented by B. S. Childs, the proto-Masoretic textual tradition is the reference text within the limits of the Hebrew text. It is considered the vehicle both for recovering and for understanding the canonical text of the OT for Christians (Childs). However, the preference for the MT is problematic in the case of coexisting different literary traditions, which we observe in the books of Samuel, Kings, Jeremiah, Proverbs, Daniel, Esther, and others. These literary stages are to be considered equally original (MT or LXX and 4QJer[bd] in Jeremiah).

The LXX tradition of books and texts is of paramount importance since, at least in many places, it was the form of the ancient Jewish Scriptures that lay before the early Christians; it is quoted in the NT and indeed throughout later Greek-speaking Christianity. Voices have been raised in recent times in favor of taking the LXX—not only its canon, but its texts—as the OT for Christians. At least for purposes of Christian biblical theology, some have proposed that the LXX should have the same weight as the MT.

7. The closing of the canon in Judaism after 70 CE

One current approach of research tends to place the setting up of the canon near 164 BCE, when Judas Maccabeus collected the scattered Scriptures (2 Macc 2:14-15), which Antiochus Epiphanes had tried to destroy (1 Macc 1:56-57). It is argued that the OT Apocrypha, Philo, Josephus, and Christian sources witness that the greater part of the Jewish communities before and after the beginning of the Christian period had access to the Hebrew canon, which is shorter than the Greek Christian canon. But even if the Hebrew canon in its main lines was established by some persons or groups in the 2nd cent. BCE, it did not become closed until much later for many (who were not necessarily "deviant") groups, among which the origins of Christianity are to be found.

The dividing line that marks a before and an after in the history of the canon, as well as in that of Judaism, does not seem to be so much the Maccabean restoration, with its rededication of the Temple, but rather the Pharisaic restoration after the destruction of the Temple in 70 CE. The Pharisaic tradition represents the main line of continuity between Temple-centered Judaism and Tanakh-centered, Temple-less Judaism. However, the sources for Pharisaic tradition in the Mishnaic period may reflect a situation either prior or subsequent to the destruction of the Temple. This has an impact on the discussions about the books whose authority was or was not debated.

Judaism prior to 70 CE was marked by a huge variety of forms. If in the Judaism of the Greek diaspora Philo could witness a conservative Judaism centered on the Torah, other devout circles of that diaspora were prepared to consider as canonical several writings such as the "additions" to the books of Daniel and Esther. These groups were not at all concerned about closing the canon of sacred books completely. Some Pharisaic circles did not rigidly apply the principle that the chain of prophetic succession had been broken in the Persian period, which in principle left the book of Sirach outside the canon.

The Pharisees represented an intermediate position between those who tended to reduce the borders of the canon to the Pentateuch (and Prophets) and those who tended to consider other books as sacred, especially if apocalyptic. The disputes concerning the canonicity of

Ezekiel, Proverbs, Qohelet, Song of Songs, and Esther were not very lengthy, in fact, for they remained debates within the Pharisees. Even within this group, discussion was restricted mostly to the book of Qohelet, which, according to the Hillelites "soiled the hands," but according to the followers of Shammai did not have this effect. Only a very small circle of Pharisees expressed some doubts regarding Song and Esther. In any case, whoever placed the canonicity of these books in doubt, as well as that of Ezekiel, Proverbs, and Qohelet, seems to have represented a minority. The majority accepted these books, following an old tradition.

In this period prior to 70 CE the distinction implied by the term *canon* between authorized and non-authorized books is very difficult to apply in the case of books such as Sirach, Tobit, Wisdom of Solomon, sections of *1 Enoch*, *Jubilees*, and some Qumran writings. Perhaps it is preferable to speak of a vast religious literature without exact limits. This approach may be vague, but perhaps gives a better idea of reality in this period than is suggested by applying the term *canon* to a collection already established in the Maccabean period.

The *formative* process of the Hebrew canon is found already almost complete in the mid 2nd cent. BCE, but the definitive and *normative* list, with the exclusion of non-canonical writings, was not drawn up until the close of the 2nd cent. CE, or at least, the final discussions about some of the books were not settled until that period. Up to that time, one must speak of "authorized" writings but not of canonical books. It is possible to speak of Jewish canon in a strict sense only from the moment in which the Pharisee-rabbinic tendency imposes itself onward. The concept of canon belongs to the normative period of Judaism and not to the formative one, when the Pharisee group was still a minority.

In reference to the period of Yabneh (JABNEH) after 70 CE, *m. Yad.* 3:5, has the statement that the books of Song and Qohelet "soil the hands." By this is meant that these books possess a special sacred character, but whether it means a "canonical" character is still debated among scholars. In any case the decision at Yabneh does not seem to have been definitive, since the discussion still continued for some time. If the expression "to soil the hands" is granted the strict meaning of a reference to a canonical book, the rabbis were doing no more than maintaining the position of the Hillel school in favor of the canonical nature of Qohelet. The sacred and perhaps canonical character of Song of Songs had never really been placed in doubt, but the fact that this book was used in secular feast or could be used in that way, had given rise to a degree of reluctance against its secular use and not so much against its canonicity.

As for the book of Esther, Rabbi AKIBA had to justify its admission into the canon based on the fact that the author enjoyed prophetic knowledge even though he was never a prophet.

With reference to Sirach, described as a "book on the border of the canon, the Pharisees were ruled by the principle of not admitting into the canon any book whose origin was considered later than the period of Simeon the Just, high priest at the time of Alexander the Great, one of the survivors of "the Great Assembly" (*'Abot R. Nat.* 1:2). Nevertheless, Sirach enjoyed some scriptural status in some circles. There are a number of indications of this: the grandson of Ben Sira considered his grandfather's writings to be on a par with the Law and Prophets (Prologue); it underwent successive Hebrew and Greek recensions in Palestine; the copies found at Masada and the Cave 2 fragments from Qumran were written stichometrically, a procedure normally reserved for books later received as canonical. Sirach continued to enjoy status in some rabbinic schools, as shown by the fact that the Babylonian Talmud quotes it, granting it the character of a sacred book.

In sum, in the Yabneh period some books were discussed, but the debate continued and the consensus on the extent of the canon did not crystallize until well into the Tannaitic period (2nd cent. CE). What happened at Yabneh was a first attempt at declaring Song of Songs and Qohelet as canonical. The canon was not something that would be established by rabbinic authority but took shape gradually. Certainly in relation to the practical needs of synagogue worship a canonical book was one fit for use in the synagogue just as previously it had been fit for use in the Temple. Song of Songs, for instance, was read on the eighth day of Passover and Qohelet at the Feast of the Tabernacles.

While it cannot be said that the canon was completely closed toward the end of the 1st cent. CE and not subject to further discussion, mainstream rabbinic tradition considered the biblical canon as virtually established. One of the intentions motivating the rabbis was to prevent groups of Jews risking the temptation of granting sacred status to the first NT writings, which were already circulating then. The apocalyptic disruptive tendencies and the Roman threat of annihilation, together with the HALAKHIC disputes of the 1st cent., may well have stimulated this fixation of the canon.

8. Criteria of canonicity

The process of establishing the Hebrew canon was guided by the basic criteria of authority and antiquity. Sacred character was accorded to books that could prove a Mosaic or prophetic origin and Davidic or Solomonic authority, going back to a period before the time when the continuous succession of prophets was finally broken in the time of King Artaxerxes (465–23 BCE) according to Josephus (*Ag. Ap.* 1.37-43). As a result, books considered as canonical had to be written before this period or before Simeon the Just according to the rabbinic tradition. The book of Daniel, edited later, succeeded in getting into the list of canonical books thanks to being written under the name of a prophet, Daniel, assumed to have lived in the Persian period.

Although Judaism did not develop a dogmatic criterion similar to the *regula fidei* or "canon of faith" in Christianity, it became increasingly necessary to set out the broad outlines of Judaism in opposition to over-restrictive currents, such as those represented by Samaritans and Sadducees, and in opposition to disruptive trends, such as those championed by some apocalyptic groups in Palestine and by others in the Jewish-Hellenistic diaspora. Later, Christian anomism and its messianic claims made also necessary to mark a clear boundary between Jews and Christians (*t. Yad.* 2, 13; *t. Sabb.* 116*a*-116*b*).

Nothing indicates that the inclusion into the canon or the exclusion from it was legislated by an official authority. It would seem rather that the rabbinic tradition was the decisive factor. Ideological criteria of canonicity do not seem to have been so important as the weight of tradition on the sacred and canonical character of a particular book. Only books and records that were continuously transmitted could find a place in the canon of Scripture.

Into rabbinic discussions on the inspired nature of a book there went such considerations as the possible secular nature of the book in question, a suspicion that weighed on the Song of Songs, and the possible contradictions of a particular book in respect of the laws or recommendations contained in the Torah, an accusation made against the books of Ezekiel (40–48) and Qohelet. Similarly, the book of Esther was accused of relating the story of a marriage between a Jewish heroine and a foreign pagan without adding any criticism at all against such a reprehensible act.

9. A tripartite or bipartite grouping of Scripture

Although scholars have moved beyond the traditional three-stage theory of the history of canon, the question of the canonization of the Hebrew Bible still remains closely related to that of its structure, bi- or tripartite, with variant formulas for referring to this structure, such as "the Law and the Prophets" or "the Law, the Prophets, and the Writings." The structure of the Hebrew Bible and of its canon guides not only the customary introductions to the OT but also to some degree the approaches to OT theology. These approaches develop on the dialectical complementarity of Law and Prophets in Judaism before the supremacy accorded to Law in the rabbinic tradition. They try also to integrate the Writings and particularly the Wisdom literature into a synthetic approach to the OT theology that takes account also of the diversity of the Hebrew Bible.

Sirach or Ecclesiasticus (ca. 180 BCE) speaks of "the law of the Most High," "the wisdom of all the ancients," and "prophecies" (Sir 38:34–39:1). The order in which Sirach subsequently praises Israel's ancestors corresponds with the order of books in the Torah and Prophets, but virtually all the Writings are absent (Sir 44–49).

The prologue to the Greek translation of Sirach (ca. 132 BCE) mentions "the Law and the Prophets and the others that followed them." The name for the third corpus of books is different in each mention: "and the others that followed them . . . and the other books of our ancestors . . . and the rest of the books." The prologue can be interpreted as reflecting a tripartite grouping of Scripture, but it can also be interpreted as reflecting a bipartite grouping: the Law and the Prophets plus other religious literature.

First Maccabees 2:50-60 contains a reference to "the law" and "the deeds of the ancestors" and alludes to the biblical traditions of the historical books and Daniel. Second Maccabees, after mentioning "the law" (2:2-3), refers to "books about the kings and the prophets, and the writings of David and letters of kings about votive offerings" (2:13-14). Second Maccabees 15:9 mentions only "the law and the prophets," but the contents of these books, especially the prophets, are not specified; so these statements cannot be used to support a precise division of the biblical books into laws and prophecies.

The "Halakhic Letter" (4QMMT, 4Q398) refers explicitly to "the b[ook of Mo]ses" (section C, lines 20-21). The 4QMMT also adds: "[And] we have [also written] to you so that you may have understanding in the book of Moses [and] in the book[s of the pro]phets and in Davi[d and the events] of ages past . . ." (C, 10-11). This writing seems to indicate a third series of biblical books, but it does not know a name for it nor does it seem to consider non-historical wisdom books that later came to form part of the collection of the Writings. On the other hand, 4QMMT seems familiar with a bipartite division of the canon: "[It is written in the book] of Moses [and in the books of the prophets] that . . ." (C, 17).

The Rule of the Community seems to point to two categories of Scripture: "as commanded by means of the hand of Moses and his servants the Prophets" (1QS 1:2-3), and "through the hand of Moses . . . and according to what the prophets have revealed through his holy spirit" (1QS 8:15-16); similarly, the Damascus Document (7:15-16).

Fourth Maccabees also speaks of "the law and the prophets" (18:10), followed by references to the narratives in the Pentateuch and the books of Daniel, Isaiah, David "the psalmist," Proverbs, and Ezekiel. It is not possible to know whether David's Psalter and the book of Daniel are included among the prophets.

In the NT the expression "the law (of Moses) and the prophets" occurs very frequently: Matt 5:17; 7:12; 22:40; Luke 16:16, 29, 31 ("Moses and the prophets"); John 1:45; Acts 13:15; 28:23; and Rom 3:21. Luke refers to "Moses and all the prophets" in 24:27, but later on to "the law of Moses, the prophets, and the psalms" (24:44). The supposition that the reference to Psalms includes the whole collection of Writings would entail seeing these terms as an expression of a tripartite canon, but such a supposition is debatable.

Philo's work *On the Contemplative Life* lists "laws and oracles delivered through the mouth of Prophets, and hymns and anything else that fosters and perfects knowledge and piety" (25) (LCL 127). Although this could point in the direction of a tripartite canon, it does not seem that this was the canon of Philo, whose works include quotations taken almost exclusively from the Pentateuch but also, although to a lesser extent, from the books of Sirach and Wisdom of Solomon, so going beyond the limits of the third part of the canon.

The evidence from Josephus in *Against Apion* could be considered as the most complete and explicit of those preserved, but its interpretation continues to bristle with difficulties (*Ag. Ap.* 1:38-40). Josephus lists twenty-two books, classified into three sections: the five books of Moses, the thirteen books written by the prophets, and "the remaining four books," which could be Psalms, Song of Songs, Proverbs and Ecclesiastes, or Job, Psalms, Proverbs, and Ecclesiastes. Here Josephus could be speaking not of divisions of the canon of his time, but of literary forms (laws, tradition, hymns, and advice) that do not correspond to canonical divisions.

These sources do not specify how many books and which ones made up the second and third parts of an allegedly tripartite canon. It is not clear whether the references to David (4QMMT; 2 Macc), hymns (Philo), or psalms (Luke) are equivalent to the "Writings," however long this last section might be. Nor is it possible to settle the question as to whether there was the idea of a canon, either open or closed, in which periods and among which Jewish groups. The possibility cannot be excluded that the tripartite canon had originally been bipartite, with the initial inclusion among the Prophets of books now found in the Writings.

10. The authority of the canonical books

The authority that some biblical books progressively attained can be seen a) in the extension of the Greek version and its first revision at the beginning of the 1st cent. BCE known through Qumran manuscripts; b) in the biblical citations contained in Second Temple and NT literature; and c) in data rendered by the Dead Sea Scrolls, such as the number of copies of each biblical book, the care taken with them or the type of writing.

Rabbinic circles of Palestine completed at the beginning of the 1st cent. BCE, a revision of the Greek text of some biblical books. The extent of this revision enables us to gain an idea of the extent of the Pharisaic canon at that time. The revision actually reached only the books of Judges, Samuel, and Kings, the additions in Greek to the book of Jeremiah, Psalms, and the book of the Twelve or Minor Prophets. The books whose

Greek version had no significant differences from the proto-Masoretic Hebrew (found in the documents of Qumran, *see* §6 above) did not need to be revised and, in fact, show no trace at all of having undergone such a revision. These books are Chronicles, Ezra, and Nehemiah. In the cases of the Song of Songs, Ruth, and Lamentations, by contrast, the whole manuscript tradition of these books does show traces of that revision. Those who revised the other books translated them for the first time. All these books were therefore recognized as sacred Scripture.

The book of Qohelet does not seem to have been translated into Greek until the end of the 1st cent. BCE. The characteristics of the Greek version of Qohelet match those of the Aquila version of the 2nd cent. CE. Until this period, rabbinic circles continued to discuss the canonicity of this book. Esther, included in the Hebrew canon, and the books of Tobit and Ecclesiasticus (Sirach), included only in the Greek Bible, do not seem to have been of any interest in the circles that carried out that revision.

The conclusion can be drawn that the circles responsible for this revision of the Greek Bible, complete at the start of the 1st cent. BCE, already had a canon of sacred books that agreed with the later rabbinic canon that lacked the aprocryphal books. The canon of twenty-two books, which does not include Qohelet and Esther, seems to comprise an old form of the biblical canon, previous to the rabbinic canon.

The explicit quotations of biblical passages contained in the oldest Jewish literature help to determine the limits of the canon as books that enjoyed enough authority to be cited in issues involving law or messianic legitimacy. The books of the Law, the Prophets, and Psalms make up the Scriptures on which Qumran legal and exegetical literature based its quotations. Among the prophets, Isaiah and Minor Prophets are more highly regarded than the books of Jeremiah and Ezekiel and the Former Prophets or historical books. The Qumran *pesharim* comment on the books of Genesis, Isaiah, Minor Prophets, and Psalms. The thematic midrashim from Qumran with eschatological content, such as *4QCatena*[a], *4QFlorilegium*, *4QTestimonia*, or *11QMelchizedek*, also quote from the Torah, Prophets, and Psalms and, among the Prophets, mainly from Isaiah and Minor Prophets.

Moving beyond the Qumran evidence, among the apocryphal or deuterocanonical books, Tobit, Judith, 2 Maccabees, 3 Maccabees, 4 Maccabees, Susanna, and Baruch present a total of nineteen explicit biblical quotations: Pentateuch (13), Amos (1), Isaiah (1), Psalms (2), Ezekiel (1), and Proverbs (1). At the end of the Second Temple period, Philo continued to quote almost exclusively from the Pentateuch: 2,260 instances (97 percent of his quotations). *Biblical Antiquities* includes twenty quotations introduced with the Lat. *dicens* (le'mor in Hebrew). All of these are taken from the Pentateuch, except for one from Psalms (99:6). Finally, the Wisdom of Solomon employs the books of Exodus, Deuteronomy, and Isaiah.

In the NT, the books explicitly quoted are almost exclusively the Pentateuch, Isaiah, Minor Prophets, and Psalms. This is especially the case in the earliest Christian writings (Mark, the double or triple synoptic tradition, Acts, Romans, and Galatians) and, in particular, of the quotations attributed to Jesus, Peter, and Stephen. Three books of the Hebrew Bible provide the text for half of all biblical citations present in the NT. These three books are Psalms, Isaiah, and a third one: Minor Prophets in Jesus' quotations, Deuteronomy in those of the whole NT, and Genesis in those of Paul.

The lists of Haftarot (the reading from the prophets) in the triennial cycle for the synagogue indicate that Isaiah and Minor Prophets were the books used most in the ancient synagogue. All synagogues must surely have possessed the whole Torah in its five vols. or "cases" (Aristeas) and some other Bible scrolls, such as Isaiah (Luke 4:20) and the Twelve Prophets. Some psalms were evidently used in the Temple, although the book of Psalms came into the synagogue service only slowly and to a relatively restricted degree.

Job and Proverbs were given special importance during the Qumran period (and even beyond the Qumran circles) and comprise the first nucleus of what would later become the collection of Writings. The book of Job is the only book outside of the Torah of which a copy written in a formal Paleo-Hebrew script has been found in Qumran (4Q101). The presence of a targum of Job among the Qumran manuscripts (4Q157, 11Q10) also demonstrates the special place that the book of Job enjoyed. The book of Proverbs is cited in Qumran texts, in pseudepigraphical writings, and by Philo. The books of Job and Proverbs ("Solomon") were employed for authoritative quotations in the letters of Paul as well as the NT Jewish Christian tractates (Hebrews and the epistles of James and 1–2 Peter).

The information on the number of manuscripts preserved in the Qumran caves of each biblical book tells us something about how highly they were regarded (at least by scribes) in the Qumran period. Among the biblical manuscripts from the Dead Sea, there are thirty-nine copies of Psalms (36 in Qumran + 3 in other caves), thirty-three of Deuteronomy (30+3), twenty-four of Genesis (20+4), twenty-two of Isaiah (21+1), eighteen of Exodus (17+1), seventeen of Leviticus (15+2), eleven of Numbers (8+3), ten of Minor Prophets (8+2). The Pentateuch, Isaiah, Psalms, and Minor Prophets are the most represented books or collections.

The distribution of books in the different caves may also be meaningful. Cave 1, which has the special feature of the scrolls having been preserved in pottery jars, has provided three copies of Psalms (1QPs[abc]), two of Isaiah (1QIsa[ab]), and one copy each of Genesis, Exodus, Leviticus, and Deuteronomy, as well as of Judges and 1 Samuel. Cave 11 also preserved important scrolls, among them six copies of Psalms (11Q5-9; 11Q11), two of Leviticus, one of Deuteronomy, and one copy of Ezekiel (11Q4).

The number of copies and the form of preservation of the manuscripts at Qumran (as well as citations in Philo or the NT) indicate that the Pentateuch, Isaiah, Minor Prophets, and Psalms were the books that had particular importance—a "canon within the emerging canon"—followed by those of the other Former and Latter Prophets (the historical books, Jeremiah, and Ezekiel) and, lagging far behind, the books in the collection of Writings.

11. Canonical and noncanonical

The biblical canon is not to be considered only as the repository of inspired works but also as the source of inspiration for new writings. Moses, David, Solomon, and the Prophets were the "authors," considered to be inspired. The Qumran parabiblical and the apocryphal and pseudepigraphic literature can be classified according to language, subject matter, or literary genre, but also as developments on the few basic scriptural collections. In this way of categorizing, narrative writings based on the books of the Torah are: *Genesis Apocryphon*, *Assumption (or Testament) of Moses*, *Life of Adam and Eve* (= *Apocalypse of Moses*), *Testament of Abraham*, and the Qumran *Book of Noah* and *Temple Scroll*. Narratives based on canonical historical works are: 1 Ezra, *Biblical Antiquities*, Paralipomena of Jeremiah, as well as the Qumran Apocryphon of Samuel–Kings. Parabiblical writings based on Hymnal Literature are: the *Apocryphal Psalms*, the *Qumran Hodayot*, and the *Psalms of Solomon*. Qumran writings as Sapiential Work (4Q416-19 and 4Q424) are based on canonical Wisdom books. The apocalyptic literature of the Enoch tradition and other Qumran writings developed on the margins or on the edge of a canon that was in process of formation. The entry of the book of Daniel into the canon gave the stamp of legitimacy to some of the apocalyptic ideas and representations that were inspired by prophetic and sapiential books already considered as Scripture, as well as by extrabiblical material.

Some of the books in the Apocrypha and Pseudepigrapha seem to have scriptural status at Qumran: *1 Enoch* and *Jubilees*, as well as Pss 151*a*, 151*b*, 154–55, and the canticle (Sir 51:13-30) found in 11QPs[a]. Tobit and the Letter of Jeremiah were probably also regarded as Scripture. The evidence thereof is similar to that previously presented about canonical books: quotations, quantity of manuscripts, or the appeal to prophetic authority.

These books are represented in Qumran by a large number of manuscripts: *Jubilees* by approximately fifteen scrolls and *1 Enoch* by twelve scrolls. Also the translation of *1 Enoch* into Greek (pap7QEn gr) suggests that it was viewed as Scripture.

The statement in 11QPs^a (col. 27:11), "all these he (David) composed through prophecy which was given him from before the Most High," clearly implies that all the compositions found in 11QPs^a, including the canticle in Sir 51:13-10 and Pss 151a; 151b; 154; and 155, are products of Davidic prophecy. Also Jude 14-15 tells us that Enoch "prophesied, saying."First Enoch and Jubilees are attributed to biblical figures and/or claim their message is from God or an angel (e.g., *1 En.* 1:2; 10:1–11:2; *Jub.* 1:5-18, 22-28, 26-29; 2:1) or from heavenly tablets (e.g., *1 En.* 81:1-2; 93:1; *Jub.* 3:8-14, 31). Some scholars assert that such claims are often characteristic of pseudepigraphical writings and may not be indicative of the authoritative status of these works among those who used them. However, the noncanonical Jewish literature forms part of the total continuum of tradition, the recognition of which corrects the tendency to consider only the two customary Testaments but not the tradition that links them together. Neglect of the so-called "Apocrypha" or "Deuterocanonicals," as well as of the Pseudepigrapha and the Qumran writings, is one of the reasons for an inadequate appreciation of Jewish tradition.

Without this noncanonical tradition of interpretation many things in the NT would have been impossible or at least very unlikely. It was the apocalyptic literature, mainly in the 2nd cent. BCE, that provided the background for much eschatological expectation and for establishing that Jesus was the fulfillment of that which the prophets long ago had said. It was Wisdom and other "intertestamental" books that identified the disobedience of Adam as the calamitous "fall," which brought sin, corruption, and death into human existence. Likewise, Wisdom and Sirach exercised a marked influence on the Christology of the NT, particularly in Paul and Matthew. Paul's concept of law depends on the interpretative tradition from OT times and into later Judaism.

The present-day perception of deterioration in some late Jewish sources is encouraged by the fact of a canon. The finality of the present canon in our Bibles leads us to think that "later Judaism" was in decline and bereft of inspiration in postbiblical times. The deprecation of later Judaism is present in much of OT theology, but the idea that late sources are religiously less reliable is now less defensible. From Daniel or the Qumran manuscripts, we can see the ways in which later Judaism worked over and reappropriated the beliefs, practices, and imagination of earlier OT books. The development of tradition *after* biblical times continues what is discernible *within* biblical times. Tradition is not only a good word for something that occurs after the Bible is revealed to a religious community, but tradition also took place within the period of the development of the canon.

12. The Christian canon of the OT

There are two different explanations of the origins of the Christian canon of the OT. The first explanation supposes Christianity to have inherited a Jewish canon of twenty-two books (which presently makes twenty-four books in the Masoretic text of the Hebrew Bible). It is said by supporters of this explanation that Christianity differed from Judaism in the way that it interpreted the Tanakh as an "Old" Testament, but the number of books and the content of the Hebrew Bible was fixed before the writings by the early Christians. The LXX version, as transmitted in Christian codices from the mid 2nd cent. CE is a collection of books, which in no way was equivalent to a supposed Jewish Alexandrian canon differing from the canon of rabbinic tradition. However, this explanation does not resolve satisfactorily the problems generated by the existence of a Christian canon of the OT, which is larger than the Jewish one, nor does it explain the possible tendencies toward an open canon in the Qumran circles as well as in other groups of the Jewish diaspora.

According to a second explanation, the Christian church did not inherit from Judaism a canon that was already closed. The church had already followed an independent road, different from Judaism, when the rabbinic canon was permanently closed. Right from the start, Christians used the Greek text as the text of the Scriptures. The NT shows great freedom in the use of different textual traditions and so reflects current practice in the period before the proto-Masoretic text (*see* §6; *see also* MASORETES; TEXT, HEBREW, HISTORY OF) was stabilized. Most of the OT quotations attributed to Jesus in the Gospels match the text of the LXX. In some cases the LXX text cited in the NT is different from both the Masoretic and the Aram. text of known targums or different from all known Greek texts. The NT reflects a textual situation previous to the great crisis of the fall of Jerusalem that accelerated the closing of the Jewish canon and the stabilization of the biblical text.

The numerous references or allusions to the Apocrypha and Pseudepigrapha in the NT show that the first Christians relied on a vast literature beyond the limits of the Hebrew canon. They refer especially to the Wisdom of Solomon, Ecclesiasticus, Baruch, 2 Esdras, and 1 Maccabees, but also to *1 Enoch*, the *Assumption of Moses* and 3 and 4 Maccabees. Although never calling specifically any extracanonical literature "scripture," Jude 14 comes close to this when referring to *1 En.* 1:9 as inspired authoritative literature. The Apostolic Fathers of the 2nd cent. churches were likewise informed by more than the current OT literature. The early church received from its Jewish heritage the notion of sacred Scriptures, but apparently not a closed canon.

The question of the OT Christian canon pivots around the Apocrypha or deuterocanonical books or expansions of books. The status of these books in the early church is uncertain. Their inclusion in Christian codices of the Greek. OT suggests that these writings were part of the early church's Bible. According to the various collections of lists of OT canons in the ancient churches, the church fathers acknowledged a broader OT canon that did Jerome. Christian scribes after Jerome included these texts in the codices of the Greek Bible. They were also included in the codices of other trans. of the Greek into *Syr.*, *Eth.*, Armenian, and other Eastern Christian languages.

A rationale must be found to explain the acceptance of the Apocrypha by an early Christian tradition that reflects the position of the NT itself. It seems most probable that the Christian canon of the OT, although more expansive than the rabbinical Hebrew canon, did in fact have an ancestry in the Judaism of Qumran and the NT era. Accordingly, the citation from the "book of Daniel the prophet" (12:10) in Florilegium (4Q174), which ascribes the book of Daniel to the prophetic corpus, corresponds with a marked feature of the Christian canon. Another hint is the fact that the Greek version of Bar 1:1–3:8 has been made by the same translator who produced Jeremiah, which indicates that both books enjoyed in some circles the same canonical consideration.

Many of these books of the Apocrypha are better understood not as interpretation of Scripture but as a continuation of it. In this sense they come closer to the concept of *scripture* than to that of postscriptural *tradition*. They are mostly books of biblical type, coming between the OT and the NT and thus symbolizing the intertestamental continuity. This could have been a factor in the acceptance of them, in contrast to documents of a more specifically "interpretative" type, such as the Qumran *pesharim*, which are not found among the Apocrypha. The Apocrypha exhibit pretensions of canonicity when they place their setting in Assyrian, Babylonian (Judith, Tobith, Baruch, and Letter of Jeremiah), or Persian contexts (Susanna, Bel and the Dragon, Additions to Daniel), thus fulfilling a basic condition for canonicity.

Apocrypha or deuterocanonical writings form a whole in which they relate among themselves and with the canonical book of Daniel. Thus, Additions to Esther treat topics that are similar to those of the book of Judith or to Daniel's dreams. The Jewish sources of 1 and 2 Maccabees are to be found in Dan 7–12, as well as in *1 En.* 85–105 and in the *Testament of Moses*. The coincidence is almost literal between Bar 1:15-18 and Dan 9:7-10, and it is contested whether Baruch is dependent on Daniel, Daniel on Baruch, or both on a common source. All of the apocryphal books often make reference to situations of persecution and (generally speaking) a context of conflict with religious idolatry, political forces, and the prevalent philosophy in diaspora circles.

The Apocrypha can be related to the world of the Jewish diaspora, the Greek speaking as well as the oriental Aramaic speaking diaspora, where Christianity spread. Those books, excepting Wisdom, were written in a Semitic language and in some cases in Aram.: Tobit and possibly the story of Susanna (4Q551), as well as the additions to Daniel, such as those Qumran writings in the Daniel tradition (4Q242; 4Q243-44, and 4Q245; 4Q246; 4Q551; 4Q252-53). Esther is also in the tradition of Aram. stories. Linguistic reasons support the existence of a Semitic original for the Additions to Esther, except for those that correspond to the edicts, redacted in Greek. As for Judith, Jerome states that he made his version from an Aram. text. These writings could enjoy special authority in circles of the Jewish diaspora.

From the rich Jewish literature of the Second Temple period Christians seem to have given preference to writings originally in Aram. or Greek, reflecting the conditions in the diaspora, rather than the Hebrew parabiblical writings reflecting conditions in the Palestinian Jewish communities. Christianity collected and transmitted Jewish "Pseudepigrapha" related primarily to pre-flood characters and to patriarchs, as well as characters from the eschatological times (prophetic sections in *1 Enoch* and *Jubilees*), which allowed for the development of a universal perspective, such as that presented by Paul in Rom 5:12 and 1 Cor 15:22 (also Phil 2:5-6). Christians did not preserve exegetical texts similar to the *pesharim* or legal ones similar to the Temple Scroll.

13. Canonical hermeneutics

The Book of Books, the Bible, is a compendium of collections of books (**ta biblia** in Greek), which can be read, recited, or commented upon in separated pieces, especially the Psalms, but also the stories, *laws*, oracles, and proverbs. But the idea of canon comprises that of totality. The biblical canon as a closed system implies today an interest in the Bible as an intertextual collection of Scriptures, which has a network of meaning that can be taken synchronically in its final, canonical form: a single biblical book is interpreted by what it means within the totality of the canon. The canon forms the context from which it is possible to construct a biblical theology and reclaim dimensions of the biblical texts that have been left aside by biblical criticism. Canonical criticism gives priority to the final or canonical form of the biblical books (or of a collection of books), in contrast to the priority granted by other methods to the study of the earliest stages in the formation of the biblical books. Canonical criticism also takes account of the community (Jewish or Christian) in which the texts of earlier periods acquired definitive and canonical form.

The major characteristic of Scripture as canon is its adaptability or relevance to the ongoing life of the community that passes it on from generation to generation;

second to this relevance is the characteristic of stability. As the stabilization process intensified, the basic Jewish hermeneutic of the biblical text changed from divine inspiration of the messages in the text to verbal inspiration of the text itself, precisely during the course of the 1st cent. of the common era.

The canon has a rhythm of closedness and openness. It is closed because it is a restricted deposit of meanings. But this deposit is open toward a non-ending history of interpretation, rereading and retelling. The plurality that is within the canon is reflected in the plurality of the Jewish and Christian traditions.

The canon is open to two polarized evaluations. 1) The Bible is often presented as a sacred Book of divine origin, but it also invites those outside a religious community to read it as a profane text, representative of a particular culture that spans one millennium of history. The Bible is a "Great Code" that contains the keys to much of the imagination in Western literature. Archetypes and symbols, which crisscross the Bible from beginning to end, confer upon it an internal dynamic and tension (law vs. prophecy) and, at the same time, a movement toward a final denouement (apocalyptic); a single archetypal structure extending from creation to apocalypse.

2) The other evaluation of the canon vindicates its theological value, which implies a plurality of theologies and encloses, at the same time, a pretension of unity: the Hebrew Bible (or OT and NT together) is to be read in its given form as a theological book. The movement that defends canonical criticism makes it into a connection between Scripture and theology and argues that the other disciplines of biblical study often distort the true canonical dimension of Scripture. Among these disciplines, the furthest from canonical criticism is the history of religion. However, this discipline does provide extensive data on ideas and religious symbols of the Persians, Greeks, and others that affected the biblical texts, and thus it helps in understanding how biblical books were interpreted in the Persian and Hellenistic periods. Study of the canonical text alone does not allow us to know, e.g., what interpretation the text of Minor Prophets had in Qumran and in Jewish apocalypticism.

Insofar as it is considered impossible to reconstruct critically a level of the text prior to the proto-Masoretic text (e.g., Qumran manuscripts; *see* §6), there is a tendency to contrast *literary authenticity*, toward which modern criticism has always strived, with *canonical authenticity*. Thus for some readers the authority of a book depends on its literary authenticity and, finally, on the divine inspiration of its author. For other readers, however, the canonical authority inheres less in the book than in the power of the tradition that recognizes it as authentic and inspired.

The setting up of the canon involved the creation of a context within which the Bible was to be interpreted henceforth. In Bible reading, whether devotional or of a more academic exercise, the canon functions (at least for Protestants, less so for Catholics) as the complete source for the proof of doctrine; no words from outside the canon—not being inspired—could have the same force. And yet, the fixing of the canon also entailed a separation of the biblical texts from their context. Once the canon was finalized, every individual book and text of the Bible became inspired, even though the interpretation of a text in an older form than the one corresponding to the final and canonical edition is perfectly legitimate and even necessary during the ongoing process of interpreting a religious book. Late developments often lose the originality of the more primitive texts that preserve the freshness of the "actual words" of the prophets or the power of the "actual deeds" that are fundamental to biblical revelation.

A canonical text is a text with authority. Whereas some philosophers and theologians propose a rehabilitation of authority and tradition, deconstructionism has undermined both rationality and tradition. Deconstruction leads eventually to abolition of canons, because new phenomena, and resistance to time and normative roles, seem to make the past obsolete. As the canon is dismantled, attention is paid to the role of noncanonical readings of canonical texts as well as readings from various contesting or marginal perspectives.

The possibility of ever achieving consensus on any real revision of the canon may be past. More important is the recognition that, against a static conception of the canon, the written text is not the final control of how a community understands or governs itself. There is a continuing process of inspired and canonical interpretation, as in the canon of the Mishnah, well beyond the closure of the biblical canon. Judaism and Christianity, as well as Islam, exhibit a similar pattern of creative development through tradition and a conviction similar to that of the Qumran community and the first Christians that divine revelation was and is not to be confined to any sacred book or inspired individual but continues into the present.

The interpretation of canon spins around a double exigency: to give a role to its formative constitution and to its normative reception. Authority inheres in the book or/and in the tradition that recognizes and confers such an authority to the book. Scripture is inseparable from interpretation, although the biblical text has preeminence over the interpreter. A Jewish approach to the canon links the Hebrew Bible with Midrash and Talmud, a linkage that has the effect of "Judaizing" the Bible. Similarly, a Christian approach to the canon links the OT with the NT, "Christianizing" the Hebrew Bible. It also links both Testaments with their interpretation in the first three cent., until the Christian canon was closed, marking its identity as distinct from the Jewish canon. *See* CANON OF THE NT.

Bibliography: J. M. Auwers and H. J. De Jonge, ed. *The Biblical Canons* (2003); J. Barr. *Holy Scripture: Canon, Authority, Criticism* (1983); J. Barton. *Oracles of God. Perceptions of Ancient Prophecy in Israel after the Exile* (1986); R. T. Beckwith. *The Old Testament Canon of the New Testament Church and its Background in Early Judaism* (1985); J. Blenkinsopp. *Prophecy and Canon. A Contribution to the Study of Jewish Origins* (1977); B. S. Childs. *Old Testament Theology in a Canonical Context* (1985); E. E. Ellis. *The Old Testament in Early Christianity: Canon and Interpretation in the Light of Modern Research* (1992); P. W. Flint. *The Dead Sea Psalms Scrolls and the Book of Psalms* (1997); P. W. Flint. "Noncanonical Writings in the Dead Sea Scrolls: Apocrypha, Other Previously Known Writings, Pseudepigrapha." *The Bible at Qumran. Text, Shape, and Interpretation* (2001) 80–123; N. Frye. *The Great Code. The Bible and Literature* (1982); A. van der Kooij and K. van der Toorn, ed. *Canonization and Decanonization: Papers Presented to the International Conference of the Leiden Institute for the Study of Religions* (1998); S. Z. Leiman. *The Canonization of Hebrew Scripture: The Talmudic and Midrashic Evidence* (1976); J. P. Lewis. "Jamnia Revisited." *The Canon Debate*, ed. L. M. McDonald and J. A. Sanders (2002) 146–62; L. M. McDonald. *The Formation of the Christian Biblical Canon* (1995); B. Metzger. *The Canon of the New Testament: Its Origin, Development, and Significance* (1987); G. W. E. Nickelsburg. *Ancient Judaism and Christian Origins. Diversity, Continuity, and Transformation* (2003); M. Saebo. *Hebrew Bible/Old Testament: The History of Its Interpretation* (1996); M. Saebo. *On the Way to Canon: Creative Tradition History in the Old* Testament (1998); J. A. Sanders. *The Psalms Scroll of Qumrân Cave 11 [11QPsª]* (1965); J. A. Sanders. *From Sacred Story to Sacred Text. Canon as Paradigm* (1991); L. H. Schiffmann. *Reclaiming the Dead Sea Scrolls. The History of Judaism, the Background of Christianity, the Lost Library of Qumran* (1994); A. Sundberg. *The Old Testament of the Early Church* (1964); E. Tov. *Textual Criticism of the Hebrew Bible*, 2nd rev. ed. (2001); E. Tov., "The Status of the Masoretic Text in Modern Text Editions of the Hebrew Bible: The Relevance of Canon." *The Canon Debate* (2002) 234–51; E. Ulrich. "The Canonical Process, Textual Criticism, and Latter Stages in the Composition of the Bible." *Studies in the Bible, Qumran, and the Ancient Near East Presented to Shemaryahu Talmon*, ed. M. Fishbane and E. Tov (1992) 267–91; E. Ulrich. *The Dead Sea Scrolls and the Origins of the Bible* (1999); E. Ulrich. "The Notion and Definition of Canon." *The Canon Debate* (2002) 21–35; J. C. VanderKam. *The Dead Sea Scrolls Today* (1994); J. C. VanderKam. "Authoritative Literature in the Dead Sea Scrolls." *DSD* 5/3 (1998) 382–402; J. C. VanderKam. "Questions of Canon Viewed Through the Dead Sea Scrolls." *The Canon Debate* (2002) 91–109; J. C. VanderKam and P. Flint. "The Dead Sea Scrolls and the Canon of the Hebrew Bible/Old Testament." *The Meaning of the Dead Sea Scrolls. Their Significance for Understanding the Bible, Judaism, Jesus, and Christianity* (2002) 154–181.

JULIO TREBOLLE

CANONICAL CRITICISM. The methodological interests of canonical criticism are framed by Scripture's performance in mediating the word of a living God for the church. From this angle of vision, the principal referent of a biblical text is not the ancient social world of its author, its intended meaning for first readers/auditors, or the reconstruction of the "real" story it narrates; rather, the goal of a faithful reading of Scripture is "knowing God." In this sense, then, a "canonical approach" to biblical interpretation is not a modern "criticism" that proposes a particular literary or historical strategy for retrieving a text's "original" meaning. While such a strategy is not at odds with the church's theological intentions for its Scriptures, the interpreter's quest for a text's original meaning is productive only when critical exegesis is the means of forming a faithful life of service to God and neighbor.

Because the interpretive practices of its practitioners turn on the theological reflection of biblical texts, canonical criticism emphasizes text-centered exegesis. The purchase of any biblical criticism is diminished if deployed in search of the horizons of ancient worlds behind the text without a complementary interest in the horizons of its current readers. Canonical criticism's primary exegetical task, then, is the illumination of a text's theological meaning within two very different settings: historical—the process that formed the biblical canon during the first four or five cent. of the Common Era—and literary-the final "shape" of the biblical canon itself. Moreover, Childs approaches the biblical canon in its final literary form, OT and NT, as a special kind of literature, the sacred Scriptures of the church, whose content when read within a worshiping community bears coherent and ongoing witness to the living God. According to Sanders, on the other hand, the historic phenomena that produced the Bible provide a hermeneutical guide to aid the interpreter when negotiating between the church's confessed beliefs about God and a changing social setting that constantly challenges its religious identity as a people belonging to God.

As guided by both these "canonical" contexts, historical and literary, biblical texts that carry different theological freight are read together by interpreters as complementary elements of Scripture's whole witness to God. The final arrangement of collections within the biblical canon is also suggestive of a logical pattern for engaging Scripture. The OT is read before picking up the NT, since the story of Israel's God is not only presumed but also frames the NT story of creation's Messiah who personifies the truth and grace of Israel's

God. Further, within the NT the fourfold narrative of Jesus' life is placed and therefore read first as foundational for a believer's theological outlook and also as the christological subtext of every other NT book. Acts is read with knowledge of the "first book" (= fourfold Gospel) in mind—what "Jesus began to do and teach" (Acts 1:1). By reading Acts with its portraits of Paul and the Jerusalem Pillars (Gal 2:9; "James, Cephas, and John"), the reader is better prepared to read the two collections of NT letters, Pauline and Pillars, with theological understanding. The Book of Revelation's "words of the prophecy" of "what must soon take place" (1:1-3) are appropriately read last as the dramatic conclusion of the Bible's story of God's restoration of the created order.

Finally, practitioners of canonical criticism are fully alert to the uses of Scripture that authorize competing, and sometimes wrong-headed, definitions of Christian faith. Rather than targeting the author's intentions for a biblical text to delimit a text's normative meaning, the church's intentions for a text are primarily cued by those reasons that led to the admission of that text into the biblical canon—that is, the historical reasons for a book's canonization and the theological role it subsequently performs within the biblical canon have greater hermeneutical value than the reconstruction of that book's meaning at the point of its origin. Accordingly, the most essential rule in regulating meaning making is not that of literary or historical criticism but the church's Rule of Faith—a grammar of theological agreements the church catholic received from the apostles who learned the Rule from the Lord Jesus. The theological "grammar" of any biblical interpretation, and its results in a congregation's common life, must agree with this Rule for it to be constitutive of Christian faith.

Bibliography: W. J. Abraham. *Canon and Criterion in Christian Theology* (1998); Brevard S. Childs. *Biblical Theology of the Old and New Testaments: Theological Reflection on the Christian Bible* (1993); Lee M. McDonald and James A. Sanders, ed. *The Canon Debate* (2002); Robert W. Wall and E. E. Lemcio. *The New Testament as Canon: A Reader in Canonical Criticism* (1992).

ROBERT W. WALL

CANOPY [חֻפָּה khuppah, סֻכָּה sukkah, עָב ʿav, שַׁפְרִיר shafrir]. A shelter used as protection from the elements in the ANE. Unlike a tent or tabernacle, a canopy is an overhead covering, made of fabric or wood, rather than one with sides.

Special kinds of shelters function as canopies in the Bible. Bridal couples were like royalty on their wedding day; they apparently were seated on a dais with a sheltering canopy overhead (Ps 19:5; Joel 2:16), just as were kings (Jer 43:10). Judith beheads Holofernes,

the chief general of Nebuchadnezzar's army, on a bed under a canopy (Jdt 13:9), and she dedicates the canopy to God (Jdt 16:19). Monumental buildings—the Jerusalem palace (1 Kgs 7:6) and Temple (Ezek 41:25)—had some sort of canopied shelter in their forecourts. "Canopy" is also projected onto the heavens as the darkness covering God's presence (2 Sam 22:12; Ps 18:11) or as the divine glory over Mount Zion (Isa 4:5). *See* BOOTH; BRIDE; BRIDEGROOM; HALL; TEMPLE, JERUSALEM; THEOPHANY IN THE OLD TESTAMENT.

CAROL MEYERS

CANTICLES. *See* SONG OF SONGS.

CAPERNAUM kuh-puhr′nay-uhm [Καφαρναούμ Kapharnaoum]. Capernaum was the center of Jesus' Galilean ministry (Matt 4:13; 8:5; 17:24; Mark 2:1; 9:33; Luke 4:23, 31; 7:1; John 2:12; 4:46; 6:17, 24, 59). Located on the northwest shore of the Sea of Galilee, the place was also known as "Tal Hum" in Arabic (the "Hill of Hum"), and "Kefar Nahum" in Hebrew (the "Village of Nahum"). Capernaum derives from the Greek spelling in Codex Alexandrinus and later traditions. Though there is archaeological evidence (pottery shards) of human activity here as early as the 3rd millennium BCE, the town reached its peak during the Late Roman and Byzantine periods, with an estimated size of ca. 13 acres and a population of ca. 1,500 people. By the 10th cent., Capernaum was reduced to an insignificant village and shortly thereafter was unoccupied until the 19th cent. During the intervening centuries it was used only by Bedouins for seasonal agriculture and grazing and as a campground for local fishermen.

Though visited by many pilgrims in antiquity, the first modern researcher to survey the site was the American scholar Edward Robinson. In June of 1838, Robinson correctly recognized the remains of the synagogue but failed to identify the site with Capernaum, which he located some 2 mi. to the southwest, at what is now known as Khirbet Minya. Since this latter site contains no remains antedating the Early Arabic periods (7th–10th cent.), most authorities readily accept the identification of the NT town with the ruins of Tal Hum. This identification was first suggested by the British explorer Charles Wilson in 1866, who thought he had found the remains of the 1st cent. synagogue mentioned in the Gospel of Luke (7:5). From this time onward, a tradition was established that became the main cause of the sacredness of the place and its attraction to Christian pilgrims.

In 1894 the ruins of the synagogue (later to be dated correctly to the 4th–5th cent.) and the western part of the site were acquired by the Franciscan Custody of the Holy Land, while some years later the Greek Orthodox Church of Jerusalem acquired the northeastern section.

Photo courtesy of Vassilios Tzaferis

Figure 1: Aerial View of Capernaum: Synagogue remains from 4th–5th cent. in center of picture.

For most of the 20th cent. (and into the 21st) the Franciscans have conducted excavations, with many interruptions, on their part of the site. While domestic structures, as well as public streets, have been exposed here, the site is best known for the magnificent synagogue and an octagonal building that has been identified by the excavators as a late 5th cent. Christian church built over the house of Peter, the apostle. The claim by the Franciscans that 1st cent. synagogue remains lie underneath the later structure has not been confirmed archaeologically.

On the other hand, the Greek Orthodox section, comprising an area of over 200,000 sq. ft., has a different story. Neglected for most of its history, it was not until 1978 that archaeologists were allowed for the first time to excavate here. The excavations continued through 1987.

Thus two separate and totally independent excavations have been conducted on the site. But it must be emphasized that the story of ancient Capernaum is one, and the results of both excavations need to be consulted.

Evidence of occupation on this part of the site goes back at least as early as the Middle Bronze Age (walls and pottery), but the major architectural remains are from the Roman through the Early Arab periods (1st–10th cent.). During this long period, Capernaum survived through a thriving fishing industry, agriculture products, and trade. The town was located on the main trade route leading to Syria from the port cities of Acco-Ptolemias and Caesarea and was a border town between the Golan and the Galilee.

Among many discoveries, two were unexpected. The first was in June of 1982 when a hoard of 282 Umayyad gold dinars was found under a courtyard stone. Made of 22=caret gold, each is about the size of an American quarter. They were minted between 696/697 and 743/744 CE. Except for the dates of the coins, they all bear the same inscriptions except one. Found in a controlled archaeological context, these coins provide a unique look into the cultural, political, and religious world at the point where Islamic and Byzantine cultures intersect.

The second surprise was found in the SW corner of the site next to the lake. Here a continuous sequence of occupation from Early Roman through the Early Arab periods (1st–10th cent.) was discovered. What was not expected were the remains of a Roman bathhouse of

John Laughlin

Figure: 2 Capernaum gold hoard as found.

the 2nd–3rd cent. A probe beneath one of its rooms revealed remains of an earlier building that was dated to the 1st cent. CE. Whether or not this earlier structure also served the function of a bathhouse is unclear.

The archaeological evidence from the Greek Orthodox property clearly indicates that during the Late Roman period, Capernaum was a well-organized and prosperous town with several large and well-constructed public buildings lining the waterfront. However, the size and extent of the town during the time of Jesus is not as clear. Without the removal of these later structures (found on both properties), which is not likely to occur, the 1st cent. town will remain relatively unknown. But its location and economy, based primarily on agriculture and fishing, must have made it important enough to have a Roman centurion stationed here as mentioned in the Gospels (Matt 8:5).

In summary, the archaeological excavations on both sides of the site have succeeded in reconstructing the history of Capernaum through archaeological data. Nearly an entire town, with its houses, courts, religious and other public buildings, has emerged from obscurity. The town suffered destruction both at the hand of humans as well as by earthquakes. The last earthquake, occurring in the 11th cent., dealt a fatal blow from which the town never recovered.

Bibliography: Virgilio Carbo. *The House of St. Peter at Capharnaum: A Preliminary Report of the First Two Campaigns of Excavations* (1972); John C. H. Laughlin. "Capernaum From Jesus' Time and Afterwards," *BAR* 19.5 (1993) 54–61, 90; Stanislao Loffreda. *Recovering Capharnaum* (1985); Vassilios Tzaferis, et al. *Excavations at Capernaum, Volume 1, 1978–1982* (1989).

JOHN C. H. LAUGHLIN

CAPHAR-SALAMA kaf'uhr-sal'uh-muh [Χαφαρσαλ– αμα Chapharsalama]. The site of a battle between the Seleucid general NICANOR and JUDAS MACCABEUS (1 Macc 7:31). The element *slm* seems to be relatively frequent in Palestinian place names, making identification difficult. One suggestion is that this was Khirbet Deir Sellam, ca. 8 km north northeast of Jerusalem, but only Arab remains have been found there. More likely is Khirbet Salama, ca. 10 km northwest of Jerusalem on the road to Beth-Horon, possibly mentioned by Eusebius (*Onom.* 153). Second Maccabees 14:16 mentions a battle at Dessau (or perhaps Lessau), but this may be a different battle at a different place.

LESTER L. GRABBE

CAPHTOR kaf'tor [כַּפְתּוֹר kaftor]. In Gen 10:14 Caphtor is mentioned as the seventh "offspring" of EGYPT. The Caphtorim, inhabitants of Caphtor (Deut 2:23), displaced the AVVIM along the southern coast of Israel near GAZA. According to Amos (9:7), Caphtor is the place from which PHILISTINES origi-

nally came, and Jeremiah (47:4) called it an island. Although based on the Table of Nations (Gen 10:14) it would seem that the Philistines came from Casluhim, most scholars prefer to relate the phrase "whence came the Philistines" with the Caphtorim. Caphtor is a well-known geographic place in the ancient Near Eastern texts. It is used in Eg. (kftiw, kftyw), Akkadian (kaptara), Ugaritic (kptr) and Greek (Καβδηρος Kabdēros) texts. The wide consensus today identifies Caphtor with Crete, an island in the Mediterranean. The Bible itself testified for a connection between Philistia and Crete (Ezek 25:16; Zeph 2:5). There is a possibility that Caphtor includes more islands in the Crete vicinity. Archaeological evidence also points to the origin of the Philistines from this region. The LXX sometimes understands Caphtor as CAPPADOCIA (Deut 2:23).

ITZHAQ SHAI

CAPITAL [כֹּתֶרֶת kothereth, כַּפְתֹּר kaftor]. An architectural element; the top member of a column, pillar, pilaster, or pier wall. In the OT, the NRSV most often translates the Hebrew word kothereth as *capital*. Kothereth is used specifically of the decorative bronze capitals on top of the pillars, Jacin and Boaz in front of the Solomonic Temple (1 Kgs 7:16ff.). One additional word is translated twice as capital in the NRSV (Amos 9:1; Zeph 2:14): kaptor. Elsewhere this latter term is translated as a flower part, calyx, and describes a decorative element of the menorah/lampstand in the Tabernacle (Exod 25:31, etc.).

In archaeological contexts, capitals of limestone, known as proto-Ionic or volute capitals, have been found at approximately ten sites in Israel and Jordan. These capitals are characterized by volutes and central triangles or bud-shaped elements suggesting a floral imagery. *See* ARCHITECTURE, OT.

JOEL F. DRINKARD, JR.

Reuben G. Bullard, Jr., Karak Resources Project
Figure 1: Volute Capital, Mudaybiᶜ, Jordan

CAPITOLIAS [Καπιτολιας Kapitolias]. Roman city identified with modern BEIT RAS, located in northwest TRANSJORDAN about 3 mi. north of IRBID. Coins indicate that it was founded in 97/98 CE. Ptolemy lists it as one of the DECAPOLIS cities, and it is included in the Province of Arabia in 106 CE. *See* RAS, BEIT.

CAPPADOCIA kap'uh-doh'shee-uh [Καππαδοκίαν Kappadokian]. A major region of central Asia Minor, extending at its largest from the Taurus Mountains and the Euphrates in the south to the Black Sea in the north and from the Upper Euphrates in the east to the Halys River and Lake Tuz in the west. Historically, the name "Cappadocia" was often applied to only a portion of this territory, with the region along the Black Sea referred to as "Pontus" and eastern portions included in Armenia. The core of Cappadocia was the high central plateau of Anatolia. It formed a central part of the Hittite territory in the mid to late 2nd millennium BCE. Under the Persians it was at first a single satrapy, then it was divided into two (Cappadocia and Pontus). Cappadocia became a semi-independent kingdom with the conquests of Alexander, and a dynasty of kings known as the Ariarthids ruled for two cent. In the 2nd cent. BCE they turned against the Seleucid overlords and championed the Roman cause, but the dynasty came to an end ca. 100 BCE. A new dynasty of Ariobarzanes was approved by the Romans; however, the royal house became entangled in the civil wars of the Roman republic, and this dynasty too ended, after only three kings. The last ruler was Archelaus I Philopatria (36 BCE to 17 CE), whose daughter married Alexander, a son of HEROD the Great of Judea. When Archelaus died in 17 CE, the emperor Tiberias turned Cappadocia into a Roman province, which is mentioned in the Bible in Acts 2:9 and 1 Pet 1:1.

LESTER GRABBE

CAPTAIN [שַׂר sar, רַב rav; סֹפֵר sofer, רֹאשׁ ro'sh, פֶּחָה pekhah; שָׁלִישׁ, shalish; χιλίαρχος chiliarchos, στρατηγός stratēgos, ἑκατοντάρχης ekatontarchēs, κυβερνήτης kubernētēs]. Typically a man with the authority of military command (an officer), but sometimes anyone in a position of authority.

In contemporary translations of the OT and NT, *captain* indicates four positions of authority: the captain of a small military unit, of an entire army, of a ship, and of the Temple guard.

A. Captain of a Small Military Unit

The most common OT term for *captain* (sar) often designates the leader of a small, sometimes elite, military unit, particularly the captain of the (royal) guard (Gen 37:36; 39:1; 40:3-4; 41:10, 12; 2 Kgs 11:4, 9, 10, 14, although rav designates the captain of the guard in Jer 52:19, 24), captain of a raiding band (2 Sam 4:2), captain of the chariots (1 Kgs 22:31-33; 2 Chr

18:30-32), and captain of fifty soldiers (2 Kgs 1:9-14; Isa 3:3) or of one hundred soldiers (2 Kgs 11:15, 19; 2 Chr 23:9-14, 20). The LXX anachronistically supplies the Greco-Roman term *centurion* (ekatontarchēs) for captain of one hundred in 2 Chr 23:14, but the terms are not parallel (*see* CENTURION).

The size of the military unit that a sar commanded is sometimes unspecified (Judg 7:25; 8:3; 1 Sam 22:2; 1 Kgs 9:22; Job 39:25). When an individual's military authority and position are ambiguous, other Hebrew terms are likely to appear: sofer, Judg 5:14; Isa 36:9; rosh, Num 14:4; pekhah, 2 Kgs 18:24; shalish, 1 Kgs 7:2, 17, 19; 2 Kgs 15:25). In the Apocrypha and NT, chiliarchos conveys this conception (1 Esd 1:9; Jdt 14:12; 1 Macc 16:19; Mark 6:21; John 18:12; Acts 21:31-33; 22:24-29; 23:10-22; 24:17; 25:23; Rev 6:15; 19:18).

B. Captain of the Army

A sar could command an entire army (Josh 5:14-15; 1 Sam 12:9; 14:50; 1 Kgs 4:13; 5:1;; 26:26; Jer 40:7). However, a rab also commonly indicates the highest-ranking officers (Jer 39:9-11, 13; 40:1-2, 5; 43:6; 52:12, 26, 30; Dan 2:14). Sar and rav can be used interchangably (2 Kgs 25:8-26:26).

C. Captain of a Boat

In the OT, rav designated the commander of Jonah's ship (Jonah 1:6). In the NT, the commanders of Paul's ship in Acts 27:11 and of the doomed trading vessels in Rev 18:17 are kubernētes.

D. Captain of the Temple Police

Luke narrates the participation of several captains of the Temple guard (stratēgos) in Jesus' arrest (22:4, 52) and the participation of a single captain in opposition to the apostles' early Christian message (Acts 4:1; 5:24-26). Although little is known about these persons, Luke portrays their duties as quasi military and not as religious. *See* ARMOR-BEARER; CENTURION; CHARIOT; RABSHAKEH; RASSARIS; TEMPLE.

Bibliography: Simon Anglim, Rob Rice, Phyllis Jestice, Scott Rusch, and John Serrati. *Fighting Techniques of the Ancient World (3000 B.C. to 500 A.D.)* (2003); Richard Gabriel. *The Military History of Ancient Israel* (2003).

THOMAS E. PHILLIPS

CAPTAIN OF THE TEMPLE [סָגָן saghan, הָאֱלֹהִים נְגִיד בֵּת, naghidh beth ha'elohim; στρατηγος τοῦ ἱεροῦ stratēgos tou hierou, προστάτης πυλῆς τοῦ ἱεροῦ prostatēs pulēs tou hierou]. Various Hebrew and Greek terms are used to designate this priestly official, "chief officer of the house of God," who commanded the Jerusalem Temple GUARD (Jer 20:1; 1 Chr 9:11; 2 Chr 31:13; Neh 11:11; 2 Macc 3:4) and was second only to the HIGH PRIEST in Temple authority. His duties included keeping order on the Temple mount and in its buildings, especially guarding the gates, supervising sentries, and guarding the Temple treasury. The MISHNAH details the places where he placed priests and Levites as night sentries and how he made rounds to supervise them. If he found them sleeping, he beat them noisily as a warning to others, and could burn their clothing (*m. Mid.* 1.1-2).

In the NT the captain/commander of the Temple appears in Acts 4:1; 5:24, 26; and Luke 22:4, 52. The plural, strategoi, in Luke 22 likely means the captain and his subordinate officers who participated in the arrest of Jesus. The close association of the captain of the Temple with the high priest in the NT and Josephus indicates that he likely was a leading SADDUCEE.

ROBERT E. VAN VOORST

CAPTIVE, CAPTOR, CAPTURE. *See* EXILE; SLAVERY; WAR, METHODS, TACTICS, WEAPONS OF (BRONZE AGE THROUGH PERSIAN PERIOD); WAR, METHODS, TACTICS, WEAPONS OF (HELLENISTIC THROUGH ROMAN PERIODS).

CAPTIVITY. *See* DISPERSION; EXILE.

CARABASION kair'uh-bay'zhee-uhn [Καραβασιων Karabasiōn]. Descendant of Bani who dismissed his foreign wife, as Ezra instructed him (1 Esd 9:34). The name is absent in Ezra 10:34-37.

CARAVAN [אֹרְחָה 'orkhah]. The caravan is a group or company (Gen 37:25; Job 6:18; Isa 21:13) that carried merchandise long distances with the use of pack animals for transport. The Hebrew word is related to both the traveler and to the "way" upon which the journey took place (Judg 5:6). Israelite caravans primarily used donkeys to transport goods from one tribal area to another. The majority of caravans noted in the OT appear to be peoples who lived in the arid desert areas of the ANE (Judg 8:11, "the way of the nomads" NIV). Traveling together provided security in barren and dangerous areas. The nomadic Ishmaelites/Midianites purchased Joseph in Gen 37 on their way to Egypt. By the 12th–11th cent. BCE the CAMEL became the transport for most caravans in the region. The Arabs of the latter OT and the NT period, Nabateans, controlled the trade that followed routes connecting the Arabian Peninsula, Babylon, Phoenician seaports, and Egypt. Important caravan routes crossed at Megiddo, bringing much wealth to Israel. The cosmopolitan nature of Israel in Amos is a direct result of the benefits from world trade connections. *See* CITY.

MICHAEL G. VANZANT

CARCASS. *See* CLEAN AND UNCLEAN.

CARCHEMISH kahr'kuh-mish [כַּרְכְּמִישׁ karkemish;

Καρχαμεις Karchameis, Καρκαμυς Karkamys]. A major city of northern Syria, located ca. 100 km (62 mi.) northeast of Aleppo, near the major crossing of the upper Euphrates River. Because of this strategic location, Carchemish was continuously occupied from the 4th millennium BCE and became a major trade and military center. Although initially independent, the city aligned itself with Mitanni in the mid 2nd millennium BCE before being conquered by the Egyptian pharaoh THUTMOSE III in the 15th cent. BCE, and then the Hittite king Suppiluliumas a little more than a century later. Carchemish became an Assyrian vassal in the 8th cent. BCE before being destroyed by King SARGON II in 717 BCE (alluded to in Isa 10:9, which lists several major Syrian cities that, like Israelite Samaria, fell to the Assyrian Empire). Carchemish is also mentioned in the Bible in 2 Chr 35:20; Jer 46:2; and 1 Esd 1:25 as the site of a famous battle in 605 BCE in which the Babylonian king NEBUCHADNEZZAR defeated the waning forces of the Assyrians and their Egyptian allies, led by Pharaoh Neco II. A few years previous, in 609 BCE, Judah's King Josiah had been killed while attempting to prevent Neco's army from marching through Israel to rendezvous with the Assyrians. As a result Judah became an Egyptian vassal, then a vassal of the Babylonians upon the Egyptians' defeat by Nebuchadnezzar. The Babylonian destruction of Judah and Jerusalem and the exile of at least Judah's upper classes followed in 586 BCE.

SUSAN ACKERMAN

CARE [שָׁמַר shamar, שׂוּם sum, דְּאָגָה de'aghah; ὁράω horaō, βλέπω blepō, σκοπέω skopeō]. Various Hebrew and Greek terms are used for a range of meanings of "care," from anxiety and sorrow (Ezek 4:16) to positive regard with interest, solicitude, and diligent concern (Luke 10:34). Care can suggest expectations of duty and obligation (Num 7:9) or personal feelings of warmth (1 Tim 3:5).

In the OT care is generally concrete. Joseph is given care of the prisoners when the chief jailer commits them to Joseph's hand (Gen 39:22). Presumably, Joseph's responsibility included their physical well-being, but perhaps also their protection and security. Pharaoh tells Moses to take care (make sure, beware) not to show his face again in the royal presence (Exod 10:28). Taking care of the holy things involves following or obeying prescribed procedures (Num 7:9).

In 2 Sam 18:3 concern (sum) is associated with the heart (לֵב lev), which for the Israelites involved thoughtfulness, since they understood the heart as a person's center. Care (de'aghah) can indicate anxiety or fearfulness as in Ezek 4:16 where God says that Jerusalem will ration bread and water with fearfulness and dismay.

In the NT a common recurrent theme is the metaphorical link between the eye seeing/watching and caring. The root horaō or "look" is used in Matt 18:10 and Luke 12:15. Other roots include blepō (to pay especially close attention to; 1 Cor 3:10; 8:9; Gal 5:15; Heb 3:12) and skopeō (to notice or look closely; Gal 6:1). Second Corinthians 4:18 uses both roots: "because we look (skopeō) not at what can be seen (blepō) but at what cannot be seen (blepō)." The term "episcopy" as one who has the responsibility of safeguarding or correct oversight is a definition of care by the church (Phil 2:4; Gal 6:1; Luke 11:35). *See* ANXIETY; PROVIDENCE; SUFFERING.

M. KATHRYN ARMISTEAD

CARIA kair´ee-uh [כָּרִי kari]. The name of a people and also the mountainous region inhabited by them in southwest Asia Minor, bounded by the Mycale mountains and the Maeander River on the north, the Salbacus Mountains on the east, the Aegean on the west and the south. The Carians were famed as mercenaries and might even have been among David's troops (2 Sam 20:23 Ketiv) and the Jerusalem Temple guards (2 Kgs 11:4, 19). The NT refers to the Carian cities of Miletus (Acts 20:15-17; 2 Tim 4:20) and Cnidus (Acts 27:7); other important cities were Halicarnasus and Caunus.

LESTER L. GRABBE

CARITES. *See* CHERETHITES AND PELETHITES.

CARKAS kahr´kuhs [כַּרְכַּס kharkas]. An attendant among King Ahasuerus' seven eunuchs, who were requested to bring him Queen Vashti (Esth 1:10).

CARMEL kahr´muhl [כַּרְמֶל karmel; Χερμελ Chermel]. Carmel is known for the DAVID and NABAL episode (1 Sam 25:2-40), as the birthplace of HEZRO, one of David's soldiers (2 Sam 23:35; 1 Chr 11:37), and ABIGAIL, whom David later married (1 Sam 25:40; 27:3; 2 Sam 2:2; 3:3). Also called Khirbet Kurmul, the city is located in the Hebron hills in Judah northeast of Khirbet Susiya and north of Moan (Ilan and Amit). *See* CARMEL, MOUNT.

JILL L. BAKER

CARMEL, MOUNT kahr´muhl [כַּרְמֶל karmel]. Because of its abundant flora, Carmel, meaning "vineyard," "garden-land," or "fruitful" (Isa 10:18; 16:10), may be used as a metaphor for beauty and fertility (Song 7:5; 2 Kgs 19:23; Isa 35:2; 37:24). Conversely, in the absence of flora during drought, Carmel is a metaphor for desolation (Isa 33:9). Mount Carmel was the meeting place between ELIJAH and the prophets of BAAL and ASHERAH (1 Kgs 18:19-40) and later a sanctuary for Elijah (2 Kgs 2:25; 4:25).

Mount Carmel, Jebel Kurmul, or Jebel Mar Elyas (Elijah), consists of a limestone ridge, stretching southeasterly from Haifa for ca. 32 km (20 mi.), dividing the Plain of ACCO in the north from the Plains of SHARON

and Philistia to the south. The highest elevation is Rom Ha-Karmel, 546 m (1,791 ft.) above sea level.

The earliest Egyptian reference to Mount Carmel may date to the reign of Pepi I (ca. 2300–2181 BCE). Other possible references to Mount Carmel, called Rosh-Kadesh (Wilson), appear in topological lists of various pharaohs, and there are further references in records of the Neo-Assyrian king SHALMANESER III.

Bibliography: A. L. Oppenheim. "Babylonian and Assyrian Historical Texts." James B. Pritchard, ed. *Ancient Near Eastern Texts Relating to the Old Testament* (1950), 265–317; F. Safar. *A Further Text of Shalmaneser III. Sumer* 7 (1951) 3–21; John A. Wilson. "Egyptian Historical Texts: Lists of Asiatic Countries Under the Egyptian Empire." *Ancient Near Eastern Texts Relating to the Old Testament* (1950) 227–64.

JILL L. BAKER

CARMI kahr´mi [כַּרְמִי karmi]. "Vinedresser." 1. Son of Reuben, ancestor of the Carmites (Num 26:6; Gen 46:9; Exod 6:14; 1 Chr 5:3).

2. Judahite father of Achan (Josh 7) or Achar (1 Chr 2:7), who violated Joshua's ban during the conquest of Jericho.

3. Probably *Caleb* instead of *Carmi* (1 Chr 4:1).

CARMONIANS kahr-moh´nee-uhns [Lat. *Carmonii*]. An ancient agricultural people in the province of Carmonia (modern Kerman) in southern PERSIA, whom HERODOTUS identifies as one of the tribes that CYRUS the Great persuaded to revolt against the Medes (*Hist.* 1.125). The Carmonians are mentioned only in 2 Esd 15:28-33, which records a vision of warfare in "the land of the Assyrians" (vv. 30, 33) between "the dragons of Arabia" (v. 29) and "the Carmonians" (v. 30), probably referring to a series of conflicts between Odenathus, prince of PALMYRA, and Shapur I, king of Persia, between 261 and 267 CE.

JOSEPH L. TRAFTON

CARNAIM kahr-nay´im [Καρναιν Karnain]. A town in Gilead, including its sacred precincts, that Judas Maccabeus destroyed (2 Macc 5:26, 43-44). Genesis 14:5 indicates that it is ASHEROTH-KARNAM.

CARNELIAN [אֹדֶם ʾodhem; σάρδιον sardion]. CARNELIAN is the first stone of the high priest's breastpiece (Exod 28:17; 39:10), one of the gems adorning the king of Tyre (Ezek 28:13), and the sixth stone, sardion, in the wall's foundation of the New Jerusalem (Rev 21:20). CARNELIAN is also used as a descriptor for God's appearance on the throne (Rev 4:3). CARNELIAN was highly valued in the ANE, and it has been found with relative frequency in biblical-period archaeological excavations, especially in the form of beads and flower-type AMULETS. CARNELIAN is a variety of chalcedony that ranges from a slightly translucent color of red to brownish-red.

ELIZABETH E. PLATT

CARPENTER [חָרָשׁ kharash; τέκτων tekton]. A skilled artisan who works with wood. Vast amounts of archaeological evidence for building with wood (stairs, second levels, furniture, doors, and gates) are found throughout the history of ancient Israel. While the meaning of the Hebrew words for hand tools that were used by carpenters is sometimes uncertain, because these words are only infrequently attested (*see* Jer 10:3 and Isa 44:13), archaeological excavations dating back to the Iron Age have produced examples of almost every type of hand tool associated with carpenters in the present day. Carpentry techniques were quite advanced (e.g., gluing, beveling, inlaying, dove-tail joining, etc.). These data suggest that carpenters were part of a skilled artisan group.

In the OT, kharash is used for any artisan of wood, stone, or metals. The combination of *artisan* (kharash) and *wood* (עֵץ 'ets) distinguishes carpenters from masons and smiths, and it occurs nine times. In each instance, the LXX uses tekton as the translation. In 2 Sam 5:11, HIRAM, king of Trye, sends carpenters to build David's palace. Likewise, in texts that describe Temple repairs, there is mention of skilled carpenters (*see* repairs of Jehoash in 2 Kgs 12, and of Josiah in 2 Kgs 22 and 2 Chr 34). Isaiah 44:13 describes the tools (string, plane, chisel, and compass) and methods used by carpenters. When these data are combined with the archaeological data, it is evident that ancient carpenters were considered skilled artisans and not common laborers. This is likely part of the reason why artisans are included in the group of Judean leaders who are deported from Jerusalem (*see* 2 Kgs 24:16; Jer 24:1; and Jer 29:2).

Only two carpenters are specifically mentioned in the NT—Joseph and Jesus (Matt 13:55; Mark 6:3). Commentators cite these references as evidence of Jesus' *humble* origins. A notable exception is Geza Vermes, who points to a latter Talmudic tradition that carpenters (identified by the word nagar) are noted for their wisdom. It is impossible to determine whether this later tradition dates back to the time of Jesus, but the archaeological and biblical evidence cited above suggest that at the very least carpenters throughout the biblical period were skilled artisans, who were separate from common laborers.

ANDREW G. VAUGHN

CARPET [שְׂמִיכָה semikhah, מַדִּין middin, צָפִית tsafith, גְּנָזִים genazim]. Various words are translated RUG or carpet in the OT, though the meaning is never certain. For example, mdd, the root of middin in Judg 5:10, has a semantic range that covers "measure" and "garments." Similar nuances pertain to Judg

4:18 (semikhah), Isa 21:5 (tsafith), and Ezek 27:24 (gezanim). Thus the precise classification of textiles into separate subgroups (clothing, cushions, carpets) seems to be more definitive in the present time than in biblical times. The NT contains no reference to carpets.

JACQUELINE LAPSLEY

CARPUS kahr'puhs [Κάρπος Karpos]. A resident of Troas, with whom Paul had left his cloak, some books, and some parchments (2 Tim 4:13). According to Eusebius (*Hist. eccl.* 4.15), a different Carpus was a bishop of Gurdos and Lydia, and martyred in Pergamum, ca. 170 CE.

CARSHENA kahr-shee'nuh [כַּרְשְׁנָא karshena']. One of King Ahasuerus' officals from Persia and Media, who advised him to replace Queen Vashti (Esth 1:14, 21).

CART [עֲגָלָה 'aghalah; ἅμαξα hamaxa]. The Hebrew word for cart is derived from the word *round*, and can refer to both two- and four-wheeled vehicles, generally pulled by oxen. The same word can be used for *cart* or *wagon*. Joseph sent wagons to fetch his father's family (Gen 45:19, 21, 27; 46:5). Judith loads the spoils from Holofernes' camp onto her carts (Jdt 15:11).

Carts often had a sacral function: The Philistines placed the ARK OF THE COVENANT on a new cart for its return to Israel, pulled by two milch cows (1 Sam 6:7-14). Later, David placed the Ark on a new cart in an aborted attempt to bring it to Jerusalem (2 Sam 6:3; 1 Chr 13:7).

In ancient Israel, carts were typically made of wood (1 Sam 6:14), but HIRAM of Tyre reportedly cast ten four-wheeled items (מְכוֹנָה mekhonah) of bronze for use in the Temple (1 Kgs 7:27-37). The typical word for *cart*, however, is not used, and whether the elaborately decorated furnishings were movable is uncertain.

Isaiah (28:27-28) and Amos (2:13) employed the image of cart wheels, used for threshing grain, as a symbol of divine judgment. *See* CHARIOT; HORSE; OX.

TONY W. CARTLEDGE

CARTOGRAPHY. *See* MAPS AND MAPMAKING.

CARVING. One of the earliest and most enduring techniques of depicting biblical narratives in the history of art is through the technique of carving.

The earliest examples of Christian carving occur on sarcophagi and wall decorations in the catacombs. The carved decoration on the sides of altars in the catacombs also told the most popular stories of Christ as Good Shepherd and Jonah.

The figural stone carving found on capitals, tympana, and the exterior walls of a medieval cathedral throughout the pilgrimage roads of England, France, and Spain taught the illiterate pilgrim the message of the Scriptures. The visual image was often one of a damning Christ, typically with Christ sitting in judgment, surrounded by the beastial symbols of the four Gospel writers. Other scenes portray the Last Judgment itself, with hideous creatures vying against angels for the souls of the deceased, as they are placed literally on scales. In the Gothic cathedrals of France, narrative carvings change significantly as Mary gains an important role in the church. Scenes in the shared life of Mary and Christ (annunciation, visitation, nativity, circumcision), along with Apocryphal stories of Mary's life, become most frequently depicted. The beasts of the tympana are replaced by decorations, or in the case of the exterior, by the gargoyles that have a functional role (water drainage) and spiritual role (ridding the demons).

The ability of the Renaissance artist to carve a metal plate, combined with the invention of the printing press, allowed previously unimaginable numbers of people to see the visual depictions created through another type of carving. Printmaking utilized the carving methods of etching and engraving to transfer ideas, propaganda, and narratives quickly and inexpensively. Life-size (and larger as in the case of Michelangelo's *David*), free-standing sculpture, patterned after those made in the antique cultures of Greece and Rome, are carved from blocks of marble.

The Baroque artist continues to carve sculptures from marble, but the intent was to reinvigorate the weakened Roman Catholic Church during the late 16th and 17th cent. Artists added emotion, drama, and spirituality to hard, cold marble, through their ability to carve naturalistic and realistic portrayals of saints, mystics, and contemporary church leaders, as well as those popular heroes from the Bible. *See* AESTHETICS; ART; CRAFTS; DESIGN.

HEIDI J. HORNIK

CASEMATE. *See* FORTIFICATION.

CASIPHIA kuh-sif´ee-uh [כָּסִפְיָא kasifya']. An unidentified site in Babylonia near the AHAVA River where the Temple servants lived during the exile (Ezra 8:17). Before returning to Judah, EZRA sent a delegation to "IDDO, the leader at the place called Casiphia," to recruit servants for the priests in the Second Temple (8:17). Ezra 8:15 makes clear Casiphians were Levites, thus suggesting that during the exile they were segregated from priests. *See* PRIESTS AND LEVITES.

ROBERT A. KUGLER

CASLUHIM kas´luh-him [כַּסְלֻחִים kaslukhim]. This is a term of debated origin, found in the ethnographic lists of Gen 10 and 1 Chr 1. The Casluhim are one of six groups of people said to have come from Egypt, from which groups the PHILISTINES originated (Gen 10:13-14; 1 Chr 1:11-12).

CASPIN kas´pin [Κασφω Kasphō]. One of five towns under Gentile attack during the Maccabean revolt. Located on the Hauran Plain, the Jewish captives were liberated and the city eventually conquered by Judas Maccabeus in 161 BCE (1 Macc 5:24-27). As the Hasmonean army proceeded to Caspin (also known as Chaspho), a group of Nabateans informed Judah of other attacks led by Timotheus on Jews in several towns, including Bozrah and Dathema. Judas subsequently slaughtered the inhabitants of Caspin, who boasted of the strength of their fortifications and supplies. *See* JUDAS THE MACCABEE.

SHERI L. KLOUDA

CASSANDER. The son of ANTIPATER, one of the generals of ALEXANDER III (the Great), who represented his father in Babylon and later became ruler of Macedonia and Greece. In Babylon, Alexander the Great (d. 323 BCE) treated him with hostility, and, according to the ancient historian Quintus Curtius (41–51 CE), Cassander participated in the poisoning of Alexander at Babylon. He explains that the poison "was brought by Cassander and delivered to his brother Iollas, and by him was put in the last draught given to the king [Alexander]" (QC, *History of Alexander* 10.10.17, LCL). He later adds that following the death of Alexander, "Antipater seized the rule of Macedonia and of Greece as well, then his son [Cassander] succeeded him, after all who were related to Alexander, even by a distant connexion, had been killed" (10.10.19, LCL). Cassander was involved in the struggles for power among Alexander's generals (or Successors, Greek = diadochai) of Alexander the Great, and eventually took control of Macedon and Greece. The conflicts of the Successors initially brought him into the role of chiliarch (cavalry commander and grand vizier) at Triparadeisus (321 BCE). After his father's death in 319 BCE, Cassander defected to Antigonus and with his support established bases in Piraeus and Peloponnese (318–17 BCE).

Following an unsuccessful attempt to invade Macedon in early 317 BCE, he later invaded it again (316 BCE) and at Pydna overthrew the vengeful and violent ruler Olympias, wife of Philip of Macedon, and mother of Alexander the Great. The Macedonians condemned her, and the relatives of her victims killed her. He later secretly killed Alexander IV, the posthumous young son of Alexander the Great and Roxane, at Amphipolis (ca. 311–310 BCE) in order to secure his power over Macedon. This was in part because Olympias had earlier used the lad to secure her power in Macedon. From 316, Cassander became the master of Macedon and promoted the memory of Philip of Macedon, and, according to Strabo, married Philip's daughter, Thessalonice, and founded the city of Thessalonica, and named it after her (*Geog. Fragments* on Book VII.21). He also notes that the ancient city of CORINTH was earlier named Potidaea and afterwards called Cassandreia after Cassander, before it was later named Corinth (*Geog. Frag.* 25; *see also* 9.1.20).

Cassander was also a leading figure in the coalition war against Antigonus (315–311 BCE) and secured the recognition of his position as general of Europe in the "peace of the dynasts" (311 BCE). He later proclaimed himself "King of Macedonians," which became his official title for the remainder of his rule. Before his death in May of 297 BCE, he was able to stabilize his rule throughout all of MACEDONIA.

Bibliography: Robin Lane Fox. *Alexander the Great* (1993/1997) 461–99.

LEE MARTIN MCDONALD

CASSIA kash′uh [קִדָּה qiddah, קְצִיעָה qetsiʿah]. Cassia bark (*Cinnamonum cassia*) was brought to the Mediterranean from Asia (Ezek 27:19). In Egypt it was part of mummification mixtures, and in ancient Israel it was used in anointing oil (Exod 30:24) and fragrances to adorn the robes of royalty (Ps 45:8 [Heb. 45:9]). *See* PERFUME; PLANTS OF THE BIBLE; SPICE.

VICTOR H. MATTHEWS

CASTANETS [מְנַעַנְעִים menaʿanʿim]. *See* MUSICAL INSTRUMENTS.

CASTLE. While fortified structures have been constructed since the earliest historical periods in the Middle East, the most impressive extant castles date from the 12th to the 18th cent. CE. These were built by the Frankish inhabitants of the Kingdom of Jerusalem and the other Crusader states (1098–1291) and Muslim dynasties—most important, the Ayyubid (1171–1260), Mamluk (1250–1517), and Ottoman (in Egypt and Syria, 1516–1918) sultanates. Major castles from the first phase of Crusader occupation between 1098 and 1187 include Karak in Jordan and Saône (Qalʿat Sahyun) in Syria. After 1187 the bulk of castle building was done by the military orders, particularly the Templars and Hospitallers. The best-preserved examples are Crac des Chevaliers (Qalʿat al-Husn) and Margat (Qalʿat Marqab) in Syria. There also exists a wide variety of Muslim military foundations, including the massive urban citadels of Cairo, Damascus, and Aleppo, isolated castles such as Qalʿat al-Jaʿbar in Syria, and the renovated Roman *castrum* at Azraq in Jordan. The need to protect Muslims making the annual pilgrimage (*hajj*) led to the construction of numerous small forts along the main routes to Mecca and Medina. *See* BULWARK; FORTIFICATION; HOLY WAR; TOWER; WALL; WAR, METHODS, TACTICS, WEAPONS.

Bibliography: Hugh Kennedy. *Crusader Castles* (1994).

MARCUS MILWRIGHT

CASTOR AND POLLUX. *See* TWINS.

CASUISTIC LAW. Casuistic or case law entered the vocabulary of biblical scholarship through Albrecht Alt,

Marcus Milwright
Figure 1: Karak Castle, Karak, Jordan

who divided most law into two categories, apodictic and casuistic. The largest cluster of casuistic laws is in Exod 21:2–22:17. A legal situation is described in a protasis (When . . .). A legal consequence, a penalty, or statement of duties is prescribed in the apodosis. Subordinate cases can be appended in "if" clauses. Alt considered casuistic law to be ideal for instructing judges. See LAW IN THE OT.

Bibliography: Alt Albrecht. "The Origins of Israelite Law." *Essays on Old Testament History and Religion*, trans. R. A. Wilson (1966) 79–132.

DALE PATRICK

CAT. Species of wild cats found presently in Israel include the caracal, the jungle cat, the wildcat, and the sand cat. The lion became extinct in the Middle Ages. The cheetah was last seen in the 1960s.

In Mesopotamian art, the LEOPARD and CHEETAH were depicted in hunt scenes. In Egypt, although the domesticated cat (*Felis silvestris*) was very popular, there is no evidence for its domestication before the 11th Dynasty.

The cat is known in the MISHNAH but is not mentioned in the OT. Nevertheless, the proximity to Egypt and Mesopotamia, and the existence of wild varieties, suggest that this animal was known in ancient Israel. See ANIMALS OF THE BIBLE.

ODED BOROWSKI

CATACOMBS. See ROME, CHRISTIAN MONUMENTS.

CATARACT [צִנּוֹר tsinnor; καταρράκτης katarraktēs]. The translation *cataracts* (Ps 42:7 [Heb. 42:8] NRSV) follows the LXX, but the Hebrew word likely means a windpipe or watershaft (*see* 2 Sam 5:8 NRSV) of some kind, with which Yahweh strikes the oceans, following the Ugaritic tsnr, which denotes a *pipe* or *shaft*.

MICHAEL OBLATH

CATCHWORD. See MNEMONIC DEVICES.

CATERPILLAR [תּוֹלַעַת tolaʿath, רִמָּה rimmah, סָס sas]. Bible translations often apply *caterpillar* (butterfly and moth larvae) erroneously to the Hebrew words חָסִיל khasil and יֶלֶק yeleq, which likely refer to nymphal stages of *locusts*, while labeling proper caterpillars as *worms*. Of the three most appropriate terms, tolaʿath is a general term, rimmah refers to maggots (as in modern Hebrew), and sas unambiguously indicates cloth moth (*Tineola bisselliella*) caterpillars. In Jonah 4:7, tolaʿath is identified as a tiger moth caterpillar.

AXEL HAUSMANN AND GÜNTER MÜLLER

CATHOLIC EPISTLES. The Catholic Epistles include James, 1–2 Peter, 1–2–3 John, and Jude. Although this collection is known by different names ("General Epistles" and "Non-Pauline Letters"), the rubric *catholic* was used to title this collection because of its universal or *catholic* address and its theological unity. Modern assessments of the Catholic Epistles underscore their literary, rhetorical, and theological diversity, and their diverse social locations. Unlike the Pauline Epistles, which are granted theological unity and importance, the Catholic Epistles are studied as a theologically incoherent collection without a strategic role to perform within the biblical canon.

This critical consensus disagrees with the underlying hermeneutics of the canonical process. The formation of this collection during the 3rd and 4th cent., indexed by Paul's reference to the Jerusalem *Pillars* (Gal 2:9), was evidently a response to the use of an extant Pauline canon. The Catholic Epistles provided a fuller picture of Christian discipleship that included not only the Pauline insistence upon a professed faith "without works" (e.g., Rom 9:30–10:13), but now complemented it with the Pillars' emphasis upon a "faith that works."

The Letter of James introduces the Catholic Epistles and facilitates a conversation between the two letter collections. This role is set out by Jas 2:22: a sinner's Pauline-like faith in God is "made complete" by the believer's Pillars-like works. The two letter collections aim at a fuller expression of how people must respond to God.

The "catholicizing" hermeneutics of the canonical process implies that the Catholic Epistles collection had this complementary intention all along—to "make complete" rather than subvert a Pauline understanding of faith (so Jas 2:22). Salvation concerns *both* the sinner's initiation into life with God and the believer's ongoing friendship with God. Appropriating either

A. Hausman and G. Müller
Figure 1: Caterpillar

epistolary collection, *Pauline* or *Pillars*, to the *exclusion* of the other will ultimately subvert the formation of Christian faith and life, which is the principal purpose of the Christian biblical canon.

The core theological themes of a "unifying theology of the Catholic Epistles," introduced by James include: 1) Human suffering tests the faith community's love for God; 2) In response to the suffering of God's people, God discloses a "word of truth" exemplified by Jesus; 3) In obedience to this word, the community must practice "pure and undefiled" behavior as the public mark of friendship with God. These purity practices include conciliatory speech, sharing goods, rescuing wayward believers, and hospitality; 4) Theological orthodoxy is made effective only when embodied in loving works; 5) Finally, the future reward of steadfast obedience to God's word is eternal life with God.

James links purity and Christian love with the familiar passage, Jas 2:14-26, in opposition to a fideism ("faith without works") that is probably shaped by overly scrupulous attention to Pauline tradition (e.g., Rom 10:9-13). Contrary to Paul's use of Abraham to promote "faith without works," James appeals to that tradition to show that the believer "is justified by works and not *sola fide*" (2:24)! James does not argue that obedient works replace earnest faith but that assertions of faith, no matter how orthodox, cannot produce divine approval of itself (2:14-17). Rather, the profession of faith (2:19*a*) is only demonized (2:19*b*) if not also embodied in merciful works (2:14-17, 20, 26) that bear public witness to the community's friendly relations with God (2:23) and neighbor (2:25). The saving works that James delineates are the purity practices that secure the spiritual (5:19-20) and physical (2:1-7, 14-17) well-being of other believers.

The Epistles of Peter then extend this pivotal claim that equates right conduct with God's redemptive will (1 Pet 3:13-17). God's people have been "reborn" to obey God in a manner appropriate to God's own holiness (1 Pet 1:13-16). God's evaluation of human conduct is a function of God's holy character that renders impartial judgments of all people (1 Pet 1:17), whether or not they have performed good works that accord with God's will (1 Pet 3:17). Although Petrine and Pauline traditions often share a common stock of ideas, the deep logic of the Petrine gospel follows James, not Paul, in asserting that God's saving grace is responsive to a people who perform good works, even though they suffer because of it.

The subtext of this claim is Christology: namely, that "Christ suffered for you, leaving for you an example that you should follow in his steps" (1 Pet 2:21). Not only is Jesus the agent of God's mercy that finds and purifies a people belonging to God; he exemplifies the obedience in suffering that has a redemptive result now (1 Pet 2:12), and is fully realized in the coming age according to 2 Peter (3:10-11).

Similarly, the theological crisis that generated the secession of *anti-christs* from the Johannine community is the divorce between the community's loving works and its inherited beliefs about Christ. The Christology of the false teachers does not engender the loving works and communal practices that mark out a purified people in a profane world. The mere profession of faith is insufficient; knowing the truth about God must be embodied in loving deeds (3:17-24), since God is love (4:7-12). A congregation that abides in the truth of God will walk in the same way that Christ walked (2:6; 3:7). This theological commitment is rounded off and concluded by Jude with an exhortation to spiritual discipline: to love God is to obey God (Jude 20-21) and to obey God is to show mercy toward others (22-23).

Bibliography: R. W. Wall. "Toward a Unifying Theology of the Catholic Epistles: A Canonical Approach." *Catholic Epistles and the Tradition* (2004) 43–71.

ROBERT W. WALL

CATHOLIC VERSIONS. *See* VERSIONS, CATHOLIC.

CATHUA kuh-th*oo*´uh [Κουά Koua, Καθουα Kathoua]. Family head whose descendants were among the Temple servants, called the NETHINIM, who returned after the exile (1 Esd 5:30).

CATTLE. The collective term *cattle*, which refers to domesticated quadrupeds, specifically bovine animals, is used in the NRSV to translate a variety of Hebrew terms, such as בְּהֵמָה (behemah, Gen 1:24), and מִקְנֶה (miqneh Gen 13:2), while the REB uses cattle most of the times to translate בָּקָר (baqar, e.g., Gen 12:16). This of course creates confusion, since there are other related terms such as "herd, flock, sheep, oxen." From context it appears that "cattle" should be applied to baqar as a collective term for cows and bulls (large cattle), as distinct from small cattle (צֹאן tso'n) and sheep. During biblical times, cattle were used mostly as beasts of burden and for traction, rather than for milk and meat. The latter two were only incidental use. Cattle were also raised for their by-products, such as dung, bones, and hide.

Unlike sheep and goats, cattle do not produce fibers for spinning and weaving. Cows are not given to wandering like sheep and goats, thus their presence in the zooarchaeological record usually indicates a more settled environment, such as a village or town.

Together with sheep and goats, donkeys, servants, camels, and tents, cattle were always considered a measure of wealth (Gen 12:16; 13:5; 20:14; 24:35; 26:14; Deut 8:13). Large herds of cattle needed large tracts of land for grazing, as alluded to in the stories about the conflict between Abraham's and Lot's herds (Gen 13) and Jacob's family in the land of Goshen (Gen 45:10; 47:6*a*). During the monarchy, the king became owner of large herds of cattle. According to the biblical account, under David special overseers were appointed for the baqar, "and over the herds that fed in Sharon was Shitrai the Sharonite: and over the herds that were in the valleys was Shaphat the son of Adlai" (1 Chr 27:29). The royal cattle were probably used as track animals, and for their by-products.

The BULLS (פַּר par) were the symbol of power and fertility. Bulls are mentioned in the OT numerous times, usually in connection with sacrifices. Sometimes the Bible uses the bull as symbol for Yahweh, and in this context employs the term אֲבִיר יַעֲקֹב ʾavir yaʾaqov (Gen 49:24; Isa 49:26) or אֲבִיר יִשְׂרָאֵל ʾabir yisraʾel (Isa 1:24). In the ancient Near East, the bull was the symbol of various gods in several cultures, a fact that must have influenced Israelite iconography and literature.

The female of the species is mentioned significantly fewer times and mostly metaphorically. In Gen 41 cows appear in Pharaoh's dream, symbolizing good and bad agricultural years. In Hos 4:16, Israel is compared to a stubborn cow, and in Amos 4:1, northern Israelite women are ridiculed when referred to as "Bashan cows."

Cows were harnessed for work. The biblical account mentions that they were used for pulling the wagon, bringing back the ark from Philistia to Judah (1 Sam 6), and they were sacrificed when they reached their destination. When the red cow was selected for the "Red Heifer ritual," she was supposed to be "without spot, wherein is no blemish, and upon which never came a yoke" (Num 19:2). *See* ANIMALS IN THE BIBLE.

Bibliography: O. Borowski. *Every Living Thing: Daily Use of Animals in Ancient Israel* (1988).

ODED BOROWSKI

CAUDA kaw´duh [Καῦδα Kauda]. An island, also called Clauda, near the southern coast of Crete, which Paul's party passed during a violent wind en route to Rome (Acts 27:16). It is probably modern Gaudos, approximately 24 nautical mi. south of Crete.

CAULKERS [מַחֲזִיקִים mahaziqim ἐνισχύον enischuon]. Seamen charged with the task of maintaining the integrity of a wooden sailing ship. The term is a participle meaning "those who make strong," and the LXX interprets it to refer to those who "strengthen the purpose" of the leaders of the sailing company, not necessarily to a class of workers. Caulkers are mentioned along with other sailing professionals in Ezekiel's oracle against Tyre (Ezek 27:9, 27), in which he predicts that Tyre will sink like a boat with all of its occupants while those on the shore watch helplessly.

BRYAN D. BIBB

CAVALRY [פָּרָשׁ parash, פָּרָשִׁים parashim; ἱππεύς hippeus, ἱππικός hippikos]. A collective term for a group of soldiers mounted on horses. Developments in bridle designs in the 8th cent. BCE allowed mounted archers to control their horses. The relative costliness of chariots, and the commanding effectiveness of cavalry, brought about the eclipse of chariots by cavalry in the mid-7th cent. BCE. The transition seems to have precipitated a shift in the meaning of parashim from a team of chariot horses to mounted cavalry; e.g., Ezek 23:6, 12; 38:4; Ezra 8:22; Neh 2:9. Only Rev 9:16 unambiguously refers to cavalry (hippikos).

WALTER C. BOUZARD

CAVE [מְעָרָה meʿarah; σπήλαιον spelaion]. Biblical and archaeological evidence shows that caves were places where people lived, took refuge, hid property, or buried the dead. Mountains, wadis, and valleys, all with caves, provide natural shelter across the interior of Israel from the hill country of the Galilee to the Dead Sea (*see* ISRAEL, GEOLOGY OF). Artificial caves could also be hewn out of the rocky terrain.

According to the biblical texts and Josephus, caves are places of refuge during times of war. The five kings of the Amorites who wage war against Gibeon take refuge in the cave at MAKKEDAH when they flee from Joshua's forces when the sun stands still (Josh 10:16). Joshua finds the kings, puts them to death, and seals them in the same cave where they hid (Josh 10:26-27). The Israelites sought refuge from the Midianites and later from the Philistines in caves, holes, tombs, cisterns, and strongholds (Judg 6; 1 Sam 13:6). David seeks refuge from Saul at the Cave of ADULLAM, and later at a cave in the wilderness of EN-GEDI (1 Sam 22:1; 24:3). When Saul hears that David is near En-Gedi, he heads towards the Rocks of the Wild Goats. Saul unknowingly enters the same cave where David is hiding. David's men encourage him to attack Saul, but David only cuts the corner of Saul's cloak—an allusion to Saul tearing Samuel's cloak (1 Sam 15:27). Josephus recounts that he hid in a cave when Vespasian captured Jotapata (*J. W.* 3.340-392).

People find shelter in caves during periods of religious persecution. Obadiah hides one hundred prophets of Yahweh from Jezebel in caves (1 Kgs 18:4). In another narrative about a prophet fleeing Jezebel, Elijah takes refuge in a cave on Mount Horeb (1 Kgs 19; *see* SINAI, MOUNT). Like Moses, Elijah meets the Lord on the mountain. According to 2 Macc 6:11, people hid in caves to celebrate the Sabbath during the persecutions under Antiochus IV (*see also* 1 Macc 2:29-38; Josephus, *Ant.* 12.273-275). When the Maccabees purify the Temple, the people recall how they had to hide in caves during the reign of Antiochus (2 Macc 10:6; see this motif in Heb 11:38; *T. Mos.* 9:5-6).

People also live in caves. LOT and his daughters settle in a cave after leaving ZOAR (Gen 19:30-38). Here the daughters sleep with their father, and each bears a son: Moab, the eponymous ancestor of the

Moabites (see MOAB, MOABITES), and Ben-ammi, the eponymous ancestor of the Ammonites (see AMMON, AMMONITES). Caves were also lairs for robbers (Ant. 14.415, 421; the NRSV renders me'arah and spelaion as "den": Jer 7:11; Matt 21:13; Mark 11:17; Luke 19:46).

Caves are places of refuge for people fleeing God's judgment and the disruption of natural order. Judahites will hide in caves in fear of God's judgment against the people's worship of idols (Isa 2:19-21). The Lord says that the survivors in Judah hiding in caves, as well as those in the open, will not be safe from the desolation of the land of Israel (Ezek 33:23-29). When the Lamb breaks the sixth seal, there is an earthquake, the sun goes dark, the moon is red like blood, and the stars fall to the earth; meanwhile, the kings, leaders, and people hide in caves, where they beg the mountains to seal them in, so they can be hidden from God and the Lamb (Rev 6:12-17).

The Bible and the archaeological record suggest that caves were used as tombs (see BURIAL). When Sarah dies, Abraham purchases the cave of MACHPELAH to use as a family tomb (Gen 23). Abraham, Isaac, Rebekah, Leah and Jacob are buried there (Gen 25:9; 49:30). The practice of burying multiple bodies in one cave tomb, a practice that existed throughout Israel's history, is perhaps echoed in biblical texts that speak of being gathered to ancestors, people, or the grave (Gen 25:8; 2 Kgs 22:20). Judith is buried in the cave with her husband Manasseh (Jud 16:23). Some tombs are artificial caves, as illustrated by the account of Jesus' burial in a tomb hewn out of rock (Matt 27:60; Mark 15:46: Luke 23:53). In a story perhaps intended to parallel the burial of Jesus in an unused tomb, Lazarus is buried in a cave covered by a stone. No other bodies are mentioned (John 11:38-44).

Caves were used in prehistoric times for shelter and burial. Shanidar Cave in Iraq provides evidence of a Neanderthal buried with flowers, but the significance of the flowers is debated. The SEFUNIM CAVES in the Carmal Mountains provide evidence of occupation dating back to the Middle Paleolithic. SHUQBA CAVE in the Wadi el-Natuf shows evidence of Musterian culture and later Natufian culture.

Possibly the most famous caves in the region are the QUMRAN caves, where the DEAD SEA SCROLLS were found in jars in 1947 by Bedouin shepherds. The area was under Jordanian control in 1949 when G. Lankester Harding and Roland de Vaux began excavating the cave where the shepherds found the first scrolls. Ten caves were discovered from 1952 to 1956.

Near Qumran other documents were found in the caves around the Wadi Murabba'at (see MURABBA'AT, WADI). Occupation of the area caves stretches back to the Chalcolithic period. Coins dated to the mid-1st cent. CE may indicate that people hid in the caves during the First Jewish Revolt against Rome. Documents

from the area date to the Second Jewish Revolt against Rome. Some letters were from Simon Bar Kochba (see also BABATHA). Remains of clothing for adults and children indicate that the caves were used by people hiding from the Romans. Roman military equipment was also found.

Caves are sites of pilgrimage as some have been associated with religious figures. In Bethlehem, the Church of the Nativity was built over caves that tradition associated with the birth of Jesus. At Hebron, a mosque stands over the traditional site of the cave of Machpelah. In Jerusalem, the Church of the Holy Sepulcher stands over a cave associated with Jesus' tomb, but the Garden Tomb is a cave that Protestants associate with Jesus' burial. In 2000, archaeologists began excavating a cave that they claim has drawings related to John the Baptist. The cave is near the traditional site of the home of John the Baptist at Ein Karim, and the graffiti on the walls has been associated with early monks. The cave appears to resemble a resevior or MIQVAH. Pottery at the site dates to the 1st cent. CE. Later pottery dates to the Byzantine Period (5th–6th cent. CE). That the site is tied to the historical John the Baptist is debatable, but the site does bear witness to Byzantine traditions related to John.

HEATHER R. MCMURRAY

CEASE, TO [שָׁבַת shavath, חָדַל khadhal; ἀδιαλείπτως adialeiptōs, κοπάζω kopazo, παύω pauō]. An action represented by a variety of Hebrew and Greek terms meaning "to stop." It is used both literally and figuratively.

In the OT, shavath can mean "to stop" (the worship of God, Josh 22:25; the end of oppression, Isa 14:4), "to cause to stop" (the temporary halt of sacrifices in the Temple, Dan 9:27), or "to rest."

Khadhal can be the act of stopping, the command to stop (stop opposing God, 2 Chr 35:21), a suspension of (or stopping in the context of) divine judgment (suspension of thunder and hail, Exod 9:29), or it can be used in a more metaphorical manner (such as the breakdown of order until Deborah became judge, Judg 5:6-7).

In the NT, the verbs pauō (the end of violence, Acts 20:1) and kopazō (with regard to the wind, Matt 14:32; Mark 4:39; 6:51) mean "to stop or cease." Adialeiptōs is used where people pray without stopping (Rom 1:9; 1 Thess 2:13; 5:17). See REST; SABBATH.

LINDA SCHEARING

CEDAR [אֶרֶז 'erez]. Like pines, cedars have needlelike leaves clustered on short branch shoots. Two types of cones, male and female, are produced on the same tree. The male is a few inches long, wormlike, and falls from the tree after pollen is shed. The female seed-bearing cone, about the size and shape of a lemon, is erect and matures in two or three years when the woody cone breaks apart in winter, releasing the scales holding the seeds. These act like gliders, ensuring wide distribution of the seeds. Seeds are viable for only a short time and germinate in cool temperatures. At high elevations and low temperatures growth is slow, and centuries are required to produce the majestic trees with their distinctive brown, resin-soaked heartwood and lighter sapwood.

Cedars of Lebanon probably never grew within the bounds of present-day Israel but were abundant on the high LEBANON MOUNTAINS ridge to the north. A tiny fraction of the original cedar forests are left and preserved in Lebanon. Natural stands of cedar also occur in Cyprus, Syria, and in the Taurus Mountains of Turkey, where ample moist air provides a receptive habitat.

Historically, the cedar of Lebanon was one of the most important building materials in the Near East. The most famous cedar building, although not the largest, was the Temple built by Solomon (1 Kgs 6). In addition, Solomon built a magnificent home for himself entirely out of cedar (1 Kgs 7) that took thirteen years to complete, six more years than the Temple. Earlier, David had built a house out of cedar (2 Sam 7:2). While cedar wood is fragrant and attractive, its chief value lies in being the only tree in the region abundant and large enough for big buildings.

A lesser-known use of cedar was in oblations for purification, as, e.g., in ritual cleansing for leprosy (Lev 14; Num 19:6). Details are not given, but it seems also likely that small pieces of cedar were used for their fragrance.

Solomon spoke about plants from the cedar of Lebanon to the HYSSOP, suggesting that the cedar was the greatest (1 Kgs 4:33). As the most majestic plant, cedars were often used metaphorically, as when prominent people were likened to cedars (2 Kgs 14:9; Ps 37:35; 92:12; Song 5:15; Amos 2:5). *See* HOUSE OF THE FOREST OF LEBANON; PLANTS OF THE BIBLE; WOOD.

LYTTON JOHN MUSSELMAN

CEDARS OF LEBANON. *See* CEDAR; LEBANON.

CEILING [סִפֻּן *sippun*]. Inner covering of a room. Used only to describe Solomon's Temple (1 Kgs 6:15, *see also* 6:9). *See* ARCHITECTURE; HOUSE; PANEL.

CELIBACY. The term *celibacy* is not found in the Bible. It derives from the Latin *caelebs*, "single, unmarried," and enters Christian theology in late antiquity. Biblical scholars use it as a synonym for sexual ASCETICISM, chastity, continence, VIRGINITY, and ABSTINENCE. This is confusing, however, for it obscures the distinct natures of these practices. Sexual asceticism, e.g., can have a different theological emphasis than sexual absti-

nence. Likewise, continence and chastity, which can be practiced within MARRIAGE, are not the same as virginity; while virginity itself can have various motivations—emulating the Virgin Mary, ritual purity, or distancing oneself from the material world. Especially in biblical studies it is important to distinguish celibacy, a way of life dependent on the absence, avoidance, or postponement of marriage, from practices whose goal is to eschew sexual activity. Indeed, most instances of sexual abstinence in the Bible occur *within* marriage (e.g., Exod 19:14-15; Lev 18:19; 2 Sam 11:11; 1 Cor 7:5; *see also* 1 Kgs 1:1-4), while the motive for biblical celibacy is rarely (if ever) sexual abstinence. Celibacy thus finds four theological justifications in the biblical tradition.

First, apocalyptic traditions from both Testaments advise against or forbid marriage in times preceding eschatological tribulation, based on the rationale that the impending crisis will render marriage difficult or impossible (Jer 16:1-9; Joel 2:16; 1 Cor 7:25-31; Rev 18:23; Luke 23:28-29). Second, and akin to this, is the argument that Christians should live celibate lives in order to devote themselves to God, free from the obligations and interruptions of married life (1 Cor 9:1-12; 1 Tim 5:3-16; *see also* Luke 8:1-3; Acts 21:9). This rationale, which parallels certain Greco-Roman moral traditions, could be used in conjunction with the apocalyptic rationale (1 Cor 7:25-40) or enhanced by messianic expectations (Luke 2:36-38; 14:15-26; 17:26-37). It is these combinations that best explain the celibacy of John the Baptist, Jesus, and Paul. A third rationale for celibacy originates in Jesus' prohibition of DIVORCE. Paul interprets Jesus to mean that if a wife leaves her husband, she must return to him or remain celibate (1 Cor 7:11*a*). In Matthew, by contrast, Jesus' prohibition prompts the disciples to ask whether a man should choose celibacy over marriage. Jesus answers by giving his qualified support to this notion, stating that such celibates have "made themselves EUNUCHS for the kingdom of heaven" (Matt 19:10-12). Finally, the synoptic Gospels teach that all who participate in the resurrection will become celibate: being immortal, they will no longer need to procreate, which is understood here (as elsewhere in antiquity) as the primary function of marriage.

Celibacy is not a decisive issue in biblical theology. Ezekiel and Hosea were married, but Jeremiah was not; and for most of the prophets there is no record of marital status. Likewise, Jesus, John the Baptist, and Paul, all of whom defend the institution of marriage, were celibate; but Peter and the other apostles were married—a fact that comes to us only incidentally (Mark 1:30 par.; 1 Cor 9:5). Further, while Jesus had no earthly wife, the risen Christ becomes the church's bridegroom (e.g., 2 Cor 11:2; *see* BRIDE OF CHRIST), and the biblical God, distinctive for his lack of a divine consort, can be pictured as Israel's husband (e.g., Jer 3:1-10).

Early in the development of Christianity, however, although not in Judaism, this relative disinterest in celibacy is reassessed in light of new ascetic tendencies. In approximately 100 CE, some church leaders were attracted to ideas of matter-spirit dualism. As a result, they promoted sexual asceticism as the true goal of celibacy, declaring it necessary for orientation to a nonmaterial God. It is this understanding of celibacy that is evidently condemned in 1 Tim 4:1-5. Of course, earlier Christians, following Hellenistic-Jewish practice, had understood sexual *abstinence* as a necessary part of celibacy. The avoidance of nonmarital sexual relations was a marker of their moral superiority over the surrounding Gentile culture (e.g., 1 Cor 6:9-11; Rev 14:1-5). But unlike their 2nd cent. counterparts, earlier Christians had not denigrated marriage or conjugal relations: both accorded with God's will (e.g., Mark 10:6-9; Rom 1:26-27; 1 Cor 7:2-4, 28, 36), and forgoing them for a life of celibacy was not a matter of avoiding evil but a matter of forgoing something good to gain something still better (Matt 19:11-12; Luke 14:26; 1 Cor 7:5, 37-38; 1 Tim 5:9-14).

Bibliography: Elizabeth A. Clark. *Reading Renunciation* (1999); Will Deming. *Paul on Marriage and Celibacy.* 2nd ed. (2004).

WILL DEMING

CELLAR [אוֹצָר *'otsar*]. The NRSV translation of the Hebrew word *'otsar* is more commonly used for "storehouse," especially associated with Yahweh's control of the elements of creation, such as the wind (Pss 33:7; 135:7; Jer 10:13), or commonly for a "treasury" associated with the palace or the Temple (2 Kgs 16:8; 1 Chr 27:27; 2 Chr 5:1). In Greek, the only reference is Luke 11:33, referring to a cellar without light. *See* HOUSE; TREASURE; TREASURY.

VICTOR H. MATTHEWS

CELSUS sel'suhs [Κέλσος Kelsos]. A Middle Platonist from the late 2nd cent., Celsus composed a systematic, searing critique of Christianity called *The True Doctrine* ('Αληθὴς Λόγος Alēthēs Logos). Celsus is known only through ORIGEN's *Contra Celsum*, which contains liberal quotations from Celsus' work in order to refute it. The reconstructed argument reveals that Celsus was well acquainted with both Christian literature as well as various forms of Christianity current in his time (e.g., "orthodox," MARCIONISM, GNOSTICISM). Celsus' polemic centers on Christian doctrine, Christianity's ambivalent relationship to Judaism, and contemporary Christian attitudes and practices. Doctrinal objections include the Christian idea that Jesus was God (which denigrates God and compromises divine unity) and the belief in fleshly resurrection (a process contrary to nature). Celsus also reproaches Christians for claiming to be the inheritors of Judaism while rejecting its laws and customs, and accuses them of sedition for refusing to participate in the Roman social order.

DAVID M. REIS

CENCHREAE sen'kruh-ee [Κεγχρεαι Kenchreai]. The eastern seaport of Corinth 6 mi. distant. The church was directed by Phoebe (Rom 16:1), and Paul sailed from there to Ephesus (Acts 18:18). Two moles were constructed in the early 1st cent. and encircled a harbor of about 30,000 sq. mi., open to the south. Warehouses, taverns, temples (Aphrodite, Asclepius, Isis) and a statue of Poseidon lined some 700 mi. of quays. Apuleius describes the ceremonies in the temple of Isis (*Metamorphoses* 11). *See* CORINTH; CULT; ISIS; PHOEBE.

JEROME MURPHY-O'CONNOR

CENDEBEUS sen'duh-bee'uhs [Κενδεβαῖος Kendebaios]. A SELEUCID general (1 Macc 15:38) under ANTIOCHUS VII (138–129 BCE), who tried to retake the Judean coastal plain and hill country from SIMON THE HASMONEAN (142–135 BCE). The Judean forces, led by Simon's sons JUDAS and JOHN HYRCANUS I, routed the Seleucids and drove them out of the disputed area (1 Macc 16:1-10). Josephus, however, records that Simon himself directed the campaign (*Ant.* 13.225-27; *J.W.* 1.52-53).

STEVEN FRIESEN

CENSER [מִקְטֶרֶת miqtereth, מַחְתָּה makhtah; λιβανωτός libanōtos]. A gold, copper, or bronze vessel holding coals from the altar fire with INCENSE on top, producing a sweet smell (Lev 10:1; 16:12; Num 16:46; Ezek 8:11). The censer was part of the test for Korah and others who mumbled against Moses and Aaron (Num 16:1-39). An angel in John's vision placed fire in a censer and threw it to earth, causing thunder, lightning, and earthquakes (Rev 8:3-5).

JESSICA TINKLENBERG DEVEGA

CENSUS [פְּקֻדִים pequdhim, מִפְקָד mifqadh, מִסְפָּר mispar; ἀπογραφή apographē, ἐπίσκεψις episkepsis, ἀριθμός arithmos]. A census in the Bible is the enrollment and numbering of a group of people, tribe, or nation for various purposes: the numbering of the seventy members of Jacob's clan who came to Egypt in the time of Joseph (Gen 46:26-27; Exod 1:1-7), taxation for ritual or governmental purposes (Exod 30:13-16; 38:24-26; Luke 2:1-5), assignment of cultic duties to clans of priestly Levites (Num 3:1-39), reckoning the number of Levites available as substitutes for Israel's firstborn males (Num 3:40-51), military counting of troops for war (Num 1:3; 26:2; 2 Sam 24:1-9; 1 Chr 21:1-6), distribution of the land of Canaan according to the size of Israelite tribes and clans (Num 26:3-56), and the counting of former exiles who returned from Babylon to Judah (Ezra 2:1-67). The three most significant census-taking events in the Bible are the wilderness census lists in Num 1 and 26, David's census in 2 Sam 24 and 1 Chr 21, and the census associated with Jesus' birth in Luke 2.

A. Census Lists in Num 1 and 26

Numbers begins with a census of the twelve tribes of Israel in the wilderness fourteeen months after the exodus out of Egypt. The census counts the males over twenty years of age who are able to go to war (Num 1:2-3). The census is part of the preparation for Israel's future military campaign into the land of Canaan. The total for all twelve tribes is 603,550. This number of male warriors would imply a total population of roughly two million people, including women, children, and the elderly. Some scholars see such numbers as historically improbable.

Theologically, the high census numbers in Num 1 testify to God's gracious blessing and partial fulfillment of the promise to give Israel's ancestors innumerable descendants. The exceedingly large numbers of available warriors also ought to have instilled confidence when Israel first came to the border of Canaan. However, Israel's confidence quickly dissipated into fear as they refused to move into the promised land in the face of the large Canaanite warriors. As a consequence, God condemned the old wilderness generation to die over the course of forty years of wilderness wandering while only their "little ones" would receive the promised land of Canaan (Num 13–14).

The second census list in Num 26 enumerated the twelve tribes of Israel once again, but with some important differences. An additional generational level of all new clan names was added, signaling the emergence of a whole new generation of Israelites. In contrast to the military purpose of the census in Num 1, the purpose of the second census was primarily to aid the fair distribution of the land of Canaan according to the size and numbers of individual tribes and clans (Num 26:52-56). A final note in Num 26:63-65 sounds the theme of the entire book of Numbers: the death of the old generation and the rise of a new generation of hope whom God would lead into the land of Canaan (Num 14:26-35).

B. David's Census in 2 Sam 24:1-9 and 1 Chr 21:1-6

Late in the reign of King David, a census of all Israelite soldiers able to go to war was ordered by David and carried out by his army commander Joab and other military leaders. In 2 Sam 24:9, Joab reported a total of 800,000 troops from northern Israel and 500,000 troops from Judah. Joab had tried unsuccessfully to dissuade David from taking the census. Why? Perhaps an ancient taboo was attached to the counting of heads. Or David may have neglected to require the payment of a ritual tax or some other ritual form of cleansing before doing the census (Exod 30:13-16). As a result of the census, God's angel sent a deadly pestilence upon the

people of Israel, killing 70,000 people. David confessed his sin for taking the census, bought a threshing floor, erected an altar, and offered up burnt offerings. David's actions stop the plague and punishment for the census (2 Sam 24:10-25).

In 1 Chr 21:1, Satan and not God is portrayed as the one who initially incited David to take the census. The Chronicler is clearly reacting to the theological problem in 2 Sam 24:1 where God incited David to take the very census that God subsequently condemned and punished with a plague.

C. The Census in Luke 2:1-5

The Gospel of Luke begins the birth narrative of Jesus with a decree from the Roman emperor Augustus that "all the world should be registered" (Luke 2:1). This census or enrollment was taken, according to Luke, "while Quirinius was governor of Syria" (Luke 2:2). This raises some historical problems in that the birth of Jesus is usually dated to 4 BCE (the year of Herod's death; see Luke 1:5). Quirinius, however, did not become the governor of Syria until a decade later in 6 CE, which is when he had a census of Judea taken, according to Josephus (*Ant.* 18.3; *J.W.* 7.253). Acts 5:37 also makes reference to this same census under Quirinius that was resisted by some Jewish rebels. Some scholars argue that the writer of Luke–Acts may have had incorrect chronological information, while others suggest that Quirinius may have been a lesser official in Syria during an earlier census in 4 BCE with a second census occurring in Judea in 6 CE.

Whatever the historical resolution, the census in Luke serves to bring Joseph and Mary from their home in Nazareth in northern Galilee to the southern town of Bethlehem for the birth of their child. In this way, the birth of Jesus becomes linked with certain OT prophecies that associate the coming of the Messiah with the house of King David, who himself came from Bethlehem (1 Sam 16:1; Mic 5:2). *See* NUMBERS, BOOK OF; QUIRINIUS; SATAN.

DENNIS T. OLSON

CENTURION sen-tyoor´ee-uhn [κεντυρίων kenturiōn, ἑκατόνταρχος hekatontarchos]. A centurion was a ranking officer in the Roman army, usually the commander over a company of 100 men or fewer. The word appears in the NT twenty-three times.

The position of centurion had a long history, since the establishment of the Republic. By the time of Julius Caesar, centurions were already reputed for their loyalty and efficiency, and he entrusted much of the operation of his forces to them. Normally they rose through the enlisted ranks after fifteen to eighteen years of service, although on occasion this level could be achieved through direct promotion, even from the emperor himself. The position was highly desired by common soldiers, and after working their way through various grades, they could aspire to the highest position, *primipilaris*. It paid as much as 17 times the rate of a foot soldier (legionary), and a career centurion could look forward to the possibility of a pension and a good retirement.

The centurion functioned somewhat like a master sergeant, with responsibilities for training and discipline, and in his duties to the tribune he functioned more like a captain. Usually the centurion had as much experience as any soldier in the army, had endured assignments all over the empire, and could have filled such diverse assignments as general oversight of building projects, posting to duty in mines and quarries, functioning as a tax collector, or as an umpire in boundary disputes. In the NT narratives, he serves as the lead officer in security patrols (Acts 21:32; 22:25-26; 23:23; 24:23; 27:1-6) or execution squads (the Gospel crucifixion narratives).

References to centurions occur in several key NT passages. If Luke's two-volume work (Luke–Acts) may be considered an argument that was designed to promote Christianity in the Roman Empire, the passages in which centurions appear, consistently support this message when the officers appear to serve in the spread of the gospel. Luke 7:1-10 presents a Roman officer in Capernaum who seeks healing for his son (servant?), as one who has faith greater than that found anywhere in Israel. Tradition suggests that he built a synagogue there. In Acts 10:1-2, Cornelius, an officer from the Italian Cohort, is said to be respected by all the Jews and is known for being pious and a God-fearer (εὐσεβὴς καὶ φοβούμενος τὸν θεὸν eusebēs kai phoboumenos ton theon). He is directed by God to invite Peter to his house, and this experience convinces Peter of the validity of the Gentile mission. In Acts, other centurions and soldiers under their command protect Paul and make it possible for him to make his way to the capital (21:32; 22:25-26; 23:17, 23). In the last appearance of a centurion (27:1, 6), Julius, a member of the Augustan Cohort, accompanies Paul safely by ship to Rome, where Paul delivers his final testimony.

The most controversial passages concerning a centurion appear in the PASSION narratives, particularly Mark 15:39. The texts disagree about the role that the officer in charge (of the crucifixion detail) actually played. According to Mark he observes Jesus' death and says (NRSV) "Truly this man is the Son of God." Matthew goes even further, attributing the *confession* to the centurion and the whole execution squad (Matt 27:54). Luke pays him the ultimate compliment by observing that he praised God and declared Jesus completely *innocent* (NRSV) or *just* (δίκαιος dikaios, 23:47).

In Mark's version (despite the fact that the majority of biblical interpreters contend that the centurion's comments before the cross function as the culmination of the gospel where the true identity of Jesus is finally revealed), some scholars express increasing doubt about the validity of this reading of the text. A lack of solid grammatical support exists for translating his words as a full Christian confession ("the Son of God"). There is also no anticipation of a central role for a Roman soldier in the story's denouement. Thus some exegetes argue that the centurion's statement is merely another ironic description of who Jesus is, "a son of God." The centurion says what is true, but on his lips it rings false, just as the earlier statements of the Jewish religious leaders do (Mark 15:26-32).

Bibliography: Lesley Atkins and Roy A. Adkins. *Handbook to Life in Ancient Rome* (1994); Earl S. Johnson. "Mark 15:39 and the So-Called Confession of the Roman Centurion." *Biblica* 81 (2000) 406–14.

EARL S. JOHNSON, JR

CEPHAS see´fuhs. *See* PETER.

CEREAL OFFERING. *See* SACRIFICES AND OFFERINGS.

CEREALS. *See* GRAIN; PLANTS OF THE BIBLE.

CEREMONIAL LAW. *See* FEASTS AND FASTS; LAW IN THE OT; PRIESTS AND LEVITES; SACRIFICES AND OFFERINGS; WORSHIP IN THE OT.

CERINTHUS suh-rin´thuhs ([Κήρινθος Kērinthus].) A Christian teacher from Asia Mminor and a contemporary of the disciple John (late 1st cent.). He was condemned as a heretic by church writers because of his unorthodox views. He taught Gnostic doctrines: that the world was not created by God but by a lesser power; that Jesus was not virgin-born but the natural son of Mary and Joseph, although he was better than other men; that the (heavenly) Christ descended on Jesus at his baptism and departed before his death; and that during his career, Jesus preached the unknown Father and worked miracles. Later church writers describe him in completely different terms: as a Judaizer who taught circumcision and the giving of the Jewish law through angels, and who expected an earthly reign of the messiah.

Bibliography: Charles E. Hill. "Cerinthus, Gnostic or Chiliast? A New Solution to an Old Problem." *JECS* 8.2 (2000) 135–72.

CHARLES W. HEDRICK

CHABRIS kab´ris [Χαβρίς Chabris]. Gothoniel's son and a magistrate of Bethulia to whom Judith presents her plan to deliver their city (Jdt 6:15; 8:10; 10:6).

CHADIASANS kay´dee-ay´shuhn [Χαδιασαι Chadi-asai, Χαδασαι Chadasai]. Possibly former residents of Kedesh. Along with the Chadiasans, they returned to Jerusalem from exile with Zerubbabel and other leaders (1 Esd 5:20).

CHAEREAS kihr´ee-uhs [Χαιρέας Chaireas]. Ammonite commander of the stronghold Gazara, and brother of Timothy, both of whom were defeated and killed by JUDAS MACCABEUS and his men (2 Macc 10:32-38).

CHAFF [מֹץ mots; ἄχυρον achyron]. In the agricultural economy of the biblical world, a major task was winnowing, or separating grains from their stalks and chaff by using a pitchfork to toss the harvested crops into the air, where the wind blew the chaff away. This image is used metaphorically to describe God driving away Israel's enemies as if they are chaff (Ps 1:4; 35:5; Isa 17:13; 29:5) or, most famously, Jesus coming with a winnowing fork in his hand to separate out the evil, or chaff, which will be burned from the good in unquenchable fire (Matt 3:11-12; Luke 3:16).

SUSAN ACKERMAN

CHAINS, IMPRISONMENT [אֵזֵק ʾazeq, זֵק zeq, כֶּבֶל kevel, מוּסְרָה musarah; ἄλυσις halusis, δεσμός desmos, πέδη pedē]. Vocabulary for assorted shackles and bonds and the state of being held by them (אָסַר ʾasar; δέω deō) may describe particular means of physical restraint. Chaining language often functions figuratively, not as description but as synecdoche or metonym, indicating the general condition or place of one's detention (e.g., Acts 24:27; Eph 6:20; Phil 1:7; Phlm 10). Mention of binding can highlight the severity of certain prisoners' custody (e.g., 2 Kgs 25:7; 3 Macc 4:9; Acts 12:6; 16:24-26; Rev 20:1-2) and heighten incarceration's potential for shaming (e.g., Nah 3:10; 2 Tim 1:16). *See* CRIMES AND PUNISHMENTS, OT AND NT; PRISON.

MATTHEW L. SKINNER

CHAIR. *See* SEAT.

CHALDEA, CHALDEANS kal-dee´uh, kal-dee´uhns [כַּשְׂדִּים, kasdim; Χαλδαίων, Chaldaiōn; Akkadian kaldu, kaldai]. A region in BABYLONIA and its inhabitants. The designation for the inhabitants, Chaldeans, is used in the Bible to refer to the last dynasty of Babylon (626–539 BCE), whose second king, NEBU-CHADNEZZAR II, conquered Jerusalem in 597 and 586 BCE, deporting many Judeans into Babylonian exile. The Chaldeans are mentioned in Isa 47–48; Jer 50–51; Ezek 11:24; 16:29; 23:15-16; 2 Kgs; Ezra; and Daniel.

References to the country Kaldu and its inhabitants begin appearing in the Assyrian royal inscriptions from the 9th cent. onward. The main tribal groups that made up the Chaldeans were the Bit Dakkuri along the Euphrates to the west and south of Borsippa, the Bit Amukani farther south, the Bit Shilani and the Bit Sa'alli in the vast southern marshes, and the Bit Yakin along the Tigris as far as the border with Elam. Though these tribal groups shared the same language and religious culture as the inhabitants of the main Babylonian cities, their political structure differed from that of the city dwellers. They were fiercely independent, more mobile, and less dependent on imperial political stability for their economic well-being. While the Babylonian city dwellers, dependent on inner-urban trade, were often pro-Assyrian during the Neo-Assyrian expansion into Babylonia, these tribal groups submitted to Assyrian power reluctantly and usually only as long as superior Assyrian forces were in their area. They repeatedly allied themselves with the Elamites and the Arameans against the Assyrians, and they put constant pressure on the major cities to revolt against Assyria, sometimes gaining control of the cities themselves. The career of Merodach-Baladan of the Bit Yakin illustrates this pattern perfectly. He submitted to TIGLATH-PILESER III in 729 BCE, but revolted when Sargon II took the throne of Assyria only eight years later. Merodach-Baladan II seized Babylon and was able to rule Babylonia for twelve years. Sargon finally drove him from Babylon in 709 BCE, but after Sargon's death he again appears on the scene to cause trouble in Babylonia for Sargon's successor, Sennacherib.

Despite strenuous and bloody campaigns against the Chaldeans and their Elamite allies during the reigns of Sennacherib and later of Ashurbanipal, Assyria was unable to pacify these tribes permanently. After the death of Ashurbanipal, the Chaldeans again gained control of the throne of Babylon, establishing the Neo-Babylonian or Chaldean dynasty. With the help of the Medes, this last Babylonian dynasty under Nabopolassar was able to destroy Assyria, capturing Nineveh in 612 BCE, and finishing off the remnants of Assyria at Harran in 609 BCE. Then after decisive defeats of the Egyptians at Carchemish and Hamath in 605 BCE, the crown prince, Nebuchadnezzar II, succeeded Nabopolassar, and extended the Babylonian conquests as far as the border of Egypt, in effect replacing Assyria as the dominant imperial power in the Near East. Following Nebuchadnezzar II's long reign, however, the Chaldean dynasty fell into rapid decline. His son Evil-Merodach and his son-in-law Neriglissar had short reigns, Labashi-Marduk was quickly removed, and Nabonidus, who seized the throne, though listed as the last member of this dynasty, was actually from Harran and hardly a Chaldean.

Despite the official use of Akkadian, the dominant spoken language of both the late Neo-Assyrian and Neo-Babylonian empires was probably Aramaic. Since most Chaldeans spoke Aramaic by the time of the exile, some late biblical writers refer to Aramaic as Chaldean.

Moreover, many Chaldeans diviners, sorcerers, and astrologers gained prominence during the Persian and Hellenistic periods, thus leading to the use of the term *Chaldean* as a designation for the practitioner of such arts. *See* ASSYRIA AND BABYLONIA.

J. J. M. ROBERTS

CHALKSTONES [אַבְנֵי־גִר ʾavne-ghir]. A metaphor for the fragility of idolatrous altars (Isa 27:9), because limestone, when heated, will convert into lime and break easily.

CHALPHI kalʾfi [Χαλφι Chalphi]. Father of JUDAS, a commander who, along with MATTATHIAS, remained to fight alongside JONATHAN (1 Macc 11:70), the Maccabean leader. Chalphi may be the same as Chapseus, whom Josephus mentions as Jonathan's father (*Ant.* 13.5.7).

CHAMBER [חֶדֶר khedher, לִשְׁכָּה lishkah, עֲלִיָּה ʿaliyyah, תָּא taʾ; γαζοφυλάκιον gazophylakion, κοιτων koitōn, παστοφόριον pastophorion, ταμεῖον tameion, θεε thee, ὑπερῷον hyperōon].

1. A private, inner room (khedher; tameion) in a large residence, such as a royal palace (Gen 43:30; 1 Kgs 20:30; 22:25; 2 Kgs 9:2; 2 Chr 18:24; Ps 105:30; Song 1:4; 3:4; Matt 24:26); at times, specifically a bedchamber (2 Sam 13:10; 1 Kgs 1:15; also koitōn, Ezek 8:12; Joel 2:16; Acts 12:20). *Chamber* is also used metaphorically to represent a constellation of stars (Job 9:9) or the realms of life/death within the "houses" of wisdom/folly (Prov 7:27; 24:4).

2. An upper room or loft (ʿaliyyah; hyperōon) in a multistoried house or temple (2 Sam 18:33; 2 Kgs 1:2; 4:10-11; 1 Chr 28:11; 2 Chr 3:9; Jer 22:13-14; Dan 6:10; Acts 20:8). In par. stories, Elijah and Elisha lodge in an upstairs guestroom and resuscitate the homeowner's stricken child (1 Kgs 17:17-24; 2 Kgs 4:8-37). Likewise, the venerable deceased disciple, Tabitha (Dorcas), is laid in an upper chamber in her home and is revived by Peter (Acts 9:36-43). Figuratively, Israel's Creator God dwells in the lofty chambers of heaven (Ps 104:3, 13).

3. A guardroom (taʾ, thee) in a palace (1 Kgs 14:28; 2 Chr 12:11) or temple (lishkah; pastophorion Ezek 40:7-36).

4. A treasury room (lishkah; gazophylakion) or storehouse compartment in the Temple precincts (Neh 10:37-39; 12:44; 13:4-9).

5. Various rooms, quarters, halls, and cells supporting palace and Temple administration (e.g., 2 Kgs 23:11; 1 Chr 9:26, 33; 23:28; 28:12; 2 Chr 31:11; Ezra 8:29; 10:6; Neh 3:30; Jer 35:4; 36:10, 12, 20-21; Ezek 40:17-46; 41:5-11; 42:1-13).

F. SCOTT SPENCER

CHAMBERLAIN [κοιτων koitōn]. The term is applied to BLASTUS, a chief advisor to Herod Agrippa I and overseer of the king's bedchamber (Acts 12:20). As a somewhat antiquated English term, the KJV used it more widely for EUNUCHS (e.g., סָרִים saris in 2 Kgs 23:11; Esth 1:10-15) and other administrators (e.g., Rom 16:23).

CHAMBERS OF THE SOUTH [חַדְרֵי תֵמָן khadhre theman]. A constellation in the southern sky, possibly the Southern Cross, Argo, or Sirius. This is the most likely meaning, given the literary context of the phrase in Job 9:9, although some argue that khadhre theman refers to the source of the southern wind. *See* STARS.

JOEL LeMON

CHAMELEON [תִּנְשֶׁמֶת tinshemeth, כֹּחַ koakh]. A small, lizardlike animal that changes its color to blend into its surroundings, the chameleon falls last in a list of swarming animals considered unclean (Lev 11:30). The Hebrew word is translated in Lev 11:18 and Deut 14:16 as "water hen," *swan*, or *ibis* in a list of birds considered unclean and, therefore, not to be eaten. The NAB translates koakh, the second animal in the Lev 11:30 list, as *chameleon*, whereas others render the Hebrew word there as LAND CROCODILE (NRSV) or sand-GECKO (REB). Ancient versions also reflect uncertain identification of this animal. *See* ANIMALS OF THE BIBLE.

EMILY CHENEY

CHAMPION [אִישׁ הַבֵּנַיִם ʾish habnayim, גִּבּוֹר gibor]. The term used to describe Goliath's status among the Philistines' warriors (1 Sam 17). Two warriors, one from each of the opposing armies, would meet in battle to determine which side would be victorious. *See* DAVID; MIGHTY MEN.

CHANNELS [אֲפִקִים ʾafiqim, יְאֹרִים yeʾorim; ἀφέσεις apheseis, πηγαί pēgai, ποταμοί potamoi, φάραγγες pharanges]. Natural or engineered conduits for WATER. Yeʾorim, an Egyptian loan-word, is often used to denote the channels of the Nile (Ezek 29:3-10). According to ancient cosmology, the channels of the SEA lay beneath the earth at its foundations (2 Sam 22:16).

CHAOS [תֹּהוּ tohu]. In the biblical worldview, an orderly CREATION is surrounded by forces of chaos. These forces are primarily described as turbulent waters (Pss 77:16; 93:3; Jer 5:22), and they are occasionally personified as a chaos dragon, LEVIATHAN (Ps 74:14; Isa 27:1), RAHAB (Ps 89:10; Job 26:12), or a Sea/River (Job 7:12; Hab 3:8).

To create the ordered world, God had to restrain these primordial waters of chaos, in some traditions by a cosmic battle to subdue the chaos dragon (Pss 74:12-17; 89:6-15; Job 26:5-14). In the account of creation in

Gen 1:1–2:4a, God divides the primordial waters (1:2), holding half of them back behind the firmament or sky, and the other half beyond the earth as seas (1:6-10). To prevent the world from collapsing back into chaos, as it did in the great flood (Gen 7:11; 8:2), God held these turbulent waters at bay behind boundaries (Job 38:8-11; Ps 104:5-9; Prov 8:27-29). The NT author of Revelation went beyond his OT ancestors to claim that God would one day eliminate the waters of chaos entirely (Rev 21:1).

THEODORE HIEBERT

CHAPHENATHA kuh-fen'uh-thuh [Χαφεναθά Chaphenatha]. A section of the Jerusalem wall that Jonathan Maccabeus rebuilt (1 Macc 12:37). This section may be the Second Quarter mentioned in 2 Kgs 22:14.

CHARACTER [δοκιμή dokimē]. In its broadest sense, character refers to the distinctive complex of qualities that distinguishes any one thing from another. In Aristotelian ethics, character is the moral center of gravity from which actions arise. In modern American usage, character is the stable, durable core of values that causes an individual to act reliably and consistently in ways that the community considers positive and admirable. The NRSV uses the English word this way in Rom 5:4, where the Greek dokimē connotes "that which has been tested and found worthy." However, there is no real biblical equivalent to the modern concept of character. In biblical texts individuals or groups who reliably and consistently act in ways approved of by God are called "righteous" (צַדִּיק tsaddiq, Gen 6:9; 7:1; δίκαιος dikaios, Matt 1:19; Mark 6:20; Luke 1:6). In both the OT and the NT, "righteousness" (צְדָקָה tsedhaqah, Gen 15:6; δικαιοσύνη dikaiosynē, e.g., Matt 5:6) refers to that moral center of gravity that enables people to be faithful (meaning trustworthy).

Because they have fully appropriated God's teaching and made it into the basis for their own actions, the righteous are not overly concerned with others' opinions of their behavior (Isa 51:7; Matt 5:6, 10). However, even those who are said to be righteous are often portrayed as acting in less than admirable ways (e.g., Noah in Gen 9:20-25 and David in 2 Sam 11:1–12:19). Righteousness, like good character, is highly desirable but not an infallible basis for good behavior. *See* FAITH, FAITHFULNESS; WORKS AND RIGHTEOUSNESS.

KATHLEEN A. FARMER

CHARACTERS, COMMON [חֶרֶט kheret]. God commands Isaiah to write on a tablet with "a man's kheret" (Isa 8:1). In its only other occurrence (Exod 32:4), kheret clearly indicates an engraving tool. Based on the expression, "writing of God" (Exod 32:16), however, translators have continued to render the Isa 8:1 phrase as "common characters."

CHARAX kair'aks [τὸν Χάρακα ton Charaka]. Town, east of the Jordan, where the Jews called the Toubiani lived (2 Macc 12:17). *See* TOB.

CHARCOAL [פֶּחָם pekham; ἀνθρακιά anthrakia]. Common fuel made from wood (Isa 44:12; 54:16) and used symbolically in Ps 11:6; Prov 26:21; John 18:18; and 21:9. *See* COAL.

CHAREA kair'ee-uh [Χαρεα Charea]. FIRST ESDRAS 5:32 name for HARSHA.

CHARGERS [פָּרָשִׁים parashim]. Spirited war horses, an emendation of *cypresses* in Nah 2:3. *See also* Isa 31:1; Jer 8:6; Rev 6:2, and HORSE.

CHARIOT [מֶרְכָּב merkav, מֶרְכָּבָה merkavah, רֶכֶב rekhev, רְכוּב rekhuv; ἅρμα harma, ῥέδη rhedē]. Two- or four-wheeled horse-drawn vehicles, used in both civilian and military contexts, primarily to transport passengers. Domesticated donkeys and horses were used to pull carts or chariots as early as the 3rd millennium BCE. During the Iron Age chariots and horses determined military superiority. Although both Israel and the military powers that dominated them possessed chariots, the neo-Assyrian and neo-Babylonian empires excelled in chariotry. Armies adapted chariots to be swift, mobile archery platforms and troop transports. As armies began to rely on cavalries, chariots became a less efficient weapon because of the expense of building them and the difficulty of maneuvering them in battle against mounted troops. In nonmilitary contexts, royalty, governmental officials, and the wealthy employed chariots to travel to their destinations.

Throughout Israel's narrative history, as well as in the Prophetic, Poetic, and Wisdom books, chariots figure prominently, as they often appear in the word pair "horses and chariots." In the OT chariots appear in the story of Pharaoh giving Joseph a chariot to ride, a sign of Joseph's position (Gen 41:43). The dread of chariots was equated with that of a whirlwind, flashing lightning, and thunder, an image associated with the "chariots of fire" that transport Elijah (2 Kgs 6:17; Sir 48:9). Such imagery becomes important in MERKABAH MYSTICISM.

In the Hellenistic period, the Seleucides used chariots, along with elephants and cavalry, to fight the Egyptians, the Romans, and the Judeans (1 Macc 1:17; 8:6; 2 Macc 13:2; 14:21). In both the Apocrypha and NT, chariots appear in apocalyptic visions (2 Esd 15:29; Rev 9:9). *See* CAVALRY; HORSE; WAR, METHODS, TACTICS, WEAPONS OF (BRONZE AGE THROUGH PERSIAN PERIOD); WAR, METHODS, TACTICS, WEAPONS OF (HELLENISTIC THROUGH ROMAN PERIODS).

MARK J.H. FRETZ

CHARISMA kuh-riz´muh [χάρισμα charisma]. Charisma is a plural noun meaning *gifts*, or specifically "gifts of healings," or *salvation*, or *celibacy*. The word appears in various forms in the Pauline tradition (Rom 1:11; 5:15, 16; 6:23; 11:29; 12:6; 1 Cor 1:7; 7:7; 12:4, 9, 28, 30, 31; 2 Cor 1:11; 1 Tim 4:14; 2 Tim 1:6), once in 1 Pet 4:10, and once in Philo's *Alleg. Interp.* 3.78.

In Rom 1:11, Paul adds the adjective "spiritual" (πνευματικόν pneumatikon) to charisma to specify "spiritual gifts." In other contexts, its meaning is fluid: e.g., scholars are divided over the specific semantic relationship between pneumatikon and charisma in 1 Cor 12.

While charisma has a diverse semantical range that makes it difficult for this word to serve as the overarching term for the concept of supernatural gifts, in the NT, the idea refers to ministry in the Spirit, based upon a humble and obedient spirit. *See* FRUIT OF THE SPIRIT; SPIRITUAL GIFTS.

Bibliography: Gordon Fee. *God's Empowering Presence: The Holy Spirit in the Letters of Paul* (1994).

BEN C. AKER

CHARITY [ἀγάπη agapē]. Word used in the KJV to mean "love," and the term is still familiar in traditional Christian wedding rituals (which draw from 1 Cor 13). *See* LOVE; SPIRITUAL GIFTS.

CHARM, CHARMER. Magical incantation; conjurer of spells. *See* AMULETS; DIVINATION; ENCHANTER; SNAKE CHARMING.

CHARMIS kahr´mis [Χαρμίς Charmis]. A city magistrate of Bethulia (Jdt 6:15; 8:10; 10:6).

CHASING. A process of decorating metal, particularly gold, for jewelry. A smith creates this effect by hammering punches into a flattened sheet of metal without puncturing it. *See* JEWELRY.

CHASM [χάσμα, chasma]. In Luke's parable of the rich man and LAZARUS, the rich man has his fortunes reversed because he failed to heed Moses and the prophets. He is forced to dwell in HADES, separated by the chasm from reward in ABRAHAM'S BOSOM (Luke 16:19-31). The image of the chasm as a place of punishment for the stars appears in Enoch's first journey across earth and SHEOL (*1 En.* 18).

HEATHER R. MCMURRAY

CHASPHO. *See* CASPIN.

CHASTISE [יָסַר yasar, יָכַח yakhakh; παιδεύω paideuō]. The family of terms associated with *chastise* (Ps 39:11; Jer 30:11; 4 Macc 18:5; Heb 12:6), which includes verb forms of *chasten* (Job 33:19; Wis 12:22)

and the nouns *chastisement* (Sir 16:12) and *chastening* (Isa 26:16). Most recent translations (e.g., NRSV) sometimes render these words as *punish/punishment*, *correct/correction*, or *discipline*. Both the Hebrew and Greek roots originally meant *instruct/instruction*, but the meaning of the terms eventually evolved to include "punishment with a view toward correction" and finally "the imposition of hardship or woe" without any reference to corrective or redemptive outcome. *See* DISCIPLINE.

DAVID R. BAUER

CHASTITY. *See* SEX, SEXUALITY; VIRGIN.

CHEBAR kee´bahr [כְּבָר kevar]. The river (or canal?) at Tel-Abib in the Chaldeans' region, where the prophet Ezekiel received a vision (Ezek 1:3; 3:15, 23; 10:15, 20, 22; 43:3).

CHECKER WORK [מַעֲשֵׂה שְׂבָכָה ma'aseh sevakhah]. A crosshatch pattern in bronze adorning the large floral capitals of the two pillars, JACHIN AND BOAZ, at the entrance to Solomon's Temple (1 Kgs 7:17), possibly resembling the pattern on the priest's checkered tunic (Exod 28:4, 39). *See* ARCHITECTURE, OT.

CHEDORLAOMER ked´uhr-lay-oh´muhr [כְּדָרְלָעֹמֶר kedhorla'omer]. The king of Elam who appears as the leader of a group of kings (Tidal, Amraphel, and Arioch) from the West, who wage battle against five "cities of the plain" in southern Israel, including Sodom and Gomorrah (Gen 14:1-2). These five cities join in rebellion against the hegemony of Chedorlaomer, so he campaigns in the Dead Sea valley until finally subduing this regional uprising (Gen 14:4-9). While the city of Sodom is being sacked, the invaders also take possession of Lot, Abraham's nephew. Word of Lot's capture comes to Abraham, who mounts an expedition to overtake the invading force. Genesis 14:15-16 reports that Abraham orchestrates a surprise nighttime attack in Dan, and harries the invaders all the way past Damascus. He reclaims the stolen bounty and brings it back to Sodom, and is rewarded by receiving the blessing of Melchizedek, king of Salem.

There has been some historical interest in this unusual story, because of the possibility of dating Abraham with a fixed historical reference. Attempts to identify Amraphel with Hammurabi, thus placing Abraham in the 18th cent. BCE, have failed. Other scholars have drawn speculative links between these king names and rulers such as Sennacherib and Merodach-Baladan, suggesting that Gen 14 is a rewriting of an original tale about the sacking of Babylon by various rulers. In any case, the narrative's purpose is to show Abraham's military, ethical, and spiritual ascendancy over the petty kings of the region.

BRYAN D. BIBB

CHEESE, CHEESEMAKING [שְׁפוֹת בָּקָר shefoth baqar]. Cheese (literally "cream from the herd") is made by curdling the milk of cows, goats, or sheep. It forms part of the list of provisions for David (2 Sam 17:29). David is also said to bring ten cheeses (literally "ten slices of milk") to his brothers (1 Sam 17:18). In Job 10:10 "cheese" is used figuratively when Job accuses God of pouring him out like milk and curdling him like cheese (גְּבִינָה givinah). *See* CURDS; FOOD; MILK.

L. JULIANA M. CLAASSENS

CHEETAH [נָמֵר namer; πάρδαλις pardalis]. Usually namer is translated LEOPARD. In Hab 1:8, where this animal is used metaphorically to emphasize the swiftness of the Chaldeans' horses, it may indicate the hunting leopard, today referred to as the cheetah, which can run as fast as 70 mi. per hour. This leopard can be trained for hunting and belongs to the cat family, although it runs down its prey rather than simply stalking and then pouncing upon it. *See* ANIMALS OF THE BIBLE.

CHELAL kee'lal [כְּלָל kelal]. An Israelite who was among the returning exiles who were forced by Ezra to give up their foreign wives (Ezra 10:30).

CHELLEANS kel'ee-uhns [Χελεοι Cheleoi]. Inhabitants of the area north of the Rassisites and the ISH-MAELITES (Jdt 2:23), probably in the eastern portion of Palestine near the Arabian Desert. Other than this reference in Judith, the Chelleans are unknown. *See* ISHMAEL; RASSIS.

CHELOUS kel'uhs [Χελους Chelous]. A town name appearing only once in the biblical corpus (Jdt 1:9) where its mention with JERUSALEM, BETHANY, KADESH, and the river of Egypt suggests a southern location. But like other towns in JUDITH that have not been located, Chelous may be a fictive place name.

CHELUB kee'luhb [כְּלוּב keluv; Χαλεβ Chaleb]. 1. A Judahite in the Chronicler's genealogy (1 Chr 4:11), the brother of Shuah and the father of Mehir. The LXX Chaleb suggests that "Caleb" (כָּלֵב) might have been in the original, or the translator misread the Hebrew.

2. Father of David's officer Ezri, who was in charge of the field workers (1 Chr 27:26).

CHELUBAI. *See* CALEB.

CHELUHI kel'uh-hi [כְּלוּהוּ keluhu]. A descendant of Bani. Ezra forced him and other men to send away their foreign wives and their children, as part of the effort to increase homogeneity in the community of returned exiles in Judea (Ezra 10:35).

CHEMOSH kee'mosh [כְּמוֹשׁ kemosh, Χαμως Chamōs]. The national deity of the Moabites, whom the OT calls "people of Chemosh" (Num 21:29; Jer 48:46). Solomon built a HIGH PLACE for Chemosh (1 Kgs 11:7; 2 Kgs 23:13), for which he is doomed (1 Kgs 11:33). Mesha, a 9th cent. BCE Moabite king, erected the MESHA INSCRIPTION, a monument to Chemosh, which credits Chemosh for allowing the oppression that MOAB experienced under Israel. It recounts that MESHA was freed from enemy kings and the land was returned to the Moabites. The inscription also describes how, in tribute to Chemosh, Mesha killed the entire population of a city.

TREVOR D. COCHELL

CHENAANAH ki-nay'uh-nuh [כְּנַעֲנָה kena'anah]. 1. Father of Zedekiah, Jehoshaphat's court prophet, repudiated in 1 Kgs 22 and 2 Chr 18.

2. A Benjaminite in the genealogy of 1 Chr 7:10, which differs from 1 Chr 8:1-40. Genealogies for Zebulun and Dan are missing in 1 Chr 4–8, but it is improbable that 1 Chr 7:6-12 originally was a genealogy of Zebulon.

CHENANI ki-nay'ni [כְּנָנִי kenani]. A Levite who supported Ezra's promulgation of the Law (Neh 9:4).

CHENANIAH ken'uh-ni'uh [כְּנַנְיָהוּ kenanyahu, כְּנַנְיָה kenanyah]. "Yahu strengthens." 1. A Levite who directed the music at the celebration of David's installation of the ARK OF THE COVENANT in Jerusalem (1 Chr 15:22, 27).

2. An Izharite appointed by David for civil duties (1 Chr 26:29).

CHENOBOSKIAN. *See* NAG HAMMADI, ARCHAE-OLOGY; NAG HAMMADI TEXTS.

CHEPHAR-AMMONI kee'fuhr-am'uh-ni [הָעַמֹּנִי־כְּפַר kefar ha'ammoni]. A town settled by the Ammonites that along, with its villages, Joshua allotted to Benjamin's tribe (Josh 18:24).

CHEPHIRAH ki-fi'ruh [כְּפִירָה kefirah]. A Hivite city (Josh 9:17), allotted to Benjamin's tribe (Josh 18:26). Its residents' descendants returned from exile (Ezra 2:25; Neh 7:29). Present-day site is Khirbet Kefireh.

CHERAN kihr'uhn [כְּרָן keran]. Seir's grandson. A chief (NIV) or clan (NRSV) of the Horites (Gen 36:26; 1 Chr 1:41).

CHERETHITES AND PELETHITES ker'uh-thits, pel'uh-thits [כְּרֵתִי kerethi; פְּלֵתִי pelethi]. The Cherethites and the Pelethites served as DAVID's palace guard under the charge of BENAIAH (2 Sam 8:18; 20:23; 23:23). They remained loyal to David in the most difficult circumstances during his reign. When David had to flee Jerusalem due to Absalom's revolt, they escorted David in his journey (2 Sam 15:18). When Sheba rebelled against David, the Cherethites and the Pelethites were among those who were called on to pursue Sheba (2 Sam 20:7). Then shortly before David's death when Adonijah attempted to take the throne, the Cherethites and the Pelethites were the only warriors who escorted Solomon to the coronation (1 Kgs 1:38-44). After David's death, they were probably assimilated into the regular army, especially since Benaiah became the commander of Solomon's army. Later on, there is a possibility that the Cherethites, spelled as CARITES, played an important role in overthrowing Athaliah and bringing Joash to the throne (2 Kgs 11:14-21).

The Cherethites appear in par. with the Philistines in two instances (Zeph 2:5; Ezek 25:16), however, they are not to be thought of as identical. The close association between the Philistines and the Cherethites comes from the fact that the Philistines are specifically associated with Caphtor (Jer 47:4; Amos 9:7), a term that can be identified with Crete or its environs, and the fact that the Cherethites are often identified as Cretans because they appear in the same region, the Negeb of Cherethites (1 Sam 30:14), as the Caphtorim/Cretans did (Deut 2:23). Some suggest that the Cherethites settled on the seacoast of Canaan much earlier than the Philistines. The term *Pelethites* appears seven times in the OT, always in association with the Cherethites, and may be another form of "Philistines," perhaps a deliberate misspelling to make David's association with the Philistines ambiguous. They were a group of Philistines who joined David during his stay at Ziklag at about the same time that a group of Cherethites did.

Bibliography: Y. Aharoni. "The Negeb of Judah." *IEJ* 8 (1958), 26–38; W. F. Albright. "A Colony of Cretan Mercenaries on the Coast of the Negeb." *JPOS* 1 (1920–1921), 187–94.

URIAH KIM

CHERITH, WADI ker'ith, wah'dee [נַחַל כְּרִית nakhal kerith]. A stream on the east side of the Jordan River where ELIJAH hid from AHAB and JEZEBEL during the drought in Israel. He remained there until the spring dried up (1 Kgs 17:2-7). Ever since the Middle Ages, scholars have debated on which side of the Jordan River this stream was located. Those who prefer the west side have argued that the Hebrew word עַל פְּנֵי 'al pene should be translated "before" or "toward" the Jordan (e.g., Gen 18:16; 25:18).

Candidates for a west of the Jordan location include 'Ain Fusail (PHASAELIS of NT times) just north of Jericho, and the Wadi Qelt near Herodian Jericho. The argument for the Wadi Qelt is based on the idea that the Arabic Qelt could have been derived from the Hebrew

kerith. A major difficulty with both of these locations, however, is that they are not really isolated but are near routes connecting the two heavily populated centers of Jerusalem and Jericho. This fact has led most scholars to prefer locating the stream on the east bank. They also argue that the most obvious reading of 'al pene is "east of" the Jordan (e.g., Eusebius *Onomast.* 174). Although the Wadi Rajib has been suggested as a possibility, most scholars have preferred the Wadi el-Yubis in the highlands of North Gilead. This wadi empties into the Jordan about 8 km south of Pella. This suggestion may make the most sense in view of the fact that Elijah was a Gileadite (1 Kgs 17:1).

RANDALL YOUNKER

CHERUB, CHERUBIM cher'uhb, cher'uh-bim [כְּרוּב keruv, כְּרוּבִים keruvim; Χαρούβ Charoub; χερουβίν Cheroubin]. 1. Winged beings, part animal, part human (Ezek 10:14; 41:18-19), associated with transporting Yahweh (2 Sam 22:11), the divine throne (Ezek 1; Rev 4:8-10), and in sacral garden contexts (Gen 3:24; Ezek 28:14). Their images were carved on the ark, tabernacle (Exod 25:18-22; 26:1), and SOLOMON'S TEMPLE (1 Kgs 6:23-28). *See* ANGEL; ARK OF THE COVENANT; MESSENGER.

MAXWELL J. DAVIDSON

2. Cherub (ker'uhb). A Babylonian city and former home of some of the returnees to Jerusalem with Zerubbabel (Ezra 2:59//Neh 7:61). Those arriving from Cherub could not be confirmed as Israelites.

3. Cherub is a personal name in 1 Esd 5:36.

STEVE COOK

CHESALON kes'uh-lon [כְּסָלוֹן Kesalon]. A city on Judah's northern boundary and west of Jerusalem. It was also called Mount Jearim (Josh 15:10).

CHESED kee'sed [כֶּשֶׂד kesedh]. Abraham's nephew (Gen 22:22). *See* KHESED.

CHESIL kee'suhl [כְּסִיל kesil]. A city in southern Judah near Edom (Josh 15:30). It is possibly the same as Bethul (Josh 19:4), Bethuel (1 Chr 4:30), and Bethel (1 Sam 30:27).

CHEST [אָרוֹן 'aron; κιβωτός kibotos]. Container for collecting money for Temple repairs (2 Kgs 12:9-10; 2 Chr 24:8-11) and for holding Temple treasures (1 Esd 1:54).

CHESTER BEATTY PAPYRI. The appellation refers to the largest discovery to date of Greek biblical manuscripts that were written on PAPYRUS, acquired in 1930–1931 by Sir Alfred Chester Beatty (1875–1968). Individual Papyri are normally cited as "P. Chester Beatty." The manuscripts are now found in the Chester Beatty Gallery of Oriental Art in Dublin, Ireland.

The Chester Beatty Biblical Papyri. Though the exact place of discovery is unknown, the papyri were likely located in a Christian church or monastery near Aphroditopolis or possibly in the Fayum. Not all parts of the eleven codices found their way to Beatty's collection. Substantial segments were acquired by John H. Scheide (Princeton), the universities of Michigan and Cologne, and the Consejo Superior de Investigaciones Cientificas of Madrid. Fragments are in Barcelona and Vienna. The Papyri are dated from the 2nd–4th cent. CE, with the majority falling in the 3rd cent.

The discovery of the Papyri challenged prevailing opinion that the format of the papyrus codex did not gain general acceptance among Christians until the 4th cent. and supplied an abundance of information on how the papyrus book was constructed. Page size ranges from about 18 × 33 cm to 14 × 24.2 cm. Some were constructed of a single gathering (quire) of papyrus sheets, while in others the gathering varies from a single sheet to five or seven. The largest codex must have counted at least 236 pages.

One of the most interesting aspects of scribal practice concerns the *nomina sacra*, namely, the contraction of a sacred word (e.g., "Jesus") to its first and last letters, marked with a horizontal line.

Since all but two (Pap. XI, XII) of the codices are dated earlier than the 4th cent., they present important evidence for the text of the Greek Bible as it existed in Egypt prior to the *traditio codicum* (the "turning in" of Christian books during the Diocletianic persecutions) and a century or more earlier than the great vellum codices of the 4th cent., namely, VATICANUS and SINAITICUS. The Papyri also demonstrate remarkable stability in the transmission history of the biblical text. For the Greek OT, their great significance lies in the fact that their text is untouched by the revisionary activity of Origen (3rd cent.) and Lucian (3rd–4th cent.), and others.

OT Papyri. Papyri VIII (containing Jer 4:30–5:24) and XI (Sir 36:28–37:22; 46:6–47:2) are the most extensive early witnesses for their respective books. Papyri IV (Gen 9:1–44:22) and V (Gen 8:13–9:2; 24:13–46:33) preserve four-fifths of the book of Genesis, a book almost absent from both Codex Vaticanus and Sinaiticus. Papyri VI (Num 5:12–36:13; Deut 1:20–34:12) is virtually free of Hebraizing corrections. Papyri VII (Isa 8:18–19:13; 38:14–45:5; 54:1–60:22) is an exceptionally good witness to the original Greek, with some annotations in Old Fayumic (a dialect of Egyptian reflected in Cop.). Papyri IX–X is most interesting among the OT Papyri. Its 3rd cent. date makes it the earliest substantial witness for Ezekiel (11:25–fin.), Daniel (1:1–12:13)–Bel (c. 4-39)–Susanna (5–subscriptio), Esther (1:1a–8:6). Pap. XII is important because of the newness of its contents: portions of Enoch, a fragment from the book of Noah, the *Peri Pascha* of Melito of Sardis, and the *Apocryphon of Ezekiel*.

NT Papyri. Papyri I (Matt 20:24–Acts 17:7) challenged the prevailing view that, prior to the 4th cent., each Gospel had circulated separately. (The order of the individual books in this codex is: Matthew, John, Luke, Mark). Papyri II (Rom 5:17–16:23; Hebrews; Corinthians; Ephesians; Galatians; Philippians; Colossians; 1 Thessalonians) remarkably reveals the placement of Hebrews among the Pauline epistles at a time when it was widely regarded as uncanonical, and its location after Romans is virtually unique. Equally uncommon is that Ephesians precedes rather than follows Galatians. Perhaps the object of greatest textual interest in Pap. II is the doxology of Rom 16:25-27, which closes chap. 15. That the Pastoral Epistles were not included in Pap. II seems certain but does not necessarily reflect doubts about their Pauline authorship. Papyri III (Rev 9:10–17:2) is at least a century older than Codex Sinaiticus and, of our early (3rd–4th cent., and before) witnesses, is the most extensive. *See* BODMER PAPYRI; CODEX; HAGIOGRAPHA; PAPYRUS, PAPYRI; SEPTUAGINT; SINAITICUS, CODEX; TEXT CRITICISM, NT; VATICANUS, CODEX; VERSIONS, ANCIENT.

Bibliography: F. G. Kenyon. *The Chester Beatty Biblical Papyri* (1977).

ALBERT PIETERSMA

CHESULLOTH ki-suhl′oth [כְּסֻלּוֹת kesulloth]. City in the territory allotted to Issachar's tribe (Josh 19:18). It is probably identical with Chisloth-Tabor (Josh 19:12) and Tabor (1 Chr 6:77).

CHEZIB kee′zib [כְּזִיב keziv]. Birthplace of Shela, third son of Judah and his Canaanite wife Shua (Gen 38:5). Possibly same town as Cozeba and ACHZIB.

CHI [χ ch]. The twenty-second letter in the Greek alphabet, which has no Phoenician prototype, and represents kh in the blue alphabets, but ks in some red alphabets. Along with the Greek letter rho (ρ r), it is often used to represent the word *Christ* (Χριστός Christos). *See* ALPHABET.

P. KYLE MCCARTER, Jr.

CHIASM ki′az′uhm. Also called *chiasmus*, a Lat. transliteration of the Greek χιασμα chiasma, referring to the Greek letter X (chi). Chiasm is the repetition of the same elements in inverted order: a-b-b′-a′; or if a middle element is present: a-b-c-b′-a′. Chiastic arrangement, conceived graphically, resembles the letter X.

Macro-chiasmus refers to chiastic arrangement covering an entire book or a large section, while micro-chiasmus refers to chiastic arrangement in a small unit, often a sentence. Although macro-chiasmus sometimes occurs in the Bible, micro-chiasmus is much more frequent.

Examples of micro-chiasmus include Isa 6:10:

Make the *mind* of this people dull   a
  and stop their *ears*   b
    and shut their *eyes*   c
    so that they may not look with their *eyes*   c´
  and listen with their *ears*   b´
and comprehend with their *minds*   a´

There is no discussion of chiasm among ancient rhetoricians prior to 400 CE. Yet chiasm frequently carries interpretive significance for biblical passages where it appears.

Bibliography: John Breck. *The Shape of Biblical Language: Chiasmus in the Scriptures and Beyond* (1994); Nils W. Lund. *Chiasmus in the New Testament: A Study in the Form and Function of Chiastic Structures* (1992); John W. Welch, ed. *Chiasmus in Antiquity: Structures, Analyses, Exegesis* (1981).

DAVID R. BAUER

CHICK. *See* HEN.

CHIDON ki´duhn [כִּידֹן kidhon]. Name of the town or the owner of the threshing floor where Uzzah died (1 Chr 13:9). A parallel text refers to the threshing floor as Nacon's (2 Sam 6:6). *See* NACON; UZZAH.

CHIEF [רֹאשׁ ro'sh, נָשִׂיא nasi', קָצִין qatsin]. Because of its long and varied social history, the Bible uses seventeen words that signify a chief or leader. Only a few of the more common terms are listed here. Of these, ro'sh (head) often indicates the head of tribes (1 Sam 15:17; Deut 33:5; Judg 10:18; 11:8, 9, 11) or even the king (Isa 7:8; Ps 18:44). A sheikh or a recognized chieftain, a nasi', is seen in the ancient contexts of Exod 22:27 and Gen 34:2. Qatsin signified a ruler of the people (Isa 1:10; 22:3; Mic 3:1, 9) or a military commander (Judg 11:6, 11). *See* PRINCE.

WALTER BOUZARD

CHIEF, HIGH PRIEST [כֹּהֵן הָרֹאשׁ kohen haro'sh; ἀρχιέρεως archiereōs]. The Aaronite priest who heads all altar priests and performs the DAY OF ATONEMENT rituals. *See* PRIESTS AND LEVITES.

CHILD, CHILDREN [יֶלֶד yeledh, יַלְדָּה yaldah (*child*), בֵּן ben (*son* or *child*), בַּת bath (*daughter* or *child*), τέκνον teknon (*child*), τεκνίον teknion ("little child"), παῖς pais (*child* or *servant*), παιδίον paidion (*child* below the age of puberty), παιδάριον paidarion ("little child"), βρέφος brephos (unborn *child, infant, baby*)].

A. Children in the OT

Children signified divine blessing. God blessed Adam and Eve to be fruitful and multiply (Gen 1:27-28). God promised Abraham many descendants (Gen 15:1-5).

Blessed was the man with many children (Ps 127:3-6) and bitter was barrenness (1 Sam 1-2; *see* BARREN, BARRENNESS).

Children were highly valued for their potential roles: contributing to the material well-being of the family, carrying on the family name, perpetuating the covenant nation's unique identity and purpose from one generation to the next (*see* FAMILY). Children were integrated from an early age into family and nation—dedicated to God, and, in the case of males, circumcised on the eighth day (Luke 2:21; *see* CIRCUMCISION). They might be named to express some aspect of God's relation to the parent or family (1 Sam 1:20). They received parental blessings, especially before a parent's death (Gen 27). Abraham's near-sacrifice of Isaac does not contradict but emphasizes the child's value for family and community: God requires Abraham to sacrifice what is most valuable, his only son, who is necessarily redeemed by a substitute sacrifice (Gen 22:1-19).

Children had to outgrow their ignorance, foolishness, and inexperience in order to fulfill their roles. Thus the stress on children's education. Proverbs 1–9 focus on parental instruction in wisdom to wean a child from adverse qualities. Children participated actively in familial and communal worship, asked questions concerning the rites observed, and repeatedly listened to the explanations of their elders, and so learned the covenant people's way of life and the underlying narrative of Yahweh's redemption (Exod 12:26-27; Deut 4:9-10). By contrast, when God chose mere youths as instruments of God's purposes, divine sovereignty and power is emphasized (e.g., 1 Sam 16:11-13).

Children's central obligation was to honor their parents (Exod 20:12). The child's obedience formed the basis of a morally and economically viable family, while insolent or violent treatment of parents was condemned (Prov 15:20; 19:26). Parental discipline was seen as necessary out of love—never anger—to save a child from destruction, and could take a harsh, physical form supposedly suited to children's irrationality (Prov 13:24; 19:18).

Children's value was not merely instrumental but fundamental, based on their relationship to the Creator: "It was you who formed my inward parts . . . in my mother's womb . . . I praise you for I am fearfully and wonderfully made" (Ps 139:13-14). Children's dependence on God was not to be outgrown: "upon you I have leaned from my birth" (Ps 71:6). Orphans, in particular, who lacked a male protector in a patriarchal society came under God's care as "helper of orphans" (Ps 10:14, 18). Sin tainted even the child in the womb (Ps 51:5), but hope for the young lay in God's redemption: "new Jerusalem shall be full of boys and girls playing in its streets" (Zech 8:5).

B. Children in the NT

The perspective on childbearing in the NT is different from that in the OT. Jesus pronounces a woe (not a blessing) on the woman who is pregnant or nursing in the coming eschatological destruction (Mark 13:17). Similarly, Paul points to the impending crisis as the reason not to enter into marriage (except to avoid sexual sin), which involves one in obligations (toward spouse and children) that distract from devotion to the Lord, and Paul never commends procreation to those already married (1 Cor 7:1-40). It is unclear whether 1 Tim 2:15, "[woman] will be saved through child-bearing provided they continue in faith, and love and holiness, with modesty," promises salvation on the basis of childbearing (viewed positively) and other commendable acts, or salvation *despite* having to go through painful childbearing (viewed negatively) as the continuing effect of sin.

Jesus' teaching that disciples are to love him more than father or mother, son or daughter, envisions conflict between parents and children over Jesus, and undermines their traditional mutual obligations (Matt 8:21-22; 10:34-37; Luke 9:59-62; 12:51-53; 14:26; contrast the emphasis on Jesus' obedience to both heavenly Father and earthly parents in Luke 2:41-51). Jesus' description of those who do the will of God as "my brother and sister and mother" (Mark 3:31-35 par.), however, implies that parent/child obligations are now located within this broader family. If children or parents lose the benefits of the patriarchal family as a result of Jesus' call to follow him, they gain even more by joining God's family: "a hundredfold now . . . brothers and sisters, mothers and children" (Mark 10:28-30). Further, Jesus' disciples are to welcome little children (not just their own) in his name, following his example (*see* below).

Jesus' teaching on discipleship does not cancel out the appropriateness of parents' instinct to give good gifts to their children, which he cites in support of trusting in the heavenly Father's benevolence (Matt 7:9-11; Luke 11:11-13). Parental care for children is also supported by Jesus' miracles for sick or demon-possessed children in response to parents' faith in Jesus (e.g., Mark 5:21-23, 35-43; 7:24-30; 9:14-29 par.; *see* CLEAN AND UNCLEAN; DEMON; DEMONIAC; HEALING; MIRACLES).

In striking contrast to children's social inferiority, Jesus teaches that children are models for entering God's reign. In Mark 10:13-16 (par. Matt 19:13-15; Luke 18:15-17) Jesus becomes indignant when the disciples try to prevent people from bringing little children to him (presumably because they were not under obligation to keep the law in anticipation of the Messiah's blessings) and instead Jesus takes them in his arms and blesses them, for "it is to such as these that the kingdom of God belongs." Children's objective, humble state, and corresponding attitude suits them for membership in God's reign, which comes to those who simply need or desire it (1 Pet 2:2). Children's innocence or another positive trait is not

implied (compare the realistic views of children in Matt 11:16; Luke 7:32; 1 Cor 3:1-2; 13:11; Gal 4:1, 3; Eph 4:14; Heb 5:13). To enter God's reign one must become like a child: humble. In Mark 9:33-37 (par. Matt 18:1-6; Luke 9:46-48) Jesus exemplifies this humility by taking a little child to himself, signifying his serving the needs of the least and becoming last of all and servant of all. echoes this teaching: one must be born from above/the Spirit, in order to see the reign of God). Jesus also teaches that whoever receives a little child in his name receives him, and thus redefines the humble task of childcare as the mark of true discipleship (*see* DISCIPLE, DISCIPLE-SHIP). Conversely, causing "one of these little ones who believe in me" (children or other social inferiors) to stumble brings judgment. Compare 1st cent. Jewish critiques of the pagan practices of abortion, exposure of newborns, and infanticide for economic and other reasons.

Similarly, uneducated children are presented as exemplary for acclaiming Jesus as the Son of David—not on the basis of their own wisdom but that which God has supplied—over the objection of the chief priests and scribes (Matt 21:15-16).

The few references to children in the NT outside the Gospels affirm children's reception of God's eschatological blessings (the Spirit is outpoured on all flesh, young and old, Acts 2:17, 38-39), inclusion in early Christian worship and communal activities (Acts 21:5), being set apart ("holy") for God as beneficiaries of God's redemptive work (1 Cor 7:14), and children's own relationship to Christ the Lord grounding their moral agency ("Children, obey your parents in the Lord!" (Eph 6:1-3; Col 3:20). The description of the parent/child relationship emphasizes the Christian parent's beneficial effect on the child: On account of a parent's faith the children are "holy" rather than "unclean" (probably referring to present or future salvation, 1 Cor 7:14-16). Household baptisms may have included children and infants (Acts 10:1-48; 16:14-15, 31-34; 1 Cor 1:16; *see* BAPTISM). Fathers are to train children "in the discipline and instruction of the Lord" (Eph 6:4), and mothers and grandparents appear to have the same informal role (2 Tim 1:5), which is to be rewarded in old age with children's care (1 Tim 5:4). Fathers who raise obedient and faithful children display the leadership quality necessary for overseeing the church with its family-like nature (1 Tim 3:4-5; Titus 1:6). There is a strong sense of children's vulnerability: fathers are exhorted not to exasperate their children and so discourage them (Eph 6:4; Col 3:21), presumably through harsh discipline. Care for orphans (and widows) in their distress is called "pure and undefiled" religion (Jas 1:27).

See BIRTH; CHILDREN OF GOD; EDUCATION; FAMILY; FATHER; MARRIAGE; MOTHER; WOMEN IN THE NT; WOMEN IN THE OT.

Bibliography: P. Balla. *The Child-Parent Relationship in the New Testament and Its Environments.* WUNT 155 (2003); G. M. Beasley-Murray. "Church and Child in the New Testament." *Baptist Quarterly* 21 (1965–1966) 206–18; M. Bunge, ed. *The Child in Biblical Traditions* (2006); J. T. Carroll. "Children in the Bible." *Int* 55 (2001) 121–34; R. E. Clemens. "The Relation of Children to the People of God in the Old Testament." *Baptist Quarterly* 21 (1965–1966), 195–205. J. Francis. "Children and Childhood in the New Testament." *Family in Theological Perspective*, ed. S. C. Barton (1996) 65–85; J. M. Gundry-Volf. "The Least and the Greatest: Children in the New Testament." *The Child in Christian Thought.* Ed. M. Bunge (2001) 29–60; W. A. Strange. *Children in the Early Church: Children in the Ancient World, the New Testament and the Early Church* (1996).

JUDITH M. GUNDRY-VOLF

CHILDBIRTH. *See* BIRTH.

CHILDLESS. *See* BARREN, BARRENNESS; CHILD, CHILDREN.

CHILDREN OF GOD [בְּנֵי הָאֱלֹהִים bene ha'elo-him; τέκνα θεοῦ tekna theou, υἱοὶ θεοῦ huioi theou]. The concept of a familial relationship between humans and God reaches back to ancient mythology and was developed variously in different eras of biblical history. It came to be used metaphorically to designate a special or privileged spiritual relationship to God. References to "children of God" or "sons of God" occur in both covenantal and apologetic contexts as they define the identity of particular peoples and communities.

    A. OT and Apocrypha
    B. Dead Sea Scrolls
    C. Philo
    D. Rabbinic Judaism
    E. Greco-Roman Religions
    F. Synoptic Gospels
    G. Pauline Letters
    H. Johannine Writings
    Bibliography

A. OT and Apocrypha

Genesis 6:4, which describes the progeny of "sons of God" (bene ha'elohim) and human women, appears to be an allusion to the primitive notion of procreation by divine beings. Even later literature describes the divine court where "sons of God" present themselves before the Lord (Job 1:6; 2:1; Ps 89:6; *1 En.* 6:2; 13:8). Human beings, however, cannot become "like one of us" (i.e., divine), "knowing good and evil" by their own initiative (Gen 3:22).

Nevertheless, the figurative or metaphorical sense of the term begins not in divine procreation but in the covenant relationship between God and Israel. God promised to make Abraham the father of a great nation through whom God could bless all the peoples of the earth (Gen 12:1-3). In the exodus God claimed Israel as "my firstborn son" (Gen 4:22-23), became "a father to Israel" (Jer 31:9), and called "my son" out of Egypt (Hos 11:1). The covenant relationship was solemnized by the sprinkling of blood (Exod 24:5-8) and the eating of a communal meal (Exod 24:11), which made the two parties one family. God gave birth to the nation through God's saving act, thereby establishing the father-child relationship with Israel (Deut 32:6, 18). The people of Israel were therefore members of the family whose head was God (Jer 12:6-7), and God loved Israel as a father loves his children (Ps 103:13; Isa 63:8-9). As the child of God, Israel was obligated to become like God, a holy people (Lev 19:2; 20:7, 26) and live according to God's directions (Exod 19:5-6; Deut 10:12-22; 14:1). Paternity also laid the basis for the hope of an inheritance; the children of God would be the heirs of the promises of the covenants (Gen 17:7-8; 18:18; 22:16-18). Israel will love and worship God, do justice, and show mercy (Deut 10:12; Mic 6:8). Israel's disobedience was a violation of this familial, covenant relationship; they were rebellious, faithless children (Deut 32:4-5; Isa 1:2, 4; 30:1, 9; Jer 3:14, 22).

The divine sonship of Israel focused in the king, through the corporate solidarity of the people, and the king's identity as the son of God extended to all of Israel (2 Sam 7:14; 1 Chr 17:13; 22:10; 28:6). To the king the Lord promised, in a psalm that was probably composed for a coronation, "You are my son; today I have begotten you" (Ps 2:7). The king of Israel was therefore the "firstborn, the highest of the kings of the earth" (Ps 89:27). God's covenant was not with the king per se but with the people of Israel.

The prophets and the later books of the OT begin to emphasize the divine sonship of individual Israelites, "children of the living God" (Hos 1:10), which comes to the fore in the Wisdom literature. Sirach counsels: "Be a father to orphans, and be like a husband to their mother; you will then be like a son of the Most High" (4:10). The righteous one has knowledge of God and "calls himself a child of the Lord" (Wis 2:13) and "boasts that God is his father" (2:16), and the unrighteous reason that "if the righteous man is God's child, he will help him and deliver him from the hand of his adversaries" (Wis 2:18). Being a child of God, therefore, arises from the covenant relationship, through which one knows God and lives rightly before God. The child of God can therefore pray to God as "Father" (Sir 23:1, 4) and seek God's protection and guidance (Sir 51:10).

Although this special status is generally restricted to the covenant community in the OT, there are intimations that God's ultimate purpose is to make all people children of God (Gen 12:3; 22:18; Isa 19:24-25; 63:16; 66:20; Zech 14:16), so that "the earth will be filled with the knowledge of the glory of the Lord, as the waters cover the sea" (Hab 2:14).

Jeremiah looks forward to the new covenant in which the Lord will put the Law within them and write it on their hearts, and they shall be God's people and know God (Jer 31:31-34). God will put a new spirit within them (Ezek 36:26). God's steadfast love lasts forever, opening the way for the hope of the fulfillment of God's purposes in the everlasting future (1 Chr 16:34, 41; Ps 100:5).

B. Dead Sea Scrolls

As the references in the Wisdom of Solomon indicate, writings during the Second Temple period reflect an increasing democratization in the concept of "children of God" and a growing restriction of the term to those who are righteous and faithful to the covenant. In view of the reverence for the divine name manifested in the Qumran scrolls, it is not surprising that Hebrew equivalents of "children of God" do not appear in them. Still, the community is designated by such phrases as "sons of light" (1QS I 9), "sons of justice" (1QS III 20), "sons of truth" (1QS IV 5), "sons of the eternal assembly" (1QS II 25), and "sons of his loving kindness" (1QH IV 32; XI 9). These circumlocutions for the divine name clearly document that the Qumran community understood itself as the righteous remnant of Israel, which was birthed by the Teacher of Righteousness and the intervention of the Holy Spirit (1QH III 1-18; VII 6-8), to become the "sons of God" in a moral sense. The Teacher of Righteousness was "a father to the sons of Grace" (1QH VII 20-21).

C. Philo

By interpreting Deut 13:18 and 14:1, Philo asserts that "they who do 'what is pleasing' to nature and what is 'good' are sons of God" (Spec. 1.318, LCL). In addition to emphasizing the moral qualifications of the sons of God, Philo offers the possibility of becoming a son of "the Word" (λόγος logos) to those who are not yet ready to become sons of God:

> But they who live in the knowledge of the One are rightly called "sons of God" . . . But if there be any as yet unfit to be called a Son of God, let him press to take his place under God's First-born, the Word, who holds eldership among the angels, their ruler as it were" (Conf. 145-47, LCL).

Here for the first time we find in one passage the concept of sons of God who merit that designation by virtue of moral uprightness or distinctive spiritual knowledge rather than by virtue of their heredity and the concept of the Word (logos) as an intermediary that helps individuals along the path to becoming "sons of God."

D. Rabbinic Judaism

M. 'Abot 3.15 attributes the following saying to Rabbi Akiba:

> Beloved are Israel for they were called children of God; still greater was the love in that it was made known to them that they were called children of God, as it is written, Ye are the children of the Lord your God (Deut 14:1).

In the Talmud, Palestinian Jewish charismatics Hanina ben Dosa and others regarded themselves as sons of God or were commended by a heavenly voice as "my son" (b. Ta'an. 24b, 25a; b. Ḥag. 15b). The rabbis debated whether Israel was and would always be the children of God or whether only those who obeyed God's will could claim this designation (b. Baba Batra 10a; Exod. Rabbah 46.4-5; Deut. Rabbah 7.9). The former view predominated. Pesikta Rabbati 5.1 reflects the debate between Jews and non-Jews, probably Christians, regarding who the children of God were:

> the Holy One, blessed be He, foresaw that the nations would get to translate the Torah, and reading it, say, in Greek, would declare: "We are the children of the Lord." And Israel would declare: "We are the children of the Lord." The scales would appear to be balanced between both claims, but then the Holy One, blessed be He, will say to the nations: "What are you claiming, that you are My children? I have no way of knowing other than that My child is he who possesses My secret lore." The nations will ask: "And what is Thy secret lore?" God will reply: "It is the Mishnah" (Braude 1968).

E. Greco-Roman Religions

Epictetus uses the phrase "son of God" often (I.3.1-3). Divine sonship is a result of the love of God and charity toward others (I.13.3; I.19.9; II.16.44). In the Hellenistic period those who possessed a divine power were called a "divine man" (θεῖος ἀνήρ theios anēr). The Mithra cult promised its adherents rebirth or adoption, as Mithras becomes the father of the initiates. Similarly, the Roman emperors were divinized as sons of God. Caesar Augustus, e.g., is hailed as "Emperor Caesar, son of God, Zeus the liberator, Augustus" (P. Oslo. 26; SB 8824).

F. Synoptic Gospels

Divine sonship in a unique sense is reserved for Jesus throughout the NT. Jesus is called both the child (παῖς pais but never τέκνον teknon) of God (Matt 12:18; Acts 3:13, 26; 4:27, 30) and the son (υἱός hyios) of God. The phrase "children of God" (tekna theou) does not occur in the synoptic Gospels, but one does find references to "sons of God" (hyioi theou, Matt 5:9, 45). Although one can readily recognize the evangelist's fingerprints on each of the passages in which these references occur, it is still distinctive that in contrast to the use of this concept in the Gospel and Letters of John there is no polemical or apologetic edge, no evidence that the term is being used to defend the standing of one group over against another. Jesus taught that being a child of God was an individual matter based on the effects of the knowledge of God in one's life, not a privileged standing conferred upon an elect nation.

In sayings attributed to Jesus, those who may be called children of God have a knowledge of God, which has led them to assume ethical qualities that show that they are becoming like their divine Father. Peacemakers are blessed because they will be called children of God (Matt 5:9), and those who love their enemies may be called children of God (Matt 5:45). The rationale offered is that God causes the sun to shine and the rain to fall on both the righteous and the unrighteous. The implicit assumption is that those who genuinely stand in a close moral or spiritual relationship to God will be like God. Therefore they will demonstrate such qualities in the way they relate to others. Jesus therefore challenged those who followed him to "be perfect (τέλειος teleios) as your heavenly Father is perfect" (Matt 5:48). The same ideas are expressed in the Lukan form of these sayings: "But love your enemies, do good, and lend, expecting nothing in return. Your reward will be great, and you will be children of the Most High; for he is kind to the ungrateful and the wicked. Be merciful, just as your Father is merciful" (Luke 6:35-36). Through this distinctive relationship, the children of God can already begin to live into the life of the age to come, so that they may even transcend marriage and procreation, and death itself, at least in a spiritual sense: "Indeed they cannot die anymore, because they are like angels and are children of God, being children of the resurrection" (Luke 20:36; 11:25-26; 1 John 3:14). Because of the assurance of the future fulfillment of this relationship, Jesus instructs his followers that they can appeal to God as their divine Father when they pray (Matt 6:9; Luke 11:2), and God will respond to them in love and mercy that exceeds that of a human parent: "How much more will your Father in heaven give good things to those who ask him" (Matt 7:11).

G. Pauline Letters

Paul uses several related phrases: "children of God" (Rom 8:16, 21; 9:8; Phil 2:15), "sons of God" (Rom 8:14, 19), "children of promise" (Rom 9:8; Gal 4:28), "children" (Rom 8:17), "seed of Abraham" (Rom 9:7, 8; Gal 3:16, 19, 29), and "heirs" (Rom 8:17; Gal 3:29; 4:1, 7). Second Corinthians 6:18 refers to both sons and daughters of God in a loose quotation, in which 2 Sam 7:14 is given a democratized interpretation.

Sonship to God is the result of salvation. Jesus, the son of God, has provided for the liberation and reconciliation of sinners so that the sinner may be adopted as a child of God: "For in Christ Jesus you are all children [lit. "sons"] of God through faith" (Gal 3:26). Conceptually, this scheme blends the experience of Israel in the exodus with the Greco-Roman practice of adoption. Because Jesus was the true seed of Abraham, by being "in Christ" the believer has become an heir of the promise made to Abraham and his descendants (Gal 3:29; Rom 4:13, 16). The concept is both corporate and eschatological. The whole creation awaits the revelation of the sons of God (Rom 8:18-21). The gift of the Spirit to believers is a guarantee of their sonship (Eph 1:14). The Spirit enables believers to call God "ABBA, Father" (Rom 8:15; Gal 4:6) and nourishes the relationship of the believer to God as child to parent, while casting out fear (Rom 8:15), interceding for the believers (8:26), and preparing them for the glorious liberty that will be theirs (Rom 8:21) when their adoption is complete (Rom 8:23; Gal 4:5). The children of God are to be imitators of their Father (Eph 5:1), children of light (Eph 5:8), and blameless instruments of God's righteousness in a wicked age (Phil 2:15). As children of God by faith in Jesus Christ, believers are not sons "by flesh" but "by spirit" (Rom 8:1-11; Gal 4:29) and enjoy freedom from bondage (Rom 8:21; Gal 4:22, 23, 26, 30, 31; 5:1). As these references indicate, one of Paul's concerns is to show that believers in Christ are heirs of the promise to Abraham. They and not Abraham's physical descendants are the true children of God.

H. Johannine Writings

The phrase "children of God" appears only twice in the Gospel of John (1:12; 11:52), but it is tied to various other metaphors in the Gospel's figurative language. The term is the Johannine community's self-designation. If the prologue to the Gospel is an elaborate chiasm, the reference to "the children of God" stands at its turning point. The children of God are not simply the physical descendants of Abraham but those who receive Jesus and believe in his name. One who comes to Jesus is "an Israelite in whom there is no guile" (John 1:47). Children of God are not born by the will of humans (John 1:13); they are born "from above," from water and the Spirit, as Jesus tells Nicodemus (John 3:3, 5). They are sustained by living water and the bread of life (John 4:10, 14; 6:32-33).

Fulfilling one of the obligations of a father, God educates his children: They are "all taught by God" (John 6:45). Jesus passed on to the disciples the teachings given to him by the Father (14:24; 17:8, 14). One's response to the Father's teaching is the criterion for identifying paternity; the children of God keep his teaching. They are distinguished as the seed of Abraham by the fact that they abide in Jesus' word (John 8:31-38).

Caiaphas' unwitting prophecy in John 11:49-50 is interpreted in 11:51-52, the only place where the phrase "the children of God" occurs in John outside of

1:12. Jesus' death was not for Israel only but so that all the children of God might be gathered. Here the reference seems to include all believers, Gentiles as well as Jews. The concern that the children of God be gathered appears in various OT references (Isa 11:12; Jer 23:3; Mic 2:12). The unity of the people of God is also a recurring concern in John (10:16; 12:32; 17:11, 21-23; 19:23; 21:11). Jesus will not leave his disciples as orphans (John 14:18). He and the Father will abide with them (John 14:23). Their status consequently changes from that of servants (John 8:35; 13:16; 15:15), to friends (John 15:15; 3 John 15), to brothers (John 20:17).

"Children of God" appears three times in 1 John (3:1-2, 10; 5:2). In the first passage it is clearly related to eschatological expectations but at the same time describes a present reality. As in John 1:12, the phrase is used in connection with being born of God. Echoing Pauline language, the elder asserts that everyone who does righteousness has been born of God (1 John 2:29). Righteousness is closely related to the standing of the children of God (3:7, 10). Their status derives from God's love (1 John 3:1) and requires that they practice righteousness. It also carried with it a hope for the future (1 John 3:2). The children of God have been born of God and have the seed of God abiding in them (1 John 3:9). As a result, they cannot continue in sin. They will love other believers (1 John 5:1-2) and keep God's commandments. They conquer "the world"; their faith is the victory (1 John 5:4).

In Johannine usage the children of God are they who believe in Jesus, have been born from God, practice love for one another, keep Jesus' teachings, do righteousness, and claim a hope in Christ for their future relationship with God, their Father. See ADOPTION; BAPTISM; CHILD, CHILDREN; FAMILY; FATHER; FATHER'S HOUSE; GOD, NT; GOD THE FATHER; HOLY SPIRIT; HOUSEHOLD, HOUSEHOLDER; HOUSEHOLD OF GOD; SON OF GOD.

Bibliography: W. G. Braude, trans. *Pesikta Rabbati* (1968) 1:93; R. Alan Culpepper. "The Pivot of John's Prologue." *NTS* 27 (1980) 1–31; Matthew Vellankical. *The Divine Sonship of Christians in the Johannine Writings* (1977); Jan van der Watt. "Family of the King: Dynamics of Metaphor in the Gospel according to John." *BibInt* 47 (2000).

R. ALAN CULPEPPER

CHILDREN, SONG OF THE THREE. *See* SONG OF THE THREE JEWS.

CHILEAB kil'ee-ab [כִלְאָב kil'av]. Second son of David, born in Hebron of Abigail, Nabal's widow (2 Sam 3:3). In 1 Chr 3:1, the name given to Daniel.

CHILIASM [χιλιασμος chiliasmos]. A type of millennialism, based on Rev 20:1-15, and taught by Apol-

linarius, which was refuted in the Second Ecumenical Council (381 CE). *See* MILLENNIUM.

CHILION kil'ee-uhn [כִּלְיוֹן kilyon]. Son of the Bethlehemites Naomi and Elimelech, who migrated to Moab. Chilion and his brother, Mahlon, married the Moabites Orpah and Ruth (Ruth 1:2; 4:9).

CHILMAD kil'mad [כַּלְמַד kilmadh]. A Mesopotamian city whose merchants traded with TYRE (Ezek 27:23). It is mentioned with Sheba and Asshur and is located near modern Baghdad.

CHIMHAM kim'ham [כִּמְהָם kimham, כִּמְהָן khimhan]. Son of Barzillai the Gileadite, who supplied David with food after David left Jerusalem during Absalom's rebellion. Barzillai asked that the reward David offered him go instead to Chimham, who apparently received a parcel of land near Bethlehem.

CHINNERETH, CHINNEROTH kin'uh-reth, kin'uh-roth [כִּנֶּרֶת kinnereth, כִּנָּרוֹת kinaroth]. Chinnereth, from the Hebrew word meaning "harp," is the inland SEA OF GALILEE that supplies the vast majority of the water flowing into the JORDAN RIVER. In the OT the site also appears to be a city on the sea's western shore, mentioned in the list of NAPHTALI's towns (Josh 19:35; 1 Kgs 15:20). The city may have given its name to the sea it adjoined (Num 34:11; Deut 3:17), or the sea, shaped like a harp and thus named, may have given its name to the city on its shore.

The site of Tel Chinnereth was excavated on several occasions during the 20th cent. and identified as biblical Chinnereth/-oth due to its strategic location in the upper Jordan Valley on the Ginnosar Plain and the pottery finds indicating habitation there from the early Bronze Age to Iron Age II.

MICHAEL OBLATH

CHIOS ki'os [Χίος Chios]. An island of approximately 850 sq. km situated in the eastern part of the Aegean Sea, approximately 10 km. from Asia Minor, and a city on the eastern coast of that island. Ancient sources note the locale's reputation for prosperity, quality wines, and claims (contested by others) of being Homer's birthplace. The Bible mentions Chios once, during the course of Paul's voyage back to Jerusalem in Acts 20:15, when his sailing party arrives "opposite Chios" to pass the night anchored within the relatively sheltered waters between the city and the mainland.

MATTHEW L. SKINNER

CHISLEV kiz'lev [כִּסְלֵו kislew; Χασελευ chaseleu]. The ninth month of the post-exilic Jewish CALENDAR, roughly corresponding to the months of November and December.

CHISLON kiz´lon [כִּסְלוֹן kislon]. The father of Elidad, who was appointed by Moses to represent the tribe of Benjamin in the distribution of Canaan among the Israelite tribes (Num 34:21).

CHISLOTH-TABOR kiz´loth-tay´buhr [כִּסְלֹת־תָּבֹר kisloth tavor]. Called CHESULLOTH in Josh 19:18, Chisloth-Tabor was a village on Zebulun's border with Issachar (Josh 19:12). Literally, the name means "loins/flanks of Tabor." The ancient village is associated with Iksal, four miles west of Mount Tabor at the northern edge of the Jezreel Valley.

CHITLISH kit´lish [כִּתְלִישׁ kithlish]. The exact location of Chitlish is unknown, although Josh 15:40 lists the town as near LACHISH in Judah's tribal allotment. Some identify Chitlish with Kentisha named on a 15th cent. BCE list of THUTMOSE III and on a 13th cent. BCE Lachish ostracon from Merneptah's reign.

CHLOE kloh´ee [Χλόη Chloē]. Chloe is mentioned only in 1 Cor 1:11 where the Greek is best translated "Chloe's people" (NRSV, NJB, REB) rather than "Chloe's household" (NIV), since family links would normally be traced through a male, even if deceased. Chloe was likely a wealthy business woman from EPHESUS whose "people" were probably business agents (perhaps freedpersons or slaves) acting for her. Those agents brought disquieting news of the Corinthian church to Paul, notably about serious splits (1:10-17; 3:5-23), triumphalism that devalued the cross (1:18–3:4; 4:8-13), and immorality (5:1–6:20).

ANTHONY THISELTON

CHOBA koh´buh [Χωβα Chōba]. In Jdt 4:4 Choba appears in a list of Israelite cities to the north of Jerusalem that were alerted to an imminent attack by the Assyrian army. The Israelites chased the fleeing enemy as far as Choba (15:4-5), indicating that the city was at the outer limits of Israelite territory. Choba is otherwise unknown outside the book of Judith, and, like other cities in the book (see BETHULIA), the site may well have been invented by the 2nd cent. author of Judith when trying to recreate a late 6th cent. BCE setting for the fictive story.

JUDITH H. NEWMAN

CHOIR. See MUSIC.

CHOSEN. The notion that God favors some individuals and/or groups over others is a central and recurring theme within the Bible. This idea eventually developed into the Christian doctrine of ELECTION, implying that some are predestined for salvation, others for damnation. However, for much of the biblical tradition, not being among those favored said little about one's ultimate disposition.

Chosenness raises a host of theological difficulties for contemporary readers who often bring egalitarian, democratic, and pluralistic sentiments to the text. Why does a loving God favor some over others, or more problematic yet, command the elimination of the Canaanites? In fact, some Jewish and Christian thinkers have argued that this idea has outlived its theological usefulness. However, these critics have failed to recognize not only the nuances of chosenness but also its centrality and pervasiveness within the Bible. Previous discussions of chosenness have often focused on specific vocabulary rather than examining it in a broader context. Thus each section below introduces the reader either to a major aspect of chosenness and/or the way the notion functions within certain parts of the OT; taken together, the reader can glimpse the larger outline of the Bible's theology of chosenness, as well as its profundity.

A. Divine Favoritism in Genesis
B. Promise Texts and Election Theologies of P and D
C. The Anti-elect
D. The Non-elect
E. Eschatological Images of Israel's Relations to the Gentile Nations
F. Election in the NT and Early Rabbinic Judaism
Bibliography

A. Divine Favoritism in Genesis

Genesis is in many ways a sustained meditation on the problems that arise when someone is mysteriously favored by God. This theme first appears in the Cain and Abel narrative in rather terse form and is given greater complexity in the following sibling stories, those of Isaac and Ishmael, and Jacob and Esau—reaching its zenith in the Joseph story. In all four of these stories a younger sibling is favored by God over the elder brother or brothers, a motif that recurs throughout the OT (e.g., Ephraim, Moses, Samuel, David, and Solomon). Furthermore, the text provides little justification for God's choice, aside from the possible exception of the Cain and Abel story, where interpreters have long argued over whether Cain's offering was inferior to Abel's (Gen 4:3-4). Yet, God's enigmatic speech to Cain focuses upon Cain's reaction to God's favoritism of Abel, not the quality of Cain's offering (Gen 4:6-7), thus highlighting the mysterious arbitrariness of God's choice.

This divine preference for the younger sibling suggests that God favors individuals not favored by human convention. But why does a tradition-bound culture like ancient Israel's preserve images of a deity who does not abide by the community's norms enshrined within its divinely ordained laws (Deut 21:15-17)? One explanation for this unusual state of affairs is that the OT time and again reveals God's power by showing how human attempts to control outcomes are subverted by God.

This recurring literary pattern might be labeled the Bible's "underdog motif." God's plan always prevails, frequently even by means of resistance to it or through those who seem to be marginal and powerless.

Another likely factor contributing to this motif's prominence is Israel's self-perception in relation to its older and more dominant neighbors, Egypt and Mesopotamia. Various biblical thinkers reacted against Mesopotamian and Egyptian religious ideas (e.g., the PRIESTLY source in Gen 1). Thus, it seems that at least part of the stress on the underdog motif, particularly the way in which younger brothers supersede their elders by divine choice, is connected to Israel's own sense of her late-born status.

Within these narratives of sibling rivalry, the non-favored brother(s) is not necessarily hated by God or excluded from God's blessing. When one looks at the language in Gen 17 and 21 describing Ishmael's status, it is clear that even though he is outside of the covenant (17:19, 21), he is barely outside it. Not only is he circumcised, thereby receiving the bodily mark of the very covenant from which he is excluded, but also he receives a special divine blessing (Gen 17:18-26; 21:12-13). Much the same can be said of Esau who prospers in life and fathers a host of progeny (Gen 36). Cain was not driven from God because he was not chosen, but rather because his jealousy drove him to kill his favored sibling.

Nor is being chosen a purely positive experience. Chosenness often brings mortal danger in its wake. Thus Abel is killed (Gen 4); Abraham, who is selected to be the father of the chosen people, is immediately driven by famine to Egypt, where his life is in potential danger (Gen 12:10-20); Isaac is nearly sacrificed to God by Abraham (Gen 22); Esau thought to kill Jacob (Gen 27:41-45); and Joseph is nearly killed by his brothers (Gen 37). This pattern of the endangerment of the chosen that usually precedes his eventual exaltation is central to both the OT and NT, as indicated by the Exodus and Gospel narratives.

Turning to the Joseph story, one encounters the idea that even within the group favored by God, some are more favored than others. While not often noticed, this idea recurs a number of times in the Bible and likely explains why the tribe of Judah and the family of David are viewed as being specially designated as the royal tribe and family, as well as why the Levites and the family of Aaron become the specially chosen groups designated for Temple service. Thus, distinctions exist even among God's one chosen people.

In these stories there is a complex interplay between divine initiative and human action. Certain of these narratives imply that human actions can help secure a person's election. For example, Jacob obtains Esau's primogeniture under duress (Gen 25:29-34), and Rebekah helps manipulate Isaac to bless Jacob rather than Esau (Gen 27). Such narratives suggest that being a morally upright person is not a prerequisite for being favored by God. Even when such elect individuals act inappropriately, as when Joseph lords his chosen status over his brothers (Gen 37), they remain mysteriously favored by God regardless of their behavior (Gen 39:2-4, 21-23). One also sees this pattern in relation to the Israelites as a whole in Exodus. God claims Israel as his firstborn son before Israel has accepted this offer (Exod 4:22-23) and only finds his choice confirmed when Israel accepts its divine commission to fulfill God's commandments given at Sinai (Exod 19–24). Even when Israel fails to respond properly to God's gracious actions (Exod 14:11-12), God continues to favor Israel.

B. Promise Texts and the Election Theologies of P and D

Ideas such as promise, covenant, and holiness are closely bound up with chosenness. Promise is a framing device within the patriarchal stories. Thus, God's promises to Abraham first mentioned in Gen 12:1-3, 7 initiates Abraham's and his descendants' special relationship to God. Elements of these promises echo like a refrain throughout Genesis (15:4-5, 16-21; 17:20; 22:15-19; 24:60; 27:28-29; 28:3-4, 13-15; 35:9-12; 48:15-16). They are composed of at least three elements: the promise of progeny, of blessing, and of land. God articulates many of these promised blessings, but several are on the lips of various human beings (Gen 24:60; 27:28-29; 28:3-4).

These promise texts articulate Israel's self-understanding of its divine election. Genesis 1–11 represents God's failed attempt to create a working relationship between humans, nature, and Godself. In the wake of this failure, God moves from a plan in which God demands equal obedience from all humans to a two-tiered plan in which most people are held to a minimal religio-moral standard (which later Judaism conceives of as the seven Noahide commandments), and one man's extended family is chosen to maintain a higher standard of religious behavior. As Gen 12:2-3 makes clear, Abraham's and thus Israel's election is closely bound up with God's larger plan to bring blessing to the whole world, even while God's purposes in choosing Abraham and his descendants are not exhausted by this linkage.

Adding to the mystery surrounding the purposes of Israel's election, the exact meaning of the *Niphal* use of ברך brk in Gen 12:3 remains hotly debated. Is this verb best rendered in the passive as "all the families of the earth will be blessed" by/through Abraham? Or, should one opt for the reflexive, "all the families of the earth will bless themselves" by Abraham? While neither translation makes it absolutely clear how all the families of the earth will receive a blessing in relation to Abraham and his descendants, other biblical texts indicate that Abraham and Israel serve as mediators between humanity and God (Gen 18:17-19; 20:7, 17; Exod 19:5-6).

Although the idea of covenant has its own trajectory of development, within the canonical text, covenant and promise are tightly woven together (e.g., Gen 15 and 17). In fact, the concepts of promise, election, and covenant are major building blocks that undergird the framework of the Pentateuch, and thus they receive extended theological attention within the Deuteronomic and Priestly sources (D and P, *see* DOCUMENTARY HYPOTHESIS). Within the confines of this entry, it is impossible to give a full accounting of the ways in which election and covenant theology mutually illuminate each other. However, a brief overview of P's and D's unique articulations of election theology seems requisite.

From a Priestly perspective, Israel's election is quite literally an election for divine service. The people of Israel living in the land of Israel become responsible for maintaining the proper environment for God to dwell among them (Num 35:34). In this theology, Israel protects the deity from offenses to his holiness, yet in so doing. Israel, and. by extension, the entire world, enjoys God's presence and the blessing that accompanies it.

Here is another instance in which one finds distinctions among the elect. Although all Israel is responsible for keeping a heightened level of moral and ritual purity, there are indeed gradations of holiness as one approaches closer to the divine presence. Thus one finds a ringlike structure in Priestly texts in which God occupies the holy of holies, with the high priest at the next level of holiness. Then come the other priests who work in the sanctuary, who in turn are followed by the Levites who maintain, move, and guard God's sanctuary. Finally, one has the other tribes of Israelites along with anyone else residing in the larger area of God's holy presence, which suffuses the land of Israel. While in some respects this scheme is hierarchical and exclusionary, in others it is quite inclusive. Since holiness is a quality Israel must maintain, even those aliens living in the land are included in aspects of the legislation (Lev 17:15-16; 19:33-34). In fact, certain Priestly texts appear to permit something akin to conversion (Exod 12:48-49).

The concept of holiness and Israel's self-understanding of its election is somewhat different in Deuteronomy. Deuteronomy contains less emphasis on the role of priests by allowing for nonsacrificial slaughter (Deut 12:20-25) and greater cultic participation by laypeople (Deut 14:22-29; 15:19-23). The view of worship and election is much less hierarchical than in the Priestly material. Rather than describing God as actually dwelling in the Temple, Deuteronomy speaks of the Temple as the place in which God will choose to establish God's name (Deut 12:5, 11). Unlike P, in D the holiness of the people of Israel living in the land makes the land holy. Thus, Deuteronomy allows aliens residing in the land to eat carrion, while Leviticus prohibits it (Deut 14:21; Lev 17:15). Most important, this holiness is not

something the Israelites earn but rather something that they are, inasmuch as God chose them (compare Lev 19:2 to Deut 14:2).

Although the spiritual outlook of Deuteronomy is generally more anthropocentric, less hierarchical, and more tolerant, there are ways in which it is more rigid. Thus, Deuteronomy contrasts Israel with the "Other" in much starker ways than one finds in the Priestly texts. Furthermore, Deuteronomy is the text most preoccupied with wiping out the pre-Israelite inhabitants of Canaan, and it also contains a list prohibiting certain other foreign groups from joining God's people (Deut 23:3-8). While Deuteronomy sees Israel as God's special people, unlike P, it is less clear what role, if any, God's people play in relation to the larger terrestrial world. While this at times leads to a kind of ethnic triumphalism (Deut 28:7-14), there is also room left for other nations to play their legitimate roles in the larger divine drama (Deut 2:1-25; 4:5-8, 19; 32:8-9). Perhaps the prophet Hosea introduces the greatest insight of D's highly developed meditation on Israel's elect status. God's connection to the people remains shrouded in mystery, because ultimately it is an affair of the heart (Hos 1-3, 11; Deut 7:7-8; 10:15).

A related theological insight noted with great vigor by D is that Israel has yet to warrant the favor it has mysteriously received (Deut 9:4-7). The notion that Israel is God's elect but has not yet demonstrated its right to the title by acts of obedience parallels Joseph, who initially misuses his elect status but nevertheless remains divinely favored. The blessings and curses found in Deut 28 reflect the two potential outcomes of Israel's election, blessing for obedience, cursing for disobedience, with no real middle ground.

P and D represent two different streams of covenantal theology. Whereas P views Israel's election as a call to serve as priestly people, D grounds election in God's mysterious love for Israel. In many ways, these two theologies of election are woven together into a new unity within Second Isaiah (Isa 40–55). This prophet of the exile (along with his counterpart Third Isaiah [Isa 56–66]) puts tremendous emphasis on the idea of Israel's election and regularly speaks of God's unfailing love for Israel (Isa 49, 54, 62). This emphasis, combined with the heavy use of the root בחר bkhr to refer to God's choosing Israel (Isa 42:1; 43:10; 44:2), is surely a further heightening of Deuteronomy's election theology (Deut 4:37; 7:7; 14:2). At the same time, Deutero-Isaiah regularly pictures Israel's election as having implications for the larger terrestrial world (Isa 42 and 49). This outward-looking view of Israel's election may well be a heightening of P's notion of Israel as a priestly nation. Interestingly enough, the centerpiece of Deutero-Isaiah's theology is a notion that both P and D affirm: in spite of Israel's failings that resulted in exile, Israel remains God's chosen people (Lev 26:43-45; Deut 4:25-31; Isa 43).

C. The Anti-elect

The Israelite idea of election presupposes three categories: the elect, the anti-elect, and the non-elect. The "elect" are God's chosen people, Israel. The "anti-elect" are those few groups who are deemed to be enemies of God and whom Israel is commanded to annihilate. However, the vast majority of foreign individuals and nations fall within the category of the "non-elect" rather than the "anti-elect." These non-elect peoples were always considered fully part of the divine economy, and, in a very real sense, Israel was to work out its destiny in relation to them, even if in separation from them.

The most prevalent anti-elect group is the Canaanite nations. God's call to annihilate these peoples and Israel's success or failure in carrying out this command occurs in a number of places in the OT (esp., within Deuteronomy and the DEUTERONOMISTIC HISTORY). These texts pose serious problems for any interpreter who wishes to argue that the models of conduct endorsed by God in the OT should indeed shape our moral universe. Certain mitigating factors, however, must be kept in mind as one seeks to understand these challenging texts. Even the harshest texts are more nuanced and ambiguous than some would concede. Thus, while Josh 10 implies that all Canaanites were killed in one fell swoop, all Canaanites were not in fact killed. Not only do Rahab and her extended family survive (Josh 2), but so do the Gibeonites (Josh 9), as well as other groups (Josh 13:1-7; 16:10; 17:12-13). Furthermore, there is evidence that later transmitters of the tradition, likely unaware that these accounts were more fiction than fact, were so troubled by this rhetoric that they softened the anti-Canaanite polemic (note Josh 11:19-20, which claims that the Canaanites were only annihilated because they rebelled against God and failed to sue for peace). Also of interest is that Achan the Israelite and his family are treated like the anti-elect once he violated God's rules concerning warfare (Josh 7). That many Canaanites are not destroyed, while some disobedient Israelites are, indicates that the book of Joshua is primarily concerned with creating communal order rather than maintaining ethnic boundaries. Clearly, ethnicity does not exclusively determine who belongs to the anti-elect.

More important yet is that neither textual nor archaeological evidence supports the notion that the Canaanites were purged in a genocidal campaign by Joshua. Judges 1–2 concedes the Israelites' failure to eliminate them, and the Deuteronomistic History, as well as texts like Hosea and Jeremiah, attributes the downfall of both Israel and Judah to the fact that they adopted various forms of illicit worship practiced by the non-Israelite peoples that they failed to eliminate. The archaeological evidence suggests there was never any mass destruction of the Canaanites by Israelites. In fact, many scholars endorse some form of the peasant revolt model to explain Israel's conquest of Canaan and assume that the majority of ancient Israelites were themselves the descendants of those Canaanites who were never destroyed.

That these narratives have little basis in actual history does not mean that they can be dismissed as unproblematic. Biblical texts that contain a rationale for something akin to genocide still demand a reckoning, even if these ideas were never fully actualized in the biblical period. Still, it is essential to evaluate the biblical text in its own historical context, uncolored by its career in postbiblical history. The question is thus: If these anti-Canaanite texts are more imaginative than historical, as the literary and archaeological evidence suggests, why did ancient Israelite thinkers generate and continue to be preoccupied by such ideas? One explanation is that texts that call on Israel to kill all the Canaanites were produced during a period of instability and powerlessness. Thus, some see these texts as a legacy from Josiah's attempted reformation (7th cent. BCE), which aimed at propagating a unified sense of identity during a politically insecure period by stifling dissent that might threaten the nascent order. Others think that they represent an exilic attempt to comprehend Israel's failure to maintain possession of the land it believed it received from God. Alternatively, this harsh rhetoric might have arisen among the exiles as a strategy for maintaining Judean social and religious identity by constructing that identity in contrast to either the Babylonians among whom the exiles lived or the Judeans who remained in the land.

Perhaps more troubling yet are the texts that deal with the Amalekites (Exod 17:8-16; Deut 25:17-19; 1 Sam 15). The condemnation of the Amalekites is phrased in terms of a cosmic battle between Israel's God and Amalek that will last throughout time (Exod 17:14-15). Furthermore, the fact that evil Haman, the mortal enemy of the Jews in the book of Esther, is textually and genetically linked to Agag, the king of the Amalekites (see Esth 3:1 and 1 Sam 15:8), may hint that even if this enemy appears outside of the land of Israel, he is to be destroyed.

The continual reuse of biblical "anti-election" theology, while troubling, reveals why such ideas appeal to the religious imagination. Fundamentally, the idea of Amalek as the incarnation of the anti-elect is an attempt to make some theological sense of recurring historical evils. Such ideas, while rightfully disturbing, should not simply be dismissed. It is essential to recognize that the notion of the anti-elect expresses a profound yearning for God's justice to prevail over evils so irrational that they seem demonic.

D. The Non-elect

While the anti-elect present the most serious challenge to election theology, the category of the non-elect contains one of the most open postures towards "the

Other" that is found in any ancient text. In Israelite legal texts, one discovers an exceedingly complex state of affairs, exacerbated because these were written and redacted over hundreds of years. While a plausible case can be made that the term גֵּר ger, translated as resident-alien or stranger, gradually evolved from its earliest uses in the covenant code in Exodus through its later uses in Deuteronomy and Leviticus toward ever greater legal inclusion of aliens, it never reaches the stage of total assimilation. The foreigner who participates in Israel's ritual and legal life still remains a resident alien. Even while Lev 19:34 declares that the stranger should be treated as a citizen and that you will love him as yourself, Lev 25:45 makes clear that the children of such resident-aliens can be acquired as perpetual slaves, unlike fellow Israelites.

Narrative materials present a variety of portraits of foreigners, which are unmatched by the legal corpora; a number of these portraits are remarkably positive toward certain foreign individuals or groups. The list of foreign figures who are treated with great respect include: the pharaoh who rules during Joseph's lifetime; the daughter of the succeeding pharaoh, who saves Moses' life (Exod 2:5-10), as well as those advisors to Pharaoh who recognize God's power in the plagues (Exod 8:19; 9:20; 10:7); Hiram, king of Tyre, who helps construct the Jerusalem Temple (1 Kgs 5); the Queen of Sheba, who testifies to Solomon's wisdom and Israel's great fortune (1 Kgs 10); the widow from Zarephath, who shelters Elijah (1 Kgs 17); Job, the wise and righteous man from the East; Cyrus, king of Persia, who conquers Babylon and decrees the return of the exiled Judeans to their land (Isa 45:1-4; 2 Chr 36:22-23); and the non-Israelite sailors in Jonah's boat who pray, sacrifice, and make vows to the Lord (Jonah 1:14-16). Some non-elect individuals, clans, or groups are closely attached to or even merged with the people of Israel. Ruth the Moabite becomes King David's great-grandmother, while Jethro the Midianite is Moses' father-in-law (Exod 2:16-22; 18:1-12; Num 10:29-32).

All of these portrayals belie the widespread assumption that Israel's sense of its own election inherently led Israelites to express contempt for the non-chosen. Indeed, a number of texts in the OT appear to challenge Israel to recognize that the non-elect often have much to teach the elect about how one should act in the world and serve God. Thus, Jethro helps Moses and the Israelites institute a more functional legal system (Exod 18). Moreover, several of these characters are juxtaposed to Israelites who are shown to be sorely lacking. Naaman the Aramean general is set against Gehazi, Elisha's greedy and disobedient servant (2 Kgs 5); Uriah, the intoxicated Hittite (belonging to one of the seven Canaanite nations that were to have been utterly destroyed), is depicted as having more sexual self-control than the sober King David (2 Sam 11); and Abimelech, king of Gerar, appears to be more pious and

God-fearing than Abraham (Gen 20). Through these contrasts, the narrators of the OT call into question the idea that one can enjoy the status of the elect without fulfilling the chosen's responsibilities, or that the non-elect cannot act in accord with God's will.

Some of these characters raise the complicated question of conversion, a word that remains problematic when applied to most of the biblical period. The idea of conversion presumes an abstraction called a "religion," comprising a series of beliefs connected to particular practices. The whole notion of Judaism as a religion probably only developed in the Hellenistic era at the earliest. Before this time, Jewish identity was marked by ethnic or tribal affiliation. Thus, groups (such as the Gibeonites in 2 Sam 21:1-14) and individuals (such as Uriah the Hittite) who sought to attach themselves to the Israelite people in antiquity frequently maintained their own foreign identities. On the individual level, total assimilation might occur over several generations as children grew up and married Israelites. The notice concerning Rahab's family in Josh 6:25, however, suggests that even an individual or small group of foreigners could remain ethnically separate while living among the people of Israel. Thus, it is more accurate to speak of individuals or groups attaching themselves (לָוָה lawah) to God's people (Isa 14:1; 56:3, 6), rather than using the term "conversion."

A related issue is whether such assimilation was easier for foreign women seeking to join ancient Israelite clans than it was for foreign men. There is substantial evidence that, in ancient Israel, the religion of the father and husband was determinative for the family unit as a whole. Thus the patriarchs all marry Mesopotamian spouses; Judah marries a Canaanite (Gen 38:2); Joseph, an Egyptian (Gen 41:45); and Moses, a Midianite or Cushite woman (Exod 2; 18; Num 12). These women all attain Israelite credentials by marrying an Israelite man. Later, Ruth the Moabite marries an Israelite man and gives birth to King David's ancestor, in spite of the prohibition in Deut 23:3-6 (Heb., vv. 3-7). Furthermore, the legislation in Deut 21:10-14 permits Israelites to take captured war brides.

On the other hand, there are a number of texts that condemn the practice of Israelite men marrying foreign women, including 1 Kgs 11, Prov 1–9, Ezra 9–10, and Neh 13. Clearly there are tensions between texts that appear to condone marrying foreign women, thereby implying such women can be assimilated into Israelite culture, and those that condemn this practice on the grounds that foreign spouses will corrupt Israel with their alien forms of worship. It may be that that these divergent passages come from different times, with earlier writers, on the whole, being more open to the assimilation of foreign women than later ones. Another possibility is that these tensions reveal a heated debate about Israelite identity, a clash between those who held a more open view and those who held a more restrictive one.

E. Eschatological Images of Israel's Relations to the
Gentile Nations

The notion of election is already articulated within
the earliest pre-exilic prophetic texts (e.g., Amos 3:1-2).
Furthermore, Hosea pioneered the love language that
became prominent in D, while First Isaiah (Isa 1–39)
explores the notion of God's holiness in ways that likely
influenced the final shape of P. In turn, authors like
Jeremiah drew on aspects of both P's and D's election
theology (Jer 2:2-4 drawing on Hosea and Lev 5:14-16;
Jer 3:1 drawing on Hosea and Deut 24:1-4). This rich
dialogue between pentateuchal and prophetic reflections reached a new zenith within Second and Third
Isaiah (40–55; 56–66), a collection of exilic and post-
exilic oracles containing some of the most strikingly
beautiful and powerful images of God's love for his
chosen people in the OT. Certain expressions within
this corpus, such as "a covenant to the people, a light
to the nations" (Isa 42:6), have received immense
attention, because Christians have understood them
as authorizing missionary efforts to bring God's word
to the whole world (Acts 14:46-47). But the question
is, to what extent, if any, did Second and Third Isaiah
envision Israel missionizing the Gentile nations?

Apart from translation issues, these expressions are
obscure enough to raise a host of interpretive issues.
Do these phrases indicate Israel's mission to the Gentile nations, or are they describing God's relationship
with Israel? Given that the larger thrust of Second
Isaiah focuses on the return of the exiled Judeans to
Zion, the expression "a light to the nations" may be
more akin to a beacon sent out to the far corners of
the earth signaling that the exile has now ended. If so,
then the addressee in this passage may be the faithful
remnant, the elect of the elect who help reanimate the
Israelite nation. Even if these expressions were taken
as addressed to the nations of the world, it is far from
certain that they should be read in a missionary way.
Perhaps God is doing something with all or part of Israel that is supposed to be witnessed by the now dazzled
nations. Or it may be that the nations recognize Israel's
God as the one true God, but this does not necessarily
connote conversion, let alone missionary activity. As Isa
49:22-26 makes clear, the nations' acknowledgment of
Israel's God often implies their humiliation and punishment, not their conversion.

While these expressions are ambiguous enough
to sustain a variety of interpretations, those who
read them in a missionary and universalistic fashion
rarely place these verses within a larger contextual
and canonical perspective. Here it helps to broaden
the frame and take account of the following texts that
enrich and complicate any discussion of the OT's view
of Gentile inclusion: Isa 2:2-4 and its close analogue
Mic 4:1-5; Isa 14:1-2; 19:18-25; 24:14-16; 25:6-7; Jer
3:17; 12:14-17; 16:19; Zeph 3:8-10; Zech 2:11-12;
8:20-23; 14:16-19; Mal 1:11, 14; the entire book of

Jonah; a number of psalms (e.g., 2, 46, 48, 87, 96, 98,
117), and many passages in Second and Third Isaiah
(e.g., Isa 42:1-7; 44:1-5; 45:14, 20-25; 49; 51:4-6;
56; 60 and 66:18-24). These various passages contain
a plethora of images, some of which are in tension or
even in contradiction with one another.

While texts like Isa 2 are rather irenic, others such
as Isa 66 envision a violent upheaval. Some speak of the
nations serving Israel (Isa 60), others of Israel or God
instructing the nations during a universal pilgrimage
to God's Temple in Jerusalem (Isa 2; Zech 8:20-23).
A number of passages that mention foreigners coming to Zion are not invoking conversion but rather
explaining that God will use these foreigners to gather
the dispersed Judean exiles and bring them home (Isa
49:22). Similarly, many of the texts that speak of foreigners acknowledging Israel's God are simply saying
that the nations will witness God's redemption of his
people Israel (Isa 52:10) and be forced to submit to
God (Isa 45:23). Of course, there are a few exceptional
texts such as Isa 19:18-25 and 66:18-24, which are
discussed below.

What generalizations, if any, can one make about
the notion of mission in the OT from this array of texts?
First, many of these passages contain a universalistic
thrust and quite a few reveal a belief in the idea that
God's relationship to Israel was part of a larger salvific
plan involving the whole world. The exact dimensions
of God's larger plan remain enigmatic. For that matter,
within the OT the idea of *salvation* implies a national
restoration rather than the later notion of individuals
receiving immortal life. Second, although many of these
texts articulate a kind of universalism in which Israel
plays a central role in God's plan, there are very few
if any texts that advocate the notion that Israel should
engage in missionary activity as this term is commonly
understood. Normally, the idea of mission is used in the
strong sense of actively proselytizing to bring others to
one's own faith. It seems, rather, that Israel's mission is
simply to be God's chosen people.

One text that might endorse human missionary
activity is Isa 66:19, although here it appears that it
may be Gentiles, not Israelites, who are engaged in
declaring God's glory to various other nations who have
not yet heard of, or witnessed, God's deeds. Even this
passage is tempered by 66:20, which has these foreigners returning Israelites still in exile to their homeland.
Thus, the OT rarely, if ever, endorses an active Israelite
mission to the Gentiles.

The question of Gentile conversion without human
agency is slightly different, and one can find more textual evidence for this idea. Sometimes the nations or
the coastlands are invoked as a way of expressing God's
cosmic scope, but some passages appear to go a bit
further. Here one thinks of texts like Isa 66:23 or Zech
14:16-19. One often overlooked fact is that while some
eschatological texts within the OT do acknowledge the

idea of foreigners worshiping Israel's God, and a few such as Isa 56:6-7 and 66:21 mention the possibility of certain select foreigners acting as cultic functionaries within the Jerusalem Temple, even these passages continue to stress God's special election of Israel, which is paired with his love of Jerusalem, Judah, and the land of Israel. Perhaps the most radical text that speaks of other nations also worshiping Israel's God is Isa 19:18-25, in which Egypt and Assyria receive titles evoking their equally special relationship to God. Here Israel's special status is maintained, but the other two nations are elevated to Israel's level.

This survey of a few select prophetic texts demonstrates how unsystematic the OT is in portraying Israel's relationship with the nations in the eschaton. Perhaps the most interesting feature of such texts is that even those passages that speak of Gentile inclusion do so not by lessening Israel's election, but rather by heightening it.

F. Election in the NT and Early Rabbinic Judaism

While major streams of NT thinking broadened the elect group to include those Gentiles who came to believe in Jesus as the Christ, this does not mean that Christianity rejected the biblical concept of election and its implied exclusivism. Early Christians did not see themselves as universalists who accepted everyone because of their common descent from Adam, but rather as particularists who found a new way to link believing Gentiles to Abraham and through him to God's elect people (Rom 4:16-18, 22-24). Christians, like their Jewish counterparts, believed that one joined the people of God by relinquishing their fallen adamic state (Rom 5:14-15).

The argument between early Christianity and what became rabbinic Judaism was over who held the proper key to repair the fractured relationship between humans and God. Was this accomplished through the giving of the Torah to the Jews at Sinai (and the dynamics of repentance and reconciliation inherent in Torah observance), or through the death and resurrection of Christ at Golgotha (with its alternative schema of divine-human reconciliation)? While various NT authors may have changed the way one joined God's people, Christianity appropriated the concept of chosenness (Rom 8:31-39; 1 Pet 2:9-10; 2 Thess 2:13).

Clearly, the NT authors, like their rabbinic counterparts, maintained the fundamentals of the OT's particularistic notion of election. Nevertheless, there are substantial differences between the NT's understanding of election and that found in rabbinic Judaism. The two traditions diverge on a number of central theological issues, including missionary outreach, the fate of those not elected, the role played by God's actions and human actions respectively, and the acceptability of God's arbitrariness.

In certain inverse ways each of the two traditions hews closer to the OT's theology in some areas and innovates in others. For example, most narratives in the OT maintain the mysterious arbitrariness of God's favoritism. New Testament authors such as Paul continue to stress this dimension of chosenness (Rom 9–11), while a number of rabbinic texts provide rationales for God's mysterious choice of Israel (*Mek.* on Exod 20:2) or of the Patriarchs (e.g., Abraham, *Gen. Rab.* 38:13) by explaining how they warranted God's favor.

On the other hand, Christianity's call to missionize the Gentiles (Matt 28:19; Mark 16:15-16; Luke 24:44-49) and its propensity to conceive of the elect as the saved standing over against the damned (John 3:18) has only tenuous grounding within the OT (Isa 65–66). But rabbinic Judaism's Noahide laws, which offer a positive place for the non-elect without their conversion, builds upon the OT's approach to the non-elect.

The most central theological claims of Judaism and Christianity are tied to each community's assertion to be God's chosen people. This should not be surprising, because election plays a very large role within the OT, which is not only the Jewish Bible but for a time was the only Scripture that early Christianity knew. Furthermore, Judaism and Christianity become utterly incoherent when they surrender their unique claims to be God's elect. While the idea of chosenness may seem arbitrary and unfair, it discloses God's close and merciful relationship toward humanity as a whole, his profoundly *personal* character.

Jews and Christians disagree over the specifics of how one defines or joins God's chosen people, what God demands from them, and the place of those not chosen in the divine economy. But just as surely both religious communities must continue to affirm the idea of chosenness. For as the Bible makes clear, God is working out his larger plan for the world through God's special relationship to Israel, his chosen people. *See* DETERMINISM; ELECTION; EXCLUSION; PREDESTINATION; PRIESTS AND LEVITES; PURPOSE, PURPOSE OF GOD; WILL OF GOD.

Bibliography: Mark Brett, ed. *Ethnicity and the Bible* (1996); Frederick E. Greenspahn. *When Brothers Dwell Together: The Preeminence of Younger Siblings in the OT* (1994); Joel Kaminsky. "Did Election Imply the Mistreatment of Non-Israelites?" *HTR* 96.4 (2003) 397–425; Jon Levenson. *The Death and Resurrection of the Beloved Son* (1993); H. H. Rowley. *The Biblical Doctrine of Election* (1950); Seock-Tae Sohn. *The Divine Election of Israel* (1991); Frank Spina. *The Faith of the Outsider* (2005); Christiana van Houten. *The Alien in Israelite Law* (1991); Claus Westermann. *The Promises to the Fathers* (1980); Michael Wyschogrod. *The Body of Faith: Judaism as Corporeal Election* (1983).

JOEL KAMINSKY

CHORAZIN koy-ray´zin [Χοραζίν Chorazin]. With Bethsaida and Capernaum, Chorazin was a town denounced by Jesus for not repenting after witnessing his deeds of power (Matt 11:21; Luke 10:13). Chorazin has been identified as Khirbet Karazeh several miles north of Capernaum (*see* Eusebius *Onom.*, 174.23). Other writings describe it as a "medium-sized" town (*t. Mak.* 3:8) with significant wheat production (*b. Menah.* 85a). Excavations of the site have unearthed domestic and public buildings, a ritual bath complex, olive oil presses, and a 3rd–4th cent. synagogue (including an Aram.-inscribed, stone "Seat of Moses" for the Torah reader). The synagogue, constructed of black basalt, faced Jerusalem; its main hall measured 65 ft. long and 45 ft. wide and features decorative friezes depicting floral motifs, grapes, an eagle, animals, and a Medusa.

Bibliography: Z. Yeivin. "Ancient Chorazin Comes Back to Life." *BAR* 13/5 (1987) 22–36.

WARREN CARTER

CHORBE kor´bee [Χορβε Chorbe]. A family head whose descendants returned from exile (1 Esd 5:12). *See* ZACCAI in Ezra 2:9 and Neh 7:14.

CHOSAMAEUS kos´uh-mee´uhs [Χοσαμαιος Chosamaios]. A descendant of Canaan who was forced by Ezra to put away his foreign wife and his children (1 Esd 9:32). The relation of 1 Esd 9:32 to the presumably par. account in Ezra 10:32 is uncertain.

CHOSEN PEOPLE. A central theological presupposition of the OT that God chose the Israelites as a special people. Christianity and Judaism each claim this title. *See* ELECTION.

JOEL KAMINSKY

CHREIA kray´uh . A unit of writing in school exercises that contains a statement or action that is attributed to a person. Chreia is used to develop the ability to structure material according to common types of argumentation, such as sayings, cause, converse, analogy, example, and the testimony of the ancients. Chreiai had numerous functions. First, they were exercises in practicing declensions. Second, they were rhetorical exercises in composition and dialectic, including recitation, inflexion, comment and objection, expansion and elaboration. Third, they have a moral function by compressing truth into very few words. A chreia displays aspects of life, thought, and action in a mode that integrates attitudes, values, and concepts with personal, social, and cultural realities. The people featured in chreiai become authoritative media of positive and negative truths about life. These "authorities" transmit social, cultural, religious, and philosophical heritage into later historical periods. Fourth, they are compact wisdom. Fifth, they provide a narrative presentation of a

key point. This includes types, noble deeds, and lifestyle. Sixth, as witticisms they are intended to amuse and entertain. Seventh and eighth, chreiai are used in polemic and refutation. Forms of chreiai include the maxim, manner of an explanation, witticism, syllogism, enthymeme, example, manner of a wish, symbolic manner, figurative manner, with a double entendre, with a change of subject, and any combination of the above.

Examples such as Mark 3:19-35; 10:17-22; Matt 12:1-8; 22:15-22; Luke 9:59-60 are concise, well-structured statements transmitting teachings within narrative frameworks about an authoritative figure.

GREG A. CAMP

CHRIST kr*i*st [מָשִׁיחַ mashiakh; χριστός christos]. Most frequently used in the NT to refer to Jesus (531 times). *Christ* is a transliteration of the Greek christos, an adjective meaning "anointed (with oil or ointment)," and often used substantively to mean "anointed one"; this adjective stems from the verb chriō (χρίω), "to anoint." The term *Christ* became early a typical designation for Jesus, so much so that it functioned as a proper name for him, thus "an apostle of Jesus Christ" (e.g., 1 Pet 1:1). Since the 1st cent. followers of Jesus have been labeled "Christian" (χριστιανός christianos; Acts 11:26; 1 Pet 4:16).

The term bore no religious significance in secular Greek. Its importance in the NT stems from Jewish texts, where it referred to the eschatological fulfillment of God's promises regarding the eternal rule of a king from the line of David. Jesus and his followers adopted its connotations of eschatological fulfillment, but replaced political dominance with an emphasis upon suffering and death in obedience to God's will. Each of the NT writers employs the term *Christ* for Jesus to combine this view of eschatological fulfillment with characteristic theological emphases.

A. The OT and Judaic Background
B. The Concept of Christ and the Historical Jesus
C. The Concept of Christ in the Christology
   of the NT
   1. Mark
   2. Matthew
   3. Luke–Acts
   4. John and the Johannine Epistles
   5. Paul
   6. Hebrews
   7. James
   8. 1 Peter
   9. 2 Peter and Jude
   10. Revelation
Bibliography

A. The OT and Judaic Background
The adjective christos is used approximately forty-five times in the LXX to translate the Hebrew מָשׁ

mashiakh (messiah), which means, as does the Greek word, "anointed (by oil)." The verb form mashakh (Greek chriō) is used for the anointing of kings, but also (rarely) for that of priests or prophets. The adjective is used of priests, who entered upon sacerdotal service by the rite of anointing (e.g., Lev 4:5, 16; 6:22; 2 Macc 1:10). Use of the term for Israel (Pss 27(28):8; 83(84):9; 105:15; Hab 3:13; Lam 4:20; and possibly 1 Chr 16:22) reveals that it does not always assume an actual rite; metaphorically it expresses Israel's special standing with God.

Ordinarily the term refers to kings who were anointed at their accession. The DEUTERONOMIC HISTORIAN uses it of Saul (1 Sam 12:3, 5; 24:7, 11; 26:9, 11, 16, 23; 2 Sam 1:14, 16); the Chronicler speaks of Jehu as "the Lord's anointed" (2 Chr 22:7, the Hebrew text has a different form of mashakh); and Isaiah refers to Cyrus as "[God's] anointed" (Isa 45:1). The majority of occurrences pertain to Davidic kings (e.g., 2 Sam 19:21; 22:51; 23:1; Pss 2:2; 18:50; 20:6; 89:38, 51; 132:10, 17), where the emphasis is upon 1) the king as appointed by God to serve as God's "viceroy" (e.g., 2 Sam 23:1); 2) the deliverance/salvation of the king (e.g., Ps. 20:6; 2 Chr 6:42); and 3) God's steadfast love toward David's descendants forever (e.g., 2 Sam 22:51; Pss 18:50; 132:10, 17).

These emphases reflect the covenant God made with David (2 Sam 7:10-16). This account of the Davidic covenant associates the concept of christos, anointed Davidic king, with the use of "SON OF DAVID," and "SON OF GOD" for Davidic kings (Ps 2:2, 7). As the moral character and political failures of many of Israel's kings led to national disasters, there emerged the hope of a future Davidic king to fulfill the promises (e.g., Isa 9:5-6; 11:1–12:6; Mic 5:3), reconcile the people to God, reestablish Israel, purge the land of oppressors and unrighteous Israelites, and bring all nations to learn of Yahweh in Jerusalem (Jer 23:5-8; 30:21-22; Ezek 37:21-23; Zech 3:8-10). This king remains a mortal, whose rule is eternal in a dynasty that would continue forever (Ps 89:3-4; Jer 17:25; 33:15-18). God addresses the king as "God," or refers to his throne as "the throne of God" (Ps 45:6-7).

Hope for an ideal monarch was intensified after the Babylonian captivity (Zech 4:1-6; 6:9-15). Although the OT never uses mashiakh/christos to refer, in a technical sense, to an eschatological royal deliverer, these expectations provided the basis for messianic hopes of the intertestamental period.

Great diversity characterizes the eschatological expectations among the Jews during the Second Temple period. Most anticipated a political ruler such as one finds in the 1st cent. BCE PSALMS OF SOLOMON. Here the term christos appears for the first time in an eschatological sense, and is used in connection with the title "son of David." This Christ will 1) eject the foreigners occupying Jerusalem (17:15, 24-25, 33); 2) judge the

nations (17:4, 31, 38-39, 47) and force them to "serve him under his yoke" (17:32); and 3) reign over Israel in wisdom (17:23, 31, 42) and righteousness (17:23, 28, 31, 35, 41; 18:8), by purging the land of unrighteous Israelites (17:29, 33, 41) so as to gather a holy people (17:28, 36; 18:9). The rule of this "christ" assumes eschatological and global aspects from its antecedents in the OT. Many of these same features are found in the PSEUDEPIGRAPHA (4 Ezra 12:31-32; T. Jud. 24:1-5) and at Qumran (1QM 11:1-18; 4QFlor 1:11-14; 4QPBless 1-7; 4QTestim 9-13).

The QUMRAN documents contain the earliest reference to mashiakh as a name. Two separate messiahs are frequently mentioned together (1 QS 9:11; Damasc. 12:23-24; 14:19; 20:1; 19:10-11; 4QTest 9-13, 14-20; 4QFlor 1:11), a priestly Messiah of Aaron (4QTest 14; 1QS 9:11), and a royal Messiah of David (4QPBless 2-5; 4QFlor 1:11; 1QSb 5:20-29). According to the DEAD SEA SCROLLS the royal Messiah will be subordinate to the priestly Messiah. Yet some texts refer to a royal Messiah as "son of God": 4QFlor 1:10-14 applies 2 Sam 7:11-14 to the Messiah; 1QSa 2:11-12 might be read as God begetting the Messiah; and 4QpsDan Aᵃ (4Q246) reads "he shall be hailed as the Son of God, and they shall call him Son of the most High."

Although Jews seem to have identified the eschatological Messiah with the SERVANT OF THE LORD in Isa 40–55, there is no firm evidence that any Jew expected a suffering Messiah. The Targum on Isa 53, which interprets the Servant messianically, construes all references to suffering as pertaining to persons other than the Messiah (e.g., the people).

B. The Concept of Christ and the Historical Jesus

Jesus was condemned to death on the charge that he claimed to be "Christ a king, that is, a political deliverer" (Luke 23:2 RSV; Matt 27:11-31). James and John imagine Jesus' role as political domination with seats of honor and authority (Mark 10:35-45). The evangelists portray Jesus tempted by political messiahship (Matt 4:1-10; 27:32-34; John 6:15). And in Acts 17:7 Thessalonian Jews accuse Paul of sedition against Caesar for saying that Jesus in his role as Christ is "another king."

The earliest strands of the gospel tradition depict a Jesus who accepted the possibility, but was reticent to claim publicly the designation "Messiah."

According to Mark 8:27-30 Jesus raised the question of his identity with the disciples. Jesus does not dispute Peter's response, "You are the Christ" (8:29 RSV), but insists that it not be publicized. Jesus immediately proceeded to teach "that the Son of Man must undergo great suffering" (Mark 8:31). The fact that a saying about the suffering of the SON OF MAN follows immediately, suggests that Jesus accepted messiahship but rejected the political associations the term had acquired in favor of a messianic content involving repudiation and death.

Caiaphas asks Jesus about his messiahship (Mark 14:61) and Jesus responds "I am." Again an assertion about the Son of Man follows: "And you will see the Son of Man seated at the right hand of Power, and coming with the clouds of heaven" (14:62). Jesus corrects the political connotations of messiahship in the direction of a heavenly transcendent (and transpolitical) reality along the lines of Dan 7. It seem likely that Jesus, himself, redefined messiahship along the lines of the suffering servant and the heavenly Son of Man figure.

Jesus responds to Pilate's questioning with more reserve, "You say so" (Mark 15:1-4). This is probably to be understood as a heavily nuanced affirmative response. Jesus construes the eschatological reign of God through God's Messiah in terms of a rule characterized by the overthrow of the powers of cosmic evil (note Jesus' indubitable practice of forgiving sin, healing sickness, cleansing unclean lepers, exorcising demons) and the repudiation of systems that privilege domination by the powerful. God's reign is accomplished through humble submission to the will of God that necessarily places the messiah-king in opposition to the power structures of religion and government and inevitably leads to his death (Mark 8:32; 14:62).

Jesus redefined the concept of messiahship that was current in his own day, away from an emphasis upon political and military rule in favor of 1) salvation from the forces of cosmic evil, such as sin, sickness, death, and uncleanness by 2) an obedience to God that involved the repudiation of the power-systems of the world, 3) a repudiation that would lead inevitably to suffering and death, but 4) finally to vindication in resurrection and glorification.

C. The Concept of Christ in the Christology of the NT

1. Mark

William Wrede (1901), argued that Mark's Gospel sought to mediate between two views of Jesus as messiah: 1) the *adoptionistic* view that Jesus became the Messiah at his postresurrection exaltation (e.g., Acts 2:36; 13:32-33; Rom 1:4; Phil 2:6-11), and 2) the *comprehensive* view, that Jesus publicly proclaimed himself messiah throughout his ministry (as in John). Since the adoptionistic view was the earliest, Wrede concluded that the historical Jesus did not consider himself to be the Messiah. Over a period of time, early Christians "pushed back" Jesus' messiahship from his exaltation to God's right hand, eventually to the beginning of his life. Mark's Gospel thus attempted to bridge the contradiction between these two understandings of Jesus' messiahship. In the narrative Jesus considered himself to be the Messiah throughout his ministry, but kept his identity a secret. Wrede's work drew scholarly attention to the theological implications of Mark's story. Throughout the 20th cent., scholars have shifted the focus of secrecy from Jesus' role as Christ to his role as

Son of God, whose divine Sonship is manifested on the cross (Mark 15:39).

"Christ" appears already in Mark 1:1, a verse that serves as a heading. The turning point between the two main units in the Gospel is Peter's confession of Jesus as Messiah. The first unit, 1:14–8:30, repeatedly raises the issue of Jesus' identity (e.g., 1:24; 3:11; 4:41; 5:7; 6:14-16), an issue that reaches its climax in Jesus' questions to his disciples (8:27-30). The narrative suggests that Peter confessed Jesus as the Christ on the basis of his mighty acts of healing, raising the dead, casting out demons, and proclaiming forgiveness of sins (e.g., 1:21-34; 1:40–2:12; 5:1-43), but failed to understand that messiahship involved submitting to the destiny of the Son of Man as one who must die, be raised, and return in glory (8:31; 13:26). In the second division (8:30–16:8), Jesus instructs his disciples about his destiny and fulfills his role as the Son of Man.

Mark also links the title "Christ" to the titles "Son of God" (1:1) and "King of the Jews/Israel" (15:32). The title "Christ," then, supplemented as it is by the notion of the suffering-dying-resurrected-returning Son of Man, clarifies the meaning of "Son of God" and "King of Israel," by indicating that Jesus is "Son of God." Jesus is perfectly obedient to the will of his Father (1:11; 14:32-44). Jesus is "King of Israel" who rules by dying on behalf of his people (10:45; 15:1-41).

2. Matthew

Matthew supports the claim that Jesus is "the Christ, the son of David, the son of Abraham" (1:1 RSV) with a genealogy. It shows that "Jesus, who is called the Messiah," brings salvation history, which began with Abraham, to its climax (1:16). As such, Jesus gives meaning and significance to the history of Israel that preceded him. The genealogy serves as the basis for Matthew's "fulfillment quotations" (e.g., 1:21-23; 4:14-16; 12:15-21), which mark events in the life of Jesus as the eschatological realization of OT passages.

Matthew associates "Messiah/Christ" with "Son of God" (e.g., 16:16; 26:63, 68) and "king/son of David" (2:1-6; 27:13-31). Jesus' messiahship is most closely tied to divine Sonship. Jesus is son of David by adoption (1:18-25) but Son of God through conception by the Holy Spirit. Matthew 22:41-46 suggests that the Christ should not be understood *ultimately* as "son of David" but in terms of another sonship, Son of God (3:17; 17:5; 27:54; 28:20). Matthew adds "Son of God" (16:16) to Mark's "the Christ" in Peter's confession and attaches a blessing: "Flesh and blood has not revealed this to you but my Father who is in heaven" (16:17). Matthew also follows the messianic confession with Jesus' prediction of the suffering-dying-resurrected son of Man (16:21). Only by divine revelation can persons know that Jesus is the Christ the Son of God (16:17), namely, that he is the one who brings God's redemptive purposes for Israel and the world to eschatological realization (1:21; 20:28; 26:26-29). Jesus knows God intimately as Father (11:25-27), and is perfectly obedient to the will of his Father (3:13–4:11; 26:36–27:54).

3. Luke–Acts

In Luke Jesus is "Christ" as the royal Son of God anointed by God (1:26; 9:20). Jesus fulfills God's plan to save the people Israel and then extend salvation to the ends of the earth (2:11; see FULFILL, FULFILLMENT). As promised in the OT (Luke 1:16-17, 67-79), salvation will begin with the poor and humble ones of Israel (1:46-55) but extend to all the nations (1:25-32). Although described in political images (1:32-33, 67-79), redemption involves the forgiveness of sins (1:77) and reconciliation to God and to others (1:16-17). Jesus dies as the royal Messiah who, by refusing to save himself, brings salvation to a condemned thief (23:36-43). Although his enemies charge Jesus with insurrection against Rome (23:2), Jesus' royal messiahship poses no threat to Roman order, for neither Pilate nor Herod found him guilty of a capital crime (23:1-24), and the Roman centurion, facing the cross, declares him innocent (23:47).

The messiahship of Jesus is largely hidden from human view (5:21; 7:49; 8:21; 9:9, 18-23; 18:34; 22:67-68) for most of the Gospel. Only the resurrected Christ can open the minds of disciples to the effect that "the Christ should suffer these things and then enter into his glory" (24:25-26 RSV). It is the resurrected Christ who assures them that "everything written about me in the Law of Moses, the prophets, and the psalms must be fulfilled" (24:44-45).

In Acts' presentation of Christ, Jesus has been "anointed" by God (drawing upon the original meaning of christos, 4:26; 10:36) to bring to fulfillment God's plan for the Messiah. In Acts the exaltation of the Christ is the saving event rather than atonement through his death, as in Mark or Paul. The exaltation fulfills Ps 110:1 (Acts 2:34-25). The exalted Jesus is "Lord," thereby empowered to dispense salvation as promise in Joel 2:28-32 (LXX).

Acts continues the story of all that Jesus *began* to do and teach (1:1 RSV) from the Gospel. In Acts the exalted Christ is engaged in repeated activity (e.g., 2:33; 9:1-18, 32-35; 22:17-21; 26:23). Thus one should not speak of an "absentee Christology" in Acts as some exegetes have done. The exalted Jesus mediates salvation through his name (e.g., 3:6; 4:10; 9:34; 16:18). Persons submit to his lordship by being baptized into "the name of Jesus Christ" (2:38; 10:48). A reconstituted Israel, with believing Jews at its core (Acts 3:17-26), supplemented by Gentiles who have faith in "Messiah Jesus" (24:24), receives salvation. Preaching about Jesus as Messiah is addressed to Jewish audiences (e.g., 2:22-36; 3:11-26; 5:45; 8:5, 28; 9:22).

Passages in Acts that seem to reflect an early adop-

tionistic Christology (Hahn), according to which Jesus became Christ at his exaltation (2:36) or will become Christ at his parousia (3:20) cannot have meant that to Luke, since Luke 2:11 declares Jesus Lord and Christ at his birth. Such texts may indicate a dynamic understanding of Jesus' messiahship: Although he was always Christ, Jesus functions as Christ in the fullest possible sense at his resurrection.

4. John and the Johannine Epistles

According to John 20:30-31 (RSV) the evangelist intends that the readers should "believe that Jesus is the Christ, the Son of God" (see SON OF GOD). The title "Christ" points to Jesus as the fulfillment of scriptural hopes for the eschatological, saving (i.e., life-giving) revelation of God (1:41-45; 4:25, 29). Jesus as the unique "Son of God" (10:22-39; 11:27; 17:1-3; 20:31) is the only one who has seen and can reveal his Father (1:14; 10:33-38; 14:6-11). Indeed, Jesus so perfectly reveals God that the gospel presents this Christ as divine (Harris), equal to "God" (1:18; 20:28). The revelation that Christ offers makes possible a personal, intimate relationship between believers and God, which John labels "(eternal) life."

Conflicts in John arise over Jesus' status as the Christ. The evangelist immediately counters the possibility that John the Baptist might be the promised messiah (1:6-9, 15, 19-28; 3:28). Jewish teachers assert hat Jesus cannot be the Christ because they know his origins, but when the Christ appears no one will know where he comes from (7:26; a tradition otherwise unknown). The Jews also "know" that Jesus comes from Galilee, but that the "scripture said that the Messiah is to be from Bethlehem (7:41-42). John's point is that earthly origin is of no significance; in fact these Jews do not know where Jesus comes from, namely, from heaven (7:29). Moreover, the Jews are offended at the Messiah's death and exaltation, since in the law the Christ "remains forever" (12:34). Such conflicts probably mirror objections faced by Johannine Christians, whose confession of Jesus as the Christ/Son of God has resulted in exclusion from the Jewish community (9:22).

The Christ of the Johannine epistles is the pre-existent Son of God (1 John 1:1-2), sent into the world as an expression of God's love (1 John 4:9; 2 John 3); and belief in "the name of his Son Jesus Christ" is the (only) basis for obedience to God's commands to love one another (1 John 3:23; 5:1-3). First John encourages fidelity to its vision of Christ against those who have left the community (2:19). The opposition "denied that Jesus is the Christ" (2:22), apparently rejecting the human reality of the Christ. First John labels these opponents "antichrists" (2:18, 22; 4:3).

5. Paul

Most occurrences of christos in the NT appear in Pauline letters. Paul usually employs the term as a proper name for Jesus. Yet even the nominal use of **christos** often retains something of its titular character.

Paul acknowledges that his understanding of Jesus as the Christ came to him from the church's earliest tradition, namely, "that Christ died for our sins in accordance with the scriptures, and that he was buried, and that he was raised on the third day in accordance with the scriptures" (1 Cor 15:3-4). Jesus is the Christ who fulfills the OT, especially in Jesus' atoning death and his resurrection. The OT witnesses to Christ (e.g., 1 Cor 10:1-13; Gal 3:16), and Christ himself "removes the veil" to make this witness perceptible (2 Cor 3:14). Paul's gospel centers on God's salvation that comes when persons place faith in Christ, resulting in the sinner's justification (i.e., establishment of right relationship with God; Rom 3:22; 5:1, 11; 10:4; 2 Cor 5:17-19; Gal 2:16). Paul's gospel urges participation in a community that, as "the body of Christ," is characterized by unity through a Christ-like humility (Rom 12:5; 1 Cor 12:12-13, 27; Phil 2:1-11).

BAPTISM involves an existential identification with the crucified Christ; accordingly, believers have been "buried with him in baptism," and should therefore consider themselves dead to sinful passions (Rom 6:1-14). Believers are now "in Christ" (an expression used 170 times). By the power of the Spirit of God (Rom 8:1, 9, 11; Gal 5:16-26) they experience a life-orientation centered in God and Christ, which will result in their resurrection from the dead (1 Cor 15:12-28, esp. vv. 21-23). As "a new creation" (2 Cor 5:17) this new existence stands in radical contrast to the sinful, self-centered orientation of human beings, who live in bondage to trespasses (Rom 5:12-21), share in the deadly curse of Adam, and would have no hope of resurrection (1 Cor 15:21-23). The concept of being "in Christ" is relational and interpersonal. It cannot be reduced to "individual mystical experience"(Deissmann), for it is actualized through participation in ecclesial communities (said to be "in Christ," e.g., 1 Thess 1:1; 1 Cor 1:2) and is expressed in moral behavior, i.e., fulfilling the "law of Christ" (1 Cor 9:21).

Although Paul emphasizes Jesus' experience of suffering, death, and resurrection (1 Cor 1, 15) and says little about earlier aspects of his earthly life or teachings, Paul mentions that the Christ was descended from David (Rom 1:1), that he was a practicing Jew (Rom 15:8; Gal 4:4), and that he instituted the Lord's Supper (1 Cor 11:23-26). Paul sometimes refers to teachings of Jesus (1 Cor 7:10-11; 1 Thess 4:15-17). Paul insists that as the Son of God (Rom 1:3; Gal 1:16) Jesus Christ spans the whole of temporal reality. Christ was the pre-existent agent of creation prior to his INCARNATION (1 Cor 8:6; 2 Cor 8:8; Phil 2:5-11). Although some scholars deny that Paul taught Christ's personal pre-existence, these passages suggest the divinity of Christ (2 Cor 4:4-6; Phil 2:6). Christ remains functionally subordinate to God (1 Cor 3:23; 11:3), is the exalted Lord who intercedes for believers (Phil 2:10-11; Rom 8:34-39), and will return from heaven as judge (Rom 2:16; 2 Cor 5:10; Phil 3:20). The disputed Pauline letters and the Pastorals present in general the same view of Christ. They add cosmic dimensions to the Christ. Christ fulfills God's eternal plan to unite the cosmos in him (Eph 1:10; 3:4, 10; Col 1:27; 2 Tim 1:9-10). Accordingly, Christ is the "image of the invisible God, the first-born of all creation" in whom and for whom all things were created (Col 1:15-20), who has now been seated in the "heavenly places" (Eph 1:10; Col 2:20), so as to reign over all "rule and authority and power and dominion" (Eph 1:20), for all things have been put under his feet (Eph 1:22). Yet Christ's death is central to his work of cosmic reconciliation (Eph 2:1-22; Col 2:20).

6. Hebrews

Hebrews represents the first attempt in Christianity to understand Jesus as a priestly MESSIAH. It combines the figures of priestly and royal Messiah (in one person). By reading Ps 110:1 (referring to a royal Davidic Messiah) in light of Ps 110:4 (referring to an eternal priest in the order of Melchizedek) the writer argues that Christ performs his priestly office with royal dignity and effectiveness (e.g., 10:11-14). Hebrews links Jesus' royal messiahship to his divine Sonship; although he was pre-existent Son and agent of creation (1:1-3; 13:8), he became Son in the fullest sense upon his exaltation (1:3-13). At Christ's kingly session God appointed him eternal high priest after the order of Melchizedek (5:5-6), thereby making possible the permanent efficacy of Christ's priestly sacrifice of himself in his death (9:15–10:26) and his intercession in the heavenly sanctuary (2:17-18; 4:14-16).

7. James

James refers to Christ only twice: in 1:1 as a proper name, and in 2:1 warning those who "believe in our glorious Lord Jesus Christ" against preference for the wealthy. James 2:1 leads some scholars to read other references to "Lord" as Christ rather than God (e.g., 5:7-9). James implicitly suggests that Christ is the king who has given the "royal law" that centers in the command to love the neighbor (2:8-13). Moral exhortations in James echo the teachings of Jesus (e.g., Jas 5:12).

8. First Peter

First Peter depicts Christians as God's holy people in the midst of pagan culture. The atoning death of "Christ" "sanctified" Christians in order to conduct themselves in purity and love (1:1-2, 14-20; 2:4-12; 4:1-6). Such moral living involves participating in Christ's destiny of suffering and subsequent resurrection glory (1:11; 2:21), a destiny predicted by the prophets who were inspired by "the Spirit of Christ within them (1:10-12).

9. Second Peter and Jude

Second Peter insists that effective Christian life in the face of challenges from false teachers is possible only through the "knowledge" of Christ (1:3, 5-6, 9, 15-20; 3:18). This knowledge is comprehensive in that it includes *memory* of the traditions regarding the earthly Jesus (1:12-21; 3:1-8), *insight* into what the exalted Christ is presently revealing (1:12-15), and *anticipation* of Christ's parousia (1:4, 11, 19; 3:1-13) when Christ will establish his eternal kingdom (a possible allusion to 2 Sam 7:12-16).

Jude emphasizes Christ's authority to reveal the truth regarding God's behavioral expectations (3, 17) and, as their "Master and Lord" (4), to make demands upon believers. As they face false teachers who reject Christ's authority, readers are encouraged to remember that God intends that they should be kept for Christ (1) and to live in anticipation of Christ's salvation ("mercy") that will come to them at the PAROUSIA (21).

10. Revelation

The entire book is a revelation from the exalted Christ, to "show his servants what must soon take place" (1:1). This Christ is the revealer of mysteries; he is responsible for what John sees regarding the churches in the present and regarding realities within the whole flow of history (Rev 4–22), especially (in accord with the perspective of the apocalyptic movement) the heavenly realities of which earthly happenings are a shadowy image. This Christ also reveals himself as the "faithful witness" (1:5) and hence as the model for the faithful testimony that John calls upon the members of the seven churches to adopt. He reveals himself, too, as the "first-born from the dead," who is thus the forerunner of Christians who suffer even unto death for their faithful witness and can, like the Christ who went before them, anticipate resurrection (2:7, 11, 17, 26-28; 3:5, 12, 21). But the experience of Christ transcends the experience of the Christians of John's churches, in the sense that Christ's death is the expiatory atonement of the LAMB of God (5:6-14), and in the sense that through his death and resurrection Christ has become ruler of the kings on earth (1:5-6). Although these kings do not know it, he is their sovereign and the ultimate actor even now in a history that is moving inexorably toward the judgment of the world by Christ, when "the kingdom of this world [will have] become the kingdom of our Lord and of his Messiah" (11:15). (References to "the Lord's Messiah" indicate that the original significance of "Messiah" as one who is anointed to reign was still operative at the end of the 1st cent.) Jesus' messiahship is developed in terms of 1) the transcendent son of Man from Dan 7 (e.g., 1:13; 14:14); 2) Jesus' sacrificial death along the lines of the Isaianic SERVANT OF THE LORD (e.g., 1:5-6; 7:14; 12:11; 19:13); and 3) Davidic sonship and the rule God promised to David's son (3:7; 5:5; 22:16; compare 2 Sam 7:12-16), thus bringing

these elements of scriptural revelation to climactic realization. *See* CHRISTOLOGY; JESUS, METAPHORS FOR; JESUS CHRIST.

Bibliography: John J. Collins. *The Scepter and the Star* (1995); Hans Conzelmann. *The Theology of St. Luke* (1961); John Dominic Crossan. *The Historical Jesus* (1991); Oscar Cullmann. *The Christology of the NT* (1963); Nils Dahl. *Jesus the Christ* (1991); Adolf Deissmann. *Die neutestamentliche Formel "in Christo Jesu"* (1892); Marinus de Jonge. *Christology in Context* (1988); James D. G. Dunn. *Christology in the Making* (1980); James D. G. Dunn. *Jesus Remembered* (2003); Ferdinand Hahn. *The Titles of Jesus in Christology* (1969); Murray J. Harris. *Jesus as God* (1992); Jack Dean Kingsbury. *Jesus Christ in Matthew, Mark, and Luke* (1981); Jack Dean Kingsbury. *The Christology of Mark's Gospel* (1983); C. F. D. Moule. "The Christology of Acts." *Studies in Luke–Acts.* L. E. Keck and J. L. Martyn, ed. (1966); Sigmund Mowinckel. *He That Cometh* (1954); Philip E. Satterthwaite, Richard S. Hess, and Gordon J. Wenham. *The Lord's Anointed* (1995); Ben Witherington III. *The Christology of Jesus* (1990); William Wrede. Greig, J. C. G., trans. *The Messianic Secret* (1971); N. T. Wright. *Jesus and the Victory of God* (1996).

DAVID R. BAUER

CHRISTIAN. *See* CHRISTIANITY.

CHRISTIAN ART. The objects created for a Christian community to learn about and to reflect upon the life of Jesus Christ may be classified as Christian art. The artist, who may or may not be a Christian, conveys a visual message for the audience. This message or meaning is conveyed in various media but most commonly in the form of painting, sculpture, architecture, and the minor arts. *See* AESTHETICS; ART; CARVING; CRAFTS; DESIGN; DRESS AND ORNAMENTATION; JEWELRY; SCULPTURED STONES.

HEIDI J. HORNIK

CHRISTIANITY. *Christianity* is not a biblical word. Its Greek equivalent, Χριστιανισμός Christianismos, is used by IGNATIUS OF ANTIOCH early in the 2nd cent. CE, in contexts that mark a clear distinction between Christianity and Judaism: "Christianity did not believe in Judaism, but Judaism in Christianity" (*Ign. Magn.* 10:3, compare 10:1, *Phld.* 6:1). The Latin *christianitas*, from which "Christianity" is directly derived, is similarly used by Tertullian (d. ca. 225), who speaks of JOHN THE BAPTIST as "a sort of dividing-line . . . at which Judaism should cease and Christianity should begin" (*Marc.* 4:33). By using a related and synonymous term, Tertullian also speaks of a "great . . . difference . . . between Judaism (*Iudaismus*) and Christianity (*Christianismus*)."

Paul does not use the word, but a similar contrast between "Judaism" ('Ιουδαϊσμός Ioudaismos) and "the truth of the gospel" underlies the account of his dispute with Peter (Gal 2:14). The use of these terms by no means implies that neither Judaism nor Christianity was in NT times a single, homogeneous unit.

The word *Christian* (Χριστιανός Christianos, "follower or partisan of Christ") is found three times in the NT. In each instance, it is used as a label for followers of Christ by Gentiles outside the movement, and may have first been used in mockery or ridicule. In Acts 11:26, Luke notes that "it was in Antioch that the disciples were first called 'Christians.'" This suggests: 1) that the name was first given by non-Christians in a Gentile milieu; 2) that by the time Acts was written, the name had become more generally used; and 3) that at that time, Christians more commonly referred to themselves as "disciples" (understood: of Jesus Christ; *see* DISCIPLE, DISCIPLESHIP). Agrippa's rhetorical question to Paul: "'Are you so quickly persuading me to become a Christian?'" (Acts 26:28) also reflects non-Christian usage and is likely said in mockery. "If any of you suffers as a Christian" (1 Pet 4:16) is also used in a derogatory setting. Already by the time of Ignatius, however, "Christian" had become an accepted and honorable title: "it is fitting not only to be called Christians, but also to be Christians" (*Ign. Magn.* 4).

A. Christianity Between Judaism and Hellenism
B. Geographical Spread
C. Structure and Organization
D. Beliefs
Bibliography

A. Christianity Between Judaism and Hellenism

The use of the distinctive name **Christianoi** clearly indicates the emergence, at most half a cent. after Jesus' death, of distinct communities who were publicly identified as followers of Christ, just as, e.g., the partisans of Herod the Great and his family were known as "Herodians" (Ἡρῳδιανοί Herōdianoi in Mark 3:6). The contrasts between Christians and Jews cited above should not be misunderstood in the light of later, especially 20th cent. ANTI-SEMITISM (*see also* ANTI-JUDAISM). They rather reflect the fact that Christianity was born in an overwhelmingly Jewish setting. The canonical Gospels rarely show the adult Jesus as moving far beyond the frontiers of Israel. Despite the success of the Gentile mission (see below), Christians remained throughout the NT period a tiny minority, often under threat (*see* GENTILES; NATIONS).

The spread of Christianity into the wider Greco-Roman world could scarcely be painless. The controversy about whether Gentile converts to Christianity should be circumcised, reflected particularly in Romans and Galatians, is only one example of tensions that were bound to arise in what has been called "the

decisive epoch of the history of earliest Christianity" (Theissen 1979, 69–110; *see* CIRCUMCISION). The relations between Jewish and Hellenistic Christianity have been differently assessed: Some have seen radical opposition between movements led by Peter and Paul, whereas others have suggested that Peter was probably "the bridge-man" who held together the diversity of 1st cent. Christianity, a spectrum of which the opposite ends were represented by Paul and James.

Paul's letters, which include the earliest extant Christian writings, show him supporting churches whose beliefs and way of life were distinct in important respects from those of both Jewish and Gentile communities. The tensions that this process caused are vividly attested, e.g., in Rom 9:1-5 (Judaism) and 1 Cor 8 (paganism). They were increased by the openness of Christian communities to persons of any ethnic origin or social status (Gal 3:28). In the Pastoral Epistles, the writer warns TITUS against "Jewish myths" (1:14). Scholars, however, differ about whether the "myths and endless genealogies" condemned in 1 Tim 1:4 are of Jewish or Gentile origin.

Within the Gospels one can trace the increasing self-consciousness of Christians communities. The context of Mark 1:39 shows that "their synagogues" means "the synagogues of the people of Galilee," but the more frequent use of this expression in Matthew (4:23; 9:35; 10:17; 12:9; 13:54; 23:34) suggests a distancing in which Jews become "them" and Christians "us." This tendency is less pronounced in Luke, while in Acts, the frequent expression "the Jews" usually refers to Jewish communities in Gentile centers (*see* SYNAGOGUE).

"The Jews" is almost equally frequent in the Gospel of John, usually, though not always, in a hostile context. This is the strongest NT evidence of the "parting of the ways" (*see* CHRISTIAN–JEWISH RELATIONS) that was soon to lead to the establishment of Christianity as a distinct entity, though one continuing (not least by its use of the Hebrew Scriptures) to acknowledge its Jewish roots. The statement: "The Jews had already agreed that anyone who confessed Jesus to be the MESSIAH would be put out of the synagogue" (John 9:22; compare 12:42; 16:2) may be anachronistic, but it indicates the extent to which Judaism and Christianity had grown apart by the time the Fourth Gospel reached its final form. The misunderstanding of the Fourth Gospel as anti-Semitic is anachronistic in a different way; attempts to avoid the expression "the Jews" in various modern translations are rarely justified.

B. Geographical Spread

The spread of Christianity by the close of the NT period is difficult to define exactly. The NT letters are occasional writings, and Christian individuals or groups may have existed in places they do not mention. Conversely, the occurrence of a place name in Acts, even associated with the visit of a Christian evangelist, does not necessarily entail the establishment of a church.

Paul's ministry was mainly associated with great urban centers, such as Antioch in Syria (Acts 13:1-2; 14:26), Corinth in Achaia (1–2 Corinthians; Acts 18:1-18), and Ephesus in Asia Minor (Acts 18:19–20:1; *see* PAUL THE APOSTLE). In the course of Paul's travels, Acts records individual or group conversions to Christianity in CYPRUS (13:12), Pisidian Antioch (13:48), Iconium (14:1), Derbe (14:21), and Lystra (14:21), and more generally the existence of churches in Syria and Cilicia (15:41). West of the AEGIAN Sea, conversions are recorded in Philippi (16:14), Thessalonica (17:4), Berea (17:12), Athens (17:34), and possibly Troas (20:7-12). Galatia is not mentioned in Acts, and the definition of the area in Asia Minor, to which Paul's letter is addressed, is a matter of dispute. Galatians 1:1 and 1 Cor 16:1, however, state explicitly that a number of churches existed in the area.

It should, however, be noted that the founders of churches in such important centers as Antioch and Rome are unknown. Christians at Puteoli (Acts 28:14) were already there to welcome Paul upon his arrival from Malta. There is archaeological evidence of Christianity in Pompeii and Herculaneum before their destruction in 79 CE.

Despite sometimes sharp differences between Christians and within Christian communities, churches were generally aware of being part of a common network, referred to inclusively as "the church" (ἡ ἐκκλησία hē ekklēsia, e.g., in Eph 5:23-32). A local church could be called "the church of God that is in Corinth" (1 Cor 1:2), suggesting a particular manifestation of a Christianity that was, in principle, universal. Local churches were kept in touch with one another by the visits of Paul and other evangelists, by messengers, and by such projects as Paul's fund in aid of Christians in Jerusalem (Gal 2:10; 2 Cor 8–9; Rom 15:25-28; *see* COLLECTION). Letters were addressed to groups of churches (Gal 1:2; 1 Pet 1:1), or have a very general address (Jas 1:1; 2 Pet 1:1; Jude 1), or none at all (Hebrews, 1 John; *see* LETTER). In Col 4:16, Paul directs that letters be exchanged between the churches in Colossae and Laodicea.

By the end of the NT period, therefore, one sees Christianity spreading westward from its home base in Judea and Galilee through Syria and Asia Minor into Achaea and Macedonia (modern Greece), Italy, and especially Rome. By the end of the 2nd cent., Christian communities had also been founded in Gaul (Lyon and Vienne), North Africa (Carthage, Alexandria), Mesopotamia (Edessa), and probably Britain and India.

C. Structure and Organization

Points of similarity have been noted between early Christian assemblies and other forms of association in Jewish and Greco-Roman society, such as synagogues, *collegia* or voluntary associations, and philosophical schools (*see* ASSOCIATIONS, COLLEGIA CLUBS). No single model corresponds exactly to what we know of the first Christian groups. There is much we do not know; there is likely to have been variety between one place and another, and changes even within the NT period. Later NT writings, notably the PASTORAL LETTERS, show increased concern with discipline, relatively fixed statements of doctrine, and the qualifications of office-bearers. There is, however, no standardization: the titles of "bishops" or "overseers" (**episkopoi**) and "elders" (**presbyteroi**) were probably interchangeable (*see* CHURCH, IDEA OF THE; CHURCH, LIFE AND ORGANIZATION OF).

In the absence of purpose-built structures, Christians, at least in Paul's churches, met in the houses of those members able to accommodate them (*see* HOUSE CHURCH). People such as AQUILA and PRISCA (or Priscilla, 1 Cor 16:19) in Corinth, or NYMPHA in Colossae (Col 4:15), acted as patrons to local Christian communities, and offered hospitality to visiting evangelists. A large city such as Corinth probably had a number of such house churches. Paul's reference to occasions when "the whole church comes together" (1 Cor 14:23) may indicate a larger gathering. Although "not many" of the first Christians, at least in Corinth, were, according to Paul, "powerful" or "of noble birth" (1 Cor 1:26), it is likely that "within the Christian community there were some members from the Christian social élite" (Clarke 1993, 130). Economic distinctions may underlie the divisions that Paul addresses in 1 Cor 11:17-22. In any case, it is clear that women played a more prominent and active role in Christian communities than would have been characteristic of Judaism, or likely in Greco-Roman society (*see* CORINTHIANS, FIRST LETTER TO THE).

D. Beliefs

By comparison with the 2nd and 3rd cent. CE, the NT as a whole bears witness to an extraordinary outpouring of creative thinking, as different writers in various ways came to terms with the impact of the Christ-event upon traditional Jewish beliefs (*see* CHRISTOLOGY; JESUS CHRIST). Marshall (2004, 717–26) has however discerned between them a "significant core of agreement and identity," presenting "a religion of redemption" expressed in a "Jewish framework of understanding," developed in a "context of mission" of which Christ, in particular his death and resurrection, was the center, issuing in a "renewed Israel," calling for a "response of faith," empowered by the HOLY SPIRIT, taking form in a community of believers governed by the commandment to love and thus to serve, and looking forward to a future in which "the fullness of salvation" would be realized (*see* LOVE IN THE NT; SALVATION; SERVE, TO). The different NT writers expressed elements of this core in widely diverse ways and with varying emphases. Yet within two generations of Jesus' death, communities based on allegiance to him, and acknowledging a family relationship to one another, had sprung up from Jerusalem to Rome.

Bibliography: A. D. Clarke. *Secular and Christian Leadership in Corinth* (1993); J. D. G. Dunn. *Unity and Diversity in the New Testament* (1977); J. D. G. Dunn. *The Partings of the Ways* (1991); M. Hengel. *Acts and the History of Earliest Christianity* (1979); I. H. Marshall. *New Testament Theology. Many Witnesses, One Gospel* (2004); G. Theissen. *The Social Setting of Pauline Christianity* (1982).

PAUL ELLINGWORTH

CHRISTIAN-JEWISH RELATIONS. For centuries most scholars asserted that Judaism and Christianity underwent a sudden and traumatic separation at some point between 70 and 135 CE. Current thinking demonstrates that the boundaries between Judaism and Christianity took centuries to develop, such that separation did not occur before the Christianization of the Roman Empire in the early 4th cent.

A. Parting of the Ways
B. Shared Beliefs
C. Areas of Tension
  1. Practice
  2. Persecution
  3. Theology

A. Parting of the Ways

The relationship between Judaism and Christianity in the first centuries of the common era has often been expressed through kinship metaphors. Historians, theologians, and exegetes in the 19th cent. often referred to Judaism as the "mother religion" that gave birth to Christianity, her "daughter religion." More recently, scholars speak of Judaism and Christianity as siblings engaged in competition with each other. The current dominant metaphor is "parting of the ways," implying a process in which a single road split into two and diverged, never to join again.

These metaphors do not take into account the diversity of early Judaism, the significant convergences between rabbinic Judaism and patristic Christianity, or the complex relationships that continued to exist between those who followed one path or another. Nor do they shed light on the date(s) of the separation or the processes that led to it. For our purposes, however, the lack of evidence for a 1st cent. "Christianity," which is separate from and in some sense opposed to "Judaism," requires us to discuss the relationships between those who believe Jesus to be the messiah (most but not all of whom will be Jewish in the NT period), and the majority of the Jewish population and its leadership, who did not share this belief.

Aside from the so-called *Testimoniuim Flavianum* by Josephus (*Ant.* 18.63), which is probably a Christian interpolation, the only references to Jesus or to his followers in the NT period are found in the NT texts themselves. These texts are hardly disinterested, factual accounts. Rather, they reflect the understanding of the early communities about Jesus' life and significance, the often difficult process of self-definition of these communities, and the pain or at least disappointment that the message was not accepted by the majority of Jews and their leadership (*see* CHRISTOLOGY; HISTORICAL JESUS; JESUS CHRIST).

B. Shared Beliefs

The NT testifies to major differences between Jews who did not believe Jesus to be the messiah and those Jews and Gentiles who did accept this belief. But it also reveals a shared belief in the one God of Israel and the sanctity of the Torah as God's revealed word, as well as similar approaches to many legal and ethical issues (*see* LAW IN THE EARLY JUDAISM; LAW IN THE NT; LAW IN THE OT; TORAH).

The commitment to monotheism emerges, e.g., in Romans, in which Paul declares that "there is no distinction between Jew and Greek; the same Lord is Lord of all and is generous to all who call on him. For, 'Everyone who calls on the name of the Lord shall be saved.'" The practice of prooftexting—supporting one's argument through the citation of biblical verses—demonstrates the belief in the Bible's sanctity and universal applicability. For example, even as Paul wants to limit the purview of the Torah in light of Jesus' appearance, he brings Genesis to bear on a rather specific syntactical argument: "Now the promises were made to Abraham and to his offspring; it does not say, 'And to offsprings,' as of many; but it says, 'And to your offspring,' that is, to one person, who is Christ" (Gal 3:16). Matthew 5:17 has Jesus declare: "Do not think that I have come to abolish the law or the prophets; I have come not to abolish but to fulfill." In keeping with this declaration, Matthew's Jesus holds forth on the subjects of murder, adultery, vows, divorce, and the "*lex talionis*" (law of retaliation): "You have heard that it was said to those of ancient times, 'You shall not murder'; and 'whoever murders shall be liable to judgment.' But I say to you that if you are angry with a brother or sister, you will be liable to judgment" (Matt 5:21-22). While Jesus differentiates his teachings from those "of ancient times," the discussion does not challenge these principles of Jewish law and ethics but rather builds upon them to propose a more stringent understanding of its teaching.

C. Areas of Tension

The NT's acceptance of these fundamental aspects of Judaism does not efface the real tensions between Jesus' adherents and those Jews who do not share their views. Among the issues at stake were Jewish practices, historical questions, and, most fundamentally, theological issues regarding the place that faith in Jesus has as a basis for relationship with God and for individual salvation.

1. Practice

The NT draws attention to two main issues pertaining to practice: SABBATH observance and CIRCUMCISION. In Matt 12:1-8, the PHARISEES chastise Jesus and the disciples for plucking grain on the Sabbath. Jesus counters with the example of King David, who "entered the house of God and ate the bread of the Presence, which it was not lawful for him or his companions to eat, but only for the priests" (Matt 12:4). The issue is not the Sabbath as such but the stringency of its requirements.

In the debate over circumcision the lines are more clearly drawn. Did Gentile followers have to undergo circumcision, that is, become members of the covenant community of Israel? Paul's letters to the Galatians show that he was adamantly opposed to Gentile circumcision, while others, such as James, believed it to be essential. In anger, he exclaims in Gal 5:12, "I wish those who unsettle you would castrate themselves!" Paul's conviction is that "in Christ Jesus neither circumcision nor uncircumcision counts for anything; the only thing that counts is faith working through love" (Gal 5:6), a view that according to Acts 10 was also shared by Peter. This belief paved the way for an alternate covenant with God, and hence helped to lay the groundwork for the eventual parting of the ways.

2. Persecution

Even though the Romans crucified Jesus, Matthew places the moral responsibility for Jesus' death not merely upon the Jews of Jesus' day but also upon subsequent generations. At Jesus' trial, Matt 27:25 has Pilate wash his hands of the affair: "Then the people as a whole answered, 'His blood be on us and on our children!'" The Gospel of John states that Jews feared expulsion from the synagogue if they openly confessed faith in Jesus (John 9:22; 16:2). Acts 8:1-3 refers to "a severe persecution . . . against the church in Jerusalem" and points to Saul, soon to become Paul, as a main perpetrator. Paul, himself, treats this hostility to Jesus' followers as evidence of his zeal for ancestral Jewish traditions (Gal 1:13).

3. Theology

At stake between the two groups is theology, specifically, acceptance or rejection of the belief in Jesus as the expected MESSIAH, the Christ, the Son of God, and the sole path to salvation. Paul puts the matter succinctly: "We ourselves are Jews by birth and not Gentile sinners; yet we know that a person is justified not by the works of the law but through faith in Jesus Christ" (Gal 2:15). In Rom 9–11, Paul struggles with the theological question of whether God's covenant with Israel is null and void since the coming of Christ. Paul concludes the Jews' refusal to accept Jesus as the messiah is part of a divine plan to allow non-Jews access to salvation: "a hardening has come upon part of Israel, until the full number of the Gentiles has come in. And so all Israel will be saved" (Rom 11:25-26).

The Gospel of John is less conciliatory. When the Jews are puzzled by and reject his message, John's Jesus declares: "You are from your father the devil, and you choose to do your father's desires. . . . Whoever is from God hears the words of God. The reason you do not hear them is that you are not from God: (John 8:43-47).

The particularities of the relationships between those who believed Jesus to be the messiah and those who did not do so may never be known. Yet the nature of these relationships as depicted in the NT texts is not merely of historical interest. The eventual separation of these two groups, developments in Christian theology and the growing power exerted by Christian churches, magnified the tensions and minimized the similarities attributed to these groups in the texts that became part of Christianity's sacred Scriptures. Certainly the deicide charge, and the charge that Jews are the children of Satan, has animated anti-Semitism for centuries, to our own day. This outcome was surely unanticipated by NT writers, despite their criticism of their fellow Jews' failure to accept Jesus as messiah. See ANTI-JUDAISM; ANTI-SEMITISM; COUNCIL OF JERUSALEM; MESSIAH.

ADELE REINHARTZ

CHRISTIAN MINISTRY. See MINISTRY, CHRISTIAN.

CHRISTIAN PAPYRI. See MANUSCRIPTS FROM THE JUDEAN DESERT; VERSIONS, ANCIENT.

CHRISTIAN YEAR, THE. The Christian year celebrates the three major events in the life and death of Jesus Christ (incarnation, resurrection, and the coming of the Holy Spirit) within the two-part structure of the lunar and solar cycles of the calendar year.

While the celebration of the Christian year can be seen as a simple reenactment of historical events, a more accurate understanding is that the year is the continual unfolding of the life of Jesus Christ in time. Thus, the ongoing eucharistic celebration of the Christian year is a daily witness to the light of Christ in the world.

A. Advent–Christmas (Incarnation)

Christmas celebrates the incarnation of Christ. The Christmas cycle is set to the solar year so that the dates of the feasts tied to it remain the same from year to year. Advent refers to the four Sundays before Christmas, which mark the preparation for the celebration of the birth of Jesus. Other holy days that are a part of the Christmas cycle are:

1. Annunciation Day, March 25
2. Epiphany, January 6
3. The Presentation, February 2

B. Lent–Easter (Resurrection)

Easter celebrates the resurrection of Christ, and it is the central feast of the Christian year. Lent is the forty-day preparatory season of Easter. In the tradition of the Western church, Easter is celebrated on the first Sunday after the first full moon on or after March 21. Because the date of Easter changes, the feasts and fasts tied to it are moveable, i.e., they do not have set dates. The major holy days of the Easter season are:

1. Maundy Thursday (the LAST SUPPER)
2. Good Friday (the cross)
3. Great Vigil of Easter; Easter Sunday (the RESURRECTION)
4. Ascension Day (40 days after Easter Sunday).

C. After Pentecost (Coming of the Holy Spirit)

The Day of Pentecost comes fifty days after Easter Sunday, and it celebrates the coming of the Holy Spirit, which initiates the work of the church in the world. On the first Pentecost: "Divided tongues, as of fire, appeared among them, and a tongue rested on each of them. All of them were filled with the Holy Spirit and began to speak in other languages, as the Spirit gave them ability" (Acts 2:3-4). After Pentecost is the longest season of the Christian year, running from the day after Pentecost until the first Sunday of Advent. *See* ADVENT; CHRISTMAS; EASTER; LENT; PENTECOST.

SUSAN E. BOND

CHRISTIANS, PERSECUTION OF. Jesus spoke to his followers about persecution (Mark 13:9-13; Luke 11:49-51; Matt 23:34-37; note John 16:2: "an hour is coming when those who kill you will think that by doing so they are offering worship to God"). Jesus himself was persecuted (Luke 4:29; John 5:16), and had endured beating, mocking, and crucifixion. His followers were warned that they could expect similar treatment from their opponents (Matt 5:10-12; 10:17-23; 24:9; Luke 21:12,16-17; John 15:18-21). However, these times were not to be feared, for they were promised the help of the Holy Spirit in threatening circumstances (Matt 24:19; Mark 13:11; Luke 12:11-12; 21:14-15)—a point stressed in the book of Acts (1:8; 2:4; 4: 8-13; 6:10; 7:55).

As predicted, real persecution beset the early church (Acts 5:17-42; 8:1; 11:19; 12:1-4; 13:45; 14:19; 16:19-24; 19:28-29). One of its most ferocious enemies was Saul of Tarsus in his pre-Christian days (Acts 8:3; 9:1-14; 22:4-8; 26:9-15). On the Damascus road "the Lord" accused Saul of "persecuting" him by attacking his disciples (Acts 9:4, 5; 22:7, 8; 26:14, 15). Paul acknowledged that he had formerly acted as a vigorous "persecutor" (διώκτης diōktēs, 1 Tim 1:13).

King HEROD Agrippa I put James, John's brother, to death with the sword (Acts 12:2), and Stephen was also martyred, praying for his enemies as he died (Acts 7:54–8:1), imitating the forgiveness that his Lord had displayed on the cross (Luke 23:34). The Acts narrative seems to justify the general statement about persecution found in the Pastoral Epistles: "All who want to live a godly life in Christ Jesus will be persecuted" (2 Tim 3:12, note also Mark 10:29-30; Gal 6:12; 2 Tim 1:8; 2:3).

In his ministry, Jesus had given counsel to his disciples. They were instructed to declare their faith in hostile settings (Matt 10:18-20; Luke 21:12-15). The apostles, after Pentecost (Acts 2; contrast Matt 26:56; Mark 14:50), had asserted their faith with boldness (παρρησία parrhēsia; e.g., Acts 4:13, 29, 31), and other Christian leaders such as Stephen and Philip had displayed similar courage and frankness as unashamed witnesses of their Lord (6:8-10; 8:4-40). Believers were called to defend their faith, offering explanations to those who raised questions or objections (1 Pet 3:15; Col 4:6; 2 Tim 2:23-26).

The apostle Paul as a Christian leader confessed his deep sense of shame in recalling his former active persecution of the followers of "the Way" (1 Cor 15:9; Gal 1:13, 23; Phil 3:6; 1 Tim 1:13). In fact, he urged believers to bless those who persecuted them (Rom 12:14; 1 Cor 4:12-13), thereby echoing the teaching of his Lord (Matt 5:44; Luke 6:27-29). He asserted that true Christians had the spiritual resources to cope with any difficulty or persecution that might befall them (Rom 8:31-39; 2 Cor 2:14-17; 9:8-11; Phil 4:19). Paul frequently noted his own sufferings as a source of encouragement to other disciples facing similar hard times (2 Cor 1:5-7; 4:8-12; 6:4-10; 12:10; Phil 4:13; 2 Tim 3:11). In like manner he held up the Thessalonians as models of noble steadfastness (2 Thess 1:4-5). He told the Colossians that he was "completing what is lacking in Christ's afflictions for the sake of his body, that is, the church" (Col 1:24). Paul accepted suffering as a means God was using to advance the kingdom and build the church, and commended the Philippians for helping him in his time of distress (Phil 4:14).

There are several references to Christ's own suffering in 1 Peter, where they are mentioned to undergird Christians confronted with social pressure and subtle persecution (1 Pet 2:18-25; 3:13-18; 4:1-2, 12-19). Job is mentioned in James as an example of patience in suffering (κακοπάθεια kakopatheia, Jas 5:10). Hebrews also provided encouragement to believers in the face of opposition by reminding them of Jesus as well as other noble servants of God in the past (Heb 12:1-4; 11:4-40). Their own sufferings (πάθημα pathēma, 10:32) held out promise of future reward (10:32-35).

In the book of Revelation a testing time is envisaged when suffering will befall Christians (Rev 2:10; 6:9-11; 13:7; 17:6). It is quite possible that John's Apocalypse was written in the reign of the Roman emperor Domitian (81–96 CE), a period in which there is no compelling evidence of widespread persecution. However, the signs were ominous; already Antipas had died for his faith as a faithful Christian witness (2:13), in loyalty to Jesus, "the faithful and true witness" par excellence (1:5; 3:14), and future hard times might be expected. The saints shared in "the suffering" (θλίψις thlipsis, 1:9; 2:9, 10; 7:14) and were called to "patient endurance" (ὑπομονή hypomonē, 1:9; 2:2, 3, 19; 3:10; 13:10; 14:12). Their suffering is noted, and future suffering anticipated (2:9, 10), but the future suffering of the impenitent and the immoral is clearly predicted as a divine judgment (2:21-23).

From Nero's time until the Decian persecutions of 250 CE, persecutions were largely local and sporadic, including those under the emperors Hadrian (117–138 CE) and Marcus Aurelius (176–180 CE). Pliny the Younger's correspondence with the emperor Trajan (111–112 CE) serves to underscore the fact that though Christianity was technically illegal, the law against Christians was not rigidly enforced. There were later persecutions under Gallus (251–253 CE), Valerian (257–260 CE), and especially Diocletian (303 CE). When Constantine came to share the throne in 306 CE persecution stopped, and when he became sole emperor in 323 CE Christians were not only tolerated but came into a place of prominence and power in the Roman Empire.

Persecution of Christians is taken seriously in the early church, but it is seen as a means of advancing the cause of Christ. Handled rightly, it is viewed as a source of blessing to those who accept it in the proper spirit: "knowing that suffering produces endurance, and endurance produces character, and character produces hope" (Rom 5:3-4). *See* MARTYR, PERSECUTION.

Bibliography: W. H. C. Frend. *Martyrdom and Persecution in the Early Church* (1965).

ALLISON ALBERT TRITES

CHRISTOLOGY. *Christology* traditionally designates expressions of, and reflections on, Jesus' religious significance in and for Christian faith. The term derives from systematic or dogmatic theology, where it designates a core traditional focus of Christian theological reflection. New Testament Christology is usually focused on the ways that NT writings articulate and reflect convictions and claims about JESUS CHRIST.

In modern scholarly study of NT Christology, generally, there are several approaches, reflecting distinguishable questions and aims. Some studies take a pronounced historical/developmental approach, the main aim being to chart a diachronic process through which the affirmations about Jesus that we see reflected in the NT came to be formulated. Other studies focus on one or more of the honorific epithets (christological titles) applied to Jesus in the NT, such as *Christ, Son of God*, and *Lord*, by using these as key indicators of Jesus' significance. This also usually involves much attention given to any pre-Christian usage of these terms. Many studies concentrate on the christological ideas of individual NT writings/writers, the concern often to portray the diversity of christological emphases in the NT, or to underscore the particular emphasis of a given writing/writer. Still other studies focus on one or more NT christological themes reflected across various NT writings, such as Jesus' pre-existence or redemptive death, and the main concern can be either historical and developmental or more of a reflective and theological focus.

Typically, Christology has meant mainly beliefs and claims about Jesus, but in recent years some scholars have also emphasized the devotional practice reflected in the NT as important evidence of Jesus' exalted status. In this article, we shall survey the main types of christological material in the NT and the key emphases about Jesus that characterize the NT. In the course of this, we shall also note briefly emphases of key NT writers/writings.

A. Key NT Materials
  1. Hymns
  2. Confessional formulas
  3. Christological titles
  4. The Gospels as "Jesus Books"
  5. Devotional Practices
B. Key Emphases
  1. Jesus and God
  2. Jesus and God's purposes
Bibliography

A. Key NT Materials

Actually, there is surprisingly little sustained exposition of Christology in most NT writings. Instead, even the earliest NT writings (letters of Paul from ca. 50 CE onward) already presuppose rather remarkable convictions about Jesus, and often these convictions are expressed in compressed forms such as hymns and confessional formulae, with which the readers are presumed to be familiar. This means that we must date the emergence of these convictions so early that they are already taken for granted as familiar to the original readers of these texts (and, hence, in need of little articulation or defense). Certainly, however, the elaboration of Jesus' redemptive work in comparison with the OT priesthood and sacrificial practices in Hebrews, and the full-scale quasi-biographical narratives of Jesus' ministry in the Gospels arguably represent more extended and notable christological texts. But, though there is not much extended explanation of Christology in the NT, there is abundant material indicating the centrality of the matter.

1. Hymns

It is very significant that several key passages in NT writings that explicitly articulate christological convictions are widely thought to be, or to derive from, early Christian odes or HYMNS. Their original use was in the context of worship gatherings, and their composition was likely prompted in settings of intense religious exaltation and inspiration. It appears that inspired songs about Jesus formed one of the earliest and most influential modes of christological expression. Several of the passages thought to preserve such songs have received considerable scholarly attention, but the primary focus here is on the NT material itself rather than a review of scholarship.

The earliest of these key passages is Phil 2:6-11. Set in the midst of Paul's exhortations to endure suffering (1:27-30), to demonstrate consideration for fellow believers (2:1-5), and live blamelessly in the world (2:12-18), these verses form a compressed narrative about Jesus' own self-humbling and obedience, and God's answering exaltation of him to a breathtaking status. Although a few have argued that vv. 6-7 were intended as a direct contrast with Adam's disobedience, most scholars take "in the form of God" (v. 6) as ascribing to Jesus some sort of pre-existent and divinelike status, from which he freely chose to descend to take "the form of a slave" and act in "human form" (v. 7). In this latter state, he further humbled himself (v. 8) and became obedient (to God) even to the point of crucifixion (*see* INCARNATION; KENOSIS; PHILIPPIANS, LETTER TO THE).

Then, in the second main part of the passage (vv. 9-11), which actually is its apex, God's exaltation of Jesus and its ultimate outcome are lyrically recounted. God has given Jesus "the name above every name" (v. 9), which must signify a participation in the very name of God. Using a remarkable adaptation of phrasing from Isa 45:23, the passage then heralds God's intention that all spheres of creation should acknowledge Jesus' as "Lord" (v. 11). Yet this universal acclamation of Jesus' unique status is all "to the glory of God the Father," reflecting the typical NT tendency to express Jesus' significance with reference to the one God of biblical tradition. But this early expression of Christology already indicates a remarkable innovation in this monotheistic tradition, with Jesus sharing extraordinarily in divine glory, and sung praise of him forming a regular part of Christian worship.

Other hymnic passages include Col 1:15-20 and John 1:1-18. In both of these texts, Jesus is also closely linked with God. In John 1:1-18 Jesus is famously referred to as the WORD (λόγος logos), and in v. 1 the Word is both with God and "was God." In context, this latter phrase must mean that the Word somehow shares in divine nature or stature (not that the Word replaces the OT deity). This passage was a major factor prompting the development of Logos christology in 2nd–3rd cent. Christian tradition. In the Colossian passage, Jesus is "the image of the invisible God, the firstborn of all creation," and is indwelt by "all the fullness of God." Both passages explicitly ascribe to Jesus a pre-existent mode (John 1:1-2; Col 1:15) and designate him as the agent through whom God created all things. Many scholars see in John 1:1-18, especially, an adaptation of OT references to the creation-role of divine WISDOM (e.g., Prov 8:22-31; Wis 7:22–10:21), or suggest a certain similarity to speculations about God's Logos in Philo of Alexandria. But both of these passages also celebrate the historic, earthly appearance of Jesus. John 1:14 famously states that "the Word became flesh" (from the Latin of this text comes the traditional term *incarnation*), and "dwelt among us," thereby in an unprecedented manner directly identifying the divine Word with Jesus. Colossians 1:18-20 portrays Jesus' crucifixion as the divinely chosen means "to reconcile to himself all things."

Several shorter NT passages are often thought to derive from hymns as well, including Heb 1:3; 1 Tim 3:16; 1 Pet 3:18-22. Ironically, however, scholars often ignore the only NT passages that are explicitly identified by their author as hymnic praise directed to God and Christ, which are in Revelation, and among which 5:9-13 is crucial. Granted, the author ascribes these songs to the heavenly court, but we may reasonably assume that they also reflect (and were intended to reinforce) worship practices of the churches with which the author was acquainted. In these particular songs, the praise focuses more on the redemptive effects of Jesus' suffering/death, an emphasis obviously linked to the author's stated purpose that readers be prepared to endure suffering (13:10; 14:12).

In addition to the oft-studied contents of these passages, it is also significant if they evidence the devotional practice of singing about or to Jesus as a component of earliest Christian worship. Such a place for songs celebrating Jesus in early Christian worship is unprecedented in the biblical, Jewish matrix of earliest Christianity, and is itself a powerful indication of the place of Jesus in early Christian life and belief.

2. Confessional formulas

Another important body of evidence comprises the compact statements commonly thought to be early christological CONFESSIONS. These are characterized by structured phrasing that seems designed for easier remembrance and recitation. Such confessions likely functioned as part of early collective worship practices, and also in other situations where believers communicated their faith and/or were arraigned before religious or civil authorities on account of it. Once again, these expressions of faith in Jesus are found in our earliest extant Christian texts (Paul's letters), where they appear without introduction or comment, indicating a wide familiarity and usage already at the time that these texts were written.

The briefest, and perhaps the earliest, "Jesus is Lord (κύριος Ἰησοῦς kyrios Iēsous)," is attested in 1 Cor 12:3 and Rom 10:9, and is also reflected in a slightly fuller form ("Jesus Christ is Lord") in the projected acclamation of Jesus by all creation in Phil 2:11. In Rom 1:3-4, many scholars perceive this two-line balanced construction as derived from another early confessional statement, this one asserting Jesus' Davidic descent and his divine affirmation as Son of God in his resurrection. It is also plausible that in passages such as Mark 8:29//Matt 16:16//Luke 9:20, and John 1:49 we have reflections of other early confessions of Jesus as *Christ (Messiah)*.

It is widely thought that an identifying feature of some confessional expressions in the NT is the use of the Greek relative pronoun, ὅς hos ("[he] who"). One example is in Rom 4:25, "[he] who was handed over to death for our trespasses and was raised for our justification." Another instance is 1 Tim 3:16, a passage whose rhythmic structure has also led some scholars to see these lines as hymnic in derivation. Here we have a more extended recitation in which Jesus is acclaimed as "revealed in flesh," divinely vindicated, proclaimed among the nations, and exalted to heavenly glory.

In 1 Tim 2:5-6, what looks like another creedal formulation includes the confession of "one God" and of Jesus as the "one mediator between God and humankind" who "gave himself a ransom for all." Also, in still other passages such as Rev 1:5-6, the rhythmic phrasing may reflect confessional formulations and practices, Jesus lauded here as the one "who loves us and freed us from our sins by his blood, and made us to be a kingdom, priests serving his God and Father."

3. Christological titles

Several honorific epithets (titles) applied to Jesus in the NT have probably been the most frequently studied evidence of early christological beliefs, sometimes to the neglect of other data. Certainly, the terms in question are significant expressions of early beliefs about Jesus. The most familiar and frequently used titles are Christ (Messiah), SON OF GOD, and LORD (*see* JESUS, METAPHORS FOR). Other notable but less frequent designations of Jesus include WORD (John 1:1-14), Image (of God, 2 Cor 4:4; Col 1:15), LAMB of God (John 1:29), and SAVIOR (e.g., John 4:42; Acts 5:31; 13:23; Eph 5:23; Phil 3:20; 2 Pet 3:2).

The confession of Jesus as "the Christ" originally both presupposed and directly laid claim to Jewish hopes for an eschatological savior-figure. In the important Jewish text, *Pss. Sol.* 17–18, we have an idealized king and the eschatological royal heir of David's throne, and this seems to have been the dominant form of messianic hope. The

Greek word Χριστός Christos translates literally the Hebrew word מָשִׁיחַ mashiakh ("anointed/anointed one," "Messiah"; *see* ANOINT; CHRIST; MESSIAH, JEWISH), which by the 1st cent. had come to function as a title for this eschatological figure (*see* ESCHATOLOGY, EARLY JUDAISM; ESCHATOLOGY, NT). So, the Christian use of the title *Christ* likely derives from the earliest setting of confession and proclamation of Jesus among Jewish circles, both in Roman Judea (Palestine) and in diaspora locations (e.g., Damascus, Antioch, Rome). Indeed, it seems very likely that even during Jesus' own ministry his followers entertained and promoted hopes of his messianic significance, and this also best explains his brutal execution by the Roman administration of Judea as "king of the Jews" (e.g., Mark 15:26). This means that "Messiah" may be the earliest confessional title, first applied to Jesus even during his own ministry by some, and used against him by others.

There is, however, no precedent for the notion that the Messiah will suffer the sort of hideous death that Jesus underwent. The radical innovation in early Christian usage of "Messiah" was to identify explicitly and emphatically Jesus' death as integral to his divinely ordained messianic mission, and to claim his resurrection and exaltation as God's glorious vindication of him as Christ (Messiah). Indeed, in NT references to Jesus' death *Christ* is used more typically than any other christological title (e.g., Rom 5:6, 8; 6:3; 1 Cor 15:3; Gal 3:13; 1 Pet 1:2, 19; 2:21; 1 John 2:1-2). It appears, thus, that in earliest articulations of the significance of Jesus' death, it was specifically as the *Christ (Messiah)* that Jesus died for us, for our sins.

Note subtle but significant differences in usage of *Christ* among NT writers. Of the 531 occurrences of the term in the NT, some 383 uses are in the Pauline corpus, some 270 of these (51 percent of total NT uses) in his undisputed letters (Romans 1–2, Corinthians, Galatians, Philippians, 1 Thessalonians, Philemon; *see* CHRIST; PAUL THE APOSTLE). This confirms that the term had already and quickly become an important item in the religious vocabulary of Christian circles. It is also clear that *Christ* is Paul's favorite christological term. In Paul, the term is used preponderantly as a name, either in formulaic expressions such as "Christ Jesus" (e.g., Rom 1:1) and "the/our Lord Jesus Christ" (Rom 1:7; 5:1), or by itself, as in "Christ died for our sins" (Rom 5:8). Yet, occasionally in Paul, we see reflections of the derivation of the term as a title, with the definite article, "the Christ" (Rom 9:5).

In some other NT writings as well, there is a notable usage of *Christ*. In particular, 1 Peter has twenty-two occurrences, mainly without the article and often in connection with references to the suffering of Jesus and of Christians (e.g., 1:11; 2:21; 3:18; 4:1, 13; 5:1). This confirms the importance of the theme of Jesus' suffering as messianic in significance across a variety of 1st cent. Christian circles.

By contrast, in all four Gospels (written a few decades later than Paul's letters) *Christ* is used far less frequently; and it is used rather consistently as a title (with the definite article). Yet each evangelist employs the term with particular nuances and emphases. Mark's opening words (1:1) include a reference to "Jesus Christ," and in 9:41 Jesus' followers are referred to as "of Christ (or Christ's)" (Χριστοῦ ἐστε *Christou este*), but thereafter the usage is "the Christ." Moreover, in all the latter cases the connections with Jewish hopes and/or with Jesus' death are clear (8:29; 12:35; 13:21; 14:61; 15:32). For Mark, Jesus is rightly "the Christ," but the author insists that what "Christ" means must be shaped very much by the events of Jesus' own ministry and passion (*see* PASSION NARRATIVES).

Matthew adopts a large number of these Markan occurrences, and also has interesting uses of his own. There is a small cluster of occurrences in the Matthean nativity narrative (1:1, 16-17; 2:1-4), which reflect the author's emphasis that he relates the birth of the Messiah. With over twice the number of occurrences found in Mark, it seems that *Christ* is an important title in Matthew, complementing Matthew's emphasis on Jesus' divine sonship.

In Luke–Acts, we have a substantial body of uses of *Christ* (twelve in Luke, twenty-six in Acts). About half of the uses in Acts are in formulaic references to "Jesus Christ" (e.g., 2:38), "Christ Jesus" (e.g., 18:5), or "the Lord Jesus Christ" (e.g., 11:17). Nearly all the other Acts uses are in passages where Jews are being urged to recognize in Jesus the fulfilment of messianic hopes, and in all these cases the term is used as a title. In some cases, OT texts are presented as prophecies of Jesus' messianic sufferings (2:31; 3:18; 17:3; 26:23), and in others a more general messianic claim is made (2:36; 3:20; 5:42; 8:5; 9:22; 18:28). In Luke as well, *Christ* is consistently used as a title (with the possible exception of 2:11), and Jesus is explicitly associated with Jewish messianic hopes (e.g., 2:26; 3:15; 4:41; 9:20). The distinctive Lukan scenes of appearances of the risen Jesus picture him identifying himself as "the Christ" whose sufferings and subsequent glorification are predicted in the OT (24:26-27, 44-47).

Only two of the nineteen uses of *Christ* in John are in formulaic expressions ("Jesus Christ," 1:17; 17:3). In other occurrences the term is a title, and Jewish messianic expectations are either alluded to or explicitly cited. In the all-important 20:31, the author's stated purpose is to promote faith in Jesus as "the Christ, the Son of God," indicating the title's importance. John refers to specifics of Jewish messianic hopes more than the other Evangelists, using these as a foil for the presentation of Jesus. In 1:19-28 and again in 3:25-30, John the Baptizer denies messianic claims for himself, but acclaims Jesus as "the Lamb of God" (1:29, 35) and "the Son of God" (1:34). The latter epithets are clearly messianic in import, as reflected in the accounts of disciples of John acclaiming Jesus as Messiah (1:41, 45, 49). Jewish messianic speculations are played off again in 7:25-44 against Jesus' true messianic identity, the crowd pictured as unable to perceive the truth of things. Likewise, in 4:25 the Samaritan woman, and in 12:34 the Jewish crowd refer to traditions about Messiah.

In all these passages, the author seeks to show that the people do not properly understand their own traditions and/or do not know enough about Jesus, and so dismiss him wrongly. In 9:22, the confession of Jesus as *the Christ* leads to synagogue expulsion, which most scholars take to reflect experiences of believers in the latter decades of the 1st cent. John alone explicitly defines *Christ* as *Messiah* (1:41; 4:25). In short, for John, Jesus' messianic status is central, and yet traditional Jewish traditions are inadequate for grasping all that Jesus' messianic status involves, and the depth of Jesus' person. In John, Jesus' messianic status is to be understood in light of his divine, heavenly sonship, and Jesus is a Messiah of truly transcendent nature.

Uses of *Christ* in the remaining NT writings basically follow similar lines. Some occurrences are in the familiar formulas (e.g., Heb 13:8, 21; 1 John 1:3; Jude 1, 17; Rev 1:1), and in others we have the term with the definite article and used as a title (e.g., Heb 3:14; 9:28; 1 John 2:22; Rev 11:15). In sum, the NT use of *Christos* reflects the deep roots of Christian faith in biblical and Jewish traditions, and the strong claim upon these traditions involved in earliest expressions of Jesus' significance.

The acclamation of Jesus as God's *Son* likewise seems to have originated in circles of believers influenced by Jewish and OT use of this expression. This term also is connected to the royal-messianic claim, and NT usage involves the royal association of divine sonship. Especially in Ps 2, God's "anointed one" (v. 2) is the divinely chosen king (v. 6), whom God addresses here also as "my son" (v. 7), and this passage is commonly seen as an echo of the Gospels' accounts of Jesus' baptismal acclamation by God as his *Son* (Mark 1:11//Matt 3:17//Luke 3:22). In OT applications of divine sonship to humans such as the king, the connotation is not ontological divinity but rather divine favor, a special authorized intimacy with God, and also the sense of a divinely authorized status and mission.

In the many applications of divine sonship to Jesus in John, e.g., this sort of connotation is evident (e.g., 3:35-36; 5:19-20). It is also likely that traditions stemming from Jesus' own references to God as *Father* were a contributing factor. But the NT applications of divine sonship to Jesus were mainly prompted, and their connotations heavily shaped, by the profound conviction that God had raised him from death and given him heavenly glory.

This helps to explain why NT references to Jesus as God's Son often hint at something more than OT uses of this category. Paul refers to Jesus' divine sonship only a comparatively few times (seventeen in the Pauline corpus, fifteen of these in undisputed letters), and the actual expression "the Son of God" is neither fixed in form nor frequently used (four times and in varying Greek word order: Rom 1:4; 2 Cor 1:19; Gal 2:20; and Eph 4:13), employed by Paul considerably less often than his many references to Jesus as *Christ* and *Lord*. Yet it is clear that Jesus' divine sonship is an important part of Paul's Christology.

Eleven of Paul's references to Jesus' divine sonship are in Romans and Galatians, the two letters where Paul engages in sustained articulation of faith in Jesus in the dialogue with biblical and Jewish traditions. This strongly indicates that for Paul "Son of God" was not a religious marketing device intended to communicate to his Gentile converts by referencing pagan notions of divine heroes and demi-gods. An examination of specific instances shows that Paul refers to Jesus as God's *Son* particularly to underscore God's central role in Jesus' appearance and redemptive actions, and Jesus' unique standing, status, and favor with God. For instance, in 1 Thess 1:9-10, Jesus' divine sonship reflects his status as the resurrected, eschatological, messianic agent of salvation from divine wrath. Similarly, in 1 Cor 15:24-28, royal, messianic imagery abounds (e.g., note the clear allusion to Ps 110:1 in v. 25). After the enthroned *Christ* has received submission of all things, then *the Son* will submit himself to God (the Father), further indicating the biblical background of the sonship category as deployed here (v. 28). In other cases, Jesus' divine sonship emphasizes God's involvement in Jesus' redemptive death (Rom 5:10; 8:32), or the high significance of the one who suffered for others (Gal 2:20; *see* ATONEMENT; CRUCIFIXION; REDEEM, REDEEMER).

In Gal 1:15-16 Paul represents as the cognitive import of the experience that radically changed him from opponent to proponent of the gospel God's revelation to him of Jesus as God's *Son*. In Rom 1:9 Paul refers to his message as "the gospel of his [God's] Son." Both passages reflect the importance of divine sonship in Paul's estimate of Jesus.

In all these cases, as with other NT uses, we have to reckon with a cognitive "backflow" from Jesus' risen and glorified status at the right hand of God, enriching and extending to new transcendent levels all previous use of divine sonship for human figures. In some NT writings, *Son* is a particularly frequent and crucial epithet for Jesus. This is evident, to cite a major example, in Hebrews. Note the contrast in the opening words (1:2) between OT revelation and that given in God's *Son*, and in the following verses the comparative contrast between the angels and Jesus as God's *Son* (1:5, 8). Likewise, in 3:6, the author contrasts Moses as servant with Christ the *Son* set over God's household. In several other instances as well, Hebrews refers to Jesus

reverentially as God's *Son* (4:14; 5:5, 8; 6:6; 7:3, 28; 10:29). Once again, in all these occurrences, *Son* connotes Jesus' high status and authority, the full extent of which is enlarged considerably in the conviction that God has exalted Jesus to heavenly glory. Jesus' sonship far exceeds anything previously imagined in biblical tradition.

But surely the greatest emphasis on Jesus' divine sonship is in the Johannine literature. John's purpose statement, previously noted (20:31), sets out *the Christ* and *the Son of God* as the two key expressions of the faith-commitment that is promoted. In other passages as well, Jesus is explicitly identified as "the Son of God" (1:34, 49; 10:36; 11:4, 27) or "the only-begotten" (unique) Son (3:16). Indeed, Jesus' divine sonship is so central that John more typically (and distinctively) refers to Jesus simply as "the Son" (e.g., 3:17, 35-36; 5:19-26; 6:40; 8:35-36; 14:13). In John, Jesus' sonship is linked to explicit claims that he was with God from before the world (1:1-2; 17:5), and came down from heaven (8:38) to do the Father's will for redemption of the world (3:16-18). Clearly, Jesus' divine sonship in John is enhanced radically by the revelatory work of the Paraclete, whom the author presents as revealing more fully Jesus' greater significance (14:25-26; 15:26; 16:12-15).

With twenty-two references to Jesus' as God's Son in its five chapters, however, 1 John unquestionably has the highest concentration of occurrences. Yet, whereas in the Gospel of John Jesus' divine sonship is the key neuralgic issue between believers and Jewish opposition, in 1 John the claim that Jesus is Son of God is advanced against those Christians whom the author accuses of serious declension from true faith, and who seem to have christological views at serious variance with what the author represents as the tradition "from the beginning (1:1-4). In subsequent Christian tradition, clearly the Johannine emphasis was influential, and "Son of God" came to represent essentially a confession of Jesus' own divinity.

Lord (kyrios) is the other christological title with very widespread usage in the NT. The term is most frequently applied to Jesus, and considerably less often to God. In Paul, e.g., approximately 180 of his 200 uses of kyrios refer to Jesus. Indeed, Paul's most frequent use of the term (approximately 100 instances) is in the expression "the Lord" (ὁ κύριος ho kyrios) as a self-standing designation for Jesus, without any other name or title (e.g., Rom 14:6, 8; 16:2, 8, 11, 12, 13; 1 Cor 3:5; 4:4-5). Clearly, *the Lord* was by itself an early Christian way of referring to Jesus. Indeed, the Greek expression appears to have had a prior equivalent in מָרֵא mare', used in Aramaic-speaking Jewish-Christian circles as a title for Jesus (a usage reflected in **marana tha** in 1 Cor 16:22). Other NT writings confirm that *Lord* quickly became a favorite christological title (e.g., Jas 1:1; 2:1; 1 Pet 1:3; Jude 4, 21).

In Matthew, Mark, and John, other than the numerous instances where the word is used in respectful address or appeal, kyrios only rarely appears to be used with the more significant confessional connotation (e.g., Matt 21:3; 22:43-45; Mark 12:36-37; 16:19-20 [in the "long ending" commonly regarded a scribal addition]; John 20:2, 13-18, 20, 25, 28; 21:7, 12). This pattern suggests that these evangelists generally avoided reading back into their accounts of Jesus' ministry the confessional language of early Christian faith. Luke, however, refers to Jesus as *the Lord* much more frequently in his account of his ministry (2:11; 7:13, 19; 10:1, 39, 41; 11:39; 17:6; 18:6; 19:8; 22:61; plus references to the risen Jesus, 24:3, 24), and thereby further attests the use of this expression as a christological formula in early Christianity.

In wider contemporary usage, kyrios could connote simply "master" (e.g., for the master of a slave), or more broadly a respectful stance toward a social superior, as a term of polite address (e.g., Matt 27:63). Likely, therefore, in at least the overwhelming number of instances in the Gospels where people address Jesus with the term (usually his followers or those seeking from him some favor) it should be understood as "Sir" (e.g., Matt 8:2, 25; 14:28; 15:22; Mark 7:28). This respectful stance is, of course, reflected in all early Christian uses of the term for Jesus; but the NT usages also witness far more profound connotations.

In illustration of this, Jesus is often referred to as *Lord* in contexts where Christian are exhorted to exhibit right behavior (e.g., 1 Thess 4:1-12; Rom 14:1-12; 16:2-20; 1 Cor 6:13–7:40). In these and the many other NT instances of usage in such contexts, the thrust of referring to Jesus as *Lord* seems to emphasize Christian behavior that is obedient to Jesus as master; his example and teachings presented as fully authoritative for them.

In NT eschatological contexts as well, Jesus is characteristically referred to as *Lord* (e.g., 1 Thess 2:19; 3:13; 4:15-17; 5:2, 23; 1 Cor 1:7-8; 4:1-5; Jas 5:7-8; Jude 14, 21). This usage likely reflects the remarkable early Christian appropriation of the OT notion of a future "day of the Lord" to refer to the eschatological return of Jesus (e.g., 1 Thess 5:2; 2 Thess 2:2; 2 Cor 1:14; 2 Pet 3:10). In these contexts as well, references to Jesus as "Lord" probably connoted much more than "master." It seems, in fact, that Jesus was ascribed the eschatological role and attributes of Yahweh. Jesus' future appearance was seen as involving judgment of all and divine triumph over all evil. This close link of Jesus with God in eschatological hopes has limited parallels in some ancient Jewish references to various agents of God (e.g., the "Elect One" in *1 En.* 37–71). But the centrality of Jesus in NT eschatological hopes is much greater, more intense, and more consistent than in any of these putative parallels.

This is rather strongly confirmed in Phil 2:9-11, which portrays God as having given to Jesus "the name above every name," with the intention that all levels of creation should acclaim Jesus as "Lord." This universal acclamation will express the recognition that Jesus has been given, and been made to share, the divine name itself, kyrios here being its Greek equivalent.

Perhaps the most significant passages where Jesus is referred to as *Lord*, however, reflect liturgical settings and actions. We noted earlier the confessional use of kyrios in acclamations set in the context of gathered worship (e.g., Rom 10:9-13; 1 Cor 12:3). The sonorous references to Jesus in Paul's letter openings and closings ("the/our *Lord* Jesus Christ," "Christ Jesus our *Lord*") are commonly thought to be intended to reflect and affirm the parlance of early Christian worship, the setting in which his letters were intended to be read aloud. Paul refers to the sacred common meal of the Christian gathering as "the Lord's supper" (κυριακòν δεîπνον kyriakon deipnon, 1 Cor 11:20) and "the table of the Lord" (1 Cor 10:21), the latter expression clearly connoting a meal with a strong worship significance, this meal directly contrasted and compared with the cult meals associated with pagan deities (*see* EUCHARIST; LORD'S SUPPER; MEALS; TABLE FELLOWSHIP). In all these references, it is obvious that the *Lord* is the risen and glorified Jesus, and there is a clear transcendent connotation to the title in these instances. It is fundamental in linguistics that usage-context is crucial for the specific meaning of words. The application of *Lord* to Jesus in the context of gathered worship is remarkable, with no direct precedent or analogy in contemporary Jewish religious practices, and surely connotes the highest significance of the term as a christological title.

Among other christological titles, perhaps "the Word," uniquely in John 1:1-14, is most familiar, and has received the largest amount of scholarly attention (compare "the Word of God," Rev 19:13). Scholars frequently explore possible relationships to Greek philosophical notions of a divine Logos (here = "reason") that pervades the cosmos and gives it an orderly operation. In PHILO OF ALEXANDRIA's writings we have another interesting adaptation of the term that seems to have been influenced by Platonic tradition, Philo's *Logos* portrayed as the presence and activity of God in/toward the creation. For Philo, however, the Logos is not really a separate being but instead represents that of God, which is perceptible by humans in particular; God himself remaining ultimately transcendent and beyond human comprehension.

The resemblances of Greek philosophy or Philo to the Logos in John, however, are few and dim at best. More typically in recent scholarship, references to personified Wisdom in OT and deuterocanonical texts are thought to be relevant (Prov 8:22-36; Wis 7:7–8:8; Sir 24; Bar 3:9–4:4; see WISDOM IN THE OT). This

Wisdom (personified as female) is portrayed as a throne-companion of God and his associate in creation of the cosmos (Prov 8:22-31; Wis 8:4-6).

In these Wisdom references we certainly have somewhat closer echoes and also a more readily available body of tradition that could have been drawn upon in John 1:1-14. For instance, note the role of the Johannine Logos in creation of the world (1:3, 10), similar to Wisdom's link to creation. Yet, whatever the relevant background of the Johannine passage, it is clear that the christological use of Logos here represents not simply the appropriation of a term or motifs but also a significant new development (see WISDOM IN THE NT).

In John we are not dealing with a conceptual category that functions to solve philosophical questions about the order of the cosmos or how God can remain transcendent while really being manifested in history. Instead, the Johannine Logos expresses far-reaching christological claims, and the use of the term is thoroughly colored and shaped by the historical figure of Jesus. It is clear, for instance, that the Logos of John 1:1-14 designates the "pre-incarnate" Son of God, the Jesus of the ensuing narrative. At several other points in John, Jesus himself is portrayed as referring to his prior heavenly status (esp. 17:5). Moreover, 1:14-17 directly claims that the Logos "became flesh" (v. 14) and is thereafter known in/as "Jesus Christ" (v. 17). So, it appears that the Johannine use of "the Logos" (unique to 1:1-14) reflects an emphasis on Jesus' significance as the uniquely full and authoritative revealer of God (esp. 1:17-18). In short, the Johannine Logos is uniquely a real person known in historical time and action, Jesus, the Son of God.

There are also a number of other christological titles or epithets less frequently found in the NT but likely of early vintage. John 1:29, 36, pictures John the Baptist acclaiming Jesus as "the LAMB [ἀμνός amnos] of God," and note 1 Pet 1:19, where Jesus' death is likened to that of "a lamb [amnos] without blemish or spot." In Revelation, of course, there are a number of references to Jesus as "the Lamb" (consistently ἀρνίον arnion, however, this term is used only in Revelation; e.g., 5:6-13; 6:1, 16; 7:9-10, 14, 17; 19:7, 9; 21:9, 14, 22-23; 22:1, 3). The lamb of Revelation was slain (5:6), and his blood is efficacious for his followers (12:11); and yet he also is a horned lamb (13:11) and triumphs over the forces of evil (17:14). Neither in Revelation nor elsewhere in the NT do we find a sentimentalization of suffering for its own sake!

A christological title used in the NT only a few times in Acts is παῖς pais ("child" or "servant"; Acts 3:13, 26; 4:27, 30). The term is also applied to Israel (e.g., Luke 1:54) and David (e.g., Luke 1:69; Acts 4:25), reflecting its frequent use in LXX Isaiah, where God's "servant," often Jacob/Israel (e.g., Isa 41:8-9; 44:1-2, 21; 45:4; 49:3) and other times unspecified, plays a major role as God's chosen instrument (42:1; 19:49:5-6;

52:13; 53:11). So, the christological appropriation of pais reflects the view that Jesus is now the chosen servant, the heir of David and the messianic figure who bears Israel's hope and destiny.

But the pattern of NT uses of pais also suggests that although it featured in early Jewish-Christian discourse, the term did not enjoy much favor in other and subsequent Christian circles. Servant apparently was not deemed a meaningful or sufficiently reverential way of referring to Jesus. Beyond the few uses in Acts, pais appears only a few more times and solely in texts that seem to preserve early liturgical usage (e.g., Did. 9:2-3; 10:2-3; 1 Clem. 59:2-4).

In 1 John 2:1, Jesus is the heavenly "advocate" or "paraclete" (παράκλητος paraklētos), and this view is likely implied also in the John 14:16 reference to the Spirit as "another advocate." Jesus' role as heavenly intercessor is also mentioned in Rom 8:34. But, of course, Hebrews develops this notion programmatically, and designates Jesus famously as the "high priest" able to act with true and final efficacy in securing redemption (e.g., Heb 2:17; 4:14-16), his own death being the sacrifice that brings genuine cleansing from sins (e.g., Heb 9:11-14, 23-28).

Hebrews (2:10; 12:2) also refers to Jesus as "pioneer/leader" (ἀρχηγός archēgos), and the same title appears in Acts 3:15; 5:31, emphasizing Jesus' role on behalf of the elect. In this last passage we also have one of a larger number of instances where Jesus is called "Savior" (e.g., Acts 13:23; Eph 5:23; Phil 3:20; 2 Tim 1:10; Titus 1:4; 3:6; 2 Pet 1:11; 2:20; 3:18), a title elsewhere in the NT applied to God (e.g., Luke 1:47; 1 Tim 1:1; 2:3; 4:10; Titus 1:3; 2:10; Jude 25). The Greek term, σωτήρ sōtēr, appears in the LXX (e.g., Ps 23:5 [Heb. 24:5]; Isa 12:2), where it translates forms of the Hebrew verb יֹשׁע ysh‘ ("to save") (see SALVATION). As Matt 1:21 indicates, at least some 1st cent. Christians were aware that the Hebrew and Aramaic forms of the name Jesus were likewise cognates of this verb. Of course, savior was also an epithet applied to various deities, and in various ruler-cults in Hellenistic and Roman periods. So, there were various resonances available for this title far wider than the somewhat sentimental connotation in modern popular piety.

It was once widely thought that Son of Man was another important christological title, and one still sees a certain residual fondness for this view among some scholars. In some earlier opinion, among ancient Jews there was a supposedly widely shared expectation of a figure bearing this title, an eschatological figure to come from heaven. Daniel 7:13-14 is the key biblical text, but the references to "the Elect One" in 1 Enoch were also deemed crucial (see CHOSEN). According to this view, "the Son of Man" was perhaps the earliest christological affirmation, the risen Jesus seen as the heavenly redeemer expected to come in glory. But for some time now it has been clear that there simply is no evidence that "the Son of Man" was ever actually a title for any such figure in Jewish expectation (*see* SON OF MAN). To be sure, the humanlike figure of Dan 7:13-14 did feature in some eschatological schemes, and the Elect One of *1 Enoch* may reflect an influence from the Daniel passage (along with passages in Isaiah). But neither 1 Enoch nor any other Jewish text uses "the Son of Man" as a fixed title. In Hebrew (**ben ʾadham**) and Aramaic (**bar ʾenosh**), "[a] son of man" is simply a way of referring to a human being, and in the OT the singular and plural forms appear often with this sense (e.g., Ps 8:5).

"The Son of Man" appears more than eighty times in the Gospels, solely in these NT texts, and only on Jesus' lips. It is never part of a confessional statement by Jesus' followers, and it is never the issue in disputations about Jesus' significance (compare, e.g., the confessional function of "Christ" in Mark 1:1, and the controversial setting in 14:61). Moreover, in every instance where Jesus uses the term (even, e.g., in Mark 14:62) one can readily substitute "I" or "me" without difficulty in the sense of the statement.

In short, the fixed use of the definite article ("*the* Son of Man") is unique to the Gospels, and carries a strong particularizing force. Indeed, this definite-singular expression appears to be a novel form, and may well derive from an equivalent Aramaic expression (**bar ʾenasha**, not found in Aramaic texts of the time) that was used by Jesus as his favored self-designation. That is, the uses of "the Son of Man" in the Gospels likely reflect a distinctive feature of Jesus' own speech that was retained out of reverence for him. But the expression did not apparently figure in early Christian confession, and certainly does not represent some supposedly early "Son of Man Christology."

In a very few cases in the NT, the term θεός *theos* ("god/God") is applied to Jesus. The unambiguous instances are in John 1:1 and 20:28. In a few other places (Rom 9:5; Titus 2:13; 2 Pet 1:1) it is more difficult to be sure whether the term is applied to Jesus or designates God (the Father). In the overwhelming number of instances, however, **theos** refers to God, whereas Jesus is more typically referred to as the **kyrios** (e.g., 1 Cor 8:5-6). Even in John, it is clear that Jesus' own divine status is linked with "the Father," and that Jesus is portrayed as subservient to the Father's will (e.g., 5:19-24). Clearly, when applied to Jesus in the NT, **theos** obviously connotes the highest type of claim about Jesus, and yet his status seems never intended to rival or eclipse the one God of biblical tradition. Moreover, the two applications of the term to Jesus in John may well reflect the strongly polemical setting and character of this text, which responds to Jewish charges that Jesus is unworthy of the sort of devotion advocated by Johannine Christians.

Understandably, christological titles have been the focus of much scholarly discussion, for they are certainly direct indicators of beliefs and claims about Jesus.

But, contrary to some, we should not assume that the titles represent discrete "Christologies," or can be played off against one another. Characteristically in the NT, one finds a number of these titles deployed, which surely indicates that they functioned as overlapping and complementary doxological statements.

4. The Gospels as "Jesus Books"

Our familiarity with the NT Gospels should not obscure their historical significance in early Christian literary history, and their particular importance as textual expressions of devotion to Jesus in 1st cent. Christianity (*see* FORM CRITICISM, NT; GOSPEL, MESSAGE). Although it is now increasingly accepted that the Gospels should be seen in the wider context of Roman-era biographical-type writings, they remain notable texts individually and collectively, comprising a distinctive Christian sub-genre. We note here how in all four of them Jesus is the authoritative voice and example, and the uniquely valid vehicle of divine purposes. By contrast, in Jewish tradition there are collections of sayings of revered teachers, from Proverbs on through the rabbinic tractate, *Pirke Aboth*. But the Gospels are powerful literary artifacts of the early Christian view of Jesus' supreme significance as the supremely authoritative figure. The extra-canonical Gospels largely confirm this centrality of Jesus (e.g., *Gospel of Thomas*, *Gospel of Philip*, *Gospel of Truth*), even if they also reflect varying versions of early Christian faith.

The Gospel of Mark is a stirring narrative that runs from Jesus' baptism by John the Baptist on through call of followers, ministry, conflict, arraignment before Jewish and Roman authorities, martyrdom, and resurrection (*see* MARTYR; RESURRECTION). In this fast-paced account, Jesus is fully authoritative in teaching and actions, which include healings, exorcisms, and even power over nature, and he is also the sole unflawed exemplar for readers (over against the shortcomings and failures of disciples). The demoniacs are the sole earthly voices that recognize Jesus' transcendent significance (e.g., 1:24, 34; 3:11; *see* DEMON; DEMONIAC), echoing God's own affirmation of his divine sonship (1:11; 9:7) over against the limited understanding of him by disciples (e.g., 4:41; 6:52; 8:14-21, 33) and the false charges of opponents (e.g., 2:7; 3:22; 14:64). The puzzlement of Jesus' followers only functions to signal for readers the higher truth of Jesus' person (e.g., 4:41; 6:52).

Moreover, the general contours of the story line of Jesus prefigure the Christian life presupposed and urged in Mark, from baptism through mission, opposition, the threat of martyrdom (e.g., 8:34-38), and eschatological vindication. If, as many scholars think, the opening words are the title of the work (1:1), this story of Jesus is the ἀρχή *archē* ("beginning/origin," "first cause") of the gospel, which is then to be preached among all nations (13:10).

The Gospels of Matthew and Luke are commonly regarded by scholars as inspired and shaped by Mark, and each can be viewed as essentially a major expansion and adaptation of a recognizably Markan narrative. This is particularly evident in Matthew, which incorporates some 90 percent of Mark. Both in Matthew and Luke the major expansions are birth narratives, resurrection-appearance narratives (*see* PASSION NARRATIVES), and a large body of sayings that is widely thought to derive from a sayings collection referred to by scholars as the "Q" source (*see* Q, QUELLE). These expansions were likely intended to provide enriched accounts of Jesus that among other concerns addressed a desire to present more of Jesus' teaching. In addition, of course, each evangelist inscribes his own emphases, and exhibits a certain authorial power in selecting, ordering, and altering material that appears largely to have been taken from a larger body of Jesus-tradition of 1st cent. provenance.

Especially since the 1960s, scholars have tended to focus on the particularities of each rendition of the Jesus-story. From his genealogy onward, Matthew, for instance, emphasizes Jesus' Jewish place in the history of Israel, Jesus' fulfillment of OT prophecy, and his royal messianic significance in particular. But the distinctives of each Gospel make it all the more significant that they also exhibit a great deal of commonality, attesting a wide appreciation for a broadly similar view of Jesus among the varying readerships for which the authors wrote.

All four canonical Gospels present similar core parameters of Jesus' activities, from baptism by John the Baptist through ministry, death, and resurrection, with a disproportionate space given to the passion and resurrection events. All four set Jesus firmly in Roman-era geography of Palestine, customs, and people, reflecting a strong concern to tie Christian faith to a real historic figure (*see* JESUS, HISTORICAL; compare, e.g., the near-timelessness of the *Gospel of Thomas*). Most obviously, and most significantly, in all four Jesus is absolutely central, the polarizing figure, the response to whom reflects one's true stance toward God's kingdom and purposes. Moreover, they all present Jesus as the Christ, God's Son, the one prophesied in the OT, the unique personal vehicle of eschatological salvation.

For all its striking distinctives, the Gospel of John fits this pattern too, a judgment reflected also in the early Christian popularity of this account and its incorporation into the NT canon. Indeed, John was probably the most influential NT writing in the development of classical christological beliefs across the first several centuries, and is rightly regarded as one of the most important christological texts in the NT. With the well-known prologue referring to the divine Word, its repeated emphasis on Jesus' heavenly origins and his uniquely direct relationship to "the Father," and the presentation of Jesus as the human embodiment of God's "glory" and "name," John explicitly presents a very high Christology. The Jesus of John's Gospel himself articulates his high status (e.g., 4:26; 5:20-29; 6:35-40; 8:56; 17:1-5), and the Johannine "voice" is notably distinctive in comparison with the Synoptics. In the references to the post-resurrection teaching activity of the Paraclete, who will glorify Jesus and lead believers into all truth about him (e.g., 14:25-26; 15:26; 16:25), we probably have the author's indication of the basis and nature of this distinctive Jesus-book. Yet John, too, firmly locates the manifestation of divine glory in the historic figure of Jesus, the narrative form of the book directly indicating the centrality of Jesus' activities and his death and resurrection.

5. Devotional practices

We have already noted the significance of hymns and the place of Jesus in early Christian worship (*see* WORSHIP, NT CHRISTIAN). In addition, there are other expressions of Jesus' centrality in the pattern of early Christian devotion. These include the ritual invocation of Jesus, for which the NT appropriates the OT expression to "call upon the name of the Lord" (e.g., Acts 2:21; Rom 10:13). This action was apparently a regular feature of BAPTISM but was also characteristic of the worship gathering generally. Indeed, Paul can refer to Christians simply as "all those who in every place call upon the name of our Lord Jesus Christ" (1 Cor 1:2). The use of Jesus' name in EXORCISM and HEALING further attests the belief in his continuing efficacy as the dispenser of divine power (e.g., Acts 3:6, 16; *see also* MIRACLES).

The designation of the common meal of Christian gatherings as "the Lord's supper," noted above, further reflects Jesus' position as the divine figure with whom believers gather in the worship setting, the risen Jesus seen as the marker and identifying presence in the Christian fellowship (*see* EUCHARIST; LORD'S SUPPER). The typical pattern of prayers to God in the NT *through Jesus* and in his name, which is already conventional in Paul's letters (e.g., Rom 1:8; and *see* John 14:13; 16:26-27) has no analogy in Jewish or pagan prayer practice, and surely further confirms Jesus' importance in the religious life of believers. In all these phenomena, we see a "binitarian" devotional pattern, in which Jesus is uniquely linked with God, not as a second or subordinate deity, and not at all at the expense of God in belief and devotion, but as the one who reflects and shares in God's glory (e.g., 2 Cor 3:18–4:4). Although often not included in discussions of NT Christology, these elements of the devotional practice reflected in the NT are important expressions of beliefs about Jesus, beliefs expressed in religious behavior.

B. Key Emphases

It is impossible to do justice here to the richness

and depth of christological emphases in the NT; so we must focus on selected key themes, which are grouped under two main headings: Jesus and God, and Jesus and God's purposes.

1. Jesus and God

As illustrated in the various christological titles already considered, in the NT Jesus' exalted status and significance is defined rather consistently with reference to God. Jesus is, e.g., the Word, the Son, the Lamb, or the Servant, of God. All of these expressions place Jesus in a unique and intimate relationship with God, and also in varying ways represent Jesus as the unique agent of divine purposes. In many cases Jesus' role as the agent of God is explicit, as in Paul's references to God having sent forth his Son (Gal 4:4-5; Rom 8:3-4). Likewise, in John Jesus speaks of himself explicitly (and distinctively) in such a manner (e.g., John 3:17; 5:36-37; 10:36; 17:8, 18), indicating both his own divine significance and yet also his complete subservience to God's will for him.

Indeed, in John and elsewhere in the NT even the most exalted expressions of Jesus' status involve associating him with God, as, e.g., in Paul's reference to "the glory of Christ, who is the image (εἰκών eikōn "icon") of God" (2 Cor 4:4), the glory of God revealed in "the face of Christ" (v. 6). We have similar statements in Col 1:15-20, where again Christ is "the image of the invisible God" (v. 15), and also in Heb 1:3, with its reference to the Son as being "the reflection of God's glory and the exact imprint of God's very being."

New Testament references to Jesus' redemptive work also typically link him with God. For example, God put forth Christ as redemptive through his death (Rom 3:24-26), God thereby demonstrating his righteousness and also his readiness to justify all who put faith in Jesus. In Christ Jesus, God has succeeded where the Law could not, sending his Son to deal with sin (Rom 8:3-4); and it is God who gave up his Son (to death) for the sake of the redeemed (Rom 8:32). Certainly, Jesus' own loving volition can also be referred to as central (e.g., Gal 2:20), but behind and beneath all that he did was God's own redemptive purpose and initiative.

Jesus' resurrection and resultant exaltation likewise are typically referred to as acts of God, as in Rom 4:24-25, where both Jesus' being handed over to death and his resurrection are ascribed to God. In his extended treatment of Jesus' resurrection in 1 Cor 15, Paul explicitly attributes it to God (v. 15), and this emphasis is further reflected in the many references to Jesus as "raised" (passive tense; e.g., 15:4, 12, 14, 17, 20). Moreover, Jesus' enthroned status over all things is by God's own action (1 Cor 15:27; Phil 2:9-11).

We noted earlier also how in NT praise and prayer Jesus is linked with God. So, e.g., in Rev 5:9-10, the heavenly court praises the Lamb for redeeming the elect for God, and then in vv. 12-14 the crescendo of worship is directed to God and the Lamb jointly. This sort of close linkage of Jesus and God in belief and devotional practice is likely the key factor that drove and demanded the subsequent doctrinal reflection that resulted in the distinctive Christian view of God as TRINITY.

In short, the linkage of Jesus with God not only defines Jesus; Jesus, in effect, redefines God, who is now "the God and Father of our Lord Jesus Christ" (e.g., 1 Pet 1:3; Rev 1:6). Because God's purposes are more fully and finally disclosed and achieved in Jesus, he effectively gives to Christian faith a significantly new perspective on God. Although (contra, e.g., Marcion, the 2nd cent. Christian teacher who rejected the OT and its deity) the God invoked in the NT is the God of Abraham, Isaac, and Jacob, in Jesus this God is also newly and distinctively revealed.

2. Jesus and God's purposes

The NT also links Jesus with virtually every purpose and main activity of God. For example, as noted already, at a very early point we have reference to the pre-existent Jesus as the agent of creation (esp. 1 Cor 8:6; and later references in Col 1:16; Heb 1:2; John 1:3). In these references, we see a firm belief that creation and redemption are profoundly linked. Although he came "in these last days" (Heb 1:2), Jesus embodies divine redemptive purposes that were formed from the beginning of creation. This means that in the NT it is not sin that sets the agenda, God responding to it; instead, God's prior intent to redeem precedes and supervenes all else (Rom 8:28-30; 1 Pet 1:20-21).

Hence, the NT notion that Jesus is predicted in the OT is not simply an instance of a quaint ancient approach toward Scripture (e.g., Luke 24:25-27, 45-47; 1 Pet 1:10-12). On a more profound level, this strong link of Jesus with the Scriptures of Israel reflects a strong conviction about the unity and coherence of divine purposes. In Jesus, God's promise to Abraham finds deepest fulfillment (Rom 15:8-9; Gal 3:16), and through Jesus all nations now are enfranchised into God's family (e.g., Gal 3:23-29). In all this, just as Jesus redefines God, so he effectively redefines the elect, who are no longer restricted to those to whom the Law has been revealed but are now all those who embrace the invitation to put faith in Jesus. Through Jesus, the unique divine Son, God now calls to adoption "many sons" who are to be formed after Christ's image (Rom 8:29). For their part, all those who trust in Christ the divine Son are entitled now also to call upon God as "Abba, Father" (Rom 8:15-17; Gal 4:4-6; see ABBA).

The Law, God's former revelation, is now seen as provisional and superseded by Christ as the manifestation of God's purposes (Gal 3:15-22). For in Jesus God has now effectively dealt with human ignorance of the Law or inability to live faithfully by it (Rom 8:3-5). As

Hebrews in particular emphasizes, the OT priesthood, sanctuary, and sacrificial rituals that formed key features of the OT approach and relationship to God are now shown to be anticipations of the ultimate priesthood and sacrifice of Jesus (Heb 3–9). Paul emphasizes that, as wide as death in Adam's descendants, so widely available is the free gift of life in Jesus (Rom 5:12-21). As death came through Adam, so now resurrection and eternal life comes through Christ (1 Cor 15:20-22). The story of Jesus is tied firmly to the OT story, and Jesus is presented as the *telos* of it all (e.g., Rom 10:4), both consummating and transcending it (*see* SECOND ADAM).

Furthermore, Jesus is also central in the NT representations of God's future purposes and actions. His resurrection is the pattern and guarantee for the resurrection of the elect (1 Cor 15:20-23, 42-49). Although believers must await their own eschatological transformation, it is enough for the present to know that they will be made like the risen Christ (e.g., 1 John 3:1-3), who at his coming again from heaven will transform believers' mortal bodies to be conformed to "the body of his glory" (Phil 3:20-21). Thus, the risen Jesus himself exemplifies and defines the embodied salvation that the elect are individually to receive.

The NT eschatological hope is explicitly fixed on Jesus' PAROUSIA, and his glorious appearance is "the day of the Lord" (1 Thess 5:1-11), the OT expression for God's decisive act appropriated to designate Jesus' return (*see* ESCHATOLOGY; SECOND COMING). It is not too much to say that in the NT all eschatological hope is linked to this event. He is the one who will return from heaven to rescue his own from "the wrath that is coming" (1 Thess 1:10). Acting with divine authority, he will send forth the angels to "gather his elect" worldwide (Mark 13:27), and at his voice the dead will rise, for God has given him resurrection power and authority to execute eschatological judgment (John 5:25-29). In all these remarkable ways, Jesus is pictured as participating directly in God's eschatological purposes, fulfilling divine expectations and roles.

In the life of faith, Jesus is not only the authoritative teacher and Lord but also the pattern. In the Gospels, he is exemplary for believers in his coming to serve and not be served (Mark 10:41-45). For Paul, likewise, Jesus is exemplary (Rom 15:7-9), especially in his readiness to humble himself in obedience to God (Phil 2:1-11). Paul makes Jesus' crucifixion and resurrection powerful events with which believers are to link themselves and be radically transformed from bondage to sin to freedom for righteousness and service (Rom 6:1-14).

It fell to Christianity of the next few centuries after the NT to wrestle intellectually with the problems of how to affirm conscientiously one God while also taking fully seriously the NT emphasis on Jesus' own divine significance. Likewise, Christians struggled with doing justice to Jesus' divine significance and the reality of his participation in human nature. In short, the richness of the NT treatment of Jesus demanded and helped to shape theological and christological debates of the first five centuries.

But the greater consistency in the NT presentation of Jesus with reference to God and God's purposes has not always been preserved well in some ancient and modern popular Christian piety, in which often Jesus effectively displaced God. Likewise, liberalizing versions of Christianity have often found it difficult to do justice to the exalted status of Jesus everywhere assumed and affirmed in the NT. It is not too much to contend that the seriousness with which Christian piety and theology continue to engage questions about Jesus in light of the NT will remain a crucial indicator of their religious integrity.

Bibliography: Richard Bauckham. *God Crucified: Monotheism and Christology in the New Testament* (1998); Maurice Casey. *From Jewish Prophet to Gentile God: The Origins and Development of New Testament Christology* (1991); J. D. G. Dunn. *Christology in the Making.* 2nd ed. (1996); Paula Fredriksen. *From Jesus to Christ* (1988); Martin Hengel. *The Son of God: The Origin of Christology and the History of Jewish–Hellenistic Religion* (1976); Martin Hengel. *Studies in Early Christology* (1995); Arland J. Hultgren. *Christ and His Benefits: Christology and Redemption in the New Testament* (1987); Larry W. Hurtado. *Lord Jesus Christ: Devotion to Jesus in Earliest Christianity* (2003); Marinus de Jonge. *Christology in Context: The Earliest Christian Response to Jesus* (1988); Frank J. Matera *New Testament Christology* (1999); Petr Pokorný. *The Genesis of Christology: Foundations for a Theology of the New Testament* (1987); Earl Richard. *Jesus: One and Many, the Christological Concept of New Testament Authors* (1988).

LARRY HURTADO

CHRONICLES, FIRST AND SECOND BOOKS OF. Chronicles begins with the first human (1 Chr 1:1), depicts the totality of Israel in genealogical form (1 Chr 1–9), upholds the united monarchy of David and Solomon as an unprecedented era of harmony, success, and national solidarity (1 Chr 10–2 Chr 9), recounts the history of the Judahite monarchy as an uneven period, a time of both success and failure (2 Chr 10–36), and concludes with the welcome news of Cyrus the Great's decree ending the Babylonian exile. In relating this long story of triumphs, temptations, and troubles, the author stresses the constancy, faithfulness, and mercy of God. Israel's fortunes may change from age to age, but the God Israel worships remains very much involved in the life of God's people.

A. What's in a Name?

The division of the work into two books (1–2 Chronicles) is not original. The book is one unit in the Hebrew. Like many other biblical books, Chronicles was originally anonymous and untitled. The most typical name ascribed to the work by the early rabbis, "the book of the events of the days," indicates that these interpreters viewed Chronicles as a book about past events—a kind of historical narrative. The other less common rabbinic name attributed to the work, "the book of genealogies," calls attention to one of the most (in)famous features of the book—the fact that it begins with nine chapters of lineages. The name of Chronicles in the LXX, *Paralipomena*, "the things left out," testifies to another early understanding of the work. Chronicles records the events left out of earlier biblical history. There are many incidents, lists, and stories in this literary work about Temple appointments, the priests, the Levites, and the Judahite monarchy that are lacking in Samuel–Kings. Saint Jerome described the book as a "chronicle," a summary of divine history. In so doing, this church father called attention both to the close involvement of the divine in the Chronicler's portrayal of ancient times and to the author's penchant for formulating condensed treatments of particular eras in Israelite history. Even though St. Jerome's nomenclature for the work has proved to be the most influential in the history of modern English interpretation, each of the other names attributed to the work also contain important insights into the book's character.

B. Relationship to Ezra–Nehemiah: The Extent of the Chronicler's History

When some scholars refer to the Chronicler's work or to the Chronicler's History, they mean the story beginning with Chronicles and ending with Ezra–Nehemiah. This older theory has come under attack in recent decades, but it is still useful to explore, however briefly, the rationale for the traditional view. The book of Chronicles ends with Cyrus's decree allowing the exiled Jews to return to Jerusalem to rebuild the Temple. The books of Ezra–Nehemiah begins with same decree, so proponents of the theory have assumed that these book form part of a greater whole, a unity that is best explained as the work of one author or editor. In promoting the theory of common authorship for Chronicles and Ezra–Nehemiah, scholars have also mentioned similar interests in genealogies, lists, the primacy of Jerusalem, the Temple, sacrifice, and the relations between priests and Levites. Seen from this perspective, the Chronicler's History covers an enormous time span, beginning with the first person (Adam) and ending with the second term of Nehemiah's governorship (Neh 13:31). In this respect, the Chronicler's History forms a long literary work that both parallels and goes beyond the scope of the earlier Primary History (Genesis through 2 Kings) that extends from the life of the first human couple (Adam and Eve) to the Babylonian exile in the early 6th cent. BCE.

At the end of the 20th cent. the consensus about authorship came undone. Many scholars, led by Japhet and Williamson, distinguish between the Chronicler's work, understood simply as the book of Chronicles, and the book of Ezra–Nehemiah, understood as the work of a different author. Seen from this perspective, the Chronicler's History begins with the first person (Adam) and ends with the Babylonian exile and Cyrus's summons to the exiled Jews to return home (2 Chr 36:21-23). In spite of the growing popularity of the theory of separate authorship, some (e.g., Blenkinsopp) have trenchantly defended common authorship. Others (e.g., Ackroyd, Eskenazi) recognize evidence for authorial diversity in Chronicles–Ezra–Nehemiah but prefer to speak of a Chronistic school, rather than to formulate a precise editorial history.

The debate about authorship has involved at least six major issues. First, scholars debate whether the LXX book of 1 ESDRAS, which begins with Josiah's reign, continues with the return, and ends with the Feast of Tabernacles (*see also* Neh 8), bears witness to an original unity between Chronicles, Ezra, and Nehemiah or represents a secondary adaptation of the same. Second, commentators disagree whether the style and characteristic language of Chronicles and Ezra–Nehemiah are similar or different. Third, some commentators view the doublet in 2 Chr 36:22-23 and Ezra 1:1-3*a* (the decree of Cyrus) as evidence for common authorship, while others view it as a secondary seam, artificially linking the two books. Fourth, some commentators think that Chronicles betrays a fundamentally different, more conciliatory, more ambitious, and more open ideology from the more restricted and limited perspective of Ezra–Nehemiah.

Fifth, some scholars discern different compositional techniques in Ezra–Nehemiah from those evident in

Chronicles. The authors of Ezra and Nehemiah call attention to sources, such as royal decrees and letters, while the author of Chronicles more closely integrates his sources into his narrative. Sixth, the organization of Ezra–Nehemiah evinces a consistent typology: project, external opposition, and eventual success, but this dialectical view of history in which one problem (rebuilding Jerusalem's Temple) after another (rebuilding Jerusalem's walls) is engaged and surmounted is said to be uncharacteristic of Chronicles. To be sure, the people of Israel are faced with substantial challenges in the story told by Chronicles, but some of those challenges result from the people's own failures and shortcomings. Judah's leadership can be Judah's own worst enemy in Chronicles (e.g., Ahaz; 2 Chr 28:1-27), but that is not the case in Ezra–Nehemiah. There, the community leaders (e.g., Zerubbabel, Jeshua, Ezra, Nehemiah) are portrayed almost entirely in positive terms and each helps the community meet the challenges of its own time.

The debate on these six issues has tilted in favor of the separate authorship theory. To be sure, there is a growing consensus that the style and characteristic language of Chronicles and Ezra–Nehemiah are fairly similar. But while a few of the differences between the theology of Chronicles and Ezra–Nehemiah may have been overstated, most agree that substantial contrasts exist between the two works and that these contrasts cannot be reduced to the different subject matters of the two books (the pre-exilic monarchy as opposed to the post-exilic province of Yehud). One work stresses the accomplishments of the Davidic monarchy and scarcely gives any attention to any non-Davidic period (e.g., the reign of Saul in 1 Chr 10:1-14) in its narrative coverage, while the other work commemorates the accomplishments of King David, mainly in the context of national liturgy and music (e.g., Ezra 3:10; Neh 12:24).

Both works are interested in genealogy, but employ genealogies in very different ways. One work sketches a very large portrait of the fullness of Israel and its many links to other peoples, especially to the other relatives and descendants of Abraham (1 Chr 1–9). In this context, it is relevant to point out that the genealogy of Judah (1 Chr 2:3–4:23) contains the most cases of intermarriage of all of the Israelite genealogies in 1 Chr 1–9. The other work is mainly concerned to employ genealogies to demarcate those who returned from the Babylonian exile and their descendants (e.g., Ezra 2 // Neh 7). Over against these "children of the exile" stand all the "people(s) of the land" (e.g., Ezra 4:4; 6:21), including (evidently) those Judahites who were not deported in the Babylonian exile. Both Ezra and Nehemiah vigorously campaign against intermarriage (Ezra 9:1–10:44; Neh 10:31; 13:23-28). Even in those cases in which the writers of both works seem to have been working with some of the same sources (e.g.,

1 Chr 9 // Neh 11), each work has gone its own way with the materials at hand. In short, one can say that each book has its own distinctive style of organization, compositional technique, and thematic concerns.

What then of the link between two books: the decree of Cyrus (2 Chr 36:22-23; Ezra 1:1-4)? At some point in the editorial histories of the two books, an attempt was made to link the two works. This linkage was probably made prior to the 2nd cent. BCE, when 1 Esdras was translated (*see* above). In this way, a historical continuum was created stretching from the primal human (1 Chr 1:1) to much of the Persian period (Neh 13).

Given the diversity of perspectives in Chronicles, Ezra, and Nehemiah, it is not surprising that some scholars who wish to explain the links between the two works (e.g., Freedman, Cross) have advanced theories of two or more redactions in the growth of these works. These modern authors affirm connections among Chronicles, Ezra, and Nehemiah, but suggest that more than one individual is responsible for all three works. In the view of a few of these scholars, the composition of Chronicles, Ezra, and Nehemiah took place in several stages stretching from the time of the Achaemenid Empire (538–332 BCE) down into the Hellenistic period.

Is it possible to draw any conclusions from all of the disagreements among scholars over the past four decades? The new theories of authorship have had practical implications for interpretation. Scholars who hold either to separate authorship or to multiple editions no longer interpret Chronicles with primary reliance upon Ezra–Nehemiah. Because Chronicles is no longer being viewed as inseparable from Ezra–Nehemiah, its characteristic concerns are no longer being forced into the mold of the point of view of Ezra or of Nehemiah. Similarly, because Ezra–Nehemiah is no longer viewed as inseparable from Chronicles, commentators have been able to explore its unique structure, characterization, and themes. The distinction between the works of Chronicles and Ezra–Nehemiah has thus allowed scholars to formulate a variety of fresh interpretations of both works.

C. Composition, Date, and Sources

By the time the Chronicler wrote in the post-exilic period, much of the literature that we associate with the OT was already written. The author draws extensively upon much of this extensive and rich literary tradition. The writer's dependence upon Genesis, Numbers, and Joshua is evident in his genealogies (1 Chr 1–9) and his dependence upon Samuel and Kings is obvious in his narration of the monarchy (1 Chr 10–2 Chr 36). The writer's indebtedness to antecedent literature is not confined, however, to his selective reuse of these literary works. Parallels with or citations from Isaiah, Jeremiah, Zechariah, Ezekiel, the Psalms, and Ruth all appear in Chronicles. Scholars generally agree that the Chronicler also had access to extrabiblical sources, but the nature and extent of these sources are disputed.

Within the postexilic period Chronicles is very hard to date. There are no specific references, no absolute synchronisms, and no extrabiblical citations that could definitively position the book within a given decade or century. Indeed, a range of over 350 years (from the late 6th to the mid 2nd cent. BCE) has been suggested for the work. Although an absolute date cannot be assigned to the book, a date past the late 3rd cent. BCE is unlikely. First, one must allow time for Chronicles or Chronicles–Ezra–Nehemiah to be brought to Egypt and translated into at least two different works (1 Esdras and *Paralipomena*). Second, *Paralipomena* is cited by Eupolemos, a Jewish-Hellenistic writer, in the 2nd cent. BCE (Eusebius, *Praep. ev.* 9.30-34). Similarly, it seems wise not to date the book too early in the Persian period, because one has to allow for earlier biblical books, such as Samuel–Kings, to be written, edited, and established in the community. For the Chronicler to make use of these works, these works had to exist by the time he wrote his own composition. For these and other reasons, many contemporary scholars date Chronicles to the mid- to late-Persian period. The most common date attributed to the composition is the 4th cent. BCE.

D. Structure

Chronicles has three major sections: the genealogies of 1 Chr 1–9, the history of the united monarchy (1 Chr 10–2 Chronicles 9), and the history of the Judahite monarchy (2 Chr 10–36). The first section, which forms a prologue to the narrative portions of the work, introduces the people of Israel—their origins, context, land, and relationships. As one can see by the sheer length of the second section, Chronicles gives pride of place to the United Kingdom of David and Solomon, presenting this as a definitive age in the history of the Israelite people. The third section of the work chronicles and comments on over three centuries in the history of the independent Judahite monarchy. Consistent with its concentration on the ties between the people and the land, the work ends when the reduced Judahite kingdom is overthrown and exiled in the Babylonian conquests of the early 6th cent. BCE.

E. Introduction to the Israelite People: The Genealogies (1 Chr 1–9)

In the ancient world, one's identity was very much tied to one's family, relationships, place of residence, and place of origin. These all provided crucial facts as to who a person was. Writing well on in the course of his people's history, it is not too surprising, then, that the Chronicler begins his story of the Israelite people with a series of lineages. The family trees are male-dominated, because the Chronicler traced family continuity through male lines. Yet, the lineages also contain considerable details about various women. In some cases, this information is provided because a given male (e.g., Abraham in 1 Chr 1:28-33) had multiple relationships (wives and concubines) and so had various offspring through multiple partners, but in other cases this information is provided because the author recognized the accomplishments of the women involved (e.g., 1 Chr 7:24). Similarly, the fact that certain women are mentioned in their own right, in addition to male relatives (e.g., Shelomit in 1 Chr 3:19), was probably due to the stature they enjoyed either in their own time or in posterity.

The total length of the genealogies is rather imposing to modern readers, but the issue of length is itself a key to understanding the author's literary designs. The breadth and depth of the lineages show that the Chronicler wished to provide his readers with an extensive, albeit not an exhaustive, portrait of the identity of his people. Because one's identity was very much tied to where one lived and to whom one was related, the Chronicler's genealogies, like many other ancient genealogies, contain numerous anecdotes about settlements, battles, migrations, and (inter)marriages (e.g., 1 Chr 2:23, 42-46, 50-55; 4:11-12, 21-23, 28-33, 39-43; 5:8-10, 11, 16, 23-26; 6:39-66; 7:21, 24, 28-29; 8:6-8, 12-13). Such details also provide contexts for the lineages themselves, helping readers to associate names with geographical settings, places, and particular incidents.

The Chronicler's genealogies begin with the first human and provide brief lineages for other peoples to whom Israel is related (1 Chr 1:1–2:2). In this respect, one sees a universal dimension in the author's thought. One can only understand Israel by understanding the peoples to whom Israel is related. Nevertheless, the main body of his work focuses upon the identity and location of the descendants of the ancestor Jacob, who is almost always called Israel in Chronicles. The very scope and structure of the genealogical system in 1 Chr 2:2–9:1 underscores the indivisibility of his offspring. The lineages are arranged according to a broad chiastic pattern.

a The peoples of the world (1 Chr 1:1-54)
  b Judah (1 Chr 2:3–4:23)
    c Simeon and the trans-Jordanian tribes
      (1 Chr 4:24–5:26)
     d The tribe of Levi (1 Chr 5:27–6:66
      [NRSV 6:1-81])
    c´ The northern tribes (1 Chr 7:1-40)
  b´ Benjamin (1 Chr 8:1-40)
a´ The Persian period inhabitants of Jerusalem
  (1 Chr 9:2-34)

Although the focus is clearly on Israel's seed, the writer does not provide a continuous set of lineages that would cover (in genealogical form) all of Israel's descendants up to his own time. Instead, he takes Israel's sons (representing various tribes) as a starting point (1 Chr 2:1-2) and repeatedly returns to this point of origin until he has managed to provide family trees for all of the groups that he thinks constitute his people. Hence, his goal was not to be entirely exhaustive—dealing with all of the twelve or more groups throughout the course of their histories. Rather, he provides readers with a sampling, perhaps what he considers to be a representative sampling, of the lineages for each of the groups and subgroups that constitute Israel. That the text repeatedly returns to Israel (Jacob) means that the author privileges the age of matriarchs and patriarchs as definitive for the genesis of his people (compare Jdt 9:2; Tob 1:1; Jub 4:1-33; Matt 1:1-2; Rom 11:1; Phil 3:4-5; *b. Pesahim.* 62*b*; *b. Qidd.* 69*a*–79*b*). The Israelite genealogies thus exhibit a cyclical quality, even though the individual tribal lineages move forward in time and the genealogies as a whole end with a list of Persian period repatriates (1 Chr 9:2-34).

Within the larger genealogical system, Judah, Levi, and Benjamin receive the most extensive attention. The very structure of the Chronicler's genealogical system thus underscores the crucial roles played by these three tribes. Levi, Israel's priestly tribe, occupies the central position, but Judah appears first and receives more coverage than any other sodality. Normally, the eldest son of Israel would be listed first (1 Chr 2:1-2), but this privilege goes instead to Judah (1 Chr 2:3–4:23), the dominant tribe of the Chronicler's own time. Within this tribe, the lineages of David, which extend all the way to the late Persian period, take center stage (1 Chr 3:1-24).

a Lineages of Judah (1 Chr 2:1-55)
    b Descendants of David (1 Chr 3:1-24)
a´ Lineages of Judah (1 Chr 4:1-23)

Just like the history of Israel (1 Chr 10–2 Chr 36), which focuses on the Davidic monarchy, the genealogies pay special tribute to David and his offspring. If the tribe of Levi has an abiding legacy in Israelite life by virtue of the ministry of the priests and Levites, the descendants of David have an abiding legacy in Israelite life by virtue of the political leadership exercised by King David's royal line. Whereas Judah's primacy is signaled by its initial position in the tribal genealogies, Benjamin's importance is underscored by its final position and its extensive lineages (1 Chr 8:1-40; 9:35-44).

Particularly interesting, given the time in which the Chronicler wrote, is the coverage devoted to Simeon, the northern tribes, and the trans-Jordanian tribes. Did all of these tribes still exist as self-standing entities? There is considerable doubt whether this was true, although it is possible that the author knew of indi-

viduals and families who associated themselves with some of these sodalities. The author himself admits that certain tribes (e.g., 1 Chr 5:25-26) had already been in foreign exile for hundreds of years. Moreover, the territory and population of post-exilic Judah seems to form a stark contrast with the territory and population ascribed to the Israelite tribes in Chronicles. Given the circumscribed borders of the province of Judah in the late Achaemenid or early Hellenistic period, the writer could easily have mentioned only Judah, Benjamin, and Levi or restricted himself to certain groups, such as the priests, within these sodalities. Yet, he continues to hold on to a larger Israelite ideal.

If genealogies can function as charters, one recognizes that the Chronicler's charter for his people is much more ambitious than the geopolitical realities of Judah in his own time might suggest. The author combs earlier biblical lineages for material relating to the various tribes and adds his own contributions (more than half of the total) to present a comprehensive portrait of the fullness of his people. One cannot do justice to the genealogical schema without recognizing that the author both adheres to an all-Israel ideal and maintains that certain tribes have played major roles in Israel's development. For the writer, the people's unity is a past, present, and future reality. In this context, it is no accident that the genealogy of the return (1 Chr 9:2-34) mentions repatriates, from Judah, Benjamin, and Levi but also from Ephraim and Manasseh (compare Neh 11:4).

The list of those in the restored community (1 Chr 9:2-34) also calls attention to the continuity between post-exilic society and the Israel of ages past. In this respect, the outer frame to the genealogies (1 Chr 1:1-54 and 9:2-34) says something about the author's view of larger divine purposes in human history. The first chapter of Chronicles reveals that Israel is kin to its neighbors, but the following genealogies (1 Chr 2–8) reveal that the descendants of Israel occupy a privileged place among the very nations to whom they are related. The list of those in the restored community (1 Chr 9:2-34) creates continuity between post-exilic society and pre-exilic society. Population shifts, war, political turmoil, natural disaster, and exile are part of history, but Yahweh's relationship with his people endures.

F. The United Monarchy

Following the precedent, if not always the exact sequence, set by Samuel–Kings, the Chronicler's coverage of the monarchy proceeds according to a fundamentally chronological outline. The reigns of kings Saul, David, and Solomon are followed by the division of the kingdom, after Solomon's death and after centuries of the Judahite monarchy. But the Chronicler's heavy reliance of Samuel–Kings can be misleading if one jumps to the conclusion that this author simply parrots his major biblical source. By means of numerous reorderings, recontextualizations, additions, omissions, and editorial comments, the author presents his own distinctive presentation of the monarchy. Paradoxically, the creative genius of the Chronicler's literary craft can be most evident in those instances in which he reworks and supplements the source material found in earlier biblical writings.

1. The legacy of King Saul: An opportunity missed

In dealing with Saul's reign, the Chronicler only relates one incident in Saul's life—the final battle in which Saul loses his life (1 Chr 10:1-14). The Chronicler's brief presentation contrasts greatly with the presentation in Samuel in which the complexities of Saul's rise, life, and demise are recounted in great detail. In the book of Samuel, David's rise overlaps with and is inevitably connected to Saul's decline, but the Chronicler pursues his own independent course. By focusing on the last conflict of King Saul's career and ignoring, for the moment, Saul's positive accomplishments, the author casts Saul's royal legacy in a negative light. Not the tribe of Benjamin as a whole but the actions of one particular Benjaminite is at issue. Because the Chronicler makes no mention of David in his depiction of Saul's demise, David is not associated in any way with Saul's downfall. To be sure, the later references to Saul indicate that the author knew that Saul's fall coincided with David's rise (1 Chr 11:2; 12:1, 2, 20, 24; 13:3). But consistent with the Chronicler's understanding of divine justice, Saul is judged according to his own actions. The cause of his demise is straightforward: Saul "did not keep the word of Yahweh" and so Yahweh "put him to death" (1 Chr 10:14). Saul's crime was to neglect the command of Yahweh and consult a ghost (1 Chr 10:13). The implication of this negative assessment is that things could have been otherwise. Israel's first king had a chance to consolidate the kingdom, but instead left it in disarray.

2. "By the people and for the people": The Rise and rule of King David

After only briefly addressing and condemning the reign of Saul, the Chronicler expends a great deal of energy depicting a most successful reign of David (1 Chr 11–29). By placing David and Solomon's achievements at the center of Israelite history, the author underscores the Davidic dynasty's centrality to Israelite life. David's ascent to power is smooth, uncontested, and highly successful. Whereas in Samuel the unification of Judah (2 Sam 2:4) and Israel (2 Sam 5:1-10) under David's command is a protracted, fractious, and bloody affair, in Chronicles representatives from all over Israel come to David immediately after Saul's death to anoint David, acclaim him king, and pledge support (1 Chr 11:1-3). To be sure, the writer acknowledges that the actual process took a considerable amount of time and effort (1 Chr 11:10–12:39), but the effect of juxtaposing Saul's death (1 Chr 10:13-14) with the acclamation of David (1 Chr 11:1-3) is to stress the new leader's positive and unifying effect on all elements of the Israelite populace. In Chronicles David does not single-handedly forge a unified Israel. Rather, the Israelites rally to David and achieve new solidarity in connection with his rule.

David's first act is to orchestrate the capture of Jerusalem (1 Chr 11:4-9), which signals the importance of his tenure as king to Jerusalem and the people as a whole. The priority given to Jerusalem as the cultural, political, and religious center of the nation is also evident in David's repeated attempts to bring the ARK OF THE COVENANT to Jerusalem early in his reign (1 Chr 13:1-14; 15:1-29). The keen concern for worship evident in David's early reign remains a constant throughout his entire life. One of the hallmarks of David's tenure is his unstinting patronage of worship, the priesthood, and music.

In retelling the story of the failed census (2 Sam 24), e.g., the Chronicler ingeniously associates the Deuteronomic mandate for a central sanctuary (Deut 12) with the divine mandate for a Jerusalem altar (1 Chr 22:1). When David repents of his sin and implores God to visit upon him, and not upon the innocent people he leads, the penalty for his wrongdoing, God relents and informs David through the prophet Gad to construct an altar to Yahweh at the threshing floor of Ornan the Jebusite (1 Chr 21:18-27). Having done so, David designates this site as the precise location for the future Temple, the home of centralized worship (1 Chr 21:28–22:1). The manner in which David confronts the error of his ways, adjusts to changing circumstances, and attempts to minimize the negative effects of his wrongdoing on others serves as a model for the Chronicler's audience. In this story, the effects of repentance lead to new blessing for the nation.

The concern for proper worship culminates in his bequeathing to Solomon a generous endowment and detailed plans for building the Jerusalem Temple (1 Chr 22; 28–29). Although David is not allowed to build the Temple himself (1 Chr 17:3-6), he does everything he can to promote this project. The king devotes great attention to Jerusalem, Yahweh's chosen city (2 Chr 6:34, 38; 12:13; 33:7), the respective responsibilities of priests and Levites (1 Chr 15; 23–24), and to matters of song and music (1 Chr 16:7-36; 25:1-31).

It would be misleading, however, to associate the Chronicler's David exclusively with worship. He is also an astute leader and military genius. The support that David receives and the counsel he receives from all quarters consolidates Israel's national solidarity, but he does not take such support for granted. He actively solicits advice from his nation's leaders and involves them in his people's work (e.g., 1 Chr 13:1-4; 15:3-13; 23:1-5; 28:1; 29:1-9). The repeated triumphs he enjoys over Israel's enemies consolidates his people's unity and enables them to meet new challenges (1 Chr 14; 18–20). The extraordinary success against Israel's neighbors ensures Israel's complete control over the land. In this way, one can see the Chronicler upholding David as a paradigmatic monarch, who succeeds where his predecessor, Saul, failed.

His bequeathing a national administration (1 Chr 23–27) to his divinely chosen son and successor ensures a smooth transfer of power to Solomon and contributes to the latter's success. In Samuel–Kings, the succession to the Davidic throne is a highly contested and drawn-out affair that divides David's own family (2 Sam 9–20; 1 Kgs 1–2). The picture is very different in Chronicles. Indeed, at the end of David's reign all Israel, including the rest of David's sons, acclaim the accession of Solomon (1 Chr 29:20-25). In his highly complimentary depiction of David's career, the author advances a coherent view of the relationships between Israelite history, politics, and cult. Yahweh, the God of Israel, is unrivaled in the heavens, yet Yahweh's dominion in the heavens has its counterpart on earth. According to the Chronicler, Yahweh chose one particular form of polity for his people—kingship—and one particular dynasty—that of David—to rule his people (1 Chr 17:7-14; 28:4-8). The one supreme God, in turn, endorsed one sanctuary—the Temple in Jerusalem—prepared for by David and built by Solomon. Chosen dynasty, chosen city, chosen Temple, and chosen Levites (1 Chr 15:2; 2 Chr 29:11) are all characteristic ways in which God institutionalizes Israel's worship.

To be sure, the survival of the Davidic kingdom and the Jerusalem Temple are not absolutely essential either to the people's continued existence or to their relationship to God. As the genealogies (*see* above) and the end of Chronicles document, the people of Israel can survive the destruction of the Temple and the kingdom centered in Jerusalem. Indeed, God can speak through foreign monarchs (e.g., 2 Chr 35:20-21) and use them to achieve his own purposes (e.g., 2 Chr 36:22-23). But in his portrayal of David's reign, the writer upholds his ideal of what Israel should be about. That vision includes an independent, unified people living in the land centered on Jerusalem and supporting the divinely authorized institutions headquartered in that city. If the reality in the Chronicler's own time fell short of the ideal, this was no reason not to commemorate the past. In the meantime, one could pray for, aspire to, and work toward better conditions in the future.

3. Solomon: king of peace and temple builder

David's hard work in securing the kingdom, rallying his people, and preparing for the Temple all come to good effect in the reign of Solomon. Like David, Solomon receives widespread popular support at the beginning of his reign. Like his father, Solomon is also an avid patron of worship. Much of Solomon's reign is, in fact, dedicated to religious matters. Unlike David, Solomon does not have to worry about an unstable country or about enemies all around. The founding father has secured the kingdom for his son. At the inception of his reign, all Israel accompanies Solomon in journeying to the Tent of the Meeting at Gibeon (2 Chr 1:2-5). In accordance with divine wishes, Solomon prepares for and supervises the construction of the long-awaited Jerusalem Temple.

Within the context of the ancient world, antiquity was viewed very positively. If things had stood the test of time, they could be valued and honored. Conversely, novelty was viewed with suspicion. After all, if the value of something was unproven, what good was it? In portraying the establishment of the new Temple under Solomon the Chronicler thus had to walk a fine line. On the one hand, he sought to buttress its antiquity by associating its site with Mount Moriah (2 Chr 3:1), the place where Abraham was asked to sacrifice his son Isaac (Gen 22:1-19). On the other hand, he presented the establishment of the Temple under Solomon as the culmination of disparate, older cultic traditions. The Temple benefits by association with antecedent religious shrines, such as the Tent of the Meeting and the ark of the covenant. These older institutions, known from the Pentateuch, found their fulfillment in the Temple (2 Chr 5:1–6:2).

The value of the sanctuary for all Israelites, repeatedly emphasized during the dedication ceremonies, is especially apparent in Solomon's prayer (2 Chr 6:19-39; compare 1 Kgs 8:31-56). In praying toward the Temple in times of trouble, Israelites can find divine compassion, forgiveness, and restitution. In his reply to Solomon's petitions, God affirms that should the people respond to calamity by humbling themselves, praying, seeking God, or returning to God, he will "hear from the heavens, forgive their sins, and heal their land" (2 Chr 7:14). It is relevant to observe that when the Chronicler wrote his work, the Jerusalem Temple's status was not unrivaled. A Samarian temple existed at the sacred place of Mount GERIZIM (compare Deut 11:29-30) and another Jewish temple existed at Elephantine in Egypt. There may well have been other Jewish temples as well. Against this background, the Chronicler emphasizes the pertinence and unique value of the Jerusalem sanctuary, no matter where Israelites may find themselves, whether at home or far away. This sacred shrine was Yahweh's designated central site of worship for all Israelites.

The Chronicler's interest in the Temple's national importance is not limited to his coverage of the united monarchy. When later monarchs, such as Rehoboam (2 Chr 12:1-12), Abijah (2 Chr 13:2-18), Asa (2 Chr 14:8-14), Jehoshaphat (2 Chr 18:28-34; 20:5-30), Hezekiah (2 Chr 30:13-21; 32:16-26), and Manasseh (2 Chr 33:10-13) respond to adversity according to Solomon's petitions, God intervenes and restores them. Conversely, when either king or people wantonly abandon God and neglect the Temple, the nation suffers.

In Chronicles the national solidarity that characterizes Solomon's accession and Temple dedication continues throughout his reign (2 Chr 8–9). There is no hint of tension between northern tribes and southern tribes until the division. This idyllic picture of inter tribal harmony has been upheld as a sign of the breadth of the Chronicler's vision, but the vision also has an edge. Because the Chronicler's portrayal of the united kingdom is so uniformly positive, it effectively impugns any person or group who would violate it. Having portrayed the establishment of Israel's normative political and cultic institutions in the time of David and Solomon, the Chronicler never reneges on their pertinence to all Israelites. His ideal of Israel is an independent nation ruled by God through Davidic monarchs, the elders of the people, the priests, and the Levites. From this perspective, those who might oppose a Jerusalem-centered view of Israelite life (e.g., many of the people in Samaria) would be opposing Yahweh's stated wishes for his people.

G. The Judahite Kingdom

Following the death of Solomon and the accession of his son Rehoboam, the northern tribes secede from southern rule (1 Kgs 12:1-20; 2 Chr 11:1-17). Whereas the author of Kings follows the course of both Northern and Southern kingdoms, the Chronicler concentrates his attention upon the tribes of Judah, Benjamin, and Levi, who make up the Kingdom of Judah (2 Chr 11). He follows the course of its history until the people are forced to leave the land in the Babylonian deportations (2 Chr 36).

1. The division and early Judahite monarchy

Largely blaming mostly Jeroboam and his entourage for the division, the Chronicler sees both the political and the cultic separation of Israel as an affront against God (2 Chr 13:4-12). Unlike the Deuteronomist (1 Kgs 11:11-13, 29-38; 14:9), the Chronicler views the Davidic promises as permanently valid for all of the Israelite tribes. Hence, the Chronicler passes over the independent history of the separatist kingdom Jeroboam founded. Nevertheless, the author shows a sustained interest in (northern) Israelite history by recording virtually every incident between north and south mentioned in Kings, as well as a number of other contacts. The Chronicler's coverage of the dual monarchies is, therefore, broadly consistent with the pattern he established in his genealogies. Israel continues to encompass all twelve tribes, but Judah, Benjamin, and Levi perpetuate the normative institutions established during the united monarchy.

The Judahite monarchy is characterized by both achievements and failures. The writer consistently documents the achievements of Judah's best kings—Abijah

(2 Chr 13:1-23), Asa (2 Chr 14:1–15:19), Jehoshaphat (2 Chr 17; 19), Hezekiah (2 Chr 29–31), and Josiah (2 Chr 34:1–35:19)—to institute reforms, reunite the people, and recover lost territories. But there are also lapses, sometimes multiple lapses, within a single reign (2 Chr 18:1–19:3; 20:35-37). The fact that a monarch, such as Jehoshaphat, can still receive positive evaluations (2 Chr 17:3-4; 20:31-33), in spite of his mixed record, demonstrates that the author did not expect perfection in human history. How well a king responded to adversity, in some cases adversity of his own making, was a critical factor in how the writer assessed royal performance.

Already during the reign of the first king of the Judahite kingdom, a prophet (Shemaiah) makes a series of appearances (2 Chr 11:1-4; 12:5-8). In the Judahite monarchy prophets play a major role in society. Whereas the Deuteronomist portrays very few active prophets in the Southern Kingdom until after the fall of the Northern Kingdom (2 Kgs 17:1-6), the Chronicler portrays many. In Chronicles, prophecy represents a vital and independent institution that checks both royal and popular regression. Prophets can provide crucial counsel in times of need (e.g., 2 Chr 19:1-3) and offer preventative medicine, whether the patient elects to take it or not (e.g., 2 Chr 15:1-7).

Communications from the prophets take both oral and written form (e.g., 2 Chr 21:12-15). To have a writing prophet comment upon one's royal career is a sign of some stature. Hence, the fact that David's actions are discussed in the works of Samuel the seer, Nathan the prophet, and Gad the seer (1 Chr 29:29-30) is itself a compliment. Conversely, the fact that the events of Ahaz's reign are only discussed in the book of the kings of Israel and Judah (2 Chr 28:27), and not in any prophetic work, is one indication of how poorly he conducted himself while in office. In the course of Judahite history, even some of Judah's better kings, such as Jehoshaphat, succumb to military, commercial, and cultic compromise (2 Chr 18:1–19:3; 20:35-37). As a divinely ordained institution, prophets limit the excess and abuse of power, sanctioning wars (2 Chr 20:14-17) or refusing to do so (2 Chr 18:4-27), praising restraint (2 Chr 12:5-8) or deriding overconfidence (2 Chr 16:7-10), encouraging reforms (2 Chr 34:22-28) or assailing idolatry (2 Chr 25:15-16). During the tenure of Jehoshaphat, trust in God is even equated with trust in God's prophets (2 Chr 20:20). In commenting on the defeat and exile of Judah, the author states that although Yahweh sent a steady supply of prophets to stir the people and priestly leaders to reform, their warnings went unheeded (2 Chr 36:14-16).

2. Regression and reform: Lowpoints and highpoints in Judahite history

The reigns of Hezekiah (2 Chr 29–32) and Josiah (2 Chr 34–35) constitute the two major high points in the history of the Judahite kingdom. Each of these monarchs lead major reform efforts, embark on major building projects (public works), attempt to rally the people (including members of the estranged northern tribes), and celebrate national Passovers. In the case of Hezekiah, his unstinting trust in Yahweh during a surprising and massive invasion by King SENNACHERIB of Assyria is rewarded by divine deliverance (2 Chr 32:1-22). In the case of Josiah, he redoubles his reform efforts (2 Chr 34:29-33) after receiving a dire warning about his nation's condition and fate from the prophetess Huldah (2 Chr 34:24-28).

Despite these and other positive indications of progress and unity during the history of the Judahite kingdom, the Chronicler does not present a historical solution to the problem of disunity within his people. In other words, the picture presented in one of the speeches of King Hezekiah (an invitation to a national Passover in Jerusalem) of a continuing rift between northern and southern tribes with some members of these tribes residing in exile (2 Chr 30:6-9) basically fits the conditions of the Chronicler's own time. In the final chapters of the book, there is no indication that either Hezekiah or Josiah permanently reunited Judah and Israel. The reforms of Hezekiah (2 Chr 30:6-11, 21; 31:1, 5, 8) and Josiah (2 Chr 34:3-7, 29-33; 35:1-19) are but temporary approximations of the ideal unity that characterized the kingdom of David and Solomon. Indeed, the very fact that a variety of Judahite monarchs attempt to reconcile members of the northern and southern tribes implies that none of these leaders effected a definitive and long-lasting solution to the problem posed by the division (2 Chr 10:1-19). The history of repeated, albeit limited, attempts at reunification during the Judahite monarchy provide, however, the Chronicler's readers with an enterprising vision of Israel to embrace. The successes achieved in former times function paradigmatically for the Chronicler's own generation. The unfulfilled legacy of the past becomes an agenda for the future.

In addition to positing some notable achievements in the Judahite monarchy, the Chronicler also depicts some lamentable declines. Major regressions occur in the reigns of Ahaz (2 Chr 28) and Manasseh (2 Chr 33:1-9). Ahaz, in fact, may be the worst king in the Judahite kingdom, because he stubbornly insists on repeating his past mistakes, much to the detriment of himself and his people (2 Chr 28:1-5, 16, 19-25). Manasseh is both the longest reigning and the worst Judahite monarch in Kings (2 Kgs 21:1-18), but he reverses course and makes amends in Chronicles. Consistent with the Chronicler's understanding of divine mercy, Manasseh repents and enjoys a significant recovery (2 Chr 33:10-19).

The Chronicler's unique treatment of Manasseh raises a larger and controversial issue in the history of biblical interpretation. Scholars commonly assert that Chronicles promotes a theology of "immediate retribution." In contrast with the picture in Samuel–Kings in which judgment is sometimes absent or long deferred, the Chronicler purportedly wishes to demonstrate that wrongdoing quickly results in punishment, while allegiance results in peace, prosperity, and success. One of the classic formulations of this tenet is articulated by the prophet Azariah, "Hear me, O Asa and all Judah and Benjamin: 'Yahweh is with you when you are with him. And if you seek him, he will be present to you. But if you abandon him, he will abandon you'" (2 Chr 15:2).

There is some merit to this scholarly assessment in that the Chronicler discerns the divine as very active in the course of Israelite history. His deity is not one who is unconcerned with or remote from the course of human affairs. Moreover, the author believes in accountability in the relations between God and his people. But this notion of accountability has itself to be put in proper historical context. Unlike many of the earlier biblical writers (e.g., Exod 20:5-6; Deut 5:9-10), the Chronicler does not believe in ancestral guilt as determining the fate of later generations. Like Jeremiah (31:29-30) and Ezekiel (18:1-32), the Chronicler thinks that justice involves each person or generation as being responsible to God for their own actions: "The person who sins, he shall die" (Ezek 18:4). In articulating this point of view, the Chronicler shares similar assumptions about reality as those present in a number of other late works, such as Job and Qoheleth (Ecclesiastes). Job could not adamantly profess innocence and Qoheleth would not complain so much about the futility of life in the manner he does if the authors believed that the actions of their ancestors determined their present standing in the world. The Chronicler thinks that each generation has to establish its own course of action before God, regardless of what previous generations may have done or not done.

Yet, a caveat must be offered here. The fact that the Chronicler believes in accountability in Israel's dealings with Yahweh does not mean that he holds to a simplistic worldview. The author neither attributes David's wars, of which there are many (1 Chr 11:4-6; 14:8-16; 18:1–20:8), nor Solomon's war (2 Chr 8:3) to divine causes. During the era of the Judahite monarchy there are again many events that the Chronicler does not overtly trace to a king's righteous or unrighteous behavior (e.g., 2 Chr 13:2-19; 14:8-14; 20:1-30; 25:11-12, 17-24; 26:6-8; 27:5; 32:1-21). In other words, the author does not see history operating mechanically, even though he sees both the divine and the human as real actors in the historical arena. The fact that God holds Israel accountable (usually through the prophets, but also through kings, priests, and Levites), and that Israel holds God accountable (usually through speeches and prayers), does not negate the freedom of others (e.g., Israel's neighbors) to act for good or for ill in relation to the people of Israel. Nor does the Chronicler attribute such actions to God; rather, he attributes them to the actors themselves. Hence, Yahweh's punishing or rewarding certain Israelite actions does not remove the randomness, injustice, or arbitrariness from the course of human history.

The Chronicler depicts divine requital for injustice and wrongdoing not simply as retributive but also as redemptive. When, for instance, God punishes King Manasseh through a personal exile to Babylon (2 Chr 33:10-11), this accountability provides the context in which the errant king repents and makes a constructive new beginning (2 Chr 33:12-13). Given that the Chronicler lived at a time in which Israelites found themselves living in many different lands, his message would not be lost on his readers. Divine mercy can mollify or avert the dire predicaments in which people find themselves, even if the people are living far from Jerusalem.

3. Destruction, exile, and a new beginning

Both Kings and Chronicles end with the Babylonian exile, but Chronicles provides much less detailed coverage of this era of decline (2 Chr 36:1-21; compare 2 Kgs 24:1–25:26). There is another important difference between the two works. The ending of Chronicles offers a more direct and clear hope for the future than does the ending of Kings (2 Kgs 25:27-30). In the final verses of his work, the Chronicler presents the decree of Cyrus commending the return of the Babylonian deportees to Judah (2 Chr 36:22-23). The emperor's declaration specifically mentions his support for the rebuilding of the Jerusalem Temple. In this manner, Chronicles contains and relativizes the tremendous tragedy of the Babylonian deportations and underscores the importance of the land to God's designs for his people. As the beginning of Chronicles introduces the people of Israel and charts their emergence in the land, the ending anticipates their return.

Bibliography: P. R. Ackroyd. *The Chronicler in His Age* (1991); J. Blenkinsopp. *Ezra–Nehemiah: A Commentary* (1988); F. M. Cross. "A Reconstruction of the Judean Restoration." *JBL* 94 (1974) 4–18; T. C. Eskenazi. "The Chronicler and the Composition of 1 Esdras." *CBQ* 48 (1986) 39–61; D. N. Freedman. "The Chronicler's Purpose." *CBQ* 23 (1961) 432–42; S. Japhet. *The Ideology of the Book of Chronicles and its Place in Biblical Thought* (1989); S. Japhet. *I & II Chronicles* (1993); I. Kalimi. *The Reshaping of Ancient Israelite History in Chronicles* (2005); G. N. Knoppers. *I Chronicles 1–9: A New Translation with Introduction and Commentary* (2004); G. N. Knoppers. *I Chronicles 10-29: A New Translation with Introduction and Commentary* (2004); M. A. Throntveit. *When Kings Speak: Royal Speech and Royal Prayer in Chronicles* (1987); H. G. M. Williamson. *1 and 2 Chronicles* (1982); H. G. M. Williamson. *Ezra, Nehemiah* (1985); J. W. Wright. "The Founding Father: The Structure of the Chronicler's David Narrative." *JBL* 117 (1998) 45–59; E. Ben Zvi. "A Sense of Proportion: An Aspect of the Theology of the Chronicler." *SJOT* 9 (1995) 37–51.

GARY N. KNOPPERS

CHRONICLES OF HOZAI (SEERS). *See* BOOKS REFERRED TO IN THE BIBLE.

CHRONICLES OF KING DAVID, RECORDS OF. *See* BOOKS REFERRED TO IN THE BIBLE.

CHRONICLES OF KINGS. *See* BOOKS REFERRED TO IN THE BIBLE.

CHRONOLOGY OF THE ANCIENT NEAR EAST. Two chronologies are employed in the study of the ancient Near East (ANE): relative and absolute. Relative chronology deals with general, nonexact dating, whereas absolute chronology deals with exact or precise dating. Archaeological layers and the materials found in them can yield a relative chronology for the stratigraphy of ancient tells. In turn, stratigraphy can establish typologies of objects, since over time the form of material artifacts changes and these can be ordered in a relative chronological sequence by comparing similar objects from different sites. Absolute chronology supplies actual dates. These are derived from ancient written sources that mention astronomical events or have links to the known classical systems of Greece and Rome. Approximate absolute dates can also be secured from scientific techniques such as radiocarbon dating (measurements of the decay of carbon isotope) or dendrochronology (study of tree-ring growth). These are approximate because the computation must allow for a statistical differential range.

Civilized societies measure time by arbitrary fixed points: e.g., BC ("before Christ") or BCE ("before the common era") and AD ("year of our Lord") or CE ("common era"). In the ANE, societies used a fixed point such as the accession year of a king. Chronographic data were kept in king lists, genealogical lists, eponym lists, chronicles, annals, and other inscriptions. These markers, in and of themselves, can only provide a relative chronology. Anchors are required in order to link the ancient chronologies with the modern system. Ancient dated observations of astronomical phenomena may provide absolute dates and thus link the ancient chronology into the modern system. The chronology of the ANE is built on synchronizations between societies who record dated astronomical observations (compared to those in Mesopotamia and Egypt) and other various societies who have their own chronologies (such as Israel and Judah).

The absolute chronology for the 1st millennium BCE ("before the Christian era") is well established by a number of astronomical observations. In Babylonia, an astronomical series of omens known as *Enna Anu Enlil (EAE)* (ca. 700 BCE, although based on earlier material) records the movements of the moon and planets. Mesopotamian astronomers of the 3rd and 2nd cents. BCE composed ephemerides that calculated and accurately predicted new moons, eclipses, and other planetary and lunar movements. In Assyria, each year received a name after an appointed official. *Limu* lists are lists of administrative officials who served annually as a magistrate (limu) at the Assyrian capital of Assur. The year of their administration was named after them. Eponym lists and chronicles were kept and periodically updated providing the basis for dating in many other types of texts (e.g., contracts, letters, annalistic inscriptions), and make it possible to date events quite precisely back to 910 BCE. Since an eclipse, which occurred June 15, 763 BCE, is recorded in the Eponym Chronicle, the lists are tied to absolute chronology. The Assyrian and Babylonian dates for the 1st millennium BCE are accurate enough to allow dating of other events in the ANE, where there is synchronism (e.g., Ahab of Israel fought against Shalmaneser III of Assyria in 853; Jehu of Israel paid tribute to Shalmaneser III in 841). For the absolute chronology of Egypt in the 1st millennium, the Persian, Hellenistic, and Roman regimes are well established, and the earlier periods can be largely determined by a dead reckoning of reigns from the beginning of the 26th dynasty back to the beginning of the 22nd dynasty, adjusted by synchronisms with Assyrian dates. One important synchronism for biblical chronology is the razzia of Sheshonq I, biblical SHISHAK, which occurred in 925 BCE (1 Kgs 14:25-28; 2 Chr 12:2-9).

The absolute chronology for the 2nd millennium BCE is less certain because it is based only on a few fixed points. In Mesopotamia, there are two lines of important textual evidence.

First, there are astronomical observations recorded in an omen series known as *Enna Anu Enlil (EAE)*. This refers to a series of astrological omens found on sixty-eight tablets, which were discovered in the library of Assurbanipal in the city of Nineveh (modern Tell Kuyunjik). The tablets date to the 7th cent. BCE (though the original series is thought by some to date back as early as the beginning Middle Bronze Age (2000 BCE). Two tablets from this series (*EAE* 20 and 21) record two lunar eclipses that occurred at specific times during the Ur III dynasty. Another tablet (*EAE* 63) is known as the "Venus Tablet of Ammitsaduqa." It records observations of the planet Venus attributed to the eighth year of this king.

Second, the Assyrian King Lists are one of the most important sources for determining absolute chronology since when combined with various sources of synchronistic information, they allow dating as far back as the Amarna period with reasonable accuracy. The astronomical evidences have been understood to suggest three possible dates for the accession year of

Ammiṣaduqa: 1702, 1646, and 1582 BCE (thus producing *high, middle,* and *low* chronologies). Often the "Middle Chronology" has been used as a compromising convenience. In recent years, a fourth system (*ultra-low*) has been proposed, arising from a study of Old Babylonian and Kassite ceramics, with Ammitsaduqa's first year being 1550 BCE. One difficulty for the ultra-low chronology is its coordination with Hittite chronology, particularly in the count of generations. However, Hittite chronology is problematic because there are no year-names, eponyms, counting of regnal years, or king lists. Eponym lists from Mari and from Kültepe (Old Assyrian period) provide more data for understanding the chronology of the early 2nd millennium, but the lists have not solved the issues. In Egypt, there are astronomical observations, in particular the heliacal rising (the appearance of Sothic star, i.e., Sirius). However, the geographic location of any reported sighting unfortunately affects reckoning of the date, creating a possible high chronology (sightings made at Memphis) or low chronology (sightings made at Elephantine). For various reasons in the study of Egyptian chronology, the low chronology has gained concensus.

The absolute chronology of the 3rd millennium is inextricably linked with that of the 2nd because records exist for the period from the fall of Babylon back to the reign of Sargon, the first emperor of Agade. Thus a late 2nd millennium chronology drags the 3rd millennium chronology down with it. There are still many uncertainties regarding the absolute chronology of the 3rd millennium BCE.

For prehistoric phases, a relative chronology is denoted by phases or cultures (e.g., Hassuna or Halaf), which are characterized by a distinctive material culture. *See* ARCHAEOLOGY; CHRONOLOGY OF THE OT; CHRONOLOGY OF THE NT.

Bibliography: G. Beckman. "Hittite Chronology." *Akkadica* 119–120 (2000) 19–32; H. J. Gasche, J. A. Armstrong, S. W. Cole, and V. G. Gurzadyan. *Dating the Fall of Babylon: A Reappraisal of Second-Millennium Chronology* (1998); H. J. Gasche, J. A. Armstrong, S. W. Cole, and V. G. Gurzad yan. "A Correction to Dating the Fall of Babylon: A Reappraisal of Second-Millennium Chronology." *Akkadica* 108 (1998) 1–4; J. J. Glassner. *Mesopotamian Chronicles* (2004); H. Hunger, and R. Pruzsinszky, ed. *Mesopotamian Dark Age Revisited* (2004); K. A. Kitchen. "The Basics of Egyptian Chronology in Relation to the Bronze Age." *High, Middle or Low? Acts of an International Colloquium on Absolute Chronology* (1987) 37–55; Manfred Bietak, ed. "Regnal and Genealogical Data of Ancient Egypt." *The Synchronisation of Civilisations in the Eastern Mediterranean in the Second Millennium B.C.* (2000) 39–32; A. R. Millard. *The Eponyms of the Assyrian Empire 910–612 BC* (1994); J. Reade. "Assyrian Kinglists, the Royal Tombs of Ur, and Indus

Origins." *JNES* 60 (2001) 1–29; D. A. Warburton. "Synchronizing the Chronology of Bronze Age Western Asia with Egypt." *Akkadica* 119–120 (2001) 33–76; D. A. Warburton "Eclipses, Venus-Cycles and Chronology." *Akkadica* 123 (2002) 108–14.

K. LAWSON YOUNGER, JR.

CHRONOLOGY OF THE NT. The attempt to construct an accurate chronological framework for the events and literature of earliest Christianity is one of the perennially problematic issues in NT studies. Since the writings of the NT are principally documents of faith and proclamation rather than historical reports, the chronological details contained within them are often incidental to their primary purpose.

A. Chronology of the Life of Jesus
1. Birth
2. Commencement and duration of ministry
3. Crucifixion and resurrection
B. Chronology of Paul's Mission
1. Sources
2. Paul's letters
3. Acts
C. Chronology of the post-apostolic age
Bibliography

A. Chronology of the Life of Jesus
1. Birth
The year of Jesus' birth can only be roughly approximated. Matthew 2:1 asserts (and Luke 1:5 suggests) that Jesus was born during the reign of HEROD (*see* HEROD, FAMILY), a reference that fixes the latest date for Jesus' birth to between March 12/13 and April 11 (the date of Passover) of the year 4 BCE. It is during this period that Herod died, according to information from Josephus (*Ant.* 17.191, 213). The story in Matt 2:1-19, however, implies that Jesus was still a very young child at the time of Herod's death, so Jesus is not likely to have been born very long before 4 BCE.

A second episode related to the time period of the nativity is the story in the Gospel of Luke of Jesus' birth during a census taken when QUIRINIUS was governor of Syria (Luke 2:1-7). Luke's account has occasioned no little amount of confusion, not least because, according to JOSEPHUS, Quirinius only assumed the governorship of Syria after 6 CE (*Ant.* 17.353; 18.1). Moreover, the governors of Syria during the final years of Herod's rule were S. Sentius Saturninus (9–6 BCE) and P. Quintilius Varus (6–4 BCE). Luke does, of course, mention in Acts 5:37 another census, which provoked an uprising led by Judas the Galilean, and this appears to be the same census of Quirinius dated to 6–7 CE by Josephus (*Ant.* 20.102; *J.W.* 7.253). In short, the reference to the census under Quirinius in Luke 2:2 does not contribute any solid information that can be used to establish a date for Jesus' birth.

Since at least as early as the 2nd cent. CE there have been a number of proposals for the exact day of Jesus' birth—such as November 18 (CLEMENT OF ALEXANDRIA, *Strom.* 1.21.145), January 6 (EPIPHANIUS, *Pan.* 51.24.1), and December 25 (HIPPOLYTUS, *Comm. Dan.* 4.23)—but these dates reflect developing tradition more than historical reality. The most that can be said from the available evidence is that Jesus was probably born sometime between 6 and 4 BCE, though perhaps as early as 8 BCE.

2. Commencement and duration of ministry
According to Luke 3:23, Jesus was "about thirty years old" when he began his public ministry. Clearly an approximation ("about") of the round number thirty may function as an indication that Jesus had attained the appropriate age of leadership (compare Gen 41:46; Num 4:3; 2 Sam 5:4; Dionysius of Halicarnassus, *Ant. rom.* 4.6.3). This age corresponds both with Luke's statement in 3:1 that John the Baptist embarked on his preaching mission in the fifteenth year of the reign of Tiberius (i.e., 28–29 CE) and with the implication of the narrative that Jesus began his own ministry shortly thereafter.

The synoptic Gospels do not provide a clear indication of the length of Jesus' public activity, though the Gospel of John implies a ministry of at least two years, covering at least three Passovers (John 2:13; 6:4; 11:55ff.). The Johannine data is complicated by the fact that the first Passover (2:13) is the setting of Jesus' Temple cleansing, an event that the author of the Fourth Gospel appears to have transposed from the end of Jesus' mission (compare Mark 11:15-17) to the beginning. If it is assumed that the Johannine chronology is influenced by theological concerns, the same is no less true of the synoptic framework. Jesus' ministry, then, may have spanned a minimum of one year and a maximum of just over two.

3. Crucifixion
While all four Gospels locate the crucifixion on a Friday, the Synoptics and the Fourth Gospel do not agree on the day of the month of Jesus' death. John 18:28 and 19:14 explicitly affirm that Jesus was killed on the Day of Preparation for the Passover (NISAN 14). The PASSOVER, then, would have been eaten on the evening of his death, but this would also have been the "dawn" of a new day, since the Jewish day began at 6 PM. In the synoptic tradition, however, Jesus celebrates the Passover with his disciples on the night before his death (Mark 14:12-16) and is crucified on Nisan 15.

Many scholars are now inclined to regard the Johannine passion chronology as more historically accurate. For example, Mark's Gospel contains several indications that its author may have been unfamiliar with the details of Jewish timekeeping and festivals (compare 12:18; 14:1). Also, some doubt that the trials and crucifixion detailed in the Markan passion narrative would have occurred on the holy day of Passover. Moreover, according to astronomical calculations, Nisan 15 (the synoptic day of the crucifixion) would have fallen on a Friday in 27 and 34 CE, years that, considering all the evidence, appear to be too early and too late, respectively, for the crucifixion. On the other hand, Nisan 14 (the Johannine tradition) can be located on a Friday in the years 30 and 33 CE. Of these possibilities, the year 30 CE is the most plausible.

B. Chronology of Paul's Mission

1. Sources

The chronology of the missionary activity and letters of the Apostle Paul, the second major figure in the early Christian movement, is difficult to determine because of the nature of the available sources. The Pauline Epistles provide at most only one absolute date from which the apostle's activity may be connected to events in world history. The narrative of Acts supplies more information, but the framework of Acts does not always agree with statements in Paul's letters, and many attribute these differences to the nature of the sources available to Luke or to his tendency to reshape earlier materials for his own theological purposes. The proper methodological procedure for discerning a chronology of Paul's life is to begin first with the Pauline letters, treating them as the only primary sources of historical information, and second, after considering the firsthand testimony of Paul, to move to Acts. Evidence from Acts may be used "to supplement the autobiographical data in the letters, but never to correct them."

2. Paul's letters

In Gal 1:11–2:14, Paul supplies a narrative of his activity prior to the writing of Galatians that reveals the following sequence of events: his apostolic commissioning (1:15-16); a three-year interval in Arabia and Damascus (1:17); "after three years" a fifteen-day visit to Jerusalem (1:18-20); a mission to Syria and Cilicia (1:21); "after fourteen years" a second visit to Jerusalem (2:1-10); and a dispute at Antioch (2:11-14). The reference to "fourteen years" in Gal 2:1 can either be counted from the time of Paul's commissioning or from the occasion of his first visit to Jerusalem. Either way, Paul may reckon partial years as "years," as was the ancient custom, so these chronological markers can designate a period ranging from just over thirteen to more than seventeen years.

To this sequence other references to Paul's evangelistic ventures and travel plans can be added. An early missionary journey to the region of Macedonia led Paul to the cities of Philippi, Thessalonica, and Athens (Phil 4:15-16; 1 Thess 1:8-9; 3:1). The Corinthian correspondence contains or alludes to a series of letters (some no longer extant; compare 1 Cor 5:9; 7:1; 2 Cor 2:3-4),

conflicts (2 Cor 1:15–2:12; 7:5-16; 10–13), and visits (1 Cor 1:11; 2 Cor 1:15-16; 12:14; 13:1-2) between Paul and the believers in Corinth. Ephesus appears to have been a center of Paul's prolonged activity in Asia (1 Cor 15:32; 16:8-9; 2 Cor 1:8). Especially helpful in determining the sequence of the letters are references to Paul's attempt to organize a monetary COLLECTION for Jerusalem from the churches of his mission in the regions of Galatia, Macedonia, and Achaia (1 Cor 16:1-4; 2 Cor 8:1–9:15; Rom 15:25-32).

The only datum from the letters that might provide the foundation for an absolute Pauline chronology is the brief mention of Paul's dramatic escape from Damascus during the reign of the Nabatean king ARETAS IV in 2 Cor 11:32-33. One proposal argues that the reference to "the ethnarch under King Aretas" in 2 Cor 11:32 can be fixed to the period of Aretas's seizure of Damascus following his triumphant campaign against HEROD ANTIPAS. This would locate Paul's escape from Damascus, as well as his ensuing journey to Jerusalem, to the period between late 36 and mid 37 CE.

3. Acts

This book adds more material, not only to Pauline chronology but also to the history of earliest Christianity in general. Information from Acts, however, is occasionally difficult to harmonize with other available evidence. Perhaps the most notorious variation concerns the number of Paul's visits to Jerusalem. In Galatians the apostle emphatically insists that he made only one trip to Jerusalem before the so-called conference visit in Gal 2:1-10; thus, the letters indicate that Paul undertook only three post-conversion visits to Jerusalem. The narrative of Acts, however, depicts Paul visiting Jerusalem five times, and the third of these visits represents a council between Paul and the leaders of the Jerusalem church.

Jerusalem Visits in Paul's Letters	Jerusalem Visits in Acts
P1 = Gal 1:18-24	A1= 9:26-30
P2 = Gal 2:1-10	A2 = 11:27-30
P3 = Rom 15:25-32	A3 = 15:1-29
	A4 = 18:22
	A5 = 21:17ff.

It is generally agreed that P1 = A1 and P3 = A5. The difficulty comes in determining which visit in Acts corresponds to P2 (Gal 2:1-10).

One common view identifies Gal 2:1-10 with Acts 15:1-29 (P2 = A3), for there are similarities in these accounts: In both, Paul and Barnabas travel from Antioch to Jerusalem to discuss the status of the Gentiles. Notable differences, however, suggest that these passages may not describe the same visit: 1) In Galatians Paul meets privately with the Jerusalem leaders (Gal 2:2), whereas in Acts the council involves the entire church (Acts 15:22). 2) In Galatians Paul is adamant that no demands were placed upon him and his associates other than remembrance of the poor (Gal 2:10), whereas A3 details a letter to the Gentile Christians obliging them "to abstain only from things polluted by idols and from fornication and from whatever has been strangled and from blood" (Acts 15:20), requirements that do not exactly match instructions on these matters in Paul's letters (compare 1 Cor 8:1).

Moreover, it is difficult to see how the conflict in Antioch recounted in Gal 2:11-14 would have arisen if the issue of commensality had earlier been settled at the Jerusalem conference. Acts 15, then, may combine two originally independent incidents involving the churches in Antioch and Jerusalem: a meeting devoted to the question of circumcision (= Gal 2:1-10) and a decree from Jerusalem that addressed the issue of dietary practices for Gentiles.

Another option equates Gal 2:1-10 with Acts 11:27-30 (P2 = A2). This solution accounts for the fact that in both Gal 2:1-10 and Acts 11:27-30 Paul and Barnabas are sent to Jerusalem as delegates of the Antioch church, as well as for the fact that the request "to remember the poor" in Gal 2:10 may allude to the role of Paul and Barnabas in delivering a relief fund from Antioch on the occasion of this visit. It is sometimes objected, however, that this famine visit does not fit Pauline chronology in other regards. While there is no extant evidence for a worldwide famine during the reign of CLAUDIUS (compare Acts 11:28), Josephus reports a great famine in Judea sometime during the procuratorships of Cuspius Fadus (44–46 CE) and Tiberius Alexander (46–48 CE) (*Ant.* 3.320; 20.51-53, 101). If Paul's second visit to Jerusalem (P2) is dated to 47–48 CE based on the Aretas datum (compare Acts 9:23-30), Acts 11:27-30 may indeed preserve an authentic remembrance of Paul's role in delivering financial assistance from Antioch. That A2 may refer to Gal 2:1-10 is also implied by the suggestion that Paul's claim, "I was eager" in Gal 2:10, alludes to a monetary collection already completed and delivered at the time of the Jerusalem conference.

A third theory, popular among some recent Pauline chronographers is that Luke transposed both the collection visit (P3) and the conference visit (P2) to different locations in his narrative, 11:27-30 and 15:1-29, respectively. According to Knox, the conference visit actually occurred during the visit reported in Acts 18:22, but because Luke desired to minimize conflicts within the nascent church and to settle the divisive issue of Gentile inclusion earlier in his history, he relocated the conference that dealt with this matter to an earlier period of Paul's missionary career.

At other points, Acts provides more promising chronological clues. The narrative of Paul's activity in Acts 18:1-18, e.g., locates Paul in Corinth during the time when "GALLIO was proconsul of Achaia" (18:12). Thanks to a fragmentary inscription from Delphi (*SIG³* 801), Gallio's possession of this office can be dated with confidence to 51–52 CE. Equally important is the allusion to Claudius' expulsion of the Jews from Rome in Acts 18:2. Claudius' edict has been connected by both ancient and modern historians with events in either 41 CE (Dio Cassius, *Roman History* 60.6.6) or 49 CE (Orosius, *Historiarum* 7.6.15-16); the latter date would, of course, correspond more closely with the arrival of Aquila and Priscilla in Corinth from Rome during Gallio's proconsulship.

Other chronologically significant references in Acts include the death of Herod Agrippa (*see* HEROD, FAMILY) (12:20-23) in 44 CE (Josephus, *Ant.* 19.343-52); the high priest ANANIAS, before whom Paul appears as a prisoner (23:1-5; 24:1) and who was replaced by Agrippa II with Ishmael in 59 CE (Josephus, *Ant.* 20.179); and Paul's trials before FELIX (23:23–24:27), procurator of Palestine, and FESTUS (25:1–26:32), who succeeded his predecessor, Felix, no later than 60–61 CE, though perhaps as early as 59 CE. These references are all important for attempts to relate Paul's activity to events in world history.

By supplementing the Pauline Epistles with information from Acts, a tentative chronology of Paul's life and letters might contain the following sequence of events, anchored in the location of Paul's escape from Damascus in 36 CE and in the identification of the conference in Gal 2:1-10 with the famine visit in Acts 11:30:

33	Paul's apostolic call
33–36	Time spent in Arabia and Damascus
36	First Jerusalem visit
	Mission in Syria and Cilicia [and Galatia?]
	First missionary journey (Acts 13:1–14:28)
44–49	Famine in Judea
47	Second Jerusalem visit; conference; delivery of relief fund from Antioch (Gal 2:1-10; Acts 11:27-30) Antioch incident (Gal 2:11-14)
50–50	Second missionary journey; travels in Macedonia and Greece
49	Claudius' edict
50–51	18-month stay in Corinth; appearance before Gallio
51–54	Extended stay in Ephesus [and imprisonment?]
54–57	Travels between Corinth, Ephesus, and Macedonia; gathering of the collection for Jerusalem
57	Third Jerusalem visit; delivery of the collection (Rom 15:25ff.); arrest (Acts 21:27-36)

| 57–59 | Two-year imprisonment in Caesarea |
| 59–62 | Trial before Festus; voyage to Rome; two-year imprisonment |

C. Chronology of the Post-Apostolic Age

The story of the chronology of the NT does not end with Paul's imprisonment in Rome, for many of the NT writings were doubtless penned during the latter half of the 1st cent. and perhaps at the beginning of the 2nd. Unfortunately, the story becomes even harder to piece together because the available sources preclude speculation on the precise chronological placement of these writings. The synoptic Gospels almost certainly betray awareness of the JEWISH WAR with Rome in 66–70 CE, either in the immediate future (Mark?) or in the past (Matthew, Luke). According to some scholars, the Johannine literature testifies to the theological development of an early Christian community over a period of at least half a century. Other writings attributed to Paul (Colossians, Ephesians, 2 Thessalonians, the Pastoral Letters) are disputed in terms of authorship, and may represent second- (or third-) generation Pauline Christianity. Although these letters may bear witness to increased institutionalization, they provide little in the way of historical data for constructing a chronology of the post-apostolic era. Finally, the book of Revelation may have been written during a period of local persecution under the emperor DOMITIAN (ca. 95 CE?).

Bibliography: Douglas A. Campbell. "An Anchor for Pauline Chronology: Paul's Flight from 'The Ethnarch of King Aretas' (2 Cor 11:32-33)." *JBL* 121 (2002) 279–302; Jack Finegan. *Handbook of Biblical Chronology*, rev. ed. (1998); Robert Jewett. *A Chronology of Paul's Life* (1979). John Knox. *Chapters in a Life of Paul*, rev. ed. (1987); Gerd Lüdemann. *Paul: Apostle to the Gentiles: Studies in Chronology* (1984); Rainer Riesner. *Paul's Early Period: Chronology, Mission Strategy, Theology* (1998); Alexander J. M. Wedderburn. *A History of the First Christians* (2004).

DAVID J. DOWNS

CHRONOLOGY OF THE OT. The chronological information available for the later stages of Israel's history is generally more accurate than that for the earlier stages, but the earliest stages generally show the most evidence of the application of theological concerns.

A. The Priestly Chronology

1. Genesis pre-history

a. From Adam to Noah (Gen 5:1-32). The Priestly genealogy provides three types of information for the antediluvian patriarchs in Gen 5:1-32: 1) the "age of begetting," of the first son, 2) the post-begetting years after the birth of the first son, and 3) the life span, which is the total of the previous figures. The MASORETIC TEXT (MT) of Gen 5:1-32 yields the following table:

Patriarch	Age of Begetting	Post-Begetting Years	Life Span
Adam	130	800	930
Seth	105	807	912
Enosh	90	815	905
Kenan	70	840	910
Mahalalel	65	830	895
Jared	162	800	962
Enoch	65	300	365
Methusaleh	187	782	969
Lamech	182	595	777
Noah	500		

Noah's age at time of flood: 600 years
From Adam to Flood: 1,656 years

Two other ancient textual traditions, the SEPTUAGINT (LXX) and the SAMARITAN PENTATEUCH (SP) provide figures at variance with the MT. The LXX adds to the age of begetting for each of the patriarchs, Adam through Methusaleh, but reduces the post-begetting years for each so that the life span figures are consistent with the MT. Similar LXX changes for Lamech leave him a life span of 753 years, 24 years less than the MT. The SP numbers are largely the same as those of the MT, except that it reduces the age of begetting for 3 patriarchs: Jared (62; MT 162), Methuselah (67; MT 187), and Lamech (53; MT 182), so that all 3 die in the year of the flood. The variance between the MT, LXX, and SP may stem from attempts to conform an earlier chronology to theological norms and boundaries. Some suggest that an older PRIESTLY chronology did exist, but that its original figures had three of the antediluvian patriarchs—Jared, Methuselah, and Lamech—surviving the flood, even though they were not occupants of the ARK. Other signs of theologically oriented editing are apparent. The significantly advanced age of begetting for Noah (500) in comparison to all other antediluvian patriarchs represents an effort to eliminate the possibility that other antediluvians would have outlived the flood, as well. Also, the extremely long life spans of the antediluvian patriarchs seem less to reflect efforts at historical exactitude and more to indicate the legendary status of these primeval figures, not unlike the life spans given for the most ancient kings of Sumer. In the end, none of the three extant versions of the antediluvian chronology can safely be regarded as reliable.

b. From Noah to Abram (Gen 11:10-26). The MT of Gen 11:10-26 yields the following table for the postdiluvian patriarchs between Noah and Abram:

Patriarch	Age of Begetting	Post-Begetting Years	Life Span
Shem	100	500	600
Arpachshad	35	403	438
Shelah	30	403	433
Eber	34	430	464
Peleg	30	209	239
Reu	32	207	239
Sereug	30	200	230
Nahor	29	119	148
Terah	70	(135)	205
Total:	290 years		

Based on the MT figures plus information in Gen 12:4; 25:7, all of Abram's postdiluvian ancestors were alive at Abram's birth, and three (Shem, Shelah, and Eber) outlived him. Both the SP and the LXX add 100 years to the age of begetting for each of the postdiluvian patriarchs, Arpachshad through Serug (50 years in the case of Nahor), in an effort to remedy this circumstance. Both also reduce the life span of each patriarch, but in varying amounts from 50 to 150 years. Again, it is not apparent that any of the three versions should be regarded as more reliable than the others.

2. Patriarchal chronology

Chronological information for the patriarchs Abraham through Joseph may be summarized in the following table:

Patriarch	Age of Begetting	Life Span	Source
Abraham	100	175	Gen 17:17; 21:5; 25:7
Sarah	90	127	Gen 17:17; 23:1
Isaac	60	180	Gen 25:26; 35:28
Jacob		147	Gen 47:9, 28
Joseph		110	Gen 50:22, 26

By using additional details found in Gen 12:4 and 47:28, we arrive at the figure of 290 years from Abraham's birth to the entry into Egypt. Neither the LXX nor the SP vary from these figures.

While absolute dates for the patriarchs are not available, various attempts have been made to associate socioeconomic circumstances and practices in the patriarchal stories with practices known from the ancient Mari documents from the Middle Bronze I period (ca. 2000–1800 BCE) or Late Bronze Age Nuzi (ca. 1550–1200 BCE). None of these comparisons has proved completely convincing.

3. From the patriarchs to the exodus

The OT provides conflicting information about the tenure of Israel in Egypt before the exodus. In Gen 15:13-16, Abram is told that his offspring would be enslaved in a foreign land for 400 years, but that they would return to Canaan "in the fourth generation." Exodus 12:40 gives the length of the Israelite sojourn in Egypt as 430 years. While the Gen 15:13 figure of 400 may be treated as a round number, the matter of the return of the fourth generation is more problematic. Moses and Aaron are the fourth generation from Jacob (Exod 6:16-20; Num 25:57-59). Allowing 40 years per generation, the resulting 160 years between Jacob and Moses is hardly equivalent to the 400 (or 430) years of the Egyptian enslavement of Israel. Probably in an effort to resolve this dilemma, both the SP and LXX of Exod 12:40 include in the 430 years both the period of Israel's enslavement in Egypt and the period "in the land of Canaan" (i.e., the patriarchal period), thereby reducing the length of the Egyptian sojourn to 215 years.

There is only one explicit extrabiblical connection for this era. The MERNEPTAH inscription from the reign of the Egyptian king Merneptah (late 13th cent. BCE), indicates that the he encountered a group of people in Palestine identified by the name "Israel." Exactly who these people were, however, how they arrived in Palestine, and what connection they had with persons so named who were at some point slaves in Egypt is unclear.

4. Summary

In the virtual absence of extrabiblical data, one is left to evaluate the Priestly chronology on its internal consistency. Yet even this task is complicated by versional differences among the MT, SP, and LXX. Most of these differences appear to be attempts by one editorial hand or another to correct various inconsistencies within the chronology. But it is unclear which of the versions (if any) is to be regarded as reliable for historical calculations.

Clearly there is a theological scheme at work in the Priestly chronology. The time between the birth of Arpachshad and the birth of Abraham is 290 years, the same as from the birth of Abraham to the entry of Jacob into Egypt. This 580-year period is bracketed by two "passages through water": the flood and the crossing of the Red Sea. Precisely at the center of the period so defined stands Abraham, through whom God has chosen to make a great nation. Again, the length of time between Abraham's entry into Canaan and the exodus is 430 years (following the SP and LXX emendations to Exod 12:40 mentioned above), which divides into two equal periods of 215 years each, one the length of stay of the patriarchs in Canaan, and one the length of stay of Israel in Egypt. Or again, if one stays strictly to the MT of Exod 12:40, the length of time between the birth of Abraham and the foundation of the first Temple in Jerusalem is, according to the Priestly chronology, 1,200 years (Abraham to entry into Egypt, 290 + sojourn in Egypt, 430 + exodus to construction of Temple, 480), a significant number with the tribal number twelve at its heart. The careful arrangement of the eras of the world, from the legendary pre-history to the numerically balanced story of the descendants of Abraham, bespeaks the Priestly conviction that God has ordered the human story so as to culminate in worship by the chosen people Israel at the chosen site of the Temple. For the Priestly writers, chronology is less about time than about theology.

B. Deuteronomistic Chronology of the Monarchy

1. Overview

The DEUTERONOMISTIC HISTORY (Joshua, Judges, 1 and 2 Samuel, 1 and 2 Kings) has its own chronological system that is different from the Priestly system. Originally, this system would most likely have had as its primary purpose the dating of contracts and other time-conditioned documents, typically by referring to the month and year of the king's reign (with or without the name of the king: e.g., "in the fourth month of the fifth year"). Throughout the history of Israel and Judah, this system appears to have been in use, although with some slight differences between the Northern and Southern kingdoms.

a. Sources. Reconstruction of the monarchical chronology uses both biblical and extrabiblical sources.

The biblical material is drawn mainly from the editorial framework of the Samuel–Kings narrative. The chronological data in LXX (Lucianic recension) of Samuel–Kings differs in some places from the MT. This variance may indicate attempts on the part of the LXX to resolve problems in the MT or, as some think, it may point to the existence of an earlier chronology from which both MT and LXX are independently derived. The biblical sources have been subjected to some editorial schematization. The use of the round number "40" throughout the early stages of the history (Judg 3:11, 30; 5:31; 1 Sam 4:18; 1 Kgs 2:11; 11:42) indicates these periods have been estimated by the use of a common round number used throughout the OT.

Extrabiblical evidence consists mainly in references drawn from Assyrian and Babylonian documents. The Assyrian *limmu* lists provide for each year of a king's reign the name of the official installed as *limmu* for the year, a highlight of the king's accomplishments within the year, and occasionally other information that can be connected to events known from other sources. The Assyrian kings also commissioned the inscription of monuments that occasionally refer to events known from the biblical record.

The Babylonian Chronicle provides an annual record of events affecting the Babylonian court, along with references to the regnal years of Babylonian and other ancient Near Eastern kings. Additionally, the Babylonian scribes recorded astronomical events such as lunar and solar eclipses that can be dated with some precision, thus providing some absolute dates around which a chronology can be built. However, the chronicle covers only the later years of the Judean monarchy.

b. Chronological fixed points. Careful comparison of biblical and extra-biblical sources yields a series of fixed points, dates for events known from both records.

Date BCE	Event	Biblical Reference	Extrabiblical Reference
853	Ahab at Qarqar vs. Shalmaneser III		Monolith Inscription
841–40	Jehu pays tribute to Shalmaneser III		18th yr of Shalmaneser III, Black Obelisk, Annals of
740	Menahem pays tribute to Tiglath-pileser III		Nimrud Inscription
734	Ahaz pays tribute to Tiglath-pileser III	2 Kgs 16:10	Summary Inscription
732	Pekah deposed, Hoshea placed on throne	2 Kgs 15:29	Summary Inscription

722	Fall of Samaria	2 Kgs 17:6a	Babylonian Chronicle
720	Second capture of Samaria	2 Kgs 6b	Sargon II, Annals of, 2nd yr.
701	Sennacherib's Campaign	2 Kgs 18–19	Sennacherib's Annals
674, 668	Manasseh pays tribute to Esarhaddon, Ashurbanipal		Esarhaddon, Prism B; Ashur-banipal, Prism C
610	Death of Josiah at Megiddo	2Kgs 23:29	Babylonian Chronicle
605	Battle of Carchemish	Jer 46:2	Babylonian Chronicle
597	First capture of Jerusalem	2 Kgs 24:12	Babylonian Chronicle

c. Terms. The scholarly discussion of monarchical chronology employs several terms that require definition.

1) Types of data. The chronological material in 1 and 2 Kings has two types: length of reign and synchronism. Length-of-reign data enumerates the length in years (or months) of a king's reign. Synchronisms indicate the year of the accession of one king in terms of the regnal year of another king. Until the fall of Samaria, the accessions of Judean kings are synchronized with reigning Israelite kings, and vice versa. Beginning with the reign of Manasseh, 2 Kings provides no further synchronistic data for Judean kings until the narrative of the fall of Jerusalem to Nebuchadnezzar, when synchronisms with the reign of Nebuchadnezzar are given for the two captures of the city (2 Kgs 24:12 and 25:8).

2) Accession year and regnal years. The portion of the year in which a king acceded to the throne is the accession year. Thereafter, each year of reign is called a regnal year. Since every king acceded to the throne in the midst of the final regnal year of the previous king, some decision must be made regarding which king would be credited with the accession year. Two options exist: "antedating" and "postdating." Antedating refers to the practice of regarding the entire accession year as the first regnal year of the new king, even the portion before the death or removal of the previous king. Postdating refers to the practice of crediting the previous king with the entire year in which he died or was removed, even though he was not on the throne for some portion of it. In postdating systems, the new king's first regnal year does not begin until celebration of the first new-year festival during which the new king is on the throne. There is no clear statement in the biblical material regarding which system Israel and Judah used, but the likelihood is that both nations practiced only postdating throughout their existence. If antedating were in practice, any contracts drawn and dated in the final year of a king's reign would have to be redrawn to reflect the new king's accession, a correction unnecessary in a postdating system.

3) New Year festival. Ancient Israel and Judah both observed a festival at the NEW YEAR that included the observation of the coronation (or anniversary of the coronation) of the king. The actual coronation of the king was held on the first New Year festival following his accession, and his first regnal year began immediately thereafter. If a king gained the throne but did not hold it until a New Year festival, the length of his reign was recorded in months, rather than in years.

New Year festivals were most likely held in the autumn of the year in both kingdoms, in the month of Tishri in Judah and Marheshvan in Israel (1 Kgs 12:32). At some point, probably during the reign of Josiah, Judah altered its calendar by moving the anniversary of the coronation to the month of Nisan in the spring of the year. (See CALENDAR.)

4) Coregencies and regnal overlaps. The term *coregency* applies to any period in which there are two kings reigning from the same throne at the same time in some sort of officially recognized arrangement of shared power. It is not clear that such was ever the case in either Israel or Judah. The Samuel–Kings narrative mentions only two occasions on which sons were placed in positions of royal leadership while their fathers were still living: Solomon's succession of David as David neared death (1 Kgs 1:38-40), and Jotham's assumption of administrative leadership when his father Azariah/Uzziah was found to be afflicted with leprosy (2 Kgs 15:5). But neither of these can truly be claimed as coregencies. But in neither case did the father continue to rule in any meaningful way.

If there are no clear cases of coregency, however, there are situations that forced the vacating of the throne by a king who continued to live well into the reign of his successor. In each case, the regnal totals for the king reflect the total number of years from accession to death, rather than from accession to abdication or removal. In addition to Jotham's succession of Azariah, the following Judean overlaps are suggested by the Samuel–Kings narrative: a) Asa (1 Kgs 15:23b); b) Jehoash (NRSV Joash; 2 Kgs 12:20), who may have survived for a period of time after being wounded in an assassination attempt (the Heb. נכה nkh literally means "struck," without necessarily connoting immediate death); c) Amaziah, who was captured in battle (2 Kgs 14:8-14). If Amaziah remained in captivity, a new king would have been placed on the Judean throne.

2. Israelite and Judean monarchies

The tables provided below depend on the MT figures, since these appear to be generally coherent; critical exceptions are noted. The discussion proceeds from more recent to more ancient periods because there is greater certainty about the later chronology than about the earlier.

a. Babylonian Period (626–538 BCE)

King of Judah	Accession Year	Regnal Years	Events or Fixed Points
Josiah	641	641–610 (31 yrs.)	610: Josiah killed at Megiddo (2 Kgs 23:29)
Jehoahaz II	610	3 months	removed from throne by Pharaoh Neco II (2 Kgs 23:30)
Jehoiakim	608	608–598 (11 yrs.)	605: Babylonian victory at Carchemish; death of Nabopolassar, accession of Nebuchadnezzar
Jehoiachin	598	3 months	March 597: First capture of Jerusalem
Zechariah	596	596–586 (11 yrs.)	July 586: Second capture and destruction of Jerusalem
Gedaliah	586	?	

The rise of a vigorous new ruler in Babylon, Nabopolassar, signaled a sea change in the geopolitics of the ancient Near East. Judah, midway through the reign of Josiah, began to look to Babylon as an ally against Assyria. In all likelihood, Josiah reorganized the annual calendar of Judah at this time, moving the observation of the king's anniversary of coronation from fall to spring. If so, Josiah's 18th regnal year (the year of Josiah's religious reform, *see* 2 Kgs 22:3) would have consisted of eighteen months, Tishri 624 to Nisan 622 BCE.

Scholars debate whether Josiah's death at the hands of Pharaoh Neco at Megiddo (2 Kgs 23:29) took place prior to the autumn of 610 or sometime in the spring of 609, as Neco was leading an Egyptian army northward toward a battle at Harran. At the news of the death of their king, the Judean "people of the land" placed Jehoahaz II on the throne (2 Kgs 23:30), but he was deposed by the Egyptian king (v. 33) after a reign of only three months and replaced by Jehoiakim. If Josiah died in 610, then the year 609 goes unaccounted in the Judean royal chronology.

Jehoiakim reigned in Judah until late 598 BCE, but died before the Babylonians captured the city. His death left Jehoiachin on the throne; he is listed as reigning only three months. The Babylonian Chronicle makes clear that the first capture of Jerusalem took place on 2 Adar (mid-March) 597 BCE, before the New Year festival. Thus Jehoiachin is not credited with a regnal year. In addition, it appears likely that the appointment of Zedekiah as king of Judah would not have taken place in time to celebrate his coronation at the New Year festival of 597, and thus the year 597–596 BCE is probably also unaccounted in the Judean chronology. Eleven years later, in the summer of 586 and in the 19th year of Nebuchadnezzar of Babylon, Jerusalem fell a

second time, and this time was substantially destroyed (*see* 2 Kgs 25:8).

b. Assyrian Period (722–626 BCE)

King of Judah	Accession Year	Regnal Years	Events or Fixed Points
Hezekiah	727	727–698 (29 yrs.)	722: Fall of Samaria (2 Kgs 18:10, 6th yr. of Hezekiah) 701: Sennacherib's western campaign (2 Kgs 18–19)
Manasseh	698	698–644 (55 yrs.)	674, 668: Manasseh paid tribute to Esarhaddon, king of Assyria
Amon	643	643–642 (2 yrs.)	
Josiah	641	641–610 (31 yrs.)	

The 2 Kings account provides conflicting synchronisms for the reign of Hezekiah. On one hand, 2 Kgs 18:1 (the synchronism with the third year of Hoshea of Israel) and 2 Kgs 18:10 (the synchronism of the fall of Samaria with the sixth regnal year of Hezekiah) would indicate that Hezekiah's accession year ended and his first regnal year began in 727 BCE. On the other hand, the synchronism of 2 Kgs 18:13 between the 14th regnal year of Hezekiah and the 701 BCE campaign of the Assyrian king Sennacherib would argue for an accession date of 715 BCE. Various attempts at solution have been proposed. Understanding the reference in 18:13 as misplaced from the account of Hezekiah's illness (2 Kgs 20:1-19) makes sense of the divine promise (20:6) to "add fifteen years" to Hezekiah's life: adding 15 years to the "fourteenth year" arrives at the twenty-nine-year length-of-reign datum provided in 18:2.

The second problem of the Hezekiah chronology is the anachronistic reference to "King Tirhakah (Taharqa) of Ethiopia" in 2 Kgs 19:9. Taharqa was born ca. 710 BCE, and so would have been much too young to be involved in the Ethiopian/Egyptian battle with Sennacherib at Eltekeh at the end of the 701 BCE campaign. This fact has led some to propose that there was a second campaign by Sennacherib against Judah, for which Taharqa was present. However, there exists neither artifactual nor inscriptional evidence for such a campaign, and it would require a 715 BCE accession date for Hezekiah, in direct conflict with the synchronism in 2 Kgs 18:2 and 18:10. More likely is the explanation that Taharqa was simply the best known of the Ethiopian kings of the era and that his name was used by the compilers of the Hezekiah narratives, rather than that of Shebitku, the Ethiopian king at the time.

c. From Jehu to the fall of Samaria (839–722 BCE)

King of Israel	Accession Year	Regnal Years/ (Length of Reign)	King of Judah	Accession Year	Regnal Years/ (Length of Reign)
Jehu	839	839–822 (18)	Athaliah	839	839–833 (7)
			Jehoash	832	832–803[793] (40)
Jehoahaz	821	821–805 (17)			
Jehoash	804	804–789 (16)			
			Amaziah	802	802–786[774] (29)
Jeroboam II	788	788–748 (41)			
			Azariah	785	785–760[734] (52)
			Jotham	759	759–744 (16)
Zechariah	748	6 months			
Shallum	747	1 month			
Menahem	746	746–737 (10)			
			Jehoahaz	743	743–728 (16)
Pekahiah	736	736–735 (2)			
Pekah	734	734–731 (4)			
Hoshea	730	730–722 (9)			
			Hezekiah	727	727–698 (29)

The revolt of Jehu against the last king of the Omride dynasty in Israel, Jehoram, probably took place in 840/839 BCE, although it is likely that preparations for the revolt were underway earlier. The Black OBELISK inscription from the Assyrian king Shalmaneser III describes the payment of tribute by Jehu, probably then still a general in the Israelite army, to the Assyrians in 841 BCE. Jehu, most likely with Assyrian backing, then conducted a coup and purge of the royal houses of both Israel and Judah, installing himself as king in Samaria, and Athaliah, a daughter of the Omride dynasty, as queen in Jerusalem. The first regnal year for both was most likely 839 BCE.

The Jehu dynasty ruled Israel until the death of Jeroboam II in 748 BCE. With Jeroboam's death, political tensions between parties that supported cooperation with Assyria and parties that opposed it erupted in civil war. Jeroboam's son Zechariah succeeded to the throne only to be removed after a month by Shallum. Shallum in turn was removed by Menahem after a reign of only six months. Neither Zechariah nor Shallum was on the Samarian throne at the New Year festival of 747, and thus the year 747–746 is unattributed to any Israelite king.

In 2 Kgs 15:30, the accession of Pekah is synchronized with the "twentieth year of Jotham," while in 2 Kgs 15:33 Jotham is credited with a reign of only sixteen years. During the civil war that eventually brought Menahem to power in Samaria in 747/46 BCE, Pekah established a rival rule, perhaps in the Transjordan, but he was unable to secure the throne in Samaria until 734, after the deaths of Menahem and his son Pekahiah. Thus, the figure of twenty years given in 2 Kgs 15:27 would represent the entire period of Pekah's ascendancy, and

not only that portion during which he controlled Samaria.

Pekah's execution by the Assyrian king Tiglath-pileser III in 731/30 BCE brought Hoshea to the Israelite throne as a vassal. After further unrest in Israel, Shalmaneser V attacked and imprisoned Hoshea in 722 BCE, according to Assyrian inscriptions. At this time, and again in 720 BCE, Assyrian kings destroyed Samaria and deported significant groups of Israelites, bringing the independent political existence of the Northern Kingdom to an end .

In the Judean chronology, the three cases (Jehoash, Amaziah, and Uzziah) in which kings were forced by circumstances to vacate the throne before their deaths fall within this period. As indicated above (§ B.1.c.4, "Coregencies and regnal overlaps") the length of reign for each king represents the years from accession to death, and is indicated in parenthesis in the table above; the year of abdication is indicated in brackets.

d. From Rehoboam/Jeroboam I to Jehu (926–839 BCE)

The period is well defined by the near-simultaneous accessions of Rehoboam in Judah and Jeroboam I in Israel (ca. 927 BCE), and ends with the revolt of Jehu in which the heads of both royal houses are assassinated (840/39 BCE), a period of 88 years. However, the total regnal years for Israelite kings of the period is 98 years, and the Judean total is 95. In addition the accession of Jehoram of Israel is synchronized with two different Judean kings: the second year of Jehoram of Judah of Judah (2 Kgs 3:1). Complicating this picture still further is the fact that the lucianic recension of the LXX provides significantly different timing, although many scholars regard the LXX figures as an attempt to correct the confused MT date.

King of Israel	Accession Year	Regnal Years/ (Length of Reign)	King of Judah	Accession Year	Regnal Years/ (Length of Reign)
Jeroboam I	927/926	927–906 (22)	Rehoboam	927/926	926–910 (17)
			Abijah	910/909	909–907 (3)
			Asa	907/906	906–9878[866](41)
Nadab	906/905	905–904 (2)			
Baasha	904/903	903–882[880](24)			
Elah	882/881	881–880 (2)			
Zimri	880	7 days			
Omri	880/879	879–869 (11)			
			Jehoshaphat	878/887	877–853 (25)
Ahab	869	868–853 (15)			
Ahaziah	853	853–852 (2)			
Jehoram	851	851–840 (12)	Jehoram	852	852–845 (8)
			Ahaziah	840	840 (1)

Ahab must have been on the Israelite throne in 853 BCE, since we know from Assyrian sources that Ahab participated in the battle of Qarqar that year. Starting with this fixed point, we suggest the following changes in the MT data: 1) That the regnal total for Ahab be shortened from twenty-two to fifteen years. While there is no textual evidence to suggest such an alteration, have suggested that the inclusion of the Elijah and Elisha cycle at this point in the Samuel–Kings narrative has disarranged the chronological data. The regnal total of fifteen years proposed here is the result of subtracting the last known date of Ahab's life (853 BCE) from the MT synchronism of Ahab's accession with the thirty-eighth year of Asa of Judah (868 BCE, 2 Kgs 1:17). 2) That Jehoram of Judah and Jehoram of Israel were the same person, son of Jehoshaphat of Judah, who succeeded his father in the south and then Ahaziah in the north when the latter died of injuries and without an heir (2 Kgs 1:17). In the wake of the shifting political and military situation between Israel and Aram (2 Kgs 6:24) Jehoram was forced to remain in the north after 845 BCE and so is credited in the Judean chronology with only eight regnal years; in fact, he was not succeeded in Jerusalem until his death in 840 BCE during the Jehu revolt. 3) That the regnal total for Omri is eleven, rather than twelve, years. The difference of a year is a product of the different times for the New Year festival in Israel and Judah. 4) That the reign of Asa was shortened by virtue of disease and incapacity, even though the king remained alive (above, § B.1.c 4). 5) That Baasha abdicated the throne two years before his death, so that his death and that of his son occurred in the same year, 880 BCE. While it is far from clear, the reference in 1 Kgs 16:13 to Zimri having destroyed the house of Baasha "because of all the sins of Baasha and the sins of his son Elah" may suggest that the two were simultaneously eliminated.

e. Saul, David, and Solomon. The reigns of Saul, David, and Solomon as described in the MT permit no chronological precision, since there is neither synchronism nor external fixed points with which to compare them. Additionally, the regnal totals for David and Solomon are given in round numbers (forty years for each; 1 Kgs 2:11 and 11:42), and the regnal data for Saul is corrupt (1 Sam 13:1). We may, therefore, provide only the broadest strokes of a chronology, positing that Solomon's reign lasted from the mid 960s until the dissolution of the kingdom in 927 BCE, and that David occupied the thrones first of Judah and then of Israel from somewhere around 1000 BCE until his death.

C. Persian Period

The chronology of the OT throughout the Persian period (539–333 BCE) is structured by the reigns of the Achaemenid kings.

Event	Date	Reference	Achaemenid King
First return to Jerusalem	538	Ezra 1:1; 5:13	Cyrus (559–530 BCE)
Reconstruction of Temple begins	520	Hag 1:1	2nd yr. Darius I (530–522 BCE)
Temple construction completed	515	Ezra 6:14	6th yr. Darius I
Ezra comes to Jerusalem	457	Ezra 7:7	7th yr. Artaxerxes I (465–424 BCE)
Nehemiah as governor in Jerusalem	444–32 BCE	Neh 2:1; 5:14	20th yr. Artaxerxes I

Because there were three kings named Artaxerxes in the list of Achaemenid kings, there has traditionally been some question as to when Nehemiah came to Jerusalem, and whether he preceded or followed Ezra. However, papyrus discoveries at the Wadi Daliyeh in 1975 have settled the matter in favor of the order described in the MT and in the table above.

The Persian Empire reached its conclusion with the victories by Alexander the Great over Persian forces, beginning with the battle of Issus in 333 BCE and concluding with the capture and death of the last Achaemenid king, Darius III, in 330 BCE.

Bibliography: W. H. Barnes. *Studies in the Chronology of the Divided Monarchy of Israel* (1981); G. Galil. *The Chronology of the Kings of Israel and Judah* (1996); A. K. Grayson. *Assyrian and Babylonian Chronicles* (1975); John Hayes and Paul K. Hooker. *A New Chronology for the Kings of Israel and Judah and Its Implications for Biblical History and Literature* (1988); J. Hughes. *Secrets of the Times: Myth and History in Biblical Chronology* (1990); J. M. Miller. "Another Look at the Chronology of the Early Divided Monarchy." *JBL* 86 (1967) 276–88; N. Na'aman. "Historical and Chronological Notes on the Kingdoms of Israel and Judah in the Eighth Century BC." *VT* 36 (1986) 71–92; E. R. Thiele. *The Mysterious Numbers of the Hebrew Kings.* 3rd ed. (1983).

PAUL K. HOOKER

CHRYSOLITE [פִּטְדָה pitdhah; τοπάζιον topazion, χρυσόλιθος chrysolithos]. It is the second stone in the high priest's breastpiece (Exod 28:17; 39:10) and the seventh stone, **chrysolithos,** (literally "gold stone") in New Jerusalem's foundation wall (Rev 21:20). It is compared to wisdom (Job 28:19); it appears as one of the gems of Eden adorning the king of Tyre (Ezek 28:13). Some English translations render the Hebrew as TOPAZ, a common, clear, gold-colored gem. The Hebrew word is probably a loan word from another language and refers to a translucent greenish-yellow stone. Currently in mineralogy, CHRYSOLITE is an interchangeable term for olivine, a green gemstone.

ELIZABETH E. PLATT

CHRYSOPRASE kris´uh-prayz [χρυσόπρασος chrysoprasos]. The tenth stone in New Jerusalem's foundation wall (Rev 21:20). CHRYSOPRASE's colors vary from apple-green to yellowish-green. This stone was rarely used in the ANE.

ELIZABETH E. PLATT

CHRYSOSTOM, JOHN. Born at Antioch ca. 347 CE and died on a forced march into Armenia in 407, John (later given the epithet "The Golden Mouth" for his eloquence in preaching) was one of the most prolific ancient commentators on Scripture. His influence on the history of interpretation has been enormous, because his voluminous writings have been better preserved than those of any Greek commentator. Unlike other ancient authors (such as Origen or Theodore of Mopsuestia), his "orthodoxy" was not later questioned. Within years of his death his writings had been translated into Latin and spread to the West.

Chrysostom's corpus comprises treatises and letters, and transcriptions (perhaps in some cases later polished by John himself) of homilies preached at Antioch (where he was presbyter from 386–398 CE) and Constantinople (bishop, 398–407 CE), which include series on Genesis, Psalms, Isaiah, and Job in the OT, the Gospels of Matthew and John, parts of Acts, and all fourteen Pauline epistles in the NT. John's "live" liturgical scriptural interpretation combines a fever to instill biblical literacy in his congregations (he complains that they know the daily race horse listing but not the names of the cities to which Paul wrote!) with impassioned moralizing, focused especially on almsgiving, prayer, and fasting.

Chrysostom was one of the emerging "orator-bishops" of the late 4th cent. (*see also* BASIL, GREGORY OF NYSSA, GREGORY OF NAZIANZUS) who united in their persons and their ministry the rhetorical education of elite Greco-Roman *paideia* (John was a student of the most famous rhetorician of his day, Libanius of Antioch) with a Christian faith that was biblically and liturgically centered. This means that not only is he an elegant and playful stylist, but he also sees in biblical texts careful rhetorical crafting in stylistic choice and in argumentation. Thus he begins most of the homily series with a *hypothesis,* a section laying out the context and plan of the writing in question. His exegetical work is pervaded by two central hermeneutical assumptions: 1) nothing in the text is accidental or immaterial (he constantly warns his hearers against "running past" details or formulas, like the epistolary prescripts to Paul's letters, that might seem insignificant); and 2) the biblical texts, written at one time and place to a particular audience, were also directed to "us," the contemporary readers. Since he was a native Greek speaker, John provides most valuable testimony to the placement (and later repositioning) of the NT writings within Greco-Roman literary culture.

Bibliography: J. N. D. Kelly. *Golden Mouth: The Story of John Chrysostom—Ascetic, Preacher, Bishop* (1995); W. Mayer and P. Allen. *John Chrysostom* (2000); M. M. Mitchell. *The Heavenly Trumpet: John Chrysostom and the Art of Pauline Interpretation* (2001).

MARGARET M. MITCHELL

CHURCH FATHERS. *See* APOSTOLIC FATHERS, CHURCH FATHERS.

CHURCH, IDEA OF THE. While the word *church* (ἐκκλησία ekklēsia) does not appear in every book of the NT—e.g., it is not found in Mark, Luke, John, 2 Tim, Titus, 1–2 Pet, 1–2 John, Jude—the concept of the church as a community of believers is reflected in each of the NT's twenty-seven books.

A. Paul

The Pauline epistles, written in the decade of the 50s of the 1st cent. CE, provide both the oldest evidence that the word *church* was used to describe communities of Christian believers and valuable insight into the nature and functioning of those communities. Five of Paul's letters (1 Corinthians, 2 Corinthians, Galatians, Philemon, 1 Thessalonians) are addressed to a church or churches, with various qualifications. Galatians is addressed to the churches of Galatia and Philemon to "Philemon . . . and the church in your house." Philippians identifies those to whom it is addressed as "all the saints in Christ Jesus who are in Philippi" (Phil 1:1) while Rom is addressed to "all God's beloved in Rome who are called to be saints" (Rom 1:7).

1. Nomenclature

A church ekklēsia is, as the etymology of the word implies (from ἐκ ek, "out," and καλέω kaleō "to call"), a gathering or an assembly, a group of those who have been called or invited. In Hellenistic Greek, the word ekklēsia was commonly used of public assemblies, especially the assembly of free men who gathered in the theater to discuss civic affairs. In Paul's usage the word *church* always designated a real assembly of people. He, however, used the terminology with specific connotations. Initially, he linked the idea of the assembly with that of ELECTION. He speaks of those who gathered in Thessalonica for the reading of his letter as those who have been chosen (τὴν ἐκλογὴν ὑμῶν tēn eklogēn hymōn, lit., "your election," from ἐκλογή eklogē "election, choosing," 1 Thess 1:4). They are the group of those who have been called and chosen as a result of the preaching of the gospel, which they had accepted. Thus describing the church of the Thessalonians with language that recalled the election of Israel (e.g., Deut 14:2; *see* Rom 9:11; 11:5, 7, 28), Paul envisioned the assembly as a reality within the history of SALVATION.

Paul spoke to the Thessalonians about other assemblies of believers, those whom he identified as the "churches of God . . . that are in Judea" (1 Thess 2:14). Paul used similar terminology when he wrote to the "church of God that is in Corinth" (1 Cor 1:2; 2 Cor 1:1; *see also* 1 Cor 10:32; 11:22; 15:9; Gal 1:13; Acts 20:28). Although expressed in Paul's Greek language, the nomenclature is remarkably similar to the language that the Qumran community used as a self-designation. Its Rule of the Community states that "no man smitten with any human uncleanness shall enter the assembly of God" (1QSa 2 IV). The same expression occurs in the War Scroll where it is said that the sixth standard carried into battle by the sons of light bears the name "Assembly of God" (1QM 4 X).

In that apocalyptically oriented community, "the assembly of God" appears to be a technical term associated with the notions of election, calling by God, and holiness or sanctification. These are the very notions associated with "the church" in 1 Thessalonians and 1 Corinthians. First Thessalonians is remarkable, not only for its multiple expressions of apocalyptic expectation (1 Thess 1:10; 2:19; 3:13; 4:13-18; 5:23), but also because of Paul's association of election terminology with an assembly largely composed of Gentiles (1 Thess 1:9). Paul writes about sanctification as God's will for that community (1 Thess 4:3-8), reminding them of God's call (1 Thess 5:24) before drawing his letter to a close. The greeting and opening thanksgiving of the First Letter to the Corinthians speak of their being called, their being called saints, and their being called into the fellowship of God's Son (1 Cor 1:2, 9; *see* Rom 1:7). In several of his letters Paul identifies the members of the church simply as "the saints" (Rom 8:27; 12:13; 15:25, 26, 31; 16:2, 15; 1 Cor 6:1, 2; 16:1, 15; 2 Cor 8:4; 9:1, 12; 13:12; Phil 4:21, 22; Phlm 5, 7). The Letters to the Romans and to the Philippians are addressed to "the saints" at Rome and in Philippi (Rom 1:7; Phil 1:1; *see* Rom 16:15; 2 Cor 1:1).

The identification of the members of the church as "the saints" represents an appropriation of terminology that had been used of Israel as God's chosen and holy people. Most likely the epithet was first used to describe Jewish Christian believers in Jerusalem (Rom 15:25, 26, 31; 1 Cor 16:1; *see* 2 Cor 8:4; 9:1, 12). Subsequently, it was used of other members of the church, including communities that were largely comprised of Gentiles. In his letter to the Romans Paul uses the image of an engrafted olive branch to explain how Gentile Christian communities could be holy. "If the root is holy," he writes, "then the branches also are holy" (Rom 11:16).

It is also likely that the "church of God" was a technical expression used by 1st cent. Palestinian Jews who considered their assemblies to be those of a community of faithful Jews who were waiting for the realization of the Kingdom of God. As such, the term was employed not only by the Qumran sectarians but also by the Christian Jews of Jerusalem and Judea (*see* 1 Thess 2:14). Paul appropriated this Jewish Christian terminology to describe the assemblies of those who had accepted his gospel and awaited the appearance of the Lord (1 Thess 1:10).

2. Defining qualities of the church

The sanctification or holiness of the church is among its defining characteristics, as it is for the community at Qumran (*see* 1QS 5II; 9V). For Paul, holiness results from God's choice, the election of the church. Because the members of the church have been chosen by God, they belong to him, they are God's holy people, the "saints" (οἱ ἅγιοι hoi hagioi, from ἅγιος hagios, "set apart, holy, consecrated"; *see* HOLY, HOLINESS, NT). The members of the church have been sanctified by Christ Jesus (1 Cor 1:2; *see* Phil 1:1) through the continuous gift of the Holy Spirit (1 Thess 4:8). At bottom, sanctification or holiness is a cultic term, designating persons or things that have been set aside for the service of God. This nuance is manifest in 1 Cor 3:16-17 where Paul describes the church as God's holy temple in which the Spirit of God dwells.

Paul remembered the church of the Thessalonians as an assembly characterized by its "work of faith, labor of love, and steadfastness of hope," the marks of the church. The faith of which Paul wrote was the believing community's living and dynamic relationship with God. For the Apostle, faith worked through and expressed itself in love (Gal 5:6). The love of which Paul wrote was the very real and active love of the other members of the community. The Apostle repeatedly addressed these believers as ἀδελφοί adelphoi (from ἀδελφός adelphos) that is, "brothers and sisters" (e.g., 1 Thess 1:4). Hence, sibling love (φιλαδελφία philadelphia) was a hallmark of the community (1 Thess 4:9). The church's eschatological orientation (1 Thess 1:10) manifested itself in the steadfastness of its hope—despite the difficulties and afflictions that Paul deemed to be inevitable (1 Thess 3:3-4).

3. Siblingship

Although the church was an assembly of believers, Paul's preferred form of direct address to the members of the churches to whom he wrote was adelphoi, "brothers and sisters" (Rom 1:13; 7:1, 4; 8:12; 10:1; 11:25; 12:1; 15:14, 30; 16:17; 1 Cor 1:10, 11, 26; 2:1; 3:1; 4:6; 7:24, 29; 10:1; 11:33; 12:1; 14:6, 20, 26; 15:1, 31, 50, 58; 16:15; 2 Cor 1:8; 8:1; 13:11; Gal 1:11; 3:15; 4:28, 31; 5:11, 13; 6:1, 18; Phil 1:12; 3:1, 13, 17; 4:1, 8; 1 Thess 1:4; 2:1, 9, 14, 17; 3:7; 4:1, 10, 13; 5:1, 4, 12, 14, 25, 27; *see* Phlm 7). This kinship terminology not only expressed the bonds of affection between the apostle and the churches to which he was writing but also the bonds that joined the members of the church together in a fictive family

and distinguished them from outsiders who did not belong to the church of God.

The fictive family ties that bound the members of the local church to one another were expressed in the gesture of affection that Paul describes as a holy kiss. He urged the members of the church at Thessalonica to "greet all the brothers and sisters with a holy kiss" (1 Thess 5:26; *see* Rom 16:16; 1 Cor 16:20; 2 Cor 13:12; 1 Pet 5:14). The affect and effect of family ties among believers extended beyond the boundaries of a single local assembly. Addressing the topic of sibling love (**philadelphia**), Paul commended the Thessalonians for the love that they had for one another, adding, "Indeed you do love all the brothers and sisters throughout Macedonia" (1 Thess 4:10).

Several of Paul's letters indicate that the fictive family relationship created by belief in the gospel and entrance into the church created specific and sometimes challenging responsibilities for the members of the church. Paul's brief note to Philemon exploits the family relationship of the members of the church (*see* GOD THE FATHER; HOUSEHOLD OF GOD). The letter was written by "Paul . . . and Timothy our brother to Philemon . . . and Apphia our sister" (Phlm 1-2). Repeatedly, Paul commends Philemon for his love. Then he makes his appeal on behalf of "my child Onesimus, whose father I have become during my imprisonment" (Phlm 10). Paul asks Philemon to take Onesimus back "no longer as a slave but more than a slave, a beloved brother" (Phlm 16).

Since the teaching of the Torah to his sons was one of a father's primary responsibilities (*b. Qidd.* 22a), rabbinic literature considered that when a man taught the Torah to another man's son it was as if he had begotten that child (*b. Sanh.* 19b). The relationship between them was that between a father and a son. For the Christian Paul, the preaching of the gospel replaced the teaching of the Torah. Because Paul had evangelized Onesimus, he considered himself to have begotten the slave, just as he considered himself to be father to the Thessalonian and Corinthian churches whose members he had evangelized (1 Thess 2:11-12; 1 Cor 4:14-17). Insofar as Paul continued to nurture the young churches, he could use maternal imagery to describe his relationship with them (1 Thess 2:7; 1 Cor 3:1-3).

Paul frequently used the kinship relationship among believers as a basis for various exhortations. Thus, the 1 Thessalonians urges the readers not to wrong or exploit a brother in this matter (1 Thess 4:6). Although some scholars take Paul's words in 1 Thess 4:6 to mean that a member of the church should not defraud another member of the church, I would argue that the matter at hand is sexuality and that his words are an exhortation to avoid adultery.

The Apostle uses the literary device of ring construction to place the entire Letter to the Galatians within the context of siblingship. The letter begins with greetings from Paul and "all the members of God's family (οἱ σὺν ἐμοὶ πάντες ἀδελφοὶ hoi syn emoi pantes adelphoi) to the churches of Galatia" (Gal 1:2). Its final salutation is: "May the grace of our Lord Jesus Christ be with your spirit, brothers and sisters" (adelphoi, Gal 6:18), underscored with an emphatic "Amen." This emphasis on siblingship in the finale of one of his letters is unique within the extant Pauline correspondence and highlights the emphasis on family bonds that undergird the argument of the entire letter.

In 1 Corinthians Paul urges the members of the church of God not to take one another to court. His argument is partially based on the bonds of kinship that exist among the members of the church. He expresses outrage that "a brother goes to court against a brother—and before unbelievers at that" (1 Cor 6:6). Family ties should prompt the members of the community to refrain from eating meat offered to idols when such conduct would be offensive to weaker members of the church: "by your knowledge the weak brother for whom Christ died is destroyed. But when you thus sin against your brothers and wound their conscience when it is weak, you sin against Christ"(1 Cor 8:11-12).

The Apostle's statement that Christ had died for the Corinthian's siblings impinges upon his words of non-commendation as he accuses the Corinthians of showing contempt for "the church of God" (1 Cor 11:22), as they celebrate their communal meal (*see* AGAPE; COMMUNION; COMMUNITY; LORD'S SUPPER; MEALS). Eating the meal in a way that expresses the social divisions within the community, as inevitable as they may be, means that the Corinthians are not celebrating the Lord's Supper (1 Cor 11:20). Rather, Paul reminds them: "As often as you eat this bread and drink the cup, you proclaim the Lord's death until he comes. Whoever, therefore, eats the bread or drinks the cup of the Lord in an unworthy manner will be answerable for the body and blood of the Lord" (1 Cor 11:26-27).

4. The Body of Christ

Paul's 1 Corinthians offers clear evidence of various issues facing a local church and perhaps some indication of its organization and membership. The letter also makes use of three striking metaphors to describe the church.

Arguing against the factionalism that threatened to break the unity of the community as its various members rallied round different leaders, Paul describes the role of himself and Apollos in the building up of the church at Corinth. He uses agricultural and construction metaphors to illustrate the cooperative roles of himself and Apollos, saying to the church: "You are God's field, God's building" (1 Cor 3:9). The agricultural imagery speaks about the complementary roles of Paul and Apollos, under God, in establishing the church as God's field. The image of the building enables Paul to speak about himself as the one who laid the foundation of the church (1 Cor 3:10) so that others might build up the church. The construction imagery depicts the diversity of the church and the complementary roles of those who build up the church. The building is ultimately identified as the holy temple of God, since the Spirit of God dwells within it (1 Cor 3:16-17).

In many ways the most striking Pauline image of the church is that of the church as the BODY OF CHRIST (1 Cor 12:12-26). Dating to the time of the Roman senator Menenius Agrippa, the image of the human body as a way of speaking about societal unity was a classical topos in Hellenistic rhetoric. Paul used the image both to speak about the unity of the single body with its many members and to speak about the many and different members complementing one another in the one body. Paul identified baptism as the means of incorporation into the single body of Christ (1 Cor 12:13) whose members include Jews and Greeks, slaves and free persons. Rather than distinctions of ethnicity and class, the diversity of charismatic figures within the church is the principal focus of Paul's attention when he describes the church as the one body of Christ.

The Apostle used the image of the body to counter the apparent claims of those who spoke in tongues and placed undue emphasis on the spiritual gift or charism that they had received at the expense of those who had received other gifts. Paul emphasized that just as the body is composed of various members, including the hand, the eye, the ear, and the less honorable members of the body—all of which belong to the one body and without which the body would not function as it should—so the church is composed of various members, each with his or her own gift (1 Cor 12:7, 11). Paul follows up his lively description of the body image by identifying apostles, prophets, teachers, miracle workers, healers, helpers, administrators, and those speaking intongues—a non-exhaustive list (*see* 1 Cor 12:7-10, 29-30, etc.)—as representative of the different charismatic figures in the church.

Paul's Letter to the Romans reprises the motif of the body of Christ. He writes: "As in one body we have many members, and not all the members have the same function, so we, who are many, are one body in Christ, and individually we are members one of another" (Rom 12:4-5). Paul does not employ the image polemically, as he did in 1 Corinthians. Nonetheless, he follows up his mention of the body with a list of spiritual gifts (Rom 12:6-8), albeit somewhat different from the various lists that appeared in 1 Cor 12. The particular gifts that Paul identifies in this passage of Romans are those of the prophet, minister, teacher, exhorter, giver, leader, and the person with compassion. The various spiritual gifts that Paul associates with the image of the church as the body of Christ express the interactive vitality of the various members of the local church.

5. Assembly of believers

Although the initial preaching of the gospel might take place in the synagogue or a workshop (1 Thess 2:9), the church required a place for the assembly of believers to gather. The salutation of the Letter to Philemon and the final greetings of 1 Corinthians suggest that these gatherings took place in the home of one of the members of the church. Thus Paul wrote "to Philemon . . . and to the church in your house" (τῇ κατ᾽ οἶκόν σου ἐκκλησίᾳ tē kat oikon sou ekklēsia Phlm 2) and conveyed greetings on behalf of "Aquila and Prisca, together with the church in their house (Ἀκύλας καὶ Πρίσκα σὺν τῇ κατί οἶκον αὐτῶν ἐκκλησίᾳ Akylas kai Priska syn tē kat oikon autōn ekklēsia, 1 Cor 16:19; see Rom 16:5; Col 4:15). Luke's description of the church in Jerusalem confirms that a house of believers was the normal venue for the gathering of the church (Acts 2:46; 12:12; see Acts 1:13-14). The BAPTISM of entire households (1 Cor 1:16; Acts 16:15, 33) and Luke's occasional reference to the household of believers (Acts 11:14; 16:31, 34; 18:8) are so many indications that the household or home was the fundamental unit of the church (see HOUSE CHURCH).

Paul's letters were read to Christians who gathered "at home" (1 Thess 5:27; Phlm 2). The preaching of the gospel, prayer, and the breaking of the bread, i.e., the EUCHARIST, were among the activities that took place in the home of a Christian. The venue in which the church gathered was a fitting locale for the use of kinship language, "brothers and sisters," that highlighted the bonds that tied Christians together. The house was also the place where breaking the bread, the eucharist could be celebrated in the context of a meal that reasonably appropriated the character of a family meal.

Archeological excavations reveal that even a relatively large family home would not be able to accommodate a large number of people. The atrium of a home in the Greco-Roman world could accommodate perhaps thirty to forty people. Larger cities, where evangelization took place over some considerable length of time, would most likely have had several house churches. The final greetings of the letter to the Romans suggest, for example, that there were at least five house churches in the imperial capital, those associated with Prisca and Aquila (Rom 16:5), Aristobulus (Rom 16:10), Narcissus (Rom 16:11), Asyncritus (Rom 16:14), and Philologus (16:15). The language that Paul employs to greet the last two groups shows that it was not only the members of a biological family or a secular household who belonged to a house church. After greeting Asyncritus, Phlegon, Hermes, Patrobas, Hermas, and "the brothers and sisters who are with them" (Rom 16:14), Paul greets "Philologus, Julia, Nereus and his sister, and Olympas, and all the saints who are with them" (Rom 16:15). The existence of different house churches, each with its own leadership cadre (see 2 John 13), may have contributed to the difficulties experienced by the churches in Jerusalem (see Acts 6:1) and Corinth (1 Cor 1:11-12). Paul does not identify by name of their patron any of the house churches in the city of Corinth but the language that he uses in the greetings of Romans and in 1 Corinthians suggests that on occasion individual house churches came together in a larger gathering or church. From Corinth Paul sends greetings to Rome on behalf of "Gaius, who is host to me and to the whole church" (Rom 16:23). The anti-social situation within the church of Corinth became apparent when they "came together as a church" 1 Cor 11:18; see 1 Cor 11:17, 20).

6. Relationship among the churches

Although the different house churches were relatively independent of one another, Paul's letters provide evidence of significant interaction among the churches. His 1 Thessalonians indicated that knowledge of the faith of the Thessalonian church was known throughout Macedonia and Achaia and beyond (1 Thess 1:7), that the love of the Thessalonian Christians extended beyond the Thessalonian church to embrace the brothers and sisters throughout Macedonia (1 Thess 4:10), and that the Thessalonian church had become an imitator of the churches of God in Judea (1 Thess 2:14). Paul's 1 Corinthians greeted the Corinthians together with all those who in every place call on the name of the Lord Jesus Christ, both their Lord and ours (1 Cor 1:2). The Second Letter is addressed to the church of God at Corinth together with all the saints throughout Achaia (2 Cor 1:1). The Letter to the Galatians was intended to be a circular letter that was to be read to the various churches evangelized by Paul in the Galatian region (Gal 1:2).

No sign of the unity among the churches was, however, as strong as the COLLECTION made in several of the Pauline foundations on behalf of God's holy people in Jerusalem. The importance of this collection is particularly underscored in Paul's Letters to the Corinthians (see also Rom 15:25-29). First Corinthians describes the practicalities of the collection. It was to be taken up on the first day of the week and put aside until such time as it could be taken to Jerusalem (1 Cor 16:1-4). 2 Cor 8–9 is an extensive plea for funds; it urges that donations to the collection be made voluntarily (2 Cor 8:3; 9:5, 7). Paul invokes the generosity of Jesus as a reason why the Corinthians should be generous (2 Cor 8:9). In addition, Paul cites the generosity of other churches in order to move the Corinthians to give generously (2 Cor 8:1-2; see 1 Cor 16:1).

This collection for the poor in Jerusalem was an expression of sibling love, a ministry or service to members of God's holy people (2 Cor 8:4; 9:1; Rom 15:25, 31; see 1 Cor 16:15). Moreover, Paul sees the collection as an "ecumenical gesture." The Corinthians' gift to the impoverished church in Jerusalem should prompt the Christian Jews of that city to pray for the ethnically mixed church of God at Corinth (2 Cor 9:14). The collection was thus a means to heal somewhat the tension between Gentile Christians and Jewish Christians. Finally, the collection was a way for members of the different churches scattered throughout the Roman Empire to express to the mother church in Jerusalem their gratitude for the spiritual blessings that they had received (Rom 15:27).

7. Organization of the local church

For the most part Paul's letters are devoid of the technical language used by the later church to describe people in leadership positions. Paul considered his own role to be that of the apostle, an evangelizer (1 Cor 1:17), one whose preaching led to the formation of a church, a gathering of believers. In this sense the apostolate could be listed first among the charisms; it was, in point of fact, the foundational charism (1 Cor 12:28). Thereafter Paul's role was to nurture the church by means of letters, the sending of emissaries like Timothy and Titus, and later visits.

Paul's letters give no indication that he assumed responsibility for appointing leaders for the churches that he would leave behind. Nonetheless, Paul's first letter, 1 Thessalonians, indicates that leaders were recognized in the church at Thessalonica within a relatively short time after it had been established. Paul urges the Thessalonians: "Respect those who labor among you, and have charge of you in the Lord and admonish you; esteem them very highly in love because of their work" (1 Thess 5:12-13). The greeting of the Letter to Philemon suggests that Philemon, in whose house the church gathered, had the leadership role within that community, as did Prisca and Aquila in the churches which met in their house both in Corinth (Rom 16:3) and in Ephesus (1 Cor 16:19).

Paul singles out ἐπισκόποι καὶ διακόνοι episkopoi kai diakonoi, "bishops and deacons" (from ἐπίσκοπος episkopos and διάκονος diakonos), literally, "overseers and servers") for particular mention among the saints in Philippi (Phil 1:1; *see* DEACON; OVERSEER). These terms designate a function, rather than serving as a title, but Paul does not write about the respective responsibilities of overseers and servers, nor does he give any indication as to who these people were. The only person identified by either of these terms in the extant Pauline correspondence is Phoebe, identified by Paul as "a deacon of the church at Cenchreae" (Rom 16:1).

On the basis of 1 Corinthians (*see also* 1 Thess 5:19), scholars often presume that the Pauline churches were rather loosely structured, i.e., "charismatically organized," on the basis of the various gifts of the Spirit to the members of the community. Paul's extensive disquisition on charisms (1 Cor 12–14) is, however, more

concerned with the harmonious interaction of those to whom the various charisms have been given than it is with setting down a plan for the organization of the church at Corinth. In the enumerated list of charisms in 1 Cor 12:28, Paul assigns the second place, immediately after that of apostles, to prophets (1 Cor 12:28). The gift of prophecy, speaking in word and/or action on behalf of God and God's people, is the only charism that appears on every one of Paul's lists (Rom 12:6; 1 Cor 12:10, 28, 29). This gift is also cited in 1 Thess 5:20. Prophecy thus appears to be a *sine qua non* of the Pauline churches.

B. Other Epistolary Texts

In the late 1st cent., 1 Timothy and the Letter to Titus promulgated in the form of a letter written under Paul's authority a number of indications as to how the church should be organized.

1. Timothy and Titus

The first few verses of the Letter to Titus intimate that Paul had left the organization of the church as a task for the future and that the organization of the church was the purpose of the document: "I left you behind in Crete for this reason, so that you should put in order what remained to be done and should appoint elders in every town, as I directed you" (Titus 1:5).

This statement of purpose suggested that the first of the tasks to be done was the appointment of elders as bishops or overseers (episkopos). Expressions such as "sound doctrine" (ὑγιής διδασκαλία hygiēs didaskalia; *see* 1 Tim 1:10; 6:3; 2 Tim 1:13; 4:3; Titus 1:9; 2:2; compare Titus 1:13) and "sure saying" (πιστὸς ὁ λόγος pistos ho logos; 1 Tim 1:15; 3:1; 4:9; 2 Tim 2:11; Titus 3:8) indicate that there was a standard of orthodoxy and a body of tradition that governed the teaching and preaching of these overseers.

Titus identifies the role of those appointed to be that of preaching sound doctrine and refuting error (Titus 1:9). First Timothy suggests that the role of the bishop was managerial: the person chosen for the task should have had experience in managing his own household so that he would be able to take care of the church of God (1 Tim 3:5). Should they rule well and be effective in preaching and teaching, the elders appointed to the function of overseer are worthy of a double honor, that is, the respect of the community and appropriate wages (1 Tim 5:17-18). An imposition of hands, perhaps by the entire group of elders, seems likely to have been the commissioning or ordination ritual (1 Tim 4:14; 5:22; 2 Tim 1:6; *see* Acts 13:3).

These two Pastoral epistles envision that the church be organized on the pattern of the Greco-Roman household. The bishop or overseer, for whom hospitality is a requisite qualification (1 Tim 3:2; Titus 1:8), is described as God's steward (θεοῦ οἰκονόμος theou oikonomos, Titus 1:7). In the Greco-Roman household the steward, generally a slave, had managerial responsibilities with regard to the household's other slaves. He assigned the tasks and coordinated the responsibilities. A similar function was to be exercised by the bishop within the church.

Like Phil 1:1, 1 Timothy mentions deacons or servers (diakonos). These must be qualified (1 Tim 3:10) and prepared for service within the household of the church (1 Tim 3:12) but their specific responsibilities are not identified within the text. Presumably they would exercise whatever functions would be assigned to them by the bishop. First Timothy seems to indicate that women are included among the servers, though some exegetes hold that the pertinent passage relates not to a function within the church but to the wives of servers (1 Tim 3:11). Paul's identification of PHOEBE as a deacon (Rom 16:1) makes it not unlikely, however, that those who would seek to organize the church under his name would include women among the deacons of the church.

First Timothy gives directives for the church's worship. The addressee called TIMOTHY is charged with being attentive to the public reading of the Scripture (1 Tim 4:13). Worship includes a variety of prayer forms, notably, supplications, prayers, intercessions, and thanksgivings (1 Tim 2:1; see WORSHIP, NT CHRISTIAN). Since there is but one God and one mediator, prayer must be offered for everyone. Kings and those in positions of civic authority are singled out as specific persons for whom prayer is to be offered. Ultimately the purpose of prayer for the authorities is the commonweal, the good of the members of the civic community (1 Tim 2:2).

In 1 Timothy directives are set down for the respective demeanor of men and women in the liturgical assembly. The epistle stipulates that men should pray without anger or argument; with respect to their outward appearance, men should pray with their hands washed and lifted up (1 Tim 2:8). With regard to their disposition, women who reverence God should be known for their good works; with regard to their physical appearance, they are to be clothed simply, without ostentatious adornment or elaborate coiffure (1 Tim 2:9-10).

Some authors see in the Pastoral's relatively long exposition on widows (1 Tim 5:1-16), the establishment of a ministerial order within the church, akin to the female deacons or deaconesses of later centuries. It is, however, preferable to take the author's effort to describe "real widows" (ὄντως χήρας ontōs chēras, from χήρα chēra "widow," 1 Tim 5:3) as an attempt to identify indigent women who should be supported by the church. The author distinguishes real widows from widows who have family to support them (1 Tim 5:4) as well as from young widows who are encouraged to marry again (1 Tim 5:14). The real widow is a widow over sixty years of age who is all alone and has only God to rely on (1 Tim 5:5). If the real widow has

lived an appropriate Christian life (1 Tim 5:5, 9-10), her name is to be put on a list (1 Tim 5:9) and she is to be supported by the church (1 Tim 5:3, 16; see WIDOW; WOMEN IN THE NT). Effectively the author of 1 Timothy has organized at least this one aspect of the church's ministry of social service, carrying out the biblical injunction to provide for the widow and orphan (e.g., Isa 1:17; compare Acts 6:1-3).

Another area of church life that 1 Timothy seeks to organize is its discipline with regard to elders, presumably those with a leadership position within the church. The church's disciplinary procedures are to be administered without partiality. Although the author does not cite Deut 19:15 as a biblical warrant for the practice, he mandates that the community should not accept an accusation against an elder except on the basis of the testimony of more than a single witness (1 Tim 5:19-20). Errant elders are to be publicly rebuked, not so much as a form of punishment but as a means of teaching the community. The chastised elder serves as a negative example for its members.

Although 1 Timothy and Titus are for the most part hortatory and legislative, 1 Tim 3:15 offers a concise theological description of the church. The author writes about, "the household of God, which is the church of the living God, the pillar and bulwark of the truth." This description capitalizes on the household structure of the church which it identifies as belonging to God (see 1 Pet 4:17). The ambivalence of the Gk. oikos, which may mean either HOUSE or HOUSEHOLD, may have led the author to specify that the oikos tou theou, the house(hold) of God, is the church of the living God (see HOUSEHOLD OF GOD). The church is an assembly that belongs to the living God. The imagery recalls the biblical motif of Israelites assembled to hear the word of the living God through Moses, God's prophet (Deut 4:10; 9:10; 18:16; 31:30). The author then uses construction imagery—perhaps capitalizing on the meaning of oikos as "house"— to describe the church's role as the guardian and promotor of the truth. The church is the solid foundation on which the truth can rest.

The Letter to Titus does not offer as finely a crafted ecclesiological statement as does 1 Timothy nor does it use the word church (ekklēsia). Nevertheless, the epistle describes the church as a community of those who await the (final) manifestation of the great God and Savior Jesus Christ (Titus 2:13). This epistle also speaks about baptism, not however as an entrance ritual but rather as a ritual of rebirth and renewal by the Holy Spirit (Titus 3:5).

2. Colossians and Ephesians

The Letter to the Colossians, whose authorship remains a subject of dispute among biblical scholars, is addressed to the saints in Colossae (Col 1:2; see Rom 1:7; Eph 1:1; Phil 1:1). It continues its description of believers as God's holy ones (Col 1:4, 12) beyond the epistolary greeting (Col 1:2), especially in Col 3:12, where the holiness of the members of the church is linked to their having been chosen and having been loved by God.

The epistle's salutation also identifies the recipients of the letter as a fictive family, as "brothers and sisters" (adelphoi, Col 1:2) as is the nearby church of the Laodiceans (Col 4:15). A few individual believers are called "brother" and are thereby identified as members of the church. These are Timothy, Tychicus, and Onesimus (Col 1:1; 4:7, 9). Among them, Tychicus is singled out as "a faithful minister" (pistos diakonos). The descriptive epithet appears to be more of a generic description rather than a designation of a specific function or office in the church. Tychicus is described as having been sent to Colossae rather than as having a permanent function among the Colossians. Moreover, the church to which he belongs is not identified (see Rom 16:1).

The Letter to the Colossians continues to speak about the church as a local assembly as did the Apostle. The letter mentions the assembly in Nympha's house (Col 4:15) and the church of the Laodiceans (Col 4:16; see 1 Thess 1:1). The text, however, goes beyond the Apostle's understanding of the church in attributing to "church" (ekklēsia) a metaphorical meaning. In Col 1:18, 24, the church is described as the body of Christ. In Romans and in 1 Corinthians both of the expressions, "church" and "body of Christ," were used to speak of the local assembly. In Col 1:18, 24, the expressions are used in reference to what might be called the universal church, the totality of believers. The church is no longer an assembly of people gathering in a single place (1 Cor 11:20); it is rather an abstract notion used to describe all believers.

With this mutation of the notion of church comes a change in the idea of the body of Christ. Paul used the metaphor to describe the unity in diversity and diversity in unity of the local church. The interaction of the various members of the body was his primary interest. In Colossians what is of interest to the author is the headship of Christ over the church. Christ is the head of the body, which is the church. The body is no longer considered as a single unit of which the head with its ears and eyes (1 Cor 12:16-17) is a part; rather, Christ is the head and the church is the torso. By describing Christ as the head of the church (Col 1:18; 2:19, the author underscores the primordial importance of Christ, Christ's authority over the church, and Christ as the source of the church's life.

The Letter to the Ephesians is essentially a theological essay on the church which uses the Colossians as its basic outline. In letter form, the epistle is addressed to the saints who are in Ephesus *and* are faithful in Christ Jesus. The *and* (kai, Eph 1:1) makes it clear that faith in Christ is central to the Ephesians' identity as members of God's holy people. The identification of believers as God's holy people is a key element in the ecclesiology of Ephesians (Eph 1:15, 18; 2:19; 3:8, 18; 4:12; 5:3, 27; 6:18). That believers are God's holy people depends on their being chosen by God, according to God's preordained plan of salvation (Eph 1:4). The predestined and everlasting character of the church is emphasized again when the mission of the church is identified as making known the richness of the wisdom of God to the rulers and authorities in the heavenly place "in accordance with the eternal purpose that he [God] has carried out in Christ Jesus our Lord. Ephesians 3 concludes with the epistle's only doxology which identifies the church as the locale in which, through Jesus Christ, eternal glory is rendered to God (Eph 3:21).

As a defining quality of the people of God, the holiness of the church is emphasized in the important but curiously mixed imagery of Eph 2:19-22 (*see also* Eph 5:27). The author begins by addressing the Gentiles who once did not belong to the body of Israel's citizens (*see* Eph 2:12) but have now become fellow citizens with God's holy people. The political imagery is then morphed into construction imagery when the church is presented as the house or household of God built on the foundation of the apostles and prophets (compare 1 Cor 3:10) with Christ as the cornerstone. Thus Christ, with his spokespersons the apostles and (Christian) prophets, is presented as the start and foundation of the church. The imagery of biological growth, with the language that would be used of the growth of the body of Christ in Eph 4:16, is employed to transform the building that is being built into a temple that is holy to the Lord in which God dwells. The complex imagery brings together the christological, theological, and apostolic elements of the church together with the idea of its growth and unity.

The epistle begins with a solemn benediction (Eph 1:3-14) which concludes with a description of believers as God's possession (περιποίησις peripoiēsis, "God's own people"). This singular expression suggests that believers are "owned" by God in much the same fashion that slaves are owned by their masters. It puts in economic terms the idea of holiness with which the benediction began (Eph 1:4). Encompassed between the idea that believers are God's holy ones (Eph 1:4) and the idea that believers are God's possession (Eph 1:14), are several notions that pertain to the nature of the church: God's holy people have been blessed with every spiritual blessing, are destined for adoption as God's children, have been pledged the inheritance of redemption, and have heard the word of truth, the gospel of salvation, with the result that they have believed in him and been marked with the seal of the Holy Spirit, their being branded, as it were, with the sign of the Spirit. This community is noted for its faith in the Lord Jesus and its love for God's holy people (Eph 1:15; compare 1 Thess 1:3).

Ephesians has taken over from the letter to the Colossians an abstract notion of the church, the body of which Christ is the head (1:23; 2:16; 4:4, 12, 15-16; 5:23, 30), but expands on the image considerably. For the author of Ephesians there is but one body, just as there is one Spirit, one hope, one Lord, one faith, one baptism, and one God and Father of all (Eph 4:4-5). Various gifts are given to the members of the church so that they might work together properly and build up the church as the body of Christ (Eph 4:12, 16). The members of the church grow and are knit together in a single body.

Thus the idea of charismatic endowment and the interaction of different members in the unity of a single body, which Paul had exploited in his use of the body image in 1 Corinthians recurs in Ephesians. Ephesians, however, attributes the charismatic gifts to the exalted Christ rather than to the Spirit (Eph 4:7-13). The reconciliation of Jews and Gentiles to God in the one body through the cross is an aspect of the unity of the church that is particularly stressed in Ephesians (Eph 2:15-16; 3:6). The ecclesial focus of this epistle is clearly emphasized when the author interprets the lordship of Christ over all things (see 1 Cor 15:25-28) as being for the sake of the church, his body (Eph 1:22-23). The author thus complements his imagery of the church as the body of Christ by adding that the church is the fullness of Christ who fills it.

One remarkable feature of the ecclesiology of Ephesians is the way that the author blends his understanding of the church with his understanding of the relationship between husband and wife. He uses a segment of a traditional household code as a literary structure, within which he embeds a striking exposition on the church (Eph 5:22-33). This exposition is a reworking of the biblical motif of the marital relationship between Yahweh and Israel (Isa 54:6-7; Jer 3:1; Ezek 16:10-14; Hosea; 2 Cor 11:3; Rev 19:7-8; 21:2, 9).

In the imagery of Ephesians the church is the bride whom Christ loves, nourishes, and tenderly cares for to the point of having sacrificed himself for her. In language that evokes both a bride's preparation for her wedding and the Christian ritual of baptism, the author portrays Christ preparing his bride so that he could present to himself a splendid bride, without spot or wrinkle or anything of that sort. Unblemished, she belongs to Christ as a holy bride. Espoused to Christ, the church owes obedience to him just as wives were subject to their husbands in the late first-century Greco-Roman household.

3. Hebrews, James, and Peter

The Epistle to the Hebrews, an exhortation rather than a letter (Heb 13:22), rarely speaks about the church. Its greatest contribution to an understanding of the church resides in the images that shaped the later church's notion of a cultic priesthood. Heb 2:12, however, makes use of a passage from Ps 22:22 [21:22 LXX] to describe the church as an assembly (ekklēsia) of those who praise the Lord. The exhortation's anonymous author uses this verse from Ps 22 since it mentions "brothers and sisters" (adelphoi, to be understood only as males in the psalm itself). This kinship language is the terminology that the author of Hebrews had used when he described sanctified believers as the brothers and sisters of Jesus, children of God (Heb 2:10-13). Ecclesial language occurs again in Heb 12:23, when the author speaks about the assembly (ekklēsia) of the firstborn. Since the firstborn within Israel especially belonged to God even though the entire nation could be described as God's firstborn (Exod 4:22-23), the imagery of Heb 12:23 describes the members of the church as the special possession of God. They share in the inheritance of Jesus, the one who is singularly the first born (Heb 1:6).

The Letter of James is another NT text that rarely mentions the "church"—only once in fact. James 5:14 stipulates that should a person in the community fall sick, then the elders of the church should be summoned so that they might pray over the sick and anoint them.

Addressed to Jewish Christians (see Jas 1:1; 2:8-12, 21), James projects a strong sense of being addressed to a well-defined community or communities. The members of the community are addressed as "brothers and sisters" (adelphoi) with a frequency that rivals the usage of Paul in 1 Thessalonians and 1 Corinthians (see Jas 1:2, 16, 19; 2:1, 5, 14; 3:1, 10, 12; 4:11; 5:7, 9, 10, 12, 19; compare James 1:9; 2:15, 4:11). Their elders are not identified merely by age (see Philo, Contempl. Life 67); rather the elders are leaders who have distinguished themselves by reason of their maturity, wisdom, and knowledge of the community's tradition(s). Some leaders in the community are described as teachers (διδάσκολος didaskalos; see 1 Cor 12:28, 29; Eph 4:11), but it is expected that they will be relatively few in number (Jas 3:1). One issue of particular concern for the author was the relationship between the rich and the poor in the fictive family that was the church (Jas 1:9-11, 2:1-7).

First Peter is one of the ten books of the NT that does not mention the word *church* (ekklēsia). The letter is addressed to a community of resident aliens (1 Pet 1:17; 2:11) who have a strong sense of their identity as a community. Its members are called "CHRISTIAN" (χριστιανός christianos, 1 Pet 4:16), relatively new language that had first been used in Antioch (Acts 11:26). Unique among the NT's descriptions of the church is 1 Peter's description of the church as a "brotherhood" (ἀδελφότης adelphotēs, 1 Pet 2:17; 5:9). Elsewhere the community is identified as the "household of God" (oikos tou theou, 1 Pet 4:17; see 1 Tim 3:15).

The community for which 1 Peter was intended had a keen sense of its own identity as God's holy people

(1 Pet 1:16-17; *see* 2:9) in contradistinction with those outside who do not obey the word (1 Pet 3:1). Its unity is predicated upon the members' humility and their love for one another (1 Pet 3:8).

First Peter 2:4-10 presents the image of the church as a spiritual temple. The author's image is composed of biblical motifs and citations from Isa 28:16, Ps 118:22 [117:22 LXX], and Isa 8:14. First Pet 2:9 constitutes a virtual title for the image that the author has portrayed: "a chosen race, a royal priesthood, a holy nation, God's own people." The four epithets are biblical descriptions of Israel that the author has applied to the church that is built on Christ as its foundation stone. This community of Jewish Christians (*see* 1 Pet 2:12) awaits the imminent eschaton (1 Pet 2:12; 4:7; 5:4).

The only identified leaders of the community are its elders who are to take their example from the text's patronymic Peter (1 Pet 1:1), willingly exercising oversight (ἐπισκοποῦντες episkopountes, from ἐπισκοπέω episkopeō, "take care, oversee," 1 Pet 5:2) over the flock, as a SHEPHERD would do, until such time as the chief shepherd appears (1 Pet 5:1-4; compare 2 Pet 2:25). The image of the community of believers as a flock and of Jesus as a shepherd is similar to the imagery developed in John 10:1-16.

One other element in the author's understanding of the Christian community that is not to be overlooked is the importance that he accords to rebirth (1:3, 23; 2:2) and baptism which, the author takes pains to point out, is not the washing of a dirty body but a means of participation in the resurrection of Jesus Christ (3:21-22).

C. The Gospels and Related Texts

Matthew is the only one of the canonical Gospels that explicitly mentions the church (Matt 16:18; 18:17 [twice]). Nonetheless, each of the four Gospels describes Jesus calling a group of disciples, leaders emerging from among them, and Jesus sending some of them out to proclaim the good news.

1. Mark

The oldest of the four Gospels, Mark, portrays a mountaintop as the locale on which Jesus selected twelve of his disciples, naming them apostles and giving them a three-fold task: to be with him, to proclaim the gospel, and to cast out demons (Mark 3:13-19a). They were apostles (from ἀπόστολος apostolos), that is, those whom he sent (ἀποστέλλω apostellō "send"; *see* Mark 6:7-13); in fact, they were sent out in pairs. Their mission was to extend Jesus' mission by proclaiming the gospel and expelling demons, the proclamation of the good news in word and in deed. The longer ending of Mark (Mark 16:9-20) portrays Jesus sending the apostles out to continue their mission after his resurrection (Mark 16:14-18, 20; *see* 1 Cor 15:5).

Throughout his Gospel, Mark continues to emphasize that this group was twelve in number (Mark 3:14, 16; 4:10; 6:7; 9:35; 10:32; 11:11; 14:10, 17, 20, 43). Despite the power struggles among them (Mark 10:35-45), the Twelve were the privileged recipients of the announcement of Jesus' impending death and resurrection (Mark 10:32-34). That the apostles were twelve in number symbolized the foundation of a new eschatologically-oriented community analogous to the twelve tribes of Israel. While Luke's Acts shows the importance of maintaining the complement of twelve after Jesus' death and resurrection (Acts 1:15-26), Matthew's portrayal of the eschaton explicates the symbolism of the number twelve: "When the Son of Man is seated on the throne of his glory, you who have followed me will also sit on twelve thrones, judging the twelve tribes of Israel (Matt 19:28; *see* Luke 22:30; Rev 21:12-14).

Within the group of twelve a select group of three, Peter, James, and John witnessed the raising of the daughter of Jairus and the transfiguration of Jesus (Mark 5:35-43; 9:2-8), asked Jesus about the coming eschaton (Mark 13:3-4), and were with Jesus in Gethsemane (Mark 14:32-42). Among the disciples, Simon, to whom Jesus gave the name Peter (Mark 3:16), emerged as the spokesperson of the disciples (Mark 8:27-30) and particularly of inner circle of three disciples (Mark 9:5-6). As spokesperson for the disciples, Peter confessed Jesus to be the Messiah in response to Jesus' questions about his identity.

Jesus told Peter and his brother Andrew that they would fish for people (Mark 1:17). Shortly thereafter Jesus entered the house of Simon and Andrew accompanied by James and John (Mark 1:29). The house/home was to become important locale in Mark's story about Jesus. Not only did Jesus work miracles in the home (Mark 1:29-31; 2:1-12; 5:35-43; 7:24-30), the home was also the place where Jesus discussed the meaning of his activity and his teaching (Mark 7:17; 9:33; 10:10-12). Jesus told the apostles and some of those who were healed to announce the good news at home (Mark 5:19-20; 6:10; compare Mark 2:11; 8:26). Meals at home were an important feature of the Markan story (Mark 2:13-17; 14:3-9, 17-25). It was in the home that Jesus referred to his disciples as his kin, his mother, brothers and sisters (Mark 3:31-35). Mark's numerous references to the house/home reflect the post-resurrection gatherings of believers at home where they experienced the powerful presence of Jesus and discussed his teachings. The setting-in-life of the traditions from which Mark's gospel was formed is parallel with the situation of the church at home, to which Paul's letters give witness.

2. Matthew

Matthew's rewrite of Mark's gospel is clearly directed to a Jewish-Christian readership. The evangelist accentuates the relationship between the twelve tribes of Israel and the Twelve (Matt 19:28) by equating the disciples with the Twelve. For Matthew, the Twelve, the disciples, and the apostles are one and the same group (Matt 10:1-2). Among the evangelists only Matthew speaks of the twelve disciples (Matt 10:1; 11:1; 20:17; 26:20). These twelve are sent out to exorcise demons (Matt 10:1) and preach the gospel (Matt 10:7).

Among the twelve, Matthew highlights the role of Peter not only by his explanation of the change of name from Simon to Peter (Matt 16:13-20) but also by the addition of a dialogue between Peter and Jesus on forgiveness (Matt 18:21-22) and the addition of a pair of sea stories which feature Peter's attempt to walk on water (Matt 14:28-33) and his finding a coin for the temple tax (17:24-27). Matthew 16:13-20 (see Mark 8:27-30; Luke 9:18-21) describes Simon Peter confessing that Jesus is the Messiah, the Son of the living God in response to Jesus' question about his identity. Responding to Simon's confession of faith, Jesus pronounces a blessing on him, proclaims that he has been the beneficiary of divine revelation, and plays on the name Peter—in Aramaic the word **Kephas** (John 1:42; 1 Cor 1:12, 3:22; 9:5; 15:5; Gal 1:18; 2:9, 11, 14) means *rock* or *crag*; Peter's name in Greek, Πέτρος Petros, is derived from πέτρα petra which means "rock" or "stone"—to say that he will build his church (ekklēsia) on the "rock," which is Peter. The image of the keys coupled with the language of binding and loosing (compare Matt 18:18) suggests that Peter is to assume the role of interpreting the Torah for those Jews who had become Jesus' disciples just as Jesus himself had interpreted the Torah for the twelve (Matt 5:17-48). Jesus' mention of the gates of Hades, which will not prevail against the church, highlights the eschatological strength of the community in which his interpretation of the Scriptures will continue to be conveyed (see Matt 7:24-27).

Matthew 18:15-18 describes how this Jewish-Christian church (Matt 10:5-6) was to deal with one of its members who had offended another. Matthew identifies the two parties as being in a kinship relationship, calling each of them "brother" (adelphos, Matt 18:15, 17). The offended person is to take the initiative in the reconciliation (see the similar use of kinship language in Matt 5:23-24). If that is unsuccessful, appeal is to be made to two or three witnesses. Should that fail, an appeal is to be made to the entire assembly (ekklēsia). Should that too fail, the offending member of the church is to be treated like an outsider, that is, like a Gentile (1 Cor 5:1-8; 3 John 10).

The finale of Matthew's Gospel describes the eleven assembled on a Galilean mountain by the risen Jesus. Judas has previously defected and killed himself (Matt 27:5). With supreme authority, Jesus commissions the eleven to make disciples from among all the nations. Their task involves baptizing the neophytes and conveying to them the very same teaching that Jesus had given to the eleven (Matt 28:16-20).

3. Luke-Acts

The Gospel of Luke, the first part of the Lukan composition, offers only subtle hints of the author's understanding of the church. It defines fictive kinship in terms of hearing the word of God and keeping it (Luke 8:21; 11:28). It alludes to the church's mission to the Gentiles by speaking about the mission of the seventy in addition to the mission of the twelve (Luke 9:1-6; Luke 10:1-17) and the sending of the servants to the countryside in the Parable of the Great Supper (Luke 14:23).

Luke develops another scene as the setting for the logion on fishing for people (see Mark 1:17; Matt 4:19). In Mark, Jesus' words are addressed to Peter and Andrew; in Matthew, to Peter and Andrew, James and John. Luke offers a story of a miraculous catch of fish (Luke 5:1-11), which culminates in a promise to Simon Peter that from then on he would be catching people (Luke 5:10). Luke's story makes no mention of Andrew and makes the sons of Zebedee the partners of Peter (Luke 5:7, 10).

The preeminent place of Simon Peter among the apostles is confirmed in the Lukan farewell discourse in the setting of the Passover meal. The literary genre normally focuses on issues pertaining to the unity and leadership of those who are to be left behind. The principal topics of Luke's farewell discourse are the leadership and mission of the apostles (Luke 22:24-37). Jesus speaks of Peter's future conversion—after the triple denial (Luke 22:34, 54-62)—and his subsequent role in strengthening the members of his fictive family. Jesus tells Simon Peter that he has prayed for him that he remain a faithful disciple, that his faith not fail.

The second part of Luke's opus, the Acts of the Apostles, highlights two aspects of the evangelist's understanding of the church, namely, his vision of the church of Jerusalem as the ideal and mother church with Peter in the initial position of leadership and his vision of the spreading of the witness to Jesus to Samaria and the Hellenistic world by means of Philip and Paul.

Peter's leadership role in the Jerusalem church is emphasized when, almost immediately after the ascension of Jesus, he stands among the brothers and sisters and takes the initiative in bringing the membership of the Twelve up to its full complement (Acts 1:15-26). Matthias was chosen for the position of overseer. After the conferral of the gift of the Holy Spirit, Peter, standing in the company of the other eleven, delivers the Pentecost speech (Acts 2:14-36). He directs those who accepted his message to change their lives and be baptized. About 3000 persons did so, thus joining the company of Jerusalem disciples (Acts 2:37-42).

Peter, accompanied by John, confirmed the Samaritan mission by going to Samaria and laying hands on those who had been baptized in order that they receive the Holy Spirit (Acts 8:14-25). Although both Peter and John witnessed to Jesus and spoke the word of the Lord to the Samaritans, only Peter is engaged in correcting the views of Simon who wanted to buy the power to confer the Spirit. After Luke had narrated the conversion of Paul (Acts 9:1-19) and the establishment of the church through Judea, Galilee, and Samaria (Acts 9:31), Peter provides a warrant for the mission to the Gentiles by having Cornelius, his family, and friends, baptized (Acts 10) and then by defending his actions in an apologia addressed to Jewish Christian believers in Judea (Acts 11:1-18).

A triad of succinct descriptions of the church in Jerusalem conveys Luke's vision of that community as the ideal church. Luke's first summary (Acts 2:42-47) of the Jerusalem church, now expanded through the addition of the three thousand who had been baptized, is that it was characterized by its devotion to the apostles' teaching, fellowship, the breaking of the bread (eucharist), and prayers (see Acts 1:14, noting the participation of women in the church, and Acts 12:5). Luke's emphasis on the breaking of the bread recalls Jesus' words that bread was to be broken in remembrance of him, an observation made by Luke alone among the evangelists (Luke 22:19).

The second summary (Acts 4:32-35) points to the centrality of the resurrection of the Lord Jesus in the testimony given by the apostles. It expands on the first summary's idea that fellowship (κοινωνία koinōnia) is expressed in the joint possession of all goods (see KOINONIA; COMMUNITY OF GOODS). Luke's comparison of Joseph and Ananias, a positive and a negative example, underscores the vital importance of sharing as a condition for membership in the community led by the apostles (Acts 4:36–5:6).

The evangelist's emphasis on the sharing of material possessions as an expression of the church's koinōnia distinguishes Luke's understanding of fellowship from that of Paul. Notwithstanding his affirmation that the sharing of material goods is a sign of the unity of the church (koinōnia, Rom 15:26; 2 Cor 6:14; 8:14, 9:13), the Apostle emphasizes that it is the believer's participation in Christ (1 Cor 1:9; 10:16), the Spirit (2 Cor 13:13; Phil 2:1), the gospel (Phil 1:5), or faith (Phlm 6) that creates fellowship within the church.

Luke's third cameo of the church in Jerusalem (Acts 5:12-16) portrays the church of the apostles as the locale of God's power at work. Signs and wonders done by the apostles and the "magic" of Peter's presence led to an increase in the numbers of those who belonged to the church. Thus, Luke's vision of the ideal church, to which members are added in baptism, is that it is characterized by the preaching and teaching of the apostles, the signs and wonders that they do, prayers and the breaking of bread, and a fellowship that is expressed in a sharing of possessions.

Luke notes that the growth of the church in Jerusalem was, nonetheless, not without its problems. To help them provide food for widows among the Hellenist believers (Acts 4:35; 6:1), the Twelve led the group of brothers and sisters in the choice of seven men to assist the Twelve. The apostles prayed over the seven and laid hands upon them, thereby commissioning them for the task at hand (Acts 6:1-6). Many scholars trace the role of servers in the church (Rom 16:1; Phil 1:1; 1 Tim 3:8-13) back to this initiative on the part of the apostles.

The second aspect of Luke's understanding of the church featured in Acts is that the preaching of the gospel message moved beyond the confines of Judea and Samaria into the world of the Gentiles. The program was announced by Jesus according to Acts 8:1. Luke specifically mentions the importance of the church in Antioch, where believers first received the name "Christian" (Acts 11:26; 13:1; 14:26; see also Acts 15:30, where it is said that Paul and Barnabas "gathered the congregation together," from συνάγω synagō, the term from which SYNAGOGUE derives). He presents Paul as the bearer of the good news to the Gentiles. Paul and his companions preached the gospel in Lystra, Iconium, and Antioch where churches were established (Acts 14:21-23; 16:5). Elders were appointed to lead each of these churches.

Paul's farewell discourse to the elders of the church of Ephesus (Acts 20:17-35) offers a sustained reflection on how Paul's ministry was to be continued after his departure. The residential leaders of the community were the overseers. Elders were made overseers by the Holy Spirit in order to shepherd the church of God, obtained through the death of Jesus. Paul's speech projects a vision of a church that will be threatened by dangers from within, the distortion of the truth by some insiders.

Acts also portrays a dynamic vision of the unity among the churches, especially their bond with the mother church at Jerusalem. Particularly important in this regard is the narrative of Acts 15, a crucial turning point in Luke's story of the church. The narrative portrays the apostolic and presbyteral college in Jerusalem recognizing the legitimacy of the mission to the Gentiles. Some Judean Christians had insisted that Gentile believers be circumcised. In response, Gentile believers sent Paul and Barnabas to Jerusalem to discuss the matter with the apostles and elders. James, the brother of the Lord, led the discussion, at the end of which a conciliatory circular letter was sent to believers in Antioch, Syria, and Cilicia. Those who gathered in Jerusalem and those to whom the letter was sent are identified by means of kinship language; they are "brothers and sisters" (Acts 15:13, 23). Luke notes that the letter was read to believers in Antioch and in the region of Phrygia and Galatia (Acts 15:30-31; 16:4-6). Luke's narrative not only recounts a stylized tale of the spread of the gospel to the ends of the earth; it also underscores the importance of the mother church in Jerusalem and the unity between that church and Gentile Christian churches.

4. The Johannine corpus

As important as the Lukan Farewell Discourse is for an understanding of the evangelist's ecclesiology, still more important is the Farewell Discourse(s) of the Fourth Gospel (John 13-17). The author's vision of the church, the community of the "beloved disciple," that would be left behind after Jesus' departure highlights the unity of the community (John 17:20-23; John 10:16) and the bond of mutual and life-giving love that has Jesus' love as its source and exemplar (John 13:34; 15:12; compare 1 John 2:7-8; 3:23; 2 John 5-6). The command that those who believe in him love one another and thus establish a bond of mutual love is one of the departing Jesus' gifts to the community. Jesus' washing the disciples' feet (John 13:2-17) projects the idea of leadership as service. The Holy Spirit, identified as the Advocate and Spirit of Truth, will be sent to them to teach them all things and remind them of all that Jesus has taught (John 14:16-17; 16:7-14). Thus, what Ferreira calls the "christological ecclesiology" of the Fourth Gospel features the revelation given by Jesus, the community's unity in their love for one another, and the sending of the Spirit into the world.

A unique feature of the ecclesiology of the Fourth Gospel is its recognition that there are those who belong to Jesus but who do not belong to the community of the Beloved Disciple. The Parable of the Good Shepherd mentions those who belong to Jesus but do not "belong to this fold" (John 10:16). The Fourth Gospel knows of the existence of the Twelve but does not accord to the group the importance that it has in the other gospels. In fact, the Fourth Gospel appears to reflect some tension between the community, for which it was written and those Christians who might be called "apostolic Christians."

The Johannine letters provide evidence of tensions among believers (*see* 1 John 1:9-11; 2:19; 2 John 9-10). Diotrephes refuses to recognize the authority of the elder, spreads false charges, refuses to exercise hospitality, and dares to take to himself the authority to expel some believers from the community (3 John 9-10). On the other hand, the Johannine community continues to enjoy a strong sense of unity. First John 1 uses a theological understanding of fellowship (κοιν-ωνία koinōnia) to speak of this unity (1 John 1:3, 6-7). Members of community have fellowship with one another, but the ground of their fellowship is fellowship with the Father and his Son Jesus Christ.

The salutation of 2 John provides a beautiful image of the church. It is written from the elder "to the elect lady and her children" (2 John 1; 3 John 4). The woman who has been chosen (ἐκλεκτή κυρία eklektē kyria) is an image of the church; her children are siblings to one another. Strikingly, 2 John does not use adelphoi,

"brothers and sisters," to refer to the members of the church, although it does refer to the children (from τέκνον teknon "child") of elect ladies (2 John 1, 4, 13). On the other hand, the sibling language abounds in 1 and 3 John (1 John 2:9, 10, 11; 3:10, 12, 13, 14, 15, 16; 4:20, 21; 5:16; 3 John 3, 5, 10).

Kinship language is language that properly belongs at home. The church of 2 John is clearly a house church (2 John 10) but it is not the only house church in the Johannine community. Second John concludes with greetings for the elect lady and her children from "the children of your elect sister" (2 John 13).

The book of Revelation recognizes the existence of the church as a local community in its series of letters to the seven churches, Ephesus, Smyrna, Pergamum, Thyatira, Sardis, Philadelphia, and Laodicea (Rev 2–3). These letters urge the local churches to greater conversion. The community of the redeemed is represented by the idealized number of 144,000, sealed out of the twelve tribes of Israel, branded with the names of the Lamb and the Father on their foreheads, and singing a new song in the presence of the Lamb (Rev 7:4-8; 14:1-5).

The last part of the book uses a pair of graphic images to portray the community of the redeemed. The church is the bride of the Lamb, the bride prepared for her husband (Rev 19:7-8). This bride is the new Jerusalem (Rev 21:2, 9-10) portrayed as the holy city in Rev 21:10-14. The names of the Twelve inscribed on the foundations stones point of this holy city highlight the apostolic origin of the church and its relationship with Israel. *See* BISHOP; BODY OF CHRIST; CHURCH, LIFE AND ORGANIZATION OF; DISCIPLES; ELDER IN THE NT; FAMILY; HOUSE CHURCH; PRESBYTER; TEMPLE.

Bibliography: R. Aasgaard. *"My Beloved Brothers and Sisters!": Christian Siblingship in Paul* (2004); R. E. Brown. *The Community of the Beloved Disciple* (1979); R. F. Collins. *The Many Faces of the Church: A Study in New Testament Ecclesiology* (2003); R. F. Collins. "The Origins of Church Law." *The Jurist* 61 (2001) 134–56; R. F. Collins. *The Power of Images in Paul* (2007); R. F. Collins. "The Transformation of a Motif: 'They Entered the House of Simon and Andrew' (Mark 1, 29)." *SNTSU* 18 (1993) 5–40; K. P. Donfried. "The Assembly of the Thessalonians." *Paul, Thessalonica, and Early Christianity* (2002); J. Ferreira. *Johannine Ecclesiology* (1998); J. A. Fitzmyer. *The Acts of the Apostles* (1998); D. J. Harrington. *The Church According to the New Testament: What the Wisdom and Witness of Early Christianity Teach Us Today* (2002); R. Michiels. "The 'Model of Church' in the First Christian Community of Jerusalem: Ideal and Reality." *LS* 10 (1985) 302–23; J. Murphy-O'Connor. *St. Paul's Corinth: Text and Archeology,* 3rd. ed. (2002); P. K. Nelson. *Leadership and Discipleship: A Study of Luke 22:24-30* (1994).

RAYMOND F. COLLINS

CHURCH, LIFE AND ORGANIZATION OF [ἐκκλησία ekklēsia]. The church according to the NT is the community gathered in Jesus' name to worship God and serve others. Rooted in the Jesus movement, the church took shape through faith in the saving significance of Jesus' death and resurrection, and found expression in various Christian communities. The NT canon bears witness to the unity and diversity of church life and organization during the 1st cent. CE.

A. The Jesus Movement and the Beginnings of the Church

1. The Jesus movement

The "Jesus movement" refers to the public ministry of Jesus and people's response to his ministry. It expresses the dynamism displayed by Jesus and his first followers as they went about proclaiming God's kingdom and working for the spiritual renewal of their people. All members of the Jesus movement were Palestinian Jews.

Jesus was born, lived, and died in the land of Israel. He read the Jewish Scriptures, participated in Jewish festivals and rituals, and observed the precepts of the Torah (even if his interpretations differed from those of other Jewish teachers). His movement began with his baptism by John, some period of spiritual testing, and the call of his first disciples.

The symbolic focal point of the Jesus movement was the kingdom of God. His first words according to Mark 1:15 (see Matt 4:17) are a good summary of all his teaching and activity: "The time is fulfilled, and the kingdom of God has drawn near; repent and believe in the good news." In teaching about God's kingdom Jesus joined together the pre-exilic belief in the present kingship of God ("The Lord is king," Ps 99:1) and the post-exilic hope for a definitive future display of God's sovereignty ("Thy kingdom come," Matt 6:10; Luke 11:2). Jesus' own person was a sign of the presence of God's reign. But he also pointed to something even greater in the future. The kingdom of God will be eschatological, transcendent, and universal. It is God's task to bring about its fullness. The NT never equates the Jesus movement or the church with the kingdom of God. However, both serve as signs of the kingdom's presence and as symbols of hope for its future fullness.

Against the background of his Jewish heritage and his convictions about the kingdom of God, Jesus invited his followers to approach God with confidence and to address God as "Father" as he did. When asked for his summary of the 613 commandments in the Torah, Jesus singled out two: love of God (Deut 6:4-5), and love of neighbor (Lev 19:18). He challenged his followers to love even their enemies (Matt 5:43-48; Luke 6:27-36). He also urged people to go to the "root" (Lat. radix) of the commandments (Matt 5:17-48), to the point of avoiding oaths and divorce, and of giving up their material possessions. Jesus showed great concern for people on the margins of Jewish society and shared meals with disreputable persons ("tax collectors and sinners") as a sign of what the banquet in the fullness of God's kingdom will be like. Moreover, Jesus holds out the possibility of divine forgiveness to all. He serves as God's agent in seeking out the "lost sheep" and restoring them to right relationship with God (Luke 15:1-32). And he insists that those who have experienced God's forgiveness should be willing to forgive those who may have offended them. The themes of intimacy with God, the primacy of the love commandment, controversial interpretations of the Torah, concern for marginal persons, and the offer of forgiveness can be attributed to Jesus with confidence and represent the core values of the Jesus movement.

Jesus was a charismatic teacher who went about Galilee and environs. If he had a home base, it was CAPERNAUM. Very early on Jesus enlisted a group of disciples to be with him and to share in his ministry of preaching and healing. Instead of prospective disciples seeking out their rabbi, Jesus summoned his disciples and they followed immediately. The inner circle constituted by the twelve apostles naturally evokes memories of the twelve tribes of Israel and suggests that the first followers of Jesus represent Israel as the people of God. The wider complement of disciples included women who played important roles in the Jesus movement (Mark 15:4–16:8;

Luke 8:1-3). Those who followed Jesus belonged to the new family of Jesus, bound together by their commitment to do the will of God (Mark 3:35).

The Gospels are remarkably frank about the failures of the Twelve. Not only do they misunderstand Jesus repeatedly but they also desert him in the hour of his passion and death. Indeed with Jesus' death it seemed that the Jesus movement was also dead. It appeared to be just another short-lived Jewish religious movement.

2. The earliest churches

With the resurrection of Jesus, however, the Jesus movement became the church of Jesus Christ. While the empty tomb was a necessary presupposition for proclaiming Jesus' resurrection, what seemed to have been more important was a series of dramatic experiences in which Jesus' followers encountered him as risen from the dead and fully alive (Matt 28:9-20; Mark 16:9-20; Luke 24:12-53; John 20:11–21:23; 1 Cor 15:3-8). Those who, a short time before, had abandoned Jesus became his public champions. The dramatic change in Jesus' followers on the basis of the appearances is the strongest argument for the reality of Jesus' resurrection from the dead. The appearances as they are narrated in the Gospels usually include a commission to proclaim the gospel to other people. While it has become customary to refer to Pentecost as the birthday of the church, one can just as well date the beginning of the church to Easter and the event of Jesus' resurrection.

According to various NT writers, what allowed the church of Jesus Christ to grow and flourish was the power of the Holy Spirit. Paul insisted that each Christian received the Holy Spirit and was obligated to use the gifts of the Spirit for the common good and for building up the church as the body of Christ (1 Cor 12:7). In Luke–Acts the Holy Spirit is a major actor in salvation history. The Spirit inspires various figures in the infancy narrative (Luke 1–2) to prophesy and provides the divine agency in the birth of Jesus (Luke 1:35). Throughout Jesus' public ministry he is led and empowered by the Spirit, having become the principal bearer of the Holy Spirit at his baptism (Luke 3:21-22a). Being "filled with the Holy Spirit" (Acts 2:4) on Pentecost, Jesus' disciples begin to prophesy and are empowered to do what he did. According to John, what made possible the continuation of the Jesus movement after the physical departure of Jesus was the Holy Spirit or Paraclete. The Paraclete served as the "stand in" or replacement for the earthly Jesus. So on Easter evening the risen Jesus says to his remaining disciples: "Receive the Holy Spirit" (John 20:22).

Several historical and sociological factors also contributed to the spread of the early Christian message and the growth of the church. The dominance of Rome throughout the Mediterranean world brought with it a peaceful interlude in the mid 1st cent. CE. Roman efforts at stopping piracy on the sea and at improving the road system on land made travel relatively easy for missionaries (but see 2 Cor 11:25-27). And the use of Greek as a common language throughout much of the ROMAN EMPIRE facilitated the communication of the Christian gospel.

Another factor that helped in the development of the church was the presence of Jews in the great cities of the Roman Empire: Alexandria, Antioch, Ephesus, and Rome. While remaining faithful to their Jewish heritage, Hellenistic Jews spoke Greek, read a Greek translation of their Scriptures, and lived in the midst of Greek and Roman culture. Their synagogues attracted not only ethnic Jews but also non-Jews (the "God-fearers" of Acts) who were impressed by Judaism because of its monotheism, high ethical standards, and community life. Luke's portrayal of Paul going first to the synagogue in any city may reflect the practice of the first Christian missionaries.

The geographical center of earliest Christianity was Jerusalem. Luke's Acts of the Apostles charts the spread of the gospel "in Jerusalem, in all Judea and Samaria, and to the ends of the earth" (1:8). The first chapters of Acts are set in Jerusalem and highlight the exploits of the apostles Peter and John, though eventually James "the brother of the Lord" emerges as the local leader. In order to arrive at a decision about the conditions under which non-Jews may enter the church, the interested parties like Paul and Barnabas hold a solemn meeting in Jerusalem (Acts 15). Throughout Paul's ministry he acknowledged the historical primacy of the Jerusalem church and organized a special collection for its poor members as a symbol of the unity between his Gentile Christian churches and their Jewish "mother church" (see APOSTLES, ACTS OF THE).

The first Christians in Jerusalem were all Jews by birth. Some were Aramaic (or Hebrew) speaking, while others were Greek speaking (Hellenists). The latter group seems to have aroused fierce opposition from conservative Jews like Saul. If Stephen's speech in Acts 7 is in any way historically reliable, it appears that the Hellenistic Jewish Christians were not much interested in Temple rituals and strict Torah observance, and held broader ideas about the scope of God's people. They were eventually forced to leave Jerusalem (Acts 8:1). Luke notes that "all except the apostles were scattered," which suggests that Hebrew Christians (the apostles) were exempted from the opposition and persecution.

Hellenistic Jewish Christians provided the impetus for the church's missionary activity. They knew the language and culture of the Greco-Roman world. When some of them encountered non-Jews at Antioch in Syria (Acts 11:19-26) who showed interest in becoming Christians, the Christian mission began to go in new directions.

Earliest Christianity was a missionary religion. The basis for such activity was Jesus himself, who worked as a traveling preacher, called disciples and sent them out to do what he did, and showed an openness to all kinds of people, including outcasts and the despised. Roman writers such as Pliny, Suetonius, and Tacitus bear witness to the rapid spread of Christianity throughout the Roman Empire. However, the number of Christians in this early period was very small. One sociologist estimates that in 50 CE there were approximately 1,400 Christians in the world, and that by the end of the 1st cent. there were approximately 7,530.

3. Did Jesus found the church?

The most decisive elements in the emergence of the church of Jesus Christ were the resurrection and the Holy Spirit. Jesus set out to proclaim God's kingdom and to prepare for its coming, not to develop a religious organization. Nevertheless, Jesus' earthly ministry did prepare for important features of the post-resurrection church.

Did Jesus found the church? Much depends on how each term is defined. Does "Jesus" mean only the earthly Jesus in his public ministry, or does it also include his passion, death, and resurrection? Does "found" mean establishing a consciously designed social organization with administrative structures and regulations, or does it refer merely to the energy or dynamism (the "Spirit") needed to transform and carry on the Jesus movement? Does "church" mean a well-defined social organization with fixed structures, or is it simply the continuation of the Jesus movement in light of Jesus' resurrection and the coming of the Holy Spirit?

The latter set of definitions fits the biblical evidence better than the former set does. How the church of Jesus Christ emerged can also be illumined by the sociological concepts of the charismatic leader and the routinization of charisma. As a charismatic prophet Jesus was convinced of his mission from God, taught on his own authority, and sought validation mainly from the one whom he called "Father" (Mark 1:22). While he attracted a number of disciples, he did not follow the religious-institutional models of his Jewish contemporaries: exclusive fellowship (*see* PHARISEES), "closed" community (QUMRAN people), or rabbinic academy (the school of YOHANAN BEN ZAKKAI). Rather, he addressed his message of God's kingdom to all kinds of people, did not set up a clearly defined organization, and emphasized mission rather than institution.

Nevertheless, there was a degree of continuity between the Jesus movement and the church. That continuity involved beliefs (about God's kingdom and Jesus as its prophet, the core ethical values), personnel (the Twelve, Peter, women), and practices (shared meals, a certain freedom regarding Jewish legal traditions). In these respects those who participated in the Jesus movement provided a basis for the church. They carried on and made "routine" the impulses set in motion by Jesus the charismatic prophet. Jesus' promise to build his church on Peter as the rock (Matt 16:18) should be read as a promise to be fulfilled after Jesus' death and resurrection.

B. The Religion of the Earliest Christians
1. Beliefs

The core of early Christian belief is summarized in 1 Cor 15:3-5: "that Christ died for our sins in accordance with the scriptures, and that he was buried, and that he was raised on the third day in accordance with the scriptures, and that he appeared to Cephas, then to the twelve." At the beginning of a long reflection on Christ's resurrection and its implications for Christians, Paul quoted a summary of the gospel that he had preached to the Corinthians and that he himself had received from his predecessors in the Christian movement. The center of this statement is the death and resurrection of Jesus. Both events are interpreted as fulfilling the OT Scriptures, and Jesus' death is given an atoning and vicarious significance ("for our sins"). In his Letter to the Romans Paul cites other already traditional statements about the sacrificial value of Jesus' death ("whom God put forward as a sacrifice of atonement by his blood," 3:25) and about his resurrection ("[who] was declared to be Son of God with power according to the spirit of holiness by resurrection from the dead, Jesus Christ our Lord," 1:4).

The same focus on Jesus' death and resurrection appears in what is generally regarded as an early Christian hymn in Phil 2:6-11. Echoing the words of the Servant Song in Isa 52:13–53:12, the hymn first describes the incarnation of Jesus as self-emptying (kenōsis) and his obedience to the Father even to the point of his shameful death on the cross. Then it celebrates Jesus' resurrection as an exaltation, in which all creation joins in confessing that "Jesus is Lord to the glory of God the Father" (Phil 2:11). Similar terms appear in credal formulas quoted in the Pastoral Epistles: "Christ Jesus came into the world to save sinners" (1 Tim 1:15); and "there is one mediator between God and humankind, Christ Jesus, himself human, who gave himself as a ransom for all" (1 Tim 2:5-6; *see* 1 Tim 3:16; 2 Tim 2:11-13; Titus 3:4-7).

Another focus of early Christian faith was Jesus as the Wisdom of God. The hymn in Col 1:15-20 first celebrates Jesus as "the firstborn of all creation" in terms taken over from or parallel to earlier descriptions of Wisdom personified as a female figure (Prov 8:22-31; Sir 24:1-22; Wis 7:22-30; *1 En.* 42:1-3). Then it proclaims Jesus to be "the firstborn from the dead" and the one in whom "the fullness of God was pleased to dwell." The theme of Jesus as Wisdom incarnate is also present in the prologues to John's Gospel ("In the beginning was the Word," John 1:1) and to the Letter to the Hebrews ("He is the reflection of God's glory and the exact imprint of God's very being," Heb 1:3). This

Wisdom-Christology reflects the fact that Jesus enjoyed a unique relationship with God as creator, and provides a theological framework for the teachings of Jesus in the Gospels.

When they looked back into the OT, early Christians found Jesus to be to the key to interpreting the Scriptures and the fulfillment of the promises made by God in Israel's sacred texts. For example, the three hymns contained in Luke's infancy narrative (1:46-55, 68-79; 2:29-32) celebrate the birth of Jesus with a pastiche of biblical phrases. The early Christians also looked forward to the second coming of Christ in glory: "Maranatha...Come, Lord Jesus" (1 Cor 16:22; Rev 22:20). They found little theological conflict between Jewish monotheism and proclaiming Jesus as "Lord." An apt summary of early Christian beliefs appears in Eph 4:4-5: "one body, one Spirit . . . one hope . . . one Lord, one faith, one baptism, one God and Father of all."

2. Rituals

The most prominent rituals of the early church were BAPTISM and the LORD'S SUPPER. The NT provides no explicit description of either rite. Rather, they are mentioned in passing, in the course of treatments of other topics. In both cases ordinary elements and actions were given new orientations and interpretations with reference to Jesus' death and resurrection.

Water baptism served as the rite of initiation into the paschal mystery and the Christian community. Rooted in Jewish rituals of purification and John's baptism, the early Christian ritual involved immersion into the death and resurrection of Jesus (Rom 6:1-4). So decisive and total was the transformation brought about by baptism that according to an early creedal statement it rendered irrelevant all ethnic, social, and gender differences: "There is no longer Jew or Greek . . . slave or free . . . male and female" (Gal 3:28). Baptism soon came to be viewed as the Christian equivalent of and replacement for circumcision as the entrance rite into the people of God (Col 2:11-12).

The meal of bread and wine known as the LORD'S SUPPER served as the rite of union with Christ and with other Christians. Rooted in the biblical covenantal and sacrificial meals and in Jesus' own custom of sharing meals with his disciples and the crowds (even "tax collectors and sinners"), the early Christian ritual involved a participation in and remembrance of Jesus' death, as well as an anticipation of the messianic banquet in God's kingdom (1 Cor 11:23-26; Mark 14:22-25; Matt 26:26-28; Luke 22:14-23). At the same time Paul perceived the significance of the Lord's Supper in defining the community as "body of Christ," and so he invoked the Lord's Supper in his efforts to dissuade Christians from participating in pagan rituals (1 Cor 10:14-22) and to avoid socioeconomic factions within the Christian community (1 Cor 11:17-34; see BODY OF CHRIST).

The Lord's Supper was most likely celebrated as part of regular community assemblies held at houses of the more well-to-do members. While the problems associated with these gatherings are treated at length in 1 Cor 11–14, we get only a glimpse of the ritual dimensions of these meetings from 1 Cor 14:26: "When you come together, each one has a hymn, a lesson, a revelation, a tongue, or an interpretation" (compare Col 3:16). It is not clear who presided over these meetings. Social conventions of the 1st cent. suggest that the owner of the house (and his wife) influenced the proceedings.

How non-Christians perceived these meetings can be seen from Pliny's letter to Trajan (10.96) in the early 2nd cent. CE. Using information extracted under torture, Pliny reported that the Christians in his province of Bithynia met before sunrise "on a certain fixed day" (Sunday?), sang "a hymn to Christ as to a god" (see Phil 2:6-11), took a solemn oath (Lat. sacramentum) to do good and avoid evil, and partook of food of "an ordinary and innocent kind" (bread and wine?).

One common religious ritual that Christians did not practice was the sacrifice of animals and other material goods (see SACRIFICES AND OFFERINGS). Such offerings were essential not only to Greco-Roman religious life but also to Jews at the Jerusalem TEMPLE. In its earliest days Christianity was such a small and insignificant phenomenon that its adherents did not have temples and altars necessary to carry out such sacrifices. Jewish Christians continued to frequent the Jerusalem Temple. However, the more important reason for the Christian failure to institute ritual sacrifice was theological: the unique and efficacious sacrifice of Christ rendered obsolete such ritual sacrifices: "he [Christ] has appeared once for all at the end of the age to remove sin by the sacrifice of himself" (Heb 9:26). By willingly offering himself as a sacrifice for sin, Christ was considered both the perfect sacrifice and the great high priest.

3. Ethics

With regard to their ethical behavior, early Christians probably did not look much different from pious Jews or "good pagans." But the theological context of their ethical teachings and practice—the will of God, Scripture, and conformity with Jesus' death and resurrection—made them distinctive. In form and content much of early Christian ethical discourse was common moral teaching. What made it distinctive was the framework in which it appeared. Paul stated the ideal in Gal 5:6: "the only thing that counts is faith working through love."

The literary forms used by early Christian teachers would have been familiar to people in the Greco-Roman world. The larger vehicles for ethical expression included the LETTER (Romans, Hebrews, etc.), the testament or farewell discourse (John 14–17; 2 Peter), and the epitome or collection of sayings (Matt 5–7;

Luke 6:20-49). Among the smaller literary forms were lists of vices and virtues (Mark 7:21-22; Rom 1:29-31; Gal 5:19-23), maxims (Rom 12:9-21; James), *chreiai* or short narratives climaxing in a saying (Mark 12:13-17), precepts and commands (1 Cor 7), and household codes (Col 3:18–4:1; Eph 5:21–6:9).

The content of early Christian ethics was shaped not only by biblical traditions and Greco-Roman morality but also by the values associated with Jesus: the command to love God and neighbor, concern for marginal persons, radical teachings (on possessions, divorce, nonretaliation), and forgiveness. There was, however, a shift in venue from the itinerant radicalism of charismatic teachers in Palestine (Jesus and his first followers) to the more settled and moderate urban life of Christian communities in the Greco-Roman world (the Pauline churches). While the earlier teachings were preserved and Jesus was presented as a model to imitate, they were now placed in a framework of what is sometimes called "love patriarchalism" in which existing social structures were taken for granted and "faith working through love" tended to focus on life within the Christian community.

Two basic, distinctive values of early Christian ethics were love of neighbor and renunciation of status. While not unique to Christianity, these values were attached to the person of Jesus as the expression of God's love for the world (John 3:16) and of Jesus' self-emptying love as the Servant of God (Phil 2:6-11). In the synoptic Gospels (Mark 12:28-34; Matt 22:35-40; Luke 10:25-28) the biblical commandment to love one's neighbor (Lev 19:18) is coupled with the command to love God (Deut 6:4-5). While in those Gospels there are many challenges to expand the notion of "neighbor" (Luke 10:25-37), in the Johannine writings (especially in the Johannine Epistles) there is a tendency to focus on fulfilling the love commandment mainly with regard to relationships within the community. Whereas in the synoptic Gospels there is frequent emphasis on reversal of status (Mark 10:31; Luke 1:46-55), in the Epistles the stress is more on life and mutual relationships within the community (Phil 2:1-5). Nevertheless, the core Gospel values of love of neighbor and renunciation of status continued to shape other values and norms in early Christian ethical teachings.

C. Paul and His Churches

1. Life in the Pauline churches

Almost half of the NT writings are attributed to PAUL THE APOSTLE, and a large part of Acts features him as the main character. When read alongside the four Gospels, these books highlight the transplanting of the Jesus movement from rural Jewish Palestine to the cities of the Roman Empire.

Pauline Christianity was largely an urban phenomenon. Paul's letters were vehicles for him to offer ongoing pastoral-theological advice to the communities that he had founded in THESSALONICA, GALATIA, PHILIPPI, AND CORINTH. He made both EPHESUS and Corinth bases of operation. Paul was primarily a founder of Gentile-Christian churches. His principle was "I do not build on someone else's foundation" (Rom 15:20). He wrote to the church at Rome (which he had not founded) in the hope of beginning a new mission in Spain. Before doing so, however, he needed to bring the proceeds of his special collection to Jerusalem (Rom 15:22-29).

From the time of his experience of the risen Christ on the Damacus Road, Paul felt a special call to bring the gospel to non-Jews "so that I might proclaim him among the Gentiles" (Gal 1:16). It is sometimes assumed from what Paul says about the Corinthian Christians in 1 Cor 1:26 ("not many of you were wise . . . powerful . . . of noble birth") that the earliest converts belonged exclusively to the lowest classes of society. However, careful analysis of Paul's references to Christians at Corinth and elsewhere indicates that Paul's converts represented a wide range of social classes from wealthy to lowly, with most of them somewhere in between. Some like PHILEMON were wealthy enough to own homes that could accommodate the meetings of the local Christian community (forty or fifty persons). Others may well have been manual laborers and slaves. The list of Christians in Rom 16:1-16 indicates the many contributions of women not only as Paul's coworkers but also as deacons (Phoebe) and even apostles (Junia). What bound together these very disparate people was their shared convictions about Jesus and the saving significance of his death and resurrection.

Paul's very short letter to Philemon provides a snapshot of life in the Pauline communities. Philemon was one of Paul's converts. He opened his home (perhaps at Colossae) to the local Christian community. He owned a slave named Onesimus (meaning "useful") who seems to have run away and so became "useless" to his master. But Onesimus sought out Paul in his imprisonment (perhaps at Ephesus), and he too became a Christian. Paul wrote to Philemon to apprise him of the situation and to ask Philemon to take Onesimus back into his household "no longer as a slave but more than a slave—a beloved brother" (Phlm 16). By his appeal to what Paul had done for Philemon spiritually and his promise to visit Philemon soon, Paul put pressure on Philemon to accept Onesimus as a fellow Christian and not simply as a slave. (Whether he expected Philemon to set Onesimus free is not clear.) Moreover, the assumption is that Paul's letter would be read publicly to the whole Christian community gathered in Philemon's own house. How could Philemon refuse Paul's request?

Besides the household, other Greco-Roman social institutions influenced life in the Pauline communities. Many Gentile converts came from the "God fearers," non-Jews who attached themselves to the local synagogue. This fact helps to explain how in his letters to Gentile Christians Paul could quote from and allude to the Jewish Scriptures and expect to be understood. Moreover, by continuing to work as a "tentmaker" Paul had the opportunity to communicate his gospel to others in the workplace. Since Christianity presented itself as a way of life, it was perceived as a philosophy and its adherents as members of a philosophical school.

Most outsiders, however, would have regarded the Pauline communities as voluntary associations. They were small groups that came together regularly and freely, developed certain distinctive rituals, and held common meals. This pattern may help to explain the otherwise puzzling reference to "bishops and deacons" in Phil 1:1, one of the very few indications regarding church officers in Paul's undisputed letters. However, the Pauline churches differed from other voluntary associations in their inclusion of persons from many different social classes, demand for total and exclusive commitment, use of the self-designation ekklēsia (which referred originally to a political assembly), and far-reaching theological claims about their identity and significance.

2. Three images of the church

One of Paul's contributions to Christian theology was his use of images of the church. Among his many images the three most prominent and influential are the Spirit-led and charismatic community, the body of Christ, and the people of God. These images were not necessarily original with Paul, and he seems to assume that his readers already know them. But no NT writer developed them as early, sharply, and extensively as Paul did.

The image of the church as the Spirit-led community is based on Paul's conviction that Jesus' life, death, and resurrection have made possible for believers a new way of relating to God (justification). Having been freed from the malevolent dominion of sin, death, and the Law, those who believe in God's promises after the example of Abraham now live under the guidance of the Holy Spirit. In Rom 8, Paul contrasts life before and apart from Christ (the flesh, death, and slavery) and life in Christ (the spirit, life, and divine filiation). As Paul says in Rom 8:14: "For all who are led by the Spirit of God are children of God."

The corollary of the church as the Spirit-led community is the image of the charismatic community. Each Christian is said to be the recipient of a divine gift or charism: "To each is given the manifestation of the Spirit for the common good" (1 Cor 12:7). Paul insists that all the charisms are activated by the Holy Spirit. They are not simply natural talents. These gifts differ and are the result of God's grace or favor. They are intended not for self-glorification but for the benefit of the whole community. They may take the forms of prophecy, faith, ministry, teaching, exhortation, generosity, diligent leadership, and cheerful compassion (Rom 12:6-8). Or they may be utterances of wisdom and knowledge, faith, healing, miracles, prophecy, discernment of spirits, speaking

in tongues (glossolalia), and interpreting tongues (1 Cor 12:8-10). Still another list includes apostles, prophets, teachers, miracle workers, healers, speakers in tongues, and interpreters of tongues (1 Cor 12:27-30). Pride of place is given to those charisms that best promote the common good. Paul generally places glossolalia low on his lists, on the grounds that without proper interpretation it does not build up the community (see HEALING; SPRIRITUAL GIFTS).

In connection with the images of the Spirit-led and charismatic community, Paul introduces the image of the church as the body of Christ: "For as in one body we have many members, and not all members have the same function, so we, who are many, are one body in Christ, and individually we are members of one another" (Rom 12:4-5; for a more extensive treatment, see 1 Cor 12:12-27). The image of the body as a means of encouraging social cooperation was often used in antiquity to describe the ideal city. Paul invoked the image of a body as a way of ensuring a level of order and harmony with the charismatic Christian community. What set Paul's usage apart from others is his insistence that the church is the body of *Christ*, not just a collection of like-minded individuals acting as a group assembled for a specific task. The risen Christ brings together the individual believers, forms them into a social organism, and animates and directs them. What makes Christians the body of Christ is their common faith and their baptism into Jesus' life, death, and resurrection. Their identity as persons "in Christ" joined together in the church distinguishes them from the "body politic" or any other social institution (see BODY OF CHRIST).

The image of the church as the people of God traces Christian identity back to God's promise to Abraham in Gen 12:2: "I will make of you a great nation, and I will bless you, and make your name great" (see ABRAHAM, NT AND EARLY JUDAISM). The image evokes God's initiative in forming biblical Israel's identity (Deut 7:6-9) and its historical, communal, and covenantal experience of God (Deut 26:5-11). Paul developed the idea of the church as the people of God first in Gal 3:6-29 (see Rom 4:1-25 for a fuller treatment) where he identifies the real children of Abraham as those (including Gentiles) who believe in God's promises. Here Jesus the Jew functions as the key to opening up membership in the people of God to non-Jews: "And if you belong to Christ, then you are Abraham's offspring, heirs according to the promise" (Gal 3:29).

Nevertheless, Paul does not regard the church simply as the replacement for biblical Israel as the people of God. In his long meditation on God's plan of salvation in Rom 9–11, Paul insists that Christian Jews like himself form the remnant that serves as the principle of continuity between biblical Israel and the church (the olive tree). Paul could not imagine the church without an organic relationship to Israel. He depicts the inclusion of non-Jews in the people of God as branches of the wild olive tree that have been grafted on to the cultivated olive tree (Israel as the people of God). While nonbelieving Israelites are now like branches cut off from the olive tree, Paul foresees their ultimate inclusion. He explains the mystery of God's plan for salvation history in this way: "a hardening has come upon part of Israel, until the full number of the Gentiles has come in. And so all Israel will be saved" (Rom 11:25-26) (*see* ANTI-SEMITISM).

These images of the church are attempts at articulating facets of the great mystery of the church. They are not mutually exclusive, and it is not a matter of choosing one over another. Paul freely joins them together. These images have exercised enormous historical influence. Reform movements throughout church history have repeatedly returned to them and held them up as the theological foundations in their programs for renewing Christian life.

3. Problems

First Corinthians illustrates some of the internal problems that Gentile Christians got themselves into, mainly on account of their faulty evaluation of various individual charismatic gifts. It also shows Paul as a pastoral theologian, giving advice to a community that he founded in light of his theological convictions. Paul regarded his letters as an extension of his apostleship. In 1 Corinthians he seemed to be responding to problems bought to his attention by emissaries and by a letter from the Corinthian Christians.

One serious problem was division within the community (1 Cor 1–4). It appears that factions had emerged on the basis of which apostle brought certain people to Christian faith and claims to superior wisdom. Paul responded by appealing to the cross as the wisdom of God and as the antithesis of worldly wisdom. Other problems included a man having a sexual relationship with his step-mother (5:1-5), lawsuits between Christians in civil courts (6:1-11), and claims that Christians should forgo marriage and practice celibacy (7:1-40). An especially divisive issue concerned eating food that had been associated with pagan cults and their sacrifices (8:1–11:1). Although Paul agreed in principle that this was a matter of indifference (since those gods do not exist), nevertheless he urged the "strong" to show pastoral sensitivity to the consciences of the "weak."

With regard to women praying and prophesying in the Christian assembly, Paul's real concern in 1 Cor 11:2-16 was that there should be order in the assembly, and that women and men should dress (or have hairstyles) in a way appropriate to their genders. In 11:17-34 Paul took issue with those who allowed the communal celebration of the Lord's Supper to be an occasion for perpetuating social and economic differences. In 12–14 Paul returned to his concern for order in the assembly and evoked the image of the body of Christ as a way of exhorting the Corinthians to respect one another's spiritual gifts. And in 15:1-58 Paul coun-

tered those who said that "there is no resurrection of the dead" (15:12) by insisting that Jesus' resurrection is the core of the gospel and the basis of all Christian hope for resurrection.

A second set of problems arose from the Jewish roots of Christianity and Paul's mission to bring non-Jews into his churches. To most observers, early Christianity looked like a sect within Judaism. Indeed, Paul may well have agreed that his "conversion" was really a move from Pharisaic Judaism to Christian Judaism. He regarded his new faith in Christ as the fullness of his Judaism, not as a new religion.

Nevertheless, Paul faced strong opposition from some of his fellow Jewish Christians. They insisted that Gentiles who became Christians should become Jews in order to be authentic Christians. They wanted such Gentiles to undergo circumcision, and to observe the Torah, especially those laws—Sabbath observance, food laws, and ritual purity—that made Jews distinctive in the Greco-Roman world. This controversy among Jewish Christians naturally confused Gentile Christians. Should they follow Paul or the so-called Judaizers? (*See* CHRISTIAN-JEWISH RELATIONS; JUDAIZING.)

In writing to the Galatians, Paul accused the rival Jewish Christian missionaries of preaching "a different gospel" (1:6), and argued that since the Galatian Christians had already received the Holy Spirit apart from the Jewish law (3:2), there was no need for them to take upon themselves the "yoke" of that law. Indeed, to do so was to submit to new form of slavery and to deny the basis of Christian freedom in Jesus' death and resurrection. Paul apparently encountered a similar problem at Philippi. Rival Jewish-Christian missionaries were advocating that Gentile Christians accept CIRCUMCISION and TORAH observance. In Phil 3:1-21 Paul responded with a mixture of scorn ("beware of those who mutilate the flesh," 3:2) and boasting about his own Jewish identity and practice ("as to righteousness under the law, blameless," 3:6). In 2 Cor 10–13 Paul answered Jewish-Christian criticisms of both his gospel and his person. The opponents were saying that Paul's "letters are weighty and strong, but his bodily presence is weak, and his speech contemptible" (10:10). Here Paul applies a kind of reverse psychology and glories in his weakness on the ground that God's "power is made perfect in weakness" (12:9).

A third set of problems involved the relationship among the churches and their unity. When Paul used the term ekklēsia, he usually referred to a church in a specific locale (at Corinth, Philippi, Rome, etc.). He regarded each community as the body of Christ and complete in itself. Nevertheless, there are elements in Paul's theology that point toward a larger conception of the unity of the churches. Paul promoted the traditional Jewish belief in one God, and contended that all humans, Jews and Gentiles alike, stood in need of salvation (Rom 1:18–3:20; *see* GOD, NT VIEWS OF).

He regarded Jesus as not only the Jewish Messiah but also as the new Adam (Rom 5:12-21) and the Lord of all creation (see SECOND ADAM; Phil 2:9-11). And he viewed all Christians as bound together by their incorporation in Christ through faith and baptism.

Likewise, Paul's missionary practice had universal dimensions. He taught that in Christ all social, ethnic, economic, and gender differences had been relativized. He took as his special mission preaching the gospel to non-Jews. He kept in touch with various communities by sending emissaries and writing letters to them. In his theology and practice Paul bore witness to his conviction that "all of you are one in Christ Jesus" (Gal 3:28).

One of Paul's key projects was the COLLECTION for members of the church at Jerusalem. He asked members of the Gentile-Christian churches that he had founded to contribute to the financial support of "the saints" at Jerusalem. He told the Galatians and Corinthians to put aside some money every Sunday for this purpose (1 Cor 16:1-4). What is often called the first Christian fund-raising letter is preserved in 2 Cor 8–9. And in Rom 15:25-27 Paul describes his plan to bring the proceeds of the collection to Jerusalem. Paul perceived the ecclesial significance of this collection not only as the opportunity for several local churches to come to the aid of another church in need but also as a symbol of unity between his Gentile-Christian communities and the Jewish-Christian community (the "mother church") at Jerusalem.

D. Later Pauline Churches

The heritage of the Pauline churches is manifest in three late 1st cent. NT works: Luke's narrative about the spread of the gospel (Acts), further reflections on the church as the body of Christ (Colossians, Ephesians), and the Pastoral Epistles (1 and 2 Timothy, Titus).

1. Acts

Luke's second volume traces the spread of the gospel from Jerusalem to Rome (1:8), shows how the great apostles Peter and Paul carried on Jesus' mission, and describes how Gentiles came to accept the gospel and became part of God's people. Acts contains historical information and tells a colorful story, though it is sometimes hard to distinguish between the two. The narrative breaks off with Paul's imprisonment (62 CE), but its composition is generally assigned to 85–90 CE. The "we" passages in the second half are often cited as proof of eyewitness testimony from Luke, the companion of Paul.

Luke's vision of the church in Acts has been a powerful factor in shaping our picture of early Christian life and organization. According to Luke, the twelve apostles are principles of continuity between the Jesus movement and the church (1:12-26). With Pentecost the community at Jerusalem became Spirit-filled and Spirit-led. But Christianity was meant for all peoples from Judea and Samaria throughout the Mediterranean world.

According to Acts, there was little or no internal conflict within the churches. The ideal of perfect harmony is expressed in summary statements early in the book (2:43-47; 4:32-37; 5:12-16). The apostles are the heroes and authoritative figures, and their lives parallel the life of Jesus described in Luke's Gospel. They are aided by deacons (6:1-6) and elders. There is great emphasis on water baptism as the rite of Christian initiation and on the "breaking of bread" as an expression of communal life.

Luke tried to show that the Christian movement posed no political threat to the Roman Empire. Whenever Roman officials investigate, they find nothing really dangerous in the churches. There is, however, a tense relationship with some Jews. The Christian mission typically begins in the local synagogue. When the apostles are driven out, they turn to the Gentiles and find success there.

2. Colossians and Ephesians

Both Colossians and Ephesians are generally regarded as Deuteropauline, that is, written in Paul's name, and reflecting developments in the latter part of the 1st cent. Those who defend direct Pauline authorship place them late in Paul's career (63–65 CE).

Written to dissuade Christians from the attractions of Judaism and the mystery religions, Colossians takes up the theme of the body of Christ and insists that Christ is the "head of the body" (1:18) and that he alone can bring new life in the Spirit (3:1-4). It presents Paul as the apostle par excellence whose sufferings are "for the sake of his body, that is, the church" (1:24). And it offers a Christian version of the Greek household code (3:18–4:1) that places relationships between husbands and wives, parents and children, and masters and slaves in the context of what is "fitting in the Lord" (3:18) (see COLOSSIANS, LETTER TO THE).

Ephesians is a revised and expanded version of Colossians. It is the closest that the NT comes to a treatise on the church. The address "in Ephesus" is missing from important manuscripts. Ephesians is important for developing further the themes of the church as the body of Christ and the locus of the risen Christ's power (1:20-23), joining the themes of the body of Christ and the people of God and describing the church formed by Christ's death and resurrection as "one new humanity" made up of Jews and Gentiles (2:11-22), emphasizing the apostles as the foundation of the church (3:1-13), stressing unity in the body of Christ (4:1-6), focusing on the teaching charisms for building up the body of Christ (4:7-16), and using the husbands-wives part of the household code to work out the relationship between Christ and the church (5:21-33). It also develops the image of the soldier of Jesus Christ (6:10-17) engaged in battle with the devil, and armed only with the "weapons" of truth, righteousness, faith, and the word of God (*see* EPHESIANS, LETTER TO THE).

3. Pastoral Letters

These three documents (1 and 2 Timothy, Titus) are called "PASTORAL LETTERS" because they are addressed to Paul's co-workers as chief pastors at Ephesus and Crete, respectively, and are largely concerned with their pastoral duties. Those who defend direct Pauline authorship place them late in Paul's ministry (63–65 CE). Those who regard them as pseudonymous place them ca. 100 CE.

The Pastorals make a sharp distinction between sound doctrine and false teaching, and propose as a positive ideal "love that comes from a pure heart, a good conscience, and sincere faith" (1 Tim 1:3-7). They often cite traditional formulas of Christian beliefs (1 Tim 1:15; 2:5-6; 3:16; etc.). They stress the value of a quiet and peaceable life, which involves praying for kings and others in high positions, and accepting Greco-Roman cultural norms about women's subordination to men (2:1-13). They insist on external respectability regarding social values and virtue.

The Pastorals promote the image of the church as "the household of God . . . the pillar and bulwark of the truth" (1 Tim 3:14). They tend to identify charisms with church offices, and link them to a rite of ordination (1 Tim 4:14; 2 Tim 1:6). They give authority and prestige to local, stable church officers. The lists of qualifications for bishops and deacons (1 Tim 3:1-13; Titus 1:7-9) and elders (1 Tim 5:17-25; Titus 1:5-6) emphasize moral probity and external respectability. How these three offices functioned together in a community is not clear.

The instructions about "real" widows in 1 Tim 5:3-16 suggest the existence of an "order" of widows for whom the community was expected to care. These women had to be over sixty years old and married only once. They must be without children or grandchildren (who would otherwise be expected to care for them), and well attested for the good works associated with women in early Christian circles (5:10). The suspicions about women in the Pastorals arose from embracing general cultural assumptions and from the support given by women to false teachers (2 Tim 3:6-7).

E. Johannine Communities

The Johannine churches represent a distinctive movement in early Christianity. There is clearly an organic historical relationship between John's Gospel and the three Johannine epistles. While probably not by the same author, they are bound together by a common theological vocabulary and outlook. Although the book of Revelation has some links with the other Johannine writings, it is better treated as a separate case.

1. John's Gospel

The Gospel of John seems to have been written for a largely Jewish-Christian community in the process of being expelled from the synagogue (9:22; 12:42; 16:2). It was the product of a group that took as its founder and patron John the son of Zebedee and/or the Beloved Disciple. It provides evidence for the activity of a distinctive school or circle that handed on and developed early traditions about Jesus, and issued in narrative that describes Jesus' career from "the beginning" (before creation) to his "hour" (his passion, death, resurrection, and exaltation).

John's Gospel has been traditionally associated with Ephesus. However, with the discovery of the Dead Sea Scrolls there has been a tendency to place at least its early phases eastward in Palestine, Syria, or Transjordan. The final form is generally dated ca. 90 CE. It reflects a strand of tradition different and most likely independent from the synoptic Gospels. It portrays Jesus as the revealer and revelation of God, and insists on both his divinity (1:1, 18; 20:28) and humanity ("the Word became flesh," 1:14; *see* INCARNATION).

When compared with other early Christian movements, Johannine Christianity seems more inward looking and mystical. It has been described variously as a sect, conventicle, or school. The sectarian tendency comes out in such sayings as John 3:11: "We speak of what we know and testify to what we have seen." Moreover, the farewell discourses that occupy most of John 13–17 are concerned mainly with how the community of Jesus' disciples is to continue when the earthly Jesus was no longer physically present among them. The advice given by the departing Jesus emphasizes keeping the commandments to believe in Jesus and to love one another. In this effort the community will be aided by the Holy Spirit or Paraclete (14:16-17, 25-26; 15:26; 16:7-15). Thus the Johannine community will survive amid hostility from "the world" and "the Jews."

The terms *world* and *Jews* are often (but not always) used negatively in John's Gospel. Indeed, *Jews* serves as a concrete example of the "world" understood as those forces in opposition to Jesus and his followers. While Jesus and his first followers were Jews, nevertheless other Jews oppose them and try to destroy the Jesus movement. The Gospel in response shows how Jesus fulfills the Jewish Scriptures and gives new meaning to the Jewish festivals. In the Passion Narrative the Jews reject Jesus and press for his death. With exquisite irony Jesus fulfills the high priest's prophecy about one man dying for his people (11:48-52) and is executed under PILATE as "the King of the Jews" (19:19) (*see* ANTI-JUDAISM; JEW, JEWS, JEWISH; WORLD).

Although John's Gospel tells the story of Jesus' public ministry ca. 30 CE, it also tells the story of the Johannine community after 70 CE as part of the contest about Jewish (and Christian) identity. John's negative comments about "the Jews" and his positive presentation of Jesus as the fulfillment of Israel's Scriptures and institutions should be read in the context of the crisis facing all Jews in the late 1st cent. CE. With the Jerusalem Temple in ruins and the Land of Israel under even greater Roman control, how was Israel's heritage to be preserved? The answer given by the Johannine Jewish Christians was: through Jesus and the community gathered around him. Other Jews rejected this answer, regarded the claims made about Jesus as blasphemous, and worked to put Christian Jews out of their synagogues.

2. Johannine Letters

Written ca. 100 CE, 1–2–3 John continue the history of the Johannine community. The author of all three letters seems to have been the person who identifies himself as "the elder" in 2 and 3 John. He is probably not the writer responsible for the Gospel. The document known as 1 John is more an essay than a letter, while 2 John was a "cover letter" to the churches to which 1 John was sent, and 3 John was a personal letter to Gaius from the elder.

First John urges members of Johannine communities (near Ephesus?) to hold fast to the commandments to believe and to love. It bears witness to what had been a traumatic schism in the Johannine movement: "They went out from us, but they did not belong to us" (2:19). The issue seems to have been a controversy over the humanity of Jesus (4:2; 5:6-7). The schismatics apparently had such a spiritual view of Jesus that they could not confess that "Jesus Christ has come in the flesh" (2 John 7). They very likely drifted away into DOCETISM or GNOSTICISM.

The second and third letters bear witness to the pivotal place of the household in the spread of early Christianity. In 2 John the elder warns the Johannine churches not to accept schismatic teachers who might appear on the local scene. In 3 John the elder praises Gaius and Demetrius for accepting his emissaries. But he criticizes Diotrephes for not accepting them and so not respecting the elder's authority. Diotrephes may simply have wished to avoid conflict; there is no indication that he was a schismatic.

3. Revelation

The book known as the Apocalypse is the record of a vision granted to "John" ca. 95 CE while in exile on the island of Patmos for preaching the gospel. He addressed this report to seven churches in western Asia Minor. The seven short letters in 2:1–3:22 indicate that some churches had lost their fervor (Ephesus, Sardis, Laodicea), others were being disrupted by "false teachers" (Smyrna, Thyatira), and still others were being harassed by the local Jewish community called pejoratively "the synagogue of Satan" (Smyrna, Philadelphia).

An even more immediate and dangerous crisis facing these communities was posed by a local political and/or religious official who was promoting the cult of the Roman emperor and the goddess Roma. This cult was part of the local civil religion, and all were expected to participate. The program caused a crisis of conscience for Christians, since they believed that the risen Jesus (and not the emperor Domitian) was really "my Lord and my God." The thrust of John's apocalypse was to call Christians to refuse to participate in this worship and to prepare to accept whatever consequences might come. John interpreted (in Rev 12–14) the crisis in cosmic and apocalyptic terms. He regarded the local official (the beast from the land) as a tool of the Roman emperor (the beast from the sea), and both of them as tools of Satan (the great red dragon). He looked for salvation in the fall of Rome (Babylon) and the appearance of the New Jerusalem coming down from the heavens.

F. Jewish Christianity

The letter of James and Matthew's Gospel represent a kind of early Christianity in more direct contact with contemporary Judaism than other NT writings. Both seem to have originated in the eastern Mediterranean world.

1. James

The implied (and perhaps real) author is James, the "brother of the Lord." While his letter contains an epistolary salutation (1:1), the body of the writing is a Jewish wisdom instruction like Sirach. The topics are typical of Jewish wisdom books: suffering, rich and poor, speech, the importance of deeds, and so forth. The name of Jesus is mentioned twice (1:1; 2:1), in a formulaic but reverential manner ("Lord Jesus Christ"). Several sayings are close to texts in the synoptic Gospels, though they are not attributed to Jesus.

James is noteworthy for its emphasis on social justice. It argues against social and economic discrimination in the Christian community (2:1-7), warns against greed (4:13-17), and excoriates the rich for dealing unjustly with their poor employees (5:1-6). It is also famous for its quarrel with at least a version of Pauline theology, and insists that "faith by itself, if it has no works, is dead" (2:17). Finally it refers in passing to "elders" who anoint the sick "in the name of the Lord" (5:14), and to the practice of Christians confessing their sins to one another.

2. Matthew's Gospel

A revised and expanded version of Mark, Matthew's Gospel is often placed in Antioch in Syria, a large Greek-speaking city with a substantial Jewish population, ca. 85 CE. It has a more Jewish flavor than Mark does, and may well have been written (like John's Gospel) in response to the challenge facing all Jews after 70 CE and the destruction of the Jerusalem Temple (21:41; 22:7; 27:25).

The Jewishness of Matthew's Gospel comes out in its preference for the term "kingdom of heaven," abundant use of OT fulfillment quotations, christological titles deeply rooted in Judaism, and conservatism regarding the Torah (5:17-20). It also presents Jesus' views on topics that were debated among late 1st cent. Jewish teachers: Sabbath observance (12:1-14), food laws and ritual purity (15:1-20), and marriage and divorce (5:31-32; 19:1-12).

Matthew was convinced that the community that took Jesus as its authoritative teacher best carried on the heritage of Israel. The polemical statements in 23:1-39 are best interpreted as directed against early rabbinic (or formative) Judaism. The passage warns Christians against adopting honorific titles being applied to Jewish teachers in "their synagogues" (Rabbi, Teacher, Father), on the grounds that "you have one instructor, the Messiah" (23:10).

Matthew 14–18 gives particular attention to the figure of Peter. Although Peter is presented as the exemplar of "little faith" in 14:28-31, he also functions as the spokesman for the disciples (17:24-27; 18:21-23), and Jesus promises to build his church on Peter as the "rock" (16:16-19).

G. Roman Christianity

Christianity came to Rome quite early, probably from Jerusalem to the large Jewish community in Rome. When Paul wrote his letter to the Romans ca. 57 CE, Christianity was already well established there. The three documents treated under this heading represent a later time, and may not be connected with one another (or with Rome). But they all deal in one way or another with persecution and suffering (*see* ROME, CHURCH OF).

1. Mark's Gospel

A long tradition associates the First Gospel with the persecution of Christians at Rome under Nero in the 60s of the 1st cent. CE. Mark has been called a passion narrative with a long introduction. It portrays Jesus as a wise teacher and powerful healer. But the shadow of the cross is present throughout Jesus' public ministry. Jesus is misunderstood and rejected by fellow Jews and disciples alike. In the passion he is abandoned by all except a few women followers (15:40–16:8). He is a suffering Messiah, and gives his life as a ransom for many (10:45). Mark's emphasis on the suffering Christ can be explained in part by his community's experience of persecution and its fear in the face of suffering to come.

2. Hebrews

The association of Hebrews with Rome is based on the closing remark in 13:24: "Those from Italy send you greetings." While ambiguous, this comment has led many interpreters to regard Hebrews as a written sermon ("word of exhortation," 13:22) directed to Jewish Christians at Rome who had grown weary of their new Christian faith and were tempted to return to Judaism. Moreover, these Christians seem also to be suffering persecution, though the author reminds them that "you have not yet resisted to the point of shedding your blood" (12:4).

Against this background the author presents Jesus as God's Son and God's Word (1:1–4:13), reflects on the priesthood and sacrifice of Christ (4:14–10:18), and urges perseverance in Christian life (10:19–13:25). At the heart of Hebrews is the insistence that Jesus is the high priest according to the order of Melchizedek. His sacrificial death is the perfect sacrifice for sins, and his willingness to offer himself made him the great high priest. His self-offering rendered obsolete the Levitical priesthood, the OT sacrificial system, and even the OT covenant. The community's directors are called "leaders" (13:17), since there is only one great high priest.

3. 1 Peter

Intended for Christians in northern Asia Minor, this letter emanated from "Babylon" (5:15), a code name for Rome. It addressed Christians suffering on account of their new faith. Peter (whether the apostle or an admirer) appeals to the new Christians' baptismal dignity, their membership in the people of God (2:9), and the good example shown by Christ the Suffering Servant (3:13-22; 4:12-19). In his parting words Peter refers to himself as an "elder" and exhorts "elders" in northern Asia Minor to "tend the flock of God" (5:1-2) until the "chief shepherd appears" (5:4). *See* APOSTLE; BISHOP; COLLECTION, NT; COMMUNION; COMMUNITY OF GOODS; DEACON; ELDERS; ELDERS IN THE NT; EVANGELIST; GOSPEL; MINISTRY; OFFERING FOR THE SAINTS; PREACHING; PROPHET IN THE NT.

Bibliography: Paul Barnett. *The Birth of Christianity: The First Twenty Years* (2005); Daniel J. Harrington. *The Church According to the NT* (2001); Wayne Meeks. *The First Urban Christians: The Social World of the Apostle Paul* (1983); Rodney Stark. *The Rise of Christianity: A Sociologist Reconsiders History* (1996); Gerd Theissen. *The Religion of the Earliest Churches: Creating a Symbolic World* (1999).

DANIEL J. HARRINGTON

CHURCH, WORSHIP OF. *See* WORSHIP, NT CHRISTIAN.

CHURCHES, SEVEN. *See* SEVEN CHURCHES.

CHUSI ky*oo'si* [Χους Chous]. A place near Egrehbeh and the Wadi Mochmur in central Palestine (Jdt 7:18). Possibly same as today's Quzah. *See* ACRABA.

CHUZA kyoo'zuh [Χουζᾶς Chouzas]. According to Luke, Chuza was an official in HEROD ANTIPAS's court and husband to one of Jesus' benefactors, JOANNA (8:3). The term used to described his position (ἐπίτροπος epitropos) suggests that he was not an ordinary administrator but a high-ranking, powerful retainer, possibly manager of Herod's estate.

CICERO. Marcus Tullius Cicero (106-43 BCE) was a prominent public figure in Rome, notable as one of the leading courtroom orators before being elected to several public offices, including CONSUL (63 BCE). Not long after the rise of the first triumvirate in 60 BCE, Cicero was exiled from Rome, and although he was able to return within two years, he never regained the same level of political influence. Unable to participate fully in politics, Cicero turned to writing works on philosophy and rhetoric. A staunch defender of the traditional ideals of the Republic, Cicero and some of his family members were murdered in the wave of assassinations that followed the rise of the second triumvirate in 43 BCE. Cicero's works, including published speeches, letters, and rhetorical and philosophical writings, have been invaluable for studies of the history of the late Republic, for understanding the genre of the letter and rhetorical theory and training, and for the glimpse they provide of philosophical debates of the time. Cicero's philosophical writings, which have a Stoic bent, became quite influential for Christian writers, notably Augustine, and remained so until the 19th cent. CE. See RHETORIC AND ORATORY.

RUBEN DUPERTUIS

CILICIA suh-lish'ee-uh [Κιλικία Kilikia]. A region and Roman province, forming the southern part of Turkey to the south of the Taurus mountain range, and facing the island of Cyprus. To the north lay Galatia and Cappadocia, to the west Lycia and Pamphylia (see Acts 27:5), and to the east Syria. There were two main parts to the region: Cilicia Tracheia ("Rugged"), a mountainous region in the west, and the fertile Cilicia Pedias ("Plain") to the east. The origin of the name may perhaps be traced back to the reign of the Assyrian king Tiglath-Pileser III (745–737 BCE) where the region of the *Hilakku* was defined to the south of Cappadocia. This may be the equivalent of HELECH mentioned in the OT (e.g., Ezek 27:11).

In the Hellenistic period Cilicia was dominated by both the Seleucids and the Ptolemies. The mountainous coastline of Tracheia made it a perfect location for pirates. This caused Rome to respond at the very end of the 2nd cent. BCE, but the pirates remained a nuisance until they were defeated by Pompey the Great in 67 BCE. The Roman province of Cilicia included an area north of the Taurus, and from 58 BCE Cyprus. Among Cilicia's governors was the orator Cicero (51–50 BCE). At the end of the republican period, in 37/6 BCE, Marcus Antonius gave parts of Cilicia to Cleopatra who retained control until the Battle of Actium (31 BCE) and Octavian's supremacy.

Cilicia Tracheia was awarded to the client-king Amyntas, a former ally of Marcus Antonius who changed sides at Actium. His death in 25 BCE brought about the incorporation of this part of Cilicia into the Roman province of Galatia. Most of Cilicia Pedias became part of the province of Syria with the provincial capital at Antioch; this situation is reflected in the grouping of Gentile Christians in Antioch, Syria and Cilicia (Acts 15:23; see also Gal 1:21). Both parts were reunited in a single province of Cilicia by the emperor Vespasian in 72 CE. Cyprus became a province in its own right.

One of the main Roman roads to Syria and the east passed through the province. From Tarsus the road ran north through the Cilician Gates in the Taurus, then westwards to Derbe, across Lycaonia to Iconium, and west to Laodicea and Ephesus in the province of Asia.

TARSUS was one of the main cities of the region (see Acts 21:39, 22:3), and under Vespasian became the provincial capital. In the late Republic the city had a thriving philosophical school; one of its luminaries was Athenodoros who had an influence on the future emperor Augustus.

Bibliography: G. E. Bean and T. B. Mitford. *Journeys in Rough Cilicia in 1962 and 1963* (1965) and *Journeys in Rough Cilicia in 1964–1968* (1970); H. Hellenkempfer. "Zur Entwicklung des Stadtbildes in Kilikien." *Aufstieg und Niedergang der römischen Welt*, vol. II.7.2 (1980) 1262–83; T. B. Mitford. "Roman Rough Cilicia," in *Aufstieg und Niedergang der römischen Welt*, vol. 2.7.2 (1980) 1230–61.

DAVID W. J. GILL

CIMMERIANS. An ancient people for whom GOMER may be an eponym (Gen 10:2; 1 Chr 1:5). Mentioned in Assyrian inscriptions.

CINNAMON [קִנָּמוֹן qinnamon; κιννάμωμον kinnamōmon). Cinnamon bark, from the laurel family (*Cinnamomum verum*), was a part of the spice trade (Rev 18:13). It was blended with myrrh and other spices to add a sweet smell to anointing oil (Exod 30:23), a perfumed bed (Prov 7:17), and the body (Song 4:14). See PLANTS OF THE BIBLE; SPICE.

VICTOR H. MATTHEWS

CIRCUMCISION [מוּל mul, מוּלָה mulah; περιτομή peritomē]. An operation performed on males—infants, children, and adults—to remove all or a portion of the foreskin (or prepuce) from the glans penis. The Pentateuch stipulates the circumcision of every Hebrew male on the eighth day after birth (Gen 17:10-11; Lev 12:2-3), every slave of an Israelite (Gen 17:12-13; Exod 12:44), and aliens who resided permanently within Israel if they desired to celebrate and eat the Passover (Exod 12:48).

Circumcision was not practiced exclusively by the Israelites. The prophet Jeremiah (9:25-26) lists "Egypt, Judah, Edom, the Ammonites, Moab, and all those with shaven temples who live in the desert" as being circumcised. The Greek historian Herodotus (2.37, 104), writing in the 5th cent. BCE, contended that circumcision originated with the Egyptians; archaeological data support the presence of the practice among the Egyptians from at least the 23rd cent. BCE. Yet, other archaeological evidence shows Syrian warriors circumcised from about 3000 BCE; thus, it may be that the practice began with Northwest Semites and extended, in turn, to Egypt.

Because circumcision played such an important role in the life and religion of the Hebrew people, it was practiced across the span of generations and the sense of its meaning grew rich with the passage of time. The OT and the NT treat the subject of circumcision in a variety of ways.

A. Circumcision in the OT

The origins of circumcision among the Hebrews are debated, though three passages from the OT are usually cited as referring in some way to the beginnings of the practice. First, at Gen 17:9-14 the Pentateuch depicts circumcision originating among the Hebrew people with Abraham as a covenantal rite with God. Given the widespread nature of the practice among Semites and others in antiquity, one probably should not regard this story as portraying the origins of circumcision per se, but rather as explaining the beginnings of circumcision among the Hebrews. Included among those circumcised in this instance were Abraham at ninety-nine years of age, every male member of Abraham's household—slave and free, and Ishmael at thirteen years of age; subsequently Isaac is depicted as being circumcised on the eighth day after his birth as narrated at Gen 21:2-4. At times scholars have argued that the story of the circumcision of Abraham and his household is an etiological account, wherein Abraham represents the Hebrew people, Ishmael signifies the Arabs, and the slaves and others stand for the various Canaanite peoples. Yet, other scholars point to ancient features of the narrative—e.g., the innovation of circumcision on the eighth day and circumcision as a sign of the covenant with God—and contend that the account of Abraham's circumcision is primitive tradition depicting something of the actual origins of the practice.

Second, Exod 4:24-26 is often regarded by scholars as the oldest account referring to the origins of circumcision among the Hebrews. In this strange story Zipporah appears to redeem Moses from the destructive powers of God (Yahweh) by circumcising their son and touching the foreskin to Moses' feet (perhaps a euphemism for the genitals). Here circumcision is thought to be of either magical or primitive religious derivation; on the one hand, serving as a sacrifice of redemption

or, on the other hand, functioning as a tribal or covenantal sign. In turn, in the OT the covenantal aspect of circumcision comes to play the dominant role in the interpretation of its meaning. Nevertheless, in this story Zipporah refers to Moses as "a bridegroom of blood . . . a bridegroom of blood by circumcision." This manner of reference to Moses leads some scholars to posit a connection between the practice of infant circumcision with the analogous practice of circumcising adults as a marital or puberty rite.

Third, Josh 5:2-9 gives the account of the males of Israel being circumcised in the wilderness prior to their celebrating the Passover as they prepared to enter and conquer the promised land. This circumcising took place at Gibeath-haaraloth, which means "the hill of the foreskins" and which is referred to after the circumcising as "Gilgal." Some scholars note that the author/editor of this story apparently wondered why the Israelites were not already circumcised, so these scholars contend that three possible answers are implicit in the narrative: 1) The Israelites were circumcised in Egypt, but in a manner that did not completely remove the foreskin; so they were circumcised a second time to roll away the disgrace of Egypt. 2) The LXX has a different text that holds that the Israelites had not been circumcised in Egypt. 3) The males who had come out of Egypt were circumcised, but their heirs who were born in the wilderness were not circumcised; it was necessary, therefore, to circumcise the males of the wilderness generation in order that they might eat the Passover. Taken at face value, the text of Josh 5:2-9 presents answer "3," which does not explain the origin of circumcision among the Hebrews.

Beyond both accounts depicting the origin and practice of circumcision and references to circumcision and circumcising in the ordinances of the law, the OT includes figurative allusions to circumcision in both Deuteronomy (10:16; 30:6) and Jeremiah (4:4). (There are also figurative allusions to being "uncircumcised"—e.g., Exod 6:30; Lev 19:23; 26:41; Jer 6:10; 9:26; Ezek 44:7, 9.) While the physical act of circumcising is never rejected in either Deuteronomy or Jeremiah (or in the passages referring figuratively to "uncircumcision"), these metaphorical references advocate a spiritual commitment to God that has ethical implications effecting the relationship of the one with a "circumcised heart" to God and other human beings.

B. Circumcision in the LXX and the Hellenistic Age

Greek culture brought significant weight to bear against circumcision. Both Greeks and Romans found the practice of circumcision loathsome, so that some Jews obscured their circumcision by a painful operation called epispasm that restored the foreskin to its natural, uncircumcised shape (1 Macc 1:15; 1 Cor 7:18; Josephus, *Ant.* 12.237-41). The embrace of Hellenistic culture by some prominent Jews encouraged the Syrian ruler Antiochus Epiphanes IV to go so far as to forbid circumcision; indeed, he made it a capital offense to circumcise Jewish children. First Maccabees (1:10-61) tells of women who were put to death because they had circumcised their male offspring. The pressure against the Jews to abandon circumcision caused circumcision to be even more important than it had been. The apocryphal *Book of Jubilees* (e.g., 1:23; 15:23-34; 30:12), reacting to the push toward Hellenization, advocates circumcision. The outcome for many Jews was that circumcision became an indispensable manifestation of the Jewish religion, for which it was worth dying. In turn, when the Maccabean Revolt broke out against Antiochus's policies, followers of Mattathias circumcised by force many Jews who had not been previously circumcised. Moreover, after the success of the revolt, several Hasmonean rulers—namely, John Hyrcanus I, Aristobulus I, and (probably) Alexander Jannaeus—forced the circumcision and Judaising of ethnic/national groups such as the Idumeans and the Itureans (Josephus, *Ant.* 13.254-58; 13.314-19; 13.395-97).

C. Circumcision in the NT

Several NT writers mention circumcision in a striking variety of ways. First, Luke refers to the circumcision on the eighth day of both John the Baptist (1:59) and Jesus (2:21). Luke associates the giving of a name to the children with their circumcision on the eighth day, which is a practice not made explicit in the OT but which may be inferred from a certain reading of Gen 21:3-4.

Second, at John 7:19-24, Jesus defends his healing of a man on the Sabbath (John 5:1-18) by forming a comparison with circumcision—arguing from lesser to greater. Jesus' defense is that since it is lawful to circumcise a child on the Sabbath, thus attending to the one bodily part in need of being put in the condition that God wills, then it is reasonable and lawful that on the Sabbath a whole body be put in the condition that God wills. Of interest here is the stipulation that while "Moses gave . . . circumcision (it is, of course, not from Moses, but from the patriarchs)," a statement which presents the phenomenon of circumcision positively in John's Gospel.

Third, in Acts, Luke refers to circumcision (and uncircumcision) in a variety of settings and ways. 1) Acts 7:8 refers to God's giving to Abraham the covenant of circumcision and to Abraham's having circumcised Isaac on the eighth day, thus recalling the scriptural origin of circumcision and emphasizing Abraham's faithfulness to the covenant. 2) Later in Acts (7:51) Luke depicts Stephen confronting his hearers, calling them "uncircumcised in heart and ears," which echoes similar OT language (Deut 10:16; Jer 6:10). 3) At both Acts 10:45 and 11:2 Luke uses the designation "circumcised" to identify Jewish Christians. These were

persons positively inclined toward the continuation of the practice of circumcision in the church, circumcision of both Jewish Christian infants and gentile converts to Christianity. 4) Circumcision forms the controversial topic (whether it is necessary to circumcise gentile converts to Christianity) that brought about the Apostolic Council of Acts 15, where a decision was made not to require circumcision of gentiles who became converts to Christianity. 5) Acts 16:3 depicts Paul, out of regard for Jews and certain Jewish Christians, circumcising the half-Jew Timothy. Finally, 6) at Acts 21:21 Luke recalls that Paul was accused of telling Jews not to circumcise their children. In summary, one sees that even in Luke's irenic narrative of the origins of the early church, notes are sounded of the controversial nature of circumcision in early Christianity.

Fourth, the bulk of the references to circumcising and circumcision in the NT occur in the corpus of Pauline writings. Paul's focus on both circumcision and uncircumcision was the result of controversies that arose in the course of his ministry. Paul preached to Gentiles, seeking to convert them to Christian thought and life and not demanding that such Gentile Christians be circumcised. Other Jewish Christians, however, did not agree with Paul and insisted that gentiles who were converted to Christianity must undergo circumcision. This dispute was the subject of the Apostolic Council that is recalled in Acts 15 and Gal 2. Despite whatever agreement was reached at the Apostolic Council, at times the circumcising Jewish Christians worked among those gentiles whom Paul had originally converted to Christianity. Such a situation occurred among the churches of Galatia. Paul responded with a pointed argument, insisting that gentile Christians must not submit to circumcision. In fact, he insisted that to undergo circumcision was to turn away from Christ as the means of relating to God in favor of Law-observance as the medium for maintaining one's relationship to God. Paul argued his point vigorously in the letter to the Galatians, and his reflections on the subject of circumcision and uncircumcision appear in other letters—Pauline and deutero-Pauline (1 Corinthians, Ephesians, Philippians, Colossians, and Titus), but especially in Romans. In essence, for Paul, because the Christian was related to God in/through Christ, there was simply no literal sense in which circumcision held meaning for Christian life. Paul's position has been dominant in the church since at least the 2nd cent. CE.

Bibliography: L. B. Glick. *Marked in Your Flesh: Circumcision from Ancient Judea to Modern America* (2005); J. Marcus. "The Circumcision and the Uncircumcision in Rome." *NTS* 35 (1989) 67–81; J. M. Sasson. "Circumcision in the Ancient Near East." *JBL* 85 (1966) 473–76.

MARION L. SOARDS

CIRCUMLOCUTION. An indirect reference to a delicate subject with evasiveness, avoiding language that is considered offensive, shameful, or taboo. Circumlocution is applied in the Bible to God, death, sex, and excrement. The following are examples: "bless God" means curse (Job 1:5, 11; 2:5, 9); "go the way of all the earth" represents death (1 Kgs 2:2); "hand" represents phallus (Isa 57:8-10; Song 5:4); "feet" (Exod 4:25; Isa 7:20) or "thigh" (Gen 47:29; Num 5:22) represents genitalia; "covering one's feet" means defecation (Judg 3:24; 1 Sam 24:4) and covering the body (Isa 6:2). Bible translations quite often employ further circumlocution (e.g., "male" for the Hebrew "urinator against the wall," 1 Sam 25:22, 34). *See* EUPHEMISM.

L. J. DE REGT

CISTERN [בּוֹר bor, בְּאֵר be'er; λάκκος lakkos, φρέαρ phrear] The Heb. bor, although variously translated by the NRSV ("pit," WELL," "cistern"), is the most commonly used term when referencing "cistern." A similar and perhaps related term, be'er, is generally more representative of the "well" (Prov 5:15), but not exclusively. The LXX uses lakkos to render bor, but occasionally phrear. Lakkos is never used in the NT, and phrear only four times (Luke 14:5; John 4:11; Rev 9:1, 2), all in reference to a shaft that opens onto the netherworld. This nuance seems to typify the use of bor in Ezekiel.

Palestinian climate and geology converged to necessitate and accommodate water storage. Limited annual rainfall produced the critical need to manage what resources were available, and thus the ancients developed systems of catchment and containment in cisterns. Cisterns were generally bulbous or pear-shaped cavities of varying sizes, normally chiseled (Deut 9:11; Neh 9:25; 2 Chr 26:10) into limestone bedrock for the primary purpose of water storage. Such factors as the quality and porosity of the limestone and its ability to retain water determined the necessity of plaster-lining the cistern. Archaeologists have excavated numerous Palestinian cisterns of both plastered and unplastered types. Jeremiah 2:13 uses the vivid metaphor of "hewing cisterns . . . broken cisterns that can hold no water" to describe the emptiness of idolatry. "Cistern" seems to be an erotic metaphor in Prov 5:15.

The BOOK OF THE COVENANT legislated the covering of cisterns to guard against animals falling in (Exod 21:33-34). Cisterns were sometimes equipped with wheels to facilitate water-drawing (Eccl 12:6).

Grain storage and refuse pits are among the secondary uses of cisterns that archaeology has validated. They were also occasionally used as places of imprisonment (Gen 37:20-29; Jer 37:17; 38:6-13). *See* WATER WORKS.

JOHN I. LAWLOR

CISTERN OF SIRAH. *See* SIRAH, CISTERN OF.

CITADEL [קִרְיָה qiryah, אַרְמוֹן 'armon, עֹפֶל 'ofel, עִיר 'ir, בִּירָה birah; ἄκρα akra]. *Citadel* describes a fortress but can be a synonym for a fortified city as a whole (Deut 2:36; 3:4; Esth 1:2) or refer to a fortification of some kind within a larger settlement (2 Kgs 15:25; perhaps 1 Kgs 16:8).

Jerusalem is a good example of both senses of the term. When David captured the city it was a walled settlement built on a hill with steep slopes on three sides so the city itself was a citadel (2 Sam 5). The psalmist points to Jerusalem's towers and walls as symbols of divinely provided security (Ps 48:12-13). Within the city was a "hill" ('ofel, NRSV "citadel," 2 Kgs 5:24) that eventually received its own fortified wall or rampart (2 Chr 27:3; 33:14). In the Hellenistic period, an area near the Temple complex was restricted and fortified (akra, 1 Macc 1:33, 36).

J. ANDREW DEARMAN

CITIZENSHIP [πολίτευμα politeuma]. No direct cognate for *citizenship* is found in biblical Hebrew, and the concept is largely absent from OT studies. It emerged in other eras and environments. The principle Greek noun is translated as "citizenship, commonwealth, conversation." A close cognate is the verb πολιτεύομαι (politeuomai); the basic notion is to act in a way reflective of one's citizenship. Other cognates include *citizen* (πολιτεία politeia), which sometimes implies the right to be a citizen, akin to *citizenship* (see Acts 22:28). The lexical domain also includes the broader term, *citizen* (πολίτης politēs), which itself derives from *city* (πόλις polis).

Citizenship refers to an individual's status within some entity, usually a socio-political structure. More generally it refers to how an individual responds to that organization's expectations of membership. Political structure in antiquity focused on cities rather than nation-states. Classics scholars have traced the emergence—especially within Greece—of political organization based upon equal, shared rights and responsibilities. Citizenship could be acquired in various ways: by being born in a specific locale, by inheritance, bestowed for some service or honor, or by purchase. This meant that individuals potentially could hold citizenship in more than one city.

The spread of Hellenism through the eastern Mediterranean introduced the notion of *citizenship* to Judaism. The OT pseudepigraphical document *Letter of Aristeas* uses politeuma to refer to the political status of the Jewish community within Alexandria in the 2nd cent. BCE; Josephus and Philo also both use the term.

The specific Gk. noun politeuma is used only one time in the NT, in Phil 3:20. Paul emphasizes that believers' true citizenship is in heaven, and their lives ought to be so focused. Such perspective mitigates other teaching Paul offers concerning political allegiance to secular authorities, such as in Rom 13:1-7.

There are two NT usages of the related Gk. verb, politeuomai, in Phil 1:27 and Acts 23:1. The first emphasizes that the demands of Christ's gospel need to be exercised or "lived out" in every dimension of a believer's life. The Lukan use of the term in Acts 23:1 is similar, describing how Paul has "lived out" his conscience before God in his social and political activities. Elsewhere Luke relates a conversation between Paul and a tribune about citizenship; they reference being a "citizen" or "Roman" (implying, "Roman citizen") in Acts 21:39 and 22:25-29. Similar claims are made in Acts 16:37-38. The possibility that Paul was not actually a Roman citizen has been vigorously debated in recent years, with some seeing the claim as a Lukan invention. The topic has puzzling dimensions, but it is unnecessary to completely reject the testimony of Acts.

The NT understanding of citizenship identified thus far draws upon Jesus' persistent teaching concerning the realm (or kingdom) of God (or heaven) and the multitude of spiritual and ethical implications that ensue (representative texts include Matt 6:19-21, 33; 25:34; Luke 12:32; John 14:1-4; 18:36). Some epistles emphasize believers' relationship with Christ in a new realm (Gal 4:21-31; Eph 2:6; Col 3:1-4; Heb 12:22-23, 28; 13:14). Other letters reapply the OT patriarchal imagery of God's people as refugees and strangers to believers in their present environment (1 Pet 1:1, 17; 2:11; Heb 11:8-16).

Bibliography: Bruno Blumenfeld. *The Political Paul: Justice, Democracy and Kingship in a Hellenistic Framework* (2001); Martin Hengel with Roland Deines. *The Pre-Christian Paul* (1991); Brian Rapske. *The Book of Acts and Paul in Roman Custody, The Book of Acts in Its First Century Setting.* Vol 3 (1994).

RAYMOND H. REIMER

CITY [עִיר ʿir; πόλις polis]. Sedentary communal existence, with basic social institutions and shared building projects, was already in place in the Neolithic period in the Middle East. Cities emerged with the development of civilizations, but the vicissitudes of climate and history meant variation in their frequency and importance. They were part of several political entities that emerged in the long sweep of Middle Eastern history, including empires, city-states, and tribal-based confederations. Fundamental change in the region came with the campaigns of Alexander the Great, which resulted in the wide-scale importation of Hellenistic culture and city planning. The Hellenistic period in the eastern Mediterranean was followed by Roman conquest and the increase of urbanization and city planning on scales previously unknown.

The common term for city in the OT (ʿir) does not preserve much specificity. It can be used for almost any settlement. Related architectural vocabulary, however, such as gates, walls, and temples, helps in defining a city. The GATE, in particular, is a place where people meet, agreements are made and witnessed, and even worship is offered. And there are also related terms for city inhabitants such as governor or mayor and elders, which indicate something of administrative structure and demographic stratification that a city may preserve.

A. Chalcolithic and Early Bronze Periods (ca. 4300–2000)
B. Middle Bronze Period (ca. 2000–1550 BCE)
C. Late Bronze Period (ca. 1550–1200 BCE)
D. Iron Age I and II (ca. 1200–975 and 975–87/86 BCE)
   1. Jerusalem
   2. Lachish
   3. Arad
   4. Samaria
   5. Hazor
   6. Megiddo
   7. Dan
   8. Extrabiblical references
E. City Symbolism and Personification in the OT
F. The Persian, Greek, and Roman Periods
   1. Hellenism
   2. Roman period
      a. Caesarea Maritima
      b. Jerusalem
      c. Other Herodian building projects
      d. The spread of Christianity
Bibliography

A. Chalcolithic and Early Bronze Periods (ca. 4300–2000 BCE)

Settlements with such things as perimeter walls, temples, and other indications of social stratification are known from the 4th and 3rd millennia BCE. Megiddo, Jericho and Arad all have Chalcolithic remains, and Ein Gedi possessed a temple shrine. Indeed, Jericho was a settlement with fortifications in the Neolithic period. It possessed a stone tower near a spring of water that could be used for defensive purposes as well as for reconnaissance, though this has been called into question.

Early Bronze Periods I–III (ca. 3000–2300 BCE) in Syria-Palestine show marked increases in urban life, including some knowledge of the systems of writing developed in the river civilizations of EGYPT and Mesopotamia. In the first half of the 3rd millennium BCE, Pharaohs of the Old Kingdom period had pyramids constructed in Lower Egypt and consolidated their political control. Early Bronze IV (ca. 2300–2000 BCE) in Syria-Palestine, however, exhibits a general decline in urban life, although there are exceptions in central TRANSJORDAN and elsewhere.

B. Middle Bronze Period (ca. 2000–1550 BCE)

The land of Canaan had a number of strong cities in the first half of the 2nd millennium BCE. Among them were BYBLOS, SIDON, DAN, HAZOR, MEGIDDO, BETH SHAN, SHECHEM, SHILOH, JERICHO, BETHEL, JERUSALEM, GEZER, LACHISH, and HEBRON. Some of these could be considered city-states, which meant that their political influence extended beyond their immediate environment and that their rulers likely bore the title "king." During this period a large, ceremonial mud-brick gate was constructed at Dan for entrance into the city. This indicates impressive human resources dedicated to the enhancement of the city's prestige. Later the gate was covered over by earthen ramparts as the city increased its defenses. The city of Hazor north of the Sea of Galilee is named in documents from MARI, at that time (ca. 1800 BCE) an influential city-state on the Euphrates in northeastern Syria. This confirms a trading network across the Fertile Crescent that was held together by diplomatic relations among various political entities. King Zimri-lim's palace at Mari had nearly 100 rooms, complete with indoor toilet facilities, a stunning example of urban architecture of the period. Hazor itself was a walled city of some 200 acres, the largest in its region.

Many cities of the period invested great effort and resources in defensive fortifications. Earthen ramparts are built to reinforce city walls. These would be needed eventually, as a number of cities were attacked and/or destroyed toward the end of the Middle Bronze Period. Chambered gates were built to control access to the city proper. Dwellings for rulers/governors and temples for the worship of Canaanite deities were part of the urban landscape. Evidence for writing is sparse in southern Canaan, but a few cuneiform tablets were discovered in the excavations at Hazor, demonstrating that a complex system of writing that helped sustain diplomacy and commerce was known in the cities. Diplomacy and commerce required various specializations, so that cities maintained scribal bureaucracies and even, where possible, professional soldiers.

C. Late Bronze Period (ca. 1550–1200 BCE)

After some political instability in Egypt and Syria-Palestine, a less intensive urban period emerged. There were, of course, cities in the Late Bronze period in Canaan, but some of the impressive Middle Bronze cities experienced destruction in the 16th/15th cent. BCE, followed by either material decline or abandonment. The pharaohs of the 18th and 19th dynasties campaigned periodically in Cisjordan, Transjordan, and Syria, establishing forms of political hegemony in the

region. They were responsible for some of the destruction in that time period. Correspondence between the Egyptian court and various governors/rulers of cities in the region, dating to the 14th cent. BCE, was discovered in Egypt in 1887. These so-called Tell el Amarna texts (see AMARNA LETTERS) are valuable indications of social relations between various cities in Canaan and their subservience to Egypt.

In the 15th cent. BCE, Megiddo was the site of a famous battle between Egyptian and Canaanite forces. HAZOR contained a series of Late Bronze Age temples, one of which had anthropomorphic and zoomorphic figures sculpted out of basalt rock. Beth Shan likewise had Late Bronze Age temples with carved figures and inscriptions in Egyptian hieroglyphics.

A major transition for all of the eastern Mediterranean begins in the 13th–12th cent. BCE. In cultural terms a transition is made from the end of the Bronze Age to the Iron Age. It can also be described as disruption, based on drought conditions and political instability, with resulting displacement of peoples and eventually new settlement patterns in the region. The Hittite and Egyptian empires show marked decline in the late 13th and 12th cent. A number of the Late Bronze Age cities, already fewer in number than in the Middle Bronze Age, are destroyed or abandoned. Resettlement may take place in the form of smaller unfortified communities or the development of new villages in the Iron Age in areas heretofore more sparsely populated. The Philistines are part of a population shift of Sea Peoples who come from Mediterranean cultures and Asia Minor to settle on the coast of Palestine ca. 1200 BCE and later. They established or resettled five cities known in the OT: Gaza, Ashdod, Ashkelon, Ekron, and Gath.

In approximately 1210 BCE, a victory stele of Pharaoh MERNEPTAH mentions an encounter with a people called Israel. With typical bombast, the pharaoh claims victory over Israel and some cities in Canaan. This is the earliest reference to an Israel in an extra-biblical text, and scholars are divided over its meaning. The reference has at least two possible connections with cities in the Late Bronze Age. First, some scholars would link the name of Israel with some unruly elements in Late Bronze Age society known as the Habiru (see HABIRU, HAPIRU). They are mentioned as raiders and troublemakers in the diplomatic letters (found at Tell Amarna; see above) sent from Canaanite cities to the Egyptian court. Some have suggested that Hebrew, a term for Israelites, is cognate to Akkadian Habiru, so that the references to the Habiru in the 14th cent. are additional evidence for tribal Israel's presence in Canaan. Whatever the best explanation of Israel's origins in Canaan, an identity with the Habiru is unlikely, just as a cognate link between the terms Hebrew and Habiru is difficult to maintain. Second, the books of Numbers, Joshua, and Judges preserve accounts of Israel's emergence in the land of Canaan. Joshua 5–11, in particular, presents the occupation of the land as a series of military defeats inflicted upon various cities and their rulers. A list of defeated cities and rulers is presented in Josh 12. Intensive archaeological and historical investigation of this matter so far has resulted in mixed results. It has proved difficult to see any corroboration of the accounts of taking Jericho and Ai (Josh 5–7), but some have seen confirmation of the process in the Late Bronze destruction layers at Lachish and Hazor (Josh 10–11). Nevertheless, it is likely that the emergence of Israel in Canaan is part of the dramatic population shifts in the eastern Mediterranean at the end of the Late Bronze Age. The narratives in Judges and 1 Samuel indicate that the Israelite tribes did not permanently occupy or did not maintain control of many of the cities (Judg 1:27-36) in Canaan until the rise of monarchy.

D. Iron Age I and II (ca. 1200–975 and 975–587/86 BCE

There is an essential overlap between the historical period of Iron Age I (ca. 1200–975 BCE) and what can be called the period of the Judges. Tribal Israel eventually emerges as the strongest political force in Cisjordan with the rise of David and then Solomon as kings in the 10th cent. (see ISRAEL, HISTORY OF). There is lively scholarly debate on the size and influence of the kingdom under David and Solomon, since there are no external corroborations to the claims of the biblical texts. Iron Age II (975–587/86 BCE) is the period of the divided monarchy and the survival of Judah at the hands of the Assyrians until Judah's own demise by the Babylonians. The Omride dynasty in Israel, as part of the divided monarchy, brought the material culture of Israel to its height in the early part of Iron Age II. From the 9th cent. BCE until the respective defeats of Israel (722) and Judah (587/86) is the classical age of Israelite and Judean cities.

1. Jerusalem

According to 2 Sam 5, David and his mercenaries took the central hill-country city of Jerusalem. That was the occasion to call the town the "City of David." Another name for the city, perhaps originally associated with the threshing floor on a high point north of the city, was Zion. The city served as the home of the Davidic dynasty and thus the capital city, first of the united monarchy and then as the head of the tribal state of Judah. A number of scholars have suggested that as David's personal property (due to the fact that he took the city) Jerusalem played a role not unlike that of Washington, D.C., the capital of the United States. Washington is not reckoned as part of any particular state and is thus a separate political entity.

David built his palace in Jerusalem. According to 1 Kgs 5–8, his son Solomon expanded the city considerably, building a temple for the Lord, the God of Israel, along with additional administrative structures. It served for some four centuries as the seat of the Davidic dynasty and nearly that long as the location of the first (= Solomon's) Temple. There are only sparse remains that can be associated with David's rule and very little from the time of Solomon. There are more substantial remains beginning in the 8th cent. BCE, including a massive wall in the western quarter of the current old city that suggests expansion of the city in the last half of that cent. (under Hezekiah?). With the fall of the kingdom of Israel in 722, a number of refugees moved south and the population of Jerusalem rose dramatically. About this same time a subterranean water channel was cut underneath the older part of the city to increase the collection of water in times of siege or other emergencies. This water channel is still preserved and open in the present and is popularly known as the Siloam tunnel.

2. Lachish

During the 9th/8th cent. BCE, Lachish was the second largest city in the state of Judah. It had massive defensive walls, the largest gate-system and the largest single building discovered so far in the kingdom of Judah. The reference to Lachish in Mic 1:13 suggests that horses and chariots were garrisoned in Lachish. Whether the rectangular pillared buildings that archaeologists have found in the strata of Iron Age II are evidence of stables (or served some other function) is a disputed matter. Lachish did have the size and social stratification necessary to support garrisoned troops. Lachish was taken and destroyed toward the end of the 8th cent. by the Assyrians and early in the 6th cent. by the Babylonians. Its Iron Age strata and material culture are important for comparative purposes as archaeologists excavate other cities of Judah. A few ostraca were discovered in the area of the excavated gate and date to the period of the Babylonian destruction. They are valuable evidence for the exchange of correspondence in pre-exilic Judah, and likely reflect the practice at Lachish of preserving written communications.

3. Arad

The Iron Age site of Arad was founded on a hill in the Negev and overlooked the ruins of the larger Early Bronze city below it. A compact site, it was eventually enclosed with walls and served as a regional center. It possessed a small shrine in its interior, complete with a sacrificial altar, two limestone incense altars, two standing stones, and a recessed inner room or "holy of holies." The date of the shrine's origins is open to question, but it was in full function by the 8th cent. BCE. Inscriptional evidence discovered at the site includes administrative texts dating to the 8th and 7th cent. BCE. They are evidence for the administrative role of Arad in storing resources and in housing administrative personnel. The fragmentary inscriptions include a reference to a

late 10th/early 9th cent., upper Hazor became a regional center with an enclosure wall, a six-chambered gate, an internal administrative quarter, and eventually a subterranean passage to the water table beneath the city.

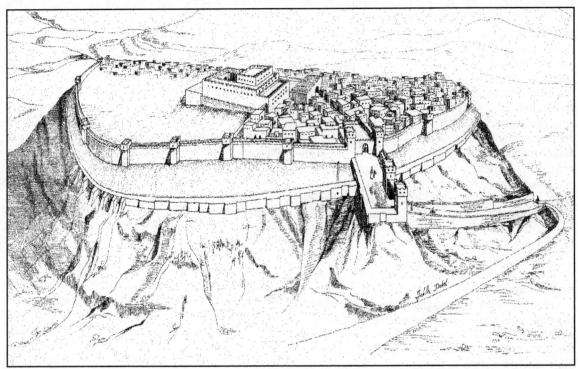

David Ussishkin, Tel Aviv University, artist Judith Dekel

Figure 1: LACHISH

"house of YHWH," which likely refers to the shrine located at the site. If so, the shrine would be the best-preserved worship center for the Yahwistic faith so far discovered in Judah.

4. Samaria

According to 1 Kgs 16:24, the Israelite king Omri bought a hill and built a capital city for the kingdom of Israel. It took its name, Samaria, from the pre-Omride owner, Shemer. Excavations carried out at the ancient ruins on the summit of the hill suggest that indeed the first major stratum of the city was constructed in the 9th cent. BCE. Thus Samaria is an Israelite city from its inception. During the reign of Ahab and his sons, the city expanded. It preserves beautiful examples of ashlar limestone masonary and typical urban architecture (storerooms, buildings associated with public and governmental tasks, and internal walls to separate sections of the city). Samaria was constructed as essentially a royal administrative acropolis. It served the dynasty of Jehu as well, and maintained a central role until the Assyrians destroyed it after months of siege.

5. Hazor

The large city from the 2nd millennium BCE was rebuilt after its destruction in the 13th cent. BCE. By the

Scholars currently debate whether these elements are to be associated with Solomon and the united monarchy or with the expansion of the Northern Kingdom under Omri and Ahab. Similar chambered gates at Megiddo and Gezer led scholars initially to associate the building expansions at all three cities with Solomon (1 Kgs 9:15). However this chronological issue is sorted out, the 9th cent. represents the pinnacle of development for Hazor (and Megiddo), apparently reflecting the influence of the Omride dynasty. Hazor was attacked, partially destroyed, and taken over by Assyria during its campaigns in the region (734–32 BCE).

6. Megiddo

As with Hazor to the northeast, Megiddo was a large city during most of the 2nd millennium and suffered decline in the transition to the Iron Age. Its first Iron Age phases were modest, but toward the end of the 10th cent. it too began to develop urban stratification, with a six-chambered gate, a city wall, and public buildings. In the 9th cent. a subterranean tunnel was begun from the south side of the enclosed city that ultimately reached the water table associated with a spring outside the city wall. This massive enterprise removed hundreds of tons of limestone bedrock. It was not the only large project to be dated about this time. A palace or governor's complex was built and rectangular, pillared buildings erected. As noted earlier, archaeologists debate the function of these latter buildings. The original excavators concluded that they were stables and that Megiddo (and Hazor, which also had them) was a regional chariot city.

7. Dan

This northernmost city of Iron Age Israel has been excavated over a period of years. In the 10th/9th

and to honor the national deity; it also shows the symbolic and cultural significance of city building as a task blessed by the gods and intended to provide order and security in a realm.

In his annals the Assyrian king SENNACHERIB describes a campaign carried out against Hezekiah and Judah in 701 BCE. He refers to shutting up Hezekiah in his city like "a bird in a cage." This may be an idiom for a siege of Jerusalem, which is otherwise described in the OT (2 Kgs 18–19; Isa 36–37). Sennacherib goes

John Laughlin
Figure 2: Iron Age II Gate, Dan

cent., its sacred precinct had a stone platform, sacrificial altar and temple. In Iron Age II, the gate had a podium for an official (king, governor, priest) to sit and in the paved-stone area nearby (plaza?) archaeologists found pieces of a monumental inscription in Aramaic, with details of the assassination of an Israelite and Judean ruler. Dan was located near the territory controlled by the Arameans, and the inscription may reflect the expansion of the Aramean king Hazael and his son in the last half of the 9th cent.

8. Extrabiblical references

From the mid-9th cent. comes a thirty-four-line inscription (*see* MOABITE STONE) from the Moabite ruler named Mesha (2 Kgs 3:4-5). In it he describes expansive building projects in his capital city such as a shrine for the national deity, an acropolis or royal quarter, palace, gates, walls, towers, reservoirs and ditches, and that he rebuilt (fortified?) other sites in his realm. The inscription is set up to glorify the king's exploits

on to report the destruction of forty-six walled cities and many villages. A basic distinction in demographics can be observed in his description. It is not unlike the manner in which cities and their "daughters," i.e., related hamlets and villages, are described in the OT (Num 32:42). In his capital city, Nineveh, Sennacherib portrayed his siege and sack of Lachish, which he carried out during his campaign against Judah. The siege was depicted in carved gypsum stone and occupied a prominent room in his palace. These exquisite carvings are now displayed in the British Museum.

E. City Symbolism and Personification in the OT

The first city-builder in the Genesis narrative is Cain, who named his construction for his son (4:17). This is perhaps the sign that he is not just a wanderer, but has strength and permanence. Among Ham's descendants is Nimrod, a mighty hunter, who is credited with building several cities in Assyria and Babylonia, including Nineveh (10:8-12). The larger cities from Mesopotamia certainly impressed the Israelites as powerful and aggressive, just the thing a renowned hunter would build and his descendants occupy. The size of a city like Nineveh would impress the later Israelites, although archaeology shows that a three-day journey just to cross it (Jonah 3:3) is certainly exaggerated. The fall of Nineveh in 612 BCE was the basis for the oracle celebrating her demise in the prophecy of Nahum. The infamous Tower of Babel grew from the resolve of people to build a city and a tower (Gen 11:4). The account is not a polemic against cities, but recognizes them as an illustration of the human quest for control.

In the Hebrew language, the primary word for city ('ir) is feminine. This fact of grammar is combined with a rich tradition of personification and symbolic portrayal. Ezekiel presents an extended allegory in which Jerusalem and Samaria are depicted as sisters whom the Lord "married" (23:1-49). The capital cities represent the independent states of Judah and Israel respectively. The book of Isaiah portrays Jerusalem in various formats including a prostitute (1:21), a daughter (1:8; 16:1; 37:22), a proclaimer of good news (40:9), a wife and mother (49:14-21; 50:1), a shining city (60:1-22), and place of pilgrimage for peoples in the latter days (2:2-4). The psalms also employ much of this symbolism for Jerusalem. In addition, interpreters describe a type of hymn in the Psalter as Zion Hymns or Songs of Zion. These psalms celebrate Jerusalem as the location of the Temple and the city of David (Pss 46–48; 122; 125; 132). Jerusalem in various roles is the chief character in the poetry of the book of Lamentations. The scope of Jerusalem's personified portrayal makes her the most frequent female character referred to in the OT.

The Temple in Jerusalem also gives rise to the traditions that the Lord "dwells" there. As put succinctly in Ps 132:13-14, God desired it for a habitation and place of rest. The ARK OF THE COVENANT, kept in the holy of holies in the Temple, was understood as the invisible seat or throne for the Lord (Exod 25:22; Isa 37:16; Ps 99:1) or as the footstool of the Lord (1 Chr 28:2; Ps 99:5). In related fashion, the city was also perceived as God's throne or footstool (Jer 3:17; 14:21; 17:12; Lam 2:1).

The last nine chapters of Ezekiel contain a vision of a transformed Jerusalem set on a high hill (Ezek 40–48). In these chapters the significance of Jerusalem as the seat of God's dwelling with Israel is depicted as the eschatological culmination of history. All the rich symbolism of Jerusalem as the city set on a hill, as the navel of the earth, and as the footstool of the cosmic Lord are brought together. Indeed, the city of Jerusalem has its name changed as a sign that a new reality has been glimpsed. The city shall be known as "The Lord is there."

F. The Persian, Greek, and Roman Periods

With the shift of power from Babylon to Persia came the opportunity for some among the Judean exiles to return to their homeland and to rebuild the Temple destroyed by the forces of Nebuchadnezzar in 587/86. The cities of Israel and Judah were not as populated in the Persian period as when the two entities were independent states. The books of Ezra and Nehemiah provide information regarding the rebuilding of Jerusalem, including the stirring account that the perimeter wall of the city was rebuilt in fifty-two days.

1. Hellenism

With his epoch-making campaigns, Alexander (the Great) of Macedon defeated the Persians and absorbed the vast holdings of their empire into his own. In the wake of his victories came the language and culture of Greece, which mixed with Semitic cultures in the Eastern Mediterranean to form a vibrant, west-Asian Hellenism ruled over by his successors. Alexander himself founded a city on the coast of Egypt that bore his name. Alexandria would become a chief city of the Mediterranean world in subsequent centuries. Its harbor had a famous lighthouse and the city developed one of the greatest libraries in antiquity.

Many cities in the former states of Israel and Judah were renamed, even as they were rebuilt or expanded. A city like Shechem was rebuilt according to Hellenistic standards and renamed in Greek Neopolis (= New City). Acco was renamed Ptolemais, Beth Shean became Scythopolis, and Rabbah of Ammon became Philadelphia, to cite just a few examples. Temples were built with marble columns decorated in either Ionian or Corinthian style. Public baths, theaters, and gymnasiums were erected in cities. In return for cooperation, some cities were granted certain rights and exemptions in relating to the Greek overlords. The famous DECAPOLIS, a collection of cities so favored, is mentioned in the NT (Matt 4:25; Mark 5:20; 7:31).

Southeast of the Dead Sea was the home of traders and pastoralists known as NABATEANS. At some point in the Hellenistic period they established their capital known as Petra in the reddish sandstone hills east of the Arabah. Even today the ruins of their magnificent tombs cut into the sandstone hills evoke awe in visitors. It was a city in which ostentatious architecture dominated, demonstrating the wealth and international contacts of the Nabateans.

2. Roman period

With the transition to Roman rule in 64/63 BCE, Syria and Palestine became the eastern edge of the so-called Pax Romana. Roman troops were stationed in the region and Roman provincial administrators sought cooperative measures with prominent local families. The latter led to the rise of Herod (the Great), son of Antipater, to various administrative posts in Palestine (37–4 BCE). Eventually he became king of the Jews and ruled over much of the territory formerly belonging to Israel and Judah, and briefly to the Maccabees. At the height of his fame he was perhaps the most recognized non-Roman of his day. His building projects were stunning achievements in the Hellenistic-Roman world and have a left a permanent mark in the region.

a. Caesarea Maritima. To honor Caesar his patron, Herod constructed a harbor city on the Mediterranean coast, Caesarea Maritima. It should be distinguished from Caesarea Philippi at the headwaters of the Jordan, which was also the beneficiary of Herod and his son Philip's largess. Both weather and tidal patterns made off-loading ships difficult at Caesarea, so Herod constructed an artificial breakwater and harbor, formed on large concrete blocks submerged to the sea floor. The city did not have an adequate supply of fresh water, so an aqueduct several miles long was constructed to bring in additional supplies. A type of flushing system took advantage of the tides to circulate sea water through channels in the city. Public baths, a hippodrome, and a theater were built to make the city an impressive introduction by the sea to Herod's realm. During Jesus' public ministry, Caesarea was the seat of Pontius Pilate, the Roman governor.

b. Jerusalem. Herod added several important public buildings to Jerusalem, making it not only the Jewish capital, but a remarkable Hellenistic-Roman city as well. It contained a family palace, but also homes of exquisite beauty belonging to the Temple priesthood and other upper-class citizens. There was a hippodrome and a theater, but most important, the Temple. In the year 20 BCE, Herod began to expand greatly the Temple area and its appurtenances. The Temple building itself could not be expanded, since its dimensions were fixed, but its materials could be upgraded and refurbished. It was reconstructed in gleaming white marble, so that its reflective brilliance could be seen for miles. The limestone platform upon which the Temple sat was expanded. A master engineer was required to plan and supervise the laying of cut limestone blocks, some of which were in excess of 20 ft. in length and weighed a hundred tons or more. A beautiful pillared portico was erected around the perimeter of the platform, which was reached by stairs ascending from the west side, a walkway through the platform from the south side and a gate on the east side. Herod's plans for the Temple area could not be completed in his own lifetime, but he was responsible for the platform extension and Temple upgrading, and his plans for Jerusalem were largely destroyed in 70 CE by the Romans, who put down a Jewish rebellion that had begun in Galilee a few years earlier. The Temple was not rebuilt, and after a second Jewish revolt in 132–35, Jews were banished from the city, its main streets were replotted according to a typical Roman plan and even the name of the city was changed to Aelia Capitolina.

c. Other Herodian building projects. Herod built magnificent temples and other public buildings in places like Caesarea Philippi, Samaria, and Hebron.

Even his family building projects in places like Jericho and the Herodium near Bethlehem contributed greatly to the village or city nearby. Remnants of his building projects can still be seen throughout the modern state of Israel and in portions of the West Bank.

d. The spread of Christianity. Christianity in the first century CE took root in some of the largest and most influential cities in the Roman Empire, including Rome. The book of Acts presents the home of the early missionary movement in Syrian Antioch (*see* ANTIOCH, SYRIAN), a town named for one of Alexander the Great's successors. It was a multiethnic city and in time became one of the largest cities in the empire. Ephesus was another city of massive proportions, possessed of a port, a great theater and for a while the largest temple in the ancient world, which was dedicated to the worship of Artemis (Diana in Roman mythology). Philippi was a Roman city, set astride a major highway. Corinth was a bustling port city. Fledgling Christian communities or house churches took root in urban areas and used the Roman communication and travel system to expand their contacts. *See* BROAD PLACE; LEVITICAL CITIES, TOWNS; VILLAGE.

Bibliography: LaMoine DeVries. *Cities of the Biblical World* (1997); Frank Frick. *The City in Ancient Israel* (1977); Volkmar Fritz. *The City in Ancient Israel* (1995); Zeev Herzog. *Archaeology of the City: Urban Planning in Ancient Israel and Its Social Implications* (1997); Gwendolyn Leick. *A Dictionary of Ancient Near Eastern Architecture* (1988); Peter Richardson. *City and Sanctuary: Religion and Architecture in the Roman Near East* (2002); Duane Roller. *The Building Program of Herod the Great* (1998); G. R. H. Wright. *Ancient Building in South Syria and Palestine* (1985).

J. ANDREW DEARMAN

CITY GATE [שַׁעַר sha'ar]. A city (a settlement with walls and one or more gates) in ancient Israel was the focal point of life in a region, serving as protection and commercial hub. The GATE was the most vulnerable part of a city's defenses (Isa 28:6), so a typical gate consisted of two to four pairs of "piers" and intervening pairs of "chambers." Some cities enhanced their defenses with a long entryway leading up to the gate at a right angle. (For examples of gates, see *NEAEHL*, 83, 167, 179, 365, 440, 503, 600, 897, 1016–17.) References to "possessing the gates" reflect their strategic importance (Gen 24:60) as well as the idea that the gate represented the whole city.

The latter also reflects the fact that a city's inhabitants had to pass back and forth between their homes and fields or other communities through the city gate. Similarly, all visitors entered through the gate (Ps 24:7-10). Therefore, gates and adjacent areas naturally served as places for all sorts of local business. Contracts were finalized and legal disputes were resolved at the city gate (Deut 17:5; 21:19; 22:15, 24; 25:7; Ruth 4:11). Several texts mention ELDERs sitting in the gate as judges and witnesses (Ruth 4:1; Job 29:7; Prov 31:23, 31; Lam 5:14), as did the king and/or his officials (2 Sam 15:1-4; 18:33–19:8). The people looked for "JUSTICE in the gate" in order to maintain the moral and ethical health of the city (Isa 29:20-21; Amos 5:10-15).

TIMOTHY M. WILLIS

CITY OF DAVID. *See* DAVID, CITY OF.

CITY OF DESTRUCTION. *See* HELIOPOLIS.

CITY OF MOAB. *See* MOAB, CITY OF.

CITY OF PALM TREES עִיר הַתְּמָרִים ['ir hattemarim]. Another name for JERICHO (Deut 34:3; 2 Chr 28:15). As one of the oldest cities in the world, Jericho grew up around a spring (Elisha's spring) that nourished a date-palm grove, earning the town this epithet.

CITY OF REFUGE. Cities of refuge were established in Israel to offer protection for those who had inadvertently killed another human being. The retaliatory justice of Israel's kinship system demanded a life for a life. When a family member was killed, a close relative became the גֹּאֵל הַדָּם go'el haddam ("AVENGER OF BLOOD") and was given the responsibility of avenging the slain person by killing the killer (Num 35:16-27; Josh 20:3; 2 Sam 14:4-11). The killer, however, could flee to a designated city, where others could hear the case. If a determination was made that no malice or intent was involved in the slaying, the killer could then enjoy the protection of the city and, while remaining in the city, was no longer subject to vengeance. The six cities designated in Josh 20:8-9, three in the Transjordan and three in Cisjordan, were strategically located so that none lay outside a day's journey from any point in Israel.

The concept of asylum in the ancient Near East was generally associated with sanctuaries. The BOOK OF THE COVENANT reflects this perspective through legislation that allows a killer to flee to a place appointed by God if the murder was not premeditated (Exod 21:12-14). The "place" marked the location of an altar, which imparted a holiness that prohibited the shedding of innocent blood. That this concept was in place as late as the United Monarchy is attested by the stories of Adonijah and Joab, both of whom took refuge by grasping the horns of the altar (although in the latter case, following Exod 21:14, Joab was taken from the altar and executed for the murders of Abner and Amasa [1 Kgs 1:50-53; 2:28-34]). The idea that an altar provided asylum has led some interpreters to propose that cities of refuge were so designated because they housed sanctuaries.

The PRIESTLY and DEUTERONOMIC legislations for cities of refuge, however, no longer directly associate asylum with sanctity. Both traditions recognize only one legitimate sanctuary. Thus, the designation of multiple sites as cities of refuge in Num 35:9-15 (Priestly) and Deut 4:41-43; 19:1-3 (Deuteronomic) precludes the location of an altar at any of the cities. The biblical legislation, instead, reflects a secularized concept of refuge based on the need to establish social structures that mitigate the cycle of retaliatory justice.

Priestly legislation (Num 35:9-29) designates six cities of refuge for those who kill someone unintentionally (בִּשְׁגָגָה bishghaghah). References to the cities of refuge (vv. 9-15, 25-28) precede and follow detailed guidelines for determining guilt and premeditation in cases of homicide (vv. 16-24). The guidelines frame culpability in terms of the use of an implement with lethal force (vv. 16-19) and in terms of malicious intent and premeditation (vv. 20-21). In both cases, the murderer is remanded to the avenger of blood for execution. Cities of refuge are then designated for the individual who kills another accidentally (22-24). The legislation stipulates that the assembled citizenry follow the guidelines on homicide and render a verdict between the accused and the avenger of blood. A decision to offer refuge then binds the citizenry to protect the accused, who remains in the city until the death of the high priest (v. 25). No reason is given to explain why the high priest's death pardons those sheltered by the city. His death is probably assumed to ransom the killer by atoning for the death of the one slain. While the high priest lives, however, the killer must remain within the city and relinquishes protection from the avenger of blood if departing during that period (vv. 26-29). A supplement to the legislation requires the testimony of witnesses (v. 30), prohibits the payment of ransom in place of the prescribed sentences (vv. 31-32), and warns that bloodshed pollutes the land (v. 33-34).

The Deuteronomic legislation complements and expands the Priestly directives but does not employ the phrase "cities of refuge." Deuteronomy 19:1-13 provides additional examples and guidelines on the issues of accidental death and murder (vv. 4-5, 11-12) and uses the phrase בִּבְלִי־דַעַת bivli dha'ath ("unintentionally") to denote the subject eligible for refuge. The passage displays a marked concern for the shedding of innocent blood, whether it be the death of the accused before judgment is rendered (vv. 6-7) or premeditated murder (v. 13). In light of this concern, Deuteronomy directs that an additional three cities may be designated if the Lord expands Israel's territory (vv. 8-9).

The actual designation of the cities in Josh 20:1-9 generally corresponds to the Priestly legislation but with a significant twist. Verses 4-5 (along with v. 6*b-c*) do not appear in the LXX version of Joshua and appear to be an editorial expansion designed to harmonize the Priestly and Deuteronomic legislation. As a result, the

Masoretic Text incorporates both operative terms for the accused—bishghaghah (vv. 3, 9) and bivli dhaʿath (v. 5)—and presents a scenario by which the elders first agree to offer refuge (vv. 4-5) until the accused can stand trial before the citizenry (v. 6).

The system of cities of refuge significantly transformed social and theological concepts of justice. The establishment of a protected space and a procedure for deciding guilt and punishment lifted retaliation and punishment from the sphere of the family to a mediating third party (whether elders or the assembled citizenry) and thereby provided a more stable platform for resolving issues of wrongful death. In addition, the associated guidelines redefined notions of guilt and culpability. While the retaliatory justice of the kinship system viewed guilt in terms of the act itself, the biblical legislation defined culpability in terms of intention. The cities of refuge therefore provided a system that recognized the gravity of taking a life but also linked punishment to intention. The fact that the accused was effectively imprisoned in the city acknowledged culpability for causing death, but the protection provided against the family avenger emphasized that matters of justice had to be decided on the basis of the intention and not the deed. *See* CRIMES AND PUNISHMENT.

Bibliography: M. Greenberg. "The Biblical Conception of Asylum." *JBL* 78 (1959) 125–32; A. Rofé. "Joshua 20: Historico-Literary Criticism." *Empirical Models for Biblical Criticism,* J. H. Tigay, ed. (1985) 131–47.

L. DANIEL HAWK

CITY OF SALT [עִיר הַמֶּלַח ʿir hammelakh]. Khirbet Qumran, the City of Salt, was one of the six cities of Judea listed in Josh 15:61-62. It is situated in wilderness and was inhabited several times beginning in the Iron Age and lasting until the BAR-KOKHBA Revolt. The Iron Age stratum has yielded a great rectangular building similar to the Israelite fortresses in the Judean and Negev deserts, and much Iron Age pottery has been recovered there.

JOSEPH RAY CATHEY

CITY OF THE SUN [עִיר הַחֶרֶס ʿir hakheres]. An Egyptian city, probably HELIOPOLIS (Isa 19:18; Jer 43:13).

CLAMP [מְחַבְּרָה mekhabbrah, ποδάγρα podagra]. Iron binder used in constructing buildings (1 Chr 22:3) and torturing prisoners (4 Macc 11:10). A wooden coupling (2 Chr 34:11).

CLAMS. Indirectly mentioned as unclean animals forbidden for human consumption, since they are water creatures without fins and scales (Lev 11:10-12; Deut 14:9).

CLAN [מִשְׁפָּחָה mishpakhah]. This Hebrew term occurs just over 300 times in the OT, translated "clan(s)" in approximately 170 instances, and "FAMILY" in most of those remaining. The latter overlaps with the translation of another Hebrew phrase for "ancestral houses" or "families" [בֵּית אָבוֹת beth ʾavoth). This confusion reflects the fluidity inherent to these designations of Israel's structural units. Ideally, the Israelite clans stand as a structural level between a TRIBE and its "ancestral houses." The names of clans are typically the names of the sons and grandsons of the founder of a TRIBE, one of the sons (or grandsons) of JACOB (*see* Num 1-4, 26). The history of the tribe of JOSEPH, like the designation of DAN as a "clan" in Judg 13:2, shows the possibility of a blurring of these distinctions. [A different term is used for the "clans" of Edom (Gen 36:15-43; 1 Chr 1:51-54); it is a homonym for the word for THOUSAND.]

A clan name designated both a large lineage group and the territory that the group controlled; the preponderance of clan names in census lists and tribal allotments (Num 1–4, 26; Josh 13–21; 1 Chr 1–9) suggests this, and the inclusion of Manassite clan names in the Samaria OSTRACA substantiates it. A clan tended to function as a collective in agricultural, legal, and military matters. Ideally then, the members of a clan felt mutually obligated to assist one another in times of need (*see* Num 36:1-12, the book of Ruth, or 2 Sam 14:1-11); however, the relative strength of those mutual obligations could wax and wane in reaction to the vicissitudes of climate and history (both local and national). Some of the biblical laws and prophetic teachings regarding unjust treatment of widows and orphans reflect the occasional neglect of such clan obligations.

TIMOTHY M. WILLIS

CLAROMONTANUS, CODEX. A 5th or 6th cent. bilingual manuscript containing the Latin and the Greek text of the letters of Paul on opposing pages and arranged in sense lines. The letters are presented in the usual sequence with the exception of Colossians preceding Philippians. On four pages between Philemon and Hebrews another scribe added a Latin list of canonical writings (*Catalogus Claromontanus*). The Greek text of the first page with Rom 1:1-7 is lacking. It is unclear where the manuscript originated. It is now kept in Paris at the Biliothèque Nationale (Gr 107, 107AB), which obtained it from the monastery of Clermont at Beauvais, France. The usual scholarly designation in critical editions is D 06. Several pages were stolen and brought to Holland during the 18th cent. but were retrieved with the help of diplomacy and police.

Bibliography: H. J. Frede. *Altlateinische Paulushandschriften* (1964).

DAVID J. TROBISCH

CLASP. *See* JEWELRY.

CLAUDIA klaw´dee-uh [Κλαυδία Klaudia]. Probably Roman, perhaps a leader of the Christian community, mentioned in 2 Tim 4:21 as sending greetings to TIMOTHY. In the *Apos. Con.* VII.46 she is reported to be mother of LINUS, an early bishop of Rome. In other traditions, she is often said to be the wife of PUDENS.

CLAUDIUS klaw´dee-uhs. Born on 1 August 10 BCE in Lugdunum (Lyons), Gaul, Tiberius Claudius Nero Germanicus was recognized by the senate as Rome's emperor on 25 January 41 CE. His reign would extend until his death (possibly by murder) on 13 October 54 CE.

Subject in his youth to sickness and physical deformities (a limp, trembling fits, speech impediments) in a society that demanded physical perfection of its rulers, Claudius had been a most unlikely candidate. According to Suetonius, Claudius' own mother Antonia had called him a *portentum hominis* ("more a bad omen than a human being"; *Suet. Claud.* 3) and his male relatives, including his nephew Gaius, who belatedly bestowed consular honors on him in 37 CE, had treated him with habitual contempt.

Claudius lacked political training and experience, but his descent from, and close connections to, the Julio-Claudian family as well as the military's intense loyalty to this house for some one hundred years convinced the senate to bestow all customary imperial powers upon him.

Claudius had grown up among books and tutors. He had devoted himself to literary studies, and was the author of histories in Greek of Carthage and Etruria (both lost) as well as a history of Rome in Latin (also lost). Claudius took a deep interest in religion, both scholarly and practical. He held a number of priesthoods. He was early in life an augur (an ancient republican priesthood) and, from 14 CE, a sodalis in the cult of Augustus. As emperor, Claudius assumed the chief priesthood (*pontifex maximus*) of Rome's traditional state religion. A measure of his devotions may taken from his consecration of an "Altar to Augustan Loyalty" in 43 CE, his celebration of the Secular Games in 47, and his extension of Rome's sacred boundary in 49.

Tacitus reports in his Annals that Claudius entreated the senate to take steps to preserve the arts of Etruscan divination by reorganizing the haruspices (11.15). Suetonius tells us that Claudius scrupulously followed traditional religious practices, including, e.g., those enjoined upon sight of an augurally significant bird (22) or the signing of peace treaties (25). On the other hand, although his attempt to introduce the Eleusinian mysteries from Athens into Rome shows him sympathetic to Greek religion (*Suet. Claud.* 25), Claudius expelled astrologers (*Tac. Ann.* 12.52), expelled Jewish/Christian agitators (*Suet. Claud.* 25; compare Acts 18:2, but compare also *Dio* 60.6.6 where Claudius prohibits

assemblies of the Jews), and outlawed the religion of the Druids altogether (*Suet. Claud.* 25).

Claudius received divine honors, including priests and temples, in the East as well as varying degrees of divine honors in other provinces, but he refused to receive worship as a god in Rome during his lifetime. Militarily and politically, Claudius was a careful and successful administrator, adding provinces (most famously Britain), founding numerous military colonies, and generously extending Roman citizenship. His mediation of Greek and Jewish disputes in Alexandria as well as his management of Judea were, on the other hand, less successful.

In Rome itself, Claudius' administration was noteworthy for an increase in the imperial bureaucracy and reliance on the services of freed slaves attached to the imperial household. Their power and influence grew at the expense of the traditional senatorial and equestrian elite, and this complicated already difficult relations with the senate.

Claudius' domestic life was dominated by his marriages, especially his third to the notorious Valeria Messalina (condemned in 48 CE; she was the mother of his son Britannicus and daughter Octavia) and his fourth to his niece Julia Agrippina, whose son Nero by a previous marriage Claudius adopted. Nero succeeded Claudius, executed Britannicus, and saw to Claudius' posthumous consecration as the god Divus Claudius. Seneca's *Apocolocyntosis* ("Pumpkinification of Claudius") offers a contemporary and cruel satire on the theme. *See* AUGUSTUS; CAESAR; CALIGULA; EMPEROR WORSHIP; NERO; ROMAN EMPIRE; ROMAN RELIGION.

Bibliography: Barbara Levick. *Claudius* (1990); Arnaldo Momigliano. *Claudius, the Emperor, and His Achievement* (1934, 1981); Vincent Mary Scramuzza. *The Emperor Claudius* (1940).

HANS-FRIEDRICH MUELLER

CLAUDIUS LYSIAS. *See* LYSIAS, CLAUDIUS.

CLAY [חֹמֶר khomer; Aram. חֲסַף khasaf; κονιορτός koniortos, ὀστράκινος ostrakinos, ὄστρακον ostrakon, πήλινος pēlinos, πηλός pēlos]. A natural type of sediment or soil composed of minerals (as well as many impurities), which are plastic and sticky when wet, but hard and indestructible when heated to a high temperature. Clay is best known for the making of POTTERY. The repeated use of clay for pottery began in the Neolithic Period (6th millennium BCE). Bricks (Nah 3:14) were also made from clay and usually sun-dried. CUNEIFORM documents were written on clay tablets. Figurines sometimes were made of clay.

Clays vary in composition of minerals and impurities and these factors affect the quality and color of the finished product. Specific clays were used for different purposes. A clay slurry, called a slip, can be used to decorate clay. When rubbed into the vessel's surface, the slip produces a certain color and sheen when the object is fired. This sheen is called "burnishing," which could also be created on vessels without slip. Clay is sometimes used as a metaphor for humans (Job 10:9; Isa 45:9; 64:8; Jer 18:6; Rom 9:19-21; *see also* Sir 33:13). In Bel 7, Daniel argues that the statue of the god Bel is made of clay, and thus cannot eat offerings given by the king.

JOHN C. H. LAUGHLIN

CLAY TABLETS. Clay tablets were the primary writing media for the CUNEIFORM texts from Mesopotamia and adjacent areas from at least the 4th through the 2nd millennium BCE. Two important sites are MARI (in Syria) and NUZI (in Iraq). The languages that used the clay tablets and cuneiform writing included Sumerian, Akkadian, Hittite, and others.

The tablets vary in size from about 1 in. square to well over 12 in. square. The clay was washed, then allowed to dry to a state where it could be held in the hand without deforming it. A wood or bone stylus was used to impress the wedge shapes which make up the cuneiform writing system. The tablets were then sun baked or kiln fired for permanence. Clay tablets were used for documents of every type: legal documents, receipts, inventories, records, literary texts, religious texts, and correspondence. Official documents were often sealed with the personal seal impressions of witnesses, and even enclosed in a clay envelope that recorded the contents of the tablet. Clay tablets were also formed into cylinders and cone shapes for special uses. *See* WRITING AND WRITING MATERIALS.

JOEL F. DRINKARD, JR.

CLEAN AND UNCLEAN. טהר thr and טמא tm' are the principal root terms for "clean, pure" and "unclean, impure." They have been translated variously: [qal] clean: pure, cleansed, purified; [pi] purify; [qal] unclean: impure, polluted, defiled; [pi] defile, pollute. Other verbal roots that are used for purity and impurity are:

ברר	brr	"purify, clean, polish"; בֹר (n) "purity, lye, soap"
זכה	zkh	"innocent"
זכך	zkk	"be bright, guiltless"
זקק	zqq	"pure" (generally of refined metals)
לבן	lbn	"turn white"
נקה	nqh	"innocent"
סדק	sdq	judicial or religious innocence
סרף	srp	"burn, smelt" (metals)
קדש	qds	sometimes "purify by bathing"
רחם	rkhs	"bathe"
כבב	kbs	"launder"

In the NT the term for *clean* is καθαρός katharos; the terms for *unclean, impure* are ἀκάθαρτος akathar-

tos and a καθαρσία akatharsia; occasionally, μιαίνω miainō, "stain, defile."

A. Old Testament
   1. Definition and description
   2. Moral impurity
      a. Idolatry
      b. Homicide
      c. Sexual sins
      d. Cultic violations
   3. Ritual Impurity
      a. Death
      b. Scale disease
      c. Sexual discharges
      d. Miscellaneous
   4. Unclean Food
   5. Purification
B. Second Temple Judaism
   1. Archaeology
   2. Late biblical texts and Apocrypha
   3. Dead Sea Scrolls
   4. Philo and Josephus
   5. Rabbinic literature
C. New Testament
   1. Synoptic Gospels and Acts
   2. Pauline literature
   3. Other NT texts
D. Rationale and Significance
   1. Old Testament
   2. Second Temple Judaism
   3. New Testament
Bibliography

A. Old Testament
1. Definition and description

Purity in the OT is a status achieved by moral integrity and ritual purification, which is required of Israel in order for God's holiness to reside among them (Num 19:20; Deut 23:24). Impurity describes not only a lack of purity but a powerful force that threatens it. Less prominently, purity can also denote physical cleanliness or the purity of refined metals.

A system of purity and impurity is found in the PRIESTLY laws of Leviticus and Numbers. The terms *ritual* and *moral* impurity, although not found in the OT, help to differentiate between types of impurity. Ritual impurity is caused primarily by certain natural functions of the human body, most of which are necessary, routine, and unavoidable. Moral impurity is incurred by violation of God's laws. Punishments for the latter are severe, and purifications include animal sacrifices. Unlike ritual impurity, however, moral impurity is not physically contagious. Both kinds of impurity are threatening to the covenant relationship that Israel has with Yahweh. Both prevent worship, and both contaminate the sanctuary and land and threaten the continued presence of Yahweh among the people of

Israel. All impurity must be purified according to specific procedures outlined in Scripture.

In ancient Israel the issue of clean and unclean is connected to the holiness of Yahweh. Holiness is the divine force that fights Israel's battles and brings God's blessing and revelation to the people (Exod 15:11; 32:29; 1 Sam 6:20; 20:12; 2 Pet 1:21). But holiness will not work unless there is purity; the community must maintain a certain level of purity in order for Yahweh to reside within it (Lev 15:31; Deut 23:14). Purity restrictions are more severe the closer one is to the sanctuary. In order to guard the holiness of the sanctuary, all Israel must be pure before entering its courts. Impurity, ritual or moral, can impinge on God's realm and bring destruction on the community. Anyone who brings impurity into contact with holiness is in danger of כָּרֵת kareth, death by divine agency (Lev 7:20-21).

2. Moral impurity

Moral integrity is often referred to as purity, and it is achieved by obedience to Yahweh. Deliberate sin brings serious penalties. Violations of any of God's commands, whether deliberate or unintentional, bring an impurity, which pollutes the sanctuary and requires a sacrifice for purification (Lev 4:1–5:13; 16:3-20; Num 15:22-31). Moral impurity is discussed in the following categories: idolatry, homicide, sexual sins, and cultic infractions.

a. Idolatry. Idolatry of any kind is considered impure by Scripture. Such activities include: creating and worshiping idols (Ezek 22:4); Baal worship (Jer 2:23); contacting the dead (Lev 19:31); and child sacrifice (Lev 20:25; Ps 106:38-39). Idolatry defiles not only the idolater but the sanctuary and the land (Lev 18:28; 20:3; Jer 32:34; Ezek 5:11; 23:38-39; 36:18; compare Josh 22:19, uncleanness of pagan land). According to the Israelite priests, impurity affects the sanctuary even if the idolater does not enter it; the deed alone is enough to cause pollution (Lev 20:3). Purifying idolatry calls for death to the idolater and destruction for all idols and their shrines (Lev 27:29; Deut 7:5, 25; 13:13-19; Josh 7).

b. Homicide. Killing an innocent human being causes a moral impurity. Murder does not include capital punishment or killing enemies in war, both of which are commanded on occasion by Scripture. Homicide defiles the land and can bring crop failure (Gen 4:10-12; 2 Sam 21:1-14; Ps 106:38; Hos 4:2-3). Purification can be accomplished only by the death of the murderer (Num 35:33) and sometimes his whole family (Josh 8:24-25). CITIES OF REFUGE were established to protect the unintentional manslayer until the matter could be properly judged (Num 35:11-12; Deut 19:1-13; Josh 20:1-9). The accused could expect asylum at the altar (Exod 21:12-14; 1 Kgs 2:29). From Israelite history, it is clear that repentance could alleviate the sentence of death, as in the case of David's murder of Uriah, but still the life of the king's child was taken and other pen-

alties incurred (2 Sam 12:10-14). (*See* CRIMES AND PUNISHMENT, OT AND NT.)

The pollution of homicide comes into relief in the law concerning the anonymous murderer. If a murdered corpse is found in a field without any indication of who the culprit is, it still causes impurity. Thus, the elders and judges kill a heifer, as a substitute for the murderer, and then wash their hands over it, swearing to their innocence and ignorance in the matter (Deut 21:1-9).

c. Sexual sins. Various sexual acts cause moral impurity: incest (Lev 18:6-18; Ezek 22:11), adultery (Lev 18:20; Num 5:13-29; Ezek 18:6-15; 33:26), homosexuality (Lev 18:22), bestiality (Lev 18:23), and remarriage to one's first spouse after an intervening marriage with another person (Deut 24:1-4). Intercourse with a menstruant causes both a moral and a ritual impurity (Lev 18:19; 20:18; Ezek 18:6). Sexual sins cause impurity to the people involved and to the land as well (Lev 18:24-30; Deut 24:4). Purification can only be accomplished by kareth (Lev 18:29).

d. Cultic violations. Pollution of a sanctuary brings about a severe impurity. This includes bringing any impure person or object into the sanctuary (Lev 12:4; 22:3), allowing holy food to mix with impure food (Lev 7:19-21), and neglecting to perform necessary purifications or sacrifices (Lev 5:2-5; Num 19:20). The Sabbath and pilgrimage festivals, e.g., Passover, are holy times in Israel and require purification of the laity as well as the priests (Num 6:10-11; Neh 13:19, 22). Not only sacrifices but agricultural priestly portions must be kept pure (Deut 26:13-14). Special occasions of divine intervention are often prepared for by purification, both ritual and moral, e.g., the Sinaitic revelation (Exod 19:10-15, 22), the Jordan River crossing (Josh 3:5), and the conquest of the Philistines (1 Sam 7:3-11). Holy personnel are not to become defiled by a corpse (certain exceptions apply; Num 6:6-7, 11; Lev 21:1-4).

Deliberate mixing of impurity and holiness is the most dangerous of all combinations. It can only be purified by kareth (Lev 7:19-21; 22:3). Sometimes punishment is an immediate divine act, such as the killing of those who offered strange fire in the sanctuary (Lev 10:1-2) or who touched the ark of God, although unauthorized (2 Sam 6:7). Unintentional pollution of sanctified things causes impurity as well but can be purified by a guilt offering with restitution and a 20 percent fine (Lev 5:15-16). In fact, unintentional transgression of any of God's laws brings about an impurity that must be purged by the same procedure (Lev 5:17-19).

3. Ritual impurity

Ritual impurity in the Bible refers to a number of physical conditions that, while often necessary for the continuance of life, prevent an individual from contact with a sacred area, personnel, food, and objects. This type of impurity falls into three categories: death, skin disease, and sexual discharges. An Israelite who has contact with any of these conditions becomes ritually defiled and must undergo purification.

a. Death. The corpse is the most impure item in the priestly system (*see* DEATH, POLLUTION OF). It conveys a weeklong contamination to anyone who touches it or shares a roof with it, and it is not purifiable (Num 19). According to Num 5:2, corpse-contaminated persons are put outside of the camp for their week of impurity, but Num 19 seems to suggest that they are in the camp undergoing purification. Persons and objects who are contaminated by the corpse must be sprinkled with special purgation water on days 3 and 7 of their impurity (*see below*, §A.5 Purification).

Related to the corpse is carcass impurity. Anyone who handles a carcass of an animal, which has not been ritually slaughtered, becomes unclean. A carcass includes the dead body of any forbidden animal (note that these animals do not convey impurity if they are alive) as well as that of any clean animal that has not been ritually slaughtered, including those that have died as prey or of old age. Touching a carcass conveys a one-day impurity that requires bathing; carrying the carcass intensifies the impurity and requires laundering as well (Lev 17:15).

b. Scale disease. Several types of skin afflictions are described in Lev 13 that cause a ritual impurity. They have in the past come under the category of "leprosy," but this should not be understood as modern LEPROSY. Rather it includes a number of specifically described skin diseases: e.g., baldness, skin eruptions, discoloration, or extreme psoriasis.

Scale disease (צָרַעַת tsara‘ath) ranks second in impurity after the corpse. This is because, like the corpse, the disease is not curable unless God decides to heal the person, as well as due to the extensive purification procedures required if healing is achieved. This disease, in fact, functions as a divine curse on several occasions (Lev 14:34; Num 12:10-15; 2 Sam 3:29; 2 Chr 26:19-20). Tsara‘ath can also be found in houses and fabrics. Here it refers to mold and fungus. The affected stones must be removed and affected fabrics burned (Lev 13:52; 14:40).

c. Sexual discharges. The most impure sexual discharge is the flow of blood from a new mother (Lev 12:1-6). Depending on the gender of the baby, this discharge renders the woman impure for one (boy) or two (girl) weeks, plus a less severe time of impurity for thirty-three days (boy) or sixty-six days (girl). During the first phase of her impurity, she may not go to the sanctuary and is contagious to other persons and various objects, including food. During the second phase, the impurity is reduced and remains threatening only to sancta (a holy place).

Irregular discharges from male or female sexual organs, e.g., gonorrhea or menstrual blood outside of a woman's period (*see* BLOOD, FLOW OF), are next on the list of intense impurities (Lev 15:1-15, 25-30).

Both of these require, first of all, healing and then sacrifices and ablutions. Regular menstrual flows and seminal emissions are purified by the wait of a week for the former, and until evening for the latter (Lev 15:16-24). Bathing is required for both, although this is an *a fortiori* inference from Scripture in the case of the menstruant. All persons with sexual discharges remain contagious to persons, beds, seats, food, vessels, and clothes for the duration of their impurity.

d. Miscellaneous. Excrement is not an impurity concern in priestly law but does become an issue in other texts. In order that the war camp remain holy and Yahweh be present among the soldiers to bring victory in battle, human waste must be eliminated outside of the camp (Deut 23:15). Ezekiel complains of defilement when he is asked to use excrement for cooking fuel (Ezek 4:12-15). Among the Dead Sea sectarians too excrement is considered impure (4Q472a; 11Q19 46.15; s*ee J.W.* 2.147-49).

While it is a physical condition, ritual purity has little or nothing to do with hygiene. In fact, it can be transferred to an individual who is simply in the same room as a corpse or a leper even where no physical contact has been made. Also, this impurity can affect houses and fabrics that have no connection to germs or disease. Furthermore, it only comes into effect when the priest pronounces it so. Most strikingly perhaps, the law is silent regarding the impurity of Gentiles; apparently they are not subject to the purity system (except the Gentile corpse, Num 31:19).

4. Unclean food

Certain animals are prohibited for food in Israel. They can be easily divided into three categories: land, water, and air. Land animals must meet two criteria to be considered clean: They must have a split hoof and must chew the cud (Lev 11:2-8). Water creatures must have both fins and scales (Lev 11:9-12). No criteria are given for fowl, but permitted birds and insects are listed (Lev 11:13-23).

The laws of forbidden foods form an interesting juncture between ritual and moral impurity. Israel's diet is usually discussed under ritual impurity, because it is not clear how the particular forbidden anmials, and not others, are connected to immorality. Nevertheless, it appears that reduction of Israel's diet to a few herbivores is based in a reverence for blood and life (Milgrom 1991). The greatest value of the dietary system lies in its forced separation of Israel from her pagan neighbors (see §D. Rationale and Significance). In any case, these laws are prohibitions; they are not unavoidable physical conditions, like, e.g., menstruation. Israel must choose to obey God's commands on the matter of diet.

5. Purification

As explained above, impurity must be purged so that it does not threaten the holiness of Israel.

Priestly law reveals a system by which impurity is purified. Purification varies in intensity, complexity, and duration, depending on the nature of the impurity. Deliberate impurities head the list, and they are purified by death. If the nation becomes inundated by impurity, Israel may be exiled from her land. Unintentional sins can be purified by repentance and sacrifices; the DAY OF ATONEMENT rites purge the sanctuary for all known and unknown sins (Lev 16:16). Next on the list are severe ritual impurities, such as scale disease, childbirth, and abnormal sexual discharges, which require complicated procedures including sacrifices. The list ends with routine, minor impurities, which do not require sacrifices but cause at least a one-day impurity and require ablutions. A table illustrates this gradation.

Impurities and Their Purifications in Priestly Law	
IMPURITY	PURIFICATION
Deliberate sin	Death (**kareth**) or exile (Lev 7:20-21; 18:28-29; 20:3-5, 22; Num 15:30; Deut 30:17-18)
Unintentional sin	Repentance, sacrifices (Lev 5:5-6; Num 15:27)
Scale disease	(After healing) 2-3 weeks of examination; sprinkling; shaving; bird rites; blood daubings, sacrifices, laundering, bathing (Lev 14)
Childbirth	Two-stage impurity: 7/14 days and 33/66 days; sacrifice, laundering, bathing (Lev 12:1-6)
Irregular sexual discharge	(After healing) 8-day impurity; sacrifice; laundering, bathing (Lev 15:3-15, 28-30)
Corpse contamination (priest)	15 days of impurity; sprinkling with purgation water; laundering, bathing (Ezek 44:26-27)
Corpse contamination	Immediate termination of Nazirite service; 8 days of impurity; (Nazirite) sacrifices; sprinkling with purgation water; shaving, laundering, bathing (Num 6:9-12)
Corpse contamination (laity)	1 week of impurity; sprinkling with purgation water; laundering, bathing, sunset (Num 5:2-3; 19:14-19)
Menstruation	1 week of impurity; laundering, bathing, sunset (Lev 15:19-24)

Handling a carcass	laundering, bathing, sunset (Lev 11:24-40)
Seminal emission	laundering, bathing, sunset (Lev 15:16-18)
Touching a carcass	bathing, sunset (Lev 11:24-40; 22:5-8)

Some of the purification activities above are based on *a fortiori* inferences from the text's prescriptions for other types of impurity. For example, Scripture does not explicitly require the menstruant to bathe, but since persons who touch her bed or seat must bathe and launder their clothes (Lev 15:21-22), it is a fair assumption that she too must bathe and launder her clothes. As a general rule, it appears that bathing is required for all ritual impurity, thus, where only laundering is stated, bathing can be assumed as well. Ritual impurity is contagious, and individuals who are contaminated secondarily must purify themselves with at least ablutions and waiting until sunset.

Certain objects are susceptible to impurity, and if contaminated must be purified. Scripture mentions: earthenware, clothes, and vessels of wood or skin or metal (Lev 11:32-35; Num 31:20, 22-23). The rabbis limit susceptible materials to these items, but some Scripture texts seem to be more inclusive (Lev 11:35; Num 19:14). Most impure items are washed, but metal vessels must be passed through fire (Num 31:22-23) and earthenware must be broken (Lev 11:33). On particular modes of purification, *see* BATHING; RED HEIFER; SACRIFICES AND OFFERINGS; WATER FOR IMPURITY.

Outside of the Priestly corpus, the biblical emphasis is primarily on purification from sin. This is achieved by repentance, sacrifices, and various punishments. Sometimes the individual is punished by various tragic circumstances, such as crop failure, exile, or death. The language of purification rituals is also used metaphorically to describe the removal of guilt: "purge me with hyssop [used for purification from a corpse], and I shall be clean" (Ps 51:9); "Wash yourselves . . . remove the evil of your doings" (Isa 1:16); "When the Lord shall have washed away the filth of the daughters of Zion and cleansed the bloodstains of Jerusalem" (Isa 4:4); "I will sprinkle clean water upon you...from all your idols I will cleanse you" (Ezek 36:25).

B. Second Temple Judaism

Second Temple Judaism was marked by a heightened concern for ritual purity. Issues of cult and purity engaged and divided Jews more so in this period than at any other time in antiquity. Purification in the Second Temple era was expected in a variety of situations. Most Jews regarded the city of Jerusalem as the holy city and purified themselves before participating in the life of the city. Many laypersons (not only priests) purified before meals, before prayer, and after impurity. Initiations into various forms of Judaism were also marked by purifications.

1. Archaeology

The excavation of the Upper City of Second Temple Jerusalem yielded many מִקְוָאֹת miqva'oth, or ritual baths (see MIQVAH, MIQVA'OTH), the most common type being a rock-cut stepped pool. Some pools allow separate paths for entry and exit. Ritual baths have been found in other parts of Israel as well, from Galilee to Masada.

Miqva'oth have also been discovered adjoining cave-tombs in this period (Reich 1987). These suggest that Jews were concerned to purify themselves immediately after corpse contamination even as several texts attest (see below). Apparently, an initial bath was performed on the first day of the week of corpse contamination to allow the individual access to society but not to the sanctuary (Milgrom 1991).

Stone vessels too are an indicator of ritual purity concerns. According to Jewish law, stone is insusceptible to impurity because it is not listed as such in Scripture, which explicitly states that cisterns are insusceptible to impurity (Lev 11:36). While some scholars maintain that purity of food and vessels was only the concern of priests, this appears unlikely. Domestic vessels, including stone mugs, pitchers, and bowls for daily meals, have been discovered in Jerusalem as well as in many rural settlements throughout the country.

2. Late biblical texts and Apocrypha

The concern for purity intensifies in late biblical texts. Gentile impurity comes into relief in this period. Ezra takes drastic measures to ensure the purity of holy seed: forcing divorce from pagan spouses (Ezek 9:2; 10:10-11). Nehemiah expels a Gentile and his belongings from the Temple and purifies the room in which he was lodging (Neh 13:8-9). Joel envisions a holy Jerusalem where non-Israelites are not welcome (Joel 4:17 [Heb.]; compare Isa 52:1). Jubilees regards any social interaction with Gentiles as defiling, and if a Jewish girl marries a Gentile, her father becomes impure (Jub 22:17; 30:10; compare J.W. 5.194). Arguments continue over the nature of this impurity, whether it is ritual or moral, but the language is definitely more physical than what is usually presented in Scripture.

In several PSEUDEPIGRAPHA, moral purification is accompanied by ritual ablutions. In the Life of Adam and Eve 11, Adam repents while standing submerged up to his neck in a river. Also, the Syb. Or. 4.165 endorses prayerful posture and water purification: "wash your whole bodies in perennial rivers" and "stretch out your hands to heaven and ask forgiveness for your previous deeds." Several texts mention washing hands in the sea or sanctifying flesh with water before prayer (Ep. Arist. 305-306; Sib. Or. 3.591-93; Jdt 12:7-8).

3. Dead Sea Scrolls

The Dead Sea Scrolls are known for a distinctive interpretation of purity: 1) Several Scrolls expand the categories of holiness and purity of the Torah, e.g., the extension of the holiness of the Temple to the entire city of Jerusalem. The Temple Scroll describes a three-day process with two baths before the impure can enter the Temple city (11Q19 45:7-12). Both the Temple Scroll and the Damascus Document prohibit sexual intercourse within Jerusalem (11Q19 45:11-12; CD 12:1-2). Hides used in Jerusalem must be from animals slaughtered as sacrifices (11Q19 51:1-6; 4QMMT B 21-26). 2) Impurity is a stronger force than in other ancient Jewish texts, as apparent from the isolation of menstruants and parturients, three-day purification periods after sexual intercourse (11Q19 48:16), and the impurity of excrement and Gentiles (1QS 5:4, 13-20; 11Q19 63:15; 4Q266 5 ii 5-7). 3) The communal food and drink, "the purity," must be harvested and eaten in a state of purity (4Q284a 1.2-8; compare 4Q274 1.5-8; 2.1; 4Q514 1 i 2, 4; compare J.W. 2.129). 4) Ritual and moral impurity are intertwined. The sinner retains both moral and ritual impurity (1QS 5:19-20), and purification is effected by both the holy spirit and ablutions (1QS 3:7-9; compare CD 10:2-3).

The site at Qumran supports the description of the Scrolls with evidence of an ancient aqueduct connecting several cisterns and immersion baths. Also 200 fragments of stone vessels have been found.

4. Philo and Josephus

Philo comments on the rigor of his contemporaries in matters of purity. After sexual intercourse and corpse contamination, he claims Jews would touch nothing until they had immersed in water (Spec. Law 3.206, 363; compare also Josephus, Ag. Ap. 2.199, 203). Although Philo stresses moral impurity and uses ritual impurity primarily in a metaphorical manner, he remains an observant Jew.

Josephus confirms the emphasis on purity in Second Temple Judaism. Before festivals all Jews entering Jerusalem apparently purified themselves (Ant. 14:285; compare John 18:28; m. Hag. 3:6). Antiochus III reportedly upheld Jerusalem's claim to purity even in nonfestival periods by forbidding impure animals or their hides to be brought into the city, and limiting Gentile access to the Temple complex (Ant. 12.145-46). Also, Josephus states that individuals with severe ritual impurities were excluded from the entire city (J.W. 5.227-32; m. Kelim. 1:6-9), and that menstruants were secluded during their times of impurity (Ant. 3:261-2; m. Nid. 7:4).

Josephus' report on the Essenes is very close to the Scrolls in the matter of purity. According to Josephus, Essenes required an initiation based on purity. After the first year of examination, a candidate was allowed to eat the pure food of the community and after two more years, the pure drink (*J.W.* 2.138; compare 1QS 6:16-22; 7:20-23; CD 15:15; 4Q265 1 ii 3-9). Essenes also bathed and changed clothes before meals (*J.W.* 2.129-31), and considered excrement ritually impure (*J.W.* 2.147-49). Furthermore, the Essenes prepared for prophetic revelation by ritual purifications (*J.W.* 2.159).

5. Rabbinic literature

Although compiled at a later date, the Mishnah, Tosefta and Talmuds are in the Pharisaic tradition and shed light on Second Temple Judaism. Many of the sages were alive during that period and comment on the extreme views of some in matters of purity (*t. Shab.* 1:7; *b. Shab.* 13a; *y. Shab.* 3ab; *m. Shab.* 1:3; compare "the impurity of a knife was more distressing to Israel than murder" *t. Yoma* 1:12; *y. Yoma* 2:1, 39d; *b. Yoma* 23b). Exaggeration aside, purity was logically a major concern in the cult-oriented society of Second Temple Judaism. Many of the early rabbis immersed every morning before prayer (*t. Yad.* 2:20; compare *b. Ber.* 22b, which is more lenient).

Rabbinic literature corroborates the concern for the purity of food. Since priestly contributions from the crops must be pure, the Mishnah requires purity before pressing but not harvesting grapes and olives (*m. Toh.* 9-10). Additionally, many of the laity, the haberim, ate food in a state of purity, and this seems to be the expectation of the Mishnah (*m. Hul.* 2:5; *m. Zabah.* 3:2; compare *t. Miqbim* 6:7).

Most helpful in rabbinic literature is the systematic organization of the laws of ritual purity and their presentation in the sixth order of the Mishnah, *Teharot*. This section provides a systematic treatment of the sources and contagion of impurity. The original sources are called "Fathers of Impurity," and persons/objects who are contaminated secondarily are "Offspring of Impurity." An impurity source can contaminate persons and vessels to at least one degree away, but can contaminate food, especially holy food, as far as four degrees away from the source. The rabbis' also describe the ritual bath, miqveh, and its reservoir, 'otsar, evidence of which date back to Second Temple times.

C. New Testament

Most of the teaching on purity in the NT centers around moral purity. All of the nineteen occurrences of akathartos in the Synoptic Gospels refer to an "unclean spirit." Pauline teaching is concerned with impurity primarily as the result of fornication. Although the laws of ritual purity are assumed as part of Scripture and therefore binding, the matter is debated throughout the NT and in some instances abandoned.

1. Synoptic Gospels and Acts

The Synoptic Gospels support the notion that observant Jews bathed or at least washed their hands before eating during the Second Temple period. Mark

says the Pharisees washed their hands before eating and that this was a "tradition of the elders" (Mark 7:3). Luke states that it was Pharisaic practice to bathe completely before eating (Luke 11:38). Mark claims that the concern to wash cups, pitchers, and kettles is prevalent among Jews (Mark 7:3). Other practices, such as, purification after impurity (Mark 1:44; Luke 2) and avoiding Gentile impurity are mentioned as well (Acts 10:38).

The synoptic presentation of Jesus on purity is ambiguous. On the one hand, he defends his disciples against the Pharisees' accusation that they do not wash hands before eating, and states that nothing thatis taken into the body from outside defiles a person. Mark even states that Jesus declared all foods clean (7:19). Jesus' apparent abrogation of ritual purity is a drastic measure, since these laws had been set forth in Scripture and carried a long tradition of observance. Furthermore, Jesus handled and raised the dead (Mark 5:41-42; Luke 7:14-15), touched and healed lepers (Mark 1:40-42; Luke 5:13) and even visited the home of Simon the leper (Mark 14:3); he performed all of these actions without apparently incurring any impurity. A woman with an irregular blood flow reached out to touch his clothes, without contaminating them, and is healed (Matt 9:18-26; Mark 6:25-34; Luke 8:40-56).

On the other hand, one cannot conclude that Jesus rejected or ignored the purity law completely. He emphasizes its moral angle (sometimes increasing its difficulty, Matt 5:17-28) and even observes many of its rituals (e.g., Jewish feasts, Temple visits). Also, he instructs his followers to listen to the Pharisees for, although they are hypocritical, they "sit in Moses' seat" and preach the truth (Matt 23:2-3; compare Mark 1:44, Jesus sends the healed leper to the priest for purification). Later, Peter seems to know nothing of Jesus' abrogation of food laws, for he refuses to eat the impure animals that are shown to him in a divine vision (Acts 10:14-16; 11:9). In fact, in the struggle of the early church to resolve the question of abandonment of all or parts of the law, no one quotes Jesus for support.

Jesus' attitude toward Gentiles too is ambiguous. On the one hand, he socializes with Gentiles and sinners (Mark 2:15-16) and even heals a Canaanite woman's child (Matt 15:21-28; Mark 7:24-30); he also commends a centurion for his faith and declares that Gentiles will be brought into the kingdom of heaven, while Jews will be thrown into darkness (Matt 8:10-12). However, he states on occasion that his mission is only to Israel (Matt 15:24), and instructs his disciples to preach only to Jews (Matt 10:5; but compare the commission to evangelize all nations, Matt 28:19).

The Apostolic Decree (Acts 15:19-21) settled the ambiguity, at least for the present, by requiring a minimum standard of cultic purity (Acts 15:28-29; 21:25). Gentile Christians are not expected to observe circumcision and all the purity rituals of Judaism, but they must abstain from meat offered to idols, from eating blood and the meat of strangled animals (not ritually slaughtered so that the blood has not been properly drained), and from unchastity.

Water BAPTISM certainly has its roots in Jewish purification traditions. Matthew states that Jews came to John "and they were baptized by him in the river Jordan, confessing their sins" (Matt 3:6, 11). As discussed above, it was not unusual in this period for penitents to perform water purification as part of their repentance process. Surprisingly, at Jesus' baptism there is a divine revelation and blessing, reminiscent of the Sinaitic revelation, which too was preceded by purification (Matt 3:16-17; Exod 19).

2. Pauline literature

The Jewish ritual purity laws were a serious obstruction to the expansion of Christianity among the Gentiles. Food laws and other rituals entrenched in Israelite practice for hundreds of years and reinforcing Israel's identity as the elect could not be easily dismissed as obsolete in the new faith. Nevertheless, Paul publically disagrees with the Jerusalem church over TABLE FELLOWSHIP between Jewish and Gentile Christians. He asserts that eating together was not a mixture of purity and impurity but a necessary activity for the growth of the church (Gal 2:11-16). He insists that the righteousness of the Christian is not based on the law but on faith in Christ (Gal 2:16). In particular, all food is inherently clean (Rom 14:14, 20). Still he exhorts Christians to be considerate of believers who are avoiding certain foods and not to offend their sensibilities, "Do not for the sake of food destroy the work of God. Everything is indeed clean, but it is wrong for any one to make others fall by what he eats" (Rom 14:20).

While not too disturbed about what Christians eat, Paul earnestly opposes impurity on a moral level. In his writings (Rom 14 excepted) akatharsia usually refers to sexual immorality, as in this text: "Therefore God gave them up in the lusts of their hearts to impurity, to the dishonoring of their bodies among themselves" (Rom 1:24). Akatharsia is often used along with porneia, "fornication" (2 Cor 12:21; Gal 5:19). As the "temple of the Holy Spirit" the church must maintain moral purity to secure the presence of God among them (1 Cor 3:16-17; 6:18-19).

Impurity is the antonym of hagiasmos, "holiness." Christians previously yielded their members to impurity but now they must pursue righteousness in order to increase in holiness (Rom 6:19; 2 Cor 7:1; 1 Thess 4:7). Paul skillfully uses the language of ritual impurity to emphasize the power of holiness through Christ. As discussed above, ritual impurity is contagious by physical contact, but Paul says that the holiness of a believer is contagious to his/her spouse and children and for this reason he advises the Christian partner not to leave the family (1 Cor 7:14).

3. Other NT texts

Several NT texts connect purification directly to salvation through Christ. By the "purification offering" of his body, Christ cleanses believers from sin (1 John 1:7). He also purifies them by his words (John 15:3; Eph 5:25-26; Tit 2:14). James emphasizes moral purification as well but expects more human effort (Jas 4:8). Pure religion, he insists, is expressed by doing good deeds and by avoiding the impurity that comes through association with "the world" (Jas 1:27).

Hebrews represents the furthest move away from Judaism in the NT. The author explicitly states that sacrifices do not cleanse from sin and regards any reversion back to the cultic laws of Moses as an insult to the supreme sacrifice of Christ on the cross. He explains that Christ's sacrifice cleanses the conscience, whereas Israelite rituals could only purify the body (Heb 9:12-14; 10:2, 22-28).

The strong trend throughout the NT, which links impurity with immorality and unclean spirits, continues in Revelation. The scarlet woman, Babylon, is portrayed as holding a gold cup that is full of abominations and the "impurity of her adulteries" (Rev 17:4). The writer declares that Babylon is a home for demons and evil spirits and describes them metaphorically as unclean birds (Rev 18:2).

D. Rationale and Significance

The biblical impurity laws have generated a fair amount of curiosity concerning the rationale behind them. It must be understood at the outset that the notion of impurity is a cross-cultural phenomenon. Societies invariably decide what is "out," and therefore impure and what is "in," or pure. Taboos of various sorts mark and enforce these barriers by labeling the undesirable element "unclean" and referring to the "in" group as "clean." Invariably, undesirable bodily conditions are attributed to demonic forces that priests attempt to neutralize by apotropoeic rituals.

1. Old Testament

Israel stands in contrast to her neighbors by eliminating the magical aspect of ancient religion and ascribing her purity laws directly to the will of Yahweh. The purity system is not accidental or magical but carries purpose and significance. The biblical rationale for clean and unclean can be discussed in the two categories used above: moral and ritual purity. Moral purity in Israel relates directly to the character of Yahweh. As God is benevolent and ethical, God's people must be likewise (Lev 19:2ff.). As God is good to them so they extend his goodness to one another. Conversely, the community must avoid evil, that which contradicts the character of Yahweh, in order to be pure.

Ritual purity carries little intrinsic value but is important as a marker separating Israel from non-Israel. Only Israel is restricted by the purity system that marks her lifestyle, even her diet, as different from her neighbors, and it forms an immovable boundary between them. Leviticus gives this rationale: "I am the Lord your God who has separated you from other people. You shall therefore make a difference between pure animals and impure" (Lev 20:24b-25). By keeping the biblical purity laws, Israel is set apart from other nations. Her lifestyle is different even to the food she eats. Exodus 34:15-16 points out the danger in eating the food of non-Israelites: Such social intercourse would undoubtedly lead to intermarriage between Israel and pagans. The food laws so restrict Israel's diet that she cannot easily socialize with outsiders or be influenced by idolatrous practices, all of which entail pagan rituals and feasts in honor of the gods.

In addition to functioning as a general marker between Israel and non-Israel, the biblical impurity laws share a common thread that is symbolically important. Together they emphasize the separation of life and death and mark Israel as a people of life who shun those who associate with death. The most impure item in the system is the corpse. Lepers, with their flaking skin and open sores, visually illustrate the process of decay. Carcasses too cause impurity. Impure animals convey contamination only when they are dead, and most of them are carnivorous. Even the discharge of genital fluids may represent death since there is a loss of life-giving forces. Those who are involved with organic processes or are at the margins of death and life, e.g., the woman in childbirth, are in a liminal state and must perform prescribed rituals to reenter the community.

Anthropologists concur that the human body is often symbolic of the community at large. Restrictions on the body often reflect the community's view of cosmic boundaries. By labeling contact with death *impure*, biblical authors may be emphasizing that Israel worships a living God, not a lifeless image. Yahweh is, rather, the giver of life, and the dead cannot praise God (Ps 115:17). Indeed, those who associate with the dead, e.g., necromancers, are to be eradicated from Israel. In addition, the Torah promises that curses and death are the result of disobedience, while an obedient people are sure to inherit blessings and life (Deut 30:15-20). Hence, what is associated with death must be avoided and restricted because it is incompatible with the holy God who gives life. Those who must of necessity contact death, e.g., to bury one's parents, must perform the duty and then purify themselves before returning to the community of the living. In a sense, Israel has put a cordon around death by restricting the community's contact with those persons and items that are exposed to it. Israel's identification with life is especially significant since many of her pagan neighbors ascribed to a cult of the dead.

From another view, impurity emphasizes the mortality of human beings. To be human is to be susceptible to impurity, to participate in processes that generate life but always ultimately end in death. God, the source of life, does not participate in this life-death syndrome. When entering the Temple, one enters God's realm where death and decay are not allowed. A standard of purity, both moral and ritual, which will activate God's holiness in Israel, is the only weapon Israel has against impurity.

2. Second Temple Judaism

Anthropologists have demonstrated that in a period of persecution a group will reinforce its boundaries and increase its purity laws. In the period of the Second Temple it seems that the crisis in Judaism brought about by Hellenization and foreign domination increased emphasis on both APOCALYPTICISM and purification on the part of pious Jews. Especially in a minority group, such as the Essenes or the Qumran sect, there is a strong concern to maintain distinct boundaries and these often surface in the form of pure-impure restrictions on the body (Douglas 1966; 1975). What is allowed into the group is carefully monitored, and the members tend to adopt rigid behavioral standards. This reinforces the separation of the members from others and preserves group identity.

3. New Testament

The early church wrestled with its heritage of purity laws from ancient Judaism. Moral purity was affirmed and its restrictions even increased on occasion. But the ritual purity laws eventually met the same fate as other Jewish rituals, including the feasts, circumcision, and the Sabbath. Since they were a marker of Jewish identity, purity rituals became problematic when Gentiles were included into the church.

Not only were the purity laws a physical hardship for the new Gentile convert, they emphasized election through genealogy rather than through faith in Christ. For example, the ancient, undergirding symbolism—that clean animals represented Israel and unclean animals represented non-Jews—now threatened the unity of the Jewish-Gentile early church. The point of Peter's vision was that non-Jews, like unclean foods, are now to be included in the kingdom of God. Also, the division that was made in the group with Jews and Gentiles eating separately was harmful to church fellowship and unity.

The transition to Gentile Christianity and full abandonment of ritual purity laws, however, was gradual. Although Jesus appears to marginalize the whole issue of ritual purity by teaching that only what comes from a person's heart will defile him (Mark 7:14-23; Matt 23:25; Luke 11:38-40), he himself appears to be an observant Jew. The apostles are shocked at the suggestion that the distinction between clean and unclean food be erased. The Apostolic Decree is a compromise that retained some of the purity restrictions of the Jewish past but abandoned others in light of the church's evangelism to the Gentiles. *See* HOLY, HOLINESS, NT; HOLY, HOLINESS, OT; PURIFICATION; SANCTIFICATION.

Bibliography: Joseph M. Baumgarten. "The Purification Rituals of DJD 7." *The Dead Sea Scrolls: Forty Years of Research* (1992) 199–209; R. P. Booth. *Jesus and the Laws of Purity* (1986); Mary Douglas. *Purity and Danger: An Analysis of the Concepts of Pollution and Taboo* (1966); Mary Douglas. *Natural Symbols: Explorations in Cosmology* (1982); Tikva Frymer-Kensky. "Pollution, Purification, and Purgation in Biblical Israel." *The Word of the Lord shall Go Forth: Essays in Honor of David Noel Freedman in Celebration of His Sixtieth Birthday* (1983) 399–414; Hannah K. Harrington *The Purity Texts* (2004); Christine E. Hayes. *Gentile Impurities and Jewish Identities: Intermarriage and Conversion from the Bible to the Talmud* (2002); Thomas Kazen. *Jesus and Purity Halakhah: Was Jesus Indifferent to Impurity?* (2002). Jonathan Klawans. *Impurity and Sin in Ancient Judaism* (2000); Bruce J. Malina. *The New Testament World: Insights from Cultural Anthropology* (1981); Jacob Milgrom. *Leviticus 1–16* (1991); Jacob Milgrom. *Leviticus 17–22* (2000) and *Leviticus 23–27* (2000); Jacob Neusner. *Purity in Rabbinic Judaism* (1994); Robert Parker. *Miasma: Pollution and Purification in Early Greek Religion* (1983); Eyal Regev. "Non-Priestly Purity and Its Religious Aspects according to Historical Sources and Archaeological Findings." *Purity and Holiness: The Heritage of Leviticus* (2000) 223–44; Ron Reich. "Synagogue and Ritual Bath during the Second Temple and the Period of the Mishna and Talmud." *Synagogues in Antiquity* (1987) 205–12. David P. Wright. *The Disposal of Impurity: Elimination Rites in the Bible and in Hittite and Mesopotamian Literature* (1987).

HANNAH K. HARRINGTON

CLEANTHES THE STOIC [Κλέανθης Kleanthēs]. Cleanthes (331–232 BCE) was a student of Zeno, the founder of STOICISM, and became the head of this philosophical school in 263 BCE. Although he composed over fifty books on cosmology, epistemology, and ethics, his only writing to survive is the *Hymn to Zeus*. This hymn praises the active principle of the world (the "Logos" allegorized as "Zeus") for establishing and maintaining the order in the universe and saving humans from their folly. The Stoic conception of the Logos is important for placing the Logos Hymn (John 1:1-18) in its religious and philosophical context.

DAVID M. REIS

CLEMENT OF ALEXANDRIA. Titus Flavius Clemens (ca. 150–210 CE) flourished in Alexandria during the reigns of the emperors Commodus (176–92) and Septimius Severus (197–211). Clement's writings exude Alexandrian features: his sources, allegorical method, middle-platonic flavor, and social location as a teacher aiming to cultivate a spiritually advanced, "Gnostic" form of Christianity. Central for Clement were: the character of faith; mastery of the passions; the relationship between God and humans; the status of Mosaic law; marriage and procreation; ASCETICISM; and martyrdom.

Eight works by Clement survive: *Protrepticus* (*Exhortation to the Greeks*), *Paedagogus* (*Christ the Instructor*), *Stromateis* (*Miscellanies*), *Excerpts from Theodotos*, *Extracts from the Prophets*, *Salvation of the Rich*, *Exhortation to Endurance* (or *To the Recently Baptized*), and a letter possibly containing a variant for the Gospel of Mark. Writings that survive as titles or fragments are *Hypotyposeis*, *On the Passover*, *On Fasting*, *On Slander*, *Ecclesiastical Canon*, *Against the Judaizers*, *On Resurrection*, and *On Continence*.

Clement's writings and those of EUSEBIUS of Caesarea constitute our main ancient sources for Clement. Eusebius describes Clement as the head of a Christian school associated with the bishop-led church in Alexandria (as Pantaneus' successor and ORIGEN's predecessor), but no persuasive evidence exists for an officially sanctioned school in Clement's day. It is better to understand Clement as one of many Christian teachers with their own "schools," resembling philosophical schools. His main Christian rivals include the followers of BASILIDES and VALENTINUS, and so-called Encratites, NICOLAITANS, Carpocratians, Phrygians, and the followers of Prodicus and MARCION. *See* GNOSTICISM.

DENISE KIMBER BUELL

CLEMENT OF ROME. A leader of the Roman church, probably during the 90s CE. Irenaeus's claim (*Haer.* 3.3.3) that he was the third bishop of Rome after Peter may be correct regarding sequence (others place him first or second), but misleading regarding the office (the position of monarchical bishop did not then exist in Rome). A late romance (the *Pseudo-Clementines*) describing him as a noble Roman citizen baptized and discipled by Peter is wholly legendary. Efforts to link him to the household of the consul Titus Flavius Clemens, or the Clement mentioned in Phil 4:3 (both very unlikely), or the Clement mentioned in the *Shepherd of Hermas* (*Herm. Vis.* 2.4.3 [8.3]) as corresponding secretary of the Roman church (a possibility) rest on nothing more than the similarity of the name. If he is, as tradition claims, the author of 1 CLEMENT, then he had a grammar school education. Nothing is known about his age or background.

Bibliography: James S. Jeffords. *Conflict at Rome: Social Order and Hierarchy in Early Christianity* (1991); P. Lampe. *From Paul to Valentinus: Christians at Rome in the First Two Centuries* (2003).

MICHAEL HOLMES

CLEMENT, FIRST AND SECOND LETTER OF. Two things attest to the importance of 1 and 2 Clement in the NT: 1) the inclusions by *Codex Alexandrinus* (5th cent. CE), which is the earliest manuscript witness; 2) the quotations as Scripture by 2nd cent. Christians. The documents circulated as letters by Clement, alleged to be the second or third bishop of Rome. There is no internal evidence to suggest authorship. The first letter was attributed to Clement in later decades of the 2nd cent. The roughly contemporary *Shepherd of Hermas* (*Herm. Vis.* 2.8.2) knows of a Clement who writes letters on behalf Roman Christian assemblies. *Second Clement* is neither a letter nor written by the author of *1 Clement*. It is a homily composed by an otherwise unknown author.

    First Clement contains important evidence about the institutionalization of early Christianity. It is often dated on the basis of circumstantial evidence to ca. 96 CE, though an earlier date, after the martyrdom of Peter and Paul ca. 64, of which *1 Clement* is an important witness (5.2-7), cannot be excluded. It is the oldest extant extra-canonical Christian letter. *First Clement* is an invaluable if rambling testament to the development of Pauline Christianity at Rome following the apostle's death. It is addressed to Christians at Corinth who have deposed properly instituted presbyter-bishops from leadership (45.6). The letter adopts commonplaces drawn from Greco-Roman and Jewish rhetorical treatments of civic concord and faction, to urge restoration of the deposed leaders. Through wedding citations drawn from the LXX and Paul's letters (especially 1 Corinthians) it reveals a Christianity at home amid popular Hellenistic philosophy and ethics, as well as Hellenistic Judaism.

    Since the publication of *Codex Alexendrinus* in the 17th cent. it has occupied a central place in debates concerning the organization of early Christian ministry. Some have discovered in the letter (40-44) evidence of a theory of apostolic succession modeled on motifs associated with the Jewish priesthood. The letter presumes governance of the Roman church supervised by a group of presbyter-bishops, rather than by a single or monarchical bishop. Strictly interpreted, *1 Clement* does not outline a regulation that extends beyond the document's immediate horizon.

    The origin and dating of *2 Clement* is uncertain. Alexandria or Rome isusually hypothesized as the setting, and the date is perhaps no later than the mid-2nd cent., since it is unaware of a single episcopacy. The document is of special importance as an example of early Christian preaching that uses Scripture, Jesus sayings, and eschatological expectation to promote a distinct Christian identity among converts who have broken with their pagan past. The Sayings of Jesus that it quotes parallel those found in the canonical Gospels and the *Gospel of Thomas*, but with differences. Some of the sayings do not appear elsewhere. The homily is an often neglected resource in reconstructing traditional sayings associated with Jesus. *See* CLEMENT OF ROME; APOSTOLIC FATHERS; JUDAISM, HELLENISTIC; MINISTRY, CHRISTIAN; ROME, CHURCH; SHEPHERD OF HERMAS; THOMAS, GOSPEL OF.

Bibliography: Barbara Ellen Bowe. *A Church in Crisis: Ecclesiology and Paraenesis in Clement of Rome* (1988); Karl P. Donfried. *The Setting of Second Clement in Early Christianity* (1974).

HARRY O. MAIER

CLEMENTINES, PSEUDO-. The *Pseudo-Clementines* are novelistic writings about Clement of Rome (an early church leader, to whom is attributed the *First Epistle of Clement*), his quest for truth, conversion to Christianity, journeys with Peter, encounters with Simon Magus, and the final recovery of Clement's family. They exist in two different 4th cent. forms: *Recognitions* (ten books, whose lost Greek text is preserved in Rufinus' Latin version, a partial translation into Syriac, and some Armenian fragments) and the *Homilies* (twenty sermons, in Greek). The Jewish Christian nature of the documents is disclosed by their anti-Pauline attitude and lower Christology.

Bibliography: Dominique Côté. *Le thème de l'opposition entre Pierre et Simon dans les Pseudo-Clémentines* (2001); F. Stanley Jones. *An Ancient Jewish Christian Source on the History of Christianity: Pseudo-Clementine "Recognitions" 1.27-71* (1995); André Schneider and Luigi Cirillo. *Les Reconnaissances du pseudo Clément: Roman chrétien des premiers siècles* (1999); Robert E. Van Voorst. *"The Ascents of James": History and Theology of a Jewish-Christian Community* (1989); Meinolf Vielberg. *Klemens in den pseudoklementinischen Rekognitionen: Studien zur literarischen Form des spätantiken Romans* (2000).

PIERLUIGI PIOVANELLI

CLEODEMUS MALCHUS klee-oh'duh-muhs mal'kus [Κλεόδημος Μαλχᾶς Kleodēmos Malchas]. A Jewish historian writing in Greek before the 1st cent. BCE. The single surviving fragment from his work concerning the Jews is quoted by ALEXANDER POLYHISTOR, JOSEPHUS (*Ant.* 239-41), and EUSEBIUS (*Praep. ev.* IX, 20.2-4). The fragment concerns Abraham's descendents through his second wife Keturah, elaborating Gen 25:1-4, and connects their exploits with Hellenistic-Roman heroes such as Heracles, a clear example of Greek-Jewish SYNCRETISM in the Hellenistic period.

MARK DELCOGLIANO

CLEOMENES. 1. Appointed by Alexander the Great (330 BCE) as administrator of Alexandria and deposed by Ptolemy I Soter.

2. As Noetus' disciple, he upheld his doctrine of modalism (3rd cent. CE) that Christ is the Father because there can be no division in the Godhead, that the Father therefore had been born and died, and that Jesus the Son is the means by which the Father is revealed to the world and humans.

EMILY CHENEY

CLEOPAS klee´oh-puhs [Κλεοπᾶς Kleopas] In Luke 24:13-32 Cleopas and another disciple of Jesus walk to Emmaus and are joined en route by the risen Jesus. He may or may not be CLOPAS, the husband of Mary recorded in John 19:25 as standing near Jesus' cross.

CLEOPATRA klee´uh-pat´ruh [Κλεοπάτρα Kleopatra]. Several queens of the Ptolemaic and SELEUCID dynasties. 1. Additions to Esther 11:1 refers to a letter concerning PURIM that Dositheus took to EGYPT during the reign of PTOLEMY and Cleopatra, apparently referring to Cleopatra II, who ruled alongside her husband and brother Ptolemy VI PHILOMETOR (174–116 BCE). According to JOSEPHUS (Ant. 13.62-73), the high priest ONIAS IV petitioned them for permission to build a temple in Leontopolis in Egypt, modeled after the Jerusalem Temple.

2. Cleopatra Thea, daughter of Cleopatra II, ruled from 150–21 BCE by marrying a succession of Seleucid kings, including ALEXANDER BALAS, DEMETRIUS II, and ANTIOCHUS VII (1 Macc 10–11).

3. Cleopatra VII (69–30 BCE) was the most famous. Following her father's death, she struggled for power with her brother Ptolemy XIII until JULIUS CAESAR arrived in Egypt in 48 BCE. Being smuggled into Caesar's bedroom one night, she endeared herself to him. Caesar appointed Cleopatra and her ten-year-old brother to be king and queen. Cleopatra married her brother, but remained Caesar's lover. Ptolemy's age left her sole ruler of Egypt.

When Caesar was assassinated in 44 BCE, Cleopatra sided with the Second Triumvirate against the Republicans. With the defeat of the Republicans in 41 BCE, Cleopatra became Mark Antony's political ally and lover. Cleopatra disliked HEROD the Great who was dependent on Mark Antony, and she took every chance to humiliate him. In 32 BCE, Cleopatra supported Mark Antony in his unsuccessful fight against Octavian. As Octavian prepared to enter Alexandria as conqueror, Cleopatra committed suicide.

KEVIN A. WILSON

CLERGY. See BISHOP; ELDER IN THE NT.

CLERK, TOWN. See TOWN CLERK.

CLIENT KINGS. See ROMAN EMPIRE.

CLIMATE. See ISRAEL, CLIMATE OF.

CLOAK [מְעִיל me'il; ἱμάτιον himation]. Translation of several Hebrew and Greek words referring to an outer garment. See DRESS AND ORNAMENTATION.

CLOISONNE. See JEWELRY.

CLOPAS kloh´puhs [Κλωπᾶς Klōpas]. Clopas is mentioned in John 19:25 in association with Mary, who is said to be the sister of Mary, Jesus' mother. He is sometimes equated with Alphaeus (Matt 10:3; Mark 3:18; Luke 6:15) and Cleopas (Luke 24:18). The connection with Alphaeus assumes that Mary the mother of James and Joses (Mark 15:40//Matt 27:56; Luke 23:49; 24:10) is the mother of James the son of Alphaeus (Mark 3:18//Matt 10:3//Luke 6:15; Acts 1:13), and is therefore Alphaeus' wife. If one assumes that only three women are named in John 19:25 (Mark 15:40//Matt 27:56), then Mary the wife of Clopas must be identified as Jesus' mother's sister. (Roman sisters were sometimes given the same name.) Hegissipus also mentions a Clopas who was Joseph's brother (Eusebius, Hist. Eccl. III.11).

Bibliography: Tal Ilan. *Jewish Women in Greco-Roman Palestine* (1995).

N. CALVERT-KOYZIS

CLOTH, CLOTHES [בֶּגֶד beghedh, שִׂמְלָה simlah, לְבוּשׁ levus, כֻּתֹּנֶת kuthoneth, אַדֶּרֶת 'addereth, שַׂלְמָה salmah, חֲגוֹרָה khaghorah; ἱμάτιον himation, ἔνδυμα endyma, ἐσθής esthēs, χιτών chitōn, στολή stolē, χλάμυς chlamys]. Cloth is fabric made of woven wool, linen, or silk to make clothing. Clothing serves a practical function as a means to cover the body, in order to preserve modesty and to keep the body warm or shaded. Clothing also serves social functions: to signal roles or social status, to distinguish gender, and to add a sense of mystery or "fashion" to one's personal appearance.

    A. Textiles
      1. Wool
      2. Linen
    B. Clothing Styles
    C. Clothing as a Social Marker
      1. Social transformations
        a. Removing clothing
          1) Voluntary removal
          2) Involuntary removal
        b. Putting on clothing
        c. Disguises
      2. Clothing and mourning practices
      3. Use of clothing as a surrogate
        for a person
    D. Metaphorical Usage
    Bibliography

A. Textiles

1. Wool

Most articles of clothing in ancient Israel were made from sheep's wool (צֶמֶר tsemer, גֵז gez, עֲמַר ʿamar; ἔριον erion). SHEEP were sheared of WOOL (Gen 38:12-13); the wool was carded and spun into fibers (Matt 6:28; "spin" νήθω nēthō); and weavers (lit. אֹרְגִים ʾorghim, "those at the loom," Isa 19:9) created woolen cloth from the fibers. Woolen fabrics were woven on a warp-weighted LOOM (many loom weights have been recovered in excavations) and stitched together using bone and bronze needles. Technical terms related to this process include: the DISTAFF (Prov 31:19, כִּישׁוֹר kishor); the spindle (Neh 3:9, פֶּלֶךְ pelekh); the "pin" used to beat up and secure the woof in the loom (Judg 16:14, יָתֵד yathedh), the "weaver's rod" (1 Sam 17:7, מְנוֹר אֹרְגִים menor ʾorghim), and the "weaver's shuttle" (Job 7:6, אֶרֶג ʿaregh).

Everyday clothing was sturdy but plain. The roughest weave, known as SACKCLOTH (1 Kgs 21:27), was worn as a sign of mourning or repentance. When garments were decorated with a variety of dyes (such as indigo or tannins) and embroidered with multicolored threads in intricate designs, they were used for formal settings such as weddings or as festal garments (Ps 45:14; Ezek 16:10). While embroidered sashes (Exod 39:29, אַבְנֵט ʾavnet) were used to bind a garment, FIBULAE (garment pins) made of bronze and iron could be attached at the shoulder, waist, or hip to hold the folds of a robe together.

2. Linen

LINEN (בַּד badh, שֵׁשׁ shesh; σινδών sindōn, βύσσινος byssinos) was considered a higher quality garment whose white color was associated with purity and the divine (Dan 10:5). Stalks of FLAX (פֵּשֶׁת pesheth) were dried (Josh 2:6), beaten, and the fibers were spun into thread. Like SILK (Rev 18:12, σιρικόν sirikon), the finest quality linen, such as that imported from Egypt, was considered a luxury item (Ezek 27:7). Most often linen was reserved for priestly robes (Exod 28:39; 1 Sam 22:18), the clothing of the upper classes (Joseph's robes in Gen 41:42; Luke 16:19), and scribes (Ezek 9:11). In the NT period, linen also was used for burial shrouds (Luke 23:53).

B. Clothing Styles

Throughout the biblical period, men wore the kuttoneth, a knee-length, wool tunic with either long or short sleeves, and a cloak or mantle (simla) was also worn to protect them against the sun and during sand storms. At least in later periods, a belt (ʾezor Jer 13:2 [NRSV "loincloth"]; Job 12:18 [NRSV "sash"]) or loincloth (khaghorah) was also worn. Women's garb was similar: a tunic and robe concealed the figure, although occasionally (as in the Beni-Hasan tomb paintings) the right shoulder was bare. An itemized list of less practical garments worn by wealthy women is found in Isa 3:18-24. Among these fashions were the VEIL, the HEADDRESS, and SASH. Given the need for ease of movement for everyday tasks like herding and farming, most clothing was draped loosely around the body. This also helped to regulate body heat and allowed for the flexibility needed to stoop or run.

The "Black Obelisk" inscription of the Assyrian king Shalmaneser III (842 BCE) depicts King Jehu of Israel wearing a fringed kuttoneth, tied with a sash, and also with hanging tassels. A pointed cap covers his head. Another Assyrian illustration from 701 BCE, however, shows Judean captives, barefooted and wearing a short-sleeved, full-length kuttoneth.

As Israel and Judah were drawn into the cultural sphere of foreign empires, the wealthy and government officials tended to adopt foreign clothing styles, a practice that Zephaniah admonishes against (Zeph 1:8). During the Hellenistic period, a charge is made against Jason, the high priest in the time of Antiochus IV, that he had forced the upper classes in Jerusalem to wear a broad-brimmed hat associated with the cult of the Greek god HERMES (2 Macc 4:12).

By the 1st cent. CE there was less concern over wearing Greek or Roman styles, such as the chiton, a long seamless, under-tunic (John 19:23), sometimes worn with a woolen cloak (chlamys) in cold weather (Matt 27:31). Paul alludes to head coverings for women (1 Cor 11:4-7), but it is unlikely that Paul is instructing the Corinthian church to adopt a Jewish tradition (see 3 Macc 4:6; Josephus, Ant. 3.270 for this custom), because Greek and Roman women regularly covered their head with a veil (Tertullian, Cor. 4; Plutarch, Quaest. rom. 267a).

C. Clothing as Social Marker

The quality, style, color, and substance of items of clothing contain socially recognizable status markers. A warrior is marked by his weapons belt (2 Sam 18:11), a scribe by his long robe (Mark 12:38), and a leper by his torn clothing (Lev 13:45). Only priests were allowed to wear linen robes with multicolored threads woven around the HEM (Exod 28:33), as well as linen undergarments (Exod 28:42; Lev 16:4; מִכְנְסֵי־בָד mikhnese vadh). Some robes (kuttoneth) were associated with a class of persons. David's daughter Tamar, e.g., as one of the "virgin daughters of the king" wears a "long robe with sleeves" (2 Sam 13:18). Garments dyed PURPLE were usually reserved for kings (Judg 8:26) or the wealthy (Luke 16:19; but see the mocking purple garb placed on Jesus in Mark 15:17-20).

1. Social Transformations

a. Removing clothing. The story of JOSEPH is characterized by a series of incidents in which clothing signals changes of social role and status. Initially, Joseph is in possession of a beautiful ornamental robe (kuttoneth) given to him by his father. But Joseph's brothers strip him of his prized robe (Gen 37:23), and Joseph's status soon changes from that of favorite son to slave. As a slave in Egypt, Joseph rises in rank in Potiphar's house until Potiphar's wife pulls off Joseph's garment (beghedh) as he struggles to get away from her embrace (Gen 39:12), and Joseph is subsequently thrown into prison. A final change occurs when Joseph proves his value to the king, and the king replaces Joseph's prison clothing with the fine linen robes (beghed shesh) of an officer in the employ of the pharaoh (Gen 41:42). Finally, Joseph is able to give his family garments as a sign of his affection and forgiveness and his ability to provide for them from the wealth of Egypt (Gen 45:22).

Ahijah illustrates another example of a change in status. He designates Jeroboam to be the king when he seizes Jeroboam's cloak from his shoulders and tears it into twelve pieces, and then instructs Jeroboam to take ten of them (1 Kgs 11:29-31). That cloak is called a "new garment" (salmah khadhasha), which suggests its value and its symbolic representation of the new nation that is about to be divided like the garment itself. Since it is torn apart by a prophet as a symbolic gesture, there is a measure of authority given to this cloth, which is shared with the king to be. Such tearing of cloth is more usually associated with mourning (see below). Ahijah could be mourning over the division of the land. However, when he gives Jeroboam the ten pieces, he bestows authority over the ten northern tribes. This action reminds readers of other symbolic divisions that call people to prepare for coming conflict (Judg 19:29; 1 Sam 11:7).

This pattern of status change illustrated by changes of clothing also appears in the PASSION NARRATIVE in Mark. The soldiers first strip Jesus of his clothing, in order to humiliate and dehumanize him. Then they place a purple cloak (πορφύρα porphyra) around his shoulders to signify in a sarcastic way his role as "king of the Jews" (Mark 15:17-18). Subsequently, he is stripped of this finery and his old clothes returned before his execution. After his crucifixion, Jesus' body is wrapped in a linen cloth (Mark 15:46, σινδόν sindon). Finally, the "young man" that reassures the women who come to the tomb is dressed in a "white robe" (Mark 16:5, στόλην λευκήν stōlēn leukēn), which is reminiscent of Jesus' pure white clothing in the TRANSFIGURATION (Mark 9:3).

1) Voluntary removal. It is clear that much of the narrative of David's rise to power, like that of Joseph, involves garments that signify a status change and an elevation of his authority. For instance, David's refusal to wear Saul's protective clothing/armor, when challenging Goliath to single combat (1 Sam 17:38), proves to be a wise strategic move on David's part, because it gives him greater freedom of movement and because it is a way of demonstrating that "Saul's way was not David's way."

Furthermore, David makes another shrewd decision to remove most of his garments in favor of very minimal attire, just the linen ephod (vadh) typically worn by priests in Exod 28:42; Lev 16:4; 1 Sam 2:18) when he brings the ARK OF THE COVENANT into Jerusalem (2 Sam 6:14, 20). As the ark approaches the gates of Jerusalem, David removes his garments and joins in the dancing with the other celebrants. A range of possibilities is attached to David's choice of minimal attire. He may be doing penance for his inappropriate transport of the ark from Kiriath-jearim, which had already caused the death of Uzzah (2 Sam 6:3-9; compare the king of Nineveh's disrobing in Jonah 3:6). It is possible that he is modeling proper behavior as a priestly figure when Yahweh (represented by the ark) is brought into Jerusalem, which sets a precedent of royal participation in ritual drama and enthusiastic worship.

In addition to the above suggestions, David may also be engaging in a visible manifestation of egalitarianism by "lowering" himself to the level of a common citizen, so that all will see that he is their equal "before the Lord." This is the opposite of what Saul had sought to do in 1 Sam 15:8-9, 15, 21, by bringing spoils and the king of the Amalekites back to Gilgal for a very visible sacrifice and celebration of their victory. Saul's disobedience had led to a rejection of his kingship, and the symbolic "tearing of the kingdom" away from his dynasty when he ripped Samuel's robe (1 Sam 15:27-28). Thus David's choice of very scanty attire in both of these episodes could be a conscious attempt to set a political tone for his reign that was very different from Saul's practice. It also marks him as a figure willing to be vulnerable before the people and before God.

Voluntary removal of one's clothing also figures into the actions of the prophet Isaiah when he uses the removal of his sackcloth and shoes (Isa 20:2) to enact his prophecy about the danger of Judah's opposition to Assyria during the Ashdod revolt of 711 BCE. Isaiah is wearing a distinctive garment—sackcloth—which is associated with mourning and repentance (see 1 Kgs 21:27; Neh 9:1; Jonah 3:5-8). His clothing may have symbolized the prophet's call for a humble stance in the aftermath of the destruction of Israel in 721 BCE and subsequent invasions of Judah by Assyrian forces (compare Mic 6:8). By removing his sackcloth and his sandals Isaiah imitates the image of the slave, defined as someone without property or identity. If they became prisoners of war and slaves, the people of Judah would share this fate.

In another example of an enacted prophecy, Jeremiah removes his linen BELT ('ezor, NRSV "loincloth") and buries it in the bank of the Euphrates, signaling the direction from which danger will come and indicating that, like his garment, the people will be buried and planted in Mesopotamia for a time (Jer 13:1-11). The term used for "belt" appears in only a few other passages (2 Kgs 1:8, Elijah's "leather belt"; Isa 11:5, a metaphoric belt; Ezek 23:15, belted Chaldeans), and may be associated with the idea of "readiness" or strength. There is a sense that a belted robe is one that has been made ready for travel or military action.

2) **Involuntary removal.** Not every instance of disrobing is voluntary. For example, the new king of Ammon uses an unorthodox method to assert his independence in an attempt to break away from Israel's influence. He has his servants shave off half of the beards from David's emissaries and cut off half of their robes (2 Sam 10:4; 1 Chr 19:4). This act shames the Israelites, symbolically emasculates them, and denies them their status as royal messengers, which usually provides diplomatic immunity.

It was apparently a common practice for warriors to strip the corpses of their enemies, taking their valuables, weapons, and food, but also their clothing (Judg 5:30). Samson killed and took away the garments of thirty Philistines (Judg 14:19). David spared Saul's life, but he cut off the corner of the king's robe in the cave at En-gedi (1 Sam 24:4-5). By cutting the king's garment, David cut away a portion of Saul's authority and indicated that he had had the king's life in his hands and had chosen to not to kill him.

Legal situations provide additional instances in which items of clothing are removed involuntarily. When a widow's male relative refuses to carry out his LEVIRATE MARRIAGE obligation, she removes his SANDAL as a sign of his loss of honor within his clan (Deut 25:5-10). Taking a garment as surety (Prov 20:16; 27:13) is a legal act, but it also has a social obligation attached. The garment, the person's only possession and the symbol of his free status, is given in pledge to guarantee that a full day's work will be done. According to the law, it must be restored to him before nightfall so that the man will not be left to shiver in the chill of the night (Exod 22:26-27; Deut 24:12-13; *see also* Matt 5:40). Thus to return the garment is considered a righteous act, and one that brings honor upon the employer. The fact that not everyone took this law seriously is demonstrated in Amos' condemnation of those who take garments in pledge or as payment of a debt (2:8) and then do not give them back, but instead choose to sleep on them before the altar of false gods.

b. **Putting on clothing.** From the beginning of the biblical narrative, putting on clothing has had significant symbolic value. After consuming the fruit of the tree of knowledge, Adam and Eve recognize their own nakedness and clothe themselves with LOINCLOTHs (khagoroth) made of fig leaves (Gen 3:7). For their transgression, they were expelled from Eden, but subsequently, God, their divine patron, "made them garments of skins" (kuttoneth) and clothed them (Gen 3:21). This gift marks the humans as God's clients and also signals that the animals, whose skins have been used for these garments, are to serve the needs of the humans in the future. Additional status-changing examples include Joseph's investiture as Pharaoh's advisor in Gen 41:42; the vesting of Aaron and his sons in priestly robes (Exod 28:3-5); Elisha putting on Elijah's mantle and then performing a series of miracles to demonstrate he had inherited the his mentor's powers (2 Kgs 2:13-25); and Ruth putting on her "best clothes" (simlah) before going to the threshing floor to meet with Boaz (3:3).

As a symbol of the covenant between them, Jonathan takes off his own robe (me'il), which is a term used primarily of priestly robes (Exod 28:31, 34; Lev 8:7; 1 Sam 28:14) or of royal robes (1 Sam 24:11; 2 Sam 13:18) and gives it to David (1 Sam 18:4). The robe is given "along with his tunic (madh the same term used for Saul's tunic that was given to David in 1 Sam 17:38), and even his sword, his bow, and his belt" (khaghorah, which usually refers to a warrior's sword-belt in 2 Sam 18:11; 20:8). Jonathan's action is symbolic of a transition of power and the legitimacy from the line of Saul to David, and it could be compared to the verbal statements made by Saul in 1 Sam 24:17-20; 26:21-25, after David spares his life.

c. **Disguises.** While clothes can function as a form of disguise, this is made possible only because of the culturally understood significance of clothing as recognizable iconic symbols of status and identity. Occasionally, putting on a garment is a form of disguise. Jacob disguises himself as his brother Esau by putting on his clothing (beghedh Gen 27:15, 27). The Gibeonites disguise themselves as weary pilgrims from a distant place (Josh 9:5-13), with dusty, patched clothes and worn-out shoes. Saul disguises himself in "other clothes" (beghedh) when he goes to meet the witch of Endor (1 Sam 28:8), but she still recognizes him. There is also some initial uncertainty about the identity of the shade drawn up through her ritual pit, but one recognizable feature was its robe (me'il). Similarly, Jeroboam's wife disguises herself when she goes to petition the prophet Ahijah to save her infant son (1 Kgs 14:1-6). Tamar exchanges the garments of widowhood for those of a prostitute in order to trick Judah into giving her the levirate marriage due to her. King Ahab disguises himself before going into battle against the Arameans by removing his royal robes and going into battle arrayed as a common soldier, while his ally, King Jehoshaphat, wore his robes of office and thus became the focus of enemy attack (1 Kgs 22:30).

Perhaps because a disguise could cause gender confusion, the law forbade cross-dressing. Deuteronomy 22:5 prohibits men wearing women's garments (simlah) or women wearing anything reserved for men as "abhorrent" to God. The story of Paghat, in the Ugaritic epic of Aqhat, contains an example of cross-dressing, but even there, Paghat dons male clothing and then slips a female garment over it all so that she is a woman disguised as a man, who is disguised as a woman (*COS* 1.103).

2. Clothing and mourning practices

The biblical text indicates that specific acts, gestures, and garments are prescribed for those in mourning. For instance, after the defeat at Ai, Joshua tears his garments and falls on his face before the ark (Josh 7:6). The victorious judge Jephthah rends his garments when he sees his daughter coming to meet him after the battle, and he realizes that he must fulfill his vow by sacrificing her (Judg 11:35). David's daughter rips her long-sleeved robe after being raped by her brother Amnon (2 Sam 13:19). Widows were expected to wear specific and recognizable garments (beghedh, Gen 38:14). Garments worn by mourners were torn as a sign of grief or were used for the specific occasion of a funeral (see Zech 13:4). It was customary for those in mourning to display their grief by wearing sackcloth (שַׂק saq; Luke 10:13, σάκκος sakkos, 1 Kgs 21:27; Isa 58:5; Jer 6:26). For example, Jacob tears his garments and puts on sackcloth after hearing of Joseph's death (Gen 37:34). David orders that Joab and "all the people" tear their clothes and put on sackcloth in mourning for the slain general Abner (2 Sam 3:31). Sackcloth was considered the principal garment for mourners and those displaying their repentance (Matt 11:21). Thus it is mentioned in the Jonah narrative as the universal garment worn by the fasting people and animals of Nineveh, as a sign of repentance and mourning for their misdeeds (Jonah 3:7-8). When Mordecai learns of Haman's plan to kill all the Jews within the Persian Empire, he tears his clothing, puts on sackcloth and ashes, and goes about the city wailing his grief (Esth 4:1). Curiously, he could not take his case to the Persian king dressed as he was, since "no one might enter the king's gate clothed with sackcloth" (Esth 4:2). One final example includes the procession of eighty men from Shechem, Shiloh, and Samaria who journey to the ruins of Jerusalem to make sacrifices. They have their beards shaved, their bodies gashed, and their clothes torn as a sign of mourning and perhaps penitence (Jer 41:5-8).

3. Use of clothing as a surrogate for a person

There are instances in the text in which an article of clothing becomes intimately tied to a person and in some cases functions as a surrogate for that person or his power when he is not present. For example, Elijah invests Elisha with power when the old prophet takes off his robe and "casts his mantle" ('adereth, referring to the prophet's "garments of hair" in Zech 13:4) over his protégé's shoulders (1 Kgs 19:19). Presumably, Elijah takes his garment back after using it as an instrument of investiture. Later, after using his mantle in a manner like Moses, who used his staff to open up the waters of the Jordan River, Elijah apparently leaves this same mantle behind when he is carried away in the fiery chariot (2 Kgs 2:8-14). Elisha assumes Elijah's power when he uses the garment to open the Jordan in the same manner as his master.

In the NT, a woman with a hemorrhage is cured when she touches Jesus' cloak (Mark 5:27-28, himation). Similarly, one of the ways in which Paul's authority as evangelist and representative of the Christian movement is certified is through the miracles performed when "handkerchiefs (σουδάριον soudarion) or aprons (σιμικίνθιον simikinthion) that had touched his skin" were carried to a sickbed and the diseased person was cured (Acts 19:11-12).

D. Metaphorical Usage

It is clothing's intrinsic function as an object of societal symbolism that also allows it to serve as a symbol of life itself. Thus, simply being clothed properly signifies well-being, as in the case of the cured demoniac in Mark 5:15. In the ancient world people seldom had multiple sets of clothing; thus garments were precious and expensive, and they would be kept for a long time. Therefore it is possible to compare one's long life with an old coat, as in Ps 102:26 where men "wear out like a garment" (see also Isa 51:6 in which the earth wears away like a garment). Similarly, one could put on an emotion or physical condition like a garment: "clothed himself with cursing as his coat" (Ps 109:18); be "wrapped in their own shame as a mantle" (Ps 109:29); or to be "wrapped in light as with a garment" (Ps 104:2); "put on garments of vengeance for clothing" (Isa 59:17), or experience how God's power can envelop one like clothing: "with violence he seizes my garment, he grasps me by the collar of my tunic" (Job 30:18). The physical world is also described as encompassed with a garment: the sky with clouds (Job 38:9); the deep (Ps 104:6); the waters of the sea (Prov 30:4). Having the proper "wedding garment" (ἔνδυμα γάμου endyma gamou) is a symbol of worthiness to enter the messianic banquet in the parable of the wedding feast (Matt 22:1-14).

God, portrayed as the divine warrior, puts on "righteousness as a coat of mail (שִׁרְיָן shiryan, Isa 59:17; see also 1 Sam 17:5; 1 Kgs 22:34), and a helmet (כּוֹבַע kovaʿ, 1 Sam 17:5) of salvation upon God's head, and God put on garments (beghedh) of vengeance for clothing, and was clad with zeal as in a cloak" (meʿil "priest's cloak" in Exod 28:4, 31). Presumably this process would be similar to the vesting of a priest, a judge, or a warrior (compare Paul's symbolic vesting in the "whole armor of God" in Eph 6:10-17 and the "breastplate of faith and love" in 1 Thess 5:8). See JEWELRY; PLANTS OF THE BIBLE; TEXTILES; WAR, METHODS, TACTICS, WEAPONS OF.

Bibliography: John R. Huddlestun. "Divestiture, Deception, and Demotion: the Garment Motif in Genesis 37–39." *JSOT* 98 (2002) 47–62; Victor H. Matthews. "The Anthropology of Clothing in the Joseph Narrative." *JSOT* 65 (1995) 25–36; O. H. Prouser. "Suited to the Throne: The Symbolic Use of Clothing in the David and

Saul Narratives." *JSOT* 71 (1996) 27–37; R. A. Schwarz. "Uncovering the Secret Vice: Toward an Anthropology of Clothing." *The Fabrics of Culture: The Anthropology of Clothing and Adornment* (1979) 24–31.

VICTOR H. MATTHEWS

CLOTHE ONESELF, TO [לָבַשׁ lavash; ἐνδύω enduō]. Clothing's function as an object of societal symbolism allows it to serve as a symbol of life itself. Garments indicate gender, membership in a community or profession, and as a metaphor encompassing both proper and improper behavior. For instance, the priest puts on special linen vestments to remove ashes from the altar and then other garments to physically transport them outside the camp (Lev 6:10-11). In Ezek 26:16 the frightened princes of Tyre remove their robes of office and "clothe themselves with trembling" as they lament their fate. False assumptions about clothing and power are found in Ezekiel's condemnation of "false shepherds," who clothe themselves in wool but "do not feed the sheep" (Ezek 34:3), and in Haggai's charge that the returned exiles' failures to gain prosperity ("clothe yourself, but no one is warm," 1:6) is a sign of God's displeasure. A spiritual transformation is equated in Eph 4:24, clothing yourself with the "new self," and Col 3:12 contains the admonition that God's "chosen ones" will cloth, themselves with the virtues of "kindness, humility, meekness, and patience." *See* CLOTH, CLOTHING.

VICTOR H. MATTHEWS

CLOUD, CLOUDS [עָנָן 'anan; עֲנָנָה 'ananah, עָב 'av, thick cloud, עֲרָפֶל 'arafel rain-cloud, עָרִיף 'arif; שַׁחַק shakhaq dust cloud, נְשִׂיאִים nesiim high clouds; νεφέλη nephelē, νέφος nephos]. Clouds sometimes bear rain (Exod 19:9; Eccl 11:3; Job 26:8; 38:22-38; Luke 12:54). Their seasonal return is associated with the Feast of the Prophet Elijah on July 20th (*see* 1 Kgs 18:44).

Clouds are a metaphor for communication between heaven and earth (Ps 18:10-11; Joel 2:2). The cloud at Sinai (Exod 19:9; Deut 4:12) and cloud filling the Tabernacle and Temple both reveal and conceal God. The "pillar of cloud" (Exod 13:21) is associated with altar smoke. The voice of God was heard out of the cloud at the Transfiguration (Mark 9:7) and provides imagery for the Ascension and for the Second Coming of Christ (Mark 13:26; Acts 1:9; Rev 1:7; see Dan 7:13). See DAY OF THE LORD; GLORY; ISRAEL, CLIMATE OF; GLORY; PILLAR OF CLOUD AND FIRE; SON OF MAN; TABERNACLE.

Bibliography: O. Keel. *The Symbolism of the Biblical World: Ancient Near Eastern Iconography and the Book of Psalms* (1978) 213–18; T. W. Mann. *Divine Presence and Guidance in Israelite Traditions: The Typology of Exaltation* (1977).

WILLIAM JOHNSTONE

CLOUD, PILLAR OF. *See* PILLAR OF CLOUD AND FIRE.

CLUB [תּוֹתָח tothakh, מַפֵּץ mappets, מַטֶּה matteh; σφῦρα sphyra, ῥάβδος rhabdos, ξύλον xylon, ῥόπαλον rhopalon, σκεῦος skeuos]. Blunt instrument used to strike a blow. Various Hebrew and Greek terms convey both military and more generic uses of the word. Job (41:29 [Heb. 41:21]) uses club (tothakh; sphyra) in the sense of weapon, saying that against Leviathan it is like chaff. Proverbs 25:18 also conjures military imagery of a war club (מֵפִיץ mefits; rhopalon) in conjunction with sword and arrows. Likewise, Isa 10:5 (matteh; rhabdos) and Jer 51:20 (mappets; skeuos) portray the club as an instrument of war. Daniel (Bel 1:26) confidently proclaims that he can defeat the dragon without a sword or club (rhabdos).

All five NT occurrences employ the more generic term for blunt instrument (xylon) to describe one of the weapons held by people who came to arrest Jesus in Gethsemane (Matt 26:47, 55; Mark 14:43, 48; Luke 22:52). *See* WEAPONS AND IMPLEMENTS OF WAR.

MARK J. H. FRETZ

CNIDUS ni'duhs [Κνίδος Knidos]. A Greek port town in the region of Caria on the southwestern tip of Asia Minor, past which Paul sailed on his way to Rome (Acts 27:7), turning southward toward Crete after winds blew him off course. Archaeologists have uncovered military and commercial harbors, temples, theaters, and a sizeable necropolis. Christian missionaries later constructed several churches there, and eventually it became the seat for a bishop. Cnidus also appears among a list of cities in 1 Macc 15:23.

KATHY CHAMBERS

COAL [גֶּחָלִים gekhalim, פָּח pakh; ἄνθραξ anthrax, ἀνθρακιά anthrakia]. The various words translated "coal" indicate charcoal or burning embers, not the mineral coal. The most common, gekhalim, always occurs in the plural and appears in Greek texts as anthrax or anthrakia (John 18:18; 21:9). Sometimes associated with theophanic appearances (2 Sam 22:9, 13 [//Ps 18:9, 13]; Ezek 1:13; 10:2), gekhalim often signifies coals for cooking (Isa 44:19), scouring (Ezek 24:11), coals from the altar (Lev 16:12), or an instrument of torture (Ps 140:10 [Heb. 140:11] and Prov 25:22 [quoted in Rom 12:20]). Pakh signifies charcoal from wood (Isa 44:12; 54:16; Prov 26:21).

WALTER C. BOUZARD

COAT [כֻּתֹּנֶת kuttoneth; χιτών chitōn]. An inner or outer garment. The inner garment usually is made of a fabric such as linen, worn close to the body, and is covered by a second layer of protective wear (Exod 28:39-40; 29:5-8; and 39:27; Lev 8:7-13). The coat that Jacob makes for Joseph is of this inner variety (Gen 37), as is the garment that the beloved has removed in Song 5:3. In the OT, the outer garment is often a COAT OF MAIL for battle (Exod 28:32 and 39:23; 1 Sam 17:5; 2 Chr 26:14; Jer 46:4; and 51:3) or vestments for the priest (Exod 28:4; Lev 16:14). Such a distinction between inner and outer coats is also made in the NT; thus, one offers both coat (chitōn) and cloak (ἱμάτιον himation) in Matt 5 and Luke 6 (NRSV: "from anyone who takes away your coat [himation] do not withhold even your shirt [χιτῶνα chitōna]," Luke 6:29). See CLOTH, CLOTHING; MANTLE; ROBE.

JESSICA TINKLENBERG DEVEGA

COAT OF MAIL שִׁרְיוֹן shiryon, סִרְיוֹן siryon; θώραξ thōrax]. A coat of mail is body armor of joined metal plates that are worn by warriors and horses. As a Hurrian loan word, the Hebrew is variously spelled with a SHIN (1 Sam 17:5, 38; 1 Kgs 22:34 // 2 Chr 18:33; 26:14; Neh 4:16 [Heb. 4:10]; Isa 59:17) or a SAMEK (Jer 46:4; 51:3 and likely, with the LXX, Job 41:5 [Heb. 41:13]). First Samuel 17:5 uses the expression siryon qasqassim. Qasqassim is normally assoc▯▯▯▯ with scaled water animals (Deut 14:9, 10; Lev 11:9, 10, 12), so it appears Goliath wore a scaled coat of mail. See WEAPONS AND IMPLEMENTS OF WAR.

WALTER C. BOUZARD

COCK זַרְזִיר zarzir; ἀλέκτωρ alektōr]. The cock appears only once in the OT. Listed among proudly striding creatures in Prov 30:29-31, the zarzir (30:31a), should probably be identified with the cock (thus the LXX; NRSV "strutting rooster" presupposes a plausible reconstruction of the Heb.). In the NT, references to the cock and its crowing are concentrated in one episode: Peter's threefold denial of Jesus (Mark 14:30, 68, 72, with par. in Matt 26 and Luke 22). In Mark 13:35, the "cockcrow" stands for the third night watch (reflecting Roman division into four watches). See BIRDS OF THE BIBLE; FOWL.

GÖRAN EIDEVALL

CODE. See COVENANT, BOOK OF THE; HOLINESS CODE; LAW IN THE OT; PENTATEUCH.

CODE OF HAMMURABI. See HAMMURABI, CODE OF.

CODEX koh´deks. The term codex, as distinct from a scroll, designates a manuscript written in book form. Though used by Romans occasionally in pre-Christian time, it is not widely employed for literary works until the 4th cent. CE. The Greek Christian Bible (LXX), however, was transmitted almost exclusively in codex form. After the 4th cent. CE parchment replaces papyrus. See ALEXANDRINUS, CODEX; BERLIN GNOSTIC, CODEX; BEZAE, CODEX; BRUCIANUS,

CODEX; CLAROMONTANUS, CODEX; EPHRAE-MI, CODEX; KOREDETHI, CODEX; SINAITICUS, CODEX; VATICANUS, CODEX; WRITING AND WRITING MATERIALS.

DAVID J. TROBISCH

CODEX ALEXANDRINUS. See ALEXANDRINUS, CODEX.

CODEX BERLIN GNOSTIC. See BERLIN GNOSTIC, CODEX.

CODEX BEZAE. See BEZAE, CODEX.

CODEX BRUCIANUS. See BRUCIANUS, CODEX.

CODEX CLAROMONTANUS. See CLAROMONTA-NUS, CODEX.

CODEX EPHRAEMI. See EPHRAEMI SYRI RESCRIP-TUS, CODEX.

CODEX KORIDETHI. See KORIDETHI, CODEX.

CODEX LENINGRAD. See LENINGRAD CODEX.

CODEX SINAITICUS. See SINAITICUS, CODEX.

CODEX VATICANUS. See VATICANUS, CODEX.

CODEX WASHINGTONIANUS. See WASHINGTON-TONIANUS, CODEX.

COELE-SYRIA [Κοίλη Συρία Koilē Syria]. "Hollow Syria." The geographic designation of this term varies greatly in the sources and over time. In its strictest geographical definition, it is the Greek name for the Beqaʾ Valley between the LEBANON and ANTILEBA-NON mountains in southern Syria. It is located north of Palestine in modern day Lebanon (1 Esd 4:48; compare Amos 1:5 [Valley of Aven]; compare Josh 11:17, 12:7 [Valley of Lebanon]). In the Hellenistic period it can refer to the southern part of the Seleucid Empire including Phoenicia and Palestine (1 Esd 2:17, 24, 27; 4:48; 6:29; 7:1; 8:67; 1 Macc 10:69; 2 Macc 3:5, 8; 4:4; 8:8; 10:11). Josephus describes Coele-Syria as extending from Egypt to the Euphrates but elsewhere uses it to refer to the Transjordanian territory over which Herod received military control from the Romans in 47 BCE.

JOHN WINELAND

COFFIN. See BURIAL.

COFFIN TEXTS. The Coffin Texts are a corpus of 1,185 magical spells to help the deceased make a successful transition to the afterlife.

Inscribed on the coffins, tomb walls, and funerary objects of wealthy nonroyal Egyptians during the

Middle Kingdom, they describe the afterlife as a place of work. In variant traditions, the deceased joins RE in his sun-boat or becomes OSIRIS, god of the dead. *See* BOOK OF THE DEAD; EGYPT.

CAROLYN R. HIGGINBOTHAM

COHORT [σπεῖρα speira]. While posted in forts and strongholds to defend the borders and maintain the peace, a Roman cohort was nominally 600 infantrymen, but in Palestine auxiliary cohorts of local soldiers could be 500 to 1,000 troops. A speira mocked Jesus (Matt 27:27; Mark 15:16; John 18:12), and John says a speira arrested Jesus (John 18:3). Luke identifies the first Gentile convert, CORNELIUS, as a CENTURION of the cohort in CAESAREA (Acts 10:1). Luke also mentions the cohort of Jerusalem protecting Paul (Acts 21:31). Soldiers from another cohort escorted Paul to his trial in Rome (Acts 27:1). *See* LEGION; WAR, METHODS, STRATEGY, TACTICS.

ADAM L. PORTER

COINS. *See* MONEY, COINS.

COL-HOZEH kol-hoh′zuh [כָּל־חֹזֶה kol-khozeh]. "Every seer." 1. Father of Shallum (Neh 3:15).

2. Ancestor of Maaseiah who lived in Jerusalem after the exile (Neh 11:5).

COLLAR [פֶּה peh]. A collar is something that encircles the neck, usually the upper part of a garment. The Hebrew peh, often translated "neck," literally means "mouth." Job 30:18 speaks of God grasping the collar of Job's tunic, and Ps 133:2 refers to oil running over the collar of Aaron's robe. Alternately, a collar may be an implement for punishment, used in conjunction with fetters or stocks (Jer 29:26), as in Ps 105:18 where "collar" translates בַּרְזֶל barzel, meaning "iron." Sirach uses the word *collar*, meaning "fetters," in a metaphorical sense to encourage the young man to submit to Wisdom (Sir 6:24, 29).

MARY PETRINA BOYD

COLLECTION, THE [λογείας logeias]. Paul organized a large ecumenical collection for the poor in the Jerusalem churches in various Christian communities under his control between 48–57 CE. His various references to this ambitious venture indicate that it was not just an "ordinary" fund-raising project (1 Cor 16:1-4; 2 Cor 8-9; Gal 2:10; Rom 15:25-27). The collection had far-reaching implications for all the parties involved, since it served as a concrete means to give expression to the unity between Jewish and Gentile Christians. However, Paul's collection should primarily be understood in terms of the ancient social convention of *benefit exchange*. Reciprocity was at the heart of all forms of benevolence within the ancient Greco-Roman and Jewish worlds. The bestowal of gifts between people always initiated the

establishment of long-term relationships that involved mutual obligations and clear status differentials between the transactors. In this regard benefit exchange provided the basic interpretative framework for Paul to come to terms with his obligation to address the needs of the poor in the Jerusalem church.

The request on the side of Peter and the leadership of the Jerusalem church, "not to forget the poor" (Gal 2:10), functioned within the framework of the reciprocal relationship between Paul as head of the Gentile mission and the Jerusalem church. Within this relationship the leadership of Jerusalem acted as the initial *benefactors* by recognizing Paul's law-free gospel, which, in turn, placed him in their debt. In response to their huge benefaction, the Jerusalem church requested from Paul, as beneficiary in this reciprocal relationship, to address the needs of the socially destitute in their midst. Through this request, the Jerusalem leadership publicly acknowledged that Paul had access to material goods and services that were not routinely available to them. The positive response from the side of Paul in particular confirmed this expectation and placed him in their debt until he delivered what he had promised.

In order to fulfill his obligations toward Jerusalem, Paul took it upon himself to organize a collection for their poor in the Christian communities in Galatia, Achaia, and Macedonia (and Asia?). By including these communities as beneficiaries in the reciprocal relationship between himself and the Jerusalem church, Paul involved them on the primary level of meaning within which he understood the collection. Benefit exchange at the same time also provided the basis for Paul's various theological reflections on this project. Therefore, aspects of the exchange receive particular attention in his letters: 1) Jerusalem's bestowal of specific spiritual benefits on Paul and his communities and their concurrent claim in terms of the establishment of a reciprocal relationship with his group (Rom 15:25ff.); 2) the religious nature of the collection as a reciprocal relationship also between God and God's people (2 Cor 8:1-6); 3) the principle of balanced reciprocity or "equality" inherent to the exchange of material gifts between Paul's communities and Jerusalem (2 Cor 8:13-15); and 4) the expected display of gratitude and prayers of thanksgiving on the side of Jerusalem after the delivery of the collection (2 Cor 9:11-15).

From Paul's point of view, his ability to realize the initial expectations of the Jerusalem church, to provide for the needs of their poor (Gal 2:10), was the basis of his socioreligious credibility within the early Christian movement. However, Paul and Jerusalem's conflicting views regarding the role and functions of the law threatened the eventual acceptance of the collection. A negative response to the collection could imply an abrupt end to the relationship between Pauline Christianity and the Jerusalem church, as the two most important "interest groups" within the early Christian movement. In anticipation of a possible rejection of the collection, Paul in Rom 15:25 offered a new theological understanding of this project over against his previous reflections that focused on securing the successful completion of this project. By shifting the emphasis from the generally accepted view to give for a return, to giving according to the principles of service and the faithful fulfilling of one's responsibilities irrespective of the response on the side of the recipients, Paul turned the collection into an "eleventh-hour success" within the framework of his own communities.

Although Luke is not well informed on the Pauline collection, in Acts 21:17 he presents us with the basic outlines of Paul's final visit to Jerusalem to deliver the collection. From the available information in this regard it may be deduced that Paul and James devised an emergency solution to ensure the eventual acceptance of the collection by the Jerusalem church. Sadly, the capture of Paul in the Temple brought an abrupt end to this imaginative project, at least from the perspective of his early Christian biographers. However, we are left with the picture of a provisional acceptance of the collection by the Jerusalem church and with Paul briefly acting out the role of their benefactor by using money from the collection to pay for the Nazarene vows of some of their members.

In spite of the unfortunate ending to the collection, this imaginative project could be described as a success, particularly within the sphere of the Pauline communities. Not only did the apostle effectively address the huge obstacles that constantly threatened the completion of the collection, but his own communities, through their sustained efforts to submit the collection as a gracious service to Jerusalem, eventually gave visible expression to their common bond of unity as believers. At the same time the Jerusalem community apparently did not reject the collection outright.

The role and impact of the collection within the early church could scarcely be overestimated. The physical effort that went into the organization and the administration of this imaginative project among the Christian communities spread out through the Roman world, in the end led to the existential involvement of most members of Paul's communities in a service for fellow believers in Judea, whom the majority of them had never even met. Obviously, these believers' basic knowledge of the system of social exchange provided an ideal foundation for Paul's theological conceptualizations of the collection. But, the fact that they were willing to give visible expression on such a large scale to their compassion for fellow-believers' plight points to the true nature of the collection as a witness to the overflowing grace of God.

Bibliography: S. J. Joubert. *Paul as Benefactor: Reciprocity, Strategy, and Theological Reflection in Paul's Collection* (2000).

STEPHAN J. JOUBERT

COLLECTIVIST PERSONALITY. Collectivist personality characterizes persons enculturated in social systems that set value on the priority of the group, on the continued embeddedness of the individual in the group, and on the precedence of group values over individual choices. Social systems that enculturate persons to act independently, to pursue individual success, and to distance self from the group in self-reliance produce individualist personalities.

Collectivism arose with the advent of the sedentary agricultural societies that followed individualistic hunter-gatherer cultures. Today, some 70 to 80 percent of the world's populations are collectivist. With the 16th cent. advent of the Puritan theology that set the individual soul at the center of religion and marketplace, neoindividualism emerged in northern Europe, marked by individual responsibility and self-determination. In this version of rather recent Western civilization, the social unit of society is not the group, the guild, the tribe, or the city, but the single, individual person. Individual human rights are given priority over the common good.

Data dealing with the contrast between collectivist and individualist societies have been collected and studied since the middle of the 20th cent. by social psychologists. Hofstede and Triandis, among others, have demonstrated the heuristic value of the collectivist/individualist contrast, which runs along a range with individualism at one extreme and collectivism at the other.

For individualists, while freedom from others and self-reliance are important values, their defining attributes are distance from in-groups, emotional detachment, and the pursuit of personal goals, while following one's internalized, individualist conscience. Individualist cultures share the belief that persons are each and singly an end in themselves, and as such ought to realize their "self" and cultivate their own judgment, notwithstanding the push of pervasive social pressures in the direction of conformity. Individualists evidence great emotional detachment from others, extreme lack of attention to the views of others, relatively little concern for family and relatives, and tendency toward achievement through competition with other individualists.

Collectivist cultures, by contrast, expect great emotional attachment to in-groups. Group goals are paramount, and socialization emphasizes the importance of dependence, submission to authority, and obedience. Collectivists are suspicious of outsiders, and are more likely to behave in an antisocial, hostile manner to strangers. They draw their strength and self-assuredness from being embedded in a group. They are anti-introspective (the group is conscience) and not psychologically minded, totally unconcerned with self-reliance and personal success. Instead, group integrity and well-being are their main concerns. Without a group, they cease to exist as healthy and meaningful persons. They are much aware of in-group/out-group boundaries that support their highly negative attitudes toward outgroup members. They almost never disagree with general in-group policy, show great emotional commitment or loyalty to in-groups, and share a sense of common fate with other in-group members. Opposition to outgroups is based on a tendency to presuppose that all out-group members are untrustworthy. Collectivists do not join many groups, but rather have an intense attachment to and identification with extremely few in-groups. Collectivists are therefore relatively well prepared for between-group competition so characteristic of Mediterranean agonistic societies. The common biblical, ethnocentric contrast between Israel and all other peoples (called "Gentiles") is typically collectivist.

There were no individualist personalities in the biblical period, although modern individualist Bible readers are often misled by the quasi individualism of elite members of otherwise collectivist societies. As ancient sources indicate, these elites were often motivated by pleasure, greed, personal needs, or power aspirations. For a contemporary example, Triandis refers to collectivist Latin American elites who indulge in all kinds of conspicuous consumption, carnivals, trade, luxury goods, and so on. The picture is not at all unlike the quasi individualism of antiquity that emerged among the urban elites who had all the qualities of collectivist personalities, yet seemed so much like modern individualists. Prophets and the throwaway people at the other end of the social scale (beggars, prostitutes, disinherited sons, orphans or children that families cannot support, who are abandoned to the streets to fend for themselves), torn from communal group moorings, might also appear as quasi individualists, yet were subject to the collectivist norms of their status.

The individual persons described in the Bible always behave as collectivist personalities. The central position of the kin unit and kin relationships in the OT is obvious. The qualities of the group founder permeate the group in all its ramifications, from Adam's willingness to dishonor God (Gen 2) and its collectivist consequences (Rom 5:12-17), to Abraham's willingness to trust in God (Gen 15), to Jacob's willingness to swindle even his brother (Gen 25, 27). To leave one's kin group, whether family or tribe, involves suffering and death. Exile was a punishment as severe as death. Group adherence and the well-being of the group are the highest priority—even in "Psalms of Individual Lament," which culturally should be more appropriately labeled: Laments of a Collectivist Individual.

The whole range of persons one meets in the NT documents are likewise collectivist personalities. Even Jesus who asks: "Who do people say that I am?" (Mark 8:27) is asking a collectivist question, seeking group input toward self-understanding. Although Paul looks like a determined individualist, a close reading of his

concerns reveals him as a typical collectivist, always seeking and requiring group approval and acceptance.

The God of the Bible is not simply "God," but the God of a specific group—whether the ancestral group rooted in Abraham, Isaac, and Jacob, or of the people Israel ("the Lord our God," Deut 6:4). For Jesus group members, God is likewise the God of Israel, who raised Jesus from the dead for us (not for me). Jesus is not personal Lord and Savior, but group Lord and Savior. Self-denial means collectivist self-denial, a willingness to break with family and friends (Mark 10:29-30; Matt 19:29; Luke 18:29-30). Such a break leads to membership in another group. Whether family or Jesus groups, the defining attributes of group adherence (in Jesus groups: being a disciple) are loyalty to the central personage(s) (called faith) and group solidarity (called love), thus enabling the new primary in-group (the church) to develop survival ability until the central person's goals would be realized. *See* INDIVIDUAL, INDIVIDUALISM.

Bibliography: Geert H. Hofstede. *Culture's Consequences: Comparing Values, Behaviors, Institutions, and Organizations across Nations.* 2nd ed. (2001); Bruce J. Malina. "Understanding New Testament Persons: A Reader's Guide." *Using The Social Sciences in New Testament Interpretation* (1996) 41–61; Harry C. Triandis. "Cross-Cultural Studies of Individualism and Collectivism." *Nebraska Symposium on Motivation 1989* (1990) 41–133.

BRUCE J. MALINA

COLONY [κολωνία kolōnia]. Before JULIUS CAESAR, colonies of the ROMAN EMPIRE were established to secure the frontiers, provide land for poor citizens, and promote agricultural development. After the time of Sulla, colonies were established in Italy to reward military veterans with land and citizenship. Julius Caesar also sent freedmen from Rome to populate colonies in other regions in order to relieve overpopulation and unemployment in Rome. According to Suetonius, he resettled 80,000 Roman citizens. Augustus established colonies around the Mediterranean in order to reward military veterans for their service. From the mid 1st cent. onward, cities were awarded the title of "colony" without receiving a settlement of veterans.

Colonies were formed either as entirely new foundations or as settlements attached to existing cities. They had the right to self-government (*libertas*), and the settlers were regarded as Roman citizens. Some colonies such as Philippi received the *ius Italicum*, the right to follow Italian legal procedures and to avoid direct taxation of land and persons (*immunitas*). Native inhabitants of colonized cities who did not possess citizenship rights were called *incolae*.

A number of cities mentioned in the NT were Roman colonies, but only PHILIPPI is identified as such

(Acts 16:12). The Greek word used by Luke (kolōnia) is a transliteration of the Lat. *colonia*. The colony at Philippi was founded by Julius Caesar and was reestablished by AUGUSTUS after the Battle of Actium in 31 BCE. Julius Caesar also founded CORINTH. Colonies founded by Augustus include Pisidian ANTIOCH, LYSTRA, TROAS, and SYRACUSE. Ptolemais (ACCO) was founded by Claudius. ICONIUM may have been founded by either Claudius or Hadrian. *See* COMMONWEALTH.

Bibliography: Adrian Nicholas Sherwin-White. *The Roman Citizenship* (1973).

GREGORY L. LINTON

COLOPHON. A scribal notation, often at the end of ancient manuscripts. It contains information about the text itself (e.g., incipit, source, number of lines, date, disposition of copy) and persons with a connection to the text (e.g., name of owner, name of scribe making the copy). Colophons appear throughout biblical literature (e.g., Jer 48:47 [Heb.]; Ps 72:18-20; Job 31:40; Sir 50:27-29; Add Esth 11:1), sometimes expanded (Jer 32:6-15), and sometimes containing attributions of authorship (e.g., David, Job).

F. W. DOBBS-ALLSOPP

COLORS. Judging from the language of both the OT and NT, the world of the Bible was not a colorful place. There is a surprising dearth of references to specific colors, and of descriptions of things or locations as colorful. Of the exceptions to this tendency, two are most significant: An extensive cluster of "color language" having to do with luxury, and another having to do with the environs and presence of God.

Colored and colorful items are frequently associated with luxury, royalty, and wealth in biblical texts. This is not surprising, in that colored goods (especially textiles, ceramics, and jewelry) were often imported and always expensive in ancient Israel. While the luxury of color is occasionally evaluated positively (e.g., the CRIMSON and PURPLE clothing of the capable wife in Prov 31:21-22), it is usually fraught with negative associations of decadence, harlotry, idolatry, and foreign influence. Notable examples include the descriptions of Ahasuerus' palace in Esth 1 and of the harlot Babylon in Rev 17–18, and various prophetic indictments of Israelite idolatry and commerce with foreign powers (e.g., Ezek 23:6; Jer 4:30).

The one context in which the luxury of colored items and fabrics meets with the broad approval of the biblical writers is that of the environs and presence of God. The intricate plans for the construction and decoration of the Tabernacle and the priestly vestments found in Exod 25–39 include the largest concentration of color language in the OT. Similarly, the detailed description of the Temple in Jerusalem found in 2 Chr 2–3 is rich with the vocabulary of color. It is noteworthy that the same colors (BLUE, PURPLE, CRIMSON) that are most common in the negatively associated contexts of human luxury are also most common in the positively associated context of the panoply of God's residences and service.

Beyond these two clusters, there are specific colors that (when not used as simple descriptors) carry their own unique biblical associations. GRAY is always associated with old age. GREEN is almost exclusively used to describe vegetation, with the accompanying associations of life and fertility. RED most often connotes blood, war, and the like. YELLOW appears only three times, all related to infection in Lev 13.

The last two colors of interest are BLACK and WHITE. References to the color black are surprisingly scarce, and almost exclusively pure description. The only exceptions are occasional references to the sky or heavenly bodies turning black as a sign of cosmic disaster (Mic 3:6; Rev 6:12). White is perhaps the more interesting of these, as it shows significant variety in its associations. White is associated frequently with leprosy and disease in the earlier texts of the OT, but also appears as emblematic of purity and in association with heavenly figures, mostly in later texts (e.g., Dan 7), and especially in the NT (e.g., the transfiguration accounts in Matt 17, Mark 9, and Luke 9, and the repeated promise of white robes to the faithful in Revelation).

D. MATTHEW STITH

COLOSSAE kuh-los´ee [Κολοσσαί Kolossai]. Access from the Aegean coast into the interior of Asia Minor (Anatolia = modern Turkey) was provided by river valleys. One of the most important was the Meander, running east from near Ephesus. About one hundred miles upstream it was joined by the river Lycus, whose valley provided the most accessible route to the central plateau and served as a major artery of east-west communication during the Greek and Roman periods. The fertile Lycus valley also encouraged settlement, and supported three prominent cities—Laodicea and Hierapolis, with Colossae a further ten miles upstream.

Four or five centuries before the time of the NT, Colossae had been populous, large and wealthy, its wealth due both to its position on the main road from Ephesus and Sardis to the Euphrates and to its wool industry. But by the early years of the Roman empire its significance had been much reduced, in contrast to Laodicea (an administrative and financial centre) and Hierapolis (famous for its hot mineral springs). There were probably substantial Jewish communities in the Lycus valley cities. In the late 3rd cent. BCE Antiochus the Great had settled 2,000 Jewish families in Lydia and Phrygia to help stabilize the region (Josephus, *Ant.* 12.147-53). Philo says that Jews were numerous in every city of Asia Minor (*Legat.* 245). And the attempt by Flaccus to seize the Temple tax in Laodicea (Cicero,

Flac. 28.68), presumably gathered from the nearby cities, suggests a large number of male Jews in the region (more than twenty pounds of gold could indicate as many as 14,000). Colossae itself could have had two or three thousand Jewish residents.

Christianity had been established there by Epaphras, a native of Colossae (Col 4:12). Though he was the principal 'apostle' for the region, Paul, appears never to have visited Colossae (Col 2:1). Presumably Epaphras was converted by Paul during the latter's lengthy mission in Ephesus. The letter to the Colossian Christians was written by Paul (or an associate), either from Ephesus, or later from Rome.

The Lycus valley was ravaged by an earthquake in 60–61 CE. Laodicea was badly damaged, but there is no reference to damage suffered by Colossae. There is some inscriptional and numismatic evidence for Colossae's continuance as a Roman city, but evidently it never recovered its former glory. The absence of Colossae from the letters of Rev 2–3 and of Ignatius, and from the subsequent history of Christianity in the region (in contrast to Laodicea and Hierapolis) suggests its greatly reduced significance. The site of Colossae has never been excavated. *See* COLOSSIANS, LETTER TO THE.

Bibliography: Clyde E. Fant and Mitchell G. Reddish. *A Gude to Biblical Sites in Greece and Turkey* (2003).

JAMES D. G. DUNN

COLOSSIANS, LETTER TO kuh-losh´uhns. The church of Colossae was founded probably in the second half of the 50s CE. It was not established by Paul himself, although he may have passed nearby on his journey through Phrygia to Ephesus (Acts 18:23; 19:1), since COLOSSAE lay on or close to one of the main East-West routes through Anatolia. Its foundation seems rather to have been the result of evangelism by EPAPHRAS (Col 1:6-7), who was a native of Colossae and who may have been responsible for the evangelism of the Lycus Valley cities (Col 4:13). Presumably Epaphras was converted by Paul during Paul's sojourn in Ephesus (Acts 19:8-10), as also another resident of Colossae—Philemon (Phlm 19); that Philemon also lived in Colossae is almost universally inferred from the par. between Col 4:9-14 and Phlm 23-24. If so, the founding of the church in Colossae may provide the only clear example of Paul's likely tactic of establishing an evangelistic center in a major city (here Ephesus) from which individual or teams of evangelists would go out to cities within striking distance from Ephesus.

A. The Church of Colossae

It is not possible to say how large the church of Colossae was when the letter was written. The reference to the church, which gathered in the house of well-to-do PHILEMON (Phm 2) implies that there were other house churches. And the house churches of Laodicea in particular may have functioned as part of the same Christian community (Col 2:1; 4:15-16). The "household rules" (3:18–4:1) also imply a household "model" for the Colossian church(es), in which both slaves and children were full members of the congregation (addressed in 3:20, 22-25; *see* HOUSEHOLD CODES).

The church was probably composed of Jews and Gentiles, though mainly of the latter. This is a deduction, inevitably somewhat speculative, from several considerations. 1. The Jewish population in the Lycus Valley cities was probably substantial. The most obvious setting in which to present the good news of a Jewish Messiah, even for a self-styled mission to the Gentiles/nations, was in the local synagogues where Gentile sympathizers (usually described as "GODFEARERS") regularly formed an accepted and respected penumbra round the local Jewish community. This is how Acts presents Paul's mission, and 2 Cor 11:24 implies a continuing association with the synagogue on Paul's part. In most cities, the earliest Christian converts likely came from this setting.

2. The implication of several passages in Colossians is that the recipients were predominantly Gentiles who through the gospel had now been given to share in privileges hitherto known only to Israel: 1:12—God "has qualified you to share the inheritance of the saints in the light"; 1:27—the "mystery" of God's purpose ("which is, Christ in you, the hope of glory") now being "made known among the nations"; 2:13—"you who were dead in the transgressions and uncircumcision of your flesh" now "made alive with him."

3. Also implied is some concern that "Greek and Jew, circumcision and uncircumcision" should mutually recognize the other's full acceptance before God "in Christ" (3:11). And 4:11 similarly implies a concern on the part of the writer to assure the recipients that Paul's own mission team reflected a similar make up of circumcision and uncircumcision.

B. The Danger Threatening the Church at Colossae

Why should Paul write (or authorize) a letter to a fairly minor church, which he had never visited? The implication of 1:7 is that news had come from Epaphras, which occasioned some anxiety. If ONESIMUS (4:9) is the slave of Philemon (Phlm 10-16), then he too could have brought news from Colossae. The references to Tychicus and Mark (Col 4:7-10), not to mention Phlm 22, also suggest a concern to maintain communication with the Colossian believers. And the warnings, which evidently form the central section of the letter (2:8-23), certainly signal an anxiety concerning the self-understanding and self-confidence of the Colossian Christians. What was the problem or danger envisaged?

1. Not a "heresy"

Most attempts to answer this question have spoken freely of "the Colossian heresy," or the Colossian "errorists," or have used similar phrases (see HERESY). Such language betrays the perspective of an established faith (an "orthodoxy") newly challenged by radicals or revisionists. But such a perspective is wholly anachronistic. Such a perspective only emerges in 2nd cent. Christianity. The "philosophy" of 2:8 and the "regulations" of 2:20 might well have been long established, beside which the gospel of Paul and the small house-meetings of believers in Messiah Jesus would have seemed brash and callow.

Nor does the letter itself suggest that the Colossian church was facing a great crisis: a group of teachers, internally or externally, endeavoring to subvert the gospel on which the church had been founded. It should not be assumed that the crisis that occasioned Paul's letter to the Galatians, or 2 Cor 10–13, provides a pattern for all the problems confronted in the Pauline letters. The continuing influence of F. C. Baur's reconstruction of Christianity's early history, as a running battle between a Petrine faction and a Pauline faction, must be recognized and challenged—in the case of Colossians at least. The contrast between the fierce denunciations of Galatians (e.g., Gal 1:6-9; 5:2-12) and 2 Cor 10–13, and the relatively relaxed tone of Colossians as a whole, including the exhortations of Col 2:8-23, indicate a quite different occasion for the letter.

The implication of 2:8-23 is that the practitioners of (an) older established "philosophy" and religious system had contrasted the "captivating" power of their own beliefs and praxis with the beliefs and praxis of the Pauline converts (2:8), had "passed (negative) judgment" on the latters' rituals and festivals (2:16), and had acted as though they themselves were umpires with the authority (of ancient tradition) to "disqualify" the Christian belief and praxis (2:18) as ineffectual and unfit for purpose. The challenge confronting the letter-writer, then, was probably so much not to counter a "false teaching" as to encourage the Colossian believers to hold up their heads in the face of a denigrating dismissal by a long-established religious system and to maintain confidence in their beliefs regarding Christ and what he had done.

What then was the older system besides which the Colossian believers found it difficult to hold up their heads? Two main answers have been offered.

2. Gnosticizing syncretism?

This was the dominant view in the latter half of the 20th cent. (see SYNCRETISM): 1) The term philosophy ("love of wisdom") had long been used of a systematic treatment of a theme, practical as well as speculative, and so for various schools of "philosophy." The term thus invites identification of the other teaching as a typically Hellenistic mix of religious philosophy. 2) The emphasis in the letter on "wisdom" (1:9, 28; 2:3, 23; 3:16; 4:5), "insight" (1:9; 2:2), and "knowledge" (1:6, 9-10; 2:2-3; 3:10) suggests a typically Gnostic (or Gnosticizing) regard for spiritual self-awareness. 3) The references to "the elements of the universe" and the cosmic powers of 2:10 and 15 likewise suggest a belief that only by establishing a right relationship with the cosmic powers can one hope to "gain entry" to the "pleroma" (2:9) and participate in the divine "fullness" (2:10)—language typical of the later Gnostic systems (see GNOSTICISM). 4) The language of 2:18 is particularly critical: it seems to indicate a practice of worshiping angels; and talk of "things seen on entering" is highly reminiscent of the "things recited," "things shown," and "things performed" (OCD[2] 716) in the initiations into the mystery religions.

The thesis fits well with a persistent view that religious syncretism was widespread in Asia Minor. There is attestation of worship of angels in western Asia Minor (BDAG 459); of at least one cult of God Most High and "his holy angels"; of associations calling themselves "Sabbatistai"; and the practice of magic was widespread. That there were Jewish elements involved in this syncretistic mix is not to be doubted; magic was a universal para-religious phenomenon at the time, and no doubt good luck charms and amulets were to be found in the household of not a few devout Jews of the period. Insofar as this broader picture is relevant to the Colossian "philosophy," it remains unclear whether it should be regarded as a Jewish syncretistic group, or as a non-Jewish group that had absorbed some Jewish elements.

On the considerations marshaled by E. Lohse, the issue is equally unclear: 1) Judaism had long been described as a "philosophy" by its influential apologists (Aristobulus, Philo, and soon Josephus). 2) Talk of "wisdom" and "knowledge" is hardly specific to or distinctive of Gnostic systems; it was widespread in Second Temple Judaism as well. 3) Although "pleroma" does become a technical term in the later Gnostic systems, the thought of divine fullness was already familiar in Hellenistic Judaism, as again Philo attests (e.g., Leg. 3:4; Gig. 47; Conf. 136; Mos. 2.238). 4) And the prepositional phrase, "worship of angels" can readily be understood as worship offered by angels, rather than worship offered *to* angels, which would fit with one of the great traditions of Jewish visionary apocalypses (Isa 6:2-3; Dan 7:10; *1 En.* 14:18-23; 36:4, 39-40).

3. The synagogue in Colossae

If the church in Colossae emerged from the SYNAGOGUE, as in Corinth and Ephesus (according to Acts 18:6-7; 19:9), then it probably appeared to the local authorities as an offshoot of the synagogue. Civil authorities tended to be suspicious of new groupings, but since the time of Caesar, the Jewish communities in Asia Minor had formally been given permission to maintain their traditional customs and rites (in reference specifically to Laodicea, Josephus, *Ant.* 14.241-42). So the new house church(es) probably appeared to watching eyes no more than an extension of the synagogues (συναγωγή synagōgē and ἐκκλησία ekklēsia were near synonyms = "assembly"; compare Acts 18:12-16). If, then, Colossians suggests that the Jesus believers were being disparaged by a venerable "philosophy," given such a history of the emergence of the HOUSE CHURCH(es), the most obvious body to warrant that description in Colossae would be one or more of the Colossian synagogues.

It is also plain, not least from subsequent history, that in the early centuries the adherents of Christianity and those of diaspora Judaism often overlapped, with church leaders regularly having to warn their flocks to avoid "Judaizing," attending the synagogue on the Sabbath, and observing the Jewish feasts (already Barnabas 3:6; Ignatius, *Magn.* 8:1; 10:3). In the light of which we should presumably allow for such an overlap among Jews, proselytes, and Godfearers, in most cities where Christianity took early root, with "church" and "synagogue" forming overlapping networks. And as the first Christian churches hardly took a uniform character (compare only the churches of Thessalonica and Corinth), so we should not assume that the diaspora synagogues were of a uniform pattern, allowing still more possibilities of overlap, interaction, and antagonism.

Such a priori reasoning chimes in well with the data of the letter itself, where a certain preoccupation with aspects of Jewish identity is evident. Colossians 1:12 has already been mentioned. The talk of "alienation" in 1:21 smacks of a Jewish perspective (as more explicitly in Eph 2:12, "aliens from the commonwealth of Israel, and strangers to the covenants of promise"), as does the repeated reference to circumcision (Col 2:11, as a positive metaphor; 4:11) and the circumcision/uncircumcision contrast (2:13; 3:11). Likewise the emphasis evidently being placed by those who passed judgment on the church in regard to food and drink (compare Dan 1:3-16; 10:3; Add Esth 14:17; *Jos. Asen.* 8:5), festivals, new moon, and Sabbaths (e.g., 1 Chr 23:31; Neh 10:33; Ezek 45:17; Hos 2:11; 1 Macc 10:34)—all characteristically had some distinctively Jewish concerns. Similarly, 2:21 ("Do not

touch, do not taste, do not handle") most probably echoes typically Jewish fears lest physical contact render impure (as in Lev 5:3), fears particularly evident in the Judaism of the period (as particularly in 1QS VI–VII and *T. Mos.* 7:9-10, "Do not touch me lest you pollute me."). Nor should the echo of the distinctively Jewish antipathy to idolatry and *porneia* ("sexual license") in Col 3:5 go unnoticed.

Similar concerns can be cited within a wider religious framework, but none of the concerns indicated above is strange to—and several are distinctive of—Second Temple Judaism ("saints," circumcision, Sabbath, antipathy to idolatry). Calendar piety, food laws, circumcision, and rejection of idolatry were not just random elements of some syncretistic cult but the norms and markers that gave Jews their identity. So the most obvious reference of the Colossian "philosophy" is to one or more of the Jewish synagogues. They probably prided themselves on the venerable age and sophistication of their religion ("philosophy"). They no doubt resented the claims being made by the Colossian church that its members, Gentile as well as Jew, were fully participant in Israel's distinctive heritage. And they presumably judged these claims to be disqualified because the Christians were not maintaining the practices that hitherto had been regarded as distinctive markers of the heritage of Abraham, Moses, David, and Elijah. The echo in 2:22 ("human commandments and teachings") of the Jesus tradition's criticism of Jewish/Pharisaic tradition (Mark 7:7/Matt 15:9) is unlikely to be accidental, and suggests a critical interaction that consciously drew on that tradition.

4. "The worship of angels"

Various 2nd cent. sources describe (or accuse) Jews of worshiping angels (*Kerygma Petri*; *Apology of Aristides* 14:4; Celsus in Origen, *c. Celsum* 1:25 and 5:6). But more characteristic of Judaism is warning against such worship (*Apoc. Zeph.* 6:15; *Apoc. Ab.* 17:2; Philo, *Fug.* 212; *Somn.* 1:232, 238; also Rev 19:10; 22:9). So if this is what Col 2:18 had in view, and the Jews indicated above (§B.3) were the target, then it must have indeed been a rather syncretistic Judaism. But since the thesis of such a syncretistic Judaism is not well attested elsewhere for this period, even by hostile witnesses like the 2nd cent. sources just alluded to, consideration has to be given to the alternative way of rendering the prepositional phrase, even if the more obvious way of taking it is as "worship offered to angels."

A subjective genitive rendering is entirely plausible ("worship rendered by angels") and has long been maintained. In the light of the preceding considerations (§B.3) it becomes all the more likely, since (as already mentioned) such worship features prominently in several Jewish apocalypses. More to the point, there is clear evidence in various Jewish sources of the period of an aspiration to join in with such worship: most strikingly in *T. Job* 48-50; *Apoc. Ab.* 17, and *Apoc. Zeph.* 8:3-4; and no less strikingly in the Qumran scrolls, notably the *Songs of the Sabbath Sacrifice* (4Q400-405). The cumulative evidence invites us, therefore, to envisage one or more Jewish synagogues in Colossae who understood their Sabbath worship as joining with the worship of the angels in heaven. The self-discipline and mortification (2:18, 23) they practiced as part of their purity, dietary, and festal traditions, they presumably regarded as requisite for such spiritual (mystical) experiences. And consequently they looked down on what must have seemed to be the relative poverty of the worship of the Jews and non-Jews who had formed a new assembly (church) in the city (*see* ANGEL).

5. The Christology of the letter

Most commentators have assumed that CHRISTOLOGY was at the heart of the issue between the letter-writer and the Colossian "philosophy." But this is unlikely. The great "hymn" (as it is usually described) in praise of Christ (1:15-20) is not set out in polemical fashion, but as grounds for the recipients' own faith and hope (1:4-5, 11-14). And the defense in 2:8-23 focuses not on Christ but on the traditions being cited (2:8), on food, drink, festivals (2:16), and purity (2:2-23). Certainly, who Christ is and what Christ has done provides the secure basis for the letter's denial of the importance of these traditions and practices (2:6-7, 9-15, 17, 19, 20; 3:1-4). But the issue is not, as often suggested, that Christ's role was being challenged by the "philosophy." The claims made about Christ are simply there to boost the Colossians' self-esteem to withstand the denigrating criticisms of their own lack of ancient tradition, of ritual, festival, and rule. The point, of course, is that what Christ had done for them and was doing in them (1:27; 3:3-4) rendered such praxis nugatory and irrelevant. But that claim, evidently, was not the point of conflict with the "cultured despisers" in the Colossian synagogue(s).

At the same time, the Colossian Christology marks a significant consolidation and step forward in Pauline Christology, including these themes: "the kingdom of [God's] beloved Son" (1:13); the cosmic sweep of the "hymn"—"all things created through him and for him" (1:16); the cosmic body identified with "the church" (1:18); he has reconciled "all things" (1:20); Christ himself as "God's mystery" (2:2); the nearest the Pauline corpus comes to a statement of incarnation— "in him the whole fullness of deity dwells bodily" (2:9); the unique expression of the Christus Victor theme (2:15); believers not only died with Christ, but already raised with him (2:20; 3:1). In Colossians we see the transition to the great Wisdom/Logos Christologies of the 2nd and 3rd cent. already well under way.

C. Who Wrote Colossians?

The answer to this question cannot be found simply by reference to the opening word of the letter: "Paul

. . . to the saints in Colossae." For the facts both that pseudepigraphy seems to have been common and accepted in the ancient world (*see* PSEUDONYMOUS WRITING), and that there was no obvious sense of authorial copyright in such ancient writings, add factors that we today are no longer in a position fully to evaluate.

Nor is the issue to be resolved simply by referring to the consensus of those who have examined the matter closely, and who have found the style of Colossians to be so different from that of undisputed Pauline letters that it cannot have been written by the same. There is the complicating factor of the secretary or AMANUENSIS. Did he simply write to Paul's longhand dictation? A skilled scribe could have used some form of shorthand; but could Paul have afforded the expense of such a skilled scribe? Possibly Paul gave his scribe an outline of what we wanted to say and left it to the secretary to pen it in his own terms and style (compare Cicero, *Att.* 3.15; 11.2, 5, 7). And what about Paul's coauthor, in this case Timothy (Col 1:1)? It is quite possible to envisage Timothy writing the letter on Paul's behalf, with Paul sufficiently content with its message to add his own personal note in his own hand at the end (4:18). This alone would be sufficient to explain the features that have hitherto pushed commentators to conclude that Colossians is post-Pauline or deutero-Pauline—not simply the differences in style but also the distinctiveness of Colossians' Christology and the emergence of new features, such as the "realized eschatology" of 2:11-12 and 3:1, and the "household rules" of 3:18–4:1. (The overlap with Ephesians is a problem more for the latter, since the consensus is that Colossians provided something of a model for Ephesians, though it may be that the same person who drafted Colossians to express Paul's views felt that much freer to use Colossians as a sort of template for the more ambitious Ephesians.)

The case for a letter written while Paul was still alive, though in prison (4:3, 10, 18) and perhaps unable to do more than add his signature (4:18), is strengthened by the other parallels—between Colossians and Philemon—the latter being regarded almost universally as written by Paul. For the closeness of the parallels between Col 4:10-14 and Phlm 23–24 is best explained by the closeness of timing of the two letters, while the differences—particularly the lack of reference to Tychicus (Col 4:7-9) in Philemon—can be explained simply by the different purposes of the two letters.

D. Where and When Was Colossians Written?

Two factors are potentially critical here: the earthquake of 60/61, which can hardly have left Colossae undamaged, and perhaps in ruins; and Paul's imprisonment (4:3, 10, 18). Since we do not know whether the Colossian church survived beyond the earthquake, we cannot simply deduce that the letter must have been written before then. But the absence of any allusion to the earthquake in the letter points more to a pre-60/61 date. That would not rule out a dating to Rome, where Paul was certainly imprisoned, and to which imprisonment the letter has traditionally been attributed. For it is just possible that Paul had been brought to Rome in time for the letter to be written (and delivered) prior to the earthquake. The request of Phlm 22 could indicate a bright hope still retained in the early days of Paul's Roman imprisonment.

In terms of closeness to Colossae, however, the more obvious candidate for place of authorship is Ephesus. It is certainly easier to envisage the slave Onesimus successfully tracking Paul down in Ephesus, only five days travel distant, whereas the distance between Colossae and Rome must have been constraining for a slave traveling without authorization and funding. Such considerations have stimulated the thesis that Paul spent some time in prison during his Ephesian mission. Acts says nothing of such an imprisonment, but passages like 1 Cor 15:32 and 2 Cor 1:8-10 can readily be interpreted as referring to a major crisis in Ephesus, possibly including imprisonment. Such a thesis need not affect any conclusions drawn regarding the authorship of the letter (§C); the conditions of Paul's imprisonment could have been as light or as severe or as varied in both Ephesus and Rome. And the time gap between a letter written during the second half of Paul's Aegean mission and one written at the beginning of Paul's imprisonment in Rome is still relatively short, so that such distinctive features as the theology of Colossians contains can be dated to either period without any disquiet. As already indicated, the differences between Colossians and the other undisputed Pauline letters are best explained by the activity of a coauthor/amaneuensis rather than by developments in Paul's own theologizing. All that the thesis of a letter written during an Ephesian imprisonment entails is a dating of Colossians to about 56, rather than, say 60/61.

E. The Outline of the Letter

Bibliography: C. E. Arnold. *The Colossian Syncretism: The Interface between Christianity and Folk Belief at Colossae* (1994); J. D. G. Dunn. *The Epistles to the Colossians and to Philemon* (1996); F. O. Francis and W. A. Meeks. *Conflict at Colossae* (1973); M. D. Hooker. "Were There False Teachers in Colossae?" *From Adam to Christ* (1990) 121–36; M. Kiley. *Colossians as Pseudepigraphy* (1986); E. Lohse. *Colossians and Philemon* (1971); E. R. Richards. *Paul and First-Century Letter Writing* (2004); T. J. Sappington. *Revelation and Redemption at Colossae* (1991); E. Schweizer. *The Letter to the Colossians* (1982); R. McL. Wilson. *Colossians and Philemon: A Critical and Exegetical Communtary* (2005).

J. D. G. DUNN

COLT [עַיִר 'ayir; πῶλος pōlos]. In the OT and NT, a colt is the offspring of a donkey. In the NT, a colt is the animal upon which Jesus entered Jerusalem prior to his crucifixion. Always rendered as "colt," pōlos appears twelve times in the NT, and only in the Gospel accounts of Jesus' triumphal entry into Jerusalem. *See* ANIMALS OF THE BIBLE.

GARY COLLEDGE

COLUMBARIA. Pigeon coops with small cubical niches. The most familiar are those in the area of MARESHAH where underground columbaria were hewn out of the soft limestone characteristic of the area. One of the many there is said to have once housed over 2,000 pigeons. Columbaria were numerous in the Hellenistic period, especially during the reign of John HYRCANUS. The sacrificial use of DOVEs may have created a need for a columbarium enterprise. *See* CAVE.

GARY COLLEDGE

COME, TO [בּוֹא bo', יָצָא yatsa', שׁוּב shuv, הָלַךְ halakh; δεῦρο deuro, ἔρχομαι erchomai, ἥκω hēkō].

One of the most frequent expressions in all of Scripture, "coming" in the OT often connotes entrance, walking, invitation, and descent. It is sometimes used to mark the covenant, as when God instructs Noah's family to come into the ark (Gen 6:18). Coming, most generally, announces themes of arrival: of people, God's presence, and prominent events. The expression is also used as an invitation to worship and praise, "O come, let us sing to the Lord" (Ps 95:1). In the NT, the theme of coming can also announce a Messianic appearance (Luke 3:16; John 4:25). Other prominent uses in the NT include invitations to follow Jesus (Matt 19:21) and believers' standing in the presence of God (Rev 15:4).

DAVID JENSEN

COMEDY. A comedy is not simply a light and amusing sequence of events; it is a play in which the main characters triumph over adversity. It can be comic in that it shows characters in their weakness or inferiority (whether moral or social). But, unlike in tragedy, the comic and "laughable is an error or disgrace [on the part of the character] that does not involve pain or destruction" (Aristotle, *Poet.* 49a34f.). While the book of Job starts and develops as a tragedy, it ends as a comedy: Job triumphs over adversity, while his friends are disgraced. Biblical examples of comedy (or comical, ridiculed characters): Ehud and Eglon (Judg 3:15-30); Esau disgracing himself by selling his birthright (Gen 25:29-34) but regaining superiority (Gen 33:1-16); Pharaoh drowned in the sea (Exod 14–15); Balaam's talking ass (Num 22:21-35); the trees choosing the thornbush (Judg 9:7-15); Haman trapped into honoring Mordecai (Esth 6; compare also 5:14 and 7:9-10); and Ahab's and the prophets' words or actions (1 Kgs 22:6, 8, 11-12, 15-18, 30). While comedy is not amusing to a victim, it is to the audience and to the characters in the text with whom the audience identifies. *See* HUMOR; IRONY; TRAGEDY.

L. J. DE REGT

COMFORT [נָחַם nakham; παρακαλέω parakaleō, παραμυθέομαι paramytheomai]. The idea of comfort is linked to a situation of grief or distress. Giving comfort to a person who has lost a beloved one belongs to ancient biblical and Jewish tradition. The verbs generally used come from the root nakham, mostly *piel*, the Greek equivalents being parakaleō and paramytheomai. Examples are found in the OT (Gen 37:35; 2 Sam 10:2f.; 12:24) as well as in the NT (John 11:19, 31).

Human comfort may be idle (Job 16:2; 21:34) if it does not open a perspective (Gen 50:21; Ruth 2:13). Lasting comfort comes from God. It is experienced by the individual (Ps 86:17; 119:76, 82) as well as by the whole People of God. "Books of comfort" are Isa 40–55 (Isa 40:1; 49:13; 51:3, 12; 52:9, but also 61:2; 66:13; Zech 1:17) and Jer 30–31 (Jer 31:9, 13). Jesus announces eschatological consolation to those who mourn (Matt 5:4; *see* Isa 61:2). Paul praises God's consolation that he experiences in all distress (2 Cor 1:3-7) and sees himself as the agent of such comfort. Good news about the communities contributes to such comfort (2 Cor 7:7, 13; 1 Thess 3:7). There will be a final consolation for the individual (Luke 16:25) as well as for the People of God, when God will wipe away every tear from the eyes of the faithful (Rev 7:17; 21:4; from Isa 25:8). *See* CONSOLATION; PARACLETE.

JOHANNES BEUTLER

COMFORTER. *See* PARACLETE.

COMING OF CHRIST. *See* ADVENT; PAROUSIA; SECOND COMING.

COMMAGENE. The kingdom of Commagene, located in southeastern modern Turkey between the Taurus Mountains and the EUPHRATES River, controlled a Euphrates crossing and important trade routes. Commagene's history is similar to other eastern kingdoms, including JUDEA, and, like them, became a Roman province.

In 163 BCE, PTOLEMY, the governor, rebelled against the SELEUCID Empire and established Commagene as an independent kingdom. Commagene remained independent until TIBERIUS made Commagene a Roman province in 18 CE. CALIGULA restored Commagene to his friend, ANTIOCHUS IV, granting it independence in 38 CE. But in 72, VESPASIAN annexed Commagene permanently to Rome. *See* MACCABEAN REVOLT; PARTHIA, PARTHIANS.

ADAM L. PORTER

COMMANDMENT [מִצְוָה mitswah; ἐντολή entolē]. Due to translators' decisions, *commandment* occurs in the English Bibles less frequently than the Hebrew mitswah. The verb designates a superior's ordering of a subordinate, the noun what is ordered. Since Yahweh/God is usually the subject, *commandment* occurs most frequently in legal and prophetic literature.

Commandments, such as the TEN COMMANDMENTS, are directly addressed injunctions concerning matters of moral gravity. Not limited in duration or to a particular person, they are incumbent on all individuals of the addressed class for an unlimited duration. The speaker assumes responsibility for the addressee's behavior, and, by implication, the addressee's welfare. The addressee owes the speaker compliance.

Jewish and Christian theology elevated commandment to the status of theological doctrine, taking cues from such generalizing uses as Deut 5:31; 6:1, 25; and 7:11. *See* LAW IN THE OT; TORAH.

DALE PATRICK

COMMANDMENTS, TEN. *See* LAW IN THE OT; TEN COMMANDMENTS.

COMMENTARY kom´en-ter-ee [Lat. *commentarius*]. First used to refer either to pupils' notes or to a speech outline, later *commentary* primarily referred to a draft written about historical events (e.g., Caesar's *Commentarii*), and then to a writing that explains the contents of a book (e.g., Julius Hyginus' late 1st cent. BCE commentaries on Virgil). Jerome is considered the first great Latin biblical commentator. After an introductory discussion of the date, provenance, and the author's purposes, the commentary explains what each verse or section means from the beginning to the end of that biblical book. *See* BIBLICAL CRITICISM; BIBLICAL INTERPRETATION, HISTORY OF; MIDRASH.

EMILY CHENEY

COMMENTARY ON THE BOOK OF KINGS. *See* BOOKS REFERRED TO IN THE BIBLE.

COMMERCE. *See* TRADE AND COMMERCE.

COMMISSION [צָוָה tsawa; ἀποστέλλω apostellō, πρόσταγμα prostagma, ἐπιτροπή epitropē, οἰκονομία oikonomia]. Authority given either by God to human leaders, by God through human leaders to other humans, or by human leaders to people, enabling those persons to complete specific tasks. In obedience to God's instructions, Moses laid his hands on Joshua and commissioned him to succeed Moses (Num 27:9, 23), especially to lead the people into the land God had promised them (Deut 31:14, 23). Nehemiah received authority from the Persian king for the task of returning the petroleum to the Temple in order to ignite the sacrifices (2 Macc 1:20). Authority from a king can also be provided in written form, as given to Ezra, allowing him and his people to return to Jerusalem (1 Esd 8:8). Paul was authorized by the chief priests specifically to go to Damascus to imprison its Christians (Acts 26:12). Paul himself refers to his preaching of the gospel as a commission because God's will, not his own, motivates it (1 Cor 9:17; 2 Cor 1:21, 2:17). Jesus empowers and instructs his disciples to carry out specific tasks: preaching about the nearness of the kingdom, healing the sick, raising the dead, cleansing lepers, and casting out demons (Matt 10:5-8); but it is unclear whether they carried out this commission during Jesus' lifetime (Luke 9:1-10; 10:1-17) or when the resurrected Jesus commissioned them to make disciples and baptize and teach these converts (Matt 28:16-20). *See* APPOINT; GREAT COMMISSION.

EMILY CHENEY

COMMISSION, THE GREAT. It is the closing pronouncement in the Gospel of Matthew (28:18-20). This is but one postresurrection directive found in the NT (*see also* Mark 16:15; Luke 24:47-49; John 20:21-23; Acts 1:8). Its significance in Matthew marks the shift from the ministry of Jesus to the ministry of the church, and implies an indefinite time period before the PAROUSIA. The universal character of the Great Commission is equivalent to Luke 24:47 and Acts 1:8. However, the procedure used in this evangelism effort is distinctly Matthean. Instead of instructing his closest disciples to preach as he did (*see* e.g., Matt 4:17; 11:1), Jesus tells them to teach and baptize, a directive that stands in contrast to some early Christian practice (*see* e.g., 1 Cor 1:17). *See* BAPTISM.

Bibliography: M. J. Wilkins. *The Concept of Disciple in Matthew's* Gospel (1989).

MICHAEL JOSEPH BROWN

COMMON. Old Testament Israel and New Testament Christianity had many common social values with those nations and cultures by which they found themselves surrounded or in which they were immersed. At the same time they attempted to maintain, in quite distinct ways, very tight social boundaries between themselves and outsiders—boundaries that demarcated what was common to the COMMUNITY itself (the "in-group") as opposed to others (the "out-group"). Such aspects have been elucidated well by recent social-science perspectives on biblical interpretation, which have sought to recognize the wider social scripts of both biblical communities. The boundary markers consisted of, e.g., table-fellowship/EUCHARIST (*see* FOOD), matters of purity (*see* CLEAN AND UNCLEAN), admission to the community (by circumcision or baptism), FAITH, language, fellowship, and spiritual distinctions. These boundaries maintained those elements common to the in-group and, for both OT Israel and Christianity, became a defining feature of those considered to be the "people of God."

A. Ethnicity
B. Common Social Values
  1. Group orientation
  2. Honor and shame
    a. Limited good
    b. Patron-client relations
C. Distinctive "In-Group" Boundary Markers
  1. OT Israel: Circumcision, table-fellowship, and purity.
  2. NT Christianity: Purity, spirit, and sacraments
Bibliography

A. Ethnicity

Ethnic distinctions exist in a context of lively social interaction and are an aspect of social organization. The concept of ethnicity has become popular as a way of talking about differences among peoples that do not depend on the anachronistic notion of "race." The features of ethnicity include:

  1. A common proper name to identify the group

2. A "myth" of common ancestry (the genealogical accuracy of the claimed descent is irrelevant)
3. A shared history or shared memories of a common past (including heroes, events, and their commemoration)
4. A common culture, embracing such things as customs, language, and religion
5. A link with a homeland, either though actual occupation or by symbolic attachment to the ancestral land (as with diaspora peoples)
6. A sense of communal solidarity

All of these features are clearly evidenced in the traditions of both OT Israel and early Christianity. The name given to the people of God in the OT is typically Israel (also Jacob or Ephraim), their significant ancestor is Abraham, the history of the community is narrated in the OT Scriptures, and their homeland, even for diaspora communities, is the promised land itself. So, too, the overwhelming concern of the OT writings are to establish the religious worship practices and appropriate customs for the community, which would stand in contradistinction to their neighbors.

In the NT period many of these features were carried over into the Christ-movement, which saw itself standing in continuity with the history and ancestry of Israel (1 Cor 10:1-13). However, there is also a marked discontinuity. The proper name for the community becomes "The Way," or "The Holy Ones/the Saints," or "The Church of God." (In part, the NT also begins to appropriate the terms *Jew* and *Israel* exclusively for believers, Rom 2:28-29; 9:6.) The homeland for the Christian is also transformed, for although Jerusalem and Judea play an important role for the nascent community, there is an eschatological hope for both a New Jerusalem (Rev 21), and a new heaven and new earth (2 Pet 3:13; Rev 21:1). The religious cult (now centerd on the identification of the hoped-for Messiah with Jesus the Nazarene), and the very nature of the newly constituted people of God created a significant disjuncture with OT Israel (John 1:13; Gal 3:26-29; Eph 2:14-22).

These same considerations are also observed within the ethnic groups of their wider social worlds where such characteristics promote notions of ethnocentrism between different groups. Here, the disparaging of another group helps promote one's own, and also maintains vital boundaries. In the 1st cent. CE, e.g., the Greeks and Romans were certainly ethnocentric (although their dislike of other peoples was not made on "racial" grounds, rather, on political, social, or religious ones). Thus the Romans thought the Greeks lacking in determination and grit, and found the Judeans antisocial and misanthropic (esp. because of their refusal to participate in imperial feast days). The Greeks, on the other hand, found the Romans vulgar and lacking in taste; and the Judeans disliked Egyptians because they found them inhospitable and intemperate.

B. Common Social Values.

Recent social-science research into ancient Mediterranean societies has also been valuable in elucidating particular *patterns* of social behavior, and has opened up windows into the social script underlying various scenarios of the OT and NT. Some of the main results of this research has indicated the importance of concepts such as group orientation, honor-shame, limited good, and patronage.

1. Group orientation

Ancient Near Eastern societies exhibited a strong in-group orientation. Here, the family group was of preeminent importance, while other group structures such as one's village, town, city, and tribe (*ethnos*) also played a major role. Individuals aligned their activities and attitudes to those of the groups to which they belonged. Typical virtues in such contexts were obedience to elders, respect for traditions, willingness to share goods with other group members (*see* COMMUNITY OF GOODS), and tendencies to represent the group in its relations to others. The word *dyadic* is sometimes applied to group-orientated personality.

2. Honor and shame

Considered to be a central value of ancient Mediterranean life, its foundational role in social relations was quite remarkable. Honor could be either ascribed (an attribute of birth or position) or achieved (gained from others in various forms of social interaction, described as challenge and response). The desire for honor was a motivating factor in much social interaction, and an individual's accruing of honor or shame would redound upon the group to which he or she belonged. Hence, the ancient Mediterranean world was intensely competitive as individuals and groups strove to promote their honor at the expense of others. The conflict-ridden nature of social interaction has been referred to as *agonistic*. Examples of honor-shame from the OT include the humiliation of David's soldiers and its response in 2 Sam 10 and Joab's rebuke to David in 2 Sam 19. In the NT, much of the social interaction between Jesus and the Pharisees described in the Gospels can be seen as agonistic, as the Pharisees attempt to criticize and undermine Jesus' credibility and ministry. Note also the conflict between Paul and the "super apostles" described in 2 Cor 10–13.

Gender was closely connected with honor and shame, especially to the extent by which women were expected to live under the authority of male family members. Women had to comport themselves with a certain dignity if their men were to preserve their honor. The seduction or violation of a woman results not only in her own shame but in gross dishonor for the men of the family, and would require heavy vengeance to restore the *status quo ante* (*see* Gen 34 and the revenge of Jacob's sons for the rape of Dinah).

a. Limited good. Ancient Mediterranean societies held to the belief that all goods (e.g., land, food, honor) were finite in quantity and could be increased only at the expense of someone else. Therefore, honorable persons worked to preserve what they had, not to accumulate more. In the OT, e.g., there is only one birthright and blessing for Isaac to hand down, and Jacob contrives to receive both (Gen 25:29-34; 27:30-40), while in the NT, John the Baptist comments of Jesus, "he must increase, I must decrease" (John 3:30). Outside the Bible, Philo asserts that the honor and regard given to deified mortals reduces the honor paid to the true God (*Ebr.,* 110; a point that Paul emphasizes in 1 Cor 10 in his critique of Christians participating in idol feasts). And Plutarch describes a person hearing an outstanding speaker and expressing envy at his success, "as though commendation were money, he feels that he is robbing himself of every bit that he bestows on another" (*On Listening to Lectures,* 44B). Hence, all goods are both limited and already distributed; a large share for one automatically means a smaller share for someone else.

b. Patron-client relations. These are social relations between individuals of differing status and are a prominent feature of Greco-Roman culture. They permit the exchange of certain resources. Typically, a person of higher status would share social, economic, and political resources and receive in return useful expressions of loyalty and honor. In some relations there may be a broker who mediates the exchange of various benefits (*See* COLLECTION, THE).

C. Distinctive "In-Group" Boundary Markers

1. OT Israel: Circumcision, table-fellowship, and purity

A critical boundary marker for OT Israel and later Jews was that of CIRCUMCISION. The rite was considered an indispensable sign of the Yahwistic covenant, and refusal to undergo the rite meant exclusion from the community (Gen 17:9-14). Evidence from extrabiblical literature shows that Jews practiced circumcision even at the risk of losing their lives (1 Macc 1:60-61), and for the majority of Jews circumcision was necessary for proselyte conversion (Esth 8:17 LXX; Jdt 14:10; Josephus, *Ant.* 13.254-58; Philo, *Migr.* 89-93). Whether or not Gentiles had to be circumcised to join the nascent Christian church was a point of contention between the Apostle Paul and other Jews in the 1st cent. (e.g., Gal 2:1-14).

TABLE-FELLOWSHIP was another critical boundary marker and, together with circumcision, became a point of contention within the early Christ-movement. For the Israelites and later Jews, the limits of acceptable table-fellowship were demarcated by the Pentateuchal laws of Lev 11 and Deut 14:3-21, together with the various halakhoth ("ways") of the oral tradition later codified in the Mishnah and Talmudic writings. Such laws and traditions were primarily concerned with the production of food and with the appropriate social-setting for its consumption. From the 4th cent. BCE to the 2nd cent. CE and beyond, there is a wealth of evidence, from Greco-Roman authors as well as Jewish sources, that Jews were zealous in keeping themselves apart from Gentiles by strict arrangements over dining (*see* CLEAN AND UNCLEAN). Eating with Gentiles was an occasion fraught with possibilities for breaching the purity code—one of the most crucial aspects of the Mosaic law for the maintenance of the separate identity of Jewish ethnicity (*see* Acts 11:2). The reason centered upon the perception of Gentiles as ritually impure. Josephus, e.g., reports that Essenes were required to take a bath after contact with a Gentile (*J. W.* 2.150), and that a Jew could not safely eat any food prepared by a Gentile for fear that it too had in some way become ritually defiled. He further implies that the very *presence* of a Gentile leads to ritual impurity (*J. W.* 14.285; 18.94).

There may have been exceptions, but those Jews who permanently gave up the prohibitions that distinguished them from Gentiles ceased to be Jews, and those who did not adhere to a strict Jew-Gentile boundary were regarded as endangering the ethnic identity of the Jewish people and were expected to either conform to or abandon Judaism altogether. In Acts 16:1-3, Luke describes Paul as succumbing to just this sort of Jewish pressure over the circumcision of Timothy.

2. NT Christianity: Purity, spirit, and sacraments

Like OT Israel, a critical boundary marker for 1st cent. Christianity was a strict regime of purity for the community. Unlike the OT proscriptions, however, believers could associate freely with "outsiders" (1 Cor 5:9-10), although immoral believers were to be ostracized from the community (1 Cor 5:11). Practical issues of personal purity are outlined in detail in 1 Corinthians, which comments upon a variety of contentious issues (such as safeguarding Christian holiness, 1 Cor 5–6; and food sacrificed to idols, 1 Cor 8–10).

Another boundary marker was that of the Holy Spirit, the reception of which was seen to bring life and reconciliation to God. It demarcated, too, those who through sonship were designated as the people of God (Rom 8:5-17; Gal 5:16-26). The sacraments of baptism and Eucharist also demarcated those of the Christ-movement. Believers are baptized as an outward sign of inner belief, a process now distinct from the Jewish rites of ceremonial cleansing; and the Eucharist stands as a communal celebration of the new covenant, cognizant of Christ's willing self-sacrifice upon the cross. *See* COLLECTIVIST PERSONALITY; FOREIGN, FOREIGNER.

Bibliography: Fredrik Barth. *Ethnic Groups and Boundaries* (1969); Bruce Malina. *The New Testament World* (2001).

MARK FINNEY

COMMON LIFE. A common life refers to the self-defining elements shared by a group of people. The framing of a common life for Jews was based on belief in shared ancestry as children of Abraham, a covenant with one God, and obedience to the Law (Torah). Nascent Christian communities built on these basic Jewish elements of monotheism and covenant, and their common life, involved TABLE FELLOWSHIP, BAPTISM, and belief that Jesus was the promised MESSIAH and fulfillment of the LAW. *See* COLLECTIVIST PERSONALITY; COMMON; COMMUNION; COMMUNITY OF GOODS.

MARK FINNEY

COMMONWEALTH [πολίτευμα politeuma, πολιτεία politeia]. A commonwealth is a type of political unit, particularly where authority resides in the people, or voluntarily united autonomous political units. *Commonwealth* is also the translation for **politeuma** in Phil 3:20 (RSV), referring to heavenly CITIZENSHIP. The NRSV uses "commonwealth" for **politeia** in Eph 2:12 to refer to the Jews as a nation. *See also* 2 Macc 13:14.

RAYMOND H. REIMER

COMMUNICATION. *See* MESSENGER; TRAVEL AND COMMUNICATION IN THE NT; TRAVEL AND COMMUNICATION IN THE OT.

COMMUNION [κοινωνία konōnia]. This term, literally "sharing," is used in the NT for the sharing of believers in fellowship together and with God. It is most common in Paul (e.g., "called into fellowship with his son," 1 Cor 1:9; *see also* Phil 3:10; 2 Cor 13:13), and is especially connected with the common meal or Lord's Supper, where Christians "share" in the "body" and "blood" of Christ (1 Cor 10:16) in a manner that is comparable, in Paul's mind, to the TABLE FELLOWSHIP of pagans with their deities, and which, therefore, Christians should avoid (1 Cor 10:21). *See* COVENANT; EUCHARIST; LAST SUPPER; LORD'S SUPPER.

DENNIS E. SMITH

COMMUNITY. The concept of community within the OT exhibits distinct changes over what may be loosely described as three significant periods: the early tribal period, the period of the monarchy, and the exilic period. In the first, community existed as a tribal theocracy and was expressed by inclusion within a named family and tribe. It was during this period that the Israelites developed a concern for adherence to TORAH as an expression of their monotheistic worship of Yahweh, which in praxis meant obedience to the pentateuchal stipulations concerning, e.g., circumcision, food laws, purity, sacrifices, festivals, and the rejection of idolatry. The Torah also established significant rights of land

ownership (framed by an understanding of the Year of Jubilee), and a concern for justice outlined in references to the alien, widow, orphan, and the poor.

The period of the monarchy, by contrast, was defined by a move to hierarchical social structures, with the king at the apex, representing God to the people. The locale of God's very presence was established within the Jerusalem Temple, the center, also, of the royal throne and authority. The changes to the community's social structures during this period were significant, and included a system of taxation, the overturning of land rights and the confiscation of land, and conscription into military or court service. The disputes over royal succession eventually led to civil war, the fracture of the nation, and prolonged hostility. The monarchical succession of the Northern Kingdom was typically seen as leading the nation away from Yahweh and was characterized especially by the reign of Ahab. Consistent prophetic announcements of impending exile were realized in 721 BCE, when the Northern Kingdom was led into Assyrian exile. The royal succession of the Southern Kingdom, Judah, fared somewhat better, with the reform movements of some of the kings (e.g., Asa, Joash, Hezekiah, Josiah) seeking a return to more traditional ideals of a theocratic community. However, kings, such as Ahaz and Manasseh, stymied these ideals. The year 586 BCE saw both the destruction of Jerusalem and the exile of the community under the Babylonians.

The period of the exile and beyond saw the community attempting to preserve certain laws and traditions by codifying and narrating them into what would later become the TANAKH. At the same time a vital oral tradition began that would be later codified as the MISHNAH and Talmudic writings. Within such a framework, many of the post-exilic community, on its return to Judea, saw a return to the temple-cult as a vital element in reestablishing community life (Haggai, Zechariah), while it is clear, too, that there were groups writing polemically concerning the ongoing rebelliousness of the community and the imminence of divine judgment (Isa 56–66). As the OT period draws to a close there is a somewhat bleak picture of community life, with Malachi on the one hand concerned about standards of community morality, and Ezra and Nehemiah on the other speaking into a situation of communal weakness and fracture. The success of the post-exilic community was made, in part, by the framework of community life put into place by Ezra, who adumbrated the role of Torah in everyday life. Nevertheless, it is also at this juncture that the faithful within the community became seen increasingly in terms of a remnant (Ezra 9:8, 13-15; Isa 10:20-22; 11:11, 16; Jer 23:3).

The NT perspective on community was influenced by that of the OT (the Scriptures of the early Christ-movement were, after all, those of the Tanakh), and, as such, there is a fundamental continuity between what was the ekklēsia, the meeting together of God's people. The major disjuncture for Christianity was predicated upon the belief that in Jesus the first disciples had received a revelation and experience of God's messiah, and the call to establish a new community around him superseded that of normative kinship or ethnic ties (Luke 12:49-53). Indeed, in including those considered unclean in 1st cent. Israel as part of a new kin-group, Jesus found himself enveloped in controversy and antagonism from other elements of the wider Jewish community (e.g., Pharisees, Sadducees, Zealots). Jesus' ministry was focused upon establishing around himself a new Israel, in some senses a restoration of the twelve tribes, and one with an eschatological dimension within the kingdom of God (Matt 19:28; Acts 26:7; James 1:1; Rev 21:12). More scandalously, for Jesus' opponents, was the idea that both Samaritans and Gentiles would be welcomed into such a community and hence into the kingdom of God (Luke 2:31-32; 7:9; 10:25-37; John 4).

The post-Easter community envisaged itself in direct continuity with the ministry of Christ, being commissioned by him to carry on his work (Matt 28:18-20), and having a concern to preserve his teaching and to hand down various traditions to subsequent generations (1 Cor 11:23; 15:1-8; 1 Thess 1:5-7). Paul's conceptual language for such a community was that of "body"; the apostle conceives of the variety of members making up a single body (1 Cor 12), that is, as a body in Christ (Rom 12:5), and more specifically as the BODY OF CHRIST (1 Cor 12:27; Eph 4:12). Such a body, as a community of faith, is also conceived as devoid of categories of ethnicity, status, or sex (Gal 3:28). So, too, the body imagery requires that the community has an internal concern for its own members (Rom 14-15; 1 Cor 8:9ff.; 12:25-26), later reflected in Luke's idea of the COMMUNITY OF GOODS. The later deuteropauline literature reflects, in part, the institutional changes that occurred in OT Israel as it moved toward the monarchical period. The Pastoral Epistles e.g., envisage church community within a framework of pastoral officers (elders, deacons etc.), who both maintained authority over others, and had a concern for the survival of particular traditions and institutions.

The thrust of the NT writings in general envisages *community* as the people of God engaged in the worship of Jesus Christ as Lord and Savior and bearing witness to an eschatological kingdom open to all. *See* CHURCH, IDEA OF THE; CHURCH, LIFE AND ORGANIZATION OF THE; COMMON; KOINONIA.

MARK FINNEY

COMMUNITY OF GOODS.

COMMUNITY OF GOODS. The sharing of resources by the early Christ-movement, seen most explicitly in Acts 2:42-47; 4:32-37, and which may be referred to in the word KOINONIA. These texts depict the importance to the community of the selling of possessions

and the even distribution of resources (especially food, although note Acts 6:1ff.). Some detect here Luke's idealizing tendency of the first generation, either as part of an OT ideal (Deut 15:4, 11), or perhaps as inspiration for his contemporaries in implementing a regime with respect to the poor that Jesus had called for in his preaching (Luke 4:16-30). Others note the influence of Greek philosophical concepts that friends have all things in common (Plato, *Resp.* 5.449C; Aristotle *Eth. nic.* 8.9.1; 9.8.2). However, similar forms of sharing are evident within both the Essene and Qumran communities (1QS VI, 13-25), and the Essenes in particular, appear to have had some influence within Jerusalem and may have provided the early Christ-movement with an exemplary model. *See* COMMON.

Bibliography: Brian Capper. "Reciprocity and Ethics of Acts." I. H. Marshall & D. Peterson, eds. *Witness to the Gospel* (1998) 499–518.

MARK FINNEY

COMMUNITY RULE. *See* RULE OF THE COMMUNITY.

COMPANION [אָח ʾakh, רֵעָה raʿah, מֵרֵעַ mereʿ, אֹהֵב ʾohav, חָבֵר khaver; μέτοχος metochos, σύζυγος syzygos]. *Companion* designates someone who lives, travels, or works with another person. Originally, the English term *companion* derives from the Latin word that means "to eat with."

The translation *companion* refers to several words in Hebrew. Companions are "brothers" (ʾakh) in Josh 14:8; Ps 38:11. Job laments that his companions ("brothers") are not loyal (Job 6:15) and that he himself is a "companion (brother) of jackals" (Job 30:29). Samson's wedding attendants are called companions (Judg 14:11, 20), and his bride is given to his companion (mereʿ) (Judg 15:2, 6). Jephthah's daughter's female companions (raʿah, raʿoth) accompany her to mourn (Judg 11:37-38; *see also* Ps 45:14). One can metaphorically be a companion (raʾah) of gluttons (Prov 28:7). Daniel's companions (Dan 2:13, 17, 18), the bride's companions (Song 1:7; 8:13), and the wife of one's youth all are referred to as khaver. Isaiah uses khaver metaphorically for someone who is a "companion of thieves." Companions can also be "beloved" (ʾohav), as in Ps 88:18 and Prov 13:20.

Of the forty-four occurrences of the term in the NT, most are translations of metochos (esp. in Heb 1:9; 3:1, 14; 6:4; 12:8). The most startling imagery of "eating together" as companions comes from the meals that Jesus had with his disciples and outsiders, including the last meal. Jesus was "handed over" by his eating companion: "the one who eats my bread has lifted up his heel against me," in order to fulfill a text from Ps 41:9 (John 13:18). In Matthew's version, Jesus embraces Judas with a fervent kiss (26:48-50), but also addresses him as "Friend" and assures him that he has come for this purpose. Jesus, according to Matthew, invites Judas to come and share the cup of death with him. True companionship is tested when death comes and Judas—like all the other disciples—did not pass that test. Jesus heeds his own directive and eats with his "enemy" and drinks with him.

A most startling usage of the term comes in Phil 4:3: "I ask you also, my loyal companion." The Greek term underlying this (syzygos), taken literally (yokefellow), refers in classical Greek to a wife as companion. Jesus taught that companionship with soldiers or those who coerce you "to go with you one mile" can, by going a second mile, be a case of "loving the enemy" (Matt 5:41-42). Paul, quoting Jesus, urges that the hungry enemy is to be your companion at the table as you drink and eat together, a moral admonition that comes to Jesus and Paul through Prov 25:21.

Companionship language is not dominant in the NT. The term "BROTHER" or "SISTER" comes apparently closer to describing the bonds that unite Christians, and even the term "FRIEND" yields to the warmer term, which also stresses the common bond to the whole family of God. Paul had no subordinates but relates to his companions as equals and stresses the preposition "syn" or "co-." The word *companion* may come as close to expressing the original as any.

WILLIAM KLASSEN

COMPASS. *See* ORIENTATION.

COMPASSION. *See* LOVE IN THE NT; LOVE IN THE OT; MERCY.

COMPLETE, TO BE [τελέω teleō]. A phrase appearing some seventy-six times in the NRSV, in the NT. It ranges in meaning from "to be perfect," "to be finished" (Luke 12:50; 14:28), and to be fully developed. It applies to tasks, people, and groups, being mature or grown up, and to communities of faith whose joy is to be complete (John 15:11; 16:24; 1 John 1:3). Paul even describes it as the pastoral task, "to work together with you for your joy" (2 Cor 2:1) in which they are "stitched together" into one. According to Paul this, "is what we pray for, that you may become perfect" (2 Cor 13:10). As a Jew Paul knew how important it is for God's people to be complete, to be one.

New Testament writers use the term καταρτίζω katartizo to describe knitting or bonding together in faith (1 Cor 1:10; 1 Thess 3:10). Likewise Jesus gave his energies to bring his disparate band of female and male disciples into one, to heal his broken people and to mend those whose lives were torn apart through suffering. In the end it was through his own alienation from God that he was able to make complete his devotion to the world. He offered a sacrifice, the benefits of which are universal. Through suffering the pain of his

brokenness he was able to achieve an ultimate union of all that is incomplete. "It is complete ("finished," NRSV)" were his last words from the cross (John 19:28-30).

Completeness is also often implied when translating the Hebrew term שָׁלֵם shalem, which has entered the English language as a greeting. *See* SHALOM.

Bibliography: Carol Newsom. *The Self as Symbol* (2003).

WILLIAM KLASSEN

CONANIAH kon´uh-ni´uh [Kethibh כּוֹנַנְיָהוּ konanya-hu; Qere כָּנַנְיָהוּ]. "Yahu has established." 1. A Levite, Hezekiah's chief officer in charge of contributions and tithes (2 Chr 31:12-13).

2. A Levitical chief under King Josiah (2 Chr 35:9).

CONCEIVE. *See* BARREN, BARRENNESS; BIRTH; CHILD, CHILDREN.

CONCENTRIC. *Concentric* denotes a PARALLELISM in the structure, syntax, or themes of a text. This parallelism may take the form either of a step- or CHIASTIC-parallelism in a few verses (e.g., 2 Thess 3:6-12) or, more properly, a ring form in pericopae (e.g., Mark 2:1–3:6) or whole books (e.g., John's Gospel). The parallelism(s) may be theologically significant or may simply be used to demonstrate literary artistry. *See* RHETORICAL CRITICISM.

L. GREGORY BLOOMQUIST

CONCISION. *See* MUTILATION.

CONCUBINE [פִּילֶגֶשׁ pileghesh]. Pileghesh is a loan word of unknown but possibly Indo-European origin. Its English translation *concubine* is unfortunate because it brings with it cultural ideas that do not seem to fit many of its uses in the OT. Scholars tend to assume that a concubine is a slave. Such an assumption is not warranted by the texts themselves. In most texts, the term appears to mean a WIFE of lower status. Bilhah, Rachel's maid, is called both "wife" (אִשָּׁה ʾishah, Gen 30:4) and "concubine" (pileghesh, Gen 35:22). In Judg 19, an unnamed concubine's partner is called both HUSBAND and BRIDEGROOM (אִישׁ ʾish; חָתָן khathan); the woman's father is called father-in-law. Concubines are named as mothers in genealogies more often than wives (Gen 22:23-24; 36:12; Judg 8:31; 1 Chr 2:46, 48; 7:14). Scholars who assert that concubines were slaves maintain that Exod 21:7-11, the law about men's treatment of designated female slaves, regulates a man's treatment of his concubines, although the term itself is not used. This stance seems to fit more with contemporary cultural assumptions about the word than with the way it is actually utilized.

In the case of Judg 19, the unnamed pileghesh seems to be free in that she moves from her husband's to her father's house. Her partner indicates emotional attachment by following her and trying to induce her to return to him. Her status as wife is shown through the fact that her rape is seen as an offense against her husband, serious enough to warrant war.

In the early monarchy, a distinction is made between wives and concubines. Both David and Solomon are accredited with more concubines than wives, perhaps indicating a harem; see also Dan 5:21, 23). When David flees from Absalom, he leaves ten concubines to care for the palace (2 Sam 15:16). After usurping the throne, Absalom publicly sleeps with these concubines to make himself "odious" in David's sight and to gain support for his cause (2 Sam 16:21-22). Once David reclaims the throne, they are shut up under guard; their status is "widowhood" (2 Sam 20:3). These instances render questionable the assumption that the concubines hold the status of slaves. In Esther, each virgin moves from the harem of the virgins to the harem of the concubines after her night with the king (Esth 2:14).

The use of pileghesh in Ezek 23:20 does not fit any of the above instances. The NRSV translates it as "paramours." It is a term applied to the Egyptians as male lovers of Oholibah, and metaphorical representative of Jerusalem. Perhaps calling them "concubine" may add an additional insult to the already offensive characterization of the Egyptians in this verse.

Bibliography: Meike Bal. Death and Dissymmetry (1988); Ken Stone. "Sexual Practice and the Structure of Prestige: The Case of the Disputed Concubines." SBLSP 32 (1993) 554–573.

MARY E. SHIELDS

CONDEMNATION. Derives from the Lat. condemnare, using the intensive prefix com and the verb damnare, "to harm, damage." In biblical usage, "condemnation" is both the declaration of guilt, usually by God acting as judge, and the resulting sentence.

The word condemnation seldom occurs in English translations of the OT. Where it does, it is usually a synonym for "judgment," as in Prov 19:29: "Condemnation [שֶׁפֶט shefet] is ready for scoffers, and flogging for the backs of fools." The idea that God judges both persons and nations is commonplace in the OT, but such judgment ordinarily occurs within the course of human history (e.g., Jer 2:31-37). Belief in eternal life is a comparatively late development (e.g., Dan 12:2, from the 2nd cent. BCE), and so, correspondingly, was the expectation of a final judgment. In subsequent centuries, a range of beliefs existed concerning the eschatological condemnation of the wicked, whether to annihilation or to eternal punishment. For example, the Jewish sectarians at Qumran were told that sinners would be "punished with fire" (1QpHab X, 5, 13), while the book of Jubilees says that the wicked are "appointed to destruction" (36:10). Such condemnation

was regarded by Jewish authors as just punishment, a sentence necessitated by the sinner's own actions, and not as a verdict rendered selectively or capriciously by God.

Condemnation is sometimes used in the English NT to translate the related words krima (κρίμα, "verdict") and krisis (κρίσις, both "decision" and "punishment"), both derived from a verbal root meaning "to divide." So krima in Mark 12:40, "They devour widows' houses and for the sake of appearance say long prayers. They will receive the greater condemnation," and krisis in John 5:28-29, "Do not be astonished at this; for the hour is coming when all who are in their graves will hear his voice and will come out . . . those who have done evil, to the resurrection of condemnation." Common elements are the verses' negative force and eschatological horizon. More often, krima and krisis are simply translated "judgment," whether in reference to the present (mostly in John, e.g., 9:39; 5:22) or the future (Rom 2:3; John 3:24). This judgment is usually but not always (e.g., Rom 11:33; Matt 12:18) negative.

Only Paul uses the intensified and less ambiguous forms katakrima (κατάκριμα) and katakrisis (κατάκρισις): Adam's "trespass led to condemnation [katakrima] for all" (Rom 5:18); "For if there was glory in the ministry of condemnation [katakrisis], much more does the ministry of justification abound in glory" (2 Cor 3:9). Paul assumes that humanity already stands under judgment, "condemnation," a situation remedied by the work of Christ. Hence the most famous use of the word, in Rom 8:1: "There is therefore now no condemnation [katakrima] for those who are in Christ Jesus." Sin's verdict, and so also its punishment, has been overturned.

Bibliography: John Collins. The Apocalyptic Imagination. An Introduction to Jewish Apocalyptic Literature, 2nd ed. (1998); Craig C. Hill. In God's Time: The Bible and the Future (2002).

CRAIG C. HILL

CONDUIT. See JERUSALEM; WATER WORKS.

CONFESSION [ὁμολογία homologia; ὁμολογέω homologeō]. Confession can involve either a public acknowledgment of sin or a declaration of something (including one's faith). Both ideas are of considerable importance in the Bible.

Confession of SIN is the dominant form of confession in the OT, where both the Hebrew noun and verb generally refer to the open admission of sin, either by the community or by the individual. Such confession is mentioned in the Pentateuch, where the penitent person was required to "confess (הִתְוַדָּה hithwaddah) the sin that you have committed" (Lev 5:5; Num 5:7). There are frequent examples of confession of sin (Num

21:7; Josh 7:19; Judg10:10; 2 Chr 33:12, 13, 19; Neh 9:2, 3), and it is mandated (Lev 26:40; Ezra 10:11; 1 Kgs 8:33-34; 2 Chr 6:36-39; 7:14; Bar 1:14). Notable examples of confession of sin include what was termed in later Christian tradition "the Penitential Psalms" (e.g., Pss 38:18; 51:3-4) and the prayers of Ezra (10:1), Nehemiah (1:6-7), and Daniel (9:4-20).

Proverbs states the general principle: the "one who confesses and forsakes (transgressions) will obtain mercy" (Prov 28:13; note Sir 4:26: "Do not be ashamed to confess your sins"). This open confession initiated God's forgiveness and could bring healing (e.g., Ps 32:5).

To confess sin involves recognizing that God is to be worshiped and obeyed by God's people: "When your people Israel, having sinned against you, are defeated . . . but turn again to you, confess your name, pray and plead with you . . . , then hear in heaven, forgive the sin of your people Israel" (1 Kgs 9:33-34; note 2 Macc 7:37). Such recognition of God moves naturally into praise and thanksgiving; the same Hebrew noun (תּוֹדָה todhah) that is rendered "confession" in Josh 7:19 and Ezra 10:11 is translated as "thanksgiving" (Pss 50:23; 95:2; 100:4), "thank offering" (2 Chr 29:31), or "thanksgiving sacrifice" (Lev 7:12, 13, 15).

In the NT the verb *confess* is used five times to speak of confession of sin (Matt 3:6; Mark 1:5; Acts 19:18; Jas 5:16; 1 John1:9). As in the OT, such confession promised God's forgiveness: "If we confess our sins, he who is faithful and just will forgive us our sins and cleanse us from all unrighteousness" (1 John 1:9). Acknowledgment of sin was necessary when false views were circulating about God and sin: "If we say that we have not sinned, we make him a liar, and his word is not in us" (1 John 1:10).

Sometimes it was necessary to seek the forgiveness of others in the community. "Therefore confess your sins to one another, and pray for one another, so that you may be healed" (Jas 5:16). A similar association of faith, forgiveness, and healing is found in the teaching of Jesus (Matt 9:2-6).

The idea of confessing one's faith is similar to the notion of bearing witness to it. In this context there is a public statement of acknowledgment that makes clear where one stands. In the book of Acts, e.g., "the Sadducees say that there is no resurrection (of the dead), or angel, or spirit; but the Pharisees acknowledge (literally, *confess*) all three" (Acts 23:8). Similarly, in his defense at Caesarea before his accusers Paul "admits" (literally, *confesses*) that "according to the Way, which they call a sect, I worship the God of our ancestors" (Acts 24:14). This is a public declaration of Christian faith made in hostile circumstances before a Roman governor. Stephen was another faithful witness who boldly confessed his faith and paid the price of martyrdom (Acts 7:58-60; 22:20).

In the Gospels Jesus insisted that his disciples were required to make an open declaration of their allegiance to him: "Everyone therefore who acknowledges (literally, *confesses*) me before others, I also will acknowledge before my Father in heaven" (Matt 10:32); the converse was also stated: "but whoever denies me before others, I also will deny before my Father in heaven" (Matt 10:33; *see* Luke 12:8-9, where the eschatological element is brought out by reference to the Son of Man's acknowledgment or denial "before the angels of God"). Such a declaration of faith in Jesus would often be difficult (note the danger of being ashamed, Mark 8:38) and subject one to persecution. Peter acknowledged Jesus as the Messiah at Caesarea Philippi (Mark 8:29), though he later denied his Lord (Mark 14:66-72).

In John's Gospel, John the Baptist is clearly presented as a witness for Jesus: "He confessed and did not deny it, but confessed, 'I am not the Messiah'" (John 1:20). He functions simply as the prophetic voice that prepares the way for Jesus, the promised Messiah (John 1:23), as predicted in book of Isaiah (Isa 40:3). As John puts it simply: "He [i.e., John the Baptist] came as a witness to testify to the light. He himself was not the light, but he came to testify to the light" (John 1:7-8).

Paul insisted that believers declare their allegiance to Christ in the form of a public "confession": "If you confess with your lips that Jesus is Lord and believe in your heart that God raised him from the dead, you will be saved" (Rom 10:9). Salvation was provided in the gospel and appropriated through faith (Rom 1:15-17); public declaration of that faith was not optional (Rom 10:10). There is a similar confession of faith noted in 1 Corinthians ("Jesus is Lord," 1 Cor 12:3; also 8:6). The importance of confessing Christ's lordship is supported by the fact that Christians were baptized "in the name of the Lord" (Acts 2:38; 8:16; 10:48; 19:5).

In 2 Corinthians Paul noted the COLLECTION of the Macedonians for the Christians in Jerusalem would demonstrate not only their generosity in sharing with the poor but also give tangible evidence of their "obedience to the confession (**homologia**) of the gospel of Christ" (2 Cor 9:13). Faith in Christ was seen as issuing in ethical consequences. In a similar way Jesus had declared that faith must issue in actual obedience to God (Matt 7:21-23; Luke 13:25-27); James too had insisted on the demonstration of one's faith by one's work (2:20-26).

The PASTORAL LETTERS present Timothy as a Christian worker who "made the good confession [of faith] in the presence of many witnesses" (1 Tim 6:12), probably at his baptism or appointment as community leader; his public testimony was seen as modeled upon that of "Christ Jesus, who in his testimony before Pontius Pilate made the good confession" (1 Tim 6:13; John 18:33-37). It was a precarious thing to declare one's allegiance in hostile surroundings (John 9:22; 12:42)! For some formulaic confessions of faith *see* Rom 1:3-4; Gal 3:27-28; 1 Tim 3:16b.

In Heb 3:1 two possible ways of understanding confession are noted: either "that which is confessed" (so NEB) or "the act of confessing" (so NEB margin); the former is preferable—"the (apostle and) high priest of whom our confession speaks." In this context, Jesus' ministry is contrasted with that of Moses; Christians profess their faith in Jesus, who is Son over the house of God, whereas Moses is only a servant in it (Heb 3:1-6). It is the continuing "confession" of Jesus Christ as their "great high priest" that the readers of Hebrews are repeatedly urged to maintain and "hold fast" (Heb 4:14; 10:23). Their trust rests in a sympathizing and merciful high priest, the victorious Son of God, who has entered the holy of holies on behalf of his people (Heb 4:14-16; 6:19-20).

In John's letters the basic confession is that Jesus is "the Son of God" (1 John 4:15). It is important to confess faith in Jesus as a real human being: "Every spirit that confesses that Jesus Christ has come in the flesh is from God, and every spirit that does not confess Jesus is not from God" (1 John 4:2-3). Such a confession stood in sharp contrast to the false teachers, who denied the reality of the incarnation: "Many deceivers have gone out into the world, those who do not confess that Jesus Christ has come in the flesh; any such person," the community is warned, "is the deceiver and the antichrist!" (2 John 7).

In the book of Revelation believers who are faithful to their Lord are encouraged with the promise that Christ himself "will confess your name before my Father and before his angels" (Rev 3:5). In Pergamum the steadfast Antipas had already suffered, being put to death for his faith (Rev 2:13), and it was quite possible that there might be others who would be thrown into prison or otherwise tested (e.g., Rev 2:10; 17:14). *See* FORGIVENESS; HERESY; MARTYR; SIN.

Bibliography: O. Cullmann. *The Earliest Christian Confessions* (1949); J. N. D. Kelly. *Early Christian Creeds*, 3rd ed. (1976); R. N. Longenecker. *New Wine into Fresh Wineskins: Contextualizing the Early Confessions* (1999).

ALLISON ALBERT TRITES

CONFIDENCE. *See* BOLDNESS, CONFIDENCE IN FAITH; FAITH, FAITHFULNESS.

CONFIRMATION. The rite in the ancient church in which baptized people received laying on of hands and anointing with oil for obtaining the Holy Spirit. In the Western church from the 5th cent. it is called **confirmatio** (confirmation). In the Middle Ages, it was understood as one's own sacramental confirmation at an "age of (moral) understanding," and after a course of instruction, and of baptismal vows. This has persisted among Roman Catholics and mainline Protestants. In the Eastern church, it is called **chrism** (anointing).

Although anointing with oil and laying on of hands at or after baptism is not explicitly witnessed in the NT, precedent for it was found in Mark 1:10 and par., where Jesus receives the Holy Spirit at his baptism; Acts 8, where the Spirit comes upon new believers when the apostles lay hands on them; and Acts 10:38, where Jesus is said to be anointed with the Spirit.

ROBERT E. VAN VOORST

CONFISCATE חָרַם kharam, יָרַשׁ yarash, לָקַח laqakh; Aram. עֲנַשׁ 'anash; διαρπάζω diarpazō]. The royal seizure of a subject's economic assets, often land, as punishment or for the king's political gain (*see* Num 27:1-10; 1 Kgs 21; Ezra 7:26; 10:8; Tob 1:20; 2 Macc 3:13). Israelite land was inalienable (Lev 25:23-24), equally distributed among the tribes as inheritance (Josh 13:1–21:25), protected by boundary markers (Deut 19:14; Prov 23:10-11) and, when held as collateral, returned in the Jubilee Year (Lev 25). Israelite kings were held to this law (Deut 17:14-20), yet Samuel cautions that kings will confiscate the best land to reward courtiers (1 Sam 8:14). Israelite monarchs legally confiscated land belonging to convicted criminals. JEZEBEL secured witnesses to represent NABOTH as a blasphemer (1 Kgs 21:8-10), a capital offense (Exod 22:28; Lev 24: 3-23; Deut 13:10; 17:5; 19:15), thus providing the legal grounds for AHAB, as the wronged party in the broken contract, to confiscate the land.

Bibliography: John Andrew Dearman. *Property Rights in Eighth-Century Prophets: The Conflict and Its Background* (1988); Christopher J. H. Wright. *God's People in God's Land: Family, Land, and Property in the Old Testament* (1990).

DEBORAH A. APPLER

CONFLATE READINGS IN THE OT. *See* TEXT, HEBREW, HISTORY OF.

CONFLICT מִלְחָמָה milkhamah, רִיב riv; ἀγών agōn, ἀγωνίζομαι agōnizomai]. Conflict in the Bible includes violence and suffering. In the OT milkhamah (from לָחַם lakham) has a range of meanings: from shoving to crowding, from conflict to antagonism; from battle to weapons of war and experts of war. The noun occurs 320 times. The verb, which occurs 168 times, means "to do battle with, to fight." Noun and verb may appear jointly; when they do, their combined force points to Yahweh's participation as a warring God with and against Yahweh's people.

The theology of war involves political strategy and often reflects divine intervention: Yahweh calls Israel and goes with them into battle, which involves God's self, character, and actions. **Milkhamah** pertains to Israel's adversaries during wilderness wanderings toward the promised land (in Exodus and Numbers), during the conquest and settlement of the land (in Joshua and

Judges), and during Saul's and David's wars (in Samuel, Kings, and Chronicles). Within Deuteronomistic framing, Yahweh supports the Israelites in war but threatens the nation with judgment when Yahweh's commandments are not followed. The Chronicler suggests a war ideology independent from the DEUTERONOMISTIC HISTORIAN in Samuel and Kings. Sometimes Yahweh fights, thus reinforcing promises of salvation from their enemies. In the divided kingdom and through the deterioration into exile, conflicts and wars intensify within Israel and between Judah and Israel (in Nehemiah, Isaiah, and Jeremiah). As displacement intensifies, apocalyptic conflicts emerge, until the people yearn for the "day of Yahweh," which provokes judgment over past and future wars against Israel. However, in apocalyptic time, both milkhamah and shalom (wholeness or peace) seem possible.

Riv, to quarrel, appears sixty-seven times in Genesis, Judges, Psalms, Hosea, Jeremiah, Nehemiah, and Isaiah. Riv and its derivatives have a variety of meanings: extrajudicial conflict specifies disputes between groups, concerning spaces, provisions, or war. Prejudicial conflict involves formulaic, accusative speech when conflict between a person and group ends in a way that is detrimental to the weaker party in the dispute. Judicial or legal conflict concerns the formal process of rendering judgment involving individuals and the society. Disruption of the legal process perverts justice in any dispute. In theological imagination among the prophets, a riv occurs when and where Yahweh is invoked during a dispute with the petitioner's enemies, or in salvific announcements or divine judgments against the nations (including Israel). Yahweh is also the object of a riv (Job's dispute with God).

In the NT, due to Hellenistic influences, conflict (agōn, agōnizomai) involves a contest or fight amid great strain, an intensity of forces, or an athletic contest. Agōn also indicates denial, a focus on provisional ends (as in athletic discipline, not asceticism). Figuratively, conflict is like running a race while bearing internal inconsistencies, personal suffering, or struggle over particular beliefs. Agōn occurs largely in the NT Letters. For example, Paul labors with great strain on behalf of the church, though supported by prayer and unity of spirit.

Agōn describes the intense, physical, mental, spiritual, and enigmatic soul-searching and suffering of Jesus at Gethsemane. The final conflict is martyrdom for Jesus; however, the goal of this loss is universal salvation.

CHERYL A. KIRK-DUGGAN

CONFUSE, TO. [בָּלַל balal, בָּלַע bala', הָמַם hamam, תִּמָּהוֹן timmahon; ταράσσω tapassō, συγχέω syncheō]. In the OT the most common words for confuse also connote mixing, destruction, noisemaking, terror, or bewilderment. God is sometimes depicted as the author of confusion. God confuses those who exhibit inordinate pride (Gen 11:7), the enemies of Israel (Exod 23:27; 1 Sam 7:10), and those who disregard the covenant through disobedience and faithlessness (Deut 28:28). Confusion results in the profusion of tongues at Babel, the defeat of enemies, and judgment for those who ignore the covenant. In some of the prophets, confusion is the result of Israel's obedience to poor leadership (Isa 3:12; 9:16). When confusion is mentioned in the NT, it often refers to the agitation and trouble caused by false teaching (Gal 1:7, 5:10). Confusion results when believers follow someone or something other than Christ and apostolic teaching.

DAVID JENSEN

CONGREGATION [קָהָל qahal, עֵדָה 'edhah; ἐκκλησία ekklēsia, συναγωγή synagōgē]. The English terms *congregation* or *assembly* or *gathering* can be used to translate a variety of terms in the OT, the LXX, and the NT.

A. Congregation in the OT, LXX, and Second Temple Judaism
B. Congregation in the NT
C. Congregational Self-designations

A. Congregation in the OT, LXX, and Second Temple Judaism

There are two commonly used roots for a gathering of people, assembly, or congregation in the OT: qahal and 'edhah. Qahal, which in its most basic sense relates to a coming-together of people, is used for a gathering of peoples or nations (Gen 28:3; 35:11; 48:4; Jer 50:9), a company engaging in war (Num 22:4; Ezek 38:4, 7, 13), a public or civic assembly (Prov 5:14; Job 30:28), a gathering of people to listen to a speaker or to engage in worship (Deut 4:10; 9:10; 2 Chr 20:5, 14; Neh 5:13), and a group of returning exiles or the restored community after the return (Jer 31:8; Ezra 10:12-14; Neh 7:66). The twenty-one occurrences of qahal in the Pentateuch occur in passages usually associated with the PRIESTLY WRITER. The author of Deuteronomy uses the term in describing those who were or were not admitted to the "assembly of Yahweh" (Deut 23:1-9). Other occurrences in Deuteronomy use qahal in reference to the "day of assembly" at Horeb or other assemblies for cultic purposes (e.g., Deut 4:10; 9:10; 18:16; 31:30). This cultic usage continues in the DEUTERONOMISTIC HISTORY (Joshua through Kings) generally. Similarly, the Chronicler tends to use the term qahal (which occurs thirty-three times) in a more formal or technical sense in reference to the complete "assembly of Israel" gathered for worship or for feasts or fasts to worship Yahweh (2 Chr 1:3, 5; 6:3, 12; 7:8; 20:5, 14; 30:2, 4, 13, 17, 23-25). It is in this cultic usage that the term qahal most clearly overlaps with the use of 'edhah in other parts of the OT.

A distinction between qahal and ʿedhah, which is apparent in places like Lev 4:13 and Num 20:2-10 (Priestly Writer), seems to be between the congregation (ʿedhah) as a designation of the people and the assembly (qahal) as a reference to the congregation coming together on a specific occasion.

The second main Hebrew term, ʿedah, is commonly used as a corporate designation for the people of Israel or for the organized gathering of the Israelites for social, political, and, especially, cultic purposes. Thus, for instance, the author of Exodus uses the term to refer to the collective body of the Israelites when Yahweh instructs the leaders (Moses and/or Aaron) to address the "whole congregation of Israel" on issues concerning the festival of Passover and unleavened bread (Exod 12), the supply of food in the wilderness (Exod 16), and the tabernacle and offerings (Exod 35). A similar usage in reference to the corporate body of Israelites continues in the Levitical code in connection with worship, including guilt offerings (Lev 4) and gatherings at the tent of meeting or tabernacle (e.g., Lev 8). The use of ʿedhah as a somewhat technical corporate designation for the people of Israel particularly stands out throughout the book of Numbers (e.g., Num 14–16).

The DEAD SEA SCROLLS attest to the continued use of qahal in the Second Temple period in a manner comparable to the OT, sometimes in reference to a gathered assembly for cultic or other purposes. Apparently influenced by Deut 23, the *Messianic Rule of the Congregation* uses qahal for the assembly of the congregation (ʿedhah), for instance (1QSa = 1Q28 2:4). The *Temple Scroll* uses qahal for the assembly gathered to engage in sacrifices during festivals, including the DAY OF ATONEMENT (11QT 16:15-18; 26:3-13). In the Teacher of Righteousness' letter to the leadership in Jerusalem (the so-called *Halakhic Letter*), the author uses the term qahal as a self-designation for the Qumran group (4QMMT). Elsewhere in the scrolls the term is sometimes used in a pejorative manner of assembled adversaries (1QM 11:16) or of the "seekers of smooth things" (the Pharisees) specifically (4QpNah 3:5, 7).

The translators of the LXX (traditionally 3rd cent. BCE) tended to use the Greek ekklēsia (from ekkaleō, "to call out, or summon") for qahal and synagōgē (from synagō, "gather together") for ʿedah. Though synagōgē was used to render both qahal and ʿedhah (e.g., Exod 16:3; Lev 4:13), ekklēsia was apparently never used to render edah in the LXX. Both Greek terms played a role in the subsequent history of self-designations among various groups of Judeans (Jews) and followers of Jesus.

B. Congregation in the NT

Some among the early followers of Jesus adopted the Greek term ekklēsia, often translated as *church* or, more appropriately, as either *assembly* or *congregation*, in reference to the gathering of Jesus-followers and, quite often, as a self-designation or title for an ongoing group or association. Chronologically, our first evidence for this usage appears in Paul's first letter "to the congregation (church) of Thessalonians" in Macedonia (1 Thess 1:1), which also happens to be our earliest surviving evidence (usually dated about 49 CE) for the Jesus-movement as a whole. Beyond his use of the term as a designation for the recipients in the letter's address, Paul employs the term a second time in praising the Thessalonians for being "imitators of the congregations (or churches) of God in Christ Jesus which are in Judea" in their endurance through suffering (1 Thess 2:14). Paul's use of "congregation" as a term for local groups of Jesus-followers in various locales is further confirmed in Paul's subsequent letters, including 1 Corinthians where it occurs twenty-two times, sometimes with the added descriptor "congregation of God" (1 Cor 1:2; 10:32; 11:16). The use of ekklēsia for a local gathering of Jesus-followers in a particular locale (rather than notions of a trans-local church, which developed later) is further clarified by Paul's reference to groups of Jesus-followers who gathered in a particular home, as in the phrase "the congregation in their house," or house-church (τῇ κατ᾽ οἶκον αὐτῶν ἐκκλησίᾳ tē kat oikon autōn ekklēsia; 1 Cor 16:19; Rom 16:5; 2 Col 4:15; *see* HOUSE CHURCH).

Some other NT authors (though not all) used the term ekklēsia to refer to a local congregation of Jesus-followers. The author of Matthew projects the term back into his story of Jesus (Matt 16:18; 18:17), the author of James incidentally mentions the "elders of the congregation" (5:14), and the elder who wrote 3 John takes it for granted that his addressees speak of their communal identity using the term ekklēsia. John the seer also calls the local groups he addresses in western Asia Minor "congregations," particularly in the opening letters of Revelation (1:4; 2:1, 8, 12, 18; 3:1, 7, 14). Similarly, the author of Luke–Acts consistently uses this idiom in his second volume to identify local gatherings of Jesus-followers at Jerusalem (e.g., Acts 5:11; 8:1-3; 11:22), at Antioch (11:26; 13:1), and at Ephesus (20:17). (There are also some apparent uses in the LXX regarding the history of the Israelites, as in Acts 7:38). A more generalizing or trans-local tendency is apparent at points in Acts, as when the author speaks of the "congregation [singular] throughout Judea, Galilee, and Samaria" (Acts 9:31). The two instances in the book of Hebrews, where ekklēsia is used of a heavenly assembly and the "assembly of the firstborn who are enrolled in heaven," do not seem to reflect Pauline usage for a local group, however (Heb 2:12; 12:23).

Other early Christian authors, including the author of *1 Clement* and Ignatius of Antioch, use the term for specific, local gatherings of Jesus-followers in a manner comparable to Paul. However, Ignatius (ca. 110 CE) provides the earliest attested use of the phrase "universal congregation," or "catholic church," in generalizing from the local congregations to a broader—apparently translocal—concept of the church (Ignatius, *Smyrn.* 8:2).

Although ekklēsia became the predominant title, we should not assume that all groups of Jesus-followers in the early period adopted the same self-designations. In fact, the evidence for congregational terminology among Jewish and other associations in the Greco-Roman world further suggests that variety of terminology from one group to the next, rather than uniformity, may have been the norm.

C. Congregational Self-designations

Although the LXX's use of ekklēsia (to translate qahal) may have played some role in Christian usage, it is important not to neglect the real-life cultural contexts of the early Christians in the Greco-Roman world, where there were many other associations and guilds who adopted similar group self-designations. Most important, the term ekklēsia was consistently used within Greek cities to refer to the political assembly of the male citizens (the institution of the people, δῆμος dēmos), as is reflected in Acts 19:39, for instance. Within the civic context of the Greek east, terms such as ekklēsia were, therefore, among the natural titles to adopt in reference to a gathering of individuals on a particular occasion or as an ongoing title for a group, guild, or association. Although not widely attested, we do in fact have at least two cases—at Aspendos in Cilicia and on the island of Delos—where an ongoing association used ekklēsia in a manner similar to some early followers of Jesus (*IGLAM* 1381–82; *CIG* 2271).

Perhaps more important, there were many other synonymous or analogous terms for a congregation or gathering of people that were adopted by occupational, religious, and ethnic-based associations of various sorts in a manner comparable to usage among the informal groups of Jesus-devotees. The practice among groups of diaspora Judeans (Jews) is instructive in regard to the variety and interchangeability of self-designations with the general meaning of "congregation." Although the term *synagogue* is attested quite often in inscriptions as a self-designation for a gathering or ongoing association of Judeans in the diaspora, there were also groups of Jews who called themselves oikos (lit. "household"), katoikountes ("settlement"), laos ("people"), ethnos, hetairoi ("associates"), and synodos. Furthermore, as with the title ekklēsia, there were also "pagan" groups with no apparent Jewish connection that used the term synagōgē as a self-designation for the association, as in the case of the "synagogue of Zeus" in Bithynia (*IApam-Bith* 35). Beyond this, there were many other similar terms adopted by Greco-Roman associations, including synedrion, synodos, koinon, hetaireia, thiasos, and mystai. Not surprisingly, we have evidence that outsiders ("pagans"), as well as both Jews and Christians themselves, could sometimes confuse these groups,

drawing on the same terminological field in describing groups of Jews or Jesus-followers (e.g., Josephus, *Ant.* 14.215-16, 235; Pliny the Younger, *Ep.* 10.97.78; Lucian, *Peregr.* 11; Ignatius, *Eph.* 12.2; 19.1; Tertullian, *Apol.* 38–39). *See* ASSOCIATIONS, COLLEGIA, CLUBS; CHURCH, IDEA OF; SANHEDRIN; SYNAGOGUE; TABERNACLE.

Bibliography: Philip A. Harland. *Associations, Synagogues, and Congregations: Claiming a Place in Ancient Mediterranean Society* (2003).

PHILIP A. HARLAND

CONGREGATION, MOUNT OF. *See* MOUNT OF ASSEMBLY.

CONIAH koh-ni′uh [כָּנְיָהוּ konyahu]. Alternate name for Jehoiachin (Jer 37:1). *See* JEHOIACHIN.

CONJURING. *See* DIVINATION; MAGIC, MAGICIAN.

CONQUER. [נָכָה nakhah, יָרַשׁ yarash; καθαίρω kathairō, κατακυριεύω katakyrieuō, κατεργάζομαι katergazomai, κρατέω krateō]. In English, *conquer* has the sense of overpowering something or someone to the point of surrender. In the OT, various verbs or phrases are translated as *conquer*. The verbs nakhah (1 Kgs 15:2; 2 Kgs 16:5), "to smite," and yarash (Judg 11:23, 24), "to inherit private property," or to "dispossess," can be translated as *conquer*. In the deuterocanonical books and the NT, the concept is found chiefly in the term nikaō, though other terms also appear. The term nikaō means chiefly "to conquer," whether it is to prevail in battle or to win in competition.

Conquer as a concept includes an obvious assumption that there are two sides, whether in war, a lawsuit, or a competition. In the OT, to conquer someone meant to defeat them. This meaning tends to hold throughout the rest of the Bible, though the means of conquest shift during the Second Temple period. Nowhere is this so pronounced as in 4 Maccabees (e.g., 1:11; 6:33; 7:4, 11; 13:7; 16:14; 17:24), where reason and endurance conquer emotions and those oppressors whose wrath the devout Jews had to endure. This notion apparently reaches a fuller fruition in Revelation, when conquerers lay down their lives like the Lamb (Rev 7:9-17). In the Johannine theology of the NT, the contest is spiritual (John 16:33), and those who conquer evil are usually engaged in an internalized battle (1 John 2:13).

L. JEAN SHELDON

CONQUEST OF CANAAN. *See* ISRAEL, HISTORY OF.

CONSCIENCE [συνείδησις syneidēsis]. Conscience (syneidēsis) is important to moral theology and practice. However, the Bible's contribution to this notion is not easily determined. There is no corresponding term in Hebrew, and where the Greek word translated by *conscience* is used by the NT, an older sense of syneidēsis as self-consciousness, especially awareness of one's guilt or negative feelings, may be all that is required by the text.

This article examines *conscience* in six sections, covering all biblical occurrences.

A. Our Notion of Conscience

Those seeking a straightforward definition of *conscience* are understandably puzzled by vagueness and inconsistency in their sources. *Conscience*, they read, is an inner voice, a capacity in the soul, a self-awareness, or a witness. Its function, they learn, is to guide conduct, give laws, or call to account, to judge against norms for all individuals and societies, or determine harmony between conduct and moral beliefs, or to excuse, justify, or sanction behavior, to render verdicts of guilt or innocence.

1. Uses of the term

Much language about conscience employs legal metaphors, invoking the roles of legislator, prosecutor, witness, and judge, and transferring those metaphors to an interior moral faculty. When concise definitions of a term are difficult, it is preferable to examine its uses. *Conscience* is employed in many familiar phrases.

Except in expressions like *the dictates* (or *the voice*) *of conscience*, the uses are negative or positive. Negatively, a conscience may be bad, unquiet, troubled, stricken, guilty, or even seared; it can have something on it or experience pangs; its owner can go against it or disobey it. Positively, consciences are good or untroubled, they are clean or clear, followed or obeyed. To do or refrain from doing something for the sake of conscience is always positive.

Many uses fit into the legal framework just noted. The legislator dictates and is obeyed or disobeyed; the prosecutor lays charges of guilt; the witness testifies to troubled or stricken feelings; the judge pronounces the defendant clear or clean. Not all uses are judicial: *seared conscience* represents vividly a nonfunctioning moral awareness, scarred by repeated wrongdoing.

2. Two aspects of conscience, and a third

Formal attempts at definition distinguish between 1) the moral sense of right and wrong, and 2) an inner feeling about the moral status of one's behavior. These two aspects are commonly found in moral theologies, where the general apprehension of moral principles, such as that "the good" ought to be pursued (what the medievals termed *synderesis*), is distinguished from the operations of conscience in assessing particular actions. Macquarrie (1970) introduces a third level, calling this a special mode of *self-awareness*, about "how it is with oneself."

The legal metaphors, while generally comprehensible, contain two problems: 1) It is too relativistic to view the individual conscience as sovereign legislator, legitimately promulgating whatever rules of conduct it wishes. The "voice" of conscience best reflects the dictates of morality, and especially in a religious context it should reinforce divine commandments. "Let your conscience be your guide" cannot mean "You legislate to yourself whatever you think right," but rather "Take seriously your commitment to moral principle and divine command; do not be swayed by power, popular opinion, or self-interest." 2) Legal proceedings are highly formalized, with roles that must not be confused: witnesses are not prosecutors, defendants are not judges. By construing conscience as a psychological faculty that performs these quasi-legal functions, we run the risk of imposing more structure and intelligibility on our inner experience than is warranted.

So in thinking about conscience we should begin with this third sense, an awareness of how it is with oneself. The reflexive awareness, about oneself, is crucial. But the awareness must have moral content: it is a self-assessment about one's moral performance, including one's attitudes about good and bad, right and wrong. In stressing self-conscious assessment in conscience, we avoid the second problem with the legal metaphors. Although there are legal strands in speaking about moral self-assessment, this self-awareness can be, and usually is, untidy and semi-articulate. We may be upset without fully knowing why, or vacillate between self-condemnation and self-justification; we may act from habit, unable to give an account of ourselves. Further, by stressing self-assessment we come closer to the heart of conscience. A general sense of right and wrong (the first sense above) is necessary, of course; but conscience cannot operate without applying the general to the particular. The operations of conscience engage the agent's own feelings about his or her behavior, not the actions of others. Conscience has to do with how it is, morally speaking, with oneself.

3. Guilt and conscience

The complex relations between guilt and shame are difficult to disentangle. However, there can be shame without guilt: one may be ashamed of one's foolishness, one's family, or one's clothes, without having transgressed any moral rules. Guilt, for its part, need not carry shame: it may trouble those whose inner thoughts do not affect their reputation or honor (although the privately guilty believer may also feel ashamed before God). The expression *guilty conscience* (conscience is not called "shamed") suggests strongly that the inward assessment is indeed about the self's own performance with respect to its duties, rather than the agent's perceived status in the eyes of others. So, if it is asserted that the shame of Adam and Eve (Gen 3:7) reveals the presence of conscience, we would want evidence of their recognition of guilt. That the Genesis account does not provide such evidence weakens the claim for conscience. But it does not follow (as often claimed) that the ancients knew only shame and not guilt (*see* section C).

B. Conscience in the Ancient World

1. Context and development

Scholarly consensus places the origin of the concept in the Greek world, although the earlier view that it arose there in a Stoic context has been abandoned. The Greek noun syneidēsis, formed from the preposition συν syn ("with") plus the verb οἶδα oida ("to know"), is commonly translated by the English *conscience*, which itself derives from the Lat. *con* ("with") plus *scire* ("to know"). The etymological sense, then, is "knowing with," knowledge in common, or shared knowledge. However, some formations from σύνοιδα synoida or *conscire* refer simply to consciousness or awareness—what C.S. Lewis calls the "weakened branch." So it is natural to translate many occurrences of syneidēsis in Greek literature in this weak sense of consciousness, without moral content.

Of interest to *conscience* is Lewis' "together branch," especially in its reflexive uses, where the knowing is shared with the self and involves the self's feelings. After a thorough canvass of the evidence, Pierce concludes that in the NT period syneidēsis

belongs to popular rather than philosophical speech, and that it refers to the agent's own behavior, specifically to *past* actions, and normally to *bad* actions. When what is present to consciousness is a guilty secret about one's past performance, we begin to approach our concept of conscience.

The full-blown notion of conscience, however, requires in Lewis' words a "great semantic shift" away from past guilty feeling toward the internal lawgiver, judging good and evil, commanding future action. What we now call moral conscience bears this shifted sense, though the term continues to include a "simmering pot" of meanings.

In what follows we distinguish within the unshifted sense of syneidēsis 1) the basic notion of self-awareness, and 2) the sense of bad or guilty feeling about the self. To distinguish these earlier meanings from 3) moral conscience in the shifted sense, "conscience" often appears here in quotation marks.

2. Biblical occurrences

Since the word for *conscience* is Greek, our evidence for the Bible's understanding of conscience is the NT and the LXX, the Greek translation of the OT. There is, however, only one LXX occurrence of syneidēsis, and one in the Greek Apocrypha (*see* §C.1). The NT, then, provides the main material for our understanding. Syneidēsis occurs thirty times, blossoming in Paul's letters with fourteen occurrences (plus a verbal form) and another eight in Pauline-related texts.

The reader seeking the Bible's view of conscience must bear in mind the various flavors of the current word. Lewis proposes that the shifted sense may be discerned in Paul, though he is uncertain whether the new meaning is already there or is only read into the text later. §D argues that the shifted meaning of syneidēsis as moral conscience is unnecessary in interpreting the NT; indeed the older, unshifted sense is often preferable. English translations sometimes recognize this, but at other times insert the word *conscience* where the original does not use it.

C. The Absence of Conscience in Much of the Bible

With no Hebrew term translatable by the word *conscience*, the concept, strictly speaking, is not to be found in the OT. While the Greek word was available to at least some NT authors, it does not appear in the synoptic Gospels or the Johannine literature.

1. The OT

The absence of a Hebrew word for *conscience* has generated two different responses. On one view, the Israelites could not have experienced anything like conscience because of their mentality: they were not introspective. Their attention was focused upon the observance of divine decrees rather than inner motivation.

A related view describes Israelite society as a shame culture, in which conduct was governed by one's perceived status before others, including God, rather than by feelings of guilt necessary for conscience.

The contrary view holds that, although there is no one Hebrew word for *conscience*, there is good evidence in many OT writings of the moral reflection involved in the processes of conscience. On this view, it is appropriate to employ the concept of conscience in translating some OT passages; on the first view this is impermissible.

In fact some translators have found it natural to use the term in certain contexts. The earliest example comes from the LXX. The Greek translators of the OT used the word syneidēsis in Eccl 10:20, "Do not curse the king, even in your syneidēsis." But the meaning is, as in the Hebrew, "even in your secret thoughts." The LXX uses the word more intelligibly in the apocryphal Wisdom of Solomon at 17:11: wickedness is "distressed by conscience." (There is also a variant reading of syneidēsis for kardia, heart, in Sir 42:18.)

In the Lat. Vulg. *conscientia* occurs twice in the OT (Gen 43:22, "it is not in our *conscientia*," NRSV, "we do not know"; and Eccl 7:23, "your *conscientia* knows that you have cursed others," NRSV, "heart," but Douay-Rheims, "conscience").

English OT translations have only recently employed *conscience*. The KJV never uses it, and the NRSV only once, in 1 Sam 25:31. Other more popular translations such as the Good News Bible employ idiomatic expressions like *clear conscience* in Abraham's representation of Sarah as his sister, Gen 20:5, 6 (NRSV, "integrity of heart"). In Job's assertions of innocence, his "conscience is clear" (27:6; LXX uses the verb synoida). Several translations refer to David's conscience in three stories. After cutting off a corner of Saul's robe, David's conscience was stricken (1 Sam 24:5); his conscience troubled him after counting the people (2 Sam 24:10); and Abigail tells him he will not suffer pangs of conscience if he refuses to take murderous revenge upon her husband Nabal (1 Sam 25:31).

More literal translations keep the Hebrew notion of *heart* in such passages, and thus remain faithful to Hebrew moral psychology. The OT concept of heart carries a complexity of meanings, having to do with the core of the person and encompassing emotive and mental states; it is thus wider in connotation than the English term. But as the seat of moral emotions and judgments, especially as present to the subject's own awareness, the heart is the place where moral self-assessment takes place. Its interior operations are secret: God alone knows the heart when others cannot (1 Sam 16:7). When David's "heart" is stricken over his conduct (1 Sam 24:5), he has reflected upon his behavior and feels guilt (even if, before his men, he also experiences shame for not respecting Saul as king)—in our words, then, he has a guilty or stricken

conscience. In the Bathsheba episode, Nathan's parable of the rich man's theft of the poor man's beloved lamb demonstrates how general moral sense is different from the guilt of conscience: David's sense of justice causes him outrage, but only Nathan's pointed "You are the man" goads him into self-reflective confession, even though the work of conscience may not be fully realized in proper repentance (nothing is said about David's "heart," 2 Sam 12:1-15).

Much evidence of the operation of conscience is to be found in the Psalms, which contain some of the greatest introspective passages in the world's literature. The innocence of conscience is illustrated in Ps 17:3 (God tries the heart in night solitude); in Ps 32 hidden sin must be acknowledged to alleviate the anguish of self-conscious guilt. It is likely that an understanding of the heart's self-reflection developed over time; the notion of the *new heart* in particular achieves prominence in exilic and post-exilic writings (the law written on the heart, Jer 31:33; the new heart of flesh, Ezek 36:25-26). Psalm 51, ascribed by tradition to David perhaps to sanitize his reputation, reveals a guilty mind aware of sin as a self-conscious condition of inner defilement rather than social transgression, and asks God to do a new thing in creating a clean heart within (v. 10).

The phenomenon of a seared or deadened conscience may be part of the meaning of the OT hardened heart (Exod 9:34) or heart of stone—but only part, for the expression can signify simply stubbornness (Ps 95:8) or even lack of any feeling or response (1 Sam 25:27).

Significantly, however, the introspective heart knows guilt but is not the source of moral direction. Such direction comes from the law and commandments of God.

2. The synoptic Gospels

We cannot know whether the synoptic writers had encountered in everyday speech the Greek word syneidēsis. We do know that they did not use it, their moral world being informed by OT sensibilities. There are, however, many references to interiority and the heart: prayer is to be in secret (Matt 6:5-6), the law is summed up in loving God with all the heart (Matt 22:37 par.); Mary treasures the events of the young Jesus' life in her heart (Luke 2:51). Further, from the heart spring words (Matt 12:34) and deeds, especially defiling sins (Matt 15:19-20 par.); and sin itself may be committed in the heart without consequent action (Matt 5:28).

As with the OT, so with the Gospels: where there is an interior self-assessment of moral performance, we may glimpse the workings of conscience. Hence the prodigal son's "coming to himself" is a realization of his having sinned (Luke 15:17-18); and the breast-beating of the tax collector (Luke 18:13) betokens the same self-realization. Since these seem to be instances of guilt rather than shame, we may invoke the notion of conscience in explaining their self-assessment. If there is shame in Peter's sudden self-awareness of having denied Jesus three times (the Lord looked on him, Luke 22:61), his bitter weeping at the sound of cock-crow may be seen as grief occasioned by conscience, and the cock as an external symbol of its operation.

The Synoptics, while reticent about Jesus' own inner life (though he was hungry, we are told nothing about his inner feelings in the temptation narratives), do comment on his compassion for the blind and sick (Matt 20:34; Mark 1:41), his anger at hardheartedness (Mark 3:5), and his amazement at unbelief (Mark 6:6). Since Jesus never asks for forgiveness or repents, we would not expect to find conscience operating within his psyche; the closest we come to internal struggle over the right thing to do is in the garden of Gethsemane (Matt 26:36-45). It would be inappropriate, however, to imagine that Jesus was consulting his moral conscience, since his entire consciousness was focused on doing the Father's will.

3. Johannine literature

John's Gospel adds nothing more to the discussion of conscience. True, the dominant motif of light is ethically important—light exposes and condemns (3:20) and reveals one's true relationship to God (3:21); Jesus as light of the world is the source of guidance (8:12). But it is far-fetched to think that the true light enlightening everyone coming into the world is conscience (1:9). As elsewhere in the Bible, the source of moral knowledge is not inner light but the commandments of God, especially in John the new commandment to love one another (13:34-35). The phrase "conviction of sin," sometimes associated with a guilty conscience, may echo from John 16:8 in some translations (NIV, "he will convict the world of guilt"), but the work of the Advocate is to prove the world wrong (NRSV), not to create guilt.

The themes of love and commandment reappear strongly in the first Johannine letter; in addition there is reference to the heart. In 1 John 3:19-22 it is not the light that condemns; rather, our own hearts sometimes do so; then the knowledge that we are from the truth, and love in deed rather than word, will reassure our hearts. The self-reflectiveness of this passage is of a piece with the Hebrew experience considered above, and once more explanation by way of conscience is natural.

Neither 2 John nor 3 John, nor the apocalyptic visions of the book of Revelation, contribute anything to the notion of conscience (the dead are judged by their deeds, not according to their conscience, Rev 20:12).

D. The Pauline Contribution to the Concept of Conscience

The Pauline use of syneidēsis, amounting to more than two-thirds of all occurrences of the concept in the Bible, is determinative of our understanding. But just what Paul means by syneidēsis, and its relation to the shifted sense of conscience, requires careful examination.

1. The Corinthian correspondence

The context for Paul's earliest use of syneidēsis is Gentile rather than Jewish, and has to do with the Christian attitude toward eating meat offered to idols. Paul's appeal to *conscience* in 1 Cor 8 and 10 means that the concept was readily intelligible to a modestly educated audience. Paul argues that, although the Christian believer is free to eat idol-meat, when such eating causes difficulties for the "conscience" of the weak, the believer should refrain. If Paul means by syneidēsis our moral conscience, his advice generates the ethical dilemma of competing consciences: the immature conscience dictates what is morally acceptable to the more robust conscience, when it should be the other way round. However, this dilemma need not arise, for syneidēsis may be read in its unshifted senses in 1 Cor 8 and 10.

a. 1 Cor 8. Clearly Paul cannot be referring to moral conscience in ch. 8, where he speaks of the "polluted" or "defiled" syneidēsis of the weak (v. 7); he means rather that the person's *self-consciousness* is defiled through association with idols. Likewise with the "wounded" syneidēsis of v. 12: It is not so much that the moral faculties of the immature are further damaged as that they *feel themselves wounded* just because they are weak. In translating v. 10's reference to the strengthening or encouragement of syneidēsis, the NRSV uses the phrase "since their conscience is weak." But Paul's meaning again refers to the weak persons' *self-understanding*; encouraged by the example of those for whom idol-meat is unproblematic, they follow suit through a false sense of themselves.

In these instances syneidēsis bears its minimal sense of self-awareness. It cannot mean negative or bad feelings, since the pollution or wounding or encouragement is not of a guilty mind. The shifted meaning of moral conscience is nowhere in sight.

b. First Corinthians 10:23-30. The minimal sense will not work, however, in 1 Cor 10. Here Paul four times uses the expression "for the sake of syneidēsis" (vv. 25, 27, 28, 29) and refers once to being judged "by the syneidēsis" of another (v. 29). Eating or not for the sake of self-understanding makes little sense. So, especially given the language of judging, it is tempting to think that moral conscience is in view here. The strong should consult their Christian conscience and refrain from eating idol-meat when it will damage the conscience of the weak. In this way the dilemma of competing consciences arises from this text.

The temptation so to read Paul should be resisted, for the older sense of syneidēsis as negative self-awareness or guilty feeling is preferable on two counts. First, this meaning gives good sense to Paul's reasoning. While the reader might think Paul is referring to the syneidēsis of the liberated eater of idol-meat in v. 25 (NRSV, "eat whatever is sold in the meat market without raising any question on the ground of conscience"), by v. 29 Paul makes it clear that he means the syneidēsis of the other person. So the passage, instead of being about consulting one's own moral sense in the decision to eat, focuses on the sensibilities of those who find eating problematic. Their negative feelings provide the reason for the stronger not to exercise their freedom to eat: as Paul has explained in ch. 8, they may stumble and fall. All the occurrences of syneidēsis in ch. 10, then, may be translated as "bad feeling." The second reason for preferring this older sense is that it dissolves the ethical dilemma. The moral conscience of the strong is not restricted or rebuked by a weaker, immature conscience. Paul is writing about how Christian freedom should deal with the immature self-perception and guilty feelings of others, not about Christian moral conscience.

c. Other incidental uses. In 1 Cor 4:4 we find a reflexive construction with the verb synoida, to be aware of oneself. "I am not aware of anything against myself, but I am not thereby acquitted" (NRSV). We may agree that, given our understanding of the shifted sense, it is helpful to refer to the apostle's "clear conscience," as does Pierce. However, Paul makes no assertions about moral conscience, but only about his own awareness of wrongdoing.

In 2 Corinthians, syneidēsis appears three times. Paul boasts at 1:12 that he has behaved properly, a boast that is also "the testimony of our syneidēsis." As in 1 Cor 4:4, his awareness of no bad feelings bears its witness to his claim. As for syneidēsis in 2 Cor 4 and 5, the common English versions misleadingly translate this by *conscience* when that concept is inappropriate. In both instances Paul is referring to the syneidēsis that others have about him. He commends himself to the syneidēsis of everyone (4:2); and he hopes that he is well known to the syneidēsis of the Corinthians (5:11). As Pierce observes, the most primitive sense of "knowing with" shared knowledge is the meaning here. Paul appeals to a common understanding of his motives.

2. Romans

From 1 Cor we would expect the language of syn eidēsis in the discussion of diet and the weak in Rom 14, but Paul makes no reference to the concept there. Instead he uses it in two different contexts: one about obeying civil authorities and the other about the law written on the heart. Intuitively, today's reader thinks of moral conscience in such settings, but the unshifted sense of syneidēsis continues to function adequately in interpreting these passages.

a. Romans 13:5. For Pierce, this well-known passage about civil obedience is normative for the entire

NT view of syneidēsis. Paul's conclusion is that one should be subject to civil authorities, pay taxes and revenue, give respect and honor (13:7). His basic reason for civil obedience is that, since God has instituted governing authorities to execute wrath on wrongdoers, submission to them demonstrates respect for God and God's good intentions toward us as citizens. Not to submit is to go against God. Paul adds, however, two more ideas to this basic reasoning. In v. 5 one should be subject, he says, "not only because of wrath but also because of syneidēsis."

These two terms, *wrath* and syneidēsis, seem to provide additional reasons for obedience. In particular, "for the sake of syneidēsis" has often been interpreted in this way; Christian moral conscience as well as respect for divine order requires submission to the authorities. That opens the door to the long debate about the relation of the Christian conscience to the state's decrees, especially tyrannical, immoral, and irreligious decrees. It is difficult to know how a well-formed Christian conscience provides reasons for subjection to such authorities. However, 13:5 may be read, not as giving additional *reasons* for civil obedience but as providing *motives* for submission. That works intelligibly with wrath, for Paul has spoken about judgment, fear, and terror in this passage, all of which motivate compliance (regardless of its moral legitimacy). The same may be said of syneidēsis in its negative sense of bad feeling. Avoiding the feeling of wrongdoing is an obvious motivator, especially for a Christian. To submit because of syneidēsis, then, is parallel to submitting because of wrath, since it is the subjective apprehension of the wrathful judgment exercised by the state. In his invocation of these two ideas, Paul is appealing to psychological prudence rather than theological principle: those who contemplate disobedience should self-consciously fear the pains of punishment.

The advantage of this reading is that it makes good sense of the passage while keeping with the unshifted meaning of syneidēsis. Whether it helps the problem of the Christian conscience in a tyrannical state is another matter. Perhaps so; at least, the removal of moral conscience as a reason for civil obedience does create space for further moral and theological reflection. Where bad feeling and fear of wrath are psychological motives, they can be assessed by what we now regard as an informed moral conscience that is able to assess particular state decrees for their contribution to well-being. Where a specific civil authority goes against divine decrees and intentions for civil society, there would be no "bad feeling" for the Christian in disobeying the state. In fact, the motive to obey God rather than human authorities would assert itself, generating bad feeling if (contrary to the situation Paul contemplates) one did in fact comply with an unjust decree.

b. Romans 2:15. The second major locus for Paul's use of syneidēsis in Romans is found at 2:15. Here the argument is that God treats Jew and Gentile alike, with impartiality. Jews are judged by the law—and not so much for their knowledge of the law, but their actions in accordance with the law. Gentiles too are judged for their actions, rather than their knowledge of the law. For while they have not "heard" the law, they may act in accordance with it: the requirements of the law are "written on their hearts," "to which their own conscience also bears witness"—and their "conflicting thoughts will accuse or perhaps excuse them" (NRSV). Commentaries refer to this as the "law of conscience," and on such a reading this passage contains an instance of the shifted sense, moral conscience. But the text does not treat syneidēsis as legislating right and wrong; that law is already written on the heart, and is the same for all human beings. Nor does syneidēsis act as moral judge: rather, the "conflicting thoughts" do the accusing or excusing. Instead, syneidēsis performs the function of witness about whether or not the legislation has been observed. It is an internal, subjective awareness about one's shortcomings—and its operation leads to those conflicting thoughts over what one knows ought to be done and the bad feeling of not having done it. Paul does acknowledge that these thoughts may indeed excuse one, but that may be because of an absence of bad feeling rather than a positive approbation upon the evaluative work of a moral conscience. Hence we may reasonably conclude not only that Rom 2:15 will work on the older sense of bad feeling, but that it lends no support to the interpretation of syneidēsis as moral conscience.

c. Romans 9:1. Paul claims to be speaking the truth in Christ, not lying, and he adds that his syneidēsis confirms this "by the Holy Spirit." Syneidēsis refers to his subjective self-awareness, opened to the work of the Spirit, which provides him with inner assurance. "I have no painful consciousness of lying."

3. Acts 23:1; 24:16

It is entirely consistent with the above that the author of Acts should make Paul confess that he has lived his life "with a clear conscience before God" (23:1), and that he does his best "always to have a clear conscience before God and all people" (24:16). The Greek adjectives are "good" (ἀγαθῆς agathēs) and "unoffending" (or "not offended," ἀπρόσκοπον aproskopon); they describe Paul's subjective self-consciousness of his moral and religious performance.

4. The Pastoral Letters

Timothy and Titus are considered here as having been influenced by Pauline thought. As in Acts, we find syneidēsis modified by two adjectives describing the content of an agent's reflective awareness: "good" (agathos, again) and "clean" (καθαρός katharos).

Both descriptors appear in 1 Tim 1:5, "love that comes from a pure heart, a good conscience, and sin-

cere faith." The pure heart forms intentions; syneidēsis denotes the subject's awareness of those intentions and associated actions. The "good conscience" of 1:19 is also associated with faith: as Timothy fulfills his promise he has nothing negative on his mind. The NRSV adds here another instance of the English *conscience* not in the original: "By rejecting conscience, certain persons have suffered shipwreck in the faith." This conjures up shifted moral conscience, but unnecessarily so: shipwreck comes from rejecting instruction and faith, which entails not being able to have a positive sense of self. Purity of "conscience" returns in 3:9 where deacons must hold to the mystery of the faith with a clean syneidēsis and in 2 Tim 1:3, where the author maintains he has worshiped God in just this way (NRSV, "clear conscience"). These instances are very close to the expressions in Acts.

Strikingly different is 1 Tim 4:2, speaking in vivid terms of liars who have cauterized their own syneidēsis (NRSV, whose "consciences are seared with a hot iron"). Unusually, we cannot render syneidēsis in terms of self-understanding or bad feeling here—or in the final occurrence in the Pastorals, Titus 1:15 (to the corrupt nothing is pure; "their very minds and consciences are corrupted"). A seared or corrupted syneidēsis is not a callous or degenerate feeling but a capacity or function that has been seriously impaired. This is as close as we come to the shifted sense of moral conscience; but even here syneidēsis does not legislate future action; instead the writer has in mind the ability to experience guilt over wrongdoing.

E. Conscience in the Letter to the Hebrews and 1 Peter

Purity and perfection are dominant concerns in Heb 9 and 10. The old order of repeated sacrifice was impotent to bring worshipers to perfection. Those rituals brought a certain form of purification, for the body and the flesh (9:10, 13), but are lacking in two ways: objectively, they do not take away sins once for all (10:1, 11), and subjectively, they do not deal with the worshiper's inner life.

The five occurrences of syneidēsis in this letter deal with the second issue, the self-awareness of the person in need of purification. Had sacrifices been effective the worshipers would have no more syneidēsis of sin, and the repetition would have ended (10:2). Here the NRSV translates syneidēsis as "consciousness," which is surely the sense. In 9:9 the same point had been made. In translating "cannot perfect the conscience of the worshiper," the NRSV treats "conscience" as a faculty in need of finishing off; more literally, however, the worshiper cannot be perfected "with respect to syneidēsis"—that is, cannot have the continued awareness of sinfulness dealt with.

The work of Christ takes care of that, cleansing our syneidēsis "from dead works to worship the living

God" (9:14). Dead works infect our self-consciousness, which when purified is freed for true worship. The believer may now come with a "true heart," a heart "sprinkled clean from an evil conscience (syneidēsis ponēras)" (10:22); once more, what is cleansed is not the conscience as evil, but the sense of oneself as wicked.

Finally, the author adds in 13:18 that he is persuaded that his own syneidēsis is good or fine (καλός kalos; NRSV, "clear"). His readers will understand that to mean that he believes himself to have subjectively appropriated the purification of Christ's sacrifice.

First Peter 2:18 enjoins the submission of slaves to masters, adding that it is to their credit if they undergo unjust suffering "because of (or for the sake of) syneidēsis of God" (v. 19). While the language recalls Rom 13, the author cannot be appealing to conscience as moral faculty or even the Romans' sense of bad feeling. The NRSV rightly translates the phrase, "while being aware of God" (this and Heb 10:2 being the only instances where it does not render syneidēsis by "conscience"). Chapter 3 speaks to all abused or interrogated Christians: they must act with gentleness and reverence, having a good syneidēsis (v. 16; NRSV, "clear conscience"). The chapter nears its close with another reference to a good syneidēsis—as the saving work of baptism. Baptism is not washing off bodily dirt, but "an appeal to God for a good conscience" (3:21 NRSV). These instances return us to the dominant use of syneidēsis in the Bible as awareness of the self with respect to wrongdoing. And given the Christian message it is fitting that here the self has come to know itself as free of guilt or wrongdoing.

Readers of the English translations should not assume that the Bible speaks of moral conscience in the shifted sense. Syneidēsis does not require translation by *conscience* except perhaps in 1 Tim 4:2 and Titus 1:15, for it is not a source of moral knowledge; sometimes it is simply self-awareness, or it is a witness to one's performance, usually negative, with respect to God's law and the commandments of Christ. If, as it sometimes seems, conscience is in decline in the contemporary world, then that decline might reflect the pronounced individualism of Western culture—an individualism ironically abetted by much of Christendom. A biblical understanding should help fashion a conscience that reflects upon moral performance in light of standards arising from beyond the self. *See* GUILT.

Bibliography: Paul W. Gooch. "'Conscience' in 1 Corinthians 8 and 10." *NTS* 33 (1987) 244–54; C. S. Lewis. "Conscious and Conscience." *Studies in Words.* 2nd ed. (1967); John Macquarrie. "Conscience, Sin, and Grace." *Three Issues in Ethics* (1970); C. A. Pierce. *Conscience in the New Testament* (1955).

PAUL W. GOOCH

CONSECRATE [קדשׁ qdsh; ἁγιάζω hagiazō]. In the OT and NT, consecration entails setting someone or something apart from others of their class. Usually consecration elevates its object's status vis-à-vis God and is equivalent to making its object holy.

Consecration in the OT. The Hebrew root associated with consecration throughout the OT is qdsh. A variety of things can be consecrated. Predetermined units of time such as the Sabbath (Gen 2:3; Exod 20:8, 11; Deut 5:12; Jer 17:22), other days of the week (Ezra 3:5), and the Jubilee Year (Lev 25:10) are routinely set apart. Periods of indeterminate length may also be established and designated as sacred (e.g., a fast, Joel 2:15). Offerings of all types are also consecrated. The firstborn of Israel are dedicated to God (Exod 13:2; Deut 15:19), as are offerings and tithes made by laity and priests (Exod 28:38; Hag 2:12). Silver, gold, and bronze from the people and from victory over enemies are also dedicated to God (2 Kgs 12:18). Temple spaces and accoutrements are consecrated (Exod 29:36-37, 43-44; 30:29; 40:9-11; Lev 8:10-11, 15; 16:19; 21:23; Num 7:1; 1 Kgs 8:64; 9:3, 7; 2 Chr 2:4; 7:7, 16, 20; 29:19). Likewise, the vestments of the priests are set apart (Exod 28:3, 41; Lev 8:30; Ezek 44:19). Other spaces may be consecrated (city gates, Neh 3:1; land parcels, houses, or fields, Lev 27:14-15, 16-19, 22; Josh 20:17; the mountain, Exod 19:23).

Groups of people are also consecrated in the OT. The entire people of Israel is set apart (Exod 19:10, 14; Lev 11:44; 20:7; Josh 3:5; 7:13; Ezek 20:12; 37:28; Joel 2:16), as are smaller groups (e.g., Jesse and his sons, 1 Sam 16:5). Priests and Levites are set apart as holy (Exod 19:22; 29:1, 33; Lev 22:9; 1 Chr 15:12, 14; 2 Chr 5:11; 26:18; 29:34; 30:3, 15). Aaronites (Exod 40:13; Lev 8:12; 21:15; 1 Chr 23:32) and Zadokites (Ezek 48:11) are especially singled out for consecration to altar service in the Temple. Even God may be made holy by proximity to God's own people (Lev 10:3) or through the people's honor of God's name (Lev 22:32; Isa 29:23). (*See* CHOSEN.)

Means of consecration in the OT vary. Most often it occurs through the presence, act, or word of God (Gen 2:3; Exod 13:2; 19:22; 29:1; Lev 10:3; 22:9), but human beings may also be consecrating agents, especially the people of Israel as a whole (Lev 11:44; 20:7; Josh 3:5; 7:13). Only occasionally may a thing have the power to consecrate; *see* especially the case of the priest's vestments (Exod 28:3; Ezek 44:19).

Consecration in the OT generally functions to make someone or something holy to God, to establish an elevated relationship with the divine that others do not share. This relationship bears rewards and responsibilities: priests receive power and material gain but also responsibility for the people's relationship with God, and prophets are favored by God yet burdened with bearing difficult messages (e.g., Jer 1:5). Consecration in the OT relates to initiating God's special relationship with Israel (Exod 19:10) and to sustaining it (e.g., through making sanctified offerings to God, Lev 22:2-3). Some notable instances reveal that consecration in the OT may also be simply a matter of setting someone or something apart for neutral, or even negative purposes: pagans can designate silver and assemblies for idolatrous worship (Judg 17:3; 2 Kgs 10:20) or God can designate the wicked for slaughter (Jer 12:3), destroyers for acts against Israel (Jer 22:7), and apostates for idolatry (Isa 65:5; 66:17).

Consecration in the NT. The key word in the NT for consecration is hagiazō, to dedicate as holy to God. The word takes its meaning chiefly from the OT, but it focuses in particular on 1) Jesus as a sanctified offering for atonement (John 10:36; 17:19), and 2) the people as sanctified by Jesus' sacrifice, the preaching of the gospel, and baptism (John 17:17; Acts 20:32; 26:18; 1 Cor 6:11; Eph 5:26; Heb 10:10). The import of consecration is, in the case of Jesus, virtually identical with the consecration associated with the OT's sacrificial offerings, while the consecration of those for whom Jesus' death occurs is similar to the election experienced by the people of Israel. Only rarely does the NT assign consecrating activity to human beings: petitioners hallow God's name (Matt 6:9; Luke 11:2); believing spouses sanctify unbelieving partners (1 Cor 7:14); believers sanctify Christ in their hearts (1 Pet 3:15); and self purification dedicates one to God (2 Tim 2:21).

ROBERT KUGLER

CONSECRATED PERSONS [קָדַשׁ qadhash; ἁγιάζω hagiazō]. The separation of a person from others of their class, usually to elevate them vis-à-vis God and make them holy. Consecrated persons in the OT include the people of Israel (Exod 19:10), smaller groups within Israel (1 Sam 16:5), priests and Levites (Exod 19:22), Aaronites (Exod 40:3), and Zadokites (Ezek 48:11). In the NT Jesus is consecrated as an atonement offering (John 10:36). Jesus' sacrifice, the preaching of the gospel, and baptism consecrate the people (John 17:17; Acts 20:32; 26:18; 1 Cor 6:11; Eph 5:26; Heb 10:10). Believing spouses sanctify unbelieving partners (1 Cor 7:14), believers sanctify Christ in their hearts (1 Pet 3:15), and self-purification dedicates one to God (1 Tim 2:21).

ROBERT KUGLER

CONSOLATION [נָחַם nakham; παράκλησις paraklēsis]. Several Hebrew and Greek words denote COMFORT or encouragement that can come from other people (Gen 27:42; 2 Sam 10:2; 12:24; Isa 22:4; Jer 16:7; John 11:19; 2 Cor 7:4), or, especially, from God (Ps 94:19; Isa 66:13; Zech 10:2; Rom 15:5; 2 Cor 1:3-4). Real consolation from God is contrasted with false comfort from magic or idolatry (Zech 10:2). Job claims it would be greater consolation to him to have

rebuke or even destruction from the true God than the empty comfort of his friends (Job 6:10; 21:2). The Holy Spirit and Jesus are special comforters or advocates. *See* PARACLETE.

KIM PAFFENROTH

CONSTELLATIONS. *See* NATURE, NATURAL PHENOMENA; ORION; SCIENCE AND THE BIBLE; SCIENCE IN THE ANCIENT NEAR EAST; STARS.

CONSTITUTIONS AND CANONS. A Syrian late 4th cent. text, which represents the most comprehensive "church order" preserved from antiquity. It is attributed to the thirteen (including Matthias and Paul; see 8.29, 32, 46) apostles and claims to be passed on through Clement.

The first six books are based on the *Didascalia Apostolorum* (from Syria, early 3rd cent.). The first part of Book 7 (1-32) is rooted in the DIDACHE. A collection of Jewish prayers (with some Christian interpolations) follows (33-38), then regulations for catechumens (39-45), a list of bishops ordained by the apostles (46), and a collection of daily prayers (47-49). Book 8 begins with a discussion of spiritual gifts (1-2, perhaps based on a lost work of Hippolytus of Rome), then draws on the Apostolic Tradition (commonly attributed to Hippolytus) to treat the selection and ordination of bishops (3-15) and duties of other clergy (16-28). Sections 29-46 contain an assortment of laws and prayers. The work concludes (8.47) with a series of canons attributed to the apostles that came to be circulated independently. It deals primarily with the ordination and duties of the clergy, and ends with a list of canonical books that includes the Apostolic Constitutions, but not the book of Revelation.

Bibliography: David A Fiensy. *Prayers Alleged to Be Jewish: An Examination of the* Constitutiones Apostolorum *(1985); W. Jardine Grisbrooke. *The Liturgical Portions of the Apostolic Constitutions: A Text for Students* (1990); Marcel Metzger. *Les Constitutions apostoliques.* Vol. I–III (1985–87).

STEPHEN WESTERHOLM

CONSUL kon´suhl [ὕπατος hypatos]. Established after the ouster of the Roman kings in 531 BCE, this chief political and military office was shared by two men elected by the *comita centuriata* for one-year terms. As consultant to the Senate, judges, and supreme military commanders (Cicero, *De legibus*) it was the highest position attainable in a political career. The position became less powerful in the late Republic, and during the empire it was appointed by the emperor.

The single biblical occurrence refers to LUCIUS as consul in a letter cited in 1 Macc 15:16, 22.

EARL S. JOHNSON, JR.

CONSUMING FIRE [אֵשׁ אֹכְלָה 'esh 'okhlah; πῦρ καταναλίσκον pyr katanaliskon]. Hebrews recalls the "blazing fire" of Sinai (12:18) when it describes God as "a consuming fire" (12:29), punishing those who fall away from faith. Deuteronomy 4:23-24 describes God as a threatening "consuming fire," reminiscent of Sinai when "God spoke to you out of the fire" (Exod 24:17), while Deut 9:3 describes God as a "consuming fire" who will defeat Israel's enemies in the promised land.

JOHN R. LEVISON

CONSUMPTION [שַׁחֶפֶת shakhefeth; ἀπορίαν aporian]. This word is a medicocentric translation of the Hebrew shakhefeth (Lev 26:16; Deut 28:22) indicating a specific physical malady. Hippocrates named the malady φθίσις (phthisis), but medicine did not understand or name it until the 17th cent. Since the precise referent of the Hebrew is unknown, it is best rendered "incurable malady" or "a malady that causes the body to waste away."

JOHN J. PILCH

CONTENTMENT [αὐτάρκης autarkēs, αὐταρκεί ας autarkeias, ἀρκέω arkeō, εὐδοκέω eudokeō]. Contentment describes an attitude of mind that is characterized by freedom from anxiety or discomfort over one's circumstances in life. In modern secular thought, contentment has been associated with having an abundance of wealth, power, friends, health, and more. But in Judeo-Christian tradition, contentment is never said to depend on the comfort of one's actual physical circumstances. Rather, contentment results from the attitude of faith and trust in God with which one confronts any or all circumstances.

The noun itself is used only once in the NRSV, as part of an argument urging the faithful to seek the "great gain" that comes from "godliness combined with contentment" (1 Tim 6:6) and to resist giving in to "the love of money" that is "a root of all kinds of evil" (v. 10). The phrase "be content/contented with" occurs occasionally in contexts indicating an individual's acceptance of what is perceived to be the will of God. Thus Paul says, "I am content with weaknesses, insults, hardships, persecutions, and calamities for the sake of Christ" (2 Cor 12:10). But in Phil 4, Paul says he has "learned to be content" with whatever he has, whether it be little or plenty, because he has learned the "secret" (v. 11) of contentment, which comes from dependence on God (v. 13).

Hebrews 13:5 tells the faithful, "Keep your lives free from the love of money, and be content with what you have," remembering that God has said, "I will never leave you or forsake you" (Josh 1:5). The faithful can be content (free from anxiety over material possessions) because they believe "the Lord is my helper; I will not be afraid" (Heb 13:6; Ps 118:6).

This is clearly the same attitude of mind Jesus describes in Matt 6:25-34 and Luke 12:22-34, though

the word *contentment* is not actually used in either text. The birds of the air and the lilies of the field are models of contentment set over against the complacency of the "rich fool" who says to himself, "Soul, you have ample goods laid up for many years; relax, eat drink and be merry" (Luke 12:19). Contentment is made possible not by the accumulation of material possessions but by selling them in order to give alms to the poor (Luke 12:33).

The prophet Habakkuk encapsulates this biblical understanding of contentment (again without using the word itself) in his poetic declaration of what it means to live by faith: "Though the fig tree does not blossom and no fruit is on the vines; though the produce of the olive fails and the fields yield no food; though the flock is cut off from the fold and there is no herd in the stalls, yet I will rejoice in the Lord; I will exult in the God of my salvation" (Hab 3:17-18).

Thus, it is clear that in the biblical tradition contentment comes from living one's life in accordance with God's intentions, with complete confidence in and dependence on God's ever-present love and grace.

KATHLEEN A. FARMER

CONTRIBUTION FOR THE SAINTS. *See* COLLECTION, THE; OFFERING FOR THE SAINTS.

CONTRIBUTIONS. *See* COLLECTION, THE; OFFERING FOR THE SAINTS.

CONTRITE [דָּכָא dakha', דָּכָה dakhah, נָכֵה nakheh]. The "contrite" are those "crushed" in "spirit" (Isa 66:2) or "heart" (Ps 51:17; also Pr Azar 1:16 [LXX 3:39]) by an awareness of their own or their people's sin and liability for divine judgment. God finds such contrition more acceptable than cultic sacrifices (Ps 51:16-17). Isaiah 57:15 and 66:2 juxtapose the transcendent grandeur of God (for whom no temple built by mortals can be adequate) with God's delight to "dwell with" (or "look to") the "contrite and humble in spirit"; their "heart" God promises to "revive."

STEPHEN WESTERHOLM

CONVERSION [שׁוּב shuv; ἐπιστρέφω epistrephō]. The biblical terms commonly associated with conversion denote a turning/returning. The wide range of views regarding what *conversion* actually entails greatly complicates attempts at understanding conversion in the Bible. The matter is further complicated by the virtual absence of the word *conversion* in English translations of the Bible and by the fact that the word *repentance* is also frequently used to translate shuv.

The turning associated with biblical conversion usually involves turning from one way of living and turning to a different way of living. While the OT focuses on the religious and social obligations of Israelites, there are references to "resident aliens" (גֵּרִים

gerim) participating in the religious and social life of Israel. Their participation required some measure of embracing the religious and social obligations of Israel (Exod 12:43-49; Num 15:11-16). The Jewish philosopher, Philo of Alexandria, frequently described resident aliens as those who had abandoned homeland, family, and friends in order to follow the people and God of Israel. Ruth is the paradigm for Philo's understanding (Ruth 1:16). Most of the turning language in the OT, however, is used with regard to Israelites returning to God. Prophets were the ones who called the people to return (Amos 4:6-13; Jer 3:12-24; Isa 55:6-9).

New Testament conversion is also understood as turning from one way of living to a different way of living. This transformation almost always involves turning to God (Acts 15:19-20; Gal 4:8-9), and it is frequently associated with repentance (Acts 3:19; 26:20). The transformation is actually more commonly referred to as "repentance" (μετάνοια metanoia) rather than "conversion." The synoptic Gospels present the inbreaking of the "kingdom of God" as the impetus for this transformation. Both John the Baptist and Jesus demand changes in the way people live their lives.

Since Acts depicts the growth of the early church, it is full of conversion stories (2:41-42; 4:4; 8:26-40; 9:35, 42; 10:1–11:18). While Paul never recounts a conversion experience like the one portrayed in Acts (9; 22; 26), he does frequently mention being "called" by God (Gal 1:11-17). Paul presents conversion as a divine calling (1 Cor 7:17-24) responded to with obedient faithfulness (Rom 1:5-6). While there is indeed much ambiguity regarding what conversion actually entails, it is clear that the biblical notion of conversion involves a change in lifestyle that results from (re)turning to the biblical God. *See* REPENTANCE.

GUY NAVE

CONVICTION [πληροφορία plerophoria, ἔλεγχος elenchos]. The full certainty with which Paul delivered his message (1 Thess 1:5); assurance concerning things unseen (Col 2:2; Heb 6:11; 10:22; 11:1). *See* BOLDNESS; COURAGE.

CONVOCATION, HOLY [מִקְרָא־קֹדֶשׁ miqra᾽ qodhesh; κλητός ἅγιος kletos hagios]. Literally, this phrase might be rendered "holy proclamation." Usage shows that its purpose was to announce the arrival of a festival day. Hence, the term is idiomatic for the day itself: the "holy convocation" or "sacred occasion" when Israel was called from its usual labors to public celebration and worship. The Sabbath itself is named as a "holy convocation" (Lev 23:3). Seven festal days are so designated in Lev 23: the first and seventh days of UNLEAVENED BREAD (vv. 7-8), Weeks (v. 21), the first day of the seventh month (v. 24), the Day of Atonement (v. 27), and the first and eighth days of Booths (vv.

35-36). In later usage, miqra᾽ referred to "reading of Scripture" or even "Scripture" itself (e.g., Neh 8:8).

JOEL B. GREEN

COOK [טַבָּח tabbakh, טַבָּחָה tabbakhah]. An individual who prepares food. Tabbakh, from the Hebrew verb "to slaughter," indicates the one who slaughters the animal for a meal (1 Sam 9:23, 24). Both males (Gen 25:29: 1 Sam 9:23) and females (1 Sam 8:13) are described as cooks in the OT. Tabbakh is also translated as "GUARD" or "executioner" (e.g., Gen 37:36). *See* BODYGUARD; COOKING AND COOKING UTENSILS; FOOD; SERVANT.

JESSICA L. T. DEVEGA

COOKING AND COOKING UTENSILS. Cooking food in the ancient Israelite household was primarily a female activity. In most households, women in the family would perform cooking tasks, while in wealthy homes, female servants might be employed. Perhaps because cooking was so commonplace, the biblical writers left few detailed descriptions of food preparation and consumption. Despite the limited textual evidence, we can assume that cooking was an essential task that occupied one or more members of the Israelite household for several hours per day, and it involved a number of complex activities requiring specialized tools and installations to accomplish.

Cooked food was required for SACRIFICES AND OFFERINGS and for sacred meals as well.

Cooking was performed in the Temple in Jerusalem, in the palace, in public bakeries, and on the road. Priests were in charge of baking bread and preparing other foods for sacred meals in kitchen facilities in the Temple precinct (Ezek 46:20, 23-24). Women were hired to bake and cook for the king's table according to 1 Sam 8:13; in Egypt, the chief baker of the royal court was a man of some importance (Gen 40:2). Professional bakers also operated in the cities of Judah, including Jerusalem, where a Bakers' Street (Jer 37:21) was presumably located near the fortress called the Tower of the Ovens (Neh 3:11; 12:38). These bakers were most likely men. Cooking activities were also performed while traveling, as during the exodus from Egypt (Exod 16:23).

The ancient Israelite diet was primarily vegetarian, and it relied on GRAIN, pulses, VEGETABLES, FRUITS, and dairy products. Breads, gruels, and parched grains made primarily from processed wheat, barley, and emmer were the staple foods in the Israelite diet. After harvesting and threshing, grains could be easily stored for use throughout the year. Grain processing was an arduous activity that could take up to several hours of work per day. Pulses like lentils, peas, and chickpeas were important sources of protein, as were dairy products like milk, soft cheeses, and butter. A variety of seasonal vegetables and fruits rounded out the diet, and seasonings like onions, garlic, and leeks as well as herbs, spices, and condiments were added to everyday soups and stews. Many cooked foods were prepared for consumption by boiling, although some could be fried in olive oil or rendered fat and prepared in other ways.

MEAT was costly (as evidenced by the food requirements of Solomon's palace [1 Kgs 4:23]) and thus usually was reserved for special occasions like festivals, banquets, sacrifices, or when receiving guests. Meat was boiled (Judg 6:19), roasted (1 Sam 2:15; Exod 12:8), or cooked in oil. There is no mention in the Bible of methods used to preserve meat, and we can assume that meat was usually prepared for immediate consumption. Archaeological excavations show that fish and fowl were more commonly consumed.

The typical ancient Israelite probably consumed three meals a day, but only the last meal—served after the agricultural work was done for the day—was a substantial hot meal. A BREAKFAST was served at home before the agricultural work was begun (Prov 31:15) and the afternoon meal, likely eaten in the fields, might include bread and parched grains dipped in vinegar (Ruth 2:14). Seasonal fruits and vegetables, along with dairy products, OIL, and WINE, were presumably consumed when they were available. The evening meal, served when the household members returned from farming, hunting, or other activities, most likely included a stew or pottage (Gen 25:29-34; 27:29; 2 Kgs 4:38-41). The story of Jesus cooking fish for a breakfast (John 21:9) possibly reflects a typical morning meal after a nighttime of fishing. The wealthy certainly enjoyed a richer and more varied diet than the commoners; Amos 6:4-6 refers to the extravagant dining habits of the rich.

Archaeological excavations at Israelite sites have shown that cooking activities usually took place in outdoor spaces associated with the household, especially courtyards. Depending on the time of year, some cooking activities may have been accomplished indoors on the ground floor or in another roofed space as well. The most commonly preserved cooking installations include hearths and bread OVENS (תַּנּוּר tannur), while artifacts related to cooking include ground stone tools and various types of POTTERY.

Based on analogies with well-preserved examples from ancient Egypt, we can assume that the Israelites used a number of tools related to food preparation and consumption made of perishable materials like wood. Because wood rots over time, the only cooking and serving vessels found in quantity in excavations in Israel are pottery containers and cooking vessels of various types. Four types of cooking VESSEL and a three-pronged fork are mentioned in 1 Sam 2:13-14, but distinguishing these vessels is difficult. Wide-mouthed cooking pots were likely used to cook stews and meat, while more narrow-necked cooking jugs were used for soups and gruels. Two-handled kraters may have been used for mixing, cooking, and serving hot stews. Meals were eaten from small bowls, and bread was likely used to scoop up food in lieu of utensils. Water, wine, milk, and other beverages were also consumed from small bowls. Ceramic griddles may have been used to bake bread; iron griddles (Lev 2:5) are not preserved archaeologically. *See* BAKE; BASIN; BOWL; CALDRON; CRUSE; FLAGON; FLASK; GOBLET.

Bibliography: Oded Borowski. *Daily Life in Biblical Times* (2003); Philip J. King and Lawrence E. Stager. *Life in Biblical Israel* (2001).

JENNIE EBELING

COPING [טֶפַח tefakh]. An architectural term in 1 Kgs 7:9, whose meaning is unclear. Elsewhere the word means "handbreadth" (1 Kgs 7:26; 2 Chr 4:5; Ps 39:5).

COPPER [נְחוּשָׁה nekhushah, נְחֹשֶׁת nekhosheth; χαλκός chalkos, λεπτός leptos]. The word *copper* is derived from Κύπρος Kypros, the name of the island of Cyprus, which is a rich source of copper ore. When alloyed with tin it produces BRONZE. In the OT, the Hebrew words are usually translated as *bronze*, since they refer to objects made of bronze. Deuteronomy 8:9 refers to the actual mining of copper, describing the "hills out of which you may dig copper." Job 28:2 mentions "copper smelted from the ore."

In the Late Bronze Age (1500–1200 BCE) copper was mined first in Cyprus, and later also in the mines of TIMNA in the Wadi Arabah, which were exploited by the Egyptians. This mining may have continued for a short while into the Early Iron Age (1200–1000 BCE), probably by groups of Midianites, but later in the Early Iron Age the mines of Khirbet en-Nahas in the East Wadi Arabah began to be exploited. Radiocarbon dating has shown that copper was mined here from as early as the 10th cent., probably by nonsedentary tribal groups, identified as KENITES by some scholars.

The copper ore was smelted onsite; copper ingots were traded with Gaza through the Beersheba Valley, and probably with Arabia as well. It is possible that King Solomon was involved in this copper trade, and that his reputation for wealth derived from this involvement. Exploitation of the copper mines of the Wadi Arabah increased greatly during the Assyrian period and was one of the main pillars of the economy of the kingdom of EDOM. The hills referred to in Deuteronomy therefore must refer to the copper mines of the Wadi Arabah.

In the NT, the word *copper* is generally used in the meaning of *copper* (actually bronze) coins (Matt 10:9; Mark 12:42; Luke 21:2).

EVELINE J. VAN DER STEEN

COPPER SCROLL. One of the most enigmatic of the DEAD SEA SCROLLS, the Copper Scroll (3Q15) is a list of buried treasure inscribed in Hebrew on three copper sheets, originally riveted together to form a single metal scroll. When it was discovered in 1952 in Cave 3 (2 km north of QUMRAN), the copper was completely oxidized, and it could not be unrolled. It was finally coated with adhesive, and then cut open for reading in 1956. It proved to contain a text that consists of sixty-four sections, each describing a treasure (usually various amounts of gold and silver), and indicating where the treasure is hidden (usually in places in or near the Jerusalem Temple or its surrounding region). Although some scholars have doubted the authenticity of the document, or dated it later than the other Dead Sea Scrolls, most accept it as genuine 1st cent. CE record of real treasure, originally belonging either to the Qumran covenanters or (more probably) to the Temple in Jerusalem. Thus the treasure may well represent part of the vast wealth of the Temple, hidden before the destruction of Jerusalem by the Romans in 70 CE (*see* TEMPLE, JERUSALEM).

Apart from this probable connection with the Temple in Jerusalem, the Copper Scroll is relevant for biblical studies in two ways: in demonstrating that Hebrew was a living language in 1st cent. Palestine, and in helping to recover the name of the pool in Jerusalem where Jesus healed an invalid (John 5:2).

The Copper Scroll is written in a type of Hebrew that is quite different from the classical literary Hebrew of the other Hebrew Dead Sea Scrolls. In fact, it represents an early form of Mishnaic Hebrew, marked, for example by the use of the preposition שֶׁל shel and the masculine plural ending -in, and thus reflects the spoken form of the language as it had developed from biblical Heb. This provides decisive evidence against the view that Hebrew was no longer a living language in the 1st cent., and that Jesus is therefore unlikely to have spoken it.

In col. 11, line 12 of the Copper Scroll, one of the hiding places is described as follows: "In Beth Eshdatain, in the reservoir [or pool]." This is probably a reference to the place described in John 5:2 as "a pool, which in Aram. [or Heb.] is called Bethesda." The Greek manuscripts of this verse vary between "Bethzatha," "Bethsaida," "Bethesda," and others, but the evidence of the Copper Scroll seems to clinch the correctness of the reading "BETHESDA."

Bibliography: George J. Brook and Philip R. Davies. *Copper Scroll Studies.* JSPSS 40 (2002); Al Wolters. *The Copper Scroll: Overview, Text and Translation* (1996); Al Wolters. "The Copper Scroll." *The Dead Sea Scrolls after Fifty Years*, ed. Peter W. Flint and James C. VanderKam (1998) 302–23.

AL WOLTERS

COPPERSMITH. *See* ALEXANDER; SMITH.

COPTIC LANGUAGE kop´tik. The adjective "Coptic" is derived from the Arabic rendering (qibti) of the Greek word for *Egyptian*, Αἰγύπτιος Aigyptios. The language comprises several dialects employed in EGYPT from the 2nd cent. CE until Arabic replaced Egyptian in the 8th cent.

Coptic represents the last stage in the long history of Egyptian language. An alphabetic script that represented vowels as well as consonants replaced the hieratic (a simpler, cursive form of hieroglyphics) and demotic script (an even simpler form of hieratic) used to write earlier forms of the language. The most common version of the Copt. alphabet supplements the twenty-four characters of the Greek alphabet with six more characters derived from the demotic script.

Coptic dictionaries list entries by their root consonants. Approximately two-thirds of the words in standard Copt. can be derived from earlier forms of Egyptian. In addition to words found only in Copt., the remaining vocabulary of Copt. texts is comprised of Greek words. Individual translators or authors may shift between a Greek word and its Copt. equivalent quite easily, which suggests that the Greek words had become part of the ordinary language. How many of the Greek meanings of a word can be transferred to its use in Copt. remains problematic.

Ptolemaic rule introduced Greek as the language of higher, level administration and learning in the 3rd cent. BCE. By the Roman period, private and administrative correspondence as well as literary composition was predominately Greek. Demotic was preserved in temples, on OSTRACA for local tax receipts, and in some private documents. Evidence for Copt. is sometimes linked to fragments of magical or astrological texts. Extensive written remains do not appear until the 3rd cent. CE, with the translation of biblical texts and other written material from Greek into Copt. The number of regional variations of the language suggests that it had developed as a spoken language before its appearance in written form. Despite its considerable Greek vocabulary, Copt. grammar and syntax remain a form of Egyptian.

Scholars have linked major dialects and variants in the language with distinct regions along the Nile valley. However, assigning distinctive locations to the six or more variations of Copt. remains a challenge for linguists. Three major divisions of Egypt account for the most prominent dialects, the Nile Delta, middle Egypt from Cairo (Heliopolis–Memphis) to al-Ashmunayn (Hermopolis), and upper Egypt, everything to the south. *Bohairic* was the dialect of the Nile Delta. Hundreds of Bohairic inscriptions were found at the monastic site of Kellia. Nonliterary text remains found in the region of Fayyum led to the classification of another dialect as *Fayyumic*. A third dialect, *Akhmimic*, is associated with upper Egypt.

The distribution, classification, and spread of dialects associated with middle Egypt continue to be debated. The most dominant dialect, *Sahidic*, can be found along much of the Nile Valley. Linguists often refer to Sahidic as "neutral" since it has the fewest idiosyncratic traits. A standard or "classical" form of Sahidic was established through 4th cent. translations of the Bible. Linguists disagree over its original locale with proposals ranging from Oxyrhynchus to Memphis or Thebes. Additional minor dialects have also been identified with middle Egypt, Mesokemic and Lycopolitan. Lycopolitan, a dialect also refered to as "subAkhmimic," occupies a region that overlaps Akhminic in the south and Sahidic. A number of Copt. treatises found near NAG HAMMADI are in this dialect or in Sahidic that includes features of it. In addition to the Nag Hammadi evidence, Lycopolitan is represented in a 4th cent. manuscript of John's Gospel and other NT fragments and in the Manichean texts of the 4th and 5th cent. from Madinat Madi.

Lycopolitan does not appear after the 5th cent. Sahidic serves as the language of the Nile Valley but is not attested in the Nile Delta where Bohairic dominates. Therefore some linguists would speak of each of these supraregional dialects as a separate Copt. language.

The Egyptian Copt. Church retains a medieval form of the Bohairic dialect in its liturgy, although the participants cannot understand the language. *See* VERSIONS, COPTIC.

Bibliography: Bentlye Layton. *A Copt. Grammar* (2000); Tito Orlandi. "Coptic Literature." *The Roots of Egyptian Christianity* (1986).

PHEME PERKINS

COR kor [כֹּר kor; κόρος koros]. The largest biblical dry measure of capacity, used for flour, wheat, and barley (1 Kgs 4:22; 5:2; 2 Chr 2:10; Ezra 7:22). There is no biblical evidence about the value of a cor. If a cor equaled the Mesopotamian *gur* (= 180 *qa*), and if *qa* was ca. 1 liter, then kor was ca. 180 liters. According to the difficult verse of Ezek 45:14 (which also uses *cor* for liquids), cor was equal to homer, which contained 10 baths, ca. 210 liters, from inscribed Iron Age vessels indicating that a BATH was ca. 21 liters. *See* WEIGHTS AND MEASURES.

RAZ KLETTER

CORBAN kor'ban [קָרְבָּן qorban; κορβᾶν korban]. In the OT, *corban* primarily denotes a gift or sacrificial offering that is consecrated to God (Lev 2:1, 4, 12, 13; Neh 10:35). In later Judaism it also introduces a vow dedicating something to God, declaring it holy by separating it from the secular sphere so that others may not benefit from it. Corban appears in the NT only in Mark 7:11, where Jesus is arguing with the Pharisees over purity practices, thus over the nature of holiness.

Citing the fifth commandment, Jesus rejects a practice allowing a son to make a vow declaring his goods holy, thereby exempting him from sharing them with his parents. Hence, Jesus effectively reconfigures holiness more as compassion toward others than as separation from the secular. *See* HOLY, HOLINESS, NT; SACRIFICES AND OFFERINGS; SANCTIFICATION.

Bibliography: Jon Nelson Bailey. "Vowing Away the Fifth Commandment: Matthew 15:3–6//Mark 7:9–13." *ResQ* 42 (2000) 193–209.

ANDY JOHNSON

CORD, ROPE [עֲבֹת 'avoth, פָּתִיל pathil; σκοινίον skoinion]. Several words for "cord" or "rope" in the Bible denote its various ritual or practical functions.

Cords are a key feature of the high priest's sacerdotal garments, serving to hold the parts of his garb together and sharing in his vestments' symbolic power that derives in part from the richness of their composition. Cords made of double-chains of pure gold (הָעֲבֹתֹת שַׁרְשְׁרֹת sharsheroth ha'abothoth) are attached to the settings of the two name-bearing onyx stones set at the shoulders of the EPHOD (Exod 28:14, 22, 24, 25; *see also* 39:3). Cords of fine blue (פָּתִיל תְּכֵלֶת pathil tekheleth) attached to gold rings join the BREASTPIECE to the ephod and the pure gold rosette (inscribed with "Holy to the Lord") to the priest's turban (Exod 28:28, 37).

Other quasi ritual uses of cord include its function as part of Judah's familial identity marker (Gen 38:18, 25) and its addition in blue to the ritual fringes on a garment (Num 15:35). Cords also appear in the Psalms and Prophetic Literature as symbolic expressions of the restraint sin or oppression impose on humankind (Isa 5:18; Pss 2:3; 129:4) and of God's loving embrace (Hos 11:4). And of course, ropes and cords appear in their simplest functions, as physical restraints (Judg 15:13, 14; 16:9, 11, 12; Ezek 3:25; 4:8), leads (Job 39:10), measuring tools (Ezek 40:3), and a means of escape (Josh 2:18).

ROBERT KUGLER

CORIANDER SEED [גַּד gadh]. The seed of the coriander plant (*Coriandrum sativum*), which is also known as cilantro and Chinese parsley, is used as a spice. Its greens may have been one of the BITTER HERBS. The term is only used in the OT to describe the appearance of MANNA (Exod 16:31; Num 11:7).

CORINTH kor'inth [Κόρινθος Korinthos]. City commanding the isthmus linking the Peleoponnese to mainland Greece. Paul worked with Prisca and Aquila for eighteen months while founding the church there (spring 50 to late summer 51, Acts 1:1-18). He made two subsequent visits (2 Cor 12:14; 13:1), on the second of which he wrote Romans. He wrote a series of letters to the community, two of which have been lost (1 Cor 5:9; 2 Cor 2:4).

Corinth's control of the harbors of Lechaeum and Cenchreae, and of the road across the 6 km-wide isthmus, enabled it to levy taxes on both north–south and east–west trade (Strabo, *Geogr.* 8.6.20). Thus from the time of Homer (*Il.* 2.570) the adjective inevitably applied to Corinth was "wealthy" (Dio Chrysostom, *Or.* 37.36). A vast plain, proverbial for its agricultural richness, stretched out to the west As host to the biennial Isthmian Games, the economy of Corinth benefited from the great influx of spectators.

The city was built on two natural terraces stepping down from Acrocorinth (575 m) to the coastal plain, but it never expanded to fill the space enclosed by the great 10-km wall erected on the optimal defensive line. Other walls 2.5 km long and approximately the same distance apart reached out to enclose the port of Lechaeum, its lifeline to the west.

Corinth has been excavated by the American School of Classical Studies at Athens since 1896. Preliminary studies appear in the *AJA* and *Hesperia*, and final reports in the series *Corinth* (1930–). In addition to a number of peripheral sites, the whole center of the city has been revealed, and the buildings that Paul saw identified.

The glorious history of Greek Corinth began in the 5th millenium BCE and came to an end when the Roman general Lucius Mummius destroyed it in 146 BCE. It is now recognized that Corinth was not "sex city" par excellence. It was not dedicated to Aphrodite, the goddess of love, and Strabo's story of 1,000 sacred prostitutes (*Geogr.* 8.6.20) rests on a misunderstanding. Moreover, the two excavated temples of Aphrodite are far too small. In the 5th and 4th cents. BCE, Athenian

writers invented words such as korinthiazesthai "to fornicate"; korinthiastēs "a pimp"; korinthia, korē "a prostitute," which were designed to make Corinth the symbol of commercial sex, but these neologisms took no permanent root in Greek.

The city that Paul knew was restored in 44 BCE by Julius Caesar as the *Colonia Laus Julia Corinthiensis*. It became the capital when Achaia was created a Roman province in 27 BCE. The province was governed by a proconsul, who served for one year, from July 1–June 30. Each city had its own municipal government, and Corinth's reflected that of republican Rome. Each year the citizens elected two senior magistrates (*duoviri iure dicundo*), who were the executive officers of the city, and two assistants (*aediles*). A 1st cent. CE inscription found east of the theater mentions an *aedile* named Erastus, who is considered to be the individual mentioned by Paul in Rom 16:23 and 2 Tim 4:20.

The first colonists were ex-slaves from Greece, Syria, Judea, and Egypt who had everything to gain. They began by robbing tombs to make a living, but the site had so much economic potential that within fifty years a number of the citizens were millionaires.

When the colonists started to build they were constrained to fit into the rectangular grid plan of long and short blocks laid down by one of Rome's finest city planners. The centerpiece was the great AGORA (15,300 sq. m). On the north side a monumental gate opened onto the road to Lechaeum. It was flanked by the north stoa and the Fountain of Peirene. A magnificent stoa ran the length of the south side in front of a number of important civic offices. The Julian Basilica marked the east side, whereas a fountain and two small temples lined the west side. In the middle of the agora was the

Todd Bolin

Figure 1: Temple of Apollo with Acrocorinth in the background

Speaker's Platform (Βῆμα bēma), where the Jews tried to arraign Paul before the Roman governor GALLIO (Acts 18:12).

Lucius Iunius Gallio was proconsul of Achaia from July 1, 51, to June 30, 52. Since he did not complete his term, leaving before winter began in late September, Paul must have met him toward the end of the summer of 51. This is a key date in the chronology of Paul's life.

The number of the inhabitants of Corinth has not been calculated satisfactorily. There is no doubt, however, that the population was extremely diverse both religiously and ethnically. The continuity of Greek cults is attested by shrines to Apollo, Athena, Aphrodite, Asclepios, Demeter and Kore, Palaimon, and Sisyphus. The worship of Isis and Sarapis witnesses to Egyptian influence. There was a temple dedicated to the Roman emperor. Philo (*Legat.* 281) attests a large and vital Jewish presence, but physical remains are sparse and late. The city recognized the Jewish community as a *politeuma*, a corporation of foreigners with permanent right of residence and governed by its own officials in its internal affairs (Acts 18:15).

Corinth had two principal recreational areas. Cranaeum was a spacious parklike suburb on the upper slopes of Acrocorinth. According to tradition, it was there, because of the crowds it attracted, that Diogenes the Cynic (ca. 400–325 BCE) lived in his barrel as a prophetic gesture of simplicity of life. "Once Alexander [the Great] came and stood over him and said, 'Ask of me anything you desire.' To which he replied, 'Stand out of my light'" (Plutarch, *Alex.,* 14). The alternative to Cranaeum was on the other side of the city. The fine swimming pool of the Lerna lay just inside the north wall. Adjoining it was the temple of Asclepios, whose dining rooms, which fronted a beautiful little square, could have been the setting for the problem of eating meat offered to idols (1 Cor 8–10).

Corinth had the honor of hosting the Isthmian Games, one of the four great pan-Hellenic festivals celebrating the worldwide unity of the Greek people. They took place biennially in April or May, and the presidency (αγωνοθετης agōnothetēs) was the supreme honor that the city could confer. The victor's crown was of dry celery. In 51, when Paul could have attended the games (1 Cor 9:24-27), the facilities at the traditional site of the temple of Poseidon at Isthmia were only being repaired, so the sporting and musical events must have taken place somewhere closer to the city. Nonetheless there would have been the same need for tents to house the great number of visitors and the wares of Corinthians who served them. Tentmakers at Corinth (Acts 18:3) had plenty of work in both manufacture and repair.

The ethos of Corinth is summed up in a proverb and a myth. The proverb was quoted by both Greeks and Romans, "Not for everyone is the voyage to Corinth" (Strabo, *Geogr.* 8.6.20; Horace, *Ep.,* 1.17.36). It meant that only the tough survived at Corinth. The myth of Sisyphus (Homer, *Od.* 11.593-600) taught them that existence was precarious and that luck counted for more than effort. Sisyphus had been a king of Corinth who enjoyed the success of a trickster, but in the underworld his task was to push a rock up a mountain. Each time he approached the summit it slipped from his hands and he had to start all over again.

Paradoxically Corinth's energetic, aggressive reputation may explain why Paul settled there rather than in placid, academic Athens (Acts 17). If he could establish a church amid the cutthroat competition of a boomtown, it would be a perfect demonstration of the power of the gospel. Later he would say that he needed no letter of recommendation other than the existence of the Corinthian church (2 Cor 3:2). Corinth also offered Paul other advantages. Merchants left regularly for all points of the compass. There would always be a group that his letter-bearers could join for security. Further, the extraordinary number of visitors to Corinth produced potential converts who would carry the gospel back to their homelands, as Epaphras did at Colossae (Col 1:7; 4:12).

The sort of workshop in which Paul worked with Prisca and Aquila (Acts 18:1-3) was scattered all over the city. They lined the streets, but were also concentrated in commercial developments. The North Market was completed not long before Paul arrived and perfectly illustrates their living and working conditions. The shops opened onto a wide, covered gallery running around four sides of a great square. They had a uniform height and depth of 4 m. The width varied from 2.8 m to 4. The wide doorway was the only source of light. There were no running water or toilet facilities. At the back, steps led to a loft lit by an unglazed window. Prisca and Aquila slept in the loft, while Paul bedded down below among the rolls of leather and canvas.

The workshop was ideal for initial missionary contacts, but for assemblies Paul needed a large private house. One of his first converts was Gaius (1 Cor 1:14), whose home was capable of holding the whole community (Rom 16:23). Presumably Phoebe offered the same facilities at Cenchreae (Rom 16:1-2). Her role as patron is perfectly illustrated by an inscription honoring her contemporary, Junia Theodora, who without any official position effectively acted as the ambassador of Lycia at Corinth, providing hospitality and smoothing official and business relationships.

There were other Christians of Gaius' social class who were wealthy and influential (1 Cor 1:26). The majority of believers were not so fortunate, but neither were they on the level of the mine and field slaves who were the very bottom of the social ladder. Sixteen members of the church at Corinth are mentioned in Acts 18:1-18; 1 Cor 1:14-16; 16:15-19; and Rom 16:21-23. This would mean that the community numbered between forty and fifty at a minimum. The vast majority had been pagans (1 Cor 12:2), but six of the named individuals were Jews.

The early 1st cent. villa excavated at Anaploga within the walls of ancient Corinth illustrates the type of well-to-do house in which Corinthian believers met for their liturgical assemblies. The quality of the mosaic floor of the dining room shows that the owner had the surplus wealth that would permit him to host the community. The dining room, however, measured only 5.5 × 7.5 m, giving a floor area of 41.25 sq. m. This is barely enough to hold the fforty to fifty members of the church, if they stood shoulder to shoulder and the space taken up by the couches is ignored. Hence, only some could be entertained in the comfortable dining room, the rest had to make do with the much inferior conditions of the atrium just outside. This discrimination thus imposed created problems at the Eucharist (1 Cor 11:17-32). *See* ACHAIA; CORINTHIANS, FIRST LETTER TO THE; CORINTHIANS, SECOND LETTER TO THE; EUCHARIST; GAIUS; GALLIO; PAUL THE APOSTLE.

Bibliography: D. Engels. *Roman Corinth. An Alternative Model for the Classical City* (1990); T. E. Gregory, ed. *The Corinthia in the Roman Period: Journal of Roman Studies* (1993); C. K. Williams and N. Bookidis, ed. *Corinth XX. The Centenary 1896–1996.* American School at Athens (2003); J. Murphy-O'Connor. *St. Paul's Corinth. Texts and Archaeology* (2002); R. M. Rothaus. *Corinth: The First City of Greece. An Urban History of Late Antique Cult and Religion* (2000); J. Wiseman. *The Land of the Ancient Corinthians* (1978).

JEROME MURPHY-O'CONNOR

CORINTHIANS, FIRST LETTER TO kuh-rin'thee-uhns. The letter of Paul traditionally known as *The First Epistle to the Corinthians* was not the first letter that Paul wrote to Christians in Corinth. In 1 Cor 5:9 he writes, "I wrote to you in my [previous] letter not to associate with immoral persons." Paul had a sustained interaction with them through oral reports and letters. He first arrived in Corinth en route from Athens in 49 or 50 CE, and ministered there for eighteen months during the proconsulship of Gallio (51–52 or 50–51). Paul wrote the "previous" letter (of 1 Cor 5:9) from Ephesus, on hearing a disquieting report of developments. In the spring or summer of 54 he wrote 1 Corinthians in part in response to an oral report of "splits" (σχίσματα schis mata) from "Chloe's people" (1:11; *see* CHLOE as well as other reports from STEPHANAS, FORTUNATUS, and ACHAICUS; 16:17). He reacts to these reports in 1:10–6:20. Paul also received a letter of inquiry from Corinth, to which he responds in 7:1–14:40. Some sections begin, "Now concerning the matters about which you wrote" (7:1; 8:1; 12:1).

Some argue that 1 Corinthians includes a collection of three or more separate letters (discussed in §B.4). This would further complicate the scope of its title. However, others argue no less strongly for the unity of 1 Corinthians. The epistle is coherent, and exponents of partition theories fail to agree precisely on where one separate letter ends and another begins. Some postulate another (third) "intermediate" letter (or part of a letter) between 1 and 2 Corinthians. If this is correct, 1 Corinthians would be Paul's second letter to Corinth, and 2 Corinthians would be his fourth.

Overview of the book. In broad terms 1 Corinthians embodies five general segments of discussion:

1. Chapters 1–4 expound the *causes and cures of "splits"* (σχίσματα schismata) within the Christian community in Corinth (1:10–4:21). Paul's diagnosis of their causes includes an exposé of a power play, coupled with a failure to appreciate the centrality of Christ and the gospel of the cross (1:10–3:4). He also ascribes the problem to a false understanding of *wisdom* and a distorted view of the role of *ministers* (3:5–4:21).

2. Chapters 5–6 convey Paul's further response to oral reports. They include a shameless attitude toward a *case of incest* (5:1-13); a grasping and manipulative use of Roman *civil law* (6:1-8); and immoral and grasping attitudes and public *conduct incompatible with Christian lifestyle* (6:9-20). Paul affirms that *bodily* life gives credibility and currency to Christian discipleship in *the public domain*.

3. Chapters 7–10 take up the letter from Corinth. Chapter 7 concerns *marriage, celibacy, widowhood, and singleness* (7:1-40). chs. 8–10 concern *"food sacrificed to idols"* (8:1). Does a robust confidence in the non-being of pagan deities permit a liberal approach to dining in pagan temples, or must the scruples of more anxious Christians decide the issue? Some regard 9:1-27 as a digression in defense of Paul's apostleship, but Paul offers a case-study of a *willingness to forego "rights"* if this helps the vulnerable.

4. Chapters 11–14 address aspects of *public worship*. Paul affirms the authority of women to lead in public prayer and in prophetic discourse, but expounds mutuality and reciprocity rather than "sameness" between the genders (11:2-16). Current ways of celebrating the Lord's Supper in Corinth do "more harm than good" (11:17). The framework of appropriating, and participating in, the redemptive events of the cross as the new Passover have become overshadowed by dining customs that divide the community (11:17-34). Paul insists on proper criteria for the exercise of spiritual gifts (12:1–14:40). Does the way in which Christians regard and use these reflect the Spirit's witness to Christ as Lord and *build up* the church as a whole and build "the other?" The chapter on love (13:1-13) forms an integral part of this argument.

5. Chapter 15 expounds *the resurrection of the dead.* Paul addresses several different problems posed by different groups. The concept, actuality, and promise of the resurrection of the dead become credible and intelligible when they are perceived to rest upon the creative and transforming act of God already exemplified and witnessed in the resurrection of Jesus Christ. It constitutes an act of divine grace and "reversal," pledged to the new humanity "in Christ" as the last Adam (15:42-52). Paul concludes the letter with arrangements for the collection, travel plans, and final greetings.

To trace this overview of content still leaves open the question of what core issues yield such a wide range of topics. Some hold that the plea for unity is the overriding concern of this epistle. Others have perceived a relapse into questionable ethical standards as a unifying theme. But this does not characterize the entire letter, and belongs to the era when writers ascribed to Corinth a Greek rather than Roman background. Julius Caesar refounded Corinth as a Roman colony by 44 BCE.

We suggest (in §B) a more complex but coherent set of factors derived largely from the very prosperity of the Roman city of Corinth and its culture of competitive self-promotion (Pogoloff 1992; Clarke 1993; Witherington 1995). Corinth boasted a vibrant, successful, self-sufficient, flourishing economy based on competitive choice and a consumerist ethos that encouraged "winners." This did not fit well with Paul's proclamation of "a crucified Christ": to the Jews an affront; to Gentiles, "folly" (1:24). Many in Corinth became Christians, but could not they construct a more triumphalist "local" theology appropriate to "winners" who reveled in "success," than Paul's preoccupation with the cross and lowly service? They wanted an emphasis on self-affirmation; freedom to choose (whether leaders or lifestyles); autonomy in ethics and church practice; and status-recognition for those with impressive "spiritual" gifts or impressive social backgrounds. Against this, Paul declares, "Let the one who boasts, boast in the Lord" (1 Cor 1:31); "let no one boast about human leaders" (3:21); "each one will receive commendation *from God*" (4:5).

A. Division and Structure of the Letter
B. Detailed Analysis of Rhetorical, Literary, Social, Cultural, Historical, and Interpretive Issues
  1. Rhetorical and epistolary forms
  2. The historical, geographical, and cultural situation: theological implications
  3. Social diversity and light from archaeological research
  4. Date of Paul's arrival in Corinth and of the writing of the letter
  5. Unity and integrity of the Letter
  6. Questions of exegetical debate and interpretation:
    a. "The splits" and issues of ministry (chs. 1–4)
    b. The case of incest, going to law, and "bodily" lifestyles (chs. 5–6)
    c. Material on the household; and "food offered to idols" (chs. 7–10)
    d. Problems in public worship: gender and attire; the Lord's Supper; and spiritual gifts (chs. 11–14)
    e. The resurrection chapter; the collection; and greetings (chs. 15–16)
C. Theological and Religious Significance of the Letter

A. Division and Structure of the Letter
Introduction: address, greeting, and thanksgiving 1:1-9
Address and greeting, alluding to the wider, translocal church 1:1-3*b*
Thanksgiving for the reader's gifts with a future eschatological focus 1:1-3

1. Causes and cures of the "splits": Power-play and status-seeking are incompatible with the gospel of the cross and its ministry 1:10–4:21
  a. Paul's appeal based on an oral report of the situation in Corinth 1:10-17
    i. The *propositio* : an appeal to mend the splits
    ii. The report of splits around actual (or hypothetical?) figures 1:11, 12
    iii. The splits are incompatible with a gospel of the cross 1:13-17
  b. The transformative power of the cross is not derived from *human* "wisdom" 1:18–2:5
    i. The cross as the criterion of the gospel and of the church 1:18-25
    ii. The social history of the congregation demonstrates the two "wisdoms" 1:26-31
    iii. Paul's mode of proclamation exemplifies the centrality of the cross 2:1-5
  c. Christ-centred understandings of *wisdom, Spirit, and spiritual* 2:6–3:4
    i. *Wisdom* redefined as revealed by God 2:6-9
    ii. The *Spirit* as transcendent, transforming, and Christomorphic 2:10-16
    iii. *Spiritual* as excluding self-centerdness and leading to maturity 3:1-4
  d. Applying these theological criteria to the church and ministry 3:5–4:21
    i. A true estimate of ministers is neither too high nor too low 3:5-9*a*
    ii. The church is God's: God's field, God's building, and God's sacred shrine 3:9*b*-17
    iii. Human judgments are fallible; wait for God's definitive verdict 3:18–4:5
    iv. All is given by grace alone; premature triumphalism has no place 4:6-13

v. Paul's pastoral care in word and deed 4:14-21

2. Issues of moral attitude and conduct that require change (also orally reported)

a. Shameless complacency over a case of incest: there are boundaries 5:1-13

b. The abuse of Roman civil law: a case of manipulation for gain 6:1-11

c. The common theme of "grasping" what is beyond the boundaries: union with Christ is to be lived out in an appropriate bodily public behavior 6:12-20

3. Paul's responses to more delicate issues raised in the letter of enquiry from Corinth: marriage, celibacy, slavery, widowhood, food offered to idols 7:1–11:1

a. Marriage, celibacy, singleness, slaves, and those widowed 7:1-40

i. Response to the Corinthian maxim cited in 7:1; the reciprocity and mutuality in marriage, and the gift of singleness 7:1-7

ii. A case for becoming married or a case for separation? 7:8-11

iii. Christians who are married already to unbelievers 7:12-16

iv. "Using" slavery or freedom in the service of the Lord 7:17-24

v. Further considerations about those not yet (or now) married: should they remain as they are? 7:25-40

b. Love for the other *versus* "my rights": the limits of "knowledge" 8:1-13

i. What does "knowledge" entailed in monotheistic faith imply? 8:1-6

ii. Freedom, "rights," and love for the other 8:7-13

c. Paul's personal example of willingness to forego "rights": everything for the sake of the gospel 9:1-23

d. Winning: a new application on self-discipline and self-control 9:24-27

e. Formative models: warning against "craving" drawn from Scripture 10:1-13

f. Covenant loyalty and participation in the Lord's Supper 10:14-22

g. Love for the other and "rights," with a case study 10:23–11:1

4. Love and respect for the other in the ordering of public worship 11:2–14:40

a. Mutual respect and self-respect in the context of gender-mutuality and complementarity 11:2-16

b. The Lord's Supper as a proclamation of the Lord's death: love and mutual respect between the influential and the vulnerable 11:17-34

c. Unity and variety of gifts freely bestowed for the purpose of building up the church and the other 12:4-11

i. Christ-centerd criteria for what is *spiritual* or *of the Spirit* 12:1-3

ii. Variety of gifts given for the single purpose of building the church 12:4-11

iii. The imagery of the body and limbs applied in favor of the vulnerable: inter-dependence and mutuality 12:12-26

iv. Fullness of gifts surpasses the capacity of any single individual 12:27-31

d. A meditation on the nature of love and call for mutual respect 13:1-13:

i. Love as the indispensable criterion for fruitfulness 13:1-3

ii. The dynamic and transforming effects of love in action 13:4-7

iii. Love as lasting into the solid future of the eschaton 13:8-13

e. Love for the other expressed as self-restrained orderedness in public worship: prophecy and speaking in tongues 14:1-40:

i. Only intelligible speech can "build up" the other person; the use of the mind 14:1-25

ii. Controlled speech: does order or anarchy signify the Spirit at work? 14:26-40

5. The resurrection of Christ and the resurrection of the dead are credible and conceivable; practical consequences for the present 15:1-58

a. *Propositio*: the reality of the resurrection of Jesus Christ, attested by public witness and by pre-Pauline tradition 15:1-11

b. First *refutatio*: the unacceptable consequences of denying the resurrection 15:12-19

c. First *confirmatio*: the resurrection of Jesus Christ as the foundation of present life and future promise 15:20-34

d. Second *refutatio*: the fallacy of the argument that "*somatic*" resurrection is inconceivable 15:35-49

i. *Exclamatio*: the folly of an inadequate view of the Creator and creation 15:35-41

ii. God's creative power through the transforming agency of the Holy Spirit 15:42-49

e. Second *confirmatio*: transformation in full in the eschatological future 15:50-57

f. The *peroratio*: the argument applied to the present 15:58

Concluding comments and concerns 16:1-24

a. The collection: participation, mutuality, solidarity with Jerusalem 16:1-4

b. Travel plans: consistent intentions, and co-workers 16:5-12

c. *Peroratio*: final exhortations and greetings 16:13-24

B. Detailed Analysis of Rhetorical, Literary, Social, Cultural, Historical, and Interpretive Issues

1. Rhetorical and epistolary forms

Research on Paul's uses of classical rhetoric emerged during the beginning of the 20th cent. However, this was largely lost from view until new interest in Paul's use of rhetorical forms reappeared in the last quarter of the 20th cent. This recent research suggests that *deliberative rhetoric* features prominently in this letter. Such rhetoric addresses issues of future policy, often for the advantage or benefit of the parties concerned. Paul's response to the Corinthian slogan "all things are lawful" well illustrates it: "not all things profit" (συμφέρει sympherei, 6:12 and 10:23. Deliberative rhetoric is also prominent in 8:6–11:1, where again Paul sets out a beneficial policy for the future. It appeals to desire and emotion as well as to thought. Paul also uses *epideictic rhetoric* of praise or blame in 4:14-21; and 11:1, 17). *Forensic* or judicial rhetoric seems to appear in the *refutatio* of 10:1-22 and 15:12-19. Paul uses a range of rhetorical resources that include antithesis, assonance, chiasmus, "code-switching" (a form of persuasive definition), *confirmatio*, diatribe, *insinuato*, irony, *narratio*, *propositio*, and *refutatio*.

However, this is not an audience-pleasing rhetoric of mere manipulative persuasion. While rhetoric in Corinth often took the form of a competitive, audience-orientated, "performance" designed *to win* a case often *against* all reason, Paul used rhetorical resources in the service of truth. He respected the givenness of apostolic tradition, Scripture, and the cross. Some postmodern writers use "rhetorical" to suggest a consumerist and socially constructed notion of "truth" shaped only by pragmatic appeals to an audience. In Corinth, as in the Sophist movement, rhetorical contests were not between *theories* but between personalities and *performers*. Roman rhetoricians in the tradition of Cicero, Quintilian, and Seneca the Elder lamented the corruption of rhetoric into an audience-pleasing competitive game, motivated by a desire for applause. Rhetoric, Seneca laments, has been debased into a vehicle "to win approval for yourself rather than for the case" (*Controversiae* 3:15; 7:8-9; 9:1). Quintilian complains that in competitive rhetoric people leap up "with a storm of ready-made applause . . . The result is empty self-sufficiency" (2:9-12). Is the gospel to be shaped by the desires of the audience for self-affirmation, or by the givenness of the apostolic proclamation of the cross (1:18–2:16)?

In 1 Cor 1–4, Paul "mimes" the role of the fool. He draws heavily on metaphors of the theater. Apostles are "a spectacle to the world" (4:9). In self-parody Paul calls himself "weak" and in disrepute, as an emissary of the crucified Christ (1 Cor 1:5; 4:8). Eloquent wisdom has no role (1:19-20; 2:1, 4), which means that the rhetorical forms attributed to chs. 5–16 remain an open question.

All the same, Paul does not disparage the use of *reason* and *argument*. The structure of 1 Cor 15 provides a model of rational argument, employing deduction, induction, inference, entailment, analogy, *reductio ad absurdum*, and *a fortiori* argument. Paul's use of argument sometimes stems from premises that appeal to reason; but often also from premises derived from Scripture and apostolic tradition. Paul uses "enthymemes," or shared premises that initiate changes of *attitude* or of *understanding*. Further, Paul's proclamation of the gospel takes the form of a *performative* or *illocutionary speech-act*: its very proclamation projects a "world" that actively transforms those who enter it. Paul meets his hearers in Corinth where their worlds of concepts or understanding can readily engage with his (1 Cor 9:19-23); but this is different from redefining the gospel to match Corinthian desires.

Some biblical scholars remain cautious about the emphasis on rhetoric in NT studies. They urge that the literary form of 1 Corinthians is that of a letter, not rhetorical discourse. It appears, however, that both epistolary and rhetorical resources are employed by Paul. Paul uses the conventional greeting-form and thanksgiving-form usually found at the beginning of letters of this period (1 Cor 1:1-9), even if filled with Christian content. Paul does not reject conventions of the non-Christian world. Only if such conventions conflict with the gospel does Paul becomes "counter-cultural."

2. The historical, geographical, and cultural situation: theological implications

Corinth saw itself as a Roman city. In 146 BCE it had challenged Rome's protection of Sparta, and Roman troops virtually destroyed the city. In 44 BCE, Julius Caesar refounded the city as a *colonia* for his veterans, and a large number of legionaries, together with freedpersons, slaves, and commercial entrepreneurs settled in Corinth over the next decades. By the middle of the 1st cent. Corinth had become a magnet that attracted businesspeople, trade, manufacture, tourism, and any who hoped to rise quickly to financial or social success. It became a vibrant, self-sufficient, and generally wealthy city, although with great variations in socioeconomic status among its people. It surpassed Athens in vitality. This ethos of independence, self-sufficiency, autonomy, and self-promotion constituted the context within which the Christian community sought to grow and to discover its identity. Some sought to reshape the gospel of the cross into an altogether more self-affirming and triumphalist religious identity; indeed, into a "Corinthian," rather than a Pauline or apostolic theology.

The geographical setting of the city provided an assured economic prosperity. Located on a narrow isthmus of barely 6 mi. across, the city boasted two harbors: Cenchreae faced East toward Asia and Ephesus: Lechaeum faced West toward Italy and Rome. The isthmus also stood between northern Greece and the Peloponnese. It stood at a four-way intersection of trade. Merchants and sailors preferred to stop off in Corinth, perhaps to move light ships on rollers across the paved diolkos between the two harbors, or otherwise to pay tolls and reload, rather than risk the storms and winds round Cape Malea at the southern tip of Greece. Trade, taxes, and business flowed into Corinth. The Peirene Fountains produced an almost limitless quantity of water not only for domestic use but also for manufacturing and the needs of tourists. Large deposits of marl and clay were utilized for the production of pottery, bricks, roof tiles, utensils, and terra-cotta ornaments. Tourists flocked in especially for the Isthmian Games. These afforded a multiplicity of spectacular attractions. Visitors brought money to buy goods, rent rooms, hire or employ carpenters, tent-makers, housekeepers, guides, bodyguards, dockers, ships, chariots, lawyers, doctors, and literate or menial slaves. The entire mood was orientated toward "success" and competitive consumerism.

What chance did Paul have when he arrived to preach "a crucified Christ; a stumbling block to Jews and foolishness to Gentiles" (1 Cor 1:23)? A crucified Christ was an *affront* (σκάνδαλον skandalon, 1:23). Christians in Corinth wished to perceive themselves as "spiritual people" (3:1-3); as "rich and reigning" (4:8-13), with "liberty to do all things" (6:12; 10:23); possessing "knowledge" (γνῶσις gnōsis, 8:1); choosing their leaders (1:12; 4:6); served by "paid professionals" (9:3-12), and possessing spectacular signs of "spirituality" (12:1-11; 14:1-25).

Christians in Corinth wanted to construct their own "local" theology. But Paul constantly reminds them they are part of a universal church, in effect one, holy, catholic, and apostolic. They are "called . . . *together with all* who call on the name of our Lord Jesus Christ in every place, both their Lord and our Lord" (1:2). To follow a self-chosen leader cheats them out of the universal resources of the church as a whole (3:18). "The body is one" (12:12), so Christians can neither disclaim membership of the body of Christ (12:15-17), nor say of other Christians, "I have no need of you" (12:21). The "weak," Paul insists, are essential to the body as a whole (12:22-24). The body must not suffer splits (12:25).

3. Social diversity and light from archaeological research

The social status of Christians in Corinth has received considerable attention. Some argue that in general Corinthians were from the least privileged laboring classes, and included many nonliterate freedpersons or slaves. By contrast others cite evidence for a wider spectrum of social standing, including some who owned businesses or possessed houses large enough to host assemblies for Christian worship. A compromise view describes the social situation in terms of the "social stratification" of Christians in Corinth. The majority were from the least privileged backgrounds, and they were regarded as "nothings" and "nobodies" in 1:27-28, and *weak* in chs. 8–10, though the meaning of *weak* may not carry this reference to class. Some Christians, however, were wealthy and influential. Seventeen prominent figures included office-holders such as CRISPUS, the synagogue ruler (Acts 18:8) and ERASTUS, city-treasurer (Rom 16:23). They included heads of households such as STEPHANAS (1 Cor 1:16 and 16:15), and householders who were able to render services to Paul or to the church, such as Crispus, and Gaius. A few were "on the rise socially," with Corinth's rapid economic upturn. But the lot of Christians was socially variable. Many were all too conscious of differences of social class, influence, patronage, wealth, and power, down to extreme poverty.

The status of slaves could vary dramatically from that of a trusted manager of a business or estate to the status of mere "property" (Lat., *res*, a thing) with no human rights. Social indicators varied along different axes of birth, influence, financial resources, benefit of a patron, business occupation, and so on. Status might be "recognized" according to different scales of values, even to criteria of supposed "spirituality." The painful division between "haves" and "have nots" (11:22) reaches its clearest focus in the "splits" (σχίσματα schismata, 11:18) that emerged in the Lord's Supper or Eucharist. Wealthy members who had houses large enough to "host" the meal followed the Roman dining customs that accommodated socially more important guests in the *triclinium* on couches, while less prestigious guests stood in the *atrium* and were served second-class food or leftovers. This practice, if it occurred, would defeat the very purpose of the Lord's Supper as a *shared participation* (κοινωνία koinōnia) in the death of Christ.

Archaeological factors at Corinth between 50 and 75 CE confirm this picture. The measurements of rooms and layout of the villas excavated in the suburb of Anaploga readily fit the above account of dining arrangements. A visitor to the site of ancient Corinth will be impressed by four outstanding archaeological features among others. First, the temple-dedications to APOLLO, Poseidon, Aphrodite, Demeter, Asklepios, and other Greco-Roman deities bring home the pluralism of religious life. Paul would have been amazed at today's appeals to pluralism as an explanation for their difficulties in Christian proclamation. Many of the temples were long-standing architectural monuments in relation to which the gospel was a newcomer. Second, many inscriptions still to be seen are in Lat., not Greek. This confirms the need to recognize the *Roman* character of many features of life. This shapes our understanding of "going to law" in 6:1-11, of dining customs in 11:17-31, and other passages. Third, coins from Paul's period witness to the wealth and cosmopolitan character of 1st cent. Corinth. They reflect trade with the Peloponnese, Asia Minor, Syria, Macedonia, and the Aegean. They confirm the importance of the Isthmian Games for tourism and for business. Fourth, several inscriptions concern significant individuals. The Babbius monument, still to be seen, witnesses to the concern of a rising star to promote his public recognition as a benefactor and his rise in status and wealth. The Erastus pavement can still be seen: "Erastus in return for his aedileship laid [this pavement] at his own expense." This was discovered east of the theater in 1929. Most consider it more than likely that it alludes to Erastus, the city treasurer of Rom 16:23.

The Peirene Fountains, the important water supply of ancient Corinth, can still be seen, along with examples of ancient paving, ancient pottery, and terra-cotta artifacts, and numerous examples of the art and craft of a vibrant, wealthy, upwardly mobile city that could export its products. There are resonances between this success-orientated, consumerist, competitive society with its complacent winners and despairing losers, and cultures of the West today. Even postmodern pluralism, fragmentation, and social constructionism are not too far removed from the Corinthian ethos of constructing everything, even religion, to meet consumer demands.

4. Date of Paul's arrival in Corinth and of the letter

The discovery at Delphi of a letter from the Emperor Claudius relating to the proconsulship of Lucius Junius Gallio is a stable marker for Pauline chronology. Four fragments of the letter were discovered in 1905; a further three in 1910; and finally two more in 1967. Most writers infer from this letter that Gallio's proconsulship ran from July 51 to June 52; some date it from July 50 to June 51 (Acts 18:12-17). On this basis Paul would have ministered in Corinth from approximately the autumn of 50 to early summer in 52.

Paul left Corinth after eighteen months, to work mainly in Ephesus for the winter of 52–53, probably through to the spring or summer of 54. Apollos traveled to Corinth during this period. The "previous" letter of 1 Cor 5:9 was written in response to bad news (perhaps from Apollos) and the spring through summer of 54 saw "intense contacts" with Corinth. Spring 54 is a likely date for the writing of 1 Corinthians in response to oral reports from "CHLOE's people" (1:11); to further news from STEPHANAS, FORTUNATUS, and ACHAICUS (16:17); and the arrival of a letter from Corinth (7:1; 8:1; 12:1).

5. Unity and integrity of the letter

Various scholars have proposed a partition theory of separate letters (ranging from two to thirteen letters) that were compiled into 1 Corinthians, of which 1:1–6:11 was independent. Other scholars argue for the unity of the letter on three main grounds: 1) Exponents of partition theories do not reflect a consensus of precisely where the breaks between letters come. 2) The subject matter of the epistle is coherent. Where contradictions or tensions are alleged to occur, patient exegesis provides *contextual* explanations for these. 3) The uncompromising tone of 1:1–6:20 stands in contrast to the more conciliatory approach of 7:1–14:40, precisely because in the former Paul remonstrates with the church on the basis of oral reports and past conduct, whereas 7:1–14:40 reflects Paul's measured and sensitive response to more complex and delicate matters about future policy of which an awareness in Corinth that there are problems is already apparent through their letter.

6. Questions of exegetical debate and interpretation

a. The "splits" and issues of ministry (chs. 1–4). Over many years different accounts have emerged of the "splits" and the names to which they are supposedly attached. Do the four slogans "I am for Apollos"; "I am a Peter person"; "I am for Paul"; "As for me, I belong to Christ" (1:12, all Greek genitives) signify two, three, or four theological parties, or no "parties" at all? In the 19th cent. F. C. Baur proposed a doctrinal division between Jewish-Christian and "Pauline" parties. But Paul nowhere expresses approval of a "Pauline" group. Perhaps 1 Cor 4:6 (NRSV, "I have applied all this to Apollos and myself") is the key to 1:12. The Greek translated *I have applied* (μετεσχημάτισα meteschēmatisa) means elsewhere *to masquerade* or *to disguise* (2 Cor 11:14) or *to transform* (Phil 3:21). Hall argues that Paul alludes to the "leaders" of 1:12 *in a disguised form*, by using the names *Paul* and *Apollos* to denote persons whom he does *not* name for reasons of pastoral tact. Chrysostom also expounded this view (Chrysostom, *Hom.* 1 Cor. 12:1). Hall sees these leaders as "Christian sophists, who combined rhetorical skill with doctrinal and ethical teaching" (2003, 18).

On ministry Paul perceives no conflict between Apollos and his own ministry (3:6-9). He warns his readers against two opposite errors. Too high a view of ministry risks personality cults (hence he uses the neuter pronoun: *What*, then, is Apollos? *What* is Paul? 3:5). But too low a view of ministers risks neglecting their necessary role as channels of divine grace: "Do not deceive yourselves . . . . All things are yours, whether Paul or Apollos or Cephas" (3:18, 21). Planting and watering are necessary *conditions* for growth that ministers undertake; but God alone, not favorite leaders, can give the growth (3:6-9).

b. The case of incest, going to law, and "bodily" lifestyles (chs. 5–6). Paul is outraged, not simply because a Christian has an incestuous relationship with his mother-in-law but no less because of the church's complacent attitude toward it. Some have argued that this "boasting" (πεφυσιωμένοι pephysiōmenoi, "puffed up," "inflated" 6:2) denotes a libertine reveling in full freedom from the law; others ascribe it to the tolerance of a prominent, wealthy Christian; still others speculate about gaining financial resources for the church through legal entailments of this immoral relationship. At all events Paul insists on the removal of the incestuous man from the church as a joint action of the congregation and the apostle (5:3-4). This is not to bring about his death, but to bring home to him his shame and to initiate his ultimate restoration (5:3-5).

Traditionally 6:1-11 has been understood as suggesting that Christians should not go to legal remedies. This is to miss the point. In Corinth, while Roman *criminal* law was administered with some safeguards for justice, Roman *civil* courts were different. Judges were accustomed to receive some kind of gift or favor to encourage a favorable hearing. Only a Christian who was sufficiently wealthy or influential to offer a financial, social, or business incentive to assist his or her case would initiate proceedings. Hence 6:1-11 continues the theme of "grasping beyond the boundaries" already introduced in 5:1-13. A wealthy Christian was seeking *to manipulate* a fellow believer into parting with goods, land, or money on the basis of superior power. Thus Paul indignantly expostulates, "How dare you!" (6:1).

This leads to further elucidations not simply of "ethics" but also of how "*bodily*" human existence constitutes a public arena for the credibility and currency of true Christian discipleship. The Christian's "bodily" existence as part of the corporate body of the church reveals itself in the public domain as "the limbs and organs of Christ" (6:15-18). Union with Christ entails not disengagement from, or indifference to, what is done "in the body" (6:12-15), but the devotion of *the whole self* in the public domain; not simply in an "inner life": "You do not belong to yourselves. For you were bought with a price. Therefore glorify God in your body" (6:19-20 NRSV). Issues of sexual attitudes and conduct belong within this frame, not simply as "ethics." Paul's use of a "list" of virtues and vices (6:9-10) is more than merely rhetorical: it instantiates instances of public or "bodily" life.

c. Material on the household and "food offered to idols" (chs. 7–10) Chapter 7 is not simply about marriage. It addresses marriage, singleness, celibacy, widowhood, and the relation between Christian vocation and "upward mobility" illustrated from being slave or freedperson. Verse 1 reflects a quotation from Corinth. "It is good for a man not to have physical intimacy with a woman." Hence the next verse begins "On the contrary" (v. 2*a*). Against the prevailing assumption in the ancient world that sexual pleasure was in effect only male, Paul implicitly recognizes the mutuality of a pleasurable intimacy: "Stop depriving each other" (7:5). A number of scholars discuss Paul's approach against the background of Stoic, Jewish, or other traditions. Paul stresses a mutual and reciprocal relationship that is distinctive in comparison with many other writers of the time.

Scholars remain divided over reasons behind Paul's apparent advice to remain single unless desire becomes a stronger distraction from devoted service than marriage itself. Are Paul's reasons contingent and contextual? Some interpret "the impending severe pressures" (7:26) and the "the external structures of the world are slipping away" (7:31) in terms of eschatological tribulation and imminence. But others argue that Paul alludes to circumstantial signs of imminent famine. Paul's main concern is whether marriage or singleness will provide more distractions from devoted Christian service. A. C. Wire (1990) insists that Paul attempts to disempower the women prophets of Corinth by confining them as afar as possible to the "private" domain of the home, but debate on this proposal is still awaited. Schrage rightly asserts that Paul does not regard marriage merely as a concession to "un-Christian longings" or as a "safety valve." Rather per v. 7:2 marriage is a good gift of God for the expression of mutual love, but it is not for all. The marriage bond is in principle life-long (7:10-14, 39), but 7:2-24 leaves room for debate about whether circumstantial "exceptions" to this principle can be defended.

The interpretation of μᾶλλον χρῆσαι (**mallon chrēsai**, 7:21) is a controversial crux: should Christians take advantage of a possible opportunity to gain freedom, or should they somehow "use" the position of a slave? Discussions are complex. Dale Martin demonstrates that to become a slave could *sometimes* bring actual status improvement and gain. Is Paul urging readers to give priority to *whatever situation* will enable best service of the Lord, rather than worrying about "bettering" personal prospects?

The social background to the controversy about "food offered to idols" is an essential key to unlock the significance of chs. 8–10. The group called "the strong" were confident that monotheistic belief underlined the "non-existence" of any reality symbolized by "idols," or by the images of pagan deities located into their temples. Moreover, many probably had social and business contacts who invited them to banquets or social meals into the precincts of a pagan temple in the normal course of social life. Were they to lose their friends and business contacts merely because "the weak" were squeamish about compromising their Christian standards by eating food dedicated to pagan deities within their temple precincts? The "weak" told a different story. They had become Christians in a world where dangerous hostile powers threatened them. Christ is Lord, and God is one, but deliberately to renew contact with pagan powers is to court disaster. On the other hand, they did not have confidence about everything that the "strong" had: perhaps they *should* eat, for opportunities to eat meat were rare for the poor. But this dilemma leaves them confused, and muddled about what Christian identity seems to mean.

Paul agrees with the inferences draws by "the strong" on a purely logical level; but insists that their horizons of debate *should* include the effect of their action on "the weak." Even if they have a technical "right" to apply their confident monotheism, often Christians must *forego their right* for the sake of *love for the other*. Paul illustrates the principle of foregoing rights in ch. 9. He has a right to financial maintenance as an apostle; but he willingly foregoes this right because to accept patronage from the influential would compromise his pastoral integrity in seeking to pay equal respect to all in the church.

d. Problems in public worship: gender and attire; the Lord's Supper; and spiritual gifts (chs. 11–14). The text of 11:2-16 concerns the HEADCOVERINGS of *both* men *and* women in public worship (11:4. Dress-codes convey "messages" far above and beyond issues of convenience. In Roman society the wearing of a head-covering by a married woman in public conveyed a message that she was not an "available" woman. It was a request to be treated with respect and a sign of self-respect. Paul affirms the authority of women to engage in prophetic discourse and to lead publicly in prayer (11:5, 6), but denies their freedom to opt out of conventions of respectability. Many infer that this denies gender-interchangeability but affirms gender equality. Interchangeability would arguably undermine the very reciprocity and mutuality that he underlines in 11:8-10. The meaning of the Greek κεφαλή (kephalē) remains highly contentious. Some contend that in this context it denotes *head* or *authority*; others advocate *source* or *origin*; a third view is that it is synecdoche for *topmost*, as a metaphor for physiological head, or one who carries a *representative* role. Three axes, namely creation-order, culture, and eschatology, all contribute to the frame of reference for understanding this passage (*see* HEAD COVERING).

The text of 11:17-34 concerns the LORD'S SUPPER or the Eucharist. Paul asserts that its manner of observance in Corinth does more harm than good (11:17). Paul understands the Lord's Supper as "proclamation (καταγγέλλετε katangellete) of the Lord's death" (11:26) in par. with "the word of the cross" in 1:18-25 and 2:1-5. Believers *participate* in it (κοινωνία koino ̄nia) as an act of *remembrance* (ἀνάμνησις anamnē ̄sis) within the framework of the new covenant (καινὴ διαθήκη kainē diathēkē, v. 25). Christians remember in the sense of "reliving" or recalling the saving events of the cross in much the same way as the people of the old covenant "relived" and recalled the saving events of the Passover, which are recited in the Passover *seder*. This does not necessarily support, however, the theory of two different primitive versions of the Eucharist: a "Jerusalem" tradition of a joyous fellowship-meal, and a solemn "Pauline" focus on Christ's death. Paul's

reservations about eating and drinking (11:22, 33-34) arise from the divisions between the "haves" and "have nots" (vv. 21-22, discussed above; *see* EUCHARIST; LORD'S SUPPER; PASSOVER; REMEMBRANCE).

The text of 12:1–14:40 concerns "spiritual gifts." Paul has already redefined *spiritual* in 3:1-4 in terms of ethics or holiness. In 12:1 the Corinthians enquire about "what is spiritual" or "what is of the Spirit" (πνευματικά pneumatika). Paul substitutes his preferred term χαρίσματα (charismata) to denote gifts that exclude self-glory (3:21). In 12:1-3 every Christian who acclaims Jesus as Lord is "of the Spirit." Many dispute the meaning of Ἀνάθεμα Ἰησοῦς (Anathema Iēsous1, 12:3*a*). Some ascribe it to a setting of persecution, or others regard it as expressing belief in the atonement (Gal 3:13) without belief in the resurrection; some regard it as a repudiation of the earthly Jesus in favor of a spiritual Christ; one scholar translates it as "May Jesus curse," as Christian vindictiveness on the analogy of pagan curse tablets (*see* ANATHEMA; CURSE).

Paul hints at a "Trinitarian" theology in 12:4-7. The main point is to hold together unity of source and will or purpose: "the same Spirit . . . the same Lord . . . the same God ..." with a diversity of modes of gifts or action (gifts of the *Spirit*; serving the *Lord*; the effective action of *God*). All gifts of the Spirit, however varied, are to promote the "building" of the church as a whole. None are for individual self-glorification. Interpretations of the gifts of vv. 8-10 remain controversial. In particular many argue that προφητεία (prophēteia) denotes applied pastoral preaching (even if it may include short ejaculatory utterances). Typically its content concerns the gospel (14:24). Paul's view of prophetic speech was worlds apart from a Corinthian view.

Speaking in tongues also remains controversial, although Paul explicitly alludes to "species" of glossolalia (12:10*c*). Some view tongues as angelic speech; others maintain the view that they denote the power to speak foreign languages; others regard tongues as ecstatic speech. Tongues are probably a precognitive outflow of longings or praise released from the subconscious mind, perhaps when the censor is bypassed. The "gift" is that of liberation, but (for Paul) only in private. Paul regards tongues as typically addressed *to God* (14:2-4) rather than embodying "messages" to a congregation (*see* PROPHECY; TONGUES).

Chapters 12–14 concern orderedness in the church, especially to ensure proper respect for "the other." Speech in public worship must be controlled. In 12:12-30 Paul reverses the image of the body and limbs to defend the vulnerable, not to defend the elite, as it was used in Menenius Agrippa's speech in Livy. The self-styled "spiritual" cannot say of "weak" Christians, "I have no need of you" (12:21); neither should less "gifted" Christians think, "I do not belong to the body" (12:16). *Tongues* are a gift, but if used in public they may make ordinary believers feel as if they are aliens and "not at home" in the congregation (14:20-25). If they feel like unbelievers, estranged or under judgment, this is inappropriate for those under grace (see BODY).

All of these issues turn on the priority of love within the church. Patient exegesis will demonstrate that ch. 13, esp. 13:4-7, forms an integral part of chs. 12–14: "Love waits patiently" (v. 4a) may reflect 14:28-32. "Love does not burn with envy" (v. 4b) may reflect 3:1-4. "Love is not inflated with its own importance" (v. 4c) may reflect 5:1; 8:1). "Love does not behave with ill-mannered impropriety" (v. 5a) may reflect 12:21; 14:28-32). "Love is not pre-occupied with the interest of the self" (v. 5b) reflects 1:12; 6:1-11. Prophetic discourse and speaking in tongues are given for ad hoc contingent needs; love abides beyond this world into the future eschatological order of reality (13:8-13; see LOVE).

e. The resurrection chapter; the collection; and greetings (chs. 15–16). The rhetorical structure of ch. 15 has been discussed in §B.1. Paul expounds the reality of the resurrection of Christ (15:1–11) as the basis for the rest of the chapter. He then provides a first *refutatio* on the unacceptable consequences of denying the resurrection (15:12-19), followed by a first *confirmatio* of the resurrection of Christ as the foundation for the promised resurrection of the dead (15:20-34); a second *refutatio* on the conceivability of the resurrection (15:35-49); and a second *confirmatio* on resurrection transformation. He concludes by applying the issues to present Christian assurance and endeavor (15:50-58).

Too many divergences of interpretation characterize this chapter to address comprehensively here, but three or four may be selected. All agree that Paul draws upon pre-Pauline apostolic tradition in vv. 1-11, and that the early creed includes Christ's burial (ἐτάφη etaphē, v. 4) to underline the genuineness of Christ's death and resurrection. But the Greek ὤφθη ōphthē (*he appeared, he was seen*, v. 5) has attracted controversy. Some argue that the verb says nothing about a *mode* of appearance; it might be subjective, like "seeing" a truth. But others insist that it alludes to appearing or being "seen" publicly. A second crux arises from multiple interpretations of "baptized for the dead" (15:29). Some perceive an allusion to "vicarious baptism" or in less stark form as "a baptism of desire" on the part of those who died before their desire was fulfilled. Others reject this view as too "sacramental" for Paul. Many see behind the verse a desire to be reunited in the resurrection with those now dead as a motive to seek baptism. It is entirely possible that the dying witness of a loved one to the assurance of resurrection may have led some to seek baptism. Verse 34 holds a key to the chapter: "knowledge of God" is the focus. For whereas "the immortality of the soul" supposedly rests upon some innate capacity of the human self to survive

death, "God gives it [the human self] a body (σῶμα sōma) in resurrection as a divine act of transformation (v. 38; vv. 42-44).

Whether we can conceive of resurrection depends not on hypotheses about the human self but upon the infinite resourcefulness of God the Creator to design and to create a "somatic" mode of existence, or existence appropriate to post-resurrection life in the kingdom of God. "Flesh and blood cannot inherit the kingdom of God" (v. 50), which has more to do with a need for transformation to holiness than with issues of "physicality." Above all, the resurrection is a transformative act in which the *spiritual body* σῶμα πνευματικόν sōma pneumatikon) has become a mode of existence that "pertains to the Holy Spirit" (Thiselton 2000, 1275), or "a body animated by, enlivened by, the Spirit of the true God" (Wright 2003). The NRSV wording, "physical body . . . spiritual body" is arguably misleading.

Issues about the COLLECTION emerge in 16:1-4. This concern may relate to "bodily" discipleship (ch. 15; also 6:12-20). Some underline its significance for Paul as a pledge of solidarity with Jewish Christians (Gal 2:10). In accord with the rest of this epistle, it relates to Paul's concern for mutuality, reciprocity, solidarity, and community. It embodies love for the other, and is no mere postscript to the rest. Chapter 16:10-12 further underlines the mutual respect of Paul and Apollos for each other, while vv. 10-24 remind us that Paul ministers collaboratively with co-workers in a supportive community.

C. Theological and Religious Significance of the Letter

This will have emerged without special pleading in §B above, especially in §B.2 and §B.6. The opening *propositio* about unity is deeply theological, as later chs. confirm. "Splits" in the church tear apart the limbs and organs of Christ. If the Holy Spirit dwells within the church as God's holy shrine, to sin against a fellow Christian becomes a kind of sacrilege. The seduction drawn from the culture of Corinth to seek a self-affirming, triumphalist construction of Christian faith is not merely a self-centered ethical aberration; it contradicts the very heart of the gospel as the proclamation of a crucified Christ. Today this contrast cannot but raise questions about social constructionism and neo-pragmatic notions of truth, as constructed by "local" communities. Chapter 13 on love expounds the highest "way" of Christian lifestyle as desire for the good of the other rather than the self or the peer group chosen by the self.

By contrast Paul sees the "affront" of the gospel as lifting people out of the narrowness of their prior horizons to experience sheer grace from God, and to look beyond the self and its desperate concerns for "recognition," to seek the good of others. At issue is not merely *individual* self-centeredness but also the corporate and communal self-centeredness of peer groups that form power groups for power play.

Many miss the *continuity* that runs through chs. 7–14, which is identified in terms of mutuality, reciprocity, and respect for "the other." Paul applied this to marriage, where his awareness of sexual mutuality is well ahead of his time (ch. 7); to the need for mutual understanding and sensitivity between "strong" and "the weak," including loving care for the most vulnerable, and recognition of one's own fallibility (8–10); to gender and mutual respect (11:2-16); to vulnerable "others" at the Lord's Supper (11:17-34); and notably to the exercise of spiritual gifts, which are given not for personal affirmation but for the benefit of all, not least by observing courtesy and reticence on one's own part in public assembly (12:1–14:40). Chapter 13 on love stands at the very the heart of these chapters.

Finally the resurrection chapter (1 Cor 15) expounds resurrection transformation as a gift of *God* to which the dead cannot contribute. This resonates with the heart of the problem in Corinth: "Who sees anything different in you? What do you have that you did not receive? If, however, you received it, why do you boast as if you did not receive it?" (4:7). Resurrection is a sheer gift bestowed upon those "in Christ"; it is not an innate human capacity. "God gives it a body" (v. 38), just as God gives life in many forms to the whole created order as its Creator. The transformation of Christians that began through appropriating the gospel (1:18-25) reaches its decisive climax in the transformation of God's sovereign act of resurrection (15:42-52).

Not surprisingly Paul has reservations about whether the preferred terms in Corinth, *wise* and *spiritual*, can readily be applied there (1:26-31; 3:1-3, 18-21; 4:8*b*). One reason is that wisdom has been re-defined in terms of the cross. "Has not God made a fool of the world's wisdom? . . . We proclaim a crucified Christ . . . God's power and God's wisdom" (1:20*b*-24). "Christ Jesus . . . became for us wisdom given from God" (1:30). These phrases exhibit the "reversals" of the cross. The cross is the criterion of the gospel and the church. Its proclamation is a performative, life-changing, act that leads to a transvaluation of human systems. First Corinthians constitutes a repreaching of the cross to those who are already Christians. Linked with this is a conflict between two very different understandings of the Holy Spirit, the *spiritual* and *prophetic*. Paul disengages signs of the Spirit from "success," and expounds "spirituality" in terms of Christ, the cross, and having the mind of Christ (2:16). In the end this is no less an epistle of God's sovereign grace than Romans. But it is worked out against the concrete background of everyday "bodily" life. Social and historical research, far from competing with a "theological" approach, in this case corroborates it, putting flesh and bones on what might otherwise be mere abstract doctrine.

Bibliography: 1. **Studies:** Edward Adams and David Horrell, ed. *Christianity at Corinth: The Quest for the Pauline Church* (2004); Karl Barth. *The Resurrection of the Dead* (1933); Alexandra R. Brown. *The Cross and Human Transformation* (1995); Andrew D. Clarke. *Secular and Christian Leadership in Corinth* (1993); Anders Eriksson. *Traditions as Rhetorical Proof: Pauline Argumentation in 1 Corinthians* (1998); Thomas W. Gillespie. *The First Theologians: A Study in Early Christian Prophecy* (1994); David R. Hall. *The Unity of the Corinthian Correspondence* (2003); Dale Martin. *Slavery as Salvation* (1990) and *The Corinthian Body* (1995); Margaret M. Mitchell. *Paul and the Rhetoric of Reconciliation: An Exegetical Investigation into the Language and Composition of 1 Corinthians* (1992); John D. Moores. *Wrestling with Rationality in Paul* (1995); Stephen M. Pogoloff. *Logos and Sophia: the Rhetorical Situation of 1 Corinthians* (1992); Gerd Theissen. *The Social Setting of Pauline Christianity* (1982); Gerd Theissen. *Psychological Aspects of Pauline Theology* (1987); Lawrence Welborn. *Politics and Rhetoric in the Corinthian Epistles* (1997); Lawrence Welborn. *Paul, the Fool of Christ: A Study of 1 Corinthians 1–4 in the Comic-Philosophical Tradition* (2005); Ben Witherington. *Conflict and Community in Corinth* (1995); N.T. Wright. *The Resurrection of the Son of God* (2003). 2. **Commentaries:** C. K. Barrett. *A Commentary on the First Epistle to the Corinthians.* 2nd ed. (1971); R. F. Collins. *First Corinthians* (1999); Hans Conzelmann. *1 Corinthians* (1975); Gordon D. Fee. *The First Epistle to the Corinthians* (1987); Richard B. Hays. *First Corinthians* (1997); Wolfgang Schrage. *Der erste Brief an die Korinther.* 4 vols. (1991–2001); Anthony C. Thiselton. *The First Epistle to the Corinthians: A Commentary on the Greek Text* (2000).

ANTHONY C. THISELTON

CORINTHIANS, SECOND LETTER TO. Letters associated with the Pauline mission grew out of the apostle's pastoral and mission activities in the communities of believers. Second Corinthians is no exception. But it is surely the Pauline letter with the most complicated set of historical, social, and communal elements behind it. It was most likely written in stages to the church in Corinth. Questions of Paul's apostolic authority and mission echo in and against such issues as a Corinthian misunderstanding of Paul's travel intentions, his harsh treatment of disloyalty, his desire to engage the church in the collection for Jerusalem, and the presence of a Jewish-Christian opposition to Paul. A profound theological presentation of Christian existence holds the whole together.

A. Structure and Content of 2 Corinthians
B. Detailed Analysis
  1. Historical concerns

A. Structure of 2 Corinthians

Assuming its basic integrity (*see* below), the canonical epistle can be divided into several sections. A rather straightforward layout disguises what is actually a rather complex letter.

Greeting 1:1-2. The opening greeting is similar to 1 Corinthians but shorter in its description of Paul and the addressees. Paul stresses the divine origin of his apostolic office. Compared with 1 Corinthians, this letter is addressed to a wider group than just those in Corinth ("all the saints throughout Achaia").

Thanksgiving 1:3-11. In the thanksgiving section (1:3-11), Paul's thanks for God's comfort in affliction corresponds to the changed circumstances of his relationship with the church, which forces him to defend his position against opponents. In this section the apologetic tone is set and the important theme of apostolic suffering is initiated.

Body 1:12–13:10. The body of the letter is filled with shifts and turns that have led many commentators to conclude that the canonical letter consists of several other letters that were stitched together at some early point. But a broad progression of topics can be discerned that unites the diverse sections.

Paul defends his change of travel plans 1:12–2:13. Changes in a travel plan (1:15-16) have caused a serious problem between Paul and the community. Paul answers the charge of fickleness or insincerity (1:17-19) and the allegation that he made his plans in a worldly way (1:12). He insists that the changes of plan (see below) were spiritually considered (1:21-22) and designed to ensure that his arrival would mean restoration of the community (1:23-24). A sorrowful letter had preceded this one (2:5; *see* below). Those who renewed their allegiance to Paul as a result are told to forgive a particular enemy who now regrets his actions. The section closes with another change of travel plans, caused by Paul's deep concern for the Christian community in Corinth,

Paul defends his apostolic authority 2:14–7:16. This long central section has at its heart Paul's defense of his apostolic office. The paradox that suffering even to the point of death is God's means of bringing the divine power of resurrection to light is integral to Paul's self-understanding. Paul's suffering, his willingness to preach the gospel without charge, and God's grace at work among the Corinthians themselves are all submitted as proof of Paul's calling (2:14–3:6). In a passage filled with OT allusions (3:7-18) Paul associates the apostolic ministry with Moses, to demonstrate that the ministry of the Spirit (the new covenant) supersedes that of the law. From all of this, Paul can insist on the authenticity of his calling to be an apostle (4:1-6): those who deny him and his message do so because of Satan. The influence of the Jewish-Christian opponents (*see* below) winds in and out of view. Suffering brackets (*see* the lists of sufferings, 4:7-15; 6:3-13) the long subsection, 4:7–6:13. Suffering is necessary in the divine plan (4:7) for establishing the cruciform life (4:10-12). The reality of Christian death is underscored along with a vivid hope in vindication and a healthy fear of judgment (5:8-9), which thrusts Paul forward in his mission (5:11-21). What follows missiologically is a call to those still opposed or unbelieving to respond to the gospel: the list of apostolic sufferings strengthens this appeal as it emphasizes again that, in contrast to the claims of opponents, Paul's sufferings mark him as the authoritative apostle. The question of how believers in the church should relate to those who continue to oppose the apostolic mission is taken up in 6:14–7:2: OT teaching about God's holiness and indwelling of the temple (now the church) substantiates a call to separate from unbelievers. But the final note in the closing subsection (7:2-16) is joy, as Paul recounts how his regret at sending the severe rebuke turned to rejoicing when Titus brought news of its redemptive effect. The note of confidence on which this section ends sets the stage for an appeal to participate in the collection.

The collection for Jerusalem 8:1–9:15. The collection for the poor Christians in Jerusalem was already in process (1 Cor 16:1). Paul provides instruction for the completion of the project, encourages the church in Corinth based on the poor Macedonian churches' efforts, and lays a theological groundwork for such sacrificial generosity. Sharing with others in the universal church amounts to a proof of authentic faith (8:8, 24; 9:13), because of Christ's own far greater self-offering (8:8-9). The story of Israel's redemption also serves as a paradigm of God's faithfulness to those willing to share rather than hoard (9:6-9). Paul hopes that successful completion of the collection will result in a unity of the church and of praise to God that spans geographical distance (9:12-15).

Paul defends himself and denounces the opponents 10:1–13:10. The tone shifts back to polemics at this point. Swirling in the air are the as yet unresolved charges against Paul, which include criticism of his physical and rhetorical unimpressiveness (2:12; 13:3), his refusal to accept support from the church (11:7-15; 12:13-17), and of his suffering (10:1, 10; 11:23-33). Paul boasts of what God has done in and through Paul. He disputes the claims of opponents to be representatives of the "super" apostles in Jerusalem, and unmasks them as servants of Satan (11:12-13). He defies a superficial equation of human weakness with sin by demonstrating through his personal experience the divine formula whereby weakness becomes the conduit for expressing God's power (12:9). The opponents' lifestyle, boasting about spiritual experiences, and their preaching for money all belie claims to spiritual authority (11:21-23), because God qualifies his servants according to the pattern of godly weakness, meekness, and humility and legitimates them by providing spiritual power for ministry (12:9-10). This section closes with a final instruction to examine the state of their faith: in view of his impending visit, those still in opposition must repent, for alignment with and obedience to the apostle is proof of one's faithfulness to Christ (13:5-8).

Closing greetings 13:11-13. The letter closes with a last plea, wrapped in benediction, to achieve reconciliation in the church and live in peace.

B. Detailed Analysis

1. Historical concerns

a. Authorship and audience and its social background. Pauline authorship of the Corinthian correspondence has never been seriously doubted. Apart from the fact that "Paul" is named in 1:1 (along with the co-sponsor, Timothy), 2 Corinthians clearly has all the stylistic marks of other Pauline letters. It is thoroughly Pauline in its presentation of justification, the law, eschatology, and Christian living. Even where questions about the unity of 2 Corinthians have led to various arguments that the canonical letter is a composite of two (or more) originally independent passages (*see* below), attribution of their authorship still goes unswervingly to Paul.

Marcion (140 CE) is perhaps the first witness to 2 Corinthians, and the Muratorian Canon included the letter. Polycarp of Smyrna in the mid-2nd cent. knows 2 Corinthians (Pol. *Phil.* 2.2; 6.2; 11.3), and Irenaeus, (ca. 180 CE) mentions 2 Corinthians by name (*Haer.* 4.28.3). Thus 2 Corinthians had a place within the Pauline corpus by the middle of the 2nd cent.

The Corinthian church (1 Cor 1:2) must be understood as a loosely related group of house churches (*see* Rom 16:23). Although the Pauline churches normally met in smaller groups in houses opened up by members (Rom 16:5; 1 Cor 16:19; Col 4:15; Phlm 2), one cannot say how many house churches made up the whole Christian community. Whether these groups came together as a "whole church" is not known (but see 1 Cor 11:20); if they did so, the small size of most houses would suggest that could only be an occasional occurrence.

Roman Corinth was strategically located to make it a commercial center, and drew people from all parts of the empire. Roman citizens were most influential, and

added to the already present Hellenistic varieties of art, philosophies, and religion, the distinctive Roman law, religions, and elements of culture. The Jewish synagogue was a fixture of the city along with mystery cults from the east that made their way to Corinth.

Repopulation by former Roman slaves after 44 BCE meant that the economy became one based on money rather than land. The city prospered, and came to be known for its religious diversity and its immorality. Sexual immorality was a familiar motif in Roman baths, at the raucous dinner parties of the well-to-do, and was even attached to a growing number of affluent women, whose most notorious examples were members of the imperial family. The elite members of the Corinthian church seem to have been Gentiles deeply invested in this style of life. Allusions to the pagan background of the Corinthian believers and references to the cultural-religious activites that they still pursued all point in this direction (1 Cor 6:10-11; 8:1–11:1; 12:2; etc.). The specific issues Paul addressed in 1 Corinthians—going to prostitutes (6:12-20), taking up lawsuits against other believers (6:1-6)—would have reflected typical behavior in Roman Corinth. The discussion about head coverings for women in 1 Cor 11 may well have sought to rein in parts of the the gender revolution among elite women, who controlled their own economic and social lives.

Though mainly Gentile, 1 Cor 12:13 indicates Christian community that was diverse in ethnic and religious backgrounds (Jew, Greek) and socioeconomic status (slave, free). Moreover, the significant role of women in worship is clear from 1 Cor 11 and 14. Jewish Greek and Latin (Roman) names are all in evidence in 1 Corinthians. Equally in evidence is a group of comparatively well-to-do householders. First Corinthians 1:26 suggests that the lower levels of the social scale were strongest numerically, but power undoubtedly resided in the hands of the few householders. First Corinthians 9 reflects Paul's sensitivity to the patron-client social relationships, which shaped commercial interactions in the empire. With wealth in the possession of a small minority, the lower classes had to forge relationships with the wealthy. Thus the client would provide services or various sorts for the wealthy patron, in return for which clients would enjoy the patron's support and protection, as long as they continued to provide faithful service on demand. Quite possibly it was just this sort of arrangement with the Corinthian church leadership that Paul sought to avoid, so that he could retain his freedom and not be shackled to the Christian householders who might then claim his obedience.

Consequently, the church in Corinth seems to have been a microcosm of the urban Roman world. The church that grew up in this turbulent environment was clearly struggling to separate itself from some of the unseemly practices that typified life there. Equally, socioeconomic and ethnic diversity, coupled with dramatic experiences of the Spirit and struggles for human power in the Christian community, combine to form the backdrop to Paul's frustrating encounters with this church.

b. Date/Location of composition, and 2 Corinthians within Paul's mission. There are two issues at stake. The first has to do with assigning the traditional tags of time and place to the letter. Making these assignments remains at the mercy of the incomplete chronology that can be reconstructed from Paul's writings and Acts. The two historical benchmarks for creating such a framework are the edict of Claudius (49 CE) and the dating of Gallio's tenure in office (Acts 18:2, 12; 51/52 CE). Working from these points, it is usually estimated that Paul departed from Corinth the first time (Acts 18:18) in 51–52 CE. After a period of travel, including a visit to Antioch, Paul begins his sustained Ephesian ministry (Acts 19:1). Standard calculations place the writing of 1 Corinthians (from Ephesus) sometime between that first departure from Corinth and the end of that Ephesian campaign (3 years, more or less; Acts 19:10; 20:31). Probably a year and a half between the writing of 1 and 2 Corinthians would be necessary for Paul's other writing and movements in relation to Corinth to fit in (see below). If 1 Corinthians was written about 54–55 CE., 2 Corinthians (perhaps initially chs. 1–9) must date to 55–56 CE. Paul wrote 2 Corinthians from Macedonia (2:13; 7:5; 8:1; 9:2), and had it delivered to the community through Titus (8:16-24).

But given the complexity of Paul's communications with this church, a second issue looms large—that of reconstructing the sequence of letters, movements, and changes associated with Paul's Corinthian mission. Behind and between the two canonical Corinthian letters lie other letters (both from and to Paul), movements, and mission plans. It is best to set these into a sequence with some discussion of the significance of each element.

First, sometime after his departure from Corinth (Acts 18:19; 51–52 CE) Paul wrote to Corinth what commentators call the "previous letter." This is alluded to in 1 Cor 5:9, where we learn that this letter took up the issue of the church's posture toward believers who engage in sexual immorality. Some have suggested that 2 Cor 6:14–7:1 represents a fragment of this "previous letter," but this is an unlikely explanation. This "previous letter" is no longer extant.

Second, 1 Cor 7:1 refers to a letter from the Corinthians to Paul ("now concerning the matters about which you wrote"), apparently delivered by the three Corinthian Christians who waited for a reply (1 Cor 16:17).

Third, our canonical 1 Corinthians (ca. 54–55 CE) responds to this letter and its questions (chs. 7–16). But at about the same time, through the less formal channels of personal reports from travelers, Paul was becoming aware of elements of disruption in the church (news from the household of Chloe; 1:11; see also 11:18; "it is actually reported that", 5:1). The presence of opposition in the church is clearly evident (4:18; 9:1-18).

At this point, two itineraries come into play:

According to 1 Cor 16:2-8, Paul communicated his plan to leave Ephesus after Pentecost, traveling through Macedonia to preach, and then making his way to Corinth for the winter before (probably) moving on to Jerusalem.

Ephesus → Macedonia → Corinth → Jerusalem

According to 2 Cor 1:15-16, however, Paul had decided instead to go directly from Ephesus to Corinth and then to Macedonia; he now anticipated also a return to Corinth following Macedonia before pushing on to Judea. Probably the second plan represents a change in Paul's thinking after 1 Corinthians was written, and plan (2) apparently superseded the earlier itinerary. But it is uncertain at what point the Corinthian church became aware of the new plan.

Ephesus → Corinth → Macedonia → Corinth → Judea

Fourth, assuming further reception of some news from Corinth to the effect that 1 Corinthians had failed to achieve its corrective goal, Paul shifted from travel plan (1) to (2), and went directly to Corinth on what has been called the "sorrowful visit" (2 Cor 2:1; fall of 54 CE). Almost certainly his attempts during this visit to correct members of the congregation met with opposition and possibly a public humiliation. The hostile reception caused him to discard plan (2) as well and return directly to Ephesus.

Fifth, upon his return to Ephesus, Paul wrote the "severe letter," in which he rebuked the community for its failure to support him (2:1-11; 7:8-13). He had hoped that this measure would spare the church another harsh visit for judgment (1:23; 2:1). Titus, who carried the letter, was charged with enforcing it as well (7:5-16).

Sixth, sometime later, probably in the summer of 55 CE, Paul left Ephesus and was preaching in Asia (2 Cor 2:12). Dangers, suffering, and a close brush with death are linked to this mission (1:8-9). Having won through to Troas, Paul found fruitful ministry opportunities but was in anguish not having received news from Titus about the Corinthian response to his written rebuke (2:12-13). So Paul pressed on to Macedonia (2:13).

Seventh, Titus finally met up with Paul somewhere in Macedonia, and delivered mixed news. On the one hand, the Corinthians had obeyed Paul and meted out punishment to the wrongdoer (2:5-11; 7:6-16). But on the other hand, Paul's shifting travel plans led to charges against him of insincerity in his commitment to the Corinthian church (1:12–2:4). At the same time, he learned of the arrival in Corinth of opponents—a group of Judaizing intruders who opposed his authority, and challenged his apostolic credentials (*see* below). Paul's response to this mixture of issues was our canonical 2 Corinthians, probably written in at least two stages and finally sent in the fall of 55 or 56 CE.

c. Paul's opponents in 2 Corinthians. One of the major issues engaged by Paul in 2 Corinthians is the disruptive presence of a distinct opposition. There is less agreement as to the identity of this group and its relation to the less clearly defined detractors of Paul in 1 Corinthians. From the numerous possibilities offered by scholars, four broad categories can be discerned: Hellenistic Jewish Christians, Judaizing Christians, Gnostics, and pneumatics influenced by a too realized view of salvation. Before deciding among the options, a brief survey of the evidence in 2 Corinthians must be made. In setting out the evidence, the recent improvement on methodology calls for the exercise of restraint in "mirror-reading" Paul's comments about opponents and careful attention to various stylistic and rhetorical features of the argument.

As the letter opens, it is clear that Paul is responding to apparent charges leveled against him, in his absence, by an opposition that is present in the community. His attitude toward the church, his abilities, and authority to serve it are being questioned. Paul is charged with being heavy-handed (1:24; 10:8), "tearing down" the community instead of building it up (10:8; 13:10), and criticized for lack of rhetorical skills (10:10; 11:6). They disparaged his weak or unimpressive physical presence (10:1), along with the way he compensated by sending fierce letters from a great distance (10:10). Paul's changes of plan were taken for a weak will and vascillating or even capricious spirit (1:17-19; 10:2). His way of writing was judged to be worldly and impenetrable (1:12-13).

Certain other specifics round out the picture of contempt for Paul by this group. Paul's sustained argument for apostolic authority in chs. 10–13 makes clear their rejection of his apostleship. They apparently regarded him as a pretender, who failed to demonstrate the signs of apostleship in the church's presence (6:8; 12:12), and who did not measure up in comparison with the Jerusalem apostles (11:5; 12:11). He lacked letters of commendation to validate his credentials (3:1-3).

One issue that often puzzles readers of the Corinthian letters is why Paul's refusal to accept financial support from the church caused so much trouble (11:7-9; 12:13). This practice could be spun in several ways. The opponents, who apparently quite happily preached for gain (2:17), alleged that this refusal of support was injurious to the reputation of the church (11:7; 12:13). It may also have been seen as deceptive, since Paul would turn around and insist that the church participate in the collection for Jerusalem (12:17-18). Behind

Paul's policy were probably two factors. On the one hand, itinerant teachers of philosophy taught for fees and were known to craft their discourses in ways that would bring the largest rewards from wealthy householders who usually sought amusement for their dinner guests. Paul might be seeking to remain free from any such associations. On the other hand, it is possible that the Corinthian church, or some of the well-to-do within it, sought to be Paul's patrons. Their financial patronage would put the apostle into the position of the obligated client. This relationship would compromise Paul's ability to lead the church he had planted.

On a number of levels, then, in 2 Corinthians Paul can be seen as attempting to respond to charges against him that had hardened into a determined stance against his authority. In and through the give and take, a profile of the opponents also emerges.

First, Paul seems unimpressed with the image these rivals had constructed of themselves. He makes much of the pointlessness of self-commendation (10:12, 18), and so prefers to let the record of his own apostolic labors speak for him. He criticizes his opponents for superficiality and emphasis on observable appearance and eloquence (5:12; 10:5, 10; 11:6). Their boasting in human achievements is cited by Paul as evidence of God's disapproval of them (10:13-17).

Second, Paul denounces their willingness to accept the financial support of the Corinthian community. This practice places the rivals in the category of those who taught for money, easily manipulated and motivated by avarice (*see* 2:17; 11:10, 12). Paul insisted, on the contrary, that his commitment to "get his living by the gospel" (*see* 1 Cor 9:14) validated his claim to apostleship.

Third, for a combination of reasons (not least of which, no doubt, was their explosive rejection of his apostleship), Paul labeled these intruders "false apostles" (11:13). Leading to this climactic judgment were charges of deceitfulness and cunning: they falsified God's word (4:2), they pretended to be apostles of Christ (11:13), and ultimately were better labeled Satan's ministers (11:15).

The last important point is the link of the opponents with Jerusalem. Though Paul would rather have avoided the sparring (11:21), his own reversion to boasting makes clear the opponents' Jewish identity and link with Jerusalem. The descriptors "Hebrews," "Israelites," "descendants of Abraham" (11:22) identify the opposition as Jews of Palestinian descent and linguistic preference. Their almost certain association with the chief apostles in Jerusalem ("the super apostles," who should be distinguished from the opponents who are "false apostles") further suggests that they were claiming to have the goodwill of the apostles as they carried out a mission against Paul in this diaspora Christian community.

These observations make it likely that they can be categorized as Judaizing Christians, similar to those who troubled Paul in the Galatian churches. The argument of ch. 3, particularly, suggests that they regarded adherence to Torah as the means of access to participation in the Holy Spirit. Although circumcision as such seems not to be the crucial issue (as in Galatians), the tenor of Paul's argument nevertheless places this group of rivals in that camp that associated covenant privilege and identity with adherence to what Paul calls (against the background of Jer 31) "the old covenant." Of the four identifications set out above, therefore, the second, Judaizing Christians, offers the best fit.

These Jewish features that identify the opponents in 2 Corinthians are lacking in 1 Corinthians. Consequently, most scholars propose that another opposition front, less well formed, and characterized by among other things an over-realized eschatology (1 Cor 4:8; 15), was responsible for the situation addressed by 1 Corinthians. The eschatology of this group might be defined as belief that the experience of the Spirit indicates full arrival of the kingdom. Believers with such spectacular spiritual gifts as prophecy and speaking in tongues considered themselves superior to others in the community (1 Cor 12–14). The outside intruders evident in 2 Corinthians represent another distinct group, but they may have found support from anti-Paul pneumatics evident in 1 Corinthians.

d. Outcome of 2 Corinthians. An eighth step in the history of Paul's Corinthian mission would have to take up the question of whether 2 Corinthians produced the results Paul intended—that is, of successfully answering the opponents' charges and regaining the respect and commitment of the church. Quite probably in the winter of 56 CE Paul made his third visit to Corinth, but this has to be surmised from the general statement of Acts 20:2-3 that Paul "came to Greece, where he stayed three months." This is almost certainly a reference to Corinth, and Paul's own reference in Rom 15:26 to the success of the collection for Jerusalem, for which he was soon to depart, suggests that 2 Corinthians achieved its purpose of restoring his authority in this church.

2. Literary issues: The integrity of 2 Corinthians

As pointed out above, the integrity or unity of 2 Corinthians has been problematic. Proponents of complex partition theories are less common than in the 19th and 20th cent., but the view that 2 Corinthians is a composite of two or more originally separate letters is still found in the literature to explain the apparent shift in tone between chs. 1–9 and 10–13. Two main factors lie behind this view. First, the structure of the letter with its various shifts and turns (*see* above) does lend itself to the suggestion that it may have been formed out of several pieces. Second, the letter (in combination with 1 Corinthians) reveals a history of letter writing that linked Paul with this community (*see* above). If 2 Corinthians were a later composite, then it might preserve

fragments of some of the intervening letters between the apostle and the community.

There are several elements that combine in discussions about literary unity. At the macro level, the letter can be divided into what appears to some to be fairly independent units. Chapters 8–9 focus on the collection and giving, and have sometimes been divided into separate documents, the first to the city of Corinth (ch. 8) and the second to the provice of Achaia (ch. 9); chs. 10–13 take up Paul's defense of his apostleship. Then there are several transition points in the letter where shifts in thought and theme have been identified: 2:13/14; 7:4/5; 6:13/14; 7:1/2. On the basis of these elements, some have gone as far as to conclude that 2 Corinthians consists of six separate passages or letter fragments that were eventually stitched into a single (our canonical) document:

> 1:1–2:13 to which 7:5-16 belongs;
> 2:14–6:13;
> 6:14–7:1;
> 8;
> 9;
> 10–13.

The origins of these various pieces are sometimes sought in Paul's "severe letter" (chs. 10–13) or in the "previous letter" referred to in 1 Cor 5:9 (6:14–7:1).

Those who maintain the integrity of 2 Corinthians—each of the above parts belonging originally to this particular apostolic communication with Corinth—generally do so on the basis of close exegesis of the transitional texts that link the dramatic shifting of hemes to the complexity of a situation that called for a variegated response.

There seems to be widest agreement that chs. 1–9 form a single letter, which Paul wrote just after Titus rejoined him (*see* 2 Cor 7:5-13), with chs. 10–13 having been written separately to address a new development, or a situation that had worsened beyond that originally reported to Paul. There is no evidence in the history of the early transmission of the biblical texts to suggest that chs. 10–13 ever had a literary life of its own. Consequently, the assumption is that the two parts were joined into a single document at a very early stage of the development of the Pauline corpus. Alternatively, it seems equally possible to envisage Paul writing 2 Corinthians in stages, over a period of weeks or months, during which the ever-changing Corinthian situation threw up one surprise after another that each required attention. This could explain the variety and shift in topics, as well as transitions that might seem rougher than would be ideal.

C. The Theological Significance of 2 Corinthians

As pointed out briefly above, 2 Corinthians bears all the theological marks of a Pauline writing. There are, nevertheless, certain features of theology that distinguish this letter, which are here divided into three categories.

1. Suffering and glory, weakness and power

Even a cursory reading of 2 Corinthians shows Paul's abiding concern to interpret his suffering. Paul provides two lists of his sufferings in 6:4-10 and 11:23-29. A particular event in which Paul came close to dying lies in the immediate past, but also served Paul's rhetorical purpose by enabling him to distinguish the marks of a true apostle from the credentials demanded by the opponents. Paul's final iteration of this theme (12:9-10; see 4:7) points out that weakness and experiences of suffering are not a contradiction to his apostolic calling as though God were displeased with the apostle. Rather they confirm Paul's apostolic authority. What seems paradoxical to some—that the real presence of the Spirit in the life of the believer or church should be accompanied by suffering—is a natural outworking of Paul's eschatology and Christology. On the one hand, the very real presence of salvation and the "guarantee" of the Spirit are features of the Christian experience of redemptive transformation in the present age marked by evil. And as a result, as long as the veil of incompleteness remains, Christian living in this world must be by faith and not by sight (5:7). On the other hand, Christ's own suffering (5:14-15) forms the pattern for the Christian experience of suffering and weakness. And Paul's ministry thus takes the cruciform shape: the truth of salvation displayed in the Christ-event is proclaimed and authenticated in and through the humanly weak but divinely strong apostolic ministry. What cannot be seen—the completion of our salvation—can, in the Spirit (1:22; 5:5), be anticipated in hope. Both death and resurrection were equal parts of Paul's experience. Suffering and weakness made Paul a vessel through which God could manifest resurrection power.

In 1:3-11 it is the theme of suffering and affliction that opens the letter. Paul stresses that God met him and his team in this dark situation and that it became a situation in which God could be experienced as the consoler and comforter. Moreover, the consolation one receives from God enables the consoled to become an instrument to others of God's consolation. There is logic in this view, but it only becomes apparent through the lens of the Christ event, in which the pattern is of movement from human weakness, through experiences of suffering, to divine vindication and empowerment, and ultimately resurrection life. What emerges in Paul's defense of his apostleship is that Spirit power and gifting now do not mean removal from this life of incompleteness, pain, and suffering; it is rather by the Spirit that the believer can endure in the midst of these things (4:10-11).

2. Salvation and the gospel

Although incomplete, salvation is a present reality (6:2). The term itself is one of several dynamic metaphors that Paul uses to describe God's healing intervention in human life. Personal experience of salvation comes by way of repentance (7:10), and Paul's ministry is understood as the means by which salvation can be extended to the world (1:6). The presentation of salvation in 2 Corinthians is shaped by the polemics with the Judaizers. Salvation is given in the context of the covenants. By drawing on the OT promise of a new covenant (Jer 31), and by showing how the gospel with its attendant promise of the Spirit-gift reflects the new covenant, Paul is able to establish the theological difference between his gospel and a view that insists on loyalty to the prior covenant established by Moses (3:7-18).

Paul shifts thereafter to the metaphor of reconciliation to explain what God the Father has done through the historical ministry of his Son to realign the "world" to himself (5:11-21). Here too the motive of the theological description is to interpret for his audience the meaning of his apostolic ministry: "God is making his appeal through us . . . be reconciled to God."

So it follows closely that the gospel, which in content is "Jesus Christ as Lord" (4:5), in Paul's thought, is the "message of reconciliation." In connection with the theme of weakness and power, it is clear that the communicator of the gospel message is not special or particularly noteworthy by sociocultural standards, for it is in human weakness that one bearing the gospel becomes an instrument of God (4:6-7). Gospel proclamation involves persuasion (5:11); yet it is not the shape of the words or the cleverness of speech that enlightens those in darkness, but the power of God expressed in and through the proclamation of the gospel (4:7).

3. Christian life and Christian death

What has already been seen of the mystery of divine power in human weakness has perhaps its most practical outworking in Paul's vision of Christian existence. What Paul describes first as his experience—receiving divine consolation in the midst of affliction (1:3-4); experiencing divine power in situations of human weakness (4:8-9; 7:4; 12:7-10)—is the broader pattern of life in Christ for all believers. Coming to terms with this reality means accepting an assessment of one's relative worthiness in God's sight and before people based not on physical or mental attributes but on Christ's death for all (8:9). Sacrifice and generosity become possible when one depends upon God for strength in weakness (4:8-9), provision in times of material need (8:9; 9:8), and life out of death (4:8-10).

Paul stresses holiness of conduct, and this requires a conscious separation from the activities and values that mark unbelievers (6:14–7:1). The OT temple background establishes the theological reasoning for this call to holiness: separation from sin, idolatry and pagan ways is the prerequisite to fellowship with God, membership in his family, and life in his presence (6:14-18).

No other passage in Paul's letters penetrates as deeply and personally into the puzzle of Christian death as 2 Cor 5:1-8. On the one hand, Paul speaks negatively of death. Death is a tearing down and dissolution of human embodiment in physicality (5:1). Human relationality is also destroyed. And this event, human death, awaits all, including those who are in Christ. On the other hand, Paul can describe Christian death almost as a rite of passage. It implies movement in God's direction, and is a necessary step or stage to fit us for existence (the "building from God" and "our heavenly dwelling") with God (5:1, 4). For this reason, death can be faced. Christ is again the paradigm—one who has undergone the negative destruction and won through to the positive renewal. Beneath the veil of the incomplete times of this present age, it is the gift of the Spirit who inspires hope in the promises and who is the guarantee of what awaits the Christian beyond death (5:5). On the strength of Paul's treatment of this element of reality, a theology of Christian death becomes a possibility and a necessity. As he sees it, as long as this age of mission continues, death is a part of life. It can be embraced courageously because it is a new beginning. *See* CORINTH; CORINTHIANS, FIRST LETTER TO THE; PAUL THE APOSTLE.

Bibliography: J. K. Chow. *Patronage and Power: A Study of Social Networks in Corinth* (1992); V. P. Furnish. *II Corinthians.* AB 32A (1984); S. J. Hafemann. *Suffering and Ministry in the Spirit: Paul's Defense of His Ministry in 2 Corinthians 2:14–3:3* (2000); S. J. Hafemann. *2 Corinthians.* The NIV Application Commentary (2000); M. J. Harris. *The Second Epistle to the Corinthians.* NIGTC (2005); R. F. Hock. *The Social Context of Paul's Ministry: Tentmaking and Apostleship* (1980); R. P. Martin. *Reconciliation: A Study of Paul's Theology* (1981); J. L. Sumney. *Identifying Paul's Opponents: The Question of Method in 2 Corinthians* (1990); J. L. Sumney. *"Servants of Satan," "False Brothers" and Other Opponents of Paul* (1999); M. E. Thrall. *The Second Epistle to the Corinthians* I: *Introduction and Commentary on II Corinthians I–VII* (1994); M. E. Thrall. *The Second Epistle to the Corinthians* II: *Commentary on II Corinthians VIII–XIII* (2000); B. W. Winter. *After Paul Left Corinth: The Influence of Secular Ethics and Social Change* (2001); B. W. Winter. *Roman Wives, Roman Widows: The Appearance of New Women and the Pauline Communities* (2003); B. Witherington III. *Conflict and Community in Corinth: A Socio-Rhetorical Commentary on 1 and 2 Corinthians* (1995).

PHILIP TOWNER

CORINTHIANS, THIRD LETTER TO. The *Third Letter to the Corinthians* is a short letter that Paul supposedly wrote in response to a letter addressed to him by Stephanas and the Corinthian presbyters. The religious leaders of the community were in great distress because of Simon and Cleobius, who were teaching that there is no resurrection of the flesh but only of the spirit, and other "Gnostic" doctrines against the body and the material world. In his reply, Paul rejects the false teaching of those "godless men" (3:38) and stresses the divine origins of the created world, the inspiration of the Israelite prophets, the reality of Jesus' incarnation, and the belief of the bodily resurrection.

In the Armenian Bible the two letters are an integral part of the letters of Paul, while in the six extant Lat. manuscripts, they are copied after the canonical letters. According to Hovhanessian, the *Third Letter to the Corinthians* was probably written in the second half of the 2nd cent., possibly against the teachings of the "Gnostic" sect of the Ophites. *See* GNOSTICISM.

Bibliography: Vahan Hovhanessian. *Third Corinthians: Reclaiming Paul for Christian Orthodoxy* (2000); Gerhard P. Luttikhuizen. "The Apocryphal Correspondence with the Corinthians and the Acts of Paul." *The Apocryphal Acts of Paul and Thecla.* Jan N. Bremmer ed. (1996) 75–91.

PIERLUIGI PIOVANELLI

CORMORANT. (*Phalacrocrorax carbo*) have been sighted on all waters in Palestine. It is thus possible that this large fishing bird was included in the biblical lists of "unclean" birds, but which Hebrew term (if any) means *cormorant?* Some modern translations (e.g., NIV and NRSV) identify שָׁלָךְ shalakh (Lev 11:17; Deut 14:17) with the cormorant. However, Driver has argued that **shalakh** signifies the fisher owl, whereas אֲנָפָה *'anafah*, occurring in Lev 11:19 and Deut 14:18 (NRSV: heron), refers to the cormorant. Different Greek terms in these passages are translated "cormorant" as well.

Bibliography: G. R. Driver. "Birds in the Old Testament: I. Birds in Law." *PEQ* (1955) 5–20.

GÖRAN EIDEVALL

CORNELIUS kor-neel´yuhs [Κορνήλιος *Kornēlios*]. A Roman army officer stationed in Caesarea and evangelized by the apostle Peter in the book of Acts. The strategic importance of Cornelius's encounter with Peter is suggested by its threefold iteration: an extensive initial account in Acts 10:1-48 reinforced by Peter's flashbacks in 11:1-18 and 15:7-11.

A. Narrator's Initial Report (Acts 10:1-48)

Cornelius is identified by a variety of occupational, social, and religious features. By profession he was a

Roman centurion, an official in charge of an eighty-soldier unit based in Caesarea Maritima, the seat of imperial rule in Judea (10:1). His regiment was part of the larger Italian Cohort (6 "centuries" = 1 cohort) and Syrian Legion (10 cohorts = 1 legion) in the region. Supervising an "Italian" company implies Cornelius's status not only as a Gentile but as a Roman citizen as well; and his rank suggests he possessed considerable wealth and standing. He further functioned as head of a sizeable household (10:2), which included slaves as well as family (10:7), and a retinue of "relatives and close friends" (10:24).

Acts emphasizes Cornelius's religious piety. Although not a full proselyte to Judaism, he "was a devout man (εὐσεβής eusebes) who feared [Israel's] God," as evidenced in his magnanimous almsgiving to "the [Israelite] people" (λαός laos) and constant praying to Israel's God (θεός theos) (10:2). This reputation as a generous, "just (δίκαιος dikaios) and God-fearing man" placed Cornelius in good favor with "the whole Jewish nation (ἔθνος ethnos)" (10:22), similar to that enjoyed by another centurion in Luke's Gospel, who loved the Jewish people and built a synagogue for them (Luke 7:1-5).

Cornelius's piety sets the stage for the ensuing narrative. While praying at three o'clock in the afternoon ("ninth hour"), a standard time for Jewish daily devotions, an "angel of God" appears in a vision, announcing that Cornelius's faithful acts "have ascended as a memorial (μνημόσυνον mnēmosynon) before God" (10:4). The heavenly messenger instructs Cornelius to find and bring back "a certain Simon . . . called Peter," lodging at a tanner's seaside home in Joppa (10:5-6). Cornelius dispatches two slaves and a "devout (εὐσεβή eusēbē) soldier" to Joppa (10:7-8).

Peter had never met Cornelius, and he would naturally be suspicious of a summons to a Roman officer's headquarters in Caesarea. As it happens, Peter is praying on the tanner's rooftop and receives an epiphany of his own, preparing him to welcome his approaching visitors. This "double vision" device, confirming divine orchestration of (unlikely) events, is similar to that which brings Ananias and Saul together in the previous chapter (9:1-18). Although initially Peter's vision seems to have little to do with Cornelius, the connection soon becomes evident. A screen lowers from heaven showing a menagerie of unclean creatures, which Peter is ordered to "kill and eat." Against Peter's protests ("By no means Lord, I have never eaten anything unclean"), the scene replays three times, culminating with the lesson: "What God has made clean, you must not call profane" (10:9-16).

"Suddenly" the screen disappears, at the moment the visitors appear at the tanner's gate, seeking Peter (10:16-18). After hearing their invitation to go to Cornelius's house, Peter hosts the messengers in his borrowed residence for the night and then accompanies them to Caesarea the next day (10:19-24). Peter's hospitality toward Gentile strangers and, in turn, the prospect of receiving hospitality in a centurion's home, inevitably includes TABLE FELLOWSHIP. Peter is beginning to accept that indeed "God has made clean" pious Gentiles like Cornelius.

This lesson becomes solidified during Peter's actual encounter in 10:24-48 with Cornelius and those gathered in his home. The scene opens with the only negative characterization of Cornelius in the narrative: upon meeting Peter, Cornelius falls at the apostle's feet and "worships" (προσκυνέω proskyneō) him (10:25). Although Cornelius worshiped Israel's God, perhaps this gesture betrays a vestige of his polytheistic heritage; or perhaps he regards Peter as a god in human form (as in Acts 14:11-18). Peter quickly sets him straight: "Stand up; I am only a mortal" (10:27; compare Acts 14:15). Then Peter and Cornelius each review the circumstances that brought them to this occasion. Peter recounts his recent revelation that God does not brand anyone unclean or profane, although he exaggerates the point by claiming an interdict against Jews' association with Gentiles (the law forbade consuming unclean food, not all contact with foreigners) (10:28-29). Cornelius rehearses his vision, which occurred "at this very hour" four days earlier, recognizes "the presence of God" among the assembly, and invites Peter to expound further on God's purpose for this meeting (10:30-33).

Peter announces his thesis at the outset of the sermon: "I truly understand that God shows no partiality, but in every nation (ethnos) anyone who fears him and does what is right is acceptable to him" (10:34-35). The description of "anyone" is tailor-made for Cornelius. Peter then explains how God's impartial purpose of reconciliation and "peace" has been fulfilled in the 1) life, 2) death, 3) resurrection, and 4) commission of Israel's Messiah, Jesus: 1) "he went about doing good and healing *all* who were oppressed," 2) suffered unjust execution "on a tree," 3) was restored to life by God's power, and 4) commissioned his followers to proffer "forgiveness of sins" to "everyone" who believes in him (10:36-43). Before Peter concludes his message, the Holy Spirit "falls upon" Cornelius's entire household, inspiring them to praise God in various tongues—just like Peter and the earliest Jewish believers at Pentecost (10:44-47). By sealing their common bond and experience, Peter offers baptism in Jesus' name to Cornelius and company, and they in turn extend hospitality to Peter and his associates "for several days" (10:48).

Understanding Acts 10 as a *conversion story* is somewhat misleading in Cornelius's case. Although his initial homage to Peter may hint at some residual idolatry, Cornelius had already accepted Israel's God as the only God and followed Jewish standards of pious conduct. Cornelius's baptism is not a sign of repentance. Cornelius's faith does expand to embrace

Jesus as God's anointed one; but there is no indication that he had been hostile to Jesus or even known who Jesus was prior to Peter's visit. The truer conversion in this story belongs to *Peter*, who undergoes a dramatic change of heart regarding the nature and scope of God's household. The significance of the Cornelius episode for Peter and the early church sharpens in subsequent retellings.

B. Peter's First Review (Acts 11:1-18)

News of Peter's sojourn in Cornelius's house reaches Jerusalem. When Peter later comes to the holy city, the "circumcised" contingent of the church calls him on the carpet for eating with "uncircumcised men" (11:1-3). Here proprieties of food and fellowship intertwine. In his defense, Peter reprises his experience "step by step"—from the vision in Joppa to the visit in Caesarea—highlighting various details and concealing others to suit his argument (11:4-17). The strongest accent falls on God's driving initiative and intention to bless the Gentiles ("Who was I that I could hinder God?" 11:17). Peter never names Cornelius in this account and discloses little new information about the centurion and his household. However, Peter now introduces conversion language (not used in 10:1-48) concerning these Gentiles' "being saved" and "granted repentance that leads to life" (11:14, 18).

C. Peter's Second Review (Acts 15:7-11)

The debate over incorporating non-Jewish converts comes to a head at the COUNCIL OF JERUSALEM. At this conference of "apostles and elders," Peter again appeals to his God-ordained encounter with Cornelius (though not by name) as proof that faithful Gentiles need not be circumcised as a membership requirement for God's people. Cornelius's experience demonstrates that the salvation of Gentiles and Jews alike ("we will be saved . . . just as they will") depends upon "the grace of the Lord Jesus," certified by God's gift of the Holy Spirit (15:7-8, 11). Although the Ethiopian eunuch (8:26-40) and a "great number" of Antioch residents (11:20-21) also represent early uncircumcised believers in Christ, Cornelius and household remain the foundational and prototypical Gentile Christians in Acts: "You know that in the early [meaning "original" ἀρχαίων archaiōn] days God made a choice among you that I [Peter] should be the one through whom the Gentiles would . . . become believers" (15:7). Simeon [Peter] has related how God *first* [πρῶτον prōton] looked favorably on the Gentiles to take from among them a people for his name." *See* CIRCUMCISION.

Bibliography: A. E. Arterbury. "The Ancient Custom of Hospitality, the Greek Novels, and Acts 10:1–11:18." *PRSt* 29 (2002) 53–72; Beverly R. Gaventa. *From Darkness to Light: Aspects of Conversion in the New Testament* (1986); Robert C. Tannehill. "'Cornelius'

and 'Tabitha' Encounter Luke's Jesus," *Int* 48 (1994) 347–56; W. T. Wilson, "Urban Legends: Acts 10:1–11:18 and the Strategies of Greco-Roman Foundation Narratives." *JBL* 120 (2001) 77–99; R. D. Witherup. "Cornelius Over and Over and Over Again: 'Functional Redundancy' in the Acts of the Apostles." *JSNT* 49 (1993) 45–66.

F. SCOTT SPENCER

CORNER GATE שַׁעַר הַפִּנָּה sha'ar happinnah, שַׁעַר הַפּוֹנֶה sha'ar happoneh, שַׁעַר הַפִּנִּים sha'ar happinnim]. First mentioned during AMAZIAH's reign and fortified by UZZIAH, it might stand at the western limit of the BROAD WALL, which enclosed the western hill of JERUSALEM, probably under HEZEKIAH (2 Kgs 14:13; 2 Chr 25:23; 26:9; Jer 31:38; Zech 14:10).

CORNERSTONE אֶבֶן פִּנָּתָה 'even pinnatah, פִּנָּה ler'osh pinnah; לְרֹאשׁ κεφαλὴν γωνίας kephalēn gōnias, ἀκρογωνιαῖος akrogōniaios]. *Cornerstone* is an architectural term that has figurative meanings and messianic nuances in the NT. The NRSV uses the term *cornerstone* eleven times. Job 38:4-6 speaks of God laying the foundations of the earth, sinking the bases on the foundation, and laying the cornerstone. This usage implies that a cornerstone is a primary stone in the building's foundation. The same imagery is found in Isa 28:16; the Lord Yahweh is "laying in Zion a foundation stone, a tested stone, a precious cornerstone (פִּנַּת יִקְרַת pinnath yiqrath), a sure foundation." Many structures, including defensive walls around towns, were built of unhewn field stones with piers of hewn stones placed at intervals. This type of construction is referred to as pier-and-rubble construction. The corners of the structure are pier walls of hewn stone. The foundation course would have the largest cornerstone, to span both sides of the corner and provide a level base for upper courses. Thus the cornerstone was critical to the stability of the whole structure.

Another OT passage may have a different architectural meaning. Psalm 118:22 states, "The stone that the builders rejected has become the chief cornerstone (lero'sh pinnah, literally, "head of [the] corner")." The phrase "head of the corner" could mean the top or uppermost stone on the corner. In this sense it would represent a stone like the keystone of an arch or the capstone of a structure. However, the meaning could also be that of the head/chief/most important stone, the corner one. Since the other architectural references in the OT refer to a foundation, it is likely that Ps 118:22 does so as well. However, Ps 118 employs the architectural term with a figurative meaning. The cornerstone clearly refers to a person.

Two other OT passages use *cornerstone* in a figurative sense. Isaiah 19:13 describes the leaders/princes (שָׂרֵי sare) of Egypt as "the cornerstones (pinnath) of its tribes." Similarly, Zech 10:4 speaks of future leaders from the tribe of Judah: "Out of them shall come the cornerstone (pinnathah), out of them the tent peg, out of them the battle bow, out of them every commander." In both passages, cornerstone refers to the most important individuals. The synoptic Gospels and Acts quote Ps 118:22. Jesus uses the passage as a messianic reference to himself (Mark 12:10-12; Matt 21:42; Luke 20:17). The quotation is a direct citation of the LXX (Ps 117:22 LXX): The context in the Synoptics is the parable of the wicked husbandmen; the tenants kill first a landowner's servants and then his son. Immediately afterward, Jesus quotes Ps 118:22 and identifies the chief priests and Pharisees as the wicked husbandmen. The quote in Acts 4:11 is in Peter's speech to the rulers and elders in Jerusalem. It treats the Psalms passage as a messianic reference to Christ.

In Eph 2:19-22, Paul uses building terminology for the household of God: believers. Ephesian Christians are members of the household of God "built upon the foundation of the apostles and prophets, with Christ Jesus himself as the cornerstone" (akrogōniaios) [Eph 2:20]. The use of foundation terminology suggests that cornerstone here also refers to the primary stone at the corner.

First Peter 2:6-7 quotes both Isa 28:16 and Ps 118:22 in reference to Christ: "For it stands in scripture: 'See, I am laying in Zion a stone, a cornerstone akrogoniaios chosen and precious; . . . but for those who do not believe, 'The stone that the builders rejected has become the very head of the corner (kephalēn gōnias).'"

JOEL F. DRINKARD, JR.

CORPORATE PERSONALITY. See ANTHROPOLOGY, CULTURAL, NT; ANTHROPOLOGY, CULTURAL, OT; COLLECTIVIST PERSONALITY.

CORPUS HERMETICUM. See HERMETICUM, CORPUS.

CORRECTIONS OF THE SCRIBES תִּקּוּנֵי סוֹפְרִים tiqqune soferim]. According to various traditions there are eighteen passages of the Hebrew text of the Bible to which early scribes made changes (emendations) for theological reasons, when it was felt adequate respect was not shown to God (e.g., Gen 18:22; Hab 1:12). There is considerable disagreement as to which passages are among the eighteen or whether these traditions are even authentic.

Bibliography: C. McCarthy. *The Tiqqune Sopherim* (1981).

TIMOTHY G. CRAWFORD

CORRUPTION [שְׁאוֹל she'ol; διαφθορά diaphthora, φθορά phthora]. Diaphthora and phthora refer to a place called The PIT or SHEOL (LXX Ps 15:10 [16:10]; Job 33:28), or to an act of corruption as in Paul's letters

where phthora is the decay of the body at the time of DEATH. Under the influence of Jewish eschatology and Greek philosophy, Paul interprets Jesus as the one who will transform the "bondage of decay" to "freedom of the glory of the children of God" (Rom 8:21), or the "perishable" of the physical to "imperishable" of the spiritual (1 Cor 15:42, 50). Luke (Acts 2:27, 31) combines the two concepts and argues that the one who is corrupted (diaphthora) will go to Hades. The Mount of Corruption (NRSV, "Destruction") was so named for Solomon's erection of sites for his foreign wives to worship their gods and goddesses, where "corruption" refers to disobedience and disloyalty (1 Kgs 11:7; 2 Kgs 23:13). *See* IMMORTALITY.

GLENNA S. JACKSON

COS kos [Κῶς Kōs]. Cos lies in the Aegean islands known as the South Sporades, off the southwest coast of Turkey, and was noted on the sea journey between Miletus and Rhodes (Acts 21:1). To the northeast lay the mainland cities of Halikarnassos (modern Bodrum) and Knidos. Although Cos is part of modern Greece, in the Roman period it was part of the province of Asia.

The island was famous for its sanctuary of the healing-god Asklepios, and its association with Hippocrates, the writer of a medical treatise. Herod the Great supported the island's post of gymnasiarch or leader of the gymnasion. Herod Antipas appears to be mentioned in a dedication by Philo Aglaos. *See* AEGEAN.

DAVID W. J. GILL

COSAM koh'suhm [Κωσάμ Kōsam]. An ancestor of Jesus, tracing him back to Adam (Luke 3:28).

COSMETICS תַּמְרוּק tamruq]. Decorating or enhancing the color or features of the human body is a common factor in the creation of personal identity and the achievement of a social standard of personal beauty or fashion.

Ancient Near Eastern texts, art, and grave goods (ointment and perfume bottles and cosmetic palettes) indicate the types of cosmetic potions and treatments used by both men and women. These include coloring the hair, skin, or nails with henna; enlarging the eyes with black kohl paint imported from Egypt; using ground up malachite or galena as eye makeup; reddening the lips and cheeks with red ochre; and mixing olive oil with a variety of herbs and spices (nard, cinnamon, frankincense, myrrh) to provide a fragrant perfume.

Since many of these products were precious and expensive (Eccl 7:1), they were stored in decorated boxes or alabaster bottles (Matt 26:7, 9; Mark 14:3) that enhanced their desirability and indicated the level of wealth of the owner (Isa 3:20). Anointing the body with oils and applying lotions and perfumes were a means of indicating a person's social station (Amos 6:6). Cosmetic treatments also could demonstrate a certain level of authority when they were combined with fine clothing or robes of office. Thus the beleaguered queen Jezebel put on a brave front in the face of the advancing army of the rebel general Jehu by painting her eyes and adorning her head (2 Kgs 9:30). An extreme example of the training required in the use of these beauty products and their application is found in the twelve-month treatment given to Esther and the other potential queen candidates in Esth 2:3-12 ("six months with oil of myrrh, and six months with perfumes and cosmetics"). Such minute attention to detail, however, was restricted to the wealthy and to members of the nobility.

For the majority, cosmetic lotions, perfumes, and ointments generally were reserved for social occasions or celebrations such as weddings or religious festivals. The injunction in 2 Sam 14:2 that those in mourning should not apply cosmetic lotions does indicate, however, that there was a level of expectation associated with personal appearance. One would also expect that careful preparations would be made when a person appeared before judges or the elders, or in anticipation of meeting a prospective husband. Note the efforts made by Ruth to enhance her appearance prior to meeting Boaz on the threshing floor (Ruth 3:3). This is paralleled in David's transformation after the death of his son when he puts on new clothes and anoints himself (2 Sam 12:20), and by Judith, who, prior to going to the "Assyrian" camp, removes her widow's garments and restores her appearance to the level she normally had displayed for her husband (festive attire, tiara, and anointing with "precious ointment" in Jdt 10:3-4). Of course, those working in the fields, at the loom, or in the manufacturing of olive oil or other products, would not have taken time to apply makeup or perfumes, except perhaps a layer of oil to protect their skin from the sun's rays. *See* EYE PAINT; HENNA; OINTMENT; PERFUME.

VICTOR H. MATTHEWS

COSMOGONY, COSMOLOGY שָׁמַיִם וָאָרֶץ] shamayim veʾarets; κοσμογονία kosmogonia, κοσμολογία kosmologia]. Where did life originate? How did it develop? Where are humans located within the universe? What is the relationship of humans to the gods? These are some of the most basic existential questions that have puzzled humans since the dawn of consciousness. They are questions that involve science, philosophy, or religion. Any attempt to answer them forces one to ponder the origins of the world, and that world begins with the individual human being, extends to nearby individuals and groups, and ultimately reaches to the remote regions of the cosmos.

The basic meaning of the term *cosmos* (κόσμος kosmos) is "order." Although first used to refer to any kind of orderly arrangement, 5th cent. BCE Greek philosophers began using it as a technical term for the

"ordered" universe. The term *cosmogony* is based on the compound Greek term kosmogonia (=κόσμος kosmos + γονία gonia), which literally means the "genesis of the ordered world." The closely related term *cosmology* (kosmologia = κόσμος kosmos + λογία logia) refers to the rational and systematic analysis of the ordered universe.

A. Purpose of Cosmology and Cosmogony
B. The Ancient Near East and Mediterranean Basin
  1. Egypt
  2. Mesopotamia
  3. Greece and Rome
C. Cosmogony and Cosmology in the OT
  1. Creator and creation
  2. Terminology and imagery
  3. Israel and the cosmos: the "Heavenly Hosts"
D. Cosmogony and Cosmology in Early Judaism
E. Cosmogony and Cosmology in the NT

A. Purpose of Cosmology and Cosmogony

All societies have struggled to comprehend and ultimately to exert influence on life at the micro and macro levels, that is on the personal and cosmic levels. The impulse behind these efforts is both existential and practical. The existential impulse is to understand the meaning of life in general and, more specifically, to find one's place in the universe. The practical impulse stems from the reality that the natural forces of the "ordered universe" sometimes have catastrophic impact on individual humans and whole societies. Humans have a need to believe that they can understand and in some way influence the world around them. Thus, the study of the origin and meaning of life and of the cosmos has always been an essential part of the human quest.

This quest for cosmological understanding is at the same time religious and scientific. Earlier generations of scholars viewed the ancient cosmologies as pre-scientific myths that in due course were supplanted by more scientific models. This approach fit quite naturally with an evolutionary model of social development. However, more recent philosophical and sociological scholarship on cosmology has found that such a dichotomy or strictly evolutionary relationship between cosmological ideas in science and religion is artificial (*see* SCIENCE AND THE BIBLE). Rather cosmological speculation equally depends on and expresses a society's understanding of itself and of the natural world. Religion and science, in whatever forms and at whatever levels they existed, served ancient peoples, and indeed many modern peoples, in a complementary manner in their quest for personal and cosmic understanding. A society's or individual's cosmological speculations are a projection of their experiences and observations of life. That is, people imagine the cosmos in ways that express their understanding of themselves and their societies. Cosmology is ultimately an analogical projection of their lives and society: cosmology reveals not only a society's understanding of the cosmos, but also its understanding of itself as an entity within the cosmos (see ANTHROPOLOGY, CULTURAL NT; ANTHROPOLOGY, CULTURAL, OT).

B. The Ancient Near East and Mediterranean Basin

1. Egypt

Although modern people prefer ordered, non-contradictory, and integrated models, ancient peoples had cosmologies that contained a vast complex of images and ideas that for them explained the cosmos. The ancient Egyptians' cosmological speculations contained what are to the modern mind seemingly conflicting images and ideas. Overall, the Egyptians, as did most ancient peoples of the Near East, imagined the cosmos as a three-tiered structure: netherworld, earthly realm, and heavenly world. Moreover, the Egyptians had at least four basic models of the cosmos. The "Celestial Bird" model imaged the cosmos as consisting of the earth and netherworld lying beneath the feet of a vast cosmic falcon. Over the falcon's head was the heavenly realm. The falcon's eyes were the sun and the moon, and the whitish speckles on its breast feathers represented the stars. This vast and mighty bird was identified as Horus, the ancient god of the heavenly realm.

The "Celestial Cow" model depicted the cosmos as a cow, the goddess Hathor. The cow was a sacred animal, so many ancient Egyptians imagined the cosmos as a vast cosmic cow. This cosmological model is presented most fully in the *Book of the Divine Cow*. The cow stood over the earth facing west, and on its belly appear the sun, moon, and stars. The celestial cow's four legs hold the sky in place above the earth. The cow consumed the sun in the evening and gave birth to it the following morning. An omen from the Egyptian COFFIN TEXTS mentions that the deceased person whom the omen was designed to help "saw Re (the sun) being born yesterday from the loins of the Celestial Cow" (Coffin Texts §335).

The "Celestial Woman" model of the cosmos is perhaps the most prominent ancient Egyptian image of the cosmos. The celestial woman is the goddess Nut who faces west and arches over the earth, balancing on her feet and hands. The celestial bodies traveled from east to west on the goddess' belly. The air-god Shu supports her midriff, while the earth god Geb (Keb) lies at the feet of Shu, stretched out between the arms and feet of Nut: "I am the soul of Shu, for whom Nut was placed above and Geb under his feet, and I am between them" (Coffin Text §77).

The "Celestial Plane" model depicts the cosmos is as a flat or convex plane. The celestial plain model stems from simple observation: the sun, moon, planets, and stars appear to rise on the eastern horizon, ascend to a level high overhead, proceed across the sky, and then descend into the western horizon.

Alongside and in conjunction with these cosmological models, the Egyptians imagined that a river or other kind of vast body of water ran across the sky. This river flowed above the head of the falcon and above the celestial plane, but it flowed on the underbelly of the celestial cow and woman. The color of the sky and the occasional rain that fell from the sky naturally led these and the other ancient peoples of the Near East to imagine that there was a vast body of water in the sky. The Egyptians imagined this celestial body of water as the Nile. The image of a celestial river stems from the importance of the Nile to ancient Egypt. The Nile was the lifeblood of Egypt. The ancient Egyptians imagined, therefore, that there was also a Nile for the celestial realm as well as for the netherworld: "You created a Nile in the netherworld, . . . you put a Nile in heaven, . . . but the true Nile comes up from the ground for Egypt" (Hymn to Aten). Each of these rivers sustained and ordered the activity in the three realms—heavenly realm, earthly realm, and netherworld—just as the Nile did for every ancient Egyptian. The many and varied Egyptian cosmologies all reflect Egyptian society and values by projecting onto the transcendent realms the patterns and structures of Egyptian society (see EGYPT).

2. Mesopotamia

In the ancient Near East each clan, city, and empire had its own explanations of the origins of the cosmos and of their particular group's place in it. The extensive literary and artifactual evidence from antiquity indicates that Mesopotamian cultures largely valued cultural continuity over radical innovation. Thus, the overall patterns in cosmological speculation persisted over time. Nonetheless, each of the ancient Mesopotamian cosmological models identifies the chief god (whoever that might be at a given place and time) as the creator and sustainer of cosmic order. The classic expression of Mesopotamian cosmology is found in the ENUMA ELISH, the Babylonian creation epic. This text narrates how the god Marduk created and structured the cosmos and thereby explains why he is the chief god in the Babylonian pantheon. After a cosmic battle with the goddess Tiamat and her forces, Marduk used the carcasses of the vanquished gods to create everything in the cosmos. He split the carcass of Tiamat in two to create the sky and the earth, and from the blood of another god, Kingu, he created humanity to serve the gods. Beneath the earth is the watery netherworld, Apsu, made from the god of that name. This tripartite cosmos is the standard ancient Near Eastern model. In fact, Marduk ultimately proclaims that he made "earth as the mirror of heaven." This myth provides the Mesopotamian explanation for how and why the cosmos is structured as it is; it accounts for the appearance and movements of the celestial bodies; and it explains humans' place and role within this structured cosmos.

Thus, while the myth explicitly states that earthly structures are patterned after the heavenly, in reality the myth represents how humans analogically project the earthly realm as they knew it onto the transcendent realms of heaven and netherworld (*see* ASSYRIA AND BABYLONIA; MESOPOTAMIA; SCIENCE, MESOPOTAMIA).

3. Greece and Rome

All ancient cosmological and astronomical texts presupposed a flat earth model. Likewise, Greek cosmology in the Homeric Age (ca. 1200–700 BCE) as attested in Homer's *Iliad* and *Odyssey* as well as in Hesiod's *Works and Days* and *Theogony* conceived of the earth as a flat land mass encircled by water, the "Okeanus" (Homer, *Iliad*, 14.246, 18.607, and 21.194; *Odyssey*, 10.467–12.6 and 24.1ff; Hesiod, *Works and Days*, 168–75). The celestial bodies rose in the eastern part of Okeanus, ran their daily courses across the sky, and in the evening descended into the western part of Okeanus. Thus, the earliest Greek images of the cosmos were very much like those of the peoples of the Fertile Crescent.

The Ionian philosophers of the pre-Socratic Age began to break away from the cosmologies that shared features with cultures of the Fertile Crescent. Instead of relying principally on religious myths, these scholars sought to explain the origin and development of the cosmos in physical terms. Thales (ca. 624–547 BCE), Anaximander (ca. 611–547 BCE), and Anaximenes (ca. 585–526 BCE) generally viewed the earth after a model that closely resembles those of the Mesopotamians and Egyptians—a land mass completely surrounded by water and suspended between the celestial and netherworldly realms, and the celestial bodies fixed to a vault overhead. Pythagoras (ca. 575–500 BCE) and his successors, the Pythagoreans, created a mathematical construction of the universe, which imagined the earth, the celestial bodies, and the universe itself to be spherical. Anaxagoras (ca. 500–428 BCE) seems to be the first scholar to arrange the planets in the following ascending order from the earth: moon, sun, Venus, Mercury, Mars, Jupiter, Saturn, and the fixed stars. PLATO (ca. 427–347 BCE) followed this model according to which the various heavenly bodies encircle the earth each in their own physical sphere with some additional intervening spheres (*Republic* 10 and *Timaeus* 38). ARISTOTLE (ca. 384–322 BCE), in his treatise entitled "On the Heavens," generally adopted Plato's system but transformed it from a theoretical model into an actual physical mechanism with a total of fifty-five spheres. According to this model, the divine sphere was the one farthest away from the earth, which itself sat at rest in the center of the cosmos. Aristotle maintained that the heavenly realm—the ethereal realm from the outer limits of the universe down to the level of the moon—is characterized by perfection and unchanging order. Each lower realm suffers from increasing disorder and corruption. In his understanding, therefore, the earth was the realm where imperfection, impurity, and disorder reigned, while the heavenly realm was perfect, pure, and entirely orderly. Aristotle's physical explanation comports completely with his metaphysical understanding of the universe. The gods ultimately reside in the ethereal realm of purity and stasis, while humans dwell on earth, the impure and chaotic realm. This geocentric cosmology, however, is most popularly identified with Claudius PTOLEMY of Alexandria (ca. 100–170 BCE). In Ptolemy's system there were a total of eight planetary spheres that account for the daily rotation of the seven planets and the "fixed stars" (note Cicero's "Dream of Scipio" in *Republic* 6.9-26; compare Cicero's *De Natura Deorum* 2.20, §52-53, and *De Divinatione* 2.43, §91). Beyond the fixed stars is the ethereal or heavenly (*caelestis*) realm. While this outermost sphere, heaven, is perfect and enduring, everything below the level of the moon is corrupt and perishing. The motionless earth situated in the middle of the universe with all else whirling around it, the geocentric model, to this day is popularly known also as the "Ptolemaic model."

The Greeks and Romans, due to advances in physics, mathematics, and astronomy, developed vastly different cosmologies from their Mediterranean and Near Eastern predecessors. These Greek cosmologies changed how humans viewed themselves and their cosmos. Religious values eventually attached to these cosmologies. Plato and his successors imaged that the several nestled spheres encircling the earth each became increasingly rarified and pure as one moved further away from earth. The old three-story universe common to so many of these cultures was being displaced, slowly and only partially in some places, by complicated Greco-Roman models. Rather than making the divine realm more remote, these models gave definition to and a rational interpretation of the space between the divine and human realms (*see* GREECE; GREEK RELIGION AND PHILOSOPHY; HELLENISM; ROMAN EMPIRE; ROMAN RELIGION).

C. Cosmogony and Cosmology in the OT

1. Creator and Creation

The Bible begins with a sentence that succinctly states the biblical editors' principal view of the cosmos: "In the beginning God created the heavens and the earth" (Gen 1:1). Cosmogony and cosmology provide the starting point for biblical and, eventually, early Jewish and Christian thought and history. Everything starts with and is set within God's creation. The Priestly Creation account in Gen 1 (*see* P, PRIESTLY WRITERS), although it has pride of place at the beginning of the biblical story, in fact was written late in the history of Israel, likely in the exilic or postexilic eras. Its authors evidently knew the widespread ancient Near Eastern myths of cosmic battle, and this account subtly draws on some of the ancient motifs of the cosmic conflict in creation. Parallels in Gen 1 with the Enuma Elish and other ancient Near Eastern accounts of the cosmic battle resulting in the creation of the cosmos include the evocative terms תְּהוֹם tehom, "deep" [Tiamat], and תַּנִּינִם tanninim, "sea monsters." Nonetheless, Gen 1 subsumes or reinterprets these old motifs of struggle between gods within a strictly monotheistic ideology, wherein God alone is the actor, and he alone transforms chaos into structured holiness: each being and place has its own specific and divinely-appointed function. Moreover, rather than taking action, God merely speaks and God's creative will is accomplished. By the end of Gen 1 divinity, humanity, and nature are at peace and in their appropriate places, and this structured holiness is ultimately deemed "very good" by the Creator (Gen 1:31). Genesis 1, therefore, presents what the biblical editors would suggest is the divine pattern for the cosmos and for civilization: God outside of creation as the only divine being, everything located and functioning in its appropriate place, and all following a holy pattern of work and rest. With Gen 1 cosmic time and historical time begin; the former remains constant and sets the unchanging standards, the latter moves onward and is subject to the vicissitudes of events (*see* CREATION).

Biblical texts from all historical periods and a variety of literary genres demonstrate that in Yahwistic circles, that is among people who worshipped Yahweh as the chief or only god, Yahweh was understood as the one who alone created heaven, earth, and all that is in them: from chaos Yahweh/God created cosmos, order (e.g., Gen 1:1, 2:4; Exod 20:11; Isa 45:12; Neh 9:6; Pss 8:3, 33:6, 146:6; Prov 3:19). According to this perspective, the Israelite and Judahite god Yahweh had no rivals, and in a world where nations claimed that their gods were the supreme beings in the universe and that all others were subject to them, the Israelites' claim for the superiority of Yahweh as creator and sustainer of the cosmos enabled them to imagine that no other nation could rival her: "So acknowledge today and take to heart that Yahweh is God in heaven above and on the earth beneath. There is no other" (Deut 4:39). Still, research has shown that phrases such as "Yahweh, God Most High, Creator of heaven and earth" and related phrases for Yahweh (e.g., "rider of the clouds" Ps 68:5;compare Ps 104:3 and "rider through the heavens" Deut 33:26) have parallels in earlier Canaanite terminology for the gods El and Baal. Thus, it is clear that the Israelites did not create these phrases but inherited many of them from earlier Canaanite traditions. Such vestiges of this Canaanite heritage emerge occasionally throughout the OT. Some ancient Israelites and Judahites imagined Yahweh as presiding over a council of divine beings in heaven (Job 1:6). Psalm 82, however, while describing just such a heavenly council, preserves

what may be an early vision of Yahweh as just one of the members of the heavenly divine council: "God stands in the council of ʾel (NRSV: "God had taken his place in the divine council;"), in the midst of the gods he passes judgment" (Ps 82:1). Here *God* (ʾelohim) likely refers to Yahweh and the term ʾel to the god El. Later the text calls on God (read Yahweh) to assume leadership: "Rise up, O God, judge the earth, for all the nations belong to you" (Ps 82:8). Similarly, Deut 32 may also contain an older image of Yahweh's role within the divine council: "When ʾelyon ("the Most High") apportioned the peoples, when he divided humankind, he fixed the boundaries of the peoples according to the number of the divine beings (lit. "sons of God"; NRSV: "gods"). The LORD's own portion was his people, Jacob his allotted share." Here ʾelyon can be understood as the proper name for the chief god of the divine council who, when pairing gods with their peoples, apportioned Israel to Yahweh. Thus, while overall biblical cosmology ascribes divinity and cosmological power to Yahweh alone, there are scattered texts within the OT that betray a more complex understanding of Yahweh's role in the cosmos.

2. Terminology and imagery

The ancient Israelite phrase for cosmos is "heaven and earth" (שָׁמַיִם וְאָרֶץ shamayim veʾarets). Such Hebrew phrases with elements representing either end of a spectrum are understood as inclusive or expressing totality. Thus, this Hebrew phrase refers to heaven, earth, and all that is in, on, between, and around them. The ancient Israelites, like their ancient Near Eastern neighbors, imagined the universe as a tripartite structure: heaven or sky (shamayim) above, earth (ʾarets) in the middle, and netherworld (שְׁאוֹל sheʾol) below (*see* EARTH; HEAVEN; SHEOL). This image of the cosmos appears throughout the OT:

> "You shall not make for yourself
> an idol, whether in the form of
> anything that is in heaven above,
> or that is on the earth beneath, or
> that is in the water under the earth"
> (Exod 20:4).
> "Where can I go from your spirit?
> Or where can I flee from your presence? If I ascend to heaven, you are
> there; if I make my bed in Sheol,
> you are there" (Ps 139:7-8).

The Hebrew word shamayim can be translated into English as either *heaven* (the realm of the gods) or *sky* (the atmosphere or celestial realm) and is related to the Akkadian term shamu or the Akkadian phrase sha—me, "place of water." The Hebrew suffix "ayim" on this term typically signifies things that occur naturally in pairs, but in this case the form is actually plural. Some scholars have understood this suffix as indicating that the ancient Israelites and Judahites had a notion of multiple heavens. It seems more likely that this plural form expresses the sky's vastness or expanse. That is to say, by using the plural form "heavens/skies," the Israelites and Judahites were stressing the vastness of the heavenly realm from horizon to horizon. In the same way the phrase "heaven of heaven" also does not indicate an Israelite belief in multiple heavens. Rather, this is how the Israelites expressed a superlative—"vast heaven," or "the highest reaches of the sky." Furthermore, the Hebrew phrase literally rendered "heaven and the heaven of heaven(s)" has also been thought by some to indicate that the ancient Israelites imagined that there were multiple heavens. But it is again probably best to understand this as referring to the vastness of heaven/sky: "heaven, indeed the vast heaven," or "the sky, even the furthest reaches of the sky." The heavens are incomprehensibly vast (Isa 40:12; Jer 31:37) and high above the earth (Isa 55:9; Ps 103:11). They extend down to and are coterminous with the surface of the earth (Deut 4:32, 30:4; Neh 1:9; compare Isa 13:5), so when one arrives at the farthest reaches of the earth, one has arrived at the boundary of the heavens (Deut 4:32, 30:4). The term *firmament* (רָקִיעַ raqia‘) denotes the atmosphere between the heavenly realm and the earth (Gen 1:6-7, 20) where the celestial bodies move (Gen 1:14-17). It can also be used as a synonym for "heaven/sky" (Gen 1:8; Ps 19:2).

When the ancient Israelites looked skyward, they, naturally, imagined that they were looking at the "floor" of heaven, and according to some of their images of the cosmos, this floor was composed of stone. "Then Moses and Aaron, Nadab, and Abihu, and seventy of the elders of Israel went up (to the top of Mt. Sinai), and they saw the God of Israel. Under his feet there was something like a pavement of sapphire stone, like the very heaven for clearness" (Exod 24:9-10). The prophet Ezekiel, in his description of the divine presence, mentioned that in his vision of God he saw "And above the dome over their heads there was something like a throne, in appearance like sapphire; and seated above the likeness of a throne was something that seemed like a human form." (Ezek 1:26). These biblical texts suggest that at least part of the Israelite mythology imagined the floor of heaven, i.e., the base of God's heavenly throne, as a stony substance. In this regard, an Akkadian text (KAR 307) likewise imagined the base of the heavenly realms as a stony substance. "The upper heavens are *luludanitu* stone . . .; the middle heavens are *saggilmut* stone . . . Bel sat there in a chamber on a lapis-lazuli throne; the lower heavens are jasper, they belong to the stars." The biblical image has, not surprisingly, parallels in the neighboring cultures.

This is only part of the picture, for in the biblical materials there is another description of the nature of the lowest level of heaven. Gen 1:6-8 suggests that the lowest level of heaven serves as a barricade against the waters of heaven. "And God said, 'Let there be a dome (raqia‘) in the midst of the waters, and let it separate the waters from the waters.' So God made the dome and separated the waters that were under the dome from the waters that were above the dome. And it was so. God called the dome (raqia‘) Sky (shamayim). And there was evening and there was morning, the second day." Although this text makes it clear that the raqia‘ is a water barrier, it does not identify the substance of which this barricade is made. The description, however, indicates that the text is referring to the vast airy expanse between the heavenly realm and the earth. Like their neighbors, the ancient Israelites thought that there was a vast body of water above the sky that was the source of the rain. The rainwater—"the waters in the heavens" (Jer 10:13, 51:16) or "above the heavens" (Ps 148:4)—may also be stored in cisterns or storehouses alongside the storehouses for the other meteorological phenomena such as wind, snow, and hail (*see* Gen 8:2; Isa 55:10; Deut 11:11, 28:12; Jer 10:13, 51:16; Ps 135:7; Job 38:22, 37). The Flood story mentions openings or windows in the sky through which this rainwater passes. "In the six hundredth year of Noah's life, in the second month, on the seventeenth day of the month, on that day all the fountains of the great deep burst forth, and the windows of the sky were opened" (Gen 7:11). Precipitation passes from the celestial body of water to earth via a window, door, or water channel (Job 38:25-27). One biblical image, therefore, identifies the lowest element of the heavenly realm as a barricade that restrains the celestial water from pouring down on earth. This parallels the Babylonian creation account, the ENUMA ELISH, which recounts that the god Marduk created the floor of heaven from the carcass of the sea goddess Tiamat and used it as a water barrier (*Enuma Elish* 4.128-41). Both the ancient Mesopotamian and the ancient Israelite cosmological images exhibit varying beliefs about the lowest level of the heavenly realm. These multiple images warn against any attempt to reconstruct the image of the heavenly realms for any of these ancient cultures. There was never one image, but several.

3. Israel and the cosmos: the "Heavenly Hosts"

The nighttime sky has always fascinated humanity. The Israelites and Judahites, like their Near Eastern neighbors, certainly were familiar with astronomy, and in fact several biblical texts mention stars or constellations by name. Unfortunately, the cosmological interests of the biblical editors did not include astronomy per se, and so there are no strictly astronomical texts in the Bible (*see* ASTRONOMY, ASTROLOGY). However, it seems from internal and external evidence that within at least a few sectors of ancient Israelite and Judahite societies people were involved with astronomical observation, speculation, and worship. The 3rd cent.

BCE Jewish apocryphal work entitled the "Astronomical Book of Enoch" (1 En. 72-82), as well as other early Jewish texts, attests extensive Jewish familiarity with astronomy. It is unlikely that Jews learned astronomy only late in their ancient history. Rather, as several texts in the OT suggest, there were people in Israel and Judah who were well acquainted with astronomy. It has become clear that at least some Israelites and Judahites of all periods looked to the cosmos and imagined that the celestial bodies were divine beings. The *Enuma Elish* (v.1-8; vii.125-31) mentions that the stars are gods, and as gods they are fitting objects of devotion. The people of Israel and Judah were no different in this matter, and several biblical texts mention their predilection to worship the celestial bodies (Exod 20:4; Deut 4:19, 17:3; 2 Kgs 17:16, 21:3-5, 23:5; Jer 8:2, 19:13, 44:17-19; Ezek 8:16; Am 5:26; Zeph 1:5; Job 31:26-28).

> And when you look up to the heavens and see the sun, the moon, and the stars, all the host of heaven, do not be led astray and bow down to them and serve them, things that the LORD your God has allotted to all the peoples everywhere under heaven. (Deut 4:19).

> He deposed the idolatrous priests whom the kings of Judah had ordained to make offerings in the high places at the cities of Judah and around Jerusalem; those also who made offerings to Baal, to the sun, the moon, the constellations, and all the host of the heavens. (2 Kgs 23:5).

> You are wearied with your many consultations; let those who study the heavens stand up and save you, those who gaze at the stars, and at each new moon predict what shall befall you (Isa 47:13).

Their dependence on an "orderly" functioning of the cosmos led ancients to worship the celestial bodies because their livelihood depended on nature, and these objects (i.e., their apparent size, movements, etc.) are related to nature's seasonal changes. Moreover, it is clear that the people thought that the stars were manifestations of gods or heavenly beings. Judg 5:20, part of a poem that may date as early as the 11th cent. BCE and that provides insight into early Israelite beliefs, mentions that during Deborah's battle against the Canaanite king Sisera the stars fought against one another as the human forces battled on earth. The stars, therefore,

are gods fighting in heaven and the outcome of their celestial battle determines the outcome of the battle on earth. Job 38:7 mentions that when God created the world "the morning stars sang together and all the heavenly beings [literally "children of God"] shouted for joy." The parallelism here of "morning stars" and "heavenly beings" indicates that this author equates the stars with the heavenly beings.

The OT seems to know of the constellation Orion and of the Pleiades. These names always occur together, and in only three places:

> (God is the one) . . . who made the Bear and Orion, the Pleiades and the chambers of the south (Job 9:9).

> Can you bind the chains of the Pleiades, or loose the cords of Orion? Can you lead forth the Mazzarot in their season, or can you guide the Bear with its children? Do you know ordinances of the heavens? Can you establish their rule on earth? (Job 38:31-33)

> The one who made the Pleiades and Orion, and turns deep darkness into the morning, and darkens the day into night, who calls for the waters of the sea, and pours them out on the surface of the earth, the LORD is his name (Amos 5:8).

The prophet Amos also knew of other stars worshipped by the Israelites:

> "You shall take up Sakkuth your king, and Kaiwan your star-god, your images, which you made for yourselves; therefore I will take you into exile beyond Damascus," says the LORD, whose name is the God of hosts (Amos 5:26-27).

Thus, there is clear evidence that at least some ancient Israelites and Judahite worshipped the stars as gods or representatives of gods (*see also* Exod 20:4; Deut 4:19, 5:8, 17:3; 2 Kgs 17:16, 21:3-5//2 Chr 33:3-5; Isa 47:13; Jer 7:18, 10:2, 19:13, 44:15-25; Zeph 1:5).

It would be incorrect to conclude from the meager evidence in the OT that ancient Israelites and Judahites were unacquainted with astronomy per se. There is, nevertheless, no explicit textual evidence of a developed astronomical "science" in ancient Israel parallel to that in Mesopotamia or Greece. While some people believed that the celestial bodies were gods, others believed that these bodies were created by Yahweh

(Gen 1:16; Ps 136:4-9, 147:4; Job 38:12-15; Neh 9:6) and that Yahweh alone established the courses of their daily and annual travels (Isa 13:10, 45:12; Jer 31:35; Ps 8:3; Job 9:7-9, 38:31-33). Solar worship was certainly a part of Israelite and Judahite religiosity as it was among other peoples of the ancient Near East. One late biblical author describes people in the act of worshipping the sun: the prophet Ezekiel saw people worshipping the sun and other gods within the precincts of Yahweh's Temple in Jerusalem.

> Then he (God) brought me to the entrance of the northern gate of the house of the LORD; women were sitting there weeping for TAMMUZ. . . . And he brought me into the inner court of the house of the LORD; there, at the entrance of the temple of the LORD, between the porch and the altar, were about twenty-five men, with their backs to the temple of the LORD and their faces toward the east, prostrating themselves to the sun toward the east (Ezek 8:14,16).

These people were facing the wrong way and had turned their backs on Yahweh and the Temple while they directed their prayers to the rising sun (Jer 2:27). The frequent references in the Bible to the Israelites' and Judahites' propensity to worship the celestial bodies only suggests that there was a developed astronomical tradition in ancient Israel comparable to the other cultures of the Near East. For strict Yahwists, however, the celestial bodies were not gods at all, but merely objects created by Yahweh and under divine control (Josh 10:12-13; Isa 38:8; Hab 3:10-11; Job 9:7, 38:7, 12). This kind of astronomical speculation was a common feature of the ancient Near Eastern cosmological imagination, and it was also a part of Israelite and Judahite religion.

The phrase "host of heaven" designates the vast assembly of heavenly beings and/or celestial bodies (Deut 4:19, 17:3; 2 Kgs 17:16, 21:3,5,; Isa 34:4, Isa 40:26; 45:12; Jer 8:2, 19:13, 33:22; Zeph 1:5; Neh 9:6; 2 Chr 18:18, 33:3, 5; see HOSTS, HOST OF HEAVEN). The phrase "Yahweh of Hosts" identifies Yahweh as leading the cosmic bodies or as presiding over the heavenly pantheon. Several passages use the image of standing before God in the sense of being in the presence of such a celestial assembly (e.g., Exod 15:11; 1 Kgs 17:1, 18:15, 22:19; 2 Kgs 3:14, 5:16; Isa 6:2; Jer 23:18, 22; Zech 3:4, 4:14, 6:5). The phrase "Yahweh of Hosts" seems to be a militaristic epithet that Yahweh inherited from the Canaanite god El as leader of the divine forces at the earliest stages of the Yahweh cult. Just as the heavenly "hosts" in Ps 29:1-2

and 148:1-5 praise God, so do the seraphim in the vision recounted in Isa 6. Isaiah himself exclaims, "Woe is me! I am lost, for I am a man of unclean lips, and I live among a people of unclean lips; yet my eyes have seen the King, the LORD of hosts!" (Isa 6:3, 5; see GOD, NAMES OF).

The OT also knows of a heavenly beings called "messengers" (מַלְאָכִים malʾakhim; e.g., Gen 21:17, 32:4; Judg 13:3; Zech 1:9-14; Ps 35:5-6, etc.), or "sons of God" or "heavenly beings" (e.g., Gen 6:2, 4; Deut 32:8; Pss 29:1; 89:7; Job 1:6, 2:1, 38:7; see ANGEL; ANGELIC HOST). These beings appear to reside with God in heaven but come to earth to act on God's behalf. The most common of these, however, is "messenger" (malʾakh). This messenger is so closely related to God, that at times they seem to merge. This messenger is the means by which God can act or be present in the material world. These heavenly messengers can take human form, as the story about Abraham and his mysterious visitors in Gen 18–19 suggests. The patriarch Jacob had a dream in which he saw "messengers of God" going up and down on a "ladder" that reached to heaven (Gen 28). Joshua had an encounter with another kind of heavenly being, the "commander of Yahweh's hosts" apparently a heavenly being who was in charge of the heavenly armies that would fight on Joshua's behalf (Josh 5:13-15).

Through the course of the biblical period, these nameless heavenly messengers began to be depicted as individuals with personal names and identities. Texts such as Ps 68:18, Deut 32:8, and Dan 7:10 all note that there is an innumerable host of celestial beings in heaven, but these beings receive personal names only beginning in the Second Temple period (roughly 539 BCE–100 CE). This is most apparent in the book of Daniel, the latest book in the OT, where these beings—angels—appear with names. This flowering of speculation on the heavenly beings during the Second Temple period was due not simply to outside influences, but to developments that had been going on within Israelite and Judahite thought for some time. The gods of the ancient Near East were first seen as Yahweh's peers, then subordinate gods, and finally "angels" created to serve the LORD. These angels eventually developed independent identities and were organized into ranks. This structuring of the cosmic beings is part of the cosmological imagination's larger attempt to bring ever more structure to the cosmos and thereby render it more intelligible and perhaps somewhat more controllable or predictable (see ANGEL; GOD, OT VIEW OF).

D. Cosmogony and Cosmology in Early Judaism

The diversity that characterized Israelite/Judahite and biblical ideas on cosmogony and cosmology continues in early Jewish texts and culture. More importantly, however, changes in the political fate of Greco-Roman era Jews had a tremendous influence in how they imagined their world and the cosmos. Even more so than the Babylonian EXILE, the conquest of the Near East by ALEXANDER THE GREAT and the subsequent Hellenization of this region had a transformative impact on Jewish culture (*see* HELLENISM). Greek culture, values, and ways of imagining the cosmos led Jews to re-conceptualize their culture and traditions. Hellenistic cosmology and concomitant religious images and ideals had a notable impact on many Jews. The Book of Daniel exhibits cosmological features that separate it from the rest of the biblical corpus. Notable in this regard is Dan 12:2-3.

> Many of those who sleep in the dust of the earth shall awake, some to everlasting life, and some to shame and everlasting contempt. Those who are wise shall shine like the brightness of the sky, and those who lead many to righteousness, like the stars forever and ever.

This text clearly suggests a new understanding of the place of the righteous—they will one day be resurrected and transferred to the heavenly realm where they take a place among the celestial bodies. This is an entirely new way of conceptualizing humanity's relationship with the cosmos during life and in the afterlife. Now rather than remain in the netherworldly realm of the dead, the righteous will ascend to heaven (*see* AFTERLIFE; DEAD, ABODE OF THE; HEAVEN). This ascent accords with Hellenistic cosmological speculation that identifies the furthest heavenly realm as the realm of purity. This is where the righteous will now one day ascend. Thus, what began as Platonic and Pythagorean images of the righteous soul longing to return to its place of origin in the ethereal realm of purity, and conceptualized in Hellenistic cosmology, has transformed aspects of early Jewish cosmology and religion. This Greco-Roman cosmology is found most fully in the writings of PHILO OF ALEXANDRIA, who sought to integrate Jewish tradition with Greco-Roman ideals and culture. Philo exhibits a thorough and accurate understanding of Greco-Roman cosmology. He knows the seven-heaven model and uses it and its attending religious values adroitly (e.g., *see Heir* 207-14, 221-24; *Cherubim* 21-25). He also noted that the soul longs to return to its place of origin in the ethereal realm of purity and permanence (*see Q. G.* 4.74; *Heir* 276). At the same time more traditional images of the cosmos persisted in early Judaism. The "Astronomical Book of Enoch" (*1 En.* 72–82), although well known in its Ethiopian version, was discovered also among the DEAD SEA SCROLLS (4QEn^ast). Some fragments of this text date to the 3rd cent. BCE and make it even older than the book of Daniel. Yet, the many copies of

it found at QUMRAN indicated that it was valued by these sectarians well into the 1st cent. CE. This text's cosmology follows old ancient Near Eastern patterns: the celestial bodies enter and exit the skies through gates, and the earth is apparently imagined as a flat plane. This text suggests that the ancient, traditional cosmology continued to serve the religious and social values of some segments of the early Jewish community. These people were either unaware of or unwilling to adopt Greco-Roman cosmologies and their concomitant religious values.

E. Cosmogony and Cosmology in the NT

The early Christian communities were heirs of both Jewish tradition as well as Greco-Roman culture. Thus early Christian texts naturally share in Greco-Roman cosmological speculation. Three texts are telling: Gospel of John, 2 Cor 12:1-4, and the Book of Revelation. John 1:1-18, the prologue to the Gospel of John, is a Hellenistic reinterpretation of the creation story in Gen 1 as recorded in the LXX translation. The account is unique to this Gospel, and its goal is to demonstrate Jesus' divinity by equating him with the powerful and creative word, the "Logos" (λόγος logos) of God. Jesus was at creation with and as God. For the Johannine Christian community, the origins of the cosmos are now even more personalized by having Jesus himself present and active "in the beginning." Their cosmology is an expression of their understanding of the cosmos and of their God's relationship to it.

In 2 Cor 12 Paul recounts a heavenly ascent to the third heaven. Heavenly ascents became a popular motif during the Greco-Roman era. These ascents typically involve a multiple heaven schema and thereby demonstrate their adoption of standard Greco-Roman cosmology. Moreover, these texts also depend on the cosmological images that locate the place of the Divine in the furthest ethereal region of the cosmos, the only place where absolute purity, perfection, and permanence reign. Ascent texts reflect the author's perception of humans' place within and access to the cosmos (*see* ASCENT TO HEAVEN; HEAVEN).

The book of Revelation, the final book of the NT and the final book of the Bible for Christians, ends with the reintegration of cultic and historic time: God and humanity are once again united in a realm of beauty, peace, abundance, purity, and permanence. However, before this blessed era can begin, the cosmic conflict must finally be resolved, a conflict hinted at in some biblical texts and evident in most ancient Near Eastern cosmological/cosmogonic texts. For the Christian reader, Revelation presents paradise restored. The sea monsters, **tanninim**, of chaos that harken back to Gen 1 and the biblical LEVIATHAN and BEHEMOTH (e.g., Isa 27:1; Ps 74:14; Job 40:15) are finally vanquished (Rev 12–13, 21). Order, "cosmos," is restored. The story ends when a new heaven and new earth appear (21:1), all things are made new (21:5), and the author can proclaim "now at last God dwells with humankind" (21:3). For Christians the book of Revelation suggests that the cosmological quest has returned humanity to the cosmogonic beginning.

Cosmology and cosmogony are the intellectual tools that humans use to structure and understand the universe around them. There is only one thing that unites human beings of all times and all places, and that is the teeming cosmos that appears overhead. As humans have tried to comprehend and even exert influence over the cosmos, their images of the cosmos have always reflected their societies. Until the most recent times, and even in our day to an extent, cosmology and cosmogony actually have said less about the cosmos and more about humans and their perceptions of themselves and their place in the cosmos.

Bibliography: Adela Yarbro Collins. *Cosmology and Eschatology in Jewish and Christian Apocalypticism* (1996); Michael J. Crowe. *Theories of the World from Antiquity to the Copernican Revolution* (1990); Martha Himmelfarb. *Ascent to Heaven in Jewish and Christian Apocalypses* (1993); Wayne Horowitz. *Mesopotamian Cosmic Geography.* (1998); Mark S. Smith. *The Origins of Biblical Monotheism: Israel's Polytheistic Background and the Ugaritic Texts* (2001); Mark S. Smith. *The Memoirs of God: History, Memory, and the Experience of the Divine in Ancient Israel* (2004); J. Edward Wright. *The Early History of Heaven* (2000); M. R. Wright. *Cosmology in Antiquity* (1995).

J. EDWARD WRIGHT

COSMOS. *See* COSMOGONY, COSMOLOGY.

COSTLY [יָקָר yqr, מִגְדָּנָה mighdanah, חֶמֶד khmd; τιμιότης timiotes, βαρύτιμος barytimos, πολυτελής polyteles, πολύτιμος polytimos]. Several terms indicating great value are rendered "costly" in the NRSV. The preciousness of materials for Solomon's building projects (1 Kgs 5:17; 7:9-11) and of goods that *sinners* seize from the innocent (Prov 1:13) is indicated by the root yqr; as is the ransom that God ironically requires to prolong a person's life (Ps 49:8). Choice gifts (**mighdanoth**) were meant to impress Isaac's prospective in-laws (Gen 24:53). The root **khmd** suggests the desirability of the designated items (2 Chr 32:27; Dan 11:38). Corals are "costly stones" juxtaposed with "lips informed by knowledge" (Prov 20:15). In Rev 18:12, imports to "Babylon" were highly prized (**timiotatos**). The great value (**barytimos**, Matt 26:7; **polyteles**, Mark 14:3; **polytimos**, John 12:3) of the ointment with which Jesus was anointed provoked the disciples' protests; but Jesus welcomed the expression of devotion.

STEPHEN WESTERHOLM

COTTON [כַּרְפַּס karpas]. Cotton (*Gossypium arboreum*) is the seed fiber of the cotton plant that grows in warm, humid climates with 3–5 in. of annual rain. The plants flower in eighty to one hundred days and then take an additional fifty-five to eighty days for the seeds to form and the cotton boll to open.

The cultivation of cotton in the ancient Near East seems to have been restricted to Egypt and Iran, although the plant is known to grow wild along river banks. It is possible that this plant was introduced into these areas as a result of trade with India, where archaeological evidence from Mohenjo Daro and Harappa in the Indus Valley indicates that cotton cultivation dates back to ca. 3000 BCE. A passage in Isaiah (19:9) refers to those who weave cotton cloth, indicating an established industry as early as the 8th cent. BCE. The Greek historian Herodotus (*Hist.* 7.65), writing ca. 500 BCE, describes Indians who wore "cotton dresses," and the use of cotton as bandages (7.181). He also referred to Indian "trees which grow wild there, the fruit whereof is a wool exceeding in beauty and goodness that of sheep. The natives make their clothes of the tree-wool" (*Hist.* 3.47).

Cotton fabric was eventually introduced into Europe by Alexander the Great in late 4th cent. BCE, but it was not widely used by the Romans.

Perhaps because of its white color, cotton fabric is referred to in two passages in Esther with the qualifying word חוּר khur, *white.* In the first instance (Esth 1:6), it is used for fine draperies that decorated the king's palace, and in the other (Esth 8:15) **khur** refers to a finely woven, white garment worn by Mordecai. *See* CLOTH, CLOTHES; PLANTS OF THE BIBLE; WHITE.

VICTOR H. MATTHEWS

COUCH [מִשְׁכָּב mishkav, מִטָּה mittah, עֶרֶשׂ ʿeres, יָצוּעַ yatsuaʿ; κλίνη kline, κοίτη koite, στρῶμα stroma]. A word used interchangeably with *bed*, at the discretion of the translator, for various Hebrew words. Couches functioned primarily as a means of reclining during meals (Esth 7:8; Tob 2:1; John 21:20), and occasionally for sleeping (Gen 49:4; Amos 6:4). *See* BED; FURNITURE; HOUSE.

VICTOR H. MATTHEWS

COUNCIL, HEAVENLY. *See* DIVINE ASSEMBLY; GOD, OT VIEW OF; HOSTS, HOSTS OF HEAVEN.

COUNCIL OF JAMNIA. *See* JAMNIA, COUNCIL OF.

COUNCIL OF JERUSALEM. *See* JERUSALEM, COUNCIL OF.

COUNCIL, THE COUNCIL, COUNCIL HOUSE koun´suhl. Terms used for judicial entities in various social, political, and religious contexts. 1. In the OT, Yahweh, the God of Israel, holds the highest place of judgment among a divine council or assembly of "heavenly beings" or "holy ones" (Pss 82:1; 89:7—"council" translates עֵדָה ʿadhath, συναγωγή synagogē in the first text; סוֹד sodh, βουλή boulē in the second; *see* SYNAGOGUE). At times, divinely commissioned human beings, such as prophets, may also "stand" in the heavenly council in order to receive special instructions for God's people (Jer 23:18-22; Amos 3:7).

2. Rulers in the biblical world typically had a royal council or advisory court comprised of military commanders and diplomatic officials (2 Kgs 9:5; 25:19; Jer 52:25; 1 Esd 2:17; Jdt 6:1, 7; 2 Macc 14:5; 4 Macc 17:17; Acts 25:12). These councilors may be described as "sitting" (יֹשְׁבִים yoshvim, 2 Kgs 9:5) in deliberative session or as "seeing the face of the king" (מְרֹאֵי פְּנֵי הַמֶּלֶךְ meroʾe pene hamelekh, 2 Kgs 25:19).

3. Occasionally, "council" represents a non-bureaucratic company, as in the violent fraternal "council" of Simeon and Levi (Gen 49:6) or the general "council of my people" associated with "the register of the house of Israel" (Ezek 13:9).

4. A metaphorical use of "council house/chamber" refers to the inner seat of thoughts and emotions experienced by the mother of the seven Maccabean martyrs: "This noble mother . . . in the *council chamber* [βουλευτήριον bouleutērion] of her own soul . . . saw mighty advocates—nature, family, parental love, and the rackings of her children" (4 Macc 15:24-25).

5. In the NT, "council" designates any local tribunals (συνέδρια synedria) before which Jesus' followers may be examined and summoned to testify (Matt 10:17; Mark 13:9).

6. Most frequently in the NT, "council" refers to "the council" or SANHEDRIN (συνέδριον synedrion), the supreme Jewish court in 1st cent. Jerusalem. In the Sermon on the Mount, Jesus warns that anyone who slanders a fellow Jew "will be liable to the council" (Matt 5:22). Jesus himself is interrogated and disciplined by the high Jerusalem council on the eve of his crucifixion (Matt 26:57-68; Mark 14:53–15:1; Luke 22:66-71; John 18:12-27), as are Peter, John, Stephen, and Paul in the book of Acts (4:1-22; 5:17-41; 6:12-15; 22:30–23:10, 28). Although the NT gives no precise numbers or roster for this council, it variously includes chief priests, elders, and representatives among the Sadducees and Pharisees. Apart from the high priests, only two other council members (βουλευτής bouleutēs) are mentioned by name. Joseph of Arimathea, an apparent sympathizer with Jesus, tended to Jesus' burial (Mark 15:43; Luke 23:50); and the venerable Pharisaic teacher, Gamaliel, advised the council to be patient in judging the early Christian apostles (Acts 5:33-39).

7. In the development of early Christian polity, some churches were governed by a "council of elders" or "presbytery" (πρεσβυτέριον presbyterion) responsible, among other duties, for authorizing gifts of ministry (1 Tim 4:14). This ruling cadre of elders reflected the tradition of wise elders on the supreme Jerusalem council and other Jewish judicial/civic bodies (*see* presbyterion

in Luke 22:66 [with synedrion] and Acts 22:5; and another term for "council of elders," γερουσία gerousia, in Exod 3:16, 18; 4:29; 12:21; 24:9; Lev 9:1, 3; Deut 21:2-19; 22:15-18; 25:7-9; 27:1; 29:9; Jdt 11:14; 3 Macc 1:8 [with πρεσβύτερος presbyteros]; and Acts 5:21 [with synedrion]). *See* CHURCH, LIFE AND ORGANIZATION OF; DIVINE ASSEMBLY.

F. SCOTT SPENCER

COUNSEL, COUNSELOR koun′suh-luhr יוֹעֵץ yoʿets, יָעַץ yaʿats; συμβουλεύω symbouleuo, βουλή boulē, συμβούλιον symboulion]. The Hebrew and Greek words have a dual meaning that is often reflected in English translations. They mean to counsel or advise, but also to put that advice into motion, i.e., to plan. *Counselor* sometimes appears to be an official position in the OT (1 Chr 26:14; 27:33; Ezra 7:28; Job 3:14). However, a variety of people give counsel, including prophets (Num 24:14; 1 Kgs 1:12), elders (1 Kgs 12:6), parents (Exod 18:19), and the people more broadly (2 Chr 20:21; 30:23). God is described as the preeminent counselor (Isa 28:29; Jer 32:19). God's decrees (Ps 119:24), Wisdom (Prov 8:14), and the messianic figure of Isa 9:6 and 11:2 share the divine quality of providing counsel. To be successful, human counsel must coincide with God's counsel (Prov 21:30). Absalom (2 Sam 15–17) and Rehoboam (1 Kgs 12) are examples of leaders who choose bad advice over good, although their choices complete God's plan. Elsewhere, God's counsel supersedes what humans have planned (Ps 33:10, 11; Isa 8:10; 19:11, 17). The words appear less often in the NT. Jewish leaders are said to counsel together to kill Jesus (Matt 26:4; John 11:53). God's counsel or plan remains supreme (Acts 5:39; Rom 11:34; Eph 1:11). *Counselor* is used in some translations for **paraklētos** (παράκλητος). *See* CHANCELLOR; CUPBEARER; PARACLETE.

SUSAN HYLEN

COUNTING. *See* MATHEMATICS; MONEY.

COURAGE. Courage is spiritual, emotional, and moral fortitude to speak and act without fear in the face of obstacles and dangers. Whereas in Greek philosophy courage is one of the cardinal virtues (Wis 8:7; 4 Macc 1:18), that an individual can naturally and independently build, courage in the Bible generally derives from the belief and hope of divine companionship and help.

In the OT *courage* is most frequently expressed by the two roots, חזק khzq and אמץ ʾmts (ἰσχύω ischuō and ἀνδρίζομαι andrizomai in the LXX), which denote "to be strong" and "to be courageous." As the conceived seats of courage, various nouns are also used to express courage. They include "heart" (לֵב lev (1 Sam 17:32; 2 Sam 7:27; 17:10; Ps 76:6; Dan 11:25; Amos 2:16; Jer 4:9; Ezek 22:14), "spirit"

רוּחַ ruakh (Josh 2:11), "soul" נֶפֶשׁ nefesh (Ps 107:56), and "hand" יָד yadh (2 Sam 4:1; Ezek 22:14). Whereas biblical Hebrew has no abstract noun for *courage*, Greek has ἀνδρεία andreia. Therefore, the LXX uses andreia and its derivatives such as ἀνδρεῖος andreios (courageous), ἀνδρειόω andreioō (to strengthen), ἀνδρίζομαι andrizomai (to be courageous), and ἀνδρείως andreiōs (courageously). The LXX also uses θαρσέω tharseō or its variant θαρρέω tharrheō (to be bold; to be courageous) to connote courage, often to translate the exhortation "Do not fear!" (e.g., Exod 14:13; 20:20; Zeph 3:16; Hag 2:5; Zech 8:13-15).

Although *courage* is mentioned throughout the OT, there are two places where the use of its terminology is concentrated: the literary context of Israel's entering the promised land and the texts related to the historical setting of the Seleucid king Antiochus IV's persecution of the Jews.

In Deuteronomy and Joshua, the combination of the two roots, khzq and ʾmts, is repeatedly used as formulaic expression. It is said that when Moses asked God to allow him to cross to the promised land, God rejected his request and told him to strengthen (khzq) and encourage (ʾmts) Joshua who would lead the people to the land (Deut 3:28). Before his death, Moses charged Joshua to be strong and courageous and not to fear or be dismayed, assuring that God would be with him and lead him (Deut 31:7-8). God also spoke personally to Joshua to be strong and courageous, assuring him of God's presence and help (Deut 31:23; Josh 1:6-9). The almost identical expression is used by Moses to charge all Israel (Deut 31:6), by the people of Israel to speak with Joshua (Josh 1:18), and by Joshua to charge the people (Josh 10:25).

A heavenly figure exhorts Daniel not to fear and says: "Be strong and courageous" (Dan 10:19). Mattathias tells his sons to be courageous and strong in the law (1 Macc 2:64). Judas encourages his army to die courageously (1 Macc 9:10). The description of Judas and his army highlights their courage (e.g., 2 Macc 8:21; 14:18; 15:10, 17). In portraying the martyrdom of Eleazar and a mother and her seven sons, 2 Maccabees repeatedly uses various expressions to praise their courage (6:27; 7:10, 12, 20, 21, 29). The courage of these martyrs is theologically elaborated in 4 Maccabees.

Several stories feature individuals whose courage is extraordinary. Abraham shows no fear in obeying God. He leaves for an unknown land and later even prepares to sacrifice his son (Gen 12; 22). Prophets endure serious hardship and persecution to deliver God's message. Each of the martyrs in 2 Maccabees fearlessly accepts torture and execution.

Some women are especially noticeable and their stories often underscore their amazing courage in contrast to timid men. Tamar risks her life and becomes the ancestor of King David through Judah, her father-in-law,

who does not keep his promise to provide a husband through LEVIRITE LAW due to his embarrassment (Gen 38). Rahab takes every risk to protect Joshua's spies who, in contrast, minimize their risks by putting a condition to their oath (Josh 2:1-24). Unlike Barak, who is afraid of going to the battlefield without Deborah, Jael, an ordinary wife, audaciously kills Sisera, who is fleeing from Barak (Judg 4:4-23). The daughter of Jephthath, without hesitation exhorts her dismayed father to do in accordance with his vow and courageously accepts death (Judg 11:29-40). Queen Esther risks her life to save her people from Haman, who, in fear, throws himself before her to beg for his life (Esther). When Uzziah, the leader of her town, agrees with the frightened people to surrender to Holofernes in five days, Judith risks her life and kills Holofernes to save her town and Israel (Judith). The courage of the mother of seven brothers described in 2 Macc 7 is most astounding. She robustly exhorts her sons not to fear but to bravely accept torture and death for the cause of their religion. She unwaveringly watches each son's torture and execution before she herself is executed (2 Macc 7).

In the NT the Greek term andreia never appears. The verb form andrizomai, which was frequently used in the LXX to translate ʾmts in the formula of exhortation, appears only once in 1 Cor 16:13, where Paul exhorts Corinthian Christians to "be courageous, be strong" in their faith. Instead tharreō or tharseō, which the LXX frequently used to translate another Hebrew formula of exhortation, "Do not fear," is generally employed. It is mostly Jesus who uses this exhortation, which is usually translated as "take heart" or "take courage." Behind this exhortation lies a belief that Jesus, in his person and ministry, represents God's presence and work. Therefore, Jesus summons the sick, "Take heart!" assuring their healing: a paralytic who is brought by others in Matt 9:2; a woman suffering from hemorrhages in Matt 9:22. When Jesus asks his disciples to summon the blind Bartimaeus, they also call him by saying "Take heart" (Mark 10:49). Jesus says to his terrified disciples in the storm, "Take heart, it is I; do not be afraid" (Matt 14:27; Mark 6:50). In the Gospel of John, Jesus tells his disciples to "take courage" in the world of persecution because he has conquered the world (16:33). In the Acts of the Apostles, Paul experiences the Lord telling him to take courage and keep witnessing for the Lord (23:11). Paul says that he maintains courage all the time because of God's companionship and help (2 Cor 5:6-10). The noun θάρσος tharsos appears once in Acts 28:15: "Paul thanked God and took courage."

Courage is often understood as proclaiming the gospel in the face of persecution, so that other terms, which primarily denote boldness (τόλμα tolma, παρρησία parrēsia), are also found in describing courage. The book of Revelation lists the cowardly among those doomed for the everlasting fire (21:8).

The NT also presents several people whose courage is extraordinary. The most important example is Jesus whose amazing courage throughout his ministry and at his crucifixion is to be emulated by all Christians. Apostles and disciples fearlessly proclaim the gospel despite severe persecutions, even confronting death. There are also several women whose courage is remarkable, such as Mary, the mother of Jesus (Luke 1–2), the woman who puts her whole livelihood in the offering box (Luke 21:2), and the woman who anoints Jesus (Luke 7:37). Among the courageous women in the NT, especially astounding is the Canaanite woman (Matt 15:21-28; Mark 7:24-30), who daringly challenges Jesus, when he has denied her request for her daughter's healing on the ground of her "ethnicity." *See* BOLDNESS, CONFIDENCE IN FAITH; GODFEARER.

SEUNG AI YANG

COURIER [רָץ rats]. A messenger who preceded the royal official (2 Sam 15:1; 1 Kgs 1:5) or who brought news from or to officials (2 Sam 18:21-26; 2 Chr 30:6; Esth 3:13-15; 8:10-14; Jer 51:31), often running or riding on horseback and carrying a written document. *See* MESSENGER; TRAVEL AND COMMUNICATON IN THE OT.

COURT NARRATIVE. Also "Court History" or "Succession Narrative"; the account of David's reign in 2 Samuel or the source underlying it, including David's dealings with Mephibosheth (2 Sam 9), the Ammonite campaign (2 Sam 10), the Bathsheba affair (2 Sam 11-12), the revolts of Absalom and Sheba (2 Sam 13–20), and Solomon's accession (1 Kgs 1–2).

Rost posited the Succession Narrative, along with the Ark Narrative and the Story of David's Rise, as a contemporary unit that explained why Solomon succeeded David as king. Rost's theory was influential in part because of its acceptance by Noth, who considered the Succession Narrative as one of the underlying sources of the DEUTERONOMISTIC HISTORY, and von Rad, who characterized it as the oldest example of Israelite historiography because of the paucity of references in it to Yahweh's involvement in human affairs.

More recently, the consensus about the existence of the Court History as an independent source has eroded. While the question of David's successor is the issue in 1 Kgs 1–2, it is hardly the prime concern of the component sections of the rest of the putative Court History. It is also impossible to delimit the source document. It has no clear beginning or end, and allusions within it require the inclusion of other texts such as 2 Sam 2:8–4:12 and 21:1-14. Some scholars eschew historical questions and instead use NARRATIVE CRITICISM to treat the present Court Narrative as entertaining literature. *See* HISTORY AND HISTORIOGRAPHY.

Bibliography: Martin Noth. *The Deuteronomistic History.* 2nd ed. (1991); Albert De Pury and Thomas Römer, ed. *Die sogenannte Thronnachfolgegeschichte Davids. Neue Einsichten und Anfragen* (2000); Gerhard von Rad. "The Beginnings of Historical Writing in Ancient Israel," in *The Problem of the Hexateuch and Other Essays* (1966) 166–204; Leonhard Rost. *The Succession to the Throne of David* (1982).

STEPHEN L. MCKENZIE

COURT OF LAW. A better expression for court of law in ancient Israel would be "gate of judgment." The space inside the city gate was so closely associated with judicial deliberation that Amos could refer to the "gate" in accusations of injustice (5:10, 15).

Ruth 4:1-12 vividly portrays judicial transactions in the gate. Boaz wants to buy property belonging to his relative Naomi and to marry her daughter-in-law Ruth. First he must persuade someone closer in the family line to renounce his right. He meets this person in the gate of Bethlehem, then gathers "elders" to witness the transaction.

Jeremiah 26 contains the most complete OT account of a criminal trial (*see* CRIMES AND PUNISHMENT). Jeremiah proclaims the destruction of the Jerusalem Temple in the Temple gate (*see* Jer 7:1-15). His audience seizes him, charging him with a capital crime. Officials come from the royal palace to act as judges; the trial takes place in the Temple gate. Jeremiah defends himself effectively, by standers support him by precedent, and he is acquitted.

Biblical legal codes (*see* COVENANT CODE; DEUTERONOMIC CODE; HOLINESS CODE.) offer glimpses of judicial proceedings. They frequently address officiating judges, supplementing laws (*see* CASUISTIC) with procedural rules and encouragement.

According to several passages (Exod 18:13-27; Deut 17:8-13, and others), cases too difficult for local judges were to be brought before Moses or "a judge and priests" for divine oracle or expert opinion. The opinion of the superior judicial authority was binding on lower courts (*see* LAW IN THE OT).

The NT community did not exercise judicial authority over members, though Paul believed it should (1 Cor 6:1-6; however, *see* Matt 18:15-20 and Acts 5:1-11). Of the few occurrences of the term *court* (Matt 5:28; 1 Cor 4:3; 6:6; Jas 2:6), none refers to the trials prominent in history (*see* LAW IN THE NT).

The SANHEDRIN was the Jewish governing council that tried Jesus (*see* Matt 26:57-66; Mark 14:53-64; Luke 22:66-71), harassed apostles, executed Stephen (Acts 6:8-15), and tried Paul (Acts 22:30–23:1-10). While the Sanhedrin's decision had the force of an indictment, Roman administrators had authority over capital crimes. Pilate condemned Jesus, and his successors sent Paul before the Roman governor (Acts 24–26).

DALE PATRICK

COURT OF THE GENTILES. The area of the Jerusalem Temple where Gentiles who conducted themselves reverently were permitted to enter. It was an open area surrounded by porches or cloisters. This court was the location of the merchants and the moneychangers whom Jesus drove from the Temple. *See* GENTILES; TEMPLE, JERUSALEM.

COURT OF THE GUARD. *See* GUARD, COURT OF THE.

COURTYARD [חָצֵר khatser]. Enclosed areas separate from but immediately surrounding a house, a palace, or the Jerusalem Temple. *See* DAVID; JERUSALEM; PERSIA; TEMPLE, JERUSALEM.

COUSIN. The English term translates, more literally, "the son/daughter of his/her uncle" (Esth 2:7; Jer 32:8, 9, 12; Lev 25:49). Cross-cultural parallels suggest that "uncle" could refer to any male relative of the preceding generation, so these are not necessarily "first cousins." Each occurrence illustrates typical legal/social obligations to near relatives: Mordecai raises his cousin Esther, after her parents die; Jeremiah redeems the property of his cousin Hanamel; and Zelophehad's daughters marry their paternal cousins to maintain their father's inheritance.

The single NT occurrence refers to Barnabas' cousin, John Mark (Col 4:10), whose assistance Paul previously rejected (Acts 13:13; 15:36-40). *See* FAMILY; MARRIAGE.

TIMOTHY M. WILLIS

COVENANT, BOOK OF THE [סֵפֶר הַבְּרִית sefer habberith; βιβλίον τῆς διαθήκης biblion tēs diathēkēs]. This title for the collection of laws in Exod 20:22–23:33 comes from Exod 24:7. The collection contains provisions governing altars to Yahweh (Exod 20:23-26), a collection of "judgments" covering crimes against persons and property (Exod 21:1–22:17), religious and moral transgressions (Exod 22:18-20, 28-31) intermixed with duties to the poor and vulnerable (22:21-27), and a table of holy times and festivals (23:10-19), followed by instructions for departure from Sinai/Horeb. Both the style and content suggest this code is the oldest in the Pentateuch. *See* CRIMES AND PUNISHMENT; LAW IN THE OT.

DALE PATRICK

COVENANT CODE. *See* COVENANT, BOOK OF THE; LAW IN THE OT.

COVENANT, DAVIDIC. *See* DAVIDIC COVENANT.

COVENANT LAWSUIT. *See* CONFLICT; LAW IN THE OT.

COVENANT, MOSAIC. *See* COVENANT, OT AND NT.

COVENANT, NEW. *See* COVENANT, OT AND NT.

COVENANT, OT AND NT [בְּרִית berith, עֵדוּת 'edhuth; διαθήκη diathēkē]. A covenant is a formal commitment made by one party to another party, or by two parties to one another; its seriousness is normally undergirded by an oath and/or rite undertaken before God and/or before other people.

- A. Covenants (berith; diathēkē) Between God and the World or God and Israel
  1. The Noah covenant
  2. The Abraham covenants
     a. The covenant regarding land
     b. The covenant regarding offspring: Isaac
     c. The covenant regarding offspring: Ishmael
     d. The covenant as the basis for the exodus
  3. The Sinai covenants
     a. The initial declaration at Sinai
     b. The confirming on Sinai
     c. The reaffirming after the making of the golden calf
     d. The restatement near the end of the time at Sinai
  4. The Moab covenant
  5. The covenant broken
  6. The new covenant
  7. The Jesus covenant
- B. Covenants (berith) Between God and Individuals or Groups
  1. The priesthood covenant
  2. The David covenant
- C. Covenants ('edhuth) as Declarations Concerning God's Expectations
- D. Covenant as a More General Term for Relationships Between God and People in the Bible
- E. Covenant As a Term For the Basis of Community Life

A. Covenants (berith; diathēkē) Between God and the World or God and Israel

Here a covenant is a solemn commitment made by God to human beings or by human beings to God or by human beings and God mutually.

1. The Noah covenant

The first covenant is made by God to NOAH, his descendants, and thus with all future humanity, including all other living creatures (Gen 6:18; 9:8-17). The covenant is a one-sided commitment on God's part, by which God undertakes never to flood the earth and thus destroy life on earth. From the point of view of the biblical writers, the creation of the world did not involve a covenant, perhaps because they thought that creation established a natural relationship between God an humanity. In human relationships there is a natural commitment of one person to another, specifically within the family. Parents do not covenant to look after their children; it is built instinctually into parenthood. But when the family relationship is extended to someone outside it, specifically when someone marries and brings a new person into the family, a covenant is involved. Covenants establish relationships where there was no relationship before. In the case of God and humanity, the natural relationship that came about by creation has been devastated by human rebellion against God and by God's destroying the world. A fresh relationship therefore needs to be established through God's covenant.

The equivalent of a rite to seal the covenant is a sign that God attaches to it. The RAINBOW that appears in the clouds after the rain, and has the shape of a bow, will henceforth not be a sign that God is acting as a warrior yet will draw attention to the fact that the rain did not continue forever but yielded to fair weather. This natural event will become one of supernatural significance. While the rainbow will thus reassure humanity that the flood will not recur, Genesis makes more explicit that it will be a sign for God: It will remind God of this undertaking. The covenant is an "everlasting" one (בְּרִית עוֹלָם berith ʿolam). As long as human life continues on earth, this covenant commitment will hold. The Noah covenant is thus significant for all humanity throughout the ages. It guarantees the security of the human and animal creation from divine destruction (though it perhaps does not rule out humanity destroying the world).

Although the Noah covenant is a one-sided commitment on God's part, it illustrates the ambiguity that often holds over whether a covenant is unconditional or conditional. God makes no reference to conditions, and earlier comments suggest that this would be no coincidence. The reason the flood came about was humanity's rebellion against God. God knows that "the inclination of the human heart is evil from youth" (Gen 8:21). It would therefore be no use making a covenant conditional on humanity's responsiveness to God. On the other hand, the covenant is preceded by statements of God's expectations of humanity (Gen 9:1-7). It is not clear how many of these statements should be seen as commands, but in some way statements of divine expectations preface God's making the covenant. God is permanently committed to humanity and will not go back on that commitment, but God does have expectations of humanity. This is confirmed by the apparent reference to this "everlasting covenant" in Isa 24:5, which identifies the everlasting covenant with "laws" and "statutes" that humanity has broken, thereby causing a curse to devour the earth.

2. The Abraham covenants

a. The covenant regarding land. Yahweh first makes a covenant with ABRAHAM to give the land of Canaan to his descendants (Gen 15:18-20; see J, YAHWIST). Here for the first time the verb for "making" a covenant is כָּרַת karath, literally "cut." The preceding ritual seems to explain it. Yahweh had repeated a promise to give Abraham the land, and Abraham had asked how he can have some assurance of this. That leads Yahweh to bid him bring various animals and birds; Abraham cuts the animals in half then falls into a deep sleep. A terrifying darkness falls, and Yahweh reiterates the promise. It will not be Abraham himself who enters into possession of the land but his descendants, after four cent. of oppression in a foreign land; it will not be fair to dispossess the Amorites yet, "for the iniquity of the Amorites is not yet complete." Then a smoking fire pot and a flaming torch, representing Yahweh, pass between the dismembered animals. This is the sign that turns the promise into a covenant and explains why one "cuts" a covenant. It is tantamount to an enacted prayer or self-curse, "If I fail to keep this undertaking, may I be cut up as these animals have been."

Paul emphasizes (Gal 3:17) that God's covenant with Abraham was simply an unconditioned promise. It did not depend on obedience to the law, which would not be given for another four cent.

b. The covenant regarding offspring: Isaac. In God's second covenant with Abraham (Gen 17; P, PRIESTLY WRITERS) the focus of the covenant lies on the promise of offspring. Like the Noah covenant, this Abraham covenant issues entirely from God's initiative but leaves ambiguous the relationship between divine commitment and human obligation. Once again, it is God who opens the conversation and does so with imperatives, then goes on to promises (Gen 17:1-2). The word for "making" the covenant is here נָתַן nathan, the regular Hebrew word for "give," while subsequently (Gen 17:7) God speaks of "establishing" it (קוּם qum); both underline the extent to which God claims responsibility for making the covenant. The fact that it is "between me and you" does not mean that both parties have equal involvement in establishing it. At no point is Abraham given opportunity to decide whether he wishes to be party to the covenant. He will simply be told something he has to do (though there will be a threat attached to failure to play one's part).

The covenant will apply to Abraham's descendants as well as Abraham himself, and the account emphasizes that like the Noah covenant, it will be an everlasting covenant (Gen 17:7, 13, 19). Yahweh also describes this as "a covenant, to be God to you and to your offspring after you" (Gen 17:7), and this comment on the mutual nature of the covenant strikes a new and far-reaching note.

The ambiguity over divine commitment and human obligation is underlined by the subsequent declaration that there is a covenant requirement laid on Abraham, but one of quite a different kind from the requirements stated in Gen 17:1. "This is my covenant, which you shall keep"; it also applies to Abraham's descendants, and to the rest of his household, including foreign slaves. "You shall circumcise the flesh of your foreskins, and it shall be a sign of the covenant between me and you" (Gen 17:10-13).

The Abraham covenant thus again parallels the Noah covenant in being supported by a sign: CIRCUMCISION. This sign, too, is given for God's sake; when God sees the sign, it reminds God that the divine covenant commitment applies to this person. Like the rainbow sign, circumcision is divinely mandated, but unlike that sign, it is humanly implemented. It can therefore be humanly ignored, though with fatal consequences: anyone who is not circumcised "shall be cut off from his people; he has broken my covenant" (Gen 17:14). The absence of the sign thus also speaks to God. The fact that Yahweh tries to kill the uncircumcised Moses but gives up when Zipporah circumcises their son (Exod 4:24-26) fits with this. Neatly but perhaps fortuitously, *be cut off* is the same verb that appears in the expression *cut a covenant*. Yahweh's willingness to be cut for failing to keep the covenant needs to be matched by human willingness to be cut, and in the absence of that, the whole person is cut. Once again "cut" is a metaphor, and the OT is not explicit on whether it means the person is to be executed, or excommunicated, or whether it means the person will lose his or her place in the register of the people of God.

The fact that humanity has the possibility of not playing its part in the working of the covenant introduces the notion of "breaking" the covenant (פָּרַר parar) rather than "keeping it"—that is, obeying it. "Breaking" the covenant could suggest annulling, making permanently ineffective, as when someone annuls a vow (Num 30:8, 13, where it is the opposite of "establish," qum). Or it could suggest violating, making ineffective at this point and imperiling but not annulling, as when someone violates a law (Num 15:31). In the broader context of the OT, Israel's recurrent breaking of the covenant does not have the effect of annulling it but rather of unleashing the sanctions that operate within the covenant's terms, as breaking a law does not make it any less of a law, though widespread breaking of a law can have that effect.

To speak of "breaking" the covenant does draw attention to the relationship between covenant and law. One way of understanding covenant is to see it as suggesting "obligation" that is imposed on oneself and/or imposed on other people. Insofar as the covenant *is* the requirement to be circumcised, it is an obligation God imposes on Abraham's offspring, like a law that must not be broken.

If one can presuppose acceptance of that obligation, when things go badly Israel can urge, "Have

regard for your covenant" (Ps 74:20), in the conviction that Yahweh "is mindful of his covenant forever" (Ps 105:8). In 1 Chr 16:15-18, David takes up this psalm in urging people to "remember [the LORD's] covenant forever ..., the covenant that he made with Abraham, his sworn promise to Isaac, which he confirmed to Jacob as a statute, to Israel as an everlasting covenant, saying 'To you I will give the land of Canaan as your portion for an inheritance.'" The next psalm observes how for all Israel's recurrent rebellions and Yahweh's consequent chastisements, "For their sake he remembered his covenant, and showed compassion according to the abundance of his steadfast love" (Ps 106:45). If the PRIESTLY narrative was composed in the exile, when Israel had indeed systematically broken the covenant and it could seem as if Yahweh had annulled the covenant, the Abraham covenant underlines the permanence of Yahweh's covenant commitment. The fact that the covenant is not explicitly dependent on a response from its beneficiaries, except for the sign of circumcision, would also be significant in this context.

c. The covenant regarding offspring: Ishmael. Does it apply to his first son, Ishmael, and his offspring, or only to Isaac and his offspring? Ishmael is circumcised along with the rest of the male members of Abraham's household (Gen 17:23-27). But before that happens, God reasserts the promise of a son to Abraham and Sarah, making clear that Ishmael does not count as the fulfillment of that promise, and declares the intention to "establish" the covenant with Isaac. Of Ishmael, God says "I will bless him," in spectacular ways, so that he becomes a great nation, "but my covenant I will establish with Isaac" (Gen 17:21).

Paul assumes there are two covenants here, though he speaks of them as covenants with Hagar and Sarah. They provide an allegorical picture of the faith in which Paul was brought up, and the faith he now holds (Gal 4:21-31). As a slave, Hagar now stands for people in spiritual slavery, and thus, paradoxically, for Mount Sinai and the earthly Jerusalem. Sarah now stands for freedom and promise, and thus for "the Jerusalem above."

d. The covenant as the basis for the exodus. When the Israelites became serfs in Egypt and groaned out, "God remembered his covenant with Abraham, Isaac, and Jacob" (Exod 2:24). "Remembering" (זָכַר zakhar) is not so much the opposite of forgetting as an indication that God now gives thought to this covenant. One aspect of the covenant promise has been amply fulfilled; Abraham's descendants via Isaac and Jacob have become a huge company. But the covenant promise also involved their coming into possession of the land of the Canaan. The time for this has now arrived. The covenant is therefore the basis for acting to release Israel so that it can return to the land not as "aliens" but to receive it as a "possession."

God adds, "I will take you as my people, and I will be your God" (Exod 6:7). The second phrase takes up the expression from Gen 17:7 (NRSV translates it slightly differently); the first phrase complements it in such a way as to introduce the two-sided "covenant formula." God's words signify an imminent nuancing of the Abraham covenant. The greater mutuality of the covenant will now mean that a commitment of Israel to God complements the commitment of God to Israel. Something of the ambiguity of the Abraham covenant will be resolved. God is still the one who takes the initiative in the words that announce the covenant and in the acts that set it up (*see* Exod 6:6), but the covenant will integrally involve a more wide-ranging response on the people's part and a mutual relationship.

3. The Sinai covenants

a. The initial declaration at Sinai. In Exod 6:6-8, Yahweh had referred to delivering Israel from serfdom, establishing the mutual relationship, and taking them to the land. When they reach Sinai, in Exod 19:1-8 Yahweh points out that the first undertaking has been fulfilled; it is therefore possible to move onto the second. This will involve Israel keeping God's covenant. The phrase recurs from Gen 17:9-10, and the people could understandably reckon that Yahweh is simply reasserting the demand for circumcision; this might link with the ease with which they agree, "everything that the LORD has spoken we will do." Actually, it will become clear that keeping the covenant will now have much broader implications.

At this point, however, Yahweh is more explicit about the special nature of the relationship that will issue from the mutual covenant commitment. Implementing the intention to "take you as my people" will mean Israel becoming Yahweh's "treasured possession out of all the peoples." That will result in Israel becoming a priestly kingdom or holy nation. The two adjectives and the two nouns form more or less synonymous pairs. Israel is separated from other peoples in such a way as to belong distinctively to Yahweh in the way that the priesthood within a people belongs distinctively to the people's deity. As such they are a nation over which Yahweh personally reigns. They are not under the rule of some other people, as they were in Egypt. They are freed from serfdom in Egypt not so that they can simply be free but so that they can be given to the service of Yahweh.

b. The confirming on Sinai. The people's initial commitment to keeping the covenant (Exod 19:8) clears the way for their meeting with Yahweh at Sinai. This is often reckoned to be *the* occasion of the making of a covenant between Yahweh and Israel, but the narrative is sparse in its reference to covenant.

In Exod 20–24 the word comes first in the requirement that Israel make no covenant with the inhabitants of Canaan or with their gods (Exod 23:32). The second

requirement explains the first. A basic obligation of some covenants is a requirement of exclusive loyalty; some political covenants or treaties require a subordinate state to show exclusive loyalty to its imperial overlord (for instance, Israel in its relationship with Assyria) and not to ally with other peoples. Analogously, Israel is expected to show exclusive loyalty to Yahweh and thus not to seek help from other deities. That is implicit in the idea of Israel being Yahweh's covenant people (e.g., Exod 19:5-6) and explicit in the first of Yahweh's Ten Words (Exod 20:2-3; *see* TEN COMMANDMENTS). Exodus 23:32 makes the link with the covenant. Exclusive commitment to Yahweh rules out covenants with other peoples because these would involve or lead to acknowledgment of their deities. Either the making of a covenant is a religious act that would require recognition of each others' gods, or close relationship with these other peoples would lead to being attracted by their gods. Israel looking at these other peoples as sources of help and strength instead of looking to Yahweh is indeed an issue in Israelite history. The Gibeonites' tricking the Israelites into a **berith** (a covenant/ treaty) implicitly involves them in a contravention of this requirement. Hosea overtly critiques Ephraim for making a **berith** with Assyria (Hos 11:12–12:1). And when Judah makes a covenant with neighbors in order to be able to resist Assyria, Isa 28:15, 18 declares that it has made a covenant with death.

The other references to covenant in the first stage of events at Sinai come in the account of the meeting between representative Israelites and Yahweh in Exod 24. This is often reckoned to be the occasion of covenant-making, but Exodus does not describe it as such, again perhaps because Exodus is clear that Yahweh and Israel are already in covenant relationship. What happens at Sinai reconfirms the covenant, specifically in light of the expectations of Israel and the undertakings that Yahweh makes to take the people to the land and care for them there (*see* Exod 20–23). Moses now reads "the book of the covenant" to the people and they make a commitment to obey Yahweh; the narrative thus repeats the scene in Exod 19:3-8, resolving the ambiguity we noted there. It is now explicit that "keeping the covenant" involves more than circumcision; it involves all this "book of the covenant" requires. The people's accepting that commitment is part of what is involved in what we might call the confirming or renewing of the covenant in the form that Yahweh has declared that it will now have, with this new requirement in light of what Yahweh has done for the people in bringing them out of Egypt.

In scholarly parlance the title "the book of the covenant" usually means Exod 20:22–23:33, or part of it; *see* COVENANT, BOOK OF THE. Exodus 20:1-17 is simply something that Yahweh "says"; it is separated from what follows by the further narrative in Exod 20:18-21, and it is often reckoned to be a later composition that has been placed at the beginning of the Sinai story because of its great importance as a summary of Yahweh's expectations. It will later become clearer that the Ten Words are the עֵדוּת 'edhuth "covenant" written by God, which is to be put into the ark; *see* Exod 31:18; 32:15-16.

The sacramental confirming of the covenant is associated with this reading of the book of the covenant. Sacrifices have already been offered, and Moses has already taken half the blood drained from the sacrificial animals and spattered it on the altar. After the people's declaration of commitment, he spatters the other half on the people themselves, saying, "See the blood of the covenant that the LORD has made with you in accordance with all these words" (Exod 24:8). The rite with the blood does not correspond to any regular worship practice, though it does recall the event narrated in Gen 15:7-21 and the idea that one "cuts" a covenant. Both Yahweh (represented by the altar) and the people are spattered with blood, sealing their commitment and bringing home the solemn undertaking that this meeting on Sinai represents. It is as if either will be torn apart for failure to keep their undertaking. The people have "made a covenant with me by sacrifice" (Ps 50:5) and the covenant blood subsequently undergirds Yahweh's promises to Jerusalem (Zech 9:11).

c. The reaffirming after the making of the golden calf. The people's making a gold calf brings about a crisis in the relationship between Yahweh and Israel as Yahweh contemplates annihilating the people. The account in Exod 32–33 does not refer to the covenant, but the incident and its aftermath implicitly raise questions about the covenant relationship. They show that Yahweh's permanent covenant with Abraham's descendants does not leave Israel able to get away with despising Yahweh. It is therefore significant that Yahweh now reaffirms a covenant commitment to Israel. Indeed, strictly and significantly this is actually the first time Yahweh makes a covenant commitment at Sinai. Yahweh did not need to do so earlier because Yahweh and Israel are already in covenant relationship. With events in Exod 32–33 having implicitly imperiled that, this is the moment when Yahweh declares, "I hereby make a covenant" (Exod 34:10).

Yet again there is some ambiguity over the relationship of divine commitment and human obligation in this covenant. On one hand, in beginning to spell out the implications of the declaration about making a covenant, Yahweh first promises to do great wonders before the people; these will be the wonders that will be involved in giving the people the land, to which Yahweh immediately goes on to refer (Exod 34:10-11). But Yahweh precedes that declaration of intent by an exhortation to "observe what I command you today" and then spells that out as involving not making a covenant with the peoples of the land (Exod 34:11-16), renewing and expanding the earlier command about

covenant-making (Exod 23:32). Once again Yahweh thus emphasizes the exclusive aspect to this covenant relationship, then continues by detailing other expectations of the people (Exod 34:17-26) in a way that overlaps with the book of the covenant. This reformulating of the requirements laid down in the book of the covenant is implicitly an act of grace on Yahweh's part. Indeed, the original revealing of expectations was an act of grace, insofar as once we know what God wants of us, we can do it; we cannot do that if we are left in the dark. Restating the expectations underlines the point. Yahweh is still reaching out in grace to Israel in being willing to do so.

So Yahweh's covenant-making (Exod 34:10) might consist in making the promise about doing wonders, or in laying down those expectations, with the promise as a preamble, or it might involve both of these. The persistence of such ambiguity in references to the covenant is of theological significance. It does not imply that Yahweh simply fails to make things clear. It rather points to the fact that the relationship between divine commitment and human obligation is inherently ambiguous, dynamic, volatile, and changeable. A covenant is not a contract, as the adversary in Job 1–2 asserts toward Job's self-perceptions about his relationship with God. The "covenant" that Leviathan would not make to serve Job (Job 41:4) would be something like a contract, but the covenant that Job had made with his eyes (Job 31:1) was an inner commitment that no one could test.

A covenant does involve a mutual commitment, but it is not exactly conditional. In this respect it rather resembles marriage. This requires that both people commit themselves to the other, but we would not say that one person makes a commitment on condition that the other does. This would underestimate the element of trust and risk in the relationship. In a contract, the conditions are calculated to minimize the element of risk and make trust less necessary. This is good practice in certain areas of life; there is nothing wrong with contracts. But we would rather marriage were not contractual and calculating in this way. In this respect the relationship between Yahweh and Israel resembles a personal relationship such as marriage more than a contract, alliance, or treaty. The recurrent ambiguity in the texts about the relationship between divine commitment and human obligation is a sign of that.

It is possible that the OT presents marriage as a covenant, though the texts that may indicate this view (Prov 2:19; Ezek 16:8; Mal 2:14) are all allusive. It also refers to a personal covenant between David and Jonathan (1 Sam 18:3), a "sacred covenant" (lit., "a covenant of Yahweh"; 1 Sam 20:8), perhaps so designated because it was "a covenant before the LORD" (1 Sam 23:18). A psalmist laments, "My companion . . . violated a covenant with me" (Ps 55:20).

After laying out those expectations in Exod 34, "the LORD said to Moses: Write these words; in accordance with these words I have made a covenant with you and with Israel" (Exod 34:27). The reference is presumably to the words in vv. 10-26. The narrative goes on to tell us that "he wrote on the tablets the words of the covenant, the ten commandments" (Exod 34:28); as the NRSV margin notes, they are literally "the ten words." Within the narrow context we would reckon that "he" is "Moses." But the chapter began with Yahweh declaring the intention to rewrite what was written on the tablets that Moses broke, so more likely the "he" is Yahweh, who was the subject in the previous verse, "the LORD said to Moses." Either way, "the words of the covenant" are here "the ten commandments," and they complement "the book of the covenant," both being integral to the covenant as statements of the obligations that Yahweh imposes and Israel accepts.

d. The restatement near the end of the time at Sinai. Near the end of the time at Sinai, Yahweh restates the point, in Lev 26 (to put it another way, Lev 26 is the HOLINESS CODE's equivalent to Exod 34). Here the relationship between Israel's obedience and Yahweh's covenant-keeping is less equivocal: "If you follow my statutes . . . I will give you your rains in their season . . . and I will maintain my covenant with you .... And I will walk among you, and will be your God, and you shall be my people" (Lev 26:3-12). "Maintain" is qum, the verb the NRSV earlier translated "establish" (Gen 6:18; 9:9, 11, 17; 17:7, 19, 21; Exod 6:4); "establish" is a more natural meaning for the verb. The promise in Lev 26:9 amounts to a renewed undertaking to make the covenant work, here in the context of the people's coming arrival in the land (compare Deut 8:18, where NRSV translates "confirm").

Leviticus 26:15 again par. Gen 17 in allowing for Israel's "breaking" the covenant, to which severe sanctions are attached. Persisting in disobedience will mean Yahweh "will bring the sword against you, executing vengeance for the covenant" (Lev 26:25). "Vengeance" overstates the affective aspect to נָקָם naqam; the Hebrew term does suggest acting with feelings, but it also presupposes that the action is the proper redress. Yahweh itemizes this redress in horrific fashion, but then declares that if the people turn back to Yahweh, "then I will remember my covenant with Jacob; I will remember also my covenant with Isaac and also my covenant with Abraham" (Lev 26:42). Remembering the covenant and thus taking action on the people's behalf is possible in the context of their wrongdoing as well as their undeserved oppression (Exod 2:24). No more than at Sinai will Yahweh annihilate them and thus "break my covenant with them; for I am the LORD their God; but I will remember in their favor the covenant with their ancestors whom I brought out of the land of Egypt" (Lev 26:44-45).

The ambiguity of the relationship between divine commitment and human obligation yet again reasserts itself. The warnings presuppose that the people have totally failed to keep their covenant obligations, and this would give Yahweh quite enough reason to terminate the covenant. The mere fact that the covenant was everlasting might not guarantee that it stays in force no matter what Israel does. Many things that God says will be everlasting such as the Temple, the priesthood, and the Davidic monarchy seem not to be everlasting. That declaration only guarantees that Yahweh is not fickle and will not have a random change of mind. This does not stop Yahweh terminating them in light of people's intransigence. But Yahweh will not "break" the covenant (Yahweh uses the verb that describes Israel's failure) let alone terminate it; perhaps "break" and "annul" end up having the same meaning in this context.

Even in this connection Yahweh will not "forget [i.e., put out of mind, ignore] the covenant with your ancestors that he swore to them" (Deut 4:31). Admittedly, at the beginning of Judges Yahweh declares, "I said, 'I will never break my covenant with you. For your part, do not make a covenant with the inhabitants of the land, tear down their altars.' But you have not obeyed my command" (Judg 2:1-2). Yahweh will therefore not drive these peoples out before Israel. Is Yahweh therefore breaking the covenant, on the basis of the fact that Israel has done so? Or does a responsive action such as that not count as breaking the covenant? On the other hand, even when Ephraim has long been unfaithful and has been chastised, "the LORD was gracious to them; he turned toward them, because of his covenant with Abraham, Isaac, and Jacob, and would not destroy them; nor has he banished them from his presence until now" (2 Kgs 13:23). "Until now" apparently implies that even the fall of Samaria and the exile of its people did not constitute such destruction or banishment. In Jer 14:21 the prophet thus feels free to urge, "do not break your covenant with us," despite our wickedness.

4. The Moab covenant

A generation on from Sinai, on the edge of the land, Yahweh commands MOSES to make a covenant with the Israelites to supplement the covenant at HOREB, by means of which the new generation will "enter into the covenant of the LORD your God, sworn by an oath, which the LORD your God is making with you today; in order that he may establish you today as his people, and that he may be your God" (Deut 29:12-13). In substance the terms of the covenant are the same, though they are adapted to aspects of life in the land in a way that reflects needs that will arise in later contexts (e.g., the people wanting a king and the problem of false prophecy). But this covenant-making also has the effect of putting the obligation of the covenant on these people who were not at Sinai. For the readers, that generation stands for each succeeding Israelite generation, and thus for them. "I am making this covenant, sworn by an oath, not only with you who stand here with us today before the LORD our God, but also with those who are not here with us today" (Deut 29:14-15).

Deuteronomy expresses more about covenant than any other book in the Bible. Indeed, although the actual occurrences of the word come chiefly in Deut 4–11 and 29–31, Deuteronomy as a whole can be seen as a covenant document, a book structured to reflect and expound Israel's covenant relationship with Yahweh (*see* DEUTERONOMY, BOOK OF). This structuring parallels that of a treaty between an imperial power and an underling such as Israel. It has been argued that it more closely resembles Hittite treaties from the 2nd millennium than Assyrian treaties from the 1st millennium and thus that it more likely reflects the work of Moses than the work of the 7th-cent. theologians whom the scholarly world has more often reckoned to be the authors of Deuteronomy, but like most aspects of the history of covenant in Israel, this question is controverted. Either way, most Israelites would presumably be unaware of the treaty background of the work, but the theologians who drafted the text perhaps found that this political arrangement helped them articulate the dynamics of Yahweh's relationship with Israel, though we should be wary of exaggerating the importance of this factor in the development of covenant thinking.

A political treaty might review the past relationship between the empire and the underling, lay down the basic requirement of loyalty to the empire, itemize specific requirements, describe the benefits and sanctions attached to compliance and noncompliance, and provide for the solemnizing and regular reading of the treaty. Deuteronomy is much longer than a treaty, but this comparison helps one see aspects of its dynamic and the way it could have communicated at least with Israel's leadership.

First, Deut 1–3 reviews the relationship between Yahweh and Israel since Sinai, as background to the reaffirmation of the covenant on the edge of the land, noting both the way Yahweh has supported Israel and the way Israel has been inclined to rebellion. Each of these is also background to the requirements that will follow.

Deuteronomy 4–11 lays down the fundamental requirement that Israel should respond to what Yahweh has done by showing unqualified commitment to Yahweh and having nothing to do with other deities. Although in a literal sense Yahweh made the covenant with the parents of the people about to enter the land, Moses declares that Yahweh did not (merely) make it with them but with this present generation (Deut 5:2-3). The NRSV translates "ancestors" rather than "parents," which brings out the fact that Deuteronomy presents every later generation of Israel as faced with

the same expectations as it portrays as binding on the Moab generation. Each generation that hears Deuteronomy read is bound by the basic expectations laid down in the Ten Words that follow in Deut 5:6-21. Exclusive loyalty to Yahweh involves making no covenant with another deity (Deut 7:2). It is the converse of the fact that Yahweh keeps covenant with those who keep their side of the commitment (Deut 7:9, 12).

The itemizing of specific requirements in Deut 12–26 is much more extensive than the equivalent section of a treaty; in a way Deuteronomy combines the form of a law code with that of a treaty. This section contains one telling reference to covenant, in the course of another comment on serving other gods than Yahweh. A person who does that "transgresses his covenant" (Deut 17:2-3; the verb is used of Achan, Josh 7:11, 15). It is another way of saying that this action involves "breaking" the covenant.

Deuteronomy 27–31 provides for the memorializing of the words of the law when the people enter the land and for their reading out on subsequent occasions, describes the blessings and curses attached to obedience and disobedience, and provides for the solemnizing of the covenant. It has been reckoned that the Festival of Tabernacles at the New Year in the Fall was also an annual covenant renewal festival, but the OT does not directly suggest this. Deuteronomy warns that Yahweh will implement "all the curses of the covenant written in this book of the law" when people have "abandoned the covenant of the LORD" by turning to other gods (Deut 29:21, 25-26). Joshua will reaffirm this at the end of his life (Josh 23:16); he also "made a covenant with the people" to confirm their commitment to exclusive service of Yahweh (Josh 24:25).

5. The covenant broken

Psalm 25:10, 14 promises that God is faithful to people who "keep his covenant and his decrees" and that "he makes his covenant known to them," and Israel needs to be able to claim, "we have not . . . been false to your covenant" (Ps 44:17). But the references to covenant in Josh 9 and Judg 2 show how it did not take Israel long to break the covenant. Solomon does the same in making marriage alliances with foreign peoples, and pays a severe penalty (1 Kgs 11:11). Elijah's critique of Ephraim is that they have "forsaken" the covenant, which sounds more far reaching (1 Kgs 19:10, 14). Hosea likewise critiques Ephraim for transgressing the covenant (Hos 8:1), specifically for doing so "at Adam," a place on the Jordan (Hos 6:7); we do not know what happened there. Ephraim's "despising" and "transgressing" the covenant, failing to keep it in mind, is the basis for the fall of Samaria and Ephraim's exile (2 Kgs 17:15, 35, 38; 18:12). "They did not keep God's covenant, but refused to walk according to his law" (Ps 78:10).

The same is true of Judah, though the narratives do not express the matter thus. Indeed, they emphasize the way Asa and his people, Hezekiah, and especially Josiah and his people made covenants that expressed an exclusive commitment to Yahweh, going back on the stance of the previous generation (2 Kgs 23:2-3; 2 Chr 15:12; 29:10; 34:30-32). The basis for Josiah's act is a "book of the covenant," earlier described (§A.3.b) as a "book of the law," a scroll found in the course of remodeling in the Temple (2 Kgs 22). The expression recalls Exod 24:7; it occurs only in these two connections. But the usual critical view has been that Josiah's actions and discovery suggest the emergence of the book of Deuteronomy. (Second Kings 23:21 relates how Josiah also celebrated the Passover in accordance with the book of the covenant, but Exod 20–24 does not mention Passover.)

On the other hand, Jeremiah does challenge Judah about its attitude to the covenant (Jer 11:1-13) and prospectively imagines other nations explaining Jerusalem's destruction by Judah's forsaking the covenant—again, perhaps a more drastic act than transgressing or breaking it (Jer 22:8-9). Likewise, Ezekiel speaks of the people having despised the oath and broken the covenant (Ezek 16:59). The people have no right to "recite my statutes, or take my covenant on your lips" (Ps 50:16). "They were not true to his covenant" (Ps 78:37). Thus on the eve of Jerusalem's fall Yahweh declares, "I will deal with you as you have done, you who have despised the oath, breaking the covenant" (Ezek 16:59). Apparently Yahweh does intend to break the covenant, though this need not mean annulling it, any more than it does when Israel breaks the covenant. And the fact that Yahweh immediately goes on to declare the intention then to bear the covenant in mind (Ezek 16:60) suggests that this is not so. Yet Yahweh's subsequent declaration of intent to establish with Israel an everlasting covenant (another one? Ezek 16:60) suggests that Yahweh's act is a very serious one.

The enigmatic Zech 11:10 perhaps also refers retrospectively to the fall of Ephraim and Judah, occasions of the breaking of "the covenant with all the peoples" (NRSV has "annulling," but the verb is the one usually translated "break"). The OT does not elsewhere refer to a "covenant with all the peoples." A covenant that benefits the nations is hardly relevant in the context; this covenant is more likely one that makes the nations Yahweh's servants in protecting and blessing Israel (compare the covenant "with" the animals in Hos 2:18; also Job 5:23). By breaking that covenant, Yahweh freed the nations to devastate Ephraim and Judah. Ezekiel 17:11-21 applies covenant language to the nations and Judah in a rather different way. Nebuchadnezzar has made a covenant (i.e., an agreement or treaty) with Zedekiah that involved Judah behaving itself, but Zedekiah has rebelled against Nebuchadnezzar. "Can he break the covenant and yet escape?" The answer is surely yes,

in some circumstances. But Zedekiah has despised and broken "my covenant" (Ezek 17:11-21). Yahweh is in covenant with Nebuchadnezzar as Yahweh's agent in ruling Judah and controlling its destiny.

6. The new covenant

Beyond the calamity of exile Yahweh declares the intention of making a new covenant with both Judah and Ephraim (Jer 31:31-34). It will be new because the thing Yahweh intends to do is different; it is new as the Sinai covenant was new over against the Abraham covenant. The Sinai covenant moved from a promise about Abraham becoming a great people to the setting up of a relationship between this people and God and a focus on giving this people the land. In addition it added a whole corpus (indeed, several corpora) of requirements to the relationship, though much of this material simply spelled out the basic expectation that the people would indeed be Yahweh's people, and exclusively so. The heart of the people's covenant-breaking thus lay in their serving of other gods.

Yahweh's intention now is to write this requirement in the people's heart. The nature of the Sinai and Moab covenants was to have Yahweh's requirements written in a book. The challenge to acknowledge Yahweh was therefore one that Israelites had to issue to one another. The work Yahweh will now do in their hearts will make this unnecessary and the covenant aim that "I will be their God and they shall be my people" will be fulfilled. The last phrase in Jeremiah's promise is "for I will forgive their iniquity, and remember their sin no more." It may indicate how Yahweh will do this writing into the people's hearts. The extraordinary nature of Yahweh's grace shown in not casting them off but rather being prepared to forgive and forget will be what finally gets to them and wins their allegiance.

Ezekiel makes the same point more sardonically. Although Judah has despised the oath and broken the covenant, Yahweh will bear the covenant in mind and in fact establish an everlasting covenant with them. That will lead to their feeling shame at their past behavior "when I forgive you all that you have done" (Ezek 16:59-63). "I will bring you within the bond of the covenant" (Ezek 20:37). He adds, "I will make with them a covenant of peace [שָׁלוֹם shalom]," a covenant that guarantees security and blessing (Ezek 34:25-31), and it "shall be an everlasting covenant with them" (Ezek 37:26). Israel will thus "come and join themselves to the LORD by an everlasting covenant that will never be forgotten" (Jer 50:5). The NRSV wording may suggest an everlasting covenant that they make and will not forget, but it would fit the other occurrences of such language if the verse again refers to an everlasting covenant that Yahweh makes and will not forget.

A particular aspect of this covenant commitment will be that Yahweh will always be speaking through the prophet (Isa 59:21). Isaiah 55:3 promises "an everlasting covenant, my steadfast, sure love for David," taking up the charge at the end of Ps 89 that Yahweh has abandoned the covenant with David and offering a distinctive response. Yahweh will be true to the covenant with David by extending its application to the people as a whole. Israel can thus be "a covenant to the people" (Isa 42:6; 49:8). This expression recalls the idea that Abraham can be a blessing. It suggests that Israel can be an embodiment for the world of what it means to be in covenant relationship with Yahweh, and thus be a means of light coming to the nations.

The Second Temple period saw Israel indeed keeping the covenant in a way they had not before. In particular, they gave up worship of other gods and worship by means of images, the key first two requirements of the Ten Words. In Ezra 10:3 the people who have married foreign women undertake to make a covenant with God to end these marriages and thus express an unqualified commitment to Yahweh alone. In accordance with the third commandment, they safeguard against wrongful use of Yahweh's name by giving up uttering the name at all, and in accordance with the fourth, they come to be committed to observing the Sabbath, which can even be seen as an everlasting covenant for Israel (Exod 31:16; Lev 24:8). Thus by NT times these requirements can be taken for granted. Conversely, by then the Jewish people are in occupation of something like the old bounds of the land, the area that belonged both to Judah and to Ephraim. Yahweh has thus kept the promise to implement this new covenant. Indeed, they are the "holy covenant" (Dan 11:28, 30), a strong way of defining them as the covenant people. Further, the spread of appreciation of Jewish religion through the diaspora means they have become a covenant to the people. Yet they are again under the domination of a foreign empire and once again need God to "remember his holy covenant" (Luke 1:72).

7. The Jesus covenant

The NT shows rather little explicit interest in covenant, though in the broader sense the concerns of covenant are embedded in the theological thinking of the NT. Luke 1:72 declares that Jesus came because God did "remember his holy covenant" and the Gospel of Mark casts Jesus' death in light of OT covenant: "My blood of the covenant . . . is poured out for many" (Mark 14:24). According to the Gospels, Jesus came to fulfill the covenant. The reference to "pouring out" and to "many" suggests a link with Isa 53 and thus ultimately with the "covenant for the people" in Isa 42:6; 49:8. The Jesus covenant will benefit the world more spectacularly than the previous versions of the covenant did. The idea of the "blood of the covenant" (Exod 24:8; Zech 9:11) is reworked in Jesus' words. In the OT, being unfaithful to the covenant could issue in the covenant-maker's blood being shed. Here, Jesus'

blood is to be shed that the covenant may become operative.

In the par. passage, Matt 26:28, Jesus adds that the pouring out of his blood brings about "the forgiveness of sins." He thus takes up Jeremiah's talk of a new covenant (Jer 31:31-34). This is explicit in a different way in the Lukan version, Luke 22:20, where Jesus speaks of "the new covenant in my blood." The text ignores the question whether God has already fulfilled the new covenant promise in the life of Second Temple Israel and uses the image of a new covenant to interpret the significance of Jesus' death. Matthew's formulation indicates the way in which this is a new covenant, because Jesus' death is of key significance for the forgiveness of the many, both Israel and the world. It will still be true that "to them belong . . . the covenants" (Rom 9:4), but people who are now "strangers to the covenant of promise" (Eph 2:12) will thus cease to be so. In keeping with this, Peter reminds Jews in Jerusalem that they are "the descendants . . . of the covenant that God gave to your ancestors, saying to Abraham, 'And in your descendants all the families of the earth shall be blessed.'" This comes about through Jesus, who calls them to turn from their wicked ways (Acts 3:25-26). That is the way they will find forgiveness.

Apostles such as Paul saw themselves as "ministers of a new covenant," whose novelty lies in its being "not of letter but of spirit" (2 Cor 3:6). This antithesis corresponds to but restates the one in Jer 31:31-34. In Paul's interpretation, the Jewish people of Paul's day have the written word, once "chiseled in letters on stone tablets," but their rejection of the gospel shows that this is all they have. When they read the old covenant, it is as if there is a veil over their minds, which is set aside only in Christ (2 Cor 3:14). Otherwise, they do not "get it." Paul thus sees the new covenant as a present reality, though he can of course recognize that the process of transformation is incomplete; further, he cannot believe that God will never take away that veil. Thus he can also see the implementation of Jeremiah's new covenant as lying at the time when God's ultimate purpose is fulfilled and all Israel is saved; "as it is written . . . 'And this is my covenant with them, when I take away their sins'" (Rom 11:25-27).

Hebrews develops the notion of the new covenant most systematically (see esp. Heb 8–9). Like the Gospels, it takes up the expression "blood of the covenant," referring specifically to the Exod 24 narrative (Heb 9:19-20) and takes it in a new direction in order to expound the significance of Jesus' death. Whereas in the OT the sacrifice involved in confirming the covenant at Sinai was separate from the regular sacrificial system, Hebrews brings these two together; it can then see the covenant sacrifice as a cleansing sacrifice (Heb 9:21-22). But the fact that Jer 31:34 speaks of forgiveness as still future shows that these cleansing sacrifices did not really "work." So "Jesus is the mediator of a new covenant" by virtue of the fact that "a death has occurred that redeems them from the transgressions under the first covenant" (Heb 9:15). The old covenant with its shortcomings (Heb 8:7-8) is thus obsolete and about to disappear (Heb 8:13). The single definitive sacrifice that Christ offered makes the regular sacrifices now unnecessary.

This puts people who believe in Jesus in a privileged position, though also in a solemn one, because the superiority of the new covenant is matched by a greater enormity involved when someone has "profaned the blood of the covenant by which they were sancti-fied" (Heb 10:29). But Hebrews has better hopes of its readers and prays that "by the blood of the eternal covenant" God may take them to complete maturity (Heb 12:20-22).

The Jesus covenant is thus a reworking of the cov-enant, analogous to the several reworkings that have preceded it. It is the means whereby the Gentile world is drawn into the covenant relationship that goes back to Abraham. There is not one covenant for Jews and one for Gentiles.

B. Covenants (berith) Between God and Individuals or Groups

1. The priesthood covenant

Malachi 2:1-9 speaks most systematically about a covenant with Levi, a "covenant of life and well-being" (shalom), which Yahweh wants to "hold" (literally, "be"). Levi himself made an appropriate response to that covenant, but his descendants have "corrupted" it. They may have done that by colluding with the unwor-thy offerings condemned in Mal 1, but in addition the priests who have married foreign women "have defiled the priesthood, the covenant of the priests and the Levites" (Neh 13:29). In this context the covenant may be the priesthood's covenant or commitment to Yahweh rather than Yahweh's to them (see PRIESTS AND LEVITES).

Similarly, Mal 2:10-16 goes on to speak of Judah "profaning the covenant of our ancestors" because it has "married the daughter of a foreign god." You have "been faithless" to "the wife of your youth" although she is "your companion and your wife by covenant." The juxtaposition of these passages suggests another reference to the involvement of Levi as well as the other clans in marriages with people committed to other gods. Apparently these marriages first involved divorce from an Israelite wife, "your wife by cov-enant": lit., "the wife of your covenant." This might imply that the first marriage was understood as a covenant or simply that the first wife was an Israelite, someone within the covenant between the people and Yahweh, whereas the new wife was outside that covenant. It is then another way of noting how such a marriage "profaned the covenant of our ancestors."

In the context of the imminent destruction of the Temple, Yahweh had declared that it would be no more possible to break the covenant with the Levites as people to minister to Yahweh than to break the covenant of day and night (Jer 33:19-22). But as usual this commitment might presuppose the unstated assumption that they stay faithful to their own cov-enant commitment.

Yahweh gives a specific covenant to Aaron's son Phinehas, because of his passionate zeal for Yahweh in killing an Israelite who took a Midianite wife (Num 25:10-13). This, too, is a "covenant of shalom," and "a covenant of priesthood," perhaps a promise that his line will always have a place in the Aaronic priesthood. The "prince of the covenant" (Dan 11:22) is likely the high priest.

2. The David covenant

In his "last words" David says that God "made with me an everlasting covenant, ordered in all things and secure" (2 Sam 23:5). The narrative has not recorded this, though one could see Yahweh's promise in 2 Sam 7 as covenantlike. More emphatically, Ps 89:3 observes to Yahweh, "You said, 'I have made a covenant with my chosen one, I have sworn to my servant David: "I will establish your descendants forever, and build your throne for all generations . . . . Forever I will keep my steadfast love for him, and my covenant with him will stand firm . . . . I will not violate my covenant, or alter the word that went forth from my lips'" (Ps 89:3-4, 28, 34). The promissory nature of the David covenant makes it comparable with the Abraham covenant.

The Judean king Abijah reminded Ephraim that Yahweh gave the kingship forever to David and his sons "by a covenant of salt" (2 Chr 13:5). We do not know the background of this expression (for which see also Num 18:19, and Lev 2:13), but it seems to underline the notion of permanency. Second Chronicles 21:7 notes that despite its wrongdoing "the LORD would not destroy the house of David because of the covenant that he had made with David." The same undertaking that made it impossible to break the Levi covenant would make it impossible to break the David covenant so that his heirs would not sit on the throne (Jer 33:19-26).

Actually Yahweh has abandoned the Davidic king: "You have renounced the covenant with your servant" (Ps 89:39). But then, according to another psalm, what Yahweh had actually said was, "If your sons keep my covenant and my decrees that I shall teach them, their sons also, forevermore, shall sit on your throne" (Ps 132:12).

C. Covenants ('edhuth) as Declarations Concerning God's Expectations

The NRSV translates 'edhuth as "covenant," which appears frequently in Exodus, Numbers, and the Psalms, and offers the alternative meanings of "testimony" and "treaty." Testimony, the traditional translation, derives from the fact that related words refer to bearing witness, but 'edhuth does not seem to have this connotation. The link with those related words suggests that 'edhuth constitutes a solemn declaration by God, but the declaration's content relates to God's expectations of Israel. The TNIV also reckons it links with the covenant and translates "covenant law." In a broad sense these expectations are indeed part of Yahweh's covenant relationship with Israel, though the occurrences of 'edhuth do not make a link with berith. In 2 Kgs 17:15 the fall of Ephraim is explained by the fact that the people "despised his statutes and his 'edhuth." Psalm 19:7 enthuses over Yahweh's 'edhuth in parallelism with enthusing over Yahweh's law, precepts, and commandment. In 2 Kgs 11:12 and 2 Chron 23:11 the priest gives the king 'edhuth—presumably some exposition of Yahweh's expectations.

The word often appears in the phrases "ark of the covenant" and "tabernacle of the covenant," so called because the 'edhuth was put inside the ark in the tabernacle (e.g., Exod 25:16, 21-22; Num 1:50-53). The ark can also be described as "the ark of the berith of the LORD" (Num 10:33; 14:44; frequently in Josh 3–6), which does make a link between 'edhuth and berith and also confirms the view that berith can often refer to Israel's commitment to Yahweh.

The nature of this 'edhuth is spelled out at the close of Yahweh's instructions about the tabernacle, when Yahweh gave Moses "the two tablets of the 'edhuth, tablets of stone, written with the finger of God" (Exod 31:18). Their content was presumably the Ten Words and/or the Book of the Covenant. On discovering the people's actions in making the gold calf, a direct contravention of a central concern of these, Moses breaks these tablets, but Yahweh subsequently undertakes to replace them (Exod 34:1, 29).

D. Covenant as a More General Term for Relationships Between God and People in the Bible

In the history of theology, the significance of covenant broadened so that it became a term for the relationship between God and Israel even where the word berith does not occur. Indeed, the original relationship between God and humanity in the garden of Eden has been seen as covenantal. Specifically, "federal theology" sees this as the "covenant of works" that was the original basis for the relationship between God and humanity. But not only does Genesis fail to refer to that original relationship as covenantal; it does not imply that the relationship was based on works but rather on the same interrelationship of God's grace and human response (Hosea 6:7 refers to Israel transgressing the covenant "like Adam," which would imply that Adam had transgressed a covenant, but many translators assume the text originally read

"at [the place] Adam" on the Jordan [so NRSV]. Isaiah 24:5 and Amos 1:9 might also be taken to refer to a creation covenant.) Thus where the OT is talking about a relationship with God that "has the character of a relationship of grace, that is to say, it is founded on a primal act in history, maintained on definite conditions and protected by a powerful divine Guardian," it can be reckoned to be talking about a covenant relationship whether or not it uses the word berith. On this basis covenant can be seen as providing the framework for OT theology. Likewise one could term the description of the mutual relationship between Yahweh and Israel in passages such as Jer 7:23; 24:7; 30:22 "the covenant formula" even though there is no explicit reference to the covenant in the context. Thus different theologians can both affirm and deny that the idea of covenant dominates the OT, and both can be right, depending on whether they are talking about covenant in the broader or narrower sense. Israel itself may have thought in covenant terms even when it did not use this language. In Neh 9–10, e.g., some commentators describe the people as a making a covenant, even though the text uses the word *covenant* only in connection with Yahweh's covenant-making and covenant-keeping (Neh 9:8, 32); it describes the community as making an "agreement" (NRSV) or "pledge" (JPS translation) (אֲמָנָה 'amanah; KJV has "sure covenant"). The prophets, too, refer to "covenant" rather infrequently; it is a matter of guesswork why this is so. But they, too, in the broader sense think in covenant terms, and this may lie behind the way they sometimes imply that they are issuing a formal charge against the people, accusing them of covenant-breaking, and warning that covenant sanctions are to be imposed on them. Yahweh thus has a רִיב riv, "indictment" or "controversy," against the people (Hos 4:1; 12:2; Mic 6:2). The form of speech would correspond to the way an imperial power brought a charge of disloyalty against one of its underlings and threatened it with punitive action. If there is a connection with covenant thinking, then this prophetic lawsuit might also be described as a covenant lawsuit.

The key theological issue that covenant raises is the relationship between divine commitment and human obligation. Covenant can put the stress on divine initiative and commitment, though it will then regard human obedience as absolutely required. Or it can put the stress on human commitment to obedience to an obligation set forth by God, though it will assume that this commitment is offered in the context of the framework of divine grace. Or it can hold these two in balance in the way marriage does; Yahweh initiates the covenant but it becomes properly operative only when humanity responds to "Yahweh's covenant." The dynamic tension between these ways of looking at the matter means God can never be taken for granted but can always be appealed to.

E. Covenant as a Term for the Basis of Community Life

The notion of covenant emphasizes the relational and communal aspect to life, expressed in human relationships and in humanity's relationship with the rest of creation. We do not live to ourselves but in mutual commitment. It has been argued that there is a close connection between covenant and "steadfast love" (חֶסֶד khesedh; see KHESED; LOVE, OT). Yahweh is one "keeping covenant and steadfast love for your servants" (1 Kgs 8:23; 2 Chr 6:14; Neh 1:5; 9:32; Ps 89:28; Dan 9:4), and khesedh is the kind of commitment that people show one another when they are in covenant. One could extend this to other classic Hebrew expressions for community values such as those listed as characteristics of Yahweh in connection with the remaking of the covenant in Exod 34:6-7. On the basis of the conviction that our human action in covenant is an imitation of God's action in covenant, one could reckon that these are the qualities of human covenantal living. On political covenants, see ALLIANCE.

Bibliography: Walter Brueggemann. *A Social Reading of the Old Testament* (1994); Walter Eichrodt. *Theology of the Old Testament.* 2 vols. (1961, 1967); Scott Hahn. "Covenant in the Old and New Testaments," *Currents in Biblical Research* 3 (2005) 263–92; A. D. H. Mayes and R. B. Salters, ed. *Covenant as Context: Essays in Honour of E. W. Nicholson* (2003); Stanley E. Porter and Jacqueline C. R. de Roo, ed. *The Concept of the Covenant in the Second Temple Period* (2003); Rolf Rendtorff. *The Covenant Formula* (1998).

JOHN GOLDINGAY

COVERINGS [כְּסוּת kesuth, מָסָךְ masakh, מַרְבַדִּים marvadim; διφθέρα diphthera, ἐπικάλυμμα epikalymma, κατακάλυμμα katakalymma, χλαῖνα chlaina]. Cloth material used for bedding or to cover openings. In passages about the Tabernacle, coverings were made from leather (Exod 26:14; 39:34). Given the degree of labor involved in weaving cloth, it may be that a woman's production of a covering for beds and furnishings signals wealth, efficiency, or careful attention to household needs (Prov 31:22). Bed coverings made of imported, colored linens serve as an enticement to the unwary or easily impressed (Prov 7:16). A shrewd person uses a stout covering to disguise an opening or cover a hiding place (2 Sam 17:19). See BED; CLOTH.

VICTOR H. MATTHEWS

COVET [חָמַד khamadh; ἐπιθυμέω epithymeō]. The Hebrew and Greek are often translated "desire," but in the final verse of the TEN COMMANDMENTS (Exod 20:17) this quaint English word *covet* appears twice with various objects. The parallel, Deut 5:21, uses two different Hebrew verbs for a rearranged set of objects. Some traditions of numbering the commandments assign number 9 and 10 to this final verse. If, however, one regards the prohibition of idolatry (Exod 20:4; Deut 5:8) as a separate commandment, all coveting must be taken as one prohibition.

The commandment has commonly been interpreted to prohibit desire for that which does not belong to a person—something like envy. The prohibition thus would belong to the tradition in biblical law and moral instruction of forbidding certain attitudes (e.g., hate, lust, greed).

Some scholars argue that **khamadh** was not an attitude but a goal-oriented action—like "machinations," "plotting." That may be how we should understand the closest par., Mic 2:2. Whichever nuance is adopted, the action of coveting is not itself a crime for which a person could be convicted. This fact differentiates the final verse from what precedes. The Ten Commandments is a moral code addressing the people of God as potential actors; most violations would be crimes, but not all.

The objects of the verb are disparate: some are property, others not. Coveting a wife, and perhaps a maidservant, would be lust; others would be envy or greed. The randomness may discourage systematization. See CRIMES AND PUNISHMENT; LAW IN THE OT.

DALE PATRICK

COW. *See* CATTLE.

COWARDICE [δειλία deilia]. A state of shameful fear. In STOIC philosophical discourse, cowardice appears as one of the cardinal vices along with folly, licentiousness, and injustice. Cowardice is the antithesis of courage, which the NT describes as one of the characteristics of a faithful disciple of Jesus. Timothy is exhorted, e.g., that God bestows a spirit of power, love, and self-discipline rather than a "spirit of cowardice" (2 Tim 1:7).

JOEL LEMON

CO-WORKER [συνεργός synergos]. A person who works in the same trade; an accomplice or associate. Paul uses the word for those who participated in some facet of the missionary effort. TIMOTHY (Rom 16:21) was a trusted associate, able to fill in when Paul could not visit a community (1 Thess 3:2) or as mediator when relations were strained (2 Cor 1:24, NRSV "workers with you"). TITUS functions in a similar fashion (2 Cor 8:23). Others, such as Prisca and Aquila (Rom 16:3, NRSV "who work with me") and Apollos (1 Cor 3:9, NRSV "servants") engaged in missionary activities independently; although they had ties to Paul's activities in Corinth and Ephesus. Paul uses the term for individuals who have assisted him as representatives of established churches, such as EPHAPHRODITUS, CLEMENT, and others at Philippi (Phil 2:25; 4:3).

Justus, who was called by Jesus, and other Jewish converts are connected with Colossae (Col 4:11), as PHILEMON (Phlm 1), Mark, Aristarchus, Demas, and Luke (Phlm 24, NRSV "fellow workers") are with their church. In addition to Prisca and Aquila, Paul mentions other associates who have apparently migrated from Asia Minor to Rome (URBANUS, Rom 16:9). The epithet indicates a general participation in missionary activities. *See* CHURCH, LIFE AND ORGANIZATION OF; MINISTRY, CHRISTIAN.

PHEME PERKINS

COZBI koz′bi [כָּזְבִּי kozbi]. Daughter of the Midianite chief Zur who married the Israelite Zimri. Both were slain by the priest Phineas, thereby averting a plague (Num 25:6-15; *see also b. Sanh* 82a).

COZEBA koh-zee′buh [כֹּזֵבָא kozeva']. Town in Judah's highlands (1 Chr 4:22). Possibly the same place as ACHZIB (Josh 15:44) and CHEZIB (Gen 38:5).

CRAFTS. Mosaics, stained glass, medieval manuscript illuminations, ceramics, metalworking, ivories, and woven tapestries are classified as crafts or minor arts to distinguish them from the major arts of painting, sculpture, and architecture. Yet, each medium served an important role in transmitting the biblical stories to various cultures throughout history.

The Neolithic plastered skull from Jericho, ca. 7000 BCE, is one of the first examples of a cult of the dead, and it suggests that the people believed in a spirit or soul, located in the head, that could survive the death of the body.

The primary decoration of churches in the Byzantine period was mosaic art. Although the technique of cut glass or stone was prevalent in the Hellenistic-Roman and Mesopotamian cultures, it was most effective for transmitting biblical and religious information between 350 and 900 CE. The reliefs in ivory and silver from the same period were very popular with Justinian. They often portrayed angels and prayers and were associated with the forgiveness of sins.

Manuscript illumination and the elegant gold and jeweled covers to Gospel books were also popular between the early 5th and 9th cent., but it continued through the 19th cent. Between the 2nd and 4th cent. CE, the vellum codex gradually replaced the roll. This had a significant effect on illustration. The illustrations done on earlier scrolls were line drawings devoid of color because the layers of pigment would have cracked and worn off as the scroll was rolled and unrolled. The vellum codex opened up the world of rich color, including gold, into what is now called manuscript illuminations. All early illuminations, Christian, Jewish, or classical were, like the mosaics, influenced by the Hellenistic-Roman painting.

Stained glass was at its most prolific in France during the Gothic period. Not only were the beautiful, multicolored rose windows placed above the entrance portals but also entire biblical narratives appeared in windows flanking the nave, transept, and side aisles. These large instructional bulletin boards of sorts begged for contemplation and reflection by the congregation. *See* AESTHETICS; ART; CARVING; DESIGN.

HEIDI J. HORNIK

CRANE [עָגוּר 'aghur]. The crane (*grus communis*) migrates to southern Judea in the winter. It is mentioned twice in the Bible (NRSV, Isa 38:14; Jer 8:7, LXX omits the word in both places). However, the sense of the Hebrew word, 'aghur, is disputed. Alternative suggestions include "thrush" (NIV) and "wryneck" (Driver). Migratory birds are certainly intended by the phrase "observe the time of their coming" in Jer 8:7. In Isa 38:14, the description of the sound made by the 'aghur is suggestive of a small bird.

Bibliography: G. R. Driver. "Birds in the Old Testament: II. Birds in Life," *PEQ* (1955) 129–40.

GÖRAN EIDEVALL

CRATES kray′teez [Κράτης Kratēs]. The deputy commander of the Seleucid citadel in Jerusalem. Sostratus, the commander of the Jerusalem citadel, appointed Crates to rule in his absence, while he and the high priest MENELAUS traveled to meet King ANTIOCHUS EPIPHANES. Crates led a band of Cyprian mercenaries (2 Macc 4:29). *See* CYPRUS.

ADAM L. PORTER

CRAWLING AND CREEPING THINGS [רֶמֶשׂ remes; ἑρπετόν herpeton]. Remes is used to indicate "every moving thing" that God allows Noah and his family to use as food (Gen 9:3) or that lives in the sea (Ps 104:25). Often understood as a more specific description for reptiles (1 Kgs 4:33) or insects, remes can also refer generically to cattle, fish, and birds as well (Gen 1:24-26, 30; 6:7, 20; 7:14, 23; 8:17, 19; Ps 148:10; Ezek 38:20; Hos 2:18). This, however, is not the same as the serpent whom God made and whose temptation of Eve and Adam in the Garden of Eden God punished by making it crawl on its belly. *See* ANIMALS OF THE BIBLE; SERPENT.

EMILY CHENEY

CREATE, TO [בָּרָא bara', יָצַר yatsar, עָשָׂה 'asah; κτίζω ktizō, ποιέω poieō]. Bara', "create," is employed only for God's activity in the OT, used by the PRIESTLY WRITER to emphasize the exalted and transcendent God (Gen 1:1, 21, 27). Though interpreted later (2 Macc 7:28; Rom 4:17) as creating out of nothing (*ex nihilo*), bara' may not originally have implied this, since CREATION in the ANE is understood as bringing order to chaos, not producing matter. **Yatsar** connotes the creative work of an artisan to "form" or "fashion," e.g., a clay pot (Jer 18:4; Isa 44:9), and by the Yahwist in the second creation account for God's sculpting humans and animals from soil (Gen 2:7, 19). ʿ**Asah**, the most general of these verbs, means "make." It is used of God, humans, and even animals and plants "producing" milk or grain (Hos 8:7), and is employed in both Genesis creation stories (1:7; 2:4*b*).

The most common term for "create" in the NT, **ktizō**, is used only for God's creative work, either of the cosmos or of the new human nature in Christ (Mark 13:19; Eph 2:10). **Poieō** carries the general sense "make" and is employed for the creative activity of God (Acts 17:24), humans (Matt 17:4), and plants producing fruit (Matt 3:10).

THEODORE HIEBERT

CREATION. The biblical concept of creation encompasses the entire world of nature, including humanity, and views this world as brought into being and sustained by God. In popular thought and biblical scholarship, however, creation is often defined more narrowly as the world of nature apart from humans, so that creation and history, or nature and culture, are talked about as if they were separate realms that could be distinguished from one another. The difference between these two definitions of creation is crucial. These meanings can easily be confused, and this confusion has frequently obscured discussions of creation in the Bible. Furthermore, biblical scholars have used the narrower definition of creation during the last century to distinguish the nonhuman realm of creation from human history and to reduce nonhuman creation to a secondary and subordinate role in biblical thought. The language and perspectives in the Bible, however, suggest that its authors neither separated creation from history so distinctly nor subordinated nonhuman creation to human history. Rather, they viewed creation as a more thoroughly integrated whole. The recovery of this biblical understanding of creation—the entire world of nature including humanity created and sustained by God—is the purpose of the analysis that follows.

A. Reconstructing the Approach to Creation in Biblical Scholarship

The role of creation in the Bible cannot properly be understood without knowing something about the way biblical scholars have approached this subject in the past. This traditional scholarly orientation to creation has become so widely accepted that until recently it has been hardly questioned, and yet it rests on assumptions that are problematic in themselves and that do not deal adequately with the understanding of creation by biblical authors. The traditional approach to creation must be described and reevaluated in order to lay the foundation for a proper analysis of creation in the Bible.

1. Marginalizing creation in past biblical scholarship

The understanding of creation in the Bible during the past cent. has been based on an approach that separated the nonhuman realm of creation from creation as a whole and reduced this realm to a secondary and subordinate position in biblical thought. This approach grows out of a deep belief in the importance of human history. It has been widely promoted under the banner of "salvation history," the story of God's mighty acts of salvation in the history of God's people. According to this viewpoint, the historical experiences of the people of God—the exodus, the settlement, the kings, the exile, and restoration in the OT, Christ and the church's mission in the NT—represent the Bible's main theme and the heart of biblical religion. This emphasis on God's presence in history has highlighted an authentic theme in biblical religion, but it is invariably linked to a deemphasis of the nonhuman world of creation. The nonhuman realm of creation is attributed lesser importance than the human realm and is viewed as the stage or arena in which the real biblical drama of God and humanity is played out. Consequently, nonhuman creation has little value in itself, plays merely a supporting role in the biblical story, and possesses only peripheral significance in biblical thought (*see* ENVIRONMENT; HUMANITY, NT; HUMANITY, OT; NATURE, NATURAL PHENOMENA; SALVATION; WORLD).

Scholars have promoted this understanding of biblical religion—its centering of history and decentering of creation (in the narrow sense)—as a key distinctive of biblical religion and as an advance in the development of human thought. By emphasizing history over nature, Israel distinguished itself from the religions of its neighbors, which took nature rather than history as the primary arena of divine activity and religious life. Thus, e.g., Israel's historical deity Yahweh is contrasted with Canaan's nature deity Baal. The historical religion of the Bible is regarded as purposeful and directed toward the goal of salvation, while the nature religions in the biblical environs are regarded as cyclical and static. Furthermore, by moving God out of nature and into history, Israel "desacralized" or "demystified" nature, opening it up to the great discoveries of scientific investigation and discovery.

This view of biblical religion has been supported by a scholarly reconstruction of Israel's actual history and of its literary traditions. According to this reconstruction, biblical history actually began with the exodus, and it was here that Israel first learned to know its God and who that God was: a God who intervenes in history to save God's people. Short biblical "creeds," such as Deut 26:5*b*-9, which centers on the exodus, were considered the oldest and most fundamental statements of biblical religion. To these literary traditions of the exodus, Israel's formative experience, were eventually added other historical traditions, including those of the settlement of Canaan, the wandering in the wilderness, the encampment at Sinai, and the patriarchs in order to complete the story of Israel's origins. Only later in its history, when Israel as a nation came into increasing contact with its larger world, did Israel come to know its God also as the God of the universe and incorporate broader creation traditions into its story. As the last literary and theological act, after its historical traditions had already come together, the primeval stories of creation were grafted onto Israel's account of its God and its beginnings. Thus the accounts of creation, the world including also the nonhuman realm of nature, were adopted as the prologue or preface to the real story of God's salvation in Israel's historical experience. In this reconstruction, the world of nature was never at the core of biblical faith: it was a late and somewhat foreign addition that remained always to some extent on the periphery of biblical thought (*see* DEUTERON-OMISTIC HISTORY).

2. Recovering the essential role of creation in the Bible

A critique of this traditional view of creation must begin with its assumptions, which derive from the modern intellectual worldview of the biblical interpreters themselves, rather than from the ancient worldview of biblical authors. The most basic claim, that creation can be neatly divided into separate realms of reality—the human and the nonhuman, history and nature—fits well with the philosophical idealism popular in Europe during the rise of modern biblical scholarship in the 19th and 20th cent., and, as will be seen in the analysis below, is inept at dealing with biblical texts. Furthermore, the reconstruction of Israelite literary traditions

and history employed to support this approach rests on hypotheses about the formation of literature derived from 19th-cent. European models, rather than from more recent views of the development of traditional epics. It is no longer possible to go behind the literary sources of Israel's origins, the YAHWIST and the PRIESTLY sources in particular, in order to claim that Israel's story—its history, literary traditions, and religious consciousness—begins at the exodus and adds creation later. It is impossible to document a shift in Israelite theology from a God of Israel to a God of the entire creation.

A brief survey of accounts of creation in the major types of biblical literature shows that biblical writers regarded the world of creation as a unified whole in which the nonhuman realm was neither separate from nor secondary to human experience. The best place to start is with the Bible's primary accounts of creation in the book of Genesis. Israel begins its story not with the exodus but with the creation of the world. This is theologically important because stories of origins such as these are charter narratives, narratives that found and establish the identity of a people. In them, beginnings function not as prologues or prefaces for the real story to follow but as defining moments that establish the essential character of a people and their world. By beginning with the story of creation, Israel's theologians claim that Israel and its God assume their identity only in relation to their place in creation as a whole, with all of its natural and cultural aspects. If the beginning of Genesis is read according to the principles by which charter narratives normally work, rather than through history-centered lenses, then the entire world of creation plays a foundational and defining role in the biblical story. The details showing precisely how the creation narratives in Gen 1–3 found a people and their world are explained in §B.1 below (*see* GENESIS, BOOK OF).

When creation is described in other biblical literature, it is characterized as an integrated whole, and it plays a foundational role in the biblical story. The Psalms contain some of the most detailed accounts of creation outside of Genesis. Typically, psalmists describe God's establishment of larger cosmic orders as the context or foundation for God's establishment of the order of the historical sphere, so that cosmic orders are closely connected, e.g., to the law (Pss 19, 93), to religious ritual (Ps 24), to the exodus and settlement (Ps 136), to the establishment of the Davidic dynasty (Ps 89), and to the rebuilding of Zion (Ps 74). The praise of God at the heart of the Psalms is expressed not just by human beings but by all members of creation (Pss 96, 97, 98, 145, 148, 150; *see* PSALMS, BOOK OF).

Israel's WISDOM literature—Proverbs, Job, Ecclesiastes—takes creation, that is, the entire world of nature, including the human and nonhuman realms, as its point of orientation for understanding how God acts and how humans should behave. For this reason, and because it does not focus on Israel's formative historical events, the history-centered scholars of the last century have considered Wisdom literature out of the mainstream of biblical thought. In fact, Israel's wisdom books share the same understanding of creation as an integrated whole with a foundational role that is found in the rest of the Bible. The traditional sayings collected in Proverbs, e.g., express the ways humans can learn to live successfully by closely observing the orders God has built into all of creation, from colonies of ants (Prov 6:6-11; 30:24-28) to the courts of kings (16:12-33; 25:1-10). When God delivers the climactic speech in the book of Job from the storm wind, God speaks about God's activity in all of creation, especially in those realms out of human reach (Job 38:1–42:6).

In Prophetic literature, creation assumes the same essential and foundational place. While the oracles of the prophets are addressed to human society and its injustices—both Israel's and its neighbors'—they describe God's restoration of justice in the human realm as grounded in God's power in the cosmic realm. The prophets believe God's control of Israel's history is predicated upon God's control of the entire universe (Jer 10:16; 32:16-25; Amos 9:5-8). This is especially emphasized by Second Isaiah (Isa 40–55), who underscores God's ability to deliver Israel from exile by placing this act of salvation in the context of God's mastery of the universe (Isa 40:25-31; 42:5-9; 51:9-11). God's work in creation in its largest sense serves as the ultimate evidence of God's power to bring order to the more particular realm of human experience (*see* PROPHET, PROPHECY).

Thus across the varieties of biblical literature and theology creation is foundational. It provides the broad horizon within which to understand God and God's activity in the world and in human history. One must be cautious in going behind these literary traditions to reconstruct their earliest stages in order to trace the origins of this view of creation to the Bible's oldest reflections. Yet those texts that have the strongest claim to antiquity, the small collection of ancient poetry spread throughout the canon, present creation in just the broad, integrated, and foundational way that is seen in the rest of the Bible. These brief archaic poems invariably integrate God's cosmic powers with God's power in the earliest events of Israelite history: the exodus and settlement (Exod 15:1-18), the Canaanite conflicts (Judg 5:1-31), the establishment of the Davidic dynasty (Ps 89), and the salvation of God's anointed and God's people (Hab 3).

B. Creation as the Entire World of Nature and Culture

The biblical idea of creation as the entire world of nature, including humanity, which is brought into being by God is nowhere illustrated better than in the Bible's primary accounts of creation in Gen 1–3.

1. The integration of nature and society in creation accounts

Unlike contemporary scientific accounts of the origins of the earth and of life on it (which divide the exploration and explanation of the beginnings of the world according to such different disciplines as astronomy, geology, biology, and anthropology), biblical accounts combine the origin and organization of all aspects of the world—including both nature and society—into a single story. And they attribute everything to divine activity. These biblical accounts are fundamentally etiological, explaining the contours of the world in which their authors lived. Differences in content, chronology, literary style, and theological perspective indicate that Genesis in fact begins with two creation stories, an account of the creation in seven days (Gen 1:1–2:4a) and an account of creation in the garden of Eden (Gen 2:4b–3:24).

The story of creation in the garden of Eden, attributed to the Yahwist (J), begins Israel's oldest epic account of itself and its origins (*see* EDEN, GARDEN OF; J, YAHWIST; SOURCE CRITICISM, OT). In this creation story, the world God creates is the world of the Israelite family farm, the natural and social environment of Israelite society. The focus of the natural landscape in this creation account is arable land (אֲדָמָה 'adhamah), land suitable for cultivation, translated "ground" in the NRSV (Gen 2:5, 6, 7, 9, 19; 3:17, 19, 23; *see* AGRICULTURE). God makes the first human/man (אָדָם 'adham) from arable land (2:7; 3:19), and God assigns humans the task of cultivating it (2:15; 3:23). The narrator's play on words—human/man ('adam) from arable land ('adhamah)—emphasizes the integral link between humanity and its landscape. This close connection has been captured with the English equivalents "earthling (from) earth" and "human (from) humus," though the most precise equivalent is "farmer (from) farmland." For the Yahwist, human identity by nature (made from arable land) and by vocation (assigned to cultivate it) derives directly from its natural environment.

The Eden narrative as a whole reflects this same focus on the origins of the agrarian Mediterranean world that defined the landscape and society of biblical Israel. The plant and animal life God creates comprises the elements of Israel's mixed agricultural economy, which was based in the cultivation of grain (עֵשֶׂב 'esev)—translated "herb" (2:5) and "plants" (3:18) in the NRSV—and tree crops (2:9), and which was supplemented with the raising of animals (2:19; *see* ANIMALS OF THE BIBLE; PLANTS OF THE BIBLE). The first humans in this account comprise the first family (2:21-24), the core unit of Israel's kinship-based society, upon which were built Israel's lineages, clans, and tribes. When the first man and woman become "one flesh" (2:24), they begin the family in two respects: with the physical act of reproduction by which the family is created and its future ensured (4:1), and with the social contract by which a new social, economic, and political kinship unit is established (*see* CHILD, CHILDREN; FAMILY; ISRAEL, SOCIAL AND ECONOMIC DEVELOPMENT OF; KINSHIP; MARRIAGE; SOCIAL SCIENTIFIC CRITICISM, OT).

The Bible's other creation narrative (Gen 1:1–2:4*a*), attributed to the Priestly Writer (P), is a later account, perhaps dating to the Babylonian exile when Israel's priests collected and edited its religious traditions (*see* P, PRIESTLY WRITER). In this creation story, the world brought into being is a cosmos that encompasses the ritual world of the Israelite priesthood (*see* PRIESTS AND LEVITES). The horizons of this world are more expansive than the world of the family farm God creates in the Yahwist's narrative, in this case including sky, sea, and land and everything that populated them. Yet the structures built into this wider universe provide the cosmic foundations for the particular religious world of Israel over which the priesthood presided.

The overall shape of the Priestly creation account, by which God creates the world in six days and rests on the seventh, establishes in the cosmos the weekly structure that mandates the observance of the SABBATH for all Israelites on the seventh day. The structure of sacred time as Israel understood it is further embedded in the universe when God creates the heavenly bodies—sun, moon, and stars—on the fourth day to divide the year into Israel's sacred seasons (מוֹעֲדִים mo'adhim; 1:14), the great festivals of Israel's liturgical year (Lev 23; *see* CALENDAR). Together with ordering cosmic time, God also orders cosmic space to provide the framework for Israel's ritual life. The spatial structure of the universe marks out the realms by which clean and unclean animals are distinguished in the Priestly dietary laws (Lev 11). Animals perfectly fitted to their native realm—sky, sea, or land (Gen 1:20-25)—are clean, while those violating these boundaries are unclean (*see* CLEAN AND UNCLEAN).

Both the Yahwist and the Priestly writer describe creation as a cosmos in which the structures of the natural world and the realities of Israelite life and religion are part of a single, coherent order. The nonhuman realm of creation is not separate from the human realm, nor is it marginal to the human drama of salvation. If anything, it is the foundation of human life and identity. Furthermore, these biblical creation accounts are not general or universal in their view of origins, as is widely claimed. Each account describes beginnings in the concrete details of the primary world of the storyteller. Thus they are etiological in aim: they explain and legitimate the particular realities of the natural and social environments of the biblical writers themselves.

In these respects, the biblical view of creation reflects a common view of creation that is shared throughout the ancient Near East. The great creation epic of Mesopotamia, ENUMA ELISH, describes the origins of the world of the Babylonians. The deity Marduk, after subduing the forces of chaos, creates an orderly cosmos and founds at its center the city of Babylon, its temple, and its rituals (*see* ASSYRIA AND BABYLONIA). In similar fashion, Egyptian creation stories establish an Egyptian world. In the creation story from Memphis, e.g., the god Ptah brings all of creation into being, including Egypt's political districts, its major temples and their offerings, and the city and temple of Memphis as the primary sacred site in the Nile Valley (*see* EGYPT). The key difference between these creation stories and the biblical accounts is not that the biblical stories reflect a historical orientation to the world while the neighboring stories reflect a natural orientation, as traditionally asserted. The world of creation in the ancient Near East, as in the Bible, is an integrated whole. The key difference lies rather in the distinctive natural and social worlds each cultural narrative creates. Each creation story, including the different ones in the Bible itself, reflects the particular lens of the distinctive world in which its author lives.

2. The place of humanity in creation

Biblical creation traditions contain two distinctive views of the role of human beings in creation. The most familiar picture is the one drawn from the Priestly account in Gen 1:1–2:4*a*, where humans are created in God's image and given dominion (1:26-28). While the meaning of humans being created in God's image continues to be debated, it is likely that the divine image is meant to convey to humans a particular role in the world rather than a particular essence or nature. Elsewhere in the ancient Near East, this expression identifies the bearer, often the king, as God's representative in the world. Taken in this way, the divine image bestows on humans a vocation: they are created to be God's representatives within the world of creation. The term *steward*, though not used in Gen 1, has been widely used by contemporary theologians to characterize this Priestly view of humanity's role in creation.

Humanity's role as God's representative, according to Priestly thought, is to exercise dominion over the earth and all of its living things (1:26, 28). To have dominion (רָדָה radhah) means to rule, as do kings over their subjects (Ps 72:8) and masters over their servants (Lev 25:43). Thus, creation is conceived as a hierarchy whose apex is occupied by humans, who hold the primary power of governance. The verb radhah, since it can be employed for both harsh and benevolent rule, does not itself define the nature of human governance of creation, but it does grant humans potent authority. If humans are to exercise this authority as God's representatives—created in God's image—then their rule must reflect the rule of God, who creates everything orderly and good (1:31). This conception of humanity as God's representative governing creation, found elsewhere in the Bible (Ps 8), is a priestly, royal image, mirroring the roles of priest and king as God's representatives in Israelite society.

The place of humanity in creation is conceived quite differently in the Yahwist's account. In this version, the first human/man (ʾadham) is made not in God's image but from arable land (ʾadhamah), literally, a farmer from farmland. And his assignment in creation is not to rule but to "till and keep" the land (Gen 2:15). The verb "till" translates עָבַד ʿavadh, that basic meaning of which is "serve," as slaves serve their masters (Gen 12:6) and as Israel serves God (Exod 4:26). Whereas the Priestly Writer saw humanity as the earth's rulers, the Yahwist presents humanity as its servants (see SERVANT; SERVE, TO). The Yahwist thus looks at creation and humanity through the eyes of the typical Israelite, the farmer, who intimately understands his dependence on creation, rather than through the eyes of the priest or king, who exercises authority and power.

The Yahwist emphasizes the interrelatedness of the human being and the rest of creation in a number of ways. Rather than set apart from creation by being the only life created in God's image, humans in J's story are made from the same material from which all other life is made: arable land, the focal point of the garden landscape (Gen 2:9, 19). The human receives the breath of life (Gen 2:7), as do all living beings (Gen 7:22). Animals and humans alike are called "living beings" (נֶפֶשׁ חַיָּה nefesh khayyah), though translators have consistently rendered this same phrase differently, thus implying an unbiblical distinction between humans and animals: "living being" for humanity in 2:7, but "living creature" for animals in 2:19 (NRSV). When the first human names the animals, this is not an act of dominion as commonly assumed (on the basis of the P story where humans are given dominion) but rather as an act recognizing the animals' individual identities and their particular relationships to humans. The Yahwist's conception of humans as members of creation rather than as its rulers is also reflected elsewhere in the Bible, in the Psalms (104) and in the divine speeches in the book of Job (38:1–42:6).

C. God and Creation

Perhaps the most fundamental fact about creation accounts in the biblical world, a fact that distinguishes the accounts from modern scientific explanations of origins, is that creation was brought into being and sustained by a divine being. This is true not just for biblical authors but for their neighbors as well. What distinguishes biblical writers from their neighbors in this regard is their focus on one God in creation. This line between the monotheism of Israel and the polytheism of its neighbors, however, is not as sharp as it is sometimes drawn. While ancient Near Eastern creation accounts are regularly populated with numerous gods, a single chief deity is primarily responsible for creation,

as is MARDUK in the Babylonian epic, *Enuma Elish*, and PTAH in the Egyptian account of creation from Memphis. And while biblical accounts describe a single creator, some include traditions of Israel's God vanquishing cosmic foes—Leviathan (Ps 74:14), Rahab (Ps 80:11)—before creating the world.

1. Creation as ordering chaos

One of the most influential doctrines of creation in the history of biblical interpretation is the doctrine of *creatio ex nihilo*, "creation out of nothing." According to this doctrine, God's prime activity at creation was bringing the substance of the universe into being where nothing had existed before, so that God is the absolute source of matter and time. This doctrine rests on interpreting the opening words of Genesis as a prepositional phrase: "In the beginning, God created the heavens and the earth." Such a view of creation is never stated explicitly in the OT; it first appears clearly only with early Jewish and Christian interpreters (2 Macc 7:28; *2 En.* 24:2; Rom 4:17; Heb 11:3). Moreover, it does not appear to represent the way beginnings were conceived in the biblical world.

The common conception of creation in antiquity, in Israel and among its neighbors, is that God's prime activity at creation was bringing order to chaos. The act of creation is not so much making matter as ordering pre-existing chaotic matter into a world that would support and sustain life. To express this idea, creation accounts in the ancient Near East customarily begin with a temporal clause describing the unformed state of things existent at creation, which becomes the material out of which the cosmos is shaped. This is just how the Yahwist's creation account begins: the opening temporal clause "When the LORD God made earth and heaven ..." (NJPS) is followed by a description of an unformed landscape (Gen 2:4*b*-6), to which God's creative work brings order and life (2:7-25). The opening of the Priestly account of creation is also most likely to be read as a temporal clause: "When God began to create heaven and earth ..." (Gen 1:1, NJPS), followed by a description of the dark watery chaos (1:2) out of which God forms the cosmos (1:2–2:4*a*).

This conception of the creator as the great "orderer" is illustrated by other biblical traditions that picture creation as a struggle between the powers of order and CHAOS. Often downplayed by biblical scholars who wish to emphasize Israelite monotheism, this struggle pits the God of Israel against a cosmic figure or figures who represent chaos. To establish the orders of creation, God must conquer a chaos monster, represented by different names and titles, but usually identified with unruly waters. The creation of the world is described in this way in Ps 74:12-17, where God subdues Sea/Leviathan, in Ps 89:6-15, where God subdues Sea/Rahab with his cohort, and in Job

26:5-14, where God conquers Sea/Rahab. Many other references to creation in the Psalms allude to this cosmic victory over chaos as the background for cosmic order (24:1-2; 93:1-5; 104:5-9). While scholars have claimed that the Priestly creation story categorically rejects this notion of cosmic conflict, the watery chaos that precedes God's creative work may be an allusion to this motif (Gen 1:2). In many instances when God's control of political and historical events is asserted, the primordial victory over chaos emphasizes God's ordering of the world in every aspect (Isa 51:9-11; Hab 3:8-15; Pss 77:12-21; 114:1-7).

2. God's relationship to creation

God's original creative acts to establish cosmic order are not viewed by biblical authors as one-time events. God is not viewed as a watchmaker, who makes a world that runs on its own. In biblical thought, God is creation's constant sustainer, preserving the orders established at creation and giving life to each new generation of living things. God's conquest of chaos at creation did not eliminate chaos; rather, God subdued it and set barriers to keep it confined and to ensure that it would not return and overwhelm the ordered world. God works continuously to preserve order and to keep the forces of chaos at bay by holding back the sea behind boundaries (Job 38:8; Ps 104:5-9; Prov 8:27-29; Jer 5:22). Should God stand back and allow the waters of chaos free reign, they would quickly engulf the world and return it to pre-creation chaos. This is just how the Priestly Writer explains the great flood, presenting it as the outbreak of the waters above and below the earth (Gen 7:11; 8:2), which God restrained at creation (Gen 1:2, 6-8).

God's constant activity to sustain and nourish creation is illustrated vividly in God's continuing role in the creation of new life. God is believed to be the source of the soil's fertility and of the harvest it produces, a belief expressed in the ritual of returning to God the firstfruits at Israel's great harvest festivals in the spring and fall (Exod 23:14-17, 19). God also creates and sustains the life of each human being in each generation. God makes the womb fertile (Gen 16:2; 29:31) and directs the development of the fetus (Ps 139:13-18; Jer 1:5). God breathes God's own breath into human beings and into animals at birth and sustains it during their lifetimes, taking it back when they die (Gen 2:7; 7:22; Ps 104:28-30).

This intimate relation between God and creation is also apparent in biblical theophanies, accounts of God's special appearances in the world, where God is regularly associated with natural phenomena. God's primary mode of manifestation in the OT is the thunderstorm, in which thunder is understood as God's voice, clouds as God's chariot, and lightning as God's weaponry. In such descriptions of God, the nonhuman imagery of the storm and the human imagery of warfare are closely intertwined. The thunderstorm is God's mode of manifestation in Israel's earliest poetry (Exod 15), in its account of God's revelation at Mount Sinai (Exod 19), and in its traditions about Jerusalem where God dwelled (Pss 18, 46). God's presence at these sacred sites attributes sacredness to the earth itself (Exod 3:5; Ps 48:2).

In spite of God's intimate involvement in the processes of creation, scholars have emphasized the absolute difference between God and creation, between creator and creature. This claim is partly the result of the traditional dichotomy, described above, by which scholars have divided creation between nature and history, emphasizing God's intimate relation with history and deemphasizing or denying God's relationship with (nonhuman) nature. It is also the result of the later philosophical conception, appearing first in Greek thought, that spirit and matter are distinct entities, and that God is spirit and creation is matter. This presumed dichotomy, however, was not present in biblical thought. God and the world of creation are in a much closer relationship in the Bible than usually acknowledged.

3. The future of creation

In Prophetic literature, God is occasionally described as devastating creation on an almost cosmic scale (Joel 2:30-31 [Heb. 3:3-4]; Zeph 1:2-3, 14-15) and as transforming it into an almost unimaginable PARADISE (Joel 3:18 [Heb. 4:18]; Amos 9:3; Zech 14:6-8). God's transformation of nature is particularly prominent in the Isaiah traditions. Isaiah of Jerusalem pictures the pacification of wild animals as a part of the reign of the righteous king in Jerusalem (Isa 11:1-9), Second Isaiah (Isa 40–55) describes the transformation of the desert to promote the exiles' return to Jerusalem (43:18-21), and Third Isaiah (Isa 56–66) mentions "the new heavens and the new earth" to picture the restoration of Jerusalem (66:22). Such images have led some to the conclusion that the prophets expected God to destroy the first creation and replace it with another.

Prophetic thought in actuality is strongly grounded in a single, original creation, which God will bring to its fullest potential. All of these pictures of transformation are parts of the concrete expectation of the restoration of the actual city of Jerusalem, with its Temple and its king, in its actual natural landscape: righteous, just, strong, secure, flourishing, and at peace. They do not point to another creation but rather describe in partly idealized form (from a human-centered perspective) the world God created at the beginning. The OT contains no theology of a fallen creation in need of redemption. The curse on the land introduced as a result of human disobedience in the garden (Gen 3:17-19) is lifted by God after the flood (5:29; 8:21-22). Prophetic visions of the future imagine a world in which Israel and its environment reflect the potential for which they were first created.

D. Cosmology: The Structure of the Universe

Biblical writers shared with their contemporaries a picture of the universe common in antiquity but strikingly different from contemporary pictures. According to biblical thought, the earth is the center of everything that exists: all aspects of creation were structured around it. The Yahwist's creation account describes only the origin of the earth and its forms of life—in particular, the landscape of the Israelite family farm—without dealing, e.g., with the skies or seas at all. In the Priestly account, which describes a more expansive cosmos, the earth has a premier position: The earth and its forms of life take center stage and the skies and heavenly bodies are put into place above it. The earth did not move—it was stable (Ps 96:10)—and the heavenly bodies moved across the sky. The sun rose and the sun set (Eccl 1:5). The entire universe, as biblical authors knew it, was essentially the earth and the natural phenomena related to it.

The shape of the earth, aside from the concrete details of the terrain of biblical Israel itself, is nowhere very precisely described. The earth appears to be a broad surface with boundaries or boarders marking its edges (Job 28:24). Some language suggests a square shape marked into four quadrants with corners (Isa 11:12; Ezek 7:2), while other expressions imply a circle, perhaps suggested by the surrounding horizon (Job 26:10). As cultures commonly organize the world with themselves and their land at its center, so Israel believed its land and in particular its capital Jerusalem to be the center of the earth (Ezek 5:5; 38:12; Pss 46, 48). As described above, Israel's accounts of creation describe the origins of the world in the concrete details of its own environment, society, and religious practices.

The earth at the center of the cosmos is entirely surrounded by waters, restrained above and below behind barriers. This cosmology is reflected in the Priestly creation story, where, on the second day, God divides the primordial waters that existed at creation (Gen 1:2), placing half above the dome (or firmament) erected above the earth and the other half below the earth (Gen 1:6-8). The waters above the earth provide the reservoir from which God summons the rains (Job 38:22, 25), while the waters below the earth are the source of springs, rivers, and seas. The earth itself is held in place above these subterranean waters by pillars sunk into them (1 Sam 2:8). As noted above, these waters are held back behind boundaries by God in order to keep them from overwhelming the earth (Job 38:8-11; Ps 104:9). Were these boundaries to be breached, as happened at the great flood, the waters would swallow the earth and return it to pre-creation chaos (Gen 7:11, 19-21).

While the cosmologies of Israel's neighbors are in their details incredibly varied, they share the basic elements of the biblical worldview, with the earth at the center of the universe, the heavens above, and the waters of chaos at the borders of the ordered world. Since this ancient cosmology is strikingly different from contemporary scientific models of the cosmos, scholars have described it as a mythic, poetic, or theological treatment of creation, rather than a scientific one. There is some truth in this claim, particularly in its theological assertion, since biblical writers saw God's activity as the source and explanation of every natural phenomenon, while modern scientists study and describe the world with a materialist methodology that sets God outside the realm of inquiry.

Yet in another sense, the biblical cosmology reflects authentic elements of the scientific endeavor. It is based on a careful observation of the orders of the world, and it represents a plausible construction of reality based on such observations, observations necessarily limited in antiquity by the naked eye and by a limited geographical purview. The impetus to observe the human environment and organize the world according to these observations is apparent not just in Israel's creation narratives but in various references to such rudimentary scientific efforts (1 Kgs 4:29-34 [Heb. 5:9-14]; Prov 25:2-3; 30:24-28). Thus biblical cosmology is better described as an integrated project, possessing an aspect of ancient science, rather than as pure myth, poetry, or theology. While scientific in a certain sense, the antiquity of such scientific efforts in biblical cosmological reconstructions must be clearly recognized. When the church has tried to defend the Bible's ancient cosmology against the advances of newer scientific work—as when the church imprisoned and persecuted the Italian astronomer Galileo for defending Copernicus's heliocentric cosmology and contradicting the Bible's geocentric one—the results have always been disastrous (*see* SCIENCE AND THE BIBLE; SCIENCE, EGYPT; SCIENCE, MESOPOTAMIA).

F. Creation in Early Christian Thought

The view of creation in the NT reflects in its essentials the OT point of view. Emerging as it did out of the Judaism of the 1st cent., the early church accepted as its Scripture Judaism's sacred texts, and its early writers explained the meaning of Jesus and of the early church in light of these texts. While describing their world on the basis of the OT point of view, early Christian writers also interpreted the OT in light of Christ, and this led to a number of adaptations of the OT picture of creation.

1. God the creator

In their references to God as the creator and to the world as God's creation, NT authors show that they are thinking and writing with the OT concept of creation in mind. God is described as the creator of the world and everything in it by many NT writers, among whom are the authors of the Gospels (Matt 24:21; Mark 13:19) and of Luke–Acts (Acts 4:24), Paul (Rom 1:20) and Paul's disciples (Eph 3:9), and the author of Revelation

(4:11). Several writers appeal directly to the accounts of the creation of man and woman in Genesis in order to make ethical claims regarding Christian practice (Mark 10:6-9 = Matt 19:4-6; 1 Cor 11:7-12). Early Christians thus take the OT understanding of creation as the basis of their thought.

Two important innovations, however, appear in early Christian texts. One of these innovations is the view that God created the world out of nothing (*ex nihilo*). Both Paul (Rom 4:17) and the author of Hebrews (11:3) appear to believe that at creation God brought the material world into existence where nothing had previously existed. In this belief, early Christians are not unique but share a point of view that emerged among Jewish interpreters in the last two cent. before the birth of Christianity (2 Macc 7:28; *2 Bar.* 21:4; *2 En.* 24:2). Whereas OT authors describe God's creative activity as the ordering of chaos by forming the world of life out of the primordial waters (as described above), their early Jewish and Christian interpreters regard God's creative activity as the making of matter. This view of creation, the doctrine of *creatio ex nihilo*, eventually became the orthodox Christian viewpoint.

A second innovation in the OT conception of creation appears among early Christian writers who held what may be described as a "high" Christology. For such NT theologians, Christ was not merely an earthly messiah but preexisted with God and participated in the world's creation (*see* CHRISTOLOGY). Paul describes Christ's role in creation in this way to the Corinthians (1 Cor 8:6). The premiere example of Christ as a cosmic figure is the hymn in Col 1:15-20, in which Christ is praised as God's co-creator of the world—"in (by) him all things in heaven and on earth were created" (v. 16)—and as God's co-sustainer of creation, preventing the world from disintegrating into chaos—"in (by) him all things hold together" (v. 17). This conception of Christ's role in creation is also present in the Gospel of John, which begins by describing Christ as co-creator in language drawn directly from Gen 1:1. For these writers, as for their OT ancestors, the world was not divided into the spheres of history and nature; rather, creation was a single whole in which the activity of God—and of Christ, for early Christians—played a creating and sustaining role.

2. Paul's conception of creation as fallen

In his letter to the Romans, Paul describes the realm of nonhuman creation as sharing the fallen fate of humanity and its longing for redemption (Rom 8:18-25). When he says "the creation was subjected to futility" (v. 20), that "the whole creation has been groaning in labor pains" (v. 22), and that "the creation itself will be set free from its bondage to decay and will obtain the freedom of the glory of the children of God" (v. 21), Paul appears to make the claim that nonhuman nature together with human nature acquired a fatal defect as

a result of human sin (Gen 3:14-19). In developing this viewpoint, Paul is giving cosmic depth to his typology of Christ as the new Adam: as sin and death came into the world through Adam, so redemption and life come through Christ (Rom 5:12-17; 1 Cor 15:20-25).

Like the idea of creation out of nothing, the notion of a fall is not found among OT writers but first emerges among their early Jewish interpreters in the last two cent. before the birth of Christianity (Sir 25:24; Wis 2:23-24; 4 Ezra 7:118). While later largely abandoned in Judaism, Paul embraces this view, and thus the fall of humanity—and nonhuman creation with it—becomes a central feature of his interpretation of Christ's purpose on earth. Just as Paul conceives of the world holistically by describing Christ's role as co-creator and co-sustainer of the cosmos (1 Cor 8:6), so he considers the entire world, human and nonhuman alike, as participating in the fall. While central to Paul, the idea of creation as fallen is not found elsewhere in the NT, and it does not therefore assume a prominent position in the NT view of creation.

3. The future of creation

The NT is deeply influenced by the apocalyptic perspective that played a prominent role in some sectors of the 1st cent. Jewish community out of which Christianity was born. Apocalyptic writers, the author of Revelation in particular, describe a dramatic intervention by God to eliminate the oppressive and destructive powers that rule the world and to restore the world to justice, prosperity, and peace. Some of this language is so emphatic—e.g., John's vision of "a new heaven and a new earth; for the first heaven and the first earth had passed away" (Rev 21:1)—that some interpreters have suggested that God would bring the first creation to an end and replace it with another. According to this perspective, the world of creation that came into existence in Genesis is only a temporary reality, to be superseded by heaven or by another reality, perhaps more spiritual in form and substance.

Christian apocalyptic writers actually take the first, original creation with ultimate seriousness. They do not expect the annihilation of creation, but its renewal and transformation. In this regard they are rooted deeply in the tradition of their OT precursors, who employed apocalyptic imagery not to describe the end of creation but to picture the restoration of the people of Israel in Jerusalem and the restoration of their natural environment as a flourishing landscape (*see* above). Early Christian writers affirm the goodness of God's first creation and God's intention to restore it to its original beauty as a part of God's redemption in Christ.

The primary Christian apocalypse, the book of Revelation, illustrates this view of creation. In his vision of God enthroned over the cosmos, John of Patmos describes those around the throne praising God as the world's creator and sustainer (4:11). The great "woes" delivered in response to the earth's turmoil are not accusations explaining these disasters as God's judgment on the earth but lamentations of creation's distress under the oppression of the forces of evil (8:13). God's judgment rests not on creation but on the Roman Empire and the demonic forces of evil that have exploited the earth and its peoples (see ROMAN EMPIRE; ROME, EARLY CHRISTIAN ATTITUDES TOWARD). The oppressive empire, represented by beasts rising from the sea (the ancient symbol of chaos; chs. 13–14), and by the ancient empire of Babylon that destroyed Jerusalem (chs. 17–18), must be subdued before creation can flourish (chs. 19–20). God's ultimate redemption is described as the city of Jerusalem descending to earth, God making a home with humanity, and all of the parts of the world of nature thriving with unimaginable vigor and life (chs. 21–22). In this, the most expansive description of redemption in the NT, God has not done away with creation but has entered it to take up residence in it and renew it (21:1-5; see REVELATION, BOOK OF).

Some elements of the transformation of creation in this image of redemption appear to push beyond the limits of the world of creation as it is described in the OT. Whereas OT writers thought of God putting limits on chaos, John of Patmos describes God eliminating it: "the sea was no more" (Rev 21:1). Building on anticipations in the OT (Isa 25:7; Dan 12:2), John expects God to do away also with death (Rev 21:4), a fervent expectation also of Paul (1 Cor 15) and other NT writers. Yet even in these visions of the transformation of creation, NT writers never expect God to replace the world of creation with another, nor do they anticipate escape to another world. For OT and NT writers alike, the world is God's, and it is in this world of creation that the purposes of God will be accomplished.

Bibliography: Bernhard W. Anderson, ed. *Creation in the Old Testament* (1984); Bernhard W. Anderson, ed. *From Creation to New Creation* (1994); William P. Brown. *The Ethos of the Cosmos: The Genesis of Moral Imagination in the Bible* (1999); William P. Brown and S. Dean McBride Jr., ed. *God Who Creates: Essays in Honor of W. Sibley Towner* (2000); Richard J. Clifford. *Creation Accounts in the Ancient Near East and in the Bible* (1994); Richard J. Clifford and John J. Collins, ed. *Creation in the Biblical Traditions* (1992); Carol J. Dempsey and Mary Margaret Pazdan, ed. *Earth, Wind, & Fire: Biblical and Theological Perspectives on Creation* (2004); Terence E. Fretheim. *God and the World in the Old Testament: A Relational Theology of Creation* (2005); Norman C. Habel. *The Earth Bible.* 5 vols. (2000–); Theodore Hiebert. *The Yahwist's Landscape: Nature and Religion in Early Israel* (1996); Jon D. Levenson. *Creation and the Persistence of Evil: The Jewish Drama of Divine Omnipotence* (1988); Karl Löning and Erich Zenger.

To Begin with, God Created: Biblical Theologies of Creation (2000); Barbara Rossing. "River of Life in God's New Jerusalem: An Eschatological Vision for Earth's Future" in *Christianity and Ecology*, ed. Dieter T. Hessel and Rosemary Radford Ruther (2000); David M. Russell. *The "New Heavens and New Earth": Hope for the Creation in Jewish Apocalyptic and the New Testament* (1996); Ronald A. Simkins. *Creator and Creation: Nature in the Worldview of Ancient Israel* (1994); Luis J. Stadelmann. *The Hebrew Conception of the World* (1970).

THEODORE HIEBERT

CREATOR. *See* CREATION; GOD, NT VIEW OF; GOD, OT VIEW OF.

CREATURE, LIVING [נֶפֶשׁ חַיָּה *nefesh khayyah;* ψυχή ζῷον *psyche zoon*]. In varying Hebrew and Greek forms, this is generally a reference to animals, often those living in water (Gen 1:20-21, 24, 30; 9:10, 12, 15-16; Lev 11:10, 46; Ezek 47:9), but sometimes to unusual beings to indicate they are living (e.g., Ezek 1:5; Rev 4:6-9). In the creation account of Gen 2:4-31, the Hebrew term is used to refer to the human after Yahweh breathed the breath of life into that creature (2:7). Presumably, animals became living creatures in a similar manner (2:19). *See* ANIMALS OF THE BIBLE; BIRDS OF THE BIBLE; CREATION; LIFE; SOUL.

EMILY CHENEY

CREDIT, CREDITOR. *See* DEBT, DEBTOR; MONEY.

CREDO, ANCIENT ISRAELITE kree´doh. In a 1938 essay and, subsequently, in his *Theology of the Old Testament*, Gerhard von Rad proposed that the biblical authors structured the larger story of Israel's sacred history around primal creedal formulations (credos). Chief among these recitations of the saving acts of God were Deut 6:20-24; 26:5-9; and Josh 24:1-13. These core confessions affirmed the divine promise to Israel's ancestors, the deliverance from Egyptian servitude, and the entry into the land. Von Rad claimed this testimony was the constitutive marrow around which legal, cultic, poetic, and other material were gathered to shape not only the first six books of the Bible, but also all that follows in OT theology. As each subsequent generation of Israelites confessed the "historical" acts of God, the old traditions were reconstituted with new and varied theological perspectives, all as a means of making explicit assertions about Yahweh. Von Rad maintained that those assertions are the proper subject matter of OT theology.

Von Rad's credo thesis has been criticized, not least because the passages upon which he relied are now generally considered to be later texts. *See* CREED; DOCUMENTARY HYPOTHESIS; SHEMA, THE.

WALTER C. BOUZARD

CREED. Formal fixed Christian creeds began to appear only in the 3rd and 4th cent., but they have their roots in biblical statements of faith. In the OT there are affirmations such as, "the LORD is our God, the LORD alone" (Deut 6:4; similarly 1 Kgs 18:39). There are also recitations of God's saving deeds, such as the one Moses tells the Israelites to pass on to their children (Deut 6:21-23).

In the NT there is the simple creedal acclamation: "Jesus is Lord" (1 Cor 12:3; Phil 2:11). Paul elaborates, "if you confess with your lips that Jesus is Lord and believe in your heart that God raised him from the dead, you will be saved" (Rom 10:9). There are two-member formulae declaring that Jesus was crucified and that God raised him up (Acts 2:23; 4:10; 5:30-31; 10:39-40). In 1 Cor 15:3-7 is a statement with four elements: Christ died, was buried, was raised, and appeared to believers. A more developed recitation is found in 1 Tim 3:16: "He was revealed in the flesh, vindicated in the spirit, seen by angels, proclaimed among the Gentiles, believed in throughout the world, taken up in glory."

Such formulations, with their poetic rhythms, were used in liturgical contexts. Jesus' command to his disciples to make disciples and to baptize them "in the name of the Father, and of the Son, and of the holy Spirit" (Matt 28:19) is clearly reflective of an early Christian baptismal liturgy. *See* CREDO, ANCIENT ISRAELITE; SHEMA, THE.

BARBARA E. REID

CREEPING THINGS. *See* CRAWLING AND CREEPING THINGS.

CREMATION. *See* BURIAL; DEATH, NT; DEATH, OT.

CRESCENS kres´uhnz [Κρήσκης Krēskēs]. 1. An associate of PAUL who left him for GALATIA (2 Tim 4:10), or as a few manuscripts read, GAUL. The reference may not be wholly positive, as Crescens' departure is part of a theme emphasizing associates abandoning the imprisoned Paul. Later tradition counted Crescens among the seventy disciples and credited him with founding churches in Mayence and Vienne.

2. Crescens (Κρίσκης Kriskēs) the Cynic, is mentioned by JUSTIN MARTYR as an opponent he refuted in public debate (*2 Apol.* 2.3). Later tradition explicitly blames Crescens for having brought about Justin's death. *See* MARTYRDOM.

RUBÉN R. DUPERTUIS

CRESCENT. *See* JEWELRY.

CRETE kreet [Κρήτη Krētē]. Crete is a large island forming the southern boundary to the AEGEAN. The Minoans, made famous through the excavation of Knossos, inhabited the island during the 2nd millennium BCE. OT references to CAPHTOR (Deut 2:23; Jer 47:4; Amos 9:7) have been linked to the Late Bronze Age Keftiu, a group that becomes prominent in Egypt during the 18th Dynasty. This group usually is linked with either Crete or the Aegean world (*see* LINEAR B). In the late archaic period Crete was celebrated for won-

David W. J. Gill

Figure 1: Ayios Titos

der-workers such as EPIMENIDES. In the Roman period it formed part of a joint province, Cyrenaica. The main Roman city was at Gortyn, which lies on the north edge of the Mesara plain in the southern part of the island. Gortyn is mentioned in a letter from Rome concerning how Jews should be treated (1 Macc 15:23). Paul sailed along the southern side of Crete on his way to Rome (Acts 27:7-16). A series of Christian communities was established on the island during the 1st cent. CE, and these formed the context for the epistle to TITUS. A church at Gortyn commemorated Titus (*see* Fig. 1, p. 789).

Bibliography: D. W. J. Gill. "A Saviour for the Cities of Crete: The Roman Background to the Epistle of Titus." *The New Testament in Its First Century Setting: Essays on Context and Background in Honour of B. W. Winter on His 65th Birthday* (2004) 220–30.

DAVID W. J. GILL

CRIB [אֵבוּס ʾevus; φάτη phatē]. A feeding trough or stall for the domesticated donkey (Isa 1:3) and oxen. *See* MANGER.

CRICKET [חַרְגֹּל khargol; ἀκρίς akris]. A winged, leaping insect with jointed legs of indeterminate species. Appearing only in Lev 11, both NRSV and NIV translate khargol as "cricket." However, the LXX uses akris, a common term for "locust." According to Lev 11:21-22, the khargol, unlike other four-legged insects, is classified as clean and therefore edible. Indeed, the akris is considered food for John the Baptist (Matt 3:4; Mark 1:6). *See* INSECTS OF THE BIBLE.

JOEL LEMON

CRIMES AND PUNISHMENT, OT AND NT. In law, *crime* is any act committed or omitted in violation of a public law. The term may connote a more serious act, in contrast to misdemeanor; however, in law *felony* bears that restricted meaning, whereas crime is comprehensive. *Punishment* in criminal law is any pain, penalty, or confinement imposed upon a person by judicial authority for conviction of a criminal act.

A. General Hebrew Terms
B. Crimes Against Persons
  1. Cain
  2. Noah
  3. Law within covenant
  4. Codified homicide law
  5. Other crimes against persons
  6. Kidnapping
  7. Family violence
  8. False witness
  9. Judicial authority
C. Crimes Against Property
  1. Theft

  2. Real property
  3. Protections of the vulnerable
D. Criminal Conversation
  1. Prohibited sexual partners
  2. Adultery
E. Apostasy, Idolatry, and Other Religious Crimes
  1. Revelation
  2. Apostasy
  3. Apologetic narrative
  4. Idolatry
  5. Other crimes
  6. Honoring the holy
F. Punishments
G. Historical Perspective
H. New Testament
  1. The kingdom of God
  2. Jesus among the criminals
Bibliography

A. General Hebrew Terms

The word *crime* is only rarely used in English translations (only four times in the NRSV); it seems to imply a rather modern idea of the "state" as the "maker" of law.

The verb *to punish* and the noun *punishment* are more common than *crime* in the NRSV. God is most often the subject of the action, though of course the court or avenger of the blood is the agent of judicial punishment.

The conceptual framework of biblical law differs from ours primarily in its theological foundation (*see* LAW IN THE OT). Israel's law has the explicit authority of God behind it. As creator, God has authority to impose behavioral norms on creatures, and as Israel's covenant partner Yahweh has the community's explicit affirmation of authority to command. The law is given by God to remedy the violence and exploitation rampant in the human community. Yahweh establishes the system of judges to exercise judgment and supplements this with divine sanctions.

Hebrew has an abundance of words denoting offenses against the order established by Yahweh and against fellow members of society. The most common general terms are formed on the roots חָטָא (ht̠ʾ), עָוֹן (ʿwn), פָּשַׁע (pšʿ), רָעַע (rʿʿ), and רָשַׁע (ršʿ).

The meaning of the verb based on ht̠ʾ is *to miss*, but this nonmoral meaning is eclipsed by its theological use, *to sin*. The nouns formed on the root all mean *sin*. The verb and noun appear in accusations (e.g., Hos 4:7; Zeph 1:17), confessions of sin by individuals (e.g., 1 Sam 15:24; 2 Sam 24:10) or the people (e.g., Exod 32:31; 1 Sam 7:6). The words cover legal and social wrongdoing as well as cultic. Some expressions so link sin with punishment that we can speak of sin entailing its own punishment, e.g., the person must die in his ht̠ʾ (e.g., Num 27:3; Deut 24:16). If the perpetrator does not suffer, his family or the larger community will (e.g.,

Exod 20:5-6; 34:6-7). The fact that a theological term is one of the most common designations for crime is a clear indication that the theocratic mindset of Scripture qualifies all wrongdoing as acting against the will of the sovereign God.

The Hebrew verb עוה ('wh) and noun ('wn) have the basic meaning of *to pervert* and *perversity*. The noun is usually used figuratively with the sense of "guilt" or "iniquity" (what makes one guilty). Since the thought world of the OT links act and consequences, the noun 'awon can mean the punishment (e.g., Gen 19:15; Jer 51:6) as well as the deed (e.g., Isa 30:13; Ezek 18:19). Just as in the case of (ht'), punishment can be passed on to later generations (e.g., Lev 26:39-40; Isa 14:21; 53:11). The term is used in confessions (e.g., Lev 16:21; 26:40-45), accusations (e.g., Isa 43:24; Jer 5:25), and prophetic judgments (e.g., Isa 13:11; Jer 2:22).

The Hebrew words based upon פשע (ps') are frequently translated *transgress* and *transgression*, though these English words have become a bit archaic. Though once popular, the translation of the noun as *dispute* and *rebellion* has proved faulty. The use of the term in such passages as Exod 22:8 indicates that the word originated as a specific term for crime. It migrated to wisdom sayings (e.g., Prov 10:12; 17:9) and calls to repent and declarations of forgiveness (e.g., Ezek 18:30-31; Isa 43:25; 44:22). It was famously used in Amos's cycle of judgments against the nations (Amos 1:3, 6, 9, 11, 13; 2:1, 4, 6).

The various words based upon the root (r'') bear the meaning of *bad*, frequently with the moral connotation of *evil*. The expression, "do evil in Yahweh's eyes," occurs frequently (e.g., Num 32:13; Deut 4:25; 17:2; Judg 2:11; 10:6; 1 Sam 15:19; 1 Kgs 11:6; 14:22). There are many similar expressions (e.g., פעל p'l, *to do*, Mic 2:1, גמל gml, *to do to*, Ps 7:5). From this root we get a word that means *evildoer* (e.g., Isa 1:4; 14:20; Jer 20:13; 23:14; Job 8:20).

The root (rs') is an antonym of צדק (zdk), *righteous* (*see* RIGHTEOUSNESS IN THE OT); it can mean *impious* and *guilty*. The noun refers first to a person who threatens (e.g., Jer 5:26; Prov 12:6) or takes the life of an innocent person (e.g., 2 Sam 4:11). In addition to murder and violence, it can mean *rebellion* (e.g., Num 16:26), oppression of the poor (e.g., Ezek 18:5), and unfair commerce (e.g., Mic 6:10-11). It is used in par. to such words as *evildoers* (e.g., Ps 28:3; 92:8), the *violent* (e.g., Ps 11:5; 71:4), the *proud* (e.g., Ps 94:2-3), the *impudent* (e.g., Isa 13:11). While not a judicial term, it is used in legal contexts (e.g., Exod 23:1; Deut 25:1; compare 1 Kgs 8:31-32). When the people confess their sin before Yahweh, they may use (rs') as well as (ht') (e.g., 1 Kgs 8:47; Ps 106:6).

Numerous other Hebrew words could be added to our list, but most are more specialized. Some are terms for evil, e.g., און ('wn), rather than crime. מעל

(m'l) has the meaning to *be unfaithful*, often with the preposition ב (b), *with*, מרד (mrd) means *to rebel*. It derives from international treaties and was applied figuratively to religious apostasy. לון (lun) has much the same meaning, though in the LXX and thereafter it has borne the meaning of *to murmur*. The Hebrew word for *deception*, שקר (shqr), describes a component of many crimes and is the subject of the ninth commandment.

B. Crimes Against Persons
1. Cain
The first crime recounted in the biblical narrative is murder: Cain's slaying of his brother Abel (Gen 4:1-16). Born into a world quite different from the Eden from which their parents were expelled, the two brothers must labor for food and fiber; moreover, they are subject to the power of temptation. As yet there is no law; right and wrong are known by intuition.

The Lord is at the center of this first crime. While no law requires sacrifice, both Cain and Abel offer sacrifices of their respective sources of livelihood. The Lord approves Abel's but not Cain's. Interpreters have often speculated that Cain offered the wrong thing, or offered the right thing in the wrong spirit. The text mentions no defect in Cain's offering, though, and a better interpretation is that the Lord arbitrarily chose one and rejected the other. God does not owe humans acceptance and blessing, and our experience testifies to a great deal of disparity.

How would Cain handle the inequity? We find him in the grip of envy (4:5); the Lord warns him to suppress it (4:6-7). Note that Cain is already under the power of sin; he must overcome it or it will compel him into crime. And, of course, it does.

The Lord acts as judge. The only witness to the crime is the killer himself, but the Lord can know things without human help: Abel's blood testifies to the crime. This is more than physical evidence; the blood, which contains the power of life, testifies to the Creator. Henceforth, murder will be a source of pollution or defilement of the land and people among whom "blood is shed."

Cain's punishment is banishment from the soil. This is symbolic: the blood pollutes the ground, so the killer can no longer farm it. Banished from the soil, he also leaves the presence of the Creator.

Now the narrative context changes: the surviving son of the original human couple becomes an alien among foreign peoples and is vulnerable to murderous attacks. The divine judge protects him with a sign that threatens vengeance; now Cain can roam without place or God.

This first crime is thoroughly ad hoc. There is no law to be broken and no prescribed remedy for violation. Yet a crime has taken place, the perpetrator is responsible and guilty, and there is punishment for the crime calculated to at least symbolize its magnitude. A threshold has been crossed, and VIOLENCE becomes common.

2. Noah

Centuries pass and God decides that the creation of humans was a mistake: "every inclination of the thoughts of (human) hearts was only evil continually" (Gen 6:5). In particular, the earth "was filled with violence" (6:11) due to humans. At first God condemns the world to annihilation (6:7) but then changes the judgment (6:8): Seeds for a revived order will be preserved amid the destruction.

When Noah offers a thanksgiving sacrifice after departing the ark, the Lord promises never again to subject the world to such wholesale, indiscriminate judgment (8:20-22). The same promise is attached to the sign of the rainbow later (9:8-17). Then God institutes a new order: humans will be feared by animals, whose meat they can now eat (but not the blood). Moreover, it is forbidden to kill humans: Both animals and humans will be held accountable for such killing. The key sentence is: "Whoever sheds the blood of a human, by a human shall that person's blood be shed; for in his own image God made humankind" (9:6). Here we have the first law. In Jewish theology this became the Noachic COVENANT. All humans are within this covenant: other peoples may not remember the covenant made with Noah, but they know that murder is wrong.

Eventually, Jewish theology ascribed most of the "second table" (murder, adultery, theft, false testimony) to this universal law because all societies have laws on these subjects. In this way, Jewish theology could appreciate the lawfulness of all humans while observing Israel's status as the people of God.

3. Law within covenant

Israel receives its law at Sinai. The people first enter into covenant with Yahweh: they vow to obey whatever Yahweh commands, and Yahweh adopts the people as God's special possession, God's holy subjects (Exod 19:3-8). This covenant will be filled out with law. Yahweh is manifest in theophany on the mountain and proclaims a series of commands (20:1-17), which condense the law to eight memorable prohibitions and two prescriptions (see DECALOGUE). Most of the prohibitions stand for aspects of criminal law. Crimes against persons are covered by the prohibition against killing and against false witness. They are, like the rest, directly addressed by Yahweh to each and every Israelite, making respecting the person of fellow Israelites a matter of personal responsibility each owes Yahweh. The violation of another community member is a sin and not only a crime.

4. Codified homicide law

In addition to the TEN COMMANDMENTS several legal codes in the Pentateuch govern the judicial process for crimes at various levels of seriousness. The first of these codes follows the Decalogue immediately in Exod 20:22–23:33. It contains a collection of criminal laws under the name "judgments" (21:1–22:20).

Leviticus contains several law codes, but the only one covering criminal law is in chs. 17–26, the HOLINESS CODE. Additional laws are given in Numbers to supplement the Holiness Code.

Deuteronomy represents Moses' laws as words before his death; the core of the discourse is a legal code designed specifically for Israel's settled life in the land of Canaan. Each code derives from a different era and from a different place and theological school. The Deuteronomic law is a revision of the Covenant Code, while the Holiness Code is part of the Jerusalem priesthood's plan for a theocratic community after the exile.

The prohibition of killing in the Decalogue is unconditional, undifferentiated, and without stated punishment. Exodus 21:12 is also unconditional and undifferentiated: "Whoever strikes a person mortally shall be put to death." This statement does not engage the addressee as a moral subject but puts the act under the death penalty. It is not a CASUISTIC LAW because it does not specify how to assess guilt or who will execute the penalty. Its force is to permit the human community to kill—to act with divine authority. The distinctions necessary for a court decision are covered in the supplemental verses (vv. 13-14). Here a distinction is made between felonious and accidental homicide, and a provision is made to protect the latter from the family member of the victim charged with killing the killer (see AVENGER OF BLOOD).

Several other passages supplement the law of the Covenant Code. Numbers 35, a Priestly document, sets up the institution of cities of refuge, six cities set aside for killers as an alternative to the cryptic "place" or "my altar" of Exod 21:13-14. The killer will flee to a city of refuge, pursued by the avenger of the blood. There will be a trial—either in the city of refuge or in the city where the killing took place—to determine whether the killer is guilty of intentional homicide or not. If the judges find the killer guilty, the avenger of the blood will put him to death.

Both Exod 21:13-14 and Num 35:16-25 describe evidence distinguishing accidental from deliberate killing. Evidence of hatred or premeditation is primary, while acts performed on the spur of the moment seem to be regarded as innocent. Only Deut 19:5 describes a self-evident accident.

According to Priestly theology, killing—"blood"—defiles the land (35:33-34). If the killing is murder, the pollution can only be removed by the death of the guilty. If the killing is accidental, killing the killer in the city of refuge would incur additional pollution. However, the killer must await atonement for the killing that took place until the "high priest" (35:32) dies.

Until that atonement, the killer is only protected in the CITY OF REFUGE. Investing the high priest's death with atoning power indicates that this law belongs to the Southern Kingdom, Judah, where the Jerusalem Temple is recognized as premier sanctuary and its priests function for the whole country.

This document has some important rules for conducting murder trials. The system of cities of refuge was set up so that "the manslayer may not die until he stands before the congregation in judgment" (35:13). Though the avenger belongs to the tradition of blood feud, biblical law seeks to subordinate self-help to communal justice.

In a trial, conviction requires at least two witnesses. If followed strictly, this rule would have limited the efficacy of court trials severely, for killing frequently takes place in secret (compare Deut 27:24). Evidence must have filled the gap.

Finally, a convicted killer could not ransom his life: he or she must die for attacking a being, who is made in the image of God (35:31). Here biblical law was revolutionary within the ancient Near East. All CUNEIFORM codes and court records from Mesopotamia and the Hittites either prescribe or allow for monetary settlement between the murderer and the family of the victim. In other words, ransom was permitted by the legal communities surrounding Israel. Israel alone held human life in such high regard that the only "payment" a killer could make was his own life. Indeed, even the accidental homicide could not offer a ransom to avoid a long stay in the city of refuge (35:32).

Deuteronomy 19:1-13 also legislates for cities of refuge. For unknown reasons, the cities do not match Num 35, and the rules of operation differ. In Num 35 the cities of refuge were LEVITICAL CITIES; not so in Deuteronomy. Although the cities are to protect accidental homicides and seem to envisage similar legal processes, one might think that the protected killer in Deut 19 could return home upon being declared innocent.

The cities of refuge are for protection of the innocent: they are designed to subordinate blood feud to judicial order. The nation is under equal danger of incurring guilt for killing an accidental homicide and for allowing the guilty to escape capital punishment.

Deuteronomy has a somewhat different conception of collective guilt from the Priestly law. In Deut 21:1-9, a ritual is prescribed for elders in a town where a slaying has taken place but the perpetrator is unknown. The crime threatens the nation with guilt, and the ritual consists of an oath of clearance and the slaughter of a heifer and hand-washing. What Priestly theology would use to remove the pollution of the land, Deuteronomy uses to plead for God's forgiveness of the nation.

5. Other crimes against persons

The Covenant Code contains provisions for other crimes against persons. Not all killing falls cleanly into premeditated and accidental. When a master kills a slave while beating him, it is punishable, but several factors distinguish it from ordinary homicide. The master has a right to beat his slave to compel him to work, whereas no citizen has that right with a fellow citizen. Moreover, slaves may not have been accorded the same value as free persons. Ancient Near Eastern law differentiated between slaves and two classes of free humans. Israelite theology in theory accorded all humans equal value and respect, but slave status may well have diminished a person in law (see Exod 21:32). This form of discrimination was reduced by the Deuteronomic Code (see Deut 15:12-18; 23:15-16).

If a person's ox killed someone, the owner was not guilty of a crime unless the animal was known to gore and the owner had not taken steps to protect the public (21:28-31). If the owner was guilty of negligence, his life could be forfeit, but he was permitted to negotiate a price for redemption.

Finally, if a homeowner killed a burglar breaking into his house, he was not guilty of felonious homicide if the killing took place at night, but was if it occurred during the day (Exod 22:2-3).

If a person injured a fellow citizen in a fight, it was not a crime, but he did owe indemnity (damages). If a pregnant woman suffered a miscarriage while witnessing a fight, the person responsible must negotiate a settlement with her husband. If the woman herself were harmed, then the case would be treated as a crime against a person (note the citation of a poetic version of the LEX TALIONIS). These few cases hardly exhaust the types of injury that would arise in law, but they could function as paradigms.

6. Kidnapping

Among the capital crimes in Exod 21:12-17, one reads, "Whoever steals a man, whether he sells him or is found in his possession, shall be put to death" (21:16 RSV; NRSV reads, "kidnaps a person"). This is kidnapping for selling into SLAVERY, not for ransom, as in the story of Joseph in Gen 37: Joseph's brothers so hated him that they planned to kill him but decided instead to sell him to slave traders. In the ancient Near East, where slaves could be traded to foreigners to make it impossible for a family to rescue the stolen member, this act was equivalent to killing. Hence, the penalty of death. The case envisaged in Exod 21:16 is of slave traders who overpowered victims and whisked them out of the country before a family could act. All the court needed was evidence of sale to convict the criminal. Deuteronomy 24:7 repeats this law.

7. Family violence

Preceding and following the condemnation of kidnapping are two violations of parents: striking and cursing (21:15, 17). One can recognize that these two capital crimes are the negative version of the commandment to honor parents (20:12). Nevertheless, penalties are certainly exorbitant. It is probable that the laws were seldom if ever applied. Parents bring the complaint, and they would have to be extremely exasperated to do so. Deuteronomy 22:18-21 provides a realistic description of the kind of situation that might provoke capital punishment of offspring. A son who is constantly unruly and violent with parents provokes the latter to appeal to the elders. Before execution, the elders would have tried to straighten him out.

Although one might regard the prohibition against *reviling* (קלל qll) God and *cursing* (ערר 'rr) a ruler as moral exhortation (Exod 22:28), at least once in biblical history it was cited as crime. When Naboth refused to sell his vineyard to Ahab, Jezebel conspired to have Naboth charged with violation of this prohibition; he was condemned and executed, and his property confiscated by the crown (1 Kgs 21).

8. False witness

The court system, designed to remedy violence and injustice, can become a perpetrator. The killing of Naboth engineered by Jezebel involved false witnesses swaying a court of Naboth's peers. In this case, false accusation was a crime against a person. However, even false accusation of theft—which entails only monetary penalty—assaults the falsely accused who had his reputation tarnished.

Deuteronomy 17:2-6 is a paradigm case of protecting the innocent from false charges. The case is apostasy—worshiping a god or subordinate being. The accused is not caught in the act, but an accuser testifies to it. If the court can confirm the charge, the accused is executed. The case ends with a warning not to convict on the testimony of one person; the accuser must be supported by one or more non-party attesters. Moreover, psychological pressure is put on witnesses by requiring them to cast the first stones; a guilty conscience might well expose a malicious accuser or an accomplice.

If a court has doubts about the truth of the charges of an accuser, they can go, according to Deut 19:15-21, to an appellate court in Jerusalem, where the parties will be examined to determine who is telling the truth. If it is determined that the accuser testified out of malice, he (or she) should be punished with the penalty that jeopardized the accused. The lawgiver cites the LEX TALIONIS to explain the penalty: life for life, eye for eye, tooth for tooth, hand for hand, foot for foot. Of course, this is metaphor; mutilation was not imposed in biblical law (with the odd exception of Deut 25:11-12). The court might, of course, decide that the accuser was testifying in good faith but had made some mistake or lacked decisive evidence; in that case, there could be no punishment of either party.

The COVENANT CODE has a set of commandments in Exod 23:1-3, 6-9 protecting the court process.

The prohibitions in 23:1-3 are directed to witnesses: You shall not spread a false report. You shall not join hands with the wicked to act as a malicious witness (v. 1). The prohibitions cited are deliberate acts of false testimony—as an accuser or a supporting witness. Both witnesses and judges must avoid the mood of the mob and class prejudice; taking bribes or allying with one of the parties will also corrupt the process.

9. Judicial authority

Several passages set up a modest judicial hierarchy in Israel, making insubordination a crime against the judicial system itself. According to Exod 18:13-27, Moses was judging all criminal and civil cases by himself, and is advised by his father-in-law to set up courts of original jurisdiction. Exceptionally difficult cases should come to Moses; he could seek a divine oracle if he did not know the answer. Numbers 11, which could well be another etiology of the same institution, also recounts the delegation of Mosaic authority to "elders."

In the Deuteronomic Code, the role of Moses seems to be taken by a court consisting of a "judge" and a multiplicity of priests (*see* 17:8-13). When the court of original jurisdiction finds a case too hard, it goes to the Jerusalem court. There is no mention of oracles in this description of the appellate court; they may have based decisions on tradition and wisdom. Their decision, nevertheless, has the force of law; the court of original jurisdiction is duty-bound to comply. Deviation is a capital crime.

C. Crimes Against Property

The Covenant Code can be divided at the end of Deut 21; beginning with 21:33 the subject changes from death and injury to persons to loss of property. Verses 21:33-36 serve as a transition; the subject of oxen remains, but now it is injury to animals. The first case is of an uncovered pit into which an animal falls. The owner of the pit pays for the loss. This is a civil penalty, not punishment for a crime. Civil law persists in the cases that follow, of an ox that gores another ox.

1. Theft

Exodus 22:1-4 contains rulings on theft. One has to do with killing during burglary; it is a crime against a person but gains its peculiar features from the occasion. The remainder prescribes repayment for theft. Biblical law treats theft more according to the pattern of a civil action than a criminal proceeding. The thief repays in kind (cow for cow, etc.), plus one or more in compensation for distress. A guilty person who could not pay, like one who could not pay off loans, would be sold into slavery to pay the bill.

The remaining laws on property (Exod 22:5-15) are either civil actions or borderline. Laws covering damage to fields and animals simply require replacement. If a person holds another's animal in trust, the bailee may avoid repayment if the animal was stolen or killed by wild animals. If there is no evidence, the bailee must take an OATH. Other disputes over ownership were also settled by oath, or perhaps by lot if an oath didn't bring resolution.

To understand the treatment of property in Israelite law, we must realize that persons and property were incommensurable in value. Moshe Greenberg was the first critical scholar to bring this to our attention, and J. J. Finkelstein reformulated Greenberg's thesis in a more secular vein. The thesis is based on the observation that no human life, except that of slaves, has monetary value placed on it in crimes against persons: The only value equal to the victim's value is the life of the killer. On the other hand, property can be replaced. In the hierarchy of beings, animals and inanimate objects are below humans, while humans are accorded infinite value by possessing the "image of God" (Gen 9:6).

Debate persists over whether such a subtle philosophical concept actually informs biblical law. Some scholars believe ancient Israelites were incapable of this level of abstraction. However, the texts bear such interpretation whether their authors appreciated it or not. Moreover, this conceptual scheme constructs a subtle, profound interpretation, congruent with mature theology.

Considering the proportion of a court docket devoted to crimes against property, one would expect more remedial law on the subject in the Pentateuch. The little section in Exod 22:1-15 is all that we have on larceny. On commercial trade, we have no criminal law, only a series of commandments urging merchants to use just weights and measures (Lev 19:35-36; Deut 25:13-16).

2. Real property
had weightier status than movable property
A family's share in the LAND was its share in the people. At the end of the conquest of Canaan, the land was divided among the tribes (Josh 13–23). Tribal territory was subdivided among families; each male member of the family should possess a share of the family's property. If a family member had to sell property due to financial distress, or other crisis, members of the extended family tried to purchase it to avoid an outsider owning a portion of the family's inheritance. If land was purchased by an outsider, according to the law in Lev 25:13-28, it reverted to the family in the Jubilee Year (once every fifty yrs.).

An individual male passed on his inheritance to his sons, the oldest receiving a double portion (*see* Deut 21:15-17). If the man had no sons, his daughters could inherit (Num 27:1-11) as long as they married within their tribe (Num 36:1-12). If the man had no children, the property passed to the nearest male kin (27:8-11). There is no criminal law covering real property. The laws cited above are laws governing primary rights

and duties. If their provisions were violated, the victim could seek redress; however, no biblical laws specify what that might be.

One of the TEN COMMANDMENTS may cover property theft tangentially: "you shall not covet your neighbor's house" (Exod 20:17*a*). The Hebrew word for COVET, חמד (hmd), means *desire*, but in some biblical passages it is closely linked to action. Micah 2:1-2 is a case in point:

> Woe to those who devise wickedness
>   and work evil upon their beds!
> When the morning dawns, they perform it
>   because it is in the power of their hand.
> They covet fields and seize them,
>   and houses, and take them;
> they oppress a man and his house,
>   a man and his inheritance. (RSV)

Coveting belongs to a stage of the theft of property. Theft of real estate is quite different from theft of movable property. Displacing the owner of the land must be done with the semblance of legality; one must use economic and judicial institutions to achieve one's goal. Prophetic condemnation of property theft implies deeper social and institutional corruption and oppression.

3. Protections of the vulnerable
The law codes have numerous provisions designed to protect the poor, widows and orphans, and sojourners. (*See* ORDER OF WIDOWS.) The Covenant Code has a set of prohibitions against oppressing the vulnerable (Exod 22:21-24; 23:9), followed by two provisions regarding lending. Loans to the poor should not entail interest: this would take advantage of the debtor's distress (*see* DEBT, DEBTOR). Clothing taken in pawn should be returned at night. These laws have the sound of moral preachments more than enforceable rights and duties. Hence, one should not be surprised to find divine sanctions (22:23-24, 27). Similar moral law exists in the Holiness and Deuteronomic Codes as well (e.g., Lev 20:9-10, 13-14; Deut 15:1-11; 23:15-16, 19-20).

Preachments protecting vulnerable members of society take on their full weight in the accusations of the prophets of judgment. We have already cited Micah's condemnation of the rich appropriating the land of the poor. Amos condemns the powerful who sell the bankrupt into slavery:

> they sell the righteous for silver,
>   and the needy for a pair of sandals. (2:6)

Probably the people sold into slavery owed money on loans and could not make the payments. There was no provision for bankruptcy in ancient law. A man would sell his children, then his wife, and finally himself. Other members of his extended family should intervene according to Lev 25:35-54, but evidently often did not. These transactions were legal; indeed, much of it was simply the enforcement of credit law. It took the prophets to expose the immoral discrepancy between a person and the monetary value that was exchanged for that life. Thus Amos and Isaiah expostulated against courts that produced such outrageous injustice, e.g.,

> Woe to those who decree iniquitous decrees,
>   and the writers who keep writing oppression,
> to turn aside the needy from justice
>   and to rob the poor of my people of their right,
> that widows may be their spoil,
>   and that they may make orphans their prey!
>   (Isa 10:1-2 RSV)

The prophetic case against the nations of Israel and Judah is not for petty theft, but of wholesale injustice, oppression in the name of the law.

D. Criminal Conversation

The title given this category is taken from Anglo-American law: it designates ADULTERY, the violation of MARRIAGE by sexual infidelity, and has the advantage of containing the word *crime*. The focal point that draws these cases together is the act of sexual intercourse; whether a crime has been committed depends upon the status of the parties.

The act of sexual intercourse is unlike any other human act in that it alone makes an exclusive claim on those engaged. The partners are supposed to be married, pledged to fidelity to their partner for life. The violation of this exclusive relationship is the crime of adultery, forbidden in the TEN COMMANDMENTS.

Marriage is grounded in creation. According to the CREATION account in Gen 2, the Lord created the whole range of animal life in search for a partner for his human, but had finally to create the being from the man's flesh. When the man awoke, he recognized the woman as "bone of my bones and flesh of my flesh" (2:23). The narrator observes "therefore a man leaves his father and his mother and cleaves to his wife, and they become one flesh" (2:24). Here we have the primal community. No other society or power has the right to violate it.

According to Genesis, ancient rulers respected the claims of marriage. According to the story in Gen 12:10-20, Abram feared the Egyptians would kill him to appropriate his beautiful wife, so he and Sarai pretended they were brother and sister. Sarai was taken into Pharaoh's house, but before he could have sexual intercourse with her the Lord intervened with plagues to warn him of his crime. He accuses Abram of deception but nevertheless returns his wife and sends them away. The pharaoh clearly recognized that the marriage bond was under divine protection.

The biblical codes are eccentric in their coverage. We have no criminal law on marriage in the Covenant Code. There is one ruling, isolated at the end of the judgments (22:16-17), which specifies the terms for resolution of a case of premarital sex. The wording says the man *seduced* the unattached girl, but the ruling would probably not differ if it were forced sexual intercourse. Since the girl is not engaged, the proposed remedy is marriage. If the girl's father does not approve of the match, he can reject it. (The girl's attitude toward the man preferably conditions her father's answer.)

Aside from this case, the Covenant Code sets out rules for the treatment of a female slave who is married into her owner's family (Exod 21:7-14). She is guaranteed the minimal rights of a married woman despite her inferior status.

1. Prohibited sexual partners

The HOLINESS CODE has little to say about the institution of marriage per se, but it has a long series of prohibited sexual partners (Lev 18:6-20, 22-23). The core of this list is women too closely related to the male addressee; sexual intercourse with them would amount to incest. Oddly, the addressee's daughter is not mentioned.

The incest list is supplemented by a disparate list of prohibited sexual acts or partners. For humanitarian reasons, a man should not marry a mother and daughter, and not be married to sisters at the same time (18:17-18). Then there is the prohibition of intercourse at a certain time of the menstrual cycle (v. 19), the only commandment concerning a prohibited act with a proper partner. Then comes adultery; here its immorality is complemented by its cultic force of defilement (v. 20). At the end of the list are male sexual intercourse and bestiality (vv. 22-23); these are condemned as "abomination" and "perversion." That's as far as the OT goes in explaining what is immoral about these acts.

In the middle of the list is a prohibition of "devoting your children to Molech by fire" (v. 21). This probably means child sacrifice to the god Molech, though there is some uncertainty. We can understand why child sacrifice is classified as a crime, but not why it is listed among sexual crimes.

The list of prohibitions is matched in Lev 20 with penalties: capital punishment or divine sanctions. Why incest taboos should be treated as judiciable is hard to say; it would seem adequate to declare such unions null and void.

2. Adultery

Adultery on the other hand, was the sort of violation for which one would expect capital punishment. A set of laws on that subject is preserved in Deut 22:13-30. Straightforward ADULTERY is condemned in 22:22: both man and woman shall be put to death, and there appears to be no prospect of mitigating the penalty. The case is simple because the violators are caught in the act. Numbers 5:16-28 proposes a ritual for resolving the case of a suspected adultery (though it only assesses the wife).

Two laws covering sexual intercourse between a betrothed woman and a man other than her future husband follow. The woman is regarded as married, so she and the man are treated as adulterers. If the violation occurs in the open country, however, the woman is accorded the benefit of the doubt. That is, it could have been coerced intercourse. This is the only legal recognition of rape that we encounter in any of the biblical laws.

Although Deut 22:23-27 speaks of a betrothed woman, it could just as well be applied to a woman who has been married for some time. That is not the case with the unusual situation treated in 22:13-21. Here a groom charges his bride with not being a virgin, and he seeks dissolution. If his charge proved true, the bride would be executed. Women destined for marriage were not to have had sexual intercourse with anyone before marriage. To save their daughter, the parents could submit a bloody sheet as evidence of the girl's virginity.

A prostitute would not be subject to the rules for brides. Deuteronomy prohibits cultic prostitution (23:17-18), though it is mentioned as practiced from time to time (e.g., 1 Sam 2:22; 2 Kgs 23:7?). However, there was "secular" prostitution that the biblical law seems to have ignored (e.g., Gen 38:15-21; 1 Kgs 3:16). Married men who had sexual intercourse with unattached women were not regarded as adulterers, as they would be now. Because ancient Israel permitted polygamy, fidelity to one woman was not expected of men, as fidelity to one man was expected of a wife. This double standard extended to extramarital sexual intercourse.

This double standard was challenged by the prophet Hosea: in 4:13b-14, the Lord cites the harlotry of daughters and brides, and then says that since it is their fathers and husbands who are fornicating with them, the women will not be punished (as their men folk would demand). Marital infidelity continued to be a subject of prophetic accusation (see e.g., Jer 2:20, 23-24, 33-35; 23:14), though often adultery is a metaphor for apostasy. Hosea introduced this metaphor, with reference to his marital experience, and it became standard in subsequent prophecy, giving the abstract sin of apostasy a more personal, intimate force.

E. Apostasy, Idolatry, and Other Religious Crimes

We have no ideal English word for the violation of the commandment (Exod 20:3) not to recognize any deity but Yahweh, the God of Israel. *Apostasy* must suffice; it means the abandonment of one's creed or party. Take it to cover an Israelite who honors another deity in worship or moral practice, or even in the interpretation of experience.

Idolatry in the strict sense is the making of an object, which is regarded as an "incarnation" of a supernatural being, and the performance of acts of worship directed to this object. This is prohibited in Exod 20:4.

The next commandment—second or third of the Ten Commandments (Decalogue) according to one's tradition—forbids taking Yahweh's name "in vain." There are several different, legitimate applications of this prohibition, some of which would be classified as crimes in the Pentateuch.

Other religious practices are not covered in the Decalogue but are of criminal magnitude within orthodox Yahwism. Divination and child sacrifice belong here.

1. Revelation

The categories of crime treated so far are common to human society; we can call them "natural" law. Those in this category are unique to Israel, obligatory for a partner to the covenant with Yahweh. Other peoples had religious laws with criminal sanctions, but not these laws. Present-day readers think of them as beliefs. However, they fit the definition of law within the Bible because the people have sworn to obey Yahweh, and these are Yahweh's commandments. In other words, the commandments have full authority according to the criteria of that legal community. Moreover, they do not depend solely on the authority of the sovereign; they are justified as fitting and advantageous to the people.

2. Apostasy

When the Israelites at Mount Sinai entered into covenant with Yahweh, a covenant that elevates them to the status of a holy nation quite unlike any other, they agreed to obey everything Yahweh commands them (Exod 19:3-8) (*see* COVENANT). The Decalogue is the first, and foremost, expression of Yahweh's will for God's people. At the head of the first table is the prohibition against having (= recognizing) any deity but Yahweh, a jealous God, who seeks the people's undivided loyalty. They were called upon to suppress their normal polytheistic inclinations; they were accustomed to a totally different regime, one in which numerous deities and spirits were given their due. Yahweh and Israel were embarked on a journey that had never before been negotiated. This struggle is going to last until Israel goes into exile.

Recognizing Yahweh alone as their God affected the life of Israel most prominently in the area of worship (Exod 34:14). Within the Covenant Code, sacrificing to another deity is a capital crime (Exod 23:20). The names of other gods are not even to be on Israelite lips (23:13).

Deuteronomy 13 is the fullest treatment of what would count as criminal violation: a prophet advocating apostasy, a family member advocating apostasy, a whole city led into apostasy. Each case is punished as a capital crime. In Deuteronomy, it should be noted, apostasy is on the order of political treason.

According to Deuteronomy, Israel is to heed only prophets who speak in the name of Yahweh (Deut 13:1-5; 18:20). A prophet who speaks in the name of another deity has committed a capital crime. Claiming Yahweh's authority for a prophet's message is no guarantee that it is true, but claiming any other authority is a crime.

3. Apologetic narrative

The pentateuchal narrative plays a special apologetic role in behalf of the first commandment. This is intimated in the text of the Ten Commandments itself: before the prohibition there is a self-introduction, "I am Yahweh your God, who brought you out of the land of Egypt, out of the house of slaves" (20:2). The Lord is known by reference to a particular history. What God did for the addressee gives grounds for trust in God's beneficent purposes. Faith is not a blind leap but a considered decision.

Let us trace this apologetic further. Exodus 20:3 is the first time in the pentateuchal narrative that the prohibition against recognizing other deities is given. To this point, no other deity is named and the few references to deities demote them to shadowy figures. Creation is ascribed to the one God, whose inconceivable power is worked upon a passive realm of being. There is one furtive allusion to the other deities (Gen 1:26); this same mysterious "we" shows up a few more times, but bears no weight.

When the patriarch Abraham and his family move to Canaan and become the human protagonists, the outsiders with whom they deal all relate to the same deity as they do. It is as if the gods of the Canaanite peoples were identified with Yahweh. The opposite will be the case in the conquest narrative.

When the family moves to Egypt and becomes a people, they are enslaved by a pharaoh who never speaks of or appeals to Egyptian deities. The Egyptians have recourse to magic but not to supernatural beings. There are no deities to attract the Israelites, who remain loyal to their ancestral God (note Exod 4:30-31). When the Israelites leave Egypt, they have several serious conflicts with Moses and Yahweh, but they do not take recourse to other gods.

Only after the people have heard the commandment do they begin to pursue other deities (Exod 32). It is as if the prohibition prompts its violation; alternatively, it redefines refractoriness as apostasy. The temptation to apostasy grows in the conquest; one of the first events on the edges of the land is the apostasy to BAAL PEOR (Num 25). This is the sort of apostasy the people were warned of before they left Mount Sinai (Exod 23:23-26, 32-33; 34:12-16). Hosea traced the long history of apostasy back to Baal Peor (9:10).

He and subsequent prophets found apostasy to be the fundamental sin of Israel and Judah (e.g., Hos 2:2-13; Jer 2:1-17; Ezek 20).

The narrative from creation to conquest shows how Yahweh alone had been the one and only God in Israel's story. As Deuteronomy puts it, the other gods are "gods you have not known" (13:2, 6). Of course, the people were familiar with these gods; they were not, however, part of their story.

4. Idolatry

Exodus 20:4 prohibits the manufacture and worship of idols of any sort. Some traditions number this the second commandment while others subsume it under recognizing other gods. A prime reason for considering it a separate commandment is that it covers actions that do not constitute apostasy. In particular, it applies to images of Yahweh as well as to other deities. It would also apply to images that are accessory, such as "golden calves" (Exod 32; 1 Kgs 12) or the cherubim in the Jerusalem Temple.

Did the prohibition apply to the ARK OF THE COVENANT? It was not an image but a plain box on which one would imagine YHWH enthroned. If the essence of an idol was that it incarnated a supernatural being, the ark is a good candidate. See the story of the ark's capture by the Philistines (1 Sam 5–6).

A significant number of passages regard idols as gods, hence idolatry as apostasy. The wording of Exod 20:3-6 does so. Verse 3 mentions "gods" in the plural, whereas v. 4 has idol in the singular; the expansion in v. 5 refers to "them," which would naturally be to "gods," though bowing down is an appropriate action for an image. *Serve*, on the other hand, is a suitable response to a god, not an image. The upshot is that the gods of v. 3 have been identified with the images of v. 4.

The prohibition of images in the Covenant Code evidences the same identification. Exodus 20:23 tells the people not to set up "gods of silver/gold" in Yahweh's presence, a designation that personifies them. Since this prohibition is followed by a command to build altars across the land at every location where revelation has occurred (20:24), the natural surmise is that the addressees are not to set up these images at Yahwistic altars. In other words, the commandment concerns public sanctuaries: Yahweh does not tolerate competitors at his worship sites. If there are no images, there will be no "gods" either. This is reinforced later by the condemnation of sacrifices to other gods (Exod 22:20) and prohibition of uttering their names (23:13). The command to build sites all over the land had the force, probably, of claiming the land exclusively for Yahweh. That is, the sanctuary dedicated to Yahweh made Yahweh the exclusive owner of the territory served by the altar.

Several collections of law have only the prohibition of images, e.g., Lev 19:4; 26:1; Deut 27:15. The use of images was probably so common in the practice of polytheism that prohibiting images made any worship impossible. However, we do have one story of prayers to Baal to light the sacrificial fire in which no images are mentioned (1 Kgs 18:20-29). This passage satirizes rituals used to arouse Baal, and images are not a part of it.

The making and worship of idols is itself the subject of much satire. Humans making gods is intrinsically incongruent. One can add the humor of using the same wood for fire and for the image (e.g., Isa 44:14-20). Moreover, the images have human features, like eyes, ears, and a mouth, but they cannot see, hear, or speak (Ps 115:3-8). Images lack any life (Jer 10:2-10). For many such reasons, idols are the height of folly.

There is much more satire of idols than of the deities they represent. It would seem that the satirists intended the reader to apply the critique of idols to the gods represented.

Once idolatry has become the subject of satire, it has declined or disappeared as a temptation. Now interpreters of the law must find reapplications of the prohibition against idolatry if the law is to continue to perform a function. One already detects some reapplication in Deut 4. Moses condemns images because they reduce God to the dimensions of a creature (4:15-18). Other peoples are allowed these objects of worship, but not Israel (4:20). Job also renounces the worship of the host of heaven (31:26-28), and adds trusting and taking pride in wealth (31:24-25). Deuteronomy 8:12-14, 17-19 seems also to associate pride in wealth with idolatry. This line of interpretation continues to this day; it has long since ceased, though, to designate a crime.

5. Other crimes

The prohibition of uttering Yahweh's name "in vain" is rather broad, applying to any inappropriate use of the divine name. One used the name Yahweh in vows, oaths, and covenants (e.g., Num 30:3; Judg 8:19; 1 Sam 20:12, 42). If one did not fulfill one's vow, oath, or covenant, divine punishment would follow. This commandment could well cover such a case.

There is, however, a more explicit application. In Lev 24:10-16, we read a case of uttering the divine name in anger. This behavior is known as BLASPHEMY. The offender was put to death by divine stipulation. If the person had used the neutral title, God, instead, punishment would be left up to God's discretion.

Some interpreters would include the use of the divine name in curses. There were legitimate uses for curses: we have them used liturgically in Deut 27 and as a warning to obey Yahweh's law in Deut 28. These are conditional curses. One could also curse an unknown thief or wrongdoer (e.g., Judg 17:2). The forbidden curse would be one with malicious intent without legal justification. Probably the condemnation of sorcery (Exod 22:18) is meant to suppress such activity.

There are ancient Near Eastern parallels to applications of this law. Failure to abide by what one has sworn to do is wrong in every society. The practice and prohibition of profanity is universal too. Even the CODE OF HAMMURABI condemns witchcraft. Thus, the third commandment is not unique to Israel. It does nevertheless depend upon revelation for its validity, if for no other reason it is Yahweh's name that is protected.

Deuteronomy 18:9-14 outlaw all means of receiving supernatural knowledge except prophecy. The lawgiver assumes that Yahweh will communicate messages to Israel only through messengers who speak in God's name; communication must be addressed and direct. The other means listed in Deut 18:9-14 and echoed in Lev 19:31 fall under the general category of divination. DIVINATION is defined as seeking to know the future or the hidden by occult means. Several entail consulting the dead; others are based on "signs" in the heavens or in the livers of sacrificial animals. Casting lots would have to be so classified as well, though Israel herself cast lots early in its history.

Deuteronomy identifies making a son or daughter "pass through fire" as a religious abomination practiced by previous inhabitants of the land (see 12:31; 18:10). This is probably child immolation, murder compounded by misguided religious devotion. In Mic 6:7, the people ask the prophet whether child sacrifice should be practiced in the name of Yahweh. Micah, of course, gives an answer that points the people in an entirely different direction. Ezekiel, however, has the deity admit that Yahweh had commanded bad laws like child sacrifice to horrify them (20:25-26). Jeremiah, on other hand, says the idea of child sacrifice had never crossed Yahweh's mind (7:31).

The HOLINESS CODE also has a law criminalizing child sacrifice. The crime is described as "giving a child to Molech" (Lev 20:2, 3, 4). The act here is apparently an act of devotion to a god named MOLECH. According to 1 Kgs 11:7, Molech was a god of the Ammonites. It is possible, though, that Molech is an altered form of **melek** (*king*), a title that could be applied to Yahweh (see Pss 5:3; 10:16, etc.). The wording of Lev 20:5 does, however, describe the act as apostasy ("playing the harlot after Molech").

6. Honoring the holy

The Sabbath commandment (Exod 20:8-11) can be criminally violated. One could perform activities that have been defined as work (see Exod 32:14) or require those under one to do it. Numbers 15:32-36 recounts a precedent for executing a person gathering firewood on the SABBATH. Legal scholars were still debating what would count as forbidden labor at the time of Jesus (see Mark 2:23-28; 3:1-6).

Failure to perform cultic duties, presumably, was criminal. For example, Israelites were expected to appear "before the Lord"—at a legitimate sanctuary, perhaps a national shrine—three times a year (Exod 23:14-17). It adds that "no one shall appear before me empty-handed" (v. 15); in other words, worshipers should render any sacrifice due. A number of sacrifices were owed by farmers and cattlemen from flocks, herds, and fields.

In Num 16, we hear of a challenge to priestly privilege (16:3) led by Korah, a Levite. The rebel position was that all the people are holy. Aaron's hereditary rights were vindicated by divine judgment on Korah and his supporters (16:31-36). One must assume every challenge to priestly authority was under threat of sanction.

F. Punishments

Neither Israel nor its neighbors punished by imprisonment (*see* PRISON). For crimes against property, the felon returned or replaced what was stolen and then compensated the victim by adding one or more of the animal or item stolen. Other types of crime prompted execution or physical punishment. A murderer was to be executed by the avenger of the blood, using a sword. When a court acted collectively to execute a capital offender, they stoned the offender; the accuser(s) cast the first stone (*see* STONING). This mode of punishment symbolized the expulsion of the wrongdoer from the community. Burning is mentioned for a few crimes involving sexual misbehavior (Gen 38:24; Lev 20:14); no explanation is offered for these exceptions. There is mention of flogging in Deut 22:18 and it is regulated in 25:1-3 (*see* SCOURGING). The *lex talionis* prescribes mutilation for bodily injuries (*see* Lev 24:19-20), but again it is not attached to any case law. Only once is mutilation prescribed in remedial rulings (Deut 25:1-3). The formula "cut off" is frequently used in the Holiness Code (e.g., Lev 20:17, 18); it may be a divine punishment or perhaps excommunication.

The religious crimes mentioned above would not be classified as crimes in modern Western societies. Even within ancient Israel enforcement was sporadic. The prophets, particularly Hosea, Jeremiah, and Ezekiel, accuse their people of routine violation of the first and second commandments. Evidently the Valley of Hinnom became so notorious for its child sacrifices (*see* Jer 7:30-34) that its name was given to hell.

We do read of occasional suppression of the worship of Baal. The most notorious purge was performed by Jehu, who slaughtered thousands of Baal worshipers invited to the temple in Samaria under false pretenses (2 Kgs 10:18-27). Hosea condemns Jehu's dynasty for the bloody events at its founding, presumably including this purge (Hos 1:4-5). There were sporadic "cleansings" of the Jerusalem Temple (e.g., 1 Kgs 15:12-13). The most significant by far was Josiah's reform (2 Kgs 23), which destroyed or covered up sanctuaries around the countryside and thoroughly cleansed the Jerusalem Temple itself. Such sporadic "reforms" do not constitute legal enforcement. The exile announced by the prophets can be understood as divine enforcement of religious crimes not enforced by law.

G. Historical Perspective

The law codes preserved in the Pentateuch derive from different periods and are suited to different polities. There are unresolved debates among scholars as to dates and contexts. The following is a moderate position that provides a coherent legal history.

Most of our documents derive from the era when the people of God exercised political power and applied their own law to the crimes that occurred in their midst. That era would be prior to the Babylonian exile. We can date the public appearance of Deuteronomy to Josiah's reform (621 BCE). The Ten Commandments may well come from the same school. The book of the covenant seems to be a cent. or more older. The Holiness Code and Priestly Law—found in Leviticus and Numbers—may preserve old Jerusalem Temple law and procedure, but its final form, granting the "high priest" supreme authority, is a design for reconstructing the Jerusalem religious community after the exile.

The Covenant Code was probably not "legislation" but a collection of teachings, regarding how to live to please Yahweh and how to decide cases involving violations of the proper ordering of society. Portions of this code may have used the Code of Hammurabi as a prototype. The rulings, however, are uniquely Yahwistic in reasoning and theology. Some of them may be idealistic—what the law should be whether it was practical or not.

The Deuteronomic Code revises the legal tradition represented by the Covenant Code; it is a "reform" document requiring a single legitimate sanctuary within Israel. This reform required a rather thoroughgoing revision of cultic practices and piety. Legal authority was also centralized and the citizen army revived.

The Priestly Law is also programmatic, restoring the religious community after the Babylonian exile. The community for which this document was designed did not regain independent political power. Judea was a minor province within the Persian Empire. However, the Jews had sufficient autonomy to preside over their own judicial system. In the diaspora, too, Jews had their own courts for cases among Jews. The law, thus, continued to be authoritative in a legal community.

However, the idealistic and hypothetical tendencies of the law took on a life of their own. Provisions of scriptural law became the subject of discussion, and new legal principles and practices arose from these discussions. Disputing "parties" or schools emerged in the Hellenistic era. Pharisees and Essenes generated a rigorous application of Torah to daily life, while the Sadducees claimed to stand by tradition. The matters that divided them were not in the area of criminal law, or not often so, but in the areas of cultic purity and holiness.

H. New Testament

The early Christian church had no legal jurisdiction and therefore produced no body of criminal law. Such authority was ceded to whatever governing authorities had jurisdiction over church members. These are said to be servants of God: "for there is no authority except from God, and those authorities that exist have been instituted by God" (Rom 13:1). The authorities enforce criminal law: government "is God's servant for your good. But if you do what is wrong, you should be afraid, for [it] does not bear the sword in vain! It is the servant of God to execute wrath on the wrongdoer" (Rom 13:4).

Jesus' message of the kingdom of God involved a critique of criminal law and a "counter" legal or moral order suited to the kingdom. The ministers of the early church adapted the uncompromising teaching of its founder and Lord to the practice of the fellowship and the lives of individual members. Forgiveness and excommunication were areas where church leaders exercised disciplinary authority.

The gospel not only offers teaching about what is a crime in the light of the kingdom that is dawning, but it also tells the story of Jesus' trial and execution as a criminal. In this case, criminal law takes on a sinister aspect, which calls for a rectification beyond history.

1. The kingdom of God

Mark summarizes Jesus' message as the "kingdom of God has come near" or is at hand (1:15). Jesus' teaching on how to live has to do with entering the kingdom. This teaching is said to be based upon Mosaic law; it could be termed an authoritative interpretation of the law.

For simplicity, we can concentrate on Jesus' teaching in the Sermon on the Mount (Matt 5–7). In Matt 5:21-48, Jesus cites Mosaic teachings and then extends the requirements beyond the rules of divine law. Some of these are criminal laws. Matthew 5:21-26 cites the law of homicide, then extends it to include anger and acrimony. These latter make one "liable to judgment." Now, however, judgment means the Last Judgment. The next case is adultery (Matt 5:27-30); Jesus extends it to include lustful thoughts. A bit later "false swearing" (5:33-37) is not extended in the same way; rather one's word should be so trustworthy that oaths are unnecessary. The *lex talionis* is cited in 5:38, and reversed: do not retaliate when hostile people afflict you.

Jesus' teaching has the effect of reclassifying all human retaliation as aggression for which one will be accountable at the Last Judgment. To live according to the norms of the kingdom is to let God enforce the law. This will entail constant forgiveness within the church fellowship (Matt 18:15-35) and disinterested love of enemies (Matt 5:43-48). The citizen of the kingdom will exercise self-control over impulses and passions.

While the early church did not have the legal autonomy of Judaism within the empire, it did have to make some decisions about admitting and disciplining members (*see* EXCOMMUNICATION). There are a number of parables and teachings about handling difficult situations. For example, Matt 18:15-20 prescribes a procedure for dealing with untoward behavior. What we do not know is whether forgiveness was available to a criminal, say a murderer or adulterer. What would happen if members of the church committed adultery and sought the forgiveness from the church? What if a member participated in an idolatrous occasion? Neither of these would be crimes against the state, but they were offenses before God. The book of Hebrews is unforgiving of "backsliders" (Heb 6:4-6; 10:26-31), Paul would have a member practicing "incest" excommunicated (1 Cor 5:3-5); and 1 John 5:16 distinguishes "mortal" (unforgiveable) sin from nonmortal (forgiveable) sin. It may have been that forgiveness for criminal acts was available at the time of conversion, but once the person had been baptized serious offenses meant excommunication.

Certain actions that would have been crimes according to Roman law were not recognized as crimes in the early church. The worship of Jesus and refusal to honor the Roman emperor was certainly such a case. So also the case of the fugitive slave, Onesimus; he left his Christian master to join Paul, at which point he converted. Paul appeals to his master, Philemon, to receive him as a brother. Paul does not mention that Onesimus has committed a capital offense by leaving.

Jesus' message of the kingdom required the church to negotiate a compromise between Jesus' uncompromising teachings and the practicalities of church governance and counseling. The NT makes only a beginning of the task.

2. Jesus among the criminals

The final chapters of each Gospel recount the trials that led to Jesus' condemnation as a criminal. They have, to be sure, other themes as well. The PASSION NARRATIVES tell the story of the suffering of Jesus so that we readers will be sympathetic. It begins with a woman anointing Jesus, then the Last Supper with his disciples, the prayer in the garden of Gethsemane, the arrest, and after his trials the carrying of the CROSS and CRUCIFIXION. The Gospels, moreover, follow the burial with accounts of the discovery of the empty tomb and Jesus' appearances.

In the middle of this narrative are the TRIALS OF JESUS, and their purpose is argumentative. The synoptic Gospels have a trial before a Jewish council known as the Sanhedrin. According to Mark and Matthew, Jesus was charged with prophesying his destruction and rebuilding of the Temple. That prophecy would amount to a messianic claim, and the high priest asks whether he claims to be a messiah. The three Gospels vary regarding his answer, but in all three the high priest deduces an affirmative. He classifies Jesus' crime as "blasphemy" (Mark 14:64; Matt 26:65).

When Jesus is delivered to PONTIUS PILATE, the Roman Prefect, there is a second trial. Here the charge is the claim to be "king of the Jews" (Mark 15:2; Matt 27:11; Luke 23:2-3; John 18:33; 19:12), a secular equivalent of a messianic claim. Pilate is supposed to discern in the charge the intent to rebel against Roman rule. This is the charge implied by the plaque posted on the cross (see INSCRIPTIONS ON THE CROSS).

We must go back to the narratives of Jesus' ministry to assess the truth of the charges. In the synoptic Gospels, Jesus does not make public messianic claims in Galilee; what claims he makes, or are made for him (transfiguration, etc.), are to be kept secret until after Jesus' resurrection (Mark 9:9, etc.). Jesus rides into Jerusalem on an ass, a rather open announcement of messiahship (Mark 11:1-10). His demonstration against the Temple may also be messianic (Mark 11:15-19). We would, thus, answer yes, Jesus does make messianic claims according to the synoptic Gospels.

The Gospel of John makes less of messiahship, more of the title "Son of God." The Sanhedrin reports to Pilate that Jesus has blasphemed by claiming to be Son of God (19:7). In this Gospel, Jesus openly makes this claim early in his ministry (John 5:16-18; 8:48-59).

In neither Gospel tradition does Jesus prepare to challenge Roman power. The coming of the kingdom is in God's hands. Humans can enter it by heeding Jesus' interpretation of the law; Jesus himself furthers it by healing. There is no discussion of either political or military actions. Pilate himself seems to know that Jesus and his followers are no threat to Roman rule because he makes no effort to arrest Jesus' disciples.

Jesus is condemned for political crimes. He is charged with making claims about himself that would cause disturbances or even open rebellion. According to the Gospel of John, the SANHEDRIN decided to eliminate him to avoid an uprising that would precipitate Roman reprisals against the entire nation: Caiaphas says, "You do not understand that it is better for you to have one man die for the people than to have the whole nation destroyed" (11:50). Evidently Jesus was the victim of the colonial division of power. The Jerusalem authorities had the task of monitoring popular movements to avoid massive Roman intervention. A strategic death now and then should eliminate dangerous charismatic leaders. A modicum of injustice was the price paid for peace.

Some aspects of the trials baffle critical historians, and it may well be that we will never know the exact story. There is no reason, though, to doubt the basic contention of the narrative; namely, that Jesus was charged as a political criminal and died with the title

"King of the Jews" over his head. The crime behind the charge may have been violation of a tendentious construction of a religious commandment. The resurrection accounts proclaim God's reversal of the judgment. See SACRIFICES AND OFFERINGS; SIN.

Bibliography: Pamela Barmash. *Homicide in the Biblical World* (2005); Hans Joachim Boecker. *Law and the Administration of Justice in the Old Testament and Ancient East* (1980); William P. Brown, ed. *The Ten Commandments: The Reciprocity of Faithfulness* (2004); Martin Buss. "The Distinction between Civil and Criminal Law." *Proceedings of the Sixth World Congress of Jewish Studies.* Vol 1 (1977); Z. W. Falk. *Hebrew Law in Biblical Times: An Introduction*, 2nd ed. (2001); J. J. Finkelstein. *The Ox That Gored* in vol. 71/2 of *Transactions of the American Philosophical Society* (1981); Tikva Frymer-Kensky. "Tit for Tat: The Principle of Equal Retribution in Near Eastern and Biblical Law." *BA* 49 (1980) 230–34; Tikva Frymer-Kensky. "Pollution, Purification, and Purgation in Biblical Israel." *The Word of the Lord Shall Go Forth: Essays in Honor of David Noel Friedman in Celebration of His Sixtieth Birthday* (1983); Moshe Greenberg. "Some Postulates of Biblical Criminal Law" *Yehezkel Kaufman Jubilee Volume* in *The Jewish Expression* (1968) 18–37; Bernard Jackson. *Theft in Early Jewish Law* (1972); Bernard Jackson. "But You Shall Surely Kill Him!: The Text-Critical and Neo-Assyrian Evidence for MT Deut 13:10." *Bundesdokument und Gesetz: Studien zum Deuteronomium* (1995); E. Otto. "Die Geschichte der Talion im Alten Orient und Israel." *Kontinuum and Proprium: Studien zur Social- under Rechtsgeschichte des Alten Orients und des Alten Testaments* (1996); Dale Patrick. "Casuistic Law Governing Primary Rights and Duties." *JBL* 92 (1973) 180–84; Dale Patrick. "The Covenant Code Source." *VT* 27 (1977) 145–57; Dale Patrick. *Old Testament Law* (1984); Dale Patrick. "The First Commandment in the Structure of the Pentateuch." *VT* 45/1 (1995) 107–18; Dale Patrick. "The Rhetoric of Collective Responsibility in Deuteronomic Law, *Pomegranates and Golden Bells: Festschrift for Jacob Milgrom* (1995); Anthony Phillips. *Ancient Israel's Criminal Law* (1970); Martha Roth. *Law Collections from Mesopotamia and Asia Minor.* 2nd ed. (1997). Moshe Weinfeld. *Deuteronomy and the Deuteronomic School* (1972); Bruce Wells. *The Law of Testimony in the Pentateuchal Codes* (2004); Bruce Wells "Lex Talionis and Exodus 21, 22–25." *RB* 93 (1986) 52–69.

DALE PATRICK

CRIMINAL. *See* CRIMES AND PUNISHMENT, OT AND NT.

CRIMSON [שָׁנִי shani; κόκκινος kokkinos]. Several terms indicating a bright red color, commonly translated *crimson*, or SCARLET, are used for textiles, except where used metaphorically, as in Isa 1:18. The DYE is obtained from the female shield louse, *Kermococcus vermilio*, which is found on the kermes oak. This expensive color is linked with blue and purple, as it is often mentioned in the construction of curtains and vestments for the tabernacle (Exod 26–39).

MARY PETRINA BOYD

CRIPPLE. *See* DISABILITY; DISEASE; HEALING; LAME, LAMENESS.

CRISPUS kris´puhs [Κρίσπος Krispos]. A ruler of the SYNAGOGUE in CORINTH who, "with his house," was baptized by Paul personally (Acts 18:8; 1 Cor 1:14). It was a major advancement in the expansion of the church to convert a Jewish official who presided over synagogue services and had authority to inflict punishment, such as excommunication or lashes.

CRITICISM. *See* BIBLICAL CRITICISM.

CROCODILE לִוְיָתָן liwyathan, לְטָאָה leta'ah]. Large, carnivorous reptile known for its flat, long, pointed head, short legs, long tail, and lizardlike body, identified as the animal named LEVIATHAN and/or BEHEMOTH in some English translations (Job 40:15–41:34, esp. 41:12-17, 22-34). The author of Job probably knew about these animals since, according to Strabo and Pliny, they could be found in the town called Crocodeilopolis near Mount Carmel. Various Hebrew and Greek words indicate lizardlike animals, and the NRSV takes leta'ah to mean crocodile in Lev 11:30. *See* ANIMALS OF THE BIBLE; LIZARD, GREAT; LIZARD.

EMILY CHENEY

CROCUS חֲבַצֶּלֶת khavatseleth]. A flower mentioned in Isa 35:1 and Song 2:1. In Isaiah it is used as a symbol of nature's abundance and in the Song of Songs to describe the beauteous maiden. The exact species of flower is uncertain. The Targum translation suggests a narcissus. Earlier studies suggested that the term referred specifically to the meadow saffron or autumn crocus based on an Akkadian cognate term habatsillatu. This Akkadian term is no longer thought to have that meaning and is now understood to actually mean "shoot."

CROSS [σταυρός stauros]. "The cross" refers to the Roman instrument of Jesus' death and thus serves also as shorthand for his death in its salvific and theological significance.

The word *cross* appears in the NT twenty-eight times, while the verb *crucify* appears fifty-four times, each with both literal and metaphorical uses. In the Gospels, the word *cross* refers to the cruel, degrading, and torturous device of execution—reserved for slaves, insurgents, and similar types—to which Jesus was nailed. It refers also, by extension, to the lifestyle of disciples, who are called to follow Jesus in the self-denial, service, and sacrificial love that led to his crucifixion (Mark 8:34). In the letters, *cross* and *crucify* point at times to the stark historical reality (Phil 2:8; Heb 12:2), but more often—and even in the historical references—the real focus is on the ironic reality that this Roman instrument of taking life was God's means of giving life.

The shadow of the cross is cast over the entire NT. Some scholars describe the Gospels as PASSION NARRATIVES with extended introductions. In Mark the cross reveals the identity of the miracle-working Son of God as the suffering Son/Messiah (15:39), who calls disciples to follow his way. In Matthew the cross demonstrates that the name "Jesus" (= "Yahweh saves") reveals his identity as the one who saves by forgiving sins, in fulfillment of Scripture (1:21; 26:28), and who exemplifies faithfulness in suffering. For Luke the cross is the culmination and paradigmatic expression of a life of filial obedience, prophetic proclamation, compassionate ministry, and innocent suffering (4:16-30; 23:26-49). For John, the cross is both the literal and figurative "lifting up" (exaltation/glorification, coronation) of the Son (3:14; 8:28; 12:32-33), and the fruition of Jesus' exemplary servant-love dramatized in the footwashing scene (13:1-20); it gives life to all who believe. In all four Gospels, the significance of the cross appears in Jesus' passion predictions, the narrative of his last meal with the disciples, and the Passion Narrative itself, all of which contain scriptural echoes (e.g., Isa 53; Ps 22).

Paul, inheriting the early Christian conviction that the cross fulfilled Scripture (1 Cor 15:3), vowed to preach nothing but Christ crucified (1 Cor 2:2), and his theology is the church's foundational *theologia crucis*. He calls his gospel "the word of the cross" (1 Cor 1:18), suggesting that all references to the gospel imply the cross—though the cross is always explicitly or implicitly linked to the RESURRECTION, which both validates and vindicates Christ's death. Paul understands believing existence (faith, hope, love) and ministry as participation in Christ's cross, or "co-crucifixion" with Christ (Gal 2:19). Baptism (Rom 6) and the Lord's Supper (1 Cor 10:14-22; 11:17-34) initiate and renew (respectively) this participation.

"The cross" therefore summarizes the historical, theological, and spiritual/ethical significance of Jesus' crucifixion in the NT.

A. Historical Reality

As historical event, the cross reveals the utter shame (Heb 12:2) and humiliation that Jesus willingly but also inevitably suffered (Mark 8:31). The NT stresses both Jesus' freedom (Phil 2:6-8; John 10:11-18b) and his obedience to God (Matt 26:42; John 10:18c;

Rom 5:19; Heb 5:8) in going to the cross, but the reality of Roman crucifixion reminds us also that Jesus must have threatened not only the religious but also the political status quo. The NT refuses to sever this political meaning of the cross from its theological significance (Mark 15:26 par.; 1 Cor 2:8).

B. Theological Significance

The theological significance of the cross lies in three principal areas: soteriology, Christology, and theology proper (the doctrine of God).

The cross is the means by which God accomplishes our salvation, often expressed as sacrifice, atonement, expiation, forgiveness, or acquittal (Mark 14:24; Rom 3:25; 1 Cor 5:7; Heb 1:3; 1 Pet 1:19; 1 John 1:7; 4:10; Rev 7:14). The earliest Christians used phrases such as "for us" and "for [our] sins" to describe Christ's death (Matt 26:28; Mark 10:45; Rom 4:25; 1 Cor 15:3; 2 Cor 5:14; 1 John 2:2). But to limit the cross to the forgiveness of sins is to ignore other aspects of the NT witness. The cross also effects covenant mediation (Hebrews), ransom/redemption/liberation (Mark 10:45; Rom 3:24; 1 Cor 6:20; Heb 9:12; Rev 5:9), exodus (Luke 9:31), reconciliation/peacemaking (2 Cor 5:18-21; Eph 2:13-16; Col 1:20), and the defeat of anti-human powers (Col 2:14-15). These complementary interpretations illustrate the breadth of human plight and divine solution revealed by the cross.

The cross also demonstrates the endurance and obedience/faithfulness of Jesus as God's Son (Rom 5:19; Heb 5:8; 12:1-3). It simultaneously manifests his sacrificial, self-giving, saving love for us (John 13; Gal 2:19-20; Eph 5:2). Thus the cross is emblematic of Christ's orientation, toward God in obedient faith(fulness) and toward humanity in self-emptying agapē, constituting thereby the quintessential covenantal act of love for God and neighbor. Thus the cross is not only revelatory of Christ's identity but is also paradigmatic of believing existence (*see* below). Christ's resurrection by God vindicates his death, but the resurrected Christ remains the crucified Jesus (Luke 24:28-35; John 20:24-29; Rev 5:6-14). As the resurrected and exalted one, Jesus is Lord (Phil 2:9-11)—which means he is to be understood within the divine identity and worshiped with God the Father—but his lordship expresses the counterintuitive power-in-weakness of the cross.

The NT interprets the cross not only as Christ's loving act but also as God's (John 3:16; Rom 5:6-8; Heb 2:9). Similarly, but perhaps surprisingly, the cross is revelatory, not only of Christ as the servant of God but also of God *qua* God. The cross reveals what true divine sonship is (Mark 15:39) and thus also what true divinity is. The cross as theophany is stressed especially by Paul, who identifies Christ's incarnation and crucifixion (his KENOSIS, or self-emptying) as the manifestation of the form of God (Phil 2:6-8). Moreover, Christ

crucified is divine wisdom, power, and holiness (1 Cor 1:18-31). Furthermore, as the cross effects the reversal of the status quo, it reveals God's identification with the lowly (1 Cor 1:18-2:5), correlating with Jesus' own ministry and demonstrating the continuity between the incarnation, Jesus' earthly ministry, and the cross.

C. Spiritual and Ethical Significance

Throughout the NT, cross-shaped or cruciform existence ("cruciformity") is the hallmark of life lived for God. Jesus, in the synoptic Gospels, ironically uses the image of Roman domination and power through crucifixion to call his followers to a counterimperial life of suffering and service. "Take up your cross" (Mark 8:34 par.)—not just once but daily (Luke 9:23)—is Jesus' dramatic call to discipleship.

For Paul, both faith and baptism are expressions of allegiance to Christ crucified and raised, and to his "body," the church. Crucifixion with Christ and to the self, world, and "flesh" (Rom 6:1-11; Gal 2:19; 5:24; 6:14) is the existential actualization of the cross in the individual's and community's life. The cross is both offensive and powerful, the source of both persecution and pride (1 Cor 1:17; Gal 5:11; 6:12-14).

The cross is therefore an icon of the fundamental shape of the Christian life, signifying practical, sacrificial, loving service rather than ambition, domination, apathy, or selfishness (Mark 9:30-37 par.; Mark 10:32-45 par.; John 13; 1 John 3:16). It also denotes love for enemies rather than vengeance, and faithfulness in suffering and persecution—even to the point of death—rather than compromise, collusion, or complaint (1 Cor 4:9-13; Heb 12:1-4; 1 Pet 2:18–4:19; Revelation). Taking up the cross is not merely an inward attitude nor a set of predetermined duties but a life-narrative that requires wisdom and discernment so that the individual and community can learn to perform acts analogous to the story of Christ, who is displayed on the cross.

In the NT, then, "the cross" is both the source and the shape of salvation; it is life-giving and life-forming. It is God's instrument of reconciliation through kenotic love rather than humanity's instrument of "peace and security" through violence. Thus the cross is inherently a divine critique of all ideologies of violence or domination (interpersonal, ecclesial, racial/ethnic, imperial), whether the proponents of those ideologies mock the cross as folly and weakness, or claim it as justification for their injustice. Simultaneously, the cross is a divine summons to radical humble service and self-giving love. *See* ATONEMENT; CRUCIFIXION; DEATH OF CHRIST; INSCRIPTION ON THE CROSS; TRIAL OF JESUS.

Bibliography: Richard Bauckham. *God Crucified* (1995). John T. Carroll and Joel B. Green, eds. *The Death of Jesus in Early Christianity* (1995); Michael J. Gorman. *Cruciformity: Paul's Narrative Spirituality* *of the Cross* (2001); Roy A. Harrisville. *Fracture: The Cross as Irreconcilable in the Language and Thought of the Biblical Writers* (2006); Richard B. Hays. *The Moral Vision of the New Testament: Community, Cross, New Creation* (1996).

MICHAEL J. GORMAN

CROSS-CULTURAL INTERPRETATION. The phrase "cross-cultural interpretation" has two meanings. Descriptively, the term refers to either 1) the use of cultural resources (such as the myths, philosophy, or concepts of the Sumerian, the Egyptian, the Jewish, or the Greco-Roman world) by biblical authors to express their understanding of God, or 2) the use of contemporary, cultural resources (such as indigenous texts or cultural frameworks) by biblical interpreters as hermeneutical tools to read the Scripture. All theological expression or interpretation is *cross*-cultural to the degree that theology and culture are not identical, though they need each other and they share some common tasks. If the cultures of the Bible and those of the interpreters are identical, cross-cultural interpretation will not be necessary; but if they do not have anything in common, interpretation will not be possible.

Prescriptively, cross-cultural interpretation refers to either 1) the fidelity of the text to complete the "hermeneutical circle" of extending the relevance of the text to the new readers, or 2) the ethical obligation of doing biblical interpretation across cultures and in a diverse community of interpreters sustained by the spiritual gifts of courage and humility. Though text and context do constrain biblical interpretation, the metaphorical nature of language empowers the text to have potential for multiple meanings. Language is embedded in a culture, therefore limited by that culture, but language, being metaphorical, does not just represent reality, it also creates reality. The process of meaning-making includes the work of representing and creating reality. Thus cross-cultural interpretation has a hermeneutical mandate of challenging interpreters to generate new life out of the old text as the text interacts with its successive readers.

There is an ethical obligation for biblical interpretation to be *cross*-cultural. Monocultural interpretation absolutizes its own reading and idolizes one's knowledge; such is the case also if one assumes a Western form of interpretation is the norm. Multicultural interpretation that advocates multiple and relative norms without engaging with one another does not constitute an ethically responsible reading—the principle of multiplicity does not make one's interpretation valid. Cross-cultural interpretation invites interpreters into a critical and dialogical process across cultures, a dialogue in which all can both accept but also transcend the limits of one's specific cultural location. *See* BIBLICAL CRITICISM; CULTURAL HERMENEUTICS; CULTURAL STUDIES.

Bibliography: Brian K. Blount. *Cultural Interpretation: Reorienting New Testament Criticism* (2004); Charles Cosgrove. *Appealing to Scripture in Moral Debate: Five Hermeneutical Rules* (2002); Daniel Patte. *Discipleship According to the Sermon on the Mount: Four Legitimate Readings, Four Plausible Views of Discipleship, and Their Relative Values* (1996); Paul Ricoeur. *Interpretation Theory: Discourse and the Surplus of Meaning* (1976); Khiok-khng Yeo. *What Has Jerusalem to Do with Beijing? Biblical Interpretation from a Chinese Perspective* (1998).

KHIOK-KHNG (K.K.) YEO

CROW [עֹרֵב ʿorev; κόραξ korax]. Strictly speaking, crows are never explicitly mentioned in the Bible. This is somewhat surprising, since the hooded crow (*corvus cornix*) must have been common in central and southern Palestine in biblical times. However, it is likely that the crow is included in the following expression: "every raven of any kind" (Lev 11:15, with a close par. in Deut 14:14). Hence, the Hebrew, which is usually translated "raven," should here (and elsewhere?) be taken in a broad, generic sense. *See* BIRDS OF THE BIBLE; RAVEN.

GÖRAN EIDEVALL

CROWN [כֶּתֶר kether, נֵזֶר nezer, עֲטָרָה ʿatarah; διά-δημα diadēma, κίδαρις kidaris, στέφανος stephanos]. The English translation of several Hebrew and Greek words for a type of headdress worn by kings, officials, and priests. It is also used metaphorically for a person's position or as a prize.

The relationships of the Hebrew words translated as *crown* is complex, because many words for headdresses occur in various combinations. MORDECAI wears the kether (Esth 6:8) and the ʿatarah (Esth 8:15), so the nature of the headdresses is unclear. Other words for headdresses include mitsnefeth (מִצְנֶפֶת, often translated as TURBAN), mighbaʿoth (מִגְבָּעוֹת, headdresses in general), peʾer (פְּאֵר, turban, GARLAND, headdress), and nezer (crown [2 Sam 1:10] or a DIADEM tied above the turban [Exod 29:6]). No clear distinction can be offered as to who can wear what. ʿAtarah can also indicate an honorable position, such as the wife who is the crown of her husband (Prov 12:4), or it can be the gray hair of old age (Prov 16:31). Mitsnefeth, mighbaʿoth, peʾer, and nezer are used for the complex headdresses of Aaron and his sons, but the first two can also be carried by a king (Ezek 21:26 [Heb. 21:31]). Whereas a kether is often from gold and an ʿatarah is from gold or from linen, in their combined form, when one is worn on top of the other, one is from gold—translated by "crown"—and the other from linen, often translated as "diadem." Mitsnefeth, mighbaʿoth, and peʾer are mostly nonmetallic and can be used as multiple layers of headdresses.

In the LXX, a similar picture arises with these terms: stephanos, the diadēma, and the kidaris. The Hebrew for kether is translated with diadēma (Esth 6:8) and ʿatarah with stephanos (Esth 8:15; Prov 16:31; Ezek 21:26). The golden crown of Jonathan is a stephanos. In the books of the Maccabees, the diadēma can be found on the heads of the successors of Alexander (1 Macc 1:9) as well as on the head of Antiochus (1 Macc 6:15). The stephanos can be combined in use with the diadēma, and with the kidaris, but the latter two can be combined as well. When combining the headdresses, the linen goes first and then the metal, followed eventually by another band worn around it.

In the NT, Jesus wears a stephanos that is woven from thorns (Mark 15:17; Matt 27:29; John 19:2.5). The Son of Man (Rev 14:14), as well as the woman clothed with the sun (Rev 12:1), wears a stephanos, as do the twenty-four elders (Rev 4:4, 10). Stephanos is also used in a metaphorical sense: a crown of glory (1 Pet 5:4), of righteousness (2 Tim 4:8), and of life (Rev 2:10). *See* CROWN OF THORNS; DRESS AND ORNAMENTATION.

KRISTIN DE TROYER

CROWN OF THORNS [ἀκάνθινος στέφανος akanthinos stephanos, στέφανος ἐξ ἄκανθα stephanos ex akantha]. According to the Gospels the soldiers carrying out Jesus' crucifixion "placed on him a woven thorny crown" (Mark 15:17). The crown, meant to resemble the laurel wreath worn by Caesar, is part of the mockery of Jesus. This mockery includes a purple cloak, a reed (symbolizing the scepter), and personal address as a so-called king (Mark 15:18-19). Sources from late antiquity describe others mocked in a similar fashion (Philo, *Flacc.* 636–39; Plutarch, *Pomp.* 24.7–8). *See* DEATH OF CHRIST; PASSION NARRATIVES.

Bibliography: C. Bonner. "The Crown of Thorns," *HTR* 46 (1953) 47–48; E. R. Goodenough and C. B. Welles. "The Crown of Acanthus (?)," *HTR* 46 (1953) 241–42.

CRAIG A. EVANS

CRUCIBLE [מַצְרֵף matsref]. A crucible is a melting pot, made of pottery, often used for liquefying silver and other refining. It is used in Prov 17:3 and 27:21 as a metaphor for the judging of a person. The participle form of tsaraf is used similarly in Mal 3:2-3. *See* MET-ALLURGY; POTTERY; SILVER; SMELT.

CRUCIFIXION kroo′suh-fike′shuhn. Crucifixion was a form of execution practiced in late antiquity, whereby a person was tied or nailed to a pole or cross and left to hang.

Crucifixion was practiced in the eastern Mediterranean long before the Romans adopted the practice. It was practiced by Persians and other peoples, such as Assyrians, Scythians, and Thracians. Alexander the Great is said to have crucified thousands (compare Curtius Rufus, *Hist. Alex.* 4.4.17). His successors continued the practice. It is not surprising that in time the Romans adopted this form of execution. It was primarily reserved for murderous or rebellious slaves (and for this reason was known as "slaves' punishment"; Lat.: *servile supplicium*).

Jewish authorities before the Roman period also practiced crucifixion. Most notorious was Alexander Jannaeus (ruled 102–76 BCE), who, Josephus tells us, on one occasion crucified a large number of Pharisees who had opposed him and had allied themselves to a foreign enemy (*J.W.* 1.97–98; compare *Ant.* 13.380). Josephus' testimony helps explain a reference in the Dead Sea Scrolls, where in one of the *pesharim* there is reference to the "Lion of Wrath" (understood to be Alexander Jannaeus) who "used to hang men alive" (4Q169 3-4 i, 7).

The Romans placed crosses along well-traveled highways, on tops of hills, and at city gates. The condemned man usually carried the cross-beam, or *patibulum* (Plutarch, *Mor.* 554A–B; Mark 15:21), sometimes with a *titulus* around his neck, declaring his name and punishment, later to be affixed to the upright cross. This cruel punishment later also befell Christians. Church historian and apologist Eusebius (4th cent.) tells of Attalus the Christian, who "was led around the amphitheatre and a placard was carried before him on which was written in Latin, 'This is Attalus, the Christian'" (*Hist. eccl.* 5.1.44).

The Gospels say that a *titulus* was placed on the cross of Jesus (Matt 27:37; Mark 15:26; Luke 23:38) and that it was written in more than one language, describing Jesus as "king of the Jews." The epithet "king of the Jews" is Roman and was originally applied to Herod the Great (compare Josephus, *Ant.* 15.409: "the king of the Jews, Herod").

Crucifixion victims were usually beaten (scourged with whips, to which hooks or sharp pieces of metal or glass were attached) and then nailed to the cross, through wrists and ankles or heels (Josephus, *J.W.* 2.306; 5.449; 6.304; *Digesta* 48.19.8.3). They were left to die, however long that took (sometimes several days). Sometimes friends and relatives were allowed to feed their loved one (Mark 15:23; John 19:28-29). Guards were stationed until the victim expired. Occasionally friends or relatives attempted to rescue the victim. The bodies of the crucified were usually left unburied, to rot and to be picked apart by birds and animals (though Roman law did permit bodies to be taken down and buried; compare *Digesta* 48.24.1, 3; Josephus, *Life* 75.420–21).

According to Cicero (*Ag. Verr.* 2.5.168) and Josephus (*J.W.* 7.203), crucifixion was the worst form of death (*see also* the disturbing comments in Juvenal, *Sat.* 14.77–78; Suetonius, *Aug.* 13.1–2; Horace,

Epi. 1.16.48; Seneca, *Dialogue* 3.2.2; 6.20.3). Indeed, the words *cross* and *crucify* actually derive from the word *torture* (Latin *cruciare*). The primary political and social purpose of crucifixion was deterrence: "Whenever we crucify the condemned, the most crowded roads are chosen, where the most people can see and be moved by this terror. For penalties relate not so much to retribution as to their exemplary effect" (Ps. Quiatlian, *Dedamations* 274; Ps. Manetho, *Aposteles notica* 4.198-200; Aristophanes, *Thesm.* 1029).

The major difference between Jewish crucifixion and later Roman crucifixion is that in the case of the former the bodies were taken down, at least if they had been crucified in lands inhabited by Jews. No corpse in the vicinity of a Jewish city was left unburied at sundown, in keeping with Mosaic Law (Deut 21:23). Moreover, strict Jewish laws regarding corpse impurity, as well as pious devotion to the dead, even criminal dead, would make it unthinkable to leave unburied bodies just outside the walls and gates of Jerusalem.

According to the Gospels, Jesus was taken down from the cross the very day he was crucified. To hasten the deaths of the two men crucified with Jesus, their legs were broken. In 1968 an OSSUARY was found at Givʿat ha-Mivtar, just north of Jerusalem (i.e., ossuary no. 4), which contained three skeletons. One of the skeletons was of a man who had been crucified, for an iron spike still transfixed the right heel bone. Fragments of wood at both ends of the spike were present. Moreover, the man's legs had been broken. The skeleton of the crucified man has been dated to the late 20s CE, when Judea and Samaria were administered by the Roman prefect Pontius Pilate. The crucified remains prove that Pilate permitted crucified Jewish criminals proper burial (as the Gospels say was the case of Jesus of Nazareth) and—if the broken leg bones are relevant—allowed them to be buried before sundown, contrary to normal Roman practice but in keeping with Jewish law and sensitivities.

In the Gospels the soldiers who crucify Jesus divide his garments among themselves (Matt 27:35; Mark 15:24; Luke 23:34; John 19:23–24). This is consistent with Roman practice (Tacitus, *Ann.* 6.29: "people sentenced to death forfeited their property"). *See* CROWN OF THORNS; DEATH OF CHRIST; PASSION NARRATIVES; SCOURGE.

Bibliography: J. A. Fitzmyer. "Crucifixion in Ancient Palestine, Qumran Literature, and the New Testament." *CBQ* 40 (1978) 493–513; M. Hengel. *Crucifixion: In the Ancient World and the Folly of the Message of the Cross* (1977); J. W. Hewitt. "The Use of Nails in the Crucifixion." *HTR* 25 (1932) 29-45; J. Zias and J. H. Charlesworth, "Crucifixion: Archaeology, Jesus, and the Dead Sea Scrolls." *Jesus and the Dead Sea Scrolls.* (1992) 273-89 + plates following 184.

CRAIG A. EVANS

CRY OUT, TO [צָעַק tsaʿaq; κράζω krazo, κραυγάζω kraugazō, βοάω boaō]. In the OT, the verb tsaʿaq refers to calling out loudly or shouting, usually in distress (e.g., Gen 27:34; 1 Sam 4:14; 2 Kgs 4:40; Isa 65:14; Jer 25:34). The sufferers may appeal for help from a powerful person such as Moses (Num 11:2) or a king (2 Kgs 6:26; 8:3), but most often the plea is to God (e.g., Exod 17:4; Judg 3:9, 15; Jonah 1:14; Ps 77:2). God attends especially to the cries of innocent victims, oppressed people, and the vulnerable: e.g., the murdered Abel (Gen 4:10), the Hebrews in Egyptian slavery (Exod 3:7), aliens, widows, and orphans (Exod 22:21-23).

The NT terms krazō, kraugazō, and boao may denote proclamation (Mark 1:3; John 1:15; 7:28; Acts 23:6; Rom 9:27), rejoicing (Matt 21:9; Mark 11:9; John 12:13; Gal 4:27), or the uproar of an angry crowd (Matt 27:23; Acts 7:57; 17:6; 19:28-34; 25:24). Outcries occur as immediate outbursts of fear or pain (Matt 14:26; Rev 12:2), indications of demonic possession (Matt 8:29; Mark 3:11; Acts 8:7), appeals to Jesus for deliverance (Matt 9:27; 14:30; Mark 9:24), and prayers to God (Luke 18:7; Acts 7:60; Heb 5:7). On the cross, Jesus invokes the psalmist's lament as he cries out in anguish to God (Mark 15:34). *See* ELI, ELI, LAMA SMABACHTHANI; LAMENT; PREACHING.

Bibliography: Richard Nelson Boyce. *The Cry to God in the Old Testament* (1988).

HAROLD C. WASHINGTON

CRY, TO. *See* MOURNING.

CRYSTAL [גָּבִישׁ gavish, קֶרַח qerakh, זְכוֹכִית zekhokhith; κρύσταλλος krystallos]. Rather than a specific substance, biblical use of the term *crystal* often refers to a quality of "clearness" or "transparency" (*see* "ice," qerakh, Ezek 1:22). In Rev 4:6 and 22:1, krystallos suggests the pureness of the "sea of glass" that surrounds the throne of God and the efficacy of "the river of the water of life" that flows from God's throne. Similarly, the New Jerusalem of Rev 21:11 takes on the radiance of God's glory, "clear as crystal" and unstained by sin. The litany comparing the value of wisdom in Job 28:12-19 to all the precious metals and jewels of the earth does seem to point to a specific product or object in its reference to "crystal" (NIV) or "glass" (NRSV) in Job 28:17 (zekhokhith). *See* JEWELS AND PRECIOUS STONES.

VICTOR H. MATTHEWS

CTESIAS. Born ca. 440 BCE, personal physician of ARTAXERXES II Mnemon (405–358 BCE), authored the *Persica*, the earliest source for Semiramis's campaigns in Media and Bactria, which later also featured ZOROASTER as king of Bactria.

Bibliography: J. Auberger. Ctesias. *Histoires de l'Orient.* Transl. and comm., Charles Malamoud (1991); R. Schmitt. "Ctesias." Vol. 6 of *Encyclopædia Iranica* (1993) 441–46.

P. OKTOR SKJAERVO

CUB kuhb [גוֹר gor, גוּר gur; σκύμνος skymnos]. Young bears, foxes, and dogs whose mothers' anger over separation from them metaphorically describes the anger of David's warriors (2 Sam 17:8), anger generally (Prov 17:12), or God's anger toward Israel's idolatry (Hos 13:8). *See also* 1 Macc 3:4. *See* ANIMALS OF THE BIBLE; BEAR.

CUBIT ky*oo*'bit [אַמָּה 'ammah]. A major measure of length, roughly the length of a human arm from the forearm to the tip of the middle finger (ca. 52 cm). *See* WEIGHTS AND MEASURES.

CUCUMBER [קִשֻּׁאִים qishu'im]. The word for cucumber appears in Num 11:5 when Israel yearned for the cucumbers they had to eat in Egypt. Garden cucumbers did not exist in the ancient Near East, so most scholars regard the referent of *cucumber* to be the muskmelon or *Cucumis melo.* For Israel sojourning in the wilderness, this sweet watery fruit would indeed be remembered as a delicacy. The reference to "a lodge in a cucumber field" in Isa 1:8 suggests the cultivation of this plant, even though the climate in Israel was not particularly suited for cultivating this type of fruit. See AGRICULTURE; FOOD; LODGE; MELON; PLANTS OF THE BIBLE.

L. JULIANA M. CLAASSENS

CULT. *See* WORSHIP, EARLY JEWISH; WORSHIP, NT CHRISTIAN; WORSHIP, OT.

CULTURAL HERMENEUTICS. The term *culture* refers to material substance, norms of behaviors, values, beliefs, and expressive symbols or representations. Culture changes across space and time. Hence, the cultural identity of persons and peoples also changes.

Hermeneutics is generally defined as the theory of interpreting a text. With the influence of Martin Heidegger's concept of *Dasein* ("historical being") and Rudolf Bultmann's *Vorverständnis* ("pre-understanding"), hermeneutics is used to designate not a methodology but a process or phenomenon of understanding meaning. Instead of focusing on the theory and method, hermeneutics focuses on the "language-event," the intentionality in the use of language, and the question regarding the meaning of meaning.

A. Role of Text and Culture in Biblical
    Hermeneutics
    Text, as in "biblical text," is an embodiment of meaning and a subject of meaning being interpreted

or read. In that sense, an interpreter is also a "text" that can be "read." Biblical "text" that is interpreted has less to do with the opaque words (signifiers) but more to do with what the words, collectively and individually, signify. A text does not exist on its own; it exists in a cultural discourse and uses a language embedded in the world of culture. A text is part of "the 'fabric' of a tale, the 'thread of discourse', the 'clothing of thought', and the 'network' of ideas" (Tyler 1987, 35).

Culture in its broad sense refers to the world of the interpreter and the context of the text. Both the interpreter and the text seek to understand each other, and both have the power to speak forth meaning. The interpreter reads the text in order to understand the meaning of the text, and the text reads the interpreter in order to inscribe a meaningful narrative and to transform the world of the interpreter. The process of understanding meaning is the interaction between the interpreter and the text, as they engage in the perpetual transaction of meaning-making with, and for, one another. Cultural hermeneutics seeks to understand the inter-interpretive reading that generates a productive and reproductive meaning.

Hans-Georg Gadamer understands the practice and process of hermeneutics as paying attention to the dialogical relationship between a text and the interpreter. The interpreter reads the text as much as the text gives meaning to the life-world of the interpreter. This mutually informing interaction between text and interpreter forms what Gadamer calls the "hermeneutical circle." The goal of cultural interpretation sees the meeting between the biblical text and the reader a necessary link in engendering life. Together with language, readers and their interpretations are the "hermeneutical bridge" to the hermeneutical circle. The writer (who is the first reader) and the readers (who are called interpreters) are coproducers of meanings of the biblical text.

Because the cultures of the interpreter and the text are fluid and mutually interactive, the meaning-making process (hermeneutics) is "a pluralistic range of possibilities" (Thiselton 1992, 55). The text is dynamic, because the same text has the power to speak to a multitude of readers and their situations. The biblical text becomes sacred in its interpretive and communicative process, since it is the assumption of the Scripture that the Holy Writer of the texts wills the sacred word to speak over time and space—and here we approach the issue of CROSS-CULTURAL INTERPRETATION.

B. Adjudicating Between Competing
    Interpretations Toward Global Interpretation
    Cultural hermeneutics advocates for contextual and indigenous interpretations of Scripture, noting that the Bible can speak to all cultures. While all interpretations are possible, competing or conflicting interpretations raise the question of which interpretations are more

plausible. Besides the virtue of humility and the ethics of shared responsibility, cultural interpretations need the theology of eschatological critique. That is, the Christ event discloses the eschatological dawning of God's truth, and also signals the open-endedness of truth and the limitation of interpreters' present knowledge. While every interpretation may be valid in its context, every interpretation is partial, and therefore its limitation is overcome through an ever-enlarging spiral process of cross-cultural (global) interpretation (*see* CROSS-CULTURAL INTERPRETATION). Communities of interpreters subject their readings to collective ideological critique in order that no one interpreter is blinded by his or her cultural assumptions. The ambiguities of an interpretation and the historicities of the interpreter, though culturally conditioned, are partially clarified and expanded through the process of global interpretation.

Cultural hermeneutics includes Scripture interpretation (reading Scripture through the lens of culture) and culture interpretation (reading culture through the lens of Scripture). The relation between Scripture and culture is a complex dialectic of values in which interpreters are both recipients, socially constructed persons, and peoples (as heirs of culture and tradition), and are also hermeneutic agents, choosers of meaning, and negotiators of values. In cultural hermeneutics, therefore, both the Scripture text and the culture provide norms of evaluation for Christian interpreters, norms that are often in tension. In the hermeneutical circle by which interpreters choose between competing plausible interpretations based on their prior understandings of Scripture and the values that are part of their cultural lens, both their understanding of Scripture and their cultural self-understanding can be transformed. *See* BIBLICAL CRITICISM; CULTURAL STUDIES; HISTORY OF INTERPRETATION.

Bibliography: Hans-Georg Gadamer. *Truth and Method* (1991); Kathryn Tanner. *Theories of Culture: A New Agenda for Theology* (1997); Anthony C. Thiselton. *New Horizons in Hermeneutics: The Theory and Practice of Transforming Biblical Reading* (1992); Stephen A Tyler. *The Unspeakable: Discourse, Dialogue, and Rhetoric in the Postmodern World* (1987); Khiok-khng Yeo. "Culture and Intersubjectivity as Criteria for Negotiating Meanings in Cross-Cultural Interpretations." Charles H. Cosgrove, ed. *The Meanings We Choose: Hermeneutical Ethics, Indeterminacy and the Conflict of Interpretations* (2004); Khiok-khng Yeo. *Navigating Romans through Cultures: Challenging Readings by Charting a New Course* (2004).

KHIOK-KHNG (K. K.) YEO

CULTURAL STUDIES. For their survival, human beings are compelled by nature to impose meaningful order upon reality. The word *culture* is broadly used to refer to the ways of life that offer systems for explaining meaning in the life-world of human society. Culture includes material substance, norms of behaviors, values, or significant virtues, beliefs, or worldview, and expressive symbols or representations.

A. Two Major Schools in Cultural Studies

The school of social sciences views culture as the "complex whole" that makes up a society. Its method of study is ethnographic; it explains systems of meaning sociologically (*see* CULTURAL HERMENEUTICS). Its assumption is that each society has its own culture; its own patterns of belief; its own ethical practices, values, and ways of life; its own institutions. All such cultural elements are formed and reformed in the changing dynamic of the historical process. The social sciences school assumes that each culture has its own way of legitimating life.

The humanities school understands culture as that which "cultivates" virtue and excellence in all human endeavors. It understands that the "ways of life" are aimed at enhancing a "cultured" society, that is, "human flourishing." Culture enables the human mind and spirit to rise above mundane societal norms and expectations in order to attain what is excellent, true, and beautiful. Matthew Arnold, e.g., believed that only culture could restore "sweetness and light" (beauty and wisdom) to society and civilization (1932, 48).

B. Cultural Coexistence, Ideological Critiques, and "Theological Culture"

Cultural studies require a commitment to cultural coexistence and ideological critique, so that ethnocentrism will be overcome, superficiality avoided, truth pursued, and diversity preserved. Culture, like theology (the interpretive meaning of God), is intertwined in the meaning of a life-world, and therefore plays a significant role in biblical interpretation. Theology can be part of a culture; culture can be a part of theology. Culture without theology is like a corpse, or worse, becomes a narcissistic demon, because it does not have spiritual resources of its own to critique and renew itself. Yet theology without culture will die, becoming anemic, because theology (and biblical interpretation) cannot feed on itself; it must feed on "the nitty-gritty" experiences of life.

Bibliography: Matthew Arnold. *Culture and Anarchy* (1932); Peter L. Berger. *The Sacred Canopy* (1967); Richard Dienst, et al., ed. *Reading the Shape of the World: Toward an International Cultural Studies* (1996); Kathryn Tanner. *Theories of Culture: A New Agenda for Theology* (1997); Khiok-khng Yeo. *Rhetorical Interaction in 1 Corinthians 8 and 10: A Formal Analysis with Preliminary Suggestions for a Chinese, Cross-Cultural Hermeneutic* (1995).

KHIOK-KHNG (K. K.) YEO

CULTURE. *See* ANTHROPOLOGY, CULTURAL NT; ANTHROPOLOGY, CULTURAL OT; CULTURAL STUDIES.

CUMIN kuh´min [כַּמֹּן kammon; κύμινον kyminon]. Cumin (*Cuminum cyminum*), of the carrot family, is a bitter-tasting seed that was used to season stews and to flavor bread. Isaiah's parable on proper agricultural methods illustrates the force involved in plowing, harvesting, and threshing: even cumin is struck with sticks to separate the seeds. Jesus ridicules the Pharisees (Matt 23:23) for their concern with the items of the tithe (dill, anise, and cumin) while failing to obey the foundation of the law (justice, mercy, and faith; compare Hos 6:6 and Mic 6:8). *See* ANISE; PLANTS OF THE BIBLE; SPICES.

VICTOR H. MATTHEWS

CUN kuhn [כּוּן kun]. A city belonging to King Hadadezer from which David took much bronze (1 Chr 18:8). *See* BEROTHAI; BRONZE.

CUNEIFORM ky*oo*-nee´uh-form. A form of writing in which one corner of a square-ended stylus is pressed into wet clay to produce a set of triangular wedges.

Each distinctive set of wedges constitutes a single sign. Depending upon the language that these signs were used to represent, they signified various linguistic units, such as words (pictograms/logograms), syllables (syllabograms), or phonemes (generally consonants) in an alphabetic system. Several Semitic and non-Semitic languages were written with various cuneiform systems, beginning as early as ca. 3500–3200 BCE, including Sumerian (primarily pictographic), Elamite, Hittite, Luwian and all known forms of Akkadian (all a combination of logographic and syllabic), and Ugaritic and Old Persian (both primarily alphabetic). *See* ALPHABET; WRITING AND WRITING MATERIALS.

Bibliography: C. B. F. Walker. *Cuneiform* (1987).

JEREMY M. HUTTON

CUP [כּוֹס kos; ποτήριον potērion]. A vessel out of which one may drink, or the actual drink. 1. Joseph's cup for drinking and divination (Gen 44).

2. A symbol of enjoyment and blessing, a metaphor for salvation (Pss 16:5; 23:5).

3. The cup filled with an intoxicating liquid that acts like a poison and is a metaphor for God's fury (Isa 51:17, 22; Rev 14:10). When Jesus speaks of the cup that he must drink (Mark 10:38-39; John 18:11), he refers to the suffering that he must undergo. That he prays to God to remove it (Matt 26:39; Mark 14:36; Luke 22:42) indicates that he interprets it to be symbolic of the wrath of God that he must bear.

4. The cup shared after the breaking of bread at the Last Supper that symbolizes Jesus' blood poured out in sacrifice to establish a new covenant (Matt 26:27-28; Mark 14:23-24; Luke 22:20).

5. The donation of a cup of cold water in Jesus' name will be rewarded by God (Matt 10:42; Mark 9:41).

I. HOWARD MARSHALL

CUPBEARER [מַשְׁקֶה mashqeh; οἰνοχόος oinochoos]. A wine taster and trusted royal advisor in Egyptian (Gen 40:1-23), Israelite (1 Kgs 10:5; 2 Chr 9:4), Assyrian (Tob 1:21-22), Persian (Neh 1:11), and other ancient Near Eastern courts. At times, Jews held this prominent position in foreign lands. According to the book of Tobit, Ahikar (Tobit's nephew) served as cupbearer and chief financial officer for Assyrian kings, Sennacherib and Esarhaddon (Tob 1:21-22; 2:10; 11:18; 14:10); and Nehemiah leveraged his position as cupbearer to the Persian ruler, Artaxerxes, to secure an appointment as governor of Judah during the period of post-exilic reconstruction.

F. SCOTT SPENCER

CURDS [חֶמְאָה khem´ah]. Curdled milk made by churning fresh milk. In the OT, curds form one of Israel's basic foods. In Gen 18:8, Abraham serves his guests curds, milk, and meat (*see also* the list of provisions for David in 2 Sam 17:29 and the drink served by Jael to Sisera in Judg 5:25). In Isa 7, curds are used in conjunction with honey. Commentators point to the dual meaning of this reference. As it is used in the context of judgment, curds may serve as a symbol of devastation. Since the grain, oil, and wine of an agricultural society have ceased to exist, the only food available is produce found in the wilderness and the few livestock kept alive by the survivors (v. 21). Alternatively, the reference to curds is reminiscent of a land flowing with milk and honey, serving as a symbol of abundance (v. 22). *See* FOOD; MILK.

L. JULIANA M. CLAASSENS

CURE, CURED. *See* HEALING; MIRACLES.

CURSE. The meaning varies in different contexts. *Curse* often denotes an utterance spoken to consign a person (or object) to harm or deprivation. Sometimes it takes the form of a prayer to God or decree from God, to bring disaster. It regularly denotes the opposite of *blessing*, often in the context of the covenant.

A. Hebrew Terms and Uses in the OT

Curse translates several Hebrew nouns and verbs. The most characteristic Hebrew stem is אָרַר (˒rr). This occurs thirty-nine times in the *qal* passive participle (˒arur) to mean *cursed* [*be*]. It stands in opposition to בָּרַךְ (barakh), *to bless*. It appears in: "Cursed be you (the serpent) above all" (˒arur ˒attah mikkol, Gen 3:14); in the curse of Cain (Gen 4:11, ˒arur ˒attah min);

and in "Shechemite Decalogue" (Deut 27:15-26), to begin each of the twelve successive curses. The remaining two most widely discussed examples are Isaac's irrevocable blessing of Jacob: "Cursed be those who curse you, and blessed be those who bless you" (Gen 27:29b); and Balaam's blessing of Israel: "Blessed be those who bless you, and cursed (arur) be those who curse you" (Num 24:9).

Other Hebrew words may be translated as *curse*, but are less distinctive. אָלָה (*'alah*) denotes a curse in the sense of the harmful effects that a curse may bring (Jer 23:10-11), or sometimes a promissory or conditional threat of evil (*see* OATH). קְלָלָה (*qelalah*) also denotes harm, but mainly as abuse or disrespect, referenced in Deut 21:22-23, which is cited by Paul in Gal 3:13. The verb form (Deut 21:22-23) prefaces the twelve *curses* of Deut 27:15-26, and explicates the covenant context of choosing *blessing* or *disaster* (Deut 30:19). חרם (*khrm*) occurs forty-eight times in the hiphil (there is no *qal* form) and twenty-nine times as a noun, but primarily in the context of war and extermination to denote an act of annihilation, or that which is banned from human use. Although the LXX translations ἀνάθεμα anathema and ἀναθεματίζω anathematizō may appear to come closer to meanings of *curse*, these more usually denote *votive offering* or *devoted*. Thus khrm is better considered under another heading (*see* DEVOTED).

B. History of Research

Building on Pedersen, Hempel (1915) drew on analogies from the ancient Near East to argue that *curse* in the OT was rooted in primitive notions of word-magic. A curse was akin to a magical incantation, often bound up with quasi-magical acts (Deut 25:9; Isa 58:9). In the Balaam narrative, a curse cannot be recalled, but must run its course inexorably by its own power (Num 22:6). Isaac cannot revoke his blessing upon Jacob (Gen 27:35). The curse upon Korah is like a contagion (Num 16:25). Mowinckel assimilated such a view (1923). Grether (1934), Dürr (1938), Ringgren (1947), and Zimmerli (1962) produced studies of "*Word*" (דָּבָר *davar* in Hebrew that seemed to give further credibility to it. He compares *the word* in the OT to "a missile with a time-fuse." Dürr viewed *word* as *kraftgeladen* a power-laden force. Eichrodt insisted that *words* once spoken, remain effective or even dangerous for a long time, "like a forgotten mine in the sea, or a grenade buried in a ploughed field." Gerhard von Rad saw it as an objective reality endowed with "mysterious power." In the 1950's successive works on *curse* by Blank (1951), Scharbert (1958), and Gevirtz (1959) assimilated many of these assumptions, and built on these foundations.

The situation largely changed in the 1960s. Brichto (1963) undertook a careful linguistic and exegetical study of *curse*, which was a model of rigorous critical research. He exposed several fallacies in Hempel. How could such prominence be ascribed to "word-magic," e.g., when Israel struggled to suppress sorcery or magic by subordinating all *powers* to the one God? Curses may indeed be irrevocable, but is not this because *God* has spoken them? Moreover *curses* often operate as *prayers* to God, with little or no thought of their operating independently on the basis of some inherent power, or being self-fulfilling. No curse can have an effect without *God's* decree behind it. Brichto concluded that the *covenant* constitutes a more decisive background than speculations about magic. The covenant framework of the awe-inspiring list of curses and blessings in Deut 27:15-26 and 28:1-6 and 16-20 appears to corroborate this.

Thiselton (1974) developed this angle of approach by proposing a further, complementary explanation for "the supposed power" of cursing or blessing in terms of speech-act theory and linguistics. The philosophers J. L. Austin, D. D. Evans, and John Searle distinguished between causal or *mechanistic* force (of the kind presupposed in theories about word-magic) and that of "institutional" performative utterances or *illocutions* (of the kind that depends upon more subtle conditions for their operative effects). In Hebrew-Christian liturgy and theology such utterances as "I appoint you," "I commission you," "I find you guilty/innocent," "I forgive you," depend upon complex conditions for their effects. The status of the speaker (e.g., whether he or she is appointed to speak for God) and the existence of an accepted procedure for pronouncing a performative utterance form two such conditions. Isaac cannot revoke his blessing upon Jacob because no illocutionary procedure existed for "unblessing," any more than a minister today can declare, "I unbaptize you," in the expectation that some solemn effect will follow. These are more likely to explain why Balaam says to Balak, "He has blessed, and I cannot revoke it" (Num 23:20). It seems unlikely that future biblical research will return to older theories of word-magic that are based on the comparative anthropology of Malinowski and Cassirer. Advances in general linguistics seem to hold the most promise for understanding cursing and blessing in the Bible.

Robert Gordon (1996) underlines the view that 1) much depends upon the status of the speaker, and 2) the covenantal context is often decisive. The covenant background has a dual significance. First, in some contexts a curse binds a person to an obligation that has a covenantal or contractual nature as a "sworn agreement" (Gen 26:28; Isa 24:6). A covenant may be sanctioned by a *curse* clause. The flying scroll of Zech 5:1-4 contains a curse that is a penalty for breach of covenant law. Second, although Israel shared with Mesopotamian texts the notion of an "indissoluble" curse, this may depend on invoking God or gods, and in both cases flexibility in terms of overriding a curse with a blessing sometimes occurs (*Gilgamesh* VII. Iii.5-iv.10). The phrase "curses of the covenant" also occurs in Qumran (CD 1:17; 1QS 2, 16; 5, 12).

C. Greek Terms and *Curse* in the NT

The Gk. terms κατάρα (katara, curse) and ἐπικατάρατος (epikataratos, accursed) occur in Gal 3:13, while ἀνάθεμα (anathema) occurs in 1 Cor 12:3 and 16:22 (*see* ANATHEMA). The meaning of 1 Cor 12:3, "No one who is speaking through the agency of the Spirit of God says, 'Jesus is cursed,'" remains controversial. The context concerns criteria for the application of the term *spiritual* or for claims that the Holy Spirit is active. Perhaps this situation is related to that of persecution, in which "Caesar is Lord" or "Jesus is cursed" would amount to renouncing Christian discipleship. Such a renunciation would hardly suggest the action of the Spirit. But this interpretation is strained beyond the context. Some suggest a possible reference to a quasi-Gnostic devaluing of the earthly Jesus, or to uncontrolled ecstatic utterance. This fits the context better, but the influence of Gnosticism in Corinth at this early date is contested, and Christology hardly becomes a key issue in 1 Corinthians. It seems more plausible to perceive in the atonement (i.e., the *curse* borne by Christ in Gal 3:13), but stopping at that point without a corresponding belief in the resurrection. This would be very compressed shorthand. One scholar interprets the Greek ἀνάθεμα Ἰησοῦς (anathema Iēsous) to mean "May Jesus [*grant*] a curse," on the analogy of "curse tablets," in which pagan worshipers appeal to their deities to *curse enemies or rivals* (Winter), but no other descriptions of the work of the Holy Spirit indicate that the Spirit might inspire a Christian to pray for such a curse; such a prayer would be evidence that the Spirit is not at work here. The abrupt reference to *curse* in 1 Cor 16:22 is surprising. But here in his final farewell Paul invokes *love* and *anathema* as characterizing the two contrasting "ways," brought into relief by an appeal to covenant loyalty, as in some traditions of the OT and Qumran (*see* ANATHEMA).

Galatians 3:13 is complex: "Christ redeemed us from the curse (κατάρας kataras) of the law by becoming a curse (katara) for us—for it is written, 'Cursed is everyone who hangs on a tree'" (NRSV). The immediate reference is to Deut 21:23 (LXX), but Paul has just cited Deut 27:26 (Gal 3:10) as an explanatory frame of reference. As in rabbinic exegesis, these are used to shed light on each other. Galatians 3:10 (Deut 27:26) states that a curse falls upon lawbreakers, while Gal 3:13 (Deut 21:23) states that a hanged man is cursed by God (Heb. קִלְלַת אֱלֹהִים qillath 'elohim, *affront to God*; LXX, κεκατηραμένος ὑπὸ θεοῦ kekatēramenos hupo theou, *cursed by God*; Paul, Ἐπικατάρατος Epikataratos, *cursed*). Traditionally this has been taken to mean that when he suffered this curse Christ underwent this curse on behalf of others, and thereby released others from the curse. Some argue that Christ's self-identification with fallen humanity is more central and more primary than curse as punishment. But in Deut 21:23 *curse* implies rejection, not merely suffering, and Paul is expounding the two Deuteronomic texts to specific effect.

Bibliography: Sheldon Blank. "The Curse, the Blasphemy, the Spell and the Oath." *HUCA* 23 (1950–1951) 73–95; Herbert Brichto. *The Problem of "Curse" in the Hebrew Bible* (1963); Anthony C. Thiselton. "The Supposed Power of Words in the Biblical Writings." *JTS* 25 (1974) 283–99; Anthony C. Thiselton. *The First Epistle to the Corinthians* (2000) 917–27 and 1350–52; Bruce Winter. "Religious Curses and Christian Vindictiveness." *After Paul Left Corinth* (2001) 164–83.

ANTHONY C. THISELTON

CURTAIN OF THE TEMPLE. *See* VEIL OF THE TEMPLE.

CURTAINS [יְרִיעֹת yeri'oth, יְרִיעָה yeri'ah, אֹהֶל 'ohel, פָּרֹכֶת parokheth; καταπέτασμα katapetasma]. The English word occurs in the plural only in the OT, most often referring to the tabernacle; specifically ten screens that house the ARK OF THE COVENANT (e.g., Exod 26 and 36; Jer 4:20). The singular form appears in both Testaments, often referring to the veil that seals off the Most Holy Place in the TABERNACLE or TEMPLE (e.g., Num 18:7; 2 Chr 3:14; Matt 27:51; Heb 6:19; 10:20). Curtain(s) is also used figuratively for the sky (e.g., Isa 40:22) or the space of the earth (e.g., Isa 54:2), exemplifying its synonymous meaning with "tent."

STEVEN D. MASON

CUSHAN-RISHATHAIM koosh'an-rish'uh-thay'im [כּוּשַׁן רִשְׁעָתַיִם kushan rish'athayim]. Cushan-rishathaim is mentioned four times in Judg 3, twice in v. 8 and twice in v. 10. In the extent text he is identified as "king of Aram-naharaim," literally "king of Aram of the two rivers." This designation would suggest that he was a Mesopotamian ruler from the north who caused trouble for Israel. The cursory nature of this brief narrative and the fact that the hero, OTHNIEL, was from the tribe of Judah make it improbable that Cushan-rishathaim was a significant northern Aramite king. With a slight textual emendation these problems subside. Instead of reading "king of Aram-naharaim" (מֶלֶךְ אֲרַם נַהֲרָיִם melekh 'aram naharayim), the text could be emended to read "King of Edom" (אֱדֹם melekh 'edhom), a plausible alteration if an early scribe transposed a resh for a dalet. Further, the term naharaim was likely a subsequent gloss, occurring in v. 8 in reference to this figure but absent in v. 10. The result is the more plausible notion that the southern hero Othniel, of the tribe of Judah, would fight against a local southern Edomite foe than that he would have battled a northern aggressor.

This emendation clarifies the use of the rare name CUSHAN as well. The term Cushan in Hab 3:7 refers to a regional Arabian Midianite tribe or to Midianites in general. In this regard, an Edomite king called Cushan would not be as implausible as would a Mesopotamian king by the same name. Whether he was an ethnic "Cushanite" is not clear; it is clear that the name would not be out of place in the context of southern Transjordan.

Cushan-rishathaim is likely not a given name, but a pejorative meaning "doubly-wicked Cushanite." The taunt expresses the enmity between the author's community and the antagonist. Since Cushan was related to Midian, an ethnic group with whom the Hebrews had had periods of intense animosity, then this enmity may have been the source of the slight. The notion of extreme wickedness may arise from an historical memory of a political-military conflict between the Hebrews and Cushan not contained in the extant biblical narratives.

RODNEY S. SADLER, JR.

CUSH, CUSHITE koosh, koosh´it [כּוּשׁ kush, כּוּשִׁים kushim, כֻּשִׁיִּים kushiyim; Αἰθιοπία Aithiopia, Αἰθίοψ aithiops]. 1. Cush, the eponymous ancestor of the nation that shares his name appears in Gen 10:6-9 and 1 Chr 1:8-10, where he is described as the eldest son of Noah's son Ham. He is presented as the primogenitor of several significant North African tribes. In the Genesis account the major Mesopotamian kingdoms are also ascribed to his lineage.

2. Cush is also the name of a certain Benjaminite mentioned as a source of anxiety for King David in the header of Ps 7:1. No further details about Cush's identity or the cause of David's complaint can be discerned in biblical narratives.

3. Cush, Cushite. Because the Hebrew term kush has been translated aithiopia in Greek and "Ethiopia" in subsequent English translations of the OT, Cush is often conflated with modern ETHIOPIA, a land to the southeast of the biblical country. More precisely, Cush refers to the geographical entity that, during the biblical period, occupied the region south of EGYPT between the first and sixth cataracts of the River Nile. Though in Scripture the term "Cush" may refer to more than one region, the only instance when it may not be definitively associated with the African nation south of Egypt or its colonies, is in Gen 10:8-12, where the story of Nimrod describes the origins of a Mesopotamian Cush, the home of the Kassites. However, even in this narrative, the author of Genesis associates the northern land with the southern Cushite Kingdom, asserting an ethnic relationship between the two geographically remote groups.

Roughly consistent with contemporary Sudan, Cush, like Egypt, was dependent upon the Nile for its survival (Gen 2:13; Isa 18:1-2, 8). Papyrus vessels that traversed Africa's largest river facilitated its trade in precious goods with Egypt and the peoples to its north (Isa 18). Such trade is the likely source of another Egyptian designation for this land, NUBIA, for it was the source of "nub," an Egyptian term for gold. It is fitting that the biblical term *Cush* is an adaptation of an Egyptian loanword (transliterated **Kush**), because Israel/Judah's persistent contact with Egypt made continued interaction with Cushites inevitable.

Cushites (**kushim**) and Egyptians (מִצְרַיִם mitsraim) had an extensive history of interrelations over more than three millennia, with elements from the southern region perhaps even colonizing earliest Egypt. Despite having common origins, relationships between the two powers were not always amicable. Though the ancestors of the Cushites initially held sway over their northern neighbor, Egypt periodically conquered and exerted hegemony over Cush and its resources, governing the nation with numerous viceroys. During a period of political instability in the wake of the decline of the Twenty-Second Libyan Dynasty and the division of the Egypt into Upper and Lower kingdoms, the tide reversed. Between 747 and 656 BCE Cushite kings Kashta, Piye, Shabaka, Shebiktu, Taharqa (biblical Tirhakah), and Tantamani of the Twenty-Fifth Dynasty governed Egypt, first from Napata in Cush and then from Egypt proper.

Cushites are described in the OT as a people who are characteristically tall, with hairless faces (Isa 18), and dark-skin (Num 12; Jer 13:23) from a region known for its luxuriant commodities (Job 28:19). The biblical authors knew the Cushites principally as soldiers participating in the Judean army (2 Sam 18), in their own Cushite-led forces (2 Kgs 19; Isa 37), or in larger Egyptian military coalitions (e.g., 2 Chr 12; 14; 16; 21; Isa 20; 43; 45). Inasmuch as they appear in Egyptian expeditionary forces in every period of the OT, whenever Judeans thought of Egypt's armies, they thought of Cushites.

Because Cushites were so frequently seen as martial forces, the *Cushite* became a biblical trope representing both divinely directed military might and the hubris that resulted from trusting in human strength (Nah 3:9). As such, Cushites served as agents of God's will (2 Kgs 19; 2 Chr 12; 21:16-17; Isa 37) and opponents of it (e.g., Isa 20:3-5). Their service in Egyptian expeditionary forces over more than a millennium was one of the principal reasons for their entrée into Palestine (2 Chr 12; 14; 16; 21).

In addition to Cushites from the region south of Egypt, there were other related groups with Cush-derived names living in the Levant. One such group was the people of CUSHAN (Hab 3:7), who inhabited a region associated with Midian. The people of

Cushan were likely a group with Cushitic ancestry that settled on the Arabian peninsula, hence the -an element affixed to their name. The "sons [or offspring] of the Cushites" compared to Israel in Amos 9:7, may refer to this or another group of Levantine Cushites also brought up to the region by Israel's God. Hence, throughout the biblical period, there is evidence of contact with descendants of Cushites dwelling near Judah's southern border.

But Cushites in Palestine also are found in Judah proper, where they lived with, married, and worked among the people of Israel/Judah. Moses' marriage to a Cushite woman (*see* CUSHITE WIFE), who was sojourning among the migrating Hebrews after the Exodus in Num 12, demonstrates that there was no prescription against such unions (and strengthens the association of Midianites and Cushites; *see* MIDIAN, MIDIANITE). The Cushite soldier who delivered news of Absalom's death to King David provides evidence that there were members of this group in Israel's armies (2 Sam 18:21-32). EBED-MELECH, the prominent Cushite courtier who convinced King Zedekiah to rescue Jeremiah from the cistern where he had been imprisoned indicates that Cushites were active as agents of Judah's monarchs (Jer 38–39). Cushites were not just foreign nationals on the border but figures fully integrated into various levels of Judahite society.

Two other figures playing key roles in biblical narratives have patronymics containing Cush-related names. Both YEHUDI (Jer 36), another courtier and scribe of King Jehoiakim, and ZEPHANIAH (Zeph 1:1), a member of the Judean royal house and a prophet, are said to be descendants of men named CUSHI, a gentilic meaning a "man from Cush." Though their Cushite heritage is not certain inasmuch as *Cushi* may be simply a personal name devoid of ethnic content, that the name occurs in patronymics abounding with otherwise consistently Yahwistic names suggests the esteem prominent Judean and even Israelite (Cush the Benjaminite, Ps 7:1, *see* 2 above) families had for Cushites.

According to the authors of books from every literary strata of the OT, Cushites came from "beyond the rivers of Cush" at the extremes of the known world to actively participate in the unfolding narratives of the OT. Their presence also is anticipated on the DAY OF THE LORD, for members of this foreign group will come with outstretched arms (Ps 68:32) full of gifts (Isa 18:7; Zeph 3:10), and they will bow before Judah's God in full submission, acknowledging that "God is with [Judah] alone, and there is no other; there is no god beside [Yahweh]" (Isa 45:14). *See* AFRICA.

Bibliography: Rodney S. Sadler Jr. *Can A Cushite Change His Skin? An Examination of Race Ethnicity and Othering in the Hebrew Bible* (2005).

RODNEY J. SADLER, JR.

CUSHAN [כּוּשָׁן *kushan*]. The term Cushan occurs once in the psalm-like prayer of Hab 3:7 (*See* CUSHAN-RISHATHAIM). Habakkuk depicts a Yahwistic theophany proceeding from the desert regions far to the south towards Judah. In v. 7 the term **kushan** is paralleled with the term Midian. When entities occur in this parallel arrangement in Hebrew poetry they should be viewed as similar or identical. Thus Cushan may be understood as a sub-tribal group of Midian, an archaic designation for the region, or, most likely as an Arabicized designation for a Cush-related group that settled in the region (*See* CUSH, CUSHITE).

RODNEY S. SADLER, JR.

CUSHION [προσκεφάλαιον *proskephalaion*]. A pillow for resting one's head while sleeping (1 Esd 3:8; LXX: Ezek 13:18, 20; Mark 4:38).

CUSHITE WIFE, MOSES' [אִשָּׁה כֻשִׁית *'ishah kushith*]. Numbers 12:1 provides the only instance when a Cushite (*see* CUSH, CUSHITE) woman is mentioned in the OT. The verse recalls MOSES' marriage to a Cushite woman, describing her identity twice by way of emphasis, and using it as a source of conflict between the lawgiver and his siblings, MIRIAM and AARON. It is evident in 12:1 that her identity as a Cushite could be presumed reason enough for these two other prominent leaders in the Hebrew migration to question her relationship to MOSES.

According to Exod 2:15-22, Moses married ZIPPO-RAH, identified as a daughter of a Midianite priest Reuel (*see* REUEL; JETHRO). Because of this, throughout the ages interpreters have wrestled with the problems represented by Num 12:1, such as 1) did Moses marry a second woman? 2) was this wife Zipporah? 3) could this wife's Cushite identity be reconciled with Zipporah's Midianite identity? Demetrius the Chronographer and Ezekiel the Tragedian explained how Moses' one wife, the Midianite Zipporah, could be identified as a Cushite. Josephus chose instead to see her as another wife from Ethiopia (*see* ETHIOPIA) taken from her land during a military campaign. It is likely, though not certain, that Zipporah is the Cushite wife, inasmuch as Midianite (*see* MIDIAN, MIDIANITE) and Cushanite (*see* CUSHAN) identity have been conflated in Hab 3:7. Accepting this, Zipporah could be identified as "Cush(an)ite," from a group descended from Cushites that dwelled in the region along the path of the Exodus.

In addition to the matter of the identification of this wife, recent scholars have also pondered if the problem caused by her Cushite identity was: 1) the woman's "race;" 2) her identity as a foreigner; 3) the authority she bore because of her priestly lineage and knowledge (Exod 4:24-26); or 4) the authority she bore because of her African heritage (*see* 1 Kgs 3:1). Though the first is unlikely due to the fact that no concept of "race" existed in the biblical period, each of the other possible problems has some merit.

An enigmatic story like this is perhaps explained by the theory that it has been redacted from two brief earlier conflict stories, one featuring just Miriam's complaint against Moses over his Cushite wife, and a second describing Miriam and Aaron's complaint over Moses' superior status. The narratives in Num 12 can be distinguished as follows:

1. Cushite Wife controversy–verses 1, 9a, 10a, 13-16.
2. Authority controversy–verses 2-5a, 6-8, 9b, 10b.

This division provides two distinct narratives with clear cycles of conflict, confrontation, and resolution. This reconstruction allows the reader to discern that Miriam's complaint about the Cushite wife evokes Yahweh's response, then Miriam's punishment. Though the cycle is clearer with stories separated, the cycle is still discernable in the extant narrative. It is only in this form that the narrative has all the elements of a formula found elsewhere in stories in Numbers: 1) complaint; 2) divine appearance; 3) divine punishment; 4) appeal to Moses; 5) Moses intercedes; 6) punishment ends.

As such, the extant story records a narrative in which an unnamed woman's Cushite identity was cause for Miriam's (and Aaron's) grievance. The story implies that the wife's identity elevates Moses' status over that of his siblings, and Miriam's (and Aaron's) complaint is met with Yahweh's disapprobation by way of a skin disease that befalls Miriam alone. Thus, the response to a grievance against a woman that bears an identity marker, Cushite, that denotes dark skin (*see* Jer 13:23), is Yahweh's punishment of another woman whose skin is transformed to be מְצֹרַעַת כַּשָּׁלֶג metsoraʿath kashalegh, "leprous, as snow" (*see* LEPROSY). "Leprous, as snow" in this instance would symbolically represent both a flaking and an unnatural absence of skin color. Miriam, because of her complaint would become pale. Rather than explicitly stating that Yahweh punished Miriam for her jealousy against this other female by "bleaching" her skin, the author engaged potent contrasting commonplace terms, כֻּשִׁית kushit (Cushite) and כַּשָּׁלֶג kashalegh ("as snow"), knowing that the audience would discern the implied irony.

Most significantly, Yahweh's response provides the theological thrust of the narrative. Were the coupling of Moses and this Cushite woman deemed inappropriate, Yahweh's response would have impugned that pair. Whatever could have been deemed problematic about the marriage of the most prominent Levite with a woman of darker skin, different ethnicity, and an alien priestly lineage, Yahweh assuages. While some unions with foreign women were categorically prohibited (e.g., Gen 28:1, 6; Josh 23:11-13), Yahweh allows a Cushite

partner for a member of the Hebrew tribe for whom purity was most critical. Though "race" would not have been an issue in biblical times and the phenotypes of Moses and his wife were likely more similar than modern interpreters would imagine, the narrative has continued relevance as it offers Yahweh's response to what some might describe as an "interracial" marriage in contemporary contexts.

An important and often unexamined implication of this passage is that there were Cushites (or Cush(an)ites) involved in the עֵרֶב רַב ʿerev rav, "mixed multitude" (Exod 12:38) that fled Egyptian captivity or joined those fleeing in the wilderness (e.g., Exod 18:1-6; Num 10:29-36; Judg 1:16, 4:11). Far from being an ethnically pure individuated human type, the group that came to be proto-Israel was already comprised of a motley assemblage of humanity. It is likely that the people of Israel and Judah continued to express varied hues due to the diverse backgrounds of their ancestors and continued intermixing throughout the preexilic period.

RODNEY S. SADLER, JR.

CUSTODIAN [παιδαγωγός paidagōgos]. A "pedagogue" was a trusted slave charged in Greco-Roman societies with taking a young boy to and from his classes and supervising his behavior there. His role was that of a GUARDIAN, guide, and disciplinarian. Paul uses "pedagogue" positively in 1 Cor 4:15, writing that many other believers are the Corinthians' "guardians," but Paul is their only "father." His meaning in Gal 3:24-25 is more controverted. The context indicates a negative use where the law of Moses is the "disciplinarian" that served to "imprison and guard" those who are "under the law." Now believers have no more need of a custodian because they have become people of God through faith.

Bibliography: J. L. Martyn. *Galatians* (1997); N. Young. "Paidagogos, The Social Setting of a Pauline Metaphor." *NovT* 29 (1987) 150–76.

ROBERT E. VAN VOORST

CUTHA kooth´uh [Κουθα Koutha]. A Temple servant whose descendants are included in a list of returnees from the Babylonian exile, released by Darius and led by ZERUBBABEL (1 Esd 5:32).

CUTH, CUTHAH kooth, kooth´uh. כּוּת, kuth; כּוּתָה kuthah; Akkadian Kutu]. Identified with the ruins at Tell Ibrahim. It was an important Babylonian cult center for the underworld deity NERGAL. Captives from Cuth, resettled by SARGON II (722–20 BCE), introduced the Nergal cult to SAMARIA (2 Kgs 17:24, 30).

CUT OFF, TO כָּרַת karath; ἀποκόπτω apokoptō, ἐκκόπτω ekkoptō]. The principal Hebrew term can mean, e.g., to cut off branches (Num 13:23) or parts of the body (Exod 4:25; Lev 22:24; Deut 23:1). Particularly important is the phrase karath berith, "to make (literally, cut) a covenant," the imagery probably derived from the covenant ritual (Gen 15:10, 18; Ps 50:5; Jer 34:18). Karath appears regularly in the intensive sense "exterminate," as in the prophetic oracles against the nations, and is commonly used when a person is "cut off" from the people or covenant community (e.g., Gen 17:14; Exod 12:15, 19; Num 9:13; 19:20).

In the NT the synonymous verbs apokoptō and ekkoptō have a more restricted range of usage: cutting off an ear (John 18:10), or branches for burning (Matt 3:10; 7:19). The latter imagery is powerfully used in Rom 11:22, 24, and even more strongly in the challenge to self-discipline in Mark 9:43, 45. The metaphor of "cutting a covenant" is not retained as such in the NT, but there are strong echoes of OT usage and theology in the savage irony of Gal 5:12 and the similar wordplay in Phil 3:2. *See* COVENANT, OT AND NT; CRIMES AND PUNISHMENT, OT AND NT; EXCOMMUNICATE.

JAMES DUNN

CUTTING LOCUST. *See* LOCUSTS.

CUTTINGS IN THE FLESH. *See* MUTILATION.

CYAMON si´uh-muhn [Κυαμών Kyamōn]. Unidentified place, facing Esdraelon, marking the boundary of the camp of Holofernes before his army advanced to Bethulia (Jdt 7:3).

CYAXARES si´aks´uh-reez [Αχιαχαρος Achiacharos]. King of MEDIA who destroyed Nineveh and captured its residents (Tob 14:15, NRSV). Cyaxares is called AHASUERUS in some manuscripts (RSV).

CYMBAL. *See* MUSICAL INSTRUMENTS.

CYNICS, CYNICISM sin´ik, sin´uh-siz´uhm. The varied "dogged" followers ("cynic" comes from Greek κυνικός kunikos, meaning "dog") of the ascetic lifestyle of the philosopher, Diogenes of Sinope (ca. 300 BCE), made their presence felt together in the public places of Mediterranean towns until ca. 550 CE. Though not named in the Bible, their relevance for understanding early Christianity has been widely debated.

Diversity within the Cynic movement is clear. Only if we rely on outside observers do Cynics appear uniform in appearance and outlook. Theirs was a world-affirming (not world-denying) asceticism. They saw their lifestyle as "natural." Like the birds and other animals, the Cynic was free from the artificiality of the quest for wealth, prestige, titillation, and the cultic reflection of society's corruption. Cynics could appear as loners, but might also be grouped, perhaps

with a teacher. Some were harsh, some easygoing.

Cynics were often highly educated, but because Cynicism was more a way of life than a philosophy, it could attract discontented artisans. Cynics often insisted that their ideals were as attainable by women as by men. They tended to skepticism in the face of fortune-telling or other unconfirmed claims to knowledge. ("Am I going to hit you with this stick or not?" asks Diogenes. "Er, not," replies the soothsayer. "Wrong," replies Diogenes, with a thwack.) Some appear agnostic, even atheistic; others seem austerely or even warmly monotheistic and convinced that their mission to change people's lives is divinely authorized. They could (like early Christians) argue among themselves and deny one another the right to the name "Cynic."

Cynics adopted varieties of shabby or bizarre dress in order to display their contempt for convention in a culture where even eating in public was shameful (*see* SHAME). Outsiders typify their garb as a double cloak, staff, and begging-bag; insiders eschew any such uniform. Some Cynics begged and slept outside; some relied on hospitality (or even a patron); some took menial jobs. A few pursued shock tactics such as public defecation and masturbation (which they asserted was as much a natural behavior among humans as among other animals), but such behavior was not the essence of the movement, as there was no set code of conduct.

Cynics taught by example, aiming for a quick conversion to their free, healthy, and authentic lifestyle ("a short cut to excellence"). With their sometimes startling behavior, jokes, illustrations from ordinary life, and vivid anecdotes (*see* CHREIAI), they challenged anyone willing to look and listen. Dio of Prusa (*Discourse* 4) tells the story of a "Good Euboean" that is comparable to "the good Samaritan" in Luke. The so-called "Stoic-Cynic DIATRIBE" seems to be a GENRE invented by 19th cent. CE philologists.

Non-Cynics tend to sum up Cynic teaching in "slogans" such as ἀσκῆσις askēsis (training), αὐτάκεια autakeia (self-sufficiency), βασιλεία basileia (kingdom), and παρρησία parrēsia (brashness, frankness); the Cynics themselves usually managed to describe themselves with few or none of these slogans.

Cynics appear in various cities. The city of Gadara in the DECAPOLIS was home to Mennipus (early 3rd cent. BCE) and Meleager (mid 2nd cent.), as well as Oenomaus (early 2nd cent. CE, a man admired by later rabbis). From the mid 1st cent. CE come Demetrius (Seneca's teacher), Demonax, Dio of Prusa, Peregrinus, and others. By the 1st cent. there is widespread evidence of a less "cultured," more plebean Cynicism independent of the intellectuals, and of wide cultural awareness of Cynic ideas. The surviving schoolbooks, the PROGYMNASMATA, are evidence of the pervasiveness of Cynicism.

Our main sources are from the late 4th cent. BCE to the 6th cent. CE. The *Cynic Epistles* are letters ascribed to Diogenes and his pupil Crates and others, dated from the 3rd cent. BCE to the 2nd cent. CE. Diogenes Laertius' *Lives of Eminent Philosophers* dates from the early 3rd CE, but its materials cover the four preceding centuries. The *Discourses* (4, 6, 8-10) of Dio of Prusa are from the late 1st and early 2nd cent. CE. We have a wide range of notes and quotations about the Cynics from Cicero, Seneca, Philo, Epictetus, Musonius, Lucian of Samosata, and many more.

No one has found analogies between Cynicism and canonical Jewish scriptures. There is ample evidence, however, of early Christian thinkers discerning considerable parallels between elements of Cynicism and of their own Christian ethos, and such parallels have been acknowledged in later times. Some scholars have preferred to find contrasts between Jesus and his followers' lifestyles and that of "the Cynics," who are usually described in a uniform and caricatured fashion. However, allowing for the diversities found inside both movements, significant similarities do emerge. There is a similar disparagement of hypocrisy, wealth, and patronage and especially of royal power. The Gospels and Cynicism share a shocking dismissal of burial conventions (Matt 8:21-22). Jesus, like a Cynic teacher, speaks in his own name, not that of God as a Jewish prophet might, nor of his own teacher, as a rabbi or a more conventional philosopher might. There is a common reliance on illustrations from life. In particular, the ethos and themes of the birds and the flowers (Luke 12:22-31) can also be found in Cynic variants of Greco-Roman discussions of busyness. When Paul became a Christian, he may have adopted a lifestyle that would have looked deliberately Cynic (e.g., 1 Cor 4:10-13).

Bibliography: E. B. Branham and M. O. Goulet-Cazé, ed. *The Cynics. The Cynic Movement in Antiquity and Its Legacy* (1996); F. G. Downing. "Jesus and Cynicism." T. Holmén and S. E. Porter, eds. *Handbook of the Study of the Historical Jesus* (2005); M. O. Goulet-Cazé. "Le cynisme ancien à l'époque impériale." *ANRW* II 36.4 (1990) 2720–2823.

F. GERALD DOWNING

CYPRESS [בְּרוֹשׁ berosh, גֹּפֶר gofer, תְּאַשּׁוּר teʾashur]. The cypress (*Cupressus sempervirens*) is a tree native to the Levant that grows up to a height of more than 15 m and is described in the OT as primarily from Lebanon. It is identified with several different terms in the OT including berosh (sometimes translated as fir); gofer; and teʾashur (translated as "PINE" in the RSV, "larch" in the NAS, and "box tree" in the KJV); and tirzah (in KJV only). Gofer was used in the manufacture of Noah's ark. Beroshim were used in the construction of the Temple of Solomon. Berosh may be a collective term for various conifers or identified with *Juniperus excelsa*. Burashu the Akkadian cognate, is translated as juniper tree. *See* PLANTS OF THE BIBLE.

Bibliography: P. J. King and L. E. Stager. *Life in Biblical Israel* (2001); M. Zohary. *Plants of the Bible* (1982).

DAVID LIPOVITCH

CYPRIAN sip'ree-uhn [ca. 200–258 CE]. As bishop of Carthage until martyred (248/249–58), Cyprian addressed Christians who lapsed under persecution but sought reconciliation with the church by making bishops, rather than confessors (charismatic authorities), the judges in reconciliation, thus enhancing episcopal authority. Cyprian denied baptism by heretics and schismatics, contending they were outside the apostolic succession and church and lacked the Holy Spirit; hence rebaptism was needed. Stephen, bishop of Rome, rejected rebaptism and defended Roman primacy. Cyprian's doctrine of the episcopate assumed shared authority of the bishops as a body. By valuing unity, Cyprian did not break with bishops who rejected rebaptism. *See* APOSTOLIC FATHERS.

NANCY WEATHERWAX

CYPROS. *See* HERODIAN FORTRESSES.

CYPRUS si'pruhs [Κύπρος Kyprus]. Paul visited this island during a missionary journey (Acts 13:4), as did Barnabas and John Mark after parting ways with Paul over a disagreement about retaining John Mark in their work (*see* Acts 15:39).

Cyprus is the third-largest island in the Mediterranean Sea (9251 sq km). It is located approximately 100 km west of Syria, 70 km south of Turkey, and some 400 km north of Egypt. The material culture of Bronze and Iron Age Cyprus—from monumental buildings to burial chambers, from pottery to seals, from copper pins to bronze cauldrons—is among the best known and most widely published of any island culture in the Mediterranean.

By the beginning of the Bronze Age (ca. 2600 BCE), excavations at several sites on Cyprus have revealed important changes in the island's economy. These include the first use of copper tools, the cart and the plow, a variety of domesticated animals and their "secondary products" (wool, leather, milk), and evidence for herding these animals (pastoralism). By adopting these technological and cultural innovations, people were able to maximize both industrial and agricultural production, ensuring a sound subsistence base. Along with the emergence of regional trade, these innovations also led to changes in the way that people thought about things, and to an increased capacity for processing and transferring information, ideas, and material goods.

Expansion in the agricultural and pastoral sectors of the economy underpinned the mining and production of COPPER from Cyprus's abundant ore deposits. Expertise in metallurgical technology is demonstrated by the quality and quantity of metal products found in both excavated sites (Kissonerga *Mosphilia*, Marki *Alonia*) and tomb deposits, the latter along the north coast (Lapithos, Bellapais *Vounos*, Vasilia *Kaphkalla*). The growing number of foreign imports into Cyprus at this time, as well as local metalworking, indicate that external demand for Cypriot copper was on the rise. By the 19th cent. BCE, cuneiform records from Mari in Syria make the earliest reference to copper from *Alashiya*, a place-name that all archaeologists and ancient historians now accept as the Bronze Age equivalent of "Cyprus."

By 2000 BCE, various states and kingdoms in the eastern Mediterranean maintained a high level of demand for imports (e.g., the CEDARS of Lebanon, the copper of Cyprus). Because tin was the metal of choice to alloy with copper in order to manufacture BRONZE, long-distance trade was stimulated even further. Technological innovations of the 3rd millennium BCE, such as the longboat and sail, facilitated the bulk transport of raw materials or manufactured goods on an unprecedented scale, while new harbor towns and diverse trading routes further promoted a budding sense of internationalism.

On Cyprus itself, people began to specialize in producing such goods as woolens and textiles, clay figurines, shell beads, gaming stones, and a variety of metal tools and implements. Recent excavations at sites such as Kissonerga *Mosphilia*, Sotira *Kaminoudhia*, Marki *Alonia*, and Alambra *Mouttes* have shown us how people lived, worked, worshiped, and died, all within the context of an increasingly complex social system. Although Cyprus never developed the type of palaces or economies that typified Levantine city-states or Near Eastern kingdoms, some people on the island were able to manage increasingly specialized levels of production, and to oversee the subsistence needs of specialists who produced surplus goods and metals for trade. By the early 2nd millennium BCE, major social changes had taken place on Cyprus, as trade and contact with outsiders helped to overcome a deep-seated resistance to social and economic stratification.

During the 2nd millennium BCE, states and kingdoms from the Near East to the central Mediterranean became involved in the production, trade, and consumption of utilitarian and luxury goods as well as a range of organic items (e.g., olive oil, wine, honey, spices). Port cities and palatial centers—Ugarit in Syria, Enkomi and Kition on Cyprus, Tell el-ʿAjjul and Tel Nami in Israel, Troy in Anatolia, Kommos and Knossos on Crete, Mycenae and Pylos in Greece—took part in this lucrative international trade, and found their political positions enhanced as a result. Copper oxide ingots, most of which were produced on Cyprus and likely served as a medium for exchange during the Late Bronze Age (ca. 1600–1200 BCE), have been recovered in contexts stretching from the Black Sea and Babylonia to Sardinia and southern France. Seaborne trade throughout the Late Bronze Age eastern Mediterranean and Near East had many dimensions: complex in nature and diverse in structure, it encompassed both state-dominated efforts and individual enterprise.

On Cyprus, several striking changes appear in the archaeological record of the Late Bronze Age: 1) urban centers with monumental buildings appear throughout the island; 2) burial practices show clear social and gender distinctions; 3) writing ("Cypro-Minoan"), on clay tablets, first appears; 4) copper production and export intensified as long-distance trading systems developed; and 5) newly built fortifications and a relative increase in weaponry indicate other kinds of change in Cypriot society. These developments reveal Cyprus's transformation from an isolated, village-oriented culture into an international, urban-centered, complex society. The successful exploitation of mineral resources and production of agricultural surpluses meant that political authority had to be centralized. Eventually, the intensified production and trade in copper made Cyprus one of the most important providers of this metal in the Mediterranean and the Near East, a situation that continued as least until the fall of the Roman Empire.

Cuneiform documents from AMARNA in Egypt and Ugarit in Syria reveal that high-level, diplomatic trade relations existed between Cyprus, Egypt, and the Levant throughout the 14th–13th cent. BCE. All these documentary records reveal the organizational efficiency, shipping capacity, and product diversity that characterized a highly specialized, well-coordinated political and economic system. This burgeoning international system brought prestige goods to Cyprus's rulers, as well as raw materials to its craftspeople, and food supplies and basic products to rural peasants and producers. Even if powerful rulers controlled local economies, the dynamics of production, trade, and consumption freed up resources for individual activities within a more structured political economy. Involvement in trade, thus, had the capacity to change economic motivations and to transform social groups. Although trade now involved both luxury goods (precious metals, semi-precious stones, ivory handicrafts) and "non-convertible" commodities (storage jars, textiles, glass) locally produced for export, the real basis of economic and political power lay in convertible goods, especially metals and the copper oxide ingots. The trade in these items was subject to tight control by powerful rulers involved in a formal gift-exchange system. Many of these rulers legitimized their position and consolidated their power by importing luxury goods that could only be acquired through the production of other goods—whether raw materials or finished products.

After ca. 1250 BCE, a series of demographic movements and site destructions associated in part with the "Sea Peoples" (*see* PHOENICIA) brought an end to the lucrative international relations of the Middle-Late Bronze ages. The "Sea Peoples," and others like them, were more a symptom than a cause of the widespread decline. Although these human displacements and cultural intermixings spelled the end of an international era, farmers and minor craftspeople remained in place in each country, with their horizons narrowed but subsistence systems still intact.

On Cyprus, the natural circumscription of the island and the growing scarcity of land and raw materials (the result of extensive plow agriculture and copper exploitation) eventually led to social divisions. The overall political and economic system, however, proved stable and the widespread collapse of other states and trading networks in the region seems to have had limited effects on Cyprus. Some of the most important developments in early iron technology took place on Cyprus at this time. While some sites suffered destruction or abandonment, the major coastal towns of Enkomi, Kition, and Palaepaphos survived, perhaps becoming new centers of authority, and managing new Cypriot contacts overseas (in the Aegean and central Mediterranean). As incoming Levantine or Aegean peoples—new migrants to the island—became "hybridized" to local Cypriot peoples and customs, copper production, and commercial enterprise became revitalized, at least in the short term. By 1050 BCE, however, the settlement patterns and political organization that had characterized the Late Bronze Age began to change, as different social and economic structures dictated the establishment of new towns that heralded the rise of Cyprus's early historical kingdoms and the island's social and commercial adjustments to the coming Age of Iron.

Bibliography: D. Bolger. *Gender in Ancient Cyprus: Narratives of Social Change on a Mediterranean Island* (2003); N. H. Gale, ed. *Bronze Age Trade in the Mediterranean.* (1991); A. B. Knapp, ed. "Production, Location, and Integration in Bronze Age Cyprus." *Current Anthropology* 31 (1990) 147–76; A. B. Knapp (with S. W. Manning and Steve O. Held). "Problems and Prospects in Cypriote Prehistory." *Journal of World Prehistory* 8 (1994) 377–452; L. Steel. *Cyprus before History: From the Earliest Settlers to the End of the Bronze Age* (2004); P. W. Wallace and A. G. Orphanides, eds. *Near Eastern and Aegean Texts from the Third to the First Millennia BC* (1996).

A. BERNARD KNAPP

CYRENE sí-ree′nee [Κυρήνη Kyrēnē]. Cyrene was located about 6 m inland from the Mediterranean Sea in the modern country of LIBYA (*see* AFRICA). It was situated on an elevated terrace about 2,000 ft. above sea level. Cyrene's fertile soil produced abundant grain, wool, livestock, olive oil, vegetables, herbs, dates, and silphium, a spice that was valued for cooking and medicine.

According to HERODOTUS (*Hist.* 4.150–58), Battus led an expedition of Dorian Greek colonists from the island of Thera to found the city ca. 631 BCE. Seven of his descendants ruled Cyrene until ca. 440 BCE. Then Cyrene was ruled by a republican government until it submitted to the rule of Alexander in 331 BCE. After Alexander's death, Ptolemy I established his authority over the region in 322 BCE. In the 1st cent. BCE, Pliny the Elder (*Nat.* 5.31) included Cyrene among the five cities of the Pentapolis. When Ptolemy Apion died in 96 BCE, he transferred the region to the Roman Senate. In 67 BCE, Cyrenaica was combined with Crete to form one senatorial province with Cyrene as the capital.

In 115–16 CE the Jewish inhabitants initiated a revolt that destroyed much of the city (Dio Cassius 68.32). Hadrian rebuilt the city, but climate changes and an earthquake contributed to its decline until the Arabs conquered the city in 642 CE.

Notable natives of Cyrene include Eratosthenes (276–ca. 194 BCE), who calculated the earth's circumference within 50 mi. of its actual distance, and Callimachus (ca. 310–240 BCE), a poet who influenced later poets such as Catullus and Ovid. Josephus described a significant Jewish population in the city (*Ag. Ap.* 2.4; *Ant.* 14.114). Notable Jewish residents include Jason (2 Macc 2:23), historian of the Maccabean revolt, and EZEKIEL THE TRAGEDIAN.

Cyrene is mentioned seven times in the NT. Roman soldiers compelled a resident of Cyrene named Simon to carry the cross for Jesus (Matt 27:32; Mark 15:21; Luke 23:26). Residents of Cyrene were among the Jewish pilgrims who heard the disciples on the day of Pentecost speaking in their own language (Acts 2:10). Jewish natives of Cyrene were among those who opposed Stephen (Acts 6:9). Jewish Christians from Cyrene preached the gospel to Gentiles in Antioch (Acts 11:20). Among the prophets and teachers in the church at Antioch was Lucius of Cyrene (Acts 13:1).

Bibliography: Shim'on Applebaum. *Jews and Greeks in Ancient Cyrene* (1979).

GREGORY L. LINTON

CYRIL OF ALEXANDRIA [ca. 375–444 CE]. A prolific commentator versed in liberal studies and divine doctrines, Cyril produced four sets of exegetical works, largely extant: 1) *Adoration and Worship of God in Spirit and in Truth*, seventeen books in dialogue form on the Pentateuch, arranged by topics showing the law's spirit satisfied by Christ; and *Glaphyra* (elegant comments), arranged by order of the Pentateuch. 2) Line by line *Commentaries on the Twelve Minor Prophets* and *on Isaiah*, following the order of the Alexandrian Bible; each book opens with its historical setting. 3) *Thesaurus, On the Holy Trinity,* and verse-by-verse *Commentary on John.* 4) *Easter encyclicals* (414–28).

Principles of ancient grammarians guided Cyril's exegesis. According to these principles, smaller sections become clear in light of the entire text, steered by the skopos (goal), and arriving at the telos (conclusion). Thus for Cyril, the Bible became one single book: its skopos was Christ; its telos was Christ's coming. False skopoi led Arians, Neoplatonists, and Jews astray. Exegesis balanced the text's physical meaning, found by explaining realia and unusual words with its spiritual wisdom (theoria), an allegorical interpretation restrained by grammar and common sense. Different text transmissions, exegetes, and Josephus were consulted.

PETRA HELDT

CYRIL OF JERUSALEM [ca. 315–386 CE]. A Jerusalemite, Cyril became a deacon at the time of the Holy Sepulchre's inauguration in 335 CE, a priest 345 CE, and a bishop by 350/351–386 CE. Thrice exiled by Arians, Cyril saw Arianism from its outbreak ca. 318 to its condemnation in 381 CE (Council of Constantinople).

Cyril's extant writings consist mainly of twenty-four lectures, written ca. 348 CE, including eighteen prebaptismal Catechetical Lectures (CL) on the creed and five postbaptismal Mystagogic Lectures (ML) on the sacraments, firmly based on the OT (twenty-two books) in its LXX version and the NT (excluding the book of Revelation) (CL 4:35-36). As every doctrinal statement must be verified in Scripture (CL 4:17; 16:24), Cyril employed the nonbiblical homoousios ("being of one substance") only in 381 CE.

Cyril read Scripture as containing the whole of doctrine (CL 5:12) and accounting for God's continuous salvation (CL 6:2). Teaching the creed and celebrating liturgy (ML 5) actualize Scripture.

The Antiochene tradition guided Cyril's perception of Scripture: sensus litteralis emphasizes the historical substance in Scripture (ML 1:2); typology provides testimonies for the salvific message (ML 1:3); theoria leads to spiritual truths not immediately obvious (ML 1:4); anagogy conveys glimpses of the Divine and leads into a moral life.

PETRA HELDT

CYRIL OF JERUSALEM, TWENTIETH DISCOURSE OF. This pseudepigraphical homily on the Dormition of the Virgin represents one of the earliest Dormition narratives of the "Coptic Type." It was composed sometime before the middle of the 6th cent. and reflects much that is typical of the early Cop. narratives, including the presence of only a few apostles and the January 16 feast day.

Bibliography: Stephen J. Shoemaker. *Ancient Traditions of the Virgin Mary's Dormition and Assumption* (2002).

STEPHEN J. SHOEMAKER

CYRUS si´ruhs [כּוֹרֶשׁ koresh; Κῦρος Kyros]. Cyrus (II) the Great established the Persian Empire (539–ca.

531 BCE), during a seminal period in the history of the Jews and the development of Judaism. Ezra and Isaiah credit Cyrus with freeing the Judean exiles in Babylon and allowing them to return home (Ezra 1:1-8; Isa 45:1) to rebuild the Temple at Jerusalem (Isa 44:28; Ezra 3:7; 4:3-5; 5:13-17; 6:3-5).

A decree attributed to Cyrus of Persia states that the exiles were to rebuild the "house of the Lord" (2 Chr 36:22-23; Ezra 1:2-4). While it is not likely that the historical Cyrus actually sent out an official proclamation to this effect (complete with biblical restoration theology), biblical accounts portray Cyrus as a ruler who had unusual sympathy and tolerance for his subjects. Cyrus' theological importance as liberator of exiles and his role in the prophesied restoration of Israel is apparent when Second Isaiah calls Cyrus "the anointed one (MESSIAH) of the Lord" (מָשִׁיחַ mashiakh; χριστός christos [Isa 45:1]).

Cyrus' early life is surrounded by legend. One story is that he was exposed as an infant but was saved by a forester (Herodotus). This motif of an infant threatened with death but saved to come back to achieve his destiny as an adult is widespread in antiquity, best known to us in the infancy accounts of of Moses and Jesus. (In addition to Cyrus, another example well known to Near Eastern scholars is Sargon I.) According to one story Cyrus was the son of the Persian king and his Median wife. We do know that Cyrus' Median great-grandfather had been the ally of Nabopolassar the Chaldean, and they together had conquered Nineveh (612 BCE) and brought down the Assyrian Empire. Cyrus was king of the region of Anshan, which was a vassal to the Medes.

Cyrus had united the Persians and Medes into one entity by ca. 550. Cyrus continued to expand his territory by military means (a famous conquest was Croesus, the king of Sardis). In 539 Cyrus' army captured Babylon. The last king of Babylonia, Nabonidus (not his son Belshazzar as Dan 5 claims), was apparently captured (not killed) and well treated. The Persian entry into Babylon was led by the general Gubaru (Gobryas) who prepared the way for Cyrus's triumphal entry two weeks later. Gubaru himself evidently died only a few days after this (*Nabonidus Chronicle* iii.22). Some have wanted to identify this Gubaru as "DARIUS THE MEDE" even though this Darius is a fictional character.

Cyrus seems to have set out to make a good impression on the Babylonians and the subject peoples. Cyrus presented himself as liberator and benefactor. A number of these claims are made in the *Cyrus Cylinder*, which seems to have been produced in Cyrus' first year. It claims that he was chosen for rule by the Babylonian god Marduk, that he protected the people of Babylonia, that he returned the statues of the gods brought into Babylon from the subject peoples by Nabonidus (during the last days of his rule), and that he allowed some peoples to return to their homes. Much of what Cyrus claims to have done was already done by Nabonidus, but it was not an unusual practice among new Mesopotamian rulers to claim for themselves the deeds of their predecessors. Further pro-Cyrus propaganda is found in the *Verse Account of Nabonidus*, which attacks Nabonidus as the opponent of the Marduk priestly establishment and hails Cyrus as its deliverer and champion (*ANET*, 312–15). Although one must treat Cyrus's own statements in official propaganda with caution, it seems likely that he allowed a return of some of the Jews to Palestine.

Because the *Nabonidus Chronicle* breaks off shortly after the conquest of Babylon, the detailed activities of Cyrus until near the end of his reign are no longer known. Like his birth, Cyrus' death is surrounded by legend: the preserved accounts do not agree and also contain fantastic elements. Yet it seems probable that Cyrus met his death in a military campaign in 530 BCE and was succeeded by the crown prince CAMBYSES. *See* EXILE; EZRA, BOOK OF; PERSIA.

Bibliography: Pierre Briant. *From Cyrus to Alexander: A History of the Persian Empire* (2002).

LESTER L. GRABBE

ABBREVIATIONS

GENERAL

*	reconstructed prototype of hypothetical word form
ANE	Ancient Near East
Aram.	Aramaic
b.	born
BCE	Before the Common Era
CE	Common Era
ca.	circa
cent.	century
chap(s).	chapter(s)
Copt.	Coptic
d.	died
D	Deuteronomist source (of the Pentateuch)
DH	See Dtr, DtrH
Dtr, DtrH	Deuteronomistic Historian
E	Elohist source (of the Pentateuch)
esp.	especially
fem.	feminine
fig.	figure
ft.	feet
g	grams
Heb.	Hebrew text
J	Jahwist or Yahwist source (of the Pentateuch)
km	kilometer(s)
lit.	literally
L	litres
Lat.	Latin
LXX	Septuagint
m	meter(s)
mi.	mile(s)
MS(S)	manuscript(s)
mg.	margin
masc.	masculine
MT	Masoretic Text
n(n).	note(s)
neut.	neuter
NT	New Testament
OG	Old Greek
OL	Old Latin
OT	Old Testament
P	Priestly source (of the Pentateuch)
par.	Parallel (used to indicate textual parallels)
pl(s).	plate(s)

SP	Samaritan Pentateuch
Str.	Stratum
v(v).	verse(s)
Vg	Vulgate
\\	between Scripture references indicates parallelism

BIBLE TRANSLATIONS

AB	Anchor Bible
ASV	American Standard Version
CEV	Contemporary English Version
CSB	Catholic Study Bible
GNB	Good News Bible
JB	Jerusalem Bible
KJV	King James Version
NAB	New American Bible
NCB	New Century Bible
NEB	New English Bible
NIV	New International Version
NJB	New Jerusalem Bible
NKJV	New King James Version
NRSV	New Revised Standard Version
REB	Revised English Bible
RSV	Revised Standard Version
TLB	The Living Bible
TNK	Tanakh

HEBREW BIBLE/OLD TESTAMENT

Gen	Genesis
Exod	Exodus
Lev	Leviticus
Num	Numbers
Deut	Deuteronomy
Josh	Joshua
Judg	Judges
Ruth	Ruth
1–2 Sam	1–Samuel
1–2 Kgdms	1–Kingdoms (LXX)
1–2 Kgs	1–2 Kings
3–4 Kgdms	3–4 Kingdoms (LXX)
1–2 Chr	1–2 Chronicles
Ezra	Ezra
Neh	Nehemiah
Esth	Esther
Job	Job
Ps/Pss	Psalms
Prov	Proverbs
Eccl	Ecclesiastes
Song	Song of Songs (Song of Solomon, or Canticles)
Isa	Isaiah
Jer	Jeremiah

Lam	Lamentations
Ezek	Ezekiel
Dan	Daniel
Hos	Hosea
Joel	Joel
Amos	Amos
Obad	Obadiah
Jonah	Jonah
Mic	Micah
Nah	Nahum
Hab	Habakkuk
Zeph	Zephaniah
Hag	Haggai
Zech	Zechariah
Mal	Malachi

NEW TESTAMENT

Matt	Matthew
Mark	Mark
Luke	Luke
John	John
Acts	Acts
Rom	Romans
1–2 Cor	1–2 Corinthians
Gal	Galatians
Eph	Ephesians
Phil	Philippians
Col	Colossians
1–2 Thess	1–2 Thessalonians
1–2 Tim	1–2 Timothy
Titus	Titus
Phlm	Philemon
Heb	Hebrews
Jas	James
1–2 Pet	1–2 Peter
1–2–3 John	1–2–3 John
Jude	Jude
Rev	Revelation

APOCRYPHA AND SEPTUAGINT

Bar	Baruch
Add Dan	Additions to Daniel
Pr Azar	Prayer of Azariah
Bel	Bel and the Dragon
Sg Three	Song of the Three Young Men
Sus	Susanna
1–Esd	1–2 Esdras
Add Esth	Additions to Esther
Ep Jer	Epistle of Jeremiah
Jdt	Judith
1–2 Macc	1–2 Maccabees
3–4 Macc	3–4 Maccabees

Pr Man	Prayer of Manasseh
Ps 151	Psalm 151
Sir	Sirach/Ecclesiasticus
Tob	Tobit
Wis	Wisdom of Solomon

PSEUDEPIDGRAPHAL AND EARLY PATRISTIC BOOKS

Ahiqar	Ahiqar
Ant. Bibl.	L.A.B.
Apoc. Ab.	Apocalypse of Abraham
Apoc. Adam	Apocalypse of Adam
Apoc. Dan.	Apocalypse of Daniel
Apoc. Ezek.	Apocr. Ezek.
Apoc. Mos.	Apocalypse of Moses
Apoc. Sedr.	Apocalypse of Sedrach
Apoc. Zeph.	Apocalypse of Zephaniah
Apocr. Ezek.	Apocrypon of Exekiel
2 Apoc. Bar.	Syriac Apocalypse of Baruch
3 Apoc. Bar.	Greek Apocalypse of Baruch
Aris. Ex.	Aristeas the Exegete
Aristob.	Aristobulus
Artap.	Artapanus
Ascen. Isa.	Mart. Ascen. Isa. 6–11
As. Mos.	Assumption of Moses
Barn.	Barnabas
2 Bar	2 Baruch (Syriac Apocalypse)
3 Bar.	3 Baruch (Greek Apocalypse)
4 Bar.	4 Baruch (Paraleipomena Jeremiou)
Bib. Ant.	L.A.B.
Bk. Noah	Book of Noah
Cav. Tr.	Cave of Treasures
Cl. Mal.	Cleodemus Malchus
1–2 Clem.	1–2 Clement
Dem.	Demetrius (the Chronographer)
Did.	Didache
1 En.	1 Enoch (Ethiopic Apocalypse)
2 En.	2 Enoch (Slavonic Apocalypse)
3 En.	3 Enoch (Hebrew Apocalypse)
Eup.	Eupolemus
Ezek. Trag.	Ezekiel the Tragedian
4 Ezra	4 Ezra
5 Apoc. Syr. Pss.	Five Apocryphal Syriac Psalms
Ep. Arist.	Epistle of Aristeas
Gk. Apoc. Ezra	Greek Apocalypse of Ezra
Gos. Pet.	Gospel of Peter
Hec. Ab.	Hecataeus of Abdera
Hist. Jos.	History of Joseph
Hist. Rech.	History of the Rechabites
Herm. Sim.	Shepherd of Hermas, Similitude
Ign. Eph.	Ignatius, To the Ephesians
Ign. Magn.	Ignatius, To the Magnesians
Ign. Phld.	Ignatius, To the Philadelphians
Ign. Pol.	Ignatius, To Polycarp

Ign. *Rom.*	Ignatius, *To the Romans*
Ign. *Smyrn.*	Ignatius, *To the Smyrnaeans*
Ign. *Trall.*	Ignatius, *To the Trallians*
Jos. Asen.	*Joseph and Aseneth*
Jub.	*Jubilees*
L.A.B.	*Liber antiquitatum biblicarum (Pseudo-Philo)*
L.A.E.	*Life of Adam and Eve*
Lad. Jac.	*Ladder of Jacob*
Let. Aris.	*Letter of Aristeas*
Liv. Pro.	*Lives of the Prophets*
Lost Tr.	*The Lost Tribes*
3 Macc.	*3 Maccabees*
4 Macc.	*4 Maccabees*
5 Macc.	*5 Maccabees (Arabic)*
Mart. Ascen. Isa.	*Martyrdom and Ascension of Isaiah*
Mart. Isa.	*Mart. Ascen. Isa. 1–5*
Mart. Pol.	*Martydom of Polycarp*
Pol. Phil	*Polycarp, To the Philippians*
Odes Sol.	*Odes of Solomon*
P. Oxy.	*Oxyrynchus Papyri.* Edited by B. P. Grenfell and A. S. Hunt.
Pr. Jac.	*Prayer of Jacob*
Pr. Jos.	*Prayer of Joseph*
Pr. Man.	*Prayer of Manasseh*
Pr. Mos.	*Prayer of Moses*
Ps.-Eup.	Pseudo-Eupolemus
Ps.-Hec.	Pseudo-Hecataeuus
Ps.-Orph.	Pseudo-Orpheus
Ps.-Phoc.	Pseudo-Phocylides
Pss. Sol.	*Psalms of Solomon*
Ques. Ezra	*Questions of Ezra*
Rev. Ezra	*Revelation of Ezra*
Sib. Or.	*Sibylline Oracles*
Syr. Men.	*Sentences of the Syriac Menander*
T. 12 Patr.	*Testaments of the Twelve Patriarchs*
T. Ash.	*Testament of Asher*
T. Benj.	*Testament of Benjamin*
T. Dan	*Testament of Dan*
T. Gad	*Testament of Gad*
T. Iss.	*Testament of Issachar*
T. Job	*Testament of Job*
T. Jos.	*Testament of Joseph*
T. Jud.	*Testament of Judah*
T. Levi	*Testament of Levi*
T. Naph.	*Testament of Naphtali*
T. Reu.	*Testament of Reuben*
T. Sim.	*Testament of Simeon*
T. Zeb.	*Testament of Zebulun*
T. 3 Patr.	*Testaments of the Three Patriarchs*
T. Ab.	*Testament of Abraham*
T. Isaac	*Testament of Jacob*
T. Adam	*Testament of Adam*
T. Hez.	*Testament of Hezekiah (Mart. Ascen. Isa. 3:13–4:22)*

T. Mos.	*Testament of Moses*
T. Sol.	*Testament of Solomon*
Theod.	Theodotus, *On the Jews*
Treat. Shem	*Treatise of Shem*
Vis. Isa.	*Use Ascen. Isa.*

Philo

Abr.	*De Abrahamo*
Abraham	*On the Life of Abraham*
Agr.	*De agricultura*
Agriculture	*On Agriculture*
Cher.	*De cherubim*
Cherubim	*On the Cherubim*
Conf.	*De confusione linguarum*
Contempl.	*De vita contemplative*
Contempl. Life	*On the Contemplative Life*
Congr.	*Decongressue eruditionish gratia*
Decal.	*De decalogo*
Decalogue	*On the Decalogue*
Curses	*On Curses (=Rewards 127–72)*
Flacc.	*In Flaccum*
Flaccus	*Against Flaccus*
Her.	*Quis rerum divinarum heres sit*
Hypoth.	*Hypothetica*
Ios.	*De Iosepho*
Joseph	*On the Life of Joseph*
Leg. 1, 2, 3	*Legum allegoriae I, II, III*
Alleg. Interp. 1, 2, 3	*Allegorical Interpretation 1, 2, 3*
Legat.	*Legatio ad Gaium*
Embassy	*On the Embassy to Gaius*
Migr.	*De migratione Abrahami*
Migration	*On the Migration of Abraham*
Creation	*On the Creation of the World*
Post.	*De posteritate Caini*
Posterity	*On the Posterity of Cain*
Praem.	*De praemiis et poenis*
Sacr.	*De sacrifciis Abelis et Caini*
Sacrifices	*On the Sacrifices of Cain and Abel*
Sobr.	*De sobrietate*
Sobriety	*On Sobriety*
Spec. 1, 2, 3, 4	*De specialibus legibus I, II, III, IV*
Virt.	*De virtutibus*
Virtues	*On the Virtues*

Josephus

Vita	*Vita*
Life	*The Life*
C. Ap.	*Contra Apionem*
Ag. Ap.	*Against Apion*
Ant.	*Jewish Antiquities*
J.W.	*Jewish War*

DEAD SEA SCROLLS AND RELATED TEXTS

1Qap Gen^{ar}	*Genesis Apocryphon*
1QH^a	*Hodayot^a or Thanksgiving Hymns^a*
1QpHab	*Pesher Habakkuk*
1QM	*Milhamah (War Scroll)*
1QS	*Serek Hayahad (Rule of the Community)*
1QIsa^a	*Isaiah^a*
1Qisa^b	*Isaiah^b*
CD	Cairo Genizah text of the *Damascus Document*

NUMBER	ABBREVIATION	NAME
1Q28a1	Qsa	*Rule of the Congregation* (Appendix a to 1QS)
1Q28b	1Qsb	*Rule of the Blessings* (Appendix b to 1QS)
3Q15		*Copper Scroll*
4Q17	4QExod-Lev^f	
4Q22	4QpaleoExod^m	
4Q82	4QXII^g	*The Greek Minor Prophets Scroll*
4Q120	4QpapLXXLev^b	
4Q127	4QpapParaExod gr	*ParaExodus*
4Q174	4QFlor (MidrEschat^a)	*Florilegium, also Midrash on Eschatology* ^{a}
4Q175	(4QTest)	*Testimonia*
4Q177	4QCatena ^{a} (MidrEschat^b)	
4Q180	4QAgesCreat	*Ages of Creation*
4Q182	4QCatena^b (MidrEschat^c)	*Catena^b, also Midrash on Eschatology^c*
4Q242	4QPrNab ar	*Prayer of Nabonidus*
4Q246	4QapocrDan ar	*Apocryphon of Daniel*
4Q298		*Cryptic A: Words of the Sage to the Sons of Dawn*
4Q385^b		*4QApocryphon of Jeremiah^c*
4Q389^a		*4QApocryphon of Jeremiah^e*
4Q390		*4QPseudo-Moses^e*
4Q394	4QMMT^a	*Miqsat Ma'aśê ha-Torah^a*
4Q521	4QmessAp	*Messianic Apocalypse*
4Q5504Qproto-Esther^{a-f}		*ProtoEsther, Aramaic, copies to*
4QFlor (MidrEschat^a)		*Florilegium (or Midrash on Eschatology^a)*
4QMMT		*Halakhic Letter*
4QpaleoDeutr		*Copy of Deuteronomy in paleo-Hebrew script*
4QpaleoExod^m		*Copy of Exodus in paleo-Hebrew script*
4QpNah		*Nahum Pesher*
4QpPss^a		*Psalm Pesher A*
4QprNab ar		*Prayer of Nabonidus*
4QPs37		*Psalms Scroll*
4QpsDan		*Pseudo-Daniel*
4Qsam^a		*First copy of Samuel*
4QTob		*Copy of Tobit*
11QMelch		*Melchizedek*
11QpHab		*A fragment of the Habakkuk scroll*
11QPs^a		*Psalms Scroll^a*
11QTemple		*Temple Scroll*
11QtgJob		*Targum of Job*

MISHNAH, TALMUD, AND RELATED LITERATURE

To distinguish between the same-named tractates in the Mishna, Tosepta, Babylonian Talmud, and Jerusalem Talmud, *m.*, *t.*, *b.*, or *y.* precedes the title of the tractate.

'Abod. Zar.	*Abodah Zarah*
'Abot	*'Abot*
'Arak.	*'Arakhin*
B. Bat.	*Bava Batra*
B. Metsi'a	*Bava Metsi'a*
B. Qam.	*Bava Qamma*
Bek.	*Bekhorot*
Ber.	*Berakhot*
'Ed.	*'Eduyyot*
'Erub.	*'Eruvin*
Git.	*Gittin*
Hag.	*Hagigah*
Hal.	*Hallah*
Hor.	*Horayot*
Hul.	*Hullin*
Ketub.	*Ketubbot*
Kil.	*Kil'ayim*
Ma'as.	*Ma'aserot*
Meg.	*Megillah*
Menah.	*Menahot*
Mid.	*Middot*
Mo'ed Qat.	*Mo'ed Qatan*
Ned.	*Nedarim*
Pesah.	*Pesahim*
Qidd.	*Qiddusin*
Sanh.	*Sanhedrin*
Shabb.	*Shabbat*
Sheqal	*Pesahim Sheqalim*
Sota	*Sota*
Ta'an.	*Ta'anit*
Tg. Neof.	*Targum Neofiti*
Yad.	*Yadayim*
Yebam.	*Yevamot*
Yoma	*Yoma (= Kippurim)*

TARGUMIC TEXT

Tg. Onq.	*Targum Ongelos*
Tg. Neb.	*Targum of the Prophets*
Tg. Ket.	*Targum of the Writings*
Frg. Tg.	*Fragmentary Targum*
Sam. Tg.	*Samaritan Targum*
Tg. Isa.	*Targum Isaiah*
Tg. Neof.	*Targum Neofiti*
Tg. Ps-J	*Targum Pseudo-Jonathan*
Tg. Yer. I	*Targum Yerušalmi*
Tg. Yer. II	*Targum Yerušalmi I*
Yem. Tg.	*Yemenite Targum*
Tg. Esth. I, II	*First or Second Targum of Esther*

OTHER RABBINIC WORKS

'Abot R. Nat.	*'Abot de Rabbi Nathan*
Gem.	*Gemara*
Gerim	*Gerim*
Mek.	*Mekilta*
Mez.	*Mezuzah*
Midr.	*Midrash*
Pesiq. Rab.	*Pesiqta Rabbati*
Pesiq. Rab Kah.	*Pesiqta of Rab Kahana*
Rab.	*Rabbah (following abbreviation of biblical book—e.g., Gen. Rab. = Genesis Rabbah)*
Song Rab.	*Song of Songs Rabbah*

NAG HAMMADI CODICES

Ap. John	*II, 1 Apocryphon of John*
Gos. Phil.	*II, 3 Gospel of Philip*
Exeg. Soul	*II, 6 Exegesis on the Soul*
Ap. John	*III, 1 Apocryphon of John*
Apoc. Paul	*V, 2 Apocalypse of Paul*
Apoc. Adam	*V, 5 Apocalypse of Adam*
Zost.	*VIII, 1 Zostrianos*
Ep. Pet. Phil.	*VIII, 2 Letter of Peter to Philip*
Melch.	*IX, 1 Melchizedek*
Testim. Truth	*IX, 3 Testimony of Truth*
Gos. Truth	*XII, 2 Gospel of Truth*

GREEK MANUSCRIPTS AND ANCIENT VERSIONS

LETTERED UNCIALS

א	Codex Sinaiticus, fourth-century manuscript of LXX, NT, Epistle of Barnabas, and Shepherd of Hermas
A	Codex Alexandrinus, fifth-century manuscript of LXX, NT, 1 & 2 Clement, and Psalms of Solomon
B	Codex Vaticanus, fourth-century manuscript of LXX and parts of the NT
C	Codex Ephraemi, fifth-century manuscript of parts of LXX and NT
D	Codex Bezae, fifth-century bilingual (Greek and Latin) manuscript of the Gospels and Acts
G	Ninth-century manuscript of the Gospels
K	Ninth-century manuscript of the Gospels
L	Eighth-century manuscript of the Gospels
W	Washington Codex, fifth-century manuscript of the Gospels
X	Codex Monacensis, ninth- or tenth-century miniscule manuscript of the Gospels
Z	Sixth-century manuscript of Matthew
Q	Koridethi Codex, ninth-century manuscript of the Gospels
Y	Athous Laurae Codex, eighth- or ninth-century manuscript of the Gospels (incomplete), Acts, The Catholic and Pauline Epistles, and Hebrews

PERIODICALS, REFERENCE WORKS, AND SERIALS

ABD	*Anchor Bible Dictionary.* Edited by D. N. Freedman. 6 vols. New York, 1992
ABR	*Australian Biblical Review*
ABRL	Anchor Bible Reference Library
ACNT	Augsburg Commentaries on the New Testament
AcOr	*Acta Orientalia*
AEL	*Ancient Egyptian Literature.* M. Lichteim. 3 vols. Berkely, 1971–1980
AfO	*Archiv für Orientforschung*
AfOB	Archiv für Orientforschung: Beiheft
AGJU	Arbeiten zur Geschichte des antiken Judentums und des Urchristentums
AJP	*American Journal of Philology*
AJSL	*American Journal of Semitic Languages and Literature*
AJT	*American Journal of Theology*
AnBib	Analecta biblica
ANEP	*The Ancient Near East in Pictures Relating to the Old Testament.* Edited by J. B. Pritchard. Princeton, 1954
ANET	*Ancient Near Eastern Texts Relating to the Old Testament.* Edited by J. B. Pritchard. 3rd ed. Princeton, 1969
ANF	*The Ante-Nicene Fathers*
ANRW	*Aufstieg und Niedergang der römischen Welt: Geschichte und Kultur Roms im Spiegel der neueren Forschung.* Edited by H. Temporini and W. Haase. Berlin, 1972–
ANTC	Abingdon New Testament Commentaries
ANTJ	Arbeiten zum Neuen Testament und Judentum
APOT	*The Apocrypha and Pseudepigrapha of the Old Testament.* Edited by R. H. Charles. 2 vols. Oxford, 1913
ASNU	Acta seminarii neotestamentici upsaliensis
ATANT	Abhandlungen zur Theologie des Alten und Neuen Testaments
ATD	Das Alte Testament Deutsch
ATDan	Acta theological danica
Aug	*Augustinianum*
BA	*Biblical Archaeologist*
BAGD	Bauer, W., W. F. Arndt, F. W. Gingrich, and F. W. Danker. *Greek-English Lexicon of the New Testament and Other Early Christian Literature.* 2nd *ed. Chicago, 1979*
BAR	*Biblical Archaeology Review*
BASOR	*Bulletin of the American Schools of Oriental Research*
BBB	*Bonner biblische Beiträge*
BBET	Beiträge zur biblischen Exegese und Theologie
BBR	*Bulletin for Biblical Research*
BDAG	Bauer, W., F. W. Danker, W. F. Arndt, and F. W. Gingrich. *Greek-English Lexicon of the New Testament and Other Early Christian Literature.* 3rd *ed. Chicago, 2000*
BDB	Brown, F., S. R. Driver, and C. A. Briggs. *A Hebrew and English Lexicon of the Old Testament. Oxford, 1907*
BDF	Blass, F., A. Debrunner, and R. W. Funk. *A Greek Grammar of the New Testament and Other Early Christian Literature. Chicago, 1961*
BEATAJ	Beiträge zur Erforschung des Alten Testaments und des antiken Judentum
BETL	Bibliotheca ephemeridum theologicarum lovaniensium
BEvT	*Beiträge zur evangelischen Theologie*

BGBE	Beitrage zur Geschichte der Biblischen Exegese
BHS	Biblia Hebraica Stuttgartensia. *Edited by K. Elliger and W. Randolph. Stuttgart, 1983*
BHT	Beiträge zur historischen Theologie
Bib	*Biblica*
BibInt	*Biblical Interpretation*
BibOr	Biblica et orientalia
BJRL	*Bulletin of the John Rylands University Library of Manchester*
BJS	Brown Judaic Studies
BK	*Bibel und Kirche*
BKAT	Biblischer Kommentar, Altes Testament. Edited by M. Noth and H. W. Wolff
BLS	*Bible and Literature Series*
BN	*Biblische Notizen*
BNTC	Black's New Testament Commentaries
BR	*Biblical Research*
BSac	*Bibliotheca sacra*
BSOAS	*Bulletin of the School of Oriental and African Studies*
BT	The Bible Translator
BTB	*Biblical Theology Bulletin*
BVC	*Bible et vie chrétienne*
BWA(N)T	Beiträge zur Wissenschaft vom Alten (und Neuen) Testament
BZ	*Biblische Zeitschrift*
BZAW	Beihefte zur Zeitschrift für die alttestamentliche Wissenschaft
BZNW	Beihefte zur Zeitschrift für die neutestamentliche Wissenschaft
CAD	*The Assyrian Dictionary of the Oriental Institute of the University of Chicago. Chicago, 1956–*
CB	*Cultura bíblica*
CBC	Cambridge Bible Commentary
CBQ	*Catholic Biblical Quarterly*
CBQMS	Catholic Biblical Quarterly Monograph Series
CANE	*Civilizations of the Ancient Near East.* Edited by J. Sasson. 4 vols. New York, 1995
CIG	*Corpus inscriptionum graecarum.* Edited by A. Boeckh. 4 vols. Berlin, 1828–1877
CSEL	Corpus scriptorum historiae byzantinae
ConBNT	Coniectanea neotestamentica or Coniectanea biblica: New Testament Series
ConBOT	Coniectanea biblica: Old Testament Series
CP	Classical Philology
CRAI	Comptes rendus del l'Académie des inscriptions et belles-lettres
CRINT	Compendia rerum iudaicarum ad Novum Testamentum
CTM	*Concordia Theological Monthly*
DDD	*Dictionary of Dieties and Demons in the Bible.* Edited by K. van der Toorn. B. Becking, and P. W. van der Horst. Leiden, 1995.
Diod. Sic.	*Diodorus Siculus.* Library of History
DJD	Discoveries in the Judaean Desert
EB	Echter Bibel
EA	El-Amarna tablets. According to the edition of J. A. Knudtzon. *Die el-Amarna-Tafeln.* Leipzig, 1908–1915. Reprint, Aalen, 1964. Continued in A. F. Rainey, *El-Amarna Tablets*, 359–379. 2nd revised ed. Kevelaer, 1978
EI	Encyclopaedia of Islam. 9 of 13 projected vols. 2nd ed. Leiden, 1954–
EKKNT	Evangelisch-katholischer Kommentar zum Neuen Testament

Enc	*Encounter*
EncJud	*Encyclopaedia Judaica. 16 vols. Jerusalem, 1972*
EPRO	Etudes préliminairies aux religions orientales dans l'empire romain
ER	*The Encyclopedia of Religion.* Edited by M. Eliade. 16 vols. New York, 1987.
ErIsr	Eretz-Israel
EstBib	Estudios bíblicos
ETL	Ephemerides theologicae lovanienses
ETS	Erfurter theologische Studien
EvQ	*Evangelical Quarterly*
EvT	*Evangelische Theologie*
ExAud	*Ex auditu*
ExpTim	*Expository Times*
FAT	Forschungen zum Alten Testament
FB	Forschung zur Bibel
FBBS	Facet Books, Biblical Series
FFNT	*Foundations and Facets: New Testament*
FOTL	Forms of the Old Testament Literature
FRLANT	Forschungen zur Religion und Literatur des Alten und Neuen Testaments
FTS	*Frankfurter Theologische Studien*
GBS.OTS	Guides to Biblical Scholarship. Old Testament Series
GCS	Die griechische christliche Schriftsteller der ersten [drei] Jahrhunderte
GKC	*Gesenius' Hebrew Grammar.* Edited by E. Kautzsch. Translated by A. E. Cowley. 2nd ed. Oxford, 1910
GNS	*Good News Studies*
GTA	Göttinger theologischer Arbeiten
HAL	Koehler, L., W. Baumgartner, and J. J. Stamm. *Hebräisches und aramäisches Lexikon zum Alten Testament.* Fascicles 1–5, 1967–1995 (KBL3). ET: HALOT
HAR	*Hebrew Annual Review*
HAT	Handbuch zum Alten Testament
HBC	*Harper's Bible Commentary.* Edited by J. L. Mays et al. San Francisco, 1988
HBT	*Horizons in Biblical Theology*
HDB	Hastings Dictionary of the Bible
HDR	Harvard Dissertations in Religion
HeyJ	*Heythrop Journal*
HNT	Handbuch zum Neuen Testament
HNTC	Harper's New Testament Commentaries
HR	*History of Religions*
HSM	Harvard Semitic Monographs
HSS	Harvard Semitic Studies
HTKNT	Herders theologischer Kommentar zum Neuen Testament
HTR	*Harvard Theological Review*
HTS	Harvard Theological Studies
HUCA	*Hebrew Union College Annual*
IB	*Interpreter's Bible.* Edited by G. A. Buttrick et al. 12 vols. New York, 1951–1957
IBC	Interpretation: A Bible Commentary for Teaching and Preaching
IBS	*Irish Biblical Studies*
ICC	International Critical Commentary

IDB	*The Interpreter's Dictionary of the Bible*. Edited by G.A. Buttrick. 4 vols. Nashville, 1962
IDBSup	*Interpreter's Dictionary of the Bible: Supplementary Volume.* Edited by K. Crim. Nashville, 1976
IEJ	*Israel Exploration Journal*
Int	*Interpretation*
IRT	Issues in Religion and Theology
ITC	International Theological Commentary
JAAR	*Journal of the American Academy of Religion*
JAL	Jewish Apocryphal Literature Series
JANESCU	*Journal of the Ancient Near Eastern Society of Columbia University*
JAOS	*Journal of the American Oriental Society*
JBL	*Journal of Biblical Literature*
JECS	Journal of Early Christian Studies
JETS	Journal of the Evangelical Theological Society
JJS	Journal of Jewish Studies
JNES	Journal of Near Eastern Studies
JNSL	Journal of Northwest Semitic Languages
JPS	Jewish Publication Society
JPOS	Journal of Palestine Oriental Society
JPSV	Jewish Publication Society Version
JQR	*Jewish Quarterly Review*
JR	*Journal of Religion*
JRE	Journal of Religious Ethics
JRH	*Journal of Religious History*
JSJ	*Journal for the Study of Judaism in the Persian, Hellenistic, and Roman Periods*
JSNT	*Journal for the Study of the New Testament*
JSNTSup	Journal for the Study of the New Testament: Supplement Series
JSOT	*Journal for the Study of the Old Testament*
JSOTSup	Journal for the Study of the Old Testament: Supplement Series
JSP	*Journal for the Study of the Pseudepigrapha*
JSPTSS	Journal of the Study of Pentecostal Theology Supplement Series
JSS	*Journal of Semitic Studies*
JTC	*Journal for Theology and the Church*
JTS	*Journal of Theological Studies*
KAI	*Kanaanaische und aramaiche Inschriften*. H. Donner and W. Rollig. 2nd ed. Wiesbaden, 1966–1969.
KAT	Kommentar zum Alten Testament
KEK	Kritisch-exegetischer Kommentar über das Neue Testament (Meyer-Kommentar)
KPG	Knox Preaching Guides
LAE	*Literature of Ancient Egypt*. WK. Simpson. New Haven, 1972.
LCL	Loeb Classical Library
LTQ	*Lexington Theological Quarterly*
MNTC	Moffatt New Testament Commentary
NA[27]	*Novum Testamentum Graece*, Nestle-Aland, 27th ed.
NCBC	*New Century Bible Commentary*
NEAEHL	*The New Encyclopedia of Archaeological Excavations in the Holy Land*. Edited by E. Stern. 4 vols. Jerusalem, 1993.
NHS	Nag Hammadi Studies
NIB	*The New Interpreter's Bible*
NICNT	New International Commentary on the New Testament
NICOT	New International Commentary on the Old Testament

NIGTC	New International Greek Testament Commentary
NJBC	*The New Jerome Biblical Commentary.* Edited by R. E. Brown et al. Englewood Cliffs, 1990
NovT	*Novum Testamentum*
NovTSup	Supplements to Novum Testamentum
NPNF	*Nicene and Post-Nicene Fathers*, Series 1 and 2
NTApoc 2:34-41	*Schneemelcher, Wilhelm. "The Kerygma Petri." In Vol. 2 of New Testament Apocrypha.* Edited by W. Schneemelcher. Rev. ed. Louisville: Westminster John Knox, 1992. 34-41.
NTC	New Testament in Context
NTD	Das Neue Testament Deutsch
NTG	New Testament Guides
NTS	*New Testament Studies*
NTTS	New Testament Tools and Studies
OBC	Oxford Bible Commentary
OBO	Orbis biblicus et orientalis
OBT	Overtures to Biblical Theology
OIP	Oriental Institute Publications
Or	*Orientalia* (NS)
OTG	Old Testament Guides
OTL	Old Testament Library
OTM	Old Testament Message
OTP	*Old Testament Pseudepigrapha.* Edited by J. H. Charlesworth. 2 vols. New York, 1983
OtSt	*Oudtestamentische Studiën*
PAAJR	*Proceedings of the American Academy of Jewish Research*
PEQ	*Palestine Exploration Quarterly*
PGM	*Papyri graecae magicae: Die griechischen Zauberpapyri.* Edited by K. Preisendanz. Berlin, 1928
PTMS	Pittsburgh Theological Monograph Series
QD	Quaestiones disputatae
RANE	Records of the Ancient Near East
RB	*Revue biblique*
ResQ	*Restoration Quarterly*
RevExp	*Review and Expositor*
RevQ	*Revue de Qumran*
RevScRel	*Revue des sciences religieuses*
RIMA	*The Royal Inscriptions of Mesopotamia, Assyrian Periods*
RSR	*Recherches de science religieuse*
RTL	*Revue théologique de Louvain*
SAA	*State Archives of Assyria*
SBB	*Stuttgarter biblische Beiträge*
SBL	*Society of Biblical Literature*
SBLAB	Society of Biblical Literature Academia Biblica Series
SBLDS	*Society of Biblical Literature Dissertation Series*
SBLMS	*Society of Biblical Literature Monograph Series*
SBLRBS	*Society of Biblical Literature Resources for Biblical Study*
SBLSCS	*Society of Biblical Literature Septuagint and Cognate Studies*
SBLSP	Society of Biblical Literature Seminar Papers
SBLSS	Society of Biblical Literature Semeia Studies
SBLSymS	Society of Biblical Literature Symposium Series
SBLWAW	Society of Biblical Literature Writings from the Ancient World
SBM	Stuttgarter biblische Monographien
SBS	Stuttgarter Bibelstudien

SBT	Studies in Biblical Theology
SEÅ	*Svensk exegetisk årsbok*
SJLA	Studies in Judaism in Late Antiquity
SJOT	*Scandinavian Journal of the Old Testament*
SJT	*Scottish Journal of Theology*
SKK	Stuttgarter kleiner Kommentar
SNTSMS	Society for New Testament Studies Monograph Series
SOTSMS	Society for Old Testament Study Monograph Series
SP	Sacra pagina
SR	*Studies in Religion*
SSN	Studia semitica neerlandica
Str-B	Strack, H. L., and P. Billerbeck. *Kommentar zum Neuen Testament aus Talmud und Midrasch.* 6 vols. Munich, 1922–6161
SUNT	Studien zur Umwelt des Neuen Testaments
SVTP	Studia in Veteris Testamenti pseudepigrapha
TA	Tel Aviv
TB	Theologische Bücherei: Neudrucke und Berichte aus dem 20. Jahrhundert
TD	Theology Digest
TDNT	Theological Dictionary of the New Testament. Edited by G. Kittel and G. Friedrich. Translated by G. W. Bromiley. 10 vols. Grand Rapids, 1964–1976
TDOT	*Theological Dictionary of the Old Testament.* Edited by G. J. Botterweck and H. Ringgren. Translated by J. T. Willis, G. W. Bromiley, and D. E. Green. 8 vols. Grand Rapids, 1974–
THKNT	Theologischer Handkommentar zum Neuen Testament
ThTo	*Theology Today*
TLZ	*Theologische Literaturzeitung*
TOTC	Tyndale Old Testament Commentaries
TQ	*Theologische Quartalschrift*
TS	Texts and Studies
TS	*Theological Studies*
TSK	*Theologische Studien und Kritiken*
TSSI	*Textbook of Syrian Semitic Inscriptions.* J. C. L. Gibson. Oxford, 1971–1982
TynBul	*Tyndale Bulletin*
TZ	*Theologische Zeitschrift*
UBS	United Bible Societies
UBS[4]	*The Greek New Testament*, United Bible Societies, 4th ed.
UF	*Ugarit-Forschungen*
USQR	*Union Seminary Quarterly Review*
UUA	Uppsala Universitetsårsskrift
VC	*Vigiliae christianae*
VT	*Vetus Testamentum*
VTSup	Vetus Testamentum Supplements
WA	*Weimar Ausgabe.* (Weimer ed.). M. Luther
WBC	Word Biblical Commentary
WBT	*Word Biblical Themes*
WMANT	Wissenschaftliche Monographien zum Alten und Neuen Testament
WTJ	*Westminster Theological Journal*
WUNT	Wissenschaftliche Untersuchungen zum Neuen Testament
ZAH	*Zeitschrift für Althebräistik*
ZAW	*Zeitschrift für die alttestamentliche Wissenschaft*

ZNW	*Zeitschrift für die neutestamentliche Wissenschaft und die Kunde de älteren Kirche*
ZTK	*Zeitschrift für Theologie und Kirche*

GREEK AND LATIN WORKS AND THEIR ABBREVIATIONS

APULEIUS

Metam.	*The Golden Ass*

ARISTOPHANES

Eccl.	*Women of the Assembly*

ATHANASIUS

Ep. fest.	*Festal Letters*

AGUSTINE

C. mend.	*Against Lying (to Consentius)*
Civ.	*The City of God*
Doctr. chr.	*Christian Instruction*
Gen. litt.	*On Genesis Literally Interpreted*
Praed.	*The Predestination of the Saints*
Trin.	*The Trinity*

CICERO

Flac.	*Pro Flacco*
Pis.	*In Pisonem*

EPIPHANIUS

Pan.	*Refutation of All Heresies*

EUSEBIUS

Chron.	*Chronicle*
Comm. Isa.	*Commentary on Isaiah*
Comm. Ps.	*Commentary on Psalms*
Dem. ev.	*Demonstration of the Gospel*
Eccl. theol.	*Ecclesiastical Theology*
Ecl. Proph.	*Extracts from the Prophets*
Hier.	*Against Hierocles*
Hist. eccl.	*Ecclesiastical History*
Marc.	*Against Marcellus*
Mart. Pal.	*The Martyrs of Palestine*
Onom.	*Onomasticon*
Praep. ev.	*Preparation for the Gospel*
Theoph.	*Divine Manifestation*
Vit. Const.	*Life of Constantine*

GREGORY OF NAZIANZUS

Ep.	*Epistulae*
Or. Bas.	*Oratio in lauden Basili*

HERODOTUS

Hist.	*Histories*

HIPPOLYTUS

Antichr.	*De antichristo*
Ben. Is. Jac.	*De benedictionibus Isaaci et Jacobi*
Chron.	*Chronicon*
Fr. Prov.	*Fragmenta in Proverbia*
Haer.	*Refutation of All Heresies*
Noet.	*Contra haeresin Noeti*
Trad. Ap.	*The Apostolic Tradition*
Univ.	*De universo*

HORACE

Ep.	*Epistles*

LUCIAN

[Asin.]	*Lucius, or The Ass*
Syr. d.	*The Goddess of Syria*

ORIGEN

Princ.	*First Principles*

PLINY THE ELDER

Nat.	*Natural History*

RUFINUS

Symb.	*Commentarius in symbolum apostolorum*

STRABO

Geogr.	*Geography*

CHARTS, ILLUSTRATIONS, AND MAPS